Volume X

Mos to Pat

NEW CATHOLIC
ENCYCLOPEDIA

SAN FRANCISCO TORONTO LONDON SYDNEY

Nihil Obstat:
John P. Whalen, M.A., S.T.D.
Censor Deputatus

Imprimatur:
✠ Patrick A. O'Boyle, D.D.
Archbishop of Washington
August 5, 1966

NEW CATHOLIC ENCYCLOPEDIA

Archbishop John Carroll, by the American artist Gilbert Stuart,
oil on canvas, 29 by 24 inches, *c.* 1805.

M

MOSAICS

Pictures or patterns formed by closely spaced polychrome or monochrome stones (tesserae) of near uniform size, natural or artificial, embedded in a binder, such as cement. In its use as architectural revetment and pavement surfacing, mosaic combines decorative qualities with a high resistance to humidity and wear. These qualities mosaic shares with related media, such as glazed tile, stone incrustation, and inlay. The latter differ from mosaic in that their units are larger and of varying sizes and shapes. The employment of these media began very early in history. An inlay depicting animal fables decorates an early dynastic harp from Ur (Museum of the University of Pennsylvania, Philadelphia). Glazed tile is found in the funerary precinct of Pharao Zoser of the Third Dynasty in Old Kingdom Egypt. It is noteworthy that the extensive and refined use of stone incrustation parallels that of mosaic during the late Roman and early Byzantine periods.

Terminology. The term "mosaic" seems borrowed from the Greek μοῦσα. In its present meaning it is of late antique origin (Spartian, *Pesc. Nig.* 6.8: "pictum de musio"; Trebellius Pollio, *Trig. Tyr.* 25.4: "pictura est de museo"; Augustine, *Civ.* 16.1.1: "quae musivo picta sunt"). The term seems to have been applied at first only to wall and vault decoration and not to pavements. A list of artisans in a decree of A.D. 337 (*Cod. Theod.* 13.4.2) includes both *tessellarii* who laid mosaic pavements and *musivarii,* makers of wall and vault mosaics. The comprehensive use of the term to include both kinds of mosaic became established gradually in the post-antique period.

Early History. The earliest recorded use of mosaic is found in Sumer. A temple façade in Warka (Biblical Erech), dating from the protoliterate period before 3000 B.C., was covered with geometric designs formed by colored cones of fired clay embedded in the walls. Luxury objects and jewelry decorated with a mosaic inlay of costly materials were produced in ancient Mesopotamia, Crete, and Egypt. However, a continuity of mosaic production on a large scale can be observed only since ancient Greece. Beyond the boundaries of European civilization the Aztecs and Mayans had developed an independent production of turquoise mosaics used on armor and luxury articles.

Ancient Greece and Rome. In ancient Greece figural scenes composed of polychrome pebbles have been found on pavements dating from the late 5th and early 4th centuries B.C. These pebble mosaics were popular in the early Hellenistic period. Some examples of rare quality have been excavated at Olynthus and Pella. Polychrome pebble pavements of decorative design were used during the archaic period. The earliest pebble mosaic is of the late 8th century; it was discovered at Gordion in Asia Minor and consists of geometric designs distributed in a blue and red pattern on a white ground.

It seems likely that the rounded shapes of pebbles and their limited polychromy as found in nature induced the Greeks to stress silhouette and outline in the design of their figured pebble mosaics. Nonetheless, certain of these display a considerable degree of modeling in the round, notably the "Stag Hunt" by Gnosis excavated at Pella.

During the Hellenistic period the development of the practice of cutting stones into small pieces of deliberate shape, called tesserae, allowed for an increase of sophistication in pictorial design akin to painting, with which the pebble mosaics had not been able to compete. An example of this technique is a panel by Sophilos depicting Alexandria personified found at Thmuis in Egypt.

Other tessellated pavements of the 3d century B.C. have been found in Morgantina. By the 2d century before Christ tessellated pavements achieved an extreme refinement in technique and pictorial conventions. Mosaics found in the palace of the Attalids at Pergamon, dating from the period before the annexation of the city by the Romans (133 B.C.), are among the finest Hellenistic pavements known. They are notable for the extremely small size of their tesserae and particularly for their rich polychromy intensified by the appearance—the earliest recorded on pavements—of glass tesserae in colors not available in natural stone. The development of a brilliant mosaic art during the Hellenistic period, attested by a limited number of originals, is corroborated by Roman copies and texts. The luxurious boats of Hellenistic rulers were decorated with mosaics. Sosos, a Pergamene mosaicist, is credited by Pliny with the invention of "the unswept floor," a subject often repeated on

Fig. 1. "The Battle of Issus," 2d century B.C., from Pompeii, National Museum at Naples, length approx. 17 ft.

MOSAICS

Fig. 2. "Bacchus," Roman mosaic from Cento Celle.

Fig. 4. Zodiac mosaic, Byzantine, 6th century, from Beisan, Palestine.

Fig. 3. "The Battle of Raphida," c. 432 to 440, in S. Maria Maggiore, Rome.

Roman mosaic pavements (*Nat. Hist.* 36.184). Roman reflections of sophisticated pictorial conventions developed in Hellenistic mosaic are found in the mosaics located in the lower sanctuary of Fortuna at Palestrina, from the period of Sulla (82–79 B.C.). One depicts a panoramic Nilotic landscape filled with human figures, architecture, and the fauna of Egypt. The other portrays a sanctuary of Neptune beneath the sea filled with fish and encompassed by a shore. The many abrupt changes in scale and orientation evident in the composition of this mosaic are in accord with its pavement location, which excludes the possibility of a consistent spatial vision on the part of the viewer.

The widespread use of mosaics in the decoration of the Hellenistic home is illustrated by the mosaic pavements located in middle-class houses in Delos of the 2d century B.C. During this century the Romans came into intimate contact with the Hellenistic world, and the Roman patricians soon adopted the practice of decorating homes with mosaic. The wealthy Campanian houses, buried by the eruption of Vesuvius in A.D. 79, were amply decorated with mosaics. In the House of the Faun in Pompeii were found pavements dating from the latter part of the 2d century B.C. (Naples Museum). Most famous is the large panel depicting the victory of Alexander over Darius at Issus (Fig. 1). It copies a Hellenistic painting, most likely by Philoxenos of Eretria. Judging from the recorded names of mosaicists on signed pavements, the artists were mainly of Greek origin.

During the period of the Roman Republic and the early Empire decorative mosaics were a popular means of pavement surfacing. Their tesserae were large, of relatively constant shape and size, and evenly laid. These decorative mosaics, whose production required no unusual talent, were called *opus tessellatum* by the Romans, who distinguished between them and the much finer *opus vermiculatum* (wormlike workmanship) comprising smaller figural panels made of much finer stones, irregularly disposed. Such smaller panels were capable of great refinements in pictorial modeling and landscape space. A number of the finest *emblemata* from Campanian houses, notably the Dioskurides panel from the House of the Faun, were mounted on plaques. The mounting indicates that they had been produced in specialized workshops and were then acquired for insertion in the pavements.

Occasionally mosaics in the towns buried by Vesuvius were used on the surfaces of walls and columns. In a small court of a house in Herculaneum an entire wall that contained a fountain and niches was decorated with mosaic. Sparkling glass tesserae depicted hounds chasing deer and vine branches and festoons set against a dark ground. On an adjacent wall appeared a panel portraying Neptune and Amphitrite. The resistance of mosaic surfaces to humidity led to their application on the walls and vaults of baths and *nymphaea*. However, the use of mosaic on a large scale can be traced only from the 2d century A.D. Remains of vault mosaics appear in the baths of the *Sette Sapienti* in Ostia and in the *canopus* of Hadrian's villa in Tivoli.

During the later Roman Empire the mosaic emblem of limited size containing figural subjects was gradually replaced by a more extensive pictorial design. This tendency involved changes toward simplification in technique and composition; it is evident in the black and white pavements popular in Italy during the 2d and 3d centuries A.D. These pavements allowed for a graphic clarity in the discernment of an expansive subject matter presented on a neutral white ground. The reduced mosaic style of late antiquity yielded masterpieces, for example, the polychrome mosaic of the Glorification of Hercules in the Tetrarchial villa at Piazza Armerina in Sicily.

Mosaic pavements were used widely in private homes and public buildings throughout the Empire. A particularly rich tradition of polychrome pavements in North Africa extends from the 1st century A.D. until after the Vandal conquest. An early North African pavement of unusual refinement was found in a villa at Zliten, dating from the later 1st century A.D. It depicts a plant scroll with various birds and animals distributed among the volutes. The extreme fineness of the work in the figured parts is indicated by the mean count of 40 to 50 tesserae per square centimeter.

Excavations that have been made at Antioch, in Asia Minor, have given evidence of a continuous mosaic production extending from the middle Empire into the early Byzantine period. A pavement showing the Seasons from the Constantinian villa in Antioch is square and sectioned into geometric fields disposed around a common center; this symmetrical mode of composition lent itself to the design of ceilings and domes.

Early Christian, Medieval, and Byzantine Mosaics. The development of mosaic as the preferred monumental art extends from early Christianity through the entire course of the Byzantine Empire. In the medieval West its use was centered in Italy and was dependent on the presence and influence of early Christian sources, as well as on the influence of Byzantium. Northern Christian Europe was acquainted with architectural mosaic until the Carolingian revival as witnessed by the original mosaic decoration of Charlemagne's Palatine chapel at Aachen. However, in the later Middle Ages mosaic as the preferred architectural decoration was replaced by sculpture, fresco, and stained glass.

The earliest extant vault mosaic in good condition is located in a modest Christian tomb beneath St. Peter's in Rome. Christ-Helios in a quadriga occupies the apex of the vault. A radiant halo surrounds the head, and the figure is displayed against a gold ground. A grapevine spreads over the golden vault, which preceded by a short period of time the construction of the church above it.

The intense polychromatic effect achieved in large interiors by the use of mosaic revetment, and especially by gold tesserae, is evident in Hagios Georgios in Thessalonica, whose mosaics date probably from the later 4th century. The most impressive of all must have been the interior of Hagia Sophia in Constantinople (532–537; 557 and after) judging by descriptions contemporary with its construction. The gold mosaic surfacing of its vaults produced a radiance that was intended to transform the experience of the architectural interior into a vision of God's heaven: "The dome covers the church like the radiant heavens" (Paulus Silentiarius).

In centralized domed buildings with mosaic interiors, churches or baptisteries, the main subject is located in the center of the dome with subordinate subjects grouped around it. In the Baptistery of the Arians in Ravenna (*c.* 500) the Baptism of Christ is so situated (Fig. 5). In the zone around the Baptism appear the

Fig. 5. "The Baptism of Christ," detail of the vault of the Baptistery of the Arians at Ravenna, c. 500.

Twelve Apostles. The dome of the Baptistery of the Orthodox (449–452) has a third zone that shows, in alternation, the four Gospel books set on altars and four ornate empty thrones (Ap 22.1–4).

The longitudinal basilica was decorated at times with mosaic on its façade. During the Middle Ages the façade of Old St. Peter's in Rome depicted the 24 Elders adoring the Holy Lamb (Ap 4.4–11). Mosaics were distributed around the interior of the basilica. The mosaics on the nave walls of S. Maria Maggiore in Rome (432–440) depict Old Testament scenes, and along the nave walls of Sant'Apollinare Nuovo in Ravenna (6th century) processions of saints move in the direction of the apse. A striking apse mosaic is preserved in Sant'Apollinare in Classe (dedicated 549). In the center of the

apse St. Apollinaris spreads his arms apart in the *orans* gesture. He is flanked by 12 lambs denoting the Apostles. Above the saint is depicted a Transfiguration rendered in symbolic terms. Christ appears in the shape of a cross enclosed in a *mandorla* that encloses a starry sky. A small bust of Christ is located at the center point of the cross. The three sheep beneath the *mandorla* symbolize the Apostles present at the Transfiguration. Elijah and Moses appear in the sky above. The mosaic decoration of the Christian sanctuary presented the illiterate devout with visual sermons whose beauty was intended to deepen the experience of faith. The mosaic panel in San Vitale in Ravenna depicting Justinian and his court illustrates an ability to represent succinct resemblances with reduced means.

In the later Byzantine period refined workmanship was particularly stressed, for instance, in the carefully modeled figures of the Deësis mosaic in Hagia Sophia in Constantinople (late 12th or 13th century). This tendency reached a peak in the portable mosaics of late Byzantium composed of extremely fine stones. Two such panels depict the 12 main feasts of the liturgical year (14th century; Opera del Duomo, Florence). The concern for the thematic distribution of mosaics within centralized interiors culminates in the decoration of the post-iconoclast cross-in-square church. In the church at Daphni (*c.* 1100) a severe Christ Pantocrator dominates the center of the dome and turns His eyes upon the devout beneath. Around Him are the 12 Apostles, and further below appear scenes from the life of Christ; the Virgin and Child occupy the eastern apse.

During the course of the Middle Ages the influence of Byzantine mosaics often reached far beyond the geographical boundaries of Byzantium. The mosaics of the Ommeyad mosque at Damascus (8th century) depict landscapes with villas, derived from ancient Roman and classicizing Byzantine sources and transmitted by Byzantine mosaicists working for Mohammedan patrons.

Byzantine influence in medieval Italy is reflected in the flourishing mosaic activity in the Veneto and Norman Sicily. The Norman kings employed Byzantine artists for the mosaic decoration of their cathedrals at Monreale and Cefalù (12th century). St. Mark's Cathedral in Venice (1063 and after), which was copied after the Church of the Holy Apostles in Constantinople, offers with its vast mosaic program perhaps the most cogent visual reflection of the interior decoration of the large churches of the Byzantine capital. The Virgin and Child in the apse of the basilica at Torcello (12th century), floating on a sea of gold, is perhaps the most striking example of Byzantine mosaic style in the West.

Rome, with its heritage of early Christian mosaics, remained an active center of mosaic production until the advent of the Renaissance. *Giotto's most monumental pictorial work was the Navicella, a mosaic 52 feet wide and 33 feet high, located on the entrance tower facing the atrium of Old St. Peter's in Rome. This mosaic may well have imitated an early Christian model. A major artistic achievement of the 13th century in Tuscany was the vast mosaic decoration of the dome of the baptistery of Florence.

From the Renaissance until Modern Times. With the advent of the Italian Renaissance and the fall of Byzantium to the Turks mosaic ceased to be a primary artistic medium. From the 15th century onward it relied mainly on conventions established by the painters. The "Death of the Virgin" in the Mascoli Chapel in St. Mark's in Venice (Fig. 7), perhaps the finest mosaic of its period (mid-15th century), illustrates this attitude. Its perspective depth explains, as in Renaissance painting, the natural spatial relationships within the panel itself; but its deep space is totally unrelated to the shape of the vault on which the panel rests. *Raphael supplied the cartoons for Luigi di Pace's mosaics in the dome of the Chigi Chapel in S. Maria del Popolo in Rome (1516). The reliance of the mosaicist on the painter can be traced in St. Mark's, Venice, during the following centuries. The 18th-century "Arrival of the Body of St. Mark" by Leopoldo del Pozzo, situated over the north door of the façade, is based on a cartoon by Sebastiano Ricci (Fig. 8). The same situation prevailed elsewhere in Italy. During this period mosaicists had little interest in medieval work. Orazio Manenti's thorough reconstruction of Giotto's Navicella (1673–75), relocated in the narthex of St. Peter's in Rome, follows Giotto only in the general features of the composition.

In the later 18th century the renewal of interest in classical, early Christian, and medieval mosaics resulted in a growth of mosaic production throughout Europe; the renewal also reached America. This revival reflected in many ways the eclecticism of the period. Early Christian mosaics were carelessly restored, as in the case of the apse mosaic of San Michele in Affricisco in Ravenna, acquired by Prussia in 1844 and transferred to Berlin. Early Christian subject matter was rendered in an unrelated contemporary style, as in Burne-Jones's pre-Raphaelite "Christ Enthroned Flanked by Angels" in the American Church in Rome. The classical pavements discovered in the excavations of the Roman towns in Campania influenced the activity of the Belloni workshop in Paris during the early 19th century.

During the 19th and the early 20th centuries churches received extensive mosaic decoration. St. Paul's in London was partially decorated with mosaics after designs by G. F. Watts and Alfred Stevens. In Paris, the apse of the Panthéon was covered with a mosaic depicting "Christ Revealing to the Angel of France the Destinies of her People," and Magne and Merson depicted in Sacré Coeur (1912–23) a Christ in Glory, the Virgin, St. Michael, and Joan of Arc. The new cathedral in St. Louis, Mo. (dedicated in 1914) is decorated largely with mosaics designed by Albert Oerken. On the whole, the style of all these mosaics is eclectic and mechanical.

At the present time mosaic is used widely as an adjunct to architecture and as an independent art. But its importance is not clearly established. The preference in contemporary art for composite media has blurred the role of mosaic as an independent medium. The recent mosaics of Jeanne Reynal, consisting of tesserae scattered here and there on rough panels of colored cement, illustrate this tendency (Fig. 9). Around the turn of the century *Gaudí used mosaic together with glazed tile and other materials in the revetment of his *art nouveau* architecture in Barcelona.

In recent church architecture, because of the increased awareness of the medieval heritage of Christian mosaics, frequent use is made of mosaic for the decoration of central areas in the sanctuary. On the whole, however, the influence of the architecture of the *International Style on recent churches and buildings in general, with its emphasis on clean wall surfaces and spatial clarity, seems to have impeded a broader role for architectural mosaic. A notable recent exception is the university library in Mexico City, designed and decorated by Juan O'Gorman. The exterior of the library is wholly covered with mosaics depicting scenes from the history of Mexico. In the bright sun these mosaics sheathe the building in a blaze of color.

Bibliography: E. W. ANTHONY, *A History of Mosaics* (Boston 1935). A. BLANCHET, *La Mosaïque* (Paris 1928). H. P. L'ORANGE and P. J. NORDHAGEN, *Mosaik* (Munich 1960). M. E. BLAKE, *The Pavements of the Roman Buildings of the Republic and the Early Empire* (Rome 1930). B. R. BROWN, *Ptolemaic Paintings and Mosaics and the Alexandrine Style* (Cambridge, Mass. 1957). D. LEVI, *Antioch Mosaic Pavements*, 2 v. (Princeton 1947). E. PERNICE, *Pavimente und figürliche Mosaiken* (Berlin 1938). M. VAN BERCHEM and E. CLOUZET, *Mosaïques chrétiennes du IVᵉ au Xᵉ siècle* (Geneva 1924). F. W. DEICHMANN, *Frühchristliche Bauten und Mosaiken von Ravenna* (Baden-Baden

Fig. 6. "Virgin Mary," Byzantine, 11th century, in Hosios Loukos, Greece.

Fig. 7. "Death of the Virgin," Michele Giambono?, mid-15th century, in the Mascoli Chapel, St. Mark's, Venice.

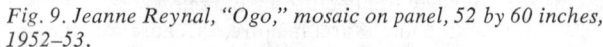

Fig. 8. "Arrival of the Body of St. Mark," Leopoldo del Pozzo, 18th century, north door of St. Mark's, Venice.

MOSAICS

Fig. 9. Jeanne Reynal, "Ogo," mosaic on panel, 52 by 60 inches, 1952–53.

Fig. 10. Louisa Jenkins, "Fourth Station of the Cross," 24 by 24 in., Mount Angel Abbey, Ore., 1953.

1958). O. Demus, *Byzantine Mosaic Decoration* (Boston 1955); *The Mosaics of Norman Sicily* (London 1950). E. Diez and O. Demus, *Byzantine Mosaics in Greece: Hosios Lucas and Daphni* (Cambridge, Mass. 1931). A. Grabar, *Byzantine Painting*, tr. S. Gilbert (Geneva 1953); *Greek Mosaics of the Byzantine Period* (New York 1964). Wilpert MosMal. M. H. Saville, *Turquoise Mosaic Art in Ancient Mexico* (New York 1922). D. Ashton et al., *The Mosaics of Jeanne Reynal* (New York 1964). **Illustration credits:** Fig. 1, Anderson-Art Reference Bureau. Figs. 2 and 4, University Museum of the University of Pennsylvania, Philadelphia. Figs. 3, 7, and 8, Alinari-Art Reference Bureau. Fig. 5, Leonard Von Matt. Fig. 6, Greek National Tourist Office, New York City. Fig. 9, Collection of the Whitney Museum of American Art, New York City.

[J. POLZER]

MOSCHUS, JOHN, 7th-century Byzantine monk and scriptural writer (known also as *Eucratas*); d. 619 or 620. He was a monk and traveler, known for his collection of vivid monastic tales entitled *Leimon* or *Neos Paradeisos* (in Latin, *Pratum Spirituale*). John began his monastic life at St. Theodosius' near Jerusalem in the third quarter of the 6th century. He made sojourns elsewhere in Palestine, Egypt, Sinai, Cyprus, Antioch, Egypt again, and finally Rome (614), usually accompanied by his disciple *Sophronius the Sophist, later patriarch of Jerusalem.

Toward the end of his life, John set down over 300 tales of edifying incidents, replete with details of the life and beliefs of the times. These are dedicated to Sophronius, but the preface indicates that Sophronius saw to their publication after John's death at Rome and his burial in the monastery of St. Theodosius. Their circulation was widespread. There are translations in Old Slavonic and Arabic; in Latin, a partial translation of the 9th and 11th centuries; in Italian, first printed in 1475; and in the Latin of *Ambrose Traversari (1423–24), published by Lippomano in 1558 and reprinted many times.

The Greek text was first printed by Fronton du Duc (1624), more completely by Cotelier (1686). French translations appeared in 1599, in 1653 by Arnauld d'Andilly, and in 1946 by M. J. Rouët de Journel. There seems to be no English translation. It is a neglected source of social and religious history, and a critical edition is needed. Sophronius and Moschus also composed a life of *John the Almsgiver, Patriarch of Alexandria, of which only a portion has survived.

Bibliography: PG 87.3:2851–3112. PL 74:119–122. Beck KTLBR 412. H. Leclercq, DACL 7.2:2190–96. Bardenhewer 5:131–135. H. Usener, ed., *Der heiligen Tychon* (Leipzig 1907). T. Nissen, "Unbekannte Erzählungen aus dem Pratum Spirituale," ByzZ 38 (1938) 351–376. E. Mioni, OrChrPer 17 (1951) 61–94, MSS; *Studi bizantini* 8 (1953) 29–36. BHG 3:1440z–42tb. I. Abuladze, ed., *John Moschus, Pratum Spirituale* (Tiflis 1960), in Georgian. H. Gelzer, ed., *Leben des heiligen Johannes des Barmherzigen* (Leipzig 1893) 108–112. N. H. Baynes and E. A. S. Dawes, trs., *Three Byzantine Saints* (Oxford 1948) 199–206. N. H. Baynes, "The Pratum Spirituale," OrChrPer 13 (1947) 404–414, repr. in his *Byzantine Studies and Other Essays* (New York 1955) 261–270.

[P. SHERWOOD]

MOSCOW

City on the Moskva River near its junction with the Moscow Canal; 135 square miles in area with a population of 5,068,000 (1964). It is the capital of the *Union of Soviet Socialist Republics and the political, industrial, and cultural center of Russia.

Early History. Moscow, a portage on the water route linking northern Russia with *Kiev and the Black Sea,

became prominent *c*. 1150. Distance and heavy forests protected it from nomadic raids, while refugees from the more vulnerable principality of Kiev to the south added to its growth; but it was burned by *Mongols under Batu Khan (1238). Prince Daniel (d. 1303), youngest son of *Alexander Nevski, received Moscow as an appanage (*c*. 1271) and was succeeded by his son Iurii (1303–25). Under Ivan I Kalita (1325–41) Moscow became the capital of the Principality of Vladimir-Suzdal, and stockades of heavy oak arose where the Kremlin now stands. Ivan obtained from the Mongols (*c*. 1328) the title of *velikii kniaz* (grand prince), and as tax collector for them he became the wealthiest and most powerful of the Russian princes. In 1299 Metropolitan Maximus (1283–1305) abandoned Kiev for Vladimir. Metropolitans Peter (1305–26) and Theognost (1328–53) often resided in Moscow. Alexis (1354–78), who assumed the title "Metropolitan of Kiev and of all Russia," began work on the first churches in the Kremlin. Prince Dmitri Donskoi (1363–89) enlarged the Kremlin, strengthening its walls with stone, so that it withstood a Lithuanian attack (1368). Dmitri was the first Russian prince to challenge the authority of the Mongols, whom he defeated in the Battle of Kulikovo (1380); Moscow succumbed to a Mongol attack in 1381, however. The city, quickly rebuilt, then expanded beyond the Kremlin and soon challenged the older *Novgorod for leadership of the emerging Russian state. During this period St. *Sergius Radonezh (d. *c*. 1429) of Holy Trinity monastery began a spiritual renaissance much needed by the Russian people after the period of Mongol domination.

The State of Moscovy. The adherence of *Isidore of Kiev to the union of the Council of *Florence led to his deposition as metropolitan (1448); his successor, John (1448–61), changed the primatial title to "Metropolitan of Moscow." The conversion of Greeks to Rome and the fall of Constantinople (1453) led Moscow to regard itself as the sole depository of the Orthodox faith. Prince Ivan III (1462–1505), who had annexed Novgorod and other neighboring territories, married Zoë, niece of the last Byzantine Emperor (1472). Later, Abbot Philothey of Eleazar monastery in Pskov, writing to Basil III (1505–33), alluded to Moscow as "the third Rome," a theory that was to become more and more important in the ecclesiastical and political history of Russia.

At this time the Russian Church had to deal with the heresy of the Nonpossessors, a group that followed St. Nils of Sorsk (d. 1508) and held that the Church should neither possess land nor coerce its members. Metropolitan Varlaam of Moscow (1511–22), who favored the Nonpossessors and opposed Basil III's remarriage, was replaced by Daniel (1522–39), who approved the remarriage; and the heretics were defeated. At the Council of the Hundred Chapters in Moscow (1551) the episcopacy asserted the supremacy of Russian Orthodoxy, as it then existed under the protection of Czar Ivan IV the Terrible, over Greek Orthodoxy. Metropolitan Philip II (1566–69), who had criticized Ivan's ruthless building of a centralized state in north Russia, was deposed and murdered in prison. Under Ivan (d. 1584), Moscow began to trade with England, and Moscovy, the English name of the city, was applied by foreigners to all Russia.

The Patriarchate. In 1589 Patriarch Jeremias II of Constantinople, visiting in Moscow, raised Metropolitan Job (1589–1605) to the rank of patriarch, an act later

Fig. 1. Dimitri Donskoi at the Battle of Kulikovo in 1380 (a), and the death of St. Sergius (b)—colored drawings on *folios 246r and 282v of a late 16th-century manuscript "Life of St. Sergius" in the Lenin-State Library, Moscow.*

sanctioned by the four Eastern patriarchs. Job assumed the title "Patriarch of Moscow and of all Russia." Patriarch Iermogen (1606–12) offered some leadership during the Time of Troubles when Moscovy declined into anarchy. Michael Romanov, the son of Metropolitan Philaret (1619–33), who had been forced to enter a monastery by Boris Godonov in 1601, was elected czar in 1613 by the *boyars* (nobles), who had united to oust the Poles and the Polish pretender in Moscow.

The monk *Nikon, patriarch in 1652, sought to make the Greek liturgical books conform more closely with the ritual used in Constantinople and caused a schism in the Russian Church. Many clergy and faithful led by the archpriest *Avvakum refused to accept these changes and became known as *Raskolniks. Nikon contested authority with Czar Alexis (1645–76), who had supported his reforms, and was deposed by a Church council at Moscow, which excommunicated the Raskolniks, or Old Believers (1666–67).

The Holy Synod. *Peter I the Great (1682–1725), who in 1712 moved Russia's capital from Moscow to the new city of St. Petersburg (now *Leningrad), regarded Moscow as the stronghold of conservative elements in Church and State. In his attempt to Westernize Russia, Peter supported the Latinized approach of the Kiev Theological Academy and usually filled vacant sees with Ukrainians. After the death of Patriarch Adrian (1700), Peter appointed *Stefan Iavorskiĭ as guardian of the patriarchal throne, but after Steven's death (1722) he did not make a new appointment. Under the Ecclesiastical Regulations of 1721, composed by the Ukranian Bp. Feofan *Prokopovich (d. 1736), the patriarchate was abolished, and the *Holy Synod, a permanent council of clergy, replaced it as governing body of the Russian Church. The members of the Synod were nominated by and held office at the pleasure of the Czar; and a secular official, the procurator of the Synod, com-

posed its agenda and sat in on its meetings. In 1723 this reorganization of the Russian Church was recognized by the other Eastern patriarchs. *Catherine II appointed more than one freethinker as procurator and made the Synod virtually a department of her government. Catherine also confiscated the lands of monasteries, which were experiencing a revival modeled after Balkan monasticism. St. Tikhon of Zadonsk (1724–83), St. Serafim of Savor (1759–1833), and Paisy Velichkovsky (1722–94) were leaders of this revival, which had its center in the monastery of Optina Pustin south of Moscow near Tula. Metropolitan *Filaret (1821–67), a notable theologian, resisted the uniformity which the procurator, General Protasov (1836–55), was imposing on the Russian Church. John Veniaminov, a missionary bishop in *Alaska, succeeded him as metropolitan (1867–79) and founded the Orthodox Missionary Society.

Revival of the Patriarchate. In 1917, under the Russian Provisional Government, a Church council in Moscow effected a far reaching reform. In November it elected *Tikhon, Metropolitan of Moscow, to the restored patriarchate and reestablished local diocesan administration in Russian sees. The reform was shortlived. In December the Communists seized Church property and closed theological schools. In 1922 Tikhon was arrested, and other members of the hierarchy were executed or deported. After Tikhon's death (1925), the government refused to allow the election of a successor, and the Russian Church was governed by administrators appointed by Tikhon before his death. *Sergius, Metropolitan of Nizhni-Novgorod, who assumed the administration of the patriarchate in 1925, sought to regularize relations with the Soviets but only brought the Church under closer government control.

The antireligious campaign was intensified in 1929 at *Stalin's direction; but World War II forced him to

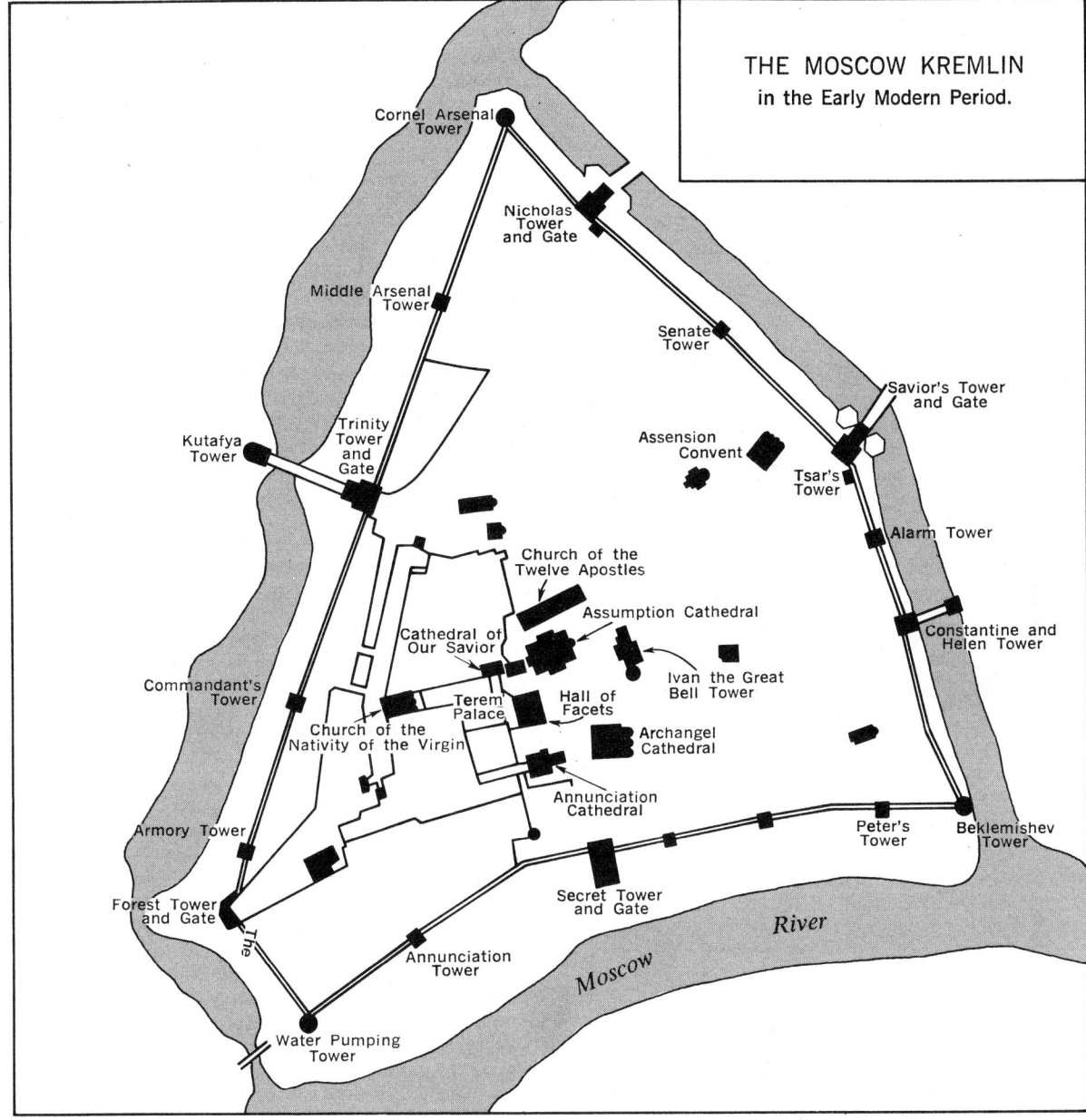

THE MOSCOW KREMLIN
in the Early Modern Period.

Cornel Arsenal Tower

Nicholas Tower and Gate

Middle Arsenal Tower

Senate Tower

Savior's Tower and Gate

Kutafya Tower

Trinity Tower and Gate

Assension Convent

Tsar's Tower

Alarm Tower

Church of the Twelve Apostles

Assumption Cathedral

Cathedral of Our Savior

Ivan the Great Bell Tower

Constantine and Helen Tower

Commandant's Tower

Terem Palace

Hall of Facets

Church of the Nativity of the Virgin

Archangel Cathedral

Annunciation Cathedral

Armory Tower

Peter's Tower

Beklemishev Tower

Forest Tower and Gate

Secret Tower and Gate

The

Annunciation Tower

Moscow   River

Water Pumping Tower

Fig. 2. Plan of the Moscow Kremlin showing the important monuments within its walls.

make concessions, and in 1943 he allowed the election of Sergius as patriarch. Sergius died in 1944, and Alexis, Metropolitan of Leningrad, became patriarch. Eight seminaries and two theological academies were reopened then. In 1965 a special department of the Soviet government was handling religious affairs.

The Roman Catholic Church in Moscow. In 1705 Peter the Great allowed Latin Catholics to build churches in Russia, but many of his successors persecuted Roman as well as Uniate Catholics, whom they suspected of having foreign political connections. For many years *Jesuits, who because of their work in education had access to intellectual circles, worked for the conversion of Russian Orthodox to Catholicism. In 1926 the French Jesuit Michael d' *Herbigny, president of the pontifical commission for Russia, reorganized the Catholic Church in Russia. But Bishop Neveu of Mos-

cow, who had left Russia in 1936, was not allowed to return as promised, and most of the Catholic clergy were arrested or deported. The Soviets sought to force members of the Uniate Church to join the Russian Orthodox Church under the patriarchate. The French church of St. Louis was served by a priest attached to the U.S. Embassy until the Russians recently insisted on his replacement by a native Russian priest (*see* MOGILEV, ARCHDIOCESE OF).

Monuments. After the Soviets restored Moscow as the capital of Russia in 1918, the city began a spectacular growth. Surrounded by modern suburbs is the old city of Moscow, dominated by the Kremlin, within which are magnificent churches, including the patriarch's cathedral of the Assumption (1326–1479). On Red Square, originally the market place, is the beautiful cathedral of St. Basil the Blessed (16th century). The

Fig. 3. The 16th-century cathedral of St. Basil the Blessed.

city also contains the University of Moscow (founded in 1755), the Tretyakov Art Gallery (from the 1880s), and other churches and palaces. Many of Moscow's older buildings were built in Italian Renaissance or baroque styles by foreign architects who worked for the czars and wealthy princes. Moscow was also a center of icon painting, and elaborate fresco cycles decorate churches and palaces.

See also ORTHODOX CHURCHES; RUSSIAN RITE.

Bibliography: W. PALMER, *The Patriarch and the Tsar*, 6 v. (London 1871–76). E. E. GOLUBINSKII, *Istoriia russkoi tserkvi*, 2 v. in 4 (Moscow 1880–1917). N. ZERNOV, *Moscow, the Third Rome* (New York 1937); *The Russian Religious Renaissance of the 20th Century* (New York 1963). A. W. ZIEGLER, *Die Union des Konzils von Florenz in der russischen Kirche* (Würzburg 1938). J. S. CURTISS, *Church and State in Russia: The Last Years of the Empire, 1900–1917* (New York 1940); *The Russian Church and the Soviet State, 1917–1950* (Boston 1953). A. M. AMMANN, *Storia della Chiesa russa e dei paesi limitrofi* (Turin 1948). S. H. CROSS, *Medieval Russian Churches* (Cambridge, Mass. 1949) 71–90. W. K. MEDLIN, *Moscow and East Rome* (Geneva 1952). G. VERNADSKY, *The Mongols and Russia* (New Haven 1953); *Russia at the Dawn of the Modern Age* (New Haven 1958). Academy of Sciences of the U.S.S.R., *Istorii Moskvy*, 6 v. (Moscow 1952–57). I. SMOLITSCH, *Russisches Mönchtum* (Würzburg 1953); *Geschichte der russisches Kirche, 1700–1917*, v.1 (Leiden 1964). G. H. HAMILTON, *The Art and Architecture of Russia* (PelHArt Z6; 1954). A. VOYCE, *The Moscow Kremlin* (Berkeley 1954); *Moscow and the Roots of Russian Culture* (Norman, Okla. 1964). H. SCHAEDER, *Moskau, das dritte Rom* (2d ed. Wiesbaden 1957). A. V. KARTASHEV, *Ocherki po istorii russkoi tserkvi*, 2 v. (Paris 1959). E. WINTER, *Russland und das Papsttum*, 2 v. (Berlin 1960). G. OLŠR, Enc Catt 8:1451–67. C. TOUMANOFF, "Moscow the Third Rome," CathHistRev 40 (1955) 411–447. **Illustration credit:** Fig. 3, Wideworld Photos.

[B. J. COMASKEY]

MOSER, JOHN, architect; b. Mannheim, Germany, 1832; d. *c.* Aug. 23, 1904. There appears to be no accurate account of his academic training or professional background; however, an obituary written by a contemporary refers to him as "a man of distinctly scholarly attainments." At the age of 16 Moser went to the U.S., and shortly after, to Canada to live for a number of years. He returned to the U.S. in 1868 to begin his architectural practice in Ohio. It is thought that Moser moved from Ohio to Anniston, Ala., in 1877 and that later he moved to Atlanta, Ga. Buildings of approximately this period attributed to him include St. Philip's Episcopal Cathedral in Atlanta and the Corn Exchange Building in Galveston, Tex.

In 1890 Moser was appointed supervising architect to the U.S. Treasury Department. While in this office Moser approved plans for a Federal building in Buffalo, N.Y. The opposition of the newly formed American Institute of Architects to the design of this project was strong and persistent and led finally to the recommendation, preparation, and enactment of the Tarnsey Bill and succeeding regulations governing the preparation and approval of designs and working documents for Federal building projects. Apparently there was no enduring personal bitterness on either side, for when the American Institute of Architects held a competition for a building project of its own, Moser submitted a design that was hailed by his colleagues of the Institute as "a very masterpiece of patient ingenuity."

Bibliography: *American Architect and Building News* 86 (Oct. 1, 1904) 1, obit. H. F. and E. R. WITHEY, *Biographical Dictionary of American Architects* (Los Angeles 1956) 430. C. MOORE, *Daniel H. Burnham, Architect, Planner of Cities,* 2 v. (New York 1921) 2:95–96, 106–110.

[P. SCHWEIKHER]

MOSER, KARL, early-20th-century Swiss architect, noted for his pioneer work in exposed reinforced concrete; b. Baden, Switzerland, 1860; d. Zurich, 1936. He studied at the Zurich College of Technology and at the École des Beaux-Arts in Paris, then taught in Zurich from 1915 to 1928. Not only did a number of modern Swiss architects receive the bases of modernism from Moser as students, but the present architectural educational system of Switzerland was derived from his efforts. Moser's architectural fame has been linked almost exclusively with his church of St. Antonius, at Basel, constructed from 1925 to 1927. There reinforced concrete was used as the structural as well as the artistic principle of design: the nave was roofed by an exposed concrete tunnel vault of rectangular rib patterning; the column supports were piers of naked concrete. When compared to A. *Perret's Le Raincy (which is of similar construction), Moser's nave appeared more factory-like and brutal. His exterior, with its freestanding bell tower, was far more successful than Perret's spire, a fact attested to by the frequent duplication of this type of tower design by later architects. Moser's St. Antonius broke new ground in the establishment of structure and form as a valid vernacular, not only in Swiss ecclesiastical architecture, but in the total development of Swiss architecture; consequently, he has been regarded as the father of modern Swiss architecture.

Bibliography: G. E. KIDDER SMITH, *Switzerland Builds* (New York 1950). A. CHRIST-JANER and M. M. FOLEY, *Modern Church Architecture* (New York 1962) 222–229. B. ZEVI, *Storia dell'*

Karl Moser, the church of St. Antonius, Basel.

architettura moderna (2d ed. Turin 1953). **Illustration credit:** Swiss National Tourist Office, New York.

[D. R. WALL]

MOSER, LUCAS, Swabian painter, apparently from Wyl (Rottweil or Weilderstadt) and documented at Ulm; fl. 1402–34. He was the first to initiate the new naturalistic style of 15th-century German painting. The only work that can definitely be assigned to this master is the St. Magdalen altarpiece at Tiefenbronn. It was made for the family Stein von Steinegg, is signed and dated 1431, and shows scenes from the life of Mary Magdalen based on the *Legenda aurea* of *James of Voragine. The style of the altarpiece, with its strong sense of three-dimensional space and volume, must have developed from the artist's knowledge of the naturalistic trends in Franco-Flemish manuscript illuminations and the early paintings of the Flemish Master of *Flémalle. The inscription that Moser painted on the frame, "Wail, O Art, wail and lament, for no one cares for thee any more," suggests that his style was so new and progressive that his contemporaries found it difficult to accept.

Bibliography: J. VON WALDBURG-WOLFEGG, *Lukas Moser* (Berlin 1939). A. STANGE, *German Painting, XIV–XVI Centuries,* ed. A. GLOECKNER (New York 1951) 12, 24. W. BOECK, *Der Tiefenbronner Altar von Lucas Moser* (Munich 1951). **Illustration credit:** German Information Center.

[E. W. HOFFMAN]

MOSES

Leader of the Israelites in their *Exodus from Egypt and their mediator in their *covenant with Yahweh at Mt. Sinai. Little is known with historical exactitude about this key figure in the history of Israel through whose efforts the motley Hebrews became a tribal confederacy and, ultimately, a monarchy. Although his existence is no longer denied by scholars, arriving at the historical substance of Moses has been made complex by authors and editors of the *Pentateuch. Factual details have long been obscured in the oral and written traditions of the cult epic celebrating the historical deeds of Yahweh.

Life. The name Moses (Heb. *mōšeh*) is of Egyptian origin (*mes, mesu,* born), perhaps originally connected with the name of an Egyptian god (as in the names Thutmose, Ahmose, etc.) that was later omitted under the influence of Israelite monotheism. A popular Hebrew etymology is offered in Ex 2.10 connecting *mōšeh* with *māšâ* [to draw forth (out of water)]. Moses was born apparently at the beginning of the 13th century B.C., the son (Ex 2.1–4; 7.7; Nm 26.59) of Hebrew parents Amram and Jochabed (Ex 6.20), with an older sister *Mariam (Miriam) and a younger (?) brother *Aaron. The account of his birth parallels the legendary story of King Sargon I of Akkad, who, deposited in a basket boat and rescued, achieved great prominence. As a ward of the Pharao's daughter, Moses doubtless pursued the academic program of an Egyptian scribe (cf. Acts 7.22). The Biblical narrative, a composite of oral and perhaps even written traditions, portrays Moses as fleeing to Madian (see MADIANITES) after killing an Egyptian in defense of a countryman (Ex 2.11–15). There he again exercised his role of champion in the cause of the seven daughters of the Cinite (Kenite) *Jethro, a Madian priest, in whose household he then resided (2.16–21). Moses married Sepphora, a daughter of Jethro, who bore him two children, Gersam (2.22)

Lucas Moser, "St. Mary Magdalen Altar," in the church at Tiefenbronn, Germany, signed and dated 1431.

"Moses Exposed on the Nile," etching by Marc Chagall (1887–   ) for a two-volume edition of the Bible, published by Tériade, Paris, 1956.

and Eliezer (18.4). On Mt. *Sinai (Horeb) Moses the shepherd experienced a theophany in the event of the *burning bush. Commissioning Moses to deliver the Hebrews from Egypt, Yahweh entrusted him with the credentials of the revelation of His identity as Yahweh, the God of Abraham, Isaac, and Jacob (3.6), together with the power to perform miraculous signs (4.1–9). In a scene somewhat inconsistent with his personality and education, Moses pleaded his ineptness for the task. Yahweh assigned a coadjutor role to Aaron (4.14–16). Before Pharao, Moses and Aaron presented in vain the case for the Hebrews, so that Yahweh punished Pharao with the 10 *plagues of Egypt (7.14–12.30). Finally Moses led the Hebrews from Egypt after the ceremonial of a *Passover meal. The journey to freedom became a flight from captors as Pharao's army attempted to recover his laborers. Moses was forced to lead the people through the only avenue of escape, the *Red Sea, into the desert. Arriving at Mt. Sinai, the people through Moses entered formally into the covenant relationship with Yahweh (Exodus ch. 19 and 24; Deuteronomy ch. 5), the terms of which are codified in the Decalogue (Ex 20.1–17; Dt 5.6–21) and the *Book of the Covenant (Exodus ch. 21–23). At Cades Moses guided the Israelite tribes through the difficult period of development. His mission accomplished, he died at Mt. Nebo without entering the promised land of Canaan (Numbers ch. 20).

Though the name of Moses has always been connected with the Pentateuch, his personal contribution to Israel was long overlooked. Outside the Pentateuch the oldest references to the Exodus make no mention of Moses. Reference is seldom made to him among the Prophets. Perhaps this is due to the Israelite mentality of eliminating instrumental causes and attributing events to

the direct intervention of Yahweh. The picture that Israelite tradition created is reflected in his subordinate characterization by later authors as the servant of God [4 Kgs 21.8; Ps 104(105).26; Mal 3.22; Bar 2.28], God's chosen one [Ps 105(106).23], priest [Ps 98(99). 6], prophet (Os 23.13; Wis 11.1), and man of God (1 Chr 23.14). In the NT, where he is the most frequently mentioned OT personality, he appears primarily as the lawgiver (Mt 8.4; Mk 7.10; Jn 1.17) who communicates God's law to man. For this reason Jesus met opposition in attempting to bring the law of Moses to final realization. As Moses proclaimed the Old Law from Mt. Sinai, the Gospel writers similarly situated Jesus on a mountain for the revelation of the New Law (*see* SERMON ON THE MOUNT). The typological prefigurement of Jesus by Moses in the Exodus events is solidly founded. Jesus used him to witness His approaching suffering and death (Mt 17.1–8; Mk 9.1–8; Lk 9.28–36). Moses is a model of faith for all Christians (Heb 11.23–29).

Iconography. Although Moses is portrayed as the father type in the Sistine Chapel, elsewhere he is more often represented in the role of savior and legislator. The striking of the rock and the revelation of the Law were the two predominant scenes until the 5th century, when other themes were introduced. The Christian community forged detailed comparisons between the activities of Moses and those of Jesus, some founded in Scripture, others in the creative imagination: e.g., between the burning bush and the virginal birth of Jesus, between the crossing of the Red Sea and Baptism (1 Cor 10.1–2), between the brazen serpent and the Crucified (Jn 3.14–15), between the manna and the Eucharist (1 Cor 10.3–4), between the striking of the rock and the piercing of the side of Christ. As a result of a misunderstanding of Ex 34.29–35 Moses was often portrayed with two horns (instead of rays) on his forehead (cf. 2 Cor 3.7). (See illustrations on facing page.)

Bibliography: H. CAZELLES, DBSuppl 5:1308–37. J. SCHREINER et al., LexThK[2] 7:648–654. E. OSSWALD, RGG[3] 4:1151–55. G. RINALDI and E. JOSI, EncCatt 8:1469–77. EncDictBibl 1558–60. R. F. JOHNSON, InterDictBibl 3:440–450. M. BUBER, *Moses, the Revelation and the Covenant* (Oxford 1946; Torchbooks, New York 1958). **Illustration credits:** Fig. 1, Mr. and Mrs. Ross W. Sloniker Collection of Twentieth Century Biblical and Religious Prints, The Cincinnati Art Museum. Fig. 2a, Dura-Europos Publications, Yale University. Fig. 2b, Anderson-Art Reference Bureau. Fig. 2c, National Gallery of Art, Washington, D.C., Samuel H. Kress Collection. Fig. 2d, Gift of Dr. Leon Kolb to Mr. and Mrs. Ross W. Sloniker Collection of Twentieth Century Biblical and Religious Prints, The Cincinnati Art Museum.

[E. ROESSLER]

MOSES THE BLACK, ST., monk; b. *c.* 330; d. *c.* 405 (feast, Aug. 28). Ethiopian by race, Moses was one of the most picturesque of the *desert fathers. First a servant or slave of an Egyptian official, he was dismissed for his immoral conduct and continual thefts, and he took to brigandage and soon gathered a gang that terrorized the district. His strength and ferocity became legendary. The details of his conversion are not known. It is thought that he took refuge from the law with some monks and was overwhelmed by their example, for he next appears at the monastery of Petra in the Desert of Scete. He found it hard to control his violence, but he was encouraged by St. Isidore, the abbot. Finally, through physical labor, mortification, and prayer, he succeeded in overcoming himself.

Moses: (a) At the edge of the Red Sea, detail of a 3d-century fresco from the synagogue at Dura-Europos, now in the National Museum at Damascus. (b) Removing his sandals before the burning bush, detail of the 6th-century mosaic on the arch of the apse of S. Vitale at Ravenna.

(c) Directing the gathering of manna, detail of a painting by the 16th-century Florentine artist Bacchiacca. From his head rise two "horns" composed of rays of light. (d) With the tablets of the Law, woodcut, 1955, by the Israeli artist Jacob Steinhardt.

*Theophilus of Alexandria heard of his virtue and ordained him a priest. When the Berbers threatened his monastery, he remained with seven companions; all but one perished. He was buried at the monastery of Dair al-Baramus, which still stands.

Bibliography: Butler Th Attw 3:435–436. ActSS Aug. 6:199–212.

[E. D. CARTER]

MOSES, CANTICLE OF

A didactic psalm that interprets the theological significance of Israel's past infidelities in the light of Yahweh's justice and mercy; attributed to Moses, it was inserted into the book of Deuteronomy (31.30–32.43) by a late redactor. This article treats the song's theme, date, and poetic genre.

Theme. The Song of Moses (Dt 32.1–43) recounts in historical retrospect Israel's infidelity to Yahweh and looks forward hopefully to His imminent, decisive intervention in the nation's life that will justify and glorify His people. Israel, prosperous in the land Yahweh has provided, has been repeatedly unfaithful to Him (32.5–6, 15–18). Forgetful of Yahweh's providential concern, Israel has forsaken Him, the nation's rock, to fear and to sacrifice to new gods, who, indeed, are "no-gods"; such gods (*šēdîm*, demons) their fathers neither knew nor feared (Dt 32.17). For this apostasy Yahweh shall punish the nation through the agency of a foreign people, notwithstanding that the latter is foolish and senseless (32.21, 27–34). Israel will suffer terror, hunger, pestilence, and destruction, presumably in the wake of an invasion. After the disciplinary punishment, Yahweh, as the avenger of His people, will again turn with compassion to Israel, whom He has definitively chosen as His inheritance among the nations of the world (32.36–43).

Date. The date of this song depends on whom one identifies as Israel's enemy, "the no-people" (Dt 32.21), whom Yahweh uses as an instrument to discipline the nation of His inheritance. O. Eissfeldt (271) believes that the exegetes since mid-19th century have been ascribing to the song too late a date, and he himself, seeing the Philistines as the "no-people," places the song in the middle of the 11th century. On the other hand, R. H. Pfeiffer (280), impressed with the wisdom terminology in the song, places its composition in the first half of the 5th century; hence, for him the "no-people" are necessarily the Babylonians whose punishment has already occurred. Others would identify Israel's enemy as the Aramaeans or Assyrians, thus giving the song a 9th- or 8th-century date. The reflective monotheism of the song (32.39), its wisdom words (32.1, 2, 6, 21, 28–29), and intense nationalistic sentiments (32.9, 19, 36–43) suggest a late date, at least a final redaction no earlier than the 6th century.

Poetic Genre. The poet looks back in historical retrospect to the nation's past much in the manner of the Psalmist in Psalms 78(79), 104(105), and 105(106). The song is didactic, aiming to teach wisdom from national history. Appearing in it are a number of wisdom words: *'imrê pî*, "words of my mouth" (32.1), *leqaḥ*, "instruction" (32.2), *nābāl*, "fool" (32.6, 21; cf. 32.15), *ḥākām*, "wise" (32.6; cf. 32.29), *tᵉbûnâ*, "understanding" (32.28), *hiśkîl*, "to have insight" (32.29), and *hēbîn*, "to understand" (32.29). The song is also prophetic in the sense that its language is that of the canonical Prophets bespeaking an unconquerable faith in Yahweh's justice and mercy. The poet employs striking images; the parallelism is regular and vigorous; and the theme is well illustrated and developed.

Bibliography: InterBibl 2:516–526. S. R. DRIVER, *An Introduction to the Literature of the Old Testament* (11th ed. New York 1905) 95–97; *Deuteronomy* (ICC; New York 1906) 344–382. A. J. LEVY, *The Song of Moses (Deuteronomy 32)* (Baltimore 1931). P. W. SKEHAN, "The Structure of the Song of Moses in Deuteronomy 32:1–43," CathBiblQuart 13 (1951) 153–163; "A Fragment of the *Song of Moses* (Deut. 32) from Qumran," BullAmSchOrRes 136 (1954) 12–15. O. EISSFELDT, *Einleitung in das Alte Testament* (3d ed. Tübingen 1964) E. BAUMANN, "Das Lied Moses (Dt. 32.1–43) auf seine gedankliche Geschlossenheit untersucht," VetTest 6 (1956) 414–424.

[B. VEROSTKO]

MOSES' ORACLES

A collection of eulogistic sayings in Dt 33.6–25 alluding to distinctive features of the individual tribes. They are enclosed by an added framework (33.2–5, 26–29) and inserted in Deuteronomy as Moses' last blessing.

The blessings of Juda, Levi, and Joseph are the most noteworthy. Juda is represented as isolated from the other tribes, weak, and in need of assistance (33.7). In contrast, Joseph (the Northern Kingdom) is strong, a prince among brethren, who has defeated the foreign enemies of Israel with his traditional military prowess; correspondingly, there is a full and elaborate blessing for him (33.13–17). The tribe of Levi is praised for fidelity at the waters of Meriba and extolled as the sacerdotal and teaching tribe; a curse is pronounced against those who hate Levi (33.8–11). The oracles have open praise or implicit good wishes for all the tribes except Simeon, of which there is no mention at all.

In relation to *Jacob's Oracles (Gn 49.1–27), the oracles of Moses are regarded by most exegetes as dependent on them, a later composition of northern provenance. In Jacob's Oracles the tribe of Simeon is mentioned, but in the oracles of Moses it is passed over in silence, probably because it had already been assimilated into the tribe of Juda. In Jacob's Oracles Levi is not blessed but rather cursed for deceitful violence against the Sichemites (Gn 49.5–7); in Deuteronomy the situation is changed: Levi, now the sacerdotal tribe, receives a blessing, which in its munificence, is equaled only by that of Joseph. It is commonly held that the oracle on Joseph describes the prevailing historical conditions of the Northern Kingdom at the time this oracle received its final form: the Northern Kingdom is flourishing, has successfully repelled a foreign invader, and is under the leadership of a Joseph tribe. Since most of the oracles, especially those of Juda and Joseph, correspond well with the conditions under *Jeroboam II of Israel (786–746 B.C.), their decisive redaction is best attributed to that time, and their exuberant praise of Joseph indicates a northern provenance.

The exordium (Dt 33.2–5) and conclusion (33.26–29) form an added framework to the blessings. In fundamental agreement with the preoccupations of the author of Deuteronomy, it links the blessings to the Sinaitic revelation and expresses a strong feeling of national solidarity; however, there is evidence that the framework is not from the *Deuteronomist's hand, since Horeb, not Sinai, is his usual name for the mountain of the Law.

As poetry, the blessings, with the exception of those of Joseph and Levi, show an archaic, lapidary style. In common with Jacob's Oracles, they are presented as a prophetic last testament to the tribes. More religious in tone than those of Genesis, they show less punning on words; without castigation or curses for any tribe, they uniformly bless.

Bibliography: EncDictBibl 1561–62. InterBibl 2:527–534. S. R. Driver, *Deuteronomy* (ICC; New York 1906) 385–417. R. H. Pfeiffer, *Introduction to the O.T.* (rev. ed. New York 1948) 278–279, 281. T. H. Gaster, "An Ancient Eulogy on Israel: Deuteronomy 33.3–5, 26–29," JBiblLit 66 (1947) 53–62. F. M. Cross, Jr. and D. N. Freedman, "The Blessing of Moses," *ibid.* 67 (1948) 191–210. O. Eissfeldt, *Einleitung in das A.T.* (3d ed. Tübingen 1964) 272–274.

[B. VEROSTKO]

MOSHEIM, JOHANN LORENZ VON,

Protestant church historian; b. Lübeck, Germany, Oct. 9, 1694; d. Göttingen, Germany, Sept. 9, 1755. Mosheim had his first experience as a teacher in the faculty of philosophy in Kiel and was professor of theology in Helmstedt from 1723. As the most influential personality in the Lutheran Church and the educational system in Brunswick, he was a decisive influence in determining the internal organization of the University of Göttingen, where he was professor and chancellor from 1747. Mosheim was a pioneer of modern church historiography, a science no longer committed to theological controversy. In theology he appears to have mediated between *Lutheran orthodoxy, *pietism, and the *Enlightenment. For Mosheim the church was not a part of the kingdom of God, but rather a purely earthbound society whose history he therefore treated not as a theological but as a secular problem. This departure from any exclusively denominational viewpoint and his striving after a strictly objective presentation of the facts, a practice hitherto unknown in ecclesiastical *historiography, combined to make him the first to succeed in overcoming the bitterly apologetic attitude of the *Centuriators of Magdeburg. Mosheim's often revised principal work, *Institutiones historiae ecclesiasticae* (Helmstedt 1755), was from the beginning geared to the practical requirements of a textbook, and its scholarly worth is limited to that of a simple inventory of facts. His *Heilige Reden* (6 v. Hamburg 1713–46) was a model for Protestant homiletics.

Bibliography: Editions. *Institutiones historiae ecclesiasticae* (Helmstedt 1755); Ger. tr. and continuation by J. von Einem, 9 v. (Leipzig 1769–78), and J. R. Schlegel and J. J. Fraas, 7 v. (Heilbronn 1770–96); further eds. in Eng., Fr., and Dutch; *Versuch einer unparteiischen und gründlichen Ketzergeschichte* (Helmstedt 1746). Literature. K. Heussi, *J. L. Mosheim* (Tübingen 1906). M. Peters, *Der Bahnbrecher der modernen Predigt J. L. Mosheim* (Leipzig 1910). J. Cohrs, "J. L. Mosheim, Institutiones historiae ecclesiasticae von 1726," in *Zeitschrift der Gesellschaft für niedersächsische Kirchengeschichte* 32 (1927) 1–49. G. N. Bonwetsch, Herzog-Hauck PRE 13:502–506. P. Meinhold, LexThK² 7:656–657. A. Wagenmann, ADB 22:395–399. M. Schmidt, RGG³ 4:1157–58.

[H. RUMPLER]

MOSLEM CONFRATERNITIES

Islamic organizations that have some similarities with religious orders in Christianity. Since the 12th century more than 30 such Moslem confraternities, often with widespread influence, have risen and fallen in *Islam, from the Qādiri fraternal order, named after a Persian mystic, 'Abd-al-Qādir al-Jīlāni, who died in Baghdad in 1166, to the Sanūsi order, founded in 1837 by an Algerian warrior shaykh, al-Sanūsi. Members of these confraternities are commonly known as *dervishes. Normally an applicant or novice (*murīd*) enters upon an initial stage (*'ahd,* covenant), passes through a course of instruction and discipline (*tarīqah,* path), and is then advanced into various stations (*maqāmāt*) of the spiritual life.

Practices and Beliefs. In these the fraternal orders differ widely. The members of an early and still popular one, al-Rifā'i, named after an Iraqi mystic Aḥmad al-Rifā'i (d. 1183), are commonly known as howling dervishes. They are distinguished by ability to perform strange feats, such as swallowing live coals and glass, holding red-hot irons, or passing knives through their bodies. Another fraternal order, al-Mawlawi, founded by a Persian, *Jalāl al-Dīn al-Rūmi (d. 1273 in Qūniyah, Konieh), is commonly known as the whirling dervishes, because of the movements they practice to stimulate ecstasy. Their ritual includes music—frowned on by Islam—and monotonous chants, with a slow whirling circular movement while the arms are extended and eyes closed. The dance ends in the fall of one after the other of the exhausted participants.

All orders join in a common ritual, *dhikr* ("remembering," mentioning God's name, Koran 33.41), which constitutes the main devotional exercise in the fraternities' quarters. The worshipers sit on the floor with legs folded in the Oriental pattern, turn their faces toward Mecca, close their eyes, and repeat the word Allah or such formulas as *lā ilāha illa Hū* (no God but He), while moving their heads from right to left. The *dhikr* is the only elaborate ritual in Islam and betrays Eastern Christian litanies as a source.

The dervish orders' quarters (*takīyah, zāwiyah*) are often called monasteries but in their social and educational functions they correspond more nearly to Protestant places of worship. In fact the corporate bodies behind them may be said to have assumed the position of the separate church organizations in Protestant Christendom. In addition to the few regular members, cloistered or wandering, the orders have numerous laymen attached to them. These continue to live in the world, observe daily prayers, and occasionally attend the *dhikr* ceremony. They are comparable to Franciscan and Dominican tertiaries. In pre-Kemalist Turkey most men had some such affiliation with one order or another. The most popular and influential of these was the Bektāshi, dating from the early 16th century and once connected with the redoubtable Janissaries. Bektāshis share excessive *Shiïte (Shī'ite) reverence for *Ali ('Alī ibn Abī Tālib) and manifest Christian theological influence. A Bektāshi branch, termed Qalandari, enjoins a life of unceasing wandering. Another dervish order called Khalwīyah (seclusion practitioners) requires of all members a stated period of retreat, with fasting to the utmost capacity of the individual and continuous repetition of religious formulas.

Position within Islam. It is clear from the above that dervish fraternities have developed practices in violation of the spirit and letter of Islam. A tradition ascribes to Mohammed the saying, "No *rahbānīyah* (monasticism) in Islam." Ṣūfī orders, as a rule, exalt their respective founders and surround them with halos of sanctity. (*See* sufism.) Miracles (*karāmāt*) are often ascribed even to the successive superiors. This power was denied Mohammed himself in the Koran. Despite orthodox Islam's disapproval, orders have always flourished. They seemed to fill the gap between the finite worshiper and the infinite worshiped. The great theologian *Algazel (Ghazzālī, al-, d. 1111), who himself practiced for a time Sufian wandering in quest of spiritual satisfaction, contributed to making mysticism palatable. But those extremists who ended in pantheism or antinomianism were accorded no toleration. A Persian mystic, al-Hallāj, who went so far as to declare, "I am the Truth," was in 922 flogged, exposed on a gibbet, decapitated, and burned by an 'Abbāsid inquisition. To the Sufis al-Hallāj became the first great martyr.

Besides introducing a form of monasticism and a ritual, dervish orders have contributed and popularized the cult of saints. Their sainthood did not preclude women. Female hagiology is headed by Rābi'ah al-'Adawīyah (d. 801) of Basra, who lived a life of celibacy, asceticism, and otherworldliness, instructing and guiding disciples in the "mystic way." When the Prophet appeared in a dream and asked her whether she loved him, her reply was: "My love of God has so possessed me that no place remains for hating ought or loving any save Him." Dervishes were evidently also responsible for introducing, or at least diffusing, the rosary beads (subḥah) as an instrument of Moslem devotion. They borrowed them from Eastern Christians, who had received them from Hindu sources. Only the puritanical Wahhābis today reject the beads, as they do the cult of saints.

A fundamental difference between Sufi and Christian monastic organizations stems from the fact that Islam, according to the learned system, is a lay religion, with no centralized authority, no hierarchy, no sacraments, no apostolic succession. This fact accounts for the self-development of the dervish orders, each in its own way, ending in a state bordering on chaos. It makes of the ulema, especially among the Sunnites, nothing but men learned in theology and canon law.

Bibliography: R. A. NICHOLSON, *Studies in Islamic Mysticism* (Cambridge, Eng. 1921). M. SMITH, comp., *Readings from the Mystics of Islām* (London 1950). D. B. MACDONALD, *Development of Muslim Theology, Jurisprudence and Constitutional Theory* (New York 1903). H. LAMMENS, *Islām: Beliefs and Institutions,* tr. E. D. Ross (London 1929), ch. 6. C. H. A. FIELD, *Mystics and Saints of Islam* (London 1910). A. J. ARBERRY, *Sufism: An Account of the Mystics of Islam* (New York 1952).
[P. K. HITTI]

MOSQUE

Moslem place of worship. The Arabic word *masǧid* (pl. *masāǧid*), literally, a place of worship, is derived from the verb *saǧada,* to prostrate one's self; the term is to be compared with Nabataean *msgd',* a votive *stele, and with Ethiopic *mesgad,* a church or temple. In Islam the mosque is also called *muṣallā,* a place where one prays (*ṣallā*) and more commonly, *ǧami'* (pl. *ǧawāmi'*), a gathering place.

Plan of the Mosque. The normal mosque consists fundamentally of a large open, quadrangular court (*ṣaḥn*) surrounded by a colonnaded portico (*muǧaṭṭā*) supported by several (often many) rows of columns, the passages between which are called *riwāq* (pl. *'arwiqa*). In the center of the court stands a large basin (*mīḍa'a*) with a fountain for making ablutions (*wuḍū'*). The covered hall on the side facing Mecca is generally much deeper, and in the wall on this side is a large ornamented niche called the *miḥrāb,* which indicates the *qibla* or direction in which one is oriented during prayer; in front of this the *imām stands while leading the prayer. In larger mosques there may be several *miḥrābs* used by different

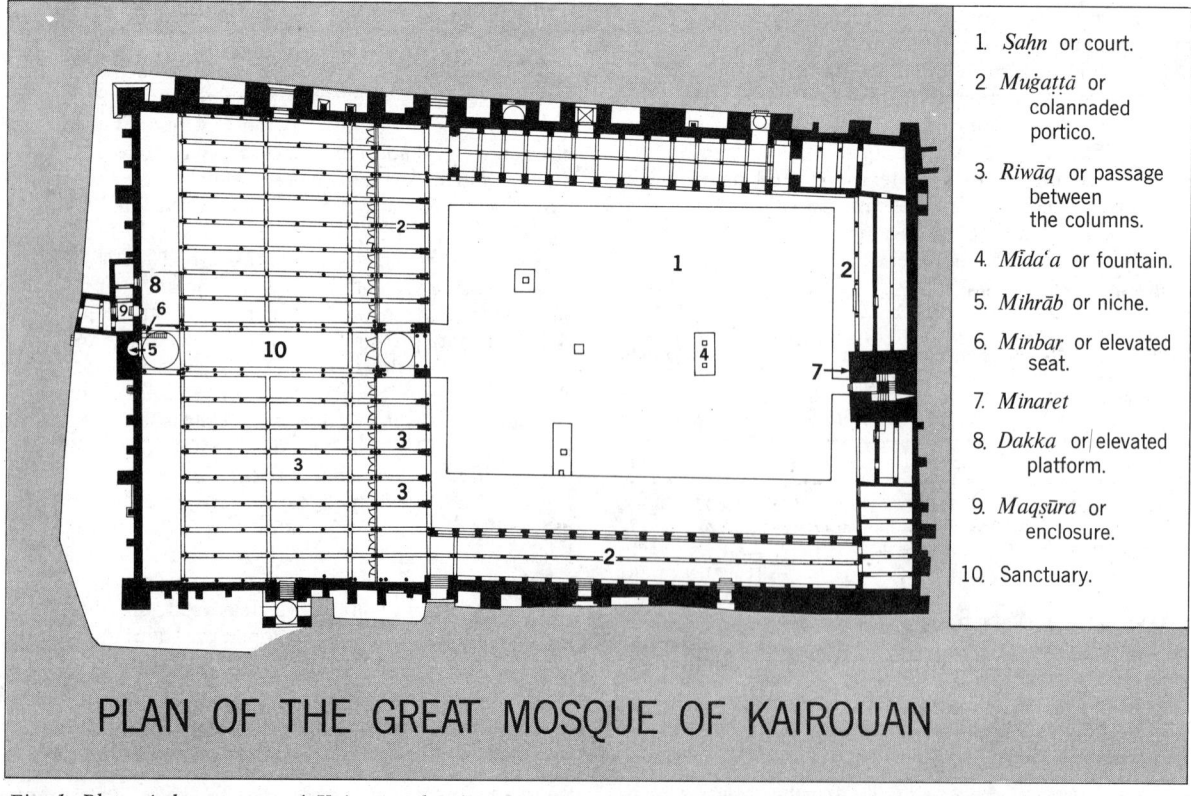

1. *Ṣaḥn* or court.

2. *Muǧaṭṭā* or colannaded portico.

3. *Riwāq* or passage between the columns.

4. *Mīḍa'a* or fountain.

5. *Miḥrāb* or niche.

6. *Minbar* or elevated seat.

7. *Minaret*

8. *Dakka* or elevated platform.

9. *Maqṣūra* or enclosure.

10. Sanctuary.

PLAN OF THE GREAT MOSQUE OF KAIROUAN

Fig. 1. Plan of the mosque of Kairouan showing the features typical of Moslem religious architecture.

"rites" (*madāhib; see* LAW, ISLAMIC). Near the *miḥrāb* stands the *minbar,* an elevated seat from which the Friday sermon (*khuṭba*) is preached; this was originally a kind of throne from which the ruler or governor might address the people and was therefore reserved, in the earliest period, for only the chief mosques. Attached to the outside wall of the building, often on the corners, stands one or more towers or minarets (*manāra, ma'dana, mi'dana*), from which the call to prayer is first sounded by the muezzin (Arabic, *mu'addin*), within some larger mosques there is also a raised platform (*dakka*), near the *minbar.* From here he repeats the call at two specified points during the Friday service. There is also a seat (*kursī*) with a desk for the recitation of the *Koran by the *qāri'* (or *qāṣṣ*). Within the *riwāq* along the *qibla* side there is in some principal mosques an enclosure (*maqṣūra*) near the *miḥrāb,* reserved for the ruler, where he may pray free from any danger of attack. In larger mosques there are a number of apartments (called also *riwāq,* or *zāwiya*), built within the extended *riwāq* or in subsidiary buildings, set aside for various purposes. These serve for study and teaching, or as living quarters for Koran readers and other personnel of the mosque, or frequently for students and those making a retreat (*i'tikāf*), whether simply during the last 10 days of *Ramadan or on a more or less permanent basis.

Early Mosques. The most important shrine in Islam is the Holy Mosque (*al-masǧid al-ḥarām*) of *Mecca that contains in its enclosure the Ka'ba, a rectangular building 40 feet by 35 feet and some 50 feet high, oriented at its corners toward the cardinal points of the compass and containing in its eastern corner the Black Stone, which has been an object of particular cult from ancient times. Around the Ka'ba is a payed area (*maṭāf*) where the *ṭawāf* (*see* HAJJ) is made. The Ka'ba was destroyed during a siege in 64/684 (i.e., A.H. 64 = A.D. 684), at which time it was already a reconstructed edifice, dating from 608, of alternating courses of stone and wood; the replacement, entirely of stone, was built by 'Abdallāh ibn al-Zubayr.

The earliest mosques of Islam were little more than open quadrangles. The house of the Prophet in Medina, where his followers gathered for prayer, consisted of an open court surrounded by mud-brick walls; against the north wall was a roofed portico (*ẓulla*) supported by palm stems; along the east wall there were built, over a period of time, nine little huts for Mohammed's wives. Where preexisting buildings were not simply taken over, as was the case in Damascus, Homs, and elsewhere, the first mosques were no more than quadrangles marked off next to the governor's or commander's residence (*dār al-'imāra*) to which walls were later added, as in Basra (founded 14/635) and Kūfa (founded 17/638). In Fusṭāṭ, the original mosque was built (21/642) by 'Amr ibn al-'Āṣ as a simple walled quadrangle with some kind of roof, possibly a *ẓulla*. (On the development of the mosque, *see* ISLAMIC ART.)

The Mosque and Worship. The mosque was, at the beginning, the center of all aspects of the community life of Islam; thus the first mosques of Medina, Basra, Kūfa, Damascus, and Fusṭāṭ were built immediately adjacent to the *dār al-'imāra* and the *dīwān* or government offices. The caliph or provincial governor received his investiture in the mosque and there acted as imām and *khaṭīb,* his *khuṭba,* or discourse, often consisting in

Fig. 2. Islamic Center Mosque, Washington, D.C. Twenty-one Moslem countries finance and sponsor the mosque, which was dedicated by Dwight D. Eisenhower in 1957.

orders for battle, etc., while the faithful were exhorted by the preaching of the *qāṣṣ* (pl. *quṣṣāṣ*). Outside the capital prayers were recited in the mosque for the Caliph or ruler as a kind of oath of loyalty; often it was in the mosque that revolutions were begun, the first open sign thereof being the substitution of another name for that of the ruler. Although it was from the outset a place in which people gathered for many purposes, the mosque rapidly took on the character of a sanctuary and came to be called, as in the most ancient Semitic usage regarding sacred shrines, the House of God (*bayt Allāh*), a name originally applied in Islam only to the Ka'ba. A particular holiness was, of course, attached to the Mosque of Medina, where the Prophet was buried; also to that of Qubā, just outside Medina, where he stopped and prayed immediately before entering the city in September 622 (*see* HEGIRA). Prayer in the mosque and the recitation there of the Koran, especially in the mosque of Medina or those associated with some renowned saint, is considered particularly meritorious. A special holiness too is associated by some with the *miḥrāb* and the *minbar,* and visitors or pilgrims will often touch them hoping to receive a blessing (*baraka*).

The Friday or cathedral mosque (*al-masǧid al-ǧāmi'*) is specifically designated within a community for the common Friday service that every male Moslem who has reached the age of reason is obliged to attend. Originally it was a community function in which the ruler led the prayer and preached the *khuṭba;* for this reason the number of cathedral mosques (early called *ḏāt manābir,* i.e., having a *minbar*) was restricted. According to some authorities there should be no more than one in a particular town; in fact, according to others there should be no cathedral mosque save in the chief

Fig. 3. Mosque of Sultan Quayt Bey, Cairo, c. 1474.

cities. With the great increase in the number of Moslems, however, and the universal need that was felt for the weekly community service, there came to be Friday mosques even in the villages; the larger centers may have several, often of considerable size. From the beginning there were many mosques besides the cathedral mosques. Numerous local and tribal mosques formed the center of both the religious and political activities of particular groups.

Again, following the ancient Arabian custom of honoring the graves of ancestors and important chiefs and the Christian veneration of the saints, a great number of mosques were built as sanctuaries over the tombs of various saints and heroes of Islam, distinguished for their piety, learning, etc., even though the association of a place of prayer with a tomb was frowned upon by many authorities. Numerous mosques were built in *Hejaz in association with events in the life of the Prophet; there and elsewhere other mosques arose in particular commemoration of *Ali ('Alī) and his descendants. The site of the temple of Solomon in Jerusalem, where the Dome of the Rock now stands, is linked both by Moslem tradition and by the name given its cathedral mosque, *al-Masǧid al-'Aqṣā* (the Furthermost Mosque), with a reference in the Koran and with the life of Mohammed.

While originally the building of mosques and their maintenance were taken as responsibilities of the government, later many were built and endowed by private individuals as pious works. As a result, the number of mosques reported to have existed at certain times in var-

ious major cities, even allowing for considerable exaggeration on the part of the sources, is truly astounding.

The Mosque and Education. Teaching in Islam has always been associated with the mosque, as the primary sciences (*'ulūm*) of Islam are concerned with the Koran, the *ḥadîth* [*see* ISLAMIC TRADITIONS (HADITH)] and the law (*fiqh, see* LAW, ISLAMIC). From early times mention is made of the *maǧlis* or *ḥalqa* (circle) of those who came to hear and receive the instruction of learned men and ascetics who taught and preached there. Teaching was done in all the important mosques, several of which had extensive libraries, and in many of the smaller ones, so that finally the term *ǧāmi'* became the equivalent of *madrasa* (school) and *riwāq* came to mean a student's living quarters. The 'Azhar Mosque was built in Cairo in 361/972, and in 378/988 the Fatimid Caliph, al-'Azīz, endowed 35 chairs of learning; the lecturers not only received ample salaries, but also were housed in rooms adjacent to the mosque. Scholars were attached likewise to the mosques of 'Amr and Ibn Ṭûlûn, also in Cairo, and to most of the important mosques throughout Islam. In many of these, stipends (some quite high) were available for students who were given lodging in or near the mosque.

Bibliography: J. PEDERSEN, EncIslam¹ 3:362–428. For further bibliog., *see* ISLAMIC ART. **Illustration credit:** Fig. 3, Lehnert and Landroch, Cairo.

[R. M. FRANK]

MOSQUERA, MANUEL JOSÉ, archbishop of Bogotá, staunch opponent of regalism; b. Popayán, 1800; d. Marseilles, France, 1853. He was a member of a distinguished family. He studied in Popayán and Quito. After being ordained, he held several posts in Popayán: rector of the University of Cauca, canon, and vicar-general. Selected archbishop of Bogotá by the congress of 1834, his selection was confirmed by the Pope, and he took over his see in 1835. From the start, he worked for the sanctification of his clergy. To this end he reorganized the seminary and made it a model for others in Spanish America; he organized the Spiritual Exercises for the priests and issued important decrees on ecclesiastical discipline. He visited all of his extensive diocese and endeavored to provide for the Christian education of youth. For this purpose he opened a secondary school run by the Jesuits; he adapted the catechism to the needs of the people of his diocese; and he helped to establish elementary schools. Mosquera tried to support the legitimate government in times of revolution, and this made many enemies for him. Since the government considered itself the heir of the Spanish crown in the exercise of patronage, the congress of 1851 passed a series of laws on religious matters that amounted to serious interference in the discipline of the Church. The archbishop of Bogotá addressed respectful but forceful messages to the congress and to the president requesting the repeal of these laws, stating that in good conscience he could not comply with them, and he asked his suffragans to work to the same end. The congress of 1852 took him to court for disobeying the laws and inciting others to do so, and he was condemned to exile and deprived of his salary. Pope Pius IX on several occasions formally approved the archbishop's conduct. Mosquera traveled to the U.S., where he was given a warm demonstration by the Catholics of New

York. He continued to France and was en route to Rome to see the Pope when he died.

Bibliography: M. M. DE MOSQUERA, *Documentos para la biografía e historia del espicopado del . . . Manuel José Mosquera,* 3 v. (Paris 1858).

[J. RESTREPO POSADA]

MOSUL, ARCHDIOCESE OF (MAUSILIENSIS),

archbishopric of the *Syrian rite without suffragans; in north *Iraq. In 1963 it had 11 parishes, 27 secular priests, 3 religious women in one convent, 713 pupils in 5 schools, and 13,000 Catholics in a population of 1,709,000; it is 29,730 square miles in area. Mosul is also the seat of a diocese of the *Chaldean rite, 2,471 square miles in area, which had 6 parishes, 14 secular and 2 religious priests, 4 men in one religious house, 24 women in one convent, 5,076 pupils in 14 schools, and 15,163 Catholics in a population of 300,000. Since the 7th century Mosul has been a metropolitanate for *Jacobites (Monophysites), who entered *Persia with the armies of Khosrau II Parvez (590–628).

The city of Mosul (population 180,000) on the right bank of the Tigris River across from *Ninive, was founded as a Christian monastery (570), which Arabs conquered (641) and made a fortress. Destroyed by *Timur *c.* 1400, it was held by the Ottoman Turks from 1638 until World War I. Until the opening of the Suez Canal (1869), Mosul was an important station on the caravan route between Europe and India.

Christianity penetrated the region in the early 2d century but the area became *Nestorian in the 5th century. After the Arab conquest Mosul was a Nestorian metropolitan see with five suffragans (7th century); the most prominent prelate was George of Erbil (Arbela) and Mosul (d. 960). The Nestorian patriarchate that entered union with Rome (1553) was located in Mosul; but it later moved to Kotchanes and reverted to schism. In 1778 Metropolitan John Hormizd and other Nestorians of Mosul became Catholic. Although suspended from his office in 1812 and 1818, John Hormizd in 1830 was confirmed by Rome as patriarch of *Babylon of the Chaldeans. Chaldean patriarchs resided in Mosul until 1947, when they moved to Baghdad. In 1960 Mosul was detached from Baghdad as a Chaldean diocese.

The Syrian rite Archdiocese of Mosul was created in 1790. In 1878 the Syro-Chaldean Seminary of St. John (Pontifical in 1882) was founded; its faculty is composed of clergy of the Latin, Chaldean, and Syrian rites. The Syrian monastery of Mar Behnam, founded in 363, is the oldest convent of Iraq.

Latin missionaries have been active in Mosul from the 17th century. The apostolic prefecture established in 1750 became a mission *sui iuris* (1896) under the Latin Archdiocese of Baghdad (Babylon). Italian Dominicans (1750–1815) were followed by French Dominicans (1856), who are still in Mosul.

Bibliography: J. M. FIEY, *Mossoul chrétienne* (Beirut 1959). W. DE VRIES, EncCatt 8:1481–82. R. JANIN, LexThK² 7:659–660. OrientCatt 161–174. AnnPont (1965) 287.

[J. A. DEVENNY]

MOTA Y ESCOBAR, ALONSO DE LA,

Mexican bishop; b. Mexico City, 1556; d. Puebla, April 15, 1625. He was educated at the Dominican convent in Mexico City, earning the doctorate in theology. After serving as a curate in Chiapas, he was sent to Spain by the University of Mexico; there he eventually became tutor to the future Philip II. After receiving his degree in Canon Law from the University of Salamanca, he returned to Mexico to become dean successively of Michoacán, Tlaxcala, and Mexico City. He twice refused appointment as bishop (of Nicaragua and later of Panama) before accepting the See of Guadalajara in 1597. His work among the Indians earned him considerable fame, particularly during the rebellion in the Serranía of Topía in 1601. Preaching to the Indian rebels in their own language, he exhorted them to remain obedient. Through a policy of care, gentleness, and justice he succeeded in pacifying them while at the same time he won the Spaniards over to better treatment of the Indians. One result of his labors was the baptism of five important caciques. In 1608, Bishop Mota y Escobar was transferred to the see of Puebla de los Angeles, where he founded several hospitals, the Colegio de la Compañía de Jesús, the convent of Trinidad, the monastery of Carmen y Santa Ines, and several chapels.

Bibliography: M. CUEVAS, *Historia de la Iglesia en México,* 5 v. (5th ed. Mexico City 1946–47).

[E. J. GOODMAN]

MOTET

A musical term of French origin, generally applied to a vocal, or vocal and instrumental, work with a Latin text intended for church use. In the Middle Ages and Renaissance, secular and political motets also were extensively cultivated, and the term fell somewhat into disrepute, though not disuse, for titles such as *Sacrae cantiones vulgo motecta appellatae* are occasionally encountered. In its earliest stages the motet was a verbal trope of the clausula (the short melisma in the chant Gradual or Alleluia)—words (*mots*) carefully underlaid to the hitherto vocalized *duplum* (second voice part). The *duplum* later changed its name to *motetus.* When a third or fourth voice was added to the existing tenor and *duplum,* it might sing the same text as the *motetus* (conductus-motet), or each voice might have a separate text. Two or three texts could be sung simultaneously without incurring practical or aesthetic objections, since the various texts were usually related to each other as well as to the feast for which the composition was intended. The tenor, whose rhythm was usually less lively than that of the upper parts, was often provided with a syllable or word indicating the source of the chant, and therefore the *organum as a whole.

Although in the 13th century the early motet was at its peak as a genuine and expressive embellishment of the liturgy, it was then also that the substitution of French secular texts for the Latin took place. By midcentury the top voice part tended to predominate because of its deliberately attractive melodic interest (Franconian style), showing the way for the more advanced methods of Petrus de Cruce, Philippe de Vitry, and Guillaume de Machaut, all of whom wrote political as well as liturgical motets. From the short-winded *ordines,* or rhythmic schemes for the tenor, the concept of *isorhythm* slowly developed, reaching a perfect, though by no means final, stage of technique in the motets of Machaut. Originally applied to the tenor only, isorhythm later pervaded all voice parts in certain

Opening of the Prelude to the choral-orchestral "Motet for a Long Offertory" by Marc Antoine Charpentier.

motets, so that they were melodically independent but rhythmically bound to a recurring pattern called *talea*. Some relaxing of this strict compositional discipline came with the motets of Guillaume Dufay and John Dunstable, whose example was influential for a considerable part of the 15th century. At this time it was not unusual to find the plainsong, skillfully decorated, in the highest voice, supported by two independent instrumental parts.

The growth of choral polyphony caused a further change in the career of the motet. Texture became much richer, progressing from density to radiance in the works of Ockeghem, Obrecht, and Desprez. Their music, known throughout Europe, set a standard of taste and technique that was to usher in the greatest era of the choral motet, culminating in the vast production of Lasso, Palestrina, Byrd, Victoria, and their contemporaries. Most of their texts were still liturgical, but some composers preferred psalm verses and other Biblical texts occasionally brought together for special reasons. Ceremonial motets for great occasions of church and state continued to emerge from time to time, and a growing interest in instrumental support can be sensed toward the end of the 16th century. The Roman composers remained faithful to the unaccompanied choral motet well into the baroque era, while the Venetians (notably G. Gabrieli and Monteverdi) were boldly experimenting in instrumentation, spatial separation of choirs, and new effects of every kind (*stile concitato*). Lully, Charpentier, and Couperin brought the choral-orchestral motet to its zenith in France; Schütz, Buxtehude, and Bach gave to Germany a rich heritage of solo and choral motets.

The term motet was occasionally applied to religious (but not necessarily liturgical) works of the classical and romantic periods, but the *Caecilian Movement brought about a new vogue for *a cappella* composition, which has continued to engage the attention of composers to the present day. The sung motet is permitted at Mass, Vespers, and any liturgical service provided the text is suitable and the music adequate.

Bibliography: M. BUKOFZER, *Studies in Medieval and Renaissance Music* (New York 1950). F. L. HARRISON, *Music in Medieval Britain* (New York 1958). Reese MusMA. Reese MusR. Buk MusB. Apel HDMus. **Illustration credit:** Bibliothèque Nationale, Paris.

[D. STEVENS]

MOTHER OF GOD

That Mary is the mother of God is a revealed fact so closely linked to Christ's salvific plan for men that since the Council of Ephesus in 431 its recognition has been the touchstone of Christian orthodoxy. If Mary is not truly the mother of God, then Christ is not true God as well as true man, and He is not the Redeemer of men. Mary is truly the mother of God if two conditions are fulfilled: that she is really the mother of Jesus and that Jesus is really God.

This article explains how Jesus is truly the Son of Mary and truly the Son of God; then it will discuss the essence of the mystery [see MYSTERY (IN THEOLOGY)] of the divine motherhood and will conclude with a brief statement on the influence of this divine motherhood on Mary's other privileges.

Son of Mary, Son of God. A woman conceives or generates a child at the very instant that God creates and infuses the soul into the properly disposed maternal ovum. Motherhood involves three elements. First, the mother generates the whole child, the being that exists completely in itself. This is why a man speaks of his mother rather than the mother of his body or his nature. Second, in generation the child receives a part of the very flesh of the parent. Hence a woman would not really generate a child if she would adopt a child or if God should create from nothing a child's body as well as his soul and place it in a human womb, where it could develop and come to term, because the child would not be from her own flesh. Finally, the child must take its origin from the maternal ovum and not from a woman's rib or heart. Eve, were the account in Genesis to be taken literally, would not have issued from Adam by way of generation.

Christ has a real human nature that His mother gave Him and this makes Him a man like other men, even though He is not a human person. He is one Divine Person subsisting in two natures: the divine nature eternally received from the eternal Father and the human nature received in time from His human mother. Can one rightly call her the mother of God from the mere fact that she gave a human nature to the Person of the *Word? Yes, because the relation of mother to child is a person-to-person relation, even though what the mother gives to her child is not the total cause of her child.

What makes Mary's motherhood essentially different from purely human motherhood is not the fact that she did something more or something different in conceiving her Child, but that her Child is a Divine Person. Instead of giving human personality to be enshrined in Mary's womb, God gives the Divine Person of His own Son as the term of Mary's maternal activity.

The early Church Fathers echo NT themes. For example, St. Ignatius of Antioch writes that God Our Lord Jesus Christ was born of Mary, who was from the seed of David. Opponents to this teaching sprang up in the early Church. *Gnosticism, which taught a redemption from the flesh through knowledge, considered the flesh an evil thing utterly beneath God's dignity. *Docetism held that Christ's body was a mere phantom. *Valentinus erroneously taught that Christ's real body was a celestial body that merely passed through Mary's body as through a channel. In his version of the NT, *Marcion has Christ appear as a full-grown man. These false teachings were ably refuted by St. Ignatius of Antioch, St. Justin, St. Irenaeus, Hippolytus, and Tertullian, but others continued to challenge this key doctrine.

Faustus of Mileve, the champion of *Manichaeism, affirmed that the virgin whom the Holy Spirit overshadowed was the earth itself and not Mary, and that later the mortal Christ became divine when He was baptized in the Jordan. In rebuttal St. Augustine speaks in his sermons of Mary as God's mother and clearly distinguishes between Mary's conceiving and that of her cousin Elizabeth.

*Arianism and *Nestorianism did not deny that Mary is the real mother of Christ, but did deny that Christ is God. In denying this primitive belief that the Incarnate Word is the uncreated Son of the Father, coequal to the Father, the Arians refused to accept Christ's divinity and as a consequence Mary's divine motherhood.

St. *Athanasius, *Arius's opponent, proclaimed Mary the mother of God (θεοτόκος, *theotokos) and buttressed the doctrine theologically by giving the first explanation of the interchange of properties known in theology as the *communication of idioms. The early 4th-century prayer, the earliest known Marian prayer, begins with the words: "We fly to thy patronage, holy Mother of God."

The direct denial of Mary's divine motherhood by *Nestorius led to the General Council of *Ephesus. Nestorius, Patriarch of Constantinople, was a disciple of Bishop *Theodore of Mopsuestia, who was in turn the disciple of *Diodore, Bishop of Tarsus. As representatives of the *Antioch school of theology, these three saw two physical persons in Christ, and the Son of God was distinct from the Son of David. Mary was for them the mother of Christ in whom the Word dwelt substantially.

In his 1931 encyclical *Lux veritatis*, in which he extended the Feast of the Divine Motherhood to the whole world, Pius XI declared that Nestorius actually asserted that the Word of God did not become man and hence Jesus Christ should not be called God, but only God-bearer, much as prophets and other holy men can be called God-bearers because of the divine grace bestowed upon them.

When St. *Cyril of Alexandria heard that Nestorius was preaching that Mary was christotokos (χριστοτόκος, mother of Christ) but not theotokos (mother of God), he took Nestorius to task in letters, sermons, and writings that defended the *Incarnation and the divine maternity. In the midst of a flurry of letters with charges and countercharges showered upon Pope *Celestine I by both St. Cyril and Nestorius, the Emperor *Theodosius II convoked the General Council of Ephesus.

At the first session, on June 22, 431, the Council fathers unanimously approved one of St. Cyril's doctrinal letters and deposed Nestorius (Denz 250–253). The enthusiastic crowds surged through the streets of the city, shouting "Holy Mary, Mother of God." The official approval of the doctrine contained in St. Cyril's letter was in effect the equivalent of a definition. Theotokos became the chant of the Christian, and the commemoration of "the glorious and ever virgin Mary, Mother of God," found its way into the liturgy of the Mass.

Mystery of the Motherhood. Turning to another question, one may inquire why God would choose to have a mother. To restore man into His own image in a still more wonderful way than He created him, the heavenly Father willed to put His own Son into the very materials of His creation in such a way that the eternal Word would restore harmony in the universe of matter and spirit and between the human and divine orders. The Son of God would become a Son of Adam, and a daughter of Adam's race would become the mother of God's own Son. St. Irenaeus develops this parallelism between the fallen angel and the disobedient virgin in Eden and the loyal angel and the obedient virgin at Nazareth, between the first Adam and the tree in paradise and the Second Adam and the Tree on Calvary.

Most Marian theologians consider the divine motherhood as the basic principle of *Mariology, but they do not agree on what constitutes the essence of the relationship between Mary and the Incarnate Word. This relationship is not merely what is called a relation of reason. It is real because it has a real subject in Mary, a real term in the Person of the Word, and a real foundation in Mary's act of generating Him. Having a Divine Person as the term of human generation exceeds the natural capacities of human nature; hence this real relation is intrinsically *supernatural.

Since divine motherhood involves the human conception of a preexistent Person, the relation of divine motherhood might even exist from the first instant of Mary's own existence, because of her predestination as God's physical mother. St. Peter Chrysologus asks why Mary, who was a virgin after Christ's birth, could not be His mother before His conception? Sylvester de Saavedra, studying the likeness between the virgin mother and the eternal Father, claimed that the root and perfection of the mother-Son relation of Mary to Christ is a grace infused into Mary's body preceding in nature Mary's generative action.

M. J. Scheeben looked rather to the relationship of the mother's union with the divine Word. The mutual giving of the Person of the Word and Mary to each other in mutual consent is a kind of divine marriage. These divine nuptials (*matrimonium ratum*) by a special grace in her soul virtually and radically bestow upon Mary the bride the divine motherhood from the first instant of

Fig. 1. The Virgin Mary as Theotokos, Byzantine relief of the 11th century, church of Santa Maria Mater Domini, Venice. A typical Eastern iconography of the Virgin as the Mother of God.

her existence. Mary's divine brideship is completed (*matrimonium consummatum*) at the Incarnation. This theory has no support in Scripture or patristic tradition.

M. J. Nicolás finds the essence of Mary's motherhood not in a relationship of union but rather in a relationship of origin and even of opposition. The proper effect of generation is separation, since the human flesh substantially sanctified is no longer Mary's flesh in the very instant in which the *hypostatic union is realized. This resulting relation of origin forms a supernatural reality that stands between the hypostatic union and the accidental union caused by sanctifying *grace.

Whatever constitutes the perfection that forms the basis for the relationship of motherhood, it must actually be in Mary, for motherhood is something that endures. Theologians commonly agree that Mary's transient generative activity is the proper foundation of her relationship to her Son. St. Thomas Aquinas affirms that some relations are founded upon what remains in the agent from the action performed (*In 3 sent.* 8.5). Nicolás explains the kind of perfection left in a mother because of her generative action. Human generative activity is a human act and therefore it has a spiritual side governed by laws based upon the very nature of man. The woman who conceives willingly performs a more perfect human act than the woman who conceives against her will.

As the divine Word assumed a nature perfect in its humanity, He accepted Mary's generative act as a perfect human act—virginal, conscious, voluntary. What remains in the agent after the transient generative action is a permanent disposition or habit, drawing the mother to her child as an immediately connatural object of knowledge and love. As the human generative act was composed of a spiritual and a material element, so does the resulting habit possess composite elements. And just as human nature is raised to the supernatural order by sharing in the divine nature (*see* DIVINE NATURE, PARTAKER OF), Mary's human motherhood is raised to the hypostatic order by sharing in the relationship of the eternal Father to the Son. Thus Mary's maternal perfection is a unique relationship, a formal image of the relationship which the eternal Father has to the same divine Son. Only the Father and Mary have generated the same eternal Person, He according to His divine nature, she according to His human nature.

From his patristic studies, Joseph Bover concludes that the mother of God would have to be a virginal mother and that only the mother of God could be a virginal mother. Aquinas bases his theology of Mary's virginity upon her assimilation to the Father in virtue of her divine motherhood (*see* VIRGIN BIRTH).

J. M. Alonso finds in the Church Fathers the thesis that the divine motherhood is a formal participation in the fecundity of the Father. He holds that the three Divine Persons in the order of efficient causality keep their distinct functions in the identity of operations and impress their personal characters on the effect produced. The supernatural form effected in Mary by the Trinitarian relation of the Father is called her personal maternal being, and is the only sanctifying form she possesses. Alonso's thesis seems to disregard papal teaching that all the divine activities that sanctify men are common to the Trinity. Then, too, one may ask how Mary can be called mother of all men if she does not possess a grace specifically the same as theirs.

Fig. 2. The Expectant Madonna with St. Joseph, painting of the School of Amiens, c. 1437. So literal a rendering of Mary's pregnancy is very rare throughout the whole scope of Christian art.

De la Taille holds that what gives a divine gift a strictly supernatural quality is the relation of union between created *obediential potency and uncreated act. Just as the Word elevated and substantially united His human nature to His Person by actuating it with His divine act of existence, so by analogy in the accidental order the Father communicates His fecundity, elevating and assimilating to Himself the foundation of Mary's human motherhood (*see* CREATED ACTUATION BY UNCREATED ACT).

Relationship to Other Privileges. The third and final question concerns the relation of the divine motherhood to Mary's other privileges. Some arguments from propriety or fitness (convenience) lack force since God enjoys perfect freedom to create or give any gift. Hypo-

Fig. 3. Madonna and Child, woodcut by Robert McGovern, American, contemporary.

thetical necessity produces certitude only when there is a necessary link between one effect and another effect that God wills to produce. When it is clearly established that Christ willed to be the perfect Son of Mary, it is logical to think that He willed to do for her everything possible as long as it was suitable to His purpose in having a mother. In like manner, if Christ willed effectively to have a perfect mother, with Himself as her only Child, then it is logical to think that this perfect mother willed to do everything possible for her redeeming Son and desired to cooperate in His Redemption to the extent that this is possible and suitable.

See also MARY, BLESSED VIRGIN, ARTICLES ON.

Bibliography: E. DUBLANCHY, DTC 9.2:2339–69. G. SÖLL, LexThK² 4:1126–27. R. LAURENTIN, *Queen of Heaven,* tr. G. SMITH (New York 1956). H. M. MANTEAU-BONAMY, *Maternité divine et l'Incarnation* (BiblThom 27; Paris 1949). M. J. NICO-LÁS, "Le Concept intégral et maternité divine," RevThom 42–43 (1937) 58–93, 230–272. W. J. BURGHARDT, "Theotokos: The Mother of God," E. D. O'CONNOR, ed., *The Mystery of the Woman* (Notre Dame, Ind. 1956) 5–33. C. FECKES, *The Mystery of the Divine Motherhood,* tr. G. SMITH (New York 1941) 13–82. M. D. PHILIPPE, "Le Mystère de la maternité divine de Marie," H. DU MANOIR DE JUAYE, ed., *Maria: Études sur la Sainte Vierge,* 6 v. (Paris 1949–61) 6:367–416, with extensive bibliog. M. SCHMAUS, *Katholische Dogmatik,* 5 v. in 8 (5th ed. Munich 1953–59; 6th ed. 1960–) 5:62–114. G. VAN ACKEREN, "Mary's Divine Motherhood," Carol Mariol 2:177–227. A. VONIER, *The Divine Motherhood,* in *Collected Works,* 3 v. (rev. ed. Westminster, Md. 1952–53) 1:327–375. J. M. ALONSO, "Hacia una Mariología trinitaria: dos escuelas," *Estudios Marianos* 10 (1950) 141–191; 12 (1952) 237–267. J. M. BOVER, "Cómo conciben los Santos Padres el misterio de la divina maternidad. La virginidad, clave de la maternidad divina," *ibid.* 8 (1949) 185–256. J. M. DELGADO VARELA, "Fr. Silvestre de Saavedra y su concepto de maternidad divina," *ibid.* 4 (1945) 521–558. S. MEO, *La Maternitá divina di Maria nel Concilio Ecumenico di Efeso* (Rome 1959). C. SPICQ, *Ce que Jésus doit à sa mère selon la théologie biblique et d'après les théologiens médiévaux* (Montreal 1959). **Illustration credits:** Fig. 1, Alinari-Art Reference Bureau. Fig. 2, National Gallery of Art, Washington, D.C., Samuel H. Kress Collection.

[P. C. HOELLE]

MOTION

Motion (Gr. κίνησις, Lat. *motus*) can be taken in a wide and in a strict sense. In the wide sense it stands for any *change, for any transition from one state or condition to another. In a strict sense it means successive and continuous change, usually spoken of as movement. Aristotle held that it is unnecessary to prove the existence of motion, since the fact is evident. This notwithstanding, motion constitutes the first and enduring problem of philosophy, and through the study of it philosophers come to significant insights into material being and into the nature of being itself. It is also of interest to psychologists, for the perception of motion—examined in scholastic and modern psychology alike—has given rise to several theories on this subject. Accordingly, the present article treats motion under two aspects, the first part dealing with it from the standpoint of philosophy, the second from that of psychology.

MOTION IN PHILOSOPHY

Originating among the early Greeks, the philosophical analysis of motion reached its fullest development in the thought of Aristotle and the scholastics. This analysis forms the conceptual background against which the characteristic approach of modern science, as well as further contributions by modern philosophers, are most easily discussed.

Early Greeks. Since the early Greek philosophers lacked precise concepts of the different kinds of being, they reduced all changes to the simplest type of motion, local motion or change of place. From the beginning they spoke of the process of becoming in this terminology: things came into being by being "separated" from an original mass, by condensation and rarefaction, or by a downward and upward path. The only philosophers to deny the possibility of change were *Parmenides and his Eleatic school. The famous paradoxes of *Zeno of Elea, for example, purported to disprove the intelligibility of local motion. Because his concept of being was absolute, Parmenides himself denied that anything could come to be. The subsequent atomists were one in denying the possibility of absolute coming into being. They reduced all change to local motion, that is, to the redistribution of atoms in space (*see* ATOMISM; GREEK PHILOSOPHY).

*Plato distinguished motion from becoming (γένεσις; *Theaet.* 152D–153E), although he usually understood motion as local motion (*Laws* 893B–894A). In *Theaetetus* (181C–182A), however, he introduced the concept of qualitative change or alteration (ἀλλοίωσιν) as one of the two types of motion. He also defined soul as "the motion which can move itself" (*Laws* 896A), and he listed psychic operations as examples of motion (*Laws* 897A). Yet he was constrained to think even of the movement of reason as similar to the local motion of a sphere and its relatively immobile central point (*Laws* 898A; cf. *Tim.* 33B–34A).

Aristotelian Concept. It remained for *Aristotle to give the first reasonably complete analysis (*Phys.* 200b 12–231a 20; 250b 11–267b 26). In this he was followed by St. *Thomas Aquinas, whose commentary on Aristotle's *Physics* is the fullest account of a philosophy of motion.

Because of his historical milieu, Aristotle had first to justify the possibility of motion by assigning principles that would account for motion in the face of the Eleatic denial. The possibility of change he saved by distinguishing being into 10 categories and into actual and potential being. For Aristotle motion was the proper formality from which to study nature and natural phenomena. No other formality, such as being or extension, can in his view reveal the nature and explain the sensible properties of matter. He maintained it necessary, however, to distinguish motions that are natural from motions that result from art, chance, or compulsion. The first kind is of fundamental relevance to his scientific study of the world.

In Book 3 of the *Physics* the famous definition of motion is given. Aristotle begins by stating the concepts to be used in its definition. Since motion spans several *categories of being, the elements of the definition must also transcend the categories; the only available prior concepts for defining motion are *potency and act. Motion must be situated midway between potentiality and full actuality. When a body is only in potency, it is not yet in motion; when it has been fully actualized, the motion has ceased. Therefore, motion consists of imperfect *act. But since imperfect act can be the termination of a motion or the starting point of a new motion, it is necessary to indicate motion as the act of a being in potency precisely as still in potency to more of the same act. Hence, motion is defined as: "the fulfilment [act] of what exists in potency in so far as it is in potency" (201a, 10).

Types of Motion. Plato had adumbrated various types of motion, but Aristotle put the classification on a scientific basis. Motions are distinguished by the goal or *terminus ad quem* (*Phys.* 224b 7). Motion does not of itself belong in the categories of being, since it is not *being, but *becoming; however, it is reduced to the category of the being in which it terminates.

Local Motion. The first, most obvious, and easiest motion to observe is change of *place, or local motion. It is divided into circular, straight, and mixed, as well as into uniform and accelerated. The nature of motion is most easily seen in local motion, and even the terms one uses to describe other types are terms applied primarily to local motion. Local motion clearly goes from term to term, from a point of departure to one of arrival. These two terms are opposed and incompatible, but admit intermediary states: thus, they are called contraries. The motion between them is continuous, or unbroken and successive, that is, traversing the intervening positions. It is divisible by reason of the extension crossed. Since an *instant is not divisible, motion cannot be instantaneous, but takes *time. Likewise, motion properly speaking belongs only to bodies, since only they have the divisibility essential to motion. Local motion of some sort is involved in all other motions, and other motions are called such by analogy with local motion.

Alteration. Qualitative motion is called alteration. It is realized only in the third species of *quality, namely, sensible qualities. Only these fit the definition of motion as continuing and successive actualization of potency. Changes occurring in the vital or psychic orders are not motions in the same sense as local change and change of sensible qualities. One speaks of the mind as "proceeding" from known to unknown, of discursive *reasoning; this, however, is only by analogy with local motion. Vital and psychic operations are not acts of beings in potency, but of beings already proximately determined to act; these operations are not the fulfillment of potentialities, but the products of potentialities already actualized (cf. St. Thomas, ST 1a, 18.3 ad 1). Further, in psychic acts there is not the successiveness characteristic of motion, nor the contrariety between the terms of the process. In *sensation the preliminary stimulation of the sensory organs is a qualitative change, but the determination of the faculty itself is not a gradual reception of act and thus is not motion. In the sensitive appetite there is motion, insofar as there is a physical accompaniment to the psychic act; the motion may be qualitative or local. Changes of moral disposition, although gradual, are not truly motions, but rather one or a series of instantaneous changes. Substantial changes are preceeded by alterations that dispose matter toward becoming a new being, but the actual generation of a new substance and destruction of the old are instantaneous, and are thereby not classified as motions in the strict sense. (*See* GENERATION-CORRUPTION; SUBSTANTIAL CHANGE.)

Augmentation and Diminution. Motion in the category of *quantity is called augmentation or growth and diminution or decrease. Augmentation does not consist of mere addition of distinct quantities to form an aggregation; such would reduce to local motion and would be augmentative, but not the motion of augmentation. The motion of augmentation must take place within the unity of a single *substance. This happens only in living beings. By nutrition these assimilate their food into their own substance and consequently achieve growth. This is a true motion. It involves some local motion, as a growing body extends spatially. It is gradual, ordinarily so slow as to escape observation. It passes through successive stages, from the smallest one cell stage to the full measure of growth determined by the specific nature. It also goes from contrary to contrary, from one positive state to another in the order of quantity. Such a motion is obviously immanent operation on the part of the living subject as agent, but it is true motion on the part of the subject as receptive of a new perfection. The opposite of augmentation is diminution or decrease.

Other Categories. The two categories of *action and passion do not constitute separate types of motion, for they are really identified with motion. Action is motion considered as being *from* the agent. Passion is the same motion considered *in* the patient. There is no motion in the category of "when" (*quando*), since time itself is the measure of motion. Nor is there motion in the category of *relation. A new relation arises as a result of a change in some other category; for instance, by reason of a change of place, a relation of proximity arises, and from change of quality in one being, a relation of similarity or dissimilarity results in another being. A mutual relation can come into being and cease to be without any change in one of the related members. Hence, change is merely incidental to relation. The categories of *situation (*situs*) and condition or vestition (*habitus*) are constituted by relations, and so do not found separate types of motion.

Reality of Motion. The objective reality of motion is known through a recognition of the various stages of actualization from the beginning to the ultimate termination of motion, even though these stages are not identified with motion. Fundamentally, each one has immediate experience of his own motions, particularly local (see below, Motion in Psychology). The paradoxes of Zeno, while purporting to disprove the reality of local motion, can be solved by an analysis of the *continuum and of the infinite (cf. *Phys.* 239b 5–240a 18). Though directed against the intelligibility of motion, they do not overturn the immediate *evidence of the fact of motion.

The reality of motion is further confirmed by the need of an efficient cause or mover. Motion is an emergence from a state of potentiality to one of actuality. This is possible only under the influence of some being in act. Even vital movement requires that one part of a living being function as agent and another part as patient, otherwise the same being would be in potency and act together. The mover must be distinct from the moved and must be proportioned to the motion produced. There must be contact, at least mediate; there is no *action at a distance. In a series of movers that are themselves moved, there is no ultimate explanation for the motion unless there be a first unmoved mover, a first cause of motion (*see* MOTION, FIRST CAUSE OF).

Motion in Modern Science. The Aristotelian requirement of a mover in act as necessary to account for motion was not easily satisfied; particularly was this the case in assigning the cause of projectile motion, such as of a stone thrown upward. Aristotle had explained the motion of the projectile after it left contact with the mover by supposing that the agent moves not only the stone, but also the surrounding air, giving the air motive power to continue projecting the stone. *John Philoponus of Alexandria in the 6th century criticized the Aristotelian theory and proposed the theory of *impetus in its stead: the mover imparts a "motive power" or energy to the projectile itself. In the 14th century *John Buridan spoke of the impetus as a qualitative power given to the body by the mover. He suggested that impetus theory could explain the motion of the heavenly bodies, once God had put them in motion. His doctrine has been assimilated into Aristotelianism and scholasticism, where impetus is explained as a quality or an instrumental power communicated by the mover. It is usually not thought to be an efficient cause of motion, but is rather seen as analogous to the internal principle of natural motion.

Ockhamist Critique. *William of Ockham reduced all physical being to the two categories of substance and quality, the only two that denoted distinct realities. The reality of local motion and position in place were thus denied, and there was no longer need to find a cause for the continuance of projectile motion. Accordingly, Ockham could deny both the original Aristotelian and the impetus theory.

Galileo's Contribution. Galileo *Galilei initiated a radical departure from such theory and study of motion. Confining himself to local motion, he stated that he had discovered by experiment certain properties of motion not hitherto observed or demonstrated. He set himself to study these properties through the method of measurement and correlation. Motion, for him, gave way to momentum, the product of the quantity of matter and velocity. Galileo identified momentum with impetus,

and this became no longer an instrument or principle of motion, but a property of motion. He was not interested in an efficient cause for the continuance of motion, but in a measurable external cause of the acceleration or retardation of motion. Therefore, observing that a velocity once imparted to a body is accelerated or retarded according to the slope of the plane along which the motion takes place, he inferred that frictionless motion along a horizontal plane is uniform and perpetual. However, since in the real world this horizontal plane is circular—the surface of the sea, the path of the heavenly bodies—then the motion of bodies continues in a circular path, rather than in a straight line. Thus did Galileo give partial formulation to the principle of inertia.

Newton and Mechanism. Sir Isaac *Newton correctly stated the principle of inertia as the first of his axioms, or laws of motion: "Every body continues in its state of rest, or of uniform motion in a straight line, unless it is compelled to change that state by forces impressed on it" (*see* MOTION, LAWS OF). From this and other axioms, Newton developed the science of mechanics, discovering in the process a formula of *gravitation that is applicable to celestial as well as terrestrial phenomena. He also studied the properties of light according to principles of motion, and in his *Optics* proposed a science of nature guided and inspired by mechanics. Newton's successors thereupon extended mechanics into every region of science, into acoustics, hydrodynamics, magnetism, electricity, heat, even into biology, psychology, economics, and sociology, at the expense of denying all that is not reducible to matter and motion (*see* MECHANISM).

Recent Physics. The use of mechanical principles as ultimate explanations of physical reality ran into difficulties in the 20th century with the advent of *relativity and *quantum theory. The Heisenberg principle of *uncertainty, according to which it is impossible in principle to measure both the position and velocity of a particle, makes it impossible to construct a mechanical model of the world. Moreover, the concept of quantum jumps is interpreted by some to involve a denial of the continuity of motion. (*See* INDETERMINISM.)

Motion in Modern Philosophy. René *Descartes recalled the common doctrine that *nature is the principle of motion and rest, but could conceive motion only as local motion. Therefore, he attempted an explanation of all material reality from a mechanical point of view, i.e., in terms of matter and local motion. He held that all that man can know of external objects are their figure, magnitudes, and motions—all modes of extension. Color, odor, taste, and other sensible qualities, in this view, are not objective. Descartes also taught that in the beginning God created a definite quantity of motion, which remains constant. Not interested in the Aristotelian or qualitative definition of motion, which he never understood, he concentrated instead on the quantity of motion, or momentum. Motion became, for him, an actual and measurable state of a body, without consideration of a potential state that is being further actualized (cf. *Principles of Philosophy,* 2.24–36).

Leibniz and Kant. *Leibniz objected to Descartes's idea that the quantity of motion in the universe remains constant; this, for Leibniz, is true rather of *force (*Discourse on Metaphysics,* 17–18). Likewise, he denied that extension is a clear and distinct idea. Extension, together with size, figure, and motion, are subjective phenomena, no less than the other sensible qualities the mechanists had rejected. Accordingly, he formulated his monadology, a doctrine in which bodies are composed of simple forces, psychic in character (*see* MONAD). The *dynamism of the system did not prevent Leibniz from interpreting bodily actions mechanically, even though they do not act upon one another. Bodies are divine machines or natural automatons (*The Monadology*, 64). The motions of bodies, however, are regulated by their preestablished harmony with one another and with souls, which act according to final causality and the divine plan of the best possible world.

Immanuel *Kant, in his precritical days, developed the monadology of Leibniz. In his definitive philosophy he defined motion as "actuation in space" (*Critique of Pure Reason,* B291). Motion is an empirical concept, since experience apprises one of something moving in space and time. But there is also a subjective element to it: the two forms of sensibility, space and time, organize the successive determinations of a movable object.

Bergson's Critique. The most searching criticism of such views was that of Henri *Bergson, who held that the scientific mind cannot grasp the reality of motion. The intellect makes static, snapshot views of various stages of a transition, thereby solidifying into discontinuous images the fluid continuity of the real. Just as a movie projector, by reason of the movement of the apparatus, reconstitutes the motion that had been immobilized in a series of still pictures, so does the mind string snapshots of reality upon an abstract "becoming" contributed by the mind itself. The mechanism of ordinary knowledge is "cinematographical." In order to grasp reality, which is duration or change itself, one must escape from the cinematographical mechanism and employ a metaphysical intuition. Since change is the essence of reality, there is no underlying subject of change; movement does not imply a mobile [see *Creative Evolution* (New York 1911); *The Creative Mind* (New York 1946)]. The mobile continuity of the real, or concrete duration, is for Bergson the subject of metaphysics. If Bergson's critique accomplishes nothing else, it at least intimates that modern thinkers, by reducing motion to a state, have allowed reality in flux to escape them.

See also PHILOSOPHY OF NATURE; MATTER AND FORM; SCIENCE (IN THE MIDDLE AGES).

Bibliography: ARISTOTLE, *Physics,* tr. R. P. HARDIE and P. K. GAYE, v.2 of *The Works of Aristotle,* ed. W. D. ROSS, 12 v. (Oxford 1908–52). THOMAS AQUINAS, *Commentary on Aristotle's "Physics,"* tr. R. J. BLACKWELL et al. (New Haven 1963). Syntopicon 1:193–217; 2:80–112. J. A. WEISHEIPL, *Nature and Gravitation* (River Forest, Ill. 1955). J. TONQUÉDEC, *La Philosophie de la nature* (Paris 1956–) 1.3. C. MAZZANTINI, EncFil 1:1676–87. S. CARAMELLA, EncFil 3:750–758.

[M. A. GLUTZ]

MOTION IN PSYCHOLOGY

The study of motion in psychology has a long and interesting history. Once it was realized that motion could be experienced when there was no physical movement and that actual physical motion might not be experienced as such, the investigation of just how man perceives movement captured the interest of psychologists. To explain these illusions, most psychologists relied upon some type of logical analysis in terms of space and time, until the significant research of Max

*Wertheimer on apparent movement showed that a new phenomenological approach was needed.

Perception of Movement. Current investigation of the perception of movement may be classified under the following headings: induced movement; autokinetic movement; direction, speed, and causality of movement; and apparent movement.

Induced Movement. In induced movement one object is displaced in relation to another, but the subject is not able to perceive which has moved. He may, for example, see the object move when in reality it is the frame that has been moved. The tendency is to interpret the figure as moving rather than the background. Also the meaning of the stimulus for the particular subject can determine which of two stimuli the subject perceives as moving.

Autokinetic Movement. Another interesting illusion of movement is the autokinetic effect, in which a stationary point of light is perceived as moving in a completely dark room. This phenomenon is explained largely in terms of nystagmus eye movements, but it is influenced also by the posture of the body, and kinesthetic sensations from the muscles. Moreover the autokinetic phenomenon is greatly influenced by social suggestibility of the subject. In both induced and autokinetic movement, the experienced movement cannot be differentiated from real movement.

Direction, Speed, and Causality. More recently it has been discovered that both direction and speed of movement depend upon the organizational factors present. It appears that the speed of movement is apprehended independently of distance or time. One peculiarity of directional movement is the trapezoidal illusion, in which a rotating trapezoid is perceived as oscillating because of the conflict in cues. Another interesting piece of research by A. E. Michotte (1881–) indicates that movement can have more complex attributes such as causality. The simulated appearance of one ball striking another is perceived as the first ball causing the second to move, even though there is no actual contact.

Apparent Movement. Of great importance in the study of the perception of movement is the phi-phenomenon, or that of apparent movement. To illustrate this phenomenon two lights are mounted side by side. First one, then the other, is turned on and off. By varying the time between the turning on of the two lights, one induces three different perceptual experiences. If the time interval is long, the first light is perceived as followed by the other. If the interval is extremely short, the two lights are perceived simultaneously. If the time interval is just right, one light is perceived as moving from position *A* to position *B*. A light is seen as moving when in fact there is no movement at all, and across a space where there is no stimulus present. The same phenomenon of apparent movement has also been reported for skin sensitivity of two successive stimuli, and for the hearing of two successive clicks.

The conditions governing the occurrence of the phi-phenomenon were investigated by Korte (1915). He found that the threshold was determined by distance between stimuli, the time interval of the succession, and the intensity of the stimuli. Moreover, the direction of the apparent movement was determined by the grouping laws of proximity and similarity. Finally the spatial arrangement of the successive stimuli may direct the apparent movement.

Theories of Perception. On the basis of the phi-phenomenon, field theorists maintain that movement is a primary sensory phenomenon not reducible to sensory attributes or to space or time. On the other hand the sensory-tonic theory of H. Werner and S. Wapner stresses the role of muscle activity in enhancing the autokinetic effect of apparent movement. The transactional functionalism theory of Ames's group and the probabilist theory of Brunswick attempt to explain the illusion of movement in terms of the cues of position, size, distance, and past experience, maintaining that these operate immediately and unconsciously.

The explanation offered by Thomistic psychologists is that movement is a *per accidens* sensible known through the operation of the internal senses, operating simultaneously in conjunction with the external senses and through physiological and psychological cues. The *imagination is the faculty that supplies the sense of movement in conjunction with the work of the senses; thus the phenomenon of apparent movement results from the work of the imagination. This faculty fuses together the successive sense impressions, e.g., moving pictures, and at the same time relates this information to the past experience of actual moving things to give an experience of movement. Such a Thomistic view can give a rational explanation of all the phenomena of movement reported in experimental psychology; yet it should be noted that what it subjects to complex analysis is in reality a spontaneous and frequently an unconscious process.

See also PERCEPTION; SENSATION; SENSE KNOWLEDGE; SENSES.

Bibliography: F. H. ALLPORT, *Theories of Perception and the Concept of Structure* (New York 1955). A. AMES, *Visual Perception and the Rotating Trapezoidal Window* (Psychological Monographs: General and Applied 65.7; Washington 1951). S. H. BARTLEY, *Principles of Perception* (New York 1958). E. G. BORING, *Sensation and Perception in the History of Experimental Psychology* (New York 1942). D. KRECH and R. S. CRUTCHFIELD, *Elements of Psychology* (New York 1958).

[J. H. VOOR]

MOTION, FIRST CAUSE OF

Experience shows that some things in the world are in motion, whereas others are at rest, and that things pass from rest to motion and from motion to rest. In view of these facts, the question arises whether each and every thing is so constituted as to be capable of both motion and rest, and can be either a mover or something moved, or whether besides things of this sort something exists that is a mover, but is itself unmoved by any other. Is there an unmoved mover that is the primal source or first cause of motion?

Scholastic philosophers commonly answer this question in the affirmative, despite the fact that many difficulties have been raised against their response, particularly since the rise of modern science and in the context of modern philosophy. In view of this situation, the present treatment is divided into two parts: the first sketches the argument advanced by scholastics to prove the existence of a prime mover; the second is a reply to objections the argument generally encounters among scientists and philosophers.

EXISTENCE OF AN UNMOVED MOVER

The scholastic proofs for the existence of a first unmoved mover are based upon an argument first proposed by *Aristotle (*Phys.* 241b 24–267b 27) and sub-sequently commented upon by St. *Thomas Aquinas (*In 7 phys.* 1–9; *In 8 phys.* 1–23) in the context of their natural philosophy. In what follows, the concepts and distinctions presupposed to this argument are first explained, then the argument itself is exposed, and some observations made on the place of such a proof in natural philosophy and its relevance to traditional proofs for the existence of God.

Presuppositions. By *motion is meant the act or process of change. This is not a disembodied energy, nor something purely and simply actual, but an actual determination of a natural body precisely as this is capable of further actuation. Motion thus conceived requires a mobile or potential subject that remains the self-same throughout the change, but becomes different from the way in which it was before the change. When a body passes from *rest to motion, motion itself begins to be in this mobile subject. Whatever begins to be does not spring from mere nothing, nor does it produce itself, but depends for its being on some active principle, called the efficient cause. The efficient cause is the mover, or active source of motion, whereas motion is an effect produced in the moved or mobile subject. Each kind of motion requires a mobile subject capable of being moved with that motion, as well as a mover able to produce the motion.

Atemporal Aspect. If the supposition is made that motion had a beginning in time and has not existed from eternity, then it is manifest that there must be a first efficient cause of motion, because anything that begins to be requires an efficient cause from which it originates. But since it is not clear from human experience or scientific reasoning that motion did have a beginning in time, the present discussion does not assume this.

Accidental vs. Essential. In order to prove by reasoning that there is a first cause of motion, a distinction should be made between motion that is caused or possessed accidentally and motion that is caused or possessed essentially. Motion is accidental when it is associated with something that merely belongs to something moved, as a color belongs to an animal and is moved accidentally when the animal moves. Motion is accidental also to something contained as a part in a whole; when the whole is moved, the part shares the motion of the whole, as a man in a boat is moved with the boat. On the other hand, motion is essential to something that is moved of itself, and not merely as part of another. Thus the motion of a stick moved by the hand, or of a thrown stone, is essential motion. Accidental motion presupposes and requires essential motion, and to the latter the argument is confined.

Mover and Moved. Several conditions must be fulfilled in order that essential motion occur. First of all there must be a distinction between the mover and the moved: whatever is moved is moved by something else. The distinction between the mover and the moved appears by way of induction from sensory experience, and also by reasoning from effect to cause. Among the things that have essential motion, some derive their motion from themselves, and others from something else; in some cases the motion is natural, whereas in other cases it is mechanical, that is, by impressed force.

It is manifest that things moved mechanically, by art or by violence, are moved by something else, that is, by a mover distinct from the moved. On the other hand, living things have in themselves an active principle or efficient cause of their own motion, by which they move themselves in different ways. They are also composed of heterogeneous parts; the part that causes motion is distinct from the part moved, as the nerves and muscles are distinct from the bones. Organisms thus move themselves by means of their parts, with the part in motion being moved by another part that is an active cause of motion. Nonliving bodies do not appear to move themselves, or to have in themselves an efficient cause of their own motion; thus they are moved by some cause that is distinct from themselves.

Reason also aids in understanding that whatever is in motion is moved by something else. Motion itself is an effect requiring both an efficient cause and a subject capable of being moved. If something is in motion and does not have the efficient cause of its motion within itself, then it is moved by something other than itself. But if it does have the cause of motion within itself, then it moves itself by means of its parts, and these are related as mover and moved. In all cases, whatever is in motion is divisible and has parts, and the whole depends upon the parts both for its existence and for its motion, whether it is moved by something else or moves itself.

Contact and Simultaneity. The second condition required for motion is that the mover and the moved must be together. Experience shows that some things are capable of causing motion and yet sometimes are not causing it, and that some things are capable of motion but sometimes are at rest. Motion requires not only a distinction between the mover and the moved, but also that mover and moved be together in place and time. The need for contact between the mover and the moved may be understood inductively, by considering the various kinds of motion, whether according to place or quality or quantity, and by reasoning in terms of cause and effect.

Local Motion. In regard to local motion, everything that is moved locally is moved either by itself or by something else. Something that moves itself has the cause of motion in itself, and so in this case it is clear that the mover and the moved are together as parts of one and the same whole. A body can be moved locally by something else in various ways, namely, by pushing, pulling, carrying, etc. Yet all these are reducible to some kind of combining or separating, because by local motion things are either brought together or separated.

Both experience and reason show that combining or separating require contact between the mover and the moved. The reason lies in the fact that the mover is the principle and cause from which the motion proceeds and begins to exist in the moved. Without contact the mover would have nothing on which to act. Since mover and moved are together and, as it were, one by contact, they share one and the same motion in different ways: the mover as efficient cause and the moved as patient or subject. Just as an effect cannot come from nothing, so it cannot come to be without some contact with its source. (*See* ACTION AT A DISTANCE.)

Alteration and Augmentation. In cases of change in quality, whatever causes alteration and whatever is altered are in contact with each other. This is clear in regard to sensory qualities and the organs of sense. For sensations of touch, taste, or smell to take place, something with the peculiar sensible quality must contact the proper organ of sense to act on it and cause the sensation, which is a kind of alteration. Sight and hearing also require contact with the appropriate sense, although in these cases the distant object first causes an

alteration in the medium, and then, through the medium, causes an alteration in the sense. Likewise, when the condition of contact is fulfilled, natural bodies interact through their physical and chemical qualities and cause alterations in each other. In change of quantity also, whether increase or decrease, there is contact between the organism and the parts that are added or lost.

Together in Time. Furthermore, mover and moved are together in time as well as in place; that is, they are simultaneous. At the same time as the mover causes motion, the moved is in motion. This is seen in the example of the hand moving the pen. The motion of the pen requires the hand as mover and contact of the hand with the pen; when and only when the hand moves the pen, the pen is moved by the hand. Mover and moved are together in place and time because they are parts of one system, and the motion is the act of both mover and moved, although in different ways: it is actively from the mover and passively in the moved (*see* ACTION AND PASSION).

Argument for a First Cause. Although man has no experimental knowledge of the prime mover, he can reason from sensible effects to the first cause of motion. It is evident from experience that something can be moved by something else in two ways. The proximate mover may itself be the source of motion, or this mover may depend upon something else. A mover that is itself the source of motion may cause the motion either directly and immediately, or through one or more intermediates, as a man can move a stone either immediately or by means of a stick in his hand. In such a case the stone is moved principally by the man, and only instrumentally by the stick, because the man moves the stick; but the stick does not move the man, nor does it move the stone unless it is moved by the man.

With facts and distinctions such as these in mind, one can propose a general argument. Many things in the world are in motion. But everything in motion is moved by something else, and mover and moved are together in place and time. The mover, in turn, is either moved by something else or it is not. In either case there must be a first mover that is not moved by anything else, but is itself as unmoved mover and the first cause of motion. Motion requires an efficient cause, and every cause that is a moved mover requires another efficient cause. Every moved mover, regardless of how many there may be in any given series, is an intermediate cause dependent upon another cause. Such a series of movers moved by something else cannot be infinite, but must terminate in a first cause of motion that is not moved by any other. If there were no unmoved mover, there would be no first cause of motion, nor any other cause, and hence no motion, which is contrary to fact.

This argument may be stated briefly in another way. Where there is motion, there must be a moved and a mover, distinct and yet together in place and time. There may also be an intermediate mover or instrument of motion. Motion is in the moved; the intermediate mover moves something and is moved by something; there must also be a first cause of motion that is unmoved by anything else, because the effect cannot be without such a cause. If anything is a mover and yet incapable of causing motion by itself, but only as moved by something else, and this in turn by something else, then such a series of moved movers cannot be infinite. It must be limited, in the sense that an unmoved mover must be the first cause of motion. Besides all the movers moved by something else, however many they may be, or of whatever kind, there must be a first cause of motion that imparts motion by itself and is an unmoved mover, independent of every other.

Role in Natural Philosophy. Questions concerning the first cause of motion may arise either in natural philosophy, or in metaphysics, or in natural and sacred theology. In natural philosophy the first cause of motion is considered only insofar as is necessary to understand motion in natural things and to determine whether the primary source of motion is or is not a natural body (*see* PHILOSOPHY OF NATURE). A body is something extended and divisible in parts that are in it and thus compose the whole. A body or extended whole is not an independent being, but depends upon its own parts for its being. A body is dependent also upon its parts for being moved, because motion requires a subject that is extended and divisible into parts. But the first cause of motion is completely independent in action, and hence also in being, because operation follows being, and the manner of acting is consequent upon the manner of being. Therefore, the first cause of motion is not a body, and does not have parts on which it depends for its being and acting. It is not composed of matter and form, nor of potency and act. It is not capable of being moved or having motion, either by itself or by something else, but is the unmoved mover of other things. Because it is unmoved, it is not a temporal being but eternal. Because it is unmoved and incorporeal, it does not cause motion mechanically, as one body moves another from without, but rather as mind or intelligence moves a body with a higher order of action. It may be true that there are many kinds of spiritual beings who are intermediate movers, in the sense that they cause motion only insofar as they are themselves moved by another mover in a way different from the movements to which material things are subject. If this is the case, however, these spiritual beings are not the first cause of motion whose existence has been proved, but are themselves moved by it.

To account for motion in the world, it is sufficient for the purposes of natural philosophy to admit one first cause of motion. One mover entirely unmoved suffices to cause motion in all things that are moved—not indeed as the only mover, but as the only first and unmoved mover—because it acts with complete independence, whereas everything that is moved in any way whatever is dependent upon an unmoved mover. Moreover, the first cause of motion is eternal and acts without detriment to itself, and so is capable of being the first cause of all motions in the world. Furthermore, the unity and the order of the world indicate that the first cause of motion is one and unique, somewhat as the orderly motion of an army indicates that there is one in command (*see* UNIVERSE, ORDER OF). To treat of the first cause more profoundly and in greater detail pertains to metaphysics and theology (*see* GOD, PROOFS FOR THE EXISTENCE OF).

First Mover and God. It is sometimes questioned whether the first cause of motion proved in natural philosophy is the being whom men call God, and whether the existence of God can be discussed or proved with the concepts and principles that pertain to natural philosophy. Although the considerations of this branch of philosophy are limited, and the first cause of motion is not included within the proper subject of natural science, yet Aristotle touched upon these ultimate problems in his *Physics,* and both St. Thomas Aquinas and Sir Isaac *Newton maintained that in natural science one should seek the first cause of motion, and treat of God inasmuch as He can be known as the cause of motion in the world. Moreover, as has been shown in the argument above, one can prove the existence of the first cause of motion through the data of experience and the principles of ordinary understanding and can show that this cause is not a natural body but an incorporeal and unmoved mover, entirely independent in action and being, and so reasonably identified with the being that men call God.

This proof from matter and motion, suggested by Aristotle and pursued by St. Thomas, has many advantages. From ordinary experience and consciousness men are aware not only of sensible motions in the world, but also of activities such as sensation, thought, and volition in themselves. Although these last are not motions in the strict sense of the term, nevertheless they are motions in the broad sense of alterations or qualitative dispositions. Sensations are initiated by sensible motions, and thoughts and volitions are in some ways dependent upon sensible motions, as they are also causes of sensible motion in man and in other things. Even thoughts and volitions are dependent on a first cause of motion, because every passing from potency to act requires a mover and ultimately an unmoved mover. It is the proper business of the natural philosopher to seek the causes of motion in natural bodies, and in order to understand his subject he must not rest content with some intermediate mover, nor with all intermediate movers—supposing that they could all be determined—but must seek the first cause of motion. Furthermore, it is only after one knows, through the study of nature, that there exists a kind of being that is not mobile or corporeal, but immobile and incorporeal (including the unmoved mover and spiritual substances), that he can show the need for a science, beyond natural philosophy, called *metaphysics (*see* BEING).

REPLY TO DIFFICULTIES

Many objections can be, and have been, raised against the line of reasoning advanced above. Such difficulties arise, not only from the special aims and methods of modern science and philosophy, but also from the concepts and principles they employ. While differences of aim or method often cause acute misunderstandings, these are usually cleared up when the proper distinctions are appreciated. Methods are proportioned to aims and objectives, and these can vary widely. Only the philosopher seeks proper reasons and first causes, and not every investigator has a philosophical interest. Differences in concept and principle are more serious, and these are so numerous that only a few fundamental ones can be treated here.

Gravitation and Projectile Motion. First of all, in regard to the principles of the argument, exceptions seem to present themselves—an indication that the principles are not universally true. Gravitating bodies do not appear to be moved by anything, nor do projectiles moving with inertial motion appear to require a mover to keep them going. Again, if a mover is required in these cases, it does not seem to be together with the moved in place and time.

Falling Bodies. It must be admitted that the cause of

motion in gravitating bodies is not clear or easily determined. Such bodies do not appear to have in themselves an efficient cause of their motion, nor do they move themselves actively by means of their parts, as living things do. It is not clear that they are moved by any force of attraction from the center of gravitational tendency, or by an efficient cause in the medium through which they pass, as a ship is blown by the wind.

Careful examination of gravitational motion shows that bodies have a constant tendency to become localized among other bodies according to a certain order, namely, that of density, with the denser bodies toward the center. This tendency is as natural as any other physical or chemical property, and is basic for the general order of the world. Ultimately, in the elements of which bodies are composed, there are certain primary tendencies in matter, such as *gravitation, electromagnetic charge, and the nuclear force, that cause all other changes in the universe, and that are explained, in the first instance, by saying that they are natural to bodies. However, this implies that they have as their cause the agent that brought these bodies into existence, whether this be some intermediate physical cause or the first cause immediately.

In light of this analysis, one can say that the essential cause of falling motion is the *agent that produces the body with its gravity, and this in a *place where gravitational motion can occur. Such motion can also be seen as deriving accidentally from whatever removes impediments, should these restrain the body from manifesting its natural tendency to fall. Beyond this, most scholastics also assign to gravity, as a *quality inhering within the body itself, some role in the causality effecting its motion. Being present in the body both locally and temporally, this can serve as the instrument of the essential mover throughout the motion, and thus preserve the principle that is under attack.

Projectiles. It is not clear exactly how a projectile continues to be moved once it has been set in motion, whether by some impulse that it derives from the principal source of the motion, or by some impression in the medium, or by both. In any case mover and moved are distinct and together at the start of the motion, and an *impetus continues to sustain the motion until it is offset by the resistance of the medium or that of other bodies. Such an impetus is analogous to the gravity of the falling body, and similarly gives basis for a reply to the objections raised. Both gravity and impetus, it should be noted, are only instrumental movers; they therefore require an essential mover to give adequate explanation for the motion they impart.

Action and Reaction. Another difficulty arises from the principle that when a body is moved there is a reaction of the moved against the mover, such that action and reaction are equal and opposite in tendency. In view of this principle it would seem that motion can be caused only by the action of one body on another, not by an incorporeal mover. To this it can be said that a corporeal mover is intermediate, and is not the first cause of motion. Action and reaction occur between bodies, but motion can be caused also by immaterial agents, such as intelligence and will. In such a case there is no reaction, because mover and moved are of a different order of being.

These and other difficulties are usually posed by those who regard the principles and concepts of Newtonian mechanics as having ontological validity and thus interpret them in a way that negates the philosophical argument already advanced. Such an interpretation, it should be noted, is not itself essential to Newtonian science, and indeed does not represent the common view of philosophers of science (*see* MOTION, LAWS OF).

Relativity and Quantum Theory. Further difficulties arise from the concepts and principles of modern physics. Motion in one observable body can be determined only in relation to another observable body. According to the principle of relativity, it is impossible to say definitively whether or not any body is in motion or at rest. Indeed it makes no difference whether one body is thought to be at rest while another is in motion. But it is important, in order to understand the case, to consider the sense in which it makes no difference which body is in motion, or whether both are in motion. The apparent motion of a body can be measured only in relation to another body, and for the purposes of mathematical formulation and calculation, abstracting as they do from many physical details, it may make no difference which body is in motion. Yet from ordinary experience one knows that there are motions, such as walking and writing, that are not merely apparent and relative but genuine and essential. It is on motions of this type that the argument for the first cause of motion is based.

Likewise, the difficulties against the argument that arise from the data and principles of *quantum theory come from the limitations of accurate measurements and the scope of mathematical formulation. Physical realities cannot be measured with complete accuracy, nor can one perform several measurements at the same time. Yet even though man's knowledge of detail is limited, still he knows many instances of essential motion that depend upon various intermediate movers; these ultimately lead to the first cause of motion.

Modern Philosophies. Difficulties arising in modern philosophies are systematic and profound. Idealists deny the distinction between knowledge and things having their own natural being, and so they do not admit a material world with its own motion, nor do they acknowledge a first cause of motion in the physical order, although they may admit a first principle in the order of logic or knowledge. Empiricists and positivists admit sensible phenomena but deny intelligible being, including genuine effects and their proper causes. Materialists hold that the sensible world is self-sufficient, either with or without rigid determinism. Agnostics and skeptics maintain that man cannot know the essential reasons of things, whether or not they have any. Ways of thought such as these do not lead to knowledge of the first cause of motion, because they are based on the denial either of the real physical world (*idealism), or of genuine effects bringing novelty into the world (*empiricism), or of the basic limitations of matter (*materialism), or of the possibility of knowing essential causes on which effects depend in being, without which they cannot be (*agnosticism, *skepticism).

See also GOD; GOD AND MODERN SCIENCE; EFFICIENT CAUSALITY.

Bibliography: E. A. SILLEM, *Ways of Thinking About God* (New York 1961). V. E. SMITH, *General Science of Nature* (Milwaukee 1958). W. A. WALLACE, "Newtonian Antinomies Against the *Prima Via*," Thomist 19 (1956) 151–192. Syntopicon 1:179–192, 543–604.

[W. H. KANE]

MOTION, LAWS OF

The three laws of *motion formulated by Sir Isaac *Newton (1642–1727) in his *Principia Mathematica Philosophiae Naturalis* (1687) systematized the science of mechanics and marked a turning-point in the history of science. Although these laws have proved extremely useful, their logical and ontological implications have been a subject of debate since Newton first formulated them. This article aims to present a representative scientific and philosophical evaluation of the laws, first explaining their more obvious content and consequences, then supplying a more detailed analysis of their meaning, and finally discussing some illicit philosophical inferences drawn from the laws that are of particular relevance to Catholic thought.

Explanation of the Laws of Motion

In the first book of the *Principia*, Newton states the three laws of motion as follows:

Law 1. Every body continues in its state of rest, or uniform motion in a straight line, unless it is compelled to change that state by forces impressed upon it.

Law 2. The change of motion is proportional to the motive force impressed, and is made in the direction of the straight line in which that force is impressed.

Law 3. To every action there is always opposed an equal reaction; or, the mutual actions of two bodies upon each other are always equal, and directed to contrary parts.

Principle of Inertia. The first law simply states what happens to a material body when it is not acted upon by external forces: it perseveres in its original state, whether this is a state of rest or one of uniform rectilinear motion. The property of matter by which it tends to conserve its present state—or conversely, its incapability of spontaneously changing that state when left to itself—is called inertia.

One can directly experience inertia in its passive aspect in the resistance met when attempting to move a weighty object from rest. The dynamic propensity of a body to continue indefinitely in uniform rectilinear motion, commonly referred to as the force of inertia, is similarly experienced in the force encountered when one is trying to alter or stop the forward progress of a moving object.

Although Newton was preceded in the enunciation of this law by C. Benedetti, B. Telesio, G. Bruno, Galileo, and C. Huygens, his is the classic formulation of the principle of inertia, and the doctrine as explained in the *Principia* is the first completely developed inertial physics.

The first law of motion can be stated mathematically in the following terms. If $\mathbf{F} = 0$, then $m\, d\mathbf{v}/dt = 0$; or, if $\mathbf{F} = 0$, then $d\mathbf{v}/dt = 0$; where $\mathbf{F}$ represents the external force, m the mass of the body, and $\mathbf{v}$ its velocity over a time period, t. The first formulation interprets motion in the modern sense of momentum, whereas the second interprets motion as velocity. When mass can be treated as a constant, as in nonrelativistic mechanics, the two formulations become mathematically equivalent.

The primary implication of the first law is that it furnishes a provisional, qualitative definition of force as "whatever changes the state of rest or uniform rectilinear motion of a body." If not a strict definition, this affords at least a criterion for force, since nonuniform, curvilinear motion indicates the presence and activity of some force. Secondly, the use of the terms "uniform" and "straight line" imply some trustworthy clock involving an isochronal repetitive process and some fixed coordinate system of reference.

Second Law. The second law is an amplification and clarification of the first. Whereas in the first Newton provides a criterion for detecting the presence of force, in the second he gives a precise method of measuring force and thus supplies a quantitative or operational definition. The term motion here indicates momentum, whose numerical value depends on the velocity and the inertial mass of the moving body. The force is directly proportional to either of these if the other remains constant. Thus the meaning of the law, simply stated, is that a force can be measured in magnitude and direction by measuring a change of acceleration. Conversely, if the mass is given, acceleration can be calculated by the measurement of the direction and magnitude of the force involved. It follows then that one can use this law to compare and measure various forces and the masses of different bodies.

Mathematically expressed, the second law states that $d(m\mathbf{v})/dt = k\mathbf{F}$ where k is a constant of proportionality and $\mathbf{F}$ and $d(m\mathbf{v})/dt$ are vectors having the same direction. This can be stated in its familiar form, $\mathbf{F} = m\mathbf{a}$, if k be set equal to unity, by a proper choice of units, if m be assumed to remain constant, and if the time rate of change of velocity (acceleration) be designated $\mathbf{a}$.

Two observations can be made on the implications of the second law. First, the "straight line" of the direction of momentum and force of which Newton speaks presents a special problem. A body of appreciable dimensionality does not move along one straight line, since it is not itself a point. Therefore this and the other laws of motion consider bodies as mass points; i.e., as if all their mass were concentrated in a mathematical point. A similar observation applies to the assumption, implicit in the first two laws, that both spatial dimensions and temporal periods can be indefinitely subdivided, so that the magnitudes associated with them can be vanishingly small. The implication of instantaneous velocities and accelerations associated with mass points reveals the theoretical character of these laws, as explained below. Secondly, the second law signals a marked variance between Newtonian physics and that of Aristotle. The laws of motion of Aristotle state only that a given force provides an object with a characteristic speed; Newton modified this by asserting that a given force always produces a definite acceleration.

Action and Reaction. Although the third law involves no new concepts, it is generally considered the most important and original of the three axioms because of the extension it gives to the concept of force. In the third law force is understood dualistically, as always involving action and reaction. Force is never found in an isolated, unilateral condition; rather, a pair of equal and opposite forces are always found together. The action and reaction of which it speaks, however, do not act on the same body. If they did, they would cancel each other, with the result that there would be no means of ascertaining the presence of any forces. The law envisages the case of body A exerting a force on body B, which in turn exerts a reaction on the original body A. This can be expressed mathematically by the equation:

$\mathbf{F}_{AB} = -\mathbf{F}_{BA}$ where $\mathbf{F}_{AB}$ and $\mathbf{F}_{BA}$ are the two interacting forces.

Two observations can also be made regarding this third law. First, it can be restated as the principle of conservation of momentum, viz, in the absence of external forces, the total change in momentum in a collision is zero. Thus, if the momentum of one body was $m_1\mathbf{v}_1$ before collision and $m_1\mathbf{v}'_1$ after collision, the change in momentum for this body is $\Delta\mathbf{p}_i = m_1\mathbf{v}' - m_1\mathbf{v}_1$ and for an n-fold collision

$$\sum_{i=1}^{m} \Delta\mathbf{p}i = 0$$

Secondly, although only the first two laws are necessary for the development of kinematics and the statics and kinetics of single particles, the third law is a necessary adjunct for the evolution of the remainder of dynamics, i.e., the statics and kinetics of rigid bodies, liquids, and gases.

LOGICAL AND ONTOLOGICAL ANALYSIS

Historically, no single physical theory has been subjected to as rigorous and exacting an analysis and evaluatory criticism as Newton's laws of motion; besides figuring in the monumental critique of Immanuel *Kant, they have also been judged (and prejudged) by such thinkers as J. d'*Alembert, S. D. Poisson, J. H. *Poincaré, C. D. Broad, E. *Mach, and B. *Russell. This section proposes an objective and neutral evaluation consonant with the philosophical position of moderate realism. It is done in five steps showing progressively that the laws are: (1) not a priori truths, (2) not evident from experience, (3) principles based on limit concepts, (4) not entirely conventional, and (5) theoretical, not experimental laws.

Not A Priori Truths. The first question to be settled is whether or not these axioms of motion are strictly intuitive principles whose truth is established solely by rational analysis, beyond refutation, and without need of *demonstration. Historically, D'Alembert, George Atwood, William Whewell, and J. L. *Lagrange held that these laws can be asserted with apriority and apodictic certainty.

The classical presentation of this view is contained in D'Alembert's *Traité de dynamique*. He declared that a body will remain at rest "as long as an external cause does not move it. For a body cannot be brought into motion of itself, since there is no reason why it should move in one direction rather than another." This basic premise he then applies to moving bodies, reasoning that a body will continue in infinite, uniform, and rectilinear motion in the absence of external causes, for then there would be nothing to determine decrease rather than increase, or deviation to the right rather than to the left.

While at first glance this seems as cogent as the principle of *sufficient reason upon which it is based, a moment of reflection reveals its fallacy. For what is to stop one from arguing in the following way: A body moving in an accelerated manner under the influence of external forces, if left to itself, should continue to accelerate indefinitely because there is no reason why it should not. Besides this, the view also involves the logical *fallacy of *petitio principii*. For D'Alembert treats changes of velocity as necessarily requiring a cause, a force, but allows changes of place without the necessity of such an external force. This basic assumption actually begs the question, for of and by themselves, neither change of velocity nor change of place deserves privileged consideration. Without recourse to direct experience, neither enjoys a purely logical primacy over the other. One can thus conclude with Eddington's evaluation of the apriority of the first law, which restates it to read: "Every particle continues in its state of rest or uniform motion in a straight line, except insofar as it doesn't."

Not Evident from Experience. Although the a priori view is no longer taken seriously, there are those who propose the first law as evident in the sense that it is clearly perceived from experience. They argue that a body at rest will obviously remain at rest if undisturbed, and that a body set in motion along a level surface will tend to move in a straight line. Moreover, the smoother the surface, the farther the object will move, and thus they reason that there is an indirect proportion between the distance the body will move and the degree of resistance offered by the surface or medium. From this, they say, one intuitively realizes that if the resistance-offering medium were eliminated completely, the body would continue to move indefinitely with unaccelerated motion.

Ordinary experience, however, belies such an inference. If the level surface sustaining any body in motion on earth were removed entirely, the body would not continue in uniform, rectilinear motion, but would fall with the acceleration due to gravity. Secondly, the observational experience of scientists yields no evidence for the existence of an absolutely nonresistive medium. The total *vacuum that is presupposed in this argument is nonexistent, at least in the sense that gravitational or electromagnetic forces seem always present in the physical universe.

Such considerations shed light on the true status of the law of inertia: it speaks of something that can exist only in the logical order, viz, force-free motion. The law states what would be verified if a moving body were isolated from everything else in the universe, and in this sense is what philosophers refer to as a counterfactual conditional. Thus N. R. Hanson would restate it to read as follows: "*If there were* a particle free of unbalanced, external forces, then it would either remain absolutely at rest, or would manifest uniform rectilinear motion *ad infinitum*" (111).

Principle Based on Limit Concepts. Newton's reasoning in establishing the principle of inertia was basically as described in the last section. Analyzing the motion of projectiles, he stated the apparently verifiable proportion: the less the resistance or the greater the velocity, the less the deviation from rectilinearity and the further the projectile will move. At this stage of his reasoning he was dealing inductively with experientially perceptible fact. He then went on, more from insight than experience, to state that one might "by increasing the velocity . . . increase the distance to which it might project and . . . diminish the curvature of the line it might describe . . . so that it might go forward into celestial spaces, [and] proceed in its motion ad infinitum" (*Mathematical Principles,* ed. Cajori, 6). Here he applied his proportion, increasing the velocity and allowing the air resistance to go to zero, until he reached the limiting case: motion ad infinitum. The first law is simply the formulation of this limiting case as a principle of motion (*see* LIMIT).

From this it should be clear that the principle of inertia, the first law of motion, is actually an inference drawn from a reasoning process that involves a limit concept. For this reason philosophers in the Thomistic tradition consider it more a physico-mathematical principle than one based directly on a study of the world of nature (cf. Wallace, 173–186).

Not Entirely Conventional. Up to this point emphasis has been placed on the first law, stressing its nonempirical character. When turning attention to the second and third laws, one finds that the approach must be reversed. There is no need to prove the physico-mathematical character of these laws, for they can be adequately expressed in mathematical equations. The effort here must be directed toward showing that these two laws are not merely arbitrary conventions, nor entirely devoid of empirical content.

Historically, there has been a tendency to consider these two axioms as purely conventional definitions, uncertifiable experimentally, and irrefutable (*see* CONVENTIONALISM). This nominalist position, held by Mach, G. R. Kirchhoff, L. *Boltzmann, and Poincaré, looks upon the second and third laws of motion as concealed definitions of force and mass respectively. The problems posed by such a position are not easily solved, but one can at least point out some general lines of solution.

Notion of Force. The claim that the second law is a mere definition of *force reduces it to a tautology. If force is identical with change of momentum, then the law is reducible to the proposition: "The changes of momentum are proportional to the changes of momentum." To show the empirical content in the second law and avoid absolute conventionalism, one need only provide a method of defining and measuring force independently of the second axiom.

It seems that this can be accomplished. First of all, some forces are psychologically perceptible through the muscular strain and stress involved in lifting, dragging, and throwing. These strains may not be the forces themselves, but they do indicate the presence of forces and they afford, independently of the second law, a basis for the concept of force. This explains the use of the term force by many thinkers before the time of Newton.

Again, there are methods of measuring forces without reference to the rate of change of momentum. For example, the elastic deformation of a spring, supplying as it does a static measure of force, is obviously independent of the second law. Yet it is not universally true that one can always measure forces without recourse to the second law. Even in these nonverifiable cases, however, the axiom does not become purely definitional, for its actual use in mechanics always involves a definite force function that has a determinate form and contains determined variables and constants.

Notion of Mass. Turning now to the third law, one can use the same process to show empirical content by pointing out how to define and measure *mass independently of this axiom. First of all, one can perceive the effects of mass in bodily sensation. For example, to move two bodies of the same size but of different substance, more exertion is required for putting one in motion than the other. The effort made is dependent on two factors: the velocity given to the bodies and the materials of the bodies themselves. This is man's primitive perception and crude measurement of the property

called inertial mass; it does not involve explicit reference to the third law.

More technically, one can measure inertial mass through experimentation with the impact of bodies. For example, when two bodies, B_1 and B_2, collide, one can assign a numerical coefficient m_{12} to B_1 and m_{21} to B_2, such that, if u_1 and u_2 be the respective velocities before, and v_1 and v_2 the velocities after,

$$m_{12}u_1 + m_{21}u_2 = m_{12}v_1 + m_{21}v_2$$

Such coefficients can be assigned for any two colliding bodies. Furthermore, by repeating the experiment, using one of the original bodies B_2 and a new body B_3, one finds a definite coefficient to be experimentally associated with each and every body. This coefficient is a measure of inertial mass. The fact that one calls such coefficients the measure of relative mass is itself definitional, but the fact that these coefficients remain constant, regardless of the velocity or the nature of the bodies involved, is not. Therefore the third law is not purely definitional, and more is involved in its formulation than mere convention (cf. Nagel, 186–202).

Theoretical Laws. Experimental laws, apart from being expressible by a mathematical relation, have a second characteristic in that they are inductive generalizations that can be verified within definite limits (*see* PHYSICAL LAWS). The latter characteristic is not found in the three laws of motion. As already explained, because these laws are based upon limit concepts and have something of a definitional character, they may be regarded as idealizations that cannot be strictly substantiated in experience.

This logical character of the axioms does not detract from their scientific value. They can still be considered as valid theoretical laws or principles. As such, they are postulates or hypotheses underlying a theory from which many consequences can be deduced that are themselves empirically verifiable, and thus are strict scientific laws. Such theoretical laws have great value in that they correlate many scientific facts, enable new phenomena to be observed, and aid in the solution of technological problems. Newton's laws of motion thus supply the foundation for a theory of mechanics that is an excellent approximation to reality, and is extremely useful for codifying the many experimental facts known about local motion. (*See* EXPLANATION IN MODERN SCIENCE.)

IMPLIED PHILOSOPHICAL PROBLEMS

The problems implied in the laws of motion, if restricted only to those involving apparent rejections of the scholastic concept of *efficient causality, arise from three sources, viz, (1) inertial motion, (2) action and reaction, and (3) action at a distance.

Inertial Motion. It is the uncritical opinion of many that the law of inertia—affirming as it does uniform, rectilinear motion without an external force—asserts that real change can occur without an explanatory cause, and thus contradicts the principle of *causality. Some would solve this problem immediately by pointing out that purely inertial motion, because it is associated with a counterfactual conditional, is only ideal and therefore needs no real cause. This solution, while of dialectical value, seems more to avoid the problem than to solve it. Furthermore, although purely inertial motion as such does not seem to exist in the physical universe, some motions are close approximations to it. For example, the motions of stars and planets, and of projectiles in very rare media, are almost uniform, and seem to be effected without an external force.

It is true that the principle of efficient causality demands an active, effective cause, not only in the beginning of such motion but also as long as the motion continues. However, such a cause is not necessarily an external force in the sense in which this term is used in mechanics. Since mechanical force is by definition the cause of acceleration, and since inertial motion involves no acceleration, there is no need of an external force. This admission, however, in no way excludes the need of some effective cause of the change that is motion itself. A real change is involved in inertial motion; the body's "being here" in one *place is continually being changed to a "being there" in another place. And this constant change, itself not self-explanatory, needs an efficient cause to explain its continuing existence.

The principle of causality merely demands, however, that there exist some efficient cause that is distinct from the motion itself and from the body that is moving. This distinction between the cause and the material body does not require that the cause be outside of the body, and thus external in the sense of a mechanical force. The cause of the motion must involve otherness, but this is verified as long as it remains distinct from the motion itself and the body that is moving.

One can arrive at a more precise notion of the efficiency involved by considering inertial motion in its totality. Experience shows that bodies in inertial motion produce effects on other bodies. For example, they communicate impetus and motion, and deform elastic bodies in collisions. Therefore such motion has associated with it some qualitative energy, a real active potency that accidentally modifies the body undergoing motion. This quality has been variously called *impetus by the medievals, momentum by R. *Descartes, and kinetic energy by G. W. Leibniz. Such impetus meets all the demands of efficient causality, and suffices to preserve the notion of continued causal action that is rejected by some on the basis of the law of inertia.

Action and Reaction. The philosophical problems arising from the third law of motion are two in number, one associated with the action of incorporeal substances on bodies, the other associated with the unidirectional character of causal action.

The action-reaction principle seems to exclude the possibility of any causation between corporeal and incorporeal being; thus it apparently invalidates the Thomistic argument for the existence of God based on motion. This difficulty is rooted in a misunderstanding of the third law of motion and its unjustified extension beyond the realm originally intended by Newton. An analysis of the law itself shows that it describes the symmetry involved in the transmission of mechanical forces. In so doing, it abstracts from movers or physical causes as these are considered in the argument of St. Thomas, but it does not reject them. In fact, Newton himself made explicit allowance for an immaterial mover, and seems to have thought it the originative source of all motion.

The second problem arises from the fact that some see the third law as invalidating the unidirectionality of the causal principle. The principle of causality, they say, asserts a one-sided dependence of the effect upon the cause, and thus explains activity without reactivity, such as required by the third law. The solution of this problem is found in a fuller understanding of causality itself. In the Aristotelian-Thomistic conception of causality, every finite and imperfect agent, precisely as finite and imperfect, suffers some change or loss in its act of causing. The reason for this is that the imperfect agent, as a composite of act and potency, is partly agent and partly patient. From this it follows that one should expect physical agents to undergo reaction from the physical bodies they act upon, in a way that it is not inconsistent with the third law.

Action at a Distance. The third and final problem related to the motion of physical bodies is that of action at a distance. It can be posed in the following terms: "Can the forces of one body act upon another body without mediate or immediate physical contact?" This problem, more associated with the notion of gravitational attraction than the three laws of motion, has two different aspects, one metaphysical, the other physical.

That action at a distance is metaphysically impossible seems to have been the opinion of Aristotle and St. Thomas; the metaphysical impossibility is still maintained by modern scholastics, although some question whether or not this is demonstrable. The argument most generally used is based on the essential accidentality of force and action. As accidents, force and action must be sustained either by the substance of the agent, or by the body acted upon, or by some intermediary; they cannot leave the agent and sustain themselves autonomously in being until coming into contact with another body. If this is the case, an action of one physical body on another, without any intermediate contact, is metaphysically unintelligible.

Regarding the physical impossibility of action at a distance there seems to be increasing unanimity of opinion. That all material activity is effected through at least intermediate contact seems presumed by contemporary physical theories, to the extent that they presuppose the existence of some type of medium. Whether this medium is conceived as the classical *ether of electromagnetics, or as a more subtle intra-atomic ether of microphysics, or as some sort of field, or as the qualitatively configurable continuum of *relativity, it appears to be basic to modern theories. Since such a medium can serve to transmit action and motion, it does not dispense with the notion of efficient causality as this is understood in scholastic philosophy. (*See* ACTION AT A DISTANCE.)

See also GRAVITATION; ENERGY; ACTION AND PASSION; SCIENCE, PHILOSOPHY OF; MOTION, FIRST CAUSE OF; GOD AND MODERN SCIENCE.

Bibliography: I. NEWTON, *Mathematical Principles of Natural Philosophy and His System of the World,* ed. F. CAJORI (Berkeley 1946). I. B. COHEN, *Franklin and Newton* (Philadelphia 1956). A. E. BELL, *Newtonian Science* (New York 1961). G. J. WHITROW, "On the Foundations of Dynamics," *British Journal for the Philosophy of Science* 1 (1950) 92–107. A. S. EDDINGTON, *The Nature of the Physical·World* (New York 1935). J. L. D'ALEMBERT, *Traité de dynamique,* 2 v. (Paris 1921). H. POINCARÉ, *The Foundations of Science: Science and Hypothesis, The Value of Science, Science and Method* (Lancaster, Pa. 1946). E. MACH, *The Science of Mechanics,* tr. T. J. McCORMACK (5th ed. La Salle, Ill. 1942). C. D. BROAD, *Scientific Thought* (London 1923). E. NAGEL, *The Structure of Science* (New York 1961). N. R. HANSON, "The Law of Inertia: A Philosopher's Touchstone," *Philosophy of Science* 30 (1963) 107–121. W. A. WALLACE, "Newtonian Antinomies Against the *Prima Via*," *Thomist* 19 (1956) 151–192. J. A. WEISHEIPL, "Natural and

Compulsory Motion," NewSchol 29 (1955) 50–81. M. JAMMER, *The Concepts of Force* (Cambridge, Mass. 1957); *The Concepts of Mass in Classical and in Modern Physics* (Cambridge, Mass. 1961). E. McMULLIN, *The Concept of Matter* (South Bend, Ind. 1963). M. B. HESSE, *Forces and Fields: The Concepts of Action at a Distance in the History of Physics* (New York 1962).

[T. D. FEEHAN]

MOTIVATION

A human motive has been defined as "that which acts as an inducement to preference or choice; that which, speaking figuratively, tends to move the will; a strong or impelling influence toward some particular object to be obtained or end to be secured. In this meaning of the word, reference is always had to some subjective precondition or tendency and never to an external force or cause" (Funk and Wagnall's *Standard Dictionary*). The definition in the *Encyclopedia of Psychology* (ed. P. L. Harriman, New York 1946) has the same import: "a goad to action; usually restricted to a more or less well-verbalized drive to behavior." More recently, motive has been defined as anything that "arouses, sustains and directs activity" (P. T. Young).

This last definition really implies that the living being is inert, roused to activity by special driving forces. The basic questions: "Why does a living being act at all?" and "Why does it act as it does?" are usually answered by analogy with physical objects: A force is required to move man or animal to action.

Instincts and Drives. The older instinct theorists had assumed that instincts are special forces expressed in rigidly determined patterns. This conception fits only insects. In vertebrates, instinctual action is never that rigid; there is always room for learning and adaptation. Eventually, it came to be thought that only the driving force is innate while the action pattern may be flexible. Thus the term drive came to be preferred to *instinct.

Both instinct and drive theories explain why man and animals act by postulating a set of biological engines, the drives. But there is a wide gap between biological drives and adult human motives, and neither drive nor instinct theories have spanned it successfully. To explain how instincts can drive to activities that do not aim at a biological goal, "social" instincts must be added to provide for adult human motivation (e.g., in the system of W. *McDougall). And in the theory of S. *Freud, where drives are so general as to account for all actions by various combinations of the sexual drive (libido) and the death instinct, a secondary organization (the ego) must be assumed to account for actions in the "conflict-free sphere of the ego." In other drive theories, also, secondary drives are added to complement primary biological forces.

Both alternatives (social instincts and secondary drives) are poor makeshifts. Social and cultural instincts cannot have a biological source—yet instincts were postulated originally because some biological force seemed necessary to explain action. In theories employing secondary drives, these are supposed to draw their energy from primary drives—yet the mode of this energy transformation is all but inexplicable. Both notions are *ad hoc* hypotheses made necessary by the inadequacy of instinct and drive theories to explain the bewildering variety of human actions.

Behavioristic Explanations. Since instinct and drive psychology had failed to account for adult human actions, should it not be possible to explain them simply, behavioristically, as man's responses to conditioned stimuli?

On the face of it, this seems an attractive alternative. The most diverse actions of the civilized adult could be explained as products of conditioned response chains. The only difficulty is to make such indiscriminate linkages plausible. Theoretically, the conditioned response is a reaction to the *un*conditioned stimulus: man or animal must learn that the conditioned stimulus announces (or belongs to) the unconditioned stimulus. But when a new motive is acquired, the new conditioned stimulus (the behaviorist's "motive") has actually never been paired with the unconditioned stimulus. A man may decide to become a painter or a poet in spite of the fact that his paintings or poems have as yet brought him neither money nor recognition. Indeed, he often has to have a paying job that will enable him to follow his avocation. How can conditioning explain, for instance, the case of Heinrich Schliemann, the famous merchant turned archeologist, who on reading Homer was struck by the thought that Troy must actually have existed? To find Troy became his dominant motive until, many years later, he could start his explorations and finally discovered its site.

Allport's "Functional Autonomy of Motives." G. W. Allport, in *Personality: A Psychological Interpretation* (New York 1937), suggested that adult motives may develop from biological needs as the result of incidental interests developed in the pursuit of instinctive goals. Though the child acts under the compulsion of biological drives, the adult acts from motives developed in the course of his growing up. According to Allport, there is merely a historical but no causal connection between the child's biological drives and the adult's social, cultural, or religious motives. The principle of functional autonomy really assumes that the individual comes to select his goals. Unfortunately, Allport does not spell out how the new motive moves to action and whether it derives its energy from the incidental association with biological drives.

Need as Motive. Since about 1940, the term need has often been used as a substitute for drive because it seems to relieve the theorist from postulating a biological source of motivation. When the meaning is extended to anything an individual deems necessary, psychological and social needs can be postulated as easily as biological needs.

A. H. Maslow, for instance, postulated a hierarchy of needs. When the physiological needs are satisfied, safety needs will emerge; and when these are largely satisfied, love needs can be experienced. Still later, the need for esteem and, finally, the need for self-actualization emerge. In addition to these five conative needs, Maslow recognizes also a "need to know" that must be satisfied before the "need to understand" can emerge. However, though a man will want the more basic of two needs when deprived in both, he may not act accordingly because, Maslow says, "there are many determinants of behavior other than the needs and desires."

This is a far more sophisticated scheme than that of most need theories. With them it has in common that needs are felt as desires. But it is not at all clear how the higher needs emerge "by slow degrees from nothingness," nor is it clear what motivates a man's actions when he goes counter to his desires.

Ethology. In recent years, European ethologists have approached instinctive motivation from a new angle. First K. Lorenz and later N. Tinbergen (*The Study of Instinct,* Oxford 1951) have reported that instinctive actions are touched off by a specific "releaser." For instance, the shadow of a bird with a short neck will make newborn ducklings run for cover, while the shadow of a bird with a long neck is ignored by them. Ethologists have also found that a few hours after hatching, chicks or ducklings will follow any moving object, be it the mother bird or the experimenter, and will keep on following on sight what has been "imprinted" in this way. These observations are interesting because they throw light on the working of instinct. At the same time, calling certain objects "releasers" does not explain their actual function. A releaser does not release a mechanical spring so that the following sequence of actions will be reeled off automatically. What is still missing is an explanation of how the releaser or the imprinting object do their work.

Definition of Motive. In accord with St. *Thomas Aquinas, a motive can be defined as "A want that leads to action." This takes into account that something must be appraised as good and so wanted, that this desire is not countermanded but leads to action. There are wants that do not lead to action either because they conflict with more important wants or because there is no action that seems suitable. A person may long for a warmer clime, a better job, a happier life; but there may be nothing he can do to bring it about.

The want that leads to action is experienced as such and arouses an action impulse that may be emotional and/or deliberate (a will impulse). Sometimes what is good (useful) is the means toward a goal that has practical value but is not pleasurable. A man may work overtime so he can pay for diagnostic tests that will indicate whether he has a malignant disease. Or, what is judged good may mean going counter to a strong desire or an instinctive tendency. The diabetic may be hungry for sweets, yet must restrict himself to a severely reduced sugar intake. A hunger strike such as Ghandhi's requires an impulse to action that goes counter to an imperative physiological need. In such a case, the action is deliberate rather than emotionally motivated. Of course, since man is a unit, a reflective judgment that something is desirable also brings with it a supporting sense judgment; but the action impulse so aroused is necessarily weaker than that produced by a strong emotional attraction.

Motive and Instinct. Neither a motive nor an instinct is a driving force, pushing man or animal to action. Rather, knowing something and valuing it arouses an urge to attain. Such wanting (whether deliberate or emotional) is an action tendency mediated by neural pathways that carry motor impulses to the appropriate muscles. And muscles contract to carry out the desired action if glycogen is available and the organism is functioning normally.

Instinctive Action. What distinguishes instinctive action from any other kind is the distinctive physiological state that sensitizes man or animal to objects offering satisfaction at this and no other time. So the salmon is content in the ocean for 4 years until the milt and roe begin to form. Only then do both male and female feel the urge to travel back to their birthplace. The physiological state brings about a felt urge that sensitizes the

appraisal of certain things needed at this and no other time. This triggers off the wanting that leads to migration, to seeking of food, mate, or bits of hay and straw for nest building. Instinctive action stops when the physiological state ceases. When the bird's eggs are ready to be laid, this urge disappears and the nest building stops.

This instinctive urge is neither a force nor is it a source of energy. It merely initiates nerve impulses that make it felt as a want and lead to action. When the desired object is found, it is appraised as good and arouses an emotional action impulse that, like every other emotion, directs action by mediating the nerve impulses that lead to a specific pattern of muscular contractions.

Instinctive activity is a disposition to a whole sequence of actions, the purpose of which is unknown to the animal. The animal knows and evaluates the thing wanted at each step in the sequence (the bird knows and wants mate, hay, nest, egg laying, and feeding of young); but the human being not only knows what he wants at each step in the sequence but also knows the sequence itself, and can act in accordance with its purpose or contrary to it. Since every motive has been defined as a want that leads to action, and the desire to act is aroused by an estimate (intuitive or reflective) and not by a physiological drive, there is no need to derive all motives from a few biological instincts. The desire to build a house, paint a picture, worship God, is the outcome of man's judgment that these things are good to do. Social, cultural, religious activities spring from rational motives, but they are for all that just as "primary," just as dependent on man's subjective evaluation, as any act in an instinctive sequence.

Rational Motives. Rational motives develop when the value of an object can be grasped by *reflection. While some inherent action tendencies (emotion and physiological appetite) take one into action without effort, a rational motive (something conceived of as useful or valuable) requires a decision to act and sustained determination to carry it out.

Since the emotional attraction produced by the reflective judgment is weak compared to the desire aroused by something inherently pleasurable, the rational decision must be affirmed against the pull of natural attractions—which accounts for the difficulty in making and carrying out such decisions. (For a fuller discussion of the scholastic doctrine, *see* MOTIVE.)

Measurement of Motivation. Though the want that leads to action must be experienced (or it could not arouse an action impulse) a person does not know all the factors that have influenced his appraisal. For this reason, one cannot reliably measure motives by asking a man about his own, even if he be willing to answer frankly. Motives have to be measured indirectly. Frequently, psychologists have tried to infer a man's motives from the values he holds. But not every value is a motive. There are values that do not lead to action. A man may consider education valuable but have no desire to continue his own. Too often, a value indicates not what a man wants for himself but what, more or less academically, he thinks is good for other people. For this reason, the *value judgment has not been particularly useful for assessing a man's motives. (See VALUE, PHILOSOPHY OF.)

Another indirect method used frequently is that of letting a man tell stories and infer from them what he would do in similar situations (Thematic Apperception Test). One of the best known methods of interpretation is McClelland's system (D. C. McClelland et al.). He scores each story for various achievement "themes" to discover the storyteller's "need for achievement" (n Ach). If desired, the same stories can also be scored for the "need for affiliation" and the "need for power." The most widely used of these is McClelland's n Ach scoring, which has a positive but highly variable relation to school grades (among boys). For girls, the "need for affiliation" seems to be more highly related to school achievement than the "need for achievement."

A more recent method of measuring motivation is Story Sequence Analysis, proposed by the author of this article. This method also employs stories but abstracts from each story an import, indicating the storyteller's opinion of the story plot and outcome. When these imports are read in sequence, they give the storyteller's convictions, his principles of action or motivational attitudes, rather than ascribing to him the emotions and actions of the story characters, as is done in other methods. Story sequence analysis has been found successful in predicting school achievement, success in teaching, and religious vocations. Since the sequence of imports gives a connected picture of the storyteller's own life situation, his goals, his problems, and their attempted solutions, this method can also be used to help the storyteller to resolve personal difficulties and increase his motivation.

See also APPETITE; EMOTION; WILL; DETERMINISM, PSYCHOLOGICAL.

Bibliography: M. B. ARNOLD, *Emotion and Personality,* 2 v. (New York 1960); *Story Sequence Analysis: A New Method of Measuring Motivation and Predicting Achievement* (New York 1962). D. C. McCLELLAND et al., *The Achievement Motive* (New York 1953). A. H. MASLOW, *Motivation and Personality* (New York 1954). C. L. STACY and M. F. DeMARTINO, eds., *Understanding Human Motivation* (Cleveland 1958). P. T. YOUNG, *Motivation and Emotion* (New York 1961).

[M. B. ARNOLD]

MOTIVATION (EDUCATION)

In its first general meaning, motivation refers to a number of different kinds of personal inner states, activities, or conditions that tend to arouse, sustain, direct, intensify, and reinforce behavior and performance. These have traditionally been distinguished from the "cognitive" mental states or processes that carry the meaning, as it were, of things as they are or as a person perceives them. These states or processes refer rather to the factors influencing how the individual wants to respond to such things, by way of being attracted or repelled by them (the scholastic appetitive faculties), by trying to gain or avoid them, by mobilizing his energies in relation to them, and by the consequent feeling of personal satisfaction in having gained or avoided them. (*See* MOTIVATION; APPETITE.) In a second meaning of the term, motivation refers to the activities of other people, intentional or not, or to the features of surrounding situations that tend to evoke in the individual a personal setting for an appropriate behavior or response. Prominent instances of this external manipulative aspect are the teacher's influence on the child learner in the classroom, the advertiser's appeal to the consumer, the personnel man's concern with worker morale and job satisfaction, and the psychiatrist's attempt to help the person handle his difficulties more effectively. Activities

relevant to these tasks commonly include the attempt to make better use of the sources of motivation that the individual brings with him by channeling or redirecting them; but often, more importantly, they involve the attempt to develop and create new sources of motivation that may be required by the broader and more mature demands of effective living. This developmental aspect of motivating the person is likely to be of special concern to those who, by vocation or profession, such as teachers, directors, child psychiatrists, and mental hygienists, have a long-range outlook for the work of motivation. This also accounts for the academic difficulty of keeping the scientific study of motivation neatly and tidily distinguished from the study of the development of the whole *personality.

Scientific Study. Of rather recent origin is the scientific study of motivation, as contrasted with the perennial humanistic, philosophical, and religious concern with motivation, by whatever name it was called, and dealing primarily with the nature of man, the essence of the good life, and the basic values of human existence. The attempt to submit motivation to the required conditions of experimental control has involved delaying difficulties. Because of its subtlety and complexity, the success of the attempt has been dependent upon the overall degree of theoretical, methodological, and technical sophistication attained chiefly by the psychologist and the educational psychologist. However, sufficient empirical facts are already available to make one aware of important distinctions in the field and the manner of reducing these, through operational definitions, to empirical observation, to see how future experimental and technical steps need to be developed, and to be able to state fairly clearly where the important problems lie that can be attacked empirically.

It is common to distinguish incentives, i.e., aspects of motivation that concern external objects, situations, or events (prizes, rewards, praise, etc.) from the internal energizing activities, states, or conditions, such as: (1) drives or organic needs, induced often by deprivation, as hunger in the experimental animal or in human volunteers in a semistarvation study; (2) social needs, assessed by rating scales or by projective tests; (3) unconscious emotional residues (complexes) left by earlier experiences (psychoanalytic assessment); (4) conscious wishes, desires and wants, suited to rating scales; (5) purposes and ideals derived from clinical or self-ratings; (6) general kinds of interests (interest inventories) that lead to preferred classes of otherwise neutral objects or activities; and (7) personal values (rating scale and clinical assessment), principles of choice between appealing alternatives of action. (*See* PSYCHOANALYSIS; UNCONSCIOUS.) It is particularly these kinds of motives that are involved in what psychologists call a hierarchy of motivational life, and to which much study has been devoted, as in continuing investigations of National Merit Scholars, for example, in trying to assess the influence of the home and social and cultural factors on the development of a strong achievement motive.

Theories. Psychologists are not all agreed that there can be no learning without motivation of some kind, but a widely accepted "drive-reduction" theory of *learning assumes that such is the case. Other psychologists, however, prefer to distinguish learning, as such, from performance, and to believe that motivation affects primarily the latter by increasing attention, for example, by reducing fatigue or monotony, by stimulating to more faithful practice and exercise, or by extending the opportunities to use the new skill or knowledge. Laboratory and classroom studies on the effect of *extrinsic* motivation, such as the use of praise or blame, reward or punishment, knowledge of progress and social competition, usually show that these are added positive factors in increasing the child's learning, but they also point out that the effect obtained varies with the difficulty of the task, the level of ability of the learner, the social background of the child, and the amount of anxiety possibly induced. There is much to be said in favor of the attempt to develop as early as possible *intrinsic* motives such as the desire to satisfy one's intellectual curiosity and the sense of personal accomplishment, progress, and competence. The effective teacher is concerned not only with immediate results but also with the means of progressively "ego-involving" the child in his educational tasks for the sake of his own ultimate motivational independence.

Bibliography: D. Rethlingshafer, *Motivation as Related to Personality* (New York 1963). D. C. Charles, *Psychology of the Child in the Classroom* (New York 1964). M. B. Arnold, *Story Sequence Analysis: A New Method of Measuring Motivation and Predicting Achievement* (New York 1962).

[W. D. COMMINS]

MOTIVE

Whatever moves the human *will, or the sufficient explanation for the act of willing in man. This article investigates the elements that move the rational *appetite from a state of potential willing to that of actually willing. The investigation, which is propaedeutic to all moral science, can be treated in two ways: the philosopher pursues the broad principles that necessarily cover and are applicable to the quasi-infinite variety of human operations, whereas the psychologist considers the same human actions in their more particular existential framework of environment, heredity, biochemistry, etc. The former's conclusions are universal, certain, and "confused," in the sense that all particular differences are fused into a broad unity. The latter's approach gives a more detailed and comparatively clearer, though less certain, picture of human acts in their concrete setting. The two methodologies, though distinct, are, however, complementary; for it is only by their dual process that any integral and sure knowledge of human actions can be gleaned.

This article limits itself to the philosophical analysis of the will's motivation, since the findings of psychology are treated elsewhere (*see* MOTIVATION; DETERMINISM, PSYCHOLOGICAL). To ensure completeness, it first considers the fact of the will's motion and its causes, then the mode of freedom in which the will is moved.

Motion of the Will. To discern the cause of the will's motion, it is necessary to distinguish between the two moments of any *motion, viz, that which physically produces the motion and that which determines it by way of *object, or term. This distinction concerns itself with efficient causality in the order of exercise, sc., to will or not, and with final causality in the order of specification, sc., to will this or that; in other words, with what moves the will as agent and with what moves it as providing its object.

The first conclusion to be seen is that in the actual execution of properly human activity, the will holds the place of first mover in man and so is itself unmoved in this order by any other human faculty. The reason is not hard to discover. Every action is by nature directed toward an object that is its *end and *good. Now, by comparison, one can see that the object of the will is a more universal end and good than the objects of man's other powers; for the will seeks the good of the whole individual, while all other potencies are inclined only to their particular perfection. Thus man is conscious that he ponders, eats, walks, etc., as he wills. The proper object of the will alone is the total good of the one willing, which is integrated by the partial goods of thinking, eating, walking, etc.

In the order of specification, however, the will cannot but be moved by other faculties. The observation that one cannot love what he does not know is here pertinent. The rational appetite is indeed thrust toward goods, but this drive must be elicited by knowledge of what is good and convenient. If a person is to be open to being and goodness, he must first be aware of reality. Certainly, man's emotional states depend on his consciousness, no matter how dim or clouded, of the pleasurable and the painful. So too, a truly human response to good (and conversely evil) must be governed to some degree at least by an intellectual insight into the goodness of things. In short, if one is to will any particular good, he must first have seen it in the light of what he has conceived as his perfection. Thus the will can operate only inasmuch as it is moved by the intellect presenting a possible good to be desired and attained.

Yet the acts of the intellect and will are exercised in the concrete existential order. Men are not subsistent spiritual faculties operating outside of the spatiotemporal dimension. It is always the will of this individual that seeks what he, as a person, wants here and now. The integral conception of a human act, then, demands recognition of man's emotional states as somewhat determinative of his will-acts. Experientially, one is aware of willing to do things precisely because of his emotional condition, of fear, desire, hate, etc. Words spoken in anger are often regretted when wrath has subsided; what was then viewed as good is now regarded with remorse. The sensitive appetites therefore have their dispositive role in shaping the will-act by molding the man willing to the present desirability of this or that particular good. *See* EMOTION; EMOTION (MORAL ASPECT).

Cause of Will's Motion. Within man, then, the will is the prime mover in the executing of his actions, while the will in turn is moved by way of object by the *intellect presenting and the passions disposing. A question remains, however, regarding the will's primacy in moving man. Here experience seems to furnish the answer. The will simply moves itself. Everyone is conscious that he wills to do and to have solely because it is his will. And, let it be added, man is not aware of any exterior force moving him physically; dispositively yes, but not as if it were compelling him to act. This appears true from the very nature of the will, because any particular good that one opts for here and now is always sought in relation to and pursuant of an all-embracive fulfillment. As the will-power is actualized in regard to all-good, it is not inconsistent that it move itself here and now to any particular good. Always the particular is contained in the universal; the commander who can order an army into battle has the power of moving a battalion into action.

While experience testifies to the self-motion of the will, reason is constrained to seek a further explanation. Granting that the will moves itself in terms of particular goods sought, because it is already actualized in regard to its universal function of being open to all-being and good, yet this primary inclination must be accounted for. The will at one time had to pass from the mere capability to the actual willing of this end. As the will is unmoved efficiently by anything within man, clearly the source of its motion must be sought in a mover exterior to himself.

The history of man testifies to the validity of this quest. Cassius might protest that "the fault, dear Brutus, lies not in our stars," but the human race has ever looked upon the celestial luminaries as forces of its destiny. Such has been a constant belief from man's primitive religious persuasions to the more sophisticated theories associated with an ever-expanding universe. Despite its popularity, however, careful study has as constantly rejected this opinion as impossible. That the heavens, atmospheric conditions, etc., have an influence on human affairs is an undeniable fact. But to dispose a man objectively in his willing is in the order of specification, and reason rightly rejects the thesis that the grossly material can efficiently actuate the spiritual, or that the inferior can activate the superior. To hold the contrary is in effect to deny the spiritual nature of man's vital principle; it is to reduce the human to the merely animal.

Indeed, the search for the necessary mover of man's will can be successfully terminated neither in the material order of nature nor even in a world of limited and finite being. The principle of *sufficient reason is here invoked. A cause, limited in itself, cannot suffice to explain an infinite effect. But man's will is unlimited in its yearning for consummation; there is no finite determination in its inclination to embrace all-being and all-good. The cause, then, of this infinite thirst, this openness to being as such, can be only what is itself unlimited, the infinite and uncaused source of all being, "to which everyone gives the name of God."

Freedom of Motion. This conclusion, of course, poses a problem in regard to the *freedom with which the will is traditionally endowed. It seems that if man is not his own first mover, then the ultimate responsibility for his actions must lie in another. It is necessary, therefore, to inspect more closely the manner, or mode, in which the will is moved, i.e., to discover whether it is activated necessarily or freely.

Specification. In the order of specification, the will-act, like all motion, is constituted formally and finally by its proper object. Moreover, the primary limitation of its action must come from its natural determination, viz, from the object that specifies it. This object is the good, or that which is convenient to the one willing. But this good, as has been seen, is presented to the will under the universal competency of the intellect. This means that the proper and adequate object of the will, naturally determining it, will be what is universally good containing within its ambit whatever possesses in any way the aspect of being and goodness. As the eye is for seeing and the hand for manipulating, so too is the will for the real possession of unlimited being and goodness. To this object the will is necessitated by the force of its nature. Whatever a man wills as his good may not be truly good, but it must be sought as constituting or contributing to his perfection. "All men seek happiness," and though at times it may be sought in the ultimate flight from the absurdity of existence, yet in the main man necessarily wills his life and his thought as necessary conditions to his fulfillment.

But beyond this basic determination to *happiness, the will remains free to choose or reject any particular good. It is true that a psychological determinism as old as Socrates posits that the will must always choose the better good. More than a trace of this theory underlies educational systems that expect the more educated person to be necessarily the better person.

Yet such a position inevitably defeats its own idealistic aim, for it limits the horizons of man by curtailing his freedom. The human mind with its universal power of penetration is apprehensive not only of being and goodness in things, but also of the imperfection and limitation native to this finite world of reality. Always the particular good presented to the will can be shown as possessing goodness, and so being desirable, or as lacking in being, and so being undesirable. The will, determined only to the universal good, is not then irresistibly drawn to anything that lacks this universal appeal. Even an abstract consideration of a being necessarily possessive of all being would not perforce move the will, since the very concept of such a being is itself contingent and so unable to move necessarily. Therefore, although the will is determined to goodness, under which aspect alone it may operate, yet, confronted by any particular object lacking a totality of goodness, it remains free.

Again, the question of man's freedom in the light of his emotional reactions has always been a matter of dispute. There are those who, conceiving man as a highly organized type of animal life, contend that, given a certain degree of emotional intensity, he must react in a determined way. There are many who delimit the extent of human liberty in the face of social and physiological factors, all of which influence man by way of emotional stimulation.

But a philosophical consideration of the principles of human action, gained not in an a priori hypothesis but through observation of human nature, ineluctably refutes any such determination of the sensitive order, while at the same time admitting its dispositive influence. For if man's powers of apprehension and appetition are really distinguished into the rational and the animal, the intellectual and the sensitive, his activity will be likewise characterized. Since it is the *person who operates by his various faculties, it is possible that his action may be threefold. His activity may be solely on the intellectual plane, as is evidenced when he is so fully integrated as to arrive at the state of maturity in which his rational nature completely controls his sensitive activity. Again, his action may be purely emotional, in which case all rational vitality is lacking, as in the child or retarded adult. Still a third state is possible, viz, when his voluntary movement runs counter to his animal inclinations. In this more common state, reason and will, though experiencing the impact of passion, are yet free to repel its influence and to hold themselves aloof from its tensions. Thus— as is implicitly affirmed in traditional social and legal thought—whenever there is properly human activity, man is free and capable of restraining the demands of sensitive nature.

Exercise. The problem of the will's freedom in the order of exercise must finally be faced. The will, as any other potential agent, must derive its actualization from a being that is itself unmoved since it is *Pure Act (*see* MOTION, FIRST CAUSE OF). Since subsistent activity would by nature be an irresistible mover, it seems clear that a will so moved could hardly retain the capacity of not moving. The will then would be necessarily moved to execution and its so-called liberty would become impossible.

In principle, the problem is solved by considering the efficacy of the First *Cause whose power extends not only to the production of all things (including the will-act) but also to the mode or manner in which such things are effected. If one is not to fall back into a discredited *occasionalism, one must grant true causality to things. Experience, moreover, is the best proof that the will is an agent that acts freely. As secondary cause, it is indeed moved to its proper operation according to the nature of its being as a participation of Being itself. Since its nature is to operate freely, it is moved freely by the sole cause of its nature. To hold otherwise, for a deistic determinism, would be to place an impossible limitation on providence. But here the human mind reaches the mystery of *infinity. Conscious of its own limitation, the human intellect strives in vain to understand how subsistent motion can be composed with liberty of *choice. Reason can demonstrate the truth of each principle, but their correspondence remains shrouded in the transcendence of the First Cause.

See also CAUSALITY, DIVINE; PREMOTION, PHYSICAL; FREE WILL; HUMAN ACT.

Bibliography: THOMAS AQUINAS, ST 1a2ae, 8, 9, 10. R. E. BRENNAN, *General Psychology* (rev. ed. New York 1952); *Thomistic Psychology* (New York 1956). H. B. VEATCH, *Rational Man: A Modern Interpretation of Aristotelian Ethics* (Bloomington, Ind. 1962).

[T. K. CONNOLLY]

MOTIVE, UNCONSCIOUS

In discussion of the influence of an unconscious or hidden motive upon the morality of human action, the term has been applied to two quite different situations, sometimes with no clear recognition that between them there is a difference that is, from the moral point of view, one not only of degree but also of kind. Sometimes the hidden motive is understood to be more or less deliberately or culpably excluded from consciousness by a kind of self-deception; at other times it indicates a motive that an automatic psychic mechanism has buried deeply in the *unconscious, where it is inaccessible under ordinary circumstances to the conscious mind but exercises a notable influence upon an individual's conscious behavior.

Self-deception. This is common enough in human experience. "It is a common and often repeated conviction of the ascetical writers through the ages that human beings are all too apt to allow their behavior to be determined by motives quite other than those which they think to be operative; and unless that assumption is accepted, all the warnings of the ascetical writers against self-deception become meaningless" (Vann, 118). In this kind of situation the hidden motive is the true end for which the agent acts, and the motive that is con-

sciously asserted is no more than a fabrication invented by the individual to permit himself to appear in his own eyes and in those of others in a more creditable light. The motive he invents is not in any true sense the cause of his acting as he does, but is simply the excuse with which he attempts to justify his action. His inadvertence to his true motive is voluntary and culpable, and it does not in any way prevent his action from being attributable to the motive that is truly operative. In this type of case, therefore, there is no question of double motivation in any proper sense of the term. There is one true motive, and the other is falsely pretexted and asserted by the conscious mind. One cannot generalize, however, and say that wherever there is self-deception that is in any degree culpable, the hidden predisposition to act in a particular way always constitutes a true end or motive in the sense in which the moralist understands the term. But it can be reasonably said that if a person does in fact act for an end that he culpably excludes from consciousness, then the camouflaged objective is the real motive of the action. There is no theoretical difficulty in harmonizing such a falsification of motivation with the teaching of Catholic moral theology regarding the structure of the human act. It is a possibility of which moralists and ascetical writers have always been aware.

The Strictly Unconscious Motive. The difficulty lies rather in integrating into the traditional concept of the human act the motive that is alleged by depth psychologists to lie in some cases more deeply buried in the unconscious through the operation of nonvoluntary psychic mechanisms. The existence of such motivation has not been established beyond doubt, but it is assumed by many and, indeed, is asserted to be a common if not indeed a normal phenomenon and one by no means reserved to those suffering from psychic disorder. However, it may appear difficult to reconcile this assumption with the view of the human act taken in traditional Christian moral thought, according to which a man is normally capable of knowing and indeed of choosing the ends for which he acts.

To avoid equivocation, a distinction must be made between the meaning given to motivation by the psychologist and by the moral theologian. The moralist generally uses the term in the sense of an end, or *causa finalis,* to which human action is directed, whereas for the psychologist a motive is more likely to signify a drive, a tendency, an urge, or an impulse to act—a meaning that is, incidentally, nearer to that given the term by St. Thomas Aquinas, for whom a *causa motiva,* or a *principium movens,* or simply a *motivum,* was identified with efficiency rather than finality. This distinction makes it possible to see that the operation of an unconscious motive (psychological) does not necessarily invalidate, or contradict, or make unreal the motive (moral) asserted by the conscious mind. The two can coexist, each contributing in a different order of causality to the same human activity but without negating the reality of the influence of the other (see Ford and Kelly 1:126).

If there exists a kind of knowledge or volition below the level of consciousness, this cannot be sufficient to account for proper human motivation or the finalization of the human act in the full sense of the word. The unconscious desire, if it exercises any influence at all, must do so in the form of impulses or urges toward activities in conformity with its bent. However, impulses or urges account for one's feeling like doing something, but they do not at all account for why he does it.

In the past the vagaries of individual impulse were regarded as mysterious, and it was considered sufficient for moral judgment to evaluate an act simply in the light of what appears in the conscious mind. Modern depth psychology has not essentially altered this situation. If its assumptions are valid, these simply make clearer the causes of the predispositions and inclinations that precede moral decision. That these influenced moral decision in some cases was not a thing unknown to the older theologians or even to the ancient philosophers. But from the fact of influence it cannot be inferred that they normally dominate or control human behavior. The conscious mind, aware of an urge or an impulse to something though unaware of its cause, evaluates what one is attracted to and considers whether it can be harmonized with one's interests as these are consciously recognized, whether it can be integrated into a pattern of life one consciously wants to realize. This rational deliberation leads to the acceptance or the repudiation of the impulse. If it is accepted, its satisfaction becomes a human motive and end; if it is rejected, it does not. The rejected impulse may continue to be felt, but its satisfaction is only desired on a level below that of deliberate volition. If it is so strong that it cannot be resisted, the hidden motive does actually dominate and control behavior, but what one does in such a case is neither human nor moral, and so has no human end or goal. But where deliberation is not frustrated, the hidden motive will do no more than account for something seeming desirable. It may explain desire on the level of sense, or perhaps even velleity in the will, but it does not account for actual choice. This must be explained in terms of the end to which one's activity is consciously directed.

Rationalization. Unconscious motivation is sometimes expounded in such a way as to make the deliberation of the conscious mind appear simply a rationalization. The conscious mind looks for and finds acceptable pretexts for doing what the unconscious wants for different and less creditable reasons, the mind's deliberation being simply a bit of stage play to hoodwink the conscience. This, however, is an unfounded assumption. The conscious mind not only finds justifying reasons to act upon some impulses, but it also finds cause to reject others. A man does not live in blind submission to his impulses and urges, whatever their source. Consider, for example, a man who has an unconscious desire to dominate and subdue others and experiences in consequence consciously felt impulses to aggressive behavior of one kind or another. Sometimes he may yield to these impulses because he judges aggression to be appropriate and reasonable in the circumstances, as well it may be; but at other times he will reject them because he sees that aggression would be unreasonable and would serve no good end. That such judgment can be sound and honest is plentifully evident from human experience.

Nevertheless, one should grant the possibility of unconsciously motivated impulses being rationalized by the conscious mind in an objectionable sense of the term. It is possible for a person to deceive himself more or less culpably in thinking that his activities are directed to the good end he alleges. But when such is the case, the spurious character of the pretexted motivation should be perceptible to the conscious mind, however deeply in the unconscious the source of the impulses may be hidden; a good examination of conscience should bring to light the fact that one's behavior is not reasonably related to the lofty ends one claims to serve.

It may also be granted that the existence of an unconscious motive can predispose an individual to rationalize his behavior in an objectionable sense. Before the time of modern psychology it was well known that men incline to find reasons to justify what they feel inclined to do. A strong unconscious motive may therefore prove an obstacle to sound moral judgment and rectitude of will, but it does not follow that these are normally made impossible.

Bibliography: J. C. FORD and G. A. KELLY, *Contemporary Moral Theology,* 2 v. (Westminster, Md. 1958–63) 1:174–200. A. PLÉ, "L'Acte moral et la *pseudo-morale* de l'inconscient," VieSpirit Suppl. 40 (1957) 24–68. E. TESSON, "Moral Conscience and Psychiatry" in *New Problems in Medical Ethics,* ed. P. FLOOD, v.3 (Westminster, Md. 1957) 85–102. C. H. NODET, "Psychoanalysis and Morality," *ibid.* 103–117. C. ODIER, *Les Deux sources consciente et inconsciente de la vie morale* (2d ed. Neuchâtel 1947). G. VANN, "Unconscious Motivation and Pseudo-Virtue," HomPastRev 57 (1956) 115–123. J. C. FORD, "Reply to Father Vann," *ibid.* 124–127. K. RAHNER, "Über die gute Meinung," GeistL 28 (1955) 281–298.

[P. K. MEAGHER]

MOTOLINÍA, TORIBIO DE BENAVENTE,

Franciscan missionary, one of the "Twelve Apostles" in Mexico; b. Benavente, León, Spain, *c.* 1495; d. Mexico City, probably in 1565. As a young man he became a Franciscan, joining the strict reformed section of the Province of Santiago. In 1523 Martín de *Valencia was

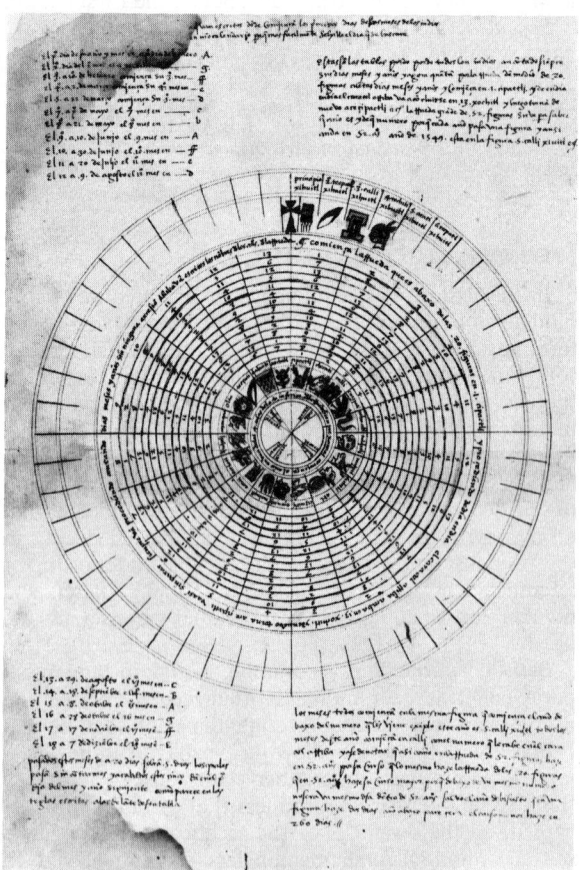

Motolinía's Aztec calendar, from a manuscript of the "Memoriales," a second copy of the now lost original.

instructed by the Franciscan minister general to choose 12 friars from the province for the first formal Franciscan mission to Mexico. Father Toribio was one of those chosen. Upon arriving in Mexico in May 1524, he took for his name the first word he learned in the Tlaxcalan tongue, *motolinía,* meaning "poverty." In June 1524, when the friars formed the Custody of the Holy Gospel, he was appointed the first superior of the Friary of San Francisco in Mexico City. In spite of the municipal officials, he maintained the authority of the Franciscan *custos* as head of the Church in Mexico. In 1525 he was appointed superior of Huejotzingo, and in 1527 he went to Honduras and Nicaragua, returning in 1529. That year he gained the enmity of the civil authorities by granting asylum in Huejotzingo to Indian leaders who had complained of heavy taxations. From 1530 to 1533 he was guardian in Tlaxcala, and traveled widely among the Indians west and north of Mexico City, helping to found the Spanish town of Puebla. In 1534 he was once more sent to Guatemala. Returning after a year or so, he was stationed as a missionary in Tlaxcala.

When the Custody of the Holy Gospel was made a province, Motolonía was appointed guardian of Tlaxcala and was instructed to write an account of the life and beliefs of the Indians in pre-Spanish times and a history of the work of the Franciscans among them. From this came his *Historia de los indios de Nueva España,* completed in 1541, his most important work. Later he wrote a related volume entitled *Memoriales.* In 1543 he was again sent to Guatemala as *custos* of a band of 24 friars. When conflicts arose with the Dominicans and several Franciscans asked to leave, he resigned his office in 1545 and returned to Mexico. In 1546 he became acting provincial in Mexico when the provincial was lost at sea; later he was provincial by election (1548–51). Little is known of his later work. In 1555 he wrote a scathing attack on the exaggerations in *Las Casas' Brevísima relación.* His last years were spent in retirement in the friary of Mexico City.

Bibliography: T. MOTOLINÍA, *History of the Indians of New Spain,* tr. and ed., F. B. STECK (Washington 1951). **Illustration credit:** The Garcia Icazbalceta Collection, University of Texas.

[F. B. WARREN]

MOTT, JOHN RALEIGH, *Young Men's Christian Association (YMCA) official, evangelical missionary, and leader in the *World Council of Churches (WCC); b. Livingston Manor, N.Y., May 25, 1865; d. Orlando, Fla., Jan. 31, 1955. He was the son of John S. and Elmira (Dodge) Mott. After graduating (1888) from Cornell University, Ithaca, N.Y., he married (1891) Leila White and became chairman of the executive committee of the Student Volunteer Movement and student secretary of the International Committee of the YMCA. In 1895 he helped to organize the World Student Christian Federation to coordinate youth groups for Christian unity, and he was its general secretary (1895–1920) and chairman (1920–28). From 1900 to 1914 he repeatedly toured the world, especially the Far East, to organize Christian youth and student movements, becoming one of the chief proponents of ecumenical Christianity. After heading the first preparatory commission for the Edinburgh World Missionary Conference (1910), he was chairman of its continuing committee until 1920, when it became the International Missionary Council with him as chairman to 1942.

Meanwhile he continued his work for the YMCA, becoming (1915) secretary of its International Committee and also of the National Council of the YMCA in the U.S. During World War I he was general secretary for

John Raleigh Mott.

the National War Work Council of the YMCA and worked with the Allied armies and among prisoners of war in Europe. From 1926 to 1946 he was president of the YMCA's World's Committee and World's Alliance. He received France's Legion of Honor, America's Distinguished Service Medal, and Norway's Nobel Peace Prize (1946).

Mott exercised an important influence on the *ecumenical movement of the early 20th century. According to C. Howard Hopkins, *History of the Y.M.C.A. in North America* (1951), "the most obvious contribution of the Y.M.C.A. to the world-wide movement that eventuated in the World Council of Churches was the person and influence of John R. Mott." He spent 50 years exemplifying the slogan adopted by the World's Alliance in 1881: that they may be one. His work with the International Missionary Council was permeated by this spirit and contributed to the formation of the World Council of Churches. In 1937 he presided over the first Faith and Order Conference at Oxford, England; a year later at Utrecht, Netherlands, he acted as vice chairman of the provisional committee to plan the projected world council. This project was delayed by war, but was crowned with success at Amsterdam in 1948, where he served as one of the presidents. Recognition of his enormous contribution to ecumenicism was given him there, when he was made lifetime honorary president of the WCC. His 16 books dealt mainly with world evangelism.

Bibliography: J. R. MOTT, *Addresses and Papers,* 6 v. (New York 1946–47). G. M. FISHER, *John Raleigh Mott* (New York 1953). B. J. MATHEWS, *John Raleigh Mott: World Citizen* (New York 1934). **Illustration credit:** YMCA, photo by Jerry Cooke.

[D. J. BOWMAN]

MOUNIER, EMMANUEL, founder of a philosophy of *personalism; b. Grenoble, April 1, 1905; d. Paris, March 22, 1950. Mounier began his active career as a professor of philosophy at St. Omer. In October 1932 he founded the journal *Esprit,* in which he applied his philosophy of personalism to the contemporary social, political, and cultural problems of the France of his day. During World War II he was a member of the Lyons resistance; was arrested (1941) but later released as a result of a hunger strike; and spent the occupation near Beauvillon, where he was a member of the *dromois maquis.* He resumed the editorship of *Esprit* after the war. Three of his works that have appeared in English translation are: *A Personalist Manifesto* (New York 1938), *Personalism* (London 1952), and *Be Not Afraid: Studies in Personalist Sociology* (New York 1954).

Mounier's personalism was based on belief in the person as a spiritual being, maintaining his existence by adhering to a hierarchy of values freely adopted and assimilated. The person lives by his own responsible activity and interior development, unifies all his activity in freedom, and by creative acts develops his individuality and vocation. The person freely involves himself in the world while maintaining a spiritual detachment from, and transcendence over, the material aspects of civilization. Personalism means "engagement in action" in contemporary civilization. Real communion is also a demand of the person; the need for it leads to neither individualism nor communism, but to a personalist communitarian society in which each person would achieve his vocation in the totality, and in which the communion of the totality would be the result of the efforts of each person.

Mounier applied this philosophy to contemporary society. For him, the capitalist economic order subordinated the person to a system of production because of the profit motive. A personalist economic order would regulate the economy according to service rendered to the members of society. This would mean in practice a type of socialism involving elimination of the primacy of the profit motive, socialization of certain sectors of industry, development of cooperative life, the priority of labor over capital, abolition of class distinctions based on division of labor or wealth, and the priority of personal responsibility over organizations.

In Mounier's thought, a personalist political order would be based upon a pluralistic society. The resulting democracy would be limited by the spiritual person and the rights of the natural societies that compose the nation. Such a democracy would be based upon autonomous societies exercising authority in their own spheres of influence and freely cooperating for national projects; it would result in a decentralization of authority and the personalization of the political order.

Bibliography: *Emmanuel Mounier: 1905–1950* (Paris 1950), also in *Esprit* 18 (1950) 721–1080. C. MOIX, *La Pensée d'Emmanuel Mounier* (Paris 1960). D. WOLF, "Emmanuel Mounier: A Catholic of the Left," *Review of Politics* 22 (1960) 324–344.

[D. WOLF]

MT. ALOYSIUS JUNIOR COLLEGE,

a junior college for women in Cresson, Pa., conducted by the Scranton province of the Sisters of Mercy of the Union. Mt. Aloysius is a development of Mt. St. Aloysius Academy, which was established in Loretto, Pa., in 1853. The Academy was transferred to Cresson in 1897 and continued as an elementary and high school until it was closed in 1961. To provide opportunities for higher education for women in the Altoona-Johnston Diocese, in September 1939 Sister Mary de Sales reorganized the original academy to include a junior college. Until 1954 the geographical distribution of students substantiated the claim that such a school was needed. After that date, however, about one-half of the students came from the Commonwealth of Pennsylvania and the rest were out-of-state or foreign students, with representatives from the Middle and Far East as well as from Central and South America.

In 1964 the 40-member faculty consisted of 3 priests, 27 Sisters of Mercy, and 10 lay teachers, who held 3 doctoral and 20 master's degrees. Five members of the faculty were candidates for graduate degrees.

Mt. Aloysius offers transfer and terminal curricula leading to the associate degree (A.A., A.S.) in arts and sciences, prelaboratory technology, merchandizing, home economics, fine arts, and nursing. The A.S. is also conferred on the executive and medical secretaries and the occupational therapist aide.

In 1941 the College was approved by the Pennsylvania State Board of Education and affiliated with The Catholic University of America. In 1943 it was accredited by the Middle States Association of Colleges and Secondary Schools.

From a class of 27 students in 1939, the enrollment increased to 330 in 1963, with a teacher-student ratio of 1 to 9. Expansion of the physical plant accompanied this growth, and a master plan provides for the addition of four buildings to the complex.

[M. S. SHIELDS]

MT. ANGEL COLLEGE,

a 4-year, coeducational, liberal arts college in Mt. Angel, Ore., the College was founded by the Benedictine Sisters, who came to Oregon from Maria Rickenbach, Switzerland, in 1882. Mt. Angel began as a normal school, and sent out its first teacher graduates in 1892. In 1915 the normal school was declared standard for training elementary teachers and has maintained that status, but as educational standards for teachers increased, the school expanded its offerings, and became Mt. Angel Women's College. It was accredited as a junior college by the Northwest Association of Secondary and Higher Schools in 1933, and as a 4-year college in 1954. In 1958, the school granted admission to men students, and subsequently became Mt. Angel College.

The curriculum of the school focuses on the liberal arts, with teacher education claiming the largest number of majors. Within this framework, areas of concentration include foreign languages, mathematics, fine arts, and drama. In order to maintain excellence in a few fields, the College has limited its major offerings to English, history, sociology, creative arts, mathematics, medical technology, and education. A specialization in gerontology, the sociopsychological study of the aging, is offered in the sociology major. An honors program has been a part of the English and history offerings since 1959. The College grants the B.A. and B.S. degrees.

Mt. Angel College is owned and directed by the Benedictine Sisters of Mt. Angel, who operate it as an autonomous legal corporation. It is under the jurisdiction of the prioress and her council. The officials elected by the convent chapter are chosen from finally professed sisters in the Benedictine community. A lay advisory board assists the sisters in their decisions, and promotes the general development of the College. The prioress is also the president of the College. The general governing of the College is under her supervision, and she is responsible for the appointment of the religious faculty members. She is assisted by the academic dean, who is responsible for the daily direction of College affairs. Faculty members share in the administrative work of the president and dean through the administrative council composed of both lay and religious members. They serve as an advisory board and aid in the interpretation of policy. In

1964 the faculty numbered 3 priests, 14 religious and 20 laymen. They held 5 doctorates, 2 professional degrees, and 20 master's degrees. College enrollment numbered 299 full-time students.

The College is financed by student tuition, the contributed services of the sisters, gifts from friends and foundations, and a small endowment.

Classes are conducted by means of seminar, dialogue, and lecture. Independent study is an integral part of many areas of study and electronic equipment is used in the foreign-language classroom. Library facilities in 1964 included 16,300 bound volumes and 250 periodicals. The College accessions 2,000 books a year.

[M. A. DIEKER]

MT. MARTY COLLEGE, a 4-year women's liberal arts college located at Yankton, S.Dak., conducted by Sisters of St. Benedict. Founded as a 2-year college in 1936, Mt. Marty has a history of development dating from 1880 when a school for Sioux Indian children was established at Yankton by Martin Marty, first bishop of the Dakotas. Marty sought help for his educational work from the Benedictine Sisters of Maryville, Mo. In addition to the group who came to Yankton in answer to his invitation, a nucleus of these sisters established a Dakota motherhouse at Zell, later moving to Vermillion, and finally, in 1887, to Yankton.

The growing Benedictine community of Sacred Heart Convent, Yankton, in 1922, opened Mt. Marty, an academy for girls, which has continued to serve the area as an accredited secondary school. Prompted by the success of this initial venture in the education of Catholic young women, the community opened Mt. Marty Junior College in 1936. During the scholastic years 1949 to 1951 the curriculum was extended to the 3d- and 4th-year level. As a 4-year liberal arts institution, Mt. Marty College conferred its first degrees on May 29, 1951. In 1961 the institution was accredited by the North Central Association of Colleges and Secondary Schools. It has accreditation from the State Department of Public Instruction, and holds membership in the National Education Association, National Catholic Educational Association, American Association of Collegiate Registrars and Admissions Officers, American Library Association, and Association for Higher Education. Mt. Marty's nursing section, established in 1961, has full state approval, and holds agency membership in both the National League for Nursing and the Conference of Catholic Schools of Nursing.

The majority of administrative officers and faculty members of Mt. Marty are members of the Benedictine community. The bishop of Sioux Falls is honorary president of the College. In 1964 the full-time faculty consisted of 19 religious and 4 lay instructors, and the part-time faculty of 2 priests, 6 sisters, and 4 lay instructors. They held 10 doctorates and 22 master's degrees. Total enrollment was approximately 330 in the regular session and 241 students in the summer session. Teacher-student ratio was 1 to 10.5. The library contained 25,000 volumes and received 219 periodicals.

Candidates for the B.A. degree may earn a major in biology, chemistry, elementary education, English, history, home economics, mathematics, social science, and music. Students may earn the B.S. degree in medical technology and nursing. In addition to its yearly scholastic program the College offers an annual summer session, an adult education program, various workshops, a yearly faculty-community study, and an annual lecture series featuring internationally known scholars. Experiments have included radio programs over local broadcasting stations and closed circuit to an adjoining hospital. Foreign language students give special instructions to local elementary school children. Mt. Marty students have received special fellowships, scholarships, and awards in areas of nursing, science, music, and English.

In 1963 the physical plant of the College comprised a triple-winged main building known as Bede Hall; two residences, Whitby Hall and Benet Home; Marian Auditorium; and Bishop Marty Memorial Chapel. Sacred Heart Hospital, situated on adjoining property, provides laboratory facilities and clinical experience for students of nursing and medical technology.

[M. KLIMISCH]

MOUNT MARY COLLEGE

Wisconsin's first Catholic liberal arts college for women, conducted by the School Sisters of Notre Dame, was founded in Prairie du Chien, Wis., in 1872 and chartered in 1913 as St. Mary's College. In 1929 it moved to an 80-acre campus in Milwaukee and has since been called Mount Mary College. Two other campuses are maintained for the education of young sisters. The College is empowered by the state of Wisconsin to confer B.A., B.S., B.S. in Education, and Ph.B. degrees. It is accredited by the North Central Association of Colleges, Wisconsin State Department of Public Instruction for Teachers' Certification, and the National Council for Accreditation of Teacher Education. It also holds membership in the American Association of University Women and other leading national organizations.

The administrative body comprises the chancellor (the archbishop of Milwaukee), a board of directors, and a board of governors composed of the president as an ex-officio member and 11 laymen. The 128 faculty members include 89 sisters, 7 priests, 32 laymen, of whom 26 hold doctorates and 80 hold master's degrees. In 1964 the total student enrollment was 1,180, with a student-teacher ratio of 8 to 1. Current income accrues from tuition, fees, the contributed services of the religious community, and the Wisconsin Foundation of Independent Colleges. Other funds—development, endowment, and alumnae—finance the expansion program.

The College offers a basic liberal arts program with majors in the humanities, fine and applied arts, and science. The occupational therapy department, approved by the Council on Medical Education and Hospitals of the American Medical Association, is one of the largest in a liberal arts college. About two-thirds of the students qualify for teaching in elementary and secondary schools; a number spend one undergraduate year abroad. Students, faculty, and alumnae have distinguished themselves in textile design and other art areas, social service, writing, and occupational therapy. The College is the executive headquarters of the Catholic Renascence Society.

In 1964 the main library housed 62,000 volumes, 500 current periodicals, a collection of all available recorded drama, microcard and microfilm materials, and a microfilm reader-printer for research purposes. Building expansion plans scheduled for completion in 1965 included a science resource center and, in addition to the usual science equipment, a planetarium, an astronomical observatory, and a greenhouse.

[M. C. DIEBELS]

MOUNT MELLERAY ABBEY, monastery of Cistercian contemplatives of the strict observance or *Trappists, Cappoquin, County Waterford, Ireland. It was founded in 1832 by 64 monks expelled from the abbey of *Melleray, France, after the revolution of 1830. The monks, mostly Irish, a few English, were under the leadership of Dom Vincent M. Ryan (1778–1845) a native of Waterford City, and former prior of the French abbey. They obtained refuge on a farm in Kerry until 1832 when Sir Richard Keane of Cappoquin offered them 500 acres of unreclaimed moorland. Nearly 10,000 volunteers from neighboring parishes helped to erect a temporary house, to fence the land and to begin its reclamation. In 1838 the Church was consecrated, but the monks lived in poverty. Yet during the Great Famine of 1847 and its aftermath they aided starving thousands. The following monasteries have been founded by Mount Melleray: 1835, Mount St. Bernard, Leicestershire, England; 1849, *New Melleray, Iowa; 1878, Mount St. Joseph, Roscrea, Ireland; 1938, *Mellifont Abbey, County Louth, Ireland; 1948, Portglenone, County Antrim, Ireland; 1954, Kopua, Hawke's Bay, New Zealand. In 1963 Mount Melleray had 125 monks of whom 48 were priests.

Bibliography: Cottineau 2:1999. A. J. LUDDY, *The Story of Mount Melleray* (Dublin 1946).

[K. J. WALSH]

MT. MERCY COLLEGE (CEDAR RAPIDS, IOWA)

A 4-year liberal arts college for women conducted by the Sisters of Mercy of Cedar Rapids, Iowa. Founded in 1928 as a junior college, Mt. Mercy initiated the third collegiate year in 1957 and conferred its first baccalaureate degrees in 1959. The College was separately incorporated in 1962.

Mt. Mercy is accredited by the North Central Association of Colleges and Secondary Schools and holds membership in the Association of American Colleges, American Council on Education, National Commission on Accrediting, National Education Association, and National Catholic Educational Association. Its program of teacher education is approved by the Iowa State Department of Public Instruction. The College is financed through the contributed services of the sisters and clergy on its faculty, participation in the Iowa College Foundation, grants, a program of annual gifts, tuition, and fees. More than 66 per cent of its alumnae contribute annually to the College.

Administration of Mt. Mercy College is through the president, who is responsible to a board of trustees composed of the mother general of the Sisters of Mercy, as chairman, and sisters and laymen elected for 6-year terms. A lay board of trustees serves in an advisory capacity. The five divisions of the College are: theology and philosophy, languages and fine arts, natural sciences and mathematics, social sciences, and service arts. In 1964 the 40-member faculty was composed of 3 priests, 23 Sisters of Mercy, and 14 laymen, holding 8 doctoral, 2 professional, and 27 master's degrees. Enrollment numbered 221 full-time and 169 part-time students in the regular session, and 122 in the summer session.

The Catherine McAuley library, with an ultimate capacity of 100,000 volumes, was erected in 1962. In 1964 it housed 19,000 volumes and received 200 periodicals. The library contains facsimiles of the *Book of Kells* and the *Book of Durrow,* and a special collection of manuscripts of poems by living poets, with letters, pictures, and personal comments from many of the writers.

Mt. Mercy's courses leading to the B.A. and the B.S. degree include liberal arts, biology, business, mathematics, music education, medical technology, home economics, social science, and social service. Students may be certified to teach at the elementary or secondary level. Student teaching is done in both the public and the parochial schools in Cedar Rapids. Students in social service do case work in social service agencies in the area. In 1963 the faculty approved advanced placement and participation in a program of study in Mexico introduced by the College of St. Thomas in St. Paul, Minn. Small seminars, independent study, and research projects are a part of College programs. Student work has been published in academic journals. Activities of cocurricular groups, honor societies, and the National Federation of Catholic College Students promote intellectual, spiritual, cultural, and social development. The annual Community Service Forum brings national figures to the campus and the city; other public lectures, art exhibits, plays, and concerts link the College to the community. In 1963 the College formulated a 10-year master plan for the development of its academic program and facilities.

Bibliography: M. I. HOLLAND, *Lengthened Shadows* (New York 1952).

[M. A. ROTH]

MT. MERCY COLLEGE (PITTSBURGH, PA.)

A liberal arts college for women founded in 1929 by the Pittsburgh Sisters of Mercy. It was established on the same site as the Academy of Our Lady of Mercy, the first academy founded by the Sisters of Mercy in the U.S. in 1844.

In April 1933 the College was chartered by the state of Pennsylvania with the right to grant baccalaureate

Mt. Mercy College, Cedar Rapids, Iowa.

degrees in the liberal arts, science, and home economics. The bachelor of science degrees in nursing and in education were later added. The College is accredited by the State Department of Public Instruction, and the Middle States Association of Colleges and Secondary Schools. The nursing department is accredited by the National League of Nursing, and the chemistry department by the American Chemical Society. Mt. Mercy College holds membership in the Association of American Colleges, American Council on Education, and National Catholic Educational Association, as well as in other professional organizations.

The bishop of Pittsburgh is the honorary president of the College, which is governed by a board of trustees composed of eight Sisters of Mercy and seven laymen. Administrative officers are the president and dean. In 1964 the full-time faculty numbered 2 priests, 34 sisters, and 21 laymen; the part-time faculty, 6 priests, 34 sisters and 19 laymen. They held 24 doctoral, 6 professional, and 62 master's degrees from colleges and universities in the U.S., Canada, and Europe. There were 839 full-time and 623 part-time students enrolled in the regular session and 1,047 in the summer session. The library housed 54,201 volumes and received 525 periodicals. It also had a special nursing collection of 1,650 volumes.

The College is financed by student tuition and the contributed services of the religious community. Small grants have been received from the National Science Foundation, the National Institute of Mental Health, and private foundations and a sizable grant from the Ford Foundation. Curricular patterns provide for general education in theology, philosophy, humanities, social sciences, and natural sciences. Major areas of study leading to B.A. and B.S. degrees include: political, natural, and social sciences; mathematics; classical and modern languages; music; speech; art; psychology; nursing; and education. The minor field either supports the major or provides a professional orientation to a career. Special vocational areas are secondary and elementary education, nursing, nutrition, speech therapy, medical technology, and medical record library science. Preprofessional courses are offered in law, dentistry, medicine, and social work.

The College offers a 4-year integrating liberal arts seminar for all students, and during the senior year, honors courses with independent study and research for superior students. Mt. Mercy was one of the first Catholic colleges to develop a program in theology, under the direction of Rev. George Tavard. Research is carried out in science (chemistry and biology), while in all disciplines, emphasis is placed on the reading of original sources and discussion. The College also provides for part-time study and off-campus centers in several religious houses. Nine buildings on the 13-acre campus provide residence, classroom, and laboratory facilities.

[M. A. HEALY]

MOUNT OF OLIVES

The Mount of Olives lies east of the city of *Jerusalem. A long ridge, running north and south for about 2 miles, separated from Jerusalem by the *Cedron Valley, it is slightly higher in elevation than the city itself. The hill is part of the central Judean range that falls off sharply to the Jordan Valley on the east and more gradually to the Mediterranean Sea on the west. The term

The Mount of Olives with the Cedron Valley in the foreground. The Basilica of Gethsemani commemorating the Agony in the Garden is in the right-center. The path going up the hill leads to Bethphage and Bethany and is approximately the scene of the triumphal entry of Jesus into Jerusalem on Palm Sunday.

"Mount of Olives" refers most properly to the southernmost of the ridge's three sections. The northernmost section is known as Mt. Scopus. The middle section is probably the site of the OT Nobe (1 Sm 21.1). The southern section, directly east of the Temple area, now called Jebel et-Tur, is, properly, the Mount of Olives, the traditional site of Jesus' Ascension into heaven. The village Kefr et-Tur, on the eastern slope, is believed to be the site of *Bethphage, while farther down the southeastern end of the slope stood *Bethany.

In the Old Testament. The Mount of Olives is mentioned only once in the OT and only in a rather late postexilic book, the Apocalypse of Zacharia (Za 14.4). But, it must be the same hill that was the scene of David's flight from Absalom (2 Sm 15.23). In Ez 11.23, the hill to the east of the city on which "the glory of the Lord . . . took a stand" after leaving the Temple must also have been the Mount of Olives. In Za 14.4, on the day of the Lord's return to Jerusalem, ". . . his feet shall rest upon the Mount of Olives, which is opposite Jerusalem to the east. The Mount of Olives shall be cleft in two from east to west by a very deep valley, and half the mountain shall move to the north and half to the south."

In the New Testament. The Mount of Olives is mentioned frequently in the Gospels, either as τὸ ὄρος τῶν ἐλαιῶν (the mountain of the olive trees) or τὸ ὄρος τὸ καλούμενον Ἐλαιών (the hill called "The Olive Grove"). The vicinity of the hill was frequented by Jesus whenever He visited Jerusalem. The road from Jericho to Jerusalem passed over this ridge. It was along this road that His triumphal entry into Jerusalem took place (Lk 19.37). When He came over the brow of the hill and saw the city, He wept because of the suffering in store for it (Lk 19.41–44). Jesus delivered his eschatological discourse while sitting on the Mount of Olives (Mt 24.3; Mk 13.3). He spent the last nights before His death on the Mount (Lk 21.37), at Bethany, or Bethphage, or in the Garden of *Gethsemani just across the Cedron (Jn 18.1) at the foot of the Mount. The Ascension of Jesus into heaven took place from the Mount of Olives, according to Acts 1.12.

Shrines and Archeology. The Mount of Olives is dotted with Christian shrines commemorating these events in Our Lord's life. Evidence of shrines and literary witnesses go back to very early times. The pilgrim Etheria, shortly before 400, mentioned that she took part in the liturgical services at Eleona, a church erected by the Empress Helena, to commemorate the spot where Our Lord taught. She mentions the place whence Our Lord ascended to heaven. She also mentions Gethsemani and Bethany. Today a modern basilica at Gethsemani is built upon the foundations of earlier churches. Halfway up the hill is a small chapel commemorating Our Lord's weeping over Jerusalem. In his excavations there B. Bagatti has found numerous *ossuaries dating from early Christianity. Farther up the hill is the church and convent of Carmelite nuns, called the Pater Noster Monastery in memory of Luke's account of the Lord's Prayer (Lk 11.1–4). On top of the hill are the restored remains of an octagonal church, now in the possession of Moslems, and believed to occupy the spot from which Jesus ascended into heaven.

Bibliography: L. HEIDET, DB 4.2:1779–93. B. BAGATTI, DB Suppl 6:688–699. H. VINCENT and F. M. ABEL, *Jérusalem Nouvelle*, v.2 of *Jérusalem: Recherches de topographie, d'archéologie et d'histoire*, 2 v. (Paris 1912–26). **Illustration credit:** Matson Photo Service, Los Angeles, Calif.

[S. MUSHOLT]

MT. ST. AGNES COLLEGE, a liberal arts college for women located in Mount Washington, a suburb of Baltimore, Md., Mt. St. Agnes was founded in 1867 by the Sisters of Mercy. In 1890 the Maryland State Legislature granted the College a charter empowering it to grant academic degrees. In 1918, however, pressure stemming from World War I obliged the College to close, although it retained its charter. In 1933 Mt. St. Agnes was reopened as a junior college and in 1946 changed its status to a 4-year college.

In 1949 the College was accredited by the Middle States Association of Colleges and Secondary Schools. The College is affiliated with The Catholic University of America and holds membership in the Maryland State Department of Education, the National Commission in Accrediting, the Association of American Colleges, the American Conference of Academic Deans, the American Council on Education, the American Medical Association, and other regional and national organizations. Administration is vested in a board of trustees. Administration officers are the president, dean, comptroller, director of admissions and student activities, and registrar. In 1964 the faculty, assisted by a staff of 12, was composed of 37 full-time and 22 part-time members, of whom 5 were priests, 22 religious, and 32 laymen. They held 11 doctorates, 6 professional degrees, and 24 master's degrees. Students numbered 425. The College is unendowed. Revenue accrues from the contributed services of the religious community and tuition fees. Further support is obtained from the Association of Independent Colleges of Maryland, of which it is a member.

Mt. St. Agnes confers the B.S. degree in medical technology, and the B.A. degree in modern languages, natural sciences, mathematics, history, psychology, sociology, speech and hearing therapy, and in elementary and secondary education. Three years of Russian are available to all students. Students may be given advanced placement, and independent study is encouraged for the superior student. A special program offering college courses to superior high school students has been offered since 1959. In 1964 Curley Library housed a collection of 31,475 bound volumes and received more than 257 newspapers and periodicals. Students also have access to the George Peabody and Enoch Pratt Libraries, the Johns Hopkins University and Hospital, the Walters Art Gallery and Peabody Institute. In 1962 Hartman House, a residence hall housing 148 students, was erected and language laboratory installed.

[M. M. THOMPSON]

MT. ST. CLARE COLLEGE. A privately controlled 2-year college for women in Clinton, Iowa, owned and operated by Sisters of the Third Order of St. Francis. When opened in 1928, the College used the same campus and facilities as Mt. St. Clare Academy, which had been operating as a high school since 1895. The College and the Academy continue to occupy the same campus, but the buildings and facilities for both institutions have expanded to accommodate 700 resident and day students.

Mt. St. Clare College is a member of the American Association of Junior Colleges and is fully accredited by the North Central Association of Colleges and Secondary Schools. Since 1947 it has been on the approved list of the attorney general of the U.S. for the admission of foreign students.

The College is located on a 110-acre estate on which 25 acres are devoted to the campus. The eight-unit complex provides residence, classroom, and laboratory accommodation, as well as facilities for the fine arts, a theater, language laboratory, speech therapy unit, and a remedial reading clinic.

The curriculum is organized in five divisions: theology and philosophy, humanities, social studies, science and mathematics, and community service. Within the curriculum are two distinct programs of studies: the transfer degree program, which includes the liberal arts, science, education, speech therapy, and fine arts; and the terminal program, leading to an associate in applied science (A.A.S.) degree, followed by students who plan to complete their education at the end of 2 years. This program includes courses in general secretarial science, medical secretarial science, general liberal arts, recreational assistanceship, and modern family living.

Mt. St. Clare provides cultural opportunities for students through the artist and lecture series sponsored by the College, and the Community Concert series sponsored by the city. The College also sponsors educational tours to places of interest in the U.S., and every 2 years organizes a summer tour of Europe, which is open to both freshmen and sophomore students.

In 1964 the 36-member faculty included 3 priests, 29 sisters, and 5 laywomen, holding 5 doctoral and 22 master's degrees. Enrollment numbered 292 in the regular session and 65 in the summer session. The library housed 18,506 volumes and subscribed to 186 periodicals.

[M. C. PHELAN]

MT. ST. JOSEPH ON THE OHIO, COLLEGE OF. A liberal arts college for women in Cincinnati, Ohio, conducted by the Sisters of Charity of Cincinnati. The pioneer group of sisters who came from Emmitsburg, Md., in 1829, founded the Academy of Mt. St. Joseph, which in 1854 was incorporated by the Ohio State legislature with power to confer academic honors and degrees. In 1906, the academy conducted courses on a college level. It was not until 1920, however, that the College began to operate as a 4-year degree-granting institution, the first Catholic college for women in Ohio.

The College is accredited by the North Central Association of Colleges and Secondary Schools and is affiliated with The Catholic University of America. It is approved by the Association of American University Women and holds membership in the American Council of Education, the American Medical Association, the National League for Nursing, and in other national, state, and professional organizations.

The board of trustees is composed of the mother superior, the College president, the dean, and five members of the community. In 1964, the administration and teaching staff included 5 priests, 38 sisters, and 40 laymen, who held 18 doctorates and 57 master's degrees. Enrollment numbered 1,047 students from 24 states and 10 foreign countries. The library housed 63,000 bound volumes and received 430 periodicals.

Besides the B.A. and B.S. degrees in the liberal arts and science, the College offers degree programs in education, nursing, and music. An integrated program of required courses provides a foundation for specialization in depth as well as vocational training and pre-professional preparation in law and medicine. The proximity of various hospitals, schools, charitable institutions, and social service agencies provides diversified opportunity for clinical practice, internship, and directed experience. The College conducts a coeducational continuing education program in evening and Saturday classes, and in summer courses. Members of the art department designed the Mater Dei Chapel on the College campus and created many of the art works found there and in other campus buildings.

[J. M. O'BRIEN]

MT. ST. MARY COLLEGE.

A 4-year liberal arts college for women in Hooksett, N.H., Mt. St. Mary College owes its beginnings to Mother Mary Francis Xavier Warde, the American foundress of the Sisters of Mercy. When the Sisters of Mercy came to Manchester in 1858, Mother Warde, realizing the need for educated women in New Hampshire, established Mt. St. Mary Academy, the first convent boarding school in the Northern New England States. The school flourished in Manchester and in 1909 was transferred to Hooksett. In 1934 it was incorporated as a 4-year college under the laws of the state of New Hampshire and empowered to grant degrees. In 1939 the College became affiliated with The Catholic University of America, and in 1945 it was accredited by the New England Association of Colleges and Secondary Schools. Mt. St. Mary holds membership in the Association of American Colleges, the American Council on Education, National Catholic Education Association, and the National Committee on Accrediting.

Mt. St. Mary is controlled by a board of trustees of seven Sisters of Mercy. The chairman is the mother general of the Congregation of the Sisters of Mercy of Manchester. The administrative officers are the president, vice president, dean, treasurer, registrar, librarian, and chaplain. An advisory board of laymen aids the sisters in the solution of problems and the formulation of future plans. In 1964 the 40-member faculty was composed of 2 priests, 28 religious, and 10 laymen, who

held 3 doctoral, 2 professional, and 22 master's degrees. Student enrollment numbered 283 students in the regular session and 158 in the summer session. Library holdings included 21,882 volumes and 158 periodicals. The College is financed by fees; the living endowment or contributed services of the Sisters of Mercy; a small endowment; and the contributions of alumnae, business, and foundations.

Mt. St. Mary College offers 4-year programs in the liberal arts and sciences leading to the B.A. degree. Programs of concentration are offered in the humanities, social and physical sciences, home economics, business, and education. In the freshman year, degree candidates concentrate on general education: theology, philosophy, English, Latin or mathematics, science, and one course selected from the field of foreign language or of science. During the next 3 years, students complete the liberal arts.

The 500-acre campus in the Merrimack Valley region provides residence and classroom facilities, science and language laboratories, a chapel, and a home practice house for home economic majors. Long-range development plans drawn up in 1960 called for a library, science building, and a residence group of four buildings that was completed in 1963.

Mt. St. Mary College has been educating women for more than 100 years. It has endeavored to instill in them the speculation of the scholar and the prudential action of the community leader. Its alumnae have been successful in graduate school; in the professions, as teachers, social workers, and dietitians; and in the world of scientific research.

[M. M. MORAN]

MT. ST. MARY COLLEGE OF NEWBURGH

Founded by the Sisters of St. Dominic in 1930 in Newburgh, N.Y., as Mt. St. Mary Normal and Training School, its original purpose was the professional education of the religious community. In 1939, to keep abreast with New York State normal schools, Mt. St. Mary reorganized its curriculum to include the liberal arts and in 1945 became affiliated with The Catholic University of America. In 1955 the University of the State of New York granted the College a provisional charter with power to grant the Associate of Arts degree upon completion of the 3-year program. In 1960, lay students were admitted and a 4-year charter sought. That same year an evening program was initiated. In 1962 the Board of Regents of the University of the State of New York empowered the institute to grant the B.A. and B.S. in Education degrees. It was henceforth known as Mt. St. Mary College.

The College is administered by a board of trustees composed of an honorary president, a chancellor, 12 Dominican sisters, and 10 Catholic laymen. They are assisted by an associate board of trustees made up of 19 laymen from professional and educational circles. The administrative officers are the president, academic dean, registrar, treasurer, and librarian. In 1964 the 31-member faculty, composed of priests, brothers, sisters, and laymen, held 13 doctorates and 18 master's degrees. Enrollment totaled 160 students. The College is financed by student tuition and fees, the contributed services of the community, and donations from friends. Although there is no appreciable endowment, grants have been received from the Atomic Energy Commission, the National Institutes of Health and the Kellogg Foundation.

Besides degrees in the liberal arts, the curriculum offers majors in the sciences and in elementary education. Students may qualify as medical technologists by completing their practicum in a hospital during a 5th year of preparation. A nursing arts program was introduced in 1964. In 1963 the Curtin Memorial Library housed 12,000 volumes and subscribed to 225 periodicals.

To extend its educational and cultural facilities to the surrounding communities, the College established the Hudson Valley International Cultural Center for the performing arts. Through its special exchange program the Center has sponsored performers from around the world in various fields of artistic endeavor.

[M. E. MAHONEY]

MOUNT ST. MARY'S COLLEGE (LOS ANGELES, CALIF.)

A 4-year liberal arts undergraduate college for women, founded in 1925 by the Congregation of the Sisters of St. Joseph of Carondelet. The Graduate School, established in 1955, and the music department are coeducational. The College operates in two locations: a 56-acre main campus in Brentwood, in the Santa Monica Mountains, and a city campus downtown. Mount St. Mary's is chartered by the state of California and affiliated with The Catholic University of America. It is accredited by the Western Association of Secondary Schools and Colleges, California State Board of Education, California State Board of Nurse Examiners, National Association of Schools of Music, and the National League for Nursing.

The College is governed by a board of trustees, a corporate body composed of nine members of the Congregation of the Sisters of St. Joseph of Carondelet, with the provincial superior as chairman. A lay advisory board of 15 members cooperates with the College in its operation and development. Administrative officers include the president, dean of the graduate school, academic dean, director of the downtown campus, registrar, and treasurer. In 1964 the 110-member faculty consisted of 9 priests, 40 sisters, and 61 laymen, holding 39 doctoral, 3 professional, and 51 master's degrees. Enrollment numbered 897 full-time and 347 part-time students

in the regular session and 800 in the summer session, including 165 graduate students, and 200 in the Sister Formation program. The faculty-student ratio was 1 to 12. The College is financed by the combined resources from endowments, gifts, tuition, fees, and the contributed services of the religious community.

The curricula provide a foundation in theological studies within the framework of the liberal arts and sciences. Recognizing the need for professional competence, the College offers programs in teaching, medical technology, and nursing, and provides preliminary courses for entrance to medical school, social work, and scientific research. Graduate programs for the master's degree are offered in education, history, and music; superior students participate in an honors program of interdisciplinary study. Courses are also offered for the Sister Formation program. Students may spend their junior year abroad at the Universidad Iberoamericana, Mexico City; Laval University, Quebec; or the University of Vienna, Austria. In 1959 the College initiated an advanced placement program for qualified high school seniors who may enroll in the regular lower division college courses. In all these programs there is a concerted effort to develop in the student the Christian wisdom to synthesize what is learned, and creativity of mind to bring such knowledge into Christian perspective.

The Charles Willard Coe Memorial Library includes the library on the Brentwood campus and the library on the downtown campus. In 1964 its collections contained approximately 75,000 volumes, as well as substantial holdings of pamphlets, maps, microfilm and microcard editions, music scores, recordings, and slides. The library regularly receives about 475 periodicals and newspapers. It has a special Newman collection consisting mainly of holograph letters, first editions, and works on Cardinal John Newman and the Oxford Movement.

The College offers an associate in arts degree (A.A.), and the Mus.B., B.A., B.S., F.F.A., M.A., M.S. in Educ., and Mus.M. degrees. The curricula are approved for California teaching credentials, licensure for nursing, and certificate for public health nursing.

Because of its location, the downtown campus is rapidly becoming recognized as a Catholic center of cultural arts. In addition to the associate of arts programs offered there, a conservatory of music and of art has been established. The Graduate School, also housed on this campus, is expanding to meet the increasing demand for graduate studies. On the Brentwood campus, the Coe Memorial Library has developed a radio and TV monitoring and recording center in order to preserve for educational, cultural, and research purposes the valuable radio and TV material that is broadcast in the Los Angeles area.

[M. G. MC NEIL]

MT. ST. MARY'S COLLEGE AND SEMINARY

Founded in 1808 by Rev. John *Dubois, Mt. St. Mary's College and Seminary is located near Emmitsburg, Md., about 70 miles north of Washington, D.C. It is operated by a corporation of secular priests whose president ex officio is the archbishop of Baltimore. It offers undergraduate degrees in both the College and the Seminary.

The history of the College and Seminary is closely interwoven with the history of the Catholic Church in the

Mt. St. Mary's College, Brentwood, Calif., campus.

U.S. during the 19th and 20th centuries. In years of service to the Church, the College is second only to Georgetown University (1789); the Seminary is second only to St. Mary's of Baltimore (1791).

Origin and Development. Fleeing the terrors of the Revolution in his native France, Dubois came to the U.S. in 1791. On Sept. 24, 1808, he cleared a tract of land on St. Mary's Mount in Maryland to begin construction of the College. For a short time, the school served as a preparatory seminary for St. Mary's in Baltimore, but within a year after its foundation 50 students of the humanities were in attendance. Dubois himself became affiliated with the Society of St. Sulpice (*see* SULPICIANS) in the first December of the school's existence, thus fulfilling a desire of 3 years to be associated with the community teaching at St. Mary's in Baltimore. In 1811 control of the college was formally transferred to the Sulpicians. The administration experienced so many financial difficulties, however, that in 1826 the Sulpicians ceded all control of the institution to Dubois, who then amicably severed his connections with the Society of St. Sulpice. By this time formal training in theology had already been introduced for students who wished to continue their studies for the priesthood.

Dubois was greatly aided in his work by Father Simon Gabriel *Bruté de Remur, later called the Angel Guardian of the Mountain. Both served in the capacity of spiritual director for Elizabeth Bayley *Seton, who lived on the Mount campus in 1809 while waiting the completion of her own settlement in St. Joseph Valley, 2 miles away. She benefited from their charity and guidance until her death in 1821. After Dubois was consecrated third bishop of New York (1826), and Bruté was made first bishop of Vincennes (1834), the Mount continued its work with such marked success that it has often been called the Cradle of Bishops. Notable among its sons in the American hierarchy are John *McCloskey (first American cardinal), John J. *Hughes (first archbishop of New York), John B. *Purcell (first archbishop of Cincinnati), and Bp. James Walsh of Maryknoll, sentenced to 20 years' imprisonment in Red China in 1960.

In 1830 Mt. St. Mary's obtained its first charter from the Legislature of the State of Maryland. It was reissued (1834) and amended (1836) on the advice of Roger B. *Taney, a good friend who later became chief justice of the U.S. Supreme Court. The charter permitted the granting of "degrees and literary honors in each and all the liberal arts and sciences as is usual in colleges and universities in this country and in Europe." A year after the foundation of the Middle States Association of Colleges and Secondary Schools in 1921, the Mount obtained accreditation from that body and has continued to enjoy its academic recognition. The College is also fully accredited by the State Board of Maryland and The University of the State of New York.

Organization. Situated at the foot of the Maryland range of the Blue Ridge Mountains, the property consists of about 1,200 acres, with facilities including 12 major buildings. Campus residence halls accommodate 700 college students and 120 seminarians, or 90 per cent of the enrollment. The government of the College and Seminary is in the hands of the council, which consists of a body of secular priests elected from the members of the faculty. The Mount is the only college in the country owned and controlled by a corporation of secular priests. A faculty of 66 is composed almost equally of laymen and priests, the latter representing 12 dioceses in the U.S. The staff holds 17 doctorates, 33 master's, and 16 bachelor degrees.

As a liberal arts college for men, the Mount seeks to offer its students the opportunity to secure their education in the environment of a small Catholic college. Mt. St. Mary's confers degrees in several curricula. The B.A. is given in classical studies; the B.S. is primarily granted for medical and dental studies; it is also conferrred in education, business, and social science. In 1964 library holdings totaled more than 94,000 volumes. A fine collection of Americana and rare books shows the progress of the printing arts.

Bibliography: M. M. MELINE and E. F. McSWEENEY, *The Story of the Mountain,* 2 v. (Emmitsburg, Md. 1911). T. MAYNARD, *The Reed and the Rock* (New York 1942); *The Story of American Catholicism* (New York 1941).

[R. R. KLINE]

MT. ST. SCHOLASTICA COLLEGE. A liberal arts college for women in Atchison, Kans., conducted by the Benedictine Sisters who came from Minnesota to Kansas in 1863. Shortly after, Benedictine priests and sisters opened two schools for the children of Kansas pioneers. These later became the twin colleges of Atchison: Mt. St. Scholastica and St. Benedict's. In 1924 Mt. St. Scholastica became a junior college under a charter from the state of Kansas and granted its first baccalaureate degrees in 1932.

The College is accredited by the North Central Association of Colleges and Secondary Schools, the University of Kansas, the Kansas Department of Public Instruction, and the National Council for Accreditation of Teacher Education for the preparation of elementary teachers. It is affiliated with The Catholic University of America, and holds membership in the American Council on Education, the Association of American Colleges, the National Catholic Educational Association, the National Association of Schools of Music, the American Association of Colleges for Teacher Education, the American Association of University Women, the Kansas Council of Church-Related Colleges, and the American Alumni Council.

The College is governed by a board of directors and administered by the president. In 1964 the faculty included 3 Benedictine priests, 40 Benedictine sisters, and 10 lay professors, holding 18 doctoral and 27 master's degrees. Enrollment numbered 459 full-time and 71 part-time students in the regular session and 577 in the summer session. Library facilities included more than 42,000 volumes and 320 current periodicals.

Mt. St. Scholastica offers the degrees of B.A., B.S., B.S. in education, B.Mus., and B.Mus.Ed. Students major in liberal and fine arts; classical and modern languages; health and physical education; home economics; mathematics; philosophy; and natural, political, and social sciences. Minors are offered in art, speech and drama, physics, and religion. In the professional and preprofessional fields, students prepare themselves for careers in home economics, dietetics, social work, medical technology, and elementary and secondary teaching.

The College sponsors study abroad. Stimulating means for achievement are seminars, independent study, advanced placement, and honors courses. In the mathematics department honor students have participated in an undergraduate research program through successive grants from the National Science Foundation.

Curricular offerings are enlarged by cooperation between the twin colleges. While St. Benedict's and Mt. St. Scholastica remain self-contained through separate faculties, rosters, and administrative policies, they nevertheless share both professors and students, particularly for the work of the junior and senior years. This cooperative policy results in greater choice of faculty personnel, larger student groups in upper classes, more specific course offerings, keener intellectual stimuli, and reduction in the duplication of laboratory equipment. As a result of its social and scholastic program, Mt. St. Scholastica has emerged with a distinct college personality: a woman's institution that combines the features of coeducation with the advantages of a Catholic woman's college.

The income of Mt. St. Scholastica College is provided largely by student fees, and gifts of alumnae, parents, and friends. The contributed services of the Benedictine faculty members constitute a continuous endowment. The College has benefited by the contribution of the Ford Foundation, and the faculty has received successive grants from the Fund for the Advancement of Education, the Raskob Foundation, and the Kellogg Foundation. Substantial awards of equipment from the Minnesota Mining and Manufacturing Company of St. Paul and the *Encyclopaedia Britannica* have provided unusual facilities in visual aids.

[M. T. BRENTANO]

MT. ST. VINCENT, COLLEGE OF

A 4-year liberal arts college for women founded in New York City in 1847 as the Academy of Mt. St. Vincent, Central Park.

Origin. Established under the direction of the Sisters of Charity of St. Vincent de Paul, the College had its origin in the educational system started in Maryland in 1810 by Elizabeth Bayley *Seton. In 1856 the Central Park academy was moved to a 96-acre campus in Riverdale, N.Y. The academy gradually introduced college courses until September 1910, when, at the request of Abp. John Farley, the sisters opened a liberal arts college with 28 students, 7 of whom were sophomores. In 1911 the Board of Regents of the University of the State of New York granted the College a charter with power to confer degrees, and henceforth the College and Academy were administered as separate organizations. The College is accredited by the Middle States Association of Colleges and Secondary Schools and by the American Chemical Society. It is affiliated with The Catholic University of America and the National Catholic Educational Association and holds membership in the American Association of University Women, American Council on Education, the Association of American Colleges, and other regional and national organizations.

Administration. In order to foster an integrated Catholic attitude toward life the College has combined a liberal and cultural education with professional studies, unified and vitalized by religion and philosophy. The motto of the College, *Bonitatem et disciplinam et scientiam doce me,* was chosen to be the guiding principle in the lives of the students. Administration is vested in a board of trustees of eight elected Sisters of Charity. Administrative officers include the president, academic vice president, dean of students, registrar, and director of admissions. In 1964 the 72-member teaching staff was composed of 7 priests, 34 sisters, and 31 laymen. They held 26 doctorates and 38 master's degrees. Between 1958 and 1963 16 religious and 6 lay faculty members have studied in European universities, and several have received grants from the National Science Foundation and the Atomic Energy Commission. Total student enrollment numbered 800 undergraduates, including an extension college of about 200 sister students for whom there are weekend classes and a summer session. The College, owned by the Sisters of Charity of New York, has no financial subsidy other than the dedicated services of the sisters. Income accrues from student tuition and fees.

Curriculum. The College offers programs leading to the B.A. degree with majors in languages, art, social and political science, and mathematics, the B.S. with majors in natural sciences and business education, or the B.F.A. Students may earn a New York State provisional certificate for teaching on the elementary or secondary level or follow a preprofessional program in law or medicine. All students follow a general program in the freshman and sophomore years. In the junior and senior years the student concentrates on a major field and professional courses. All programs include a core of philosophy and theology.

Although there are some large lecture groups, many small classes, discussion groups, directed research projects, and seminars are held in each field. In 1964 a library containing 45,000 volumes and two periodical rooms with a total of 295 periodicals was available to all students. Under faculty direction students participate in the Eastern Science Conferences, American Chemical Affiliates, White House Conferences, and the Mock United Nations General Assemblies.

About 50 per cent of the graduates each year matriculate at institutions of higher learning for graduate study. Graduate awards include Fulbright scholarships, Woodrow Wilson Fellowships, and New York State Regents College Teaching Fellowships. The College ranks first of all women's colleges in the U.S. in the number of accredited women chemists.

[M. C. LYNCH]

MOUNTAINS, SACRED. The vastness of mountains, their summits often enshrouded in mists and clouds and seemingly touching the sky, their deep and pathless forests, their sheer cliffs, gloomy gorges, and dark caves, the intensity of their thunderstorms with blinding lightning and deafening echoing thunderclaps, are awesome phenomena even to modern man. It is not surprising, therefore, that many peoples have regarded mountains as objects of enormous and mysterious powers. The personification of mountains as divinities

View of Mt. Olympus, home of the gods of Greek legend.

is found in the New World as well as in the Old. However, the concept of mountains as the dwelling places of gods, of spirits, and of the dead, and as the center of the universe and the starting point of creation, is still more widespread. In Greek mythology and religion, e.g., Mt. Olympus was the home of the gods. In Mesopotamia, the mountain was looked upon as the abode of the god who "dies" in the dry season but comes forth with the revival of nature; as the home of the dead; as the source of life-giving rain and of natural life in general. The mountain was not only the abode of chthonian divinities, but was also a means of communication with the gods of the sky. Accordingly, temples were often built on heights. Thus the ziggurat of Mesopotamia is best interpreted as a kind of temple constructed in imitation of a mountain. Mountains have an important role in the Bible. It is significant that the greatest theophanies from *Sinai to *Thabor took place in mountain settings and that the theophany in each case endowed the mountain with a sacred character. Finally, the mountain is often used in the Old Testament and elsewhere as a peculiarly appropriate symbol of divine power, changelessness, eternity, protection, and justice.

Bibliography: M. ELIADE, *Patterns of Comparative Religion* (New York 1958) 99–102, 374–379. M. ELIADE and K. GALLING, RGG³ 1:1043–44. J. SCHILDENBERGER, LexThK² 2:219–220, with bibliography. E. STOMMEL, "Berg," ReallexAntChr 2:136–138, with bibliography. J. A. MacCULLOCH, "Mountains, Mountain Gods," Hastings ERE 8:863–868. **Illustration credit:** Courtesy of the Royal Greek Embassy, Press and Information Service.

[M. R. P. MC GUIRE]

MOURA, ANTÔNIO MARIA DE, Brazilian regalist, subject of a controversy between the Holy See and the Brazilian Empire; b. Vila Nova da Rainha do Caeté, Minas Gerais, 1794; d. Rio de Janeiro, March 12, 1842. Nothing is known of his family because he was abandoned at the door of Captain Caetano José Nascentes, who raised him and took care of his education, sending him to Coimbra, Portugal. There Moura was ordained and then graduated in law (1819). On his return to Brazil, he entered political life, a normal career for priests at the time in Brazil, and demonstrated the regalistic ideas he had learned at the University of Coimbra. In 1830 he was elected to represent his native province in the legislature, where he stayed until 1837. He was also professor of law in São Paulo.

He became a center of controversy in 1833, when the Brazilian government named him major chaplain and bishop of Rio de Janeiro and the Holy See did not give its approval. Rome's attitude was based on two regalistic projects that Moura had supported in 1831 and on information that he suffered from paralysis and was suspected of avarice and drunkenness. The Brazilian government did not accept the explanations of the Holy See, saying that they were rash and exaggerated. Negotiations went on until 1835, when Rome questioned merely his orthodoxy. A formula of abjuration was then prepared for Moura to sign. At this point, however, two facts decided the Holy See to refuse Moura's nomination. The first was a project presented in the Brazilian legislature by Estêvão Rafael de Carvalho, asking for separation of the Brazilian Church from Rome and investing the government with supreme authority over it; although not approved, this project revealed how far the regalists intended to go. The second was the exchange of letters between the Minister of Justice and Moura, with a consequent refusal of the latter to sign the above-mentioned abjuration. From then on Moura's cause was lost, even though the regent of the empire, Diogo Antônio *Feijó, a well-known liberal and regalist, carried on the fight and threatened separation from Rome to get Moura confirmed as bishop. The prudence of the Brazilian parliament, however, closed the matter for the time being. Moura finally withdrew his nomination in 1839, and the Brazilian Empire, for appearance sake, asked the Pope to make Moura bishop "in partibus infidelium." Gregory XIII, however, commenting on the attitudes of the bishop-elect, made him only a domestic prelate of His Holiness. On Sept. 3, 1839, the bishop newly elected by the government, Manuel do Monte Rodrigues de Araújo, was proclaimed in a secret consistory as bishop of Rio de Janeiro and major chaplain.

Bibliography: M. Cardozo, "The Holy See and the Question of the Bishop-Elect of Rio, 1833–1839," *Americas* 10 (1953–54) 3–74. Jerônimo de Avelar Figueira de Melo, "Dissídio entre Feijó e a Santa Sé," *Anais do segundo Congresso de história nacional . . . 1931,* v.2 (Rio de Janeiro 1934–46) 97–174.

[T. BEAL]

MOURNING CUSTOMS (IN THE BIBLE)

Conventional forms of displaying grief in the ancient Near East at the death and burial of a relative or an important public figure or in times of general calamity or personal affliction. Funerary rites of mourning were considered as obligatory as burial itself, and to be deprived of them was held to be a curse (Jer 16.4, 6; 22.18–19; 25.23). The ritual mourning was carried out by the deceased person's relatives (Gn 23.2; 50.10; 2 Sm 11.26; Ez 24.16–18) and by all others affected by the death (1 Sm 25.1; 28.3; 2 Sm 1.12; 3.31). Their lamenting was often aided by hired men (Am 5.16; 2 Chr 35. 25; Eccl 12.5) and women (Jer 9.17–21; 2 Chr 35.25).

The rites began as soon as death occurred (3 Kgs 13.29; cf. Mk 5.38), while the body was being prepared for interment [*see* BURIAL, II (EARLY CHRISTIAN)], or when news of death arrived (Gn 37.34; 2 Sm 1.17); and they continued usually for 7 days (Sir 22.11; 1 Sm 31.13; Jdt 16.29). The cases of longer mourning (70 days for Jacob, including 40 days for embalming, Gn 50.7; 30 days for Aaron, Nm 20.29, and for Moses, Dt 34.8) are exceptional and show Egyptian influence.

The customs of general and funerary mourning in use among the Israelites were in vogue also among other peoples of the ancient Near East. They were characterized by various forms of self-affliction and by loud wailing. Mourners tore their garments and put sackcloth on their bodies (Gn 37.34; 2 Sm 3.31). They went barefoot (2 Sm 15.30) and with heads uncovered (Ez 24.17, 23), neglected ordinary care of the body (2 Sm 14.2; 19.24; Dn 10.3), sat on the ground (Jb 2.13), put dust and ashes on their heads (Jos 7.6; 2 Sm 13.9), beat their bare breasts (Is 32.12), and restricted food and drink (2 Sm 1.12; 1 Mc 3.47). The practice, however, of shaving one's head and gashing one's body for the dead, though known in Israel (Jer 16.6), was forbidden in the Law (Lv 19.28; 21.5; Dt 14.1).

The most characteristic mourning rite was the lamentation. Besides short repeated cries, such as those recorded in Am 5.16; 3 Kgs 13.30; Jer 22.18 ("Alas! Alas, my brother! Alas, sister! Alas, Lord!"), there were longer formal dirges (Heb. *qînôt*), composed in the limping meter of three accents followed by two, sung by

Mourners at a funeral, fragment of an Egyptian relief, probably from Memphis, late Eighteenth or early Nineteenth Dynasty, c. 1350 B.C. Above and below the group of mourners are tables stacked with foodstuffs to be placed in the tomb.

professional mourners to the accompaniment of music on the flute (Jer 48.36; cf. Mt 9.23). Ancient dirges, such as those of David for Saul and Jonathan (2 Sm 1.17–27) and for Abner (2 Sm 3.33–34) and of Jeremia for Josia (2 Chr 35.25), were collected and used as models in later times (1 Mc 9.21). With deep emotion these poems laud the dead and bewail their fate but express no spiritual hope.

Whatever sacrificial or magical intentions may have been connected with these rites among pagans, there is no good reason, in the light of Israel's monotheistic faith, to attribute such intentions to the Israelites, although they too were influenced in their vehemence and sadness by the prevailing view of life after death. *See* AFTERLIFE, 2; SHEOL (ABODE OF THE DEAD). A tendency to restrict and to spiritualize mourning can be observed in Jl 2.13; Sir 38.16–23.

Some of the Israelite burial and mourning customs of OT times continued to be practiced in the NT period: at the home of Jairus in Capharnaum (Mk 5.22–24, 35–43); at Nain (Lk 7.11–15); at the home of Martha and Mary in Bethany (Jn 11.1–46); and at the death of Tabitha (Dorcas) in Joppe (Acts 9.36–42). Our Lord's Resurrection from the dead worked a change in the tone and spiritual motivation of mourning: death is now conquered (1 Corinthians ch. 15), Christians do not mourn "as others who have no hope" (1 Thes 4.13), for they look toward a "New Jerusalem," where "death shall be no more; neither shall there be mourning" (Ap 21.2, 4). The Christian dead have merely "fallen asleep in the Lord" (Acts 7.59; 1 Cor 15.6, 18; 1 Thes 4.12; cf. Mt 9.24), so that for the early Christians a burial place was a "dormitory" (the original meaning of κοιμητήριον—cemetery).

Bibliography: De Vaux AncIsr 59–61. F. Nötscher, *Biblische Altertumskunde* (Bonn 1940) 93–96. G. Stählin, Kittel ThW 3:148–155, 829–851. H. Schmidt, RGG³ 6:1000–01. EncDictBibl 1570–73. **Illustration credit:** Courtesy of the Detroit Institute of Arts.

[M. A. HOFER]

MOURRET, FERNAND,

ecclesiastical historian; b. Eygalières (Bouche-du-Rhône), France, Dec. 3, 1854; d. Paris, May 28, 1938. Fernand Maria Émile Mourret completed his classical education and studied law at Aix-en-Provence. After the obligatory military service, he practiced law for a short time and in 1879 entered the seminary of St. Sulpice at Issy, near Paris. In 1883 he joined the *Sulpicians and was sent to study in Rome, where he was ordained (Dec. 22, 1883). Severe illness forced him to interrupt his graduate studies in Rome after 1 year. Too frail for seminary work, he devoted the next 10 years to less arduous tasks. He taught in the major seminary in Avignon (1894–96) and was then appointed to teach philosophy in the seminary of St. Sulpice in Issy. In 1898 he was transferred to the Sulpician theological school on the Rue de Regard, Paris, where he taught apologetics, dogmatic theology, and sacred eloquence. In 1902 he began to teach ecclesiastical history, the subject with which his name remains associated. His principal works, all published in Paris, were: *La Vénérable Marie Rivier* (1898); *Leçons sur l'art de prêcher* (1909); *Le Mouvement catholique en France de 1830 à 1850* (1917); *Les Directions politiques, intellectuelles et sociales de Léon XIII* (1920); and *La papauté* (1929). *Le Concile du Vatican, d'après des documents inédits* (1919) made use of the papers of M. Icard, former superior of St. Sulpice. In conjunction with J. Carreyre, Mourret published *Précis d'histoire de l'Église* (3 v. 1924). Mourret's best-known work is *Histoire générale de l'Église* (9 v. 1914–27), written to provide his students with an up-to-date textbook. Essentially it represents the history courses conducted by Mourret, but for the contemporary period it constitutes an original work that remains authoritative, especially for French history. The first 8 volumes (to 1878) have been translated into English by Newton Thompson as *A History of the Catholic Church* (1931–57). Mourret was an eminent professor, noted for his extensive knowledge, vivacity, and clarity, and he won renown, too, as a professor of homiletics and a spiritual director. He was extraordinarily kind and accessible.

Bibliography: *Bulletin Trimestriel des Anciens Elèves de S. Sulpice* (Paris 1903).

[E. JARRY]

MOUTON, JEAN,

Renaissance polyphonist; b. Haut-Wignes, near Boulogne, *c.* 1459; d. Saint-Quentin, Oct. 30, 1522. He was a choir boy at 7 years, and served after ordination at Notre Dame, Nesles (1477–83), later receiving canonries at Thérouanne and Saint-Quentin. During his artistic career he held posts as choral director at Amiens cathedral (1500); master of the children at Saint-André, Grenoble (1501–02); and singer in the chapels of Anne de Bretagne (1509), Louis XII (1513), and Francis I (from 1515); and was cited favorably by Leo X, Alfonso I of Ferrara, *Glareanus, Morley, and others. His compositions comprise about 16 Masses, 5 Magnificats, 110 motets (including political ones), and 20 chansons. His style is essentially contrapuntal, but has a delicate texture, achieved through frequently paired voices, a clear, concise form, and flexible, calm melodic lines. He transmitted the Josquinian tradition (*see* DESPREZ, JOSQUIN), together with his personal style, to his most famous disciple, *Willaert, founder of the Venetian polychoral school.

See also MUSIC, SACRED, HISTORY OF, 4.

Bibliography: P. Kast, MusGG 9:679–686. A. C. Minor, *The Masses of Jean Mouton*, 2 v. (Doctoral diss. microfilm; U. of Mich. 1951). J. M. Shine, *The Motets of Jean Mouton* (Doctoral diss. unpub. New York U. 1953). E. E. Lowinsky, "The Medici Codex," *Annales Musicologiques* 5 (1957) 61–178. J. Ravell and S. Broman, Grove DMM 5:921. Roland-Manuel v.1. Reese MusR.

[I. CAZEAUX]

MOUVEMENT RÉPUBLICAINE POPULAIRE (MRP)

A liberal and Catholic party in *France. Its antecedents can be found in the thought of such men as H. F. R. de *Lamennais, J. B. H. *Lacordaire, C. F. R. de *Montalembert, and Albert de *Mun, but also in two small groups of the period before World War II, *La Jeune République* and the *Partie Démocrate Populaire*. Highly influential also was Marc *Sangnier and his magazine *Le Sillon*. In a real sense, however, the MRP was the product of the French resistance movement during World War II. Georges Bidault, who became chairman of the clandestine National Council of the Resistance, as well as other leaders, thought vaguely in terms of a Christian alliance. But a young university student, Gilbert Dru, gave the movement its form and its direction. After he was executed by the Germans in 1944 his work survived under the leadership of Bidault; the party emerged, first as the Republican Movement of Liberation, then as the Popular Republican Movement.

Program. The party program is based upon Catholic principles of ethics and social justice and is critical of both capitalism and socialism, although it embraces aspects of both. The postwar French system of *family allowances was largely the work of the MRP. The MRP is unreservedly democratic and republican and has warmly endorsed the unification of Europe in which one of its leaders, Robert *Schuman, played a vital role. In most respects the MRP has been on the moderate left side of the political spectrum. However, as a Catholic party, it has always espoused the cause of government subsidies for Catholic schools, an issue on which the historical left of France has been in strong disagreement.

Strength. The MRP emerged from the resistance with considerable strength. In the elections of October 1945 it received 24.8 per cent of the national vote and in

June 1946 it emerged as the strongest party of France with 28.1 per cent. In November 1946 it was still formidable with 25.9 per cent. These results did not represent its true strength, however. Of the three foremost political parties immediately after the liberation, the Communists, the Socialists, and the MRP, the MRP was relatively most acceptable to conservative voters. But when the traditional conservative and middle-of-the-road parties reappeared the MRP was abandoned by a large part of its following. By 1951 it had lost half its supporters and descended to a mere 12.4 per cent of the vote. Subsequently it declined to 10.9 per cent in 1956 and 8. 9 per cent in 1962. In the elections of 1958 a split occurred between Bidault, until then the principal leader, and most of his colleagues over the burning Algeria question. Bidault formed a new party called the Christian Democrats, but this proved abortive and the Christian Democrats disappeared soon after the election. Both wings of the party together obtained 11.5 per cent of the vote that year.

The MRP participated in most governments of the Fourth Republic. In particular, during a major part of the period, the foreign ministry was occupied first by Bidault and later by Schuman. The last government prior to the return to power of Gen. Charles de Gaulle in 1958 was headed by another MRP leader, Pierre Pflimlin. The MRP entered the first De Gaulle government and remained in it until 1962, when it found itself in strong opposition to De Gaulle's nationalistic European policy. Even after leaving the government, its opposition was not as total and systematic as that of the Socialist and Communist parties. In particular the MRP opposed any coalition or cooperation with the Communists. A new and young leadership attempted to revitalize the party, but without making substantial progress. In spite of its loyal cadres, the MRP suffered from erosion on both its flanks; on the left because as a Catholic party it was either unacceptable or only barely acceptable to the Socialists, and on the right because of its opposition to De Gaulle. The majority of the party leadership has strongly favored a union of the center parties into one single party; since this goal has not been achieved, the party has found it difficult to make a comeback.

See also CHRISTIAN DEMOCRACY; POLITICAL PARTIES, CATHOLIC; SOCIAL MOVEMENTS, CATHOLIC, 2.

Bibliography: M. EINAUDI, *Christian Democracy in Italy and France* (Notre Dame, Ind. 1952). M. P. FOGARTY, *Christian Democracy in Western Europe, 1820–1953* (Notre Dame, Ind. 1957).

[R. G. NEUMANN]

MOVEMENT FOR A BETTER WORLD, a religious movement to infuse in individuals and groups the spirit of mutual charity and unity that provides the basis for the social presence of Jesus: "For where two or three are gathered together for my sake, there am I in the midst of them" (Mt 18.20). The movement was inaugurated by Pius XII and blessed by his successors John XXIII and Paul VI. In a radio message of Feb. 10, 1952, Pope Pius called himself the "herald of a better world willed by God" and asked for a renewal of the structures of society [*Dal Nostro cuore* ActApS 44 (1952) 158–162]. The founder and first international director, Riccardo Lombardi, SJ, of Rocca di Papa, Italy, answered the plea. Since 1952, through Father Lombardi's initiative, promoting groups of the movement have been established on every continent.

The promoting group consists of specially trained priests, brothers, sisters, and lay people who strive to practice the asceticism of the movement. This asceticism of mutual charity and unity is the exercise of seeking always and at all times truth and the common good. It implies that there must be unity in holding to the truth with the intellect and in seeking the common good with the heart and will. This exercise is aided by the social presence of Jesus. Charity creates the climate for the practice of this asceticism. The means used to stimulate it is a retreat varying from 8 to 10 days. The three parts of the retreat, based on the doctrine of the Mystical Body of Christ, emphasize the necessity of a great apostolic effort in the contemporary world, the inner renewal of apostolic men in relationship to God and neighbor, and the total apostolic effort that must be made in the Church in all areas of activity and on all social levels.

Bibliography: R. LOMBARDI, *Towards a New World* (New York 1958); *Esercitazioni per un mondo Migliore* (Rome 1958), Eng. in prep., outline and format of the Better World Retreats; *The Salvation of the Unbeliever,* tr. D. M. WHITE (Westminster, Md. 1956); *Rifare il mondo* (2d ed. Rocca di Papa 1959); *Orientamenti fondamentali* (11th ed. Rome 1957); *La dottrina marxista: esposizione e discussione* (3d ed. Rome 1956); *La storia e il suo protagonista* (3d ed. Rome 1947).

[R. L. BENNETT]

MOYË, JOHN MARTIN, BL., founder of religious congregations of women and missionary in China; b. Cutting, Lorraine, Jan. 27, 1730; d. Trier, Germany, May 4, 1793 (feast, May 4). John, the 6th of 13 children born to John Moyë and Catherine Demange, was educated at the Collège of Pont-à-Mousson, the Jesuit College of Strasbourg, and the Seminary of Saint-Simon in Metz. After his ordination in 1754, Father Moyë devoted himself as vicar to pastoral work in the Diocese of Metz for 17 years. To secure free education for village children, he founded the Congregation of the Sisters of Divine Providence in 1762. He was appointed superior of the Seminary of Saint-Dié in 1767, but 2 years later he asked to join the *Paris Foreign Missionary Society. On March 28, 1773, he arrived in Chengtu, the capital of Szechwan in southwestern China, to work under Bp. François Pottier, the Vicar Apostolic. His missionary field covered half of Szechwan and the province of Kweichow. For 10 years he worked with tireless and inventive zeal, baptizing pagan children in danger of death, writing books of devotion, and organizing exercises of piety. In 1782 he established an Institute of Christian Virgins to care for the sick and to give Christian instruction to Chinese women and children in their homes.

Physical exhaustion and the opposition to his apostolic methods manifested by his five co-workers caused him to ask to return to France in 1784. Lorraine again became the field of his apostolate and the Sisters of Divine Providence his special care. Within the decade, the French Revolution created grave religious problems. Father Moyë gave counsel and generous help to the persecuted nonjuring priests and the religious forced from their cloisters. To save the congregation he had founded, he moved the Sisters of Divine Providence to Trier in 1791. The advance of the French army, however, caused its suppression the next year. Restored in

1816, the congregation numbered 116 convents by the end of the century, and in 1866 the Sisters made a foundation in San Antonio, Texas. Father Moÿé died in the týphus epidemic that spread to Trier in 1793. Pope Leo XIII approved the introduction of his cause on Jan. 14, 1891. The heroicity of his virtue was proclaimed May 21, 1945, and he was beatified Dec. 27, 1954, by Pope Pius XII.

Bibliography: ActApS 38 (1946) 287–290; 46 (1954) 734–737, 739–740; 47 (1955) 33–39. J. MARCHAL, *Vie de M. l'abbé Moÿé de la Société des Missions Étrangères, foundateur de la Congrégation des Soeurs de la Providence en Lorraine . . .* (Paris 1872). G. GOYAU, *Un Devancier de l'oeuvre de la Sainte-Enfance: Jean-Martin Moÿé, missionaire on Chine, 1772–1783* (Paris 1937). R. PLUS, *J. M. Moÿé . . . des Missions Étrangères: fondateur des Soeurs de la Providence* (Paris 1947). E. HERRGOTT, LexThK² 7:666, with bibliog. A. P. FRUTAZ, EncCatt 8: 1493–94. M. G. CALLAHAN, *The Life of Blessed John Martin Moÿé* (Milwaukee 1964).

[G. M. GRAY]

MOYENMOUTIER, ABBEY OF, former Benedictine monastery located in the Vosges Mountains on the upper Meurthe River in eastern France. It was founded toward the end of the 7th century by St. *Hidulf, a monk at Saint-Miximin and auxiliary bishop of Trier, who, having left Trier, settled as a hermit on the site that was to become Moyenmoutier. Others joined him and formed a small monastery situated midway between five others, consequently known as *medianum monasterium* or Moyenmoutier. In its long history (11 centuries) Moyenmoutier was influenced by reform movements emanating from the Abbey of *Gorze, and later, from *Cluny. One of its outstanding sons was *Humbert of Silva Candida. To counteract the evils brought by the system of commendatory abbots, it joined (1601) with the Abbey of Saint-Vanne at Verdun in forming the great congregation of Saint-Vanne et Saint-Hydulphe, which was suppressed by the French Revolution in 1790.

Bibliography: MGS 4:87–92. Cottineau 2:2008–09. Potthast Bibl 1:733. GallChrist 13:1398–1407. G. ALLEMANG, LexThK² 7:666. H. LECLERCQ, DACL 12.1:380–390, on its foundation and early abbots.

[C. DAVIS]

MOYLAN, STEPHEN, Revolutionary War soldier; b. Cork, Ireland, 1734; d. Philadelphia, Pa., April 13, 1811. As the son of John Moylan, a prosperous merchant, he was educated in Paris. He came to America in 1768, and settled in Philadelphia where he established himself as a successful merchant. In 1771 he helped to organize the Friendly Sons of St. Patrick, serving as its first president. He was an opponent of British legislation before Lexington and Concord, and he enlisted in the Continental Army outside Boston in 1775. As muster-master and aide-de-camp to George Washington, he dispatched privateers to prey on British shipping. He was appointed to the office of commissary general by the Continental Congress in June 1776. He proved to be unsuited to this function, and submitted his resignation within a few months. Thereafter he volunteered as a regimental cavalry commander. He raised a light horse organization in Pennsylvania and served as its colonel at Valley Forge. Moylan participated in many of the Revolutionary campaigns; he was with Anthony Wayne in the Bulls Ferry expedition, with Nathaniel Greene in the Carolina campaign, and

with Lafayette at Yorktown. His career was marred by quarrels with his commander, Casimir Pulaski, as a result of which Moylan was court-martialed. He was acquitted, however, and later was vindicated, succeeding to Pulaski's cavalry command (1778) and being brevetted brigadier general (1783). After the war he returned to his business in Philadelphia, where he became registrar of Chester County (1792) and commissioner of loans of Pennsylvania (1793).

[J. L. MORRISON]

MOZAMBIQUE

Largely agricultural country of southeastern *Africa, 297,731 square miles in area, bordering on the Indian Ocean, north of the Republic of South Africa and south of Tanzania. After its discovery by Vasco da Gama in 1498, it served as a way station for the Portuguese en route to India around the Cape of Good Hope. Later it was a source of slaves for Brazil. Its boundaries were definitely established only in 1891. In 1951 it became an overseas province of Portugal. The preliminary figures in the 1960 census indicated a population of 6,600,000, which included 25,000 whites, 12,500 mulattoes, and 1,600 Asiatics. About 14 per cent were Christians (including 100,000 Protestants), 10 per cent Moslems; the rest of the population remained pagan.

Portuguese Jesuits initiated mission activity in the 16th century. Gonçalo da *Silveira, SJ, was martyred in 1561 after baptizing the rulers of Monomotapa and 300 persons in the court. Dominicans entered the area in 1577. Until 1612 the Portuguese territories in this

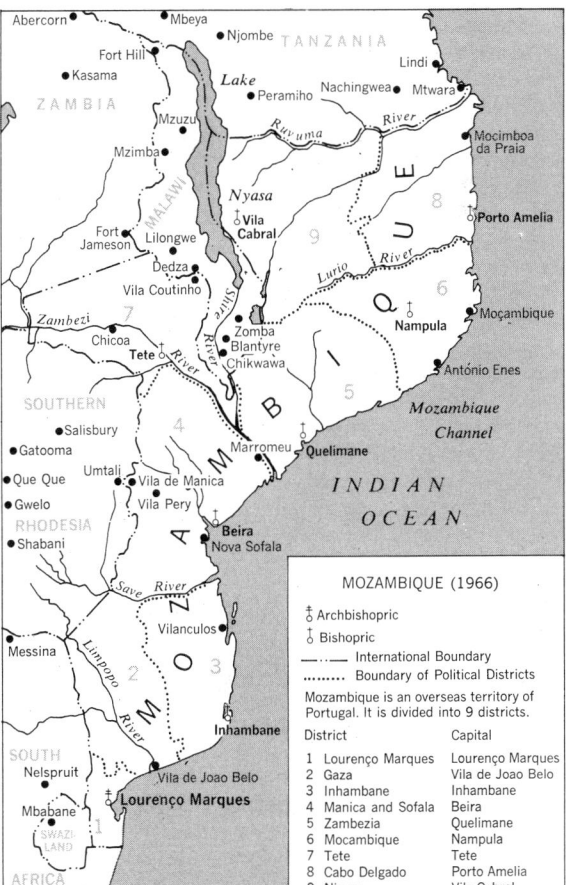

MOZAMBIQUE (1966)

‡ Archbishopric
† Bishopric
—··— International Boundary
········ Boundary of Political Districts

Mozambique is an overseas territory of Portugal. It is divided into 9 districts.

District	Capital
1 Lourenço Marques	Lourenço Marques
2 Gaza	Vila de Joao Belo
3 Inhambane	Inhambane
4 Manica and Sofala	Beira
5 Zambezia	Quelimane
6 Mocambique	Nampula
7 Tete	Tete
8 Cabo Delgado	Porto Amelia
9 Niassa	Vila Cabral

section were attached to the See of *Goa in India; thereafter they formed a separate prelature *nullius*. During the 17th century Dominicans evangelized the Monomotapa region, whose king was baptized in 1652. The Jesuits returned, and other orders joined in the apostolate in the interior, while chaplains served the Catholics in the coastal settlements. Decline began in the 18th century; it was accelerated by the anti-Jesuit policies of *Pombal. Missionaries kept decreasing in number. Portugal's suppression of religious orders in 1834 made the situation worse and by 1855 no missionaries remained. A change for the better occurred in 1881 when the Jesuits resumed their work. Franciscans arrived in 1898. By 1910 there were 71 missionaries, mostly Portuguese. The mission suffered again from the extreme anticlericalism of the Portuguese regimes (1910–25). Since the Portuguese concordat with the Holy See (1940), progress has continued at an accelerated rate.

The hierarchy was created in 1940 when *Lourenço Marques, the capital, became the seat of an archdiocese and metropolitan see for the country. Its suffragan dioceses in 1964 were Beira (created in 1940), Inhambane (1962), Nampula (1940), Porto Amelia (1957), Quelimane (1954), Tete (1962), and Vila Cabral (1963). Archbishop Teódosio de Gouveia of Lourenço Marques received the red hat in 1940, the first prelate south of the Sahara ever to be named cardinal. The number of Catholics rose from 4,000 in 1900 to 60,000 in 1936, and to 850,000 in 1963, when there were 490 priests, 80 seminarians, 410 brothers, 650 sisters, and 342,000 students in Catholic schools.

Bibliography: F. DE ALMEIDA, *História da Igreja em Portugal,* 4 v. (Coimbra 1910–22). L. KILGER, *Die erste Mission unter den Bantustämmen Ostafrikas* (Münster 1917). M. DE OLIVEIRA, *História eclesiástica de Portugal* (2d ed. Lisbon 1948). A. BRASIO, *Monumenta missionaria africana,* 7 v. (Lisbon 1952–56). G. L. ROMMERSKIRCHEN, EncCatt 8:1494–96. R. WENZEL, *Portugal und der Heilige Stuhl* (Lisbon 1958). R. PATTEE, *Portugal na África contemporânea* (Coimbra 1959), with full bibliog. J. DUFFY, *Portuguese Africa* (Cambridge, Mass. 1959); *Portugal in Africa* (Cambridge, Mass. 1962; pa. 1963). A. DA SILVA REGO, *Llções de missionologia* (Estudos de ciências políticas e sociais 56; Lisbon 1961). A. MÉNDES PEDRO, *Anuário Católico do Ultramar Português (1960): Annuaire Catholique de l'Outre-Mer Portugais* (ibid. 57; 1962), Fr. and Port. on opposite pages. *Bilan du Monde* 2:619–622. Centro de Estudos Políticos e Sociais, Lisbon. Missão para o Estudo da Missionologia Africana, *Atlas missionário português* (Lisbon 1962). AnnPont has annual data on all dioceses. For further bibliography, *see* AFRICA.
[R. PATTEE]

MOZARABIC RITE

The name that designates the liturgical rite Christians used on the Iberian Peninsula down to the end of the 11th century. The rite is known by many titles. The Rite of Toledo and Mozarabic remain the most commonly accepted designations today. The meaning of the title "Mozarabic" is uncertain. The rite itself existed in Spain before the arrival of the Arabs, and it is difficult to find any subsequent Arabian influence in the rite. The title seems to refer to the fact that the rite lingered on in the part of Spain under Arabian influence after it had been abandoned in Christian Spain.

History. In spirit and substance the Mozarabic rite is a Western liturgy. Its most evident influences are Gothic and Roman. The Gothic source is traced to the beginning of the Visigothic rule at the end of the

6th century, the Roman influence probably to consultations of Rome in liturgical matters even earlier and to the first preachers of the gospel from Rome. The controversy concerning the total orthodoxy of the rite, its susceptibility to Adoptionist interpretations, is still an open question.

The decline of the Mozarabic liturgy dates from the 11th century. That was a period of centralization that expressed itself also in an effort toward a more uniform practice in liturgy. The Roman rite was decreed for Spain by Rome. In 1080 the Council of Burgos ordered the adoption of the Roman rite. The decrees, even though championed by some of the rulers, met with opposition. There was a stormy period of efforts at enforcement and of resistance. Finally a compromise was agreed upon whereby six parishes of the "Mozarabic" Christians in Toledo would officially keep the old rite. However, there is evidence that it lingered on in many places for a good while after that time. Eventually, even in these six parishes, the rite was used only on special occasions, and finally, it was abandoned. Sporadic attempts were made to revive the rite, whether as a historical monument or in the name of national pride is not clear. García de *Cisneros, who became archbishop of Toledo in 1495, had editions of the Missal and Breviary prepared. He founded the Mozarabic chapel in the Cathedral of Toledo, which perpetuates the rite to the present time. In fact, this chapel is the only place where the rite is found regularly celebrated today. There is daily Eucharistic celebration but no Communion for the people. It is celebrated once or twice a year at the Talavera chapel in Salamanca.

Celebration of the Mass according to the Mozarabic rite at the cathedral in Toledo, Spain. The celebrant is kissing the pax instrument, which will then be proferred to those in attendance in the choir.

But even in these places only the Eucharist and the Divine Office are in the Mozarabic rite; all other Sacraments, blessings, and functions are celebrated according to the Roman rite.

Sources. Mozarabic manuscripts date from the 8th to the 11th centuries. All the most important ones have been published mainly by M. *Férotin. The fundamental sources are: (1) The *Missale mixtum,* a complete Missal published in 1500 (PL 85); (2) *Missale omnium offerentium,* an abridged Missal and Office book, with some miscellaneous matter: preparations for Mass with explanations of the prayers, a calendar, and Martyrology (PL 75:530–569); (3) *Liber Sacramentorum Mozarabicus,* containing mostly prayers for the priest celebrant only (see Férotin); (4) Antiphonal, found in the *Missale mixtum;* (5) *Liber commicus* or *Liber comitis,* a Lectionary [ed. G. Morin, *Anecdota Maredsolana* 1 (Maredsous 1893)]; (6) *Liber Ordinum,* a Pontifical, a Ritual, and some Mass texts, including also homilies to be read at the office (see Férotin); (7) *Breviarium gothicum,* a complete Breviary published in 1502 (PL 86). An interesting feature of the Mozarabic manuscripts is their frequent indications of the authors of the hymns and liturgical texts.

Mass. The order of Mass begins with the preparatory prayers, some said during the vesting and others at the altar. The latter resemble those of the Roman rite but are somewhat expanded. The chalice and paten are purified, the wine and bread prepared with appropriate prayers. After these preparations there is the Introit, Gloria (omitted during Advent and Lent), and an Oration. The Oration often relates to the Gloria with little reference to the feast or season. This is typical of the Mozarabic liturgy.

The reading service begins usually with a lesson from the Old Testament. This is followed by a responsory. The Epistle and Gospel are then read. There is no responsory after the Epistle, only the quiet prayers and blessing in preparation for the reading of the Gospel; a Psalm and Alleluias, Lauda, follow the Gospel, however.

During the chanting of the Lauda the offertory prayers are recited. In an earlier time the faithful made offerings of bread and wine, and during this rite the Sacrificium, similar to the Roman Offertory Antiphon, was sung. Following this come seven prayers, many of which vary with the seasons or the feast. The first is a simple call to prayer. The second asks God to accept the prayers. Here is found a listing of names, the commemorations. The third prayer is one of intercession. The fourth is a peace prayer, a prayer for reconciliation with one's brothers before the gift is offered. Here the celebrant kisses the paten and gives it to the deacon and there is an exchange of the kiss of peace. The fifth prayer begins with the Preface dialogue, continues through the Preface, Sanctus, and a post-Sanctus oration. There follows the prayer that includes the formula of Consecration. The sixth prayer is a number of reflective prayers, some of which are Epicleses. There is a second Elevation. The Creed (on Sundays and certain feasts) is recited here, and is followed by the breaking of the host into nine parts, each representing a mystery of Christ from His Incarnation to His ruling as Risen Lord. There follows a commemoration of the living. The seventh and last prayer is the Our Father. The response Amen is made to each

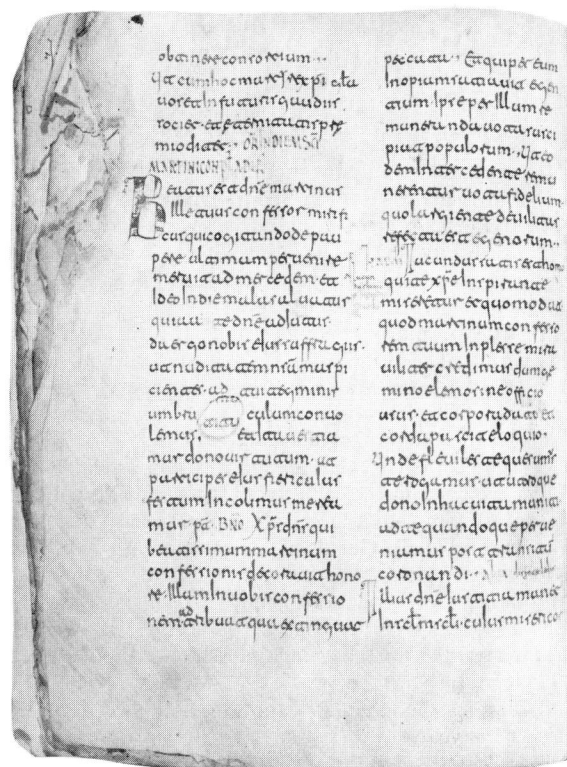

Folio from an "Orationale Gothicum" containing prayers for non-Eucharistic Mozarabic services (Add. MS 30.852, fol. 16v). The manuscript was found in the monastery of San Domingo de Silos, near Burgos, Spain, and is thought to date from the 9th century.

phrase of the Our Father with the exception of "give us this day our daily bread" to which the response is "because you are God." As in the Roman rite the prayer ends with a long reflective commentary on the last petition of the Our Father. This is followed by the Commingling. There is inserted here a pre-Communion blessing, sometimes in as many as five phrases.

After the Communion of the celebrant there is a call to Communion for the faithful. The Mass is concluded with a thanksgiving prayer, the dismissal, a prayer in honor of Mary, and a final blessing that dates from the 16th century.

Church Building. The earliest type of church of the Mozarabic period indicates Eastern influence. The plan was a Greek cross with a rectangular sanctuary. The horseshoe arch typical of Spanish architecture was evident in the earliest buildings of the period, before the Moorish influence. The early style was developed somewhat in its purity in the sections of Spain not under the influence of the Moors and is called, accordingly, Asturian. The churches of the later Mozarabic period are quite diverse in structure but most show marked Moorish influence. This "mixed" style is what is usually referred to as Mozarabic architecture.

Bibliography: F. CABROL, DACL 12.1:390–491. M. FÉROTIN, *Le "Liber ordinum" en usage dans l'église Wisigothique et Mozarabe d'Espagne du Ve au IXe siècle (Monumenta Ecclesiae liturgica* 5; Paris 1904); *Le "Liber Mozarabicus sacramentorum" et les manuscrits mozarabes (ibid.* 6; Paris 1912); *Histoire de l'abbaye de Silos* (Paris 1897); "Deux manuscrits wisigothiques de la bibliothèque de Ferdinand Ier," BiblÉcChartes 62 (1901)

374–387. A. A. KING, *Liturgies of the Primatial Sees* (Milwaukee 1957) 457–631. **Illustration credits:** Fig. 1, William Neufeld. Fig. 2, Courtesy of the Trustees of the British Museum.

[R. F. LECHNER]

MOZARABIC RITE, CHANTS OF

The repertory of chant used in the Visigothic liturgy of the medieval Church in Spain. This chant style burgeoned and came to full bloom between 550 and 650 and was firmly fixed at the time of the Arab invasion (771). It is called Mozarabic because the term describes a Christian living under Arab or Islamic domination (711–1085), and because its principal MSS date from this period. The principal surviving musical codices of the Visigothic-Mozarabic liturgy are preserved in the cathedral of Toledo; in San Domingo Abbey, Silos; in San Millán Abbey, Cogolla; in the cathedral of León; and in the University of Santiago de Compostela. These codices, copied in the 10th and 11th centuries, contain an almost complete musical repertory of the Visigothic Church of Toledo that dates back to the 6th, 7th, and early 8th centuries. The most precious of them is the Antiphonary of León. According to some scholars, this is an early 10th-century copy of an original MS of King Wamba written for the Toledo parish of St. Leocadia in 672. It begins with the feast of St. Ascisclus (Nov. 17) and contains the Office and the Mass for the entire ecclesiastical year.

The office for Christmas, Antiphonary of León, housed in the Libro Cantoral of the cathedral at León. Above each line of text can be seen the Mozarabic neumes.

Notation. Mozarabic chant had its own musical notation, but the notation of these codices is illegible for the reason that there is not a single musical codex of the Mozarabic period that is copied upon lines of the musical staff. When in the 11th century the Gregorian codices without lines were transcribed into codices with lines, Spanish musicians did not do the same for their own melodies. As a consequence, the Visigothic-Mozrabic neumes are legible only to the extent of the number of their notes. There is no means of determining the relations of tonal height within the notes of a neume, nor its melodic connection with the preceding and following neumes. The melodic treasury incased within the neumes is undecipherable without the help of a later diastematic notation. Such notation was found for 20 or so of the actual melodies preserved. In 12 folios of the MS of the *Liber Ordinum* of the Monastery of San Millan an Aquitainian superimposed system was substituted for erased Mozarabic neumes. The comparison of these folios with the Mozarabic neumatic notation of the same pieces in the MS of the *Liber Ordinum* of the San Domingo monastery of Silos served as a key to decipher the existing melodies. These melodies show that Mozarabic chant was monodic and of a free rhythm and modality equal to that of *Gregorian chant. They exemplify syllabic, neumatic, and melismatic styles.

There are two classes of script in Mozarabic notation: the horizontal and the vertical. The horizontal script pertains exclusively to the codices of Toledo and to a very fragmentary Portuguese codex of Coimbra. In these codices the neumes incline to the right. The codex of Silos and the Antiphonary of León are in vertical scripts. Both the horizontal and vertical scripts originated, however, in the scriptoria of Toledo.

Diffusion. Through the efforts of Charlemagne and the promulgation of the *Lex Romana,* France sacrificed her own liturgy and chant for the liturgy and chant of Rome. The effect of this edict in Spain paralleled the success of the reconquest. The *Lex Romana* did not triumph in Aragon until 1071 and became successful in Navarre, Castille, and Leon only in 1076. The Spanish Mozarabic rite was finally suppressed by Rome in 1089, except for six parishes in Toledo where it was allowed to continue. Here it struggled along with much difficulty and became almost extinct until Cardinal *Ximénes de Cisneros became archbishop of Toledo. He received a concession from Pope Julius II in 1508 to found the Mozarabic chapel of Corpus Christi in the cathedral church of Toledo. The service books edited by him preserve some Mozarabic melodies in corrupt form, but these books have little value since the original melodic treasury was already undecipherable.

Bibliography: C. ROJO and G. PRADO, *El canto mozárabe* (Barcelona 1929). G. PRADO, "Mozarabic Melodics," *Speculum* 3 (1928) 218–239. H. ANGLÈS, *La música española* (Barcelona 1941); NewOxHMus 2:81–91. P. WAGNER, "Der Mozarabische Kirchengesang," *Gesammelte Aufsätze zur Kulturgeschichte Spaniens* 1 (Spanische Forschungen der Görresgesellschaft 1; Münster 1928) 102–141. **Illustration credit:** MAS, Barcelona.

[I. WORTMAN]

MOZART, WOLFGANG AMADEUS

A principal composer of the classical period and of all time; b. Salzburg, Austria, Jan. 27, 1756 (baptized Johannes Chrysostomus Wolfgang Theophilus); d. Vienna, Dec. 5, 1791. Mozart's father, Leopold, had been a respected composer and violinist in the employ of the archiepiscopal court of Salzburg. As a small boy Mozart already displayed amazing talents as violinist and harpsichordist, even as composer. In 1769 he

Wolfgang Amadeus Mozart, by Quenedey after a portrait from life.

entered Archbishop Colloredo's service. There he had frequent opportunities for writing sacred music, yet he resented increasingly the confining environment of a small ecclesiastical state, and this resentment was aggravated by travels to important musical centers throughout Europe. The inevitable break between the archbishop and the young musician occurred in 1781. Mozart then settled in Vienna, always hoping for a desirable court position. As late as 1790 he applied for an appointment to the Austrian court, stating in his application that "from my childhood on I have been familiar with the church style." The desired appointment did not materialize. That Mozart wrote virtually no sacred music after leaving Salzburg is attributed in part to this failure, but also to the curtailment of church music during the age of *Josephinism.

Mozart was essentially a believing and practicing Catholic, as seems certain from many of his letters (see Einstein, 77–81). He saw no conflict between his religious beliefs and Freemasonry in which he became involved in 1784, taking an active part in its affairs and providing a number of compositions for Masonic occasions—e.g., Cantatas K. 429, 471, 623; *Masonic Funeral Music,* K. 477. The "Masonic virtues" of tolerance, brotherly love, steadfastness, and silence also figure in the libretto of *The Magic Flute,* an opera generally interpreted as a Masonic allegory. Objections against liturgical use of Mozart's sacred compositions have often been voiced, in the 19th century and today, chiefly because of their allegedly "worldly" or "operatic" nature. Such a view can largely be explained by the fact that his operas and his instrumental music have always been more widely known. Many features that simply represent Mozart's own style, and that of his period, when encountered in his sacred works remind some listeners of his secular music. To this day, however, his church music regularly receives liturgical performances in Austria and Southern Germany.

Sacred Works. Both individual Mass movements and complete Masses from Mozart's childhood and adolescence have been preserved, e.g., the *Kyrie,* K. 33 (1766), and the *Missa Brevis,* K. 49 (1768). Many early works

(e.g., the incomplete *Missa Brevis,* K. 115) indicate that he had studied the sacred music of *Eberlin and Michael *Haydn, especially their works in strict (contrapuntal) style; yet few of his own compositions are consistently in this style. Strict contrapuntal writing (the *stile antico* of which Padre *Martini was considered a master) represented a challenge to the young composer but was in Mozart's idiom united with other elements, especially the prevailing Italian church style—the *stile moderno,* in which one melodic line was prominent, and often quite florid, with orchestral accompaniment.

Masses. The *Missa Solemnis,* K. 139, a substantial early work, has a large orchestra with timpani and four trumpets. Other important settings include the *Missa in honorem SSmae Trinitatis,* K. 167, in which there is no vocal solo writing; the *Missa Brevis* in C, K. 220, in an essentially homophonic style; K. 257, the "Credo Mass" (so-called because of the recurring exclamation "Credo, credo"); the "Coronation Mass," K. 317, written for a small pilgrimage church near Salzburg; and the great but incomplete Mass in C-minor, K. 427 (1783). Some portions of this last, especially the *Laudamus te* with its florid solo passages in Neapolitan style, have been cited as evidence of the "operatic" quality of his sacred music. Other sections, however, are severely contrapuntal, some in five- or eight-part choral writing. Much of the music is serious, full of dramatic tension, expressing the sacred text with eloquence and sincerity. The unfinished Requiem, K. 626, completed by his pupil Franz Süssmayer, has become his best-known sacred work. During his last years Mozart thought often of death; he seems to have felt that the Requiem, commissioned under rather mysterious circumstances, was to be his own funeral Mass, and the setting is consistently in keeping with the text.

Other Liturgical Music. Among other extended sacred works are two settings of Vesper Psalms and Magnificat, K. 321 and 339, and several litanies, K. 109, 125, 195, 243. His smaller sacred works, especially the motets, show great variety. The Introit *Cibavit eos,* K. 44 (Bologna 1770), is a study in the *stile antico,* based on a Gregorian *cantus firmus. Other motets, e.g., the Offertory *Inter natos mulierum,* K. 72, reflect the musical idiom of the young composer's home environment. Motets in the purely soloistic Italian style were written when an occasion called for them. One such, *Exsultate, jubilate,* K. 165, composed for the *castrato* Rauzzini, consists of three arias, ending with the well-known *Alleluia.* His last motet, *Ave verum corpus,* K. 618 (1791), scored for four voices, strings, and organ, still appeals widely because of its simplicity and sincerity. There are also 17 church or "Epistle" sonatas, short compositions for strings and organ, with wind and timpani parts added in some instances. In the Salzburg cathedral these compositions were traditionally performed between the Epistle and the Gospel (*see* ORGAN MUSIC).

Style. Many stylistic characteristics of Mozart's sacred works are found also in his secular music. Some Mass movements are in sonata form (suggested especially by the *Kyrie - Christe - Kyrie* text). Characteristic themes may recur throughout a movement. Melodic structure, the harmonies, and instrumentation found in Mass and Offertory frequently resemble those of symphony and opera. No more than in J. S. *Bach's age did composers

Holograph MS of Mozart's "Ave Verum Corpus" (1791), in the Austrian National Library at Vienna (CPV 18.975, v. 3).

of Mozart's draw rigid distinctions between sacred and secular style, though counterpoint (the "Palestrina style") was considered especially suitable for the Church, particularly during Advent and Lent. Mozart's style developed and matured along similar lines in sacred and secular works. Thus parallel prominence is given to wind instruments and use of chromaticism in Mozart's later sacred works (C-minor Mass, *Requiem*) and in symphonies and concertos from the same period. Skillful counterpoint distinguishes many of his later works, especially after 1782, when his acquaintance with Baron Swieten led to renewed interest in the music of Bach and *Handel. While he impressed his own style characteristics on his sacred music, Mozart did observe many conventions found in liturgical music of his age, among them the use of a figured bass (by then largely obsolete in secular music), and the traditional fugal endings of *Gloria* (*Cum Sancto Spiritu*) and *Credo* (*Et vitam venturi saeculi*).

See also MUSIC, SACRED, HISTORY OF, 6.

Bibliography: *Werke: Kritisch durchgesehene Gesammtausgabe,* 74 v. in 69 (Leipzig 1877–1905; repr. Ann Arbor 1951–); *Neue Ausgabe sämtlicher Werke* (Kassel 1955–), edition of the Internationale Stiftung Mozarteum in Salzburg; *The Letters of Mozart and His Family,* ed. and tr. E. ANDERSON, 3 v. (London 1938). Literature. O. E. DEUTSCH, *Mozart: A Documentary Biography,* tr. E. BLOM et al. (Stanford 1965). A. EINSTEIN, *Mozart: His Character, His Life, His Work,* tr. A. MENDEL and N. BRODER (New York 1945). E. BLOM, *Mozart* (London 1935). K. G. FELLERER, *Mozarts Kirchenmusik* (Salzburg 1955). Fellerer CathChMus. R. G. PAULY, *Music in the Classic Period* (New York 1965). K. GEIRINGER, "The Church Music," *The Mozart Companion,* ed. H. C. R. LANDON and D. MITCHELL (New York 1956) 361–376. L. VON KÖCHEL, *Chronologisch-thematisches Verzeichnis . . . Mozarts,* ed. F. GIEGLING et al. (6th ed. Wiesbaden 1964), the basis, since 1862, of "K numbers" or "Köchel listing" universally adopted in place of opus numbers (which Mozart rarely used) for identification purposes. F. LIPPMANN, MusGG 9:699–839. W. HUMMEL, "Mozart Gesellschaften," *ibid.* 839–842, includes Mozarteum. **Illustration credits:** Fig. 1.

Museo teatrale alla Scala. Fig. 2. Austrian National Library, Vienna.

[R. G. PAULY]

MRAK, IGNATIUS, second bishop of *Marquette, Mich.; b. Hotovle, Carniola, Austria, Oct. 16, 1818; d. Marquette, Feb. 1, 1901. After education at the Royal Gymnasium and the Seminary of Laibach (Ljubiljana), he was ordained there Aug. 3, 1837. Influenced by the work of his countryman Frederic *Baraga, Mrak sought admission (1845) to the Diocese of Detroit, Mich. Upon arriving there, October 1845, he was immediately sent to assist another countryman, Rev. Francis *Pierz, at Arbre Croche (Harbor Springs). Two years later Mrak was given his own mission at La Croix (Cross Village) with Middletown (Good Hart), Castor Island (Beaver Island), and Manistee (Manistique) included. Here and later at Grande Traverse the missionary spent 13 years ministering to the Indians of the lakelands. Much to his dismay, Mrak was chosen (1868) to succeed Baraga as bishop of Sault Ste. Marie and Marquette. He was consecrated in the metropolitan cathedral at Cincinnati, Ohio, Feb. 7, 1869, wearing secondhand regalia.

Devoted to a life of simplicity, Mrak continued his work among the Indians and struggled to meet the pioneer needs of the Church in Upper Michigan. He made special efforts to improve the calibre and education of his missionary clergy and opened Catholic schools wherever possible. He also organized elected lay boards to assist pastors in the material administration of their parishes. Because of a painful rheumatic condition, he resigned his see (1878), which then had 20 priests serving 27 churches with missions and a Catholic population of 20,000. Appointed titular bishop of Antinoe, Mrak returned to his beloved Indian missions. During the last 9 years of his life he remained at Marquette, where he performed chaplain duties at St. Mary's Hospital. Mentally alert to the end, the old missionary made his last public appearance in August 1899 at the consecration of Marquette's fourth bishop, Frederick Eis, whom he had ordained.

Bibliography: Archives, Diocese of Marquette, Mrak Papers. A. I. REZEK, *History of the Diocese of Sault Ste. Marie and Marquette,* 2 v. (Houghton, Mich. 1906–07).

[C. J. CARMODY]

MUARD, MARIE JEAN BAPTISTE, founder of the Society of *St. Edmund; b. Vireaux (Yonne), France, April 24, 1809; d. La Pierre-qui-Vire (Yonne), France, June 19, 1854. After studies at the major seminary in Sens, he was ordained (1834) and spent the next 6 years in parochial ministries. He was eager to become a missionary, but his bishop refused him permission to go to China. In 1843 he founded at the ancient Cistercian monastery in Pontigny (Yonne) a group of diocesan missionary priests, known originally as Prêtres Auxiliaires, Missionaires de St. Edmond, and later as the Society of St. Edmund. Muard remained at Pontigny until 1848. During this period he gave stability to the community and composed its rule. After sojourning in Rome and Subiaco he returned to France and in 1850 founded the monastery of Sainte Marie de La Pierre-qui-Vire near Avallon (Yonne). This community, which belongs to the Benedictine congregation of Subiaco, became an abbey in 1884. Muard continued an active apostolate until he fell ill after preaching a mission at Saint-Étienne. He died a few days later. His process for beatification opened in Rome in 1928.

Bibliography: *The Life of Jean Baptiste Muard,* v.9 of *Library of Religious Biography,* ed. E. H. THOMPSON, 9 v. (London 1867–86). L. BRULÉE, *Life of the Rev. Mary John Baptist Muard,* tr. I. ROBOT (New York 1882). J. BOUCHARD, *Vie du R. P. Muard,* 2 v. (Paris 1893). L. VEUILLOT, *Le R. P. Muard* (Paris 1901). D. HUERRE, *Jean-Baptiste Muard* (Saint-Léger-Vauban, Yonne 1950). G. BERNOVILLE, *Le Père Muard* (Paris 1942). V. F. NICOLLE, *Historical Sketch of the Society of St. Edmund* (Burlington, Vt. 1943). P. LOUSIN, *Revue Mabillon* 51 (1961) 179–191.

[G. E. DUPONT]

MUENCH, ALOISIUS JOSEPH

Cardinal and diplomat; b. Milwaukee, Wis., Feb. 18, 1889; d. Rome, Italy, Feb. 15, 1962. He was the oldest of six children of immigrant German parents. After studies at St. Francis Seminary, Milwaukee, he was ordained June 8, 1913, and served as assistant at St. Michael's Church, Milwaukee, and at the University Chapel, Madison. He received a master's degree (1919) from the University of Wisconsin and studied at the University of Fribourg, Switzerland, receiving his doctor's degree *summa cum laude* in the social sciences. Before returning to the U.S. he spent a year auditing classes at Louvain, Cambridge, Oxford, London, and the Sorbonne. In 1922 he was appointed to St. Francis Seminary, Milwaukee, where he served as professor of dogma and as rector. On Aug. 10, 1935, he was named third bishop of *Fargo, N.Dak., and on Oct. 15, 1935, he was consecrated in the Gesu Church in Milwaukee by Abp. Amleto Cicognani, Apostolic Delegate to the U.S.

Assuming his new duties at the height of the Depression, Muench proved himself an able administrator. He organized the Catholic Church Expansion Fund to save many mortgaged and indebted parishes and to provide capital funds for future expansion. He founded a diocesan newspaper, established diocesan seminary scholarships, organized a priests' mutual aid fund, convoked the first synod in the diocese, and published a synodal book of diocesan legislation. Active in many social conferences and organizations, he was a staunch supporter of the *Catholic Central Union (Verein) and was prominent in the *National Catholic Rural Life Conference, serving two terms as its president. With two priests of the Fargo diocese, William T. Mulloy and Vincent J. Ryan (both later bishops), Muench edited a sociological work, *Manifesto on Rural Life.* He was a member of the pontifical commission for The Catholic University of America, Washington, D.C., and of the episcopal Commission for Peace among Peoples, as well as of the international organization Pax Romana. Throughout his 23 years as bishop of Fargo he wrote an annual Lenten pastoral letter for distribution among his flock. The most famous of these, "One World in Charity" (1946), was a plea for just treatment of our former enemies, and it condemned the Morgenthau plan of restricting Germany to a rural economy. A translation of this letter found wide distribution in Germany.

In February 1946 Pius XII appointed Muench apostolic visitator to Germany; shortly thereafter Secretary of War Robert P. Patterson named him liaison consultant for religious affairs to the military governor of Germany. In this capacity he was advisor to Gen. Lucius Clay and his successors on matters involving the Catholic Church and the American Army of Occupation. He also functioned as administrator of the Vatican mission established by the Pope to provide for the spiritual and material needs of the refugees, expellees, and displaced persons in Germany. The *National Catholic Welfare Conference also appointed Muench to serve as military vicar delegate for the Catholics serving in the American Armed Forces in Germany. In November 1949, in anticipation of Germany's independence and sovereignty, Pius XII named Muench regent of the apostolic nunciature in Germany, and a year later granted him the personal title of archbishop. On March 6, 1951, when Germany became

Cardinal Aloisius Joseph Muench.

sovereign, Muench as papal nuncio was the first diplomat to present his credentials to the West German government; he was named dean of the diplomatic corps. In gratitude for his varied and signal services to the German people, Theodore Heuss, President of the West German Republic, conferred upon Muench Germany's highest honor, the Grand Cross of the Order of Merit (Dec. 20, 1957).

John XXIII on Dec. 9, 1959, created Muench a member of the College of Cardinals with the title of St. Bernard at the Baths. He was the first American to serve actively as a cardinal in the Roman Curia. He was a member of the Sacred Congregations of Religious, Rites, and Extraordinary Affairs, as well as protector of a number of religious communities. He died in Rome at Villa Salvator Mundi, after receiving personally the apostolic blessing of John XXIII; his remains were interred in St. Mary's Cemetery, Fargo.

[G. M. WEBER]

MUGHALS

A Moslem dynasty ruling India between 1526 and 1858, claiming descent through *Timur (Tamerlane) from the Mongol family of *Genghis Khan. The dynasty was founded by Babur, who led an army of some 10,000 men from Afghanistan into the Punjab in 1526. Much of northern India had been ruled by the Moslem sultanate of Delhi since the 13th century. Babur defeated the forces of Sultan Ibrahim Lodi at Panipat and, before his death in 1530, conquered a large portion of north central India. His son Humayun lacked resolve and was forced into exile in Persia in 1544 by Ser Shah, an Afghan rebel. By 1555, however, he succeeded in recapturing Delhi and Agra. Humayun's son Akbar (1556–1605) was the real founder of the Mughal Empire. After 15 years of constant warfare he had won all of northern India except southern Sind; in a second phase between 1586 and 1601 he annexed Kashmir, Baluchistan, Qandahar, Khandesh, Berar, and parts of Ahmednagar and Orissa. At the time of his death he ruled the most spacious empire that India had ever known.

Akbar was a shrewd and foresighted administrator who won his subjects' allegiance. His policy was to conciliate the Hindus even to the point of favoring Moslem-Hindu syncretistic sects. He abolished the traditional Moslem poll tax, freely admitted Hindus into the army and other imperial service, and minimized the influence of the Moslem clerics (Arabic *ulamā'*). He ruled that taxes should never exceed one-third of the subject's gross product and he set up a system of checks on the efficiency of provincial governors. Akbar's successor Jahangir (1605–27) indulged in extravagant expenditures and was inattentive to government and the security of the frontiers. The reign of his son Shah Jahan (1627–

Mughal Emperor Shah Jahan (1627–66), builder of the Taj Mahal; Mughal miniature of the 17th century.

66) marked the zenith of Mughal art and architecture, culminating in the Taj Mahal; but his large-scale building programs and badly planned military campaigns reduced the imperial treasury. Shah Jahan also showed signs of bigotry toward non-Moslems. In 1657 he fell ill and his sons Aurangzeb and Dara Shirkuh fought over the succession. In 1658 Aurangzeb emerged victorious and imprisoned his father in the fort at Agra until his death.

The reign of Aurangzeb (1658–1707) is justly regarded as the foremost cause of the decline of the Mughal Empire. He magnified Shah Jahan's bigotry and reversed most of Akbar's policies. He tried to demand a general conversion to Islam, introduced censorship, excluded Hindus from imperial service, put to death the Sikh guru (*see* SIKHISM), and thoroughly upset the revenue system by inordinate taxation. Although in his time the empire attained its greatest territorial extent, revolt was gathering in many districts. Decline set in swiftly. Puppet sultans controlled by favorites or court factions succeeded to the rule, and independent dynasties, as in Hyderabad, Oudh, and Bengal, emerged. The Marathas of the Deccan revolted and in 1737 were at the gates of Delhi. In the north Nadir Shah of Persia occupied Mughal territories and, in 1739, defeated the Mughal army. Persian and Afghan forces then allied themselves with most of the Indian Moslem rulers against the Marathas, who were alienating their own Hindu allies through cruelty and extortion. The Marathas were defeated in 1761, but it was a hollow victory for the Mughals. Neither they, even with their allies, nor the Hindus could establish a unified state.

The Portuguese had come to India early in the 16th century, but their influence had been superseded by the Dutch and the British. The foundation of the British East India Company in 1600 began British trade ascendancy, and in the course of the 17th century India became a pawn in European diplomatic games. Avenging the "Black Hole of Calcutta" incident, Robert Clive led an expedition that made the British *de facto* rulers of Bengal. When the Mughals joined forces with the Marathas and other Indian rulers to oppose British expansion, Warren Hastings, the British governor of Bengal (1772–85), reversed policy toward them with the goal of preserving British India intact. French intrigues and the attacks of Pindari bandits goaded on by the Marathas provided a justification for further British action, until after the Maratha War of 1817–19 Britain became paramount in India. The threat of Russian intervention, the Sikh uprisings, and especially the Sepoy Mutiny of 1857 brought about the final phase. Bahadur Shah II, the last of the Mughal emperors, was involved in the mutiny. When Delhi fell he was tried and condemned to exile, and the government of India was transferred from the East India Company to the British Crown.

Bibliography: G. B. MALLESON, *Akbar and the Rise of the Mughal Empire* (Oxford 1903). W. H. MORELAND, *India at the Death of Akbar: An Economic Study* (London 1920); *From Akbar to Aurangzeb: A Study in Indian Economic History* (London 1923). W. IRVINE, *Later Mughals*, 2 v. (Calcutta (1921–22). T. G. P. SPEAR, *Twilight of the Mughals* (Cambridge, Eng. 1951). **Illustration credit:** Courtesy, The Cleveland Museum of Art.

[J. KRITZECK]

MUHLENBERG, HENRY MELCHIOR, organizer of the Lutheran Church in Colonial America; b. Einbeck, Hanover, Germany, Sept. 6, 1711; d.

Trappe, Pa., Oct. 7, 1787. Educated under the influence of *Pietism at Göttingen University, Hanover, Muhlenberg was sent to America in 1742 in response to appeals from Lutheran colonists.

Despite the fact that the center of Muhlenberg's activity was in southeastern Pennsylvania, his travels and correspondence extended his influence to the entire Atlantic seaboard. He strengthened existing congregations and helped to organize new ones, secured additional clergymen from Europe and began to train a native ministry, united ministers and congregations in a synodical organization (1748), and through his reports to Europe (the so-called Halle Reports) secured financial and other assistance. Mühlenberg's three sons achieved prominence: Peter (1746–1807) was brigadier general in the American Revolution; Frederick (1750–1801) was first speaker of the U.S. Congress; and Henry Ernest (1753–1815) was a botanist as well as a clergyman.

Bibliography: *The Journals of Henry Melchior Muhlenberg,* tr. T. G. TAPPERT and J. W. DOBERSTEIN, 3 v. (Philadelphia 1942–58). P. A. W. WALLACE, *The Muhlenbergs of Pennsylvania* (Philadelphia 1950), bibliog. 321–342.

[T. G. TAPPERT]

MUINTIR NA TIRE, an Irish community movement, founded in 1937 by Father John M. Hayes, designed especially for the needs of rural people. It aims to utilize the neighborly relations that are inherent in the Irish background as a means to social progress and development. Although people are well acquainted with neighborliness between individuals and families, they are not always familiar enough with communitywide effort. It is desirable that neighborliness should mature into community spirit. This requires a realization that the people of a parish can choose certain goals to be achieved and can work toward them by united and deliberate action. This approach to community development has been confirmed by international experience as is clear from United Nations reports.

The parish is the unit of organization. A parish "guild" includes all in the parish who accept the aims and constitution of Muintir na Tire and are willing to take part in its work. It may include men, women, and youth who have left the primary school. Sections are formed for the purpose of selecting the parish council. In a rural parish there are usually sections for farmers, laborers, business and professional men, women, and youth. Muintir na Tire is not a rival of other specialized organizations for teachers, trade unionists, farmers, traders, and the like. It might be said that each of these organizations is interested in its own particular brick in the social edifice while Muintir na Tire is interested in the mortar that holds them together. It seeks to create as many situations as possible in which men and women, young and old, can take part fully and on terms of equal status in projects of joint concern.

Muintir na Tire has frequently been ahead of state-sponsored reforms. It organized the first Irish summer schools in agriculture and domestic economy. What is known as the Parish Plan for Agriculture was a Muintir na Tire idea. Similarly, the first Irish campaign for the eradication of bovine tuberculosis was made by the guild of the founder's own parish. Parish halls, playing fields, and shelter-belts can be seen by all, but the works of the guilds are not always visible. Their scope includes educational, recreational, social, and economic, as well as other means for attaining unity at the grass roots.

Bibliography: G. F. THOMASON, "Muintir na Tire's Role in Irish Community Development," *Studies* 51 (1962) 408–418.

[J. NEWMAN]

MUKDEN, ARCHDIOCESE OF (FOMTIENENSIS), metropolitan see since 1946, in northeast *China. The city of Mukden (Shen-yang) is also the capital of Liao-ning province. According to statistics for 1950, the latest available, the archdiocese, 10,833 square miles in area, had 27 parishes, 33 secular priests, 141 women in 2 convents, and 11,800 Catholics in a population of 5 million. Its seven suffragans, with 285 priests, 448 sisters, and 138,500 Catholics in a population of 24 million were: Ch'ih-feng, Fu-shun, Ch'eng-te (Jehol), Chi-lin (Kirin), Ssu-p'ing (Szepinkai), Yen-chi, and Ying-k'ou; all but Ch'ih-feng (1949) and Ying-k'ou (1949) were created dioceses in 1946.

From 1725 the Jesuits sent Chinese priests into Manchuria occasionally to visit immigrant Christians there. The Vicariate Apostolic of Liao-ning, which was detached from the Diocese of *Peking in 1838, lost the Vicariate of *Mongolia in 1840 and, as the vicariate for Manchuria, was left with Mukden, Chi-lin, and Hei-lung-chiang provinces. In 1898 Chi-lin and Hei-lung-chiang became the Vicariate of North Manchuria. The Vicariate of South Manchuria became that of Mukden (1924–46). The first Manchurian priest was ordained in 1869. In 1900 the Boxer Rebellion did great damage to the Church in Manchuria. The recent emigration of Japanese and Koreans has reduced the number of Catholics. In 1949 care of the archdiocese was transferred from the *Paris Foreign Mission Society to Chinese secular clergy. Ssu-p'ing (1929), Fu-shun (1932), and Ch'eng-te (1938) were carved from Mukden as vicariates.

Bibliography: *Annuaire de l'Église catholique en Chine* (Shanghai 1950). MissCattol 302–308. E. PECORAIO, EncCatt 8:1487–88. AnnPont (1965) 288–289.

[J. KRAHL]

MULCASTER, RICHARD, educator, author, tutor to Edmund Spenser; b. Cumberland, England, *c.* 1531; d. Essex, April 15, 1611. Although Mulcaster was born into a family of modest means, a number of Mulcaster's ancestors had held positions of consequence at Court, while others were scholars and landowners. Educated at Cambridge and Oxford, in 1556 he received an M.A. degree from the latter, where he attained eminence as a scholar in Greek, Latin, Hebrew, and Arabic. As a result of his unusual accomplishments, Mulcaster was appointed first headmaster of Merchant Taylors' School, London, a post he held until 1586. For the next 10 years, he disappeared almost completely from public notice, except in 1588 when he appeared briefly as examiner for Merchant Taylors' School. In 1596 he became headmaster of St. Paul's School, London, where he remained until August 1609. From then until his death, he served as rector of Stanford Rivers in Essex.

Following his resignation as headmaster of Merchant Taylors' School, Mulcaster wrote two outstanding educational treatises: *Positions, Wherein those Primitive Circumstances be examined, which are necessarie for the Training up of Children either for skill in their Booke or Health in their Bodie* (1581), which constitutes the aggregate of Mulcaster's educational theories and principles, and *Elementarie, which entreateth chieflie of the right Writing of the English tung* (1582), which contains his views on speaking, reading, writing, and teaching the English language, on which he placed emphasis both as a medium of instruction and a subject of study.

Mulcaster advocated 5 years of elementary school during which a good foundation should be laid in the vernacular. He insisted that the school give special attention to reading, writing, drawing, and instrumental music in preference to Latin (which he considered of little value to the majority of boys) and permit only those who showed special ability for advanced training to proceed beyond the elementary school. He urged the moderate use of physical exercise, emphasized morality and good manners, suggested conferences between parents and teachers, demanded that teaching methods be uniform and that elementary school teachers be the best prepared and the highest paid.

Mulcaster also advocated a 5-year grammar, or secondary, school in which Latin, Greek, Hebrew, poetry, history, and oratory should be the basic subjects with special emphasis on moral training and physical exercise. He recommended that universities be divided into faculties to ensure adequate specialization and was the first to propose the practical organization of teacher training colleges in England. He insisted that girls receive at least an elementary education but that their curriculum be limited strictly to reading, writing, and music.

Although he made no provision for the study of the natural sciences, because of his insistence on the vernacular, he is considered the forerunner of the sense realists.

Bibliography: *Elementarie* (London 1582), also ed. T. CAMPAGNAC (Oxford 1925); *Positions* (London 1581), also ed. R. H. QUICK (London 1888); *Educational Writings,* ed. J. OLIPHANT (Glasgow 1903).

[C. A. SMITH]

MULDOON, PETER JAMES

Bishop; b. Columbia, Calif., Oct. 10, 1862; d. Rockford, Ill., Oct. 8, 1927. He was the eldest son of Irish immigrant parents, John and Catherine (Coughlin) Muldoon. After attending the public schools of Stockton, Calif., he continued his studies at St. Mary's College, St. Mary, Ky. In 1881, he entered St. Mary's Seminary, Baltimore, Md., for his philosophical and theological training. He was ordained for the Archdiocese of Chicago by Bp. John Loughlin of Brooklyn, N.Y., on Dec. 18, 1886. A favorite of Abp. P. A. *Feehan, he acted as his chancellor and secretary from 1888 to 1895, when he was appointed pastor of St. Charles Borromeo Church, Chicago. The recognition accorded the young American-born priest was resented by some of the Irish-born clergy of the archdiocese, and a few vented their hostility on him and flouted the authority of the archbishop.

When Abp. Patrick A. Feehan and his auxiliary, Alexander J. McGavick, declined in health, Muldoon was consecrated titular bishop of Tamassus and auxiliary of Chicago in Holy Name Cathedral on July 25, 1901, by Cardinal Sebastian Martinelli, Apostolic Delegate to the U.S. Martinelli's presence was construed as Rome's approbation of the young bishop and an ad-

monition to his detractors. Six days after his consecration he was appointed vicar-general of the archdiocese.

Feehan died on July 12, 1902, and Muldoon, the administrator, was one of the candidates for the vacant

Bishop Peter James Muldoon.

see. However, in January 1903, Rome transferred Bp. James E. Quigley of Buffalo to Chicago. Five years later, the Diocese of Rockford was erected from territory of the Archdiocese of Chicago, and Muldoon was named bishop of the new see. He was a candidate for the See of Chicago when Quigley died in July 1915, but Rome appointed George W. Mundelein, auxiliary Bishop of Brooklyn. In December 1916, Muldoon was consulted about accepting the vacant See of Monterey-Los Angeles, Calif., but he expressed his preference to remain in Rockford. There followed 5 months of confusion and frustration. The appointment of Muldoon to the West was made, the bulls were issued, and the wire services informed, but the bishop refused to act until an answer was received from Rome on his recent petition to remain in Rockford. In May 1917, Rome finally acquiesced, and Muldoon remained in his diocese.

During his years as a bishop in Chicago and Rockford, Muldoon played a prominent role in the movement for social reform, gaining a reputation as a friend of labor and a defender of labor unions. When the American Federation of Catholic Societies, under the inspiration of Peter E. Dietz, a prominent labor priest, established a social service commission in 1911, Muldoon was appointed chairman. As chairman of the National Catholic War Council (1917–18), he became a nationally known figure. This organization, designed to coordinate all Catholic activities in furthering the war effort, brought Muldoon into close association with members of other religious groups and governmental agencies. His forcefulness and diplomacy ensured the success of the council and prompted Cardinal James Gibbons to propose a peacetime organization comparable to it. Muldoon, as one of the new committee members, submitted a program to the hierarchy at their meeting in September 1919. It was approved, though not unanimously.

Rome at first viewed the new organization favorably, but when dissatisfied American bishops complained to the pope, the original approbation was qualified and then revoked. On his ad limina visit in 1920, Muldoon pleaded the case of the National Catholic Welfare Council; later Bp. Joseph Schrembs of Cleveland, Ohio, was dispatched to Rome to defend the new organization. The Holy See finally gave unqualified approbation, and the new agency was continued under the title of *National Catholic Welfare Conference (NCWC).

During the formative years of the NCWC Muldoon was chairman of its Social Action Department and commanded attention locally and nationally in the social reform movement. Muldoon's death in 1927 came after an illness of several months.

Bibliography: A. I. ABELL, *American Catholicism and Social Action: A Search for Social Justice, 1869–1950* (New York 1960). M. WILLIAMS, *American Catholics in the War* (New York 1921). F. G. MCMANAMIN, "Peter J. Muldoon, First Bishop of Rockford, 1862–1927," CathHistRev 48 (1962) 365–378. **Illustration credit:** Herzog Photographers, Rockford, Ill.

[F. G. MC MANAMIN]

MULLANPHY, JOHN, philanthropist; b. Enniskillen, County Fermanagh, Ireland, 1758; d. St. Louis, Mo., Aug. 29, 1833. He joined the Irish brigade of the French Army in 1778, but returned to Ireland in 1789 to marry Elizabeth Browne of Youghal, County Waterford. They immigrated to America in 1792 and lived in Philadelphia, Pa., and in Baltimore, Md. In 1798 the family moved to Frankfort, Ky., where Mullanphy opened a bookstore in addition to establishing himself in commerce. Early in 1804 he moved to St. Louis in the upper Louisiana territory. Mullanphy's fortune stemmed from two major sources: the advantageous purchase of low-priced cotton in New Orleans, La., just prior to the end of the War of 1812, and the resale of that cotton in England immediately after the war; and the acquisition of real estate in and around St. Louis. The Mullanphy family devoted much of its effort to good works. It was instrumental in establishing several institutions and religious orders in St. Louis: the Religious of the Sacred Heart (1827); the Sisters of Charity of Emmitsburg, Md. (1828), who founded Mullanphy Hospital (now De Paul Hospital), the first Catholic hospital west of the Mississippi; the Visitation Nuns (1844); the Sisters of St. Joseph of Carondolet; St. Ann's Lying-In and Foundling Asylum (1844–45), the first of its kind west of the Mississippi; and the Society of St. Vincent de Paul (1845). Of the Mullanphys' 15 children, the only surviving son was Bryan Mullanphy, who continued the family philanthropy. He was elected mayor of St. Louis on the Democratic ticket in 1847 and later appointed judge of the St. Louis circuit court; he died unmarried in 1851. He left one-third of his estate to found the Mullanphy Emigrant and Travelers' Relief Fund to aid poor and needy travelers going West; in 1934 the fund became associated with the National Traveler's Aid Society.

[A. L. COCHRAN]

MULLANY, AZARIAS OF THE CROSS, BROTHER, educator, author; b. near Killenaule, County Tipperary, Ireland, June 29, 1847; d. Plattsburg, N.Y., Aug. 20, 1893. Patrick Francis Mullany immigrated to Deerfield, N.Y., in 1857. While attending Assumption Academy, Utica, N.Y., he chose the vocation of his teachers, the Brothers of the Christian Schools; he was professed in 1862. He was assigned in 1866 to Rock Hill College, Ellicott City, Md., as a teacher of mathematics. He was president of the college (1879–86) and worked with such educators as Daniel Coit Gilman, Herbert Baxter Adams, and Andrew D.

White. He moved to De La Salle Institute, New York City, in 1888, where his lectures and writings made him one of the best-known Catholic religious in America. He helped to organize Catholic reading circles and was a founder of the Catholic Summer School of America at Plattsburg. Although limited by ill health and inadequate formal education, he mastered nine languages and became a specialist in varied fields of knowledge, notably literature and philosophy. A frequent contributor to Catholic periodicals and the *International Journal of Ethics,* his chief writings were *An Essay Contributing to the Philosophy of Literature* (1874), *The Development of Old English Thought* (1879), *Aristotle and the Christian Church* (1888), *Books and Reading* (1889), and *Phases of Thought and Criticism* (1892). Posthumously, many of his articles and reviews were compiled as *Essays Educational, Essays Philosophical, Essays Miscellaneous* (1896).

[B. R. WEITEKAMP]

MÜLLER, ADAM HEINRICH, German social philosopher; b. Berlin, June 6, 1779; d. Vienna, Jan. 17, 1829. A Protestant by birth and early education, he became a Catholic in 1805. He entered the Austrian government service in 1813 and served as consul-general in Leipzig and at various European conferences.

Müller's writings include *Elemente der Staatskunst* (1809), *Versuche einer Neuen Theorie des Geldes* (1816), and *Von der Notwendigkeit einer Theologischen Grundlage der Gesamten Staatswissenschaften* (1819). Müller has been called the founder of the romantic school of economics, but he is really its only representative. Against the rational and mechanical concepts of classical economics, he proposed a romantic, organic system. He emphasized authority and tradition, and proposed a restoration of an idealized feudalism, which was corporate, Christian, and authoritarian. He was also, however, a proponent of a strong national state that would represent the soul of a people.

Müller's economics was characterized by metaphysical concepts rather than operational tools. He emphasized the social character of money, arguing that it was money only in the moment of transaction. Capital he described as the link between the past and the future. He emphasized the inclusion of spiritual capital within the concept of wealth.

Because Müller's economics could not be used for purposes of analysis, he exercised little influence on later work. His influence came from his social ideas, which were generally opposed to democracy, republicanism, internationalism, liberalism, and humanitarianism. He clearly influenced Othmar *Spann's universalism and is generally credited, despite his theology, with being a precursor of Nazi political thought.

[J. P. MC KENNA]

MÜLLER, JOHANN, German physiologist and anatomist; b. Coblenz, July 14, 1801; d. Berlin, April 28, 1858. As the son of a prosperous shoemaker, he had the leisure and finances to complete his medical and scientific education at the University of Bonn and at Berlin where he studied under K. A. Rudolphi. Having considered and abandoned the idea of entering the priesthood, Müller returned to Bonn, eventually becoming professor of anatomy, physiology, and pathology (1830–33). He held a similar post at Berlin (1833–

58). He was the first great experimental physiologist in Germany, and through his teaching inspired and trained a large group of distinguished workers. Among them were R. Virchow, R. Remak, T. *Schwann, F. Henle, E. Du Bois-Reymond, and H. *Helmholtz, all of whom extended Müller's influence for many decades after his death. Müller diverted the currents of *Naturphilosophie,* in which he had at first immersed himself, and which had assumed inordinate force and oblique meanings in Germany under Goethe and L. Oken. Müller did this by enlisting the physical sciences and experimentation for the solution of biological phenomena, despite his firm acceptance of Aristotle's *vitalism and *teleology. He established the law of specific nerve energies; that is, a certain nerve always renders the same response regardless of the stimulus applied to it. This led him and his disciples to much valuable research in sense physiology. His most enduring influences arose from his classic *Handbook of Human Physiology* (tr. London 1842), which originally appeared in German in two volumes (1833–40). Besides covering current physiology, it embraced his own personal discoveries. His later years (1840–58) were successfully devoted to research on evolution, morphology, anatomy of lower vertebrates, paleontology, and marine biology.

Bibliography: E. Nordenskiöld, *History of Biology,* tr. L. B. Eyre (new ed. New York 1935).

[L. P. Coonen]

MULRY, THOMAS MAURICE

First president of the Superior Council of the U.S. Society of St. Vincent de Paul, businessman; b. New York City, Feb. 13, 1855; d. there, March 10, 1916. Of Irish-Dutch extraction, he was the second of 14 children born to Thomas Mulry and Parthenia (Crolius) Mulry, of New York City. He was educated in parochial schools and at De La Salle Academy and as a young man took night classes at old Cooper Union. In 1872, after the family's second brief venture into farming in Wisconsin, he became associated with his father as an excavation contractor in the firm of Mulry and Son, New York. In 1880 Mulry married Mary E. Gallagher, Hunter College graduate and teacher in New York public schools. The couple had 13 children; 4 of them joined the Society of Jesus, and one became a Sister of Charity. The contracting business of Mulry and Son prospered, with the younger Mulry eventually taking over active management. As a moderately successful business man, he expanded his interests to include banking, insurance, and real estate, becoming president of the Emigrant Industrial Savings Bank in 1906.

After becoming a member of the Society of St. Vincent de Paul at 17, Mulry continued throughout his life to exercise this layman's charitable vocation, accepting offices from the presidency of St. Bernard's Parish Conference, 1880, to the presidency of the Superior Council of the U.S., 1915. Under his leadership, Vincentians relinquished an earlier position of aloofness and entered into cooperative effort with other public and private welfare agencies. Mulry permanently influenced the Catholic charities movement in the U.S. He fought the abuses inherent in almshouse care of dependent children and notably succeeded in improving conditions and standards of placement care. His plea for moderation all but ended the long controversy between advocates of insti-

tutional care and proponents of foster home care. *The Government in Charity* (1912), his principal publication, vigorously affirmed the state's responsibility to encourage and work cooperatively with private charitable agencies, but opposed excessive secularization of social welfare work. Under his direction special programs were initiated: summer outings and camps for needy boys and girls; the Catholic Home Bureau, which stimulated Catholic home placement programs; and the Catholic Boys' Club movement. National unification of the St. Vincent de Paul Society, attributable in part to Mulry's leadership, was achieved with the establishment of the Superior Council of the U.S. in 1915.

Although principally identified with the Vincentian organization, Mulry achieved recognition in the broader welfare community. He was among the founders and a vice president of the National Conference of Catholic Charities; helped establish the Fordham School of Social Service; founded St. Elizabeth's Home for Convalescent Women and Girls; and was a member of the Board of Governors of the New York Catholic Protectory. In 1907 he was elected president of the National Conference of Charities and Correction. Pres. Theodore Roosevelt named him to be one of a committee of three to organize the First White House Conference on Children (1909).

Bibliography: J. W. Helmes, *Thomas M. Mulry: A Volunteer's Contribution to Social Work* (Washington 1938). D. T. McColgan, *A Century of Charity,* 2 v. (Milwaukee 1951).

[D. Baker]

MULTITUDE

Considered absolutely and in the broadest sense of the term, unspecified plurality, hence intelligible only as opposed to some kind of *unity. Often usage connotes, in addition to mere plurality, a collectivity or superior kind of unification embracing a plurality of more ultimate units, as when one speaks of "a multitude." The more properly metaphysical notion refers to a nonnumerable plurality. This article discusses the origin of the notion, its various analogies, and its uses in philosophy and theology.

Origin. In the order of development of the various analogical uses of this term, the first refers to the kind of plurality that is grasped in immediate sense experience, such a rudimentary and ultimate experience that no further analysis seems capable of altering the basic content or interpretation. Prior to any notion of number, this plurality of material things is available to the sense of touch, to sight, and to hearing. The ability to grasp such a plurality as a collective set is sometimes referred to as number sense, but this precedes the formation of the number concept since number, taken concretely, is a measured material multitude. This prime analogate of multitude, pertaining to material entities only, manifests finer distinctions within it. Thus some pluralities are not perfect in the sense that their parts cannot be perfectly distinguished, e.g., the fingers of the hand, distinct yet joined. Again, some multitudes are irreducible, e.g., a group of men, whereas others are not, e.g., several pieces of wax that can be melted together to form one. This latter instance indicates that plurality is due to materiality, to quantity, and not to formal differences that characterize the individual members who constitute the multitude.

Analogies. Plurality requires some kind of distinction, for without distinction there is simple *identity under which only unity can be found. Confining one's thought to perceptible, physical multitude, it makes little difference whether the elements of the collection are substantial individuals or mere parts, whether they be of the same type or species or simply diverse in kind. Almost any degree of physical separation or any kind of actual separation will suffice to found such a multitude, but some sort of dividedness based on the distinctions proper to quantified matter is required. Since distinction itself is based on some mode of opposition that sets one element over against another, the ultimate foundation of physical multitude can be found in the fact that in extended matter one part is not the other: "this here" is not "that there." This opposition, a difference in *quantity, is sometimes called *situation (*situs*). The parts of such a quantitative multitude can be understood as units; and when the collection is compared to a representative unit, the *number, or relative measure, of the collection can be determined. This kind of multitude is opposed to, and yet, in some way, composed of, units that can be signified by the numeral "1."

Following a somewhat similar line of development, it is possible to conceive of multitude in another, analogous, sense based on some mode of formal *opposition. Consequent upon opposition, formal distinctions can be made, and thus *division and plurality or multitude in a formal sense. This notion of multitude is often called transcendental and is opposed to transcendental unity or unity of *being itself, since form is the principle of entitative unity. Aristotle distinguished four modes of formal opposition: contradiction, contrariety, privation, and relation. Any of these may found a formal distinction and hence transcendental multitude—"transcendental" because not limited to any category but analogically common, as the term being is common. Clearly the notion of multitude changes as the basis of opposition changes, but in any case the correlative unity is a kind of nondividedness in being itself and hence not a standard for quantitative measure or enumeration. A formal, or transcendental, multitude cannot be counted in any sense of the term, whereas material, or quantitative, multitude is the proper subject of enumeration.

Philosophy and Theology. In philosophical thought the opposition between unity and multiplicity appears in many guises. The problem of the one and the many is one of the most fundamental metaphysical issues: how can being be one, i.e., common to all that is, and yet be the obvious multitude that it is? The Eleatics tended to regard multiplicity as an illusion of the senses (*see* GREEK PHILOSOPHY). *Plato found a unity in the transcendent Idea in which the sensible multitude participates, and *Aristotle resorted to a theory of *analogy to preserve both undeniable facts. The solution of I. *Kant, unique in its time, required a synthesizing activity of the mind that alone could attain intelligible unity in phenomenal multiplicity by the imposition of its own categories and connectives. The same issue reappears in epistemology as a dispute between *nominalism and *realism, in the philosophy of logic as the problem of *universals, in the philosophy of nature as the problem of *monism versus pluralism, and in philosophical theology as *pantheism versus monotheism. Even in the philosophical considerations of mathematics, which seems to concern itself with quantitative plurality, there is a reflection of the problem in questions about the formation of the number concept.

In theology the concept of transcendental multitude is quite important inasmuch as all distinction and hence plurality of nonmaterial being must be formal. Any speculation about the pluralities of *angels involves transcendental multitude, and each angelic individual can be understood as formally distinguished from all others. Likewise, in Trinitarian theology, the divine Persons are distinguished by a relational opposition that is itself transcendental and so the multiplicity in the Persons must be analogically transcendental. Apparently the image-making power of the human mind and the necessity for material signification create the impression that such multiplicity is subject to counting.

Bibliography: D. J. B. HAWKINS, *Being and Becoming* (New York 1954), ch. 7. F. SLADECZEK, "Die spekulative Auffassung vom Wesen der Einheit in ihrer Auswirkung auf Philosophie und Theologie," *Scholastik* 25 (1950) 361–388. D. GARCIA, "De Metaphysica multitudinis ordinatione et de tribus simpliciter diversis specibus ejusdem secundum divi Thomae principia" DivThomP 31 (1928) 83–109, 607–638; 32 (1929) 43–56.

[C. F. WEIHER]

MUN, ALBERT DE, orator, parliamentarian, organizer, and journalist, who helped to launch Catholic *social movements in France; b. Lumigny, Feb. 28, 1841; d. Paris, Oct. 6, 1914. Until his 30th year, Count de Mun followed a family tradition of military service by training at Saint-Cyr and serving first in Algeria, then in France. His experiences during the Franco-Prussian War and the Paris Commune of 1871 prompted him to dedicate his life to the re-Christianization of his country and to an apostolate of social reconciliation. Organizations that he founded among members of the aristocracy, employers, and workers translated Catholic principles into a force for social change through research studies, publications, congresses, and action programs. Although limited in their appeal by a paternalistic orientation, clubs for young workers organized with the help of fellow officers and aristocrats offered spiritual, educational, and social activities to many thousands and aroused anticlerical opposition. In the Chamber of Deputies, where he served from 1881 until his death, except for a 4-month period, De Mun was a pioneer in the struggle for social legislation. His eloquence as "the workers' deputy" won him membership in the Académie Française and, when a heart condition kept him from the rostrum, he continued his militant crusade for the Church and workers as a journalist.

Bibliography: M. LYNCH, *The Organized Social Apostolate of Albert de Mun* (CUA Stud. in Sociol. 36; Washington 1952). T. P. NEILL, *They Lived the Faith* (Milwaukee 1951).

[M. LYNCH]

MUNCH, EDVARD, one of the greatest Norwegian painters and graphic artists; b. Loreiten, Dec. 12, 1863; d. Sköyen, near Oslo, Jan. 23, 1944. He was the son of a military surgeon. From 1885 to 1889, in Paris, he underwent the influence of the Postimpressionists. From 1891 on, he worked on the "Frieze of Life," the core of his creative effort, which centered on themes of love, death, and the eternal in man. The finished work was exhibited in the 1897 "Salon des Indépandants" in Paris. There followed a second version of the same

Edvard Munch, self-portrait as a young man.

theme in 1903–04, and a third one in 1906 for the German Theatre (Max Reinhardt). The exhibit of his pictures in the hall of the Berlin Artists Association in 1902 ("Puberty"), accompanied by the protests of reactionaries, made him famous. From 1895 to 1905 he produced some significant graphic works that show the same theme as his paintings. Besides expressive elements, they contain symbolical elements. Between 1909 and 1915 he painted the murals of the University of Oslo (one is the "Sunrise"), which depict the stages of man's life. From this time on, his approach to the world and to man became more positive and closer to nature. He worked intensively to the very end of his life. There are innumerable replicas of his most important sketches.

His influence on the "Bridge" painters and other Expressionists is generally overrated. The more important among his followers, such as *Kirchner and Kokoschka, received some inspiration from him, but for the most part they went their own ways.

Among his graphic works are "The Kiss," etching (1895); "The Sick Girl," lithograph (1896); "Sadness," drawing (1896); "The Kiss," drawing (1897). Among his paintings are "The Cry" (1893), "The Vampire" (1894), "The Dead Mother" (1899), "Girl on the Bridge" (1901), and "Marat's Death" (1906). His most important exhibits were: Kunsthaus, Zurich (1922); Museum of Modern Art, New York (1950); Haus der Kunst, Munich (1954). The most important collection of his work is at the Munch-Museum, Oslo.

Bibliography: K. GLASER, *Edvard Munch* (Berlin 1918). D. HODIN, *Edvard Munch* (Stockholm 1948). G. SCHIEFLER, *Verzeichnis des graphischen Werks*, 2 v. (Berlin 1907–28). J. H. LANGAARD and R. REVOLD, *Edvard Munch* (Stuttgart 1963). **Illustration credit:** Norwegian Embassy Information Service.

[W. GROHMANN]

MUNDELEIN, GEORGE WILLIAM

Cardinal, third archbishop of Chicago, Ill., archdiocese; b. New York City, July 2, 1872; d. Chicago, Oct. 2, 1939. He was the only son of Francis and Mary (Goetz) Mundelein, who sent him to St. Nicholas parochial school on Manhattan's lower East Side. Because his family had only modest means, friends helped him through De La Salle Institute and Manhattan College, New York City, from which he received the B.A. degree in 1889. A fellow classmate, Patrick J. Hayes, and he decided to study for the priesthood. It is not altogether clear why he decided to study for the neighboring Diocese of Brooklyn, N.Y. He spent 3 years at St. Vincent's Seminary in Beatty, Pa., and completed his training at the Propaganda College, Rome. He was ordained in Rome by Bp. Charles McDonnell of Brooklyn on June 8, 1895, and offered his first Mass at St. Peter's Tomb.

On his return to Brooklyn, he was appointed McDonnell's associate secretary and administrator of the Lithuanian Church at Williamsburg. In December 1897 he became diocesan chancellor, and 9 years later was made a domestic prelate, an unusual distinction in those days. The Arcadia, a group of Catholic scholars known for their literary attainments, elected him to membership on April 20, 1907. At the request of McDonnell, Mundelein was named titular bishop of Loryma and auxiliary bishop of Brooklyn and consecrated on Sept. 21, 1909, in St. James Procathedral. He resigned as chancellor to become rector of the Cathedral Chapel of Queen of All Saints, where he supervised the building of a church, school, and rectory, combined in one Gothic structure. He also directed the erection of Cathedral College of the Immaculate Conception, the preparatory seminary.

Archbishop of Chicago. On Dec. 9, 1915, Mundelein was chosen to be the third archbishop of *Chicago. Only 43 years old, he was the youngest archbishop in the U.S. His enthronement in Holy Name Cathedral

George William Mundelein.

took place on Feb. 9, 1916, with the apostolic delegate, Abp. Giovanni Bonzano, presiding. A civic reception was tendered him at the Auditorium Theatre on February 13 at which the new archbishop spoke, promising to bring the name of his predecessor Abp. James E. Quigley "permanently and prominently before every man, woman, and child in the diocese." This pledge was fulfilled 3 months later when a pastoral letter of May 14, 1916, announced the building of Quigley Preparatory Seminary, a project the clergy and people enthusiastically supported. While this building was under construction Mundelein planned a major seminary, which the archdiocese had needed since August 1868 when the seminary department of the University of St. Mary of the Lake had been closed. A site was found near Area, Ill., and when the diamond jubilee of the archdiocese and the silver jubilee of the archbishop's ordination were celebrated in April 1920, the project for a new major seminary was announced. The purse given to the archbishop for his jubilee was used to begin construction of the philosophy buildings. During the next 14 years St. Mary of the Lake Seminary added 14 buildings in Georgian architecture to its plant on the shores of Lake Eara in Lake County. In 1924 the town of Area changed its name to Mundelein, and the school became known as Mundelein Seminary. Ten years later, the Congregation of Seminaries and Universities recognized St. Mary of the Lake Seminary as a pontifical faculty of theology with the privilege of conferring the doctorate in theology. Mundelein always took special interest in the seminary and collected rare books, manuscripts, autographs, coins, vestments, chalices, and pictures for its museum, library, and chapels.

Another of Mundelein's notable accomplishments was the organization of Catholic Charities in March 1918, by which he united the diverse charitable activities of the archdiocese and prompted support for them. He never forgot that he had been a poor boy and always expressed affection for the underprivileged. Each year at Christmas he personally paid for a complete outfit of clothing and shoes for 100 needy children. Toward the end of his life he said to the members of the Holy Name Society: "The trouble with us in the past has been that we were too often allied or drawn into an alliance with the wrong side. Selfish employers of labor have flattered the Church by calling it a great conservative force, and then called upon it to act as a police force when they paid but a pittance of wages to those who worked for them. I hope that day is gone by. Our place is beside the poor, behind the working man."

Cardinal. All Chicago rejoiced at the news on March 2, 1924, that its archbishop would be elevated to the College of Cardinals in the consistory of March 24. When Mundelein was in Rome to receive the red hat, he began preparations to hold the 28th International Eucharistic Congress in Chicago from June 20 to 24, 1926. More than a million Catholics, including 12 cardinals, 64 archbishops, 309 bishops, 500 monsignors, and 8,000 priests made this congress one of the greatest religious demonstrations ever witnessed in the U.S. In 1928, when Pius XI appealed for help in building the new Propaganda College in Rome, Mundelein responded with a check for $1,500,000, underwritten by the generous mission contributions of his priests and people. In 1934 he celebrated his episcopal silver jubilee in Rome, where he purchased a building for the

Collegio S. Maria del Lago, a house for postgraduate students. Three years later on May 18, 1937, he condemned the religious persecution undertaken by Hitler and the Nazi party. His description of the Fuehrer as "an Austrian paperhanger" brought protests at the Vatican and Washington.

A personal friendship developed between Mundelein and Pres. Franklin D. Roosevelt. When the new Outer Drive Bridge, Chicago, was dedicated on Oct. 5, 1937, the President was his luncheon guest. In October 1938 Mundelein served as papal legate to the eighth national Eucharistic Congress in New Orleans, La. While in Rome to report to Pius XI, he celebrated the beatification Mass for Frances Xavier *Cabrini, whose funeral Mass he had offered in Chicago in 1917. After the death of Pius XI in February 1939, Mundelein participated in the conclave that elected Cardinal Eugenio Pacelli as Pius XII on March 2, 1939. Seven months later Cardinal Mundelein died suddenly of a coronary thrombosis and was buried in a crypt behind the main altar in the seminary that bears his name.

Bibliography: P. R. MARTIN, comp., *The First Cardinal of the West* (Chicago 1934). E. T. REGAN, *100 Years: The History of the Church of the Holy Name* (Chicago 1949). G. W. MUNDELEIN, *Letters of a Bishop to His Flock* (New York 1927). **Illustration credit:** Chicago Historical Society.

[H. C. KOENIG]

MUNDELEIN COLLEGE

A 4-year liberal arts college for women in Chicago, Ill. Founded in 1929 at the request of Cardinal George Mundelein, Archbishop of Chicago, America's first skyscraper college for women is conducted by the Sisters of Charity of the Blessed Virgin Mary. A charter granting the right to confer collegiate degrees was granted

Mundelein College skyscraper, Chicago, Ill.

by the state of Illinois in November 1929, and the College was opened to students in September 1930 with an enrollment of 250.

The 15-story classroom building houses laboratories, studios, chapel, gymnasium, swimming pool, and a 1,250-seat theater. In 1934 the College converted a Chicago mansion into a library, in 1962 opened Coffey Hall to provide on-campus housing for 206 students, and in 1963 added a dormitory for 500 students.

Mundelein College is accredited by the North Central Association of Colleges and is affiliated with The Catholic University of America. It is approved by the State Department of Education, the State Teacher Certification Board, National Council for Accreditation of Teacher Education, National Association of Schools of Music, and the American Association of University Women. The College holds membership in the Federation of Illinois Colleges, National Catholic Educational Association, American Council on Education, Association of American Colleges, American Association of Colleges for Teacher Education, Association of Illinois Colleges, National Committee on Accreditation, and the National Educational Association.

Mundelein's board of trustees is composed of the mother general, the members of her curia; and the College president. Administrative officers include the president, a lay vice president, academic dean, dean of students, registrar, and secretary-treasurer. In 1964 the 112-member faculty was composed of 44 Sisters of Charity and 68 laymen, who held 43 doctoral, 2 professional, and 77 master's degrees. Enrollment numbered 1,149 full-time and 117 part-time students in the regular session and 839 in the summer session. Mundelein is an independent, gift-supported institution without capital endowment other than the contributed services of the religious faculty.

In 1964 as the result of a 2-year self-study, the College announced a number of changes effective in 1965. Included are a modified 3-3 system, with three 11-week terms and three courses during an average term; more intensive liberal arts study with one-half of the entire program devoted to basic studies in humanities, social and natural sciences, fine arts, theology, and philosophy; broad areas of concentration replacing traditional majors and minors; and tutorial programming for honors students. Curricula lead to the B.A., B.S., and B.F.A. degrees.

Classes are ordinarily small with lecture, discussion, and seminar methods freely employed. Electronic teaching aids include a language laboratory and closed-circuit television.

Mundelein College offers advanced placement courses for high school students, graduate study at city universities during seniors' last undergraduate semester, and a continuing education and degree-completion program for mature women. There are opportunities for study abroad through the Institute of European Studies; for science research at the Argonne National Laboratories, and for teacher education in an NCATE approved program.

[M. I. GRIFFIN]

MUNDWILER, FINTAN, second abbot of *St. Meinrad, Ind.; b. Dietikon, Zurich, Switzerland, July 12, 1835; d. St. Meinrad, Feb. 14, 1898. He studied at the claustral school at *Einsiedeln, entered that mon-

astery in 1854, and was ordained in 1859. With Martin *Marty, later abbot and bishop. Mundwiler was sent (1859) to the newly founded monastery of St. Meinrad, where he served as rector of the school and first prior (1870). Upon Marty's nomination as vicar apostolic of the Dakota Territory, Mundwiler was elected second abbot of St. Meinrad (Feb. 3, 1880). During his term of office St. Meinrad experienced many difficulties, including the destructive fire of 1887, the struggles to rebuild, and certain internal dissensions. With tact and moderation Abbot Fintan brought about a renewal in observance, the reconstruction of the abbey, and an increase in the school enrollment. Under him St. Meinrad's daughterhouse, New Subiaco in Arkansas, was made an abbey (1891), and St. Joseph's Abbey in Louisiana was founded (1889). He was the first president (1881) of the Swiss-American Congregation of *Benedictines, and he composed the congregation's first statutes.

Bibliography: Archives, St. Meinrad Archabbey, Einsiedeln, Conception Abbey, St. Joseph's Abbey, and New Subiaco Abbey. A. KLEBER, *History of St. Meinrad Archabbey, 1854–1954* (St. Meinrad, Ind. 1954).

[C. DAVIS]

MUÑECAS, ILDEFONSO DE LAS, famous guerrilla in the war for Peruvian independence; b. San Miguel, Tucumán, date unknown; d. near Lake Titicaca, 1816. He studied at the University of Córdoba, being ordained and receiving a doctorate in theology at the end of the century. He completed his religious education in Europe and returned a few years later to establish himself in Cuzco as rector of a parish. A strong partisan of the emancipation of the Spanish colonies in America, he took part in the subversive movements in Cuzco that culminated in the uprising of Aug. 3, 1814, headed by the Indian leader Mateo Pumacagua and the Creoles Pinelo and Angulo. When the action was extended to Upper Peru, Muñecas joined the group marching on La Paz, accompanying Pinelo as chaplain and personal adviser. The capture of that city was due in great part to Muñecas, who cleverly came to an agreement with its inhabitants. When the patriots were defeated a short time later and La Paz was once again occupied by the King's troops, he sought exile among the aborigines of the altiplano. Determined to continue the struggle, he succeeded in forming among the aborigines a band of guerrillas with which he harrassed the royalists for 2 years. Finally, defeated by a party that went out in pursuit of him, he was taken prisoner in May 1816. As he was being taken to Peru by order of the Spanish authorities, he was shot by one of the soldiers who was escorting him.

[H. SANABRIA FERNÁNDEZ]

MUNGUÍA, CLEMENTE DE JESÚS, Mexican prelate and scholar, active in the defense of the Church during the Liberal reform and the period of Emperor Maximilian; b. Los Reyes, Michoacán, Nov. 21, 1810; d. Rome, Dec. 14, 1868. He graduated in law and practiced the profession in Morelia and Mexico City from 1838 to 1841, when he was ordained to the priesthood. He then served in various ecclesiastical posts of the Diocese of Morelia, including those of vicar-general and vicar of the curia. In 1843 he was named rector of the seminary, where he had taught, and he brought this institution to a high level of academic and scientific activity. Munguía was elevated to the bishopric of Michoacán in 1850. In 1853 he was named president of the council of state by the dictator *Santa Anna. With the victory of the Ayutla revolution, he vigorously defended the Church against the Liberal reformers and was exiled in 1856 by President Comonfort. Returning to his diocese the following year, he declared himself in favor of the Plan of Tacubaya, which called for the derogation of the liberal constitution of 1857 and set in motion the War of the Reform. At the conclusion of the war in 1861, which resulted in victory for the Reform party under Benito Juárez, he was again sent into exile. With the beginning of the French invasion of Mexico, he returned to Morelia in 1863 as its first archbishop. He soon incurred the enmity of Emperor Maximilian because of his outspoken views on the rights of the Church. He was one of the prelates who signed the Manifest of Dec. 29, 1864, urging the government not to legislate in religious matters without a previous concordat with the pope. He also protested against the Law of Religious Tolerance; but disillusioned in his hopes under the Emperor, he went to exile again in 1865 and spent his last days in Rome. A prolific writer, he left 14 volumes, ranging from a course in universal jurisprudence (1844) to a synthesis of the philosophy of thought and expression (1852), in addition to numerous essays and addresses.

Bibliography: E. VALVERDE TÉLLEZ, *Bio-bibliografía eclesiástica mexicana, 1821–1943,* 3 v. (Mexico City 1949).

[J. A. MAGNER]

MUNICH

City of 1,100,000 inhabitants on both banks of the Isar River, 25 miles north of the Alps, in south Germany; capital of *Bavaria, seat of the Archdiocese of Munich and Freising (*Monacensis et Frisingensis*), former residence of the Wittelsbach (1255–1918).

It was an independent cloister (*Munichen*) when first mentioned in 1158. Duke Henry the Lion destroyed the bishop's bridge over the Isar at Freising (20 miles north of Munich), as well as his customs house, mint, and salt works, moving bridge, customs house, and the salt trade with *Salzburg to Munich. Prosperity from trade occasioned the building of St. Peter Church (*c.* 1170) and the establishment of the new parishes of Our Lady and the Holy Spirit (1271), Munich's only three parishes until 1800. The influential group around the antipapal Emperor *Louis IV the Bavarian (1314–47) included *Marsilius of Padua, *John of Jandun, and the Spiritual Franciscans *Michael of Cesena and *William of Ockham. Under the Catholic Wittelsbachs, especially Albert V (1550–79), *William V (1597–97), and *Maximilian I (1597–1651), with Jesuit help, Munich was a stronghold of the Catholic reform. Munich suffered heavily in the Thirty Years' War. Subsequently it has had a long history as a center of culture and art. Adolf *Hitler made an unsuccessful putsch there (1923), and a four-power conference in Munich dismembered Czechoslovakia before World War II (1938).

The Archdiocese of Munich and Freising is the successor of the See of Freising, which St. *Boniface estab-

The 15th-century brick cathedral at Munich, Germany, as viewed from the tower of a nearby Gothic church.

lished in 739 as a suffragan of *Mainz (suffragan of Salzburg after 798). St. *Corbinian (d. *c.* 730), an Irish monk bishop, had founded a monastery in Freising, where there had been Christians from Roman times. The many cloisters in the area contributed to religious, cultural, and economic life: Weihenstephan, *Tegernsee, Isen, Scharnitz-Schlehdorf, and Innichen (founded in 769 by Duke Tassilo for the Slav missions). Bishop Arbeo (764–783), an ally of the Carolingians from Lombardy, fostered religious and cultural life and had the relics of Corbinian translated to Freising from the south Tyrol. Synods combated private churches (756) and established parishes (798) where diocesan priests replaced monks (800). A cathedral chapter of canons, mentioned in 842, gradually replaced the cathedral cloister. *Leidradus of Lyons studied in the cathedral school. The book of donations compiled by Kozroh under Bishop Hitto (811–834), the first such work in Germany, is a source for Freising's early history. The first German hymn was composed under Erchanbert (836–854), and Anno (855–875) at the Pope's request sent an organ to Rome. The Slavic mission of St. Methodius was expelled, and Freising's Gallican liturgy became Roman. Cathedral and library burned under Waldo (883–906), but the king granted Freising the bridge and the salt toll to pay for reconstruction. St. *Lantbert (937–957) repaired the damages of the Hungarian invasions. The politically influential Abraham (957–993) collected MSS, including perhaps Fréising's Old Slavic texts. In the investiture struggle most of Freising's bishops sided with the Emperor.

At the end of the episcopacy of Freising's most important prelate, *Otto (1138–58), the toll bridge was moved to Munich. Under Otto II (1184–1220), who completed the rebuilding of the cathedral after a disastrous fire, an episcopal history was begun. The cathedral chapter sided with Louis IV against the popes at Avignon. In the 15th century the University of *Vienna influenced intellectual life in Freising, which was overshadowed by the humanist school of St. Peter in Munich; the historian Veit Arnpeck (d. 1495), who studied in Vienna, showed no signs of humanist influence. Bishop Sixtus von Tannberg (1473–95) began an urgently needed reform, and the Wittelsbach maintained Catholicism during the Reformation. The seminary was begun in 1688. Veit Adam (1618–51), the first *prince bishop, and Johann Franz Ecker (1695–1727) kept church life at a high level; but the Enlightenment and royal absolutism were too strong for Ludwig Joseph (1769–88) and Joseph Konrad (1790–1803), the last of Freising's prelates. The domain of Freising was secularized by Bavaria in 1802.

The court bishopric in Munich (1789) was suppressed in 1805, but efforts to establish a see in the center of secular authority succeeded with the concordat of 1817 and the papal bull of 1818. The Archdiocese of Freising was formed from the suppressed Sees of Freising and Chiemsee, the provostship of Berchtesgaden, and the parts of the Archdiocese of Salzburg in Bavaria, and had as suffragan sees *Augsburg, *Regensburg, and Passau. The Church of Our Lady of Munich became the cathedral, and its collegiate chapter (1492–1803) was replaced by a metropolitan chapter. Archbishop Lothar Anselm von Gebsattel (1821–46), who repaired the spiritual damages after secularization and the vacancy of the see, built semi-

naries at great personal expense. He obtained from Louis I (1825–46) the restoration of orders to their cloisters: Benedictines in *Scheyern and St. Boniface in Munich; Franciscans; and Capuchins. Karl August von *Reisach (1846–55) defended the Church from State tutelage, especially in the episcopal conference at Freising (1850), whose petition to the king was drawn up by the learned Friedrich Windischmann (1811–61). Maximilian II extricated himself by having Reisach made a cardinal in the Roman Curia. Gregor von Scherr (1856–77), formerly abbot of *Metten, had to contend with official anti-Catholic feelings and discrimination, the antipapal stand of J. I. von *Döllinger, and troubles following *Vatican Council I. Döllinger and Johann *Friedrich made Munich a center of *Old Catholics. Michael von Rampf (1825–1901), Vicar of Munich under von Scherr and his successor the historian Abp. Antonius von Steichele (1878–89), resisted Minister Johannes von Lutz and the *Kulturkamp; von Rampf became bishop of Passau (1889–1901). Church-State relations improved after the episcopal conference at Freising (1887); and Abps. Antonius von Thoma (1889–97), Franz Joseph von Stein (1898–1909), and Franziskus von Bettinger (1909–17, cardinal in 1914) devoted themselves to pastoral problems resulting from aggressive free thought, to a Catholic press, to education, and to charity. Michael von *Faulhaber (1917–52, cardinal in 1921), who continued this work, was an opponent of national socialism (1933–45). Cardinal Joseph Wendel (1952–60), previously bishop of Speyer, under whom was held the World *Eucharistic Congress (1960), was succeeded by Cardinal Julius Döpfner, formerly bishop of Berlin.

Munich was heavily bombed in World War II, but has been in great part restored. The brick Gothic cathedral (1468–88) has two famous towers, 324 feet high with cupolas. The cathedral of Freising (1161–1205), made Gothic in 1480 and modified in 1621 and 1724, has a remarkable crypt of four naves. Munich has no Romanesque churches and only three Gothic churches (for the most part made baroque). The older churches were built by cloisters and by private endowment. The 19th-century churches of Louis I are a group apart: St. Ludwig, St. Boniface, and All Saints. Almost all religious orders in Germany have houses in Munich, and there are many cloisters, churches of interest, and pilgrimages in the archdiocese. Catholic groups are active and conduct extensive charitable works. More than 60 parish churches have been built in Munich since 1900.

In 1963 the archdiocese, 4,622 square miles in area, had 1,253 secular and 526 religious priests, 793 men in 54 religious houses, 6,394 women in 403 convents, and 2,043,500 Catholics in a population of 2,500,000. Its suffragans are Augsburg, Passau, and Regensburg.

Bibliography: C. MEICHELBECK, *Historia Frisingensis*, 2 v. (Augsburg 1724–29). K. G. FELLERER, *Beiträge zur Musikgeschichte Freisings* (Freising 1926). *Die katholische Pfarreien Münchens in ihrer historische Entwicklung* (Munich 1935). O. BREITER, *Das kirchliche München* (Munich 1951). J. STABER, *Volksfrömmigkeit und Wallfahrtswesen des Spätmittelalters im Bistum Freising* (Munich 1955). G. SCHWAIGER, *Die altbayerischen Bistümer Freising, Passau und Regensburg zwischen Säkularisation und Konkordat, 1803–1817* (Munich 1959). A. W. ZIEGLER, LexThK² 4:351–353; *Monachium* (Munich 1958). R. BAUERREISS, LexThK² 7:675–676. **Illustration credits:** Fig. 1, German Information Center, New York City. Fig. 2, G. E. Kidder Smith.

[R. BRANDLMEIER]

The church of St. John Capistrano, Munich, designed by the German architect Sep Ruf. It is a notable example of the contemporary-style churches constructed in Munich and elsewhere in Germany since World War II.

MUNICH, UNIVERSITY OF

An autonomous Bavarian institution of medieval origin situated in the German Federal Republic. It is under the jurisdiction of the Ministry of Education and partially financed by the State of Bavaria. It is officially known as the Ludwig Maximilian University of Munich.

Original Foundation in Ingolstadt. Although at the request of Ludwig, Duke of Bavaria, Pope Pius II on April 19, 1458, had issued the bull approving the establishment of a *studium generale* at Ingolstadt, first site of the University, political disturbances stemming from the Duke's conflict with the Emperor, Frederick III, delayed the foundation until 1472. On June 26 of that year the University, composed of the four Faculties of Arts, Theology, Philosophy, and Law, was formally inaugurated under the chancellorship of the bishop of Eichstädt, in whose diocese Ingolstadt was located. Modeled on the University of *Vienna, Ingolstadt nevertheless had some special features of its own: (1) there was no division into nations and consequently no student rights, although provided for in the original charter (1458); (2) the Faculty of Arts was divided into two distinct *viae,* or sections—the nominalists and the realists—each with its own dean, council, and *matricula* (in 1478 Duke Ludwig obliged these two *viae* to unite, with the right to one Faculty vote only); and (3) in keeping with the papal bull, degree candidates were obliged to take an oath of obedience to the Holy See. This was the first instance of external control imposed on the University, although internal control was common in European institutions. The University was administered by the rector, chosen in turn from each of the Faculties and elected by the masters; a general council composed of deans of Faculties and the rector; and the Faculty councils.

In 1494 Duke Ludwig's son, Duke George, founded the Collegium Georgianum for 11 needy students to be supervised by a regent. Although similar institutions existed in connection with the University of *Paris, the Collegium Georgianum represented a departure from German custom, according to which colleges were for masters teaching at the university. In time other similar student colleges were opened for the various Faculties. The University was sustained mainly by large endowments accruing from holdings of the clergy and religious orders and also by additional revenues that were donated by Pope Adrian VI and by Pope Clement VII.

Shortly after its founding, the University warmly espoused humanism and counted among its professors some of the most outstanding scholars of the day: the humanist and poet Conrad *Celtis; Jakob Locher, surnamed Philomusos; Johann Turmair, called Aventinus from his birthplace in Italy, whose *Annales Boiorum,* a history of Bavaria, translated into German (*Bayerische Chronik*) became the first important history in the German language; and the moralist Paulus *Laymann.

During the Reformation Duke William IV and his chancellor, Leonhard von Eck, strove to preserve intact the orthodoxy of the University. In this endeavor they were assisted by Dr. Johann Maier (generally known as Eck from his birthplace), who became the foremost opponent of the Reformation and who, during the Counter Reformation, succeeded in making Ingolstadt a stronghold of Catholicism in southern Germany just as Wittenberg was the center of Lutheranism in the North. In 1549, with the approval of Pope Paul III, Duke William IV of Bavaria appointed several Jesuits to the Faculties of Theology and Philosophy, among them the theologians Peter *Canisius and Alfonso *Salmerón. Other distinguished Jesuits associated with the University at this time were the Spanish theologian *Gregory of Valencia and the controversialist Jakob *Gretser. By 1688 the Jesuits were in full charge of the Faculty of Philosophy, a position that they held until their suppression in 1773.

Despite political disturbances, particularly those resulting from the Thirty Years' War (1618–48), the University continued to be a center of learning throughout the 17th century when it counted among its professors such men as Christoph *Scheiner, inventor of the pantograph, who also perfected the helioscope and is credited with discovering the sun's rotation and sun spots; Jakob *Balde, the "German Horace," poet and professor of rhetoric; and the jurists Kaspar Manz and Christopher Berold.

Transfer to Munich and Later Development. During the second half of the 18th century a rationalistic spirit infiltrated into the University through the influence of Joseph Adam, Baron of Icksätt, who headed the institution. This trend was later reinforced by the activities of Adam Weishaupt, a professor of Canon Law, who sought to make the University a center of the Enlightenment through the Illuminati, a secret society that he had founded. The organization was later dissolved and Weishaupt dismissed. Financial difficulties, however, interrupted the smooth functioning of the institution; and on May 17, 1800, by order of the elector Joseph Maximilian, later the first King of Bavaria, the University was transferred to Landshut, where in 1802 it was officially named the Ludwig Maximilian University. On Oct. 3, 1826, by order of Ludwig I, the University was moved to Munich, its permanent location, where it first occupied a former Jesuit college. In 1840 the University took possession of the classical edifice constructed by Andreas Gärtner, which extended along the famous Ludwig- and Amalienstrassen in one of the most beautiful sections of Munich. There it became internationally known as a center of culture and research. During World War II the University suffered heavy losses from the air attacks of 1944–45, when more than 70 per cent of the buildings were destroyed, including the library with a large part of its bound volumes, manuscripts, and rare book collections. Reconstruction was begun after World War II to provide for the constantly growing postwar enrollment.

In 1965 the University was composed of the Faculties of Theology (Catholic), Law, Economics, and Social and Political Sciences (including business administration and forestry), Medicine (including dentistry), Veterinary Medicine, Philosophy (including liberal arts, journalism, musicology, and education) and Natural Sciences (including mathematics, food technology, and pharmacy), and the Institute of Physical Education. State diplomas are issued in all Faculties based on state examinations. Degrees include the licentiate and doctorate in theology, and the doctorate in all other Faculties. The academic staff (1965) numbered approximately 500 full-time and 400 part-time members; student enrollment totaled more than 20,000 men and women. The library housed 800,000 bound volumes and the Döllinger collection.

Among the outstanding scholars associated with the University during the 19th and 20th centuries were the philosophers Franz von *Baader (1765–1841) and Friedrich von *Schelling (1775–1854); the chemist Baron Justus von Liebig (1803–73); the theologian and historian Johannes Joseph Ignaz von *Döllinger (1799–1890); the Byzantine philologist Karl *Krumbacher (1856–1809); the physicist Wilhelm Konrad Röntgen (1843–1923), who received the Nobel prize in physics (1901) for discovering the X ray; the political economist Ludwig Brentano (1844–1931); the patrologist Otto *Bardenhewer (1851–1935); the art historian Heinrich *Wölfflin (1864–1945); the Roman philologist and critic Karl Vassler (1872–1949); the surgeon Ernst Ferdinand Sauerbruch (1875–1951); and the medieval Latin philologists Ludwig *Traube (1861–1907) and Paul *Lehmann (1884–1964).

Bibliography: H. RASHDALL, *The Universities of Europe in the Middle Ages,* ed. F. M. POWICKE and A. B. EMDEN, 3 v. (new ed. Oxford 1936). L. BOEHM, LexThK² 7:676–678.

[M. B. MURPHY]

MUNICH METHOD IN CATECHETICS,

an adaptation to catechetics of the psychological steps of learning and teaching, developed by J. F. Herbart and T. Ziller. The Munich catechists formulated their method in six principal and secondary steps: presentation, explanation, application and preparation, aim, and synthesis. The primary steps in the teaching procedure correspond to three steps in learning on the part of the pupil (viz, perception, understanding, and practice). Furthermore, there is direct appeal to the cognitive and appetitive powers of the learner: to the senses and imagination in the "presentation," to the intellect in the "explanation," and to the will and emotions in the "application." These principles of learning have their roots in the psychology of Aristotle and were formulated by St. Thomas Aquinas as the bases for all learning and teaching. A story, usually from the Bible, containing a doctrinal or moral truth is presented by the teacher; explanation of the religious elements to be learned is followed by practical application to daily living. The inductive process of teaching from the known to the unknown, from the concrete to the abstract, was a major improvement over the hitherto prevailing word analysis of the catechism answers.

For the use of this method in the U.S., *see* RELIGIOUS FORMATION, 1.

Bibliography: H. W. OFFELE, *Geschichte und Grundanliegen der sogenannten Münchener katechetischen Methode* (Munich 1961). For more complete bibliographical data see L. LENTNER et al., eds., *Katechetisches Wörterbuch* (Freiburg 1961).

[J. B. COLLINS]

MUNIFICENTISSIMUS DEUS.

On Nov. 1, 1950, Pope Pius XII defined the Church's doctrine of the *Assumption of Mary into heaven. The phrase *Munificentissimus Deus* (Most Bountiful God) both entitles and begins the document of definition, an apostolic constitution.

Apart from its survey of various descriptions and defenses of the Assumption, and the definition itself, this papal bull has established itself as a milestone in the history of *Mariology for: (1) the capital significance which the Pope gives to the universal contemporary belief in the Assumption as evidenced by the almost unanimous concurrence of the bishops of the world when he asked their opinion: "This outstanding agreement of the Catholic prelates and the faithful . . . by itself and in a way altogether certain and free of all errors, manifested this privilege as a truth revealed by God and contained in that divine deposit which Christ has delivered to His Spouse to be guarded faithfully and to be taught infallibly"; (2) the lack of systematic appeal to Holy Scripture as basis for the proclamation. The Pope states that all the "proofs and considerations of the Fathers and theologians are based on the Scriptures as their ultimate foundation," but he does not analyze individual texts (as did Pius IX in *Ineffabilis Deus,* the definition of the *Immaculate Conception).

It is noteworthy that (1), despite the long history of differences on the meaning of the *Proto-evangelium (Gn. 3.15), he forthrightly applies the text to Mary; (2) without any exegetic reservation he alludes to "theologians and preachers who, following in the footsteps of the Fathers, have been rather free in their use of events and expressions taken from Sacred Scripture"; (3) with approval he refers to St. Bonaventure who applied to Mary "in a kind of accommodated sense" words of the Canticle (8.5) which helped to justify, in the original sermon, belief in the Assumption.

Then, after drawing practical moral consequences from this belief, the document concludes with the solemn statement: "We pronounce, declare, and define it to be a divinely revealed dogma that the Immaculate Mother of God, the ever Virgin Mary, having completed the course of her earthly life, was assumed body and soul into heavenly glory."

Bibliography: PIUS XII, "Munificentissimus Deus," ActApS 42 (1950) 753–771; Eng. *Catholic Mind* 49 (Jan. 1951) 65–78. B. CAPELLE, "Théologie de l'Assomption d'après la bulle 'Munificentissimus Deus,'" NouvRevTh 72 (1950) 1009–27. Davis CDT 170–179, with bibliography. SacTheolSumma BAC 2:2.201–223.

[J. W. LANGLINAIS]

MUNOZ, VICENTE,

Franciscan architect; b. Seville, Spain, 1699; d. Salta, Argentina, Sept. 8, 1784. He entered the convent of Buenos Aires as a Franciscan novice on July 7, 1741. Muñoz directed the building of the church of San Francisco in Buenos Aires, begun in 1730 with plans formulated by Andrés *Blanqui, SJ. Since the church was not inaugurated until 1754, Muñoz probably carried out the major part of the work. Years later, when the convent was rebuilt, he again acted as builder and director. Muñoz also directed the work on the chapel of Terciarios de San Roque in Buenos Aires. Muñoz, called to Córdoba to complete work on the cathedral (begun in 1690 by architect José González Merguelte and continued in 1729 by Blanqui), probably designed its majestic dome, equalled in beauty by few works in all America. In 1759 he moved to Salta to direct the work of the new Franciscan church. Although there is no documentary proof that the plans were by Muñoz, the similarity of the dome to that of the cathedral of Córdoba suggests that he was the author. In 1882 the forward part of this church was completely remodeled by Luis Giorgi, and at present Muñoz is credited with the design of San Francisco de Salta only from the transept back. Although there is no proof that he planned the buildings mentioned above, it is certain that he was their builder, a fact that attests to the exceptional quality of his skills as a technician.

Bibliography: G. FURLONG, *Arquitectos argentinos durante la dominación hispánica* (Buenos Aires 1946). M. J. BUSCHIAZZO, *Historia de la arquitectura colonial en Iberoamérica* (Buenos Aires 1961).

[M. J. BUSCHIAZZO]

MÜNSTER, SEBASTIAN, Hebraist, geographer, and cosmographer; b. Nieder-Ingelheim, Germany, Jan. 26, 1488; d. Basel, Switzerland, May 26, 1552. In 1505 he entered the Franciscan Order and studied Greek and Hebrew under K. *Pellicanus in the Franciscan monastery at Ruffnach. At a later date, however, probably about 1524, he became a convert to Lutheranism. In 1524 he became professor of Hebrew at the University of Heidelberg, and from 1528 to the time of his death he was a professor of the same subject at the University of Basel. His well known illustrated works on geography and cosmography were first published in German at Basel in 1544; later they passed through numerous editions in Latin and the principal European languages. He edited the *Biblia Hebraica,* 2 v. (Basel 1534–35) with a Latin translation of the same, and his Hebrew text of the Book of Tobit (Basel 1542) was used in the *Polyglot Bible of London.

Bibliography: V. HANTZSCH, *Sebastian Münster: Leben, Werk, wissenschaftliche Bedeutung* (Leipzig 1898). O. CLEMEN, RGG³ 4:1182–83. R. ALMAGIÀ, EncCatt 8:1519. H. BARDTKE, LexThK³ 7:687–688.

[C. H. PICKAR]

MÜNSTER, UNIVERSITY OF

An institution of higher learning in the State of North Rhine-Westphalia, Germany (Federal Republic). It was founded in 1773 as a university through the efforts of the Münster Secretary of State, Franz Friedrich Wilhelm von *Fürstenberg, and the Prince Bishop Max Friedrich von Königsegg-Rothenfels. On May 28, 1773, the University of Münster received papal recognition and in October the approval of the Kaiser himself. Official dedication took place on April 16, 1780. Financial resources accrued from Münster religious houses (a Jesuit college and a Benedictine convent, Sanctae Mariae trans aquas), which had been suppressed with papal approval. The curriculum of the four Faculties of Philosophy, Theology, Law, and Medicine partly stemmed from the philosophical-theological instruction of the Jesuits in the Gymnasium Paulinum established in 1588. The secularization of the ecclesiastical state of Münster in 1803 gave rise to heated debates regarding the nature of the formerly Catholic institution. The administrator of the diocese, Clemens August von Droste-Vischering, in opposition to the Prussian government, demanded that the character of the University be Catholic, and at least the Theological Faculty be controlled by the bishop to safeguard the religious character of the University. This demand led to the closing of the University in 1818 and the temporary suspension of the Theological Faculty in 1820. In 1818, instead of the University, an institute (called an academy since 1843) was established with two Faculties: Philosophy and Catholic Theology. The statutes of 1832 effected the reorganization of the institution and granted the Faculty of Theology the right to graduation; they granted the same right to the Faculty of Philosophy in 1844 and 1895 respectively. They also regulated the relationship of the bishop with the Faculty of Theology, but bypassed the question of whether the institution was to be denominational or to have absolute religious equality.

From 1848 on, Johann Georg Müller tried to reclaim the academy as a religious institution; in 1856 the representative assembly of Westphalia pressed the Prussian government to establish the institution as a Catholic university. The expansion of the Faculty of Philosophy in 1875 meant the end of the previously Catholic institution. This was interpreted as stemming from the *Kulturkampf.* The year 1875 was in fact the turning point in the restoration of the University, completed in 1902 with the founding of the Faculty of Law and Political Science. In 1907 the institution received the title Wilhelms University of Westphalia; in 1914 the Evangelical-Theological Faculty was established; in 1925 the Faculty of Medicine, including Dentistry, was added; and in 1948, the Faculty of Mathematics and Natural Sciences, including pharmacy. During World War II almost all University buildings were destroyed or severely damaged, but since 1947 they have been rebuilt. In the early 1960s the Faculty of Philosophy included schools of liberal arts, psychology, musicology, and education. On Jan. 1, 1961, the University ordinances went into effect. In 1964 the University comprised 6 Faculties, and approximately 110 institutes, seminars, and clinics connected with the different Faculties, and maintained an 800,000 volume library.

The University of Münster is under the jurisdiction of the Ministry of Education of North Rhine-Westphalia and is supported by State funds; it is governed by the rector and senate, the former elected to office for 1 year. Students pay tuition and attend an academic year from November to July. The language of instruction is German. State examinations are provided in law, medicine, dentistry, food technology, pharmacy, and teaching on the secondary level. Diplomas are conferred in chemistry, geology, business administration, mathematics, physics, psychology, journalism, and economics. The M.A. is granted in arts, and doctorates are awarded in theology, law, political science, medicine, dentistry, philosophy, and natural science.

The number of students in 1818 was 378, in 1902 it was 870. After the restoration of the University, enrollment increased sharply: the largest number of students before 1945 had been approximately 5,000; in

Münster University, Faculty of Law and Petri-Kirche (St. Peter's Church).

1963 the University numbered more than 14,000 students with 130 full-time professors. In 1963 approximately 500 students attended the Catholic theological faculty, which offers 16 full professorial chairs. In addition to the Catholic Theological Seminar, established in 1885, there are institutes for Christian Social Science (1951), for studies on the missions (1952), and the Catholic Ecumenical Institute (1961). The *Theologische Revue,* published since 1902 by the Catholic theological faculty, reviews new theological publications. Other University publications include: *Jahresbericht über das akademische Jahr,* an annual report of the academic year.

Bibliography: C. F. KRABBE, *Relation über die Studienanstalten in Münster* (Münster 1854). A. PIEPER, *Die alte Universität Münster, 1773–1818* (Münster 1902). A. EITEL, *Von der alten zur neuen Universität in Münster* (Münster 1953). J. HERRMANN, *Die Universität Münster in Geschichte und Gegenwart* (2d ed. Münster 1950). E. HEGEL, *Die katholisch-theologische Fakultät Münster in ihrer geschichtlichen Entwicklung, 1773–1961* (Münster 1961). R. STUPPERICH, *Die evangelisch-theologische Fakultät der Universität Münster* (Münster 1955). K. E. ROTHSCHUH, *Kleine Geschichte der medizinischen Fakultät der Universität Münster* (Münster 1957).

[E. HEGEL]

MÜNSTER IN WESTFALEN

Capital of Westphalia, in northwest Germany; the scene of the signing of the Peace of Westphalia (1643–48), ending the Thirty Years' War. In 1963 the Diocese of Münster (*Monasteriensis*), suffragan to *Cologne since its creation in 805, had 1,396 secular and 132 religious priests, 832 men in 52 religious houses, 8,034 women in 512 convents, and 1,949,000 Catholics in a population of 3,413,000; it is 5,714 square miles in area. The medieval see was bordered by Cologne, *Utrecht, and *Osnabrück.

St. *Ludger (d. 809), the first bishop, built a *monasterium* in Mimigernaford, which by 1068 was called Münster. Until Liudbert (d. 870) the bishops were also abbots of *Werden; *Liesborn was one of several cloisters of canonesses established in connection with important parish churches. Around the strongpoint of the cathedral from the 10th century grew up a merchant settlement. In the *investiture struggle the bishops sided with the empire until 1118. After the Concordat of *Worms (1122) the secular authority of the bishops became strong, and from 1173 the city was administered by a bishop and cathedral chapter (restricted to the nobility). The cathedral school founded by Ludger enjoyed a humanist revival with Rudolf von Langen (1438–1519), who had been educated under the *Brethren of the Common Life; and Münster ranked with Deventer as a leading school of west Germany. Protestantism entered in the 1520s, and only the cathedral, collegiate churches, and cloisters remained Catholic. Münster suffered under the *Anabaptist reign of terror (1534–35) of King Jan Bokelson of Leyden, until the city was regained by Bp. Franz von Waldeck (1532–53), who was sympathetic to Lutheranism. Catholicism was strengthened under Bp. Johann von Hoya (1566–74), a Tridentine reformer, and Bps. Ernst (1585–1612) and Ferdinand of Bavaria (1612–50), who made Münster a bulwark of Catholicism in northwest Germany until Napoleonic times.

The work of Jesuits (who took over the cathedral school in 1588), Capuchins (1612), and Observant Franciscans (1613) was completed under the militant

Christoph Bernhard von Galen (1650–78), who consolidated the secular power of the bishop. Vicar-general Franz von *Fürstenberg made the Jesuit college a regional and denominational university (1773), opened a theater (1775), and with Bernard *Overberg reformed the school system. The Circle of Münster around Fürstenberg and Princess *Gallitzin made the city a center of the Catholic Reform. Following secularization (1803) Clemens von *Droste zu Vischering administered the vacant see from 1807. After its restoration and reorganization (1821) the diocese had to cope with the *Kulturkampf and problems of industrialization. Cardinal von *Galen (1933–46) heroically opposed the neopagan errors of National Socialism. In 1958 part of the see went to the new Diocese of Essen. Notable members of the Catholic theological faculty associated with Münster's university were G. *Hermes, J. T. H. *Katerkamp, A. *Berlage, J. *Schwane, J. *Pohle, F. J. *Dölger, F. *Hitze, F. *Diekamp, J. *Mausbach, and J. *Schmidlin.

Ludger built a cathedral (torn down in 1377), and Erpho (1085–97) consecrated a second one (1090) whose late Romanesque nave was rebuilt on the old foundations (1225–64). The cathedral chapter founded by Ludger was suppressed in 1811. Collegiate churches dissolved in 1811 were: the old cathedral, established by Burchard (1098–1118); St. Liudgeri, noted for a late Romanesque nave (*c.* 1200) and a Gothic choir (1383); St. Martini, which has a Gothic nave (1350); and St. Mauritz (*c.* 1080), to which a Gothic choir was added (1471). Münster has many medieval churches, badly damaged in World War II but almost all restored. Secular monuments include the Gothic town hall where the Spanish-Dutch peace was signed in 1648. In Münster are located the motherhouses of several women's congregations as well as houses of other religious orders.

Bibliography: *Westfälisches Urkundenbuch (bis 1325),* v.1–8 (Münster 1847–1913), Index (1921). *Die Geschichtsquellen des Bistums Münster,* 8 v. (Münster 1851–1937). *Quellen und Forschungen zur Geschichte der Stadt Münster,* 8 v. (Münster 1898–1936); NS I, 1–2 (1960–62). L. SCHMITZ-KALLENBERG, *Monasticon Westfaliae* (Münster 1909). J. O. PLASSMANN, *Geschichte der Stadt Münster* (Münster 1925). M. GEISBERG, *Die Stadt Münster,* 7 v. (Bau- und Kunstdenkmäler der Prov. Westfalen; Münster 1932–), v.7 Index. *Handbuch des Bistums Münster,* ed. H. BÖRSTING and A. SCHRÖER, 2 v. (2d ed. Münster 1946). J. PRINZ, *Mimigernaford-Münster* (Münster 1960). W. RAHE, RGG³ 4:1177–79. A. SCHRÖER, LexThK² 7:683–687.

[A. SCHRÖER]

MÜNZER, THOMAS, revolutionary 16th-century Anabaptist leader who fatefully influenced the Catholic and Protestant attitude toward the Anabaptist movement; b. Stolberg, Germany, before 1490 (1468?); d. Mühlhausen, Germany, May 27, 1525. After studying at universities in Leipzig and Frankfurt an der Oder, he was ordained and served for a time as convent chaplain. At the Leipzig Disputation in 1519 he met Luther, who recommended that Münzer serve a church in Zwickau (1520). In this socially unstable environment Münzer came under the influence of Nicolaus Storch and his Zwickau prophets, which led him to accept direct communication with God, rejecting Luther's reliance on the written word. Expelled from Zwickau (1521), he wandered about central Europe until he was invited in 1523 to serve a church in Allsted in Electoral Saxony. Münzer proved to be a successful and eloquent preacher. He produced the first complete German lit-

Thomas Münzer.

Writers (Philadelphia 1957). G. Franz, RGG³ 4:1183–84. E. Iserloh, LexThK² 7:689–690. **Illustration credit:** Archiv Für Kunst und Geschichte.

[G. W. FORELL]

MURABBA'ĀT, a wadī in the Judean Desert about 11 miles south-southwest of Wadi Qumran. In December 1951 Bedouins from the same Ta'âmireh tribe that had made the original discovery of the *Dead Sea Scrolls at Qumran in 1947 offered new manuscripts for sale to the archeologists in Jerusalem. They were persuaded to lead the archeologists to the site of the new discoveries, which proved to be four large caves about half way up a 600-foot cliff in a wild gorge of the Wadi Murabba'āt. An expedition to these caves was immediately organized by Father R. de Vaux of the *École Biblique in Jerusalem and G. L. Harding of the Jordanian Department of Antiquities. The excavation of these almost inaccessible caves from January 21 to March 3, 1952, proved extremely difficult but very rewarding. Four levels of occupation were uncovered: Chalcolithic (4000–3000 B.C.), Middle Bronze (2000–1600 B.C.), Iron II (900–600 B.C.), and Greco-Roman. Perishable materials of great antiquity, such as wooden vessels and the remains of rush mats, were found for the first time in Palestine. The caves were principally places of refuge. During the period of the Second Revolt (A.D. 132–135) they were occupied by a group of the Jewish insurgents against Rome. Two letters sent by their leader, Simon *Bar Kokhba, are among the many valuable documents recovered from the caves.

Bibliography: P. Benoit et al., *Les Grottes de Murabba'ât* (DiscJudDes 2; 1961).

[W. V. E. CASEY]

MURAT, JOACHIM, king of Naples; b. Labastide-Murat (Lot), France, March 25, 1767; d. Pizzo (Catanzaro), Italy, Oct. 13, 1815. His father, an innkeeper, became the manager of the estates of *Talleyrand-Périgord. For a time Joachim studied at the seminary in Toulouse. His record during the French Revolution was undistinguished. His star rose and set with that of *Napoleon I. After serving Bonaparte as a brilliant cavalry commander and as an accomplice in the *coup d'état* of November 1799, Murat was made a marshal of France and grand duke of Berg. In 1800 he married the first consul's youngest sister, Caroline. As King Joachim Napoleon of *Naples (1808–15) he ruled as an enlightened despot, ended feudalism, established order, and promoted the welfare of his subjects, many of whom chafed under French domination. Murat supported Napoleon's annexation of the *States of the Church and the arrest of Pope *Pius VII (1809). Murat's later concern for the unification of *Italy was prompted partly by his desire to end the papal temporal power. A restless soldier, King Joachim seized Capri but failed to capture Sicily, where English forces protected the Bourbon dynasty. After accompanying Napoleon on the Russian campaign and fighting at Leipzig, he entered into secret negotiations with *Metternich to salvage his kingdom from the disintegrating Napoleonic empire. In return for Austria's promise to secure from its allies a guarantee for the maintenance of his kingdom, Murat agreed by treaty (Jan. 11, 1814) to withdraw his support from Napoleon and to renounce his

urgy, which anticipated Luther and influenced liturgical development. Involved in agitation against local authorities, Münzer organized a secret confederation consisting of peasants and miners from neighboring Mansfeld. In a command performance sermon preached July 13, 1524, he vainly attempted to win John of Saxony, brother of Frederick the Wise, to his plan to establish a theocratic state. Opposed by Luther and forbidden to preach, Münzer fled to Mühlhausen, where he aided Heinrich Pfeiffer in making the city a center of the peasant revolt. He soon joined a roving, undisciplined, and poorly equipped army of peasants whom he encouraged with his apocalyptic preaching. Captured and tortured after their rout at Frankenhausen (1525), he recanted his political and religious views before execution. Replacing Luther's justification by faith with justification by suffering and Luther's distinction between the two kingdoms with theocratic millennial hopes, Münzer obtained religious certainty through dreams and visions. When these proved delusions he collapsed. Erroneously considered the typical Anabaptist by the Protestant reformers and the typical chaotic consequence of the Reformation by Catholics, Münzer became a symbol, distorting both Protestant and Catholic interpretations of the Reformation. His later popularity among Marxists as an early Communist is based upon a misinterpretation of the records.

Bibliography: *Werke,* ed. G. Franz (in press at Gütersloh). G. W. Forell, "Thomas Münzer, Symbol and Reality," *Dialog* 2 (1963) 12–33. C. Hinrichs, *Luther und Müntzer* (Berlin 1952). M. M. Smirin, *Die Volksreformation des Thomas Münzer und der Grosse Bauernkrieg,* tr. H. Nichtweiss (2d ed. Berlin 1956). G. H. Williams, ed., *Spiritual and Anabaptist*

claim on Sicily. When the allies failed to recognize him, he declared war on Austria but was routed at Tolentino (May 2, 1815), and fled to France. In a final attempt to seize Calabria, the deposed monarch invaded southern Italy. At Pizzo he was captured, tried, and executed.

Bibliography: J. N. MURAT, *Lettres et documents pour servir à l'histoire de Joachim Murat, 1767–1815*, 8 v. (Paris 1908–14). A. H. ATTERIDGE, *Joachim Murat: Marshal of France and King of Naples* (New York 1911). N. CORTESE, EncIt 17:149–150, with photo. A. VALENTE, *Gioacchino Murat e l'Italia meridionale* (Turin 1941). H. ACTON, *The Bourbons of Naples, 1734–1825* (New York 1958).

[R. J. MARAS]

MURATORI, LODOVICO ANTONIO, Italian historian; b. Vignola, Italy, Oct. 21, 1672; d. Modena, Jan. 23, 1750. He began his brilliant scholarly career in 1695 as Doctor of the Bibliotheca Ambrosiana in Milan. Declining other offers, such as that of Victor Amadeus II who wanted him for the University of Turin, Muratori returned to Modena in 1700 as ducal archivist. There he devoted himself to the history of the political life of the *Este family; his work *Antichità estensi* (2 v., Modena 1717, 1740), the basis of his fame as a historian, grew out of his several studies on the current legal struggle between Pope *Clement XI and Emperor Joseph I for possession of the city of Comacchio. At the suggestion of Apostolo Zeno, Muratori began collecting the works of historians of the Italian Middle Ages, *Rerum Italicarum scriptores* (27 v., Modena 1723–38; v.28 posthumously pub. in 1751; 2d ed., Città di Castello 1900). This work, together with his other publications of sources, *Antiquitates Italicae medii aevi* (6 v., Milan 1738–43) and *Novus thesaurus veterum inscriptionum* (6 v., Milan 1739–43), marked Muratori as the founder and initiator of modern Italian historiography. In his 12-volume *Annali d'Italia* (Milan 1744–49), deliberately patterned on *Mabillon's annals of the Benedictine Order, Muratori did not succeed in really elaborating his source material, but his *Annali* do represent the first large-scale attempt at a unified view of Italian history. A conscientious priest as well as a historian, Muratori was

Lodovico Antonio Muratori.

unswerving in his recognition of ecclesiastical authority in purely theological questions, but he consistently and trenchantly held that historical criticism should be brought to bear on the secular phenomena of the Church.

This brought him into conflict with current ecclesiastical opinion in regard to the power of the *papacy and the cult of the saints (*see* HAGIOGRAPHY). His moderate reformist ideas, especially his demand for freedom of science and scholarship, even in questions of religion, mark him as a representative advocate of "enlightened Catholicism" [see especially his work *De ingeniorum moderatione in religionibus negotio* (Paris 1714)].

Bibliography: Works. *Opere*, 36 v. (Arezzo 1767–80; 2d ed. in 48 v. Venice 1790–1800); *Scritti inediti di L. A. M.* (Bologna 1872; 2d ed. 1880); *Epistolario di L. A. M.*, ed. M. CAMPORI, 14 v. (Modena 1901–22); *Corrispondenza tra L. A. M. e G. G. Leibniz*, ed. M. CAMPORI (Modena 1892). Literature. G. F. SOLI MURATORI, *Vita del proposto L. A. M.* (Venice 1756). É. AMANN, DTC 10.2:2547–56. T. SORBELLI, *Bibliografia Muratoriana*, 2 v. (Modena 1943–44). F. COGNASSO, EncCatt 8:1523–27. S. BERTELLI, *Erudizione e storia in L. A. M.* (Naples 1960). E. COCHRANE, "M.: The Vocation of a Historian," CathHistRev 51 (1965) 153–172.

[H. RUMPLER]

MURATORIAN CANON. Discovered by L. A. *Muratori in the Ambrosian Library at Milan in 1740, the Muratorian fragment is the oldest known canon of the NT. The Milan copy, which seems to have come from Bobbio, is hardly older than 8th century. Mutilated at both ends, it contains 85 lines. Four fragments, probably of the 11th and 12th centuries, were found at Monte Cassino.

The date of composition is clear from lines 74–77: "Very recently [*nuperrime*], in our times, Hermas wrote the *Shepherd,* when his brother, Bishop Pius, was sitting in the chair of the Church of the City of Rome" (*see* HERMAS, SHEPHERD OF). The pontificate of Pius I was about A.D. 142–155.

The poor Latin suggests that the original was Greek. Also, the neuter plural subject with singular verb (*alia plura . . . recipi non potest:* lines 65–67) is normal in Greek, but barbarous in Latin. Most of the literature of the Roman Church at this time was in Greek. Yet Latin also had begun to be used by the end of the 2d century, and there were at that time Latin translations of at least part of Scripture. Moreover, the play on words in lines 67–68, *fel cum melle misceri non congruit,* could not be made in Greek. Perhaps the translator substituted a current Latin saying for a different original.

It is uncertain who composed this canon. Clement of Alexandria, Melito of Sardes, Polycrates of Ephesus, Pope Victor, Pope St. Zephyrinus, and St. Hippolytus have been suggested as possible authors. The last, the first antipope, is the most favored. From the way it speaks of the city, the canon seems to have been written at Rome. It uses a tone of authority, which would accord with one who claimed to be pope; e.g., it says firmly that some works attributed to St. Paul "cannot be received in the Catholic Church," and, "We receive only the Apocalypses of John and Peter." Moreover, the canon strongly argues, against the Roman priest Caius, that St. John the Apostle wrote both the fourth Gospel and the Apocalypse. The arguments used are thought to come from Hippolytus. M. J. Lagrange [RevBibl 42 (1933) 182] cites Denys bar-Salibi, a 12th-century Syrian: "Hippolytus says that John, writing . . . 13 Epistles, wrote them to seven churches" (cf. lines 48–50 of the canon). Yet these arguments are not conclusive; the author might be merely citing general belief, or decisions of authority. Nor would Hippolytus have used a tone of

First page of the 8th-century fragment of the Muratorian Canon in the Biblioteca Ambrosiana (MS I, 101 sup.).

authority before c. 217, when he laid claim to the papacy. But that was not soon after the papacy of Pius I (cf. lines 74–77). For the contents, see BIBLE, III (CANON), 3.

Bibliography: Quasten Patr 2:207–210. Altaner 158–160. H. LECLERCQ, DACL 12.1:543–560. M. J. LAGRANGE, Histoire ancienne du Canon du N.T., pt. 1, Introduction à l'étude du N.T. (pts. 1, 2, 4, Paris 1933–37); "L'Auteur du Canon de Muratori," RevBibl 35 (1926) 83–88; "Le Canon d'Hippolyte et le Fragment de Muratori," RevBibl 42 (1933) 161–186. **Illustration credit:** Biblioteca Ambrosiana, Milan.

[W. G. MOST]

MURBACH, ABBEY OF, former Benedictine abbey in Upper Alsace, near Colmar, France, on the Murbach River; one of the most important German abbeys of the Middle Ages. It was founded a little before 728 by Count Eberhard, and St. *Pirmin of *Reichenau. It soon received great prerogatives: vast possessions, *exemption from episcopal jurisdiction, and autonomy under the Holy See. Murbach enjoyed its finest era in Carolingian times, when it had an important community, schools, and a rich library. Deserted in the 11th century during the *investiture struggle, it was quickly reestablished during the 12th century; its beautiful church, of which some parts still remain, was built at that time. During the 13th century the abbot ranked among the princes of the Empire, and Murbach was imperial territory. But at the end of that century the abbey suffered a decline—a decline even more pronounced in the 14th century when the abbey would accept only noblemen. *Common life was abandoned in the 15th century. From the 14th century the prince abbots of Murbach were also the abbots of Lure, in the Diocese of Besançon; and in 1560 Pius IV permanently united the two monasteries, both then held in *commendation. The affiliation of Murbach with the Swiss Benedictines in 1666 and then with the congregation of Strasbourg in 1715 proved to be vain attempts at restoring the common life. In 1764 the monks obtained the right to become secular clerics (see SECULARIZATION OF CLERICS) and moved to the neighboring town of Guebwiller. A riot on July 26 and 27, 1789, destroyed this chapter of *canons composed exclusively of noblemen.

Bibliography: A. GATRIO, Die Abtei Murbach im Elsass, 2 v. (Strasbourg 1895). M. BARTH, Handbuch der elsässischen Kirchen im Mittelalter, v.2 (Archives de l'Église d'Alsace 12; Strasbourg 1961) 519–1190, esp. 886–897, with abundant and up-to-date bibliog. O. FELD, LexThK² 7:693–694.

[J. CHOUX]

MURI, ABBEY OF, Benedictine abbey, formerly in Aargau, Diocese of Basel, Switzerland; since 1845 in the former Augustinian monastery of Gries in Bolzano, Italy. It was founded in 1027 by the Hapsburgs as a family cloister and settled from *Einsiedeln. The first prior, Reginbold (1032–55), built the convent. The church, a Romanesque three-nave, flat-roof basilica with two towers, was consecrated in 1064; and in 1065 the provost became an abbot. In 1082, as the customary of *Fruttuaria was introduced from *Sankt Blasien, Muri was detached from the Hapsburgs, who became advocati. The abbey came under imperial (1114) and papal (1139) protection. The Acta Murensia, begun c. 1150, offer data on the early Hapsburgs. In the 14th century fire damaged the abbey twice; in 1431 the right of advocatus went to the Swiss Confederation. Pontifical privileges were granted to the abbots in 1507. The Reformation brought Muri, which had accumulated extensive possessions, to the brink of ruin; but Abbot Johann Jodokus Singeisen (1596–1644) applied Tridentine reforms, helped found the Swiss Benedictine Congregation (1602), and raised Muri to new heights. In 1622 the abbey became exempt from the bishop of Constance. Placidus Zurlauben (1684–1723) was made a prince of the empire (1701) after he acquired new lands, making Muri the richest abbey in Switzerland. Decline began with restrictions by the Helvetic Republic, and secularization by Aargau occurred in 1841. Austria offered a refuge to the monks in Gries; the abbot, however, retains his title of Muri. Since 1841 the abbey has cared for the Swiss Gymnasium in Sarnen. The buildings in Muri now house a mental institution; and the church, which was rebuilt (1694–97), now serves a parish. The stained-glass windows, as well as the library went to Aargau.

Bibliography: M. KIEM, Geschichte der Benediktiner-Abtei Muri-Gries, 2 v. (Stans 1881–91). H. STEINACKER, "Die ältesten Geschichtsquellen des habsburgischen Hausklosters Muri," Zeitschrift für die Geschichte des Oberrheins, NS 23 (Heidelberg 1908) 387–420. O. HUNKELER, Abt J. J. Singeisen (Diss. Fribourg 1951). R. AMSCHWAND, Abt A. Regli und die Aufhebung des Klosters Muri (Diss. Fribourg 1956); LexThK² 7:694.

Sarnen Jahresbericht (1955–56). Kapsner BenBibl 2:242. Cottineau 2:2020–22.

[A. MAISSEN]

MURIALDO, LEONARDO, BL., founder of the *Pious Congregation of St. Joseph (Turin); b. Turin, Italy, Oct. 26, 1828; d. there, March 30, 1900. He studied theology in the university of Turin, where he obtained a doctorate (1850) and was ordained (1851). He then devoted himself to the education of poor boys, and in 1857 he became director of the oratory of San Luigi, offered to him by St. John *Bosco. To improve his pedagogical talents and to familiarize himself with the French school of spirituality, Murialdo attended the seminary of St. Sulpice in Paris (1865–66). Upon returning to Turin he was named rector of the Collegio Artigianelli, which aimed to supply poor youths between the ages of 8 and 24 with Christian education and with training in some trade. Under Murialdo's leadership the school gained a high reputation for its modern methods of vocational guidance and for its superior teaching staff.

In 1873 Murialdo founded the Pious Congregation of St. Joseph (Turin) and became its superior general. As one of the first in Italy to promote the Catholic worker movement, he established in Turin Catholic workers' unions (Unioni Operaie Cattoliche, 1871) and began the weekly publication *La Voce dell'Operaio*. To effect the Christian renewal of society and win liberty for the Church, Murialdo participated actively in the Opera dei Congressi, served on Catholic committees, and initiated many Catholic associations. At the sixth Catholic Congress in Naples (1883) he established a national federation of societies to improve the press and founded the monthly *La buona stampa*. In beatifying him (Nov. 3, 1963) Paul VI remarked that the Church was exalting not only his personal virtues but also "the social force that these virtues clothe." Murialdo's remains are venerated in the church of St. Barbara in Turin.

Bibliography: E. REFFO, *Il teologo L. Murialdo* (Turin 1903; 6th ed. Rome 1964). G. VERCELLONO, *Vita e spirito del Servo di Dio teologo L. Murialdo* (Bergamo 1941). J. COTTINO, *Il beato L. Murialdo* (Pignerol 1963). F. BEA, *Beato L. Murialdo* (Rome 1963). A. MARENGO, *Contributi per uno studio su L. Murialdo educatore* (Rome 1964).

[G. MILONE]

MURIEL, DOMINGO, Jesuit philosopher and canonist; b. Tamanes, near Salamanca, Spain, 1718; d. Faenza, Italy, Jan. 23, 1795. He entered the Society of Jesus in 1734, and was sent to Rio de la Plata in 1748. As professor of philosophy in Córdoba, he introduced the so-called "new or Cartesian philosophy." He was subsequently a professor of moral theology and Canon Law, rector of the Colegio of Monserrat, and secretary to the provincial. In 1762 he was selected as procurator at the courts of Madrid and Rome; he was in Spain at the time of the expulsion of the Jesuits in 1767. During his exile in the Papal States, he was rector and provincial of the province of Paraguay with headquarters in Faenza. The general opinion of his holiness was such that the cause of his beatification was initiated soon after his death. No less distinguished for his knowledge than for his sanctity, he wrote the *Fasti novi orbis et ordinationum apostolicarum ad Indias pertinentium breviarium* (Venice 1786), and *Rudimenta Juris Naturae et Gentium* (Venice 1791), as well as several unpublished

writings in the archives of Italy and Spain, such as the "Collectanea dogmática de saeculo XVIII" and "Monumenta historica, chronologica, dogmática ab anno 1776 ad annum 1780." Among Muriel's published writings that do not, however, bear his name is his *Lettre à l'auteur de l'article jésuite dans le Dictionnaire Encyclopédique* (1766). He wrote also the *Breve noticia de las misiones vivas de la Compañía de Jesús en la Provincia del Paraguay* (1766).

Bibliography: G. FURLONG, *Domingo Muriel* (Buenos Aires 1934); *Domingo Muriel, S.J., y su Relación de las misiones* (Buenos Aires 1955).

[G. FURLONG]

MURILLO, BARTOLOMÉ ESTEBAN, painter of the "golden age" of Spanish baroque; b. Seville, 1617 (baptized Jan. 1, 1618); d. Seville, April 3, 1682. He was a devout man who for a time aspired to the priesthood; his daughter became a Dominican and his son a Franciscan. Orphaned at an early age, he earned a livelihood by painting cheap religious pictures until he studied (1642–45) at the royal galleries in Madrid under *Velázquez, from whom he learned a great deal. Murillo then became the favorite artist of Seville's aristocratic class and the universally popular interpreter of the Immaculate Conception. His first effort on this theme (in the Seville museum) resembles the earlier *Ribera in grandiosity; such works, at Aranjuez and the Prado (Madrid), adumbrate the *rococo. Among Murillo's other renowned works are "The Angels' Kitchen" (Louvre), "St. Elizabeth Healing the Sick" (La Caridad, church and hospital of San Jorge, Seville, where he worked as a Brother of Charity), "St. Francis with the Crucified Christ" (Seville museum), and a great "Vision

Murillo, "The Immaculate Conception," canvas, in the Museo Provincial, Seville.

Murillo, "Little St. John," canvas, in the Prado, Madrid.

of St. Anthony" (Seville cathedral). His religious work is distinctively baroque in its brilliant coloring and preference for beauty that tends toward intimacy and prettiness, and away from classical perfection and the spiritual realities (the *estilo vaporoso*). This same spirit marks his paintings of childhood, such as "Children with A Shell" and "Little St. John" (Prado); and his secular subjects (mostly in the Alte Pinakothek, Munich) are unique in Spanish painting as clearly foretelling the spontaneity of composition, lightness of movement, and decorativeness of the 18th century. The best of these is the charming genre piece, "The Women at the Window," or "The Duenna" (National Gallery of Art, Washington, D.C.)

See also BAROQUE ART; ROCOCO ART.

Bibliography: G. C. WILLIAMSON, *Murillo* (London 1902). A. F. CALVERT, *Murillo* (London 1908). A. MUÑOZ, ed., *Murillo* (Leipzig 1943). A. L. MAYER, *Murillo* (Klassiker der Kunst in Gesamtausgaben 22; 2d ed. Stuttgart 1923); Thieme-Becker 25: 285–287. G. KUBLER and M. SORIA, *Art and Architecture in Spain and Portugal and Their American Dominions, 1500 to 1800* (PelHArt Z17; 1959). O. F. L. HAGEN, *Patterns and Principles of Spanish Art* (Madison 1943). G. JEDLICKA, *Spanish Painting*, tr. J. M. BROWNJOHN (New York 1964). **Illustration credits:** Photo MAS, Barcelona.

[R. J. VEROSTKO]

MURNER, THOMAS, satirist and vigorous foe of Luther; b. Oberehnheim, Alsace, Dec. 24, 1475; d. there, Aug. 22, 1537. He entered the Order of Friars Minor Conventual at 15 and was ordained at 19. Between 1495 and 1502 he traveled in France, Germany, and Poland, studying at Freiburg, and receiving the M.A. degree at Paris, and the Th.B. at Cracow. He returned to Strassburg in 1502. In 1506 Emperor Maximilian I made him poet laureate. He criticized in satire the abuses of the Church, and welcomed the reformers until they attacked dogmas and tradition. From this time he became the champion of Catholicism at Strassburg against Lutheranism and at Lucerne against Zwinglianism. The Peace of Zurich in 1529 stipulated that Murner be brought to trial before judges of the Protestant cantons, but he fled to the Palatinate. In 1530 he returned to Oberehnheim, where he remained until his death. Murner represents the contrasts of his age. He was ardent for reform yet crude in his writings; passionate for novelties but an advocate of tradition; frivolous and grave, restless and tormented with the contradictions of the time.

Murner's works include *Chartiludium logicae* (Cracow 1507); *Ludus studentum Friburgensium* (Frankfort 1512); *Arma patientiae, Germania nova, Narrenbeschwörung* (Strassburg, 1519); *Der lutherischen evangelischen Kirchendieb und Ketzerkalender* (Lucerne 1526); translation of the *Defense of the Seven Sacraments* by Henry VIII (Strassburg 1522); *Causa helvetica orthodoxae fidei* (Lucerne 1528).

Bibliography: Sbaralea 4.3:132–136. T. VON LIEBENAU, "Documenta quaedam circa vitam Fr. Thomae Murneri O.M. conv.," ArchFrancHist 5 (1912) 727–736; 6 (1913) 118–128. *Bibliographia Franciscana* 6 (1938–39) 477. Wadding S 216. J. LEFFTZ, LexThK² 7:695–697. R. NEWALD, *Elsässische Charakterköpfe aus dem Zeitalter des Humanismus* (Colmar 1944).

[R. J. BARTMAN]

MURPHY, FRANCIS PARNELL, governor of New Hampshire; b. Winchester, N.H., Aug. 16, 1877; d. Nashua, N.H., Dec. 19, 1958. Francis, the son of Patrick E. and Ellen (Lambert) Murphy, was born on a farm. He entered the shoe manufacturing business as a packer and rose through supervisory and managerial posts with the Child Chamberlin Company of Newport, R.I., and its successor, the W. H. McElwain Company, Manchester, N.H. He married Mae Herrick, of Newport, in 1902; they had five children. In 1923, as vice president and director of J. F. McElwain, shoe manufacturers of Nashua, he was one of three partners responsible for the firm, which employed the largest group in the state (4,500 workers).

As a Republican, Murphy was elected to the General Court in 1931 and served as chairman of the Ways and Means Committee. In 1932 he was a delegate to the Republican national convention, and the following year he was elected to the Governor's Council. In 1936 he survived a Democratic landslide in the nation and in the state to become governor for the first of two consecutive terms (1937–40). During his tenure the legislature created the New Hampshire state police and approved an interstate compact for flood control, which was ultimately superseded by the Federal Flood Control Act of 1938. After the hurricane of 1938, which caused damage in New Hampshire estimated at about $50 million, Murphy effectively supported flood control projects in the Merrimack and Connecticut watersheds. In Murphy's second term, the introduction of the merit system for state employees brought New Hampshire's practices in line with Federal requirements for departments receiving Federal aid.

In 1942, 2 years after leaving the governor's office, Murphy ran for the U.S. Senate as a Democrat, but was defeated. Thereafter he retired from public life, but until his death, he remained active in his company.

[F. L. BRODERICK]

MURPHY, FRANK, jurist, public official; b. Harbor Beach, Mich., April 13, 1890; d. Detroit, July 19, 1949. He was the third child of John F. and Mary (Brennan) Murphy, and was educated at local public schools and at the University of Michigan, where he received an A.B. and LL.B. in 1912 and 1914 respectively. He taught at the Detroit College of Law until World War I, during which he served as lieutenant and captain with the 4th and 85th Infantry Divisions in France. After brief service with the Army of Occupation in the Rhineland, Murphy sought further legal training at Lincoln's Inn, London, and at Trinity College, Dublin.

He reestablished himself in Detroit by 1919, and became chief assistant to the U.S. District Attorney for that city. He taught law at the University of Detroit from 1922 to 1927. As a Democratic candidate, Murphy was elected judge of the Recorders' Court in Detroit in 1923. His first term was followed by reelection, then by two successive terms as mayor of the city. President Franklin D. Roosevelt named him Governor General of the Philippine Islands (1933–35) and High Commissioner (1935–36) when the Islands became autonomous. In 1936 he was elected governor of Michigan, and served during one of the most trying periods of industrial agitation in that state's history. His handling of the sit-down strikes in Flint earned him national recognition; his refusal to disregard either property rights or human interests brought both censure and applause, but later judgment generally approved his stand.

He was named U.S. attorney general by President Roosevelt in 1939; while serving in this office he inaugurated an administrative law study and set up a civil rights division, adding materially to the strength of the Department of Justice. In 1940, Roosevelt appointed Murphy to the Supreme Court, where he served until his death. As associate justice, he joined the liberals on the bench. His opinions, described as subordinating strict precedent to an altogether human ideal of justice, were especially eloquent in civil rights cases and in those involving federal-state relationships. Never married, Murphy was sometimes described as combining an active political and social career with the private life of an ascetic.

Bibliography: T. W. ARNOLD, "Mr. Justice Murphy," *Harvard Law Review* 63 (1949) 289–293. E. GRESSMAN, "Mr. Justice Murphy: A Preliminary Appraisal," *Columbia Law Review* 50 (1950) 29–47; "Mr. Justice Murphy," *Michigan Law Review* 48 (1950) 742–744. J. P. FRANK, "Justice Murphy: The Goals Attempted," *Yale Law Journal* 59 (1949) 1–26.

[M. C. KLINKHAMER]

MURPHY, JOHN, spiritual director, preacher; b. Dublin, Dec. 29, 1710; d. Dublin, July 3, 1753. He was the son of Bryan Murphy, tallow chandler of Thomas Street, Dublin, and Alice McMahon. Bryan, deprived of his father by the Williamite wars, through apprenticeship had been brought up a Presbyterian, but returned to the Church on his deathbed. John showed early promise, was sent to Santiago in 1727, and then went to Salamanca, where his brilliance, linguistic ability, and ascetic spirit made a notable impression. Ill health compelled his return to Dublin, where he was ordained. His priestly ministry was remarkable for charity, preaching that attracted many non-Catholics, and extraordinary influence with the crowds in a time of many riots. Tireless in counteracting the effects of the Charter Schools, in providing for orphans, in caring for the wayward, he undermined a weak constitution by his unremitting apostolate in Dean Swift's Dublin, coupled with his self-mortification. Though a canon, he remained always an assistant priest in his native parish of St. Catherine. In 1750 he visited Rome to solicit help in the struggle against the Charter Schools and received the D.D. degree. His funeral evoked an extraordinary manifestation of public grief, noted by the Protestant press of the day.

Bibliography: *An Account of the Life . . . of Rev. John Murphy, D.D.* (Dublin 1753).

[J. J. MEAGHER]

MURPHY, JOHN BENJAMIN, one of America's outstanding surgeons; b. near Appleton, Wis., Dec. 21, 1857; d. Mackinac Island, Mich., Aug. 11, 1916. He was educated in Chicago at Rush Medical College and interned at the Cook County Hospital. After 2 years of graduate study in Vienna, Murphy returned to Chicago to begin practice. From 1884 he lectured on surgery at Rush Medical College.

Murphy pioneered in many areas of surgery and won early recognition by the invention of the Murphy button (1892), a mechanical device for making rapid and accurate intestinal and gastrointestinal anastomosis. By indefatigable efforts he became one of America's leading surgeons, one who had worldwide recognition. He studied the surgery of the lungs and nervous system, and, in his later years, he became interested in bone and joint surgery. It was as a teacher, however, that Murphy exerted his greatest influence.

Murphy was deeply religious and scrupulous in his religious obligations. Although invariably kind and courteous, he was associated with numerous controversial events that brought him criticism from the medical profession. Despite this, he was elected president of the American Medical Association (1910). Murphy's most noteworthy works are *General Surgery* (1911) and *The Surgical Clinics of John B. Murphy, M.D., at Mercy Hospital, Chicago* (5 v., 1912–16).

Bibliography: L. E. DAVIS, *J. B. Murphy: Stormy Petrel of Surgery* (New York 1938).

[L. M. ZIMMERMAN]

MURPHY, JOHN JOSEPH

Publisher and printer; b. County Tyrone, Ireland, March 12, 1812; d. Baltimore, Md., May 27, 1880. His parents, Bernard and Mary (McCullough) Murphy, immigrated to Delaware when John was 10. After attending New Castle Academy, Del., he learned printing in Philadelphia and about 1835 moved to Baltimore where he established a book and stationery store. He married Margaret E. O'Donnoghue (1852), who died in 1869; they had seven children. During his publishing career, which began in 1836, he issued 1,458 editions of 817 titles, the peak year being 1860 with 91 imprints. Spiritual reading and devotional works constituted the largest category with 100 entries, the most famous being Cardinal Gibbons's *The Faith of Our Fathers,* which sold more than 2 million copies. As the publisher of documents pertaining to the dogma of the Immaculate Conception he was awarded a papal gold medal in 1855; for the *Acta et Decreta* of the Second Plenary Council of Baltimore (*see* BALTIMORE, COUNCILS OF), he was given the title of "Typographer of the Holy See." In the field of serials, he published the *U.S. Catholic Magazine*

(1842–49), later absorbed by the *Catholic Mirror*. He launched one of the earliest Catholic juveniles, the *Catholic Youth Magazine* (1857–61), and was the publisher (1859–61) of the *Metropolitan Catholic Almanac and Laity's Directory*, begun (1833) as the *U.S. Catholic Almanac*. The Murphy imprint appeared on many speeches, especially of those of congressmen, on five by Jefferson Davis, for example, and on several by Stephen Douglas. For a quarter of a century he published for the Maryland Historical Society of which he was a member. The Murphy firm was dissolved in 1943 and the New York firm of P. J. *Kenedy took over the assets.

[E. P. WILLGING]

MURPHY, WILLIAM MARTIN, founder of Independent Newspapers, Ireland's most important newspaper group; b. Bantry, Ireland, Nov. 21, 1884; d. Dublin, June 26, 1919. Son of Denis Murphy, a building contractor, and Mary (Martin) Murphy, he was educated at Belvedere, the Jesuit college in Dublin (1896–1901). He worked in a Dublin architect's office until his father's death brought him back to Bantry at the age of 20 to manage the family business. His enterprise expanded the scope of the firm, which built churches, schools, and bridges throughout Ireland as well as railways and and tramways in Britain and on the Gold Coast. He became member of Parliament for Dublin and president of the chamber of commerce.

In 1904 he acquired three Dublin daily newspapers and in January 1905 replaced them with the *Irish Independent*. Two years later he launched the *Sunday Independent* and *Evening Herald*. Murphy built up Independent Newspapers through a stormy period of Irish history. He led Dublin employers in a decisive struggle with trade unions, culminating in the 1913 lockout. Three years later the Easter Rebellion left the city ablaze around his office. When bombardment leveled Dublin's center, he purchased a block of ruined buildings and on their site erected his newspaper offices. The outlook of the Murphy newspapers has always been strongly Catholic. While they enjoy a reputation for unbiased reporting of national events, they are also regarded as an influential medium of communication on Catholic affairs in Ireland. Murphy wrote one book, *The Home Rule Act 1914 Exposed* (Dublin 1917).

See also CATHOLIC PRESS, WORLD SURVEY, 14.

Bibliography: J. SWEETMAN, *The Irish Industrial Question* (Dublin 1914). A. WRIGHT, *Disturbed Dublin* (London 1914).

[S. O'HANLON]

MURRAY, DANIEL, archbishop of Dublin; b. near Arklow, County Wicklow, April 18, 1768; d. Dublin, Feb. 26, 1852. After studies at the Irish College in Salamanca, Spain, he was ordained (1792) and then served as a curate in Dublin and Arklow. At the request of the aged Abp. John *Troy of Dublin, Murray was consecrated his coadjutor bishop with the right of succession (1809). A man of gentle manner and moderate views, Murray was active at a critical time for the Church in Ireland. He was president of St. Patrick's College, Maynooth (1812–13). His deep involvement in the veto controversy caused him to visit Rome in 1814 and again in 1815 to oppose granting the British government a veto over Irish ecclesiastical appointments. Largely because of Irish opposition, the veto proposal was dropped. As archbishop of Dublin (1823–

52), Murray devoted much attention to providing schools and hospitals, especially for the poor. With Mary *Aikenhead he founded the Irish Sisters of Charity (1811). Under his patronage Catherine *Mc-

Daniel Murray.

Auley introduced the Sisters of Mercy in Ireland, and Frances *Ball established the Ladies of Loretto in Dublin. Murray encouraged the Irish Christian Brothers to work in his diocese. During the struggle for Catholic *Emancipation, Murray was an active supporter of the Catholic Association. His political views were always Whig rather than nationalist. Usually he avoided political controversy, but he did not hesitate to oppose Daniel *O'Connell during the agitation to repeal Ireland's legislative union with England. Murray cooperated with the government in establishing the Commission for Charitable Donations and Bequests (1844–45), despite O'Connell's opposition. Murray also upheld the government's program for higher education (the so-called godless colleges) against O'Connell, Abp. John Mac-Hale, and the majority of the bishops. Successive British governments sought Murray's advice on matters concerning Catholics.

Bibliography: W. MEAGHER, *Notices of Life and Character of . . . Murray, Late Roman Catholic Archbishop of Dublin . . .* (Dublin 1853). J. T. GILBERT, DNB 13:1249. P. BOYLAN, *Souvenir of the Centenary of the Death of Most Rev. Daniel Murray* (Dublin 1952).

[K. B. NOWLAN]

MURRAY, PATRICK, theologian; b. Clones, County Monaghan, Ireland, Nov. 18, 1811; d. Maynooth, Nov. 15, 1882. He entered Maynooth in 1829 and was elected a Dunboyne scholar, which meant 3 years of graduate study. He was appointed to a chair in theology and occupied it until his death. His major theological work, *De Ecclesia Christi* (3 v. Dublin 1860–66), was long a source book for Catholic controversialists. He was intensely interested in the theological education of the laity and wrote four volumes of *Essays, Chiefly Theological* (Dublin 1850–53) for this purpose. At his death he was prefect of the Dunboyne Establishment, revered for his kindliness as a professor, for his holiness of life and for his intellectual gifts.

Bibliography: D. COGHLAN, CE 10:646–647.

[A. ROCK]

MURRAY, PHILIP, U.S. labor leader; b. Lanarkshire, Scotland, May 25, 1886; d. San Francisco, Calif., Nov. 9, 1952. When he was 16, he and his father, mother, and nine brothers and sisters immigrated to the U.S., settling in a small coal-mining town near Pittsburgh, Pa. He immediately went to work in a local mine as a helper, pursuing his studies at home in the evenings. An argument with a checkweigher led to his discharge from the mine, and he was ordered out of the camp owned by the coal company. His fellow miners rallied to his support and a strike was voted, but hunger forced the miners back to work after little more than a month. Murray, put on a train bound for Pittsburgh, was ordered by company agents not to return. "I never had another doubt as to what I wanted to do with my life," he recalled in later years. He was elected (1912) a member of the executive board of the United Mine Workers of America and became vice president (1920) of the union, serving in that capacity for more than 20 years.

When the drive to unionize the giant steel industry was launched with the help of other, established unions, Murray became chairman (1936) of the vast effort. Within a year and a half after the drive was started, the U.S. Steel Corporation, largest steel firm in the world, agreed to negotiate and sign a wage agreement. Subsequent contracts signed during Murray's lifetime brought substantial wage benefits and security to the steelworkers and their families. He served as president of the new union, the United Steelworkers of America, until his death. Under his leadership 2,500 local unions were founded and the union grew to a maximum strength of 1 million members.

In November 1940 Murray was elected president of the Congress of Industrial Organizations, a post he held until his death. He served on numerous governmental committees under Presidents Franklin D. Roosevelt and Harry S Truman and was regarded as a labor statesman in the truest sense of the word. He believed that most labor problems could be solved by reasonable men around the conference table, where he used effectively his vast knowledge of facts covering the whole field of industry and economics. For him, industrial unionism was the key to permanent economic security for workers. He is buried in a small cemetery on the outskirts of Castle Shannon, Pa., a small mining community where he once worked as a miner.

[G. G. HIGGINS]

MURRAY, THOMAS C., playwright; b. Macroom, County Cork, 1873; d. Dublin, March 7, 1959. He was educated in Cork and at St. Patrick's Training College, Drumcondra, Dublin, and taught in primary schools in Cork and Dublin. He was headmaster of Inchicore Model School from 1915 until retirement in 1943. His reputation rests entirely upon his plays, almost all of them first produced at the Abbey Theatre, Dublin. His first play, *The Wheel of Fortune,* was produced (1909) by the Cork Little Theatre, which Murray had founded with Terence MacSwiney, Con O'Leary, and Daniel *Corkery. Murray's first notable work was *Birthright* (1910), a powerful study of the murderous conflict caused between two brothers on a small farm when the elder is disinherited by his father; this arises from the failure of the father, gnarled and twisted by the land struggle, to realize that the next generation seeks a better life on the land. *Maurice Harte* (1912) is a variation on the same theme and deals with the tragedy

caused by Maurice's parents when, fearful of the disgrace of having a "spoiled priest" in the family, they force him to continue his clerical studies. The next success, *Spring* (1918), handles tragically the theme of

Thomas C. Murray.

rural avarice; *Sovereign Love* (1913) had failed in attempting a comic treatment of the same theme.

Murray's reputation as an Abbey Theatre dramatist perhaps reached its peak with *Autumn Fire* (1924), a full-length tragedy about a hale old farmer, a widower, who marries a young girl and is then incapacitated by an accident. The attraction of the wife for his son and the spiteful gossip of his relatives make him believe the worst; but there is no resolution of the tragedy, beyond the estrangement and suffering of all three.

In these plays and in the one-act tragedy, *The Briary Gap* (1928), in which a young woman, abandoned by her seducer and repelled by a narrow-minded priest, is driven to suicide, Murray is at his best in realistic depiction of Irish rural characters, speaking vivid yet simple dialogue. His other plays do not display the same power and are marred by faults that are present to a slighter degree in these; a tendency toward melodrama, a lack of structural inventiveness, and a certain failure of vitality at moments of crisis. He remains, nevertheless, one of the best realistic dramatists of the Abbey Theatre between 1910 and 1928. "It was a sociological age," wrote A. E. Malone, historian of the Irish Theatre, "and the problems of the social system pressed heavily upon the general mind. . . . The younger playwrights everywhere examined that conscience in the theatre." Murray managed to do this for Ireland while preserving a high sense of artistic integrity. His other plays are *Aftermath* (1922), *The Pipe in the Fields* (1927), *The Blind Wolf* (1928), *A Flutter of Wings* (1929), *Michaelmas Eve* (1932), *A Stag at Bay* (1934), *A Spot in the Sun* (1938), and *Illumination* (1939). *Spring Horizon* (1937) was his only novel.

Bibliography: A. E. MALONE, *The Irish Drama* (London 1929). L. ROBINSON, ed., *The Irish Theatre* (London 1939). **Illustration credit:** courtesy, Cork University Press.

[R. MC HUGH]

MURRAY, THOMAS EDWARD, business executive, inventor, nuclear expert; b. Albany, N.Y., June 20, 1891; d. New York City, May 26, 1961. He received his B.S. in mechanical engineering from Yale

University in 1911. He joined the Metropolitan Engineering Company, of which his father was president, and distinguished himself as an inventor. He received more than 200 patents during his career. After his father's death in 1929, he became president of the company and later board chairman of Thomas E. Murray, Inc., and of Murray Manufacturing Corporation. He was a director and member of the finance committee of the Chrysler Corporation, receiver for the Interborough Rapid Transit Company, and a trustee of the welfare fund of the United Mine Workers, and of several banks. In 1950 he resigned from these positions to become one of the first members of the U.S. Atomic Energy Commission. Murray favored the development of tactical rather than strategic nuclear weapons and urged a program of underground testing. He opposed the emphasis on thermonuclear weapons, and proposed the stockpiling of small weapons as an alternative. He also sought a balanced public-private plan of development of nuclear power for peaceful purposes. A Democrat, Murray, was not reappointed by President Eisenhower at the expiration of his term in 1957. However, he was immediately appointed as a consultant by the Joint Congressional Committee on Atomic Energy, and from that position continued to advocate his program. He received honorary degrees from many universities and colleges. Among his awards were the Stevens Institute medal, the Laetare medal of Notre Dame, the Engineer of the Year medal of the Yale Engineering Association, and the Irish Historical Society medal. He was a fellow of the American Institute of Electrical Engineers, a fellow of the American Society of Mechanical Engineers, a knight of St. Gregory, and a knight of Malta.

[D. E. MARLOWE]

MURRI, ROMOLO, Italian priest, sociologist, politician, publicist, Modernist; b. Montesampietrangeli (Ascoli Piceno), Aug. 27, 1870; d. Rome, March 12, 1944. After ordination (1893) he studied at the University of Rome, founded the Catholic periodical *Vita nuova,* participated in the origins of the Federazione universitaria cattolica italiana, and adhered enthusiastically to the Catholic social movement and to *Christian Democracy (see SOCIAL MOVEMENTS, CATHOLIC, 5). Cultura sociale,* a periodical begun by him in 1898, advocated a new political and social direction for Catholic activity. Soon he came into conflict with the leadership of the Opera dei Congressi and its president, Giambattista Paganuzzi, and guided a group, composed mostly of young persons, that was eager for independence and for predominance in the entire Catholic movement. Murri was unable to reach an understanding even with the second (social) group of the Opera, the one most open and disposed to collaborate, because of the ever more direct intervention of the Holy See in the Catholic social movement during the last years of Leo XIII. The widening of the conflict induced Pius X to suppress the Opera dei Congressi and to reorganize on other bases Italian *Catholic Action. Murri became discontented, partly because he was not placed in charge, and founded the Lega democratica nazionale, condemned by Pius X in 1906. Passing from the political to the doctrinal field, Murri showed himself favorable to philosophico-theological *Modernism, in rebellion against the hierarchy. In 1907 Murri was suspended

a divinis, and in 1909 he was excommunicated. Some of his best disciples then abandoned him. He continued his conflict in the new *Rivista di cultura,* the organ of the Lega democratica nazionale. Turning again to political life, he was elected a deputy (1909) and joined the extreme left. After losing all his political influence, he devoted himself to writing for the liberal press. Murri was a very talented man and a prolific author who could arouse enthusiasm, but who was incapable of directing a movement or collaborating with one. He returned to the Church in 1943.

Bibliography: P. SCOPPOLA, "R. Murri e la prima democrazia cristiana," *Il Mulino* 6 (1957) 99–115; "Il modernismo politico in Italia: La Lega democratica nazionale," in *Rivista storica italiana* 69 (1957) 61–109; *Dal Neoguelfismo alla Democrazia cristiana* (2d ed. Rome 1961); *Crisi modernista e rinnovamento cattolico in Italia* (Bologna 1961). B. BROGI, *La Lega democratica nazionale* (Rome 1959). F. CARAFFA, EncCatt 8:1534–35.

[A. MARTINI]

MUSIC, ARTICLES ON

The scope of the articles on music in this encyclopedia embraces the relation of music to religion and worship and the historical manner in which music has entered the life of the Church. Religious music itself, although not always forming a part of church worship, is included on the ground that it also arises from man's desire to express musically some aspect of his religious beliefs. Articles on specifically religious forms, such as sequences, oratorio, responsory, antiphon, motet, *organum, falso bordone,* and spirituals, are included; but no general coverage of music as a science and an art is intended. Technical information on the elements of music (harmony, rhythm, counterpoint, for example) must be sought in standard music reference works.

The composers and music scholars accorded individual biographies were selected according to the following criteria: (1) those who wrote specifically for Church services; (2) those who wrote religious music regardless of their religious beliefs; (3) those who influenced the history of church music by their teachings and writings; and (4) Catholics who contributed significantly to general music history or repertory. It will be noticed that the first three are musicoliturgical categories, and the fourth, historical. In this purview not all composers who were baptized Catholics were selected, and space limitations did not permit inclusion of all important Protestant or non-Catholic composers since the Reformation. Because of the nature of the encyclopedia, special emphasis is placed on the sacred music of those composers who, like Mozart, F. J. Haydn, or J. S. Bach, wrote in all media and genre.

The relation between man's aesthetic nature and his religious sensitivities is treated in three general articles: MUSIC (PHILOSOPHY), which lays the aesthetic basis for the discussion; MUSIC AND RELIGION, which treats of the role of music in a worshiping group; and MUSIC, SACRED, which examines the specific problem of the relation between music and Christian worship. MUSIC, SACRED, HISTORY OF may be considered the central music article in the encyclopedia since it surveys the development of church music in its classic chronological phases. Several of the more important aspects of this complicated problem are singled out for more extended treatment in particular articles, such as: MUSIC, SACRED, LEGISLATION ON; MUSIC EDUCATION IN THE U.S.; GREGORIAN CHANT; CAECILIAN MOVEMENT; MASS, ROMAN,

MUSIC OF; DIVINE OFFICE, ROMAN, CHANTS OF; ORGAN; ORGAN MUSIC; CHOIR; CHOIR MUSIC; HYMNS AND HYMNALS. The music of each of the Western rites—Mozarabic, Milanese (Ambrosian), and Gallican—is treated separately; and BYZANTINE RITE, CHANTS OF, and MUSIC, HEBREW, describe two important non-Western traditions. MUSIC, SACRED (U.S.); MUSIC, SACRED (CANADA); and LATIN AMERICA, MUSIC IN, chronicle the development of church music in specific areas that could not be treated fully in the general survey article.

The great advances in musicology, especially in the uncovering of new information on the history of music in the Middle Ages and the Renaissance and in the continued reappraisal of the known sources, have opened up fresh areas for sacred music scholarship and brought to light new treasures in the Church's musical heritage. The emergence of the discipline of ethnomusicology, with its current concentration on primitive and non- or para-Christian musical folkways, has yielded scientific certitudes for untutored assumptions in still more recondite research regions. Thus, an encyclopedia published in the mid-20th century has obvious advantages over previous works of reference. The very range of its resources, however, necessitates a judicious selection of materials and a rigid limitation on the wordage available for each topic. The music bibliographies, prepared with a view to representing both the author's authority and the reader's requirements (and, in the case of early composers, modern editions, if available, of his works), resolve the impasse between the claims of breadth and the claims of depth.

[R. G. WEAKLAND]

MUSIC (PHILOSOPHY)

Initially music (Lat. *musica,* Gr. μουσική [τέχνη]) was employed in a broad sense to signify any human art over which the nine Muses presided. It was then gradually restricted in meaning to signify the fine art of combining vocal and instrumental sounds into rhythmic, melodic, and harmonic structure. It is generally regarded as the most moving emotionally of all the arts. Since the concern of philosophers with music is summarized in their attempts to arrive at ever more precise

Detail from "Parnassus," a fresco completed by Raphael in 1510 in the Stanza della Segnatura, the Vatican Palace, showing Apollo, as the symbol of music, surrounded by the Muses and playing the viola da braccio.

definitions, this article explores in a summary fashion the positions of a number of philosophers on the nature of music.

Greek Thought. Among available documents, the fragments of the Pythagoreans are the oldest. Their principal interest in music was to discern the mysterious role of number in the physicomathematical order. By means of this investigation, they discovered three important truths about music: (1) tonal intervals can be described by fixed numerical relations; (2) harmony is produced by contraries (namely, high and low sounds); and (3) an analogy exists between geometric and musical harmony inasmuch as (*a*) musical harmony has a continuity similar to the continuity of various geometric figures and solids, and (*b*) musical harmonies can involve inverted proportions. (*See* PYTHAGORAS AND PYTHAGOREANS.)

Plato. The divine origin of harmony and rhythm was emphasized by *Plato. Thus God has produced in man the natural inclination to produce harmony and rhythm, not at random, but ultimately in imitation of spiritual harmony (*Ion* 534D, E). Mathematics, according to Plato, is of considerable help in making a clear delineation of rhythms and harmonies (*Rep.* 400). In the *Laws* (812C), he describes music as "the movement of melodies imitating the soul agitated by the passions."

Aristotle. In general, *Aristotle accepts what his predecessors have said about music (*Pol.* 1340a 14–19; 1340b 5–10; 1341b 8–15, 23–40). In his extended consideration of music in the *Politics* (1339a 11–1342b 33), he discusses the role of music in the education of youth, and in this context manifests certain formalities about music not previously recognized or made explicit. Aristotle agrees with the common view that music imitates the movement of human emotions (*Poet.* 1447a 20–25; *Pol.* 1340a 19–1340b 10). But since human emotions are related to human action, music imitates artistically human action as well, and therefore should first be examined in a general consideration of all the arts (*Poet.* 1447a 14–17).

In the extant writings of Aristotle there is not much treatment of music distinctively as an art form. In some agreement with Plato, Aristotle recognizes that the formal principles for disposing musical matter are derived from mathematics; arithmetic provides number, which ensures proportion within and among rhythms and harmonies, and geometry serves as the foundation for conceiving and achieving musical coherence (cf. *Phys.* 194a 8; *Meta.* 1004a 6–8). Because of this special relation between music and mathematics, music is a distinct science and art (*Anal. post.* 76a 9–15, 23–25). Yet music has something in common with the arts of epic, tragedy, comedy, dithryambic poetry, dancing, and painting (*Poet.* 1447a 20–1447b 15; 1448a 1–18; 1449a 1–12). From the general science of poetics, music derives the distinction of meters and their capacity for mutual order with a view to signifying epic, tragic, or comic action (*ibid.*). In this way, music can be understood to signify the order of human emotions as related particularly to these three types of action.

Since man is naturally inclined to be iambic in speech, Aristotle maintains that the iamb is the natural meter (*ibid.* 1449a 24–27). The external use of the iamb, however, is traceable to the human inclination to resolve problems; and the iamb contains the sign of indecisiveness (the "arsis" or light measure) as its first part, the sign of decisiveness (the "thesis" or weighty measure) as its second part. Thus iambic music, or music wherein the iamb is the architectonic and regulating meter, is especially apt to help man develop his natural propensity to speak and move decisively, and, indirectly, to judge decisively (*Pol.* 1340a 16–19; 1340a 40–1340b 14; 1341a 3–9).

Aristotle goes on to discuss the musical "modes," which are established by the proportion of harmony to rhythm (*Pol.* 1341a 17–1342b 17). Thus the Doric mode is the best for the training of young persons because the Doric harmonies have the best proportion to iambic meter, whereas the proportion of the Lydian harmonies to the iamb is not very clear and is, therefore, more suitable for very young children and elderly persons (*Pol.* 1342a 1–1342b 30).

Plotinus and the Prescholastic Tradition. *Plotinus starts his examination of music by observing that its ulterior purpose is to bear the listener beyond nature, to the highest beauty, whereby the soul, being beautified, becomes like God (*Enneads* 1.6.6). More generally, however (and here Plotinus makes explicit a truth generally presupposed in Aristotle's discussions), music has the poetic purpose of making man attentive to some truth that should be examined (*ibid.* 4.4.40). This it accomplishes by binding his irrational appetites. As regards the signification of the meters, Plotinus notes that the art concerning sounds is analogous to "intelligible rhythm" (*ibid.* 5.9.11).

The contributions of St. *Augustine to traditional doctrine on music are considerable. Observing the proportion between musical continuity and the muscular control exercised by the singer, he describes music as "the science of good modulation." Since this proportion has a similar effect upon the listener, he goes on to say that music is the science moving man "by the preserved dimensions of tempi and intervals" (*Musica* 1.2–3). On the basis of the foregoing, music is a principle whereby man can know, analogously, the harmony of God's government (*Epist.* 166.5.13); and, from the knowledge of the immutable numbers in music, one can analogize to immutable Truth (*Musica* 6; *Retract.* 1.11).

In addition to his extensive consideration of the relation between mathematics and music, *Boethius distinguishes three types of music: (1) mundane, found especially in the phenomena of the heavens; (2) human, which gives the incorporeal vivacity of reason to the body and reconciles the rational and irrational parts of the soul; and (3) that which enables instruments to serve melody (*De instit. mus.* 1.2). According to his description of "human" music, then, one purpose of music is to counteract sluggishness in the body and its faculties (*ibid.* 5.2).

Whether Boethius arrived at this conclusion on his own or because of his close friendship with *Cassiodorus is hard to discern. One of the best read and most extensive writers on music during the early Middle Ages, Cassiodorus was more interested in proportion and harmony as achieved in musical works than under their strictly mathematical aspects. He describes music as "the discipline which examines the differences and accords among mutually congruous things, that is, sounds" (*Comm. in Ps.* 97). The suggested analogous supposition of the term "sounds" is confirmed by his tenet that sonorous music is the symbol of all physical and moral harmony (*Epist. ad Boeth.*). This harmony is readily discerned in the first-accomplished, although nonprimary, effect of music, namely, pleasure in the experience of bodily well-being and of the soul's love for the body. Indeed, there is a mysterious bond between musical pleasure and supreme happiness, because aesthetic joy is a symbol of happiness in heaven; the satisfaction of the soul in music is especially analogous to the beatific vision because of the similarity in the respective effortless acts of the intellect (*De anima* 12).

Within its own scope, music frees man from the cares of life, distracts him from his occupations and preoccupations, and raises him to fully interesting activities (*Epist. ad Boeth.*). Cassiodorus held that, by promoting fortitude, the Dorian mode promotes also modesty and chastity. By the use of harmonies of a range lower than those employed by the Greeks, the Phrygian mode can animate the soul to fight against evil, while the Lydian mode comforts the person who feels defeated (*ibid.*). According to Cassiodorus there are three parts of music, namely, harmony, rhythm, and meter (*ibid.*). Vocal music should observe the notes, pauses, accents, pedal melody, and "composition" of the phrase (*ibid.*). Finally, he mentions the fact that natural overtones and natural undertones are contained in the human voice as focused on distinct mid-range tones, and that this fact constitutes the basic meaning of "symphony" (or "sounding together").

High Scholasticism and Grosseteste. Most of St. *Albert the Great's important observations on music are contained in his *Commentary on Aristotle's Politics* (bk. 8). In addition to his many references to Aristotle's doctrine on music, St. *Thomas Aquinas made a theological application of the Aristotelian summation, with further analyses, in his *Commentary on Psalm 32*.

The coherence of the tradition concerning music up to and including Aquinas is rather clear. *Robert Grosseteste, however, introduced a subtle confusion that served to obscure this solid tradition for at least 6 centuries. As summarized by De Bruyne (*Études d'Esthétique médiévale* 3:139–148), Grosseteste teaches that there are five fundamental proportionalities, identically repeated in a whole, from which is derived "all beauty, that is, all 'concord,' whatever the magnitudes may be." This fundamental, universal, metaphysical principle is as true of plastic beauty as it is of sonic beauty (*De luce* 59). The five proportionalities are at the basis of harmony in the musical arts: music, dancing, and poetry (*ibid.*). Both sonic and visible forms can be represented by simple figures (*De gen. sonorum* 8). All these forms are reduced to movements, which can be measured and ordered according to the principles of spatial proportionality, as well as by time measures (*De artibus liberalibus* 2). One and the same discipline concerns the proportions in singing and in the movements of the body (*ibid.* 3). All artistic compositions, however, are regulated by the number 10 and the simple relations that it contains, and the ethical effects of music are based upon the concordance between the proportionality in the soul and the proportionality of sensible nature (*ibid.*).

*Thomas of York and *Roger Bacon extend Grosseteste's position, Bacon holding that music is the fundamental art, since, without it, grammar and the other arts of the trivium cannot possibly be learned with any thoroughness (*Opus majus* 4).

Here one has an attempted philosophical justification of formalistic music, that is, music without pulsation (or genuine modulation). The truths partially contained in Grosseteste's position are that the proportions established by number do regulate artistic production; that geometry is a discipline that enables the artist to establish coherence (taken in its full analogous meaning) in the work he produces; and that what is directly imitated is natural movement (especially human motion). But by reducing all these truths to mathematical proportions, Grosseteste tends to destroy the hierarchy of artistic signification.

Renaissance and Modern Developments. A reaction against this position was manifested early in the *Renaissance by M. *Ficino, who held that "love is the master of all the arts," including music. Later G. *Vico taught that, like poetry, music has divine and heroic characteristics; it is the expression of "the most violent passions of the nascent human race," and that, therefore, music is the first expression of man, coming before words and the reflections of the "pure mind" (*Scienza nuova*). Apparently, then, Vico was restoring the analogous signification of music; yet his dialectical language prevents one from establishing this point with certainty. He arrived at Roger Bacon's cited position, yet based upon another principle.

For G. W. *Leibniz, music is "a hidden arithmetical exercise of the mind not knowing how to number itself" (*Epist.* 154). According to Immanuel *Kant, music is "a charming game concerned with the sensations of hearing" (*The Critique of Judgment* 1). He doubts whether it is truly an art, since it is "the pleasure which culture incites [the game of thoughts being the effect of a quasi-mechanical association] and, judged by reason, it has less value than any of the other *beaux-arts*" (*ibid.*). Finally, music is "a continuous commotion and excitation of the soul" (*ibid.*).

Friedrich *Schlegel seems to revive Vico's position by holding that, since music expresses the most profound sentiments, it is analogous to philosophy. Arthur *Schopenhauer expands this doctrine by teaching that music has an absolute primacy over the other arts because of its inconfutably metaphysical character. Unlike the other arts, music represents the will, rather than ideas. It is an immediate objectivization. Richard *Wagner rejects Schopenhauer's conclusions, but agrees with him in his general position that music manifests the profound essence of things, especially the tragic aspect of human existence. Friedrich *Nietzsche carries the implicit pessimism of these tenets to its logical extreme by holding that, since music is a Dionysian rather than a plastic-Apollinean art, it is concerned with the world of drunkenness and dreaming.

Recognizing that the foregoing positions involve almost a complete denial of music as a discipline, Eduard Hanslick maintains that the expression of sentiments does not constitute the content of music, and that specifically musical beauty consists only in sounds and their artistic arrangement. Paul Hindemith and Igor Stravinsky have espoused Hanslick's theory as accenting the most important aspect in the act of composing.

The Nature of Music. As is evident from the foregoing, direct contributions to an essential definition of music seem to have ended with the propagation of Grosseteste's ultimate reduction of music to mathematics. From his predecessors, however, one can glean its basic elements and say that music is the art which, through the use of modulation and the mathematical delineation of rhythms and harmonies (and, possibly, with the aid of established modes), imitates human emotions as engaged in epic or dramatic action, with the direct aim of recreational contemplation, which indirectly promotes man in the moral good. This definition corresponds with the general position taken by critics and others on the nature of music.

Mention should finally be made of scholars and composers who have developed the science of music under its mathematical and acoustical aspects. In fact, a knowledge of this development, together with a thorough acquaintance with the works representing the whole history of music, and a knowledge of contemporary acoustical research, are all needed for a full appreciation of the philosophical tradition concerned with this subject.

See also ART (PHILOSOPHY); LIBERAL ARTS; MUSIC, SACRED; MUSIC AND RELIGION; MUSIC EDUCATION IN THE U.S.

Bibliography: J. PORTNOY, *The Philosopher and Music: A Historical Outline* (New York 1955). E. DE BRUYNE, *Études d'esthétique médiévale*, 3 v. (Bruges 1946). A. M. MOSCHETTI, Enc Fil 3:770–779. Eisler 2:190–191. W. D. ALLEN, *Philosophies of Music History* (New York 1939, repr. 1962). *History of Music in Sound*, ed. G. ABRAHAM et al., 10 v. (New York 1953–59). O. THOMPSON, ed., *The International Cyclopedia of Music and Musicians*, rev. N. SLONIMSKY (5th ed. New York 1949). **Illustration credit:** Alinari-Art Reference Bureau.

[F. C. LEHNER]

MUSIC, HEBREW

The present article deals primarily with Hebrew music in Biblical times, and its ancient liturgical use as seen in the light of discoveries made in the first half of the 20th century. But it covers also the history of Hebrew music in its liturgical aspect from antiquity to the present time.

HEBREW MUSIC OF BIBLICAL TIMES

The main source of knowledge about Hebrew music, the "Musica Hebraeorum," is the Old Testament. The interpretation of the Biblical texts remained hypothetical until modern times, and there was a tacit consensus that one had to rely entirely upon the scanty Biblical passages that mentioned the use of musical instruments. A great deal of guesswork had been accumulated concerning the ancient Hebrew names for musical instruments, and the study of Biblical music remained the exclusive domain of theologians and linguists.

Musical Instruments Known from Archeology. A new era of paleo-musical research was inaugurated with modern archeology, which brought to light some well-preserved musical instruments of antiquity, such as the famous lyres and oboes of Ur (Mesopotamia), the trumpets of the tomb of Tut-ankh-Amon (Egypt), and the αὐλοί (oboes) of Greece, besides a large number of pictorial representations or sculptures of ancient musical instruments. Although the civilizations of Mesopotamia, Egypt, and Greece were situated at the outer radius of the Land of the Bible, their musical instruments and the modes of playing them could not always be considered representative for the descriptions given in the OT. The soil of ancient Palestine was generally considered void of pictorial or archeological evidence of musical instruments because of the Hebrew law prohibiting pictorial art. A recent inventory by Bathyah Bayer (see bibliog.) provides some reliable information on this point. Based

Fig. 1. Hebrew captives from Lachish playing lyres, fragment of an alabaster relief from the palace of Sennacherib at Nineveh, 7th century B.C.

HEBREW MUSIC

Fig. 2. Bronze oil lamp excavated in Israel, with a decorative handle showing a lulav, a menorah, and a shofar, 4th century A.D.

Fig. 3. Final page of Johann Reuchlin's book "De accentibus et orthographia linguae hebraicae," published in 1518. The page shows three of the Hebrew reading accents (Yatiw, Pasiq, Legarme) with the musical motives in a 4-part setting by Johann Böschenstein. It is the first melodic transcription of the Hebrew accents according to the Azkenasic use.

on the excavation reports of Greater Canaan (Palestine, Transjordan, Syria, and Lebanon) published since mid-19th century, Bayer's work lists no less than 280 archeological items, among them about 130 actual sound instruments, mostly clappers, bells, and bone tubes (flutes), and also an ivory horn and a conch horn. The number of items has already been increased since the latest excavations in Israel (1964). Modest as they are, these findings (e.g., the *Bar Kokhba coins from 132–135 with lyres and trumpets, hitherto the earliest pictorial evidence) help to widen the musical path into antiquity from the 2d Christian century back to the 19th century B.C. and allow a comparison of these artifacts with the literary records of the corresponding periods in the OT. The rest of the evidence is supplied by a third source, namely the still living folk traditions of the Near East, which, thanks to their static nature, may reflect the actual style of music in the distant past and thus furnish a clue to many a buried treasure. Equipped with recently developed research methods of modern ethnomusicology, one may probably find added significance in the often-quoted Biblical texts and thus reconstruct a more lifelike picture of ancient Hebrew music.

The instances of musical documentation are, however, few and disconnected in time and space. Some forms of worship are mentioned, related to musical traditions (e.g., the postexilic Temple service, idealized as going back to David and Solomon), as well as numerous names of instruments, and some incidence of liturgical singing and ritual dancing. Even some actual songs are interspersed in the books of the OT, such as the song of Lamech (Gn 4.23–24), the Song of the Well (Nm 21.17–18), the Song of the Red Sea (Ex 15.2–18; *see* MOSES, CANTICLE OF), the Song of Debora (Judges ch. 5; *see* DEBORA, CANTICLE OF), and David's Lament (2 Sm 1.19–27).

Musical Instruments of the Bible. The first Biblical mention of music, in Gn 4.21, which provides a rough classification of musical instruments into stringed and (reed-) wind instruments, states that Jubal was "the forerunner of all who play the harp (*kinnôr*) and the pipes (*'ûgāb*)." In addition Jubal's proper name itself indicates a third group of instruments, i.e., the natural horns of animals such as the ram's horn (*šôpār*), called also *yôbēl* or *qeren*. In the later books of the Bible, three categories of musical instruments are associated with three classes of citizens: (1) the priests, or *kōhǎnîm*, entitled to blow the horns and trumpets; (2) the professional Temple musicians or Levites, playing the lyre (*kinnôr*) and harp (*nēbel*); and (3) the folk (Israel) using the reed pipes and flutes (*ḥālîl*). These instruments were supplemented by self-sounding bronze gongs or cymbals (*ṣilṣāl*) and bells (*pa'ǎmôn*), which, because of their magical connotations, were used only by the highest Temple officials within their caste (Ex 28.35–36; 1 Chr 16.5). The Biblical drum (*tōp*), mentioned in Gn 31.27, is often associated with female societies and their ritual dances (Jgs 11.34) and with the prophets of the local altars of sacrifice, the "*high places" (1 Sm 10.5). Women also had their special forms of antiphonal singing in two alternating groups (Jgs 5.11; 11.40).

Of the ancient triad of instruments, i.e., *kinnôr*, *'ûgāb*, and *šôpār*, only the *šôpār* survived from Jewish antiquity (in the New Year and Atonement services of the synagogue). The lyres and harps have continued to live

in the memory of mankind as the sublime sound symbols of the Davidic Psalter and of the splendor of the traditional Salomonic Temple orchestras (1 Chr 15.16), whereas the folk instruments—the pipes and flutes—held their place in paraliturgical ceremonies, popular feasts, and processions (1 Sm 10.5). The traditional names of these wind instruments, given (in the *Talmud) as, *'ûgāb, ḥālîl, magrēpâ*, and *'ǎbûbā'*, were used sporadically from earliest Biblical times to the later Talmudic period and may have been representative for quite distinctive classes of musical wind instruments.

Shofar. The sound of the shofar (*šôpār*, ram's horn), shrouded in mystery and strong symbolism and connected primarily with the sacrifice of Isaac (Gn 22.13) and his redemption through the appearance of the ram, is perpetuated in the sound of its horn. Its magical quality is behind the events of Mt. Sinai (Ex 19.6–19), of the fall of Jericho's walls (Jos 6.4, 5, 20), Gedeon's battle (Jgs 7.16), and the procession with the ark of the covenant (2 Samuel ch 6). In Nm 10.1–10 the silver trumpet (*ḥǎṣôṣᵉrâ*) makes its appearance in competition with the natural horn and reaches a temporary significance at the magnificent Temple services in the time of the monarchy (2 Chr 5.12–13).

Stringed Instruments. The Biblical *kinnôr* is neither a harp nor a violin but a lyre of Assyrian origin, with an irregular trapezoid shape. It developed into the chief Temple instrument of the monarchical period, and its use spread northward through the Syrian provinces into Greek-speaking lands, where it was known as the λύρα or κιθάρα. Its sister instrument, the *nēbel* (harp), with its bowed or triangular shape and open frame, penetrated southward from the Assyrian homeland into Egypt and East Asia. Both *kinnôr* and *nēbel* are frequently mentioned in the OT, (*kinnôr*, 42 times; *nēbel*, 27 times), mostly as the noble attributes of the Levite guild of Temple musicians. The lyre called *'āśôr* (10-stringed), as mentioned in Ps 32(33).2; 91(92).4 and 143 (144).9 is the *Psalterium decacordum* of St. Jerome's letter to Dardanus. The stringed instruments called *sabkā', pᵉsantērîn*, and *qîtrôs* in Dn 3.5, 7, 10, 15 may have been ancient Hebrew forms of lyre and harp to which Greek-Aramaic names were given.

Wind Instruments of Bamboo (Cane, Reed). These instruments, like flutes and pipes, originated in the peasant culture of Western Asia, where they are still played, apparently without major changes in material or design. Several designations are known: *'ûgāb*, for the nomadic period; *ḥālîl*, for the Kings' and Prophets' period; and *'ǎbûbā'*, for the Talmudic period. Unfortunately, the Biblical sources do not allow a more precise classification of these names according to the flute, clarinet, or oboe families of wood-wind instruments. Yet, with the help of archeological evidence, it may now be safely stated that all three types had been in use since nomadic times; such basic materials as cane, bone, or clay were employed in their construction. Excavated specimens indicate that their earliest forms vary between those of whistles with a central hole—sometimes in an anthropomorphic outline—and the more musical structures of single tubes or of a pair of pipes with two or more fingerholes. Occasional details, such as the conical or cylindrical shape of the tube, a notched or bell-like mouthpiece, or the number and distribution of finger holes, may contribute to a more precise classification. In addition, the post-Biblical names of the so-

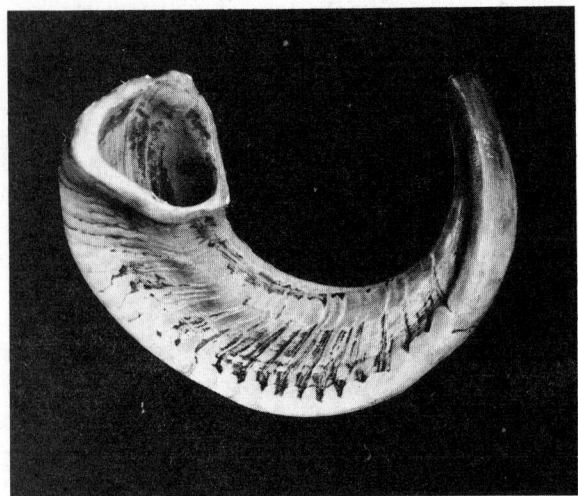

Fig. 4. A 20th-century ram's horn shofar.

called organ of the Orient, the *magrēpâ,* and the *hirdô-lîn* (the Greek ὕδραυλις, water organ), as mentioned in the Talmudic treatise 'Arakhin (10–11), as well as the *Sumpônyâ* (bagpipe or panpipe?) of Dn 3.5, 10, 15, may be included here.

LITURGICAL SONG

The evolution of Jewish liturgy reflects the major events of Biblical history. According to Lv 9.22, Aaron offered the various sacrifices that are described in the postexilic priestly writing. During all phases of these preexilic periods the folk preferred the decentralized form of natural stages on the peaks of mountains, consecrated to local deities and administered by groups of folk prophets. As a part of their profession, the prophets employed small instrumental bands with such instruments as harp, drum, flute, and lyre, as described in 1 Sm 10.5–6. The role of music as a means of prophetic inspiration may be gathered from Samuel's words to Saul that, under the influence of sound, the prophets would start to prophesy and Saul together with them, and that he would "be turned into another man."

Temple and Synagogue. According to the Book of Chronicles, which represents postexilic thought, a great change took place through the unification of worship in the Temple of Solomon (*c.* 962–922 B.C.). Here cultic action which set minute regulations for the divine service required a thorough organization of the Temple musicians (Levites), and included a professional music school. At that time the Psalter already served as the base of the musical liturgy, which was performed by magnificent choirs and massive orchestras of harps and lyres (2 Chr 15.17–24; 16.4–43). After the Babylonian exile (587–538 B.C.) new spiritual forces that were then at work were associated with Ezechiel and Nehemia, but chiefly with Ezra the Scribe. The power of the Book began to make itself felt against animal sacrifices; the idea of individual prayer, study, and meditation replaced the former ritualistic convention. Ezra's introduction of weekly public readings from the Scriptures was a departure of great significance, for it helped to develop the melodious recitation of the Biblical texts and with it the whole system of reading accents—the Bible cantillation. The practice also invited the active partici-

pation of the layman and eventually led to the foundation of small houses of assembly, or *synagogues; these gradually developed into new centers of worship in a growing antagonism toward the Temple service. In these small synagogues the final transformation of sacrifice into prayer took place; prayers were then recited at corresponding hours around the day, with added commentaries, psalms, supplications, and benedictions—an order that since then has been at the base of the liturgical life of both the Jewish *Diaspora and early Christianity. Here also are the common roots of their respective musical forms of liturgy. These forms developed in three directions: psalmody, lesson, and prayer (i.e., the chanting of the lyrical parts of the OT, e.g., Psalms, Job, and Proverbs, the reading of the prose parts of the OT, and the singing of the post-Biblical hymns and prayer songs). From these practices the chant of the Diaspora synagogue took its start, as did Gregorian chant (*see* JEWISH LITURGY).

Psalmody. The litanylike chanting of the Psalms was closely shaped to their literary form of parallel half-verses displaying two versions of one poetic image; e.g., "The heavens declare the glory of God, / and the firmament proclaims his handiwork" [Ps 18(19).1]. Following this poetical double-structure, the melodic formula was organized around a central tone line that was broken up only to mark the syntactical points of the sentence—the opening, middle and ending—with small melodic flourishes. Performance was antiphonal or responsorial, in various degrees of combinations. The Psalm formulas were adapted also for the Biblical books written in plain prose and were accordingly enlarged to fit the irregular prose sentences. This system of ecphonetic accents was eventually accepted by early Christianity for the chanting of psalmody and lesson; thus the system was perpetuated with the start of Gregorian and Byzantine chant and the history of Western music.

Scriptural Lesson. The reading of the Biblical prose necessitated a more elaborate system of reading accents in neumatic notation that would represent punctuation and melodic formulas at the same time. Three chief schools of Hebrew grammarians, the Masoretes (*see* MASORA), worked on the critical edition of the OT, beginning *c.* A.D. 500 (completion of the Talmud) with the older Palestinian school. The work continued with the eastern (Babylonian) school, and culminated in the western (Tiberian) school system as laid down in the codex of Aaron *ben Asher (A.D. 895). In this final version the accents were organized in groups of disjunctive and conjunctive types, i.e., in *reges* and *servi,* spinning a dense net of interwoven motifs over the literary texts. When the system of Tiberias came into practice, the Jews in the Diaspora countries were already reorganized into major geographical zones represented mainly by the Oriental communities (Yemen, Irak, Iran, etc.), the Spanish (Sephardic) Jews of the Mediterranean countries, and the central European (Ashkenazic) communities. The latest doctrine was not accepted equally at all the distant points of dispersed Jewry. This fact accounts, *inter alia,* for the great variety of musical dialects observable in the present forms of Bible cantillation. Strangely enough, it seems that the most distant communities in western Europe have best preserved the elaborate Tiberian system, as can be seen in the early musical notation of Bible accents in the Hebrew grammars of the humanists J. *Reuchlin (1518) and S. *Münster (1524). The Oriental and Sephardic communities reveal a closer relation to the older Babylonian system of cantillation. In various ways, both have adapted their original melody to the Arabic or Persian song and ornamental technique prevailing in their host countries.

The performance of these reading accents (*ta 'ămēhammiqrā'*) was in the hands of a nonprofessional representative of the congregation, the *še'lîah-ṣibbûr.* Responses, when required, were sung not by a special choir but by the entire congregation. The potential participation of everyone (except women) may account for the general knowledge of the Biblical and prayer literature, of their tunes and liturgical functions, possessed by Jews all over the world, and this has constituted an important means of perpetuating their musical traditions.

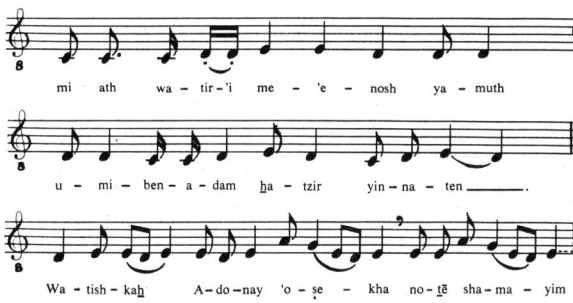

Prayer Tunes. The beginnings of Hebrew hymnody date back to the 6th century (Jose ben Jose) and reach a first peak with the poet Eleazar Kalir (*c.* 750, in Palestine). These hymns and prayers (*piyyuṭim*) formed the basis of the newer cantoral music in the synagogue. They also necessitated a professional performer, the cantor (*ḥazzān*). The creative periods of Hebrew poetry were centered in Moorish Spain of the 11th and 12th centuries, with poets such as *Judah ben Samuel ha-Levi, Abraham and Moses *Ibn Ezra, and Ibn Gabirol (*Avicebron); in the 16th-century Cabalistic school (*see* CABALA) of Safed (Upper Galilee), with such poets as Solomon Alkabetz, Isaac *Luria, and the great Israel Nadjara (1555–1628; his song book *Zemirot Yisrael,* Venice 1599). Finally, in the 18th century, one finds the renewed Cabalistic movement of *Ḥasidism. It took its start in southern Russia and had as its founder the Baal Shem-Tov (d. 1760), whose teachings revitalized Jewish thought, poetry, and song and continue to influence them.

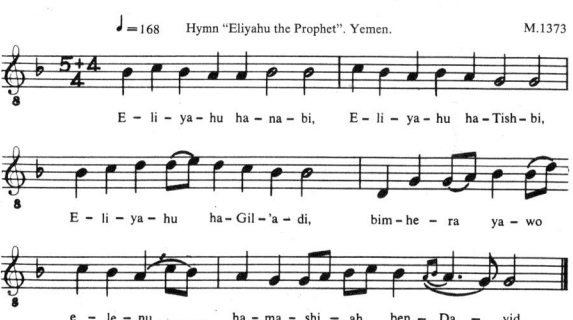

Meanwhile, the *ḥazzān* or *cantor in synagogue service, as the soloist performer of the prayer tunes, had developed an individual singing style, a richly ornamented melody based on the expressive vocal technique of improvisation—an old Oriental heritage. Here are to be found the roots of the ecstatic songs without words (*niggûnîm*) which are connected with the mystic religious movement of Ḥasidism. Whereas in the Mediterranean countries Jewish song had absorbed much of the Arabic technique of *maqām* improvisation, Jewry in eastern Europe developed its own form of model melodies, or *Steiger* (e.g., *Ahava rabba, Adon malakh*), which have since served as sources for innumerable variants of cantoral melodies. In the so-called Mi-Sinai songs, snatches of ancient Hebrew melodies are interwoven with more recent ones and serve as remembrance motifs of the Sinai homeland.

Medieval Writings on Jewish Music. The medieval literature on Jewish music starts with *Sa'adia Gaon

(892–942). In his *Kitāb al-amanāt* (Bagdad 933) he presented new aspects of the ancient Greek doctrine of rhythm as an ethical value. Of the Spanish-Jewish school of poets there were, among others, Moses Ibn Ezra (1060–1139), who, in his history of that school of literature, mentioned the names of some 60 poets; he also developed a system of poetry in his *Poetica* in accordance with the newly acquired Arabic forms of poetic meters. Among medieval Jewish philosophers who wrote on music were *Maimonides (1135–1204) in his *Responsas* 129 and 143; Shem-Tov Falaquera (1220–92) in his *Sepher ha-Mevakkesh;* Abu'l Salt Umaja (1134) in his treatise on music; Abraham Abulafia (1240–90) in his *Gan Naʻul;* Profiat *Duran (1403) in his *Maʻăseh ʼepōd;* and *Levi ben Gerson (d. 1344) in his *De numeris harmonicis* (1342; Coussemaker ScriptMus MA 3:10). This last work was commissioned by Philippe de *Vitry.

The Renaissance and Baroque. In Italy during the 16th century a number of famous Jewish musicians and philosophers were connected with the court of the *Gonzagas at Mantua. The greatest personality among them was Salomone de Rossi (*c.* 1560–*c.* 1632), author of madrigals and canzonettas, chamber sonatas (after 1607), and a famous collection of motets of three to eight voices on Hebrew Psalms and prayer texts, *Salmi e cantici ebraici* (*Haššîrîm ʼăšer li-Shᵉlômōh,* Venice 1623). Other Jewish madrigalists of this period included: David Città (fl. 1616); Anselmo de Rossi (fl. 1618); Allegro Porto (fl. 1619–25). Among the instrumentalists were Abramo dell'Arpa (1566), harpist, singer, and actor; his nephew, Abramino dell'Arpa (fl. 1587), and the lutists Gianmaria da Cornetto (14 pieces in H. Gerle's lute book, *Ein neues sehr künstliches Lautenbuch,* 1552) and Jacchino Massarano (1599). Among Jewish writers at Mantua were Yehuda Moscato (*On Lyre Playing,* 1589), and Leone de'Sommi (*Dialoghi sull'arte rappresentativa*). Leone da Modena (1571–1648), the dominant personality and a man of wide culture, wrote pamphlets on Jewish music and a preface to Salomone de' Rossi's *Salmi;* he founded a Jewish academy of music in the ghetto of Venice and was its director (1629–39). There was also the great disciple of Moscato, Abraham Portaleone (1542–1612), with his often-quoted description of Biblical music and musical instruments, *Shiltē haGibborim* (Mantua 1512; repr. in A. Kircher, *Musurgia universalis,* 1650, and partly in B. Ugolino's *Thesaurus,* 1744).

The Reform Movement. With the fall of Mantua in 1628 and the plague in 1630, the great era of the Italian-Jewish symbiosis of art and music came to a sudden end, though musical activities continued on a more modest scale within the Jewish congregations where singing fraternities performed hymns and Hebrew cantatas, some of which have been preserved (see I. Adler). These groups at Mantua, as well as similar ones at Prague, Regensburg, Nikolsburg, Amsterdam, Offenbach, and Maenza, seem linked by their liberal trend to the period of emancipation (18th–19th centuries). At this point, a liturgical reform movement began; its objective was to coordinate the synagogue song with the contemporary oratorio style of choral singing developed by F. J. *Mendelssohn, Franz *Schubert, and others. The most influential collections of such harmonized services were those by S. Sulzer (1840, 1865), S. Naumbourg (1847), A. Baer (1877), L. Lewandowski (1870,

1876, 1882), and the American cantor E. Stark (1909, 1913). Artistic settings of synagogue services by contemporary composers have been produced by Lazare Saminsky (1926), Joseph Achron (*c.* 1927), Ernest Bloch (1930), Frederick Jacobi (1930), Darius Milhaud (1947), and Leon Algazi (1952). To these may be added the *Haggadah* by Paul Dessau (1936), the *Kol Nidre* by Arnold Schoenberg (1938), and a number of religious cantatas by Israeli composers, among them Uria Boskovitch, Paul Ben-Haim, Marc Lavri, Mordechai Seter, and Joseph Tal.

Music in Modern Israel. Contemporary Israeli music is conditioned by certain trends. The genuine musical folklore, brought into Israel by immigrants of many lands and different communities, is one of these. More than 70 communities, many of them from Oriental Islamic countries, are to be found in Jerusalem alone; they are the last singers of the age-old religious chant and song. The monumental research done in this field by Z. Abraham Idelsohn has been continued by Robert Lachmann (d. 1939) and E. Gerson-Kiwi at the Jerusalem Archives of Oriental Music, and will be carried on at the Research Center for Jewish Music at the Hebrew University in Jerusalem. The history of musical thought and theory in Hebrew music, has been extensively explored by H. Avenary and E. Werner.

The new Israeli folk song and dance developed during the last 60 years of resettlement, predominantly in the communal settlements (*kibbutzim*), reflect a multiple interaction of traditions. As to texts and melodic motifs, the folk song leans heavily on the Bible and on Biblical chant and, lately, also on Arabic patterns of folk tunes.

Modern Israeli art music has aspired to combine Eastern melody with the latest Western compositional techniques. Art music in Israel started with composers of the Russian school, such as Joel Engel, Joachim Stutschewsky, and Marc Lawry, and it has continued with composers of the Western neoimpressionistic school (Erich Walter Sternberg, Paul Ben-Haim, Hanoch Jacobi, and Karel Salomon). Another group, represented by Oedon Partos, Uria Boscowitch (d. 1964), and Mordechai Seter explores new combinations between Eastern ways of composition and Western means of presentation. The first contributions to electronic music have been made by Joseph Tal; and those in 12-tone and "chante" systems, by a younger group (Abel Ehrlich, Heinz Alexander, Ben Zion Orgad, Yeheskiel Braun, Yizhak Sadai, and Shlomoh Yaffe). For nearly all of them, the spiritual chant of the Bible and of prayers has become a source of a thorough artistic reorientation.

Bibliography: R. A. WATERMAN et al., comps., "Bibliography of Asiatic Music," *Music Library Association Notes* 5 (1947–48) 354–362, 549–562. A. SENDREY, *Bibliography of Jewish Music* (New York 1951). A. Z. IDELSOHN, *Thesaurus of Hebrew-Oriental Melodies,* 10 v. (Leipzig 1914–32); *Jewish Music in Its Historic Development* (New York 1929; repr. 1946); *Jewish Liturgy and Its Development* (New York 1932); "Parallelen zwischen gregorianischen und hebräisch-orientalischen Gesangsweisen," *Zeitschrift für Musikwissenschaft* 4 (1922) 515–524. C. SACHS, *The Rise of Music in the Ancient World, East and West* (New York 1943); *The History of Musical Instruments* (New York 1940); *The Commonwealth of Art* (New York 1946). E. WERNER, *The Sacred Bridge* (New York 1959); New OxHMus 1:313–324. E. WERNER and I. SONNE, "The Philosophy and Theory of Music in Judeo-Arab Literature," HebUCAnn 16 (1941) 251–319; 17 (1942–43) 511–572. H. G. FARMER, "Mediaeval Jewish Writers on Music," *MusRev* 3 (1942) 183–189; *Maimonides on Listening to Music* (Bearsden, Eng. 1941); *Sa'adyah Gaon on the Influence of Music* (London 1943). R. L. LACHMANN, *Jewish Cantillation and Song in the Isle of Djerba* (Jerusalem 1940). H. AVENARY, *MusGG* 7:224–261; "Formal Structure of Psalms and Canticles in Early Jewish and Christian Chant," *MusDisc* 7 (1953) 1–13; "Magic, Symbolism and Allegory in Old-Hebrew Sound-Instruments," *Collectanea Historiae Musicae* 2 (1957) 21–31; "Hieronymus' Epistel über die Musikinstrumente und ihre altöstlichen Quellen," *Anuario Musical* 16 (Barcelona 1961); "Pseudo-Jerome Writings and Qumran Tradition," *RevQum* 4 (1963) 3–9; "Études sur le cancionero judéo-espagnol, XVIᵉ et XVIIᵉ siècles," *Sefarad* 20 (1960); *Studies in the Hebrew, Syrian and Greek Liturgical Recitative* (Tel-Aviv 1963). E. GERSON-KIWI, *DBSuppl* 5:1411–68; *Grove DMM* 3: 304–313; "Synthesis and Symbiosis of Styles in Jewish Oriental Music," *Studies in Biblical and Jewish Folklore*, ed. R. PATAI et al. (Bloomington, Ind. 1960); *MusGG* 7:264–280; "Halleluia and Jubilus in Hebrew-Oriental Chant," *Festschrift Heinrich Besseler* (Leipzig 1961) 43–49; "Religious Chant: A Pan-Asiatic Conception of Music," *Journal of the International Folk Music Council* 13 (1961) 64–67; "The Legacy of Jewish Music through the Ages: Review," *In the Dispersion*, v.3 (Jerusalem 1963); "On the Musical Sources of the Judaeo-Hispanic Romance," *MusQ* 50 (1964) 31–43; "Musicology In Israel: A Survey of Its Historical Development," *Acta Musicologica* 30 (1958) 17–26. P. GRADENWITZ, *The Music of Israel* (New York 1948); *Music and Musicians in Israel* (rev. ed. Tel-Aviv 1959). I. ADLER, in *Encyclopédie de la musique*, 3 v. (Paris 1958–61); *La Pratique musicale savante dans quelques communautés juives en Europe aux XVIIᵉ et XVIIIᵉ siècles* (Doctoral diss. Paris 1963). B. BAYER, *The Material Relics of Music in Ancient Palestine and Its Environs: An Archeological Inventory* (Tel Aviv 1963). C. H. KRAELING and L. MOWRY, *NewOxHMus* 1:282–312. A. M. ROTHMÜLLER, *The Music of the Jews* (London 1953; repr. Gloucester, Mass. 1962). G. VINAVER, ed., *Anthology of Jewish Music* (New York 1955). W. O. E. OESTERLEY, *The Jewish Background of the Christian Liturgy* (Oxford 1925). G. BIRKNER, "Psaume hébraïque et séquence latine," *Journal of the International Folk Music Council* 16 (1964) 56–60. M. WEGNER, *Die Musikinstrumente des alten Orients* (Münster 1950). H. HICKMANN, *Musik des Altertums: Aegypte* (Musikgeschichte in Bildern 2; Leipzig 1961). S. CORBIN, *L'Église à la conquête de sa musique* (Paris 1960). **Illustration credits:** Fig. 1, Courtesy of the Trustees of the British Museum. Fig. 2, Miriam Schloessinger Collection, New York City. Photo-Frank J. Darmstaedter.

[E. GERSON-KIWI]

MUSIC, SACRED

Vatican Council II's *Constitution on the Sacred Liturgy* (Dec. 4, 1963) in ch. 4 gives a concise code of sacred music (*musica sacra*), without all the details given in previous Roman documents (notably Pius XII's encyclical *Musicae sacrae disciplina,* Dec. 25, 1955; and the Instruction *Sacred Music and the Sacred Liturgy,* Sept. 3, 1958).

The Role of Music in Liturgy. Chapter 4 begins by reaffirming the role of sacred music: "The musical tradition of the universal Church is a treasure of inestimable value, greater even than that of any other art. The main reason for this pre-eminence is that, as a sacred song united to the words, it forms a necessary or integral part of the solemn liturgy." Thus any discussion of Catholic Church music must turn in great part on its function. This is described by the *Constitution* as triple: "expressing prayer more delightfully" (*orationem suavius exprimens*), "fostering unity of minds" (*unanimitatem fovens*) and "enriching sacred rites with great solemnity" (*ritus sacros maiore locupletans sollemnitate*). While this division of functions is neither complete nor devoid of overlapping, it does call attention to several values found in music generally, and it relates them to worship: the first suggests the role of music as "true art," insisted on in Pius X's motu proprio of 1903; the second stresses the socializing function of

the liturgy; the third is a reminder of the stately and sacral qualities that befit public worship. This triple emphasis is by no means academic; against the "populists," who tend to focus only on the social or participational aspect of liturgy, it is a needed reminder that in public worship more than a minimal awareness of solemnity is in order.

The *Constitution* speaks of the "ministerial function of music in the liturgy," rather than of "the handmaid of the liturgy," as Pius X had done earlier. This ancillary role and some of its implications had often been resented by musicians, who were pleased with the more significant term "ministerial." Both words, however, throw light on an obscure area. For while music must not be belittled as something adventitious, neither can its place in liturgy be altogether autonomous. Music for worship must be controlled by the requirements of those who are to use it as a means of prayer. Thus, in the normal heterogeneous parish, if music is to fulfill its ministerial function, it must not be entirely unrelated to the people's preparation of sensitivity; altogether avant-garde or esoteric music would, accordingly, be in place only in a more cultivated or specialized situation. Nor, on the other hand, should the artistic level of liturgical music be low, and this for obvious reasons. It seems evident that this artistic-vs.-popular tension implies a zone of relativity, and can hardly be expected to achieve more than an unstable, shifting resolution.

The Role of the People. At the same time, the *Constitution* insists, more explicitly than its predecessors had done, on the role of "God's people" in the liturgy, recalling also the "hierarchical" (art. 28, 30, 32). The people's part will, of necessity, be commonly restricted to unisonal music. Gregorian chant is acknowledged as specially suited to the Roman liturgy (*liturgiae romanae proprium*), and "other things being equal" (*ceteris paribus*) should be given "pride of place" (*principem locum*). In this context it is not clear what *ceteris paribus* means; however, in view of the notably smaller stress placed on Gregorian chant in the *Constitution*, as compared with previous documents, it would appear that its place of honor is in great part speculative. At the same time, article 117 expresses the desire for new chant editions and for "an edition containing simpler melodies, for use in small churches."

Article 121 invites composers to "produce compositions which have the qualities proper to genuine sacred music, not confining themselves to works which can be sung only by large choirs, but providing also for the needs of small choirs and for the active participation of the entire assembly of the faithful." While in previous Roman documents popular hymnody had been allowed and occasionally encouraged, this new statement extends the use of music sung by the people. Following the *Constitution*'s appearance and to fill its demands, a great number of "People's Masses" in the vernacular appeared; these were of vastly unequal merit. Many settings for Psalms also have been published, notably those of Joseph Gelineau, SJ, Lucien Deiss, CSSp, S. Somerville, Guido de Sutter, Jan Vermulst, and Haldan D. Tompkins.

The Choir. "Other kinds of sacred music, especially polyphony, are by no means excluded from liturgical celebrations" (art. 116). It is evident that such music presupposes choirs, and the *Constitution* insists that "choirs must be diligently promoted" (art. 114). The earlier stress on Palestrina does not appear. To what extent this more elaborate music belongs in the liturgy will depend very much on the choral resources of individual churches; thus, article 114 adds "especially in cathedral churches." The same article insists, too, that "whenever the sacred action is to be celebrated with song, the whole body of the faithful be able to contribute that active participation which is rightly theirs, as laid down in Art. 28 and 30" (these two articles do not specify the parts, though they include at least responses and acclamations). Traditionally, the choir's role is to provide music that is meant to be listened to and contemplated (e.g., the music between the proclamation of Epistle and Gospel).

Instrumental Music. Instrumental music is given a wider range of use, following the severe restrictions set down (but, in subsequent practice, unevenly obeyed) by the motu proprio of Pius X. The special privilege of the pipe organ in the Latin Church is upheld, "for it is the traditional musical instrument which adds a wonderful splendor to the Church's ceremonies and powerfully lifts up man's mind to God and to higher things." The 1958 instruction had explicitly excluded the "electronic" organ (64), and the *Constitution,* by singling out the "pipe organ" (*organum tubulatum*), seems to continue the prohibition.

Other instruments require "the knowledge and consent of the competent territorial authority" and may be used "only on condition that the instruments are suitable, or can be made suitable, for sacred use, accord with the dignity of the temple, and truly contribute to the edification of the faithful." This article (120) gives cross references that indicate a deemphasis on uniformity in favor of fostering "the genius and talents of the various races and peoples." This broad missiological principle will need special application when Western countries are had in mind. Accordingly, after the *Con-*

King David with his harp, surrounded by musicians playing medieval instruments, miniature from a 12th-century French manuscript (MS lat. 6755(2), fol. Av).

stitution appeared, a tentative use of popular instruments (guitar, percussion, and others) was noted in several countries. Musicologists, among others, welcomed the freedom to use more instruments, especially with baroque and other music.

Religious, Nonliturgical Music. Nothing is said in the *Constitution* about the category discussed in the 1958 instruction, "Religious Music." This was described (54) as music that, while not suited to liturgical functions, "still tends to arouse religious sentiments in those who hear it and to foster worship." While its proper place, according to the instruction, is the concert hall, it may be admitted, within certain conditions, even into church though not during liturgical functions. Obviously, there is no accepted line of demarcation here. It may be that, with the new insistence on participation, the more elaborate polyphonic Ordinary settings will be increasingly performed in sacred concerts rather than during the liturgy.

The place of emotion in sacred music adds another complication. Whatever system of aesthetics one finds acceptable, artistic worth can never be measured in quantitative terms, as though the higher the pulse rate or blood pressure in one's response, the better the music. Nor is the special "uplift" required in sacred music susceptible of easy measurement or phenomenological analysis. Nor, on the other hand, is the catch phrase "it's too beautiful to be liturgical" a satisfactory principle, since it reflects a Manichaean or puritanical viewpoint. Common sense and tradition suggest that, while music must be appealing and moving, liturgical music requires some measure of sobriety, restraint, modesty. The Christian's acceptance of his creaturely condition must go hand in hand with his grateful awareness of redemption and vocation as a son of God. Thus, sacred music should reflect both glory and humility, celebration and sacrifice, thanksgiving and penance, and, at least to some degree, should embody these Christian beliefs and attitudes.

Aesthetics and the History of Sacred Music. The Church Fathers, as Quasten and Gérold have shown, were not without reservations regarding the use of music in church. While the very early Church adopted much of its psalmody from the Jewish tradition with no noteworthy self-consciousness, there arose the problem of secular music in the pagan environment. Certain instruments and modes had, even in classical Greek times, been associated with idolatry and licentiousness, and some of the Fathers, at times under Neoplatonic influences, tended to be reluctant and cautionary.

According to Franco of Cologne (writing about 1260), the scholastics "have treated sufficiently of plainsong and have fully explained it to us both theoretically and practically" (*Ars cantus mensurabilis*). While much of this speculation had to do with technical matters, not a little dealt with the ethical character of the Gregorian modes. The problems of the profane element in sacred music were exacerbated by the birth of polyphony and its extensive development. Session 22 of the Council of Trent denounced such abuses—"the mixture of lascivious or impure" elements either "in organ or instrumental playing or in singing." In 1749 Benedict XIV, in his *Annus qui,* condemned abuses connected with the operatic style. In the 20th century, starting with Pius X's motu proprio of 1903, the Church has several times addressed itself officially to sacred music as a whole, usually with explicit warnings against profane styles or elements. It is noteworthy that the *Constitution on the Sacred Liturgy* takes an altogether positive approach. This appears to be because of the general mood of *aggiornamento* and "open" Christian humanism embodied in the person of John XXIII, and may be in part owing to acceptance of some elements of relativity; for, after much experience and the findings of anthropology and missiology, it now seems clear that cultural context has a great deal to do with one's response to music, and that what may sound "liturgical" to one group may not be equally acceptable to another. Thus, quick generalizations are unwarranted.

Bibliography: J. GELINEAU, *Voices and Instruments in Christian Worship*, tr. C. HOWELL (Collegeville, Minn. 1964). J. SAMSON, *Musique et chant sacrés* (Paris 1957). J. QUASTEN, *Musik und Gesang in den Kulten der heidnischen Antike und christlichen Frühzeit* (Münster 1930). C. J. MCNASPY, "The Sacral in Liturgical Music," in *The Renewal of the Liturgy* (New York 1963). J. McKINNON, *The Church Fathers and Musical Instruments* (Doctoral diss. unpub. Columbia U. 1965). F. ROMITA, *Jus musicae liturgicae* (Rome 1947). **Illustration credit:** Bibliothèque Nationale, Paris.

[C. J. MC NASPY]

MUSIC, SACRED (CANADA)

The story of music in Canada, like that of music in the U.S., is not a record of steady progress from a primitive to a sophisticated style. The first white Canadians were not illiterate but citizens of the high French baroque, and every subsequent wave of immigration from Europe has carried with it the elements of the mother country's culture prevailing at that moment. The first Canadian music was sacred music, whether the incantations of the aborigines or the plainchant of the missionaries is in question. In either case there was a prehistory or an inherited tradition, the one as mysterious as the provenance of the natives themselves, the other identifiable with 16 centuries of Christian life.

Native Music. Very little is known about Indian chants in use at the time Canada was colonized by the Europeans—beyond the four Micmac songs of *c.* 1570 that only *Lescarbot, the first historian of Canada, mentions (unfortunately, without indication of their rhythm). In 1928, however, the well-known folklorist Marius Barbeau listed some very interesting songs found among Indian and Eskimo tribes still untouched by civilization. The singers were accompanied by drums in varied rhythms that, strangely enough, rarely synchronized with melodies using a pentatonic scale (in descending motion: E-D-C-A-G). While missionaries testified to the unusual musical aptitude of the natives in absorbing the Christian melodies, it is clear from the evidence that neither the Indian nor the Eskimo melos exerted any influence on the character of ensuing Canadian musical style.

Before Confederation (1867). During the colonial period both French and English influences contributed to the development of Canadian sacred music. For the French missioners music was the prime instrument of religious instruction. They taught their Indian subjects how to chant, to master Western scales, to handle musical instruments; they also translated the texts of Mass and church hymns into native dialects and composed vernacular lyrics for French melodic settings. Such was the Huron Christmas carol *Jesous Ahatonhia* thought to be the work of Noël de Brébeuf. Baron

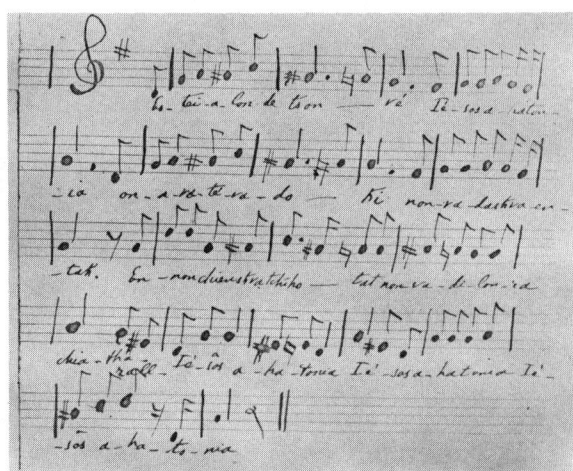

MS copy of the Huron Christmas Carol "Jesous Ahatonhia" in the Archives of the College Sainte Marie, Montreal.

de Poutrincourt, commander of Port Royal, Nova Scotia, was evidently the first Canadian to create original music; according to Lescarbot "he composed (1610–12) some of the music regularly used at divine service." It is stated by another writer that René Ménard (1604–*c.* 1666), a missioner claimed by both Canada and the U.S., had composed some motets in 1640. The earliest composition preserved, however, is a section of plainchant melody written by Rev. C. A. Martin (1648–1711) for the feast of the Holy Family. Martin may have composed also the two Masses of that period preserved at the Hotel Dieu, Quebec. A Gradual, Processional, and Vesperal were published in Quebec (*c.* 1800–02); and a new collection of hymns in 1818. The first organ in Canada had been installed in Quebec in 1663.

The first wave of French settlers after the explorers and missioners brought farmers and fishermen led by the entrepreneur Jean Talon, and with them a rich repertory of folk songs and dances, as well as the instruments to accompany them. Thus, from the early 18th century to the early 20th, French Canadian music was marked by exuberant folk song characteristics as much as by sacred themes. The best energies of the people, however, were expended on the problem of mere survival in a hostile wilderness. Hence professional training was unavailable during this period. Despite such handicaps a number of composers, chiefly of church music, emerged from this background, among them J. Quesnel, F. H. Glackemeyer, C. Sauvageau, C. M. Sabatier, J. J. Perreault, and J. B. Labelle.

Anglo-Saxon Tradition. Like their French neighbors, English settlers, scattered over an immense territory, had to overcome the hardships of colonization before there was opportunity for creative musicianship. Moreover, several sects, notably the Quakers and the Methodists, considered music as profane and even proscribed the use of organ at worship. On the other hand, the English were natural organizers and quite early formed choral groups whose expanding repertory included the more popular choral classics and created a market for new works. Moreover, every English garrison had its regimental band (often led by a German), and in this way much of the European light classical music, probably in poor transcriptions, was promulgated in Canada.

The choir of St. Michael's Cathedral School of Music, photographed in 1937, with Msgr. J. E. Ronan directing.

After Confederation. Following establishment of the Commonwealth, composers of French and English backgrounds developed new trends after their own traditions. Among the French-oriented, some followed the established norms (such as C. Lavallée, G. Couture, A. Fortier, and J. A. Tremblay), while others, among them F. A. Laliberté, C. Champagne, G. D. Tanguay, H. Gratton, and G. Cusson, showed remarkable originality in use of folk song and in other experimental ways. Still others, such as M. Blackburn, J. P. Couture, J. Vallerand, M. Perrault, C. Pépin, and P. Mercure, are identified with the progressives.

Standing in the forefront of musical life ·among Anglo-Canadian musicians are Sir Ernest MacMillan, by reason of his educational leadership, his development of the Toronto Symphony, and his compositions, including settings of French-Canadian and Indian folk songs; and Healey Willan, because of his many students and large corpus of sacred choral compositions. Others of their persuasion are W. MacNutt, G. Ridout, E. Rathburn, G. A. Bales, R. Fleming, and H. Freedman (all Willan disciples), I. Applebaum, W. H. Anderson, and A. Whitehead. Serial (tone row) techniques are explored in the work of B. Pentland, J. Weinzweig, A. Brott, A. Twa, N. Chotem, H. Somers, and J. Beckwith. The neo-Canadian school, whose constituents aspire to a synthesis of all the diverse currents, ethnical and technical, is represented by Q. MacLean, A. Walter, W. Kaufmann, C. Morawetz, and U. Kasamets, among others.

Development of musical awareness and appreciation among Canadians is reflected in the output of books and periodicals; the professional orchestras (notably at Halifax, Montreal, Toronto, Winnipeg, and Vancouver); the National Youth Orchestra, *Les Jeunesses Musicales;* the civic choral groups (such as the outstanding Mendelssohn Choir, Toronto); the excellent Protestant church choirs, particularly in Ontario; the singing societies of German, Russian, Jewish, Ukrainian, Polish, and Czech centers; the conservatories and university music schools; and the recurrent music festivals.

Sacred Music since the Motu Proprio (1903). Training, of admirable quality, in church music scholarship and performance is offered in many seminaries and scholasticates for men and religious institutes for women, and particularly in the schools of church music flourishing in the four leading French-speaking universities: Quebec (Laval), Montreal, Ottawa, and Sherbrooke. The Benedictine Abbey of St. Benoît-du-Lac, a notable center of Gregorian culture, has to a great extent set the tone for all Canada in theoretical and practical chant studies. Its curriculum has been adopted by the universities mentioned above, as well as by specialized institutes and choir schools, such as L'École Vincent d'Indy, Outremont; L'École Normale de Musique, Westmount; L'Action Musicale Liturgique, St. Hyacinthe; La Maîtrise de Québec, Les Petits Chanteurs du Mont-Royal; and the Cathedral Schola Cantorum, Toronto. Summer extension courses are offered annually at Regina, Saskatoon, London (Ont.), Toronto, Ottawa, Montreal, Quebec, Moncton, Halifax, and St. John (Newfoundland). The influence of St. Benoît-du-Lac, implemented by the Ward Method (*see* MUSIC EDUCATION IN THE U.S.) has resulted in a marked increase in both appreciation and performance of liturgical music in the lower schools as well.

The 20th-century musico-liturgical revival has also brought international recognition to several choirs, such as that of the monks at St. Benoît-du-Lac, the Schola Cantorum of the Grand Seminary of Montreal, Les Petits Chanteurs du Mont-Royal, the Schola Cantorum of Toronto, the Palestrina Choir of Ottawa, the Choir of Nôtre-Dame d'Acadie and that of L'Université Saint-Joseph, both of Moncton. It has likewise promoted the publication of a number of periodicals, hymn collections, and studies, among them *Rhythmique grégorienne* by G. Mercure, OSB; *Traité d'accompagnement grégorien* by E. Lapierre; and *La Musique sacrée dans nos paroisses* by J. Martel, OMI. Finally, the gradual replacement of Latin by the vernacular as the language of worship has given marked impetus both to congregational singing and to the creation of new liturgical settings for congregational use.

A National Music. Thanks to the labors of many generations of music makers, solid traditions in both the sacred and secular areas are gradually emerging. It cannot be stated, however, that an authentic Canadian musical idiom is near. The development of Canadian music was hampered in the early period by pioneering conditions, particularly the scattering of settlers over immense stretches of land and the great distances between settlements, which made each town a closed circle and precluded the public appreciation, enlightened criticism, exchange of views, and even competition that a composer needs. Such obstacles to a national expression have largely disappeared with the development of modern means of communication and the influence of the Canadian Broadcasting Corporation programs. On the other hand, a national art must reflect the distinguishing traits of a people, and this presupposes a national homogeneity, whereas the Canadian populace is composed of heterogenous ethnic groups still strongly attached to the parent culture. Hence, until these groups merge into one society, the Canadian composer will tend to reflect the soul of his fatherland—if indeed he is not tempted to a rootless cosmopolitan manner. With time and continued creativity, however, a Canadian style may be achieved on the rich resources of folk and art music that are available to music makers.

Bibliography: H. KALLMANN, *A History of Music in Canada, 1534–1914* (Toronto 1960). E. MACMILLAN, ed., *Music in Canada* (Toronto 1955). L. SAMINSKY, *Living Music of the Americas*

(New York 1949). C. M. Barbeau, *Répertoire de la chanson folklorique française au Canada* (Ottawa 1962–). Canadian Broadcasting Corp., *Catalogue of Canadian Composers*, ed. H. Kallmann (rev. ed. Ottawa 1952). Canadian Music Library Assoc., *A Bio-Bibliographical Finding List of Canadian Musicians . . .* (Ottawa 1961). Sisters of St. Ann, *Dictionnaire biographique des musiciens canadiens* (2d ed. Lachine, Que. 1935). See also *Encyclopedia Canadiana*, ed. J. E. Robbins, 10 v. (Ottawa 1960), articles on "Church Music," "Folk Music," "Music," "Musical," "National Songs," and "Opera."

[J. MARTEL]

MUSIC, SACRED (U.S.)

The history of sacred music in the U.S., like that of general music, is a study as variegated as the plurality of cultural and religious backgrounds represented in the nation's early settlers and later immigrants. While American music thus was far from being indigenous in its first manifestations, in its development it has exhibited a continuing (if uneven) surge for freedom from its European motherland together with a growing self-awareness and involvement with native sources of inspiration. Colonial America's first music was music related to denominational worship; today, significantly influenced by current liturgical, theological, and ecumenical developments, the music of America's churches continues its process of adaptation.

Music in the Missions. The music of 16th- and 17th-century Europe was brought to America by Spanish and French missioners, chiefly Franciscan, Dominican, and Jesuit.

In Spanish Domains. Spanish foundations dating from 1598 in New Mexico achieved a high degree of development in the areas of organ music, choir schools, and vocal polyphony that involved "note" singing a century before it was practiced on the Eastern seaboard. Fray Cristóbal de Quiñones (d. April 27, 1609) and numerous other friars were responsible for these initial musical endeavors. One of the first collections of authentic Indian melodies was that of Fray Felipe Arroyo de La Cuesta. Again in the California missions the Franciscan padres introduced the music as well as the language and customs of their native Spain. Plainchant predominated, but some figured Masses and motets, also homophonic in structure and with a high incidence of thirds, sixths, dominant sevenths, and occasional diminished chords, were in the mission repertory. The absence of ornamental solo sections and of repetitions of text helps to distinguish this mission music from its later liturgical counterpart in Eastern centers. Part-music was written on a single five- or six-line staff, with a system of colored notation to distinguish voice parts: tiple (soprano), white notes outlined in red; contralto, white notes outlined in black; tenor, solid red notes; bass, black notes.

Mission life in the 18th and early 19th centuries dictated the musical usage, since natives were encouraged to live within the mission compound. The daily musical program was scheduled as follows: *Cantico del Alba* (morning prayer), chanted upon rising; the *Alabanza* (the Commandments, Sacraments, and other catechetical material recited or sung in Spanish); the Mass in plainsong or figured Latin settings; the *Alabado* (song of divine praise); the *Bendito* (grace before and after meals); and the *Angelus*. At sundown the mission populace gathered for the *Doctrina* and the *Alabado* in the native Indian tongue, and during the day chosen singers chanted the Divine Office. The whole day was thus permeated with sung prayer, and even after sundown an evening of song and dance was common. Instruments used were the violin, viola, cello, bass, flute, trumpet, horns, guitars, drums, and triangle. After congregational singing in the form of simple psalm tones and antiphonal chants was established, a formal choir was trained. The

Fig. 1. One of four pages devoted to music in the autograph MS of Father Felipe Arroyo de la Cuesta written at Mission San Juan Bautista, California, in 1819. This shows an Indian text set to the music of a Mission hymn.

repertory consisted of Propers for Sundays and principal feasts (simplified settings by Padre Narciso Durán), Masses in chant or homophonic settings, and Latin hymns for Benediction and special feasts. Padre Durán encouraged instrumental accompaniment to sustain pitch and wrote in simplified scale patterns using the *F* clef with needed accidentals. Although concrete evidence of the music in the Southwest, Texas, and Florida is scarce, it may be assumed that the same pattern was followed wherever the Spanish missioners penetrated. With the collapse of the Spanish missions (1833–34) their music fell into obscurity and therefore failed to influence directly the course of church music in America.

In French Domains. The pattern of mission life prevailing on the West Coast was unknown in northeastern U.S. and Canada. The missioner spent his days in the midst of the Indian nations. Tribes remained tribes, not guests of the mission enclosure. As in Spanish territory, however, one of the chief problems was that of communication—especially of religious truths. Often the basic facts were imparted through hymns—either the setting of Christian texts to native melodies or, as later happened, native dialects to European melodies. Various teaching aids were devised, such as the Quipii, a knotted cord signifying certain doctrinal ideas; the Order of Songs, pictures suggesting the subject of each hymn stanza; the Notched Stick, arbitrary engraved characters used to direct prayers and hymns; and Syllabaries, which were signs used to indicate sounds, thus obviating the task of teaching the Indian a foreign tongue. Extant hymnals (1830–70) use the Indian vernacular with the title of the melody indicated in a European language. Contents include Latin hymns, *cantiques* (common tunes), English hymns, and some original tunes. In use today is the Huron carol *Jesous Ahatonia*, probably composed by Jean de Brébeuf, one of the *North American martyrs. One Midwestern missioner, the Italian Samuel *Mazzuchelli, OP, made such headway with his Wisconsin Winnebagos that they learned to chant Sunday Vespers with alternating verses in Latin and their vernacular. Because of the language barrier, however, none of these apostolic-cultural endeavors had any influence on the course of American church music.

Protestant Beginnings (17th Century). The pilgrims of New England relied upon English hymnals for their worship services. The *Ainsworth Psalter* contained unaccompanied unison settings of metrical psalms—one note to each syllable in binary rhythm (*see* PSALTERS, METRICAL; HYMNS AND HYMNALS). When the Salem and Plymouth communities joined the Massachusetts Bay Colony (1691), the *Bay Psalm Book* gained ascendancy and continued to constitute New England's singing staple for the next century. In the Anglican settlements there was a struggle for popularity between the "Old Version" (*Bay Psalm Book*) and the more poetic New Version of the Psalms of David (1696) of Tate and Brady. Both versions were later replaced by the hymnody of English writers, such as Isaac Watts. Two non-English communities, the Ephrata Cloister, near Lancaster, Pa., and the *Moravians (Unity of Brethren) centered in Winston-Salem, N.C., maintained a high level of musical activity in the 18th century. Relying heavily on European material, the Ephrata group developed antiphonal singing to an art, whereas the Moravians performed choral, chamber, and symphonic works (not necessarily religious) of European masters. Another center of musical activity was the camp meeting. The revival movement among various denominational dissenters generated the folk hymn, a combination of secular folk tune and religious text, as leaders sought to replace the "placid" Puritan psalm with a heartier type of group singing. Folk hymns in turn were succeeded by the popular *gospel song, a commercial, individually composed hymn.

Catholic Hymnody (18th Century). Formal publication of hymnals for Catholic use was not initiated until 1787. Credit is due to Benjamin Carr (1768–1831), influential musician, teacher, hymn composer, and music publisher, for his pioneer publications. Numerous other hymnals, however, came with immigrating Catholics, and with this influx of hymnals came a threefold western European influence: (1) postbaroque concerto style with its specified elements, i.e., melodic and harmonic reiteration, alternaticn of solo and chorus sections, and ornamentation of melodic lines (in this way a pseudo-Neapolitan *bel canto* style was implanted in the hymnals); (2) Viennese classical form and presentation of thematic material, whose unskilled and inartistic handling resulted in a monotonous tonic-dominant harmony with "Alberti Bass" accompaniment; thus Viennese orchestral idiom was exploited in the form of numerous orchestrated Masses, but, in an attempt to imitate the masters, most composers simply exaggerated the means; (3) adulation of the self-styled composer who was the enthusiastic and zealous but all too often untrained hymn tune writer and compiler. Catholic hymnody suffered both musically and textually as a result of one or more of these factors. Moreover, the defensive mood of the post-Tridentine period penetrated liturgical music, and at the same time Catholics were deprived of the heritage of the German chorale. Congregational singing was almost entirely replaced by the solo voice, quartet choirs, and lengthy organ solos. Degeneration became complete when hymnals proudly displayed "religious" texts set to popular secular compositions.

Nineteenth-Century Trends. The 19th century felt the surge of political and artistic nationalism. Composers, such as *Gottschalk, incorporated "American" elements in their works, e.g., Indian melos, spiritual tunes, ragtime rhythms. Arthur Farwell (1872–1952), recognizing the role of imitation in the early stages of creativity, sought freedom from European domination and answered *Dvořák's challenge to explore native folk music with the foundation of the Wa-Wan Press for the advancement of American music. Henry Gilbert (1868–1928) shared Farwell's interest, his deep love for all folk music manifesting itself in a heavy reliance on American Indian lore. Gilbert preferred to "seek his own hat" rather than wear "a borrowed crown." An 18th-century predecessor, William Billings (1746–1800), had championed the same cause with an unusual display of musical creativity, and his fuguing tunes became basic source material for later composers, such as William Schuman. Charles Ives (1874–1954), successor to Farwell and Gilbert, realized their ideals. Rejecting conventional musical structure, Ives introduced polytonality, polyrhythms, tone clusters, functional intervals, and jazz effects, and his use of native folk music as his germinal musical idea initiated a truly creative trend in American music.

Fig. 2. Watercolor birthday greeting for Jacob Van Vleck, Moravian minister-musician at Bethlehem, Pa., 1795. The painting, in the collection of the Moravian Historical Society, Nazareth, Pa., shows Van Vleck playing for a group of Moravian sisters or girls from the Bethlehem Boarding School, where he was an instructor.

In Protestant Communions. Protestant church music reflected a twofold trend during the Victorian period: the use of the dignified hymn, and the popularity of gospel songs. Three basic elements in the religious milieu are recognizable: (1) the evangelical movement headed by the Wesleys; (2) the *Oxford Movement, fostering a return to ancient faith and practice; and (3) the Modernist movement, which sought complete involvement of man in liturgical worship. Hymnody drew heavily on the poetry of Cardinal J. H. *Newman, E. Caswall, F. W. *Faber, and John Mason Neale; initially, however, less attention was focused on the music. The Oxford Movement encouraged the revival of the Latin hymns, folk song carols, plainsong hymns, and German chorales, which were adopted according to local American needs. A simultaneous concern for performance led to the utilization of secular part-song techniques as evidenced in the works of the English composers J. B. Dykes, J. Barnby, and J. Stainer. The Victorian feeling for antiquity led to extreme sentimentalism, musical and religious. Lowell Mason (1792–1872), well known for his hymns "Nearer My God To Thee," "My Faith Looks Up to Thee," and "From Greenland's Icy Mountains," stands in the forefront of American musicians of this period, by reason of his labors for music education in the public schools, with special emphasis on sound choral training. His hymns, like those of Thomas Hastings (1784–1872) and W. B. Bradbury (1816–68), are still used in churches today. The oratorios *St. Peter* (John Knowles Paine, 1839–1906) and *Hora novissima* (Horatio Parker, 1863–1919) represent the peak of religious music of the period. The Parker work, for mixed chorus and orchestra, and based on St. Bernard's poem *Contemptor mundi,* was his first internationally recognized success. Critics paid Parker the highest of 19th-century accolades in comparing it with the works of such composers as Palestrina, J. S. Bach, and Josquin Despres, while choral societies in England and America performed the work frequently.

In Catholic Worship. Catholic music of the 19th century seemed as deeply entrenched in European operatic style as ever. The influx of English and Irish Catholics, lacking valid liturgical traditions, continued the deterioration of Church music. Quartet choirs and orchestral ensembles seemed the ideal at this time. Gregorian chant was scarcely known in the U.S. Mass composers of the period assumed the romanticist symphonic style, with no attempt to differentiate between secular and church expression. The *Caecilian Movement, initially a reform group in the German-speaking countries, found strong support in German parishes of the Middle West. Restoration of plainsong and classic polyphony was their main concern, and their desire for objectivity of expression challenged the lush romantic composition of the period. While the group fostered revival of the older German hymns, the vernacular hymn was relegated to extraliturgical services. The movement must be credited with stemming the tide of shallow, operatic church composition; by severing itself from the general musical development of the country, however, it gradually deteriorated to a system of stereotyped reproduction of musical patterns.

Contemporary Church Music. American church musicians of the 20th century have resisted the influx of secular tunes as a basis for liturgical music, while leading secular composers have turned to religious themes

Fig. 3. Signature page of the autograph MS of Lou Harrison's "Mass for Voices, Trumpet, Harp, and Strings" in the Collection of the Library of Congress.

for their inspiration, e.g., Stravinsky's *Symphony of Psalms,* Virgil Thomson's *Symphony on a Hymn Tune,* and Paul Creston's *Threnody* and *Three Mysteries,* with their steady reliance on chant themes (*see* MUSIC, SACRED, HISTORY OF, 8.) The late 1940s witnessed a resurgence of Mass settings by such composers as Roy Harris, Samuel Barber, Roger Sessions, Aaron Copland, and others. Copland's *a cappella* masterpiece *In the Beginning* reveals close adherence to scriptural text, as does Randall Thompson's *Peaceable Kingdom,* a mixed chorus setting of eight texts from Isaia. Alan Hovhaness skillfully employs religious texts (and sometimes the monody of the Middle East) in such works as his well-known *Alleluia* for mixed voices, *30th Ode of Solomon* for baritone and orchestra, cantata, *Shepherd of Israel,* the *Magnificat* for four voices, chorus, and orchestra, and his many motet settings of Psalm verses. Norman dello Joio's opera *The Triumph of St. Joan* follows the same trend, but he uses religious melodic resources also in a number of instrumental works: *Variations, Chaconne and Finale,* whose themes are derived from chant; *Piano Sonata No. 3* based on the Gregorian *Mass of the Angels;* and *Fantasia on a Gregorian Theme,* for violin and piano.

Gian Carlo Menotti's *Amahl and the Night Visitors, Saint of Bleecker Street,* and *Death of the Bishop of Brindisi* are further evidences of this religious interest. Other 20th-century composers utilizing similar materials include Ross Finney, Peter Mennin, John J. Becker, Theodore Chanler, and Louis Mennini. Russell Woollen has developed an individual style within the contemporary dissonant idiom. His handling of chantlike rhythms and thematic material in his *Mass for Boys Voices and*

Organ, Mass in the Major Mode, and *Missa Melismatica* testifies to his unification of divergent musical styles. He has contributed to the American musical scene also as educator, virtuoso, and composer of such secular works as *Sonata for Piano Duo, Toccata for Orchestra,* and an opera, *The Decorator,* a 1959 television production. Another influential composer-teacher is Leo Sowerby of the College of Church Musicians in Washington, D.C., best known for his anthems and contemporary organ music. His religious music includes the choral work *Canticle of the Sun* (Prayer of St. Francis) and *Throne of God,* based on the Book of Revelation.

Within the churches themselves there has been a multiple development: (1) congregational music using German chorale form and sung in unison; ancient motets adapted to congregational singing; Gregorian chants and hymn settings by contemporary writers; and (2) selections for the trained choir—an artistic repertory capable of expressing meaning congenial to the worship by the larger group. *The Anglican Hymnal* (1940) contains the old Latin Office hymns in English, hymns by American authors, translations from Orthodox and German Pietist sources, and German chorales.

The motu proprio of Pope St. Pius X (1903) restated the role of music in Catholic worship, admitting for use "everything good and beautiful . . . in the course of the ages." This decree, on the one hand, gave a final impetus to the revival of Gregorian chant, initiated earlier by the Benedictine monks of Solesmes (*see* SOLESMES, MUSIC OF). On the other hand, it heralded the return of Renaissance polyphony and encouraged modern composition. The liturgical movement, through its interest in the congregation's participation, has occasioned the reexamination of musical means and materials. The chant has come to be recognized as the highly artistic and difficult work it is, demanding the appropriate assignment to choir or partial use by the congregation. Hymnody has received perhaps the closest scrutiny. A purging of 19th-century romanticist endeavors and a reconsideration of the wealth of Reformation and pre-Reformation hymns has caused an artistic advance in hymnal publication. Contemporary composers, native and European, have been encouraged to explore the area of congregational music.

Outlook for American Church Music. The future of American church music seems bright. Musicians, liturgists, clergy, and laity are deeply aware of the strong relation between the liturgical service and its music. A precise definition of the roles of the clergy, people, and choir will impose a specific repertory for each. The organist seems to be highlighted in a manner unknown since the baroque era. Instruments other than the organ are again to be considered for their specific artistic contribution. Balance and choice present the principal questions: balance among congregational unison song, choir selections, and solo organ music; and choice, for, as each era breaks from its predecessor, a new surge of material demands discriminating evaluation. Informed criteria for this evaluation are indispensable if truly creative music is to play its role in the deepening of the liturgical experience. The Instruction of 1958 and the Constitution on the Sacred Liturgy (1963) indicate a direction for guidance of this balance and choice so necessary for the life of American church music.

Bibliography: Fellerer CathChMus. W. DOUGLAS, *Church Music in History and Practice* (rev. ed. New York 1962). R. N. SQUIRE, *Church Music* (St. Louis 1962). R. M. STEVENSON, *Patterns of Protestant Church Music* (Durham, N.C. 1953). L. W. ELLINWOOD, *The History of American Church Music* (New York 1953). W. T. MARROCCO and H. GLEASON, eds., *Music in America, 1620–1865* (New York 1964). H. W. FOOTE, *Three Centuries of American Hymnody* (Cambridge, Mass. 1940, repr. Hamden, Conn. 1961). Chase AmMus. P. H. LÁNG, ed., *One Hundred Years of Music in America* (New York 1961). O. DA SILVA, ed., *Mission Music of California* (Los Angeles 1941). J. V. HIGGINSON, "Hymnody in the American Indian Missions," *The Papers of the Hymn Society XVIII,* ed. W. W. REID (New York 1954). *A Short Bibliography for the Study of Hymns,* ed. J. R. SYDNOR, ibid. XXV (1964). C. VERRET, *A Preliminary Survey of Roman Catholic Hymnals Published in the U.S. of Amer.* (Washington, D.C. 1964). *Alonso de Benavides' Revised Memorial of 1634,* ed. F. W. HODGE et al. (Albuquerque 1945). L. M. SPELL, "Music Teaching in N.Mex. in the 17th Century," *New Mexico Historical Review* 2 (1927) 27–36. L. B. SPIESS, "Benavides and Church Music in N.Mex. in the Early 17th Century," JAmMusSoc 17 (1964) 144–156. L. SAMINSKY, *Living Music of the Americas* (New York 1949). **Illustration credits:** Fig. 1, Reproduced by permission of the Bancroft Library. Fig. 2, Old Salem, Inc., and The Moravian Music Foundation. Fig. 3, Reprinted with the permission of the copyright owner, Peer International Corporation.

[C. VERRET]

MUSIC, SACRED, HISTORY OF

The historical development of music in Christian worship is intimately connected with the history of liturgy on one hand and with the general history of music on the other. Until the late Middle Ages there is no history of music except that related to the liturgy. After that time, in addition to liturgical music, religious music that was not intended primarily for public worship can also be found. Such music, then, is a part of the history of sacred music, although it is not always a part of the history of liturgical music (see section 2, below). This article proceeds historically from the sporadic accounts of the use of music in the early Church through the golden age of chant and the growth and development of polyphony to the beginnings of a more modern art, and discusses current problems.

1. EARLY CHRISTIAN MUSIC

There is no doubt that the early Christian communities simply continued the musical practices of the Jewish synagogues they had been accustomed to attend.

Music in Apostolic Times. For the fore-Mass and the morning and evening gathering that developed into the Divine Office the synagogue practice served as the model. Readings from Scripture were followed by Psalm singing. At least the differentiation between the roles of the *cantor and congregation was a clear one. The cantor was also permitted a kind of improvised, charismatic song of joy. It is difficult to determine whether in Eph 5.19 St..Paul is referring to three different types of musical pieces in the Christian community or is using three terms to describe one and the same phenomenon: ψαλμοῖς καὶ ὕμνοις καὶ ᾠδαῖς πνευματικαῖς. In Col 3.16 he uses, however, the same division. It must be remembered that the Jewish synagogues in the diaspora had already adopted the Greek language, and Hellenistic musical practices could also have made inroads into the traditional chants.

Theories of Jewish Origins of Gregorian Chant. All critics agree that the descriptions of musical practice in the Jewish temple have nothing in common with Christian chant. The most difficult problem is to ascertain the degree to which the Gregorian chant known today has been influenced by Jewish chants, specifically from the synagogue practices of the time of Christ. In answering this question, certain facts must be considered: the first notated sources for Gregorian chant come from the 9th century (before that time only literary references to music exist); there is no way of finding out the exact nature of Hebrew chant in the early Christian centuries. Even if one assumes that the Gregorian melodies as written down for the first time in the 9th century go back in basic form for several centuries as an oral tradition, there is no exact parallel in Hebrew chant with which to compare it. The assumption that several Jewish groups have retained an oral tradition untampered by Western practice for almost 2 millennia seems difficult to accept. The Hebrew literary forms, especially the antithetical structure of the Psalms, were carried into early Christian practice. Beyond this, all one can say is that the general musical system common to the Jewish, Syriac, and Hellenized communities became the musical system for early Christianity. The fragment of the Oxyrhynchos papyrus (3d century), which contains a fragment of a hymn written in classical Greek notation, shows that the musical practice was of the type associated with the Near East basin, i.e., diatonic and based on modal formulas related to the octoechos, and had nothing in common with the descriptions and few musical fragments of classical Greek music that have survived.

Descriptions of Musical Practices in the Early Patristic Period. The improvised, charismatic song—associated especially with the Alleluia—continued in Christian worship, although the dangers of pride and theatricality are often alluded to. A distinction in this regard between the roles of cantor, lector, and deacon is often difficult. In the West, it was Gregory who took the melismatic song from the deacon. The general musical practice, however, was of the litany or refrain type (called responsorial; see RESPONSORY). After verses of the Psalms sung by a cantor, the congregation sang a simple refrain. In addition to this practice, there is an allusion in St. Basil to the practice of dividing the congregation into two groups for alternating verses of the Psalms; Basil maintains that this practice was not unique to his region. Various sources for the origin of this practice are given, with Ambrose being cited as the originator of the practice in the West (see Augustine, *Conf.* 9.7). Although the Eastern Church had developed free hymnody and poetry as a part of the liturgical service (see especially St. Ephram), the West was slower to adopt such a practice. After the time of Ambrose, hymnody became a structural part of the Divine Office in addition to Psalms and Biblical lessons. The first allusion in the West to the manner of Psalm singing, which was to become the standard medieval practice, namely the taking over of the responsorial refrain into the antiphonal or alternating style, is found in Cassian (early 5th century). From the 5th century on, less is known of the manner in which the people participated at services; the reason for this lack is that the purpose of the surviving descriptions was to recount monastic and basilical practices.

Attitudes toward Music among the Fathers. The rejection of all musical instruments from Christian worship is consistent among the Fathers. These were associated with pagan, orgiastic rites. For this reason the descriptions in the Old Testament of the temple worship with different kinds of instruments were interpreted allegorically. The heavy influence of Platonic musical aesthetics can be found in the Fathers, especially in Clement of Alexandria and Chrysostom (probably through the writings of Philo). Plato insisted on the need to control the music of the community in order to protect morals. Once the proper number for music was found, it should not be abandoned. The Psalms, thus argued Chrysostom, were divinely given to the Church and were the inspired word. They were the earthly reflection of the divine harmony. In general, the Fathers could be divided into two classes in their attitude toward music: those who accepted it and its beauty, provided the *vox* and *mens* were in agreement (Basil, Cassiodorus, and Benedict); and those who feared the pleasures of music as contrary to the ascetical Christian ideal (Jerome is the supreme example).

Families of Chant. Concommitant with the rise of the various families of Western rites there arose families of Western chant: *Ambrosian, *Gallican, *Mozarabic, and *Gregorian. They all show musical relationships to the contemporaneous *Byzantine chant and a certain interdependency among themselves that musicologists have not accurately determined.

See also MUSIC, HEBREW; CANTOR IN CHRISTIAN LITURGY; PSALMODY; RESPONSORY; ANTIPHON; CONGREGATIONAL SINGING.

Bibliography: H. HUCKE, LexThK² 4:429–433. T. GEORGIADES, RGG³ 4:1207–17. H. LECLERCQ, "Chant romain et grégorien," DACL 3.1:256–311. B. STÄBLEIN, "Choral," MusGG 2:1265–1303; "Frühchristliche Musik," *ibid.* 4:1036–64. E. WERNER, *The Sacred Bridge* (New York 1959). T. GÉROLD, *Les Pères de l'Église et la musique* (Strasbourg 1931). E. WELLESZ, *Eastern Elements in Western Chant* (Oxford 1947). H. ANGLÈS, "Latin Chant before St. Gregory," NewOxHMus 2:58–91. J. QUASTEN, *Musik und Gesang in den Kulten der heidnischen Antike und christlichen Frühzeit* (Münster 1930).

[R. G. WEAKLAND]

2. MONOPHONIC MUSIC TO 1200

The oral traditions of the Christian communities and monasteries (until the invention of musical notation in the 9th century) must have varied greatly one from another. If Pope Gregory the Great at the beginning of the 7th century attempted to bring some order into the liturgical makeup, it is hardly conceivable, given the means of communication of the times, that any uniformity could have been attained in music. The founding of the Roman *schola cantorum and the erecting of monastic chapters at the major basilicas gave life to a Roman chant tradition that became more and more subtle and complex. Darkness still shrouds much of the story as no musical MSS from the period are available. That the reign of the Byzantine popes in the 7th century also had an influence on music can only be surmised.

The Carolingian Period. Before the Carolingian period there was no attempt to keep a musical unity in Christendom, but the concept of Holy Roman Empire included liturgical—and thus musical—imitations of Roman usages. Cantors and liturgical books were brought up to the Carolingian court for diffusion of the Roman practice throughout the empire. The different Gallican usages were to be suppressed in favor of the *cantilena romana,* although Walafrid Strabo (b. 808), a generation later, mentions that those with an ear for music could still recognize the old Gallican tunes in the revised hymnody.

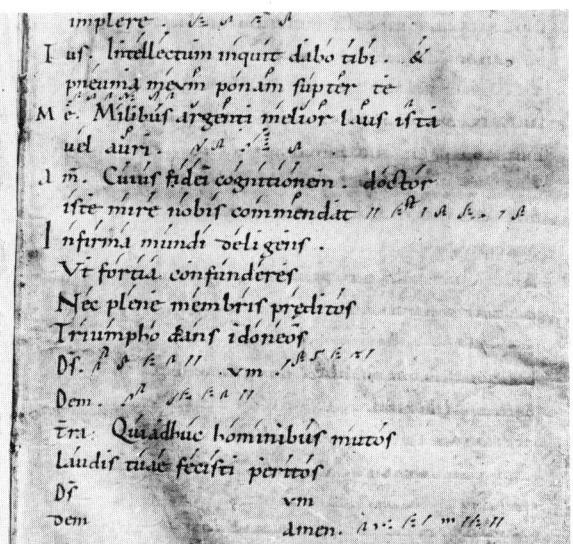

Fig. 1. Portion of a page from a 10th-century manuscript of trope texts and music (Vienna, Aust. Nat. Lib., Collected Codex 1609, fol. 5r, detail).

The first Western music that is written down and can be subjected to a critical analysis is *Gregorian chant. MSS containing the chant appear all over the Empire beginning with the late 9th century. Whether it was the original Roman chant brought north, or a hybrid of Roman and local Gallican practices remains a disputed question, although the latter theory is the more convincing. From the theoretical treatises beginning with the mid-9th century, the actual fragments from the same century, and the full MSS of the 10th century, it is clear that the musical repertoire of that time was a vast one and highly developed. The *Ordines romani* show the numerous adaptations of Roman liturgical practice as well as the need for skilled cantors and leaders (called *primicerius* and *secundicerius*). The music recorded is not that sung by the people, but by the trained *scholae* of clerics and monks. The *antiphonale missarum* or Graduale for the Mass chants and the *antiphonale* for the Office chants contained most of the music needed for the complete year. When the teaching of this standard repertoire resulted in considerable inconvenience, *tonaria* were developed. In them the chants were arranged by modal similarities for easier memorization and reading. The special chants reserved to the soloists were written in the *cantatorium*. The survival of many copies of these books from the 10th century onward makes possible an accurate history of liturgical music from that time. However, not only do we know nothing of the music of the people at this point of history, but we are also totally ignorant of nonliturgical or folk music before the 12th century.

Additions to the Standard Repertoire. The chant repertoire was soon augmented by freely composed additions of texts and melodies that gave birth to *tropes and *sequences. The need for new outlets for the creative imaginations of the post-Carolingian cantors must have come as a result of the rigidity of the standard repertoire. The tropes and sequences permitted the introduction on a given feast of more popular elements and more local allusions. Although there is some evidence that a basic repertoire of these new pieces somehow made its way across the Empire, the differences in the extant collections from various abbeys are large. It is clear that the lengthening of the services by long processions and incensations may have contributed to the need for more music not provided by the standard repertoire. St. Martial at Limoges, France, and Sankt Gallen in present Switzerland were renowned sources for this activity.

Liturgical Drama. Out of the dialogue trope, especially that which preceded the Introit, there arose the liturgical drama. See LITURGICAL DRAMA (MUSIC). Again, it permitted more popular and more didactic elements to enter the liturgy and provided opportunity for freer creativity on the part of the composer. These dramas became larger and larger until they separated entirely from the liturgy.

Other New Compositions. The special talents of the composer from the Carolingian period until the 12th century and beyond also found outlets in the composition of *rimed offices. As new feasts were introduced, experimentation with verse texts and rhythmical patterns found its counterpart in music. The numerous processions connected with monastic services gave birth to a special book called the *processionale*. In it could be found new responsories and antiphons to be sung on special feasts as well as metrical *conductus* or processional hymns. The influence of the growing secular forms that culminated in the troubadours could also be seen in the Latin *planctus* or laments (reaching their peak in those by Abelard) and the new vernacular *laudi, cantigas, and Geisslerlieder*. These new popular forms became especially prominent after the 13th century. During this entire period new compositions of the Ordinary of the Mass in chant continued, both troped and untroped.

Special Chant Traditions. Within the Gregorian tradition one cannot distinguish families as markedly different as were the Gregorian and Ambrosian, for example, but different religious orders and different localities did develop traits peculiar to themselves. Thus the Beneventan tradition in Italy differed from the German not only in notation but in many particular usages. In England the early Gregorian practices merged with new elements after the Norman invasion to form a chant dialect called Sarum (see SARUM RITES, CHANTS OF). The Cistercian reform also affected music and many of the more elaborate chants were brought into simple patterns. The Dominican chant also has its peculiar flavor.

Gregorian chant continued to be used in services long after the new elements listed above and the use of polyphonic music took over the major interests of composers. As it came down through the centuries, this chant was constantly affected by secular music of the times and by contemporary styles and idioms. Attempts to restore it to its pristine vigor have been constant. It can be said, however, that it reached its apogee in the Carolingian and post-Carolingian period and never regained the subtlety evidenced in the earliest MSS of that time. It was only natural that composers, after exhausting the musical means of one style, should have turned so avidly to the possibilities of the new polyphony.

See also TROPE; SEQUENCE; LITURGICAL DRAMA (MUSIC); MASS, ROMAN, MUSIC OF; DIVINE OFFICE,

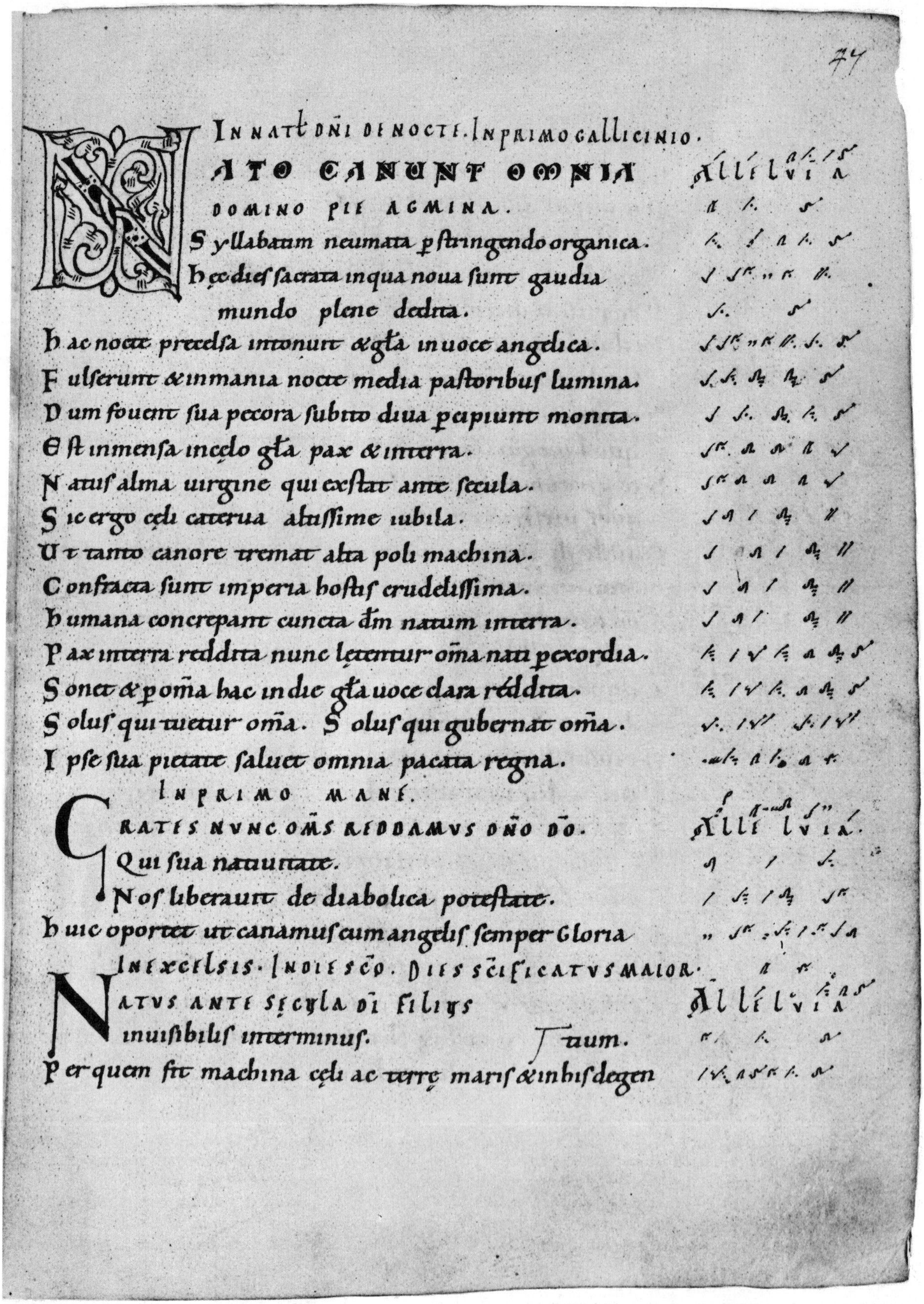

74

IN NATĻ DŅI DE NOCTE. IN PRIMO GALLICINIO.

NATO CANUNT OMNIA   Alleluia

DOMINO PIE AGMINA.

Syllabatim neumata p stringendo organica.

Hæc dies sacrata in qua noua sunt gaudia

mundo plene dedita.

Hac nocte precelsa intonuit ægla in uoce angelica.

Fulserunt & inmania nocte media pastoribus lumina.

Dum fouent sua pecora subito diua pcipiunt monita.

Est inmensa in celo gła pax & in terra.

Natus alma uirgine qui exstat ante secula.

Sic ergo celi caterua altissime iubila.

Ut tanto canore tremat alta poli machina.

Confracta sunt imperia hostis crudelissima.

Humana concrepant cuncta dm natum in terra.

Pax in terra reddita nunc letentur oma nati pcordia.

Sonet & poma hac in die gła uoce clara reddita.

Solus qui tuetur oma. Solus qui gubernat oma.

Ipse sua pietate saluet omnia pacata regna.

IN PRIMO MANE.

GRATES NUNC OMS REDDAMVS DŅO DO.   Alleluia

Qui sua natiuitate.

Nos liberauit de diabolica potestate.

Huic oportet ut canamus cum angelis semper Gloria

IN EXCELSIS. IN DIE SCO. DIES SCIFICATVS MAIOR

NATVS ANTE SECVLA DI FILIVS   Alleluia

Inuisibilis interminus.   Tuum.

Per quem fit machina celi ac terre maris & in his degen

Fig. 2. Texts of Christmas sequences with Sankt Gallen neumes set along side, page from the "Salzburg Graduale" written at the Abbey of Sankt Peter in Salzburg in 1060, now in the Austrian National Library (Codex 1845, fol. 47r).

ROMAN, CHANTS OF; RIMED OFFICE; GREGORIAN CHANT.

Bibliography: Apel GregCh. H. ANGLÈS, "Gregorian Chant," NewOxHMus 2:92–127. J. HANDSCHIN, "Trope, Sequence, and Conductus," ibid. 128–174. S. CORBIN, L'Église à la conquête de sa musique (Paris 1960). A. GASTOUÉ, Les Origines du chant romain (Paris 1907). Ursprung. Wagner GregMel. **Illustration credit:** Figs. 1 and 2, Picture-Archives, Austrian National Library.

[R. G. WEAKLAND]

3. POLYPHONIC MUSIC: ORIGINS TO 1450

The 9th century, the era of the *Carolingian renaissance, with its palace school and liturgical reforms, had also provided the first example of written counterpoint in the anonymous treatise *Musica enchiriadis* (Gerbert ScriptEcclMusS 2:168). There is no certain evidence as to what extent either written or unwritten part music may have existed before then.

Early Organum. The examples in *Musica enchiriadis* are all syllabic, note against note, and very short. They are called *organum, the name given until c. 1250 to all the various styles of polyphony that involve a liturgical melody and added voice parts. Some, called "strict," proceed in simple parallel motion at the fourth or fifth; others, called "free," have oblique motion as well.

A gap of more than 100 years occurred before the next important treatise, a chapter in *Guido of Arezzo's *Micrologus* (c. 1040), where counterpoint is more firmly established by introducing the concept of planned contrary motion at the cadences (*occursus*): major 2d or 3d to unison. Examples reveal also the crossing of parts; and free organum is preferred to strict. Outside the theoretical treatises, the largest number of examples of polyphony—about 164 organa—is found in the 11th-century MS Corpus Christi College 473, called the *Winchester Troper.*

The music of *Winchester* confirms the theorists' statements on contrary motion, but the pitches cannot be transcribed accurately since the example are written with staffless (cheironomic) neums. Two other MSS, Lucca 603 and Chartres 109, are written with neums on staves; hence their music can be transcribed accurately with regard to pitch but not to rhythm. The striking example from the Chartres MS ignores the theorists' rules of perfect consonances in order to build lines with color and strength.

Toward the year 1080, the start of a renaissance that was to last through the 12th century made its appearance with some of the finest Romanesque buildings, the *Chanson de Roland,* the earliest *troubadours, and the first substantial growth in polyphony. Four MSS from the Limoges district, probably from the monastery of St. Martial [Bibliothèque Nationale lat. 1.1139 (late 11th century), BN 1.3459, 3749 (12th century), and British Museum add. 36881 (early 13th century)] contain polyphonic works. Most are written with neums that are heighted or on a staff (diastematic), so that the pitches are clear. Transcription of rhythm, however, involves so much guesswork that scholars differ widely in their interpretation. The most striking device is the lengthening of the chant, or tenor, notes to sometimes as long as 26 notes of the added voice (as in *Jubilemus exultemus,* BN 1.1139, fol. 41), so that actual preception as melody is excluded. It sounds more like a series of drones at various levels, a method later developed by the Notre Dame school. On fol. 60′ of BN 1.1139, the upper voice of the *Benedicamus Domino* is troped, i.e., has its own separate text added to the melody and text of the liturgical tenor (*see* TROPE). This device qualifies it as an example of the early *motet, a polyphonic form that was to become prominent during the 13th century. In the melismatic passages of many pieces the beginnings of masterful contrapuntal technique appear. These passages alternate sensitively with the note-against-note passages and lose the angularity of more primitive counterpoint. The quality of melody, however, differs from chant, with many melodic sequences and sweeping descents. Extraordinary passages like those below contain some of the earliest examples of exchanged voices, called *Stimmtausch,* as well as imitation.

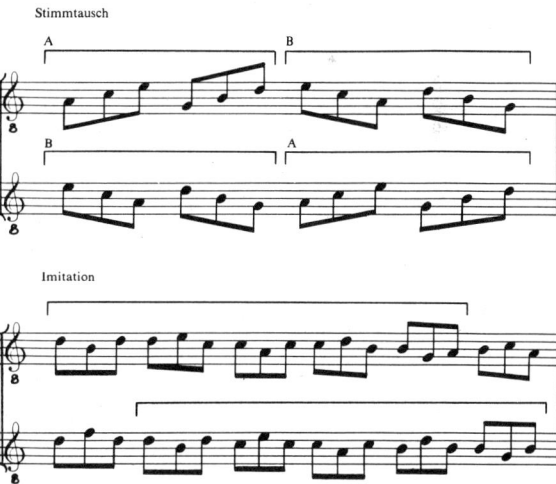

Another MS, copied c. 1140, the Codex Calixtinus in the cathedral library in Compostela, Spain, has 20 two-part *organa* and the oldest known three-part piece, *Congaudeant catholici.* The middle voice appears to have been interpolated later; some parts of it function as a filler, being without melodic interest.

The Ars Antiqua (The Old Art). The first contrapuntal school to produce music of international acclaim was that of Notre Dame, which flourished in and near Paris during the late 12th and early 13th centuries. Its music

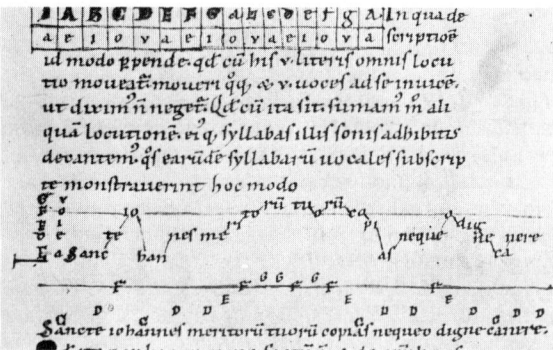

Fig. 3. Letter-notes on lines in a 12th-century manuscript of Guido of Arezzo's "Micrologus" preserved in the Austrian National Library, Vienna (Codex 51, folio 40 verso).

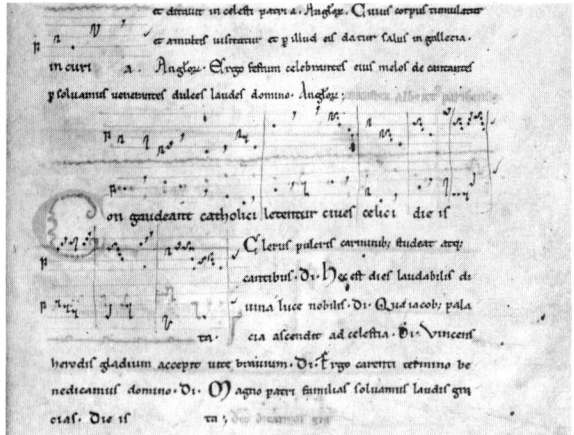

Fig. 4. The beginning of "Congaudeant catholici" in the Codex Calixtinus (fol. 185r, detail), at Compostella.

may be found in three 13th-century MSS: Florence *Biblioteca Laurenziana* Pl. 29.1 (F), and Wolfenbüttel *Bibliothek* 677 (W¹) and 1206 (W²), each containing over 190 closely written pages of polyphony. As this music was performed in monasteries and cathedrals throughout Europe, large and small collections may be found in 60 or more other MSS copied as far away as Spain, England, and Bavaria. Although not all the rhythmic problems have been worked out, most of the transcriptions done recently are faithful enough to convey the poetical aspects of the music and warrant performance in church, concert, or recording.

The original Notre Dame collection was called the *Magnus liber organi* (Great Book of Organa), and, according to the English theorist known to musicologists as Anonymous IV (Coussemaker ScriptMusMA 1:342), it included settings for the feast days of the entire ecclesiastical year written by the composer *Léonin and partly rewritten by his successor, *Pérotin. Anonymous IV stated that the *Magnus liber* was in use at the cathedral of Paris until his own day (c./1280); this, however, is not proof that it originated there. The *Magnus liber* has not survived, but the organa common to all three Notre Dame MSS, as well as those common to F and W², are considered by Husmann to have belonged to that original collection (MusQ 49:311–330).

Léonin and his successors set the Proper rather than the Ordinary of the Mass, together with the solo parts of the Gradual and Alleluia and some responsorial sections of the Office, leaving the choral parts of the service to be sung in unison as on the nonfestive days of the year.

The chief difference between a Saint-Martial and a Notre Dame *organum* was that the latter was organized according to one of six repeated patterns of rhythm called *modi*.

These patterns were varied at irregular intervals by omitting a weak beat (*fusio modi*), inserting a rest (*pausatio*), or by breaking a note into several quick ornaments (*fractio modi*); these variations, however, never obscured the patterns. The syllabic sections of the tenor could stretch out beneath the upper melisma in even longer drones than at Saint-Martial, sometimes lasting 40 measures. The added voice or voices crossed and recrossed one another as in the earlier styles of organum, though by Pérotin's time the phrases had become short and clear-cut. Phrases usually began and ended on perfect consonances, touching unisons midway. The perfect consonances appeared, too, on most accented beats, the other beats carrying any of the other intervals.

New in Notre Dame was the treatment of the melismatic sections of the chant tenor, reshaped rhythmically into one of the *modi*, often a slower *modus* than that of the added voice. These sections were called *discantus* or *clausulae*. The measuring of both or all voices, together with the heritage of unifying devices from Saint-Martial and Léonin, made possible the construction of really interesting works in three parts by Pérotin and his contemporaries. Before the turn of the century, Pérotin wrote the first four-part works, *Viderunt* (F, fol. 1) and *Sederunt* (W¹ fol. 1). The *clausulae* form the link with the two later periods of the *Ars antiqua,* as many were transformed into motets by adding texts to the upper voices. Later, original motets were composed. Starting as a sacred form, the motet underwent secular influence, and love songs, often frivolous and imaginative, were added to the liturgical tenors or even combined with sacred verse in another voice. The counterpoint continued to gain its marvelous linear liberty, which combined with increasing vertical subtlety.

The rhythmic changes occurring during the 12th and 13th centuries kept the notational systems in an almost constant state of flux. Among the theorists were *John of Garland, *Walter Odington, *Johannes de Grocheo, as well as the above mentioned Anonymous IV. Two theorists undertook important reforms of notation. In the mid-13th century, *Franco of Cologne facilitated exactness in reading by assigning definite time values to the conventional note forms then in use (*Ars cantus mensurabilis;* see Coussemaker ScriptMusMA 1:117). At the end of the century, *Petrus de Cruce introduced further notational innovations to facilitate distinction among the smaller note values.

The Ars Nova (The New Art). A new musical spirit appeared early in the 14th century. The six rhythmic patterns of the 12th- and 13th-century *modi,* which had long served as means of unification, now became a prison. The musical idea of the 14th century usually found expression in complicated rhythms, often with iambic and trochaic figures in the same phrase. Triple rhythm had been the norm during the time of the *ars antiqua,* with duple as the exception; now both were the norm, with the duple indicated at first by red notation (e.g., MS BN 1.146, *Le Roman de Fauvel*), later by time signatures. Sometimes one voice alternated rapidly with rests in the other (the "hocket"). The first musical canon had appeared in France in 1288 and was followed by many others.

The traditional employment of rhythmic figures as unifying devices continued, however, in a new way. The 13th-century patterns (*ostinati*) were replaced by whole complicated phrases, sometimes as long as 10 measures, which were repeated several times with fresh pitches (isorhythm). The working out of so much that was new in counterpoint and organization involved a temporary neglect in the setting of words, the latter becoming a mere pretext, sometimes, for the setting of multiple lines.

In a time of profound change it is inevitable that there be modernists and conservatives. Many of the innovations were condemned by the *Docta sanctorum* (1322) of Pope John XXII. Composers were accused of arbitrary interruptions in melody, addition of frivolous vernacular texts to the sacred chants, and, in general, of preferring modern to ancient music. The *Docta sanctorum* went so far as to regulate technical details, permitting only the Pythagorean 4th, 5th, and 8ve (octave) in counterpoint, over a chant tenor that must be rhythmically unaltered. Although parts of this letter are understandable in view of the bold procedures that were just beginning, it is unfortunate that it was written before the characteristic 14th-century works had appeared. Those who drafted it could not realize how the new style would be made to speak in a work as august as Guillaume de *Machaut's Mass (transcribed in 1949 by G. Van, in CorpMensMus 2). This great monument of the 14th century, the first known polyphonic Mass to be written by one person, combines solid tradition, in its isorhythmic foundation, with wild audacity, especially in its astounding rhythms and intervals. The Kyrie, Sanctus, and Agnus Dei have sections with isorhythm in all voices, some contrasting sharply with others in speed. The Gloria and Credo prolong the *conductus* tradition, alternating between marching block chords and held chords. The whole disconcerting and exalting work is united by five or more motifs, some appearing in each movement.

Machaut brought high refinement, astonishing melodies, and unexpected chromatics to the other forms that he inherited—the *lai, complainte, virelai, rondeau, ballade.* His double ballade has two simultaneous texts. His motets, like the Mass, have the traditional base of isorhythm, though in extremely complex phrases, which are sometimes repeated in diminution. His works can be found in over 30 MSS, most of them transcribed by Friedrich *Ludwig.

Among composer-theorists, two leaders of the new movement were Philippe de *Vitry and *Johannes de Muris. Vitry introduced the term *Ars nova* (c. 1325) as the title to a treatise that, however, deals mainly with notational rather than musical innovations (see Coussamaker ScriptMusMA). In his compositions there are numerous complete chords, some tonal cadences, and passages with consecutive thirds. Both composers frequently raised the 7th degree to function as leading tone (*musica falsa*), and sometimes even the 4th degree in the same cadence, as leading tone to the dominant, forming a cadence with a strangely modern sound (Burgundian cadence). The tracts of Johannes de Muris are available in Coussemaker ScriptMusMA, Gerbert ScriptEcclMusS, and Strunk SourceR.

The period between Machaut and *Dufay, known as that of the mannerists (see Apel NotPolyMus 403–435), produced much secular and some sacred music with even more complicated rhythms than before, with a tendency for recherché combinations and picturesqueness. Composers in France were Baude Caurdier (fl. *c.* 1400), Jean Tapissier, Cesaris, Grimace, and many others.

The passage below by Cesaris (from *Polyphonia sacra,* ed. C. van den Borren, 174–175), has a concentrated treatment of motives suggestive of Webern. Much of this music has recently been transcribed by G. Reaney.

Some music for religious dance, appearing in a MS at Sens, consists of a liturgical Gradual reshaped isorhythmically, with indications for the steps (J. Chailley, 21:18).

In Italy the first part of the 14th century saw French *ars nova* influence, with copies of French works in Italian MSS; later there was influence of French on Italian forms. This period is represented by Giovanni da Cascia (1300–50) and Jacopo da Bologna. Little sacred music has survived. Composition in the last part of the century was dominated by the blind organist of Florence, Francesco *Landini (1325–97), who astonished and moved everyone by the speed and delicacy of his playing on the portative organ and who won the laurel crown reserved for poets and emperors. He introduced some of the complexities of Machaut's style, to which he added an Italian sweetness of melody. His contemporaries were Partolino da Padua, Paolo Tenorista, Ghirardello da Firenze, and Johannes *Ciconia, among many others. A typical style involved moving two voices together, the upper one with added ornaments, as in Bartolino's setting for the Credo (in G. de

Van, *Les Monuments de l'Ars Nova*). The consecutive thirds are noteworthy.

For further examples of this music, see N. Pirrotta and L. Ellenwood (in bibliog.). Important manuscripts are MS Torino Bibl. Naz. J II 9 (ed. Hopper) and MS Firenze Bibl. Laur. Squarcialuppi Pal. 87 (ed. J. Wolf). The chief theorists were *Marchettus of Padua, who wrote a comparison of French and Italian notation, *Pomerium musica mensurata* (Gerbert ScriptEcclMusS 3:121), *Prosdocimo de Beldemandis (Coussemaker ScriptMusMA 3:218), and *Ugolino of Orvieto (see F. X. Haberl, in bibliog.). Ugolino clarified some of the rules of *musica falsa.*

In 14th-century England, Worcester appears to have been the important center. The chief English contribution was the use of the 6th chord in parallel motion, with the liturgical chant in the lowest voice (discant). There was much reciprocal influence between England and France. The composer who dominated early 15th-century England was John *Dunstable (d. 1453), musician and astronomer. His music, although essentially in the style of the French *ars nova,* avoided that school's artificial modernism, having a transparent beauty and naturalness destined later to characterize the works of the early Renaissance.

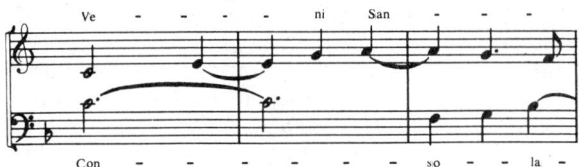

Others of the early 15th-century English school were the insular composers Cooke, Damett, and Sturgeon, and the Continental ones, Lionel *Power and Bedingham. A MS known as Old Hall, at the Catholic College of St. Edmonds, contains Mass parts and hymns by many of these composers (ed. A. Ramsbotham and H. Collins). Dunstable's complete works were edited by M. Bukofzer for *Musica Britannica.* Also in *Musica Britannica* (v.55) is a collection of 15th-century English carols in two and three parts, which were assembled from a number of MSS. Most are in English, the rest in Latin.

Bibliography: F. Ludwig, *Repertorium organorum . . . et motetorum . . .* (Leipzig 1910), descriptive catalogue of the

Notre Dame and allied manuscripts. F. GENNRICH, *Bibliographie der ältesten . . . Motetten* (Darmstadt 1957). C. VAN DEN BORREN, ed., *Polyphonia sacra* (rev. ed. University Park, Pa. 1963). N. PIRROTTA, ed., *Music of Fourteenth-Century Italy* (Corp MensMus 8; 1954). G. REANEY, ed., *Early Fifteenth-Century Music* (ibid. 11; 1955). G. DE VAN, ed., *Les Monuments de l'Ars Nova*, fasc. 1 (Paris 1938). H. TISCHLER, ed., *The Earliest Motets*, CorpMensMus v.30 (in press), 12th- and early-13th-century motet collections. F. LANDINO, *Works*, ed. L. ELLINWOOD (Cambridge, Mass. 1939). J. CHAILLEY, *Histoire musicale du moyen âge* (Paris 1950); "Un Document nouveau sur la danse ecclésiastique," *Acta musicologica* 21 (1949) 18–24. W. G. WAITE, *The Rhythm of Twelfth-Century Polyphony* (New Haven 1954), with transcriptions of two-part organa in W¹. H. HUSMANN, *Die Drei- und vierstimmigen Notre-Dame-Organa* (Leipzig 1940), with transcriptions of three- and four-part organa; "The Origin and Destination of the *Magnus liber organi*," tr. G. REANEY, MusQ 49 (1963) 311–330. E. THURSTON, *The Conductus Compositions in Manuscript Wolfenbuttel 1206* (Doctoral diss. microfilm; N.Y.U. 1954), with transcriptions of *conductus* in W². Y. ROKSETH, *Polyphonies du XIIIᵉ siècle*, 4 v. (Paris 1935–39), with transcriptions of a large 13th-century motet collection. U. KORNMÜLLER, "Musikleben des Ugolino von Orvieto," *Kirchenmusikalisches Jahrbuch* 10 (1895) 19–40. F. X. HABERL, "Bio-bibliographische Notizen über Ugolino von Orvieto," *ibid.* 40–49. J. HANDSCHIN, "The Two Winchester Tropers," JThSt 37 (1936) 34–49, 156–172. L. TREITLER, "The Polyphony of St. Martial," JAmMusSoc 17 (1964) 29–42. Reese MusMA. NewOxHMus v.2. Apel NotPolyMus 201–202, list of medieval theorists who discussed notation. Strunk SourceR. Coussemaker ScriptMusMA. Gerbert ScriptEcclMusS. H. HÜSCHEN, MusGG 1:679–702. H. BESSELER, *ibid.* 702–729. **Illustration credit:** Fig. 3, Picture-Archives, Austrian National Library. Fig. 4, MAS, Barcelona.

[E. THURSTON]

4. POLYPHONIC MUSIC, 1450–1600

The Middle Ages developed a strong organized and measured rhythm. The 15th and 16th centuries saw this trend enhanced by melodic as well as rhythmic fluidity into a contrapuntal art never surpassed.

Music of Northern France and the Low Countries. With the coming of the Guillaume *Dufay generation, paraphrasing of the chant in Mass compositions became widespread (*see* MASS, ROMAN, MUSIC OF). Often, however, the chant melody was so extensively elaborated as to be hardly recognizable. Composition in the treble-dominated style continued. Complete Mass Ordinaries began to appear in profusion, and *cantus-firmus* treatment became a chief method of unification. In a *cantus-firmus* Mass of this period, the chosen melody, sacred or secular, was normally presented by the tenor in relatively long time-values, while the other voices wove constantly fresh polyphony about it.

One method of composition much utilized, especially in hymns, was *fauxbourdon,* in which the unwritten middle part moved in parallel fourths with the upper part. The result was largely a series of 6/3 and 8/5 chords, in contrast to later Italian *falso bordone,* which, commonly applied in 16th-century *psalmody, employed mainly chords in root position but was similarly chordal (with florid cadences), recitativelike, and given to repetition. Common cadences in the period were the "under-third" (sometimes wrongly called the "Landini sixth"); the "octave-leap," in which the bass leaps up an octave while the tenor crosses below it, and the so-called "Burgundian cadence," which has two different, simultaneously sounding leading tones. The polyphonic flow might occasionally be interrupted by fermata-marked block-chords to emphasize words of special importance.

Sources. The most extensive sources for sacred polyphony dating from *c.* 1420 to *c.* 1480 are seven codices compiled at Trent, then under Germanic control. They contain over 1,800 compositions, most of them sacred. An example of a more accurate but smaller source (containing 339 works) is the famous MS Q15 at Bologna.

Composers. Jean Brassart and Arnold de Lantins joined the papal choir in 1431. Arnold's three-voice Mass is among the early complete settings of the Ordinary after *Machaut (see section 3 of this article). Guillaume Dufay was one of the greatest exponents of French music, regardless of period. He wrote in all the forms and used all the techniques of his day. His Mass on *L'Homme armé* may be the first in the long list of *cantus-firmus* Masses based on that celebrated tune. *Cantus-firmus* style gradually replaced the treble-dominated in the Masses of Dufay. His compositions in sequence- and hymn-form illustrate the systematic alternation of plainsong and polyphony, a technique also applied in some of his separate Mass movements.

The tenors of a number of chansons of Gilles Binchois and Antoine Busnois were used as *cantus firmi* in Masses by later composers. Binchois's motets and Magnificats contain much *fauxbourdon*-like writing. Johannes Okeghem, who enjoyed a reputation for excellence among his contemporaries, is the acknowledged master of the latter part of the 15th century, as well as the composer of the earliest surviving polyphonic Requiem setting. Okeghem often conspicuously avoided the clear phrase formation found in compositions by Dufay and Busnois, and preferred to keep the flow of polyphony constant. His style is characterized by grand, sweeping melodic lines.

Renaissance Style. The small total range that was typical of medieval polyphony, and abetted the frequent crossing of voices, went hand in hand with a sharp differentiation of the individual parts—whether in rhythm, in melody, or in the timbres of the performing media. As a wider range came into use, crossing became less frequent and differentiation between the voices less sharp. The growing homogeneity of the voices eventually resulted in the establishment of imitation as the standard technique of the late Renaissance. As to form, the larger structures that were widely cultivated included not only the Mass but also the *Magnificat, of which whole cycles were written in all the modes (often two examples of each).

Mass Compositions. During the Renaissance, a tendency developed to write complete Mass Ordinaries. The cyclic Mass, in which the sections are related to each other, resulted from an effort to unify the Mass as a whole. Two main types, the *cantus-firmus* Mass and the "motto" Mass (which involves the use of a head motif), were already being used in the early 15th century. The parody Mass, which is based, not on a single melody, but on the several voices of a polyphonic model, came to be favored by 16th-century composers. The 15th and 16th centuries are notable also for the development of the organ Mass. Here, in certain movements, alternate verses were represented by music solely for organ, the other verses being sung in plainsong (*see* ORGAN MUSIC).

Theorists. The 12 treatises of Johannes Tinctoris (*c.* 1435–1511) form a *summa* that affords insight into the musical theory of the entire Renaissance. Other theorists active *c.* 1480 were Franchino Gaforio, whose

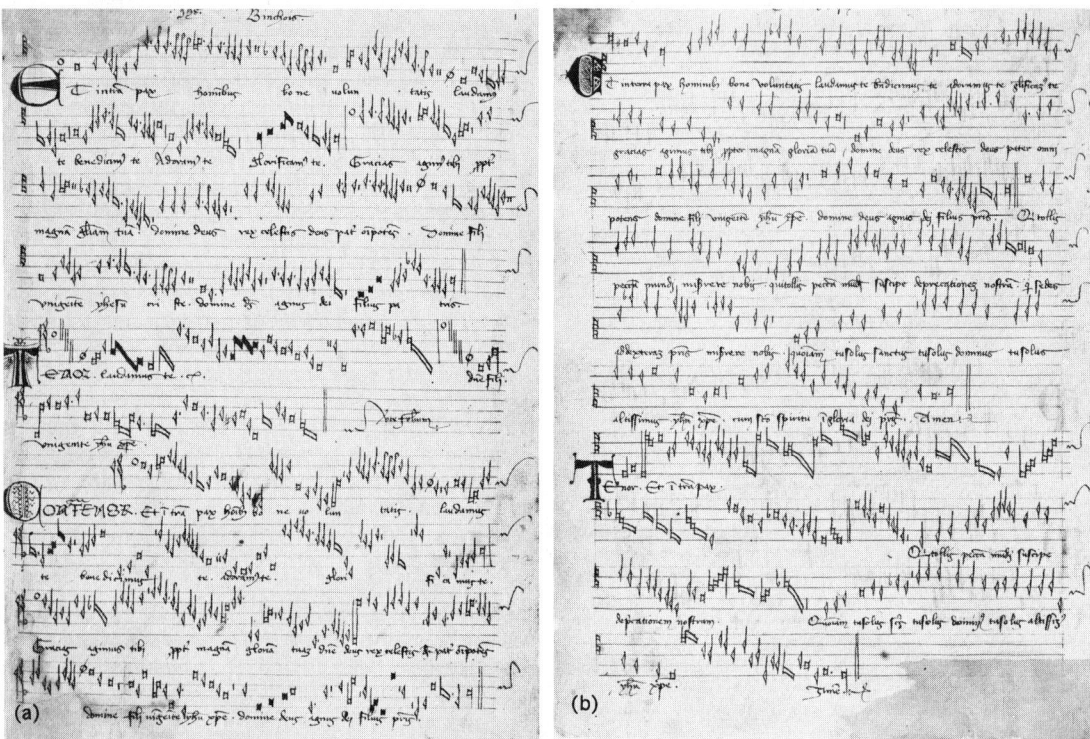

Fig. 4. Polyphonic music (1450–1600): (a) "Et in terra pax" of Binchois, French manuscript, c. 1436 (MS Canon. Misc. 213, fol. 60v). (b) "Et in terra pax" of Dufay, same MS (fol. 1r). (c) Guillaume Dufay and Gilles Binchois, miniature, 15th-century manuscript of "Le Champion des Dames" (MS Fr. 12476, fol. 98r); they are shown with a small portable organ and a minstrel's harp.

important contributions include his eight rules of counterpoint and theory of proportions, the Spanish Bartolomé Ramos de Pareja, and the German Adam of Fulda. Pietro Aaron, who wrote in the vernacular, desired consistent indication of accidentals and emphasized practical terminology. The Swiss Henricus Glareanus gave separate identity to the Ionian, the Aeolian, and their plagals in the traditional system of ecclesiastical modes. Virtually all these provided equivalents for major and minor. Giuseppe Zarlino recognized the difference in effect of major and minor harmonies. He also gave 10 rules for underlying words to polyphonic music. Among other important Renaissance theorists were Francisco de Salinas, Domenico Pietro Cerone, and Adrianus Petit Coclico.

Music Printing. The first important printer of music other than plainsong was Ottaviano dei Petrucci of Venice. His sacred publications include some 15 collections of Masses and about 15 of motets and other sacred works, such as *Lamentations and *laude.*

Franco-Netherlandish Composers (c. 1490–c. 1560). In the period of Josquin *Desprez practically every basic feature of Renaissance music that did not already exist made its appearance. A fusion of the art impulses of Italian and Franco-Netherlandish music was in process and produced the underlying musical style of the late Renaissance. The characteristic qualities of the new music were molded by a large group of singularly gifted composers, all vigorously active at about the same time. Of these, Jacob Obrecht, Alexander Agricola, Heinrich Isaak, Loyset Compère, Josquin Desprez, Antoine Brumel, Pierre de La Rue, Antoine de Févin, Jean Mouton, and Carpentras were outstanding. One of the prominent features of Obrecht's Masses is his breaking of a *cantus firmus* into segments and employing each one repeatedly, reserving a complete consecutive presentation for the tenor or some other voice toward the end. Isaak's monumental *Choralis Constantinus (Constantiensis)* is the first comprehensive polyphonic setting of Propers of the Mass spanning the whole Church year. It includes the Propers for all Sundays and for certain feast and saints' days. Of interest among the works of Compère are two "substitution" Masses. Such works consist of a series of motets, each intended to replace a liturgical Mass movement. Josquin Desprez was the foremost composer of the early Renaissance, serving also as a transition to the late Renaissance. Although he is at his very best as a motet composer, where he is not restricted to one text, Desprez is still a central figure in the field of the Mass. His works in this form collectively illustrate all the basic Mass techniques of the entire Renaissance. Here, as elsewhere, his technical virtuosity is such that contrapuntal complexity in no way interferes with apparent spontaneity.

Post-Josquin Period. After Josquin's death, his style was further developed and disseminated throughout Europe by Netherlandish composers. The Franco-Netherlandish style took root on foreign soil, producing masters such as Palestrina in Italy, Victoria in Spain, Senfl in Germany, and Byrd in England. A general trend toward simplicity in French writing is evident in the post-Josquin period. A distinct tradition that developed in the French Mass showed a tendency toward chordal writing and a resulting clarity of text. "Word painting"—an attempt to depict actual words through musical devices—gained in popularity. All these trends were

evident in the works of a group now known as the "Paris school," of which Claude de Sermisy and Pierre Certon, both of the Sainte-Chapelle, and Clément Jannequin were the leading representatives. The three most important composers of sacred polyphony in the period between Josquin and Lasso were Nicolas Gombert, Clemens non Papa, and Adrian Willaert. In the sacred music of Gombert, pervading imitation is a pronounced trait. Clemens, a prolific writer of motets, composed three-part settings for the *Souterliedekens,* or "Little Psalter Songs," an extremely popular collection of monophonic settings of the 150 Psalms in Dutch rhymed verse, originally intended for Catholic use outside the church. Willaert spent his last 35 years at St. Mark's in Venice. His main contributions to sacred polyphony in Italy were: (1) the establishment of Franco-Netherlandish technique in church music; (2) the development of choral antiphony; and (3) the cultivation of a "modern" style emphasizing faultless declamation of the text. Other important composers of sacred music in Italy during this period were Costanzo Festa (who spent nearly 30 years in the papal service), Jakob Arcadelt, Nicolò Vicentino, Philippe *Verdelot, Jachet Berchem, Jacques Buus, and Cipriano de *Rore. Claude Goudimel, who remained for the most part in France, composed works for Catholic use prior to his becoming a Huguenot c. 1460.

Council of Trent and Church Music. In 1562 a canon was approved at the Council of Trent that banned from church music all seductive or impure melodies, all vain and worldly texts, and all outcries and uproars, and decreed that the words be clearly understandable (*see* MUSIC, SACRED, LEGISLATION ON). A minority attempt to restrict the Mass to monophonic setting was rebuffed. Tendencies, already present, toward carefully observing Latin accentuation and curtailing melismas purely on artistic and humanistic grounds, were confirmed by the Commission of Cardinals, which sat following the Council. In response to a need for shorter and simpler polyphonic Masses, the *Missa brevis,* which happened to conform to the requirements of the Commission, became common. The prestige of plainsong temporarily declined, partly owing to a change in musical ideals to which Gregorian chant no longer conformed.

Late Renaissance Music in Italy (c. 1560–c. 1600). Probably one of the influences persuading the Council to retain polyphony in the Church was the frequent performance at its early sessions of the *Preces speciales* of Jacobus de *Kerle. Kerle, Palestrina, Animuccia, Lasso, and Rosselli contributed to the investigation by composing contrapuntal Masses. Among the works of Giovanni Animuccia are two collections of *laude spirituali.* *Laude* were canticles of praise to be sung in the evening before the image of the Virgin, a practice dating from the 13th century. The sacred works of Palestrina have long been regarded as embodying the ideal application of polyphony to music for the Catholic Church. They represent the last stage in the development of a style that systematized the handling of dissonance and the use of certain time values in particular rhythmic contexts. Palestrina's predilection for symmetrical structure and quiet harmonies is reminiscent of the Josquin style. Although Palestrina's 105 surviving Masses are, as a group, his greatest contribution, his numerous motets and related works include some of his finest compositions. Among other composers of

Fig. 5. Title page of volume 4 of Orlando di Lasso's work, "Patrocinium Musices," from the edition of 1576. Volume 4 of the work is devoted to four-, five-, six-, and eight-voice settings of the "Magnificat."

Fig. 6. Two pages (a and b) from volume 4 of Orlando di Lasso's "Patrocinium Musices" as they appear in the edition of 1576. These pages show the beginning of one of the composer's four-voice settings of the "Magnificat."

sacred music active at Rome were the madrigalist Luca Marenzio, Giovanni Maria Nanino, Felice Anerio, and Annibale Zoilo.

Other Italian centers made noteworthy contributions. At Modena, Orazio Vecchi wrote sacred works much affected by secular traits. Mantua fostered Giaches de Wert and Giovanni Gastoldi. At Milan, Vincenzo Ruffo, encouraged by Cardinal Borromeo, wrote much in a preponderantly choral style with the specific purpose of meeting the wishes of the Council of Trent, while Orfeo Vecchi, foreshadowing the 17th century, provided his Masses with *basso continuo*. Among other important composers were Marco Antonio Ingegneri at Cremona, Carlo Gesualdo (Prince of Venosa) at Naples, and Giovanni Matteo Asola and Costanzo Porta in cities near Venice. The Venetian composers, as a group, dedicated their best efforts to the motet rather than to the Mass. Andrea Gabrieli and his nephew, Giovanni, both organists at St. Mark's, wrote distinguished polychoral motets.

Renaissance in Spain and Portugal. Spanish music in the 15th century was strongly influenced by that of France, and, increasingly, of Italy. The two greatest Spanish composers of sacred music in the late Renaissance were Cristóbal de Morales and Tomás Luis de Victoria. Although Morales based his work on Franco-Netherlandish models, he achieved an individual style marked at the same time by starkness and richness. Victoria belongs stylistically with the Roman school, though his writing tended more toward abrupt and vigorous lines and leaps uncharacteristic of the Palestrina style. Other composers of sacred music in 15th- and 16th-century Spain were Johannes Cornago, Johannes Urredo (actually Wreede, a Fleming), Juan del Encina, Diego Ortiz, Francisco Querrero, and Juan Pablo Pujol.

In Middle Europe. German sacred music with Latin text shows, on the whole, extreme conservatism in the 15th century, while leaning heavily on Franco-Netherlandish precept. Three features characterize the sacred polyphony to about 1500: (1) a tendency to fall into closed, uneven periods, as opposed to the smooth, unceasing flow of Franco-Netherlandish music; (2) continuous activity of all four voices, as opposed to the Western preference for varying the texture by means of passages for two or three voices; and (3) awkwardness in the treatment of rhythm. The most important sacred composer in the early period was Heinrich Finck, who quite transcended the general run. German sacred composition of the 16th century continued to be strongly influenced by Franco-Netherlandish models, and later also by Italian. The leading native Germanic composers of the century were Ludwig Senfl and Hans Leo Hassler. More important and influential, however, was a Walloon at the court of Albert V of Bavaria, Orlando di Lasso. His motets for four or more voices display much chordal writing mingled with the polyphony (the breakdown of pervading imitation being well under way); a feeling for harmonic propriety, made evident by the many chord roots that progress by leaps of fourths and fifths; and the inclusion of the third or fifth of a chord much oftener than in Palestrina. Lasso, unlike Senfl, employed Gregorian chant in very few of his Masses, the great majority of them being parodies of works by himself and other composers. Among the Netherlanders active at the Hapsburg court were Kerle, Jacob Vaet, Philippe de Monte, Jacques Buus, Jacques Regnart, and Carl Luython. The Slovene Jacob Händl (Jacobus Gallus), also in Hapsburg employ, was active principally in Bohemia. His *Opus musicum* is a collection of motets for the whole liturgical year. The German Thomas Stoltzer was active mainly in Hungary. By far the most brilliant native musical development in the East was that of the Poles, among whom Waclav of Szamotuł, Nicholas Gomółka, and Nicholas Zieleński are outstanding.

Music in England. England was one of the leading musical nations about 1450. After mid-century, however, the English tended increasingly toward an insular conservatism, culminating in the works of William Cornysh, Robert Fayrfax, and others. Fayrfax, relying heavily on pure counterpoint, made much less use of imitation than Josquin. The greatest English composer in the early 16th century was John Taverner. The polyphonic lines in his Masses show greater freedom and complexity than those of his contemporaries, yet many of the same technical features are evident—frequent changes in vocal registration, repetition of melodic fragments by varying voice groups, and instances of *fermata*-marked block chords. Important composers of the period after the formal break between England and the papacy in 1534 were Christopher Tye, Robert White, John Shepard, and Thomas Tallis. All wrote works with both Latin as well as English texts, and it is not always possible to tell whether a piece of Tudor church music with Latin text was intended for the Roman Catholic service or the Anglican, in its earlier stages. The finest Elizabethan composer of Latin church music was William Byrd. His *Gradualia* is the last of the great Renaissance Proper cycles, the others being those of Isaak and Händl. Among other Elizabethan composers of Latin sacred polyphony were Alfonso Ferrabosco I, Thomas Morley, John Wilbye, Richard Deering, and Peter Philips.

Bibliography: Reese MusR. NewOxHMus v.3. Fellerer Cath ChMus. **Illustration credits:** Fig. 4*a*, Bibliothèque Nationale, Paris. Fig. 4*b* and *c*, Reproduced by permission of the Bodleian Library, Oxford. Figs. 5 and 6, Reid Music Library, University of Edinburgh.

[G. REESE]

5. THE BAROQUE PERIOD

All the music of the baroque period is dominated by opera, which began with the early *favole in musica* of J. Peri (1561–1633), G. Caccini (*c.* 1546–1618), and especially *Monteverdi (1567–1643), and which, with the opening of the first public opera house in Venice in 1637, became the first music to appeal to large audiences and hence to be influenced by popular taste. Nothing in baroque music, from Monteverdi to J. S. *Bach, can be understood without knowing something of the over-

whelming popularity of opera and the way in which all other music reflected its influence to a greater or less degree. Baroque style, in the words of W. Apel,

is characterized chiefly by the thorough-bass technique, leading to a texture of two principal contours, melody and bass, with the intervening space filled in by improvised harmony [on a keyboard instrument—organ or harpsichord, the so-called 'continuo']. In Germany, however, the contrasting style of true polyphony not only persisted but reached, in Bach, its very acme of perfection and greatness. A third principle of Baroque [music] style is the *stile concertante,* that is, contrasting effects, a principle which expressed itself in the abrupt changes of the early canzona as well as in the solo-tutti alternation of the concerto grosso and in the echo-effects of vocal and of organ music. Other basic conceptions of Baroque music are improvisation and ornamentation. Lastly, mention must be made of the final establishment of tonic and dominant as the principal chords of harmony . . . . [Apel HDMus 1950, 77.]

In Italy. Composers of liturgical music in the first decades of the 17th century followed two methods of composition: the *stile antico,* which preserved features of the 16th-century style of choral writing, and the *stile moderno.* All the leading composers of the 17th and 18th centuries, from Monteverdi to Antonio *Lotti, wrote works in *stile antico.* The *stile moderno* first appeared in G. *Gabrieli's polychoral motets for St. Mark's, Venice, which blend and contrast solo, choral, and instrumental groups—large-scale motets containing many striking effects of chromatic harmony and instrumental color. A representative collection of liturgical music published by Monteverdi in 1610 includes a Mass in *stile antico* with organ continuo, Vespers of the Blessed Virgin (responsory, five psalms, hymn, and two settings of the Magnificat), and other pieces designed, according to the title page, "for princely halls and chapels." The Vesper items are much influenced by Gabrieli. In the psalms the musical treatment is changed for each verse, the verses being frequently separated by *ritornelli.* Generally the psalm tones are retained as *canti firmi,* accompanied by vocal and instrumental counterpoints; but they are also set in *falso bordone,* i.e., reiterated chords under the melody in the rhythm of the words. In the other pieces of the collection the new style of writing for solo voices is evident; virtuoso ornamental passages underlie the meaning and mood of the texts. The *Sonata sopra Sancta Maria* shows the growing

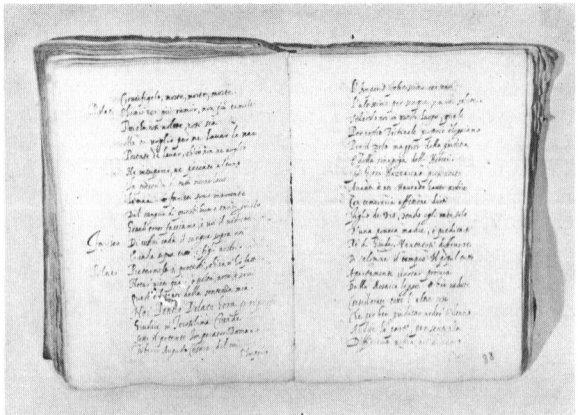

Fig. 7. Manuscript libretto by an unknown author for a 16th-century sacred oratorio, "La Passione di Cristo."

importance of instrumental music for church use. Although it is not a liturgical work, the 11-fold repetition of a plainsong by a solo soprano gives it a quasi-liturgical air almost completely belied by the independent music for two violins, viola, cornetti, trombones, and organ.

Monteverdi's contemporaries and successors generally abandoned the use of the plainsong *cantus firmus*. They preferred two *concertato* styles: the one using only solo voices with or without instruments, which came to resemble the secular cantata in its forms and its use of instrumental *ritornelli;* and the "grand" *concertato*, employing one or more choirs and groups of instruments, mainly intended for the new baroque churches. André Maugars (*c.* 1600–40), a French viol player visiting Rome in 1624, has left descriptions of performances of such works with as many as eight lofts erected around the nave, each containing its own instrumental or vocal group, and all directed by the composer from the middle of the church. Despite their apparent complexity, these compositions were held together by a very simple, even banal, harmonic structure. The most extravagant work of this sort was the 53-part Mass of Orazio *Benevoli (1605–72) for the consecration of Salzburg cathedral, requiring two 8-part choirs, two string ensembles, two of wind instruments, and two of brass.

By the end of the 17th century the operatic styles reigned supreme. The rise of Neopolitan opera saw the introduction of solo arias in the motet, which by this time could mean any piece of music set to a Latin text (other than those of the Mass Ordinary) and often denoted forms that were in fact *cantatas of several movements. In the hands of *Leo (1694–1744), *Durante (1684–1755), *Feo (1685–1745), and other 18th-century composers, the Mass was expanded into a huge cantata in which independent choruses and arias were combined with instrumental movements. An overture frequently served as an introduction. The liturgical consequences were disastrous. As J. A. Jungmann describes it:

> The liturgy was not only submerged under this ever-growing art but actually suppressed, so that . . . there were festive occasions which might best be described as 'church concerts with liturgical accompaniment'. . . . Texts which could be chosen at random—as was permitted after the elevation—were transferred to other places in the Mass. On the other side, the celebrant often tried to continue with the offertory even while the choir was still singing the *Credo,* or to restrict the singing of the preface and *Pater noster* to the initial words so as to leave the rest for the music and the organ. [The Mass of the Roman Rite (New York 1951) 1:149.]

The church music of the Austrian and south German composers of the baroque was deeply influenced by that of the Italians, many of whom visited or resided for long periods in the chief cities. The works of the Germans, however, and particularly those of J. J. *Fux, show a more strongly contrapuntal approach.

In France. The development of church music in France was much influenced by the requirements of the court, the artistic and cultural center of the nation. Louis XIV preferred to attend a low Mass, which did not allow time for elaborate settings of the Ordinary. Yet, since music was considered an essential part of a ritual performed in the King's presense, a compromise was made in the so-called *Messe basse solonnelle:* the performance of motets for voices and instruments dur-

Fig. 8. Seventeenth-century Italian upright harpsichord. The folding doors are decorated with religious subjects.

ing certain parts of the service. The influence of the Italian *concertato* may be seen in the motets of Henri *Dumont (1610–84), director of the Chapelle Royale from 1663. From the mid-17th century, Italian styles and forms dominate French music. Marc Antoine *Charpentier (1634–1704), a pupil of *Carissimi and director of the Dauphin's chapel, wrote Masses, motets, and *Leçons des Ténèbres* for soloists, chorus, and instruments. The Tenebrae settings are a remarkable example of musical interference with the liturgy: texts intended to be chanted by a lector are set as cantatas and drawn out to 10 times their length by constant verbal repetition. Jean Baptiste *Lully (1632–87) brought to the motet the pomp and brilliance of the French form of opera, of which he was virtually the sole creator: the *tragédie-lyrique*. His *Miserere* and *Te Deum* are scored for full operatic band including trumpets and drums. Operatic overture, double choirs, solo aria, and recitative are blended with instrumental interludes to produce some of the most elaborately brilliant church music ever written. Michel de *Lalande (1657–1726) extended the style of Lully's motets to the Mass Ordinary, of which he wrote 12 settings. Despite an almost Handelian grandeur, his music has a seriousness and a perception of the religious meaning of his texts and their relevance to the liturgy that Lully's works lack. François *Couperin (1668–1733) wrote in the highly ornamental style called rococo (or *stile galante*); his chief works for liturgy are psalms (treated as cantatas, each verse having a separate movement) and *Leçons des Ténèbres*.

Protestant Music. The music for all Protestant churches in this period contrasts sharply with that composed for the Catholic liturgy in that it includes vernacular music for the congregation as an essential part of liturgical worship.

Lutheran Germany. The development of German Lutheran choral music was profoundly influenced by the congregational hymn, or *chorale* (as it came to be called when used in choral compositions). Michael *Praetorius (1571–1621) published nine volumes entitled *Musae Sioniae* containing 1,200 of his compositions based on *chorales*, using *concertato* styles, contrapuntal forms, and simpler treatments such as duets and solo arias. Johann Schein (1586–1630) and Samuel Scheidt (1587–1654) continued the *concertato* treatment, emphasizing the textual meaning by melodic and harmonic features. The greatest figure before Bach, Heinrich *Schütz (1585–1672), seldom used *chorale* melodies (though he made a book of harmonizations for a metrical *Psalter), preferring, by reason of his Italian training under Gabrieli, a dramatic approach that, while indebted to both Gabrieli and Monteverdi, was profoundly personal and deeply felt. The works in *Sacrae Symphoniae*, published in three volumes (1628, 1647, and 1650), utilize all the techniques of the early Italian baroque, ranging from solo settings of Psalms to mighty polychoral motets.

Fig. 9. Page from a 17th-century manuscript (Huntington MS 461, fol. 5r) of songs in English by Thomas Weelkes, John Mundy, Thomas Tallis, and other English composers.

The Lutheran Church had continued the older method of reciting the Passion narrative to a special chant while punctuating it by polyphonic settings of the "crowd" portions of the text. Later composers developed this into the "oratorio-Passion" by introducing orchestral and organ accompaniments and inserting sections with nonliturgical texts. Stages in this development are represented by the *St. John Passion* (1643) of Thomas Selle (1599–1663); *St. Matthew Passion* (1667) of Christian Flor (1626–97); and *St. Matthew Passion* (1673) of Johann Theile (1646–1724). Schütz's Passions stand apart: they have no instrumental accompaniment, and, apart from the opening and concluding movements, the chorus sings only "crowd" passages, the rest being sung to a quasi-Gregorian type of recitative.

By the end of the 17th century, Italian opera was a strong influence on German church music. The blending of the various choral forms based on *chorale* tunes had produced a large composite type of composition that later came to be called cantata. A Hamburg pastor, Erdmann Neumeister (1671–1756), published texts for what he called "reformed" cantatas. Regarding the cantata as a "fragment of an opera," he discarded all Biblical passages and hymn texts in favor of poetical paraphrases that could be set as recitatives and *da capo* arias. His texts roused much opposition, and many composers mingled them with texts and musical forms from the older style; the cantatas of J. S. *Bach are the greatest representatives of this. The Passion story was also given "operatic" treatment and poetical paraphrased texts; such works, however, were no longer liturgical but concert hall music. Bach's Passions represent a compromise between the earlier and the new forms; he retained the complete Biblical text but added *chorales*, choruses, and arias that had non-Biblical texts.

Anglican Music. English composers were slow to incorporate the new vocal styles of the Continent. Up to the civil war, despite some experiments in music for the Chapel Royal by William Child (1606–97) and Monteverdi's pupil Walker Porter (1595–1659), the older polyphonic style continued in the "full" and "verse" forms of the anthem and service. At the Restoration (1660) Charles II imported music "in the French style," with instrumental sections for violins, and had Pelham Humfrey (1647–74), John Blow (1649–1708), and Henry *Purcell (1659–95) trained in up-to-date European techniques. The church music of these men and particularly of Purcell is equal to anything of its period on the Continent in technical expertise, while preserving a peculiarly English type of melody and harmony. After Purcell and with the appearance of Italian opera in London, Anglican church music speedily copied Italian models. *Handel's *Chandos Anthems*, while revealing acquaintance with Purcell's work, are wholly Italianate in style and form.

See also BAROQUE, THE.

Bibliography: Buk MusB. S. CLERCX, *Le Baroque et la musique* (Brussels 1948). R. HAAS, *Die Musik des Barocks (Handbuch der Musikwissenschaft* 3; New York 1928). A. HARMAN et al., *Man and His Music* (New York 1962). Láng MusWC. Apel HDMus. **Illustration credits:** Fig. 7, Museo Teatrale alla Scala. Fig. 8, The Metropolitan Museum of Art, The Crosby Brown Collection of Musical Instruments, 1889. Fig. 9, The Huntington Library, San Marino, California. Fig. 10, Courtesy of The Royal Opera House, Covent Garden; Houston Rogers.

[A. MILNER]

Fig. 10. Scene from the 1962 Covent Garden (London) production of Handel's "Alcina," with Joan Sutherland.

6. THE CLASSICAL STYLE

Characteristics peculiar to the classical period emerged around 1750, reached a high point of artistic expression in the works of Haydn and Mozart, and evolved into Romanticism in the works of Beethoven and Schubert.

New Style Sources. Sources of the style were the experiments of the Mannheim composers with new orchestral devices, the interest of the Viennese composers in formal structures, and the melodic and harmonic freedoms of the Italian composers of opera and cantata. The Church composer assimilated all of these styles—often more instrumental and theatrical than religious—and applied them to liturgical texts. The style is basically dramatic, and is founded on a balanced formal structure that permits the tensions inherent in musical contrasts, both tonal and melodic, to evolve in a logical but emotionally moving way. Historically, the style is cast against the intellectual background of the *Enlightenment: it combines the rational temperament of that movement with its *Josephinism, and reflects both its strained Church-State relationships and its attempts at reform.

The Mannheim School. Musical activity reached tremendous heights throughout Europe. Composition, performance, and circulation of new music in general showed clearly the intense musical life Europe was experiencing at this time. The rise of the Mannheim School in the mid-18th century brought a new orchestral style and performance into music that would be as important as the Viennese interest in sonata form in building the Viennese classical style. Two leading composers of religious music in the Mannheim circle who attempted a combination of formal aspects and high expressiveness were Franz X. *Richter and George *Vogler. The period around 1750 and shortly thereafter provides a transitional stage in Church music from the baroque contrapuntal style with thorough-bass accompaniment to a more expressive vocal and instrumental style that also emerged with national elements. The orchestral concept dominated the Masses, Vespers, litanies, Offertories, and psalms written in the new style.

Southern Influences. The influence of Italian opera and cantata conventions moved north during the middle part of the 18th century. The Neapolitan use of simple harmonies with highly ornamented melodic lines rendered the liturgical texts dramatic and full of pathos. Niccolò *Jommelli, Baldassare *Galuppi, Domenico *Cimarosa, and Giovanni *Paisiello wrote in this style. By building on the foundations of the cantata form and its sectional structure, these Italian composers lost sight

Fig. 11. Concert in a Venetian convent, painting, c. 1782, by Francesco Guardi. The scene depicted is in one of the four convents or "ospedali," which were celebrated during the 18th century for their excellent orchestras.

of the unity of liturgical texts and imposed on them the concerto principle. Vivid orchestrations, the aria and *bel canto*—all characteristic of the Neapolitan stage—found their way into liturgical music since the same composers who wrote for the theater wrote for the church. It was a simple process to combine this trend with *Empfindsamkeit* (highly expressive technique) of Germany to achieve a new style, neither baroque nor yet fully classical. Typical of the merging of the operatic with the instrumental idioms are the works of Johann Adolph *Hasse, a German composer who, like many others, lived and studied in Italy. He wrote his 100 operas in the same style as his many oratorios and Masses. But not all composers favored the new style. Many still wrote in the strict contrapuntal style of "stile antico." For example, Johann *Albrechtsberger and Georg *Pasterwitz and others continued to write in the polyphonic idiom of previous generations. Their works show but slightly the influence of the new melodic concept.

The Viennese Classics. A reconciliation of the Italian operatic tendencies with Northern instrumental writing matured in the Viennese composers. Here, the element of balance in a logical form combined with expressionism in melody reached its peak. After 1770 religious music also was affected by these elements. For example, to give balance and unification, parts of the Mass received cyclic treatment, i.e., the music of the first Kyrie

would be repeated for the third Kyrie and again for the *Dona nobis pacem* of the Agnus Dei. This created an A-B-A form in the Kyrie and made that Mass a rounded form. The first and final sections of the Gloria and the Credo were treated in similar fashion. Sonata and rondo forms were worked into the larger sections with a fugue acting as a coda. The cantata elements remained, however, and arias were standard fare for the *Et incarnatus est,* and the Benedictus; the orchestral accompaniment knits the work into a homogeneous whole. All joined to form in the classical period a definite ecclesiastical style that was both religiously inspired and musically satisfying. These composers were writing church music in their own contemporary style and were using their talent and craft to produce artifacts that were consistent with the philosophy that surrounds the celebration of the liturgy during the Classical period. For this reason they were musically superior to the uninspired, academic compositions of those composers adhering to the old polyphonic style.

Mozart and Haydn. With the emphasis given to symphonic writing, it is not surprising that Classical sacred music found its zenith in Wolfgang Amadeus *Mozart and Franz Joseph Haydn. In early works they were careful to express the general meaning of the text, repeating syllables, words, and sections of the text when musical reasons demanded. Haydn experimented with techniques of form and even tapped the store of folk song. In the case of Mozart, one can discern a marked change in his style after he left Salzburg. His first compositions reflected the examples of Johann *Eberlin and a stronger influence from chamber music and the Neapolitan style. The Masses he wrote from 1758 to 1782 show a unique ability to blend elements of German classicism and form with Italian lyricism. The unfinished C-Minor Mass (K.427) illustrates the new church style: it is a successful assimilation of the forementioned principles. His great *Requiem* is considered to be the epitome of his church style, if not of all Viennese sacred music. The vocal idiomatic writing that Mozart gave to his religious music can be compared with the symphonic and orchestral principles that Haydn contributed. The vocal solo did not interest Haydn as much as did the vocal quartet. Using remnants of the concerto-grosso form, he contrasted the quartet against the tutti of the full choir. In his earlier works, he had used polyphony infrequently, with the exception of specific choral fugues. After a 14-year lapse, Haydn returned to writing sacred music, using a polyphony integrated into the expanded use of the orchestra. His six monumental Masses written between 1796 and 1802 make extensive use of sonata principles, canon and fugue—all with a full participation of the orchestra. Unlike Mozart, Haydn wrote two oratorios. After his visit in England, he returned to write his *Creation,* a work that reflects the exuberance of Nature, an idea characteristic of the Enlightenment. Although the naïve representation of natural phenomena was criticized, the oratorio was tremendously suc-cessful as a combination of symphonic and choral elements. Because of its success, Haydn composed his second, *The Seasons,* that was equally well received. In these last works of Mozart and Haydn the pinnacle of classical sacred music was reached: the emergence of a style that united the polyphonic choir and the symphony orchestra is significant. If operatic traces can be detected, it is only because these elements were necessary parts of the composer's vocabulary.

Beethoven and Schubert. The Viennese classical style was carried on by Ludwig von *Beethoven and Franz *Schubert. Beethoven's C-Major Mass (1803) is so reminiscent of the Viennese style that it could be called a companion Mass to Haydn's works. It has all the fresh, heroic ideals of Beethoven's early creative period. Even in his *Missa Solemnis* one can see the influence of Haydn's symphonic cohesion. The large individual parts of this Mass are conceived with oratorio principles of grandness. Schubert, too, participated in this direct stylistic line with the Viennese church style. His early Masses exhibit the sectional treatment of the text, but show the lyrical quality peculiar to all of his works. In his last two Masses (A flat and E flat), the music tends to be Romantic because of the harmonic color and moving lyricism characteristic of Schubert's writing. Classical elements, however, can be seen in the balance and reserve inherent in the structural make-up of the works.

The Influence of Josephinism. The high classical Viennese church style was not without its opponents. The conservatives who favored the "stile antico" have

Fig. 12. Page of the holograph manuscript of Mozart's Requiem" (K. 626) preserved in the Austrian National Library, *Vienna (Cod. 17561). Left unfinished by Mozart's death in 1791, it was completed by his pupil Süssmayer.*

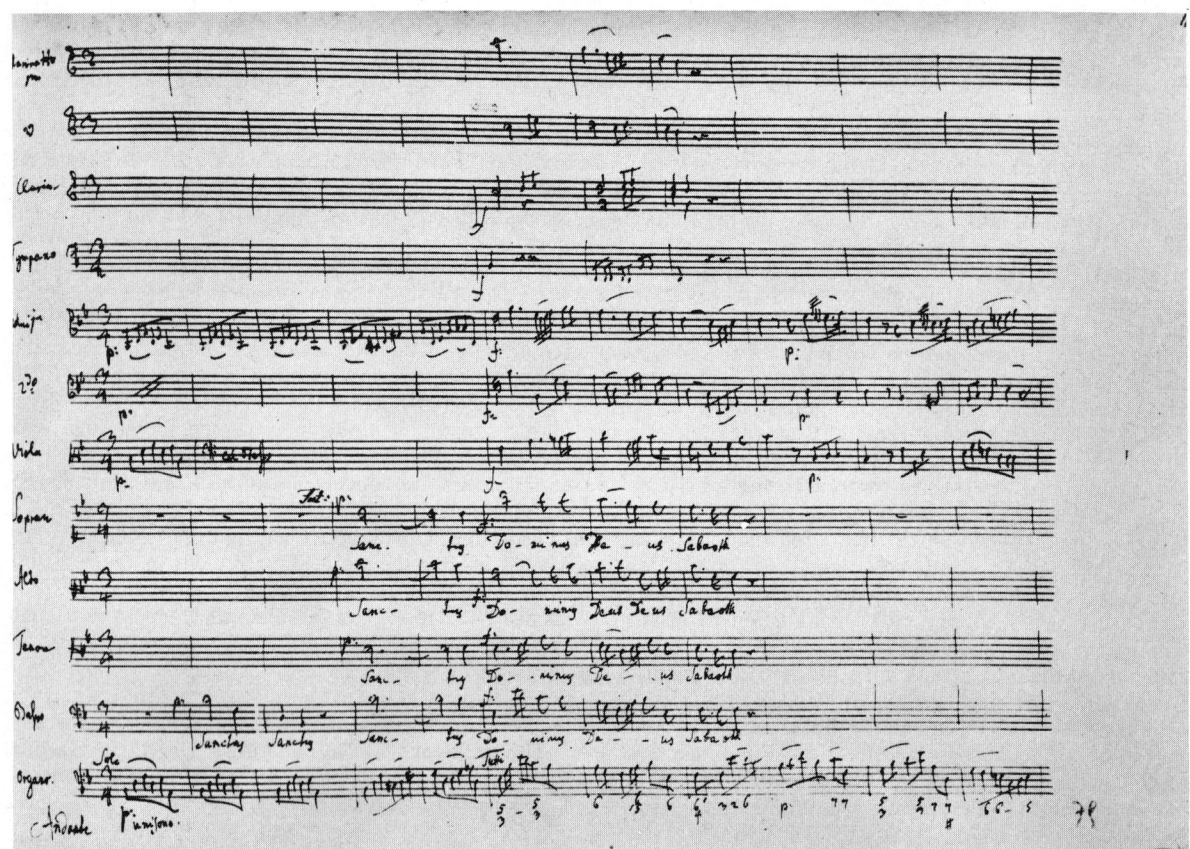

Fig. 13. *A portion of the Sanctus in the holograph manuscript of Haydn's "Lord Nelson Mass" preserved in the* Austrian National Library, Vienna (Cod. 16479). *It was composed between July 10 and Aug. 31, 1798.*

already been mentioned. The restoration of liturgical propriety took place under the decrees of Joseph II of Austria (*see* JOSEPHINISM). As a child of the Enlightenment's philosophy, he wanted to simplify the celebration of the liturgy in Austrian churches. Because of the large number of churches in Vienna, schedules were devised to regulate the hours of worship to avoid duplications. Vespers and Compline were curtailed considerably in diocesan churches together with many popular pious exercises. To establish a vernacular hymnody during the celebration of liturgical functions, a German hymnal was prepared by Johann Kohlbrenner in 1777; it was promulgated in all of Austria by 1783. The German sung mass (*Singmasse*) can trace its origins to this decree. While instrumental church music was not totally restricted, the use of concerted music was regulated. The symphonic Mass was too well rooted to be easily discouraged and dispensations were occasionally granted for its performance. Archbishop Collaredo (*see* MOZART) suppressed instrumental music in his see, but later (1787) permitted its performance on special feasts. It was under his direction that Michael *Haydn reinstituted the sung Gradual (1782). Haydn composed many Graduals in a simpler chordal style with instrumental accompaniment that replaced the "Epistle sonatas." The whole trend of Josephinism reform of church music was the simplification of the liturgy to encourage better communal worship. It did not deter, however, countless second-rate composers from imitating

the Masses of Haydn and Mozart well into the middle of the 19th century.

Bibliography: D. J. GROUT, *A History of Western Music* (New York 1960). Fellerer CathChMus. Láng MusWC. R. G. PAULY, "The Reforms of Church Music under Joseph II," MusQ 43 (1957) 372–382; *Music in the Classic Period* (Englewood Cliffs, N.J. 1965). Ursprung. **Illustration credits:** Fig. 11, Alte Pinakothek, München. Figs. 12 and 13, Austrian National Library, Vienna.

[F. J. MOLECK]

7. ROMANTICISM

The revival of religious interest that took place during the opening years of the 19th century is mirrored in the music of the period. The most important romanticist trend was the use of all musical devices to project a subjective attitude toward religion in sacred music. Especially among French and Italian composers opera was the most popular means of musical expression, and the line between what was appropriate for the stage and what for the choir loft was not sharply drawn. The new harmonic resources developed by C. P. E. Bach and Mozart, most clearly evident in Mozart's *Ave Verum Corpus* and *Requiem*, widened the range of emotional expression but also led to secular and sentimental styles. The romanticist interest in exoticism found religion an "effect," as is shown by inclusion of church scenes on the operatic stage or the use of the *Dies Irae* in secular instrumental compositions by Berlioz, Liszt, and Rachmaninoff. Although "national styles" in church music were discernible, nationalism as such played a minor role in Catholic church music during this century.

Concerted Mass. The aesthetic of symphonic church music, dominant in the later 18th century, remained in force during most of the 19th. In the typical concerted Mass of these periods, liturgical considerations were subordinated to musical exigencies: the chorus sang to orchestral accompaniment; passages of text were excised, troped, or repeated for subjective emphasis or to round out musical forms; and sections were allocated to soloists whose parts sounded like operatic arias or ensembles. The degree of romanticist content in concerted church music varied from composer to composer. Latent in Mozart's later works, it was developed by Cherubini, Lesueur, and Hummel, continued in the music of Schubert and Weber, and reached its peak in the works of Thomas, Gounod, and Rossini. Later composers such as Liszt, Franck, and especially Bruckner, Dvořák, and Fauré, treated the musical devices of the time with more restraint and better taste.

Concerted Masses are objectionable on liturgical grounds because of text repetition, settings of the priest's intonations, virtuoso demands on the musicians, orchestral accompaniment, and length—all of which distract the congregation from the action of the Mass; yet the works in this genre by Schubert, Bruckner, Dvořák, and Fauré are an integral part of the musical treasure of Catholic-inspired music and are eminently suitable for concert performance. The merits of concerted Masses should be judged by comparison with the Masses of Maillart and Farmer, early editions of *St. Basil Hymnal*, and the *Tantum Ergo* derived from the Sextet in Donizetti's *Lucia di Lammermoor*. The *Missa Solemnis* of *Beethoven and the rediscovery of J. S. Bach's *B-minor Mass* inspired the composition of large concerted Masses and similar works for the concert hall rather than for the church. The Requiems of Cherubini, Berlioz, Schumann, Verdi, and Dvořák, despite their liturgical texts, should be classed as oratorios.

Oratorio. The rise of choral societies and music festivals during the 19th century provided a steady demand for new oratorios. The founders of the romantic Protestant oratorio were Spohr and Mendelssohn. The sentimental chromaticism of Spohr and the "Victorian" complacency of Mendelssohn's religious music permeates most of these later works. Brahms, with his roots in the older German contrapuntal tradition, created in his *German Requiem* the best Protestant successor to the great works of Schütz, J. S. Bach, and Handel. Oratorio was less popular in Catholic countries. Deserving of study are the oratorios of Lesueur, which anticipate those of Dubois, Saint-Saëns, and Massenet. Fauré's *Requiem* is a virtual transfiguration of these intimate oratorios. Gounod's *Rédemption* and *Mors et Vita* (written for England) and Franck's *Les Béatitudes* are the leading large-scale French oratorios. The greatest Catholic oratorios of the period are those by Elgar. Also of interest are "religious" operas such as Saint-Saëns' *Samson et Dalila*, Massenet's *Le Jongleur de Notre Dame*, and d'Indy's monumental *La Légende de Saint Christophe*.

Organ. The rediscovery of J. S. Bach's organ works served to rescue organ music from the virtual desuetude into which it had lapsed during the classical period. Protestant organ music is best represented by the sonatas of Mendelssohn, the late chorale preludes of Brahms,

and the works of Reger and Karg-Elert. Liszt's organ works are significant among those by Catholic composers. During the latter part of the 19th century, France was the center of organ playing. Though Franck's works stand at the peak, many excellent organ compositions were written by Guilmant, Widor, and Vierne. Subsidiary centers of organ composition and performance were in Brussels (Lemmens), Munich (Rheinberger), and Rome (Bossi). *See* ORGAN MUSIC.

Other Forms. Concerted Masses were generally restricted to court and cathedral churches with professional singers and musicians. In smaller parishes the principal music consisted of the simple *Landmessen* and Masses in the style of Michael Haydn and Hummel of the Viennese classical school. Though Catholic hymns continued to be written during the 19th century, little of enduring value was created. Most of them contain sentimental chromatic harmonies, are operatic in style, or resemble salon romances (e.g., Lambillotte's hymns with piano-style accompaniments); and for these reasons they are proscribed in many U.S. dioceses.

Protestant church music assumed a variety of forms. Spohr and Mendelssohn were the models for the "Victorian" Anglican church music of Goss, Barnby, and Stainer. Excellent hymns, especially of the processional type, were written in England. In popular Protestant hymnody the rugged "Sacred Harp" and the sentimental or martial *gospel songs were peculiarly American contributions (*see* HYMNS AND HYMNALS). A major revival of sacred music occurred in Russia. About 1830 Bortniansky's Italianate anthems began to be supplanted by the Germanic tonal chant harmonizations of Lvov and Bakhmetieff. The influence of Glinka and "The Five" (Balakirev, Borodin, Cui, Moussorgsky, and Rimsky-Korsakov), especially in their scoring of folk songs, led to modal harmonizations of the traditional chants and of compositions in modal style by Kastalsky, Rachmaninoff, Ippolitov-Ivanov, Grechaninov, and others.

Reform of Catholic Music. Notable attempts were made during the century to reform Catholic church music, chiefly by reintroducing Renaissance sacred polyphony, which had been rediscovered through such sources as Baini's biography of Palestrina; the studies of Renaissance polyphony by Thibaut, Kiesewetter, and

Fig. 14. Title page of the first printed edition of Beethoven's "Mass in C Major" (Op. 86). Composed in 1807, the Mass was first published in 1812 with a dedication to Prince Ferdinand Kinsky.

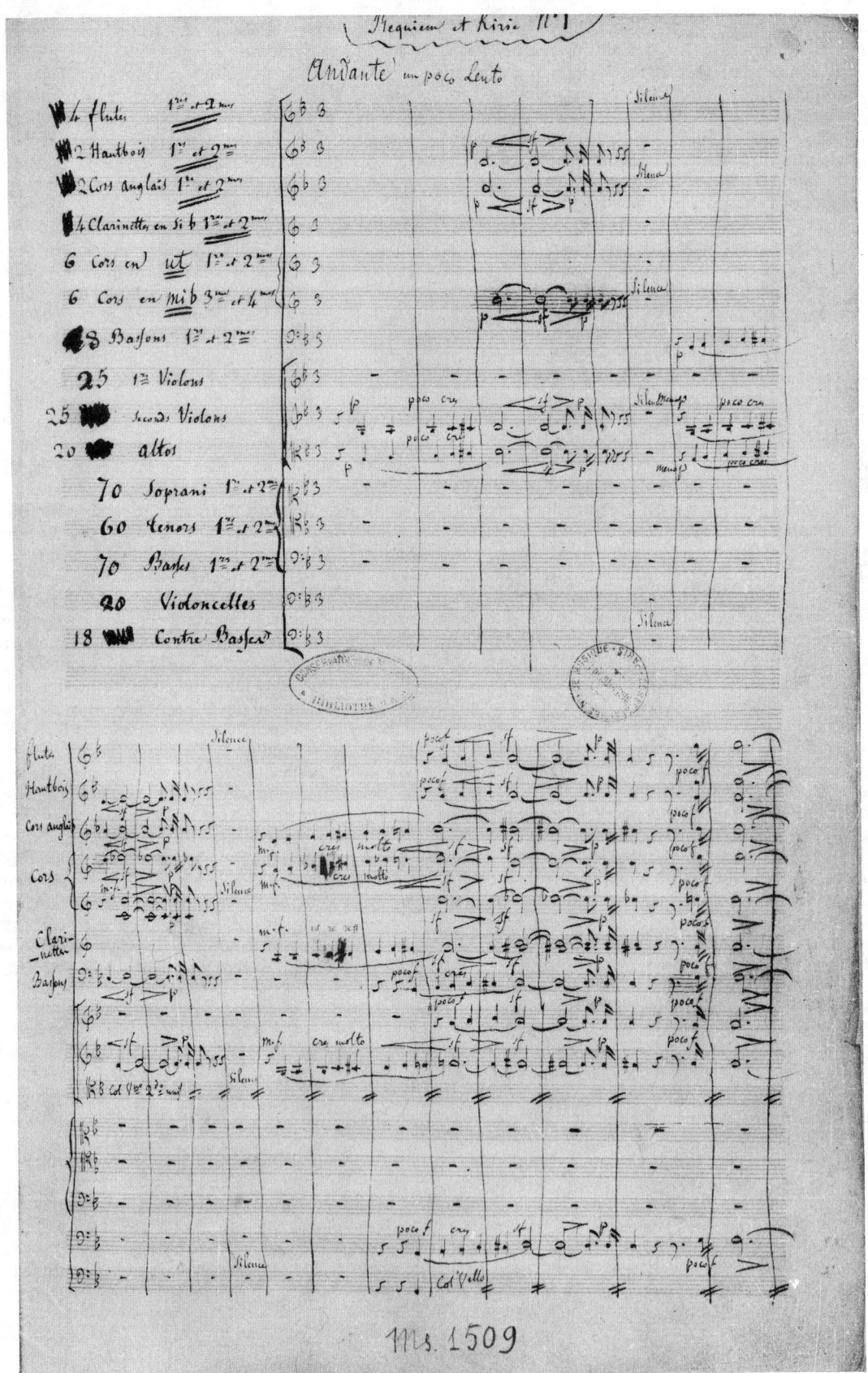

Fig. 15. The opening page of the holograph of Hector Berlioz' "Requiem" (Cons: MS 1509, fol. 31).

Winterfeld; the collections of 16th-century vocal music by Choron, Commer, Proske, Maldeghem, and others; and the composition of new music in this restrained contrapuntal style (*see* CAECILIAN MOVEMENT). Munich (Aiblinger, Ett, Rheinberger) and Regensburg (Proske and Haberl) were the focal points of reform, and the Caecilian Society, founded by F. X. Witt in 1868, was the most influential reform group; but parallel movements were found in every land, and the reform ideal was formally approved by Pius IX in 1870. The most enduring monument of 19th-century Catholic musical scholarship was the restoration of Gregorian chant, largely through the labors of the Benedictine monks of *Solesmes under the leadership of Dom Guéranger. The chief legacies of Solesmes are the *Paléographie musicale* (1889–), a collection of facsimiles of early MSS; a theory of chant rhythm; and the Vatican edition of the chant (*see* CHANT BOOKS, PRINTED EDITIONS OF).

Musicology. Neither the Caecilian reforms nor the Solesmes studies would have been possible without the emerging discipline of historical musicology. Musicology's task was not to illustrate how music had "progressed," but to investigate the music of the past on its own merits and to publish collections and scholarly studies of early music. Besides the publications cited above in the fields of Renaissance and Gregorian music, other landmarks of 19th-century research and publishing activity were the incomplete general histories by Ambros and Fétis; Fétis's *Biographie universelle* of musicians; Eitner's *Quellen-Lexikon,* a census of music MSS; Coussemaker's anthology of medieval treatises on music; and the prolific writings of Riemann. Nationalism stimulated the publication of *Denkmäler* (monuments of music) in the Germanic lands, and in England, France, Italy, and Spain.

Although the 19th-century investigations of Renaissance church music were handicapped by an almost total misunderstanding of 16th-century performance practice, this was outweighed by the creation of a climate of opinion in which music of the past was found worthy in its own right and, because of its lack of association with the 19th-century styles of the concert hall, opera house, or salon, was best suited for divine worship. The labors of the musicologists were crowned by Pope St. Pius X when he declared in his motu proprio of 1903 that the most suitable styles of church music were Gregorian chant and Renaissance polyphony—in that order.

The Church Composer. Relations between the Church and the composer, however, had reached a low point by the beginning of the 20th century, and only in organ music was significant creative work produced. On the one hand, the Church was devoting her resources to more urgent educational, missionary, and social endeavors; on the other hand, congregational (and too often, clerical) preference was for melodious Masses and sentimental hymns. Then, too, the individualism implicit in romanticism tended to alienate the composer from the emerging emphasis on the doctrine of the Mystical Body, with its corollary in "collective," participated worship. Composers of stature disdained to write for the limited uses of the parish church, and in their sacred compositions they favored Gregorian chant and Renaissance polyphony, thus reflecting both Caecilian ideals and the romanticist penchant for the archaic, but also

rejecting the idiom of the day and the role of style-setter of music to come.

See also CHOIR MUSIC; ORGAN MUSIC; CONGREGATIONAL SINGING; GREGORIAN CHANT; CANTATA; ORATORIO; CAECILIAN MOVEMENT; ROMANTICISM, LITERARY; ROMANTICISM, PHILOSOPHICAL.

Bibliography: Fellerer CathChMus. A. EINSTEIN, *Music in the Romantic Era* (New York 1947). Ursprung. A. OREL, "Die katholische Kirchenmusik seit 1750," *Handbuch der Musikgeschichte,* ed. G. ADLER, 2 v. (2d ed. Tutzing 1930; repr. 1961) 2:833–864. A. SCHERING, *Geschichte des Oratoriums* (Leipzig 1911) 382–624. **Illustration credits:** Fig. 14, Gesellschaft der Musikfreunde, Wien. Fig. 15, Bibliothèque Nationale, Paris.

[R. M. LONGYEAR]

8. POST-ROMANTICISM

Post-Romanticism in music signifies, basically, both an idiom (advanced tonal chromaticism) and a historical period of transition. It bridges 19th- and 20th-century styles and ends, approximately, with the death of Gustav *Mahler in 1911. It is therefore introductory to the history of sacred music in the 20th century, which is a period more properly characterized by the development of new technical resources, including atonality and polytonality, and the application to music of such aesthetic concepts as Impressionism and Expressionism. For liturgical music the motu proprio of St. Pius X, *Inter pastoralis officiae* (Nov. 22, 1903), was the key document. Its influence, while profound, was less complete than had been hoped, and attention to its ideal of "the restoration of all things in Christ" was seriously retarded by World War I. Nevertheless it must ultimately be assessed in terms of its permissive if reserved attitude toward modern music, its effect on later papal pronouncements, and three general developments accelerated by its impetus: (1) the revival of chant as an ideal for choral and congregational singing, (2) the practical study of chant in seminaries, and (3) the establishment of schools for the professional study of chant as well as of church music in other styles.

The "Traditional School." The musical idioms of Romanticism (see section 7, above) and Post-Romanticism achieved a valid and permanent popularity that impeded any mass espousal of later styles. That a "traditional school" of Catholic church-composers should gain ascendancy was therefore not surprising; but musicians such as *Refice, *Perosi, and *Yon, competent and dedicated though they were, remained apart, both from major figures of the era (*Schoenberg, *Bartók, Stravinsky) and from such minor but still "mainstream" composers as K. Szymanowski (1882–1937), Charles Ives (1874–1954), or *Villa-Lobos (1887–1959). Contributing further to the Church's loss of vital contact with contemporary trends were: her global concern with problems other than those of an often esoteric new music, the almost total secularization of 20th-century musical art, and changing sociological patterns, particularly that of patronage.

In France the transition from a lingering Romanticism to authentically modern liturgical styles was facilitated by continuing interest in the organ as a church instrument (*see* ORGAN MUSIC). Conservatives such as *Vierne and *Widor prepared the way for progressive successors as diverse as the gifted but essentially minor Jean Langlais (1907–) and the more controversial but influential Olivier Messiaen (1908–). The latter's organ cycles have attracted particular attention (e.g., *La Nativité du Seigneur*, 1935). He has produced important orchestral, chamber, and didactic works and numbered among his composition pupils such members of the later avant-garde as Pierre Boulez (1925–) and Karlheinz Stockhausen (1928–).

After Debussy. Impressionism offered composers of liturgical music a break with Romanticism free from involvement with expressionism and unmitigated dissonance; clear roots in the modality of chant and the structural principles of Gothic polyphony; and seemingly unlimited possibilities of adaptation to a continuing chant revival. Claude *Debussy (1862–1918), as the genius of French Impressionism, evolved a highly distinctive, sensuous, musical language, sometimes with neopagan implications (he was once rebuked by the archbishop of Paris for a production of *Le Martyre de Saint-Sébastien*). "Les Six," following Debussy, Ravel, and Satie, developed sophisticated personal styles that were indebted, in part, to the neoclassic elements in the work of Stravinsky. Three of the "Six" took some account of religious values, as can be seen in such works as Darius Milhaud's setting of texts from Pope John XXIII's encyclical *Pacem in terris* (1963); Arthur Honegger's *Le Roi David* (1921), and *Poulenc's Mass in G Major (1938), *Gloria* (1961), and *Sept Répons des Ténèbres* (1963).

The "New" Music. Contemporary trends in Catholic church music, as seen from the vantage point of 1965, involve aspects of traditionalism, nationalism, and the kaleidoscopic variety of techniques, idioms, ideologies, and ideals that have figured authentically in 20th-century developments: e.g., dodecaphony, panserialism, neomodality, neomedievalism, aleatory and electronic experimentation, and eclecticism. Jazz and other popular or folk elements are not considered here, though their influence and the cleavage between "serious" music and the demands of a large public for entertainment music cannot be denied. Further, with the growth of ethnomusicology and the flowering of a new ecumenical spirit, mention may be made of the African *Missa Luba* and the possibilities it suggests. Traditions and directions assimilated from Eastern rites and cultures have been explored in Western secular music more extensively than in sacred contexts (e.g., Henry Cowell's *Koto Concerto*, 1964), although Alan S. Hovhaness's *Magnificat* "combines Middle Eastern melos with Latin spirituality" to the satisfaction of a following who find in this American composer of Armenian descent a significant contemporary voice.

Traditionalism. Western traditionalism in liturgical music has concerned itself with preserving what it regarded as the twin ideals of a Romantic harmony "purified" of chromaticism and a texture that would be at least quasipolyphonic in "neo-16th-century" style. Difficult aesthetic problems are involved here; yet it must be said that while diatonicism, for example, may have at least transient validity within virtually any contemporary idiom, the "neo-" styles must be infused with special inspiration to achieve viability in sacred as well as in secular music, a fact that naturally applies also to genuinely new styles.

Nationalism. Nationalism in music tends of its nature, to some extent, to move away from the universalism of a catholic ideal. Yet the healthily secular Romanticist art of B. *Smetana represented the Czech spirit so au-

thentically that from related roots could grow the Post-Romanticist works, both sacred and secular, of Leoš *Janáček (1854–1928), whose *Slavonic Mass* transcends mere regionalism. In Spain, Manuel de *Falla, though a devout Catholic, wrote no sacred music; whereas in Hungary, Zoltán Kodály (1882–) is revered not only for nationalistic leadership (including pioneer musicological research, partly with Bartók, into Magyar folklore) but also for a varied and substantial *oeuvre*, including the deeply felt, Post-Romanticist *Missa brevis*, a work appreciated internationally. (It has even been choreographed.)

Other Influences. Contemporary idioms, styles, and techniques have found their way rather easily into music of broadly sacred implication, less easily into functional liturgical works, such as Stravinsky's *Symphonie de psaumes*, regarded by many as his masterpiece. The neo-medievalism of Stravinsky's *Mass* (1948) is naturally different from that of *Hindemith's last work, 1963; each setting is thoroughly representative not only of the personal style of the composer but also of the 20th century; whereas such a work as the *Missa Salve Regina* of Langlais (1949), however imposing, seems "neo-Dufay-Debussy" in inspiration and effect. All three compositions differ spiritually from Carl Orff's simplistic,

Fig. 16. Opening page of the holograph MS of Igor Stravinsky's "Symphonie de psaumes" written to commemorate the 50th anniversary of the Boston Symphony Orchestra, 1941. The manuscript is in the Library of Congress.

secular, neomedieval excursions. The English school has produced from its conservative-eclectic sources several Mass Ordinaries acceptable to moderately progressive elements in both Catholicism and Anglicanism, e.g., the Mass in G-minor of *Vaughan Williams (1872–1958) and the *Missa in honorem Sancti Dominici* of Edmund Rubbra (1901–   ), both *a cappella;* while Britten in his *War Requiem* (1962) has created a contemporary ritualistic work internationally admired, if unacceptable to the most intransigent of the avant-garde. More restricted in scope and inspiration has been the neomodality of the Belgian organist-composer Flor Peeters (1903–   ), whose work as teacher, lecturer, and performer in behalf of improved standards places him in the vanguard of a noble Catholic militia too numerous to name.

Varied influences (Harvard University, Walter Piston, Nadia Boulanger) have been brought to bear on the American priest-composer Russell Woollen (1923–   ). He has reserved his more advanced ideas for secular works, using an accessible neomodalism for Mass Ordinaries that explore possibilities of congregational participation and other specialized problems. Unisonal settings with organ accompaniment have proved effective in fostering a moderate modernism like that of the Langlais *Missa in simplicitate* or a more ruggedly dissonant style (the Roger Sessions *Mass: in English*, with the exception of the Kyrie). Composers in many countries have contributed settings in varying textures to a repertory of contemporary Mass Ordinaries and Propers that the new vernacular usages may relegate to liturgical, if not necessarily to musical, oblivion despite their merit.

Atonality. While of highest significance in the general development of 20th-century music, atonality has found little liturgical acceptance. The dodecaphonic expressionism of Alban Berg and Schoenberg has remained all but completely foreign to the religious milieu, although Schoenberg's opera *Moses and Aaron* has invited continuation of his search for new musico-dramatic values. Ernest Krenek has staked a pioneer liturgical claim for the 12-tone technique with his *Missa duodecim tonorum* (1957). A stronger ultimate influence, however, may be that of Anton von *Webern. For although neither his own fervent Catholicism nor his intimate knowledge of medieval and Renaissance sacred music deflected him from commitment to an austere modernism too uncompromising for present liturgical usage, several later composers have found ways to adapt the principles of his pointillistic serialism to functional liturgical music.

Aggiornamento. The later avant-garde, as such, has remained almost completely apart from liturgical problems, and electronic music is presumably proscribed from Catholic services. But the vitality, exuberance, and inventiveness (if not always the reverence and mysticism) of many among the most advanced composers have been a source of hope and continued interest, even though a new liturgical music has yet to emerge. While awaiting the grace of a 20th-century *Okeghem, *Victoria, or *Bruckner, the Church of the 1960s has addressed itself to problems centering around (1) the challenge of lay *participation and *congregational singing; (2) the need for adaptation to new vernacular usages on the part of both choir and people; (3) a closing of the cultural gap dividing popular and "classical"

modern musical activity, in order that the representative Catholic composer may find his rightful place in the Church of the *aggiornamento.*

See also MUSIC AND RELIGION; MUSIC, SACRED (CANADA); MUSIC, SACRED (U.S.).

Bibliography: P. COLLAER, *A History of Modern Music,* tr. S. ABELES (Cleveland 1961). J. MACHLIS, *Introduction to Contemporary Music* (New York 1961), contains bibliog. of 161 titles and works in Eng. K. G. FELLERER, *Soziologie der Kirchenmusik* (Cologne 1963). J. SCHELL, *Aesthetische Probleme der Kirchenmusik im Lichte der Enzyklika Pius' xii. Musicae sacrae disciplina* (Berlin 1961). MusQ 51 (Jan. 1965), a special issue: "Contemporary Music in Europe." J. GÉLINEAU, *Voices and Instruments in Christian Worship,* tr. C. HOWELL (Collegeville, Minn. 1964) 199–203. W. J. LEONARD, ed., *Liturgy for the People* (Milwaukee 1963). **Illustration credits:** Fig. 16, Copyright 1941 by Russicher Musikverlag; Renewed 1958. Copyright and Renewal Assigned to Boosey & Hawkes. Courtesy, Boston Symphony Orchestra.

[F. J. BURKLEY]

MUSIC, SACRED, LEGISLATION ON

Since apostolic times the Church has been careful to regulate the use of music at sacred services, encouraging fitting music and prohibiting unbecoming songs and chants.

History of Legislation. The directions of the Church on sacred music during the early Christian centuries are contained in documents of a liturgical and disciplinary nature, rather than in separate acts of legislation on music. The first successor of St. Peter to write on music was Pope St. Clement (92–101), who regulated the use of chant. Only after Pope Leo IV (847–855) are separate documents on music to be found. In his *Una Res* he commanded Abbot Honoratus of the monastery of Farfa and his monks to sing only Gregorian chants.

In the Fathers. The Fathers of the Church forbade worldly and pagan music but commended worthy Christian songs and chants. They prohibited musical instruments that were associated with pagan music—the harp and lyre—and excluded lascivious and worldly songs as well as chanting by women, since this was a characteristic of pagan worship and was thought to foster sensuality rather than piety. The Fathers sought to encourage spirituality and devotion by the use of psalmody, for this allowed participation of the faithful in the worship of the church.

Conciliar Action before Trent. The Councils and synods of the Church have frequently legislated on sacred music. Those held before the 14th century concerned themselves with the following questions: the entry of laymen into the office of singing the liturgical chant, the preservation of texts from Sacred Scripture, and the exclusion of hymns and songs that contained heretical teachings, the preservation of the traditional chant of the Church, the condemnation of worldly and theatrical songs in church and cemetery (especially on the occasion of vigils and funerals), and the exclusion of worldly dances and themes. Principal among these councils and synods were those at Laodicea (343–381), Braga (561), Tours (567), III Toledo (589), Autun (650), Cloveshoe (747), Aachen (816), Rome (853), Trier (1227), and Rouen (1235). In 1324–25 Pope John XXII spoke from Avignon in the bull *Docta sanctorum patrum* and warned against the introduction of unbecoming elements in polyphony. Subsequent synods and councils reiterated the need to guard against the introduction of profane songs in the vernacular and unbecoming and worldly texts.

The Council of Trent. The reform of the liturgical books following the Council of *Trent (1545–63) involved the reediting of the missal and breviary. (*See* CHANT BOOKS, PRINTED EDITIONS OF.) Further, the *Ceremonial of Bishops,* which contains directions for the conducting of pontifical ceremonies, was revised under Clement VIII and published in 1600. It described the rites and ceremonies to be observed at Masses, Vespers, and other sacred functions, as well as the rights of precedence. It contains many references to music.

The legislation of the Council of Trent concerning music was enacted at the 22d, 23d, and 24th sessions. The principal points discussed centered upon the nonliturgical character of some church music, the curtailment and unintelligibility of liturgical texts, and the insertion of nonchurchly vernacular songs, as well as worldly and lengthy organ compositions. These abuses were to be eliminated from the churches and care was to be given to the musical and liturgical education of clerics. Provincial councils were to determine the legislation in these matters, as seemed fitting according to particular circumstances.

After Trent. Legislation following the Council of Trent may be divided into two classes: general laws and particular indults for religious communities or dioceses. Only the laws that had general applicability will be listed here. They are the following: Alexander VII, *Piae Sollicitudinis,* 1657; Congregation of the Apostolic Visitation, 1665; Declaration of Cardinal Carpegna, 1692; Roman Council at the Lateran Basilica, 1725; *Instructio Clementina,* 1731; Clement XII, "Musicians in Pagan Worship," 1733; Benedict XIV, *Annus Qui,* 1749; Pius VI, "Choral Functions," 1791; Declaration of Cardinal Zurla (1824); Cardinal Odescalchi, "Notification," Declaration of Cardinal Patrizi, 1842, and Nov. 18 and 20, 1856; Congregation of Sacred Rites, *Romanorum Pontificum,* 1883; Congregation of Sacred Rites, "Regulations for Sacred Music," 1884; Congregation of Sacred Rites, *Quod Sanctus Augustinus,* 1894; Congregation of Sacred Rites, "Regulations for Sacred Music," 1894; Congregation of Sacred Rites, encyclical letter to the bishops of Italy, 1894.

It can be said that the sources for the legislation on church music in effect at mid-20th century began with the motu proprio of St. Pius X, Nov. 22, 1903. The important documents between 1903 and the Constitution on the Sacred Liturgy of Vatican Council II are the following: Canon 1264 of the Code of Canon Law, 1918; *Divini cultus sanctitatem;* Pius XI, Dec. 20, 1928; *Musicae sacrae disciplina,* Pius XII, Dec. 25, 1955; and "Instruction on Sacred Music and Sacred Liturgy," Congregation of Sacred Rites, Sept. 3, 1958. The decrees in these documents have been brought together and implemented by chapter six of "Constitution on the Sacred Liturgy," Vatican Council II, Dec. 4, 1963; motu proprio of Paul VI, Jan. 25, 1964; and Instruction of the Congregation of Sacred Rites, Sept. 26, 1964. For the U.S. the following two documents are of importance: Bishops' Commission on the Liturgical Apostolate, "Directives for the Use of Vernacular at Mass," Oct. 29, 1964, and "A Memorandum on Music for the Vernacular Liturgy," November 1964. From these sources the Church's regulations concerning the Mass, its participants and its music can be summarized.

Spirit of the Legislation. It is the mind of the Church that the faithful take an active part in both sung and recited Masses.

Sung Mass. Specific directions for participation in sung Mass are found in the 1958 "Instruction on Sacred Music and Sacred Liturgy" (par. 24–27), in which these three stages in the progress of the faithful toward active participation are given: (1) chanting of the liturgical responses, (2) singing of the parts of the Ordinary, and (3) chanting some of the Proper of the Mass. These same directives are found in the "Constitution on the Sacred Liturgy," in a general manner, in paragraphs 14, 30, and 112 to 121. Paragraph 30 states: "To promote active participation, the people should be encouraged to take part by means of acclamations, responses, psalmody, antiphons and songs, as well as by actions, gestures, and bodily attitudes. And at the proper times all should observe a reverent silence."

Recited Mass. The 1958 instruction (paragraphs 28–34) outlines four stages by which the participation of the faithful in recited Mass may be accomplished: (1) by saying the easier liturgical responses, (2) by answering the parts said by the server, (3) by reciting with the celebrant parts of the Ordinary, and (4) by reciting sections of the Proper, i.e., Introit, Gradual, Offertory, and Communion. Moreover, participation is to be effected by the singing of "hymns clearly suited to the respective parts of the Mass."

Vernacular Settings. The "Constitution on the Sacred Liturgy" has made allowance for the introduction of the vernacular languages into the parts of celebrant, ministers, choir, and congregation. The bishops of the U.S. have allowed the use of English for parts of the Proper (Introit, Gradual-Alleluia-Tract, Offertory, Communion) and the Ordinary (Kyrie, Gloria, Credo, Sanctus-Benedictus, Agnus Dei). New melodies for these English texts must be approved by diocesan music commissions, but new melodies for the chants of the priest and ministers and the Our Father sung by the people together with the celebrant must be approved by the National Conference of Bishops.

The concern of the bishops of the U.S. is expressed in the following statement: "Because of the danger that unsuitable musical settings for the vernacular will be used, it is strongly recommended that each Bishop, with the assistance of the Diocesan Liturgical and Music Commissions, exercise strict supervision over the melodies used for the Ordinary and Proper chants of the Mass, while encouraging composition of such music and legitimate experimentation. It seems most important at this stage that no approval be given to any settings for the Ordinary of the Mass which exclude the participation of the people" (Bishops' Commission on the Liturgical Apostolate, "A Memorandum on Music for the Vernacular Liturgy").

Basic Norms. The norms for music used at liturgical services were laid down by Pius X in the motu proprio of 1903. They are "holiness, true art, and universality." The specific types recommended are *Gregorian chant, classical polyphony, and approved modern compositions. Pope Pius XI repeated these principles in 1928, as did Pius XII in *Musicae sacrae disciplina.* But Pius XII enumerated distinctions between liturgical music and religious or sacred music, and made provision for the performance of sacred music at nonliturgical occasions. The 1958 Instruction clarifies certain points on sacred concerts (par. 55), but in general preserves the norms of Pius X, Pius XI, and Pius XII. The "Constitution on Sacred Liturgy" (par. 112–121) contains the basic norms on sacred music. Moreover, it makes provision for adapting native elements, especially in mission lands, into sacred music (par. 39–40, 119).

Bells and the Use of Instruments. Pius X opposed the use of instruments in church (motu proprio, par. 15–21) and Pius XI continued this policy, but Pius XII in *Musicae sacrae disciplina* (par. 58–61) relaxed this prohibition, allowing instrumental music that was executed artistically. *Bells are treated in the 1963 instruction, with instruments, in paragraphs 60, 68, 81–83, 97, 98d, and 101 to 103. The "Constitution on Sacred Liturgy" treats them in paragraph 120.

Use of the Organ. The motu proprio of Pius X (par. 15–18) encouraged the use of the *organ both as an accompaniment for the singing and as a solo instrument. *Divini cultus sanctitatem* (ch. 8) gave specific directions as to the correct manner of playing the organ. *Musicae sacrae disciplina* (par. 58) stated that the organ holds preeminence over all other instruments in church. The 1958 instruction (Par. 61–64) distinguishes between the pipe organ, harmonium, and electric organ. The electronic organ had previously (July 13, 1949) received a broader sanction from the Congregation of Sacred Rites than was stated in the 1958 "Instruction," according to which "the electronic organ may be tolerated temporarily." The 1958 instruction (par. 80) restricted the playing of the organ during those parts of the Mass when the celebrant prayed in a loud voice, in order that the readings might be heard clearly by the faithful.

Choirs and Women in Choirs. The motu proprio of Pius X stated that whatever singing does not pertain to the celebrant and sacred ministers "belongs properly to the choir of clerics, and that if singers are laymen they are substitutes of the ecclesiastical choir." Pius X stated that the singing must be, for the greater part, choral music, and that solos must never absorb the greater part of the liturgical text. In paragraph 13 he stated that "women cannot be admitted to the choir." This law was not well obeyed, especially in the U.S., where, as a result, women sang in choirs with the tacit permission of the bishops. Pius XI refrained from speaking on the subject, but Pius XII in *Musicae sacrae disciplina* (par. 74) modified the legislation of St. Pius X and allowed the use of mixed choirs or choirs of women or girls, so long as they remained outside the sanctuary and behaved in a suitable manner. The 1958 instruction especially mentioned choirs of men and women or of women or girls as being allowed (*see* CHOIR; CHOIR MUSIC).

Concerning Personnel. The motu proprio of Pius X (par. 12–14) described the office of choir members as a liturgical one and mentioned the high moral and spiritual qualities that should be possessed by those who sing in church, since they are substitutes for clerics. Pius X spoke of the proper attire of singers as that of cassock and surplice. He advocated the training of boys for the singing of the soprano and alto parts. Boys were to be trained in choir schools at cathedral and parochial churches, and they were to sing with the men. The 1958 instruction outlined the Christian qualities that should be present in the lives of singers, directors, organists, musicians, and composers, as well as the necessary musi-

cal and liturgical training required for the proper performance of their duties.

Sacred music is to be an integral part of seminary and religious training; and talented individuals, provided they possess the other required qualities, are to be given special training in order that they may foster true liturgical music.

Bibliography: P. M. FERRETTI, *Papal Documents on Sacred Music* (Washington 1928). A. HANIN, *La Législation ecclésiastique en matière de musique religieuse* (Paris 1933). R. F. HAYBURN, *St. Pius X and the Vatican Edition of the Chant Books* (Los Angeles 1964); *Digest of Regulations and Rubrics of Catholic Church Music* (rev. ed. Boston 1966). J. F. MYTYCH, *Digest of Church Law on Sacred Music* (Toledo, Ohio 1959). A. PONS, *Droit ecclésiastique et Musique sacrée*, 4 v. (St. Maurice 1958–61). F. ROMITA, *Jus musicae liturgicae* (Turin 1936). *Les Enseignments pontificaux: La Liturgie*, ed. Moines de Solesmes (Tournai, France 1954). Liturgical Conference, *Manual for Church Musicians*, ed. P. J. HALLINAN (Baltimore, Md. 1964). K. WEINMANN, *Das Konzil von Trient und die Kirchenmusik* (Leipzig 1919). Reese MusR. Fellerer CathChMus.

[R. F. HAYBURN]

MUSIC AND RELIGION

This article treats the link between music and religious cult as the expressed affirmation of a supernatural order. The first part of the article analyzes the process of sacralization and secularization in Occidental Christian music. The second part surveys the role of music in the non-Christian rituals of both the nonliterate or primitive cultures and the high civilizations of the Far and Middle East.

The very fact of religion implies community action in the form of prayer or ritual; it implies cultic activity in the broadest sense of the term. Inasmuch as religion is inseparably linked with an apperceptive knowledge concerning a divine "Other" and to the extent that this knowledge presupposes a discriminatory power (which, in turn, is identical with man's ability to name things), language is a necessary part of the religious phenomenon. Cult is present together with the religious phenomenon and exists primarily through the audible word since the divinity, once named, must be called upon repeatedly. For it is the word that, by means of its double characteristic of designation and perceptibility, forges peoples into a community under the sign of religion. But since this word is not used for the natural purposes of ordinary language, it becomes song—music.

Now religion and music relate to one another in singing the same way that language relates to its intonation within the religious community. A word used in cult is a religious declaration of one kind or another. If it is spoken plainly and naturally, it merely serves to bring about the audible communication of this declaration. Through its intonation in song, however, there emerges an effect that cannot be deduced from speaking alone. Voice, tonal voice, is not absolutely necessary for speaking. Only articulation is required for that. By contrast, singing is impossible without tonal voice. This element of intonation transforms simple speech—expression of a person—into song, which is the vocal embodiment of the community.

The person is immediately made manifest through the phenomenon of speech. This faculty, the ability to articulate, is an exclusive and immediate property of man. Between articulation and the human person there is no mediating element. Between song and the human person, on the contrary, there is a third term, the tone, which acts as a mediator. The tone is a "something" that is not specifically human, for even nonhuman things, animals and instruments, can produce a tone. Thus, whereas the mere fact of language is the immediate—and the only immediate—mode of appearance for the spiritual and thus for the person, song can capture the spiritual only by first incarnating and objectifying it, as it were, by using something material: the tone. At the same time this incarnate cultic language also actualizes the community qua community engaged in worship. It is true that architecture presents something visible and objective in the proper sense of the word, and thus it too actualizes the community; yet it does so in a relatively independent fashion, for in architecture the speaking being is only presupposed but, as such, does not actually produce the edifice in the way it produces the song or tonal speech. Song appears, then, as a synthesis of something immediately manifest and something corporeal, between person and community, between language and architecture, as it were. To the extent that the person (understood in a broader sense than the explicit meaning that Christian usage gives this term) is encountered simultaneously with the religious phenomenon, it provides man with the ground of possibility for bringing song (as participating in language) and religion into immediate correlation.

In the Christian West

Christianity was proclaimed in the Greek and Latin languages. In the West—to which this consideration is limited—the language of worship has been Latin ever since the 3d century. Its basic stock was taken from Sacred Scripture. Both the Latin and Greek translations of these Scriptures were entirely in prose. Even such texts as the Psalms were rendered in straightforward speech. Likewise, the accessory prayers that belong to the liturgical action were in prose form. Thus, prose may be designated as the primary liturgical language layer of Christian divine service.

Liturgical texts done in verse acquired acceptability only with the passage of several centuries. They did not crowd out the primary layer but were inserted between the prose texts. Verse is poetry and, as such, of human creation. Christian religious poetry is like a response that the believers give in their own words to the religious event that stirs the community from within. Thus again, verse may be designated as the secondary language layer in liturgy and contrasted with the prose, which is the primary layer.

Monophonic Music. The prose intoned in divine service—and also the poetry (hymns) to the extent that it gained admission into the liturgy—during the 1st millennium or, more exactly, up to Carolingian times, was Latin plain chant. This chant was modeled after the Latin language: it exploited the linguistic gestures of Latin's natural course of movement but did not enter into the sense coherence, the word meaning, of the language. It did not interpret the content of the language. In other words, this chant did not manifest itself as an attitude formed by the person toward the word. The melody was simply like a form-fitting vessel of the language, a musical vehicle of the word.

Polyphony. Polyphony came into the liturgy not through the primary but through the secondary language layer. From Carolingian times on people began to execute the newly emerging Latin Church poems, *Sequences, and later *tropes in a polyphonic manner. The cultivators of this new music were the recently Christianized Germanic peoples. Naturally, Latin was not the mother tongue of these new nations. In fact, even the Romance, or Latin, peoples had acquired independent vernacular dialects. Consequently, the language of the Church was no longer understood by the people at large. The intoned sacral word, which was already considered as inherently divine, holy, and untouchable, was now conceived altogether as a nonliving language. It was hypostasized; it was no longer regarded as speech at all but rather as something primarily existent, necessarily given. With this attitude the task of music was also changed: music was no longer the vessel of a linguistic gesture but a rigid edifice, consisting of chords, into which the word was introduced as something given.

With the course of time this early polyphony, which at first dealt only with the secondary language layer, acquired some measure of independence, so that it could be applied to the primary layer also. People began to dissect even the already extant melodies of sacred plain chant into single long notes, transforming them into the so-called *cantus firmus and building a polyphonic block of harmonies around each single note. It is thus that first (since the 12th century) the Proper and later (since the 14th century) the Ordinary chants of the Mass were set to music.

This polyphonic interpretation of the primary liturgical language as something divine and unapproachable became in subsequent centuries a new musical vehicle of meaning that, this time in polyphony, recaptured the linguistic gestures of the Latin language and, at the time of the Counter Reformation, led to the highpoint of Latin Church music in the works of *Palestrina and *Lasso. Their works still treat the (Latin) word epigraphically, so to speak, as something unapproachable.

Protestant Music. Through the Reformation, preaching came to occupy the center of liturgical action. Luther grounded himself in Sacred Scripture as the spoken word; he built upon the German language. The language of church service was now understood; it was re-enacted also as a meaningful content. In German—as in the other modern languages—speaking, as an act supported by personal liability and responsibility, became the express structure of the language. Unlike Latin, however, such speaking does not lend itself immediately to musical intonation, as the embodiment of a singing community. This latter function was taken over by the Evangelical church-song or chorale. Thus, the primary language layer was divested of music, in that the scriptural prose was now heard as immediate and ordinary speech. And it was the secondary language layer that became the monophonic church-song embodying the community. It was this layer also that became the primary layer musically, which assumed the function of the Latin liturgical chant. Consequently, polyphonic art-music now appeared as a third entity, but one that was nevertheless rooted in the Evangelical Church service. This art-music found two opposite realizations, both of which, however, constitute the essence of Protestant religious music. First, Heinrich *Schütz took the Biblical language, the primary layer that was divested of music, and made it the material of his compositions. Next J. S. *Bach, used, as in the art-

Plucked-fiddle players before the Lamb of God, miniature from a manuscript of Beatus' Commentary on the Apoc- *alypse written for the Abbey of Santo Domingo de Silos, Spain, c. 1091–1109 (Brit. Mus. Add. MS 11695, fol. 164).*

music of the early Middle Ages, mainly poetry rather than Bible texts for his music.

This new stratification of music took place within Catholic services too as soon as the vernacular languages were drawn into it. In the 18th century the vernacular became the basis of church music naturalized in the Catholic Church also, while polyphonic art-music assumed an autonomous role in the liturgy similar to the one it played in the Evangelical Church.

Sacred and Secular Music. The sacral is what is blessed or consecrated. By itself, only the word is genuinely sacral. The profane, i.e., the natural, world is always consecrated "in the name of," through the naming word. Considered in isolation, in its unwrought materiality, music is profane. Only through the word does it become sacred music. This circumstance is the prerequisite for the genesis of a kind of music that, although not sacral, is nevertheless consecrated secular music. From the musical element alone, no clear distinction can be drawn up between truly sacred or even generally spiritual works on one hand and secular works on the other (otherwise such phenomena as musical contrafacts would be incomprehensible). It is not the autonomous musical element but, above all, the content, the disposition, the purpose that the music serves, that makes a work spiritual or secular.

The primarily profane element in music is the polyphonic-instrumental element. This element, however, can be incorporated into the sacral domain; it can be consecrated, so that it can appear in worship either as a language-bound or even as a purely instrumental music. The process of gradual consecration of this profane musical element through the sacral word constitutes, from the 9th century on, the history of our Occidental music. Since the time of Bach, music, even language-bound music, was conceived from the instrumental point of view. Insofar as Bach made the profane or polyphonic-instrumental element the chief vehicle for an eminently religious expression, which then inherited the place of the hitherto language-bound music, this element became consecrated.

In the meanwhile, through opera and autonomous instrumental music, secular music became very powerful (especially in Catholic regions). From then on, contrary to what it had been before, secular music became normative for the spiritual also. Nevertheless, this new secular musical vehicle—regardless of its incorporation of new, and one might say, yet unconsecrated elements—presupposes its centuries-old relationship to the sacral word; it carries the traces of its provenance; it has historical memory through which it remains consecrated.

The Viennese classic composers F. J. *Haydn, *Mozart, *Beethoven, standing on Catholic soil, derived their art from this secular music. But they fused it again with the great, sacral tradition of Occidental music that had been fecundated by the instrumental element once before (by Bach). They accomplished the last step: they transformed the specifically religious music into a generally spiritual music of profound Christian anchorage. Symbolic of this is Beethoven's *Missa Solemnis,* which was conceived not only according to the spirit of Christianity, but over and beyond that, according to the specifically liturgical reality of the Mass.

During the 19th century, with the advent of private, subjective, and bourgeois elements, the state of affairs was changed radically. The sacral was no longer inherent in the new musical vehicle of meaning, as it had been up to the time of Beethoven's death. It is for this reason that even the religious music of this epoch functions only as a mirror, reflecting the private relation of each composer to religion.

The ecclesiastical and for the most part sociologically motivated tendency of contemporary times toward liturgical renewal influences also the musical reshaping of the divine worship. Over and above the possibility of free polyphonic composition, and beside the more emphatically favored cultivation of the music of the past, the need for a new monophonic liturgical chant in the vernacular together with new church songs becomes particularly pressing. That the old liturgical melodies, which are bound too much to the Latin texts, cannot simply be taken over as they are is evident to everyone. But even the creation of new melodies—especially for prose texts—presents problems whose magnitude should not be underestimated.

See also MUSIC, SACRED, HISTORY OF, 1–8; MUSIC (PHILOSOPHY).

Bibliography: NewOxHMus v.1–2. Fellerer CathChMus. Ursprung. Láng MusWC. Reese MusMA. Reese MusR. Buk MusB. G. REESE and R. BRANDEL, eds., *The Commonwealth of Music* (New York 1965). W. D. ALLEN, *Philosophies of Music History* (New York 1939; repr. 1962). J. GÉLINEAU, *Voices and Instruments in Christian Worship,* tr. C. HOWELL (Collegeville, Minn. 1964). J. SAMSON, *Musique et chant sacrés* (Paris 1957). T. GEORGIADES et al., "Musik," RGG³ 4:1195–1224. T. GEORGIADES, *Musik und Sprache: Das Werden der abendländischen Musik, dargestellt an der Vertonung der Messe* (Berlin 1954).

[T. GEORGIADES]

IN NON-CHRISTIAN RITUALS

Under this heading is reviewed the relation of music to the religious practice in both primitive and highly civilized societies isolated from Christian influences.

Primitive Cultures. Religion in all its manifestations plays an important part in the musical life of the world's nonliterate or primitive cultures. The dominant characteristic of the music of these cultures—African Negro, American Indian, Australian aboriginal, paleo-Siberian, Oceanian, etc.—is its existence entirely in oral tradition, without notation, from which results a high degree of simplicity and homogeneity of style. Typically, in these cultures, music is associated closely with the supernatural; and the simpler a tribe, the greater, usually, is the proportion of the music that is in some sense religious.

The ways in which music is associated with aspects of religion are many and go far beyond the mere use of music in ceremony. A few examples must suffice. In those areas of Asia and the Americas in which shamans become entranced in order to communicate with the supernatural, music is the device that produces the trance. Sympathetic magic appears in situations in which stylized—that is, musical—versions of animal calls are performed in order to bring the animal to the hunter or in which instruments made of animal hide and bone are played in order to assuage the spirit of that animal. Calendric songs, sung at particular times of the year, are used by many societies, including those of eastern Europe, to assure successful harvests. Music also universally accompanies ceremonies with religious significance, such as those celebrating rites of passage from one stage of social development to another, e.g., birth, puberty, marriage. Indeed, in some cultures music occupies the role of a special language for communication with the supernatural. Its importance in religion can also be documented by the fact that in many cultures, religious music is the most complex as well as representative of the most archaic styles.

The specific origin of musical material in nonliterate cultures is, of course, obscure. In general these cultures usually ascribe religious songs to composition by individuals in a dream or in the process of some other supernatural process, or they present mythological data to account for the origin of their songs, claiming, for instance, that they were transmitted by an early culture, hero, or founder of the tribe. Specialists in religion—priests, shamans, medicine men—are frequently also the specialists in music composition and performance. In some cultures, however, such as that of the Plains Indians, any man can compose songs or learn them in visions, just as anyone can communicate directly with supernatural powers.

Although nonliterate cultures normally do not have a theory of music that can be stated verbally by informants, there are examples in which the particular role of music in religion is stated or can be empirically deduced. For instance, among some Indian tribes the most important religious experience for an individual is a vision, in which a guardian spirit appears and gives important advice. The spirit often teaches the visionary songs, which may be required by the tribe as evidence of an authentic vision.

In northern Australia the people of Yirkalla have ceremonial songs that are learned a few at a time by the men as they grow older, so that only the oldest know all ritual songs. These songs are accompanied by a drone pipe, and the relation of the various notes of the scale to that of the drone is different for the songs of each clan. Thus, cosmological and ceremonial differences can be reflected in structural differences in the music of even the simplest cultures. At a more advanced level West African deities have their special cults, each of which has its particular type of drums and drum rhythms of great complexity. This practice has been carried into the Afro-American voodoo cults of Brazil and the Caribbean. Musical instruments often have religious significance. For example, the bull-roarer in Australia is thought to represent the voice of ancestors. The making of instruments associated with rituals is itself an elaborate ceremony that is thought to give life and power to the instrument.

The Arapaho, a typical North American Indian tribe, have a number of types of religious songs: (1) songs of age-grade ceremonies; (2) songs learned in visions; (3) songs of the sun dance, their main ritual, which can be identified by their larger range and greater intricacy; (4) songs of the ghost dance, a ceremony imported with its songs from the Great Basin tribes to the West; (5) songs to accompany the modern and Christian-influenced Peyote ceremony, in a musically distinct style. Speaking very generally, religious music tends to retain older style elements than does secular music. Changes of songs and errors in performance are thought to invalidate ceremonies. Thus, even in a unified style, such as that of the Negroes of Surinam, it has been found that the religious songs are older, that is, more closely similar to West African music, than other songs.

Beyond the tendency to preserve older materials, little may be said in general about the styles of music used by nonliterate societies in religious contexts. The variety of styles is tremendous. New Zealand Maoris sing extended chants revolving about one note. Ellice Islanders have choral recitations in half-spoken performance. American Indians use their simplest as well as their most complex styles for religious song: the ghost dance songs are among the simplest of the Plains, while the Pueblo Indians' katcina-dance songs (dances of ancestors) are the most intricate in North America. In contrast to modern Western culture, nonliterate societies tend to have, by far, more religious than secular songs. In contrast with the West, also, nonliterate cultures, if they have instruments at all, use them as ceremonial paraphernalia par excellence. The variety of musical styles is also reflected in the texts. Words of religious song extend from detailed and lengthy chronicles of tribal mythology to brief supplications of a deity, and to meaningless though fixed syllables.

Oriental Civilizations. The art music of Japan, China, Indonesia, India, and the Islamic nations include religious music of many kinds. Special genres of music, such as chanting, are reserved for religious use, but in many cases music with religious connotations does not differ appreciably in style from the secular music of the same culture. The most prominent religions of the Asian civilizations are Islam, Hinduism, and Buddhism. Generally speaking, these religions do not make so wide or so specific a use of music in worship as does Christianity, and on the other hand, music is not so completely tied to ritual and ceremonial life as it is in the typical nonliterate culture. Music does play a great role in the cosmology of ancient Asian nations. Precise tuning of instruments, for example, was regarded as essential to the order of the universe in ancient China. The classical music of India even today exhibits ritual aspects as well. Thus, many of the *ragas* (scales or melody skeletons on which improvisation is based) are to be played only at specific times of day or under particular conditions. The task of the Indian musician is to uphold the order of the universe. The idea that music has a role or power far beyond that of providing aesthetic pleasure is widespread in the Orient.

The kinds of religious music vary greatly. We find monophonic chants that have some superficial similarity to Gregorian chant, but we know also orchestral music performed on metallophones and other percussion instruments, and there are intermediate gradations as well. No generalizations regarding the overall character of sacred Oriental music versus that of secular music can be proposed.

Chinese Buddhist music embodies elements of Tibetan and Indian influence. Chanting is frequently within a small tonal range, and occasionally it may be performed in parallel thirds or fourths or accompanied by cymbals. Responsorial singing is known and can result in overlapping and polyphony. Japanese Buddhist music has several genres and an elaborate music theory. Two main modes, *ryo* (roughly Lydian) and *ritsu* (roughly Dorian), are used. Services consist of chanting and speaking by priests, and the main subdivisions are marked by strokes on gongs and bells. Quite in another vein, festivals and dances are associated with Buddhist evangelism in the vernacular languages. The influence of China on Japanese Buddhist music can be seen in the fact that in the 9th century Japanese monks annually journeyed to the Chinese monastery of Yü-shan, where they could study the proper way of singing praise to Buddha.

A form of chant is used also to recite the Rigvedic hymns in India. Here a semispoken form of performance encompassing three distinct pitches separated by major seconds is common. Rare today, but associated with the larger offerings and sacrifices, is the Samaveda, whose chants have a much wider melodic range. In contrast to the Rigveda, the music of the Samaveda departs greatly from speech, disregarding linguistic principles and revealing greater rhythmic variety and, occasionally, extremely melismatic passages. Instrumental music and dance also figure in the Vedic ceremonies. In Indonesian rituals the gamelan orchestras, consisting largely of xylophones, sets of gongs, and other percussion instruments, though now largely part of secular life, play an important role. In Bali the gamelan orchestras were originally used only in ceremonies connected with cremation.

Since Moslems do not have ceremonies or services similar to those of Christianity, Islam does not have religious music in the Western sense of the word. Nevertheless, music has many religious associations. Most important are the chanting of the Koran and the call to prayer. The latter, originally a simple announcement shouted in the streets, became a stylized, dirgelike, melismatic kind of chant. At times throughout its history Islam was influenced by "purists" who tried to eliminate music from religious as well as secular life. The various dervish orders and the special developments of Islam in numerous countries and cultures brought forth many kinds of music and dance that, while often outwardly secular, have religious connotations. Throughout Oriental civilizations the essentially religious nature of music is recognized, and the distinction between strictly sacred and absolutely secular music is difficult to make.

Bibliography: NewOxHMus v.1. B. Nettl, *Music in Primitive Culture* (Cambridge, Mass. 1956). C. Sachs, *The Rise of Music in the Ancient World* (New York 1943); *The Wellsprings of Music* (The Hague 1962). A. P. Merriam, *The Anthropology of Music* (Evanston, Ill. 1964). J. Kunst, *Ethno-musicology* (3d ed. The Hague 1959), contains comprehensive bibliog. W. P. Malm, *Japanese Music and Musical Instruments* (Rutland, Va. 1959). H. H. Roberts, *Ancient Hawaiian Music* (Honolulu 1926). F. Densmore, *Chippewa Music*, 2 v. (Washington 1910–13). W. Rhodes, *Music of the American Indian, Northwest, Puget Sound* (Washington 1954). **Illustration credit:** Courtesy of the Trustees of the British Museum.

[B. NETTL]

MUSIC EDUCATION IN THE U.S.

The training of youth in music theory and practice, with special reference to U.S. Catholic schools, is reviewed in this article.

The Church's patronage of music in every age is based upon the functional concepts of sacred music as "handmaid of the liturgy," as Pope Pius X termed it in his 1903 motu proprio. Secular music as well as liturgical is, however, recognized by the Church as benefiting the emotional and volitional faculties of human nature; as Pius XII wrote, in the encyclical *Musicae Sacrae Disciplina* (1955), "Music is among the many and great gifts of nature with which God, in whom is the harmony of the most perfect concord and the most perfect order, has enriched men." Thus, instruction in music should be an integral part of the Catholic educational tradition.

Early History. Monastery choir schools from the 9th to the 12th centuries provided the earliest systematic music education under Christian auspices. These were functional schools, preparing members of religious orders for participation in the liturgy. Although liturgical repertory was their objective, instruction in music reading and theory was a basic step toward this goal. Indeed, the development of our Western system of notation evolved from choir school instructional techniques. After the 12th century similar schools developed in cathedral cities, and many have perdured to recent times, e.g., the Vienna choir school, in which *Haydn and *Schubert were educated. In return for their services as choir members, men and boys received a complete academic education, admittedly musical in emphasis.

Earliest ventures in Catholic music education on the North American continent were a choir school for boys founded in 1524 at Texcaco, Mexico, by the Franciscan friar Pedro de *Gante, and a similar school for French and Indian boys begun at Quebec in 1635 by the French missionary Paul LeJeune. Padre José Mariano Elizago established a conservatory of music in Mexico in 1825. *See* MUSIC, SACRED (CANADA); LATIN AMERICA, MUSIC IN.

The absence of liberal music training in early American public education (i.e., on the English-speaking Eastern Seaboard) betrays both the persistent reality of the struggle for survival and the "iconoclastic" Puritan-Calvinist influence. In their first stage American public schools were in fact religious schools under Protestant direction. The first effort to introduce music in the public school curriculum—in Boston, 1835—is credited to Lowell Mason. In general, Catholic schools in the U.S. followed the public school program, though there is evidence that music was not entirely ignored. Bl. Mother Seton's Sisters of Charity, the Ursulines in New Orleans, and other American and European communities entering the work of education in this country included modest music courses in their curricula. Every convent school had its music department, in which young women studied piano, harp, guitar, and mandolin and sang the simple and frequently sentimental melodies of the early 19th century, seemingly oblivious to the classical Haydn and Haydnesque Masses, nonliturgical but musically sound staples of parish services. *See* MUSIC, SACRED (U.S.).

Development. Music education in Catholic schools took a new direction when the Catholic Normal School of the Holy Family (later Pio Nono College) was founded at St. Francis, Wis., by Rev. Joseph *Salzmann with the encouragement of John Martin *Henni, first bishop of Milwaukee. In this pioneer school for teachers, music courses were conducted by John *Singenberger, who had absorbed the traditions of the German *Caecilian movement and founded the first American Caecilian society at St. Francis in 1873. (*See* MUSIC SOCIETIES IN THE U.S.) For over 40 years the Caecilian movement dominated liturgical music in German parishes of the Middle West at the hands of choirmasters and organists who exerted a strong influence for good liturgical music in the schools of the area. Although its impact was thus limited, it prepared the way for wider acceptance of the church music reform ordered in 1903 by Pius X.

In response to this papal directive, Mother Georgia *Stevens, RSCJ, in collaboration with Mrs. Justine B. Ward, who dedicated her life and fortune to the cause of good music in Catholic schools, founded the Pius X school of Liturgical Music at Manhattanville College of the Sacred Heart, New York City, in 1906. Eminent authorities on Gregorian chant and polyphony came from Rome and from the Abbey of *Solesmes to conduct intensive liturgical music courses attended by religious and lay teachers staffing parochial schools, Catholic high schools, and colleges throughout the country. The institute was affiliated with the Pontifical Institute of Sacred Music in 1954.

The founding of the Gregorian Institute of America by Dr. Clifford A. Bennett in 1941 inaugurated another advance in Catholic music education. The institute (now based at Toledo, Ohio) began its work with the Catholic Choirmasters' Course, a series of correspondence lessons in various aspects of liturgical music. At the completion of the home-study portion of the course, students attended summer sessions under world-famous experts in church music. Affiliation with the University of Montreal in 1947 enabled students to work toward the baccalaureate degree. The degree program was transferred in 1953 to Laval University, Quebec. Further enrichment of the course is provided through affiliation with the Gregorian Institute of Paris, and through study programs available at the Abbey of Solesmes and other European centers of liturgical music. A publications department established in 1945 and numerous recordings of lectures, ceremonies, and musical works extend the educational influence of the Gregorian Institute to parish choirs and parochial schools in all parts of the nation.

The National Catholic Music Educators Association, founded in 1942 by Msgr. E. J. Goebel and Dr. Harry Seitz, and based at The Catholic University of America, Washington, D.C., has become another force toward improvement of Catholic music education. Acting with professional confidence and competence, the NCMEA has aided diocesan school authorities to arrive at a keener appreciation of music in the schools, especially by means of its publication, *Musart,* and by the activities of its affiliated diocesan units, and annual national conventions in which liturgical leaders and music educators lecture and hold clinics and demonstrations in their special fields for thousands of teaching delegates.

During the first century of their existence Catholic schools confined music instruction largely to preparation for liturgical participation and the simple recreational aspects of music. As parish schools were organized into diocesan systems under the guidance of superintendents delegated by local ordinaries, interest in comprehensive music programs began to develop. Diocesan and community music supervisors and teachers have devised courses of study covering music education for various age and grade levels and providing guidance for teaching vocal and instrumental music, with appropriate emphasis upon music reading and music theory. By 1964 almost every U.S. diocesan system had a music program that was based on an approved music text for elementary schools and usually supplemented by the development of instrumental activities in bands and orchestras.

Textbooks. Catholic schools at first depended upon typical public school instructional material, supplementing this with hymns and Gregorian Masses for liturgical participation. It soon became apparent that textbooks designed specifically for Catholic schools would simplify the task of coordinating sacred and secular music in the school program. Four major series have been developed in response to this need. First in the order of publication is the "Ward Method" (1914; in 4th ed. 1964) by Mrs. Justine B. Ward, published by the Catholic Education Press. Other series integrating sacred and secular music in graded elementary school courses are: *To God through Music,* prepared by the Sisters of Providence of St. Mary-of-the Woods, Ind., under the supervision of Sister M. Lourdes, SP, and published by the Gregorian Institute (1953–59); *Music for Life,* prepared by a committee of teachers of the Archdiocese of Hartford, Conn., under the chairmanship of Sister M. John Bosco, RSM, and published by McLaughlin-Reilly Company (1953–64); *We Sing and Praise,* edited by Sister Cecilia, SC, Sister John Joseph, CSJ, and Sister Rose Margaret, CSJ, and published by Ginn and Company (1957–62).

In Secondary Schools. Music is still of extracurricular status in American Catholic high schools. Bands, orchestras, and choral groups flourish, and young participants receive valuable training and performance experience, often under competent professional directors. City, state, and diocesan music festivals and competitions sharpen taste and self-criticism and provide further incentive to artistic excellence. Formal courses in music theory, appreciation, and history are seldom offered as electives, though progress in this direction is discernible in individual schools and systems. Private instruction in instrumental and vocal music is available in most private and many parochial and diocesan high schools.

In Colleges and Seminaries. Most Catholic colleges offer undergraduate music programs. Since music education graduates usually accept teaching or supervising posts in public or Catholic schools, the influence of music as an academic discipline thus further permeates the field of American education. A number of Catholic universities offer graduate music programs leading to the M.A. or Ph.D. degree in musicology, performing arts, or music education. Solid training in Gregorian chant and other forms of liturgical music, in music history and appreciation, and in methods of teaching music, is also provided for future music educators in the *Sister Formation program inaugurated during the 1950s in novitiates and juniorates of American religious communities.

Students in the nation's minor and major seminaries have traditionally been trained in the art of plainchant and the rubrics of worship. The *Menti nostrae,* Pius XII's apostolic exhortation on seminary education (1950), however, enjoins a broadened curriculum to include studies in the liberal and cultural disciplines such as are provided in the preparation for any other profession. Accordingly, in addition to intensified work in strictly liturgical music, electives are gradually being introduced to provide background in the whole range of music, and, for musically gifted students, opportunities for professional lessons off the campus. In the spirit of *Menti nostrae* the Seminary Committee of

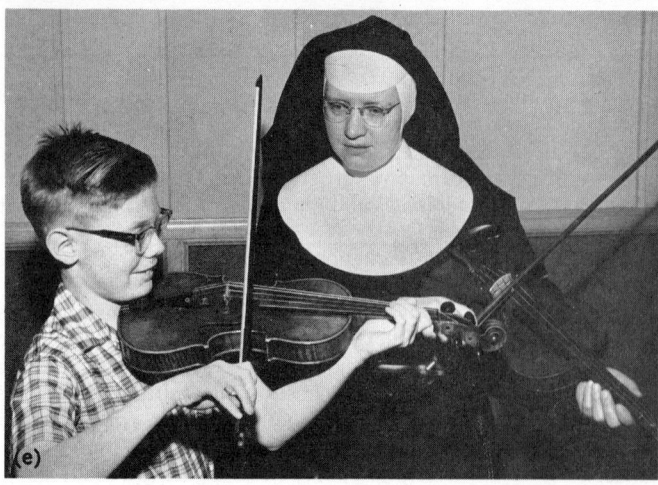

Music education: (a) Music methods class at the University of Dayton. (b) Chorus practice at Manhattanville College of the Sacred Heart, Purchase, N.Y. (c) The Symphony Orchestra of Central Catholic High School, Fort Wayne, Ind. (d) A string group from the orchestra of Mary Queen of Peace School, St. Louis. (e) Violin instruction at St. Coletta School, Jefferson, Wis. (f) Fourth-grade music class at Mary Queen of Peace School.

the NCMEA Liturgical Department has been elaborating a syllabus coordinating music education with the pastoral and liturgical formation of future priests.

See also MUSIC, SACRED, HISTORY OF, 7, 8; MUSIC, SACRED (U.S.).

Bibliography: Archives, Pius X School of Liturgical Music, Manhattanville College, Purchase, N.Y. *Musart* (1948–). M. R. MOORE, "Music in Early American Catholic Schools," Cath EdRev 60 (1962) 577–587. J. E. LAMEK, *Music Instruction in Catholic Elementary Schools* (Washington 1933), somewhat outdated. D. W. SHAUM, *The Music Program in Catholic Colleges and Universities in the United States* (Washington 1961). Catholic University of America, *Proceedings of the Workshop on Music Education (Teaching)*, ed. J. B. PAUL and R. H. WERDER (Washington 1954–). R. M. MURPHY, *An Historical Survey of the National Catholic Music Educators Association* (Washington 1963). National Catholic Music Education Association, *Partial Proceedings of the Eighth National Convention* (Washington 1955). A. P. BRITTON, "Music Education: An American Specialty," *One Hundred Years of Music in America,* ed. P. H. LÁNG (New York 1961) 211–229.

[C. WARD]

MUSIC SOCIETIES IN THE U.S.

Professional organizations for musicians concerned with Catholic liturgical music have existed in the U.S. from the period of the *Caecilian movement, activated in Germany in 1868 to foster the reform of sacred music and revival of chant and Renaissance polyphony. Most significant of such groups in the U.S. was the American Caecilian Society, founded in 1873 at the Catholic Normal School of the Holy Family, St. Francis, Wis., under the sponsorship of Bp. J. Martin *Henni of Milwaukee by Rev. Joseph *Salzmann and J. B. *Singenberger. Singenberger, who had joined the faculty of this pioneer teacher-training institute directly after completion of his studies with F. X. *Witt and F. X. *Haberl, leading spirits of the reform movement in Germany, patterned the American group after the parent Caecilian Society. At subsequent conventions in major cities, programs of good Church music were performed in collaboration with local choirs, thus introducing compositions of polyphonic and Caecilian composers and developing higher liturgical and artistic standards. Its publication, *Caecilia,* spread its reforming influence further, besides enlarging the available repertory of Renaissance and contemporary Church music. Although its membership was confined largely to Church musicians in German areas, the society did much to prepare the way for the directives of Pope St. Pius X's 1903 motu proprio on sacred music before its decline set in c. 1900.

The Society of St. Gregory of America, the inspiration of N. A. *Montani, filled the gap left by the waning Caecilian Society. It was planned in 1913 at an informal meeting in Baltimore, Md., organized the following year at the Catholic Summer School of America, Cliff Haven, N.Y., with the help of Very Rev. Ernest R. Dyer, SS, Msgr. Leo P. Manzetti, and Rev. John Petter, and approved by a papal rescript of May 1, 1915, for the purpose of promoting the cause of sacred music according to the decrees of the Church. It was governed by an executive board that met annually, and was composed of affiliated diocesan guilds that came together for national conventions. Publications included its quarterly, the *Catholic Choirmaster,* and the "White List" of liturgically acceptable compositions, with approved supplements. The Liturgical Medal was granted

from time to time to Catholic lay musicians for significant contributions to Church music.

In August 1964 the officers and executive boards of both societies, meeting in Boys Town, Nebr., effected a merger, naming the new society the Church Music Association of America. Rt. Rev. Rembert G. Weakland OSB, archabbot of St. Vincent Archabbey, Latrobe, Pa., was chosen president of the new group. Other officers were Rev. Cletus Madson, St. Ambrose College, Davenport, Iowa, executive vice president; Rev. Richard J. Schuler, St. Thomas College, St. Paul, Minn., general secretary; and Frank Szynskie, treasurer. The two periodicals *Caecilia* and *Catholic Choirmaster* also became one at this founding meeting.

Another influential group is the National Catholic Music Educators Association, which claims broad membership among teachers and liturgists desiring to promote closer integration between school and church music and to foster research in this area of music education (*see* MUSIC EDUCATION IN THE U.S.). Catholic church musicians are represented also in several interdenominational societies working to promote high standards in church and school music, foster research, or develop individual musicianship. Among these are the American Guild of Organists, which grants certificates of associate, fellow, and choirmaster to artists of demonstrated qualifications; the Hymn Society of America, which promotes the creation of new hymns and research in hymnody; the American Musicological Society, devoted to research in theory and history of music; the Music Educators National Conference, which concentrates on school-music techniques; and the American Society of Composers, Authors, and Publishers, which protects the performance rights of its members. American church musicians also participate in the International Society for Musical Research, the International Society for Contemporary Music, and the International Federation of Little Singers, which affiliates boy choirs from many countries. On the feast of St. Cécilia, Nov. 22, 1963, Pope Paul VI created an international *Consociatio* for Sacred Music and promulgated its statutes. Its patron is the incumbent prefect of the Congregation of Rites, and its objective is cooperation among the several national church music societies.

See also MUSIC, SACRED (U.S.).

Bibliography: J. V. HIGGINSON, "The American Caecilian Society," *Catholic Choirmaster* 28 (1942) 107–109; "History of the Saint Gregory Society," *ibid.* 26 (1940) 57–59, 160–163; "Pope Paul VI on the Consociatio for Sacred Music," *ibid.* 50 (1964) 104–105. E. E. NEMMERS, *Twenty Centuries of Catholic Church Music* (Milwaukee 1949). L. W. ELLINWOOD, *The History of American Church Music* (New York 1953). *Catholic Choirmaster* 50 (1964), "Jubilee Issue 1914–1964."

[J. V. HIGGINSON]

MUSIL, ROBERT

Austrian novelist and dramatist; b. Klagenfurt, Nov. 6, 1880; d. Geneva, Switzerland, April 15, 1942. He was the son of Alfred, a college professor, and Hermine (Bergauer), both of well-to-do, middle-class, intellectual background and both baptized Catholics. Robert later converted to Protestantism so that he could marry a divorcee. After attending elementary schools in Steyr and Brünn, he entered the military school at Eisenstadt and later the Vienna Technical Military Academy. He had a short career as an officer. After a period as an assistant at the Stuttgart Technical College, he studied philosophy, psychology, and mathematics in Berlin, where he obtained his Ph.D. in 1908 with a dissertation against the positivism of E. Mach. For a time he was a free-lance writer, then (1911–14) librarian at the Vienna Technical College, after which he became editor of the Berlin *Neue Rundschau*.

During World War I Musil served as an officer, first for 2 years of the Austrian southern front, then as publisher of a soldiers' newspaper that was also an important intellectual organ. Until 1922 he was employed in the Austrian civil service and then once again took to free-lance writing in Vienna under rather difficult living conditions. During this time he was supported by his devoted wife, Martha (Heiman), a divorcee of Jewish ancestry. Musil wrote free-lance in Berlin (1931–33) and in Vienna until 1938, when he voluntarily immigrated to Switzerland in protest of *National Socialism. His sojourn in Switzerland was made possible principally through the help of the Protestant pastor Robert Lejeune. Musil died in obscurity and won world recognition only after the edition of his complete works by Adolf Frisé.

Musil's first novel, *Die Verwirrungen des Zöglings Törless* (1906), caused something of a stir because of its revelation of some of the more furtive aspects of adolescence among cadets, but his book *Vereinigungen* (two tales, 1911) met with no success at all. The well-structured and psychologically profound short stories "Grigia" (1923) and "Die Portugiesin" (1923) won some recognition, as did *Drei Frauen*, which contained these two stories and "Tonka" (1924). The play *Die Schwärmer* (1921) and the farce *Vinzenz und die Freundin bedeutender Männer* (1924) have never succeeded on the stage. All this work was ultimately only an intensive preparation for his one great lifework, the novel *Der Mann ohne Eigenschaften*, which was never completed (v.1 1930; v.2 1933; v.3 was published by his wife in 1943 from surviving notes; in the complete edition of his works a fourth volume was compiled from other fragments). This enormous novel, which tries to encompass the whole of the last year of peace of the Austrian monarchy (called "Kakanien" as a play on the adjective "kaiser-königlich"—the full form of the ubiquitous "k.k."), presents a unique synthesis of loving criticism and a satirical dissection of that most remarkable of states. Without being directly autobiographical, Musil summed up in the person of the principal character, Ulrich, all the experiences of his own life, a life that, according to the Protestant critic Heinz Flügel, was not entirely irreligious: "To the extent that Robert Musil without hypocrisy reminds us in his novel of the as yet unaccomplished designs of God, he perhaps contributes more to the renewal of Christian hope than do those who use the alleged heterodoxy of Musil's concept of God as a pretext to avoid answering his call to a really positive Utopia" [*Herausforderung durch das Wort* (Stuttgart 1962) 53]. Although Musil did not strive for the tense, sculptured style of epic prose, the quality of his work equals that of *Proust's *A la recherche du temps perdu* and *Joyce's *Ulysses*. He was as well a master of the essay form (e.g., *Nachlass zu Lebzeiten*, 1936).

Bibliography: *Gesammelte Werke in Einzelausgaben*, ed. A. Frisé, 3 v. (Hamburg 1952–57), contains also his diaries and letters. K. Dinklage, ed., *Robert Musil. Leben. Werk. Wirkung* (Vienna 1960). W. Berghahn, *Robert Musil in Selbstzeugnissen und Bilddokumenten* (Hamburg 1963), with bibliog.

[E. Alker]

MUSPILLI, an incomplete Old High German alliterative poem of 103 lines, in Bavarian dialect. It is preserved on three pages at the front and back of a 9th-century MS from *Sankt Emmeram, containing the pseudo-Augustinian *Sermo de symbolis contra Judaeos*. The MS is now in Munich. The title, inappropriately supplied by the first editor, is from an obscure compound occurring in line 57 meaning either "doom" or "judgment on the world" or "destroyer of the earth," i.e., fire. The poem is compiled from two apocryphal Christian themes: the perilous journey of the soul and the psychopomps to particular judgment; and the battle, signs, and General Judgment elaborated under Eastern influence from Apoc 11.3, 7. *Muspilli* runs as follows: Angels and devils contend for the possession of departing souls; let sinners prepare against this encounter; let men also know that there will be a General Judgment heralded by signs including the apocalyptic battle between Elias and Antichrist; let all avoid sin, especially kin-slaying, and be ready for resurrection when Christ appears with his cross at Judgment. Scholars debate the poem's alleged paganism, its unity, and its vocabulary, notably the words *muspille,* line 57, and *weroltrehtwison,* line 37. All admit the genius of its unknown author.

Bibliography: Sources. MS Munich Clm 14098, s. ix. T. W. Braune, *Althochdeutsches Lesebuch*, ed. K. Helm (13th ed. Tübingen 1958). Literature. J. K. Bostock, *A Handbook on Old High German Literature* (Oxford 1955). H. Schneider, "Muspilli," ZAlterlit 73 (1936) 1–32. G. Baesecke, "Muspilli II," *ibid.*, 82 (1948–50) 199–239. A. C. Dunstan, "*Muspilli* and the Apocryphal Gospels," *German Life and Letters* 11 (1957–58) 270–275.

[L. K. Shook]

MUSSET, LOUIS CHARLES ALFRED DE, poet and dramatist; b. Paris, Dec. 11, 1810; d. there, May 2, 1857. After attending the Collège Henri IV, he unsuccessfully tried law and medicine. His *Contes d'Espagne et d'Italie* (1830), whose spirit of melancholy and satire revealed the influence of Byron, won immediate attention. While in Italy with George Sand (1833–34), he produced *Les Nuits* (1835–37) and *Lorenzaccio* (1834), the best tragedy of the Romantic theater. His *Confession d'un enfant du siècle* (1836) is a reasonably accurate reflection of the attitudes of many toward the religious and social adjustment that marked Romanticism. He was not only the best poet of love produced by the Romantic movement, but also was its most successful dramatist; his plays are still performed regularly in France. Although with the *Lettres de Dupuis et Cotonet* (1836–37) he officially renounced Romanticism, he was destined by temperament to remain closely associated with it. In 1852 he was elected to the French Academy despite protests about his love affairs. Musset always wanted to accept Christianity but he was hindered by his weakness. Unlike *Hugo and *Lamartine, he did not construct a quasi-philosophical system, but tried to explain metaphysical problems by the distorted concept of love that obsessed him. Like *Vigny, he complains of God's indifference to man's plight, but he is unable to accept Vigny's stoicism as an alternative. *L'Espoir en Dieu* (1838) is simply a restatement of Jean Jacques *Rousseau's contention that God reveals Himself to the human heart and not to the mind. *Lorenzaccio* provides the best insight into Musset's inner conflict, the age-old struggle of a burdened soul yearning for assurance of forgiveness. Like his creator, Lorenzaccio recognizes the beauty of virtue and the horror of sin, but refuses to believe that God will forgive him. Musset, the keenest student of psychology among the major Romantic poets, paradoxically remained incapable of analyzing and solving his own problems.

See also ROMANTICISM, LITERARY.

Bibliography: *Oeuvres complètes,* ed. M. ALLEM (Paris 1933–38). P. VAN TIEGHEM, *Musset: L'Homme et l'oeuvre* (Paris 1944). H. D. SEDGWICK, *Alfred de Musset, 1810–1857: A Biography* (Indianapolis 1932). P. GASTINEL, *Le Romantisme d'Alfred de Musset* (Paris 1933). M. ALLEM, *Alfred de Musset* (Paris 1948). H. LEFEBVRE, *Alfred de Musset, dramaturge* (Paris 1955).

[C. LOMBARD]

MUSSO, CORNELIUS,

theologian; b. Piacenza, April 16, 1511; d. Rome, Jan. 9, 1574. He joined the Conventual Franciscans at Piacenza, studied at the University of Padua, and taught metaphysics at the University of Pavia and theology at the University of Bologna. He was consecrated bishop of Bertinoro in 1541, and was transferred to Bitonto in 1544. Musso gave the inaugural address at the Council of Trent, and thereafter played a considerable role in the procedural sessions. He took a particularly active part in the discussions on the sources of revelation, original sin, justification, and the Sacraments. At the end of the Council, he returned to his diocese to begin the work of reform. Opposition from the court of Naples forced him to give up this work and resign his see in 1572. His sermons fill eight volumes. Musso is faithful to Bonaventure and Scotus in theology; his chief works are: the *De Deo Uno et Trino* (Venice 1585), *Commentaria in b. Pauli Epistolam ad Romanos* (Venice 1588), and *De Divina Historia Libri III* (Venice 1585, 1587).

Bibliography: G. ODOARDI, EncCatt 8:1564–65. H. JEDIN, LexThK² 7:706. R. J. BARTMAN, "Cornelius Musso, Tridentine Theologian and Orator," FrancStudies 5 (1945) 247–276. G. ODOARDI, "Fra Cornelio Musso, O. F. M. Conv. Padre, oratore e teologo al Concilio di Trento," *Miscellanea Francescana* 48 (1948) 223–242, 450–478; 49 (1949) 36–71.

[P. FEHLNER]

MUSSOLINI, BENITO

Italian statesman; b. Dovia (Forlì), Italy, July 29, 1883; d. Dongo (Como), April 28, 1945.

Career to 1922. Benito Amilcare Andrea Mussolini was the firstborn of a poor, working-class family. His formal education, never systematic, began at the school conducted by the Salesians in Faenza. Later he attended the Giosuè Carducci college (1894–98) and the normal school at Forlimpopoli, from which he received a teaching license for elementary schools (June 1901). In 1900 he had enrolled in the Italian Socialist party. When he failed to answer the call for obligatory military service (1902), he fled to Switzerland until 1904. This Swiss sojourn, centered at Lausanne, exposed Mussolini for the first time to an ideological "underground" made up of obscure Italian political refugees and European professional revolutionists. In search of work and ideas, he plunged eclectically into 19th-century philosophy and ideology, reading the works of such men

as Schopenhauer, Nietzsche, Stirner, and Blanqui. In Switzerland also he made his apprenticeship as a socialist journalist and ideological polemicist. His early writings reflect a violent temperament giving vent to antimilitaristic, antimonarchical, antidemocratic, and antireligious passions. In his youthful thought and action Mussolini seems to have undertaken a private war against God and country. Following a general royal amnesty, he returned to Italy and was enrolled in the Bersaglieri corps of the Italian army (1905–06). After his discharge Mussolini plunged back into his activity as an extreme socialist and journalist, while teaching French in a private preparatory school at Oneglia on the Italian Riviera. Some of his most virulently anti-Christian views and frequently scurrilous attacks on Catholicism appeared under the pseudonym of "Vero Eretico," with which he signed his contributions to the weekly socialist paper of Oneglia, *La Lima.* His reputation within north Italian socialist circles was growing. In 1909 he was offered the post of secretary of the labor syndicate of Trent and was made editor of the socialist weekly, *L'Avvenire del Lavoratore.* The Tridentine region, then part of the Hapsburg domain, was the battleground of a three-cornered political struggle between Italian irredentists, socialists, and Catholic groups. Mussolini had a brief hostile encounter with Alcide de *Gasperi, editor of the Catholic *Trentino,* for whom he was to nourish a lifelong hatred. He was expelled from Trent as a subverter of the political order and religious peace of the Austro-Hungarian Empire. In 1910 he returned to Forlì and entered into a common-law marriage (regularized in 1915) with Rachele Guidi, by whom he had five children.

From 1910 to 1912 Mussolini laid the foundation for his brief leadership of the Italian Socialist party. He founded and edited at Forlì an incendiary revolutionary organ, *Lotta di Classe,* through which, contrary to the reformist tendencies of the official national leaders of the party, he continued to agitate his personal brand of activistic socialism. During 1911, with Italy engaged in the Libyan war, he organized violent ultrapacifist demonstrations and was arrested for inciting sabotage of the war effort. Found guilty of antinational activity, he was condemned to a 1-year prison term, later reduced to 5 months, which he served in the jails of Forlì and Bologna. Upon his release he found himself famous in Italian socialist circles. Whereas his first participation in a national congress of the Italian Socialist party (1910) had been a fiasco, his activity at the congress in 1912 carried the day for the extreme socialist line against the reformist right (Bissolati, Bonomi) and the moderate center (Turati, Treves). His personal triumph was capped by his succession to the editorship of the party's official organ, *Avanti!* From 1912 to October 1914 Mussolini was almost undisputed as *duce* of Italian socialism. The outbreak of World War I, however, brought a completely new turn to Mussolini's life and career. From an extreme internationalist-neutralist position, he veered suddenly toward a nationalist-interventionist, war-mongering posture by exhorting Italy to throw in her lot on the side of the Entente. On Oct. 24, 1914, he was expelled from the Socialist party and was forced to abandon the editorship of *Avanti!* Quickly (Nov. 14, 1914) he launched his own daily, *Popolo d'Italia,* which to the end of his career remained his official mouthpiece. Mussolini served on the Italian front from August 1915 to February 1917, when he was seriously wounded. After hospitalization, he was discharged from active military duty. His political battles were soon resumed, first on the pages of *Popolo d'Italia* and then in political organizational work.

In 1919 and 1920 Italy was gripped by disenchantment over the "mutilated victory," social discontent, political agitation, and new revolutionary ferment—a situation ready-made for Mussolinian activism. In March 1919 Mussolini and a small group of political friends founded in Milan the Italian National Fascist party, whose aims were as obscure as its program was eclectic (nationalist, syndicalist, revolutionary, republican, etc.). The party grew slowly into a north Italian movement, whose members came chiefly from the middle classes, and whose support derived apparently from certain large industrial and agrarian interests. From 1920 to 1922, with its changes of program and tensions within the ranks of *fascism heightened by contrasting political elements, social currents, and ideological tendencies, Mussolini alone held the party together and molded it into a single-minded "state within the State." The "March on Rome" (Oct. 28, 1922), which Mussolini directed from Milan, represented the victory of a new political strategy that neutralized the leaders of the liberal and socialist Italian ruling class (Giolitti, Bonomi, Turati), even as it held at bay the forces of political Catholicism organized in Don Luigi *Sturzo's *Partito Popolare.* In October 1922 only the Italian monarchy could have spared Italy the collapse of her liberal parliamentary regime. But King Victor Emmanuel III chose to collaborate with the "Fascist Revolution." Instead of having Mussolini arrested for sedition, he called him to Rome and installed him as prime minister of Italy. Mussolini's assumption of power (Oct. 30, 1922) marked the end of an Italian era. During the ensuing 2 decades and more the history of Italy centered on Mussolini.

From 1922 to 1945. After a period of trial and error at authoritarian rule, which culminated with the assassination of the socialist parliamentary leader Giacomo Matteotti (June 1924), Mussolini began to dismantle the entire structure of the Italian liberal state. The shift from a personal authoritarian rule to an all-encompassing *totalitarianism was achieved during the decade that began with Mussolini's speech of Jan. 3, 1925, proclaiming the dictatorship, and ended with his speech of Oct. 2, 1935, launching the fascist attack against Ethiopia. The fascistization of all aspects of Italian public life was an accomplished political fact when, on May 9, 1936, the Duce proclaimed the new fascist Italian Empire from his balcony in the Roman Palazzo Venezia. On that day Mussolini's power and prestige seemed supreme; yet it was then that symptoms of decline began to appear. For from 1922 to 1934 Mussolini had been shrewdly cautious to safeguard the original image he had created at home and abroad of fascism as a conservator of law and order against social subversion and international lawlessness. Despite his verbal violences and occasional shows of force against the West, Mussolini had not detached Italy from her unofficial entente with the Anglo-French international leadership. The Ethiopian War (1935–36) acted as a catalyst. At its close Mussolini's Italy was closer to Nazi Germany, which had not openly opposed his imperialistic designs, than to France and England, which had half-heartedly led the League of Nations into a "sanctionist" posture vis-à-vis fascist aggression. The ideological manifestoes preceding the formation of the Axis, the signing of the Anti-Komintern Pact (November 1936), and the Italian-German military alliance, known as the "Pact of Steel" (May 1939), revealed that Mussolini, deluded by success, was becoming an active instrument of Adolf *Hitler's ambitions. Mussolini's sponsorship of *anti-semitism and *racism in 1938 in a land that had been singularly free of biological and cultural prejudice marked the beginning of the end of the shaky moral consensus he had won from his people.

When Mussolini caused Italy to enter World War II (June 1940) on the side of Germany, he sealed his own fate and that of fascist Italy. Against the almost unanimous opposition of all classes of Italians, Mussolini launched his country, militarily unprepared and morally uncommitted, into a war whose stupendous scope eluded his personal and political comprehension. As dictator he placed his country in a tragic situation in which it feared victory on the side of its ally more than defeat on the side of its enemy. Mussolini's vaunted Machiavellianism proved its own nemesis.

Disasters in the field (1942–43) profoundly disillusioned the Italians about the Duce's political wisdom and moral responsibility. The *coup d'état* of July 25, 1943, was the work of a cabal within the fascist grand council led by Dino Grandi, but it extended to almost every sector of the official classes, including the King. It stripped Mussolini suddenly of power and marked the real close of his political career. The last phase of his life (July 1943–April 1945) was an anticlimax. As the nominal ruler of the north Italian fascist Republic of Salò, Mussolini lived in the shadow of the crumbling Third Reich (1944–45). Mussolini's summary execution at the hands of extremist partisans acting in the name of the "Corpo Volontari della Libertà," a branch of the Italian antifascist resistance movement, has been regarded as "an act of revolutionary justice" beyond appeal. It closed a career lived violently during an Italian and European era of war, revolution, and terror.

Very few, if any, Italian political leaders of the 20th century have played so significant a role and exerted so fateful an influence at home and abroad as did Mussolini. His public life was a complex alternation of successes and failures, involving the rise and fall of an ideological regime that was at first associated with his name and that later characterized the European totalitarian phenomena of fascism and *national socialism. Throughout his life Mussolini's political and ideological features underwent, or at least manifested, violent mutations, changing from socialism to fascism, from quasi anarchism to statism, from defeatist pacificism to militarism, from syndicalism to nationalism, from anticlericalism to official confessionalism; but his character remained unaltered. Never, perhaps not even at the height of his power, did he cease being a rebel against the humanistic tradition of Europe and against the fundamental values of Christian ethics. Irreligious and anticlerical, Mussolini viewed the Church merely as an organization, a powerful institution whose "secular" persistence and influence had little or nothing to do with her spiritual mission. His part in reconciling

Church and State in Italy through the *Lateran Pacts (1929) was crucially important, but his motivation was basically political. His relations with the Church (1930–40) reveal clearly that he seldom if ever responded to the call of moral principles or of religious and spiritual forces. His career was essentially a ceaseless agitation within an expanding sphere of activistic nihilism.

See also ITALY; PIUS XI.

Bibliography: For preliminary orientation in the vast bibliography on Mussolini, see P. ALATRI, *Le origini del fascismo* (Bologna 1961) 286–302. I. DE BEGNAC, *Palazzo Venezia: Storia di un regime* (Rome 1950) 681–688, cites titles on Mussolini and fascism not mentioned by Alatri and other biographers. For Mussolini's own works, writings, and speeches, see *Scritti e discorsi*, 13 v. (Milan 1933–40), an incomplete official collection; *Scritti e discorsi adriatici*, ed. E. SUSMEL, 2 v. (Milan 1942–43); *Gli ultimi discorsi* (new ed. Rome 1950). For a postwar attempt at an exhaustive collection of Mussolini's works, see *Opera omnia*, ed. E. and D. SUSMEL, 32 v. (Florence 1951–59). Mussolini's "classic" statement on the "doctrine of fascism" first appeared as an article in the EncIt 14:847–851. Autobiog. material of varying value is found in the following works of Mussolini: *My Autobiography* (London 1939), highly tendentious. The self-portrait written by Mussolini in 1911–12, *La mia vita* (Rome 1947) is authentic and revealing; other details on Mussolini's early life and activity appear in his biog. of his brother, *Vita di Arnaldo* (Rome 1932). See also the following by Mussolini: *Il Trentino veduto da un socialista: Note e notizie* (Florence 1911); *Il mio diario di guerra* (Milan 1923); *Storia di un anno: Il tempo del bastone e della carota* (Milan 1944), which is also in Eng. ed. under the title of *The Fall of Mussolini* (New York 1948). E. LUDWIG, *Talks with Mussolini* (Boston 1933); *Hitler e Mussolini: Lettere e Documenti* (Milan 1946). On the early life and socialist career, still unsurpassed, G. MEGARO, *Mussolini in the Making* (New York 1938). G. PINI and D. SUSMEL, *Mussolini: L'uomo e l'opera*, 4 v. (Florence 1953–55), detailed, oversympathetic. Different facets of the Duce's character and activity are highlighted in the following: G. DORSO, *B. Mussolini alla conquista del potere* (Turin 1949). P. MONELLI, *Mussolini piccolo borghese* (Milan 1950). G. SALVEMINI, *Mussolini diplomatico* (Bari 1952). C. F. DELZELL, *Mussolini's Enemies: The Italian Anti-Fascist Resistance* (Princeton 1961), excellent. F. W. DEAKIN, *The Brutal Friendship: Mussolini, Hitler, and the Fall of Fascism* (New York 1962). I. KIRKPATRICK, *Mussolini: A Study in Power* (New York 1964). R. DE FELICE, *Mussolini*, v.1, *Il rivoluzionario* (Turin 1965). For contrasting assessments of Mussolini's religious policy, with particular reference to the relations between Church and State in Italy under fascism, see L. SALVATORELLI and G. MIRA, *Storia d'Italia nel periodo fascista* (4th ed. Turin 1956) 419–505. A. C. JEMOLO, *Chiesa e stato in Italia negli ultimi cento anni* (Turin 1948) 589–686. G. DE ROSA, *Storia del Partito Popolare* (Bari 1958). L. STURZO, *Italy and Fascismo* (New York 1927). D. A. BINCHY, *Church and State in Fascist Italy* (New York 1941).

[A. W. SALOMONE]

MUSURUS, MARCUS, post-Byzantine humanist influential in the dissemination of Greek learning to western Europe; b. Candia (Herakleion), Crete, *c.* 1470; d. Rome, 1517. During his youth Musurus went to Venice, and *c.* 1486 he was in Florence studying under the famous Greek humanist John, or Janus, *Lascaris. Later he was again in Venice as an intimate associate of the Aldine circle and principal editor of the Aldine Press. After contributing to the *Etymologicum magnum* of *Calliergis, Musurus edited the *editio princeps* of Aristophanes, published by *Manutius in 1498. In 1503 Musurus was appointed professor of Greek at the Venetian-controlled University of Padua, and his 6 years in that post (together with his subsequent teaching in Venice) constitute a milestone in the development of Greek studies in western Europe. His students included many of the most famous Hellenists of the age, for example, Girolamo *Aleandro, John Conon, Germain de Brie, and even the great *Erasmus, who at-

tended Musurus's lectures at Padua. In 1509 the War of the League of Cambrai forced him to withdraw to Venice, where he remained until 1516. During that period he completed his edition of Plato, which for the first time made readily available the original Greek text of the *Dialogues*. In 1516 he was summoned by Pope Leo X to participate in the newly formed papal Greek institute in Rome.

Under Musurus's direct supervision no less than 11 or 12 first editions of important Greek authors were published by the Aldine Press, among them the *Lexicon* of Hesychius and the celebrated edition of Plato. His editorial and teaching activities together enable Musurus to rank as one of the most influential Hellenists in the entire history of the revival and dissemination of Greek letters in western Europe during the *Renaissance.

See also CATHOLIC PRESS, 16.

Bibliography: R. MENGE, "Vita Marci Musuri" in *Hesychii Alexandrini Lexicon*, ed. M. SCHMIDT, 5 v. (Jena 1858–68) 5:1–57. E. L. J. LEGRAND, *Bibliographie hellénique*, 4 v. (Paris 1885–1906; repr. Brussels 1963) 1:cviii–cxxiv. D. J. GEANAKOPLOS, *Greek Scholars in Venice: Studies in the Dissemination of Greek Learning from Byzantium to Western Europe* (Cambridge, Mass. 1962), 111–166, most recent biog.

[D. J. GEANAKOPLOS]

MU'TAZILITES

The earliest important theological school of *Islam. The name (Arabic *mu'tazila*) is derived from the verb *i'tazala*, meaning "to separate oneself from." The first Mu'tazilites were political, those who "separated themselves from" both *Ali and his opponents in the quarrel over the legitimacy of his succession to the caliphate. Later the term indicated the position that the Moslem grave sinner was neither believer, unbeliever, nor hypocrite, but simply a sinner (*fāsiq*).

History. The founders of the Mu'tazilite school were Wāsil ibn 'Atā' (d. 748) and 'Amr ibn 'Ubayd (d. 762), both of Basra. But Abu'l-Hudhayl al-'Allāf (d. 840) was the true founder of Mu'tazilite dogmatics. Other prominent members of the Basra school were Mu'ammar, Hishām al-Fuwatī, al-Aṣamm, and al-Nazzām. The Baghdad school was founded by Bishr ibn al-Mu'tamir (d. 826), and included such men as Thumāma ibn Ashras and Ibn Abī Du'ād. Under the Caliphs Ma'mūn, Mu'taṣim, and Wāthiq, Mu'tazilism was the state theology, and its teaching that the *Koran was created was enforced by a kind of inquisition (*miḥna*). The Caliph Mutawakkil was hostile to the Mu'tazilites, and from his time on the school gradually declined, though it long maintained centers in the eastern part of the empire. After the Mongol invasions it survived mainly among the Zaydites of *Yemen, where it still exists.

Teachings. There are divergencies in doctrine among the many Mu'tazilite doctors, yet nearly all have held the fundamental position expressed in the five basic principles commonly attributed to the Mu'tazilites. The first, pure monotheism (*tawḥīd*), is the most important principle of Mu'tazilism, since it is the source of almost all its doctrines. God is one in the strictest sense. Anthropomorphisms are to be denied, or, when they occur in the Koran, are to be interpreted symbolically. The attributes commonly assigned to God have only a figurative meaning and are in no way realities in or distinct from the divine essence. The Koran is created. There is no beatific vision. Several solutions are proposed to the problems of creation and of God's relation to the created world.

The second principle concerns divine justice ('adl). God is supremely just. He always does what is best for His creation. He cannot will evil; hence man is personally responsible for his own moral acts. The Mu'tazilites insisted strongly on man's free will, a position that was practically rejected by later "orthodox" Moslem theology. The third principle, called "the promise and the threat" (al-wa'd wa'l-wa'īd), begot discussions concerning the final lot of the believer, sinner, and infidel; the nature of faith and unbelief; grave and light sins; legal questions in general; and the authenticity of traditions. The fourth was the intermediate state of the grave sinner (al-manzila bayna'l-manzilatayn). This is not clearly distinct from the two preceding principles. But the discussion of the grave sinner's state involved lengthy consideration of the caliphate and of the legitimacy of the first four caliphs. The fifth principle dealt with commanding good and forbidding evil. The expression is Koranic (e.g., 3.106, 110). Disapproval of evil must be by word and deed, and even by the use of the sword. This was little discussed as time went on. The general framework of these five principles left much room for refinement and difference of opinion, and later discussions often developed into philosophical disputes.

Significance. The Mu'tazilites have sometimes been called rationalists, freethinkers, or liberals of Islam. They were rationalists only in the sense that they used rational argument in their teaching. To this they were forced by the necessity of defending Islam against the dualists (Manichaeans) and the followers of other religions, many of whom became halfhearted converts to Islam. It later became the practice of "orthodox" writers to vilify the Mu'tazilites in every possible way. Their writings were destroyed, so that the only surviving Mu'tazilite manuscript, apart from works preserved in Yemen, is the *Kitab al-Intisār*, edited by Nyberg in 1925. Certain Zaydite manuscripts in Yemen may lead to a better knowledge of the Mu'tazilites and their teaching. By their polemic they certainly saved Islam from its early adversaries, and by their use of reasoning and philosophy they founded the science of *Kalām. They also contributed much to the development of the sciences of Koran exegesis, jurisprudence, and tradition. Far from being liberal, they showed much intolerance when themselves protected by the state. They played an important role in the development of Moslem theology and profoundly influenced many of the "orthodox" theologians. Since the time of Muḥammed 'Abduh, the great Egyptian reformer (d. 1905), there have been indications of a revival of interest in the Mu'tazilites among Moslem thinkers, and even of a return to some of their principal theses. This "neo-Mu'tazilism" could have far-reaching effects on the development and direction of modern Islam.

Bibliography: H. S. NYBERG, EncIslam¹ 3:841–847; *The Shorter Encyclopedia of Islam* (Leiden 1953) 421–427. A. N. NADER, *Le Système philosophique des Mu'tazila* (Beirut 1956). *Kitāb-al-Intisār* (*Le Livre du triomphe et de la réfutation d'Ibn al Rawandi l'nérétique*), Arabic text and French translation of Nyberg's 1925 edition referred to in the text. R. CASPAR, "Le Renouveau du Mo'tazalisme," *Mélanges de l'Institut Dominicain d'Études Orientales du Caire* 4 (1957) 141–202. *See also* the relevant bibliographies under ASH'ARĪ, AL-; KALĀM.

[R. J. MC CARTHY]

MUTH, CARL

Journalist; b. Worms am Rhein, Jan. 31, 1867; d. Reichenhall (Bavaria), Nov. 15, 1944. His parents were devout Catholics, and his father's occupation as church painter brought young Carl early into contact with the problems of art and religion. Muth took 6 years of his Gymnasium studies in Algiers, where the whole spiritual and intellectual ferment of French Catholicism was revealed to him under the influence of Cardinal Charles *Lavigerie. Muth abandoned early plans for mission work to devote himself to the study of political science and German philology in Giessen, Berlin, and Strassburg. During this time he contributed to the *Mainzer Journal,* was editor (1893–95) of the daily *Der Elsässer*

Carl Muth.

(Strassburg), and published the family magazine *Alte und Neue Welt,* in which he concerned himself principally with the problem of modern literature. In an article "Wem gehört die Zukunft" (1893), he opposed the superstitious belief in progress inherent in materialism and began considering for the first time the possibilities of overcoming the "literary inferiority" of the Catholics in Germany, so as to liberate church and theology from their isolation.

With his polemical works published under the pseudonym of Veremundus (*Steht die katholische Belletristik auf der Höhe der Zeit?*, and *Die literarischen Aufgaben der deutschen Katholiken,* 1899), he launched the "Catholic literary controversy" in which he had to fight on two fronts, against the intellectually unambitious in his own camp and against the "Enlighteners" hostile to the Church (*see* LITERARY REVIVAL, CATHOLIC). He was severely critical of the literary backwardness of Catholic writers and critics, whom he reproached for "apathy and unconcern for the general artistic endeavors of the nation," denominational prejudice, moral and pedagogical narrowmindedness, and "a positively unbelievable prudery." Simultaneously Muth opposed *Modernism and its naturalistic and materialistic aberrations, proposing instead an idealistic philosophy. He won the debate with his key work, *Wieder-*

geburt der Dichtung aus dem religiösen Erlebnis (1909), directed particularly against his principal opponent Richard von Kralik and Viennese neoromanticism ("The Gral").

A stay in Paris brought Muth into contact with the *renouveau catholique;* this contact was crucial for his later development. The magazine *Hochland* (a monthly publication "for all fields of knowledge, literature, and art"), which he founded in 1903 to cope with the grave perils and difficulties besetting German Catholic literature, aimed at a "new encounter between Church and culture." Until World War I, *Hochland*'s interests were mainly literary; only in 1916 did the magazine begin to devote attention to political and social problems (*see* CATHOLIC PRESS, WORLD SURVEY, 11). Muth became a champion of the concept of democracy within the still predominantly monarchically minded German Catholicism of those days. The essay "Res publica" (1926) typifies his political stand; it is a call to Catholics to become aware of their political responsibility and to cooperate actively in the fashioning of the new social order.

Muth believed that Europe's survival was dependent on the solution of the social question, on whether it would be possible to imbue Social Democracy with the sentiments and impulses of Christian brotherliness (*see* SOCIAL MOVEMENTS, CATHOLIC, 3). He made an urgent appeal to all Christians (in "Die Stunde des Bürgertums," 1930) to abandon their antisocialist prejudices and to the socialists to get rid of their anti-Christian resentments. Muth was forthright in his opposition to the rising tide of National Socialism (in *Das dritte Reich und die Sturmvögel des Nationalsozialismus,* 1931). *Hochland* maintained its stand even after Hitler had come to power, and was banned only in 1941. It resumed publication in 1946 and is (as of 1965) in its 57th year of publication in Munich, under the direction of Muth's long-time associate Karl Schaezler.

Bibliography: K. ACKERMANN, *Der Widerstand der Monatsschrift Hochland gegen den Nationalsozialismus* (Munich 1965), with bibliog. *Wiederbegegnung von Kirche und Kultur in Deutschland: Festschrift für Karl Muth* (Munich 1927). **Illustration credit:** Kösel-Verlag, Munich.

[O. B. ROEGELE]

MUTILATION

A theological term that in general denotes damage done to the living human body, but is not uniformly defined in current moral manuals. Some definitions are so worded as to restrict the notion to surgical amputations and excisions. Others, somewhat broader in scope, include in addition any suppression or diminution of bodily function, however induced. But in view of recent papal teaching, and in the light of the advances of modern medicine, it seems advisable to extend the definition to include any procedure that either temporarily or permanently impairs the natural and complete integrity of the body or its functions. This extension of concept does not of necessity make for a more rigorous moral theology. However, it facilitates the understanding of moral solutions that could otherwise prove puzzling.

Fundamental Principle. Basic to any question of mutilation is the theological fact that our right of dominion over our lives and bodies is not unrestricted. As a creature of God, man is custodian, not proprietor, of his physical being, and consequently he may dispose of his bodily members only within the limited scope of their natural finality. As Pius XII explained this truth,

> . . . [man] is not absolute master of himself, of his body or of his soul. He cannot, therefore, freely dispose of himself as he pleases. . . . [He] is bound by the immanent teleology laid down by nature. He has the right of *use*, limited by natural finality, of the faculties and powers of his human nature. Because he is a user and not a proprietor, he does not have unlimited power to destroy or mutilate his body and its functions. [ActApS 44 (1952) 782.]

Implicit, however, in the Pope's denial of unlimited right of self-disposal is the acknowledgment of some limited right in this regard. This restricted right emerges initially from the essential superiority that the total person enjoys in relation to any corporeal part. For as an integral part of the unified complexity that is the human person, each bodily member is by nature ordained to the total good of that personal whole. This part-for-whole relationship is implied in the "immanent teleology" to which Pius referred. Consequently it follows that the principle of *totality is centrally relevant to the question of mutilation. The principle was thus stated by Pius immediately after the words quoted above:

> By virtue of the principle of totality, by virtue of his right to use the services of his organism as a whole, the patient can allow individual parts to be destroyed or mutilated when and to the extent necessary for the good of his being as a whole. He may do so to ensure his being's existence and to avoid or . . . to repair serious and lasting damage which cannot otherwise be avoided or repaired.

It is currently a matter of theological dispute whether Pius XII intended to assert that only the principle of totality can be invoked as a valid norm for determining the licitness of any mutilation.

Kinds of Mutilation. Mutilations that damage or destroy the generative function are called contraceptive mutilations; they are treated specifically elsewhere (*see* STERILIZATION; ANOVULANTS; CASTRATION; HYSTERECTOMY; OVARIOTOMY; VASECTOMY).

Noncontraceptive mutilations include all types of mutilation that do not damage or destroy the generative function. Moreover, there is a morally relevant difference in the purpose for which a mutilation may be performed: it may be for the benefit of the patient or for the benefit of another; as these circumstances change, the applicability of the principle of totality also varies.

For the Patient's Benefit. Frequently it happens that a bodily member, other than one designed for procreation, becomes a serious threat to the life or general good health of the patient. When such is the case, and when sound medical judgment considers it necessary, surgical removal of the offending member is readily justified by the principle of totality alone. Usually mutilation of this kind becomes necessary and licit because disease or malfunction has made one part of the body malignant with respect to the total composite. However, even a healthy member may on occasion become hostile to the welfare of the whole, e.g., if one's foot were inextricably chained to the floor of a blazing room. Thus, the principle of totality sometimes provides for the sacrifice of even a healthy part of the body when by its mere presence or normal function that part constitutes a grave threat to life or health.

Prophylactic surgery, i.e., that calculated to prevent future danger rather than to avert a present threat, may also at times be permissible. Removal of a healthy appendix, for example, on the occasion of laparotomy performed for some other legitimate reason, or removal of an apparently healthy uterus together with malignant ovaries, may be justified on the grounds that with relatively little added risk, a probable source of future danger to the patient is eradicated.

*Cosmetic surgery, i.e., surgery performed solely for the aesthetic purpose of improving a patient's physical appearance, ordinarily qualifies theologically as a form of mutilation whose licitness is determined in accordance with the principle of totality.

The use of anesthetics, narcotics, hypnosis, etc., which deprive one temporarily of the use of reason, also entails mutilation, which is altogether licit when medically indicated for the patient's benefit.

For Benefit of Others. It must be conceded that deliberate mutilation suffered for another's benefit cannot find justification according to the principle of totality. As Pius XII insisted, the subordination of part to whole predicated of the integral parts of the physical human body does not characterize the relationship existing between individual persons and the moral body which is society, or even the mystical body. To maintain the contrary would lead to conclusions of an inadmissible totalitarian kind. Hence if mutilation for altruistic motives is ever to be vindicated as a virtuous act, some other relevant principle must be utilized.

A number of respected theologians have recourse, therefore, to the principle of fraternal charity or love, which stipulates that all members of the human race relate to one another as essentially equal. By virtue of this mutual relationship, one's neighbor is essentially neither superior nor inferior but rather "another self." Consequently, reasonable administration of one's body does not seem to exclude certain limited sacrifice of bodily integrity in the interests of another's welfare.

Blood transfusions, heterologous skin grafts, etc., are regarded by some theologians as extraneous to the concept of mutilation, since they do not diminish bodily integrity to any considerable degree and because the "borrowed" elements soon replace themselves. It would seem preferable, however, to classify these procedures as minor mutilations, since they do have some slight effect upon bodily integrity and imply some degree of administration of one's body. Beyond any doubt such procedures, however classified theologically, are licit in ordinary circumstances. Human experimentation (*see* EXPERIMENTATION, MEDICAL) entailing some sacrifice of bodily integrity, or perhaps some risk to life for the benefit of others, represents a form of mutilation. So do *organic transplants from living donors. Both these forms of mutilation depend for their justification, to the extent that they can be considered legitimate, on the principle of charity.

Bibliography: ActApS 22 (1930) 565; 44 (1952) 779–789; 45 (1953) 673–679, 747. E. F. HEALY, *Medical Ethics* (Chicago 1956). J. P. KENNY, *Principles of Medical Ethics* (2d ed. Westminster, Md. 1962). J. PAQUIN, *Morale et médecine* (Montréal 1960). G. KELLY, "Pope Pius XII and the Principle of Totality," ThSt 16 (1955) 373–396; "The Morality of Mutilation: Towards a Revision of the Treatise," ThSt 17 (1956) 322–344.

[J. J. LYNCH]

MUTIS, JOSÉ CELESTINO

Spanish priest, physician, and naturalist; b. Cádiz, 1732; d. Bogotá, Nov. 11, 1808. As the son of Julián Mutis and Gregoria Bosio, he was descended from the old Mut family of Mallorca. After finishing studies in grammar, philosophy, and theology in the Real Colegio de San Fernando, he attended the University of Seville, where he received degrees in philosophy and medicine. In 1757 he went to Madrid and, after his degree was recognized, taught anatomy. Under Barnades he studied natural sciences and mathematics, to which he devoted the rest of his life. In 1760 he was to be sent to London and other university centers at government expense, but he preferred to become the physician of Pedro Mesía de la Cerda, recently appointed viceroy of the kingdom of New Granada. Mutis, inspired by the Swedish botanist Von Linné (Linnaeus), wanted to begin his *Historia natural de las Américas.* Years later, Von Linné, enthusiastic about Mutis's discoveries in New Granada, paid him this tribute: "Gratulor tibi nomen inmortale, quod nulla aetas unquam delebit."

In Bogotá Mutis dedicated himself to the practice of medicine and on March 13, 1762, instituted the teaching of mathematics in the Colegio Mayor del Rosario, where he himself taught for 2 years. However, he never neglected his study and observation of nature, according to his *Diario de observaciones,* which he kept for almost 30 of the 48 years he spent in Colombia. Botany, entymology, and mineralogy were always his first interests. He wanted not only to make discoveries but also to apply his knowledge to the rudimentary colonial economy and to medicine. He was the first to explain Newton's theories in America and to defend the doctrines of Copernicus. While charged with informing the viceroys on matters of education and economy, he brought about noteworthy moves toward progress. He kept up a scientific correspondence with outstanding European scholars, who respected and admired him. Mutis was known especially for his study of quinine (Chinchona) and for the establishment of various species and their pharmacological classification. His labors are summarized in the *Historia de los árboles de la quina,* a posthumous work published in Madrid in 1828. Many valuable plants

José Celestino Mutis.

native to Colombia were discovered and classified by him. In 1772 he was offered an outstanding position in Spain, which he refused because he did not want to abandon his botanical studies and because he had a still-unrealized vocation to the priesthood. Mutis was finally ordained at the age of 42.

As early as 1763 he had suggested that the King of Spain organize a botanical expedition to New Granada, a land rich in untapped natural wealth. It was not until 1783, and with the firm backing of the archbishop and Viceroy *Caballero y Góngora, that the expedition was formed under Mutis's direction. The King named him botanist and astronomer, and the Academies of Stockholm and Paris elected him corresponding member. The accomplishments of the expedition were enormous. A thorough study of the natural wealth of Colombia was undertaken by the group, which included Eloy Valenzuela as vice-director; José Camblor, scrivener and geographer; Diego García, OFM, specimen collector; and Pablo Antonio García, an artist. By 1806 the expedition counted 11 professional and correspondent members, 10 master painters, and 5 officers. In 1802 Mutis underwrote the cost of erecting the first astronomical observatory of Spanish America; this observatory still exists in Bogotá. Its first director was the learned Caldas. The same year Mutis reactivated the College of Medicine, founded the chair of chemistry in the Colegio del Rosario, and encouraged the formation of the Patriotic Society of Friends of the Country. He was spiritual director of the monastery of Santa Inés. At his death he had spent 48 years in Colombia and had dedicated all his efforts to the scientific and political growth of the country. His manuscripts, prints and engravings, anatomies, botanical descriptions, zoological and mineralogical collections, and his herbarium of 20,000 plants were sent to Spain in 1816. In 1954, through a joint effort of the governments of Spain and Colombia, a deluxe edition was begun of the *Flora de la real expedición botánica del Nueva Reino de Granada,* a glory of American science.

Bibliography: G. HERNÁNDEZ DE ALBA, *La vida y la obra de José Celestino Mutis* (Madrid 1951); ed., *Archivo epistolar del sabio naturalista, José Celestino Mutis,* 2 v. (Bogotá 1947–49); ed., *Diario de observaciones de José Celestino Mutis, 1760–90,* 2 v. (Bogotá 1957–58).

[G. HERNÁNDEZ DE ALBA]

MUZI, GIOVANNI, bishop of Città di Castello and first papal representative to come to the Americas; b. Rome, 1772; d. Spoleto, 1849. With independence, it became necessary for the Spanish American republics to conduct their own ecclesiastical affairs with the Holy See. In 1822 a Chilean envoy, Archdean José Ignacio *Cienfuegos, arrived in Rome and requested that a nuncio be sent to Chile with ample powers to settle the many critical problems of the Church there. Since Chile was not yet recognized as an independent country, it was decided to send an apostolic vicar, or non-diplomatic representative of the Holy See. Muzi, auditor of Nuncio Pablo Leardi in Vienna since 1817 and a former theology professor of the Roman College, was chosen for the mission. He was named titular archbishop of Filipos and was given faculties for Chile and for all Spanish American countries. These faculties included the naming and consecrating of bishops without further recourse to Rome.

The Muzi Mission, as it became known, left Genoa on Oct. 5, 1823, with Gian Maria Mastai, later Pius IX,

as chaplain to the archbishop, and Giuseppe Sallusti, who wrote a history of the mission, as secretary. Muzi's reception and later expulsion from Buenos Aires, his 8-month stay in Santiago, and his visit to Montevideo belong to the church history of these countries. Before returning to Genoa, where he arrived June 25, 1825, Muzi wrote a *Carta apológetica* (Córdoba 1825) defending his mission against his many critics. In Rome the archbishop gave the first detailed report on the condition of the Church in the various countries he visited.

After the personal failure of his mission, he retired from the papal diplomatic service and accepted the bishopric of Città di Castello where he published an important work of local history, *Memorie ecclesiastichi e civili di Città di Castello* (7 v. 1842–44). He was consulted regularly on Spanish American Church problems by the Congregation of Extraordinary Ecclesiastical Affairs. A special report he had compiled on his mission to America was lost until recently, but it has been located in the Vatican Archives.

Bibliography: P. LETURIA, *Relaciones entre la Santa Sede e Hispanoamérica,* 3 v. (Rome 1959–60). P. LETURIA and M. BATLLORI, *La primera misión Pontificia a Hispanoamérica, 1823–1825* (StTest 229; 1964).

[W. J. COLEMAN]

MUZIO, GIROLAMO, humanist and polemicist; b. Padua, Italy, March 12, 1496; d. near Florence, 1576. His reputation as a humanist and a writer enabled him to serve various secular and ecclesiastical princes. He received a pension from Pius V. His secular works include verses and two studies on chivalry, *Duello* (1550) and *Gentiluomo* (1575). More important are his religious polemics. To refute the assertions of Pier Paolo *Vergerio, Bishop of Capodistria, who fled to Switzerland in 1549, Muzio published correspondence he had had with Vergerio and his associates. In 1551 he published *Mentite ochiniane,* against Bernardino *Ochino. Muzio entered into polemics with Heinrich *Bullinger and others. His *Lettere cattoliche* (1571) describes the evils besetting the Church.

Bibliography: P. PASCHINI, EncCatt 8:1580. Mercati-Pelzer DE 2:1090. F. BABINGER, LexThK² 7:715.

[E. A. CARRILLO]

MYCONIUS, FRIEDRICH, one of the leading Protestant reformers in central Germany; b. Lichtenfels am Main, Dec. 25, 1490; d. Gotha, April 7, 1546. While attending Latin school in Annaberg, Myconius (also called Mecum) encountered Johann *Tetzel, the indulgence preacher, and was offended by him. Myconius joined the Franciscan Order, but failed to find assurance of God's grace in the monastic way of life. In 1524 he fled to Electoral Saxony. He was active as an evangelical preacher in Zwickau and Buchholz and in August 1524 went to Gotha. He reformed the church order, participated in the official church and school visitations in Thuringia in 1527 and 1533, attended the Marburg Colloquy in 1529, contributed to the Nuremberg Concord of 1536, and helped in the negotiations at Schmalkalden in 1537, Frankfurt and Nuremberg in 1539, and Hagenau in 1540. In Melanchthon's place he made a trip to England in 1538 for union efforts with the English Church. He helped to introduce the Reformation in Annaberg and Leipzig in 1539 upon the death of Duke George.

Bibliography: F. MYCONIUS, *Geschichte der Reformation,* ed. O. CLEMEN (Leipzig 1914); *Der Briefwechsel des Friedrich*

Mykonius, 1524–1546, ed. H. U. Delius (Tübingen 1960). P. Scherffig, *Friedrich Mekum von Lichtenfels: Ein Lebensbild aus dem Reformationszeitalter* (Leipzig 1909). R. Jauernig, RGG³ 4:1229–30.

[L. W. Spitz]

MYCONIUS, OSWALD,

Swiss humanist and reformer; b. Lucerne, Switzerland, 1488; d. Basel, Oct. 14, 1552. Myconius (originally Geisshäusler) was educated at Rottweil, Bern, and at the University of Basel (1510–14). He came to Zürich as a teacher in 1516. In 1518 his influence was decisive in securing the election of his friend Huldrych *Zwingli as people's priest of Great Minster. He began intensive study of the Bible in 1520 and went to Lucerne in that same year to teach. His departure in 1522 was occasioned by his open espousal of the Reformation. After a brief sojourn in Einsiedeln, he returned to Zürich in 1523 to assist Zwingli in his reform of the city. In 1531 he moved to Basel, there to succeed *Oecolampadius as antistes of the city in August 1532. In addition to writing commentaries on several books of the Bible, he wrote a brief biography of Zwingli in 1532, prepared the Basel Confession of 1534, and contributed to the formulation of the First Helvetic Confession of 1536 (*see* CONFESSIONS OF FAITH, PROTESTANT).

Bibliography: K. R. Hagenbach, *Johann Oekolampad und Oswald Myconius* (Leben und ausgewählte Schriften der Väter und Begründer der reformirten Kirche 2; Elberfeld 1859) 309–462. O. E. Strasser, RGG³ 4:1230.

[C. Garside, Jr.]

MYSTERIES OF THE LIFE OF JESUS.

These mysteries may be approached in several ways: as objects of faith, commemoration, or praise, and in this sense mystery; or, under the aspect of event. Considered in this latter light, mysteries are episodes that happened in time and place during the earthly life of the historical Jesus from His Incarnation to His Ascension. Mysteries are contingent in fact, and in spite of their historical uniqueness (Heb. 9.26) and contingency (Jn 3.16; 1 Jn 4.10) they have a universal meaning for the salvation of mankind; for the Word who spoke on Creation Day (Jn 1.10) took on a historical form (Jn 1.14), underwent successive development, and had a human destiny; hence, the mystery of Christ does not lie in that He is God, but that He is God-Man.

When mysteries are contemplated as events, they cannot be falsely sublimated so that Christ's created activities ultimately become merely supernatural actuations of His humanity; nor can they be demythologized so that the divine action is reduced to merely natural causality. The events of the whole life of Jesus, each in its own way, find meaning and reach their climax in the mystery of the cross and Resurrection, by which man is saved (Rom 3.23–24; 1 Jn 2.2; Acts 4.10–12). It is in the contemplation of the mysteries as events in the life of Jesus that one finds Him man's exemplar for imitation in the mystery of His lowliness, obedience, holiness, and love (Jn 13.6).

Bibliography: Denz "Systematic Index," E5b. T. E. Clark, "Some Aspects of Current Christology," *Thought* 36 (1961) 325–343. D. M. Stanley, "The Conception of Our Gospels as Salvation-History," ThSt 20 (1959) 561–589. K. Rahner, *Theological Investigations*, tr. C. Ernst (Baltimore 1961) 1:149–200. J. Daniélou, *Christ and Us*, tr. W. Roberts (New York 1961) 128–153. L. Malevez, *The Christian Message and Myth*, tr. O. Wyon (Westminster, Md. 1960).

[M. D. Sablone]

MYSTERY (IN THE BIBLE)

Exegetes of the "History of Religions" school (e.g., W. Bousset and R. Reitzenstein) have suggested that the Pauline use of μυστήριον (Gr. for "mystery") to refer to salvation in Jesus Christ was a borrowing from the pagan mystery religions as part of an attempt to make Christianity understandable to the Greek world (*see* MYSTERY RELIGIONS, GRECO-ORIENTAL). Today, however, it is more widely recognized that "mystery" was an ancient Hebrew theological term that was current in Jewish circles at the time of Christ. This article explains the concept of mystery in the OT, in non-Biblical Jewish thought, and in the NT.

In the Old Testament. In the Septuagint (LXX) the word μυστήριον occurs some 21 times; it appears only in the postexilic books (Tobit; Judith; Daniel; Sirach; 2 Machabees), normally translating the Hebrew word *rāz* (borrowed through Aramaic from Old Persian), which is generally in the plural. There are other Greek synonyms for mystery in these late books, including κρύπτα and ἀπόκρυφα, "secrets, hidden things." In tracing the idea of mystery, one must begin long before the postexilic period with the Hebrew concept of *sôd*, a word which is never translated by μυστήριον. This Hebrew word seems to have originally meant "council, assembly"; but ultimately it came to designate what was decided in a council, namely, "counsel," particularly "secret counsel," and thus "mystery."

Preexilic Period. One of the early theological uses for *sôd* was in reference to the heavenly council. H. W. Robinson, F. Cross, and others have shown that there was a common Semitic belief in an assembly of heavenly beings that decided the fate of the world. In pagan thought it was an assembly of the gods; in Hebrew thought it was an assembly of angels presided over by Yahweh who had the dominant role in making the decision [Jb 1.6–12; Ps 81(82).1]. There is probably a reference to the heavenly assembly in Gn 1.26, "Let us make man in our image and likeness"; and in Is 40.1 Yahweh's imperative is addressed to the angelic court.

The power of the heavenly *sôd* to enact decrees concerning men gave it practical importance in Hebrew life. The decisions on high were made known to the people by the prophet who was introduced through visions into the sessions of the heavenly assembly. Isaia's call consists of his seeing the heavenly assembly where God is asking the angels, "Whom shall I send?" (Is 6.8). When Michea, son of Jemla, is asked by the King of Israel to prophesy, he answers by telling what he saw in the heavenly assembly (3 Kgs 22.19–22). Amos announces almost as a proverb that God will surely not do anything "until He has revealed his *sôd* to His servants the prophets" (Am 3.7). To know the heavenly *sôd* (council, counsel) became the criterion for distinguishing a true prophet from a false prophet. Jeremia says scornfully of the false prophets, "For which of them has stood in the *sôd* of Yahweh and seen and heard His word?" (Jer 23.18; see also Jb 15.8).

Postexilic Period. This concept of a prophet's being introduced into the heavenly council and its mysterious counsels was the basis for the importance attributed to heavenly secrets in postexilic Judaism. The Persian loanword *rāz* made its way into Aramaic and Hebrew, alongside *sôd*, to express the concept of mystery. The number of individuals who claimed to have seen the heavenly mysteries increased, as did the types of mysteries that were reported.

In Daniel ch. 2 *rāz* ($\mu\nu\sigma\tau\eta\rho\iota\sigma\nu$ in the LXX) is used eight times to refer to Nabuchodonosor's dream and its symbolic contents. No wise man can unravel such mysteries, but only God in heaven who reveals mysteries can make known what shall be. Here "mystery" is employed in what shall become a very frequent usage: a vision of the future given to man by God, in symbols. In apocalyptic literature it will often be an angel who interprets this mystery for the chosen seer, but sometimes God Himself speaks.

The Book of Sirach says that God's secrets, like the vicissitudes of life and the working of providence, are beyond human knowledge (Sir 11.4) and it warns man not to investigate such things (3.21–22). Occasionally, to the humble, God will reveal His secrets [4.18; 42.18–19; 3.19 (Hebrew)], as He did in the past to Isaia (48.24–25). It is in Sir 4.18 that one meets, for the first time, Wisdom as God's agent in revealing mysteries. Besides God's plan for men, mysteries in Sirach include astronomical and meteorological phenomena (43.32) and the secret actions of men, often evil (1.28–29). One way for men to come to a knowledge of mysteries is through a study of ancient traditions found in the Law, and in the teaching of the wise men and the prophets (39.7; 47.15–17).

In the Hellenistic outlook of the Book of Wisdom, the mysteries of God include His plans for the afterlife (Wis 2.22). The origins of Wisdom are classified as mysteries (6.22), and Wisdom herself is initiated into the knowledge of God (8.4). Some of the language of the mystery religions appears in this book (12.5; 14.15) but chiefly by way of attack on these religions. Solomon is pictured as the example of a man to whom God has given true knowledge of a variety of mysteries (7.17–21).

In non-Biblical Jewish Thought. There are important uses of mystery in extra-Biblical literature. In investigating these it will be useful to distinguish between apocryphal writings in general and the Dead Sea Scrolls in particular.

Apocrypha. The sobriety of the mystery passages in the canonical literature is appreciated when one studies the noncanonical literature. Dating from the 2d century B.C., Enoch presents a fascinating variety of mysteries: (1) evil mysteries (9.6–8; 10.7; 16.3), such as those taught to women by the evil angels—an echo of Gn 6.1–4; (2) cosmic mysteries and their relation to men (41.3; 60.11–22)—an angelic guide introduces Enoch to these astrological secrets; (3) mysteries of God's will and human actions (63.3; 83.7; 84.3)—a special mystery is the judgment God will render on man's deeds (103.2; 68.5); and (4) the mystery of the Son of Man, the Elect One, hidden in God's presence before creation (48.6; 62.7), who shall be revealed on the day of judgment (62.1) to pour forth the secrets of wisdom and counsel that God has entrusted to him (53.1; 62.2).

From A.D. 60 to 150 a series of apocalypses (2 Baruch; 3 Baruch; 4 Ezra) gives witness to the last Jewish developments in the use of "mystery" parallel to the usage of the NT. In 2 Baruch are described the visions accorded to Baruch amid the ruins of Jerusalem after the city had fallen to the Babylonians. The term "mysteries" is used for these visions and for their interpretation. The mysteries include cosmic phenomena (48.2–3;

see also 3 Baruch 1.8), as well as the happenings of the last time (2 Baruch 81.4; 85.8).

In 4 Ezra are found the visions of Ezra about the fall and rise of Jerusalem. Throughout his life, Ezra had received revelations of the mysteries of God pertaining to the future in store for Jerusalem and the world (6.32–33; 10.38); and in this he was privileged like Moses who also saw "the secrets of the times" (14.5). Some of these mysteries revealed to Ezra are to be kept secret (12.36–37; 14.6 for Moses).

The Dead Sea Scrolls. In the Qumran *Dead Sea Scrolls (henceforth DSS) also, one finds mysteries playing an important role. The Hebrew word most frequently used is *rāz*, sometimes occurring in parallelism with *sôd; nistārôt* (hidden things) also occurs.

The first type of mystery we may distinguish in the DSS concerns God's providence as it affects angels, men, and the future of Israel. In 1QM 14.14 God's "marvelous mysteries" concern the elevating and casting down of the angels. Evil persons are under the dominion of the Angel of Darkness "according to the mysteries of God until the final time set by Him" (1QS 3.20–23; 4.18). On a more personal level the author of 1QH (9.23–24) says to God, "You have chastised me in the mystery of your wisdom." The death of the just in the final war against evil will be according to the mysteries of God to test the eagerness of others (1QM 16.11; 17.8–9). To the Teacher of Righteousness have been revealed secrets concerning the future found in the words of OT prophets (1QpHb 7.1–5); it is perhaps this figure who speaks in 1QS 11.3–4, "He made my eye contemplate His wonders; and the light of my heart, the mystery to be."

A second set of mysteries in the DSS concerns the community's own interpretation of the Law. If we remember that the Qumran community thought of itself as an assembly or council, this use of "mystery" may be related to the origins of the term as the secret counsel of a council. The ideal of intimate union between the sectarians and the angels is a theme of the DSS, and the community's council on earth was considered to be a reflection of the angelic council in heaven (1QS 11.8). Thus, in 11.5–7 one initiated into the community comes to know God's marvelous mysteries, a wisdom hidden from wise men, a fountain of glory hidden from any worldly assembly. In CDC 3.12–14 we hear that to faithful Israelites God revealed the hidden things in which all Israel had gone astray, and then by a process of historical selection the Qumran community became God's final repository of those hidden commands whose observance is necessary for eternal life (3.18–20). Those who are fully accepted as members are to be made "wise in the marvelous and true mysteries amidst the men of the community" (1QS 9.18–19), but they must keep these hidden from the noninitiated (4.6; 1QH 5.25–26). The author of the hymns seems to have a special role: "You have set me up . . . as the interpreter of knowledge in your marvelous mysteries to test the seekers of truth and to try the lovers of discipline" (1QH 2.13–14).

Thirdly, the cosmic and meteorological mysteries are also mentioned in the DSS (1QH 1.11–12, 21; 12.11–13).

Fourthly, there are evil mysteries. *Belial has his own evil *sôd* (1QS 4.1), his own hostile mysteries (1QM 14.9); and according to these "mysteries of iniquity" men deform the works of God in their guilt (1QH 5.36).

However, all this is doomed to perish. On the trumpets that will give the signal in the great war against evil will be written: "The mysteries of God for the destruction of evil" (1QM 3.8–9). *See* BIBLE, III (CANON), 4, 5.

In the New Testament. Because of the special use St. Paul makes of mystery, it will be useful to study his epistles separately, after having investigated the use of the term in the rest of the NT.

Outside the Pauline Writings. The word μυστήριον occurs in one logion in the Gospels, a parallel passage in Mk 4.10–12; Mt 13.10–13; Lk 8.9–10, which is found between the parable of the sower and its explanation. The setting of this logion is not original, but it does concern parables: "To you is granted the mystery ["mysteries" in Matthew and Luke] of the kingdom of God; but to those who are outside everything is in parables." The fluctuation between the singular and the plural reminds us of the fluctuation in Hebrew between the use in singular of *sôd* and the use in the plural of *rāz*. This use of "the mystery of the kingdom of God" is to be associated with the use seen above where divine providence and its working for the salvation of men comes under the rubric of God's marvelous mysteries. It is to be noted that Enoch 41.1 speaks of "the mysteries of the heavens and how the kingdom is divided." That only the specially selected are given to know the mysteries is consonant with the whole history of the concept of mystery. (*See* PARABLES OF JESUS.)

In Ap 1.20 mention is made of the mystery of the seven stars seen in the right hand of *Alpha and Omega; and in 17.5–6 the prostitute astride the scarlet beast is a mystery, as is her name. As said above, in Daniel and in the Jewish apocalypses "mystery" was often used to characterize symbolic visions and their interpretation. In particular, mystery as applied to the symbol of the stars may be an echo of the cosmic mysteries. In Enoch 43.1–4 the mysteries of heaven include the stars, which have names given them by God. The names of the stars are the names of the saints on earth, just as the stars of the Apocalypse stand for the *angels of the churches. A parallel to Ap 17.5–6 may be found in Enoch 60.10 where the explanation of *Leviathan and *Behemoth is called a mystery; and in 3 Baruch 3 one of the "mysteries of God" is the *dragon of evil.

It is said in Ap 10.7 that with the trumpet of the seventh angel God's mystery will be completed, as He announced to His servants the Prophets. The last clause echoes the use of *sôd* in Am 3.7 (see also 1QpHb 7.1–5). As previously mentioned, the secret will of God concerning the end of time was one of the standard mysteries.

Pauline Writings. The earliest occurrence is in 2 Thes 2.7 where, in reference to the signs of the last times and the appearance of the man of lawlessness, it is said, "The mystery of lawlessness is already at work." This is a reference to the economy of evil. While mention is made of evil mysteries in Sirach and Enoch, the best parallel is in the DSS where the evil spirit is permitted to function until the end time according to the mysteries of God. The very expression "mystery of iniquity [i.e., lawlessness]" occurs in the DSS.

Next, there are five (or six) occurrences of "mystery" in 1 Corinthians, and here the Pauline doctrine of salvific mystery is beginning to take shape. In 1 Cor 2.7 Paul speaks of "a hidden wisdom of God in a mystery, a wisdom which God predetermined before the ages for our glory, which no one of the rulers of this world had known." The emphasis is on the wisdom of God hidden in a mystery, and this wisdom is God's plan for man's salvation in Jesus. As Pauline thought and theological vocabulary progresses, the emphasis will pass over to the mystery, and wisdom will become an attribute of mystery. Connections between wisdom and mystery have been seen in the OT. In 1 Cor 2.10 Paul says that this wisdom hidden in a mystery has been revealed to us through the Spirit. In both Sir 48.24–25 and Dn 4.6 God's mystery is revealed through the workings of His spirit.

Paul refers to himself as one of the "stewards of the mysteries of God" in 1 Cor 4.1. The context does not clarify this use of mystery. "Mysteries of God" is a frequent expression in the DSS; and in 1Q 36.16 mention is made of "men in custody of Your mysteries."

In contrasting various gifts with the gift of charity, Paul mentions in 1 Cor 13.2 the gift of being "acquainted with all the mysteries and all knowledge." (*See* CHARISM.) When Enoch receives a revelation, it is frequently said, "He showed me all the mysteries of . . ." (Enoch 41.1; 52.2; etc.). Thus Paul is speaking of a gift of revelation given to special figures like apocalyptic seers.

In 1 Cor 14.2 Paul says that he who speaks in a tongue is not understood, but through the Spirit he utters mysteries. It is difficult to decide whether "mysteries" here means unintelligible language or hidden truths. In 1 Cor 15.51 Paul announces the resurrection of the dead at the last trumpet as a mystery. It has been shown that mystery was connected with judgment in Enoch and connected with the afterlife in Wisdom.

There is, finally, a dubious occurrence of mystery in 1 Cor 2.1 where Paul describes how he came preaching the μυστήριον or μαρτύριον (witness) of God. The textual evidence is divided between the two readings, and it is not possible to decide with certainty which is correct.

The word mystery occurs twice in Romans. In Rom 11.25 Paul reveals the mystery that Israel has been blinded until all the nations come to believe in Jesus, but ultimately all Israel will be saved. Once again mystery is applied to the divine economy of salvation. We recall that in 4 Ezra the vision of the ultimate redemption of Jerusalem was described as a mystery. In Rom 16.25 Paul speaks of his preaching of Jesus Christ in terms of a mystery kept secret for long ages but now brought into the open and by means of the prophetic writings made known to the Gentiles. Whether this final salutation of Romans is authentic has been questioned. If it is genuinely Pauline, this is the first of Paul's equation of the mystery with Jesus Christ, an equation that is a specification of the larger mystery of God's plan of salvation. Paul mentions the prophetic foreknowledge of the mystery, a feature that has been seen as part of the most ancient Hebrew concept of mystery.

It is in the Captivity Epistles, Colossians and Ephesians, that the Pauline mystery finds its fullest expression. The equation of the mystery with Christ, seen in Romans, becomes standard: in Col 1.26–27 the mystery is identified as "Christ among you, the hope of glory"; in Col 2.2–3 Paul speaks of "the mystery of God, Christ, in whom are hidden all the treasures of wisdom and knowledge"; and in Col 4.3 and Eph 3.4 he speaks of "the mystery of Christ." Once again it is said that this mystery, which in previous generations was not made known to men, has been revealed to the Apostles and Prophets in the Spirit. Perhaps the closest parallel for this is in Enoch 48.6; 51.3; 62.7, where it is said that the Elect One, the Son of Man, was chosen and hidden in God's presence before creation to be revealed to the elect in the end time. There are good Qumran parallels for the expressions in these Epistles connecting knowledge and wisdom with mystery. One notices that Paul, who began with "wisdom hidden in a mystery" (1 Cor 2.7), has come around to a mystery in which wisdom is hidden.

The special characteristic of the mystery in Ephesians is the collective aspect of the salvific plan in Christ, as in Eph 1.9–10: "the mystery of His will . . . to gather all things in Christ, both heavenly and earthly in him." This includes the subjection of the hostile angelic powers to Christ. The three references to "mystery" in Eph 3.2–11 constitute the longest single Pauline treatment of the topic, and pull together most of the themes that have already been pointed out.

A special use of "mystery" is found in Eph 5.32, where Paul cites Gn 2.24 and says, "This is a profound mystery, and I interpret it as referring to Christ and his Church." "Mystery" is used here, as by 2d-century Christian writers, especially Justin, to refer to a deeper meaning of a Scripture passage. In Sir 39.2–7 and 1QpHb 7.1–5 the theory that the hidden things of God can be found in the ancient Scriptures is propounded.

In Eph 6.19 mention is made of "the mystery of the gospel," which is but a variant of the mystery of Christ, since the gospel announces salvation for all in Christ.

In the Pastoral Epistles "mystery" is found in 1 Tm 3.9 and 16: "the mystery of faith" and "the mystery of religion." What is meant is the doctrinal content of faith or religion which involves, as 3.16 indicates, a belief in Christ from His Incarnation to His glorification. Thus, the mystery in 1 Timothy is once more God's plan of salvation for men effected in Jesus Christ.

In summation, the NT and Pauline use of mystery is varied with many of the same modalities found in the pre-Christian Semitic use of mystery. The predominant use concerns God's salvific plan for men in Jesus [see REVELATION, CONCEPT OF (IN THE BIBLE)], even as the origin of mystery in the OT seems to have been the divine plan for men as formulated in the heavenly council. Once granted the uniqueness of Paul's concept of Jesus, there is nothing in the Pauline mystery passages by way of vocabulary and thought pattern that cannot be explained from the Jewish background without recourse to the pagan mystery religions.

Bibliography: H. A. A. KENNEDY, *St. Paul and the Mystery Religions* (London 1913). D. DEDEN, "Le 'Mystère' paulinien," EphemThLov 13 (1936) 403–442. H. RAHNER, "Christian Mysteries and Pagan Mysteries," *Greek Myths and Christian Mystery,* tr. B. BATTERSHAW (New York 1963) 3–45. K. PRÜMM, DBSuppl 6:10–225. R. E. BROWN, "The Pre-Christian Semitic Concept of 'Mystery'," CathBiblQuart 20 (1958) 417–443; "The Semitic Background of the N.T. *Mysterion,*" *Biblica* 39 (1958) 426–448; 40 (1959) 70–87.

[R. E. BROWN]

MYSTERY (IN THEOLOGY)

A hidden reality or secret. More specifically, in the theology of revelation, a truth that man cannot discover except from revelation and that, even after revelation, exceeds human comprehension. In addition to this primary meaning, which will be discussed in the present article, the term has other connected meanings that should be kept in mind: (1) in soteriology, the great redemptive acts of God in history, especially in Jesus Christ (*see* MYSTERIES OF THE LIFE OF JESUS); (2) in the theology of worship, the sacramental reenactment of the redemptive deeds of Christ (*see* SACRAMENTS, THEOLOGY OF; MYSTERY THEOLOGY).

History of the Notion. While the complete history of the term has yet to be written, the following high points may be noted.

Greek Fathers. The term μυστήριον is used by the Greek Fathers in many senses. They include the following:

1. The salvific counsels of God, hidden from all eternity in the divine mind, but partly manifested through His Prophets and especially through Christ.
2. The great salutary interventions of God in history, whereby He executes His salvific designs, including especially the decisive events of the Incarnation, Passion, and Resurrection of Christ.
3. The hidden senses of Scripture, especially the typological sense of the OT, which looks forward to Christ and the Church.
4. The Sacraments, as ritual continuations of God's salvific actions in Christ. This sacramental use of the term μυστήριον did not become established until the 4th century, when the mystery religions were no longer serious competitors of Christianity.
5. The pagan cults and rites, e.g., those of Eleusis, Attis, Osiris, Cybele, and Mithra (*see* MYSTERY RELIGIONS, GRECO-ORIENTAL).
6. In some of the Alexandrian writers (notably Clement), certain esoteric doctrines that, for fear of profanation, should be restricted to an elite among the faithful.
7. In Gregory of Nyssa, objects of mystical knowledge, such as were revealed to Moses and Paul in their ecstasies.
8. Especially in the 4th-century Fathers (Gregory of Nazianzus, Gregory of Nyssa, Chrysostom, etc.), a revealed truth that even to faithful and educated Christians remains obscure by reason of its sublimity.

This last use of the term is particularly important in view of the later development of the notion. The theme of God's incomprehensibility, already set forth by Philo Judaeus in the 1st century, was strongly emphasized by the orthodox Fathers of the 4th century in opposition to the Eunomians, who maintained that God had so revealed Himself that the Christian believer could fully understand His essence. The anti-Eunomian Fathers developed a markedly negative (or "apophatic") theology, insisting on the total otherness and immeasurable majesty of God. As Rudolf Otto noted in his work, *The Idea of the Holy* [tr. J. W. Harvey (2d ed. New York 1958)], Chrysostom provides some of the finest expressions of the sense of the "numinous" in ancient Christian literature. With apt illustrations from the Bible, Chrysostom shows how the mysterious presence of the revealing God gives rise to sentiments of consternation, mental disarray, and trembling due to a combination of fear and delight.

In the 6th century, Pseudo-Dionysius the Areopagite made effective use of the vocabulary of the mystery religions to inculcate a sense of holy awe. His mystical works, translated into Latin by John Scotus Erigena (c. 850), were to influence the great scholastics, including Thomas Aquinas.

Latin Fathers and Doctors. In the West the Greek term μυστήριον, especially where it referred to Christian sacred rites, was generally translated by *sacramentum*. But *mysterium* also was used, both to designate the pagan mystery cults and to signify hidden truths, including the hidden meanings of Scripture. St. Augustine uses *sacramentum* and *mysterium* almost interchangeably, but with slightly different connotations. *Sacramentum* refers primarily to the outwardly visible rite or symbol; *mysterium,* to the hidden meaning behind it.

The medieval tradition was, on the whole, quite faithful to Augustine in its handling of the terms. Often *mysterium* was used to denote the spiritual or allegorical significance of Scripture.

St. Thomas Aquinas, relying on the etymology of the word, takes note of hiddenness or secrecy as fundamental to mystery (*In Isaiam,* prol.). In his theology, the *divina mysteria* are truths hidden in God, knowable to man only under the veils of *faith. Very frequently in Thomas's writings *mysterium* occurs as the object of the verb *credere*. Following the Biblical practice, he normally applies the term mystery not to the inner being of God, but to His redemptive counsels, whether already executed or still to be accomplished in eschatological times. Only on rare occasions does he call the Trinity a mystery, and then principally in connection with the Incarnation, which he terms "the most excellent of all mysteries" (ST 1a, 57.5 obj. 1). For example, in ST 1a2ae, 1.8 he distinguishes between the "secret of the Godhead" (*occultum divinitatis,* i.e., the Trinity) and the "mystery of Christ's humanity." Except in passages referring to the Eucharist, Thomas practically never calls the Sacraments mysteries. The consecrated wine, he says, is rightly called "mystery of faith" (*mysterium fidei*) because the blood of Christ is not apparent to the senses (ST 3a, 78.3 ad 5).

19th Century. During the controversies with various rationalistic movements, mystery gradually emerged as a technical term in the Catholic theology of revelation. The semirationalists maintained that human reason, at least when sufficiently schooled under the tutelage of revelation, was in principle capable of comprehending and demonstrating all the dogmas of faith. From this it would follow that faith, in the sense of an assent to testimony, would not be required on the part of those who had reached full intellectual maturity. The doctrines of the leading semirationalists were severally condemned (Denz 2738–40, 2828–31, 2850–61). The Syllabus of Errors, reaffirming this stand, rejected the fundamental tenets of semirationalism (Denz 2909–14).

Vatican Council I, climaxing this development, solemnly defined that there are "true mysteries properly so called," i.e., dogmas of faith that cannot be "understood and demonstrated by a properly cultivated mind from natural principles" (Denz 3041). In the chapter corresponding to this definition, the Council explained that by strict mysteries it meant truths "hidden in God that cannot be known unless divinely revealed" (Denz 3015) and that "by their nature so transcend a created mind that even when communicated by revelation and accepted in faith, they remain covered by the veil of faith itself and as it were shrouded in obscurity, so long as in this mortal life 'we are exiled from the Lord, for

we walk by faith and not by sight' " (Denz 3016; cf. 2 Cor 5.6–7).

The Council, in the passage just quoted, seems to imply that there will be no more mysteries in heaven, when the light of glory replaces the dimmer light of faith. This classical position of Catholic theology—which is also that of St. Thomas (*In 1 epist. ad Cor.* 2 lect. 1)—is supported by various Biblical texts in addition to the one cited by the Council (e.g., 1 Cor 13.9–12; 1 Jn 3.2). Nevertheless, it is well to note, as K. Rahner has several times insisted, that no created intellect can be elevated to the point where it will have absolutely comprehensive knowledge of God (cf. Denz 3001). Not even in heaven will God be appropriated as an object by the dynamism of the human *ratio*.

While stressing the negative note of incomprehensibility, Vatican I took pains to point out that "reason, enlightened by faith, when it diligently, reverently, and modestly inquires, by the gift of God, attains some understanding of mysteries, and that a most profitable one" (Denz 3016). Such understanding is achieved by comparison of mysteries with things naturally known, with one another, and with the final destiny of man. In this way one may perceive the harmony between the natural and supernatural orders, the mutual coherence among the truths of faith, and the meaningfulness of the mysteries for man in his earthly pilgrimage. Although the concepts by which one knows mysteries are only remotely similar to the realities for which they stand, they afford a knowledge that is fully valid so far as it goes. Indeed, the contemplation of mysteries in this life can provide a kind of faint anticipation of the eternal vision enjoyed by the blessed.

Further Speculation. In the struggle against rationalistic tendencies in the 19th century the notion of mystery was gradually modified. Whereas the Fathers and medieval Doctors, thinking of mystery as something hidden within a sacramental presence, were inclined to regard the Incarnation as the supreme mystery, the 19th-century theologians, concentrating on the features of transcendence and obscurity, more frequently held with M. Scheeben that the Blessed Trinity is the "mystery of mysteries." In line with this tendency, Leo XIII referred to the dogma of the Trinity as "the greatest of all mysteries, since it is the fountain and origin of all" [*Divinum illud munus;* ActSSed 29 (1897) 645].

In current Catholic teaching, three classes of divine mystery are commonly recognized. These are discussed below in the order of ascending sublimity.

Natural Mysteries. Naturally knowable truths that remain obscure because we lack proper and positive concepts of the realities involved are natural mysteries. While such mysteries may be found in the created order (e.g., animal instinct, human free will), they are preeminently verified in God, by reason of the extreme deficiency of the created analogies by which we know Him. For example, the divine freedom is far more a mystery than human freedom, for our experience affords no clue as to how freedom can be present in an immutable subject.

Supernatural Mysteries in the Wide Sense. Truths concerning the created order that are not knowable without revelation but that, once revealed, are free from any special obscurity are supernatural mysteries in the wide sense; e.g., the primacy of the Roman pontiff in the Church. Such a fact, being dependent on God's free disposition, could not be known without revelation, but after being revealed it has an intelligibility comparable to that of other juridical notions.

Supernatural Mysteries in the Strict Sense. Those truths that cannot be known without revelation and that, even after revelation, remain obscure to us by reason of the sublimity of their object are supernatural mysteries in the strict sense. Three principal mysteries are normally recognized as belonging to this class: (1) the Trinity (Denz 3225), which is the mystery of the communication of divine life within the Godhead; (2) the Incarnation (Denz 2851), which is the supreme supernatural communication of the divine life to a created nature; and (3) the elevation of finite persons to share, through grace or glory, in the divine life (Denz 2854). All other supernatural mysteries (e.g., original sin, the Eucharist, the Church as a supernatural communion, predestination) are commonly held to be reducible to the three central mysteries just named.

Supernatural mysteries in the strict sense, since they concern realities of the divine order, are beyond the comprehension of any created intellect. Their special obscurity comes from the fact that they have to do with God, not merely under those aspects in which He is directly mirrored by creatures (as, for instance, His goodness is reflected in the goodness of creatures), but precisely under those aspects wherein, thanks to His immeasurable transcendence, created analogies break down (*see* ANALOGY, THEOLOGICAL USE OF). Because the generation of living creatures only remotely resembles generation within the Godhead, we cannot reason from the former to the latter. Even after revelation, we cannot see the inner grounds that account for the fact. Revelation tells us that there is a plurality of Persons in God, that one of them has become man, and that men are called to be sharers of God's inner life. But it does not explain how such things can be.

During the early part of the 20th century a controversy arose as to whether man could know without revelation that there are any strict mysteries in God. Many competent theologians (e.g., C. Pesch, I. Ottiger, H. Dieckmann) replied in the negative, but others (e.g., R. Garrigou-Lagrange, M. D. Roland-Gosselin) held that man can definitely establish that there must be in God perfections that lack any counterpart in the created order, so that man could not learn them without revelation or, even after revelation, understand their internal possibility.

Apologetical Considerations. Apologetics must show that the Christian notion of strict mystery is meaningful and credible. This task is necessary, for modern rationalism and scientism have sometimes claimed that in view of the unlimited possibilities of rational and scientific progress, all truths of revelation can eventually be reduced to strictly demonstrative knowledge.

To this object one may reply, with K. Rahner, that the human mind is so structured that it necessarily grasps particular limited objects against the horizon of the unconditioned and indefinable, the Absolute. Since this Absolute is the ground of all intelligibility, the human mind, even before it is the faculty of comprehension, is the faculty of mystery. The revealed mysteries of Christianity enrich man's knowledge of the Absolute by certifying that God can communicate His divine life and draw near in grace without compromising His utter transcendence. But because all these truths have reference to the inner being of the Absolute, which outstrips objective concepts, the Christian mysteries can never be rationally or scientifically demonstrated.

Religious phenomenology, by showing that the notion of mystery is a constant feature of human religion, has underscored the value of mystery. All vital religions, as R. Otto recognized, live off a numinous experience of the divine presence, which arouses sentiments of awe and fascination. Men have always suspected that if God communicates with man, He must do so in a mysterious way, imparting deep and inscrutable secrets. Scheeben was therefore able to argue that the mysteries of the Christian faith, far from making it incredible, support its claim to be God's supreme self-revelation. If Christianity were devoid of mystery, he added, it could not stir and hold men as it does.

Approaching the question from another point of view, modern personalistic philosophers (such as M. Scheler, G. Marcel, and J. Lacroix) have shown that an element of mystery is inseparable from genuinely personal knowledge. Spirit as such is never deductively proved or experimentally verified; it is normally discerned through the signs by which it freely manifests itself. When a man reveals himself to a friend, he opens up something of the mystery of his own being. If God wishes to reveal Himself and draw man into friendship, He must share with man His own inner mystery. The human relationship of personal intercommunion therefore provides a fruitful analogy by which to approach the revealed mystery of man's *supernatural communion with God. In this perspective mystery appears less as a particular datum of revelation than as a dimension in which the entire relationship of revelation and faith unfolds.

See also REVELATION, THEOLOGY OF; SYMBOL IN REVELATION; ACCOMMODATION; APOLOGETICS; DOGMATIC THEOLOGY; FAITH AND REASON; FIDEISM; HERMESIANISM; METHODOLOGY (THEOLOGY); SEMIRATIONALISM; THEOLOGY; TRADITIONALISM.

Bibliography: General. A. MICHEL, DTC 10.2:2585–99; Eng. tr., C. J. MOELL, *Mystery and Prophecy* (pa. West Baden Springs, Ind. 1954). C. COLOMBO, EncCatt 8:1131–35. K. RAHNER, Lex ThK² 4:593–597; Fries HbThGrdbgr 1:447–452; "Über den Begriff des Geheimnisses in der katholischen Theologie," *Schriften zur Theologie,* v.4 (Einsiedeln 1962) 51–99. R. GARRIGOU-LAGRANGE, *De revelatione per ecclesiam catholicam proposita,* v.1 (4th ed. rev. Rome 1945). M. NICOLAU, SacTheolSumma BAC 1.2. M. J. SCHEEBEN, *The Mysteries of Christianity,* tr. C. VOLLERT (St. Louis 1946). *Le Mystère: Semaine des intellectuels catholiques,* Paris, Nov. 18–25, 1959 (Paris 1960).

History of the notion. B. NEUNHEUSER, LexThK² 7:729–731, with literature. F. CAVALLERA and J. DANIÉLOU, Introduction to J. CHRYSOSTOME, *Sur l'incompréhensibilité de Dieu* (SourcesChr 28; Paris 1951). P. VISENTIN, "*Mysterium-sacramentum* dai padri alla scolastica," *Studia Patavina* 4 (1957) 394–414, with literature. A. M. HOFFMANN, "Der Begriff des Mysteriums bei Thomas von Aquin," DivThomF 17 (1939) 30–60. J. M. A. VACANT, *Études théologiques sur les constitutions du concile du Vatican,* 2 v. (Paris 1895).

[A. DULLES]

MYSTERY RELIGIONS, GRECO-ORIENTAL

The word "mysteries," as used in this article, signifies the secret cults of Greco-Roman antiquity permeated by Orientalism. They form two groups. (1) Autochthonous Greek cults; in Roman times only those of Eleusis and of Dionysus—with Orphism as a branch of the latter—were still important. (2) Oriental cults;

only the Phrygian and Egyptian cults developed into the complete form of a mystery religion, whereas the Syrian Adonis cult did not reach this stage. The mysteries of Mithras have their own ideology and their own history. Therefore, they are treated separately near the end of the article.

A first question is whether the mysteries, in respect to origin, can be thought of as a whole. The answer must be affirmative, except for Orphism and Mithraism, both of which were artificial creations. The three Oriental cults, along with the Eleusinian mysteries of Demeter, belong to the same eastern Mediterranean group and have a prehistoric origin. Their unifying principle is their fertility aspect, typical of the cults of agricultural populations. Occupying a central place is a female figure, fertility personified; closely connected with her is another figure, fecundity, i.e., actual fertility or its products. This second figure, her partner, undergoes in his own person the dramatic change of the seasons in nature from yearly birth to yearly death. In Eleusis this partner is a young woman; in the Oriental types of this religion, a young man. The table shows in broad outlines the origin of the most important forms of the mystery cults out of a probable prehistoric root and their distribution. The first two lines are self-explanatory. The third line contains the names under which the fertility deities appear in the 1st millennium in those countries that became the point of departure for the later Hellenistic mysteries.

Chief Focal Areas. Four great focal points of fertility religion may be distinguished: ancient Crete, North Anatolia (Phrygia), Syria, and Egypt. This fourfold grouping contains many secondary focal points that are omitted in this article for the sake of brevity. The form of the fertility rite found in Syria goes back to the Sumero-Babylonian cult of Ishtar and the myth of Dumuzi-Tammuz, the existence of which is already attested for the 3d millennium B.C.

Ancient Crete. The copious data furnished by archeological excavation on Creto-Mycenean civilization show that, while the phenomenon of life stood in the forefront of thought and feeling, there are only very few traces of those excesses (e.g., the reaper vase of Knossos) such as are often connected with living fertility religions. According to present knowledge it seems that all religion here is dominated by an apparently single female deity ruling simultaneously three realms: the kingdom of animals and plants (better perhaps, of all growth), the abode of the dead, and the domain of war. The last function may be a part or a concomitant function of her role as goddess of the royal palaces and of the kings themselves. Images on seals depict religious dances of priestesses. They express a belief in the epiphany of the goddess and her male partner. At her entrance all vegetative life starts moving ecstatically. The sarcophagus of Hagia Triada shows a death cult combined with the veneration of a fertility and earth goddess. The name of Dionysus has been deciphered on one of the tablets in Linear Script B as part of a theophoric cognomen. It is, however, uncertain whether this member of the old Cretan pantheon already possessed the essential traits of the classical Dionysus and also, whether he may be considered the partner of the great goddess of nature. Neither of the two hypotheses can be wholly rejected. In any case, the Eleusinian Demeter, goddess of the fertility of the earth, is one of the most important descendants of the ancient Cretan nature goddess. The dramatic element characterizing the Eleusinian cult has its prototype in the partly ecstatic cult of ancient Crete. This assumption, which is more or less the opinion of M. P. Nilsson [*The Minoan-Mycenaean Religion and its Survival* (2d ed. Lund 1950)], revives an old thesis of P. Foucart. Further research of the Minoan tablets may be expected to clarify ancient Cretan correlations, for both Eleusis and Dionysus, though for the latter

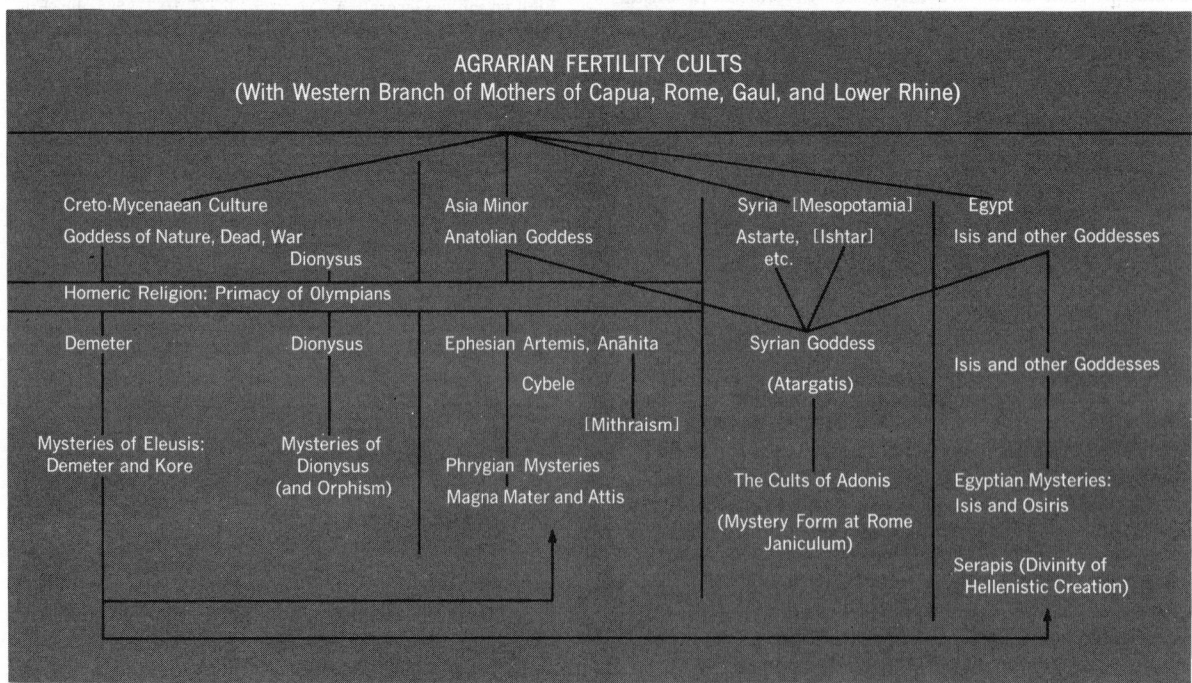

Agrarian fertility cults (with Western branch, Mothers of Capua, Rome, Gaul, and Lower Rhine).

the correlation Asia Minor—Thrace seems to be the more important.

North Anatolia. In the culture cycle of North Anatolia, rock carvings in the vicinity of the old Hittite capital (near Ankara) depict two deities that, on account of the flowers they offer each other, were formerly dubbed god and goddess of spring and considered as prototypes of the later couple Cybele-Attis. These Hittite deities are now recognized as complex in nature, representing the sun goddess of Arinna and the Hittite representative of the Hurrian weather god Teshub. Nevertheless, there remains the motif of a "sacred marriage," which often points to a fertility cult, and in the numerous train of one of the two deities a direct ancestor of the later Cybele has been recognized. The orgiastic element, characteristic for the pair Attis and Cybele at an early date, may have been present at this early stage of the Anatolian cult; but the Phrygian invaders of Asia Minor from Thrace certainly strengthened it. The Artemis of Ephesus is but an offshoot of this Anatolian mother. She was worshiped only incidentally and in secret rites. Their details are not known.

The goddess Anahita, in reality an East Anatolian deity whom the Persians worshiped, has been inserted in the third row of names, since her cult in Asia Minor spread westward at an early date and she appears in company with Mithras. The similarity between Cybele and Anahita—the two were often interchanged—led at times even to a local fusion of the concomitant figures of both Attis and Mithras, although they had nothing in common with each other [cf. W. Wüst, "Mithras" in Pauly-Wiss RE 15.2 (1932) 2135–].

Syria. The Syrian fertility goddess bears different names in different places of worship. Especially important is the goddess called in Greek the consort of Adonis of Byblos (likewise Aphrodite), and the *Dea Syria* of Hierapolis, also called Bambyce, Atargatis (i.e., the Atar of Attis). Conformities in ceremonial, particularly the emasculation of male followers, prove that the principal figure of this cult kept much of the nature of the old Anatolian goddess. Likewise, the old Mesopotamian Ishtar lives on in the Syrian Astarte, as is evident also from the close correspondence between Adonis of Byblos and the old Mesopotamian Dumuzi-Tammuz. Since, in the final development of the Egyptian myth, Isis finds the body of Osiris in Byblos, the clear mythological connection between the Syrian and Egyptian pair of vegetation deities is thereby indisputably confirmed.

Egypt. In Egypt the fertility aspect is found not only in Isis but, considering the connection between gods and animals, also in Hathor. The latter was represented as a horned cow or else—a case of incompleted iconographic anthropomorphism—with a cow's head. But in Egypt itself, and especially in the Egyptian component of Hellenism, Isis and her partner Osiris were destined to have a far greater influence.

Mythicoritual Development of the Basic Vegetation Duality. A mother goddess does not occupy the supreme role in cult, as she did in Crete, among any of the Near Eastern peoples where such a female divinity is found. Everywhere male deities have the leading place. Thus, in Mesopotamia several great gods, e.g., Anu, Enlil, Ea, Marduk, Ashur, tower above the goddess Ishtar, notwithstanding her position as mistress

of life, who appears now as virgin, now as wife and mother, while her lover Dumuzi-Tammuz shares the tragic fate of all nature heroes. In Syria at Bambyce, beside the goddess one finds the god designated as Attis—and as the superior figure. The whole ritual as represented on coins shows that he is not conceived as having a secondary position, as the Phrygian Attis and the later Adonis of Byblos had. Lucian's description in his *De Dea Syria* makes this clear.

The same is true of the female successor of the North Anatolian mother goddess, named usually after the many individual mountains in the forests of which she was thought to roam, but less frequently after towns. The invasion of the Phrygians, a people related to the Greeks, brought her into contact with a religious sphere that assigned the chief role to a male deity. And the mountain mother surely had to take a subordinate position herself wherever the Greek colonists of Asia Minor seized power. Thus, in Homer the Idaean Mother—the "Mother of Mt. Ida" of the Trojans—is represented as being closely connected with Zeus, but as subject to him. Copious archeological evidence from the mountain dominating Ephesus, of later date but clearly pre-Christian, has confirmed the different relative positions of mistress of nature and high god. A whole row of reliefs depict the triad Zeus, with beard; the Great Mother, with tympanon and other emblems and flanked by lions; and the youth Attis. One of the inscriptions of Ephesus expressly mentions Zeus as the autochthonous, or ancestral god. Hence, it may be concluded that the Greeks did not favor the elevation of Attis to the status of a true god, as is to be noted here and there in Phrygia as a result of his assimilation to Men, the moon god; nor did they favor the loose relationship of Attis and Cybele, which will be discussed below.

In the chief centers of population the cult of the Great Mother had extensive temple possessions and was under the control of a hierarchic priesthood that often politically administered the temple territory. It is sufficient to mention the temple-states of Ma (i.e., mother), Commagene, Bambyce, Hierapolis Castabala, and also the theocratic state of Ephesia. But the fact that a supreme deity of the stature of Zeus was being recognized at the same time proves that these fertility cults were not to be regarded as the total expression of religion but rather as elements in the whole religious complex of the area. That is very important for the understanding of their precise nature after their expansion westward, especially in the Roman Empire. The individual Oriental cults could not, and probably did not, wish, of their own accord at least, to compete with Christianity. They were part of the total potential of paganism that under imperial leadership wished to prevent Christianity from conquering souls.

Common Elements in the Mystery Cults. Their original structural likeness was not lost in later development, although naturally the cults emanating from a single point of departure came to differ considerably in details. The similar course of historical evolution makes it possible to sketch the nature of this group of Oriental cults together, at least with regard to their main features.

It is appropriate to start with the myth, since it contains so many common elements. In every case there is a basic pair of deities dissimilar in rank. Of these two, the female figure embodies fertility itself, whereas her male companion (who is intended to portray fecundity, the result of fertility, i.e., the abundant growth of plants and animals) is represented sometimes as her son, sometimes as her lover, and hence exhibits a peculiar hybrid character. This basic personification opened the road for further mythology, and it was a road that could not help leading into many byways.

O. Kern has given the following explanation. In the subtropical regions that are regarded as the home of the mysteries, namely, Asia Minor, Egypt, and the Aegean area, the change from the winter stagnation of nature into sprouting vegetation and the still greater change seen in the decline of growth in summer as a result of heat and drought usually occur abruptly and are full of contrasts. These contrasts, with their very disquieting effects on the feelings, found expression in emotional outbursts, and the more so as men pictured to themselves the proximate cause of the death, assumed as real, that the mythological being representing biological life was destined to undergo. Typical for Phrygia is the legend of the death of Attis, circulating with many variations; he emasculates himself out of remorse for his unfaithfulness toward his mistress, the Great Mother. In Syria, Adonis dies during the hunt, killed by a wild boar. In Egypt, Osiris succumbs to the snares of Seth, who symbolizes the hot desert wind that is so dangerous to most plants.

When once this stage was reached in the construction of the myth, a psychologically simpler motivation followed. A double set of feasts, often gathered in a cycle, mourning the disappearance of vegetation and again hailing its reappearance, was established. Instead of a merely mild, sympathetic feeling for the impersonal decay of nature, one could now abandon himself to personal grief at the tragic death of a being regarded as a youthful and handsome person. This personal relation gave a new emphasis to the joyous feast that belonged to the whole series of religious celebrations. These expressions of religious emotion were publicized by mass actions and not by individuals. In this way primitive celebrations honoring demigods of vegetation became great public festivals in their area of origin.

However, intense excitement could easily lead in two directions to sexual excesses. Cruelty and lust are passions that are psychologically closely related. It seems that in prehistoric times it was considered a service to the community to give to the Mistress of Nature the sacrifice of sexual power through emasculation. This may be compared to sacred prostitution, which represented an offering to the powers of fertility, and was often regarded as a magic act. Research has confirmed for many of these cults the emasculation of priests even of the highest class, although it is difficult to ascertain how widespread this practice actually was in later historical times. In many places, e.g., in the service of the Magna Mater of Pessinus, the emasculated high priest was called Attis and therefore as such was the companion or attendant of the goddess. This peculiar fact has led to the opinion that the emasculation of cult personnel, long practiced as a fertility sacrifice, was transferred to the myth of the god, thus providing the mythical αἴτιον (explanation) for the ancient rite.

The Element of Secrecy. All the cultic phenomena mentioned have been postulated on fairly solid ground

for the early part of the 1st millennium B.C., and for the areas of origin of the Oriental group of the later Hellenistic mysteries. If the god occupying the primary position in the pair of vegetation divinities in northwestern Asia Minor is called Zeus, the insertion "Homeric religion" on the table is justified. The Indo-European tribes that fused with the original inhabitants of the Aegean area and founded the Greek people looked upon these ecstatic fertility rites as foreign and strange. The knightly and warlike class of nobles of the archaic and legendary period immortalized by Homer gave a tone to the religious sphere and kept itself aloof from the whole world of chthonic cults. Hence, since the older religious element was pushed into the background in Greece, it was in Greece itself that psychological necessity gradually led to secrecy. The autochthonic population, keeping strictly to the ancient forms of worship (e.g., in Eleusis) came to practice them apart and surrounded them with a wall of silence.

But even in Greece it is not likely that this esoteric factor, necessitated by circumstances, was the sole reason for the origin of secrecy. An added reason may have been the fact that the rites had a partly sexual character, as is obvious from the pronounced biological mentality from which they derived their origin. This is also why many women's cults (e.g., the Thesmophoria at Athens and the cult of the Bona Dea at Rome) were closed to men. Some authors, K. Kerényi, e.g., have tried with much insight to show that male societies were at the root of the ancient secret cults. This hypothesis is manifestly untenable in the case of the most important cults (e.g., that of Eleusis), since they were open to both sexes from the outset, although their priestly functions were in the hands of women. Lastly, wherever eschatological hopes came to be connected with the performance of the rites, a certain awe for the latter, which were said to conceal something sublime, tended to encourage the practice of secrecy on the part of all. At Eleusis, it is true, this hope itself is not part of the secret but only the ritual way for becoming a sharer in it.

THE ELEUSINIAN MYSTERIES

The early Christian writers, especially Clement of Alexandria, are severe in their criticism of the Eleusinian Mysteries (see Clement of Alexandria, *Protrept.* 2.21.2).

General Characterization and Early History. This cult may claim a detailed treatment because of the long tradition of supporting evidence and its important role in the classical period. It seems very probable that, at the beginning of the 3d century B.C., the Hellenistic form of the Egyptian mysteries was fashioned on the Eleusinian by Timotheus, a member of the Eleusinian priestly family of the Eumolpids, and that a similar imitation may be assumed in the case of the final elaboration of the cult of the Magna Mater and Attis under the early Roman principate.

Thus the Eleusinian ritual may be regarded as a typical and historical Greco-Oriental mystery religion. It includes the Dionysiac mysteries, the second mystery cult rooted in early Greek religion. Specialists such as Wilamowitz-Moellendorff hold that the latter was not merely the only mystery cult still active in imperial times, but that it was very important. The discoveries in the Roman cemetery under St. Peter's at Rome have shown that in the later years of the 2d century A.D. Dionysian emblems had replaced Egyptian ones. Although this fact may be explained as a matter of fashion, it tends to reveal in any event a newly awakened interest in Dionysus as a porter god and god of the nether world—aspects of the deity that were stressed in the mysteries.

The Eleusinian mysteries belong to a cycle of feasts performed in two stages, a year apart, or even in three stages, thus requiring a total period of 3 years if performed according to rule. The three stages are: initiation ($\mu\acute{\nu}\eta\sigma\iota\varsigma$), dedication ($\tau\epsilon\lambda\epsilon\tau\acute{\eta}$), and full revelation of the mystery ($\dot{\epsilon}\pi\acute{o}\pi\tau\epsilon\iota\alpha$). A person could take part in these ceremonies only once, but it was not a civic duty to participate. It is not certain whether famous Athenians, who were deeply interested in ancestral beliefs, such as the tragedian Aeschylus, were mystai of Eleusis. Yet the Eleusinian celebrations were considered to have an importance and to bring honor to the city. Eleusis, originally, was not connected with Athens; it was an independent and significant place, the residence of a king. The foundations of the citadel reach back partly to the beginning of the 1st millennium B.C. The place of worship was structurally connected with the royal stronghold situated on the top of the adjacent height.

By the early 7th century B.C., Eleusis had lost its independence to Athens. As a result, the administration of the cult passed into the hands of Athenian officials, who respected the old customs, as ancient religious sentiment demanded. Thus, they permitted the old Eleusinian families, among which certain ritualistic functions were hereditary, to retain their rights and privileges, reserving for themselves, however, the power of appointing the high priest.

The Celebration of the Mysteries. The celebration of the mysteries was connected with Athens in the following manner. The preliminary ceremonies were held in Athens and were somewhat modified. But the second and third stage of the ceremonies, which took place in September (Boedromion) and could be held only in Eleusis, began with a solemn procession from Athens to Eleusis.

The dominant theme of the myth is the mother love of Demeter for her daughter Kore—this generic name being apparently older than the individualized name Persephone. Many who might be indifferent to other features of this myth could still appreciate this beautiful human motif. Everywhere else the core of the myth is not mother love but sexual love between man and woman, and only in the Egyptian mysteries is this sexual love the love between husband and wife (Isis and Osiris). In Egypt a child, the boy Horus, is added to this couple, but that is only a side aspect of the myth and does not affect it in any essential way, as it does in part at Eleusis. Actually, however, as regards the symbolism of the Eleusinian Kore, the dominant feature is her relationship to Pluto, the god of death. Kore, the bride whom he captures, represents the final destiny of all vegetative life, indeed of all earthly life, and thus can portray human death in an allegorical manner. The other associations with her and her mother, intended and aroused by the mysteries, become more meaningful only when both become mediators of a better life after death.

The Eleusinian hope is the high point of the so-called Homeric *Hymn to Demeter,* where in 5.479–481 the lot of the initiated in the hereafter is pictured as more pleasant than that of the non-initiated. Several verses later, they are called the blessed on whom the pair of exalted and chaste goddesses bestow their loving care. The same word blessed ($\ddot{o}\lambda\beta\iota o\varsigma$) describing the lot of the initiates is used by Pindar (Frg. 137, ed. Bergk) and Sophocles (Turchi, no. 152). The word $\ddot{o}\lambda\beta\iota o\varsigma$ has about the same sense as the word $\mu\alpha\kappa\acute{\alpha}\rho\iota o\varsigma$ used in the two accounts of the Sermon on the Mount (Matthew ch. 5; 3– ; Luke ch. 6; 20–). But whereas this word, as used by the Evangelists, praises as blessed the way of life made possible by the New Covenant, the sole title to Eleusinian blessedness is initiation. There is no question of atonement. Only the worst criminals were excluded from initiation, a point severely criticized already in antiquity.

Opinions differ respecting the performance of the rites in the second and third stages and also respecting the precise arrangement of the interior of the sacred building. Benches for spectators, cut out of rock and still recognizable today, prove that participants in the cult engaged in liturgic actions that were visible to all. Literary allusions to emotions of fear manifested by the spectators, and likewise the express mentioning of a descent ($\kappa\alpha\tau\alpha\beta\acute{\alpha}\sigma\iota o\nu$) by Asterius (*Hom.* 10; PG 40:324B) suggest the dramatic performance of the moving legend of the rape of Persephone by Pluto. Clement of Alexandria (*Protrept.* 2.21) has preserved for us the so-called password ($\sigma\acute{\nu}\nu\theta\eta\mu\alpha$) of Eleusis. It is a formula to be repeated by the candidate for final admission, who had to show thereby that he had passed the intermediate stage. Thus one learns the main actions. The formula runs: "I have fasted, I have drunk of the sacred cup [$\kappa\nu\kappa\epsilon\acute{\omega}\nu$], I have taken [the things] from the sacred chest, having tasted thereof I have placed them into the basket and again from the basket into the chest." The fasting and drinking from a ritualistic container evidently aim to imitate ceremonially the fasting of Demeter out of sorrow for the disappearance of her daughter, as related in the legend, and also the drink with which she refreshed herself after having been cheered by the indecent jests of her maid Baubo.

Fertility Aspects of the Rites. In his account, Clement of Alexandria puts the Baubo scene before the cultic action and criticizes it harshly. The handling of the anonymous things ($\dot{\alpha}\pi\acute{o}\rho\rho\eta\tau\alpha$) suggests that they were symbols of female and male sexuality. The dual containers, differentiated by the names "chest" and "basket," seem also to confirm this view. This assumption seems logical and is confirmed by other intimations of the Church Fathers.

This explanation of the last act of the *synthema,* or password ceremony, which is described in such cryptic language, seems sound for intrinsic and extrinsic reasons. (1) Such an act is in keeping with a fertility cult. Other secondary Eleusinian rites contain this feature, as the call to the earth: $\ddot{\nu}\epsilon$, $\chi\acute{\nu}\epsilon$, "rain, conceive" (Proclus, *In Tim.* 40E). (2) This action is appropriate to the second stage of the rites. (3) Certain finds in the temple of Demeter at Priene, a kind of affiliate of Eleusis, similar to the one established especially in Alexandria, show a marked sexual emphasis. These finds suggest directly the use of the female sexual sym-

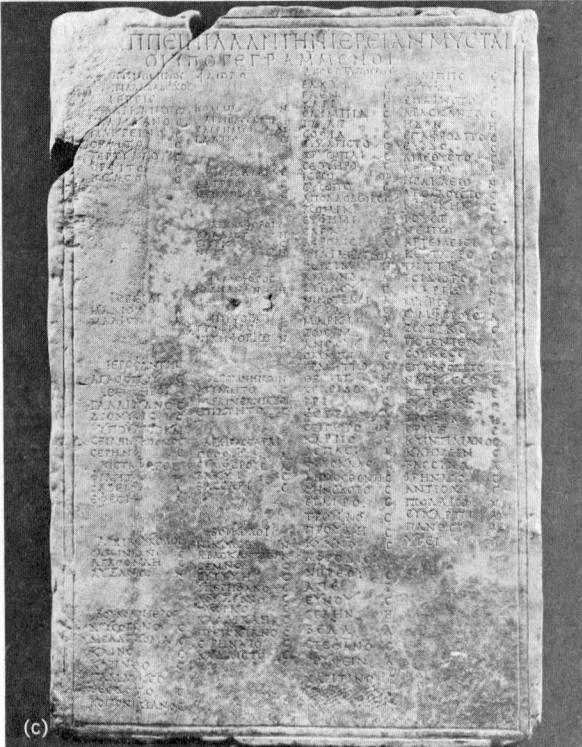

(a) Initiation at Eleusis, detail of the "Lovatelli Urn" in the Museo delle Terme, Rome. (b) Girl undergoing the ordeal and bacchante, detail of a fresco in the Villa of the Mysteries, Pompeii, c. 50 B.C. (c) Bacchic inscription on the marble base for a marble statue, 2d century A.D., discovered in the Roman Campagna. The unique importance of this inscription is that it sets forth the structure of a Bacchic

"Thiasos," and lists the functions of the members from the highest to the lowest. (d) Aion, Roman marble relief, 2d century A.D., in the Museo e Medagliere Estense, Modena, Italy. The figure is interpreted as reflecting syncretistic religious and philosophical concepts of late antiquity, showing connections with Orphism, the fire theology of the Chaldaean Oracles, and Mithraism.

bols as a means of initiation. The simultaneous use of the male symbol is the more easily explained, since the latter plays a central role in the Hellenistic mystery rites that exhibit a more or less close dependence on Eleusis.

The procedure at the third stage, revelation (ἐπόπτεια), is known through independent and credible assertions of early ecclesiastical writers and Fathers. Two acts are mentioned. The first is the "hierogamy," or sacred marriage between the high priest (hierophant) and priestess (cf. Gregory of Nazianzus and Proclus; Turchi, nos. 32–). It was probably intended to symbolize the mythical nuptials of Demeter and Iasion on the thrice-plowed field (Hesiod, *Theog.* 969–972), itself the mythical symbol of the sacred marriage of heaven and earth. Hippolytus furnishes important additional information. The priest raised a freshly cut ear of wheat—obviously the fruit of this sacred marriage—with the loud cry: "The exalted goddess bore a holy boy, the strong one bore a strong child" (Turchi, no. 130). As a confirmation of the prehistoric age of this rite and of the relation of the nucleus of the Eleusinian cult actions to the early farming stage of culture, it is to be noted that the same rite has been found in North Africa and in the period preceding the spread of the Indo-European culture in the West (cf. D. J. Wölfel in König, *Christus,* 1:340–).

Thus, one sees that at Eleusis hope in a better life to come and improvement of material welfare, which is so dependent on the fruits of the earth, are closely connected. St. Paul has pointed out an association of ideas between wheat and the hereafter (1 Cor 15.37). Eleusinian eschatology, however, did not embrace precisely what for Paul was the symbolism of the sprouting seed, namely, bodily resurrection. The quasi-official formulation of the Eleusinian hope in the Homeric *Hymn* is remarkably modest. It does not look beyond a life in the lower world, and even for this it dares to promise the initiates, as opposed to non-initiates, only a gradual improvement in their lot.

Evaluation and Later History. Yet these rites gave their initiates the consolation that there was at least one form of divine worship that showed some interest in the great question of the beyond. The official cults of the Greek states ignored this problem. The Olympians enjoyed their own blessedness without caring for the future lot of men. M. J. Lagrange has given the noblest interpretation of the Eleusinian Mysteries; one should not speak blindly of magic here, but should regard the whole procedure as an act of trust in the power of the "august goddesses." But despite the consolation furnished by the rites and the veneration they enjoyed from age itself, they could not withstand critical examination. The comfort could be only as real as the persons of the divinities themselves.

However, later classic times and especially the Hellenistic age recognized fully the symbolic-mythical values contained in the rites. Not only in Athenian but in all ancient literature, Eleusis was renowned as an inalienable jewel of the city of Athens, a symbol of its cultural contributions, the first and most basic of which was the raising of cereals. Even after the mysteries had lost all credence in ancient Greece, including Attica itself, they were still celebrated with pomp as old folk customs, with a feeling for history and with a treasuring of the past for its own sake. During the

several revivals of Greek culture, beginning with the great efforts of Hadrian, the mysteries' power of attraction was proved again and again, especially in the case of the Romans who took pleasure in becoming initiates. Alaric destroyed a great part of the sanctuary in A.D. 395, and the celebration of the rites was forbidden by the laws of Theodosius the Great in the same period.

The Cult of the Great Mother, or Magna Mater

Within a limited space it is not possible to cover all vegetation or fertility cults that have mystery elements. However, the cult of the Great Mother deserves formal treatment, being both so representative and so important. The early Greeks were already familiar with the mother of Zeus (Μήτηρ ʽΡέα), simply as mother of the gods, a figure undoubtedly related to the mother goddess of Asia Minor. But this Greek Rhea has no partner of such dubious and uncertain status as Cybele's partner Attis. When, therefore, the Phrygian goddess with her companion Attis asked for admission, as was inevitable in a commercial town such as Athens as a result of the influx of immigrants from Asia Minor, the new mother goddess was not identified simply with Rhea but had to be satisfied, like all foreign cults, with a place outside the city walls.

But apparently, already before the Persian wars, some traits of the Asian form of the mother cult had been introduced into the Greek worship of Rhea. This has psychological probability in its favor, since Pindar praises the venerable Asian Mother in one of his Olympic odes (on Hiero). In the Hellenistic Age, the worship of the Magna Mater is conducted at the Peiraeus in full Asiatic style by the ὀργεῶνες (i.e., men who celebrate the *orgia*) with the assistance of a special cult personnel. There is mention of a priestess of Attis and a couch (κλίνη) that she must prepare for the god. This act may represent the mourning over the dead Attis, who previously seems to have been honored by joyous dances around a throne. Plato was familiar with the exotic ritual of enthronement (ἐνθρονισμός) as part of the initiation of the followers of the Magna Mater, the corybantes (*Euthyd.* 429D).

Eight hundred years after Plato, in the 4th century A.D., when *taurobolia* were celebrated in Athens in honor of the Magna Mater, the Asian mother definitely entered the Greek pantheon and had Demeter and Kore beside her as companion goddesses—a situation that would have been unthinkable in early times.

The Cult of Magna Mater in the Roman Period. The Romans knew Adonis at an early time in their history, partly through the Greeks of south Italy, and partly through the Etruscans. In 205 B.C., in the crisis of the Second Punic War, they introduced the cult of the Asian Mother from Pessinus in Galatia. The Phrygian cult was given a place on the Palatine, opposite the later house of Livia, but the astute heads of the Roman state allowed only one annual public celebration: the lustration of the image of the Magna Mater in the Almo stream, which had no connection with the fate of Attis. The cult, in the form given it by the Emperor Claudius, who was interested in religious antiquities, is known through its incorporation in the Roman religious calendar as well as through archeological representations, e.g., on a sarcophagus in S. Lorenzo fuori le mura. In order to understand the performance of the cult in this later and elaborated form, one must remember the personality of Attis as the representation of the nature cycle and also the basic structure of his myth as outlined earlier in this article. A pine tree, which was intended to represent the hero, profusely decorated as a tree of spring and adorned with an image of Attis, was carried in procession (Firmicus Maternus, *De errore prof. rel.* 22). At the same time, the tree, since it was an evergreen, may have symbolized his ostensibly newly assumed life, though the myth says nothing about this. Then the procession with the image of the Magna Mater was carried out with much greater pomp. Quite apart from these public ceremonies, secret rites were also performed. As in Eleusis, these were obviously based on ritualistic imitation of events in the myth. Firmicus Maternus mentions a ceremony of mourning the dead (*ibid.* 23), probably but not necessarily referring to Attis, and an anointing of the throat of the candidates with oil, with the accompanying words: "Take courage, mystae, you belong to a god who has been saved, and he will also be your salvation from toil." Even more valuable is the formula reported in common by both Firmicus Maternus and Clement of Alexandria: "I have eaten from the *tympanon* [drum], I drank from the *kymbalon* [cymbal]"—both are instruments employed in the worship of the goddess. Whereas in Firmicus the words "I became a mystes of Attis" follow immediately, Clement mentions (*Protr.* 2.15) two more mystic acts: "I carried the *kernos,* I slipped into the bridal chamber." The *kernos,* a container having several parts and found already in ancient worship, was employed as something intended obviously to produce its effect as an archaic rite. The last statement quoted gives a key at least to the general meaning.

Evaluation and Later History. Obviously the rite was intended to impress upon the mystai the subjective certainty of having been united in a special way with the goddess, as in a mystic marriage or, on a more modest plane, as Lagrange has proposed, as a personal servant of the Great Mother. It seems clear that the strong motivation of hope present in this cult, a hope in harmony with the religious interests of the Greco-Roman period, probably served as a foundation for a belief in a higher and better life beyond the grave. It would thus be in the line of the Eleusinian ideology. The rhetorical vehemence with which Firmicus, the chief source, criticizes such rites must be understood in the light of the times. But the Christian polemist is right in reminding the believers in these mysteries that the whole activity has no real value or meaning, since it is based entirely on myth. In form and content the sacred formulae are essentially an imitation of the Eleusinian "symbol." Formally they are a synopsis of the rites that the candidate for membership had to undergo before he could be admitted to the final initiation. In content these rites are modeled on the myth, as the containers chosen for food and drink are the drum and the cymbal. These instruments were said to have been used by the goddess on her mythical journey through the mountains of Asia Minor and hence were employed also in the public processions in honor of Cybele.

Something original, something as yet without analogy in any Greek cult, is mentioned by Prudentius (*Peristeph*). In some 80 verses he describes the cere-

mony of the *taurobolium in the cult of the Magna Mater. It deserves notice here because the rebirth mentioned in the pertinent inscriptions as the expected effect has often been compared with the rebirth that is promised as an effect of Baptism (Ti 3.5). But the *taurobolium* aimed at a restoration of physical forces only through the blood of a bull. The general atmosphere of the rite is not one of spiritual hopes, and it is occasionally taken over as a rite beneficial for the common good (*pro salute Caesaris*). All the Western evidence dates from the 2d century A.D. on.

THE MYSTERIES OF DIONYSUS

Between the Eleusian and the Dionysian mysteries there are several important differences. The cult of Eleusis keeps its external structure unchanged, primarily because it is bound to a definite locality, but the cult of Dionysus varies considerably in place and time. The significance of the two Eleusinian divinities is already evident from the Homeric poems; and in addition to the data furnished by archeology, a considerable body of relatively clear information is found in early Christian literature.

As regards the secret worship of Dionysus (i.e., mystery rites that go back to the pre-Hellenic period), the evidence comes in part from widely separated places and is difficult to correlate. Furthermore, the evidence is open to serious question on the historical side and refers to markedly different periods. Yet Dionysus is a divinity who is clearly the object of a mystery cult. This is evident from his local origin and his myth, scanty as it is, as well as from the nature of the god as revealed by the sum of all available data—and especially by the data preserved in the form of his cult.

According to Greek legend, Dionysus came to Greece from Thrace (as in Euripides's *Bacchae*) and also by sea (as is recalled in the role of the vehicle in the form of a ship employed in the Athenian Dionysia). The recently established connection of this god with ancient Cretan religion tends to confirm that he was not out of harmony with the Greek fertility worship and was integrated into it at an early date. The restriction of the domain of Dionysus to wine, and more specifically to viticulture, is found in certain ancient writers, e.g., Diodorus, who have spun out long myths on Dionysus as the god of wine. Relying on this evidence, H. Jeanmaire thinks he can clarify more sharply the particular function of this god and his cult. The difficulty is that among the late mythographers it is hard to distinguish between earlier and later myths. The Orphics elaborated the saga of the birth of the god into a confused pattern of stories in order to obtain a foundation for their profound speculation. The older saga tells of the tragic death of the god's mother, Semele, and it is highly suggestive that this name means earth, as P. Kretschmer has established. The desire to see Zeus cost her her life.

The myth relates matters that normally belong to child rearing, but with this difference, that the people engaged in this task are naturally mythical persons. Thus Hermes entrusts the care of the child to the nymphs, but it soon escapes from its nurses. This incident provides the Boeotian cult of Dionysus, at least in the later period, with the motif of a search in the mountains for Dionysus by the Thyads. The latter are but other names for the frenzied female attendants of the god, the Maenads, who personify in the cult the nymphs assigned to the care of the child by Hermes.

The birth of a god who, like Dionysus, is so closely connected with vegetation and belongs to the old pair of fertility divinities, must be followed by a death. Accordingly, Philochorus, a specialist in the history of religion writing in the early Hellenistic age, mentions a tomb of Dionysus within the temple precinct of Delphi. The ceremonies devoted to the awakening of the god to a new birth took place, however, only every 3d year. This was a very awkward situation, since Dionysus was regarded as being temporarily in residence at Delphi, substituting for Apollo, who was thought to spend the winter with the Hyperboreans.

The love affair between Dionysus and Ariadne is typical of the vegetation myth: Ariadne's early death is the counterpart of the disappearance of Persephone. The myth, which in the elaborate literary form given it by poets such as Nonnus (5th century A.D.) tells of Dionysus' journey to India, is very late. It is merely a reflection of Alexander's Indian campaign.

Spread of the Cult and Its Special Features. The older myths of the journeys of Dionysus reflect the early propagation and the peculiar nature of the cult. This cult, manifestly an ecstatic one from the outset and under the strong influence of women, was spread successfully despite the opposition of political authorities, as indicated in the story of the revenge of Dionysus on the Theban King Pentheus. Euripides in his *Bacchae* describes this revenge in detail. Bacchus (Dionysus) induces Pentheus to search for the Maenads who are roving about Mt. Parnassus, but they take him for an animal and tear him to pieces. This is, at the same time, one of the earliest accounts of the rite of omophagy. During the winter and early spring, female worshipers of Dionysus used to roam about Parnassus, hunting down wild animals, tearing them apart, and eating their raw flesh.

Phrygia furnishes more convincing evidence than does central Greece for the ceremony of the awakening of Dionysus. Here he passes for a god hibernating in the realm of Persephone—a slight mitigation only of the idea of the death of the vegetation god, who in spring is brought in with great pomp at the feast of the *Katagogia* [cf. Wilamowitz-Moellendorff, *Die Religion der Griechen* (Leipzig 1932) 2:373–   ]. In the Hellenistic period there is mention of a state-controlled cult of Dionysus at Miletus, in which raw flesh was eaten, evidently a civilized continuance of ancient savage customs, but subsequently placed under state control (*ibid.* 372). The mad celebrations in the Parnassus region, which were intended also to awaken the god Dionysus, did not exclude men completely but were the special privilege of women. In this respect, because of the esoteric tendency present, the celebrations in question fall within the general framework of the mystery cult.

The time after Alexander witnessed a general revival of Dionysian worship. For Egypt, there is proof for the spread of secret Dionysian rites in the fact that Ptolemy Philopator took measures to bring even the privately conducted rites of Dionysus under his control. A royal decree ordered those in possession of initiation formulas to register them in person with the government; obviously the government feared excesses. About the same time this cult, which for a long time

had been prevalent in southern Italy, exhibited a new development, characterized by violence, sexual excesses, and even murder; and it spread to Rome itself. Therefore the Roman Senate took prompt and severe action, as is recorded in the extant inscription on bronze, the *Senatus consultum de Bacchanalibus* and by the historian Livy (39.14.1).

The Pompeian Evidence. Nevertheless, more moderate forms of the rite were allowed to continue, as is proved by the series of paintings in one of the halls of the so-called Villa dei Mysteri (also called the Villa Item). The connection with the cult of Dionysus is certain, since in this cycle of paintings Dionysus, with his familiar attribute the *thyrsus,* or stàff, and reposing on the bosom of his beloved Ariadne, occupies the commanding place. This obviously mythical scene may be considered as expressing the inner meaning of the mystery that is to be dramatically presented. As the precise portraiture indicates, the actors include not only definite persons, such as the mistress of the house, but also, along with them and without sharp distinction, mythical beings such as Silenus and Pan. A winged form, whether a mythical figure or a personification of the mystic rite ($\tau\epsilon\lambda\epsilon\tau\acute{\eta}$), lays the lash upon the back of a woman. This scene is framed first by the unveiling of the phallus, the initiation proper, and secondly by the solo dance of a woman. If it was intended to symbolize the joys of the hereafter to be expected from participation in the initiation, this dance, not perhaps positively licentious and yet not especially exalted in character, bears witness to the typically pagan concept of the future life. In any case, the series of scenes in the Villa Item, whether representing an initiation into a mystery or simply a bridal ceremony, is characteristic of a Greco-Roman Dionysian ritual, with an emphasis on sensation and surprise.

This set of paintings of the Villa Item, notably the initiation rite proper (i.e., the unveiling of the phallus), is paralleled by a series of so-called Campanian reliefs, and M. I. Rostovtzeff has interpreted the paintings of the Casa Omerica in Pompeii as having much the same content. Accordingly, it seems assured that some kind of mystery cult of Dionysus flourished in the vicinity of Naples in the 1st century A.D. Whether the inscription of Agripinilla describes genuine Dionysiac worship or refers to more or less licentious revels under the cloak of mystery rites is not clear (see Nilsson GeschGrRel 2:343–344). By this time the Hellenistic mystery religion had developed a kind of "common liturgical language" with fixed formulas.

Problems of Interpretation. The real secret seems to be the sexual element, but sublimated as a symbol of all fertility. However, the striving to come into closer contact with the mystery divinities is difficult to explain, especially in the case of Dionysus, when one looks for the precise reason why Dionysus should be a particularly fitting mediator of hopes for the hereafter. Heraclitus of Ephesus, reflecting on the riotous scenes during the Dionysia in his city in the 5th century B.C., states in one of his customary obscure utterances: "They celebrate the grape feast in honor of Hades." But he says this as one who sees more deeply than the common man, and he says it with pensive melancholy in the light of the contrast between festive joy and the frailty of all vegetative and earthly life. In any case, the cycle of Dionysian myths, while to a limited degree symbolizing growth, offers far less expectation of salvation than is the case in the Oriental group.

A ritualistic drama commemorating the annual awakening and passing of vegetation, as mentioned earlier, maintained itself in a few places only, e.g., in Delphi and in Phrygia. Even this fact would hardly be known, unless historians such as Plutarch with antiquarian interests had reported it. Dionysus was surnamed from the outset Lyseus as a symbolic personification of or as the mythical giver of wine. All that ancient speculation itself associated with this title exhibits an attempt at a theological interpretation of this metaphor, which has interest chiefly because, beneath the play of legend, it reveals the religious aspirations and longing for salvation on the part of pagan souls.

ORPHISM

The myth of the child Dionysus already pointed in the direction of the Dionysus of Orphism. The latter figure, it is true, has received a highly complex elaboration and is overladen with fantastic myths that cannot be told here in detail. And yet Orphism is so important that some attention must be given it in this article. It was certainly a combination of opposites and had a bad name in antiquity because of its practice of licentious rites and its strange manner of life. Orphism, the origins of which continue to be warmly debated, alone among the mystery religions—except perhaps Mithraism and the Egyptian mysteries because of their emphasis on eschatology—possessed a complete system of doctrine, and was concerned with the dissemination of knowledge. All other mysteries, being essentially forms of worship, aimed only at producing certain dispositions of mind and vague hopes.

Earlier History. In the modern investigation of mystery religions, Orphism has long occupied a special place through the importance assigned to it by Plato. Whether the latter agrees with the opinions he introduces from Orphism is not always clear from his words. It is to be assumed rather that he merely wishes to praise the general character and line of thought that he quotes in support of his own doctrines, e.g., the belief in retribution in the hereafter and therefore in the meaning of human life as involving moral responsibility.

In support of such a view of life Orphism created a profound myth. It can be traced back to an origin in single individuals and in the first place to Onomacritus, who lived in the age of the Pisistratids (6th–5th century B.C.). The lot of man is viewed as a miserable result of an original sin, yet one not committed by man but by his mythical ancestors. According to Orphic teaching men are formed out of the ashes of the Titans, sons of Uranus and Gaia, therefore, of a pre-Olympian race of gods. They had been destroyed by the lightning of Zeus because they had committed the outrage of tearing to pieces and devouring his child Dionysus, all except his heart. Athena brought the heart to Zeus, who in turn swallowed it and produced another Dionysus, namely, the Dionysus of Orphism. The Papyrus Smily, also called the Papyrus Gurob after its place of discovery in Egypt (Kern, *Orph. Frg.* 31), dates from the 3d century B.C. and confirms the earlier myth. In mentioning the playthings of the child Dionysus; it tells of the Titans tearing him to pieces. They fell upon him

while he was playing a child's game, amusing himself with the apples of the Hesperides. This tends to prove its existence at an earlier date in the Greek area, the sole source for its spread to Egypt. It is very interesting to note that writers under the early Empire are the first to tell that the Titans had devoured the limbs of the child.

Orphism, in keeping with the formal, artificial character of its origins, left free scope for further development and personal transformation. But as opposed to the view of I. M. Linforth, it must be maintained that closed Orphic associations, therefore societies of mystai, existed already in classical Greek times. In the Hellenistic age, the Papyrus Gurob—perhaps because it was the cult legend of one of the Dionysian societies that by order of Ptolemy Philopator was required to turn over religious documents—appears to confirm the existence of mysteries under Orphic influence. However, Orphism in this period seems to have been the object of scholarly study rather than a living and active cult.

Later History and Evaluation. An Orphic book of hymns dating from the early imperial age seems to be the work of certain societies, especially in the city of Pergamon, where a shrine has been discovered in which deities praised in the hymns were worshiped. But the manner of worship that the book indicates has nothing to do with a mystery religion so far as almost all external rites described are concerned. The cosmogony of Orphism—which is intended to include its theogony and anthropogony—was fully elaborated apparently only at a late date and is known exclusively from Neoplatonic sources. It gives an important place to the primitive cosmic egg. This motif is not a mythical Greek fabrication but belongs to the earliest mythological cosmogony and can be traced back to very early prehistoric cultures. In the Roman imperial age it was connected with the figure of Aion. The Aion of Modena is of the greatest value historically. It is a figure so loaded with attributes as to leave an unaesthetic impression; but to the men of late antiquity, to which it belongs, it served as a symbol of the esoteric wisdom underlying the outward representation. The so-called Orphic passports for the dead, found in Crete and south Italy, contain instructions for a confession of innocence similar to those with which the ancient Egyptians provided themselves for their meeting with the judge of the dead in the other world. Connection with Egypt, accordingly, has been suggested for this Orphic phenomenon (see Prümm, DBSuppl 6:72).

MITHRAISM AND OTHER ORIENTAL MYSTERIES

At the outset, it may be stated that there are certain analogies with Orphism. These analogies are found in the form of its origin and in its emphasis on doctrinal content. Mithraism, like Orphism, was founded by specific individuals. Magi, Persian priests from north and east Persia and from the highlands of Cappadocia, consciously influenced by the tendencies toward a union of Greek and Oriental religious elements, created this cult in the 4th–3d century B.C. The Oriental basis was primarily Persian popular religion and not Persian Zoroastrianism. Zoroaster had condemned all gods of the popular religion without being able to extirpate them. The Magi put the Indo-Persian deity Mitra, conceived as a noble figure and given certain features of the Babylonian sun-god Shamash, in the center of a theogonic and cosmogonic myth. The name Mitra means truth, faithfulness, or contract. (*See* MITHRAS AND MITHRAISM.)

Sources of Mithraism. In the absence of literary sources, the myth must be interpreted essentially from the monuments, a relatively large number of which have been preserved. The fairly copious monumental evidence is to be explained in part from the nature of the places of worship. The latter were artificial grottoes, imitations of natural caves, which were low and small and could accommodate only a few dozen worshipers. No Mithraic association had more than 100 members, and most of them had a much smaller number. Since the worshipers were mostly soldiers, the *Mithraea,* or shrines of the cult, have been found especially on the frontiers—hence, in Britain, along the Rhenish and Danubian Limes, and in Africa and Asia. Dura-Europos on the Euphrates was a flourishing center of Mithraism. After the abandonment of the military frontiers under various pressures, these shrines, often wholly or partly subterranean, no longer occasioned special interest, and thus much of their content was left intact. Obviously Rome as a military center and world capital with a large percentage of foreigners in its population has revealed many Mithraic shrines, though these may not have been used simultaneously. Archeological investigation has identified more than 50. Ostia, possibly more Orientalized than Rome, has yielded 18 *Mithraea,* a relatively large number, even if they are usually small.

The Mithraic Myth. The doctrine of Mithraism, a combination of Greek theogony and an Iranian myth, is concerned with the origin of fertility from a celestial bull. The god, born out of a rock, who enters an already existing pantheon of the Greek type, brings this bull from the kingdom of the moon and kills him. This triumph of youthful force was given a typical iconographic form by a great artist and this form was never changed: a representation of Nike bringing a sacrifice of thanksgiving after victory. This achievement of Mithras made Mithraism an appropriate religion for soldiers. Further mythical scenes beside the main picture show another battle of Mithras, this time with the Sun (*Sol, Helios*), who finally receives him in friendship and takes him to heaven in his chariot. The last scene undoubtedly embodies the hope that is impressed in seven ceremonial stages (Raven, Nymph, Soldier, Lion, Persian, Sun-runner, Father): an expectation of an afterlife in the sky, which gained ground under the Empire, because an underworld hereafter came to be felt as gloomy and repulsive.

Mithraic Ritual. The whole interior of the Mithraic shrine is arranged for holding a meal in the ancient way, with participants reclining on couches—hence the benchlike structures along the side walls. The meal consisted of bread and water. But neither the meal nor the Mithraic baptism—exclusively a form of purification as found in many religions—was the essential element of Mithraic ritual. The all-important feature was the tests of courage required for admission to the higher degrees. They are represented in formidable fashion in the *Mithraeum* of Capua and partially also in that found under the church of St. Prisca in Rome. An inscription from the latter mentions a *cauterisatio,* the branding with the sign of the god, a ceremony that Tertullian compares with Confirmation. A recently dis-

covered *Mithraeum* at San Marino (Castelli Romani) exhibits beautiful cultic scenes, the official publication of which is still awaited (1965).

For the higher speculations associated with Mithraism, the *Borysthenic Discourse* of the famous Sophist Dio Chrysostom (b. *c.* A.D. 40; d. after 112), is repeatedly cited. He describes a cosmogony and an anthropogony, including a kind of original sin of man, in the sense of Plato's *Phaedrus,* but with emphasis on the Stoic doctrine of universal conflagration. However, it is not known to what extent this is his own personal doctrine (cf. Nilsson GeschGrRel 2:688). The age and origin of the figure of Aion, which is often represented separately along with the bull scene and which resembles the Orphic Aion of Modena, are doubtful. The opinion of F. Cumont, who would have Aion dominate the whole pantheon, has lost ground. The figure is now identified rather with Ahriman himself, the evil principle of Mazdaism, and it seems that a place was found for this worship in Mithraism.

Other Oriental Mysteries. It is not necessary here to deal in detail with the cult of Adonis—which never became a fully developed mystery religion—and with the Egyptian mysteries, since their more important aspects were covered earlier in the article and in particular in the treatment of the Mysteries of Eleusis. Attention was called also to the possibility of connecting the congratulation of the mystai on "the god that has been saved," which is directed perhaps to the mystae of the Magna Mater, with the mystae of Osiris. Since the various mysteries had so much in common, it is very much to the point to refer to a passage in the *Metamorphoses* of Apuleius. It makes a journey to the elements or the stars the core of the mysteries of Isis. This journey was probably intended to be an actual anticipation of the eventually expected real journey to the stars (see *Met.* 11.23).

RELATIONS WITH CHRISTIANITY

The question of the relations between the mystery religions and Christianity arose in the 19th century as a result of the simultaneous operation of two factors, namely, the systematic scholarly investigation of the history of the mystery religions by classical philology and archeology and the decline in the belief in the historical reliability of the New Testament revelation as a consequence of so-called liberal and historical exegesis. Within the limits of this article, only the high points concerning the question of relationship can be treated. For detailed coverage, see the bibliography following this article.

New Testament Evidence and Its Interpretation. In contrast to the Old Testament, where a specific warning is given against Adonis worship, the Gospels mention the Magi; and this in itself might well be interpreted as containing an allusion to a mystery cult, namely, that of the Persian Mithras (cf. Matthew ch. 2). On the basis of the copious evidence for the employment of Semitic equivalents in the Qumran texts for the Greek *mysterion,* it is clear that the mere use of the term *mysterion* does not mean that St. Paul consciously wished to imply a connection between Christian and pagan use of the term, to say nothing of any positive approval of any Christian connection with pagan mysteries whether in their forms of worship or in their literary or written presentations. Paul uses the word *mysterion* nearly always in the singular, while by contrast the pagan mysteries are nearly always mentioned in the plural. The following point is more significant. Paul employs the singular form *mysterion* in the sense of the secret, hidden design of God in its totality. There is no emphasis on the cult aspect.

Christian Mystery and Pagan Mystery. Forms of worship, namely, the Sacraments, may be included in the term *mysteria* as found in 1 Cor 4.1; but in that case, as incorporated into the plan of salvation as a unity and in subordination to the Apostles' mission of serving as ambassadors of Christ (2 Cor 5.19, 20).

Even among Catholics, a certain school of exegesis has maintained that Paul saw the tragic experiences of the heroes of the mysteries as a divine pedagogy for the pagans to prepare them for the message of salvation, and from that point of view intended to represent, as opposed to the pagan mystery cults, the real and true mystery. However, this is unlikely for several reasons. The ancient mysteries do not represent a historical fact, but a regularly recurring annual rhythm. In Christian worship "representation" is not a theatrical and mimic one in a series of separate acts, but is centered as one single moment, the redemptive and decisive act of the Lord on the cross. Finally, in Christian worship this remembrance of a real fact is not connected with specific seasons (at least in apostolic times), but takes place every Sunday, and continues to be observed even after the institution of the main liturgical feasts with Easter as their center.

The Apostle's various admonitions against revels, banquets, etc., cannot be interpreted as referring specifically and literally to the mysteries; at most they are concerned with the excesses occasioned by the public and private worship of Dionysus (Rom 13.13; Eph 5.18). Some exegetes suspect an implied condemnation of the mysteries in the reminiscence in 1 Cor 12.1 of a "magic urge" on the part of hearers to certain cults. Such scholars adopt this view because they believe that Paul, with the idea of the "dumb idols" vividly in mind, is perhaps thinking of those divinities whose emotional worship presents a certain resemblance to excesses connected with phenomena at Corinth. A more likely reference to pagan mysteries is to be found in the heresy of Colossae [see DBSuppl 6 (1960) 218–222].

Bibliography: The literature on the mystery religions is voluminous and, given the difficulties presented by the sources, on many points there is no unanimity among scholars. The older literature in this field, furthermore, is dominated, in general, by a tendency to regard Christianity as largely, if not exclusively, an adaptation of the pagan mysteries.
General works. N. TURCHI, *Fontes historiae mysteriorum aevi hellenistici* (Rome 1923). R. FOLLET and K. PRÜMM, "Mystères," DBSuppl 6 (1960) 1–225; *Religionsgeschichtliches Handbuch* (new ed. Rome 1954) esp. 213–356 and 843–846. [These comprehensive studies by the contributor give full details and furnish copious bibliography]. O. KERN and T. HOPFNER, "Mysterien," Pauly-Wiss RE 16. 2 (1935) 1209–1350. U. VON WILAMOWITZ-MOELLENDORFF, *Der Glaube der Hellenen*, 2 v. (Berlin 1931–32). Nilsson GeschGrRel. [The contents of these last two standard, comprehensive works can be easily controlled through the excellent indexes.] F. CUMONT, *Lux perpetua* (Paris 1949).
Special works. P. FOUCART, *Les Mystères d'Éleusis* (Paris 1914). G. MYLONAS, *Eleusis and the Eleusinian Mysteries* (Princeton 1961), with good bibliog.; however, he rejects interpretations given by a number of other scholars. M. P. NILSSON, *The Dionysiac Mysteries of the Hellenistic Age* (Lund 1957). M. I. ROSTOVTZEFF, *Mystic Italy* (New York 1927). H.

JEANMAIRE, *Histoire du culte du Bacchus* (Paris 1959). A. BRUHL, *Liber Pater. Origine et expansion du culte dionysiaque à Rome et dans le monde romain* (Paris 1953). O. KERN, *Orphicorum fragmenta* (Berlin 1922). I. M. LINFORTH, *The Arts of Orpheus* (Berkeley 1941). W. K. C. GUTHRIE, *Orpheus and Greek Religion* (2d ed. London 1952). J. CARCOPINO, *Aspects mystiques de la Rome païenne* (Paris 1941). H. GRAILLOT, *Le Culte de Cybèle Mère de Dieu, à Rome et dans l'Empire romain* (Paris 1912). M. J. LAGRANGE, "Attis et le Cristianisme," Rev Bibl 28 (1919) 419–480. G. NAGEL, "Les Mystères d'Osiris dans l'ancienne Égypte," *Eranos-Jahrbuch* 11 (1944) 145–166. A. J. FESTUGIÈRE, *Personal Religion Among the Greeks* (Berkeley 1960). M. P. NILSSON, "The Syncretistic Relief of Modena," *Symbolae Osloenses* 24 (1945) 1ff. For the Mysteries of Mithras, *see* MITHRAS AND MITHRAISM. On the relations of the mystery religions and Christianity, in addition to K. PRÜMM, "Mystères," 173–225 *op. cit.*, see H. PINARD DE LA BOULLAYE, *L'Étude comparée des religions*, 3 v. (5th ed. Paris 1929) 1:361–544. K. PRÜMM, *Der christliche Glaube und die altheidnische Welt*, 2 v. (Leipzig 1935). L. DE GRANDMAISON, *Jesus Christ: His Person, His Message, His Credentials*, 3 v. (New York 1935–37) v.3, esp. 349–377. M. J. LAGRANGE, *Introduction à l'étude du Nouveau Testament*, pt. 4, *Critique historique*, pt. 4.1, *Les Mystères: L'Orphisme* (2d ed. Paris 1937) esp. 187–224. C. COLPE, *Die religionsgeschichtliche Schule: Darstellung und Kritik ihres Bildes vom gnostlischen Erlösermythus* (Göttingen 1961). C. VAGAGGINI, *Il senso teologico della liturgia* (2d ed. Rome 1958); Eng. *Theological Dimensions of the Liturgy*, tr. L. J. DOYLE (Collegeville, Minn. 1959).
Illustration credits: Fig. 2*a* and 2*b*, Alinari-Art Reference Bureau. Fig. 2*c*, The Metropolitan Museum of Art. Fig. 2*d*, Galleria, Museo e Madagliere Estense, Modena, Italy; photo by Carlo Orlandini.

[K. PRÜMM]

MYSTERY THEOLOGY

The doctrine proposed by O. *Casel concerning the active presence of Christ's redeeming action in the Sacraments, especially in the Eucharist.

Casel's Theory. In more than 100 articles, letters, and works from 1918 to 1941, Casel never ceased to develop, to clarify, and to defend a doctrine that he deemed adequate to express the teachings of the Fathers and the most ancient liturgies and that he based on the notion of *mysterium*. The most explicit exposition of this doctrine can be found in his work *The Mystery of Christian Worship* (Westminster, Md. 1962; originally published in German in 1932). He says: "The mystery means three things and one. First of all it is God considered in Himself as the infinitely distant, holy, unapproachable, to whom no man may draw near and live. . . . And this all-holy one reveals His mystery, comes down to His creatures and reveals Himself to them; yet once again *in mysterio*, that is to say, in a revelation by grace to those whom He has chosen, the humble, the pure of heart" (5). "For St. Paul μυστήριον is the marvellous revelation of God in Christ. . . . Christ is the mystery in person, because He shows the invisible Godhead in the flesh" (6). "Since Christ is no longer visible among us, in St. Leo the Great's words, 'What was visible in the Lord has passed over into the mysteries.' We meet His person, His saving deeds, the working of His grace in the mysteries of His worship. St. Ambrose writes: 'I find you in your mysteries' " (7). "The content of the mystery of Christ is, therefore, the person of the God-man and His redeeming act for the salvation of the Church; it is through this act that the Church is integrated into the mystery" (12).

It is precisely in the mystery of worship that this integration of the Church in the mystery of Christ takes place. "As a participation in the life and truth of God, this divine reality infinitely surpasses all abstract teaching. It could not be encompassed in a doctrine; it had to find expression in symbols. Cultic symbols, then, are necessary modes of expression; they do not have a purely pedagogical value, but are bearers of divine salvation. Thus the mystery of Christ finds its necessary incarnation in the mystery of worship" ["Glaube, Gnosis und Mysterium," JbLiturgwiss 15 (1941) 276]. "The [cultic] mysteries are a working out and an application of Christ's mystery. God, who revealed Himself in the man Christ, continues after the Ascension of Christ to act on earth through Christ the high priest according to the ordinary economy of communicating grace in the Church, namely, the mystery of worship, which is nothing else but the prolongation of the God-man's action on earth" (*The Mystery of Christian Worship* 27).

Although essentially in conformity with the best tradition explicated in Pius XII's *Mediator Dei* and Vatican Council II's *Constitution on the Sacred Liturgy*, Casel's teaching comprised two elements that in time gave rise to violent controversies. These controversies at least have gradually shown what in Casel's position was of passing value and what represented a permanent theological acquisition.

Pagan Mysteries. Casel placed his teaching against the perspective of the mystery cults of the ancient Hellenic Mediterranean world. He certainly did not claim that the pagan mysteries exercised a direct influence on the organization of Christian worship. He nonetheless insisted that the use of the same terms by both indicated a fundamental analogy, not indeed on the level of objects, but on that of ways of expression. "The language of the ancient mysteries was used unhesitatingly to express to some extent the unfathomable content of what she [the Church] possessed; indeed many ancient forms and customs were taken over to enrich and adorn the simplicity of the Christian ritual" (*The Mystery of Christian Worship* 34).

This aspect of Casel's theory was subjected to lively attack, notably by K. Prümm and J. M. Hanssens, who rejected any influence of pagan mystery terminology in Christian liturgy and believed the Christian use of the term mystery had to be interpreted solely in accordance with its Biblical meaning: a divine secret communicated by revelation. One may say that Casel's theory has been greatly undermined by subsequent research done on the mystery cults. It seems well established that the latter contained no precise doctrine on the participation of the mysteries in the divine life, even less on the intervention of savior-gods. On the contrary, D. Deden and G. Söhngen appear to have solidly proved the continuity of the Christian doctrine of mystery with the Biblical tradition, notably the Pauline texts.

Presence of the Redemptive Act. Casel, however, put the accent on the active reality of the mystery of salvation to the point that the very presence of the saving act becomes reactualized in the liturgy. He based the necessity for this reactualization on the fact—to him indisputable—that tradition understands man's participation in the mystery of salvation as implying and demanding a real but mystical participation in the life and death of Christ. It demands a life and a death of Christ in the very sacramental act; this is how we share in His act of salvation. Some of Casel's expressions seem to imply a reactualization of even the historical aspect of the redemptive act. Despite his lack of precision, his thought was very firm on this point. He did not insist on

such historical contingencies, but his fear of seeing the realism of the mystery-presence reduced, and his inability to use a more conceptual way of thinking prevented him from accepting the approach of other theologians, even of those who were less distant from his own conception than he recognized. However, his disciples, notably V. Warnach and B. Neunheuser, thought they were able to be faithful to him and yet propose explanations with more delicate nuances and more in conformity with classical theological modes of expression.

Controversy and Progress. Both aspects of Casel's doctrine came in for criticism; his harshest critics were J. B. Umberg and K. Prümm, who rejected not only his theory of the Christian mystery's relationship to the pagan mystery cults, but also his conception of the mystery presence.

The traditional character of Casel's doctrine and its conformity with patristic teaching have also been the object of discussions. It can now be considered as established (L. Monden, E. Schillebeeckx, and J. Betz) that the Fathers

> . . . regard sacramental grace as an ontological participation in the glorified existence of Christ by means of a real configuration to the mystery of His passion and death. In particular, they hold the Mass to be the reactualization, the representation (in the etymological sense of the word) of the sacrificial act of Christ on the cross for His Mystical Body. They therefore clearly and indubitably affirm the *fact* of a presence of Christ's death as a saving act in the mystery of Christian worship. Beyond this they do not go. One does not find in their writings a speculatively elaborated theory of the Sacraments; they do not provide any indications as to the *how* of the mystery presence. [Monden 188.]

The compatibility of Casel's doctrine with St. Thomas Aquinas's theology was also discussed. Casel himself did not seem certain that his teaching was in accord with Thomas. G. Söhngen, the first theologian to attempt the integration of a modified Caselian doctrine in the perspective of classical theology, considered Casel's thought at least foreign to Thomas's teaching.

Such was not the opinion of E. Schillebeeckx, who took up and deepened the views of A. Vonier and E. Masure. Because of the hypostatic union, all that Christ's humanity experienced was assumed by the Divine Person whose acts do not suffer the limits of duration. Consequently, the effect of each act will be realized when the Divine Will, eternally actual, determines that it should be realized. It is primarily through the Sacraments and the other mysteries of worship instituted by the Church that the redemptive mystery is brought to us according to the will of Christ. Summarizing Schillebeeckx's thought, J. Gaillard writes (541):

> In the liturgical mysteries we have, at one and the same time, the actual presence of the transcendent element and the virtual presence of the total act (passion, resurrection, etc.) always acting, though its transitory elements belong definitively to the past. The historical salvific act is thus attained by the mysteries, either in itself as far as its permanent element is concerned, or by divine power as far as its purely temporal element is concerned. Liturgical mysteries are truly the celebration and manifestation of the historical redeeming act, even though their actual content is only the *mysterium,* i.e., the permanent element and the instrumental power.

Moreover, the Thomistic teaching on the sacramental character as a participation in the priesthood of Christ ensures "the real foundation for this unity [of the various liturgical mysteries] and therefore occupies a key position in Catholic sacramentalism. Because of the sacramental character, the symbolic worship of the Church becomes a *mysterium;* by this *mysterium* the Sacraments are Christ's own actions in and through the Church" (Schillebeeckx 670).

Bibliography: A complete list of Casel's works (211 nos.) may be found in A. MAYER et al., eds., *Vom christlichen Mysterium* (Düsseldorf 1951). For the study of the various controversies, the essential work remains T. FILTHAUT, *Die Kontroverse über die Mysterienlehre* (Warendorf 1947), Fr. *La Théologie des mystères* (Paris 1955). G. SÖHNGEN, *Symbol und Wirklichkeit im Kultmysterium* (Bonn 1937); *Der Wesensaufbau des Mysteriums* (Bonn 1938). V. WARNACH, "Zum Problem der Mysteriengegenwart," *Liturgisches Leben* 5 (1938) 9–39. B. NEUNHEUSER, "Mysteriengegenwart: Ein Theologumenon inmitten des Gesprächs," ArchLiturgwiss 3 (1953) 104–133; "Ende des Gesprächs um die Mysteriengegenwart?" *ibid.* 4 (1956) 316–324; "Dom Odo Casel and Latest Research," DownRev 76 (1958) 266–273. L. MONDEN, *Het Misoffer als Mysterie* (Roermond 1948). J. BETZ, *Die Eucharistie in der Zeit der griechischen Väter* (Freiburg 1955–61) v.1.1. E. MASURE, *The Sacrifice of the Mystical Body,* tr. A. THOROLD (London 1954). A. VONIER, *A Key to the Doctrine of the Eucharist* (1925; reprint Westminster, Md. 1956). E. H. SCHILLEBEECKX, *De sacramentele heilseconomie* (Antwerp 1952). C. DAVIS, "Dom Odo Casel and the Theology of Mysteries," *Worship* 34 (1960) 428–438; *Liturgy and Doctrine* (New York 1960). D. DEDEN, "Le 'Mystère' paulinien," EphemThLov 13 (1936) 405–442. J. UMBERG, "Mysterien Frömmigkeit?" ZAsz Myst 1 (1926) 351–356; "Die These von der Mysteriengegenwart," ZKathTh 52 (1928) 357–400; "Sacramenta efficiunt quod significant," *ibid.* 54 (1930) 92–105. J. M. HANSSENS, "Estne Liturgia cultus mystericus?" PeriodicaMorCanLiturg 23 (1934) 112–132, 137–160. K. PRÜMM, *Der christliche Glaube und die altheidnische Welt,* 2 v. (Leipzig 1935); *Christentum als Neuheitserlebnis* (Freiburg 1939). J. GAILLARD, "La Théologie des Mystères," RevThom 57 (1957) 510–551.

[I. H. DALMAIS]

MYSTICAL BODY OF CHRIST

The phrase "Body of Christ," as applied to the Church, is both Pauline and patristic, but the adjectival modifier "mystical" is neither. As far as known, the phrase *Mystical* Body is first used to designate the militant Church in Latin theological writings of the second half of the 12th century; and the first official document using it is Boniface VIII's bull *Unam Sanctam* (Nov. 18, 1302, Denz 870–875). From the time of the *Eucharistic controversies in the 9th century until *c.* 1150, the Latin phrase *Corpus mysticum* occurs frequently, but it always means Christ's Eucharistic Body. In this Eucharistic meaning there is at work a profound awareness, chiefly Augustinian in inspiration, of the intimate link between Christ's Eucharistic (i.e., mystical) Body, and His Church Body, often called at this time Christ's true Body (*verum Corpus*). The connection is this: the mystical Eucharistic Body, as a sacramental mystery, both signifies and realizes the "true" or Church–Body of Christ. From *c.* 1150 onward, *Berengarius's errors touching Christ's Eucharistic Presence occasioned by way of reaction such an emphasis on the identity of Christ's Eucharistic Body with His "physical" Body (see Denz 700), that the *Eucharist began to be called Christ's "true" Body (*verum Corpus*); and, by a gradual inversion of the two earlier formulas, Christ's Church-Body began to be called His Mystical Body to distinguish it from His true physical Body present in the Eucharist. At first, the qualifier "mystical," applied to the Church-Body, kept its traditional Eucharistic resonances; the Church-Body is thought of as a "mystically" or sacramentally signified and realized Body. With the passage of time, how-

ever, this Eucharistic sense of the qualifier "mystical" gradually disappeared. In St. Thomas this dissociation of the adjective "mystical" from its Eucharistic context seems already well begun (see ST 3, 8.1 and 8.3); and by the time of the Reformation the Eucharistic connection was wholly lost. For the meaning attached to the term today, see Pius XII's encyclical *Mystici Corporis,* par. 58.

St. Paul. Exegetes are not wholly agreed (1) on the origin and meaning of the Pauline theme "Body of Christ"; (2) on the relation between 1 Corinthians and Romans, where the theme occurs only occasionally, and the later captivity epistles (Colossians, Ephesians), where the theme is central and combined with the new themes of "Head" and "plenitude."

Origin of Theme. Although some exegetes see its origin in the popular Stoic commonplace likening the cosmos or the state to an organism (see 1 Cor 12.12–30; Rom 12.4–5), while others prefer to appeal to the Gnostic myth-motif of the Primal Heavenly Man, still it remains most probable that the primary source of the Pauline Body of Christ theme is to be found within the resources of Christian revelation and life, and within the framework of Judaic habits of thought and of expression. This last view is set forth here.

In his presentation of *salvation history St. Paul sees Christ as the countertype of *Adam. Just as "the first man, Adam" (1 Cor 15.45) was the head of mankind in its catastrophic fall, so Christ, "the last Adam, became a life-giving spirit" (*ibid.*) to the new mankind, restored according to "the likeness of the heavenly man" (1 Cor 15.49; see Rom 8.29). See in general 1 Cor 15.20–28; 45–49; Rom 5.12–21. Because Christ, risen and glorified after the victory in His own Body-Person over sin, death, and hell, is "the beginning" (Col 1.18; 1 Cor 15.20, 23), i.e., not merely a fresh start in time, but a total fontal beginning of new life, He is the Head of the new humanity in whom all live anew.

In this Adam-Christ parallel St. Paul is using a Hebraic category of thought, namely, the so-called "corporate or inclusive personality." To the Hebraic mind the father-head of a family or nation is looked on as fulfilling a real-representative role compassing and including all his issue; he acts in their name and stead and holds their destiny in his own person and work. His descendants in turn are their forefather, in the sense that his destiny unfolds itself in their lives. This way of thinking history enabled the Hebrew to pass in thought and language from the One to the Many in him, and vice versa. Such inclusiveness, when applied to Christ's Person and work, supposes His oneness with man's flesh and blood, but is grounded primarily in His mission, held from His Father, to be the Man who is the beginning of the new age and the new creation; whose saving acts, once done in history's center, have meaning and make destiny for the Many compassed in His Body-Person; and whose Spirit-filled Manhood is now in glory qualified to invest sacramentally the Many, as they appear in the unfolding of time, with the new life which is His once and forever.

To appreciate the realism of St. Paul's *soteriology, one must recognize how forcefully he stresses the role of the Man Jesus in salvation history (see Rom 5.15; 1 Cor 15.21; 15.47; 1 Tm 2.5). To St. Paul *salvation in Christ is neither Greek nor Gnostic in aiming at any final emancipation from the body; rather it presses for the integral renewal of the old man in his totality. This is possible only through union with the Man Jesus and with His saving work, wrought in His Body-Person; this is possible only through a sharing in His passage from His lowly Body of death, wholly like (sin apart) man's own natural style of existence, to His new Body of life in glory. In Christ's own life the Body of sin and death, which He took on Himself at His Father's behest, was broken in death (see Rom 8.3), and in a critical reversal of the old world's momentum this same Body, now "spiritual" and "life-giving" (1 Cor 15.44–58) is dowered with all the newness of life through the Spirit (Rom 1.4). To be saved one must share in His way and level of life; one must be wholly conformed to "the body of his glory" (Phil 3.21; see 2 Cor 3.18); one must "bear the likeness of the heavenly man" (1 Cor 15.49). The Body of Jesus, the living Body-Person, has then the decisive role in the work of man's salvation; and it is into that Body, passing and passed from death to glorious life, that Christians are baptized (see Rom 6.3–11; Gal 3.27; 1 Cor 1.13–15) in a union the reality of which belongs to a new final order that in this present world is still hidden (Col 3.3) and only beginning. By Baptism in faith the whole Christian man, himself a body-person, begins his sharing in the new life of the Man Jesus, and this sacramental union, inaugurated in Baptism and consummated in the Eucharist, tends right from the start, even in this world, toward the "spiritual body" that will transform man's "natural body" (1 Cor 15.44; see Rom 6.8; 8.11).

The Pauline theme of the Body of Christ has thus primarily a soteriological provenience and meaning. It always involves a reference to the individual Body of Christ, i.e., to Him who has borne death up in His own Body onto the cross, and who enters into heaven to become the bearer of new life in His glorious Body. The mode of this most unique of unions by which the glorious Christ compasses in Himself all Christians as His members, is something St. Paul is not much concerned with. What he does stress is: (1) the tremendous reality and intimacy of this inward-outward union, without prejudice to the distinct personalities, Christ's and man's; (2) the prime ground of the union in the dead and risen Savior, the Man Jesus (see Col 2.17); (3) the wholeness of the term of the union, i.e., the individual member is a body-person; and (4) the many members who are Body together, or "fellow members of the same body" (Eph 3.6).

Relation of Great Epistles to Captivity Epistles. The main lines of the development of the theme in Romans and 1 Corinthians (1 Cor 6.12–20; 10.17; 12.12–30; Rom 12.4–5) are substantially continued in the later captivity epistles (Col 2.11–13, compared with 1.22; 3.9–11; Eph 2.14–16; 4.4–6). However, the latter combine new traits with the earlier Body of Christ theme, thus enriching it with a fusion of new elements. The new emphases are the following: (1) the Body is now personified and practically identified with the universal Church; (2) the glorified Christ appears as the Head of the Church-Body and is thus clearly distinguished from it; and (3) the Body theme is associated with a more cosmic dimension of salvation, a development that is manifested by its linkage with the term "plenitude." Body of Christ now designates the object of Christ's redemptive love; He is the "savior of the body" (Eph 5.23), of which Christians are "the mem-

bers" (5.30). This Body is a living organism, hierarchically structured, which holds together all Christians and which "attains a growth which is of God" (Col 2.19; see Eph 4.16). This Body is "the Church" (Col 1.18, 24; Eph 1.22–23; 5.23–33); Christians are its "members" (Eph 4.25); and Christ is its "Head" (Col 1.18; 2.19; Eph 1.22; 4.15–16; 5.23). Lastly, this Body is associated with the theme of "plenitude" (Col 1.18–2.3; 2.9; Eph 1.23; 4.13–16).

In the Head-Body combination, the term Head is used in a twofold metaphorical sense: (1) superior authority or leader (Col 1.18; Eph 1.22; 5.23); (2) source of the energies of life and growth (Col 2.19; Eph 4.15–16). The origin of this thematic combination is not easy to discern. However, the term Head, meaning superior authority, is a Biblical metaphor, which St. Paul applies to Christ, apart from the Body theme, first in 1 Cor 11.3, and then later in Col 2.10. In the latter case St. Paul calls Christ the Head of the cosmic "Powers," thus countering certain false speculations, current at Colossae, that placed Christ on a level with these "Powers." Once Christ is thus thought of as Head in this sense, the metaphor could be conveniently combined with the Body theme, with Christ becoming the authoritative Head, the glorious Lord, ruling His Body the Church. The Head-Body combination once thus made, could admit a further metaphorical coloration with the use of the term Head to signify the vital principle of nurture and of growth in a living body, a usage which St. Paul could have taken over from his Hellenistic milieu, especially from the Stoics or from contemporary medical language.

The splendid passage in Eph 5.22–32 is a synthesis of all the ideas on the Church as Body and Christ as Head, with the exception of the Head understood as principle of the Body's life and growth.

Members of the Body. For St. Paul only the baptized faithful are members of the Body. He emphasizes the charismatic diversity in unity of the various members of Christ's Body in His one Spirit (1 Cor 12; Rom 12.3–8). The faithful are "fellow-members of the same body" (Eph 3.6), not in despite of their differing *charisms, but because of them. The members' various gifts (see 1 Cor 12.7) are meant to conspire under the one Spirit, their author and mover (1 Cor 12.7–11; see Eph 4.7), to serve and adorn the whole Body (Rom 12.3–8; 1 Cor 12.7; 14.12, 26). This unity in diversity is a permanent characteristic of the structure and life of Christ's Body (1 Cor 12; Rom 12.3–8).

Spirit and Body. That Christ's Body is intimately joined to the Spirit is clear from the way St. Paul coordinates "one body and one Spirit" (Eph 4.4; see Eph 2.16.18). The Spirit that is the life principle of the new economy is the Spirit who quickens the Body of the risen Christ, and through Him, the Christian (1 Cor 15.44–49; see 1 Cor 6.17). The Spirit of Christ (Rom 8.9; Gal 4.6; Phil 1.19; see 2 Cor 3.17) is the inward life-giving principle, sovereignly building up and forming the Church as the living Body of Christ (1 Cor 12.3–11, 13). The Spirit is given in Baptism (1 Cor 6.11; Ti 3.5).

Fathers. The *mystery of the Church as Christ's Body found congenial expression in the Fathers (notably Origen, Hilary, Athanasius, Chrysostom, Cyril of Alexandria, and Augustine), although often they treat it less in itself than in the elaboration of other doctrinal themes, e.g., the *Incarnation, the *Redemption, the divinization of the Christian, and the Eucharist. Here only certain general patristic orientations will be indicated.

(1) St. Ignatius of Antioch touched the heart of this mystery when he urged the faithful of the Church of Magnesia to "a union both according to the flesh and according to the spirit" (*To the Magnesians*, 1.2; see *To the Smyrnaeans*, 12.2). The key patristic belief that Ignatius expresses here is this: that the empiric Church-Body that the Fathers knew so well as churchmen and as faithful is Christ's Spirit-quickened Body; that the great mystery that the Father had in mind since eternity is now being realized, with a beginning finality, in the continuing work of Christ in His Body, the present Church. In the early Church "the appeal to the Church's holiness was born of the fact that men took the visible Church seriously" (J. Ratzinger, *Volk und Haus Gottes in Augustins Lehre von der Kirche,* München 1954, 65). The grace of the new economy is profoundly incarnational, an embodied grace, because the Church's "beginning and first-fruits is the flesh of Christ" (Augustine, *In epist. Ioh.* 2.2, PL 35:1990). The principle that the Fathers used in their reflections on the mystery of the visible Church is "the sacramental principle, which marks the necessary union between the visible sign and the hidden reality, . . . a principle as dear to the West as to the East" (J. Daniélou, "Μία Ἐκκλησία chez les Pères grecs des premiers siècles," in *1054–1954: L'Église et les Églises,* Chevetogne 1954, 1.139).

(2) A second patristic constant is this: "the great and glorious Body of Christ" (Irenaeus, *Adv. Haer.* 4.33.7, PG 7:1076) is the one sphere of Christ's Spirit ever "realizing the will of the Father in men and renewing them from their old way into the newness of Christ" (*ibid.* 3.17.1, PG 7:929). "For," says Paul, "God has established in the Church Apostles, prophets, teachers, —and all the other effects of the Spirit's working, in which those who do not come together in the Church, have no share. . . . Where the Church is, there is the Spirit of God; and where the Spirit of God is, there is the Church and all grace. And the Spirit is truth. Wherefore those who have no share in the Spirit . . . do not drink of the shining water flowing from the Body of Christ . . . ." (*ibid.* 3.24.1, PG 7:966). It is to "Christ's own Spirit" (Cyril of Alexandria, *In Ioh. Evang.* 17. 20–21, PG 74:561) that is primarily due the varied and total inward-outward life of Christ's Body, in which each member has his proper energies and role suiting him to serve the interplay of faith and hope and love in the communion of the saints; it is to the Spirit likewise that is due the Body's splendid holiness. These patristic convictions are condensed in an Augustinian formula still current: "What the soul is to the body of a man, that the Holy Spirit is to Christ's Body which is the Church" (*Serm.* 267.4, PL 38:1231). Indeed these patristic affirmations were so urgent and so massive that they opened up genuine problems. Faced with certain heterodox puritan movements such as *Montanism and *Donatism, the Fathers were challenged to save not merely the appearances, but the reality of the "Una Sancta," the One Holy Body of Christ. Among the troublesome problems that they thus had to grapple with were these: (a) how is the grave sinner, especially a heresiarch, to be thought of as having place and role within the glorious Body of Christ; (b) in what measure is the Spirit, with His grace, at work outside the Church's frontiers, particularly in the Sacraments of the schismatic and heretic?

(3) Another significant orientation is the indissoluble association that the Fathers proclaimed between Christ's Eucharistic Body and His Church-Body, with the Eucharist being the supreme symbol and the chief realization of the inward-outward unity of the Church-Body. To the Fathers it was unthinkable to accord the Eucharist a kind of independent treatment apart from its chief effect, which is the in- and con-corporation of Christ's members in His one Body. To partake of the Eucharist meant to be embodied into the Church. Communion in the sacred "things" or elements of the Eucharist (*communio sanctorum* in the real-sacramental sense) meant communion with Christ and with the saints who are His members (*communio sanctorum* in the masculine-personal sense). For St. Augustine, writes Ratzinger, "what makes the essence of the concrete Church is this: that she celebrates and is the Body of Christ" ("Herkunft und Sinn der Civitas-Lehre Augustins," in *Augustinus Magister,* Paris 1954, 2.978). Augustine, who here, as elsewhere, dominates the whole development of medieval *ecclesiology, says: "If then you are the Body of Christ and His members, your mystery is laid on the Lord's table; you are receiving your own mystery. . . . Be what you see, and receive what you are" (*Serm.* 272, PL 38:1247–48).

(4) One last patristic orientation. At times some Fathers give the term "Body of Christ" a meaning and an extension different from that of St. Paul, to whom Christ's Body is a visible Body, sacramentally and hierarchically structured, and composed of baptized Christians as its members. St. Augustine, e.g., more than once makes the Body of Christ comprehend all the saints "who are to be born and to believe in Christ from Abel himself until the end of time" (*In Psalm. 90 serm.* 2.1, PL 37:1159). The Church-Body thus understood as reaching out and comprising in a solidarity of Christian faith all the saints of both covenants, old and new, is a theological construct, due mainly to the Latin Fathers. St. Augustine and St. Gregory the Great were deeply influential in impressing this development on later Western ecclesiology.

Although the Fathers found it useful to express in this way the continuing unity of the whole historical economy of salvation, nevertheless they had a deep sense of the newness and originality of Christianity and were quite aware that the Church of the OT was but an imperfect, preparatory stage, a kind of childhood minority with respect to the adult Church of the NT. But in their effort to stress the overall economy of salvation in the one Christ, what held their attention, at least from St. Augustine onward, was rather the invisible line of inward Christian grace; whereas the continuing embodiment, itself a grace, of that same inward grace in both the OT and the NT, was much less satisfactorily integrated into a balanced synthesis. This orientation tended to view the mystery of salvation from a metahistorical and an asocial plane. In affirming that the OT saints, by their faith in the Christ to come, were really Christians and members of His Body, St. Augustine explained that "the times have changed, but not the faith . . . ; the signs have varied, but the faith abides" (*In evang. Ioh.* 45.9, PL 35:1722, 1723). This Augustinian orientation occasioned in subsequent Western theology a bias toward an un-Pauline disembodiment of Christ's Body, toward a one-sided view of Christ's Body as an interior community of grace with Christ, whose headship is thus limited to an invisible inpouring of grace. The question left unanswered is this: what has the fullness of the times (Heb 1.1–2) brought to the fullness of the mystery; and wherein lies the fulfillment within the acknowledged continuity (Col 2.17)?

Medieval Period. St. Augustine's authority dominates the ecclesiology of the early and high scholastic periods. As in the patristic age, so too here there are no formal treatises of ecclesiology. The pertinent matter is distributed piecemeal, not only in the various questions of the summulists (*see* SENTENCES AND SUMMAE), but also in liturgical, homiletic, and exegetical writings.

In the 12th century the dominant description of the Church is the Body of Christ. This designation, although allowing a variety of meaning and extension as in the Fathers, still has its central reference and focus in the visible Catholic Church. However, the elaboration of the theme "Body of Christ" commonly emphasizes the inward community of grace in Christ, without any special effort to integrate the sociojuridic aspect of the Church into the Body of Christ. Such a one-sided concern marks an inchoative dissociation of sensibility and interest with respect to the total mystery, i.e., the theandric reality of the Body of Christ. The reasons of this practical dissociation are the following: (1) the patronage of the Augustinian tradition in ecclesiology; (2) the then visible Church as a reality, peacefully forming and framing life, unchallenged by any significant heresies; (3) the beginnings of Canon Law as a separate discipline, with sociojuridic questions in ecclesiology falling gradually to its purview, while the more inward elements of the Church were appropriated to speculative dogma.

The 13th century does not fundamentally alter the orientations and emphases of the 12th. The scholastics of this period, beyond doubt, had a sound sense of the theandric nature of the Body of Christ (see, e.g., St. Thomas, ST 1a2ae, 108.1; 3a, 60.6; 3a, 62.6). This fact is discernible, for instance, in the physico-instrumental causality assigned by St. Thomas to Christ the Head in His humanity (ST 3a, 8.1 ad 1), a role that Augustine never attributed to the Man Jesus (see G. Philips, "L'influence du Christ Chef sur son corps mystique suivant s. Augustin," in *Augustinus Magister,* Paris 1954, 2.805–815); it is perceptible, too, in the strongly affirmed ecclesial dimension of the Eucharist, which is "the Sacrament of Church unity" (St. Thomas, ST 3a, 67.2), and whose reality is "the unity of the Mystical Body" (ST 3a, 73.3), or "the Mystical Body of Christ which is the society of the saints" (ST 3a, 80.4).

It is clear enough, however, that in practice the 13th-century theologians were more interested in the inward grace of the Christian Body than in the Christian embodiment, itself a grace, of that inward grace. What commanded their attention was the inwardness of grace. This fact is discernible in various ways:

1. In the Augustinian view that "the ancient Fathers belonged to the same Body of the Church as we do" (St. Thomas, ST 3a, 8.3 ad 3). Citing the Aristotelean dictum that "each thing appears to be that which preponderates in it" (ST 1a2ae, 106.1), and rightly holding that "the grace of the Holy Spirit" (*ibid.*) is the chief element in the New Covenant, St. Thomas concludes that the saints of the Old Covenant "in this respect belonged to the

New Testament" (*ibid.,* ad 3). This theological construct uses "Body" in a quite un-Pauline way.

2. In the treatment of Christ's Headship—and of the correlative membership or incorporation of the faithful—principally from the viewpoint of the Head's invisible inpouring of interior grace (St. Thomas, ST 3a, 8.3 corp. and ad 3) and of the member's inward adhesion to the Head through faith and love.

3. In the tendency to look on the heavenly Church in a way analogous to the Augustinian consideration of the Church of the New Alliance, i.e., to attend to what is "principal" in it, namely, the soul's vision of the Triune God, without a firm enough evangelical emphasis on what is "secondary," i.e., the whole man, according to the Biblical anthropology, gloriously sharing in his risen body in the new life with his fellows (see St. Thomas, *In 3 Sent.* 26.2.5, sols. 1–2 compared with ST 1a2ae, 106.1 corp. and ad 1; 1a2ae, 107.1 ad 3).

14th to the 19th Century. The 14th and 15th centuries mark the beginnings of a separate treatise on the Church, often the work of canonists and arising chiefly under the sign of controversy. The 16th-century Reformers, with their liquefaction of the Church as the social sign and bearer of salvation, and with their radical dissociation of any empirical Church from the true Church of the saints or the predestined, led the Catholic controversialists to counter by stressing the visible Church as the social means of salvation and by de-emphasizing some of the older Augustinian themes judged less useful to mark the visible reality of the NT Church. *Bellarmine, e.g., distinguishing between the "body" and the "soul" of the Church, and between the various ways of pertaining to them, singly and jointly, (see *De Eccl. Mil.,* ch. 2), gives a value to the element "body" in which, at the rare extreme, the visible elements, i.e., "the external profession of the faith and sharing in the sacraments" (*ibid.*), seem to acquire almost a consistency by themselves. The Church, which is "a society, not of angels, nor of souls, but of men" (*ibid.* ch. 12), has for "its form, not interior faith, . . . but exterior, i.e., the confession of faith" (*ibid.* ch. 10). In this Bellarminian emphasis, which admittedly considers only very extreme cases, the meaning of "body" becomes almost the opposite of what that term so often stressed in the medieval scholastics, i.e., the inward grace-filled company of the Christian saints. At the same time the older Augustinian ecclesiology continued its way unflaggingly, chiefly in more speculative theological writing.

It is symptomatic that neither orientation was very successful with the theological problem of the grave sinner's place in Christ's Body; and that often the solution, phrased in embarrassed language, resulted in a partial dissociation of the visible Church and the Mystical Body.

19th Century. J. A. *Möhler (1796–1838) contributed decisively to a recentering of the theology of the Mystical Body, much more truly in his *Symbolik* (5th ed. 1838) than in his earlier brilliant but one-sided essay, *Die Einheit in der Kirche* (1825). In *Die Einheit* Möhler romantically describes the Body of the Church as "the concentration of love" (no. 64), thus assigning a dynamism to grace that is inward-outward in its orientation; "the whole social structure of the Church is nothing else but the embodied love" (*ibid.*) of the community of the faithful, itself fashioned by the Spirit of the Lord. In *Symbolik,* however, Möhler resolutely makes the redemptive Incarnation the guiding principle of his ecclesiology. The visible Body of the Church is presented as a theandric mystery, patterned on Christ as its paradigm (*see* THEANDRIC ACTS OF CHRIST), and charged with continuing His work and His way among men until He come. Möhler thus establishes a fruitful and harmonious interplay of life between the Church as the bearer of salvation and the Church as the company of the saints; under both aspects—that of the saving energies of Christian grace and that of the new life of salvation in Christian grace—the Church is an embodied grace, both sacramental and social.

Möhler's sounder orientations were usefully elaborated by several theologians who in one way or another underwent his influence and who had a metempiric affinity of spirit with him. They are Carlo *Passaglia (1812–87), Klemens *Schrader (1820–75), J. B. *Franzelin (1816–86), and the celebrated M. J. *Scheeben (1835–88). The work of the first three of these, although today not well known, was solid and influential.

Church Documents. According to the Church's ordinary teaching, the Mystical Body on earth is identical with the Roman Catholic Church. For pertinent documentation, especially papal, see S. Tromp, v. 1; Denz (31st ed.) 2319; and the letter of the Holy Office *Suprema Haec,* Aug. 8, 1949 [see AmEcclRev 127 (1952) 307–311].

In the Mystical Body there are associated in an indissoluble alliance of mission Christ's Spirit and Christ's Apostles, serving together, each in their vastly different ways, the one sovereignly, the other ministerially, the continuing work of Christ's redemptive love, and thus forming and sustaining the visible company of Christ's saints on earth. Within the one Body, embodying both the saving energies of Christ's gracious mission and the new life of those saved by Christ's grace, there is a mutual interpresence and interplay of life between the Church as the society that saves and the Church as the community of the saints.

Among more recent documents stressing this orientation see Leo XIII, *Satis cognitum,* June 29, 1896 (Act SSed 28:708–739); *Divinum illud munus,* May 9, 1897 (ActSSed 29:644–658); and Pius XI, *Mortalium animos,* Jan. 6, 1928 (ActApS 20:5–16).

For the present status of the doctrine, see Pius XII, *Mystici Corporis,* June 29, 1943 (ActApS 35:193–248); and Vatican II, *Constitutio Dogmatica de Ecclesia, Lumen Gentium* 7–8.

Theological Questions. Among many questions engaging theological reflection are the following:

1. The eschatology of the Mystical Body, both as a Body and as a whole.
2. The grades of membership in Christ's Body on earth, with membership understood as an inwardoutward grace, i.e., as a participation in the grace of the Body. The problem of grave sinners (*see* MEMBERSHIP IN THE CHURCH).
3. Is the role of the Spirit more than an appropriated one? Is there need to postulate a created soul?
4. The best way to describe the unity between Head and Body, without exaggerating or attenuating its

realism, and without slighting the fact that it is a union between persons and an incarnational union, i.e., an inward-outward, sacramental and social union.

See also SOCIETY (IN THEOLOGY); ABIDING IN CHRIST; BROTHER IN CHRIST; INCORPORATION IN CHRIST; SOUL OF THE CHURCH; COMMUNION OF SAINTS; OFFICE, ECCLESIASTICAL; PAUL, APOSTLE, ST.; CHURCH, ARTICLES ON.

Bibliography: P. BENOIT, "Corps, tête et plérôme dans les épîtres de la captivité," RevBibl 63 (1956) 5–44. L. CERFAUX, *The Church in the Theology of St. Paul,* tr. G. WEBB and A. WALKER (New York 1959). J. A. T. ROBINSON, *The Body: A Study in Pauline Theology* (London 1952). F. MALMBERG, *Ein Leib - Ein Geist* (Freiburg 1960). S. TROMP, *Corpus Christi quod est ecclesia,* 3 v.; v.1 (*Introductio generalis*) *The Body of Christ Which is the Church,* tr. A. CONDIT (New York 1960) v.2 *De Christo capite mystici corporis* (Rome 1960) v.3 *De spiritu Christi anima* (Rome 1960). H. DE LUBAC, *Corpus Mysticum: L'Eucharistie et l'église au moyen-âge* (2d ed. Paris 1949). M. SCHMAUS, *Die Lehre von der Kirche,* v.3.1 of *Katholische Dogmatik* (5th ed. Munich 1955–58). É. MERSCH, *The Whole Christ,* tr. J. R. KELLEY (Milwaukee 1938; London 1949). H. SCHLIER and J. RATZINGER, LexThK² 6:907–912.

[F. X. LAWLOR]

MYSTICAL MARRIAGE

Mystical marriage or spiritual marriage (also espousal to Christ) is a figure used to denote the state of a human soul living intimately united to God through grace and love. In a broad sense, mystical marriage is applicable to all unions of souls loved by God and drawn to Him, as in the case of virgins solemnly consecrated, religious in vows, and all other souls espoused to Christ (2 Cor 11.2). More properly, and in a more restricted sense, mystical marriage refers to what is recognized in mystical theology as "trans-

"The Mystical Marriage of Saint Catherine," an early impression by the 14th-century artist Barna da Siena.

forming" union between a soul and God, requiring extraordinary graces, and to which God calls only a few particularly privileged persons, e.g., SS. John of the Cross and Teresa of Avila. The latter (*Interior Castle*, 7 Mansions, ch. 2) and the former (*Spir. Cant.*, stanzas 12–27) recognize the "transforming" (permanent) union as distinct from and higher than mere spiritual bethrothal (transitory). Mystical marriage constitutes a consummate union of love; a total possession, a fusion of "lives"—the soul is made one with God, made divine, by participation, without losing its identity. It is a total union involving the transformation of the substance of the soul by sanctifying grace, and the transformation of the faculties by divine light and love (*Ascent of Mt. Carmel* 2, 5, 6). The initiative in this matter and the choice of souls to whom this union is granted belong to Christ. It is permeated with His transcendence; its action and effects are of the Holy Spirit. Though this union is not of its own will, the soul "adheres to Christ with all its strength; lives for Him; allows itself to be ruled by Him," according to St. Bernard of Clairvaux (*In Cant. Serm.* 85, 12).

It is a union that comprises the elements of a certain continuous awareness of the presence of the Divine Spouse; a consciousness of His assistance in the higher operation of intellect and will. These and other characteristics notwithstanding, we find St. Teresa admitting that she did not know with what to compare it—since it is so sublime a favor and brings the soul such great delight (7 Mansions).

The model of mystical marriage is the union of the Humanity of Christ with the Verbum—a union perfect in charity and absolute in continuity. Mary, the Bride of Christ par excellence, is its greatest exemplar in this life.

The figure of marriage significantly portrays that intimate union of a completely dedicated soul (bride) to Christ (Bridegroom). Its basis is found in Holy Scripture, e.g., marriage was a common image of the union of Jahweh and His people Israel (Os 2.19). It was a figure familiar to the Fathers of the Church. St. Ambrose referred to consecrated virgins as "married to God" (*De Virg.*, I, c.8, n.52). Jesus called Himself the "Bridegroom" (Mt 9.15); and St. Paul writes: "For I betrothed you to one spouse" [Christ] (2 Cor 11.2).

Mystical marriage is always related to the mystery of Redemption, which was accomplished objectively through the Redeemer, Christ the Bridegroom; and is realized subjectively in the soul-bride, through Baptism and sanctification. Redemption enters into the very essence of mystical marriage; it gives it a salvific value. In this life, it bestows upon the soul in "transforming" union, a "taste" of the joy of consummated love with her Divine Bridegroom in the Beatific Vision (Ap 21.2).

Bibliography: DictSpirAscMyst 2.2:1643–2193. P. LEJEUNE, DTC 2.2:1616–31. TERESA OF ÁVILA, *Obras completas*, new rev. ed. E. DE LA MADRE DE DIOS, 3 v. (BiblAutCrist 74,120, 189; 51–59) v. 2; *Complete Works*, ed. SILVERIO DE SANTA TERESA and E. A. PEERS, 3 v. (New York 1946) v. 2, "Interior Castle." JOHN OF THE CROSS, *Complete Works*, ed. SILVERIO DE SANTA TERESA and E. A. PEERS, 3 v. (Westminster, Md. 1963) "Ascent of Mount Carmel" and "A Spiritual Canticle of the Soul." J. J. MCMAHON, *The Divine Union in the Subida del monte Carmelo and the Noche oscura of Saint John of the Cross* (Washington 1941). BERNARD OF CLAIRVAUX, *Opera*, ed. J. LECLERCQ (Rome 1957–   ) 2 v. to date. C. MARMION, *Sponsa Verbi: The Virgin Consecrated to Christ*, tr. F. IZARD (St. Louis 1925). P. KETTER, *Christ and Womankind*, tr. I. MCHUGH (2d ed. rev. and enl; Westminster, Md. 1952). **Illustration credit:** Museum of Fine Arts, Boston.

[A. A. BIALAS]

MYSTICAL PHENOMENA

In popular usage, the term mystical phenomena is sometimes used to embrace all those unusual and mysterious phenomena that surpass the known, normal powers of the human soul and imply the operation of some being superior to the soul or of some unfamiliar factor within the human soul. So understood, the subject would belong to the field of parapsychology, which investigates phenomena of this kind in religion and mysticism, spiritualism, occultism, diabolism, psychology, physiology, physics, and chemistry (Omez, 11–17).

In Christian spirituality, however, the term is taken in a stricter sense and includes only: (1) those internal and external manifestations that ordinarily proceed from the authentic mystical activity of a soul (concomitant mystical phenomena); and (2) the extraordinary graces, charisms, or miracles that sometimes accompany mystical activity but are not essentially related to mystical operations as such (charismatic mystical phenomena). Concomitant mystical phenomena are called ordinary mystical phenomena and are supernatural *quoad substantiam;* charismatic mystical phenomena are called extraordinary and are supernatural *quoad modum* [R. Garrigou-Lagrange, *Christian Perfection and Contemplation* (St. Louis 1937) 235–238].

From the point of view of Christian spirituality an authentic mystical contemplation of the purely natural order is a contradiction in terms, and an intimate experience of God can occur only through grace (J. Maritain, *Les Degrés du savoir*, 4th French ed., 534). However it would seem that an authentic mystical experience and the concomitant phenomena are possible among non-Christians who possess a high degree of sanctifying grace and sufficient intensity of charity. Moreover, it is possible that certain persons, psychologically so gifted, may enjoy a profound awareness of God that although less intense than authentic mystical experience, is yet beyond the religious experience of the average believer. Into this latter category would fall numerous Buddhist, Hindu, and other non-Christian "mystics" whose experiences are tentatively explained by some parapsychologists as a *psi*-function of the human soul [Omez, 20–26; H. Brémond, *Prière et Poesie* (Paris 1926); A. Wiesenger, 3–96].

The present treatment of mystical phenomena is restricted to those manifestations that ordinarily proceed from authentic mystical activity (concomitant mystical phenomena) and those extraordinary psychosomatic manifestations that sometimes occur in authentic mystics (charismatic mystical phenomena).

Concomitant Mystical Phenomena. The concomitant phenomena vary with the degree of intensity of mystical activity and serve as an indication of the soul's progress in the mystical life, although each soul does not necessarily experience all the concomitant phenomena or even all the phenomena proper to a given stage, for mystical activity is the work of God, who can lead souls as He will. Moreover, mystical activity is possible in the life of a person who is not in the mystical state. Theologians commonly agree that mystical activity is essentially an experience of God, more or less intensely felt through the operation of the gifts of the Holy Ghost; and since the gifts themselves pertain to the supernatural organism of the spiritual life, whatever proceeds from the activity of the gifts should be classified as concomitant and ordinary phenomena.

The division of concomitant mystical phenomena given by St. Teresa of Avila (cf. *Interior Castle,* 4th–7th Mansions) has been adopted by most theologians since her time. She lists the mystical phenomena in connection with the various grades of mystical prayer, and the same approach is used by St. John of the Cross and St. Francis de Sales (cf. *Treatise on the Love of God* ch. 6–7). [For the mystical activity of the active life, see John of St. Thomas, *The Gifts of the Holy Ghost* (New York 1951); G. G. Carluccio, *The Seven Steps to Spiritual Perfection* (Ottawa, Canada 1949); J. Maritain, *Prayer and Intelligence* (London 1928).]

The following are the principal and concomitant mystical phenomena, from the beginning to the end of the mystical state:

1. An intuition of God or divine things, as distinct from discursive knowledge, with a profound penetration of divine mysteries.
2. An experimental or quasi-experimental knowledge of God or divine things. This is the essential phenomenon of the mystical life and is usually accompanied by spiritual joy, interior absorption in God, disdain for wordly pleasures, and a desire for greater perfection (cf. Poulain, 2, 5–6; Arintero, 2, 3).
3. Passive purification of the senses, which presupposes the active purgations of senses and spirit (*see* PURIFICATION, SPIRITUAL).
4. Continued awareness of the presence of God, accompanied by "sleep" or suspension of the faculties, filial fear of God, love of suffering, divine touches, spiritual sensations, flights of the spirit leading to ecstasy, wounds of love, and interior communications (see St. Teresa, *Interior Castle* 5th–6th Mansions; Arintero, 2:4, 7).
5. Passive purgation of the spirit (see St. John of the Cross, *Dark Night;* Arintero, 2:184–204).
6. Total death to self, heroism in the practice of virtue, joy in persecution, zeal for the salvation of souls, and relative confirmation in grace.

Charismatic Mystical Phenomena. Extraordinary mystical phenomena do not occur in the normal development of the spiritual life, but proceed from a supernatural cause distinct from sanctifying grace, the virtues, and the gifts of the Holy Ghost. Therefore they are classified as charisms (*gratiae gratis datae*) and since charisms neither presuppose grace in the soul of the individual nor flow from sanctifying grace, they are no proof of the sanctity of the individual. Some charisms are true miracles; others are supernatural in cause but do not necessarily surpass the powers of created nature and thus are called "epiphenomena" of the mystical life and are "paranormal" in relation to mystical activity (cf. the charisms listed in 1 Cor 12.4, which pertain to the apostolate).

Considered exclusively as paranormal, extraordinary phenomena could be attributed to one of three possible causes: God, occult natural powers, or diabolical influence. Hence the rule established by Pope Benedict XIV in *De Beatificatione et Canonizatione Servorum Dei:* No phenomenon is to be attributed to a supernatural power until all possible natural or diabolical explanation has been investigated and excluded. The difficulty involved in discerning the cause of paranormal mystical phenomena is that the psychosomatic structure can react to stimuli in a limited number of ways. Sometimes the same psychic or bodily reaction will occur in a seizure of hysteria as in a true mystical ecstasy (e.g., visions, locutions, or revelations). In many instances the most that can be concluded is that a phenomenon could have proceeded from God, from some occult natural power, or from a diabolic influence. In view of the foregoing, the following statements serve as rules of discernment concerning paranormal phenomena:

1. No extraordinary phenomenon may be attributed to a supernatural, i.e., divine, cause as long as a natural or diabolical explanation is possible.
2. The extraordinary phenomenon is not of itself an indication of the sanctity of the individual, for God could grant charisms to a person in mortal sin and even work miracles through such persons.
3. Normally it would be temerarious to petition God for charisms or miracles, since none of these phenomena flow from sanctifying grace, the virtues, and the gifts of the Holy Ghost; and privileges of this kind could in fact be damaging to the spiritual life of an individual.
4. No extraordinary phenomenon is necessary for the attainment of sanctity.
5. The extraordinary phenomena, when they come from God, are generally classified as *gratiae gratis datae,* and are primarily for the good of the faithful and not for the one who receives them, although accidentally the individual may benefit from them.
6. Because of the impossibility of identifying the cause of some of the extraordinary phenomena, the investigator should consider primarily the effects of the phenomena on the life of the individual who has experienced them. (For the signs of the spirit of God, the diabolic spirit, and the human spirit see Arintero, 2:7; Royo-Aumann, 28.)

Is it possible that a person could be subject to the influence of several of these spirits at the same time? Or in other words, could a true mystic be subject to diabolical influence at the same time that he is acting under the impulses of the gift of the Holy Ghost? Or is it possible for a person to be acted upon by a gift of the Holy Ghost (a truly mystical operation) and at the same time suffer from a pathological mental or organic condition? The answer to these questions can best be stated in a series of conclusions:

1. Any deliberately willed phenomenon that involves a defect in any virtue is incompatible with the perfection of charity that constitutes Christian perfection and sanctity.
2. Any phenomenon that flows from the weakness of the individual or from any other cause that is not deliberately willed may coexist with mystical phenomena, so that a genuine mystic may exhibit truly neurotic or psychotic symptoms.
3. It is possible that a true mystic may, with God's permission, be given over to the influence and power of the devil (diabolical obsession).

4. Any person, even one in mortal sin, could be the recipient of any of the *gratiae gratis datae* or be the instrument of God in working a miracle.

Since grace does not destroy nature, but perfects it (cf. St. Thomas Aquinas, ST 1a, 1.8 ad 2), and since each person is unique, certain individuals will be better or worse disposed for the perfection of virtue by reason of temperament and other characteristics that influence the workings of grace. Because of these predispositions, certain types will be more inclined to manifest paranormal phenomena, charisms, or truly mystical phenomena. Thus, the choleric and the melancholic temperaments are more receptive to ecstasy, trance, visions, raptures, revelations, and locutions (see St. Teresa, *Book of Foundations,* ch. 7); the sanguine temperament is more disposed to interior touches, caresses, consoling visions, or any phenomenon of the affective order. The history of spirituality shows that women are more prone to illusion than men, and more women among the saints have been remarkable for extraordinary phenomena. Other factors that dispose for extraordinary phenomena are a vivid imagination, uncontrolled emotions, badly regulated mental prayer, exhausting mental labor, and excessive austerities.

Charismatic Phenomena. The following are the principal charismatic phenomena.

Visions. By visions we mean the perception of an object that is naturally invisible to man. Visions can be divided into corporeal (perception by bodily eyes), imaginative (result of a phantasm in the imagination), or intellectual (result of intelligible species impressed on the intellect). *See* SPECIES, INTENTIONAL. Corporeal and imaginative visions may be caused by some natural power or by the devil, and therefore such possibilities must be investigated. The intellectual vision could not be caused immediately by the devil, who has no direct access to the human intellect, but it could proceed from a natural or a supernatural cause (*see* VISIONS).

Locutions. These are interior illuminations by means of words or statements, sometimes accompanied by a vision and seeming to proceed from the object represented. They can be divided into auricular (words heard with the bodily ear), imaginative (words perceived in the imagination), and intellectual (concepts perceived immediately by the intellect). Unlike prophecy, locutions are generally for the consolation or enlightenment of the one who receives them and thus differ from *gratiae gratis datae* in the strict definition. Auricular or imaginative locutions could proceed from any one of three causes: natural, diabolical, or supernatural; intellectual locutions could proceed from natural or supernatural causes. *See* LOCUTIONS.

Revelations. These are manifestations of hidden truths that are not normally accessible to man. Truly mystical revelation is usually accompanied by the gift of prophecy and its interpretation requires the gift of *discernment of spirits. Revelations may be absolute (simple statement of a truth or mystery), conditioned (usually a threat or promise based on some condition), or denunciatory (a condemnation or threat of punishment). Private revelations may proceed from a natural, a diabolical, or a supernatural source, and even if the revelation is supernatural in origin, the seer may unwittingly distort its meaning. *See* REVELATIONS, PRIVATE.

Reading of Hearts. The knowledge of the secret thoughts of others or of their internal state without communication is known as reading of hearts. The certain knowledge of the secret thoughts of others is truly supernatural, since the devil has no access to the spiritual faculties of men and no human being can know the mind of another unless it is in some way communicated. But knowledge of the secrets of another's heart may be conjectured by the devil and transmitted to a person, or they may be surmised by a deluded individual who takes his conjectures to be supernatural illuminations.

Hierognosis. This is the ability to recognize a person or object as holy or blessed and to distinguish what is genuinely so from what is not. A similar phenomenon with regard to holy objects is sometimes found in sinners and therefore the phenomenon is not necessarily supernatural but could also proceed from a diabolical power.

Flames of Love. These are burning sensations in the body without apparent cause. They admit of degrees: simple interior heat (usually a sensation around the heart, which gradually extends to other parts of the body), intense ardors (when the heat becomes unbearable and cold applications must be used), and material burning (when the heat reaches the point of scorching the clothing or blistering the skin, especially around the heart). This phenomenon could be caused by the devil or some pathological condition and therefore is not necessarily to be attributed to a supernatural cause.

Stigmata. These phenomena are the spontaneous appearance of wounds and bleeding that resemble the wounds of Christ. Sometimes the entire body is covered with wounds, as if from a scourging, or the forehead is punctured as if by thorns. These wounds usually appear during ecstasy and the wounds do not become inflamed or infected. Stigmatization could be produced by natural causes (autosuggestion, hypnosis, fraud), by the devil, or by supernatural power. *See* STIGMATIZATION.

Tears of Blood and Bloody Sweat (Hematidrosis). The effusion of blood from the eyes, as in weeping, or from the pores of the skin, as in perspiring, could be caused by the devil or it could be the effect of some physical or psychic pathology.

Exchange of Hearts. The substitution of the heart of the mystic for the symbolic heart of Christ, or the bestowal of a ring to designate the mystical espousal or *mystical marriage, could also be effected in an imaginative vision.

Bilocation. This phenomenon is the simultaneous presence of a material body in two distinct places at the same time. It is physically impossible that a physical body can be in two places at the same time by a circumscriptive presence, although this is denied by Leibniz, Suárez (*De Eucharistia,* 48.5.4), and Bellarmine (*De Sacramento Eucharist.,* 3.3.662). True bilocation with circumscriptive presence could not occur even by a miracle. What is miraculous in this phenomenon is that while the physical body is circumscriptively present in a given place, the same body is present by a sensible representation in a distinct place.

Agility. This is evidenced in the instantaneous movement of a material body from one place to another without passing through the intervening space. The agility could only be apparent if the movement were not instantaneous, but simply faster than the human eye could follow.

Levitation. This is the elevation of the human body above the ground without visible cause and its suspension in the air without natural support. It may also appear in the form of ecstatic flight or ecstatic walk. True levitation cannot as yet be naturally explained. Apparent levitation has been witnessed at spiritualistic séances and in certain cases of psychosomatic pathology. (See Thurston.)

Compenetration of Bodies. This occurs when one material body appears to pass through another material body. It is generally held to be philosophically impossible although much remains to be learned concerning the quantity, weight, and distribution of parts in a body. In the apparent compenetration of bodies, one of the bodies could be an immaterial representation of a body; or it is possible that a body might enjoy the anticipated quality of subtlety that is characteristic of a glorified body.

Bodily Incombustibility. This is the ability of bodies to withstand the natural laws of combustibility. It may be due to some occult natural cause or to the devil. If mystical, it could be interpreted as a testimony of the holiness of the individual or, in cases of a test by fire, of the truth of doctrine.

Bodily Elongation or Shrinking. Sudden reduction or increase in size of the body may occur for no apparent reason. This is said to have occurred in spiritualistic séances (see Thurston, 192–208) and could also be caused by occult natural powers or by the intervention of the devil. It is not generally accepted as a mystical phenomenon because of its morbidity and apparent lack of purpose.

Inedia. This is an absolute and total abstinence from all nourishment beyond the limits of nature. Some investigators are not convinced that inedia is necessarily miraculous.

Mystical Aureoles and Illuminations. Resplendent light may emanate from the body of an individual, especially during ecstasy or contemplation. It is considered an anticipation of the radiant splendor of a glorified body. Illumination and phosphorescence have been verified of certain plants and animals.

Sweet Odors. These have been noted as emanating from the living or dead body of a person. They are classified as miraculous by Benedict XIV, although the phenomenon could be caused by the devil or by autosuggestion. If it is a true mystical phenomenon, it is interpreted as the sign of the sweet odor of glory and a testimony to the holiness of an individual.

Blood Prodigies, Bodily Incorruptibility, and Absence of Rigor Mortis. These phenomena are well attested in the lives of the saints. Many cases could possibly have a natural explanation or be caused by diabolical power. Some are accepted as true mystical phenomena and testimonies from God concerning the holiness of an individual; others seem to be purely morbid and serve no spiritual purpose.

Bibliography: BENEDICT XIV, *Doctrinam de servorum Dei beatificatione et beatorum canonizatione* (Rome 1757). A. FONCK, DTC 10.2:2599–2674. JOHN OF THE CROSS, *Complete Works,* ed. SILVERIO DE SANTA TERESA and E. A. PEERS, 3 v. (Westminster, Md. 1953). TERESA OF ÁVILA, *Complete Works,* ed. SILVERIO DE SANTA TERESA and E. A. PEERS, 3 v. (New York 1946). A. F. POULAIN, *The Graces of Interior Prayer,* tr. L. L. YORKE SMITH (6th ed. St. Louis 1950). A. SAUDREAU, *The Degrees of Spiritual Life,* tr. B. CAMM, 2 v. (New York 1907); *The Mystical State* (New York 1924). J. MARÉCHAL, *Studies in the Psychology of the Mystics,* tr. A. THOROLD (London 1927). A. FARGES, *Mystical Phenomena Compared with Their Human and Diabolical Counterfeits,* tr. S. P. JACQUES (2d ed. London 1926). J. G. ARINTERO, *The Mystical Evolution in the Develop-ment and Vitality of the Church,* tr. J. AUMANN, 2 v. (St. Louis 1949–51). A. ROYO, *The Theology of Christian Perfection,* tr. J. AUMANN (Dubuque 1962). R. GARRIGOU-LAGRANGE, *The Three Ages of Interior Life,* tr. T. DOYLE, 2 v. (St. Louis 1947–48). A. TANQUEREY, *The Spiritual Life* (Westminster, Md. 1945). H. THURSTON, *The Physical Phenomena of Mysticism* (Chicago 1952). A. WIESINGER, *Occult Phenomena in the Light of Theology* (Westminster, Md. 1957). E. UNDERHILL, *Mysticism* (12th ed. rev., Meridian Bks., New York 1960). Z. ARADI, *The Book of Miracles* (New York 1956). R. OMEZ, *Psychical Phenomena* (Twentieth Century Encyclopedia of Catholicism 36; New York 1959). J. MARITAIN, *Distinguish to Unite or the Degrees of Knowledge,* tr. G. B. PHELAN, from 4th French ed. (New York 1959).

[J. AUMANN]

MYSTICAL UNION may be described as the relationship between a person and God in the highest degrees of the mystical life. Ordinarily, mystical union is said to have three stages: prayer of union, prayer of ecstatic union, and prayer of transforming union (*mystical marriage).

In the prayer of union the soul is deeply aware of God's presence. All the internal powers of the soul, including the memory and imagination, are captivated and occupied with God. This union, usually of short duration, is marked by the absence of distractions, and the certainty of being deeply united to God.

The prayer of ecstatic union differs from the prayer of union in that the external senses are also suspended or captivated. As the intensity of the mystical union grows, it becomes so great that the body cannot withstand it and so falls into ecstasy. In this union the Holy Spirit, acting through His gifts, so intimately and ardently unites the soul to God that the natural weakness of the subject cannot withstand the intensity of the light and love communicated. The soul falls into ecstasy, and this causes the body to experience an alienation of the senses.

In the prayer of transforming union (mystical marriage) there is a complete transformation of the soul into the Beloved. God gives Himself to the soul and the soul gives itself to God in a certain consummation of divine love, so that the soul shares in God's life as fully as is possible in this life. This union is more or less permanent; the soul is more conscious than ever of the Blessed Trinity. The soul is absorbed in seeking the honor of God, eagerly desiring to undertake anything or suffer anything that God may will.

Bibliography: TERESA OF AVILA, *Interior Castle, in Complete Works,* ed. SILVERIO DE SANTA TERESA and E. A. PEERS, 3 v. (New York 1946) v.2. JOHN OF THE CROSS, *The Living Flame of Love,* tr. D. LEWIS (New York 1912). A. ROYO, *The Theology of Christian Perfection,* tr. and ed. J. AUMANN (Dubuque 1962).

[N. LOHKAMP]

MYSTICI CORPORIS

Pius XII issued the encyclical *Mystici corporis* [Act ApS 35 (1943) 193–248] on June 29, 1943. The encyclical was in part a reaction against a vague and diffuse tendency discernible in some quarters of Catholic theology, especially in the years between the two world wars, toward what has been labeled a romantic vitalism or biologism in *ecclesiology. Nonetheless the encyclical is primarily a positive document, designed to present a doctrinal view of the militant Church as the Body of Christ (pars. 11, 90). Its obvious effort to synthesize the achievements of the past, both theological and magisterial, around the theme of the Body of Christ supports the view that the document's chief concern is not merely terminological exactitude but doctrinal formation.

Among the chief orientations found in the encyclical the following deserve notice: (1) there is a decisive turning away from a non-Incarnational and asocial concept of Christian *grace, which tends to regard grace's outward dimension as a purely provisional and transient reality; (2) hence the socio-sacramental reality of the Church as the communal life of grace is itself a true component of the total Christian grace, and thus Christ's Church Body cannot be the anomaly of a nonbody in which the vital relationships between Head and members tend to be unchurched; (3) this theandric ecclesiology is grounded on a pneumatology in which the role of Christ's Spirit, insofar as He is at once immanent in and transcendent to Christ's Church Body, is analogous to His role in Christ's physical Body, i.e., He is sent to invest Christ's Church, in whole and in its parts, with Christ's own life and energies, and thus to assimilate it, Body and members, to Christ, its paradigm and Head; (4) Christ is the "sustainer" of His Body (51–52), its *hypostasis in some mysterious sense, without prejudice to His own transcendence or to the distinct personalities of His many members.

Against this larger background it is easier to situate the following positions of the encyclical: (1) the identification of the Roman Catholic Church with the *Mystical Body of Christ on earth; (2) the delineation of the inward-outward grace of membership in a way clearly affirming the outward factors, without, however, any unilateralism; (3) the refusal to admit any basic dislocation between the Church of law and the Church of love, indeed the affirmation of the complementariness of the pneumatic and the juridic missions in the Church; (4) finally, the strong sense of Christian communion, or of the total common life of the Church, conceived as an inward-outward total grace, with a variety of members gifted in Christ, comprising both the lowly and the exalted, each serving together in his way the upbuilding of the Body in Christian love.

The encyclical concerns itself chiefly with the NT "militant Church" (1); hence it does not stress the OT ἐκκλησία as the forerunner of the NT Church Body of Christ, nor is any special relief given to the heavenly Jerusalem as the final realization of the Church's earthly pilgrimage. The encyclical does not attend to the question whether the NT "Body" theme has, over and above its assured metaphorical sense, a prior realistic sense, related to Christ's real Body, dead to sin on the cross, risen again to new life, and now gloriously reigning in heaven. The profound nexus between Christ's Eucharistic Body and His Church Body, though by no means passed over (81–84, 18), is not as centrally placed in the encyclical as, e.g., in patristic ecclesiology. The question is left open whether the Holy Spirit may be considered the soul of the Mystical Body in any proper sense (see SOUL OF THE CHURCH).

It has been noted that the encyclical omits the Biblical theme of the Church as the *people of God and to that extent constricts the overall viewpoint from which the mystery of the Church can profitably be regarded. The metaphorical theme of God's people is proposed as a useful complement to the Body theme, particularly advantageous in that it enables the theologian to reflect better on the historical continuity between the two covenants, old and new, and between the two covenant peoples, according to God's total plan of *salvation. Any effort, however, to invest the Biblical theme of the Body of Christ with theological disfavor, as an infratheological construct, or to dislodge it from its notable place among the many Biblical themes or images cumulatively employed and required to draw out that measure of fruitful understanding that man may reach in this life of the mystery of Christ's Church, is a disservice marked for failure.

See also CHURCH, ARTICLES ON.

Bibliography: J. HAMER, "Signification et Portée de l'Encyclique *Mystici Corporis*," *L'Église est une communion* (Paris 1962) 11–34. F. MALMBERG, "Die Enzyklika *Mystici Corporis*: Dogmatischer Wert und innere Struktur," *Ein Leib-Ein Geist* (Freiburg 1960) 43–54. A. MICHEL, DTC, Tables générales 1: 1116–18. W. BARTZ, LexThK² 7:731–732. Davis CDT 1:291–293.

[F. X. LAWLOR]

MYSTICISM

A term used to cover a literally bewildering variety of states of mind. Perhaps the most useful definition is that given by Jean *Gerson: "Theologia mystica est experimentalis cognitio habita de Deo per amoris unitivi complexum" (Mystical theology is knowledge of God by experience, arrived at through the embrace of unifying love). There are three points to notice: (1) the use of the term mystical theology (which was traditional in the Church until comparatively modern times) associates the mystical state with, while distinguishing it from, natural theology, which enables man to arrive at some knowledge of God by natural reason; also from dogmatic theology, which treats of the knowledge of God arrived at by revelation. (2) We do come to know God through mystical theology. (3) This knowledge is obtained not by intellectual processes but by the more direct experience implied in the term "unifying love."

Non-Christian Mysticism. This article is concerned primarily with Catholic mysticism, but it is necessary to recognise that Catholics and Christians in general have no monopoly of mysticism. Indeed, every religious tradition has its mystical aspect, and we cannot do adequate justice to the subject of Catholic mysticism without seeing something of the background from which it sprang. Just as in the realm of Biblical scholarship exegetes have come to recognize that we cannot isolate the Jewish experience from the larger context of Egyptian and Babylonian religion, so we have to see the whole development of Christian mysticism in the light of a common human striving.

Thus, within the remote world of China an early teaching maintained that man's highest purpose was the quest of *Tao,* which was regarded as the Ultimate Reality, source of all that is, pervading and harmonizing all natural phenomena. Hence, for man, *Tao* is the exemplar of conduct and man can find himself only by some kind of identification with it.

The process by which this identification is achieved bears a remarkable resemblance to the traditional teaching of Christian mysticism. First comes a process of purgation. In the words of Lao Tzŭ: "Only one who is eternally free from earthly passions can apprehend the spiritual essence of *Tao.*" After this stage comes the condition in which the achievement of virtue is not a self-conscious, self-regarding effort but rather a connatural state. The final stage is reached when harmony with Tao is fully realized. In this condition, man is the unresisting vehicle of *Tao,* so that he is able to rise above the limitations of matter and the laws of the physical universe.

On the other hand, it must be insisted that in much Chinese speculation, especially in the writings of Lao Tzŭ, there is no idea of "religion" as we understand the term, no sense of a personal relationship with God, or of obligations to him. In fact, the end of the mystical way for the Taoist might well seem to be an absorption into some pantheistic system (*see* PANTHEISM). It is hardly surprising that, to all intents and purposes, Taoism became amalgamated with *Buddhism.

Of *Hinduism, it is unnecessary to speak here, except to mention the possible influence that Indian ideas had on the Greek tradition through Pythagoras, and hence on Plato and *Neoplatonism. Neoplatonic influence on the Christian tradition through *Plotinus and *Proclus is undeniable. It was recognized that nothing made life more worth living than to look upon Beauty, not just in its partial and imperfect realizations, but in itself.

There is a kind of universal tradition embracing a metaphysics "that recognizes a divine reality, substantial to the world of things and lives and minds; and a psychology that finds in the soul something similar or even identical with divine reality; and an ethic that places man's final end in the imminent and transcendent Ground of all being." (See A. Huxley, *The Perennial Philosophy,* introduction.)

Is Mystical Experience Open to All? Yet, if the foregoing were true, the problem at once arises, why is the recognition of this universal reality so partial and fragmentary? What is it about the mystics that enables them to pierce through the veil that conceals from so many others the essential truth and goodness and beauty of God Himself? In the words of one of the mystics quoted by Huxley (*ibid.*):

> O my God, how does it happen in this poor world that thou art so great and yet nobody finds thee, that thou callest so loudly and nobody hears thee, that thou art so near and nobody feels thee, that thou givest thyself to everbody and nobody knows thy name? Men flee from thee and say they cannot find thee; they turn their backs on thee and say they cannot see thee; they stop their ears and say they cannot hear thee.

There has been much debate whether the full mystical experience is possible for all men or whether it is open only to those of a certain temperament. Dom Cuthbert Butler, a recognized authority, argued that the traditional Christian view, which had been lost to sight during the 18th and 19th centuries, is that all men are called to a specifically mystical way of knowing and loving God. In favor of this view he quoted Bishop John Hedley, who argued that contemplation is the chief act of the heart of man, for the heart flowers in the act of charity, and contemplation is charity that is actual, pure and flowering under the movement of the Holy Spirit. It differs from ordinary prayer, yet is not extraordinary in the sense that humble souls cannot aspire to it. It is not a miraculous activity, but is simply the perfection of supernatural prayer, ordinarily given by God to those who remove obstacles to it and avail themselves of the requisite means.

R. Garrigou-Lagrange protested against the view that there are two ways of perfection: an ordinary way, intended for all, and an extraordinary one of prayer and mystical life, to which all fervent souls are not called

by God. On the contrary, there is only one unitive way, not of its nature extraordinary, to which, by docility to the Holy Spirit, generous souls are led to perfection. Nevertheless, it must be acknowledged that because of a lack of proper guidance or because of other unfavorable circumstances, or because particular individuals are strongly inclined to exterior activities, some generous souls may not arrive at the mystic life during the span of an ordinary lifetime. This, however, Garrigou-Lagrange considered to be accidental.

Accidental or not, Abbot Butler recognized the situation to be so common that, through no fault of the individual concerned, the circumstances of life may, and often do render the experience of mystical union all but impossible. He cited St. Gregory's complaint that by becoming pope he had lost the gift of contemplation he had enjoyed in the monastery, and concluded there is much to be said for the view that there are not one or two "unitive ways" but many, just as there are many mansions in our Father's house.

One of the problems raised by much mystical literature is that far too many authors seem anxious to achieve a basic classification of states, into which, like some bed of Procrustes, the diversified experiences of a whole host of highly individualized personalities must be made to fit. The all but infinite variety of physiological conditions, intellectual endowments, social background, educational equipment, and the like, render it unlikely a priori that the way to God will be precisely the same even for any two persons, let alone for a whole mass of people. It seems desirable, therefore, to maintain flexibility of mind in trying to evaluate the accounts that different mystics give of their experiences, even while we recognize that, as the fundamental qualities of human nature remain unchanged, so there is likely to be a rough parallelism between any two sets of experience.

The Role of Grace. Certainly an absolutely essential starting point for all is the desire to arrive at whatever the goal may be and a consequent willingness to undertake whatever steps may be required to attain that goal. Yet even this starting point itself implies some faint recognition of what the goal is. "You would not be looking for me if you had not found me," as Pascal expressed it. Already the process of turning away from what is not God in order to come to God has begun; already God is "drawing" the soul to Himself. It is here that we begin to encounter what is probably the crucial problem in any discussion of mysticism—the cooperation between the soul and God. This is, of course, only a specialized form of a larger problem (*see* GRACE AND NATURE), but it calls for particular treatment here.

Without going into the question of the possibility of genuine mystical experiences for those who do not belong in any external sense to Christianity (though the modern view tends to be that such grace may be more widely available than was once thought), all Christian writers agree that where genuine mystical experiences occur they are the direct result, not of any efforts of the mystics themselves but of a special grace over and above the ordinary graces available to all Christians.

Some chosen souls appear to enjoy more than the ordinary gift of faith and the power to love and serve God. They seem to enjoy a supernatural knowledge and love beyond that of other generous souls, as though in some manner they participated more fully in God's own knowledge and love of Himself, and thus shared more intimately in the life of the Blessed Trinity and of the blessed in heaven. In their case, grace appears to do more than cooperate with their human effort. It is as though God produces in them a knowledge and love that exceeds all that can be felt or expressed by the faculties, although it is experienced by the soul.

The whole mystery of the relationship between any human soul and its Creator, at any phase and therefore especially at the stage of mystical union, springs from the nature of man's being. Dependent as he is on the creative act of an eternal Creator, an act that is described in its temporal effects as an act of conservation, man's whole conscious life is passed in a space-time world; yet he is more than a "pilgrim of eternity." The roots of his being, at a level deeper than consciousness, are to be found in the very Being of God Himself. Because of original sin, the consciousness of God that would seem to be connatural to man, has become fitful and obscure. It can be restored only by a rigid process of "purgation," a deliberate effort to turn away from this space-time world of everyday experience to concentrate on the eternal reality of God.

Precisely because so much of our conscious life is inextricably bound up with this world of sense, the process of purgation is a painful one. Hence follows the dark night of the senses, then the dark night of the soul, in the course of which the personality is detached from that absorption in temporal, material reality that has become connatural to man. Hence comes, too, the traditional insistence on the *via negativa,* the attainment to some knowledge of God by seeing Him as the denial of all that is commonly thought and felt by human beings through the ordinary channels. In this "cloud of unknowing," the mystic learns God by unlearning, so to say, everything that is not God. Moreover, unlike the objects of ordinary knowing, God is not the passive object of the mystic's contemplation. Rather is He the active inspiration, an overwhelming Power to whom the mystic submits, freely and therefore not inertly. The surrender becomes an immense enrichment, simply because the knowledge and love of God is the consummation of man's purpose.

The Mystic's Knowledge of God. St. Thomas Aquinas developed what has come to be accepted as the classic explanation of what we may call the mechanics of the intellectual communication implicit in the experience of mystical union. Human knowledge begins with some sense awareness. On this raw material—the colored shapes, the sounds and feelings, the scents and tastes produced by physical and chemical interaction between an external object and the sense organ—the intellect works to "abstract" the idea or concept that is the specific object of normal, human rational activity. Out of changeable phenomena is derived the changeless concept. By linking together these abstract ideas the mind makes judgments, it reasons, and infers. Ordinarily in the act of thinking, the concept is never entirely free of a penumbra of images or phantasms, be they no more than the words in which we normally clothe our ideas. (Yet we do distinguish between the word and the idea, as is shown by those occasions when, as we say, we are trying to find the right word to express what is in our minds.)

In the highest forms of intellectual activity, it does seem that the image becomes less and less helpful, and can indeed be a positive nuisance. The most obvious example is provided by mathematical reasoning. The geometrical figure, the algrebraic formulas are necessary to begin the process; but the stage is reached sooner or later when what we are thinking of bears only the remotest relation to what can be pictured: the curve is replaced by the formula, which is seen to bear less relation to what it purports to describe than do the stenographer's notes to the rhetorical cadences of the speaker, or the notes of a musical score to the symphony or sonata as it is created by the composer or performed by the orchestra.

Perhaps there was some way of knowing that began with an immediate activity of intellect, without any previous stage of sensation and abstraction. Since any created nature is finite and liable to imperfection, only by special divine help would human nature be able to abide permanently in the enjoyment of a situation calling for the complete integration and subordination of all its faculties to the purposes of the spiritual side of its being. Having lost that preternatural endowment, man, of himself, is no longer capable of that intellectual awareness of God which, if awareness is to be adequate, must obviously be free from the distorting effects of imagery. God is pure spirit and is therefore not to be described in language drawn from sense experience.

But there seems to be no reason in the nature of things why, in some cases and for special reasons, God should not confer a grace that might restore a person temporarily to that condition of perfection that man enjoyed before the Fall. We may presume that whereas in an unfallen state man's preternatural endowments would enable him to enjoy such an immediate awareness of God while still retaining his normal consciousness, direct awareness is not possible in the fallen state except at the price of a suspension of normal consciousness. In St. Thomas's words:

> In contemplation, God is seen by a medium which is the light of wisdom elevating the mind to discern the divine . . . ; and thus the divine is seen by the contemplative by means of grace after sin, though more perfectly in the state of innocence. [*De ver.* 18.1 ad 4.]

The foregoing remains no more than a theory, but as far as it goes, it is a coherent explanation and serves as at least a useful working hypothesis. It helps us also to understand why the mystic, after his experience, is invariably incapable of describing what happened or even, it would seem, of remembering anything at all except that something did happen. Thus St. Augustine says:

> Thy invisible things, understood by those that are made, I saw indeed, but was not able to fix my gaze thereon; my weakness was beaten back, and I was reduced to my ordinary experience (*Conf.* 7.23).

Moreover, as F. L. Mascall says (*Christ, the Christian and the Church,* 61):

> When the soul tries to describe this object to itself, when it tries to relate this knowledge to knowledge obtained by normal means, and above all when it tries to tell other people about it, it is faced with an enormous problem of translation and interpretation.

A. F. Poulain, in an exhaustive treatise on this subject, includes examples of some remarkable ways in which mystics interpreted their experiences. Thus St. Mechtild apparently declared that Christ had told her in a vision that the virtue of patience was especially dear to Him because *patientia* combines *pax* and *scientia;* St. Catherine of Siena claimed to have had a vision in which Our Lady revealed that she was *not* conceived immaculate! In individual cases, of course, it is possible to doubt whether any genuine mystical experience did in fact occur; but it is equally possible to suppose that, in attempting to translate into normal language and thought the contents of some mystical illumination, even a saint must be reduced to an ordinary way of thinking.

Validity of Mystical Experience. At this point, the question may well be asked, by both the skeptic and the sincere believer, whether there may not be some validity in R. A. Vaughan's unkind definition: "Mysticism is that form of error which mistakes for a divine manifestation operations of a merely human faculty." How can the mystics be said to "know" something that cannot be expressed in words and communicated to others, or rendered explicit by the mystics even to the mystics themselves? Perhaps it must be admitted that mystical experiences cannot be "justified" or authenticated by and in themselves. But this is not to say that there is no answer to the question here raised.

There is danger of concentrating too closely on mystical experience as an isolated phenomenon, dissecting the statements of this or that individual mystic, and so losing sight of the whole history of the subject. For in the words of William James: "There is about mystical utterances an eternal unanimity which ought to make a critic stop and think."

First, there is the general background of the long line of Christian mystics to be considered. The intellectual equipment, temperamental qualities, and educational opportunities of such men and women as SS. John, Paul, Augustine, the Pseudo-Dionysius, SS. Gregory, Bernard, Teresa of Avila, and John of the Cross, to say nothing of the English and German mystics, were so vastly different that one might expect differing approaches to mystical activity and widely dissimilar consequences. Yet, despite immense difference in detail, there is an almost monotonous sameness about their general attitudes to the basic matters of moral conduct and religious beliefs. If mystical experience were no more than a self-induced trance, and if the alleged intuition of a divine reality were sheer hallucination, it is remarkable that these baseless and purely subjective phenomena should be under the control of a persisting framework of ideas and beliefs.

Forgetting for the moment the specific problem of the authenticity of mystical experiences, one might look at normal Christian belief and practice. We believe that this world of material substance and rational and moral activity is but the surface of an unfathomed abyss of energy, eternally operative and effective.

"The weariness, the fever and the fret" that make up the conscious content of normal human experience cannot be understood save in relation to an external existence, which is the deepest reality. From that deepest reality man has come, to live out his little day, realizing, as best he may with the help of God, the perfection for which he was made. Even apart from the assurance of revelation, there is what is described by Dean Inge as "the raw material of all religion, and perhaps of all

philosophy and art as well, namely that dim consciousness of the *beyond,* which is part of our nature as human beings." At the heart of the Christian message is the doctrine that the world of man and the world of God, time and eternity, meet and blend in the Incarnate Word. Our reasons for believing this have nothing to do with mysticism.

Mysticism, on the other hand, has a history of experience in which the mystic claims to have been in immediate contact with the Ground of Being, known in an intellectual way that is free from imaginative content, and incapable of normal conceptualization. Further, the result of the total experience is not so much a deepening of understanding as a sort of fusing of personalities. Hence the prevalance of language and imagery drawn from the common experience of human love, an experience leading to physical union in which the lovers seek to express an identification of interests, desires, joys, and delights as symbolizing a longing for union of personality. It is not given to mortals to achieve such union; but, from the accounts the mystics have left, it would seem that somehow it is achieved in the highest form of their experience, sometimes even described as a "mystical marriage." Now human love is a powerful revealer of personality. Through love one comes to know another in a profounder way than by the ordinary exchange of social contact. (It is not without significance that we speak of a man's "knowing" a woman in sexual intercourse.) The difference between God's self-revelation in what may be called the ordinary ways—through the Prophets, the teaching Church—and what is given to the mystic in his special experiences may well be that, in the latter, there is a fusing of will and intellect in one act, analogous to but immeasurably fuller than the communion of souls that is experienced in human love.

Recalling Gerson's definition—"knowledge of God arrived at through the embrace of unifying love"—we might suggest that, in the mystic's experience, there is a complete coordination of both intellect and will, directed toward God, who is the perfect and adequate end of their activity. Hence, it can be seen why the effect of mystical contemplation is not merely, not even primarily, an illumination of the intellect but chiefly a deepening of the whole personality, an enriching of character, a development of virtue. It is this fact that, in the end, is the guarantee of the mystic's claim. For in the authentic mystic, we have a man or woman who is invariably distinguished for integrity, candor, and sensitivity of conscience. At the state of ordinary awareness, he shares our ideals, our beliefs, our principles of conduct. It is conceivable that, in some cases, the mystic's alleging of his experience of God is a piece of self-deception, hallucination, hysteria, megalomania, and the like. But it is absurd to suggest that all the mystics are so deceived all the time. Once it is admitted that some of the mystics may be right sometimes, that some of them genuinely "experience God" in an act wherein the whole of their spiritual nature, will and intellect, is operating at the highest level attainable by man (and then only with the special assistance of God), there is sufficient ground for claiming the mystics as witnesses, in a sense eyewitnesses, to the ultimate truth after which the rest of us are dimly groping.

Bibliography: From an almost limitless selection, the following brief list gives a representative picture. W. R. INGE, *Christian*

Mysticism (London 1899). A. THOROLD, *An Essay in Aid of the Better Appreciation of Catholic Mysticism* (London 1900). W. JAMES, *The Varieties of Religious Experience* (New York 1902). R. M. JONES, *Studies in Mystical Religion* (London 1909). A. F. POULAIN, *The Graces of Interior Prayer,* tr. L. L. YORKE SMITH (St. Louis 1950). A. B. SHARPE, *Mysticism: Its True Nature and Value* (St. Louis 1910). E. UNDERHILL, *Mysticism* (12th ed. rev. Meridian Bks. New York 1960); *The Essentials of Mysticism* . . . (New York 1920). E. C. BUTLER, *Western Mysticism* (London 1922). F. VON HÜGEL, *The Mystical Element of Religion,* 2 v. (2d ed. London 1923). R. OTTO, *Mysticism East and West,* tr. B. L. BRACEY (New York 1932). J. CHAPMAN, *The Spiritual Letters* . . . , ed. R. HUDLESTON (2d ed. London 1935). R. A. KNOX, *Enthusiasm* (New York 1961). D. KNOWLES, *The English Mystical Tradition* (New York 1961). S. SPENCER, *Mysticism in World Religion* (Baltimore 1963). F. C. HAPPOLD, *Mysticism: A Study and an Anthology* (Baltimore 1963), excellent bibliog.

[T. CORBISHLEY]

MYSTICISM IN LITERATURE

A consideration of the place of mysticism in literature poses some initial difficulties in the matter of definition (for the characteristics of mysticism, properly so called, *see* MYSTICISM). It should therefore be these qualities that imbue works which can properly be called both literary and mystical. The habit is quite current, unfortunately, for any literary work to be called "mystical" as long as it manifests a deep religious attitude or experience, deals with the supernatural or even the preternatural, or sees nature as a veil that at once conceals and reveals the Absolute. In the strictest sense, mysticism is the direct, intuitional experience of God through unifying love. There have been and are mystics in this strict sense outside the Catholic Church, even among non-Christians (e.g., the Mohammedans or pagan Greeks). Such experiences, however, are difficult to identify. When absorptions in the Soul of the universe or in some universal Mind are described, it is difficult to determine whether these are an experience of a personal God in charity. Oftentimes there is question only of a religious experience in the realm of ideas and feelings. Without prejudging the mystical quality in this strict sense in the writings of Blake, Huysmans, Emerson, or Goethe (to take these as representatives of different literatures), it seems possible and even necessary to distinguish their vague and often pantheistic-tinged absorption from the more effective union with a personal God that gives depth and fire to the writings of such mystics as St. *John of the Cross, St. *Francis of Assisi, and St. *Catherine of Siena.

It may not be an oversimplification to say that the first type of mysticism is an "I–It" relationship, the second an "I–Thou" realization, and that consequently from this second more intimate confrontation a more profound, moving, and universally significant literature would be expected to arise. This expectation is largely fulfilled in the writings of the "I–Thou" mystics; the frustration that so often hampers the efforts of these mystics to state their experiences arises from the very fact that their union with God in intuitive love has been so intimate, so unique, so literally ineffable that it defies capture in human words.

"I–It" Mystics. The whole course of world literature has been definitely shaped by those who wrote what may be called mysticism in a broad sense. This mysticism is specified by an intense realization of the difference between things of this world and the great otherworldly spiritual realities. Since many of these writers receive

separate treatment in this encyclopedia, they cannot be singled out here for extensive consideration. To give but a sampling, and restricting mention to those who are of acknowledged literary importance, there are from ancient times and up to the 12th century *Plato and *Plotinus, *Philo Judaeus, *Avicebron (Ibn Gabirol), and *Maimonides; (Moses ben Maimon) in later times, Samuel *Coleridge and *Blake in England, Jonathan *Edwards and *Emerson in the U.S., Johann *Herder and *Klopstock in Germany, and the Symbolists (*see* SYMBOLISM, LITERARY) in France. Many more, without being clearly Christian, have spoken eloquently of a world beyond sense, and their collective testimony to these invisible realities has been a force constantly and powerfully working against the materialistic and positivistic influences that always threaten to infiltrate a literature written by sense-fettered and earth-bound men.

"I–Thou" Mystics. It is, however, with mystics in the strictest sense of the word that one enters the realm of a literature that is unique in its intrinsic beauty and significance. The Epistles of St. Paul and St. John and the Apocalypse open the way to the subsequent attempts of Christian mystics to recount in human language the sublimity of their experience of direct knowledge of God. St. Paul distills the literary difficulty that all Christian mystics have faced when he states (almost in complaint) that he was "caught up into paradise, and heard secret words, which it is not granted to man to utter" (2 Cor 12.3). His account of his raptures and visions is nevertheless magnificent prose. St. Augustine hints at something of the same difficulty in expressing the ineffable when he says: "Thee when first I saw, Thou liftedst me up, that I might see there was something which I might see, and that as yet I was not the man to see it" [*Confessions,* tr. Watts (London 1912) 1.373]. But Augustine overleaped the barrier of expression to give the world in the *Confessions,* and indeed in much of his other work, abiding literary masterpieces. The influence of *Neoplatonism gave a distinct literary quality to the work of Dionysius the Areopagite (*see* PSEUDO-DIONYSIUS), one of the great shapers of subsequent Christian mysticism.

The Middle Ages saw a great flowering of mysticism. Most of the accounts of mystical experience are superb in the fervent tenderness and modesty that make them gems of affective literature. Such, for example, is St. *Bernard of Clairvaux's sermon on the Song of Songs:

> I confess, then, though I say it in my foolishness, that the Word visited me, and even very often. But although He very frequently entered into my soul, I have never at any time been sensible of the precise moment of His coming. I have felt that he was present. . . . You will ask, then, how, since the ways of His access are thus incapable of being traced, I could know that He was present? But he is living and full of energy, and as soon as He has entered into me He has quickened my sleeping soul, has aroused and softened and goaded my heart, which was in a state of torpor, and hard as a stone. He has begun to pluck up and destroy, to plant and to build, to water the dry places, to illuminate the gloomy spots, to throw open those which were shut close, to inflame with warmth those which were cold, as also to strengthen its crooked paths and make its rough places smooth, so that my soul might bless the Lord, and all that is within me praise His holy Name. [*Life and Works,* ed. J. Mabillon (London 1896) 4.457.]

Others whose prose possesses this literary charm were *Richard of Saint-Victor, St. *Bonaventure, and St.

*Dominic; there were also mystics who were great poets, such as St. *Thomas Aquinas, whose majestic hymns (e.g., *Pange lingua* and *Sacris solemniis juncta sunt gaudia*) are obviously the fruit of his own mystical prayer.

The literary qualities of the English *mystics have often been adverted to. There is a simplicity and charm to their recounting of their experiences, which recalls the Franciscan influence that stemmed so largely from St. Francis of Assisi himself (*see* FIORETTI, THE) and from the *Laudi* of his followers (*see* RELIGIOUS ORDERS, LITERARY INFLUENCE OF). But there is much Augustinian influence at work, too, as may be seen in the anonymous *The Cloud of Unknowing* (between 1345 and 1386). Other true masterpieces of the English school are Walter Hilton's *The Scale of Perfection*, Julian of Norwich's *Revelations of Divine Love,* and Richard Rolle's poems.

On the Continent, Jan van *Ruysbroeck introduced a superb symbolism in his *The Book of the Sparkling Stone* and spoke with great ardor in *The Adornment of the Spiritual Marriage*. The same intimate fervor is manifest in the works of St. *Bridget of Sweden and St. Catherine of Siena. The great German mystics, such as *Mechtild of Magdeburg and St. *Hildegarde of Bingen, had profound literary influence. But it is to Spain that one looks for the greatest mystical literature, beginning with the Catalan, Ramón *Lull, and culminating in the rich prose of St. *Teresa of Avila and the sublime poetry of St. John of the Cross.

One of the seminal literary achievements of the mystics was in developing and deepening (if not in originating) various symbolical "frames" for the account of their experiences. Such, for example, are the symbols of the ladder, the pilgrimage, and, with particular in-

fluence, the bold symbols of earthly wooing, love, and marriage as analogues of the divine union. But even more fruitful for deeply affective and intimately moving revelation has been the mystics' constant meditation on the Passion of Christ. It has been *this* intimacy that has given the "I–Thou" mystics the source of the superb literature produced by them. They, like (but how much more profoundly than) their paler "I–It" counterparts, speak in a chorus of loving testimony to the reality (in truth, a *personal* reality) of the God with whom they had achieved direct, intuitive knowledge through unifying love. That they were not able to speak of this experience more often in what are called the accents of literature lay in the fact, as Julian of Norwich said in her *Revelations of Divine Love,* that "Ah, hard and grievous was His pain . . . for which pains I saw that all is too little that I can say; for it may not be told."

Illustration credit: Courtesy of the Trustees of the British Museum.

[H.. C. GARDINER; E. E. LARKIN]

MYSTICS, ENGLISH

The great flowering of English mysticism was in the 14th century, with such writers as Walter *Hilton, *Julian of Norwich, Richard Rolle (*see* ROLLE DE HAMPOLE, RICHARD), and the nameless author of *The *Cloud of Unknowing*. It was the full and final growth of a tradition of devotion and speculation that had begun soon after the Christianization of England with Bede; in many of his homilies and commentaries we find his learning in the Scriptures and the Fathers expressing itself in an affective prose that tells of a progress through prayer and contemplation to an immediate perception of God's nature. In Bede's writings we find the germ of the devotions to the Sacred Heart, to the Passion and to the mysteries of Our Lady, for which later medieval England was to become famous.

Development. From the earliest days of the Anglo-Saxon Church, contacts with Ireland, though not always amicable, had existed. No doubt the Irish contributed to the growth of the body of highly individual prayers, especially those to the crucified Savior, found in such pre-Conquest compilations as the Books of Cerne and Nunnaminster. *The Dream of the Rood,* a much earlier composition, is beyond question the finest contribution of Old English literature to Christian devotional writing. One further circumstance in the religious life of the times, a trait shared with Ireland, helped to mold the forms and the thought fully expressed only centuries later: England became celebrated for its great numbers of hermits and anchorites. It may be that the Norman Conquest, which for a time excluded most Englishmen from ecclesiastical preferment, gave impetus to the solitary life of contemplation. Certainly in the 11th century and onward, we have much evidence to show that this life was pursued by many.

In the simple illiterate hermit Godric of Finchale, poet of the love of Christ and His Mother, we have a successor to the great tradition of Caedmon. Godric's contemporary, Christina of Markyate, though she wrote nothing, survives in her biography as an intrepid seeker for graces which she gained only by a total denial of the world. Some of the greatest figures in the English Church of this time wrote treatises which became standard among those vowed to anchoritic contemplation.

The prayer before the prologue in the 14th-century MS of "The Cloud of Unknowing" (MS Harl. 674, fol. 17v).

Special mention must be made of St. Anselm's Latin *Meditations*, St. Aelred's Latin *Mirror of Love* and St. Edmund's French *Mirror of Holy Church*. Their fruitfulness is witnessed by the speed with which they were turned into English, and the wide circulation such translations gained. In the early 13th century there appeared a wholly original English work, the **Ancrene Riwle*, in which the traditions of vernacular prose writing were given new life. The *Riwle* is only one of a number of contemporary guides to the solitary life of contemplation. The "Katherine Group" of English spiritual writings show that the author of the *Riwle* was not alone in his revival of English prose. Until the very end of organized religious life in the mid-16th century, the *Riwle* continued to be read, adapted, copied, and quoted. Many works which gained an independent fame in the 14th and 15th centuries, such as *The Chastising of God's Children, The Poor Caitiff* and *Disce Mori*, derive inspiration from it; and its study is today essential to those who would understand the individual genius of the spiritual thought of the age.

Religious Poetry. The religious life of medieval England is, indeed, singular in the West for the huge body of vernacular religious poetry, almost all of it anonymous, which has come down to us. It is still fashionable to regard much of it, the poems of love for Our Lady in particular, as derivative alike in language and inspiration from profane songs of courtly love; but this view is objectionable in many ways. It is equally arguable that courtly literature owes much of its inspiration to religious models, and the evidence, in England alone, provided by such very early lyrics as those of Godric and the evocative quatrain upon the Crucifixion quoted by St. Edmund in the *Mirror*, shows that the Franciscans were far from being the first to make popular songs about the love of God. Even before Richard Rolle we have such poems as Thomas of Hales's *Love Rune* to witness to the survival of long-established traditions. In Rolle, though we may think his reputation as a contemplative exaggerated, in his own times and ours, we find an unrivaled poet of the sweetness of divine love. The author of the *Cloud* and Walter Hilton both make adverse criticisms of the type of devotion which Rolle popularized, showing that it could lead to a superstitious veneration of "consolations," real or imagined, for their own sake; but they were themselves in some respects Rolle's debtors. He helped to preserve and adapt the style in which they wrote, and there are few who study the *Cloud* and *The Scale of Perfection* without having first known Rolle's *Incendium Amoris* and his English treatises and poems. Who the author of the *Cloud* was we do not know, nor is his identity important. His teachings, partly inspired by Pseudo-Dionysius and Richard of Saint-Victor, on the steps in contemplation and prayer that will lead to an immediate union with God, to "deification," aroused hostility. Doctrinally, the *Cloud* and its constellation of minor treatises, *Privy Counsel* and the rest, resemble principally John Ruysbroeck among Western mystics. Walter Hilton, the solitary turned Augustinian canon, is more sober, more academic, less original in his manner of presentation; nonetheless his writings established themselves in the 15th century as authoritative guides to contemplative prayer.

Ecstatic Mysticism. Quite apart from these two is their contemporary, Julian, the anchorite of Norwich

Woodcut title page of "Rycharde Rolle hermyte of Hampull in his Contemplacyons of the drede and loue of God, with other dyuerse tytles." Printed at London by W. de Worde, c. 1529.

whose *Revelations* show her to have been England's one great ecstatic mystic. This she does not claim for herself: her book merely records a series of mysterious visions, granted to her over a short period early in life, and the doctrine she drew from them after long pondering. What she teaches of the Incarnation, the Passion, Redemption, and damnation, makes comparison of her with Hadewijch, Mechtild of Magdeburg, and Catherine of Siena not inappropriate.

Until the ruin of organized Catholic life, and afterwards, these mystics continued deeply to influence the country's life and thought, as St. Thomas More and Augustine Baker, among many others, show us; but they had written for an age which had died, and it was not until the 19th century revived men's reverence for the medieval world that they were able again to show students of spiritual life the paths towards God which they, no less than the saints of the Counter Reformation, had followed to their goal.

See also ENGLISH LITERATURE, 2.

Bibliography: D. KNOWLES, *English Mystics* (London 1927); *The English Mystical Tradition* (New York 1961). W. R. INGE, *Studies of English Mystics* (London 1906). St. Margaret's lectures for 1905–06; to be read with caution. M. WARD, ed., *The English Way: Studies in English Sanctity from St. Bede to Newman* (New York 1933). E. COLLEDGE, *Medieval Mystics of England* (New York 1961). **Illustration credit:** Library of Congress, Rosenwald Collection.

[E. COLLEDGE]

MYTH, LITERARY

The investigation of "literary" myth is not limited to those forms that are found in highly developed civilizations with a written literature. As a matter of fact, it is essential for an exact understanding of myth to give special importance to primitive and archaic cultures because the more sophisticated forms of the so-called high civilizations frequently conceal or cloud myth's true nature and function.

Definition. In a very general way, myth can be defined as a story about the holy. Already in the oldest Greek texts where the word occurs, it is used—though not exclusively—for narrative or story, and at an early period it became the technical expression for the traditional stories about the gods. The evolution of the concept of myth, partly of a merely semantic nature, and partly caused by a changing religious consciousness or attitude, is very instructive with regard to the present confusion in the use of the term.

The Greek term $\mu\hat{v}\theta os$, which means word, is derived from the Indo-European root *meudh* or *mudh*, i.e., to reflect, to think over, to consider. This seems to indicate an original stress upon the deeper content of the word, the definitive and final expression of a reality. However, the opposition between $\mu\hat{v}\theta os$ and $\lambda\acute{o}\gamma os$, introduced by the *Sophists, who disbelieved—or misunderstood—the stories about the gods, gave later on a rather pejorative connotation to $\mu\hat{v}\theta os$. Xenophanes made a radical criticism of the mythologies as related by Homer and Hesiod. Theagenes of Rhegion interpreted them allegorically, whereas Euhemerus invented a pseudohistorical explanation of myth, which, to this day, continues to be called after him (*euhemerism). Plato repeatedly equated myth with legend or fairy tale, although he himself used myths as appropriate means to convey a mystery. Aristotle regarded myth as a product of fancy and fabulation. All these authors, to be sure, knew myths mainly through the literary transformations of the poets, where legendary and etiological elements are plentiful. In Lucian $\mu v\theta o\lambda o\gamma\epsilon\hat{\iota}v$ means to lie, to tell tall stories. This Hellenistic conception is typical also for the Judeo-Christian tradition: myths were discredited fictional narratives and were rejected as absurdities and falsehoods, if not as abominations and diabolical inventions.

Renewed Interest Since the Renaissance. With the revival of classical antiquity, the Renaissance renewed the interest in myth. Natalis Comes considered myth to be a symbolical or allegorical expression of philosophical speculations. *Vico, a remarkably independent figure in an era of rationalism, interpreted myth as a spontaneous reaction of primitive man to natural phenomena, but also as a poetic expression of historical events. His interpretation combined allegorical explanation and historical reductionism. The Romantic movement gave much emphasis to the religious factor in myth, e.g., J. G. *Herder and especially *Schelling, who saw myth as a necessary stage in the self-revelation of the Absolute. In the second half of the 19th century, the systematic and comparative study of religions, then first established as a science, although naturally interested in myth, still largely shared the old prejudices of the *Enlightenment. Max Müller's (1823–1900) ingenious and widely popular, but rather extravagant, thesis about myth as a disease of language is well known, but even *Frazer, an arduous and rather well-informed

student of religions, regarded myths as mistaken explanations of human or natural phenomena. *Rationalism called myth everything that did not agree with its own concept of reality. For W. Wundt (1832–1920) it was a product of imagination; for L. Lévy-Bruhl (1857–1939), of a prelogic, a primitive mentality.

The neo-Kantian philosopher *Cassirer attempted to evaluate the mythical function in the structure of human consciousness. He rejected the allegorical interpretation and stressed the autonomy of myth as a symbolic form and an interpretation of reality: it was the primitive intuition of the cosmic solidarity of life. *Freud, *Jung, and their psychoanalytical schools gave a new impetus to the study of myth by pointing out the striking similarities between their content and the universe of the unconscious. Their error, all too often, was to reduce myth altogether to the dynamics of the unconscious.

The 20th-Century Developments. In the mid-1960s, philosophers such as K. Jaspers (1883–   ) and P. Ricoeur (1913–   ) give a very positive evaluation of myth as an expression, or as a cipher, of the transcendent, a language of being. It was, however, the diligent study of primitive religions, where myths exist in a more or less unadulterated form as living and functional religious values, that proved to be the determining factor in the new understanding of myth. Although, in the common acceptance of the word, myth still belongs more or less to the world of imagination, there is a growing awareness of the fact that myth is par excellence the language of religion. Anthropology, ethnology, phenomenology, and the history of religions, completing the insights of sociology, psychology, philosophy, and folklore, are instrumental in the modern revalorization of myth.

From the works of scholars such as J. Baumann (1837–1916), A. E. Jensen (1899–1965), and M. Eliade (1908–   ), it is easy to extract a synthetic view of myth, although not so easy to define or to describe it in such a way as to take care of the variety of forms and types of myths resulting from its intricate development. Fundamentally, myth is the sacred story of a primordial event that constitutes and inaugurates a reality and hence determines man's existential situation in the cosmos as a sacred world. Myths deal with the so-called limit-situations of man, as expressed in the great mysterious moments of his existence: birth, death, initiation. But they make them transparent for their sacred meaning, referring them to a divine prototype that happened in mythical time, or, rather, mythical no-time.

Recognition of Sacred Character. It is this sacred character that distinguishes myth from related literary types: saga, legend, and fairy tale, although, in fact, it is rather difficult to discover pure myths. Most myths, by the time they are recorded, appear as hybrid literary types, and it is not always simple to make out where myth ends and legend begins. Sagas, and to a certain extent also legends, are founded on something that really, or at least supposedly, happened in time, whereas myths deal with metahistorical events. Fairy tales, however, have no fundamental relation whatsoever to time or reality. But myth has this relation in an eminent way because it founds reality, brings a reality into time. Moreover, as Eliade, among others, has convincingly shown, fairy tales and legends are often secularized myths. There is no doubt that myths are primary; no longer understood, they ceased to be revelations of a mystery or expressions of a mode of being in the world, but became diversions told for entertainment. However, their initiatory character very often can still be recognized. One could say, in a certain sense, that myth becomes less and less myth when it becomes more and more literature, because it enters a process of secularization in which it is blended and embellished with many nonmythical elements. But even in its highly sophisticated forms as a literary work of art, myth cannot be understood unless its religious nature is first recognized.

R. Pettazzoni has given due importance to the fact that the Pawnee and other North American Indian tribes make a distinction between true and false stories. According to this distinction, which can easily be substantiated and corroborated with evidence from archaic peoples all over the world, myths are true stories that deal with the holy and the supernatural, whereas false stories, those that have a profane content, are just make-believe.

It is important, however, to stress the difference between the truth of myth and its historical veracity. Myth, of its very nature, repels historicity, because the event it relates happened before history began, in an eternal instant. Myth, therefore, is not some sort of garbled history; it tells what really happened, not in time, but in the beginning, in the era of the gods. It is the story of a primordial event that accounts for the way a reality came into existence, i.e., began to exist in time. If myth is true, it is because it deals with what is real par excellence, because it deals with the reality that accounts for what exists in time and space. It reveals the true nature and structure of the *hic et nunc* realities by relating them to a metaempirical reality. It reveals the deeper, authentic meaning of life by showing how this particular mode of being in the world came about. In general one might say that the etiological concept, and consequently the etiological criticism of myth, misses the point, because it misunderstands the true nature of myth. Myth does not explain as much as it reveals and is unconcerned about apparent contradictions, because such contradictions exist in the empirical realm only. Historical and logical precision are irrelevant in the world of myth, because myth expresses not an erudition but a consciousness of a reality. It expresses what, in the religious consciousness of the believer, is true and valid.

The distinction between true and false stories in archaic cultures is also a distinction between sacred and profane. Myth is holy because its protagonists are gods or superhuman beings who intervene in the universe and establish it as an ordered cosmos. Myth is holy also because of the sacredness it makes present. Already the mere recitation of the myth results in the supernatural being present *hic et nunc*, and in this way mediates to those who hear it an insight into the holy ground of empirical or phenomenological reality. Usually this recitation is restricted to certain periods of sacred time. Frequently it is performed in the course of cult ceremonies, in which the myth is then the ἱερὸς λόγος, by certain authorized members of the community only, priests or elders. There may be certain taboos involved with the recitation too, e.g., the presence of women. Myth is not common property; one has to be initiated into it. Usually the stories about the gods are known thoroughly to certain experts only, who have the task of initiating the boys coming of age into the sacred traditions of the tribe.

Exemplary Character. Another fundamental characteristic of myth is its exemplarity. The intervention of the gods in this world, related in the myths, is paradigmatic and normative for man's behavior, ritual as well as social. One could say that myth prescribes for man the mode of being in the world, which it reveals to him: his place in time and space, his participation in the world of animals and plants as well as in the society of men, his cosmic dimension, the laws that govern the specific nature of his human existence, etc. The order the gods established, because it is powerful and holy, because it is reality, has to be safeguarded. Their deeds, because they constitute reality, life, salvation, have to be faithfully repeated, and therefore they become models for all significant human activities. This explains why archaic man is fundamentally imitative and traditional: he wants to secure the power of his actions and gestures by patterning them after the powerful deeds and gestures of the gods. The order of the cosmos and the regularity of its phenomena are reflected in the sacred norms that determine social relations and ethical behavior, as well as ritual procedure. Moreover, since the model is no part of the temporal, but some sort of an eternal instant, it remains paradigmatic and can be repeated over and over again in time. For archaic man, reality is a function of the imitation of a mythical archetype.

Myth and Ritual. The exemplary nature of myth is most evident in the ritual reenactment of a holy, primordial event. As suggested above, the recitation of a myth is in itself already some sort of a ritual because of the solemnity connected with the recitation: "Der rezitierte Mythus ist immer ein Schöpfungswort" (G. van der Leeuw). Very often, however, the recitation of the myth is accompanied by a dramatic representation of the event that it relates. The ritual execution of the myth makes the primordial creative event infinitely repeatable and hence continuously present in time. By reenacting the deeds of the gods that brought about reality, life, fecundity, etc., man is able effectively to maintain or renew them. Ritual projects man into the era of the gods, makes him contemporary with them, and lets him share in their creative work.

This close association between myth and ritual has given origin, ever since W. Robertson Smith (1846–94), to widely opposed theories about the nature of their mutual relationship. Is myth the offshoot or description of the corresponding ritual, or is it, on the contrary, some sort of libretto or script for the dramatic representation in ritual? Both theories have found very articulate defenders. The first one, in particular, has been brilliantly proposed and widely popularized by the English myth and ritual school (S. H. Hooke) and the Scandinavian school of Uppsala (Mowinckel). However, it seems that they do not always escape successfully the pitfall of some sort of pan-ritualism, which attempts to reduce almost everything to a ritual origin. In a certain sense the opposing theories carry on a sterile discussion, because, historically speaking, it is impossible to substantiate any linear or genealogical evolution from ritual to myth, or vice versa. All agree that at the present time one can find examples of primary rituals as well as of primary myths, but nothing allows one to project this present situation into the origin. True enough, at a certain stage of the development of religious consciousness it is possible to find the awareness that a myth sanctions a rite. But since myth, as B. K. Malinowski (1884–

1942) put it, vouches for the efficiency of a rite, this awareness may very well be an a posteriori etiological interpretation. It would be hazardous to conclude from this to the chronological priority of the ritual. Myth certainly is not fundamentally an etiological explanation of a ritual or a rationalization of an existing custom. It would be wrong to reject the possibility, or even the fact, that in the later development of both myth and ritual the former assumed the function of explaining or justifying obscured aspects of the latter, but to accept as the origin of myth a rite that has to be explained would leave no alternative to the shaky theory of the magical origin of religion. (*See* RELIGION; RELIGION IN PRIMITIVE CULTURE.)

Neither myth nor ritual really explains anything; rather, they express in parallel, more often intertwined, and always mutually complementary ways the fundamental religious experience of archaic man in a cosmos that reveals the creative presence of the gods. It does not make too much sense, for example, to say that the recitation of the *Enuma Elish* by the Babylonian priests at the Akitu festival served the purpose of explaining the ceremonies. Rather, it is the presence, within its temporal reenactment, of the ideal, eternal model. The mystery of creation is expressed simultaneously in word and in imitation. The ritual in the strict sense of the term presents the event, and the myth relates this presentation to its transcendental model and meaning. The concomitant myth, in a certain sense, identifies the ritual reenactment with its divine prototype, and, by so doing, intrinsically determines or prescribes the process to be followed.

The dichotomy of myth and ritual seems to be a recent phenomenon. For primitive man they were not two things brought together, but two aspects of one reality, one experience expressed in the two fundamental forms of human expression: word and gesture, each one clarifying, complementing, and requesting the other. Really primary is the divine model or archetype as it is revealed in the reality of the cosmos and of life. "We must do what the gods did in the beginning," says the Śatapatha Brāhmana, and this old Indian adage is valid all over the world. Even where myth, because its justifying or etiological character is obvious, can be proved to be chronologically secondary to the rite, it would still be imperative to distinguish between the formulation and the content of the myth. Myth and ritual are not to be separated; where they are, myth enters a process of secularization and ritual becomes superstition.

Types of Myth. Myths are usually classified according to their subject matter: cosmogonic, theogonic, and anthropogonic myths, Paradise myths, myths of Fall and Flood, soteriological or eschatological myths. The various types can, of course, be further subdivided typologically; the cosmogonic myth, for example, could be further divided into myths of emergence, of the earth-diving type, of struggle with the primordial dragon, of dismemberment of a primordial being, etc. Such divisions have their practical usefulness but are quite artificial, and there would be a good case for reducing all myths, if not to a single type, at least to one prototype. Indeed, all myths have a very definite common denominator: they deal with the beginnings of realities—the origins of the world and of mankind, of life and death, of the animal and vegetable species, of culture and civilization, of worship and initiation, of society, its leaders and institutions. The only apparent exception, the eschatological myth, in fact also deals with the restitution of creation in its original purity and integrity. Because it reveals how the totality of the real came into being, the cosmogonic creation myth is the prototypical one, continued and completed by the other myths.

Myth and the Bible. Where the word myth is mentioned in the Bible, almost exclusively in the NT, it is invariably in the pejorative sense of fiction, old wives' tale, lie, or error. Typical is the well-known text of 2 Tm 4.4: "They will stop their ears to truth, and turn to myth." It is obvious, however, that this negative attitude is nothing more than a conformity with the prevalent use of the term, together with a rather exclusivistic religious absolutism. Foreign religious traditions are not false because they are myths; they are called myths because they are, or are supposed to be, false. This does not necessarily imply a fundamental incongruity between Holy Scripture and myth, as myth is understood. The incongruity is not between Bible and myth, but between Bible and falsity.

It is evident that the narratives of Genesis about the creation of the world and of man, about Eden and the Fall, etc., are not really history in the ordinary sense of the word, but very much stories about events that took place "in the beginning," events that constituted the cosmos as a reality, and about man in his specific mode of being in the world, his existential situation as a created, mortal, sexed, and cultural being. If it could be substantiated that the story of Genesis ch. 1 was recited at the Hebrew New Year's festival, this association between the creation myth and the annual ritual of cosmic renewal would be a further confirmation of its mythic character. Other examples of this association between narrative and ritual—with the essential difference that the mythical archetype is replaced by an historical prototype—are the Exodus story, reenacted in the Passover ceremony, and the mystery of Christ's redemptive sacrifice and Resurrection, renewed in the Eucharistic celebration of the Mass.

The Bible, as a literary work, has a tradition that includes myth as a literary genre and does not reject mythical patterns from other civilizations. This is not surprising; what is surprising is the remarkable restraint Israel used in this regard. One could say that, in a certain sense, the authors of the Bible demythologized to a great extent whatever myth they used. In the cultural and civilizational context of the Bible, the use of mythical language in order to express the supernatural and transcendental content of a religious message is self-evident. Because myth reveals in a dramatic way what philosophy and theology try to express conceptually and dialectically, it adapts itself naturally to the expression of an active divine presence in the cosmos. Because myth is not limited by the laws of logic, it expresses naturally the divine reality as something that transcends thought in a *coincidentia oppositorum*. Because myth takes place in a nontemporal era, it presents naturally a transtemporal or metahistorical event that never happened, but always is, *ab origine*.

With regard to the mythical outlook of religious man, there is, however, in the Judeo-Christian tradition a totally new factor. Although mythical patterns remain discernible, the decisive events are no longer extra-temporal, but, in a very real sense, historical: God intervenes effectively in human history. Myth reveals the existence of the gods as the ground of all created reality, but the Bible reveals God's activity on the scene of time. In myth, as in Platonism, time is but the moving image of unmoving eternity, a never ceasing repetition of creation through a process of periodical regeneration. But in the Judeo-Christian tradition time is creation itself in the act of being accomplished. Historical events have a value in themselves because they mark God's interventions in time. They do not mark a recurrence of archetypes, but a new, unique, and decisive moment in an irreversible process. The message of the Prophets, for example, is much more about these interventions of God in history than about His presence in the cosmos. As a matter of fact, one could very well, with Tresmontant, define the *nabi* (prophet) as one who has the understanding of the sense of history. Here again there is an implicit demythologization in the Bible.

Creation, Fall, and Flood can be said to be events of the beginning, but not the Exodus, the passage of the Red Sea, the crossing of the Jordan, the invasion of Canaan. These are historical events. Again, the mythical pattern is discernible in the ritual repetition of creation of those events as well as in the liturgical year that periodically repeats the events of the Nativity, life, death, and Resurrection of Jesus. But, although the reactualization is obvious, especially in the Sacraments, this repetition is nevertheless, in the awareness of the believers, a remembrance of an historical fact, an *ephapax* that already achieved its soteriological end "once and for all." In 2 Pt 1.16–18 one can see the importance given to this historical aspect by early Christianity, and again it is in opposition to myth: "We were not following fictitious tales when we made known to you . . . Jesus Christ, but we had been eyewitnesses . . . . We ourselves heard . . . .. We were with him . . . .."

After *Strauss, *Renan, and others in the 19th century, Rudolf Bultmann (1884–   ) stressed the mythical character of the NT and the need to demythologize the Christian kerygma, i.e., to strip it from its obsolete, mythological elements, caused mainly by Hellenistic gnosticism and Jewish apocalyptic ideas, in order then to interpret it anthropologically or existentially. Since this question is extensively dealt with in other articles, a few general remarks will suffice here (*see* DEMYTHOLO-GIZING; FORM CRITICISM, BIBLICAL; LITERARY GENRES, BIBLICAL). Sometimes demythologization really stands for deliteralization, a nonliteral interpretation or understanding of an imagery that became inappropriate because it was based on an outdated, mistaken, or incomplete knowledge, e.g., an erroneous cosmology. This is, of course, what respectable theology did throughout the ages, and it is imperative as long as the message is not evacuated with its expression. Insofar as myth, for Bultmann, is to conceive and to express the divine in terms of human life, the only alternative to some sort of *re*-mythologization seems to be complete silence. Finally, demythologization sometimes stands for an effort to salvage in the narratives of the NT the historical kernel from its so-called "mythical husk." To assess critically what is strictly historical and what is not is certainly to be commended. But to distinguish does not mean to separate or to oppose. What is denounced as mythical garb may be a necessary or at least a convenient instrument to reveal the historical event as a theophany. To eliminate myth in this sense would be disastrous because both myth and fact are demanded

by—and coinstrumental in—the revelation of divine presence in history. As such they validate each other.

See also MYTH AND MYTHOLOGY; MYTH AND MYTHOL-OGY (IN THE BIBLE).

Bibliography: J. DE VRIES, *Forschungsgeschichte der Mythologie* (Freiburg 1961). M. ELIADE, *Patterns in Comparative Religion,* tr. R. SHEED (New York 1958); *Myths, Dreams, and Mysteries* (New York 1961); *Myth and Reality* (New York 1963). T. J. SEBEOK, ed., *Myth: A Symposium* (Bloomington, Ind. 1958). H. A. MURRAY, ed., *Myth and Mythmaking* (New York 1960). R. CAILLOIS, *Le Mythe et l'homme* (Paris 1938). B. MALINOWSKI, *The Myth in Primitive Psychology* (London 1926). A. E. JENSEN, *Myth and Cult among Primitive Peoples,* tr. M. T. CHOLDIN and W. WEISSLEDER (Chicago 1963); ed., *Mythe, Mensch und Umwelt* (Bamberg 1950). W. NESTLÉ, *Vom Mythos zum Logos* (Stuttgart 1940). E. CASSIRER, *Philosophy of Symbolic Forms,* tr. R. MANHEIM, 3 v. (New Haven 1953–57) v.2. H. M. and N. K. CHADWICK, *The Growth of Literature,* 3 v. (Cambridge, Eng. 1932–40). C. G. JUNG and C. KERÉNYI, *Einführung in das Wesen der Mythologie* (Amsterdam 1941). R. QUENEAU, ed., *Histoire des littératures,* 3 v. (Encyclopédie de la Pléiade 1, 3, 7; Paris 1955–58) v.1. R. PETTAZZONI, *Essays on the History of Religions,* tr. H. J. ROSE (Leiden 1954). H. BAUMANN, "Mythos in ethnologischer Sicht," *Studium generale* 12 (1959) 1–17. G. VAN RIET, "Mythe et vérité," in his *Problèmes d'épistémologie* (Paris 1960).

[F. DE GRAEVE]

MYTH AND MYTHOLOGY

The myth is a narrative that portrays an event. What marks the narrative as a myth are both the characters appearing in it and the influence of the event on the structure and order of the existence or life assumed. The time in which the mythical event takes place is therefore of basic meaning for every other time.

Precise Definition. If attention is concentrated on the characters appearing in myth, there is a tendency to define myth simply as a narrative or story concerned with gods. However, such a definition needs certain qualifications. Myth, it is true, usually deals with gods or divine beings (daemons, angels, and others), but a story about gods in itself is by no means necessarily a myth. The territory of genuine mythical literature is abandoned as soon as a people has reached the cultural stage in which, through its love of stories, it creates ever new and more exciting tales about its favorite gods, ascribing unusual traits or features to them and furnishing details concerning their complicated adventures or escapades. Such stories about gods lead to creative literary art and serve merely for entertainment.

The genuine myth deals with incidents and actions, with struggles and afflictions, with death and resurrection, with defeat and victory, in which the god endures his lot and reveals his nature. The myth, therefore, is not a divine biography. While in biography the essential and the unessential are combined, the myth is concerned in its narrative exclusively with the character and range of activity of the god, focusing attention on his relation to the cosmos and to man. If the myth, for example, tells of a divine child, this is not to be understood as the beginning of a continuing story, which later covers his full growth and development. The divine child is identical with the god himself, and his activity corresponds to the activity that the god carries out according to his nature.

The nature of the myth is revealed in Kerényi's definition of it as the "story of beginnings." The myth tells about a god and, in so doing, gives an account of origins. In the mythical event a condition or an order is introduced and is realized in a foundation. The myth as such adduces in etiological fashion the reason that the condition or order exhibits the precise form that it has and not another. Yet it should be emphasized that the reason intended is to be regarded first as ἀρχή (beginnings) and then as αἴτιον (cause). The relation between the mythical event and the consequent order connected with it has not occurred by chance or in any external way, but order itself has sprung from the content of the event in the process of its happening.

Myth and Time. There is a correspondence between the original character of the myth and the kind of time in which the mythical event takes place. The myth is thought of as true insofar as no doubt is present that the mythical event actually took place. However, it did not happen in the real time in which the history of the given people has developed. The time of the myth transcends historical time. Its time is not prehistoric time, but primeval time, and, in respect to eschatological myths, not the future but the last days, the end of time.

Primeval time comes before all other time; although the time of origins, it has the peculiarity that it can never be actual past. In a certain measure it is constantly present, since the organization and form of existence is rooted in it. If one lives as a hunter or as a farmer in harmony with the changing rhythm of nature or lives within the given social order and condition, he is firmly moored in the primitiveness that the mythical events of the primeval time have established. If one wishes to understand the conditions of existence, he must, consequently, put himself back directly; he cannot proceed to understanding solely through analysis. Explanation is always found in what is behind, in the primeval time that is immediately accessible through myth.

Myth and Cult. The dialectic inherent in the circumstance that the mythical happening is always found before every time, and yet is likewise present in every time, forms the background for the proper function of myth, namely, its participation as λεγόμενα (things said) in cult. There can be myths without connection with cult, having become completely detached from cult and given a continued life as stories only. Nevertheless myth, not only in most cases, but also by virtue of its nature as the narrative or history of origins, is so closely connected with cult that its function in cult belongs to its definition. In the cultic action the original event becomes present, and primeval time becomes the now or lives again through repetition. The god performs anew his order-founding act, he fulfills anew his destiny, or takes on anew his sphere of existence.

There is much to justify the view that cult is earlier than myth and that therefore, ordinarily, cult does not form around myth; conversely, myth derives its origin from cult. However, in that case it is impossible to know how the thought, without which the whole cult action is connected, originated. In any event, this special kind of cultural form goes far back in human history, and it may be assumed that it belongs to a time in which man was able to express himself better by other means than language, namely, by dance, gestures, attitudes, and primitive types of music. Therefore, the basic events and experiences that created society were not preserved through linguistic formulations or in memory, but were passed on through a repeatedly new enactment in the institution of cult. When man then attained a cultural level that enabled him, with the help of language, to construct connected formulations of his thought, spoken

elements received a constantly increasing role in cultic action. A ἱερὸς λόγος was created. While it participates in a sense in the cult action, the function of the ἱερὸς λόγος is not to inform or to explain, but rather to put an action into operation. It is only at this stage that a meaningful narrative is composed, which, in etiological fashion, explains the individual parts in the cultic action. As the λεγόμενα (things said), it is a parallel structure that accompanies and harmonizes with the δρώμενα (things done) in cult.

MYTH, SAGA, LEGEND, AND MÄRCHEN

Myth, as a special kind of primitive narrative, must be distinguished from other similar narrative forms. However, the distinction can be made only in a general way, for it must be emphasized that the boundary lines cannot always be sharply drawn. The narrative can slip over easily from one form into another, and the same motifs can be found in the different forms. Nevertheless, distinction contributes to better understanding.

Saga. While the myth is primitive history and is concerned with establishing order in the structure of existence, saga is more closely bound to a locale and is connected with definite historical events and places. The time in which the saga events take place is in the past of the given people, and the persons portrayed are for the most part heroic figures who ostensibly have played a decisive role in great events. Often, but by no means always, an actual historical event underlies the saga, but it is then so embellished or forced to fit such fixed schemata that the separation of what is strictly historical in the content is hardly possible.

If a cult develops around the hero of the saga, he becomes the object of religious worship or his actions are magnified into the deeds of a savior. Saga is thus transformed into myth. In another respect also the creative possibilities of saga are freer than those of myth. Thus, without losing its character as saga, it can be enriched with new features and expanded into a whole saga cycle. It is not connected with cult, but in general serves rather as a form of entertainment; and in this respect it admits additional elements and alterations.

Like myth, saga often has etiological meaning, but the explanation that it gives, in contrast to that of myth, is actually an αἴτιον (cause), and its object is usually a local phenomenon: the giving of a name, a custom connected with a place, a geographical feature, and similar things. The etiological factor, however, is rarely the main concern of saga; it is introduced rather as a supplementary observation of an explanatory addition.

Legend. The term legend comes from the period of the early Church when it was customary, especially in monastic communities, to read accounts of the saints or martyrs at divine service or on their feast days. Hence it is clear that legend, as well as saga, is a narrative that is based on historical events and persons, but that enriches and embellishes its material through the free play of the imagination. Hence the special tone of the legend is also clear of itself. Legend is religious in character and is intended in a special way to have an edifying effect. Its characters, accordingly, are always figures ideal in piety, models worthy of reverence, who inspire admiration and imitation.

Accordingly, it is not strange that the various legends have common traits. The similar kind of piety, the same examples of god-fearing actions, holy renunciation, and martyrlike pathos recur in legend after legend. Legend as a kind of narrative is not restricted to Christianity in antiquity and the Middle Ages. A legendary literature was created universally around great religious personalities, and their image was transmitted to later times in the form of the legendary biography (cf. the legendary life of Buddha). Finally, given the religious character of a legend, it can appear also in forms that approach the myth. Furthermore, terminology in this respect is not sharply fixed, and one can employ the expression cult-legend as a synonymous designation for the word myth.

Märchen. The root of *Märchen* is entirely different. In contrast to all other kinds of narratives it is not concerned with real persons or events, but establishes its own world and its own time. The *Märchen's* setting is an indefinite place—"east of the sun and west of the moon"—and its events occur at an indefinite time—"there was once." It has no relation to the world or time in which actuality is the characteristic feature.

Consequently, it operates under other laws than those of the real world. Everything is quite different, yet the *Märchen* does not abandon itself to confusion and caprice. On the contrary, its happenings are subject to inflexible laws. This fixity finds expression also in its style. The structure of the *Märchen* is strict, and it is dominated throughout by schematic features, as, for example, repetition, triple groupings, suspense, and similar devices. However, the *Märchen* and the myth are closely related in their origin. In both forms of narrative the same primitive view of the world and of life is clearly present. But what in the myth takes place in the sphere of reality is, in the *Märchen,* consciously elevated into the realm of fantasy and its regulated play. Accordingly, the *Märchen* of its nature is fundamentally harmless, although the most horrible things can transpire in it.

At the risk of oversimplification, it may be said that, while all four narrative forms operate with the same motifs, each operates in a wholly different manner, and in one peculiar to itself in each case. In the saga, the theme is handled usually in tragic fashion; in the legend, to serve the purpose of edification, and in the *Märchen,* primarily to give pleasure. The myth alone understands its theme to be origin and foundation.

CLASSIFICATION OF MYTHS

The classification of myths can be attempted only in broad lines, and the assignment of specific myths to specific categories is often open to question. Nevertheless, the setting up of a scheme of classification is indispensable if one wishes to get a concrete and clear understanding of myth.

Cosmogonic Myth. By definition, this type of myth deals with origins, and by its nature it is always cosmic in scope. The cosmogonic category of myths is the basic group with which the remaining groups are combined in various ways. The cosmogonic myth tells of the origin of the cosmos either through a direct act on the part of the creator or through emanation from a primeval being or nature. The act of creation can be carried out by the High God alone or in cooperation with other mythical beings—or sometimes with the primeval man or with an evil adversary. However, the High God can also withdraw into the background, either because he is outside the myth or because, after his primitive act of

creation, he leaves the further work of creation to be accomplished by other powers.

The process of creation can be represented as an intellectual act whereby God alone, through his thought, word, or will calls the world into existence, or it can be conceived also as a craftsman's shaping of preexistent matter. If, on the other hand, the origin of the world is thought of as an emanation process, the cosmogonic myth then speaks usually of a long and highly imaginative development in which a primeval being is divided or split up to constitute a multiform world.

Theogonic Myths. The creation of the gods is the theme of special myths. These describe how the polytheistic world of the gods originated as a creation of a High God, or how a first divine pair became the ancestors of the subsequent world of the gods. Accordingly, the theogonic myths can be regarded also as a part of a cosmogony, the *Theogony* of Hesiod being the best known example. The appearance of the gods is itself a part of the general development of the cosmos, and generations of gods can arise that replace each other—often in dramatic ways. The relation of the High God to the world of gods that he has created is never a hostile one. On the contrary, the High God has withdrawn into his heavenly realms, in which he has an untroubled existence, while other divinities, who may be characterized in some respects as intermediate beings, must preserve and guard the created cosmos.

Anthropogonic Myths. The origin of men frequently plays an important role in mythology. The cosmogonic and theogonic myths then form only the prologue to an anthropogony. But the opposite type of myth is also found, in which the entrance of men into the world does not play even the slightest role and is therefore insignificant. Again, in many other myths, man is portrayed as a special or unique being, either in the form of a powerful primeval man who helped the creator god in his further work, or as a central figure of divine origin who was created to rule over the cosmos. Anthropogony can be emphasized also in a more naturalistic fashion: man, like the plants, has grown out of the earth or has been born of stone, or formed as a figure from clay. In the Orphic myths man sprang from the ashes of the Titans as a dualistic unity of soul and body. Universally, anthropogonic myth, with inventive imagination, depicts the contemporary view of the nature and function of man.

Myths of the Primitive State of the Cosmos and Man. Myths dealing with this theme not only describe the original state of the cosmos, but are intended especially to furnish information on the processes that led to subsequent and present conditions. Many myths tell how death came into the world. This happened through a chance event, through disobedience, through some clumsiness or carelessness, or because a command was not observed. With death, evil also came into the world. Man must suffer and work hard; he has fallen from his primitive happy state into evil snares and has become subject to stern conditions. The various cultural spheres have their origin also in events of the mythical primeval time. The structure of society is to be traced back to primeval happenings, the present laws are of divine origin, and the great bearers of civilization founded the patterns and regulations of the various professions, even when they often had to overcome in decisive battles powers threatening them.

Savior Myths. The myth of the savior-god is closely connected especially with the mystery cults and is often a further development of earlier agricultural myths. Underlying all differentiating details, there is an extraordinarily widespread and strikingly uniform schema. The god is the object of an evil attack on the part of evil powers and is put to death in tragic circumstances. The good powers, however, inaugurate countermeasures and the god is restored to new life, often in connection with his conquest or dominion over the kingdom of the dead.

Eschatological Myths. Eschatological myths have a much less extensive distribution. They postulate a definite conception of the nature of history and occupy themselves with speculations on its end. They usually portray the final time as a period of dramatic cosmic events that point to the coming of the hero-god and in which judgment will be rendered on good and evil. The events of the final time lead to a new creation and to the establishment of a state of bliss, which is often conceived as the restoration of the happy condition lost in primeval time.

Mythological Systems. In origin, myths are short, limited narratives that, according to the occasion, relate an appropriate mythical event. However, if the myth-forming period of a people is approaching its end and the store of myths has become so rich that even contradictory traits or elements are present, theological speculation begins to operate. An effort is made to combine the myths into a system of homogeneous character, and to remove aberrations or disharmonies, in order to give the total myth complex the appearance of a theologically consistent whole. This development is often accompanied by a somewhat depreciatory attitude to the original "naive" form, and the mythological system subjects the content of the individual myths to thorough allegorical interpretation.

The systematization of myth, therefore, is an indication that the myth has lost its proper character. Men no longer believe in the literal reality of the myth, but regard it as the expression of "eternal" truths. The myth is transformed into a philosophical theorem; its personal and active forces are now only the cloak for abstract, metaphysical concepts; and the views on the nature of existence and on the nature of man have actually become nonmythical. The realities of existence are no longer ascribed to primeval events. Accordingly, the appropriate form of expression, namely, the visualizing dramatic narrative of myth, is lost also, and its place is taken by metaphysical definition and philosophical argument. In other words, the mythological system is the transitional stage from true myth to metaphysical speculation.

The Origin and Development of Mythology

D. *Hume (1711–66) made the study of myths a field of scientific investigation. As opposed to the Deistic ideas of a "natural religion," he maintained that mythological concepts are a kind of primitive explanation of nature and that their origin is to be sought in the sphere of the emotions. Hope and especially fear are the factors that impel men to formulate mythico-religious concepts.

Influence of Idealism and Romanticism. German Idealism and Romanticism, as a reaction against the Enlightenment, rediscovered myths and evaluated them primarily from an aesthetic point of view as poetical or literary creations. The mythical composition was regarded as an independent product of intellectual life, an independent contribution of the creative imagination. On the speculative-philosophical plane, F. W. *Schelling (1775–1854), especially, raised myths to a position of central importance. The principles that are found in the mind of God as a unity penetrate human consciousness by a kind of metaphysical process. They split apart in opposition and tension, and at this stage they are best called myths.

Wundt, Otto, Cassirer, and Tillich. The Religio-Historical School in the second half of the 19th century, under the leadership of H. *Usener (1834–1905), went back to the ideas of Hume. W. *Wundt (1832–1920), however, made a new advance in the investigation of myths. He regarded the emotions as the sources of myths. But the possibility of the emotions' leading to mythical ideas is to be ultimately ascribed to the imagination. Through the apperception of things as persons, it is possible for man to objectify his emotional states. Wundt, nevertheless, did not yet have clearly in view the specific elements in the feelings and imagination that produce myths.

In this regard R. *Otto (1869–1937) made a supplementary contribution. His description of the emotional states, by which man is affected in the presence of the numinous, is characterized especially by his view that religious feeling is something specific. The primary thing is the emotional state. The myths merely cluster about it as creations of the imagination. Moreover, at the same time, they are by-products that can harden into a shell, and the shell can prevent the development of a genuine religious attitude or disposition.

E. Cassirer (1874–1945) investigated the phenomena of myths more from an epistemological than from a psychological point of view. According to his conception, the myth has its own nature; and beside art, language, and science it constitutes one of the symbolic forms of intellectual life. It builds its world according to its own laws and derives its specific value from the association of meaning inherent in itself. On the other hand, for Cassirer, the symbolism of the myth remained a kind of primitive understanding of life that gave rise to scientific knowledge and its development.

Here P. Tillich opposed Cassirer. Myth, according to Tillich, falls in the category of the unconditioned or of the being other-worldly to which the religious act is directed. The myth chooses its own objects, which it sets up as symbols of the unconditioned. Insofar as the unconditioned is a reality, the myth in its symbolic orientation to the unconditioned is also real. Tillich emphasizes that the myth does not select its symbols arbitrarily. The creation of symbols is governed by the law that the symbol itself participates in what it is to symbolize.

Freud and Jung. Finally psychoanalysis made important contributions to the understanding of the myth. S. *Freud (1836–1939) considered myths the expression of suppressed desires. He enunciated a psychological law according to which suppressions precipitate themselves in a symbolic expression, a discovery that has served as a basis for the psychoanalysis of the meaning of dreams. Of considerable influence also has been Freud's idea of the origin of civilization out of primeval events, and of primeval sin, the permanent consequence of which he called the Oedipus complex.

Symbol formations, understood and evaluated on a purely individual basis, are interpreted by C. G. *Jung (1875–1961) as an authentic expression of superindividual truths of life, the starting point for the life of the individual ego. With the help of his concept of the collective unconscious and of archetypes as the forms under which it makes its appearance, Jung attempted to break through the barriers of individual psychology and to make dreams and myths function as the symbols in which hidden transcendence as such manifests itself in the world of human consciousness. Jung's ideas have had fruitful influence on contemporary mythological research.

Bibliography: G. LANCZKOWSKI, LexThK² 7:746–750. J. SLØK et al., RGG³ 4:1263–78, with bibliog. H. J. ROSE, A Handbook of Greek Mythology (6th ed. New York 1958) 1–16. H. USENER, Götternamen (3d ed. Bonn 1948). W. WUNDT, Völkerpsychologie (3d and 4th ed. Leipzig 1923–26) v.4–6. S. FREUD, The Interpretation of Dreams (1900–01) in Standard Edition of the Complete Psychological Works, ed. J. STRACHEY, 24 v. (London 1953–   ) v.4–5; Das Unbehagen in der Kultur (Vienna 1930), tr. J. RIVIÈRE; Civilization and Its Discontents (London 1930). B. MALINOWSKI, The Myth in Primitive Psychology (London 1926). R. OTTO, The Idea of the Holy, tr. J. W. HARVEY (2d ed. New York 1958). E. CASSIRER, Mythical Thought, v.2 of The Philosophy of Symbolic Forms, tr. R. MANHEIM, 3 v. (New Haven 1953–57). C. KLUCKHOHN, "Myths and Rituals: A General Theory," HarvThRev 35 (1942) 45–79. M. ELIADE, The Myth of the Eternal Return, tr. W. R. TRASK (Bollingen Ser. 46; New York 1954); Myths, Dreams, and Mysteries, tr. P. MAIRET (New York 1960). D. BIDNEY, "The Concept of Myth and the Problem of Psychocultural Evolution," AmAnthropologist 52 (1950) 16–26. H. ABRAHAMSSON, The Origin of Death (Uppsala 1951). C. G. JUNG and K. KERÉNYI, Einführung in das Wesen der Mythologie (4th ed. Zurich 1951). W. F. OTTO, Gesetz, Urbild und Mythos (Stuttgart 1951). E. BUESS, Die Geschichte des mythischen Erkennens (Munich 1953). J. L. SEIFERT, Sinndeutung des Mythos (Vienna 1954). H. KNITTERMEYER, Das Problem des Mythos (Wilhelmshaven 1955). W. BASCOM, "The Myth Ritual Theory," JourAmFolklore 70 (1957) 103–114. T. J. SEBEOK, ed., Myth: A Symposium (Bloomington, Ind. 1958). R. T. CHRISTIANSEN, The Migratory Legends (Helsinki 1958).

[J. SLØK]

MYTH AND MYTHOLOGY (IN THE BIBLE)

The affirmation of the presence or absence of myth in the Bible depends largely on the definition of myth. In the light of modern Biblical research, if the term is correctly understood, there is no reason why it could not be legitimately used in reference to the interpretation of a number of Biblical passages. On the definition and nature of myth, see MYTH AND MYTHOLOGY above.

In the Septuagint the Greek word μῦθος (myth) occurs only in Sir 20.19, where, however, it has the meaning of proverb. The NT condemns myths (μῦθοι) as so many "fables" (1 Tm 1.4), "old wives' tales" (1 Tm 4.7), "commandments of men," incompatible with the truth (2 Tm 4.4; Ti 1.14), and "fictitious tales" (2 Pt 1.16). Consequently, until recently scholars generally tended to exclude myth from the Bible. It was alleged that Israel's staunch monotheism was incompatible with the polytheism essential to myth, that its linear approach to historical phenomena ran counter to the cyclic pattern of myth. Biblical authors had, indeed, sometimes utilized mythical motifs for the sake of poetic ornamentation (Is 14.12–15; Ez 28.12–19); one might even grant that occasional myths had found their way into the Bible together with something of the mythical mentality that had inspired them (e.g., in Gn 2.4b–3.24), but these

had been so purged and transformed in the process that they hardly deserved the name of myth.

With a reappraisal of the nature of myth, however, and a growing tendency to consider polytheistic elements as accidental to mythopoeic mentality, more and more authors have begun to affirm the presence of myth, or something akin to myth, in the Bible. They refer to passages such as the *Yahwist's *creation story and his account of *paradise and the *fall of man, of the *deluge, and of the *tower of Babel, the many references to Yahweh's slaughter of, or domination over, the primeval sea monster, etc. (See ABYSS; CHAOS; LEVIATHAN; DRAGON.) These passages, it is argued, are neither historical (i.e., derived from human testimony based on direct observation of the events) nor properly theological (i.e., deduced by discursive reasoning process). They take place in primeval times; their main actors share many of the characteristics of mythical personages; and they constitute an attempt to explain contemporary phenomena. Yet one hesitates to apply, without reservation, the term myth to these passages because of the important differences between them and their counterparts outside Israel. There is no doubt that the purging of all polytheistic traits (and consequently of all theogonies and theomachies) and the incorporation of these narratives into a basically historical pattern make myth in the Bible something quite unique. Furthermore, the existence of a religious festival in Israel that might have served as the cultic context for the reenactment of these myths is doubtful. Recent efforts on the part of the Scandinavian School to make of the Hebrew Feast of the *New Year and the Feast of *Booths (Tabernacles) the occasion for the recitation of Biblical myths [see S. Mowinckel, Psalmenstudien (v.2 Kristiania 1922)] have not found general acceptance. However, whether or not one admits the presence of myth in the Bible depends largely on how one defines it. If myth is taken to mean no more than a popular explanation in figurative language of certain natural phenomena, there is no reason why the term cannot be applied to a number of Biblical passages.

See also DEMYTHOLOGIZING.

Bibliography: EncDictBibl 1584–88. H. CAZELLES and R. MARLÉ, DBSuppl 6:246–268. G. LANCKOWSKI and H. FRIES, LexThK² 7:746–752. S. MOWINCKEL and R. BULTMANN, RGG³ 4:1274–82. G. STÄHLIN, Kittel ThW 4:769–803. H. FRANKFORT et al., The Intellectual Adventure of Ancient Man (Chicago 1946), later pub. as Before Philosophy (pa. Baltimore 1959). C. HARTLICH and W. SACHS, Der Ursprung des Mythosbegriffes in der modernen Bibelwissenschaft (Tübingen 1952). E. O. JAMES, Myth and Ritual in the Ancient Near East (New York 1958). B. S. CHILDS, Myth and Reality in the O.T. (Naperville, Ill. 1960). J. BARR, "The Meaning of Mythology in Relation to the O.T.," VetTest 9 (1959) 1–10. J. L. McKENZIE, "Myth and the O.T.," CathBiblQuart 21 (1959) 265–282.

[L. F. HARTMAN]

MYTH AND REFLECTIVE THOUGHT

Myths as concrete, graphic narratives of the divine and its world are a religiohistorical phenomenon, reflecting also a morphological aspect of cultural development. In their actual existence they point to a datum that must be considered fundamental for solving the general problem of the nature of man.

Although in very different ways, the narratives generally designated as myths furnish basically information on the world as a whole, on the ultimate questions of human existence, on the meaning and end of life, in short, on matters to which only the most concentrated application of reflection gives access. However, the general experience of investigators is "that all questioning of the Primitives for information in respect to reflective thinking is wont to be unsuccessful" [P. Schebesta, *Die Negrito Asiens* (Vienna 1957) 2.2:35]. Do the myths, then, represent a preliminary form of an, as yet, nonreflective and immediate *consciousness in relation to the world as a whole, to a world view? And if so, to what extent and in what way is this possible?

If one begins with an actual phenomenon, something similar confronts him. In his conscience he chooses the good, that which accords with man in relation to the whole. The concept of the good and the whole is therefore essentially proper to conscience. This means, however, that the concepts proper to conscience, which are revealed in their characteristic content by reflection, are those that presuppose a relation to a whole that is itself first discerned only by reflection. The reality of conscience can be said to refer, therefore, to a spiritual dimension within man, even before reflective thought becomes occupied with a full elaboration of its content and thus makes its reality evident. In this way the possibility arises for a nonanalogical, graphic form of discourse, viz, myth, to become actual. Accordingly, myth is nothing but the immediate consciousness, expressed by language in a state that is still vague and imprecise, of ultimate relations or, in a total way, of human existence as conditioned in matter, life, society, and culture. This grounding of reflective thought in conscience gives the answer to that open and persistent aporia in philosophy regarding the possibility, in respect to content, of the basic relationship or connection that becomes evident in the thinking of thinking, i.e., of the problem that has entered the history of philosophy under the heading of *innatism (*ideae innatae*). Mythical thinking reveals itself as a constituent factor of thinking in general.

This indication of the mythical structure of man, however, raises the question of the truth and the manner of appearance of myth. One can examine the truth of the myth directly from the basic data of conscience and indirectly by means of a morphological investigation of the material of the myth's content. Accordingly, the truth in the myth dealing with origins consists in this, that man, whether in nonreflective speech or in silence (silence, insofar as it is of the same origin as speech), possesses the consciousness of his divine origin and of the divine character of the world, mankind, and history as derived from that same origin. However, myth is untrue and defective if its mythical elements are separated from their whole and are made independent—a process that can be discerned by cultural and religio-morphological study of the polytheistic forms of religion and their myths.

Myth as the constituent element of theory immediately connected with consciousness, arising out of the attitude or reaction to the world, is therefore in its truth or untruth—the transitions, at times, are necessarily fluid since there are no obvious boundaries in the defining consciousness—of decisive meaning for every age. For since man has his being in the mythical structure, the given myth is not only decisive for the possibility and truth of theory (the world view interpreted as world outlook) but also for the application that in weal or woe determines history. In fact, one might even say that man always has a world view that cannot be demythologized. In this sense reflection has before it a twofold task: (1) to investigate in what way, being mythically determined and established itself, it can find the true myth and translate it into its reality as a recognition of truth; (2) to discover in what forms myths, withdrawing into veiled silence, brought, and bring, truth and untruth to actuality in history and in the present age.

Bibliography: E. Cassirer, *Philosophy of Symbolic Forms* 3 v. (New York 1953–57) v.2. W. Dupré, "Die methodologische Bedeutung von Sprache und Mythos und das Weltbild der Bambuti," *Festschrift Paul Schebesta* (Vienna 1963). M. Eliade, *Aspects du mythe* (Paris 1963). A. Andwander, *Zum Probleme des Mythos* (Vienna 1964), with copious bibliog.

[W. DUPRÉ]

NABATAEANS

A people of North Arabia who were of historical importance and developed a high civilization from the end of the 4th century B.C. to the 2d Christian century. This article summarizes their history and civilization. For Nabataean religion, *see* ARABIA, 3.

Nabataean History. The royal title in inscriptions is *mlk nbṭw,* "king of Nabatu." The word Nabatu designates not the country, but the tribe, or rather the eponymous hero of the tribe. The personal names *Nbṭ* and *Nbṭ'l* (*Nabaṭel,* God has revealed Himself) are South Arabic. Of Arabic origin also are most of the names borne by the Nabataeans, who are therefore not to be identified with the Nabayate of the chronicles of Assurbanipal (the Nabaioth of Gn 25.13 and Is 60.7), who were Aramaeans; the root *nbṭ* is quite distinct from the root *nby.* The Nabataeans made their appearance in history only *c.* 312 B.C. Antigonus, one of the generals of Alexander the Great, sent two expeditions against these nomads, who lived by raising cattle, by the incense traffic of Arabia Felix, and by the sale of Dead Sea bitumen to Egypt. Although *Petra, the "Rock" on top of which they hoarded their wealth, was captured for a short time, the Nabataeans kept their independence against the Ptolemies and later against the Seleucids. At the time of the Machabees they were still nomads. In 2 Mc 5.8 mention is made of "Aretas, king of the Arabians," i.e., of the Nabataeans; he probably had his capital at Petra. According to 2 Mc 12.10–12 and 1 Mc 5.24–26 (cf. 9.35), the Nabataeans were living along the desert border of Transjordan. Beginning with Aretas II (*c.* 100), an almost complete list of the Nabataean kings can be reconstructed. His son Obodas I triumphed over the Hasmonaean King Alexander Jannaeus in *c.* 93 B.C. and over the Seleucid King Antiochus XII in 85 B.C. According to J. T. Milik it was this Obodas to whom the title of "god" was given and in whose honor the city in the Negeb containing his mausoleum was named Oboda (Avdat). Obodas II seems to have been a "do-nothing" king. Under Aretas III the Nabataeans were masters of Damascus from 84 to 72 B.C. They then interfered, without success, in Judean affairs, siding with Hyrcanus II against Aristobulus II. In 64 B.C. Pompey created the province of Syria and charged his successor Scaurus with the subjection of the Nabataeans. About

62 B.C. Scaurus advanced to the gates of Petra, but Aretas III bought him off with a large indemnity. Malichos I (*c.* 60–30 B.C.) and Obodas II (30–9 B.C.) are known only through their quarrels with Herod the Great. Syllaios, the all-powerful minister of Obodas II, guided and perhaps intentionally misled Aelius Gallus, the Roman governor of Egypt, during the latter's expedition, ordered by Augustus, into Arabia Felix (25–24 B.C.). But Augustus succeeded in diverting trade via Egypt, the Red Sea, and the Indian Ocean, to the detriment of the caravan route from Dedan via Petra to Gaza. Aretas IV (9 B.C. to A.D. 40) was obliged to ask Augustus to confirm his royal title, but placed after it the epithet *rḥm 'mh,* "who loves his people," thus expressing national feeling. He gave one of his daughters in marriage to Herod Antipas, his neighbor in Perea, but the Jewish tetrarch repudiated her (*c.* 27) in order to marry his sister-in-law Herodias (Mt 14.3).

It is doubtful whether the Nabataeans were masters of Damascus when St. Paul fled the city, whose gates were guarded by "the ethnarch of King Aretas" (2 Cor 11.32; cf. Gal 1.15–18, where Arabia probably means Hauran or the Decapolis). The event occurred probably between A.D. 36 and 39. Tiberius (A.D. 14–37), hostile to Aretas, certainly did not concede the Damascus region to him, and there is nothing to suggest that Caligula (A.D. 37–41) did so. The absence of any coins of that city in the name of the emperors between 33–34 and 62–63 proves nothing, considering the rarity of Damascene bronzes for the Augustan Age. The city had not ceased to be part of the province of Syria, and the ethnarch must have been the head of the Nabataean colony of Damascus. The gates were those of the neighborhood where Paul resided and were situated, according to certain indications, in the present "Christian quarter." The kingdom of Aretas began only at Bosra, but to the south it extended as far as Hegra, where there are many inscriptions dated during his reign. His son Malichos II also controlled the oasis of Duma. However, the port of Leuke Kome, on the eastern side of the Red Sea at the latitude of Hegra, was held by the Romans, who collected one-fourth of the value of all merchandise imported. In 66, Malichos II sent 6,000 men to Titus in Ptolemais (*Accho) for service against Judea. His son Rabbel II seems to have lost control of Hegra *c.* 76 and then made Bosra his capital. Bosra was chosen by Trajan as the legate's residence when Nabataea was captured by Cornelius Palma and transformed into a province of Arabia (A.D. 106). Gradually the people ceased to think of themselves as Nabataeans.

Nabataean Civilization. Power remained in the hands of the royal family, and the prime minister was given the title of brother of the king. The queens were called sisters of the king. Despite his progressive sedentarization, the king remained close to his subjects, and sometimes accounted for his actions to them. Attire did not include the tunic. Banquets were frequent, the guests gathering in groups of 13. The kingdom was divided into districts, each administered by a strategos.

Language and Inscriptions. From the time the Nabataeans settled in Idumea they borrowed the language of the local population, first for written and then for oral use. This language was a prolongation of the Aramaic of the empire, like Judeo-Aramaic (Daniel, Qumran) or Palmyrene, but with a marked conservative tendency. The relative pronoun is *di* and not *d';* the suffix of the third person masculine plural is *hom* and not *hon,* etc. There were many Arabisms, especially at Hegra, which was near Dedan with its Lihyanite (North Arabic) dialect. From the 2d century on, other Arabs, such as the Safaites and the Thamudaeans, penetrated into the province of Arabia, and the inscriptions became increasingly crammed with Arabic expressions. In fact the text bearing the most recent date (328) is almost entirely in Arabic. At first Nabataean script did not differ from Aramaic script (cf. the 3d century B.C. inscription of Halasa in the Negeb which names a certain "Haretat king of Nabatu"). About 100 B.C., however, Nabataean script underwent an evolution marked by elongation of forms and closing of curves (as in the two inscriptions of Aslah at the entrance of the gorge of Petra, the second dating from Year 1 of Obodas I). The elongation was less marked in the Hauran, and one may wonder whether the inscriptions of the high place of Si', from the Herodian epoch, are not really Aramaic. On the other hand, authentic Nabataean inscriptions are known from both sides of the Red Sea, from Sinai, from the Damascus region, and from as far distant a country as Italy.

Nabataean Art. This is an offshoot of Greco-Oriental art. It is possible only to mention here the temples of the high place of Si', east of Sueida, or the sanctuary of Khirbet Tannur dedicated to the Edomite god Qos; their ornamentation, if not their groundplan, is fundamentally akin to that of Palmyra in the last centuries B.C. and first Christian centuries, or that of Parthian Mesopotamia. More characteristic are the so-called Nabataean capitals, with corners in the shape of horns that began as Corinthian capitals deliberately left unfinished. Stone blocks of small size were used for the construction of buildings and dams. In the rock-cut tombs and living quarters the sandstone walls were drafted slantwise, giving them a corded aspect. From the architectonic point of view, facades of the rock-hewn tombs at Petra and Hegra are noteworthy; those surmounted by crenelations or by two facing "staircases" are unique. Some of the facades at Petra imitate those of a temple. The most beautiful façades, of late Hellenistic (baroque) style, may well be earlier than A.D. 106. The Nabataean sanctuaries were of three sorts: those completely open, a survival of the old Semitic *haram;* those of Arabic type,

Nabataean tomb, called el-Deir, "the Monastery," cut into the side of a cliff on a peak to the west of Petra (end of 1st century).

with a small cubical cella in the middle of the area; and those of Syrian style, with tripartite cellas. Finally, mention should be made of a very delicate variety of Nabataean pottery, decorated with stylized plant motifs.

Bibliography: DIODORUS SICULUS, tr. R. M. GEER, 2:48; 19:94–100 (LoebClLib; 1935, 1944). STRABO, 16:4.18–26. *Periplus of the Ponti Euxini,* in A. DILLER, *The Tradition of the Minor Greek Geographers* (Lancaster, Pa. 1952) 118–138, text. K. DEICHGRÄBER, Pauly-Wiss RE 9A.1 (1961) 947, fragments of Uranios, *Arabica,* preserved by Stephen of Byzantium, JOSEPHUS, *Ant.* 13–18. Articles on recent excavations by G. and A. HORSFIELD, N. GLUECK, P. PARR, P. C. HAMMOND, D. KIRKBRIDE, J. STRUGNELL, C. H. H. WRIGHT, A. NEGEV, etc. in QAntiqPal, AnAmSch OrRes, BullAmSchOrRes, BiblArchaeol, PalExplQ, *Annual of Dept. of Antiquities of Jordan,* IsrExplorJ, etc. J. T. MILIK and H. SEYRIG, "Trésor monétaire de Murabba'ât," *Revue numismatique,* ser. 6, 1 (1958) 11–26, on the coins. J. STARCKY, "Pétra et la Nabatène" DBSuppl v.7, full bibliog.

[J. STARCKY]

NABIS, the name of a small group of artists working in Paris between 1889 and 1899; the name is taken from the Hebrew for "prophet." The oldest member and spokesman for the group was Paul *Sérusier, who discovered *Gauguin in his pre-Tahitian stage and passed on his discovery to the rest. In a reaction against Impressionist naturalism they preferred to paint in flat, high-keyed color, often representing subjects with Symbolist overtones. Sérusier proclaimed that "to copy nature exercises the eye and hand but it fatally enfeebles the memory of forms. . . . Art is a means of communication among souls." Also included in the group were Maurice *Denis, *Bonnard, Vuillard, Maillol (who later turned to sculpture), and Willibrord *Verkade, a Dutch convert to Catholicism. Verkade wrote around 1890 that he thought he heard a battle-cry from studio to studio, "Walls more walls to decorate; the end of easel painting! There is nothing but decorations." He and the two other Catholics in the group, Denis and Sérusier, maintained lifelong communications and their correspondence was published in Denis's *Journal*. But the eclectic inspiration of the group was not sufficient to make the movement much more than a passing phase. Vuillard and Bonnard gradually developed a decorative mode of *Impressionism called *Intimisme*.

Bibliography: C. CHASSÉ, *Les Nabis et leur temps* (Lausanne 1960), extensive bibliog. P. SÉRUSIER, *L'ABC de la peinture* (Paris 1942). M. MALINGUE, "Petits et grands Nabis," *L'Oeil* 62 (1960) 36–46. G. MAUNER, "The Nature of Nabi Symbolism," *Art Journal* 23.2 (1963–64) 96–103. F. SELVIG, "Les Nabis: Prophets of the Vanguard," *Art News* 61 (Dec. 1962) 34–37, *passim*.

[P. M. LAPORTE]

NABUCHODONOSOR (NEBUCHADREZ-ZAR), KING OF BABYLON

Reigned Sept. 7, 605, to 562 B.C. On the 1st of Elul, upon the death of his father, Nabopolassar, Nabuchodonosor II ascended the throne of the Neo-Babylonian Empire. The spelling of his name as Nabuchodonosor in the Vulgate and Douay Version has its basis in the Septuagint spelling, Ναβουχοδονοσόρ, which has the vowels of the original name approximately correct but incorrectly has an "n" for an "r" as the third last consonant. The original Akkadian name is *Nabū-kudur-uṣur* [O Nabu, protect the border (or, the heir?)]. *See* NEBO (NABU). The Hebrew Masoretic Text has the name either as *neᵇbukadreṣṣer* (so usually in Jeremia) or less correctly as *neᵇbukadneṣṣer* (so elsewhere).

The OT and several ancient historians, such as Josephus, mention Nabuchodonosor, as do many dedicatory inscriptions of his buildings; but the details of his reign were unknown until the recent publication of the Babylonian Chronicle by the British Museum. In 608–607 B.C., Nabopolassar and Nabuchodonosor (then Crown Prince) led the Babylonian forces against the mountainous country north of northwestern Mesopotamia. The next year saw another Babylonian invasion of southern Armenia and of the cities in the vicinity of *Carchemish, the city on the Euphrates where Pharao *Nechao (Necho) had established himself after defeating King *Josia of Juda at *Mageddo (Megiddo; see 4 Kgs 23.29) and invading Syria. In the late spring of 605, after Nabopolassar had returned to Babylon, Nabuchodonosor defeated Nechao at Carchemish and again at Hamath on the Orontes. Just as Syria lay open to the Babylonian advance, Nabopolassar died in Babylon on the 8th of Ab (Aug. 15), and Nabuchodonosor returned to the capital city. The following year he was back in Syria, where he subdued *Ascalon (Ashkelon) and began to make inroads into Juda. An unsuccessful invasion of Egypt in late 601 forced Nabuchodonosor to return to Babylon to recoup his strength.

At this point King Joachim of Juda (609–598), who had paid tribute to Babylon for 3 years, rebelled and thus committed a fatal error. After conquering northern Arabia, the Babylonians advanced against Jerusalem in 598–597. Joachim died soon after the siege began, and his 18-year-old son, *Joachin, inherited the crown. After 3 months Jerusalem fell (March 16, 597), and its new King was taken to Babylon. Joachim's brother Sedecia was elevated to the throne by Nabuchodonosor. His 10-year reign (597–587) was marked by continual agitation and sedition. By 589, inflamed with fierce patriotism and bolstered by promises of Egyptian support, Juda had pushed itself into open and irrevocable revolt.

Nabuchodonosor immediately reacted and besieged Jerusalem in late 588 or early 587. On the 9th of Tammuz (July 30), 587, the city fell. Shortly afterward, it was completely destroyed, and its inhabitants were deported to Babylonia. Juda was organized into the provincial system of the empire, and its population of poor peasants was governed by Godolia (Gedalia), a former chief minister of Sedecia.

Although there is a gap in the Babylonian Chronicle extending from the 11th year of Nabuchodonosor's reign (594–593) to the 3d year of Neriglissar's (557–556), it is known from an inscription that Nabuchodonosor led his armies in an unsuccessful invasion of Egypt in 568. Nabuchodonosor's long reign saw Babylonia rise to its zenith as a world power. Temples, public buildings, palaces, and canals were built not only in Babylonia itself, but in the other cities of the realm. The German archeologists of the "Deutsch-Orient Gesellschaft," headed by Dr. R. Koldewey, began excavating the site of the city of *Babylon in 1899. The careful method employed yielded the ruins of the city that was once the capital of a world empire. After a reign of 43 years, Nabuchodonosor was succeeded by his son *Evil-Merodach. No historical value is to be attached to the Nabuchodonosor of the Book of Daniel or that of Judith.

Bibliography: EncDictBibl 1595–98. M. LEIBOVICI, DBSuppl 6:286–291. F. GÖSSMANN, LexThK² 7:861–862. P. NOBER, Enc Catt 8:1592–95. D. J. WISEMAN, *Chronicles of Chaldean Kings, 626–556 B.C., in the British Museum* (London 1956). W. F. ALBRIGHT, "The Nebuchadnezzar and Neriglissar Chronicles," BullAmSchOrRes 143 (1956) 28–33. D. N. FREEDMAN, "The Babylonian Chronicle," BiblArcheol 19 (1956) 50–60. J. BRIGHT, *A History of Israel* (Philadelphia 1959) 304–311, 324–326. M. NOTH, *The History of Israel,* tr. P. R. ACKROYD (2d ed. New York 1960) 280–294.

[D. L. MAGNETTI]

NABUCO DE ARAUJO, JOAQUIM, Brazilian writer and abolitionist; b. Recife, Aug. 19, 1849; d. Washington, D.C., Jan. 17, 1910. He was the son of José Thomaz Nabuco de Araujo, prominent jurist and statesman.

He devoted his outstanding oratorial talent to the abolition of slavery. After his election to the Chamber of Deputies at the age of 30, he consistently brought the subject of slavery to the attention of his peers. He thereby sacrificed his political career, since both political parties and the landed interests opposed any debate of the subject. He then turned to journalism and wrote *O Abolicionismo,* a study of the economic problems related to the extinction of slavery. With the Liberal party's conversion to bettering slave conditions, his popularity grew, and he regained his seat in Parliament. His elections were nationally significant because of the independence shown by the district leaders against orders from the government. He obtained Pope Leo XIII's support for his campaigns.

A law abolishing slavery was passed May 13, 1888. There was popular rejoicing, but the proponents of a republic in Brazil felt their hour had come. Eighteen months later a republic was proclaimed. Although he was urged to join the new order, Nabuco remained a monarchist.

Two of his books are Brazilian classics: *Minha formação,* his autobiographical study of his youth, and *Um estadist do imperio,* a biography of his father that is also the constitutional history of the epoch. As a historian, Nabuco is powerful and lucid. His style is noted for the charm and suavity he introduced into a language sometimes called granitic.

As Brazilian Ambassador to the United States he devoted the last years of his life furthering Pan-Americanism.

Bibliography: C. NABUCO, *The Life of Joaquim Nabuco,* tr. and ed. R. HILTON et al. (Stanford 1950).

[J. NABUCO]

NABU-NA'ID (NABONIDUS)

Last king (555–539 B.C.) of the Neo-Babylonian empire. Nabu-na'id ([the god] Nabu is exalted), or as he is called in classical sources, Nabonidus, came to the Babylonian throne in a palace revolution and introduced innovations in both politics and religion that soon won for him the hatred of the Babylonian priesthood. Their hostility contributed to his downfall on Oct. 13, 539, when Babylon fell to *Cyrus, King of Persia, without a battle.

Aramaean by origin and strongly influenced by his Aramaean mother, Nabu-na'id fostered a religious movement that aimed at replacing *Marduk, the head of the Babylonian pantheon, with the moon-god Sin, and most likely in the form of the Aramaean moon-god Teri, whose cult center was at *Haran. This alienated the Babylonian priests and showed that in religious matters Nabu-na'id ran counter to some of the deepest Babylonian traditions.

In politics he likewise displeased at least one faction in Babylon, for he was strongly pro-Assyrian and referred to the kings of Assyria as "my royal ancestors." Even more unconventional was his action in making his son Bel-šar-uṣur regent in Babylon, while he himself resided for 10 years at the oasis of Tema in the Arabian desert.

Many solutions have been offered to the problem of Nabu-na'id's bizarre activities. He was not, as was once proposed, an antiquary incapable of ruling, or a religious fanatic heedless of consequences. It seems more likely that he attempted, with boldness and originality, to unite the Aramaeans with the Babylonians against the growing menace of the Persians. Beside his political motivation, a certain religious idealism probably inspired this last of the Babylonian kings.

With the coming of Cyrus the Great into Babylon Nabu-na'id seems to have been exiled to eastern Persia. But his legend lived on. Behind the more illustrious name of *Nabuchodonosor (Nebuchadrezzar), Nabuna'id appears in the Jewish traditions that are incorporated in Dn 2–5 (*see* DANIEL, BOOK OF). Likewise in Herodotus's account of the last Babylonian dynasty his two Labyneti seem to involve a confusion between Nabuchodonosor and Nabu-na'id. However, in a fragment of the *Dead Sea Scrolls Nabu-na'id utters in his own name a pious prayer to the God of Israel referring to his 7-year illness at Tema and to the futility of his earlier prayers to his pagan gods.

Bibliography: P. GARELLI, DBSuppl 6:269–286. L. HARTMAN, EncDictBibl 1592–94. J. LEWY, "The Late Assyro-Babylonian Cult of the Moon and its Culmination at the Time of Nabonidus," HebUCAnn 19 (1946) 405–489. A. L. OPPENHEIM, "Babylonian and Assyrian Historical Texts," Pritchard ANET 305b–314a. D. N. FREEDMAN, "The Prayer of Nabonidus," BullAmSch OrRes 145 (1957) 31–32.

[W. L. MORAN]

NACCHIANTI, GIACOMO (NACLANTUS),

theologian; b. Florence, *c.* 1500; d. Chioggia, March 6, 1569. In 1518 he joined the Dominican Order and in 1544 was named bishop of Chioggia. During the first phase of the Council of Trent he intervened vehemently, although not always opportunely. Besides opposing the privileges accorded by the council to mitred abbots, he attacked the propositions of those council fathers who wanted to place simple tradition on a plane with inspired Scripture, describing them as impious. Three days later he submitted with exemplary humility to the final decree. For a time his teaching remained suspect, and an inquiry was conducted in Nacchianti's diocese in 1548 and 1549. After the favorable outcome of the inquiry, Nacchianti played an important role in the 1562 session of the council. He contributed to the disciplinary discussion on the question of bishops' residing in their dioceses and the doctrinal discussion on the Last Supper as a sacrifice. When he returned to his diocese after the council, he applied its decrees zealously. His principal works, printed originally in Venice (1567), are the *Ennarrationes in Epist. ad Ephesios, Ennarrationes in Epist. ad Romanos, Sacrae Scripturae medulla,* and the *Tractationes XVIII theologales variae.* Though faithful to St. Thomas, Nacchianti nonetheless fused abundant scriptural material into a synthesis of his own.

Bibliography: Quétif-Échard 2.1:202–203. A. PIOLANTI, Enc Catt 8:1596–97. M. M. GORCE, DTC 11.1:2–3.

[W. D. HUGHES]

NADAL, GERÓNIMO,

Jesuit theologian, special emissary of St. Ignatius Loyola in promulgating the Constitutions of the Society of Jesus throughout Europe; b. Palma, Majorca, Aug. 11, 1507; d. Rome, April 3, 1580.

Nadal studied with Ignatius at Alcalá in 1526 and again at Paris from 1532 to 1535, but refused to make the Spiritual Exercises. He was ordained at Avignon, received his doctorate in theology, and in 1538 returned to Majorca, where he taught theology. In 1542, after reading a letter written by Francis Xavier from India, he began to think about the society in Rome and finally joined Ignatius there in 1545. He entered the society on November 29 of that year. He became so closely associated with Ignatius that he is variously referred to by authors as Ignatius's "voice and soul," "heart," "arm," "second mind," "alter ego," and the "second founder of the Jesuits."

Nadal became the first rector of the first Jesuit college, that of Messina in Sicily, in 1548. His educational program there led eventually to the development of the Ratio Studiorum. In 1552, he began a life of travel from one end of Europe to the other, under four successive generals, promulgating the newly written constitutions of the society, acting as vicar-general, assistant, visitor, and peacemaker. Twice rector of the Roman College, he took part in the Diet of Augsburg and was a papal theologian at the Council of Trent.

Although unknown among spiritual writers, Nadal breathes throughout his many works, in great part unpublished, the special spirit of the Society of Jesus. His teaching on prayer is especially illuminating, particularly on the relationship between prayer and action.

Bibliography: G. NADAL, *Epistolae,* 4 v. (MonHistSJ; 1905). M. NICOLAU, *Jeronimo Nadal, S.J. 1507–1580: Sus obras y doctrinas espirituales* (Madrid 1949). J. F. CONWELL, *Contemplation in Action: A Study in Ignatian Prayer* (Spokane 1957). J.

BRODRICK, *The Progress of the Jesuits, 1556–79* (New York 1947).

[J. F. CONWELL]

NAGASAKI, ARCHDIOCESE OF (NAGASAKIENSIS)

Metropolitan see since 1959, whose seat is in the seaport of Nagasaki on the west coast of Kyushu Island, south *Japan. In 1964 the see had 60 parishes, 65 secular and 42 religious priests, 233 sisters, and 76,300 Catholics in a population of 1,677,500; it is 1,619 square miles in area. Its four suffragans, which had 298 priests, 848 sisters, 25,000 students in 93 schools, and 50,000 Catholics in a population of 18,128,000, were Fukuoka (created in 1927), Hiroshima (1959), Kagoshima (1955), and Oita (1961).

When the Apostolic Vicariate of Japan, created in 1846 and entrusted to the *Paris Foreign Mission Society, was divided into north and south vicariates (1876), Nagasaki became the seat of the latter. When the Vicariate of Central Japan was created (1888), Nagasaki's jurisdiction was restricted to Kyushu and the Goto and Ryukyu Islands. With the establishment of the hierarchy in Japan (1891), Nagasaki became a diocese, suffragan to *Tokyo. In 1927 Kagoshima and Fukuoka were detached from Nagasaki's jurisdiction. In 1959 Nagasaki became an archdiocese.

Nagasaki was probably named after Nagasaki Kotarô, a late 12th-century ruler. The Jesuit Gaspar Vilela built a church of All Saints in Nagasaki (*c.* 1569), which soon was a Christian city. From 1571 Nagasaki was the terminal port in Japan for Portuguese ships from *Macao. In 1580 the Christian daimio Omura Sumitada donated the city to the Church; but after Hideyoshi's anti-Christian edict (1587), Nagasaki became an imperial city. Alessandro *Valignano, the great organizer of Jesuit missions in Japan, visited Nagasaki. The bishops of Japan's first see, erected in Funai (now Oita) in 1588, as a rule had to reside in Nagasaki. After Bp. Luis de Cerqueira (1598–1614), who founded a seminary in Nagasaki (1601) and ordained 15 Japanese priests, persecution and Japanese isolation brought about the end of the Japanese episcopacy.

Christian missionaries returned to Nagasaki in 1863 under the auspices of the Paris Foreign Mission Society and discovered many descendants of the early Christians. Bernard Petitjean (1866–84), the first occupant of the Vicariate of Japan, founded a seminary for Japanese clergy. Jules Cousin (1885–1911) held the first synod of Japan in Nagasaki (1890). Jean Combaz (1912–26) dedicated the largest church in the Far East at Urakami in Nagasaki; it was destroyed by the atom bomb of 1945 but was rebuilt by 1959. Januarius Hayasaka (1927–37) was the first Japanese bishop of Nagasaki. In 1962 a shrine was built on the hill of Nishizaka near Nagasaki for the 26 martyrs who were crucified there in 1597 (*see* JAPAN, MARTYRS OF).

The archdiocese had in 1964 an archdiocesan minor seminary founded in 1875, four minor seminaries of religious orders, a junior college with 200 girls, 12 high schools with 5,374 students, 3 elementary schools with 798 pupils, and 36 kindergartens with 6,513 children. There were 2 archdiocesan hospitals, 5 orphanages, 36 nurseries, and a home for the aged.

Bibliography: E. PECORAIO, EncCatt 8:1598–99. *Catholic Directory of Japan, 1962–63* (Tokyo 1962). MissCattol 407–408. J. VAN HECKEN, *The Catholic Church in Japan since 1859,* tr. and rev. J. VAN HOYDONCK (Tokyo 1963). H. CIESLIK, "Zur Geschichte der kirchlichen Hierarchie in der alten Japanmission," NZMissw 18 (1962) 42–58, 81–107, 177–195; "The Training of a Japanese Clergy in the 17th Century," *Studies in Japanese Culture* (Tokyo 1963) 41–78. AnnPont (1965) 292. **Illustration credit:** Japan National Tourist Organization.

[A. SCHWADE]

View of the harbor of Nagasaki, Japan, with one of the old Catholic churches in the foreground.

NAGLE, NANO (HONORIA)

NAGLE, NANO (HONORIA), educator, foundress of the Presentation Sisters; b. Ballygriffin, near Mallow, County Cork, Ireland, *c.* 1718; d. Cork, April 26, 1784. She was the eldest of seven children of Garret Nagle and Ann Mathew, members of the remnant of the dispossessed Catholic landowners and *Jacobites in politics. During an unexplained change in family fortunes (*c.* 1728), she was sent to France. On her father's death (*c.* 1746), she returned to Dublin with her mother and sister Ann. Since 1733 Dublin Catholics in addition to struggling against the disabling *penal laws had had to contend against a new threat to the faith, the heavily endowed government-supported exploitation of poverty, contrived through the Charter Schools and their proselytizing institutions. The discovery that her sister Ann had disposed of a dress-length of silk—Nano liked to be fashionable—to help the poor, followed shortly afterward by Ann's death, fired her determination to devote the remainder of her life to God in the service of the poor. The first step was a return to the family home to begin her apostolate in the immediate district. However, overwhelmed by the immensity of the problem compounded of poverty and ignorance, she entered a convent in France, but not for long. Solemnly advised by her Jesuit director, she returned to begin a school in a mud cabin in Cove Lane, Cork, *c.* 1754 or 1755. In 9 months, at a time when Catholic schools were illegal, 200 girls were attending. In 1757 she was aided by a

Nano Nagle.

considerable inheritance, and within 2 years she was conducting seven schools, five for girls and two for boys, that provided a rudimentary secular education, religious instruction, and an assiduous preparation for the encounter with Christ in the Sacraments. To expand and make permanent this apostolic work for the poor she introduced the Ursuline nuns in 1771, at great cost to herself. But her heart was set on the specific needs of the Irish apostolate, and so she founded in 1775, with a very few companions, the Society of the Charitable Instruction, "which excluded every exercise of charity, which was not in favour of the poor" (Walsh), and which, after her death, grew into the famous Presentation Order. An inspiration to the men of her time, this small, physically weak woman radiated a Pauline energy in her zeal for the Christian education of youth.

Bibliography: T. J. WALSH, *Nano Nagle and the Presentation Sisters* (Dublin 1959). M. R. O'CALLAGHAN, *Flame of Love: Life of Nano Nagle* (Milwaukee 1960).

[J. J. MEAGHER]

NAGLE, URBAN, or Edward J., dramatist, orator, pioneer in the apostolate of the theater; b. Providence,

Urban Nagle.

R.I., Sept. 10, 1905; d. Cincinnati, Ohio, March 11, 1965. After public and parochial schooling, he graduated from La Salle Academy and Providence College and received a Ph.D. (1934) from The Catholic Uni-

versity of America, Washington, D.C. He was professed as a Dominican friar on Aug. 19, 1925, and ordained on June 15, 1931. Subsequently he served as a professor at Providence College, the editor of the *Holy Name Journal,* and chaplain for the Dominican Sisters' motherhouse at St. Mary of the Springs, Columbus, Ohio.

Nagle devoted the first 20 years of his priestly life to the drama, while fulfilling other assignments. In 1932, with Thomas F. Carey, OP, he founded the Blackfriars Guild. Five years later they established the Blackfriar Institute of Dramatic Arts at Catholic University, which later became the Speech and Drama Department. As one of the cofounders of the Catholic Theatre Conference (1937), Nagle served for 25 years on its board of governors, and was honored in 1961 with its Father Dineen Award (*see* CATHOLIC THEATRE MOVEMENT). From 1940 to 1951 he was the moderator of the Blackfriars Guild in New York City, which operates the oldest off-Broadway theater.

Nagle's principal dramas were *Barter* (1929), a Longmans Green prize play; *Catherine the Valiant* (1931); *Savonarola* (1938), selected as one of the Ten Best Plays of the 1941–42 season by the New York *Herald-Tribune; Lady of Fatima* (1948); and *City of Kings* (1949), a Christopher prize play. Aware of the apostolic potentiality of radio and television, Nagle was a speaker on many religious programs, particularly the "Hour of Faith" and the "Catholic Hour." His book of essays, *Uncle George and Uncle Malachy* (1946), is a compilation of some of his addresses. His *Behind the Masque* (1951) details his work in theater and other media of communications.

Bibliography: W. ROMIG, ed., *The Book of Catholic Authors,* 5th ser. (Grosse Pointe 1957).

[J. B. LARNEN]

NAGOT, FRANCIS CHARLES, religious superior; b. Tours, France, April 19, 1734; d. Emmitsburg, Md., April 9, 1816. He made his classical studies at the Jesuit college in his native city. In 1753 he entered the Little Community of Saint-Sulpice, Paris. He was accepted as a candidate for the Society of St. Sulpice, and ordained on May 31, 1760. In 1760 he was appointed to teach theology at the major seminary in Nantes, and he earned his doctorate in theology from the University of Nantes, with which the seminary was affiliated. In 1768 he was recalled to Paris and made superior of the Little Company. Two years later he became superior of the Little Seminary of Saint-Sulpice. In 1789 he was appointed vice rector of the Grand Seminary of Saint-Sulpice and named one of the 12 assistants of the superior general. He was sent to London in 1790 to arrange with Bp. John Carroll for the foundation of a seminary in the new Diocese of Baltimore, Md. Nagot, having been designated superior of the group, arrived in Baltimore with three Sulpician priests and five students. On July 18, 1791, they occupied One-Mile Tavern at North Paca Street, on the site of the present St. Mary's Seminary, the first Catholic seminary in the U.S. In 1806 Nagot opened a minor seminary at Pigeon Hill, Pa., but in 1809 this seminary closed and·the students were transferred to Mt. St. Mary's, Emmitsburg, Md. Shortly after observing his sacerdotal golden jubilee, Nagot resigned as superior of Mt. St. Mary's. He continued to live at the seminary until his death. The best known of his five published works is the *Vie de M. Olier* (1818).

Bibliography: L. BERTRAND, *Bibliothèque sulpicienne*, 3 v. (Paris 1900) v.2.

[C. J. NOONAN]

NAGPUR, ARCHDIOCESE OF (NAGPURENSIS),

metropolitan see since 1953, in Maharashtra State, central *India. In 1963 it had in 72,680 square miles 16 parishes, 50 secular and 26 religious priests, 46 men in 3 religious houses, 196 women in 11 convents, and 16,500 Catholics in a population of 14,288,000. Its suffragan Amravati (created in 1955) had 14 parishes, 27 priests, 107 sisters, and 16,500 Catholics in a population of 8,400,000 in an area of 31,464 square miles. Priests from *Goa visited Nagpur in 1820, and in 1839 Irish military chaplains resided in Kamptee and Jaina, to be joined later by missionaries of Annecy from the Vicariate Apostolic of Vizagapatam (a diocese in 1886). Nagpur, a diocese (1887–1953), came under British rule in 1853. Evangelization of the native people began in 1897; the first Indian prelates were E. D'Souza, MSFS (1951–64) and L. Raymond (1964–). The city of Nagpur, with a population of 644,000, has a state university which was founded in 1923.

Bibliography: *The Catholic Directory of India, 1962* (Allahabad, India 1962). AnnPont (1964) 292.

[E. R. HAMBYE]

NAHMANIDES (MOSES BEN NAHMAN)

Talmudist, Biblical commentator; b. Gerona, Kingdom of Aragon, Spain, c. 1195; d. Acre, Palestine, c. 1270. According to the acrostic formed by his title and name, Rabbi Moses ben Nahman, he was called "the RaMBaN," in official non-Jewish documents, "Maestre Bonastrug de Porta," and "Gerondi" from his birthplace.

Life. In addition to his rabbinical duties, first at Gerona and then at Barcelona, Nahmanides seems to have practiced medicine. He was the father of a family that included, besides his daughters, a son who died early in life, a son named Solomon, and another named Nahmān. The most noteworthy episodes in his career were his unsuccessful attempt, c. 1232, to conciliate the factions that warred over *Maimonides' *Guide for the Perplexed,* and his celebrated disputation in 1263 at Barcelona with Pablo Cristiá, OP, often styled erroneously "Pablo Christiani."

Fray Pablo, a convert from Judaism, had undertaken to demonstrate the truth of Christianity from Jewish sources and had enlisted the authority of Jaime I of Aragon to arrange a disputation with Nahmanides. Freedom of speech was stipulated for this debate, but both sides published accounts claiming victory. Nahmanides' account gave such offense that he was arraigned, sentenced to 2 years' banishment, and his pamphlet was burned. Attempts were made to increase this sentence; Pope Clement IV intervened on the side of severity, although he forbade the execution or mutilation of Nahmanides.

On Sept. 2, 1267, Nahmanides arrived in Jerusalem where he spent his remaining years in exile; he died, probably at Acre, and was buried at Haifa, close to the grave of Jehiel of Paris.

Writings. At 15 Nahmanides began to write supplements to the Code of Rabbi Isaac Alfāsī and soon followed these with writings intended to defend that master against Rabbi Zerahiah ha-Levi Gerondi and Rabbi Abraham ben David. Nahmanides is the author of glosses on a long list of Talmudic treatises and of at least three works of halakah. As he had defended Alfāsī in his youth, so in his maturity Nahmanides defended the 9th-century "Laws of the Ancients" against Maimonides, although, in a letter to the conservative rabbis of France, he praised the merits of Maimonides. His "Letter on the Sanctity [of Marriage]" opposed the disdain for human impulse which, he felt, Maimonides had adopted from "that Greek," Aristotle. Nahmanides wrote commentaries on the Canticle of Canticles, on the Book of Job, and, in exile, on the Pentateuch; he published a sermon preached in the presence of the King of Castile. Three letters written during his exile have survived. He commented on the *Book of *Yesirah* and possibly on other cabalistic texts. He wrote also liturgical poems and prayers.

Exegetical Postulates. As early as his defense of Alfāsī, Nahmanides set down in his "Wars of the Lord" a principle Aristotle would not have disavowed: "There is in the art [of commenting] no such certain demonstration as in mathematics or astronomy" (Schechter, 112). The authority of the ancient rabbis, he held, deserved respect: "Though their words are not quite evident to us, we submit to them." Despite his "desire and delight to be the disciple of the earlier authorities," even the "pure wine of their wisdom" must give way to evidence. He was unwilling to be "a donkey carrying books." Hence, "when their views are inconceivable to my thoughts, I will plead in all modesty, but shall judge according to the sight of my eyes" (*ibid.,* 111, 112). One instance of such independence is his rejection of the dictum of Rabbi Simlai that there are 614 precepts in the Law. "How to number the commandments," wrote Nahmanides, "is a matter on which I suspect all of us [are] mistaken and the truth must be left to Him who will solve all doubts" (*ibid.,* 112). Since Rabbi Simlai's text is merely "homiletical," the solution given is optional—a line of argument to which he had recourse in his disputation with Fray Pablo. Another crucial assertion of Nahmanides in the course of that debate is that the date of the appearance of the Messiah has less importance for Jews than Christians imagine. In his *Date of the Redemption* Nahmanides argued that to be faithful to the Mosaic Law under Christian rule is more difficult, and thus more meritorious, than in the days of the Messiah.

Theological Opinions. Nahmanides was content to enumerate three basic Jewish dogmas: the world has been created, God exercises providence, and God possesses a knowledge that is also foreknowledge and omniscience. But Nahmanides' thought is rich in unconventional solutions. God, identical with His Glory and Presence, is the author not only of conspicuous miracles such as the 10 plagues of Egypt, but also of miracles so frequent and constant that they escape all notice. The Torah (Mosaic Law) knows that all things are miraculous and attributes "nothing to nature or to the order of the world" (Schechter, 119–120). Apart from the Torah "there would be no difference between man and the lower animate species"; even Christians and Moslems, thanks to translations, are "heirs of the Torah" and this is why they too are civilized (*ibid.,* 122). The soul of man exists before its life in the material body and a soul can animate successively more than one body. Thus in a levirate marriage a child can inherit the soul of his actual father's deceased brother; and it is with justice that the iniquity of the father falls on his children in whom his guilty soul lives anew (*ibid.*, 118).

Naḥmanides deplored his exile in moving terms: "I am banished from my table, far removed from friend and kinsman . . . with the sweet and dear children whom I have brought up on my knees, I left also my soul." But he knew the solace of the Psalmist too: "The loss of all this and of every other glory my eyes saw is compensated by having now the joy of being a day in thy courts [O Jerusalem]!" (*ibid.*, 109, 110).

Bibliography: S. SCHECHTER, *Studies in Judaism* (1st ser. Philadelphia 1920). On the disputation between M. Naḥmanides and P. Cristiá, see C. ROTH, "The Disputation of Barcelona (1263)," HarvThRev 43 (1950) 117–144. G. VAJDA, *Introduction à la pensée juive du moyen âge* (Paris 1947) 110, 152, 153, 165, 210, 232, 233.

[E. A. SYNAN]

NAHOR, name of two men in the patriarchal traditions. The first Nahor (Heb. *nāḥôr*) is the son of Sarug (of the line of Sem) and the father of Abraham's father *Thare (Gn 11.22–25); as an ancestor of Abraham, he is mentioned in Luke's *genealogy of Jesus (Lk 3.34).

The other Nahor is the son of Thare and brother of Abraham and of Lot's father Aran (Gn 11.27–28). Like Jacob (35.23c) and Ismael (25.12–16), he is the father of 12 sons: 8 from his wife Melcha and 4 from his concubine Roma (22.20–24). Perhaps the names of his wife Melcha (Heb. *milkâ*, queen) and his sister-in-law *Sara (Heb. *śārâ*, mistress, lady) are to be connected with the Akkadian *malkatu* (queen) as a title of the goddess Istar (*see* ASTARTE) and *šarratu* (queen) as a title of the moon-goddess and thus derived from the names of the local deities of *Haran.

The eight sons of this Nahor by his wife Melcha appear to be the eponymous ancestors of Aramaean tribes or places: Us, Buz, Camuel, Chased, Hazau, Pheldas, Jedlaph, and Bathuel. Us (Heb. *'ûṣ*) is listed among "the sons of Aram," i.e., Aramaean tribes, in Gn 10.23, and a certain "land of Us" is the fatherland of Job (Jb 1.1), inhabited by the *bᵉnê qedem* (sons of the East, i.e., Easterners; Jb 1.3). The tribe of Buz is mentioned, with Dedan and Thema, in Jer 25.23 as one of the tribes of the desert (see also Jb 32.2). Chased (Heb. *keśed*) is the eponymous ancestor of the Chaldeans (Heb. *kaśdîm*), an Aramaic people of the Syrian Desert [*see* CHALDEANS (IN THE BIBLE)]. A tribal name similar to Hazau (Heb. *ḥăzô*) is found in the Assyrian inscriptions. Bathuel is the father of *Rebecca and *Laban (Gn 24.15, 29), and Laban is called "an Aramean of Phaddan-Aram" (25.20). The sons of Nahor by his concubine Roma are Tabee, Gaham, Thahas, and Maacha (22.24). Tabee (Heb. *ṭebaḥ*) appears also as the name of a town near Damascus (2 Sm 8.8). Maacha (Heb. *ma'ăkâ*) is the name of a region and a tribe south of Damascus (Jos 12.5; 13.11; Dt 3.14). These names serve to connect Israel vertically and horizontally with other peoples of the ancient Near East.

Nahor's own name is probably to be connected with the place called *Nuḥuru, Niḥaru,* or *Niḥaran* in the Old-Assyrian tablets and *Til-Naḫiri* (Mound of Nahor) in the Mari tablets. This place was near the ancient city of Haran and was perhaps the same as "the city of Nahor" mentioned in Gn 24.10. Nahor is presented as a polytheist in the Bible; in the covenant made between Jacob and Laban the latter swears by "the gods of Nahor," and Josue alludes to Nahor's religion when he tells the Israelites that their forefathers "served other gods" (Jos 24.2).

Bibliography: R. DE VAUX, "Les Patriarches hébreux et les découvertes modernes," RevBibl 55 (1948) 321–347, esp. 323–324. W. F. ALBRIGHT, *Recent Discoveries in Bible Lands* (New York 1956) 73. G. E. WRIGHT, *Biblical Archaeology* (rev. ed. Philadelphia 1963). R. T. O'CALLAGHAN, *Aram Naharaim: A Contribution to the History of Upper Mesopotamia in the Second Millennium B.C.* (Rome 1962). InterDictBibl 3:497–498. H. JUNKER, LexThK² 7:765. EncDictBibl 1600–01.

[E. MARTIN]

NAHUM, BOOK OF

A collection of oracles exulting over the fall of *Ninive, capital of Assyria, enemy of Yahweh and His people.

Division and Content. The book consists of five literary units, as follows: (1) An alphabetic psalm (1.2–10). The acrostic, however, is incomplete and the order somewhat disturbed. It describes a theophany of Yahweh, destroying His enemies and protecting those who trust in Him. The form and content of this section differ from the rest of the book. Many scholars, accordingly, hold that it is not Nahum's work; it may be earlier or later. The editor who collected Nahum's oracles and who is responsible for the present book probably inserted this psalm. As an introductory poem, it provides the proper light for viewing Ninive's fall. (2) An oracle of doom against an Assyrian king, probably Sennacherib who invaded the land in 701 B.C. (1.11, 14). (3) An oracle of consolation for Juda (1.12–13; 2.1, 3). The theme common to these verses is hope and comfort for Juda; she will no longer suffer from Assyria. Some scholars regard these verses as additions to Nahum's poetry. The evidence for this view is not very forceful. (4) Two poems on Ninive's fall (2.2, 4–14; 3.1–3). The

God speaking to Nahum and his disciple, illuminated capital "O" to the Book of Nahum in the early 13th-century "Great Bible of Demeter Nekcsei-Lipocz" in the Library of Congress, Washington, D.C. (Pre. Acq. MS 1, Vol. II, fol. 189). The artist has given God the Father the usual iconographic attributes of Christ.

first is a vivid war song that describes with great effectiveness the storming and plundering of Ninive and the flight of her people. The second poem opens with a cry of woe for Ninive. The description of the confusion of the stricken city is remarkably effective. (5) Two short satires on Ninive's fall. The first (3.4–7) depicts Ninive as a harlot; she will receive the punishment imposed on a harlot. The second satire (3.8–19) recalls the fate of *Thebes (Noh), the ancient Egyptian capital. Ninive is no better; a similar destruction awaits her. Assurbanipal, the Assyrian king, captured Thebes in 663 B.C. Ninive fell to the Babylonians and Medes in the late summer (July–August) of 612 B.C.

Composition, Date, and Teaching. The Book of Nahum is a collection of oracles, edited like the other *prophetic books of the OT. Nahum's oral preaching probably took place during the period 626–612 B.C. Some modern authors have proposed a different view of the book; they consider Nahum a cultic work, a thanksgiving liturgy over the accomplished fall of Ninive or a rogation liturgy praying for its fall. It is likely that Nahum was a temple prophet and perhaps associated with Josia in the work of reform. But the textual evidence for these interpretations is scant.

Nahum is a thoroughgoing Israelite, a patriot who proclaims Yahweh's fidelity to His vine (2.3). More than once he affirms Yahweh's universal lordship of history. He always relates Ninive's punishment to the sins of Assyria. Nahum's prophesying coincided with Josia's reign, the period of great *Deuteronomic reform. This may explain the absence of any reference to Israel's sins. Another explanation may simply be that not all of Nahum's oracles have been preserved.

Bibliography: A. GEORGE, DBSuppl 6:291–301. EncDictBibl 1601–02. B. VAWTER, *The Conscience of Israel* (New York 1961) 219–221. J. P. HYATT, "Nahum," *Peake's Commentary on the Bible,* ed. M. BLACK and H. H. ROWLEY (New York 1962) 635–636.

[J. MORIARITY]

NAILS, HOLY

Term used to designate the nails with which the Roman soldiers fastened Jesus to the cross. Though their history and present location are uncertain, the holy nails are regarded with veneration by Christians because of their connection with the *Crucifixion of Jesus.

The Roman manner of crucifixion was by means of ropes or nails or both together. The narratives of the *Passion of Christ in the Bible, with their bare statement of the event, do not specify whether ropes or nails were used in the Crucifixion of Jesus. More informative are the accounts of the resurrected Christ; that of John explicitly states that Jesus' hands carried the mark of the nails (Jn 20.25, 27), while that of Luke, according to the commonly accepted text, states that the feet, too, carried such marks (Lk 24.39). The Septuagint translation of Ps 21(22).17 (traditionally taken as a messianic psalm) as "They have dug [ὤρυξαν] my hands and my feet" helped to establish the view that the feet of Jesus also were nailed to the cross.

In regard to the feet, the iconography of Christian tradition shows three successive stages: the earliest representations of Jesus on the cross (on the carved door of Santa Sabina, Rome, and the *crucifix in St. Martin's cathedral, Lucca, Italy—both from the 5th century) show only the hands of Jesus nailed to the

cross; from the 6th to the 12th century each foot is represented as nailed separately to the cross; from the 13th century onward the image of Jesus on the cross is generally depicted with only one nail piercing both feet, with one foot on top of the other. Yet the witness of iconography, far removed from the actual event, has followed custom based on uncertain traditions. The Holy *Shroud of Turin indicates that the feet of Jesus were nailed, but it does not give clear evidence whether they were nailed separately or together. However, it would have been difficult for executioners to pierce both feet of a condemned man with a single nail; hence it seems probable that Jesus' feet were nailed separately.

The history of the holy nails is less certain than their number. St. *Helena is credited with having found the holy nails when she discovered the true cross of Jesus. According to St. *Gregory of Tours (PL 71:710) two of the nails were used to make a bit for the bridle of Constantine's horse, and another was used to decorate his statue. At present some 30 nails, each purporting to be one of the original holy nails, are venerated throughout the world. Which, if any, of these is authentic will probably never be determined because of the maze of devotion and emotion that has accumulated around them.

Bibliography: J. W. HEWITT, "The Use of Nails in the Crucifixion," HarvThRev 25 (1932) 29–45. L. H. GRONDIJS, *L'Iconographie byzantine du Crucifié mort sur la croix* (2d ed. Brussels 1947). C. E. POCKNEE, *Cross and Crucifix in Christian Worship and Devotion* (London 1962). J. BLINZLER, *The Trial of Jesus,* tr. I. and F. MCHUGH (Westminster, Md. 1959) 264–265. P. BARBET, *A Doctor at Calvary,* (New York 1954). W. BULST, *The Shroud of Turin,* tr. S. MCKENNA and J. J. GALVIN (Milwaukee 1957) 38, 49, 62. H. THURSTON, CE 10:672.

[M. W. SCHOENBERG]

NAIN, a town in Galilee, south of Nazareth, at the north foot of the Hill of Moreh (the latter mentioned in Jgs 7.1). Although it was probably inhabited since early Israelite times, Nain is not referred to in the OT. It is mentioned only once in the Bible—in Lk 7.11 as the town where Jesus raised a widow's son from the dead (7.11–17). All the NT Greek MSS give its name as Ναΐν (Nain), and the little Arab village that was on the site until the Israeli war of 1948 was still called Nein. A Jewish midrash connects the town's name with the words, "and the land was pleasant (nā'ēmâ)," that occur in Jacob's blessing of Issachar (Gn 49.15), in whose tribal territory the town lay (see Dalman 191). Perhaps St. Jerome knew of this tradition when he spelled the town's name as Naim in the Vulgate. The ruins of the Byzantine church and the Crusader church on the site have not yet been excavated.

Bibliography: C. KOPP, *The Holy Places of the Gospels,* tr. R. WALLS (New York 1963) 236–241. G. H. DALMAN, *Sacred Sites and Ways,* tr. P. P. LEVERTOFF (New York 1935) 185, 190–192, 210. D. C. PELLET, InterDictBibl 3:500. Abel GéogrPal 2:394–395.

[G. H. GUYOT]

NAIROBI, ARCHDIOCESE OF (NAIROBIENSIS),

metropolitan see since 1953, in southeast *Kenya, East Africa. In 1963 it had in 13,488 square miles 77 parishes, 8 secular and 107 religious priests, 109 men in 31 religious houses, 195 women in 36 convents, and 140,000 Catholics in a total population of 1,030,140. Its 7 suffragans, which had 146 parishes,

380 priests, 834 sisters, and 872,600 Catholics in a population of 7,793,000, were: Eldoret (established 1959), Kisii (1960), Kisumu (1953), Kitui (1963), Marsabit (1964), Meru (1953), Mombasa (1965), and Nyeri (1953); and the Prefecture Apostolic of Ngong, with 3 parishes, 7 priests, 9 sisters, and 2,070 Catholics in a population of 60,000. Nairobi is also the capital of Kenya.

The diocese of Nairobi succeeded to the Vicariate Apostolic of *Zanzibar. The Augustinian convent on Zanzibar founded by Vasco da *Gama in 1499 was dispersed by Arabs in 1698. Holy Ghost Fathers labored in the vast Prefecture Apostolic of Zanguebar (1860), a vicariate in 1883, the seat of which moved from Zanzibar to Nairobi in 1933. The see has widespread educational, medical, and welfare facilities; and the Society of St. Vincent de Paul and the Legion of Mary are active. The major seminary of Langata is one of the best in Africa. Protestants, who began missionary activity in 1899, number about the same as Catholics. Islam is strong, especially along the coast. Since 1959 the Orthodox metropolitan of East Africa has resided in Nairobi. The Kikuyus, disillusioned with the Mau Mau, offer the Church a field of expansion.

Bibliography: *The Catholic Directory of East and West Africa 1961* (Nairobi 1961). AnnPont (1964) 292.

[J. J. O'MEARA]

NAJRAN, MARTYRS OF, 5th- and 6th-century Christians put to death in South Arabia (feast in the Roman Martyrology, Oct. 24). St. Arethas and his companions were martyred in Najran, a town in northern *Yemen and a center of South Arabian Christianity. Before 520, the South Arabian Prince *Dhū Nuwās (Dunaan), a convert to Judaism, revolted against the Aksumite Ethiopians who ruled the Arabs and Jews of Yemen. He seized the capital, Zafar, massacred the garrison and clergy, and turned the church into a synagogue. In 523 (or late 524) he blockaded Najran, but impatient of a long siege, he offered an amnesty in return for capitulation. Despite the warnings of the aged Prince Arethas, the people agreed. Dhū Nuwās pillaged the Christians, exhumed and burned the corpse of Bishop Paul, set fire to the church, cast 427 priests and deacons, monks and consecrated virgins into a furnace at the bottom of a ravine, decapitated Arethas and 200 (or 340) others among the chiefs and nobility, and massacred more than 4,000 of the common people who refused to declare that "Christ is a man and not a God." The atrocities were halted when the Aksumite King Elesbaan and his army defeated the forces of Dhū Nuwās and annihilated the power of the Yemenite Jews; unfortunately he used barbaric cruelty in the process. Though the Najran martyrs were undoubtedly Christians, it is not clear to what extent they may have unwittingly been Monophysites.

Bibliography: BHO 99–106. ActSS Oct. 10:661–762, 919–920. J. PÉRIER, DHGE 3:1650–53, brief critical appraisal of the sources. J. RYCKMANS, *La Persécution des chrétiens himyarites au sixième siècle* (Istanbul 1956).

[W. J. BURGHARDT]

NALDI, ANTONIO, Theatine canonist and theologian; b. Faenza (Ravenna), Italy, date unknown; d. Rome, 1645. He entered the Theatines at Venice in 1588. Little else is known of his life, except that he was much esteemed by his contemporaries for his virtue. His known works are: *Summa seu relationes practicae notabiliores casuum fere omnium conscientiae* (Rome 1635) and *Annotationes practicae ad varia juris pontificii loca ex novissimis constitutionibus apostolicis breviter excerptae, nonnullis etiam disceptationibus suis quibuscumque materiis obiter insertis* (Rome 1633).

Bibliography: Hurter Nomencl³ 3:1209. F. BONNARD, DTC 11.1:18–19. *Dizionario universale delle scienze ecclesiastiche,* ed. C. L. RICHARD, 10 v. (Naples 1843–53) 7:22.

[P. F. MULHERN]

NAMATIANUS, RUTILIUS, the last truly Roman poet; fl. *c.* 420. He was of Gallo-Roman parentage, and he held office under the Emperor Honorius as *magister officiorum* (412) and *praefectus urbi* (414). In his elegiac poem *De reditu suo,* of which one book and part of a second are extant, he described his journey from Rome to southern Gaul, which he undertook in September 416 or 417. Rutilius reflected the mind of the old pagan aristocracy in Rome still dedicated to the *Dea Roma* and the city's cultural mission. In the poem, besides providing interesting descriptions of the city itself and the coast of Etruria, he reflected the pagan resentment toward Judaism, monasticism, and the barbarians, particularly the general Stilicho, who had burned the Sibylline Books.

Bibliography: J. W. and A. M. DUFF, eds., and trs., *Minor Latin Poets* (LoebClLib) 753–829. J. HAMMER, OxClDict 596. E. S. DUCKETT, *Latin Writers of the Fifth Century* (New York 1930). P. DE LABRIOLLE, *Revue des Études Latines* 6 (1928) 30–41. J. CARCOPINO, *ibid.* 180–200.

[F. X. MURPHY]

NAME, BAPTISMAL. Canon law (CIC c.761) requires pastors to give children Christian names, adding these names whenever parents object to substitutions. The right of selecting the name belongs to the parent(s), the guardian, or the sponsor, but the obligation of giving the name is the pastor's (see Second Plenary Council of Baltimore, *Acta* 232, 233). For historical treatment, *see* NAMES, CHRISTIAN; NAMES, MEDIEVAL.

Bibliography: E. G. WITHYCOMBE, *The Oxford Dictionary of English Christian Names* (New York 1947). Abbo 1:761. Woywod-Smith 654.

[M. A. WERNER]

NAME OF GOD

The Biblical use of the names for God provides a valuable insight into the richness and complexity of Semitic thought. For the Semitic peoples, an unnamed thing was a nonexistent thing; names were considered to identify and describe the very being and function of their bearers (Eccl 6.10; Gn 1.3–10; 27.36; Is 40.26). A man's name represented him wholly, was his alter ego. To know a name was to be able to exercise influence over the owner by using it. To change a man's name was to show one's power and authority over him (4 Kgs 23.34: cf. Gn 2.19–20; Dt 28.10). To cut off a man's name was the same as destroying him [Jer 11.19; Ps 82(83).5].

In religious matters, knowledge of the name of a god was considered the most effective way of establishing contact with him. The priests of Baal tried to obtain Baal's intervention by the repeated shouting of his name

(3 Kgs 18.26–28). In Israel, where one also called upon the name of the Lord (3 Kgs 18.36–37), belief in the magical properties of the divine name never took root. The divine name was not a carefully guarded secret, whereas secrecy was an essential feature of magical names and formulas. Moreover, the Lord had freely revealed His name and commanded that He be addressed by it and by no other (Ex 3.15; 23.13). It was a name that should not be profaned (Ez 36.21). Legislation against its misuse was quite explicit (Ex 20.7).

The divine name was evocative, not only of God's being, but of His relationship with His people. He is not the God of a land, nor of a particular city, but the God of the people of Israel, into whose life He intimately penetrated. In Israel His name was held in great esteem, and became an all-embracing part of the religious life of the nation. The "name of the Lord" was loved (Ps 5.12), praised (7.18; 148.13), and used in prayer (Jer 14.21); it was blessed (Jb 1.21), proclaimed (Dt 32.3), and thanked [Ps. 96(97).12]. Israel lived and acted in His name (Mi 4.5), trusting in His help and interest [Ps 123(124).8]. The divine name was synonymous with God's glory [Is 42.8; Jer 10.6; Ps 101(102).16]. Prophets spoke "in the name of the Lord," with all His authority and power (Jer 11.21).

The Temple was built to honor the Lord's name (2 Sm 7.13; 3 Kgs 8.16, 29). Not only did the Temple bear His name (Jer 7.10, 14); it was also His name's abode (Dt 12.5, 21). All nations would honor the Lord's name in Jerusalem (Jer 3.17). Isaia declared (30.27) that the divine name comes from afar to punish Assyria. Such personifications reconciled the transcendence of Yahweh with His presence in the Temple. Eventually, Yahweh was referred to simply as "the Name" (Lv 24.11) without any further specification.

See also EL; ELOHIM; ELYON; JEHOVAH; ADONAI; SHADDAI; YAHWEH.

Bibliography: H. GROSS, LexThK² 4:1127–29. W. EICHRODT, *Theology of the Old Test.,* tr. J. A. BAKER (London 1961–   ). E. JACOB, *Theology of the Old Testament,* tr. A. W. HEATHCOTE and P. J. ALLCOCK (New York 1958). J. P. E. PEDERSEN, *Israel: Its Life and Culture,* 4 v. in 2 (New York 1926–40; reprint 1959). P. VAN IMSCHOOT, *Théologie de l'Ancien Testament,* 2 v. (Tournai 1954–56). T. VRIEZEN, *An Outline of Old Testament Theology,* tr. S. NEUIJEN (Newton Centre, Mass. 1958).

[R. T. A. MURPHY]

NAMES, CHRISTIAN

A person's Christian name is usually the given name added to the family, tribal, or local designation to distinguish one from the other members of the family. The custom of distinguishing a person's first name from the family name is late in development, though many Romans had two or three names paralleling the family name. Ancient and early medieval man usually had one name, and was distinguished from others by reference to his father or to his town or place of origin. Among ancient peoples generally, a name was considered the identification of the essence, nature, or function of an individual, rather than merely a distinguishing appellation. This is true of Biblical names and of those found among non-Hebrew nations. It is exemplified in the name given to Christ by divine order: "You shall call his name Jesus, for He will save His people from their sins" (Mt 1.21); and to Simon, son of Jonah, by Christ: "You are Peter and upon this rock [*petra*] I will build my Church" (Mt

20.18). This relation between a name and the function or significance of the bearer is illustrated by the use of the word "name" itself to signify the presence or the power of God, whose nature or inner being was unknowable (Ps 20.2; Jer 6.10; Mal 1.6, 11, 14; 2.5), as well as of Christ as the Son of God (Mc 9.38–39; Mt 7.22).

Early Christian Names. There is no evidence that the primitive or early Christians changed their names on receiving Baptism; in general they had the names of the people or nation among whom they were born, and in the New Testament there are many names of converts derived from those of the pagan gods or Greco-Roman cult. This fact is further borne out by the Christian names discovered on inscriptions found in the catacombs and cemeteries of Rome and elsewhere, down to the 4th and 5th centuries, and is true likewise of the martyrs, confessors, and bishops mentioned in early Church history.

The first certain evidence of a change of name inspired by Christian belief is supplied by Ignatius of Antioch (d. *c.* 110), who refers to himself as "also called Theophorus," or the God-bearer (*Epist. ad Eph.*). The claim of Pope Damasus I (366–384) on an epigram (7) that the Apostle to the Gentiles had changed his name from Saul to Paul at Baptism is not substantiated by Acts, where he is called Paul in 11.18; but the name Saul is still used in 13.9. *Cyprian of Carthage (d. 258) speaks of two bishops and a confessor who had changed their names respectively to Peter, Paul, and Moses; and *Dionysius of Alexandria (d. 264) says that many Christians took the names of Peter and Paul, and particularly of John, the well-beloved disciple, out of veneration for the Apostles (Eusebius, *Hist. eccl.* 7.25.14). Eusebius further witnesses to the fact that in Palestine five Egyptian martyrs rejected their pagan names out of hatred for idolatry and called themselves Elia, Jeremia, Isaia, Samuel, and Daniel (*De mart. Palest.* 11.8). Cyprian of Carthage added Caecilianus to his name in honor of the priest who converted him; and Eusebius of Caesarea, that of the martyr *Pamphilus, who had been his friend and mentor. Inscriptional evidence shows that this custom was common.

Early Baptismal Names. It is not known when Christians generally began to give their infants Christian names at Baptism. The people of Antioch are said to have called their children after Bp. Meletius of Antioch (360–381); but *Ambrose of Milan (*De virg.* 3) and *John Chrysostom at the close of the 4th century complained that Christians were giving their children names haphazardly, and suggested that they consider giving them names of illustrious men and women who had earned credit with God (PG 50:515). *Theodoret of Cyr witnesses to the fact that people gave children the names of martyrs to provide them with protectors (*Graec. affl. cura* 8.67). However, the Arabic canon 30 of the Council of Nicaea I (325) is a much later falsification; and evidence for a change of name such as that of the martyr St. Balsamus to the name Peter, as recorded in his vita, is questionable.

The name of Mary found in St. Paul's Epistle to the Romans (16.6) and in several early catacomb inscriptions is probably the feminine of the Roman Marius, and does not seem to have been in general usage among early Christians, probably out of special reverence. This seems true also of Joseph. John is found frequently in Italy after the 4th century, but is rare in Gaul and almost unknown during this period in Germany and Spain. Peter and Paul were used widely as Christian names after the 3d century. Gradually, with the recognition of Christianity as the religion of the Empire, names connected with the doctrines of the faith, such as Anastasius (resurrection), Athanasius (immortality), Redempta, Reparatus, and Renatus (redemption, rebirth in Baptism), Salutia and Soteris (salvation) appear regularly in Christian inscriptions on tombs and monuments. Likewise, names connected with the Christian feasts are common, such as Epiphanius, Natalio, Pascasius, Pentecoste, Quadragesima, and Sabbatius (H. Leclercq, DACL 12.2:1513). The name Martyrius appears in the 4th century and is widespread in both Greek and Latin.

Names are taken from Christian ideas, such as Quodvultdeus (God's will), Theodulus (God's servant), Deusdona, Deusdedit, and Adeodatus (God's gift), as well as from virtues, such as Agape (love), Pistis and Fides (faith), Elpis and Spes (hope); many imitate the names of the martyrs and confessors indicating Christian attitudes as well, such as Irene (peace), Victor and Victoria, Vincentius, Gaudentius and Hilarius, Caelestinus and Felicissimus. Nevertheless in the lists of bishops attending the early councils and synods, along with specifically Christian names, there are still many pagan names, even those of the gods, indicating that there was no uniformity of practice or tradition in the adoption of Christian names. The continuance of the use of pagan names in late antiquity was based on local usage that included dignified names such as Aequitas, Probitas, Pietas, Melite, Hedone, Jucundus, and Elegans, as well as such inelegant names as Alogius, Fugitivus, Importunus, Calumniosus, Malus, Foedula, Stercus, and Stercorius—in the past opprobrious names given to Christians by pagans in the period of persecution.

Evidence of the changing of names on conversion is clear in the 5th century. For example, Acacius, Bishop of Constantinople, changed the name of Athenaïs to Eudocia on her Baptism before she married the young Emperor Theodosius II (421). St. Euthymius, the 6th-century Palestine monk, changed the name of barbarian chieftain Aspebet to Peter, and Bp. Innocent of Tortona had changed his name from Quintus on becoming bishop. Also, Bede speaks of King Cedwalla's being baptized as Peter (*Hist. eccl.* 5.7).

Christian Gaul. In Gaul to the end of the 4th century, Christian inscriptions record only Greek and Latin names, but between the 5th and 7th century, there is a gradual ascendancy of Germanic names. The historian Gregory of Tours (538–594) illustrates the intermixture of Greco-Latin and barbarian names: his grandparents were George and Leocadia; his parents, Florentius and Armentaria; his brother was Peter, and his sister was married to a Justinus; his uncle was Gondolfus; and his nieces, Eustenia and Justina. The clergy in general seem to have been recruited from Gallo-Roman families and had Roman names, as did many of the officials and administrators under the *Merovingians, since they were allowed to live under Roman law by a constitution of Clothaire (*tit.* 58. *lex* 1) attested by the Council of Tours (567). Germanic names prevailed even though at Baptism such barbarian

princes as Hermegild and Caedual were given the names of Peter and John. Waldo took the name of Berchtramnus, and Favo became Allowinus (Gregory of Tours, *Hist. Franc.,* 5.39; 8.32).

With the conquest of the various parts of Europe and North Africa, the barbarian names gradually took preponderance, although among princes and the educated, some Roman and many hybrid names persisted. In the royal families of the Visigoths, Burgundians, Ostrogoths and Franks, Saxons, and Celts similar sounding names were handed down from one generation to another. Thus in the family of King *Clovis and the Burgundian Princess Clothilde, the first syllable Gund was repeated in the names Guntharius, Gundovaldus, Guntchramnus; and Chlodo was echoed in Chlodebaudus, Chlotharius, Chlodomerus, and Chlodovaldus; while feminine names ran to Chlodobergis and Chlodesinda, Theodovaldus, and Theodechildis.

Saxons, Celts, and Slavs. In Anglo-Saxon England the prefix Aethel in names such as Aethelstane, Aethelbald, Aethelfrith, and Aethelheard is common among bishops and princes, as are the names Aelfred, Aelfhere, and Aelfric; princes and abbesses are Aelfled and Aethelflaed. Aldfrith and Aldgisil vie with Ceolfrith, Ceolnoth, Ceolred, and Ceowulf. Similar combinations are evidenced by Eadbald, Eadbert, Eadburga, and Osgar, Osmund, Oswald, and Wulfhelm, Wulfric, and Wulstan. Saxon names are reflected also among freedmen and serfs, and the changeover to Norman names (11th–12th century) was a political issue.

Although the pagan names were retained among the Celts in Ireland, an attempt was made to reconcile them with similar sounding Latin names. Thus the pagan Diarmaid became the Latin Jeremias; Seanachan was Biblicized into Jonathan; but names such as Brigid, Ita, and Deirdre were soon Christianized by belonging to native saints. Mary was originally brought into Gaelic as Muirē; but when the Normans came in the 11th century, there was a transfer from Marie to Moira or Maureen. A similar metamorphosis overtook John, which had become Eoin or Owen in Gaelic, but became Sean when the Norman form Jean was introduced, while Sheila was the Irish equivalent Julie.

Among the Slavs similar developments are met after the 7th century when the King of Bosnia, Rudoslav, married a Roman Princess and called their son Petroslav, who in turn had a son Paulimir. Byzantine names continued the Greco-Roman tradition and affected contiguous nations as they became Christian. Other Oriental people reflect in their first names the Christian names current in the ambience of the apostles who converted them.

Saints' Names at Baptism. Insistence on the giving of a Christian name at Baptism was not regularized before the councils and Rituals of the 14th century, when the names in the martyrologies, legends of the saints, translations of relics, pilgrimages, romances and histories of the Crusades, and the morality plays popularized Old and New Testament names as well as those of the martyrs and saints of the early Church. In northern Europe in the 15th century, the names of Joseph and Mary came into common use; in Spain and Greece people had not hesitated to employ the names Jesus and Christ.

With the Renaissance in Europe there was a return to pagan names, and a similar phenomenon is noticeable in the Byzantine world among scholars. The emphasis on Christian names received impetus from the Council of Trent (sess. 25) which insisted on the orthodoxy of the veneration of saints against Protestant denial. The Roman catechism of the Council and the Roman Ritual (1614) strongly urged priests not to allow parents to give their children strange, laughable, obscene, or idolatrous names. Contemporary discipline in this matter instructed the parish priest to persuade people to give children a saint's name, and if they refused, to enter both the given name and that of a saint in the baptismal register (CIC c.761).

Title Churches and Guilds. Roman title churches took their names originally from the donors or the locations; in the late 4th and 5th centuries these names were canonized as those of saints. However, churches that preserved the relics of a saint or in which there was a special connection with a martyr or Christian truth were named after that subject, though the church itself was dedicated to God. Thus churches of the Anastasia or Resurrection, of the Savior, and of the Cross were erected in Jerusalem; and, with some confusion, churches in other cities were given similar names.

Later Christian antiquity and the early Middle Ages saw churches dedicated in honor of the great figures of the Old Testament, of the Apostles, or of other holy persons of the New Testament, usually with a legendary connection such as those of SS. Lazarus, Mary Magdalen, Dionysius (French, Denis). The translation of relics, pilgrimages to Rome and the Holy Land, and the legends of the saints also influenced the selection of patrons for guilds and brotherhoods, as well as the cultivation of special saints by religious orders, such as Mary Magdalen and Peter among the Cluniacs; the Blessed Virgin among the Premonstratensians and Cistercians; John the Baptist by the Templars and Hospitallers; and among the knightly orders appeared the names Lawrence, Ulrich, Vitus, Aegidius, Michael, George, Nicholas, Catherine of Alexandria, Barbara, and Margaret of Antioch. With the regularized process for the canonization of saints, countries, cities, and dioceses, as well as princes, bishops, and republics selected their particular patron saints. Since 1630 most of these patrons have been acknowledged with rescripts by the Congregation of Rites.

In the second half of the 19th century a systematic collection and historical evaluation of patron saints was begun, but in the selection of patrons for particular activities or assistance, both historical fact and legend still played a part. In contemporary times the popes have appointed certain saints as universal patrons; thus St. Joseph, as the Patron of the Universal Church and of the Laborer; Aloysius Gonzaga, for students; Camillus of Lellis and John of God, for the sick, doctors, and nurses; Paschal Baylon, for Eucharistic societies and sacramental brotherhoods; the Curé d'Ars, for pastors; John Chrysostom, for preachers; Alphonsus Liguori, for confessors and moral theologians; Vincent de Paul, for charitable works; Francis of Assisi, for Catholic Action; Francis de Sales, for the press; Theresa of Lisieux, for world missions; Frances of Rome, for fliers; and Christopher, for automobile drivers. Popular selection still honors St. Barbara for vocations; the Three Kings, for travelers; Margaret of Antioch and Gerard Majella, for the pregnant; Gallus and Sigismund of Burgundy, against fevers; and Lucy of Syracuse and

Clare of Assisi, for eye diseases. However, the universal recourse to patron saints in every aspect of life that pervaded the Middle Ages was destroyed with the Protestant Reformation.

Papal Names. There is no evidence for the change of name on the part of a new pope before *John II (533–535), whose original name was Mercurius. Both Roman and Greek names appear almost indiscriminately in the early list of popes. John XII (955–963) changed from Octavian; Gregory V (996–999), from Bruno; Sylvester II (999–1003), from Gerbert; Peter of Pavia took the name John XIV (983–984); and Peter of Albano, Sergius IV (1009–1012). After that, it became the custom for the pope to take a new name, although Adrian VI (1522–23) and Marcellus II (1555), retained their original names.

Religious Names. There is evidence that, from at least the 6th century, aspirants for the monastic way of life changed their names on entrance into religious life. In the Oriental Church, the custom grew of taking the name of a saint whose first initial was the same as one's given name; thus Basil would take the name of St. *Bessarion. During his probationary period or novitiate, the candidate would write the life of his patron saint for his menologion, in order to be able to imitate the saint more perfectly. Behind the change of name was the determination to cut oneself off from one's worldly identification and one's former way of life, as well as a complete dedication of the new man to the service of Christ. This custom seems to have influenced the papal change of name, which became the rule in the 11th century. Most congregations of nuns, sisters, and brothers, as well as a number of religious orders and congregations of men, still retain this practice.

Bibliography: H. LECLERCQ, DACL 12.2:1482–1553. J. GEWIESS et al., LexThK² 7:780–783. W. DÜRIG, ibid. 784. J. B. LEHNER and W. DÜRIG, ibid. 8:187–192, patron saints. H. LESÊTRE, DB 4.2:1669–77. N. TURCHI et al., EncCatt 8:1917–19. H. USENER, *Götternamen* (3d ed. Bonn 1948). E. SCHLENKER, *Die Lehre von den göttlichen Namen* (Freiburg 1938). W. DÜRIG, *Geburtstag und Namenstag* (Munich 1954). F. BOND, *Dedications and Patron Saints of English Churches* (London 1914). H. DELEHAYE, *Les Origines du culte des martyrs* (2d ed. Brussels 1933). H. SCHAUERTE, *Die volkstümliche Heiligenverehrung* (Münster 1948). R. L. POOLE, "The Names and Numbers of Medieval Popes," EngHistRev 32 (1917) 465–478. P. RABIKAUSKAS, "Papstnamen und Ordnungszahl," RömQuartalsch 51 (1956) 1–15. F. KRÄMER, ibid. 148–188. F. BOCK, RGG³ 5:49–50. J. JUNGMANN, LiturgJb 4 (1954) 130–148. T. KLAUSER, *Christlicher Märtyrerkult, heidnischer Heroenkult und spätjüdische Heiligenverehrung* (Cologne 1960). F. G. HOLWECK, *A Biographical Dictionary of the Saints* (St. Louis 1924). P. WOULFE, *Irish Names and Surnames* (Dublin 1923). *National Catholic Almanac* (Paterson 1965).

[F. X. MURPHY]

NAMES, MEDIEVAL

The last traces of the Roman system of personal nomenclature scarcely outlasted the 6th century in the West. Under the empire the "three names" (*praenomen, nomen,* and *cognomen*) that had earlier sufficed to designate the citizen were often swelled by the multiplication of *cognomina* to an unconscionable number. Reaction to this extravagance created a welcome for the principle observed by the barbarian invaders, that the individual had but one name. Even in thoroughly Romanized areas this name itself was, from the 5th century onward, increasingly likely to be of Germanic origin: in Gaul the proportion of Germanic to other names—1 to 3 in the 5th century—had become 3 to 1 by the 7th century, and 4 centuries later the few Greek and Roman names in use were almost all those of scriptural saints. Though vernacular forms naturally differed from language to language and though local popularity, such as that of *Alan* in Brittany, *Baldwin* in Flanders, and *Edward* in England, might affect distribution, the dominant names were then common to most of the countries of Christian Europe. Their universality was further emphasized by the fact that in written documents the same standard Latin forms translated them everywhere.

Various circumstances combined to restrict the number of names in general use during the Middle Ages. The sources of Germanic name formation had dried up by *c.* 850, and resistance to other innovating influences was protracted; e.g., the Church generally favored only names with religious associations. Of the names actually current at any given time, fashion concentrated popularity on relatively few: more than half the Englishmen named in 13th-century records are called *John, William, Robert, Richard,* or *Henry.* Once a name had gained favor, its success was prolonged by the custom, copiously attested for the English landowning classes but almost certainly not peculiar to them, whereby the name given to a child at Baptism was that of one of the godparents, unless long-standing family tradition or devotion to a particular saint dictated another choice. The continued vogue of the five names mentioned above actually raised to nearly two-thirds the proportion of 14th-century Englishmen bearing one or another of them.

In everyday life people who had received the same name at Baptism might be known by differing hypocoristic or diminutive forms of it, and this must generally have been the case when, as often happened in the later Middle Ages, the same baptismal name was borne by two or more living children of the same parents. However, in documents in which the same Latin form rendered both the baptismal name itself and all the variant hypocoristics, confusion between namesakes could be avoided only by the addition of identifying particulars, or surnames.

Surnames, as thus defined, appear in French documents toward the close of the 10th century. At first they were used only occasionally and as a means of separating persons of the same name mentioned in the same instrument; later they occurred in contexts in which no such need for differentiation is apparent. They fall into four main classes. The first, which identify the bearer by reference to his parentage, are often collectively described as patronymics (a term that does not exclude metronymics); the second class indicate the individual's occupation, status, or nationality; the third are toponymics, or locality names, taken from his place of abode or origin; and the fourth are sobriquets alluding to his personal characteristics, physical or moral.

Early surnames are essentially personal and are by no means constant. The same person might be known at different times and in different places by different surnames, and scribes seem sometimes to have deliberately selected the one that was most apt in the circumstances of the transaction they were recording. The name par excellence of the individual was that he had received at Baptism; it remained fixed throughout his life except in the very rare cases in which it was changed by the bishop at Confirmation.

The processes by which surnames became hereditary are obscure, and generalization is not easy. It seems to be agreed that in all countries a tendency in this direction is observed among the nobility before the humbler classes; in the southern parts of individual countries before the northern; in town before country; and in France (early in the 11th century) and England (among the Norman invaders) before Germany. But one must wait until 1267 for a London jury to declare of a convicted felon, variously known as Cantebrigge and Derby, that he "ought, as they understand, to have his father's surname and thus to be called Roger de Cantebrigge."

It was certainly very slowly that surnames came to be conventionally regarded as hereditary; and in all countries there were long periods of transition during which some members of society had hereditary surnames, some had personal surnames, and some had no surnames at all. The stages in the transition are very roughly marked by changes in scribal practice. At their first appearance surnames are subjected in Latin documents to such Latinization as they will admit; but later there is a growing tendency to leave them in the vernacular. The significance of this, so far as patronymic surnames are concerned, may be deduced from 13th-century decisions of the English court of Common Pleas that *Gilbertus filius Stephani* and *Johannes filius Walteri* were inadmissible ways of naming Gilbert Fitz Estevene and John Fitz Wauter, whose respective fathers were not named Stephen and Walter.

Bibliography: E. W. FÖRSTEMANN, *Altdeutsches Namenbuch,* 2 v. in 3 (v.1, 2d ed., v.2, 3d ed. 1900–16), v.1, *Personennamen.* G. E. COKAYNE, *The Complete Peerage . . .,* ed. V. GIBBS et al., v.3 (London 1913), app.C. E. G. WITHYCOMBE, *The Oxford Dictionary of English Christian Names* (2d ed. Oxford 1950). A. DAUZAT, *Dictionnaire étymologique des noms de famille et prénoms de France* (Paris 1951). P. H. REANEY, *Dictionary of British Surnames* (London 1958).

[L. C. HECTOR]

NANCHANG, ARCHDIOCESE OF (NANCIAMENSIS), metropolitan see since 1946, in southeastern *China. The city of Nanchang (Nan-ch'ang) is the capital of Kiangsi (Chiang-hsi) civil province. According to statistics of 1950, the latest available, the see was 27,027 square miles in area and had 18 parishes, 13 secular and 23 religious priests, 47 women in 4 convents, and 26,000 Catholics in a population of 4,870,000. Its four suffragans, Kan-chou, Chi-an, Nanch'eng, and Yü-chiang, all created in 1946, had about 50 parishes, 136 priests, 78 sisters, and 69,600 Catholics in a population of 9 million.

Matteo *Ricci preached in Nanchang (1595). In the mid-17th century Franciscans, Dominicans, and Jesuits labored in Kiangsi province. The area suffered from persecution during most of the 18th and 19th centuries. Kiangsi came under the apostolic administrator Pierre *Lambert de la Motte (1659), and was incorporated in the Diocese of *Nanking (1690), which was under the Portuguese *padroado.* (*See* PATRONATO REAL.) The vicariate apostolic, erected in 1696, was subjected to the coadjutor bishop of Fu-chien in 1732 after a 17-year vacancy. In 1838 the Vicariate of Kiangsi and Chekiang was entrusted to Vincentians, to be divided in two again (1846). In 1879 Kiangsi was further divided into north and south vicariates. North Kiangsi, from which was detached the Vicariate of East Kiangsi (1885), was called Kiukiang in 1920, when it ceded some territory to Chi-an, and Nanchang from 1924 until 1946 when it became an archdiocese.

Bibliography: *Annuaire de l'Église catholique en Chine* (Shanghai 1950). MissCattol 371–374. A. Pucci, EncCatt 8: 1606–07. AnnPont (1965) 293–294.

[J. KRAHL]

NANCY

Capital of Meurthe-et-Moselle department in northeast France, on the left bank of the Meurthe River, near rich iron deposits. Almost all the 130,000 inhabitants (1964) in the city and the 90,000 in the suburbs are Catholics. Until 1766 Nancy was the capital of the duchy of Lorraine. In 1777 the Diocese of Nancy (*Nanceiensis*) was detached from that of Toul and made suffragan to *Trier. It was united with Toul, Saint-Dié, and Verdun as a suffragan of *Besançon in 1801; since 1824 it has been united with Toul. Since 1865 the bishops have worn the famous rationale of Toul. In 1963 the diocese had 641 parishes, 678 secular and 85 religious priests, 141 men in 18 religious houses, 1,287 women in 148 convents, and 626,138 Catholics.

Nancy. In the late 11th century the town formed around the Duke of Lorraine's castle, beside which there was a Benedictine priory for some time. There was only one parish, dedicated to St. Evre, Bishop of Toul, until the late 16th century, when an expansion began that required new parishes (seven in 1789). The Dukes of Lorraine supported the development of religious houses, especially in the early 17th century after the Counter Reformation. A diocese was requested in 1597 and a primatial chapter was founded in 1602, but it was only after France annexed Lorraine that Nancy

Nancy, Place du Gouvernement and church of Saint-Evre.

became a see. Religious foundations disappeared in the Revolution, except the hospital Sisters of St. Charles (founded in 1652), who now have eight motherhouses. Under *Louis-Philippe's July monarchy (1830–48) there was a Catholic renaissance in Nancy, where *Lacordaire founded the first house of restored Dominicans in France (1843). The monumental history of the Church by R. F. *Rohrbacher (d. 1856), professor at the major seminary, influenced the formation and spread of *ultramontanism in French-speaking countries. Bishop C. M. A. *Lavigerie (1863–67) revived diocesan institutions. The *Dictionnaire de théologie catholique,* undertaken at the seminary of Nancy (1897), was directed by A. *Vacant, E. *Mangenot, and E. *Amann, priests of Nancy. Nancy has schools for the blind and for deaf mutes. The university, founded in Pont-à-Mousson (1572), moved to Nancy (1768).

The Church of Notre-Dame de Bonsecours (1738–41) has a statue of Our Lady (1505) made for Duke René II to commemorate his victory over Duke Charles the Bold of Burgundy in 1477; it also houses the tombs of Stanislaus Leszczynski (d. 1766), King of Poland and Duke of Lorraine, and his Queen, Catherine Opalinska (d. 1747). The Church of the Cordeliers (1485–87), also built by Duke René to commemorate his victory, has a ducal chapel (1609–12) with tombs of the dukes. The vast classical cathedral (1703–42), with three naves, has in its treasury a chalice, paten, gospel book, and liturgical comb of St. Gauzelin (d. 962), Bishop of Toul.

Toul. On the Moselle River, 13 miles west of Nancy, Toul (with *Metz and Verdun) was a famous medieval bishopric and the see of Cardinals of *Lorraine. Capital of the *Leuci,* it was evangelized in the 4th century by Bishop St. Mansuetus and had 11 other sainted bishops, including *Aper and *Gerard. St. *Gauzelin in 927 received the titles of prince of the Holy Roman Empire and count of Toul. The Holy See appointed many Italian prelates to Toul from 1278 to 1668, when the right of appointment went to the king of France. Guillaume *Fillastre held the see (1448–60). The former cathedral, in Gothic (13th–15th century), has a famous portal.

Bibliography: C. Pfister, *Histoire de Nancy,* 3 v. (Nancy 1902–09). H. Leclercq, DACL 12.1:602–621. G. Allemang, LexThK² 10:230–231. AnnPont (1965) 294. **Illustration credit:** French Embassy, Press and Information Division, New York City.

[J. CHOUX]

NANINO, GIOVANNI MARIA, Renaissance teacher and composer of the Roman school (also Nanini); b. Tivoli, Italy, *c.* 1545; d. Rome, March 11, 1607. He appears to have been a student of *Palestrina, whom he succeeded as *maestro di cappella* at St. Mary Major in 1571. He held a like position at San Luigi de' Francesi 1575–77, then he entered the papal choir as a tenor, and was *maestro* from 1604 to 1606. Renowned as a teacher, he numbered among his students F. Anerio, G. Allegri, A. Cifra, S. Landi, and others. Nanino was particularly facile in the composition of canon, and in style he adhered closely to the principles of Palestrina. He published three volumes of madrigals, one of spiritual canzonettas, and one of motets; most of his output remains in MS, including Masses, Lamentations, psalm settings, and many other sacred works, together with valuable pedagogical treatises on counterpoint.

Bibliography: G. M. NANINO, motets and madrigals in *L'arte musical in Italia*, ed. L. TORCHI, 7 v. (Milan 1897–1908) 2:1–30. G. RADICIOTTI, *Giovanni Maria Nanino* (Pesaro 1909). R. J. SCHULER, *Caecila* 90 (1963) 46–68. G. D'ALESSI, MusGG 9: 1256–58. Reese MusR. Baker 1144–45.

[F. J. GUENTNER]

NANKING, ARCHDIOCESE OF (NANCHIMENSIS),

metropolitan see since 1946, in east *China. The city of Nanking (Nan-ching) is the capital of the civil province of Kiangsu (Chiang-su). Statistics for 1950, the most recent available, showed the see, 7,000 square miles in area, to have 17 parishes, 37 secular and 10 religious priests, 10 men in 3 religious houses, 33 women in 4 convents, and 32,500 Catholics in a population of 6 million. Its four suffragans, Hai-men (created in 1946), Shang-hai (1946), Su-chou (1949), and Hsü-chou (1946), had 343 priests, 805 sisters, and 280,000 Catholics in a population of around 29 million.

In 1599 Matteo *Ricci fixed his residence in Nanking, where he was joined in 1609 by a fellow Jesuit, Vagnoni, who built a church there (1611). The many conversions were ended with a persecution that began in 1626. In 1660 Nanking was one of several vicariates entrusted to Bp. Ignatius Cotolendi, who was succeeded (1674) by the first Chinese bishop, Gregory Lo (Lopez), OP, consecrated in 1685 (d. 1690).

In 1690 were created the dioceses of *Peking and Nanking, suffragan to *Goa (as was *Macao) and under the Portuguese *padroado*. With the creation of Chinese vicariates in 1696, the Nanking diocese was reduced to the provinces of Chiang-su, An-hui, and Honan (made a vicariate in 1844). Jesuit missions and their seminary, founded in 1681, suffered from the *Chinese Rites controversy, persecution, and the suppression of the Society; and the bishop's residence was moved to Shang-hai. The Diocese of Nanking was reduced to a vicariate apostolic (1856–1946), from which the Vicariate of An-hui was detached (1921). In 1924 the first national synod of bishops of China was held in Shang-hai under Abp. Celso Costantini, the first apostolic delegate to China. In 1926 Bp. Simon Tsu, SJ, first vicar apostolic of Hai-men, was one of six Chinese bishops consecrated by Pius XI in Rome. The Prefecture of Hsü-chou (1931) and the Vicariate of Shang-hai (1933) were created out of Nanking. The Chinese-Japanese war (1937–45) did much damage to Catholic churches and schools in Nanking, which has been in the care of Chinese secular clergy since 1936.

Bibliography: A. PUCCI, EncCatt 8:1607–09. MissCattol 338–343. *Annuaire de l'Église catholique en Chine* (Shanghai 1950).

[A. TSEU]

NANNING, ARCHDIOCESE OF (NANNIMENSIS),

metropolitan see since 1946, in southern *China. The city of Nanning (Nan-ning) is the capital of Kuang-hsi-chuang Autonomous Region. According to statistics for 1950, the latest available, the see was 46,332 square miles in area and had 21 churches, 26 secular priests, 63 sisters, and 7,584 Catholics in a population of 6 million. Its suffragan Wu-chou had 25 priests,

14 sisters, and 12,000 Catholics in a total population of approximately 3 million.

Kuang-hsi Province, part of the Diocese of *Macao, was assigned to François *Pallu to administer (1659) and incorporated in the Diocese of *Nanking (1690), which was under the Portuguese *padroado*. See PATRONATO REAL. It was made a vicariate apostolic in 1696 but, without a vicar, returned to the jurisdiction of Macao. In 1850 the Prefecture Apostolic of Kwang-tung was formed, comprising Kuang-hsi, Hainan Island, and French Kuang-chou with Fort Bayard. From this was detached the Prefecture of Kuang-hsi (1875), which became a vicariate (1914) called Nanning from 1924 until 1946, when it became an archdiocese. It ceded territory to Lanlung (1922) and Wu-chou (1930). Outbreaks claimed the lives of Christians in 1856, 1897, and 1898. The archdiocese is entrusted to the *Paris Foreign Mission Society.

Bibliography: *Annuaire de l'Église catholique en Chine* (Shanghai 1950). MissCattol 389–390. A. PUCCI, EncCatt 8:1614. Ann Pont (1965) 294.

[J. KRAHL]

NANTES, EDICT OF

A proclamation issued by *Henry IV of France, April 13, 1598, providing a measure of toleration, civil rights and liberties, and security for French *Huguenots. It contained 92 general articles signed by the King April 3, 1598, 56 particular or secret articles signed May 3, and 3 brevets. The first brevet gave an endowment of 45,000 crowns annually for the support of the clergy and churches of the Reformed Church; the second gave 180,000 crowns a year for the upkeep of garrisons in the fortified towns; the third distributed 23,000 crowns to certain Huguenot leaders. According to the general and particular articles: Roman Catholicism was restored and reestablished where it had previously been practiced, and any interference with divine service was forbidden; members of the Reformed religion were permitted to live without restriction anywhere in France and were allowed freedom of religious worship wherever they had been permitted to worship publicly by the edicts of 1577, 1596, and 1597, and in two towns in every bailiwick; they could not conduct services within 5 leagues of Paris, but services could be held in the homes of Huguenot nobles; they were granted complete civil liberties, including the right to hold public office and attend colleges and academies; they were permitted to hold synods and political meetings; special tribunals were authorized to settle disputes between Catholics and Huguenots, the one in the Parlement of Paris to consist of 10 Catholics and 6 Protestants, the provincial parlements to have an equal number of Protestants and Catholics; the salaries of Protestant ministers were paid and some financial aid was provided for their colleges; the Huguenots were given 100 security areas or towns for 8 years, the King was to pay the cost of the garrisons, and the governors of these towns were to be nominated by the King with the consent of the churches. The edict was registered in Paris and Grenoble in 1599; in Dijon, Toulouse, Bordeaux, Aix, and Rennes in 1600; but not until 1609 in Rouen.

The edict was a compromise only. The "Politiques," who were particularly responsible for it, asserted that religious toleration was a matter of expediency rather than a matter of principle. The Catholic clergy opposed the granting to the Huguenots of freedom of conscience, civil liberty, the right to ecclesiastical assemblies, and state subsidies for the Protestant Church. The Protestants were unhappy about limitations imposed upon them, and fearful that the edict would be violated after Henry's death. The lease on the fortified towns was renewed in 1611 and thrice more until 1624, but soon after Henry's assassination (1610) there were violations of the edict: discrimination against Huguenots in employment, their exclusion from some professional schools, restrictions on public worship, destruction of some Protestant churches. An uneasy truce developed into open conflict. After the fall of La Rochelle in 1628, *Louis XIII, on the advice of *Richelieu, issued the Edict of Alais (1629), depriving the Huguenots of all political rights and razing fortifications, but preserving religious liberties. After the peace of Alais, however, there was a gradual deterioration of the Huguenot religious position. Restrictions against them were more open under *Louis XIV, who revoked the edict on Oct. 18, 1685.

Bibliography: J. VIÉNOT, *Histoire de la réforme française*, 2 v. (Paris 1926–34). J. FAUREY, *L'Édit de Nantes et la question de la tolérance* (Paris 1929). J. ORCIBAL, *Louis XIV et les protestants* (Paris 1951). W. J. STANKIEWICZ, *Politics and Religion in Seventeenth-Century France* (Berkeley 1960). Pastor 23:157–164.

[D. R. PENN]

Students singing at Nanzan University Festival.

NANZAN UNIVERSITY, THE CATHOLIC UNIVERSITY OF NAGOYA

The Catholic University of Nagoya, Japan, is the largest element in the Nanzan Educational Institution (*gakuen*). This complex includes a university, a boys' junior and senior high school, a girls' junior and senior high school in Nagoya, a boys' junior and senior high school in Nagasaki, the college church, and a Divine Word Seminary (*see* DIVINE WORD, SOCIETY OF THE). The coeducational university has an enrollment of 2,707 students of whom only 140 are Catholics, including 46 seminarians.

Nanzan (nan: south; zan: mountain) originated in the 1926 directive of the Congregation for the Propagation of the Faith that strongly urged the Prefect Apostolic, Joseph Reiners, SVD, on his transfer from Niigata to the newly created Vicariate of Nagoya, to take effective steps for the Catholic education of youth in that area. At that time there was only one parish church in the vicariate, which embraced five civil prefectures of nearly 12,000 square miles, with some 400 Catholics in a population of 5½ million. Reiners established the Nanzan Boys' Middle School in 1932 and entrusted it to the Divine Word Fathers. After World War II, Aloysius Pache, SVD, principal of the school, transformed it from a college to a full-fledged university in what is now the Nanzan Educational Institution. While establishing the school complex, as first president of Nanzan he purchased the 27-acre Rakuen tract of land for the expansion of the University which plans to accommodate 3,500 students.

In 1963 the University was reorganized into the three faculties of arts and letters, foreign languages (English and Spanish), and economics. Special features are the anthropology department and the language laboratory. This latter, established by Franz Giet, SVD, in 1951, was the first speech laboratory in Japan and served as a model for similar installations in schools throughout Japan. Monumenta Serica, an institute of research in Chinese cultural history, is attached to the University. The M.A. and Ph.D. degrees are conferred by the anthropology, economics, and English departments. Students may obtain a teacher's license, approved by the civil authorities, in English, French, German, sociology, and commerce. Language courses are held for the general public during the summer.

The curriculum follows one introduced after World War II from the U.S. Nanzan is recognized by the Ministry of Education and is also accredited by the Organization of Private Universities in Japan. The University has a faculty of 172 members of whom 75 are Catholic, including 37 religious. Full-time teachers sign no contract with the school. Once employed they must be retained until the 65-year retirement age. The highest administrative authority is invested in the chairman of the board of trustees. The University is supported by tuition, fees, contributions from the Divine Word Society, Catholic friends in the U.S. and in Europe, and an annual contribution from the Propagation of the Faith. Student admission is determined by a competitive entrance examination in English, Japanese literature, sociology, and mathematics. The Anthropological Institute conducts research in the prehistory of Japan and Asia. The staff of the economics department does extensive research in contemporary problems. There is also active research in the education of the blind. A library containing 80,000 volumes has an ultimate capacity of 300,000.

Nanzan University publishes *Academia,* a quarterly journal of the Nanzan Academic Society that includes every academic field; and *Collectaneae Universitatis Catholicae Nanzan,* which contains academic works in ethnology, linguistics, anthropology, and philosophy. Available in this series are Dr. Martin Gusinde's Japanese version of *Die Twiden* and the *Ainu Bibliography,* and the Japanese translation of Wilhelm M. *Schmidt's *Mutterrecht.* Other publications are the *Nanzan Bungaku,* annual literary journal; *Monumenta Serica;* and the *Nanzan Herald,* an informational English paper for friends abroad.

The motivating force of the institution is summarized in the motto: *Hominis Dignitati.* Students of pagan and materialistic background attend courses in philosophy and religion where they hear for the first time in their lives man's purpose and final end.

[A. J. HOTZE]

NAPLES

City in south Italy, on the Tyrrhenian Sea; a bishopric (*Neapolitanus*) from very early times and a metropolitan see since the 10th century. In 1963 the archdiocese, 50 square miles in area, had 1,577,000 Catholics (almost the entire population), 734 secular and 702 religious priests, 1,125 men in 112 religious houses, and 3,030 women in 290 convents. Its four suffragans, which had 681,770 Catholics, 552 priests, and 484 sisters, were: Acerra (established in the late 11th century), Ischia (whose first known bishop appears in 1179), Nola (whose first known bishop was St. *Felix, d. c. 260), and *Pozzuoli (founded in Apostolic times).

City. Naples (*Neapolis*) was founded in the 7th century B.C. by Greeks, and flourished as the center of Greek culture in Italy during the Roman Empire. Christianity reached Naples early, but the only extant relics of its origins are the so-called tomb of Vergil, the Roman grotto of Posilipo, and the catacombs of St. *Januarius, the city's patron.

After the fall of Rome, Naples was invaded by Odoacer and by the Goths; it was taken by the Byzantine *Belisarius (536), by Totila (542), and again by Byzantium (553), and was besieged by the Lombards (581, 592, and 599). After 661 it was a duchy dependent on Byzantium. Independent in the late 8th century, it had to fight off Saracens and Lombards. Pope John VIII, however, excommunicated the duke-bishop Anastasius II for allying with the Saracens. In 1139 the Normans captured Naples, and in 1194 the Hohenstaufen took it because of its opposition to Constance, wife of Emperor Henry VI. Independent again in 1197, it held out until 1220 against Frederick II, who in 1224 founded in Naples the first state university, where St. Thomas Aquinas taught (1272–74). Rebelling against Conrad IV in 1250, Naples appealed to Innocent IV. Innocent died in Naples (1254), and his successor, Alexander IV, was elected there. The city was subject to *Manfred in 1256; and in 1266, as a papal fief, it fell under the bad government of Charles of *Anjou. In 1281 the Castel Nuovo was built, and in 1282, after the *Sicilian Vespers, Naples became the capital of the Kingdom of Sicily. Under Angevin rule until 1441, the city underwent an artistic revival under French influence, illustrated by the Gothic cathedral and Gothic churches of S. Clara and S. Lorenzo Maggiore, S. Maria Incoronata, and other churches; the artists P. *Cavallini, S. *Martini, the Sienese sculptor Tino di Camaino, and *Giotto.

Angevin rule was replaced in 1442 by Alfonso V of Aragon, who beautified Naples. After the war of 1503 between France and Spain, Naples became a Spanish province under a viceroy. A rebellion in 1547 rejected the Spanish Inquisition but had to accept the Roman Inquisition. Viceroy Peter of Toledo suppressed schools and cultural activities in retaliation; but the philosophers B. *Telesio, T. *Campanella, and G. *Bruno, the physicist Giambattista della Porta (1538?–1615), and the adventurous poet Giambattista Marino (1569–1625) show that intellectual life continued. In general, however, the educated class wasted itself in forensic

disputations and juridical decisions in an era of interminable controversies between Church and State. In 1647 the Masaniello revolt against bad government was soon suppressed. The War of the Spanish Succession brought the Austrian Hapsburgs to Naples (1707–34) before the kingdom regained independence under the Bourbons. Charles IV (1734–59), later Charles III of Spain (1759–88), widened streets, built palaces, and instituted charitable foundations such as the hostel for the poor and the porcelain factory of Capodimonte; but this revival was ephemeral and neither met the needs of the times nor measured up to the work of monarchs elsewhere. In the 17th and 18th centuries Naples had several noteworthy and original artists—the man of letters Giambattista Caracciolo (1695–1765); the painters J. *Ribera Lo Spagnoletto, Mattia Preti (1613–99), Salvator Rosa (1615–75), Bernardo Cavallino (1622–54), Luca Giordano (1632–1705), Francesco Solimena (1657–1747), and Sebastiano Conca (1679–1764); and the musicians G. *Paisiello, A. *Scarlatti, and D. *Cimarosa. Naples became the capital of the French Parthenopean Republic (1799) and was a Napoleonic kingdom under Joseph Bonaparte (1806–08) and Joachim *Murat (1806–15), after which the Bourbons occupied the throne until Garibaldi made the city part of united Italy (1860). The papal Concordat with Naples was suspended between 1788 and 1818.

Archdiocese. Christian origins date from c. 100, and catacomb paintings based on the *Shepherd of *Hermas* indicate a fully developed Christian community, but there were no early martyrs of Naples. The basilicas built in Naples and Capua by Constantine were the only ones the Emperor erected south of Rome. Bishop Maximus (d. 362 or later) had been exiled for his faith by Constans I, and sometime earlier there was a Bishop Asprenas of Naples. Contacts of Neapolitan bishops with Rome were frequent; and refugees from the Vandals in Africa arrived in Naples in 439. Reduce, bishop during the Lombard siege of 581, gave valuable codexes to the episcopal library. Sergius (718–747) accepted the archiepiscopal dignity from the patriarch of Constantinople but then submitted to Rome. The Iconoclastic controversy (see ICONOCLASM) made itself felt in Naples, and in 860 Nicholas I called Bishop Athanasius to a council in Rome against the archbishop of Ravenna. Stephen II (767–800) sent some of his clergy to *Monte Cassino to study, and the school of Naples produced notable literary figures in the late 9th and the 10th centuries. Naples became a metropolitan see after *Capua (966) and *Benevento (969), yielding civil preeminence as well to those duchies. Neapolitan bishops contributed to the establishment of Norman rule. In 1294 Celestine V resigned the papacy, and Boniface VIII was elected in Naples. In the *Western Schism, Naples under Joanna I of Anjou sided with the antipope Clement VII (1381), with Urban VI (1386) under Charles of Durazzo, and again with Clement (1386) under Louis II of Anjou. Five archbishops recognized Rome and four recognized Avignon; two recognized the antipope John XXIII of Pisa (1411–15).

Archbishop Alessandro *Caraffa in 1497 translated the relics of St. Januarius from Montevergine to Naples, and Alfonso Caraffa in 1565 held a diocesan synod instituting reforms of the Council of Trent. Gian-Pietro Caraffa became Pope Paul IV and Antonio Pignatelli

Naples, catacombs of St. Gaudiosus, detail, 5th or 6th-century fresco of St. Sosius and a jeweled cross; Sosius was martyred with Naples' patron, Januarius.

became Innocent XII. Several archbishops came from the *Caracciolo family. Sisto Riario Sforza (1848–77) received *Pius IX as an exile in Naples, and he himself, because of his opposition to the annexation of Naples to the Kingdom of Italy, was exiled until 1866.

Neapolitan monasteries date from c. 400, that of Lucullano (founded c. 492), with a library that included St. Jerome's original translations of the Bible, being especially noteworthy. Greek monasteries were numerous, and in the early 9th century two monasteries were founded by the Duke of Naples and his widow. The Book of *Lindisfarne (c. 700) is based on the Neapolitan liturgy. The catacombs of St. Januarius lost importance with the translation of the saint's relics to Benevento (831), but bishops continued to be buried there, and its paintings offer a study of Christian art from the 2d to the 10th century. The catacombs of St. Gaudiosus contain early mosaics. Little remains of the catacombs of St. Ephebus. The tomb of Bp. St. Severus, who corresponded with St. Ambrose, shows Milanese influence. Some ancient mosaics of the Baptistery of S. Giovanni in Fonte (c. 400) remain. Constantine's basilica, called S. Restituta c. 850, had five naves and no transept. It was modified considerably with the building of the Angevin Gothic cathedral in 1294. The basilica built by Bp. Stephen I (499–501) was completely destroyed, giving place to the Angevin cathedral. Parts of other early basilicas remain.

Bibliography: H. ACTON, *The Bourbons of Naples (1734–1825)* (London 1956); *The Last Bourbons of Naples (1825–1861)* (London 1961). G. DORIA, *Storia di una capitale: Napoli dalle origini al 1860* (Milan 1958). H. LECLERCQ, DACL 12:691–776. D. MALLARDO and G. CARANDENTE, EncCatt 8:1631–44. U. M. FASOLA et al., LexThK² 7:856–859. AnnPont (1964) 295, 1413. **Illustration credit:** Pontificia Commissione di Archeologia Sacra.

[G. A. PAPA]

NAPOLEON I

French general, emperor; b. Ajaccio, Corsica, Aug. 5, 1769; d. Saint Helena, May 5, 1821.

Early Years. Napoleon was the son of Charles and Laetitia (Ramolino) Bonaparte. His father was thriftless and fickle, but his mother was economical, orderly, morally austere, religious in the Corsican manner, and very severe. The maternal influence over the Christian upbringing of her unruly, taciturn son seems not to have been profound. In 1780 Napoleon received chastisements from his mother when he refused to attend Mass, but this did not increase his devoutness. His great-uncle Lucien, an archdeacon, was more adept in conciliating wisdom with thrift than in preaching fervor. At the military school in Brienne, which he entered in April 1779, the boy was industrious and avid to learn, but quarrelsome and increasingly aloof. He remained attached to Father Charles, who prepared him for First Communion, but was much less edified by the other Minims who taught him and who celebrated Mass in 10 minutes, according to him. In 1784 he transferred to a military school in Paris where the technical training was first class, but the religious formation revolved too much around external practices imposed by school discipline and reflected the 18th-century spirit that penetrated the institution. The young cadet had to attend Mass each weekday and high Mass, Vespers, and catechism class on Sunday; he had to receive Holy Communion bimonthly and go to confession monthly. His independent spirit and his already weakened faith found this conformism irritating. The crisis that caused Napoleon's detachment from the Church was intellectual rather than moral. Pleasure did not attract him. His meager income reduced him to a poor, austere mode of life. On his own testimony books were his sole debauchery; so enticing were they that he often deprived himself of food to purchase them. He nourished himself on the ancient classics and still more on such modern authors as Rousseau, Voltaire, Montesquieu, Mably, and Reynald. As a result the rationalism of the *Enlightenment penetrated his spirit and displaced his weakly rooted Christian beliefs. During his stay at the artillery school of La Fère, he ceased to approach the Sacraments and received them no more until his deathbed. He subscribed to the principles of 1789 and sided with the *French Revolution.

Napoleon continued to regard Corsica as his true homeland. He reserved for it the first display of his revolutionary fervor in order to install there the new revolutionary regime, which his family supported. His brother Joseph *Bonaparte was elected a member of the Directory, and his uncle Joseph *Fesch took the oath upholding the *Civil Constitution of the Clergy in order to become vicar to Bishop Guasco; but Napoleon himself failed to obtain a military command. The Bonapartes came into conflict with Pascal Paoli, who opposed the Revolution, and had to flee to France (June 1793).

From 1793 to 1799. The uprising in southern France in favor of the Girondins supplied the young artillery captain with an opportunity to reveal his military genius. Toulon, which had fallen into English hands, was reconquered thanks to a plan devised by Napoleon. This success won him the favor of *Robespierre, the rank of general at the age of 22, and the command of the artillery in the French army in Italy. After July 27, 1794 (9 Thermidor), Napoleon was branded as a follower

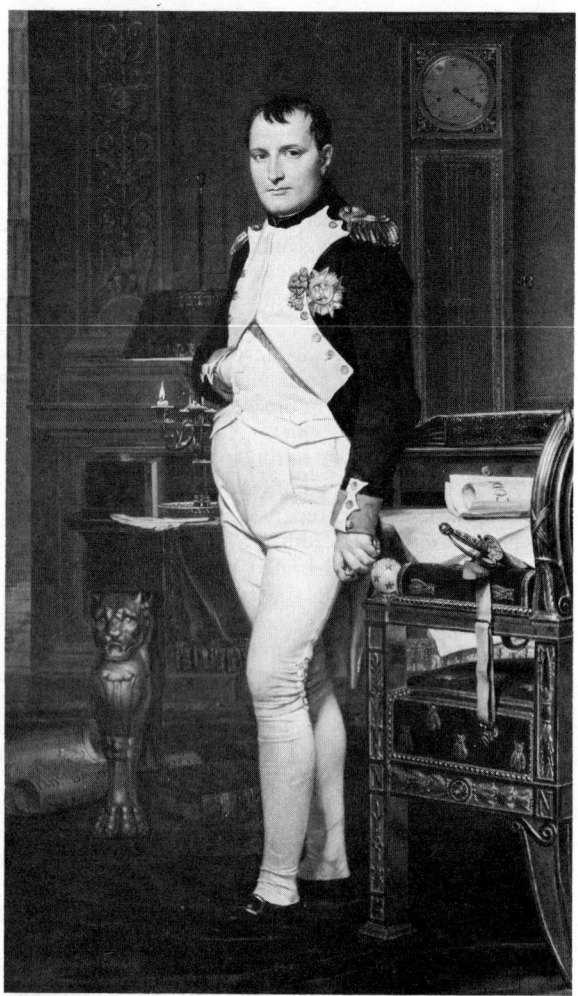

"Napoleon in his Study," by Jacques Louis David.

of Robespierre, stripped of his rank, and arrested. He then offered his services to Paul Barras and subdued the royalist insurrection (October 1795). As a reward Barras named him general of a division and commandant of the army of Paris. Barras, however, distrusted the savior of the Republic and tried to control Napoleon by turning over to him his mistress, the widow Josephine de Beauharnais. Bonaparte became passionately attached to this woman and entered a civil marriage with her (March 9, 1796) once he had been made general in charge of the army in Italy. Both of them could have had recourse to either the refractory or the constitutional priests, but neither of them troubled to do so. Josephine continued to attend the sermons of the constitutional Bishop Belmas at St. Étienne du Mont; yet this woman of fashion regarded morality lightly. Her religion was nothing but vague sentimentality (*see* JOSEPHINE, EMPRESS).

Italian Campaign. During the war in Italy Napoleon learned from experience the social realities that he must take into account in formulating his political policies and military strategy. Despite his limited resources he confronted an offensive by new Austrian armies. To protect his rear he had to win the support of Italian Jacobins and at the same time to placate the Catholic populace, which threatened to rise against the French Revolutionary troops. Napoleon was so much impressed

by the attachment of the Italians to the Church that he refused to obey the Directory's orders to march on Rome and "smash the throne of stupidity." After a first campaign in Romagna he stopped at Bologna and there signed with the Holy See an armistice guaranteeing papal neutrality while assuring himself of a war contribution of 21 million francs (June 20, 1797). After negotiations at Paris failed to effect definitive peace, a second campaign conquered Romagna and the *Legations, but Bonaparte refrained from proceeding farther and informed *Pius VI that he could remain undisturbed in Rome. Napoleon promised also to provide protection for the Pope and the Church, because "it is my special concern that no one make any change in the religion of our fathers." On his own initiative General Bonaparte reopened negotiations and concluded the Treaty of Tolentino (Feb. 19, 1797) without conforming to the Directory's instructions. This pact severed from the *States of the Church only the Legations, Ancona, and Avignon. The Pope retained sovereignty over the rest of his territories, but paid 33 million francs as war indemnity, which was "equivalent to ten times Rome." This consoled the French government for these territorial concessions.

Religious Policy. No question arose concerning a bull retracting papal condemnations of the Civil Constitution of the Clergy and requiring Catholic support of the revolutionary regime. Napoleon declared that he had not spoken about religion. He was convinced that an agreement on this point could not be reached with the basically anticlerical Directory. On this subject he had already framed his basic policies of inviting priests to preach obedience to the government, consolidating the new constitution, reconciling the constitutional with the refractory clergy, and leading the majority of Frenchmen back to religion. At that moment, however, the situation did not seem to him propitious to put his ideas into operation. Napoleon's project for Italian unification encountered Catholic opposition because the Jacobins with whom he dealt to create the Cispadine Republic and then the Cisalpine Republic practiced an antireligious policy contrary to his views. The general sought unsuccessfully to moderate the Cisalpine government and the regional commissioners. But after his departure these men followed their own wishes. The discontent provoked by their anti-Christian action contributed largely to the uprising of 1799, which caused the collapse of a regime imposed by the French invader. Bonaparte heeded the lessons taught by this experience. It was not Catholicism as such that he intended to respect, but popular sentiment. His policy in the Egyptian campaign, during which he favored Islam, was inspired by the same selfish and realistic outlook.

Religious Restoration in France. Religion counted for naught in the *coup d'état* of Brumaire (Nov. 9, 1799), contrived by *Sieyès for financial and political motives. But Bonaparte, whose military cooperation had seemed indispensable for the success of this operation, asserted himself as head of the consular government and gave to it a personal orientation. For reasons of domestic and foreign policy he intended to regulate the religious question. Before he could start a campaign to terminate the war then raging, he had of necessity to pacify the Vendée region. Thanks to *Bernier, he succeeded by granting to the Vendeans religious liberty in the Treaty of Montfaucon. Logic dictated that the same freedom should extend to the whole nation. The decree of 28 Nivôse (Jan. 17, 1799) provided it and yet demanded from priests no more than fidelity to the constitution. On the other hand, another decree (Dec. 30, 1799) sought to dissipate the bias against the French Revolution in the papal conclave then meeting in Venice and to combat Austrian influence in the conclave by prescribing exceptional honors for the remains of Pius VI. For the moment these half measures had to suffice, because the First Consul was not yet firmly established in power. He preferred to wait until further military victory strengthened his authority before putting into effect his full program. His discourse to the clergy in Milan (June 5, 1800), which became widely known, indicated that he would discuss with the Pope a complete reconciliation between France and the Church. Not until the victory at Marengo, however, did he reveal the plan already matured in his mind and charge Cardinal Carlo Martiniana of Vercelli to transmit his proposals to Pius VII.

Religious Outlook. Napoleon was undoubtedly more eager to promote his own policy than the interests of the Church, but the extent to which his policy corresponded with his personal dispositions toward Catholicism is disputed. From this time until his exile to Saint Helena, his contradictory statements can be invoked in opposite senses; but since these utterances varied according to the circumstances and the questioners and the effect Napoleon wished to obtain, they cannot be taken literally or interpreted as proof of his religious disquiet. Napoleon was basically an enlightened despot in the 18th-century style, nourished by the philosophers of that period. Like Voltaire, he judged religion necessary for the populace. His Deism, his belief in the immortality of the soul, and his religious sentimentality came from Rousseau and Robespierre. He did not believe in Catholicism as the one true religion. For him all religions possessed some value; all should be admitted in places where they exist; and all should be utilized for the good of the state. He believed in controlling religion but not in imposing it on others. As a son of the French Revolution he was faithful to the principles of 1789. At the same time he was willing to derive from *Gallicanism other principles that permitted the ruler to limit papal interventions. His religious practice remained external, official, and restricted to attendance at Sunday Mass, an obligation from which he excused himself in the army, because the army, which idolized him, had no need of cult or chaplains. (*See* CATECHISM, IMPERIAL.)

Concordat of 1801. Napoleon's plan of religious restoration was part of his plan for a general restoration in France. Since the population as a whole clung to Catholicism, he sought to satisfy it while utilizing its religion. He believed that public opinion did not demand the restitution of ecclesiastical goods alienated during the Revolution. As for the clergy, he considered that a subsistence salary would be sufficient compensation. Napoleon judged also that national unity required ending the schism caused by the Civil Constitution of the Clergy. His policy of reconciliation aimed to produce neither victor nor vanquished and obliged him to maintain a balance between the bishops of the *ancien régime* and the constitutional bishops by forcing both groups to resign. Thereupon the First Consul would name the entire new hierarchy. In doing so he planned to select some bishops from the *ancien régime* prelates and some from

the constitutional hierarchy and to amalgamate them with new elements. He wanted to retain from the Revolution the division of dioceses according to civil districts, or departments, while reducing the number of dioceses lest the budget become too burdensome and disaffect the public. The same realism that dictated all these measures obliged Napoleon to have recourse to the Pope in order to disavow the error committed by the Civil Constitution in 1790 and to prevent the reappearance of religious divisions. Therefore he recognized Pius VII's authority, but on the condition that the Pope recognize the legitimacy of Napoleon's government. He admitted also the Pope's authority to remove bishops and to appoint others in their stead. In accordance with the principles of 1789, however, he insisted that all cults must enjoy liberty and that Catholicism must not be the state religion. His plan envisioned finally that the liberty accorded Catholic public cult should be submitted to such police regulations as seemed necessary.

After laborious negotiations *Pius VII and Napoleon reached agreement in the *Concordat of 1801. But this text masked rather than dissolved their differences. Quickly the First Consul incorporated the *Organic Articles into the Concordat, severely restricting its scope.

Conflict with Pius VII. Much graver than the causes of conflict to which the application of the Concordat gave rise was the fundamental opposition between Napoleon Bonaparte and the Pope. The former lacked a spiritual sense; the latter was essentially a spiritual man. Despite their mutual sympathy, even affection, the two men were bound to come into conflict. Conciliating though he was, the Holy Father would not compromise his principles even when his independence was jeopardized. Napoleon perceived this at the time of his coronation as emperor (Dec. 2, 1804). The Pope, fortified only by vague promises, agreed to come from Rome to Paris and to allow modifications in the traditional ceremony. On the eve of the event Josephine, who wanted an indissoluble religious marriage lest she be later repudiated, explained to the Pope the details of the couple's civil marriage. Pius VII then insisted that this irregular situation be rectified immediately if he were to participate in the coronation next day. Napoleon had to consent to have his union blessed by the Church, but did so only on condition that Cardinal Fesch, his uncle, officiate at the marriage without witnesses and that this matter be kept shrouded in secrecy similar to that of the confessional. Pius VII returned from his journey to France without obtaining any of the religious advantages he sought, except for some secondary ones.

To the difficulties presented by the French concordat were added those caused by the Italian concordat (1803). In some respects the latter was more favorable to the Church, since it recognized Catholicism as the state religion; but this good feature was offset by the Melzi decrees. Napoleon's coronation as king of Italy (1805) speeded the introduction into northern Italy of French laws and institutions that were inspired by the spirit of the French Revolution. Moreover, Pius VII refused to conclude the German concordat proposed by the Emperor Napoleon for the ecclesiastical reorganization of Germany.

The extension of the French Empire and the resultant wars hastened the crisis, which became acute after 1810, between the Pope and the ruler who wanted to be the successor of Caesar and Charlemagne. Although Napoleon invoked his "system," neither his foreign nor his religious policies conformed to fixed, preconceived notions. Instead his ideas were in continual flux and were modified according to the needs of the moment. It was not his ill-defined system that guided Napoleon but the "force of things." At the same time his military victories and the ever-widening scope of his conflicts accentuated his autocracy. In his policy and strategy Italy played a key role. He was attached to the peninsula also because to it he owed his start toward fame and because the memories of imperial Rome were always dear to his heart. The debarcation of the allied forces at Naples previous to the battle of Austerlitz obliged him to hold Italy to protect his rear. Therefore in 1806 he integrated Naples, Venice, and the duchies with the Kingdom of Italy and extended to these regions the provisions of the Italian concordat and the French legal code. This provoked Pius VII's protests.

Imprisonment of Pius VII. Up to this point Napoleon had not occupied the remaining States of the Church. Now he demanded that the Pope expel foreign agents and close his ports to the allies. So tense did the situation become that Fesch was recalled from Rome and Consalvi resigned as papal secretary of state (June 17, 1806). Once Napoleon had crushed Prussia and concluded peace with Russia at Tilsit, he increased his demands on the Pope. To prevent any opening in the Continental Blockade, whose aim was to ruin England's economy and force its capitulation, Napoleon ordered Pius VII to close his ports to the British. He even asked the Pope for military aid against the heretics, "our common enemies." As father to all Christians Pius VII repulsed this ultimatum. Bayane's attempt at negotiation failed. Napoleon then ordered Gen. François de Miollis to occupy Rome (Feb. 21, 1808). He decreed the annexation of the States of the Church to the French Empire (May 16, 1809); and when Pius VII retaliated by excommunicating the perpetrators of this sacrilege, he ordered General Radet in July to remove the Pope from Rome and then to conduct him as a prisoner to Savona, in northern Italy.

One last step that remained was to bring the Supreme Pontiff to Paris to make him pope of the Great Empire. But nothing could weaken Pius VII's resistance. When he was deprived of his liberty and his advisers, he refused to exercise his papal powers or to institute bishops canonically. Thenceforth the struggle centered on this last point. As vacant sees multiplied, Napoleon tried vainly to end this impasse by turning to the French episcopate. An ecclesiastical committee was convened in 1809 to find a solution, but it disappointed him.

Second Marriage. To complicate matters still more, Napoleon sought to assure himself a male heir by ridding himself of Josephine and marrying a girl with royal blood. Two decisions of the Parisian diocesan and metropolitan ecclesiastical officials, which were correctly rendered, declared Napoleon's marriage on the eve of coronation null. The first decision was based on defect of form; the second was based on defect of form and also on Napoleon's merely simulated consent to the marriage contract. A controversy followed concerning the competence of these diocesan tribunals. Among the Roman cardinals then in Paris one group was convinced that the solution of this case pertained to the Pope and refused to assist at the Emperor's marriage to Archduchess Marie Louise of Austria (April 1810). The reprisals

against these "black" cardinals did not in any way promote the success of the mission of Cardinals Giuseppe *Spina and Carlo Caselli, who were sent to Savona to work out a settlement with Pius VII.

Institution of Bishops. To circumvent the difficulties caused by Pius VII's refusal to give canonical institution to newly named bishops, Napoleon nominated to the See of Paris Jean *Maury and caused the diocesan chapter to confer on him the powers of vicar capitular. Pius VII ruined this scheme by sending secretly to Paris a brief that declared Maury's powers null. In his fury the Emperor ordered the Pope kept in closer confinement and began a police persecution against clerical resistance.

The emotion roused by the Maury affair convinced Napoleon of the need to solve the problem. He appointed a second committee to find a solution, but it had recourse to subterfuges. At a solemn gathering (March 11, 1811) Monsieur *Émery defended papal authority so courageously that the Emperor displayed his admiration. A delegation of bishops to Savona shook Pius VII's resolve for a short time, but it had no lasting result because the Pope revoked his concessions concerning canonical institution by a metropolitan. Napoleon then resigned himself to convoking the imperial council of 1811. There the bishops as a group resisted him, but individually they bowed to his will. When another delegation went to Savona, Pius VII conceded to the metropolitan, acting in the Pope's name, the power of instituting bishops after 6 months. Napoleon demanded a change in this last point, but Pius VII refused. The situation thus had arrived at a new deadlock.

Concordat of Fontainebleau. Napoleon had the Pope transferred to Fontainebleau, near Paris (June 1812), in the expectation that a victorious military campaign in Russia would permit him to overcome finally the resistance of the "old imbecile." After returning from the disastrous Russian expedition, the Emperor was more determined than ever to succeed by extracting from the Holy Father a new concordat. Pius VII signed the so-called *Concordat of Fontainebleau, but this text was intended only as a preliminary one that would serve

NAPOLEONIC EMPIRE IN 1812 ON THE EVE OF THE INVASION OF RUSSIA

◫ The French Empire   ▥ Allies of Napoleon in 1812
▨ Satellite States of the French Empire   ▢ Independent Nations.

Map showing the conquests of Napoleon I.

as the basis for a later definitive agreement, provided everything were kept secret. When Napoleon in bad faith published this document as if it was a concluded concordat, Pius VII withdrew the concessions envisaged by him as the basis of the accord. As military defeat overwhelmed him, Napoleon freed the Pope (Jan. 21, 1814). During the Hundred Days he tried vainly to regain the Holy See's friendship; but Waterloo rendered Msgr. Izoard's mission useless.

Last Years. In writing about Napoleon's religious attitude during his exile at *Saint Helena (1815–21), Las Cases, Gourgaud, Bertrand, and Marchand have contradicted one another. Their accounts leave a mixed impression. In his last testament the Emperor expressed a desire to die in the Catholic religion that he had inherited from his forebears and to receive before death Viaticum, Extreme Unction, and whatever else was customary in similar cases. According to Bertrand he was motivated solely by a belief that this would "promote public morality." Not all historians accept this interpretation. Napoleon died on May 5, 1821, after receiving the ministrations of Abbé Vignali on May 1. Pius VII was the one responsible for sending a chaplain to Saint Helena after the European powers refused to heed the papal request to mitigate Napoleon's sufferings. The Pope had not forgotten that Napoleon had reestablished religion in France. Because of the "pious and courageous effort of 1801," Pius VII had long since forgiven the subsequent wrongs at Savona and Fontainebleau, which he described as mere errors of a spirit carried away by human ambition, whereas the Concordat was a Christian, heroic, and beneficial action.

See also FRANCE.

Bibliography: J. LEFLON, *La Crise révolutionnaire, 1789–1846* (Fliche-Martin 20; 1949). A. LATREILLE, *L'Église catholique et la révolution française*, 2 v. (Paris 1946–50); *Napoléon et le Saint-Siège, 1803–1808* (Paris 1935). V. BINDEL, *Histoire religieuse de Napoléon*, 2 v. (Paris 1941). L. MADELIN, *Histoire du Consulat et de l'Empire*, 16 v. (Paris 1937–54). Dansette v.1. E. E. Y. HALES, *The Emperor and the Pope* (New York 1961). S. DELACROIX, *La Réorganisation de l'Église de France après la Révolution* (Paris 1962–). Schmidlin v.1. A. THEINER, *Histoire des deux concordats de la république française et de la république cisalpine conclus en 1801 et 1803*, 2 v. (Bar-le-Duc 1869). A. BOULAY DE LA MEURTHE, *Histoire de la négociation du Concordat de 1801* (Tours 1920); *Histoire du rétablissement du culte en France 1802–05* (Tours 1925). M. ROBERTI, *Milano capitale napoleonica*, 3 v. (Milan 1946–47) v:1. A. FUGIER, *Napoléon et l'Italie* (Paris 1947). L. GRÉGOIRE, *Le Divorce de Napoléon et de l'Impératrice Joséphine: Étude du dossier canonique* (Paris 1957). G. GOURGAUD and C. J. F. T. DE MONTHOLON, *Mémoirs pour servir à l'histoire de France sous Napoléon. écrits à Sainte Hélène, par les généraux qui ont partagé sa captivité, et publiés sur les manuscrits entièrement corrigés de la main de Napoléon*, 8 v. (Paris 1823–25); ed. D. LACROIX, 5 v. (new ed. Paris 1905). M. J. E. A. D. DE LAS CASES, *Mémorial de Sainte-Hélène*, 4 v. in 8 (London 1823), separate Eng. and Fr. eds. with same title and format; ed. J. PRÉVOST, 2 v. (Paris 1935). H. G. BERTRAND, *Cahiers de Sainte-Hélène, janvier-mai 1821*, ed. P. FLEURIOT DE LANGLE (Paris 1949). **Illustration credit:** National Gallery of Art, Washington, D.C., Samuel H. Kress Collection.

[J. LEFLON]

NAPOLEON III

Emperor of France; b. Paris, April 20, 1808; d. Chislehurst, England, Jan. 9, 1873. He was baptized Charles Louis and was the third son of Louis and Hortense Bonaparte (then King and Queen of Holland) and the nephew of Napoleon Bonaparte. He was forced by the Congress of Vienna to spend his early manhood in exile. Educated in a Bavarian Gymnasium, he acquired Swiss citizenship. As a member of the *Carbonari he took part in a local Italian revolution (1830–31) against the Austrian Hapsburgs. The combined efforts of his mother and Cardinal Mastai (later *Pius IX) were required to rescue him from capture and possible execution. He afterward attempted two ill-fated *coups d'état* against the bourgeois government of the Orleanist King Louis Philippe. Pardoned after the failure of his coup of 1832 at Strasbourg, Louis Napoleon visited Boston, Mass. (1836–37), before going to England to await the death of his mother. The attempted coup of 1840 at Boulogne led to his imprisonment at the Ham fortress near the Belgian border. With the help of Dr. Henru Conneau, he escaped (1846) to England, where he established important political and social connections. In 1848 he served as a constable in London during the Chartist demonstration.

As an intellectual, Louis Napoleon was influenced by the socialist ideology of *Saint-Simon. He wrote several treatises, two of which foreshadowed his political and socioeconomic policies, which would place him among the first rulers to cope with problems emerging from the industrial revolution. His *Napoleonic Ideas* advanced a constructive social and economic program for the French people. In *The Extinction of Pauperism* he advocated a regulated economy and social hierarchy, ideas that led later critics to label him a protofascist.

In 1848 the February and June Revolutions in France spelled the permanent end of monarchy and ushered in the Second French Republic. A constitution was adopted in November, and, assisted by the Napoleonic legend, his own versatile appeal and program, and the fear of socialism, Louis Napoleon was elected president for a terminal 4-year term. He had won Catholic support by promising, after negotiations with *Montalembert, to protect religion, grant the Church freedom of education, and guarantee the freedom and authority of the Pope, then in exile at Gaeta. As president, he dispatched troops to occupy Rome and permit the return of Pius IX, and he recommended the Falloux Law on education (*see* FALLOUX, FRÉDÉRIC ALFRED PIERRE DE). The constitution enabled the conservative Legislative Assembly to control the executive, but imprudent decisions in limiting the suffrage and in granting presidential power to appoint army and police chiefs made possible Louis's coups of 1851 and 1852. The first coup granted Louis sweeping powers to revise the constitution, while the coup of 1852 established the Second Empire. Montalembert broke with him, but Louis *Veuillot and Bishop *Maret led most Catholics to support his imperial claims. Republican opposition was subdued, and in 1853 the Emperor married the beautiful Spanish Countess Eugenie de Teba. Three years later the Prince Imperial, Louis Napoleon (1856–79), was born, assuring succession to the throne.

The domestic policy of Napoleon III stimulated the progress of the industrial revolution. A network of railroads and a banking system contributed to national unity, while the economy was bolstered by government credit at home and in imperial territory. Banking developed with great vigor. Government banks (the Crédit Foncier and the Crédit Agricole) and the private Crédit Mobilier encouraged industrialization, commerce, urban development, and agricultural growth. The Bank of France centralized the banking structure. The Cobden Treaty of 1860 with England committed France to a

Napoleon III, portrait by Alfred Dedreux (1810–60).

policy of free trade. It was less remunerative than expected, but a public works program averted economic dislocation and made possible the prefect G. E. Haussmann's beautification of Paris. In 1864 the government permitted the rise of labor unions with rights of strike and bargaining.

Relative peace and prosperity were conducive to the growth of French culture and the contributions of L. *Pasteur in science, F. M. de Lesseps in engineering, C. P. *Baudelaire and G. *Flaubert in literature, J. Offenbach and G. Courbet in the arts, and J. Garnier in architecture. Catholicism flourished despite the growing differences between Liberal Catholics and the ultramontanists (*see* ULTRAMONTANISM). Numerous religious congregations of women were authorized, and French missionaries, such as the *White Fathers in Algeria, labored in many parts of the world, especially in southeast Asia. *Lourdes became an international shrine of pilgrimage.

Ambitious overextension in the field of foreign affairs led France to disaster. Among Napoleon's imperial ventures, the Crimean War was particularly expensive in lives and money and brought questionable diplomatic gain. The War of Italian Liberation (1859–60) revealed that France alone could not control the balance of power. Theoretically committed to the *risorgimento, Napoleon was fearful of alienating Catholic support, and consequently his maintenance of French troops in Rome deprived the United Italian armies of their most desired prize. Only with the withdrawal of these troops in 1870 was the last remnant of the *States of the Church occupied. The Mexican expedition (1861–67) terminated in the execution of "Emperor" Maximilian,

the withdrawal of French troops, and loss of prestige. Imperial expansion into Indochina and Algeria led to a century of tension and eventual expulsion. In 1863–64 Polish patriots waited in vain for French help. Only Rumania, which achieved autonomy, profited from Napoleon's idealistic belief that he could act as the arbiter of European destiny. Overconfidence and preoccupation with unsound foreign ventures blinded him to the rise of a powerful Prussia. The French defeat in the Franco-Prussian War (1870–71) resulted in the capture and exile of the Emperor and the humiliating Treaty of Frankfurt. France never wholly regained the prestige attained by Napoleon during his 22 years of rule.

Bibliography: A. L. GUÉRARD, *Napoleon III* (Cambridge, Mass. 1943). *Oeuvres de Napoleon III,* 5 v (Paris 1854–69). P. GUÉRIOT, *Napoleon III,* 2 v. (Paris 1933–34). P. DE LA GORCE, *Histoire du Second Empire,* 7 v. (Paris 1894–1905). J. MAURAIN, *La Politique ecclésiastique du Second Empire de 1852 à 1869* (Paris 1930). É. OLLIVIER, *L'Empire libéral: Études, ré cits, souvenirs,* 18 v. (Paris 1894–1918). F. COGNASSO, EncCatt 8: 1628–33. Dansette v.1. R. W. COLLINS, *Catholicism and the Second French Republic* (New York 1923). **Illustration credit:** French Embassy Press and Information Division, New York City.

[R. J. MARAS]

NARBONNE, a city of 35,899 (1962) in the Diocese of Carcassonne, south France, 5 miles from the Mediterranean. The Roman colony *Narbo Martius* (118 B.C.) on the site of a Celtic emporium gave its title to the civil province *Narbonensis I.* The location of the forum is known and portions of the capitol, amphitheater, and walls of the Late Empire remain. The capital of medieval *Septimania,* Narbonne was held successively by the Visigoths (462), Saracens (c. 718), and Franks (759); c. 900 it passed to a local viscountal dynasty which disputed control of it with the archbishops. On May 25, 1508, Louis XII of France annexed it to his domains.

Gregory of Tours dates its first bishop, Paul, c. 250. Recognized as a metropolitan see in 422, it exercised jurisdiction in Catalonia from c. 800 to c. 1100 and had 9 French suffragans c. 1300. Though the See of *Toulouse was detached from its province in 1317, the bishoprics of Alet and Saint-Pons were added in 1318 and Alais in 1694. At the exile of Abp. A. R. de Dillon (1762–90) and the suppression of the archbishopric (1790), it had 11 suffragans; but it was not reconstituted in 1802 when much of its diocesan territory went to Carcassonne. Since 1822 the archbishop of Toulouse has joined *Narbonensis* to his title.

From c. 250 to 1790 the episcopal succession numbers 74 names, of which four are doubtful. Its archbishops include St. *Theodard (d. 893), *Arnaldus Amalrici (d. 1225), Guillaume *Briçonnet (1507), and Cardinal John of *Lorraine (d. 1550). Archbishop Gui Foulquoys (1259–61) became Pope Clement IV (1265–68); and Giulio de Medici (1515–23), Pope Clement VII (1523–34). In late 1415 negotiations to secure the abdication of the Avignon Pope Benedict XIII took place in Narbonne. Episcopal councils assembled there in 458, 589, 788 (Adoptionism?), 883, 902, 947, 990, 1043, 1045, 1054 (Truce of God), 1090, 1128, 1134, 1211, 1227 (Albigensians and reform), 1243 (Inquisition), 1374, 1430, 1551, and 1607. Its ecclesiastical architecture includes the former Cathedral of St. Just (13th–14th century); the Basilica of

St. Paul–St. Serge (13th–15th century), adjoining a 4th-century necropolis where excavations were made in 1942 and 1946; the former abbey church of Notre-Dame de Lamourguier (13th century), housing the lapidary museum; and the archiepiscopal palace (13th–14th century), now housing the municipal collections.

Bibliography: P. CARBONEL, *Histoire de Narbonne* (Narbonne 1956). GallChrist v.6. L. SIGAL, *Les Premiers temps chrétiens à Narbonne d'après l'archéologie* (Narbonne 1947). H. LECLERCQ, DACL 12.1:791–878. *Congrès archéologique de France* 112 (1955) 433–502. EncWA 5:605. *Guide pratique des catholiques de France* (11th ed. Paris 1963) 4:477–487.

[H. G. J. BECK]

NARDI, JACOPO, historian, statesman; b. Florence, 1476; d. Venice, 1593. Patriot and admirer of Savonarola, he held several official positions after the expulsion of the Medici in 1494. He continued in public service until the reinstatement of the Medici in 1530, when he was exiled and his property confiscated. He defended the Florentine exiles at Naples in 1535 against Francesco Guicciardini, but without success. He spent the rest of his life mainly in Venice, where he died in poverty. Among his many works are *La vita di Antonio Giacomini*, and two comedies reminiscent of Plautus, *L'amicizia* and *I due felici rivali*. He is best known for his *Istorie della città di Firenze*, based in part on the *Diario* of Biagio Buonaccorsi and covering the period 1494 to 1538. Although written with an obvious republican bias, it has a high moral tone and is a good record of events in which Nardi himself participated.

Bibliography: J. NARDI, *Istorie della città di Firenze*, ed. A. GELLI, 2 v. (Florence 1858). A. PIERALLI, *La vita e le opere di Jacopo Nardi* (Florence 1901). G. TOFFANIN, *Il Cinquecento*, v.6 *Storia letteraria d'Italia* (4th ed. Milan 1950) 440–442, with bibliography. M. LUPO GENITLE, *Studi sulla storiographia fiorentina alla corte di Cosimo I De' Medici* (Pisa 1905).

[V. LUCIANI]

NARSES, general and last Byzantine governor of Italy; b. Armenia?, *c.* 475; d. Rome (Constantinople?), *c.* 575. He was a slave and eunuch at the Byzantine court. In 532 he broke the Nika rebellion against *Justinian by distributing money among the leaders. In 535 he suppressed a rebellion in Alexandria. He was made imperial treasurer in 538, and was sent to Italy to assist and control the victorious Byzantine general *Belisarius against the Ostrogoths. Rivalry between the two generals led to the capture and devastation of *Milan by the barbarians, and Narses was recalled to Constantinople in 539. In 551 he returned to Italy as a general with more than 30,000 troops; he defeated the Ostrogoths twice in 552, slaying their leaders, Totila in one battle and Teia in another. In 554 he defeated the Franks near Capua on the Volturno, thus delivering Italy from the barbarians. As supreme military and civil governor, he then restored order to the devastated country. *Justin II (565–578) dismissed him, but rather than return to Constantinople Narses retired to a villa near Naples, as the *Lombards invaded Italy. Pope John III invited him to return to Rome. Nothing is known of Narses' last years.

Bibliography: PAUL THE DEACON, *De Gestis Langobardorum* 2:1–5 in PL 95:477–483. Baronius 10:86, 146, 151, 221, 247–248, 257–258. E. STEIN, *Histoire du Bas-empire*, ed. J. R. PALANQUE, 2 v. (Paris 1949–59) 2:356–360; 599–611.

[J. VAN PAASSEN]

NARY, CORNELIUS, priest, controversialist, translator; b. near Naas, Co. Kildare, Ireland, *c.* 1660; d. Dublin, March 3, 1738. After being educated locally, he was ordained in Kilkenny in 1684, went to Irish College, Paris, graduated doctor of laws from the University of Paris, and became tutor in London to the Earl of Antrim. He was appointed parish priest of St. Michan's, Dublin, *c.* 1700, and composed a catechism for the use of his parish (1705), to which he introduced the Dominican and Poor Clare nuns. In 1717 he translated the New Testament with practical liturgical intent. He wrote a "powerful memorial" (Lecky) on the subject of the oath of abjuration, called *The Case of the Catholics of Ireland* (1724). Nary's literary activity included an ambitious *New History of the World* (Dublin 1720); translations from the French; writings on *Unigenitus;* and among others, replies to one George Synge, *Charitable Address to All Who Are of the Communion of Rome* (1728). An active member of the diocesan chapter, he figured in domestic controversies.

Bibliography: J. WARE, *Works*, ed. and tr. W. HARRIS, 3 .v. (Dublin 1739–64) 2:299. N. DONNELLY, *History of Dublin Parishes* (Dublin n.d.) 3:50–55. W. E. H. LECKY, *History of Ireland in the 18th Century*, 5 v. (London 1893).

[J. J. MEAGHER]

NASHVILLE, DIOCESE OF (NASHVILLENSIS)

Suffragan of the metropolitan See of *Louisville, Ky., coterminous with the state of Tennessee, was separated from the Diocese of Bardstown (now Louisville) on July 28, 1837. It was the most destitute of the 17 sees erected in the U.S. up to that time. In all its 42,022 square miles the first bishop, Richard P. Miles, OP, found only 300 Catholics, one little church, and not a single priest to help him. In 1851 the Dominican sisters arrived in Memphis and established St. Agnes Academy, which has since become *Siena College (1921). By 1860, when Miles died, there were 13 priests, 14 churches, 9 parish schools, an orphanage, and about

HOLY ROSARY CATHEDRAL

Fig. 1. Holy Rosary, Nashville, Tennessee's first Catholic church, 1821.

Fig. 2. St. Mary's, old cathedral, Nashville. Dedicated 1847.

12,000 Catholics. The second bishop, James Whelan, OP, established St. Cecilia Academy at Nashville (1860) to which was later added Aquinas Junior College (1961). The diocese suffered greatly during the Civil War, and after 3 years Whelan resigned (1863). Reconstruction was carried on by Bp. Patrick A. *Feehan (1865–80), who built 22 churches, introduced 8 religious orders, and increased the number of priests from 9 to 25. In Nashville the Sisters of Mercy opened a girls' school, and the Franciscan fathers took charge of St. Mary's and other parishes in Memphis, where in 1871 the Christian Brothers erected a boys' school (later *Christian Brothers College) and the Good Shepherd sisters began a school for girls (1875). The yellow fever epidemics of the 1870s decimated the diocese; in Memphis alone 19 priests, 23 sisters, and 3 brothers died.

After Feehan was transferred to Chicago, Sept. 10, 1880, Joseph Rademacher became Nashville's fourth ordinary, June 24, 1883. Three hospitals, 13 churches, and 5 schools were built before he was transferred to Fort Wayne, Ind. (1893). During the 29-year rule of

the forceful Bp. Thomas S. Byrne (1894–1923) the first diocesan synod was convoked (1905), and many institutions were founded. Byrne promulgated the law that Catholic children must attend Catholic schools with the result that even as late as 1963 about 90 per cent of the diocese's children were in Catholic schools. New religious orders brought into the diocese included the Paulist and Josephite fathers, the Daughters of Charity, and the Little Sisters of the Poor. In the 11-year administration of Byrne's successor, A. J. Smith (1924–35), native vocations and frequent Communion were promoted. The Poor Clares founded a monastery, and 15 churches and 6 schools were built. During the episcopacy of William L. Adrian, begun in 1936, three synods were held; a newspaper, the *Tennessee Register,* was established; and many lay organizations were formed. In 1963, despite the growth of Catholicism, Catholics numbered only 83,588 in a total population of 3,600,-000. They were organized in 75 parishes, 31 missions, and 76 stations, served by 154 priests, of whom 29 were religious. There were also 54 brothers and 546 sisters helping to staff the diocese's 3 colleges, 13 high and 57 elementary schools, 5 general hospitals, 2 orphanages, and 2 homes for the aged.

Bibliography: V. F. O'DANIEL, *The Father of the Church in Tennessee, Richard Pius Miles, O.P.* (New York 1926). G. J. FLANIGEN, *Catholicity in Tennessee, 1541–1937* (Nashville 1937).
[G. J. FLANIGEN]

NASSAU-SIEGEN, JOHAN MAURITS VAN, liberal governor of Pernambuco during the Dutch occupation; b. Dillenburg, Germany, 1604; d. Siegen, 1679. He served in the Low Countries under Frederick Henry and took part in many battles. In 1636 he was chosen to govern the region of Brazil from Rio Grande do Norte to Alagôas, which the Dutch West India Company occupied between 1630 and 1635. He began consolidating the conquest with the taking of Ceará and Sergipe, but failed in the attempt to occupy Bahia (1638). He occupied Mina, or Dahomey (1637), a center for Negro slave traffic on which the sugar plantations of Brazil were dependent. In setting up his civil government, Johan Maurits tried to obtain the collaboration of the subjugated Luso-Brazilians, who were all Catholics. He guaranteed them freedom of worship despite the intransigency of the Calvinist preachers who wished to prevent this. Due to this conciliatory attitude, Dutch Brazil prospered. The same attitude was manifested toward the Sephardic Jews who had migrated to Brazil from Holland and there had impediments put in the way of their religious and commercial activities by the Calvinists. Johan Maurits, a true man of the Renaissance, introduced to Brazil the literary men, scientists, and painters of Holland and Germany. Through his financial aid, studies of tropical diseases were made, and cartography was advanced; he also commissioned paintings of men, animals, and landscapes of the region. In 1641 he occupied Maranhão in northern Brazil, and Angola and São Tomé in Africa. In 1644 he returned to Holland where, at The Hague, he built "Mauritshuis." He then went to Germany; he was made a prince of the Empire in 1653.

Bibliography: L. DRIESEN, *Leben des Fürsten Johann Moritz von Nassau-Siegen* (Berlin 1849). C. R. BOXER, *The Dutch in Brazil, 1624–1654* (Oxford 1957).
[J. A. GONSALVES DE MELLO]

Fig. 3. New Cathedral of the Incarnation, Nashville. Dedicated 1914. Copied from the old Church of San Martino ai Monti, Rome; tower after that of St. Damaso Church.

NATAL, ARCHDIOCESE OF (NATALEN-SIS),

located in the state of Rio Grande do Norte, Brazil; created a diocese in 1909; raised to an archdiocese in 1952. In 1964 it had two suffragan dioceses, Mossoró (1934) and Caicó (1939). The first parish in the area was founded about 1600, but the area remained largely mission territory. The Jesuits, and later the Carmelites and Capuchins, catechized the Indians until Pombal secularized the missions. After 1748 the number of parishes began to increase. During the 19th century the work of the Capuchins, particularly Frei Serafim de Catânia, was outstanding in the state. In the 20th century the Church has assumed leadership in social and economic projects for this extensive, underdeveloped region plagued by periodic droughts. Apostolic Administrator Eugênio Sales de Araújo began the Natal Movement to raise the religious, economic, and cultural level of the people, especially those in the interior, by coordinating all such efforts. From this came the Northeast Regional Secretariat, which, under his direction, coordinated the activities and plans of all the dioceses. Rural syndicates were founded that brought together more than 25,000 agricultural workers. Educational radio programs reach more than 2,000 schools with 35,000 pupils. Thus Natal became the center of a varied modern apostolate in the northeast. Among its innovations was the entrusting of the direction of the parish of Nísia Floresta to four sisters. Among the orders working in the province in 1964 were Missionaries of the Holy Family, Capuchins, Marists, Salesians, Lazarists, and Franciscans.

1963 STATISTICS

Area	Population	Parishes	Clergy	
			Sec.	Reg.
Natal	711,145	34	39	17
Mossoró	299,820	18	24	11
Caicó	166,293	10	14	5

Bibliography: L. DA C. CASCUDO, *História do Rio Grande do Norte* (Rio de Janeiro 1955). R. DE LA PAZ, *A Diocese de Mossoró* (Fortaleza, Brazil 1939).

[O. VAN DER VAT]

NATALIS, ALEXANDER

Theologian, historian, polemecist (known also as Alexandre Noël); b. Rouen, Jan. 19, 1639; d. Paris, Aug. 21, 1724. In 1654 Alexander entered the Dominican Order at Saint-Jacques in Rouen. He undertook his ecclesiastical studies in 1656 at Paris, received the baccalaureate in 1671 and the licentiate in 1673, became a master of theology in 1674, and was appointed a doctor of theology at the Sorbonne in 1675.

After taking his academic degrees, he taught philosophy and theology for the Paris province of his Order, was regent of studies for his own and other provinces (1673–?), and was provincial of his province (1706–10). He tutored J. N. Colbert, son of the minister of Louis XIV.

In 1675, when John Launoi of the Parisian faculty of theology equated the payment of *annates with *simony and questioned the Aquinian authorship of the *Summa Theologiae,* Alexander defended the payment of an-

nates and vindicated the authorship of Aquinas in the work, *Summa S. Thomae vindicata.* He also wrote his *Dissertatio polemica de confessione* (1678) and the *Dissertationum ecclesiasticarum trias,* which included his thoughts on episcopal supremacy over priests, clerical celibacy, and the Vulgate (1678).

Alexander's success as a lecturer in history prompted him to compose his great historical work *Selecta historiae capita et in loca ejusdem insignia dissertationes historicae, chronologicae, criticae, dogmaticae* (1676–86). Volumes covering the Church's first 10 centuries were praised highly, but those dealing with the 11th and 12th centuries aroused indignation in Rome because of their Gallican tinge. In 1684 Innocent XI condemned the entire work as well as the *Summa . . . vindicata,* the *Trias,* and Alexander's polemical dissertation on Confession. The penalty of excommunication was threatened for reading, retaining, or printing these works. A second prohibition came in 1685 with the condemnation of the volumes of the *Selecta historiae capita* devoted to the 13th and 14th centuries. The Dominican Master General Monroy deprived Alexander of all his privileges, but the French government interceded for him in Rome. Nevertheless, in 1687 a third prohibition censured the volumes of the history dealing with the 15th and 16th centuries. Benedict XIII withdrew the prohibition of Alexander's works (1724) and Benedict XIV removed the excommunication on the use of all editions (1754); yet the books are, to this day, listed on the Index, except the edition of the *Selecta . . . capita* of July 8, 1754, with notes and animadversions by Roncaglia (see Hänggi, 161).

In 1686, Alexander turned to theology, writing his *Theologia dogmatica et moralis secundum ordinem Catechismi Tridentini* (1693), his last major work. It was intended not only for the theologians, but also for parish priests, confessors, and preachers. In its preface, he indicated a desire for reconciliation with Rome. He published many short treatises (mostly in French), engaged in polemics with the Jesuits, especially Gabriel Daniel, on *probabilism, *laxism, and *Molinism. The controversy was eventually stopped by the King. Alexander also entered the *Chinese rites controversy: his *Apologie des Dominicains missionaires de la Chine* (1699) was followed by *Conformité des cérémonies chinoises avec l'idolatrie grecque et romaine* (1700).

In 1701, he dedicated himself to providing guideposts for preachers, writing a literal and moral commentary on the New Testament (1703–10). In 1701 he became suspect of Jansenism by signing the *Cas de Conscience,* maintaining that absolution could be given to a cleric who declared that he held on certain points the sentiments of "those called Jansenists," especially that of respectful silence on the question of fact (*see* JANSENISM). He later wrote letters of explanation and made a retraction.

His third conflict with Rome arose over the bull *Unigenitus* (1714), not because he was a Jansenist, but because, with Archbishop Noailles, he thought some of Quesnel's condemned propositions were representative Thomistic thought; he considered the bull not the work of the Pope, but of the Molinists. Alexander's name was included in the list of "Appellants" to the next general council.

In his last years, blind and worn out, he lived at Saint-Jacques, Paris. On the feast day of St. Dominic in 1724, he renounced his appellancy, less than a month before he died at peace with the Church.

Bibliography: A. HÄNGGI, *Der Kirchenhistoriker Natalis Alexander (1639–1724)* (Fribourg 1955). D. A. MORTIER, *Histoire des Maîtres Généraux de l'Ordre des Frères Prêcheurs,* 8 v. (Paris 1903–20). Quétif-Échard 2.2:810–813.

[J. A. DOSHNER]

NATCHEZ–JACKSON, DIOCESE OF (NATCHETENSIS–JACKSONIENSIS)

Suffragan of the metropolitan See of New Orleans, La., coextensive with the state of Mississippi, an area of 46,340 square miles. The diocese was erected on July 28, 1837; in 1963 it numbered more than 67,400 Catholics in a total population of about 2,178,240. The first bishop, John Joseph Chanche, arrived in Natchez May 18, 1841, and found only two priests and no churches within his vast jurisdiction. Natchez, Vicksburg, and some places along the Gulf Coast had small groups of Catholics, with a few more scattered throughout the state, but numbers of them had not seen a priest for many years. Chanche, traveling throughout his diocese by stagecoach, river steamer, and any other means available at that time, worked vigorously for 11 years. By the time of his death, July 22, 1852, the basic structure of the fine Gothic cathedral had been completed in Natchez, and churches had been erected in nine other places; there were 10 priests, a girls' orphanage, and plans for several other churches. His successor, James O. Van de Velde, SJ, arrived Nov. 23, 1853, but about 2 years later an accident led to his death on Nov. 13, 1855.

The third bishop, William H. *Elder, arrived on May 30, 1857, to direct the see, which, despite the paucity in numbers and the poverty of the Catholics, made heartening progress in the years following the Civil War. When in 1880 Elder was transferred to Cincinnati, Ohio, as coadjutor archbishop, the diocese had 19 priests, 48 churches, 15 parochial schools, and a Catholic population of 12,500. During the episcopate of Francis Janssens, who was consecrated for Natchez May 1, 1881, St. Mary's Cathedral, Natchez, was completed and solemnly consecrated on Sept. 19, 1886; missionary work among the Negroes and Indians in the state was advanced; and the number of Catholics had increased to 15,000, with 30 priests, 60 churches, and 26 parochial schools to care for their needs. When Janssens was transferred to New Orleans in 1888, Thomas Heslin was consecrated fifth bishop on June 18, 1889, and served until his death Feb. 22, 1911. His administration was characterized by slow but healthy growth. The sixth bishop was John E. Gunn, SM (1911–24), an eloquent speaker and effective administrator, who directed the establishment of nine new parishes and many mission chapels throughout the state.

On Oct. 15, 1924, Richard Oliver Gerow was consecrated seventh bishop of Natchez. A steady growth has marked his administration, during which the number of parishes has doubled and the number of priests more than doubled, while three Catholic hospitals, a monastery of cloistered Carmelite nuns, a lay retreat house, and a seminary of the Oblates of Mary Immaculate have been established, and other religious works inaugurated. In 1948 new chancery offices at Jackson, including administrative offices and bishop's residence, were completed and on July 22 of that year the bishop transferred his residence from Natchez to Jackson. The name of the diocese was changed to Natchez-Jackson on Dec. 18, 1956, and St. Peter's Church in Jackson was named as cocathedral. By 1963 the diocese numbered 88 parishes, 190 priests, 52 brothers, and more than 400 sisters. There were 48 elementary schools, 26 high schools, 3 hospitals, 2 schools for nurses, and 2 orphanages under Catholic auspices.

Bibliography: R. O. GEROW, *Catholicity in Mississippi* (Natchez 1939).

[R. O. GEROW]

NATHAN, name of a prophet in the days of *David and *Solomon; the name also of one of David's sons. The Prophet Nathan (Heb. *nātān,* shortened form of a theophoric compound, such as *nātan-'ēl,* "God has given [a son]") dissuaded David from building a temple and gave him the important oracle that promised perpetuity to the Davidic Dynasty (2 Sm 7.1–29). He reproved David for his adultery and murder of Uria (2 Sm 12.1–15). According to the Biblical *Chronicler, it was with Nathan's concurrence that David ar-

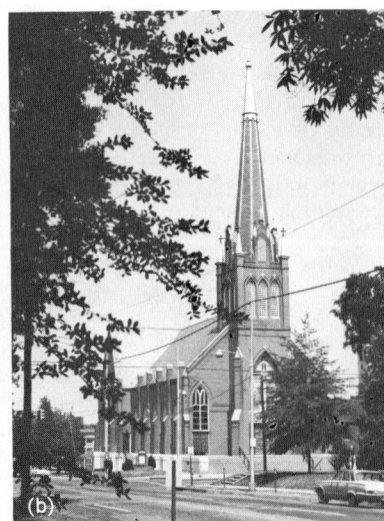

Natchez-Jackson: (a) St. Mary's Cathedral, Natchez; (b) St. Peter's Church, Jackson; (c) Bp. John J. Chanche.

ranged the musical service for the sanctuary (2 Chr 29.25). Nathan supported Solomon in his bid for the throne (3 Kgs 1.10–45). According to 1 Chr 29.29 and 2 Chr 9.29 Nathan wrote a history of David and Solomon.

Nathan, son of David (2 Sm 5.14), is probably the ancestor of the family mentioned in Za 12.12. St. Luke (3.31) traces the lineage of Jesus through this Nathan rather than through Solomon.   [F. BUCK]

NATION

The term nation suffers from the ambiguity arising from a conflict between popular usage and attempts at scientific precision. Etymologically, the word is derived from the Latin *nasci* (to be born); given this derivation, one might expect it to be applied to a group of common racial or biological origin. This is often the case in popular usage when the term is used interchangeably with race or stock. Even in scholarly usage, however, the term owes something to its etymology, at least in the sense that a person derives a cultural heritage from his national or ethnic group. For each human person, this social group provides the "generative milieu" and "may be thought of as a co-parent of the individual's personality, and especially of his intellectual self, even as his progenitors are the parents of his physical self" (Wright, 70–71).

Sociologists and political scientists have attempted to refine the concept and to distinguish the nation from other human groupings, e.g., *race, tribe, people, *state. Actually, the nation is a relatively modern phenomenon characterized by the emergence of large groups of men sharing "a fellowship in socially relevant values and the common will to assert this fellowship within the society of nations" (Messner, 474). This sense of fellowship emerges from common historical experiences and presupposes a common territory and a common *culture and *social institutions.

Sociological Aspects. The elements that help to build up a sense of national *community include common language, religion, cultural forms, economic interests, geography, and common historical experiences involving common trials and triumphs. The presence of any one or several of these in combination does not of itself guarantee the formation of a nation. The key factors are the emergence of a "we feeling," a sense of community, and a consequent will to national self-assertion in relation to other groups (*ibid.* 485). In other words, it is not the factual existence of the various elements in combination, but the social meaning attributed to them by the people who share them that gives self-consciousness and unity to the group. Thus, the common territory is thought of as "our native land," as the soil for which national military heroes have fought and died, as the subject of patriotic songs and poetry. Economic interdependence through division of labor and exchange within a common market area gives rise to many other relationships that cement the sense of common interests. A common tongue is the medium for a common literature that speaks of the common experience of life and expresses the highest human aspirations in a distinctive mode. Religion provides a common interpretation for the socially relevant moral values shared by the group.

Political Dimension. Quite commonly, during the last 2 centuries, the will to self-assertion on the part of a national group has taken the form of "political self-determination" or the alleged right of the national group to exist as a separate political unit or state, independent of and equal to other, already existing polities. This political dimension of nationality is the natural outgrowth of the fact that the nation, like the human person, can become conscious of its own identity only through relationships with other groups that are in many respects similar, yet distinct. Just as interacting persons form a community with common institutions for common ends, so interacting nations form a community and require a political form. Historically, the western European nations became nation-states under the dynamic influence of economic, social, and political developments that permitted them to be viable political units. Economic developments widened the area of markets beyond the old localistic bases; strong monarchs, allied with newly emergent middle-class entrepreneurs, built strong, centralized governments and established permanent bureaucracies to conduct the affairs of state. Gradually, as *democracy replaced *monarchy and as improved communications made possible the awakening and continuous upbuilding of national consciousness, the nation-state reached the culmination of its development and became the basic political unit of the modern Western world.

Nationalism. National consciousness frequently is expressed in a sense of pride in the achievements of a people, in devotion to the building up of the institutions of the common life, and in great sacrifices for the defense or liberation of the nation. In fact, this devotion has at times become a secular religion whose chief dogma is "my country, right or wrong," and has been at the heart of the demand for "national self-determination" in the political sphere (*see* NATIONALISM). This slogan is more powerful among peoples with some degree of national consciousness who have been forced to live under political rule that has not provided an environment of freedom for the development of national culture. Such development requires a good measure of political stability that can be achieved only when the political unit is viable, that is, capable of effective government. This in turn requires an adequate economic base, competent leadership, and sufficient political consensus to guarantee unity and social cooperation.

International Interdepedence. In mid-20th century the factors that make for political viability are not necessarily coextensive with those that make for national self-consciousness. As modern technology has made possible the extension of Western political and economic influence throughout the world, old societies and new political units have been drawn into increasing interdependence on the economic, cultural, social, political, and military levels in a world community that is still groping to establish effective international political institutions (*see* INTERNATIONAL RELATIONS). In the absence of such institutions for the preservation of peace, order, and justice in these relationships, national groups have at least an apparent justification for their claim to "national self-determination" on the one-nation, one-state principle. Their only hope for preserving their identity seems to be in creating political machinery that they can control. Yet the realities of political and economic life, in eastern Europe after World War I, for example, or in contemporary Africa, often frustrate this type of national self-assertion. The "wars of national liberation" of the newly emerging nations have often led to disillusionment and frustration because the newly created "states" could not prove themselves politically viable.

Ethical Aspects. The near-universal influence of nationalism in the contemporary world and the persistence of demands for political self-determination on a national basis pose the problem of the legitimacy of national aspirations, especially as these affect international relations. The contemporary universality of the phenomenon might indicate the "naturalness" of the nation as a social group. To what extent is the existence of nations a reflection of a common human need? Is the nation a "natural society" in the sense of traditional Catholic social philosophy?

Relation to Human Nature. As already indicated, the "natural" character of the nation springs from its fulfillment of the need of the human personality for a community within which to grow and to be formed through the reception of a social and cultural inheritance (*see* SOCIETY). On the natural plane, the formative influence of this "generative milieu" engenders a sense of gratitude, of devotion, of loyalty, and of willingness to sacrifice for the good of the community to which a person owes the social dimension of his being. This loyalty is a sort of filial piety, a sense of indebtedness to the fatherland, in short, the virtue of *patriotism. Supernaturally, this patriotism is a form of preferential *charity through which a person responds with gratitude and loyalty to the social group that is instrumental in the perfection of his personality, through which he in turn renders full worship to his Creator. In this sense, the nation is a natural group; it meets a need of human nature; it is not artificially contrived or founded; a person is born into it and receives his nationality without any voluntary action on his part.

Relation to Social Development. But, if the nation is natural, why is it a relatively recent historical phenomenon? Unlike the family or even the political society, the nation seems to be dependent on historical circumstances for its emergence as an identifiable human form. An analogy with the development of the sense of individual identity and of the uniqueness of each human person will clarify the point. The general recognition of the dignity and uniqueness of each human person, although this has always been a fact and although it is one of the basic tenets of Christianity, is only now dawning on the conscience of mankind and being articulated in the demand for the acknowledgment and protection of universal human rights (see John XXIII, *Pacem in terris,* 39–45). Similarly, each nation—the result of a unique combination of cultural, geographic, economic, linguistic, and religious elements—is in a position to make a unique contribution to human civilization once its people have become aware of this uniqueness. The virtue of patriotism by which they love this national "good," since it is love, impels them to share this good with others and to respect the unique contributions that other nations also make to the common human patrimony. In contrast, exaggerated nationalism is in reality a form of group egoism that emphasizes differences, exclusivism, and intolerance. Hence, true patriotism is pacifying, whereas nationalism tends toward conflict and leads to *totalitarianism in one form or another.

Because of its uniqueness, each nation has a right and even a duty to preserve itself and to work for conditions conducive to its preservation and growth. In some circumstances of history, this may require political autonomy. But if circumstances do not permit the establishment of a viable political unit, the well-being of the nation itself indicates the necessity to join with other groups in the creation and maintenance of a viable political system that can guarantee to all its component groups the order and peace essential for healthy national life and development.

Relation to the International Common Good. As a society, the nation is not "perfect" in the Aristotelian sense; that is, it does not possess in itself all the means necessary for the fulfillment of its own proper ends. Even large and well-established nation-states are no longer self-sufficient, but need the assistance and protection of an international authority with a scope of power proportioned to the worldwide nature of many contemporary problems. As John XXIII remarked in *Pacem in terris,* "Today the universal common good poses problems of worldwide dimensions, which cannot be adequately tackled or solved except by the efforts of public authorities endowed with a wideness of powers, structure and means of the same proportions: that is, of public authorities which are in a position to operate in an effective manner on a worldwide basis. The moral order itself, therefore, demands that such a form of public authority be established" [Act ApS 55 (1963) 293]. It seems to follow that national groups, whether they have a separate political existence or constitute a group within a larger political framework, are obligated in *social justice to cooperate in the creation and functioning of the international institutions necessary to achieve the common good on which their own perfection depends, a good that John XXIII defined in *Mater et Magistra* as embracing "the sum total of those conditions of social living whereby men are enabled to achieve their own integral perfection more fully and more easily" [ActApS 53 (1961) 417].

See NATIONALISM; STATE, THE.

Bibliography: M. H. BOEHM et al., EncSocSc 11:231–252. J. T. DELOS, *La Nation,* 2 v. (Montreal 1944). J. MESSNER, *Social Ethics: Natural Law in the Modern World,* tr. J. J. DOHERTY (new ed. St. Louis 1964). *Race: Nation: Person* (New York 1944). P. RIGA, *Peace on Earth* (New York 1964), a comment on *Pacem in terris.* L. L. SNYDER, ed., *The Dynamics of Nationalism* (Princeton 1964). J. J. WRIGHT, *National Patriotism in Papal Teaching* (Westminster, Md. 1943; repr. 1956), esp. 27–72 and bibliog.

[T. A. CORBETT]

NATIONAL ASSOCIATION OF EVANGELICALS

A voluntary association of American Protestant evangelistic denominations, churches, schools, organizations, and individuals, who are united without executive or legislative control on the basis of a commonly accepted statement of faith. The purpose of the Association is to provide national identification for evangelicals, fellowship in cooperative witness, and service in every major field of evangelical concern. The occasion for the foundation of the Association was dissatisfaction among evangelical Protestants with the Federal Council of Churches of Christ in America (1905–50; *see* NATIONAL COUNCIL OF THE CHURCHES OF CHRIST IN THE U.S.A.).

They objected that the Council had admitted to its membership a large number of "liberals" who, in their philosophy and theology, were un-Biblical and even anti-Biblical; that it had deliberately omitted or purposely neglected to include provisions for the preservation of all the values inherent in historic Protestantism; and that it had forced evangelicals to take protective measures to ensure their liberty in preaching the Gospel and in carrying out their church programs.

The first organized effort of evangelicals to unite among themselves was the formation in 1929 of the regional New England Fellowship. Its success led to a meeting of evangelical leaders in Chicago, Ill., Oct. 27–28, 1941, and the unanimous decision to call a national conference in St. Louis, April 7–9, 1942. Representatives from approximately 40 denominations agreed at the St. Louis meeting "to organize an Association which shall give articulation and united voice to our faith and purposes." In May 1943 at Chicago a constitutional convention worked out a statement of faith, which was built on the Bible as the supreme authority in all matters of belief and conduct. With this creedal basis the convention then adopted a permanent constitution. In 1964 the Association had among its members 40 complete denominations, and individual churches from 40 other denominations, as well as 2 million individuals from many churches. Headquarters are located in Wheaton, Ill., and seven regional offices in various parts of the U.S. Central to the Association is the Office of Public Affairs in Washington, D.C., which keeps a watch on legislation, the infringement of religious liberties, religious persecutions, and other matters of evangelical interest. The monthly magazine, *United Evangelical Action,* is the official publication of the Association. Typical members are the *Assemblies of God, a pentecostal, missionary denomination composed of approximately 8,000 self-governing churches with 515,000 members located in every state of the U.S. and in many foreign countries.

Eleven commissions and five affiliated service organizations of the Association operate in many fields of evangelical concern. Among the more important are: the Evangelical Foreign Missions Association, which serves 58 member mission boards who have more than 6,000 missionaries in 108 countries; the National Religious Broadcasters and Radio-TV Commission, which aids its constituents in the field of Gospel broadcasting; the Evangelical and Spiritual Life Commission, which gives assistance in the important area of evangelistic efforts; the Church Extension and Home Missions Commission, which gives help in the establishment of local churches; and the Social Action Commission, which coordinates the work of evangelical social welfare agencies.

Bibliography: J. D. MURCH, *Cooperation without Compromise* (Grand Rapids 1956).

[R. MATZERATH]

NATIONAL CATHOLIC CONFERENCE FOR INTERRACIAL JUSTICE, a federation, founded in 1960, of more than 60 *Catholic Interracial Councils and similar organizations. Each member group retains its autonomy and responsibility for its own program. The Conference was organized to assist local councils and other Catholic institutions in developing

leadership, programs, and professional race relations staffs. Its representation of the councils on the national level is particularly important. It encourages Catholics to become more active in efforts to attain racial integration. The central office in Chicago is a clearinghouse and a source of publications, program aids, and technical skill. The programs of its national meetings are of general interest. A field office in New Orleans is concerned with the special problems of race relations in the South. The Conference is supported by contributions from member organizations, donations, and foundation grants. Particularly notable were its service as a secretariat for the first National Conference on Religion and Race, held in Chicago during January 1963, which was attended by 700 religious leaders of all denominations; and its organization of Catholic participation in the March for Jobs and Freedom at the national capital on Aug. 28, 1963.

[J. J. O'CONNOR]

NATIONAL CATHOLIC EDUCATIONAL ASSOCIATION

A voluntary association of more than 14,000 Catholic educational institutions and educators organized for the purpose of improving Catholic education at all levels. As stated in its constitution, it is dedicated to the principle that "Christian education embraces the whole aggregate of human life, physical and spiritual, intellectual and moral, individual, domestic and social, with the goal of elevating it and perfecting it according to the example and teaching of Christ."

Founded in 1904 as the Catholic Educational Association of the U.S. (CEA), it united three separate organizations: the Educational Conference of Seminary Faculties (1897); the Association of Catholic Colleges (1898); and the Parish School Conference (1902). In 1927 the CEA changed its name to the National Catholic Educational Association (NCEA).

Much of the inspiration and organization are attributed to Rt. Rev. Msgr. Thomas J. *Conaty, rector of The Catholic University of America, and Rev. Francis W. *Howard of Columbus, Ohio. Conaty became bishop of Los Angeles in 1903, and his successor at The Catholic University, Most Rev. Denis J. *O'Connell, became the NCEA's first president general and served from 1904 to 1908. Howard was secretary general from 1904 to 1928 and president general from 1929 to 1936.

During World War II and subsequent years, when crowded campuses and new areas of knowledge made heavy demands upon educational institutions, the NCEA owed much to its presidents general, the Most Rev. John B. Peterson (1936–43) and the Most Rev. John T. McNicholas, OP (1946–49), and to its chief administrative officers, Rt. Rev. Msgr. George *Johnson, secretary general (1929–43), and Rt. Rev. Msgr. Frederick G. Hochwalt (1944–   ).

The objectives of the NCEA are: (1) to promote the quality of Catholic education at all levels; (2) to provide Catholic education with national and regional representation; (3) to enable Catholic educators to work together for professional growth in administration and in scholarly attainment; to encourage graduate and professional study for priests, brothers, and sisters, and stimulate their active participation in national, regional, and local educational associations, non-Catholic as well as Catholic; (4) to foster cooperation between Catholic educational bodies and other agencies (to this end, the NCEA is represented at approximately 100 meetings of educational associations each year in the U.S. and at frequent international meetings); (5) to stimulate educational research; (6) to enable Catholic education to interpret itself to the public through its meetings and its publications.

In the beginning the CEA had only three departments: for seminaries, colleges, and parish schools. In 1964 it had seven departments: major seminary, minor seminary, college and university, superintendents, secondary school, elementary school, and special education for the physically and mentally handicapped. In addition, there are two autonomous sections: the vocation section, dedicated to attracting young men to the priesthood; and Sister Formation, to enhance the spiritual, intellectual, and professional preparation of sisters and to encourage graduate education for teaching sisters.

Each department annually elects its own officers and two delegates to the general executive board, plans programs, holds meetings, and issues publications. The general officers of the association are the president general, vice presidents general (one for each NCEA department), and the executive secretary, who is the chief administrative officer elected by the executive board for a 3-year term and eligible for re-election.

In its first 10 years the Association acquired 1,909 members. This was a period of heavy Catholic immigration from Europe and the establishment of many new Catholic schools. In order to make the NCEA's services available for information regarding recognized academic standards, Msgr. Frederick G. Hochwalt, who joined the Washington office in 1944, sought to bring more schools into the Association. From 3,418 reported in Dec. 1945, the membership increased to approximately 14,000 in 1964. Virtually all major seminaries, colleges, universities, and secondary schools and four-fifths of the elementary schools are members of the NCEA. Of the total membership approximately 12,000 are educational institutions and about 2,000 are individuals. The annual convention of the NCEA, usually held in April, customarily attracts more than 15,000 priests, religious, and laymen.

When the NCEA came upon the scene, American Catholic education rather strictly followed the parochial structure of the Church, and schools existed almost in isolation. Through the NCEA cooperation to meet regional and national needs was effected. The NCEA was also instrumental in providing the professionalization required by schools serving the Catholic community as it moved from immigrant status to that of full participation in the Republic.

As a means of extending information and assistance, the quarterly *National Catholic Educational Association Bulletin* is sent to all members. Each department issues regular periodicals or newsletters to its members. The NCEA publishes a number of directories and handbooks of primary value to Catholic educators.

[M. IRWIN]

NATIONAL CATHOLIC OFFICE FOR MOTION PICTURES

This organization formerly known as the National Legion of Decency, is the official national film office of the Catholic Church for the U.S. (*see* MEDIA OF SOCIAL COMMUNICATION, II, 1). Under the supervision of the Episcopal Committee for Motion Pictures, Radio, and Television, the Office directs and promotes the film apostolate among U.S. Catholics. Established by the hierarchy (April 1934), the Legion of Decency played a prominent role in the development of the Church's view on motion pictures. At the same time the evolution in ecclesiastical teaching that has taken place under the pontificates of Pius XI, Pius XII, John XXIII, and Paul VI has, in turn, effected significant changes in the Legion's own approach to the motion picture apostolate. The present focus of its program under the direction of the National Catholic Office reflects that teaching, especially as it is found systematized in the encyclical *Miranda prorsus* and in *Vatican Council II's *Decree on the Media of Social Communication*.

There are two principal phases to the Office's modern film apostolate. First, by means of a biweekly publication of motion picture ratings, critical reviews, and relevant information, it provides a guidance service on the moral and aesthetic values of current films. Second, through its educational division, the National Center for Film Study, the Office promotes and services film-educational projects in schools, colleges, seminaries, and parishes. These services include the production and distribution of educational materials as well as the organization of courses, conferences, and workshops on the Seventh Art. Both phases of the Office's program have as their objective the formation of such discriminating taste and judgment in the movie patron that his moral and aesthetic sensibilities will be adequately refined, and the encouragement of the authentic artist to create films reflecting a Christian vision of man. Finally, once each year the Office invites the faithful, through their bishops, to renew their voluntary pledge of support to this film apostolate.

Origins and Early Years. Today one of more than 40 fully established national Catholic film offices throughout the world, the Office was, at its inception in the spring of 1934, a unique Catholic institution on the international scene. For several years prior to that date, Americans of all faiths were seriously discontented with the moral quality of the movies. In the face of this mounting public resentment the American film industry had adopted (March 1930) a code of ethics aimed at self-regulation. But 3 years later the original spirit of this code had been lost and with it any real effectiveness in its application.

At its annual meeting in November 1933 the U.S. hierarchy, calling for industry reform, approved a national campaign for the moral improvement of film production. A committee of bishops was appointed to plan the campaign. In April of the following year, the National Legion of Decency was established as an official Church agency charged with the responsibility of directing an organized crusade for better films. The Legion was to be guided by a permanent Episcopal Committee for Motion Pictures.

The Legion crusade enjoyed immediate support not only in Catholic circles but also from hundreds of thousands of Protestants and Jews. The effect upon the moral quality of production was substantial. By 1938 the executive staff was able to report that 93 per cent of all films released that year (496 out of a total 535) had been found morally unobjectionable either for family or for adult viewing. The immediate success of the crusade was so extraordinary that on June 29, 1936, Pius XI had already been prompted to publish his encyclical letter on motion pictures, *Vigilanti cura*. Expressing appreciation to the American bishops and faithful for this "holy crusade," this "excellent experiment," the Pope commended imitation of it to the rest of the Catholic world. Pius XII, in his encyclical letter *Miranda prorsus* 21 years later, renewed the declaration of his predecessor that "it is absolutely essential for Bishops to set up a permanent national office" for films.

The American experiment, which had thus influenced the Catholic world at large, was, during the ensuing years, to benefit from the work and experience of other national offices but particularly from the carefully developed teaching of Pius XII in his allocutions on the *Ideal Film* and in *Miranda prorsus*. (*See* MEDIA OF SOCIAL COMMUNICATION, II, 1.)

Changing Climate of the Postwar Years. In the decade after World War II the Legion became aware of the emergence of a widespread indifference and even hostility to its program. The reasons for this postbellum attitude were complex. For the majority of those not Catholic any species of *censorship had become anathema and un-American. In spite of its long record of opposition to government film-censorship, the Legion was considered to be the most powerful unofficial censorship force in the country. Certain activities (such as theater boycotts) on the part of well-intentioned Catholics and organizations associated with the Church reinforced this conviction. At the same time the film industry was facing bankruptcy because of the successful challenge television was making for the entertainment dollar. To meet this competition, producers introduced more and more mature subject matter into their films; in some cases maturity was merely a guise for salaciousness and those responsible for it supported the anticensorship movement.

Some Catholics, as well, had lost interest in the Legion; some even became outspoken in their criticism of it. In its 3d decade of operation the Legion faced a new generation of Catholics. Many of them were college and university graduates who became dissatisfied with the alleged restrictive and negative approach of the Legion to the film medium. Such an approach, they argued, was creating for the Church in America the singularly un-Catholic reputation of being the repressive censor and policeman of the Seventh Art rather than its patroness. Moreover, the Legion's overly simplified system of classification, which had been devised when motion pictures were for the most part escapist entertainment, was judged totally inadequate to satisfy the new need for a mature Christian evaluation of the screen. In the matrix of commercial competition with the new marvel of television, the film was fast becoming the most important medium for the communication of ideas.

The annual pledge of the Legion came under special fire, not only because of its negative "I condemn" approach, but more so because of what was considered to be an arrogant disregard for Christian conscience and a properly motivated commitment, which so frequently attended the annual administration of the pledge in too many parishes. Not a few theologians began to worry about the false consciences as well as the moral confusion being created by this lack of intelligent pastoral instruction. They were also concerned that some preachers were, without warrant, elevating the Legion's classifications from the status of moral guides to that of ecclesiastical laws seriously binding in conscience. The publication of *Miranda prorsus* (Sept. 8, 1957) impelled the Legion to bring its program up to date. In the light of Pius XII's teaching, a modernization of the Legion's work, which had been under study and review for several years previously, was judged essential in order to dispel confusion and regain broad Catholic support for the film apostolate.

The New Legion. From the fall of 1957 until the summer of 1964 the Legion gradually underwent carefully planned and important changes. From the outset special attention was devoted to the board of reviewers and consultors. They were increased in numbers and, more important, in quality. The system of classifications was substantially revised to make provision for mature subject matter and treatment in films. The Legion was authorized by the Episcopal Committee to recommend and promote the more outstanding films. This new policy of recommendation, at first restricted to family films, was subsequently broadened to include any film in an approved category. The old pledge was replaced with a new version whose text summarizes the major themes of *Miranda prorsus*. Moreover, with the cooperation of the bishops a special campaign was directed to pastors in order to eliminate confusion about the pledge and its obligations. In 1965 the title of the organization was changed.

During all this period the executive staff made serious efforts to promote the cause of film education in schools, colleges, seminaries, and parishes. Finally this positive program became a permanent reality with the establishment (August 1964) of the National Center for Film Study as the educational affiliate of the Legion. The new Office has not only regained the broad support of Catholics but also enjoys the respect and interest of Americans generally and of educators and film-makers in particular. The critical reviews published by the Office in its *Catholic Film Newsletter* are influential, its educational services are widely used, and its support and endorsement of individual films is hoped for by all major film producers.

Administration. An executive secretary and an assistant executive secretary are the administrative officers of the Office. Their work is supervised by the five-member Episcopal Committee for Motion Pictures, Radio, and Television, which acts on behalf of the entire body of the U.S. hierarchy. Through this committee the executive staff makes an annual report to all the bishops. In addition, each diocese has a diocesan director who has the responsibility of promoting the Office's apostolate in his area.

In the work of film evaluation the executive staff of the national office is assisted by the volunteer services of a large committee of qualified reviewers. It includes lay and clerical educators from every branch of education—primary, secondary, college, and university; motion picture critics and other professional laymen, including many who are engaged in various areas of the mass media; parish priests; student counselors; husband-wife teams; and the Motion Picture Department of the *International Federation of Catholic Alumnae. Films are usually screened privately for the Office and in advance of public release. No film of any consequence is classified without a qualitative analysis of the written opinion of at least 30 to 40 (and frequently even more) of these reviewers.

The first task of the National Center for Film Study, the educational affiliate of the Office, is to assist in the program of encouraging public support for meaningful, entertaining, and artistic films. Reviews of currently released movies of more than average merit are prepared by the center as well as detailed guides for films deserving special study. The center also provides information, ideas, and news about film educational activities. A second responsibility of the center is to prepare and distribute all those materials required for the servicing of film educational projects around the country. A priest director and a lay executive secretary, with the advice of a board of directors and consultors, administer the work of the center.

Classification System. The Office's system of classification (1965) is based upon the directives of *Miranda prorsus* and is substantially similar to that followed today by most national Catholic film offices. There are four subdivisions to the "A" or "morally unobjectionable" category: A–I, for general patronage; A–II, for adults and adolescents; A–III, for adults; and A–IV, for adults, but with reservations. The "B" classification is used for films considered to be "morally objectionable in part for all." The "C" or "condemned" rating is applied to films found to be totally incompatible with Christian moral values or standards of decency.

In addition to assigning a classification to each film reviewed, the Office gives special attention to the better films. Those which are recommended receive a critical review in depth and the others briefer reviews in the *Catholic Film Newsletter.*

The Pledge and Moral Responsibility. The pledge, which Catholics are invited to renew each December, has always been an important aspect of the Office's program for the film apostolate. The original pledge formula was issued in April 1934. By November of the same year the Episcopal Committee introduced a revised version that was in general use for many years. After the publication of *Miranda prorsus,* the text of the pledge was again revised in order to incorporate in capsule catechetical form the principal points of the Church's teaching concerning films.

Of all the mass media, motion pictures are generally recognized to be the most potent for influencing the moral and cultural values of a people and even of the world community. This influence is particularly significant on the young. In a free society the problems that arise because of the irresponsible use of the power of the film medium must be controlled, not by government censorship (except in the case of obscenity), but by the exercise of personal responsibility. This is the principle fundamental to National Office policy in the matter of the pledge.

The pledge does not add any new obligations in conscience. Much less does it change the Office's normative guides into binding ecclesiastical laws. The content of the pledge is no more than a summary of already existing obligations from the natural moral law and the Christian imperative of charity.

The purpose of the pledge is to provide Catholics with the annual opportunity of making a free and corporate witness to their faith in those matters that pertain to a mature and truly Christian choice of film entertainment. During the celebration of the Paschal Liturgy the faithful solemnly renew their Baptismal promises as a sign of the new life they have received in and through the Risen Christ. During the celebration of the Advent Liturgy, which prepares again for the coming of the Word of God, the Catholic renews the promises of the National Office pledge as a sign of the mature witness to which those confirmed in the Lord have been consecrated by His Spirit.

See also EROTIC LITERATURE.

Bibliography: The *Catholic Film Newsletter* and film classifications available from National Catholic Office for Motion Pictures, 453 Madison Ave., New York, N.Y. 10022. Film educational materials and information available from National Center for Film Study, 1307 South Wabash Ave., Chicago, Ill., 60605. H. C. GARDINER, *Catholic Viewpoint ˜on Censorship* (New York 1958; rev. ed. Image Bks. 1961). G. KELLY and J. C. FORD, "The Legion of Decency," ThSt 18 (1957) 387–433. *The National Legion of Decency: Thirty Years of Christian Witness, a Review and Preview,* statement of the Episcopal Committee for Motion Pictures, Radio and Television, April 15, 1964 (Washington 1964). E. MCANANY and R. WILLIAMS, The Film Viewer's Handbook (Glen Rock, N.J. 1965).

[P. J. SULLIVAN]

NATIONAL CATHOLIC PHARMACISTS GUILD OF THE U.S., an association of Catholic pharmacists, was organized in 1962. Before that date there were some diocesan associations of Catholic pharmacists in various parts of the U.S. One of these, the Catholic Pharmacists Guild of St. James of the Diocese of Fall River, Mass., presented to its bishop, the Most Rev. James L. Connolly, a plan for a national pharmacists' organization. With the bishop's approval, and with the cooperation of the officers of other diocesan guilds, the St. James Guild sponsored a national membership campaign that resulted in an organizational meeting in New York City on Sept. 19, 1962, with 21 diocesan representatives present. The decision was reached to form a national guild and the following were elected as officers: Timothy P. Keating, New Bedford, Mass., president; Clarence H. Winkelmann, Clayton, Mo., vice president; and Ursula E. Heyer, Baltimore, Md., secretary. The National Catholic Pharmacists Guild, now affiliated with the National Council of Catholic Men, meets twice a year and publishes a monthly newsletter.

[T. P. KEATING]

NATIONAL CATHOLIC RURAL LIFE CONFERENCE, an association of Catholics dedicated to the spiritual and material well-being of rural people; using both natural and supernatural means, it strives to enrich their lives and to assure their salvation. The Conference (NCRLC) was formed in November 1923 at a meeting of 80 rural-minded pioneers, convened by Edwin V. *O'Hara, later bishop of Kansas City. Three years previously, he had become head of a new rural life bureau of the *National Catholic Welfare Conference. From contacts thus gained, he laid the groundwork for the larger movement, which became the NCRLC. The Conference established its own central office at St. Paul, Minnesota, and appointed Father James A. Byrnes the first executive secretary. His successor from 1940 to 1958 was Msgr. Luigi G. Ligutti of the Diocese of Des Moines, Iowa. The national office was moved to Des Moines in 1940. In its early years, the Conference was largely an organization of clergy, meeting annually for the purpose of studying rural issues and formulating statements of policy. Its *Manifesto on Rural Life* (Milwaukee, Wis. 1939) was especially important. In more recent years, it has enlisted memberships from thousands of lay persons whom it serves through 125 diocesan rural life directors and 1,600 rural life chairmen in various Catholic organizations (1964). It publishes a monthly bulletin, *Catholic Rural Life,* and several leaflets and booklets about rural issues. Liturgical and devotional activities are promoted to provide the basis and motivation for the Conference's social and economic programs. By a decree of the Congregation of Rites, Feb. 22, 1947, St. *Isidore the Farmer was named the heavenly patron of the NCRLC, which promotes devotions, including three annual novenas, in his honor. The Conference also encourages sacramental blessings of soil, seed, and flocks in spring ceremonies and thanksgiving for God's bounty on the feast of Our Lady of the Fields, celebrated with that of the Assumption on August 15 and on the national Thanksgiving Day. To accomplish its goals of order and justice in economic and social matters, the Conference cooperates closely with local religious and secular organizations in promoting community development committees, cooperative marketing associations, credit unions, and educational institutions. It maintains close contact with the Congress and the Administration through a Washington office. Its Office for International Affairs, established in 1958 under the direction of Msgr. Ligutti, promotes international conferences and keeps in touch with the UN *Food and Agriculture Organization.

Bibliography: R. P. WITTE, *Twenty-Five Years of Crusading* (Des Moines 1948). E. W. O'ROURKE, "The Catholic Church in the Rural Mid-West," *Catholic Church, U.S.A.,* ed. L. J. PUTZ (Chicago 1956) 202–210.

[E. W. O'ROURKE]

NATIONAL CATHOLIC SOCIAL ACTION CONFERENCE (NCSAC), an organization founded to stimulate, guide, and assist American Catholics to undertake *social action to make sound principles operative in American *social institutions. It succeeded the *Catholic Conference on Industrial Problems, founded in 1922 through the initiative of the Department of Social Action of the *National Catholic Welfare Conference, which continues to provide headquarters for NCSAC.

The founding national convention, held at Chicago in 1957, had been preceded by meetings at Cleveland and New Orleans in 1955 and 1956. Louis F. Buckley, then with the Social Security Board, who had served 10 years as president of the older body, became the first president of NCSAC. Prominent among the founders were Msgr. George G. Higgins, director of the NCWC Department of Social Action, and Edward Marciniak, then editor of *Work,* a publication of the Catholic Labor Alliance of Chicago. The membership of NCSAC includes about 25 affiliated organizations and about 400 lay and clerical members who are engaged in Catholic social action. The special interests of individual members include the labor movement, management, industrial relations, rural and urban life, the cooperative movement, professions, adult education, civil rights, interracial justice, and diocesan social action. Annual conferences with speakers and workshops encourage exchange of information and experience. These meetings also stimulate the formation of new organizations in specific fields. Awards are presented by NCSAC in recognition of significant contributions to social action.

[L. F. BUCKLEY]

NATIONAL CATHOLIC WELFARE CONFERENCE (NCWC)

An "agency of the Archbishops and Bishops of the United States to organize, unify and coordinate Catholic activities for the general welfare of the Church." More popularly, however, this organization, known by its initials NCWC, is generally thought of in terms of its secretariat headquarters in Washington, D.C. There an eight-story building, singular in the capital city because of the three-story statue of Christ, the Light of the World, gracing the facade, houses a staff of 19 priests and about 240 lay people who tend to routine functions of great import to the Church in the U.S.

History. The NCWC traces its origin to the National Catholic War Council, a wartime committee of the Catholic archbishops of the U.S. At the beginning of World War I, Cardinal James Gibbons of Baltimore, Md., had given his assurance to Pres. Woodrow Wilson that the Catholic resources would be mobilized to assist in the war effort. At the time, the Chaplains' Aid Association, the Knights of Columbus, and numerous other Catholic organizations were already seeking permission from the government to launch different types of war work. But while there was no dearth of Catholic activity, there was a lack of coordinated leadership, a factor which caused the U.S. government much difficulty. In 1917, keenly conscious of the need for a coordinated program among Catholic organizations, John *Burke, CSP, director of the Chaplains' Aid Association, approached Gibbons to propose a general meeting of all Catholic societies to devise a unified and coordinated plan of action. Gibbons favored the idea, as did Cardinal William O'Connell, of Boston, Mass., and Cardinal John Farley, of New York. Burke, therefore, quickly assembled 115 Catholic representatives, among whom were 42 bishops, representatives from 27 societies of men and women, and members of the Catholic press. As Burke's plan for coordination was discussed, some fear was expressed that a new type of organization would usurp the work of existing societies. The fears were adequately dispelled, and after long debate the delegates passed a resolution recommending the establishment of a national coordinating committee to be known as the National Catholic War Council.

Gibbons, quick to act on this resolution, wrote to the American hierarchy proposing the formation of the War Council, with all the archbishops of the U.S. as its Administrative Board, and with a committee of four bishops to direct ordinary activities. When the hierarchy endorsed the plan, the first committee, appointed in December 1917, consisted of Bp. Peter J. *Muldoon, of Rockford, Ill.; Bp. Joseph *Schrembs, of Toledo, Ohio; Bp. (later Cardinal) Patrick *Hayes, of New York; and Bp. William T. *Russell, of Charleston, S.C. Burke was then chosen to direct and coordinate the activities of the War Council and effect a harmonious liaison with governmental and other national agencies; with the approval of the superior general of the Paulist fathers, he was released for this work. The War Council, quickly establishing a reputation for effectiveness, set up committees for men's and women's activities to obtain governmental recognition for war work. This recognition gave Catholic societies equal status with non-Catholic groups that had traditionally been designated by the government as the only private agencies to be involved in governmental welfare programs. One group to receive such recognition was the Overseas Committee of women. These women traveled to France immediately after the war to serve the American troops, in much the same manner that the United Service Organizations (USO) did later. As the war drew to a close there was no doubt that the War Council had fulfilled its purpose. It had also instilled in American Catholics a deep consciousness of their resources, their strength, and their responsibility, and provided a plan of Catholic unity and coordination that was to affect the history of the Church in America, and indeed, in other parts of the world.

After the armistice of 1918, when wartime measures were discarded in favor of reconstruction and rehabilitation, the War Council faced an uncertain future. However, the intervention of Benedict XV ensured the continuation of NCWC. February 1919, in a letter to the American hierarchy assembled in Washington, D.C., for their first formal meeting since the Third Plenary Council of Baltimore in 1884, the Pope asked them to join him in working for the cause of peace and social justice in the world. The bishops responded by resolving to meet annually and by means of a continuing committee to foster Christian principles, particularly in the fields of education and social action, and to keep in contact with all vital issues on the American scene relating to the Catholic Church. Expressing his pleasure, Benedict XV replied: "This is truly a worthy resolve and with the utmost satisfaction we bestow upon it our approval." On Sept. 24, 1919, therefore, the bishops of the U.S. resolved: "that an organization be formed of the Hierarchy to be known as the National Catholic Welfare Council and its duties and powers to be indicated by those present: and, that an Administrative Committee composed of seven members of the Hierarchy be elected by the National Catholic Welfare Council to transact all business between meetings of the National Catholic Welfare Council and to carry out the wishes of the National Catholic Welfare Council as expressed in the annual session." By secret ballot the members chose from a slate of 15 candidates the following 7 members to serve as the Administrative Committee: Cardinal Gibbons. honorary chairman; Abp. Edward J. *Hanna of San Francisco, Calif., chairman; Bishop Muldoon, vice chairman; Abp. Austin *Dowling of St. Paul, Minn.; Abp. (later Cardinal) Dennis *Dougherty of Philadelphia, Pa.; and Bishops Russell and Schrembs.

Reflecting the awakening sensitivity of the American hierarchy for problems and issues reaching far beyond the confines of any one diocese, the plan for this committee of bishops provided that the affairs of the Church would be discussed and policies established at the annual meeting of the hierarchy. The Administrative Committee would serve, in between general meetings, as the agent of the bishops, deputized to implement these policies. The Administrative Committee, however, realized the limitations of time and resources, foreseeing that the mass of work they envisioned would be too much for any ordinary, who also has the care of a diocese. In December 1919, therefore, the committee took over the War Council and its staff, set up a national

National Catholic Welfare Conference headquarters, Washington, D.C.

headquarters in Washington, D.C., and unanimously elected Burke to fill the post of executive secretary.

In its beginning stages the NCWC had to withstand various tests. The first major one arose from a confusion about the exact status of NCWC in relation to a bishop in his own diocese. As a national organization representing the combined thinking of bishops, the NCWC loomed in the minds of some as a dictator of Church policy, a new type of ecclesiastical jurisdiction impinging on the autonomy of an ordinary. This very point had been thrashed out in the first annual meeting of the bishops, and it was clear from the beginning the bishops never intended that NCWC play such a role. Fears, however, persisted and even Rome was affected by the anxiety. In 1922, therefore, the Holy See, threatening to suppress the organization if it were the type some feared it to be, asked the bishops for a clarification. Through lengthy correspondence with the Pope and by personal representation in Rome, the Administrative Committee permanently clarified two fundamental points: first, the NCWC is a voluntary organization, depending for membership and support on the free choice of each bishop: second, the NCWC possesses no ecclesiastical jurisdiction or compulsory authority. The only authority of NCWC is the moral suasion it draws from the consensus of the bishops of the U.S. Any bishop, however, may choose to align himself or not with the policies or practices of the organization. While the nature of NCWC had been clarified, its name still left a few lingering doubts. The Holy See, therefore, requested that the term council be changed to conference.

During the more than 40 years of its existence, the NCWC has demonstrated the validity of its basic ideal of coordination and unification. It has also inspired the foundation of 42 national bishops' conferences fashioned after its same basic pattern. These conferences vary in many details of organization and activity, but the central theme pervades them all, the fulfillment of the collective responsibility of the bishops within a given country.

Organization. Every year each bishop, residential or titular, who serves or has served the Church in the U.S., its territories, or possessions, is invited by the dean of the hierarchy to attend the annual meeting of the bishops in Washington, D.C. At this meeting the bishops elect for a 1 year term 10 of their members to serve on the Administrative Board of NCWC. To them are joined ex officio the American cardinals, and together all act on behalf of the bishops during the time between the annual meetings. No elected member may serve on the Administrative Board for more than five consecutive terms, but he may be reelected after an absence from the board. The Administrative Board annually chooses its own officers and designates from among its membership an episcopal chairman for each department of NCWC. Each episcopal chairman in turn may choose an assistant and adviser bishop to aid him in the work of his department. These, however, have only a voice, not a vote, in the deliberations of the board. The American cardinals serve ex officio, that is, they have full vote in all matters but do not have portfolio.

In general the function of the Administrative Board is to act as the executive agency of the bishops in all matters referred to it at the annual meeting and to execute the mandates and commissions of the bishops. In particular, the members of the board supervise the work of the departments, issue an annual report of departmental activities to each bishop just prior to the annual meeting, and make recommendations to the body of the bishops. They meet in executive sessions twice a year, once just prior to the annual meeting of the bishops and again immediately after Easter. The chairman of the board presides over the executive department, which in turn has responsibility for the supervision and coordination of the various departments. A general secretary acts as the chief administrative officer for the board. It is his responsibility to supervise the day-to-day activities of the departments and to ensure office unity.

Activities. The charge given to the NCWC by its original charter was to act as a representative for the bishops and to use its facilities for the general welfare of the Church. This charge has been carried out, with varying degrees of success, by the seven departments serving under the executive office: Education, Press, Social Action, and Legal, all founded in 1919; Lay Organizations, comprised of the *National Council of Catholic Men and the *National Council of Catholic Women; Immigration, founded in 1920; and Youth, established in 1940. To each department has been added over the years offices and bureaus to deal with specialized fields of concern to the Church. Through the activities of these departments the Church in the U.S. gives evidence of its unity on a very practical level. One of the first instances of unified activity occurred during the days of prohibition. The Federal government proposed certain regulations for obtaining altar wine for sacramental purposes. Almost immediately telegrams poured in from bishops and priests from all over the country with different and sometimes contradictory suggestions, causing much confusion among government officials. Proceeding on the instruction of the Administrative Board, NCWC representatives met with government officials to work out a suitable procedure.

Education. The Education Department provides better liaison, sometimes for the government in educational matters, but most frequently with schools and educational associations, both Catholic and non-Catholic. In general the department directs its resources to the growth and development of Catholic schools, functioning as a coordinating agency and as a medium for the exchange of points of view and educational materials. It also must safeguard the interests of Catholic schools, particularly in matters relating to Federal legislation.

Legal and Social Action. The Legal Department keeps abreast of all legislative and judicial developments that affect the Church either favorably or unfavorably, especially those involving religious and moral issues and the ever-present Church-State question. The Social Action Department was established to further the teachings of Leo XIII on labor and social questions. It serves, therefore, as a clearinghouse for the dissemination of the best thought in the field of social action: industrial relations, international relations, interracial relations, rural life, social work and charities, and the study of communism. The principal tools for this work are the encyclicals of the popes and the statements of the American bishops on social and economic matters. In later years the Social Action Department attached to itself the Family Life Bureau (1931) to develop and coordinate family life programs and projects, and the Bureau of Health and Hospitals (1948), which concerns itself with Federal legislation and national policy concerning health measures.

Press. In 1919, when American Catholics were a small and widely scattered minority in the U.S., the bishops felt keenly the need for information on the life and thinking of Catholics not only over the country, but over the world. Above all they wished to strengthen communications with Rome. To this end they established the Press Department, a bonafide, accredited news-gathering agency known in journalistic circles as NC News Service. By 1964 it was the largest religious news service in the world, releasing its dispatches to all English-language Catholic newspapers in the U.S. and Canada, to many Catholic magazines, and to the Catholic press in 63 countries of the world. In 1941 the Press Department initiated *Noticias Catolicas,* a Spanish and Portuguese edition of the New Service. For 23 years this service provided Catholic news to the entire press of Latin America. Then, in 1964, when it became evident that a Latin American news agency could not work effectively from Washington, D.C., the Press Department transferred *Noticias Catolicas* to Lima, Peru, where it functions as an independent news service for Latin America.

Immigration. Many obstacles confronted the immigrant to the U.S., particularly the Catholic immigrant who was often regarded by Americans as a threat to the dominant Protestant culture that once prevailed in the U.S. In facilitating the migration of these foreigners, and in protecting the faith of the Catholic immigrant, the Immigration Department developed into a national immigrant aid organization ranking with all others, sectarian and nonsectarian, and fully recognized by the U.S. Office of Immigration. To the immigrant has been added the refugee, a situation resulting in involved technicalities in U.S. laws on immigration. The department has necessarily become involved in case work, handling over 50,000 cases a year, cases involving immigration, deportation, naturalization, and citizenship.

Lay Organizations. Leo XIII had urged that the laity take an active part in the duty of teaching, and Pius X had applied the term Catholic Action to the apostolic works of the laity. In 1919 the American bishops gave an organizational form to lay activity in the U.S. by establishing the Department of Lay Organizations. This department became a means of federating lay groups which could, under the guidance of ecclesiastical authority, take an active role in the mission of the Church. The two councils that comprise this department, the National Council of Catholic Men (NCCM) and the National Council of Catholic Women (NCCW), foster the participation of the laity in the apostolate of the hierarchy. They channel to their affiliates in the dioceses of the country information from the departments and bureaus of NCWC; provide unity and cooperation of the clergy and laity in national and international movements and conferences; and stimulate the study and appreciation of Catholic principles in education and social, economic, and political life. In providing these services, both councils function in parallel lines through a pattern of diocesan and deanery councils. In 1964, there were 66 archdioceses and dioceses affiliated with NCCM and 116 with NCCW. In 1948 to develop the special apostolate among nurses, there was attached to the NCCW the National Council of Catholic Nurses (NCCN). Operating in 107 archdioceses and dioceses, the NCCN directs its programs to the spiritual welfare, professional advancement, and cultural development of Catholic nurses in both Catholic and non-Catholic hospitals.

Youth. Also in the area of lay activity, and with an eye to training future lay leaders, is the Youth Department. This department, established in 1940, serves as an instrument for reaching both American Catholic youth and the professional and volunteer adults working with them. It has three main objectives: to exchange information on the philosophy, organization, program, and methods of Catholic youth work; to promote the National Council of Catholic Youth as a federating agency for all approved Catholic youth groups; and to contact and evaluate national governmental and nongovernmental youth organizations and youth-serving agencies.

The college and university section includes the *National Federation of Catholic College Students (NFCCS) and the National Newman Club Federation. The NFCCS is a federation of the undergraduate students of Catholic colleges and universities for the promotion of lay leadership through cocurricular and intercampus programs. The National *Newman Apostolate is a federation of Catholic students in non-Catholic colleges and universities. Its 460 campus centers promote religious education and provide leadership training.

In the area of the lay apostolate the voluntary nature of NCWC affiliation stands out boldly. The departments gain diocesan affiliates not by an enforced mandate from national headquarters, but only by proving the merits of their programs and by showing the advantages of federation. Misinterpretation of federation has slowed the work of the departments, but it has also forced them to strive continually to provide better and expanded services to local affiliates.

Other Bureaus and Offices. New developments in the life of the Church or the country have prompted the establishment of new bureaus and offices within the permanent secretariat of the NCWC. In 1938 the Bureau of Information was activated as an information and public relations agency to give a true picture of the Church to Americans, particularly by servicing the secular press. In 1945, after the United Nations Organization Conference in San Francisco, Calif., the NCWC set up an Office for UN Affairs in New York. As an accredited observer organization to the United Nations, this office has access to special briefings and documentations, through which it keeps NCWC departments informed on UN developments. In 1949, as more and more visitors from other lands traveled to the U.S. on student and government programs, the Foreign Visitors Office was established for their assistance and orientation. In 1960, in answer to a special plea from the Holy See, the U.S. bishops set up the Latin America Bureau to put at the disposal of the Pontifical Commission for Latin America the resources of the Church in the U.S., both clerical and lay. The program, among other things, is directed to the construction of seminaries and the strengthening of education through the staffing of schools and the improvement of mass communications.

Other groups, operating under the aegis of NCWC, but organized as separate legal entities, include the *Catholic Relief Services—NCWC and the National Catholic Community Service. The Catholic Relief Services (CRS) was established by the bishops in 1943 to cope with war rehabilitation problems overseas. Each year since its founding CRS, relying for its resources on the Catholic people of the U.S., has channeled hundreds of millions of dollars of food, clothing, and medicine to needy people all over the world. In addition to the basic relief program, CRS is directing its resources to technical assistance and community development in many countries to meet the changing needs of the people. The National Catholic Community Service (NCCS) was established by the bishops to service the men and women in the armed forces of the U.S. It accomplishes this goal as one of the six member agencies of the United Service Organizations (USO).

Both CRS-NCWC and NCCS are subject to the Administrative Board of NCWC. Some committees, however, have been established by the general body of bishops and therefore are directly subject to that body rather than to the Administrative Board. These committees concern themselves with such matters as the liturgical movement, Propagation of the Faith, Confraternity of Christian Doctrine, migrant workers, decent literature, and other specialized fields. Despite this different line of organization, these committees are an integral part of NCWC.

The National Catholic Welfare Conference has been succinctly described as the "expression of our unified faith." The unity among U.S. Catholics for which the NCWC can claim no small credit comes not as a result of any ecclesiastical jurisdiction that it possesses. No such wedge for acceptance of its programs has ever been among its resources. Rather, its voluntary character—the complete freedom of any bishop to align himself or not with its programs and policies—has forced NCWC to prove its own worth on the merits of the service that it renders to the Church. This factor has been one of its greatest challenges through the years of its existence. Bishops, priests, and laity have risen to that challenge, and the success of NCWC stems from the sensitivity of the American bishops to their collective responsibility as a national conference of bishops and manifests itself in the voluntary unity of the bishops and laity of the country.

[F. T. HURLEY]

NATIONAL CONFERENCE OF CATHOLIC CHARITIES

An association of local and diocesan Catholic agencies, was founded by 17 laymen and 9 clerics at The Catholic University of America in 1910. According to a brochure published by the Conference, it provides "a national service to . . . diocesan agencies; it interprets their work on a national scale; it represents . . . Catholic Charities on national and local issues, and today, increasingly, in international matters . . . ."

Establishment and Early Years. Credit for establishment of the Conference belongs to the lay leadership of the St. Vincent de Paul Society. All the 17 laymen in the founding group were members of the Society. The principal framers included Thomas M. Mulry, President of the Superior Council of New York City in 1910, and Edmond J. Butler, a member of the same Council. Clerical founders included Msgr. William J. Kerby, of The Catholic University of America; Rev. Francis Foy, of Nutley, N.J.; Msgr. D. J. McMahon, of New York City; Rev. M. J. O'Connor, of Boston, Mass.; and Msgr. William J. White, of Brooklyn, N.Y. The initiative, however, for establishing the Conference came from Brother Barnabas of The Brothers of the Christian Schools in New York. Long active in the service of youth, he had become convinced that the work of Catholic charitable organizations was impaired by a lack of regular communication among themselves and of opportunity for the interchange of ideas. Associated for years with Mulry, he had repeatedly discussed with him the desirability of an annual meeting of Catholic charity workers from all over the U.S. When the Society of St. Vincent de Paul at its meeting in Richmond in 1908 warmly endorsed such a conference, Brother Barnabas wrote to Bp. Thomas J. Shahan, Rector of The Catholic University of America, urging him to sponsor it. Shahan agreed and an organizational meeting was held on Feb. 19, 1910.

This organizing group agreed to found a national conference, and its first general meeting, attended by about 400 delegates, was held at The Catholic University of America, Sept. 25–28, 1910. Bishop Shahan was elected president and held that office until 1929. Monsignor Kerby served as secretary until 1920, when he was succeeded by Monsignor John O'Grady.

Catholic leaders in charitable work at the time shared the view of their non-Catholic colleagues that social work should not be content with alleviating distress but should aid clients in removing conditions that caused poverty and destitution. This view implied professionalization of social work. Accordingly, the early meetings of the Conference strove to overcome the comparative isolation of the individual Catholic agencies from each other and from the experience and methods of non-

Catholic groups. They aimed also to improve standards for those engaged in Catholic social work. To promote its goals, the Conference sponsored local, regional, and national conferences of Catholic agencies; encouraged establishment of Catholic schools of social work, established the *Catholic Charities Review* (1916); and carried on a program of information service, research projects, and occasional publication dealing with specific problems.

The Conference met biennially at Catholic University until 1920. Thereafter it met annually, moving from one city and region of the U.S. to another. Establishment in 1916 of a committee of diocesan directors of charity as one of the permanent national committees of the Conference was the beginning of the close relationship between diocesan directors and the Conference and gave a marked impetus to integration of Catholic charitable activities at the local and diocesan levels.

An obvious obstacle to the success of the Conference during its early years was the inadequate representation at the biennial meetings of the Catholic sisterhoods who carry on about 75 per cent of Catholic charitable activities. Persuaded that greater participation by the sisterhoods would benefit them and Catholic charities generally, Monsignor O'Grady arranged for a meeting of representatives of religious communities to coincide with the Conference meeting of 1920. From this meeting there developed the National Conference of Religious within the framework of the National Conference of Catholic Charities (*see* NATIONAL CONFERENCE OF RELIGIOUS ON CATHOLIC CHARITIES).

1930 to 1960. Improvement of standards for social workers continued to be a major concern of the Conference during its first 2 decades. The respective merits of the volunteer and professional in social work were regularly debated as well as the need for proper training of the volunteer worker. Mr. Robert Biggs, of the St. Vincent de Paul Society in Baltimore, and Dr. Charles P. Neill, of Catholic University, were foremost in stressing the need of training not only for relief of distress but for elimination of its causes. From 1940 and through the early 1950s, the deliberations at the annual meeting reflected concern lest the professionalization of social work may have been accompanied by a loss of its "spiritual component," and leaders of the Conference emphasized the importance of Christian charity as the guiding beacon and standard in Catholic social work.

Although the annual meeting remained one of the Conference's principal avenues of influence, regional meetings began to be common after 1930 and by 1948 were an important part of the Conference's activities. Their success reflects, on the one hand, the growth of influence of the National Conference, and on the other, a desire of participants for greater opportunity to exchange ideas and experiences than was possible at the annual meetings with their crowded agenda.

The Great Depression of the 1930s, with its widespread distress and the social legislation that it occasioned, gave impetus and new direction to the work. The Conference had always been committed to social reform and lent its support to a wide variety of Federal social legislation. It supported, for example, a Federal housing program for low-income families in the 1930s, contending that slum conditions increased the burden of charitable organizations and that housing reform was a key to the rehabilitation of the urban community. The Conference, however, opposed the means test (that is, making aid depend upon proof of need), and in its support of old-age benefits argued for a program that would distribute benefits to the aged as a matter of right, rather than on proof of need. However, in its support of legislation, the Conference constantly took the position that government, in all its welfare programs, should foster and develop the private agencies, rather than supplant them. Throughout the 1940s and 1950s, the Conference advocated a more active Catholic interest in welfare legislation with a view of supporting needed legislation and of ensuring that in such legislation the position and function of the private agency be safeguarded.

Publications. From the outset the Conference had hoped to foster a strong program of research. The publication of a *Directory of Catholic Charities* (Washington 1922) was the result of a long and continuing effort to get a factual picture of Catholic charities in the United States. Kerby's *The Social Mission of Charity* (New York 1921), O'Grady's *Catholic Charities in the United States* (Washington 1931) and Msgr. John M. Cooper's *Children's Institutions* (Philadelphia 1931) began to meet the need for a literature on Catholic social work. The Conference's committee on Standards of Family Case Work in Diocesan Agencies in 1926 published a useful report entitled, "A Program for Family Service in Diocesan Agencies." In 1934 the Conference began publication of an information bulletin that would keep diocesan directors aware of the rapidly developing social legislation and its provisions, and circulated a series of informational bulletins among Catholic child-care institutions. After World War II it began circulation of a new information bulletin dealing with such topics as child-welfare legislation, socialized medicine, international relief, housing, and juvenile delinquency. After 1950 the Conference sponsored a new series of studies on particular aspects of social work, which included such titles as *The Housemother,* by M. Charles, RSM; *Gannondale: A Self Study of an Institution,* by Beatrice M. Faivre; *A Study of the Aging in a Cleveland Parish,* by Mary Therese, OP; and *Older People of St. Boniface Parish* by Janet Bower, Ph.D.

Bibliography: National Conference of Catholic Charities, *Proceedings* (Washington 1911). St. Vincent de Paul *Quarterly* (New York 1895–1916). *Catholic Charities Review* (Washington 1917–). J. O'GRADY, *Catholic Charities in the United States: History and Problems* (Washington 1931). M. T. BOYLAN, *Social Welfare in the Catholic Church* (New York 1941). D. T. MC-COLGAN, *A Century of Charity,* 2 v. (Milwaukee 1951). D. P. GAVIN, *National Conference of Catholic Charities, 1910–1960* (Milwaukee 1962).

[D. P. GAVIN]

NATIONAL CONFERENCE OF CHRISTIANS AND JEWS

Founded "to promote justice, amity, understanding and cooperation among Protestants, Catholics and Jews and to analyze, moderate and finally eliminate intergroup prejudices which disfigure and distort religious, business, social and political relations, with a view to the establishment of a social order in which the religious ideals of brotherhood and justice shall become the standards of human relationships." The National Conference of Christians and Jews (NCCJ) was an attempt to counteract the religious intolerance that marked the 1920s in the U.S. In 1928 the presidential campaign,

with its anti-Catholic prejudice, induced members of the Federal Council of Churches to form a committee that later became the National Conference of Christians and Jews. Chief Justice Charles Evans Hughes, Newton D. Baker, S. Parkes Cadman, Roger Williams Straus, and Carlton J. H. Hayes were the founders and first officers; Dr. Everett R. Clinchy, executive director.

The NCCJ is not an interfaith movement; it does not aim at religious syncretism or engage in common worship, but endeavors to guard against religious indifferentism. As a civic organization of religiously motivated people, the NCCJ strives through education and discussion to promote civic cooperation and mutual understanding among men of good will of all religious, ethnic, and racial groups without compromise of religious beliefs. Its basic philosophy stems from the Judeo-Christian ethic of the equality of all men, while its technique is educational involvement of many heterogeneous groups to bring about better understanding and cooperation in matters of common social and civic concern. Fundamental to the whole idea of the NCCJ is the conviction that the equal worth of all men is a moral responsibility that must be accepted and lived up to by all individuals; all institutions; and all racial, religious, and ethnic groups.

The NCCJ functions through three national cochairmen, a Catholic, a Protestant, and a Jew, respectively; a president and executive vice president; and a board of governors and of trustees. There are 65 regional NCCJ offices, each with Catholic, Protestant, and Jewish cochairman and a board composed of Catholics, Protestants, and Jews. Each office, working within a general program framework, cooperates with schools and colleges, parents, youth, management, labor unions, police, community leaders, and clergy to promote the objectives of the NCCJ. Brotherhood Week, first suggested by Hugh L. McMenamin, a Roman Catholic priest, of Denver, Colo., illustrates the year-round effort of the conference. This observance, designed as a period of intensive effort to have the people of the U.S. rededicate themselves to the principles enunciated in the Preamble to the *Declaration of Independence, spread to thousands of communities.

The educational work of the conference has been carried on primarily through workshops, discussion groups, and clergy dialogues. Special projects of the NCCJ include: religious freedom and public affairs, which aims to promote better understanding through techniques for peaceful handling of differences; the merit promotion project, which attempts to reduce discrimination in employment and promotion because of racial, religious, or ethnic origin; and a parent-centered project on rearing children of good will, designed to make parents aware of their transmission of prejudice to children. Work with police and community leaders to promote respect for the rights of all citizens has become a phase of conference activity, as has work with young people and mass media.

Bibliography: J. E. PITT, *Adventures in Brotherhood* (New York 1955).

[J. M. EAGAN]

NATIONAL CONFERENCE OF RELIGIOUS ON CATHOLIC CHARITIES, an organization

within the National Conference of Catholic Charities (NCCC) that represents the religious who conduct charitable institutions. In 1919 Msgr. John O'Grady, Assistant Secretary of the National Conference of Catholic Charities, made a nationwide visitation of welfare institutions conducted by religious. At the time these institutions were undertaking about 75 per cent of the charitable work done by Catholics in the U.S. During this tour O'Grady came to realize how virtually isolated were the religious who conducted these institutions and how much they needed opportunities for meeting and exchanging ideas with others active in welfare work. In conjunction with the 1920 biennial session of NCCC, O'Grady arranged for a special conference of religious active in social and charitable work. At this conference a decision was reached and a committee formed to arrange similar conferences at regular intervals. Sister Miriam Regina, SC, was elected chairman of the committee and Sister M. Celestine, OSF, secretary.

The committee, called the National Conference of Religious (NCR), functioned informally within the NCCC for a number of years, and in 1947 became an advisory group to the NCCC on matters pertaining to the welfare activities of religious. Since that date the standing committee of the NCR has held three meetings annually, in different dioceses, and has continued its participation in the annual meeting of the NCCC. From its establishment NCR members have taken an active part in the general program of NCCC, serving on its board of directors and on regular and special committees, planning and conducting workshops, and contributing both to the *Catholic Charities Review* and to the special studies sponsored by the NCCC.

The discussions and publications of the NCR reflect both the widened participation of the sisterhoods in the work of the NCCC, and the changing methods and scope of social work. During the early years of NCR its discussions focused around the institutional care of children, but gradually they were broadened to include the specialized needs of a wide range of particular groups and the training required of those who would deal successfully with them. Its publications are on such topics as the chaplain's function in a Catholic institution, sisters in social service, adoption practices, exceptional children, day care of children, and maternity homes.

A persistent concern of the NCR has been the encouragement of youth to undertake works of personal, charitable service in their homes, parishes, and neighborhoods. Participating institutions were encouraged to welcome young volunteers and to train them adequately to meet the needs of those whom they would assist. The NCR has regularly emphasized the necessity of keeping charity and its personal element at the center of social service.

[B. M. FAIVRE]

NATIONAL COUNCIL OF CATHOLIC MEN (NCCM)

A national federation of organizations of Catholic laymen (NCCM), established in 1920 under the National Catholic Welfare Conference (NCWC) and mandated by the American hierarchy to promote and service the development of the lay apostolate and Catholic Action.

Membership and Government. The NCCM's member organizations include parish societies, interparochial societies, state-wide organizations, diocesan federations, and national organizations. The majority of NCCM's programs and services are channeled to its affiliated organizations through diocesan and deanery councils. The NCCM seeks to establish in every diocese a unifying federation of all the men's organizations in that diocese. These diocesan federations are generally known as Diocesan Councils of Catholic Men. The diocesan council forms subordinate counterparts to itself called deanery councils, to which the parish and interparochial organizations are affiliated.

Direct affiliation of local and state men's organizations is permitted where there is no diocesan federation affiliated with the NCCM. Individual "Associates" may pledge themselves to support the work of the council through annual associate dues, prayers, and active participation in the organized lay apostolate. National Catholic men's organizations are affiliated with the NCCM directly also on the national level. Approximately 10,000 men's organizations with a total membership of nearly 9 million are affiliated with the NCCM.

The NCCM is governed by a general assembly consisting of the presidents of diocesan councils and national organizations, who in turn elect an executive board composed of 16 members. Since the beginning of Vatican Council II, the NCCM's policies have been related to the major areas of renewal in the Church's life, namely, liturgy, Scripture, ecumenism, catechetics, and social action. Their direction is carried out through a staff of 35 trained professionals. The national office is located in Washington, D.C., with a branch office for radio and television in New York City.

Objectives and Activities. The major objectives of the NCCM are to federate Catholic men's organizations into a common agency; to develop, promote, and service programs of apostolic action related to contemporary issues; to serve as an informational service link between the NCWC and laymen's organizations; to be a central clearinghouse for information on Catholic laymen's activities; to promote and coordinate lay cooperation in national matters affecting the Church; to help existing Catholic men's organizations to work more effectively in their own localities; to cooperate in furthering the aims of all approved movements in the interest of the Church and society in general; to participate in national and international movements related to its goal; and to bring about a better appreciation of Catholic principles and ideals in the social, economic, educational, and civic life of the U.S.

The major areas of the NCCM's apostolate include: (1) religious activities, such as spiritual and apostolic formation, pastoral assistance, liturgy, and retreats; (2) communications—by means of parish libraries, promotion of the NCCM's radio and television programs, and cooperation with the Legion of Decency and the National Office for Decent Literature; (3) civic and social action—in areas of race relations, migratory labor, employment and problems of the "dropout," urban redevelopment, rural life, cooperation in community affairs, and educational programs on the Church's social encyclicals; (4) legislation—local, state, and national laws relating to current issues such as civil rights, education, the aged, social welfare, labor, and agriculture; (5) family life—family retreats, Cana conferences, family-life institutes, and religious practices and instructions in the home; (6) youth—cooperation with diocesan and parish youth directors, sponsorship of youth leadership training courses, and promotion of recreational and educational facilities; (7) public relations—internal news letters; bulletins; and press, radio, and television releases on organizational programs; (8) international affairs—the fostering of foreign students and visitors; educational programs on the United Nations; study clubs; and meetings on foreign affairs, missions, underdeveloped countries, and world peace; (9) organization and development—training through the NCCM's leaders' course in the lay apostolate in affiliated organizations, and through the speakers' bureau and membership drives.

Although the NCCM develops and recommends a wide variety of programs, its major effort is directed towards assisting its affiliated organizations to carry out programs developed locally. Once local affiliates have formulated their own program goals, the NCCM provides advice and informational materials. Special program aids are developed periodically on major areas of concern for the lay apostolate. These include "The Leaders' Course in the Lay Apostolate" (for adults and youth), which aims at educating and motivating laymen in their vocation as Christians in the world, and alerting them to some of the basic issues in the temporal order that require their action; the "Program on the Mass" and the "Mass Commentators' Training Course," which provide parish priests and laymen with practical tools for furthering those parts of Vatican Council II's *Constitution on the Liturgy* that call for a better understanding of the liturgy and for training and using commentators in community Masses; the "Release from Racism" kit, which offers materials and program suggestions designed to mobilize Catholic men's organizations on the race issue; and three separate kits of materials on "Federal Aid to Education," which provide information and facts on the Catholic school system.

In addition, four regular publications supply continuous service to the NCCM's affiliated organizations: *Alert Catholic Men, Program and Training, Executive Newsletter,* and *Highlights*. Other materials and services for various aspects of council activity are provided in its "Program Manual for Parish Meetings," an annual "Publications List," and a "Convention Advisory Service." In its program of leadership training and weekend retreats, the NCCM provides intensive study and training in the lay apostolate for a small group of lay leaders in an atmosphere of prayer, combined with liturgical and scriptural services. A lay professional on the staff serves as codirector for these weekend retreats. The NCCM maintains a library of Catholic films and is responsible also for all regularly scheduled national Catholic network radio and television programs, the best known of which is the National Broadcasting Company's "Catholic Hour," instituted in 1930. These programs, intended for Catholics and non-Catholics, reach a weekly audience of 6 million.

One of the NCCM's important functions is to represent American Catholic laymen in other national and international organizations and meetings. The NCCM is the U.S. representative to the International Federation of Catholic Men, to the International Office for Catholic Radio and Television (UNDA), and is associated with the permanent board of directors of the World Congresses of the Lay Apostolate. The NCCM maintains liaison with the United Nations through its affiliation with the U.S. Mission to the UN and the UN's Department of Public Information. Personnel of the NCCM participate in conferences and meetings of government, religious, and secular organizations on subjects related to NCCM's interests in youth, family, the aging, race relations, labor, civil rights, international affairs, and urban redevelopment. The NCCM also testifies before Congressional committees on subjects of moral concern to its membership, and on national issues of interest to all citizens, such as federal aid to education, migratory labor, and obscene literature.

[M. H. WORK]

NATIONAL COUNCIL OF CATHOLIC NURSES

The National Council of Catholic Nurses of the United States of America was organized at the request of the Administrative Board of Bishops of the National Catholic Welfare Conference. In April 1938, Cardinal Pizzardo, Prefect of the Congregation of Religious, wrote to the American bishops stating that it was the wish of His Holiness, Pius XI, that Catholic nurses be enrolled in a Catholic association of nurses. Such organizations were to be formed for the "mutual religious and moral aid of the members, instructing them on the moral and religious duties of their profession" and were "in no wise to be considered unions for the furthering of professional interests."

The Council was formally organized in Chicago, on June 10, 1940, at a meeting presided over by Most Rev. Joseph F. Rummel, Archbishop of New Orleans, Episcopal Chairman of Lay Organizations, NCWC. Seven archdioceses and twenty-one dioceses sent representatives to this meeting, at which a constitution was adopted and officers were elected. The first president was Mary Kelly (Mullane) of the Archdiocese of Detroit.

The Council operates under an elected board with a spiritual director appointed by the episcopal director of lay organizations, NCWC. Membership is through affiliated diocesan organizations with provision for individual members to join the National Council directly if no diocesan organization exists in their areas. Originally, only registered professional nurses were eligible for membership, but the Council was opened to licensed practical nurses in 1960. The National Council became affiliated with the International Committee of Catholic Nurses (CICIAMS) in 1953.

The objectives of the Council are the spiritual, professional, and material welfare of Catholic nurses; the fostering among all nurses of the spirit of charity in the care of the sick; the provision of an agency through which Catholic nurses can speak corporately in matters of common interest to their profession; and the promotion of programs of voluntary care of the indigent sick. These objectives are carried out through the programs of diocesan councils—retreats for nurses; lectures and discussions on moral ethics, nursing trends, implications of new drugs, treatments, research and technological developments; volunteer services to the indigent sick, to clinics, to parochial school systems, etc.—and through a national convention held in the even years and regional meetings in the odd years. The Council's quarterly magazine, *The Catholic Nurse,* is designed to keep Catholic nurses abreast of medical, nursing, and Church developments that affect their lives and to foster a Christian concept of patient care. The Council represents the International Committee at meetings of the United Nations Children's Fund and the World Health Organization when they are held in the United States.

[D. N. KELLY]

NATIONAL COUNCIL OF CATHOLIC WOMEN (NCCW)

A federation of 14,000 Catholic organizations representing approximately 10 million women in 120 dioceses in the U.S. The National Council of Catholic Women (NCCW) is governed by a board of directors, one from each ecclesiastical province in the U.S., elected at national conventions. The board elects from its membership an executive body consisting of a president, three vice presidents, a secretary, a treasurer, and a member-at-large, each for 2-year terms. The Military Council of Catholic Women, a member group organized in 1957, has active affiliates in Germany, England, France, Italy, Spain, Morocco, and Okinawa.

Origins. In 1919, with approval of Benedict XV, the bishops of the U.S. established the National Catholic Welfare Conference (NCWC) to promote Christian life in the nation and to further the cause of Christ and His Church. In 1920 the NCWC's Department of Lay Organizations was divided into the National Council of Catholic Men (NCCM) and the National Council of Catholic Women, which at that time had only 90 affiliated organizations. As a federation of existing organizations, the NCCW is designed to unite Catholic women's organizations for the strength and prestige that unity gives; to channel from the NCWC to affiliated organizations information and material in the fields of religion, education, family life, social action, and international relations; and to offer assistance to affiliated organizations through correspondence, and by means of programs, national conventions, regional institutes, and conferences.

Activities. The NCCW is a service agency. Through its national headquarters, staffed by an executive director and assistants in various fields, it offers to affiliated organizations as much or as little as they need or wish. One important service, provided through the National Committee System, reaches from national, through diocesan and deanery chairmen, to the parish or local groups. The national chairman and vice chairman for each national committee are appointed by the NCCW president. In turn, diocesan committee chairmen are appointed by the diocesan president for all national committee program areas selected by the bishop for the particular council. Committee programs feature the application of Christian principles in areas of spiritual development, family life, community, and national and international concerns. Special cooperation is afforded the *Confraternity of Christian Doctrine, Catholic Charities, the National Catholic Community Service, *Catholic Relief Services, NCWC, the National Catholic Resettlement Council, and the *National Catholic Rural Life Conference. The NCCW also promotes a continuing program of traffic safety.

The NCCW is required by its constitution to meet in convention biennially to conduct its business and elect its governing board. In alternate years, regional leadership training institutes are held in strategic areas to give women from all 50 states an opportunity to attend. The aim is to train Catholic women leaders for participation in the work of the Church and community and to provide a means for the expression of their views.

Convention resolutions and statements of the NCCW play a strong role in supporting positive leadership and guiding public opinion. As with most American leaders, members of the NCCW are concerned with the shortage of schools, teachers, and scientific, technological, and other facilities in both the public and the church-related schools.

The Christian principles of the dignity of the person, the brotherhood of man, and racial and religious equality have consistently been supported by the NCCW. In January 1963, at the invitation of Pres. John F. Kennedy, NCCW representatives met with other leaders of the Catholic, Protestant, and Jewish faiths to examine the role of churches and synagogues in eliminating racial discrimination from their own institutions and communities. The NCCW took immediate steps to implement the conference by conducting leadership institutes throughout the U.S. to give a comprehensive background of the historical, social, and economic as well as religious aspects of the race problem, and to provide means for carrying out organized programs in the different areas.

The NCCW represents U.S. Catholic women at national and international meetings of government and nongovernment agencies concerned with the welfare of women or the moral and religious welfare of mankind. Council observers attend sessions of the United Nations (UN) and the United Nations Educational, Scientific and Cultural Organization (UNESCO). The NCCW is affiliated with the World Union of Catholic Women's Organizations (WUCWO) and cooperates with Inter-American Catholic Action and the Inter-American Catholic Social Action Confederation in such problem areas as human rights, poverty, education, housing, birth control, status of women, and atomic test-ban treaty. Other international projects include a study of the problems of the Latin American and other developing nations, home hospitality for foreign students and visitors, and assistance to the needy in cooperation with Catholic Relief Services. These programs include medical care and training in nutrition for mothers, the purchase of local food for families, a constant supply of new and used clothing to needy children, a self-help project in Hong Kong for widows with dependent children, and the support of orphans and abandoned children in Korea.

Publications of the NCCW include *Focus,* a comprehensive guide for the study and discussion of Latin America; *Proceedings* of national conventions; *UN Newsnotes,* covering events at the UN, its specialized agencies, and in international movements, and excerpts from significant papal statements; the *Word,* a monthly magazine published by the NCCW as a major public relations channel—informative, interpretative, and entertaining; *Yearbooks,* with background information, resources, program suggestions, and committee outlines; and *WUCWO Bulletins.*

[M. MEALEY]

NATIONAL COUNCIL OF THE CHURCHES OF CHRIST IN THE U.S.A.

A federation of Protestant, Eastern Orthodox, and National Catholic Churches affiliated with the *World Council of Churches. Its membership (reported as 40,-605,228 communicants in 1964) represents about two-thirds of the total Christian church population in the U.S. that is not Roman Catholic.

Historical Development. The American counterpart of the world *ecumenical movement had two phases: the formation of new churches through organic merger and the cooperative federation of many denominations for the sake of greater efficiency. Since 1900 the principal denominational cooperatives have been the Federal Council of Churches, organized in 1908, and the National Council of Churches, which succeeded the Federal Council in 1950.

When the Federal Council was formed, its 28 member churches included *Baptists, *Methodists, and *Presbyterians, but the number was only a fraction of the total Protestant population. Its basis of union was modeled on the principles of American democracy. According to its constitution, the Federal Council was to express the fellowship and catholic unity of the Protestant denominations, with a view to bringing them into united service for Christ and the world. Although the largest, the Federal Council was only one of several like agencies that sought to bridge the denominational differences in American Protestantism. They had all been founded to make their work more effective. But this was not enough. As the agencies evolved their programs, they found overlapping and divisions of responsibility. Closer cooperative action was needed. Further study and negotiation were finally terminated in 1941 at a historic Atlantic City, N.J., conference that recommended "creation of a single cooperative agency to succeed all of the existing national councils." This met with enthusiastic acceptance, and after 9 years of planning the National Council of Churches was established in

The Interchurch Center, New York City, housing the offices of the National Council of the Churches of Christ in the U.S.A.

Cleveland, Ohio, Nov. 28 to Dec. 1, 1950. Delegates of 29 Protestant and Orthodox bodies joined forces to express their common faith and witness of cooperation with one another.

The preamble of the constitution they adopted stated, "In the providence of God, the time has come when it seems fitting more fully to manifest oneness in Jesus Christ as Divine Lord and Savior, by the creation of an inclusive cooperative agency of the Christian Churches in the United States of America." This prelude has since become the guiding norm for the 12 national interdenominational groups that agreed to unite in the interest of improving their influence and effectiveness. Among these groups, the largest was the Federal Council, and the most recent was the Protestant Radio Commission, established in 1947. The other 10 bodies, with their founding dates were: the Foreign Missions Conference of North America (1803 and 1911); the Home Missions Council of North America (1908); the International Council of Religious Education (1922), actually an outgrowth of a national Sunday School Convention (1832); the Missionary Education Movement of the U.S. and Canada (1902); the National Protestant Council on Higher Education (1911); the United Council of Church Women (1940); the United Stewardship Council (1920); Church World Service (1946); Interseminary Committee (1880); and the Protestant Film Commission (1947). Among the contributing factors that helped to shape the National Council was the growing interest in social studies, which showed that American denominationalism was often less doctrinal than cultural and ethnic. Its divisiveness, therefore, could be resolved at least partially by active collaboration in the externals of church life without infringing on the creedal autonomy of the different churches.

Constitutional Structure. The National Council is incorporated pursuant to the laws of the State of New York. Units of the Council are allowed to remain incorporated under the law of a state or of the national government: but this permission does not modify their relationship or obligations to the national body.

Eleven purposes are specified in the constitution, of which the most important is to continue and extend the functions of the original merging societies, along with the *Student Volunteer Movement and the United Student Christian Council that joined after 1950. Each of the other 10 aims is directed to the more general scope of the Christian religion:

1. To manifest more fully the oneness of the Church of Christ according to the Scriptures and to further the efforts of the member churches in proclaiming the Gospel of Jesus Christ to the end that all men may believe in Him
2. To encourage the study and use of the Bible
3. To carry on programs for and with the churches by which the life of the Church may be renewed and the mission of the Church may be fulfilled
4. To foster and encourage cooperation, fellowship, and mutual counsel among the churches for the purposes set forth in this Constitution
5. To assist the churches in self-examination of their life and witness in accordance with their understanding of the will of God and of the Lordship of Jesus Christ as Divine Head of the Church
6. To further works of Christian love and service throughout the nation and the world

7. To study and to speak and act on conditions and issues in the nation and the world which involve moral, ethical, and spiritual principles inherent in the Christian Gospel

8. To encourage cooperation among local churches and to further the development of councils and other organizations in agreement with the Preamble of this Constitution, and to maintain cooperative relationships with such bodies

9. To establish and maintain consultative and cooperative relationships with the World Council of Churches; other international, regional, and national ecumenical organizations; and agencies related to the churches in the United States

10. To establish specific objectives and to carry forward programs and activities for achieving the purposes herein stated

Constituent membership in the Council is conditioned on acceptance of its principles and aims, as set forth in the constitution. A religious body becomes a member upon approval by a two-thirds majority vote of the member communions present and voting at a General Assembly, and a corresponding vote of the representatives from the churches. Besides full-fledged membership, the Council admits participation by other organizations, such as state councils of churches, and boards and agencies of communions that are not members of the Council. They are given recognition as affiliates with the privilege of sharing in work being carried forward by the national body. Moreover any group or society that the General Board recognizes as maintained for distinctly Christian purposes may be connected with the Council in the role of a "related movement," or at least "in fraternal relationship." But always the secondary affiliations must work in accord with its constitution and bylaws to retain recognition by the National Council.

The basic governing body of the Council is the General Assembly, whose membership consists of officers and past presidents of the Council, as well as representatives of the constituent communions. They include seven delegates for each denomination plus one for each 70,000 communicant members, with the stipulation that at least one-fourth be laymen, laywomen, or young people preferably not in the employ of the churches or church organizations. Each constituent denomination may nominate further delegates as being representative of its interests and concerns. Members of the Assembly are appointed or elected for 3-year terms. Between meetings of the General Assembly, the Council is governed by a General Board, which has the full power of the Assembly except the right to amend the constitution or to elect denominations to constituent membership. The internal structure of the Council and the whole of its complex activity are carried on through units established under authority of the General Board.

One passage in the certificate of incorporation reveals the Council's concern not to infringe on the freedom of its constituency. "It shall have no authority or administrative control," the document reads, "over the communions or churches which become its members or its affiliated or co-operating bodies. It shall have no authority to prescribe a common creed, or form of church government, or form of worship, or to limit the autonomy of such communions or churches."

Achievements and Guiding Principles. Historians of the National Council point to its remarkable achievements in spite of numerous hazards. Thus in the early years of the Council, an organized group of laymen, seeking special privilege, offered the Council the alternative of unlimited financial support for a pact of silence on social issues, or deprivation of its lines of support. Another crisis that the Council is still facing is periodic attack by extremists who charge the officers and spokesmen with theological heresy, atheism, lack of patriotism, and communism. Yet the churches have stood by the Council and joined in its defense.

High among the achievements of the National Council have been the statements it regularly issues on a wide variety of subjects—theological, sociocultural, and political. These have ranged from "Christian Principles of Economic Life" to "Responsible Parenthood," and from "Public Funds for Public Schools" to an "Advisory Policy Statement on Religious Broadcasting." Such statements serve the purpose of creating a notable image of unity both within the churches belonging to the Council and before the American people. In the words of Roy G. Ross, who guided the Council as general secretary during the first 12 years of its existence, "the Council is respected by government as the primary agency of the churches for liaison on matters touching the relations of church and state and programs serving the common weal." Certainly the impact of the Council's philosophy has been deeply felt through its periodic declarations on matters of national concern.

The cause of religious unity has been advanced through the Council's dependence on the World Council of Churches as the principal worldwide agency for ecumenical policy, strategy, and program planning, and on the International Missionary Council and World Council of Christian Education as supplementary agencies in their respective fields. When the first two bodies merged in 1961, this was partly (if not mainly) the result of assistance from the National Council; and the growing concern of the churches for moral and spiritual values in public education is due largely to the steady effort of the Council's leadership to stem the tide of secularization in American life.

In a more tangible way, the Council has undertaken the cause of Christian unity by forming a permanent committee to study the problem of denominationalism and to recommend ways of fostering reunification. One result has been a number of significant mergers of large denominations. Two examples are the *United Church of Christ, formed in 1957 by a union of the Evangelical and Reformed with the Congregational Christian bodies; and the American Lutheran Church, organized in 1960 through a merger of the American Lutheran, the Evangelical Lutheran, and United Evangelical Lutheran denominations (see LUTHERANS IN NORTH AMERICA).

On the local level, the National Council has helped the state and community councils do work that would otherwise have been quite impossible. Through its Division of Home Missions, "churches on wheels" are provided for several hundred thousand migrant farm workers in some 30 states. Interdenominational committees of the Council's Division of Christian Education administer the preparation of Sunday school curriculum outlines used by thousands of church groups. The division also syndicates Sunday school lessons to newspapers and magazines through "National Council Religious Features." The U.S. Army and Air Force are among the heaviest purchasers of National Council audio-visual materials on such varied subjects as premarital counseling, foreign missions, international church relief, and the training of youth leaders.

On the Council's yearly calendar are more than 20 religious observances, including a Universal Week of Prayer in January, Race Relations Sunday in February, World Day of Prayer on the First Friday of Lent, May Fellowship Day to foster closer relations among Christian Women, Rural Life Sunday on Rogation Sunday, Christian Education Week beginning the last Sunday in September "to make people aware of Christian education responsibilities in the home, church and community," Communion Sunday in October, and Share-Our-Surplus Week during the Thanksgiving season.

Hundreds of religious radio and television broadcasts reach Americans through the Council's Broadcasting and Film Commission, and on the education front the National Council gives executive leadership to the United Christian Youth Movement, which embraces more than 10 million young people.

Among the hopes and prospects that the Council leadership has for the future, the most prominent is its desire to expand the "work of reconciliation" with religious bodies that do not belong to the Council. Such reconciliation, officials say, should first be made with Protestants and Orthodox who do not cooperate with the National Council, notably those in the Baptist and Lutheran tradition who are unsympathetic with "unionism." Equally urgent is the felt need for collaboration "with our brethren in the Roman Catholic tradition from whom we of both the Protestant and Orthodox traditions have been separated for long centuries. We must proceed on the assumption that all these who acknowledge Jesus Christ as Lord and Saviour are brothers."

Underlying the external operations of the National Council is a theology of the Christian faith that sees in the ecumenical movement the rise of a second Reformation. On one hand, it recognizes that churches are steadily moving toward the goal of organic unity; but on the other hand it believes that this goal should be reached without sacrificing the values gained out of the first Reformation.

Bibliography: Sources pub. by the National Council include: *Christian Scholar* (quarterly), Commission on Christian Higher Education. *Information Service* (weekly), Bureau of Research and Survey. *Memo* (monthly), Commission on Christian Higher Education. *National Council Outlook* (monthly), Office of Public Relations. *Newsletter* (quarterly), Office for Councils of Churches. *Publisher* (bi-monthly), Office of Publication and Distribution. *Religious Newsweekly* (weekly), Office of Public Relations. *Religious Radio and Television Newsletter* (bi-monthly), Broadcasting and Film Commission. *Rural Missions*, Division of Foreign Missions. *Together* (quarterly), Division of Foreign Missions.

[J. A. HARDON]

NATIONAL FEDERATION OF CATHOLIC COLLEGE STUDENTS,

a federation founded in 1937 for lay undergraduate students in U.S. Catholic colleges and universities. Students affiliate with the Federation (NFCCS) through student government organizations on the various campuses. The Federation, however, unites efforts of individual units through a national office with headquarters in the National Catholic Welfare Conference building in Washington, D.C.; national officers; national secretariats; and an annual national congress.

The purpose of the Federation is twofold: (1) "to stimulate thought and action on the significant contemporary issues in order to promote personal commitment to the work of the Church and to the perfection of society, and (2) to represent with national and international impact the opinions of Catholic College students on these issues" (Art. II, NFCCS Constitution, 1962).

In 1964 the Federation had a membership of 100,000 students in more than 125 Catholic colleges and universities throughout 15 regions. Campuses are represented regionally and nationally by two elected delegates who voice opinions of their constituents on policies and programs and avail their campuses of facilities of the national organization. Regions of the Federation are represented in the national council by two delegates. Five national officers compose the executive committee of the NFCCS.

Federation programming is centered in four secretariats located on member campuses. They deal in social action and in international, religious, and student affairs; prepare programs for campus adoption; and serve as a referral agency for student inquiries.

The NFCCS is the only national Catholic federation of students in Catholic colleges. Programs administered by the national organization are geared to transcend areas already covered by local campus clubs and personnel. In addition NFCCS can take part in national projects not open to nonaffiliated campuses and individuals. Its work is administered and directed solely by students and its annual national congress gives a united voice to the U.S. Catholic college students. The congress serves to instruct delegates concerning work of the secretariats, the availability of materials, and modes of program implementation. Students participate in workshops conducted by the secretariats and in plenary sessions dealing with problems and projects of national scope.

Special NFCCS committees include those directed to the interests of the foreign student, the foreign correspondence exchange program, forensic information center, the scholarship program, and a travel program. Among its national commissions are the Catholic Action Study Bureau (CASB), Confraternity of Christian Doctrine (CCD), commissions on industrial relations, liturgy, missions, family life, international relations, Mariology, and student government.

The Federation is a constituent unit of the College and University Section of the National Council of Catholic Youth (NCCY), and an affiliated federation of Pax Romana, an international movement of Catholic students. The NFCCS official newspaper is the *Forum*.

[M. TREACY]

NATIONAL FEDERATION OF CATHOLIC PHYSICIANS' GUILDS,

an association of Catholic physicians in the U.S., founded in 1932 to promote spiritual aims and ideals as they apply to members of the medical profession. The guild members participate widely in parish and diocesan activities. Among other services, they often assist in parish pre-Cana and Family Life instructions and help provide general health care for the religious and clergy. Guild members make an annual retreat and observe the feast day of St. Luke, the patron of physicians, with a White Mass.

The national federation sponsors programs of medical education and research and encourages guild members to give short- and long-term service in foreign mission areas. It also sponsors a newsletter, *Guilds in Action,* and an official journal, *The Linacre Quarterly* (named after Thomas *Linacre, a learned English physician of the 16th century). To promote the philosophy and ethics of medical practice, the journal publishes articles on medical science and Catholic theology, written by medical specialists and moral theologians.

When founded in 1932, the federation had 11 local guilds. In 1964 there were 104 guilds with 7,000 members.

[W. J. EGAN]

NATIONAL FEDERATION OF ST. APOLLONIA GUILDS, a federation of Catholic dentists' guilds organized in 1928 in Boston, Mass., to encourage spirituality among guild members, to spread devotion and knowledge of St. Apollonia, the patron of dentists, to raise professional standards and ethics, to support and maintain organized dentistry, and to practice charity along professional lines. Impetus for establishment of the federation was supplied by the *Apollonian,* a quarterly magazine published and distributed nationally by the Boston guild, which was founded in 1920 and was the first guild of Catholic dentists in the U.S. Two years after the establishment of the federation, delegates met at Buffalo, N.Y., to adopt a constitution and bylaws. Each guild in the federation is autonomous, holds regular meetings, conducts an annual closed retreat, and designs its own program to serve the needs of its community and diocese. Among outstanding guild activities have been the equipping, maintaining, and staffing of free clinics in hospitals, homes for the aged, convents, orphanages, and other institutions. In many dioceses, guild members examine parochial school children annually and conduct educational programs in high schools to interest students in dentistry as a career.

[P. J. BRUEL]

NATIONAL HOME AND SCHOOL SERVICE

A Catholic association devoted to the welfare of children and youth. The National Home and School Service is an expansion, in organization and services, of the Committee on Parent-Teacher Associations, established in 1931 under the auspices of the National Council of Catholic Women. In 1951, to avoid infringement upon a similar copyrighted title, the name was changed to the Committee on Home and School Associations, and in 1961 it was modified to National Home and School Service.

Between 1950 and 1960, the impact of larger enrollments, school facility expansion, and the increased interest and active participation of parents in local educational policies, necessitated a revision of the services offered. Programs were formulated that would more effectively meet the concerns of parents, administrators, and educators, as well as the needs of children and youth.

In September 1960, the National Catholic Home and School Association was inaugurated as a clearinghouse for Catholic parent-teacher groups as well as for individuals. It functioned under the joint sponsorship of the National Council of Catholic Women and the National Council of Catholic Men, with the Department of Education of the National Catholic Welfare Conference and the National Catholic Educational Association. It continued under this joint sponsorship until 1963 when it became the exclusive responsibility of the National Council of Catholic Women. Since 1960, as a national center for home and school activities, it has serviced approximately 1,200 subscribers.

The objectives of the National Home and School Service are based on the recognition that a partnership of home and school is indispensable, and that the coordinated efforts and support of all those involved in and concerned with the welfare and education of the child— parents, teachers, and administrators—are essential. These objectives are facilitated by educational programs designed: (1) to aid parents in acquiring self-understanding, to help them assume their proper role in the education of the child, and to enhance their understanding and knowledge of child growth and development; and (2) to effect mutual understanding and greater cohesiveness between home-school relationships in creating an environment both stimulating and satisfying to the child. Cooperation with the National Catholic Education Association and representation at national and regional meetings helps strengthen parental cognizance of trends in education.

Program guides for study-discussion groups, lectures, panels, workshops, and films, as well as monthly bulletins, all of which follow a yearly theme, implement the program. The most important function of the National Home and School Service, however, is that of being the sole national center for Catholic school–connected groups or individuals. In this capacity, it provides help, information, and materials for home and school activities, recognizes the necessity for regional and national planning in education, and endeavors to provide leadership for optimum educational experiences for each child.

[M. M. BRESNAHAN]

NATIONAL OFFICE FOR DECENT LITERATURE (NODL)

In December 1938 the Catholic hierarchy of the U.S. established the NODL. Its purpose as stated by the episcopal committee was "to set in motion the moral forces of the entire country . . . against the lascivious type of literature which threatens moral, social, and national life." The NODL was not envisioned as an exclusively Catholic movement, but was and is a service organization that coordinates activities and supplies all interested groups with practical information gathered from the aggregate experience of many organizations actively working on literature programs. It also issues a quarterly bulletin containing current information on activities, programs, and procedures throughout the country. Finally, it prints each month a list of magazines and pocket-size books judged objectionable for youth. NODL does not review hard-cover books, but only publications available to youth at nominal prices. It does not enter the field of adult reading.

Publications are evaluated according to a code for youthful reading, which deems those publications objectionable that (1) glorify crime or the criminal, (2) describe in detail ways to commit criminal acts, (3) hold lawful authority in disrespect, (4) exploit horror, cruelty, or violence, (5) portray sex facts offensively, (6) feature indecent, lewd, or suggestive photographs or illustrations, (7) carry advertising, which is either offensive in content or promotes products that may lead to physical or moral harm, (8) use blasphemous, profane, or obscene speech indiscriminately and repeatedly, or (9) hold up to ridicule any national, religious, or racial group.

A publication is first evaluated by a competent reviewer. The majority of reviewers are Catholic, but some are Protestant or Jewish. Regardless of creed, those sincerely interested in the welfare of youth are invited to join NODL's reviewing board. If the reviewer finds the publication objectionable for youth according to the code, the magazine or paperback book is re-reviewed by five other critics. If all six consider the publication in violation of the code, the publication is listed as "Disapproved for Youth." NODL never declares a publication to be obscene or pornographic. Such a decision must be made by the courts. NODL believes, however, that some list compiled by competent reviewers and based on an objective code is necessary to help parents and interested groups.

NODL recognizes that it should not be merely negative in character, and accordingly, to foster good reading, it publishes a list of "Acceptable Pocket-Size Books for Youth." This list is revised periodically and has received widespread approval. At the same time, NODL does not believe that fostering good reading habits is the complete solution to the problem. Such a program can effectively cultivate a taste for good literature in only a portion of youth, and furthermore presupposes good home and school training. The community also has a responsibility to neglected, unwanted, and retarded children. Publications that emphasize the lurid, the sensational, and the violent add to the burden such children already have in striving to live a normal life. NODL advocates the enactment of adequate, constitutional legislation to remove the worst of the offensive material. Moreover, it reaffirms the democratic right of any citizen to protest in a legal manner against the sale of publications he considers objectionable for youth. Further, NODL defends the right of parents, teachers, pastors of souls, and others charged with the welfare of youth to counsel and direct their families, their students, and their flocks in this matter.

[J. J. HOWARD]

NATIONAL SHRINE OF THE IMMACULATE CONCEPTION

The largest Catholic church in the U.S. and the seventh largest church in the world, erected in Washington, D.C., under the direction of the American bishops.

At the Sixth Provincial Council of Baltimore (1846) the bishop of the U.S. chose Mary as patroness of the U.S. under her title of the Immaculate Conception. In 1914 Bp. Thomas *Shahan, fourth rector of The Catholic University of America, Washington, D.C., received the approval of Pius X for the project of the National Shrine. Five years later the firm of Maginnis and Walsh, with Frederick V. Murphy associate, was chosen as architects; the chief creator of the final design was Charles Maginnis (1867–1955). In 1954 the firm became Maginnis and Walsh and Kennedy. Eugene F.

National Shrine of the Immaculate Conception.

Kennedy, Jr., was architect for the erection of the superstructure.

Early studies and a model in Gothic design were rejected in favor of one that was contemporary and original but in the spirit of Byzantine and Romanesque architecture. While drawing upon tradition, the architect attempted to create an ecclesiastical building that was distinctively American. On Sept. 23, 1920, Cardinal James Gibbons laid the cornerstone of the Shrine on a site adjacent to the campus of The Catholic University. By 1931 the crypt church and some of the crypt areas had been completed; between 1954 and 1959 the exterior of the upper church was built. Six years later, 10 of the 11 chapels planned had been added to the exterior; the interior was still unfinished.

The building is in the form of a Latin cross, 459 feet long, 240 feet wide at the transepts. The height is 120 feet to the peak of the roof, 237 feet to the top of the dome, and 329 feet to the top of the bell tower. The seating capacity is 3,500; total capacity is 6,000. The Shrine was built without structural steel, entirely of masonry, as were medieval cathedrals. The Knights Tower (bell tower) adds a strong vertical accent to the overall composition of the Shrine. On the tiled dome, huge gold symbols of Our Lady appear against a blue background.

Notable among the 137 separate pieces of sculpture on the exterior are two figures by Ivan *Městrović. All of the artistic details of the Shrine were planned by an iconography committee, including theologians, historians, and artists. The sculpture of the east wall explains the theme of faith; that of the west wall explains charity. The north wall features contemplatives, and the art of the façade centers around Christ and Our Lady.

The interior of the main church contains a long row of high Roman arches leading to the sanctuary. In the north apse, on the high curved wall, there is a 3,500-square-foot mosaic of Christ in Majesty by John de Rosen. Below, five apsidal chapels dedicated to the glorious mysteries of the rosary have been completed with marble and brilliant mosaics. Ultimately, the walls of the Shrine will be covered with marble, and the domes, filled with mosaics; 10 chapels will flank the nave. In 1965 four chapels had been built in the transepts, while the east and west apses, to contain 10 rosary chapels and two great mosaics, were expected to be completed within 5 years. Of the total of 176 stained-glass windows planned, 64 had been installed, including three rose windows.

The crypt church is a low, vaulted room with massive arches focusing attention upon the main altar, an isolated block of golden Algerian onyx. The crypt's marbles, golden mosaics, and ceramic tiles are rich in doctrinal and historical meaning but are discreetly subordinated to the table of sacrifice. In the crypt area there is a chapel for confessions, a chapel and replica of the Grotto at Lourdes, a chapel of St. Pius X, a chapel in which Bishop Shahan is buried, and a chapel of Our Mother of Good Counsel, with several additional ones planned. Memorial Hall contains marble columns and walls inscribed with the names of certain donors.

On Nov. 20, 1959, after the completion of the upper church, the National Shrine was dedicated by Cardinal Francis Spellman of New York in the presence of 4 other cardinals and more than 200 archbishops and bishops. The dedication was the largest ecclesiastical ceremony in the history of the Church in America and was listed by the secular press as one of the 10 major events of world news in 1959. In the years following the dedication, the Shrine was visited by 1 million people annually. It maintains a full schedule of daily and Sunday Masses, daily confessions, and regular services. It provides guides and services for pilgrims and visitors. It also publishes a bulletin, *Mary's Shrine*. Under the direction of the bishops, the Shrine is staffed by a director and an assistant director, who are diocesan priests, and by a group of Oblates of Mary Immaculate, who act as assistants to the director.

Bibliography: W. P. KENNEDY, *The National Shrine of the Immaculate Conception* (Washington 1922). B. A. MCKENNA, *Memoirs of the First Director* (Washington 1959). T. J. GRADY, AmEcclRev 136 (1957) 145–154; 137 (1957) 400–409; 141 (1959) 217–231. **Illustration credit:** Reni Photos.

[T. J. GRADY]

NATIONAL SOCIALISM

National Socialism (Nazism) in Germany had no definitive, systematically developed, or organized intellectual program and no firmly constructed set of concepts and values. As an ideology it was characterized by lack of unity and even by stark contradictions among its various elements. It was in these respects in sharp contrast to Bolshevism.

Neither the original 25-point program of the Nationalsozialistische Deutsche Arbeiterpartei (NSDAP), formulated in 1920 by Gottfried Feder (1883–1941), nor the *Mein Kampf* (1925–26) of Adolf *Hitler, nor the *Mythus des 20. Jahrhunderts* (1930) of Alfred Rosenberg (1893–1946) offered any politically, socially, culturally, or religiously grounded *Weltanschau-*

ung. Even before 1933, the National Socialist program, with its formulas for agitation, had been silently put aside, while Rosenberg's book, which Hitler had never read, had come to be considered simply a "private work." *Mein Kampf* was indeed widely circulated, but was not regarded seriously enough. The National Socialist ideology was a mixture, for common consumption, of extremely nationalistic, popular, and anti-Semitic thought with strongly imperialistic and militant tendencies. This ideology charged the state with the task of preserving the so-called Nordic-Aryan race, for the right to leadership was regarded as racially determined and assigned, with adequate living space (*Lebensraum*) and even world domination, to the Germanic "master race."

Totalitarian Character. Fortified by the "will to power" (F. Nietzsche), National Socialism combined its claim to complete and sole power in the state (*totalitarianism) with the demand that life should be radically reoriented toward permanent "complete mobilization" (total war). Christianity, described as "alien to the race" and unheroic, was to be replaced by a pseudo religiosity designated as *Gottgläubigkeit* (belief in God). A conglomerate ideology was offered as a substitute religion. By affirming the undisguised cult of power and force as historically justified strength, National Socialism denied all moral values and, to the same extent, revealed itself as pure *nihilism.

National Orientation. Under Hitler's influence, the term national, which had been especially attractive in middle-class circles, lost its original meaning. Aggressive *nationalism served as an ideological disguise for the obsession with self that formed the real core of Hitler's outlook. Since he saw the NSDAP only as a form of personal allegiance to himself—as the idealized Germanic representation of fate and loyalty—it is more correct to speak of Hitlerian than of National Socialist ideology. The determining factor of this ideology lay in the logical realization of the *Führerprinzip* (leadership principle) in all political, social, and cultural spheres.

During his years in Vienna (1907–13), Hitler's thinking was shaped to a decisive degree by the spirit of Richard *Wagner (1813–83); he never lost the impression made on him by Wagner's world, an ambiguous mixture of ambition—partly revolutionary, partly political, and partly artistic—and of *anti-Semitism and vegetarianism. In Vienna, Hitler assimilated the extreme anti-Semitism associated with the Alldeutsche group and Georg von Schönerer, and the concept of "noble races" taught by the religious sectarian Jörg Lanz von Liebenfels (1874–1954). The latter considered himself the founder of a new order of Knights Templar of Nordic persuasion and advocated, in his journal *Ostara* (founded 1905), a creed of "racial purity." Lanz later considered himself the father of National Socialism, but in 1938 he was officially forbidden to write. He has since been cited as the one "who gave Hitler his ideas" (W. Daim).

Behind the militant ideological imagery of Hitler was an unhistorical and popular biological concept of nationality (*Volkstum*). Hitler's sociorevolutionary naturalism was directed, like Bolshevism but unlike Italian *Fascism, toward the destruction of traditional forms of society. Even after 1933 the most frequently employed term for describing the National Socialist ideology and its basic aims was *völkisch*. Insofar as National

Socialism is not to be reduced to pure opportunism or the naked struggle for power, it was nationally oriented.

Social Darwinism. An important ingredient of this primitive philosophical mixture was the Social Darwinism developed toward the end of the 19th century from teachings on "racial characteristics" then current (A. Ploetz, A. Tille). Rejecting socialistic theories about milieu and accepting the older *racism of J. A. de Gobineau (1816–82) and Houston Stewart Chamberlain (1855–1927), this doctrine was based on the "natural law" of the survival of the fittest in the struggle for existence. Actuated by biologism and aggressive imperialism, it gave rise to recommendations for planned population controls and for the "cultivation" of a "master race." The demand for *Lebensraum* in Europe for "Greater Germany," motivated by the racially grounded German claim to leadership in world affairs, was to be fulfilled at the expense of foreign nations (through emigration and annihilation). This goal was pursued by employment of the old ruse of establishing absolute hostility against one particular group and excluding it from the national community. This myth of the enemy race was the counterpart of the myth of the enemy class in the Bolshevist theory of domination. In addition, Rosenberg contributed highly confused anticlerical ideas in his advocacy of the renewal of "Nordic belief."

Reactionary Romanticism. Around this mixture of National Socialist ideas were grouped still other related ideas already widely disseminated, especially among German intellectuals: the social romanticism of the youth movement, the idealized memories of experiences at the front during World War I (reviving the military community structure), misconceived German idealism, and unpolitical aestheticism. The concept of leadership (*Führerideologie*) circulated in innumerable leagues and youth associations found ready acceptance in a Germany torn by parties and factions, in which liberal democratic political and social forms were dismissed as examples of "Western alienation" and "middle-class decadence." There was a noteworthy receptiveness to the romantic glorification of the peasantry (*Blut-und-Boden*) in opposition to socialism and to older concepts of a "Prussian" or national socialism—extending from Fichte to Oswald Spengler's *Preussentum und Sozialismus* (1920)—as opposed to an international world-revolutionary Marxism. The national-revolutionary fantasies of the writer Arthur Moeller van den Bruck (1876–1925) produced visions—corresponding to the title of his book, *Das Dritte Reich* (1923)—of an empire "in the spirit of the soul of the race." Here was the notion of the "young nations" needing *Lebensraum* in order to grow (*see* GEOPOLITICS).

Combined with the principle of leadership and forcibly elevated in 1933 to the rank of political doctrine, the vaguely defined content of the National Socialist ideology became a dangerous weapon. Allowing the Nazi leaders a peculiarly ambiguous lack of commitment and readiness to change—only the hostility to the Jews with its gruesome consequences remained constant—this popular national ideology formed the theoretical basis of the totalitarian and criminal government of Germany from 1933 to 1945.

See also GERMANY.

Bibliography: H. ARENDT, *The Origins of Totalitarianism* (New York 1951). M. BROSZAT, "Die völkische Ideologie des National-sozialismus," *Deutsche Rundschau* 84 (1954) 53–68. H. BUCH-HEIM, *Das Dritte Reich: Grundlagen und politische Entwicklung* (Munich 1958). H. CONRAD-MARTIUS, *Utopien der Menschenzüchtung: Der Sozialdarwinismus und seine Folgen* (Munich 1955). E. FRAENKEL, *The Dual State: A Contribution to the Theory of Dictatorship* (New York 1941). K. VON KLEMPERER, *Germany's New Conservatism: Its History and Dilemma in the 20th Century* (Princeton 1957). F. NEUMANN, *Behemoth: The Structure and Practice of National Socialism, 1933–1944* (New York 1944). J. F. NEUROHR, *Der Mythos vom Dritten Reich: Zur Geistesgeschichte des Nationalsozialismus* (Stuttgart 1957). E. NOLTE, *Der Nationalsozialismus in seiner Epoche* (Munich 1963). E. G. REICHMANN, *Die Flucht in den Hass: Die Ursachen der deutschen Judenkatastrophe* (Frankfurt 1956).

[R. MORSEY]

NATIONALISM

Nationalism may be defined as a sentiment unifying a group of people—a *nation, as the Swiss, Russians, or Japanese—who have a real or imagined common historical experience and a common aspiration to live together in the future as a separate group. In the contemporary world this unifying sentiment is usually expressed in loyalty to the nation-state (the political entity), whatever the government; in love of the native land, although only a part of it may be known to the nationalist; in pride in the common culture and economic and social institutions, although these may not be understood; in preference for fellow nationals in contrast to disregard or dislike for members of other groups; and in zeal not only for the nation's security but also for its glory and expansion. In its most modern and developed form nationalism requires, as Jean Jacques *Rousseau advocated in the 18th century, almost absolute devotion to and conformity with the will of the nation-state as this is expressed by the ruler or rulers (autocratic or democratic). When nationalism has developed to this point, its adherents often strive for or boast of the superiority of their nation's culture if not its military power.

The fact is that contemporary men think of themselves as Frenchmen or Englishmen, Chinese or Japanese, Mexicans or Cubans, Nigerians or Ghanians. They seldom recall their common membership in the human race as they stress their national identities and differences. If in remote areas, as in parts of Africa, this is not yet true, relentless forces seem to be driving them into national communities, conditioning them to be nationalists. An outstanding Argentinian reformer, Ricardo Rojas, pleaded for national education to "restore the national spirit . . . and save the Argentine school from the foreign clergy, from foreign gold, and from foreign books" [quoted in A. P. Whitaker, *Nationalism in Latin America* (Gainesville, Fla. 1962) 41]. From the beginning of the 20th century children in the schools of the U.S. have often been required to pledge allegiance to their flag, the symbol of "one nation indivisible." In 1955 a statesman of Israel, Abba Ebban, asserted before the United Nations General Assembly his country's right to limit entry to those "men and women the central passion of whose lives shall be devoted to Israel's flag, loyalty to Israel's independence, zeal for Israel's welfare and security, and a readiness to defend her against all assaults from near or far" (*New York Times,* Oct. 4, 1955). The English-Polish-Jewish historian, Sir Lewis Namier, thought that for every man "the native land is his life-giving Mother, and the State raised upon the land his law-giving Father" [*England in the Age of the American Revolution* (2d ed., New York 1961) 18]. The "true believer" of the 20th century became the nationalist who, in the phrase of the French Royalist newspaper, *L'Action Française,* "places the fatherland above everything" [quoted in W. C. Buthman, *The Rise of Integral Nationalism in France...* (New York 1939) 291]. During World War II men of many nations felt like the Japanese, Kazan Kayahara, who spoke for his compatriots, "If necessary for the preservation of our State, we are ready to lay down our lives any moment for it is the most sacred of all treasures we have in this world" [quoted in D. Brown, *Nationalism in Japan* (Berkeley, Calif. 1955) 229].

ORIGINS

What are the roots of this sentiment? A contemporary answer is that nations are the groups with which men now identify themselves for their protection, for satisfaction of their basic material needs, and for the achievement of their highest creative goals. Another contemporary answer is that national states govern the daily lives of men, tax them, police them, adjust their disputes, take care of them in times of weakness, and protect them against foreign dangers. Still a third answer is that *culture is now not local or universal but predominantly national; when men create, they speak or sing in national tongues; when they play, they play in national sports; and when they dream, they dream of national achievements and national triumphs. But these answers are only descriptions of the present national groupings and sentiments of men. They do not reveal how nationalism began, developed, and became the powerful force it has.

Nationalism as an Attitude. In a psychological sense, as David Potter has observed, nationalism "is a tendency, an impulse, and attitude of mind, rather than an objective, determinate thing" ["The Historian's Use of Nationalism and Vice Versa," AmHistRev, 67 (July 1962) 926]. Attitudes vary with time and place, and with the individual and the group. The devotion citizens give to their respective nations, national interests, ideals, and states is of differing degrees of intensity, of diverse qualities, and given for many different reasons. Moreover, men form other kinds of groupings based on religious, ethnic, racial, class, and sectional unities and diversities. They have other loyalties, to their churches, families, crafts, and professions. They often seek realization of their material interests as individuals, through their local communities, or in far-distant international organizations. Their cultures, as manifested in creative arts or manners of living, are rooted deeply in the past when nations as such did not exist; at times they reflect local or international origins. Finally, division and conflict arise not only out of national but also out of individual, class, ideological, and many other differences; for violence may occur within as well as between nations, in riots, revolutions, and civil wars.

Ascribed Sources of National Identity. Nationalists have engaged in many fancies. They have believed that Divine Providence, nature, or historical forces have singled out their nation or destined it to be independent and supreme. They have supposed that geography, climate, and natural boundaries have determined nations and set them apart from each other. They have imagined that their nations arose because of racial differences and inequalities or that (as the Marxists believe) nations

have arisen out of the bourgeoisie's search for profits and markets [J. Stalin, *Marxism and the National and Colonial Question,* ed. A. Fineberg, (Moscow 1935) and A. D. Low, *Lenin on the Question of Nationality* (New York, 1958)]. They have ascribed inherent characteristics to various peoples that set them apart as nations. And they have thought (with some reason) that language differences have set peoples apart in national groups [H. L. Koppelmann, *Nation, Sprache und Nationalismus* (Leiden 1956)].

There may be truth in each of these explanations, especially in that based upon obvious differences in language; but evidence for most of them is nonexistent, scanty, or inconclusive. Though various nations have believed themselves to be chosen by Divine Providence, they can adduce no proof; and the messages of the great religions, as Christianity and Mohammedanism, are for all men without regard for nationality: "Here there is not 'Gentile and Jew'" (Col 3.11). There is little evidence that geography and climate determined the origin or development of nations as such or conditioned men to be loyal exclusively to their respective nations; historically, men have lived in and been loyal to many kinds of secular communities, to tribes, city-states, and empires. "Natural boundaries," so far as the evidence permits generalization, turn out to be the boundaries toward which some nations have moved through war and diplomacy, and many nations have no such boundaries. On the basis of recent biological and anthropological research, *race can no longer be considered a serious explanation of national groupings and behavior. Individuals within nations do seem to share common or national social customs and habits of mind, but despite much study social scientists have not been able to isolate these and arrive at any scientific conclusions. "National character" does not appear to be inherent: individuals of different nations appear to have similar characteristics; the characters of individuals within nations vary widely; and the "national character" of individuals within nations seems to be constantly changing, e.g., the orderly and quiet Englishman of the 20th century is far from his unruly and boisterous ancestor in Tudor England [see W. Buchanan and H. Cantril, *How Nations See Each Other* (Urbana, Ill. 1953) and H. C. J. Duijker and H. N. Frijda, *National Character and National Stereotypes* (Amsterdam 1960)]. Nations and nationalism have been used to forward economic and other interests not only by the bourgeoisie but also by workers and farmers, and a good many nobles and clergy have been national patriots; hence, a class interpretation of nationalism is too simple. Languages do divide men; but several languages are spoken within some nations (Switzerland and India), and the same languages are spoken by people of different nations (Great Britain and U.S., or Spain and most Latin-American nations).

Nationalism is the product of history, of nurture, not of nature. Nations and nationalism appeared comparatively late in history, and men are not born with love of nation inherent in them. Loyalty and patriotism were strong in the Greek city-states and in the Roman Republic and Empire; they are not unknown in primitive tribes. Children must learn to love their "fatherlands" [J. Piaget and A. M. Weil, "The Development in Children of the Idea of the Homeland and of Relations with Other Countries," *International Social Science*

Bulletin 3 (1951) 561–578). What we now know as nations and nationalism originated and developed in late Western and modern history out of the institutions, the ideas, and the conditions that existed during the past 6 to 7 centuries.

HISTORY IN THE WEST

From about 1100 to 1600 in Western Europe, the medieval monarchs acquired large territorial domains, primarily by war, diplomacy, and marriage. Over these they ruled, establishing common laws and courts, collecting taxes, and raising troops. In short, they imposed a common or national authority over particular territories and the people or peoples inhabiting them. Through hundreds of years there arose among the inhabitants of these territories—e.g., the French or the English—a feeling of common history, common tragedies and glories, a consciousness of common needs of trade and defense, and usually a common language. Here, then, were bases for nations and the emerging sentiment of nationalism.

Rise of Popular Nationalism. During the 18th century individuals of the middle classes increasingly began to feel that the nation belonged to them. This was not a new phenomenon; nor was it a feeling restricted to the middle classes, since a good many nobles and clergy felt the same way. But during the 18th century more and more members of the middle classes believed more and more strongly that their ownership of property gave them a stake in the nation. If the nation belonged not only to the king but also to the property-owning people, these people had an interest in the national welfare and should have a voice in national affairs. Voltaire wrote, "When those who possess, like myself, fields and houses, assemble for their common interests, I have a voice in this assembly. I am a part of the whole, a part of the community, a part of the sovereign. Here is my fatherland" [*Oeuvres complètes* (Paris 1785–89) 42.264].

When men possessed a fatherland, they were citizens, not mere subjects; and being citizens, they could demand or give to themselves rights and privileges. This, in part, was what actually happened during the English, American, and French Revolutions of 1688, 1776, and 1789. Many men, or at least those who owned property, had new reasons to be devoted to the nation. Popular nationalism, as distinguished from dynastic loyalty, was beginning. Soon all inhabitants, at least all native inhabitants of a nation, were considering themselves citizens entitled to national rights such as those guaranteed by the English unwritten and the American and French written constitutions. And, in turn, as the nation afforded rights and benefits, the citizens were patriotic, that is, national-minded. The "organizer of victory" of the French Revolution, Lazare Carnot, expressed the feeling of many national patriots when he wrote in 1793, "Oh France! Oh my fatherland! Oh great people, truly great people! On your soil I had the honor to be born; I could not cease to belong to you without ceasing to exist. You contain all the objects of my affection; the work that my hands have helped begin; the old virtuous man who sired me, my unblemished family; the friends who know the depth of my heart. . . ." [in H. F. Stewart and P. Desjardins, eds., *French Patriotism in the Nineteenth Century (1814–1833)* (Cambridge, Eng. 1923) 51].

The great wars of the French Revolutionary and Napoleonic eras accelerated the process in Western lands. Frenchmen, Englishmen, Germans, and Spaniards believed themselves threatened or oppressed, feared foreigners, and warred against each other with national armies. Fear intensified national hatreds and led to greater reliance upon national governments. These national governments, in consequence, acquired more and more power, more and more prestige, and gave promise of a better future. The nation became the vehicle of men's hopes and their fortress against fear, the symbol of better times to come, a refuge in time of trouble.

Inculcation of Nationalism. The governments of nation-states, to satisfy the most ardent patriots, began consciously to make good citizens, to force all citizens into the national molds. The more they acted, the more nationalist their citizens became and the more these citizens demanded national institutions and national ways of living. National governments made the churches and even religion national. By military conscription and the *levées en masse* they created national armies. Through the establishment of national school systems they fostered national patriotism. Laws, courts, and taxes all became increasingly national rather than local or provincial. Citizens thus were conditioned to be interested in their nation, their nation-state, their common national needs and aspirations. And often they responded enthusiastically. They celebrated the winning of national independence or national freedom on national holidays, and they sang the praises of their nations in a *Rule Britannia*, a *Star Spangled Banner*, a *Marseillaise*, or a *Deutschland über Alles*.

Through the 19th and 20th centuries almost every activity and idea seemed to conspire to promote nationalism. Ideas reenforced the emerging national institutions and cultures. These institutions and cultures fostered national ideas. How could men enlarge their opportunities and freedoms and shield themselves against the misfortunes of everyday life or the threat of foreign enemies? Through unity of thought and action within their own nations. What emperor or king, noble, or priest had once provided in the way of protection and encouragement, the independent, ambitious national state seemed to be able to do and to do more completely and efficiently. Outside the state, though increasingly brought within it, economic forces and cultural influences worked toward the same national ends.

Railroads stitched the Italian boot, making possible the economic cohesiveness upon which Mazzini, Garibaldi, and Cavour could politically unify Italy. In the U.S. Henry Clay's "American System" and similar schemes brought the sections closer together. Everywhere tariffs were erected to protect national economic interests. Banking systems became national and, later, great industries became national in the distribution of their plants and sales. During the 19th century national governments aided chiefly business. During the 20th century they came to assist workers and farmers as well, as the latter demanded and usually obtained protection against foreign labor or crops, social insurance or crop loans, and minimum wages or parity prices. They, too, began to have a stake in their nation-states and to become national-minded.

By the second half of the 20th century almost everything the citizen heard and saw seemed to reenforce his nationalism. The press, radio, and television tended to become national in ownership and coverage. Schools taught national citizenship. The French school child learned the geography of France as a landowner comes to know his property, and the American child was taught to believe in the U.S. as a land of "liberty and justice for all." [The literature on school training is voluminous, but see B. Pierce, *Citizens' Organizations and the Civic Training of Youth* (New York 1933).] Historians, as the authoritarian Heinrich von Treitschke of Germany, the republican Ernest Lavisse of France, and the democratic George Bancroft of the U.S., wrote and taught proud national histories. Literature, cooking, and sports became national and were judged by national criteria. Even science and music, written in international notation and symbol, became Russian, German, French, or American in tradition. To make certain that national rather than other values prevailed, patriotic (often also secret) societies in nearly every country demanded with some success that foreign influences be rooted out, that only "good national" or "100 per cent national" ideas be permitted.

CONTEMPORARY NATIONALISM

From the latter part of the 19th century the nationalism that had developed earlier in western Europe spread over the world, deepening and intensifying everywhere. Europeans carried not only their trade, their diseases, and their guns to Africa, Asia, and the Americas; they carried also the spirit of nationalism.

New Nations. The later Asian, African, and Latin-American nationalisms developed in many respects like those of Europe, but there were differences as well. Perhaps because they were sparked more by common dislike or fear of foreign oppression than by common hope for achievement of liberties, the new nationalisms usually contained less fervid and less united support of national governments than had the European. Each of the new nationalisms, the Indian or the Indonesian, the Algerian, the Ghanian, or the Nigerian, differs in character. But certain tentative generalizations can be hazarded. In several cases, as in Egypt and some other African nations, national leaders held socialist (or populist) views; and often students, who had learned of Western democratic rights and liberties in Europe, were the most passionate advocates of national independence. Nearly always the middle classes, so instrumental in the development of European nationalism, were weak in comparison to the European middle classes and, though nationalist in sentiment, played a lesser role than did their counterparts in Europe. In some cases, for example, in Japan and Turkey, military officers who had been trained in Western Europe or by European teachers were ardent nationalist leaders. Often the inferior status and the political and economic oppression of "colored" peoples led to resentment or national hatred toward former or present white imperial rulers. In many cases so-called capitalist or Communist powers, as the U.S., the U.S.S.R., and mainland China, have tried to develop and to use nationalist feeling in their own national interests. Throughout Asia and Africa peoples were newly encouraged by the Covenant of the League of Nations and the Charter of the United Nations to ask for "self-determination" and for freedom and equality. In several of the new African nations, however, the peoples, still loyal chiefly to their tradi-

tional tribes, had not acquired by the 1960s the national feeling that leaders sought to instill.

Reliance on National Power. Men do not necessarily love the hand that feeds them or worship their benefactors. Indeed, some men in most nations have fought against the pervading nationalism and resisted the power of the leviathan national states. The reality remains, however, that over the world men have become increasingly national-minded. When the Negro in the U.S. in the 1950s and 1960s wanted equality, he demanded action by the national government because he thought he could not get this equality through any other agency. When in the 1950s and 1960s Poles and Hungarians wanted restoration of their rights, they believed that they had to throw off Russian domination and once more win national independence. When from World War I onward some Latin-American peoples desired higher standards of living, they demanded national action against Yankee "imperialism." When many Asian and African peoples after World War II sought freedom, they rebelled against English or French domination and sought to establish their own independent nation-states. When modern peoples everywhere, in fear or in hope, sought security from domestic and foreign threats, they turned first to their national governments, or worked to establish them. For the achievement of basic needs, for the winning of civil rights and cultural privileges, and for fundamental order and safety, the nation-state had become the modern means, the most powerful and effective means men understood and employed.

Dangers. The dangers that arise from nationalism are principally two. The loyalty men give to their nations sometimes turns into idolatrous worship, becomes exclusive and all-encompassing [C. J. H. Hayes, *Nationalism; A Religion* (New York 1960)]. This occurs particularly in wartime, e.g., during the French Revolution and the two world wars of the first half of the 20th century. Nationalism then becomes a religious crusade that is intolerant, aggressive, and hostile, stifling thought and leading to persecution within the nation. Pius XI termed it "an ideology which clearly resolves itself into a true, real pagan worship of the state—a statolatry which is not less in contrast with the natural rights of the family than it is in contradiction to the supernatural rights of the Church" [*Non abbiamo bisogno*, ActApS 23 (1931) 302]. Crusading zeal also leads to *war, the second danger. Nationalists tend to seek glory and expansion for their nations. In so doing, they conflict with the nationalists of other nations. International conflict results. Nationalism as exemplified by most European nations before 1914 was one cause of World War I, and the belligerent nationalism of Nazi Germany, Fascist Italy, and Shinto-worshiping Japan led directly to World War II. Just after the beginning of hostilities in 1939, in his first encyclical, Pius XII remarked that excessive nationalism "leaves the stability of international relations at the mercy of the will of rulers, while it destroys the possibility of true union and fruitful collaboration directed to the general good" [*Summi Pontificatus*, ActApS 31 (1939) 554].

Dangers of nationalism lead men of good will to seek alternatives. Three alternatives appear possible for the last third of the 20th century: (1) regional federations coupled with an effective international organization, (2) the establishment of a world state in which national cultures may remain but national states are deprived of their power to war, (3) the spread of a world religion in which the ethical goals preclude violence. None of these alternatives, although they have long been the dream of minorities, appears to attract sufficient numbers of people for its realization. Until one of them is believed to offer the freedom and hope, protection and security that the nation now does, nationalism will continue to exist and to increase in intensity. Opponents of nationalism who wish to work toward one of the alternatives, federation, world state, or world religion, would have to see that it touches the interests of individual men as closely and intimately as the national state now does. This, at present, they do not seem to do, but when they do, they might recall times before nationalism arose. Men have had other loyalties; nationalism has varied with time and circumstance; and under other religious, political, economic, and social conditions, new or different, even world loyalties may arise.

See also COLONIALISM; IMPERIALISM; PATRIOTISM; PEACE, INTERNATIONAL.

Bibliography: F. CHABOD, *L'idea di nazione*, ed. A. SAITTA and E. SISTAN (2d ed. Bari 1962). C. J. H. HAYES, *Essays on Nationalism* (New York 1926); *The Historical Evolution of Modern Nationalism* (New York 1931). F. O. HERTZ, *Nationality in History and Politics: A Study of the Psychology and Sociology of National Sentiment and Character* (New York 1944). R. JOHANNET, *Le Principe des nationalités* (new ed. Paris 1923). H. KOHN, *The Idea of Nationalism: A Study in its Origin and Background* (New York 1944). F. MEINECKE, *Weltbürgertum und Nationalstaat: Studien zur Genesis des deutschen Nationalstaates* (7th ed. Munich 1928). Royal Institute of International Affairs, *Nationalism: A Report by a Study Group of Members of the Royal Institute of International Affairs* (London 1939). B. C. SHAFER, *Nationalism: Myth and Reality* (New York 1955). L. L. SNYDER, *The Meaning of Nationalism* (New Brunswick, N.J. 1954). G. J. WEILL, *L'Europe du XIXᵉ siècle et l'idée de nationalité* (Paris 1938). J. J. WRIGHT, *National Patriotism in Papal Teaching* (Westminster, Md. 1943). F. ZNANIECKI, *Modern Nationalities: A Sociological Study* (Urbana, Ill. 1952). Two bibliographies are K. W. DEUTSCH, *Interdisciplinary Bibliography on Nationalism* (Cambridge, Mass. 1956) and K. S. PINSON, *A Bibliographical Introduction to Nationalism* (New York 1935).

[B. C. SHAFER]

NATIONALIZATION

A term that is generally used interchangeably with the term socialization in the literature of social ethics, denoting ownership, or the acquisition of ownership, of property, usually productive, by a national state or by a lesser political society within a national state. When nationalization occurs, the rights of ownership are exercised through an agency of government. The property in question is publicly owned and controlled.

The following are examples of nationalization: the state farms of the U.S.S.R., the railroads of England, the state liquor stores in certain parts of the U.S., the New York State Barge Canal, and the Bank of England. These properties are all publicly, not privately, owned and managed.

Expropriation must be carefully distinguished from nationalization; for, although it often serves as a step toward nationalization, the two are not always or necessarily connected. In recent years there have been several instances of expropriation of large landed estates by governments for the purpose of redistributing and thus increasing private ownership of land. This kind of expropriation without nationalization has taken place in Italy since World War II.

At times nationalization is effected simply through reservation to itself by government of certain kinds of properties or productive activities before they have ever been in the domain of private economic enterprise. An example of this is the production of materials that can be used for the generation of nuclear power. At other times a government will appropriate to itself only a certain segment of an industry, e.g., long-distance trucking, leaving the rest of the industry in private hands.

In recent decades acts of nationalization have been quite common. Nationalization of nearly every kind of productive property is practiced by the U.S.S.R., by Communist China, and by their satellites. Most of the colonial lands that have received political independence since the end of World War II have nationalized large segments of their economies, especially basic industries, such as steel production. In England the Labor party pursued a policy of nationalization when it won control of Parliament after World War II. At that time the coal mining and steel industries were converted into public properties.

What are the moral principles governing nationalization? First of all, nationalization is not morally wrong in itself. If the common good requires nationalization, then nationalization is morally justifiable. This is the norm for determining the morality of any act of nationalization. Normally industries and business enterprises should not be owned or operated by government, but if governmental intervention is necessary for the common good, nationalization may be resorted to, but only if less extreme measures, such as partial limits upon the freedom of the private owners, are inadequate.

Therefore, the Catholic Church takes the position that nationalization should not be employed as a normal and ordinary social policy but only when measures short of nationalization cannot effectively provide for the common good. The Church fears that the reckless use of nationalization may open the door to governmental tyranny. In each instance, then, it must be proved that nationalization alone can accomplish what must be done to satisfy the demands of the common good. And, if the act of nationalization involves expropriation, compensation must be made to the expropriated owners according to the norms of commutative justice.

Bibliography: J. MESSNER, *Social Ethics* tr. J. J. DOHERTY (new ed. St. Louis 1964). M. L. EBERDT and G. J. SCHNEPP, *Industrialism and the Popes* (New York 1953). J. Y. CALVEZ and J. PERRIN, *The Church and Social Justice: The Social Teachings of the Popes from Leo XIII to Pius XII*, tr. J. R. KIRWAN (Chicago 1961).

[C. A. ELLER]

NATIONS, TABLE OF THE

The genealogies of Japheth, Ham, and Sem, as given in Genesis ch. 10 and commonly referred to as the Table of the Nations, represent an effort to explain the origin of the peoples, tribes, and certain cities of the ancient Near East. The redactor presumes the unity of the human race, and is especially concerned with recording how the genealogy of Sem descends to Phaleg (Gn 10.25), one of the direct ancestors of Abraham (Gn 11.18–26).

Literary Considerations. Discrepancies in the table indicate a lack of literary unity. Saba, Hevila, and Lud

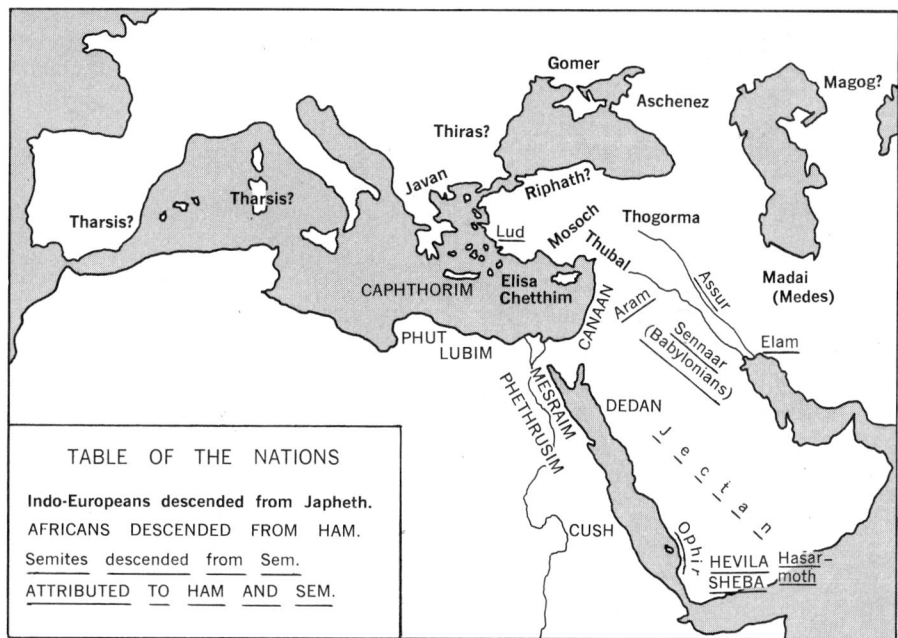

TABLE OF THE NATIONS

Indo-Europeans descended from Japheth.

AFRICANS DESCENDED FROM HAM.

Semites descended from Sem.

ATTRIBUTED TO HAM AND SEM.

in different verses descend from different progenitors (cf. v. 7 and 13 with v. 28–29 and 22); Canaan is territorially more extensive in v. 15–18 than in v. 19. One can distinguish two styles. Stereotyped expressions introduce and close three enumerations of names (v. 2 and 5; 6 and 20; 22 and 31): this uniformity is absent in other passages, especially in v. 8–12 and 25, which are in an anecdotal style. The parallel and symmetric formulas are characteristic of the Pentateuchal *priestly writers (P). Scholars generally distinguish two sources: to P belong v. 10.1a, 2–5, 6–7, 20, 22–23, 31, 32; to the *Yahwist (J) belong v. 10.1b, 8–12, 13–19, 21, 24–30. The basic source used is P; J is incomplete here.

Structure. Considering only the original P document, the table presents a harmonious division of the peoples and tribes of the ancient Near East. It is basically geographical, though at times, it reflects political and historical relationships. Several anomalies point to the artificial grouping of each genealogy. Despite the statement in v. 6, modern ethnology does not link non-Semitic Mesraim (Egypt) and Semitic Canaan to a common ancestor. The Japhetites, about whom the author relates the least (v. 2–5), are spread from Madai (the *Medes in northwestern Iran) to *Tharsis (in the region of the western Mediterranean). The Hamites (v. 6–20) include the then-known peoples of northeastern Africa and several tribes of southern Arabia; Canaan is placed here because of its onetime political subjugation to Egypt. The Semites (v. 21–31) include the Assyrians, Aramaeans, Hebrews, and non-Semitic Elamites, peoples closer to the Patriarchs and the regions from which they originally migrated. Lud (v. 22), i.e., Lydia in western Asia Minor, is out of place in this list of Semites, just as the Sumerian and Babylonian cities (v. 8–12) are out of place in the list of the Hamites. The whole chapter serves as an introduction to the genealogy of Abraham (Gn 11.10–26); hence, the descendants of Noe's eldest son, Sem, are listed after those of his other sons.

Time of Composition. Since the Philistines, who invaded the coast of Southern Canaan in the first quarter of the 12th century B.C., appear in the list, a date of composition after 1200 B.C. is required. The Cimmerians (Gomer) and Scythians (Aschenez), known to Israel only in the 8th and 7th century B.C., are also in the list (v. 2–3); Lydia, which became an independent empire about the early 7th century, is included too (v. 22). Consequently, the table, at least in its present form, must have been composed after this time. Other secondary factors point to the exilic period as the probable time of composition. The author's preoccupation with the linking of all races and nations to Noe is a tribute to the Creator's greatness, an acknowledgement of His universal primacy, since man's reproductive powers are a blessing from Him.

Bibliography: J. PLESSIS, DBSuppl 1:765–774. J. SIMONS, "The 'Table of the Nations' (Gen. 10): Its General Structure and Meaning," *Oudtestamentische Studiën* 10 (1954) 155–184. G. VON RAD, *Genesis: A Commentary,* tr. J. H. MARKS (Philadelphia 1961) 135–141; *Old Testament Theology,* tr. D. M. G. STALKER, 2 v. (New York 1962–   ) 1:161–163. J. CHAINE, *Le Livre de la Genèse* (Paris 1951) 147–159.

[N. L. VAILLANCOURT]

NATIVISM, AMERICAN

Described by its historian (J. Higham, 4) as "intense opposition to an internal minority on the ground of its foreign (i.e. "un-American") connections." Major nativistic traditions in the U.S. include anti-Catholicism, antiradicalism, and the cult of Anglo-Saxon superiority; its major historical contribution has been the restriction of immigration.

Historical Beginnings. The ideological elements in U.S. nativism, which account in part for its anti-Catholic tradition, include the Protestant origins of 12 of the colonies; Protestant hostility to early Catholic rulers in Maryland; and the secularist ideology animating revolutionary leaders, most of whom regarded Catholicism as outmoded European obscurantism. Antiradicalism was stimulated by conservative horror at European upheavals, especially the French Revolutions of 1789 and 1870 and the Russian Revolution of 1917, and the resultant desire to preserve the U.S. from similar disturbances. Belief in Anglo-Saxon superiority was heightened by fear of loss of power through the growth of immigrant political strength.

The economic and social aspects of nativism include ethnic rivalries; resentment of immigrant competition for labor rewards; anxiety of older immigrants to increase their standing as Americans by discrimination against newer groups; business fear of unionization, countered by business benefits from immigrant labor; and political expediency, directly through exploitation of popular causes or through readiness to employ any weapon for the destruction of dangerous antagonists, and indirectly, by fabricating nativist issues to divert attention from real and disruptive questions (as the Know-Nothing uproar was used to distract the public from the slavery controversy).

Sectionally, nativism assumed different forms. Easterners in a comparatively rigid social structure both opposed the rise of alien elements and feared immigrant conquest of the cities. The prewar South feared European subversion of American institutions, notably slavery, by English abolitionists and by Catholics who might be expected to obey the renewed papal condemnation of slavery by Gregory XVI. J. L. Chapman's *Americanism versus Romanism* (1856) is typical of the latter nativist school. The immigrant was welcomed in the West and post-Civil War South, particularly where communities were rapidly expanding or not fully formed, but as the frontier situation disappeared, competition bred hostility. Frustrated agrarian crusaders tended to seek a simple cause for their failure and found in Catholic, Jew, or immigrant a convenient scapegoat as their fears focused on an alien, depraved Europe and the seemingly foreign-dominated East [see, e.g., C. Vann Woodward, *Tom Watson* (1938)]. Orientals offering cheap labor inspired Pacific coast nativist riots, leading to a 10-year Chinese exclusion act (1882, reenacted 1894, made permanent 1904), the effective commencement of immigration exclusion.

Major Periods of Prevalence. Increasing tensions with revolutionary France, including the expectation of war, led to the imposition of security measures by the Alien and Sedition Acts of 1798. These included the Naturalization Act, extending the prenaturalization period from 5 to 14 years (the old system was restored in 1802); the Alien Act, authorizing the president to expel aliens merely on suspicion of treasonable inclinations or belief in their being a threat to the public safety (this expired in 1802); and the Alien Enemies Act, empowering the president in wartime to imprison or deport enemy subjects. Aimed at Pres. John Adams's Francophile Jeffersonian critics, many of whom were of alien origin, the acts endangered Irish exiles in particular, since their forcible return to British dominions could result in their destruction for United Irishmen affiliations. Although the main struggle and prosecutions took place under the Sedition Act, the Federalist regime remained strongly hostile to Irish radicals, and its minister to London, Rufus King, sought to prevent their coming to the U.S. The identification of John Adams with restrictionist measures was the more tragic in view of his previous history of friendship for Irish patriotic aspirations (see his *Novanglus*), but the violent, incendiary tones of the journalists of the day, coupled with his fear of a Paris-style uprising, led him to become one of the champions of alien repression.

1830 to 1860. The swift economic and territorial expansion of the U.S. brought with it a certain rootlessness and the craving for simple moral solutions. The intellectual simplicity of the religious revivalism that swayed Jacksonian America made for a firmness of moral standard, but it also carried the seeds of intolerance toward faiths alien to itself. The same spirit looked for clear-cut issues in the problems of the day and led to a rapid growth of American conspiracy consciousness that continued for more than a century. The secrecy of Masonic proceedings and of the Catholic confessional became prime targets for the conspiracy seeker, and the anti-Catholicism of the revivalist preachers exacerbated the tendency to see in the Church an anti-American menace. Thus the mob burning of the Ursuline Convent at Charlestown, Mass., on Aug. 11, 1834, was the sequel to three violently anti-Catholic sermons delivered in Boston the previous day by the Presbyterian clergyman Lyman *Beecher.

Anti-Masonry first emerged following the unaccountable disappearance of William Morgan (September 1826), a renegade Mason who proposed to publish the secrets of the order. Anti-Masonry forces organized a political party in New York State (1830) and contested the next presidential election under the banner of William Wirt, who carried only Vermont. Ambitious politicians (W. H. Seward, Thurlow Weed, Thaddeus Stevens) used the party in their own interest and abruptly deserted it when voters lost interest in the issue. After 1836 the party disappeared. The European origins of Masonry were among the aspects of the order under attack, but it was chiefly its role as precursor of nativistic parties that won anti-Masonry its significance in U.S. history.

Even movements of purely American origin, such as Mormonism, suffered persecution at the hands of their neighbors for divergence from the American religious norm and for economic discrimination against "Gentiles" during these years, but the most bitter hostility was reserved for Catholicism. The 1830s saw the emergence of a stream of anti-Catholic propaganda in magazines, newspapers, pamphlets, and books. These included pleas for curbing Catholic immigration, opposition to Catholic schools and officeholders [e.g., "Brutus" (Samuel F. B. Morse), " Foreign Conspiracy Against the Liberties of the United States" (1834)], and organs avowedly seeking the conversion of Catholics, of which the *American Protestant Vindicator* (1834–42), edited by Rev. W. C. Brownlee proclaimed itself the champion. Brownlee and his followers maintained they could save the "wretchedly deluded votaries" of Catholicism only by a zealous exposure of the alleged iniquities of that religion. Such exposés wasted little space on purely doctrinal controversy, but were devoted to revelations of plots hatched in Austria and elsewhere for the enslavement or mass murder of American Protestants by immigrant Catholic hordes, agitation against Catholic schools then becoming popular among many non-Catholics, and allegations respecting the sexual morals of nuns and clerics.

Some anti-Catholic crusaders sought to the best of their ability to keep such charges as they made within the realm of the verifiable, but in popularity and number they were far outstripped by the myth-makers. A craving for pornography without attendant guilt feelings was satisfied by a perusal of many anti-Catholic tracts that

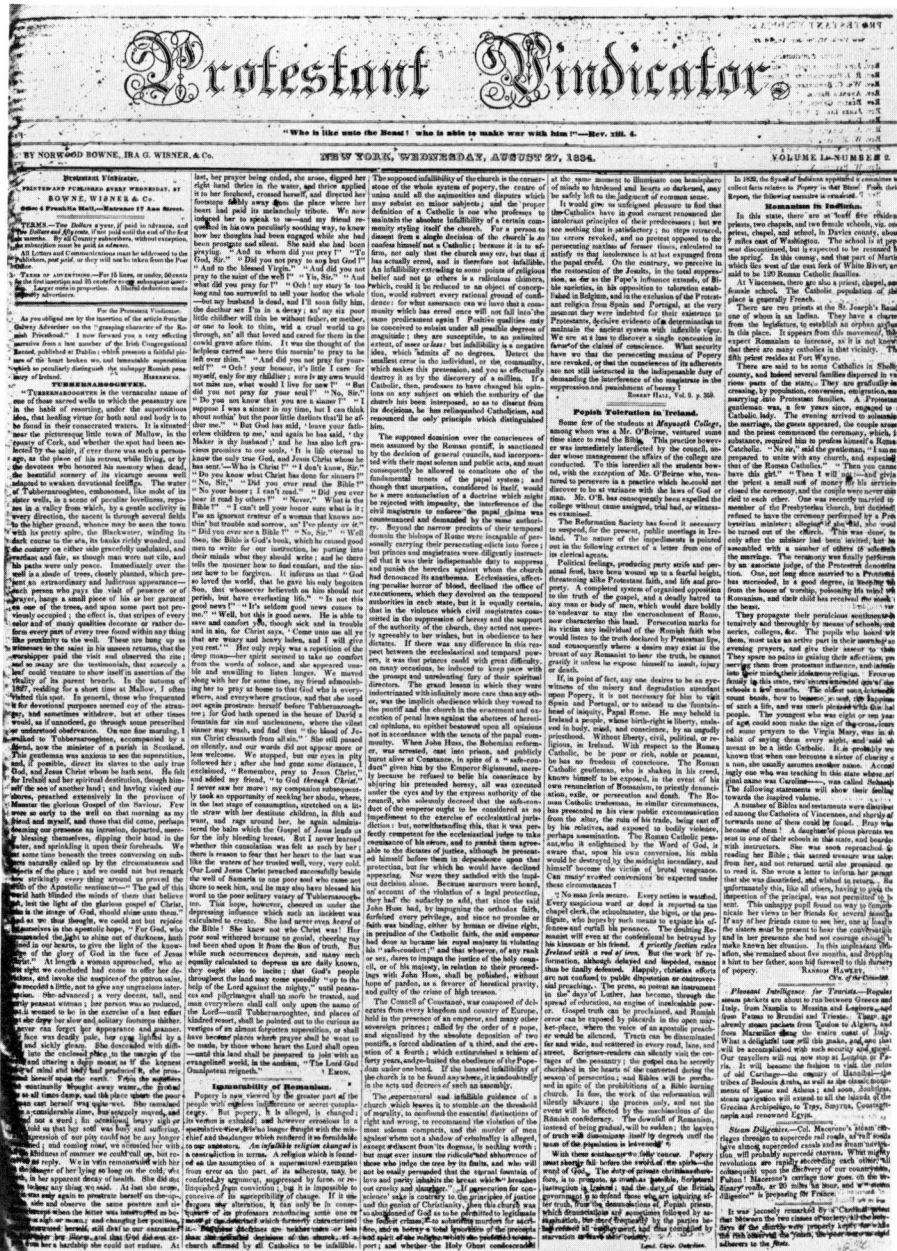

First page of the "Protestant Vindicator" for Aug. 27, 1834. The headlines "Immutability of Romanism," "Popish Toleration in Ireland," and "Romanism in Indiana" are typical of the sentiments communicated throughout the history of the newspaper.

in their efforts to attract an audience were an easy prey to the temptation for bawdy improvisation on the themes of convent and confessional, as exploited by priests for purposes of sexual outlet. The most celebrated of these publications, the *Awful Disclosures of the Hotel Dieu Nunnery of Montreal* (1836) and its sequel, both allegedly the work of an ex-inmate, Maria Monk, branded the institution in question as a nest of debauchery, infanticide, murder, and rape, all described in detail and profusely illustrated. Actually, Maria Monk was an impostor of apparently deranged mind, whose persuasively written work was probably the offspring of overzealous Protestant ministers into whose hands she fell. Her charges were extensively examined and refuted by public-spirited Protestant writers, notably Col. William L. Stone, no friend to Catholicism. But the book, even after the lapse of Maria Monk into drunkenness, prostitution, and theft (she died in prison in 1849), was reprinted many times for dissemination in anti-Catholic crusades.

Clashes between Protestant and Catholic mobs fanned the flames, as did the American renewal of Orange-Catholic hostility originating in Ireland. Catholic protests against reading the King James Bible in public school, and demands for public aid to parochial schools also added fuel to the controversy. Chief areas of anti-Catholic sentiment in this phase were New York City and Philadelphia, Pa., where in the summer of 1844, 20 died and 100 were injured in Orange-Catholic riots. The Irish Great Famine (1845–52) sent 1,250,000 starving Irish immigrants to the U.S. between 1845 and 1855. Since their destitution prevented migration to the West, they choked the Eastern cities, radically and suddenly altering them. Native American opinion, while philanthropically disposed to assist the impoverished in Ireland, was dismayed at the hitherto unparalleled experience of a pauper immigration on such a scale, and as the political bosses sought to make capital from the new arrivals, anger mounted. The Native American party (founded 1845) and its successor (the Know-Nothing, or American, party of the 1850s) called for drastic changes in naturalization laws. *Know-Nothingism reached its greatest strength in 1855, but it split on the slavery issue, with the Southern forces left in control. Former President Millard Fillmore, the party candidate in 1856, carried Maryland alone, after which the party declined. The Civil War, in which many immigrants distinguished themselves, destroyed nativism for a time; war hysteria was turned against "Copperheads."

The nativistic character of Know-Nothingism was revealingly illustrated by the fact that the Know-Nothings specifically exempted Louisiana Catholic Creoles (some of whom joined the party) from charges of participation in the Catholic conspiracy against the U.S. Because the Creoles, unlike Maryland Catholics, had maintained a separate identity in the face of Catholic immigration, their "American-ness"—of which, on the slavery issue, they gave proof—was therefore unquestioned. On the other hand, descendants of English or Irish colonial settlers attracted suspicion because they permitted themselves to be the summit of a Catholic social ladder of which the pauper Irish immigrants were the base.

1886 to 1896. Increased immigration, intensification of the labor-capital struggle, and concern over the strength of Catholic political bosses contributed to a renewal of nativism in the late 1880s. Antiradicalism and anti-Catholicism joined in protest against Cardinal James Gibbons's championship of the *Knights of Labor, which, led by the Catholic Terence V. Powderly, reached its zenith in membership in 1886. The Haymarket bomb-throwing in Chicago, Ill. (May 1, 1886), unleashed a tide of antilabor sentiment not restricted to the anarchists associated with the incident. Foreign-born leadership in labor and socialist and anarchist movements became the focus of protest, while the *American Protective Association (APA) revived the anti-Catholic issue, utilizing the old methods of propaganda and issues of attack as well as enmity to the Knights of Labor. The APA declined after 1896. Meanwhile, labor unions themselves were swinging toward immigration restriction in their opposition to the challenge of foreign labor. In 1897 the American Federation of Labor (AFL) officially endorsed the demand for a literacy test, thereby joining hands with Boston intellectuals banded together in the Immigration Restriction League, whose most vociferous spokesman in Congress was Sen. Henry Cabot Lodge. Pres. Grover Cleveland's veto of a bill embodying the literacy provision (February 1897) frustrated their efforts, and nativism suffered a setback following the return of prosperity and the redirecting of nationalism by the Spanish-American War and its attendant climate of expansionism.

1905 to 1930. Nativism in the late 19th and early 20th century was marked by a more sophisticated intellectual racism than the earlier crude glorification of the Anglo-Saxon. Social Darwinism was adapted to assign to the immigrant the role of unfittest in his native country; eugenics was employed to assail "degenerate breeding-stocks"; and anthropology, classifying the races under Nordic (fair longhead), Alpine (roundhead), etc., rather than national categories, was pressed into service as part of the nativist's intellectual equipment. Glorification of the Nordic race and lamentation for the corruption introduced by immigrants of "inferior" racial origin were the themes of Madison Grant's *The Passing of the Great Race* (1916) that, largely ignored at first publication, became widely influential after the war. Such ideas, filtered through to the political world, led to a new departure in nativist attitudes as they were renewed; henceforth hostility was turned chiefly against the Mediterranean peoples, who had been immigrating in substantially increasing numbers in recent years. Ironically, those most bitterly assailed as factors liable to cause degeneration of the American people included Southeast European Jews, Southern Italians, and Greeks, whose ancestors had laid the foundations of western Judeo-Christian civilization.

Anti-Catholicism was kept alive, notably in the South, by such journals as *Tom Watson's Magazine* and the *Menace* (whose circulation reached a peak of 1,500,000 in 1915). Aggressive nationalism mounted during the war years against the hitherto largely unassailed German-Americans, and later against pacifists, socialists, anarchists, and radicals of all kinds. In the high tide of retreat from internationalism after the war, the great red scare of 1919 [see Robert K. Murray, *Red Scare* (1955)] included both a widespread deportation of Soviet sympathizers by Attorney General A. Mitchell Palmer and violent physical assaults on left-wing groups, notably the Industrial Workers of the World (IWW), by such nativist elements as the American Legion. In 1920, writes Higham (p. 263), "while the redemption of the alien ebbed . . ., the old drive for the rejection of the immigrant passed all previous bounds."

Anti-Semitism, supplanting anti-Catholicism in the nativist response to the radical challenge, found expression in the widely disseminated and fraudulent "Protocols of the Elders of Zion," which laid the Bolshevist successes in Russia at the door of the Jews. The *Dearborn Independent* (1919–27) was perhaps the spearhead of the anti-Jewish attack. The revived *Ku Klux Klan, however, was undiscriminating in its nativism; Negroes, Jews, Catholics, and the foreign-born of all kinds came literally under its lash. The new motion picture industry gave assistance to the Klan by a production glorifying its predecessor of Reconstruction days based on Thomas Dixon's *The Clansman* (1905) and entitled *Birth of a Nation* (released 1915). The anti-Catholic aspect of the Klan first came to prominence in 1920 and flourished thereafter. Its power flowed far beyond the South to the Middle West and Far West, and membership at its apogee reached 5 million (Indiana and Oregon being areas of outstanding strength). Scandals tore it asunder after 1925; in its heyday the outrages charged against it, including murder, had come to an impressive figure.

This national fever of xenophobia received congressional acknowledgment in the revival of immigration restriction. The AFL, its nativism aggravated by reaction to the IWW challenge, continued to agitate in this cause. Congressmen who enjoyed labor support tried to catch the immigrant vote as well, but rural nativist forces, led by the anti-IWW, anti-Japanese Congressman Albert Johnson of Washington, demanded suspension of immigration. A compromise measure, restricting immigrants to 3 per cent of each nationality in the population according to the 1910 census, became law (May 19, 1921). Thus was born the quota system, a feature of all subsequent restrictionist legislation. The literacy test had been embodied in legislation passed over Pres. Woodrow Wilson's veto in 1917.

The quota was altered to 2 per cent of the 1890 census for each nationality group, and the maximum quota halved from 357,000 (1924); the maximum quota was further reduced to 150,000 a year with apportionment by nationality on the basis of the national population situation in 1920 (a provision of the 1924 law, but not actually effected until 1929). Satiated by this revolutionary alteration in U.S. immigration policy, nativism (or 100 per cent Americanism, as it called itself) waned in this postwar phase. The nomination of Gov. Alfred E. Smith of New York by the Democrats for the 1928 presidential election rekindled some of the flames, but without significant effect; the administration candidate, Herbert Hoover, was invincible regardless of his opponent. Smith's nomination was in itself testimony to nativism's losses.

After 1930. Sporadic outbreaks of nativism accompanied the Depression years, notably as an American accompaniment to the rise of European Fascism. The anti-Semitic campaigns of Rev. Charles E. Coughlin, whose radio addresses led his superiors to silence him, had their Protestant equivalent in the diatribes of Rev. Gerald L. K. Smith, former follower of Louisiana demagogue Huey Long. An undercurrent of racism was kept alive by the anti-Negro agitators of the South, notably Sen. Theodore G. Bilbo of Mississippi. Publisher William Randolph Hearst, Elizabeth Dilling, and others sought to foment a second red scare in 1934–35, and the sensitive area of education once more became the focus of witch-hunts against alleged seduction of the innocent [see Walter Metzger, *Academic Freedom in the Age of the University* (1955)]. Meanwhile, the American Civil Liberties Union recorded the greatest "variety and number of serious violations of civil liberties" since the war. Seven state legislatures enacted teachers' oath statutes, but this was a measure of the failure to fulfill nativist promise, as far more had been debated. The crusade, fascist in character, identifying mild liberals with Communists, proved immediately ugly but ultimately it was somewhat harmless.

World War II destroyed anti-Semitism as a political force in American life, but brought with it much injustice to Japanese-Americans, interned for the duration. In a Supreme Court decision [*Korematsu v. U.S.* (1944)] Japanese exclusion from the West Coast was upheld. The burden of proof of loyalty was thrust upon the unfortunate Japanese-Americans, although the Court, in *Ex parte Endo* (1944), denied that a person of proved loyalty could be detained. Many innocent Americans of Japanese extraction suffered socially, as well as from the danger of internment. The House Committee on Un-American Activities, an instrument of nativism by definition, was given permanent status in 1945.

With the advent of the cold war, nativism obtained a fresh lease on life. The Communist ideology of America's chief antagonist, the U.S.S.R., offered easy rewards to the superpatriot who chose to confine himself to fighting the cold war at home. The third red scare shook America to its foundations and culminated in the McCarthy hearings. Sen. Joseph *McCarthy of Wisconsin attracted perhaps the greatest body of support and opprobrium for his exploitation of the disloyalty issue; the better entrenched Sen. Patrick *McCarran of Nevada employed the scare for the preparation of nativist legislation that would outlast it. The Internal Security (McCarran) Act of 1951 forced Communists and Communist-front bodies to register as agents of a foreign power, dedicated to overthrow the U.S. government by violence, thus rendering them liable to imprisonment under the Alien Registration (Smith) Act of 1940. The Smith and McCarran Acts tightened control on aliens, the latter measure excluding from the U.S. any member or foreign member of a totalitarian organization (in practice this has not been employed against Fascists). The McCarran-Walter Act (1952) codified existing immigration laws, increasing their rigidity; screening measures were introduced to weed out subversives. Both McCarran bills became law over presidential veto.

The destruction of many innocent reputations through congressional investigation and the demoralization of the diplomatic and military arms of government through the same process ultimately brought about McCarthy's overthrow (1954). The ensuing revulsion and McCarran's death (1953) ended the most violent phase of latter-day nativism. Many political and social legacies remained, however, and small Fascist organizations (e.g., the John Birch Society) continued to manifest extreme nativism. Anti-Catholic propaganda declined during the cold war, except among a small, though much publicized, minority. The most celebrated of these was Paul Blanshard, who sought to identify the Kremlin with the Vatican in the public mind. Blanshard's liberal origins, combined with the antilibertarian aspects of Catholicism cited by him, placed an attractive gloss on what was merely a reassertion of the old charge that Catholicism was un-American; his works fostered a suspicion of Catholics among liberals of shallow mind. Blanshard avoided the usual charges of clerical immorality and Catholic conspiracy for the mass murder of Protestants; this concession to modern standards of objectivity was not imitated by the anti-Catholicism evoked by the Democratic nomination for the presidency of another Catholic, John F. Kennedy. Although nativism may have accounted for some votes against Kennedy, his election and subsequent assassination probably destroyed anti-Catholicism as a force in American life. By the national character of his appeal, in life and after death, Kennedy offered proof of what nativists had so long denied, namely, that a descendant of pauper, "undesirable" immigrants could prove himself a representative and patriotic American.

Effects on U.S. The nativism written on the statute books since 1921 did much to isolate the U.S. from currents of world opinion and the realities of foreign situations, a particularly perilous contribution in terms of the country's international responsibilities. It constituted a denial of the freedom and receptivity of American society, two traits whereby the U.S. came to enjoy her role as a leader in the spread of democracy and liberty. It fostered a negative nationalism, founded on hatred, that continued to corrode a true patriotism; it became an ally of the cause of discrimination against, and segregation of, American Negro citizens. By making conformity a virtue, nativism immeasurably eroded the force of one of the traditions that had built America—a constant readiness to respond to the challenge of the unknown.

Effects on Catholicism in U.S. Although few Catholics were driven from their faith by nativist outbreaks, a heavily nativist climate probably had more corrosive effects, notably in the South and parts of the West where Catholics lacked numbers to give one another moral reassurance. The Catholic response to nativist attack at times lacked wisdom, but seldom courage. It also had less pleasant features. Thus Catholics failed to unite with other minority groups under attack, e.g., Negroes and Jews, but rather tended, especially in the 20th century, to welcome the turning aside of nativist wrath in other directions. Intergroup hostility among immigrants themselves abetted this tendency. Ultimately, it is to be feared that nativism fostered in American Catholicism an intense zeal to cleanse itself of the un-American stigma at all costs. During the slavery crisis, Catholics, regardless of Gregory XVI's teachings, temporized on the slavery issue and strongly denounced the un-Americanism of the abolitionists. A century later, Catholics had so readily identified themselves with the prevailing impulse to conform to the American attitude, that, for instance, "the American Church," in Richard Hofstadter's phrase, "absorbed little of the impressive scholarship of German Catholicism or the questioning intellectualism of the French Church" [*Anti-Intellectualism in American Life* (1963), 138]. Moreover, the Protestant nativist, who clamored for further restriction of immigration and saw in every liberal academic a Communist incendiary, found allies among the Catholics, who had formerly been targets for his most bitter bigotry. The tragedy lies in the fact that nativism, taken at its word, was confounded with truly American patriotism even by its former victims.

Bibliography: R. A. BILLINGTON, *The Protestant Crusade, 1800–1860* (New York 1938). C. J. BARRY et al., Symposium on Nativism in CathHistRev 44 (1958) 137–164. O. HANDLIN, *Race and Nationality in American Life* (Boston 1957). M. A. JONES, *American Immigration* (Chicago 1960). M. L. HANSEN, *The Immigrant in American History* (Cambridge, Mass. 1940). M. A. RAY, *American Opinion of Roman Catholicism in the 18th Century* (New York 1936). J. HIGHAM, *Strangers in the Land: Patterns of American Nativism, 1860–1925* (New Brunswick, N.J. 1955). **Illustration credit:** Library of Congress.

[O. D. EDWARDS]

NATIVITY OF CHRIST.

The date of the birth of *Jesus Christ can be calculated only approximately; the most probable date seems to be about the year 7 or 6 B.C. It is well known that the calculations of *Dionysius Exiguus upon which the system of determining the year of Christ's birth is based are in error. Matthew 2.1 says that the birth of Christ took place in the days of King *Herod (the Great). It is known from *Josephus that Herod died in the spring of the year 4 B.C. In the 15th year of Tiberius, Jesus was about 30 years old (Lk 3.23); this would be the year A.D. 28–29. One may date Christ's birth more precisely from the information given by Lk 2.2 that the birth took place at the time of the census under Cyrinus. Cyrinus was Publius Sulpicius Quirinius, who was governor of the province of Syria. During his

The Nativity of Christ, woodcut, 1958, by the contemporary Japanese artist Ryusei Furukawa (1894–   ).

administration a census took place in Judea previous to the incorporation of that kingdom into the province of Syria upon the deposition of Archelaus in A.D. 6. This census took place while Caesar Augustus was ruling the Roman Empire (30 B.C.–A.D. 14). The relationship of the census under Quirinius to the imperial census is a matter of perplexity for historians. Perhaps Quirinius inaugurated the census under a special commission in 6 or 7 B.C. after his first term as governor and completed it by a better known census during his second term, A.D. 6 to 12. No further precision of the date can be made, since the date of December 25 does not correspond to Christ's birth but to the feast of the *Natalis Solis Invicti*, the Roman sun festival at the solstice.

According to Matthew and Luke, Jesus Christ was born in Bethlehem, a village in Judea about 6 miles south of Jerusalem, slightly to the west. The place is mentioned in the Gospel account to show Christ's Davidic ancestry, since Bethlehem is the city of David. The fact of the birth at Bethlehem is not stated anywhere else in the NT; the account in Jn 7.40–42 implies the ignorance of the people regarding the birth of Christ in Bethlehem. There was no apologetic reason for the Gospel writers to invent the Bethlehem birthplace merely to confirm Christ's Davidic origin, since the popular belief at the time did not suppose that the Messiah would come from Bethlehem. There is no written evidence in Jewish tradition for the Bethlehem birthplace of the Messiah before the 3d century A.D. The popular thought in Our Lord's time was that the birthplace of the Messiah was unknown, and that when He came, He would present Himself in such a way that no one would know where He came from. Since it would have served no useful purpose for the early Christians to invent Christ's birth in Bethlehem, one must conclude that He was actually born there. Mi 5.1 is obscure.

Bibliography: J. BLINZLER, LexThK² 2:422–425. A. BEA and U. HOLZMEISTER, EncCatt 4:1011–20. Robert-Tricot 2:123–146. U. HOLZMEISTER, *Chronologia vitae Christi* (Rome 1933). H. U. INSTINSKY, *Das Jahr der Geburt Christi* (Munich 1957). B. BOTTE, *Les Origines de la Noël et de l'Épiphanie* (Louvain 1932). **Illustration credit:** Mr. and Mrs. Ross W. Sloniker Collection of Twentieth Century Biblical and Religious Prints, The Cincinnati Art Museum.

[R. L. FOLEY]

NATIVITY OF MARY

Sacred Scripture mentions nothing specifically about Mary's conception and birth. What is known of her nativity derives principally from the Apocrypha—books that are generally unreliable historically but that sometimes incorporate genuine traditions, some of which have found their way into the Church's liturgy.

In the Apocrypha. The oldest (c. A.D. 150) and basic Apocryphon referring to Mary's nativity is entitled Birth of Mary: Revelation of James [Papyrus Bodmer V] or, more popularly (since Postel, 1552), Protoevangelium of James. Its anonymous and probably Judeo-Christian author, indignant at anti-Marian calumnies of the time, glorified the Virgin *Mother of God in what amounts to a primitive Mariology. The opening five chapters of the work describe the miraculous, though not necessarily "immaculate," conception and birth of Mary. Joachim and Anne, a wealthy couple elderly and childless, beseech God to remove the humiliation of sterility and grant them a child. Each is assured separately by an angel that their prayers had been heard, and Mary is born after 7 [9] months. Some versions and recensions of the Protoevangelium, understanding the angel's assurance to Joachim in a past tense, suggest a virginal conception in Anne's womb. Later pertinent Apocrypha (Gospel of Pseudo-Matthew, probably 8th–9th centuries; Gospel of the Birth of Mary, a shortened form of Pseudo-Matthew; a Syriac-Armenian Infancy Gospel; and some Coptic Lives of the Virgin) all rest on and repeat evidence of the Protoevangelium.

Mary's Birthplace and Davidic Descent. According to Lk 1.26 Mary was living at *Nazareth when she conceived her divine Son. In the absence of further scriptural data some presume that Nazareth would have been her own birthplace. In much later Apocrypha (e.g., Gospel of the Birth of Mary), Nazareth is given as the home of Joachim and Anne. The Protoevangelium of James supposes that Mary was conceived and born in Jerusalem, a tradition supported by later writers and by remnants of a small oratory (c. A.D. 300) in Jerusalem, above which the 5th-century basilica of St. Anne was built.

It is still disputed whether Mary, like Joseph, was of David's line. Some see the genealogies in Matthew ch. 1 and Luke ch. 3 as referring only to Joseph's forebears, not Mary's. They point out that Elizabeth, Mary's relative, was of Aaronitic descent (Lk 1.5), which might indicate that Mary too was of a priestly family. However, a tradition going as far back as Ignatius of Antioch (*Eph.* 18.2; 20.2; *Rom.* 7.3; *Smyrn.* 1.1) and Justin Martyr (1 *Apol.* 32; *Dial.* 43.45, 100, 120), based on NT texts that seem to refer to Christ's descent from David according to the flesh [Lk 1. (27), 32, 69; Rom 1.3)], testify to Mary's Davidic lineage; cf. also Tertullian *De carne Christi* 22; Augustine *Cons. Evang.* 2.2.4; Pseudo-James; and Pseudo-Matthew. More probably, then, Mary's parents were descendants of David, and Mary's Son was the Son of David according to the flesh, not merely legally through the putative fatherhood of Joseph.

See also ANNE AND JOACHIM, SS.; BIBLE, III (CANON), 5; IMMACULATE CONCEPTION; MARY, BLESSED VIRGIN, ARTICLES ON.

Bibliography: M. LINDGREN-TRIDELL, "Der Stammbaum Maria aus Anna und Joachim," *Marburger Jahrbuch für Kunstwissen-schaft* 11–12 (1938–39) 289–308. A. MERK, "Das Marienbild des Neuen Bundes," in *Katholische Marienkunde*, ed. P. STRÄTER, 3 v. (Paderborn 1947–51) 1:44–84. O. CULLMANN, "Infancy Gospels," in *New Testament Apocrypha*, ed. E. HENNECKE et al. (Philadelphia 1963–) 1:363– . A. RUSH, "Mary in the Apocrypha of the N.T.," Carol Mariol 1:156–184. DB 4:780–781.

[E. MAY]

NATURAL LAW

A *law or rule of action that is implicit in the very *nature of things. The term is sometimes used in the plural form to designate laws that regulate the activities of nature in both the organic and the inorganic realm (*see* PHYSICAL LAWS). More properly, however, it is applied exclusively to man and designates a rule of conduct that proceeds from human nature as rational. For St. Thomas Aquinas, "natural law is nothing other than the participation of eternal law in rational creatures" (ST 1a2ae, 91.2); thus Aquinas conceives it as the imprint of God's providential plan on man's natural reason.

This article is divided into three main sections. The first treats of the historical development of the concept of natural law; the second provides a Thomistic analysis of the concept; and the third discusses the place of the concept in contemporary theology and philosophy. (For specific applications of the concept, *see* NATURAL LAW AND JURISPRUDENCE; NATURAL LAW IN ECONOMICS; NATURAL LAW IN POLITICAL THOUGHT.)

HISTORICAL DEVELOPMENT

Although natural law has always been perceived in its basic content by human beings, its concept has been formalized, elaborated, articulated, and systematized only with the growth and development of philosophy. The historical evolution of this doctrine may be conveniently traced through five periods: (1) the pagan period, corresponding to that of the Greco-Roman world and extending from *Heraclitus to St. Paul; (2) the Catholic and scholastic period, extending from St. Paul to Hugo *Grotius; (3) the Protestant and post-scholastic period, extending from Grotius and S. von Pufendorf (1632–94) to J. *Bentham; (4) the period of decline, corresponding to the rise of positivism and extending from Bentham and D. *Hume to F. Gény (1861–1959) and R. Stammler (1856–1938); and (5) the contemporary period of revival, extending from Gény and Stammler to the mid-1960s.

Greco-Roman Period. There is evidence of the idea of a universal divine law binding on man in Oriental literature, such as that of China, long before the rise of philosophy in the West. But the origin of a natural-law doctrine, with its elaboration as an unbroken, continuous development, is first to be found among the ancient Greek poets and historians. Thus Sophocles (c. 497–406 B.C.), Thucydides (c. 460–400 B.C.), and Xenophon (c. 427–355 B.C.) presented a concept of the natural law that is divine, universal, and known to all.

Greek Philosophers. A development of this early Greek notion appears in the writings of Heraclitus, who held that the natural law is eternal and immutable, the foundation of human laws (*Fragments* 102, 112–116). Other Greek philosophers, such as *Plato, elucidated this doctrine (*Laws* 715, 884–910; *Rep.* 419–445). It was left to Plato's student *Aristotle, however, to clarify the distinction between natural law and law that is humanly enacted (*Eth. Nic.* 1134b 18–1136a 9; *Rhet.* 1373b 1–18).

Such Greek philosophers used observation and experience to discover an order in the universe that they associated with a predictable, regular recurrence of events. Traceable to the activity of animate and inanimate matter, this recurrence is in response to an ordering principle or law that rules the cosmos. But man also is part of the cosmos and hence subject to an ordering law, which in his case is the right or just by nature. Morals and human law, for the Greeks, thus have their foundation in the harmony of nature or the natural law. This law exists independently of human will and has universal validity. It provides objective principles and ideals to which human beings must conform, by their very nature, as part of the cosmos.

Functionally, therefore, natural law affords a measure for the wise, the good, the just, the prudent, and the happy man. It provides too a basis for an idealized political and social order. It also makes possible the distinction between the category of divine, universal, and unchangeable law and that of human, politically enacted, and variable law. But the idea of natural law at this stage of its evolution tends to subordinate the individual to the Greek city-state. Even for Aristotle, individual man achieves the perfection of his human nature through law only in the good order of the city-state, which is analogous to the cosmic order (*Pol.* 1252a 1–1253a 38).

The doctrine of natural law reached its highest development in the pagan world within *Stoicism, the philosophical movement founded by Zeno of Citium (*c.* 336–*c.* 264 B.C.). Characteristic of Zeno's teaching and that of other Stoic philosophers, such as Chrysippus (*c.* 280–*c.* 208 B.C.), was the thesis that man is a citizen of the world. Thus emphasis was placed on the nature of man as such and not merely as related to political society. A broader society consequently results from human nature itself, which is subject to the law of right reason. The individual thus comes to be recognized as a moral unit who is governed by universal law, which prescribes a pattern of behavior that is discoverable by reason. In this way, law and justice are seen as transcending the confines of the city-state.

Roman Thought. After the military conquest of Greece by Rome *c.* 146 B.C., the Stoic idea of natural law began to infiltrate the Roman world. *Cicero played an important role in interpreting and disseminating this idea. For him, natural law is the highest reason implanted in nature, transcending space and time; it is eternal and unchangeable, the same in Rome as in Athens. Coming from God, it commands what is to be done and forbids what is to be avoided. It precedes written law and the state. More specifically, it embodies basic principles (e.g., the right of self-defense against aggression), regulates justice (giving to each his due), and promotes the common good. It also forbids fraud and theft.

Whereas among the Greeks the philosophy of natural law was directed mainly, though not exclusively, toward human conduct in general, among the Romans it was related chiefly to the juridical and legal orders. The natural right, or the just by nature, therefore became the *ius naturale* of the Roman jurists, i.e., a speculative body of universal moral ideas and principles.

The *ius civile,* or body of legal precepts, was applied exclusively to Roman citizens. But eventually, after Rome became a great maritime and trading center, it became necessary to supplement the *ius civile* with the *ius gentium,* or body of law for foreigners. As positive law, the *ius gentium* was constructed from the common denominator of principles obtaining in the various legal systems of countries from which foreigners came. The policy of using this common denominator was rationalized on the grounds that it was only the implementation of the *ius naturale,* the expression of universal reason.

By the end of the classical age of Roman jurisprudence, i.e., about 300 years after the death of Cicero, hundreds of texts had referred to *ius naturale, naturalis ratio,* and *rerum natura.* Thus Ulpian (d. A.D. 228), the great Roman jurist, stated that insofar as the *ius civile* is concerned, slaves are not regarded as persons; nevertheless, this is not true under natural law because under that law all men are equal (*Digest* 50.17.32). Ulpian was obviously referring to the natural law when he wrote that the precepts of the law are to live honestly, to harm no one, and to render each his own (*Institutes* 1.1.3; *Digest* 1.1.10). Most Roman jurists, such as Gaius (2d century A.D.), oriented the legal order toward the natural law primarily by following the standard of objective right reason as manifested in experience (*Institutes* 1.156, 158).

Catholic and Scholastic Period. Although the Fathers of the early Christian Church generally emphasized the supernatural law of theology rather than the natural law of philosophy, there were several notable exceptions. Among these were St. *Paul, St. *John Chrysostom, St. *Augustine, and St. *Isidore of Seville, all of whom borrowed Stoic ideas in describing the interrelationship between natural and supernatural laws. The Stoics had been uncertain as to whether the ultimate source of natural law was personal and divine or whether it was immanent in nature in the sense of *pantheism. It was impossible for them to synthesize natural law with the myths of the pagan religions of their time. In this area, the Fathers of the Church, and later the scholastics, were able to supply new insights based on supernatural revelation.

Early Christianity. St. Paul, the Apostle of the Gentiles, wrote that the natural law is inscribed in the hearts of all men, even though all do not have the Law (of Sinai) of divine revelation (Rom 2.12–16). St. John Chrysostom taught that the natural law is promulgated through man's conscience, which supplies the basis of human law (*Ad pop. ant.* 12). According to St. Augustine, the *ius naturale* comes from a personal, all-wise, and all-powerful God, the same God who has authored the Christian Scriptures; hence natural law is not derived from nature in the pantheistic sense (*Civ* 11.4.2). St. Isidore of Seville held that all laws are either divine or human and that *ius naturale* is the law observed everywhere by the instinct of nature, such as that ordaining the marriage of man and woman, the procreation and rearing of children, and the like. It is not human positive law (*On Laws* 4).

Canonists. The canonists, especially as seen in the *Decretum* of *Gratian, were chiefly responsible for transmitting the interrelationship between natural and supernatural law that had been worked out by the Fathers to the golden age of scholastic philosophy. According to Gratian, all justice is founded on natural law, which is of divine origin (*Decretum* 1). This law goes back to the beginning of mankind; its content is to be found in the Ten Commandments and the Gospel, which dictates the golden rule of doing to others what one wishes done to oneself. A decade after Gratian, the canonist *Rufinus referred to the natural law as the divine power that nature implants in man, impelling him to do good and avoid evil (*Summa Decretorum*).

Thomistic Concept. But it remained for St. *Thomas Aquinas to perfect the idea of natural law. This he did by distinguishing in the natural law of the Stoics and in the *ius naturale* of the Romans the *lex aeterna* and the *lex naturalis.* The eternal law is the divine providence governing the cosmos, man, and matter, both animate and inanimate. It proceeds from the intellect and will of God. Natural law is that part of the eternal law that is applicable to man alone. Natural law is in accord with man's nature (ST 1a2ae, 91.2–4).

Subrational creatures and inanimate matter must obey the eternal law, but man can disobey it because he has freedom as to moral choice. However, he ought to obey the eternal law, i.e., the part that governs him, or natural law; for otherwise he violates his nature. Thus did Aquinas correct the error of Ulpian, who is quoted in Justinian's *Digest* (6th century A.D.) as having declared that the law of nature is not peculiar to the human race but belongs to all creatures (1.1.1–4). Ulpian had made the natural law (a part) identical with the eternal law (the whole). According to Aquinas, *ius naturale* becomes *lex naturalis* insofar as it relates to man. By this semantic change he gave rationally discovered law a statutory connotation, while insisting that natural law has the same source as supernatural law.

But Aquinas did not destroy the rational basis of the pagan, Aristotelian-Stoic doctrine of natural law by substituting the authority of supernatural law, in the sense of truth revealed in the Bible, in its place. Rather, to use a metaphor, he taught that the single coin of divine law is stamped on one side by the supernatural law of Judeo-Christian theology, accepted on faith, through grace, as the word of God, and on the other side by the natural law of philosophy, perceived by reason. Inasmuch as both laws emanate from a single source, they can never be in conflict.

Later Thought. In the 14th century, the Thomistic view of natural law was challenged by some. Thus, *Duns Scotus wrote that *lex naturalis* has no intrinsic connection with the essence of God and hence can be different from what it happens to be (*Op. Oxon.* 1.8.5. 22–23). *William of Ockham held that natural law is wholly the product of divine will; it is divine positive law, or supernatural law, since God is primarily absolute and omnipotent will (*Quodl.* 1.10.3; 1.13). Both deviated, therefore, from the Thomistic idea of natural law by eliminating intellect and reason from its authoritative basis.

But in the 16th century, reason was restored to the doctrine of natural law by Spanish jurist-theologians such as Domingo de *Soto (*De iustitia et iure* 1.5.2) and Francisco *Suárez (*A Treatise on Law and God the Lawgiver* 2.6.5). These thinkers affirmed that the ultimate source of the natural law is in the divine will and intellect; and its proximate principle, in the essence of man. They also emphasized a historical-analytical and comparative-empirical approach that gave content to natural law, particularly in the field of international relations.

Protestant and Postscholastic Period. The outbreak of the *Reformation in the 16th century initiated a new period in the history of the doctrine of natural law. The term natural law had been so long embedded in the thinking of the Western world that philosophers and jurists continued to use it after the Reformation, although they attributed to it an essentially new and heterogeneous content.

Insofar as the theology of the Reformation affirmed the private interpretation of the Scriptures, it led to the rejection of the idea of objective truth in the areas of both supernatural and natural law. The *conscience of the individual became more than the source of personal moral responsibility; it became the measure of truth in all matters of right and wrong, good and evil. Subjective theories of natural law, detached from the element of experience, began to postulate the existence of a state or condition of nature in which man lived before he constructed politically organized society. In this state of nature, there was a "law of nature." Unlike the natural law, the law of nature was not related chiefly to conduct in general or to the legal or theological order, but rather to the political order. This emphasis accompanied the rise of political problems with the emergence and growth of national states and churches.

Law of Nature School. According to the law of nature school, man perceives the natural law by his subjective faculty of reason, which contemplates human nature as an abstract essence existing in a vacuum, apart from time and place. Man determines the content of the law of nature not by induction but by a purely deductive process. (The scholastics had made use of induction here, studying the standard of right reason in relation to historical and contemporary experience.)

The law of nature school exalted the autonomy of the individual faculty of reason; that this led to an excessive *subjectivism is evidenced by the basic disagreement within the school over the state of nature, the content of the law of nature in this aboriginal condition, and its fate once man established politically and legally organized society by a social contract.

Grotius. The contributions of Hugo Grotius effected the transition between the scholastic and the law of nature concepts of natural law. Like the scholastics, Grotius believed in the existence of objective right reason, with resulting immutable principles, and in God as the highest source of natural law (*De iure belli ac pacis* 1.1). Unlike them, he held that the natural law could exist even without a personal and divine Law-Giver, since it had a sufficient basis in reason alone. He also stressed individualism, *rationalism, and the social aspect of rational human nature in reference to natural law (*ibid.* 1.3.8). But he did not go so far as to hold that the social nature of man is the sole source of natural law.

Grotius erred in believing that man once lived in a state of nature under a law of nature that could be derived from man's essence. He taught that it was possible to deduce by strict logic a complete system of principles with universal validity and from these to develop an all-sufficient code of legal rules (*ibid.* prol.) He thus failed to distinguish the immutable aspects of the natural law, the mutable conclusions that result from the application of immutable principles to changing factors, and the positive law that implements both types of principles. Under his law of nature doctrine, therefore, natural law lost the flexibility and dynamism it had enjoyed in the prior periods.

Pufendorf. Samuel von Pufendorf first articulated the concept of the law of nature in its pure or classical form. For him, the *ius naturale* is related to God's will, not to His essence. It is not a participation in the divine law eternally present in God's essence, as Aquinas taught, but came into existence only when God created man, with his impulse toward sociability. The sociable capacity of man is the sole proximate source of natural law, the starting point of speculation in this sphere (*De iure naturae et gentium* 2.3).

Pufendorf considered reason so autonomous that in effect civil law, both substantive and procedural, became natural law, even though in theory he distinguished between natural law and positive law. For him, natural law is only a model law, advisory but not mandatory. Hence the state enacts positive law so that the natural law may be obeyed (*ibid.*).

Hobbes and Locke. The great divergence among the various adherents of the law of nature school may be seen by comparing the views of T. *Hobbes with those of J. *Locke. Hobbes saw the state of nature as a state of war of all against all, in which the life of man is solitary, poor, nasty, brutish, and short. The basic norm is self-preservation, springing from natural law, which is a dictate of right reason regarding things to be done or omitted for the preservation of life and limb. The first fundamental law of nature is that peace be sought, and all other natural laws are derived from this. Morality is rooted, therefore, in peace; this is the reason why agreements must be kept (*Leviathan* 13).

According to Hobbes, the law of nature prescribes that man should form the civil state in order to preserve the fundamental right to life. In establishing the state, however, man surrendered his freedom, equality, and the right to everything he had enjoyed in the state of nature, physical survival alone excepted. This was done by a covenant. The will of the resulting omnipotent state is based on the fundamental principle that agreements must be kept. Man may not morally resist the state because its enactments are natural law. Indeed the state, as the authoritative interpreter of both natural and supernatural law, was transformed into a mortal god in a literal sense. If there is a conflict between a command of the state and the private moral judgment of the individual, Hobbes advises the latter to go to Christ by martyrdom (*ibid.* 18).

But for Locke, contrary to Hobbes, the historical state of nature was a condition of peace, good will, and mutual cooperation. Man enjoyed the right of freedom and equality, as well as the right to work and own property. The law of nature dictated justice, but the authority of civil society was necessary to enforce it. Politically organized society resulted from a *social contract, but the continuing obligation of obedience on the part of the people depends on the proper observance of that contract by the sovereign (*Second Treatise on Civil Government* 19).

For Locke, the natural law is a dictate of practical common sense—a nominalistic symbol for the rights of the individual, reflecting his self-interest. These rights do not emanate from the natural law by intrinsic necessity; rather, they limit the political sovereign and should be enforced by human positive law (*ibid.* 9).

Others. Conceptions of the state of nature and the law of nature found therein were expressed by J. J. *Rousseau (*The Social Contract* 1.8, 2.6, 4.2), C. *Thomasius (*Fundamenta iuris naturae et gentium*), C. *Wolff (*Institutiones iuris naturae et gentium* 2), and others. The term law of nature became so ambiguous that it was used to justify such divergent theories as enlightened despotism, state absolutism, and the omnipotence of the democratic state. The ultimate position was that each individual's reasoning faculty manufactures natural law rather than discovers it.

Kant. The law of nature school ended with I. *Kant, who introduced a new doctrine of natural law. Kant showed that the state of nature was only a historical fiction to explain the foundation of the civil state, since man had always lived in a social state. He struck a decisive blow at the philosophy of the law of nature, which had been ascendant for the prior 2 centuries. In particular, he maintained that man cannot reach the ideal, or perfect, law by a process of pure reason (*The Philosophy of Law* 1; *Introduction to the Metaphysics of Morals* 4.24). Although the formal, subjective elements of the reasoning process do not come from experience, they are valid only insofar as they are referred to experience. Thus did Kant restore the empirical factor to the doctrine of natural law.

Kant projected an individualist idea of natural law in its final and highest form. Freedom of will became the ultimate, supreme, immutable value, a natural inborn right that included all natural rights. He reconciled the conflict between the equally free wills of the various individuals in society by a *categorical imperative—a universal law directing that each individual should so act that the free exercise of his will would enable him to live without interfering with the like freedom of others. Under this theory, natural law is not a part of an eternal law, although the natural law supplies the immutable ideal of freedom upon which the categorical imperative is constructed. The categorical imperative is imposed by a necessity inherent in the very idea of freedom. For Kant, the legal order has no connection with the moral order.

Period of Decline. The natural law tradition reached a high degree of prestige at the end of the 18th century, but gave way in the 19th to *positivism, which held the authority of the state to be supreme in every sense. The reasons for this decline may be enumerated as follows.

Various Factors. First, even before the dawn of the 19th century, D. *Hume laid the groundwork for the widespread assault on natural-law doctrine. A skeptic, he proclaimed that the human mind can never attain the essences of things and that it cannot determine what is intrinsically morally good or evil. Morality is not a matter of idealism but is determined by the sentiment of approval, itself related to the useful. According to Hume, the moral law has no basis in the rational and social nature of man and has no connection with immutable verity.

Second, positivism was promoted by the individualist utilitarians, such as J. *Bentham (*Treatise on Legislation* 13). In place of idealism, Bentham substituted the notion of utility as measured by the greatest good or by the happiness of the greatest number, taking happiness in the sense of personal satisfaction and advantage (*see* UTILITARIANISM). Bentham sought consciously to build a new body of law. He was the forerunner of John Austin (1790–1859), who created the analytical school of jurisprudence, a school widely influential among Anglo-American jurists.

Third, the historical school, founded by F. K. von *Savigny, contributed indirectly to the rise of positivism. It maintained that natural, or ideal, law springs spontaneously from the spirit of a people and is reflected in custom. It is a higher law, found and not made. For this school, customary law, like natural law, limited the authority of the political sovereign to make law. Yet the historical school was positivist in its ultimate philosophy, for it believed that customary law was the result of the will of the people yielding to nonrational impulses and responding to historical necessity rather than to right reason. It fostered positivism by maintaining that only human positive law exists, and this based on human will that is uninhibited by reason.

Fourth, positivism was advanced by the newly emerging science of *sociology, which had its origin in the writings of positivist philosophers such as A. *Comte. Assuming a mechanistic view of the physical universe based on mathematically demonstrable laws that control the activity of nature, it regarded moral and social laws as analogous to the law of gravitation. Sociological jurisprudence later abandoned this approach.

Correctives to the Law of Nature. From the viewpoint of the scholastic doctrine of natural law, it is understandable, however, why the analytical, historical, and sociological schools were able to attract a following. Each of these schools in its own way corrected a deficiency of the pseudoconcept of natural law that had been developed in the 17th and 18th centuries. Whereas Aquinas had visualized man as a rational and social animal who relies on both reason and experience and needs a legal order enforced by a temporal sovereign, the law of nature school overemphasized subjective reason in its analysis. These reactions against the law of nature school were therefore quite legitimate, even though they had little to do with the natural-law doctrine of Aquinas.

The analytical school focused attention on legal analysis and the logical interdependence of legal rules and precepts; it stressed the fact that law is in the external forum and should be enforced by the sovereign. The historical school restored the factor of experience. The sociological school reintroduced the element of the social status of man and the means-ends aspect of law, as maintained by Aquinas. Each of these schools erred, however, by concentrating on one factor to the exclusion of others and by refusing to accept any immutable moral value, such as the dignity of the individual.

Other factors that contributed to the rise of positivism included the search for an explanation to justify absolute political sovereignty in both domestic and foreign affairs, the thrust of moral *relativism related to anthropological studies, the rejection of a priori postulates by the physical sciences, and mistaken ideas about human *evolution, *empiricism, *pragmatism, and materialistic psychiatry.

Period of Revival. A reaction against the sterility and ineffectiveness of positivism began with a revival of natural law doctrine. This revival was led by F. Gény, the neoscholastic (see EncFil 2:645–646), and R. Stammler, the neo-Kantian (see *ibid.* 4:929–930). Both emphasized the sociological aspects of the natural law, an emphasis that has continued throughout the contemporary period.

Scholastic Circles. Gény began the revival in France by considering the social life of the individual as a moral phenomenon governed by the natural law as understood by Aquinas. He used the Thomistic doctrine of natural law to provide a much-needed equitable and sociological interpretation for European codes. Gény's notions received great encouragement from Pope Leo XIII, especially through his encyclicals relating to political and social matters, such as *Libertas* (1888) and *Rerum novarum* (1891), and by succeeding popes (*see* SCHOLASTICISM, 3).

Renewed interest in the scholastic doctrine of natural law as this relates to the legal and social orders began in the U.S. in the 1920s and 1930s. Law reviews sponsored by universities such as Fordham, Detroit, Marquette, Georgetown, and Notre Dame became channels for an ever-growing literature.

The *American Catholic Philosophical Association established a committee on the philosophy of law in the early 1930s that arranged an annual forum for the presentation of papers relating to natural law and the solution of legal and social problems. These expanded further the body of natural-law literature.

The revival of natural-law doctrine was enormously accelerated by the experience of two world wars. After World War II, it was manifest that such a doctrine alone could provide an authoritative basis for upholding the intrinsic dignity of the individual against ruthless dictatorship. The quest for political and legal justice resulted in the rediscovery that there is a moral order and that this springs from an authority beyond the human will.

Interest in the doctrine of the natural law is evidenced in the U.S. by the *Journal of the American Bar Association,* the *Natural Law Forum* of the University of Notre Dame, and the *Catholic Lawyer,* published by the St. Thomas More Institute for Legal Research of St. John's University, New York. Southern Methodist University, Dallas, sponsors an annual symposium on natural law; and Loyola University, New Orleans, an institute on natural law as related to the solution of some contemporary social problem.

The revival of natural-law doctrine has been widespread in Latin America, especially in Argentina and Mexico; in Europe, particularly in Italy, Germany, France, and Spain; and in the Orient.

Nonscholastic Circles. Stammler initiated a revival of the neo-Kantian doctrine of natural law. For him, the content of the natural law is wholly changeable and changing, dependent upon the social ideals and conditions of a particular time and place. Through natural law, all possible individual goals of the community of freely willing men are to be harmonized. He thus reconciled the idea of natural law with the notions of evolution and utility.

The more recent neo-Kantian development in the field of legal philosophy has been led by Giorgio del Vecchio (1878– ; see EncFil 1:1454–56). His position is closer to the Thomistic than that of Stammler. Indeed, the position of Del Vecchio represents the minimal deviation from scholastic doctrine in the modern revival. He admits the existence of a divine Law-Giver who has given man a supernatural law by revelation, but he does not relate this Law-Giver to the natural law. He derives the elements of transcendence and immutability for his juridical idealism from the essence of man rather than deriving them from the divine will and intellect.

Other nonscholastic doctrine of natural law has taken a non-Kantian direction, rejecting any immutable, transcendental, objective ideal of conduct to which man should conform his behavior. Exponents of this type of natural-law doctrine, such as M. R. Cohen (1880–1947), accept the existence only of relative ideals for human conduct. But these ideals do exist a priori in an objective order and do not arise solely from facts. The "ought" stands in juxtaposition to the "is." In ultimate analysis, the ideals are rational and change very slowly.

Other contemporary natural-law writers, such as L. L. Fuller and Jerome Hall, deviate more markedly from the scholastic idea of natural law. They believe that there are ideals for the evaluation of man's conduct, but that these are principally generalizations of what will best advance the social interest.

Bibliography: B. F. BROWN, ed., *The Natural Law Reader* (New York 1960). G. DEL VECCHIO, *Philosophy of Law,* tr. T. O. MARTIN (Washington 1953). A. PASSERIN D'ENTRÈVES, *Natural Law* (London 1951). D. FITZGERALD, "The 'State of Nature' Theories of the 17th and 18th Centuries and Natural Law," ProcAmCathPhilAs 32 (1958) 161–172. J. F. GARCÍA, "The Natural Law," *ibid.* 22 (1947) 1–18. C. A. HART, "Metaphysical Foundations of the Natural Law," *ibid.* 24 (1950) 18–28. J. MARITAIN, *The Rights of Man and Natural Law,* tr. D. C. ANSON (New York 1943); *Man and the State* (Chicago 1951). Notre Dame Univ., *Natural Law Institute: Proceedings,* v.1–5 (1947–1951). R. POUND, "The Revival of Natural Law," *Notre Dame Lawyer* 17 (1941–42) 287–372. H. A. ROMMEN, *The Natural Law,* tr. T. A. HANLEY (St. Louis 1947).

[B. F. BROWN]

THOMISTIC ANALYSIS

Natural law, as can be seen from its history, has been the subject of much controversy. A partial explanation for this is that advocates of natural law have frequently ignored its ontological basis and adopted as their starting point what they considered the distinctive characteristic of human nature. As each proponent had his own concept of human nature, it was inevitable that each would have his own peculiar philosophy of natural law. Yet when viewed in isolation from its ontological origin, human nature itself furnishes norms that have little more than psychological validity. *Confucius and his early disciples recognized this. Thus the opening sentence of the Confucian classic, *The Unvarying Mean,* reads: "What is ordained of Heaven is called the essential nature of man; the following of this essential nature is called the natural law; the cultivation and refinement of this natural law is called culture." The Confucian view is close to that of St. Thomas Aquinas, who held that natural law is a participation of the eternal law in man, and that positive law consists in variable determinations of immutable fundamental principles as these are applied to the varying conditions and circumstances of social life. For both Aquinas and Confucius, positive law, itself an integral part of cul-

ture, is a development and implementation of the God-given natural law that man bears within him.

This part of the article presents an analysis of the concept of natural law based on the philosophy of St. Thomas Aquinas. It discusses the relation of natural law to eternal law and positive law, the essentials of natural-law doctrine, the effects of natural law, man's awareness of the law, and its various confirmations in divine revelation and in papal teaching. More recent philosophical positions that are relevant to contemporary developments in theology are discussed in the third part of the article.

Relation to Eternal Law and Positive Law. Eternal law, natural law, and positive law, though distinct from one another, form a continuous series that may be compared to a tree. The eternal law is its hidden root; the natural law is its main trunk; and the different systems of positive law are its branches.

All systems of human law contain, in varying proportions, natural principles and positive rules. The former are not made but are merely declared by human authority; therefore they may not be abrogated. In the words of Pope Leo XIII:

> Of the laws enacted by men, some are concerned with what is good or bad by its very nature; and they command men to follow after what is right and to shun what is wrong, adding at the same time a suitable sanction. But such laws by no means derive their origin from civil society; because just as civil society did not create human nature, so neither can it be said to be the author of the good which befits human nature, or of the evil which is contrary to it. Laws come before men live together in society, and have their origin in the natural, and consequently in the eternal, law. The precepts, therefore, of the natural law, contained bodily in the laws of men, have not merely the force of human law, but they possess that higher and more august sanction which belongs to the law of nature and the eternal law. [*Libertas praestantissimum,* June 20, 1888.]

Of the positive rules of law, the same Pontiff said:

> Now there are other enactments of the civil authority, which do not follow directly, but somewhat remotely, from the natural law, and decide many points which the law of nature treats only in a general and indefinite way. For instance, though nature commands all to contribute to the public peace and prosperity, still whatever belongs to the manner and circumstances, and conditions under which such service is to be rendered must be determined by the wisdom of men and not by Nature herself. [*Ibid.*]

Thus, positive law is nothing more than an implementation of the natural law that must vary with the changing circumstances and conditions of social life.

Essentials of Natural-law Doctrine. Fundamental to St. Thomas's philosophy of natural law is the distinction between the speculative reason and practical reason (*see* SPECULATIVE-PRACTICAL). The natural sciences are the work of the speculative reason; natural law, on the other hand, is a "dictate of the practical reason." "The precepts of the natural law are to the practical reason what the first principles of demonstrations are to the speculative reason, because both are self-evident principles" (ST 1a2ae, 94.2). Just as *being is what first falls under the apprehension of the speculative reason, so *good is what first falls under the apprehension of the practical reason. For the practical reason is directed to action, and every agent acts for an end that it regards as good. Hence the first principle of the natural law is: good is to be done and evil is to be avoided. "All other precepts of the natural law are based upon this: so that whatever the practical reason naturally apprehends as man's good or evil belongs to the precepts of the natural law as something to be done or avoided" (*ibid.*).

Both the speculative and the practical reason attain the same degree of certainty with regard to *first principles, but not with regard to the conclusions drawn from these principles. St. Thomas makes a point of this difference:

> For, since the speculative reason is concerned chiefly with necessary things, which cannot be otherwise than they are, its proper conclusions, like universal principles, are true without fail. The practical reason, on the other hand, is concerned with contingent matters, which are human actions; consequently, although there is some necessity in its general principles, the more we descend to matters of detail the more frequently we encounter defects. [ST 1a2ae, 94.4.]

Thus, for St. Thomas, it is vain to expect the same certainty in judicial decisions as in the physical sciences, but it would be rash to deny altogether the existence of universal principles that constitute the natural law.

Content of Natural Law. St. Thomas defines the natural law as the participation of the eternal law in the rational creature (ST 1a2ae, 91.2). It should be noted, however, that the participation to which he refers is limited and defective. "Human reason cannot have a full participation of the dictate of the Divine Reason, but according to its own mode, and imperfectly" (91.3 ad 1). In other words, man's natural participation of the eternal law consists in the knowledge of certain general principles, not of particular decisions relating to individual cases.

Moreover, since generality admits of infinite degrees, the precepts of natural law cannot be numbered exactly. All such precepts are conclusions deduced from the primary precept that good is to be done and evil avoided. As these conclusions become more and more remote, they shade off into the sphere of human law; therefore, there can be no clear-cut borderline between natural and human law. That is why St. Thomas maintains that the natural law can be changed by way of addition and is capable of unlimited growth (94.5).

There seems to be little point, however, in classifying the precepts of the natural law into secondary and tertiary, as some authors do; apart from the primary precept, all conclusions derived from this are simply more or less remote. For St. Thomas all the moral precepts of the Old Law pertain to the natural law in the sense that all are consonant with reason, although all do not pertain to natural law in the same way (100. 1). Of the Ten Commandments the first three (according to the enumeration in common use among Catholics) pertain also to divine positive law inasmuch as man needs instruction by God to enable him to perceive their consonance with reason; the remaining seven pertain to the natural law not only in the sense that they are consonant with reason, but also inasmuch as this consonance does not require revelation to be known. The latter precepts are among the most proximate conclusions from the primary principles. "Honor thy father and thy mother" is a concretization of "good is to be done," and the remaining six Commandments are concretizations of "evil is to be avoided." All are among those things "that the natural reason of every man, of his own accord and at once, judges should be done or avoided" (*ibid.*). Other precepts of the Old Law pertain also to natural law, even though their rightness is not

immediately apparent. An example is "Honor the person of the aged man" (*ibid.*), which is among the more remote conclusions. For St. Thomas, the two most immediate conclusions deducible from the primary precept are: "Thou shalt love the Lord thy God" and "Thou shalt love thy neighbor"; all the precepts of the Decalogue are referred to these (100.3 ad 1).

Besides moral precepts, St. Thomas mentions two other types, namely, the ceremonial and the judicial (or juridical). The ceremonial precepts are determinations of the natural law whereby man is directed to God, whereas the juridical precepts are determinations of the natural law whereby man is directed to his neighbor. Unlike conclusions, determinations belong not to the integral body of the natural law but to positive law, whether divine or human. There is no question that the ceremonial precepts, which deal with the ways and forms of worship, belong to divine positive law. As to the judicial or juridical precepts, although most are determinations of the natural law, some may be conclusions (however remote) of the natural law, and therefore constitute an integral part of it.

Determination vs. Conclusion. The distinction between a conclusion and a determination is clearly expressed by St. Thomas: "The law of nature has it that the evildoer should be punished; but that he be punished in this or that way, is a determination of the natural law" (ST 1a2ae, 95.2). Similarly, it is a conclusion of the natural law that he who injures another should compensate him; but exactly how to compensate him is a determination that can be laid down by positive law and is subject to change. For instance, the following law is found in Exodus: "When a man steals an ox or a sheep and slaughters or sells it, he shall restore five oxen for the one ox, and four sheep for the one sheep" (21.37). Such a prescription is certainly not a part of the natural law, because it is not evident to natural reason. The case is different with the following: "You shall not molest or oppress an alien, for you were once aliens yourselves in the land of Egypt" (Ex 22.21). "You shall not wrong any widow or orphan" (22.22). "The innocent and the just you shall not put to death" (23.7). "Never take a bribe, for a bribe blinds even the most clear-sighted and twists the words even of the just" (23.8). Whether these are referred to as moral or juridical precepts, they are conclusions of the natural law whose rectitude is apparent to man's reason.

While determinations form no part of the natural law, their proper function is to implement the natural law. An instance of this is found in the modern law of restitution. The natural law demands that one who is unjustly enriched at the expense of another should restore whatever benefits he has derived from his unjust act. In order to implement this dictate of natural reason, American judges have invented the fiction of "constructive trust." As Justice B. N. Cardozo has put it, "When property has been acquired in such circumstances that the holder of the legal title may not in good conscience retain the beneficial interest, equity converts him into a trustee" (225 N.Y. 380, 386). More recently, Judge C. S. Desmond has said that "a constructive trust will be erected whenever necessary to satisfy the demands of justice. Since a constructive trust is merely 'the formula through which the conscience of equity finds expression,' its applicability is limited only by the inventiveness of men who find new ways to enrich themselves by grasping what should not belong to them" (299 N.Y. 27). Here positive law serves the natural law as a faithful and efficient handmaid.

The cases of constructive trust furnish also an apt illustration of the function of *synderesis, *conscience, and *prudence and their mutual workings with respect to natural law. It is the role of synderesis to perceive the principles of natural law: the principles here involved are that no one should enrich himself unjustly at the expense of another and that, if he does, he should be required to restore the benefits to the latter. It is the role of conscience to recognize that, in this or that particular case, a particular party is unjustly enriched. Finally, it is the role of prudence to devise or choose the best means of implementing the demands of justice. The interworkings of these functions in the jurist are seen at their best in the courts of equity, which had their origins in the English chancellor, who was at the same time "the keeper of the king's conscience." No doubt many of the chancellors were steeped in the Christian tradition of the natural law.

Effects of Natural Law. Among the principal effects of the natural law are its obligation and its sanction.

Obligation. The obligation of natural law arises from two sources: (1) it is rooted in the essential order of things, and (2) it is ultimately made not by man but by God. Of all creatures, man alone is endowed with a moral law and with reason to discern its obligations. He is aware that it is precisely this ingrained moral law that distinguishes him from the lower animals. It is the badge of his natural nobility. To obey the dictates of this moral law is to be true to his own nature. To play false to his nature, on the other hand, is to fall lower than brute animals, who, although devoid of rationality and a sense of obligation, follow instinctively the laws of their nature.

Regarding the provenance of law's obligation from God, Immanuel Kant observed: "Two things I contemplate with ceaseless awe; The stars of heaven, and man's sense of law." This expresses more than a cosmic emotion that springs from the feeling of harmony between macrocosm and microcosm; the awe of which Kant speaks comes also from an awareness, at least implicit, of God the Supreme Lawgiver. When one is aware that the same God who established the order of the universe also instituted the internal order of man's nature, his vision is like that of David, who saw the whole universe radiant with the glory of God (Ps 18.24). The laws that the Lord has written in man's heart, however, convey more than Kant's categorical imperatives; they are also a perennial delight. This high vision defies all human expression and imagination; yet one sure effect of it is that man's desire and will are "revolved, like a wheel which is moved evenly, by the love which moves the sun and the other stars" (Dante, *Paradiso,* 33.142).

Sanction. Only a portion of the natural law can be adopted and enforced by human law with its external sanctions. To take a simple instance, human law can forbid adultery with penal and civil sanctions. But Christ said that "anyone who so much as looks with lust at a woman has already committed adultery with her in his heart" (Mt 5.28). This, too, belongs to the natural law; but human law is too clumsy an instrument to take cognizance of such cases. Does this mean that the natural law is without a sanction of its own? If so, it would be ineffectual. In fact, however, natural law is

more effective than human law. In the first place, virtue is its own reward; and vice, its own punishment. One simply cannot be virtuous without being happy, nor can one sin without being miserable. Man's natural end is complete self-realization, that is, being entirely true to his nature. *Virtue promotes this cause, whereas *vice frustrates it. As a Chinese proverb has it, "there is no happiness like that of doing good." And it is equally true that there is no hell like sinning. Herein lies the intrinsic sanction of the natural law.

Again, natural law is sanctioned by the law of spiritual causality: one reaps what one sows. "Do men gather grapes from thorns, or figs from thistles? Even so, every good tree bears good fruit, but the bad tree bears bad fruit" (Mt 7.16–17). In saying this, Christ merely restated part of the natural law. For it does not take a special revelation to know that "God's mill grinds slowly but surely," as the Greeks observed. *Lao Tzŭ put the same truth in this way:

> Vast is Heaven's net;
> Sparse-meshed it is, and yet
> Nothing can slip through it.

Finally, since God is supremely just, real virtue (especially when hidden) will not go unrewarded any more than deliberate and unrepented viciousness will go unpunished. The Christian law of mercy does not abolish this fundamental law of divine justice: on the contrary, it reveals the nature of this justice more fully, gives man a chance to begin anew, calls him to repentance, and enables him to meet its obligations. Christ did not come to destroy the natural law, but to fulfill it (cf. Mt 5.17). As a consequence of His coming, the Christian's obligation to fulfill the law has increased immeasurably. For unless his justice exceeds that of those who know not Christ, he shall not enter the kingdom of heaven.

Awareness of Natural Law. From the foregoing, one may conclude that the natural law is not external to man but is ingrained in his nature. Its primary precept of pursuing good and avoiding evil and its immediate conclusions are indemonstrable; yet they are self-evident principles of the practical reason. Thus it is not by logical or empirical reasoning that the natural law is established. Man knows it by a direct intuition provided by synderesis. Conscience, on the other hand, is the act that applies this general knowledge to a particular situation. If, for instance, a person sees a little child crawling into a well, he sees immediately that it is his duty to hold the child back and save its life, no matter whose child it may happen to be. This awareness is the working of conscience. If, moreover, one fails to rescue the child and it is drowned in the well, he feels remorse. This, too, is the working of conscience, which, having given the command in the first instance, applies its sanction for failure to carry it out.

The foregoing example was used by *Mencius to illustrate his insight that every man has an intuitive perception of what is right and what is wrong and a natural inclination or aptitude for the good. The former seems to correspond to synderesis; the latter, to conscience. Synderesis is the legislator that declares the law, and conscience is the judge who applies it to particular cases.

Since the elementary principles of the natural law are innate in human nature, evidences of it appear even in primitive law. Yet there is a growth in the content of natural law with the progress of civilization. As the human mind becomes more and more enlightened, it becomes capable of devising new and more effective methods of ascertaining the truth and implementing the natural law. Similarly the human heart, refined by the developments of arts and letters, grows in sensitivity to new values and needs of humanity; as a consequence it prompts legislators and judges to draw new conclusions from the first principles of the natural law. In this way, new natural rights have emerged in the course of history and have been recognized, though not made, by human law. One example is the "right of privacy," which the Georgia Supreme Court recognized in 1905 for the first time in American jurisprudence as a right "derived from the natural law." Obviously, the court was conscious of what it was doing, for it declared, through Judge Cobb, that "the right of privacy has its foundation in the instincts of nature. It is recognized intuitively, consciousness being the witness that can be called to establish its existence" (*Pavesich v. New England Life Insurance Co.*, 122 Ga. 190).

Divine Revelation and Papal Teaching. The natural law is independent of any divine revelation. Its first principles are common to all men and are not the exclusive possession of the Judeo-Christian tradition. However, there can be no question that Christian writers have been greatly aided by revelation in their discovery of the natural law and natural rights. This point was brought out clearly by Chancellor James Kent in *Wightman v. Wightman* (Chancery Court of New York, 1820. 4 Johnson Ch. 343). Pronouncing the nullity of the marriage of a lunatic, Chancellor Kent said:

> That such a marriage is criminal and void by the Law of Nature, is a point universally conceded. And, by the Law of Nature, I understand those fit and just rules of conduct which the Creator has prescribed to Man, as a dependent and social being; and which are to be ascertained from the deductions of right reason, though they may be more precisely known, and more explicitly declared by Divine Revelation.

It is truly characteristic of her catholicity that the Church has persistently "affirmed the value of what is human and is in conformity with nature," notwithstanding her teaching on original sin. Pius XII, the greatest jurist among the modern popes, never tired of speaking of the natural law. In his address to members of the International Convention of Humanistic Studies (1949), he observed:

> She [the Church] does not admit that in the sight of God man is mere corruption and sin. On the contrary, in the eyes of the Church, original sin did not intimately affect man's aptitudes and strength, and has left essentially intact the natural light of his intelligence and his freedom. Man endowed with this nature is undoubtedly injured and weakened by the heavy inheritance of a fallen nature, deprived of supernatural and preternatural gifts. He must make an effort to observe the natural law—this with the powerful assistance of the Grace of Christ—so that he can live as the honor of God and his dignity as man require.

Starting from the essential nobility of human nature, the Pope went on to say:

> The natural law—here is the foundation on which the social doctrine of the Church rests. It is precisely her Christian conception of the world which has inspired and sustained the Church in building up this doctrine on such a foundation. When she struggles to win and defend her own freedom, she is actually doing this for the true freedom and for the fundamental rights of man. In her eyes these essential rights are so inviolable that no argument of State and no pretext of the common good can prevail against them . . . .. It cannot touch these rights for they constitute what is most precious in the common good.

Pius XII saw that the chief source of confusion and disorder in the 20th century lies in the deliberate abandonment of the natural law. In his very first encyclical, *Summi Pontificatus,* he asserted:

> One leading mistake We may single out, as the fountainhead, deeply hidden, from which the evils of the modern state derive their origin. Both in private life and in the state itself, and moreover in the mutual relations of race with race, of country with country, the one universal standard of morality is set aside; by which We mean the natural law, now buried away under a mass of destructive criticism and of neglect.

This has become possible because in some states, at least, the pernicious doctrine of state absolutism has prevailed, with the result that the state has actually usurped the position of God. When the Author of the natural law is set aside, there can be no room for the natural law, which, as Pius XII insisted, "reposes, as upon its foundation, on the notion of God, the Almighty Creator and Father of us all, the Supreme and Perfect Law-giver, the wise and just Rewarder of human conduct."

Bibliography: J. C. H. WU, *Fountain of Justice* (New York 1955). J. MESSNER, *Social Ethics: Natural Law in the Modern World,* tr. J. J. DOHERTY (new ed. St. Louis 1964). M. T. ROONEY, *Lawlessness, Law, Sanction* (Washington 1937). Notre Dame Univ., *Natural Law Institute: Proceedings,* v.1–5 (1947–51). J. D. WILD, *Plato's Modern Enemies and the Theory of Natural Law* (Chicago 1953). P. J. STANLIS, *Edmund Burke and the Natural Law* (Ann Arbor 1958). A. G. CICOGNANI, *Canon Law,* tr. J. O'HARA and F. BRENNAN (2d ed. Westminster, Md. 1947; repr. 1949).

[J. C. H. WU]

CONTEMPORARY THEOLOGY AND PHILOSOPHY

One distinction that is indispensable for understanding the place of natural law in contemporary theology and philosophy is that between the ontology of natural law, or its existence, and the epistemology of natural law, or the knowledge of principles that may be said to constitute it. It seems from the dissent that takes place in contemporary discussions of natural law that there is more disagreement over the epistemology than there is over the ontology.

Protestant Criticisms. S. E. Stumpf suggests such a distinction when he asserts that contemporary Protestant thought is fundamentally critical of natural-law theory although it does not repudiate the theory completely. For the Protestant, the disagreement arises from a philosophy that is based on the accessibility of nature to man's rational powers, an accessibility that he is unwilling to admit. For him the "Catholic" natural law is associated with the Thomistic notion of the analogy of being, according to which the natural law is defined in terms of the eternal law that exists in God. The promulgation of this law, as has been explained above, is made in the rational nature of man and the application of its principles, whether primary, secondary, or tertiary, to contingent situations is made by the consciences of men in their practical prudential judgments. For many Protestants, this explanation places too much importance on stable natures and rational powers, and not enough upon the ambiguity in every moral situation. Reinhold Niebuhr's criticism of what he calls "classical, catholic, and modern natural law concepts" proceeds along these very lines. He insists that these concepts do not allow for the historical character of human existence because they are radicated in a classical rationalism that did not understand history. These concepts, for Niebuhr, do not appreciate the uniqueness of the historical situation or the accretions that came into the definition of natural law through history. The general principles are too inflexible, and the definitions of these general principles are too historically conditioned. Niebuhr does not deny an "essential" nature of man, but the profoundest problem for him is the historical elaboration of man's essential human nature, on the one hand, and the historical biases that have insinuated themselves into the definition of that essential human nature, on the other.

A second criticism, for Niebuhr, is the tendency in the classical theory to make the law of love an addition to the law of obligation, with the result that the one deals with the determinate possibilities and the other the indeterminate possibilities of good. In his view, clear lines between determinate and indeterminate possibilities cannot and should not be drawn. Niebuhr illustrates this by saying that justice is an application of the law of love for which the rules are not absolute but relative. All such rules are applications of the law of love and do not have independence apart from it. They would be autonomous only if they were based upon an "essential" social structure, and there is no definition of such an essential structure of community except the law of love. Stumpf makes this the cardinal point of criticism between the Protestant and Catholic conceptions of natural law. The ground of ethics is love even for the natural man and such love is the fulfillment and completion of the law. Love and grace are not dimensions of the supernatural order only, but justice is infused and transfigured by love. The Protestant conception, then, is fundamentally the confrontation of man with the God of judgment and love commanding him, not through the mediation of abstract primary, secondary, and tertiary principles, but subjecting him to the single imperative of love. No law mediates between man and God—only love—and this love is the natural law for the very reason that love is the law of man's essential human nature.

Different Views of Reason. It should be seen at once that all Catholic and many Protestant theologians would admit an essential human nature, but even there the word "essential" demands quotation marks and precise refinements of meaning. R. E. Fitch, Dean of the Pacific School of Religion, is quoted in a footnote of an article by A. R. Jonsen "Arguing Ethics" [*Homiletic and Pastoral Review* (Jan. 1964) 302], where reference is made to two entirely different views of reason that are possible in any discussion of natural law. For the Catholic, the stress is on the reason that is Aristotelian, classical, ordered, and universal; for the Protestant, the emphasis is on the reason that is individualistic, inquiring, and experimental. Fitch says that both are needed and no one will question that conclusion. The combination of the two stresses might be assisted by the suggestive use of the term prismatic analysis in connection with the formation of the practical prudential judgments of the individual conscience. It can readily be seen how the most general principles of law passing

through this individual human prism receive all the colorations, the ambiguities, the obstacles, and the helps from the particular existential historical moment of their passage. For the person who leans toward a somewhat complete situationalism, no law passes through the human prism but the law of love; anything else that he might designate as law is not exigent and obligatory but guiding and tentative, provisional and contingent (*see* SITUATIONAL ETHICS). The position of the moderate situationalist is one that appreciates both the imperative of obligation and the imperative of love, while giving full validity to all the contingent factors in the ambiguous ethical situation. Between the divine transcendence and the ever-changing human situation, J. C. Bennett places the "middle axioms," which seem to be employed to mediate between more general norms and the unique structural situation. Niebuhr speaks of "enduring structures of meaning and value" that must be assured a valid role in the ethical choice. Will Herberg finds some clarification of these conceptions of the "enduring structures of meaning and value" of Niebuhr and the "middle axioms" of Bennett by citing Edmund Burke, who has this to say about natural rights:

> These metaphysical rights, entering into common life, like rays of light which pierce into a dense medium, are . . . refracted from a straight line . . . [and] undergo such a variety of refractions and reflections that it becomes absurd to speak of them as if they continued in the simplicity of their original direction. ["Conservatives, Liberals and the Natural Law, II," *National Review*, June 19, 1962.]

Philosophical Presuppositions. The fundamental disagreement on natural-law theory, therefore, is rooted in philosophical presuppositions on the nature of law, on the nature of man, on the very meaning of "natural." The signification of a theory of natural law for the Roman Catholic, the Protestant, and the secular humanist will be conditioned from the very start by these philosophical presuppositions. In fact, almost all theological disagreements find their ultimate sources of division in philosophical premises. To those inclined to regard metaphysical knowledge as not so respectable a knowledge as that of the empiriological sciences, the intelligibility of nature, of man, of law, and of God will be regarded with increasing skepticism. All these obstacles that are profoundly philosophical will make difficult the acceptance even of the existence of natural law at its barest minimum. When, in addition to the difference in philosophical presuppositions, the differences in theology concerning the nature of original sin and its consequences for the nature of man are studied, it can be more clearly seen why natural law for the Catholic has been a dialectical tool. It stands to reason that he can employ this tool effectively only if he constantly appreciates these philosophical and theological differences.

Catholic Theology. Natural law has understandably been of interest to the Catholic theologian, who has always interested himself in the mutual relation of reason and faith and is convinced that God operates in history through the natures of things and especially through the nature of man. He presumes that man's nature has not been deformed by original sin and that his intellect and will are capable of constructing a natural theology and a moral philosophy that is valid and is complemented by supernatural theology and a moral theology. In light of this presumption, he does not hesitate to study essential human nature and to discover certain conformities and deformities with respect to it. Unfortunately, the principal obstacle to the acceptance of natural law in modern times is the mistaken notion that this law belongs to the Catholic Church and no other. Yet it is undeniably true that the Catholic Church has been the most vigorous defender of natural-law theory in areas ranging from property rights to contraception and from the problems of medical ethics to those of nuclear warfare.

With the gradual lowering of moral standards, however, the Church has given more of her magisterial attention to the claims of nature and justice. J. Fuchs, in *Lex Naturae zur Theologie des Naturrechts* (Dusseldorf 1955, 9–12), shows that since the reign of Pius IX the term natural law has been employed with increasing frequency in the documents of the Church. The term is constantly mentioned in the allocutions and discourses of Pius XII on the issues of peace and war, on political organizations, and on the obligations of the many professions, especially medicine and law. Yet the fact that the Church has been concerned to defend the natural and to relate it to the supernatural does not make the natural itself supernatural. The natural law is the basis and foundation for the supernatural code of ethics found in moral theology, where the additional evidence for certain forms of ethical conduct derives from Biblical sources and from tradition. At times the papal documents refer to elevated human nature, to human nature supernaturalized by grace; where this is done, however, the texts are clear, and such citations do not permit a reader to conclude that the argument from reason has been so substantially undermined that only Catholic faith provides a valid and cogent ground for ethical conduct. The interrelation between faith and reason on the precise question of the probative value of evidence from natural law is most certainly ground for debate among Catholic theologians, but no one of them would deny completely all probative value and all cogency to a natural-law argument.

Charge of Vagueness and Ambiguity. A fundamental criticism, especially from circles outside the Church, points to the difficulties in the presentation of the natural law; the presentation seems to be indeterminate and unsatisfactory, at least as its defenders formulate it. Again, the evidence that the defenders of natural law adduce may not be cogent in the light of differences in moral beliefs and practices at different times and places. N. Bobbio, in "Quelques arguments contre le droit naturel" [*Le droit naturel* (Paris 1959) 175–190], suggests this criticism when he remarks that philosophers are inclined to deny that the natural law is natural, whereas legal scholars tend to deny that it is a law. The response for the Thomistic supporters of natural law is that it is both natural and genuinely a law, that it is verifiable as natural and valid in an authentic meaning of law. Robert Gordis points out the dilemma of those who stand outside the dominant tradition of natural law but are sympathetic to its value. He refers to Robert M. Hutchins's observation that natural law appears to many to be "a body of doctrine that is so vague as to be useless or so biased as to be menacing." For such persons the vagueness and ambiguity of terms such as nature and natural have been always a part of the history of ideas. For them

the opinion of Leslie Stephens may not be the cynical exaggeration that it is for others: "Nature is a word contrived in order to introduce as many equivocations as possible into all theories, political, legal, artistic or literary, into which it enters." Critics of natural law are ready to add to the catalogue of meanings given to "nature." D. G. Ritchie, in *Natural Rights* (2d ed. London 1903, 20–47), has a chapter "On the History of the Idea of Nature in Law and Politics"; Erik Wolf's *Das Problem der Naturrechtslehre* (Karlsruhe 1955) gives nine meanings for "nature" in the context of natural law alone; and Philippe Delhaye's *Permanence du droit naturel* (Louvain 1960, 9–21) has an introduction that explains at least 20 meanings of "nature."

This testimony to the vagueness and ambiguity of the term nature was not unknown to the proponents of natural law from their examinations of its meaning for the Stoics, John Duns Scotus, Bishop J. Butler, Hume, and Rousseau. Despite the plurality of meanings of "nature" and "natural," the Hastings *Encyclopedia of Religion and Ethics* does refer to natural law, placing the principal emphasis on the physical laws of nature and some emphasis on the natural moral law. The proponent of natural law insists that nature, with or without the premise of a God, does manifest design and order—whether reference is to the nature of physical bodies or to the rational nature of man. In man there is a determinate nature that has not changed in essentials in the 20th century. Aristotle's affirmation of the invariability of natural law that goes with nature, as contrasted with the variability of civil law that goes with man's free will, is just as strongly made by the modern proponent of natural moral law. From the study of human nature, the ordered structure of its parts, the relation and co-relation of its tendencies and appetites, the subordination of vegetative and sentient orders to the rational, conclusions are drawn concerning the rightness and wrongness of certain acts. This analysis of human nature is enormously complicated and sophisticated, but it is a possibility for man.

Contributions of Anthropology. As helps in this analysis, tradition, revelation, and authority are more acceptable for some than for others. For all, however, the traditional elaboration of natural law must be supplemented by materials from cultural anthropology. Thomistic ethicians have an important function in the incorporation of these contributions. In "Human Evolution: A Challenge to Thomistic Ethics" [*International Philosophical Quarterly,* 2 (1962) 50–80], Charles Fay shows how some of the changes resulting from man's biocultural evolution may so transform the relation between man and nature (e.g., atomic energy, polymer chemistry) that certain acts may receive a different moral evaluation. R. H. Beis, in "Some Contributions of Anthropology to Ethics" [*Thomist* 28 (1964) 174–224], considers the several advantages that a knowledge of anthropology holds for the ethician and discounts the anxiety of those who consider that anthropology supports only ethical relativity. In fact, Beis finds contradictions in the position of anthropological ethical relativity when it attempts to assume values of its own.

The philosopher-theologian, interested in a firm foundation for his natural-law position, is not unconscious of the advances in the contributions of anthropology to ethics. He is encouraged to recognize that anthropology does not scientifically establish ethical relativity. However, there is need for introducing into the natural-law presentation many more findings of anthropology, for these can help clarify the distinction between what is universal and invariable in human nature and what is relative and conditioned by the circumstances of cultural development. F. E. Crowe, in "The Irreplaceable Natural Law" [*Studies* (Summer 1962) 268–285], shows that St. Thomas affirmed the changeability of human nature when he considered human nature concretely and realistically existing in each individual as it is subjected to biocultural evolution as well as to *individuation. To say that this mutability of human nature is an ontological accident is not to deny the importance of an ontological accident. Even grace is an ontological accident, but it has the effect of changing man in a very significant way. Likewise, the ontological accident introduced into concrete, realistically existing human nature may introduce essential differences into morality. For example, the ontological accident of the married status of one party changes a sin from fornication to adultery, which are specifically different sins. These ontological accidents that bring about essential differences in morality are more appreciated by the natural-law proponent who has studied the sources of cultural anthropology. Beis adverts to the several values of these sources by observing that anthropological knowledge places human nature in its proper perspective; thus it makes the ethician aware that, while existing human nature is enculturated, there is still something proper to human nature and something derivable from culture.

Other Disciplines. It may be overoptimistic and naïve to consider that there can be more fruitful agreement on natural law by further clarification of the two aspects of human nature, the absolute and invariable, and the relative and conditioned. If the former has been emphasized in the past, the latter is not being ignored in the present. This is especially so in contemporary discussions of natural-law jurisprudence.

Again, the modern ethician and theologian who introduces references to natural law in medical morality or in sexual ethics does not ignore scientific facts that are relevant. The discussion of the licit use of *anovulants in certain pathological conditions raises many questions for whose answer the ethician is ready to accept all the scientific help he can get. Do the anovulants sterilize by the suppression of ovulation or not? If they do (and almost all commercial advertising for the anovulants say as much), what conditions will warrant an indirect sterilization? What conditions are considered to be pathological? What are the limitations on the meaning of pathology? Does pathology confine itself to the physical, somatic, organic side of human nature, or should psychological factors also be considered? The modern ethician and theologian of natural law takes into account all relevant scientific data and frequently finds the lack of consensus not among ethicians and theologians but among scientists themselves. For example, concerning the oral contraceptive pills, there are some doctors who state that the pill does not induce temporary sterility but merely results in ovarian "repose." Others call this "poor science" and refer to the literature of commercial drug firms describing the pills as "extremely effective in inhibiting ovulation," in "inducing temporary sterilization," etc.

Where does this disagreement on the part of science leave the ethician and theologian of natural law? Since the moralist must wait for the judgment of competent medical men, there is little wonder why his own judgment must be tentative and hesitating. Little wonder, too, why there is confusion generated among the less informed in situations such as these.

Role of the Church. To avoid such confusion, the Catholic Church has always maintained that the natural law is an object of its teaching authority and that its guidance is necessary for an adequate knowledge of the natural law. Gerald Kelly, SJ, refers to the moral (not physical) necessity of revelation in this regard. In other words, the guidance of the Church is a practical, or moral, necessity for obtaining an adequate knowledge of the natural law. When it is considered that the natural law is sufficiently promulgated, according to its proponents, if there is promulgation of its primary and secondary precepts in such a way that no one can be invincibly ignorant of these, this alone leaves so much to be discovered by man himself that, without the assistance of some guide and authority, his search would not be very satisfactory. Kelly mentions the position of most theologians regarding the moral impossibility of observing the natural law without grace and cites a professor of dogmatic theology who once told him that he thought this moral impossibility of observing the natural law without grace is so unique as to be practically a physical impossibility. Kelly then remarks that he had come to the same conclusion about the moral impossibility of adequately knowing the natural law without grace—i.e., that this moral impossibility is so unique as to be practically a physical impossibility. The reader should be able to agree or disagree with this position, especially regarding the more remote principles of natural law, from the experience of those around him of all degrees of culture and education.

See also NATURE; MAN; LAW; LAW, PHILOSOPHY OF.

Bibliography: C. W. KEGLEY and R. W. BRETALL, eds., *Reinhold Niebuhr: His Religious, Social and Political Thought* (New York 1956). *Handbook of Christian Theology*, ed. M. HALVERSON and A. H. COHEN (pa. New York 1958). J. COGLEY et al., *Natural Law and Modern Society* (Cleveland 1963). L. R. WARD, "Natural Law in Contemporary Legal Philosophy" Proc AmCathPhilAs 33 (1959) 137–143. S. BERTKE, *The Possibility of Invincible Ignorance of the Natural Law* (CUA Studies in Sacred Theology 58; Washington 1941). R. D. LUMB, "Law, Reason and Will," *Philosophical Studies* 10 (1960) 179–189. G. P. GRANT, *Philosophy in the Mass Age* (New York 1960).

[T. A. WASSMER]

NATURAL LAW AND JURISPRUDENCE

The philosophy of the natural law is predicated upon the existence of an objective moral order, within the scope of human intelligence and the capacity of human virtue, upon which the peace and happiness of personal, national, and international life depend, and to which all human beings, civil societies, and voting majorities are bound in conscience to conform.

According to this philosophy human beings are endowed by their Creator with certain natural rights and obligations to enable them to attain in human dignity their divine destiny. These natural rights and obligations are inalienable precisely because they are God-given. They are antecedent, both in logic and in nature, to the formation of civil societies and the casting of ballots. They are not granted by the beneficence of the state, democratic or otherwise; consequently the tyranny of the state, democratic or otherwise, cannot destroy them. In fact it is the moral responsibility of the state, through the instrumentality of its civil law, to acknowledge their existence and protect their exercise, to foster and facilitate their enjoyment by the wise and scientific implementation of the natural law with a practical and consonant code of civil rights and obligations.

Search for Objectivity. The construction and maintenance of a *corpus juris* adequately implementing the natural law is a monumental and perpetual task demanding the constant devotion, the clearest intelligence, and the most mature scholarship of the legal profession. For the fundamental principles of the natural law, universal and immutable as the human nature from which they derive, require rational application to the constantly changing political, social, economic, and technological conditions of dynamic civil society.

The application of the natural law postulates change since the circumstances of human existence necessarily change. It is inconsistent with unquestioning complacency in the *status quo*. It demands a reasoned acceptance of the good and a rejection of the bad, in all that is new, and advocates a critical search for the better. It postulates constant scrutiny of the data of history, sociology, politics, economics, psychology, biology, medicine, and other pertinent human knowledge. It insists that effort toward improvement of the *corpus juris* be made in the light of the origin, dignity, and destiny of man and in the knowledge of the origin, nature, and purpose of the state.

The relationship between natural law and civil law or, as it is popularly denominated, between morals and law, is the prime problem of jurisprudence. It is a particularly difficult and delicate problem in a society such as the pluralistic American society in which large groups of citizens sincerely differ, theologically and philosophically, about the morality of many activities and institutions and about the proper public policy of the state concerning them.

Americans were once divided upon the moral and legal issues of human slavery. They were later divided upon the moral and legal issues of racial discrimination. They have been divided over the moral and legal issues concerning capital and labor, compulsory military service and thermonuclear weapons, loyalty oaths and flag salutes, prize fighting and gambling, Bible reading and prayers in public schools, the equal treatment of children in private schools, the use of alcoholic beverages, the control of obscenity, and many other moral-legal questions.

Despite their shared reverence for the sanctity of human life, for the sacredness of marriage, for the holiness of the marriage act, for the dignity of children, the fact is that Americans have been divided over civil laws and public policy respecting marriage and divorce, monogamy and polygamy, adultery and fornication, prostitution and homosexuality, artificial contraception and insemination, abortion and sterilization, the adoption of children, suicide and euthanasia, capital punishment, and even the questions of blood transfusions or medical aid to sick or dying children.

Possibly some of the differences will never be solved to the satisfaction of all, but will be determined from time to time merely by majority vote. Nevertheless the peace and good order of a pluralistic society demand

that it sincerely strive to resolve its differences, as best it can, with civil dialogue and mutual respect, on sound moral and legal principles.

Law and Morality. Americans desire a civil society and a legal system founded upon valid principles of morality. The philosophy of the Declaration of Independence epitomizes and expresses this desire. It appeals in express terms to God, the Creator, the Supreme Judge of the World, and expressly commits the young American nation to His divine providence, basing its claim to freedom upon inalienable rights bestowed by God.

Morality Influencing Law. The moral law comes from God. The civil order depends upon the moral order. The good society cannot be based upon police power alone. For it is morality that imposes the obligation in conscience to obey civil law. Without such obedience the enforcement of civil law, the administration of justice, and the preservation of liberty would be impossible. It is a fact of human experience that the majority of people, in the majority of their actions, habitually obey the law of the land, not out of fear of police sanctions, but because they recognize that they are morally bound to do so. The moral obligation to obey civil law is the foundation of a decent and free society.

Civil law, accordingly, must respect the natural law. Man-made law cannot validly command the violation of any God-given obligation, nor can it validly prohibit the exercise of any God-given right. Law must be just. An unjust law cannot, of itself, bind the human conscience. An unjust law is, in reality, no law at all, but merely an act of governmental violence and a species of immoral force. At various times and places men have been forced to submit to immoral laws. For almost 100 years in America the abomination of human slavery was enforced by law. An immoral law contradicts conscience. Conscience and the natural law repudiate immoral civil laws.

This is not to say that each individual is sufficient unto himself to determine arbitrarily which laws he will obey and which he will disregard. In cases of genuine doubt, it is reasonable to presume that civil laws, enacted under the safeguards of constitutional processes, are consonant with the natural law. Nevertheless, a palpably immoral law cannot bind the human conscience. There is a moral right to disregard it. There may be a moral obligation to resist it to the death. In the face of a clear and irreconcilable conflict between the natural and the civil law, between morals and law, we must obey God rather than man.

The great body of American law is based upon the natural law. The incorporation of sound moral principles has been the most conspicuous factor in the development and refinement of American common and constitutional law. A simple example is seen in the fundamental axiom of *criminal law: that, except for reasonable minor exceptions, the overt act does not make a criminal unless his mental state is criminal—*actus non facit reum nisi mens sit rea*—which was a principle of moral theology long before its adoption by criminal law. Similarly, with understandable exceptions, the moral principle of personal responsibility, based upon the premise of freedom of the will, constitutes the foundation and determines the superstructure of all of American criminal and civil law. The legality of American free society is essentially predicated upon morality.

The refining influence of morals upon American law is evident in the development of *equity; in the evolution of the law of contracts and torts; in the explication of the law of theft, from larceny through embezzlement to false pretenses; in the law of sales, from the crude *caveat emptor* to decent dealing; in the law of agency, from mere authority to fiduciary obligations; in the law of property, from raw power to social duties; in the law of industrial relations, from laissez-faire rugged individualism to fraternal responsibilities; in American constitutional law, from allowance of human slavery to the statutes initiating freedom and equality; in the law of equal protection, from maintenance of racial segregation to the legislation upholding human dignity; in the law of procedural and substantive *due process; and so with many other principles and precepts of American common and constitutional law.

Law Encouraging Morality. But the moral order depends upon the legal order also. Civil laws are necessary for the recognition and the implementation of morals in organized society. Without the support and the sanction of civil law, many moral obligations could not be fulfilled, and many moral rights could not be protected against the encroachments of the unscrupulous and the machinations of the malicious. The law and the police power of the state are necessary to protect the vast majority of the people in their fixed intention and obligation to observe the precepts of the moral order.

Furthermore, the law must do more than protect those obvious moral rights and obligations upon which all men easily agree. It must do more than enforce the immediately evident principles of the natural law about which there is a general consensus. The law has an educative as well as a coercive function. The law cannot escape the perplexing task of advancing from the immediately evident and universally conceded principles of morality to the derivative principles that depend upon mediate and empirical evidence. Law is a practical and progressive science. It must specify and apply particular principles of morality by enacting specific and particular rules and standards that do not bask in the sunlight of universal agreement. The law is frequently relegated to the dimmer light of argument and controversy; sometimes, unfortunately, to the semidarkness of strident partisanship and bitter emotionalism. In light or in darkness, the law must relentlessly express, as best it can, the public morality and the common good of society. Moral sensitivity must characterize public opinion, objectivity must prevail in the legislative process, and scholarly wisdom in the judicial process.

Public Morality. Fundamental to the concept and purpose of civil law is the fact that legality and morality, while interrelated and interdependent, are not identical. Their respective fields overlap, but they are not coextensive. Many crimes are sins, and many sins are crimes, but crime and sin are not the same thing. Certain crimes, such as the so-called public-welfare offenses that are penalized as overt acts regardless of the mental state, can be committed without sin; certain sins, such as simple lying or solitary masturbation, can be committed without crime. But lying that involves fraud or libel or masturbation that involves public indecency are both sins and crimes. They are sins because they are immoral. They are crimes because they offend that aspect of the common good of civil society that is properly called public morality. It is not the purpose or function of civil law to prohibit or penalize an immoral act simply because it is immoral. The end or purpose of civil law is the public or common good of civil society. In the field of morals, therefore, the scope of civil law is not the area of purely private morality, but of public morality.

It is not easy to delineate with precision the specific fields of public and private morality. It is difficult to draw a sharp line that will clearly and satisfactorily distinguish those moral actions that properly fall within the legislative competence of the state and those that are properly beyond it. In such a task reasonable men may differ, and their opinions may vary from time to time and from culture to culture. The distinction is certainly not the difference between publicity and secrecy. The publicized lie is not a crime. The secret murder is. The distinction is between those actions that primarily concern the actor as an individual, and those actions that concern the neighbor or the community in such a way as to affect substantially the common good of civil society.

The field of public morality is by no means confined to criminal law; it embraces also the areas of civil law, such as contracts, torts, property, equity, commercial and industrial rights, and especially constitutional law. It is helpful for understanding of public morality to consider a number of obviously immoral actions punished as crimes by mature and civilized states.

Murder, manslaughter, rape, mayhem, assault and battery violate the personal rights of others to life and bodily integrity; kidnaping and false imprisonment violate the personal rights of others to liberty and locomotion; robbery, larceny, embezzlement, and false pretenses violate the personal rights of others to property; arson and burglary violate the personal rights of others to habitation and enclosure; libel violates the personal rights of others to reputation; bribery and perjury pervert the administration of justice and obstruct the preservation of liberty; commercialized vice corrupts the citizenry and offends the public decency; riots disrupt the public peace and order; treason invades the security of law itself. All the above rights and values are essential to a just and ordered liberty, that is, to the common good of organized civil society. All immoral actions, therefore, that militate against such rights and values are in the field of public morality and properly subject to state legislative power.

Private Morality. It is a misleading half-truth to say that the state cannot legislate morality. Every state can, should, and does in fact legislate in the field of public morality. Society could not exist without such legislation. The whole of American law is witness to the fact. But the state should not, and usually cannot, legislate in the field of purely private morality.

Purely internal acts of virtue and of vice constitute a large part of the field of morality, of the good or evil human life, but the state is utterly incompetent to legislate concerning purely internal acts of virtue or of vice and seldom attempts it. Moreover, apart from purely internal acts, the state should not attempt to legislate concerning those overt acts that are in the field of purely private morality. The nature of the state indicates that its legislative competence extends only to that part of morality that affects the common good of civil society and that is properly called public morality. In view of this limitation, and in this sense only, it may be said that it is not the state's business to legislate morality.

The stability of the marriage bond, many rights and obligations of the married, the care of legitimate and illegitimate children, the rights of the unborn, the protection of youth from corruption, the prevention of sexual promiscuity and venereal disease, the curtailing of alcoholism and drug addiction, the safeguarding of the poor from fleecing by gambling syndicates, and the general condition of fundamental sociomoral standards are matters that clearly affect the public or common good of society. For that reason they are properly within the scope of civil law and public policy.

Nevertheless the American states differ substantially in their laws and public policies concerning marriage, divorce, separation, abortion, adoption, adultery, fornication, prostitution, homosexuality, contraception, gambling, alcohol, narcotics, capital punishment, etc. It is submitted that these differences reflect disagreement on one or more of the following three questions: whether the given activity is immoral; if immoral, whether it is in the field of private or public morality; if in the field of public morality, whether this or that public policy is the proper or prudential way to handle the immoral activity.

Inalienable Human Rights. The philosophy of the natural law postulates a number of fundamental human rights and obligations that are absolute and inalienable and that must be protected by civil law. Among such rights are those to life, worship, marriage, property, labor, speech, locomotion, assembly, and reputation. The "absolute" character of such rights creates a difficulty for those who do not understand natural-law philosophy.

Such rights are absolute in the sense that they derive from human nature. They are not mere gifts from the state. The state is bound to protect them and cannot destroy them even though, at times, states have physically prevented their exercise. Legalized human slavery prevented the exercise of these fundamental human rights, but it did not destroy the rights themselves.

Limited. Fundamental human rights are not absolute in the sense that they are unlimited in scope. It is a commonplace in the philosophy of natural law that human rights, even the most fundamental, are limited. They are limited in the sense that they are subject to specification, qualification, expansion and contraction, and even forfeiture of exercise, as the equal rights of others and the requirements of the common good reasonably indicate.

Some typical limitations upon the scope of the fundamental human rights enumerated above are as follows. Life may be forfeited upon just conviction of a capital crime. The right to it is qualified by the right of others to legitimate self-defense, is subject to the right of the state to reasonable prevention of crime, and may be endangered in the waging of a just war. The right to Worship may be qualified by reasonable restrictions as to time, place, and circumstance; and hence, e.g., prayer meetings may be prohibited at high noon in the middle of Times Square. That to Marriage may be specified and qualified by reasonable restrictions as to age and consanguinity—but not by so-called miscegenation statutes that conflict with the essential right (*see* MARRIAGE, U.S. LAW OF). The right to Property may be qualified, contracted, or expanded, by reasonable *zoning laws, antitrust legislation, wage and hour and safety regulations. The right to Labor may be specified and

qualified by reasonable licensing requirements, sanitary regulations, wage and hour and safety regulations. *See* WELFARE LEGISLATION (U.S.). Speech may be restricted by reasonable laws concerning incitement to crime, libel and slander, *obscenity, and the divulgence of information to the enemy in time of war (*see* FREEDOM OF SPEECH AND PRESS, U.S. LAW OF; DEFAMATION, U.S. LAW OF). Locomotion may be qualified by reasonable passport rules and immigration laws. The right of Assembly may be qualified by reasonable requirements in the interest of public health, safety, and order. The right to Reputation may be qualified by reasonable laws requiring testimony in public trials, allowing fair comment on public affairs and officials, requiring the disclosure or reporting of embarrassing contagious diseases. These are simply random examples of typical limitations upon the scope of a few obvious, natural and inalienable rights. All such rights are subject to similar limitations.

If the scope of natural rights were subject to unreasonable or arbitrary limitation, either by the fiat of a dictator or a democratic majority vote, then they would be subject to simple extinction and could not be said to be absolute. If, however, the scope of natural rights is subject only to reasonable limitation for the sake of the common good, then indeed they are not subject to simple extinction and can properly be said to be absolute. Reasonable limitation of scope is a proper condition of natural and inalienable rights.

The human person, in his essential nature, is not merely an individual being. He is also a social being living with his fellows in an organized society that is subject to political, economic, technological, and social change. His natural rights—and corresponding obligations to respect the natural rights of others—are both individual and social. To consider him solely as an individual would lead to anarchy. To consider him solely as a social unit would lead to totalitarianism. But his individual-social nature, adequately considered, leads inevitably to the conclusion that his natural rights are absolute, in the sense explained, because he is an individual for whose rights good governments are instituted. Reasonable reflection leads also to the compatible conclusion that his natural rights are limited in scope, in the sense explained, because he is also a social person obliged by nature to contribute to the common good of human society.

Immutable. Confusion is created also by the universal and immutable character of fundamental principles of natural law. Such principles are as universal and immutable as the human nature from which they are derived. When properly understood, they suffer no exceptions.

The four monosyllables, "Thou shalt not kill," are sometimes used to express a fundamental secondary principle of the natural law. If these four words were to be taken in simplistic literalness, they would not indicate a universal and immutable principle, because there are circumstances in which killing is obviously permissible.

The quoted words merely indicate the natural law principle that is adequately expressed as, "Thou shalt not kill or inflict bodily harm upon any human being *unjustly.*" This principle is universal and immutable. In its negative aspect, it prohibits the immoral killing or inflicting of bodily harm upon self or other human beings. In its positive aspect, it commands a reasonable preservation of life and bodily integrity. Therefore, acts of legitimate self-defense, defense of others, warfare, executions for crime, corporal punishment, surgery, vaccination, anesthesia, strenuous sports are relevant to the principle if they are justifiable.

The justification of such acts will depend upon the norm of morality, i.e., conformity with or difformity from human nature individually and socially considered, upon the nature of the act, the circumstances of the action, and the motives of the actor. But the principle "Thou shalt not kill or inflict bodily harm upon any human being unjustly" remains universal and immutable.

This is not to say that the determination of such moral and legal justification is automatic or without difficulty. A particular question of the justifiability of self-defense may be extremely difficult in regard to both morals and law, without the slightest doubt being cast upon the universality or immutability of the principle. The solution of such problems gives rise to the sciences of morality and lawmaking.

A principle of morality or of law is not without value because its application to particular cases is difficult. The American constitutional phrase "due process of law" indicates a legal principle (declaring and enforcing a principle of natural law) that has taxed the judicial mind for centuries. And the development of the legal concept of due process of law has occasioned influences of natural law on jurisprudence. The natural law, which says that a human being may not be deprived of his life unjustly, is recognized and enforced by the civil law, which says that a human being may not be deprived of his life without due process of law. In close cases, moralists and legalists of reasonable but finite mentalities may differ about the application of justice and due process. General principles alone do not decide particular cases; but particular cases cannot be decided without them.

Conclusion. Difficulty is sometimes engendered by a failure to distinguish between a principle of the natural law and a rule of the civil law. The former is universal and immutable, the latter is not. A principle of natural law can be known by man, because he can know his nature and essential relationships; but a principle of the natural law cannot be made, changed, or destroyed by man because he cannot make, change, or destroy his essential nature. Conversely a rule of the civil law must be made and may be amended or repealed by man's legislative or judicial process. Thus a rule of the civil law lacks the universality and immutability of a principle of the natural law. This is the precise reason why rules of civil law, as they are enacted, amended, and formulated from time to time and from circumstance to circumstance, should always be consonant with the principles of natural law. It is why the natural law constitutes the general norm to measure the justice or injustice of civil law.

Among the changeable and changing rules of civil law are: the rule of consideration in contracts, the rule of hearsay in evidence, the rule of recording in property, the rule of witnesses in wills, the rule of strict liability in torts, the rule of "retreating to the wall" in crimes, and hundreds of others, from the rules governing statutes of limitations to traffic rules and minor procedural regulations. As rules, they have a certain generality, but they are subject to exceptions, and they require change, gradual or drastic, as time, circumstance, and wisdom

demand. They are practical and subsidiary means whereby the civil law, more or less efficiently, applies the principles of the natural law to human beings living in the constantly changing political, economic, technological, and social conditions of civil society.

Three factors have contributed to the confusion and misunderstanding concerning the impact of natural law upon civil law. First, the misuse of natural law terminology, in the 19th and early 20th centuries, in support of laissez-faire rugged individualism—seen in many old Supreme Court decisions that piously exalted property and contractual rights to the detriment of other basic human rights and the genuine needs of the common good. Second, the lack of familiarity of members of the legal profession with the writings of the natural law philosophers and reliance upon secondary, unscholarly sources of information. Third, an unfortunate propensity, on the part of enthusiasts of natural law, to claim too much for their philosophy. The naive proposition "All we have to do to solve our practical problems is to apply natural law" is similar to the false panacea "All we have to do is to apply the Constitution."

The natural law itself is inadequate to solve the complex problems of a dynamic human society. It requires implementation by civil law; and such implementation involves not merely argumentation and research, but validation even by trial and error. The search is for the best civil laws to act for the personal and the common good.

Bibliography: R. F. BÉGIN, *Natural Law and Positive Law* (CUA CLS 393; Washington 1959). J. ELLUL, *The Theological Foundation of Law,* tr. M. WIESER (Garden City, N.Y. 1960). Center for the Study of Democratic Institutions, *Natural Law and Modern Society* (Cleveland 1963). A. L. HARDING, ed., *Natural Law and Natural Rights* (Dallas 1955). F. S. C. NORTHROP, "Philosophical Issues in Contemporary Law," *Natural Law Forum* 2 (1957) 41–63. M. T. ROONEY, *Lawlessness, Law, and Sanction* (Washington 1937). L. STRAUSS, *Natural Right and History* (Chicago 1953). J. C. H. WU, *Fountain of Justice* (New York 1955).

[W. J. KENEALY]

NATURAL LAW IN ECONOMICS

The term natural law has been used in economics to designate both normative and explanatory, or analytical, systems of thought. Normative natural-law doctrines are ethical systems for deriving rules for human conduct. Analytic natural-law systems purport to explain the nature and operation of the economic system on the basis of some inherent necessity. Applied to normative systems, the term natural law has been elastic enough to embrace both scholastic economics and Benthamite utilitarianism; applied to analytic systems it encompasses classical economics at the one extreme and Marxian economics at the other. Yet while a system may be predominantly normative or predominantly analytic, it is not exclusively one or the other. A normative system presupposes an explanatory theory for analyzing economic phenomena; and the proponents of an explanatory natural law, rarely content to remain at the level of pure analysis, tend to elevate their conclusions into norms of ethics and canons of policy.

The Scholastic Doctors. For the scholastic doctors the natural law was jurisprudential and ethical. It was law. It imposed on men the moral and ethical obligation to follow the dictates of reason (*recta ratio*) as it interpreted the imperatives of the situation in which they found themselves. Implicit and fundamental to scholastic economics, as well as to its sociology and politics, was a belief in the solidarity of human society based, in the first instance, on a philosophy that saw men as possessed of a common nature with a common origin and destiny that could be attained only through cooperation; and in the second instance, on a theology that revered men as brothers in Christ and children of God. Against this background the concept of the public, or common, good was pivotal, as it applied to social relationships.

To put the matter briefly, the obligations of the natural law in a concrete economic situation were practically determined for the scholastic economists of the 16th century by answering the question, What does the common good require? And once this question was asked, the need for an explanatory, or analytic, economic theory became evident. The scholastic jurists were seeking practical rules for conduct. In matters relating to exchange, for example, their purpose would not have been served by responding that the natural law required equality between the value received and the value surrendered. The scholastic doctor had to go further and ask what kind of value is in question and how it is measured or determined; i.e., to give meanings to his norms he had to elaborate an explanatory theory of economic value. The late Joseph A. Schumpeter, citing Luis Molina as typical of 16th-century scholastic economists, says that he "clearly identified natural law, on the one hand, with the dictates of reason (*ratio recta*), and with what is socially expedient or necessary (*expediens et necessarium*), on the other. . . . He definitely married natural law to our rational diagnosis, with reference to the Common Good, of the cases—whether individual contracts or social institutions—which we observe in research or practice" [J. A. Schumpeter, *History of Economic Analysis* (Oxford University Press 1954) 109].

For all who advocated any of its various forms, the natural law implied some vision of an economic order and some necessity with respect to its operation and maintenance. For the scholastics, the natural physical laws imposed a rigid necessity on inanimate nature: free-falling bodies in a vacuum accelerate at an unvarying rate because the laws of physical nature require it. But the natural moral law governing man obliged, but did not compel, him to follow the dictates of reason as it interpreted for him the moral imperatives of a given situation. Thus in the scholastics' conception, the economic order was not the automatic result of laws inherent in economic phenomena; man remained a self-governing maker of his own economic order, with the responsibility of asserting his authority, as circumstances might require, over economic reality. The distinction between the kind of necessity imposed on inanimate nature by the natural physical laws and on men by the natural moral law tended to become blurred when the concept of natural law came to be applied to economic analysis.

The Natural-law Economists. Four groups that proposed natural-law systems of economic analysis deserve discussion: the physiocrats, the classical school of economists, the utilitarians, and the Marxists. To the first of these, however, we shall advert only in passing. They had little influence on subsequent economic thought, and what is said about the classical school is broadly applicable also to them. As a representative of the clas-

sical school we shall discuss explicitly only the position held by Adam Smith.

Adam Smith. Any attempt to discuss the natural-law aspects of Adam Smith's economic analysis courts error because his *Wealth of Nations* fails to make explicit the details of his philosophy. But a vision of the economy as a quasi-mechanical system seems to have remained always at the periphery of his thought. Consideration of the epoch-making achievements in the physical sciences must have aided both Smith and the physiocrats in achieving, independently of each other, what was perhaps their greatest contribution to economic science, a view of the economy as a unified system. The planets, despite their wide-swinging and apparently unrelated courses, had been shown to be parts of a system and to follow predictable paths in obedience to laws that human reason had discovered and formulated. From inanimate to social nature must have seemed a short step. The economy, when closely observed, was seen also to be a system. Did it not also obey laws that, when discovered and stated, would introduce order into the apparent chaos of the self-seeking activities of individual men? In taking this step, that is, in formulating economic laws, Smith and his successors, and especially their popularizers, tended to impose on human beings in their economic relationships a necessity that approached the response of inanimate nature to its physical laws. This statement, if understood to describe an explicit and conscious attitude of either Smith or the major economists in the classical tradition, goes too far. They clearly recognized that men are free, but the tendency to clothe economic behavior with mechanical qualities seems to be almost visibly operating just below the surface of their analysis. This appeal to nature, when yoked to David Ricardo's cold logic, helps to explain the rigid dogmatism with which later generations of noneconomists invested the propositions of classical economic theory.

In Smith we may distinguish a normative ethic, an analytic natural law, and a natural order. A major task of the normative natural law, i.e., of reason guiding both society and its members, was abolition of "all systems either of preference or restraint," thus permitting the simple and obvious system of natural liberty to operate of its own accord. The result would be an economic order of maximum efficiency in which men were rewarded in accordance with the value of their economic contribution. The law (here we have the explanatory natural law) that achieves and maintains this order is essentially intrinsic to the economic system. Its impelling force is the self-interest of the individual members of society, coupled with their equally natural propensity to cooperate through exchange, to truck and barter, with other men. Its policing force is the discipline of the free market. Thus the forces that make for establishment and maintenance of economic order have ceased to be man and society acting in conscious response to the dictates of reason. It has become inescapable law written by providence in human nature at the level of instinctive response.

This does not imply that Smith advocated either an unrestrained self-interest or considered man as amoral in his economic affairs. Professor O. H. Taylor, who brought to the study of Smith both a sympathy for his liberalism and an unusual understanding of the natural-law tradition (and to whom this exposition is indebted) has shown that Smith's "simple and obvious system of natural liberty" assumed that exchange would always take place within a system governed by a moral code that required justice and advocated benevolence in human relations and within a framework of competitive markets that based economic reward upon service to the community. It does imply that Smith overemphasized the automatic character of the economic system and that by linking mechanistic analysis both with natural law and providential design on the one hand and with optimum utilization of economic resources on the other, he laid the foundation of a business philosophy that relieved society of its obligation to strive to make its economic system reflect the requirements of social justice. As this business philosophy became a major determinant of public policy in the 19th century, it also became and remained for generations an obstacle to social reform.

Utilitarianism. Benthamite utilitarianism (Jeremy Bentham, 1748–1832) replaced self-interest with a pleasure-pain calculus as the wellspring of human motivation: the character of economic response remains automatic, for men choose what gives pleasure; they flee from pain. Utilitarianism, of course, rose above the cruder concept of pleasure. There was room in the concept for Brahms as well as for beefsteaks, but not for much else. Beatitude, of course, is the end of all human striving. But if we equate with pleasure all efforts to attain it, including the necessary self-denial, utilitarianism loses all its meaning. Whereas Smith made economic welfare consist in an increase of the product of a nation's labor, utilitarianism saw it as the greatest good (the greatest pleasure) of the greatest number. To the state fell the task of maintaining whatever social cooperation was needed for attaining this common good. Since men are attracted by pleasure and deterred by pain, the business of achieving the common good becomes a matter of the state's devising appropriate incentives and sanctions. And as the state must direct its citizens, it must also choose their goals. Thus liberalism, in a utilitarian setting, acquires a new meaning; it justifies unlimited intervention in economic matters and makes the state the arbiter of the economic satisfactions of its citizens, and through pleasure-pain incentives and deterrents it reduces the populace to automatons.

Utilitarianism and the scholastic view of the normative natural law have this in common: both place in the public authority the ultimate responsibility for assuring the common good. But they are light years apart in their view of what constitutes the common good. The scholastic doctors could be thoroughly utilitarian when it came to achieving economic goals. They asked what the common good requires. But economic goals held a place in their hierarchy of values that made the economic process itself instrumental. Utilitarianism, however, adopts a view of welfare that excludes everything that gives depth and meaning to human living. The jurisprudence of liberalism is reduced to mathematical computations and interpersonal comparisons of unquantifiable satisfactions. For these reasons the welfare economics that utilitarianism sponsored has been relatively disappointing.

Marxism. It would be more accurate to regard Marxism as a natural-law (analytic) sociology rather than as economics. The determinism underlying Marx's interpretation of history relates not only to the economic system, but to the whole social order. It is basically economic, however, for with Marx it is the character of economic phenomena that shape and determine all other institutions. Little need be said here beyond pointing out that for Marx the economic system dominates men, and not vice versa, and that the system is driven irresistibly by class conflict to revolution, the overthrow of capitalism, and to the victory of the proletariat. Like the natural law of the classicists, Marxism leads logically to abdication of responsibility. For the classicist, human direction of the system was unnecessary; welfare had been assured by the invisible hand. For the Marxian, to the extent that he remained wholly consistent, human direction was futile; the march of history was ordained and irresistible.

Contemporary Aspects. Natural-law thinking, whether of a normative or analytic nature, is largely discredited in economics today. The normative natural law, of which Catholics in the scholastic tradition are the more important advocates, is discredited partly because it is not widely understood. A more important reason is the failure of many writers in this tradition, most of whom are advocating social reforms, to wrestle with the economic realities of problems they consider. Too often they seem content to argue from natural-law premises that some socially desirable end should be achieved and having established this conclusion to their satisfaction, fail to consider the economic problems involved. The fact that men have the responsibility of assuring justice in economic relationships does not cause the economic problem to disappear. There is an economic science precisely because economic goods are scarce in relation to human wants. Successful reform can occur only within the limits of economic feasibility. The rehabilitation of a normative natural law will require a better command of economic theory by its proponents. Natural law has been discredited in an analytic sense on the basis of experience. While there are economic laws, i.e., observed or inferred relationships between economic realities, nothing in their nature assures that they will automatically produce an efficient and equitable economic order. Experience demonstrates the opposite. They may be manipulated for private advantage by those who acquire power positions in the economy. Economics today is almost wholly scientific; i.e., it devises tools for economic analysis and explores relationships between economic phenomena without pronouncing on the desirability either of goals or policy. Economists now are asking whether this cultivation of pure economics has not gone too far and whether there is sufficient inquiry among economists about the ends of economic activity and the requirements for and constituents of a sound economic order.

Bibliography: J. A. Schumpeter, *History of Economic Analysis,* ed. E. B. Schumpeter (New York 1954). O. H. Taylor, *A History of Economic Thought* (New York 1960); "Economics and the Idea of Natural Laws," *Quarterly Journal of Economics* 44 (1929–30) 1–39. P. Strure, "L'Idée de loi naturelle dans la science économique," *Revue d'économie politique* 35 (1921) 294–317, 463–482. W. L. Davidson, *Political Thought in England: The Utilitarians from Bentham to J. S. Mill* (New York 1916).

[L. C. Brown]

NATURAL LAW IN POLITICAL THOUGHT

*Natural law has been a perennial theme for political philosophers; and even in mid-20th century, after 150 years of critical analysis, it retains an interest and vitality. The concept of natural law originated in the classical period, reached its highest development in late medieval and early modern times, and continues to be significant, especially in legal theory and in the ideology of *Christian Democracy and other movements of Catholic inspiration. In the course of 2,500 years, the appeal to certain fixed universal principles that can be perceived in *nature and in human nature has taken a variety of forms and served a number of functions; but as long as men have sought justifications for the political order beyond those of tradition and revelation, the appeal to nature and natural law has remained an element in political thought (*see* STATE).

Classical Period. It was the breakdown of the traditional order in the period following the Persian Wars and the immediate confrontation of widely varying political systems that first gave rise to the appeal to nature in ancient Greece. In the search for an ethical and legal standard, the participants in the political discussions of 5th-century Athens made use of the concept of nature (*physis*) that had been used in earlier scientific speculation to explain the ultimate constituent elements of the universe. In Thucydides's history of the Peloponnesian Wars and in the opening pages of Plato's *Republic,* there are images of the then current Sophist doctrine that by a natural law the strong do and should rule the weak. Surviving fragments of Sophist writings also indicate that some argued that all men were equal by nature and that social as well as moral distinctions were purely conventional. In his *Republic* *Plato attempted to respond to both these criticisms, arguing for a natural order of reason over the passions in the individual and of the more rational over the less intelligent in society. *Aristotle based his defense of slavery on a natural inequality among men and appealed to the nature of man as the basis for government and private property. Equally important for the history of the theory was Aristotle's teleological method, his attribution of an inherent purposiveness and intelligibility to nature. Yet neither Plato nor Aristotle developed a full-fledged natural law theory as such. For Plato law was associated with the rigid and inadequate legal rules of the contemporary Greek city-state; it appeared to be a second-best compromise when the rule of the wise could not be assured. In his *Nicomachean Ethics* Aristotle wrote of a natural justice invariable among gods but variable among men (1134b); in the *Politics* he described law as "reason free from passion" (1287a), and in the *Rhetoric* he alluded to a universal or common law "in accordance with nature" (1373b). Yet it is only in the writings of the Stoics that the term "law of nature" was used, and a systematic theory of a higher law based on nature developed.

Emerging in Greece after the breakdown of the Greek city-state and the triumph of the Macedonian Empire, *Stoicism became the dominant philosophy of the ruling classes of the Roman Empire and profoundly influenced the formulation of *Roman law. According to Stoic thought man participated in divine Reason, which permeated the universe; and it was in the common possession of reason, considered both as a moral and intellectual faculty, that all men were equal by nature. Stoic thought on natural law thus departed in theory from the elitism of Plato and Aristotle, although in practice *Cicero, whose *De republica* and *De legibus* are the principal sources for Stoic natural law theories, rejected democracy and argued for the rule of a rational elite. A similar hesitancy to apply the practical consequences of the theory characterized the attitude of Cicero and the Roman lawyers toward a possible conflict between the natural law and existing legal institutions, such as slavery, that were viewed as contrary to the natural equality of all mankind.

Christian Development. Christianity gave a different basis to the doctrine of *equality—the moral responsibility of every man to God—and a different appeal as the basis of political legitimacy—the will of God. Christianity had a higher law, but it was not the law of nature; it was that of divine revelation (*see* REVELATION, THEOLOGY OF). The early Christian attitude toward nature was ambiguous. On the one hand, nature (and especially human nature) had been corrupted by *original sin. The pagan philosophers without the guidance of revelation were steeped in sin, which would adversely affect their ability to attain moral truth. As Tertullian put it, "not Athens, but Jerusalem" (*De praescriptione haereticorum,* ch. 7). On the other hand, nature was created by God, who as a purposive and intelligent Being had established an ordered universe. Moreover, St. Paul, who was familiar with Stoic thought, had written, "When the Gentiles who have no law do by nature what the Law prescribes, these having no law are a law unto themselves. They show the work of the Law written in their hearts" (Rom 2.14–15).

In their confrontation with classical culture, the Fathers of the Church ultimately adopted the latter attitude and incorporated the natural-law doctrine as part of the Christian tradition. St. *Augustine himself, despite his emphasis on the opposition of nature and grace, often referred to the natural law in his writings. However, the Stoic teaching about the original equality of all men received a different formulation in Christian teaching. The Fathers saw equality as the condition in the Garden of Eden and attributed all forms of domination and government, property, and slavery, to man's fall from grace. As this instance demonstrates, the relation of natural law to revelation was not clear in early Christian writings; and as late as the writings of the canon lawyers of the 12th and 13th centuries, the natural and the divine law tended to be equated.

It was the genius of St. *Thomas Aquinas in the 13th century to distinguish divine law, in the sense of revelation, from natural law, in the sense of those moral imperatives that man can perceive with his reason in an ordered universe created by God. Aquinas drew on Aristotle to affirm the natural character of government and to relate Aristotelian teleology to the natural law in a hierarchy of ends and inclinations in human nature corresponding to the principal precepts of the natural law. In a famous passage (ST 1a2ae, 94.2) he described these as existence; self-preservation; the family; and education, society, and (natural) religion.

The appeal to the natural law had more force in the Middle Ages when it was associated directly with God's will than in Roman times when it was simply a philosophic theory. Yet despite Aquinas's argument that human laws contrary to natural law are null and void (ST 1a2ae, 95.2.), it was not widely used for the purpose of invalidating existing laws or practices. Laws were sometimes opposed by referring to natural and divine law (retaining the canonist confusion of the two), but the most common appeals were to the positive law of the Church or to traditional feudal rights. The natural law decreed human equality, but there was no demand for the abolition of slavery; and the belief in a hierarchical universe, derived ultimately from Neoplatonist sources, tended to justify a hierarchical social order as a part of the nature of things. Yet in the late Middle Ages the doctrine of the original natural equality of all mankind was also cited to reinforce the development of representative institutions in both Church and State, and appeals were made in both canon and civil law to the principle that all those affected by governmental decisions have a natural-law right to give their consent, either through representatives or (more often) tacitly.

Modern Period. Aquinas had asserted the limits of human reason and the importance of the divine law as a guide and a supplement to the natural law; but at the same time, in emphasizing the rational character of the moral law and the powers of the human reason to attain truth, he had helped to lay open the possibility of the assertion of a naturalist and rationalist morality without recourse to revelation, or for that matter, to God. The late scholastics had asked whether the natural law was so firmly based in reason that even God himself could not change it, and *Grotius (1583–1645), the first of the modern theorists of international law, argued in 1625 that the natural law would still exist "even if we should concede that which cannot be conceded without the utmost wickedness, that there is no God" (*De Jure Belli ac Pacis,* prolegomena). Although one can exaggerate the secularism of early modern theories of natural law, there is no doubt that the medieval link between the natural and the divine law was broken once there was disagreement after the Reformation as to the content of revelation. In fact, it appeared for a time that the Reformers' suspicion of reason and the natural man would end all reference to the natural law by Christian writers. However, the need for a common standard in a religiously divided Christendom compelled those who wrote works of political theory to appeal to it and to develop theories as to its origin and content that were less specifically religious than those of the Middle Ages.

In the works of Thomas *Hobbes (1588–1679) the term natural law was used to describe a set of maxims for self-preservation, and a hypothetical state of nature replaced the Judeo-Christian Garden of Eden. God entered only as the enforcing sovereign of revealed law, not as the eternal reason of Thomism. John *Locke (1632–1704) borrowed the state of nature from Hobbes, but combined it with a theory of natural law that was derived from St. Thomas by way of the Anglican divine Thomas *Hooker (1553–1600). Although there are problems in relating Locke's theory of natural law to the empiricism of his *Essay Concerning Human Understanding,* the recent discovery of a manuscript copy of his *Essays on the Law of Nature* makes it clear that his theory of natural law was more traditional than Hobbesian. A novel element, however, was his strong emphasis on the right of private property as decreed by the natural law.

In the 17th-century theories, the natural law served the important function of providing a ground for legitimacy in a political theory. For Grotius the requirements of the social nature of man were the source of the binding force of international law. For Hobbes, man's drive to preserve himself made obedience to the sovereign a moral obligation. For Locke, the natural rights of man provided the basis for consent to government and the limits upon the exercise of power. In all three cases, too, the natural law was seen as prescribing a fundamental

equality among men that was not simply a characteristic of some earlier lost state—although in Hobbes's theory, this equality was more physical than moral. In the same century, new scientific advances undermined whatever arguments for hierarchy could be drawn from analogy to the structure of the universe. Natural law arguments were drawn from human nature, not from nature in general.

It was as a theory of consent and equality that natural law, as transformed by Locke into natural rights, achieved its most widespread acceptance in the 18th century. In the *Declaration of Independence (1776) and the Declaration of the Rights of Man (1789), it became a central feature of the ideologies of the American and French Revolutions; and subsequently it provided the intellectual background for the early court decisions that established the American doctrine of judicial review (*see* POLITICAL THOUGHT, AMERICAN).

Yet at the very time that it attained its greatest influence the theory of the law of nature was subjected to a series of attacks that led to a rapid decline in its influence. In England David *Hume (1711–76) in his *Treatise of Human Nature* (1740) took issue with the notion that any values could be derived from the facts of nature or human nature, while the utilitarians such as Jeremy *Bentham (1748–1832) argued that moral and legal principles were better derived from their effects on society than from anything inherent in nature. On the Continent, Immanuel *Kant (1724–1804) posited a sharp dichotomy between the facts of nature and the realm of moral obligation, and attempted to draw conclusions about law and morality from the nature of legal and moral obligation rather than from the nature of man. In the 19th century, the positivists attempted to separate legality and morality to the detriment of natural-law theory, which had considered them as closely related (*see* POSITIVISM IN JURISPRUDENCE). The theory of evolution and new anthropological research also revealed that the nature of man was not as fixed and unchanging as the defenders of natural law had assumed. By the end of the 19th century, the only political theory that made use of natural law was that contained in the papal social and political encyclicals, which continued to speak in terms of Thomistic natural-law theory (*see* SOCIAL THOUGHT, PAPAL).

Natural Law Revival. In the 20th century, particularly since the 1930s, there has been a marked revival of interest in natural law as it relates to political theory. A variety of different factors account for this. The excesses of the Nazi regime suggested the need for a higher standard beyond that of the positive law, and after World War II the UN Declaration of Human Rights was justified by some as an attempt to set down natural law obligations binding on governments (*see* HUMAN RIGHTS). The neo-Thomist revival, and especially the writings of Jacques Maritain (1882–), modernized the theory of Aquinas and placed greater emphasis on the development in history of new insights into the implications of the natural law, thus partially coming to terms with the evolutionist critique. In terms of practical effect, the most important development was the organization of Christian Democratic parties in Europe and more recently in Latin America, whose programs are couched in natural-law terms borrowed from the papal encyclicals and the writings of Maritain. Proposals such as family allowances, worker participation in management, guarantees of the right to organize trade unions, and, more recently, religious freedom and a nuclear test ban treaty have been advocated as conclusions from the natural law. In the area of personal morality with implications for public policy, artificial birth control, sterilization, and divorce have been opposed as prohibited by the same law. Among the areas currently in dispute among natural-law theorists of Thomist inspiration are the extent of the limits on property rights that may be imposed by the state, and the morality of nuclear warfare.

Aside from legal theorists, there are few non-Thomist political philosophers who use the vocabulary of natural law. Yet much of the writing about politics and morals is based on an implicit or explicit conception of the nature of man and the prerequisites for the full expression of human potentialities. To speak about the dignity of man or the necessity of human freedom is to assert a goal for society and the political order that is related to certain universal and constant values inherent in the nature of man. That these moral and legal conceptions vary in different societies proves only that the perception and application of these goals and the choice among them in the common situation of conflict of one with another remains difficult. Ultimately the problem remains the one that puzzled the Greeks: how to find the one in the many, a constant principle in a world of change, a measure that is neither too rigid nor too vague to provide a standard for positive law and government and a basis for political obligation. The answer that the Greeks first conceived—a law of nature—continues to appeal to political theorists, among them many who are not aware of the type of argument they are using.

See also LAW; POLITICAL THOUGHT, HISTORY OF.

Bibliography: A. PASSERIN D'ENTRÈVES, *Natural Law: An Introduction to Legal Philosophy* (New York 1951), the best general survey of the topic with an excellent bibliog. Center for the Study of Democratic Institutions, *Natural Law and Modern Society* (Cleveland 1963). E. S. CORWIN, *The "Higher Law" Background of American Constitutional Law* (Ithaca, N.Y. 1955). J. MARITAIN, *Man and the State* (Chicago 1951); *The Rights of Man and Natural Law,* tr. D. C. ANSON (New York 1943). H. A. ROMMEN, *The Natural Law,* tr. T. P. HANLEY (St. Louis 1947). L. STRAUSS, *Natural Right and History* (Chicago 1953).

[P. E. SIGMUND]

NATURAL ORDER

The terms natural and natural order have been used extensively in modern theology to distinguish as sharply as possible what is meant by supernatural and supernatural order. While this contrast and correlation has had a long history in Catholic theology, its modern usage and emphasis appear to stem from the middle of the 19th century. Confronted with the spread of philosophical naturalism as well as various theories of natural religion, the theologians began to make the notion of the supernatural a fundamental category of systematic theology. As used in this context the notions natural and natural order serve to underline clearly the transcendent character of the divine order and the gratuitous character of the order of grace, which they incorporate into the notion of the absolute supernatural. The natural order, therefore, would be defined as a created order in which man would be directed to an end or destiny that is strictly proportionate to his capacities, powers, and exigencies. This end would be God as known through reason. In contrast the absolutely supernatural would

be that which completely transcends the capacities, powers, and exigencies of created or creatable nature. The notion of the natural order played a very important role in the systematic treatment of such areas as apologetics, revelation, and grace. It enabled the theologian to bring out clearly the transcendence of the divine order and the gratuity of man's call to the beatific vision as well as his elevation by God's grace.

In recent years, however, there has been considerable questioning and debate over the exact content of this theological notion of natural as contrasted with supernatural. The basis of the criticism lies in the fact that the usage is built upon a more precise, specific, and detailed definition of natural than is legitimately possible. It is argued that historical man is a reality whose total actual nature can be known only through revelation. Revelation helps us to discern some elements proper to the natural order. Rational analysis discloses other elements. Hence while nature and grace are clearly distinct, nothing can be defined in such specific detail that a kind of clear and proven horizontal line could be drawn between the natural and the supernatural.

The theological opinion that gave rise to this critique began with the fact that God has called historical man to the beatific vision. From this fact it is argued that this divinely given vocation is not something merely logical awaiting some future actualization. Rather it is a fact; it is real and must have an impact on man that influences the very structure of his nature. Hence the supernatural, while gratuitous, is rooted in man from the very beginning of his existence. By reason of this he has a tendency to the beatific vision and a resonance of it in his very being. It is this situation that Karl Rahner describes as "the *supernatural existential." If, therefore, the supernatural is already present in man in the sense described, there is no element of his nature that is not in some way touched by it. Hence the difficulty or even impossibility of saying what precisely is natural and so belongs to the natural order. In all this it should be noted that the protagonists of this position do not reject the possibility that God could create intelligent beings and not call them to the beatific vision.

Bibliography: S. OTTO, "Natur," Fries HbThGrdbgr 2:217–219. H. DE LUBAC, *Surnaturel: Études historiques* (Paris 1946) 325–395. M. J. SCHEEBEN, *Nature and Grace,* tr. C. VOLLERT (St. Louis 1954). K. RAHNER, "Concerning the Relationship between Nature and Grace," *Theological Investigations,* v.1, tr. C. ERNST (Baltimore 1961) 297–317. J. P. KENNY, "Reflections of Human Nature and the Supernatural," ThSt 14 (1953) 280–287.

[E. M. BURKE]

NATURALISM

A movement within American philosophy affirming that nature is the whole of reality; that man has his origin, growth, and decay within nature; and that nature—defined as that which is amenable to scientific investigation—is self-explanatory. The term is used also (1) for an ethical doctrine teaching that *morality consists in living according to nature or to biological impulse; (2) for the aesthetic doctrine holding that art must imitate nature (*see* AESTHETICS; NATURALISM, LITERARY); and (3) for the religious belief that identifies nature with the Godhead (*see* PANTHEISM). This article is concerned with the philosophical position known as American naturalism, treating of its history and its salient characteristics, and concluding with a critique from the viewpoint of theistic realism.

History. As a philosophical attitude, naturalism is not indigenous to America. Its European roots are evident in British *empiricism and in the *positivism and sociologism of August *Comte and Ernst *Mach. Nowhere but in the U.S., however, has the term naturalism been commonly used to designate a particular set of philosophical views. Yet naturalism arrived relatively late on the American scene. It arose as an alternative to the *idealism dominant in American thought during the last quarter of the 19th century and influential during the first 2 decades of the 20th. By the 1930s, naturalism had clearly replaced idealism as the predominant trend in American philosophical thinking.

The first major expression of the naturalistic temper in the U.S. is to be found in the *Life of Reason* (5 v. New York 1905–06) of George *Santayana. Other systematic expressions are subsequently to be found in Roy Wood Sellars' *Evolutionary Naturalism* (Chicago 1921), Frederick J. E. Woodbridge's *Nature and Mind* (New York 1937), and James B. Pratt's *Naturalism* (New York 1938). Contributions that also must be mentioned are those of Morris R. Cohen (*Reason and Nature*, New York 1931), Clarence I. Lewis (*Mind and World Order*, New York 1929), and William P. Montague (*The Ways of Things*, New York 1940).

Of American naturalists, however, John *Dewey is the most important, not only because of his significant contribution to the doctrinal development of naturalism but also because through him naturalism has come to exert a strong influence on public education and consequently on the American mind generally. The history of American naturalism is strikingly reflected in Dewey's own intellectual development as he moved from an early defense of idealism, confident that the new discoveries in biology and psychology could be incorporated into an idealistic framework, to an outright naturalism, presented as the only outlook compatible with the modern scientific world view. The mature naturalism of Dewey not only is apparent in his later works such as *Experience and Nature* (Chicago 1925) and *The Quest for Certainty* (New York 1929), but it is reflected also in the writings of his disciples, particularly in the articles of his cocontributors to the platform volumes, *American Philosophy Today and Tomorrow* (ed. H. M. Kallen and S. Hook, New York 1935) and *Naturalism and the Human Spirit* (ed. Y. H. Krikorian, New York 1944). Many of the contributors to these two volumes subsequently developed themes first presented there. Although American naturalism at mid-century is not to be identified with the authors represented in these symposia, it is evident that they well represent this tendency in American thought. Of the contributors to these volumes, three of Dewey's disciples may be singled out as representative of the naturalistic interest and temperament, viz, S. Hook, E. Nagel, and J. H. Randall, Jr.

Sidney Hook (1902–), long associated with the Washington Square College of New York University, has written extensively on social questions. His works include: *John Dewey: An Intellectual Portrait* (New York 1939), *Reason, Social Myths, and Democracy* (New York 1940), *Education for Modern Man* (New York 1950), and *The Quest for Being* (New York 1961). Ernest Nagel (1901–), who has taught at Columbia University since 1930, has written principally

in the philosophy of science and has done much to refine the naturalist's concept of science. His important works are: *Sovereign Reason* (New York 1954), *Logic Without Metaphysics* (New York 1957), and *The Structure of Science* (New York 1961). John Herman Randall, Jr. (1899–), has lectured at Columbia since 1925. Randall has been notably influenced by Woodbridge as well as by Dewey. A historian of philosophy and perhaps more metaphysically inclined than most naturalists, Randall's major contributions to naturalism are his volumes *Nature and Historical Experience* (New York 1958) and *The Role of Knowledge in Western Religion* (Boston 1958).

Characteristics. The principal notions that underlie naturalism may be explained by sketching its characteristic teachings, i.e., its method, epistemology, anthropology, pragmatism, empiricism, ethics, and philosophy of value.

Method. Most of the proponents of naturalism present it as a tendency, an outlook, or a frame of mind, rather than as a system. Two basic theses underlie all naturalistic investigation. The first affirms that whatever happens in nature is dependent in some fundamental way on the organization of bodies located in space and time, and the second insists that the "scientific method" is the only means of obtaining reliable knowledge. Naturalists, on the whole, are found to be rather ambiguous in stating the nature of scientific method, but most would admit of its analogical predication. In a broad sense, scientific method is regarded as nothing more than the use of "critical intelligence." Hence the disciplines of sociology and economics, as well as history in some of its phases, are regarded by the naturalist as genuinely scientific.

Epistemology. Epistemologically the naturalist must be considered to be a realist, in the sense that he holds that the objects of knowledge are extramental and that they exist as they are perceived to be, although nominalistic and Kantian tendencies can at times be discerned in some naturalists. Metaphysically, the naturalist presents himself as antidualistic, objecting to the distinctions between the natural and supernatural, between man and nature, mind and body, and appearance and reality. He will accept the designation "materialist" if he is allowed to distinguish between reductive materialism and his own. Reductive materialism, as the naturalist defines it, reduces mental events immediately to the physical, whereas nonreductive materialism, or naturalism, affirms merely that every mental event is contingent upon the organization of certain physical events. The naturalist is careful to avoid suggesting that an idea is nothing but "a potential or tentative muscular response" or that pain is nothing but "the passing of an electric current through a nerve fiber." But he does assert that the relation between the occurrence of ideas or pains and the occurrence of physiological manifestations is a contingent or causal one. As to the existence of God, immortality, separated souls or spirits, cosmic purpose or design, these are denied by the naturalist "for the same generic reasons that he denies the existence of fairies, elves, leprechauns, and an invisible satellite revolving between earth and moon." There is no evidence for any of them.

Anthropology. As to his teaching on man, the naturalist grants that man is unique among animals in ability and accomplishment but denies that he occupies a special place in nature. Between man and his animal ancestors there is only a difference of degree, not one of kind. Consciousness, like the other phenomena, can be described empirically, at least in its effects, and accounted for in terms of matter and the organization of matter. Presupposed by the naturalist is a theory of biological evolution according to which nature in its evolutionary process regularly gives rise to operations and functions on newer and higher levels. Consciousness and thought are regarded as two such higher operations. They have their sole cause in the organism in which they appear. Admittedly, thought and consciousness are distinct from any previous products of an evolving nature, but the factors from which they arose are no different, except for their particular organization, from the factors whence physical, chemical, and biological processes arose.

Pragmatism. By temperament the naturalist is oriented toward the practical. With the pragmatist he agrees that knowledge, if it is to be considered meaningful, must have practical consequences. But whereas C. S. *Peirce and W. James would be reluctant to identify pragmatism with any one method, the naturalist, particularly in the *instrumentalism of John Dewey, identifies experimental science as the perfect example of the intimate connection between theory and practice, between knowing and doing. For the naturalist, mind or intelligence exists as a problem-solving power, and this function is regarded as more important than its theoretical employment. Science, insofar as it is the most perfect form of intelligence, takes on the status of instrument par excellence.

Concerned with the application of critical intelligence to the social, political, and economic problems of the times, the naturalist is contemptuous of fixed codes theologically or philosophically derived. He regards religion and traditional philosophy as impediments rather than as aids to social progress. Although he looks upon belief in God as a dangerous drain on social energies, he does not deny a certain sociological value to religion. But he does deny that it produces knowledge that can be subjected to rigorous criticism. What is valuable in religious witness, the naturalist asserts, can be derived from other sources.

Empiricism. Although the naturalist by disposition eschews systems, he has nevertheless, by adopting an empiricist attitude toward the problems of substance, efficient causality, and final causality, produced a consistent metaphysics with consequences in the moral and civic orders. By defining substance as a logical category, as that segment of the process called reality upon which man chooses to fasten his attention, and by adopting D. Hume's analysis of causality, the naturalist has ruled out the question of the origin of the universe. Because situations are always encountered as particular, concrete, and determinable, one can never experience anything that might be called "the Universe." The Universe, or Nature, has no meaning except in the sense that it might be considered a locus for all processes. The meaning of any process, according to the naturalist, is the way it functions in its context. Now what has no context can have no function and hence no meaning. The Universe has no discoverable context, since one experiences it neither as a whole nor as coming to be. Hence the question of its origin is a meaningless question.

Ethics. The implications for ethics are apparent. Since, according to the naturalist, there is no transcendent end for man, values must be found within the social context. As Krikorian has written, "the source of motivation for humanity must be found within the natural setting of its existence . . . rather than in something which is neither verifiable nor approachable." Values are relative because the most one can determine is "how best" he can do something under a particular set of circumstances. What is best absolutely is beyond one's knowledge. Man cannot determine what is best in the ultimate context, because the ultimate context is beyond discovery. Hence the good of a situation has to be determined on the basis of the defect to be rectified. Each situation will give rise to its own good. There will be no fixed absolutes as the supernaturalist would suppose. The imposition of fixed or transcendent ends is simply a sign of an emotional grappling for certainty where certainty is impossible.

Values. In the realm of values the naturalist has been primarily a philosopher of ethics or an epistemologist, rather than a moral philosopher in the traditional sense. His concern has been with the question of how values ought to be determined. Although all naturalists are agreed that scientific procedure ought to be employed in ethics, there is no general agreement as to what constitutes scientific procedure. The naturalist recognizes that normative propositions cannot be determined by the same procedure employed in verifying questions of fact. He admits also that the use of data derived from the physical and behavioral sciences does not constitute an ethics as scientific. Most naturalists find the problem of how to determine values scientifically a particularly vexing one. Confronted with the problem, many fall back on custom or inclination as a guide in determining what is morally best or resort to some form of *utilitarianism. But most naturalists admit that custom or inclination is not a sure guide; the whole point of the naturalist's concern with morals has been to get away from subjectivism. Utilitarianism is likewise found unsatisfactory, because it begs the question as to which of the ends and relationships human beings naturally cherish, or which of the values they normally institute, are desirable in the long run; it also fails to take into account the empirically discernible fact that man acts out of motives of duty. Admittedly naturalistic ethics is incomplete.

Critique. In evaluating the work of the American naturalist, the validity of many of his insights must be acknowledged: for example, his insistence on starting with experience, his interest in social and political questions, his concern for an enlightened and critical morality, his emphasis on clarity and the useful function that *linguistic analysis can perform in achieving clarity, and his demand that the philosopher shun any special witness, such as that which might be provided by intuition or religious faith. The naturalist's attack on idealism, his repudiation of the Cartesian dichotomy between mind and body, his criticism of some prevailing ethical and religious conceptions of nature are features that are not reserved to naturalism but are part of a common *realism and can therefore be accepted.

But what cannot be accepted is the naturalist's principal thesis that the boundaries of scientific knowledge are the boundaries of certain knowledge. Nowhere does the scientist himself proclaim that his method is the only one productive of reliable knowledge. Science includes no such treatment of epistemology or values as one finds them in naturalism. The naturalist's defense of his position is not a scientific defense but is based on an appeal to common sense and to the data of history.

The naturalist rightly attempts to rule out anything that has no claim to genuine knowledge, but in doing so he has assumed that philosophy has produced no certain knowledge. Also, he has implicitly denied that there is truth or falsity in philosophical knowledge. Again, the naturalist's employment of history is selective. The history of philosophy is not merely a record of discord. It also discloses amid the diversity of opinion and the prevalence of conflict a core of common philosophical experience that exhibits a remarkable unity. Étienne Gilson has clearly shown in his *Unity of Philosophical Experience* (New York 1937) that similar approaches to perennial problems yield strikingly similar results. It seems, therefore, that the task of "critical intelligence" is not the wholesale repudiation of philosophy but the sifting of diverse opinions to determine what is valuable in them.

The naturalist's thesis that traditional philosophy and theology, especially during their period of ascendancy in the Middle Ages, have exercised a retarding influence on science is belied by recent developments in the history of science and technology. There is a growing body of evidence, accumulated since the pioneer work of P. *Duhem and L. Thorndike, to show that medieval philosophy and theology, far from impeding the development of science and technology, actually laid the groundwork, through discussions of science and scientific method, for the so-called scientific renaissance of the 17th century. Also indefensible is the assumption that the distinction between God and nature inevitably leads to an antagonism in which man's temporal ends are slighted. Although theism in some of its forms may result in a neglect of temporal values, the history of Christianity, in every age, is replete with examples of concern for specifically human ends (*see* MAN, NATURAL END OF).

From an epistemological point of view, the naturalist's delimitation of reality to nature is a consequence of an uncritically assumed empiricism. In adopting the empiricist's solution to the problems of *substance and *causality, the naturalist has automatically ruled out the possibility of reasoning to a transcendent cause of nature or of recognizing the spiritual component of man. By following Hume, the naturalist opens himself to the same charges that are brought against that 18th-century philosopher, namely, that in atomizing experience he falsifies the fact that things are not given in isolation but in a dynamic interrelation with other things, both conferring and receiving action. Against the naturalist it can be argued that a respect for the empirical origins of knowledge does not oblige one to turn his back upon the generic traits of existence that can be discovered through reflection and by means of inference. Nor does an acknowledgment of the contingent and novel blind one to the unity and connectedness that also are features of nature. Finally, the naturalist's commitment to empiricism has rendered him impotent in precisely the area in which he has most wanted to succeed, the area of values. Naturalistic

ethics as yet remains a program rather than an accomplishment. In a certain sense, this last remark can be made of the whole of naturalism, which in its positive character at times seems to be saying no more than "Let us be scientific!"

See also VALUE, PHILOSOPHY OF; SCIENCE, PHILOSOPHY OF; RATIONALISM.

Bibliography: P. ROMANELL, *Toward a Critical Naturalism* (New York 1958). J. D. COLLINS, *Three Paths in Philosophy* (Chicago 1962), a critique of naturalism from the standpoint of a theistic realism.

[J. P. DOUGHERTY]

NATURALISM, LITERARY

A literary mode that developed in the latter half of the 19th century out of attempts to interpret the human condition according to contemporary scientific thought and method. When first introduced into literary discussions in the mid-19th century, the term was generally used as roughly synonymous with "realism." In spite of this early confusion and ready interchangeability of the two terms, naturalism is now generally distinguished as a specific outgrowth of realism, as well as its most extreme form. Realism and naturalism both predicate a close fidelity to everyday reality, but naturalism goes beyond realism chiefly in its underlying commitment to some deterministic view of human conduct. (*See* DETERMINISM, PHYSICAL; DETERMINISM, PSYCHOLOGICAL.)

Outgrowth of Realism. Realism, the more generic of the two terms, cannot be rigidly confined to a period in literary history inasmuch as elements of it are to be found to some degree in all literary traditions. Its emergence in the 19th century as a more or less well-defined movement was influenced by a large number of factors, among them the growth of science and secularism, the social disruptions wrought by industrialism, and the revolt against the Romantic literary tradition (*see* ROMANTICISM, LITERARY). As a reaction against the romance novel, it aimed to use the "real" or the "actual" as a norm, to avoid all manipulation of the probabilities of real-life experience, all idealization and reshaping of reality according to moral, aesthetic, or other preconceptions; this meant, in short, to present life "as it is" and with all possible objectivity. Although the intellectual, economic, and social conditions in most countries of the Western world fostered an indigenous growth of literary realism, it was in France that it achieved its earliest distinction. By 1830 *Stendhal, Merimée, and *Balzac were already writing in the realistic mode, and by the 1860s, when naturalism was just beginning to emerge, the realistic novel in France had already reached its ultimate refinement in *Flaubert's *Madame Bovary* (1857).

Naturalism, too, first rose to prominence and received its most important theoretical formulations in France during the 1860s, '70s and '80s, but before the end of the century naturalistic writing had achieved a broad currency throughout Europe and was already in evidence in America. Even more emphatically than realism, naturalism was influenced by contemporary secular and scientific attitudes, which the philosopher *Comte and the biologist *Darwin, the critic *Taine, and the physician Claude *Bernard typified and quickened. As with realism, it is difficult to gauge the extent to which French example accounts for the international scope of naturalism, for the scientific premises upon which it was based had already been promulgated throughout the

Western world. On some writers, such as the Irishman George Moore (1852–1933) and the American Frank Norris (1870–1902), the influence of *Zola is direct and demonstrable. But the naturalism of many writers, including Thomas *Hardy, Stephen Crane (1871–1900), and Theodore *Dreiser, is much more clearly the consequence of a given temperament and experience responding to certain local conditions and a pervasive scientism. Still, the fact remains that whatever the impetus it received from contemporary science, naturalism as a literary movement could readily flourish only where the existent literary tradition provided a suitable climate. As implied above, that tradition was nowhere more congenial than in France, and it was there that naturalism enjoyed its earliest and, for many years, most notable flowering.

However significant the impact of science upon the development of realism, in the movement of naturalism the scientific outlook became the underlying rationale. Indeed, in the unmitigated naturalism of Zola, who in *Le Roman expérimental* (1880) gave the movement its major theoretical statement, the term implies not only a deterministic view of man but also an elaborate attempt to apply the methodology of Bernard's *Introduction à l'étude de la médecine expérimentale* (1865) to the technique of the novel. In its fullest expression, then, naturalism is distinguished from realism by both its orientation to some necessitarian ideology and its method of documented "scientific" analysis.

As the movement extended beyond the early French naturalists—the brothers Goncourt and Zola—and beyond the borders of France, there appeared innumerable deviations from the kind of naturalism they professed to practice. With the appearance of the works of various other theorists—such as Spencer, Haeckel, Nietzsche, Marx, Loeb, Freud, Pavlov, Jung—private and public convictions were variously deflected; and under the influence of one or more of these thinkers, many novelists tended to emphasize some specific determinant, such as man's heredity and biological compulsions, his economic, social, or political environment, his libido or conditioned reflexes or unconscious memories. Or they might (as the more skilled naturalists generally did) see man as determined by a fearful combination of such forces—by the biological, environmental, and psychological imperatives combined and interacting.

Art of the Naturalist. The more discriminating and subtle the mind and art of a naturalistic writer, in fact, the more likely it is that his sense of the forces bearing upon man's condition will be complex rather than simplistic, conditional rather than absolute. The naturalism of many later writers, consequently, does not necessarily preclude man's free choice, but rather implies that whether man has free will or not, in most cases his life is determined by factors he neither knows nor can control. It is this fatalistic condition that principally makes for the fairly consistent grimness, the prevailing pessimism of naturalistic fiction. It should be stressed, however, that such forces are beyond the control of their victims chiefly because of their bumbling confusion, their lack of intelligent awareness. The literature of naturalism, as a result, is notoriously deficient in characters of intelligence and objectivity, intensely conscious of their fate and fully aware of its determinants.

Nevertheless we do find that for some naturalists [the American James T. Farrell (1904–), for example]

the possibility of free choice and conscious self-determination is both an ideal and attainable. Though Zola did not admit free will, even he insisted that his determinism was not "fatalistic," that by recognition and control of the coercive forces of his existence man could alter his conditions and ultimately create an ideal social order. In the work of writers such as *Hemingway and *Faulkner, whose fiction generally reflects a strong naturalistic bias, the postulate of free will and choice of alternatives nevertheless results in fiction strikingly existentialist in character when the protagonist is endowed with self-consciousness, intelligence, and objectivity (*see* EXISTENTIALISM IN LITERATURE). In general, intelligence and objective awareness may be taken as limits that naturalism can seldom trespass and still remain convincingly deterministic. For even though characters so equipped may fail in their attempts to resist the powers that would shape their destinies, their failures are now in a significant degree failures on their own terms. It is probably only on this borderline between the deterministic forces acting from within or without and a conscious knowledge of and resistance to them that the naturalistic novel can again discover the possibilities of the tragic.

In the technical presentation of this fictive material, moreover, the deviations from the documentary technique of the Goncourts and Zola are even more recalcitrant to generalization. For although the "typical" naturalistic novel tends to be relentlessly factual, to seem unselective and studiedly objective, naturalistic fiction, considered in its later developments especially, manifests in fact a wide variety of styles and techniques. The style of Stephen Crane, for example, is at once impressionistic, poetic, and symbolic, whereas the fiction of Frank Norris reveals a strong proclivity to the romantic and melodramatic as well as the symbolic. Both Crane and Dreiser, moreover, intrude their feelings and opinions ruthlessly into their fiction, Dreiser overtly by periodic speculative disquisitions or sentimental rhapsodies, Crane somewhat more subtly by his excessive and distortive irony. In practice, then, the only factor that may be consistently identified in naturalistic fiction is the author's underlying conviction that man's destiny, for whatever "natural" reason, is irresistibly determined—or virtually so—by forces beyond his power.

Influence of Naturalism. Outside France naturalism exerted its strongest influence upon the national literatures of Germany (especially the drama of *Hauptmann and Arno Holz); Sweden (the drama and fiction of *Strindberg); Denmark (the criticism of *Brandes); Norway (the social drama of *Ibsen and Björnson); Italy (where it went under the name *verismo* and achieved its most important expression in the work of *Verga); England (the fiction of George Moore and George Gissing); and the U.S. The movement of naturalism, moreover, has probably affected the literature of all modern nations to the degree that they have been caught up in the intellectual currents and crises that have so profoundly disturbed the religious and humanistic traditions of the Western world during the last century.

In assessing the literary achievement of both realism and naturalism, there can be no doubt that, being less formulaic in their interpretations of human nature, realists such as *Flaubert, Turgenev (1818–83), *Tolstoi, *Dostoevskiǐ, *Conrad, and Henry *James achieved the more notable successes. The naturalists, on the other hand, in spite of many literary excesses and failures, nevertheless produced a body of literature of considerable power and durability. Even granting that naturalism probably succeeds best when it deviates most from rigid scientific premises and doctrinaire assumptions, the fact remains that many of the naturalistic perspectives and techniques have powerfully influenced and deeply enriched subsequent fiction.

Bibliography: L. Ahnebrink, *The Beginnings of Naturalism in American Fiction* (Cambridge, Mass. 1950), with bibliog. M. Josephson, *Zola and His Time* (New York 1928). G. W. Meyer, The Original Social Purpose of the Naturalistic Novel," *Sewanee Review* 50 (1942) 563–570. E. Stone, ed., *What Was Naturalism?* (New York 1959). C. C. Walcutt, *American Literary Naturalism* (Minneapolis 1956). H. C. Gardiner, *Norms for the Novel* (rev. ed. Garden City, N.Y. 1960), esp. pt. 2. R. Dumesnil, *L'Époque réaliste et naturaliste* (Paris 1945). L. J. Henkin, *Darwinism in the English Novel: 1860–1910* (New York 1940). W. Linden, ed., *Naturalismus* (Leipzig 1936). P. Martino, *Le Naturalisme français: 1870–1895* (Paris 1930).

[J. X. Brennan]

NATURE

From the Latin *natura* (Gr. φύσις), a term with many related meanings in philosophy and with extensive applications in theology. Among philosophers it is commonly taken to mean the essence of a thing as this is the source of its properties or operations; more strictly, however, it is a primary and per se principle of motion and rest that is found in natural things as opposed to artifacts. It is sometimes used in the more restricted sense of human nature, for which meaning *see* MAN, 3. Theologians use the term in opposition to grace or to supernature, particularly when discussing human nature, and in opposition to person, particularly in Trinitarian theology and Christology. This article treats the concept in a general way and in two stages, the first dealing with nature in philosophy, the second with nature in theology.

NATURE IN PHILOSOPHY

Since nature is the proper subject of the *philosophy of nature, the major emphasis in this part of the article is on nature as studied in natural philosophy. Topics treated include the primary meanings of the concept, its development among the Greeks, modifications in it occasioned by the rise of modern science, an Aristotelian analysis of its meaning in natural philosophy, and various secondary meanings.

Primary Meanings. On Nature (Περὶ φύσεως) is the title under which the writings of the pre-Socratics have been handed down to posterity. Some doubt exists as to what precisely was the first meaning, but it is generally admitted that at least an early and important use of the term φύσις was to designate the primordial stuff or underlying substratum persisting through all *change. It is likely that the early Ionian philosophers imagined the world as developing in an orderly fashion from within, somewhat as a living being, and hence the primary substance would have been viewed, though indistinctly, as a source of activity. Thus φύσις was an intrinsic principle that accounted for the ceaseless change or *becoming of things. Moreover, the very process of becoming, it seems, was itself called φύσις, a term that is etymologically related to φύω, to grow (cf. Lat. *natura* and *nascor*). Finally, at some later date the term was applied to the changing things themselves taken in their totality. This is possibly the most common sense of nature in modern usage and was probably the

meaning of φύσις intended in the title Περὶ φύσεως. (For Aristotle's account of the etymology and the meanings of φύσις, see *Meta.* 1014b 16–1015a 19.)

Greek Development. The attempt of the Ionians of the 6th century B.C. to explain all becoming in terms of one material principle (e.g., water or air or fire) reached its logical conclusion in *Parmenides with the very denial of nature as process. For Parmenides all being must be one and exclude all nonbeing; as such it is perfectly immutable, and only as such is it knowable; all change is but sensory illusion. After Parmenides, there was an attempt to reconcile *being, stable object of intellect, with the becoming of sensory experience. Fundamental reality remained immutable; it was, however, multiple: the four elements of *Empedocles; the "seeds," infinite in number, of *Anaxagoras; the atoms of Leucippus and *Democritus. These particles, in motion, combined and separated, and as such were principles of change and of a multiplicity of changing compounds. The atomists, with their homogeneous particles differing only in size and shape, interpreted all change in terms of movement in space ("void") and all sensible qualities, such as color, in terms of quantitative differences (*see* ATOMISM). They have been considered as forerunners to modern science. So too have the Pythagoreans, who, from the 6th century B.C., had been seeking to explain the world in the light of numbers.

The claim to find the ultimate explanation of reality in the random motions of corporeal elements, i.e., in nature and chance, was strongly opposed by *Plato. If nature means the primary source of becoming, what is truly nature, for him, could only be what is really first, and that is intelligence and art. Thus, with Plato, nature in the commonly accepted sense gave way to divine soul, and chance to divine direction (*Laws* 888E–899D). Finality, introduced as conscious design, was lodged in a principle (soul) distinct from the purely corporeal. Likewise, the intelligibility of sensible bodies was to be sought beyond them, in the changeless, purely intelligible Ideas, of which they are imperfect imitations (*Phaedo; Rep.* 449–540). The order of the sensible world could be seen, too, in terms of the a priori principles of pure number. As for the changing imitations considered in themselves, of these there could be no science, but only a likely account.

Nature was reinstated as a true principle and a real source of explanation within the material universe by *Aristotle, who thus restored the philosophy of nature to the rank of a *science (*scientia*). Aristotle continued the naturalist tradition of the pre-Socratics, his science being qualitative rather than mathematical, empirical rather than rationalist. It was far from being a mere return, however. After Plato there was form to be reckoned with. In Aristotle the natural world becomes intelligible in itself only because nature is identified with form in matter—with form now seen as the actuality of matter—even more properly than with matter itself (*see* MATTER AND FORM). This form becomes the origin of activity, and matter, considered in itself, is reduced to a principle of mere passivity and receptivity. The realization of form in matter is the goal of natural activity, and although there are various combinations and separations of elements, it is always for the sake of a form; hence, the teleological view, as opposed to the mechanistic, remains dominant. But purpose is now found in the unconscious workings of form as well as in the conscious activities of rational soul. Although Aristotle conceived the natural universe as impregnated with and illuminated by form, for the ultimate explanation he too reached beyond nature. It is the desire to imitate the fully actual reality of Pure Form that, in the final analysis, explains all the ceaseless processes of nature.

Later Modifications. Both the Platonist and the Aristotelian view of nature extended into the Middle Ages. The early period was largely Neoplatonist, but in the 13th century the commentaries of St. *Albert the Great and especially of St. *Thomas Aquinas brought the Aristotelian doctrine of nature into the foreground.

In the 16th and 17th centuries, the rapid development of the new empirico-mathematical science was accompanied by an emphatic rejection of *teleology: the conception of natures tending to ends. At first, change was Platonistically explained by an inherent, creative principle (*natura naturans*) animating and directing the world of nature (*natura naturata*)—terms that go back to the Latin translation of *Averroës. *See* WORLD SOUL (ANIMA MUNDI). Before long, however, under the influence of F. *Bacon, J. *Kepler, G. *Galilei, R. *Descartes, I. *Newton, and others, the account became thoroughly mechanistic. With the rejection of the geocentric astronomy and the adoption of the universal law of gravitation, the qualitatively differentiated world of Aristotle gave place to a totally homogeneous universe. Purely qualitative differences, such as color, were considered to be functions of quantitative structure, and were soon dismissed as mere appearances to a sentient mind. Matter as potency was replaced by matter as mass and extension. All change was reduced to the motion of smallest parts in space; all causality, to prior events, i.e., to prior motions, identical causes being followed by identical effects. The spontaneous activity of bodies gave way to the idea of force (impact, attraction) and the impulse toward ends was displaced by inertia, the disposition to remain always the same. Nature thus became, for the scientist and the philosopher of nature alike, a mechanical system of inert, homogeneous mass-bodies, situated in space and time, moved by external forces, and utterly devoid of all but quantitative properties. (*See* MECHANISM.)

In the 20th century, the adequacy of purely mechanistic principles of explanation has been seriously questioned for the biological and psychological sciences. Further, the scientific theories of evolution along with the physicist's conception of matter as energy have made more generally acceptable a view that was already to some degree in evidence in the philosophies of G. W. *Leibniz and G. W. F. *Hegel, viz, the idea of nature as internally active and engaged in process. This conception, to which in some instances has been added the idea of aim, has found philosophical expression in the works of such thinkers as H. *Bergson, S. *Alexander, and A. N. *Whitehead.

Aristotelian Analysis. A fuller presentation of the Aristotelian concept of nature, which has been generally adopted by scholastic thinkers, entails considering his definition of nature, nature as passive, nature as active, end as nature, and related concepts.

Definition of Nature. Aristotle (*Phys.* 192b 8–32) reached his definition of nature by way of a comparison of the things that exist by nature (viz, animals and their parts, plants and simple bodies) with those that exist by other causes, in particular by art. The former are seen to have within them a tendency to move, i.e., to change. The artifact as such has no such tendency. It has an inclination to change only accidentally insofar as it is made of a natural substance. Nature, then, concluded Aristotle, is the principle or cause of being moved and being at rest in that in which it is primarily, by reason of itself and not accidentally.

"Being moved" implies passivity. Strictly speaking, the principle that constitutes a thing as a mover is a nature only when the mover by its activity is itself moved. Also, *motion here includes any kind of corporeal change, accidental or substantial; it excludes, however, spiritual operations, such as intellection. "Rest" implies the attainment of the end to which the movement was directed. The phrase "by reason of itself and not accidentally" excludes such cases as the doctor who cures himself. The art of medicine is, in this case, intrinsic but accidental to the one who is being cured, considered as such.

Nature as Passive. Nature, thus defined, was identified by Aristotle first (*Phys.* 193a 10–30) with *matter taken as the substratum of change, i.e., as the passive, potential principle of being moved. In opposition to the pre-Socratics, Aristotle conceived of the ultimate material principle (primary matter) as being of itself bereft of all form, purely passive, pure potentiality. The matter, however, from which becoming proceeds, taken in its concrete existence, is always determined matter. The substantial form currently possessed, determining the matter in a particular way, always limits and defines matter's immediate potentialities. This is true both for the potency of primary matter for new substantial forms and more obviously for the accidental receptivities characteristic of any given being. Furthermore, since the form already possessed by the matter can be the source of certain activities as well, the matter on which a natural agent operates, just as it is never pure potency, need not be entirely passive. Its activity, in fact, may run contrary to the aim of the agent.

Nature as Active. It is especially with *form, however, that Aristotle is concerned to identify nature (*Phys.* 193a 30–b 19). The ancients, not distinguishing the two principles of matter and form, had conceived of their primordial stuff as already determined and capable of activity. Once substantial form is disassociated from matter and recognized as principle of essential determination, source of activity, and end of generation, it becomes obvious that form more than matter deserves to be called nature. Nature, then, as active principle of movement, is substantial form. (Note that, although one says "Nature acts," strictly speaking it is the composite substance that acts in virtue of its nature.)

Form is the source of two different types of activity in nature. First and more obviously, form is the intrinsic source of the vital activities of the living body. As such, it is known as *soul. And as such it is a nature, since, by these activities, the living being is itself moved. The soul, in fact, is the primary source of activity whereby one part of the heterogeneous composite moves another part. Moreover, all the vital activities are either movements themselves (e.g., growth) or essentially connected with movements (e.g., sensation) or they presuppose movements (e.g., intellection). The soul, however, is also the principle of generation, an activity that is essentially directed to another substance. But even as such, it is a nature, insofar as the movement takes place within the same species, if not within the same individual (*Meta.* 1032a 15–26).

Second, form is the intrinsic source of the spontaneous activities characteristic of a given body, e.g., a chemical element (*Gen. et cor.* 323b 2–324b 25). Inanimate bodies, not having differentiated parts, do not move themselves. Their activities, on the contrary, are directed to other bodies that in turn may affect them. The forms, in this case, satisfy the requirement of interiority in the definition of nature insofar as they are parts within a system of interrelated active and passive potencies.

In Aristotle's cosmology, however, there are certain movements of bodies that do arise from an intrinsic source (*Phys.* 254b 33–255b 31), as in his example of a body falling to the ground—a movement that does not appear to require an external agent (*see* GRAVITATION; MOTION, FIRST CAUSE OF). In this case, however, nature functions as a principle of activity without constituting the thing as a mover. The body, in fact, does not move itself, part moving part, as does the living thing. For Aristotle, rather, the movement arises spontaneously from the impulse of the form toward what is appropriate to it, which, in this instance, is a suitable environment. (For a study of this conception in conjunction with the theories of gravity and relativity, see J. A. Weisheipl.)

End as Nature. Whether a movement is natural or not cannot always be determined by sole reference to the active and passive principles. The determining factor is ultimately the *end of becoming, and this too is nature (*Phys.* 193b 13–19, 194a 27–32).

Nature, in one sense, has been identified with the receptive and determinable principle. There are, however, in the world of nature, potencies that are not natural: the capacity of a natural body to take on an artificial form, or the capacity to be altered by some violent action. The natural potency differs from these in that it is a positive inclination to an act that perfects or fulfills the being so inclined, or else contributes to the good of the species or even to the good of the universe as a whole. The passive principle in nature, moreover, is normally related to a natural *agent, through the activity of which it is brought to act. The activity of natural agents is accounted for by the tendency of the form in nature to actualize and bring to completion what is potential either within the same individual or beyond. The natural agent, then, actively tends to that good or perfection to which the potential principle is passively inclined. Furthermore, the natural agent, fixed in its species by its form, is also determined by this same principle with respect to specific goals, which it attains for the most part (*see* CHANCE; INDETERMINISM). Thus the acts to which it naturally directs matter by its activity are determinate acts. It is in this sense that a nature is said to act for an end. (Obviously, the end as a good is more easily recognized in the activity of living beings than it is in the workings of the inanimate world.) Consequently, it is the act or form, considered as the end to which a natural being tends either actively or passively, that determines whether a process is or is not in accordance with nature. And in those cases where the good of the whole is in opposition to the good of the individual (as in the case of corruption), it is the former that takes precedence as a determining principle. (*See* FINALITY, PRINCIPLE OF.)

The form considered as end, furthermore, is itself properly called nature. It is a principle of becoming, and one that, in the essential order of things, is prior even to the passive and active principles as such. It is also intrinsic, insofar as natural movements are for the sake of the form (*finis cui*) from which they spring. In fact, the natural form seeks its own preservation and development within the individual; it tends by generation to its own continuance, as a specific form, in other individuals; and ultimately, by realizing its specific ends, it contributes to the order and preservation of the universe, i.e., to the good of the whole of which it is a part.

Related Concepts. Art, *violence, and *chance are all active principles that presuppose nature but operate outside the order of natural finality. See ART (PHILOSOPHY).

Secondary Meanings. From nature meaning the form or essence that is the end of generation, the word has been extended to signify any essence whatsoever without reference at all to becoming (see Thomas Aquinas, *In 5 meta.* 5.822–823). This sense, as applicable to any being, material or immaterial, is frequently conveyed by the terms definition and quiddity. A meaning somewhat closer to the original is that of essence as the source of any activity, whether of physical movement or of spiritual operation (*De ente* 1). This sense, too, is sometimes conveyed by the term substance. For a fuller discussion of these concepts, *see* ESSENCE; FORM; DEFINITION; QUIDDITY; SUBSTANCE. For a treatment of laws of nature, *see* PHYSICAL LAWS; NATURAL LAW; and for the principle of the uniformity of nature on which such laws are based, *see* UNIFORMITY.

Bibliography: Syntopicon 2:225–250. A. GUZZO and V. MATHIEU, EncFil 3:789–811. C. FABRO, EncCatt 8:1682–83. J. B. METZ, LexThK² 7:805–808. R. G. COLLINGWOOD, *The Idea of Nature* (New York 1960). A. N. WHITEHEAD, *The Concept of Nature* (Cambridge, Eng. 1920; repr. 1930). J. A. WEISHEIPL, *Nature and Gravitation* (River Forest, Ill. 1955). A. MANSION, *Introduction à la physique aristotélicienne* (2d ed. Louvain 1946). S. O'FLYNN BRENNAN, "Physis: The Meaning of Nature in the Aristotelian Philosophy of Nature," *Thomist* 24 (1961) 383–401.

[S. O'FLYNN BRENNAN]

NATURE IN THEOLOGY

Clarification of the concept nature has enriched the development of theology and the understanding of the Christian faith. It has given a more accurate understanding and depth to the theology of the Trinity, Incarnation, Redemption, Mystical Body, the Church, Mary, and man. Historically, the notion of nature has been focal in every era: from the Trinitarian-Christological controversies of Christian antiquity, through the grace disputes of Pelagianism and Protestantism, to Modernism and existentialism. The term nature is not met in the Old Testament nor does the concrete mentality of the Semites lend itself to an abstract and transcendental concept of nature, predicable of God, angels, man, and irrational creation. Though the word nature, φύσις, is used in the New Testament, its meaning must be determined in each instance from the context. St. Augustine was hampered in his efforts to preserve the supernaturality of grace by his notion of nature in its primary etymological sense of *natus,* born. Although he maintained man's condition prior to the Fall to be "natural," the Doctor of Grace is not calling into question the supernaturality of that condition but is affirming the "original" characteristic of that state. In the decrees of the Councils of Ephesus and Chalcedon and in the writings of the contemporary Fathers there is a gradual precisional evolution of the term nature. St. Thomas Aquinas made a major contribution to Catholic theology by clearly distinguishing between *grace and nature, fixing the boundaries of the *natural order and the *supernatural order. The contribution of current theologians would be their emphasis on the concrete, historical, and social aspects of nature.

In contemporary theology the term nature is used in two senses. (1) In a general sense, nature refers to the created universe (rational or irrational or both) with determined laws of interdependence and God as its source and end. (2) In a specific sense, nature includes not only the philosophical definition as that which determines a being's species and proper activity but a deeper understanding from revelation of the concrete nature of man, angel, and God. The following consideration of nature in theology is divided according to these two senses of the term.

Nature in a Specific Sense. The philosophical understanding of nature has already been treated extensively in this article; it may now proceed to a consideration of the contribution of revelation and theology.

Human Nature. Man does not know precisely just what human nature is or exactly how far it extends. Philosophy through experience and reflection gives him certain definite concepts about nature, but he never knows exactly when he has included too much or too little in his concept. Theology goes beyond philosophy and sees nature as being from God and directed to God in special ways, as including *supernatural and grace-qualified factors, and as being in a historical-social situation where new experiences in man's process of realization help man understand what is of his essence and what is contingent. Man is always historically becoming, and therefore his understanding of concrete nature is also permanently *in via.* Philosophy, then, can give a well-grounded concept of the nature of man, but it is for theology with revelation to further consider man's nature in its supernatural context.

Three major constants appear in Catholic theological understanding of human nature. (1) Man is the *image of God. Because of its special similarity to God, human nature has an immediate ordination to Him. Human nature itself, therefore, will ever constitute a moral principle for judging human behavior. (2) Mankind is one: it has not only an essential unity by human nature but an even greater unity in Adam and Christ. Therefore, the previously mentioned conformity-with-nature moral principle must be understood not merely of the individual man but also of all men as one. Moreover, this oneness of mankind offers the natural foundation for the law of love of neighbor and has important consequences for the Church's social teaching. (3) The unity of human nature is one of the most distinctive characteristics of the Judeo-Christian conception of man, combining the two apparently heterogeneous worlds of matter and of spirit. History has shown that Christian insistence on man's fundamental unity is the sole effective remedy for monism, whether in the form

of an idealistic spiritualism or of an empirical materialism. Even the Christian has not found it easy to avoid tendencies that overemphasize now one and now another aspect of man's enigmatic nature.

Man, in his capacity of incarnate spirit, has a place in the divine plan that surpasses his nature. Even though this human nature considered abstractly is not altered by its history, it must ever be borne in mind that abstract human nature never did nor does exist. The whole spiritual and cultural history of man testifies that man continually experiences new modes of realization and understanding of his nature. Theological consideration of human nature must never stop with an examination of human nature as such, but must always include concrete human nature with its history centered in its *elevation in Christ (*see* MAN, 4).

Angelic Nature. Theology confirms philosophy's stand that human nature, incarnate spirit, crowns the material universe. However, above human nature is the angelic nature: "You have made him [man] a little less than the angels" (Ps 8.6). The existence of created beings of a purely spiritual nature is unknown to philosophy. In fact, the very concept carries with it the connotation of the unreal and the unrealizable to modern man. Catholic theology, seeing the wonderful completion of the material universe in the manifold degrees of perfection, confirms the becomingness of a similar gradation in the spiritual universe. Man occupies the lowest place in this universe of spiritual beings, having a more perfect nature than what is purely material but still partially dependent upon matter. In accordance with the general providence of God, governing the inferior through the superior, angels have definite roles to fulfill in the lives of men and in the ordering of the whole material universe (*see* ANGELS, 2).

Theology of the Trinity and Incarnation. In expressing its belief in supernatural realities, the Church does not bind itself to any particular philosophical system. This is brought out most clearly when it presents its two most fundamental mysteries, the Trinity and the Incarnation, in terms of nature and person. In the formulation of these mysteries, these terms are analogies to be understood only in the light of the revealed reality. The foundation for the analogical application of the terms nature and person to these mysteries rests on a minimal number of philosophical presuppositions. Nature simply refers to that which constitutes the internal unity of anything. Person says nothing more than separateness from everyone and everything else—hence *incommunicability. The precise meaning of these terms in the dogmatic formulas is grasped by the Church only by reflection on the very mysteries of the Trinity and the Incarnation. Because of the necessarily partial character of any expression of a supernatural reality, faith seeking understanding has always sought, and eventually used, other analogies to complement the nature-person analogy, e.g., those based on mutual relations, human mind, and human love.

The mystery of the Incarnation reveals a concrete, individual, human nature without a human personality. In the presence of this mystery, Catholic theology has been perennially confronted with the yet unanswered question of the relation of nature and person. Philosophy is usually content with the identification of the concrete, individual, existing nature and the person. Some contemporary trends in theology suggest a reexamination of this philosophical position, not only on an ontological, but also on a psychological plane.

Nature in a General Sense. Two questions are raised in theology by nature in a general sense: (1) concerning the relation between the natural and supernatural orders, and (2) concerning the different states of nature.

Natural and Supernatural Orders. By the natural order is meant the natural disposition and relationship of creatures among themselves and to God, the extrinsic author and end of everything within the order. Man with his natural faculties seeks to attain a perfect, mediate possession of God. This end man could attain by human activity in the material universe in accordance with the norm of the order—the natural law. By the supernatural order is meant the supernatural disposition and relationship of creatures among themselves and to God, the extrinsic author and end of everything within the order. Jesus Christ, His human nature elevated by the *hypostatic union and sanctifying grace, beatific vision and love, is the one mediator between God and man and is therefore the intrinsic author and end of everything in this order. Man is elevated by a sharing in the divine nature (sanctifying grace) and in the infused divine powers (theological virtues). By union with Christ and corresponding activity in accordance with the norm of the order—the divine positive law—man can attain an immediate possession of God through beatific vision and love.

Though the natural order is not a *de facto* order, still theology is concerned with that order because of its manner of elevation. The supernatural does not imply the suppression of the natural but rather its supereminent realization. Hence the adages: "The supernatural is not opposed to but above nature"; "Grace does not destroy but perfects nature." These principles must, however, be carefully understood, for they contain a certain equivocation. The supernatural is not a perfection of nature within the order of nature. The Christian humanist is often tempted to view the supernatural as though it were simply a supreme realization of natural perfection. Central to the Christian message is the absolute incapability of nature to attain to the supernatural, for the supernatural is a perfection of a higher order than the natural. The supernatural, to be sure, is the full realization of nature but in a perfection that transcends the natural order completely. The Christian way of death-resurrection is one not merely of removing sin but also of transcending the natural for a greater openness to the supernatural received as grace—pure gift. Supernatural grace, therefore, is not some superstructure, imposing itself on human nature and disturbing the order of pure nature. Grace, it is true, is unexacted by man's nature, but God created man so that he *could* receive this gift and receive it as such: as an unexpected, unexacted gift.

The point of contact between the natural and supernatural orders is human nature, for only man, abstracting from the angels, is capable of being elevated to the supernatural order. This capacity in human nature is referred to as *obediential potency. Theology clearly distinguishes this capacity in human nature for the supernatural, which God alone can fulfill, from all of man's other natural capabilities, which he himself can carry out. The existence of such an obediential potency in human nature is known to man only through revelation of the fact of actual supernatural elevation. Still this openness of the human spirit for the supernatural indicates not only a nonrepugnance but even a becomingness for the supernatural elevation. The conception, then, of obediential potency is not to be seen in its purely negative aspect as freeing man from the contradiction of a supernatural-natural union, but more positively as an inner, conditional ordination to the supernatural. This openness of spirit is central for one's understanding of the scriptural doctrine that man is made in the image and likeness of God.

States of Nature. Even though, historically, nature never existed without the supernatural elevation, nature connotes a perfection complete in itself and hence could exist in a purely natural state. Theologians distinguish five different possible states of nature: (1) *pure nature, with no *preternatural or supernatural elevation; (2) integral nature, with preternatural endowments; (3) elevated nature (the original state of man prior to the Fall), with preternatural and supernatural gifts; (4) fallen unredeemed nature, incapable of attaining its end because of sin; (5) redeemed nature, superabundantly restored to its original elevated state by the *Redemption of Jesus Christ. Even though the last is the only actual state of human nature known to man on earth, there would seem to be no intrinsic impossibility for the actual existence of the other states. In fact, some theologians see a certain appropriate completeness of the universe in positing the actual existence of these other states of nature on planets other than the earth.

God's Glory. "God saw that all He had made was very good" (Gn 1.31). Only the whole of God's creation contains the divinely intended manifestation of His goodness. *See* GLORY OF GOD (END OF CREATION). Every area of human endeavor contributes its proper insight into the glory of God discovered in nature. The scientist encounters the beauty of nature in its manifold variation, generous richness, and prodigious creativity. The philosopher discovers in nature an underlying permanence and unity that preserve a most wonderful order in the whole. Only theology attains to the ultimate harmonization of nature's multiplicity and unity in its Creator, who has revealed Himself to be one in nature and triune in personality. This triune Deity has, moreover, offered to share with all created nature His own harmonious multiplicity in unity. This properly divine beauty is shared in immediately by the more excellent angelic and, through Christ, human natures, mediately by all nature "because creation itself also will be delivered from its slavery to corruption into the freedom of the glory of the sons of God" (Rom 8.21).

See also BAIUS AND BAIANISM; DESTINY, SUPERNATURAL; DIVINE NATURE, PARTAKER OF; JESUS CHRIST, II (IN DOGMATIC THEOLOGY); JESUS CHRIST, III (SPECIAL QUESTIONS); PERSON (IN PHILOSOPHY); PERSON (IN THEOLOGY); SUPERNATURAL EXISTENTIAL; TRINITY, HOLY; VOCATION TO SUPERNATURAL LIFE.

Bibliography: Y. E. MASSON, DTC 11.1:36–44. J. ALFARO, LexThK² 7:809–810, 830–835. H. LESÈTRE, DB 4:1488–90. H. KUHN and S. OTTO, Fries HbThGrdbgr 2:211–221. EncDictBibl 1426–29; 2604–05. I. M. DALMAU, SacTheolSumma BAC 2.2. I. SOLANO, *ibid.* 3.1. R. LE TROQUER, *What Is Man?* tr. E. E. SMITH (New York 1961). K. RAHNER, *God, Christ, Mary and Grace,* tr. C. ERNST (his *Theological Investigations* 1; Baltimore 1961). J. B. HAWKINS, "On Nature and Person in Speculative Theology," DownRev 80 (1962) 1–11.

[M. J. DORENKEMPER]

NAU, FRANÇOIS NICOLAS, Orientalist and patristic scholar; b. Thil, France, May 13, 1864; d. Paris, Sept. 2, 1931. Nau attended the major seminary of Saint-Sulpice, Paris (1882–94), where he obtained the baccalaureate in theology and Canon Law. After having been ordained for the Diocese of Paris on Dec. 17, 1887, he studied the natural sciences at the Institut Catholique of Paris (1887–94); received the licentiate in mathematics (1889) and physics (1890) at the Sorbonne; and taught mathematics and astronomy at the Institut Catholique (1890–1930). In 1889 he began the study of Syriac under Abbé *Graffin and later applied himself also to Hebrew and Aramaic under Auguste Carrière (1892–95). In 1895 he published a Syriac astronomical text, *The Book of the Ascent of the Spirit* by Bar Hebraeus, with a French translation. Thereafter, until his death, he was a prodigious editor of Syriac texts, chiefly published in the *Patrologia Orientalis,* which he and Graffin founded in 1899. With Graffin he served as assistant editor (1905–11) and editor (1911–16) of the *Revue de l'Orient Chrétien.* The list of his publications occupies 27 pages of fine print in the *Journal Asiatique.* In 1896 he became a member of the Société Asiatique, and from 1912 a member of its council. In 1903 he was made an honorary *chorbishop by the Maronite patriarch of Antioch.

Bibliography: I. ORTIZ DE URBINA, EncCatt 8:1692. M. BRIÈRE, "L'abbé François-Nicolas Nau," *Journal Asiatique* 223 (1933) 149–180.

[L. F. HARTMAN]

NAUCLERUS, JOHN, German humanist and historian; b. probably in Württemberg, *c.* 1425–30; d. Tübingen, Jan. 5, 1510. Nauclerus (properly Verge or Vergenhans) acted as tutor and counselor for the future Duke Eberhard V of Württemberg from 1450 to 1459, serving also as pastor and canon of Brackenheim. He was provost of Stuttgart (1465–72) and possibly was active at the Universities of *Paris and Basel. Nauclerus was instrumental in the founding of the University of *Tübingen (1477) and taught Canon Law there, functioning also as rector and then, from 1483 to 1509, as chancellor and provost. About 1504 he wrote *Memorabilium omnis aetatis et omnium gentium chronici commentarii,* covering the years from the creation of the world to his day. The work divides history into ages and counts 63 generations to the birth of Christ and 51 from Christ to 1501. Written in annalistic style, Nauclerus's history reflects the spiritual attitude of the Middle Ages, unaffected by the humanistic spirit of his own age. It shows a strong predisposition for affairs in his homeland, for Church matters and papal proceedings; but it is a valuable source for the contemporary period. Unpublished until after Nauclerus's death, the history was edited by *Melanchthon and printed in Tübingen in 1516. It had such great success that it went through nine editions before 1617. Besides his administrative work and his literary undertakings, Nauclerus was a canon lawyer and sought a compromise between local custom and Canon Law.

Bibliography: Works. *De Symonia* (Tübingen 1500); *Memorabilium . . . commentarii,* 2 v. (Tübingen 1516). Literature. P. JOACHIMSEN, *Geschichtsauffassung und Geschichtschreibung in Deutschland unter dem Einfluss des Humanismus* (Leipzig 1910) 1:91–104. J. W. THOMPSON and B. J. HOLM, *History of Historical Writing,* 2 v. (New York 1942) 1:426. H. TÜCHLE, Lex ThK² 7:845.

[C. R. BYERLY]

NAUMBURG, city on the Saale River in Saxony, central Germany. The bishopric of nearby Zeitz (founded 967–968 together with Magdeburg) was moved to Naumburg· (1027–32) away from attacks from Bohemia, and a cathedral was built before 1050. Bishops of the 11th and 12th centuries, as imperial princes, were frequently absent; and from 1285 their residence was in Zeitz. Protestantism spread easily, and Julius von *Pflug (1541–64) needed force to secure his see from the Lutheran Nikolaus von *Amsdorf. A diet in 1561 attended by 12 Protestant princes failed to reconcile Calvinist and Lutheran lords or agree about the Last Supper, but members refused to attend the third session of the Council of *Trent.

The city was destroyed by fire in 1472 and 1532 and sacked by the Swedes in 1636. Bishops Dietrich (1111–23), Udo I (1125–48), *Wichmann (1148–54, afterwards bishop of Magdeburg), and Udo II (1161–86) founded many monasteries; *Pforta is nearby.

Naumburg has many architectural monuments, the most famous being the cathedral of SS. Peter and Paul (Romanesque and early Gothic, 12th to 14th century),

Ekkehard and Uta, two of the founders, statues in the west choir of the cathedral at Naumburg, Germany.

The 13th-century west choir of the cathedral at Naumburg. Statues of founders can be seen at gallery level.

which has two choirs, the east (completed in 1300) and the west (1250–70). The early Gothic sculpture of the west choir, particularly the 12 statues of the cathedral's founders and patrons and the realistic Passion scenes in relief, by an unknown master, can be matched only in *Bamberg. The two west towers (207 feet high) and the two east towers (184 feet high, with baroque cupolas) are Romanesque-Gothic.

Bibliography: *Urkundenbuch des Hochstifts Naumburg*, ed. E. Holtermann (Magdeburg 1925). H. Bergner, *Naumburg and Merseburg* (2d ed. Leipzig 1926). K. Schöppe, *Naumburger Chronik* (Naumburg 1929). W. Bunke, LexThK² 7:846–847. W. Schlesinger, *Kirchengeschichte Sachsens im Mittelalter*, 2 v. (Cologne 1962). **Illustration credits:** Fig. 1, Marburg-Art Reference Bureau. Fig. 2, German Information Center, New York City.

[E. P. COLBERT]

NAUSEA, FRIEDRICH (GRAU), theologian; b. Waischenfeld (hence he is called Blancicampianus), Upper Franconia, *c.* 1490; d. Trent, Feb. 6, 1552. He studied at Leipzig (1514); Pavia (1518); Padua, where he obtained the doctorate in law (1523); and Siena. He interrupted his theological studies to accompany Cardinal L. *Campeggio on his trip as legate to combat heresy in Germany. On the way, Nausea tried at Bretten to win P. Melanchthon back to the Catholic faith. Named pastor at Frankfurt in 1525, Nausea had to withdraw because of Protestant pressure, and from 1526

until 1533 he labored fruitfully at Mainz as cathedral preacher and as a writer [*Centuriae IV homiliarum* (Cologne 1530)]. Ferdinand I called him to Vienna in 1534 and made him court preacher. There he became coadjutor in 1538 and successor in 1541 of Bp. J. Fabri. In 1540 and 1541 he took part in the religious discussions at Hagenau and Worms. By word and in writing Nausea worked against the spread of the Reformation and sought the reform of the Church, above all through the renewal of the bishops and priests. He ordered the visitation of his parishes [*Pastorialium inquisitionum elenchi tres* (Vienna 1547)], sought a better training of future priests [*Isagogicon de clericis ordinandis* (Vienna 1548)], and looked after the catechizing of the people [*Catechismus Catholicus* (Vienna 1543)]. By means of suggestions for reform and an extensive literary and personal activity, he paved the way for the Council of Trent, in which he participated for the first time in 1551. At the Council he argued in favor of *Communion under both species and marriage of the clergy. Unfortunately, death soon ended Nausea's reforming influence.

Bibliography: É. Amann, DTC 11.1:45–51. H. Gollob, *Friedrich Nausea: Probleme der Gegenreformation* (Vienna 1952). H. Jedin, "Das konziliare Reformprogramm Friedrich Nauseas," HistJb 77 (1958) 229–253. R. Bäumer, LexThK² 7:847.

[E. ISERLOH]

NAVARRE, CATHOLIC UNIVERSITY OF

Founded in Pamplona, Spain, by *Opus Dei as a center of higher learning (Estudio General de Navarra), the University officially opened with the Faculty of Law in 1952. Other faculties followed: Medicine and a School of Nursing (1954); Philosophy and Letters (1955); Science (1957); Journalism (1958); and Engineering (1960), which was established in the neighboring city of San Sebastian. The ecclesiastical Faculty of Canon Law was established in 1959; and in 1958, a School of Business Administration and Management was incorporated with the University.

In August 1960, in accordance with the 1953 Spanish concordat, the "Estudio General de Navarra" was erected as a Catholic university by the Holy See, and, under the title it now bears, "Universidad de Navarra," became the first independent university in Spain. Encouraged by the existence of this university, the Spanish government signed an agreement with the Holy See on April 5, 1962, establishing the precise conditions for the validity of degrees granted by Church universities, and on Sept. 8, 1962, granted recognition to all existing faculties. Thus the University of Navarre opened a new epoch of educational freedom in Spain and terminated the state monopoly which had existed since the 19th century.

After recognition as a Catholic university, it established a Faculty of Pharmacy, a School of Architecture, and institutes of liberal arts, modern languages, and social sciences. Although the plan of studies in some faculties follows that of Spanish universities, the directing body tries to incorporate the best foreign university traditions; the administration has adopted the tutorial system, elective courses, and seminars. Each year international summer courses are organized in Spanish language and culture; journalism; current affairs; and specialized areas of scientific, medical, and technical nature.

The chancellor, who is the president general of Opus Dei, supervises the direction of the University, which is controlled by a board of governors. This consists of the rector, vice rector, director of studies, secretary general, administrator, and the deans of directors of the various faculties and institutes of the University. The rector of the University in 1964, Prof. José Maria Albareda, was one of the leading Spanish figures in the world of science. He had been secretary general of the Spanish Institute of Scientific Research since its inception and was also a member of the Pontifical Academy of Sciences. Each faculty is governed by a board, which consists of the dean, vice dean, the secretary, and the professors. The students are represented on these boards. In 1964 there was a teaching staff of 230 members, of whom the majority were laymen. All held doctorates and were dedicated to both teaching and research.

The University is open to all students regardless of race, creed, or nationality. Of the 2,500 students enrolled in 1964, about 300 were foreign students mainly from Latin America, although there was a substantial minority from the underdeveloped countries in Africa and Asia in which the University takes a special interest. The University has, moreover, established a system of scholarships, 25 per cent of which include free education. Spanish students may also take advantage of the state scholarships. The University, which receives no grants from the Spanish government, is financed principally

Original site of Faculty of Philosophy and Letters at the Catholic University of Navarre, Spain.

by the "Asociacion del Estudio General de Navarra." Generous help is also provided by the provincial governments of Navarre and Guipuzcoa and by the municipalities of Pamplona and San Sebastian. Since its foundation in 1952, University facilities have expanded. Besides the faculty buildings begun in 1960, there are seven residence halls, three for men and four for women. The Schools of Medicine and Science adjoin the provincial hospital.

The University publishes two journals, *Ius canonicum* and *Revista de Medicina,* and has begun several series of books on civil and Canon Law and medieval and modern history. There are departmental libraries in the humanities, geography, social sciences, medicine, and biology. Library holdings in 1964 totaled 118,000 volumes.

[J. A. PANIAGUA]

NAVARRETE, DOMINGO FERNÁNDEZ,

Dominican missionary, polemicist, archbishop, and primate of the West Indies; b. Castrogeriz, Spain, 1618; d. Santo Domingo (Hispaniola), Feb. 16, 1686. After religious profession at Peñafiel on Dec. 8, 1635, and higher studies at Valladolid, Navarrete volunteered for the Philippines, and arrived there on June 23, 1648. A decade later he transferred to the China field (Macao, July 14, 1658), working in Fukien and Chekiang provinces until the outbreak, in 1665, of the disastrous Regency persecution. Internment of the mission personnel at Canton (March 25, 1666) made possible a collective conference to adopt uniform directives of pastoral action for the China Church, a program in 42 articles. In an interchange of argumentative briefs with the Jesuit apologists through 1668 and 1669, Navarrete opposed implementation of Alexander VII's permissive ruling of 1656 for the Rites (art. 41), but in the end gave written adherence to an earlier text of the Jesuit practices (Sept. 29, 1669). Three months later, however, he secretly left Canton and set out for Europe, arriving at Lisbon on March 19, 1672. While mission procurator at Madrid, he began composition of a massive trilogy dealing with the culture, peoples, and Christian penetration of the Chinese Empire and characterized by trenchant strictures on Jesuit methods there. Besides its controversial chapters, the first volume, *Tratados historicos, politicos, ethnicos y religiosos* (Madrid 1676), contains a spirited account of the missionary's travels and adventures (Eng. tr., Churchill, 1704); the second, *Controversias antiguas y modernas,* more combative in spirit, was suppressed by the Inquisition in 1679. Two years earlier its author had left for the Spanish Indies

(July 17, 1677), having been nominated to the archiepiscopal See of Santo Domingo. Consecrated on April 4, 1682, he spent the remaining 4 years of his life in an embattled effort to raise the standard of colonial morals, aided in this struggle for reform by the local Jesuits, whose zeal he praised in successive reports to the Crown. (*See* CHINESE RITES CONTROVERSY.)

Bibliography: *The Travels and Controversies of Friar Domingo Navarrete 1618–1686,* ed. J. S. CUMMINS, 2 v. (London 1962). Quétif-Échard 2.2:720–723.

[F. A. ROULEAU]

NAVARRO, JUAN, Renaissance musician, composer of Vesper psalms and Magnificats; b. in or near Seville, *c.* 1530; d. Palencia, Sept. 25, 1580. He is not be confused with the Franciscan missionary in Mexico who subscribed himself Juan Navarro Gaditanus, i.e., native of Cadiz (*see* LATIN AMERICA, MUSIC IN). After singing in the ducal choir at Marchena (1549), moving thence to Jaén and Málaga (1553), and an unsuccessful attempt to succeed Cristóbal de *Morales (with whom he had studied) as musical director at Málaga, he was chapelmaster at Ávila cathedral (1565–66) and then transferred (Nov. 7, 1566) to Salamanca cathedral, where he worked closely with Francisco de *Salinas, the blind organist and theorist. Thereafter he served (1574–78) as Ciudad Rodrigo cathedral musicmaster and from 1578 until death in the same capacity at Palencia. Highly esteemed in Rome, he was one of only two Spanish choirmasters whose opinion the nuncio was advised to consult on candidacies for the papal choir in 1574. His *Psalmi, Hymni ac Magnificat* (Rome 1590) were favorites in Portugal and Mexico as well as Spain.

Bibliography: M. H. ESLAVA, ed., *Lira sacro-hispana,* 5 v. in 10 pts. (Madrid 1869) v.1.2, Magnificats and psalms. F. PEDRELL, ed., *Salterio Sacro-Hispano* (Barcelona 1905), psalms. H. ANGLÈS, *Catàleg dels manuscrits musicals de la Collecció Pedrell* (Barcelona 1921). R. STEVENSON, *Spanish Cathedral Music in the Golden Age* (Berkeley 1961); MusGG 9:1297–99. G. CHASE, "Juan Navarro Hispalensis and Juan Navarro Gaditanus," MusQ 31 (1945) 188–192.

[R. STEVENSON]

NAVEL. The navel of the earth is a mythological and religio-geographical concept of a center, which is frequently associated with a manifestation and objectivization of the sacred in hills and mountains. This idea led to the establishment of places of worship on mountains or to the building of temples on artificial mounds. Numerous traditions are familiar with a holy mountain in the center of the world, whose top touches heaven and whose roots extend into the regions below the earth. It forms the *axis mundi,* which joins the three cosmic domains—heaven, earth, and lower world. The world mountain serves as the center of the world, about which the stars turn and upon which the gods dwell. Its summit forms the "navel of the earth." Since the requirements of cult transfer the cosmic world mountain into a concrete earthly environment, the navel becomes a definite center, as Delphi in Greece, and the Kaaba or "highest place" in Islamic tradition. Traces of this idea of a center are present also in the Bible. Jerusalem is spoken of as a middle point (Ez 5.5), Mount Garizim is described as the "navel of the earth" (Jgs 9.37), and the name of Mount Tabor (Jos 19.22) is etymologically related to Hebrew *tabūr* (navel; Ez 38.12). Rabbi ben Gorion

cites the Jewish tradition according to which the rock of Jerusalem is the foundation stone of the earth, i.e., the "navel of the earth"—a concept that Christianity transferred to Golgotha.

Bibliography: M. ELIADE, *Patterns in Comparative Religion,* tr. R. SHEED (New York 1958) 231–238. J. LEWY, "Tabor, Tibar Atabyros," HebUCAnn 23 (1950–51) 357–386. G. LANCZKOWSKI, RGG³ 4:1285–86, with bibliog. H. V. HERMANN, *Omphalos* (Orbis Antiquus 13; Münster 1959). H. G. QUARITCH WALES, *The Mountain of God* (London 1953). A. J. WENSINCK, *The Ideas of the Western Semites concerning the Navel of the Earth* (Amsterdam 1916).

[W. J. KORNFELD]

NAXOS, ARCHDIOCESE OF (NAXIENSIS), metropolitan see since 1522, following the Turkish conquest of *Rhodes. The seat of the Latin archdiocese is on the island of Naxos (170 square miles) in the Cyclades north of Crete in the Aegean Sea. Naxos was a Venetian duchy (1207–1566) and was under the Turks (1579–1829) before it became part of Greece. In 1961 the archdiocese (532 square miles) had 29 parishes, 12 secular and 3 religious priests, 4 men in one religious house, 34 women in 2 convents, and 4,000 Catholics in a population of 51,000.

Naxos was a see by 451 and was made suffragan to Rhodes under Emperor Leo VI (886–911). The Latin diocese was established in 1208; in the 17th century Jesuits and Capuchins had some success among the Greek Orthodox on the island. In 1803 the Greek Orthodox Sees of Naxos and Paros were united as Paro-Naxia. In 1919 the Latin archdiocese was united with the Latin See of Andros-Mykonos-Tenos which itself had had a complex history. Andros had been a bishopric by 459, suffragan to Rhodes by 630 and to Athens *c.* 900. The Greek Orthodox See of Andros became an archbishopric under the Patriarchate of Constantinople *c.* 1700; since 1821 it has been united with the See of Syros except when a bishopric (1833–1900). The Latin Diocese of Andros (1208) was administered by a vicar (1702–1824) until united with the See of Mykonos-Tenos. In 1400 the Latin Diocese of Mykonos was united with that of Tenos, a bishopric since the 6th century and a Latin diocese since the 13th century.

The three suffragans of the Latin Archdiocese of Naxos have 22 parishes, 22 secular and 4 religious priests, 34 sisters, and 8,136 Catholics in a population of 296,000; they are Chios, Santorin, and Syros (which has administered Melos since 1698). Chios, Christian from Apostolic times, had a bishop by 450; the Latin diocese dates from 1322. Santorin, a see by the 4th century, had only a Latin bishop from 1207 to 1566, when the Greek Orthodox see was restored. Syros, a see by the 9th century, had only a Latin bishop from 1207 to 1833, when the Greek Orthodox see was restored.

Bibliography: G. HOFMANN, *Vescovadi cattolici della Grecia* (OrChrAnal 715; 1938); EncCatt 8:1698. H. LECLERCQ, DACL 12.1:1019–21. S. VAILHÉ, DHGE 2:1802–04. AnnPont (1965) 297.

[E. P. COLBERT]

NAZARENE, title applied to Jesus, whose "own town" (Lk 2.39) was *Nazareth. He is called the "Nazarene" (Gr. Ναζαρηνός) in Mk 1.24; Lk 4.34; etc., or "Nazoraean" (Gr. Ναζωραῖος) in Mt 2.23; Jn 19.19; etc.—these two adjectival forms being synonymous. The word is used with evident contempt in Acts 24.5, where the followers of Christ are described as "the Nazarene sect."

The designation of Nazarene given to Jesus in Mt 2.23 creates an exegetical problem, for it is said to fulfill "what was spoken through the prophets." The following three suggestions have been offered as explanations of what Matthew intended by this reference to the OT. (1) Matthew relates Nazarene to *nazirite, a word designating a man set apart, holy, consecrated to God (cf. Nm 6.1–21); the description is certainly true of Christ, although He was not a nazirite in the technical sense. (2) Others see a reference here to Is 11.1, where the Messiah is described as "a sprout growing out of his [Jesse's] root." Now there is some connection phonetically and perhaps even etymologically between Nazareth (Gr. Ναζαρέτ, Ναζαρέθ) and nēṣer, the Hebrew word used in Is 11.1 meaning shoot or sprout, though Matthew would then be offering little more than a play on words. (3) Finally, many hold that Matthew refers to a general truth seen by Christians in the OT (note that he uses the plural, "prophets"), that the Messiah was to be despised and held in contempt; see especially Is 53.2–4 (see SERVANT OF THE LORD ORACLES); Psalm 21(22); and Ps 68(69).8–9. This prediction is already fulfilled by Christ's residence in the small unimportant town of Nazareth: its inhabitants were held in such low esteem (Jn 1.46) that to be called a Nazarene was to be the object of disdain and contempt.

Bibliography: EncDictBibl 1615–16. F. Prat, *Jesus Christ: His Life, His Teaching, and His Work,* tr. J. J. Heenan, 2 v. (Milwaukee 1950) 1:115–116. H. H. Schaeder, Kittel ThW 4:879–884. W. F. Albright, "The Names *Nazareth* and *Nazoraean,*" JBiblLit 65 (1946) 397–401.

[A. LE HOULLIER]

NAZARENES (BROTHERHOOD OF ST. LUKE),

a group of 19th-century German painters inspired by Christian faith and German nationalism to paint in imitation of the Italian Quattrocento masters. Although they predated the full Romantic movement, their spirit is one of studied return to another age as an ideal, with the additional sentimental confusion of religio-ethical and aesthetic values. The leader of the Brotherhood was Johann Friedrich Overbeck (1789–1869), who as a disciple of Friedrich *Schlegel was converted to Catholicism (1813). Protesting the academic instruction at the Vienna Academy, Overbeck, with Franz Pforr and Ludwig Vogel, left Germany for Rome in 1810, intending to revive Christian fresco painting in the "simple and pure" style of *Perugino and *Raphael. They lived a communal life in the convent of San Isidoro, where they were joined by other disciples: W. von Schadow, the Veit brothers, J. D. Passavant, J. Führich, Schnorr von Carolsfeld, and Peter von Cornelius (1783–1867). As a group they produced two murals: a "Joseph in Egypt" cycle (Casa Bartoldi 1816), and a "Dante and Tasso" cycle (Villa Massimi 1817–27). Overbeck and Cornelius are known also for their individual works, e.g., Overbeck's fresco in the Portiuncula, Assisi. Although these two later renounced the ideals of the brotherhood, its spirit lived on in English *Pre-Raphaelitism.

Bibliography: G. Dehio, *Geschichte der deutschen Kunst,* 4 v. (Berlin 1934) v.4. H. Focillon, *Le Peinture aux XIXe et XXe siècles du réalisme à nos jours* (Paris 1928). M. Howitt, *Friedrich Overbeck,* 2 v. (Freiburg 1886). A. Kuhn, *Peter Cornelius und die geistigen Strömungen seiner Zeit* (Berlin 1921). H. Geller, *Die Bildnisse der deutschen Künstler in Rom 1800–1830* (Berlin 1952). K. Simon, Thieme-Becker 7:432–438. P. F. Schmidt, *ibid.,* 26:104–106.

[M. M. MICHELS]

NAZARETH

City nestled among the hills of Galilee. It is not mentioned in the OT literature, or in the Talmud, or by Josephus. It is referred to frequently, however, in the NT because Jesus came from that city and was known as the *Nazarene. Although it is called a city, it is quite small. The name is spelled in different ways in the NT. Most frequently it is Ναζαρέτ or Ναζαρέθ, but it occurs also as Ναζαρά, Ναζαράτ, or Ναζαράθ.

It was at Nazareth that the angel Gabriel brought to Mary the message that she was to be the mother of the Savior (Lk 1.26). Mary and Joseph left there to go to Bethlehem, where Jesus was born. Then the Holy Family returned to Nazareth after their flight into Egypt (Mt 2.23). There Jesus spent the years of His hidden life (Mt 2.23; Lk 2.39, 51). During His public life Jesus seldom visited Nazareth because He was not well received there (Lk 4.16–30). That Nazareth was not highly regarded may be inferred from the question of Nathaniel, from neighboring Cana, "Can anything good come out of Nazareth?" (Jn 1.46).

During the 1st century Nazareth was inhabited not only by Jews, but also by Christians, some of whom, it seems, were relatives of Our Lord. In the early 4th century Joseph of Tiberias had been commissioned by Constantine to build churches for Christians in the Jewish towns and villages of Galilee. We may suppose that he built a church at Nazareth because of the town's intimate connection with Jesus. In 634 the Moslems occupied Nazareth and made life difficult for its Christians. In the 12th century the Crusaders made Nazareth into an episcopal city, but it did not remain so for long, because the city soon fell back into the hands of the Moslems. The Franciscans established a convent in the city in 1390, but only since 1620 have they been able to remain there permanently. Since 1948 Nazareth has been within the confines of the State of Israel.

Of the many shrines commemorating events of the NT, the two most important are the House of St. Joseph

Modern Nazareth from the south. The ancient city occupied the site now covered by the cluster of buildings below the crest of the hill, near the center of the photograph.

and the Sanctuary of the Annunciation. In the preparations for constructing a new basilica over the spot where the Annunciation took place, a systematic excavation was conducted by B. Bagatti. He has shown that here, underneath the church built in 1730 by the Franciscans, which had been removed to give place to the new basilica, there was a church built by the Crusaders. Earlier than this, there was a 5th-century church that in turn had been preceded by a Christian structure from as early as A.D. 200. Numerous graffiti were found on the plaster walls and on the plastered surfaces of loose stones, made by early Judeo-Christians. Of special interest is one of the graffiti containing, in Greek, the opening words of the angelic salutation, "Hail, Mary."

Bibliography: EncDictBibl 1616–18. B. BAGATTI, "Ritrovamenti nella Nazaret evangelica," *Stud. Bibl. Franc. Liber Annuus* 5 (Jerusalem 1954–55) 5–44; DBSuppl 6:318–333. S. SALLER, "Recent Work at the Shrine of the Annunciation at Nazareth," CathBiblQuart 25 (1963) 348–353. C. KOPP, *The Holy Places of the Gospels,* tr. R. WALLS (New York 1963) 49–86. **Illustration credit:** Matson Photo Service, Los Angeles.

[S. MUSHOLT]

NAZARETH COLLEGE, a 4-year liberal arts college for women founded in Kalamazoo, Mich., in 1924. Its origins go back to 1889, when the Congregation of the Sisters of St. Joseph was established in Kalamazoo by the Very Reverend Frank A. O'Brien. In 1891 the Sisters founded Nazareth Academy as a secondary school for girls and as a training school for sisters. The extension of the program of studies to the college level in 1912 led to its formal organization in 1924, when a charter was granted by the state of Michigan.

The College is affiliated with The Catholic University of America. It is accredited by the North Central Association of Colleges and Secondary Schools, State of Michigan Department of Public Instruction, and Michigan College Association. It holds membership in the Association of American Colleges, American Council on Education, Michigan College Foundation, and other professional organizations. Nazareth is under the patronage of the bishop of Lansing. The board of trustees comprises the seven administrative officers of the Nazareth religious community. The board of advisers numbers 14; there are 5 executive officers: the president, dean, registrar, dean of women, and treasurer. In 1964 the 49-member faculty numbered 1 priest, 27 sisters, and 21 laymen, holding 7 doctoral, 4 professional, and 33 master's degrees. There were 313 full-time and 125 part-time students in the regular session and 426 in the summer session. The library housed 33,619 volumes and received 215 periodicals.

Nazareth College offers programs in the arts and sciences leading to the B.A. and B.S. degrees. The curriculum provides a general education in the humanities and science as well as specialization in a chosen area of knowledge. Through electives in the upper division, provision is made for professional preparation in medical technology, dietetics, art, music, elementary and secondary education, and home economics. Concentration is offered in philosophy, English, Latin, French, Spanish, biology, chemistry, mathematics, history, sociology, art, and music.

A development program begun in 1958 has added classroom, residence, and administration facilities to the College campus. A master plan provides for the construction of a new library, a speech and language building, an auditorium, and a gymnasium.

[M. DE P. DEHN]

NAZARETH COLLEGE OF KENTUCKY

A 4-year liberal arts college for women in Nazareth, Nelson County, Ky. The College traces its origin to Nazareth Academy, established in 1814 by the Congregation of the Sisters of Charity of Nazareth. The original foundation, a log cabin near Bardstown, was used until 1822 when the establishment was transferred to its present location. In 1829, the General Assembly of Kentucky granted the charter under which the College operates today. An amendment to this charter was secured in 1920 in order to render explicit the degree-granting powers implicitly contained in the original document.

Normal or education courses were first offered at Nazareth to prepare sisters for teaching in the parochial schools conducted by the congregation. Courses on a junior college level were opened to both lay and religious students in 1921. In 1940, the College attained senior college status by incorporation in Nazareth College, Louisville, now known as *Catherine Spalding College.

In December 1962, upon the successful completion of the Institutional Self Study and Periodic Visitation, formal recognition as a distinct 4-year college was granted by the Southern Association of Colleges and Schools. Nazareth College is affiliated with The Catholic University of America and holds membership in the American Council on Education, the Association of American Colleges, the Association of Higher Education, the National Catholic Education Association, and the Southern Association of Colleges for Women. It has the official recognition of the Kentucky Association of Colleges, the Kentucky State Department of Education, and the U.S. Department of State for Exchange Students, and is approved by the office of the attorney general of the U.S. for foreign students.

The organizational pattern of Nazareth College comprises several distinct units: a college, an academy (the campus secondary education laboratory school), a postulate, a novitiate, a juniorate, a retired faculty house, and a motherhouse, the residence of the board of trustees. These units are so integrated that they form a single-purpose institution, namely, an individual college for the Christian higher education of younger women, both lay and religious.

The control of the College is vested in a board of trustees, which bears full and complete legal responsibility for the College as a corporate entity. The board of trustees chooses the president of the College, who is responsible to the board for the administration of the College. In 1964 the 58-member faculty was composed of 1 priest, 48 sisters, and 9 laymen; faculty members held 11 doctorates and 28 master's degrees. Total enrollment numbered 456 students representing 27 states and 18 foreign countries in the regular sessions and 436 in the summer session. The principal support of the College is the dedicated life service of the religious community. Other yearly sources of income include tuition, an annuity of $15,000 from the board of trustees, and $31,000 from investments. The College curriculum is designed to ground the students in the liberal arts while at the same time offering opportunities for training in the professional fields open to women today. Courses leading the B.A., B.S., and Mus.B. degrees are offered in the fine and applied arts, the natural and social sciences, modern languages, physical and health education, dietetics, home economics, and elementary, secondary, and business education. Special training is provided in speech therapy.

O'Connell Hall, named for Sister Ellen O'Connell, the first directress of Nazareth Academy, is the center of academic activity. Among the nine other buildings on the campus are the Carroll library, which in 1963 housed 34,000 volumes and subscribed to 350 periodicals, and the research laboratory, a unit of the Institutum Divi Thomae (Cincinnati, Ohio), in which faculty and students engage in cancer research. The St. Vincent de Paul conventual church (1854) is one of the oldest buildings on the campus.

[A. G. MC GANN]

NAZARETH COLLEGE OF ROCHESTER,

a 4-year liberal arts college for women operated by the Sisters of St. Joseph, in Rochester, N.Y. The College was founded Sept. 24, 1924, at a time when women were rapidly assuming more active roles in professional, business, and civic life. Enrollment increase obliged the College to move to a larger campus in 1932 and again in 1942, when it transferred to Pittsford, a suburb of Rochester. Nazareth is accredited by the Board of Regents of the University of the State of New York and Middle States Association of Colleges and Secondary Schools. It is recognized by the American Medical Association and holds membership in the American Council of Education, Association of American Colleges, American Association of University Women, and other national educational organizations.

The College is governed by a board of trustees and a lay advisory board. The bishop of the diocese is the chancellor of the College. In 1964 the 86-member faculty consisted of 2 priests, 44 sisters, and 40 laymen, holding 25 doctorates and 53 master's degrees from American and European universities. Total enrollment numbered 898 full-time and 197 part-time students in the regular session and 446 in the summer session. The library housed 63,616 volumes and received 471 periodicals.

Although Nazareth has no substantial endowment, income accrues from several sources: tuition, the contributed services of the religious community, the alumnae and parents' associations, the Nazareth College Guild, gifts from foundations and corporations, friends of the College, and bequests.

The curriculum, which is based on the liberal arts, offers courses leading to the B.A., B.S., and M.A. in humanities; fine arts; natural sciences; modern languages; elementary, secondary, art, music, and business education; social work; and speech correction. Preprofessional courses are given in law and medicine. Teaching methods combine lecture, seminars, and independent study for superior students. Through a program of cooperation, Nazareth College and *St. John Fisher College for men share faculties and facilities in certain areas. In 1950 Nazareth College expanded its program to include graduate studies. Alumnae studies show that one-third of Nazareth's graduates enter the teaching

profession, and more than one-third undertake advanced work within 5 years after graduation. Many enter industry, business, and science.

To accompany increasing needs, between 1958 and 1964 a building program has provided a library, two residence halls, a language laboratory, and a speech clinic. A fine arts building, auditorium, and chapel are in the planning stage.

[E. M. SCHREINER]

NAZARIUS OF LÉRINS, ST., abbot; b. 584?;

d. 629? (feast, Nov. 18). He appears in the abbatial list as 14th abbot of *Lérins. Little is known about him. Like his predecessors at Lérins, Nazarius labored to root out the remaining vestiges of pagan worship into which the district frequently lapsed. He is said to have despoiled a sanctuary of Venus near the monastery and to have established there a convent for women that flourished until the Saracen raids of the 8th century. His name is inscribed in the Gallican calendar of saints.

Bibliography: GallChrist 3:1193. P. MEYER, "La Vie latine de saint Honorat et Raimon Féraut," *Romania* 8 (1879) 481–508. Chevalier BB 2:3291.

[B. F. SCHERER]

NAZIRITES, persons consecrated to God through a

special vow. The basic text concerning the Nazirites (Heb. *nāzîr,* from the root *nzr,* to separate, closely related to *ndr,* to vow) is Nm 6.1–21, according to which they have a threefold obligation: to abstain from wine and all fermented drink (*see* RECHABITES; Jer 35.5–8), to leave their hair uncut, and to avoid all contact with dead bodies. The first provision seems to be a reaction of Israel's nomad background against the agricultural life adopted in Canaan, seen as a corrupting influence, and the third is connected with ritual purity; the second provision is undoubtedly a very ancient practice, but one to which it is difficult to assign an explanation.

Although Nm 6.1–21 belongs to the priestly tradition (*see* PRIESTLY WRITERS, PENTATEUCHAL), and is, therefore, a recent text, it is certain that it codifies a very ancient custom. The vow of the Nazirites is mentioned in several historical and prophetical texts of the Bible and seems to have taken different forms in the course of time. The earliest texts that speak of it, Jgs 13.4–5, 7, 13–14; 16.17 (Samson), 1 Sm 1.11 (Samuel), and Am 2.11–12, present the consecration of the Nazirites as lifelong, and as resulting from a divine call. Of the three obligations of the Nazirites given in Nm 6.1–21 only the one concerning the hair is mentioned in the cases of Samuel (1 Sm 1.11) and Samson (Jgs 13.5)—though abstinence from wine is imposed on Samson's mother—and only the one concerning wine in Am 2.11–12. The practice of the Nazirite vow was certainly still known in the later period of the OT (1 Mc 3.49–51) and in NT times; and it is mentioned in Josephus and in the Talmud. St. Paul made a vow of this kind at Cenchrae (Acts 18.18) and offered the prescribed sacrifices along with four others, at the Temple of Jerusalem (Acts 21.23–24). Some think that St. John the Baptist was also a Nazirite (Lk 1.15).

Nazirites are found, therefore, throughout Biblical history. One must see in this practice a particular manifestation of religious asceticism, and also, in the early period of Hebrew history, a symptom of the reaction of Yahwism against the Canaanite influence.

Bibliography: M. JASTROW, "The *Nazir* Legislation," JBiblLit 33 (1914) 266–285. De Vaux AncIsr 466–467. EncDictBibl 1618. G. RINALDI, EncCatt 8:1714–15.

[A. L. BARBIERI]

NE TEMERE

The words *Ne Temere* (lest perhaps) are the opening words of a decree concerning the juridical form of marriage. After consultation with the commission of cardinals, assigned the task of codifying the law of the Church, the decree was issued by Pope Pius X through the Congregation of the Council on Aug. 2, 1907, to take effect on Easter Sunday, April 19, 1908 (CIC *Fontes* n4340).

The *Tametsi decree* (Nov. 11, 1563) of the 24th session of the Council of Trent had already established a juridical form necessary for the validity of marriage. *Tametsi* stated: "Those who shall attempt to contract marriage otherwise than in the presence of the parish priest or of another priest authorized by the parish priest or by the Ordinary and in the presence of two or three witnesses, the Holy Council renders absolutely incapable of thus contracting marriage and declares such contracts invalid and null, as by the present decree it invalidates and annuls them."

Despite the *Tametsi* decree, and despite further clarifications from the Roman congregations and the wide faculties given to ordinaries and their delegates, there still remained great need for further amplification and legislation in the Church with regard to the form of marriage.

Clandestine marriages continued to be contracted. This often condemned practice presented many moral as well as legal problems. The decree *Tametsi,* however, had not been published everywhere so that it had not become effective throughout the universal Church. Where it had been published doubts remained concerning the proper pastor before whom a marriage was to be contracted. Finally, the *Tametsi* decree had made no exemption from the law for baptized non-Catholics. The last difficulty had been somewhat alleviated by the decree *Matrimonia quae in locis* of Benedict XIV, which exempted baptized non-Catholics from the juridical form of marriage (Nov. 4, 1741). This decree was issued originally for Belgium and Holland only, but was later extended to other parts of the world and then applied to all places where the *Tametsi* decree had been promulgated.

In his declaration, Benedict XIV referred to the widespread doubts and anxieties that troubled bishops, pastors, and missionaries concerning the validity of non-Catholic and mixed marriages. To settle the various difficulties once and for all while abolishing any contrary law or custom, the *Ne Temere* decree made the following provisions: (1) All Latin-rite Catholics were bound to the juridical form of marriage when they married Catholics. (2) Non-Catholics were exempted when they married among themselves. (3) The "communication of privilege" admitted by Benedict's declaration was henceforth abolished, so Catholics were bound to the juridical form when they married non-Catholics, except in Germany and Hungary as a result of the constitution *Provida* given by Pope Pius X to Germany and later extended to Hungary. (4) The juridical form re-

quired the presence of the local ordinary or pastor or a priest delegated by either. These ministers could validly assist at all marriages within the territorial limits of their respective jurisdictions. The presence of at least two other witnesses was required. (5) In imminent danger of death, if neither the ordinary nor pastor nor a delegate of one of these could be present, marriage could be contracted validly before any priest and two witnesses for the sake of peace of conscience or the legitimation of offspring. (6) In places where the local ordinary, pastor, or delegate could not be present and the absence had endured for at least a month, marriage could be contracted before two witnesses without the presence of a priest. Moreover, the *Ne Temere* decree, in the interest of good order, determined that marriages ought to be celebrated in the parish of the bride.

The legislation on the canonical form of marriage as laid down by the decree *Ne Temere* was later substantially adopted by the Code of Canon Law, which went into effect on May 19, 1918. The one major difference between the legislation of the Code of Canon Law and the legislation contained in the *Ne Temere* concerned persons who had been baptized in the Catholic Church but who later lost their identification with the Church. The *Ne Temere* decree made no exception for these persons with regard to the canonical form of marriage. The Code of Canon Law provided for them in canon 1099.2, exempting non-Catholics who had been baptized in the Catholic Church provided one or both of their parents were non-Catholics and provided they were raised from infancy outside the Catholic Church.

Finally, on Aug. 1, 1948, Pope Pius XII eliminated the exemption afforded by the latter part of the abovementioned canon 1099.2. This final ruling concerning the form of marriage became effective on Jan. 1, 1949.

Bibliography: E. FUS, *The Extraordinary Form of Marriage According to Canon 1098* (CUA CLS 348, Washington 1954). J. CARBERRY, *The Juridical Form of Marriage* (CUA CLS 84; Washington 1934). W. BOUDREAUX, *The "ab acatholicis nati" of Canon 1099.2* (CUA CLS 227; Washington 1946). A. MARX, *The Declaration of Nullity of Marriages Contracted Outside the Church* (CUA CLS 182; Washington 1943).

[W. VAN OMMEREN]

NEALE, LEONARD, second archbishop of the Baltimore, Md., Archdiocese, president of Georgetown College, Washington, D.C.; b. Port Tobacco, Md., Oct. 15, 1746; d. Baltimore, June 18, 1817. He was born of an old Maryland family, son of William and Anne Neale. At about the age of 12, he was sent to Europe to obtain his education under Catholic auspices, a privilege he could not enjoy in the colony. After his course at St. Omer's in French Flanders he entered the Society of Jesus on Sept. 7, 1767. At the time of the suppression of the Society in 1773 he was a priest and still engaged in the study of theology. He then went to England and from there to Demarara in British Guiana as a missionary.

In 1783, Neale returned to Maryland and was assigned to the mission of Port Tobacco. When the yellow fever plague of 1793 in Philadelphia took the lives of Lorenz Graessel, who had been named coadjutor bishop of Baltimore, and Francis Anthony Fleming, OP, Neale went to Philadelphia and was soon named its vicar-general by Bp. John Carroll. During Neale's ministry in that city, he met Miss Alice Lalor and helped her to found the first community of Visitation Nuns in the U.S.

In 1798 Carroll called Neale to the presidency of Georgetown College. While retaining this post, he was selected as Carroll's coadjutor and was consecrated bishop of Gortyna in the procathedral of St. Peter's in Baltimore on Dec. 7, 1800. This was the first time this ceremony was performed in the U.S. Neale joined Carroll in 1803 in writing to Gabriel Gruber, superior of the Jesuits in Russia, to present the petition of the former Jesuits to be joined with the Society of Jesus still existing in White Russia. Moreover, Neale's support of this project continued until the viva voce restoration was effected in 1806. He likewise rejoiced with the Jesuits at their final and complete restoration throughout the world in 1814.

On the death of Carroll, Dec. 3, 1815, Neale succeeded to the metropolitan See of Baltimore, receiving the pallium from Pius VII the following year. One of his first acts was to request from the Holy See the formal approval of the Visitation community at Georgetown. His episcopate was sorely tried by schisms in Philadelphia and Charleston, S.C. Burdened by these troubles, he sought a coadjutor and selected the Sulpician, Ambrose Maréchal. The latter's appointment as titular bishop of Stauropolis on July 24, 1817, came about a month after the archbishop's death. Neale is buried in a crypt beneath the altar of the convent chapel of the Visitation Convent in Georgetown, Washington, D.C.

Bibliography: M. BRISLEN, "The Episcopacy of Leonard Neale," HistRecStud 34 (1945) 20–111. P. K. GUILDAY, *The Life and Times of John Carroll, Archbishop of Baltimore, 1735–1818* 2 v. (Westminster, Md. 1954). A. M. MELVILLE, *John Carroll of Baltimore* (New York 1955).

[J. M. DALEY]

NEAMTU, ABBEY OF,

14th-century Rumanian monastery, outside the town of Targu Neamt, northeast Rumania, in Moldavia. Targu Neamt was once an important fortress, built in 1210. Later, Neamtu Abbey was founded at the site of a hermitage there. The monastery became one of the largest, richest, and most famous monastic foundations in *Rumania. During its golden age it had 2 churches, 10 towers, and over 600 monks. It was enlarged and enriched by Stephen the Great, Prince of Moldavia (1457–1503) and became a center for pilgrims and tourists.

Bibliography: I. CRĂCIUNAS, "The Monastery of Neamt, the Center of Monasticism in Moldavia," *Mitropolia Moldovei și Sucevei* 38 (1962) 343–353, in Rumanian. S. PORCESCU, "Cultural Activity of Neamt in the 15th Century, *ibid.* 477–506, in Rumanian.

[J. PAPIN]

NEANDER, JOHANN AUGUST WILHELM,

German Protestant church historian; b. Göttingen, Germany, Jan. 17, 1789; d. Berlin, July 14, 1850. He studied theology at Halle, where the writings and personal influence of *Schleiermacher contributed to his conversion from Judaism. He changed his name from David Mendel to Neander (new man) when baptized (1806). After teaching at Heidelberg (1812), Neander went in 1813 to the University of Berlin, where he lectured on church history and the New Testament. He was noted for his pioneer authorship of Protestant church history monographs, among which were *Über den Kaiser Julianus und sein Zeitalter* (1812, translated as *Julian the Apostate,* 1850); *Bernhard von Clairvaux* (1813); and *Chrysostomus* (1822). His numerous monographs led to his very influential six-volume church

history, to A.D. 1431 (1826–52), which appeared in various English translations. It portrayed the subject as a conflict between the spirit of Christ and the spirit of the world. Rejecting the pragmatic school's view of Christianity as a set of rationalist or supernatural doctrines, Neander employed a dialectical form of historical interpretation. His "pectoral theology," named from his motto, "It is the heart that makes the theologian," induced him to emphasize the providence of God and to portray individuals in great detail. His writing tended to be pietistic, lacking in synthesis, and based on a concept of the Church as merely a group of individuals juxtaposed.

Bibliography: *Werke,* 14 v. (Gotha 1862–67). P. SCHAFF, *Saint Augustin, Melanchthon, Neander* (New York 1886). G. UHLHORN, Herzog-Hauck PRE 13:679–687. EncRelKnow 8:95–96. W. NIGG, *Die Kirchengeschichtsschreibung* (Munich 1934). K. SCHOLDER, RGG³ 4:1388–89.

[L. J. SWIDLER]

NEBO (NABU),

one of the more important minor deities of the Babylonian-Assyrian pantheon. The god Nebo (Akkadian Nabû, the called) appears in the Code of *Hammurabi in the early 2d millennium B.C. as son of the national god *Marduk and tutelary deity of the city Borsippa (to the south of the city of *Babylon) and of its temple Ezida. In later documents he is characterized as the divine scribe, writer and bearer of the "tablets of destiny" that enshrine the decrees of the gods. In accordance with this role, he was considered patron of the scribal art and of human learning.

The cult of Nebo originated and remained strong in *Babylonia, where it played an important part in the annual New Year Festival at Babylon; during this time, his statue was borne from Borsippa to Babylon, where it was honored together with that of Marduk. It is to this festival that the satirical words of Is 46.1 refer: "*Bel [i.e., Marduk] bows down, Nebo stoops, their idols are upon beasts and cattle." Though the worship of Nebo was adopted in *Assyria, the intermittent anti-Babylonian feeling there prevented his attaining the prominence he enjoyed in Babylonia.

The name of the god is found in the OT as a theophoric element in several Babylonian proper names of the period preceding and during the Exile: Nabuchodonosor (Nebo, protect the son, Jer 21.2 and *passim*), Nabu-zardan (Nebo gave offspring, Jer 39.9 and *passim*), Nabu-sezban (Nebo, save me! Jer 39.13), and—in a form altered by the piety of Biblical scribes—Abdenago (Servant of Nebo, Dn 1.7 and *passim*).

See also MESOPOTAMIA, ANCIENT, 3.

Bibliography: EncDictBibl 1619. F. NÖTSCHER, LexThK² 7: 755–756. A. DEIMEL, *Pantheon Babylonicum* (Rome 1914), s.v. Nabû. K. L. TALLQVIST, *Akkadische Götterepitheta* (Helsingfors 1938), s.v. Nabû. Prichard ANET² 331–334.

[R. I. CAPLICE]

NEBO, MOUNT,

one of the summits to the east of the northern end of the Dead Sea. It owes its significance to its associations with Moses. According to the Biblical accounts (Nm 27.12–14; Dt 32.48–52; 34.1–8) Moses went to the top of this mountain at the express command of God; there he had his final view of the Promised Land, and there he died. From the Biblical passages it is clear that Mt. Nebo must be a headland of a region known as Abarim and Phasga. The precise headland, however, is known only from tradition. Witnesses of that tradition are Eusebius,

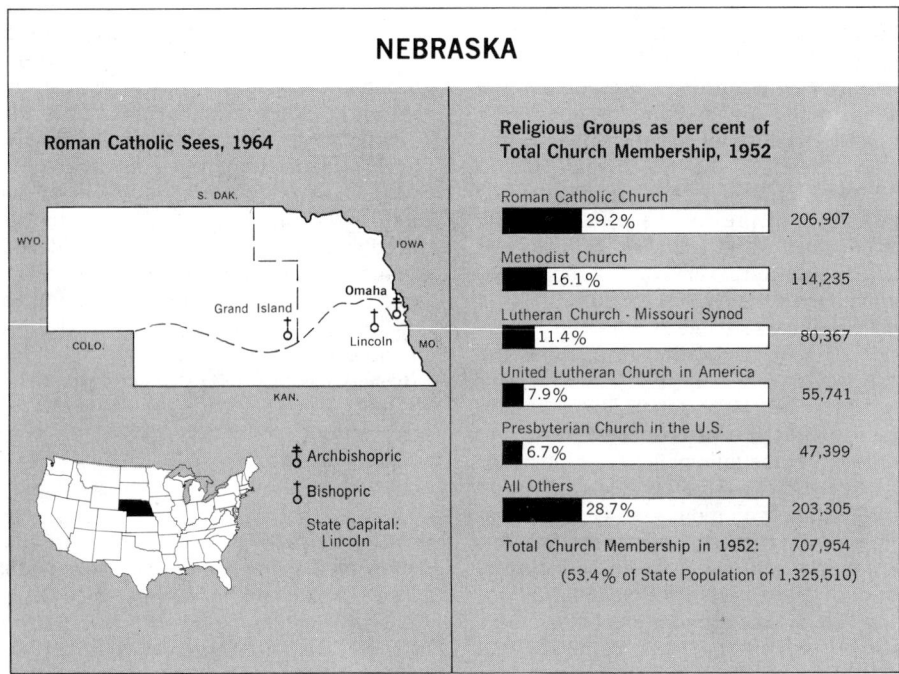

NEBRASKA

Roman Catholic Sees, 1964

S. DAK.

WYO.

IOWA

Omaha

Grand Island

COLO.

Lincoln

MO.

KAN.

✠ Archbishopric

✠ Bishopric

State Capital:
Lincoln

Religious Groups as per cent of Total Church Membership, 1952

Roman Catholic Church
29.2%   206,907

Methodist Church
16.1%   114,235

Lutheran Church - Missouri Synod
11.4%   80,367

United Lutheran Church in America
7.9%   55,741

Presbyterian Church in the U.S.
6.7%   47,399

All Others
28.7%   203,305

Total Church Membership in 1952:   707,954

(53.4% of State Population of 1,325,510)

Church-membership statistics were compiled by the Bureau of Research and Survey of the National Council of the Churches of Christ in the U.S.A.

Jerome, Aetheria, and Peter the Iberian. A church and monastery of Moses were erected on the traditional site during the Byzantine Period (4th to 8th centuries A.D.). The witnesses claim that the church served also as a memorial of the burial of Moses. Explorations since 1864 and excavations since 1933 have revealed many interesting details regarding these monuments. An archeological report has been published in S. J. Saller's and H. Schneider's, *The Memorial of Moses on Mount Nebo* (3 v. Jerusalem 1941 and 1950). The modern name for that site is Siyâgha, which is most probably an Aramaic term meaning "the monastery." Since 1933 the site has been linked by a road with the town of Madaba (*Medaba) about 6 miles to the southeast.

Bibliography: Abel GéogrPal 1:379–384. K. Hopf, LexThK² 7:861. EncDictBibl 1620.

[S. J. SALLER]

NEBRASKA

A state in the Great Plains region of central U.S., admitted to the Union (1867) as the 37th state. It is bounded by the Mississippi River on the northeast and east, by South Dakota on the north, Iowa and Missouri on the east, Kansas on the south, Wyoming on the west, and Colorado on the southwest. The capital is located at Lincoln; Omaha is the largest city and an important center for meat packing and meat processing. After World War II the state's economy was diversified by the manufacturing of machinery, chemicals, and meat products.

History. Although Nebraska was part of an area that formerly was controlled at different times by Catholic Spain and France, little missionary activity occurred before 1838. The Franciscan Juan Mingües, however, met his death probably in the close vicinity of present North Platte in the disastrous Villasur ex-

pedition of 1720. After 1838 occasional itinerant missionaries, mostly Jesuits traveling up or down the Missouri or along the Oregon Trail to or from the Northwest, visited Nebraska. In 1857 the Holy See established the Vicariate Apostolic of Nebraska coterminous with the territory, and 2 years later James M. O'Gorman, prior of the Trappists at New Melleray, Iowa, became its first vicar apostolic. The state comprises *Omaha, erected as a diocese in 1885 and established as an archdiocese in 1945; the Diocese of *Lincoln, erected in 1887; and that of *Grand Island, which was erected in 1912 with the see originally located at Kearney and which was transferred in 1917 to Grand Island.

Population. In a total population of 1,325,510 in 1952, Catholics constituted 15.5 per cent; Protestants, 37.2 per cent; Jews, 0.6 per cent; and all others, 46.7 per cent (*see* CHURCH MEMBERSHIP, U.S.). By 1961 the Catholic percentage had increased to 17.7 per cent, with Catholics numbering about 250,000 in the state's total of 1,411,656.

Education. Parallel with a system of tax-supported schools is a system of Catholic education from the elementary level to collegiate and professional schools. In 1964 more than 39,000 pupils were educated in 147 Catholic elementary schools; and about 10,800, in 42 secondary schools. Two Catholic colleges for women, St. Mary's (1923) and Duchesne (1880), and Creighton University (1878), all in Omaha, enrolled nearly 5,000 students. Although the state constitution prohibits any allotment of public moneys in support of sectarian instruction, in general a cordial relationship has existed between the parochial school systems and the office of commissioner of education, which supervises teacher certification, programs of study, and maintenance of academic standards. Statutory or constitutional law forbids auxiliary services to parochial school pupils.

Church-State Relations. References to and provisions affecting religion are incorporated in the state constitution and in acts of the legislature and the judiciary.

Constitution. Nebraska is governed by the Constitution of 1875, as amended. The preamble states that the people are "grateful to Almighty God for our freedom." Article 1, sec. 4, provides for religious freedom. No preferences may be given by law to any religion and no religious test may be required for holding office. No person may be disqualified from being a witness because of his religious beliefs, "but nothing herein shall be construed to dispense with oaths and affirmations."

Sectarian instruction is not allowed in institutions supported in whole or in part by public funds, and no religious test may be required of a student or teacher for admission to or continuance at such public school or institution (art. 7, sec. 11). Property not owned or used for financial gain or profit is exempt from taxation when it is used exclusively for religious purposes (art. 8, sec. 2).

Executive, judicial, and legislative officers and members must take an oath or affirmation before entering upon their official duties (art. 15, sec. 1).

Marriage and Divorce. Marriages of men under 18 and women under 16 are forbidden except in certain cases of pregnancy. The consent of parents is needed for men under 21 and women under 18. A license and blood test are required. Certain public officials and clergy may perform the ceremony. Common-law marriages are not recognized. Indian marriages, according to Indian custom, are lawful if contracted prior to April 8, 1913.

Marriages are void if either party is bound by a prior subsisting marriage; if a party is insane, an idiot, or afflicted with venereal disease; if the parties are related by blood in any degree of the direct line, and up to and including first cousins.

Marriages may be annulled on the grounds of nonage, force, fraud, insanity, idiocy, physical incapacity.

The grounds for absolute divorce are: adultery; physical incompetency at the time of marriage; a sentence to imprisonment for life or for more than 3 years; willful abandonment or utter desertion for 2 years; habitual drunkenness; incurable insanity with a 5-year confinement immediately preceding the filing of the petition; extreme cruelty; gross, wanton, and cruel refusal or neglect of the husband to provide suitable maintenance for the wife when he is able to do so. The decree is not final for 6 months. There are no restrictions on remarriage. *See* MARRIAGE, U.S. LAW OF; DIVORCE (U.S. LAW OF).

Abortion, Birth Control, Sterilization. The law forbids *abortion unless two physicians advise it as necessary to preserve the life of the woman. An illegal attempt is punishable by imprisonment for up to 1 year or a fine. If the mother, vitalized embryo, or fetus dies, there is a sentence of from 1 to 10 years. Advertising drugs for abortion is forbidden.

The law restricts *birth control. The advertisement or sale of contraceptives is forbidden, but exceptions are made for physicians and pharmacists. The sale and publication of medical standards that treat the topic and the teaching of it in regularly chartered medical schools is permitted (*see* CONTRACEPTION; ANOVULANTS).

The law provides for *sterilization in the case of mentally deficient persons in the Beatrice State Home. Feebleminded people are sterilized before release, after a proper hearing. Persons adjudged feebleminded, imbeciles, and those afflicted with hereditary epilepsy or insanity must be sterilized before they are permitted to contract marriage.

Property and Taxation. Religious and charitable organizations may incorporate under articles 6 and 15 of title 21 of the Religious Corporations Act. The bishop, with two subordinate clergymen and two laymen, may incorporate and hold property for the benefit of the Church.

Real and personal property of religious societies and charities not run for profit is exempt from taxation.

There are no mortmain provisions.

The restrictions on fundraising outside of one's home county include the obtaining of a certificate and the issuance of receipts to donors. But the provisions of this act do not prohibit churches and like charitable organizations from soliciting in the immediately adjoining counties where part of their membership resides.

Prisons and Reformatories. Regulations may be made to give prisoners in county jails copies of the Bible. Upon the release of any prisoner from the Nebraska Penal and Correctional Complex, the warden furnishes, at the expense of the state, a Bible to each convict who can read.

Holidays and Sunday Observance. Christmas and New Year's Day, Labor Day, Thanksgiving Day, February 12, February 22, April 22, May 30, July 4, October 12, and November 11 are legal holidays. Transactions made on holidays are valid. When a holiday falls on Sunday, the next succeeding business day is a holiday. The sale of beer on Sunday is optional. Liquor sales during an election are forbidden. Under certain conditions, baseball and public dancing are forbidden.

Morality, Public Health, and Safety. No state condones polygamy. Disturbance of a religious meeting is punishable by a fine up to $20. The licensing statutes for the practice of the basic sciences do not affect members of any church in the practice of their religious tenets, provided they do not prescribe or administer drugs or medicine, or perform surgical or physical operations, or assume the title of, or make themselves out to be physicians or surgeons. The county boards may make and enforce regulations to prevent the intro-

Sod house, Dale, Nebraska, 19th-century photograph. It was here that Mass was first said in Custer County, Nebraska, by Father Phelan of Grand Island, 1886.

duction or spread of contagious, infectious, and malignant diseases in their respective counties.

Various Constitutional Freedoms. When religious worship is made a public exhibition in the form of a seance for gain on the stage or at a carnival, fair, circus, or show, it is not a religious liberty guaranteed by the constitution (*Dill v. Hamilton* 291 N.W. 62).

Guarantees of freedom of religion, speech, and assembly are fundamental rights but are not absolute in all their aspects; thus an act motivated by religious belief or thought to be a proper exercise of free speech does not necessarily preclude criminal liability [*Holdridge v. U.S.* 282 F (2) 302].

Bilbiography: H. W. CASPER, *The Church on the Northern Plains, 1838–1874,* v.1 of *History of the Catholic Church in Nebraska* (Milwaukee 1960–). J. C. OLSON, *History of Nebraska* (Lincoln 1955). O. H. ZABEL, *God and Caesar in Nebraska . . . 1854–1954* (Lincoln 1955). *Revised Statutes of Nebraska, 1943* (reissued Lincoln 1956). *Nebraska Digest, 1855 to Date* (St. Paul, Minn. 1939–). **Illustration credit:** Fig. 2. Courtesy of the Custer County Historical Society, Broken Bow, Nebraska.

[H. W. CASPER]

NECESSITY

Necessity signifies something fixed or determined that must be, or be so, and cannot be otherwise. Man cannot think that to be is the same as not to be, nor can he at once both affirm and deny the same of the same. Thus some awareness of necessity is included in the *first principles of human thought. However, a more distinct knowledge of necessity and its diverse kinds is attained with the notion of *causality. A cause is something that influences the being of another, or upon which something must follow with dependence in being. To know in the full sense of genuine understanding is, by common consent, to know the proper cause or necessary reason of being, on account of which something is, or is so, and cannot be otherwise.

When necessity is considered in regard to being or that which is, it is opposed to *contingency or corruptibility. A changeable thing, as such, is not a necessary being. Considered in relation to knowledge, necessity is opposed to *opinion or *probability, whereas in action it is opposed to *freedom.

Origins in Aristotle. In order to explain the meaning of necessity, *Aristotle lists examples according to the different kinds of causes (*Meta.* 1015a 20–1015b 16). Something may be necessary as a concurrent cause of being and life, as respiration is necessary for an organism. Furthermore, something may be necessary for the attaining of a good or the avoiding of an evil, as a journey may be necessary, or the taking of medicine. Again, force or violence have necessity, and also whatever is effected by force or violence. In general, that is necessary which cannot be otherwise, whether by reason of an intrinsic cause, such as matter or form or intrinsic nature, or by reason of an extrinsic cause, whether final or efficient. Just as in logical demonstrations necessary conclusions follow from necessary premises, so that which is necessary may be either an effect having a necessary cause, or a cause that is necessary of itself and not dependent upon another cause. In ancient times the heavenly bodies were thought to be necessary beings of incorruptible nature, yet dependent upon another cause. The first cause of all is itself uncaused. This is the strictly necessary being, the one that is purely actual and immutable.

Scholastic Doctrine. Considerations such as these, together with many others, were elaborated in the works of the medieval scholastics, among which the teaching of St. *Thomas Aquinas is most representative. They taught that God is the only necessary being not dependent upon any other cause. God is subsistent being and intelligence. In Him being and essence, or nature, are identical, and so He is, or exists, with the most absolute necessity (ST 1a, 3.4).

Necessity in Creatures. Furthermore, the scholastics taught that God created the world of bodies and intelligent spirits by the free exercise of His omnipotence, not from eternity but at the beginning of time, and not by necessity of His nature, or out of need for them, but out of generosity and benevolence (ST 1a, 19.3; 44.1). Hence the world is contingent upon God's good pleasure, and constantly depends in being on the Creator, without whose conserving act it would cease to be. Nevertheless, even in contingent beings there is something necessary, and there is nothing so contingent that it does not have necessary aspects (ST 1a, 86.3). Speaking of creatures as they are according to their own being and natures, spiritual beings together with their essential properties are strictly necessary and cannot be otherwise by any power within themselves. Material beings also are strictly necessary as regards matter and motion in general. Although particular bodies are contingent and corruptible, still in the course of nature they do not come from nothing, nor do they pass into nothing, but the corruption of one is the generation of another. Matter as the primary subject of change can be neither generated nor corrupted, nor can the general principles of motion cease to operate by any defect in themselves. The course of nature is neither chaotic nor perfectly regular; it includes many kinds of events and products that occur with regularity, as well as many that are incidental and accidental. Events and products that occur with regularity have determined efficient and material causes, and they share the necessity of their causes. Incidental and accidental occurrences, although undetermined or casual in particular, are necessary concomitants in the world order. (Cf. *C. gent.* 2.30.)

Natural Necessity. Because the course of nature is not perfectly regular, and because in particular cases the materials required for a process might be lacking or indisposed, or the agent might be prevented from producing its regular effect, the question was raised about the possibility of a philosophy or science of nature (*see* PHILOSOPHY OF NATURE). Do natural things have principles, causes, or elements that can be discovered and by which they can be explained scientifically? This question was answered in the affirmative from two points of view. In the first place, it was thought that the various species of natural things are distinguishable empirically by differences that are distinct and irreducible and that occur with sufficient regularity to manifest the definable natures with their consequent properties. These natures are changeable and corruptible as they are found in individuals, but when understood abstractly and according to their essential principles, they are necessary and universal. In the second place, the orderly processes of nature attain great natural advantages that are regularly produced and that are the ends or goals of natural activity. If one supposes that the natural end which is usually attained will in fact be attained, then certain other things are necessary, namely, certain materials to be determined or actualized by certain agents. To this there is no exception, and therefore it was maintained that from this point of view natural science is possible. It was thought that man can attain knowledge of natural things that is necessary and universal, not merely in regard to the general aspects of nature, but also in regard to the distinct species with their parts and interrelations. In order to attain a more detailed knowledge of nature, the scholastics undertook some experimentation and measurement, but progress was slow and few appreciated the importance of quantitative considerations. What was more characteristic of their thought was that while acknowledging that matter and motion are necessary, they sought a reason for this necessity in the end or final cause, which they admitted to be only conditionally or hypothetically necessary. Their cardinal point was that if the end is, or is to be, then the antecedents must be, without exception, in the order of nature. (Cf. *In 2 phys.* 15.)

Mathematical Necessity. Necessity in the objects of mathematics was held to be clearer and stronger than that in physical things (*see* MATHEMATICS, PHILOSOPHY OF). The mathematician abstracted from sensible matter and motion, and considered quantitative beings merely as they are imaginable and intelligible. Mathematical numbers and figures were considered as existing only in the mind of the mathematician, and were constructed in the mind out of their known principles and elements. Hence they were regarded as more clearly and certainly known than physical things, and it was thought that many of their properties could be demonstrated as necessary. For many centuries mathematics was regarded as the paradigm of necessary and universal knowledge. (Cf. *In Boeth. de Trin.* 5.2; 6.1.)

However, the scholastics did not admit that in either physics or mathematics one considers forms or essences absolutely, according to their strictest necessity. This is the business of the metaphysician, who relates effects to their ultimate causes, whether of being or of truth and goodness, and tries to explain all things in relation to their strictly necessary cause, namely, God. (*See* METAPHYSICS.)

Moral Necessity. The scholastics pointed out a likeness between the necessity found in physical processes and that found in moral actions (*see* ETHICS). In a physical process there is unconditioned or absolute necessity on the part of the matter and the agent, and conditioned or hypothetical necessity on the part of the goal that is or is to be attained by determined means. So also in moral action there is absolute necessity in the principle that each man desires to be humanly happy, and hypothetical necessity to choose the reasonable good and avoid evil in order to achieve genuine happiness. The desire for *good is naturally determined, not free, but together with reason it is the principle of free *choice of the means to happiness. Yet freedom of choice might be impeded or lessened by ignorance and emotion. (Cf. *In 6 eth.* 3.1142–52.)

Logical Necessity. Necessity was admitted also in the purely logical order of mental operations. The mind begins to function and so must first apprehend its own object, called *being, and then something opposed to being, which might be *nonbeing or this as opposed to that. Then with natural necessity man judges that being is not nonbeing, or this is not that. Thus he attains the first principle of thought, called the principle of *contradiction, which is not a supposition but an axiom, that is, a necessary, self-grounded, or self-evident principle. Likewise, after one knows whole and part, he must judge with natural necessity that the whole is greater than the part. In regard to these primitive concepts and principles the mind is naturally determined by the clearest *evidence, and so error is here impossible. From principles that are known to be true and necessary, one can by valid reasoning draw conclusions that are also true and necessary (*see* DEMONSTRATION). In formal logic it is sufficient that the consequence or logical connection between the principles and the conclusion be valid and necessary, according to the laws of reasoning based on the axioms or postulates of the system. The necessity in this case is not absolute but hypothetical: if a valid conclusion is to be reached, the premises must be thus or so; and if the premises are thus or so, this conclusion must follow because it is the only one permitted by the axioms, all others being excluded. (Cf. *In 1 anal. post.* 13; *In 2 anal. post.* 7.)

Nonscholastic Thought. During the scholastic period there were many thinkers, both Platonists and nominalists, who rejected the moderate *realism of Aristotle and his medieval followers. Nominalists emphasized the contingencies in sensory experience, and neglected or denied the intelligible necessities of being, with its necessary reasons and causes. Platonists did not look for intelligibility in the sensible world, but rather in the world of transcendent ideas and spiritual realities. (*See* NOMINALISM; PLATONISM.)

Cartesianism. At the beginning of the modern period, R. *Descartes endeavored to make a complete break from the methods and principles of ordinary thought and traditional philosophy. He chose to proceed not from knowledge of something that is necessary and universal, such as the principle of contradiction, but from the particular fact of his own thought, which he identified with his own being. Thereafter, he went step by step from one clear and distinct idea to another, without seeking in all cases a rational or intelligible connection between his ideas.

The method and teachings of Descartes resulted in opposing tendencies of *rationalism and *empiricism, and of *idealism and *materialism, with attempts to unite both tendencies in various forms of *monism.

Rationalism and Empiricism. B. *Spinoza and G. W. Leibniz developed the rationalist tendencies into a deterministic view of God and the world. According to these thinkers, necessity was opposed to freedom only when it resulted from external domination or compulsion, not from internal determination. God is free because He is self-determined, and all nature is determined by God. Hence everything is necessary and nothing contingent, nor is there genuine freedom of choice in God or man.

T. *Hobbes, J. *Locke, and D. *Hume also defined freedom as lack of external compulsion. Hume maintained that everything has a cause, and denied *chance, but held that man does not know necessary causes in nature. Kant saw that this restriction of human knowledge to *phenomena threatened the validity of physical science as developed particularly by I. *Newton. Hence, in order to defend this kind of science, Kant attributed the elements of necessity and universality to the structure of the mind that knows, rather than to the thing known. He held that the mind has necessary ways of knowing, antecedent to all experience of particular things, and maintained that the essences of things and their necessary causes are speculatively unknowable. However, he admitted that the acknowledgement of God and freedom, morality, and immortality are practically necessary for a good life.

Idealism and Materialism. This strain of subjectivism was further developed into idealism by J. G. *Fichte, F. *Schelling, and G. W. F. *Hegel to the point where the inner necessity of the idea was identified with the outer necessity of historical fact. Communists now interpret the Hegelian dialectic as a determined order of materialistic evolution that eventually and inevitably will favor themselves.

Formalism. Many contemporary logicians and mathematicians profess to have no interest in principles that are true and necessary. They employ terms that are defined only by the postulates of the *axiomatic system they freely invent, and frankly acknowledge that one cannot know whether the systems in actual use are either complete or self-consistent.

Critique. This brief account shows that modern ways of philosophical thought are far removed from the natural realism of Aristotle and the scholastics. Nevertheless, universality and consistency remain the goals of thought, and these necessarily exclude self-contradiction. It appears impossible to doubt the necessity of the principle of contradiction, or the ability of the human mind to know *truth, and to discover in some cases, at least, the necessary reasons and causes of being, without which things cannot be as they are or as they ought to be. In such knowledge of the necessary reasons and causes of being, genuine *science, *philosophy, and *wisdom are commonly thought to consist.

See also CONTINGENCY; POSSIBILITY; DETERMINISM, PHYSICAL.

Bibliography: G. JALBERT, *Nécessité et contingence chez saint Thomas d'Aquin et chez ses prédécesseurs* (Ottawa 1961). J. CHEVALIER, *La Notion du nécessaire chez Aristote et chez ses prédécesseurs* (Paris 1915). J. MARITAIN, "Réflexions sur la nécessité et la contingence," *Angelicum* 14 (1937) 281–295. Syntopicon 2:251–269. A. GUZZO and V. MATHIEU, EncFil 3:828–837. Eisler 2:259–271.

[W. H. KANE]

NECESSITY OF MEANS. Something is said to be necessary with the necessity of means when it fulfills the function of *means* to an end; hence it is intrinsically related to the nature of the subject necessitating it. This necessity belongs to the ontological order.

Necessity of means can be absolute or relative. It is *absolute* when it excludes the possibility of being supplied by something else; e.g., sanctifying grace is necessary for the beatific vision by absolute necessity of means. Absolute necessity of means is also called metaphysical necessity.

Necessity of means is *relative* when it does not exclude the possibility of being supplied by something else. Thus Baptism of water is necessary for salvation by a relative necessity of means; in fact, under certain conditions, Baptism of desire (*in voto*) can remit original sin. Similarly the Church is necessary for salvation by absolute necessity of means, but *membership in the Church is necessary only by relative necessity of means, because, if one is invincibly ignorant of the Church and at the same time, through the Church's invisible *mediation, one possesses faith and sanctifying grace, one can be saved without being a formal member (*see* MEDIATION OF THE CHURCH). Relative necessity of means is also called physical necessity.

In more theological language, absolute necessity of means demands the presence of a thing that is the means in its full reality (*in re*), whereas relative necessity can be satisfied by the desire for it or *votum (*in voto*).

See also NECESSITY OF PRECEPT; SALVATION, NECESSITY OF THE CHURCH FOR.

Bibliography: F. LAKNER, LexThK² 7:862–863.

[M. EMINYAN]

NECESSITY OF PRECEPT. Something is said to be necessary by necessity of precept when it is required by a positive will of the superior or legislator. Hence the quality or entity in question is not intrinsically related to the nature of the subject requiring it, but only extrinsically, i.e., by the free determination of another subject.

This necessity belongs to the *moral* order, and not to the metaphysical order; hence it ceases to urge when it is physically or morally impossible to satisfy it. Thus to hear Mass on Sunday, being imposed by a positive law of the Church under pain of mortal sin, is necessary by necessity of precept. If a dispensation is obtained from the legitimate authority, or if the law cannot be fulfilled except with grave inconvenience, or if it is physically impossible to fulfill it, the law ceases to urge.

The Catholic Church, for instance, is said to be necessary for *salvation not only by necessity of means, but also by necessity of precept. Christ set up the kingdom of God on earth, which is the Church, and entrusted it to the Apostles and their successors. All must have the Gospel of the kingdom preached to them and be baptized in order to form part of this kingdom, and those who refuse cannot be saved (Mk 16.16). Similarly Baptism is necessary for salvation not only by necessity of means but also by necessity of precept, namely, by the positive will of Christ and by the law of the Church.

See also NECESSITY OF MEANS; SALVATION, NECESSITY OF THE CHURCH FOR; VOTUM.

Bibliography: J. SCHMID and F. LAKNER, LexThK² 7:1056–59. É. AMANN, DTC 11.1:55–56.

[M. EMINYAN]

NECHAO (NECHO), second or, according to another reckoning, sixth pharao (609–594 B.C.) of the Twenty-sixth, or Saite, Dynasty of Egypt. He is noted for his temporary restoration of the ancient Egyptian empire in Asia, followed by his decisive defeat by the Babylonians at Carchemish in 605 B.C. In Biblical history this Pharao's intervention had a profound effect on the future course of Israel's history. During his reign King Josia of Juda fell in battle; his sons were reduced to vassals; and Jerusalem itself was besieged and captured.

Psammetichus I (663–609 B.C.), Nechao's father and fourth head of Saite House in the Delta, is often called

Nechao, bronze statuette, Twenty-sixth Dynasty.

the liberator of Egypt. He had spent his long reign restoring the unity and power of Egypt that had been lost by decay and anarchy and by the Assyrian conquest of the land. His plan to restore the ancient Egyptian empire in Asia he was forced to leave for his son Nechao to carry out.

Nechao, in his reign's first year, when the destruction of Ninive (612 B.C.) by the Medes and Babylonians had left Syria free of Assyrian domination, invaded Palestine, captured Gaza and Ascalon (Jer 47.1–7), and proceeded north toward Syria. At *Mageddo (Megiddo) King *Josia of Juda made an attempt to stop him but lost his life in the battle (4 Kgs 23.29–30). The Egyptian army advanced as far as Haran (Harran), then returned south, recrossed the Euphrates, and set up headquarters at Rebla. In Palestine, Joachaz, son of Josia, had succeeded his father; but after he had ruled only 3 months, Nechao deported him to Egypt and enthroned Eliakim, another son of Josia, to whom he gave the *throne name of Joakim. The Pharao imposed on Joakim a heavy tribute of 100 talents of silver and 1 talent of gold (4 Kgs 23.29–35).

The new Asian empire of Egypt was of short duration. In a series of encounters the Babylonians under King Nabopolassar (626–605) and his son *Nabuchodonosor (605–562) gradually drove the Egyptians back to *Carchemish, where in 605 B.C. they inflicted a decisive defeat on them (Jer 46.2–6). After an even more overwhelming defeat at Hamath on the Orontes, Nechao retreated to the Delta, leaving Syria and Palestine under Babylonian control. However, in 601, when Nabuchodonosor attempted to invade Egypt, Nechao was able to check him at the Egyptian border. This aroused new hopes in the pro-Egyptian party in Jerusalem; but when the Babylonians laid siege to the city in 598, the Pharao made no attempt to give help.

Among his commercial enterprises, Nechao constructed two fleets, one in the Mediterranean and one in the Red Sea. He failed in his efforts to excavate a canal joining the Nile and the Red Sea. A more successful venture was his dispatching a ship with Phoenician mariners to sail around Africa, a feat that they accomplished in 3 years. Nechao was succeeded by his son Psammetichus II (594–588 B.C.).

Bibliography: J. YOYOTTE, DBSuppl 6:363–393, with extensive bibliog. M. PIEPER, Pauly-Wiss RE 16.2 (1935) 2167–69. EncDict Bibl 1620–21. A. H. GARDINER, *Egypt of the Pharaohs* (Oxford 1961). **Illustration credit:** The University Museum of the University of Pennsylvania.

[J. A. GRASSI]

NECKER, JACQUES, financier and man of politics; b. Geneva, into a family from Pomerania, Sept. 30, 1732; d. Coppet, near Geneva, April 9, 1804. He came to Paris while he was young and began his banking career with a fellow Swiss, Vernet, who in 1762 gave him financial help with which to become a cofounder of the Thellusson-Necker bank, soon the foremost in France. Its owners became rich by grain speculation and daring enterprises. In 1764 Necker married Suzanne Curchod, who established a flourishing salon. He defended the French Indies Company in 1769, but the loss of the colonies frustrated his efforts. In 1772 he officially left banking and in 1773 received a prize from the Académie Française for his eulogy of J. B. *Colbert, in which he sketched an ideal minister of finance. In 1775 he attacked the liberal economic policy of *Turgot with respect to the grain trade, and his wife's salon hailed him as a man of state. In 1776 he became director of the royal treasury and on June 29, 1777, director general of finance. He was unable to join the royal council as finance minister because he was a Protestant. He fostered his own reforms and continued some of Turgot's in the provinces, but he was a banker believing in government control, not an economist or a politician. He floated loans to remedy deficits. His *Compte rendu* in 1781, which had the approval of Louis XVI, made public the bad state of France's finances, pointing out at

Jacques Necker.

the same time with figures the nobles and others responsible. They forced him out of office in May 1781. But public opinion was behind him, and he strengthened his position in 1784 with the 3 v. *De l'administration des*

Aug. 26, 1788, but he again showed defects—indecisiveness, doctrinairism, intolerance of opposition. He called the Estates General, but for financial reforms. For 2 hours he lectured it with figures. The court dismissed him July 11, 1789, but public opinion and the fall of the Bastille hastened his return. On August 6 he became first minister of finance. Opposition to him grew, however, and when the Assembly abandoned him Sept. 18, 1790, there was no reaction. He left Paris quickly and went to Coppet with his wife, daughter (Mme. de Staël), and nephew. He failed in his efforts to keep himself prominent by writing: *Sur l'administration de M. Necker, par lui méme* (1791), *Du pouvoir exécutif dans les grands états* (2 v. 1792), and *De la révolution française* (4 v. 1797). A number of his writings were published in London and translated into English. He wrote *De l'importance des opinions religieuses* (London 1788), translated into English (Boston 1796).

Bibliography: E. Lavaquery, *Necker, fourrier de la Révolution, 1732–1804* (Paris 1933). E. Chapuisal, *Necker* (Paris 1938). A. M. Ghisalberti, EncIt 24:486–487. P. Jolly, *Necker* (Paris 1951). J. Lough, *Introduction to Eighteenth Century France* (London 1960). **Illustration credit:** New York Public Library, Picture Collection.

[W. E. Langley]

NECROLOGY

A list or register in which the names of dead members, associates, and benefactors of religious communities or capitular and collegial bodies were inscribed so that prayers might be offered for their souls on the anniversary of their death.

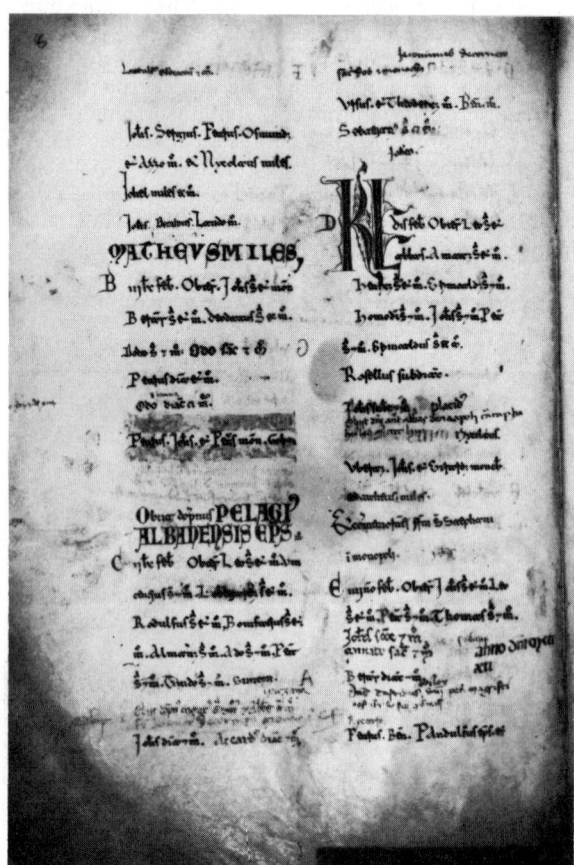

Folio from a mid-12th-century necrology at Monte Cassino (MS 47, fol. 278v) inscribed with names of deceased persons to be commemorated January 29 to February 2.

Though the necrology eventually assumed its own proper form and use, it originated in the *diptychs

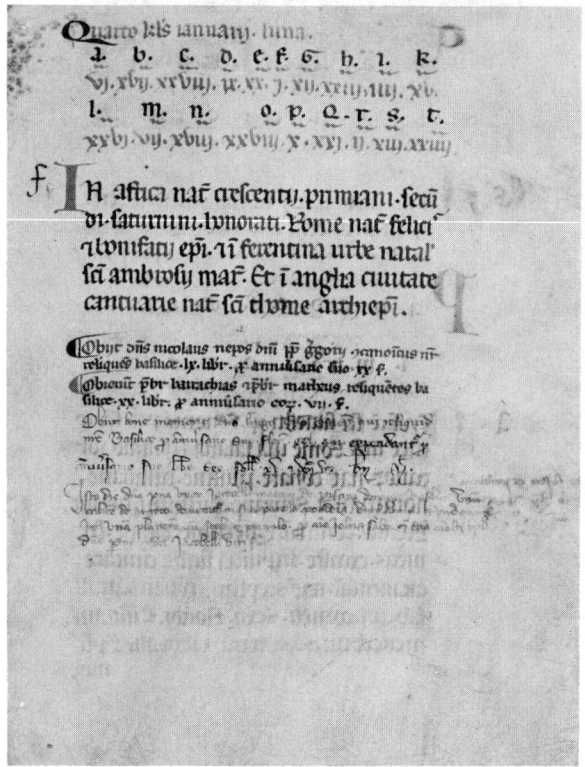

Folio from a 13th- or 14th-century necrology, "Il Martyrologium benefactorum Basilicae Vaticanae" (fol. 185r).

from which were read the names of those to be commemorated during Mass. In the 7th century the list of the dead, by then become impossibly long, began to be limited to those directly related to the community and was arranged according to the day of death. At first these lists were inserted in liturgical books already in existence, in *Sacramentaries, calendars (Fig. 1), and *martyrologies. Then, as the necrology became longer, it was drawn up as an independent register following the plan of a calendar with obits arranged according to the day of the month (Fig. 2). This form began to be used late in the 8th century. Eventually the list of the dead was read with the martyrology during the canonical hour of Prime. It is probably for this reason that the register was often called *martyrologium* in the Middle Ages. Other common names were *liber obituum, liber defunctorum, necrologium,* and *obituarius.* In a few cases the name *liber vitae* was used, though this term usually referred to the living. In its final form, attained by about 1100, the necrology included the names of deceased members of the community, the deceased of communities that had entered a fellowship of prayer, servants, and benefactors.

Of somewhat different form were the *Annales necrologici,* in which the names of the dead were noted year by year, either as part of the annual notice in a chronicle or in a register especially given to this purpose, e.g., the Fulda Annals 779–1065 (MGS 13:161–215).

The necrologies of the Middle Ages have proved a useful source for the historian and the philologist. They are still in use by some religious orders and various charitable societies that commemorate the anniversaries of deceased members.

Bibliography: Sources. Description. Wattenbach 1:437–460. Potthast Bibl 2:807–842. *Inventaire des obituaires belges* (Brussels 1899), suppl. by U. BERLIÈRE in *Bulletin de l'Académie royale des sciences, de lettres et des beaux-arts de Belgique, commission royale d'histoire* 72 (1903) lxxxiii–cxii. Wattenbach-Levison 1:64–67.

Editions. MGNecr 1–5. *Necrologi e libri affini della provincia Romana,* ed. P. EGIDI, 2 v. (Fonti per la storia d'Italia 44–45; Rome 1908–14). *Necrologio del Liber confratrum di S. Matteo di Salerno,* ed. C. A. GARUFI (ibid. 56; 1922). *I necrologie Cassinesi,* ed. M. INGUANEZ (ibid. 83; 1941–). *Recueil des historiens de la France, Obituaires,* ed. G. GUIGUE et al., 5 v. (Paris 1902–33).

Literature. F. X. WEGELE, *Zur Literatur and Kritik der fränkischen Nekrologien* (Nördlingen 1864). E. EBNER, *Die klösterlichen Gebets-Verbrüderungen bis zum Ausgange des karolingischen Zeitalters* (Regensburg 1890). A. MOLINIER, *Les Obituaires français au moyen âge* (Paris 1890). H. LECLERCQ, DACL 12.2:1834–57. A. PRATESI, EncCatt 9:20–22. A. FRANZEN, "L'Obituaire de St.-Victor de Xanten," RHE 61 (1961) 36–41. F. ZOEPFL, LexThK² 7:873–874. **Illustration credits:** Fig. 1, Archives of Monte Cassino. Fig. 2, Archivio Capitolare di S. Pietro.

[M. M. SHEEHAN]

NECROMANCY

NECROMANCY, a form of magic employed for calling up the spirits of the dead, or demons, to foretell the future or to accomplish some other act in the natural world that would otherwise be impossible. The practitioners from ancient times to the present have usually belonged to a special class of priests or seers. Necromancy, in various forms, has had a world-wide distribution. It had an important place in the Assyro-Babylonian and Egyptian civilizations, and a well-known example is found in the Old Testament. The Greeks were familiar with it, as is indicated by the elaborate ritual used by Odysseus in calling up the spirits of the dead (*Odyssey* 11.23–332), and by the role assigned to the departed in temple medicine. It was current also among the Etruscans and Romans. Although necromancy was severely condemned by the Church, repeated references are made to the practice in the Middle Ages and the Renaissance, and a considerable body of writings on the subject is extant. The traditional necromancy was made famous by the Faust legend and its literary treatment by Marlowe and Goethe.

See also MAGIC; DIVINATION.

Bibliography: H. J. ROSE, Hastings ERE 4:775–780, esp. 778. Prümm RelHdbh 380–383. T. HOPFNER, Pauly-Wiss RE (1935) 16.2:2218–33. Hastings ERE, index volume, see "necromancy." Thorndike, see index in each volume.

[T. A. BRADY]

NEEDHAM, JOHN TURBERVILLE

NEEDHAM, JOHN TURBERVILLE, antiquarian and naturalist; b. London, Sept. 10, 1713; d. Brussels, Dec. 30, 1781. His father was a London barrister who, at his early death, left a considerable fortune. The family was Catholic, and Needham began his formal education at the English College at Douai in 1722. He became a teacher of rhetoric there, was ordained in 1738, and, 2 years later, went to England as director of the Catholic school at Twyford. After a brief interlude in Portugal he returned to London, where, in 1747, he became the first English Catholic clergyman to be elected a fellow of the Royal Society. From 1743 he published papers and books on scientific matters, but he is known chiefly for his controversy with the Abbé Lazzaro *Spallanzani. Needham defined in a new way the old problem of the spontaneous generation of life:

he suggested that a sealed vessel could be heated to kill all life within it, and then if life appeared within the vessel it must have originated spontaneously. However, Needham found that such life did appear, and Spallanzani found that it did not. Although later generations have viewed this as an impasse, Needham's contemporaries found Spallanzani's arguments the more convincing.

Needham attracted attention also by his attempt, in 1761, to interpret an Egyptian inscription in terms of Chinese characters. He was elected a fellow of the Society of Antiquaries of London in that same year, but Jesuit scholars refuted his interpretations.

From 1751 to 1767 Needham traveled as tutor to various Englishmen. In 1768 he settled in Brussels as director of a government-established literary society, which became the Imperial Academy in 1773. He was appointed as a canon in the collegiate church of Dendermonde, a position that he exchanged for a canonry in the collegiate and royal church of Soighies in Hainault. His election to many learned societies implies that he had the respect of his contemporaries.

[D. H. D. ROLLER]

NEERCASSEL, JOANNES VAN

NEERCASSEL, JOANNES VAN, bishop of Castoria *in partibus,* and sixth vicar apostolic of the Dutch Mission; b. Gorcum, 1623; d. Zwolle, June 6, 1686. After studies in Cuyck, Louvain, and Paris, where he joined the Congregation of the Oratory, he was ordained in 1648. He became vicar-general of the archbishopric of Utrecht in 1653, coadjutor of Vicars Zacharias de Metz in 1661 and Balduinus Cats in 1662. He succeeded Cats in the next year. His was a brilliant, somewhat capricious personality, formed in the Berullian school and inclined toward Jansenistic rigorism. Of his writings, *Amor poenitens* (1683) was censured by the Index in 1690; the *Tractatus de sanctorum . . . cultu* (1675) was criticized for disparaging the cult of the saints; and the *Tractatus de lectione Scripturarum* (1677) was reproved for allowing the reading of the Bible in the vernacular. Though he signed the anti-Jansenist formula of Alexander VII without restriction, he had relations with the Abbey of *Port-Royal and invited Antoine *Arnauld to settle down at Delft.

Bibliography: R. R. POST, ed., *Romeinsche bronnen* (The Hague 1941–). L. J. ROGIER, *Geschiedenis van het katholicisme in Noord-Nederland,* 3 v. (Amsterdam 1945–47) v.2.

[P. POLMAN]

NEGEB

NEGEB, a mostly barren region, of vague boundaries in OT times, lying south of Bersabee toward the desert of Sinai. "Parched land," as the Hebrew name (*negeb*) signifies, it forms the southern half of modern Israel, extending in the form of an inverted isosceles triangle to an apex on the Gulf of Aqaba. N. Glueck, in explorations of this area since 1952, uncovered more than 500 sites that were once inhabited. That the area could be inhabited at all was a result of the skill and industry of its peoples in managing a meager water supply at various times during its history. There is no evidence of a more adequate rainfall during any past age to account, as some have supposed, for the periods of its population.

The Negeb has served as a bridge between East and West since the 4th millennium B.C. and was the scene of intermittent populations that flourished and declined over the centuries. There was a long period of settlement beginning just before the time of the Hebrew Patriarchs. Glueck's findings have created new respect for geographical references in the Patriarchal and Exodus narratives that were formerly dismissed as unreal. Abraham frequently wandered into the Negeb (Gn 12.9; 13.1, 3; 20.1); Isaac (Gn 24.62) and Jacob (Gn 37.1; 46.5) dwelt there. At the time Abraham journeyed there, he would have found inhabited sites and places of pasturage already existing. After the patriarchal age, numerous settlements disappeared. While the Israelites were in the Desert of Pharan, spies passed through the Negeb, and their discouraging report caused the people to spend a generation in the area (Nm 13.25–14.38; 1.19–40). David, fleeing from the jealous Saul, spent much time in the northern portion of the Negeb. *Amalecites inhabited the Negeb, and the OT tells of their wealth of cattle in the stories of Saul's and David's victories over them (1 Sm 15.9; 27.9).

Glueck has shown that the region was much more settled during the 2d millennium B.C. and the period of the Judean monarchy than was once believed. From the time King Solomon began his commercial expansions to the south in the 10th century B.C., Judean fortresses and sites dotted the Negeb till the time of the Babylonian captivity in the 6th century B.C. During the 6th and 5th centuries B.C., the northern part of the Negeb was occupied by *Edomites and became part of their kingdom of Idumea. The central and southern parts of the Negeb were occupied by the *Nabataeans from 100 B.C. to A.D. 100. This people had an absolute genius for utilizing every drop of rain water. They dug cisterns, damned wadis, terraced slopes to arrest any erosion of soil, and brought the Negeb to its most intensive stage of cultivation. The region continued to be inhabited until the 7th Christian century. Glueck's work exposed cisterns by the thousands. Today the Israeli are cleaning out these cisterns and putting the Nabataean waterworks back into use. Continuing efforts at irrigation and planting give promise that the area of the Negeb may once again sustain life as it did in Biblical times.

Bibliography: N. GLUECK, *Rivers in the Desert* (New York 1959). EncDictBibl 1625.

[F. F. BERGEWISCH]

NEGRI, ADA, Italian writer; b. Lodi, Feb. 3, 1870; d. Milan, Jan. 11, 1945. She earned her living as a teacher, and when her first collections of poetry were published (*Fatalità*, 1892; *Tempeste*, 1894), she was hailed as the poet of the new society of the working man. Her poetry expressed the misery and the sorrow of the poor who still had courage to bear the adversities of modern life. The social implications of this early poetry made her something of a champion of the working people, a class from which she herself had come. With marriage and motherhood, however, her inspiration and manner changed. With *Maternità* (1904), *Dal Profondo* (1910), and *Esilio* (1914), she withdrew more within herself and dealt with feminine emotions and experiences in contrived works that are neither greatly inspired nor very original. In her prose works (e.g., the collection of short stories, *Le Solitarie,* 1917; and the autobiographical *Stella Mattutina,* 1921) Negri is often a capable realist, excelling in descriptions of feminine passions and torments, physical and emotional. The basis of much of both her prose and poetry is her own life—her experiences as a school teacher and her

devotion to poetry and social causes. This autobiographical emphasis is often too heavy, especially when her topic is treated emotionally.

Her later collections of poetry, *Libro di Mara* (1919), *Canti dell'isola* (1925), *Vespertina* (1930), *Il Dono* (1935), and *Fons Amoris* (1939–43), reflect a progressive turning away from social revolt and its allied subjectivism and a perceptible movement toward Christian faith, in which she found a source of patience, reconciliation, and peace.

Bibliography: *Tutte le opere,* 2 v. (Milan 1954–56). B. CROCE, *La letteratura della Nuova Italia,* 6 v. (Bari 1914–45) v.2. L. RUSSO, *I narratori* (Milan 1951).

[A. J. DE VITO]

NEGROES, CATHOLIC SCHOLARSHIPS FOR, an organization founded in 1946 by Mrs. Roger L. Putnam, under the patronage of Cardinal Richard Cushing, Archbishop of Boston. The primary purpose of this endeavor is to help young Negroes to obtain a good training in the arts and sciences whereby they can not only help themselves but also, when their training has been completed, return to their own people and help them also. Beneficiaries, however, are not required to devote themselves to their own race when they are ready to establish their life's work.

Lack of funds, which always fall short of the genuine need for aid, somewhat restricts the group in its activity. However, resources are sufficient to award scholarships ranging from $100 to $600 to about 115 students in colleges throughout the U.S. These annual grants, which total more than $20,000, accrue mainly from small donations that the Putnams generously fortify.

By 1956 Catholic Scholarships for Negroes had aided 123 young people to occupy responsible positions in a wide variety of fields: medicine, law, homemaking, social work, priesthood, sisterhood, education, and chemical research. One of the first graduates received a teaching fellowship in electronics at Harvard University, Mass., and two were Fulbright scholars: one at Heidelberg, Germany; the other at the University of Aix-en-Provence, France.

Since the scholarship fund has never been large, grants in aid cannot cover all expenses. The administrators of Catholic colleges, however, have helped out greatly here, sometimes waiving all tuition and fees for a complete 4-year education. Many of the students increase their resources by doing outside remunerative work, such as baby-sitting for families in the college vicinity or doing light housework in return for their room and board. The students are not expected to reimburse the association for the money received through these grants-in-aid, but they are asked to contribute $3.00 in annual dues toward helping other students.

Despite the organization's title, grants are not limited to Catholics; several scholarships are granted each year to non-Catholics. All, however, must be well prepared academically, have good character references, and meet in full the requirements for admission to the college of their choice.

Among its summer activities each year the association sponsors the education of a group of Negro sisters from three communities: the Sisters of the Holy Family, New Orleans, La.; the Franciscan Handmaids of Mary, New York, N.Y.; and the Franciscan Sisters of Baltimore City, Baltimore, Md. These sisters, who number about 20 and are chiefly candidates for the master's degree, receive special preparation for teaching.

Sometimes the organization engages in a special project: in the summer of 1964 it paid the expenses of a sister from Immaculate Heart College, Los Angeles, Calif., to accompany the Massachusetts adults who supervised student work in Mississippi; and sent one student to the Goethe Institute in Montreal, Canada. Since 1947 the organization has spent $253,512.84 in student aid.

[R. J. DEFERRARI]

NEGROES IN THE U.S., I
(HISTORY OF)

According to the census of 1960, there were 18,871,831 Negroes in the U.S., constituting 10.3 per cent of the total population. Biologically, American Negroes represent a fusion of many African peoples and of white and American Indian strains as well. It is estimated that about 80 per cent have some admixture of the latter strains, received since the arrival of their ancestors in the New World. Culturally, however, despite their African origin, the traits of American Negroes are derived principally from the host society. Their *race distinguishes them only physically; so far as they exist at all, the so-called *race differences that are used by some to justify *prejudice against the Negro or other *minorities in the U.S. are due, not to innate psychological factors, but to participation in distinctive subcultures that have developed in the course of American history. From the beginning, *racism in the form of color prejudice was much more serious in the Anglo-Saxon than in the French or Spanish colonies. It was deepened by the emotions aroused in defense of *slavery and by the violence of the Civil War. After emancipation, therefore, Negroes continued to occupy an inferior, castelike position, concentrated as they were in the rural South in conditions of economic poverty and cultural deprivation. Their rejection by whites, on the one hand, and their consciousness of a common condition and status, on the other, provided a basis for the eventual growth of solidarity and the emergence of a Negro minority group with its own characteristic institutions and leadership.

The history of the Negro in the U.S. can be divided into three chronological periods: from 1619 to 1865, 1865 to 1940, and 1940 to the time of this writing (1964). The first was the period of Negro slavery with its economic, social, political, and moral consequences and its abolition during the Civil War. The second was the period of Reconstruction and the restoration of white rule in the South, the beginnings of Negro protest, and the economic change resulting from World War I. The last period involves the changes in the position of the Negro in American society after World War II.

Negro Slavery. Importation of Negroes to the English colonies began in 1619, when a Dutch ship brought 20 Negroes to Jamestown, Va. Since slavery was not then recognized by English law or custom, these Negroes were indentured servants. By the end of the 17th century, however, slavery in the English colonies had evolved as a legal institution either through statutory enactment or *de facto* recognition by all colonial governments.

Of the 697,628 Negro slaves in the Thirteen Colonies in 1770, only 40,000 lived in the Middle and New England colonies where the predominance of commerce and manufacturing made slave holding on any large scale uneconomical. In the agrarian South, where slavery was economically advantageous, there were approximately 656,000 slaves by the end of the colonial period. The greatest impetus to the constant increase in the number of slaves imported annually was their unlimited supply, their relative cheapness, and the permanency of their status. The majority were employed in agriculture under a communal, capitalistic enterprise called the plantation system. It has been estimated that 12 to 15 million slaves were brought to the New World from the 16th and through the 18th century.

The expedience of the slave system gradually led to its acceptance and later its rationalization by both Catholics and Protestants. The "Christianizing influence"

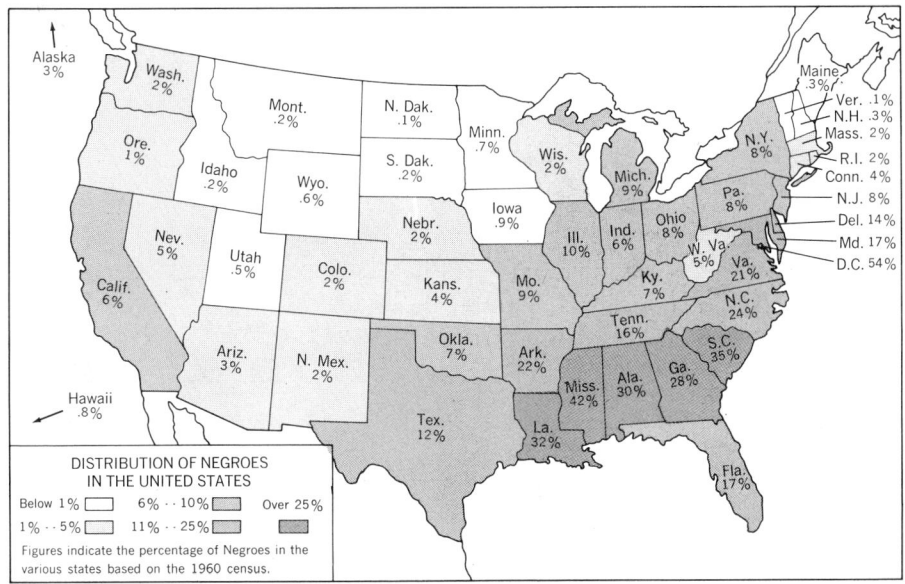

Fig. 1. Map showing areas in the U.S. with significant Negro population.

that slavery afforded and the conviction that slavery was the Negro's "natural condition" were argued as sufficient justification for Negro enslavement. The most articulate religious opposition to slavery came from the Quakers, who urged their members to manumit their slaves.

Early Opposition to Slavery. Considerable antislavery sentiment developed during the Revolutionary era. Recognition of the inconsistencies between slavery and the philosophy of the rights of man led Thomas Jefferson and Benjamin Franklin to declare slavery an evil and to urge its abolition. Similar convictions led to the organization of antislavery societies in every state during the post-Revolutionary period. These organizations advocated immediate manumission of slaves and the abolition of the slave trade. Legislation was enacted for this purpose in Pennsylvania, Rhode Island, Maryland, and South Carolina. After 1790, with the growth of concern for property rights, the movement for human freedom was undermined and could not be sustained.

The controversial nature of slavery was evident at the Constitutional Convention of 1787. Agreement was reached only after considerable debate and compromise. It was agreed that three-fifths of the slave population should be counted in the apportionment of representation, as well as in the levy of direct taxes, that a national ban on the slave trade should become effective after 20 years, and that fugitive slaves should be returned to their owners.

Conditions in the South. The trend toward a decline in slavery was reversed after 1800. By 1820, slavery was considered essential to the economic well-being of the South. The decennial census reports show that the number of slaves rose from 697,624 in 1790 to 2,009,043 in 1830 and to 3,954,760 in 1860. Since the majority of these were concentrated in the South, the increase was obviously related to the demand for cotton. This demand increased steadily with the spread of the industrial revolution. The plantation system became entrenched as the most profitable and productive system of organizing land, labor, and enterprise for the production of the western world's most marketable commodity.

Despite the risks involved in generalizing about the condition of slaves under the system, it must be acknowledged that there was indisputable exploitation of human and natural resources. Conditions were certainly far from idyllic, as maintained by some supporters of slavery, nor were they in all instances as brutal and cruel as alleged by opponents. Everywhere, however, slavery was a system of regulations and controls implemented by slave codes that made chattel of human beings. The daily life of the plantation slave was hard and monotonous. Food and shelter were of the crudest type. Opportunities for recreation were few and came principally during the summer "lay-by," the Christmas season, and wedding celebrations. The life of urban slaves, of whom there were approximately 400,000 in 1850, was less rigorous. Those with talent and training were often hired out by their owners and worked in semiskilled and skilled trades.

Social institutions among slaves were generally unstable. The slave family, without legal basis, was always unstable, for the slave trade operated against it. Permanency was largely a matter of chance, depending entirely upon the moral and religious practices of the owner.

Fig. 2. Unique American watercolor, c. 1800–25, probably from South Carolina, showing what is thought to be a slave wedding. Elements of costume, the cane used by the dancing man, and musical instruments are types used in West Africa, from which slaves had been brought directly to Charleston since the early 18th century.

Education of slaves was proscribed by law in most slave states, where it was considered a potential danger to the preservation of slavery. In spite of its proscription and the conviction of many that Negroes were uneducable, many owners gave their slaves some instruction. In a few cities, schools for Negroes were surreptitiously maintained. Thus, large numbers of Negroes, slave and free, were literate prior to 1860.

Religious worship and church activities were permitted, provided proper precautions were taken to assure that no efforts were made to instruct slaves in those states where instruction was proscribed. Occasionally slaves were compelled or allowed to attend the owner's church, where surveillance was possible and the dissemination of incendiary ideas could be prevented. The Methodists and Baptists exerted the greatest influence upon plantation Negroes, although these churches and others were ultimately enlisted by the slave interests to defend slavery on religious and scriptural bases. There were few Catholic slaves apart from those of the Catholic regions of southern Louisiana and southern Maryland.

Negro reaction to the servile status was indicated by the number and frequency of planned or attempted uprisings between 1800 and 1860, by appeals from the platform by free Negroes in the antislavery movement, and by the persistent fear of slave revolts by whites. Among the more significant slave uprisings were the Gabriel Prosser revolt in Virginia in 1800, the Denmark Vesey revolt in South Carolina in 1822, and the Nat Turner revolt in Virginia in 1831; none of these was successful. Slave revolts occurred also aboard ships engaged in the coastwise slave trade. Reactions such as these indicate the falsity of the image of the slave as happy, contented, and docile.

Free Negroes. In addition to the Negro slave population, there were 59,000 free Negroes in 1790; 319,000 in 1830; and 480,000 in 1860. Approximately 45 per cent of these lived in the South, chiefly in urban centers such as Baltimore, Charleston, New Orleans, and Mobile, primarily because these centers afforded superior social and economic opportunities. Similar concentrations developed in Philadelphia, New York, and Boston. Free Negroes were free either because they were born of free parents, had been manumitted by benevolent owners, or had been able to purchase their freedom. Fear of slave uprisings and of an unlimited number of free Negroes, who constituted a threat to slavery, resulted in statutory restrictions against manumission after 1830.

Conditions under which the free Negroes lived varied greatly. Some were able to accumulate real and personal property and to become respected members of their communities. The vast majority, however, faced many forms of economic hardship, restriction, and opposition, especially in the South, from competing white workers. In the North, free Negroes gave considerable attention to self-improvement and intellectual advancement. They established schools, benevolent societies for mutual aid to members in time of need, and, under the leadership of Richard Allen, David Coker, and Absalom Jones, an independent Negro church. Free Negroes were active also in antislavery and abolitionist movements which, by 1830, had developed rapidly in the North and West as an outgrowth of the general humanitarian crusade of the era. Among them, Robert Purvis, Samuel Cornish,

John Russwurm, Harriet Tubman, and Frederick Douglass served as founders, officers, or agents in national and regional antislavery organizations. Douglass and Sojourner Truth were especially effective on the platform, while Cornish and Russwurm made their contribution through the incipient Negro press.

The Antislavery Movement. Although the extreme faction of the antislavery movement led by William Lloyd Garrison became the most famous, other more moderate evangelical and humanitarian factions led by Theodore Dwight Weld, Arthur and Lewis Tappan, and C. C. Finney played significant roles in opposing slavery. All factions worked to eradicate slavery, although they differed with regard to immediacy and method. Utilizing both the platform and the press, they declared war on slavery.

The antislavery issue had deep implications for the churches. It resulted in the division of the Methodist and Baptist churches into northern and southern branches. Quakers, Presbyterians, and northern Methodists gave leadership and direction to the antislavery movement. Only a few Episcopalians and Catholics became involved. Catholics tended to regard slavery as a political issue with which the Church should not become involved. Individually, some priests condemned slavery; others defended it. On the whole, Church leaders were conservative, held slavery not incompatible with natural law, and opposed abolitionists as enemies of religion and public order.

The antislavery movement became associated with the movement for colonization of Negroes abroad. It gained the support of northerners, who believed that it would serve the best interests of free Negroes, and of southerners, who welcomed the opportunity to rid the section of free Negroes. The American Colonization Society, organized in Washington, D.C., in 1817, was the most effective organization in the movement. African colonization failed primarily because of the enormity of the job and because of articulate opposition by free Negroes. The establishment of *Liberia on the west coast of Africa and the emigration to it of approximately 12,000 Negroes were the only tangible accomplishments of the effort.

After 1830, issues involving slavery were increasingly injected into national politics. During the next 3 decades, discussions of public policy concerning slavery in the western territories, the admission of new states to the Union, and the rendition of fugitive slaves became controversial issues. National policies that threatened the existence or expansion of slavery were opposed by the southern states in the name of states' rights. Sectional fears and irreconcilable interests resulted in a complete breakdown in communication. The appeal to arms followed in 1861.

The Civil War inevitably involved many issues pertaining to the Negro. The chief of these were the enlistment of Negro soldiers and the emancipation of slaves. Despite pressure from Radical Republicans during 1861 and early 1862, emancipation was successfully resisted by President Lincoln. He also refused to enroll Negro volunteers in the Army until late 1862 when pressure from northern war governors, Union military reverses, and the impending issuance of the Emancipation Proclamation forced a reversal of policy. It is estimated that 180,000 Negroes had enrolled in the Union Army and 30,000 in the Navy by the end of hostilities.

Reconstruction to World War II. Reconstruction after the Civil War greatly altered the southern political and social order. Three constitutional amendments—the 13th, 14th, and 15th—granted freedom, citizenship, and suffrage to Negroes. To southerners, the most unacceptable aspect of Reconstruction was participation of Negroes in political affairs, for after 1868 all southern constitutional conventions and legislatures contained some Negro members. Negroes served as legislators, lieutenant-governors, sheriffs, recorders of deeds, and justices of the peace. There were 22 Negroes elected to Congress, 2 of them senators.

Allegations of Negro domination of southern politics are unfounded, and conventional appraisals of the Reconstruction as "a blackout of honest government" have been challenged by some competent historians. While recognizing the existence of incompetence and corruption in the South, as in other sections of the nation, the revisionist historians emphasize the significance of the achievements of Reconstruction governments, such as the enfranchisement of poor whites, the establishment of social welfare facilities and free public schools, and the framing of new constitutions.

White Supremacy. The failure of Radical Reconstruction and the "redemption" of the South by southern whites, resulted in a series of measures to eliminate Negroes from political life. After 1876, narrow Supreme Court interpretation of the Civil War amendments and a decline of northern interest in southern Negroes resulted in the return of white supremacy to the South and in the nullification of the gains that had been made by Negroes between 1865 and 1875. Congressional efforts to protect Negroes in the exercise of suffrage were invalidated by the Supreme Court; the Civil Rights Act of 1875 protecting the right of Negroes to use public facilities without discrimination was declared invalid; and school segregation was held not inconsistent with constitutional guarantees.

Unburdened of fear of intervention by northern politicians and the Supreme Court, the South proceeded to readjust relations between the races. One aspect of this readjustment was the establishment of a color-caste system rejecting all claims of social equality on the unscientific assumption of Negro mental and physical inferiority. Color-caste was reinforced by Jim Crow statutes that prohibited association of the races in all areas—recreation, employment, transportation, education, and residence. The "separate but equal" doctrine, enunciated by the Supreme Court in 1896, gave judicial sanction to the system. While Jim Crow legislation supported the caste system, southern legislatures eliminated Negroes from politics between 1890 and 1910. Poll taxes, property and moral qualifications, tests of literacy and understanding, and grandfather clauses were devised and interpreted to disfranchise Negro voters. Throughout the period, most southern Negroes remained dependent on a new plantation economy that was not very different from the old.

At the beginning of the 20th century, therefore, most Negroes lived under a legalized system of segregation and discrimination with little protection for personal or property rights. For example, the lynching of 3,300 Negroes between 1882 and 1903 indicates their general lack of safety and security.

Beginnings of the Negro Protest. Negro reaction to the return to servile status varied from programs of

Fig. 3. "Benediction in Georgia," lithograph, 1916, George Bellows. Exemplifying a kind of latter-day abolitionism, this print protests against a sanctimonious white supremacy that used the notorious chain-gang system of convict labor as one of its instruments.

accommodation to strong movements of protest and revolt. Booker T. Washington, the great accommodationist, advocated vocational and industrial education of the masses in order to provide a measure of economic security more urgently needed than political and social rights. His approach was supported by southern whites as the answer to demands for the education of Negroes. Other Negro leaders rejected Booker Washington's program as too restrictive. They contended for full civil rights, including the exercise of the franchise and opportunities for education in the liberal arts. With W. E. B. DuBois as leader, this group established the Niagara Movement in 1905 to mold opinion in support of a drive for equal rights. Although the Niagara Movement was short lived, it identified the Negro intellectual with Negro protest, and enunciated the basic goals of American Negroes, which remain little changed in the 1960s.

The National Association for the Advancement of Colored People (NAACP) was organized in 1909 by a group of Negroes and white liberals who reacted against the existing pattern of racial violence and discrimination. It continued the organized protest of the Niagara Movement. Its objectives were complete equality, justice in the courts, and an impartial suffrage. Largely through its efforts, the Supreme Court, in the next 3 decades, began to interpret the Civil War amendments in the spirit of the framers.

Another form of protest, under the leadership of Marcus Garvey, reached its zenith in the 1920s. Garveyism, a type of black nationalism, appealed largely to the Negro masses, who were urged to reject white American society and to establish a country for Negroes in Africa. Although the colonization effort was a failure, Garveyism contributed significantly to the development of race pride and represented the first mass protest movement among American Negroes.

Demographic and Economic Change. Significant changes in the social and economic life of Negroes occurred between 1918 and 1940. Before 1914, the majority of southern Negroes lived on plantations under conditions approximating slavery. During and after World War I, more than a million Negroes migrated to northern industrial areas to find more lucrative employment, better educational opportunities, and freedom from fear of violence. Concurrently, there was migration from rural to urban areas within the South. Migration and urbanization initiated a transformation in the employment patterns of Negroes.

During the 1930s, urban Negro workers were especially depressed, for with economic discrimination and without seniority, they were the first fired and the last hired. Unemployment forced many to live on relief. Communist efforts to capitalize on this plight were generally unsuccessful. Except for a few intellectuals, American Negroes were not revolution-minded and were determined to obtain justice and equality within the framework of the American democratic system.

The Negro in the 1960s. The anomalous position of the Negro in contemporary American society is reflected by advancement and widening opportunity on the one hand, counterbalanced by continuing patterns of discrimination and caste on the other. By census definition, a Negro is any person who has any known trace of Negro ancestry, regardless of how racially indistinguishable he may be. In physical traits, Negroes range from pure Negroid to pure Caucasoid. The once large mulatto element has declined since 1920; increased racial pride among Negroes and "passing" of persons indistinguishable as Negroes have contributed to this decline. The extent of "passing," though difficult to determine, has been estimated at 20,000 to 30,000 persons a year. The desire to escape restrictions of color and caste is facilitated by geographical mobility and urban anonymity. Despite the disappearance of many who might be classed as Negroes, the Negro population increased 25.4 per cent during the decade, 1950 to 1960, as compared with an 18.5 per cent increase for the total population.

The distribution of the Negro population has changed radically since 1900, when 90 per cent of it was concentrated in the South. With increased northward and westward mobility, only 58 per cent remained there by 1960. Census statistics also reveal continued urban mobility among Negroes, 73.2 per cent of whom lived in urban areas in 1960. The majority are concentrated in large cities. Eleven of these—New York, Chicago, Philadelphia, Boston, Washington, D.C., Los Angeles, New Orleans, St. Louis, Detroit, Baltimore, and Cleveland—have Negro populations of 200,000 or more. In these cities the Negro masses are concentrated in the central city, where blighted residential areas, abandoned by upwardly mobile whites and Negroes, are scattered through and around the central business core.

Occupational Status. Urbanization has had a notable impact on the economic status of Negroes. The manpower shortages created by World War II enabled Negroes to gain employment in occupations from which they had been previously excluded. In spite of expanding opportunities, flagrant inequities persist because of racial discrimination. In 1961, a report of the U.S. Civil Rights Commission cited known discrimination in training and employment opportunities offered by the armed services, in apprenticeship training programs, in referral services of state employment services, and by employers, including the Federal government.

Occupational discrimination contributes to the high Negro unemployment rate, which is 2 to 3 times the national average, and to the large income differential between Negro and white workers. In 1962, the median income of Negro workers was $3,233, or 55 per cent less than the $5,830 of white workers. This represented only a 1 per cent decline in the differential from 1947 to 1962. Further indication of the disparity between the earning potential of Negroes and whites under prevailing practices was the estimate that, in 1962, the Negro worker with a 4-year college education could expect to earn a smaller lifetime income than a white worker with an 8th-grade education.

Two promising attempts to deal with this problem were the establishment of national and state fair employment practices commissions and of the President's Committee on Equal Employment Opportunity. The Federal Fair Employment Practices Commission (FEPC) was a byproduct of World War II, when it was established by Pres. Franklin D. Roosevelt to combat discriminatory practices in industry. Although it fell short of its goal, it succeeded in increasing Negro employment and in encouraging the establishment of similar commissions in northern states.

Social Status. Racial segregation and discrimination in American society have resulted in the evolution of the Negro community with its own social institutions. Although white society tends to assign all Negroes to a lower class status, the Negro population has its own *social class system with upper, middle, and lower classes. The Negro upper class has a long tradition of education and culture. It is characterized by good family background and personal security. A sizable Negro middle class has emerged, which has profited most from improved educational opportunities, especially in higher education, and from increased opportunities in professional, technical, and clerical employment. In civic responsibility, respect for law, morals, housing, recreation, and dress and other personal habits, the Negro middle class conforms to the same standards as its white counterpart.

It is the Negro lower class, which constitutes a majority of the Negro population, that is best known to most whites. This group is composed of farm laborers, sharecroppers, migratory laborers, unskilled workers, servants, and domestics. Lower-class Negroes are marginal workers with little economic or personal security; they are seldom able to maintain minimum standards in health or housing, have little formal education, and contribute disproportionately to crime and delinquency rates.

Although educational opportunities for Negroes have expanded considerably since the late 1930s, serious deficiencies remain. In the South, where the greatest inequities exist, as late as 1950, 1 in 5 Negro adults had completed no more than 5 years of formal schooling, only 2 in 5 had any high school education, and nearly 3 times as many Negroes as whites were functional illiterates. In the North, twice as many Negro adults as white adults had no high school education. Since 1954, educational opportunities and facilities for Negroes have shown a great deal of improvement. As a group, however, it is estimated that American Negroes trail whites by nearly a generation in educational development. Discrimination and segregation, *de jure* and *de facto*, contribute significantly to this lag. (*See* NEGROES IN THE U.S., II.)

In housing, even more than in education, there is considerable racial discrimination and segregation in all sections of the nation. Housing available to the majority of Negroes, as compared with that available to whites, is insufficient, inferior, and more expensive. Necessity, rather than choice, has forced the great majority of Negroes to live in or near the central city in ghettos that continue to expand and deteriorate with the in-migration of rural Negroes to urban centers in the North and South. The concentration of large numbers of low-income families in overcrowded, substandard housing contributes substantially to numerous social, moral, and health problems. It is often difficult also for upper- and middle-class Negroes to find housing commensurate with their incomes. President Kennedy's "open occupancy" order of 1962 and state and local ordinances banning discrimination in housing are promising steps taken to meet this problem.

Social Disorganization. Although the lives of a large number of Negro families, especially in the upper and middle classes, are stable and secure, low economic status, lack of education, and the substandard housing of a majority of Negroes produce a disproportionate number of social and health problems. Family disorganization, *illegitimacy, *juvenile delinquency, and *crime are often problems of low-income groups. Similarly, disease and mortality rates reveal a Negro-white differential. There has been a steady decline in the Negro mortality rate since 1900, but in 1960 it was still 37 per cent greater and life expectancy 6.1 years less than for whites. High rates of mortality and desertion contribute significantly to family instability and disorganization, especially among lower-class Negroes. Loss of the wage earner has resulted in twice as many (1 in every 5) urban Negro families as white families having female heads of households. Absence of the discipline and authority of a father in the home, frequent absence of the mother, and inadequate housing that is crowded beyond the limits of safety and decency have resulted in high illegitimacy rates. In some cities, 1 in 5 live births is illegitimate among Negroes, as compared with 1 in 50 among whites. Illiteracy, unemployment, poverty, double standards of justice, racial prejudice, and frustrated ambitions are major factors contributing to delinquency and crime. In this problem area, it is the doubly disadvantaged, depressed lower-class group that contributes to the magnitude of the burden.

The Negro Church. Outside the family, the Negro church is the most influential social institution in the Negro community. It has long identified itself with movements for racial advancement. The long-standing identification and acceptance of the Negro minister as leader of his people in social as well as spiritual problems provided a basis for the leadership role of the Negro ministry in the *civil rights movement after World War II. The vast majority of Negroes in both North and South are members of the Baptist Church; the second largest number are of the Methodist faith. In addition to other organized religious bodies to which varying numbers of Negroes belong, there are the independent Negro churches, many of them "storefront" or "house" churches, in which rural Negroes in urban areas, especially in the North, find a form of worship similar to that which they knew in the rural South. (*See* NEGROES IN THE U.S., III.)

Political Status. The Negro's political position, in which the Negro church has always taken an active interest, improved after 1940. Increased registration of Negro voters, increased Negro candidacy for elective offices, and more frequent appointment of Negroes to high level administrative positions attest to this fact. The underlying factors are mass migration of Negroes to urban centers outside the South, new Federal statutes designed to protect voter rights, court decisions against discriminatory electoral practices, and presidential support for equal suffrage. Outside the South, there was an increase from 2 to 3 million Negro voters between 1950 and 1960.

In the South, where political restrictions against Negroes are rooted in tradition, there has been steadily mounting reaction against political exclusion. From 1952 to 1962 the number of registered Negro voters increased from approximately 1 million to 1.7 million, largely as a result of an intensified voter registration drive sponsored cooperatively by Negro civil rights organizations. Action by the Kennedy administration to eliminate barriers at the polls supported and encouraged it. The Civil Rights Acts of 1957, 1960, and 1964 gave legislative support to the effort. Southern extremists have attempted to block voter registration through discriminatory and dilatory registration procedures, economic reprisals, and other forms of intimidation. Evidence of substantial discriminatory disfranchisement of Negroes in 160 counties in 8 southern states was cited in the 1961 report of the U.S. Civil Rights Commission.

The increase in the number of Negroes in elective and appointive positions is another indication of the improved political status of the Negro minority. Even in some southern cities, Negroes have been elected to local boards and municipal councils. The trend is more pronounced in local and state governments outside the South, and in the Federal government. At the national level, the Kennedy administration gave recognition to the Negro minority by appointing qualified Negroes to high level administrative and judicial posts, as well as to top diplomatic posts as chiefs of missions in European countries. Five Negroes were also elected to Congress in 1962.

The Civil Rights Movement of the 1960s. The effort to improve the political position of the Negro minority in the U.S. is only one aspect of the drive by Negro Americans for full civil rights. An intensification of this drive during the early 1960s has been called the "Negro Revolution." Negroes seek first-class citizenship, with all its attendant rights, privileges, and responsibilities, as a basic goal. Most of all, they demand that neither color nor racial origin shall be determinants of the scope of their participation in American life. In this, they have had the advantage of new court decisions that have struck blow after blow against the legal supports of the color-caste system. The U.S. Supreme Court has nullified restrictive covenants, which sought to legalize residential segregation and similarly designed restrictions upon interstate travel, educational facilities, and public facilities owned by state and local governments. A growing conviction that statutory provisions and judicial decisions of themselves would not guarantee full civil rights led to a shift in strategy from complete reliance on litigation to use of direct action as well. This gave the movement a new militancy and a sense of urgency clearly indicated in the slogan—"Freedom Now"—of the March for Jobs and Freedom held in Washington, D.C., on August 28, 1963.

The Negro protest movement, born of World War II idealism, has been spearheaded by the "New Negro."

Fig. 4. Portion of the crowd of 210,000 participating in the March for Jobs and Freedom, Washington, D.C., August 28, 1963, in an effort to promote civil rights legislation.

Neither an outside agitator, a Communist, nor a product exclusively of the North, he is a courageous, and often very intelligent person, who is willing to risk his life, personal freedom, and future for the cause of human freedom and dignity. Able and courageous national leaders, such as Roy Wilkins, Martin Luther King, and James Farmer, have forcefully presented, each in his own way, the cause of the Negro minority to the American people in terms of national, international, and moral responsibility. In addition, mass demonstrations by American students, largely Negroes; economic boycotts; and other forms of nonviolent resistance are relatively new forms of protest. They have added such terms as "sit-in," "kneel-in," and "freedom ride" to the American vocabulary.

To some Negroes, the slow progress toward complete freedom and equality appears both hopeless and undesirable. These are the Black Muslims. Although united with other protest groups in their rejection of Negro inferiority and of gradualism in Negro-white relations, the Black Muslims advocate Negro superiority and supremacy, as well as the withdrawal of American Negroes from American life rather than integration into it. They distrust the American dream of democracy and the intentions of the dominant race to implement it. Their appeal has been largely confined to the lowest socioeconomic class, whose frustration and insecurity have brought impatience with other Negro protest movements.

In short, after more than a century, the story of the Negro in the U.S. is still one of struggle for freedom. It is a continuing struggle to make the American promise of freedom and equality for all Americans a reality. The efforts to implement this dream for Negroes has assumed various forms—revolt, protest, litigation, and direct action in defiance of unjust laws. Experiences of the middle years of the 20th century indicate that full realization of this goal requires not only new policies and approaches, but also basic changes in the racial attitudes of most Americans.

Bibliography: J. H. FRANKLIN, *From Slavery to Freedom* (2d ed. New York 1956). E. F. FRAZIER, *The Negro in the United States* (rev. ed. New York 1957). E. GINZBERG, *The Negro Potential* (New York 1956). M. J. HERSKOVITS, *The Myth of the Negro Past* (New York 1941). G. MYRDAL, *An American Dilemma,* 2 v. (New York 1944). W. G. DANIEL, ed., "The Relative Progress of the American Negro since 1950," *Journal of Negro Education* 32 (1963) 311–516. **Illustration credits:** Fig. 2, Abby Aldrich Rockefeller Folk Art Collection, Williamsburg, Va.; Fig. 3, Philadelphia Museum of Art; Fig 4, Photo—Clifton Cabell.

[B. H. NELSON]

NEGROES IN THE U.S., II (EDUCATION OF)

The education of Negroes in the U.S. began in 1619 with the arrival of the first Negroes in America. The history of the education of Negroes before the Civil War falls into two periods: (1) from the introduction of slavery to the climax of the insurrectionary movement about 1835 and (2) when the industrial revolution had changed slavery from a patriarchal to an economic institution and intelligent Negroes subsequently made so many attempts to organize servile insurrections that the pendulum began to swing the other way. Four periods after the Civil War should be noted: (1) the Reconstruction, (2) the compromise, (3) pressing demands from World War I to 1954, and (4) the 1954 Supreme Court decision and its sequels.

ANTEBELLUM PERIOD

The early antebellum period started with the informal education of slaves and ended with repressive measures about 1835.

Religious and Philanthropic Activities. Religious groups in the 17th century established societies for the education of Negroes and for the opening of schools. The Jesuit missionary Paul Le Jeune in 1634 described his teaching of the alphabet to a Negro. Toward the end of the century the *Code Noir* (1685), the French law regulating slavery, placed the responsibility for the enlightenment of slaves on their masters.

At the turn of the 18th century the first philanthropic organization for the distinct purpose of the "enlightenment of the Negro," the Society for the Propagation of the Gospel in Foreign Parts, was organized within the Church of England. Key personalities during this period were: Rev. Samuel Thomas of Goose Creek Parish in South Carolina, the first school master under this program; Thomas Bray, promoter of Negro education through the establishment of the first educational foundation for the benefit of the Negro in North America (1701); and Elias Neau, benefactor of the first school in New York City in 1704.

Working in the same field were, concurrently, French and Spanish Catholic missionaries, whose liberal ideas embraced the granting of certain privileges to slaves, including their education. In fact the educational activities of these pioneers provided the impetus for the education of slaves by other religious groups. In New Orleans, La., the Ursuline nuns established a school for Negroes in 1734 after less formal efforts to teach Negroes and Indians. (*See* TRANCHEPAIN, MARIE ST. AUGUSTIN MOTHER.)

The Quakers, who earlier had protested slavery in the Colonies, provided the first permanent and well-developed schools devoted to the education of Negroes. Leaders in later efforts to provide education for Negroes included Anthony Benezet, a teacher in Philadelphia, Pa., who worked with the Quakers to provide more effective education for Negroes and who left his fortune to establish a school; Thaddeus Kosciuszko, the Polish general who gave property to be used for the purchasing, liberation, and education of slaves in trades and in moral responsibility; and John Woolman, a Quaker minister who commended those who taught Negroes and attacked policies and practices that forestalled their education.

The period following the Revolutionary War witnessed the establishment of schools for Negroes in several cities: the New York African Free School (1786); a private school in Boston (1798); a school in Henrico County, Va., bequeathed by Robert Pleasants (1800); the first school house for colored children in Washington, D.C., erected by three colored men, George Bell, Nicholas Franklin, and Moses Liverpool (1807); a school for colored girls in Georgetown, D.C. (1820); the first seminary for colored girls in the District of Columbia (1827); a day school in Baltimore, Md., opened by Rev. William Livingstone in connection with the St. James African Church; and St. Frances Academy for Girls in Baltimore, founded by the *Oblate Sisters of Providence, the first religious order for colored women in the U.S. and elsewhere.

Repression. Negro insurrections, which certain forces in the country attributed to the education of the Negroes who learned of the French Revolution and of the exploits of Toussaint L'Ouverture, halted the rapidly expanding educational facilities and opportunities. The disturbances in Camden, N.J. (1816), and Charleston, S.C. (1822), led by Denmark Vesey, resulted in restrictive legislation prohibiting the instruction of slaves and in some states of any Negroes. The Nat Turner insurrection in Southampton County, Va. (1831), led to further restrictions: closing all schools open to Negroes, limiting communication of slaves with one another and with free Negroes, and in some cases prohibiting religious worship. Despite these measures the education of Negroes in the South continued. Southern communities in some instances maintained schools "in defiance of public opinion or in violation of the law." However, an objective appraisal of the status of Negro education before the Reconstruction indicates that conditions combined to give little educational opportunity to the Negroes.

POSTBELLUM PERIOD

After the Civil War the concern of the Federal government for the education of former slaves resulted in governmental efforts that were paralleled by the programs of religious and philanthropic agencies, which together encouraged a pattern of segregated education.

Reconstruction. Although the Federal government established the Freedmen's Bureau in 1865, approval for its operation in education came only a year later. During the 5 years of its existence, 4,239 separate schools for Negroes were established. The bureau also served as a stimulating and coordinating agency for the work of private organizations and did noteworthy work in the opening of high schools and normal schools. The closing of the Freedmen's Bureau in 1871 forced agencies concerned with the education of Negroes to close some schools and to concentrate efforts in a limited number of educational centers.

The Reconstruction period saw the establishment of the George Peabody Fund, the first of new foundations without secular or sectional restrictions. Specifically, the fund provided (1) direct assistance to salaries of Negro elementary teachers, (2) aid toward the extension of school terms, (3) stimulus for the establishment of public school education for both races in the South, and (4) a concern for improved teacher training.

The colleges and universities for Negroes established during the decade following the Civil War were primarily under private auspices although three Southern states (Mississippi, Virginia, and South Carolina) made provisions during the 1870s for the higher education of Negro Youth under the first Morrill Act of 1862. Congress later granted funds for agricultural experiment stations, none of which was located in a Negro college in the South.

Patterns of segregation in higher education developed with the legislation requiring segregated public schools, although they did not include specific references to colleges. Among educational developments by religious groups was the opening of a seminary in Baltimore, Md., in 1876 by Cardinal James Gibbons, assisted by Bp. Herbert Vaughn (later cardinal), who was then touring the U.S. for the purpose of preparing candidates for the priesthood in St. Joseph's Society of the Sacred Heart for College Missionaries, now known as the *Josephite fathers.

Compromise. The brilliant spokesman for Negro rights, Frederick Douglass (1817–95), a former slave abolitionist, maintained that all discrimination should be removed and full equality of opportunity secured through education and legislation. However, the withdrawal of Federal troops and the gradual restoration of power to the former slaveholders whose concept of the new South accepted first and second class citizenship, brought increasing conflict between Negroes and whites. Separation of the races and restrictions on participation were keynotes of the new policy. A movement toward conciliation gained momentum in 1895 with Booker T. Washington's Atlanta (Ga.) speech, to which the term Atlanta Compromise has been applied. Washington maintained that racial harmony was possible through agreement regarding the roles of the races; and many Negroes and whites, Northerners and Southerners, supported his emphasis on industrial education for Negroes. W. E. B. DuBois, however, attacked the Compromise and insisted that the education of Negroes should not be different from that of whites and that college education with an intellectual emphasis should be afforded Negro youth.

The separation of races received legal sanction in the case of *Plessy v. Ferguson* (1896), which held that "separation of the races did not necessarily imply inferiority of either race to the other and was a reasonable exercise of the State's police force."

The opening years of the 20th century witnessed philanthropic agencies' increased interest in Negro education. The John F. Slater Fund (1882) had become the second agency in this field. During a 10-year span (1902–12) five foundations provided support for Negro education: (1) the General Education Board (1902), which offered aid to private colleges and universities for teachers' salaries, support of critic teachers and state agents for Negro schools; (2) the Anna T. Jeanes Fund (1907), which provided limited assistance to public schools for Negroes, especially for county supervisors of rural schools; (3) Carnegie Foundation (1911), which made available funds especially for the building of libraries; (4) the Phelps Stokes Fund, which lent support for surveys of Negro education and work with Negro schools and colleges; and (5) Julius Rosenwald Fund (1912), which made a major contribution to the construction of schools for Negroes with the stipulation that citizens share in costs.

Two important developments in the Catholic Church were (1) the establishment, in 1907, of the Catholic Board for Mission Work among the Colored People, a board composed of archbishops that delegated general responsibility for Catholic missionary activity among Negroes and has paid the salaries of many teachers engaged exclusively in colored missionary work and (2) the work of Mother Mary Katherine *Drexel, foundress of a new religious congregation, authorized and guided by Abp. Patrick J. Ryan of Philadelphia, Pa. This new Congregation, the *Blessed Sacrament Sisters for Indians and Colored People, under Mother Mary Katherine's leadership, established 48 elementary schools, 12 high schools and the first and only Catholic University for Negroes in the U.S., Xavier University of Louisiana in New Orleans.

Pressing Demands from World War I to 1954. Major educational developments in Negro education between World War I and World War II included the expansion of school enrollments, improved school facilities, and increased financial support; in addition there was a growing concern with the gap in the quality of education afforded under the separate but equal policy. The performance of Negro recruits in army examinations, the rejection rate of Negro draftees, the demands of returning servicemen for equality of opportunity, industrialization, urbanization and migration all called attention to the educational desert that existed for Negroes in most of the South. Southern states refused to admit Negroes to state colleges and embarked on a plan of out-of-state tuition grants to Negro residents for the pursuit of graduate and professional education in private colleges for Negroes.

Negroes sought expanded opportunities for study; the strategy involved the use of the courts. For 20 years in a series of court cases Negroes probed for a complete breakthrough toward the goal of equal opportunity in education. Initially, higher education provided the test situations. The *Pearson v. Murray* decision in Maryland in 1936 led to the opening of state graduate and professional schools to Negroes in all Southern states except Alabama, Florida, Georgia, Mississippi, and South Carolina.

The decision of the U.S. Supreme Court in *Missouri ex. rel. Gaines v. Canada* (1938) set a new interpretation of "separate but equal," in the requirement that the same educational opportunity be available to all residents of a state. In the 9 years following the Gaines decision most state systems established graduate and professional schools in the state colleges for Negroes as alternatives to the admission of Negroes to the state universities for whites. Then, in *Sipuel v. Board of Regents,* the U.S. Supreme Court (1948) ruled that states must provide equal opportunity for education within their borders. States recognized that establishment of separate graduate and professional schools of equal calibre in each state would be financially impossible. Efforts to secure congressional approval of a southern regional pact failed.

The decision of the Supreme Court in *Sweatt v. Painter* (1950) and *McLaurin v. Oklahoma State*

Regents (1950) made segregation within the school a test of equality. Twelve Southern states then accepted Negro students in graduate and professional schools, under court order; two states complied voluntarily. There followed test cases involving undergraduate education in which additional aspects of equality such as convenience and cost to the pupil were reviewed by the courts.

The Brown Decision and Its Sequels. The attack on segregation in education moved to the lower grades, and in the *Brown v. Board of Education,* or the School Segregation Cases (May 17, 1954), the separate but equal ruling was overruled in the Supreme Court's declaration that segregation by race *per se* is inconsistent with the equal protection of the law and unconstitutional. A year later the Supreme Court ordered school systems to implement the 1954 decision "with all deliberate speed." Since then continuous litigation has been the pattern.

Since 1954 Northern and Western states have been under attack for policies of racial segregation in public education. Charges have included discriminatory transfer practices, overcrowding of Negro schools, bias in special programs and site selections, and the lack of equipment in schools primarily serving Negro students. In *Taylor v. Board of Education of New Rochelle, New York* (1964), the court found that deliberate gerrymandering existed and thus the plaintiff had been denied equal protection under the law. Other cities involved in litigation include Highland Park, Mich.; Philadelphia, Pa.; Chicago, Ill.; and St. Louis, Mo. Efforts to resolve the issues without court action have been attempted.

Title IV (Desegregation of Public Education) and Title VI (NonDiscrimination in Federally Assisted Programs of the Civil Rights Act of 1964) directly affect the education of Negroes. Under the provisions of Title IV, the U.S. commissioner of education is directed to report on the status of desegregation in public education in the U.S., to provide technical assistance to school systems and institutes and in-service training for school personnel, and to facilitate the process of desegregation. In addition, the attorney general may initiate legal proceedings to assure the orderly achievement of desegregation in public education.

Under the provisions of Title VI of the Civil Rights Act of 1964, programs and activities that receive Federal assistance may not segregate. Federal assistance to education includes college facilities, construction, research grants and equipment, impacted areas school construction and assistance, school lunch and school milk programs, vocational educational activities and economic opportunity (antipoverty) programs. Recipients of Federal aid must give assurance that "no person shall be excluded from participation, denied any benefits or subjected to discrimination on the basis of race, color, or national origin." There has been a significant amount of compliance with these regulations.

The Economic Opportunity Act, in its provisions for a job corps, work-training programs, work-study programs, and an adult business education program, is expected to contribute to the improvement of the education of Negroes. The broad attack planned by these programs on educational problems from preschool through adulthood should counteract influences that are basic to learning difficulties.

The Elementary and Secondary Education Act of 1965 (public law 89–10), which became law on April 11, 1965, sought to improve the quality of education of lower income families in which category a large percentage of Negro families falls. Its provisions include: the establishment, expansion, and support of special programs; the extension of library resources and instructional materials; the establishment of centers to provide a diverse range of experiences for children and adults; special counseling and guidance; remedial reading courses; and continuing adult education.

The Higher Education Act of 1965 provided further support for the improvement of the education of Negroes through Community Service and Continuing Education (Title I), for attacking the problems relating to housing, poverty and government; for Library Assistance and Training and Research (Title II); for strengthening developing institutions with a National Teacher Fellow Program and cooperative agreements (Title III); for Student Assistance in Educational Opportunity Grants, student loans, work study and NDEA Program Improvement (Title IV); for a National Teachers Corps (Title V); and for Educational Media Equipment (Title VI) and Construction of Facilities (Title VII).

The future of the education of Negroes in the U.S. depends on the cooperative activities of all segments of the population in the movement to implement the expressed objective of the U.S., which is equal educational opportunity for all.

See also CIVIL RIGHTS, U.S. LAW OF; CHURCH AND STATE IN U.S. (LEGAL HISTORY), 4; NEGROES IN THE U.S., I; NEGROES, CATHOLIC SCHOLARSHIPS FOR.

Bibliography: W. DUNNE, "The Roman Catholic Church: The Rationale and Policies Underlying the Maintenance of Higher Institutions for Negroes," *Journal of Negro Education* 29 (Summer 1960) 307–314. U. LEAVELL, "Trends in Philanthropy in Negro Education," *ibid.* 2 (1953) 38–52. W. A. Low, "The Education of Negroes Viewed Historically" in *Negro Education in America: 16th Yearbook of the John Dewey Society,* ed. V. A. CLIFT (New York 1962). U.S. Commission on Civil Rights, *Civil Rights under Federal Programs* (C.C.R. Special Publication No. 1; Washington 1965); *Equal Protection of the Laws in Public Higher Education, 1960* (Washington 1961); *Civil Rights—U. S. A. Public Schools, Cities in the North and West, 1962* (Washington 1962); *Civil Rights—U.S.A. Public Schools, Southern States, 1962* (Washington 1962). C. G. WOODSON, *The Education of the Negro Prior to 1861* (New York 1915). M. N. WORK, *Negro Year Book, 1931–32* (Tuskegee, Ala. 1931).

[C. L. MILLER]

NEGROES IN THE U.S., III (RELIGION OF)

In many respects the religious life of Negroes seems to parallel that of the white community. Although concentrated largely in the churches of the *Baptists and *Methodists, the two largest Protestant denominations among the whites, Negroes are represented also in varying degrees among other Protestants, Roman Catholics, and a variety of sects and cults. It is frequently noted that their patterns of worship, organization, and doctrine resemble those of their white counterparts, except that their worship is often characterized by greater emotional expression. J. R. Washington, in *Black Religion,* contends that the differences are more significant than is usually acknowledged; however, the scope of this article does not permit full discussion of the different interpretations of the various aspects of the religious life of Negroes. The bibliography includes some of the important recent interpretative works.

History of Chief Religious Institutions. The religious life of Negroes in the U.S. contains few elements transferred from their African home. Although there has been much debate over the extent to which African customs and ideas were retained by the slaves, it appears that religious traits were quite thoroughly blotted out of their memories. Uprooted from tribal connections and deliberately "stripped of [their] social heritage" (Frazier, 1–), the African slaves retained little from their native culture. In the New World, the slaves were gradually indoctrinated with a general Christian worldview. By the time they were emancipated, the Negroes were eager to erect their own independent institutions, and they formed denominations patterned after those of American Protestants.

In the early years of slavery, many masters were reluctant to allow slaves to be baptized, because they feared that making them Christians might entail an obligation to free them. When they were reassured that they would not lose their property, they came to see that Christianizing slaves made them more tractable. In the 18th century, more direct effort was made to evangelize Negro slaves. Anglican missionaries were active in this endeavor in the first half of the century; and after the *Great Awakening, Baptists and Methodists extended their aggressive revivalism to the Negroes. Preaching by the latter groups tended to be highly emotional; instruction was minimal; and only the simplest elements of the gospel were presented.

The Negroes established relatively few of their own churches prior to the Civil War. Slaves ordinarily attended the church of their masters, but were segregated in the balconies. Apart from regular church services, white ministers or Negro exhorters addressed assemblies of slaves; but after the Nat Turner insurrection of 1831, great caution was exercised to keep such gatherings under supervision. Such independent churches as existed before 1860 were composed of free Negroes. In the Revolutionary era Baptist churches were begun at Savannah, Ga., and Petersburg, Va., and about 1809 at Philadelphia, Pa., New York City, and Boston, Mass. In general, however, most Negroes in the North (slave or free) belonged to predominantly white churches. A Protestant Episcopal church was formed in Philadelphia in 1791; and in the next year, a Methodist Epis-

The first Negro Baptist church in the U.S., in Savannah, Ga., 19th-century photograph, reproduced from "History of the Negro Church" by Carter G. Woodson.

copal Church. A few years later, the African Methodist Episcopal Zion Church followed. In 1870 the Negro Methodist churches of the South united to form the Colored Methodist Episcopal Church. Thereafter other groups splintered off from these parent bodies.

General organizations of the Baptists came later. Not until 1886 was the body formed that was the forerunner of the present National Baptist Convention, U.S.A., Inc. In 1916 a branch from this became the National Baptist Convention of America. These constitute the two largest Negro denominations today, and from them have come several smaller offshoots. The *Presbyterians first organized a general body of Negro churches in 1870, when the Colored Cumberland Presbyterian Church was established.

Distribution in Major Protestant Bodies. In 1960 the Bureau of Census reported about 19 million Negroes in the U.S., nearly three-fourths of whom were affiliated with some religious body. The great majority belonged to Baptist and Methodist groups, and more than two-thirds of them were concentrated in five bodies. The *Yearbook of American Churches* (1965) reported as follows: National Baptist Convention, U.S.A., Inc., 5,500,000 (1958); National Baptist Convention of America, 2,668,799 (1956); African Methodist Episcopal Church, 1,166,301 (1951); African Methodist Episcopal Zion Church, 770,000 (1959); and the Christian Methodist Episcopal Church, 444,493 (1961).

At least another million members were scattered in about 30 other all-Negro Protestant bodies of various denominations. About 600,000 more were affiliated with predominantly white denominations. The Methodist Church, for example, had nearly 400,000 Negroes in its membership, of whom about 360,000 comprised an all-Negro conference called the Central Jurisdiction. In 1964 the quadrennial meeting of the Methodist Church voted to work toward absorbing all of the Negro churches into the other regional conferences as soon as possible.

The United Presbyterian Church incorporates its Negro churches into the regular presbyteries and synods, and there are a fair number of churches having at least token integration. In 1964 Rev. Edler G. Hawkins was the first Negro minister to be elected moderator of the general assembly of the United Presbyterian Church in the U.S.A. The Presbyterian Church, U.S. (Southern), generally has separate synods and presbyteries for Negro churches. In the American Baptist Convention, there are many congregations with some Negro members, and since 1964 the denomination has made special efforts to persuade member churches to become integrated. Many Negro churches are also affiliated with their regular associations and conventions. There are virtually no Negroes in the Southern Baptist Convention. Episcopalians, Congregationalists, and Lutherans have integrated Negro churches into their regular organizations, but the number of such churches among them is fairly small.

Catholic Negroes. Some Negroes were Roman Catholics from the Colonial period of American history, but these were confined principally to Louisiana and Maryland. No special effort was made to win Negroes to Catholicism prior to the Civil War. The first Negro church among the Roman Catholics was St. Francis Xavier in Baltimore, Md., formed in 1863. The Second Plenary Council of Baltimore (1866) determined to es-

tablish Negro churches and schools. In 1871 the *Josephite Fathers began to concentrate on missions to Negroes, and they were subsequently aided by the *Blessed Sacrament Sisters for Indians and Colored. In 1874 a Negro priest, James A. *Healy, was appointed bishop of the Diocese of Maine. His brother, Patrick F. Healy, was president of Georgetown College (later University) from 1874 to 1882. The number of Negro converts to Roman Catholicism was small for many years, and there were few Negro priests; the Baptist and Methodist churches seemed more congenial to the Negro people. After World War II, however, there was a steady increase of Negro converts. By 1965 it was reported that there were more than 700,000 Negro communicants in Roman Catholic churches. *See* NEGROES IN THE U.S., IV (APOSTOLATE TO).

Negro Sects and Cults. Just as the freedom of the American environment encouraged denominational divisions and the initiating of new religious movements among white people, so the Negro people have developed numerous denominations, sects, and cults. Toward the end of the 19th century, the holiness movement began to make an appeal to Negroes (*see* HOLINESS CHURCHES). In 1897 the Church of God in Christ was established; by 1960 it numbered 413,000 adherents. Other movements of the pentecostal-holiness type include the Apostolic Overcoming Holy Church of God, Triumph of the Church and Kingdom of God in Christ, the Church of the Living God, the Apostolic and Pentecostal Church, and others (*see* PENTECOSTAL CHURCHES). These range in size from about 75,000 to fewer than 1,000 members. In addition to these groups, there are countless storefront churches and a number of cults with special emphases.

Among the more unusual cults is that of the Black Muslims. Started by W. D. Fard, a "prophet" of obscure origins, the movement has been led largely by Elijah Mohammed since 1934. This movement rejects Christianity as a white man's religion. Encouraging antagonism toward whites, it teaches that the Negro can work out his own salvation in this world by segregation rather than integration with white society. Inspired by a common hostility toward whites, the members manifest a high degree of dedication and discipline; and drug addicts, alcoholics, and prostitutes are reported to have been rehabilitated through its ministrations. In 1961 C. Eric Lincoln reported that this group was "America's fastest growing racist sect" (4), having then a membership that was reputed to be larger than 100,000.

Another bizarre group is that of the Peace Mission Movement, founded by the American Negro who called himself Father Divine. Combining features of faith-healing and holiness movements, it has attracted many adherents. Begun in Sayville, N.Y., it received an impetus after the arrest of Father Divine for disturbance of the peace. The sudden death of the judge who sentenced him to a fine and imprisonment was hailed as a divine punishment and lent dramatic support to the extravagant claims made by the leader. Father Divine claimed to be God and encouraged his followers to pray to him and worship him as divine. Those who belong to the movement are required to refrain from smoking, drinking, sexual immorality, and racial prejudice; and a remarkable degree of discipline is maintained by the group.

Negro Ministry. A major problem of the Negro churches has been that of securing a trained ministry. Only a small percentage of pastors have college training, and the great majority have only high school education or less. The dearth of capable young men interested in the ministry has continued through the 1960s, constituting one of the most critical factors in the situation of the Negro churches. For many years the Negro minister was the leader of his people; by the mid-20th century, however, Gunnar Myrdal noted that "as a class Negro ministers are losing influence, because they are not changing as fast as the Negro community" (875). Nevertheless, quite a few ministers have exhibited outstanding abilities. Martin Luther King, Jr., was the recipient of the Nobel Peace Prize in 1964. Howard Thurman, Dean of the Chapel at Boston University, is reputed to be one of America's finest preachers. James H. Robinson, pastor of a Presbyterian church in Harlem, New York City, gave the Beecher Lectures on Preaching at Yale Divinity School. Benjamin E. Mays, who served for years as president of Morehouse College in Atlanta, Ga., is outstanding as a minister and as an educator. Although these examples indicate the ability of Negroes to attain first rank, the fact remains that too few men of high caliber seem disposed to consider this calling. Moreover, the church, once the primary social center of Negroes and the main outlet for talents of leadership—now has many competitors; as Negroes rise in the educational scale, the functions of the church change and, according to some, its significance dwindles.

Bibliography: N. R. BURR, "The Negro Church," *A Critical Bibliography of Religion in America,* 2 v. (Religion in Amer. Life 4; Princeton 1961). S. C. DRAKE and H. R. CAYTON, *Black Metropolis: A Study of Negro Life in a Northern City* (New York 1945). A. FAUSET, *Black Gods of the Metropolis: Negro Religious Cults of the Urban North* (Philadelphia 1944). E. F. FRAZIER, *The Negro Church in America* (New York 1964). S. HARRIS and H. CRITTENDEN, *Father Divine: Holy Husband* (Garden City, New York 1953). R. F. JOHNSTON, *The Development of Negro Religion* (New York 1954); *The Religion of Negro Protestants* (New York 1956). *The Journal of Negro History* (Lancaster, Pa. and Washington 1916–   ). C. E. LINCOLN, *The Black Muslims in America* (Boston 1961). F. S. LOESCHER, *The Protestant Church and the Negro* (New York 1948). B. E. MAYS and J. W. NICHOLSON, *The Negro's Church* (New York 1933). G. MYRDAL, *An American Dilemma,* 2 v. (rev. ed. New York 1962) 1:858–878. J. R. WASHINGTON, JR., *Black Religion: The Negro and Christianity in the United States* (Boston 1964). W. D. WEATHERFORD, *American Churches and the Negro: An Historical Study from Early Slave Days to the Present* (Boston 1957). C. G. WOODSON, *The History of the Negro Church* (Washington 1921).

[N. H. MARING]

NEGROES IN THE U.S., IV (APOSTOLATE TO)

The Catholic Church's apostolate to the Negro has had a double function—spreading the faith among non-Catholic Negroes and fostering its practice by the Catholics among them.

Developments to 1866. In the colonial period, the Catholic Church and the Negro came into contact only in Maryland and in the Spanish territories of Florida and Louisiana. Although the Jesuits and Carmelites worked among the free Negroes and slaves, there was no special apostolate. In the postrevolutionary period, while the Church's few priests sought to preserve the faith of the native Catholics and the increasing number of immigrants, no major convert work was undertaken.

White and Negro Catholic exiles from Haiti's 1793 revolution settled in Baltimore, Md., Charleston, S.C., and New Orleans, La. Migrants from Maryland developed a Catholic center on the Kentucky frontier. Exiled from France in 1791, the *Sulpicians began work among Baltimore's Haitian Negroes. By 1796 Rev. Louis W. *Dubourg, later bishop of New Orleans, was using the basement chapel of St. Mary's Seminary as the center of worship for Catholic Negroes. In 1828 Rev. Jacques Nicholas Joubert de la Muraille (d. 1843) began a school for the instruction of this group; he was responsible for the foundation of the *Oblate Sisters of Providence, the first Negro sisterhood in the U.S. Four novices, one from Cuba and three from Santo Domingo, made their first promises on June 2, 1829. The community was approved by Gregory XVI in 1831, and the sisters took simple vows on July 2, 1832. Their chapel, built in 1836, became for all practical purposes the parish church and the first Negro Catholic church edifice in the U.S. Increasing in size, the congregation took over the basement of St. Ignatius church, the Chapel of Bl. Peter Claver, in 1857. Through the efforts of Michael *O'Connor, SJ, former bishop of Pittsburgh, Pa., funds were collected in 1863 to establish their own parish and a year later St. Francis Xavier's church, under the care of the Jesuits, was formally dedicated.

With the assistance of a white French woman, Marie Jeanne Aliquot, the second community of Negro sisters was established by two Negro women, one a Santo Domingan refugee, directed by Rev. Étienne Rousselon. The Congregation of Sisters of the *Holy Family was inaugurated in New Orleans on Nov. 21, 1842. In Kentucky Rev. Charles *Nerinckx attempted (1824) a biracial community with the Sisters of *Loretto, but the Negro part was discontinued by his successor, Rev. Guy Chabrat. Although Bp. John *England had shown concern for the Negroes in his diocese, he was forced to close his Negro school, opened in 1835, after a year because of the threats of anti-Abolitionist mobs. In Pittsburgh Bishop O'Connor blessed (1844) the short-lived Chapel of the Nativity of the Blessed Virgin for Negroes. In the District of Columbia, Rev. Charles I. *White began raising funds in 1863 and opened Bl. Martin de Porres Chapel on Feb. 11, 1866. Originally cared for by the Jesuits, it was turned over to Rev. Felix Barotti from the Brignole-Sale College in Genoa, Italy, under whose direction it grew into St. Augustine's Church, dedicated in 1876. Xavier *Weninger, SJ, with funds from King Louis of Bavaria, helped Rev. Adrian Hoecken, SJ, to open (1866) St. Ann's church and school for the Negroes of Cincinnati.

After 1866. With the Church hampered by an anti-Catholic milieu, a shortage of priests and religious, swelling numbers of immigrants to care for, lack of financial support, and the absence or weakness of Catholic influence in the areas of heavy Negro population, the Negro apostolate relied mostly on individual efforts. These, while sincere, were, with few exceptions, transient in effect.

Episcopal Efforts. The Second Plenary Council of *Baltimore (1866) attempted to unify these individual efforts and to establish a coordinated approach. The Apostolic Delegate, Abp. Martin J. *Spalding, and others hoped that one man, preferably with the status of bishop, would be appointed to direct the Negro

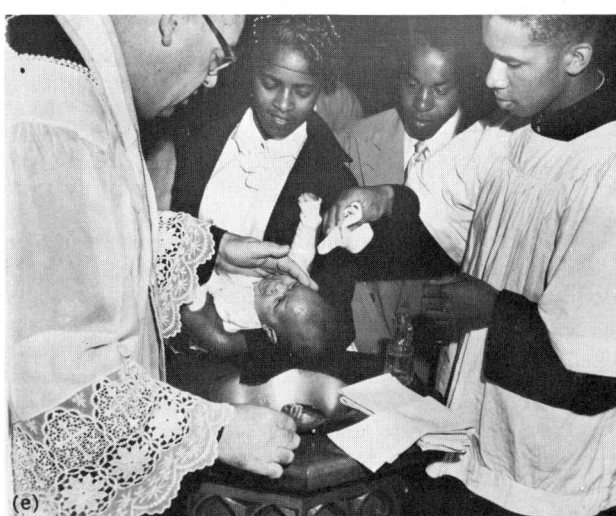

Apostolate to the U.S. Negroes: (a) Ordination of a priest.
(b) Group baptism. (c) Backyard conversation with a Joseph-
ite Father. (d) Class for converts. (e) Infant baptism. (f)
Instruction in a first-grade classroom.

work. But the opposition of Abp. Peter R. *Kenrick, who feared that this would lead to divided diocesan authority, defeated the plan. The council did urge zeal in bringing Negro converts either into already existing congregations or into special churches of their own, whichever would be most efficacious under local circumstances. An appeal was made to bishops and religious superiors in America and to the Catholic regions of Europe for help in supplying the needed manpower. The bishops were specially urged to devote immediate attention to these matters in their provincial councils. Patrick N. *Lynch, Bishop of Charleston, opened (1868) St. Peter's church for Negroes. In Louisville, Ky., Rev. John Lancaster *Spalding constructed (1870) St. Augustine's church as a Negro center. Work for the Negro had been going on in St. Louis in a gallery chapel of St. Xavier's church since 1858, but the Jesuits finally were able to open St. Elizabeth's Church for Negroes in 1873.

After the Tenth Provincial Council of Baltimore (1869), the work of the Negro missions in the U.S. was entrusted by Pius IX to St. Joseph's Foreign Missionary Society of Mill Hill. This group had been founded (1866) in England by Rev. (later Cardinal) Herbert *Vaughan. The first group of four priests arrived in Baltimore on Dec. 5, 1871. They were solemnly installed in St. Francis Xavier's Church on Dec. 10, 1871, by Archbishop Spalding. Up to 1892 the *Mill Hill Missionaries had charge of eight churches in Baltimore, Washington, Charleston, and Louisville and had established in Baltimore a major seminary, St. Joseph's (1888), and a minor seminary, Epiphany Apostolic College (1889). With Mill Hill at work on three continents, some felt that the American group should become independent and concentrate on the Negro missions. Under the leadership of Rev. John R. Slattery and the auspices of Cardinal James *Gibbons these men formed (1893) St. Joseph's Society of the Sacred Heart (*Josephite fathers) to work solely for the Negroes in America.

At the Third Plenary Council of Baltimore (1884) the *Commission for Catholic Missions among the Colored People and the Indians was instituted, and it inaugurated a yearly national collection. These funds have made possible a more rapid expansion of the apostolate. Further help came after the bishops' meeting of 1906, when the *Catholic Board for Mission Work among the Colored People was established under Rev. John E. Burke as director. His successor, Rev. Edward C. Kramer, was particularly helpful in supporting the sisterhoods in the work.

Religious Orders. The Oblates (numbering 320 sisters in 1965) and the Holy Family Sisters (322 members) were joined by other communities. The *Franciscan Sisters of Mill Hill began work among Negroes there in 1881. The *Mission Helpers of the Sacred Heart were formed in Baltimore (1890) to help on the Negro Missions. The *Franciscan Sisters of Glen Riddle, Pa., began work in Baltimore in 1890. Mrs. Margaret Murphy of San Antonio, Tex., established St. Peter Claver's school (1888), and formally brought into existence the Sister Servants of the *Holy Ghost and Mary Immaculate (1893). The greatest single addition came through Katherine *Drexel of Philadelphia. She devoted her family fortune and her life to the missions by founding the *Blessed Sacrament Sisters for Indians

and Colored People (1891). They conduct *Xavier University of Louisiana in New Orleans, which began as a Catholic institution of higher learning for the Negroes on Sept. 27, 1915, and in 1965 had more than 800 students in its college and graduate departments. The third community of Negro nuns was founded in Savannah, Ga., by Mother Mary Theodore Williams (1917), under the direction of Rev. Ignatius Lissner, SMA; in 1965 the Congregation of Handmaids of Mary included 68 professed members. Through the years other communities of religious women have not only undertaken Negro mission work, but have also made positive efforts to make their communities biracial.

Notable early increases in the communities of men working in the field came with the addition of the *Holy Ghost fathers (1881), the Society of *African Missions (1907), the Society of the *Divine Word (1906), and other secular and religious priests who entered the field. By 1928 there were 196 priests in charge of 188 churches for 197,523 Negro Catholics, of whom 19 per cent were in the North and West; in 1935 the numbers had increased to 243 priests, 210 churches, and 228,894 Negro Catholics, 31 per cent in the North and West.

Negro Priests. The development of a Negro priesthood in America was slow in starting. The first three priests were the *Healy brothers, sons of an Irish father and a mulatto mother: James Augustine, ordained (1854) in Paris for the Diocese of Boston, Mass., and consecrated bishop of Portland, Maine, June 2, 1875; Alexander Sherwood, ordained in Rome for Boston (1858); Patrick Francis, ordained a Jesuit in Belgium (1864). Augustus Tolton, the son of slave parents, was ordained in the Urban College of Propaganda in Rome (1886) and worked in Quincy and Chicago, Ill. The first Negro ordained in the U.S. was Charles Randolph Uncles, a Mill Hill father who was ordained in Baltimore (1891) and was one of the five priests forming the Josephite fathers. Archbishop John *Ireland in St. Paul ordained Stephen L. Theobald (1910) as the first American-trained diocesan priest. The major step forward was taken by the Society of the Divine Word, which inaugurated (1920) the present St. Augustine's Seminary of Bay St. Louis, Miss., for the training of Negro candidates for their community. Their first candidate, Maurice Rousseve, SVD, was ordained May 23, 1934. By 1965 there were 61 other Divine Word Negro priests, two of whom became bishops. The total number of living priests of the Negro race has grown from 6 in 1935, 38 in 1944, 62 in 1957, 120 in 1961, to 159 in 1965, 49 of these being diocesan priests.

Negro Leadership and Interracial Developments. In the wider area of development of Catholic Negro leadership and interracial relationships, the first major national organization was the Congress of Colored Catholics. The first congress (1889) in Washington, D.C., attended by outstanding Negro Catholics and church leaders from all over America, discussed the needs of the Negro and sought to devise ways of bettering religious and social conditions. Congresses were held yearly until 1894, in Cincinnati, Philadelphia, Chicago, and Baltimore. In Mobile, Ala., four Josephite priests and three Negro laymen organized (1909) the *Knights of Peter Claver to provide "Catholic fraternalism, Christian charity, and insurance protection for Negro Catholics." By its 50th anniversary this group had more than 12,000 members in 226 councils and courts in the U.S. It has not only supplied financial support to the missions, but also helped train leaders for interracial work. In July 1918 at Techny, Ill., the *Catholic Student Mission Crusade was organized to interest Catholic students in the missions through lectures and writings, by prayer and self-denial, and by mission giving. From its earliest days it showed a strong interest in the Negro missions. It did much to bring an awareness of the religious and social needs of the American Negro to Catholics on the high school, college, and seminary levels, particularly under the influence (1930–42) of John T. Gillard, SSJ.

To secure appointments of trained Catholic Negroes in the camps during World War I, a protest group was organized in Washington. This continued to function after the war and evolved into the Federated Colored Catholics of the U.S., which held its first convention in 1925. A split between eastern and western factions in 1932 led to the development of the National Catholic Interracial Federation for the West, while the eastern group maintained the original name. Both groups gradually moved into a new organization that was primarily the development of John *LaFarge, SJ. After his transfer from Negro mission work in Maryland to an editorial post on *America* in New York City, he began (1927) the Catholic Laymen's Union with a group of Negro Catholic business and professional men in Harlem, New York City. They sought adequate preparation for leadership in the community through study and personal sanctification. The group was sufficiently developed to step into the breach caused by the split in the Federated Colored Catholics and to cooperate in forming the *Catholic Interracial Council in New York on May 20, 1934. At about the same time a group of priests, LaFarge included, met in Newark, N.J. (Nov. 12, 1933), to form the Clergy Conference on Negro Welfare. They wanted to answer the challenge of the migrating Negroes by making priests and nuns more aware of the new opportunities to gain Negroes for Christ. This parent Northeast Clergy Conference extended its influence by the development of the Richmond Clergy Conference, the Mobile Clergy Conference, and the Mid-West Clergy Conference, all of which, by personal contact and newsletter, helped to develop interest in fulfilling the Church's obligations to the Negro. They contributed to the organization (1940) of the Catholic Conference of the South, which sought means in accord with Christian principles to eliminate segregation and to meet the problems of increased urbanization and industrialization, mechanized agriculture, and a broader democracy. More important, they all created an atmosphere in which the work of the Catholic Interracial Council could spread throughout the nation. By 1965 there were more than 110 councils and allied groups in operation, through which "conscientious, educated, and intelligent Catholics of both races, working together methodically under competent spiritual direction" tried to combat race prejudice and to attain social justice for the whole social group regardless of race. The need for coordination of these proliferating activities and a centralized fact-gathering and evaluating group for the most effective channeling of Catholic interracial activities resulted in the formation

at Chicago of the *National Catholic Conference for Interracial Justice (1960), with a full-time Southern Field Service (1961). Much has been accomplished, indirectly through the bishops, in desegregating and integrating parishes, schools, and hospitals and, directly, by organizing national and local workshops, developing the National Conference on Religion and Race, and setting up the program of "Project Equality," by which various dioceses have marshaled the force of their buying power to require firms with which they do business to demonstrate an employment program of equal opportunity.

Other Catholic organizations, such as *Friendship House, which was founded (1938) in Harlem by Baroness Catherine DeHueck and spread out to Chicago, Washington, Portland, Ore., and Shreveport, La., seek to be interracial community centers staffed by volunteers to carry on works of spiritual and temporal mercy and to preach racial justice and charity by living it. A similar approach is used by Fides House, established (1940) in Washington, and the *Catholic Worker Houses of Hospitality, founded by Dorothy Day, which also supply food and shelter for the needy of all races.

Accomplishments. Catholic leaders have tried to set the atmosphere for complete and Christian integration for many years. Francis Janssens, when bishop of Natchez, Miss., in 1887, drew a clear and objective picture of the Negro problem and the Catholic Church and strongly recommended the development of a Negro Catholic clergy. Archbishop John Ireland of St. Paul, Minn., spoke out eloquently and frequently for the rights of the Negro in America and in the Church. The statements of the bishops of the U.S. in 1943 and 1958 stressed the moral and religious character of the race question and the need for political, economic, educational, and social equality. Cardinal Lawrence Shehan of Baltimore in his pastoral letter (March 1, 1963) on racial justice pointed out that Catholics had been all too slow in correcting their shortcomings in the field of racial justice, and for this reason "we have a special obligation to place ourselves in the forefront of movements to remove the injustices and discriminations which still remain."

More and more Catholics have come to the fore in working for the removal of injustices and discrimination: in the March on Washington (1963), in Selma and Montgomery (1965), and in Chicago (1965). In these instances the presence of priests, nuns, and brothers in the ranks of the demonstrators served both as witness to the commitment of the Church in the struggle for Negro rights and as a balance to hold in check the extremists of either side. Less spectacularly but effectively, Catholics have worked in the field of civil rights, of fair employment, of equal housing, and educational opportunity.

Sectional Differences. Differing local circumstances largely determine what can be done. In the deep South, *New Orleans had the leadership of Abp. Joseph F. *Rummel, who endeavored to bring about a broadly based integration as steadily as the environment would allow. In 1944 at Xavier University he stressed that education and economics had to be the basis for sound progressive achievement for the Negro. By 1949 he had integrated the archdiocesan Holy Name societies, the sodalities, and the Councils of Catholic Men and Women. In that year he cancelled the Holy Name jubilee observance when the City Park Commission would not allow an integrated participation. In his pastoral letter of March 1953, he stated that there was no segregation in the kingdom of heaven, nor would there be any in the churches of New Orleans. In his 1956 pastoral he declared segregation morally wrong and sinful, violating justice and charity. Finally he ordered the desegregation of Catholic schools in 1962, enforcing his decrees with the penalty of excommunication.

In the Southwest Abp. Robert E. Lucey of *San Antonio, with both Mexican and Negro minorities under his jurisdiction, has been a vocal and practical leader. He declared in 1942 that "the liberty of our brother is not the freedom to suffer and endure in poverty and squalor, but rather the liberty of a child of God to live in peace and security. Democracy has no meaning where special privilege and injustice prevail." In 1945 he attacked the Texas poll tax and sought adequate state child labor laws. In 1951 he rebuked Catholics who were followers and tolerated the race prejudice of people they were supposed to lead. Quietly but firmly he has integrated all phases of his archdiocese in conformity with his spoken statements.

The Middle West had the stimulus of Cardinal Joseph Ritter, who in both *Indianapolis, Ind., and *St. Louis, Mo. (after 1946), integrated his churches and schools, meeting opposition with the threat of excommunication. *Chicago had the pioneering efforts of its auxiliary Bp. Bernard J. Sheil and Cardinal Albert *Meyer, who not only spoke strongly but developed administrative procedures and active Negro parishes in areas of Negro concentration and integrated parishes, schools, hospitals, and social services.

Since 1946 *Washington, D.C., a border area, under Abp. Patrick A. O'Boyle has been outstanding in the continued development of Negro Catholic participation in all phases of parochial and diocesan life without major incidents or setbacks. In his 1963 pastoral the archbishop stressed that no Catholic with a good conscience could deny the Negro the legitimate opportunity to secure proper housing, equal opportunity for a job, proper and adequate welfare assistance, and full participation in public and private educational facilities. He championed the Negro cause in Vatican Council II by asking for "forthright and unequivocal condemnation of racism in all forms."

Program and Goals. The Negro apostolate has been conceived in terms of its goals and the dominant type is that which the Third Plenary Council of Baltimore emphatically recommended. This approach is based on a church located in a Negro community or subcommunity for service to it, with its own pastor and, if possible, a parochial school and other services. Several other types of approach have been used, particularly the racially mixed parish. A Negro neighborhood that has a mission center or parish has a potential non-Catholic audience and usually some Catholic Negroes who need, prefer, or will avail themselves of its services. The fulfilment of the apostolate requires further instruction and training of converts, as well as the pastoral care of Catholics older in the faith who live within the boundaries of the mission or parish. Gaining the attention of prospective converts and instructing them in the faith fills much of the time of most priests attached to the missions and parishes that were by

design or are now *de facto* serving larger or smaller Negro congregations. These establishments are the main and the most fertile sources of converts and effective agents of vital follow-up work. Catholic schools in Negro neighborhoods have been valuable adjuncts to missionary and pastoral programs and have often been bridges to the surrounding non-Catholic groups, as well as auxiliaries to the pulpit and the altar. A steadily increasing number of parishes in racially changing parts of large cities, both in and outside the South, offer pastoral services to incoming Catholic Negroes and facilities of their schools to the children of well disposed non-Catholics, and endeavor by other means to reach the latter. More and more of these are automatically becoming Negro parishes, with an accented missionary program. In addition, informational, catechetical, and social centers, in cities with scattered Catholic Negro residents, are offering them and non-Catholics special services of a religious nature that lead to their assimilation into the local parishes.

The achievements of the apostolate, as measured by the number of Catholic Negroes, are impressive; between 1890 and 1965 Catholic Negroes increased numerically at least sevenfold; the total Negro population, less than threefold. In 1965 converts and their descendants constituted at least 400,000 of the approximately 750,000 Negroes who were Catholics. This calculation allowed for no defections among the offspring of the 125,000 Negroes reported as Catholics in 1890 or for discounting this improbably high figure. In 1965 one out of 25 Negroes was a Catholic; in 1890, at best one out of 80. In that year 27 priests were largely engaged in ministering to Negroes, 24 small churches had been provided for them, and about 85 small schools. The framework was only slowly enlarged during the next 20 years; the annual yield of converts first exceeded 1,000 in 1910. Thereafter, as more and more priests were assigned to the apostolate, many new churches and schools were established, all at an accelerating rate. In 1964 more than 800 priests were in charge of 525 Negro congregations, each with its church, and 350 with schools; that year 13,495 Negro converts entered the Church. Conversions had steadily increased over the years and in the same ratio as the number of priests engaged in this ministry increased.

In 1965 half of the Catholic Negroes (375,000) were in the Southern and border states. But the majority of Catholic Negroes living in other states were the products of the Southern missions. Since 1917 the heavy stream of migrants to Northern and Western cities has heightened the challenge and multiplied the opportunities of the apostolate there. Its main stress, however, is still in the South, where 488 of the 520 Negro missions and parishes, 255 of the 520 parochial and high schools, and 460 of the 780 priests are engaged in this ministry.

See also NEGROES IN THE U.S., III.

Bibliography: *Reports of the Secretary of the Commission for Catholic Missions among the Colored People and the Indians, Baltimore, 1889–1925* (Washington 1926–), annuals. J. T. GILLARD, *The Catholic Church and the American Negro* (Baltimore 1930); *Colored Catholics in the U.S.* (Baltimore 1941). A. S. FOLEY, *God's Men of Color* (New York 1955). E. P. MCMANUS, *Studies in Race Relations* (Baltimore 1961). J. T. LEONARD, *Theology and Race Relations* (Milwaukee 1963). **Illustration credit:** Courtesy of *Josephite Harvest.*

[P. E. HOGAN; J. B. TENNELLY]

NEHEMIA

Jewish governor of Judea under the Persians. He succeeded in having the fallen walls of Jerusalem rebuilt. Before he was governor, Nehemia (Heb. *nᵉḥemyâ*) was an official at the court of the Persian King *Artaxerxes I (465–424 B.C.). The conditions under which the Palestinian Jews then lived were far from ideal. The defenses of the capital Jerusalem lay in ruins, and the Jews themselves were subject to harassment and oppression by their predatory neighbors. Hearing of these conditions and moved by pity for his people, Nehemia obtained credentials from the King and set out in the 20th year of Artaxerxes for Jerusalem, where he remained for 12 years (445–433 B.C.) as governor (*peḥâ* in Neh 5.14, 15, 18; 12.26; *tiršātā'* in Neh 8.9; 10.2): Neh 2.1–8; 5.14.

His first major accomplishment was to rebuild the wall of Jerusalem, despite the threats and various stratagems of the neighboring governors, *Sanaballat (Sanballat) of Samaria, *Tobia the Ammonite, and Gossem (Geshem) the Arab, who accused him of rebellion against the king (Neh 2.10, 19; ch. 4; ch. 6). In Neh 7.15 it is said the wall was completed in 52 days, but the period of 2 years and 4 months that Josephus (*Ant.* 11.5.8) allows for this is a much more plausible length of time.

During this time, famine and usurious exactions of the upper classes brought the poorer people crying to Nehemia for relief (Neh 5.1–5). Prompt action by the governor—his request to the assembled leaders, with pointed reference to his own unselfish example—led to the restoration of lands and houses to the indigent (Neh 5.6–13; see also 5.14–19). Next, Nehemia resettled a tenth of Judea's population, moving them into the newly fortified Jerusalem (Neh 7.4–5; 11.1–2). The dedication of the city's wall is described (in the Chronicler's style) in Neh 12.27–43.

In 433 B.C., Nehemia returned to Artaxerxes (Neh 13.6). Sometime after that, but before the King's death in 424, Nehemia came again to Jerusalem as governor. This time he was noted principally for correcting abuses. He drove Tobia from a room that had formerly served as a Temple storeroom but had been given to Tobia for his personal use (Neh 13.4–9); reinstated the practice of tithing for the support of the Levites (Neh 13.10–14); enforced observance of the Sabbath (Neh 13.15–22); and prohibited marriages with foreigners, to prevent such marriages from leading the Jews into idolatrous practices (Neh 13.23–27). He also expelled the son-in-law of Sanaballat from the Jerusalemite priesthood (Neh 13.28–29).

Comparatively little else is known of Nehemia. According to Neh 7.2 he placed his brother Hanani in charge of Jerusalem. In Sir 49.13 he is praised for restoring Jerusalem's defenses. The "memories of Nehemia" cited in 2 Mc 1.36 associate him with a discovery of fire-producing νεφθαρ (naphtha), and in 2 Mc 2.13 it is said that he founded a library and collected various books: (1) about kings (the OT books of Josue through Kings?), (2) Prophets, (3) David's writings (Psalms), and (4) royal letters (of the Persian kings) concerning votive offerings. One Talmudic reference identifies him (incorrectly) with Zorobabel (*Sanhedrin* 38a), and another credits him (wrongly) with the completion of the book of Chronicles (*Baba Bathra* 15a). For the Book of Nehemia, *see* CHRONICLER, BIBLICAL.

Bibliography: EncDictBibl 1626–27. H. SCHNEIDER, LexThK² 7:868–869. K. GALLING, RGG³ 4:1395–96. H. H. ROWLEY, "Nehemiah's Mission and Its Background," BullJRylLibr 37 (1955) 528–561. A. FERNÁNDEZ, *Un hombre de carácter: Nehemías* (Jerusalem 1940).

[N. J. MC ELENEY]

NEHEMIA, BOOK OF, Biblical book whose principal narratives relate: (1) the return of Nehemia, an official (cupbearer) at the court of the Persian King Artaxerxes I (464–423 B.C.) to the province of Juda; (2) the work of Nehemia and the Jewish People in rebuilding the walls of Jerusalem, despite economic difficulties and the opposition of the Samaritan Governor *Sanaballat and others; (3) the reading of the Law by the priest-scribe Ezra and the renewal of the covenant with God by the Jewish community; (4) the rehabitation of Jerusalem; (5) the return of Nehemia to Jerusalem after an interval at the Persian court and his correction of abuses discovered upon his return. For a more complete treatment of this book, *see* CHRONICLER, BIBLICAL.

[N. J. MC ELENEY]

NEIGHBOR, means the person to be loved as oneself in fulfillment of all the demands of the second part of the Ten *Commandments (Lv 19.11–18; Ex 20.12–17; Dt 5.16–21). The Hebrew word commonly used was *rēa'*, signifying friend, companion, or fellow. In the OT neighbor usually connoted someone associated with a person by tribal or national bonds, i.e., one's compatriot (thus, the parallels in Lv 19.11–18: *'amīt,* compatriot; *'am,* kinsman; and *bᵉnê 'ammekā,* sons of your people). Job's final protestation of innocence (Job ch. 31) indicates, however, that in the highest type of Israelite morality one's neighbors included also one's servants and farm workers (v. 13–15, 38–40a), the poor and helpless (v. 16–23), traveling strangers (v. 32), and even one's enemies, in whose misfortune Job never took pleasure (v. 29–30).

This noble apologia foreshadowed the morality demanded by Jesus Christ in Mt 5.43–48, where Our Lord broadened the concept of neighbor to include enemies and persecutors, who were the beneficiaries of God's creative care along with the rest of mankind. Henceforth, a neighbor, for a Christian, was not one who belonged to the same clan or religious community, but simply one's fellow man, even if he were a sinner (Lk 6.27–35). For a Christian to love only his friend (the basic meaning of the OT *rēa'*) would make him no different than a sinner, who does as much. The Christian, since he professes to be God's son, i.e., to be like his Father, who is "kind towards the ungrateful and evil" (Lk 6.35b), must pattern his attitude toward men upon God's love for all mankind. The parable of the Good Samaritan (Lk 10.25–37) graphically exemplifies this principle. By a paradoxical twist Christ identifies the Samaritan, a member of a race hated and shunned by the Jews, as the prime example of merciful concern for one's afflicted enemy, in contrast to the cruel negligence of the priest and Levite for one of their own people. The Samaritan is the true Christian.

Romans 12.14–21 and 13.8–10, interpreted in conjunction with 1 Cor 13.4–7 and Gal 3.28; 5.14, show that St. Paul's concept of a Christian's neighbor extended to every member of the human family, which was being made "one in Christ Jesus" (Gal 3.28). Even a limited vengeance, permitted, yet kept from being excessive by the law of exact retaliation (Ex 21.25), was no longer permissible for a Christian; it clashed with God's act of *redemption of all men through Christ's death. The Lord had pardoned sinners; the pardoned must bear with those who offend them (Col 3.12–15; 1 Jn 4.7–11). In the fully developed Christian morality, therefore, one must "overcome evil with good" (Rom 12.21) and, following God's lead, love as one's neighbor even an enemy.

See also ENMITY.

Bibliography: EncDictBibl 1377–85. H. F. BECK, InterDictBibl 3:534–535.

[J. E. FALLON]

NEILL, CHARLES PATRICK, economist, arbitrator, public official; b. Rock Island, Ill., Dec. 12, 1865; d. Washington, D.C., Oct. 3, 1942. His parents, James and Julia (Walsh) Neill, settled in Austin, Texas, in 1871. After attending the University of Notre Dame, Ind., and the University of Texas, Austin, Neill graduated from Georgetown University, Washington, D.C., in 1891. He taught at Notre Dame until 1894, when he began to study for his Ph.D. at Johns Hopkins University, Baltimore, Md. After receiving his degree in 1897, he joined the faculty of The Catholic University of America, Washington, D.C., where he served as professor of economics until 1905. He married Esther Waggaman of Washington in 1901.

Under Pres. Theodore Roosevelt, Neill served as recorder for the commissions that handled labor difficulties in the anthracite industry. He was U.S. commissioner of labor (1905–13) under Presidents Roosevelt and William Howard Taft, and Pres. Woodrow Wilson named him commissioner of labor statistics (1913) in the new department of labor. In these posts Neill provided Federal mediation services in railroad labor disputes, and he drafted the basic Newlands Act (1913) in this field. His investigation of the meat-packing industry resulted in a Federal inspection law in 1906, and he prepared an exhaustive report on child labor as the basis for congressional legislation.

Neill's reputation as an arbitrator led him to specialize in this area after he left the department of labor in 1913. He was employed (1915–39) by the Southeastern Railways to handle labor problems, arbitrated some 3,000 issues in 1917–18, and served on the U.S. railroad board of adjustments from 1919 to 1921. Neill was also concerned with industrial safety and promoted state workmen's compensation laws. His work and his charitable activities as a member of the Board of Charities of the District of Columbia and a trustee of the Girls' Reform School brought him an LL.D. (1908) and the Laetare medal (1922) from the University of Notre Dame. He was an active club member and a leader in several professional societies, including the American Statistical Association, of which he was elected president in 1916.

[J. L. MORRISON]

NELLIGAN, ÉMILE, French-Canadian poet; b. Montreal, Dec. 24, 1879; d. there, Nov. 18, 1941. His father was Irish, his mother French-Canadian. He made little progress in school, and in March 1897 withdrew from the Collège Sainte-Marie in Montreal. Because of his hypersensitive, artistic nature, he was already living in a world of dream where poetry was the only reality, and while still a student (1896) he published in a Montreal magazine, *Le Samedi,* nine poems that gave evidence of unusual talent. After 1897 his association with the outside world was largely restricted to attendance at meetings of the École Littéraire de Montréal, of which he had become a member in February 1897. Nelligan's poetic career was brief. Consumed by melancholy and a horror of reality, he retreated more and more into his world of dream. At the age of 19, he had to be committed to an institution for the mentally ill. He was then taken to the Retraite Saint-Benoît, and, in October 1925, to the Saint-Jean-de-Dieu hospital, where he spent the rest of his life. His collected poems first appeared in 1904. The originality of Nelligan's verse within the framework of Canadian literature can not easily be overestimated. "Le Vaisseau d'or" and "La Romance du vin," two of his most famous poems, make this manifest. While the older Canadian poets of the second half of the 19th century had been influenced by the French Romantics, Nelligan found his models in *Baudelaire, *Verlaine, Maurice Rollinat, and Georges Rodenbach. His poems brood over the spiritual drama of a man striving to escape his tragic destiny by a flight into an ideal world where love, music, religious emotion, a return to the innocence of childhood, and even to a greater degree, the terrifying encounter with death might bring him peace and contentment. Nelligan's achievement as a poet is impressive. The diversity of his rhythms, the beauty of his imagery, the musical quality of his verse, and the success with which, in spite of the limited range of his intellectual and emotional experience, he has given expression to the sufferings and aspirations of his tormented soul make him the first truly modern poet in the history of French-Canadian literature.

Bibliography: É. NELLIGAN, *Poésies complètes, 1896–1899,* ed. L. LACOURCIÈRE (Montreal 1952); *Émile Nelligan et son oeuvre,* pref. by L. DANTIN (3d ed. Montreal 1932). P. WYCZYNSKI, *Émile Nelligan: Sources et originalité de son oeuvre* (Ottawa 1960).

[J. M. CARRIÈRE]

NĚMCOVÁ, BOŽENA, Czech novelist; b. Ratibořice, northeastern Bohemia, Feb. 4, 1820; d. Prague, Jan. 21, 1862. Early in her life, and with no formal education, Němcová left her small native town, located on the hereditary estates of the Dukes of Zaháň, and traveled with her husband through the Slovak-speaking northern part of Hungary, through Bohemia and Bavaria to Prague. Although handicapped by this rootlessness and by poverty, she participated in the literary and political life of the times—an epoch that witnessed the rise of nationalism after the Napoleonic wars and culminated in the revolutionary year of 1848. On friendly terms with *Erben and the other enthusiastic students and imitators of the folklore that then dominated Czech literature, she joined Erben for a time in collecting and editing Czech and Slovak fairy tales.

Driven by ever-increasing personal and family difficulties, Němcová turned to more realistic expression in such novels as *Divá Bára* (Crazy Barbara) and *V zámku a podzámčí* (In the Castle and Near It). They proved perhaps not as realistic as she thought they were; they were influenced to a great extent by contemporary Czech authors whose insight into the heart was combined with open moralizing. After the frustration and disillusionment of 1848, Nemcová became increasingly attracted to the memories of her own happy girlhood. The resultant work, *Babička* (1855, Grandmother), is a classic of Czech literature. It was only partially autobiographical and certainly not realistic; it is rather a dream, full of vivid memories and pensive poetry. It is firmly anchored in the cycle of the liturgical year. There is hardly a mystery or tenet of the Christian faith that was not a pillar of the world in which the heroine and the persons around her lived and moved. The Duchess of Zaháň, introduced into the work perhaps as a symbol of "enlightened" thought, sees herself defeated by the ideals and beauty of Němcová's ancient yet ever new world.

Bibliography: F. CHUDOBA, *A Short Survey of Czech Literature* (1924). F. KUBKA and M. NOVOTNÝ, *Božena Němcová* (Prague 1941). M. OTRUBA, *Božena Němcová* (Prague 1962).

[B. CHUDOBA]

NEMESIS, half-chthonian, half-Olympian Greek

goddess. By the 6th century B.C., she already had a temple at Smyrna in Asia Minor and was worshiped at an early date in Attica, where she was honored at Rhamnus and identified with Adrastea, "she from whom no escape is possible." Very soon, however, the idea of *nemesis* (retribution) predominated, although Plato still mentions the goddess as "the messenger of Dikē" or Justice (*Laws* 717D) and the concept in this sense had already assumed an important place in Herodotus and Aeschylus.

Of the three types distinguished by S. Ranulf—misfortune-punishment, caprice of the gods, and jealousy of human prosperity—Aeschylus retains only the first. However, he includes the third to the extent of showing that excess of prosperity leads to a "disproportion," *hybris,* which itself deserves punishment. (Cf. his *Persians* 821–822 and the whole *Oresteia*.) He regards *nemesis* not as vengeance or jealousy, but as an implacable penalty for excess or impiety, and as one sent by Zeus, eternal principle of justice. Herodotus, on the contrary, represents the popular point of view, that the gods could not bear to have man too happy. This is the explanation that Solon gives to Croesus after the latter's defeat. Philosophers condemned this kind of anthropomorphism as unworthy of divinity. Plato outlawed envy from the circle of the gods (*Phaedrus* 247A; cf. *Timaeus* 29E) and, in spite of the ancient precept "not to think higher than becomes a man," he urged man to imitate divinity to the best of his power.

Bibliography: H. J. ROSE, OxClDict 601. S. RANULF, *The Jealousy of the Gods and Criminal Law at Athens* (London 1933). J. COMAN, *L'Idée de la némésis chez Eschyle* (Paris 1931), esp. p. 10. H. HERTER, Pauly-Wiss RE 16.2:2338–79.

[E. DES PLACES]

NEMESIUS OF EMESA

Bishop of Emesa (now Homs), early Christian psychologist; fl. *c.* 390–400. Apart from his treatise *On the Nature of Man*, nothing is known of his life, but there is no reason for identifying him with Nemesius, pagan governor of Cappadocia (*c.* 383–389), the friend and correspondent of St. Gregory of Nazianzus. Several Greek manuscripts of his work and excerpts quoted by *Maximus the Confessor call him a bishop. Nemesius, a man of considerable culture, was acquainted with philosophical and medical literature, and was critical and independent in his judgment of doctrines. Although Origen, Basil the Great, and especially Greg-

ory of Nyssa had written of man and the soul, Nemesius composed the first *summa* of Christian psychology in the East. The work is a compilation, with extensive borrowings from Galen and the philosophers; but the material is assessed from a Christian viewpoint before being admitted into a remarkable synthesis that is neither Platonic nor Aristotelian, but Christian in character.

The opening chapter criticizes the concepts of man advanced by Plotinus and Apollinaris, Aristotle, and Plato, and then emphasizes the place of man in the plan of creation. Since man bridges the spiritual and the material worlds, he occupies a privileged place and has a corresponding obligation to live up to the dignity God has given him. This requires a correct concept of what the soul is (ch. 2). Here neither Plato nor Aristotle provides an adequate doctrine: one making the soul too independent of the body, the other reducing the soul to little more than a quality of the body. Nemesius concludes that the soul is an incorporeal entity, subsistent in itself, immortal, and yet designed for union with the body, and discovers in Ammonius Saccas and Porphyry the best explanation of that union (ch. 3): the soul is not changed in the union nor does it become corruptible with or through the body, and yet it makes one being with the body. A certain parallel for such a unique union Nemesius finds in the union of the Divine Word and the human nature in the Incarnation. He has no clear statement on the origin of the soul, and seems to believe in a species of preexistence totally devoid of Platonic myth or of the errors of *Origen.

After a detailed study of the powers of the soul, based on Galen's divisions of the brain, and on anthropological doctrines of the Stoics, Aristotle, and others (chapters through which the scholastics became acquainted with much ancient tradition), Nemesius lays the foundation for a Christian philosophy of free will and human acts. Although he depends on Aristotle's *Nicomachean Ethics* for many details, such as the classification of human acts (ch. 29–), the power of choice (ch. 33–), Nemesius establishes, as a specifically Christian approach, the fact that free will is a concomitant of reason: "If the creature is endowed with reason, it is master of what it does, or else the power to deliberate and choose is pointless; and if it is master of its actions, it must by all means possess free will" (ch. 41). Changeableness, also, is a mark of the creature, even in its rational nature. The psychology of the human act propounded by Nemesius was perfected by *Maximus the Confessor (580–662); as passed on by the Syrian Mose bar Kepha, *Anastasius Sinaita, and *John Damascene, it became an important part of scholastic doctrine [cf. RechThAMéd 21 (1954) 51–100; and O. Lottin, *Psychologie et morale aux XIIᵉ et XIIIᵉ siècles,* v.1 (Gembloux 1957) 393–424].

The treatise came to be ascribed to St. Gregory of Nyssa (who had written a work "On the Making of Man"), and was known under his name to the Western scholastics in the Latin translations of *Alphanus of Salerno (d. 1085) and Burgundio of Pisa (*c.* 1160), although some sentences were also known to the scholastics under the name of Remigius.

Bibliography: Gilson HistChrPhil. Quasten Patr 3:351–355. W. TELFER, *Cyril of Jerusalem and Nemesius of Emesa* (Philadelphia 1955). É. AMANN, DTC 11.1:62–67. E. SKARD, Pauly-Wiss RE Suppl. 7 (1940) 562–566. I. BRADY, "Remigius-Nemesius," FrancStudies 8 (1948) 275–284.

[I. BRADY]

NEMROD (NIMROD)

A legendary hero, great hunter, and reputed first conqueror of all Mesopotamia (Gn 10.8–12). His name (Heb. *nimrōd*) is reflected in Nimrud, the modern name of ancient Calah (Chale), which he "built" (Gn 10.11). Various identifications have been proposed, of which Tukulti-Ninurta I seems most likely.

The literary background of Gn 10.8–12 is rather complicated. Nemrod appears only in Gn 10.8–12; 1 Chr 1.10; Mi 5.5. Of these, 1 Chr 1.10 simply quotes Gn 10.8, and Mi 5.5 uses "the land of Nemrod" as a poetic term for Assyria. Genesis 10.8–12 belongs to the *Yahwist portion of the Table of the *Nations (ch. 10). It thus dates from *c.* the 10th century B.C. and seems to be merely a remnant of a longer narrative about Nemrod. According to v. 7 of the P account (*see* PRIESTLY WRITERS, PENTATEUCHAL), which now forms the structure of ch. 10, Chus (Ethiopia), the son of Ham, has five sons, none of whom is Nemrod. *See* ETHIOPIANS (CUSHITES). In the stylistically distinct v. 8, Chus is said to be the father of Nemrod. As E. A. Speiser has pointed out, Chus in v. 8 might refer to Mesopotamia and especially to the Cassites. The "land of Sennaar," in v. 10, is southern Mesopotamia or Babylonia.

The proverb in v. 9, "Like Nemrod, a mighty hunter before the Lord," is not quoted elsewhere, nor is there any other record of a mighty hunter and ruler in Mesopotamia called Nemrod. Various attempts have been made to identify Nemrod with some ancient king. (For a convenient summary of the older identifications that have been proposed, none of which has proven fully satisfactory, see Speiser.)

G. von Rad [*Genesis*, tr. J. H. Marks (Philadelphia 1961) 142–143] has adopted Sethe's suggestion of *Amenhotep III (1402–1364). As an Egyptian ("Mesraim"), Amenhotep could be called a son of Ham, though not of Chus. He was known as *neb ma re* (found as Nimmuris in the Amarna letters), and boasted both of his expedition to the Euphrates and of his hunting exploits.

Speiser has rightly objected that the Biblical notice does not really suit an Egyptian ruler who reigned long before Calah was founded (probably shortly before or after 1250 B.C.) and whose influence in Mesopotamia was ephemeral at best. There is no evidence that Amenhotep III ever reached any of the cities attributed to Nemrod in Gn 10.11. Speiser's identification of Nemrod with Tukulti-Ninurta I (*c.* 1233–1199) is attractive. The name "the trust [or the help] of the god Ninurta" could have been shortened to Ninurta, and this could in turn underlie the form Nemrod. The examples adduced by Speiser, while not decisive, tend to support his suggestion. After a short interregnum, Tukulti-Ninurta I succeeded Shalmaneser I (*c.* 1265–36), the probable founder of Calah, and was the first Assyrian to conquer Babylon and rule all of Babylonia. He sponsored great building projects in his capital, *Assur (Asshur), and in *Ninive (Nineveh), and eventually built a new but short-lived capital, Kar-Tukulti-Ninurta, not far from Ninive. (*See* MESOPOTAMIA, ANCIENT, 2.)

This career, which would not be equaled by that of another Assyrian until *Tiglath-Pileser III, some 5 centuries later, may be mirrored in Gn 10.8–12. There are difficulties, among them the validity of equating Chus with Cassite (especially since Tukulti-Ninurta

conquered the Cassite ruler of Babylon and carried off the statue of his god Marduk). But, while Speiser's suggestion has not been proved beyond doubt, it represents the best hypothesis on the basis of the available evidence. Tukulti-Ninurta I is the most likely candidate for the role of the Biblical Nemrod.

Bibliography: E. A. SPEISER, "In Search of Nimrod," *Eretz-Israel* 5 (1958) 32*–36*, includes bibliog.

[K. G. O'CONNELL]

NENNIUS, historian; b. supposedly North Wales. Nennius (Nemnius) is thought to have been a pupil of Elbodugus (d. 809), who had been bishop of Bangor. Nennius's *Historia Brittonum* was edited by T. *Mommsen (MGAuctAnt 13:111–122) from 11 manuscripts. As there is no complete form of the *Historia* now extant, the text must be critically reconstructed. An important Irish translation made in the 11th century remains the best authority on the work as a whole. The *Historia* professes to give a sketch of British history to the 8th century; this is followed by lives of St. Patrick and of King Arthur and the *mirabilia* of Britain. This is the earliest mention of Arthur and his exploits and forms the point of departure for all serious students of that cycle (*see* ARTHURIAN AND CAROLINGIAN LEGENDS). The date of composition is still a matter of dispute. Some of the *mirabilia* listed occur also in the earliest strata of the Mabinogion and in early Welsh poetry. F. Lot has shown how Nennius utilized a Mercian genealogy of kings compiled in 796.

Bibliography: H. ZIMMER, *Nennius vindicatus* (Berlin 1893). L. DUCHESNE, "Nennius retractatus," *Revue Celtique* 15 (1894) 174–197. Kenney 152–155. Manitius 1:240–242. R. THURNEYSEN, *Zeitschrift für celtische Philologie* 20 (1936) 97–137, 185–191. F. LOT, *Nennius et l'Historia Brittonum* (Paris 1934). R. I. BEST, *Bibliography of Irish Philology and Manuscript Literature: 1913–1941* (Dublin 1942) 2092–2102.

[R. T. MEYER]

NEO-AFRICAN LITERATURE

The meeting between Negro-African culture and that of the West is the seedbed of Neo-African literature, which has recently flourished in Africa south of the Sahara and on the west coast of both Americas, including the Caribbean. In contrast to orally transmitted Negro-African folk literature, which is, for the most part, the work of anonymous authors, Neo-African literature is written, the work of known authors, most of whom still write in European languages. It differs from the older colonial literature, which was based exclusively on European models, in that its style is characterized by a number of African techniques: imagery from the realm of magic, rhythmic rather than dramatic structure, intensification through repetition, "imperativism" (commanding the future to become present by incantation), and African adaptation of European languages and speech modes.

Tradition and Innovation. These stylistic elements may be a direct link with tradition, as, for instance, in the mission literature in African languages; they may be taken unconsciously from folklore preserved by unreflective transmission, as, for instance, in Afro-American literature in the U.S.; or they may be adopted and employed quite consciously, as in *Négritude* poetry (literally "Negro-ness," a term coined in 1939 by Aimé Césaire to describe the retrospective awareness of the heritage of traditional African cultural values). Neo-

"Awakening Africa," welded steel sculpture, by Vincent Kofi, Ghana.

African literature thus is not specified by the color of the skin or by the particular language of its creators, but by its style. At present, it is still directed predominantly toward demands for freedom and against colonial, social, and individual guardianship.

Pull of Western Literature. Two opposing trends present themselves. The first is the attempt of the literature to reject African traditions of style and meaning and to integrate itself with Western literature. It is represented as "disciple literature," which ranges from great early works, such as the novel *Chaka*, by Thomas Mofolo (c. 1875–1948), to works that are mere imitations of Western literature. In the sociocritical novels of the South African Peter Abrahams (1919–   ), *Mine Boy* (1946), *The Path of Thunder* (1948), *Wild Conquest* (1950), and *A Wreath for Udomo* (1956), and those of Ezekiel Mphahlele (1919–   ), *Down Second Avenue* (1959), African stylistic elements decrease from work to work, as they do also in the works of René Maran (1887–1959), whose first work, *Batouala* (1921), was a forerunner of *Négritude*.

Rebellion Against Colonialism. The opposing trend aims consciously to strengthen African stylistic devices at the expense of Western ones. Thus there arose as early as 1928 the "Afro-Cuban poetry" as a re-Africanization of the imitative colonial literature that preceded it. Its most important authors are Nicolás Guillén (1902–   ) author of *Songoro Cosongo* (1931), *El son entero* (1947), and *La paloma de vuelo popular* (1948); E. Ballagas (1908–54); and Marcelino Arozarena (1912–   ). But it was *Négritude* poetry that brought about the real change (1939–47), beginning with the works of Aimé Césaire (1913–   ), *Cahier d'un retour au pays natal* (1939), *Les Armes miraculeuses* (1946), *Soleil cou-coupé* (1948), *Et les Chiens se taissaient* (1956), *Ferrements* (1960), and *Cadastre* (1961). Contemporary poets were Léopold Sédar Senghor of Senegal (1906–   ), author of *Chants d'ombre* (1945), *Hosties noires* (1948), *Éthiopiques* (1956), and *Nocturnes* (1961); and Léon Damas (1912–   ), with *Pig-*

ments (1937), *Graffiti* (1952), and *Black Label* (1956). *Négritude* poetry has been called by Jean-Paul Sartre the "only great revolutionary poetry of our time." The Africanization of stylistic techniques, raised to a principle and spread from the Caribbean to West Africa, helped to enkindle, on both sides of the Atlantic, anticolonial intellectual fervor.

Younger poets in the Congo who write in French have been particularly caught up in this movement. Such are Gérard-Felix Tchicaya U Tam'si (1931–   ) in *Feu de brousse* (1957), and *A Triche-coeur* (1958); on the Ivory Coast, Bernard Dadié (1916–   ) in *La Ronde des jours* (1956); in Madagascar, Jacques Rabémananjara (1913–   ) in *Les Dieux malgaches* (1947), *Antsa* (1948), and *Lamba* (1956); in Haiti, René Depestre (1926–   ) in *Minerai Noir* (1956), and others.

The power of expression and rhythmic complexity of Afro-Caribbean novelists like George Lamming (1927–   ), *In the Castle of My Skin* (1953), The *Emigrants* (1954), *Of Age and Innocence* (1958), and *Season of Adventure* (1960); Victor Reid (1913–   ) in *New Day* (1949), *The Leopard* (1958); and Jacques Roumain (1907–   ) in *Bois d'ébène* (1945), and *Gouverneur de la rosée* (1944), are even surpassed in Africa by Camara Laye of Guinea (1928–   ), who uses subtle symbols, e.g., in *Enfant noir* (1953), and *Le Regard du roi* (1954), and by the sarcastically humorous Mongo Beti of the Cameroons (1932–   ) in *Le pauvre Christ de Bomba* (1956), *Mission terminée* (1957), and *Le Roi miraculé* (1958).

Two Nigerians write in the magical tradition. Daniel Olorunfemi Fagunwa (1910–   ) has produced *Ogboju ode ninu igbo irunmale* (1950), and Amos Tutuola (1920–   ) is author of *The Palm Wine Drunkard* (1952), and *My Life in the Bush of Ghosts* (1954). Birago Diop of Senegal (1906–   ) follows the tradition in *Les Contes d'Amadou Koumba* (1947), as do Djibril Tamsir Niane of Guinea in *Soundjata* (1960), Benjamin Matip of the Cameroons (1932–   ) in *A la belle Étoile* (1962), and Paul Lomami-Tshibamba of the Congo (1914–   ) in *Ngando* (1948).

African life, present and past, is depicted by the Nigerians Chinua Achebe (1931–   ) in *Things Fall Apart* (1958), and *No Longer at Ease* (1960), and Cyprian Ekwensi (1921–   ) in *Jagua Nana* (1961); by Ferdinand Oyono of the Cameroons (1929–   ) in *Un vie de boy* (1956); by Paul Hazoumé of Dahomey (1890–   ) in *Doguicimi* (1938); and by Nazi Boni of Volta (1914–   ) in *Crépuscule des temps anciens* (1962).

The Theme of Conflict. The conflict with the modern world, with Christianity, with the social and political situation, and with intellectual acculturation is a frequently recurring theme. It is taken up in South Africa by Bloke Modisane (1924–   ) in *Blame Me on History* (1963); Alex LaGuma (1925–   ) in *A Walk in the Night* (1962); and Alfred Hutchinson (1925–   ) in *Road to Ghana* (1960); in Nigeria by Onuora Nzekwu (1928–   ) in *Wand of Noble Wood* (1961), and *Blade among the Boys* (1962); on the Ivory Coast by Bernard Binlin Dadié (1916–   ) in *Climbié* (1956), and Sidiki Dembele in *Les Inutiles* (1960); in Sierra Leone by William Conton (1923–   ) in *The African* (1960); in Dahomey by Olympe Bhêly-Quénum (1928–   ) in *Un Piège sans fin* (1960); in Senegal by Ousmane Socé

(1911–) in *Karim* (1935), and *Mirages de Paris* (1937), and by Semben Usman (Sembène Ousmane, 1923–) in *Ô Pays, mon beau peuple* (1957).

Poets writing in English include Gabriel Okara (1921–) and John Pepper Clark (1935–) of Nigeria, and George Awoonor-Williams (1935–) of Ghana. The dramatists are the Nigerians Wole Soyinka (1934–), e.g., *A Dance in the Forest* (1960), and John Pepper Clark, e.g., *Song of a Goat* (1961). The works of Abbé Alexis Kagame of Ruanda (1912–), such as *La Philosophie bantu-rwandaise de l'Être* (1956), offer an analysis of the philosophical assumptions of Neo-African literature, as do the essays of L. S. Senghor. Neo-African literary journals are, among others, *Présence Africaine* (Paris), *Black Orpheus* (Ibadan, Nigeria), *Abbia* (Yaoundé, Cameroons), and *Transition* (Kampala, Uganda).

See also SOUTH AFRICAN LITERATURE.

Bibliography: Anthologies. L. SÉDAR SENGHOR, ed., *Anthologie de la nouvelle poésie nègre et malgache de langue française* (Paris 1948). L. HUGHES, ed., *The Poetry of the Negro, 1746–1949* (Garden City, N.Y. 1953). J. JAHN, ed., *Schwarzer Orpheus* (4th ed. Munich 1964); *Das junge Afrika: Einundvierzig Erzählungen afrikanischer Autoren* (Munich 1963); *Afrika erzählt* (Frankfurt a. M. 1963). P. RUTHERFOORD, ed., *African Voices: An Anthology of Native African Writing* (New York 1960). G. MOORE and U. BEIER, eds., *Modern Poetry from Africa* (Penguin; Baltimore 1963). L. HUGHES, ed., *Poems from Black Africa* (Bloomington, Ind. 1963). Commentaries. J. JAHN, *Muntu: An Outline of the New African Culture,* tr. M. GREENE (New York 1961). G. MOORE, *Seven African Writers* (London 1962). T. MELONE, *De la négritude dans la littérature négro-africaine* (Paris 1962). L. KESTELOOT, *Les Écrivains noirs de langue française: Naissance d'une littérature* (Brussels 1963). **Illustration credit:** Courtesy, Harmon Foundation, New York City.

[J. JAHN]

NEOCAESAREA. Three bishoprics bear the name Neocaesarea in the early Church: (1) Neocaesarea in Bithynia. The exact location is uncertain, but it was probably in the western part of Bithynia mentioned in 1 Peter 1.1. Two of its bishops attended synods in Constantinople: Olympius (*c.* 381) and Cyriacus (518). (2) Neocaesarea in Pontus Polemoniacus. Here Origen's distinguished student, St. *Gregory Thaumaturgus, was bishop *c.* 240 to 270. According to St. *Gregory of Nyssa, the Church in Pontus suffered persecution under Emperors *Decius and Galerius. When peace was restored, Gregory Thaumaturgus christianized pagan festivals, gathered the relics of martyrs, fixed days for commemorating their triumphs, and inspired his flock to erect churches. An important synod between 314 and 325 enacted legislation that affected the catechumenate for many years and barred the *clinici* from the priesthood on the ground that they had received Baptism more from fear of death and judgment than from dedication to Christ. Some ruins, fragments of inscriptions, and sculptures remain as witnesses to the once flourishing church. (3) Neocaesarea on the Euphrates in northern Syria. This was a military garrison in Augusta Euphratensis, whose fortifications were strengthened under *Justinian I. *Theodoret of Cyr (GCS 44:31) mentions Paul, Bishop of Neocaesarea, who had suffered for the faith, as being present at the Council of *Nicaea I.

Bibliography: W. RUGE, Pauly-Wiss RE 16.2 (1935) 2409–13. W. M. RAMSAY, *The Historical Geography of Asia Minor* (London 1890). A. VON HARNACK, *Die Mission und Ausbreitung,* 2 v. (Leipzig 1906) v.2. H. LECLERCQ, DACL 4.2:2298; 12.1:1103. A. KREUZ, LexThK² 7:876. AnnPont (1964) 631–632.

[H. DRESSLER]

NEOCLASSICISM

The term is properly applied to modern "classicisms," i.e., to the best that modern literatures have produced under the dominant inspiration of Greco-Roman literature and thought. It implies a doctrine of imitation, an aristocratic concept of art, a sense of elegance in form and proportion, a tendency toward concentration and economy and control of artistic means. It holds that the poet is not only born but must also be made; to genius must be added technique, theory and doctrine, learning, and critical acumen. It therefore encourages the study of ancient poetics and the formulation of corresponding rules and precepts for modern authors.

Neoclassicism is a consequence of the Renaissance revival of ancient letters and the enthusiastic effort by the modern nations of Western Europe to endow their vernacular literatures with the splendors of the age of Pericles and the age of Augustus. Only when this is achieved—so runs the argument—can a literature (or a nation) claim to be ranked as great. And when it is achieved, emulation tends to become rivalry; equality and independence are proclaimed through quarrels between the ancients and the moderns, or a battle of the books, and the bestowing of a classical honorific title upon a modern literary epoch: the Age of Leo X, the *Siglo de Oro,* the *Siècle de Louis le Grand,* and the like.

Mediterranean Neoclassicism. The earliest such achievement occurred in Italy in the first half of the 16th century, considered by the Italians as their equivalent of the age of Augustus. It represents the flowering of a rich and complex culture which, since *Petrarch, had lovingly assimilated classical culture, made it contemporary and alive, and infused it permanently into the thought, life, and creative processes of the elite. The greatest literary work of the time is *Ariosto's *Orlando furioso* (1516). Its vivid world of color and movement within a vast but controlled structure is presented with a sharp sense of the realities of human nature viewed with mature indulgence, a charming sense of humor, and a gentle irony. Its effortless and serene cult of perfect form reveals a pure High Renaissance neoclassicism, never to be achieved again. (*See* ITALIAN LITERATURE, 1).

In Spain *Cervantes' *Don Quixote* (1605) fuses classical and Italian Renaissance themes and ideals with a rich native popular tradition to produce the first great novel. A powerful sense of life pervades this work, crowded with personages of all classes and types and with multiple episodes, adventures, interpolated tales, and dominated by the firmly drawn antithetical figures of the knight and his squire. The novel moves constantly on two or more conceptual levels and the resultant tensions generate the action and organize it in perspective and depth. Cervantes, like the best of his contemporaries such as *Calderón of the *Siglo de Oro,* represents a baroque neoclassicism. (*See* SPANISH LITERATURE, 2.)

In France neoclassicism reaches its height in the theater, with *Racine and *Molière. Greek models now equal Roman models in importance; Italian and Spanish influences are strong; native popular elements yield to a learned aristocratic tradition conscious of rules and

*Woodcut of a battle scene in Ariosto's "Orlando Furioso,"
printed in Venice (1562) by V. Valgrisi.*

reason; French history and French life are banished in favor of universal or general topics and characters. The heroes are passionate and deeply human and speak an impeccable poetic language. France's neoclassicism, like Spain's, is baroque, but more concentrated and controlled, less local and picturesque. (*See* FRENCH LITERATURE, 3.)

The three Mediterranean neoclassicisms were followed by still other classical revivals or pseudoclassicisms of lesser merit and duration—in the work of Vittorio Alfieri (1749–1803), Nicolás Fernández de Moratín (1737–80); in the drama of *Voltaire—or an isolated talent or genius such as André Chénier (1762–94) or *Leopardi.

Neoclassicism in England and Germany. England is the only nation to apply the term neoclassicism to a period of its literary history, that of *Dryden and *Pope; and the title has a slightly pejorative flavor—it might more honorably have designated the age of the Elizabethans and *Milton. Both Dryden and Pope derive their doctrine from French *classicisme,* hence the name. They are keenly aware of the native tradition and of the ancient and Renaissance sources from which it drew enrichment, but from all this wealth they take only what can be made to conform to the new ideas of order, decorum, good taste, and good sense. The age of reason (*empiricism) that they initiate worships clarity and "wit," places a new emphasis on the expression of social ideals, separates morality from religion, affects a tone

of moral dryness and purely lay skepticism, turns naturally to mockery and satire. Above all it is attentive to the laws of form, to the cadenced and compact expression of its essentially commonplace and conservative ideas. Theirs is an "enlightened" neoclassicism. (*See* ENGLISH LITERATURE, 5, 6.)

The Germans come late to their Renaissance and their *Klassik,* and at a moment that coincides with the development of *Sturm und Drang.* Their neoclassicism is in part a reaction against the French, in part a sort of escapist exoticism, like their interest in the Middle Ages or the Orient. It has theoretical foundations in archeology and art history and it involves sentimental pilgrimages and attitudinizing among famous ruins. It draws its central inspiration from the beauty and nobility of Greek thought and art, characterized in Johann Winckelmann's famous phrase as "noble simplicity and tranquil grandeur" (*eine edle Einfalt und eine stille Grösse*). It finds its best literary expression in works by *Schiller, *Hölderlin, and *Goethe. But these names suggest that German neoclassicism never achieved dispassionate objectivity or a rigidly controlled formal structure. It remains intensely personal, and deeply involved in contemporary issues. It is readily accommodated with the Gothic, the picturesque, the medieval, the sentimental, the revolutionary. It is, in the last analysis, a Romantic neoclassicism. (*See* GERMAN LITERATURE, 4, 5; ROMANTICISM; GOTHIC REVIVAL).

Neoclassicism is a very complex European phenomenon that is still being reassessed by contemporary scholarship, particularly on the basis of penetrating stylistic analysis of individual authors and stricter definition of period styles and outlooks.

Bibliography: G. HIGHET, *The Classical Tradition* (New York 1949). P. MOREAU, *Le Classicisme des romantiques* (Paris 1932). H. PEYRE, *Le Classicisme français* (New York 1942). H. HATZ-FELD, "A Clarification of the Baroque Problem in the Romance Literatures," ComparLit 1 (1949) 113–139; "Mis aportaciones a la elucidación de literatura barroca," *Revista de la Universidad de Madrid* 11 (1963) 349–372, lists Hatzfeld's other studies on this problem. R. F. JONES, *Ancients and Moderns* (St. Louis 1936). M. PRAZ, *Gusto neoclassico* (Florence 1940). W. KOHL-SCHMIDT, *Form und Innerlichkeit* (Bern 1955). **Illustration credit:** Library of Congress, Rosenwald Collection.

[C. B. BEALL]

NEOCLASSICISM (IN ART)

In painting, sculpture, and architecture the term neoclassicism is applied to any style that revives formal and iconographical values associated with ancient Greece and Rome; for example, neoclassical elements are found in the art of the Carolingian era and the Renaissance and in the baroque works of Nicolas *Poussin and Inigo *Jones. Specifically neoclassicism is that style that predominated from about 1750 to 1850, and whose effects were felt throughout Europe and America.

The style may be characterized as a striving for simplicity and order through a sense of clear geometric programs of space and volume; precise, hard-edged forms; a linear technique; severe (even harsh) lighting; and a shallow, uncluttered organization with strict attention to planes. Iconographically, themes were taken from mythology and legendary history, stoical subject matter being preferred. These features were seen as the essence of antique art. Fascination with the Greco-Roman world approached a mania with successive publications of aesthetic theory and archeological investigation. Excavations began at Herculaneum (1738) and

Pompeii (1748) and were followed by Giovanni Battista *Piranesi's publication of his *Views of Rome* (1748). The chief spokesman of the movement, Johann *Winckelmann, looked upon as the first modern art historian (*Reflections on the Imitation of Greek Art,* 1755; *History of Art among the Ancients,* 1764), attracted to Rome such painters as Anton Raphael Mengs (1728–79), Pompeo Battoni (1708–87), Maria-Joseph Vien (1716–1809), Gavin Hamilton (1723–98), Angelica Kauffmann (1741–1807), and the American Benjamin West (1738–1820), who introduced the mode into Britain with such works as "Agrippina with the Ashes of Germanicus" (1766, Yale University). It was Vien's student Jacques Louis *David, however, who was to achieve the quintessence of neoclassical ideals in his "Oath of the Horatii" (1784–85, Louvre) with its unyielding stoicism and severe, hard, relieflike execution that marked the final abandonment of the *rococo sentiment and softness that had lingered in the art of the earlier painters. David, in later life, and his followers (excepting Jean Auguste Dominique *Ingres, 1780–1867) became overly concerned with the trappings of archeological exactitude and their work, vitiated by romantic tendencies, ceased to be truly neoclassical.

Although sources and inspiration were the same for architecture, the major areas of practice were in France and England. James Stuart's and Nicholas Revett's *Antiquities of Athens* (v.1 1762) proved immensely influential, as did the works of Ange Jacques Gabriel (1692–1782), and Claude Nicolas Ledoux (1736–1804). Indeed the same progression can be seen in architecture as in painting. The pseudo-neoclassicism of West and Gabriel led to the purified forms of David and Ledoux. The latter's working with interrelationships of stark, solid geometric forms with a minimum of ornamentation produced an abstract style known as romantic classicism, romantic in its nostalgic sensitivity toward antiquity and classical in its formal clarity. Sir John Soane (1753–1837) was the major proponent in England, while in America, Benjamin Henry *Latrobe (1764–1820) produced what Hitchcock has called "one of the finest ecclesiastical monuments of Romantic Classicism" in the Baltimore Cathedral (1805–18, now Basilica of the Assumption of the Blessed Virgin Mary).

See also CHURCH ARCHITECTURE, 8; ART, MODERN EUROPEAN, 1.

Bibliography: J. SUMMERSON, *Architecture in Britain, 1530–1830* (4th ed. PelHArt Z3; 1963). E. KAUFMANN, *Architecture in the Age of Reason* (Cambridge, Mass. 1955). H. R. HITCHCOCK, *Architecture: 19th and 20th Centuries* (2d ed. PelHArt Z15; 1963). F. NOVOTNY, *Painting and Sculpture in Europe, 1780–1880* (PelHArt Z20; 1960). E. WATERHOUSE, *Painting in Britain, 1530 to 1790* (2d ed. PelHArt Z1; 1962). H. HAWLEY, *Neo-classicism: Style and Motif* (Cleveland 1964). **Illustration credit:** Archives Photographiques, Paris.

[R. G. CARROTT]

Jacques Louis David, "Oath of the Horatii" (1784–85), 10 ft. 8¾ in. by 13 ft. 10½ in., Musée du Louvre.

NEO-GUELFISM, the program of Italian Catholic liberals during the *Risorgimento who stressed the relation between the Church and civilization and led the reform-unification movement from 1843 to 1848. Some Italians used the term Neo-Guelfism in derision, but its followers accepted it. These opponents, the Neo-Ghibellines, thought the temporal power of the papacy a hindrance to Italian unification. They were fewer in number and less noted than the Neo-Guelfs, whose ranks included such scholars and writers as *Balbo, *Capponi, *Manzoni, *Tosti, and Carlo Troya.

The leading Neo-Guelf was Vincenzo *Gioberti. In his most famous book, *Del Primato Morale e Civile degli Italiani* (1843), he reminded his countrymen of their former greatness, proposed liberal reforms, and a unification plan that envisioned a federation of the independent states of the peninsula with the pope as president and the king of Sardinia as military defender. The book was popular and influential. It appealed to moderates who disapproved of *Mazzini. The book also inspired Balbo to write *Le Speranze d'Italia.* The future *Pius IX discussed both books with friends. Soon after his elevation to the papacy (1846), he began a series of reforms in the *States of the Church that attracted much attention, and helped the progress of reform in other Italian states.

The effectiveness of Neo-Guelfism quickly subsided after the revolution of 1848, and very little interest was shown thereafter in federation. Even in 1843 not all Neo-Guelfs accepted Gioberti's main notion of the pope as president of Italy. Balbo and others preferred Charles Albert as king. When Pius IX proposed a customs union and a federation with Tuscany and Piedmont, Charles Albert proposed a defensive league, which conflicted with the Pope's position as a spiritual leader. After the decline of Neo-Guelfism, Italians turned to the leadership of Piedmont for the unification of Italy.

Bibliography: G. F. H. and J. BERKELEY, *Italy in the Making,* 3 v. (Cambridge, Eng. 1932–40). B. CROCE, *History of Europe in the Nineteenth Century,* tr. H. FURST (New York 1933); *Storia della storiografia italiana nel secolo decimonono,* 2 v. (3d rev. ed., Bari 1947) v.1. E. PASSERIN, EncCatt 8:1743–45.

[M. L. SHAY]

NEO-KANTIANISM

A term employed in the history of philosophy to designate the sustained attempt, by a number of groups and from different points of view, to reconstitute the thought of Immanuel *Kant as the basis for a philosophy that would meet the problematic and speculative exigencies of the second half of the 19th century. It was primarily a German movement, with centers at a number of German universities; it was not exclusively so, however, for its influence was felt in England, France, Italy, and, with the emigration of Ernst *Cassirer, one of the last great representatives of the movement, in the U.S. Otto Liebmann (1840–1912), in his work *Kant und die Epigonen* (Stuttgart 1865), is credited both with the decisive initiation of the current and with the coining of its rubric, "back to Kant," for he concluded the studies of the work of J. G. *Fichte, F. W. J. *Schelling, G. W. F. *Hegel, A. *Schopenhauer, etc., which comprise the book, with this phrase. The rubric cannot be taken, however, as indicating a single unitary movement, for there existed a great diversity of opinion as to the doctrines of Kant

to which return should be made. Moreover, even when some degree of consent was achieved on this point, various interpretations of the favored doctrines were offered. These interpretations were not always wholly self-consistent or consistent with each other; nor, finally, were they authentic interpretations of Kant that realized all the potentialities of his thought. On the whole, the cultural pressure of *positivism tended to make the Neo-Kantians place an excessively narrow interpretation on Kant's philosophy.

Historical Background. The historical background of the Neo-Kantian movement is provided by positivism, toward which Neo-Kantianism exhibits an ambivalent attitude. On the one hand, its central motive is a rejection of the positivist claims; on the other, it exhibits the influence of positivism in many facets of its doctrines and methods. Thus, it repudiates the attitudes of positivism as dogmatic and antiphilosophical; at the same time, it accepts the central thesis of positivism, i.e., that physicomathematical science provides the paradigm of all valid forms of knowledge. In accordance with this view, it conceives the philosophical task as the critical investigation of the conditions that make this kind of knowledge possible and valid. This conception of the task of philosophy constitutes the real point of contact and reference between Neo-Kantianism and Kant; for Kant had conceived philosophy as the critical examination and determination of the a priori principles and structures that render experience of the physical world and action in the moral sphere possible and provide the basis for scientific, ethical, and preferential discourse. At the same time, Neo-Kantianism devotes considerable attention to the tradition of Romanticism, which it criticized and rejected far more forcibly than it did positivism (*see* ROMANTICISM, PHILOSOPHICAL). Romanticism had directed sharp criticism against physicomathematical science on the basis of the abstractness intrinsic to it; it had proposed instead a conception of philosophy as concrete knowledge, free from and unlimited by such abstractness. Romanticism had, in its own way, claimed Kant as progenitor; Neo-Kantianism rejected this claim as spurious, pointing out that the essence of Kantian method was scientific rigor, a quality conspicuously lacking among the Romantic philosophers. Its return to Kant was an effort to preserve the positivist ideal of a philosophy as scientifically rigorous as a physicomathematical discipline and, with this, the Kantian transcendental values. The historical development of the movement is determined by its efforts to realize this ideal in the various areas of speculative interest.

Principal Currents. The principal currents comprising the Neo-Kantian movement, or at least conventionally allied with it, are (1) the realist current, whose principal exponent was A. Riehl; (2) the psychological current, represented by L. Nelson, the follower of the psychologist J. F. Fries; (3) the metaphysical current, a chief representative of which was the same Leibmann who is credited with originating the Neo-Kantian motto; (4) the logical current, called the School of Marburg because its center was at that university, led by H. Cohen and counting as its chief figures P. Natorp and E. Cassirer; (5) the value theory current, called also the School of Baden, including among its adherents such distinguished figures as H. Rickert, W. Windelband, H. Münsterburg, and, by a looser connection, W. Dilthey; and finally, for the sake of completeness, (6) the physiological current, associated with the researches of H. A. von Humboldt and the relativistic current of G. Simmel. The important figure of Bruno *Bauch was dominant in the movement for many years; though formed in the School of Baden and always devoted chiefly to its theoretical interests, he exercised, through his editorship of the important journal *Kantstudien,* a guiding influence over all the currents of the movement. From the point of view of theoretical interest, clarity of development, and distinction of achievement, the logical School of Marburg and the value-theory oriented School of Baden are the outstanding elements of the Neo-Kantian movement.

Alois Riehl. The realistic current found its chief exponent in Alois Riehl (1844–1924), whose chief work, *Der philosophische Kritizismus* (2 v. Leipzig 1876–87), was the basic document of the movement. Riehl strikes a characteristic note of all Neo-Kantians by his resolute rejection of metaphysics as a philosophical science. Philosophy, for him, is a science of experience and what does not fall within experience can find no expression in philosophical discourse. At the same time, he rejects, *en bloc,* all the idealistic and Romantic interpretations of Kant; these assign an exclusive role to the subject, which, in Hegel's phrase, takes the world onto itself. Riehl returns rather to Kant's original distinction and insists that from the subject can be derived only the form of knowledge; the content of knowledge must come from experience, and ultimately from sense experience. It must be noted that, while returning to this original Kantian distinction, Riehl tends to overlook the many difficulties to which it had given rise and the efforts made, in the idealistic tradition, to meet these difficulties. Riehl is one of those who was forced by the cultural pressure of positivism to impose an excessively narrow interpretation on Kantian thought. For Riehl, the Kant of the *Critique of Pure Reason* is very nearly the only Kant, and philosophy becomes identical with the theory of knowledge and its adjunct problems. He remains strictly faithful to Kant in that he conceives the theory of knowledge in gnoseological, and never in psychological, terms.

Leonard Nelson. The last-mentioned attitude sets Riehl in contrast with the psychological current, the chief exponent of which was Leonard Nelson (1882–1927). Nelson, professor at Göttingen from 1919 until his death and founder of the Neo-Friesian School, proposed, on the model of Jakob Friedrich Fries (1773–1843), to develop the critical *gnoseology of Kant on psychological bases and in accord with a strict psychological method. The author of many studies and editor of the journal of the Neo-Friesian School (*Abhandlungen der Friesschen Schule*) for a number of years, Nelson is best known, perhaps, for his contributions to this journal questioning the possibility of the theory of knowledge—in much the same sense as Riehl had proposed to make such a theory the exclusive concern of philosophy. Nelson's criticism is based on the fact that this theory would presume to offer a criterion for determining the validity of knowledge, while the status of such a criterion would be entirely ambiguous. On the one hand, it could not itself be knowledge; nor, on the other hand, could it fall outside the sphere of knowledge, since a criterion, to be used, must be known. His solution was to return to the simpler and immediate elements of conscious-

ness that could become the object of psychological treatment. The entire process of the Kantian critiques was thus recast in psychologically descriptive terms—and not only the processes of knowledge but such ethical principles as the categorical imperative as well. Nelson enjoyed a considerable influence, but this waned rapidly during the period between World War I and World War II.

Otto Liebmann. The metaphysical current of Neo-Kantianism found its chief exponent in Liebmann. The fame of his early work *Kant und die Epigonen* tends to place in the shade his more positive and constructive work, precisely the work that establishes him as the leading figure of the metaphysical current of Neo-Kantianism. His avowed purpose was to develop the basic problems of Kantianism in such a manner as to achieve a synthesis between the demands of criticism and those of metaphysics. It might also be said that he sought to carry criticism beyond the point where Kant had left it to build a systematic metaphysics that would be faithful to the conditions laid down by the critical philosophy. An idea of what he meant by metaphysics may be gathered by his assertion that, whereas physics deducts facts from laws, the role of metaphysics is to determine the why of all that happens in nature and experience. Metaphysics in this sense is possible only if it is at the same time critical, by which he meant that it proceeds by a hypothetical consideration of the essence of things. Yet his would be a metaphysics relative to the human mind, since the critical attitude demands that, at every point in the construction of that metaphysics, the conditions of human understanding be taken as limits and terms of reference. Liebmann made a like condition for the unity of ethical theory and the critical attitude. There are no absolute values, since values are relative to the valuing subject; yet, with constant reference to that subject, it is still possible to achieve an ethics of transcendental value.

Otto Liebmann.

Marburg School. Equally adamant in its opposition to the "psychologization" of Kant and inclined in an antimetaphysical direction was the School of Marburg, perhaps the most distinguished of the Neo-Kantian groups. It was a school in a very true sense, for it had a physical location, identifiable personnel in constant and explicit communication with each other, and a commonly accepted goal and method. Founded by Hermann Cohen (1843–1918), it retained during its

Hermann Cohen.

entire career the stamp of his personality and the direction he imparted to it. Cohen also attracted men of high caliber both in their formation and scholarship and in their theoretical capacity. The most eminent of these were Paul Natorp (1854–1924) and Ernst Cassirer (1874–1945), the last-named bringing international prestige to the group by his masterly historical work and his well-researched and carefully articulated speculative efforts. An excellent account of the school and its work is provided by Natorp in his essay "Kant und die Marburger Schule," *Kantstudien* 17 (1912) 193–221.

The direction given by Cohen and characteristic of the school throughout its career is logical and methodological; its main link with Kant is the *Critique of Pure Reason*. The chief concern is the determination of the logical-transcendental conditions of science. Among these, it assigns a prominence to the logical structures that condition experience, tending to dissolve *intuition into the logical processes and no longer assigning it an autonomous position and function; it thus truncates a goodly portion of the *Critique of Pure Reason*. The diminishing of the elements of immediacy in experience tends to throw into clearer relief the controlled methodological procedures of science and to reveal science as less and less dependent on the "given" element in experience. The logical processes of thought tend more and more to determine the object completely, though never, in keeping with the notion of the "thing-in-itself," entirely encompassing it.

Though concentrated in the area of science and pure reason, the attention of the Marburg School also embraced the areas of ethics and aesthetics, achieving notable insights in both. It tended to absorb the phenomenon of religion into the ethical area, a tendency already perceptible in Kant, though not explicit in his intention. The ethical field, in turn, was largely socialized by both Cohen and Natorp and, subsequently, by other members and adherents of the school.

Another notable characteristic of the Marburg School was its constant interrelation of theoretical and historical interests. Its theoretical works exhibit a high degree of erudition and historical sense, and its historical works are distinguished by the way in which they are related to, and made to serve, the clarification of theoretical problems of philosophy. Cassirer especially distinguished himself in this way.

Baden School. No less eminent in its personnel and achievements was the School of Baden. This current of Neo-Kantianism numbered among its representatives the historian of philosophy W. Windelband (1848–1912), the theoretician of value H. Rickert (1863–1936), and the incomparable W. *Dilthey (1833–1911), whose work was predominantly in the theory of history and of culture. In justice to Dilthey, it should be noted that his achievement places him outside the limits of any school and establishes him as an original thinker in his own right.

The general character of the School of Baden may best be indicated by contrasting it with that of the Marburg School. The Baden School was convinced of the necessity of a critical study of culture and values at least as philosophical as that sought for the sciences of nature in the Marburg School. It was convinced, moreover, that the instruments necessary for such a work were present in the critical philosophy of Kant, and especially in the *Critique of Judgment*. Windelband's reflections on history and his contraposition of history to the natural sciences as equal areas of knowledge and investigation led him to establish a classification of the sciences into nomothetical and idiographic. The natural sciences are defined as nomothetic because they seek to establish the laws of nature; the sciences of culture are called, by contrast, idiographic because they seek the form of cultures. The natural, or nomothetic, sciences generalize particular facts that are considered typical instances of a single species, whereas the idiographic sciences are individualizing, seeking the form of a particular culture or expressive work.

Windelband's student Rickert continued this line of thought, seeking to advance beyond his teacher by establishing the difference between natural and cultural sciences on a more formal basis; this formal basis was the reference of the sciences of culture to value in the sense in which R. H. Lotze (1817–81) had defined that term. The cultural sciences have value as their formal object. On this basis, Rickert undertook the elaboration of a general theory of value. (*See* VALUE, PHILOSOPHY OF.)

This tendency was carried to its culmination by Dilthey both in theory and in practice. For Dilthey the "sciences of the spirit" (i.e., of value, culture, and history) are gnoseologically anterior to the sciences of nature; indeed, all science is a product of historical experience and expression. Dilthey developed a psychological basis for the sciences of the spirit that involved a subtle theory of the hermeneutics of the historical document. He applied his theories with great perception in such works as his *Leben Schleiermachers* (2 v. Berlin 1867–70), which revealed the potential of biography in the history of ideas and offered a new conception of cultural biography.

Influence. The influence of Neo-Kantianism may be seen in every major figure in German thought to the end of the 19th century. In England a "return to Kant" movement is to be found in Robert Adamson (1852–1902), in France in C. B. *Renouvier (1815–1903), and in Italy in Francesco Fiorentino (1834–94).

See also KANTIANISM; CRITICISM, PHILOSOPHICAL.

Bibliography: G. VARET, *Manuel de bibliographie philosophique,* 2 v. (Paris 1956) 1:476–490. I. M. BOCHEŃSKI, *Contemporary European Philosophy,* tr. D. NICHOLL and K. ASCHENBRENNER (Berkeley 1956). Copleston v.7. H. LÜBBE, LexThK² 7:911–913; RGG³ 4:1421–25. K. VORLÄNDER, *Kant und sein Einfluss auf das deutsche Denken* (2d ed. Bielefeld 1922). A. DENEFFE, *Kant und die katholische Wahrheit* (Freiburg 1922). **Illustration credits:** German Information Center, New York.

[A. R. CAPONIGRI]

NEO-LATIN LITERATURE

By Neo-Latin literature is meant the great mass of writing produced by authors of the *Renaissance, *baroque, and modern periods (from c. 1300 to 1800). It is at its most natural in Italy, but the contributions made in France, the Low Countries, Germany, Poland, Scotland, Hungary, and England (more or less in that order) are likewise significant.

The heterogeneity of authors (aristocrats, tailors' sons, adventurers, bishops, diplomats, professors, littérateurs) is matched by that of the genres themselves: history, science, philosophy, biography, drama, the essay, the novel, epic, lyric, satire, pastoral, verse-epistle, the elegy—all these and more are represented in vast profusion.

This literature is cosmopolitan and international—books written in Latin at Rome might be published at Lyons, sold in Amsterdam, and read in London.

PROSE

The prose writing of the period characterized as Neo-Latin demands prior attention for its sheer bulk, if for no other reason. As a matter of convenience, it is here discussed under the following categories: history, philosophy, correspondence, oratory, and other forms.

Historical Writing. Modern historical writing began in Renaissance Latin literature: for the first time since *Ammianus examination of cause and effect, based on the study of primary sources, replaced the mere chronicle. At the same time rhetoric became a pronounced element in historical style: as the humanists modeled their style in essays and letters on Cicero, so too they modeled their historical style on Livy (for long works) or Sallust (for brief monographs).

One of the earliest and most famous of such historical works is the *Historia populi Florentini* of Leonardo *Bruni, papal secretary and later chancellor of Florence. It is a careful, unprejudiced account (from 80 B.C. to A.D. 1402) based on conscientious use of the Florentine archives, informed (like many Renaissance histories) with a strong republican feeling. Its style is Livian—clear, colorful, fluent, and readable. Bruni's *Rerum suo tempore gestorum commentarius* is a Sallustian monograph on the events of the period from 1378 to 1444; its most remarkable passage is that describing the bloody massacre at the Milvian Bridge in Rome (1402).

Another historian of Florence was *Poggio Bracciolini, who, like Bruni, was a papal secretary and later chancellor of Florence. His *Historia Florentina,* though not a monograph, covers only the events from 1350 to 1455. Poggio was both more and less a historian than Bruni: he gave more intimate details but was far less

interested either in annalistic completeness or in constitutional development.

Venice received its due in the huge but incomplete *Rerum Venetarum Decades* of Marcantonio Sabellico (1436–1506). While Sabellico was aware of the importance of evaluating sources, his skill in their use was not so marked as Bruni's or Poggio's.

Also worthy of note is the brilliant Sallustian monograph of Angelo Poliziano (1454–94), entitled *Coniuratio Pactiana.* It recounts the *Pazzi plot to murder Lorenzo the Magnificent and his brother at Mass; it is one of the minor masterpieces of the Renaissance Latin literature of Italy.

The best-known Latin history produced in the British Isles is the *Historia Scotorum* of George *Buchanan, greatest of the 16th-century Scottish humanists and a Latin poet of force and originality. The book (which in Buchanan's own words, aimed at ridding Scottish history of "Inglis lyis" and "Scottis vanitie" alike) remained the standard history of Scotland until the end of the 18th century.

The enormous *Historia sui temporis* of Jacques de *Thou, diplomat, scholar, and man of the world, deals with the years 1543 to 1584 in no less than 138 books. It is unquestionably the most important historical work produced in France during the 16th century. De Thou's connection with the royal court of Henry III and Henry IV and with men of eminence in France and elsewhere gave him access to confidential documents of all sorts; of these he made thorough and expert use.

Philosophy. Among philosophers, three groups are clearly discernible: one evincing a purely humanistic interest in philosophy, with strong emphasis on Stoic ethics; another devoted to *Platonism; and a third that continued the medieval tradition of *Aristotelianism.

Most typical of the first group is Francesco *Petrarch, who opposed *Averroism, dialectic, and natural philosophy, and fostered an educational ideal compounded of the eloquence of Cicero, the sobriety of *Stoicism, and the piety of *Augustinianism.

The Neoplatonist movement is associated with the Medici entourage at Florence. They were repelled not only by the practical aims of the humanists but also by the scientific approach of the Neo-Aristotelians. The Neoplatonists opposed both extremes with an eclectic amalgam of Platonism and Christianity. Their intention was to produce neither the man of the world nor the scientist, but the devout intellectual.

Most influential of the Neoplatonists was Marsilio *Ficino. Certain that total harmony existed between Platonism and Christianity, he devoted a lifetime to the elucidation of Christian doctrine by means of Platonic concepts. Ficino quite literally believed that Plato had been divinely inspired; the study of the Platonic dialogues was not merely a matter, then, of literary or antiquarian or intellectual interest, but a Christian duty.

The Neo-Aristotelianism of the Renaissance was not (as in the Middle Ages) the basis for the study of logic, natural philosophy, and theology, but formed the foundation of the natural sciences (especially medicine) and mathematics: it is natural and significant that Alessandro Achillini was equally famous as anatomist and Aristotelian.

But as *Neoplatonism became increasingly influential, its attacks on Neo-Aristotelianism became more powerful. As a result, Neo-Aristotelians tended to concentrate more and more on the ethical implications of their studies and on creating an original philosophy that would emphasize personal values and yet be in accord with the rapidly emerging natural sciences. This aim is notable from the time of Pietro *Pomponazzi. The purpose was, clearly, to fight the Neoplatonists with some of their own weapons without relinquishing the secular basis of Neo-Aristotelianism.

Correspondence. Among forms of prose in Neo-Latin literature, one of the most important and rewarding is correspondence. Newsletters were written in Latin for international circulation (the *Mercurius Gallo-Belgicus* is a well-known example), but these were too general in nature and too exclusively political in content to be satisfactory. The result was that Renaissance men of letters corresponded with friends in their own and other countries with energy, persistence, and fluency: nothing else in all the literatures of Europe gives a clearer picture of the unity resulting from a common training, common interests, and the use of a common international language. No one, perhaps, was more skilled in the use of that language, no one was more cosmopolitan, than the Italianate Dutch Anglophile Desiderius *Erasmus of Rotterdam, whose letters fill 12 large octavo volumes.

Petrarch's collection is one of the largest and most important. This collection appears in groups: the *Familiar Letters,* the *Various Letters,* the *Letters of His Old Age,* and the *Untitled Letters.* Petrarch tells us that he destroyed over 1,000 letters that he considered below standard; for all that, the total number of letters in the four collections far exceeds the number of Cicero's.

As has often been pointed out, Petrarch was the first man since the fall of Rome to leave, in this way, a detailed account of his life and times. Some of the best-known passages in Petrarch's voluminous works occur in the letters: his famous description of his home and garden at Vaucluse, the narrative of his visit to Mount Vesuvius, and that of his ascent of Mount Ventoux with his brother Gherardo. The first of these is often quoted to illustrate Petrarch's modern love for natural scenery.

The letters of Coluccio *Salutati, chancellor of Florence, are not so numerous as Petrarch's; even so, they run to 25 books. They are even more important than Petrarch's as source materials for social and political history, though less interesting as literary works: they are frequently written in medieval officialese.

The letters of Bruni are extant in 10 books. They were famous during the 15th century for the excellence of their style, and are still worth reading for lively descriptions of cities and country estates and for acute, and often amusing, comments on life and character and narratives of travel.

Poggio is the most striking figure in Neo-Latin literature during the first half of the 15th century. His are the liveliest letters imaginable, and the topics of some are well known to everyone who has ever dipped into the literature of humanism: the burning of the Hussite *Jerome of Prague in 1416 at Constance, public baths in Germany, German drunkenness, discoveries of classical manuscripts in German monasteries, and the like. The entire collection is marked by a vigor and urbanity quite unparalleled in the earlier period of humanism.

One of the most extensive collections (37 books) of letters is that of the man who "combined the accomplishments of a scholar with the insidiousness and bru-

tality of a brigand," Francesco *Filelfo. For the history of Italian education and of classical scholarship they are of considerable importance, for Filelfo taught at almost every major center of learning in Italy and described his experience in detail. Scores of purely personal letters discuss Filelfo's hopes for new appointments, the amount of his salary in successive posts, the financial difficulties caused by the princely manner in which he lived, his violent quarrels, his insolent demands on patrons for money, and much more. These letters are violent and crude, but never dull, pious, or prosaic.

Neo-Latin literature includes also the letters of Enea Silvio Piccolomini of Siena (1405–64). After a busy life of public service and private pleasure, Piccolomini turned to the Church in 1447, and became Pope *Pius II in 1458. His Latin writings fill a large folio volume; to the modern reader the most interesting are the *Commentarii* (an account of his own times), a history of Bohemia in the style of Livy, a comedy (*Chrysis*) in the manner of Terence, and above all the letters (1431–54), which fill four large volumes in the *Österreichischen Geschichtsquellen,* ed. R. Wolkan (Vienna 1909–20). Quite apart from their usefulness as primary sources of history, they also contain innumerable passages in which a remarkably cool observer describes the character and analyzes the motives of Europe's most important personages.

We now come to three of the most famous humanists of the 15th century—Ficino, Poliziano, and Giovanni *Pico della Mirandola. The correspondence of Ficino runs to 375 folio pages of small print. Many of the letters are brief notes to friends reporting the progress of a new book or complaining about a dilatory printer. An astonishingly large number discuss the nature of friendship; such *epistulae amatoriae* are quite common in Renaissance Latin correspondence and almost form a separate literary type.

The second member of this trio, Poliziano, one of the brightest ornaments of both Italian and Neo-Latin literature, wrote letters covering the period from 1487 to 1494. These shed light on the most remarkable period of his career and include letters of consolation, answers to requests for information or help, brief friendly scraps, notes on the progress of new books, views on Latin style and diction. The most famous is that in which he describes the death (1492) of Lorenzo de' Medici; the most attractive is one in which he replies to a precocious young lady named Cassandra Fedele, who had steeled herself to write to the great man.

The third Medicean is Pico, of whom Poliziano wrote, "Upon this man—demigod, rather—Nature bestowed every possible gift. He was tall, well-built, and remarkably handsome. His mind was acute, his memory prodigious, his industry immense. It is hard to tell whether he was more famous for talent or virtue." Unfortunately, only 47 of Pico's letters are extant, and all are rather disappointing: they had been heavily censored by his nephew Gianfrancesco.

No other collection of 16th-century letters gives a more vivid picture of the Rome of *Leo X than that of Cardinal Pietro *Bembo of Venice, notorious as the Ciceronian purist who advised Giacopo Sadoleto to avoid the shoddy Latin (*nugae*) of the Vulgate. Undoubtedly, Bembo's purism has been exaggerated. He loved the times in which he lived, and spent a happy and successful career within the Church.

His friend, Aonius Palearius (1503–70), ended his life at the stake as a heretic. Of Palearius's four books of letters, some give news of mutual friends, some return thanks for favors done, some report on his reading; the most characteristic are those that give us information on the administration of Lucca (a strong center of the Italian reform movement).

Oratory. An extensive field of Renaissance Latin literature was that of oratory; the spoken word was more important, when books were rare and newspapers nonexistent, than it is now. Latin speeches abound in all periods of the Renaissance, but they are especially common during the 15th century: we still possess complimentary flourishes addressed to visiting prelates or princelings, university addresses delivered at the beginning of a course on, say, Vergil, congratulations to a pope on his accession, set discourses on philosophical topics, funeral orations, marriage orations, orations published as open letters, and so on. A few are important for historical, literary, or other reasons; the vast majority, however, were occasional and ephemeral.

A typical collection of speeches appears in the first third of the *Orationes clarorum virorum*, published at Venice in 1559. In the first 53 *folia* are 15 complimentary addresses; none is of much importance, it is true, but all are well written and fairly interesting to read. An excellent example is the speech delivered by Bernardo *Giustiniani on the accession (1471) of Sixtus IV: it is a piece of excellent classical Latin prose; it has, furthermore, considerable historical importance, for amid all the compliments appears much detailed information on the political and military position of Europe in the 1450s and early 1460s.

The remainder of the same volume is devoted to 16 funeral orations, a form of oratory little suited to modern tastes. It is true that such speeches contain information hard to find elsewhere and, in so far as style is concerned, are irreproachable; but the eulogies pall and grow wearisome. Practically all those that are extant follow a rigid pattern. Poggio's third, for instance, runs as follows: (1) introduction, (2) birth and early training of Niccolo de' Niccoli, (3) general panegyric, (4) specific panegyric, (5) cause of death, (6) peroration. The same scheme appears in Giambattista Giraldi's oration on Pope Innocent VIII; Marcantonio Sabellico's on Zaccaria *Barbaro; and Celio Calcagnini's orations on Beatrice of Hungary, Ippolito d'*Este, Alfonso d'Este, and Ercole *Strozzi.

Eight marriage orations appear among the twenty extant speeches of Filelfo. These *orationes nuptiales* have a highly stylized form, well illustrated in Filelfo's third. It contains (1) a panegyric of the honorable state of matrimony, (2) famous wives of antiquity, (3) panegyric of the bride's family, (4) panegyric of the groom's family, (5) peroration. Few marriage orations are of any interest at all.

More important than this sort of writing is the oration *On the Dignity of Man* by Pico: this work "contains ideas that are of major importance in the thought of Pico and in the thought of the Renaissance" (Kristeller). The fundamental doctrines of Pico, as expressed in the *De hominis dignitate* and elaborated in subsequent works, are four: (1) *humanism is in no way a repudiation of the thought of the Middle Ages; (2) knowledge is a unity, so that the only road to truth lies through a vast effort of syncretism; (3) every philosophic and every religious doctrine contains a secret, esoteric teaching; (4) all earlier religions and philosophies merely adumbrate Christianity.

Of real importance are some of the orations delivered at the beginning of an academic year at universities— Philipp *Melanchthon's are worth the attention even of modern pedagogues.

Other Forms. There are at least a dozen other highly developed forms of Renaissance Latin prose, which can only be mentioned in passing: works of invective, such as those of *Scaliger; philosophical dialogues, such as those of Jacopo *Sadoleto; satirical dialogues, such as those of Leone Battista *Alberti; biographies, such as those of Paolo Giovio; innumerable pamphlets, broadsides, and essays on a huge variety of subjects; works of literary theory or criticism, such as those of Lilio Gregorio Giraldi; volumes on legal and political theory, such as those of Jean *Bodin; works on pedagogy, such as those of *Comenius; works on every contemporary aspect of physical science, such as those of *Copernicus, *Brahe, and *Kepler; antiquarian treatises, such as those of Flavius *Blondus; and encyclopedic works from Guglielmo da Pastrengo's in the 14th century to Daniel Georg Morhof's in the 17th. To list all the materials available for study in these fields would produce a major bibliographical monograph.

DRAMA

The first true plays of modern Europe were the comedies and tragedies of the Renaissance Latinists. Although the tradition of Latin drama was not so important nor so continuous in Renaissance Latin literature as that of other genres the amount of drama produced was still impressive.

Comedy. The earliest humanist comedy was the *Philologia* of Petrarch, no longer extant: in writing to Cardinal Giovanni *Colonna, Petrarch called it a work of his extreme youth. It was, no doubt, modeled on the Latin comedies of Terence, but beyond that one can say little about it.

Much later Pier Paolo *Vergerio tried his hand at comedy with a play called *Paulus* (c. 1390): Plautus was the model for this play, and, considering the morals of some of the characters, it is astonishing that Vergerio should have described the play as being written "to improve the character."

A clearer moral aim appeared in the *Poliscene* of Bruni, written about 1395. The conventionality of the plot did not prevent the author from displaying a good Latin style, a certain amount of comic suspense, and effective wit.

Better known today (at least by name) is the *Philodoxus* of Leone Battista Alberti, a tour de force attributed by its youthful author to a nonexistent writer of antiquity called Lepidus; it was not until much later that the hoax was uncovered. The plot is the standard "boy-meets-girl" story in ancient form; as in *Paulus* there is grossness, and situations for which the kindest word would be "ambiguous."

The *Chrysis* of Piccolomini was not intended to improve the character of its audience. Its purpose was to amuse the cultivated humanist who had read Terence and Plautus and was aware that life is not always conducted on simple moral principles.

The comedies mentioned so far have been individual *jeux d'esprit*—the authors in question tried their hands at a single play, perhaps experimentally, and then passed on to other interests. Tito Livio de' Frulovisi (c. 1400–60), however, wrote no less than six comedies, thereby earning the title of the first modern playwright.

Latin comedy flourished elsewhere in Europe: in the first half of the 16th century primarily in Germany and the Low Countries, and here the most famous name is Macropedius (Georg van Langeveldt, 1475–1558), whose 12 plays reveal sharp observation of human frailty, much bourgeois realism, and considerable *vis comica*. It is evident that the plots of many of his plays were derived from Teutonic folklore.

In the second half of the 16th century the chief center for Latin comedy was the University of *Cambridge. Here plays employed the plot of intrigue characteristic of Greco-Roman New Comedy; these, too, presented stock characters again and again. More important elements were the characteristically insular and English flavor, and the clear influence of Italian vernacular comedies. Some of these plays have more than historical interest: the anonymous *Laelia* (1594)—a Neo-Latin *Twelfth Night*—is highly entertaining.

Tragedy. Modern tragedy in the vernacular did not develop until the late Renaissance, and then in only a few countries. The Neo-Latin tragedians, though seldom successful, did, at least, prepare the way by anticipating the models, the themes, and the errors of vernacular dramatists.

The earliest modern tragedy was the Latin *Ecerinis* of Albertino Mussato of Padua (1261–1329), a work for which the author was crowned poet laureate when Petrarch was still only 10 years old. The play is modeled, understandably, on Seneca: rhetoric and declamation, blood and horror permeate it; but the Senecan skill in construction and care for unity of effect are present also. The *Ecerinis* is based on the life and incredible cruelties of Ezzelino III of Padua, and is the first of many Neo-Latin tragedies drawing on contemporary personalities and events.

Cambridge produced tragedy as well as comedy. The best-known play here was the *Ricardus Tertius* of Thomas Legge (1535–1607), a typically Senecan work filled with violence and crime. Marlowe and Greene almost certainly knew the play, and it is possible that Shakespeare had read it: the famous wooing scene in *Richard the Third* is not mentioned in Holinshed, but appears in *Ricardus Tertius*.

Biblical Drama. A remarkable aspect of Renaissance Latin literature was the suddenly appearing Latin Biblical drama of the 16th century, especially in the Low Countries and Germany. The great majority of the plays were written by Protestants and almost every Protestant religious playwright was a propagandist.

Two names are especially memorable—those of the Scottish George Buchanan and the German Nicodemus Frischlin (1547–1590). In 1542, while teaching at the Collège de Guyenne, Buchanan produced, for the edification of his pupils, a Latin Biblical drama Senecan in tone but Greek in structure: the Greek form is natural, since the story of Jephtha's daughter bears a close resemblance to that of Iphigenia. The *Jephtha* acquired contemporary fame, but for the modern reader it has little interest. The case is different with the plays of Frischlin. They are vivid dramatic sketches or scenes rather than full-blown *pièces de théâtre;* but the characterization is lively, the dialogue interesting, and the

structure neat. They are anti-Catholic, and were intended for the edification of Frischlin's pupils.

POETRY

The mass of Neo-Latin poetry extant is formidable. Much of it can be dismissed as nothing more than verse composition; but there remains a large body of verse distinguished by variety and quality: Giovanni Quatrario appears at the lower end of the scale, and Giovanni Pontano at the higher.

The great number of Neo-Latin poets and versifiers of the Renaissance and later periods confined themselves to forms of poetry devised by the ancients. Naturally, there was much experimentation within the limits of these forms, but no example anywhere of any major new development. The poets confined themselves to the lyric in its various forms, to various types of heroic (i.e., hexameter) poetry, and to the many varieties of occasional verse. In all these forms the care devoted to style and versification was prodigious.

Lyric. Today we use the term lyric often for fairly brief love poems; among Greeks and Romans, however, lyric poetry developed three distinct forms—choric, personal (melic), and elegiac.

Choric. This form is represented in Greek by the elaborate odes of Pindar. It rarely appears in Latin literature except in the choruses of early tragedy and again in those of Seneca, in both places in attenuated form. Personal lyric appears in Greek in the fragments of Alcaeus and Sappho; in Latin, in Catullus and (especially) Horace. The occasional and reflective lyric, written in the elegiac meter, appears in Greek at its best and worst in the *Greek Anthology;* in Latin it reached its zenith in the poetry of Propertius, Tibullus, and Ovid.

The Neo-Latinists observed the practice of the Romans: choric lyric on the grand scale appears only in drama, personal lyric is well represented, and elegiac poetry is enormously popular.

Personal Lyric. One of the earliest collections of personal lyric is the posthumous *Odes* of Filelfo, who firmly believed that his Latin style was superior to that of the ancients; his odes are, in fact, vigorous, but bombastic and awkward.

In the eight books of poems by Giovanni Antonio Campano (1429–77), the majority are elegiac and occasional; but the slighter personal lyric is not neglected: hendecasyllabic poems, for example, present us with a pleasant series of "nothings by Sylvanus Urban."

The 18 amatory hendecasyllabic poems that appear in the *Epigrammata* of Michele Marullo (1453–1500) form an attractive lyric sequence addressed to an early sweetheart called Neaera. Whether Neaera was real hardly matters, any more than does the actual existence of objects of the Elizabethan love songs. Equally pleasant are the brief poems in hendecasyllabics, Asclepiadeans, and iambics addressed to a variety of friends and enemies.

With Giovanni Pontano of Naples (c. 1424–1503) we come to one of the most famous names in Renaissance Latin literature. His brief personal lyrics are of three types—amatory poems, brief but formal literary odes, and poems addressed to his friends and family; these are in the *Parthenopaeus, Hendecasyllabi, Iambici,* and *Lyra.* His Latin verse, modeled though it is on classical types, has its own characteristic flavor. In the amatory poems of the *Hendecasyllabi* there is a vivid picture of the freedom of manners at the holiday resort called Baia; the place had a reputation for being licentious even in Cicero's day. But Pontano's Latin Muse is seldom lewd and frequently the verse is graceful.

The formal odes are less attractive: the panegyrics of Alfonso of Aragon in *Lyra* 7 and 10 are closer to Pontano's heart than to the modern reader's. *Lyra* 3 and 4 are lyric versions of a theme recurrent in Pontano and Sannazaro alike—the praise of nymphs in various beautiful scenes around Naples.

The poems addressed to friends are, naturally, miscellaneous in content. Pontano sympathizes with a contemporary on his advancing years, invites friends to dinner on St. Martin's Day, congratulates Marullo on gaining the affections of a girl he calls Septimilla. None is of great importance, but all are pleasant to read.

A descendant of an old Florentine family was Ercole Strozzi of Ferrara (1481–1508), son of an even more famous father, Tito Vespasiano Strozzi. Almost all Ercole's verses are in the hexameter or elegiac meters; but a fair number of poems appear in hendecasyllabics, iambics, Sapphics, and Asclepiadeans. Many of these are ephemeral bits and pieces: the poet praises the artfulness of Luigi Pittori's Latin epigrams, flatters Alfonso d'Este and Lucrezia *Borgia, and the like. More important than all of these is a sequence of eight religious odes on the Virgin Mary and Christ; the Sapphic ode *In gloriosam Virginem,* with which the series ends, is a sincere hymn of praise.

There are many other excellent Italian Neo-Latinists, such as Giano Anisio, Giovanni Cotta, Celio Calcagnini, Francesco Maria Molza, Giambattista Giraldi, Giambattista Pigna, and Elio Giulio Crotti. Of the scores of Neo-Latin poets outside Italy, Johannes Secundus, George Buchanan, Paulus Melissus, and Jakob *Balde deserve special notice.

Of all the poems of Johannes Secundus (1511–36), the Low Countries' major Neo-Latin poet, the Horatian *Odes* are the least known—quite undeservedly, since they contain many a striking phrase or well-knit stanza. The formal, courtly odes are elaborate, resounding, and dignified, without any of the pompousness and turgidity that Filelfo would have thought proper to their occasions. The reflective odes are attractive and especially Horatian; the best, perhaps, is the Alcaic ninth, addressed to Pierre Bausan.

These poems, although excellent, have been overshadowed by the famous lyric sequence called *Kisses,* a work that has found a huge number of imitators among both Latin and vernacular poets: Pierre de *Ronsard, Lazare de Baïf, and Kasimierz *Sarbiewski imitated individual poems, while Remy Belleau, Jean Dorat, and Gervais Sepin wrote whole sequences called *Kisses, Glances, Sighs,* and the like. The collection— addressed to Neaera, a blonde courtesan whom the poet had met in Spain in 1534—consists of 19 short poems in a variety of meters, a cycle describing 19 varieties of kiss from the most chaste to the most voluptuous.

Buchanan is, as earlier noted, Scotland's best-known Neo-Latinist. Even Samuel Johnson regarded Buchanan's poetry as one of the great achievements of Renaissance Latin literature; earlier, Scaliger the Younger had called him the greatest Latinist in Europe, and Wordsworth considered one of Buchanan's lyric poems "equal in sentiment if not in elegance to anything in Horace."

The best-known of German writers of Latin lyric is Paulus Melissus of Franconia (1539–1602). His *Emmetra* is unique in Neo-Latin literature as one of the very few attempts (aside from tragedy) at choral or Pindaric lyric on a grand scale. One of the poems, *Ad Rosinam,* is a startling but courageous attempt to employ choral lyric in amatory poetry. The *Melica* consists of the more conventional sort of personal lyric.

There is space only to mention the Jesuit poet Jakob Balde of Alsace, a true baroque virtuoso; as an example of virtuosity his work has few equals in Neo-Latin literature. His meters are Horatian and his themes equally so. He is at his best in such a reflective lyric as *Bona Mens* (The Clear Conscience), in which form, diction, and theme are all Horatian; the poem is not a cento of platitudes, but an honest statement of firmly held belief.

Elegiac. The third form of lyric is elegiac. The elegiac couplet is often employed for a whole sequence of poems in which the poet narrates the course of a real or imaginary love affair. The situations are conventional and Ovidian, but may be varied ad libitum.

In Cristoforo Landino (1424–1504) we meet another member of the Florentine school of Neoplatonists, author of an elegiac sequence of poems addressed to a woman called Sandra. Landino first saw her in Rome in 1443 and describes how he was overwhelmed by her beauty. The sequence develops along conventional lines, often in a frigid manner; at no time does any poem overstep the bounds of the strictest propriety, for Sandra was in all probability the wife of a prominent member of the Medici family: Landino's pose of the adoring lover was a courtly gesture only.

Still another Florentine poet was Alessandro Braccesi (1445–1503) whose *Amores* was dedicated to Guido da Montefeltro. The love sequence dealing with a girl named Flora, is similar to Landino's *Xandra,* but considerably more elaborate. In 30 poems, many rather too long, Braccesi tells the usual tale of ups and downs from the lover's first sight of his lady to the final separation.

Outside Italy the only important elegiac love sequences are those of the German Conrad *Celtis and the Belgian Johannes Secundus. The four books of Celtis's *Amores* constitute four cycles, with four apparently real heroines. Book 1 is devoted to an affair with a Polish girl of Cracow named Hasilina, book 2 to an affair with the venal Elsula of Nürnberg; in book 3 Celtis is in Mainz with Ursula, in book 4 in Lübeck with Barbara. There is much Ovidian reminiscence, but it is noticeable also how much is derived from Italian Neo-Latin models. Yet Celtis's work is not wholly derivative.

In 1531 or 1534 Johannes Secundus met and fell in love with a brunette beauty of Malines named Julia. There can be little doubt of Julia's effect on the poet's emotions. Even though the situations described are entirely conventional, Secundus writes with a fervor and sincerity that carry conviction: the third poem should be read by anyone dubious of the intrinsic value of Renaissance Latin literature.

From the earliest days of the 15th century to the latest of the 17th, Neo-Latin poets and versifiers poured forth an endless succession of volumes of miscellaneous elegiac poems, usually entitled *Poemata, Carmina, Elegiae,* or, more often, *Sylvae.* Individual love poems appear by the hundred, as do poems on the poets' lives, feelings, circumstances, and hopes. More and more commonly, too, as the 16th and 17th centuries progressed, a poet would gradually build up a collection of epigrams, usually of one or two elegiac distichs. Here the most famous name is that of John Owen (1560–1622), one of the last authors to publish exclusively in Latin.

Heroic. The heroic hexameter, although commonly associated with the epic, is sufficiently flexible to be employed for a number of different sorts of serious poems. These may be briefly noted as the epic itself, occasional poems, verse epistles, philosophical poems, didactic verses, verse satires, and pastoral verses.

In epic proper Petrarch's long heroic poem *Africa*, on Scipio's defeat of Hannibal, is more often adversely criticized than read. Its Latinity and versification are faulty. The poem as a whole is pedestrian and pompous; but there are episodes that read well in excerpt and possess a certain dignity.

A far better Latin poet than Petrarch was Mapheus *Vegius. As a youth of 20 he composed a remarkable supplement to Vergil's *Aeneid*. He attempted a brief epic of approximately 500 lines on the conversion of St. Anthony and also *Vellus Aureum (Golden Fleece)*. Vegius achieved a fine fluent hexameter and a convincing manner.

Basinio de' Basini (1425–57) is almost unreadable. His *Hesperis* (13 books, in 6,948 hexameters) relates the life and exploits of Sigismondo Pandolfo Malatesta of Rimini, and is marred by almost every sort of fault to which the epic form is liable.

Even less enthralling are three epics by Baptista Mantuanus (1448–1516)—a seemingly interminable theological epic called *Alfonsus*, a 5,000-line poem called *The Victory of Gonzaga* celebrating Francesco Gonzaga's defeat of the French in 1495, and another 5,000-line poem called *Agelaria,* which traces the history of the family of Hernando Consalvo (*el gran capitán*).

The *De Partu Virginis (The Virgin Birth)* of Jacopo *Sannazaro is the first epic so far mentioned that is worth reading in its entirety for its own sake. This is a little epic, arranged in three books and extending to only 1,443 lines. Sannazaro's inveterate paganism permeates it. It is true that among the Italian Neo-Latinists this poet writes the most limpid verse; but the incessant use of pagan elements is incongruous in a Biblical setting.

The accusation of excessive Vergilianism has frequently been leveled at the *Christiad* of Marco Girolamo *Vida. But we must judge Vida by the standards and practice of his own century (and of almost every century except the 20th); moreover, we cannot condemn him for imitation of Vergil in one breath, and in the next breath praise Milton for even more palpable imitation, not only of Vergil, but of Vida himself.

Occasional Verse. Of the many occasional (commemorative) uses of the hexameter, four dominate, namely, epithalamium, genethliacon, epicedium, and panegyric.

A typical epithalamium is a 260-line poem by Gabriele Altilio (*c.* 1440–1501), celebrating the wedding of Giangaleazzo *Sforza of Milan and Isabella, daughter of Alfonso II of Naples. Although Altilio is not a first-rate poet, he stands high in the second rank: he displays skill, taste, and refinement; his command of Latin is extensive and exact; his diction, although a little affected, is always precise.

A characteristic genethliacon is a poem of 251 hexameters addressed by Johann Stigel (1515–62) to the infant son of Johann Friedrich II of Saxony and Duchess Elizabeth. The poet congratulates the parents of the child, describes the christening ceremonies, the knightly combats celebrating the birth, and the rustic merrymaking in the Saxon villages, concluding with a prophecy of the golden age that will arise with the child's coming of age.

Typical of epicedia are two poems composed by Strozzi on the deaths of Cesare Borgia and his own father; both poems are lugubrious and panegyrical.

The panegyric proper is sometimes interesting and more lively. There are scores from which one might choose, but it will be enough to mention one, that of the Prussian Albert Voigt (*fl.* 1580). His *Mauricius,* extending to 2,467 hexameters, is violently anti-Catholic in tone, dealing largely with the Spanish conquest of the Netherlands. Much of the vituperation derives from Juvenal, and the work is as much hymn of hate as it is panegyric of Prince Maurice of Nassau.

Verse Epistle. More interesting and significant than these largely ephemeral poems is the verse epistle, modeled on the *Epistulae* of Horace. Of the *Epistulae metricae* of Petrarch, one critic said that if they had been written in Italian, they would long ago have been recognized generally as one of Petrarch's most important works. The three books contain 67 verse letters addressed to 36 different people: those most frequently addressed are Petrarch's generous patron, Cardinal Giovanni Colonna, the courtier Marco Barbato of Sulmoa and Naples, the soldier Giovanni Barrili of Naples, Cardinal d'Aube, and the polymath Guglielmo da Pastrengo; oddly, only one letter is addressed to Boccaccio. The themes are similar to those of the prose letters—public affairs, ethics, the nature of poetry, and personal matters. The largest group consists of poems of autobiographical interest.

Philosophical Poetry. A fair number of Neo-Latin philosophical poems, written in the manner of Lucretius, are extant, some of more than antiquarian interest.

Of particular note is the *Zodiac of Life* of Marcellus Palingenius (i.e., Pier Angelo Manzolli; *c.* 1500–43), a crypto-Protestant of Ferrara; when the book was posthumously published in 1549, the poet's body was exhumed and burned as a heretic's. Manzolli's pessimism had led him to deny not the existence, but the eternal happiness of the soul. To most modern readers the most important parts of this long poem are those passages of virulent satire directed against contemporary life and manners. A similar poem is the *Immortality of the Soul* of Aonius Palearius. More orthodox in content are the *Principles of Nature* of Scipione Capece (d. 1562) and the *Garden of Philosophy* of Basilio Zanchi (1501–58).

Didactic Verse. In didactic verse the Neo-Latin poets, particularly the Italians, reached a standard seldom achieved before and probably never approached since. No subject was too unlikely for these venturesome poets; and although some of the resulting works are worthless, there are many that should not be brushed aside without consideration.

Three of the major works of Pontano are didactic. The *Urania* deals in a Lucretian manner with the heavenly bodies' influence on the earth and their alleged influence on human life; the verses are enlivened by digression and myth, simile and metaphor, and a great many contemporary allusions and references. The *Meteora* (on weather) is what the title suggests. The *Garden of the Hesperides* (on the growing of oranges and lemons) is the pleasantest of the earlier Italian didactic poems.

Probably the best didactic poems ever produced in Italy are a group by Vida. The early *Game of Chess* (1513?) is a witty and entertaining work. More thoroughly didactic are *The Silkworm* (1524?) and *The Art of Poetry* (1527); the latter found a brilliant translator in Christopher Pitt (1725).

Didactic poetry flourished outside Italy throughout the 16th and 17th centuries, and includes Tycho Brahe's *Urania,* Buchanan's *Sphaera,* Scévole de Sainte-Marthe's *Paedotrophia,* Nathan Chytraeus's *Mundus,* and Du Fresnoy's *Geographia.*

Satire. Satire is less widely represented in Neo-Latin literature than one would have expected. Characteristic are the 100 satires (each of 100 lines) of Filelfo. The first poem (*Sat.* 1.1), like Juvenal's first, is a raucous declaration of war on immorality, cruelty, and fraud. Another, *Sat.* 1.6, is a bitter sneer at a contemporary whom Filelfo calls "Nicholas Nobody," a poem almost as virulent as those (2.3; 5.7) directed at Poggio. Attacks on monks satirize their ambition (5.3), superstition (3.4), and immorality (2.5). The immorality of women is attacked in *Sat.* 1.9, that of men in *Sat.* 4.2. Some of the satires are ethical (1.4; 4.7–8). The poems cited represent the perennial themes of Neo-Latin satire.

Pastoral. Pastoral poetry, largely but not exclusively modeled on Vergil's *Eclogues,* represents the most popular literary vogue of Neo-Latin poetry. Between 1300 and 1800, over 200 Neo-Latinists wrote from 1 to 20 eclogues apiece; a complete anthology would fill over 3,000 octavo pages. Amid the hundreds of pastorals extant, it is found that the old genre developed new forms (the fisherman's eclogue, the sailor's eclogue, etc.) and new uses (e.g., satirical eclogue, humorous eclogue, religious eclogue); and it could be used as a medium to celebrate public events, rejoice over personal good fortune, or lament personal losses.

Conclusion. The abundance, vitality, and variety of Neo-Latin literature is astonishing, and the number of literary genres represented (the above discussion mentions only a few) no less so. Authors were men who took an active part in the development of political, religious, philosophical, literary, and pedagogical ideas all over Europe. This literature is thus international in interest and its history is continuous from the early 14th century to the close of the baroque age.

Bibliography: G. TIRABOSCHI, *Storia della letteratura italiana,* 9 v. (2d ed. Modena 1787–94). P. A. BUDIK, *Leben und Wirken der vorzüglichsten lateinischen Dichter des 15.–18. Jahrhunderts,* 3 v. (Vienna 1828). D. BUCHANAN, *De scriptoribus Scotis,* ed. D. IRVING (Edinburgh 1837). F. A. ECKSTEIN, *Nomenclator philologorum* (Leipzig 1871). L. MÜLLER, *Geschichte der klassischen Philologie in den Niederlanden* (Leipzig 1869). G. VOIGT, *Die Wiederbelebung des classischen Alterthums,* ed. M. LEHNERDT, 2 v. (3d ed. Berlin 1893). W. PÖKEL, *Philologisches Schriftsteller-Lexikon* (Leipzig 1882). G. MANACORDA, *Della poesia latina in Germania durante il Rinascimento* (Rome 1906). Sandys 2. A. SCHROETER, *Beiträge zur Geschichte der neulateinischen Poesie Deutschlands und Hollands* (Berlin 1909). G. BOTTIGLIONI, *La lirica latina in Firenze nella seconda metà del secolo xv* (Pisa 1913). A. SAINATI, *La lirica latina del rinascimento* (Pisa 1919). G. ELLINGER, *Geschichte der neulateinischen Literatur Deutschlands im 16. Jahrhundert,* 3 v. (Berlin and Leipzig 1929–33). G. BERTONI, "Umanisti Portoghesi," *Giornale storico della letteratura italiana* 114 (1939) 46–49. L. BRADNER, *Musae Anglicanae* (New York 1940). D. C. ALLEN, "Latin Literature," *Modern Language Quarterly* 2 (1941) 403–420. P. O. KRISTELLER, *The Philosophy of Marsilio Ficino,* tr. V. CONANT (New York 1943). P. VAN TIEGHEM, "La littérature latine de la Renaissance," *Bibliothèque d'Humanisme et Renaissance* 4 (1944) 177–418. Cosenza DictItHum. L. MARTINES, *The Social World of the Florentine Humanists, 1390–1460* (Princeton 1963). W. L. GRANT, "European Vernacular Works in Latin Translation," *Studies in the Renaissance* 1 (1954) 120–156; *Neo-Latin Literature and the Pastoral* (Chapel Hill 1965).

[W. L. GRANT]

NEO-ORTHODOXY

A Protestant theological movement, originating in the dissent of such men as Karl Barth from the liberal Protestant view of religion (*see* BARTHIANISM). To Barth and his associates, to whose thought the name dialectical, or crisis, theology was first given, religion based on experience is no religion at all. Against the religion of experience, therefore, they invoked those tenets of the Reformation that tend to make the qualitative distance between God and man appear infinite and not susceptible of being overcome.

The "orthodoxy" of these positions, then, consists in adherence to themes such as the incompetence of human reason in attaining knowledge of God. In fact, this noetic armature of the doctrine of man's depravity is the rallying point of this school of thought, with a correlative, the absolute need of divine grace for man's salvation. Theologians of this persuasion emphasize also the inflexibility of God's judgment against sin.

The "new" factors of what typifies neo-orthodoxy consist in methods and emphases either not available to or eschewed by Protestant orthodoxy of the 17th and 18th centuries. Adherents of the latter tended to be fundamentalist in their view of the Biblical text, in contrast to the neo-orthodox, who avail themselves of the benefits of modern criticism in their use of the Bible. Even in strictly doctrinal matters the new school could be called "impressionistic," in the sense that some doctrines of the Reformation receive an entirely personal treatment at their hands, e.g., predestination according to Barth. Neo-orthodoxy, essentially a protest against the humanistic elements that had, to the mind of its proponents, spoiled Protestantism and made it "liberal," is unintelligible outside this context. This accounts, for example, for the tendency among these theologians habitually to express the attributes of God in such a way that every "Yes" is balanced off by an equally emphatic "No."

If reaction against creeping *anthropomorphism, thought by the neo-orthodox to be the malady of liberal Protestantism, is the point of the movement's origin, it is, paradoxically, also the factor of cohesion—for neo-orthodoxy is by no means a single, carefully articulated thought system. Certain names are, to be sure, identified with it, but not with the rigor of a species to its genus. Each of the two major branches of the Reformation is represented among the neo-orthodox. Among the Calvinists, Barth is most characteristically so. In fact, in the spectrum of neo-orthodoxy Barth holds a place quite clearly distinguishable. Distrust of natural theology as a possible path to God and the correlative suspicion of the theological relevance of the analogy of being are epitomized in his thought. The critical freedom with which the neo-orthodox view their progenitors in the Reformation comes to a climax in him too, for it is evident throughout his *Church Dogmatics* that only the Scriptures are, in principle, to be accepted as normative—and this to the exclusion even of the authority of John Calvin. In Barth the transcendent majesty of God and the lightning power of his word are trumpeted to the extent that his critics have questioned the possibility of his putting into true focus the doctrines of reconciliation (justification) and redemption (the term he uses for the final liberation of man in God).

G. Aulén makes the most systematic case for neo-orthodoxy outside the Lutheran tradition (he himself belongs to the school of Lund). What Barth shouts from house tops, however, Aulén, together with others such as E. Brunner, recites in a lower register. The touchstone is the attitude toward the use of reason in gaining knowledge about God. Aulén is not so absolute as Barth; neither is he enamored, however, of any mixing of theology and metaphysics.

P. Tillich and R. Niebuhr are sometimes called neo-orthodox; it appears, however, that America does not have the right climate for purebred orthodoxy. These two theologians, though they evolved with and in the same direction as Barth for some time, finally came to adopt a position whereby theology is seen as exercising a mediating function between the church and the world. In this case it would have to accord reason an important function in the verifying of theological data.

Bibliography: W. M. HORTON, *Christian Theology, an Ecumenical Approach* (rev. and enl. ed. New York 1958). J. MACQUARRIE, *Twentieth Century Religious Thought* (New York 1963).

[M. B. SCHEPERS]

NEOPHYTE, from the Greek νεόφυτος, meaning newly planted, is a term found once in the NT (1 Tm 3.6). It came into use in the Church to designate those newly converted from paganism or from any non-Christian sect, and later, by extension, was applied to those recently admitted to the religious or clerical states. The term in its earlier use contained an obvious allusion to the new planting or engrafting of the convert by Baptism into the Mystical Body of Christ. In the early Church neophytes constituted a relatively more numerous portion of the Church's membership. The disciplinary severity of the times and the need for a more thorough preparation for the duties of the Christian life not only caused the *catechumenate to be prolonged, but also led to the observance of a period of special postbaptismal formation. In the course of time a relatively greater proportion of the faithful were born into the Church and received their early religious formation from infancy. This made a prolonged catechumenate less necessary, and, in fact, with the changing circumstances brought about by the peace of Constantine and the reception of great numbers of converts, it became a practical impossibility. This led, especially in the period of the Christianizing of the Germanic tribes, to a shift in emphasis from pre- to postbaptismal training, and the formation of the neophyte, as distinguished from that of the catechumen, received greater attention (*see* CATECHETICS).

According to the prescription of St. Paul, a neophyte was not to be made a bishop (1 Tm 3.6) because of the moral vulnerability to which he was likely to be subject in consequence of the insufficiency of his formation. The Council of Nicaea (325) extended this prohibition to include ordination to the priesthood, the Council of Sardica (343) to the diaconate, and later custom to the reception of all the Orders and even of tonsure. The status of neophyte was recognized as constituting an impediment to the reception of Orders, and before the Code many canonists regarded it as a true irregularity (*see* HOLY ORDERS). The length of the period during which one is disqualified from the reception of Orders is not specified in law but is left to the judgment of the ordinary.

In missionary countries the need for a postbaptismal period during which the neophyte requires special guidance and formation is recognized (*see* CATECHESIS, MISSIONARY).

Bibliography: H. LECLERCQ, DACL 12.1:1103–07. R. NAZ, DDC 6:997.

[P. K. MEAGHER]

NEOPHYTE (IN THE EARLY CHURCH)

The term used to describe a newly baptized Christian, adapted from St. Paul's reference (1 Tim 3.6) to one "newly planted" (νεόφυτος) in Christ. The use of the word was extended later to describe those newly admitted to the clerical or monastic life (Gregory I, *Epist.;* PL 77:784); and in both senses it passed into CorpIurCan (D.48.1.2). It is also used more generally to refer to someone newly engaged in a particular work or career.

St. Paul cautioned against the laying of hands on neophytes to make them bishops, lest their lack of experience in the faith render them arrogant or deficient; and the Council of *Nicaea I (325) formally condemned the ordination or consecration of a neophyte as an abuse that encouraged clerical ambition or promoted the vanity of the people who desired to have a prominent personage as their bishop. *Jerome (*Ad Oceanum;* PL 22:663), *Gregory of Nazianzus (PG 35:1090), and *Gregory I (PL 77:1030–37) also inveighed against this practice, although during the 4th and 5th centuries there were notable exceptions, such as Ambrose of Milan, Augustine of Hippo, Synesius of Cyrene, and Nestorius of Constantinople.

In the 4th century the term covered catechumens who had put off the reception of Baptism until adulthood and upon being baptized, usually on the vigil of Easter or Pentecost, were clothed in white garments for 8 days, given the *traditio legis Christi,* the kiss of peace (*osculum pacis*), anointed for confirmation, and admitted to reception of the Eucharist.

During the Middle Ages special care was paid to converts who through their change in religion were frequently deprived of position. Richard, the prior of Bermondsey, founded a hospital of converts in 1213; this was imitated by the Dominicans at Oxford, and Henry III established a *domus conversorum* in London for catechumens and neophyte Jews. The Council of *Basel in 1431 prescribed a manner of procedure for neophytes (Mansi 29:99–101). St. *Ignatius of Loyola occasioned the erection of a *casa dei neofiti* at Rome in 1543, and *Gregory XIII built the house still standing near the Church of the Madonna dei Monti for the same purpose (May 20, 1580).

Local councils in the New World prescribed that after their Baptism converts should be given special instructions including the four prayers *Pater, Ave, Credo,* and *Salve Regina* (Conc. of Mexico, 1555,

c. 1; Synod of Quito, 1570). While the first political junta in Mexico (1524) had apparently forbidden the giving of the Eucharist to Indian neophytes even as Viaticum, *Paul III declared that the Indians were true human beings endowed with reason and should be admitted to the Sacraments (*Veritas ipsa*, June 2, 1537), and in 1567 the Council of Lima prescribed the giving of Paschal Communion and Viaticum to the neophytes. A similar problem in India was settled by *Alexander VII (Jan. 18, 1658). In 1645 and 1656 Propaganda declared that the Chinese neophytes were obliged to observe the Church's law concerning the reception of the Sacraments and fasting. In modern missionary work, special care is given to the post-baptismal formation of neophytes.

In the development of Canon Law the status of a neophyte was considered an irregularity (*ex defectu fidei*) for the reception of orders; but the Code treats it as merely a simple impediment (CIC cc.987n6, 542n2).

Bibliography: S. DA ROMALLO and N. KOWALSKY, EncCatt 8:1741–43. P. WESS, LexThK² 7:876. H. LECLERCQ, DACL 12.1: 1103–07. J. SCHMIDLIN, *Catholic Mission Theory*, tr. M. BRAUN (Techny, Ill. 1931).

[J. BEAUDRY]

NEOPLATONISM

In the strict sense, Neoplatonism designates the particular form that *Platonism took on at the end of the ancient era, from the 3d to the 6th centuries after Christ. In a broad sense, it designates the currents of thought before or after this period that offer some analogy with one or other of the characteristics of Platonism at the end of the ancient era. The treatment in this article discusses the place of Neoplatonism in the history of ancient thought, the history of Neoplatonism, and the relationships between Neoplatonism and Christianity.

Characteristics of Neoplatonism. Neoplatonism, taken in the strict sense, exhibits three principal characteristics. First it is an exegesis of Plato's *Dialogues*, coupled with an attempt to systematize even disparate texts by appealing to a hierarchy among levels of reality. Then it is a method of spiritual life. Finally, and notably in the case of *Proclus, it is a pagan theology seeking to systematize, and attain a rational grasp of, the revelations of the gods.

Recent historical studies seem to conclude that these characteristics are not new and that Neoplatonism existed already at the time of ancient Platonism, indeed even during Plato's life. The interpretations of Plato proposed by A. J. Festugière and Léon Robin authorize such a view. Following W. Theiler's discovery of a form of Neoplatonism deriving from Antiochus of Ascalon and Posidonius, C. J. de Vogel and Philip Merlan found in the ancient Academy, i.e., in the works of Aristotle and of Plato himself, the existence of a hierarchy among the levels of reality and the modes of knowledge (the good, the ideas, souls, nature, and matter). Again, the history of allegorical interpretation has shown that pagan theology was also very traditional. Thus what is called Neoplatonism would quite simply be identified with Platonic scholasticism.

Although this view merits serious consideration, it should not obfuscate what is new and irreducible in late Platonism as compared with ancient Platonism, namely, the desire to arrive at complete systematization and absolute internal coherence. During the 2d century, immediately before *Plotinus's work, the philosophical tradition was overburdened with heteroclite and incoherent elements. Even Antiochus of Ascalon added doctrinal elements, borrowed from *Aristotelianism and *Stoicism, to Platonic teaching. Moreover, there was a tendency to merge philosophical syncretism with a religious syncretism that made equal acknowledgement of all revelations capable of providing salvation for the soul. This was the epoch of pagan, Christian, and Jewish *Gnosticism.

Reacting against such a confusion, Plotinus invited man to interior simplification and unification. In this he was heir to Stoicism, which proposed the attainment of spiritual coherence by way of recollection and conversion to the divine Word, immanent in man, as well as in all other things. The immanence of the Word was assured by a total blending or complete interpenetration of the Word and matter.

Neoplatonism thus transferred the spirit of Stoicism to the Platonic universe. Everything is in all: each level of the hierarchy of things contains the whole of possible reality, but under a different aspect. The One contains all things, as do also the Intellect, the Soul, or the sensible world, but each hypostasis contains the whole of reality in its own way. In the One, all things are potentially present; in the Intellect they are compenetrated in an immediate intuition; in the Soul they are unfolded as in rational discourse; in the sensible world, they are mutually exterior, like sensations. The conversion, then, consists in reascending to a mode of knowledge that is even more unitive, in such a way as to arrive at a coincidence, in mystical ecstasy, with the Absolute from which these levels of reality and these modes of knowledge proceed. The system of things and the life of the soul are animated with the same movement of procession and conversion, unfolding and concentration.

History of Neoplatonism. At the beginning of the 3d century, at Alexandria, Plotinus had pursued the courses of Ammonius Saccas, who was the teacher also of *Origen, the Father of the Church. Plotinus was strongly influenced by his teacher and later, in Rome, taught "according to the spirit of Ammonius." In default of precise knowledge of the doctrines professed by Ammonius, Plotinus must remain for us the founder of Neoplatonism, i.e., the movement for interior unification just described.

Porphyry's Influence. With *Porphyry, a disciple of Plotinus and his successor at Rome, a decisive turning point was reached. While preserving the purely Platonic message of his teacher, Porphyry returned to the earlier traditions and held that religious revelations, too, could make the way of salvation known. He is the first known philosopher to comment upon the *Chaldaic Oracles*, a long poem composed during the era of Marcus Aurelius. This pretended to expound a divine revelation that, beside theurgic practices aimed at leading the soul to the heavenly world, proposed a theological system inspired by Platonism and Pythagoreanism. It taught that after a supreme, transcendent God, endowed with intellect and will, came a second God, the Demiurge, and a whole hierarchy of astral divinities. Because of Porphyry's influence, these *Oracles* were to become the bible of Neoplatonism. However, taken literally, their teachings were hardly compatible with the doctrine of Plotinus.

Iamblichus and Proclus. All later Neoplatonism can be defined as an attempt to achieve a systematization among Plotinianism, the *Chaldaic Oracles,* and the *Orphic Hymns.* In opposition to Porphyry, with a view to safeguarding the transcendency of the One (strongly maintained by Plotinus), and by taking account of even the smallest details in the text of the *Oracles,* his successors multiplied the intermediary hypostases and the levels of reality. At the beginning of the 4th century, the Syrian, *Iamblichus, became the initiator of this new exegetical method. Although he taught in Syria, after his death (*c.* 330) the greater part of his disciples formed a group at Pergamum in Mysia. From this school came the writings of Emperor Julian and the treatise of Sallust entitled *On the Gods and the World.* The tradition of Iamblichus seems to have been introduced at Athens during the second half of the 4th century.

At the beginning of the 5th century, Syrianus and Proclus, the representatives of this tendency, constructed a vast system which brought Platonism, Chaldeanism, and *Orphism into unison. Two basic principles dominate this synthesis. The first is the principle of analogy: while developing the unity represented by the immediately higher level of reality, each level of reality imitates this unity; everything is in all, according to more or less unified modes. The second principle is that of mediation: to imitate transcendent unity, each level of reality is endowed with a ternary structure, which, departing from unity, unfolds itself and goes on to return to unity because of conversion; to become itself, it must leave itself. In 529, the Emperor Justinian decided to bring an end to the school at Athens, the last bastion of paganism in the Christian empire. The head of the school, Damascius, then took refuge with his disciples near King Chosroes in Persia.

Damascius was the last great Neoplatonist. His *Questions and Solutions Concerning First Principles* constitute a profound criticism of Neoplatonism. The notion of the Absolute is for him very problematic. If the Absolute does not have any relation with anything else, it can no longer be the Principle. By the very claim that the Absolute is utterly unknowable and undefinable, the relation of other things to the Absolute is undefinable, and the whole metaphysical edifice of Neoplatonism comes in danger of crumbling.

Effect in the West. If the East was dominated by the tradition of Iamblichus, the Latin West knew only the tradition of Porphyry and Plotinus. This is true of pagan authors—Firmicus Maternus, *Macrobius, and Martianus Capella—as well as of Christian writers—Marius Victorinus, Ambrose, Augustine, *Calcidius, and Claudianus Mamertus. *Boethius alone, who wrote at the beginning of the 6th century, came under the influence of the schools at Athens and Alexandria. Even at Alexandria, the influence of Iamblichus's tradition was disseminated slowly and in moderate form. At the beginning of the 5th century, Hypatias and Synesius knew only Plotinus and Porphyry. Only at a later date did Hierocles, Hermias, Ammonius, Olympidorus, and Simplicius follow courses given at the school in Athens; and the Neoplatonism that they professed was always more sober, of a more moral character, and more scientific than that professed by their teachers: Syrianus, Proclus, or Damascius. Moreover, from the 6th century onward, the school became predominantly Aristotelian and Christian.

Neoplatonism and Christianity. From Plotinus to Damascius, Neoplatonism was always anti-Christian. Attacking the Christian Gnostics, Plotinus simultaneously combatted specifically Christian notions, as, for example, that of creation. Porphyry and the Emperor Julian wrote treatises against the Christians that provoked refutations from Eusebius of Cesarea and Cyril of Alexandria.

From the middle of the 4th century onward, however, Christian thought was strongly influenced by Neoplatonic philosophy and mysticism. In the East, Basil of Cesarea, Gregory of Nyssa, Synesius of Cyrene, and *Nemesius of Emesa, and, in the West, Marius Victorinus, Ambrose, and Augustine, made abundant use of Plotinus or Porphyry, frequently without citing them. In the 5th century, *Pseudo-Dionysius borrowed his hierarchical universe from Proclus. In the East, this direct influence of Neoplatonism continued throughout the Byzantine period, notably up to Psellus (11th century), Michael Italicos (12th century), Nicephoros Gregoras (14th century), and Gemistos Plethon (15th century). Plethon played a role in restoring Neoplatonism to the West in the course of the Italian Renaissance, at the court of the Medici. In the West, from the high period of the Middle Ages onward, Neoplatonism was accepted through the works of Ambrose, Augustine, Boethius, Calcidius, and Macrobius. In the 9th century, *John Scotus Erigena translated the writings of pseudo-Dionysius and Maximus the Confessor, and, in his *De divisione naturae,* combined the Proclean Neoplatonism of pseudo-Dionysius with the Porphyrian Neoplatonism of Augustine.

Arabian Thought. From the 12th century onward, Neoplatonism entered the medieval West by another route, namely, that of *Arabian philosophy. In fact, the texts of the Greek philosophers had been translated into Syriac by Nestorian Christians at the school of Edessa (431–439), and once they had been propagated in Persia, they were translated into Arabic during the 9th century, after the establishment of Baghdad. Under the influence of these translations, Arabian philosophy became a Neoplatonic interpretation of the works of Aristotle. Once it came into Spain during the 12th century, this Arabian philosophy placed Christian thought into renewed contact with Neoplatonism.

From the 12th century onward, Latin translations from Arabic or Greek gave Christian theologians a direct knowledge of Neoplatonic works, namely, the *Liber de Causis* (translated during the 12th century), the *Theology of Aristotle,* the *Elements of Theology* by Proclus, and Proclus's commentary on the *Parmenides,* translated by William of Moerbeke in the 13th century. Having received a strongly Platonized thought from the Christian tradition, certain theologians of this era, reading these Neoplatonic texts, regarded Platonism as naturally Christian.

Later Mysticism. The influence of Neoplatonism reached its apogee, at the end of the 13th century, in the writings of certain German Dominicans, all disciples of *Albert the Great, namely, *Theodoric of Freiberg, Berthold of Mosburg, *Nicholas of Strassburg, and especially Meister *Eckhart. Under the influence of this current, mysticism in the Rhine region developed also through the writings of *Henry Suso, *Tauler, and *Ruysbroeck. This German Neoplatonism was to become one of the sources of modern thought through the work of *Nicholas of Cusa, who transformed the metaphysics of Proclus into a method of knowledge that sought an ever deeper vision of the unity of the universe.

All these Byzantine, Latin, Arabian, or Germanic currents of Neoplatonism were united in the Italian Renaissance, which produced the great attempts at religious and philosophical unity by Giordano *Bruno and Tommaso *Campanella. During the modern era, the Platonic tradition was to be perpetuated both in England by the *Cambridge Platonists and in the *Siris* of Berkeley (1744); and in Germany by the *idealism of Schelling and Hegel.

Evaluation. The encounter between Neoplatonism and Christianity thus conditions the entire history of Western philosophy. During the patristic period, it provided an apt vocabulary for theology. The Trinitarian theology of Marius Victorinus, Basil of Cesarea, Augustine, and Synesius borrowed formulas from Porphyry, enabling it to express the unity of substance in the Trinity of hypostases. The Porphyrian expressions concerning the union of the soul and the body were of equal service in the formulation of the dogma concerning the hypostatic union, that is, a union without confusion of natures. In this regard, Nemesius has been a most valuable witness.

Yet, from the patristic era onward, Neoplatonism has had an influence on Christian teachings concerning the spiritual life that is highly disputable. The ancient tradition went from the humanity of Christ to the knowledge of the Father; it took ecclesiastical experience, i.e., the effect of the Holy Spirit in the Church, as its point of departure to attain God. Neoplatonism, on the contrary, pretended that an immediate and experimental knowledge of the transcendent God is possible. While making the necessary corrections in this matter, St. Augustine and St. Gregory of Nyssa were led to a like doctrine. From this there would result, in teachings on mysticism, a disequilibrium between the doctrine on union with God and the doctrine on the mediation of the Incarnate Christ. Pushed to the extreme, the danger makes its appearance in such writings as those of Meister Eckhart, who held that "the uncreated spark" of the soul is coeternal with the Ineffable.

Bibliography: T. WHITTAKER, *The Neo-Platonists: A Study in the History of Hellenism* (2d ed. Cambridge, Eng. 1928). A. H. ARMSTRONG, *An Introduction to Ancient Philosophy* (3d ed. London 1957). P. HENRY, *Plotin et l'Occident* (Louvain 1934). P. P. COURCELLE, *Les Lettres grecques en Occident* (new rev. ed. Paris 1948). A. J. FESTUGIÈRE, *Contemplation et vie contemplative selon Platon* (Paris 1936). L. ROBIN, *Les Rapports de l'être et de la connaissance d'après Platon* (Paris 1957). W. THEILER, *Die Vorbereitung des Neuplatonismus* (Berlin 1930); *Die chaldäischen Orakel und die Hymnen des Synesios* (Halle 1942). C. J. DE VOGEL, "On the Neoplatonic Character of Platonism and the Platonic Character of Neoplatonism," *Mind* 62 (1953) 43–64. P. MERLAN, *From Platonism to Neoplatonism* (2d ed. The Hague 1953). Fondation Hardt, pour l'études de l'antiquité classique, v.5, *Les Sources de Plotin* (Geneva 1960). H. LEWY, *Chaldaean Oracles and Theurgy* (Cairo 1956). C. SALLUST, *Concerning the Gods and the Universe,* tr. A. D. NOCK (New York 1926). DAMASCIUS LE DIADOQUE, *Dubitationes et solutiones de primis principiis,* ed. C. E. RUELLE (Paris 1889). R. ARNOU, DTC 12.2:2258–2392. P. SHOREY, *Platonism, Ancient and Modern* (Berkeley 1938). W. D. GEOGHEGAN, *Platonism in Recent Religious Thought* (New York 1958).

[P. HADOT]

NEO-PYTHAGOREANISM

The Pythagorean school of philosophy became extinct in the 4th century B.C., but there continued to be "exoteric" Pythagoreans who cultivated an ascetic way of life modeled on the supposed practice of Pythagoras himself. References to them are found in Middle Comedy (in Diels, *Frg. Vorsokr.* 1, no. 58E), and the moralizing tractates preserved in Stobaeus [ed. F. G. A. Mullach, *Fragmenta Philosophorum Graecorum* 2 (Paris 1867) 1–129]. Pythagoreanism had been originally perpetuated only by oral teaching, and the succession was broken in the 4th century. Therefore, when the school was revived in the 1st century B.C., especially at Alexandria and Rome, it became eclectic, drawing on the doctrines of various schools. Thus, Sextus Empiricus gives two accounts of the Neo-Pythagorean number doctrine, the first of which (10.261–281) is Platonic, and the second (10.281–284), Stoic. Diogenes Laërtius (8.24–33) preserves a good, though brief, statement of Neo-Pythagorean tenets quoted from Alexander Polyhistor. Alexander discusses number symbolism, teachings on souls and *daimones,* the structure of the world, the kinship of man with gods and animals, and rewards and punishments in a future life. He does not mention transmigration of souls, but this doctrine is attested elsewhere.

Number Symbolism. Number symbolism is characteristic of Neo-Pythagorean thought. Some members of the sect used only the monad (Stoic), while others also introduced the undefined dyad (Platonic). In this and other respects, Neo-Pythagoreanism was not unified in doctrine. It was a movement rather than a well-defined school, and it is therefore not always easy to tell who was a Neo-Pythagorean and who was not. For instance, the work of Pseudo-Timaeus of Locri contains nothing specifically Pythagorean, and Ocellus Lucanus could as easily be regarded as a Peripatetic.

Moral Precepts and Practices. After number symbolism, moral precepts are the most characteristic mark of Neo-Pythagorean writings [e.g., Iamblichus, "Golden Verses," *Vita Pythagorae,* ed. A. Nauck (Leipzig 1884)]. The doctrine that all living things—gods, men, animals—are akin led to many practices: abstinence from meat and fish, the use of linen rather than woolen clothing, the cultivation of self-control and friendship, and the careful observance of piety toward the gods. Some members of the school believed that the air was full of souls and divine spirits (*daimones*), that dreams are a reality, and that burial rites are very important [see F. Cumont, *Recherches sur le symbolisme funéraire des Romains* (Paris 1942)]. Some advocated an examination of conscience every evening. Agatharchides mentions three ways in which men become better: by making themselves as like the gods as possible; by doing good deeds; and by death, which frees the soul from bodily contamination. It is not surprising that such men looked down upon others with less high ideals and that, like the contemporary early Christians, they were regarded with suspicion, particularly in Rome, where all foreign religions were mistrusted.

Some Neo-Pythagoreans also practiced magic or worse, at least in popular opinion. P. Nigidius Figulus, whose piety Cicero extolled (*Ad Fam.* 4.13), used boys as mediums in the recovery of treasure (Apuleius, *Apol.* 42); and Vatinius, whom Cicero accused of sacrificing boys to the Manes (*In Vat.* 14, and *Schol. Bob.* ad 1), was a member of Nigidius's circle.

Apollonius of Tyana. The best-known Neo-Pythagorean is *Apollonius of Tyana, born about the beginning of the Christian Era. According to his biographer Philostratus, he substituted hymns and prayers for blood offerings, forbade the use of meat and wine, ate vegetables, wore linen, never bathed or cut his hair, practiced holy silence and sexual purity, and thus was united to the gods. He acquired magic powers as well as knowledge of the future and the past, including that of his own previous incarnation (Philostratus, *Vita Apoll.* 3.23; 6.21). The letters ascribed to him reveal Apollonius as he seemed to his immediate followers before the time of Philostratus. Apollonius was clearly a powerful personality living in a believing age, and he appealed to the learned as well as to the simple. Even some Christians respected him, for Sidonius Apollinaris (*c.* A.D. 432–480), Bishop of Clermont, transcribed for a friend a revised version of a Latin translation of Apollonius's biography (*Epist.* 8.3). There were undoubtedly other similar Neo-Pythagorean teachers of whom we know nothing.

Evaluation of Neo-Pythagoreanism. There is little philosophy in all this. Neo-Pythagoreanism was most conspicuously a religious movement, as its general character and concerns make clear. The Neo-Pythagoreans were often at odds with contemporary society, but, at the same time, the movement embodied several characteristic features of the religious life of the Empire: mysticism and occultism, belief in miracles, asceticism, stern morality, and the close union of the believers within their own group.

Neo-Pythagoreanism was absorbed into Neoplatonism, as is evident from the writings of Numenius (*c.* A.D. 150–250), who regarded the teachings of Pythagoras and Plato as practically identical, and from the lives of Pythagoras by Iamblichus and Porphyry. At an earlier date, it certainly influenced Philo Judaeus's terminology and it affected Christian thought through Clement of Alexandria. The latter often mentions Pythagoras, but largely as he was known through the Neo-Pythagorean writings.

See also ASCETICISM (NON-CHRISTIAN); GREEK PHILOSOPHY (RELIGIOUS ASPECTS); NEOPLATONISM; PYTHAGORAS AND PYTHAGOREANS.

Bibliography: Sources. *Ocellus Lucanus,* ed. R. HARDER (Berlin 1926). *P. Nigidii Figuli operum reliquia,* ed. A. SWOBODA (Vienna 1889). E. A. LEEMANS, *Studie over den wijsgeer Numenius van Apamia mit uitgave der fragmenten* (Brussels 1937). Other works. Ueberweg 1:513–524. R. DODDS, OxClDict 603. R. BEUTLER, Pauly-Wiss RE (1937) 17.2:2361–80. M. P. NILSSON, *Geschichte der griechischen Religion* (2d ed. Munich 1955–) 2:396–407. A. SCHMEKEL, *Die Philosophie der Mittleren Stoa* (Berlin 1892). A. DELATTE, *Études sur la littérature pythagorienne* (Paris 1915).

[H. S. LONG]

NEOSCHOLASTICISM AND NEOTHOMISM

Terms frequently used to designate the revival of *Thomism in the 19th and 20th centuries (*see* SCHOLASTICISM, 3). Even before *Aeterni patris* of *Leo XIII Catholic scholars eager to promote a *Christian philosophy tended to identify scholasticism with Thomism and vice versa. The historical studies of M. *De Wulf revealed some differences among 13th-century scholastics, but these he dismissed in order to obtain a common body of philosophical teachings, which he and others called *philosophia perennis.* For De Wulf, *philosophia perennis,* "elaborated by the Greeks and brought to perfection by the great medieval teachers, has never ceased to exist even in modern times" (CE 10:746). Recognizing that Thomism was too narrow

a term to designate a perennial philosophy, he preferred to speak of scholasticism and neoscholasticism. For him, neoscholasticism eliminated false or useless notions in 13th-century scholasticism, such as celestial movers, the incorruptibility of celestial bodies, their influence on terrestrial events, the diffusion of sensible "species" throughout a medium and their introduction into the organs of sense. The generally accepted view of neoscholasticism was expressed by De Wulf in his *Scholasticism Old and New,* tr. P. Coffey (Dublin 1907). It is retained in the titles of certain Catholic philosophical journals, e.g., *The New Scholasticism, Revue néo-scholastique* (1894–1909), *Revue néo-scholastique de philosophie* (1910–45), and *Rivista di filosofia neoscolastica.*

Later historical studies, notably by P. *Mandonnet and by É. Gilson, revealed profound differences among medieval scholastics that could not be dismissed. Moreover, a single body of philosophical thought called *philosophia perennis* could not be found to exist among the Greeks, medieval scholastics, and contemporary scholastics. The view of De Wulf and the Louvain school was discredited by Gilson and others. Neoscholastic and Neothomist thought were frozen in safe manuals during the crisis of *Modernism. Instead of using scholastic and Thomistic principles to solve modern problems, as was the wish of Leo XIII, neoscholastic manuals were, for the most part, content to provide a philosophical foundation for the study of theology. Narrowness and lack of vitality helped to give a pejorative sense to the terms neoscholasticism and Neothomism.

Profounder studies of the texts of St. *Thomas Aquinas frequently revealed discrepancies between the authentic teaching of St. Thomas and views presented as Neothomistic. Thus many Thomists felt that the prefix "neo" could be understood as a negation of true Thomism. For this reason, J. Maritain wrote: "I am not a neo-Thomist. All in all, I would rather be a paleo-Thomist than a neo-Thomist. I am, or at least I hope I am, a Thomist" [*Existence and the Existent,* tr. L. Galantière and G. Phelan (New York 1948) 1].

Neothomism, like Thomism itself, is only one philosophical and theological school within the whole of scholasticism. Moreover, both terms have been used in a favorable and in an unfavorable sense. In a pejorative sense they signify a type of modern thought that is narrow, irrelevant, or unfaithful to the true mind and spirit of the great thinkers of the Middle Ages. In a favorable sense they signify living thought that is both faithful to the great masters of the Middle Ages and relevant to modern problems.

See also SCHOLASTICISM, 3.

Bibliography: M. DE WULF, CE 10:746–749. P. DEZZA and G. SANTINELLO, EncFil 3:874–880.

[J. A. WEISHEIPL]

NEOT, ST., monk, hermit; d. *c.* 900 (feast, July 31). After ordination he moved from *Glastonbury Abbey to Cornwall in western England where he lived as a hermit. According to legend he became the friend of *Alfred the Great; the story of the burned cakes and Alfred is first found in a history of the Shrine of St. Neot in Cornwall. He went on a pilgrimage to Rome to pray for Alfred's victory over the Danes. Neot was buried in Cornwall, but later his body was moved to St. Neot's in Huntingdonshire. It is possible that there were actually two saints of the same name, one a Celt from Cornwall, the other an Anglo-Saxon.

Bibliography: ActSS July 7:325–340. W. Böhne, LexThK² 7:877. BHL 2:6052–56. R. Wuelcker, "Ein angelsaechsisches Leben des Neot," *Anglia* 3 (1880) 102–114. J. Asser, *Life of King Alfred, together with the Annals of Saint Neot Erroneously Ascribed to Asser,* ed. W. H. Stevenson (Oxford 1904) 256–258, 296–299. F. Wormald, ed., *English Kalendars before A.D. 1100* (London 1934–   ). Zimmermann KalBen 2:518–521.

[R. T. MEYER]

NEPAL, kingdom in the Himalayas between India and Tibet, 54,500 square miles in area, and governed since 1951 by a constitutional monarchy. The population, estimated in 1964 at 9,000,000, adhered mostly to *Hinduism or Lamaist *Buddhism (*see* LAMAISM). The ruling family was Hindu, and the state was officially Hindu. Protestants had perhaps 500 members. The number of Catholics was very small. Christianity entered Nepal when Jesuit missionaries passed through the country from 1628 onward, but they did not establish themselves there, although King Pratap Malla invited them to do so in 1679. Nepal became in 1703 part of the Capuchin mission to Tibet. The eastern and central sections were evangelized, until the Gurkha conquest (1765–68) caused the Capuchins and their converts to withdraw to Bettiah in Bihar, India. Thenceforth the country was closed to foreigners. Ecclesiastically it was placed under the jurisdiction of the Vicariate Apostolic of Tibet and Hindustan in 1784 and from 1808 under various Indian jurisdictions, until in 1919 it was subjected to the newly created Diocese of Patna. All citizens are now permitted to practice their own religion, and Christian missionaries are permitted to work in the country under certain restrictions. Since ancient times, however, conversion from Hinduism has been forbidden. This ban was given full legal status in 1963, when foreigners who were found guilty of proselytizing among Hindus were made subject to expulsion after a 1-year imprisonment. Converted Nepalese Hindus continued to be regarded as Hindus and could be punished by imprisonment up to 3 years. Jesuits from the U.S. and India were permitted in 1951 to open a high school for boys, for which the government provided the site. A Catholic school for girls, operated by sisters, opened in 1955; it was attended in 1965 by King Mahendra's eldest daughter.

Bibliography: E. D. Maclagan, *The Jesuits and the Great Mogul* (London 1932). L. Petech, ed., *I missionarii italiani nel Tibet e nel Nepal,* 4 v. (Rome 1952–53). Clemente da Terzorio, *Le Missioni dei Minori Cappuccini,* 10 v. (Rome 1913–38) v.9. H. Davis, *Nepal, Land of Mystery* (London 1942). *Bilan du Monde* 2:622–623.

[E. R. HAMBYE]

NEPHTHALI (NAPHTALI), eponymous ancestor of one of the Israelite tribes. Nephthali was the sixth son of Jacob, and born of Bala, Lia's maid; he was thus the full brother of *Dan, a relationship probably suggested by the fact that the territories of these two tribes were contiguous. The name (Heb., *naptālî*) is given a popular etymology in Gn 30.7–8, where it is connected with the idea of cleverness or wrestling.

The Palestine territory of the tribe of Nephthali extended from the southern end of the Lake of Genesareth to Mt. Hermon in the north, with the upper Jordan and the Lake of Genesareth serving as its eastern border; it was bounded by Issachar and Zabulon in the south and by Aser in the west (Jos 19.32–39). The proverbial fertility of its land is alluded to in *Moses' Oracles (Dt 33.23).

According to Jgs 1.33 the tribe of Nephthali was not able to subjugate completely the Canaanite elements in the territory that fell to it, though these were eventually absorbed into the tribal strain. The tribe figures prominently in the important engagement against Sisera, the Canaanite leader; Barac, the only military leader of Nephthali named in the Bible, was chosen by *Debora to lead the Israelite coalition (Jgs 4.6, 10; 5.18). The tribe is also found fighting against the *Madianites in the days of Gedeon (Jgs 6.35; 7.23).

Nephthali's position, as one of the peripheral tribes north of Manasse and Ephraim, left it exposed to the constant peril of marauding bands and hostile neighbors. Weakened by Syrian attacks, it was overcome and taken into captivity by the Assyrian warlord, *Tiglath-Pileser (Theglath-Phalasar) III (*c.* 732 B.C.; see 3 Kgs 15.20; 4 Kgs 15.29).

The future glory promised to this region in the prophecy of Isaia (Is 8.23–9.1) Matthew sees fulfilled when the saving ministry of Jesus began in eastern Galilee (Mt 14.13–16).

Bibliography: EncDictBibl 1628–29.

[R. BARRETT]

NEPOS OF ARSINOË, 3d-century Millenarianist and bishop of Arsinoë (modern Medinet El Faiyûm, Egypt); author of liturgical hymns and of a Judaizing view of the Apocalypse called a *Refutation of the Allegorists.* Though lost, this book is described by Eusebius of Caesarea (*Hist. eccl.* 7.24, 25) as having been refuted by Bp. *Dionysius of Alexandria (d. 265) in a two-volume tract, *On Promises.* Nepos propounded a Millenaristic viewpoint in which he interpreted the promises made to the saints in the Scriptures as due to be fulfilled on this earth during a 1,000-year reign of the just, in which man's physical powers would be given full satisfaction. Dionysius first held a 3-day conference to dispel the effects of this doctrine among the Egyptian bishops, then wrote his refutation. But the disciples of Nepos apparently initiated several schismatic movements that explain the Church's generally reticent attitude toward allegorical interpretation of the Scripture. Nepos's views also witness to the continuance of Judaistic tendencies in the Church of the 3d century.

Bibliography: J. Kirchmeyer, LexThK² 7:878. É. Amann, DTC 11.1:68–69. Quasten Patr 2:103–104. L. Gry, *Le Millénarisme* (Paris 1904) 101–107. C. L. Feltoe, ed., *The Letters of Dionysius of Alexandria* (Cambridge, Eng. 1904) 106–126.

[J. BENTIVEGNA]

NEPOTISM, the practice of popes and other ecclesiastics (and hence of any person in a position of authority) of showing special favor to relatives or other interested parties. It is associated particularly with certain popes, some of whom understandably placed their relatives in positions of trust in times of crisis. First-degree papal nepotism, or the selecting of a nephew or relative for curial office, goes back to Pope Adrian I (722–795), who made a nephew *primicerius,* or senior "Judge Palatine." Examples occur more thickly from the 10th century onward; thus Innocent III (1198–1216) turned to his own family, particularly to his brother Richard, in order to bring the fractious Roman commune to heel. Dante (*Inf.* 19.31) characterized Pope Nicholas III (1277–80) as "greedily advancing" the *Orsini family; more justifiably, perhaps, he also attacked (*Inf.* 19.52–81; 27.85–129) Pope Boniface VIII (1294–1303), since Boniface's pontificate was notably preoccupied with the aggrandizement of the *Gaetani family and the relentless harrying of the rival *Colonna family. Thus in early 1295 he made his favorite nephew Benedetto Gaetani a Cardinal, at the end of the year honoring similarly two other nephews, Giacomo Gaetani Tommasini, a Franciscan, and Francesco Gaetani, a married man separated from his wife, as well as another relative, the curial poet *James Gaetani Stefaneschi. The Avignon cardinals and popes, particularly Clement V and Clement VI, consolidated the tradition [see B. Guillemain, *La Cour pontificale d'Avignon* (Paris 1962) 156–164, 171–175], to the great disgust of Petrarch [*Epistulae sine nomine* 11, ed. P. Piur, *Petrarcas Buch ohne Namen und die päpstliche Kurie* (Halle 1925)]. However, if the development of papal *provision aided the popes in beneficing relatives, it must be remembered that one of the less well-known complaints against the system was that it cut across "episcopal nepotism"; as Bp. Grandison of Exeter (1328–69) put it, "I have for many years been unable to provide for my nephews and retainers" [A. J. Bannister, *The Cathedral Church of Hereford* (London 1924) 182 n.2]. The golden age of nepotism came with the Renaissance popes: Callistus III (1455–58) called the *Borgias from Spain; Sixtus IV (1471–84) spread his favors among *Della Rovere, Sansoni, Bassi, and *Riario relatives; the Borgia, Alexander VI (1492–1503), made his son Cesare chancellor of the Church and sought to carve for him a hereditary state in central Italy; Leo X (1513–21) impoverished the Church in attempting to conquer Urbino for his nephew Lorenzo de' *Medici. The trend was stemmed to some extent by the bull *Admonet nos* of Pius V (1567), but second-degree nepotism, or the conferring of favors instead of offices, was to continue until the constitution *Romanum decet pontificem* (1692) put an end to its grosser aspects; in the meantime papal families such as the *Aldobrandini, *Borghese, *Barberini and Pamphili had benefited hugely.

Bibliography: E. ROTA, EncCatt 8:1762–63. P. FERRARIS, Mercati-Pelzer DE 2:1123. G. SCHWAIGER, LexThK² 7:878–879.

[L. E. BOYLE]

NERESHEIM, ABBEY OF,

in Württemberg, south Germany; its patrons are SS. *Ulrich and *Afra of *Augsburg. Founded for canons by Count Hartmann of Dillingen (1095), it was settled by Benedictines from *Petershausen (1106) and *Zwiefalten (1119). In 1497 it joined the *Melk reform and in 1685 the Augsburg Congregation of the Holy Ghost. In the 17th and 18th centuries it had close ties with the Jesuit University of Dillingen and sent professors to the lyceum in Freising and the University of *Salzburg, while it had its own school of philosophy and theology and a gymnasium (to 1806). Secularized in 1803 and awarded to the princes of Thurn and Taxis, it was restored as an abbey in 1920. The baroque cloister (1694–1714) has rich stucco-work; the church (1745–98), B. *Neumann's most mature work, has cupola frescoes by Martin Knoller (1769–75). The humanist Abbot Benedikt Maria Angehrn (1755–87), cousin of Prince-abbot Beda Angehrn of *Sankt Gallen (1767–96) and imperial administrator of *Sankt Ulrich in Augsburg (1778–82), was opposed by the monk Benedikt Maria Werkmeister (b. 1745; d. 1823), a talented scholar who championed the Catholic Enlightenment and had ties with I. H. von *Wessenberg. The monk K. Nack wrote a history of the abbey (Neresheim 1792).

Bibliography: P. WEISSENBERGER, LexThK² 7:879–880.

[P. WEISSENBERGER]

NERGAL,

a god of the Assyrian-Babylonian pantheon, appears originally to have been a manifestation of the sun-god Shamash, embodying in particular the destructive properties of the latter; he was considered ruler of the underworld and lord of death, pestilence, war, and inundation and was represented in literature and art as a lion. Among the cuneiform tablets discovered at el-Amarna is a partially preserved poem telling of his assumption of power over the underworld from his spouse, the goddess Ereshkigal.

The principal cult-site of Nergal was the Babylonian city of Cutha (modern Tell Ibrahim, northeast of Babylon), where the temple E-meslam was dedicated to him. After the fall of Samaria to Assyria in 721 B.C. and the exile of its inhabitants to Assyria, settlers from Cutha were transplanted to Israel, and there they introduced the worship of Nergal (4 Kgs 17.24–30). The name of the god is found in the OT (Jer 39.3, 13) as a theophoric element in the Babylonian name Nergal-sarezer (Akkadian *Nergal-šar-uṣur,* "Nergal, protect the king").

See also MESOPOTAMIA, ANCIENT, 3.

Bibliography: A. DEIMEL, *Pantheon Babylonicum* (Rome 1914), s.v. Nergal. K. L. TALLQVIST, *Akkadische Götterepitheta* (Helsingfors 1938), s.v. Nergal. Pritchard ANET 103–104.

[R. I. CAPLICE]

NERI, PHILIP, ST.

Catholic reformer and founder of the Oratorians; b. Florence, July 21, 1515; d. Rome, May 26, 1595 (feast, May 26). Philip, son of Francesco, a Florentine lawyer, and his wife Lucrezia da Mosciano (d. 1520), grew up with his two sisters, Caterina and Elizabetta, in the care of a loving stepmother. He was both popular and pious as a boy, and was found often with the Dominicans at St. Mark's, where he talked with the friars and learned to revere *Savonarola, who was executed in Florence in 1498.

Apostle of Rome. Philip's family sent him, at 17, to his uncle, Romolo, a merchant of San Germano (now Cassino), who was willing to take Philip into his business and eventually to leave it to him. The prospect of a prosperous commercial career repelled Philip, who wished by then to give his life directly to God. With this intention, he left for Rome (1533), where he lodged with a Florentine, Galeotto del Caccia, whose two small sons he tutored. Already Philip was eating and sleeping little, and praying much. From 1535 until 1538 he followed courses in philosophy at the Sapienza University and in theology at Sant' Agostino, earning high praise as a student. Instead of becoming a priest, as expected, Philip abandoned his studies, and for 13 years followed what was, for that time, an unusual, even idiosyncratic, vocation—that of a layman, entirely on his own, devoting himself exclusively to prayer and the Christian apostolate. He meditated on the Gospels; he prayed, sometimes, it seems, in ecstasy; he frequented the Catacombs (a reflection of his interest in the primitive Church); he persuaded friends and acquaintances to turn to Christ. In 1548 under the spiritual direction of Persiano Rosa, he organized some laymen into the Confraternitá di SS. Trinità to assist poor and convalescent pilgrims. This grew into the celebrated hospital of S. Trinità dei Pellegrini. The background of this activity must be remembered; corruption in the Church at Rome, an indifferent clergy, a people paganized by the Renaissance, a Reformation movement in the North attracting the loyalty of whole nations, and a reforming council just convening at Trent.

Father Rosa urged that he could serve the Church better as a priest, and on May 23, 1551, Philip was ordained. He lived for some years at the church of S. Girolamo della Carità with other priests and exercised a distinctive apostolate in the confessional. For the further instruction and sanctification of his penitents he arranged, in the afternoons, informal talks, discussions, and prayers in a room above the church. He also led excursions to other churches, often with music and a

"Madonna and Child Appearing to St. Philip Neri," oil painting by the Venetian artist Giovanni Battista Piazzetta (1682–1754).

picnic on the way. In 1559, his "Pilgrimage to the Seven Churches" brought censure from Paul IV and the temporary suspension of all Philip's works. He seems to have aroused jealousy, and he was represented as encouraging plots against Paul IV, fomenting a sect, and holding "conventicles." The more moderate reformer Pius IV succeeded in this same year (1559), and Philip was back in favor.

Development of the Oratory. Several of Philip's followers became priests and from 1564 they lived as a community at the church of S. Giovanni dei Fiorentini, where they prayed and ate together (but took no religious vows) and celebrated the Eucharist and preached regularly. This was the beginning of the Oratory, as it is now known. Its distinctive feature was the popular daily afternoon service of four informal talks, interspersed with vernacular prayers and hymns. The talks concerned the spiritual life, Scripture, Church history, and the study of a saint's life. *Palestrina, one of Philip's followers, contributed musical settings for scriptural readings, hymns, motets, and *laudi spirituali* (hence the term Oratorio). The multivolume *Annales Ecclesiastici* of Caesar *Baronius, whose standard of critical scholarship was high for his times, grew from his regular talks in the Oratory.

Persecution reoccurred in 1567 when it was reported to Pius V that the Oratory was an assemblage of heretics, where laymen preached and sang vernacular hymns. But the intervention of Cardinal Charles *Borromeo saved the Oratory. In 1575 Pope Gregory XIII, a friend to Philip, formally approved the new "Congregation of the Oratory," as a group of priests living in community without vows, for prayer and preaching. The small, dilapidated church of S. Maria in Vallicella was given to the congregation, and on the site was built a large new one, which has continued to be known as the Chiesa Nuova, and to be the church of the Roman Oratory. Philip was the first provost (superior); he was succeeded by Baronius.

Until Philip died, his advice was continually sought. Visitors, including many cardinals, thronged his room, and (SS.) *Ignatius of Loyola, *Camillus de Lellis, John *Leonardi, Charles Borromeo, *Felix of Cantalice, and *Francis de Sales delighted in his friendship. As an influence in the Counter Reformation Philip has been justly counted with the Jesuits and the Council of Trent, on the grounds that as the "Apostle of Rome" he was foremost in converting to personal holiness many of those most influential in the central government of the Church. Philip has been considered an eccentric buffoon studying to mortify himself and proud Renaissance gentlemen into humility; a suspect leader of an evangelical reform movement; a saint around whom miracles were constantly occurring; a holy founder of 45 oratories now in existence; and an exponent of real, living, personal faith. Invariably Philip's humility, his gaiety, his personal attractiveness, and his fervent attachment to the Person of Christ have been noticed.

John Henry Newman felt his attractiveness, joined the Oratory, and founded the first English-speaking house (Birmingham). Philip was beatified by Paul V (1615) and canonized by Gregory XV (May 12, 1622).

Bibliography: Butler Th Attw 2:395–399. R. Bäumer, LexThK² 7:881. C. Gasbarri, EncCatt 5:1327–31; *Filippo Neri, santo romano* (2d ed. Rome 1944). L. Ponnelle and L. Bordet, *St. Philip Neri and the Roman Society of His Times,* tr. R. F. Kerr

(New York 1933), list and discussion of sources. A. CAPECELATRO, *The Life of Saint Philip Neri . . .*, tr. T. A. POPE, 2 v. (new ed. New York 1926). G. INCISA DELLA ROCHETTA et al., eds., *Il primo processo per san Filippo Neri,* 3 v. (StTest 191, 196, 205; 1957–60). A. BAUDRILLART, *Saint Philippe Néri, 1515–1595* (Paris 1939). P. G. BACCI, *Vita di Sto Filippo Neri* (Verona 1624); Eng. *Life of St. Philip Neri,* ed. F. I. ANTROBUS, 2 v. (rev. ed. St. Louis 1903). V. J. MATTHEWS, *St. Philip Neri* (London 1934). L. BOUYER, *The Roman Socrates,* tr. M. DAY (Westminster, Md. 1958). **Illustration credit:** National Gallery of Art, Washington, D.C., Samuel H. Kress Collection.

[J. CHALLENOR]

NERIGLISSAR, King of Babylon 560–556 B.C., son-in-law of *Nabuchodonosor (605–562). Neriglissar and Neriglassar are forms of his name that appear in the Greek sources; his Babylonian name was *Nergal-šar-uṣur* [O (god) *Nergal, guard the King]. A man of the same name (which appears in the Bible as Nergal-sarezer, Heb. *nergal śar'eṣer*) who was one of the high officers at the capture of Jerusalem in 587 B.C. (Jer 39.3, 13) may well have been the one who later became King Neriglissar. In August 560, after having Nabuchodonosor's son *Evil-Merodach (562–560) assassinated, Neriglissar usurped the throne of Babylon. In 556 he led an army into western Cilicia (southeastern Asia Minor) to repel an attack on this distant border of the Neo-Babylonian Empire. His son and successor, Labashi-Marduk, was overthrown after a reign of less than 2 months (May and June 556) by *Nabu-na'id (556–539).

Bibliography: EncDictBibl 1631. W. F. ALBRIGHT, "The Nebuchadnezzar and Neriglissar Chronicles," BullAmSchOrRes 143 (1956) 28–33.

[R. KUGELMAN]

NERINCKX, CHARLES, frontier missionary, founder of the Sisters of Loretto; b. Herffelingen, Belgium, Oct. 2, 1761; d. Ste. Genevieve, Mo., Aug. 12, 1824. The son of Sebastian, a successful physician, and Petronilla (Langendries) Nerinckx, he was the eldest of seven sons and seven daughters, many of whom entered religious orders. He studied philosophy at the University of Louvain, Belgium, and was ordained Nov. 1, 1785. After a decade as parish priest in Mechlin and Meerbeek, he spent another 10 years administering the Sacraments from various hiding places, notwithstanding the rigors of the French Revolution. In September 1803, through Princess Amalia *Gallitzin, he offered his services to Bp. John Carroll, arriving at Baltimore in November 1804. He was sent to Georgetown College (now University), Washington, D.C., to study, then to Kentucky to join Stephen T. *Badin, until that time the only priest in that vast mission field. Nerinckx arrived at Bardstown, Ky., in July 1805; he worked for the next 7 years with Badin, and then alone in various parishes. During his 19 years in the state he built 14 churches. In 1809 he organized the first Holy Name Society in Kentucky, and in 1812, with two young women, founded the Sisters of *Loretto, the first native American community. He made two trips to Europe, returning with valuable paintings and religious supplies. He also brought over the first Jesuits to work in the West, among them Pierre Jean *De Smet. Disagreement with Bp. Guy Chabrat over the rule of the Sisters of Loretto prompted him to withdraw in 1824 to Missouri, where death overtook him before he could realize his hope of working with the Indians. In 1833 his remains were returned to the motherhouse he had established at Loretto, Ky.

Nerinckx was noted for his great strength and his devotion to duty. As it took 6 weeks to cover his mission stations, he spent his days in the saddle, his nights in the

Charles Nerinckx, pioneer missionary in Kentucky.

woods, often in physical danger. Although regarded as stern, he was gentle when instructing children and slaves. His uncompromising stand against the evil practices of the frontier caused friction, and later critics mistakenly accused him of proneness to Jansenistic tendencies. Several Latin manuscripts indicative of his scholarship and hundreds of his letters have been discovered in the Mechlin diocesan archives; many other letters are preserved in the Baltimore archdiocesan archives.

Bibliography: W. J. HOWLETT, *Life of Rev. Charles Nerinckx* (Techny, Ill. 1915). C. P. MAES, *Life of Rev. Charles Nerinckx* (Cincinnati 1880). H. MAGARET, *Giant in the Wilderness* (Milwaukee 1952). J. H. SCHAUINGER, *Stephen T. Badin* (Milwaukee 1956). R. J. PURCELL, DAB 13:428–429. M. J. SPALDING, *Sketches of the Early Catholic Missions of Kentucky, 1787–1827* (Louisville 1844). A. C. MINOGUE, *Loretto Annals of the Century* (New York 1912).

[J. H. SCHAUINGER]

NERO, ROMAN EMPEROR, A.D. 54 to 68; b. Anzio, Dec. 15, 37; d. Rome, June 9, 68. He was adopted in 50 by the Emperor Claudius, who had married his own niece, Agrippina, Nero's mother. In 53 Nero married Octavia, the daughter of Claudius. When Claudius was poisoned in 54 on the orders of Agrippina, Nero was presented to the soldiers as the new emperor. For the first 5 years his reign was popular, owing to the careful guidance of *Seneca and Burrus. In 55 when Agrippina threatened to side with Britannicus, the son of Claudius, against him, Nero had him poisoned, and in 59, weary of his mother's demands, he had her murdered. In 62 he divorced Octavia and married his mistress. In this same year Burrus died and Seneca retired; their place was taken by Ofonius Tigellinus, who converted the last years of Nero's rule into a reign of terror. Nero the Hellenophile surrounded himself with Greeks and Orientals; he was also an enthusiast for the arts and extravagant spectacles, which together with his tendency to autocracy cost him the support of conservative Romans. Despite the relief measures he provided for those left destitute, he was blamed for the fire of July 18, 64, that broke out in the Circus Maximus and destroyed half of Rome. Nero turned the blame on the Christians, according to *Tacitus, and many of them were put to death by cruel tortures. Peter and Paul were martyred in Rome under Nero, but the year of their death is uncertain. A conspiracy against Nero in 65 under Calpurnius Piso failed, but in 68 the armies under Julius Vindex at Lyons and Servius Sulpicius Galba in Spain revolted. Deserted by the pretorian guards and condemned to death by the senate, Nero killed himself.

Emperor Nero, an unflattering portrait carved on marble disc.

Bibliography: A. Momigliano, CAH 10:702–742. M. A. Levi, *Nerone e suoi tempi* (Milan 1949). E. Hohl, Pauly-Wiss RE Suppl 3:349–394. H. U. Instinsky, LexThK² 7:881–882. **Illustration credit:** Alinari-Art Reference Bureau.

[M. J. COSTELLOE]

NERSES

The name of many Armenian churchmen and officials, five of whom are discussed in this article.

Nerses the Great, St., 4th-century Armenian Catholicos or patriarch; b. Cappadocia, 333 or 337; d. Khakh, on the Euphrates, 373 (feast, Monday after the 4th Sunday after Pentecost). Nerses was the son of Athanakines and Bambish, the sister of King Diran, and close relative of St. *Gregory the Illuminator. He was educated in Cappadocia and married a Mamikonian princess, who bore him a son, *Isaac the Great, and died a few years later. In the early years of the reign of King Arshak II, he returned to Armenia, served as a royal counselor and custodian of the royal sword, and was chosen the catholicos by popular acclamation after the death of Patriarch Shahak. He was consecrated at Caesarea in Cappadocia, the metropolitan see for *Armenia, by Eusebius (or possibly Dianos) in 353, and he initiated a reform of the Armenian church with a synod held at Ashtishat. He promulgated decrees prohibiting marriages between close relatives, denounced pagan practices, and introduced positive legislation regarding fasting and monastic life. He also erected schools, convents, hospitals, asylums, and churches in imitation of Cappadocian ecclesiastical activities. King Arshak deposed him for condemning the scandals of the court, and from 360 to 362 he appealed for aid in Constantinople. He returned to Armenia (364 or 368) and was restored as catholicos by King Pap after Arshak had been betrayed to the Persians by members of his entourage. Nerses rebuilt the churches destroyed by the Persians. In 372 he took part in a synod at Caesarea, but he was apparently poisoned at the King's command for denouncing the royal family's evil ways. His career is described by Faustus of Byzantium (*History*), whose narrative must be used with caution.

Nerses II Astaraketzi, Armenian catholicos from 548 to 557. He called the Synod of Dwin (554–555) at which 18 bishops participated and condemned the Khoujik sect imported into Armenia by merchants infected with both Nestorianism and Manichaeism. The 38 canons of the synod are important for the development of Armenian teaching on the Sacraments and monastic life.

Nerses III, Armenian catholicos from 642 to 661. Endowed with a Byzantine education, Nerses built the patriarchal palace and the church of St. Gregory in Vagarshapat and received the title *Schinogh* or builder. He attempted to win the Armenian Church to the Chalcedonian viewpoint on the question of the two natures in Christ, but he had to cede before the opposition of Theodore Rschtuni and returned to his original bishopric at Taykh.

Nerses of Lambron, St., bishop of Tarsus in Cilicia; b. Lambron, Cilicia, 1153; d. Tarsus, July 14, 1198 (feast, Monday after 3d Sunday after Assumption). The son of Oshin II (d. 1168), Prince of Lambron, Nerses was educated in the Armenian monasteries of Skewra and Siav-Liarn, and spoke Armenian, Greek, Latin, and Syrian. His granduncle Nerses IV ordained him in Hromkla, and he changed his name from Smbat to Nerses and retired to a solitude. At the request of Gregory IV Tegha, he accepted the archbishopric of Tarsus in 1175; he was selected as an ambassador by King Leo II to greet Frederick Barbarossa. On Frederick's death in the river Saleph (1190), he took the young Prince Frederick under his protection. He participated in reunion efforts with Rome and Byzantium, gave the opening discourses at the Synods of Hromkla (1179) and Tarsus (1196), and undertook an embassy to Constantinople in 1197. Of his 33 preserved writings, those devoted to the liturgy, Biblical commentaries, preaching, and Church discipline are the most significant. He also translated into Armenian a number of patristic works including the Rule of St. Benedict, the Dialogues of Gregory the Great, and the Ekthesis of Epiphanius of Constantia, as well as the Syro-Roman legal code. Some of his works have been edited and translated into German by Max zu Sachsen, K. Bruns, E. Sachau, and F. Finck.

Bibliography: V. Inglisian and M. van den Oudenrijn, LexThK² 7:882–884. G. Amaduni, EncCatt 8:1768. H. G. Beck, RGG³ 4:1403, Nerses IV. H. F. Tournebize, *Histoire politique et religieuse de l'Arménie* (Paris 1910); DHGE 4:297–298. J. B. Emine. tr., in *Collection des historiens anciens et modernes de l'Arménie.* ed. V. Langlois et al., 2 v. (Paris 1867–69). R. Grousset, *Histoire de l'Arménie* (Paris 1947). É. Amann, DTC 15.1: 538–540. J. Marquart, *Philologus* 55 (1896) 213–227. N. Akinian, AnalBoll 67 (1949) 74–86, Nerses the Great. G. Capuletti, *Sancti Nersetis Clajensis opera,* 2 v. (Venice 1833). F. Nève. *L'Arménie chrétienne et sa littérature* (Louvain 1886). A. Ter-Mikelian, *Die armenische Kirche in ihren Beziehungen zur byzantinischen* (Jena 1892). P. Dzoulikian, *Proche-Orient chrétien* 11 (1961) 36–43, Nerses IV and Nerses de Lambron. P. Tekeyan, *Controverses christologiques en Arméno-Cilicie* (OrChrAnal 124; 1939).

[N. M. SETIAN]

NERSES GRATIOSUS (SNORHALI), archbishop (catholicos) 1166–73, saint in the Armenian Church; b. Cilicia, 1102; d. Hromkla, 1173 (feast Aug. 3). Nerses IV Klayeçi, called Šnorhali or "the Gracious," was educated by his uncle Catholicos Gregory II and the great Armenian doctor Stephen Manuk. Nerses succeeded his brother, Gregory III Pahlavuni, as catholicos and had his residence at Hromkla, on the Euphrates. He was a competent theologian and worked (1170–72) with *Manuel I Comnenus for the reunion of the Byzantine and the Armenian Churches. Manuel sent the Byzantine theologian Theorianus to Hromkla for theological conferences at which Nerses and several bishops accepted the Chalcedonian formula concerning the two natures in Christ, despite the opposition of Syrian delegates. Nerses also accepted the Byzantine calendar for the main ecclesiastical feasts to convince Patriarch *Michael III Anchialus (1170–78) of his orthodoxy. He became an ardent defender of the traditional doctrines of the Armenian Church against *Monophysitism and was quoted in this context by Pius XII in the encyclical *Sempiternus Christus rex* (1951). He was one of the early leaders in the Armenian literary renaissance. Among his writings are a complaint over the fall of Edessa (1144), Biblical commentaries, and encyclical letters treating of canonical matters. He was noted as a poet and writer of sacred hymns. His *Twenty-four Hour Prayers* (the daily prayers of St. Nerses) was translated into 32 languages of the Christian world. Before he died he named the younger of his two nephews, both bishops, to succeed him. The elder, however, imprisoned his cousin and had himself consecrated catholicos under the name Gregory IV Tegha. (For bibliography, *see* NERSES.)

[J. M. BUCKLEY]

NESTLE, EBERHARD, Lutheran Biblical scholar and Orientalist, b. Stuttgart, Germany, May 1, 1851; d. there, March 9, 1913. He earned his Ph.D. at the University of Tübingen. From 1883 to 1898, he was professor successively at Ulm, Tübingen, and Ulm. From 1898, he was professor and then superior at the Evangelical Seminary at Maulbronn. His early studies concerned chiefly the Septuagint, but the last 20 years of his life were spent mostly on the Greek NT. In 1898, he published his critical Greek NT, constructed essentially by choosing the common reading from the editions of C. *Tischendorf, B. F. *Westcott and F. J. A. *Hort, and R. F. Weymouth (later, when completed, that of B. Weiss), with variants in the apparatus. Adopted by the British and Foreign Bible Society in 1904, this text became practically a new Textus Receptus, and has since been revised by his son, Erwin Nestle, with the apparatus radically changed (1927) and the text improved (1941). He also proposed to publish a parallel Hebrew-Greek OT, but did not live to complete it. In addition, he published numerous grammars and Biblical aids.

Bibliography: H. HAAG, DBSuppl 6:424–426. J. SCHMID, Lex ThK² 7:884.

[D. W. MARTIN]

NESTOR, Russian chronicler; b. *c.* 1056; d. *c.* 1114. He was a monk of the Pecherskii Cave Monastery of Kiev from 1073 until his death. Of his origin and life little is known, but he is accepted as the author of the lives of St. Theodosius, Abbot of the Pecherskii Caves, and of the martyrs, Princes Boris and Gleb of Kiev. A tradition long persisted that Nestor was the author of the *Povest vremennykh let* (Narration of Bygone Years), known as *The Russian Primary Chronicle* (trans. S. H. Cross, Cambridge, Mass. 1930), the first Kievan account of early Russia. This chronicle is a mixture of didactic and historical elements interspersed with Byzantine and other sources often of legendary character. The main sources of native origin were the story tellers and perhaps the *byliny,* old ballads and epic songs. The description of the reigns of Princes Vsevolod (d. 1093) and Sviatopolk II (d. 1113) is that of an eyewitness. Modern historians do not consider Nestor the actual author of the chronicle, although some Russian scholars are of the opinion that material previously collected by the monk Nikon was revised by Nestor and was then used by another monk to compile a new redaction at the request of Prince Vladimir Monomach (d. 1125). The language of the chronicle is Old Bulgarian with some influences from the Kievan dialect.

Bibliography: M. D. PRISELKOV, *Nestor letopisets* (St. Petersburg 1923). N. K. CHADWICK, *The Beginnings of Russian History: An Enquiry into Sources* (Cambridge, Eng. 1946). K. BESTUZHEV-RIUMIN, *On the Composition of the Russian Chronicles until the End of the 14th Century* (St. Petersburg 1869), in Russian.

[B. B. SZCZESNIAK]

NESTORIAN CHURCH

After the condemnation of Nestorius at Ephesus in 431 and the agreement reached between *John of Antioch and *Cyril of Alexandria in 433, the teaching of the Antiochene school on the two natures in Christ as developed by *Diodore of Tarsus, *Theodore of Mopsuestia, and *Nestorius was definitively checked in the West. In the East, however, partly through historical accident and partly through political expediency, Nestorian doctrine became the official teaching of the Persian Church, whose missionary activities over a number of centuries were to rival those of Rome itself.

Christian Origins in Persia. Very little is known about the introduction of Christianity into Persia. The "Parthians and Medes and Elamites, and inhabitants of Mesopotamia" (Acts 2.9) who were in Jerusalem on the first Pentecost must have taken home some knowledge of the new faith. Later Greek, Syrian, and Persian legends variously maintain that the Apostles Peter and Thomas preached to the Parthians and that Thaddaeus, Bartholomew, and Addaeus (*Addai), one of the 72 Disciples, evangelized Mesopotamia and Persia. An ancient chronicle notes the destruction of a Christian church by a flood at Edessa in 201. It is quite possible that the first real Christian communities were founded in 260, when, after the defeat of Valerian, many Christians with their priests and bishops were carried off from Coelesyria into Mesopotamia. The inner organization of the Persian Church was effected by Papa bar Aggai, who was bishop of the royal city *Seleucia-Ctesiphon in the last decades of the 3d century and the first decades of the 4th.

Under the relatively weak Arsacids (c. 247 B.C.–A.D. 224) Christianity was largely tolerated, but when the Sassanids (224–651) came to power, conversions from Zoroastrianism were regarded as a capital offense. This opposition to Christianity was sharpened in the 4th century, when it became the official religion of the Roman Empire. The Christians were subject to intermittent and, at times, violent persecutions. For 40 years (348–388) no patriarch, or catholicos, could be elected to the See of Seleucia-Ctesiphon. Since no theological school could be erected in Persian territory and the schools of Antioch, Alexandria, and Constantinople were so far distant, it was extremely difficult to provide instruction for future priests.

The problem was partially solved by James, Bishop of *Nisibis, a Roman city near the Persian frontier. On his return from the Council of Nicaea in 325 he founded a theological school at Nisibis and entrusted its direction to the future saint and Doctor of the Church *Ephrem the Syrian. The school flourished until 363, when Nisibis was handed over to the Persians by the Emperor Jovian after Julian's disastrous campaign against Ctesiphon. Transferred to Edessa, the school became famous for its adaptation of Aristotelian philosophy to theology and for its translations of Greek works into Syriac.

In 399, when Yazdgard I became King of Persia, Emperor Arcadius sent Bishop Maruthas of Martyropolis to congratulate him on his accession. Maruthas, a Mesopotamian and a skilled physician, was able to win the monarch's favor for the Christians. With the help of his governors, Yazdgard (also Yazdagrid) in 410 convoked a synod at Seleucia under the direction of the Catholicos Isaac. The plenary session that was held February 1 with 40 bishops in attendance adopted the Nicene Creed and the principal disciplinary decrees of Nicaea and of the provincial synods that completed it. Toward the end of his reign Yazdgard was influenced by the *Magi, who were alarmed by the spread of Christianity; and he ordered the destruction of Christian churches and the exile of Christians themselves. Though he died soon after giving this order, the persecution was continued by his son, Vahrām V (421–438). When the Persians demanded the return of Christians who had fled into Roman territories, war broke out. In the treaty of peace that followed, *Theodosius II obtained from Vahrām (also Vaharam, Bahram) a promise of freedom of conscience for Christians in Persian lands, and at the same time he guaranteed a similar liberty for Mazdakites living within the Roman Empire.

The Persian Church Becomes Nestorian. A synod held in 424 under Patriarch Dadisho' with 36 bishops present decreed that the Persian catholicos was subject only to the tribunal of Christ. This implicit declaration of independence from the Church of the West was followed in later years by the adoption of the dubious Christological doctrines of Theodore of Mopsuestia and Nestorius. In its teaching on Christ the school of *Edessa, where the Persian clergy were educated, was essentially Antiochene; that is, it so stressed the distinction between the two natures in Christ as to give the impression, even if unintentional, that there was no really personal union but only one that was moral or accidental. At the time of Nestorius's condemnation, *Rabbula, a violent opponent of Nestorius, was bishop of Edessa. On his death in 435 he was succeeded by Ibas, head of the school at Edessa and staunch defender of Theodore of Mopsuestia. In 449 at the "Robber Synod" of *Ephesus Ibas was deposed on the basis of a letter that he had written to the Persian Bishop Mari of *Seleucia-Ctesiphon (433 of 436), in which he defended Diodore of Tarsus and Theodore of Mopsuestia while rejecting Nestorius. Though Ibas was reinstated at Chalcedon (451) after anathematizing Nestorius, his letter was condemned at the Council of *Constantinople II (553) as one of the "Three Chapters." On the death of Ibas in 457 Narses, who had succeeded him as head of the school of Edessa, was driven from the city by the Monophysites. Going to Nisibis, he founded a school there that continued to keep alive the teachings of

Theodore and Nestorius on the two natures in Christ. The college eventually accommodated some 800 students and became so famous that Pope *Agapetus I and *Cassiodorus thought of founding a similar one in Italy.

When the Catholicos Dadisho' died in 456, he was succeeded by Bâbôe (457–484). His position was sought by Bar Sauma, Metropolitan of Nisibis, patron of Narses, and friend of King Peroz. At court Bar Sauma urged the advantages of a married Christian clergy, a project favored by the Magi, and a Christian teaching or doctrine (Nestorianism) that would be different from that of the Roman Empire. In 484 Bâbôe was arrested because of a letter he had written to Constantinople that was intercepted at Nisibis. When he refused to "prove" his loyalty to the King by worshiping the sun, he was cruelly executed. Bar Sauma's hopes of obtaining the catholicate were, however, shattered by the death of King Peroz shortly after that of Bâbôe.

In 485 Acacius was elected patriarch, and in February of the following year he held a synod at Seleucia in which the Antiochene, or Nestorian, formula for the dogma of the two natures in Christ was adopted and permission was granted to deacons and priests to marry even after ordination. In 497 a synod held by the Catholicos Bābai extended this permission to bishops and the catholicos.

During the 6th century the Nestorian Church was torn by a long schism (521 or 522–537 or 539), a violent persecution (540–545) under Chosroes (Khusro) I (531–579), and by various ecclesiastical scandals. Order was restored through the reforms of the great Patriarch Mar Aba (540–552), but his successor, Joseph, was deposed for simony and oppressing his subject priests and bishops. When the Catholicos Gregory I died in 609, Chosroes II ordered the confiscation of his goods and forbade the election of a successor. The see was vacant until 628. At a synod held by the Nestorian bishops in 612 without the presidency of a patriarch, the Christology of the energetic monk Bābai the Great was adopted. Unlike other earlier Nestorian formulas, that of Bābai can in no sense be interpreted in a way that would make it harmonize with the decrees of the Council of Chalcedon.

In 628 Chosroes was assassinated, and his son Kavādh II came to the throne. A secret convert to Christianity, the new king permitted the Nestorians to elect a catholicos, Ishojabh (also Ishō'jab; 628–644 or 646), but he died after 6 or 8 months of a troubled reign. Yazdgard III (631–651), the last of the Sassanids, was unable to muster sufficient forces to ward off the attacks of Islam and in 637 saw the fall of his capital city Seleucia-Ctesiphon.

Monasticism and Missionary Endeavors. Despite the frequent persecutions from without and the scandals, schisms, and dissensions from within, the Nestorian Church showed a remarkable vitality under the Sassanids, especially in the growth of monastic institutions and in the founding of numerous missions. Already in the 3d century there were hermits in Persia leading ascetical lives in solitude. In the writings of *Aphraates in the following century mention is made of the "sons" and "daughters of the covenant," men and women dedicated to study and prayer, leading celibate lives in a community. This native monastic movement was influenced by the ideals and practices of immigrant monks from Egypt. The great organizer and reformer of monasticism among the Nestorians was Abraham of Kashkar (501–586). After traveling in Egypt and spending some time in Nisibis, he established a retreat on Mount Izlā. Numerous other monasteries were founded by his disciples. A distinctive characteristic of Nestorian monasticism was the active interest that the monks took in the physical and spiritual needs of their countrymen.

The missionary labors of the Nestorians were partially due to the persecutions to which they were subject. Driven from their homes, they established new centers of Christianity in remote parts of the kingdom or in foreign lands. But they also engaged in active proselytizing along the great trade routes leading to the north, south, and east. Before the Arab conquest of Persia they had brought Christianity to Yemen and the eastern coasts of Arabia. Other missionaries were active on the islands of Socotra and Ceylon and in South India, as is evidenced by Pahlavi inscriptions of the 6th and 7th centuries on stone crosses found at St. Thomas's Mount near Madras and at Kottayam in Travancore. The liturgical language of these churches was Syriac; and their theology, Nestorian. During this period there were Nestorian churches, bishops, and even metropolitans in the great caravan cities of Central Asia, including Merv, Herat, and Samarkand.

The first Nestorian missionaries reached China in 631. Four years later one of them, Olipan, visited Emperor T'ai Tsung in his capital of Changan, more recently known as Si-gnan-fu or Sian. He received permission to preach the "Luminous Doctrine," as Christianity was then known in China. During the course of the next century several monasteries and a metropolitanate were established. The early history of this mission has been recorded on the so-called Nestorian monument erected in February 781 and discovered in 1625 at Chou-chih, 50 miles southwest of Si-gnan-fu. An edict of Emperor Wu Tsung issued in 845 primarily against the Buddhists caused serious harm to the Nestorian Church in China, and by the 10th century Christianity had completely disappeared from the empire.

Nestorians under the Moslems. The conquest of Persia by the Arabs brought 2 centuries of relative peace and prosperity to the Nestorians. The Moslems granted the Christians, who were monotheists and to a great extent Semites like themselves, freedom of worship and the right to make converts among the Persians. Realizing their own cultural inferiority, they employed Christian scholars to translate the writings of the ancient Greek philosophers into Arabic and were thus able to acquire the Hellenic culture that they later communicated to the Christians of the West. But Moslem rule also had its disadvantages. Ordinary Christians were forced to accept a lower position in society and to pay a special tax. The Nestorian catholicos came to be regarded as the civil head of his community, especially after the patriarchate was moved to Baghdad, and this increased the rivalry for election. But, despite these difficulties, the missionary activities of the Nestorians continued to flourish, especially under Timotheus I (780–823). Missionaries sent out by him made numerous converts in Tibet and Chinese Turkestan, who were to be of great importance because of the connections these peoples had with the Mongols.

Portion of a charter of protection granted to the Nestorian Church by the Caliph Muktafi II of Baghdad in 1138 (Rylands MS Arab 669); it confirms the election of the Nestorian Patriarch 'Abdīshō III.

One of the sons of Genghis Khan (1162–1227) married a Christian princess of the Keraits, and she became the mother of his two most famous grandsons, Kublai (1216–94) and Hulagu Khan (1217–65). Hulagu's favorite wife was a Christian, and Mangu, grand khan from 1251 to 1259, is said to have been baptized by an Armenian bishop. Under Mongol rule Christian missionaries were again able to enter China, and the Nestorians had an archbishop in the Mongol capital of Cambaluc, later Peiping.

After falling into the hands of the Seljuk Turks in the 10th century and then passing through a period of political anarchy, Persia was subjected to the Mongols by Hulagu Khan in 1258. In 1281 Mark, a Mongolian monk and son of an archbishop, who had come to Baghdad to visit the center of Nestorianism, was named catholicos and took the name of Yabhalaha III. Of a kindly disposition, he ruled the Nestorian Church through a stormy period under seven Mongol kings and had the consolation of baptizing some of them. His hope that the Mongols would join forces with the Christians of the West to crush Islam was doomed to failure. After a period of vacillation the Mongols turned to Mohammedanism rather than to Christianity, finding it more compatible with their own barbaric customs. Under the Moslem Timur (1379–1405) the Persian Christians suffered a terrible persecution. All those who failed to escape to the mountains were put to the sword, and very little is heard of the Nestorians in these areas until the accession of 'Abbas the Great in 1582.

Reunions with Rome. The Crusades provided various contacts between the Churches of the East and the West, and these in turn led to more or less successful attempts at reunion with Rome. Negotiations were frequently conducted through Franciscan, Dominican, and, in later centuries, Jesuit missionaries, but not always with sufficient understanding and prudence. In the spring of 1235 the Dominican William of Montferrat was sent by Gregory IX to the Catholicos Sabrīshōʻ V, who had shown some interest in a reunion. This embassy proved to be fruitless, but soon after it a Nestorian archbishop, probably from Damascus, on the occasion of a pilgrimage to Jerusalem made his submission to the Holy See and was congratulated by Pope Gregory IX in a letter dated July 29, 1237. In 1304 the Catholicos Yabhalaha sent to Rome from Maragha a profession of faith through a Dominican returning to Italy, but his desire for reunion was frustrated by the Nestorian clergy who checked the efforts of Latin missionaries to bring it about. In 1340 Elias, Archbishop of Nicosia in Cyprus, made a profession of faith in which he upheld the authority of the Holy See, but it was only in 1445 that a reunion of the Nestorian Church in Cyprus was officially recorded in Rome. This is to be found in a bull of *Eugene IV, which he promulgated after the Metropolitan Timotheus had made his profession of faith before the archbishop of Colossae.

In a bull of April 8, 1330, John XXII urged the Dominican Jourdain de Séverac, whom he had appointed bishop of Quilon on the Malabar coast, to work for a return of the Christians of that area to union with Rome. Nothing is known of the success of this venture except that c. 1347 there was a Latin church in the city. In 1498 the Portuguese came to India, and in 1503 the Malabar Christians asked for their protection. These Christians were gradually freed from their Nestorian errors and formally united with Rome. In 1599 a synod convoked at Diamper by Alexis Menezes, Archbishop of Goa, decreed a unification of the hierarchy and a revision of the liturgical books of the Malabar Christians to bring them into greater conformity with the Roman ritual. The decrees were enforced by the Portuguese, but the policy was a failure since many Catholics broke with Rome and joined the Nestorians. Through the efforts of Jesuit and Carmelite missionaries, however, nearly 250,000 of the Malabar Christians remained united with the Holy See.

In 1551 a group of Nestorians eager for reunion met at Mosul and delegated Sullāqā, superior of the monastery of Rabbān Hormizd, near Alkōsh, to go to Rome. There he made his profession of faith and on April 28, 1553, received the pallium and the title of Chaldean patriarch. He returned to the East with two Maltese Dominicans to help him with the work of reunion. After taking up residence at Diárbekr, he was imprisoned and executed at the beginning of 1555. The united Chaldeans chose as his successor 'Abdīshō, the metropolitan of Jeziret ibn-Omar (Beit-Zabdaï), who went to Rome and received the pallium from Pius IV.

During the 17th and 18th centuries reconciliations with various Nestorian groups continued to be made. In the 19th century the Nestorians were greatly di-minished in numbers. Their chief center was around Lake Urmia in the mountainous regions of northwestern Persia. In the 1830s and 1840s they were frequently attacked and massacred by the neighboring Kurds. During these same decades they were visited by English and American Protestant missionaries, and toward the close of the century, by Russian missionaries as well. During World War I their numbers were further diminished by marauding bands of Turks, Kurds, and Moslem Persians. Many fled from the mountains of Kurdistan to the plains of Mesopotamia, then occupied by the English. In 1933, after Iraq's declaration of independence, many Nestorians fled to Syria. Of this once vast and apostolic Church there are only a relatively few survivors today: 80,000 in Iraq, Iran, and Syria; 5,000 in India; and another 25,000 in the Americas.

Bibliography: J. CHAPMAN, CE 10:755–759. G. OUSSANI, CE 11:712–725. J. LABOURT, CE 3:559–561; *Le Christianisme dans l'empire perse* (Paris 1904). Latourette. R. LEYS, LexThK² 7:887–888. M. GUIDI, EncIt 24:680–684. F. NAU, *L'Expansion nestorienne en Asie* (Paris 1914). E. TISSERANT, DTC 11.1:157–323. M. JUGIE and G. DE VRIES, EncCatt 8:1780–87. **Illustration credit:** John Rylands Library, Manchester, England.

[M. J. COSTELLOE]

NESTORIANISM

A development of the Antiochene theology as it had been formulated by Eustathius of Sebaste, Diodore of Tarsus, and *Theodore of Mopsuestia in reaction to Arianism and Apollinarianism. It is clearly dyophysitic (*duo physeis,* or two natures in Christ), in contrast with the explanations of St. *Cyril of Alexandria, who held that in Christ there was one nature (*mia physis*), in which teaching Cyril's opponents detected Apollinarian echoes.

Nestorian Teaching. The doctrine of Nestorius is known through fragments of his letters and sermons preserved in the Acts of the Council of *Ephesus, frequent citations in the works of St. Cyril of Alexandria, fragments of a personal apology (*Tragoedia*) composed after his deposition but before 439, and through the text of another apology, *The Bazaar of Heracleides,* written toward the end of his life and preserved in an interpolated Syrian version. Further information is offered by such opponents as John *Cassian (*De Incarnatione Domini contra Nestorium* of 429–430) and St. Cyril (*Adv. Nestorii Blasphemias* of 430), who convinced their contemporaries and posterity that Nestorius was a heretic.

Some modern historians, such as A. Harnack, F. Loofs, J. Bethune-Baker, and L. Duchesne, have sought to reestablish Nestorius's good name, saying that he was not necessarily a Nestorian; and A. Grillmeier believes that underlying the Nestorian formulas, even though these are contestable or plainly heterodox, there are valuable theological suppositions.

Christology. The Christological thought of Nestorius is dominated by Cappadocian theology and is affected by Stoic thought. Although it was not devoid of speculative value, nevertheless, in its attempt to avoid Arianism and Apollinarianism, Nestorianism did not reflect the true tradition of the Church. This fact was recognized by the early historians, such as Socrates (*Hist. Eccl.* 8.29.30); for in his *Bazaar of Heracleides,* Nestorius asserted that the key word *Theotokos had not been used by the Fathers.

Nestorius never spoke of "two sons," nor did he consider Christ as simply a man (*purus homo*); hence it was improper on the part of Eusebius of Doryleum to accuse him of the *Adoptionism of Paul of Samosata, a theology that saw Christ as a man who through his sufferings and virtues attained the dignity of a Son of God (Bewährungstheologie).

Cyril spoke of one sole nature (*mia physis*) in Christ, a nature that could be understood in the way that Cyril intended: as a concrete, existent subject. But Nestorius defined a nature in the sense of *ousia*, or substance, and distinguished precisely between the human nature and the divine nature, applying in his Christology the distinction between nature (*ousia*) and person (*hypostasis*), which was currently in use in the trinitarian theology. Remarking that "wherever the Scriptures mention the economy [of salvation in the Incarnation] of the Lord," they attribute His birth and Passion not to the divinity but to humanity, Nestorius refused to attribute to the divine nature the human acts and sufferings of Jesus (*Epist. ad Cyrillum*). This statement represents the crux of the disagreement between Cyril and Nestorius; it makes it probable that if their ideas and vocabulary could have been neatly clarified and defined, the argument as well as the schism could have been avoided.

The Theotokos. Nestorius refused to call Mary the *Theotokos* (God bearer), which proved to be the starting point for the whole quarrel. He held that to call Mary the Mother of God would be in effect to say that the divine nature had been born of a woman; Mary had begotten only a man, to whom the Word of God was united. Nestorius would agree to say *Theotokos* (Mother of God) only on the condition that one said at the same time *anthropotokos* (mother of man); for him the right word was *christotokos* (mother of Christ).

While distinguishing between the natures, Nestorius still affirmed their union. He would not consent to speak of "two sons"; but he spoke of a conjunction, a voluntary union, or one of accommodation, and gave the impression of believing in a union in the psychological or moral order rather than that of a metaphysical nature. This would be an extrinsic union like that of a temple with the divinity inhabiting it, of clothing and the wearer, or of an instrument (*organon*) and the user. Certain of these examples, such as that of the temple, are found in the Scriptures and in tradition.

Nestorius affirmed the close union and conjunction of a concrete human nature with the divinity, and the termination of that union is the *prosopon* or person of Christ, God and man. This involves a central point of difference between the theology of Nestorius and that of Cyril as well as that which the Church made its own at the Council of *Ephesus and in subsequent tradition.

St. Cyril. For Cyril, who justly drew support from the Creed of Nicaea, the unique subject is the Word (*Logos*) incarnate, become man in such fashion that it can be said that it is the Word that is born, lives, suffers, and dies in the flesh; there is no distinguishing between the Word and Christ. Nestorius on the other hand made a distinction between the *Logos* (the divine nature) and Christ (the Son, the Lord), which he saw as a result of the union of the divine nature and the human nature. Christ for him was like the total of two natures or the expression of their union, rather than the unique divine subject of the Incarnation. Nestorius spoke likewise of

a "*prosopon* of union," the result of the union of the two *prosopa*, the divine and the human.

There is no doubt that Nestorius used the term *prosopon* (which meant originally the mask or representation of a person in the Greek theater) in expressions that recall the "communication of idioms," and he used formulas that Cyril might have employed; but the metaphysical foundation behind this use of "nature" and "person" was insufficient to protect the personal unity represented by the *"Word Incarnate."*

According to É. Amann, Nestorius could not imagine a nature without its own subsistence, or which was not a concrete hypostasis or personality. He did not clearly comprehend the distinction between the concept of real existence and that of independent subsistence. According to G. Prestige, Nestorius was not able to reduce to a unique, clearly differentiated person the two natures of Christ, which he nevertheless distinguished with such admirable realism.

The Nestorian Church. After the Council of Ephesus a strong Nestorian party existed in eastern Syria around the theological school of Ibas of Edessa, who was apparently a convinced Nestorian. After the theological peace achieved in the agreement of 433 between Cyril of Alexandria and John of Antioch, a number of bishops who rejected that agreement drew closer to the Syrian Church of Persia, which officially adopted Nestorianism at the Synod of Seleucia in 486. The Nestorians were expelled from Edessa in 489 by the Emperor Zeno and emigrated to Persia. It was thus that the Nestorian Church broke away from the faith of the Church of Constantinople and the Byzantine Empire.

The Nestorianism of the Persian Church was greatly strengthened at the synod of 612 when it adopted the heterodox principles of the catholicos, Babai the Great: two natures, two *hypostaseis*, one sole *prosopon*; the term *theotokos* was formally excluded. This Church continued to flourish in spite of periods of persecution under the Sassanids, and even after the invasions of the Turks and Mongols. Its strength is witnessed by its theological schools at Seleucia and *Nisibis; its monasticism; and missionary expansion in Arabia, India (Malabar), Turkistan, Tibet, and even in China, where the bilingual inscription (in Syrian and Chinese) of Si-ngan-fu attests its presence in 781. The invasion and bloody persecution by Tamerlane (1380) almost destroyed the Nestorian Church, which today is greatly reduced in size in Iraq, Iran, and Syria and has a number of congregations in the U.S.

A reunion of the Nestorians of Cyprus with Rome took place in 1445. In 1553 the Nestorian patriarch John Sulaqua professed the Catholic faith at Rome and was recognized as patriarch of Mosul. The union thus achieved continues today. Since 1696 the Chaldean patriarch has the title patriarch of Babylon. The Chaldeans number about 180,000 adherents. The Nestorians of Malabar, reunited with Rome in 1599, have some 1,300,000 communicants and use the old Syrian liturgy of Addai and Mari (*see* MALABAR RITE).

Bibliography: NESTORIUS, *Nestoriana*, ed. F. LOOFS et al. (Halle 1905); *Le Livre d'Héraclide de Damas*, tr. and ed. F. NAU et al. (Paris 1910), Eng. tr. *The Bazaar of Heracleides*, tr. and ed. G. R. DRIVER and L. HODGSON (Oxford 1925). J. F. B. BAKER, *Nestorius and His Teaching* (Cambridge, Eng. 1908). F. LOOFS, *Nestorius and His Place in the History of the Christian Doctrine* (Cambridge, Eng. 1914). É. AMANN, DTC 11.1:76–157. A. GRILLMEIER, Grill-Bacht Konz 1:120–202; "Das Scandalum oecumenicum des Nestorius," *Scholastik* 36 (1961) 321–356. P. T. CAMELOT, Grill-Bacht Konz 1:213–242; *Éphèse et Chalcédoine*, v.2 of *Histoire des conciles oecuméniques* (Paris 1962). L. I. SCIPIONI, *Ricerche sulla Cristologia del Libro di Eraclide di Nestorio* (Fribourg 1956). F. NAU, *L'Expansion nestorienne en Asie* (Paris 1914). E. TISSERANT, DTC 11.1:157–323. Latourette 2.

[P. T. CAMELOT]

NESTORIUS

Patriarch of Constantinople and heresiarch; b. Germanicia in Euphratesian Syria, after A.D. 381; d. Libya, after 451. Of Persian parenthood, Nestorius studied in Antioch and entered the monastery of Euprepios, where he was ordained. He penetrated deeply into the Antiochene theology, although it is doubtful that he became a disciple of *Theodore of Mopsuestia. An orator, he was selected by *Theodosius II to succeed Sisinnius as bishop of Constantinople and was consecrated April 10, 428. A zealous opponent of *Arianism and *Pelagianism, he corresponded with Pope *Celestine I on the Pelagianism of *Julian of Eclanum, then residing in Constantinople.

Nestorius inaugurated a vast theological quarrel by preaching against the title *Theotokos, or Mother of God, given to the Virgin Mary, claiming she should be called rather the Mother of Christ. His doctrine was challenged by Eusebius of Doryleum, still a layman, who posted a contestatio, or rebuttal, on the doors of *Hagia Sophia in Constantinople, charging Nestorius with the errors of *Paul of Samosata. Nestorius wrote to Pope Celestine to explain his teaching on the Christotokos, and Eusebius sent the Pope copies of the bishop's sermons. Meanwhile *Cyril of Alexandria, disturbed by agitation on the part of Egyptian monks, sent two letters to Nestorius warning him of the heretical implications in calling Mary only the Mother of Christ and not the Mother of God. Cyril finally sent a dossier of the argument to Celestine, who in a Roman synod (August 430) summoned Nestorius to retract within 10 days and charged Cyril with executing this sentence. After a synod at Alexandria in which Nestorius' teaching was condemned (November 430), Cyril wrote a third letter to Nestorius to which he adjoined 12 anathemas (*capitula*) requesting Nestorius's acquiescence and signature. Nestorius in turn charged Cyril with *Apollinarianism and called upon the Emperor Theodosius II to convoke a council to settle the matter. The Council of *Ephesus met in June 431, but Nestorius refused to appear before it when Cyril, charged by Pope Celestine with acting as his legate, took over the presidency. In a session on June 22, 431, Nestorius was condemned as a heretic and despite charges of irregularity in the Council's proceedings, Theodosius deposed Nestorius and relegated him to a monastery from which, at the insistence of *John of Antioch, he was sent into exile to Petra in Arabia (436) and finally to the Great Oasis in Libya, where he died.

In 435 Theodosius ordered the writings of Nestorius to be burnt; hence only fragments of his sermons, letters, and treatises have been preserved. They were edited by F. *Loofs in 1905. His *Bazaar of Heraclides*, discovered in 1895 in a Syrian translation, is an autobiographical defense of his teaching in which he claims that his doctrine was identical with that of Pope *Leo I and *Flavian of Constantinople. Its literary form attests Nestorius' eloquence, and its plea for charity and forgiveness have caused a reestimate of his guilt as a heretic, although the doctrine known as *Nestorianism took its rise from his preaching. A fragment of an earlier defense, known as the *Tragedy* of Nestorius, written probably between 431 and 435, has been preserved in Greek, Latin, and Syriac, and a number of his letters and sermons have been published in the literature dealing with the Council of Ephesus.

Bibliography: NESTORIUS, *Nestoriana: Fragmente,* tr. and ed. F. LOOFS et al. (Halle 1905). É. AMANN, DTC 11.1:76–157. I. RUCHER, Pauly-Wiss RE 17.1:126–137. Quasten Patr 3:514–519. M. JUGIE and G. DE VRIES, EncCatt 8:1780–87. ActConcOec 1.1.1–6. J. F. BETHUNE-BAKER, *Nestorius and His Teaching* (Cambridge, Eng. 1908). R. V. SELLERS, *Two Ancient Christologies* (London 1940). P. GALTIER, "Nestorius mal compris, mal traduit," Greg 34 (1953) 427–433.

[P. T. CAMELOT]

NETHERLANDIC LITERATURE

The Netherlandic language, of the West Germanic dialects, is spoken in the Netherlands, northern Belgium, and in northernmost France. In the Netherlands the official language is called Dutch; in Belgium and northern France, Flemish. Flemish is almost purely Low Franconian, while Dutch is Low Franconian with Low Saxon and Frisian traits. There are no remains of Old Netherlandic save some names in Latin charters and two lines in Old West Flemish, dating from the 11th century. Written Netherlandic in the Middle Ages shows rather strong dialectal differences, so that West and East Flemish, Brabant, Limburg, and Hollandic dialects are recognizable in addition to the language of the eastern provinces. In the 17th century the Hollandic dialect dominated and gave its particularities to modern Dutch, while in the south, Flemish became the language of northern Belgium.

Medieval Literature. Literature in the Low Countries appeared early in the 12th century with the legend of *St. Servaes* by Henric van Veldeke (*c.* 1140–90). Then followed pre-courtly romances, the finest of which is the tale of *Karel ende Elegast* (1200–30), whose hero was a romantic vassal of Charlemagne. Under the influence of the Crusades, Oriental tales appeared around 1250, e.g., *Floris ende Blanceflor* (see CRUSADE LITERATURE). The first Arthurian romances were written by *Jacob van Maerlant (see ARTHURIAN AND CAROLINGIAN LEGENDS). The authors of chivalric literature were mostly clerics and even ordinary citizens, since *feudalism never flourished in the Lowlands. Animal fables were beloved, for their didactic flavor agreed with the needs and taste of the burghers, who were powerful in a time when in most other countries knighthood was at its height (see CHIVALRY; ROMANCE, MEDIEVAL). About 1149 Magister Nivardus from Ghent produced a Latin epic, *Isengrinus,* and in the middle of the 13th century the *Esopet* appeared, a translation of Aesop's fables. This genre culminated in the epic *Reinaert* (early 13th century), a satire on weak princes and bad priests. The greatest moralist was Jacob van Maerlant, of whose many followers Jan van Boendale (1285–1365) is best known.

Besides legends and fables, the citizens enjoyed reading or listening to the noteworthy deeds of their princes and ancestors, and a rich chronicle literature developed. *Troubadour songs were scarce, whereas folk songs flourished. Religious poetry consisted mainly of Christmas songs, some of which have a high poetic value. Mystical poetry was written by the nun *Hade-wijch, prose by the widely known Bl. Jan van *Ruysbroeck. The monasteries fostered the spreading of legends in which the merciful assistance of the Virgin Mary was stressed (e.g., *Beatrijs, Theophilus*). Marking the end of the Middle Ages, four courtly dramas, the so-called *abele spelen* (beautiful plays), represented the oldest secular theater of western Europe (*Esmoreit, Gloriant, Lanseloet van Denemarken,* and *Van den Winter ende van den Somer*).

Humanism and Renaissance. During the 15th and the beginning of the 16th century, the literature of the Lowlands gradually evidenced the influence of *Humanism and the *Renaissance. The increasing quantity of literature produced by the citizens themselves reflected middle-class attitudes and emotions. The people still loved religious prose and poetry, and especially plays that emphasized religious problems. Two of these are true works of art: *Mariken van Nieumegen* (*c.* 1500) relates the story of a girl who lived with the devil, but whose soul was saved through the help of the Blessed Virgin, and *Elckerlijc* (*Everyman), written probably by the Carthusian monk Petrus Dorlandus (1454–1507), was translated into English.

Printing made literature accessible to a greater number of people and made possible the *Volksboeken* (popular books), in which the stories of Alexander, Troy, and Floris and Blancheflor were retold and illustrated with rough woodcuts. Adventurous travelogues (e.g., *Mandeville), stories based upon popular legends (e.g., *The Four Haymons Children*), and chronicles were also widespread. The tale of the humorous rascal Thyl Ulenspiegel, reflecting the same mocking spirit as the *Reynaert* of former days, was most widely read. Poetry was found in large collections: many poems dated back to an earlier period. The songs of the Franciscan preacher Joannes Brugman (1400–73) and of Sister Bertken (d. 1514) embodied a practical mysticism reminiscent of the spirituality of the *Brethren of the Common Life.

Most important were the so-called Rederijkerskamers (Guilds of Rhetoric), whose members established strict rules for the writing of poetry. They favored allegories, and although the contents of their works still reflected much of the medieval mind, their language, embellished with classical names and metaphors, showed the influence of humanism. The Rederijkerskamers flourished mainly in the South, where Anthonis de Roovere (1430–82) and Cornelis Everaert (1485–1556) wrote several allegorical plays. The priest Matthijs de Castelein (1485–1550) wrote a *Conste van Rhetoriken* (1548, Art of Rhetoric) and Colijn van Rijssele composed *Spiegel der Minnen* (Mirror of Love), the first bourgeois drama in the Netherlands (early 16th century). Several of the Rederijkers were influenced by the Reformation, which spread quickly through the Lowlands and established various Protestant sects, notably the Calvinists and Baptists. Concurrent with the religious struggles was the political uprising (1568) against Philip II's absolutism. Large collections of historical poems that were sung by the people as comfort in their distress, the so-called *Geuzenliederen* and the songs of Adriaen *Valerius' *Nederlandtsche Gedenck-clanck* (1626), reflect the emotional strength of the people, and are still sung in school and home. The southern Lowlands was the center of power until after the fall of Antwerp in

1584, when prominent Protestants who had fled to the north continued the fight that ended in the independence of the northern provinces (1648). The south remained under foreign rulers until 1815.

During these turbulent times the true spirit of the Renaissance penetrated the literature of the Lowlands, appearing first in the poems of Jan van der Noot of Antwerp (1539–c. 1600), who became a Calvinist in 1566, only to return in 1578 to the Catholic Church. He wrote an epic, sonnets, odes, elegies, and prose, and was strongly influenced by the French poet *Ronsard. Prose writing became an art in itself and was done with the utmost care following the example of the classics. Dirck Volkertszoon *Coornhert and *Marnix van St. Aldegonde wrote philosophic and polemic prose; the painter Carel von Mander (1548–1606), a refugee from the south, composed his *Schilderboek* (1604, Painters' Book) on the model of the Italian *Vasari's *Vite dei piu eccelenti pittori, scultori e architetti* (1550). Hendrik Laurensz Spiegel of Amsterdam (1549–1612) presented Catholic-humanistic philosophy in his long poem *Hertspieghel* (1694, Mirror of the Heart). Love for his mother tongue impelled him to write the first Dutch grammar, in cooperation with his friend Roemer Visscher (1547–1620), author of the first Dutch emblemata (*see* EMBLEM BOOKS).

The Golden Age. These authors paved the way for the next generation, which achieved Holland's "golden age." The five greatest poets of this period reach the highest level of world literature. Jacob Cats (1577–1660), a moralist storyteller, combined Calvinistic philosophy and practical wisdom in his iambic poems. "Father Cats" was read in every Dutch family and many Dutch proverbs originate from his works. Constantijn *Huygens also was of the didactic school.

The "last of the minstrels," Pieter Corneliszoon Hooft (1581–1647), traveled in France and Italy and returned

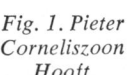

Fig. 1. Pieter Corneliszoon Hooft.

a full-fledged Renaissance poet, who wrote in pursuit of beauty and tolerance. His sonnets and love songs are notable for their musical rhythm and rich vocabulary. His prose shows the influence of Tacitus, whose works he translated. Best known is his *Nederlandse Historien* (1642–47), an account of the Dutch uprising against Spain. In addition Hooft composed the first pastoral play in Dutch, *Granida* (1605). His drama, *Gheeraerd van Velzen* (1613), expresses the opinion that the murder of a prince who has violated the rights of the people is justified as long as it is not motivated by personal revenge. In *Baeto* (1617), the prince is seen as his people's servant. Finally Hooft showed that he had not lost the common touch in *Warenar* (1616), a comedy after Plaudus's *Aulularia* a colorful picture of the life of the burghers of Amsterdam. Joost van den *Vondel, the greatest representative of *baroque literature in the Netherlands, lost contact with Hooft after being converted to Catholicism.

An early representative of romanticism was Gerbrand Adriaens Brederode (1585–1618), whose lyrical poetry is of enduring freshness and beauty. Like Hooft, he knew intimately the life of the ordinary people, and pictured it in a farce, the *Klucht van de Koe* (1612, Farce of the Cow), a masterly mixture of realism and humor, and in his comedies *Het Moortje* (1615, The Mooress) and the *Spaanschen Brabander* (1618, from the Spanish novel *Lazarillo de Tormes*), wherein he painted a realistic portrait of a boasting southerner who embellishes a drab life with his vivid imagination. This period produced as well several minor poets whose works are of considerable value. The fervent Calvinist Jacobus Revius (1586–1658) wrote songs and sonnets in strong poetic language. The clergyman Dirck Rafaelsz Camphuysen (1586–1627) represented liberal Protestantism with his popular *Stichtelijke Rijmen* (1624, Devotional Rhymes), which was reprinted more than 50 times during the century. Joannes *Stalpaert van der Wiele wrote from the Catholic viewpoint, while Jan Starter (1594–1626), author of the first Dutch musical, composed secular songs. The last prominent poet of this century was the pietistic artist Jan Luyken (1649–1712), a follower of Jakob *Böhme; Luyken wrote texts for his own etchings and based religious meditations on everyday scenes. His works have a high artistic value, the poems and illustrations expressing the same lyric, deeply religious spirit.

Prose also made great strides in this period. The *Statenbijbel*, the official translation of the Bible (1626–37), composed by a committee of scholars and linguists from both south and north, had a strong impact on the Dutch language (*see* BIBLE IV, 25). In the latter half of the century Geeraerdt Brandt (1626–85) wrote a *Historie der Reformatie* (1671). He also is the author of the oldest biographies of Hooft (1677), Vondel (1682), and Admiral de Ruyter (1685). While the northern provinces could boast an extremely rich literature, the south had only a few writers: Justus de *Harduwijn and Boetius à Bolswert (*c.* 1580–1633), author of an allegory of life as a pilgrimage (1627); Adriaen *Poirters and Michiel de Swaen (1654–1707), whose comedy *De gecroonde Leersse* (1688, The Crowned Boot) is still performed. None of these authors achieved complete success, mainly because of the poor economic situation of their suppressed country. At the end of the 17th and the beginning of the 18th century the Lowlands were no longer a world power; endless wars had proved England's supremacy.

Rationalism and Classicism. It was in this period that *rationalism and classicism dominated the arts as well as literature (*see* NEOCLASSICISM). Rich merchants imitated the aristocracy and engaged court poets, who wrote long, laudatory poems on the occasions of birth, marriage, or death. Pastoral descriptions of the mansions and their symmetric gardens were likewise a favored topic. The Catholics Jan Baptist Wellekens (1658–1726) and Lucas Schermer (1688–1711) excelled in this genre. A late echo of Marnix's *Biecorf* is Jacob Zeeus's (1686–1718) anti-Catholic satire *De Wolf in't Schaepsvel* (1711, The Wolf in the Sheepskin). The former Catholic Willem van Swanenburg (1678–1728) also wrote antipapal songs. The best poet of this period was Hubert Poot (1689–1733), whose pastoral songs gave, for the first time, a personally experienced feeling for nature (*see* ARCADIANISM). The best prose writer was Justus van Effen (1684–1735), who introduced spectatorial literature. His free and natural style contrasts happily with the lushness of the *baroque. This simple style, embodying everyday speech, also characterizes the work of the comedy writers Thomas Asselijn (1620–1701) and Pieter Langendijk (1683–1756), who dramatized the vices of their fellow citizens with gentle humor.

Sturm und Drang and Sentimentalism. Toward the end of the 18th century, Dutch literature, until then under either French or English influence, received new stimuli from the German *Sturm und Drang* movement and from *sentimentalism, both reactions against the formalized literature of the Age of Reason (*see* GERMAN LITERATURE, 5). The political situation, influenced by French revolutionary tendencies, introduced a new emotional tone into literature. Two parties were in conflict: the conservatives or Orangists who wanted to keep the Prince of Orange as a *stadtholder,* and the progressives or Patriots, who fought for a free republic. The Orangist Hieronymus van Alphen (1746–1803) was the first to insist that sentiment has a proper role in literature. He was the author of the first Dutch cantata and of children's poems that are familiar to every Dutchman. Jacobus Bellamy (1757–86), a fervent Patriot, retained simplicity in his lyrics, but wrote fiery *Sturm und Drang* songs on his ideals of freedom. With Rhynvis Feith (1753–1824), pure sentimentalism entered into Dutch literature: lovers weeping on tombs and dying of melancholy. More controlled sentiment is found in the novels of Maria Elisabeth Post (1755–1812), who glorified the "noble savage," but the most significant authors of the period were the coworkers Elisabeth Wolff-Bekker (1738–1804) and Agatha Deken (1741–1804). Their novels *Sara Burgerhart* (1782) and *Willem Leevend* (1784–85) were the first modern Dutch psychological novels, revolving around the problems of sentimentalism and religion, written with a fine sense of humor and typical Dutch realism; they portray middle-class life with all its nuances.

Repercussions of the French Revolution were felt in the Lowlands, whence the Prince of Orange was forced to flee to England while the French troops helped the Patriots. Under Napoleon, the Lowlands became part of the French Empire, but after his defeat, the Congress of *Vienna united south and north as one United Kingdom under Willem I. This unification proved too artificial and after a short struggle, the south received its desired independence in 1830. From then on, the new Kingdom of Belgium and the Netherlands developed separately. But their literatures remained related and romanticism flourished in both countries.

Literature in the North. In the north, Willem Bilderdijk (1756–1831) broke down the last strongholds of rationalistic thinking: he poured out his religious and political feelings in epics and lyrics, and his influence as a conservative historian reached far into the 19th century. He sought rapport with Catholics in his *Aan de Roomsch-Katholieken dezer dagen* (1823, To the Roman Catholics of These Days). His opposite, Anthony C. W. Staring (1767–1840), expressed his liberal ideas in concise poems. In the latter part of the 19th century, many authors explored new territory, principally that of national history. Under the influence of Walter Scott, Jacob van Lennep (1802–68) used historical topics for his popular novels; Aarnout Drost (1810–34) adopted a more spiritual approach; and Reinier Cornelis Bakhuysen van den Brink (1810–65) wrote carefully researched historical essays designed to better acquaint his people with their glorious past. The greatest author in this genre, however, was Louise Geertruida *Bosboom-Toussaint, whose novels reveal her complete acceptance of Protestantism.

Under English influence, Nicolaas Beets (1814–1903) wrote the first genuinely humorous prose. Published under the pseudonym Hildebrand, his *Camera Obscura* (1839), which mixed realistic and sentimental short stories of middle-class life, established his wide popularity and won him many followers up to the end of the century. What Beets did in prose, the liberal clergyman Petrus Augustus de Genestet (1829–61) did in poetry. For generations his half-sentimental, half-humorous poems, inspired mainly by scenes from family life, were most frequently read and recited.

Finally, the critical essay developed with Jacob Geel (1789–1862), the first Dutch author in this genre. He was followed by Everhardus Johannes Potgieter (1808–75), the most important figure of the period. In 1837 Potgieter became one of the founders of *De Gids* (The Guide), which, in his hands, soon became the leading literary magazine. He emphasized the glory of the 17th century at the expense of mediocrity of his own time, hoping thus to stimulate the people; to the same end he introduced foreign authors (e.g., the American, Nathaniel Hawthorne) to the Dutch public. Potgieter's political poems as well as his prose reveal a humanistic liberalism (e.g., *Aan New York*, 1841). After having left *De Gids* he wrote *Florence* (1867), a long poem picturing Dante as the ideal citizen.

Potgieter collaborated with Conrad Busken Huet (1826–86), whose exemplary literary studies, *Litterarische Fantasiën en Kritieken* (collected 26 v., 1881–88), are still important for both style and generally accurate assessments. Huet's standard works on the cultural history of Belgium and the Netherlands are *Het Land van Rubens* (1879) and *Het Land van Rembrandt* (1882–84). A much weaker talent was that of the liberal Protestant clergyman Allard Pierson (1831–96), who in *Intimis* (1857) gave an account of his experience in the Catholic city of Louvain in order to provide the Dutch with a better understanding of Catholicism. His *Geschiedenis van het Katholicisme* (1868) and books on *Israel, Hellas,* and *Johannes Kalvijn* (1887–91) are standard works.

Continuing the tradition of these liberal authors, Carel Vosmaer (1826–88) represents the revival of classical studies and the growing cult of beauty; several of his novels and his excellent translations of the *Iliad* (1880) and the *Odyssey* (1888) are noteworthy. Eduard Douwes *Dekker, writing as "Multatuli," was more radical and leaned toward socialism; he had an immense influence on the next generations. Not only the liberals wrote political poetry; conservative voices also were raised. Isaac de Costa (1798–1860), a Portuguese Jew and pupil of Bilderdijk, became a Calvinist and the main figure of the "Reveil" movement, which emphasized the emotional quality of religious life in contrast to rigid dogmatism. Da Costa expressed his political, antirevolutionary ideas in a widely read pamphlet, *Bezwaren tegen den Geest der Eeuw* (1823, Objections Against the Spirit of This Century), and in political poems. He pointed out that estrangement from God was a danger for the nation.

During the 18th century Catholicism had played a minor role in Dutch cultural life, but after the French Revolution Catholics were granted the same rights as other citizens. J. M. Schrant (1783–1866), still a rationalist, tried to reconcile reason and religion. Three men, the convert Joachim le Sage ten Broek (1775–1847), his militant follower Jan J. F. Wap (1806–86), who fought *ultramontanism and the Jesuits, and Cornelis Broere (1803–60), tried to lift Catholic life to a higher intellectual level. But the chief impulse toward the revival of Catholic influence in art and literature came from the Bilderdijk-disciple J. A. *Alberdingk Thijm.

Literature in the South (Belgium). In the south Jan Frans Willems (1793–1846), supported by the Dutch King Willem I, urged his countrymen, whose Flemish language had been suppressed for centuries, to use their mother tongue instead of French and to look to the north for support in their fight against French supremacy. He tried to organize resistance and is rightly called "the father of the Flemish movement." He was joined by Hendrik Conscience (1812–83), whose nationalistic historical novels *De Leeuw van Vlaanderen* (1838, The Lion of Flanders) and *Jacob van Artevelde* (1849) gave his people self-confidence and pride in their past. Flanders' greatest poet, Guido *Gezelle, rejected Willems's call and strove for a Flemish culture independent of the north. From his school came the Rev. Hugo Verriest (1840–1922), the professor who inspired young Albrecht Rodenbach (1856–80), an ardent fighter for Flemish national pride and independence (e.g., *Gudrun*, 1882).

The Rise of Naturalism. In the Netherlands and in Belgium a reaction against declining literary romanticism was ushered in by *naturalism, individualism, and impressionism. Marcellus Emants (1848–1923), Hélène Swarth (1859–1941), and Jacques Perk (1859–81) were the forerunners of the new literary generation that founded the magazine *De nieuwe Gids* (1885, The New Guide) in the north, and *Van Nu en Straks* (1893, From Now and Later) in the south. *De Nieuwe Gids* vigorously charged that Dutch literature was lagging far behind the literatures of other countries. Its young editors themselves splendidly exemplified the ability of the Dutch to create literary works of high quality. Willem Kloos (1859–1938) wrote expressionistic, pantheistic sonnets that are among the Dutch classics. The essayist Albert Verwey (1865–1937) reevaluated literary figures of former times in forceful prose, while his poems expressed a mild Spinosism. (*See* SPINOZA, BARUCH). Frederik van *Eeden, however, was an ethical idealist.

Connected with this group or inspired by its enthusiasm were the Catholic-born Lodewijk van Deyssel (pseud. for Karel J. L. Alberdingk Thijm, 1864–1952), who had begun his career as a naturalistic writer (e.g., *De kleine Republiek,* 1889). In his essays he could be sarcastic as well as ecstatic, and it was he who ridiculed the mediocre poetic idols of a former generation. Herman Gorter (1864–1927) showed in his lyrical poem *Mei* (1889, May), written under the influence of Shelley and Keats, that beauty alone is not sufficient for the life of the soul. He became a socialist, and testified to his new ideals in the epic *Pan* (1907–16). Jacobus van Looy (1855–1930) was the first modern Dutch author to delve into child psychology (e.g., *Jaapje,* 1917). His colorful style (e.g., *Proza,* 1889) befitted one who was a painter as well. Louis Couperus (1863–1923), whose novel *Eline Vere* (1889) pictured decadence in aristocratic society, is recognized as one of the best novelists of this era. His novels about ancient Rome and Alexander the Great reflect the discord in the soul of the author who denounced God, yet felt His power. The plays of Herman *Heijermans were concerned with socialist ideology on the stage.

Henriette Roland Holst van der Schalk (1869–1952), the greatest woman poet of the time, first wrote humanistic sonnets (1885), but gradually her socialistic idealism expressed itself in a poetic play (*Thomas More,* 1912) and in several long poems. Later she left Marxism and became a Christian Socialist, embodying her farewell to Communist ideology in the epic *Heldensage* (1927, Heroes' Legend). Her biographies of Rousseau (1912), Garibaldi (1920), Tolstoi (1930), and Rosa Luxemburg (1935) are standard works. Pieter Cornelis Boutens (1870–1943) wrote Neoplatonic poems and reworked the medieval legend *Beatrijs* (1908). These authors had no common positive ideal and even among the editors of the *Nieuwe Gids* a split was inevitable. Verwey, more socially orientated than the hyperindividualistic Kloos, founded his own periodical, *De Beweging* (The Movement, 1905–19), around which he assembled many poets of the next generation, such as P. N. van Eyck (1887–1954) and Arthur van Schendel (1874–1946). Van Schendel was most famous for his romantic novels *Een Zwerver verliefd* (1904, A Wanderer in Love) and *Een Zwerver verdwaald* (1907, A Wanderer Lost the Way). His best novel, *De Waterman* (1933) pictures in masterly style Holland's landscape and its damp, hazy atmosphere as well as its silent, philosophical inhabitants. To this group also belong the poet J. C. Bloem (1887–) and Israel Querido (1872–1932) whose novels are inspired by the life of the people of Amsterdam, and by stories of the Orient.

Catholic authors published an excellent monthly, *De Beiaard* (The Carillon, 1916–25), under Gerard Brom (1882–1959). During the first decades of the 20th century, however, socialism was the chief inspiration of poets and novelists. The most popular poet was Carel S. Adama van Scheltema (1877–1924), the most remarkable was Abraham van Collem (1858–1933), and the most beloved novelist was A. M. de Jong (1888–1943), a former Catholic, who pictured boys' life in his famous *Merijntje Gijzen* (1925–38). Geerten Gossaert (pseud. for E. C. Gerretson, 1884–1958) represented Protestantism, following the tradition of the 17th century in his poems, while Adriaan Roland Holst (1888–), who does not belong to any group, despaired of mankind's betterment and longed for the happiness of Elysium.

After the World Wars—in the North. Literature after World War I was marked by pessimism and confusion. A vague humanism appeared in the periodical *De Stem* (The Voice) of Just Havelaar (1880–1930) and Dirk Coster (1887–1956). The "classic" poet of this period was Marinus Nijhoff (1894–1953). A more individualistic group consisted of Herman van den Berg (1897–), the first Dutch expressionistic poet; Hendrik Marsman (1899–1940), who wanted to dominate expressionism; and Hendrik de Vries (1896–), who showed the influence of Edgar Allan *Poe; and the neoromanticists J. W. F. Werumeus Buning (1891–1958), Jan Slauerhof (1898–1936), and especially Menno ter Braak (1902–40), the principal essayist of the period, who was keenly intellectual and even cynical. A weaker, but more scholarly talent was that of the essayist Edgar du Perron (1899–1940). Simon Vestdijk (1898–) utilized psychological background in his prose and poetry. Johan F. Bordewijk (1884–) gave a picture of fascist education in *Bint* (1934), and of Rotterdam's burghers in *Karakter* (1938).

Novels on rural themes offered an escape from distress and the threat of war. They were written by the Protestant, Anne de Vries (1899–) in *Bartje* (1936), by the Catholic, Antoon Coolen (1897–1961), and by Herman de Man (pseud. for S. H. Hamburger, 1898–1946), a Jewish convert. Albert Helman (1903–) captured in his work the atmosphere of his native Surinam. Henriette van Eyck (1897–) tried to see the world in a humorous light and A. den Doolaard (pseud. for C. Spoelstra, 1901–) described life in foreign countries. Many authors, especially female writers, sought relief from the troubles of the times in childhood memories: Margot Antink (1869–1957) wrote *Sprotje* (1906–09), and later, together with her husband Carel Scharten (1878–1950), *De Jeugd van Francesco Campana* (1924, The Childhood of Francesco Campana). Others working in this genre were Ina Boudier-Bakker (1875–) with *Kinderen* (1905, Children), Top Naeff (1878–1953) with *Letje* (1926), and Carry van Bruggen (1888–1932) with *Het Huisje aan de Sloot* (1921, The Little House near the Ditch). The Catholics, who could now freely express their feelings and convictions, formed a strong group in which the pessimist Gerard Bruning (1898–1926), Jan Engelman (1900–), and Gabriel Smit (1910–) were the best poets, and Anton van Duinkerken (pseud. for W. J. N. A. Asselberg, 1903–) strove to spread Catholic culture through his poetry and essays. Socialist literature became more polemic and was represented by Theun de Vries (1907–) in a historical novel, *Rembrandt* (1931), and in the anti-Catholic *Doctor José droomt vergeefs* (1933, Doctor José Dreams in Vain); by Maurits Dekker (1896–1962), best known for his revolutionary novel *Brood* (1933, Bread); by Johan Brouwer (1898–1943), author of the historical novel *Filips Willem;* and by Jef Last (1898–), whose extreme leftist views are revealed in novels and poetry.

Victor van Vriesland (1892–), a poet and essayist, belongs to no group or school, whereas Anthonie Donker (pseud. for N. A. Donkersloot, 1902–) writes poetry in the traditional style of the school of 1880. World War II left its tragic traces in the poems of Jan Campert (1902–43) and in the prose of Ed Hoornik (1910–). The war, however, minimized political and religious differences and tended to bring various groups together. Authors of humorous prose, who wrote in an effort to escape the nightmare of war and its memories, were Godfried Bomans (1913–), Annie M. G. Schmidt (1911–), and Simon Carmiggelt (1913–). Poets such as Gerrit Achterberg (1905–), M. Vasalis (pseud. for M. Droogleever Fortuyn-Leenmans, 1909–), and the Catholic Bertus Aafjes (1914–), best known for *Een Voetreis naar Rome* (1946, A Journey on Foot to Rome), and, of the younger generation, Gerrit Kouwenaar (1923–), Remco Campert (1929–), and Cees Nooteboom (1933–); prose writers such as Anna Blaman (pseud. for J. P. Vrugt, 1905–60), Hella Haase (1918–), and Bert Schierbeek (1918–)—all show that partisan camps do not exist in the latest literature. Perhaps this augurs well for the future of Netherlandic literature.

In the South. The south went through the same evolution as did the north, but the editors of *Van Nu en Straks* never were so individualistic as those of *De nieuwe Gids*. From the beginning they aimed to give Flemish an equal standing with French. Among its editors, August Vermeylen (1872–1945), author of literary essays and a symbolic novel, *De wandelende Jood* (1917, The Wandering Jew), wanted to make Flanders' culture part of European culture; Prosper van Langendonck (1862–1920), a devout Catholic, showed the power of the Flemish language in his half-romantic, half-modern poetry; Emanuel de Bom (1868–1953) published the first naturalistic novel in Flanders, and the convinced anticlerical Cyriel Buysse (1859–1932) presented naturalistic themes with fine craftsmanship. Catholics grouped around the leading periodical, *Dietsche Warande en Belfort* (1900–).

The greatest authors, however, did not emerge until the next generation. First among them is Stijn Streuvels (pseud. for Frank Lateur, 1871–), whose village novels are excellent. Herman Teirlinck's (1879–) first great novel, *Mijnheer Serjanszoon Orator didacticus* (1908) is a reaction against naturalism; an expressionist in other works, especially in drama, he pictured Flemish city life as touched by decadence; works of his, such as *Het ivoren Aapje* (1909, The

Fig. 2. Stijn Streuvels (Frank Lateur).

Ivory Monkey), are similar to those of Louis Couperus (1863–1923). Symbolism found an outstanding representative in Karel van de Woestijne (1873–1929), who struggled between sensualism and a mystic longing

for God, a tension he expressed in poetic prose and in limpid poems. The principal Catholic poet, Karel van den Oever (1879–1926), wrote under the slogan "All for Flanders; Flanders for Christ." With Jan van Nijlen

Fig. 3. Felix Timmermans.

(1884–) he represented a modern mysticism. Following them was the priest Cyriel Verschaeve (1874–1949), who wrote lyric poetry, drama, and prose (e.g., *Jezus*, 1940).

World War I did not break the Flemish spirit, but made the Flemish love of country more conscious. This is best represented by the popular Felix *Timmermans, whose *Pallieter* (1916), *Boerenpsalm* (1935, Peasant Psalm), and many short stories picture colorful Flemish country life. Ernest Claes (1885–) wrote in the same genre. More modernistic is the work of Paul van Ostayen (1898–1928), e.g., *Music-Hall* (1916). René de Clercq (1877–1932) published militant poems on the rights of the Flemish, such as *De Noodhoorn* (1916, The Distress-Horn), as well as popular folksongs. Lode Baekelmans (1879–) pictures the life of the poor in his native Antwerp. Wies Moens (1898–) became known for *Celbrieven* (1920, Cell Letters) in which he expressed his trust in humanity. Achilles Mussche (1896–) writes in the same spirit. Marnix Güsen (pseud. for Jan A. Goris, 1899–), wrote essays and cynical novels, criticizing the Catholic Church and in particular Catholic education. An accent on social and humanitarian problems appears in the novels of Gerard Walschap (1898–) and Lode Zielens (1901–44). Willem Elsschot (pseud. for Alfons de Ridder, 1882–1960) wrote keenly cynical prose and poetry, as in *Villa des Roses* (1913) and *Kaas* (1933), although in *Tsjip* (1934) there is a reflection of his confidence in the future. Among the best poets is the expressionist, Gaston Burssens (1896–). The ideas of *Van Nu en Straks* were further propagated by the group that edited the journal *'t Fonteintje:* Maurice Roelants (1895–), author of psychological novels such as *De Jazzspeler* (1928), Raymond Herreman (1896–), Richard Minne (1891–), and Karel Leroux (1895–). A flight from crude reality is a recurrent motif in the novels of Raymond Brulez (1895–) and Maurice Gilliams (1900–); the latter is, however, above all, a lyric poet, as are Paul Verbruggen (1891–), Albe (pseud. for Renaat A. Joostens, 1902–), Dirk Vansina (1894–), and Pieter G. Buckinx (1903–). The best lyric poet of this period is Karel Jonckheere (1906–), whose work is neoromantic, as is that of

Jan Vercammen (1906–) and of André Demedts (1906–); the latter's prose and poetry express a deep trust in God.

After World War II the greatest novelist was Filip de Pillecijn (1891–1962). His romantic works reflect a longing for beauty and a love for all that is good and noble, as in *Blauwbaard* (1931, Bluebeard). In *Mensen achter de Dijk* (1949, People Behind the Dike) he portrays Flemish farm life. Johan Daisne (pseud. for Herman Thiery, 1912–) is inspired principally by the cinema; Louis-Paul Boon (1912–) pictures proletarian life; Piet van Aken (1920–), Hugo Claus (1929–), and Ward Ruyslinck (pseud. for Reimond de Belser, 1929–) continue Flanders' great tradition of picturesque writing. Together with many others, these authors have fulfilled Vermeylen's wish, and enabled the literature of Flanders to rival the best of contemporary Western Europe.

Bibliography: J. TE WINKEL, *De ontwikkelingsgang der Nederlandsche letterkunde,* 7 v. (2d ed. Haarlem 1922–27). G. KALFF, *Geschiedenis der Nederlandsche letterkunde,* 7 v. (Groningen 1906–12). J. PRINSEN, *Handboek tot de Nederlandsche letterkundige geschiedenis* (2d ed. The Hague 1920). F. BAUR, et al., eds., *Geschiedenis van de letterkunde der Nederlanden,* 9 v. (s'Hertogenbosch 1939–52). G. KNUVELDER, *Handboek tot de geschiedenis der Nederlandse letterkunde,* 4 v. (2d ed. 's Hertogenbosch 1957–61). J. C. BRANDT-CORSTIUS, *Geschiedenis van de Nederlandse literatuur* (Utrecht 1959). C. G. N. DE VOOYS and G. STUIVELING, *Schets van de Nederlandse letterkunde* (Groningen 1963). T. WEEVERS, *Poetry of the Netherlands in Its European Context, 1170–1930* (London 1960). R. F. LISSENS, *De Vlaamse letterkunde van 1780 tot heden* (Amsterdam 1954). G. HERMANOWSKI, *Die moderne flämische Literatur* (Bern 1963). T. COOPMAN and L. SCHARPÉ, *Geschiedenis der Vlaamse letterkunde* (Antwerp 1910). **Illustration credits:** Fig. 1, The Netherlands Information Service, New York. Figs. 2 and 3, Belgian Government Information Center, New York.

[J. I. MENDELS]

NETHERLANDS

The Netherlands, known also as Holland, is one of the Low Countries in northwestern Europe, along with *Belgium and Luxembourg. With a land area of 13,000 square miles, the country had a population exceeding 12 million in 1965, the highest population density in the world. Since 1815 the government has been a constitutional monarchy. In the early Christian era Batavian and other Germanic tribes inhabited the Low Countries, which eventually became part of Charlemagne's empire. Most of the area belonged to Germany after 870 and constituted a dependency of the Kingdom of Lotharingia. As the central power declined, a number of separate lay and ecclesiastical territories arose. After 1384 the Dukes of Burgundy brought the region gradually under their control. The Netherlands fell to the Hapsburgs in 1477, when Mary of Burgundy married Maximilian, Archduke of Austria and later emperor. In 1555 Emperor Charles V made over the Netherlands, along with Spain, to his son Philip II. In 1579 the seven northern provinces proclaimed their independence, which was recognized by the Treaty of Westphalia in 1648. The southern provinces remained under Hapsburg control as the Spanish or Austrian Netherlands. In 1795 the patriots set up the Batavian Republic in the Netherlands, and in 1806 Napoleon I made his brother Louis king of Holland. In 1815 the Congress of Vienna joined Holland with the Austrian Netherlands to form the Kingdom of the Netherlands.

The union lasted until the revolution of 1830, which resulted in the independence of Belgium.

CHURCH HISTORY TO 1559

At the beginning of the Christian era Roman control and civilization in these regions did not reach much farther north than to Maastricht and Heerlen and thence southwestward to the North Sea. Christianity may have been introduced in the 2d and 3d centuries by soldiers, officials, merchants, and slaves, but not in any systematic way. The first bishop appeared only in the 4th century; he was the Armenian St. Servatius (Sarbatios), who had his see at Tongeren (c. 346–359). He was buried at Maastricht in the Church of St. Servaas. At the Council of Rimini (359) Servatius was a defender of orthodoxy. But the Frankish occupation and colonization of the superficially Romanized frontier regions put an end to whatever Christianity existed there.

Missions before Charlemagne. Mission activity started anew after the Baptism of King Clovis in 496 at Reims. Bishop *Vedast (Vaast) labored in the Artois; Falco, in Tongeren; and Eleutherus, in Tournai. More to the north St. *Amandus was the first missionary bishop; he became bishop of Maastricht (c. 649), to which town the bishops of Tongeren, already before Monulphus (558), had moved their residence. From then on Irish, Anglo-Saxon, and Frankish missionaries established themselves in newly founded monasteries and devoted themselves to the mission of the north. Between 625 and 730, 21 new monasteries were founded, mostly in the Romanized south. From Maastricht S. *Lambert (670–705) and, after the translation of the residence, from Liège St. *Hubert (705–727) preached the gospel in Brabant. In Frisia, the region north of the Rhine and the Meuse, Christianity could not penetrate before the Frankish conquest, which came tentatively in 689 and decisively in 719. The isolated endeavors of the Anglo-Saxons St. *Wilfrid of York (678) and Wicbert (688–689) failed because of the Frisian-Frankish war. But already in 690 the Northumbrian St. *Willibrord (d. 739) and his companions had started systematic evangelization. Willibrord was appointed bishop of Utrecht by King Pepin II in 695 and was approved and consecrated by Pope Sergius I.

Many Anglo-Saxon missionaries crossed the North Sea, including St. *Boniface, who became the second bishop of Utrecht (753) and was murdered by the Frisians at Dokkum (June 5, 754); St. *Willehad, who later was bishop of Bremen; Liudger; St. *Lebuinus; and many others. They were supported in their efforts by the Frankish royal power, and were aided by monks already in the region. By c. 800 the Low Countries were fully Christianized. *Utrecht was the most important diocese, and like Liège, was a suffragan of the Archdiocese of Cologne. To the north and the east, parts of the newly won territories were brought under the supervision of the Dioceses of Münster and Osnabrück. The southern regions belonged to the Archdiocese of Reims and to the Dioceses of Noyon-Tournai, Cambrai, and Terwaan (Thérouanne).

The 9th Century. *Charlemagne contributed greatly to the growth of the territorial, juridical, and financial independence of the Sees of Utrecht and Liège by extending and reinforcing their rights of immunity. The raids of the Normans (810, 834–837, 880–882) wrought wholesale destruction of churches (Utrecht before 858) and monasteries, including *Egmond and Maastricht. Bishops Hunger (854–866), Odilbold (870–899), and *Radbod (900–917) had to live in exile in Odilienberg near Roermond and in Deventer. Bishop Balderik (918–976) was finally able to rebuild the cathedral, chapter-houses, and the monastery in the ruined town of Utrecht.

Secular Role of Bishops. From 925 the Low Countries were part of the German kingdom. Accordingly, in conformity with the German (Ottonian-Salic) system, the bishops of Utrecht and Liège in the course of the 10th and 11th centuries found themselves endowed with secular rights and privileges; they were even entrusted with the civil rule of counties. They became princes of the empire, trustworthy defenders of the king's power against counts and dukes who were striving to free themselves from royal control. Thus in Utrecht Bishop Ansfried of Hoey (995–1010) received royal territory and judicial rights; Bishop Adalbold (1010–26), a county in Drente and Teisterbant; Bishop Bernold (Bernulfus; 1027–54), two more counties, demesnes, and regalian rights. These secular territories given to the bishop of Utrecht up to 1054, the so-called Sticht, together with all pertinent judicial, political, and military rights, were acquired as a result of a deliberate imperial program to create ecclesiastical secular territories as powerful institutional counterparts in the political balance of the German empire. Liège arrived at the same stage under Bishop *Notker (972–1008). Some monasteries, such as Thorn and

Fig. 1. Medieval tower of the abbey church at Rolduc.

Elten, also became political entities, directly subjected to the empire.

This political position forced the bishops to resort to military action against rebellious imperial vassals, such as the prefect Balderik or Count Diederik III of Holland. This intricate mingling of ecclesiastical and secular interests profoundly influenced the spiritual orientation not only of the bishops, but also of the higher clergy, monks, nuns, common people, and nobility. Even their personal relations to God were affected by these political, feudal, juridical, and hierarchial factors that dominated everyday life.

Gregorian Reform. Utrecht was one of the acknowledged strongholds of the imperialists during the *investiture struggle. Bishop William (1054–76) signed, as the third important man, the act of deposition of Pope *Gregory VII. Bishop Conrad (1076–99) was as closely connected with the old imperial system as were his Liège confrères Henry of Verdun (1075–91) and Otbert (1091–1119). The abbots of St. Paul's Abbey in Utrecht and of Egmond Abbey, who had not been influenced by the spirit of the *Cluniac Reform in its Gregorian implementation, were firm supporters of the imperial cause. Egmond was not transferred into the possession of the Holy See by the owner of the monastery, Count Diederick VI of Holland, before 1140.

The northern Low Countries were more interested in the moral than in the political aspects of the *Gregorian Reform. Everywhere a strong enthusiasm was in evidence for the newly discovered evangelical ideals of apostolic life (poverty and preaching). Among the chief promoters of this spiritual renewal was St. *Norbert of Xanten (c. 1080–1134), founder of the *Premonstratensians. The Canons Regular of St. Augustine (at Rolduc from 1112) and the Benedictines also attracted numerous new members. Hitherto there had been only three monasteries in the northern regions, but from this period they multiplied rapidly and effected an enthusiasm for the Christian life among the laity. The heretical preaching of the layman *Tanchelm (c. 1100) near Antwerp advocated an extreme moral reform, extending to revolt against the clergy, the liturgy, tithes, and the administration of Sacraments by unworthy priests.

Only after 1100 did the archbishops of Utrecht begin to move slowly in the Gregorian direction. Godebold (1114–27), the first to leave the imperial party, approved wholeheartedly the Concordat of *Worms (1122). The concordat, as applied to Utrecht, meant that there would be no more foreigners in the see, no more imperial nominations, but instead free election by the five chapters of Utrecht and by the cathedral chapter of Liège of native candidates, such as Andreas of Cuyk (1127–39) and Harbert (1139–50) for Utrecht, and of natives of Namur, Louvain, Jülich, Leien, and other towns of the area for Liège. The rise of new powers was manifested in the ardent struggle among the princes of Holland, Guelders, and Cleves and the chapters and the municipal communities of Utrecht and Deventer at the election of Herman of Hoorn (1150–56).

In other respects, however, the period after the Concordat of Worms was not sharply distinguished from the preceding one. The spread of monasteries in the

Low Countries continued in a more concentrated form. The Benedictines, for example, founded 17 monasteries between 1122 and 1215. The transition to monasteries with a more severe rule (Canons Regular, Norbertines, Benedictines) indicated an intense interest in monastic life. The 14 *Cistercian convents for nuns that were established within 50 years demonstrated the important role of women in this movement. The newly created double *monasteries for men and women eventually became independent foundations.

From the Third Crusade to the Western Schism. The religious zeal inspired by the Crusades led to the birth and spread of new military orders. The Knights of *Malta, the *Teutonic Knights, and the *Templars founded their own houses in the Low Countries, mostly in the years 1240 to 1260.

In the Low Countries several leading lords, as well as the populace, took an active part in the *Crusades: Dirk VI of Holland (1139); Floris III of Holland and his son William, and Otto of Guelders were in the army of *Frederick I, Barbarossa (1184). Bishop Otto (1216–27) and his men, and Count William of Holland, together with the Frisians, fought the Moslems at Damietta (1217). But the crusaders were diverted at times to serve secular purposes, as when the Frisian crusaders were employed to fight the rebellious Stedingers, who did not wish to pay tithes to the archbishop of Bremen (1234). Crusaders were used also to capture (1248) the town of Aachen, site of imperial coronations, for the Roman King, *William IV of Holland.

Emperor Frederick Barbarossa again appointed bishops (Geoffrey of Rhenen, 1156–78; Baldwin of Holland, 1178–96) who followed him in his battles against the Pope and against the lay nobles. At the time of the double election in Germany (1198), the bishops of Utrecht and Liège, like their Rhenish colleagues, supported the Guelf candidate, until finally the German Emperor *Frederick II was eliminated as a determining factor in ecclesiastical policy. The electoral chapters, however, were to find the emperor's place taken increasingly by the neighboring territorial princes of Holland and Guelders, and later by the popes during the Avignon period. Many secular considerations, such as conflicting international or territorial political interests, now determined the election, appointment, deposition, or translation of bishops.

Synodal records and statutes, nevertheless, reveal a continuing interest in liturgy, discipline, administration of Sacraments, celebration of feasts, ecclesiastical organization, and monastic life. Around 1350 there were 100 days that were celebrated as solemnly as Sundays, an anomaly in a world that was steadily becoming urbanized and commercialized. The *mendicant orders began *c.* 1230 to come to the new towns in Holland, Brabant, and Utrecht, and provided the people with appropriate spiritual care. The rise of the *Beguines reflected the interplay of religious and social factors (surplus of women). Among the important spiritual phenomena in this period were the Eucharistic miracle at Amsterdam (1345), the hysterical preoccupation with death by the Flagellants and the Dancers (1347), the observantist movement in the convents, and the *Devotio Moderna, which at the end of the 14th century found a promoter of European significance in Gerard *Groote of Deventer (1340–1384). *See* BRETHREN OF THE COMMON LIFE; WINDESHEIM; THOMAS À KEMPIS; IMITATION OF CHRIST; SPIRITUALITY OF THE LOW COUNTRIES.

The Low Countries did not produce theologians or philosophers of world fame, but they did supply many scholars who played important roles at the universities of Paris, Cologne, Louvain, and Heidelberg. Included among them were *Marsilius of Inghen (d. 1396), *Henry of Gorkum (d. 1431), and Heymericus de Campo (d. 1460). Only Wessel *Gansfort (1419–89) acquired international importance; his treatises later won the admiration of Martin Luther.

1378 to 1559. During the *Western Schism the Low Countries supported *Urban VI and the Roman line of claimants, apart from a short period of neutrality at Liège dictated by Philip of Burgundy. The concordat of Pope Martin V with the German nation (1418) meant for the Low Countries a considerable restriction in papal *provision and appointments. The estates of Utrecht, the chapters, the nobility, and the citizens of the towns of the Sticht thereafter played the most important role in the election of the bishop of Utrecht, their spiritual and temporal lord.

Political differences were the main cause of the first Utrecht schism (1423–1433–1449), in which the western part of the diocese (Nedersticht) supported the cause of the papal appointee Zweder of Kuilenburg, while the eastern districts (Oversticht) followed their elected candidate Rudolf of Diepholt. The whole conflict was essentially a Burgundian affair, since Duke Philip of Burgundy was pushing into the northern territories. Burgundian influence kept growing stronger through the centralization that Philip initiated. His illegitimate son David received the See of Utrecht (1457–96), and his nephew Louis of Bourbon, that of Liège (1455–82). Eventually nearly all the northern regions came under Philip's control. In the same way Frederick of Baden (1496–1517), a grandnephew of Philip the Fair, Duke of Burgundy, was appointed for Utrecht by his uncle the Roman Emperor Maximilian I, who on this occasion received a papal privilege of free appointment. But the Burgundian-Hapsburg family abandoned Frederick when he compromised himself by negotiating with France, and the see was given to another Burgundian protégé, Philip of Burgundy (1517–24). Henry of Bavaria, the next bishop, was not even consecrated. Unable to resist Burgundian pressure, he surrendered in 1528 to Emperor Charles V the temporal territories and rights held by the See of Utrecht since 1054. This marked the end of the Middle Ages in the Netherlands.

From a religious point of view this end was occasioned by the progress of the *Reformation. The evangelical, a dogmatic-moral orientation of northern *humanism, supported by the practical mentality of the Devotio Moderna, the aversion against quibbling scholasticism, and the ever-sharper criticisms of ecclesiastical abuses prepared the way for the new doctrines. The new critical philological method of Erasmian theology manifested itself in a context of vehement attacks on the old scholastic system and met with severe resistance at the University of Louvain. Precisely because of his personalistic humanism, Desiderius *Erasmus of Rotterdam (1469–1536) was not the man to reconcile the doctrinal controversies of his age.

The specifically Dutch form of the new theology was not Lutheranism but Sacramentarianism (Hinne

Rode, Cornelis Hoen); but the popular spiritualistic movement of the *Anabaptists attracted many of the lower classes. Government repression, however, quelled the revolutionary excesses and forced Anabaptism to adopt a withdrawal from public activity (Quiet Baptists; *Mennonites). It was French *Calvinism that caused the separation of more than half the population from the Church by identifying the cause of reformed religion with the struggle for political independence and for the preservation of national rights against the dominating policy of Spain.

FROM 1559 TO 1795

The most obvious sign of the centralizing, absolutist Hapsburg policy, culminating in the final unification of the Netherlands under Charles V, was the concordat of 1559, which King *Philip II of Spain, ruler of the Netherlands, extorted from Pope *Paul IV. Already at the secularization of Utrecht, Charles V had acquired an obvious right of episcopal nomination, and Bishops William of Enckenvoirt and George of Egmond were no longer regarded as having any significant authority. Real power and jurisdiction rested with the higher clergy and the chapters. Since the spread of Lutheranism was not restrained by the imperial edicts, a more efficient ecclesiastical organization was needed. By the bull *Super universas* (May 12, 1599) the Holy See created three new ecclesiastical provinces: *Cambrai (with Arras, Tournai, Namur, and St. Omer as suffragans); *Mechelen (with Ypres, Ghent, Bruges, Antwerp, Bois-le-Duc, and Roermond); and Utrecht (with Haarlem, Deventer, Middelburg, Groningen, and Leeuwarden). The nominees of Philip II were far from ideal; the only bishops outstanding for ability and virtue were Nicolas de Castro of Middelburg, Cunerus Petri of Leeuwarden, and Wilhelm Lindanus of Roermond.

Origins and Spread of Protestantism. The Netherlands region needed reformation urgently. The number of priests increased considerably in the 15th century. By the end of this century there were about 6,000 secular and 3,000 religious priests, 1,600 parishes, and 75 collegiate churches with 1,200 canons; but 25 per cent of these priests did not observe the law of celibacy, and most of them had received poor theological training. As a result the parish priests and the regular clergy were unable to refute Lutheranism and Calvinism with effective arguments or to hold their flocks together. Young priests with the training advocated by the Council of Trent were lacking everywhere in the Low Countries because of the absence of seminaries.

Chapters and magistrates, opposed as they were to the new organization of dioceses, delayed the holding of a council of the Archdiocese of Utrecht until 1565. Prelates and chapters accepted the Tridentine doctrinal decrees, but not until 1568 did they submit to the disciplinary measures, which curtailed their jurisdiction. The projected new seminary was not erected.

In this unfavorable situation all plans for Catholic reform came to nought even before the rebellious Calvinist minorities invaded Holland and Gelderland in 1572 and in the name of freedom and of reformed religion cut short all organized Catholic life. Subsequently the Calvinists won by military force the remaining northern provinces in which the reformed religion was sometimes introduced with violence (Martyrs of *Gor-

Fig. 2. Façade and tower of the cathedral at Utrecht.

Fig. 3. Jan Steen, "Moses Striking the Rock," oil on canvas, 37¾ by 39½ inches.

kum, and of *Alkmaar). In Utrecht Catholicism was liquidated between 1579 and 1580; with the death of Archbishop Schenck (Aug. 25, 1580) the hierarchy in this ecclesiastical province came to an end. The worthy Bp. Govert van Mierlo of Haarlem (d. 1587) had to flee from the Calvinistic terror in May 1578 and was never able to return to his see. His cathedral chapter continued his work, however, and became an important center of missionary activity until 1703. The bishop of Deventer died in May 1577; the bishop of Middelburg, in May 1573; and the bishop of Groningen, in October 1576. Cunerus Petri of Leeuwarden was banished in April 1578. Philip II nominated others in their places, but these nominees did not receive papal confirmation and were therefore of no importance in the regions where Calvinists were preponderant. Brabant and Limburg did not belong to the rebellious Calvinistic federation until *c.* 1630. The hierarchy was preserved at Bois-le-Duc until 1632, and at Roermond until 1801. In these two dioceses the Tridentine reforms were introduced with such ease and success that Catholicism has remained strong in these regions to the present time.

Catholic Reform. A solution for the inadequate ecclesiastical organization was found when Sasbout Vosmeer (d. 1614), a secular priest belonging to a patrician family of Delft, was appointed vicar-general for Utrecht (1583) and for Middelburg (1584). In his administration Vosmeer was subject to the newly erected nunciature at Cologne until 1596 and after that, to the nuncia-

ture at Brussels. In 1592 Vosmeer became vicar apostolic; he received episcopal consecration in 1602. This appointment indicated clearly that the Holland mission was directly under Roman control. From 1622 until 1908 it was under the Congregation for the Propagation of the Faith. Vosmeer's good example stimulated a handful of young priests to devote themselves under very difficult circumstances to missionary work around Delft. Willem Coopal, vicar of the chapter in Haarlem from 1592, was the soul of the missionary activity in northern Holland. Utrecht and Oldenzaal later became important regional missionary centers. As a result of this missionary endeavor many Catholic villages are found today in regions that are almost entirely Protestant. In Drente, Groningen, and Friesland, however, the great shortage of zealous priests allowed these regions to become almost completely Protestant. The regular clergy could fill the need only partially; until 1614, for example, there were only 15 Jesuits in the Dutch mission. The situation changed for the better a few years later. By 1630 there were nearly 100 religious and 300 secular priests at work. The increase was due to the newly founded seminaries at Cologne (1602) and Louvain (1617). Later priests came also from Douai. The Vicars Apostolic Philippus *Rovenius (1614–51) and Johannes *Neercassel (1663–86) distinguished themselves by concentrating all their forces on pastoral activity. Rivalry between regular and secular clergy adversely affected the results.

Restrictions on Catholics. The Netherlands has never been subjected to the imposition of Protestantism by force, nor was the Reformed Church an officially established one (*see* REFORMED CHURCHES). Catholics were excluded from political offices, magistracies, and guilds, but judicial officers in nearly every town allowed Catholics to hold religious services in private homes, garrets, and barns for a financial consideration. Despite these disabilities, important Catholic artists contributed to the glory of the Dutch golden age. The convert and poet Joost van den *Vondel, the painter Jan Steen, the architect Hendrik de Keyser, and the musician Joannes *Stalpaert van der Wielen, are only the most famous among a great number. The 17th century was not dominated by a Calvinistic cultural hegemony, but the official repression, the exclusion from social life and from certain forms of trade and industry affected more and more the personal and collective honor and vitality of Catholics. Under the circumstances it is not surprising that Catholicism in the Netherlands declined until it comprised only a third of the population in 1726. Around 1700 the leading merchants, industrialists, and intellectuals were Protestants, and the gentry were ready to go over to Calvinism. The poverty-stricken and the proletariat had done so from the very beginning. Catholics were to be found in the middle class, among the shopkeepers and artisans. Only in the 18th and 19th centuries did immigration from Westphalia change this pattern. The distilling of gin and the preparation of tobacco and other products and, later, the manufacture of textiles enabled these Catholic immigrants to acquire considerable wealth.

In view of the unfavorable position of Catholicism in the United Provinces, the division in Catholic ranks caused by the Schism of *Utrecht is all the more regretable. After 1702 the Estates of Holland no longer permitted the presence of a vicar apostolic appointed by Rome. This left Catholics without a legitimate leader. No new bishops were appointed, the Sacrament of Confirmation was not administered, churches were not consecrated, and there was only a perfunctory supervision from Brussels by an Italian nuncio acting as vice-superior of the Dutch mission. After the death in 1727 of the vicar apostolic J. van Bijleveldt the only form of ecclesiastical organization was that of nine archpresbyterates: Holland, Zeeland, Friesland, West Friesland, Utrecht, Gelderland, Twent, Salland, and Groningen. This organization remained unchanged until 1853.

SINCE 1795

The recent history of the Catholic Church in the Netherlands begins in 1795; it can be subdivided at the years 1853 and 1914.

1795 to 1853. After the patriots turned the Netherlands into the Batavian Republic (1795–1806), the religious situation changed. A decree of the Batavian National Assembly (Aug. 5, 1796) ended the extremely close union of the State with the privileged Reformed Church. The introduction into the Netherlands of the principles of the *French Revolution legally emancipated the suppressed Catholics and gave them the opportunity to become magistrates. In the National Assembly (March 1796) 25 per cent of the members were Catholics. Brabant was admitted to the Batavian Republic, but Limburg and Zeeuws-Vlaanderen were annexed to France. This resulted in the abolition in 1801 of the Diocese of Roermond, whose territory was divided between Aachen and Liège. The Vicariate Apostolic of Breda was created in 1803. This new freedom profited Catholics. Churches were restored, and new ones could be built. Priests were no longer required to seek government permission in order to function. The erection of seminaries in Breda, Bois-le-Duc, Warmond, and 's-Heerenberg (1798–99) made it possible to educate the clergy of the Netherlands on native soil.

King Louis Bonaparte (1806–10) changed this freedom into a new kind of Gallican servitude by creating a department of cult and by demanding control over such ecclesiastical affairs as the education and payment of the clergy, the administration of churches, and the projected reestablishment of the hierarchy. The annexation of the Kingdom of Holland to France (1810–13) was only a brief interlude. During it the Diocese of 's-Hertogenbosch was reestablished, but its bishop could not take possession of his see because of opposition from the local clergy. Breda was annexed to the See of Mechelen. Van Maanen, Goubeau, and Van Gobbelschroy, who served as advisers to King William I (1813–39), learned the ideas of Louis Napoleon and maintained in practice the provisions of the French *Concordat of 1801 and the *Organic Articles. P. G. van Ghert, influenced by the views of *Hegel regarding the state, aimed to form a national Church under governmental supervision. To this end he created the college of philosophy at Louvain (1825), where seminarians would imbibe the spirit of *Febronianism before studying theology. These projects caused such a serious conflict that King William I asked for a new concordat (1827). This document abolished the concordat of 1801 for Limburg and established on paper the organization of dioceses. But it was not put into effect fully because Protestants and anticlericals opposed it and because the Catholic clergy disliked any agreement that gave the crown preponderant influence in the nomination of bishops and canons. The northern Netherlands remained a missionary district.

King William II (1840–49), who was strongly influenced by Johannes Zwijsen, a priest in Tilburg, favored the Catholic desire to found new monasteries and to start Catholic schools and social care; but he did not succeed in putting the concordat of 1827 into effect. As a result of the separation of Belgium from the Netherlands the Vicariate Apostolic of Limburg was separated from Liège (1840), Zeeuws-Flanders was annexed to the Vicariate Apostolic of Breda (1841), and the vicars apostolic of Breda, Bois-le-Duc, and Roermond received the episcopal dignity (1842). The reestablishment of the Catholic hierarchy had to await the constitution of 1848, which granted freedom of education and of ecclesiastical organization.

Catholics cooperated with liberals for the principles of unrestricted political freedom. For a generation the Catholic laity had been stimulated by the publications of J. Le Sage ten Broek, whose periodical *De Godsdienstvriend,* begun in 1818, was influenced by Hugues Félicité de *Lamennais in its ultramontane outlook. Influential also were Professors Cornelis Broere and Franciscus van Vree of Warmond, who strove for a Catholic cultural revival by founding *De Katholiek* (1842) and the Catholic daily *De Tijd* (1845). Differences in politicoecclesiastical thought brought into

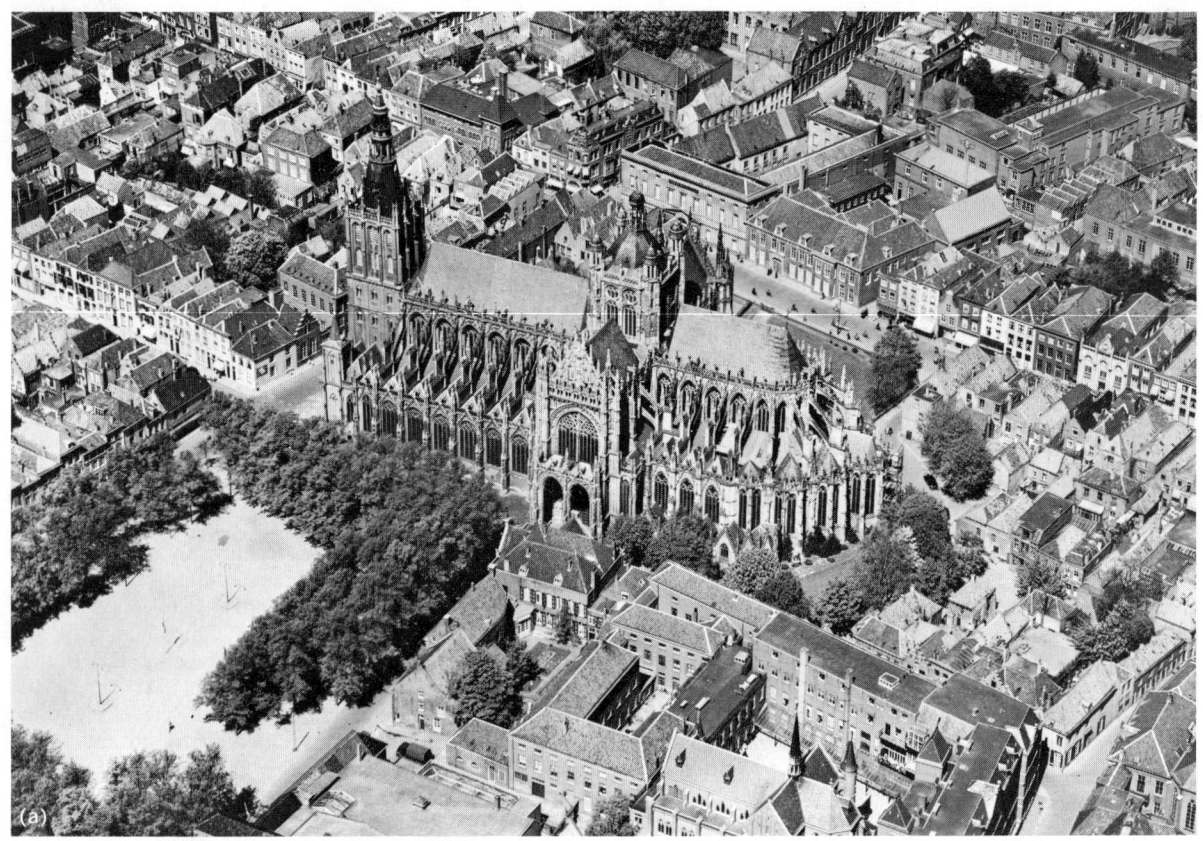

Fig. 4. Netherlands: (a) The cathedral of St. John in Bois-le-Duc, the finest example of Gothic church architecture in the Netherlands. (b) A new Catholic church in Haarlem, designed in a severe contemporary style.

being two groups of Catholic laymen. A conservative group, Gallican in spirit, centered around the department of cult and favored government influence in ecclesiastical affairs. A second group, composed of younger persons, gathered around *De Tijd* and strove for complete separation of Church and State. The latter group received the support of most of the professors at Warmond, and of Bishop Zwijsen, the vicar apostolic of Bois-le-Duc.

The conservatives requested the reestablishment of the hierarchy, but the progressives and liberals actually obtained it in 1853 as a logical consequence of the principles of freedom contained in the constitution of 1848. The ideas formulated by Bp. C. A. von Bommel of Liège influenced the papal bull *Ex qua die arcano*, in which Pius IX restored the hierarchical organization of 1559. The Archdiocese of Utrecht was made the metropolitan see. Its archbishop, Johannes Zwijsen, was made administrator of Bois-le-Duc. Suffragan to Utrecht were the Dioceses of Haarlem, Breda, and Roermond. The Vicariates of Megen and Grave, erected in 1801 for the Netherlands sections of the suppressed Dioceses of Roermond and Liège, were associated with Bois-le-Duc.

Protestants joined with conservatives who opposed the Liberal premier Jan Thorbecke. Their vehement reaction caused the fall of Thorbecke (1853) and led to the promulgation of an innocuous decree requiring a bishop to ask for official admission before taking up residence in his see.

1853 to 1914. During these 6 decades Catholics tended to dwell in cultural isolation. A common past as a religious minority, the increasing centralization of ecclesiastical authority in Rome, and Pius IX's teachings in *Quanta cura* and in the *Syllabus of Errors* (1864) promoted among these Catholics an attitude of separation from the world, modeled on the outlook of the French publications *L'Univers* and *La Croix*. Ultramontanism found strong support in the Netherlands. With the exception of Bp. Franciscus van Vree of Haarlem, the hierarchy concerned itself with ecclesiastical administration and pastoral works, and it did not engage in scientific or theological discussions. Original scholarly productions were few. The most important ones were those of Cornelis Broere in theology, W. Nuyens in history, J. A. *Alberdingk Thym in literature, and T. Borret in archeology. Catholics played a more important role in music, architecture and sculpture because of the work of Pierre Cuypers, Louis Royer, and the three Strackés.

The Catholic alliance with the Liberals in politics bore good fruit, but it did not endure because of the disinclination of the Liberals to put into effect the results of 1848 and to grant to Catholics complete freedom and government subsidies for Catholic elementary schools (1857, 1878). Hermann Schaepman (1844–1903), priest, poet, and politician, was mainly responsible for the conservative direction taken by Catholics. In 1880 he became a member of the second chamber of the Estates-General, and he published *Proeve van een Program* (1883), which provided the basis for the political organization of Catholics in *Rooms Katholieke Staatspartij* (1896). In conjunction with Abraham *Kuyper, the Protestant political leader, Schaepman established a Catholic-Protestant coalition to oppose the influences of *liberalism. By combining the struggle

for widening the suffrage with the school issue at the time when the constitution was revised (1887), Schaepman discovered the road that led to the granting of general suffrage and to the equating of public and private education in the distribution of public funds (1917). In his later years Schaepman followed the directives of Pope Leo XIII concerning social problems and collaboration with non-Catholics. Alfons Ariëns, the pupil of Schaepman, founded the Association of Catholic Laborers (*R. K. Werkliedenvereniging*), which formed the nucleus of the present-day *Katholieke Arbeiders Beweging*. Henri Poels strove after 1910 for the social emancipation of the workers in Limburg.

After Leo XIII's death (1903) there was in the Netherlands, as elsewhere in the Church, a reaction against appeasement, free scientific research, and irenic spirituality. The concentration on purely spiritual matters gave rise to a very intense Eucharistic life and interest in the liturgy. At the same time the reaction against *Modernism promoted *Integralism. The eager vigilance of Integralists, such as M. A. Thompson, a priest who edited the Rotterdam Catholic daily newspaper *De Maasbode* (1897–1912), stigmatized all efforts for parliamentary and social democracy and all ecumenical and irenic colloquies as traitorous collaboration with a libertine world.

Since 1914. The 20th century has been notable for the revival of Catholicism. There has been a remarkable development of efficient Catholic organizations in the spiritual and secular spheres. Parishes have been created and churches built. The foundation of the Catholic University of *Nijmegen (1923) and of the Catholic School of Economics in Tilburg (1927) were the most outstanding events in the progress of Catholic higher education. Several monasteries were built. Catholic hospitals and other charitable works increased in number. Missionary zeal intensified. The apostolate of Christian culture gained a wide following.

This organized Catholicism has drawn serious criticisms from younger intellectuals, such as Willem Asselbergs (alias Anton van Duinkerken), who fought as hard against the "heresies" of humanism and vitalism as against Catholic attitudes of self-sufficiency and triumph. The generation after Schaepman was so willing to continue his policy of political alliance with Protestants that a Catholic, Charles Ruys de Beerenbrouck, was prime minister in three cabinets (1918–22, 1922–25, 1929–33). To an increasing degree Catholics have also sought closer relations with the socialists; they have blamed Catholic politicians for conformism to traditional principles that did not offer any solution for mounting economic and social problems at the national and international levels. The decline of effective democracy led some Catholics to look with favor on Italian Fascism and, to a lesser extent, on German National Socialism, and to form *De Nieuwe Gemeenschap* and *Zwart Front*.

World War II reunited all elements in a common resistance to the German occupation of the country. Johannes de *Jong, Archbishop of Utrecht, later cardinal (1945), was recognized universally as the leader in the resistance to the ideology of National Socialism. In 1941 membership in the *Nationaal-Socialistische Beweging* was forbidden. It was during this period of occupation that Catholics and Protestants began the colloquies that have effected a healthful change in the spiritual climate and that have promoted the *ecumenical movement. The ideals of political cooperation after World War II tried to break through the bastions of confessional parties and to formulate a comprehensive national policy. The Catholic bishops, however, have preferred to retain existing Catholic organizations, but they have revealed also an awareness of the shortcomings of isolationism (*Episcopal Mandate,* 1954).

An ecumenical spirit has been growing since 1954. Catholics have been participating to a greater extent in national, political, and cultural life. Religious discrimination has been on the decline. Important historical syntheses by L. J. Rogier have destroyed the remnants of the former ghetto mentality and have stimulated Dutch Catholicism to self-conscious thought and action. At Vatican Council II Cardinal Bernardus Alfrink and others gave evidence of the vigor and universality of outlook characteristic of Netherlands Catholicism in the second half of the 20th century.

Statistics. The Archdiocese of *Utrecht is the metropolitan see for the entire Netherlands. Its six suffragan dioceses are Breda, Haarlem, Roermond, 's-Hertogenbosch (or Bois-le-Duc), Groningen, and Rotterdam (the last two erected in 1955).

Total 1963 population was 12,042,000. In 1961 Catholics constituted 40.4 per cent of the inhabitants; *Netherlands Reformed, 28.3 per cent; Reformed, 9.3 per cent; other denominations, 3.6 per cent; and persons without religious affiliation, 18.4 per cent. Nearly

88 per cent of the Catholics fulfilled their Easter duty in 1962. In 1650 nearly half the population was Catholic; but in 1726, about one-third. According to the 1809 census, 38.1 per cent were Catholics. In 1899 the Catholic percentage was 39.

In 1963 there were 1,717 parishes, 4,015 secular and 4,280 religious priests, 2,235 major seminarians (1,590 being religious), 8,470 religious men in 435 houses, and 32,680 religious women in 1,182 houses.

Catholic elementary and secondary schools, which receive financial support from the government, numbered 37 per cent of all schools at these levels and enrolled 42 per cent of all students. The University of Nijmegen had 4,300 students; and the School of Economics at Tilburg, 1,350. The 124 Catholic hospitals had 25,000 beds. Catholics published 33 daily newspapers, 19 newspapers appearing at least once a week, and 366 periodicals of a religious, cultural, or scientific character. There were 54 Catholic publishing houses (*see* CATHOLIC PRESS, WORLD SURVEY, 19; NETHERLANDIC LITERATURE).

Bibliography: A. G. WEILER et al., *Geschiedenis van de Kerk in Nederland* (2d ed. Utrecht-Antwerp 1963). R. R. POST, *Kerkelijke verhoudingen vóór de Reformatie van c. 1500 tot c. 1580* (Utrecht 1954); *Kerkgeschiedenis van Nederland in de Middeleeuwen,* 2 v. (Utrecht 1957). S. AXTERS, *Geschiedenis van de vroomheid in de Nederlanden,* 4 v. (Antwerp 1950–60). L. J. ROGIER, *Geschiedenis van het katholicisme in Noord-Nederland,* 3 v. (Amsterdam 1945–47). P. GEYL, *The Revolt of the Netherlands, 1555–1609* (London 1932; 2d ed. New York 1958); *The*

Fig. 5. Map of the Netherlands showing the Roman Catholic sees, 1966.

Netherlands in the 17th Century, 2 v. (New York 1961–64). L. J. ROGIER and N. DE ROOY, *In vrijheid herboren: Katholiek Nederland, 1853–1953* (The Hague 1953), revised as, L. J. ROGIER, *Katholieke herleving* (2d ed. The Hague 1962). Latourette Christ 19th–20th Cent v.1, 2, 4. É. DE MOREAU, DHGE 7: 519–756. J. A. DE KOK, *Nederland op de breuklijn Rome-Reformatie: Numerieke aspecten van protestantisering en katholieke herleving in de Noordelijke Nederlanden, 1580–1880* (Assen 1964), with summary in Eng. G. BROM, DTC 12.1:79–96. S. VAN DER LINDE et al., RGG³ 4:1460–71. P. H. WINKELMANN, LexThK² 7:952–955. *Bilan du Monde* 2:676–687. AnnPont has annual data on all dioceses. **Illustration credits:** Figs. 1, 2, and 4, Netherlands Information Service, New York City. Fig. 3, John G. Johnson Collection, Philadelphia.

[Å. G. WEILER]

NETHERLANDS REFORMED CHURCH

The Calvinistic Reformed Church in the *Netherlands, *Nederlandse Hervormde Kerk* (NHK), came into existence at a general synod convened by King William I in 1816 shortly after the political restoration of the country. The roots of this Church go back, however, to the 16th-century Reformation. Synods between 1571 and 1619 established the doctrinal alignment and discipline of the Reformed Church in Holland. Accordingly the NHK inherited as its confessional literature the *Confessio Belgica* (1561), the Heidelberg Catechism (1563), and the canons of Dordrecht on predestination (1619). *See* CONFESSIONS OF FAITH, PROTESTANT. At this time the NHK adopted a presbyterian form of ecclesiastical government, with an annual synod to enact legislation. Synodal decrees had to be submitted to the monarch for approval. Greater autonomy was granted in 1852, and all controls were removed in 1876.

Internal troubles, which plagued the NHK from its inception, corresponded to some extent to the current political controversies between liberals and conservatives. Thus, in reaction to the liberal interpretation of the binding force of confessions, a revival movement arose in the 1830s. Under Hendrik de Cock (1801–42) a group of these revivalists separated in 1834 from the NHK and formed the Christian Reformed Church, *Christlijke Gereformeerde Kerk* (CGK). Much more serious was the break that resulted from a long-standing controversy between the "modernist" and "orthodox" parties. The latter group, led by Abraham *Kuyper, professed fidelity to the original tenets of the Calvinist reformation and protested the corruption of these beliefs by the "free-thinkers." Kuyper founded the Free University of Amsterdam (1880) and formed, with his disciples, the Reformed Mourning Church, *Gereformeerde Kerk* (1886). When many of the CGK joined Kuyper's movement in 1892, the Reformed Churches in the Netherlands, *Gereformeerde Kerke in Nederland* (GKN), originated. Within the NHK, meanwhile, tensions between the "ethical" party under A. J. T. Jonker and the "free-thinking" party of Niemeyer led to further divisions. All efforts to achieve real unity before World War II proved fruitless, but the shared experiences during the Nazi occupation created an *entente* that culminated in a new church order (1951).

In 1965 the NHK had some 3 million members, about one-third of the country's population. The GKN, with somewhat less than 700,000 followers, represented about 7 per cent of the inhabitants. The CGK had about 60,000 adherents. All three groups are Calvinist in theology and are organized in the traditional synodal manner. Each congregation elects a consistory composed of elders and deacons, and each local congregation has the right to call a minister to serve it. Synods are of three kinds: (1) synods of various classes, (2) provincial synods, and (3) general or national synods. There are also committees to coordinate the missionary, social, and other activities of the Churches. *Barthianism has recently had a great impact, especially in the NHK.

See also REFORMED CHURCHES; REFORMED CHURCHES IN NORTH AMERICA.

Bibliography: W. F. DANKBAAR, EvangKL 2:1589–96. S. VAN DER LINDE and K. H. MISKOTTE, RGG³ 4:1465–67, 1469–71. W. SCHATZ, LexThK² 7:864. F. THYSSEN, *ibid.* 2:1149.

[M. B. SCHEPERS]

NETTER, THOMAS, Carmelite theologian, generally known as Thomas Netter of Walden; b. Saffron Walden, Essex, England, *c.* 1370; d. Rouen, France, Nov. 2, 1430. At an early age he entered the *Carmelite Order at London where he was ordained in 1396. His subsequent studies at Oxford brought him into contact with Wyclifite teaching, the logic of which at first attracted him. He soon discovered, however, that J. *Wyclif was "an open counterfeiter of Scripture" and devoted much of his energy to refuting Wyclif and eliminating Lollardy. His main work on this subject, *Doctrinale fidei catholicae contra Wiclevistas et Hussitas,* was written *c.* 1421 at the request of Henry V. He was present at the trials of *Oldcastle and other *Lollards and is reputed to have criticized Henry V for not proceeding more vigorously against Lollards; the same issues led him into controversy with Peter *Payne at Oxford. At the councils of *Pisa and *Constance he served as a delegate for his order, of which he was elected provincial for England in 1414. In 1419 he was sent by Henry V as envoy to Vladislav, King of Poland; Alexander, Duke of Lithuania; and Michael, Grand Master of the Teutonic Knights. Three years later he attended Henry V on his deathbed and preached the sermon at his funeral. Appointed confessor to the young Henry VI, Netter accompanied the King to France in 1430, and died in Rouen, where he was buried. Though Netter is notorious in English tradition as the hammer of the Lollards, he is remembered among the Carmelites as a distinguished scholar and restorer of the order's discipline.

Bibliography: B. ZIMMERMAN, ed., "Epistolae Waldensis," in *Mon. Hist. Carmelitana* (Lerins 1907) 444–482. J. MERCIER, DTC 15.2:3505–06. Knowles ROE 2:146–148. Emden 2:1343–44. J. A. ROBSON, *Wyclif and the Oxford Schools* (Cambridge, Eng. 1961).

[D. NICHOLL]

NEUMANN, BALTHASAR, one of the most important German baroque architects (baptized Eger); b. Cleb, Bohemia, Jan. 30, 1687; d. Würzburg, July 18, 1753. By profession Neumann was an artilleryman and engineer but was chosen by the prince-bishop of Würzburg for architectural service in connection with plans for a new palace at Würzburg. He began in collaboration with other architects, among whom were Maximilian von Welsch and Johann Lukas von Hildebrandt. Gradually he assumed charge of the direction so that, for all practical purposes, the complex of the Würzburger Schloss (1720–44) may be considered to be his

The principal façade of the Schloss at Würzburg, designed by Balthasar Neumann and built 1720–44.

The double-towered west façade of the pilgrimage church of Vierzehnheiligen, built 1743–72, after plans by Balthasar Neumann.

own creation. Neumann's works, which include palaces and houses, churches and monasteries, bridges and streets, are imposing. They demonstrate his mastery over the spatial problems of concern to architecture in his time—the central axis, curved ground plans, and coulisse-like perspectives. The Residenz at Würzburg, the grand staircase at Bruchsal (1732), and the pilgrimage church of Vierzehnheiligen (begun 1743) may be considered to be his masterpieces. They are truly representative of the last phase of the baroque, or the rococo, if one wishes to accept the latter as a term designating a style immediately following the baroque.

Bibliography: *Die Briefe Balthasar Neumanns von seiner Pariser Studienreise 1723*, ed. K. LOHMEYER (Düsseldorf 1911); *Die Briefe Balthasar Neumanns an F. v. Schönborn*, ed. K. LOHMEYER (Saarbrücken 1921). P. J. KELLER, *Balthasar Neumann* (Würzburg 1896). M. H. VON FREEDEN, *Balthasar Neumann: Vom Wirken und Schaffen des grossen Baumeisters* (Amorbach 1960). E. VON CRANACH-SICHAR, Thieme-Becker 25: 411–416. **Illustration credits:** Fig. 1, German Information Center, New York City. Fig. 2, Hans Retzlaff.

[L. A. LEITE]

NEUMANN, JOHN NEPOMUCENE, BL.

Bishop; b. Prachatitz, Bohemia, March 28, 1811; d. Philadelphia, Pa., Jan. 5, 1860. He was the son of Philip and Agnes (Lebis) Neumann. He was educated in Budweis, Bohemia, at the gymnasium of the Pious Workers, and entered the diocesan seminary in 1831. Two years later he transferred to the school of theology at the Charles Ferdinand University, Prague, Bohemia. Upon completing his seminary studies in 1835, he was not immediately ordained because the Diocese of Budweis was sufficiently staffed with priests. Having resolved to become a missionary in the U.S., he decided to set out even before ordination. He landed in New York with but one suit of clothes and a dollar; he was accepted into the Diocese of New York and ordained by Bp. John Dubois June 25, 1836. After serving 4 years in the region of Buffalo, N.Y., Neumann entered the Congregation of the Most Holy Redeemer and took his vows at Baltimore, Md., on Jan. 16, 1842. He was the first Redemptorist to be professed in America. Following appointments as assistant parish priest in Baltimore and pastor of St. Philomena's parish in Pittsburgh, Pa., he was named viceregent, and later vice provincial, of all Redemptorists in the U.S. During his 2 years in these posts (1847–49), he placed the Redemptorists in the forefront of the parochial school movement. He subsequently served as consultor to the vice provincial and pastor of St. Alphonsus parish, Baltimore.

Neumann was named bishop of Philadelphia by Pius IX, and was consecrated in Baltimore by Abp. Francis Patrick Kenrick on March 28, 1852. During Neumann's episcopacy, over 80 churches were constructed in the diocese. He organized the parochial schools into a diocesan system and increased the number of pupils almost twentyfold within a few years. He established the Forty Hours devotion on a diocesan basis and made yearly visitations that took him into every parish and mission station. Among the teaching orders he introduced into his diocese were the Holy Cross Sisters, the Holy Cross Brothers, the Sisters of Notre Dame de Namur, the Immaculate Heart Sisters, and the Christian Brothers. He founded the Sisters of the Third Order of St. Francis in Philadelphia and the preparatory seminary at Glen Riddle, Pa. The construction of SS. Peter and Paul Cathedral, Philadelphia, was begun by him. Neumann wrote many articles for Catholic newspapers and periodicals but did not always sign his writings. Among his published works were *Kleiner Katechismus* (1846), the larger *Katholischer Katechismus* (1846), and *Biblische Geschichte des Alten und Neuen Testamentes zum Gebrauch der katolischen Schulen* (1849). His heavy burden led Pius IX to give him a coadjutor, Bp. James F. Wood, in 1857.

Neumann, small of stature and humble in manner, possessed organizing ability and a knowledge of six modern languages. Many openly admired his saintliness during his lifetime. After his death, stories of his hidden virtues and of favors obtained through his intercession led the Philadelphia diocesan authorities to examine his life history. This ordinary process was succeeded by the apostolic process in 1897. On Dec. 11, 1921, Benedict XV solemnly declared the heroicity of Neumann's virtues. On Oct. 13, 1963, Neumann became the first American bishop to be beatified.

Bibliography: M. J. CURLEY, *Venerable John Neumann, CSSR, Fourth Bishop of Philadelphia* (Washington 1952). J. A. MANTON and F. A. NOVAK, *Venerable Bishop John Nepomucene Neumann* (St. Paul 1960). **Illustration credit:** Venerable Bishop Neumann Center, Philadelphia.

[M. J. CURLEY]

NEUMANN, THERESA

Mystic and stigmatic; b. Konnersreuth, Bavaria, April 9, 1898; d. there, Sept. 18, 1962. Her parents were simple country folk, who gave their daughter a thoroughly Christian education. Father Naber, the pastor of Konnersreuth and her spiritual guide, noticed nothing remarkable about her in childhood. In her early years she suffered an illness that left her somewhat irritable and nervous, and she was, moreover, subject to frequent attacks of vertigo. After completing her elementary schooling, she was employed in 1912 as a servant by a neighbor, Max Neumann. On March 10, 1918, a fire broke out on the adjacent farm. This terrified Theresa, but she was capable of taking part in the activity organized by Neumann to keep the flames away from his home. For 2 hours she handed up pail after pail of water to dampen the buildings. Then a pail suddenly slipped from her hand. She could "do no more." Her legs became numb; in her back she felt a pain as if something had pinched her. This condition continued, so that she was able to undertake only lighter tasks on the farm. However, in April she was compelled by her employer to resume heavier work. While she was mounting the stairs of a cellar, carrying a sack of potatoes, her legs suddenly gave way and she fell backward, striking her head against a stone ledge. Unfit for strenuous labor, she returned to her mother's home where she helped with the housework.

Her sufferings, however, did not cease, and at this time her character underwent transformation, and she became melancholy and irritable. Everything seemed to annoy her, and she was frequently provoked to such fits of temper that she became unbearable to her family. In April 1918 she entered the hospital at Waldsassen, but she left after a stay of 7 weeks without showing any improvement. On the contrary, her symptoms were noticeably aggravated; her violent spasms became stronger and more frequent. Her sight weakened until May 17, 1919, when, she found upon emerging from a severe convulsive attack that she was "blind." About this time Theresa also suffered anaesthesia of the entire left side of her body, and was deaf in her left ear. For 3 months she was subject to paralytic attacks in her left arm. Toward Christmas 1922 she experienced a violent

Bl. John Nepomucene Neumann.

Theresa Neumann, photograph made during her last years.

pain in her throat that made it impossible for her to swallow solid food. After October 1918, when she became bedridden, her body was often covered with sores and abscesses. In November 1925, she had appendicitis, and a year later, pneumonia. From all these illnesses she was cured without medical help, a circumstance that she and her friends attributed to the miraculous help of God.

Phenomena. The Lent of 1926 marked a new stage in Theresa's life. At that time she began to have "Friday ecstasies" in which she saw in vision the Passion of Christ, with many details not mentioned in the Gospel. This vision did not constitute a continuous spectacle, but was broken down into about 50 separate episodes (stations). The duration of these varied from 2 to 15 minutes. In the intervals between particular stations she would fall first into a state of "absorption," in which her mind resembled that of an infant and the simplest notions were unintelligible to her. This was regularly followed by a state of "exalted repose," in which Theresa might speak, perhaps using unaccustomed turns of phrase, or she might communicate Christ's counsels and orders to others or announce future events. The Friday ecstasies were associated with the stigmata on her hands and feet and left side.

Interpretation. The cause of the strange phenomena in Theresa's life can be discussed without calling into question the possibility of her sanctity, and there has, in fact, been a long and heated controversy on the subject.

Theresa's marvelous recoveries from her various illnesses could have been miraculous, but the certain judg-

ment that they were seems unwarranted, especially if they are considered in the light of the principles followed by the Congregation of Rites in examining miracles. There is insufficient evidence either that alleged organic illnesses existed or that their cure could not have been effected by natural forces. Regarding her Friday ecstasies, their supernatural character cannot be confidently affirmed according to the rules laid down by Benedict XIV and by mystical authorities such as SS. Teresa of Avila and John of the Cross. It is for this reason that a number of ascetical theologians, such as Professor Westermayr, Dom Mager, OSB, Father Bruno, OCD, and others, have vigorously opposed what they called the mysticism of Konnersreuth.

Again, stigmatization carries with it no guarantee of its miraculous origin. It could well have been, it seems, a natural effect of her "ecstatic emotion." The first appearance of her stigmata, their gradual slow evolution, their changing shape, their strict dependence upon the emotion, the manner in which Theresa treated them, etc., all seem to favor this theory. Moreover, an impressive number of modern theologians believe that *stigmatization as such can be explained without a direct miraculous intervention on the part of God. Her visions also are susceptible of a natural psychological explanation, and indeed there are elements in their content that give rise to theological objections to attributing a divine origin to them.

Her prolonged fasting provides a greater difficulty. It is claimed that from September 1927 until her death she took no nourishment. Unfortunately, Theresa's family never allowed the thorough examination of this point that the Catholic hierarchy insistently demanded. The refusal to cooperate with the Church on this decisive point created serious suspicions. The observation of Theresa's fasting by four Franciscan nuns for a 2-week period during July 1927 was accomplished in conditions that make it impossible to regard it as a guarantee that Theresa's fast was absolute.

Bibliography: R. Biot, *L'Énigme des stigmatisés* (Paris 1955). J. Deutsch, *Ärzliche Kritik an Konnersreuth: Wunder oder Hysterie?* (Lippstadt 1938). H. Heermann, "Um Konnersreuth," ThGlaube 24 (1932) 215–228. H. C. Graef, *The Case of Therese Neumann* (Westminster, Md. 1951). F. von Lama, *Therese Neumann: A Stigmatist of Our Days,* tr. A. P. Schimberg (Milwaukee 1929). P. Mansion, "Thérèse Neumann et autres stigmatisés," *Saint-Luc médical* (1933) 387ff. N. G. McCluskey, "Darkness and Light over Konnersreuth," *Priest* 10 (1954) 764–774. B. Poray-Madeyski, *Le Cas de la visionnaire stigmatisée Thérèse Neumann* (Paris 1940). F. L. Schleyer, *Die Stigmatisation mit den Blutmalen* (Hannover 1950). P. Siwek, *The Riddle of Konnersreuth,* tr. I. McCormick (Milwaukee 1953); "Why Write Theresa Neumann?" *Priest* 12 (1956) 725–733; "Konnersreuth Again," *ibid.* 13 (1957) 506–511; "Some Mystical Phenomena," *ibid.* 14 (1958) 488–493, 590–598, 664–672; "The Two Stigmatists Padre Pio and Theresa Neumann," *Revue de l'Université d'Ottawa* 28 (1958) 105–129. J. Teodorowicz, *Mystical Phenomena in the Life of Theresa Neumann,* tr. R. Kraus (St. Louis 1940). L. Witt, *Konnersreuth in Lichte der Religion und Wissenschaft* (Waldsassen 1927). F. Gerlich, *Die stigmatisierte Therese Neumann von Konnersreuth,* 2 v. (Munich 1929).

[P. SIWEK]

NEUTRALITY

Under traditional *international law, participants in a legally recognized *war were termed "belligerents." All nonbelligerent states were automatically placed in the category of "neutrals." Belligerents were accorded rights and charged with duties under the law of war. Neutrals operated under a separate legal regime designed to limit their influence on the conduct of wars to which they were not parties. Violations of the duties of neutrality were considered to be international delinquencies and could even furnish an injured belligerent with justification for expanding the war to include the offending neutral.

The Concept before World War I. There was, however, always a certain inconsistency in the theory of neutrality. The law of neutrality is dependent on the law of war. The politics of neutrality is dependent on the politics of war. In the traditional international law that developed between the Treaties of Westphalia of 1648 and World War I, the scholastic concept of "just war" was never seriously applied. War became accepted as a factual phenomenon without normative implications. The task of international law was not to control recourse to war but rather, first, to determine when the "legal status of war" began and ended and, second, to lay down prescriptions concerning its conduct. In these circumstances, it was somewhat misleading to say that non-neutral behavior engendered a right to extend the war to the non-neutral party. A belligerent was always at liberty, legally, to do so for any or no reason. Rather, the significance of the law of neutrality was that it ensured the operation of a special body of law that presumably was mutually beneficial to belligerents and neutrals. Neutrality was, in a sense, really more a political than a legal matter, even though an impressive "law of neutrality" was being developed, particularly with regard to maritime trade and blockades. Moreover, given the generally limited nature of wars prior to 1914, there was an underlying assumption that, generally speaking, states had no legitimate reason for meddling in the conflicts of others. All this was changed by World War I.

After World War I. The principal legal consequence of World War I was that the *League of Nations and subsequent international constitutional documents created a presumption against unilateral first recourse to force. A "just war" approach reappeared wherein "legal" and "illegal" or "aggressive" wars were distinguished. The great political consequence of the war was the appearance of totalitarian systems whose ends and means were so extreme that neutrality toward efforts to resist them was considered to be no longer normatively justifiable or, at least, not preferable.

The radical changes in the law, politics, and morality of neutrality were dramatically demonstrated by the dilemmas of U.S. foreign policy at the beginning of World War II. The whole U.S. legal tradition was heavily weighted in favor of neutrality, and isolationism had been the hallmark of traditional U.S. foreign policy. World War II broke out as a result of acts of aggression that patently violated the international legal order established after 1918 and violated in ends as well as means the basic values to which the U.S. was devoted. Yet it took a combination of a violation of America's own principles and laws of neutrality by Pres. Franklin D. Roosevelt and the Pearl Harbor attack to bring the U.S. into the war.

After World War II. The status of neutrality as a legal, political, and moral institution is uncertain. Were the United Nations collective security system to operate as planned, there would be no right or duty of neutrality in a UN enforcement action. Even in less clear "police actions," such as the defense of Korea and

the interventions in the Middle East and the Congo, there might be some difficulty in defending a "neutral" attitude. On the other hand, the Cold War and the ideological character of most contemporary conflict have created the problem of "neutralism," connoting to some a pejorative meaning, but to others a legitimate "third force" concept of "unalignment." Thus, according to one's ideological preferences and attitudes toward the UN, "neutrality" may be legal and good, legal but bad, or a preferable independent status and attitude.

The status of neutrality is further complicated because the very idea of a "legal status of war," sharply distinguished from a status of peace, increasingly gives way to a more realistic recognition of the spectrum of conflict that characterizes so much of contemporary *international relations. Wars of "indirect aggression" that are met with unacknowledged counterinterventionary participation in conflicts of a mixed civil-international character are the most familiar forms of recourse to force today. Neutrality with respect to such conflicts is almost impossible for the principal powers, and the practice of states has emphasized vagueness and flexibility rather than precision and doctrinal dogmatism in dealing with third-party interventions in them.

Thus as long as the law with respect to force drifts between the institutions and principles ideally established by the UN Charter and the facts of international life, and as long as the normative presumption against interference in wars is overcome by ideological and other factors, there is little likelihood that the law of neutrality, once a cornerstone of enlightened programs in support of international order, will be possessed either of great clarity or importance.

See also INTERVENTION; WAR, MORALITY OF.

Bibliography: W. W. BISHOP, *International Law, Cases and Materials* (Boston 1962) 861–901. H. W. BRIGGS, ed., *The Law of Nations: Cases, Documents and Notes* (2d ed. New York 1952). C. G. FENWICK, *International Law* (3d ed. New York 1948) 623–659. C. C. HYDE, *International Law,* 3 v. (2d ed. Boston 1947) 2224–2384. M. S. MCDOUGAL and F. P. FELICIANO, *Law and Minimum World Public Order* (New York 1962) 384–519. L. OPPENHEIM, *International Law,* ed. H. LAUTERPACHT, 2 v. (New York 1955–57). J. STONE, *Legal Controls of International Conflict: A Treatise on the Dynamics of Disputes and War-Law* (New York 1954) 380–416. R. W. TUCKER, *The Law of War and Neutrality at Sea* (Washington 1957).

[W. V. O'BRIEN]

NEVADA

Lies mostly in the Great Basin of the intermountain region of western U.S. and is frequently referred to as the sagebrush or silver state; its Spanish name means snow-clad. The riches of its Comstock Lode (discovered in 1859) has yielded over $1 billion in silver and gold. Its area of 110,540 square miles makes it seventh among the American states in area. Nevada became a territory in 1861; statehood followed in 1864.

History. The formal beginning of Roman Catholicism in the area dates back to Aug. 16, 1860, when according to the diary of Abp. J. S. Alemany of San Francisco, Calif., "Rev. H. Gallagher is sent to the mission of Carson Valley." Just 2 years earlier Rev. Joseph Gallagher (1821–87), his brother, had offered Mass in such places as Genoa, Carson City, and probably in Virginia City, but his pioneer efforts were impermanent. A more solid foundation was laid by Rev. Hugh Gallagher (1815–82), who established the first Catholic congregation in the Mormon town of Genoa and erected

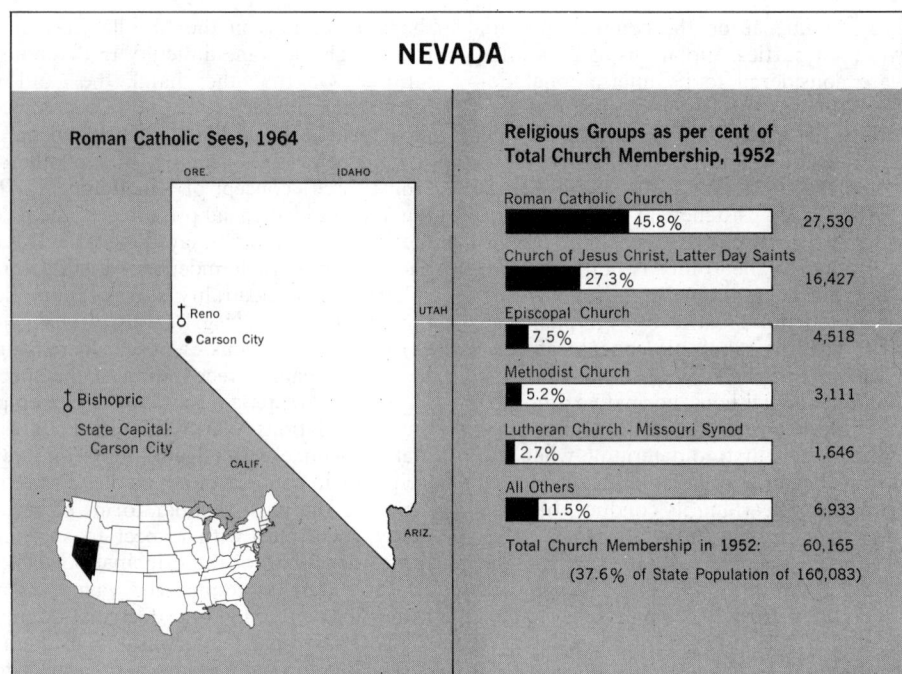

NEVADA

Roman Catholic Sees, 1964

ORE.   IDAHO

☦ Reno
● Carson City

UTAH

☦ Bishopric

State Capital:
Carson City

CALIF.

ARIZ.

**Religious Groups as per cent of
Total Church Membership, 1952**

Roman Catholic Church
| 45.8% | 27,530 |

Church of Jesus Christ, Latter Day Saints
| 27.3% | 16,427 |

Episcopal Church
| 7.5% | 4,518 |

Methodist Church
| 5.2% | 3,111 |

Lutheran Church · Missouri Synod
| 2.7% | 1,646 |

All Others
| 11.5% | 6,933 |

Total Church Membership in 1952:   60,165

(37.6% of State Population of 160,083)

Church-membership statistics were compiled by the Bureau of Research and Survey of the National Council of the Churches of Christ in the U.S.A.

the first Catholic church there in 1860. Other churches followed at Carson City and at Virginia City, the latter directly on the Comstock Lode, center of Nevada's mineral riches. The gold miner who became a bishop, Patrick *Manogue, was the builder of three successive churches in Virginia City and served as pioneer pastor there for 20 years (1861–81) before his consecration in 1881 as coadjutor bishop of the Diocese of Grass Valley, Calif. (the see city was later moved to *Sacramento). He continued as pastor in Virginia City until he succeeded to the See of Grass Valley in 1884. Nevada was included in the ecclesiastical territory assigned to the newly erected Vicariate of Marysville, Calif. (1860), and much of its territory was included in the subsequent Diocese of Grass Valley (1868). With the erection of the Diocese of Sacramento (1886), eight counties of the state of Nevada were included in the new diocese. On March 27, 1931, the Diocese of *Reno, which is coextensive with the state of Nevada, came into being.

Population. In a total state population of 160,083 in 1952, Catholics constituted 17.1 per cent; Protestants, 19.6 per cent; Jews, 0.8 per cent; and all others, 52.5 per cent (*see* CHURCH MEMBERSHIP, U.S.). In 1961 the state population stood at 285,278; of these 17.5 per cent were Catholic. They were served by nearly 100 priests and there were 2 high schools (1,234 students) and 11 elementary schools (4,122 students) under Catholic auspices. In addition, more than 6,300 students received religious instruction on released time programs.

Church-State Relations. References to and provisions affecting religion are incorporated in the state constitution and in acts of the legislature and the judiciary.

Constitution. Nevada is governed by the Constitution of 1865, as amended. "Perfect toleration of religious sentiment shall be secured, and no inhabitant of said state shall ever be molested, in person or property, on account of his or her mode of religious worship"

(ordinance); and the people are "grateful to Almighty God for our freedom" (preamble).

Article 1, sec. 4, provides for liberty of conscience, forbids preferences to any religion, and states that no one shall be considered incompetent as a witness because of religious opinions, "but the liberty of conscience . . . shall not be so construed, as to excuse acts of licentiousness or justify practices inconsistent with the peace, or safety of this State."

"All impeachments shall be tried by the Senate, and when sitting for that purpose the senators shall be upon oath or affirmation" (art. 7, sec. 1). Real and personal property of corporations formed for religious purposes is exempt from taxation (art. 8, sec. 2).

All officers—legislative, executive, ministerial, and judicial—must take an oath or affirmation, which, if an oath, ends in the words "so help me God" (art. 15, sec. 2). Teachers in public schools and universities must take the oath or affirmation (art. 11, sec. 5).

"No sectarian instruction shall be imparted or tolerated in any school or university that may be established under this Constitution" (art. 11, sec. 9). "No public funds of any kind or character whatever, state, county, or municipal, shall be used for sectarian purpose" (art. 11, sec. 10).

Marriage and Divorce. Marriages of men under 18 and women under 16 are forbidden except in certain cases of pregnancy. The consent of parents is needed for men under 21 and women under 18. A license is needed, but there is no provision for a blood test. Certain public officials and clergy may perform the ceremony. Common-law marriages are not recognized.

Marriages are void if the husband forces the woman into marriage and is later convicted of the act as a criminal offense; if either party is bound by a prior subsisting marriage; if the parties are related by blood in any degree of the direct line, up to and including first cousins. Marriages may be annulled on the grounds of fraud, nonage, want of understanding, and when there is ground for annulling or declaring a contract void in equity.

The grounds for absolute divorce are: impotency at marriage and continuing to the time of action, adultery, willful desertion for 1 year, conviction of a felony or infamous crime, habitual gross drunkenness after marriage incapacitating the party from contributing his or her share to the support of the family, unexcused neglect on the part of the husband to provide the common necessities for a period of 1 year, insanity for 2 years prior to the action, and when the parties have lived apart for 3 years. There are no restrictions on remarriage. *See* MARRIAGE, U.S. LAW OF; DIVORCE (U.S. LAW OF).

Abortion, Birth Control, Sterilization. The law forbids *abortion unless it is necessary to preserve the life of the mother or child. Every person who with intent to produce a miscarriage prescribes, supplies, administers, or advises the woman to take drugs or uses or causes to be used instruments to produce a miscarriage is guilty of abortion and may be imprisoned from 1 to 5 years. The sale of drugs to produce a miscarriage is a misdemeanor if there is knowledge of intent.

The law restricts *birth control by making it unlawful to advertise goods to prevent conception, but there is no statute prohibiting the sale of such (*see* CONTRACEPTION; ANOVULANTS).

There is no reference to *sterilization in the state code.

Property and Taxation. Religious and charitable societies may incorporate under chapter 85 of the Nevada code. There is also a Corporation Sole Act under which the Roman Catholic Church may incorporate; the legal title to property is vested in the bishop, who is the corporation sole by virtue of his office. The corporation sole has continual perpetual succession. Nothing in Nevada law prevents the incorporation of a parish as a corporation sole.

Real and personal property of religious societies and parishes not run for profit is exempt from taxation.

The real estate held by a religious corporation may not exceed 1 block in any town or city, and 10 acres in the country. Exceptions include all property owned prior to March 2, 1867, and land held by a corporation sole.

There is no fund-raising statute.

Prisons and Reformatories. The board of state prison commissioners must provide for the holding of divine services in the state prison on each Sunday and for that purpose may secure the services of one or more ministers of the gospel; the expense thus incurred may not exceed $520 a year. The board must also furnish each convict with a copy of the Bible and other books and papers conducive to the well-being of the prisoners.

Holidays and Sunday Observance. Christmas and New Year's Day, Labor Day, Thanksgiving Day, any day appointed by the president or governor, May 30, July 4, October 31, and November 11 are legal holidays. When a holiday falls on Sunday, it is observed the next day. When the performance of an act fixed by law or contract falls upon a holiday or nonjudicial day, it may be performed on the next business day.

Morality, Public Health, and Safety. No state condones polygamy. A person who willfully disturbs and interrupts a religious meeting is guilty of a misdemeanor. The chapter on healing arts and basic sciences does not apply to Christian Science practitioners acting within the limits of their respective callings. None of the laws of the state regulating the practice of medicine or healing may be construed to interfere with treatment by prayer or with any person who administers to or treats the sick or suffering by mental or spiritual means; any person who selects such treatment for the cure of disease may not be compelled to submit to any form of medical treatment or to removal to any isolated hospital or camp without his consent, provided the sanitary and quarantine laws of the state are complied with. The same condition applies to the prevention of blindness from ophthalmia in newborn babies and to tuberculosis cases as long as the person is quarantined in a proper place and complies with the sanitary laws and regulations.

Various Constitutional Freedoms. A statute prohibiting the outdoor advertising of hotel and motel rates was found not to prohibit free speech [*Viale v. Foley* 350 P (2) 721].

Bibliography: T. K. GORMAN, *Seventy-Five Years of Catholic Life in Nevada* (privately printed; Reno 1935). H. L. WALSH, *Hallowed Were the Gold Dust Trails* (Santa Clara 1946). J. B. MCGLOIN, *Eloquent Indian: The Life of James Bouchard, California Jesuit* (Stanford 1949), for details on Manogue. *Nevada Revised Statutes* (Carson City 1957–   ).

[J. B. MC GLOIN]

NEVERS, capital of Nièvre department, central France, on the right bank of the Loire River; the seat of a bishopric since *c.* 500. In 1963 the diocese (*Nivernensis*) had 230 priests, 310 sisters, and 230,000 Catholics in a population of 245,000; it is 2,660 square miles in area. The motherhouse of the Sisters of Charity and Christian Instruction, founded in 1680, is in Nevers.

Under the Old Regime, Nevers was the capital of the county Nivernais, which had not been a Gallo-Roman *civitas*. It appears only in 825 and seems to have been formed out of *Auxerre and other *pagi*. It went from hand to hand until the Burgundy family made a hereditary county of it shortly before 990. The counts were vassals of the duke of Burgundy and, from 1015, of the king. A peerage duchy in 1464, Nevers went to the *Gonzaga family.

A 6th-century baptistery has recently been excavated beneath the cathedral. Tauricianus, the first known bishop, appears in 517, his diocese carved from that of Auxerre. The composite-style Cathedral of St-Cyr and St-Julitte (10th–16th century) is the only one in France with two opposite apses. Strange to say, its patrons are eastern saints, whose relics, brought to the West *c.* 400 by SS. *Amator and Sabinus, in part fell to the lot of the cathedral of Nevers. The Church of St-Étienne (1063–97) is pure Romanesque and quite solemn. Pilgrims come to Nevers to venerate the remains of St. Bernadette *Soubirous (d. 1879), who entered the Sisters of Charity there in 1866.

The diocese, a departmental bishopric in 1790, not restored by the *Concordat of 1801, was restored in 1822 as suffragan to *Sens; it corresponds to the department. Its history, poorly studied to date, offers nothing noteworthy and has no place in a general history. By tradition several of its bishops, who include St. *Deodatus (*c.* 680) and Pierre *Bertrand (1320–22), are called saints. Nevers had the misfortune to have as bishop the half-crazy Gilles Spifame, who made a profession of Calvinism in his cathedral on Easter Sunday, 1558, became a Protestant pastor, married, and was finally executed in Geneva for forgery.

Diocesan abbeys include the Augustinian St-Martin (8th century), the Premonstratensian Bellevaux (1188) ruined by Calvinists in 1562, and the Benedictine Notre-Dame (date unknown). The 6th-century Corbigny was once in the See of Autun; and La *Charité-sur-Loire (706), given to Cluny (1056), with one of the most beautiful Romanesque churches in the Loire area, was formerly in the Diocese of Auxerre.

In 1223 the Latin bishops of Bethlehem took refuge in Clamecy (in the present diocese), keeping their title and being nominated by the counts and bishops of Nevers until 1801.

Bibliography: BEAUNIER. *Abbayes et prieurés de l'ancienne France*, ed. M. L. BESSE (Paris 1905–41) 6:103–120. A. MASSÉ, *Histoire du Nivernais* (Paris 1938). H. DE FLAMARE, *Le Nivernais pendant la guerre de Cent ans*, 2 v. (Paris 1913–25). H. LECLERCQ, DACL 12.1:1152–67. E. JOSI, EncCatt 8:1793–96. AnnPont (1964) 299.

[E. JARRY]

NEVILLE, GEORGE, archbishop, statesman, and patron of learning, who played an important role in politics and in the spread of *humanism; b. *c.* 1433; d. Blyth, Nottinghamshire, England, June 8, 1476. A son of Richard, Earl of Salisbury, he went to Balliol College, Oxford, receiving his B.A. in 1450, and his M.A. 2 years later. Having been made acolyte and sub-deacon in 1453 and ordained priest in 1454, he collected a large number of ecclesiastical benefices, and from 1453–57 and 1463–72 he was chancellor of *Oxford University. Neville was bishop of *Exeter (1456–65), when he became archbishop of York, and was chancellor of England (1460–67 and 1470–71). After the Yorkist restoration of 1471, he was placed in the Tower of London, pardoned, and then imprisoned at Hammes near Calais (1472–75). In politics Neville followed his brother Warwick, the kingmaker, rather than play an independent role. In the field of humanism his activity was that of a patron; the humanists in his household included John *Shirwood, later bishop of Durham. He also stimulated Greek studies by collecting Greek MSS and befriending the scribe Emanuel of Constantinople, who copied Greek texts for him.

Bibliography: F. GODWIN, *De Praesulibus Angliae commentarius*, 3 v. (London 1616) 1:471–472; 2:63–69. J. TAIT, DNB 14:252–257. R. WEISS, *Humanism in England During the Fifteenth Century* (2d ed. Oxford 1957) 141–148. Emden 2: 1347–49.

[R. WEISS]

NEVIN, JOHN WILLIAMSON, American Protestant theologian; b. Upper Strasburg, Pa., Feb. 20, 1803; d. Lancaster, Pa., June 6, 1886. He graduated from Union College, Schenectady, N.Y. (1821), and entered Princeton Theological Seminary, N.J., where he studied under Archibald Alexander and Charles Hodge. Through Hodge he became interested in the works of August Neander and began the study of German. In 1830 Nevin became professor of Biblical literature at Western Theological Seminary, Pittsburgh, Pa., where he was noted as an extreme abolitionist. Differences with the administration led to his resignation in 1840 to accept a professorship at the German

John Williamson Nevin, portait by Jacob Eichholtz, 1841, in the Fackenthal Library, Franklin and Marshall College, Lancaster, Pa.

Reformed Seminary, Mercersburg, Pa. Nevin's historical studies and sympathy for the German tradition, as well as his Old School background, made him a champion of the doctrine and liturgy of the Heidelburg Catechism against the "new measures" of revivalists. In 1844 he published *The Anxious Bench*, the first appeal of the Mercersburg theology, which emphasized the heritage of the Reformed Church from Catholicism. The following year he and Philip Schaff were co-defendants before the Synod of Pennsylvania on charges of Puseyism. In 1846 Nevin published his best-known book, *The Mystical Presence*, an attempt to restore the traditional Reformed understanding of the Lord's Supper against prevailing Zwinglian views. His important works on *The History and Genius of the Heidelburg Catechism* and on *The Church* followed in 1847. With Schaff he founded in 1849 the *Mercersburg Review*, which became the chief organ of their movement. Nevin established a tradition of doctrinal loyalty, liturgical renewal, and ecumenism; but the Mercersburg movement was never wholly accepted by his church. In 1861 he left the seminary to become a professor at Franklin and Marshall College, Lancaster, Pa.; he served as its president from 1866 to 1876.

Bibliography: T. APPEL, *The Life and Work of John Williamson Nevin* (Philadelphia 1889). J. H. NICHOLS, *Romanticism in American Theology* (Chicago 1961). D. DUNN, *A History of the Evangelical and Reformed Church* (Philadelphia 1961). **Illustration credit:** The Historical Society of the Evangelical and Reformed Church.

[R. K. MAC MASTER]

NEW ABBEY (SWEETHEART), former Cistercian abbey, situated 7 miles south of Dumfries, Scotland, in the Diocese of Galloway. It was founded April 10, 1273, by Dervorgilla, the widow of John de Balliol, and dedicated to St. Mary, and was the last *Cistercian abbey to be built in Scotland until 1946. The monks called it Sweetheart (or *Dulce Cor*) because the foundress, a grandniece of two Scottish kings and the mother of another (John Balliol 1292–96), had her husband's heart embalmed after his death and kept in her presence; and this, following her own death in 1289, was buried with her in the new abbey she had founded. The abbey was colonized from *Dundrennan, and like its nearby motherhouse, suffered badly in the Anglo-Scottish wars of independence (1296–1306). After the disaster of Flodden in 1513, the monks placed themselves and their property under the protection of Lord Maxwell, which action undoubtedly saved the buildings from destruction by the reformers in 1559–60. Its last abbot, Gilbert Broun, was forced into exile when the abbey with its revenues was annexed to the crown in 1587, but he returned twice to defend the old religion, was finally arrested, and died in exile in 1612. In 1624 the abbey was erected into a temporal lordship for Robert Spottiswoode, who styled himself Lord New Abbey. It is now a ruin.

Bibliography: J. M. CANIVEZ, ed., *Statuta capitulorum generalium ordinis cisterciensis ab anno 1116 ad annum 1786,* 8 v. (Louvain 1933–41) 3:91, 201; 6:690. J. S. RICHARDSON, *The Abbey of Sweetheart* (2d ed. Edinburgh 1951). S. CRUDEN, *Scottish Abbeys* (Edinburgh 1960) 73–74.

[L. MACFARLANE]

NEW APOSTOLIC CHURCH

Created in 1863 as the result of a schism within the *Catholic Apostolic Church, by the 1960s it had become one of the largest sects in Germany. Of its estimated 600,000 adherents, about four-fifths lived in Germany, but there were members also in England, Canada, Switzerland, Holland, France, Australia, South Africa, the U.S., and South America.

Some members of the Catholic Apostolic Church in North Germany began to be concerned about the survival of the church when 6 of its 12 apostles had died by 1860. They rallied around Heinrich Geyer, who believed that the deceased apostles should be replaced by new ones; when he began to choose such successors, he was excommunicated by the parent body. The dissenters organized the Universal Christian Apostolic Mission whose name was changed to the New Apostolic Church in 1906. The leading role in the new sect was soon filled by F. W. Schwartz, who supplanted Geyer as head of the organization in 1878. Influenced by the *Calvinism of the Dutch Reformed Church, Schwartz reversed the Catholic tendencies of the original Catholic Apostolic Church. His successor, Fritz Krebs, appointed himself chief apostle (*Stamm-apostel*) and reduced the authority of the other apostles. He chose his own successor, Hermann Niehaus, who served as chief apostle for 25 years after Kreb's death in 1905. The sect sent missionaries throughout the world and reported 300,000 members by 1932. The number of apostles was increased beyond 12 so that there would be one apostle for each administrative area. J. G. Bischoff became chief apostle after the death of Niehaus,

and despite some schisms the New Apostolic Church almost doubled its membership during his administration. He died in 1960 and immediately after his death 27 apostles elected Walter Schmidt chief apostle.

The 4,000 New Apostolic congregations are tightly organized through a hierarchy headed by the chief apostle. In addition there are apostles, bishops, district elders, and local pastors and evangelists. They have world headquarters at Frankfort, Germany. As in Mormonism this sect allows the reception of baptism, communion, and sealing by proxy for the dead (*see* LATTER-DAY SAINTS, CHURCH OF JESUS CHRIST OF). Only an apostle can confer the sacrament of "sealing," which is known also as the baptism of fire. Those who are sealed can share in the first resurrection and participate in the rule by Christ during the millennium. Worship services in the New Apostolic Church are austere and resemble the Calvinist order of worship. Almost all traces of the Catholic liturgical emphasis of the parent body have disappeared. The church is adventist, authoritarian, and aggressively mission-minded. A schism by 11 apostles in 1956 claimed 50,000 adherents. These dissenters reject baptism for the dead and have tried to restore a more Catholic liturgy. There are several smaller dissenting groups, such as the Apostolate of Jesus Christ and the Dutch *Apostolisch Genootschap.* In 1964 the New Apostolic Church reported 14,762 members in 162 congregations in the U.S., where its evangelistic efforts have been directed toward the German-American community.

Bibliography: K. ALGERMISSEN, *Christian Sects,* tr. J. R. FOSTER (New York 1962) 25–34.

[W. J. WHALEN]

NEW BRITAIN, in *Oceania, the largest island in the Bismarck Archipelago northeast of *New Guinea, 13,000 square miles in area. William Dampier, its discoverer, in 1700 gave it its name, which was changed to New Pomerania while it was a German colony from 1884 until after World War I. Since 1921 it has been under Australian mandate as part of the Trust Territory of New Guinea. After being part of the Vicariate Apostolic of Central Oceania from 1836, and that of Melanesia from 1844, New Britain, with other islands in the archipelago—the *Solomon Islands (until 1897–98)—became a separate Vicariate Apostolic of New Britain (1889). It was renamed New Pomerania (1890), and Rabaul (1922) after its chief town. In 1957 the Vicariate of Rabaul was divided, and that of Kavieng in *New Ireland created. Thenceforth Rabaul's jurisdiction was restricted to New Britain and neighboring islands.

Catholic mission progress was slow and difficult because the Melanesian natives were still in the early stone age cultural level, and because Wesleyan missioners had preceded the Catholics. Slight success rewarded the efforts of the *Marist Fathers, who came in 1844, and those of the Milan Foreign Missions Institute (merged later with the *Pontifical Institute for Foreign Missions). In 1882 the area was entrusted to the *Sacred Heart Missionaries (MSC) and, since 1922, to their province of Lower Germany. Louis *Couppé, MSC, the first vicar apostolic, came to New Britain in 1888 and developed the mission on a very sound basis after abolishing the "religious districts." He was not discouraged by catastrophes such as the murder of two priests, three brothers, and five sisters in the Baining Mountains (Aug. 13, 1904). In 1912 he founded the Daughters of the Immaculate Conception, a native sisterhood that had more than 70 members in 1964. At his death (1926) the vicariate had some 23,500 Catholics. Despite World War II, which resulted in a Japanese invasion and the deaths of 58 missioners, 23 of whom were murdered, growth caused the division of the vicariate in 1957. In 1964 among New Britain's 110,000 inhabitants 70,000 were Catholics, served from 44 mission stations by 60 priests (2 being natives), 47 brothers, and 177 sisters.

Bibliography: *Pioniere der Südsee,* J. HÜSKES ed., (Hiltrup 1932). L. McDOUGALL, *MSC Missions* (Sydney 1945). *Seventy-five Glorious Years, 1882–1957* (Vunapope, New Guinea 1957). R. W. ROBSON, *Handbook of Papua and New Guinea* (2d ed. Sydney 1958). AnnPont (1964) 762. For further bibliog. and map, *see* OCEANIA.

[J. GLAZIK]

NEW CALEDONIA, an island 7,218 square miles in area, situated east of Queensland, Australia, and south of *New Hebrides in *Oceania. Together with the Chesterfield Islands, Huon Islands, Loyalty Islands, Bélep Archipelago, the Isle of Pines, and Walpole Island it forms civilly the French territory of New Caledonia, and ecclesiastically since 1847 the Vicariate Apostolic of New Caledonia; in 1966 it became the Archdiocese of Nouméa with suffragan sees at Port Vila (*New Hebrides) and Wallis-Futuna. Catholic missions in the vicariate have been entrusted to the *Marist Fathers. Bishop Guillaume Douarre, together wth four other Marists, founded the mission at Balade (1843). In 1847 Brother Blaise Marmoiton, whose cause for beatification was introduced in 1919, was slain; and the other missioners were expelled for 4 years. France annexed New Caledonia (1853), an event that allowed the mission security to develop, but gradually changed its character. The main island became a penal colony, on which 11,000 *libérés* remained as settlers. French governors proceeded to attract colonists and to exploit the extensive mineral resources. The native Melanesians were forced back with the increase of the white population, consisting almost entirely of French Catholics. When successive vicars apostolic expressed distress at the ill effects of these changes on native life, they met anticlerical opposition in government circles and bowed finally to the inevitable. They reorganized the mission to care for growing numbers of Europeans, as well as the Melanesian tribes and some 11,000 immigrants from Vietnam, Indonesia, the Wallis Islands, and elsewhere.

Protestant evangelization in this area began in 1834, when Polynesian catechists came to the Loyalty Islands. English-speaking missioners from the London Missionary Society organized this mission 2 decades later. National and religious tensions led them to entrust it to the *Société des Missions Évangéliques* of Paris toward the end of the century, although the London Missionary Society did not withdraw finally until 1921.

In a total 1964 population of some 81,000, Catholics numbered 55,000 (28,000 Europeans, 23,000 Melanesians, 4,000 belonging to other races, mainly Polynesian). There were 65 priests (11 native), 67 brothers (16 native), 260 sisters (132 native), 33 quasi-parishes, and 9,550 students in 119 Catholic schools. Protestants totaled about 23,000 (20,000 Melanesians, 1,200 Tahi-tians, 2,000 Europeans). There were also about 3,000 Mohammedans.

Bibliography: P. O'REILLY, *Caledoniens* (Paris 1953). Ann Pont (1964) 759. For additional bibliog. and map *see* OCEANIA.

[J. E. BELL]

NEW GUINEA

Tropical island in *Oceania, north of *Australia. Its 341,424 square miles make it the second largest island in the world. Sighted by the Portuguese in 1511, the island was discovered and claimed by Spain in 1527. In the 17th century the Dutch claimed an indefinite territory and formally annexed the western half in 1828. The east was explored by the English in the 18th century, but because of the forbiding climate, the dense forests, and difficult terrain, no European power did much to develop the country until the late 19th century. In 1884 England established a protectorate over Papua, the southeast territory, and Germany established the colony of Kaiser Wilhelmsland in the northeast; in 1885 the Dutch adjusted their territory to the new claims. During World War I the Australians captured Kaiser Wilhelmsland and administered it first as a mandate territory of the League of Nations and then as a trust territory of the United Nations. Dutch New Guinea was ceded to *Indonesia in 1963 and was renamed Irian Barat, or West Irian. The population (1963) was established at 2.8 million. Of this total, northeast New Guinea had 1,500,000; Papua 550,000; and West Irian 750,000. There were about 1,150,000 Christians (800,-000 Protestants) and 20,000 Moslems; the rest were pagans.

New Guinea was included in the Vicariate Apostolic of Melanesia, created in 1844 and entrusted to the Marist Fathers. Within 6 years slaughter and disease brought the mission to an end before any missionaries landed on New Guinea itself. The Milan Foreign Mission Society received the area in 1852 and suffered a similar fate. In 1881 the vicariate was entrusted to the Sacred Heart Missionaries (MSC), who from *New Britain founded the first New Guinea mission on Yule Island (1885). The area, under British-Australian influence, had already been visited by Protestant missionaries, and government authorities impeded normal development of the mission by creating exclusive territorial spheres of influence for the various Christian missionary groups. By 1964 there were in Papua the Vicariates Apostolic of Port Moresby, Samarai, and Yule Island, all staffed by the MSC, and the Prefectures Apostolic of Mendi, staffed by Capuchins, and Daru, staffed by Montfort Fathers.

Kaiser Wilhelmsland was entrusted to the Divine Word Missionaries (SVD) as a prefecture apostolic in 1896. Protestant missionaries had preceded them, and the German government had imposed spheres of religious influence. The missionaries laid out extensive coconut plantations and later added cocoa and coffee plantations that made the missions partially self-supporting. During World War II more than 100 priests, brothers, and sisters were killed. In 1964 a regional major seminary was erected at Madang. By then the area was divided ecclesiastically into the Vicariates of Alexishafen, Wewak, Mount Hagen, and Goroka staffed by the SVD, Aitape staffed by Franciscans, and Lae staffed by the Mariannhill Missionaries. The Prefecture Apostolic at Vanimo was staffed by the Passionists.

Dutch New Guinea became a prefecture apostolic in 1902 and was entrusted to the MSC. By 1964 there were two vicariates. Merauke in the south was staffed by MSC, and Sukarnopura (formerly Hollandia and then Kota Baru) in the north was staffed by Franciscans. The Prefecture Apostolic of Manokwari in the Vogelkop is cared for by the Augustinians.

In 1963 the entire island had about 350,000 Catholics, served by 420 priests, 130 major and minor seminarians, 195 brothers, and 365 sisters. The Church maintained more than 1,270 schools with about 62,700 pupils.

Bibliography: A. Dupeyrat, *Papouasie: Histoire de la mission, 1885–1935* (Paris 1936). A. Freitag, *Glaubenssaat in Blut und Tränen* (Kaldenkirchen, Ger. 1948). MissCattol 438–439, 467–473. Bilan du Monde 2:645–650. AnnPont has annual data on all vicariates and prefectures. For further bibliography and map, *see* OCEANIA.

[R. M. WILTGEN]

NEW HAMPSHIRE

A New England state in northeast U.S., one of the Thirteen Colonies, admitted to the Union (1788) as the ninth state. It is bounded on the north by Canada, on the east by Maine and the Atlantic Ocean, on the south by Massachusetts, and on the west by the Connecticut River and Vermont. Concord is the state capital; and Manchester, the largest city.

History. Originally a dissenting offshoot of the Massachusetts Bay colony, New Hampshire became a separate royal colony in 1680 and in the aftermath of independence established itself as a sovereign state, always retaining its Protestant bent. Under the revised constitution of 1784, the state retained a religious test that excluded Catholics from the major offices in the state government. The constitution also authorized towns to support "public Protestant teachers of piety, religion, and morality" (art. 6). The number of Catholics in the state was negligible until the influx of Irish

settlers in the wake of the famines of the mid-1840s. Their presence was resented; in 1855 Gov. Ralph Metcalf, elected by the Know-Nothing (nativist) party, made a vigorous anti-Catholic speech to the legislature. But the agitation died down quickly, and the Know-Nothings quietly disappeared as the newly founded Republican party solidified its ranks for the election of 1860. In 1877 constitutional changes abolished substantially all the religious qualifications for public office, and in 1936 the state had a Catholic governor, Francis P. *Murphy. The Diocese of *Manchester, coextensive with the state, was established in 1884 by a division of the Diocese of *Portland, Maine.

Population. Even before the peak of Irish immigration had passed, French Canadians had begun to enter New Hampshire. But the great majority attracted by jobs in the textile, shoe, and paper industries, came later (1885–1925), settling mainly in Manchester, Nashua, Berlin, and Somersworth, with smaller groups elsewhere. As newcomers, they were forced to accept low wages and long hours; and influenced by the opposition of the Canadian hierarchy to the Knights of Labor, they tended not to join labor unions. More than most immigrant groups, the Franco-Americans retained their separate existence. The proximity of the state to Canada made intercourse between the two communities easy, and the strength of mutual bonds discouraged movement out of the region. In the 1960s Franco-Americans made up about a quarter of the state's population, the highest proportion in the U.S. Other immigrant groups —Italians, Germans, Poles, and Lithuanians—all predominantly Catholic, had helped to increase the Catholic body to about 237,000 in a total population of approximately 613,000. In 1952, when the state population was 533,242, of whom 35.6 per cent were Catholics, Protestants accounted for 16.8 per cent; Jews, 0.6 per cent; and all others, 47 per cent (*see* CHURCH MEMBERSHIP, U.S.).

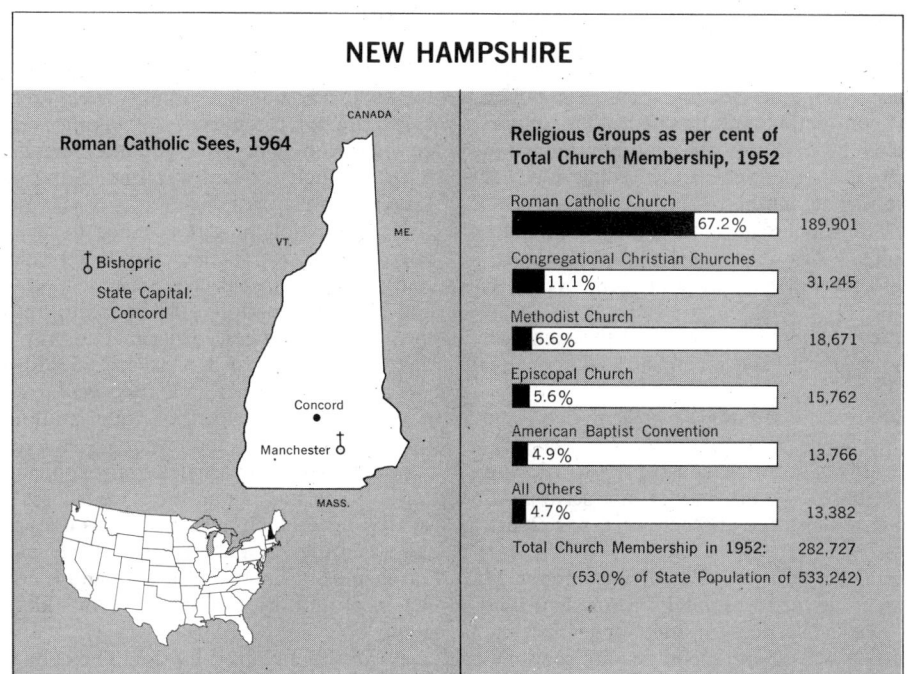

NEW HAMPSHIRE

Roman Catholic Sees, 1964

CANADA

VT.   ME.

☩ Bishopric
○

State Capital:
Concord

Concord ●
Manchester ○ ☩

MASS.

Religious Groups as per cent of
Total Church Membership, 1952

Roman Catholic Church
67.2%   189,901

Congregational Christian Churches
11.1%   31,245

Methodist Church
6.6%   18,671

Episcopal Church
5.6%   15,762

American Baptist Convention
4.9%   13,766

All Others
4.7%   13,382

Total Church Membership in 1952:   282,727
(53.0% of State Population of 533,242)

Fig. 1. Church-membership statistics were compiled by the Bureau of Research and Survey of the National Council of the Churches of Christ in the U.S.A.

Fig. 2. Administration building of St. Anselm's College, Manchester, N.H., founded 1887.

Education. In 1964 St. Anselm's College, founded (1887) in Manchester by the Benedictines, had a total enrollment of about 1,300 students, and 3 small Catholic colleges for women—Notre Dame in Manchester, Mt. St. Mary's in Hooksett, and Rivier in Nashua—had a combined enrollment of about 1,000. There were also 72 elementary schools (24,450 students) and 20 high schools (5,577 students) under Catholic auspices, with more than 30,000 additional students receiving religious instruction on released-time programs.

Church-State Relations. References to and provisions affecting religion are incorporated in the state constitution and in acts of the legislature and the judiciary.

Constitution. New Hampshire is governed by the Constitution of 1784, as amended. The right of conscience is inalienable (part 1, art. 4). Freedom of religion is recognized, but it does not include disturbing the public peace or others in their religious worship (part 1, art. 5). Part 1, art. 6 states that public worship is to be encouraged and "that the several towns, parishes, bodies corporate, or religious societies, shall, at all times, have the exclusive right of electing their own public teachers, and of contracting with them for their support and maintenance." Members of one sect do not have to support teachers of another sect, and the law may not subordinate one sect to another.

"No person, who is conscientiously scrupulous about the lawfulness of bearing arms, shall be compelled thereto, provided he will pay an equivalent" (part 1, art. 13).

The senate tries impeachments with all the members sworn to try the case truly and impartially (part 2, sec. 38).

Governors, councilors, senators, representatives, and military or civil officers (town officers excepted) must take an oath or affirmation that ends in the words, "so help me God." Quakers or others who are scrupulous about swearing may substitute another form (part 2, art. 84).

Marriage and Divorce. Marriages of men under 14 and women under 13 are absolutely forbidden. The consent of a judge is needed for men under 20 and women under 18. A license and blood test are required. Certain public officials and clergy may perform the ceremony. Common-law marriages are not recognized.

Marriages are void if either party is bound by a prior subsisting marriage; if the parties are related by blood in any degree of the direct line, and up to and including first cousins; and by nonage. Marriages may be annulled on the statutory ground of nonage and on any common-law grounds.

The grounds for absolute divorce are: impotency, extreme cruelty, the conviction of a crime and imprisonment for more than 1 year, treatment that could seriously injure health or reason, drunkenness for 2 years, the joining of a religious sect that believes the relation of husband and wife is unlawful, refusal to cohabitate for 6 months, nonsupport, desertion, and various types of absenting oneself. Remarriage is subject to no statutory regulations. *See* MARRIAGE, U.S. LAW OF; DIVORCE (U.S. LAW OF).

Abortion, Birth Control, Sterilization. The law forbids *abortion unless it is necessary to preserve the life of the mother. An attempt to procure a miscarriage is punished by imprisonment up to a year or a fine up to $1,000. An intent to destroy a quick child is punishable by imprisonment up to 10 years and a fine of $1,000. If the woman dies, the person responsible under the statutes is guilty of murder in the second degree and is punished accordingly.

The law restricts *birth control. New Hampshire has no statutes concerning birth control or contraceptives as such (*see* CONTRACEPTION; ANOVULANTS). Its statutes dealing with obscene literature and minors may be construed to include the regulation of contraceptives.

The law provides for *sterilization. If the superintendent of the state or county institution judges that it is in the best interests of the inmate and of society, he may have the patient sterilized if he follows the correct procedure. This includes patients with hereditary forms of insanity that are recurrent, idiocy, imbecility, feeblemindedness, or epilepsy. Therapeutic sterilization is permitted. Certain safeguards must be followed.

Property and Taxation. Religious and charitable associations may incorporate under the Voluntary Corporations and Associations Section of the code. Charitable corporations may establish and maintain common trust funds. The bishop and other trustees are deemed bodies corporate for the purpose of taking and holding property for the church. Real and personal property of religious societies and charities, not run for profit, is exempt from taxation.

If a donation or gift is made to an unincorporated religious society, such society is considered a corporation so far as may be necessary to take, hold, manage, and use the donation, gift, or grant; but the income of the donations, gifts, or grants to any such unincorporated society may not exceed $5,000 per year.

The commissioner of public welfare, upon application and after investigation, may authorize the temporary solicitation of money or other valuables and the temporary sale of articles for bona fide religious, benevolent, and philanthropic purposes and may issue certificates of such authority. This does not apply when the soliciting organization has a permanent residence or place of business in the state and is authorized under the local authority of a mayor or alderman or selectmen.

Prisons and Reformatories. The code states that "the rules and regulations established for the government of any prison, house of correction, or public charitable or reformatory institution shall provide for suitable religious instruction and ministration to the inmates." Furthermore, "the inmates shall have freedom of religious belief and freedom to worship God according to the dictates of their consciences; but this shall not permit anything inconsistent with proper discipline and management, or any expense beyond that made under the preceding section."

Holidays and Sunday Observance. Christmas and New Year's Day, Labor Day, Veterans Day, Thanksgiving Day, February 22, the 4th Monday in April, May 30, July 4, October 12, election day, and November 11 are legal holidays. When any holiday falls on Sunday, the following day is observed as a holiday. Sunday sales are forbidden except for the necessities of life. As a general rule the sale of intoxicating liquor is forbidden on Sunday and election day, but the statutes make exceptions.

Morality, Public Health, and Safety. No state condones polygamy. On the Lord's Day, within the walls of any house of public worship or near the same, no person must behave rudely or indecently, either during the time of public service or between the forenoon and afternoon services.

The section dealing with communicable diseases states that it should not be construed to restrict in any manner the individual's right to select the mode of treatment of his choice; it may not require the physical examination or medical treatment of a patient who in good faith relies on spiritual means or prayer for healing as long as the sanitary and quarantine laws, rules and regulations relating to infectious, contagious, and communicable diseases are complied with. In general, all children must be vaccinated before entering public school. In *State v. Drew* 192 Atl. 629 (1937) the court held that a parent who refused to send his child to school because of a statute prohibiting the attendance of nonvaccinated children was guilty of an offense against the statute requiring school attendance.

Various Constitutional Freedoms. In *Chaplinsky v. State of New Hampshire,* 62 Sup. Ct. 7.66, the court held that the conviction of the accused under the statute punishing the use in a public place of words

Fig. 3. Administration building of Notre Dame College, Manchester, N.H., founded 1950.

likely to cause a breach of peace did not substantially or unreasonably infringe upon freedom of speech.

The New Hampshire statute requiring a license for conducting a parade on the public street and vesting the licensing board with discretion was found not in violation of the 14th Amendment's guarantee of freedom of worship, speech, press, and assembly (*Cox v. New Hampshire* 61 Sup. Ct. 762).

Bibliography: R. H. Lord et al., *History of the Archdiocese of Boston . . . 1604–1943,* 3 v. (New York 1944). M. St. L. Kegresse, *A History of Catholic Education in New Hampshire* (Doctoral diss. unpub. Boston U. 1955). R. B. Dishman and D. C. Knapp, *A New Constitution for New Hampshire* (Durham, N.H. 1956). J. D. Squires, *Granite State of the United States,* 4 v. (New York 1956). *New Hampshire Revised Statutes Annotated, 1955* (Rochester, N.Y. 1955). *West's New Hampshire Digest, 1760 to Date* (Boston 1951–).

[F. L. BRODERICK]

NEW HAVEN THEOLOGY, or Taylorism, refers to the 19th century New England theological system that originated with Nathaniel William *Taylor, professor at Yale Divinity School, New Haven, Conn. (1822–58). An exposition of Puritan theology, it was the most influential and controversial since that of Jonathan *Edwards. Using rational philosophy, Taylor devised a system that dealt with human responsibility and featured freedom of the will. Taylor, called "the Pelagianist" by some Calvinists, taught that there is a native sinlessness in man, an ability in him to renovate his own soul, and self-love, or the desire for happiness, is the source of all voluntary action. Although he considered himself to be in the Edwards tradition, Taylor's views represented a serious departure from strict Puritan Calvinism (*see* GREAT AWAKENING). His teaching that man's acts are not necessitated, but free, because man may act "in a contrary way at all times," was interpreted by many as a denial of Calvinism's cardinal tenet on the absolute sovereignty of God. Moreover, his belief that man may be motivated to a conversion of life seemed contrary to the Calvinist doctrine on "Divine Benevolence." When resistance to these ideas mounted, a fellow Congregationalist, Bennett Tyler, led the opposition, founding a new Divinity School in Hartford, Conn., to teach "traditional Puritanism."

In addition, Presbyterian opposition was strong and even more consequential. Charles Hodge of Princeton Divinity School wrote vehement attacks against "the novelties of New England Theology"; those who agreed with him became known as the "Old School" within Presbyterianism. Many younger clergymen and revivalists who found Taylor's teachings appealing and useful in their work were referred to as the "New School." The two groups exchanged accusations of heresy; disagreements on other issues arose frequently, especially on the missions where cooperation with the Congregationalists was fostered and a plan of eventual union drawn up. Here the Old School charged that the New School and Congregationalist influences had subverted Presbyterian order and that innovations had crept into their worship. By 1837, when a general assembly was held in Philadelphia, Pa., the controversy had reached its peak. The Old School dissolved completely the plan of union with the Congregationalists and cut off several New York New School synods. When these asked for readmittance and were refused, they formed their own assembly, to which all the New School group affiliated themselves, causing a schism that lasted 32 years. By 1880 Taylor's views were generally rejected by all. However, his insistence that divine governance must be understood in a way that includes man's moral responsibility paved the way for the later transition from rigid Calvinism to "Liberal Orthodoxy" in America.

Bibliography: F. H. FOSTER, *A Genetic History of the New England Theology* (New York 1963). S. E. MEAD, *Nathaniel William Taylor, 1786–1858: A Connecticut Liberal* (Chicago 1942).

[T. HORGAN]

NEW HEBRIDES, a rugged archipelago largely of volcanic origin in *Oceania northeast of *New Caledonia and west of the *Fiji Islands, 5,700 square miles in land area. Together with the Santa Cruz Islands, 380 square miles in area, and the small groups known as the Banks Islands and Torres Islands, they constituted the Vicariate Apostolic of New Hebrides Islands, erected in 1904; in 1966 they became the Diocese of Port Vila. The natives are Melanesians. Great Britain and France govern the area jointly through the condominium of the New Hebrides, except for Santa Cruz, a British protectorate.

Protestant missioners began in 1839 the first effective evangelization at the cost of many lives. *Marist Fathers (SM) came from New Caledonia early in the 19th century, but concentrated Catholic efforts waited until 1887, when Bp. Hilarion Frayasse, SM, sent four missioners and several native helpers, with the urging and help of the French government. Progress was slow. By 1938 Catholics numbered 2,600; Protestants, 10,000; pagans, 30,000. Protestant missionary groups, which directed 274 schools in 1964, remained mostly English-speaking and very influential. Catholic missions were associated with the French language, the tongue used in their schools. The 1964 population of *c.* 60,000 was well over 90 per cent native, with a few thousand British and French, the latter being more prominent numerically and economically. Protestants numbered 40,000; Catholics, 9,700 (7,100 natives), served by 26 priests, 1 brother, and 86 sisters.

Bibliography: V. DOUCERÉ, *La Mission catholique aux Nouvelles-Hebrides* (Lyons 1934). AnnPont (1964) 759. For additional bibliog. and map *see* OCEANIA.

[J. E. BELL]

NEW IRELAND, about 2,800 square miles in area, the largest island after *New Britain in the Bismarck Archipelago to the northeast of *New Guinea in *Oceania. Mariners from the Netherlands were the first to land in this section of Melanesia. The Marquis de Rays established on its west coast the colony of Port Breton, to which he sent four expeditions with more than 500 colonists. From 1884 until the end of World War I the island was a German colony named New Mecklenburg. Since 1921 it has been an Australian mandate, part of the trust Territory of New Guinea. Ecclesiastically it pertained successively to the Vicariates Apostolic of Western Oceania (1836–44), Melanesia (1844–89), New Britain (1889–1922), and Rabaul (1922–57). In 1957 the Vicariate Apostolic of Kavieng, chief town in New Ireland, was created, and entrusted to the North American province of the *Sacred Heart Missionaries. Besides New Ireland and adjacent islands, it includes in the Bismarck Archi-

pelago, the Admiralty Islands (800 square miles), and the small Duke of York Islands, which have had missioners since 1912. The vicariate covers 89,000 square miles of the Pacific Ocean.

Wesleyan missioners arrived first, as in New Britain. The first Catholic mission was started in 1902 by the Sacred Heart Missionaries, and progressed so well that it survived World War I without serious damage. G. Peekel, K. Neuhaus, and other missioners have made significant scientific contributions to ethnology, botany, and linguistics. World War II brought Japanese occupation and considerable destruction to the missions. Since that time the Cargo Cult has been very detrimental to the Catholic faith, especially on the island of Manus. In 1964 Catholics constituted about 40 per cent of the 60,000 inhabitants of the Kavieng vicariate, about 40,000 of whom dwelt in New Ireland, and 20,000 in the Admiralties. There were 18 priests, 5 brothers, and 25 sisters attending 17 mission stations and a large leper colony on Anelaua Island. (For map *see* OCEANIA.)

Bibliography: AnnPont (1964) 753. For additional bibliog. *see* NEW BRITAIN; OCEANIA.

[J. GLAZIK]

NEW JERSEY

A Middle Atlantic state, one of the Thirteen Colonies, admitted to the Union as the third state on Dec. 18, 1787. It borders on New York, Pennsylvania, Delaware, and the Atlantic Ocean, and has an area of 7,836 square miles. In 1960 its population of 6,066,782 gave it eighth rank among the states. Its heavily urbanized (nearly 90 per cent) pattern of settlement gives it a population density exceeding 12,000 per square mile in the vicinity of New York City. Six cities have a population exceeding 100,000, including Newark, the largest (405,220); Jersey City (276,101); Paterson (143,663); Trenton, the capital (114,167); Camden (117,159); and Elizabeth (107,698). With a high per capita income, the state's economy is based primarily on manufacturing, with tourism along its Atlantic coast as an added source of revenue.

Population. In 1952 Catholics constituted 36.8 per cent of the state's population. Jewish congregations, with 4.8 per cent, exceeded any individual Protestant denomination, but together Protestants numbered 16.1 per cent. Methodists, Presbyterians, Episcopalians, and Lutherans were most numerous among Protestants. Those claiming no religious affiliation amounted to 42.3 per cent. (*See* CHURCH MEMBERSHIP, U.S.)

Education. School attendance is compulsory between the ages of 7 and 16. In 1960 about 738,068 students were enrolled in the public elementary schools, and 364,644 in the high schools. The state contains 5 universities, including Princeton and Rutgers, the state university; 26 colleges; and the Institute for Advanced Study. In 1960 the Catholic Church operated 440 elementary schools with an enrollment of 239,518; 93 secondary schools with an enrollment of 39,956, and 6 colleges, including Seton Hall University of South Orange, with an enrollment of 14,904. A 1941 statute permits local boards of education to provide at public expense for the transportation of children to parochial and private schools. This law was upheld by the U.S. Supreme Court in the *Everson* decision of 1947. *See* CHURCH AND STATE IN THE U.S. (LEGAL HISTORY), 4.

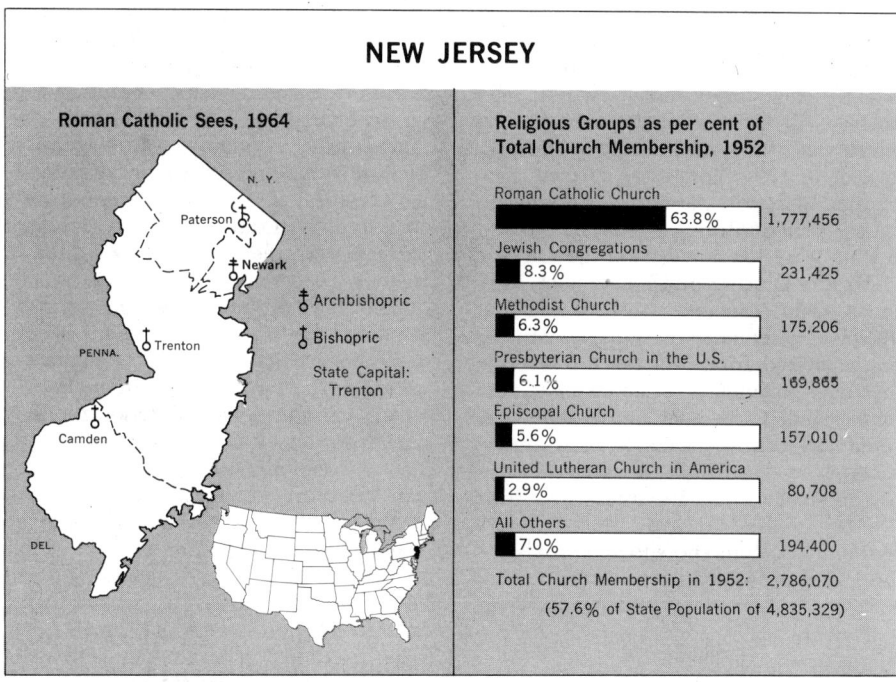

NEW JERSEY

Roman Catholic Sees, 1964

N. Y.

Paterson

Newark

PENNA.   Trenton

Camden

DEL.

Archbishopric
Bishopric
State Capital: Trenton

Religious Groups as per cent of Total Church Membership, 1952

Roman Catholic Church — 63.8% — 1,777,456
Jewish Congregations — 8.3% — 231,425
Methodist Church — 6.3% — 175,206
Presbyterian Church in the U.S. — 6.1% — 169,865
Episcopal Church — 5.6% — 157,010
United Lutheran Church in America — 2.9% — 80,708
All Others — 7.0% — 194,400

Total Church Membership in 1952: 2,786,070
(57.6% of State Population of 4,835,329)

Church-membership statistics were compiled by the Bureau of Research and Survey of the National Council of the Churches of Christ in the U.S.A.

History. After the English assumed control from the Dutch in 1664, New Jersey was divided into West Jersey, a Quaker stronghold, and East Jersey, whose fortunes were tied to New York City. Proprietary government ended in 1702, when the Jerseys were united as a royal colony. Its geographic position and large Tory population gave it a leading role in the American Revolution, and it was an important defender of the small states in the Federal Constitutional Convention of 1787.

Early Catholicism. Until the middle of the 19th century Catholics were neither numerous nor significant in New Jersey. Catholic immigration was discouraged by legal and social conditions indicated by Queen Anne's instructions to Governor Cornbury in 1702 directing him to grant liberty of conscience to all "except papists" and requiring administration of a test oath to prevent "dangers which may happen from popish recusants." This atmosphere continued into the postcolonial period. The state constitution, adopted in 1776, excluded an established church and guaranteed to everyone "the inestimable privilege of worshiping Almighty God in a manner agreeable to the dictates of his own conscience," but it guaranteed only that "no protestant inhabitant . . . be denied the enjoyment of any civil right merely on account of his religious principles" and that "all persons professing a belief in the faith of any protestant sect . . . shall be capable of being elected into any office of profit or trust or being a member of either branch of the legislature." These provisions were not removed until a new constitution was drafted in 1844.

Catholic settlers came to New Jersey in some numbers, especially as the glass and iron industries were developed, and their settlements were tended by Jesuit missionaries working out of St. Joseph's Church in Philadelphia and "riding the circuit" through New

Jersey. The most noted of these early priests was Rev. Ferdinand *Farmer, who from 1758 to 1786 ministered to the scattered Catholics of Greenwood Lake, Mount Hope, Macopin, Charlottenburg, Ringwood, Basking Ridge, Trenton, and Salem.

19th and 20th Centuries. By 1814 the number of Catholics in Trenton had increased sufficiently to build a small church, which was dedicated to St. Francis by Michael Egan, first bishop of Philadelphia. In 1820 the Catholic community in Paterson received its first pastor, Rev. Richard Bulger, who built a church there the following year. Paterson became a diocese in 1937. Newark's first parish, St. John's, was established in 1826, and its church dedicated in 1828. *Newark became a diocese in 1853 and an archdiocese in 1937. The years following the War of 1812 were a time of rapid industrial and commercial development in New Jersey. Catholic immigration, especially from Ireland and Germany, increased with the railroad and canal building that began in the 1830s. By 1853, when the first diocese was organized in New Jersey, the city of Newark had three churches, the original St. John's; St. Mary's, for the Germans; and the new St. Patrick's. In Trenton there were two: St. John's and St. Francis of Assisi (the original St. Francis) for the Germans. In the entire state there were 30 churches, with at least as many mission stations, all tended by 30 priests.

The ecclesiastical status of New Jersey changed several times. When the Diocese of Baltimore was erected in 1789, the state was included in its jurisdiction, and there is a record of a visit paid to Trenton by Bp. John Carroll in September 1803. When the Dioceses of Philadelphia and New York were established in 1808, New Jersey was divided between them. Belonging to New York was "the eastern part of the province of New Jersey closest to" it. Attached to Philadelphia was "the western and southern part of the province of New

Jersey." Following the recommendation of the Second Provincial Council of Baltimore (1833), the Holy See, on June 18, 1834, redefined the boundaries of all the dioceses in the U.S.; New Jersey, however, remained divided between New York and Philadelphia until, by act of Pius IX on July 29, 1853, the Diocese of Newark, designated suffragan to New York, was formed. The rapid growth of the Church in the new diocese led to its division by Leo XIII on July 15, 1881. Fourteen counties of the state were separated from the Diocese of Newark to form the Diocese of *Trenton. In 1937 the Holy See once again rearranged the ecclesiastical map of New Jersey. The counties of Passaic, Morris, and Sussex were separated from Newark to form the Diocese of *Paterson (December 9); Camden, Atlantic, Cape May, Cumberland, Gloucester and Salem were taken from Trenton to form the Diocese of *Camden (December 9); Newark was raised to the rank of archdiocese and metropolitan of the province (December 10).

Church-State Relations. References to and provisions affecting religion are incorporated in the state constitution and in acts of the legislature and the judiciary.

Constitution. New Jersey is governed by the Constitution of 1947, as amended. The preamble states that "we the people . . . grateful to Almighty God for the civil and religious liberty which He hath so long permitted us to enjoy, and looking to Him for a blessing upon our endeavors to secure and transmit the same unimpaired to succeeding generations, do ordain and establish this Constitution." Article 1 provides for freedom of religion and right of conscience. It declares that "there shall be no establishment of one religious sect in preference to another; no religious or racial test shall be required as a qualification for any office or public trust." However, the members and officers of the legislature and state officers must take an oath or affirmation before entering upon their duties (art. 4, sec. 8; art. 7, sec. 1). All impeachments are tried by the senate, whose members must be under oath or affirmation (art. 7, sec. 3). The constitution exempts from taxation real and personal property used exclusively for religious purposes and not for profit (art. 8, sec. 1).

Marriage and Divorce. Marriages of men under 18 and women under 16 are forbidden, except in certain cases of pregnancy, and the consent of parents is needed for men under 21 and women under 18. A license and blood test are required. Certain public officials and clergy may perform the ceremony. Common-law marriages contracted after Dec. 1, 1939, are not recognized, and marriages are void if the parties are related by blood in any degree of the direct line, up to but not including first cousins. Marriages may be annulled if either party is bound by a prior subsisting marriage or is incapable of consent; other reasons include nonage, forbidden degrees of relationship prohibited by law, or physical incurable impotency. Absolute divorce may be granted on grounds of adultery; willful, obstinate, and continued desertion for 2 years; or extreme cruelty. There are no restrictions on remarriage. *See* MARRIAGE, U.S. LAW OF; DIVORCE (U.S. LAW OF).

Abortion, Birth Control, Sterilization. The law forbids *abortion. Any person who maliciously or without lawful justification administers, prescribes, advises, or directs a pregnant woman to use a drug or instrument with intent to cause or procure a miscarriage is guilty of a high misdemeanor. If the woman or child dies there is a fine of not more than $5,000 and imprisonment for not more than 15 years. Instruments for abortion are not to be exposed for view or sale.

The law "regulates" *birth control by statute in New Jersey. A person cannot without "just cause" display instruments for *contraception or advertise them; so doing constitutes disorderly conduct. The intent is to regulate rather than prohibit the sale of contraceptives (*see* ANOVULANTS).

The law prohibits therapeutic *sterilization if it conflicts with a person's religious beliefs.

Property and Taxation. Religious and charitable associations may incorporate under the chapter entitled "Corporations and Associations Not for Profit." The New Jersey code has specific statutes for various religious denominations. The Roman Catholic Church can incorporate at the diocesan or parish level. Action by the board of trustees must be approved by the bishop, which in effect gives him supreme control through his trustees. The real and personal property of religious societies and charities, used exclusively for these designated purposes, and not run for profit, is exempt from taxation. The exemption on parsonages is limited to an amount not exceeding $5,000. The land exemption is limited to 5 acres.

Prisons and Reformatories. There is nothing in the code concerning chaplains or religious services. The case of *McBride v. McCorkle* 130A (2) 881 involved a plaintiff in a New Jersey prison who was denied the opportunity to hear Mass because he was in a segregated cell block, whose members were not allowed to attend Mass. The court ruled that this was necessary to preserve order and discipline and declared that "if the plaintiff has lost any right, it has come about by his own hand."

Holidays and Sunday Observance. Sunday, Christmas and New Year's Day, Good Friday, general election days, Thanksgiving Day, Saturday after 12 noon, February 22, May 30, July 4, October 12, November 11, and any day designated by the president or governor for fast or prayer or as a bank holiday are legal holidays. If a holiday falls on Sunday, the following Monday is a holiday. Business may be transacted on holidays, except for Sundays, with some exceptions. The sale on Sundays of automobiles, furniture, and clothing is forbidden. Certain forms of recreation are allowed, and the retail sale of alcohol is optional.

Morality, Public Health, and Safety. No state condones polygamy. A person who disturbs a religious assembly is deemed a disorderly person. The chapter on abuse and cruelty toward children may not be construed to deny the right of a parent or guardian, having the care and control of the child, to treat or provide treatment for an ill child in accordance with the religious tenets of any church, as authorized by other statutes of the state, provided that the laws relating to communicable diseases and sanitary matters are not violated. The board of education may exempt a pupil from physical examination or from immunization if the parent objects thereto, in a signed written statement, upon the ground that it interferes with the free exercise of his religious principles. In *State v. Perricone* 181 A (2) 751 (1962), however, it was held that the refusal of parents on religious grounds to submit their infant child to blood transfusions necessary to save his life or mental health amounted to statutory neglect. The law protected from criminal prosecutions persons acting pursuant to their religious beliefs in matters involving child welfare, but it did not render the state helpless in protecting children. In *Hoener v. Bertinato* 171 A (2) 140 (1961), it was ruled that an unborn child's rights to life and health are entitled to legal protection even though the child is not viable.

Persons may treat themselves in accordance with the religious tenets of their church, provided that the laws, rules, and regulations relating to communicable diseases and sanitary matters are not violated. The law relating to the practice of medicine and surgery in general do not apply to persons practicing healing by spiritual, religious, or mental means if no material medicine is prescribed or used and no manipulation or material means are employed.

Various Constitutional Freedoms. An injunction restraining a union from distributing circulars proclaiming that a manufacturer's beverages were nonunion made was found to be an infringement of the union's freedom of speech and press under state and Federal constitutions, notwithstanding the absence of strikes or disputes between the manufacturer and his employees [see *E. L. Kerns Co. v. Landgraf* 16 A (2) 623]. A New Jersey ordinance required persons who sell newspapers upon the highways and in the public places of Atlantic City to procure a permit and comply with regulations imposed by the director of public safety and approved by the city commissioner. These regulations, which were neither enumerated in the ordinance nor determined with the solemnity or publicity of an ordinance, were found to violate the free speech and free press provisions of the Federal and state constitutions [see *Herder v. Shahadi* 14 A (2) 475].

Bibliography: I. S. KULL, ed., *New Jersey: A History,* 4 v. (New York 1931). W. S. MYERS, ed., *The Story of New Jersey,* 5 v. (New York 1945). J. M. FLYNN, *The Catholic Church in New Jersey* (Morristown, N.J. 1904). W. T. LEAHY, *The Catholic Church of the Diocese of Trenton* (Princeton 1907). *New Jersey Statutes (Annotated) 1937* (St. Paul, Minn. 1939–). *West's New Jersey Digest* (Newark, N.J. 1954–).

[J. H. BRADY]

NEW JERUSALEM CHURCH

Known also as the New Church or the Swedenborgian Church, organized in London, England, in 1787 by students of the theological writings of Emanuel *Swedenborg (1688–1772). Swedenborg himself never organized a church or even a group. The first organizer in London was Robert Hindmarsh, a Methodist. Subsequently ministers were ordained and other groups recognized; in 1789 the first General Conference of the New Church met in the chapel at Great Eastcheap.

Swedenborgian doctrine was introduced into the U.S. in 1784; the first congregation was organized in Baltimore, Md., in 1792. By 1817 the number of existing societies was sufficient to form a General Convention of the New Jerusalem, which met that year in Philadelphia, Pa., where the current president resides at the local Swedenborgian church. A separate body of Swedenborgians was formed in 1890, and in 1897 took the name of the General Church of the New Jerusalem with headquarters in Bryn Athyn, Pa. This group considers itself more faithful to the ideas of Swedenborg, has its own school system, and in government is similar to the *Episcopal Church. The General Convention churches are more liberal in doctrine, more active in ecumenical cooperation, and are congregational in church polity. Membership in the *National Council of the Churches of Christ in the U.S.A. presents a problem to Swedenborgian churches because of their unusual doctrine on God: He is One and is "the Lord and Savior Jesus Christ, in whom is the Father, Son and Holy Spirit" (*Adoramus,* a non-creedal formula used in many churches). This seems to be a Trinity of Person, not of Persons; the matter, however, is under study by a church committee. Other distinctive doctrines are derived from Swedenborg's spiritual writings, although local option determines the selection for any individual congregation. Some consider him the heaven-sent revealer of the true spiritual meaning of Scripture; others look upon him much as Lutherans consider Martin Luther or Roman Catholics regard the Greek Fathers. Swedenborgian doctrines more commonly held include the belief that Sacred Scripture is God's Word, revealing Jesus Christ as the "Divine Human" by faith, in whom men are saved; the New Jerusalem is a symbol of a new spiritual era in man's life, heralded by Swedenborg's spiritual interpretation of the Word; and man is a free spirit temporarily clothed with a material body; death releases him into the world of God and angels, where he makes his final free choice of heaven or hell.

Thus a Swedenborgian is a Christian who finds in the writings of Swedenborg a meaning of life that points the way to growth of mind and spirit, resulting in a life of loving service to others. He enters his church by baptism or confirmation, or simply with a letter of transfer from another Christian church. In 1964 worldwide membership was estimated at about 40,000. Many Swedenborgians enroll in other local churches where no local Swedenborgian church exists. The General Convention in America now lists 80 churches and book depots, 51 ministers, and 5,800 members. The Convention has a national church in Washington, D.C., and a famous memorial chapel at Portuguese Bend, Calif. The General Church is much smaller and concentrates its activity mainly at Bryn Athyn, where it has a cathedral, an academy, and a theological seminary. Other seminaries for the General Convention are at Cambridge, Mass., and Islington, London.

The Swedenborg Foundation in New York publishes and distributes his theological writings, often donating sets of his works to libraries, clergymen, and scholars. Publications of the church include: the monthly *New Church Messenger* and the annual *Journal of the General Convention.*

Bibliography: M. BLOCK, *The New Church in the New World* (New York 1932). W. WUNSCH, *An Outline of New Church Teaching* (New York 1926). H. KELLER, *My Religion* (New York 1964).

[D. J. BOWMAN]

NEW MELLERAY, ABBEY OF

In July 1849 the Cistercian (Trappist) monks of Mount Melleray, County Waterford, Ireland, accepted the invitation of Bp. Mathias Loras of Dubuque, Iowa, to establish a foundation on 500 acres of timber and prairie land presented to them 12 miles southwest of Dubuque and 18 miles west of the Mississippi River.

Of the original 16 who embarked from Ireland in

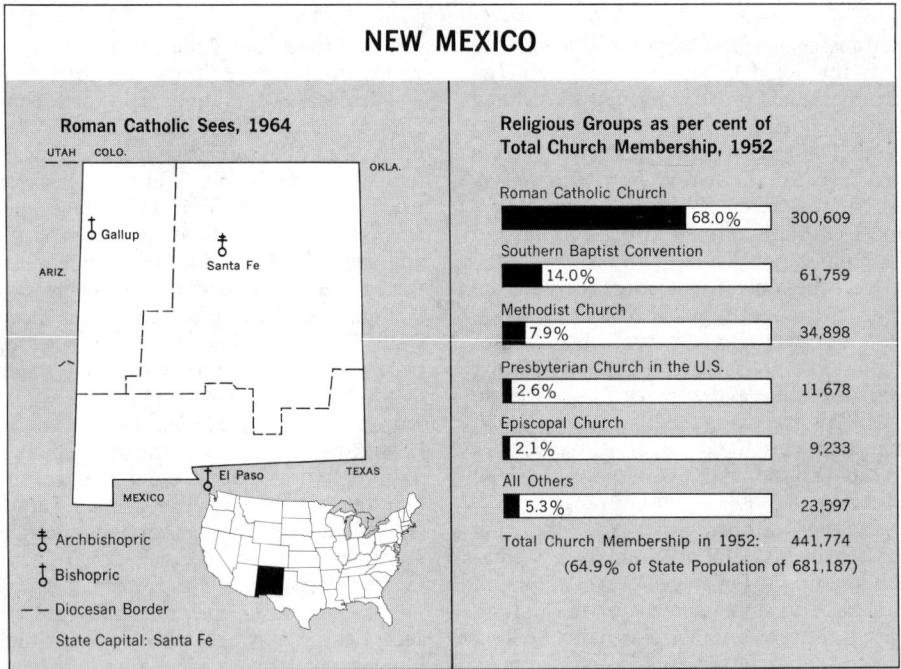

NEW MEXICO

Roman Catholic Sees, 1964

State Capital: Santa Fe

‡ Archbishopric

† Bishopric

-- Diocesan Border

Religious Groups as per cent of Total Church Membership, 1952

Roman Catholic Church	68.0%	300,609
Southern Baptist Convention	14.0%	61,759
Methodist Church	7.9%	34,898
Presbyterian Church in the U.S.	2.6%	11,678
Episcopal Church	2.1%	9,233
All Others	5.3%	23,597

Total Church Membership in 1952:   441,774
(64.9% of State Population of 681,187)

Church-membership statistics were compiled by the Bureau of Research and Survey of the National Council of the Churches of Christ in the U.S.A.

September 1849, six died of cholera on the steamboat between New Orleans and St. Louis, an omen of the adversity, poverty, and hard labor that were to mark so much of New Melleray's history. However, two monks molded in such circumstances were Clement Smythe, second bishop of Dubuque (1857–65), and James O'Gorman, Vicar Apostolic of Nebraska (1859) and later first bishop of Omaha.

In 1863 New Melleray was raised to the status of an abbey and additional farm acreage was gradually accumulated. Two wings of the monastery were erected by 1870 in the style of the Pugin revival of 13th-century Gothic.

Two long-lived superiors, Alberic Dunlea and Bruno Ryan, governed from 1897 to 1944, during which time the abbey managed to survive another lean cycle of indebtedness and scarcity of vocations. From 61 members in 1860, the community was reduced in 1918 to 17 aged monks responsible for the monastery and its 3,000 acres. But Dom Bruno lived to see the erection of a new guesthouse wing, the dispelling of all debt, and a community of more than 50 men.

From 1944 to 1954 three abbots held office, Albert Beston, Eugene Martin, and Vincent Daly, under whom New Melleray's fortunes improved. A post-World War II increase of vocations among former servicemen raised the community to 135, including 40 priests. A building project was inaugurated, doubling the abbey's size, and the farm program was intensified and modernized. A foundation comprising about 25 monks was established in the Ozarks of southern Missouri in 1950. In 1954 Dom Philip O'Connor assumed office as abbot.

Bibliography: M. ALBERIC, *Compendium of the History of the Cistercian Order* (Trappist, Ky. 1944). M. M. HOFFMAN, *Arms and the Monk* (Dubuque 1952). C. W. WHALEN, *The Trappist Way* (Peosta 1946). A. J. LUDDY, *The Story of Mount Melleray* (Dublin 1946).

[C. O'CONNOR]

NEW MEXICO

State situated on the mountainous plateau of southwestern U.S. and admitted to the Union (1912) as the 47th state. The state is bounded on the north by Colorado, on the east by Oklahoma and Texas, on the south by Texas and Mexico, and on the west by Arizona. The capital is Santa Fe, and the largest city is Albuquerque. The most important river of the state is the Rio Grande, known in Spanish times as Rio Bravo del Norte; it is the major irrigation source and the area of most extensive farming. The state's mineral wealth is considerable, including zinc, copper, gold, and lead; in 1960 it ranked first in the nation in the production of uranium ore, potassium salt and perlite; third in manganic ore; and fourth in natural gas. By the 1960s the development of military establishments and atomic energy centers had aided the state's economy and given employment to large numbers. Tourists, attracted by the climate and beauty of the state, which contains millions of acres of national forests, constitute a chief source of income. Many Indian pueblos remain almost as they were in the 13th century and are part of New Mexico's complex cultural pattern—Indian, Spanish, and American.

History. The ecclesiastical history of New Mexico began with the planting of the cross there by the expedition of Francisco Vázquez de Coronado (1540), although the small expeditions of Cabeza de Vaca and Fray Marcos de *Niza may have entered the area previously (*see* CONQUISTADORES). With Coronado were several Franciscan friars, two of whom stayed on after the expedition withdrew to Mexico in 1542. Of these two, Juan de *Padilla became the protomartyr of the U.S., and Juan de la Cruz was killed in New Mexico a short time later.

Although several small unauthorized parties entered New Mexico during the 50 years following the Coronado expedition, it was not until 1598 that a full-scale colonizing expedition moved in, under the leadership of Juan de Oñate, who was accompanied by Franciscan missionaries from Mexico City. When their missionary efforts among the Indians showed good results, the Spanish Crown determined to support the colony. Sante Fe was founded (*c.* 1610) as the capital of New Mexico. Constant tensions between civil and ecclesiastical authorities and increasing discontent among the Indians culminated (1680) in the Pueblo revolt led by Popé. This concerted and well-organized uprising cost the lives of 22 missionaries and many of the Spanish settlers; New Mexico was not permanently reconquered and the missions reestablished until 18 years later.

During the 18th century the increasing number of Spanish settlers gradually changed New Mexico from an Indian to a Spanish settlement. By the end of the century the Spaniards outnumbered the Indians four to one. The area was visited twice (1730, 1760) by the bishops of Durango, and in 1787 secular clergy was introduced into the four most important Spanish towns. After 1821, when the ties between Spain and Mexico were broken, the Franciscans gradually disappeared, and in 1833 Bp. Antonio Zubiria turned the missions over to the secular clergy.

On Aug. 18, 1848, Gen. Stephen Watts Kearny raised the American flag in Santa Fe, initiating the era of American control. As an American territory, New Mexico did not remain long under Mexican ecclesiastical jurisdiction; in 1850 it was made a vicariate apostolic, and in 1853 *Santa Fe became a diocese and later (1875), an archdiocese. During this entire period of advancement the Church in New Mexico was ruled by John Baptist *Lamy, who was consecrated in 1850 and resigned in 1885. Under his guidance the Mexican clergy were replaced mainly by Frenchmen. The Sisters of Loretto founded the first Catholic school for girls (1852); the Christian Brothers established (1859) a school for boys, which became St. Michael's College (1947); and the Sisters of Charity opened the first Catholic orphanage and hospital in Santa Fe (1865). In 1940 a second diocese was formed and included a large section of northern Arizona; Bp. Bernard T. Espalage was installed as the first bishop of *Gallup.

Population. In 1952 Catholics constituted 43.6 per cent of the state's total population of 681,187; Protestants, 20.5 per cent; Jews, 0.2 per cent; and all others, 35.7 per cent (*see* CHURCH MEMBERSHIP, U.S.). In 1961 the estimated Catholic population was 359,159, approximately 39.3 per cent of the state's total population.

Education. In 1964 St. Michael's College and the coeducational College of St. Joseph on the Rio Grande, Albuquerque (1940), enrolled about 1,500 students. There were 26 high schools (4,870 students) and 81 elementary schools (19,781 students) under Catholic auspices; approximately 47,800 additional students received religious instruction on released-time programs.

Church-State Relations. References to and provisions affecting religion are incorporated in the state constitution and in acts of the legislature and the judiciary.

Constitution. New Mexico is governed by the Constitution of 1912, as amended. The preamble states that the people are "grateful to Almighty God for the blessings of liberty." Article 2, sec. 11 provides for freedom of religion; a person may not be denied rights because of his religion, nor may preferences be given by law to any religion. The senate tries all impeachments, and during such trials the senate members must be under oath of affirmation (art. 4, sec. 35). A citizen's right to vote, hold office, or sit on a jury may not be abridged because of religion (art. 7, sec. 3). "Perfect toleration of religious sentiment shall be secured, and no inhabitant of this state shall ever be molested in person or property on account of his or her mode of religious worship" (art. 21, sec. 1). Church property not used for profit is exempt from taxation (art. 8, sec. 3).

"No religious test shall ever be required as a condition of admission into the public schools or any educational institution of this State, either as a teacher or student, and no teacher or student of any such school or institution shall ever be required to attend or participate in any religious service whatsoever" (art. 12, sec. 9).

Persons elected or appointed to any office must take an oath or affirmation before entering upon their duties (art. 20, sec. 1).

"The use of wines solely for sacramental purposes under church authority at any place within the state shall never be prohibited" (art. 20, sec. 13).

Marriage and Divorce. Marriages of men under 18 and women under 16 are forbidden except when authorized by the court. The consent of parents is needed for men under 21 and women under 18. A medical exam-

St. Christopher, tempera over gesso on a pine panel, by José Rafael Aragón, who worked in New Mexico from 1830 to 1850; a work typical of the state's religious folk art.

ination is required. Certain public officials and clergy may perform the ceremony, or it may be performed in accordance with the rites of any religious society. Common-law marriages are not recognized.

Marriages are void if the parties are related by blood in any degree of the direct line, and up to but not including first cousins.

The grounds for absolute divorce are adultery, impotency, cruel or inhuman treatment, pregnancy of the wife at the time of marriage by one other than her husband without the husband's knowledge, abandonment, conviction of a felony, habitual drunkenness, incurable insanity for 5 years, incompatibility or failure of the husband to support his wife according to his means, station in life, and ability. There are no restrictions on remarriage.

A legal separation may be obtained if the parties are permanently separated and no longer live and cohabit together. *See* MARRIAGE, U.S. LAW OF; DIVORCE (U.S. LAW OF).

Abortion, Birth Control, Sterilization. The law forbids *abortion unless two physicians deem it necessary to preserve the life of the mother or to prevent serious and permanent bodily injury. Criminal abortion consists of administering to any pregnant woman any medicine, drug, or other substance, or operating upon her, or using any method or means whereby an untimely interruption of her pregnancy is produced, or attempted to be produced, with intent to destory the fetus. Such abortion constitutes a fourth degree felony; but if the woman dies, it is a second degree felony.

There are no references to birth control, contraception, anovulants, or sterilization in the state code.

Property and Taxation. Religious and charitable associations may incorporate as nonprofit corporations under the chaper entitled "Associations Not For Profit." There are provisions for a corporation sole that may continue up to 100 years. Title vests in the corporation sole. Parishes may incorporate also.

Real and personal property of religious societies and charities, not run for profit, is exempt from taxation. But a property tax is imposed on any part of ecclesiastical property that is not being used for purposes of religious worship and instruction. Property acquired with a tax lien is not exempt from that lien.

There are no mortmain statutes or fund-raising statutes.

Prisons and Reformatories. There are no statutes concerning chaplains or religious matters.

Holidays and Sunday Observance. Christmas and New Year's Day, Labor Day, Thanksgiving Day, February 22, May 30, July 4, October 12, and November 11 are legal holidays. Certain other days are school holidays. When the holiday falls on Sunday, the next day is deemed a holiday. Most of New Mexico's blue laws were repealed in 1963. The sale of alcoholic beverages on Sundays is optional under county or municipal control.

Morality, Public Health, and Safety. No state condones polygamy. Disturbance of a lawfully assembled religious society gathered together in public worship is considered a petty misdemeanor. The act concerning basic sciences of the healing arts does not apply to Christian Scientists, nor does the practice of medicine act affect or limit in any way the practice of the religious tenets of any church in the ministration to the sick or suffering by mental or spiritual means. Exemption from immunization is possible upon the presentation of affidavits from an officer of a recognized religious denomination, stating that the child's parents or guardians are bona fide members of a denomination whose religious teaching requires reliance upon prayer or spiritual means alone for healing.

Various Constitutional Freedoms. In *Lujan v. U.S.,* 209 F (2) 190, it was held that it is no deprivation of religious freedom to inquire concerning a person's particular beliefs or tenets.

Bibliography: F. A. Domínguez, *Missions of New Mexico, 1776,* tr. E. B. Adams and A. Chávez (Albuquerque 1956). J. B. Salpointe, *Soldiers of the Cross* (Banning, Calif. 1898). F. V. Scholes, *Church and State in New Mexico, 1610–1650* (Albuquerque 1937); *Troublous Times in New Mexico, 1659–1670* (Albuquerque 1942). B. Segale, *At the End of the Santa Fe Trail* (Milwaukee 1948). P. Horgan, *Great River: The Rio Grande in North American History,* 2 v. (New York 1954). *New Mexico Statutes, Annotated, 1953* (Indianapolis, Ind. 1954). *New Mexico Digest, 1852 to Date,* 6 v. (St. Paul, Minn. 1948). **Illustration credit:** Fig. 2, Collection, Museum of New Mexico. Photo by Laura Gilpin.

[F. WARREN; W. E. MC CARTHY]

NEW-MOON FEAST, HEBREW. In ancient Israel the first day of each month, i.e., the day after the new moon was sighted, was a feast day with ordinances similar to those of the *Sabbath, with which it is linked in several passages (e.g., 4 Kgs 4.23). It has not been demonstrated, however, that the two were in fact originally connected. The monthly feast is not mentioned in the festival calendars of the Pentateuch, but in Nm 28.11–15 the sacrifices for it are prescribed in detail. The antiquity of the feast is clear, however, from allusions in the Prophets (Is 1.13–14; Os 2.13; Am 8.5), and a New-Moon dinner at the royal court, requiring ritual purity for participation, is described in 1 Sm 20.5–29. Like the Sabbath, it was a day of rest from work.

The New-Moon Day was observed throughout OT times (e.g., Ezr 3.5; Neh 10.33) and in NT times as well (Col 2.16), but it gradually lost its importance and disappeared from Jewish life. In later Biblical times only the first of the 7th month, Tishri, retained its prominence (Lv 23.24–25; Nm 29.1–6) and was observed with special solemnity: rest, trumpet blasts, a holy convocation, and sacrifices. This solemnity may reflect an earlier time when this day was a new year's day. The much later Hebrew Feast of the *New Year, Rosh ha-Shanah, retained the characteristic trumpet blast of the 1st day of Tishri. But the New Moon Day of Tishri is never mentioned in the Bible as a new year feast.

Bibliography: H. Eising, LexThK² 7:916–917. N. Turchi, EncCatt 8:1748–49. De Vaux AncIsr 469–470. K. Kohler, JewishEnc 9:243–244. A. Caquot, "Remarques sur la fête de la néoménie dans l'ancien Israël," RevHistRel 158 (1960) 1–18.

[G. W. MAC RAE]

NEW NORCIA, ABBEY OF, a Benedictine abbey *nullius* (*Novae Nursiae*), in Western *Australia, about 80 miles north of *Perth, of which it is a suffragan. It was founded (1846) by a Spanish monk, Rosendo Salvado, for the evangelization of Australian aborigines. After living 3 years among these primitive nomads, Dom Salvado (1814–1900) visited Europe (1849) in search of missionaries. While in Rome he was appointed bishop of Port Victoria (now Darwin). Before he could return, his entire flock abandoned the region for southern goldfields, whereupon the Pope permitted him to return to New Norcia. Bishop Salvado and his young Spanish community built a monastery, and cleared the land for agriculture. They established schools, built cottages for married natives, and introduced them to farming and handicrafts. In March 1867 Pius IX made the monastery an abbey *nullius* and a prefecture apostolic. On a visit to Rome (1900), Bishop Salvado arranged for its affiliation with the Spanish province of the Subiaco Congregation of *Benedictines. His successor, Dom Fulgentius Torres (abbot 1902–14), found a changing social situation. With the coming of European settlers and a decline in the number of natives, the abbey had to provide for the spiritual needs of a white, rather than a colored, population. In the North, however, Abbot Torres established a new mission to aborigines in 1908 on the Drysdale River. Succeeding abbots were Anselm Catalan (1914–51) and Dom Gregory Gomez (1951–   ).

Bibliography: J. T. McMahon, *The Salvado Story* (Perth 1956). AnnPont (1964) 728.

[J. G. MURTAGH]

NEW ORLEANS, ARCHDIOCESE OF (NOVAE AURELIAE)

Metropolitan see erected April 25, 1793, as the Diocese of Louisiana and the Floridas by Pius VI upon the application of King Charles IV of Spain. The vast territory of the original diocese, except for the area under the jurisdiction of the Diocese of Baltimore, stretched from the Rocky Mountains to the Atlantic and from Canada to the Gulf of Mexico. The territory, detached from the See of Havana, was previously part of the older Diocese of Santiago de Cuba, under whose jurisdiction the Louisiana colony had passed in 1762. Before that date, Quebec had spiritual jurisdiction over French colonial Louisiana. After the 1849 Provincial Council of Baltimore recommended additional ecclesiastical jurisdictions, Pius IX on July 19, 1850, raised New Orleans to the rank of metropolitan see. The first suffragan dioceses were those of Galveston, Tex.; Mobile, Ala.; Natchez, Miss.; and Little Rock, Ark. In 1963 the province embraced, besides the metropolitan see, the Dioceses of Mobile-Birmingham; Natchez-Jackson; Little Rock; and, in Louisiana, Alexandria, Lafayette, and Baton Rouge. The archdiocese includes 10 civil parishes (counties) in southeast Louisiana in addition to that portion of St. Mary's Civil Parish lying east of the Atchafalaya River. According to the U.S. census of 1960, the total population within these 7,577 square miles was approximately 1,132,600, of whom about 40.9 per cent were Catholic.

Early History. The parish church with the longest uninterrupted history is St. Louis Basilica, whose origin extends practically to the founding of New Orleans in 1718. The first Mass in what is now the archdiocese was offered nearly 20 years earlier, on March 3, 1699, by Rev. Anastase Douay, a Franciscan missionary, with the expedition of Pierre Le Moyne, Sieur d'*Iberville, who established the power of France in the Lower Mississippi Valley. On a later expedition to Louisiana with Iberville, the Jesuit Paul du Ru put to use his fragmentary knowledge of the tribal languages of the Bayagoula, Ouma, and Natchez Indians by preparing a rudimentary catechism for their instruction. By early spring of 1700, Du Ru was supervising the construction

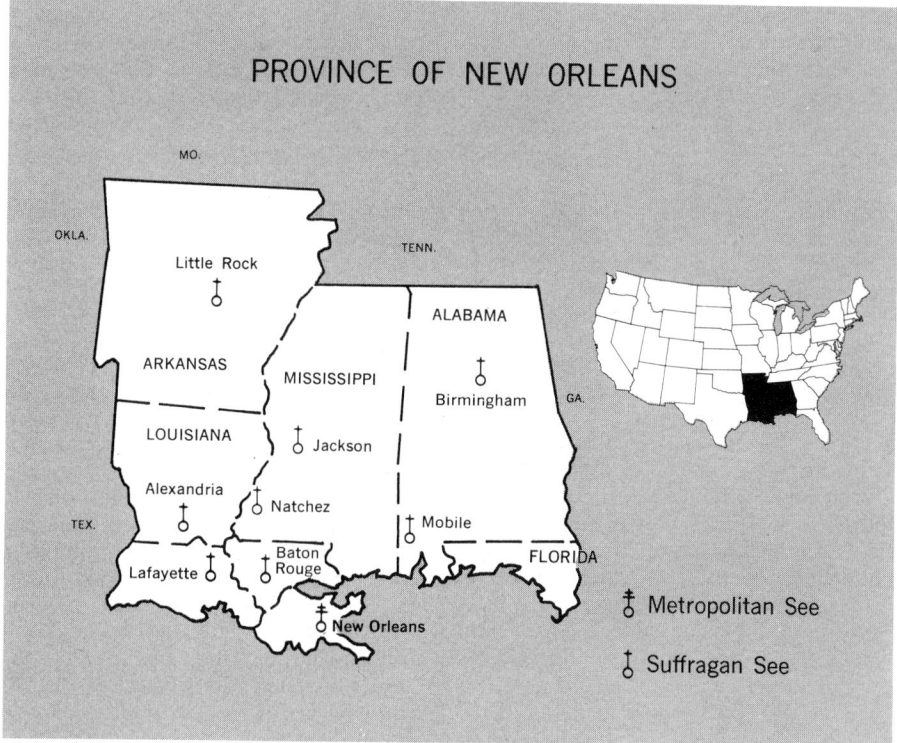

Fig. 1. Province of New Orleans, comprising one archdiocese called the metropolitan see and six dioceses called suffragan sees. The archbishop has metropolitan jurisdiction over the province.

Fig. 2. St. Louis Basilica, New Orleans.

of a small church in an Indian village situated close to the present community of Bayou Goula in Iberville parish.

The Church made little progress during the 5 years (1712–17) when Antoine Crozat, French financier, attempted to exploit the region. The Council of the Marine in 1717 recommended turning the colony over to John Law's Company of the West and its successor, the Company of the Indies (or Mississippi Company). In accordance with the charter issued by the regent, Philip II, Duke of Orleans, religious affairs were included in the activities of the Company of the West from 1717 to 1731. Occasionally priests, known as concession chaplains, were among the personnel assigned to the land grants in the colony. More important than the concessions, however, was the founding of New Orleans as the new capital of the colony by Jean Baptiste Le Moyne, Sieur de *Bienville, brother of Iberville, in 1718. The plan for the city, laid by Adrien de Pauger, provided for a church and presbytery where these were finally located, but divine services were held only in improvised and inadequate quarters until April 1727, when the first substantial St. Louis parish church was finally completed.

Various secular, Carmelite, Jesuit, and Capuchin priests labored in the colony during its formative years. The first Capuchins were Bruno de Langres, who arrived in New Orleans towards the end of 1722, and Philibert de Vianden, who took charge of the district from the Chapitoulas, a few miles above the original boundaries of the city, to Pointe Coupée, including Les Allemands, the German Coast, and the intervening concessions. Les Allemands had a chapel, dedicated to St. John, on the west bank of the Mississippi as early as 1724. In April 1723, Bruno was replaced as superior

of the Capuchin missions in Louisiana by Raphael de Luxembourg, who was also vicar-general of the bishop of Quebec. Raphael established, in 1725, the first school for boys in New Orleans, but it lasted only 5 or 6 years. Nicolas Ignace de Beaubois, founder of the Jesuit missions in New Orleans, induced the Ursulines of Rouen, France, to establish a military hospital and school for girls. The pioneer group of Ursulines reached New Orleans on Aug. 6, 1727, and began the educational enterprise that has continued without interruption to this day. In 1722, the Jesuits, who contributed notably to the spiritual and economic well-being of the area, undertook the spiritual jurisdiction of the Indians in the colony, a responsibility entrusted to them by Bp. Louis Duplessis-Mornay of Quebec. Their endeavors were supported in large measure by an extensive indigo and sugar plantation adjacent to New Orleans. In July 1763, while Michael Baudouin was superior, the Jesuits were dispossessed of their property and banished from Louisiana. Their departure, some 10 years before the society was suppressed, seriously hampered and retarded the growth of the Church in colonial Louisiana.

After 1776, Church affairs in New Orleans bore a definite Spanish stamp. Cirillo de Barcelona, chaplain of the Spanish expedition against the British in West Florida, was consecrated auxiliary bishop for the Louisiana colony on March 6, 1785. Shortly before leaving for his consecration in Cuba, he appointed his assistant Antonio de *Sedella temporary pastor of St. Louis. For decades thereafter, Sedella, known as Père Antoine, was the center of controversy in the area.

First Bishops. When the Diocese of Louisiana and the Floridas was created in 1793, Luis Ignacio de *Peñalver y Cárdenas was consecrated as first ordinary and arrived in New Orleans on July 17, 1795, marking the beginning of home government in Church affairs. Peñalver noted in a report to the Spanish government that of the 11,000 Catholics in New Orleans, only about 400 performed their Easter duty. He instituted a number of necessary reforms, combated religious indifference and Voltaireanism, and established parishes in such places as the Poste des Avoyelles, Many (Neustra Señora de Guadalupe at Bayou Scie), and Monroe. Meanwhile, the parish church in use since 1727 had been destroyed in the great fire of 1788 and a new structure, the future Cathedral of St. Louis, was completed in 1794. Although renovated several times, it remains substantially the same building, still in use as the cathedral. In December 1964 it became a minor basilica.

In 1801 Peñalver was transferred to the Archdiocese of Guatemala and jurisdictional quarrels, interdiction, and threats of schism marked the next 15 years in New Orleans. Père Antoine was at odds with Rev. Patrick Walsh and Canon Thomas Hassett, who attempted to administer the diocese during the episcopal vacancy; the wardens of the cathedral (*marguilliers*), after assuming control of church temporalities in 1805, waxed more and more arrogant; and, to complicate matters further, Spain ceded Louisiana back to France, which, in turn, sold it to the U.S. in 1803. Aware of the territorial transfer, the Holy See decided not to send Bishop-elect Francisco Porro y Peinado to Louisiana, and on Sept. 1, 1805, placed it temporarily under the spiritual supervision of Bp. John Carroll of Baltimore, Md. Carroll in time named the chaplain of the Ursulines, Jean Olivier, his vicar-general, but the latter's authority was openly challenged by Père Antoine and the cathedral wardens. Finally, on Aug. 18, 1812, Rev. Louis William *Dubourg, president of Georgetown College and founder of St. Mary's College in Baltimore, was named administrator apostolic by Archbishop Carroll. It was Dubourg, complying with Andrew Jackson's request, who officiated at a Te Deum in St. Louis Cathedral following the U.S. victory over the British at the Battle of New Orleans on Jan. 8, 1815.

On Sept. 24, 1815, Dubourg was consecrated in Rome, and Louisiana finally had a bishop, after an interregnum of nearly 15 years. Dubourg, however, remained in Europe for the next 2 years, enlisting priests and seminarians, as well as the services of the Religious of the Sacred Heart, and helping in the formation of the organization that eventually became the Pontifical Society for the *Propagation of the Faith. Upon arriving in the U.S., Dubourg went to St. Louis, Mo., and returned to New Orleans only in late 1820. The next year he called a synod, which was attended by 20 priests. On March 25, 1824, Joseph *Rosati, CM, was consecrated as Dubourg's coadjutor, but his administration of the Church in New Orleans amounted to supervision at a distance, since he resided in St. Louis. A significant event of the period was the arrival of the Sisters of Charity from Emmitsburg, Md., to staff the Poydras Asylum in New Orleans. Dubourg resigned in mid-1826 and died in 1833 as archbishop of Besancon, France.

Dubourg's resignation left the lower end of the Mississippi Valley without a resident bishop and was the signal for further disorders, which the annual visits of Rosati could not completely control. Rosati, appointed bishop of St. Louis in 1827, in time recommended a fellow Vincentian for the See of New Orleans, and Leo Raymond de Neckère was consecrated in St. Louis Cathedral on June 24, 1830. His regime was brief, for he was stricken with yellow fever and died on Sept. 5, 1833. A few months before (April 21, 1833), he had established New Orleans's second parish, St. Patrick's, to accommodate the Irish immigrants and other English-speaking people of the city. He had also invited to the diocese the Sisters of Our Lady of Mount Carmel from Tours, France, but they arrived after the bishop's death, and settled in Plattenville on Bayou Lafourche.

Archdiocesan Growth, 1850–1935. A remarkable period of Church expansion coincided with the growing importance of New Orleans as a center of commerce and expanding population. The city, emerging as fourth largest in the nation, increased in population from 29,737 in 1830 to 102,193 in 1840. The diocese covered the entire state, and had a total population approaching 300,000, served by 26 churches and 27 priests, when Anthony *Blanc became fourth bishop, Nov. 22, 1835.

Blanc. During the 25 years Blanc administered the see, the number of churches increased to 73, and priests to 92. He established Assumption Seminary on Bayou Lafourche, two colleges, nine academies and schools, four orphanages, a hospital, and a home for girls. Under the guidance of Etienne Rousselon, Vicar-General, the Sisters of the Holy Family were founded (1842) as a diocesan Negro community to teach, care for orphans, and tend to the aged of the colored race. Blanc invited five communities of nuns to the diocese: the Sisters Marianites of Holy Cross (1848); the Sisters of St. Joseph of Bourg (1856); the School Sisters of Notre Dame (1856); the Sisters of Our Lady of the Good Shepherd (1859); and the Dominican Sisters, who, however, did not arrive from Cabra, Ireland, until 4 months after his death. The Redemptorist fathers established themselves (1843) in Lafayette, then part of New Orleans Diocese, where German, Irish, and French immigrants had settled. The Jesuit fathers opened the College of the Immaculate Conception in 1849 on a plot of ground that had once formed part of the plantation of which they had been defrauded in 1763. The Congregation of Holy Cross came (1849) to stabilize St. Mary's Orphan Boys' Home, which had been opened by Adam Kindelon, first pastor of St. Patrick's. Rev. Cyril De la Croix organized the first conference of the Society of St. Vincent de Paul after a layman, William Blair Lancaster, brought a manual of the society to New Orleans (1852).

Blanc called two diocesan synods and two provincial councils. After a long and severe struggle with the church wardens, culminating in the withdrawal of the clergy from the cathedral (1843), he abolished the trustee system. During the recrudescence of *Nativism, he was the target of polemics and abuse in the press, but a loyal laity, represented by the Catholic Temperance Society, rallied to his defense. In litigation with the wardens, the Louisiana supreme court upheld the position of the bishop (1844). Three years after Blanc became archbishop of New Orleans in 1850, his jurisdiction was reduced about 22,000 square miles by the erection in the upper part of the state of the Diocese of Natchitoches, but the Catholic population of the archdiocese was decreased by only 25,000. After his death on June 20, 1860, the archdiocese was administered by Father Rousselon until the arrival of Archbishop-elect Jean Marie *Odin from Galveston, Tex.

Odin. The second archbishop took possession of his see only a few days after the bombardment of Ft. Sumter on April 12, 1861, Louisiana having already seceded from the Union and joined the Confederacy. During the Civil War, the archbishop's position was an extremely

Fig. 3. St. Louis Basilica, interior.

delicate one, calling for infinite tact and diplomacy. The times grew more trying after the city was occupied by Federal troops on May 1, 1862. Union forces wrought considerable damage on Church properties in such places as Pointe Coupée and Donaldsonville, and the war years witnessed a disruption of religious and educational work in Thibodaux, Convent, Plaquemine, Grand Coteau, and elsewhere. Reconstruction was no less trying. but Odin continued, within limitations, the expansion program of his predecessor.

During the archbishop's visit to Europe in 1863 in search of men and money for his diocese, the Marist Fathers accepted his invitation to labor in Louisiana. In 1867 the Oblate Sisters of Providence, a Baltimore community of Negro nuns. began staffing a home for dependent children. The Little Sisters of the Poor opened their home for the aged poor after a committee of pious women, called Les Dames de la Providence. asked for their help in maintaining a home for the aged founded in 1840. The Brothers of the Sacred Heart came to New Orleans from Mobile in 1869. The archbishop invited the Sisters of Mercy, who began their visits to the parish prison, city workhouse. boys' house of refuge, and the insane asylum in 1869. The first Benedictine convent in the archdiocese was opened (1870) in the German national parish of Holy Trinity, New Orleans. The nuns arrived from Covington, Ky., and later established a motherhouse in Covington. La.

After numerous requests for assistance, Odin finally obtained a coadjutor with right of succession. He was Napoléon Joseph Perché, who had been chaplain of the Ursulines for many years, founder (1842) of the first Catholic newspaper in Louisiana (*Le Propagateur Catholique*), and vicar-general of the archdiocese. He was consecrated in St. Louis Cathedral on May 1, 1870, and succeeded to the see when Odin died in France, May 25, 1870.

Perché and Leray. Like his predecessors, Perché invited several communities to the archdiocese: the Sisters of Perpetual Adoration, now known as the Sisters of the Most Holy Sacrament, who arrived at Waggaman in 1872; the Sisters of Christian Charity, who established themselves at St. Henry's convent, New Orleans, in 1873; and the Discalced Carmelite Nuns, who arrived in 1877. In addition, Archbishop Perché approved the founding of a diocesan community, the Sisters of Immaculate Conception, organized on July 11, 1874, in Labadieville with Elvina Vienne as first superior. Soon after his installation as head of the see, Perché also inaugurated a costly program of church building, school construction, and parish foundations that contrasted sharply with the record of his predecessor. These expenses, plus financial aid to families impoverished by the Civil War, caused the archdiocesan debt to soar to $590,925, of which $257,080 was due European bondholders.

Weakened by age and infirmities, and overwhelmed by the tremendous debt, the archbishop asked for a coadjutor. The Holy See appointed Francis Xavier Leray of Natchitoches, who became archbishop upon Perché's death on Dec. 27, 1883. Leray's chief concern as coadjutor and as ordinary was the reduction of the archdiocesan debt, so his administration was practically without building or expansion programs. The only new community established in the archdiocese was that of the Poor Clare Nuns (1885). Upon his death on Sept.

Fig. 4. *St. Joseph's Abbey, St. Benedict, La.*

23, 1887. Leray was succeeded by Francis Janssens. the Dutch-born bishop of Natchez.

Janssens. The new archbishop received the pallium from Cardinal James Gibbons on May 8, 1889, although he had actually taken possession of the archdiocese on Sept. 16, 1888. He invited the Benedictines of St. Meinrad's Abbey in Indiana to open a seminary for the training of priests. Luke Grüwe. OSB, established (1890) what later became St. Joseph's Abbey (St. Benedict, La.), and Janssens dedicated the seminary on Sept. 3, 1891. The archbishop welcomed Mother Frances Xavier Cabrini to New Orleans and encouraged her to establish (1892) a house primarily to assist Italians who had begun to migrate in large numbers to the city. In 1893, he asked the Sisters of the Holy Family to care for dependent or neglected Negro boys, and thus started the present Lafon Home for Boys, one of several institutions named for the local Negro philanthropist Thomy Lafon.

Janssens was greatly esteemed throughout the archdiocese, which numbered 341,613 in the centennial year of 1893. He encouraged spiritual ministrations to patients at the leprosarium at Carville, La. When the hurricane of 1893 swept the Louisiana Gulf Coast, Janssens went among the Italian, Spanish, and Malay fishermen in the island settlements in a small boat to comfort them; he later helped them to rebuild their homes. He promoted devotion to Our Lady under the title of Prompt Succor. The corporate structure of each parish, as it exists today, was determined in 1894 when each parish was legally incorporated with the archbishop, the vicar-general, the pastor, and two lay directors as board members. Janssens was the first ordinary to promote native vocations on a large scale; his predecessors generally had depended on priests and seminarians from Europe, and had leaned heavily on religious to staff new parishes. He sponsored the Catholic Winter School, opened parochial schools, and launched a dozen new parishes. Alarmed at the defections from the faith among the colored, he established St. Katherine's (1895) as a Negro parish, but on a temporary basis, since he did not wish to promote racial segregation. He died June 9, 1897, while en route to Europe in the interest of the archdiocese.

Chapelle. Placide Louis *Chapelle, sixth archbishop of New Orleans, was transferred from Santa Fe., N.Mex., in February 1898. In concern over the archdiocesan debt, he ordered the annual contribution of 12 per cent of the revenues of each parish for 5 years. This helped in the eventual liquidation of the long-standing debt, although it aroused the displeasure of some pastors. Chapelle's relations with his priests, many of them born and educated in France, were hardly improved by his extended, though necessary absences as apostolic delegate extraordinary to Puerto Rico and Cuba, and later as apostolic delegate to the Philippine Islands. It was evident that he needed an auxiliary and one was provided when the pastor of Annunciation Church in New Orleans, Gustave Rouxel, was consecrated on April 9, 1899. In 1898 the archbishop, in his anxiety to economize, withdrew aid from the preparatory seminary at St. Benedict. On the other hand, he opened a theological seminary (1900) in an existing building next to St. Stephen's Church, New Orleans, with Fathers of the Congregation of the Mission as professors. Some 12 parishes and missions were established during Chapelle's regime and the Dominican fathers began (1903) their ministry in the archdiocese. Chapelle died a victim of yellow fever, on Aug. 9, 1905.

Blenk. The next ordinary, James Hubert Blenk, SM, was well known to the archdiocese long before his appointment on April 20, 1906. He had served as bishop of Puerto Rico, former auditor and secretary to the apostolic delegation to the West Indies, rector of Holy Name of Mary Church, and president of Jefferson College, Convent, La. Blenk, an ardent promoter of Catholic education, set up (1908) the first archdiocesan school board and appointed the first superintendent of schools. The preparatory seminary was again placed under the care of the Benedictine fathers of St. Joseph's Abbey (1908), but the theological courses were discontinued (1907) at the seminary opened by Chapelle. Most major seminarians of the archdiocese matriculated at Kenrick Seminary in St. Louis and St. Mary's Seminary in Baltimore, or studied abroad. In September 1904 the Jesuits started a small college in New Orleans, which in 1911 was amalgamated with the College of the Immaculate Conception and became *Loyola University. Blenk designated (1908) St. Mary's the normal school for women religious engaged in teaching in the archdiocese. In time *St. Mary's Dominican became an accredited Catholic woman's college.

French Benedictine nuns, forced to leave their country, settled (1906) in Ramsay under the guidance of Paul Schaeuble, OSB, who had become first abbot of St. Joseph's in 1903. The Sisters Servants of Mary, having left Mexico during the Carranza revolution, found refuge also in the archdiocese and inaugurated (1914) their ministrations among the sick and bedridden in the city. The sisters of the Society of St. Teresa of Jesus, likewise refugees from Mexico, began teaching at St. Louis Cathedral school in 1915. That same year, the archbishop urgently requested Mother Katharine Drexel, foundress of the Sisters of the Blessed Sacrament for Indians and Colored People, to undertake the education of Negro youth in New Orleans. In 1917 the sisters opened a normal school and the following year they were authorized by the state legislature to conduct colleges and confer degrees. The sisters launched *Xavier University of Louisiana in 1925. For further ministration to the colored population, the archbishop solicited the services of St. Joseph's Society of the Sacred Heart (Josephites) and the Holy Ghost Fathers, assigning six parishes to the former and one to the latter. In

1911 the Brothers of Christian Schools purchased St. Paul's College, Covington, from the Benedictine Fathers. In 1912 the Ursulines, under the supervision of their chaplain, François Racine, moved from their third convent building to a new site on State Street where, 10 years later, the national shrine of Our Lady of Prompt Succor was erected.

Early in his administration, Blenk strengthened lay groups. He organized (1906) the State Board of Holy Name Societies, the Louisiana State Federation of Catholic Societies (1909), and the Federation of Catholic Societies of Women of Louisiana. He promoted the Catholic Order of Foresters, the Knights of Columbus, and the Knights of Peter Claver. The growth of the population in the archdiocese, especially in southwest Louisiana, made a division expedient. Partition was effected Jan. 11, 1918, shortly before Abp. John William Shaw was promoted to the New Orleans see. Jules Benjamin Jeanmard, administrator of the archdiocese following the death of Blenk (April 15, 1917), was named first bishop of the new Diocese of Lafayette. The area of the archdiocese was reduced by about 11,000 square miles, 40 church parishes, and a population of about 300,000.

Shaw. One of Shaw's first actions was to invite the Oblates of Mary Immaculate, with whom he had worked closely as bishop of San Antonio, Tex., to administer St. Louis Cathedral and to take charge of the churches and missions in Livingston parish. In 1919 the Sisters of Charity of the Incarnate Word, from San Antonio also, came to teach at St. Francis de Sales parochial school. In 1920 Archbishop Shaw, with his chancellor August J. Bruening, began to lay plans for a financial campaign for the erection of a major seminary. With the help of laymen, the campaign realized close to $1 million and Notre Dame Seminary, staffed by Marist Fathers, became a reality in September 1923. In Baton Rouge, the Sisters of St. Francis of Calais opened Our Lady of the Lake Hospital (1923). Franciscan fathers returned to the archdiocese on July 21, 1925, when they took charge of the newly established parish of St. Mary of the Angels in the city, and missions of the Lower Coast. The Sisters of the Holy Ghost and Mary Immaculate arrived from San Antonio in September 1926 to teach the Negro children of St. Luke's School, Thibodaux. Shaw encouraged the endeavors of Catharine Bostick and Zoe Grouchy in the establishment of the Missionary Servants of the Most Holy Eucharist of the Third Order of St. Dominic, a community intended for religious instruction of the children in public schools and for social relief work. In 1928 the Society of the Divine Word took over the mission stations on both the east and west bank of the lower Mississippi River. In 1931 the Jesuits purchased the old Jefferson College in Convent and converted it into Manresa House for laymen's retreats.

Father (later Bishop) Maurice Schexnayder began Newman Club work in 1929 at Louisiana State University, one-third of whose student body was Catholic. Monsignor Peter M. H. Wynhoven established (1925) Hope Haven for orphaned and abandoned boys, later placed under the Salesian Fathers of St. John Bosco. Opposite Hope Haven, Madonna Manor for small boys replaced St. Mary's and St. Joseph's Orphanages. Wynhoven, in addition to many other assignments, also reorganized the social services and charities of the archdiocese by setting up (1924) Associated Catholic Charities. In 1922 Shaw convoked the sixth synod, the first in 33 years. In 1932 he launched the official diocesan paper, *Catholic Action of the South*, with Wynhoven as first editor in chief. It replaced the *Morning Star*, which had been published between 1878 and 1930.

Shaw's last years were burdened by problems of the financial depression of the 1930s. Some archdiocesan funds were frozen in local banks and several parishes found it difficult to meet the high interest due on monies borrowed during the 1920s. Nevertheless 33 new parishes were opened between 1919 and 1934. After a brief illness, Shaw died on Nov. 2, 1934, and Jean Marius Laval, who had been consecrated auxiliary (1911) to Blenk, became administrator.

Development since 1935. The history of the archdiocese since mid-1935 is coextensive with the tenure of Joseph Francis *Rummel, its 13th ordinary and 9th archbishop, who was transferred from Omaha, Nebr., on March 9, 1935, and installed in New Orleans May 15. He intensified and accelerated existing movements, proposed and promoted new projects, sponsored the eighth National Eucharistic Congress (1938) and numerous regional and national conventions, and issued authoritative statements on social problems. He launched a series of successful financial campaigns, insisted on a sound fiscal policy for each parish and institution, reorganized and expanded the archdiocesan administration, and promptly implemented decrees of the Holy See.

Parochial and Educational Growth. When Rummel was appointed to New Orleans the Catholic population of the archdiocese was conservatively estimated at 361,882, out of a total population approaching 1 million. There were then 132 resident parishes, 97 missions, and 451 secular and religious priests. By 1960, the Catholic and the overall populations had increased by about 66 per cent, the number of parishes 40 per cent, and the priests 25 per cent. Insufficient vocations to the priesthood hindered the archbishop from establishing more parishes as a steady rise in population brought demands for churches, schools, and other institutions, especially in suburban areas. Nevertheless, well over $100 million of building contracts were let, the majority after World War II, and at least half were

for schools, convents, and school-allied buildings. The Youth Progress Program was launched on Jan. 21, 1945, for the expansion of high schools for boys, recreational facilities, and a boys' protectory. Twelve years later, the oversubscribed Diocesan Campaign of Progress made possible a $2 million seminary at St. Benedict to accommodate 400 students, a new central administration or chancery building, four centers for Newman Clubs at state and private colleges and universities, and a projected home for the aged. Between these two campaigns, which were carried out by volunteer laymen under the guidance of their pastors, parishes of the archdiocese memorialized the dual observance of Rummel's silver jubilee as a bishop (1953) and his golden jubilee as a priest (1952) by contributing $1 million for the erection of St. Joseph's Hall of Philosophy which raised the capacity of Notre Dame Seminary to 150.

In 25 years, the Catholic school population more than doubled, reaching 90,546 in 1961. Contributions to the missions totaled $3,600,000 from 1935 to 1960. Under the leadership of Msgr. Edward C. J. Prendergast, of Father (later Bishop) Robert E. Tracy, and after 1945, of Msgr. Gerard L. Frey, the Confraternity of Christian Doctrine (CCD) became one of the most dynamic forces in the archdiocese. Its released-time and other catechetical classes reached 50,559 public elementary grade children; Junior Newman Club programs, 8,932 students in public junior and senior high schools; vacation schools, 4,590; while CCD active and associate members numbered 7,504 and 5,799 respectively. The CCD also sponsored courses in theology for laymen, closed retreats for parochial eighth-grade pupils and for public school children, a committee for religious, junior CCD groups for high school–age members, 1,734 lay teachers in parish schools of religion, and the Cana and pre-Cana conferences to which Rummel gave impetus in 1957.

New communities of men entering the archdiocese were Missionaries of Our Lady of La Salette (1938), the Maryknoll fathers (1944), and the Brothers of the Good Shepherd (1955). Communities of women returning to the archdiocese or settling in it for the first time included the Religious of the Presentation of the Blessed Virgin Mary (1949); the Poor Sisters of St. Francis Seraph of the Perpetual Adoration (1951); the Daughters of Jesus (1952); the Religious of Our Lady of the Retreat in the Cenacle, who opened (1958) Maria Immaculata Retreat House; and the Oblate Sisters of Providence (1958). Rummel organized the Archdiocesan Council of Catholic Men although, in time, its program was more or less assumed by the Archdiocesan Union of Holy Name Societies. The Archdiocesan Council of Catholic Women was even more successful as the Catholic Daughters of America and the St. Margaret's Daughters augmented their courts and circles. New organizations, groups, and agencies established since 1935 include the Catholic Evidence Guild, the Catholic Maritime Club, the Catholic Physicians' Guilds in New Orleans and Baton Rouge, the Catholic Students' Mission Crusade, the Catholic Youth Organization, and other recreational-cultural groups for teen-agers and young adults, the Catholic Committees for Boy and Girl Scouts, Borromeo Clubs, Serra Clubs in the see city and in the capital, the Seminary Guild, the Council of Catholic School Cooperative Clubs, the Council of Home and School Associations

Fig. 5. Eucharistic Congress, 1938, City Park, New Orleans.

in Baton Rouge, the Catholic Women's College Committee, the Legion of Mary, the St. Thomas More Catholic Lawyers' Association, the Catholic Accountants' Guild, the Catholic Nurses' Guild in Baton Rouge, the League for Laymen's Retreats, a secular institute known as Caritas, Ozanam Inn, and the St. Vincent de Paul Store.

Other Areas of Progress. In addition to the usual curial posts, the diocesan administration includes an appreciably expanded ecclesiastical tribunal; commissions for sacred music, ecclesiastical art, and the liturgy; a diocesan building commission, appointed at the time of the seventh diocesan synod in 1949; a Catholic Bureau of Information; directors for the Legion of Decency; the deaf-mute apostolate, and hospitals; and a Catholic Laymen's Foundation. The Catholic Council on Human Relations, an organization of Catholic laymen designed to promote interracial justice and charity, held its first meeting in March 1961.

Through the years Rummel was a staunch champion of the underprivileged and promoter of social justice. He opposed "right to work" bills introduced in the state legislature during the sessions of 1948 and 1954; led a movement to maintain reasonable rent controls after World War II; accepted Negro applicants at both minor and major seminaries; racially integrated the Archdiocesan School Board, the Councils of Catholic Men and Women, the Sodalities, and the Holy Name Societies; recommended Negro laymen and laywomen for papal honors; issued his pastoral "Blessed Are the Peacemakers" in March 1953, decreeing an end to various forms of segregation practiced over the years in many parish churches; upheld the Supreme Court decision of May 17, 1954, which ruled segregation in public schools unconstitutional; and in a pastoral dated Feb. 11, 1956, declared racial segregation morally wrong and sinful. Regrettably, his stand on these socio-moral issues proved unpopular among many otherwise representative Catholic laymen.

On Aug. 14, 1961, John XXIII named Bp. John P. Cody of Kansas City–St. Joseph, Mo., coadjutor archbishop with right of succession and also erected the Diocese of Baton Rouge, the 38th to be carved out of the original territory of the Diocese of Louisiana and the Floridas. On the occasion of the observance of his 60th anniversary of ordination to the priesthood, May 24, 1962, Archbishop Rummel announced that, at his request, Archbishop Cody had been appointed apostolic administrator of New Orleans. Cody succeeded to the see at Rummel's death on Nov. 8, 1964. He was transferred to Chicago, Ill., on June 16, 1965, and his successor, Philip M. Hannan, auxiliary bishop of Washington, D.C., was installed in New Orleans on Oct. 13, 1965.

Bibliography: Archives, Archdiocese of New Orleans. Archives, St. Louis Cathedral, New Orleans. R. BAUDIER, *The Catholic Church in Louisiana* (New Orleans 1939). C. M. CHAMBON, *In and around the Old St. Louis Cathedral of New Orleans* (New Orleans 1908). E. A. DAVIS, *Louisiana, the Pelican State* (Baton Rouge 1959). C. L. DUFOUR, ed., *St. Patrick's of New Orleans, 1833–1958* (New Orleans 1958) commemorative essays for the 125th anniversary. A. E. FOSSIER, *New Orleans: The Glamour Period, 1800–1840* (New Orleans 1957). M. GIRAUD, *Histoire de la Louisiane française,* 2 v. (Paris 1953–58) v.1, *Le Règne de Louis XIV, 1698–1715;* v.2, *Années de transition, 1715–1717.* T. L. SMITH and H. L. HITT, *The People of Louisiana* (Baton Rouge 1952).

[H. C. BEZOU]

NEW ROCHELLE, COLLEGE OF

A 4-year liberal arts college for women, chartered in 1904 as the College of St. Angela, and renamed the College of New Rochelle (New Rochelle, N.Y.) in 1910.

Origin. The College evolved from the Ursuline Seminary for Girls, which was established in 1897. The foundress of the College of New Rochelle, Mother Irene Gill, OSU, Provincial of the Ursuline Nuns of the Roman Union, showed foresight and vision when she purchased the charred ruins of Leland Castle, built in Westchester County in 1855 as a hunting lodge called "Tally-Ho Inn," and established the nucleus of a liberal arts college for young women. The first class had nine students. In 1963 enrollment numbered over 900 resident and nonresident students, who occupied 13 large Tudor-Gothic stone buildings surrounding the original "Castle."

Curriculum. From its early years the College gave both the B.S. and B.A. degrees. In 1951, however, it limited the program to a single course of studies leading to the B.A. degree. Based on an integration-concentration plan, the curriculum provides a general education in the humanities and sciences centered on the disciplines of theology, philosophy, and history. There are 16 fields of concentration, which include the liberal and fine arts; the natural, social, and political sciences; modern languages; and speech-English. Courses leading to certification in elementary and secondary education are also available. Graduates receive a representative number of fellowships and scholarships annually, and about 35 per cent go on to graduate school. The library, which in 1964 housed more than 78,000 volumes and received 425 periodicals, is the hub of the seminar program required in the junior and senior years. The College faculty numbered 124 members, and included 6 priests, 51 religious, and 67 laymen. The faculty-student ratio was 1 to 10. In 1959 a visiting professorship was established with the endowment of the Anna V. McCarthy Chair, made possible by a gift from the late Miss McCarthy. This has enabled the College to profit from the lectures and seminars of American and foreign scholars. The Chair has been occupied by the Belgian theologian Augustin Leonard, OP; the English philosopher Paul Henry, SJ; and by Dietrich von Hildebrand, professor of philosophy.

The erection of the Mother Xavier Memorial Fine Arts and Administration building in 1960 provided additional facilities for the art, speech, and music departments as well as a language laboratory. Four large residence halls, a chapel, a dining hall with cafeteria and social lounges, and a sports building provide facilities for the nonacademic phases of education. Besides a guidance program, which provides opportunities for the student to receive help when needed, priests, religious, and laymen are available to individual students who seek their advice. In addition, informal faculty coffee hours, colloquies, and "talks without chalk" make possible the interchange of ideas among faculty and students. A student advisory board, established in 1910, has since given way to an All-College Council, which encourages greater interaction among administration, faculty, and students.

The College holds membership in the National Students Association (NSA) and in the *National Federation of Catholic College Students (NFCCS). Intercollegiate activity is evidenced in debating, dramatic productions, sodality congresses, joint meetings of language clubs, and other formal and informal ways.

The distinctive aim of Ursuline educators—to prepare women who will act as a leaven in society—is realized through the 6,700 College alumnae who are active in civic and parochial affairs throughout the country. Within the last 5 years, more than 60 graduates have given 1 year to the home or foreign missions, teaching, doing parish work, or staffing information centers.

The College holds its charter from the Board of Regents of the University of the State of New York and is a member of the Middle States Association of Colleges and Secondary Schools. It holds membership in the American Academy in Rome, the American Association of University Women; the American Council on Education; the American Library Association, and other national and regional education organizations.

Administration. From 1904 to 1949, the administrative power of the College was exercised by the dean under the presidencies of Rev. Michael C. O'Farrell (1904–18), Rt. Rev. Msgr. Joseph F. Mooney (1918–23), Rt. Rev. Msgr. John P. Chidwick (1924–35), Rt. Rev. Msgr. Cornelius F. Crowley (1935–37), and Rt. Rev. Msgr. Francis Walsh (1938–49). In 1949, the first on-campus president, Mother Dorothea Dunkerley, OSU, was appointed, and held office until 1957. The board of trustees is composed of members of the Ursuline Community, a number of laymen, and a representative of the cardinal. Other administrative officers include the dean, registrar, and treasurer.

[M. A. GALLIN]

NEW TESTAMENT LITERATURE

The NT, comprising 27 books, forms a unit of literature that complements the OT and completes the written record of God's revelation to mankind (*see* OLD TESTAMENT LITERATURE). The present division of NT writings is by no means chronological. Under the influence of the OT division of historical, didactic, and prophetical works, a similar division was made in early Christendom for the NT writings, and this became stabilized at the Council of Trent (EnchBibl 59). Thus, for the historical section there are the four Gospels and Acts; for the didactic section, the 14 Epistles of Paul, the 2 Epistles of Peter, the 3 of John, the Epistle of James, and the Epistle of Jude; and for the prophetic section, the Apocalypse of St. John.

Literary Genres. The NT writings fall under various categories of literary style. They are not, however, literature in the sense of a conscious effort for style, artistry or imitation, and perpetuation of a given literary school or age. They were all written originally in Greek, and they pertain to the Greco-Roman culture of the 1st Christian century. They employed the κοινή or commonly spoken Greek language of the day (*see* GREEK LANGUAGE, BIBLICAL). From the viewpoint of borrowings there was practically no dependence on the literature of this period, and quotations from secular authors are very few (from Menander in 1 Cor 15.33, from Epimenides and Aratus in Acts 17.28, and from Epimenides in Ti 1.12). Dependence, such as there is, is entirely upon the OT literature, which is quoted more than 300 times, mostly from the Septuagint. Poetic forms, when they occur, seem to derive from the OT Prophets and Psalmists and from liturgical hymns, as in the prologue of St. John's Gospel (Jn 1.1–13) and St. Paul's eulogy on charity (1 Cor 13.1–13), rather than from any affected imitation of contemporary styles. The preaching and teaching of Christ is recorded in the Gospels in the spirit and style of the Prophets and in the rabbinical mode of teaching common at that time.

Thus, there are genres of the sermon, the parable, and the dialogue, which are utilized to great advantage by the Evangelists. The epistolary style, which occurs especially in the Pauline Epistles, is dependent upon the contemporary form for letter writing; but this does not mean that it was a slavish imitation of style after the manner of Plato or Cicero or Epicurus, all of whom deliberately wrote in this manner to express their opinions and teachings. The *diatribe, virtually a sermon, designed not merely to instruct but to convert the listener or reader, was the most familiar form for philosophical writing. It was no doubt used by Jewish preachers of the *Diaspora, and it was certainly employed by their Christian successors. The apocalyptic style, so common to the Prophets and to rabbinical teachers in times of persecution, was fully developed in the early Christian teaching on the *Parousia and especially in the Apocalypse.

The modern trend of studying literary genres opens even wider the lists of categories of styles into which scholars place the individual books and their parts. Whatever the final analysis, however, the fact remains that the books developed more from the psychological need to express in writing and to perpetuate the religious teachings of the early Christian preachers than from a conscious attempt to imitate or borrow from contemporary secular or religious authors. The first task of the Church was to convert men to faith in Jesus, and the second was to instruct converts in the Christian life. The teaching of Christ was presented in a form well-suited for memorizing. Oral catechesis, as seen in the type of St. Peter's preaching in Acts ch. 2–3, was the basic means of promulgating the faith. As ritual developed, there was a gradual incorporation of the Christian message into liturgical rites, which then became source material for the inspired writer. As the Church grew, it was inevitable that the primitive oral catechesis should be put into writing. Tradition attests to a gradual growth of a NT Biblical *canon [*see* BIBLE, III (CANON), 3]; samples of it already appeared among the Apostolic Fathers, and more complete lists were used in the mid-2d century. *See* LITERARY GENRES, BIBLICAL; FORM CRITICISM, BIBLICAL.

Development. While the earliest beginnings of most of the NT books are shrouded in darkness, two basic collections can be traced: the four Gospels and the Pauline Epistles, exclusive of the controversial Epistle to the Hebrews. Although an Aramaic Matthew, supposedly written for the *Judaeo-Christians of Palestine *c.* A.D. 50, is mentioned in early tradition (Papias, Irenaeus, and the Anti-Marcionite Prologue) as first among the Gospels, its larger Greek version nevertheless appeared much later (after 70?) and was based not only on the Aramaic Matthew but also on the Marcan Gospel and the so-called Q Document that was used also by Luke. Mark, who was Peter's interpreter, wrote from memory, probably after the death of Peter (64 or 67), for Gentile Christians of Rome, or according to some, in the late 50s. Luke, the companion of Paul, is said to have written for the Gentiles of Achaea sometime after Mark's Gospel, which he used, hence *c.* 60 to 62 or after 64 or 67, depending on one's choice of Mark's date, or according to some after 70. Matthew and Mark are more impersonal in tone and probably were used for liturgical purposes. Luke's Gospel is more literary, and his objective was a more historical narration. On the interdependence of these three Gospels and their similarities and dissimilarities, *see* SYNOPTIC PROBLEM. The Gospel of St. John, whose author is not mentioned by name in his Gospel, but is referred to as the "disciple whom Jesus loved," was written, according to ancient tradition, while the author was in Asia Minor at Ephesus toward the end of the 1st Christian century. Its purpose was to confirm and deepen the faith of Christian converts. It has the tone of a polemic against Judaism. The question of identifying the author as St. John is still mooted in many circles today.

The Acts of the Apostles, as it were, a fifth Gospel, treating of the deeds mostly of Peter and Paul, was written by the same man who wrote the Third Gospel (see Acts 1.1), sometime after this Gospel, toward the end of St. Paul's life. There is some doubt about the final form of Acts since it has come down to us in two text forms—a shorter but more polished Alexandrian text and a verbose Western text presumably rewritten *c.* 150.

The history of the composition of the Gospels and Acts indicates that while the sayings and deeds of Christ and His Apostles began to be recorded in writing some time between 10 and 20 years after the Resurrection, they were not given the full authority of Scripture, as was granted to the OT and some of the Pauline writings, until late in the 1st century.

The Pauline corpus of Epistles, mostly addressed to a particular community or group of communities, served the needs of the mission by instructing, edifying, and removing misunderstandings. Three of the Epistles, however, the so-called *Pastoral Epistles, are addressed to officials. The First Epistle to the Thessalonians was written from Corinth at the beginning of 52; hence it is perhaps the first of Paul's letters and thus the oldest of the NT inspired writings. The rest of the Epistles probably followed in this order: 2 Thessalonians (late 52); Galatians (54); 1 Corinthians (spring of 57); 2 Corinthians (autumn of 57); Romans (winter of 57–58); Colossians, Philemon, Ephesians, and Philippians (61–63); 1 Timothy, Titus, and 2 Timothy some time between A.D. 63 and Paul's death (64 or 67), if these three Epistles were really written by him.

From this synopsis it can be seen that it is possible that most of Paul's writings appeared before the Gospels, unless one accepts a very early date for Mark and Luke, i.e., before 62. Some of the Pauline writings were soon accepted on the same plane as the inspired writings of the OT, as can be seen from 2 Pt 3.15. Not all the Pauline Epistles are acknowledged by modern scholars as Paul's work. The Pauline authorship especially of the Pastoral Epistles and of Ephesians is challenged, to say nothing of the most controverted of all, the Epistle to the Hebrews.

The *Catholic Epistles (James; 1 and 2 Peter; 1, 2, and 3 John; and Jude), so called because most of them were destined more for the Church at large than for an individual person or community, are less epistolary in character and are regarded more as tracts or instructions. Also, whether the names ascribed to them are actually those of the author, or perhaps the names of the persons whose teachings are reflected in them, or merely pseudonyms, is one of the disputed questions connected with several of these epistles (*see* ANONYMITY AND PSEUDONYMITY). The canonicity of many of them (James, Jude, 2 Peter, 2 and 3 John) was once disputed. These Epistles are variously dated in the second half of the 1st century, depending on whether one accepts or rejects the authorship of the men to whom they are ascribed.

The authorship of Hebrews and Apocalypse has the longest history of dispute and controversy. Hebrews is more of a treatise than a letter. Many doubt that Paul had anything to do with it, or, if so, only indirectly. According to those who maintain strict Pauline authorship, it is dated between 63 and 67. Other scholars look upon it as a work written some time between 70 and 90. The Western Church did not accept it as Paul's work until the middle of the 4th century, whereas the Eastern Church considered it Pauline as early as the 3d century.

The Apocalypse likewise suffers in identifying its author and in understanding its literary genre, to say nothing of coping with its message. Unlike Hebrews, the Apocalypse met with much opposition in the Eastern Church as late as the 6th century, whereas the Western Church always accepted it as true Scripture. Early tradition accepted St. John the Apostle as its author, but there is no unanimity among modern Catholic scholars on its authorship. A too literal interpretation of the visions in terms of actual historical periods led to confusion and distrust of the book in times past.

Regardless of the controversies that persist to the present day in consideration of the authorship, the authenticity, the integrity, the time of composition, the mode of literary genre of some of the NT literature, all these writings are nonetheless truly revered and accepted by the Church as being inspired and canonical and containing Christ's message to mankind.

See also the articles on the individual books of the NT.

Bibliography: J. N. SANDERS, "The Literature and Canon of the NT" in *Peake's Commentary on the Bible,* ed. M. BLACK and H. H. ROWLEY (New York 1962) 676–682. Wikenhauser NT Intro. R. A. MacKENZIE, *Introduction to the New Testament* (New Testament Reading Guide, v.1; Collegeville, Minn. 1960). J. HUBY, Robert-Tricot 1:382–474. Robert Feuillet v.2. Cath CommHS 18–21, 40–44, 752–759.

[B. A. LAZOR]

NEW THOUGHT

A movement embracing any form of modern belief in the practice of mental healing other than those associated with traditional Christianity. The name came into vogue in 1895 and was used as the title of a magazine published for a time in Melrose, Mass., to describe a "new thought" about life, based on the premise that knowledge of the real world of ideas has marvelous power to relieve people of various ills.

History. The movement began with the work of Phineas P. Quimby (1802–66), of Portland, Maine, who practiced mental and spiritual healing for more than 20 years and greatly influenced Mary Baker *Eddy, foundress of *Christian Science. At first Quimby practiced unqualified mesmerism; the client would sit opposite the doctor, who then held the person's hands and looked him intently in the eye. As the patient went into a mesmeric sleep, Quimby spoke to him and talked him out of his ailment, often manipulating the affected part with hands that were moistened for greater efficiency. Later, Quimby became convinced that disease was simply an error of the mind and not a real thing, so that mesmerism could be dispensed with and equal, or even better, results assured. In time he claimed that his only power consisted in the knowledge he had that sickness is illusion and in the ability to communicate this assurance to others. In a circular addressed to the sick, Quimby thus described his own system: "My practice is unlike all medical practice. I give no medicine, and make no outward applications. I tell the patient his troubles, and what he thinks is his disease; and my explanation is the cure. If I succeed in correcting his errors, I change the fluids of the system and establish *the truth, or health. The truth is the cure.* This mode of practice applies to all cases."

Quimby organized no society, but persons whom he had helped adopted his method, passing it on to others with additions and changes of their own. Two of his followers, Warren F. Evans and Julius A. Dresser, gave systematic form to his ideas; they are regarded as the intellectual founders of New Thought and its allied movements. Evans published six books on the subject, of which the most significant were *The Mental Cure* (1869), *Mental Medicine* (1872), and *Soul and Body* (1875). According to Evans, disease has its roots in wrong belief. Once that is changed, disease is cured. A devoted Swedenborgian, he had long been familiar with the writings of G. *Berkeley and other idealists (*see* SWEDENBORG, E.). His own character and personal experiences further led him to a point where he was ready to apply an extreme form of idealism to the healing of disease. Dresser, cured by Quimby in 1860, began his major work in mental healing in 1882 in Boston, Mass., where Dresser and his wife, Annetta, were competing with Mrs. Eddy. When Dresser's clients were curious to learn how they had been healed, he obliged with a series of 12 class lectures, which included a study of the divine immanence and a consideration that the spiritual life is continuous, that men already live in eternity. "To realize that our real life is spiritual was to overcome the illusions of sense-experience with its manifold bondages." Dresser's son and biographer popularized his father's teaching.

Evans and Dresser remained faithful to the memory of Quimby, whereas Mrs. Eddy disclaimed all dependence on her benefactor, whom she called "an ignorant mesmerist." Mrs. Eddy's followers became organized in a tightly knit society, the Church of Christ, Scientist; the disciples of Quimby founded numerous small groups under different names, such as Divine Science, Unity, Practical Christianity, Home of Truth, and the Church of the Higher Life. Before the turn of the century, these came to be known as New Thought and in 1894 the first national convention was held. In 1908 the name National New Thought Alliance was adopted and 6 years later the organization became international. Its membership was extended to all the major countries of the world.

Basic Principles. Although New Thought did not substantially change after the time of Quimby, Evans, and Dresser, there was an expansion of scope to cover a broader perspective than healing sickness. The Declaration of Principles, adopted by the International Alliance

in 1917, begins by affirming "the freedom of each soul as to its choice and as to belief." Accordingly no creedal profession is necessary. "The essence of the New Thought is Truth, and each individual must be loyal to the Truth he sees. The windows of his soul must be kept open at each moment for the higher light, and his mind must be always hospitable to each new inspiration."

Allowing for a monistic interpretation of the universe, the declaration states, "We affirm the new thought of God as Universal Love, Life, Truth and Joy, in whom we live, move, and have our being, and by whom we are held together; and His mind is our mind now, that realizing our oneness with Him means love, truth, peace, health, and plenty." In the same strain, taking monistically Christ's words about the kingdom within us, New Thought asserts that "we are one with the Father" (*see* MONISM).

In keeping with Quimby's theory of the mind's influence, it is held that "Man's body is his holy temple. Every function of it, every cell of it, is intelligent, and is shaped, ruled, repaired, and controlled by mind. He whose body is full of light is full of health. Spiritual healing has existed among all races in all times. It has now become a part of the higher science and art of living the life more abundant."

Consistent with its stress on present well-being, New Thought believes that "Heaven is here and now, the life everlasting that becomes conscious immortality, the communion of mind with mind throughout the universe of thoughts, the nothingness of all error and negation, including death, the variety in unity that produces the individual expressions of the One-Life." All this is to be understood against the background of an idealism that some have traced to G. W. F. *Hegel and others to Berkeley. "We affirm," the declaration concludes, "that the universe is spiritual and we are spiritual beings."

New Thought considers itself a form of Christianity, while denying the Trinity, original sin, and the divinity of Christ. It proposes instead a cosmic hypostatic union that reflects the Christology of David *Strauss. "Every man is an incarnation of God," New Thought teaches, "anyone who recognizes this and lives in conscious and harmonious union with Spirit, automatically becomes Christ."

Unlike other denominations that emphasize mental health, such as Christian Science, New Thought permits dual membership; many of its adherents are active church-goers in the more liberal Protestant denominations.

Bibliography: M. BACH, *The Unity of Life* (Englewood Cliffs, N.J. 1962). H. E. CADY, *Lessons in Truth* (rev. ed. Lee's Summit, Mo. 1955). H. W. DRESSER, *Health and the Inner Life* (New York 1906); *A History of the New Thought Movement* (New York 1919). E. HOLMES, *New Thought Terms and Their Meanings* (New York 1942). R. PEEL, *Christian Science: Its Encounter with American Culture* (New York 1958).

[J. A. HARDON]

NEW ULM, DIOCESE OF (NOVAE ULMAE), established Nov. 18, 1957, comprising 9,863 square miles of the 15 most western counties—Big Stone, Brown, Chippewa, Kandiyohi, Lac Qui Parle, Lincoln, Lyon, McLeod, Meeker, Nicollet, Redwood, Renville, Sibley, Swift, and Yellow Medicine—of the metropolitan See of *St. Paul, Minn. Alphonse J. Schladweiler, pastor of St. Agnes parish in St. Paul, was appointed (Nov. 28, 1957) the first bishop of the new diocese and was consecrated in the cathedral of St. Paul (Jan. 29, 1958) by Abp. William O. Brady. The following day the diocese was canonically erected, and Bishop Schladweiler was installed at Holy Trinity Cathedral in his see city of New Ulm.

The first church in New Ulm, begun in 1858, was destroyed before completion during the Sioux uprising in 1862. Alexander Berghold became the first resident pastor (January 1869). In 1870 a second edifice was blessed in honor of the Holy Trinity. Construction of the third church (later the cathedral) was begun in 1890; the Romanesque structure was blessed in 1893. The diocese is distinctly rural. Most of the parishes are in small towns with numerous farm parishioners; some parishes are totally rural. Within the diocesan boundaries only two cities, New Ulm and Willmar, have a population of more than 10,000 (1960 census).

When the diocese was established, the 68,904 Catholics (285,394 total population) were served by 98 priests in 86 parishes and 9 missions, and there were 37 primary schools, 7 secondary schools, 2 hospitals, and 1 home for the aged. By 1964 a chancery office and bishop's residence, two parishes, two homes for the aged, and another hospital had been added to the diocesan facilities. Catholics then numbered 71,823 (286,711 total population), and there were 1,381 students in the 6 high schools and 10,040 in the 40 elementary schools under Catholic auspices. An additional 10,372 students received religious instruction under released-time programs.

Bibliography: J. M. REARDON, *The Catholic Church in the Diocese of St. Paul* (St. Paul 1952). P. H. AHERN, ed., *Catholic Heritage in Minnesota, North Dakota, South Dakota* (St. Paul 1964).

[G. B. KUNZ]

NEW YEAR, HEBREW FEAST OF THE

Among the neighbors of ancient Israel the New Year's festival was an event of profound religious significance. In Judaism, too, and hence within the Israelite tradition, New Year's Day (*rō'š haššānâ*, the beginning of the year), which falls on the 1st day of the 7th month (Tishri, September-October), has been observed with great solemnity at least as far back as the 2d Christian

Jews in Jerusalem celebrating the Feast of the New Year in their home.

century (Mishnah). Distinctive of the liturgy are the frequent blasts on a shofar horn (*šôpār*) and the recitation of passages from the Pentateuch, the Psalter, and the Prophets that speak of God's kingship, His merciful mindfulness of man, and the shofar. According to the Mishnah, the day is also one of divine judgment on the works of men, a conception that later found expression in the liturgy and created the mood of joy tempered with fear and sorrow characteristic of the feast. A question later disputed among the rabbis was whether the feast was not also a commemoration of the day of creation.

Seen against this historical background, the ambiguity of the Biblical evidence is unexpected, and it creates the unresolved problem of the Hebrew New Year's feast. Many scholars consider the Jewish feast a relatively late innovation. They stress the lack of all explicit reference to such a feast, not only in the OT, but in Jewish sources prior to the Mishnah, which simply adhere to the Biblical text (Lv 23.23–25; Nm 29.1–6), if they mention a feast on the 1st of Tishri at all. Even the expression *rō'š haššānâ* occurs only once in the entire OT (Ez 40.1), and then it refers to neither a day nor a feast. The Biblical feast on the 1st of Tishri, which is attested only in late texts, seems to be of postexilic origin and therefore to have arisen at a period when the new year began in the spring; it could not therefore be a New Year's feast. Besides, it shares with the later Jewish feast only the date and (probably) the horn blasts.

Against the view that the autumn harvest festival was a New Year's celebration before the Exile, it is urged that this feast looks not ahead, but back, in joy and gratitude for the harvest; the garnering marked an end, not a beginning (note its position in the old calendar of Ex 23.14–17; 34.18–25). In fact, in Ex 23.16 the feast is explicitly put "at the end of the year" (literally "at the going out of the year," which is often taken to mean "at the beginning of the year," even by those who reject a New Year's feast, but who then insist there is no evidence that the temporal reference had any bearing on the nature of the feast; however, in Akkadian the same verb is used of a period of time past as opposed to one "entering," i.e., beginning).

However, the argument from silence—and this is the main one against the antiquity of the Hebrew New Year's feast—is treacherous, the more so here in view of the meager documentation on Israel's religious calendar; one may compare the silence of numerous texts of the Assyrian *takultu* ritual, which until recently could only be inferred to be part of the *akîtu* festival. Also, unless the Jewish feast derives from an older tradition, not only does its origin remain a mystery, but it presents the enigma of a New Year's feast being established in the autumn, long after the religious calendar began in the spring. Probably, therefore, the feast prescribed for the 1st of Tishri in Lv 23.23–25 celebrated the New Year. The text, however, yields little information about the feast itself except that it was to be a day of rest with a *zikrôn terû'a* (see below), a convocation of the people, and sacrifices (cf. Nm 29.1–6). Perhaps there was also a reading of the Law (cf. Neh 7.73b–8.18). The feast must have originated when the year began in the autumn and therefore before the Exile.

At this period, however, the only autumn festival now known was that of the ingathering. The postexilic distinction of the 1st of Tishri (New Year's feast), the 10th of Tishri (Day of Atonement), and the 15th to the 22d of Tishri (Feast of Booths) must represent a splintering of the ancient harvest festival, a development that, independently of the problem at hand, the accumulation of feasts in the autumn, unparalleled before the Exile, also suggests. As to the difficulty of "at the end of the year" in Ex 23.16, it must first be remarked that the time element would hardly have been mentioned were it not relevant for the character of the feast. Moreover, in a later recension of this calendar, the expression is changed to "the turn[ing point] of the year" (Ex 34.22), which allows for a feast that celebrates a beginning as well as an end: the two aspects are not mutually exclusive. That the autumn festival did in fact look ahead as well as back is indicated by a number of unquestionably ancient rites in the time of the second Temple that were clearly intended to ensure fertility in the year ahead: the procession around the altar and the water libation (cf. Is 12.3–6), which, as similar rites elsewhere show, were meant to produce rain; the covering of the altar with branches to symbolize—and produce—growth from the ground, etc.

The New Year's feast was, therefore, a time of joy [for the details, see BOOTHS (TABERNACLES), FEAST OF], but also of a certain anxiety, as the people looked to the rains that must soon follow if plenty was to be theirs again. Hence the rites to produce fertility. There were also penitential observances (cf. the later Day of *Atonement) to placate God for the sins of the previous year and to obtain his blessing on the new one. Probably too, in Jerusalem under the monarchy, God's kingship was proclaimed (see ENTHRONEMENT FEAST), and therefore in the acclamation of the people and the shofar blasts (both may be included under terû'a) in one of the so-called enthronement Psalms [Ps 46(47).6], the source of the terû'a in Lv 23.24 might be found, though why it is called a "reminder" (zikrôn) and what exactly it meant after the Exile remain obscure.

The existence of another New Year's feast in the spring, the Feast of *Passover or of Unleavened Bread, which is defended by some scholars, does not seem very probable and is generally denied.

Bibliography: N. H. SNAITH, *The Jewish New Year Festival: Its Origin and Development* (London 1947). E. AUERBACH, "Neujahrs- und Versöhnungsfest in den biblischen Quellen," VetTest 8 (1958) 337–343. A. MICHEL and H. CAZELLES, DBSuppl 6:597–645. J. B. SEGAL, *The Hebrew Passover from the Earliest Times to A.D. 70* (New York 1963). De Vaux AncIsr 502–506. H. GROSS, LexThK² 7:910. EncDictBibl 1636–37. For additional bibliography, see ENTHRONEMENT FEAST. **Illustration credit:** Israel Information Services, New York.

[W. L. MORAN]

NEW YORK

One of the original 13 states of the U.S., situated in the Middle Atlantic region, 30th in area and 1st in population (1960) among the 50 states. It is bounded on the north by Lake Ontario, the St. Lawrence River, and Canada; on the east by Vermont, Massachusetts, and Connecticut; on the south by New Jersey, Pennsylvania, and the Atlantic Ocean; and on the west by Pennsylvania, Lake Erie, and the Niagara River. Roughly triangular in outline, the state is about 326 miles from east to west and 300 miles from north to south; it includes Long Island and Staten Island on the Atlantic coast. It has a total area of 49,576 square miles, including 1,632 square miles of inland waters. New York's capital city is Albany. In addition to New York City, the principal centers with a population of 100,000 or more are Buffalo, Rochester, Syracuse, Yonkers, Albany, and Utica.

History. Long before New York became known as the Empire State, it was the home of a mighty confederacy of Indian tribes made up of the Mohawks, Oneidas, Onondagas, Cayugas, and Senecas. This union of Indians was known to the French as the Iroquois and to the English as the Five Nations (later Six when the Tuscaroras joined in 1715). Successful in dominating the other Indian tribes of the area, they also terrorized European settlers and missionaries and exercised an important influence on the colonial history of this area.

Colonial Period. The first Europeans to come into contact with the Five Nations were the French, who occasionally sent vessels up the Hudson to trade with the Indians after the discovery in 1524 of New York Bay and the river by Giovanni da *Verrazano, a Florentine in the service of Francis I of France. By July 1609 French efforts to lay the foundations of New France and to spread Christianity had penetrated to Lake Champlain, thereby arousing the hostility of the Iroquois, who for years thereafter held the balance of power between the English and the French in America.

In September 1609 Henry Hudson, an English mariner employed by the Dutch East India Company to search for a new passage to the East Indies, entered New York harbor in the "Half Moon" and followed the river that bears his name as far north as the present site of Albany. On the basis of this claim, the Dutch colony of New Netherland was founded in 1624, when the first permanent settlers consisting of about 30 families, mostly Walloon, arrived. The population had grown to 200 or more by 1626, when the government of the province was fully established with power vested mainly in a director-general and council. Soon after, Manhattan Island was purchased from the Indians for 60 guilders ($24), and Ft. Amsterdam was erected at its lower end and the settlement there made the seat of government. Although the charter of 1640 declared that "no other Religion shall be publicly admitted in New Netherland except the Reformed . . .," these Dutch Calvinists were less virulent in their opposition to Catholicism than their New England brethren. In fact, Isaac Jogues, SJ, was rescued from the tortures of the Iroquois by the Dutch at Ft. Orange and brought to New Amsterdam in the fall of 1643, where he was kindly received by Gov. William Kieft (see NORTH AMERICAN MARTYRS). Nevertheless, the paucity of Catholic settlers—Jogues found only two in the town—continued during the entire period of Dutch rule despite the fact that the total population of the province increased from 2,000 to 10,000 between 1653 and 1664.

New Netherland passed into the hands of the English when, in March 1664, Charles II erected it with additional territory into a province and awarded it to his brother, James, Duke of York, who became its lord proprietor. The conquest of the Dutch colony was completed without fighting when, on September 8, Gov. Peter Stuyvesant formally surrendered to the English. This marked the beginning of brighter prospects for Catholic settlement in the province henceforth to be known as New York. The conversion to Catholicism in 1672 of the royal proprietor, the future James II, was soon reflected in the directives he issued for the government of his American domain. In 1682 he appointed a Catholic, Col. Thomas *Dongan, as governor and instructed him to accede to the long-standing demand of the colonists for a representative assembly. When the new governor arrived in New York in August 1683, his party included an English Jesuit, Thomas Harvey, who was later joined by two other priests and two lay brothers of his society.

Dongan, an administrator of considerable ability, lost no time in summoning the assembly that in October 1683 passed the bill of rights that he had proposed. This *Charter of Liberties and Privileges, containing a guarantee of entire freedom in religion, placed the Catholic governor of New York with Roger *Williams, the *Calverts, and William *Penn as the chief promoters of religious freedom in colonial America. During the remainder of Dongan's term of office, the various denominations had their respective houses of worship, and the little Catholic chapel in Ft. James was the first site where Mass was regularly offered in New York by the Jesuits who ministered to the relatively few Catholic settlers. It was Dongan's plan to counteract the influence of French missionaries by seeking additional English Jesuits to take up work among the Indians to the north, an area that he felt rightly belonged to the British crown. But his official career was brought to an end before the English Jesuits could carry out the policy regarding the Indians of New York.

After the English revolution of 1688 and the accession of William and Mary, the American colonies were thrown into a ferment of excitement. In New York the German-born Calvinist Jacob Leisler led an armed rebellion in May 1689, which ushered in a reign of terror. The policy of religious toleration in New York was soon replaced with restrictive measures against Catholics; the former Governor Dongan was hunted as a traitor, and the Jesuits were compelled to flee the colony. With the establishment of the Church of England by law in four of the leading counties of New York in 1693, the long dark night of penal legislation descended upon the few Catholics who were courageous enough to remain in the province. Although Leisler was removed and executed in 1691, anti-Catholic legislation continued to be multiplied under Henry Sloughter, the new governor, and his successors. An act of 1700 made it a crime for a priest to be found in New York, and anyone who harbored a priest was subject to a fine of 200 pounds. Perhaps no other single incident better illustrates the intensity of colonial anti-Catholic rancor than the reception accorded the Acadians, or "French Neutrals," expelled from their homes in 1755 and distributed among the colonies from Massachusetts to Georgia. Of the quota sent to New York, the adults were bound out as indentured servants and the children assigned to Protestant families. Unquestionably this persecution and proscription of Catholics in the colony not only sufficed to keep their numbers from increasing but also tended to discourage any who might have possessed the faith from announcing the fact. These dismal conditions were to obtain until after the Revolution, and Mass was not celebrated in a public manner until offered by the chaplains of the French troops who were sent to aid the colonies in their struggle. Meanwhile, affairs in the colony generally were concerned chiefly with the defense of the northern frontier and the rising disaffection of the colonists with the English government's colonial policy.

Revolutionary War. The quickening spirit of rebellion against the mother country's political and economic measures undoubtedly drew increased strength from the prejudice aroused by the passage of the *Quebec Act in June 1774. In colony after colony pulpit and press warned that the "popery act" that secured for Canada freedom for the exercise of the Catholic religion was a serious menace to colonial Protestantism. The first colonial flag run up in New York in place of the English colors bore on one side the inscription "George III-Rex. and the Liberties of America.—No Popery." It is small wonder, then, that Catholics found their position a difficult one, faced as they were with the dilemma of deciding on which side to cast their lot as the colony moved to make common cause with the revolutionists. On July 9, 1776, the delegates to the New York provincial congress adopted the Declaration of Independence and formally committed the province to the rebel cause. Undoubtedly the Catholic colonists were aware that many of the most vigorous opponents of the British policy of coercion had been the bitterest persecutors of "papists." On the other hand, their experience with the British government offered little hope for religious liberty or anything like political and social equality. In the end the greater number of Catholics chose to cast in their lot with the revolutionists and only a few of them joined the loyalist group. The patriotic part played by American Catholics in the revolutionary struggle and the aid of Catholic France and Spain marked a weakening of the anti-Catholic bias. However, when Congress advised the several states to adopt constitutions, the New York convention meeting for that purpose at Kingston on March 6, 1777, adopted an amendment to the naturalization clause, proposed by John Jay, which effectively excluded foreign-born Roman Catholics from citizenship. Not until 1806 was this offensive clause abrogated. Nevertheless, the period of Catholic proscription was drawing to a close; and when on Nov. 25, 1783, the British forces finally evacuated New York City, such Catholics as were in the city at the time began to assemble once again for the open celebration of their religion.

Postrevolutionary Period. With the coming of peace, a new life began for the inhabitants of New York, who numbered nearly 234,000 including about 1,500 Catholics. In the years that followed remarkable gains were made in the social and economic fields, characterized by systematic colonization, the extension of agriculture, the development of manufactures, the growth of commerce and transportation, and the improvement of educational facilities. These were only temporarily checked by the War of 1812, which was vigorously opposed by New York, and by the later Civil War. A greatly accelerated rate of economic development characterized the postwar years. Agriculture, manufacturing, commerce, transportation, merchandising, banking, and allied fields all received new impulses. Rapid urbanization, too, marked this period as floods of immigrants poured into factory towns and industrial centers, making the social problems of this era more numerous and more complex. The solution of such problems as the exploitation of immigrants; unfair labor practices; inadequate provision regarding public

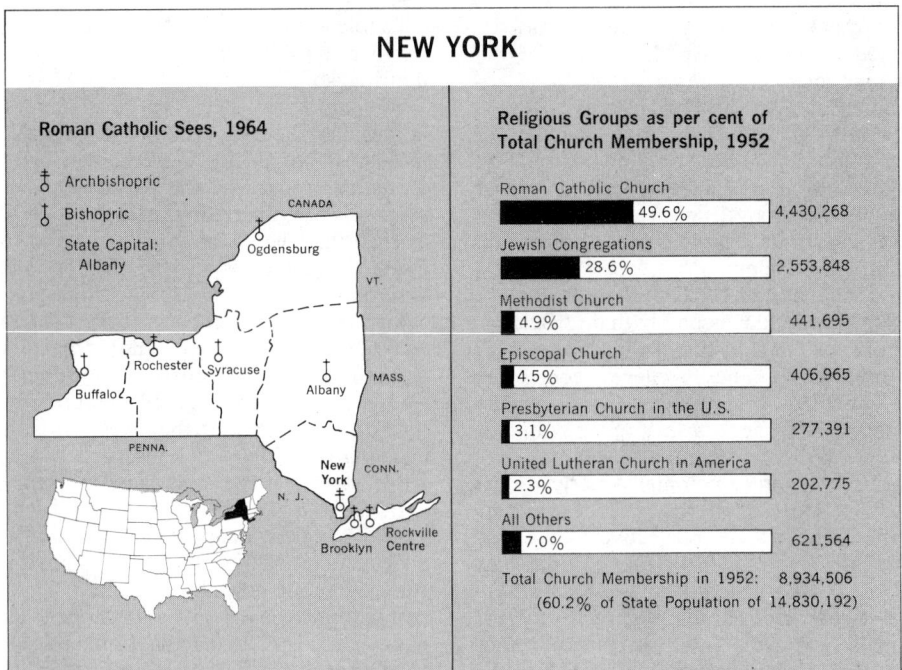

NEW YORK

Roman Catholic Sees, 1964

‡ Archbishopric
○

‡ Bishopric
○

State Capital:
Albany

Religious Groups as per cent of
Total Church Membership, 1952

Roman Catholic Church		
49.6%		4,430,268
Jewish Congregations		
28.6%		2,553,848
Methodist Church		
4.9%		441,695
Episcopal Church		
4.5%		406,965
Presbyterian Church in the U.S.		
3.1%		277,391
United Lutheran Church in America		
2.3%		202,775
All Others		
7.0%		621,564

Total Church Membership in 1952: 8,934,506
(60.2% of State Population of 14,830,192)

Church-membership statistics were compiled by the Bureau of Research and Survey of the National Council of the Churches of Christ in the U.S.A.

housing, health, education, and old age; corruption in politics; increase in crime; and, especially during the recurrent economic depressions, widespread unemployment, became the concern of political leaders, writers, publishers, reform organizations, professional groups, and individual citizens. On the whole, the program of state legislation resulting from these developments was quite progressive. Alfred E. *Smith, a Democrat and the first Catholic governor of New York, played an important role in bringing about reforms during the four terms he occupied the office.

Population. New York's heterogeneous population has created a pluralistic culture that tolerates marked differences in social position, economic status, and religious belief. Since 1820 it has been the most populous state in the Union and its rate of increase in population rose from 9.6 per cent in 1900 to more than 11 per cent in 1950. Moreover, since 1920 New York has also had a higher percentage of foreign-born residents than any other state. In 1952 Catholics constituted 29.9 per cent of the total state population of 14,830,-192; Protestants accounted for 13 per cent, Jews 17.2 per cent, and all others 39.9 per cent (*see* CHURCH MEMBERSHIP, U.S.). The Catholic population is organized under the Province of New York, which includes the Archdiocese of *New York and its suffragan sees at *Albany, *Brooklyn, *Buffalo, *Ogdensburg, *Rochester, *Rockville Centre, and *Syracuse.

Education. Free elementary schools were provided as early as 1633 during the period of Dutch control, and higher education had its beginning with the founding of King's College (Columbia) in 1754. In 1965 the educational system of the state included both public and private institutions: university, college, secondary, elementary, and professional and special schools. Responsibility for this comprehensive system is vested in the New York State Education Department, which grants charters, exercises supervision over all institutions incorporated in the state, and determines state educational policy. The Board of Regents of the University of the State of New York is the legislative body for determining educational policy, subject to the approval of the legislature. In 1948 the State University of New York was created by the legislature and assumed responsibility for all state-financed institutions of higher education in New York. With the creation of the University of the City of New York in 1960, the public institutions of the city inaugurated additional graduate faculties.

Of the approximately 4 million students enrolled in the elementary and secondary schools of the state in 1964, about 900,000 were in elementary and secondary schools under Catholic auspices. The colleges and universities of the state included 42 Catholic institutions with a total enrollment (1964) of nearly 54,000. Fordham University (1841) was the first Catholic institution for higher education in New York, and the College of New Rochelle (1904) was the first Catholic college for women chartered in the state. Although no direct public financial aid is received by the parochial and private institutions of the state, pupils enrolled in these are eligible for benefits such as bus service and for college and university students, scholarship aid and, under the 1961 Scholar Incentive Program, tuition assistance.

School attendance is compulsory between the ages of 7 and 16, inclusive, and free schooling may be obtained by all persons up to the age of 21.

Church-State Relations. References to and provisions affecting religion are incorporated in the state constitution and in acts of the legislature and the judiciary.

Constitution. New York is governed by the constitution of 1895, as amended. The preamble states that the people are "grateful to Almighty God." Article 1, sec. 3 states that "the free exercise and enjoyment of religious profession and worship, without discrimination or preference, shall forever be allowed in this state to all mankind; and no person shall be rendered incompetent to be a witness on account of his opinions on matters of religious belief; but the liberty of conscience hereby secured shall not be so construed as to excuse acts of licentiousness, or justify practices inconsistent with the peace or safety of this state." Senators, or judges of the court of appeals, or the major part of either try impeachments; and the senators or judges must be under oath or affirmation when doing so (art. 6, sec. 10).

Public money or property may not be used to aid denominational schools, ". . . but the legislature may provide for the transportation of children to or from any school or institution of learning" (art. 11, sec. 4).

Most members of public office must take an oath or affirmation and "there shall be no other test for holding such office" (art. 13, sec. 1).

Real or personal property used exclusively for religious purposes may be exempt from taxation if not operated for profit (art. 16, sec. 1).

Courts having jurisdiction over a child should try to place him in the custody of persons of the same religious persuasion where it is practicable (art. 6, sec. 32).

Marriage and Divorce. Marriages of men under 18 and women under 16 are forbidden except in certain cases of pregnancy. The consent of parents is required for men under 21 and women under 18. A license and blood test are required. There is a 3-day waiting period. Certain public officials and clergy may perform the ceremony. Common-law marriages contracted after April 29, 1933, are not recognized.

Marriages are void if either party is bound by a prior subsisting marriage or if the parties are related by blood in any degree of the direct line and up to but not including first cousins. Marriages may be annulled on the grounds of nonage, want of understanding, physical incapacity, force, fraud, duress, incurable insanity for 5 years, a 5-year disappearance in which the party is believed to be dead and a diligent search has been made.

The only ground for absolute divorce is adultery. Limited divorce is granted for adultery, cruel and inhuman treatment, unsafe and improper conduct, abandonment, and failure to support the wife. The guilty party may not remarry during the life of the plaintiff unless the court granting the divorce allows it after a lapse of 3 years and on proof of uniformly good conduct. *See* MARRIAGE, U.S. LAW OF; DIVORCE (U.S. LAW OF).

Abortion, Birth Control, Sterilization. The law forbids *abortion, whether attempted or successful, unless it is necessary to preserve the life of the mother or child. A woman is liable to imprisonment for the killing of the child in an attempted miscarriage and is guilty of manslaughter in the second degree. The manufacturing, giving away, or selling of drugs or instruments to procure a miscarriage is a felony.

A 1965 law allows "the sale or distribution of any instrument or article, or any recipe, drug or medicine for the prevention of conception." However, *birth control devices may be sold only in licensed pharmacies; they may not be advertised or displayed, or sold to persons under 16. (*See* CONTRACEPTION; ANOVULANTS.)

There are no references to *sterilization in the state code.

Property and Taxation. New York devotes a whole book (v.50 of McKinney's *Consolidated Laws*) to Religious Corporation Law. The Roman Catholic churches may incorporate with the archbishop or bishop, the vicar-general of the diocese, the rector of the church, and two laymen acting as trustees. Property is held in trust; but in order to mortgage, lease, or sell any of its real property the trustees need the bishop's permission. Charitable corporations may incorporate under the General Corporation Law. Certain real and personal property of religious societies and charities, not run for profit, is exempt from taxation.

No person having a husband, wife, child, or descendant or parent may by his or her last will or testament devise or bequeath to any benevolent, charitable, literary, scientific, religious, or missionary society, association, corporation or purpose, in trust or otherwise, more than one-half part of his or her estate, after the payment of his or her debts; and such devise or bequest is valid to the extent of one-half and no more. The validity of a devise or bequest for more than one-half may be contested only by a surviving husband, wife, child, descendant, or parent.

New York's extensive fund-raising provisions concerning both professional and nonprofessional fund raisers do not apply to religious corporations organized under the Religious Corporation Law.

Prisons and Reformatories. Section 146 of the New York Correction Law allows every minister of the gospel having charge of a congregation in the town wherein any prison is located to visit the prison at pleasure.

Prisoners have freedom of worship, and religious services on Sunday are allowed. But in the case of *Brown v. McGinnis* [180 N.E. (2) 791 (1912)] concerning Black Muslims, it was held that freedom of religion is not absolute, but rather a preferred right, which cannot interfere with laws enacted for the preservation, safety, or welfare of the state. In *Pierce v. La Vallee* [293 F (2) 233, 2d Cir. (1961)] it was held that a petition alleging discriminatory treatment because of religion started a civil action entitling the Black Muslim plaintiffs to relief under the Federal Civil Rights Act. In *Sostre v. McGinnes* [334 F (2) 906 (1964)], the second Circuit Court held that state authorities, including state courts, had to be given an opportunity to propose workable rules and regulations that would permit the Muslim inmates to carry out their religious practices as far as possible within the limits of prison discipline.

Holidays and Sunday Observance. Christmas and New Year's Day, Labor Day, election day, Thanksgiving Day, days appointed by the president or governor as holidays, February 12, February 22, May 30, July 4, October 12, and November 11 are legal holidays. Half holidays are from noon to midnight on Saturdays on which no holidays fall. When the holiday falls on Sunday, the next day is a holiday. A 1965 law authorizes family businesses to operate on Sunday if the proprietor observes another day of the week as his Sabbath, if he keeps his store closed on that day, and if he has no one outside his immediate family working in the store on Sunday. Most forms of entertainment are allowed after 1:05 P.M.

Old St. Patrick's Cathedral, Mott Street, New York City, from a copy of the "New York Mirror" of the 1830s.

Morality, Public Health, and Safety. No state condones polygamy. A person is guilty of a misdemeanor if he willfully disturbs a religious meeting or prevents another by threat or violence from performing religious acts. It is a misdemeanor to allow the presentation of living characters representing the divine Person. Under the compulsory education law and subject to the rules and regulations of the board of regents, a pupil may, consistent with the requirements of public education and public health, be excused from such study of health and hygiene as conflicts with the religion of his parents or guardian. The statutes on medical practice may not be construed to affect or prevent the practice of the religious tenets of any church. In *Santos v. Goldstein* [227 N.Y.S. (2) 450 (1962)] the supreme court held that the refusal of parents to consent to a blood transfusion for their child, although operative procedure might have made a transfusion essential for the safety of the child, warranted finding that the child was "neglected" within the Domestic Relations Court Act. But the court also said that its finding in no way implied that these parents failed in their duty to the child in any other respect. In *re Vasko* [263 N.Y.S. 552 (1933)] the court held that there had been no abuse in ordering an operation to permit removal of an eye of a 2-year old child as recommended by medical experts, when parents arbitrarily refused to allow it.

Various Constitutional Freedoms. In *People v. Nahman* [70 N.Y.S. (2) 29] it was held that bearing placards with legends thereon is a means employed for the dissemination and communication of ideas to others and is embraced within the concept of "freedom of speech" protected by the Federal First Amendment. An ordinance requiring advance permission to disseminate information and opinion either by speech or by the handing out of pamphlets or the use of plac-

ards or the like, on the streets, was found violative of the constitutional guarantees of freedom of religion, speech, press, and assembly [*People v. Kieran* 26 N.Y.S. (2) 291].

An ordinance of the Village of Southampton prohibiting solicitation and distribution of pamphlets or advertising matter on private property without first obtaining the occupants' consent was held not unconstitutional as applied to persons distributing religious literature [*People v. Brown* 27 N.Y.S. (2) 241].

Bibliography: E. H. ROBERTS, *New York: The Planting and Growth of the Empire State.* 2 v. (Boston 1887; repr. 1904). N.Y. State Hist. Assoc., *History of the State of New York,* ed. A. C. FLICK, 10 v. (New York 1933–37). D. M. ELLIS et al., *A Short History of New York State* (Ithaca, N.Y. 1957). *Documentary History of the State of New York,* comp. E. B. O'CALLAGHAN, 4 v. (New York 1849–1851). J. R. BAYLEY, *Brief Sketch of the Early History of the Catholic Church on the Island of New York* (New York 1853; repr. 1870). J. D. G. SHEA, *A History of the Catholic Church within the Limits of the United States,* 4 v. (New York 1886–92). J. T. ELLIS, *American Catholicism* (Chicago 1956). *McKinney's Consolidated Laws of New York,* 2 v. (Brooklyn, N. Y. 1954). *Abbott New York Digest, 1794 to Date,* 8 v. (Rochester, N.Y. 1944). **Illustration credit:** The New York Historical Society.

[M. P. CARTHY]

NEW YORK, ARCHDIOCESE OF (NEO-EBORACENSIS)

Metropolitan see, comprising the boroughs of Manhattan, Bronx, and Richmond, in New York City, and the counties of Westchester, Putnam, Dutchess, Rockland, Orange, Sullivan, and Ulster. Within this area of 4,717 square miles, there were (1963) 1,704,350 Catholics in a total population of 4,980,000. The diocese was created April 8, 1808; the archdiocese, July 19, 1850. The dioceses suffragan to New York included Albany, Brooklyn, Buffalo, Ogdensburg, Rochester, Rockville Centre, and Syracuse. These, along with Newark, Paterson, and part of Trenton, in New Jersey, made up the territory of the original see. In the first division (1847), the creation of the Dioceses of Albany and Buffalo cut off the northern and western sections of the state: in the second (1853), the new Sees of Brooklyn and Newark removed Long Island and New Jersey. Since 1861, when the boundary between Albany and New York was readjusted, the limits of the archdiocese, with the exception of the period from 1885 to 1932, when the Bahama Islands were under the jurisdiction of New York, have remained unchanged.

COLONIAL PERIOD

From the time that Giovanni da *Verrazano discovered New York Bay (1524), the area has had Catholic associations. The explorers Estevan Gomez and Samuel de *Champlain preceded Henry Hudson in sailing both the southern and northern waters of the state.

Dutch. The Dutch settlement of New Amsterdam was only a year old when the Franciscan Joseph d'Aillon, probably the first priest to enter the state, visited the Niagara region (1627). Thereafter Jesuits established missions among the Iroquois. René Goupil became the first martyr within the confines of the state (1642); his companion, Isaac Jogues, suffered martyrdom in 1646, with John de Lalande, at Ossernenon (Auriesville). *See* NORTH AMERICAN MARTYRS. Fathers Claude Dablon and Pierre Chaumonot built a chapel where Syracuse now stands (1655). Two years later Father Simon Le Moyne

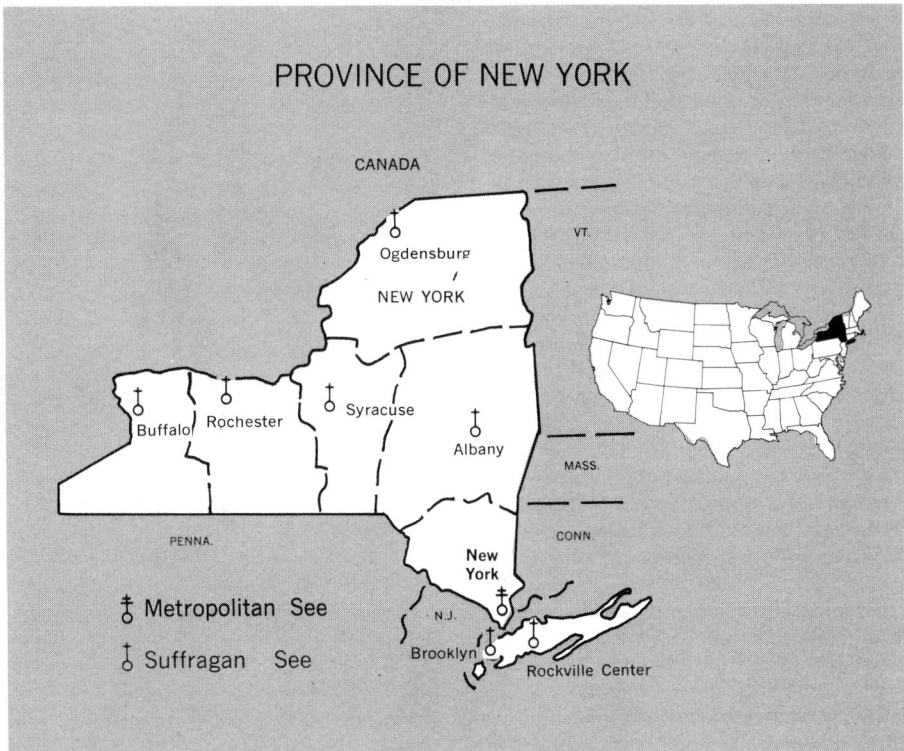

PROVINCE OF NEW YORK

Fig. 1. Province of New York comprises the Archdiocese of New York, called the metropolitan see, and seven dioceses, called suffragan sees. The archbishop has metropolitan jurisdiction over the province.

came downriver to minister to a few Catholics, both Dutch and French, in New Amsterdam, and probably to offer Mass there, on a French ship and in the settlement.

English. Apart from the converts made by the Jesuits among the Indians, Kateri *Tekakwitha being the most famous example (1676), very few Catholics were to be found in the colony when the Dutch ceded it to the English in 1664. The former, while establishing the Reformed Church, had been mildly tolerant; the latter, especially under the Catholic governor, Thomas *Dongan (1683–88), were for a time even more generous. Dongan's Charter of Libertys and Privileges granted religious freedom, thereby enabling the Jesuits who arrived about this time—Fathers Thomas Harvey, Henry Harrison, and Charles Gage—with two lay brothers to assist them, to celebrate Mass and to set up a short-lived Latin school near the present Trinity Church.

The overthrow of King James II in England and Jacob Leisler's rebellion in New York put an end to such tolerance. Penal laws, similar to those in Britain, thereafter specifically excluded Catholics from the rights of citizenship and banned their priests from the colony under pain of perpetual imprisonment and of death upon escape and recapture. In 1709 the Jesuits were forced to abandon their missions among the Iroquois, and barely a trace of Catholics, Indian or white, is discernible for the rest of the colonial period. John Ury, a nonjuring Protestant clergyman, suspected of being a Catholic priest and a leader of the "Negro Plot" of 1741, was executed, along with several Spanish Catholic Negro slaves. A number of exiled French-Acadian Catholics entered New York in 1755 but were scattered through

the colony under indenture and soon lost to history as Catholics. A band of Scottish Catholics settled in the Mohawk Valley (1773) under Father John MacKenna, the first resident priest since Dongan's time. As loyalists they moved to Canada in the course of the American Revolution. Probably as early as 1775 Father Ferdinand *Farmer, SJ, began periodically to visit New York City to say Mass secretly for a handful of Catholics in a loft on Water Street. Father de la Motte and other French naval chaplains, one with Washington's troops on the site of the present archdiocesan seminary in Yonkers, celebrated Mass for Catholics of the area during the Revolution. It was not, however, until the state constitution of 1777 guaranteed religious liberty and the British evacuated New York that Father Farmer could openly enter the city in 1784.

In October of the same year Charles *Whelan, an Irish Capuchin, arrived in New York where he began to say Mass in the house of José Roiz Silva, a wealthy Portuguese merchant; he became the nucleus of a congregation of about 200 Catholics. In the whole state, so the prefect apostolic, John Carroll, estimated (1785), there were about 1,500 Catholics. New York was, until 1800, capital of the republic, and the small Catholic body was augmented by official representatives of Catholic European powers, in whose houses chaplains also celebrated Mass, and by the few Catholic members of Congress. Led by Hector St. John de Crèvecoeur, the French consul, and taking advantage of a state law of 1784 permitting any religious denomination to organize as a body corporate, they set up The Trustees of the Roman Catholic Church in the City of New York. Crèvecoeur, with £1,000 advanced by Thomas Stoughton, the Spanish consul general, and the latter's business partner, Dominick Lynch, bought the unexpired leases of five lots of the Trinity Church Farm. There, on Oct. 5, 1785, the Spanish ambassador, Don Diego de Gardoqui, officiated at the laying of the cornerstone of the mother church of New York, Old St. Peter's, on Barclay Street. In the very method of its establishment, St. Peter's was to be the prototype in a half century of trustee difficulties for the American Church.

With the arrival in late 1785 of another Capuchin, Andrew Nugent, the possibility of gross abuse in the system became apparent. Nugent, with a group of trustees and parishioners, soon created a faction against Whelan which, despite a hurried visit of Carroll to New York, caused the first schism in the American Church and the departure of Whelan from the city. Although Nugent had the satisfaction of opening St. Peter's on Nov. 4, 1786, he in turn antagonized the trustees and was suspended by Carroll, who made a second visit to the city in 1787. Nugent lost his post through legal action by the trustees and was succeeded by a Dominican, William *O'Brien.

For a decade thereafter O'Brien maintained harmony. He toured Cuba and Mexico to collect funds and furnishings for the infant church. In periodic yellow fever epidemics he ministered heroically to victims. In his time a second church. St. Mary's in Albany (1798) was built. St. Peter's free school was opened (1800), the first of its kind in New York and the recipient of public funds after 1806. Elizabeth Ann Seton, later foundress of the Sisters of Charity, was received into the Church in 1805.

DIOCESE

On April 8, 1808, Pope Pius VII created the Diocese of New York and appointed Richard Luke Concanen, an Irish Dominican resident in Rome, first bishop.

Concanen. Concanen, destined owing to the Napoleonic Wars never to reach his see and to die in Naples (June 19, 1810), empowered John Carroll, now archbishop of Baltimore, to appoint a vicar-general for New York. Thus, in October 1808, Anthony *Kohlmann, accompanied by a fellow Jesuit, Benedict *Fenwick, and four scholastics, arrived from Maryland as administrator. Although the two priests found St. Peter's congregation to be composed mainly of Irish-Americans, they preached in French and German as well as in English and soon attracted a flock so numerous (14,000) that on June 8, 1809, Kohlmann laid the cornerstone of the second church in the city, St. Patrick's, intended as a cathedral for the first bishop. In the same year he founded the New York Literary Institution, a college that prospered until the recall of most of the Jesuits to Maryland in 1813. In 1812 three Ursuline nuns from Ireland opened an academy and free school. In 1813 a group of exiled French Trappists started an orphan asylum in the building vacated by the Literary Institution. Again promise was abortive: the Trappists returned to France in 1814, and the Ursulines sailed for Ireland 2 years later. Meanwhile Kohlmann was recalled to Maryland (1815), 2 years after winning, in a celebrated case before the Court of General Sessions, a favorable decision respecting the seal of Confession which set a precedent in American law. On May 4, 1815, old St. Patrick's Cathedral, Mott Street, was dedicated by Bishop Cheverus of Boston.

Fig. 2. St. Patrick's Cathedral, New York City.

Connolly. Six months later John *Connolly, who had been an Irish Dominican living in Rome at the time he was consecrated second bishop of New York on Nov. 6, 1814, arrived in his see. He found about 15,000 Catholics in a population of 100,000, only three churches, and four priests in a diocese covering the whole of New York State and the northern half of New Jersey. Compelled to act as bishop, parish priest, and curate, he succeeded in opening another free school in the basement of St. Patrick's (1816). He also introduced Mother Seton's Sisters of Charity to the city (1817), made long visitations of his diocese (1817 and 1820), and established nine additional churches. New York State was growing rapidly, becoming after 1820 the most populous in the Union. Construction of the Erie Canal (1817–25) attracted thousands of Irish laborers for whom the bishop could not provide priests. He had no seminary and noted sadly what he considered the repugnance of American youth to the ecclesiastical state. His problems multiplied when public aid for church schools was ended in 1824 on account of alleged misuse of funds by the Bethel Baptist Church corporation. Moreover, he lost probably his ablest assistant when Benedict Fenwick was withdrawn from New York by his Jesuit superiors (1817). He also had to contend with strained relations with some of his clergy, and especially with the trustees who controlled the churches. Fathers Charles Ffrench and Thomas Carbry, supporting the bishop, were in open and sometimes scandalous opposition to Fathers Peter Malou and William Taylor, who were on the side of the trustees. So acrimonious did the debate become that the trustees sent Taylor to Rome to complain against and possibly to supplant the ordinary. Bishop Plessis of Quebec was directed by the cardinal prefect of the Congregation of Propaganda Fide to visit New York (1820) and report on the trouble. The departure from the diocese of the priests who led both factions and the suspension of Malou brought an uneasy peace; but it further depleted the ranks of the clergy.

When Bishop Connolly died, Feb. 6, 1825, the diocese fell to the care of his vicar-general, John *Power, who, since his arrival from Ireland in 1819, by his moderation of the trustee dispute and by his ability generally, had won the affection of all parties and the expectation that he would succeed to the see. In the 21 months of his administration he reinstated Malou, founded New York's first Catholic newspaper, the *Truth Teller* (1825), built a new orphan asylum under the care of the Sisters of Charity (1826), and dedicated a third church in the city, St. Mary's (1826). The appointment, therefore, of John *Dubois, president of Mt. St. Mary's College and Seminary in Emmitsburg, Md., as third bishop in 1826 came as a somewhat unwelcome surprise to the preponderantly Irish congregations in New York. They viewed him as a Frenchman, incapable of fluent English, and seemingly, as a former Sulpician, imposed on them by Archbishop Maréchal of Baltimore and the Sulpicians there. The new bishop's first pastoral letter (July 1827), in which he sought to refute such suspicions, got a cool reception.

Dubois. In the summer of 1828, when Dubois made a 3,000-mile tour of visitation, there were only 18 priests in his vast diocese to minister to a population of nearly 150,000 Catholics. Shortly thereafter (1829), in order to secure both priests and funds for a seminary, he journeyed to Rome and Paris. Two years later, having been unsuccessful in recruiting additions to his clergy but with about $18,000 in financial aid from the Congregation of Propaganda and the Society for the Propagation of the Faith, he was able to lay the cornerstone of a seminary at Nyack, N.Y. (1833). Within slightly more than a year the building was destroyed by fire, uninsured and a total loss. Subsequent attempts to establish a seminary in Brooklyn and in Lafargeville were equally disappointing. The trustees of the cathedral frustrated Du-

bois's effort (1829) to set up a school for boys under a religious brotherhood, and in 1834 they refused to accept a successor to their pastor, Thomas Levins, whom he had suspended. They even threatened to withhold the bishop's salary.

Distracted by such internal dissension, the Catholics at the same time became targets of a renascent bigotry. Already in 1824 the recently introduced Orange Society had provoked an anti-Catholic riot in Greenwich Village. Ten years later, in the same neighborhood, men of St. Joseph's Parish guarded by night the work of building their church, and in 1835 armed parishoners prevented a threatened attack on the cathedral. Editorials in the *Protestant,* the *Awful Disclosures* of Maria Monk, William Brownlee's "American Protestant Association," and Samuel Morse's "Native American Democratic Association" all fomented hatred. Bishop Dubois shunned controversy, but his priests were not so reticent. John Power and Felix Varela in the *Truth Teller,* Thomas Levins and Joseph Schneller in the *Weekly Register and Catholic Diary,* and Constantine Pise in the *Catholic Expositor* vigorously rebutted the Protestant press. In Philadelphia, Father John Hughes was making a public mark in debate with a Presbyterian minister, John Breckenridge.

In 1837 Dubois, debilitated by his struggle with the trustees, by age, and by crippling attacks of rheumatism, accepted the appointment of this same John *Hughes as his coadjutor, with right of succession, and consecrated him in St. Patrick's Cathedral on Jan. 7, 1838. From the outset the coadjutor proved master of the situation. Long familiar with the abuses of trusteeism in Philadelphia, he successfully appealed to the congregation of the cathedral against their truculent trustees (1839) and thus dealt the system a blow from which it was never to recover in New York. In the same year Dubois resigned diocesan management to his coadjutor and entered a reluctant retirement. He died on Dec. 20, 1842. Despite the travail of his administration, the Catholic population of his diocese had risen by one-third, the number of clergy had tripled, and there had been a fourfold increase in churches. To care for German immigration, rapidly increasing after 1830, he had welcomed the Redemptorists into the diocese, encouraged the building of St. Nicholas's Church in the city, and provided a superintendent of the scattered German communities in the person of Father John Raffeiner.

ARCHDIOCESE

Under Hughes the See of New York, like the city itself, was to gain preeminence in America. In the two decades after 1840 about 70 per cent of the more than 4 million immigrants to the U.S. entered through the port of New York. Many of them, Irish and Germans uprooted by famine and revolution, were Catholics who settled in the city or were drawn along the Hudson and Mohawk valleys to the cotton and woolen mills, iron and tanning industries, and construction on the Croton Aqueduct and the Hudson River railroad. In 1851 alone, 221,213 Irish landed in New York.

Hughes. For the protection of these immigrants, Hughes encouraged the formation of the Irish Emigrant Society, the Emigrant Industrial Savings Bank, and an immigrant commission of the state legislature. He denounced the importation of Irish secret societies, the foreignism of Young Irelanders and their radical press,

Fig. 3. St. Mary's Church, New York City.

as well as the too-swift Americanization advocated by such native converts as Orestes *Brownson. He fought sectarian proselytism preying upon the immigrants' destitution, and, controversially, Catholic projects to settle them on western lands. They so swelled the population of the diocese that it was split in 1847 by the erection of the Sees of Albany and Buffalo. New York was raised to an archdiocese in 1850, and restricted again in 1853 to its present (1963) size by the creation of Brooklyn and Newark. Yet at the time of Hughes's death in 1864, the churches and chapels in this now reduced territory outnumbered by over 20 those for the whole area of 1840, and the number of priests had more than tripled. The archbishop had established St. Joseph's Seminary (1840) and St. John's College (1841), both at Fordham, N.Y., promoted the founding of the North American College in Rome (1859), welcomed the opening of Manhattan College, New York City (1853), and planned a provincial seminary at Troy.

Bishop Hughes's reputation as a formidable controversialist, already proved in the Breckenridge debate, was further publicized in sharp and sometimes bitter exchanges with Mayor James Harper, Colonel William Stone, "Kirwan" (the Reverend Nicholas Murray), Horace Greeley, James Gordon Bennett, Senator Lewis Cass, Erastus Brooks, and Orestes Brownson. In 1840, the bishop led a campaign to regain for the eight Catholic free schools of New York City a proportionate share of the common school fund. His argument before the Common Council, while unavailing, drew attention, as did his endorsement of a slate of candidates favorable to the Catholic claims in the state election of that year, to the injustice of a situation whereby the professedly nonsectarian, but actually Protestant and privately controlled, Public School Society received state funds at the same time that Catholic schools were excluded from such benefit. Two years later the state legislature, by extending the common school system of the rest of the state to the city, spelled the eventual demise of the Society. The apparent failure of the Catholics forced them back upon their own meager resources. Led by Hughes, they established 38 new free schools and academies before the end of his episcopate.

The aggressiveness of their bishop, while inspiriting his socially inferior, largely immigrant, and hitherto rather supine flock, excited nativist alarm. A mob smashed the windows of the cathedral and of the bishop's house in 1842. Two years later, armed Catholics, with Hughes's encouragement, again had to defend the cathedral and themselves from a repetition of the nativist riots in Philadelphia. Anti-Catholic sentiment also accounted for the election in 1844 of James Harper as mayor on the Native American ticket, and for the origin in New York in 1852 of the Know-Nothing party (see KNOW-NOTHINGISM). The city, while fervently greeting the revolutionist, Louis Kossuth, in 1851, treated shamefully a papal nuncio, Archbishop *Bedini, 2 years later. National absorption in the issues leading to the Civil War helped to dissipate prevalent bigotry. Archbishop Hughes, who in 1846 had declined a request of President Polk that he intercede with the Catholic Mexicans at the outset of the Mexican War, readily accepted in 1861 a commission of his friend William Seward, Secretary of State, and of President Lincoln to visit Europe and there represent the Union cause. The Catholic laity of New York, largely Irish, while deprecating abolition-

ism, as did their archbishop, contributed impressive numbers and valorous service, particularly in New York's famous 69th Regiment, to the Union forces. Their religious communities, especially the Sisters of Charity and the Sisters of Mercy, were among the first nurses of the battlefield. Moreover, it was mainly the personal appeal of the archbishop himself, at the request of Governor Horatio Seymour, that quelled the notorious New York draft riots of 1863.

John Hughes died on Jan. 3, 1864, leaving a well-ordered archdiocese and ecclesiastical province. Improvements had been effected through the legislation of the first two New York diocesan synods (1842 and 1848) and three provincial councils (1854, 1860, 1861). Hughes had organized a diocesan chancery (1853), patronized 10 new religious communities, and rescued church property from the mismanagement of lay trustees. His flock had increased in numerical strength and by the accession of notable converts in what appeared to be an American counterpart of the Oxford movement. They had an articulate press as represented by Brownson's *Quarterly Review,* the *Freeman's Journal,* the *Metropolitan Record,* and Father Isaac *Hecker's *Catholic World.* Archdiocesan charities were advanced by the founding of a pioneer conference of the Society of St. Vincent de Paul and the opening of St. Vincent's Hospital. A local branch of the Society for the Propagation of the Faith was established. The cornerstone was laid for the boldly conceived new St. Patrick's Cathedral, and the archbishop had come to be recognized as a figure of national prominence.

McCloskey. The importance of New York in the nation and in the universal Church received recognition during the next episcopate (1864–85) in the elevation of its archbishop to the cardinalate. John *McCloskey— a native of New York, consecrated coadjutor to Hughes in 1844, transferred to Albany as its first bishop in 1847, and installed as fifth bishop and second archbishop of New York on Aug. 21, 1864—became America's first prince of the Church in 1875. The ceremonies of investiture of the new cardinal, and the dedication, 4 years later, of the new cathedral received unprecedented publicity, attesting the change in public sentiment toward the Church. This was further evidenced by the election in 1880 of William R. Grace as first Catholic mayor of the city. The cardinal, unlike his predecessor, mild-mannered and benign, stood as a public figure mainly on account of his rank. During his irenic administration the archdiocese experienced more than a double growth in the number of churches, clergy, and schools. Significantly, as immigrants raised the Catholic population of towns along and east and west of the Hudson, 58 of the 90 new churches were built outside New York City. Holy Rosary Mission was founded (1884) to minister to the large proportion of Catholics among the more than 6 million immigrants who debarked at Castle Garden between 1861 and 1890. To provide for Catholic Italians, arriving in steadily increasing numbers after 1880, the first church exclusively for their use was entrusted to the Pallottine Fathers (1884).

The national complexion of the clergy was also changing. Hitherto, although 107 priests had been ordained from St. Joseph's Seminary in Fordham (1840–61), a major proportion of the New York clergy was recruited in Europe, especially in Ireland. With the opening of St. Joseph's Provincial Seminary in Troy (1864–96), the 741 priests ordained there for the various dioceses of the ecclesiastical province were almost all native Americans. From 1864 to 1885 approximately 16 religious communities of priests, sisters, and brothers arrived to assist them. Charitable works increased proportionately, notably with the opening of the New York Foundling Hospital under the Sisters of Charity, the first institution of its kind in the U.S., the New York Catholic Protectory for delinquent children, Father John *Drumgoole's Mission of the Immaculate Virgin for homeless waifs, and a rapid multiplication of conferences of the St. Vincent de Paul Society. Elsewhere signs of confidence and maturity appeared in the founding of Hecker's Catholic Publication Society, P. J. Hickey's popular *Catholic Review,* and John Gilmary *Shea's United States Catholic Historical Society. Although the third and fourth diocesan synods (1868 and 1882) and the fourth provincial council (1883), which the cardinal convoked, did not effect all the executive reorganization and pastoral adaptation necessary in a fast-changing archdiocese, his untroubled administration stands in contrast to those of his predecessor and successor. Enfeebled in his last years, he relied increasingly upon the assistance of a coadjutor archbishop until his death on Oct. 10, 1885.

Corrigan. The coadjutor (since 1880), Michael A. *Corrigan, immediately succeeded to the archbishopric. One of his first acts was to convoke the fifth New York diocesan synod (1886), the decrees of which, in 20 titles and 264 numbers, were so thorough and brought such efficiency into diocesan administration and discipline, that the four subsequent synods of his episcopate (1889, 1892, 1895, 1898) could add little to them. The Catholic population almost doubled during Corrigan's administration (1885–1902). Over 5 million immigrants entered the country between 1881 and 1890, followed by almost 4 million in the next decade, the majority now coming from Catholic sections of Europe. As early as 1886 the archbishop, in a report to Rome, noted among the foreign-language-speaking Catholics in New York City some 60,000 Germans, as many Bohemians, 50,000 Italians, 25,000 French, 20,000 Poles, and lesser numbers of French-Canadians, Spaniards, Greeks, and Lithuanians. By 1902 non-English-speaking Catholics in New York had the services of over 100 priests of their respective nationalities and more than 50 churches. The Italians alone, the largest group among them, had 50 Italian priests and 20 churches and chapels, as well as the ministrations of the recently arrived Pallottine sisters, Mother Cabrini's Missionary Sisters of the Sacred Heart, the Scalabrinian fathers, and the Salesians. The Blessed Sacrament fathers came to work among the French-Canadians and the Assumptionists among the Spanish-speaking. During the same period the total number of churches and chapels again more than doubled, as did the number of diocesan and regular clergy. Eight new religious communities of men and sixteen of women, two of them, the Sisters of Divine Compassion and the Dominican Sisters of St. Rose of Lima, founded in New York, began work in the archdiocese. Despite the severe depression of 1893 to 1896, a model seminary, the new St. Joseph's in Dunwoodie was built. Corrigan also inaugurated a trend toward specialization in the work of the clergy by establishing the New York Apostolate, a Confraternity of Christian Doctrine, a superintendent and an association of diocesan charities, a diocesan superintendent of schools, examining boards for teachers, and school commissioners for the various districts of the archdiocese.

Catholic education was a hotly debated issue of the day. The archbishop had the satisfaction of promulgating in his synod of 1886 the instructions of the Third Plenary Council of Baltimore (1884) on the necessity of parochial schools. He doubled the number of such schools within his own jurisdiction and rallied New York patronage as the main support of a national Catholic summer school (1892). He viewed with distrust, as harmful to the concept and growing system of Catholic schools, such compromise solutions as the Faribault-Stillwater experiments of Abp. John Ireland of St. Paul and the *Poughkeepsie plan in operation in his own archdiocese since 1873. His conservative position on this question, and on others such as membership of Catholics in secret societies, Irish nationalism, the Catholic University in Washington, and the prevalence of a heterodox *Americanism, led to disagreement with other members of the American hierarchy, particularly Archbishop Ireland, and to an ecclesiastical *cause célèbre* in New York. Edward *McGlynn, rector of St. Stephen's Church and long an opponent of separate schools, in 1886 actively associated himself with the mayoral campaign of Henry George, to whose radical land and tax theories he publicly subscribed. Refusing to obey the archbishop's prohibition of such political engagement, McGlynn was repeatedly suspended and eventually removed from St. Stephen's. Subsequently excommunicated for failure to account in Rome for his insubordination and his adherence to the Georgian economic theories, he and his supporters bitterly denounced the archbishop and the Roman authorities. The affair, exploited by a sensational newspaper press, focused unwarranted attention on personalities and withdrew it from more substantial and positive elements of growth of the Church in New York. Despite the furor the archbishop, characteristically, held to a routine of efficient diocesan administration. He oversaw construction of the seminary in Dunwoodie, completed the spires of his cathedral and projected its Lady Chapel, and planned, before his death on May 5, 1902, a preparatory seminary.

Farley. His successor, John M. *Farley, auxiliary bishop since 1895, was installed as fourth archbishop of New York on Oct. 5, 1902. Astutely pursuing a policy of conciliation, dramatically emphasized in his returning from Rome in 1904 with the nomination to monsignorial dignity of eight of his priests (an unprecedented number and some of them former partisans of McGlynn), he soon overcame the residue of disunion in the ranks of the clergy. The beginning of monthly days of recollection for priests in the same year, the opening of Cathedral College as a preparatory seminary in 1903, and a doubling of the number of priests of religious communities were also to add vigor and numbers to the clergy, so necessary to cope with a still mounting population. Although before the end of his administration (1918) the trend of older residents away from Manhattan toward Brooklyn and New Jersey had begun, immigration was still to account for a rise of about 200,000 in Catholic population. In a decade (1901–10) that greeted nearly 9,000,000 immigrants, of whom 1,285,349 came in 1907, the peak year in American immigration history, Italians continued to constitute the largest segment of Catholics. Only a few months after his ac-

Fig. 4. Medal commemorating the centenary of the founding of the Diocese of New York.

cession the archbishop presided at a meeting of his Italian clergy to discuss the problem. Of the slightly more than 100 new churches he established, over a third were for the care of Italian-Americans. The Holy Ghost fathers began their ministry among the Negroes of Harlem, and in 1912 Mother Drexel's Sisters of the Blessed Sacrament opened their first school for Negro children there.

The era also saw the ebbing of debate over Catholic education. The archbishop, created a cardinal in 1911, strongly supported the rather precarious fortunes of The Catholic University of America, the infant National Catholic Educational Association, and the organization of the College of New Rochelle, the first Catholic college for women in the state. While the Catholic population of the archdiocese rose by about 20 per cent, church schools and their enrollments doubled in number; two priests were appointed superintendents of parochial schools. Approximately 2,000 Catholic teachers in the public schools were united in an association called The Workers for God and Country. Other signs of vitality appeared in the publication, under the auspices of Dunwoodie Seminary, of the highly respected *New York Review* (1905–08), the first scientific Catholic theological journal in the U.S., and the *Catholic Encyclopedia* (1907–14), largely under the cardinal's patronage. These years also marked the corporate conversion of the Anglican Friars and Sisters of the Atonement, the beginning of the laymen's retreat movement, and public celebration of the centenary of the diocese. The Lady Chapel of the cathedral was completed and the entire edifice solemnly consecrated. The Catholic Foreign Mission Society of America (*Maryknoll) established its headquarters and seminary in the archdiocese; and the local Society for the Propagation of the Faith was reconstituted and contributions to the missions rose from a few thousand dollars annually to over a quarter of a million by 1918. An attempt to coordinate all other charities of the archdiocese in an organization known as the United Catholic Works was arrested by the outbreak of World War I.

Before Cardinal Farley died, Sept. 17, 1918, the entrance of the U.S. into the war tested the resources of the archdiocese. The cardinal founded the New York Catholic War Council, which sponsored a soldiers' and sailors' club, a women's Catholic patriotic club, and a Catholic hospital for shell-shocked patients. His auxiliary bishop (since 1914), Patrick J. *Hayes, was appointed by the Holy See bishop ordinary of the U.S. army and navy chaplains (1917). He so effectively recruited and organized the corps of Catholic chaplains that by the end of the war there were 1,523 priests, in 5 vicariates, under his jurisdiction. Of the 1,023 Catholic chaplains already commissioned by Nov. 11, 1918, the 87 from New York formed a contingent more than twice as large as that from any other diocese. Bishop Hayes also made personal appeals in behalf of the Liberty Loans and was a director of a Knights of Columbus drive that raised nearly $5 million for work among servicemen.

Hayes. On March 10, 1919, in the same year that a fellow native of New York's lower East Side, Alfred E. *Smith, became the first elected Catholic governor of the state, the former auxiliary was named to the See of New York as its fifth archbishop. Five years later he received an enthusiastic reception, replete with ticker-tape parade from the Battery, when he returned from Rome a cardinal. During the 19 years of his administration the Catholic population of the archdiocese fell from over 1,250,000 to about 1,000,000. This was the result of the gradual decline in immigration during the 1920s and a sharp drop during the Depression years of the thirties, as well as an accelerated exodus of Catholic families to metropolitan areas beyond his jurisdiction. The number of churches, nevertheless, increased by one-sixth; schools, by one-half; and the clergy, by one-third. Charitable institutions and services had continued to multiply, often with overlapping and duplication of activity and at the expense of economy and efficiency. Three months after his accession the new archbishop announced a detailed survey of the more than 200 welfare agencies of the archdiocese, and in the following year he coordinated them all under a secretary for charities, at the head of a corporation entitled Catholic Charities of the Archdiocese of New York. The new organization was commended by the New York State Board of Charities (1920) as "the most significant and important event of the year in the field of charitable work." It quickly assumed a position of leadership among private welfare organizations throughout the country and served as a model for other dioceses. Supported by a special gifts committee of the laity and an annual parish appeal that soon netted over $1 million yearly, Catholic Charities successfully met the challenge of the severe financial depression following the stock market collapse of 1929 and earned for its founder the popular title Cardinal of Charity.

Never a dynamic public figure, the cardinal spent the last years of his life in semiretirement. He did, however, introduce the Catholic Youth Organization to the diocese (1936), patronize the literature committee that bore his name, and promote a Catholic theater movement. The heart ailment which seriously restricted his activities eventually resulted in his death, Sept. 4, 1938.

Spellman. On April 15, 1939, Pope Pius XII appointed Francis J. Spellman, then auxiliary bishop to Cardinal O'Connell of Boston, sixth archbishop of New York. Seven years later, the same pontiff named him to membership in the College of Cardinals. The new ordinary brought to New York fresh spirit and talent. He had been educated in theology as a seminarian in Rome and had had experience in chancery, archival, and journalistic pursuits as a young priest in Boston. He had been trained in diplomacy in the Vatican secretariat of state, and in pastoral administration as an auxiliary bishop. With his capacity for work and practical judgment, a Celtic flair for invention and improvisation, and Roman *savoir-faire,* Spellman soon became a symbol and spokesman of the American Church.

In 1939 the parishes and welfare units of the archdiocese bore a burden of individual debts aggregating some $28 million. Schools, hospitals, and other charitable institutions needed modernization and enlargement. Shifting populations required new parishes. In the first 4 months of his administration the archbishop ordered a survey of the debt situation, amalgamated liabilities, and financed, on an archdiocesan level and at a saving of over $500,000 yearly, the total debt. As a long-range effect of the operation, the chancery became a sort of central and readily accessible bank for the entire parish system. The process of coordination and adaptation continued in a thorough reorganization of the archdiocesan matrimonial tribunal, expansion and relocation of the chancery and administrative offices in spacious quarters dedicated to the memory of former archbishops of New York, the convoking of a diocesan synod (1950), and the establishment, for all parishes and institutions of the archdiocese, of a central purchasing agency, a consolidated insurance service, and a building commission. The purchasing agency, serving also the national Catholic Relief Services in its aid to 64 foreign countries, in 1963 directed an expenditure of about $1 million a month, while the building commission in the first 22 years of its existence supervised construction valued at more than $400 million.

Part of the building program involved the creation of 30 new parish units, consisting usually of church, school, convent, and rectory, particularly in suburban areas. From 1939 to 1961 the Catholic population of the archdiocese rose by more than 50 per cent, as a result almost exclusively of the immigration of over 600,000 Puerto Ricans, 72,000 of whom came to New York in 1953 alone. The problem they posed was not so much one of providing new churches in the metropolis, where most of them settled, but of absorbing the newcomers into already existing congregations. To facilitate the process the cardinal created the office of Coordinator of Spanish Catholic Action, supervising an intensive program of Spanish-language study by priests, seminarians, sisters, and brothers. By 1961 one-third of the parishes of the archdiocese offered special services for Spanish-speaking Catholics. The sharp rise in population and a growing need of priests in other than parochial assignments made new demands on the clergy, whose rate of increase, 30 per cent for the diocesan and 40 per cent for the regular clergy, fell behind that of the laity. To obtain greater numbers the cardinal appointed a director of vocations, as coordinator of information and guidance services for prospective seminarians and postulants. To perpetuate

and bring up-to-date Archbishop Corrigan's ideal of clerical education, Spellman renovated the academic facilities of the archdiocesan seminary, most notably in the addition of a new and modern library.

The development of Catholic education in general, among other indices of growth and maturity during the period from 1939 to 1961, drew public attention and concern to the Catholic community. On the elementary level, new schools and the reconditioning of older structures doubled capacity, so that by 1961, 35 per cent of all school children in the area of the archdiocese were in Catholic schools. Mainly through the construction of large, centrally located diocesan high schools, capacity on the secondary level more than tripled, while 5 new colleges helped to double the enrollment of the 10 existing in 1939. In addition, under the auspices of the Confraternity of Christian Doctrine, more than 100,000 students in public elementary and high schools were registered (1961) in parish programs of released-time and after-school classes. School construction, accompanied by rising academic standards and an intensive teacher-training program subsidized in part by the cardinal, accounted for a major share of the archdiocesan building schedule. Begun in 1939 with a projected expenditure of $10 million, interrupted by World War II, it was intensified thereafter to a climactic, archdiocesan Cardinal's Campaign of 1960–61 that resulted in almost $40 million in pledged contributions.

The war itself taxed the energies of the archdiocese, pledged to the national effort by the archbishop in the first hours of struggle. In 1939 the Holy See appointed him military vicar, in succession to Cardinal Hayes, of the armed forces of the U.S. This made him responsible for what was to become, with Catholics constituting a high proportion of American military personnel and their commissioned and auxiliary chaplains numbering about 5,000, the largest see in the world. Approximately 250 priests of the archdiocese served as chaplains. The vicar himself, after reorganizing and expanding the military ordinariate, traveled nearly 100,000 miles on four tours of military stations that took him to every front, a practice he continued in the Christmas seasons that followed the war years, during the Korean conflict, and thereafter. Intimate association with the troops and with statesmen, and his widely read books, in prose and verse and including a highly successful novel, that resulted in large part from his war experiences were the beginning of a world reputation and influence. Charity on an international scale continued after the war from headquarters in New York of NCWC Catholic Relief Services, the Catholic Committee for Refugees, and the Bishops' Resettlement Committee for Refugees, as well as of the Catholic Near East Welfare Association, both the national and diocesan Society for the Propagation of the Faith, and from the cardinal's personal identification with missionaries and his benefactions in the course of world travel. Charity at home met the problems of war and postwar years through a revitalization of Catholic Charities. With new central offices from which it supervises—through its departments of family service, child care, health and hospitals, youth activities, and youth counseling—nearly 200 welfare agencies, this organization had by 1961 an annual budget of over $4,500,000, realized at an overhead for appeal and administrative expenses of less than 5 per cent. Catholic

Charities also extended its services to pioneer in the field of mental and emotional health. In the modernization and enlargement of charitable institutions, as well as the construction of 12 new hospitals, homes for the aging, and child care centers, it has been responsible for a large part of the building program. Two annual social events, the Cardinal's Christmas party and the Alfred E. Smith memorial dinner, have helped to finance respectively the modern New York Foundling Hospital and the expansion of St. Vincent's Hospital into a medical center. In other areas of development and adaptation, a family life bureau, an apostolate for non-Catholic hospitals, regional adult information centers, and a bureau of information and radio and television communications were newly established in the archdiocese.

Cardinal Spellman supervised a remarkable growth and consolidation of Catholic Charities; he was a sponsor of the *New Catholic Encyclopedia* and patron of *The Catholic Encyclopedia for School and Home*, the latter an archdiocesan project. He has taken uncompromising positions on such controversial issues as the exclusion of Catholic citizens from the benefits of Federal aid to education (1949 and 1961), a strike of cemetery workers in his own archdiocese, the trend toward moral irresponsibility in the film industry, the global threat and domestic subversion of Communism, racism, and the indiscriminate identification abroad, even by European Catholics, of America with materialism. In fall 1966 Spellman offered his resignation, but Pope Paul asked him to continue as archbishop of New York.

Bibliography: J. T. SMITH, *The Catholic Church in New York,* 2 v. (New York 1905). L. R. RYAN, *Old St. Peter's, the Mother Church of Catholic New York, 1785–1935* (United States Catholic Historical Society 15; New York 1935). M. P. CARTHY, *Old St. Patrick's, New York's First Cathedral* (New York 1947). HistRecStud. J. R. HASSARD, *Life of the Most Reverend John Hughes, D.D., First Archbishop of New York* (New York 1866). J. M. FARLEY, *The Life of John Cardinal McCloskey, First Prince of the Church in America, 1810–1885* (New York 1918); *Memorial of the Most Reverend Michael Augustine Corrigan, D.D., Third Archbishop of New York* (New York 1902). R. I. GANNON, *The Cardinal Spellman Story* (New York 1962). **Illustration credits:** Fig. 2, Museum of the City of New York. Fig. 3, Custombook, Inc., The Custom Building, South Hackensack, New Jersey. Fig. 4, courtesy of Walters Art Gallery, Baltimore, Md.

[J. A. REYNOLDS]

NEW YORK LATIN SCHOOL, conducted by English Jesuits in New York City during the administration of Gov. Thomas *Dongan (1683–87). Little definite information is available about the institution. It is generally believed to have been founded in the autumn of 1684 by Father Thomas Harvey, who had accompanied the Irish Catholic governor to New York in 1683, and Father Henry Harrison, who joined Harvey the following year. Later, two Jesuit brothers and a third priest, Charles Gage, arrived and probably assisted in the School, which was located on the site of the present Trinity (Episcopal) Church. While contemporary documents call it a Latin school, most likely elementary subjects also were taught. Details of the curriculum, however, are not known, nor can the number of students enrolled be determined. It is nevertheless certain that prominent English and Dutch families sent their sons to the school.

When in 1687 the colony of New York was merged with the Dominion of New England, Dongan lost his office and withdrew from the city. With the departure of their sponsor and protector, the little community of Jesuits began to break up. Possibly the school closed its doors as early as 1687. Certainly it did not survive the violently anti-Catholic Leisler's Rebellion of 1689, which drove the last English Jesuit from the colony. Like the few short-lived Catholic schools in Maryland, the school in New York testifies to the efforts of colonial Catholics to provide a religious education for their children despite great difficulties.

Bibliography: T. F. O'CONNOR, "A Jesuit School in Seventeenth Century New York," *Mid-America* 14, or NS 3 (1932) 265–268. G. G. STANDER, "Jesuit Educational Institutions in the City of New York (1683–1860)," HistRecStud 24 (1934) 209–275.

[F. X. CURRAN]

NEW ZEALAND

New Zealand, which forms part of *Oceania in the Pacific Ocean, was discovered and named by the Dutch explorer Abel Tasman in 1642. Captain James Cook visited and mapped the area from 1769. Its 104,000 square miles comprise the two large islands (North Island, South Island), Stewart, Chatham, and several smaller islands. New Zealand, which became a British colony in 1840, was granted responsible government in 1856. It is now a self-governing state in the Commonwealth. The southern sections were settled systematically from the British Isles. Its 1963 population of 2,575,000 included 167,000 Maoris and 14,000 Pacific Islanders. About 34 per cent of the population were

Fig. 1. New Zealand, ecclesiastical divisions.

Episcopalians, 23 per cent Presbyterians, 7 per cent Methodists, and 14 per cent Catholics.

Catholic Origins and Growth. The Vicariate Apostolic of Western Oceania, created in 1836, included New Zealand and was entrusted to the *Marist Fathers (SM), with Bp. Jean *Pompallier as the first vicar apostolic. New Zealand was then a no-man's land inhabited by some 100,000 Maoris and 1,000 Europeans, mostly of British origin. British Protestant missionaries had been working with success among the Maoris since 1814. After Pompallier learned from Bp. John Polding of Sydney, Australia, that Thomas Poynton, his family, and about 20 other Catholics were living in the far northwest of New Zealand, he landed near Poynton's house on the Hokianga (Jan. 10, 1838). In 1839 he transferred his headquarters to Kororareka, the chief port for whaling ships. Near here the British governor Hobson established the capital after arranging the Treaty of Waitangi (1840), whereby many native chieftains recognized the suzerainty of Queen Victoria. French Marists made progress among the Maoris. By 1843 there were 12 mission stations.

The Vicariate of Western Oceania was divided in 1842 to create the Vicariate of Central Oceania, including New Zealand. In 1846 Philip Viard, SM, was consecrated coadjutor to Pompallier and laid the cornerstone of St. Patrick's Cathedral in Auckland, the capital until supplanted by Wellington in 1867, where Pompallier made his headquarters after Hone Heke's rebellion in the far north (1845–46).

Pompallier's differences with Marist superiors led Rome to divide New Zealand in 1848 into the Dioceses of Wellington and Auckland. Viard and the Marists were given Wellington, the southern region. In 1850 Pompallier returned to Auckland from Europe with 10 clerics and 8 Sisters of Mercy from Carlow, Ireland.

From 1859 North Island suffered from land disputes between Europeans and Maoris, followed by warfare in Taranaki and the Waikato. During and after these wars British soldiers, who included many Irish Catholics, were demobilized and settled in the country. The ensuing Hau Hau outbreaks, extending to the east coast, lasted until 1871, when they were crushed with the aid of friendly tribes. The Maori missions went into an almost total eclipse until their revival in 1881 under the Marists in the south and the *Mill Hill Missionaries in the north. Bp. John Luck of Auckland (1882–96), an English Benedictine, reorganized the Maori mission in his diocese.

Gold discoveries in 1861, combined with the absence of hostile Maoris, led to the rapid development of Otago and Southland. Many of the numerous immigrants were Irish miners who came from Australia. D. Moreau, SM, founded the Dunedin mission on South Island in 1861. In 1869 Otago and Southland were formed into the Diocese of Dunedin. The first bishop was Patrick Moran (1869–96), who had been Vicar Apostolic of the Eastern District on the Cape of Good Hope, South Africa. He arrived in 1871 with 1 priest and 10 Dominican sisters from Dublin. When Moran encountered strong anti-Catholic sentiments in Otago, where Presbyterianism was dominant, he followed a policy of taking the offensive. During his episcopate he created a Catholic school system, began construction of a Gothic cathedral (not yet completed), and started *The New Zealand Tablet*, a Catholic weekly, which still flourishes.

Fig. 2. Blessed Sacrament Cathedral, Christchurch, New Zealand, completed 1905.

Michael Verdon, who succeeded Moran in the See of Dunedin (1896–1918), had been the first president of St. Patrick's College, Manly, Australia. With the support of the other bishops, he opened Holy Cross Provincial Seminary in Mosgiel (1900) and served as its first president.

The territory now occupied by the Diocese of Christchurch on South Island received its first resident priest (1840–51) in the French settlement at Akaroa. The town of Christchurch, which had been colonized in 1850 as an Anglican settlement, had no resident priests until 1860. In 1887 the Diocese of Christchurch was created; it included the provinces of Canterbury and Westland, the latter province being transformed by gold discoveries after 1865. John Grimes, an English Marist, became the first bishop (1887–1915). He was notable for his organizing ability and devotion to the liturgy. Besides establishing a good Catholic school system, he completed a new cathedral by 1905. Holy Name Seminary was opened in Christchurch in 1947.

Current Status of Catholic Church. Since 1896 New Zealand has formed one ecclesiastical province with the Archdiocese of *Wellington as the metropolitan see. Its suffragan sees are Auckland, Christchurch, and Dunedin. The country remains under the jurisdiction of the Congregation for the Propagation of the Faith.

In 1964 New Zealand had 267 parishes, 525 churches, 483 diocesan and 311 religious priests, 240 seminarians, 359 brothers, and 2,538 sisters. Most numerous among the religious institutes for men in 1963 were the Marist Fathers (with 311), Marist Brothers (194), Redemptorists (38), and Trappists (26). The Sisters of Mercy had 866 members, the Congregation of Our Lady of the Missions had 318, and the Sisters of St. Joseph of the Sacred Heart, 218.

Catholics numbered 364,000, about one-seventh of the population. Nearly one-fifth of the Maoris were Catholics. Three Maoris were priests, and many were religious. About 62 per cent of the Catholics were regularly attending Mass. There was one adult convert for every 193 Catholics.

While New Zealand was organized in provinces, each province had charge of education within its confines. Most provinces subsidized denominational schools.

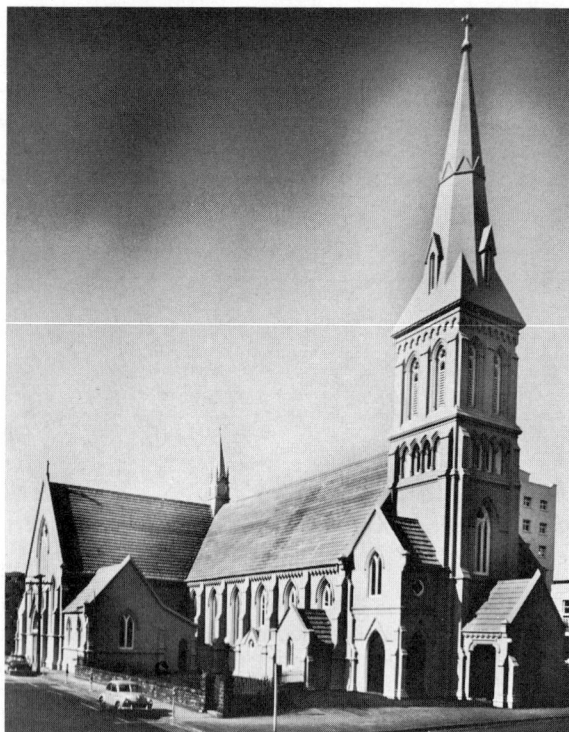

Fig. 3. St. Patrick's Cathedral, Auckland, New Zealand.

After the abolition of the provinces in 1876, the central government cancelled this aid and organized a national system of free, secular, and compulsory schools. Catholics have set up their own school system on the primary and secondary levels only. These schools receive no support from the state except for a few fringe benefits. Catholic schools conform to the state syllabus in secular matters and prepare pupils for public examinations. At the state universities there are six Catholic residence halls and Catholic chaplains.

Fig. 4. Te Atatu church, near Auckland, New Zealand.

Catholics opened their first primary school in Auckland in 1841 and their first secondary school in Northcote, Auckland, in 1849. In 1964 there were 49,000 students in 276 Catholic primary schools and 15,400 in 62 secondary schools. There was also one training college for teachers.

There were 9 Catholic hospitals, 7 orphanages, and 26 other charitable institutions. Government subsidies are supplied for hospital building costs and for part of the support of patients.

Catholic political parties do not exist. In public life Catholics have not exercised an influence proportionate to their numbers. Church-State relations have been peaceful. No preference or discrimination is shown to any religious or racial group.

The two Catholic weeklies are *The New Zealand Tablet,* published in the Diocese of Dunedin, and *Zealandia,* in Auckland. The *Marist Messenger* is a monthly devotional periodical (*see* CATHOLIC PRESS, WORLD SURVEY, 20).

Bibliography: J. B. F. POMPALLIER, *Early History of the Catholic Church in Oceania,* tr. A. HERMAN (Auckland 1888). P. F. MORAN, *History of the Catholic Church in Australasia* (Sydney 1897). A. MONFAT, *Les Origines de la foi catholique dans la Nouvelle Zélande* (Lyon 1896). J. J. WILSON, *The Church in New Zealand,* 2 v. (Dunedin 1910–26). F. REDWOOD, *Reminiscences of Early Days in New Zealand* (Wellington 1922). P. T. McKEEFRY, *Fishers of Men* (Auckland 1938). Latourette v.5, 7. Sisters of Mercy, *Gracious Is the Time* (Auckland 1952). M. C. GOULTER, *Sons of France* (Wellington 1957). L. G. KEYS, *Life and Times of Bishop Pompallier* (Christchurch 1957). V. J. McGLONE, *Fruits of Toil* (Carterton 1957). *Bilan du Monde* 2:651–655. *The Official Year Book of the Catholic Church of Australasia* (Sydney 1963–64), annual. AnnPont has annual data on all dioceses. **Illustration credits:** Fig. 2, F. E. McGregor, Christchurch. Fig. 3, Selwyn Rogers, Auckland. Fig. 4, *Zealandia.*

[M. MULCAHY]

NEW ZEALAND LITERATURE

Most 19th-century New Zealand writing is now of merely historical interest. Occasional prose works, like Samuel Butler's *First Year in Canterbury Settlement* (1863), merit attention, but no enduring fiction was produced, and the verse is pallidly minor Victorian. An upsurge of national feeling in the 1890s inspired more individualistic poetry from W. Pember Reeves (1857–1932) and Jessie Mackay (1864–1938), and some interest attaches to the pre-1920 novels of William Satchell (1860–1942).

New Zealand literature proper began in the 1920s when native-born writers liberated themselves from the exile tradition. From this period date the best stories of Katherine Mansfield (1888–1923) and the early poems of R. A. K. Mason (1905–) and A. R. D. Fairburn (1904–57). The novels of John Mulgan (1911–45), Iris Wilkinson ("Robin Hyde," 1906–39), and John A. Lee (1891–) charted hitherto unexplored areas of national life, while in his short stories Frank Sargeson (1903–) employed a sensitive style based upon local colloquial speech. Mason, Fairburn, Charles Brasch (1909–), Denis Glover (1912–), and Allen Curnow (1911–) brought New Zealand poetry to maturity in the 1930s. In following decades, they and their successors, among them Kendrick Smithyman (1922–) and Louis Johnson (1924–) produced poetry either neo-Wordsworthian or academic in character and, in the main, humanistic in spirit.

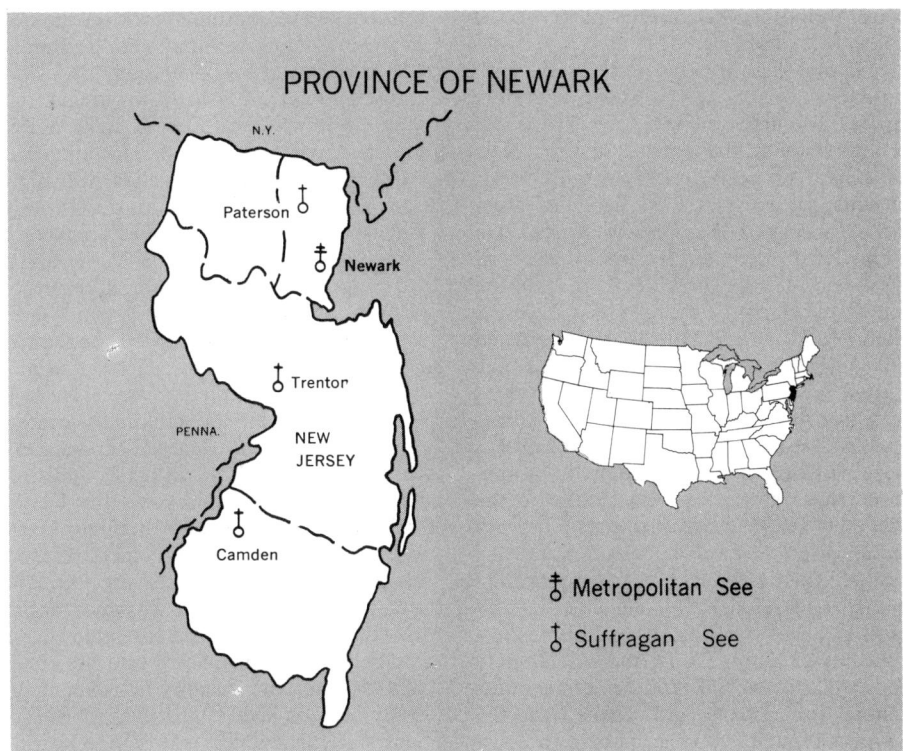

PROVINCE OF NEWARK

‡○ Metropolitan See

↓○ Suffragan See

Province of Newark, which comprises the Archdiocese of Newark, known as the metropolitan see, and three dioceses known as suffragan sees. The archbishop has metropolitan jurisdiction over the province.

After World War II, fiction developed rapidly. The novels of Ruth France (1913–   ), Guthrie Wilson (1914–   ), Janet Frame (1924–   ), Errol Brathwaite (1924–   ), Barry Crump (1935–   ), and Sylvia Ashton-Warner cover a wide variety of subjects and techniques. The short story was enriched by A. P. Gaskell (1913–   ), Helen Shaw (1913–   ), and Maurice Shadbolt (1932–   ); literary criticism increased in sophistication after the foundation of the literary quarterly, *Landfall*, in 1947.

As a minority group (one in seven), Catholics contributed little to early New Zealand writing, although some polemical pamphlets and apologetic books were issued by the clergy, and one or two pioneers like Thomas *Bracken made some impact using a conventionally Victorian style. The first important Catholic poet, Eileen Duggan, published her first book, *Poems*, in 1921. After World War II, other notable Catholic poets appeared—James K. Baxter (1926–   ), perhaps the finest of his generation, M. K. Joseph (1914–   ), W. H. Oliver (1925–   ), Mary King (1904–   ), Charles Doyle (1928–   ), and Father J. E. Weir (1935–   ), among them. Catholic novelists of the 1930s, such as the prolific Nelle Scanlan and Pat Lawlor (1893–   ), wrote light popular fiction; this strain has been continued by Ruth Park (1920–   ), Darry McCarthy (1928–   ), and Frank Bruno (1909–   ). More serious novels, concerned with moral values, have been produced by M. K. Joseph, Frances Keinzly (1922–   ), Pat Booth (1929–   ), and Roderick Finlayson (1904–   ), who has also written notable short stories about the Maoris. Catholics have contributed worthily to serious scholarship in the historical writings

of Sir James Hight (1872–1958) and W. H. Oliver. Mary Goulter has described the country's missionary and agricultural past, and Lillian G. Keys has written the monumental *Life and Times of Bishop Pompallier* (1957), New Zealand's first Catholic missionary.

Bibliography: E. H. McCORMICK, *New Zealand Literature* (London 1959). J. C. REID, *Creative Writing in New Zealand* (Auckland 1946). J. STEVENS, *The New Zealand Novel, 1860–1960* (Wellington 1961).

[J. C. REID]

NEWARK, ARCHDIOCESE OF (NOVARCENSIS)

Metropolitan see comprising Essex, Hudson, Bergen, and Union counties in the northeastern part of New Jersey, in area (541 square miles) the smallest of all the dioceses in the 50 states. Its total population is 2,892,000, of whom Catholics number 1,512,322, placing Newark as the fourth largest U.S. see in population, following Chicago, Boston, and New York. The Province of Newark, coterminous with the state of New Jersey, includes the suffragan Dioceses of Trenton, Paterson, and Camden.

Administration. Before the erection of Newark as a separate diocese suffragan to New York in 1853, Catholics of the northern counties of New Jersey belonged to the New York Archdiocese, while the southern half of the state was included in the Diocese of Philadelphia, Pa. The religious history of New Jersey in the colonial period and the early republic was largely Protestant, although small groups of Catholics were ministered to by Jesuit missionary priests, among them Ferdinand *Farmer, Lorenz *Grässel, and Leonard *Neale, and six parishes were established in various parts of the state in the period from 1814 to 1827.

With the advent of thousands of German and Irish Catholic immigrants into New Jersey towns, the Holy See erected Newark as a diocese on July 29, 1853, and included in its jurisdiction the entire state of New Jersey with its 40,000 Catholic inhabitants. In 1881, 14 central and southern counties were detached from Newark when the Diocese of Trenton was erected. On Dec. 9, 1937, Pius XI divided Trenton into the Sees of Trenton and Camden, and the three northern counties of Passaic, Morris, and Bergen were removed from the Newark jurisdiction and assigned to the newly erected Diocese of Paterson. The following day, December 10, Newark was raised to the status of an archdiocese.

Bayley. James Roosevelt *Bayley, a convert to Catholicism, served as first bishop of Newark from 1853 to 1872, when he was named archbishop of Baltimore. His episcopate in Newark was devoted largely to the founding and staffing of religious institutes of every kind. The diocesan priesthood was augmented, and the beginnings of an educated Catholic laity were provided by the establishment of *Seton Hall College (now University) in South Orange, N.J., in 1856. This institution included the major Seminary of the Immaculate Conception from 1862 to 1927. The Benedictines, Passionists, Conventual Franciscans, and Jesuits were the earliest men's orders brought into the diocese to assist the diocesan clergy. A new community of Sisters of Charity was formed by Bayley in Newark in 1859, moving its headquarters to Convent Station the next year. Other early communities of sisters who engaged in teaching, hospital, and orphanage work were the Benedictine Sisters, the School Sisters of Notre Dame, the Sisters of Mercy, the Sisters of St. Joseph, and the Dominican and Franciscan Sisters. The Brothers of the Christian Schools entered the diocese to conduct boys' classes in a number of the parish schools.

Corrigan. The second bishop, Michael Augustine *Corrigan, was vicar-general of the diocese when he succeeded Bayley in 1873 and served until 1880, when he was transferred to New York. Faced with numerous financial problems at Seton Hall and in the parishes, Corrigan raised funds and donated large sums from his family estate. He introduced additional religious communities, including the Second Order Dominican Sisters, Sisters of the Good Shepherd, and Franciscan Brothers.

Wigger. A native of New York, Winand Michael *Wigger was ordained for the Newark diocese and engaged in parish work until he was named third bishop of Newark in 1881, a position he retained until his death on Jan. 5, 1901. During his administration he unsuccessfully backed a school aid bill in the Assembly (1892–93) to give state aid to parochial schools. Under his direction work was begun on the new Cathedral of the Sacred Heart, on ground purchased by Bayley. By 1901 the number of Catholics had increased to 300,000 and priests totaled 265; of these 75 were religious.

John Joseph O'Connor. Having been born in Newark, June 11, 1855, and ordained in 1877, the fourth bishop taught at Seton Hall and at the seminary, and served as seminary rector, vicar-general, and pastor, until his appointment to the episcopate in 1901. He headed the Diocese of Newark until his death there on May 20, 1927. During his 26-year episcopate, additional funds

were raised to continue work on the new cathedral. In 1926, the major Seminary of the Immaculate Conception was moved to Darlington.

Thomas Joseph Walsh. Newark's fifth bishop and first archbishop was born Dec. 6, 1873, at Parker's Landing, Pa., and ordained for the Buffalo, N.Y., Diocese in 1900, where he was chancellor until appointed bishop of Trenton in 1918. He was tranferred to Newark in 1928 and ruled as its first archbishop from Dec. 10, 1937, until his death on June 6, 1952. He initiated a campaign for a new seminary building and chapel at Darlington (1936), organized the Mt. Carmel Guild to supervise social work, and in 1951 founded an archdiocesan newspaper, the *Advocate.* He also began a drive in 1950 for funds to complete Sacred Heart Cathedral and initiated work on the building's interior.

Thomas Aloysius Boland. The second archbishop was born in Orange, N.J., in 1896 and ordained in 1922. He taught at Seton Hall and the Darlington seminary and served as chancellor, auxiliary bishop (1940), and bishop of Paterson (1947–53), before being installed as archbishop of Newark on Jan. 14, 1953. Under him, Mt. Carmel Guild was reorganized in 1954 and its work extended to aid the blind, the deaf, and other handicapped groups. Serra International was introduced in 1954 and the sodality movement organized on an archdiocesan level in 1957. The Cathedral of the Sacred Heart, which is French-Gothic in design, was consecrated on Oct. 19, 1954. In 1961 a development campaign was inaugurated to provide eight new high schools, four homes for the aged, and a philosophy house at the major seminary. By 1964 there were 1,177 priests, including 358 religious, serving the archdiocese, as well as 3,244 sisters and 205 brothers.

Institutional Development. In addition to Seton Hall University, conducted by the archdiocesan clergy and

Cathedral of the Sacred Heart, Newark, N.J.

lay associates, the archdiocese contains St. Peter's College, Jersey City, conducted by the Jesuit Fathers, and Caldwell College, conducted by the Dominican Sisters of Caldwell. Besides its main campus at South Orange, Seton Hall also operates University College, Newark, and Seton Hall-Paterson, for undergraduate students; the School of Law at Newark, and the Colleges of Medicine and Dentistry at Jersey City. Associated with St. Peter's College is St. Peter's Institute of Industrial Relations, also located in Jersey City.

At the archdiocesan major Seminary of the Immaculate Conception at Darlington, near Ramsey, the course of studies extends over 6 years and includes philosophy and theology. The students receive the A.B. degree from Seton Hall University at the end of their second year. Through an additional affiliation with The Catholic University of America, Washington, D.C., a selected group of fourth year theologians receive the S.T.B. degree each year. The minor seminary, Seton Hall Divinity School, has been located on the South Orange campus of Seton Hall University since 1862. Students in high school and freshman and sophomore years of college who are preparing for the priesthood attend special classes at Seton Hall Preparatory School and University before proceeding to the major seminary.

In 1964 there were 54 secondary schools in the archdiocese, with a total student enrollment of 24,255. Elementary schools, mostly parochial, numbered 224 with an enrollment of 147,236. The 9 Catholic hospitals in the archdiocese—St. James's and St. Michael's, in Newark; St. Elizabeth's and Alexian Brothers' Hospital, in Elizabeth; St. Mary's in Hoboken; St. Francis', in Jersey City; St. Vincent's, in Montclair; St. Mary's, in Orange; Holy Name, in Teaneck—have a combined capacity of 2,324 beds and 319 bassinets. Eight children's homes and orphanages have a total capacity of 852; three homes for the aged, 406 guests; three residences for women, 160 guests; six day nurseries, 325 children. St. Joseph's Home for the blind is located in Jersey City.

Associated Catholic Charities, with headquarters at the chancery office and a branch at Paramus, includes among its activities the supervision of adoptions and the operation of three shelters for unwed mothers. Mt. Carmel Guild provides special services for the handicapped in cooperation with the Department of Special Education of Seton Hall University and the Archdiocesan School Office. The Guild operates four hearing and speech centers and four psychological guidance centers. It also supervises extensive programs for the blind, deaf, and mentally retarded (two centers for the blind, four for the deaf, four catechetical schools for the deaf, and one center for the mentally retarded).

Organizations. The archdiocese is divided into 266 parishes and missions, 40 of which are conducted by members of religious orders (Benedictines, 6; Capuchins, 3; Carmelites, 9; Conventual Franciscans, 2; Dominicans, 2; Franciscans, 7; Third Order Regular, 2; Jesuits, 1; Oblates, 1; Pallotines, 3; Passionists, 2; Salesians, 2). Noteworthy among the many archdiocesan commissions, societies, and projects are the Apostleship of the Sea (with one director and two assistant port chaplains); the Apostolate for Vocations (holding two annual Vocation Weeks at Seton Hall for high school and elementary students); a Catholic Home Study Course (religious instruction sent by mail to interested

non-Catholics: a project of the major seminary); the Commission for Sacred Music (conducting annual Demonstration Mass of liturgical music by elementary school children); the Institute of Sacred Music (with branches for priests, sisters, organists, and choir directors); the Pius XII Institute of Social Education (for education in Catholic principles of social justice); and an Audio-Visual Library (providing rental, loan, and sale of audio-visual equipment for catechetical and other educational purposes).

The *Advocate,* the official weekly newspaper of the archdiocese, serves also as the official publication of the Diocesan of Paterson. An official diocesan directory has been issued annually since 1957.

Bibliography: H. G. J. BECK, *The Centennial History of the Immaculate Conception Seminary, Darlington, N.J.* (Privately printed, Newark 1962). J. M. FLYNN, *The Catholic Church in N.J.* (Morristown, N.J. 1904). C. D. HINRICHSEN, *The History of the Diocese of Newark, 1873–1901* (Doctoral diss. unpub. CUA 1962). *The Summit of a Century: The Centennial History of Seton Hall University, 1856–1956* (South Orange, N.J. 1956). **Illustration credit:** Fig. 2, *The Advocate,* Newark, N.J.

[W. KELLER]

NEWBATTLE (NEWBOTTLE), ABBEY OF,

former *Cistercian abbey in the county of Midlothian, old Diocese of Saint Andrews, Scotland (Neubotle, i.e., a new dwelling). It was founded by *David I and his son Henry, Nov. 1, 1140, and dedicated to St. Mary; it was the first daughterhouse of *Melrose. Its later acquisitions included a coal mine and a quarry, which provided the monks with a useful source of income. The abbey was badly damaged by the English in 1385, 1544, and 1548. In 1560 its Abbot, Mark Ker, subscribed to the reformed religion and secured the Abbey's properties for his son. The east range of the Abbey is now incorporated into Newbattle Abbey College.

Bibliography: *Registrum S. Marie de Neubotle,* ed. C. INNES (Edinburgh 1849). *Royal Commission on the Ancient and Historical Monuments and Constructions of Scotland: Counties of Midlothian and West Lothian* (Edinburgh 1929). J. M. CANIVEZ, ed., *Statuta capitulorum generalium ordinis cisterciensis,* 8 v. (Louvain 1933–41), 5:750–751; 6:406, 689–690; 7:37. G. W. S. BARROW, "Scottish Rulers and the Religious Orders, 1070–1153," *Transactions of the Royal Historical Society,* 5th ser. 3 (1953) 94–95. Easson 65.

[L. MACFARLANE]

NEWBERY, JOHN,

publisher and merchant; b. Waltham St. Lawrence, Berkshire, England, 1713; d. London, Dec. 22, 1767. At 17 John, son of a farmer, was apprenticed to a printer, William Carnan, of nearby Reading. On Carnan's death Newbery inherited a share in the business and expanded it so successfully that by 1744 he transferred it to London, where he established (1745) permanent headquarters at The Bible and Sun in St. Paul's Churchyard. He published works by Dr. Johnson, Christopher Smart, Tobias Smollett, and Oliver Goldsmith. He was fond of children and began to produce books for them—the first person, so far as is known, to specialize in juvenile publications. Many of his attractive little books were bound in a characteristic "Dutch flowered paper," with designs in several colors. *A Little Pretty Pocket Book* (1744), *The Lilliputian Magazine* (1752—a miscellany rather than a true magazine), *Mother Goose's Melody* (c. 1760), and *Goody Two Shoes* (1765) are representative titles. Newbery certainly wrote much of the material himself, but the authorship of some of the titles that he published remains a tantalizing puzzle.

Newbery was a likeable, kindly man and a benefactor of impecunious authors, as both Goldsmith and Johnson had occasion to discover. But he was a businessman to the core; he overlooked no possible opportunity to advertise his wares, including patent medicines.

In recognition of his part in the development of children's books, the influential U.S. publisher Frederic Melcher established the Newbery Medal (1921), an award given annually by children's librarians of the U.S. for the most distinguished book for children by an American author published during the previous year.

See also CHILDREN'S LITERATURE.

Bibliography: DNB 14:312–314. I. SMITH, *A History of the Newbery and Caldecott Medals* (New York 1957).

[E. SHEEHAN]

NEWMAN, JOHN HENRY

Apologist, theologian, cardinal; b. London, Feb. 21, 1801; d. Birmingham, England, Aug. 11, 1890.

LIFE

He was the eldest of the six children of John Newman, an unsuccessful London banker, and Jemima Fourdrinier, the daughter of a well-to-do middle-class French Protestant paper manufacturer. The other children in order of birth were Charles Robert (1802), Harriet (1803), Francis (1805), Jemima (1807), and Mary Sophia (1809). Newman entered the private boarding school at Ealing in 1808. Although his life at home had been warm and happy, in 1816 the bank with which his father was associated failed, and from then on the family was in reduced circumstances. Newman's sisters were sent to their grandmother, but he continued at Ealing. This event profoundly affected the entire family; the father died in 1824.

As a Protestant. Newman's early religious orientation was toward Calvinism and Fundamentalism. In 1816, however, shortly after the failure of the bank and the subsequent catastrophe at home and apparently in connection with an illness that profoundly disturbed him, Newman went through a 5-month period that he later referred to as conversion. At that time a friend introduced him to Thomas Scott's *The Force of Truth* and Milner's *Church History.* The first convinced him of the divinity of Christ, and the second introduced him to the Fathers of the Church of the 4th and 5th centuries. He concluded that God willed him to lead a life of celibacy. There was apparently a complete change in the vision he had of himself. The nature of this spiritual crisis is somewhat obscure, but he emerged from it as a different person. He considered the experience to have been a turning point in his career. He gained a profound awareness of the presence of God. The beginnings of an intellectual foundation for his moral convictions stem from this period. He emerged with a love for the Fathers of the Church and a fear and abhorrence of Rome and the papacy, which seem to have come from his reading of Newton's *On the Prophecies.* His new insights produced certain basic contradictions that would engage him for the next 30 years.

University Life. Newman matriculated at Trinity College, Oxford, in December 1816 and took up residence there the following June. While there, he made the acquaintance of John William Bowden, who was to be his close friend and frequent support until Bowden's death in 1844. He and Bowden undertook the publication of a literary magazine called *The Undergraduate* in 1819. Newman won a scholarship at the end of his first year and gained a reputation as a student. In the schools examination in November 1820, to the surprise of all, he failed to achieve honors in either the mathematical sciences or the classics. He retained his scholarship, however, and determined to stay on at Oxford until he would take Holy Orders.

Newman tried the schools examination at Oriel in 1822 and was elected a fellow at Oriel on April 12 of that year. It was there that he met Edward Bouverie Pusey, Richard Whatly, Edward Copelston, Edward Hawkins, and Thomas Arnold. He was ordained deacon on June 13, 1824. The following October his father died.

Newman accepted the curacy of St. Clement's, which he retained until his appointment as public tutor of Oriel in 1826. He was ordained as an Anglican priest May 29, 1825. He served as public examiner in classics in the B.A. degree for the university in 1827–28 and was given the vicarage of St. Mary's, the university church, in 1828. He served as the university select preacher (1831–32) and that same year relinquished his college tutorship.

When Richard Hurrell *Froude was elected to a fellowship at Oriel in March 1826, he and Newman became close friends. In 1832 Newman accompanied him on a Mediterranean cruise needed for Froude's health. Then, while traveling alone through Europe, Newman was beset by long and dangerous illness in Sicily. During his convalescence he made several trips to Catholic shrines and churches in Europe; it was on his return to England that he wrote his famous poem "Lead Kindly Light."

Oxford Movement. Shortly after his return (July 1833) to England the question of disestablishment of the Anglican Church was introduced before Parliament. Newman, Froude, John *Keble, and William *Palmer threw themselves into the task of writing tracts and dissents of the church. The following December the *Tracts for the Times* began to appear. Of these, there were eventually 90, of which 26 were written by Newman.

The Tractarian movement, with Newman at its head, evoked considerable criticism on the part of both the bishops and the priests of the Church of England. Hurrell Froude took as active a part in the movement as he was able, suffering as he was from tuberculosis, which forced him to live away from England. Froude died in the beginning of 1836, a serious loss to Newman, who depended on him for support in the *Oxford Movement, as the Tractarian movement came to be called, as well as for his spiritual insights and warm friendship.

The next few years were a time of tremendous intellectual activity for Newman. He was engaged in writing the tracts as well as preparing the sermons he preached at St. Mary's, later published as the *Parochial and Plain Sermons.* In 1838 he became the editor of the *British Critic,* a magazine that was a platform for expression for those members of the Anglican Church who had Catholic sympathies. It was at this time too that Newman began his serious studies of the Fathers of the

Church. Following his famous *Tract 90,* which was an attempt to interpret the Thirty-nine Articles of the Church of England in a Catholic sense, he was censured by the authorities of the University of Oxford as well as by 24 bishops of the Anglican communion. As a consequence, in 1841 Newman retired to Littlemore, part of the parish of St. Mary's. Having refurbished a small stable and several outhouses, in which he and several companions lived according to a daily rule of life, he began a life of prayer and fasting for the purpose of clarifying his opinions about the Church Catholic. In 1845 he wrote his *Essay on the Development of Christian Doctrine* and made the decision to become a member of the Roman Church. He was received into the Roman Catholic Church by Dominic Barberi, an Italian Passionist, on Oct. 9, 1845, in the small private chapel at Littlemore. Many of the companions living with him in Littlemore became Catholics at the same time, but Keble, Pusey, and Newman's own family remained members of the Church of England.

As a Catholic. Newman and his convert companions left Littlemore in February 1846. They took up residence at the old Oscott College, renamed Maryvale by Newman. It was near the residence of Bp. Nicholas P. *Wiseman, who was then living at the new Oscott College not far from Maryvale. Wiseman took on the direction of the new community, and through his encouragement Newman decided to become a priest of the Roman Catholic Church. He and Ambrose St. John, one of his Littlemore companions, left England for the College of Propaganda in Rome in September 1846. There they had their first introduction to systematic Catholic theology, which lasted for about 1 year. Newman was ordained priest on Trinity Sunday 1847. He offered his first Mass on the Feast of Corpus Christi 1847.

Founding the Oratory. Before returning to England, with the encouragement of several of his Roman friends and of Pius IX as well, Newman and his companions went to the Oratory of St. Philip Neri at Santa Croce to learn the rule and customs of the Oratory.

After returning to England on Christmas Eve 1847, Newman established the first Oratory in England at Birmingham the following Feb. 2. His influence among the Catholics and recent Anglican converts was very great. He was joined in the Oratory by Frederick W. *Faber and other converts from the Church of England. After a falling out of no great consequence, Newman encouraged Faber to open an Oratory in London. This he did in May 1849, while Newman stayed behind to undertake the instruction of the factory workers of Birmingham.

Rome's restoration of the English hierarchy in 1850 gave rise to a wave of antipapal feeling among the members of the Church of England. The no-popery campaign was assisted indirectly by the return of Wiseman to England as the cardinal archbishop of Westminster, preceded by his famous but misunderstood pastoral letter *From Out the Flaminian Gate.* Newman wrote a number of letters of explanation to newspapers under the pen name *Catholicus.* The Oratorians came under severe attack by the no-popery forces, perhaps because during this time a new house for the Birmingham Oratorians was under construction at Edgbaston. The Protestant Alliance fomented the antipopery campaign in England by providing a chapel for Giacinto

Achilli, a married former Dominican priest, who came to London in 1850 after refusing to do penance for his scandalous behavior in the previous positions he occupied in Italy. He published a book, *Dealings with the Inquisition,* which was popular and widespread in the Anglican communion. In an article in the *Dublin Review,* Wiseman criticized Achilli and exposed a number of his previous sexual irregularities; he also encouraged Newman to make a more direct criticism in the sermons he was preaching in Birmingham (later gathered together as *The Present Positions of Catholics in England*). With the support of the Protestant Alliance, Achilli brought a case of criminal libel against Newman. Convicted of libel in June 1852, Newman, through his lawyer, moved for a new trial. Although the move was not granted, the delay provided time for the public's temper to cool so that Newman was released after he paid a fine of £100 plus trial expenses amounting to approximately $60,000. The costs of the trial were borne by Newman's friends in England, Europe, and America. It was a moral victory for Newman.

An Irish University. Throughout this troublesome period Newman was developing his idea on the nature of education. He delivered a series of lectures on university education in London in 1852. They were delivered to fulfill a promise he had made in 1851 to Dr. P. *Cullen, Archbishop of Armagh, and later Cardinal Archbishop of Dublin, that he would accept the rectorship of a new Catholic university that Cullen was determined upon for Ireland. Disappointed over his failures to begin the new university in Ireland, he tendered his resignation to the Irish bishops. The university lectures that he had delivered in London 6 years earlier were amplified and completed during his stay in Ireland and were eventually published as his *The Idea of a University.*

Papal Authority. During his stay in Dublin there was also anxiety at home because of several differences of opinion that arose between the Oratories of London and Birmingham. Newman was accused of trying to dominate the London Oratory and thereby reduce its autonomy; his reputation suffered because of the disputes between himself and Faber. Faber became more and more identified with the ultramontane movement among English Catholics. Because of his criticism of Faber's handling of the London Oratory and of his peculiar, perhaps saccharine, attitude toward spirituality, Newman not only was accused of disapproving ultramontanism but was held suspect of disloyalty toward the prerogatives of the pope himself.

Partly as a theological conviction and partly by way of reaction to the antipopery movements in England, a number of Catholic intellectuals expressed the belief that the temporal power of the pope was essential to the constitution of the Church. There had been an increasing centralization of authority in both disciplinary and doctrinal matters in the person of the pope during the 19th century. In the 1850s there was a growing movement in favor of a strong formal declaration of papal infallibility. Although Newman did not publicize his grave reservations about the direction of this movement, he did refuse to participate in the demonstrations that were organized to support it.

Upon his return from Ireland in 1858 he was asked by the English hierarchy to take over the editorship

Cardinal John Henry Newman, chalk drawing by George Richmond, c. 1840, in the National Portrait Gallery, London.

of a Catholic periodical entitled *The Rambler*. Shortly after he assumed its editorship, he prepared an essay of his own entitled *On Consulting the Faithful in Matters of Doctrine*. This essay was delated to Rome, and subsequently Newman had to resign from the editorship of the magazine. The matter was not finally cleared up, nor was Newman finally exonerated, until 1867.

In 1864 Charles Kingsley attacked the Roman clergy in general and Newman in particular, alleging that both held the view that truth has no value. Newman felt the attack totally unjustified and undertook a defense of himself and the Roman clergy. Writing in weekly installments for publication in a newspaper, Newman defended his own conversion in a series of essays later published together as the *Apologia pro vita sua*. It caught the public interest and reestablished Newman's significance and importance in the religious life of England. The entire work was completed in 2 months.

After his plans to found a Catholic center at Oxford failed, Newman set his mind to preparing a statement on the relationship between faith and reason to be valid not only for the intellectuals but for the common man as well. His thoughts on this crucial topic were finally published as *The Grammar of Assent* (1870); It was designed to justify the faith of the ordinary man who was often unable to formulate his faith for himself.

The year that the work appeared in print Vatican Council I was holding its sessions. There was a growing eagerness on the part of H. E. *Manning and W. G. *Ward, together with the ultramontane faction in England, to see the doctrine of papal infallibility defined in the strongest possible terms. Newman's position on papal infallibility was that, before being defined, such a doctrine should be given more time to mature. He asserted that he belived in papal infallibility from the day he became a Catholic and was never opposed to the definition of the doctrine as such, but felt the definition to be inopportune. He asserted, however, that should the Council adopt a definition, he would be the first to conform.

Newman was personally invited by Pius IX to attend the sessions of the Council, but he asked to be excused. His request to be excused was misunderstood, but it was based on his desire to remain in the Oratory and to avoid the pomp necessary to such large ecclesiastical gatherings.

The result of the Council was a definition of infallibility in precisely the way that Newman had always believed it, and far less rigoristic than was desired by Manning and Ward. Subsequent to the definition there was enormous political criticism raised by conspicuous lay members of the Anglican church. William Ewart Gladstone launched an aggressive attack against the dogma of infallibility as well as against the Catholic Church as a whole. It was felt that his criticism voiced the opinion of many members of the Church of England. Since Manning's defense of the dogma was unconvincing, Newman wrote one of his own, his famous *Letter to the Duke of Norfolk,* which was warmly received by both the Church of England and the Roman Church, and won the approval of Manning and Ward. A faulty translation was forwarded to Rome, however, and was misunderstood by Cardinal A. *Franchi, who asked Manning to have Newman make some corrections. But Manning wrote Franchi a heated defense of Newman, which brought the two men together in friendship. After Manning's vote of confidence, Newman's prestige in Rome increased considerably.

Cardinalate. After suffering one of the most severe trials of his later years in the death of Ambrose St. John in 1875, Newman experienced one of his greatest vindications in 1879, when Bp. W. B. *Ullathorne informed him that the new pope, Leo XIII, wished to bestow on him the dignity of cardinal and would permit him to continue to live in his Oratory. Though Newman was then 78 and in precarious health, he made the trip to Rome to receive the honor. The previous year, 1878, his old college, Trinity of Oxford, had made him its first honorary fellow. He paid another visit to Oxford as a cardinal and preached in St. Aloysius Church there.

Newman continued to live at the Oratory in the simple manner to which he had become accustomed. He suffered an illness in 1888 and was weakened by several falls. He offered his last Mass on Christmas Day 1889. Until then he was alert and shared the community life with the other fathers of the Oratory. He presided over the close of the school term of 1890. Shortly thereafter he died quietly. The words engraved on his memorial stone were of his own choosing: *Ex Umbris Et Imaginibus In Veritatem.*

DOCTRINE

It is not easy to characterize any one of the principal doctrines that go to form the Newman corpus. The principal contribution of Newman to religious thought is his extraordinary ability to gather insights and express them in so complete a way that no aspect of them is left untouched. His thought is developmental. He was not schooled in the traditional scholastic method, nor was he attached to pure speculative reason, which, he often feared, had a tendency to outstrip the facts on which it exercised itself. His principal orientation from his earliest days was formed mainly by his daily reading of Sacred Scripture. Later in his career, especially in the Oxford days, he developed an intense interest in the Fathers of the Church. His doctrine reflects the scattered notices of doctrine that are characteristic of both Scripture and the Fathers. Whatever systematization they enjoy in his writings is due largely to the necessity of polemics or in rare cases to his truly unified and well-articulated theory of the development of doctrine. The doctrines discussed below have been selected as perhaps more characteristic of his thought than others upon which he has made observations, but which seem to be less central to his principal religious thought.

Scripture. Apart from *Tract 85* (*Holy Scripture in its Relation to the Catholic Creed*) and certain articles published in 1884, Newman's thoughts on Scripture are scattered throughout all his works. Two problems seemed to form the basis of his doctrine on Scripture: the inspiration of Scripture and its interpretation. Against the rejection of inspiration and inerrancy that characterized Anglican Scripture study after the time of A. P. Stanley and B. Jowett (1855) and the difficulties raised by the rapidly advancing positive sciences, Newman taught (at least in 1861–63) that the Scriptures were all inspired, as were their authors. In his writings at that time (collected by J. Seynaeve from the Birmingham Oratory archives and published in 1953 as *Newman 1861–1863 Inspiration Papers*), he examined the documents of the magisterium, the internal scriptural evidence, and the testimony of the Fathers and theologians on scriptural inspiration and concluded (before Vatican Council I) that the books of Scripture are directly inspired but that there was no formal definition by the Church making their inspiration a dogma of faith. Subsequently he said that one is bound to believe in the inspiration of the sacred authors (Trent) and of the books themselves (Vatican I). For him, the Church's magisterium is the unique and infallible interpreter of the Bible. As a matter of fact, the gift of inspiration requires as its complement the gift of infallibility. Inspiration, however, pertained only to those sections dealing with faith and morals. There are some grounds for believing that there was a direct but implicit condemnation of Newman's view on this in *Providentissimus Deus,* but that Leo XIII refrained from mentioning his name out of respect for him.

Newman felt that the whole of Scripture, in all its parts (Vatican I), is inspired, but not all the elements in each of these parts (*totaliter sed non tota*). Possibly *obiter dicta* were included in the books by the human author; these may not be inspired, according to Newman. The final interpretation of Scripture and its sense, however, must be left to the Church's magisterium. Two principles seem to dominate Newman's method of exegesis: the first is the conviction that Scripture is essentially a work of religion, not of science or history; the second is his "sacramental principle" based on the belief that all the works of God are one and that less important elements of these works (the visible world) are shadows, figures, types, signs, and promises of the more important elements (the invisible world). It may be in terms of this latter principle, as a matter of fact, that he interpreted the theory of instrumental causality in the exploration of his theory of inspiration, rather than in terms of the developed scholastic notion, which he may never have fully accepted or, perhaps, understood.

Newman taught the unity of the two Testaments and the progressive fulfillment of the Old through additional revelation finally to be completed by the New, resulting in a unity founded on Christ. He preferred the mystical or allegorical interpretation of the Alexandrian Fathers to the literal interpretation of Antioch, but later in his life he found it necessary more frequently to use criticoliterary methods. For him, Scripture may contain several senses, but the identification of them may not be left to the personal taste or intellectual disposition of the interpreter. He rejected polysemia, or metasemia, i.e., the theory that there may be a multiplicity of literal senses in a single text. Two scriptural senses are distinguishable in Newman's theory: the literal sense and the mystical sense. The latter, in turn, contains two other senses: the typical sense founded on the facts, events, and persons described, and the *sensus plenior* that belongs to the words themselves. Newman did not regard Scripture as a teaching instrument but rather as a standard of orthodoxy against which the catechesis of the teacher is compared and to which the apologist appeals for the proof of his doctrinal formulations.

Tradition. Newman's doctrine on tradition is developed within the theological context of the continuity of churches that he sees to exist between the pagan, Jewish, and Christian dispensations. There have been "revelations," at times to pagan poets as well as to Jewish Prophets, which are finally summed up in Christ. The initial revelations God made to mankind gradually became part of the deposit of faith and may be found within the structure of the Church Catholic. The Church is not always fully conscious of all the elements of its deposit of faith but is always under its influence by way of what might be called vacant vision. It is the vision the Church has of those aspects of its doctrine that are not completely formulated but yet exist within its life. The Christian revelation that found its summation in Christ is somewhat the same as but somewhat different from the general revelation that was given to mankind under both pagan and Jewish dispensations. Even amid the varieties of Christian traditions that now exist, it is possible to perceive the true tradition that was in existence at the beginning and still exists. The basic link that exists between the Christian and Jewish dispensation is the link of prophecy. Prophecy is uttered in the Old Testament and fulfilled in the New. The continuity between the Jewish dispensation and the Christian is so close that the one can be said to have become the other. Within the dispensations is a continuity of tradition.

Tradition is a variety of uniform custom. For Newman it is something silent but living. It is similar to a river before the rocks intercept it. There seems to be no definite shape or form given to the waters until the stream is intercepted by obstacles, at which time it comes to life. Tradition is a habit of opinion in the Church. It is something the Church reflects upon, masters, and expresses, depending on the emergency it faces. It is something that is necessarily unwritten. It is too much alive and too much part of the Church's very nature to be able to be committed entirely to

writing. Tradition would seem, then, to be identified almost with the life of the church itself.

Types of Tradition. In the early Church it was unnecessary and even undesirable to formulate the elements of tradition into doctrines. As the ages of the Church followed each other, as the distance from apostolic times increased, and as the fervor and devotion of later times began to wane, there was need for a gradual and ever more sophisticated formulation of the belief of Christians. With the rise of heresies and attacks on the Church from both friends and enemies, an additional reason for the formulation of doctrine arose. It soon became necessary to develop a means of testing whether a given formulation of doctrine being spread among the Christian people was in fact part of the apostolic tradition. The test that applies to determine whether or not a given aspect of tradition is apostolic is the following: "Whatever doctrine the primitive ages unanimously attest, whether by consent of Fathers, or by Councils, or by the events of history, or by controversies, or in whatever way, whatever may fairly and reasonably be considered to be the universal belief of those ages, it is to be received as coming from the Apostles" (*Via Media* 1:50). For Newman there are two kinds of tradition: episcopal tradition and prophetical tradition. Episcopal tradition is the definite set of beliefs that have been passed on from bishop to bishop and have been called to the attention of each Christian. It is surrounded by a body of explanations of its meaning. On the other hand, prophetical tradition cannot be contained in a code or a treatise, but is rather a body of truth that pervades the entire Church like the atmosphere. Sometimes it is the same as episcopal tradition; other times it develops into legend or fable. It is partly written and partly unwritten, partly the interpretation and partly the supplement of Scripture (*ibid.* 1:249). The obligation to believe the content of the creed and tradition is wider than the development of the creed and tradition itself. The Christian's duty of obedience to the creed is far wider than the extension that can be given to the meaning of the creed.

True tradition is to be perceived not by purely historical methodology, since historical evidence reaches only part way in the determination of what the Church's doctrine is. It is not history that makes a person a Catholic, but rather the Church's dogmatic use of history in which the Catholic believes. The dogmatic use of history involves the use of Scripture, tradition, and the ecclesiastical sense. No doctrine can be disproved by history, but by the same token no doctrine can be proved simply by history. There is a standard of Catholic doctrine and it is to be found in the early Fathers of the Church. The ultimate test of whether or not a doctrine is apostolic is whether the early Fathers believed that it was part of the tradition of the Church in their own age. True tradition can be recognized if there is an unbroken line of testimony in its behalf from Father to Father. True tradition will be ancient tradition. The Church's use of history will show with regard to a true tradition that whenever the past ages have spoken at all they have spoken in witness to it. Tradition is not wholly identified with the creed or with Scripture but is the system of faith and ordinances each generation receives from the preceding one.

With regard to the existence of a body of doctrine separate and independent from the Scripture, i.e., the question of constitutive tradition, Newman's final belief was that there is a formulated creed that existed from the beginning apart from Scripture and that Scripture itself is part of a wider concept, which he finally came to call tradition. Scripture takes for granted certain sanctions, doctrines, and messages necessary for salvation that, if not found in Scripture, must be sought outside of it. Scripture by its structure and its own teaching presumes the existence of a tradition outside itself. Newman did not enter into the question of whether the truths that are contained outside Scripture are substantive additions or whether they are simply developments that come from the early Church's commenting on Scripture. He left open the question whether there are matters of faith contained in the extrascriptural deposit or simply matters of conduct or discipline. However, it does seem from the notes added to his published works, in the editing he did toward the end of his life, that throughout the major part of his writing career he had the belief that all revealed doctrine is contained in Scripture. It is clear from the autobiographical writings that Newman had read St. Robert Bellarmine and had a clear notion of what theologians today call constitutive tradition. His final stance on the question of constitutive tradition was that there is a body of doctrine not contained in Scripture, not indeed opposed to it, but independent of it and separate from it.

Both the Church and tradition are considered by Newman to be interpreters of Scripture. Both tradition and Scripture, in turn, are interpreted by the infallible magisterium of the Church. Tradition, however, is not limited by Scripture or by the creed. It is wider than either, is developmental in nature, and requires an assent of faith that is coextensive with its entire developmental capacity.

There was at the beginning a definite lack of formulation of doctrine in the ante-Nicene Church. This is in no way an indication that the doctrines later formulated did not exist in the first 4 centuries, nor does it indicate that such doctrines were not part of the tradition or were not recognized as part of it. An explicable silence with regard to doctrine in the early Church is not an evidence either for or against the doctrine. Especially because of devices such as the *Disciplina Arcani* and the three modes of the Economy identified by Newman it is reasonable to expect that there would be a lack of formulation of doctrine in the early Church. The modes of the Economy according to Newman are as follows: (1) in some cases, concealing the truth when it could be done without deceit; (2) in some cases, stating the truth only partially; and (3) in some cases, representing it under the nearest form possible when an inquirer could not possibly understand it exactly. The *Disciplina Arcani* is an example of the first mode of the Economy; the answer that Christians believe in only one God to the question "Do Christians believe in the Trinity" would be an example of the second mode; and the representation of angels with wings would be an instance of the third Economical mode, designed to fit the context of the knowledge of a people to whom Christianity was preached for the first time.

Newman takes notice of certain cautions to be employed in interpreting the Fathers as sources of tradition. Complexity, with the attendant possibility of misunderstanding, follows from the very nature of the Church as king, prophet, and priest. Its simultaneous exercise of this threefold function is often confusing to the uninitiated. In addition to this, one should be aware that the Fathers often speak the truth in a context of their own age and culture; one should avoid the danger of confusing actual mistakes on the part of the Fathers in interpreting Scripture with their true traditionary teaching. Newman stresses the danger of oversystematizing tradition to the point where reason exceeds the positive evidence. Finally, he cautions against the danger of reading the words and thoughts of the expositors of tradition within the context of a later age.

Sources of Apostolic Tradition. According to Newman the several sources of apostolic tradition may be divided into negative and positive sources. As negative sources, Newman singles out heresies and the influence they have had on the formulation of doctrine. He points out that an attack on an aspect of the Church's life usually results in the formulation of a doctrinal statement to display the orthodox attitude. Silence is another negative source. It is the peculiar reticence of certain past times with regard to important doctrines. The reticence must be explained, often by a later formulation.

There are several positive sources of evidence mentioned in Newman's writings: the testimony of individuals, of theologians, and of the schools, the literary expression of an age, and the testimony of the Fathers, of the bishops of the Church, of the magisterium, and finally of the popes.

The diversity of sources of information concerning tradition led Newman, in his structured thinking on tradition, to formulate what he took to be the basis of the proof from tradition. The basis of any proof from tradition, however, must be that the early Church thought that such a thing was correct, and the early Church must have known (*Discussions and Arguments* 149). The certitude possible from a study of tradition is nonhistorical certitude. One must not expect irrefragable proof for all the points of doctrine now existing in the Church, since many of these were formulated only gradually.

In the attempt to implement such a proof, Newman formulated the argument from convergence of evidence. This argument is based partly on Butler's theory of analogy. There is a significant original contribution made by Newman based in part on Butler and in part on the rule of Vincent of Lérins: *Quod semper, quod ubique, quod ab omnibus creditum est.* Although it is impossible in practice to apply the rule of Vincent of Lérins absolutely, it is possible to observe a center toward which a number of independent pieces of information gravitate. It is inconceivable that this center to which they converge could be error; it must be truth. There is a metaphysical element in the argument from convergence of evidence that transcends the elements of the argument itself. Whereas the final certitude that may be arrived at from an array of testimony is moral-historical, the convergence of independent testimonies introduces a metaphysical element into the proof. Whereas moral certitude may be gained from the facts of the case, the convergence of the facts must be explained on a metaphysical basis that is wider than the historical evidence alone.

Nature of Belief. Newman's doctrine on how Christians give reasonable belief to the doctrines of Scripture and tradition is to be found partly in the *Oxford University Sermons* and fully developed in *The Grammar of Assent*. The context within which his theory of belief was articulated was the problem raised for the large numbers of uneducated Christians, who give their assent to the doctrines of Christianity, by the theory enunciated by John Locke that the real lover of truth will not admit any proposition with greater assurance than will be warranted by the logical proofs on which it is built. Newman recognized that in practice the vast majority of Christians do not base their assurance of faith on a well-reasoned body of logical propositions or proofs. The question he asked was how the assent of faith that characterizes these Christians is a rational and therefore reasonable act of faith.

Newman gathered the factors involved in the solution to this question from a close analysis of the mental acts involved in holding propositions of any kind, including religious. He described these acts as three: doubt, which is interrogative in form and asks a question; inference, which is conclusionary in form and conditional since it rests on premises; and assent, which is assertive in form and is categorical, since it implies the absence of conditional premises. He further distinguished between notional and real assent. Notional assent is given to propositions that are abstract and general and contain terms that refer to things that do not exist as such. Real assent, on the other hand, is given to propositions that are made up of singular nouns and of terms that stand for things that are external to man. Real assent is more vivid and forceful than notional. Notional assent is given to propositions of profession, credence, opinion, presumption, or speculation. Notional assent contemplates its own creations instead of really existing extramental realities. With regard to giving assent to dogmas, a real assent given to them results in an act of religion; a notional assent given to them results in a theological act. Every religious man is to a certain extent a theologian, and no theology can exist without the presence of religion.

The key to the understanding of Newman's theory of belief is the distinction he made between the acts of assent and of inference. Inference is conditional and is based on conditional verification. Assent, on the other hand, is to some degree independent of inference. The strength or validity of the act of assent does not depend directly on the strength or validity of the conditional inferences that precede it. This distinction establishes the possibility of a strict assent to a proposition that is not inferentially verified by correspondingly strong inferences. Assent is either simple, when it is exercised unconsciously, or complex, when it is made conscious and arrived at deliberately. Both forms, however, are to some degree independent of the inferences that precede them.

Inference deals always with comparisons of propositions so that the conclusions drawn are abstract and can be applied to concrete matters only with probability, not with certain proof. Assent, however, is unconditional and is applied unconditionally to concrete reality. The question arises how it is possible to pass from inference to assent. In this Newman depended heavily on Bp. J. *Butler's theory of analogy. From it he established an argument that is somewhat different from Butler's and transcends it: the argument from the accumulation of probabilities that are each independent of the other and perhaps too tenuous to lead to assent separately or perhaps too subtle and circuitous to be able to be converted into syllogisms or too numerous and various for such a conversion even though it is possible to convert them. It is the unconscious working together of the various parts of a mosaic gradually taking form before one's mental eye, rather than the strict Aristotelian logical deduction characteristic of other epistemological approaches to the problem of assent. Drawing conclusions from such probabilities and giving the assent of belief to the pervading conclusion contained within them, but never consciously formulated, requires the operation of a special sense that Newman called the illative sense. It is by means of this illative sense that the ordinary uneducated man can have a real certitude of the fundamental truths of religion without demonstrative proofs. To prove that the doctrines to which Christians give assent are part of the authentic tradition of the apostolic age, it must be shown that current Christian doctrines have developed from the apostolic age in such a way that they are identical even though they have undergone change.

During his Anglican years Newman was eager to establish the identity between the Anglican communion and the Church of the first 4 centuries. To do this he undertook a serious historical study of the Fathers. At the time of his conversion in 1845, he was in the final page proofs of *An Essay on the Development of Christian Doctrine*. It was an attempt to explain both the fact of change in the Church and its direction as well, with the result that the Anglican Church could be identified with the ante-Nicene Church. It led Newman to quite an opposite conclusion, however: that the Anglican Church was not the same as the Church of the first 4 centuries, but that the Roman Church was. The *Essay* is divided into two parts, the first having to do with doctrinal developments in themselves, and the second with doctrinal developments relative to doctrinal corruptions. Newman's theory of the development of doctrine is based on his belief that it is characteristic of an important and vital idea to live in the mind that has received it and to become an active principle that leads to a number of self-reflections and applications of the idea to other ideas as they develop. He listed five kinds of development: political, logical, historical, ethical, and metaphysical. A Christian idea is no less an idea because it is Christian. There is, accordingly, an antecedent argument in favor of the development of Christian ideas and therefore of Christian doctrine. There is need for an infallible guide to determine the direction of the development, but development there must be.

The essential characteristics of true development of a doctrine within Christianity are the following: preservation of type, continuity of principles, power of assimilation, logical sequence, anticipation of its final configuration, conservative action on its past, and lasting vigor.

The significance of Newman's doctrine of development cannot be overemphasized in modern theology.

Attempts at formulating theories of development of doctrine in the 20th century draw heavily on Newman's original insights. His theories on tradition and the nature of belief underlie much modern speculation in fundamental dogmatic theology. The religious insights of Newman have never been exploited fully. In the 20th century it has become possible, because of the availability of his published writings and the 20,000 or more letters he wrote during his life, to come to a better understanding of his religious genius and the meaning it has for the present time.

Bibliography: *Collected Works*, 25 v. (New York 1890–1927); *The Letters and Diaries of John Henry Newman*, ed. C. S. DESSAIN (New York 1961–); *Autobiographical Writings*, ed. H. TRISTRAM (New York 1957). G. BIEMER, *Überlieferung und Offenbarung: Die Lehre von der Tradition nach J. H. Newman* (Freiburg 1961). A. J. BOEKRAAD and H. TRISTRAM, *The Argument from Conscience to the Existence of God according to J. H. Newman* (Louvain 1961). L. BOUYER, *Newman, His Life and Spirituality,* tr. J. L. MAY (New York 1958). O. CHADWICK, *From Bossuet to Newman: The Idea of Doctrinal Development* (Cambridge, Eng. 1957). C. DAWSON, *The Spirit of the Oxford Movement* (New York 1933). R. A. DIBBLE, *John Henry Newman: The Concept of Infallible Doctrinal Authority* (Washington 1955). H. FRIES, *Die Religionsphilosophie Newmans* (Stuttgart 1948). J. GUITTON, *La Philosophie de Newman* (Paris 1933). F. KAISER, *The Concept of Conscience according to J. H. Newman* (Washington 1958). M. NÉDONCELLE, *La Philosophie religieuse de J. H. Newman* (Strasbourg 1946). J. SEYNAEVE, *Cardinal Newman's Doctrine on Holy Scripture* (Louvain 1953); DB Suppl 6:427–474. M. TREVOR, *Newman: The Pillar of the Cloud* (Garden City N.Y. 1962); *Newman: Light in Winter* (Garden City, N.Y. 1963). J. H. WALGRAVE, *Newman the Theologian,* tr. A. V. Littledale (New York 1960). W. P. WARD, *The Life of John Henry Cardinal Newman* (New York 1912). H. TRISTRAM and F. BACCHUS, DTC 11.1:327–398.

[J. P. WHALEN]

LITERARY INFLUENCE

Newman exercised a profound influence on the literature of the English-speaking world and on the whole Western literary community. His works not only survive; they are also actively studied. The collected edition has been reprinted often. Important single works, such as *The Idea of a University, Apologia pro vita sua,* and *The Grammar of Assent,* are available in numerous editions in many languages. New collections of his letters, memorabilia, diaries, and notes continue to appear regularly. Learned articles, monographs, and full-length studies of Newman's views on theology, philosophy, church history, education, and literature testify also to the quality of enduring vitality found in his writings.

Newman has been classified chiefly as a didactic or apologetic writer, and his specifically literary achievement is often described as the fashioning of a style perfectly suited to his rhetorical intentions. Recently, however, literary scholars have studied the aesthetic elements of the structure and style of his books and of individual sermons, essays, and poems. Thus, in the symposium *Newman's Apologia: A Classic Reconsidered* (New York 1964), it was pointed out that the *Apologia* is more than an objective history of Newman's religious opinions and a reasoned argument supporting the validity of his doctrinal claims. It is also, and just as importantly, a spiritual autobiography marked by aesthetic distance, dramatic structure, a delicate handling of perspective and tone. In short, in his *Apologia* Newman also *creates* an image of a soul working out its eternal destiny. Similar studies of *The Idea of a University* and of individual sermons such as "The Second Spring" emphasize the point that Newman's art is, in Dwight Culler's phrase, "a mediatorial form," that is, one that infuses imagination and intuition into the world of fact and reason.

Poetry and the Novel. Newman's reputation as a writer of expository prose has overshadowed his valuable contributions to poetry, the novel, and literary theory. Despite their Victorian accent, his verses and hymns, particularly "Lead Kindly Light," still appeal to the meditative reader. His long poem, *The Dream of Gerontius* (1866), is greatly admired for its fervor and sonority as well as for the accuracy with which it expresses the Christian theology of death. Newman's novels were closely related to the experiences of his own conversion. In *Loss and Gain* (1848) Charles Reding, in part at least the alter ego of the author, is shown in his pilgrimage toward the Catholic Church. Here, Newman's sensitive rendering of the Oxonian atmosphere, his unerringly accurate psychological observation, his power of dramatizing religious argument, have earned for him the distinction "of being the only eminent Victorian who could write a confessional novel of spiritual autobiography in high spirits as well as high seriousness" (Margaret Maison, *The Victorian Vision,* 1961). *Callista* (1856), a historical fiction set in 3d-century North Africa, also explores the psychology of conversion, but with special attention to the pagan milieu. Alfred Duggan characterized *Callista* as "unique, like the mind that composed it: unique, astringent, remorseless, unforgettable," a view that sums up the book's 20th-century reputation. In both novels aspects of Newman's religious experiences that were later to be revealed more directly in the *Apologia* are encountered.

Theory of Literature. Newman's writings on literature, most of them delivered as lectures contained in *The Idea of a University* (3d edition), offer pregnant theories about literary style and literary history in the plan of a liberal education. "Thought and speech are inseparable from each other," he wrote. "Matter and expression are parts of one: style is a thinking out into language. . . . The style really cannot be abstracted from the sense . . . .." He regarded literature as the book of man, just as science was the book of nature, and theology the book of God. Thus for Newman the study of literature was a study of natural man in his historical processes. In making this point Newman redirected Catholic higher education toward a humanistic rather than utilitarian path.

Newman's greatest influence, however, is the action of his own personality on readers and, particularly, on writers. H. Belloc and G. K. Chesterton, Graham Greene and Evelyn Waugh, Ronald Knox and Christopher Dawson, each according to his temperament, has experienced the shock of Newman's commitments and reflected the light of his intuitions.

Bibliography: R. A. COLBY, "The Poetical Structure of Newman's *Apologia pro vita sua,*" JRelig 33 (1953) 47–57. C. F. HARROLD, *John Henry Newman: An Expository and Critical Study of His Mind, Thought and Art* (London 1945) 440–452. J. J. REILLY, *Newman as a Man of Letters* (New York 1925). A. S. RYAN, "Newman's Conception of Literature" in *Critical Studies in Arnold, Emerson and Newman* (U. of Iowa Humanistic Studies VI, No. 1; Iowa City 1942). F. TARDIVEL, *La Personalité littéraire de Newman* (Paris 1937).

[F. X. CONNOLLY]

NEWMAN APOSTOLATE

The work of the Church on the campuses of secular universities and colleges. While its first objective is the religious education, pastoral care, and apostolic formation of Catholic students attending secular colleges, it is deeply concerned with the presentation of Catholic thought and culture to the whole university community. This article gives a brief history of the origins and development of the Newman movement and of the national organizations that have been established to promote its growth.

Beginnings. The first Newman Club was formed at the University of Pennsylvania in Philadelphia in 1893. Timothy L. Harrington, a medical student at the university, was primarily responsible for its organization. In his undergraduate days at the University of Wisconsin in Madison, he had belonged to the Melvin Club for Catholic students. Finding no similar organization at the University of Pennsylvania, Harrington elicited the interest of others in the medical and dental schools, and after receiving the approval of P. J. Garvey, pastor of St. James Church, in whose parish the university was located, proceeded with its organization. It was Harrington who suggested the name Newman Club in honor of Cardinal John Henry Newman, the English scholar and churchman who had died just 3 years before. Harrington became the first president of the Newman Club. Of the first officers of the Newman Club, Harrington and two others, James J. Walsh and his brother Joseph, later became men of such prominence in Catholic affairs that they were listed in the *American Catholic Who's Who*.

In addition to establishing an organization for Catholic collegians under the direction of a chaplain, these pioneers began a threefold program—religious, intellectual, and social—that still remains basic to the Newman Apostolate; they chose Cardinal Newman as their patron. The accusation has been made that Newman has been patron of this apostolate in name only. But in fact Newman's spirit, Newman's ideas and ideals have had a continuing influence on the development of the movement; and he has often provided the one source of unity in an apostolate carried on in diverse circumstances and at differing stages of development.

Newman Hall and St. Bede's Chapel at the University of Pennsylvania, Philadelphia, as they looked shortly after the founding of the first Newman Club.

For almost 50 years after this first Newman Club was formed at Pennsylvania, the work of the Church for those attending secular colleges was carried out almost entirely within the framework of similar student organizations, more and more of which came to be called Newman Clubs. At times and in some places these clubs might not even have an officially recognized chaplain. Carlton J. H. Hayes, recalling his early days at Columbia, observed that a classmate of his "did found a Newman Club, but it was a strictly lay organization; and what outside clerical instruction we occasionally got was bootlegged to us, so-to-speak, by a brave Jesuit and scholarly editor of the *Catholic Encyclopedia*, the late Father John Wynne." Hayes further noted that a metropolitan federation of clubs, formed by faculty advisers, was "without benefit of clergy." Usually, however, a chaplain was appointed by the bishop, though in many instances only by a casual general directive to "look after the students at the college."

The year after its foundation, the Newman Club at Pennsylvania sponsored a lecture by Bp. John J. Keane, then rector of The Catholic University, Washington, D.C. The lecture, "The Outcome of Philosophic Thought," was given in the university chapel to a large audience that included a professor of philosophy (an Episcopalian minister) and many of his friends. A few years later the Penn Newman Club sponsored a lecture by Cardinal James Gibbons. Then gradually the social program grew, and after the middle of the 20th century Newman Clubs were said to be noted more "for tea-dances than theology."

Early Developments. Although the Newman Club was the sole Catholic program in most places until after World War II (and still is at small schools), as far back as 1906 other patterns began to develop. In 1906 Henry C. Hengell was appointed by Abp. Sebastian G. Messner of Milwaukee to serve the Catholic students at the University of Wisconsin in Madison as full-time chaplain. That same year, Abp. Patrick W. Riordan of San Francisco asked the Paulist Fathers to provide a full-time chaplain for the University of California at Berkeley. In 1910 St. Paul's Chapel at the University of Wisconsin and Newman Hall, with its St. Thomas Chapel, at Berkeley, were built. Student organizations were maintained on both campuses and the scope of the Newman work was greatly enlarged. There was, for all practical purposes, a university parish at Wisconsin and California. The chaplain gave his full time to the Newman Apostolate and became acquainted with the university. He found some of the faculty anxious to cooperate with religious groups for the welfare of the students. He came to be viewed as the Catholic chaplain of the university, rather than as restricted to the group of students who belonged to the Newman Club.

Question of Religious Education. The appointment of full-time chaplains led to other developments. As priests came to understand better the religious needs of the campus community and developed a better perspective of the role of the Church and the Church's responsibility in this community, they saw that the apostolate was an educational one. Pastoral concern would in one sense always be first; Catholic students' salvation was to be achieved through the sacramental grace and liturgical worship of God in His Church. But their salvation and Christian perfection would normally be attained only if the knowledge and understanding of their faith was commensurate with their secular knowledge. Formal educational programs were imperative; and given the circumstances, credit courses in religion were a practical necessity if many students were to take them.

In 1915 arrangements were made by the Paulists in charge of the Newman Foundation at the University of Texas to teach Bible courses for which university credit would be received. Protestant groups at the University of Texas had been offering such courses for a number of years; and after a full-time Catholic chaplain had been appointed, similar arrangements were approved for a "Catholic Bible Chair."

A similar plan, developed in 1919 at the University of Illinois, was initiated by the Catholic chaplain, John A. O'Brien, in cooperation with Protestant chaplains. The university senate, petitioned to allow university credit for religion courses, gave approval, but with the stipulation that each religious foundation be chartered by the State of Illinois as a school of religion and that certain standards regarding facilities and personnel be met. Having purchased a frame house on campus with borrowed money, O'Brien obtained the charter from the state and in 1920 offered three courses for Catholic students. In his efforts to provide adequate and permanent facilities, however, he precipitated an open controversy that affected the development of the Newman movement for many years to come.

Catholic Foundation Controversy. O'Brien's project for the Catholic educational foundation at the University of Illinois had the approval not only of Bp. E. M. Dunne of Peoria, the diocese in which the university is located, but of Abp. George W. Mundelein of Chicago and the other bishops of Illinois. In an address before the state convention of the Knights of Columbus on May 12, 1925, appealing for financial help to build the Catholic foundation at the university, O'Brien stressed the educational role of the foundation as a supplement to the secular education offered by the university. A few months later (Aug. 22, 1925) appeared the first of a series of articles in the Jesuit weekly *America* that continued periodically for the next several months to attack secular education, Catholics attending secular colleges and universities, and, in a particular way, O'Brien's concept of the Catholic foundation. The attitude of *America* was perhaps summed up in an editorial comment of March 20, 1926:

> *America* has repeatedly gone on record as heartily in favor of ministering to the spiritual needs of Catholics at secular colleges and universities. What *America* opposes is undue extension of the Newman Club idea into the educational field of those institutions.

This attitude was shared by many at that time and for many years to come. Archbishop Michael J. Curley of Baltimore was particularly outspoken against the Catholic foundation plan and openly stated that those who were backing it "are waging a secret hypocritical warfare against the best interests of the Church in America. . . . The whole movement is decidedly inimical to the Church of Jesus Christ. It matters little who the authors are. Luther and Arius were both priests."

As a result, bishops who shared such an evaluation (and it seems that for years, most did) merely tolerated Newman Clubs as a necessary evil, as something purely remedial—much like prison chaplaincies—and made it clear that their only purpose was to safeguard the faith of students who should not have been at secular col-

Celebration of Mass in St. Bede's Chapel (1964).

leges anyway. Any efforts to provide a positive program of religious education was considered as calculated to attract to secular colleges students who would otherwise have gone to a Catholic college. The few studies made during those years had consistently shown there were three primary reasons for Catholics' attendance at secular schools: financial necessity (particularly in publicly supported institutions), proximity to home (financial considerations often entering in again), and availability of courses not offered in Catholic colleges. It could, of course, be shown that many Catholics were in secular colleges for less worthy reasons, though these were actually in the minority. Nevertheless, the conviction persisted that a Catholic foundation at a secular university would be harmful to Catholic colleges—and so they were not established until the second half of the 20th century. It is noteworthy that, except for priests directly involved in the Newman movement and an occasional layman, the Jesuit editors of *America* were the first to speak out openly to urge reversal of the stand taken by their predecessors 35 years earlier. In May 1960 they wrote:

> Some way must be found to insure that Catholic students on secular campuses share to the greatest possible degree in the positive benefits of Catholic higher education. . . . What is required is a new kind of Newman Club, more on the scale of a Catholic Institute. This would be complete with library, lounges, study facilities, lecture halls, seminar rooms, and above all, a faculty competent to create the scholarly climate of Christian culture that attracts and challenges students. . . ."

The official acceptance of the educative role of the Newman apostolate came in 1962, when the college and university department of the National Catholic Educational Association (NCEA) amended its bylaws to provide associate membership for Newman educational centers. Since that time Newman concerns have been an integral part of the annual NCEA convention, and the Newman Apostolate is seen as an important arm of Catholic higher education.

The *America* editorial and the acceptance of Newman by the NCEA were symbolic of a more general change in attitude toward the Newman movement. Several factors had brought about this change, the most obvious being the fact that 2 Catholics out of 3 were in secular institutions while most Catholic colleges had capacity enrollments. Other factors also played a part: bishops' awareness that many vocations were coming from the secular campus; assumption by Catholic faculty of secular colleges and former Newman students of prominent roles of lay leadership in parish and diocese; an increase in the number of priests, brothers, and sisters doing graduate work at secular universities. Each in its own way served to break down the prejudice that the secular university was totally inimical to Catholic life and values. Along with this, and perhaps even more important, was the general change that had taken place in the social status of Catholics and of the Church in America, and the resulting weakening of the earlier ghetto mentality of the Catholic community and the more positive evaluation of facets of American culture and of American institutions. Another factor was the impact of the national organizations formed to promote the Newman Apostolate. Helping in a variety of ways, these national groups helped most, perhaps, just by being national rather than local, and thus bringing the importance of the Newman Apostolate to the attention of the whole American Church. The first of these got its start in the early 20th century.

Federation of College Catholic Clubs. In the spring of 1915 there was a series of meetings at which representatives of five Catholic clubs from New York City colleges gathered to discuss the formation of a federation of such clubs. The clubs included the Barat Club of Hunter College, New York City; the Newman Club of the College of the City of New York; the Newman Club of Columbia College, New York City; the Craigie Club of Barnard College, New York City; and the Catholic Club of Teachers' College, New York City. The purpose of the federation was to join for mutual assistance in preserving and strengthening the Catholic faith of club members. On Oct. 28, 1915, students and faculty members of these same five colleges met at the home of Mrs. Jacob L. Phillips, New York, formally organized the Federation of College Catholic Clubs (FCCC), and elected its first officers: president, Prof. James A. Kieran of Hunter College, New York City; vice president, Prof. Alexis I. DuPont Coleman of the College of the City of New York; and secretary, Frank W. Demuth, a graduate student at Columbia, New York City. At the first annual conference, held the following July at the Catholic Summer School at Cliff Haven, N.Y., 50 delegates from 11 college clubs were present. In addition to the original five, there were delegates from Smith College, Northampton, Mass.; New York University; Adelphi College, Garden City, N.Y.; Brooklyn Polytechnic Institute, New York City; Princeton University, N.J.; and the University of Pennsylvania, Philadelphia. A similar federation, organized earlier (1908) at Purdue University, Lafayette, Ind., made up mostly of Catholic Clubs in the Middle West—the Catholic Students' Association of America—remained in existence until World War I. Its member clubs later joined the Federation of Catholic College Clubs.

One of the reasons that the FCCC, which in 1938 became the Newman Club Federation, continued to flourish and eventually supplant the Catholic Students' Association of America, can be found in the appointment of John W. Keogh, who had become chaplain general of the FCCC in 1917.

Keogh had been the first full-time chaplain at Pennsylvania, and remained chaplain of the federation until 1935. He traveled from one end of the country to the other urging the formation of Newman Clubs and the appointment of chaplains. Where Newman Clubs were already established, he urged affiliation with the federation. He was a man of priestly integrity and orthodoxy, and his concern for the Church and the salvation of souls could never be questioned. When he relinquished the post of national chaplain, the federation had withstood its greatest period of opposition and was ready for a new period of development.

For more than 25 years after its organization, this federation of Newman Clubs had at best been tolerated by the ecclesiastical authorities. In several instances the local ordinary refused to appear at an annual convention held in his diocese. On one occasion the bishop agreed to meet the student officers at his home—and then proceeded to excoriate them for attending secular colleges. Then, in 1941, with the formation of the National Council of Catholic Youth at the behest of the Holy See, the Newman Club Federation was accepted as a full member of the college and university section, and thus received the formal approbation of the American bishops. Permanent headquarters were established at the National Catholic Welfare Conference (NCWC) building in Washington, D.C., and a part-time executive secretary had a desk in the NCWC Youth Department. Eventually a full-time executive secretary was engaged, and in 1952, Thomas A. Carlin, OSFS, was appointed as the first priest to direct the national office.

John Henry Cardinal Newman Honorary Society. The 1938 convention in Washington occasioned the formation of another national organization related to the Newman movement. For several years a special honor key for outstanding service to the Newman movement had been conferred by the federation. Now it was decided to bring these honorees into a permanent society, to form, as it were, an elite group devoted to the furthering of the Newman movement, as well as to provide local groups with a means to confer special recognition for outstanding service. After 1950 the John Henry Cardinal Newman Honorary Society brought national attention to the Newman movement by conferring annually the Cardinal Newman award on a distinguished Catholic layman. This award recognizes an individual for some special contribution to the work of the Newman Apostolate or for his special exemplification of its goals and ideals. Among those who have received this award are Clare Booth Luce, Mr. and Mrs. Frank Sheed, Dr. Jerome Kerwin, Sen. Eugene McCarthy, Dr. Carlton J. H. Hayes, Dr. Helen C. White, Benjamin G. Raskob, and Dr. George Shuster.

National Newman Chaplains Association. Following World War II, the number of full-time chaplains increased rapidly. With this growth of full-time chaplains, a professional association for Newman Chaplains was organized in 1950 during the national convention held in Cleveland. While recognizing the voluntary character of affiliation with the Chaplains Association, as with all affiliation to the national Newman movement, the association seeks, in the words of its brief charter, "to set standards for educational and pastoral programs by discussion and agreement; and to implement them by mutual assistance."

Through the conferences held at the time of the annual convention and through the regular meetings of the association's advisory board and executive committee, a consensus has developed on a number of points regarding the basic philosophy of the Newman Apostolate. A number of publications and (since 1962) a training school for new chaplains, as well as an institute for new chaplains during the annual meeting, have made it possible to assist newly appointed chaplains and to guide them by commonly accepted principles of operation. The importance of the educational function of the Newman Apostolate and the educational role of the chaplain in his work on the secular campus have been stressed, but always within a framework of the basic pastoral ministry of the Newman chaplain.

Role of the National Chaplain. Following Keogh's long term as national chaplain, the tenure of this post has varied. Until 1942 the national chaplain was elected by the voting delegates at the national convention, much the same as the other officers of the federation. After the inclusion of the Newman Federation in the NCWC in 1941, the episcopal moderator for Newman was appointed by the episcopal chairman of the youth department, and he in turn now appoints the national chaplain. For several years the term of office was for only 1 year; but on petition of the Chaplains Association in 1951, it was approved that the term of office should be 2 years and that the Chaplains Association should present a preferential list of names to the episcopal moderator.

Over the years many outstanding priests have given leadership to the Newman movement through the office of national chaplain. Donald Cleary of Cornell University, Ithaca, N.Y., chaplain from 1940 to 1944, wrote the first Newman Club manual and played an important role in obtaining the official recognition for the Newman Federation in its affiliation with the NCWC. Three national chaplains, making substantial contributions to the work when holding the post, were later to focus attention on the Newman Apostolate by their appointments to the episcopacy. Within 18 months, and while each was an active Newman chaplain, Leonard P. Cowley of the University of Minnesota, Minneapolis, was named auxiliary bishop of St. Paul; Paul J. Hallinan, director of Newman Clubs in Cleveland, became bishop of Charleston and was later named first archbishop of Atlanta; and Robert E. Tracy of Louisiana State University, Baton Rouge, became auxiliary bishop of Lafayette, La., and later first bishop of Baton Rouge. Identified so closely with the work, they served in a particularly effective way to bring the Newman Apostolate to the attention of their fellow bishops.

In addition to being informal episcopal witness for the Newman Apostolate, Bishop Hallinan became episcopal moderator of the national Newman work in 1960 and gave decisive leadership to the movement for 3 years.

In 1965 the role played by the national chaplain was assumed largely by the priest in charge of the national office at the NCWC, when the one holding this position became assistant director of the youth department and director of the National Newman Apostolate.

National Newman Alumni Association. At least as early as 1920 Newman Alumni Clubs had been formed to offer a program of continuing religious education to its members and to support the work of the Church on campus. For many years these clubs belonged to the national federation on the same basis as the campus clubs, and their members were a strong force in the leadership of the federation. In line with the policy to make the federation truly a student organization, these alumni clubs withdrew from the federation in 1957 to form the National Newman Alumni Association as an affiliate organization to the federation. Provision has been made for individual memberships in the association as well as club membership. The alumni seek to promote the work of the apostolate, particularly by assisting in the national public relations program.

National Newman Foundation. In an effort to obtain funds for the many needs of the Newman Apostolate, to ensure responsible control of such funds for the welfare of the Church, and to prepare for the growing financial needs of the future, the Chaplains Association petitioned the bishops of the NCWC administrative board in November 1959 to approve a plan to set up a national foundation as a nonprofit corporation. This proposal was approved and a charter for the foundation was issued by the District of Columbia in May 1960. For several months it was directed by a temporary board of trustees made up of Newman chaplains. In December 1962 control of the foundation was turned over to a permanent board of 20 laymen and 6 clerics who hold official positions in the National Newman Apostolate. Besides seeking funds from individuals and commercial and industrial firms, the National Newman Foundation also seeks grants for specific projects from other foundations.

National Newman Association of Faculty and Staff. Recognizing that many contributions can be made to the Newman Apostolate by the Catholic faculty members and others on the administrative staffs of our secular colleges and universities, a national association for such persons was begun in 1959, primarily as a means of communication with the Catholic faculty in secular institutions. Governed by a desire to keep organization to a minimum, the development of this segment of the apostolate has proceeded slowly, though on a local level there are many instances of strong faculty participation in the local Newman program.

National Newman Apostolate. Thus, over the years six national organizations were established to further this work of the Church on the secular campus. Except for the special approval given to the foundation, for many years only the National Newman Club Federation had the formal approval of the American hierarchy. When the federation was first organized in 1915, it was technically a federation of student clubs. In fact, it was an organization run by faculty, alumni, and chaplains; it was not until 1938 that the federation constitution allowed an undergraduate student to hold national office and not until 1942 that a student could become president of the federation. When formally recognized by the bishops, the federation was placed in the youth department of the NCWC, and for 20 years the work of the national Newman movement was carried on under the fiction that this was an exclusively student operation. The welfare of Catholic students was indeed the principal concern of the Newman movement, but as has been seen, there were certainly other than student organizations set up to promote this apostolate.

Recognition of developments that had already taken place led Abp. John F. Dearden of Detroit, as episcopal chairman of the NCWC youth department, in consultation with Bishop Hallinan as episcopal adviser to the Newman movement, to reorganize the national Newman work under the umbrella title of the National Newman Apostolate, and to give formal approval to these various national organizations as component units of the national apostolate.

In April 1962 this recognition was formalized by Abp. John J. Krol, who had succeeded Archbishop Dearden in the youth department post, and who established the National Newman Apostolate as a full section of the youth department. Charles Albright, CSP, who has been serving as executive secretary for the federation, became the first coordinating secretary of the national apostolate. A former student officer of the federation was named his assistant as executive secretary for the student federation.

Thus from a student club at the University of Pennsylvania and a struggling federation of Newman Clubs barely tolerated by Church officials, a major apostolate in the American Church has developed—approved and encouraged by the American bishops, carried on by and concerned with every portion of the university community. With the proportion of students attending publicly supported institutions increasing each year, it has become increasingly obvious that the Newman Apostolate must hold a place of importance if the Church in America is to have an educated laity who are not religiously illiterate. Since mid-20th century there has been a phenomenal increase of full-time chaplains, Catholic centers, and university parishes, with nuns, brothers, and laymen joined to the staffs of such centers, assisting the chaplains in their educational and pastoral roles. Some critics still see a great disproportion between the personnel attached to Catholic colleges and universities and the number of priests and religious involved in the Newman Apostolate. One mark of success has been that bishops and priests from other countries are studying the American scene and adapting the Newman Apostolate to their own needs and circumstances.

Bibliography: W. J. WHALEN, *Catholics on Campus* (pa. Milwaukee 1961). **Illustration credits:** Peter Dechert, Bryn Mawr, Pa.

[C. ALBRIGHT]

NEWMAN ASSOCIATION, the national organization for Catholic university graduates and professional people of Great Britain, with headquarters in London. It aims to encourage the educated Catholic laity to take a full part in the life of modern society in an apostolic spirit, to enable the talents of experts in various fields to be placed at the service of the Church and of society at large, to facilitate the study of problems encountered by Catholics engaged in various professional and intellectual disciplines, and to assist and encourage Catholics to take a full part in the life of the universities at both student and graduate levels. The Association has more than 40 circles, mainly in university towns, and works also through national specialized groups, e.g., the Theological Studies Group, Legal Studies Group, and Philosophy of Science Group. It conducts a program of adult education through study groups, lectures, regional conferences, publications, etc.; undertakes social action through its circles or other constituent groups; represents Catholic graduates and professional persons in various national bodies, whether Catholic, interdenominational, or neutral; and encourages members and constituent circles and groups to participate in the promotion of the liturgical and ecumenical movements. The Association is a member of the Mouvement International des Intellectuels Catholiques of *Pax Romana.

[J. A. BRYDEN]

NEWTON, SIR ISAAC

Physicist, mathematician, and natural philosopher; b. Woolsthorpe, Lincolnshire, England, Dec. 25, 1642; d. Kensington, March 20, 1727. Newton, posthumous child, was the only son of Isaac Newton, a prosperous yeoman farmer. The remarriage of Isaac's mother further increased the family's property, and he inherited a competent estate at her death. After attending the grammar school at Grantham, he was matriculated at Trinity College, Cambridge, in 1661.

Undergraduate Investigations. Despite modifications and reforms initiated in the 16th century, the curriculum when Newton arrived at Cambridge remained substantially the scholastic curriculum of the Middle Ages. As generations before him had done, Newton began his undergraduate career with the study of logic, ethics, and rhetoric, a foundation on which a thorough study of Aristotelian philosophy was to be built. The notes in which these studies were recorded have survived. Newton, however, could not remain in ignorance of the new intellectual currents of the 17th century. His notes on the peripatetic philosophy broke off unfinished, and in a large empty space in his notebook he began, about the beginning of 1664, a new set of notes labeled *"Quaestiones Quaedam Philosophicae."* Under the heading he entered a slogan: "Amicus Plato amicus Aristotelis magis amica veritas." The notes are from Descartes,

A portrait of Isaac Newton by Godfrey Kneller, dated 1702.

Galileo, Gassendi, Boyle, Hobbes, H. More, and others. Newton's new friend *veritas* was the mechanical philosophy in which the scientific revolution had chosen to clothe its discoveries.

In the *Quaestiones* Newton, while still an undergraduate, digested what had been accomplished so far, and in them he began to formulate the questions his scientific career would be devoted to answering. At much the same time he became acquainted with mathematics. By the end of 1664 he had assimilated all that the mathematical tradition could offer him, and taking his initial stimulation from Descartes's geometry, he was beginning to push beyond the existing study of mathematics toward the calculus. When Newton took his B.A. in 1665, he had not told anyone of his progress in natural philosophy and mathematics. No one knew that perhaps the most extraordinary undergraduate career in the history of university education was being completed, and no one learned at the time of the startling discoveries concerning light, gravity, and mathematics with which he crowned his studies during the following year.

Among the topics discussed in the *Quaestiones* was color. With the publication of Descartes's philosophy, which had proposed to replace the qualitative Aristotelian conception of nature with a quantitative mechanical one, the problem of color had become virtually a test case for the mechanical philosophy. Descartes himself had undertaken to show that the physical reality behind a sensation of color is not a real color in a body but a mechanical motion of tiny round corpuscles turning upon their axes. As far as color was concerned, the revolt against Aristotle was less complete than it seemed, for however much Descartes had altered the conception of quality, he had continued to think of colors as modifications wrought on light, which in its pristine form appears white. Newton's undergraduate notebook records the first suggestion that colors may appear, not through a process of modification, but rather through one of analysis. By the beginning of 1666 he had elaborated the idea into a full conception of colors and had confirmed it with experiments.

When Isaac *Barrow, the first occupant of the Lucasian chair of mathematics at Cambridge, retired, Newton was appointed to succeed him. He chose to deliver his first set of lectures, in the spring of 1670, on optics.

Theory of Color. The *Lectiones Opticae* expanded a short essay of 1666 into a full and complete treatment embodying virtually all the experiments and concepts that were ultimately to form Book I of the *Opticks*. White light was shown to be a heterogeneous mixture of rays, each disposed to exhibit one color and no other and able to withstand modification by any known means. Since each species of ray has a different index of refraction, a beam of white light can be analyzed into its constituent parts (by a prism, for example) to produce the phenomena of colors. Reflections can also analyze a beam of white light, as Newton's experiments on the colors of thin plates demonstrated. Basic experiments with the colors of thin plates had been included in the essay of 1666, and these were expanded by 1672 into a paper nearly identical to Book II of the *Opticks*. Although the *Opticks* itself was not to appear until more than 30 years had passed, everything it contained except the passages on thick plates and on diffraction, together

with the "Queries," had been formulated either before the publication of Newton's first paper or within 2 months of its appearance. Although Newton maintained a corpuscular conception of light and rejected undulatory theories both in 1672 and later, his *Opticks* was not concerned with this question. He contributed a new conception of color to optics; it has survived all changes of opinion on the nature of light.

In the spring of 1670 Newton announced his theory of color in his initial lectures. There is no evidence whatever to suggest that it was comprehended; his later lectures on mathematics and mechanics also failed to stimulate any response. Meanwhile the theory had led him to conclude that refracting telescopes could never be perfected; therefore he constructed the first reflecting telescope. When the Royal Society in London heard of the telescope, they asked to see it. Gratified by its success, Newton also sent a condensed version of his theory of color to them in February 1672. The publication of the paper involved a personal crisis of major dimensions. Newton was torn by conflicting emotions. On the one hand he wanted public recognition of his work; on the other he feared ridicule to the point that only with difficulty could he bring himself to publish. Inevitably the reaction to his paper was not completely favorable. It can hardly be maintained that he was subjected to a torrent of criticism or even of comment. Over a period of 6 years he had scarcely a dozen replies to make, most of them brief. Furthermore, none of the criticisms effectively challenged his theory, so that he was always fully in command of the situation. Nevertheless Newton's composure gave way. To Hooke's critique he replied with abusive insults, and he responded to Huygens's mild letter with such warmth that *Huygens declined further discussion. Within 18 months of the original publication Newton had severed his correspondence with Henry Oldenburg, secretary to the Royal Society, and had sullenly retired to his cloister. Plans for the publication of a mathematical work were dropped. In 1675 the realization that *Hooke and others had accepted his views restored his confidence sufficiently to induce him to submit his observations on thin plates and his hypothesis of light to the Royal Society, though not to the public. But a new set of criticisms, directed to the paper of 1672 by English Jesuits in Liège, first Linus and ultimately Lucas, upset him anew. The correspondence reached its climax and its conclusion with an untempered, almost paranoiac outburst, and Newton, severing his ties with the scientific community, withdrew into a silence that he maintained, with only a few exceptions, for more than 6 years. The *Opticks*, ready in 1672 and intended for publication, finally appeared in 1704.

Mechanics. The occasion of Newton's reemergence was a visit from Halley in 1684. Following a conversation with Hooke and Wren, Halley had come to seek Newton's aid in determining mathematically the orbit traced by a moving body attracted by a centripetal force that varies inversely as the square of the distance. He learned that Newton had solved the problem, demonstrating that under such conditions an elliptical orbit must be followed; and as a result of that visit the *Principia* ultimately appeared.

Newton's interest in such questions was not new. It can be traced to his undergraduate days, when the reading of Galileo and Descartes stimulated entries in the

Quaestiones devoted to mechanics, including cosmic mechanics. Galileo's work had been prompted by the necessity of a new system of mechanics to support the Copernican system. If his concept of inertia reconciled terrestrial mechanics with a moving earth, it did not settle the questions of celestial mechanics. Indeed, celestial mechanics constituted the major lacuna in the emerging structure of the new scientific world view. *Kepler had shattered the perfect circles and the crystalline spheres of ancient astronomy. What then kept the planets in their orbits? Descartes's vortices, which did not, to be sure. take account of elliptical orbits, had been intended to explain the cosmic order in mechanical terms. Newton's undergraduate *Quaestiones* picked out the defects of the Cartesian explanation.

Shortly thereafter he defined successfully the mechanical elements of orbital motion—a projectile constantly turned from its inertial path by a sufficient centripetal force would trace a closed orbit. Could the centripetal force be identical with the gravitating force by which heavy bodies fall to the earth? Computing the acceleration of gravity from the pendulum and calculating that it would decrease as the square of the distance, Newton imagined gravity to extend to the orbit of the moon and compared it with the deviation of the moon from a rectilinear path. As he later remarked, he found it to "answer pretty nearly." The concept of universal gravitation was contained in the calculation; the *Principia* was not. Between the raw idea employed in 1666 and the *Principia* stood a number of obstacles that Newton was not yet able to leap—the demonstration, which Halley asked for, that an elliptical orbit would follow from the inverse square law; the demonstration, which alone allowed him to compare the force of gravity on the surface of the earth to the force attracting the moon, that a sphere in attracting external bodies acts as though its mass were concentrated at its center; a complete treatment of mechanics in which both celestial and terrestrial phenomena could be explained from the same principles. All these things Newton lacked in 1666, and if he was then forging the mathematical tool that could supply them, he had not yet employed his instrument to that end. It was not by accident that the *Principia* did not appear in 1666.

For much of the decade following, Newton was absorbed in mathematical, optical, and chemical research. In 1679 Hooke, the successor to Oldenburg as secretary of the Royal Society, tried to engage him in a scientific correspondence. In refusing, Newton mentioned casually an experiment to prove the diurnal rotation of the earth—a body let fall from a high tower should fall to the east of the foot of the tower because of its initially higher tangential velocity. In a sketch accompanying the notion he showed the trajectory of fall, a spiral ending at the center of the earth. Hooke was unable to resist the temptation to correct. The path of a body imagined to fall unimpeded through the earth, he pointed out in reply, would be, not a spiral ending at the center, but "a kind Elleptueid" returning to the original height from which the body was dropped. Never one to accept criticism lightly, Newton broke off the correspondence, which he had not wanted in the first place, but he later admitted that its stimulation first led him to work out the demonstration of the elliptical orbit. That demonstration, however, was only one of the missing pieces. Moreover, Newton was then engaged in chemical

studies, and he was still nursing the psychological scars left by the Lucas correspondence. The *Principia* did not appear for some years.

The Principia. By 1684 the situation had changed. Newton began to think again of publication; he made at least a tentative start on a mathematical treatise. He took up anew the study of mechanics for his Lucasian lectures in the autumn. Entirely by accident Halley came to visit him in August and found a Newton receptive as he had not been for 6 years. Not only did Halley receive the propositions on the ellipse, but he learned also of a treatise on motion. The Royal Society requested that Newton submit it to them, but the treatise that Newton set to work on was far more than the Royal Society or Halley dreamed of. As early as December 1684, Newton was writing to John Flamsteed for observations pertinent to Book III; already he had projected the work in its final dimensions. In the spring of 1687 he sent the manuscript of the last book to Halley, and in the summer the *Philosophiae Naturalis Principia Mathematica* was published.

The *Principia* did far more than announce the law of universal gravitation. A treatise on mechanics, terrestrial and celestial, it synthesized and completed the 17th-century science of mechanics and applied it to the solution of major questions hitherto unsolved. In Book I Newton enunciated the basic laws of mechanics as they are still taught. To the principle of inertia, conceived by Galileo and Descartes, he added the concept of force. Descartes's attempt to mechanize natural philosophy by the action of particles in motion did not satisfy Newton.

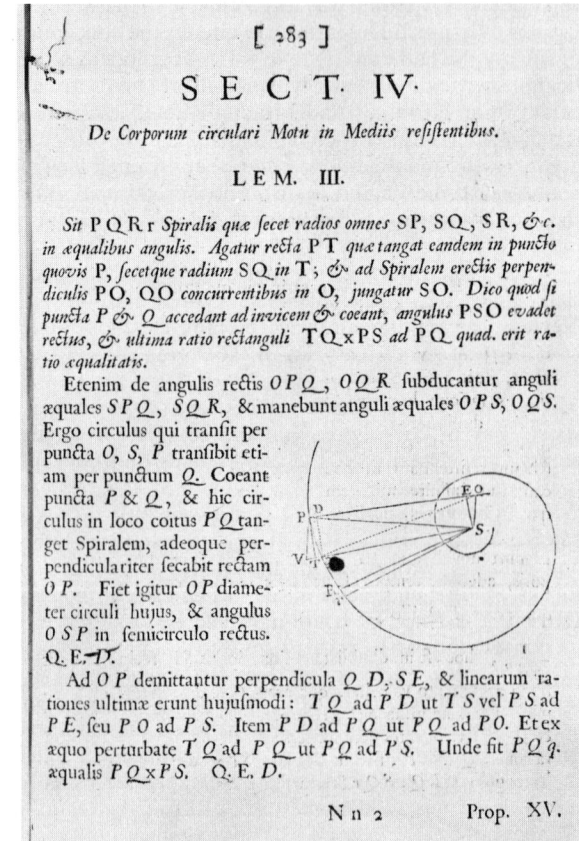

A page from the first edition of "Philosophiae Naturalis Principia Mathematica" (1687).

He returned rather to the work of Galileo, who had described motion in exact mathematical terms. The distinguishing feature of Newton's conception of force was its mathematical definition. Force is whatever causes a body to accelerate; it is measured by the product of the mass of the body and its acceleration. As a necessary correlative to the concept of force, the concept of mass, distinguished clearly from weight, also received its definition in the *Principia*. Book I of the *Principia* developed a theoretical science of mechanics for bodies moving in a vacuum. Book II considered movement in resisting media. Book III applied the principles arrived at to the description of the solar system, of comets, and of tides, and, by handling these phenomena successfully, further demonstrated the validity of the principles.

The concept of force was at once the central contribution of the *Principia* and the chief obstacle to its acceptance. The mechanical philosophy of the 17th century, which had its chief source in Descartes, explained phenomena in kinetic terms. The physical world was held to consist of matter in motion, and any explanation that could trace a phenomenon to the action of moving particles had reached the ultimate factor. Even in the hands of its master, Descartes, the mechanical philosophy descended all too easily to the invention of imaginary microscopic machines in which unseen cogs turned invisible wheels to grind out nature's phenomena. In Newton's philosophy the ultimate factor was dynamic rather than kinetic; forces replaced moving particles. Since force now acquired an exact mathematical expression, the change operated to make science yet more quantitative and less qualitative. Although Descartes had rejected qualitative Aristotelian philosophy to assert that matter and extension are equivalent, his vortices were described, and could only be described, in qualitative terms. The force of gravity, on the other hand, was a mathematical abstraction from the observed motions of planets and terrestrial bodies. The nature of gravity was a question that might be ignored or postponed; bodies move *as though* they attract each other with a force proportional to the product of their masses and inversely proportional to the square of the distance between their centers of gravity. Exact observation advanced side by side with exact calculation in Newtonian science.

In the discussions that followed the publication of the *Principia*, Newton insisted on the mathematical validity of gravity as a conclusion independent of the ontological status of gravity. In speculations, such as the "Queries" attached to the *Opticks*, he affirmed his belief in the existence of forces as more than mathematical abstractions. The "Hypothesis of Light" of 1675, still under the influence of the kinetic mechanical philosophy, attempted to reduce phenomena, including gravity, to the impact of ethereal particles. Newton had not yet arrived at a clear conception of force. Once he had, he either dispensed with an *ether in his speculations or recast the ether in a new mold. In the second English edition of the *Opticks* (1717), he traced gravity again to the operations of an ether, not a kinetic ether, however, in which the ultimate agent was a moving particle, but a dynamic ether composed of particles mutually repelling each other. Newton was convinced that particles of matter must also attract and repel each other with another range of forces distinct from the force of gravity. The cohesion of bodies, capillary action, the expansion of gases, various chemical reactions, these and other phenomena could be explained only by such forces. He did not, however, succeed in reducing them to exact quantitative treatment, and relegating their discussion to writings explicitly labeled as speculations, he bequeathed their investigation to his successors.

Mathematics; the Leibniz Controversy. The least fully published aspect of Newton's work was his mathematics, although it was to mathematics that he first directed the full strength of his genius, and in mathematics that he first reaped its harvest. By far the greatest bulk of his early manuscripts are devoted to mathematics. In 1665, the year of his bachelor's degree, he had already advanced beyond the first steps of differentiation and integration to which his predecessors had attained, and he had begun to elaborate the fluxional *calculus. By 1669 he had reduced his discoveries to a treatise, and early in the 1670s he was preparing to publish them. At this point the paper on colors in the *Philosophical Transactions* revealed the terrors involved in publication, and he drew back. Although the fact of his mathematical genius could not be kept secret, he did not publish his work until the *Opticks* in 1704, which contained two short treatises as an appendix. By that time the controversy with *Leibniz had already begun. While Newton had remained silent, Leibniz also had carried earlier discoveries forward into the calculus, and unlike Newton he began to publish in 1684. The world of mathematics learned the calculus from Leibniz; it adopted his method and his notation. By 1690 Newton wished to assert his claim. He furnished Wallis with the information about his method that appeared in volume II of Wallis's *Opera* in 1693. Finally, with the encouragement of others he plunged into the priority controversy. The assertion was made that Leibniz's work was so much plagiarism stemming from visits to England and correspondence with Newton in the 1670s. Leibniz and his followers replied in kind. Newton himself did not appear publicly in the battle, but he furnished the ammunition to combatants such as Keill and even helped to prepare their bombshells. When the Royal Society appointed a committee to investigate and report, Newton, the president of the society, silently prepared the report and had it published as the committee's impartial judgment. He even reviewed the report anonymously in the *Philosophical Transactions*.

The controversy plays an unhappy light upon Newton's character. It is not too much to say that it dominated the final 25 years of his life. Once aroused, he stalked Leibniz remorselessly, refusing to cease even when his antagonist died. He left behind an incredible stack of manuscripts in which he polished and polished again the bitter attacks on Leibniz that were to appear under the names of others. He was unable to banish the issue from his mind. When he tried to follow other studies, it intruded upon his consciousness by force; and any number of manuscripts on other topics were interrupted by furious paragraphs against the German mathematician. Nor was the priority dispute an isolated case in his life. Hooke, Lucas, and Flamsteed were all attacked with equal, if not equally sustained, fury. The publication of the paper on colors in 1672 and the discussion that followed revealed a deep, indeed an unappeasable, insecurity; when challenged in any way, Newton gave way to terror and could only lash out blindly in self-defense. The fundamental fact of his character was the tension between his genius and his inability to rest secure in it.

Newton's whole attention was not devoted to science. His interest in alchemy is well known, although it would appear that Newton himself considered it a study belonging to natural philosophy. He wrote extensively on theology, adopting a position not far removed from *theism. Newton rejected the doctrine of the Trinity as irrational and tried to define a natural theology from which revelation was removed. But he was a religious man and a firm believer in God, and he certainly regarded himself as a good Christian.

Newton believed that it appears "from phenomena that there is a being, incorporeal, living, intelligent, omnipresent" (*Opticks*, 3d ed., 1721, 344). In fact, God does not only conserve His creation, He actively intervenes to maintain it. In the *General Scholium* to the second edition of the *Principia*, Newton concluded that since God exists always and everywhere, He constitutes duration and space. Infinite space is the divine sensorium in which God perceives and comprehends all things. Yet Newton seems to avoid the extreme of *pantheism: for him, God constitutes absolute space and time, by His omnipresence and eternity, but He is not identified with them.

Newton's writings on apocalyptical prophecies were not mystical or chiliastic in any sense, but more exercises in deciphering cryptograms. Closely allied were his historical studies, which brought forth a new, though abortive, system of human chronology removing several centuries from the annals of man as they were then generally received.

Newton was twice elected to Parliament, representing the University of Cambridge. In 1695 he was appointed warden of the mint and 4 years later became master, a position which he held for life. He served as president of the Royal Society from 1703 until his death. Newton was knighted by Queen Anne on the occasion of her visit to Cambridge in 1705. He is buried in Westminster Abbey.

Influence. By common agreement Isaac Newton is included in any list of the half-dozen supreme geniuses of the human race. Attaining intellectual maturity just as the scientific revolution of the 17th century was approaching its culmination, he was able to digest the pioneering work of his predecessors in physics and mathematics, to carry it to a higher level of perfection, and to apply his discoveries to the solution of critical problems. In his work the scientific revolution attained a coherent defensible conception of nature as a whole which could, and did, supplant the much attacked Aristotelian philosophy; hence the phrase "Newtonian synthesis." More than any other man, Newton defined and demonstrated the ideal that scientific investigation continues to pursue today—the mathematical description of natural processes. Reacting against the Cartesian demand for necessary causes, he returned instead to a pattern already suggested by men such as Kepler and Galileo; and in the *Principia* he demonstrated the superior power of a mathematical science content to describe and not to explain. Although 2½ centuries of continued investigation have necessarily led modern science to a far more profound description of nature, science continues to work within the framework he defined. Nor has his influence been confined to the world of science. As the growth of natural science has been the supreme fact of modern intellectual history, so the work of Newton, its first great synthesis, may stand as its symbol in respect to other areas of thought. Through his works, a modified version of the Cartesian dualism of matter and spirit gained general currency. The central questions of modern philosophy, such as the problem of epistemology, have sprung from these metaphysical premises. The Christian religion, too, has felt his impact. Many factors have contributed to remove Christianity from the central role it once played in the life and thought of Western civilization, but among the intellectual factors none even approaches the impact of natural science. However little he may have desired that end himself, Newton contributed to it. No area of thought has stood immune to the influence of science. When one considers the role of technology in the world today and its dependence on science, one can legitimately extend Newton's influence beyond the intellectual sphere. Indeed, considering his work both in itself and as the leading representative of modern science as a whole, it can be affirmed that no other man has exercised a comparable influence on the course of modern civilization.

Bibliography: I. B. COHEN, *Franklin and Newton* (Philadelphia 1956), with Rosenberger, the best introduction to Newton. F. ROSENBERGER, *Isaac Newton und seine physikalischen Principien* (Leipzig 1895). A. KOYRÉ, "The Significance of the Newtonian Synthesis," *Archives Internationales d'Histoire des Sciences* 3.1 (1950) 291–311; "La Gravitation universelle, de Kepler à Newton," *ibid.* 4.2 (1951) 638–653. D. BREWSTER, *Memoirs of the Life, Writings, and Discoveries of Sir Isaac Newton* (Edinburgh 1855). L. T. MORE, *Isaac Newton: A Biography* (New York 1934). A. R. HALL, "Sir Isaac Newton's Note-book, 1661–65," CambHistJ 9 (1947–49) 239–250. A. R. and M. B. HALL, "Newton's Theory of Matter," Isis 51 (1960) 131–144. R. S. WESTFALL, "The Development of Newton's Theory of Color," *ibid.* 53 (1962) 339–358; *Science and Religion in Seventeenth Century England* (New Haven 1958). J. E. HOFMANN, *Studien zur Vorgeschichte des Prioritätstreites zwischen Leibniz und Newton und die Entdeckung der höheren Analysis*, AbhBerlAk Mathematisch-naturwissenschaftliche Klasse, No. 2 (1943). H. W. TURNBULL, *The Mathematical Discoveries of Newton* (London 1945). D. T. WHITESIDE, "Patterns of Mathematical Thought in the Later Seventeenth Century," *Archive for History of Exact Sciences* 1 (1960–62) 179–388. Copleston v.5. **Illustration credits:** Fig. 1, National Portrait Gallery, London; Fig. 2, Library of Congress.

[R. S. WESTFALL]

NEWTON, JOHN, military and civil engineer; b. Norfolk, Va., Aug. 24, 1823; d. New York City, May 1, 1895. He was converted to Catholicism in early manhood. Upon graduation from the U.S. Military Academy in 1842, Newton entered the Corps of Engineers, and aided in the construction of fortifications and harbor works along the Atlantic and Gulf Coasts. Before the Civil War, he had been chief engineer of the Department of Pennsylvania with the rank of captain. During the Civil War he became a commander of military operations rather than an engineer and, as a brigadier general (later major general) of volunteers, took part in numerous actions, including the command of the I Corps at Gettysburg. He was brevetted colonel, brigadier general, and major general in the Regular Army. After the war, he returned to the engineers as lieutenant colonel, and was responsible for the construction of the defenses of New York Harbor, improvements to the Hudson River, and the clearing of the underwater obstructions from Hell Gate Channel. After retirement as brigadier general (1887), Newton was appointed commissioner of public works in New York City, where he developed means of steam drilling for the clearance of rock pinnacles from New York Harbor. He became president of the Panama Railroad Company (1889), a position he retained until his death. He was a member of the National Academy of Science.

Bibliography: G. W. CULLUM, *Biographical Register of the Officers and Graduates of the U. S. Military Academy* (3d ed. rev. Boston 1891–). DAB 13:473–474.

[D. E. MARLOWE]

NEWTON COLLEGE OF THE SACRED HEART,

a liberal arts college for women in Newton, Mass. Newton was founded in 1946 by the Religious of the Sacred Heart at the request of Abp. (later Cardinal) Richard Cushing. In March of the same year, the College was chartered by the State of Massachusetts and empowered to grant all degrees except those of doctor of laws and doctor of medicine. The College, however, grants a B.A. degree only. It is accredited by the New England Association of Colleges and Secondary Schools and affiliated with The Catholic University of America. The board of trustees consists of members of the religious community who are assisted in the forming of financial and scholastic policy by a board of advisors made up of clergy and laymen. Administrative officers are the president, dean, treasurer, director of admissions, and registrar. In 1964 the faculty, which numbered 67, included 1 priest, 45 laymen, and 21 religious. They held 25 doctorates, 1 professional degree, and 29 master's degrees. Newton is small enough to maintain a sense of unity and large enough to stimulate diverse interests and opinions. In 1964 enrollment totaled 663 students with a faculty-student ratio of 1 to 10. The library housed 55,000 volumes and received 382 periodicals. Holdings increased at the rate of 5,000 volumes a year. Except for the contributed services of the religious community, the College is without endowment and relies on student fees for operating expenses.

The curriculum is based on the liberal arts, with primary importance attached to philosophy and theology. Special features include a 4-semester study of Western culture required for freshmen and sophomores, a lecture course in which faculty members from all departments cooperate with speakers from other campuses. Areas of special interest are political, natural, and social sciences; the arts; religion; and mathematics. Another special feature is a major in modern languages, which requires a 4-year study of one language, 3-year study of two other languages, and a basic knowledge of a fourth. The College has a cooperative program with Boston College, which offers its lecture and laboratory facilities for students taking courses in physics and mathematics. In the major fields lecture, seminar, and independent study programs are pursued at the discretion of the faculty members.

[C. E. MAGUIRE]

NEWTOWN MANOR SCHOOL.

About 1653 Ralph Crouch, a layman, established a school at Newtown, St. Mary's County, Md. Crouch, who had been in the Novitiate of the Society of Jesus at Watten, Belgium, for some time, around 1640 came to assist the Jesuit Fathers in the Maryland Mission. The school, which opened in 1653, was made possible by a provision in the will of Edward Cotten: "I doe give all my female cattle and their increase forever to be disposed of . . . unto charitable uses . . . the stocks to be preserved and the profits to be made use of to the use of a Schooll." He expressed his desire that "if they shall think convenient . . . the Schooll [shall] be kept at Newtown" (*Maryland Land Records,* Liber 1, 46–48). In a letter dated Sept. 4, 1662, Crouch stated, "I affirme boldly alsoe that on my part I did (as appeared to all my neighbors) as much as lay in mee, fulfill the will of the deceased [Cotten], in remoueing my teaching of schoole to the New Towne: and there was ready some years to teach, eyther Protestant or Catholikes" (*Archives of Maryland,* 49, 20–22).

Crouch returned to Europe in 1659 and was readmitted into the Jesuit Novitiate at Watten as a coadjutor brother. He died at Liège Nov. 18, 1679. The school, however, was still in operation in 1662, when it was mentioned in the trial of Francis Fitzherbert, SJ, and perhaps until at least 1667, since an item in the estate of Robert Cole, of Newtown, contains provision for "the Childrens Schooling" (*Archives of Maryland,* 41, 566–567; 57, 206).

In 1668 William Bretton and his wife Temperance sold Newtown Manor to the Jesuits, who in 1677 opened a school for humanities at the site. In a 1681 letter of the English Provincial, John Warner, reference is made to a school opened 4 years earlier under the direction of the Jesuits Francis Pennington and Michael Forster, who were assisted by Brothers Gregory Tuberville and John Berboel. That the School was more than a "Three R's Academy" is indicated by the fact that the pupils were admitted into European colleges. Two boys sent to St. Omers, Belgium, from this school in 1681 were Robert Brooke, the first native-born Marylander to become a Jesuit, and Thomas Gardiner. Thomas Hothersall, a Jesuit scholastic, who used the alias Slater in the Maryland Mission, taught grammar and humanities at the school from 1683 until his death in 1698. Although the school at Newtown Manor seems never to have fully developed, it kept alive the idea of an education under Catholic auspices and maintained, as it were, the franchise for later and fuller developments.

Bibliography: T. HUGHES, *History of the Society of Jesus in North America: Colonial and Federal,* 3 v. (New York 1907–17) v.2. J. M. DALEY, *Georgetown University: Origin and Early Years* (Washington 1957). E. W. BEITZELL, "William Bretton of Newtown Neck, St. Mary's County," *Maryland Historical Magazine* 50 (1955) 24–33; "Newtown Hundred," *ibid.* 51 (1956) 125–139.

[J. M. DALEY]

NIAGARA UNIVERSITY

A coeducational institution conducted by the Congregation of the Mission (*see* VINCENTIANS). The University was founded Nov. 21, 1856, by John Joseph *Lynch, CM (later Archbishop of Toronto, Canada) under the auspices of John *Timon, CM, first Bishop of Buffalo. Located first in Buffalo, N.Y., primarily as a seminary, it was transferred to its present site when Lynch purchased 300 acres on Monteagle Ridge near Niagara Falls; on May 1, 1857, with John Monaghan, CM, and six students, he moved into a brick inn that was on the property. In June 1861, the board of trustees incorporated the establishment under the title of the College and Seminary of Our Lady of Angels. Increasing enrollment caused the Vincentian Fathers to build an addition to the brick building, for which ground was broken on April 4, 1862. A fire, in which one seminarian lost his life, destroyed the main structure on Dec. 5,

1864. By 1868 a new building plant, begun in 1865, was completed. A large section of the first floor of the south wing became the library in 1923, and a small gymnasium was added to the north wing in 1927. Upon relocation of the seminary in the Diocese of Albany in 1961, the old seminary building was renamed Clet Hall and used as a dormitory.

Under Robert E. V. Rice, CM, fourth president of the College, the New York State Legislature granted a charter on April 20, 1863, authorizing the institution to confer baccalaureate degrees. An act of the legislature elevated the College to university status on Aug. 7, 1883. On the following October 10 the Niagara medical school opened in the city of Buffalo, followed by the establishment of a law school in the same city on Oct. 1, 1887. Both schools have since been amalgamated into the University of Buffalo.

Under its charter, Niagara conducts the Seminary of Our Lady of Angels; the colleges of arts and sciences, business administration, and nursing; the school of education, the graduate school, and the evening division, which offers associate degrees. Accredited by the Middle States Association of Colleges and Secondary Schools and the National League of Nursing, Niagara also holds membership in other prominent associations of higher education. In 1956 the Congregation of Seminaries and Universities issued a decree for Niagara's canonical erection as a pontifical university.

The University is administered by a president, executive vice president, vice president for financial affairs, academic vice president, deans of the various schools and departments, and a registrar. In 1964 the full-time institutional staff consisted of 42 priests, 4 sisters and 67 laymen. There were 36 part-time instructors. Of the staff, 36 held doctorates, 10 held professional degrees, and 69 had master's degrees. Total enrollment was 1,992 students. The University has approximately 6,000 alumni of whom about 1,200 are priests. Besides programs in liberal arts and sciences, the undergraduate college offers pre-law, pre-dental, and pre-engineering courses. It conducts a TV credit program leading to a degree and participates in the TV Continental Classroom. Advanced placement is open to superior students who qualify by examination. Graduate programs that lead to M.A. or M.Sc. degrees include chemistry, secondary education, English, guidance, history, natural sciences, and philosophy.

There are four campus publications. The oldest of these is the weekly *Niagara Index* (1870), a student publication. The third oldest Catholic college paper in the U.S., the *Crusader,* has been published each semester since 1935 by the seminarians of Our Lady of the Angels. It chronicles major activities of the seminary and publishes materials concerning the alumni and writings contributed by them. The *Aquila,* dating from 1937, is a literary quarterly containing short stories, poetry, and treatises on philosophy and science written by the students. An alumni magazine, the *Eagle,* is published three times a year.

On the campus, besides Clet Hall (1865), there are four dormitory buildings: Alumni Hall, which contains faculty offices and the College chapel (1888); Perboyre Hall (1909); the student center (1949); De Paul Hall of Science (1962); and the library (1964), which housed 65,000 volumes and received 537 periodicals.

[I. F. MOGAVERO]

NIBELUNGENLIED, THE

The earlier title of this *epic was probably *Der Nibelunge Nôt.* It was written about 1200 by an unidentified author, almost certainly an Austrian, and, earlier opinion notwithstanding, an educated man, probably a cleric under Wolfger von Ellenbrechtskirchen, Bishop of Passau (1191–1204). The epic contains thematic and stylistic echoes of medieval literature in German, French, and Latin, and frequently reflects the courtly attitudes of the Hohenstaufen era in which it received its final form.

Despite the author's attempt to create a courtly atmosphere, the *Nibelungenlied* is not a court epic, nor is it Christian, though it reflects some aspects of Christianity (e.g., the celebration of Mass). From the standpoint of content and ethics, it shows kinship with sagas, originating in the migration period (*c.* 375–500), and known in differing versions from the *Lieder-Edda,* the *Prosa-Edda,* the *Thidrekssaga,* and a 16th-century chapbook: *Das Lied vom hürnen Seyfried.* Thirty-three manuscripts of the *Nibelungenlied* are totally or partially extant; the earliest (not the original) dates from the beginning of the 13th century, the latest from the beginning of the 16th. All complete manuscripts except k contain a sequel in rhymed couplets, *Die Klage,* which is of later composition and inferior craftsmanship. The principal manuscripts are *A* (Munich), *B* (St. Gall, now generally considered closest in form and content to the lost original), and *C* (Donaueschingen).

Development of the Epic. Though popular in the Middle Ages, the epic disappeared until 1755, when the *C* manuscript was rediscovered at Hohenems in Vorarlberg. Much scholarship has been expended on attempts to trace the development of the *Nibelungenlied* from lay to epic. Wide acceptance has been accorded to Heusler's theory that it developed in several stages (none of them extant) from two separate alliterative lays of Frankish origin, a *Brünhildlied* and a *Burgundenlied,* dating from the 5th or 6th century. Adherents of this theory postulate as the immediate predecessor of the *Nibelungenlied* a hypothetical *ältere Nôt,* composed in Bavaria or Austria about 1160, and containing a brief version of the *Brünhildlied* as prelude to a longer account of the *Burgundenlied.* Attempts to find historical prototypes for the *Brünhildlied* have thus far been unconvincing, but there is no doubt as to the historical basis of the *Burgundenlied.* In 437, the Huns (not under Attila) destroyed the Burgundian kingdom on the Rhine, slaying the nobles; in 453, after his marriage to the Germanic maiden Hildico, Attila died. Legend quickly combined and distorted the two facts, asserting that Hildico had killed her husband to avenge her brothers. Centuries later, someone, perhaps the author of the *ältere Nôt,* united this legend with the account of Siegfried's death in the *Brünhildlied,* making the necessary changes: Kriemhild (Hildico) no longer kills her husband to avenge her brothers; she kills her brothers to avenge her first husband (Siegfried). Recent scholars have devoted their efforts with increasing frequency to aesthetic criticism, and a new appreciation of the literary merits of the epic and of the technical skill of its author is evolving.

The Story of the Epic. The 39 *Âventiuren* (cantos) of the *Nibelungenlied,* as we know it, are divided into two roughly equivalent parts: *Âventiuren* 1–19 describe the

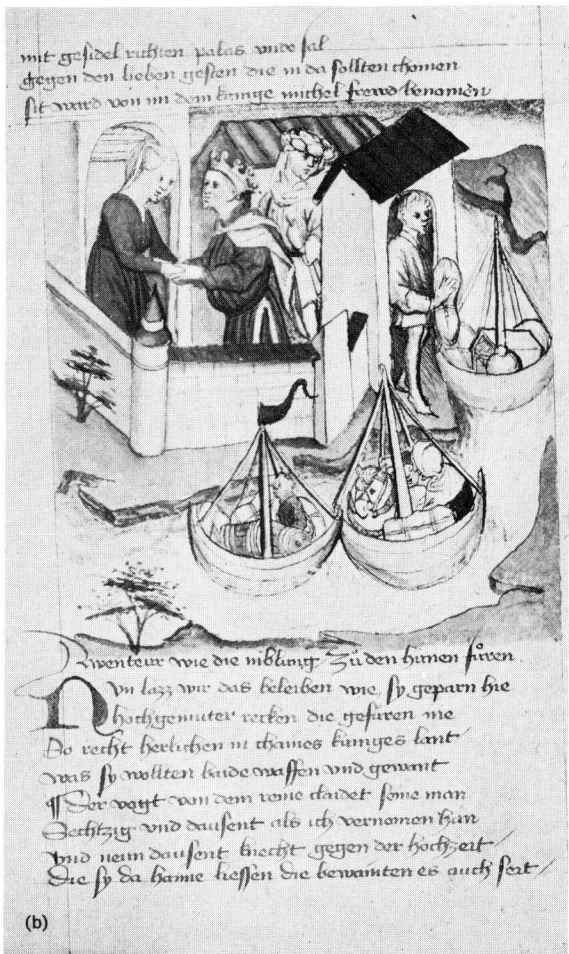

Miniature from the earliest known illustrated manuscript of the "Nibelungenlied," dated 1435 (Deutsche Staat. Bibl. Ms. Germ. fol. 855, folios 49 r. and 98 r.). (a) An incident in Âventiure 12: messengers returning to the Burgundian court at Worms after having invited Siegfried and Brünhild to a festival. (b) A moment in Âventiure 25: farewells at the Burgundian court as the Kings and their retinue leave for Etzel's court.

death of Siegfried; Âventiuren 20–39, the destruction of the Burgundians. The story is as follows. At Worms, Kriemhild, sister of the Burgundian Kings Gunther, Gernot, and Giselher, is wooed by Siegfried of Xanten, who has slain a dragon, seized its treasure, and, except for one spot on his back, been made invulnerable by its blood. Pretending to be Gunther's vassal, Siegfried, rendered invisible by the *Tarnkappe*, performs in his stead three feats of skill that Brünhild of Iceland has made the conditions of marriage. He thereby wins Brünhild for Gunther, and Kriemhild for himself. After the double wedding, Brünhild, refusing to submit to Gunther, is again subdued by an invisible Siegfried, who takes her ring and girdle and gives them to Kriemhild. Siegfried and Kriemhild depart for Xanten, returning to Worms 10 years later at Brünhild's insistence. Kriemhild quarrels over precedence with Brünhild, who considers her the wife of Gunther's vassal. Indignant, Kriemhild reveals that it was Siegfried, not Gunther, who subdued Brünhild, and shows the ring in proof. To avenge Brünhild, Hagen, Gunther's vassal, kills Siegfried, having first, through deceit, learned from Kriemhild the secret of his vulnerability. Kriemhild swears vengeance. Fearing that she will use Siegfried's treasure to this end, Hagen sinks it in the Rhine.

Part two begins when Rüdeger requests Kriemhild's hand for Etzel, King of the Huns. Kriemhild accepts, viewing the marriage as a first step toward vengeance. Thirteen years later, she invites her kinsmen to visit her at Etzel's court. Shortly after their arrival, they are attacked by Kriemhild's henchmen, with fearful losses on both sides. When only the principals are left, Dietrich von Bern conquers Gunther and Hagen, and leads them in fetters to Kriemhild. She has Gunther slain, and herself strikes off Hagen's head when he refuses to reveal the location of her sunken treasure. The poem ends when Kriemhild is slain by Hildebrand, who is Dietrich's vassal.

See also LITERATURE, ORAL TRANSMISSION OF; SAGA.

Bibliography: *Das Nibelungenlied,* ed. H. DE BOOR (Bremen 1959) text of *B* MS. *The Song of the Nibelungs,* tr. F. G. RYDER (Detroit 1962). A. HEUSLER, *Nibelungensage und Nibelungenlied* (5th ed. Dortmund 1955). F. W. PANZER, *Das Nibelungenlied: Entstehung und Gestalt* (Stuttgart 1955) good general introduction; nothing comparable in English. M. THORP, *Study of the Nibelungenlied* (Oxford 1940) history of research, 1775–1937. B. WACHINGER, *Studien zum Nibelungenlied* (Tübingen 1960). T. ABELING, *Das Nibelungenlied und seine Literatur* (Leipzig 1907) bibliography. W. KROGMANN and U. PRETZEL, *Bibliographie zum Nibelungenlied und zur Klage* (2d ed. Hamburg 1959). **Illustration credit:** Deutsche Staatsbibliothek, Berlin.

[M. F. MC CARTHY]

NICAEA I, COUNCIL OF

The first general council of the Christian Church, convoked by Emperor *Constantine I, probably toward the close of 324, and lasted from May 20 or June 19 to *c.* Aug. 25, 325.

Background. After his victory over Licinius (September 324), Constantine, Emperor of the East, found his provinces seriously disturbed by religious controversy, spearheaded by the Alexandrian priest *Arius and his bishop, *Alexander. The dissension apparently began about the year 318, or somewhat later, when Arius was publicly rebuked by Bishop Alexander for teaching that the Word was not coeternal with the Father but had a beginning of existence; otherwise, Arius said, there would be two "unbegotten" principles. If, then, the Word had a beginning, He could not be of the same nature as the Father; He must, like other creatures, have been made from nothing. Nor can He be called the true and natural Son of God; at best He is the adopted Son. It follows that the Word, as a creature, is in fact the first and most perfect of creatures and is subject to change and sin. He did save mankind, but because He was utterly faithful to God's grace. Arius seems to have denied that the Incarnate Word had a human soul. The deep roots of his doctrine are discoverable in his master, *Lucian of Antioch, and it is understandable that Arius's fellow disciples at Antioch, called Collucianists were among the first fervid promoters of *Arianism.

Unwilling to change his position, Arius had to appear before a synod of almost 100 bishops of Egypt and Libya convoked by Bp. Alexander *c.* 320. Remaining unmoved, he was excommunicated by the synod, as were his followers, Bps. Secundus of Ptolemaïs and Theonas of Marmarica, and some of the Alexandrian clergy and virgins. As usual, Alexander sent encyclical letters in the synod's name to the more distinguished bishops, explaining and refuting the errors of Arius, notifying them of his excommunication and requesting them to avoid communion with him. These letters affirm, especially on the basis of John ch. 1, that the Word is coeternal with the Father, truly God, God's only begotten Son.

Expelled from Alexandria, Arius went to Coelesyria to fellow disciples, prominent among whom were Paulinus of Tyre and Theonas of Laodicea. *Eusebius of Caesarea gave him a friendly welcome. In Nicomedia, whose bishop, *Eusebius, lent him unfailing support, he wrote the *Thalia* (Banquet), a long rhapsody, at least partly in metric form, in which he incorporated his theological ideas. With his growing number of supporters he held a synod, which issued encyclical letters against Alexander. This situation continued during the persecution waged by Licinius against the Christians (321–324) and was of serious concern to his conqueror, Constantine.

Captivated by Christianity, Constantine wanted to give it the protection of the state; for, in line with the old Roman idea, he regarded himself as Pontifex Maximus of Christianity, "bishop in matters external" (*Vita Const.* 4.24). As such, he thought it his task to settle a controversy that was upsetting the politico-religious unity of his Christian empire. Theologically incompetent despite the assistance of his adviser Bishop *Hosius of Córdoba, Constantine wrote to Alexander and Arius enjoining silence in this nuanced matter, which seemed to him to have no relation to Christian dogma. Hosius, who took the Emperor's letter to Alexander, returned unsuccessful. When another synod in Antioch late in 324 failed to effect the desired unity, the Emperor decided to settle the controversy by a general synod of the more important bishops of the world. He hoped that such a synod would also solve the paschal controversy concerning the date of *Easter. There were still *Quartodecimans who followed Jewish custom; and although most of the bishops celebrated Easter on Sunday in honor of the Resurrection, even some of these, to determine the lunar cycle, consulted the Jews, who did not follow the astronomical computation as did the Christian churches. Constantine wanted to eliminate these differences by establishing the date of Easter independently of the Jews.

The Council. The Council opened at Nicaea in Bithynia (modern İznik, northwestern Turkey in Asia), in Constantine's palace, with an address by the Emperor. About 300 bishops were present (the number 318 reported by *Ambrose of Milan and *Hilary of Poitiers is symbolic: cf. the 318 servants of Abraham, Gn 14.14), and almost all were from the eastern half of the Empire: more than 100 came from Asia Minor, about 30 from Syria-Phoenicia, fewer than 20 from Palestine and Egypt. Prominent figures were Hosius of Córdoba (who presided with the delegates of Pope Sylvester, the Roman priests Vitus and Vincentius), Alexander of Alexandria (accompanied by his secretary and future successor, the deacon Athanasius), *Eustathius of Antioch, *Marcellus of Ancyra, Eusebius of Caesarea in Palestine, Leontius of Caesarea in Cappadocia, *Macarius of Jerusalem, Eusebius of Nicomedia, Caecilianus of Carthage, and some "confessors" who had suffered in the persecution of Licinius. In the beginning at least, Constantine was honorary president and even intervened to ensure peaceful discussion.

Nave and apse of Hagia Sophia in Nicaea.

Doctrinal Definition. Doctrinal issues were the Council's first concern. Arian-minded bishops proposed a formula of faith (contents not extant) that was indignantly rejected by the vast majority. Then Eusebius of Caesarea proposed the baptismal creed of his own Church, the oldest eastern creed now known. Its orthodoxy gained it general approval, but a majority of the bishops insisted on certain additions that would counter the Arian errors more clearly and explicitly. The first, ἐκ τῆς οὐσίας τοῦ πατρός, directly contradicted the Arian affirmation that the Son, not genuinely begotten, did not proceed from the very essence, or nature, of the Father, but only by the Father's will, like other creatures. The second addition, γεννηθέντα οὐ ποιηθένα, confronted Arius's statement that the Son is not so by nature, but is "made" by the Father. The third addition, ὁμοούσιον τῷ πατρί, comprised the most significant word of the creed, the sword of division for decades after the Council.

Not a Biblical word, ὁμοούσιος appears for the first time in Gnostic literature: they are ὁμοούσιοι who belong to the same category of nature. Since in strict generation the son has the same nature as his father, there is always ὁμοουσία here; this the Arians denied to the Word with understandable logic because they denied His generation. The word ὁμοουσία affirms that the Word is God as the Father is God, and this because He is the Father's true Son. And if this affirmation is linked with the first article of the creed, "one God Father," it is clear that the Nicene Creed proclaims numerical identity of the Father's nature and the Son's. The creed does no more than mention the Third Person, for the divinity of the Spirit was not at issue. (*See* HOMOOUSIOS.)

The Nicene Creed was the first dogmatic definition of the Christian Church and through the ages has served as a tessera of orthodoxy. Almost all the expressions used are scriptural, with the addition of certain words that are philosophical in origin. The meaning of Scripture is made clear in the light of tradition. The Son's divinity in its strict sense is defined.

Easter Question and Canons. As for Easter, the Fathers decreed (1) that all Christians should observe it on the same day, (2) that Jewish customs should not be followed, and (3) that the practice of the West, of Egypt, and of other Churches should remain in force, namely, of celebrating Easter on the Sunday following the first full moon after the vernal equinox.

Nicaea promulgated 20 disciplinary decrees (cf. Con OecDecr 5–15). In later times certain Syriac and Arabic canons (*pseudonicaeni*) were falsely attributed to the Council. Canons 15 and 16 forbid bishops, priests, and deacons to involve themselves in the affairs of another diocese or locality. Canon 4 orders that bishops be appointed by all the other bishops of the province, and in case of difficulty, by at least three; the appointment was to be ratified by the metropolitan bishop. Canon 5 declares that provincial synods are to be held twice a year, presumably under the metropolitan, to examine excommunications inflicted by bishops. The famous canons 6 and 7 ratify the traditional prerogatives of Eastern Churches.

The bishop of Alexandria has power over Egypt, Libya, and Pentapolis, after the fashion of Rome's quasi-patriarchal authority. Here is the seed of the patriarchate: the patriarch has under him all the metropolitans of the entire region. The age-old privileges of Antioch, Aelia (rebuilt as Jerusalem), and other Churches are ratified, but it is not clear whether the privileges in question are merely honorary.

Some canons have to do with the dignity of the clergy: the ordination of eunuchs (c.1), of those insufficiently tested since Baptism or proved unworthy (c.2), of those who have denied the faith in persecution (c.10), and cohabitation of clerics with other than relatives or women beyond suspicion (c.3). Canon 13 confirms the ancient practice of giving Communion to penitents at the hour of death. A twofold criterion is set up for the admission of heretics (c.19): those who have not erred on the doctrine of the Trinity, such as the Novatians, are to be reconciled without repetition of their Baptism; the followers of *Paul of Samosata, however, are to be rebaptized, since it is not clear that they confess the Trinity. Deacons are warned (c.18) to give precedence to bishops and priests. On Sundays and the days of Pentecost, the faithful are to stand for the liturgy, not kneel (c.20).

Aftermath. It is not certain how long the Council lasted, though it was probably for several weeks, at the close of which Constantine bade the fathers farewell. Only two bishops, Secundus of Ptolemaïs and Theonas of Marmarica, refused to sign the creed and the accompanying anathema. With Arius, they were exiled to Illyricum. Constantine confirmed the decrees of Nicaea, proclaimed them laws of the Empire, and wrote a letter to the bishops of Alexandria and other absent bishops expressing his joy that harmony in faith had been achieved. While Constantine lived, none of the friends of Arius who were dissatisfied with the doctrine of Nicaea dared to attack the Symbol directly. The Eusebians (Eusebius of Nicomedia and his supporters) maneuvered rather to remove the more influential representatives of Nicaea from the scene by political strategy; conspicuous proof of their success is discoverable in the exiling of Eustathius of Antioch and Athanasius even under Constantine.

Of the Acts of the Council, there are preserved only the Symbol with the added anathema against the Arians, the disciplinary canons, lists of the bishops in attendance (extant in different languages and not always consistent), and the synodal letter notifying the Alexandrian Church of the excommunication of Arius and his followers.

Although Nicaea's judgment on Arianism was clear and conclusive, it was a sign of contradiction and cause of serious division in the East until 381, primarily because of the word ὁμοούσιος. In their opposition to the Council and to the expression, Arians and Semi-Arians were in agreement.

The so-called *Acta* of Nicaea used by Gelasius of Cyzicus (PG 85:1191–1360) and the Coptic Acts edited by E. Revillout, *Le concile de Nicée d'après les textes coptes et les diverses collections canoniques* (2 v. Paris 1876, 1898), are apparently spurious. The extant documents of Nicaea have been edited by H. G. Opitz, *Athanasius Werke* 3.1 (Berlin-Leipzig 1934). For the canons, see Hefele-Leclercq 1.2:528–620, and ConOecDecr v.5–15; for the list of bishops, H. Gelzer, H. Hilgenfeld, and O. Cuntz, *Patrum nicaenorum nomina* (Leipzig 1898), and E. Honigmann, "Une liste inédite des Pères de Nicée," *Byzantion* 20 (1950) 63–71; for the decree on Easter, Pitra IurEccl 1:435–436, and H. Leclercq, DACL 13.2:1549.

Bibliography: Hefele-Leclercq 1.1:335–632. G. BARDY, Fliche-Martin 3:69–176. M. GOEMANS, *Het algemeen concilie in de vierde eeuw* (Nijmegen 1945), ch. 2–3. I. ORTIZ DE URBINA, *Nicée et Constantinople* (Paris 1963); *El símbolo niceno* (Madrid 1947). V. C. DE CLERCQ, *Ossius of Cordova* (Washington 1954). J. N. D. KELLY, *Early Christian Creeds* (2d ed. New York 1960) 205–230. **Illustration credit:** National Council of Catholic Men.

[I. ORTIZ DE URBINA]

NICAEA II, COUNCIL OF

The seventh ecumenical council of the Church, and the last to be recognized by the Eastern Church, August to October 787.

History. When Emperor Leo IV died prematurely on Sept. 8, 780, any hope of ever restoring the veneration of *images—a practice forbidden in Byzantium for more than a century and a half—appeared impossible. The entire state machinery and the high offices of the Church were in the hands of men committed to *iconoclasm; the army, which Emperor *Constantine V Copronymos, the most passionate iconoclast of all, had so often led to victory, remained jealously devoted to his memory. Yet when Empress *Irene assumed power in 780 in the name of her son, Constantine VI, who was still a minor, she was determined to restore the veneration of icons throughout the Empire. A plot, vigorously repressed, enabled her to get rid of ministers and other personages hostile to iconoduly. She then contacted Pope *Adrian I (*sacra* of Aug. 29, 784), informing him of the intention of the Byzantine government to convoke a general *council and requesting him to send duly empowered representatives. Furthermore, to remove the main obstacle to such a council, Patriarch *Paul IV was replaced as patriarch by the Empress's own secretary, *Tarasius.

The order convoking the council was promulgated throughout the Eastern Empire at the beginning of 786. Rome had welcomed this step on the part of the Greeks and sent a delegation of two members of the Roman clergy: a secular cleric and a religious, namely, the archpriest Peter and the hegumen Peter of the Greek monastery of San Saba. There were no other representatives from the West. The Byzantine episcopate sent 350 of its members. On Aug. 1, 786, the Council opened in Constantinople itself, in the basilica of the Holy Apostles, in the presence of the sovereigns, but elements of the imperial guard broke into the church, forcing the Council's temporary dissolution. But Prime Minister Stavrakios transferred or disbanded all regiments that had mutinied, and the Empress transferred the Council to Nicaea in Bithynia, where it opened on Sept. 24, 787.

The sessions, eight in all, lasted 3 weeks, and all except the last were held at the church of Hagia Sophia in Nicaea. Patriarch Tarasius, not the papal legates, presided, but the legates signed all documents first and were always listed first.

The Council had to decide immediately about the iconoclastic bishops, of whom many were present. Could the Council recognize their right to be seated? It took the first three sessions to dispose of this burning question, for the monks—numerous and active—opposed with determination the Council's decision to recognize the iconoclasts once they had abjured their heresy before the assembly. The next two sessions (Oct. 1 and 4) established the legitimacy of the veneration of icons through an examination of scriptural and patristic tradition. The sixth session (Oct. 5 and 6) dealt with Rome's demand that the great synod held at Hiereia in 754 be condemned. The seventh session (Oct. 13) climaxed debate by fixing the terms of the dogmatic decree ($\H{o}\rho o\varsigma$) that proclaimed belief in the efficacy of the intercession of *saints, in the legitimacy of the veneration of icons or statues, i.e., veneration or relative cult as opposed to the cult of latria (*see* WORSHIP) which is the highest adoration, and due God alone. Twenty-two disciplinary canons were appended to this dogmatic definition. The Empress—not without ulterior political motives—wished to associate the people of the capital city with the decisions of the Council and therefore decided to close the Council by a sort of apotheosis, having all the fathers come to Constantinople for an eighth session in the Magnaura palace itself. On October 23 all gathered before the sovereign, who addressed the assembly herself and then had the decree of faith proclaimed; she then signed it, even before her son, Constantine VI, and the Roman legates. The *Acta* of the Council became the law of the state; their strict enforcement was to assure the Byzantine Church, despite some harassment by the old heresy, a respite of some 30 years. The Council thus marked the end of the first period of iconoclasm.

Acts of the Council. Though the East was virtually restored to peace by the Council, the appearance of the *Acta* in the West caused considerable uproar. It is not very probable that the actual text of the proceedings had been submitted to Pope Adrian I for approval, even though Patriarch Tarasius had reported to him on what had transpired at the Council. The *Acta* themselves reached the Holy See in a translation containing grave errors on essential points, even going so far as to represent the fathers of Nicaea as saying the opposite of what they had actually defined. *Charlemagne, kept in ignorance of what had occurred in the East and still smarting from the wound to his self-esteem caused by the rupture of the engagement of his daughter Rotrude with the young Emperor Constantine VI, submitted to the theologians of his court, including *Alcuin, the translation of the *Acta* that the Pope had sent him. The astonishment of his experts was so great that the Monarch—who was more interested in condemning the Byzantine Emperor, whose rank and title within Christendom he coveted—commissioned a refutation in a work called the *Capitulare de imaginibus*, or the *Libri Carolini*. Charlemagne then convened a great council at Frankfurt of 350 bishops who, in the presence of papal legates, condemned the Council of Nicaea. A special embassy brought to Rome an extract of the *Libri Carolini*, as well as a letter in which Charlemagne adjured the Pope to deny approval of the Council of Nicaea. In 794 the Pope replied in a memorandum that refuted in detail the complaints of the Frankish court, though with moderation. But the Holy See still did not give immediate approval to the *Acta* in question, for Constantinople refused to give Rome satisfaction in other matters, e.g., restitution to Rome of those Italian and Illyrian territories and patrimonies transferred to the Patriarchate of *Constantinople by Emperor Leo III in 733. Even in the East the Council was not recognized until 843; its ecumenical status was not actually confirmed until the Council of *Constantinople IV in 869–870. Moreover, the Patriarch *Photius was able to complain in the synod of 879–880 that Rome had still not recognized its authority. However, Nicaea II was recognized almost immediately by the legates at the session of Jan. 26, 880, and soon after by Pope *John VIII in person, as a result of his reconciliation with Photius. The insertion of the Council of Nicaea II, after 880, into the formula of the papal profession of faith was the Western Church's seal of recognition of its ecumenical status.

Bibliography: Sources. Mansi 12:991–1154; 13:1, for the Acts. *Ibid.* 12:951–990; 13:759–820, for various documents. Jaffé E 2448, 2483, pontifical letters. Duchesne LP 1:486–523, for Pope Adrian I. Dölger Reg 341–347, 349, imperial letters. Grumel Reg 351–359, patriarchal Acts.
  Literature. Hefele-Leclercq 3.2:601–798. H. LECLERCQ, DACL 7:263–267. G. FRITZ, DTC 11.1:417–441; Tables générales 665–666. G. OSTROGORSKY, "Rom und Byzanz im Kampfe um die Bilderverehrung. Papst Hadrian I. und das VII. Oekumenische Konzil von Nikäa," *Seminarium Kondakovianum* 6 (1933) 73–87. Ostrogorsky 156–165. Fliche-Martin 6:107–120. E. HAMMERSCHMIDT, "Eine Definition von *Hypostasis* und *Ousia* während des VII. Allgemeinen Konzils," *Ostkirchliche Studien* 5 (1956) 52–55. P. VAN DEN VEN, "La Patristique et l'hagiographie au concile de Nicée de 787," *Byzantion* 25–27 (1955–57) 325–362. L. USPENSKIJ, "Sedmoj vselenskij sobor i dogmat ob ikonopočitanii [The 7th ecumenical council and the dogma of the cult of images]," *Zurnal Moskovskoj Patriarchii* fasc. 12 (1958) 40–48, in Russian. R. BÄUMER, LexThK² 7:967–968. J. M. A. SALLES-DABADIE, *Les Conciles oecuméniques dans l'histoire* (Geneva 1962). On the *Libri Carolini.* K. HAMPE, "Hadrians I. Vertheidigung der zweiten nicaenischen Synode gegen die Angriffe Karls des Grossen," NeuesArch 21 (1895) 83–113. G. HOCQUARD, *Catholicisme* 2:586–588. H. SCHADE, "Die *Libri Carolini* und ihrer Stellung zum Bild," ZKathTh 79 (1957) 69–78. G. HAENDLER, *Epochen karolingischer Theologie* (Theologische Arbeiten 10; Berlin 1958). K. BAUS, LexThK² 6:1020–21.

[V. LAURENT]

NICARAGUA

Central American republic located approximately 375 miles from the Panama Canal and 375 miles from Mexico, bounded on the north by Honduras, on the south by Costa Rica, on the east by the Atlantic Ocean, and on the west by the Pacific Ocean. It has an area of about 57,145 square miles and a population of about 1,600,000. The population is concentrated along the Pacific coast; the major cities are Managua, León, and

ECCLESIASTICAL NICARAGUA, 1964
105 Parishes: 1,239,280 Catholics
‡ Archbishopric   ⊕ Bishopric
● Vicariate Apostolic or Prelacy nullius
The capital of Nicaragua is Managua.

Granada, and the chief port is Corinto. The climate is generally hot and humid except in the mountainous region. Nicaragua has two great lakes and a number of rivers that flow into the Atlantic. The volcanic chain near the Pacific coast is always active but not dangerously so. Nicaragua is an agricultural and cattle-raising country whose exports are cotton, coffee, sugar, timber, and meat; it also has gold and copper mines.

History. Christopher Columbus, on his fourth voyage to the New World, discovered the Atlantic portion of the territory on Sept. 12, 1502; Gil González d'Avila discovered the Pacific portion 20 years later. In 1524 the conquest was accomplished by Hernández de Córdoba, who founded the cities of Granada and León. The monetary unit of the country, the cordoba, was named after him. During the colonial period Nicaragua suffered from the depredations of English pirates; in defense against them Rafaela Herrera became a national heroine.

Nicaragua formed a part of the Captaincy General of Guatemala until 1821, when along with the rest of the provinces of Central America (except Chiapas, which was annexed to Mexico), it became independent and joined the United Provinces of Central America. In 1836 the federal pact was dissolved, and after many vicissitudes Nicaragua became an independent republic in 1845. In 1855 it was invaded by William Walker, who, after seizing the country, was driven out by Nicaraguan and Central American troops. Four years later, when his new attempt to invade Central America failed, Walker was shot in Honduras.

The country enjoyed a peaceful period under the Conservative rule until 1893, when a *coup d'état* put in power Gen. José Santos Zelaya, a man of liberal ideas, educated in Europe. Despite the beneficial reforms that he introduced into the country, he governed it for 17 years with a dictatorial iron hand. Upon Zelaya's fall, Nicaragua went through another convulsive period until a new armed rebellion brought the Liberals back to power in 1929. The U.S. played an important role in Nicaraguan politics from 1909 until the occupation forces were finally withdrawn in 1933. In 1937 Anastasio Somoza gained dictatorial power and held it to his death in 1956. Since then Nicaragua has enjoyed a period of respite or perhaps of transition.

Christianization and the Religious Orders. The people of Nicaragua are almost all Christians, and the majority are Catholic. Catholicism came to Nicaragua with the discovery and was established with the conquest. The first chaplain arrived with Gil González d'Avila in 1522, and in 1524 the first Franciscan church was founded in Granada. Bartolomé de *Las Casas first visited Nicaragua in 1530 and returned in 1532 with four other Dominicans to found the convent of San Pablo at the request of Bishop Osorio. During the colonial period the Jesuits also established themselves in Nicaragua. After independence, and particularly in the 20th century, the number of religious orders in the country multiplied. Among them are the Spanish Franciscans, Italian Franciscans, Dominicans, Jesuits, Capuchins, Salesians, Christian Brothers, Redemptorists, Piarists, Benedictines, Augustinian Recollects, and the order of Jesús Divino Obrero, which runs a reformatory in Managua. Secular priests from Canada have charge of the national seminary, which was originally founded by the Dominicans in León and transferred to the capital in 1950. The

Atlantic coast remains a mission area, and there the Capuchins maintain churches, schools, and a seminary.

Religious orders of women in Nicaragua include four native congregations founded since 1950: the Doctrineras, the Siervas Misioneras de Cristo Rey, the Misioneras Catequistas Lumen Criste, and the Siervas de Nuestro Señor. Among the foreign congregations serving in Nicaragua are the Missionaries of the Sacred Heart, Sisters of the Assumption, Josephites, Sisters of Charity of the Blessed Virgin of Mercy, Oblate Sisters of Divine Love, Oblates of the Sacred Hearts, Franciscans, and others. They serve in primary and secondary schools, care for the seminary, an orphanage, a sanitarium, and almost all the hospitals located in the country.

Ecclesiastical Organization. In 1527 the first bishop was named for the province of Nicaragua. However, Fray Pedro de Zúñiga died in Cádiz before setting out for his see and was succeeded by Diego Álvarez de Osorio, who took possession of the bishopric in León in 1532. Since that time the area of Nicaragua has been divided into one archbishopric, five dioceses, and one vicariate apostolic. The lack of vocations is a major problem for the Church in Nicaragua. Much hope is placed in the seminary, which has increased its student body to about 100.

Educational and Charitable Institutions. The religious orders have been active in establishing educational institutions in the country. The Jesuits, Salesians, Christian Brothers, and Piarists have schools for both primary and secondary education. In 1960 the Jesuits founded in Managua the first Catholic university in Central America, the Universidad Centroamericana. It includes the following professional faculties: civil engineering, electrical engineering, veterinary medicine, law, and business administration. There is also a national university in León.

Among the charitable institutions operating in Nicaragua are Cáritas, which is supported from the U.S.; Catholic Action, which in addition to spiritual work runs a dispensary for poor children; and the Congregación Mariana, which does catechetical work. The Legion of Mary also functions in the area.

There are four Catholic presses: that of the archdiocese, of the Salesians in Granada, the reformatory in Managua, and the Christian Brothers in León. There are two Catholic weeklies: *El Observador* in Managua and *El Trabajador* in Granada. Managua also has a Catholic radio station.

The Modern Church. There is complete separation between Church and State in Nicaragua, and cordial relations are maintained between them. The Holy See maintains as its representative to the government an apostolic nuncio who is considered by the other ambassadors as permanent dean of the diplomatic corps. The country has a number of shrines to which pilgrimages are made: Nuestro Señor de Esquipulas in La Conquista, Carazo; San Jerónimo in Masaya; Santo Domingo de Guzmán in Managua; La Vírgen de la Inmaculada Concepción in El Viejo, Chinandega; Nuestro Señor de Esquipulas in El Sauce, León; and La Vírgen de la Purísima Concepción in Granada.

Protestantism was introduced along the Atlantic coast in mid-19th century by Englishmen from Jamaica. Not until the 20th century did Catholic missionaries begin intensive work in that area. Protestant sects began their penetration of the Pacific area after World War I and have increased their activities since 1945. The most active groups are Baptists, Evangelists, Seventh-day Adventists, Mormons, Anglicans, and Moravians.

Important Figures. Outstanding among the Nicaraguan hierarchy have been Bishop *Pereira y Castellón of León, Bishop Lezcano y Ortega, first archbishop of Managua, and Azarías Pallais (d. 1957), known for his scholarship and sanctity. In the literary world Rubén *Darío achieved worldwide fame as a poet and a linguist. Salomón de la Selva (1893–1958) was another famous poet, as were Alfonso Cortés Azarías Pallais, Pablo Antonio Cuadra, Joaquín Pasos (1915–47), Ernesto Mejía Sánchez, Carlos Martínez Rivas, Ernesto Cardenal, Fernando Silva, Ernesto Gutiérrez, and Eduardo Zepeda Henríques, all in the 20th century. A literary movement begun in Nicaragua in 1928 and called "Vanguardia," was led by José Coronel Urtecho and Luis Alberto Cabrales.

Bibliography: O. CUADRA DOWNING, ed., *Nueva poesía nicaragüense* (Madrid 1949). J. D. GÁMEZ, *Historia de Nicaragua* (Managua 1889; 2d ed. Madrid 1955).

[E. GUTIÉRREZ]

NICCOLÒ DI BARTOLOMMEO DA FOGGIA,

Italian Romanesque sculptor active in 1272 in Apulia. His only documented work, a pulpit at Ravello, marks the last phase of *Romanesque art in Apulia and parallels the pulpits done in Tuscany by the most important sculptor from southern Italy, Niccolò *Pisano. Niccolò, the son of Bartolomaneo of Foggia and therefore probably born in that town, signed the marble and mosaic pulpit of the cathedral of San Pantaleone, Ravello, with the inscription, "Ego Nicolaus de Bartholomeo de Fogia marmorarius hoc opus feci," naming as donors the wealthy patricians Nicola Rufolo and his wife, Sigilgaita della Marra. The pulpit is of the shape traditional in southern Italy, a rectangular structure carried on six columns that rest on the backs of lions. A bust of the Virgin and Child and heraldic birds and beasts of Byzantine inspiration executed in mosaic on a gold ground, and Cosmatesque inlay, form a colorful contrast to the controlled foliate decoration, sculptured in marble, that borders the polychrome panels or springs luxuriantly from the capitals. The most unusual feature of the pulpit is the bust of a crowned woman, sculptured in the round, who smiles as she gazes out from the upper edge of the pulpit; it has been variously identified as a portrait of Sigilgaita in Byzantine dress or as a personification of the Church. A parallel in the Exultet Roll of Gaeta may be cited for the latter interpretation, as also a more idealized bust of a woman from the pulpit at Scala near Ravello. That the Ravello head was intended for its present position is suggested by the form of the crown, which resembles the foliate ornament on the pulpit. Two relief busts are placed within the spandrels of the trefoil arch forming the entrance to the pulpit and immediately below the crowned head. These seem to be influenced by classical coins or cameos. Beneath the reading desk of the pulpit are two grinning heads of a man and woman. The Ravello pulpit reveals the hand of an artist brought up within the circle of the court of Frederick II, whose art retains its classicizing, proto-Renaissance dignity only

Niccolò di Bartolommeo da Foggia, pulpit in the cathedral at Ravello, Italy, signed and dated 1272.

in the enigmatic crowned head, lapsing into Romanesque idiom in other details.

Bibliography: H. DECKER, *Romanesque Art in Italy,* tr. J. CLEUGH (New York 1959) 62–63. **Illustration credit:** Alinari-Art Reference Bureau.

[M. M. SCHAEFER]

NICE (FRANCE), chief town of the French Alpes-Maritimes Département and bishopric; founded in the 3d century B.C. by colonists from Marseilles and named Nikaia (victory). A port for Roman military stores during the Punic Wars, Christianity spread there quickly from Marseilles and penetrated the Alpes-Maritimes province. There was a bishop in Nice in the 4th century who sent two delegates to the Council of Arles (314); and the first known bishop, Amantius, took part in the Council of Aquileia in 381. St. *Leo I united the bishopric of Cimiez (Cemenelum) to Nice and the union of the two sees was confirmed by Pope *Hilary I (461–468). Devastated by the barbarians, Nice was restored during the Carolingian empire, became a possession of the Counts of Toulouse, then of the House of Anjou, and in the 11th century an independent republic. Ceded to Savoy in 1419, it was reunited to France in 1860.

In 1962 the city had 244,360 inhabitants; the diocese had 550,000 Catholics out of 632,000 inhabitants, with 241 parishes, 367 secular and 99 religious priests, and 22 seminarians.

Bibliography: H. LECLERCQ, DACL 12.1:1168–79. R. LATOUCHE, "Nice et Cimiez," *Mélanges F. Lot* (Paris 1925) 331–358; *Histoire du Comté de Nice* (Paris 1932).

[A. DANET]

NICENE CREED

A profession of faith agreed upon, although with some misgivings because of its non-Biblical terminology, by the bishops at *Nicaea I (325) to defend the true faith against *Arianism. It is basically a Baptismal creed of Syro-Palestinian origin into which have been interpolated anti-Arian clauses, including the word *homoousios (at the urging of *Hosius of Córdoba and *Constantine I), and to which have been appended four anathemas. Structurally, the creed (Denz 125, 126) is a brief, tripartite Trinitarian statement, stressing the *consubstantiality of the Son, His *Incarnation, redeeming death, and *Resurrection. It concludes simply with "and in the Holy Spirit" followed by the anathemas that condemn typical Arian slogans oft repeated in *Arius's *Thalia,* e.g., "There was when He was not." Though scholars previously maintained that the Creed of *Eusebius of Caesarea was the model of the Nicene, it is now generally admitted that Eusebius's creedal profession at Nicaea I was motivated by his desire for rehabilitation and was not intended to be a proposal of a basis for a conciliar creed.

The first witness to what is popularly known as the Nicene Creed, sometimes called the Niceno-Constantinople Creed (Denz 150), is found in the acts of the Council of *Chalcedon (451). Herein the Niceno-Constantinople Creed is attributed to the bishops of *Constantinople I (381), whose amplification of the Nicene produced the Niceno-Constantinople. But careful literary analysis reveals the impossibility of the latter's dependence on the former. There are significant omissions in the Niceno-Constantinople, while there are also additions doctrinally insignificant in light of the errors of the day, together with minor differences in word order and sentence structure pointlessly made if the Nicene-Constantinople is the Nicene expanded. Furthermore the Niceno-Constantinople contains longer sections on the Person of Christ and the Holy Spirit, as well as articles concerning belief in the Church, Baptism, the resurrection of the dead, and eternal life. The majority of scholars until recently either denied any connection of the Niceno-Constantinople with Constantinople I or opted for a purely accidental association through supposed creedal professions made by *Cyril of Jerusalem or Nectarius at the Council. For those adhering to the traditional explanation of the Niceno-Constantinople Creed's connection with the second ecumenical Council, the creed found in *Epiphanius of Constantia's *Ancoratus* (374) would surely be the Niceno-Constantinople's paradigm did not some scholars with good reason suppose that the Nicene, rather than the Niceno-Constantinople, stood in the text. The antinomies seem best resolved by the fact that before Chalcedon, creeds other than the Nicene were referred to as Nicene because of their basic fidelity in doctrine to the Nicene. Thus Constantinople I may be said to have adopted and promulgated the Niceno-Constantinople, already in existence in the Baptismal liturgy, not as a new creed or as the Nicene literally expanded, but as the Nicene faith in substance, better adapted to combat the errors of the day.

The Niceno-Constantinople's recitation at the Eucharist began apparently at Antioch under the Monophysite Patriarch *Peter the Fuller (d. 488); its use in the West dates from the third Council of *Toledo (589), when possibly the *filioque was inserted. The Niceno-Constantinople's place in the Roman liturgy is due to the efforts of Emperor *Henry II, who persuaded Pope *Benedict VIII to enjoin its recitation on Sundays and on feasts of which mention is made in the Creed.

See also CHRISTOLOGICAL CONTROVERSY, EARLY; CREED; GENERATION OF THE WORD; LOGOS; WORD, THE.

Bibliography: I. ORTIZ DE URBINA, LexThK² 7:968–969; 7:938–940; *El símbolo niceno* (Madrid 1947). J. N. D. KELLY, *Early Christian Creeds* (2d ed. London 1960) 205–262.

[T. RYAN]

NICEPHORUS II PHOCAS, BYZANTINE EMPEROR,

963 to 969; b. 912; d. Constantinople, 969. He came of a celebrated family of Cappadocian aristocrats and generals, and he rose to command of the Byzantine armies under Emperor *Constantine VII Porphyrogenitus (d. 959), and in the reign of Romanus II recovered Crete after 134 years of Saracen occupation. On the death of Romanus II (963), he was proclaimed emperor, and he married the widowed Augusta Theophano and became protector of her infant sons Basil II and Constantine VIII. In 6 years of government he liberated all Cilicia, including Tarsus, and overran Syria almost unopposed. He conquered Cyprus in 965, and Antioch in 969. In 966 he invited the Russian Prince Svjatoslav to attack Bulgaria, a useful buffer state, thus leaving a difficult situation in the Balkans for his successor. His dispute with *Otto I the Great over the Byzantine possessions in Italy is described in the *Legatio* of Liutprand of Cremona, Otto's ambassador in Constantinople.

A great general, Nicephorus lacked popular support in his capital because of his introduction and maintenance there of a large body of Armenian troops, the increased taxation required to sustain his military operations, and the reforms he made for the limitation of monastic properties. He was a close friend of St. *Athanasius the Athonite, and he was deeply religious, even ascetic, and favored the monastic foundation on Mt. *Athos. A conspiracy headed by his comrade-in-arms John Tzimisces (later *John I Tzimisces), to which his own wife Theophano seems to have been privy, came to a climax on Dec. 10, 969, when Nicephorus was brutally murdered.

Bibliography: H. HUNGER, LexThK² 7:972. G. L. SCHLUMBERGER, *Un Empereur byzantin au Xe siècle. Nicéphore Phocas* (new ed. Paris 1923). Ostrogorsky 250–263. P. CHARANIS, Dumb OaksP 4 (1948) 55–61, monasteries. M. CANARD, *Histoire de la dynastie des H'Amdanides de Jazîra et de Syrie,* v.1 (Paris 1953).

[R. JENKINS]

NICEPHORUS I, PATRIARCH OF CONSTANTINOPLE, ST.,

reigned April 12, 806, to March 13, 815; Byzantine theologian and historian; b. Constantinople, *c.* 758; d. in exile near Chalcedon, June 2, 828 (feast, March 13). Nicephorus stood in the forefront of the battle against *iconoclasm. His father, Theodore, of noble lineage and an imperial secretary to Emperor *Constantine V, had twice suffered torture, degradation, and banishment in defense of the veneration of images and had died in exile. Under *Tarasius, afterward his predecessor in the patriarchate, Nicephorus became, like his father, an imperial secretary (between 770 and 780) and as such took part in the Council of Nicaea II (787). Some time later he retired to a monastery, without, however, becoming a monk, possibly because he had fallen out of favor at court or wanted leisure for study. He was chosen head of the largest poorhouse in Constantinople, perhaps by Emperor Nicephorus I at his accession (802), and 4 years later he was made patriarch against the advice of Theodore the Studite; but he soon joined forces with Theodore against Emperor Leo V in the controversy over iconoclasm. In 815 he was deposed and exiled near Chalcedon. He used his time to produce anti-iconoclastic treatises (*see* BYZANTINE CHURCH, HISTORY OF). After his death his bones were translated to Constantinople by Methodius (847) and interred in the church of the Holy Apostles on March 13, his feast day in both the Greek and Roman Churches; the Greeks also observe the day of his death, June 2.

Two of his principal dogmatic works dealing with the iconoclastic *horos* and *florilegium* of patristic texts of 815 are still unedited. His *Apologeticus major* and *minor* and three *Antirhetikoi* or Diatribes (813–820) are important for the excerpts they preserve of Emperor Constantine's writings favoring iconoclasm. Nicephorus's works are important for the critique of patristic sources that he introduces into his theological arguments. He wrote also a history, the *Breviarium* or *Historia syntomos,* covering the years 602–769. The authenticity of several canonical and poetical works attached to his name is disputed.

Bibliography: O. Volk, LexThK² 7:971–972. PG 100:201–850. C. G. de Boor, ed., *Nicephorus . . . opuscula historica* (TB; 1880). L. Orosz, ed., *The London Manuscript of Nicephoros "Breviarium"* (Budapest 1948). R. P. Blake, *Byzantion* 14 (1939) 1–15. V. Grumel, RevÉtByz 17 (1959) 127–135. Pitra SpicSol 1:371–503; 4:292–380. Beck KTLBR 490–491. R. Janin, DTC 11.1:452–455. G. Moravcsik, *Byzantinoturcica,* 2 v. (2d ed. Berlin 1958) v.1. P. J. Alexander, *The Patriarch Nicephorus of Constantinople* (Oxford 1958). R. M. Mainka, "Zum Brief des Patriarchen Nikephoros I von Konstantinopel an Papst Leo III," *Ostkirchliche Studien* 13 (1964) 273–281.

[M. J. HIGGINS]

NICEPHORUS BLEMMYDES,

Byzantine monk, theologian, advocate of reunion; b. Constantinople, 1197; d. Emathia, near Ephesus, 1272. In 1205 he left Constantinople, soon after its fall to the Crusaders (1204). In the course of several years he acquired encyclopedic knowledge through his studies at Prusa, Nicaea, Ephesus, Smyrna, and other cities. In 1223 he became a member of the clergy of Nicaea. In 1232, at Nicaea, and in 1234, at Nymphaeum, he took part in the theological discussions with the Latin legates. He composed a tract defending the Greek position, which occasioned the failure of the negotiations then and again in 1250. He was entrusted with the education of the future Emperor Theodore II Lascaris and of George Akropolites, founded the monastery of Emathia near Ephesus (1248), and refused the bishopric of that city as well as the patriarchate of Nicaea offered to him by his former pupil Theodore. Toward 1256 he accepted the conciliatory attitude toward the Latins adopted by the Emperor, apparently influenced by the *Dialogues on the Procession of the Holy Spirit* written by Nicetas of Maronia, and he interpreted the phrase "per filium" in an anti-Photian sense. However, in his autobiography, writtten in 1264, he repudiated any compromise with the Latins.

Preserved in two recensions, the autobiography is the chief work of his abundant literary production, which included two controversial tracts on the procession of the Holy Spirit, a testament for his monks "Against the filioque," commentaries, scholia on the Psalms with an interesting introduction ($\pi\rho oo\iota\mu\iota o\nu$) on ecclesiastical chant, an encomion of St. John the Evangelist that is a dogmatic dissertation on Johannine theology, and several manuals of philosophy.

Bibliography: PG 142. V. Grumel, DTC 11.1:441–445; *Catholicisme* 2:85–86. H. G. Beck, LexThK² 7:970. M. Jugie, EncCatt 2:1719. Beck KTLBR 671–673. G. Mercati, *Bessarione* 31 (1915) 226–238; *Opere minore,* 5 v. (StTest 76–80; 1937–41); ". . . Commento del Salterio," *Biblica* 26 (1945) 153–181. H. I. Bell, "The Commentary on the Psalms," ByzZ 30 (1929–30) 295–300.

[I. DALMAIS]

NICEPHORUS GREGORAS,

Byzantine historian and man of learning; b. Heracleia Pontica, 1295; d. *c.* 1359. He went to Constantinople at the age of 20. There, under the educational guidance of the Patriarch Glykys and the Grand Logothete Theodore Metochites, the latter the outstanding scholar of the period, Gregoras soon distinguished himself as a man of learning, particularly in astronomy. He also became influential in court circles. But the triumph of *Hesychasm, against which Gregoras fought a losing battle, led to his confinement in the monastery of the Chora. Released in 1355, he died not long after (1359).

Gregoras was the author of numerous works devoted to a variety of subjects: theology, astronomy, hagiography, philosophy, history, grammar, and many letters (ed. R. Guilland, Paris 1927). Among his works the best known is his *Roman History* (ed. L. Schopen and I. Bekker, 3 v. Bonn 1829–55). Divided into 37 books, it covers the period from 1204 to 1359 and includes, besides the political history of the period, lengthy excursuses on the intellectual and theological activities of the author. The significance of Gregoras in the cultural life of Byzantium in the 14th century cannot be fully appreciated, however, because most of his works still remain unedited.

Bibliography: R. Guilland, *Essai sur Nicéphore Grégoras: L'Homme et l'oeuvre* (Paris 1926). G. Moravcsik, *Byzantinoturcicia,* 2 v. (2d ed. Berlin 1958) 1:450–453, with latest bibliog.

[P. CHARANIS]

NICETAS CHONIATES,

incorrectly called Akominatos, younger brother of Michael Choniates, theologian, important Byzantine historian; b. Chonae (Phrygia), 1140; d. Nicaea, 1213. As a child he went to Constantinople to study under the guidance of his elder brother. Entering civil service, he became governor of Philippopolis, where he witnessed the destruction caused by armies of *Frederick I Barbarossa on the Third *Crusade. He served as imperial secretary under *Isaac II Angelus. After the sack of Constantinople by the Crusaders in 1204, Nicetas fled to the court of Theodore I Lascaris in Nicaea, where he turned to writing. Nicetas proved to be one of the better theologians of the time. As a model for his "Treasury of Orthodoxy" he used the "Panoply of Dogma" by Euthymius Zigabenes. Nicetas's chief work is a Chronicle of 21 books covering the period from 1118 to 1206. In this work he used the treatise of Eustathius of Thessalonica in describing the capture of that region by *Normans in 1185. Because of his power of vivid description, he was considered the most brilliant historian of medieval Byzantium after *Psellus; Nicetas was a fervent Greek patriot, reflecting the rising tide of Byzantine nationalism. He was unusually objective and reliable despite his experiences with the Crusaders' armies. His works helped to make the epoch of the Comneni one of the most brilliant and flourishing periods of Byzantine historiography.

Bibliography: PG 139:319–1057, 1101–1447; 140:9–282, 1221–45. Ceillier 14:1176–77; Table 2:208. L. Petit, DTC 14.1:316–318; 16:20. Krumbacher 281–286. Beck KTLBR 663–666. Ostrogorsky 311–313.

[M. C. HILFERTY]

NICETAS DAVID,

the Paphlagonian, 10th-century disciple of Arethas, rhetor and prolific writer of encomia on Apostles, saints, and martyrs. His main work is the life of the Byzantine Patriarch *Ignatius, which seems to have been composed in 907. In opposition to *Photius he presents his hero as a true saint who had never yielded to the pressure of civil authorities or become unfaithful to his principles. Nicetas considered the patriarchs who succeeded Ignatius as unworthy because they shared Photius's lust for power: Stephen, Anthony, Nicholas, and Euthymius. He branded the last three as almost heretics because they had sanctioned the third and fourth marriages of the Emperor *Leo VI.

As a radical opponent of tetragamy (fourth marriage) he composed a treatise against the Patriarch Euthymius and the Emperor and, disgusted by the fact that even his teacher Arethas had been induced to approve the tetragamy, Nicetas retired to a hermitage near Media on the Bulgarian frontier. Suspected of espionage, he was arrested and brought to Constantinople. Because of his writings against the Patriarch and the Emperor he would have been severely punished had he not been saved by the intercession of the Patriarch Euthymius, who let him become a monk in his monastery of Agathos. As a monk Nicetas chose the name of David; he stayed in the monastery until 910. He devoted the rest of his life to the writing of homilies and encomia. These writings were attributed to another Nicetas, called the philosopher, but this attribution is wrong. Nicetas, the rhetor and philosopher, should be identified with the author of the life of Ignatius; but the opinion that he was bishop of Dadybra is likewise false. This error was caused by a misinterpretation of the abridged form of his monastic name David in a manuscript. Nicetas seems to have written most of his compositions between 913 and 963. His life of Ignatius was later introduced into the anti-Photian collection and used by the opponents of Photius in their campaign against the second patriarchate of Photius and the repudiation of his immediate successors.

Bibliography: K. M. LOPAREV, "Zhitie," *Russkiĭ Arkheologicheskiĭ Institut: Izvĭestĭiă* 13 (1908) 173–181. Mansi 16:209–296, Vita Ignatii, 409–458, anti-Photianist collection. PG 105:488–574, Vita Ignatii; *ibid.* 15–487, homilies and encomia. ActSS April 3:ix–xvi, app., St. George. A. VOGT, ed., "Deux discours inédits de Nicétas de Paphlagonie," *Orientalia Christiana* 23 (1931) 5–97. P. KARLIN-HAYTER, ed., "Vita S. Euthymii," *Byzantion* 25–27 (1955–57) 1–172. F. DVORNIK, *The Photian Schism* (Cambridge, Eng. 1948). R. J. H. JENKINS, "A Note on Nicetas David Paphlago and the Vita Ignatii," DumbOaksP 18 (1965).

[F. DVORNIK]

NICETAS OF REMESIANA

Bishop and distinguished ecclesiastical writer; b. place and date unknown; d. after A.D. 414. Remesiana has been identified with the site of the modern Yugoslavian village of Bēla Palanka, east of Nish (the ancient Naissus). Although of Greek origin according to his name (the Latinized form of Νικητής), he was entirely Western in outlook and temperament and wrote excellent Latin. In 398 and 402 he visited his friend Paulinus of Nola, and the latter's *Propempticon* (*Carmen* 17), written on the occasion of his departure following the first visit, is the chief source for his life. According to a reference preserved in St. Hilary (*Frg. hist.* 15) he was already a bishop in 366–367, and the mention of his name in the letter of Pope Innocent I to the bishops of Macedonia (Innocent I, *Epist.* 22) dated Dec. 13, 414, indicates that he was still living at that time. Gennadius (*De viris illustribus* 21) furnishes valuable data on his writings, although his account is very brief.

Nicetas's chief work, the *Competentibus ad baptismum instructionis libelli sex,* a manual of instruction for baptismal candidates, is preserved only in fragments, but, fortunately, the sections covering *De ratione fidei,*

De potentia Spiritus Sancti, and *De symbolo* are rather long. Basing himself solidly on the teachings of the Council of Nicaea and making full use of the *Catecheses* of St. Cyril of Jerusalem, he defended the consubstantiality of the Son against the Arians and the consubstantiality of the Holy Spirit against the Macedonians. His commentary on the Creed employs the term *communio sanctorum* for the first time, and it has an important place in the history and exposition of the symbol. The sermons, *De vigiliis servorum Dei* and *De psalmodiae bono* (or *De utilitate hymnorum*), were already recognized as genuine by the Maurist Luc D'Achéry in 1659. The first deals with the celebration of the vigils of Saturdays and Sundays, and the second stresses the importance of the singing of psalms or hymns at these vigils. In the second work, the *Magnificat* is assigned to St. Elizabeth (9, 11). Nicetas is probably the author of the little treatise *De diversis appellationibus Christi;* but the arguments adduced to identify the *Ad lapsam virginem libellus,* assigned to him by Gennadius, with the pseudo-Ambrosian *De lapsu virginis consecratae* are not convincing. Paulinus of Nola praised Nicetas as a writer of hymns and said that he taught the barbarian Bessi and Scythians to glorify Christ in song, but no hymn has survived with his name. Despite the advocacy of Dom G. Morin and A. E. Burn, there is no solid evidence for making him the author of the **Te Deum.*

Bibliography: *De vigiliis,* ed. C. H. TURNER, JThSt 22 (1920–21) 306–320; *De utilitate,* ed. C. H. TURNER, *ibid.* 24 (1922–23) 225–252. A. E. BURN, *Niceta of Remesiana: His Life and Works* (Cambridge, Eng. 1905). Dekkers CPL 646–652. Cross ODCC 953–954, with bibliog. E. PETERSON, EncCatt 8:1838–39. P. T. CAMELOT, LexThK² 7:974–975, with bibliog. Altaner 458–459. Bardenhewer 3:598–605. U. MORICCA, *Storia della letteratura latina cristiana,* 3 v. in 5 (Turin 1928–34) 2.2:1148–63.

[M. R. P. MC GUIRE]

NICETAS STETHATOS,

Byzantine controversialist, mystical writer; b. c. 1000; d. c. 1080. He received his epithet of *stethatos* or *pectoratus* (the lionhearted) when he openly rebuked Emperor *Constantine IX Monomachus for his immorality. When Nicetas was 14 years old, he became a monk of *Studion monastery, where he became a devoted disciple of *Symeon the New Theologian. He was driven from the monastery for a time when he honored Symeon as a saint after his death. In the conflict (1053–54) between *Michael Cerularius and *Humbert of Silva Candida (see EASTERN SCHISM), Nicetas played a leading part in support of Cerularius but was forced by the Emperor to an insincere recantation of his attacks against the Roman Church. Of his polemic on this occasion, the *Dialexis* and *Antidialogus* became the nucleus of a later comprehensive compilation on the azymes, or unleavened bread, and the *Synthesis against the Latins,* which attacked the *filioque, was later to be included in *Nicetas Choniates' *Thesaurus of Orthodoxy.* Stethatos' principal contribution to mysticism was his *Life of Symeon the New Theologian,* written to establish Symeon's sanctity against his detractors, but incidentally setting forth Nicetas's own ascetical and mystical views. Along this same line he published Symeon's works with an introduction, and composed *Against the Saint's* [i.e., Symeon's] *Accusers.* Independent writings on mysticism included a treatise on the soul and the *Spiritual Paradise.* These and his other essays on mysticism and miscellaneous subjects reveal an ascetical and mystical system that followed very closely that of his master.

Bibliography: Works. *Dialexis, Antidialogus, Synthesis,* v.2 of *Humbert und Kerullarios,* ed. A. MICHEL, 2 v. (Paderborn 1924–30); life of Simeon the New Theologian, in *Un Grand mystique byzantin: Vie de Syméon le Nouveau Théologien, 949–1022,* ed. with Fr. tr. by I. HAUSHERR and G. HORN (Orientalia Christiana 12; Rome 1928). Literature. M. T. DISDIER, DTC 11.1:479–486. Beck KTLBR 535–536. H. G. BECK, ByzZ 53 (1960) 132–133.

[M. J. HIGGINS]

NICETIUS OF TRIER, ST.,

bishop; b. probably Limoges, France; d. Trier, Germany, Dec. 5, 566 (feast, Dec. 5). A *Benedictine monk and abbot, he was called to Trier *c.* 525 by the Frankish King Theodoric I (d. 534). He renewed his diocese by reform of clergy and promotion of monasticism, and also by the rebuilding of churches fallen into disrepair, especially the cathedral. He is considered one of Trier's greatest bishops. Nicetius was active at several *Merovingian synods, taking part in those of Clermont-Ferrand in 535, Orléans in 549, Toul in 550, and Paris in 551. He fearlessly denounced the transgressions of Kings Theodebert I (d. 547) and of Clotaire I (d. 561). Clotaire banished him for his outspoken criticism in 560, but he was restored with honors the following year by King Sigebert I (d. 575). His correspondence with the Lombard Queen Clodiswind (d. 570) and the Byzantine Emperor *Justinian I is evidence of his wider influence. He is buried in the church of St. Maximin in Trier.

Bibliography: K. BAUS, LexThK² 7:941–942. Mabillon AS 1:184–187. BHL 2:6090–92. Chevalier BB 2:3314. Zimmermann KalBen 3:397–398.

[P. VOLK]

NICHOLAS I, POPE, ST.

Pontificate, April 24, 858, to Nov. 13, 867; b. *c.* 819–822; d. Rome (feast, Nov. 13). The son of the *regionarius* Theodore, he was ordained a subdeacon by Pope *Sergius II and a deacon by *Leo IV. He served in the Curia under *Benedict III and was elected pope on Benedict's death. He was consecrated at St. Peter's in the presence of Emperor *Louis II. In his efforts to establish the authority of the papacy, Nicholas faced three major crises in the government of the Church.

A synod at Aachen on April 29, 862 (Mansi 15:611–17), had authorized the repudiation of Theutberga, the wife of *Lothair II, the King of Lorraine. Another synod at Metz, in June 863, attended by papal legates, recognized Lothair's marriage to Waldrada, but the Pope, suspecting bribery, reversed the judgment and excommunicated the participating prelates (*Annales Bertiniani* 863). This occasioned an attack upon him early in 864 by Archbishops Gunthar of Cologne (d. 873) and Theutgaud of Trier (d. 868), who in turn were deposed by the Pope. Although Lothair and Theutberga were officially reconciled in 865, as late as Oct. 30, 867, Nicholas felt it necessary to demand evidence that Lothair had truly taken back his wife (Jaffé E 2884). It was the Pope's firm contention in this conflict that the Holy See could judge even the most powerful of temporal rulers when they were guilty of transgressing the moral law.

The extent of metropolitan authority was another source of conflict during his reign. Following the deposition of Bishop Rothad II of Soissons (d. 869) in 862 by Archbishop *Hincmar of Reims and his suffragans, the Pope decreed an examination, which in January 865 resulted in Rothad's restoration (MGEp 6:379–401). Here, for the first time, Nicholas referred to the *False Decretals, which gave broad authority to the papacy. The demurral of a Soissons synod in 866 to rejudge the case of the deposed cleric Wulfad, first brought censure from the Pope, but eventually Nicholas found Hincmar's explanation satisfactory (Jaffé E 2823, 2881). These cases, together with the Pope's earlier deposition of John VIII of Ravenna, helped to establish the authority of Rome over the sees of the West.

The success of the Byzantine missionaries *Cyril and Methodius in evangelizing Moravia after 863 caused Nicholas to invite them to Rome; and he always took an active interest in Church affairs in the East. Upon the forced abdication, late in 858, of *Ignatius, Patriarch of Constantinople, and the receipt of the systatic letters of his successor *Photius, the Pope, on Sept. 25, 860, dispatched legates to investigate the matter (Jaffé E 2683). When in the spring of 861, in a synod at Constantinople, they recognized Photius, Nicholas disowned his envoys, and on March 18, 862, insisted upon a Roman trial (Jaffé E 2691–2692). At Rome, probably in the summer of 863, the synodal action was revoked (Jaffé E 2819). Although on Sept. 28, 865 (Jaffé E 2796), the Pope offered the possibility of a new examination, the sending of a papal mission to Bulgaria and of a harsh note to Photius, both on Nov. 13, 866 (Jaffé E 2812, 2814), so infuriated the Patriarch that a synod assembled by him in August-September 867 at Constantinople deposed the Pope (Grumel Reg 482). Nicholas's own death spared him knowledge of this action and subsequent events (*see* EASTERN SCHISM). One of his last letters complained bitterly of the Greek attitude toward the Roman Church (Oct. 23, 867; Jaffé E 2879).

Bibliography: Jaffé E 1:341–368. MGEp 6:207–240, 257–690. Grumel Reg 1.2:72–95. Duchesne LP 2:151–172. J. ROY, *St. Nicholas I,* tr. M. MAITLAND (London 1901). Mann 3:1–148. F. A. NORWOOD, "The Political Pretensions of Pope Nicholas I," ChHist 15 (1946) 271–285. F. DVORNIK, *The Photian Schism* (Cambridge, Eng. 1948); "The Patriarch Photius and the Roman Primacy," *Chicago Studies* 2 (1963) 94–107. T. SCHIEFFER, LexThK² 7:976–977. É. AMANN, DTC 11:506–526.

[H. G. J. BECK]

NICHOLAS II, POPE

Pontificate, Dec. 6?, 1058, to July 19–26, 1061; b. Gerard, in Lorraine or French Burgundy, date unknown; d. Florence, Italy. He was made bishop of Florence in 1045. When Pope *Stephen IX died in Florence (1059), Benedict X (John of Velletri) was proclaimed pope on April 5 by a group of the Roman aristocracy, the *Tusculani, opposing the reform group of the Roman Curia led by Hildebrand, later *Gregory VII. The cardinals, however, did not recognize Benedict's election. Under the influence of Hildebrand and with the support of the German court and of Duke Godfrey of Lorraine and Tuscany, Nicholas was formally elected in Siena. With a show of force, Godfrey brought Nicholas to Rome, where he was enthroned

Jan. 24, 1059, after Benedict had fled. According to contemporary, although somewhat partisan, reports, he was the first pope to be crowned with the *camelaucum,* the original form of the *tiara.

Nicholas was a strong adherent of the party of papal reform and was influenced by Hildebrand, *Humbert of Silva Candida, and *Peter Damian. He was a man of personal integrity, capable in ecclesiastical and political matters, and devoted to the contemporary renovation of the Church that laid the groundwork of the *Gregorian reform. Attempting to eliminate political influence in papal elections, he proclaimed the *election decree of 1059, promulgated at the Lateran Council, known as the decretal *In nomine Domini* in the citation by Gratian (CorpIurCan D.23 c.1). Its authorship, once attributed to Humbert, is now disputed. The decree was the starting point for new papal election legislation, and its system remained fundamental to all later election laws. Clearly the new decretal made the *cardinal bishops the essential electors. In legislating this norm the practice of the early Church was restored, since in that period the neighboring bishops of a vacant see usually made the first choice of the candidate and presented him to clergy and people for acclamation and consent. On the other hand, it was this restriction of the election right to the cardinal bishops that caused great opposition and had to be changed after Nicholas's death (*see* POPES, ELECTION OF).

The Roman synods of 1060 and 1061, as well as other papal decretals, make clear the spirit of reform. In particular Nicholas legislated against clerical marriage (*see* CELIBACY, HISTORY OF) and *simony and restricted the influence of the laity on *proprietary churches. He tried to restore the *common life for the cathedral clergy and reformed the administration of ecclesiastical properties, forbidding abuses and improper alienation. Beginning with his reign, dispensation from marriage impediments (post-factum dispensations) gained in importance. This was also part of the reform to secure the validity of marriages and to reduce annulments, particularly because of the impediment of consanguinity (*see* MARRIAGE, CANON LAW OF, 3). In those times a dispensation was given after the marriage had been consummated. A typical example of the Pope's dispensation practice was the sanation of the marriage of Duke William of Normandy with his cousin, whom he had married in spite of a prohibition by Pope *Leo IX. Nicholas also favored the positive tendencies of the *Patarines, who opposed the dissolute practices of the higher clergy and aristocracy of Milan. There, usually only the sons of patrician families were appointed to clerical offices. Many of them were married priests, who often successfully tried to have their sons appointed to ecclesiastical offices. In 1055 Nicholas sent Peter Damian and Anselm of Lucca (*Alexander II) to Milan to reform the Church.

Nicholas further made peace (Melfi, August 1059) with the Norman princes of southern Italy, *Robert Guiscard and Richard, who were confirmed in their conquests and who in turn promised support of the papal reform in their domains. Nicholas's forceful renovation of the Church aroused opposition, particularly that of the Roman Emperor *Henry IV and the German bishops, led by *Anno II of Cologne. A German synod held in 1061 tried to nullify many of the Pope's reform decrees, but Nicholas did not live long enough to become involved in the struggle between *imperium* and *sacerdotium* that followed his reign.

Bibliography: Jaffé L 1:557–566. L. DUCHESNE, *Les Premiers temps de l'état pontifical* (3d ed. Paris 1912), Eng. tr. A. H. MATHEW (London 1908). A. CLAVEL, *Le Pape Nicolas II: Son oeuvre disciplinaire* (Lyons 1906). Mann 6:226–260. A. FLICHE, *La Réforme grégorienne,* 3 v. (Louvain 1924–37), v.1. G. MICCOLI, "Il problema delle ordinazioni simoniache e le sinodi Lateranensi del 1060 e 1061," StGreg 5 (1956) 33–81. Seppelt 3:37–49. H. G. KRAUSE, *Das Papstwahldekret von 1059 und seine Rolle im Investiturstreit* (StGreg 7; 1960). W. M. PLÖCHL, *Geschichte des Kirchenrechts,* v.2 (2d ed. Vienna 1962). B. SCHMEIDLER, "Zum Wahldekret Papst Nikolaus II. vom Jahre 1059," *Historische Vierteljahrschrift* 31 (1937–39) 554–560.

[W. M. PLÖCHL]

NICHOLAS III, POPE

Pontificate, Nov. 25, 1277, to Aug. 22, 1280; b. Giovanni Gaetano Orsini, Rome, between 1210 and 1220; d. Soriano, near Viterbo, Italy. Little is known of his career before his appointment as cardinal by *Innocent IV in 1244, but the *Orsini family was one of the most powerful *Guelf families in Rome. In 1261 *Urban IV named him rector of Sabina (*see* SUBURBICARIAN DIOCESES) and protector of the *Franciscans. He also played a significant role in papal diplomacy, being chosen a member of the commission of cardinals that invested Charles of *Anjou with the Kingdom of Sicily in 1265. In 1276 he was a member of the commission that sought to negotiate a settlement between Charles of Anjou and the German King, *Rudolf I of Hapsburg, in the dispute over possession of the Sicilian kingdom. Elected pope to succeed *John XXI after a 6-month vacancy, Nicholas initiated a number of administrative reforms within the Church and in the operation of the *States of the Church.

He was anxious to restore papal and Roman control over the city of Rome and to eliminate foreign rulers. To this end he issued the *Constitutio super electione senatoris Urbis* on July 18, 1278, which forbade entrusting the government of the city to foreign senators, a measure specifically designed to end the Angevin domination. Nicholas also undertook reforms in the papal administrative machinery, the most important of which concerned procedures of the papal chancery. He sought to improve the quality of the college of cardinals by a series of distinguished new appointments.

This pontificate was marked by a number of attempts to resolve longstanding disputes. The union of churches decreed at the second Council of *Lyons in 1274 having failed to materialize because of the inability of the Eastern Emperor to enforce its requirements on his subjects (*see* EASTERN SCHISM), Nicholas demanded strict enforcement and the use of stronger means to secure obedience. The union was viewed as the first step in the raising of a great Crusade to recapture the Holy Land, but its failure and the distracted state of European politics prevented the realization of these plans. Nicholas was asked to settle the *poverty controversy that had divided the *Franciscans into Conventuals and Spirituals; his solution was contained in the bull *Exiit qui seminat* (Aug. 14, 1279), which together with *Clement V's bull *Exivi,* has remained the basis of the Franciscan observance. Finally the Pope endeavored to end the conflict over possession of Sicily and, after lengthy negotiations, arranged a treaty that appeared to satisfy the claims of the Angevin and Hapsburg parties without infringing upon the rights of the papacy.

The treaty was signed in May 1280, but the conflict broke out again after Nicholas's death. Nicholas established the permanent papal residence in the *Vatican and enlarged its palace and gardens. He was buried in the Chapel of St. Nicholas, which he built in *St. Peter's Basilica.

Bibliography: *Les Registres de Nicolas III*, ed. J. Gay and S. Vitta, 2 v. (Paris 1898–1938). A. Demski, *Papst Nikolaus III* (Münster 1903). R. Sternfeld, *Der Kardinal Johann Gaëtan Orsini* (Berlin 1905). E. Amann, DTC 11.1:532–536. S. Runciman, *The Sicilian Vespers* (Cambridge, Eng. 1958) 182–190. D. P. Waley, *The Papal State in the 13th Century* (New York 1961). Seppelt 3:539–558, 618–622.

[J. M. Muldoon]

NICHOLAS IV, POPE

Pontificate, Feb. 22, 1288, to April 4, 1292; b. Girolamo Masci, at Lisciano, near Ascoli, Italy, Sept. 30, 1227; d. Rome. Nicholas was the first pope to develop a coherent policy for administering the lands that comprised the *States of the Church. A man of humble origins, he joined the *Franciscans as a young man, studying at Assisi and Perugia, later becoming provincial of the Dalmatian province (1272) and finally succeeding St. *Bonaventure as minister general of the order (1274). His ability attracted papal attention, and in 1272, Pope Gregory X employed him on a mission to invite the Greek Church to attend the Second Council of *Lyons, to be held in 1274. In 1278 Pope Nicholas III appointed him cardinal, and in 1281 Martin IV named him bishop of Palestrina.

Nicholas, the first Franciscan to attain the papal office, was elected after a vacancy that had lasted for almost 11 months after the death of *Honorius IV. The college of cardinals had been split between pro- and anti-Angevin factions (*see* SICILIAN VESPERS), each seeking the election of a pope favorable to its cause. Nicholas was a compromise candidate agreed upon by the two factions. He refused his first election, Feb. 15, 1288, and accepted the papal throne only after a second election. Like the other popes of the late 13th century, he was faced with the unresolved Sicilian problem. He personally favored the Angevin party (*see* ANJOU) and annulled the treaty of 1288 that had confirmed Aragon's possession of the island kingdom.

Reflecting the interests of his order, Nicholas was anxious to expand the Church's missionary work, sending friars to Persia, China, and Ethiopia [*see* MISSIONS, HISTORY OF (MEDIEVAL)]. In the East these activities were also connected with his desire to launch a new crusade, especially after the fall of Acre (1291).

Finally, Nicholas recognized the lack of an administrative policy that would provide a basis for governing the States of the Church. Having determined the requirements of such a policy, he allied the papacy with the powerful *Colonna family, paving the way for an alliance between the papacy and one of the strong factions at the root of the unrest within the Papal States. The most immediate threat to peace was the decline of the republican communes there and the rise of the signories. These politically unstable governments increased the turmoil because they aroused violent opposition that often erupted in armed conflict. To encourage more ecclesiastical interest in the problem of administering the Papal States, Nicholas issued the decree *Celestis altitudo potentie*, July 18, 1289, assigning one-half of the papal revenues to the college of *cardi-

nals. This action not only recognized the increasing importance of the cardinals, but also encouraged them to pay closer attention to the administration of the Papal States, which provided a large part of these revenues. But at the time of his death Nicholas had not yet been able to execute his policy, and the breakdown of papal government continued. He had, however, indicated how this might be halted. (For illus., see following page.)

Bibliography: *Les Registres de Nicolas IV*, ed. E. Langlois, 2 v. (Paris 1886–1905). O. Schiff, *Studien zur Geschichte Papst Nikolaus IV* (Berlin 1897). Mann 17:1–246. S. Runciman, *The Sicilian Vespers* (Cambridge, Eng. 1958). D. P. Waley, *The Papal State in the 13th Century* (New York 1961). **Illustration credit:** Leonard Von Matt.

[J. M. Muldoon]

NICHOLAS V, POPE

Pontificate, March 6, 1447, to March 24, 1455; b. Tommaso Parentucelli, Sarzana, Nov. 15, 1397; d. Rome. Thomas, the son of a doctor, had to abandon his studies at Bologna on being orphaned. Thereupon he acted as tutor in two wealthy Florentine families, and was thus influenced by the humanistic and artistic ferment of that city. After finishing his studies at Bologna, he entered the household of Bp. Niccolò *Albergati of Bologna, whom he served faithfully for 20 years, accompanying him to Rome, Florence, and elsewhere, profiting by the example of his saintly patron. After Albergati's death (1443), *Eugene IV first made Parentucelli bishop of Bologna, which being in revolt refused

Pope Nicholas V, portrayed as St. Sixtus II, entrusting the treasure of the Church to St. Lawrence. Detail of a 15th-century fresco by Fra Angelico in the Vatican.

Pope Nicholas IV as a donor, kneeling at the feet of the Virgin; detail of a mosaic by the artists Jacopo Torriti and Jacopo da Camerino, A.D. 1290, in the apse of the basilica of St. John Lateran at Rome.

him entry; Eugene then sent him on missions to Germany. There he successfully mitigated antipapal opposition and was made cardinal in December 1446.

On Eugene's death (1447), Parentucelli was elected pope. Proclaiming a policy of peace, he dismissed the mercenary troops; conciliated by concessions various Roman families, even allowing the rebuilding and partial refortification of Palestrina; and granted Bologna practical independence. Poland was attached to the Holy See by further concessions; Frederick III of Austria was won to Nicholas's cause by the Concordat of Vienna (1448) and a promise of imperial coronation, fulfilled in 1452. Frederick consequently withdrew his safe-conducts from the rump council of Basel, which then went to Lausanne. Nicholas agreed to extremely generous conditions for its dissolution, letting it accept the antipope Felix's resignation, "elect" Thomas Parentucelli pope, and decree its own dissolution. With the end of the council, Nicholas rehabilitated all its members in their dignities and made Felix cardinal with a pension (1449).

In 1450 Nicholas proclaimed a Jubilee, which drew pilgrims from all Western Christendom, and served at once to strengthen devotion, to reestablish the papacy as the center of the Church, and to improve both papal and Roman finances. The occasion was marred by an outbreak of plague, during which Nicholas left the city, and by a traffic disaster on the Ponte Sant'Angelo in which at least 172 people were trampled to death. The few, but worthy, cardinals he created included *Nicholas of Cusa, the promoter of reform in Germany.

The Pope's chief claim to fame is the impulse he gave to the *Renaissance in Rome. He made, and in great part carried out, elaborate building plans (including a renovation of the Leonine city) in a Rome that was in ruins after more than a century of neglect. The stational churches, various palaces attached to basilicas, bridges, and roads, as well as the city's fortifications, were rebuilt, and in many parts of the Papal States fortresses were erected. To decorate his buildings he invited artists from many nations, especially from Florence. The best known was Fra *Angelico, some of whose work still remains in the chapel of S. Lorenzo in the Vatican. The Pope's commissions encouraged the art of tapestry, the ornamentation of rich vestments, and gold and silver work.

However, his principal interest was books. His agents searched for rare codices in most countries, an army of copyists was employed to multiply them, and some of the most celebrated humanists labored in their correction and translation. The writings of Herodotus, Thucydides, Homer, Polybius, Strabo, and other authors of Greek antiquity, as well as many works of the Greek Fathers, were rendered into Latin, and thus made available to those who did not read Greek. In his literary pursuits Nicholas spent vast sums of money and was generous to a fault to the humanists, several of them Greek refugees, who thronged to the papal court. Unfortunately, while most were above reproach, some were more pagan than Christian and a disgrace to the Church that employed them. At his death Nicholas left a library of 807 Latin and 353 Greek MSS, a very large collection for that day (see VATICAN LIBRARY).

The year 1453 was disastrous for the Pope. In January he forestalled a plot against his life, becoming in consequence more timorous than ever; he had all the ringleaders executed. In May the Turks captured Constantinople, and the fleet of papal and Venetian ships (the latter with orders not to annoy the Turks) was too late to help. His health also deteriorated. He tried to rally Western Christians to a crusade, but the effort was ineffectual. With the same objective, he invited the Italian States to meet in Rome to arrange a treaty of peace. The meeting failed, but prepared the way for private diplomacy, leading to the peace of Lodi (1454), in which Nicholas and finally all the States acquiesced. The States, however, were not willing to risk their wealth for the protection of Christendom.

Nicholas, a man of unstained life, vivacious, but simple in manner, had the artistic spirit to appreciate all forms of art and to harmonize them, giving architecture the first place. His importance in the arts and in literature cannot be overestimated. In a deathbed speech he claimed that he had patronized the arts, not for personal fame but, by making Rome outstanding, to strengthen religious allegiance. His policy of "peace by concession" was breaking down as his reign ended, for the princes did not share his ideals.

Bibliography: Sources. VESPASIANO DA BISTICCI, *The Vespasiano Memoirs: Lives of Illustrious Men of the XVth Century,* tr. W. G. and E. WATERS (London 1926). B. SACCHI, *Platynae historici,* ed. G. GAIDA in Muratori RIS² 3.1:328–339. G. MANETTI, *Vita Nicolai V summi pontificis ex manuscripto codice Florentino* in Muratori RIS 3.2:907–960. Literature. Pastor 2:1–314. M. CREIGHTON, *A History of the Papacy During the Period of the Reformation,* 5 v. (London 1882–94) v.2. E. Müntz, *Martin V – Pie II, 1417–1464,* v.1 of *Les Arts à la cour des papes pendant le XVᵉ et le XVIᵉ siècle,* 3 v. (Paris 1878–82). E. MÜNTZ and P. FABRE, eds., *La Bibliothèque du Vatican au XVᵉ siècle* (Paris 1887). Seppelt 4:307–326, 490–493. V. ILARDI, "The Italian League . . .," StRen 6 (1959) 129–166. **Illustration credit:** Alinari-Art Reference Bureau.

[J. GILL]

NICHOLAS V, ANTIPOPE,

May 12, 1328, to Aug. 25, 1330; b. Pietro Rainalducci, at Corvaro (Rieti), Italy; d. Avignon, Oct. 16, 1333. After 5 years of marriage, he became a Franciscan at Aracoeli in Rome. During the *Avignon Papacy, Emperor *Louis IV the Bavarian arranged for his election by the people of Rome in opposition to Pope *John XXII, who was residing in Avignon. Louis granted Nicholas approval within the Empire (making him the last imperial antipope), but since Nicholas had only a few followers, his cause was hopeless. He followed the Emperor to Pisa but finally submitted to John on Aug. 25, 1330, in Avignon. Here he was kept in semidetention until his death.

Bibliography: K. EUBEL, HistJb 12 (1891) 277–308. A. MERCATI, StTest 134 (1947) 59–82. G. SCHWAIGER, LexThK² 7:979.

[G. J. DONNELLY]

NICHOLAS I, EMPEROR OF RUSSIA,

b. Tsarskoe Seloe, Russia, June 25 (O.S.; July 7, N.S.), 1796; d. St. Petersburg, March 2, 1855. Nicholas, the son of Czar Paul I and Sophia Dorothea of Württemberg, succeeded his brother *Alexander I as ruler in December 1825. His motto during his 3 decades as sovereign was "Orthodoxy, Russianism, nationalism." To put his policy into effect he sought to crush liberalism and maintained a rigid censorship and control over education. Yet these years witnessed a flowering of Russian literature, graced by the writings of Pushkin, Gogol, Dostoyevsky, Tolstoy, and others. The Czar's expansion efforts won most of Armenia and the area at the mouth of the Danube, but it involved Russia eventually in the disastrous Crimean War (1853).

In his dealings with the Orthodox Church, Nicholas professed to restore harmonious relations, but he actually increased its dependence on the state. Catholics of the Latin rite who belonged to traditionally Catholic ethnic groups were tolerated, but Stanislav Siestrzencewicz-Bohucz, who had been Alexander I's chief instrument for controlling Latin Catholics, was deposed as metropolitan of *Mogilev (1826). Catholics belonging to the *Eastern Churches saw their union with Rome destroyed by Nicholas, who disapproved the continued existence of Catholic Ukrainians and Byelorussians. Joseph Semashko, an Eastern-rite priest, drew up the plan to incorporate his coreligionists into the Orthodox Church. After the Union of *Brest was declared void (1839), the *Ukrainian (Ruthenian) rite Catholics were subjected to the schismatic *Holy Synod.

The uprising in *Poland (1830) caused Nicholas to contact *Gregory XVI, who condemned the violence of the revolution and urged Catholic Poles to be submissive to legitimate authority (February 1831). When the Emperor expressed dissatisfaction with this admonition as too weak, the Pope dispatched a stronger brief to the Polish bishops, *Superiori anno* (June 9, 1832). Previously Gregory XVI had complained about Russia's treatment of Catholics. In 1847 Pius IX concluded a concordat with the Emperor (*see* UNION OF SOVIET SOCIALIST REPUBLICS).

Bibliography: C. DE GRUNWALD, *Tsar Nicholas I*, tr. B. PATMORE (New York 1955). A. BOUDOU, *Le St-Siège et la Russie, 1814–1883*, 2 v. (Paris 1922–25). Schmidlin, v.1, 2. R. LEFÈVRE, "S. Sede e Russia e i colloqui dello Czar Nicolà I nei documenti vaticani," *Miscellanea historica pontificia* 14 (1948) 156–293. A. M. AMMANN, *Storia della Chiesa russa e dei paesi limitrofi* (Turin 1948). E. WINTER, *Russland und das Papsttum*, 2 v. (Berlin 1960–61) v.1. W. GIUSTI, EncCatt 8:1853–55. B. STASIEWSKI, LexThK² 7:997–998.

[R. F. BYRNES]

NICHOLAS, STUDITE ABBOT, ST.,

Byzantine monk and anti-Iconoclast; b. Kydonia, Crete, 793; d. Constantinople, 868 (feast, Feb. 4). He joined his uncle Theophane, a Studite monk in Constantinople, at the age of 10 and was sent by the Abbot Theodore (*see* THEODORE THE STUDITE, ST.) to study in a school under the jurisdiction of the monastery. He became a monk and priest, and he followed his abbot into exile during the iconoclastic persecution (*see* ICONOCLASM). After flogging and ill-treatment he was imprisoned for 3 years at Smyrna. In 821 he was freed, and aided by his brother Titus, he rejoined the monastery after the invasion of Crete by the Saracens and the massacre of his family (*c.* 826). Exiled anew in 829, he took refuge on the outskirts of Constantinople. In 846 he succeeded Naucratius as abbot and was forced out of the monastery again, but he returned to office in 853. In 858 he was among the first to oppose the depositions of the patriarch (St.) *Ignatius and the nomination of *Photius. There followed a new exile, deposition, and imprisonment. He died shortly after being reinstated (867); he was 75. As was the practice, his biography emphasizes the miracles he had accomplished. It was written in 916 under the fourth successor to Nicholas and is a most interesting document of the period aggravated by the later iconoclastic struggles and the affair of Photius. It

is also a valuable source of precious information concerning the customs of the times.

Bibliography: F. COMBEFIS, ed., *Vita*, PG 105:863–926. ActSS Feb. 1:544–557. T. NISSEN, *Byzantinisch–neugriechisches Jahrbuch* 14 (1937–38) 331–339. G. DA COSTA-LOUILLET, *Byzantion* 25–27 (1955–57) 794–812. E. V. DOBSCHÜTZ, ByzZ 18 (1909) 70–72.

[I. DALMAIS]

NICHOLAS I, PATRIARCH OF CONSTANTINOPLE

Patriarchate, March 1, 901, to February 907, and *c.* May 15, 912, to 925; b. Constantinople, 852; d. there, May 15, 925 (feast, in the Greek Church, May 15). Nicholas was born of an Italian slave on the private estates of Patriarch *Photius and entered a career in the civil service; but as a close friend of Photius he was involved in his fall (886) and became a monk. Having been chosen as secretary (*Mysticus*) by the Emperor *Leo VI he was appointed patriarch of Constantinople in 901. Nicholas's correspondence reveals the finer side of his complex character, his charity and forbearance in appeasing the strife over the Emperor's four marriages, the so-called tetragamy; his prudence in dealing with abuses; and his zeal for converting the barbarians of Cis- and Trans-Caucasia. He was deposed in 907 either for opposing Leo VI's fourth marriage or for treasonable dealings with a rebel—eyewitness sources differ. Recalled either by Leo shortly before death or by Emperor Alexander (912–913), Nicholas headed the board of regency for the minor *Constantine VII Porphyrogenitus, but experienced great difficulties. By taking a savage revenge on *Euthymius I, who had replaced him as patriarch, he alienated many among the clergy, and he was opposed by the party in the state loyal to the Macedonian dynasty and the Queen Mother Zoë, who had been forced into a convent with Nicholas's connivance. Thus the Byzantine state was disturbed by conflict between the Nicholaites and Euthymians.

During the rise of *Romanus Lecapenus (920–944) Nicholas used his position as regent to arrange a marriage between his ward, Constantine VII, and Romanus's daughter Helen, and conducted a diplomatic correspondence with the Bulgarian Czar Symeon in favor of a peace treaty. He achieved a reconciliation with Euthymius before the latter's death (917) and undertook a campaign to restore unity to the Church. In a synod (920) he issued a decree of union settling the question of more than one marriage, by legislating that a second marriage was on a par with a first, that a third was subject to stringent regulations, and that a fourth was equivalent to living in sin. However, an influential group demanded the intervention of the Holy See, and Nicholas requested the Pope to send legates to reassert the original decision of Pope *Sergius III (904–911) on Leo's fourth marriage, which, Nicholas said, had then become the decision of all (Grumel, *Regestes*, 675), namely, that a fourth marriage was against Byzantine law and the Byzantine sense of propriety, yet a dispensation was granted for the good of the State, the need of a settled succession in a legitimate heir. Pope *John X (914–928) complied, and thus in 923 ended the schism between the Euthymians and Nicholaites. Nicholas was canonized by the Byzantine Church. His literary remains consist of sermons on notable occasions, the decree of union, and his diplomatic letters.

Bibliography: PG 111:9–392. Mai SpicRom 10:161–440. CMedH² v.4.1. Beck KTLBR 550. K. BAUS, LexThK² 7:995. G. MORAVCSIK, *Byzantinoturcica,* 2 v. (2d ed. Berlin 1958) v.1. Ostrogorsky 190, 230–236. A. A. VASILIEV, *A History of the Byzantine Empire* (2d Eng. ed. Madison, Wis. 1952). J. DARROUZÈS, ed., *Epistoliers byzantins du Xᵉ siècle* (Paris 1961). R. J. H. JENKINS, *Acta antiqua Academiae Scientiarum Hungaricae* 11 (1963) 145–147; "Three Documents Concerning the *Tetragamy,*" DumbOaksP 16 (1962) 229–241; "A Note on the *Letter to the Emir* of Nicholas Mysticus," *ibid.* 17 (1963) 399–401. P. KARLIN-HAYTER, "La Préhistoire de la dernière volonté de Léon VI," *Byzantion* 33 (1963) 483–486.

[M. J. HIGGINS]

NICHOLAS III, PATRIARCH OF CONSTANTINOPLE, 1084 to 1111.

Of unknown origin, called Grammaticus, Nicholas became a monk in the urban monastery of Prodromos and in 1084 succeeded the deposed Eustratius Garridos as patriarch. His career was devoted to intense administrative and canonical activity. He attempted to regulate the difficult questions, raised by the Metropolitan Leo the Chalcedonian (1084–86), who opposed the employment of sacred objects for other than a religious purpose as a form of *iconoclasm, including the use of the Church's jewels to supplement urgent needs of the imperial treasury as requested by Emperor *Alexius I. Nicholas opposed imperial attempts to promote bishoprics to the rank of metropolitan sees, and frequently intervened in strengthening monastic discipline, as in the case of the Wallachian shepherds on Mt. *Athos. He condemned the monk Nilus (1094) and the *Bogomil heretics of Constantinople, as well as their leader, the physician Basil (1110).

He was probably the author of a monastic *Typikon,* adapted from that of St. Sabas and attributed to Nicholas of Constantinople, and he laid down canonical responses for Baptism, marriage, confession, fasting, and established a rite for the Proscomide, i.e., the preparation of the holy gifts at the beginning of the Liturgy. Despite his original antiunion convictions, in a synod held in September 1089, and in a letter to Pope Urban, he went on record as favoring a resumption of relations with the papacy, but he proved intransigent in the controverted questions regarding the *filioque, unleavened bread, and the Roman primacy.

Bibliography: PG 119:859–884; 127:972–984; 131:39–48; 138:937–950. Pitra SpicSol 4:487–495. Grumel Reg 1.3:938–998. V. GRUMEL, "Un Document canonique inédit du patriarche Nicolas III," ÉchosOr 39 (1940–42) 342–348; LexThK² 7:986. W. HOLTZMANN, "Die Unionverhandlungen zwischen Kaiser Alexios I und Papst Urban II im Jahre 1089," ByzZ 28 (1928) 38–67. Beck KTLBR 660–661. R. JANIN, DTC 11.1:614–615.

[I. DALMAIS]

NICHOLAS OF AARHUS, BL.,

Danish ascetic; b. Jutland, *c.* 1150; d. Aarhus, Denmark, 1180 (feast day now unknown). Nicholas, or Niels, was a bastard son of King Canute V Magnusson (d. 1157). He spent some years at the Danish court, but later retired to his estates near Aarhus, where he led a simple and saintly life. Legend praises his chastity and charity. He was regarded as one of the patron saints of Aarhus although he was probably never formally canonized or beatified. There was an unsuccessful process initiated in Rome in 1254, and in connection with this a number of miracles were recorded.

Bibliography: M. C. GERTZ, ed., *Vitae Sanctorum Danorum,* 3 v. (new ed. Copenhagen 1908–12) 3:391–408. N. HANSEN, *Vore Helgener* (Copenhagen 1917) 173–175. J. OLRIK, *Dansk biografisk Leksikon,* 27 v. (Copenhagen 1933–44) 16:615–616.

[H. BEKKER-NIELSEN]

NICHOLAS OF AUTRECOURT

Scholastic theologian; b. Autrecourt (Ultricuria), near Verdun, France, *c.* 1300; d. Metz, shortly after 1350. Having obtained his degree in arts at Paris, he became a bachelor of theology. In 1340 *Benedict XII cited Nicholas to the papal court at Avignon on suspicion of teaching erroneous doctrines. On May 19, 1346, *Clement VI condemned Nicholas and ordered his works to be burned in public. His surviving writings are nine letters to Bernard of Arezzo, of which only two are complete; one letter to Giles of Medonta; a question, *Utrum visio creaturae possit naturaliter intendi;* and an important treatise, *Ad videndum an sermones Peripateticorum fuerint demonstrativi,* usually designated by the opening words, *Exigit ordo* or *Satis exigit ordo.* The complete treatise is extant in one manuscript only. In the prologue he states clearly that he does not intend to establish any positive teaching but only to examine the main Averroist doctrines and to test the validity of their demonstrations. He asks that the reader not accept as a fact the eternity of the world or atomism or any of the statements he makes in proving that the peripatetic conclusions are, at best, only probable and, at worst, quite false. He also asks that men not spend their whole life investigating the sayings of *Aristotle and his commentators; rather let them adhere to the sacred Christian law and the articles of faith. The judges at Nicholas's trial for heresy rejected such assertions as mere subterfuge (*excusatio vulpina*).

In his attack on *Aristotelianism and Averroism Nicholas began with two principles: that all knowledge comes from sensation and that there is only one valid criterion of certitude, namely, the basic principle that contradictories cannot at one and the same time be true. However, the senses do deceive man, and it is often difficult to reduce arguments to the principle of contradiction. Therefore, in most cases one must be satisfied with probabilities. Nicholas applied these principles in criticisms of Averroist-Aristotelian physics, of the theory of knowledge, and of causality. Concerning physics, generation and corruption as described by Aristotle cannot be proved; atomism, which Aristotle rejected, is just as probable an explanation. Nicholas's method was either to prove a doctrine contrary to that held by Aristotle or to prove an Aristotelian argument to be insufficient. Concerning knowledge, Nicholas first proves that there is not a single intellect for all men (*see* INTELLECT, UNITY OF). He then shows that man is certain of his sensations, of his feelings, and of principles known by means of terms. He is aware of the objection that evidence and truth are not identical. In reply he asserts that, since the intellect desires truth, deprivation of truth would be a violation of universal goodness and man's desires would be in vain. Nicholas did not deny *causality, but he did deny its demonstrability. The doctrines expressed by

Nicholas were not unique; *John of Mirecourt, a contemporary, taught many of them. It is difficult to assess the influence of Nicholas because of the condemnation of 60 of his theses in 1346 and his abjuration in 1347 (ChartUnParis 2:576–587). After his condemnation he is supposed to have fled to the court of *Louis IV, the Bavarian.

Bibliography: J. R. O'DONNELL, "Tractatus universalis magistri Nicholai de Ultricuria ad videndum an sermones Peripateticorum fuerint demonstrativi," MedSt 1 (1939) 179–280; "The Philosophy of Nicholas of Autrecourt and the Appraisal of Aristotle," *ibid.* 4 (1942) 97–125. J. LAPPE, *Nicolaus von Autrecourt: Sein Leben, seine Philosophie, seine Schriften* (Beitr GeschPhilMA 6.2; 1908). J. R. WEINBERG, *Nicolaus of Autrecourt* (Princeton 1948). M. DAL PRA, *Nicolà di Autrecourt* (Milan 1951); "La fondazione del'empirismo e le sue aporie nel pensiero di Nicolà di Autrecourt," *Rivista critica di storia della filosofia* 5 (1952) 389–402. E. MACCAGNOLA, "Metafisica e gnoseologia in Nicolà d'Autrecourt," RivFilNeosc 45 (1953) 36–53. W. P. SUHOW, "Nicolaus von Autrecourt und die altgriechischen Atomisten," *Bibliotheca classica orientalis* 4.5 (Berlin 1959) 318.

[J. R. O'DONNELL]

NICHOLAS OF BASEL, layman, heretical Beghard; d. Vienna, *c.* 1395. Preaching in the Rhine region near Basel (*see* BEGUINES AND BEGHARDS), he proclaimed himself inspired, and insisted that he was endowed with authority to govern the use of episcopal and priestly powers. He taught that submission to his direction was necessary for attaining spiritual perfection and that his followers could not sin even though they committed the worst crimes and disobeyed both Church and pope. K. Schmidt considered him the author of the *Bericht von der Bekehrung Taulers* (ed. Strasbourg 1875), which attributed the conversion of Johannes *Tauler (1300–61) to the *Gottesfreund vom Oberland* (Friend of God of the Upper Rhine), whom Schmidt identified as Nicholas of Basel. This theory has now been generally abandoned. Nicholas was burned at the stake with two of his followers.

Bibliography: H. DENIFLE, "Der Gottesfreund vom Oberland und Nikolaus von Basel," *Historisch-politische Blätter für das katholische Deutschland* 75 (1875) 17–38, 93–122, 245–266, 340–354. E. W. MCDONNELL, *Beguines and Beghards in Medieval Culture* (New Brunswick, N.J. 1954). W. MÜLLER, LexThK² 7:981–982.

[A. CONDIT]

NICHOLAS OF CLAIRVAUX, monastic author and courtier; b. county of Champagne, early 12th century; d. *c.* 1176. Nicholas, educated at the Benedictine abbey of Montiéramey near Troyes, entered the abbey of *Clairvaux in 1145, and became secretary to St. *Bernard of Clairvaux. He was expelled in 1152, but found favor at the courts of Pope *Adrian IV and Count Henry I of Champagne. By 1160 he was prior of St. Jean-en-Châtel in Troyes, and he may have become abbot of Montiéramey shortly before his death. His extant works, minor but indicative of monastic culture, are 19 sermons, edited with the works of *Peter Damian; over 60 letters; 2 Offices (still unpublished), and 10 sequences.

Bibliography: Sources. Sermons, PL 144, and see O. J. BLUM, *St Peter Damian* (Washington 1947) 42–45. Letters, mostly in PL 196:1589–1654. M. D. CHENU, "Platon à Cîteaux," ArchHist DoctLitMA 29 (1954) 99–106. J. LECLERCQ, "Les Collections de sermons de Nicolas de Clairvaux," RevBén 66 (1956) 269–302. J. F. BENTON, "Nicholas of Clairvaux and the Twelfth-Century Sequence," *Traditio* 18 (1962) 149–179; "Nicolas de Clairvaux

à la recherche du vin d'Auxerre," *Annales de Bourgogne* 34 (1962) 252–255.

[J. F. BENTON]

NICHOLAS OF CLAMANGES

Christian humanist and theologian; b. Nicholas Poillevillain, Clamanges (Champagne, Diocese of Châlons), *c.* 1360; d. Paris, 1437. At the age of 12 he entered the College of Navarre in Paris, where he pursued literary and theological studies. He quickly won renown and made many lasting friendships in the circle of the humanists—at court, John of Montreuil, James of Nouvion, Gonthier Col, and later Nicholas of Blaye; at the papal court in Avignon, John Muret and John of Moccia. In 1393 he became rector of the University of *Paris, where his friends and colleagues included *Peter of Ailly and Jean *Gerson. Urged by his friends, he went to Avignon, where in 1397 he became papal secretary under the antipope *Benedict XIII. Having escaped death during the plague of 1398, he returned to Langres. Although he was deeply involved in the political pressures surrounding the *Avignon papacy, Nicholas nevertheless seriously promoted measures for ending the *Western Schism. After Benedict's escape from Avignon, Nicholas rejoined him until the second withdrawal of obedience of 1408. He then returned to France permanently, residing in Langres, Valprofond, and Fontaine au Bois. In 1432 he returned to the College of Navarre in Paris; he engaged in writing till his death.

Above all Nicholas was a distinguished man of letters, an authentic Christian humanist. His was not a combative temperament; he never took sides directly in the factions that tore France asunder or the parties that divided the Church. It was by his letters and treatises that he intervened in the affairs of his century. Of his 151 extant letters, 138 were edited by J. Lydius, the others by A. Coville. Of his treatises, *De fructu eremi* and *De fructu rerum adversarum* were written *c.* 1408 at the time of his trials. Literary works include a tale and several poetic pieces, e.g., *Descriptio et laus urbis Januae, Deploratio calamitatis ecclesiasticae, Descriptio vitae rusticae, Descriptio vitae tyrannicae.* His other works treat of the internal strife in France (*De lapsu et reparatione justitiae* and the *Oratio ad Galliarum principes*) or deal with the Schism and the misfortunes of the Church, especially his *De ruina et reparatione ecclesiae* and *De praesulibus simoniacis.*

His vehement but justified criticism of the morals of ecclesiastics has sometimes caused Nicholas to be considered a precursor of the *Reformation. But such was not the case. His critiques were no harsher than those of Peter of Ailly or Dietrich of *Nieheim. He was neither a revolutionary nor a pagan. Although greatly influenced in his style and arguments by the ancient writers whom he cited abundantly, he always returned to the Scriptures and his reflections and counsels are authentically Christian. Also extant are several beautiful prayers, a commentary on Isaias, *De filio prodigo, De novis festitatibus non instituendis,* and *De studio theologico,* in which he voices his deep conviction: We must not belabor the word of God; with it we must nourish our souls and give it abundantly to others.

Bibliography: *Opera omnia,* ed. J. M. LYDIUS (Leiden 1613); *Le Traité de la ruine de l'église,* ed. A. COVILLE (Paris 1936).

A. COVILLE, *Recherches sur quelques écrivains du XIVᵉ et du XVᵉ siècle* (Paris 1935). J. LECLERCQ, *"Les Prières inédites de Nicolas de Clamanges,"* RevAscMyst 23 (1947) 171–183. E. VANSTEENBERGHE, DTC 11.1:597–600. G. MOLLAT, *Catholicisme* 2:1165. A. COMBES, EncCatt 8:1844. R. BÄUMER, LexThK² 7:983–984.

[P. GLORIEUX]

NICHOLAS OF CUSA

Cardinal and bishop of Brixen (Bressanone, Italy), ecclesiastical politician, philosopher, theologian, and mathematician, also known as Cusanus; b. Kues (Lat. Cusa), part of the town Bernkastel-Kues on the Moselle, Diocese of Treves (Trier), Germany, 1401; d. Todi in Umbria, Italy, Aug. 11, 1464.

Life. After studies at Heidelberg and Padua, Cusanus took the doctorate in Canon Law in 1423. He probably taught for a few years at the University of Cologne after 1425, and in 1428 and 1435 refused calls made upon him by the recently founded University of Louvain. His period of greatness began in 1432, when he went to the Council of Basel to defend the claims of Ulrich of Manderscheid to the archdiocesan See of Trier against Bishop Raban of Speyer, who was named to the see by the Pope. Although he lost the case, the publication of his work on ecclesiastical law, *De concordantia catholica,* in which he supported the superiority of the general council over the pope, caused him to become one of the most respected members of the council. In the course of the year, relations between Eugene IV and the council became worse. Finally a break came over the question of a site for a proposed council for reunion with the Greeks. One of the presidents, Cardinal Giuliano Cesarini, led a minority group, which included Nicholas, in endorsing the Pope's choice of a place in Italy; when Eugene moved the council to Ferrara, Cusa left Basel. His leaving the conciliar radicals and joining forces with the Pope was a decisive point in his life. It was not, as many of his former friends claimed, a change of party based on convenience, but rather a genuine change of attitude stemming from his newly acquired understanding that the unity of the Church could be guaranteed only by the papacy.

In the winter of 1437–38, he was a member of the papal legation to Constantinople to win the Greek Emperor and the hierarchy of the Greek Church over to the papal plan and to bring them to Italy. From the early summer of 1438 on, he worked so indefatigably in Germany for the cause of Pope Eugene at meetings with emperors and princes—until the concluding of the Vienna Concordat (1448)—that A. S. Piccolomini, later Pius II, referred to him as the "Hercules among Eugene's followers." In acknowledgment of his great services, Eugene's successor, Nicholas V, created Cusa a cardinal. In March 1450, the Pope gave him (in disregard of the recently concluded concordat) the Diocese of Brixen, and himself consecrated Cusa, who had become a priest between 1436 and Oct. 11, 1440.

Toward the end of the Jubilee Year, the Pope made him his legate to Germany with a threefold task: to invigorate the religious life of the people by preaching the Jubilee indulgence; to reform the religious and diocesan clergy; and to work for peace. This official journey, lasting from Dec. 30, 1450, to March 1452, was the high point of Cusa's life. The legate visited many cities and cloisters in a circle tour of Vienna, Magdeburg, Haarlem, and Trier, preached often to clergy and laity, held provincial and diocesan synods at which he published his reform decrees, made visitations, and disposed authoritatively of questions placed before him. Utilizing competent coworkers, he conducted his journey as a gigantic parish mission (cf. J.

Nicholas of Cusa before St. Peter, detail of Cusa's monument by A. Bregno (1456), Church of St. Peter in Chains, Rome.

Koch, *Nikolaus von Cues und seine Umwelt,* Heidelberg 1948, 116–148).

Around Easter, 1452, he took over his diocese, and he held office until his death. During the 5 years he actually reigned, he not only established the finances and holdings of the diocese on a sound basis, but strove to make it a model diocese through such measures as frequent episcopal sermons, diocesan synods, and visitations of parishes and cloisters. If he met opposition here, he encountered even more when he attempted to regain his land rights as a prince, in accordance with the medieval practice. Since Duke Sigmund of Austria, who as Count of Tyrol was protector of the Church in Brixen, would allow no encroachment on his own property rights, a conflict ensued and the cardinal was eventually defeated. Fearing that the Duke intended to kill him, Cusa fled from the episcopal city in June 1457 and took refuge in the fortress of Buchenstein in the Dolomites. In the fall of 1458 he left his diocese altogether. His attempt to return after the Congress of Mantua (1459) ended, after the Duke's short siege of Cusa's castle at Bruneck in the Puster valley, with Cusa's promise to meet all his adversary's demands. Pius II regarded the actions against the cardinal as an insult to the Holy See and began ecclesiastical proceedings against Sigmund. Since the latter would not relent, he was excommunicated and the province of Tyrol placed under interdict. Only after the death of Cusa and that of his papal benefactor was the long and bitter feud terminated and the papal censure finally removed.

The last years of the cardinal, however, were by no means solely occupied by this unfortunate strife, for the Pope assigned him many important tasks. Without enumerating these, one may say that Nicholas was an influential adviser of Pius II. Nicholas's body was buried in his titular church of St. Peter in Chains, but his heart reposes in the hospital for the poor that he, his father, and sister built in his native Kues. According to a letter to the archbishop of Trier (Brixen, Dec. 14, 1453), in which he made known his intention to give to the poor whatever God gave him, he used the income from his benefices toward the hospital's construction, completed in 1458 (deed for the foundation: Rome, Dec. 3, 1458). Whereas much that the cardinal wrote and accomplished was short-lived, this institution endures to the present. Since the hospital contains his library, which is still priceless despite the losses it has suffered, it is a center for scholarly research.

Works. It is amazing that with all his extraordinary activity in ecclesiastical affairs Nicholas still found time to write. He had the singular gift of being able to concentrate on the tasks that confronted him and yet to be completely relaxed in his leisure, reading the Fathers, as well as contemplating philosophical, theological, and mathematical problems—often writing down his solutions with remarkable facility. Only his most important works can be mentioned here. On Feb. 12, 1440, in Kues, he finished his first philosophical work *De docta ignorantia* (On Learned Ignorance). This document presupposes the Christian faith and proposes to show that man's knowledge of God is only ignorance. His second work, which was purely philosophical and was written about 1442, examines the extent of possible knowledge for man and is entitled *De coniecturis.* Since in his view an exact concept of truth is not possible for man, Nicholas calls every positive statement about truth "conjecture." In the summer vacation of 1450, Nicholas wrote four dialogues under the general title of *Idiota,*—including *De sapientia* (2 books), *De mente,* and *De staticis experimentis*—and two mathematical treatises. The fall of Constantinople (1453) inspired him to write the religious treatise *De pace fidei,* and in his involuntary retreat in the castle at Buchenstein (1457–58) he wrote an essay concerning the problems of human knowledge, *De beryllo.* The works penned in Rome in the last years of his life—*De non aliud* (1462), *De venatione sapientiae* (1463), *De ludo globi* (1464), and *De apice theoriae* (1464)—reflect, for the most part, conversations in the household circle of his friends and young associates. In addition to these there are approximately 300 (mostly dated) sermon outlines and notes (1430–59). (See index by J. Koch, Cusanus-Texte I. Predigten 7. Heidelberg 1942, 48–194.) Separately handed down are the sermon the cardinal gave on June 5, 1463, at the investiture in the Benedictine convent at Monte Oliveto (Umbria, Italy), and the moving letter he wrote a few days later to the novices (G. von Bredow, "Das Vermächtnis des Nikolaus von Kues," SBHeidel 1955, 2 Abh.).

Thought. Nicholas's writings are, in their entire approach, nonscholastic; thus he cannot be located in any theological school of his time. He relies on the Neoplatonic Christian tradition, which originated with *Proclus and *Pseudo-Dionysius, and came down by way of *John Scotus Erigena and the School of Chartres to Meister *Eckhart, without identifying himself with any school. Nicholas rejects the scholastic method of questions, arguments pro and con, etc., and develops a new style of philosophical essay. This itself is the expression of Cusa's firm conviction that all human knowledge is inaccurate and that truth can be attained only by "infinitely many steps." The medieval ideal of the *Summa,* in which each question and answer has its determined place, no longer exists for him. A factor that played a decisive role in Cusa's mathematical as well as his philosophical essays was the idea—which occurred to him on his voyage from Constantinople to Venice (1437–38) and seemed to him like a "gift from above"—that contradictions will be resolved in infinity (*coincidentia oppositorum*). With the aid of this principle he believed that he, though a mathematical dilettante, could solve the twofold problem of the quadrature of the circle and the transformation of a circular arc into its length by simple construction.

Learned Ignorance. The discovery of this principle, above all, led him to his new method of "learned ignorance." Nicholas developed this first in the light of man's knowledge of God. He began with the Neoplatonic concept of God as an absolute unity. He preferred this concept to others, because the notion of the Triune is the fundamental concept of Christian theology. Absolute unity is infinite. Since no relationship between the infinite and the finite permits a comparison, and man's discursive thinking depends upon comparison, God is inaccessible to such thought. Is God so remote from man's knowledge that all statements made by Christian philosophers and theologians about Him are empty of content? According to the teaching of St. *Thomas Aquinas, the analogy of being furnishes concepts that help man overcome the infinite chasm that separates him from God. This method

Nicholas did not adopt as his own, because he did not accept its supposition, viz, the philosophy of being.

The method Cusa developed was a method of investigation through symbols (*symbolice investigare*). A symbol, by its very nature, relates to something it symbolizes. It does not represent a concept, but rather an image. Where does one get symbols? Nicholas answers: The human intellect either conceives symbols in itself or it creates them. An object is known to be as it is only when it owes its existence to the human intellect. It is for this reason that Nicholas chooses his first symbols from geometry. From a given straight line, a triangle, a circle, and a sphere are "unfolded." These are already contained potentially within the line itself. Thereupon, Nicholas asks one to make a double transcendence, i.e., a double venture beyond the finite. With the first step he arrives at the infinite straight line—there is only one—that does not contain within itself a potentiality for triangle, circle, and sphere, but rather, simultaneously, is really infinite triangle, infinite circle, and infinite sphere. This infinite geometric formulation is not only unimaginable but also beyond rationality, since the contradictions, straight and curved, are resolved in it (*coincidentia oppositorum*). In the second transcendence one must abstract from all quantity and raise himself to the absolute, simple infinity of God. He stays with this in "ignorance," but it is "learned ignorance," because, in symbols, one somehow touches God's infinity. It is as if he sees through a mirror darkly (1 Cor 13.12). The symbol points out that God's infinity in this way is unity, a unity that is simultaneously absolute fullness and that contains within itself implicitly (*complicite*) all opposites in absolute simplicity. Yet, in his *De coniecturis,* Cusa changed this doctrine by holding that God is infinitely above the coincidence of opposites.

The Cosmos. Although Cusa's development of geometric symbols is open to criticism [see M. Feigl, Div Thom F22 (1944) 321–338], symbolic theology, to which Nicholas devoted much thought to the end, is itself worthy of study. Especially profound and penetrating is the insight contained in *De ludo globi.* When God created the world He "unfolded" Himself, but in otherness, in such a way that all creatures are somehow images of God, although they have only a "contracted" being. The universe participates in God's infinity insofar as it has no given limits in space and time. It is also a unity, although not an absolute unity like God, but rather a contracted one that contains a potentially infinite variety and differentiation that is all implicitly within it. The "self-unfolding" of the universe can be seen in two ways. First, it develops step by step. This idea of a stepwise, hierarchical cosmos Nicholas could have taken from tradition. What was new was the thought, which G. W. *Leibniz was later to systematize, that all steps are so connected with each other that the world displays an uninterrupted continuity from the least elements to the highest spirits. The second consideration begins with the idea that everything that really exists is individually determined. If the universe is evidenced in the individual, the latter is similarly representative of the universe.

Nicholas breaks fundamentally, as one can see, with the ancient and medieval concept of the world. If the universe is infinite in space, then it has no immovable center. Earth is a planet among planets and not inferior to the others. It has a special place in that it is the habitat of man, whose nature is more perfect than that of other inhabitants of the visible world.

Man. Human nature is a world in miniature, a microcosmos—an idea first expressed in Greek natural philosophy. Nicholas, however, went further, speaking of man as a "human god" and a "second god." This is not for him the expression of a proud Renaissance consciousness, but rather the interpretation of the words God used to create man according to His own image (Gn 1.27). Nicholas sees this likeness above all in the creative power of the human intellect. Just as God is the Creator of the real world, so is man not only the creator of his world of concepts (including mathematical concepts), but also the inventor of many things for which he does not find a pattern in nature but only in his own intellect. Also, in this regard, he is like the Creator who encompasses all things within Himself. Man is finally like God in that he possesses freedom of will, although unlike God in that this freedom includes the possibility of choosing evil. Man can make of himself an angel or a beast; both are contained potentially in human nature. His moral responsibility is to develop within himself a likeness to the triune God.

Other Contributions. Nicholas was a universal thinker who illuminated and contributed to many areas of scientific endeavor without being a specialist in these fields. His contributions to astronomy and mathematics were significant. Through his "thought experiments" with the balance, he earned himself a place in the history of scientific methodology. The first geographical map of central Europe was inspired by him. So, too, can the first catechetical chart in the German language be traced to him. Above all he was an important legal historian who recognized the illegality of the *Donation of Constantine and the Pseudo-Isidorian decrees; he wished to have the ancient sources of Germanic law compiled in a unified German law, and he was able to support his claims for the restoration of his rights as a prince-landowner through an exact knowledge of the documents in his episcopal archives concerning the development of the territory of the Church in Brixen. His all-embracing spirit set as a lifetime goal the reestablishing of a complete harmony in everything, but this grand scheme was destined to remain an unaccomplished ideal.

See also RENAISSANCE PHILOSOPHY.

Bibliography: Works. *Opera,* ed. J. FABER (Paris 1514; reprint Basel 1565), first, almost complete edition; *Opera omnia,* ed. E. HOFFMANN and R. KLIBANSKY, 14 v. (Leipzig 1932–), new critical edition; *Schriften des Nikolaus von Cues in deutscher Übersetzung,* ed. E. HOFFMANN (Philosophischen Bibliothek; Leipzig 1936–); *The Vision of God,* tr. E. GURNEY-SALTER (New York 1928); *Oeuvres choisies de Nicolas de Cues,* tr. M. P. DE GANDILLAC (Paris 1942).

Literature. Copleston v.2. Gilson HistChrPhil. P. ROTTA, Enc Fil 1:1379–84. E. VANSTEENBERGHE, *Le Cardinal Nicolas de Cues . . .* (Paris 1920). H. BETT, *Nicholas of Cusa* (London 1932). E. MEUTHEN, *Die letzten Jahre des Nikolaus von Kues* (Cologne 1958). P. MENNICKEN, *Nikolaus von Kues* (Leipzig 1932). M. P. DE GANDILLAC, *La Philosophie de Nicolas de Cues* (Paris 1941), Ger. *Nikolaus von Cues: Studien zu seiner Philosophie und Philosophischen Weltanschauung* (Düsseldorf 1953). P. E. SIGMUND, *Nicholas of Cusa and Medieval Political Thought* (Cambridge, Mass. 1963). V. MARTIN, "The Dialectic Process in the Philosophy of Nicholas of Cusa," *Laval Théologique et Philosophique* 5 (1949) 213–268. E. MEUTHEN, *Das Trierer Schisma von 1430 auf dem Basler Konzil: Zur Lebensgeschichte des Nikolaus von Kues* (Buchreihe der Cusanus-Gesellschaft, ed. J. KOCH and R. HAUBST, v.1; Münster 1964). *Mitteilungen und Forschungsberichte der Cusanus-Gesellschaft,* v.1 (Münster 1961–), v.1 contains good *Cusanus-Bibliographie,* suppls. in succeeding vols. **Illustration credit:** Alinari-Art Reference Bureau.

[J. KOCH]

NICHOLAS OF DINKELSBÜHL

German theologian; b. Dinkelsbühl, Germany, *c.* 1360; d. Vienna, Austria, March 17, 1433. He attended a good Latin school, probably in the Carmelite monastery of his native town, and in 1385 went to the University of *Vienna, which had only the preceding year been staffed with a theology faculty. He was awarded the master of arts degree and the licentiate in 1389 and began theological studies while lecturing in the arts faculty. In 1392–93 and again in 1397 he was dean of the arts faculty. He received his licentiate in theology in 1408 and the degree of master of theology in 1409. For more than 40 years he lectured at Vienna; he was made rector of the university in 1405–06 and was dean of the faculty of theology in 1418, 1425, and 1427. He continued brilliantly, if with little originality, the tradition of his more famous teachers *Henry Heinbuche of Langenstein and *Henry of Oyta. Nicholas was celebrated as the *lux ex Suevia,* and Peter of Pirchenwart (d. 1436) called him in his obituary "a veritable second founder of our University." In 1405 he became canon of St. Stephen's and in 1425, confessor to Duke Albrecht V (d. 1439) of Austria, whose ecclesiastical policy he had successfully supported. As an ambassador of the Duke, Nicholas was active from 1414 to 1418 at the Council of *Constance, where he greeted the Emperor *Sigismund on his entry into the city on Dec. 24, 1414. He represented the German nation at the assembly that elected *Martin V pope in 1417, ending the *Western Schism. In an oration addressed to Martin V, he begged especially for Martin's support of the reform movement initiated by the Abbey of *Melk, a reform of which Nicholas was one of the founders and pioneers. As a member of the Holy Office, he was especially involved in the trial of *Jerome of Prague. The testimonial he compiled on the "scandalous tenets" of the Dominican John of *Falkenberg nevertheless reveals Nicholas's natural disposition to be a mediator. In 1427 he was commissioned by Martin V to preach to the *Hussites. Nicholas not only came out in favor of *conciliarism, as his class and rank would dictate, but he was a voluminous writer of important sermons on the subject, aside from his academic lecturing and research activity. His manuscripts have been preserved in Vienna, Munich, Melk, Klosterneuburg, Graz, and Vorau; and although they number more than 1,000, only a few have been edited. He wrote the usual commentaries on the *Sentences,* among which the *Quaestiones Mellicenses* are outstanding, and also commentaries on the Scriptures. Here he was following the scholastic tradition, which likewise set the style for his general sermons. He showed an original talent in his treatises and sermons on the ecclesiastical policy questions of his time, the Hussite heresy, and conciliarism. His *Avisamenta vel Reformationis methodus* deals with monastic reform; and another group of manuscripts includes various works, such as *De praeparatione ad missam.* Nicholas's remains are buried in the Cathedral of St. Stephen in Vienna.

Bibliography: A. MADRE, *Nikolaus von Dinkelsbühl: Leben und Schriften* (BeitrGeschPhilMA 40.4; 1965), important work for any serious study. K. BINDER, LexThK² 7:984–985. A. LHOTSKY, *Quellenkunde zur mittelalterlichen Geschichte Österreichs* (Graz 1963) 331–335. G. KOLLER, *Princeps in ecclesia* (Graz-Vienna-Cologne 1964). H. HÜHN-STEINHAUSEN, EncCatt 8:1844–45. P. UIBLEIN, MitteilIÖG 73 (1965).

[H. WOLFRAM]

NICHOLAS OF FLÜE, ST.

Farmer, politician, father of 10 children and then hermit, whose influence saved Switzerland from disruption in 1481; b. at what is now Flüeli, near Sachseln, Obwalden, March 21?, 1417; d. in the Ranft, a nearby ravine, March 21, 1487 (feast, in Switzerland, Sept. 25; elsewhere, March 21). The first child of a devout and relatively wealthy couple, Klaus (as he was usually called) was a remarkable lad, given to praying unostentatiously, and early influencing his companions. As a youngster he fasted every Friday, and this was increased to four times a week, probably soon after a vision he had at the age of 16. This vision of a tower rising up from the Ranft deeply impressed him and made him long for a solitary life. In the 15th century there was already conscription among the Swiss, and Klaus was drafted into the army for the Zurich wars (1440–44) and the Thurgau war (1460). A fellow con-

St. Nicholas of Flüe, a portrait statue in wood carved c. 1504. Because this statue was made only about 20 years after the death of the saint, it may have been carved by someone who actually knew him.

script recorded that Klaus "did but little harm to the enemy, but rather always went to one side, prayed, and protected the defeated enemy as best he could." During the Thurgau campaign he put a stop to the burning of the Dominican convent of St. Katharinental near Diessenhofen, where an Austrian garrison had taken refuge. Probably not long after the Zurich war Klaus married Dorothea Wyss from Oberwilen. His longing for the life of a hermit had seemingly become quiescent, but it was still latent and caused an inner conflict that became acute about 20 years later. Owing to gaps in the Obwalden archives, most of Klaus's political and judicial activity must remain unknown, but, on his own admission, he had considerable authority as a judge and councilor. He said he did not remember ever having been unjust or a respecter of persons. Despite his obvious ability he despised temporal honors and contrived to prevent his election as Landamman. About 1463, family life became a burden to him and, advised by a priest friend, he found temporary relief in devoting much time to meditation upon the Passion. Troubled by irremediable events, which were proving obstacles to his peace of mind, he withdrew from politics about 1465. The longing to become a hermit made itself felt ever more acutely; and, convinced that it was what God wanted of him, Klaus wrested the permission from Dorothea to leave her. Three and a half months after the birth of their fifth son Nicholas, who was to become a priest and doctor in theology, Klaus left home, on Oct. 16, 1467. Fearing local opposition, he set off to cross the frontiers, but near Liestal a seemingly supernatural intervention made him retrace his steps. His first attempt at eremetical life was made on the forsaken Klisterli Alp in the Melchtal. This came to nought, thanks to the curious, scoffing visitors who came to see him. Klaus repaired to the Ranft, to the site of the tower of his youthful vision, quite near his home. For the remaining 19½ years of his life he abstained completely from food. Neighbors helped him build a log cabin; a year later, however, it was the local authorities, who, after having set guards to watch him and convince themselves that he and his fast were genuine, constructed a hermitage and an adjoining chapel. In 1469, Thomas Weldner, auxiliary Bishop of Constance, came to test Klaus and to consecrate the chapel. Churchmen and politicians came to ask his advice, and people in great numbers consulted him in their troubles. Even his wife, with whom he had clearly a deep understanding, was among the visitors to the hermitage. Friendly, affectionate, and thoughtful, he had a remarkable gift for encouraging the sad and depressed. To all he was known as "Brother Klaus." Owing to his efforts, the quarrelling cantons came together at the Diet of Stans in Dec. 1481; and when, during the assembly, they were on the point of returning home to settle matters by arms, his advice to the delegates, transmitted by Heinrich am Grund, the parish priest, restored peace. Nicholas was buried at Sachseln, where his body still lies. He was canonized in 1947, and is venerated by Catholics and Protestants alike. His importance as a figure of peace and brotherhood can hardly be exaggerated. Owing to his unique visions and prodigious memory he has attracted the attention also of psychologists.

Bibliography: R. DURRER, *Bruder Klaus*, 2 v. (Sarnen, Switz. 1917–21). K. VOKINGER, *Bruder Klaus: Sein Leben* (Stans, Switz. 1947). F. BLANKE, *Bruder Klaus von Flüe: Seine innere Geschichte* (Zurich 1948). M. L. VON FRANZ, *Die Visionen des Niklaus von Flüe* (Zurich 1959). G. R. LAMB, *Brother Nicholas* (New York 1955). **Illustration credit:** Verlag Jos. Reinhard, Sachseln.

[T. BOOS]

NICHOLAS OF GORRAN, preacher and exegete; b. Gorran, Dept. Mayenne, France, 1232; d. Paris, *c.* 1295. He entered the Dominican Order at Le Mans, but spent almost his whole life at the Dominican monastery of Saint-Jacques in Paris. For some years he was the confessor of King Philip the Fair. He wrote commentaries, glosses, and postils on the whole Bible, with special concentration on the NT. His *Commentaria in IV Evangelia* was often reprinted, the first edition being among the incunabula (Cologne 1472). His *Postillae in epistolas canonicas septem* was first published as a work of St. Thomas Aquinas (Paris 1543).

Bibliography: Quétif-Échard 1.1:437–444. Hurter Nomencl³ 2:416. ArchFrPraed 14 (1944) 50–52; 22 (1952) 396, 404. M. M. GORCE, DTC 11.1:614.

[L. F. HARTMAN]

NICHOLAS HERMANSSON, ST., bishop, hymnographer; b. Skäninge, *c.* 1326; d. Linköping, Sweden, May 2, 1391 (feast, July 24). Having studied in Paris and Orléans, he was canon in Uppsala, 1350; archdeacon in Linköping, 1360; and bishop of that diocese in 1374. He had educated *Bridget of Sweden's sons, and in 1384 Vadstena, the motherhouse of the *Bridgettines, was founded in his diocese. He is regarded as the greatest of the hymnographers of medieval Sweden. He was an important and stern churchman and at times opposed the royal power. The cult of St. *Ansgar became popular in Sweden through his efforts. In 1414 his canonization was attempted without result but in 1499 Rome gave permission for his relics to be translated; the translation was carried out in 1515.

Bibliography: BHL 2:6101–03. *Svenska män och kvinnor* (Stockholm 1942–) v.5. Butler Th Attw 3:178–179. J. METZLER, LexThK² 7:987. T. LUNDÉN, *Sankt Nikolaus av Linköping kanonisationsprocess: Processus canonizacionis beati Nicolai Lincopensis* (Stockholm 1963).

[H. BEKKER-NIELSEN]

NICHOLAS OF LYRA, French theologian and exegete; b. Lyre, Normandy, *c.* 1270; d. Paris, *c.* 1349. He joined the Friars Minor at Verneuile (*c.* 1300) and later studied and received the doctorate at Paris; by 1309 he was a professor at the Sorbonne, where he taught for many years. One of the best equipped Biblical scholars of the Middle Ages, he fully mastered Hebrew, was familiar with the Jewish commentators, notably *Rashi (1030–1105), and was indebted also to many others, particularly St. Thomas Aquinas. Deploring the state of Biblical studies in his time, he set out to change them. His chief work, *Postillae Perpetuae, sive Brevia Commentaria in Universa Biblica,* set forth the literal sense of Scripture, which he considered the most important and decisive one and the foundation of all mystical interpretations. His exposition was lucid and concise, and his observations, always original, were judicious and sound. Nicholas was highly esteemed and widely read on account of his sound scholarship and judicious interpretations. The *Postillae* was the first Biblical commentary to be printed (Rome 1471–72) and soon became the favorite manuel of exegesis. Martin Luther frequently used Nicholas's works and was indebted to them for his rabbinical knowledge. Nicholas

St. Nicholas of Myra, devotional picture or fragment of an altarpiece by Carlo Crivelli, 15th-century.

taught no new doctrine but returned to the same sound exegetical principles repeatedly laid down by the early Fathers and the schoolmen. Their efforts had failed because of the adverse tendencies of the times, but Nicholas carried out these principles effectively. H. Hailperin says he may be called the greatest early Bible scholar after Jerome.

Bibliography: H. LABROSSE, "Sources de la biographie et oeuvres de Nicolas de Lyre," *Études Franciscaines* 16 (1906) 383–404; 17 (1907) 489–505, 593–608; 19 (1909) 41–52, 153–175, 368–379; 35 (1923) 171–187, 400–432. C. V. LANGLOIS, "Nicolas de Lyre, frère mineur," HistLittFranc 36 (1927) 355–400. H. HAILPERIN, *Rashi and the Christian Scholars* (Pittsburgh 1963) 137–246, 249–260, 282–357, excellent notes and bibliog. A. KLEINHANS, LexThK² 7:992–993.

[J. J. MAHONEY]

NICHOLAS OF MYRA, ST., bishop of Myra in Lycia, first half of the 4th century (feast, Dec. 6; translation of relics to Bari, May 9). No historically trustworthy evidence of his ancestry or the events of his life exists, except for the fact of his episcopate. Legends have him born in the Lycian town of Patara, imprisoned in the Diocletian persecution, and present at the Council of Nicaea I and fix his death date at 345 or 352. *Justinian I built a church in his honor in the early 6th century (Procopius, *De aedificiis* 1.6), and Basil the Macedonian, an oratory in the imperial palace about 870. In the West, the first pope to bear his name built a basilica in his honor in the Lateran (*c.* 860). His cult was brought to Germany by the Byzantine Princess Theophano, wife of Otto II (973–983). It came to Italy with the theft in 1087 of his body by Italian soldiers and its "translation" to Bari. More than 2,000 churches are dedicated to him in France and Germany, and about 400 in England. Russia, Sicily, Lorraine, and Greece honor him as patron. The principal miracle-legends deal with his liberation of three unjustly imprisoned officers; his secret provision of dowries for three poor girls; and his deliverance of three innocent youths condemned to death. The oldest documentary evidence of the Nicholas legends is an 11th-century MS in Karlsruhe Library. The dowry legend was combined in Germany with local folklore to make St. Nicholas into the bringer, on the eve of his feast, of secret presents for children; in the English-speaking countries his name was corrupted into Santa Claus, and the legend became associated with Christmas Eve.

Bibliography: G. ANRICH, *Hagios Nikolaos,* 2 v. (Leipzig 1913–17). **Illustration credit:** Courtesy, the Cleveland Museum of Art.

[A. G. GIBSON]

NICHOLAS ORESME, French theologian and a founder of modern science and mathematics; b. Normandy, Diocese of Bayeux, *c.* 1320; d. Lisieux, July 11, 1382. A student of theology at Paris in 1348, he was grand master of the Collège de Navarre by 1356. In 1362 he was canon of Rouen and in 1364 dean of the cathedral. Some time before 1370 he became chaplain of King Charles V. He was consecrated bishop of Lisieux in 1378.

There are recent editions of some of his writings, but others are extant only in manuscripts and early editions. He wrote both in Latin and in French. At the request of Charles V he translated into French the *Nicomachean Ethics, Politics,* and *De caelo* of Aristotle and the pseudo-Aristotelian *Economics.* These translations were important in the development of the French language. Oresme's theological writings include *Contra astronomos judiciarios,* with a French adaptation *Livre de divinacions,* in which he argues against astrology and the magic arts, and a Christological treatise, *De communicatione idiomatum in Christo.*

Oresme is best known as a scientist, mathematician,

Nicholas Oresme presenting the book to King Charles V of France, detail of a miniature in a 14th-century manuscript (Brussels MS 9505–6, fol. 2v) of Aristotle's "Nicomachean Ethics" translated for the King by Oresme.

and economist. His most original scientific ideas are contained in two French works, *Traité de la sphère* and *Livre du ciel et du monde*. Against Aristotle he held, on the ground of the omnipotence of God, the possibility of many universes and the movement of man's universe in space. He questioned the Aristotelian theory that the earth is at rest while the heavens rotate about it, pointing out that motion is relative to the observer: the heavens appear to revolve around the earth, but the opposite may appear to an observer in the heavens. He was a precursor of Copernicus in holding that the appearances are explained more simply by supposing the daily motion of the earth than the motion of the heavens. Although Oresme saw no obstacle to this theory in Scripture and answered objections to it, he did not hold it as certain; in the end he accepted the traditional opinion.

Oresme's contributions to mathematics include the notion of fractional powers and rules for operating them. He prepared the way for analytical geometry by his use of graphs and algebraic functions to represent variations in the intensity and extension of qualities, such as heat and motion. Oresme's *De origine, natura, jure, et mutationibus monetarum* was the first scientific study of the problem of money.

Bibliography: Works. *Traité de la sphère* (Paris 1508); *Tractatus de latitudinibus formarum* (Paris 1482), an abridgement of the unedited *Tractatus de figuratione potentiarum et mensurarum difformitatum; Le Livre du ciel et du monde*, ed. A. D. MENUT and A. J. DENOMY, MedSt 3 (1941) 185–280; 4 (1942) 159–297; 5 (1943) 167–333; *The De Moneta of Nicholas Oresme and English Mint Documents*, tr. C. JOHNSON (New York 1956); *Quaestiones super Geometriam Euclidis*, ed. H. L. BUSARD (Leiden 1961); tr., *Le Livre de Éthiques d'Aristote*, ed. A. D. MENUT (New York 1940); *Le Livre de Yconomique d'Aristote*, ed. A. D. MENUT (Philadelphia 1957). Studies. L. F. MEUNIER, *Essai sur la vie et les ouvrages de Nicole Oresme* (Paris 1857). P. M. M. DUHEM, *Études sur Léonard de Vinci*, 3 v. (Paris 1903–16; repr. 1955) 3:346–405; *Le Système du monde*, v.7 (Paris 1956), *passim*. A. MAIER, *Die Vorläufer Galileis im 14. Jahrhundert* (Rome 1949), *passim*. A. C. CROMBIE, *Augustine to Galileo: The History of Science, 400–*

1650 (Cambridge, Mass. 1953). G. W. COOPLAND, *Nicole Oresme and the Astrologers: A Study of His Livre de divinacions* (Liverpool 1952). M. CLAGETT, *The Science of Mechanics in the Middle Ages* (Madison, Wis. 1959), *passim*. **Illustration credit:** Bibliothèque Royale, Brussels.

[A. MAURER]

NICHOLAS PAGLIA, BL., disciple of St. *Dominic, preacher, founder of priories at Trani, Perugia, and, perhaps, Todi; b. Giovinazzo, near Bari, Italy, 1197; d. Perugia, Feb. 11, 1255 (feast, Feb. 14). While studying law at *Bologna, he heard (St.) Dominic preach (1218) and joined the Dominican Order. He was twice provincial of the Roman province, from 1230 to 1235, and in 1255. In 1231 *Gregory IX appointed him to reform the overly strict Benedictine monks of *Sant' Antimo. He was present (1233) at the translation of St. Dominic's body. Prudent, charitable, and compassionate, especially to fellow religious, as superior he preached fraternal charity and joy and asked for willing, loving obedience. His relics repose under the high altar at Perugia. Leo XII beatified him, March 26, 1828. He is pictured, once by Fra *Angelico, with rods (authority), a book (learning), and church models (founder).

Bibliography: B. ANDRIANI, *Il Beato Nicola Paglia da Giovinazzo* (Molfetta 1959). A. WALZ, LexThK² 7:996–997.

[B. CAVANAUGH]

NICHOLAS OF PRUSSIA, BL., Benedictine monk; b. Prussia, *c.* 1379; d. monastery of San Niccolo del Boschetto, near Genoa, Feb. 23, 1456 (commemoration, Feb. 23). He made his vows on Feb. 6, 1414, under Abbot Louis Barbo (d. 1443) in the reformed monastery of Santa Giustina in Padua. Subsequently, he lived for a time in San Giorgio, Venice, and in *San Benedetto di Polirone near Mantua before going to Genoa, where he was made prior and novice master by 1430. He was noted for his zealous observance of the monastic rule, his holiness of life, and his gift of miracles. His relics are at San Giuliano d'Albaro, near Genoa. His cult is not approved.

Bibliography: Zimmermann KalBen 1:247–249. F. G. HOLWECK, *A Biographical Dictionary of the Saints* (St. Louis 1924) 741–742. A. ZIMMERMANN, LexThK¹ 7:588. J. JANUENSI, *Vita* in Pez ThesAnec 2.3:309–340.

[M. F. MC CARTHY]

NICHOLAS OF STRASSBURG, Dominican theologian and mystic; fl. 1323 to 1329. A member of the German province, he was a contemporary of *John of Sterngassen, Gerard of Sterngassen, and Meister *Eckhart. He may have studied theology in Paris. Before 1323 he wrote a *Summa philosophica* (5 bks.; MS Vat. lat 3091), in which he synthesized the doctrine of *Albert the Great and *Thomas Aquinas. Between 1323 and 1329 he was lector at the priory in Cologne and vicar of the master general in reforming the German province. During the process against Eckhart in 1326 he defended his confrere and exonerated his doctrines. When the archbishop of Cologne renewed charges against Eckhart in 1327, Nicholas was also implicated. During the crisis he was excommunicated, possibly out of revenge, by a confrere, Hermann of Höchst; but the Pope absolved him completely that same year. His best-known work is *De adventu Christi*, written about 1323. Some scholars have called it a "plagiarism" because it is a compilation drawn from two treatises by *John (Quidort) of Paris. Although he was a popular preacher, only 13 German sermons

"Miracle of St. Nicholas of Tolentino," by Giovanni di Paolo (c. 1403–82), tempera on wood, 20½ by 16⅜ inches.

are extant; they reflect a practical approach and a sound theological piety.

Bibliography: M. Grabmann, *Mittelalterliches Geistesleben*, 3 v. (Munich 1926–56) 1:392–431. E. Filthaut, LexThK² 7:998. H. Denifle, "Der Plagiator Nicolaus von Strassburg," Denifle-Ehrle Arch 4:312–329. Stegmüller RS 1:272.

[J. F. Hinnebusch]

NICHOLAS OF TOLENTINO, ST., patron of the Holy Souls; b. Sant' Angelo (near Fermo), 1245; d. Tolentino, Sept. 10, 1305 (feast, Sept. 10). Struck by the unusual precocity and piety of this son of Campagnone and Amata de Guarutti, the bishop of Fermo admitted him to minor orders and a canonship when he was still only in early boyhood. A sermon on the text 1 Jn 2.15–17 ("Do not love the world . . .") determined Nicholas to renounce the prospect of ecclesiastical eminence. He entered the Augustinian monastery at Sant' Angelo and had as his novice master there Father Reginaldo, the man who had preached the sermon.

From the beginning, Nicholas was an outstanding religious. Ordained at Cinguli in 1271, he served briefly there and in other houses of his order over a 4-year interval. Then he went to Tolentino, where he spent the remaining 30 years of his life. The developing urban life that characterized 13th-century Europe led to a decline in morality and religion. At Tolentino Nicholas worked hard to counteract this tendency. He not only preached daily to the people in the streets, he sought them out in their homes, in the hospital, and in prison. His rare power of persuasiveness in speech was bolstered by the authority that his reputed miracles gave his words. He became an increasingly popular confessor and edified his people particularly by the great devotion with which he said Mass. They put much trust in his intercession for departed souls, though it is uncertain whether the tradition of long standing according to which he is invoked as "Patron of the Holy Souls" goes back to his own times.

The process of his canonization, begun in 1325, was not completed until 1446 because of the troubles of the *Avignon papacy and the *Western Schism. A basilica, adorned with important 14th-century frescoes, enshrines the saint's body at Tolentino. The body, except for the severed arms, lay hidden beneath the basilica until its rediscovery in 1926, when it was formally identified.

Bibliography: Sources. ActSS Sept. 3:636–743. *Analecta Augustiniana* 3 (1909–10) 236–237, decree of canonization, 471–472, initiation of process; 13 (1929–30) 40–53, rediscovery of body. Literature. JORDAN OF QUEDLINBURG, *Liber vitasfratrum,* ed. R. ARBESMANN and W. HÜMPFNER (New York 1943). *Augustiniana* 6 (1956) 143–144. N. CONCETTI, *Vita di S. Nicola da Tolentino* (Tolentino 1932). Butler Th Attw 3:524–527. PIUS XII, "Quinque ante saecula," ActApS 38 (1946) 274–276. A. P. METZGER, "The Great Patron: St. Nicolas and the Suffering Souls," *The Tagastan* 15 (1952) 8–11, 49. **Illustration credit:** John G. Johnson Collection, Philadelphia.

[J. E. BRESNAHAN]

NICHOLAS TREVET, Dominican theologian, historian, humanist; b. Somerset, England, *c.* 1265; d. after 1334. The son of a justice in eyre, Sir Thomas Trevet (d. 1283), he entered the *Dominicans, studied at Oxford before 1300, and succeeded *William of Macclesfield, OP, as Regent Master at the university (1303–07). His *Quaestiones disputatae, Quodlibeta I–V,* and commentary on Genesis and Exodus belong to this period. In 1307 the general chapter of his order at Strasbourg gave special commendation to these Biblical commentaries and the Master General, Aymeric, urged him to complete his commentary on the Pentateuch. Later he wrote a commentary on Leviticus and sent it to Aymeric. Between 1307 and 1314 he lived in Paris, gathering material for his *Annales sex regum Angliae* (1135–1307), for his future Latin *Historia,* dedicated to Hugh of Angoulême, archdeacon of Canterbury, and for his last work, the *Cronycles,* written in Anglo-Norman (one version being dedicated to Princess Mary, sister of Edward II who was a nun of Amesbury Abbey). Returning to England, he resumed teaching at Oxford (1314–*c.* 1317) and developed a humanistic interest in the ancient classics. He commented on Seneca's *Declamationes (Controversiae)*— which he dedicated to John of Lenham, OP, confessor to Edward II (before 1314)—as well as on Boethius, Cicero, and Virgil. At the request of Nicholas of Prato, Papal Legate to England and dean of the College of Cardinals, he wrote a commentary on the *Tragedies* of Seneca; he was commissioned by Pope John XXII to write a commentary on Livy. He wrote also the earliest commentary on St. Augustine's *De civitate Dei,* later replaced in popularity and excellence by the work of his junior contemporary *Thomas Waleys. In 1324 he was lector of the Dominican Priory in London. He must still have been alive in 1334, since he mentions in the Anglo-Norman *Cronycles* that the reign of John XXII was 19 years.

Although not an original or speculative thinker, he was a pioneer in Biblical theology, historical accuracy, classical philology, and Christian humanism. His commentaries on Scripture revived Biblical studies in the Order of Preachers, and his interest in classical authors stimulated the renaissance of humanism in Europe. The popularity of his writings, which include approximately 30 works, is attested to by the more than 300 MSS that are extant.

Bibliography: *Il commento di Nicola Trevet al Tieste di Seneca,* ed. E. FRANCESCHINI (Milan 1938). Quétif-Échard 1.2: 561–565. Emden 3:1902–03. D. A. CALLUS, LexThK² 7:999–1000. C. L. KINGSFORD, DNB 19:1161–63. Glorieux L 1:246–254. Stegmüller RB 4:6032–38. F. EHRLE, "N.T., sein Leben seine *Quodlibet* und *Quaestiones ordinariae,*" *Festgabe Clemens Baeumker,* BeitrGeschPhilMA (1923) 1–63. R. J. DEAN, "Cultural Relations in the Middle Ages: N.T. and Nicholas of Prato," StPhilol 45 (1948) 541–564. B. SMALLEY, *English Friars and Antiquity in the Early 14th Century* (New York 1961).

[J. A. WEISHEIPL]

NICHOLAS OF VERDUN, Mosan goldsmith of the late 12th century; b. Verdun?, between 1130 and 1150; d. Tournai?, after 1205. His classicizing style and typological iconographic programs are transitional to the early Gothic. His earliest certain work is the so-called Klosterneuberg Altar (1181; Klosterneuberg, Austria), formerly a pulpit or ciborium containing 45 plaques executed in engraving and champlevé enamel. After the destruction of the abbey the altar was reconstructed in 1331 as an altarpiece with two wings. Six plaques in the style of the early work and enamels were added, and the verse inscriptions dividing the zones were lengthened. The altarpiece now consists of 51 plaques, each with an inscription, arranged in three zones according to a complex theological program for which there is no exact prototype. The upper tier contains scenes "ante legem," the middle "sub gratia," the lower "sub lege," except for the final six plaques, which deal with the Last Judgment. Style and technique are dependent upon the tradition of goldsmith's work in the Meuse valley and Cologne regions, while antique influence, already apparent in *Renier of Huy's work, can be seen in many figures. The relatively simple setting used for the altar's complex iconographic program gives way to a greater use of metal sculpture in the Shrine of the Three Magi (1181–*c.* 1220, Cologne Cathedral), which contains on its two long sides figures of Prophets by Nicholas. The hollow folds of the garments and easy grace of the poses are suggestive of the later Chartres and Reims classicizing figure style. In his final signed and dated work, the Shrine of the Virgin

Nicholas of Verdun, plaque with the "Crossing of the Red Sea," detail of the Klosterneuberg Altar, finished 1181.

(1205, Tournai Cathedral), enamel work plays only a subsidiary role.

Bibliography: F. RÖHRIG, *Der Verduner Altar* (Vienna 1955). S. COLLON-GEVAERT et al., *Art Roman dans la Vallée de la Meuse aux XIe et XIIe siècles* (Brussels 1963). **Illustration credit:** Austrian Information Service, New York City.

[M. M. SCHAEFER]

NICHOLAS, HIRAM CHARLES, founder and first president of the Council of Profit-Sharing Industries; b. Cincinnati, Ohio, July 19, 1893; d. Orrville, Ohio, April 23, 1950. In 1933 Nicholas became president of the Quality Castings Co. of Orrville, Ohio, a gray-iron foundry that had been closed by the Depression. Observing that the amount of defective castings was high, he introduced for foremen a bonus program designed to reduce scrap. Encouraged by its success, he decided to extend similar programs to all employees. After some experimentation, he adopted a profit-sharing plan that almost from its inception paid to employees bonuses amounting to about 35 per cent of their regular wages; at the same time, it increased returns to the stockholders.

Nicholas became an enthusiastic promoter of profit sharing and organized the Council of Profit-Sharing Industries, becoming its first president in 1947. He recognized that profit sharing can never substitute for skilled management, good wages, or sound industrial relations; but he maintained that when united with these, it can enhance the incomes of both workers and owners and build a spirit of vigorous cooperation. Nicholas married Helen Issenmann in 1921 and was the father of 8 children.

[A. YONTO]

NICLAES, HENDRIK, founder of the "House of Love," or Nicolaites or Familists; b. Münster, Westphalia, 1502; d. 1580. At Münster Niclaes (Nicholas) attended Latin school and worked in his father's business. At the age of 27, when he was suspected of Lutheran beliefs, he moved to Amsterdam, where he was under suspicion of being a "Münsterite." In 1541 he established a business at Emden, East Friesland, and gathered some followers. He was imprisoned, but escaped and went to the Netherlands, London, and Cologne. He wrote more than 50 pamphlets dealing with his prophecies and mystical pantheism and also carried on a literary dispute with David *Joris. About his relationship with the latter, an opponent said: "David George layed the egg and Henry Niclaes brought forth the chicken." He does not seem to have had any other Anabaptist connections. Niclaes emphasized an actual righteousness and holiness, which was practised in the "House of Love." Connected with this was an attempted degree of enlightenment and divinization. He had some followers in England and the Netherlands, among whom was the printer Christoffel Plantijn of Antwerp. By the end of the 17th century the Nicolaites had disappeared.

Bibliography: F. NIPPOLD, "Heinrich Niclaes und das Haus der Liebe," *Zeitschrift für die historische Theologie* 32 (1862) 321–402. R. M. JONES, *Studies in Mystical Religion* (London 1909). G. H. WILLIAMS, *The Radical Reformation* (Philadelphia 1962). K. ALGERMISSEN, LexThK² 4:21. G. BAREILLE, DTC 5.2:2070–72.

[C. KRAHN]

NICODEMUS, a Pharisee and apparently a member of the *Sanhedrin who showed himself interested in and favorable to the message of Jesus. He is known only from the fourth Gospel. Nakdemon ben Gurion, a wealthy Jew mentioned in the Talmud as helping in the laying up of stores against the coming Roman siege of Jerusalem (*Gittin* 56a; see also *Ta'anith* 19b, 21a on a Hebrew etymology giving his Greek name), bore a Hebraized form of the name Νικόδημος (prevailing among the people), but he is hardly to be identified with the Nicodemus of the Bible. John's Gospel relates how the latter, "a ruler of the Jews" and "a teacher in Israel," came to Jesus "at night" to converse with Him—a conversation in which Jesus stressed the necessity of a spiritual rebirth by water and the Holy Spirit for entering the Kingdom of God (Jn 3.1–21). Thereafter John refers to Nicodemus as "he who had come to Jesus by night," i.e., secretly (Jn 7.50; 19.39). On one occasion when some of the Pharisees wished to have Jesus arrested, Nicodemus spoke in His defense and suggested in vain that Jesus should be given a hearing (Jn 7.50–52). When Jesus was taken down from the cross, Nicodemus assisted *Joseph of Arimathea in preparing His body for burial, for which he contributed a large amount of myrrh and aloes (Jn 19.39–40).

Bibliography: EncDictBibl 1638. H. C. KEE, InterDictBibl 3:547. S. MENDNER, "Nikodemus," JBiblLit 77 (1958) 293–323.

[E. MAY]

NICODEMUS THE HAGIORITE, b. Naxos, 1748; d. Mt. Athos, July 14, 1809. He was baptized Nicholas; he made his studies at Smyrna and retired to Naxos in 1770 to escape Turkish reprisals. In 1775 he entered Mount *Athos, where he took the name Nicodemus. An encounter with Macarius of Corinth in 1777 confirmed his scholarly aspirations and he was persuaded to prepare an augmented edition of Macarius's *Philocalia,* or collection of oriental patristic texts dealing with mental prayer. This edition had a great influence on the revival of *Hesychasm and the *Jesus Prayer. His revised edition of Macarius's work on frequent Communion was condemned by Procopius of Smyrna in 1785, but his position was accepted as orthodox by the Synod of Constantinople in 1819.

Nicodemus, a prolific writer, contributed to the development of hagiographical, liturgical, scriptural, mystical, and canonical interest in the Oriental churches. His most important work, the *Pedalion,* or *Rudder of the Ship of Knowledge,* is a commentary on Greek canon law, which manifests certain anti-Roman tendencies. These are usually attributed to interpolations by its editor, the monk Theodoritus, though Nicodemus elsewhere manifests obvious prejudices against Roman ecclesiastical institutions. Nevertheless to stimulate the cultivation of mental prayer he published, in modern Greek, adaptations of both the *Spiritual Combat* of Lorenzo *Scupoli and the *Spiritual Exercises* of *Ignatius Loyola. His *Philocalia* (Venice 1782), or collection of writings on spiritual sobriety, and his *Enchiridion of Counsels* (Venice 1801), or doctrine of the custody of the five senses, the imagination, and the heart are of major influence in the contemporary Greek spirituality.

Nicodemus was solemnly canonized a saint of the Greek Church on May 31, 1955. A third edition of the *Philocalia* (Athens 1958) caused a considerable revival of interest in his writings.

Bibliography: E. CANDAL, EncCatt 1:454. V. GRUMEL, Lex ThK² 4:1321; DTC 11.1:486–490. P. MEYER, "Beiträge zur Kenntnis der neueren Geschichte und des gegenwärtigen Zustandes der Athosklöster," ZKirchgesch 11 (1889) 395–435, 539–576. L. PETIT, "La Grand controverse des Colybes," ÉchosOr 2 (1899) 321–331. M. VILLER, RevAscMyst 5 (1924) 174–177.

[G. A. MALONEY]

NICODEMUS OF MAMMOLA, ST., Calabrian-Greek ascetic, monastic founder; b. Cirò, *c.* 900; d. Mammola, March 25, 990 (feast, March 12). While still a youth, he became a Basilian monk in the famous monastic eparchy of the Mercurion, under the spiritual guidance of St. Fantino, who also directed St. *Nilus of Rossano. Later on, he withdrew to Mt. Cellerano, where for many years he lived a strict ascetic life. His virtue attracted many disciples, so that the hermitage of Cellerano became a large monastic community. About 975 he moved to the region of Gerace. Subsequently he built in the woods near Mammola a monastery that after his death in 990 was dedicated to his memory. His relics are venerated in the principal church of Mammola, whose patron saint he has been since 1630. A life, written by the monk Nilus at the end of the 12th century, is the principal source for his biographers.

Bibliography: A. AGRESTA, *Vita di s. Nicodemo Abbate* (Rome 1677). A. AROMOLO, *Vita di s. Nicodemo di Cirò* (Cirò 1901). V. ZAVAGLIA, *Vita del santo padre nostro Nicodemo* (Mammola 1961). V. SALETTA, *Vita inedita di s. Nicodemo di Calabria dal cod. Messan. 30* (Rome 1964).

[M. PETTA]

NICOLAITES, or Nicolaitans, members of a libertine sect of the early Church. John praises the church of *Ephesus for detesting "the works of the Nicolaites" (Ap 2.6); he scores the church of *Pergamum for harboring "some who hold the teaching of the Nicolaites," and describes them as adherents of the teaching of *Balaam (Ap 2.14–15; cf. Nm 31.16 with 25.1–2; 2 Pt 2.15; Jude 11). The same tendency is doubtless meant in Ap 2.20–24: the church of Thyatira is blamed for tolerating a self-styled prophetess whom John calls *Jezabel (4 Kgs 9.22), since she led Christians astray with her teachings about fornication and the eating of meat offered to idols (see Acts 15.20–29: these were two of the points on which James enjoined Gentile Christians to follow Jewish practice; see also 1 Corinthians, ch. 8–10). The Nicolaites seem, accordingly, to represent an excessively liberal or even antinomian outlook, possibly abusing the teachings of St. Paul on freedom (1 Cor 10.23), appealing to an esoteric knowledge that John sarcastically called "the deep things of Satan" (cf. 1 Cor 2.10). One of the serious problems that faced Christians at this time was precisely to what extent they might participate in the social and economic life of the Roman Empire, which involved attending sacrificial banquets and easily resulted in immoral practices (though the "fornication" of the Nicolaites might here mean metaphorically faithlessness to the true God).

There is no reason to link the Nicolaites with the deacon Nicholas (Acts 6.5), as Irenaeus (*Adv. haer.* 1.26.3; 3.11.1) and other Fathers have done; Clement of Alexandria (*Strom.* 2.20; 3.4) reports a story that a saying of Nicholas was misinterpreted by the Nicolaites in appealing to his authority. The existence of the Nicolaites (antinomian Gnostics) mentioned by these and other Fathers and their relationship to the Nicolaites of Apocalypse are problematic.

In the Middle Ages advocates of clerical celibacy, e.g., Cardinal Humbert (*C. Nicetam* 25), called their opponents Nicolaites.

Bibliography: É. AMANN, DTC 11.1:499–506. J. MICHL, LexThK² 7:976. G. KRETSCHMAR, RGG³ 4:1485–86. A. ROMEO, EncCatt 8:1859. EncDictBibl 1638–39. A. VON HARNACK, "The Sect of the Nicolaitans and Nicolaus the Deacon in Jerusalem," JRelig 3 (1923) 413–422.

[E. F. SIEGMAN]

NICOLAS, JEAN JACQUES AUGUSTE, French lay Catholic apologist; b. Bordeaux, Jan. 6, 1807; d. Versailles, Jan. 17, 1888. He was a lawyer at Poitiers and Bordeaux, then head of a division under the minister of cults Frédéric de *Falloux (1849–54), inspector of public libraries (1854–60), judge in the tribunal of the Seine (1860–67), and counselor at the court in Paris (1867–77). After this he lived in retirement at Versailles until his death. Almost all his numerous writings were in the field of apologetics and were inspired by contemporary circumstances. His principal work, *Études philosophiques sur le Christianisme* (4 v., 1842–45; 26th ed., 1885), was composed to resolve the doubts of his father-in-law, who desired to return to the faith; it was very successful, brought the author to the attention of Falloux, and was honored with a letter from Pius IX. In reply to the *Méditations* by the Protestant François *Guizot, Nicolas wrote *Du Protestantisme et de toutes les hérésies dans leur rapport avec le socialisme* (1852). After the cure of his daughter, which he attributed to the Blessed Virgin, he published an original work, *Nouvelles Études philosophiques sur le Christianisme* (4 v., 1855–60), whose three parts examined Mary's role in the divine plan, in the Gospels, and in the Church. When *Renan wrote his *Vie de Jésus,* Nicolas published in refutation *La Divinité de Jésus-Christ* (1864) and *L'Art de croire* (2 v., 1866). After the Franco-Prussian War he denounced the social evils of his homeland in *L'Etat sans Dieu* (1872). As a remedy he proposed the alliance of throne and altar in *La Révolution et l'ordre chrétien, Jésus-Christ, introduction à l'Évangile étudié et-médité à l'usage des temps nouveaux* (1875), *La Raison et l'Évangile* (1876), and *Études sociales sur la Révolution* (2 v., 1890). Subsequent to a visit to Rome he defended papal temporal sovereignty in *Rome et la papauté* (1882). His final work, *Étude historique et critique sur le P. Lacordaire,* was not at all favorable to the celebrated Dominican. The writings of Nicolas were not notable for theological profundity or critical historical sense, but their popularity made him one of the century's leading apologists.

Bibliography: P. LAPEYRE, *A. Nicolas, sa vie et ses oeuvres* (Paris 1892). E. BIRÉ, *Études et portraits* (2d ed. Paris-Lyon 1913) 289–311. J. CARREYRE, DTC 11.1:548–555.

[J. DAOUST]

NICOLE, PIERRE

Jansenist theologian; b. Chartres, Oct. 19, 1625; d. Paris, Nov. 16, 1695. He studied philosophy at Paris, where he took his master's degree in 1644, and then turned his attention to theology, receiving his baccalaureate from the Sorbonne in 1649. His relatives among the nuns at *Port-Royal arranged for him to join the group of men who shared the ideas of the recently deceased Abbé Saint-Cyran (*see* DUVERGIER DE HAURANNE, JEAN) and operated a school for boys near the convent. Nicole taught literature and formed a friendship with the brilliant Antoine Arnauld, younger brother of Mère Angélique (*see* ARNAULD), Abbess of Port-Royal, and spiritual director of the nuns. Nicole collaborated with Arnauld on many writings, although often Arnauld's part was merely to give his approval. These writings are published among the 43 volumes of the collected works of Arnauld (Lausanne 1775–83).

Nicole was a close collaborator with Pascal and was so highly regarded as a writer that many read him despite their lack of interest in his generally religious subjects. His writings are chiefly polemical and were often published under pen names. He wrote much in defense of *Jansenism and against the Jesuits, though his posthumously published writings on grace are far from Jansenistic. Despite its good qualities, his writing against the quietists, produced at the request of Bossuet, goes to extremes in the rejection of mysticism. He defended also the position of the *Maurists on monastic studies against A. J. de *Rancé, founder of the Trappist reform.

Though far more moderate than most of the Jansenists both in substance and in style, Nicole is characteristically Jansenist in his commitment to endless controversy and his love for fine distinctions. He probably originated the famous distinction between doctrine and fact with which Port-Royal tried to evade the condemnation of the five propositions from the *Augustinus, which they were willing to accept as erroneous but not as contained in the book. Although he was refused Sacred Orders by his bishop, he leaped to the defense of clerics not so ready with the pen when they were attacked for rejecting the condemnation of the five propositions. He was constantly trying to enlist St. Thomas

Aquinas in defense of his case, and even wrote a book entitled, *Conformity of the Jansenists and the Thomists concerning the Five Propositions.*

Among his numerous writings a few are especially deserving of mention. His fame was established by his Latin translation of the *Provincial Letters* of Pascal, published with notes and additions under the name of William Wendrock. He wrote extensive scholarly works against the Calvinists in defense of transubstantiation and the Real Presence, as well as a more general attack on Calvinist positions that produced a whole literature of controversy. Perhaps his greatest work is his *Essais de morale,* which first appeared in four volumes, and were printed, emended, added to, and reprinted again and again until the edition of 1753 filled 14 volumes. The weakness of human nature and the incapacity of the natural man for virtue dominates his characteristic Jansenism in morality. In response to attacks on Jansenism he wrote two works that were later published together and give important details of life at Port-Royal, *Les Imaginaires et les visionnaires ou dix-huit lettres sur l'hérésie imaginaire.*

Bibliography: J. CARREYRE, DTC 11.1:634–646. Bremond 4:418–588. Hurter Nomencl³ 4:444–448. L. WILLAERT, LexThK² 7:948–949.

[A. ROCK]

NICOMACHUS FLAVIANUS, statesman and scholar, one of the last champions of ancient paganism; b. *c.* 334; d. 394. Like his close friend *Symmachus, he held a series of high offices in the imperial administration. He was one of the most learned members of the circle of pagan intellectuals who hoped to restore the old Roman religion and its institutions. His paganism, like that of his group, reflected the influence of Porphyrian Neoplatonism, being a syncretistic ensemble of various cults and practices. He translated Philostratus's Life of *Apollonius of Tyana into Latin, and he himself was an expert in augury and other forms of divination. In 392 he became an ardent supporter of the usurper Eugenius, declaring that all signs pointed to a great victory of Eugenius and his army over Theodosius and to the destruction of Christianity. Even before the final defeat and death of the usurper in 394, Nicomachus seems to have committed suicide.

Bibliography: P. C. DE LABRIOLLE, *La Réaction païenne* (6th ed. Paris 1942) 351–352. J. GEFFCKEN, *Der Ausgang des griechisch-römischen Heidentums* (rev. ed. Heidelberg 1929) 160–162. O. SEECK, Pauly-Wiss RE 6.2:2506–11.

[M. R. P. MC GUIRE]

NICOMEDIA

Ancient city of Bithynia in Asia Minor, modern Izmit, Turkey. From the 3d to the 1st century B.C. it was the capital of Bithynia; later, the titular See of Bithynia Prima. Nicomedia was founded by King Zipoetes, whose son Nicomedes I made it his capital (*c.* 264 B.C.) and adorned it with numerous magnificent buildings. At the turn of the century Hannibal sought asylum at his court. Nicomedia remained the capital of Bithynia even after King Nicomedes III (or IV) willed the country to Rome (74 B.C.). *Pliny the Younger in his letters to Trajan speaks of the senate house, an aqueduct that he had built, a forum, and the temple of Cybele. As capital of the province Nicomedia was one of the first cities in northern Asia Minor to be Christianized. The first bishop of Nicomedia was Prochorus. Under Marcus Aurelius, Bp. *Dionysius of Corinth wrote a letter to the faithful of Nicomedia (*c.* 170) warning them against the heresies of Marcion. Origen lived there with his benefactor, Ambrose (*c.* 240); and the Emperor *Diocletian built there an imperial palace, a hippodrome, a mint, and an arsenal. *Constantine I was brought up there; the pagan philosopher Libanius taught there; and *Lactantius served as tutor to the children of the Emperor. There was a Christian Church close to the imperial palace, which was destroyed (303) when Diocletian initiated a severe persecution of the Christians of Asia Minor and hundreds were martyred. Under Maximinus Daia, in 312 the persecution in Nicomedia took the lives of many faithful members of the clergy. Among the latter the most prominent were Bishop Anthimus and the priest Lucian of Antioch.

In the mid-4th century Bp. Eusebius of Nicomedia granted asylum to Arius, thus making the city a center of *Arianism. Two of its Arian bishops, Eudoxius and Demophilus, became archbishops of Constantinople. A Novatian sect settled in Nicomedia toward the end of the century. To the metropolitan See of Nicomedia (325) belonged the Dioceses of Chalcedon, Prusa, Apollonias, Hadrianoi, Caesarea in Bithynia, Nicaea, Chios, Neocaesarea, and Prusias; in the 7th century it was listed as seventh among the metropolitan sees of the Patriarchate of Constantinople.

During the 4th century Nicomedia suffered an invasion of the Goths and an earthquake (Aug. 24, 354), which ruined most of its buildings; fire completed the catastrophe. The city was rebuilt during the reign of *Justinian I (527–565) but subsequently was destroyed by the Shah Khusru (Chosroes) II. In 711 Pope *Constantine I visited the city, and in 1073 John Comnenus was proclaimed emperor there. In about 1330 the Sultan Orkhan captured the city and restored its ramparts, parts of which still display the two epochs of Nicomedia's history, the Roman and the Byzantine. Nicomedia continued to be a metropolitan see until 1923; since then it has been a Latin titular bishopric.

In a journey through Asia Minor in 1555 H. Dernschwam recognized walls and foundations of the ancient city but could not identify them [*Tagebuch einer Reise nach . . . Kleinasien,* ed. F. Babinger (Munich 1923) 154–156, 238]. No systematic excavations have yet been attempted at Nicomedia; however, some remains of buildings and inscriptions came to light in 1937. A contemporary portrait of Diocletian is of great interest; other finds have not yet been published.

Bibliography: B. KOTTER and O. FELD, LexThK² 7:1001–02. R. JANIN, ÉchosOr 20 (1921) 168–182, 301–319; DHGE 9:20–28. V. SCHULTZE, *Altchristliche Städte und Landschaften,* v.2.1 (GÜTERSLOH 1922) 244–305. H. LECLERCQ, DACL 12.1:1236–45. W. RUGE, Pauly-Wiss RE 17.1 (1936) 468–492. F. K. DÖRNER, *Inschriften und Denkmäler aus Bithynien* (Berlin 1941) 1–106, bibliog.

[G. LUZNYCKY]

NIDER, JOHANN, Dominican theologian, writer, diplomat, reformer; b. Isny (Württemberg) *c.* 1380; d. Nuremberg, Aug. 13, 1438. Nider (Nyder, or Neider) entered the Order of Preachers at Colmar *c.* 1400, and under the saintly Conrad of Prussia was formed in the spirit of strict observance. Following his novitiate, he began his philosophical and theological studies at the University of Vienna and completed them at Cologne, where he was ordained. He soon became celebrated as a preacher throughout Germany and Switzerland. Nider attended the Council of Constance, participating in the debates over the doctrines of Hus. In 1423 he became professor of theology at the University of Vienna, and attracted many disciples by his reputation. He was prior of Nuremberg, 1425–29. Throughout Germany he preached the reform initiated by Bl. Raymond of Capua and furthered by Bl. John Dominici. Nider was prior of the convent of strict observance at Basle, 1429–36, and from 1429 to 1438 was vicar over all the reformed priories in Germany. In 1431 he went as theologian to the Council of Basle, which sent him as legate to the Bohemian church. In Bohemia he preached against the Hussites and attempted to reunite those who had broken communion with Rome. He was conciliar legate in 1434 to the Diet of Ratisbon. In 1436, on completion of his term as prior of Basle, he returned to the University of Vienna, where he was elected dean of the faculty of theology.

His principal work, the *Formicarius* (5 v., 1517), was written in 1437. It is a collection of anecdotes and dialogues, a rich source for the religious history and political mind of the first part of the 15th century. It also contains long developments on diabolical activity. His other works are the *Praeceptorium divinae legis* (17 editions before 1500), *Tractatus de contractibus mercatorum* (8 editions before 1500), *Alphabeticum divini amoris,* which was later attributed to Gerson; *De modo bene vivendi,* erroneously thought to be a work of St. Bernard, and many other moral and ascetical works.

Bibliography: Quétif-Échard 1.2:792–794; 2.2:822. K. SCHIELER, *Magister Johannes Nider, aus dem Orden der Prediger-Brüder* (Mainz 1885). A. WALZ, EncCatt 8:1868–69. M. M. GORCE, DTC 11:851–854.

[J. F. QUIGLEY]

NIEBUHR, BARTHOLD GEORG, historian and statesman; b. Copenhagen, Denmark, Aug. 27, 1776; d. Bonn, Germany, Jan. 2, 1831. The son of the explorer Carsten Niebuhr, he studied in Kiel University and then entered the Danish civil service, first as secretary to Finance Minister Schimmelmann and later as assessor and director of the East India Bank. His political hostility to revolutionary and Napoleonic France and his enthusiasm for the German national movement led him to accept Baron Heinrich vom Stein's invitation to enter the Prussian finance administration. Niebuhr's opposition to Karl von Hardenberg (d. 1822) forced his retirement from politics in 1810. Out of the lectures he delivered at Berlin University in 1810 on Roman history and archeology grew, in the following years, his *Römische Geschichte* (3 v. Berlin 1811–12, 1832; Eng. tr. *Roman History,* 1928–42), which was epoch-making in the development of European historical thought. During the War of Liberation, Niebuhr urged a greater role for Prussia in the organization of Germany and thus became the first great champion of "Borussianism." From 1816 to 1823 he was again active in politics. His negotiations as Prussian chargé d'affaires to the *Holy See, especially the negotiations on administrative problems of the Catholic Rhineland, which had fallen to Prussia, led to a *concordat in 1821. On his return to Germany, Niebuhr declined an invitation to the University of Berlin and settled in Bonn, where he was active as an independent teacher until his death in 1831. During these years in Bonn, Niebuhr revised the *Römische Geschichte* into its final form and with this work laid the foundation for the modern empirical science of history. Taking his cue from suggestions of Friedrich August Wolf (d. 1824) in the field of classical philology, Niebuhr was the first historian to use the methods of textual criticism on a large scale in the examination of the credibility and genuineness of sources.

Bibliography: Works. *Römische Geschichte*, 3 v. (new ed. Berlin 1873–74); *Briefe*, ed. D. Gerhardt and W. Norvin, 2 v. (Berlin 1926–29), continued by D. Gerhardt and E. Vischer; *Politische Schriften*, ed. G. KÜNTZEL (Frankfurt 1923). Literature. H. NISSEN, ADB 23:646–661. F. SCHNABEL, *Niebuhr* (Heidelberg 1931). E. KORNEMANN, "Niebuhr und der Aufbau der altrömischen Geschichte," HistZ 145 (1932) 277–300. H. VON SRBIK, *Geist und Geschichte vom deutschen Humanismus bis zur Gegenwart*, 2 v. (Munich 1950–51) 1:210–220. G. P. GOOCH, *History and Historians in the Nineteenth Century* (2d ed. New York 1952) 14–23. K. SCHOLDER, RGG³ 4:1458.

[H. RUMPLER]

NIEBUHR, HELMUT RICHARD, Protestant theologian and educator; b. Wright City, Mo., Sept. 3, 1894; d. Greenfield, Mass., July 5, 1962. He was born of Gustave and Lydia (Hosto) Niebuhr, and was the younger brother of Reinhold Niebuhr. After graduating from Eden Theological Seminary, Webster Groves, Mo., in 1915, he was ordained a year later in the Evangelical and Reformed Church. Niebuhr married Florence Marie Mittendorff on June 9, 1920. He obtained his B.D. at Yale Divinity School, New Haven, Conn., in 1923, and his Ph.D. at Yale University in 1924. In 1931 he joined the faculty of the Yale Divinity School, where his major interest was the relationship of Christian faith to civilization. Although he was not as well-known as his brother, his thought commanded wide attention. While acknowledging the need for the Church and Scripture, he warned against their deification "as though the historical and visible church were the representative of God on earth, as though the Bible were the only word that God is speaking." He sought more of an I-Thou relation between God and man, and felt that Protestant theology could best minister to the Church by resuming "the general line of march represented by the evangelical, empirical, and critical movements." Theological formulas were for him "not the basis of faith but only one of its expressions and that not the primary one." His works include *The Social Sources of Denominationalism* (1929), *The Kingdom of God in America* (1937), *The Meaning of Revelation* (1941), and *Christ and Culture* (1951).

Bibliography: "Portrait," *Life* (Dec. 26, 1955) 140:39–40. "Remembered Mentor," *Christian Century* (July 25, 1962) 79: 905.

[E. DELANEY]

NIEDERALTAICH, ABBEY OF, in the Bavarian Benedictine Congregation, Diocese of Passau; on the left bank of the Danube near the mouth of the Isar. Since the 12th century it has been called *Altaha inferior* to distinguish it from the nearby Abbey of Oberaltaich (*Altaha superior*). The Agilulfinger dukes founded it before 750 and settled it with monks from *Reichenau, who brought with them the Burgundian cult of St. *Maurice, patron of the church. Niederaltaich colonized and evangelized the Bavarian

forest, Bohemia, Moravia, and Hungary, settling *Kremsmünster (777). Ruined by the Hungarian wars, it was reduced to a group of canons by 1000. Bishops *Pilgrim of Passau and *Wolfgang of Regensburg included it in the *Gorze-Trier-Regensburg reform. Under St. *Godard (d. 1038), later bishop of Hildesheim, Niederaltaich headed a reform, settling or reviving *Tegernsee, *Hersfeld, Ossiach, Bakonybel, Ostrow (St. Iwan), Brevnov, and *Olomouc (Olmütz). St. *Günther was a missionary and colonizer, and Bl. Richer became abbot of Monte Cassino; *Judith was one of several women recluses at Niederaltaich. The abbey lost its free imperial status (857–1156) in the investiture controversy and was put under the bishop of *Bamberg. Abbot Herman (1242–73), compiler of the *Annales Altahenses*, restored the abbey to its former prestige. Eight of Niederaltaich's monks were requested as abbots at a time when the old religious orders were in decline. Rebuilt after the ruin of the Thirty Years' War, the abbey was destroyed with its library in fires (1659, 1671). Abbot Joscio Hamberger (1700–39) revived it and had the baroque church built. The abbey was secularized (1803) but resettled from *Metten (1918) and united to the Priory of Innsbruck-Volders (1927) before it became an abbey again (1930). Its Ecumenical Institute has a leading role in the *ecumenical movement.

Bibliography: G. LANG, *Die Heiligen und Seligen von Niederaltaich* (Metten 1941). R. BAUERREISS, LexThK² 7:950–951.

[E. M. HEUFELDER]

NIEDERMÜNSTER (ALSACE), CONVENT OF, former abbey of nuns in the Diocese of *Strasbourg; founded before 710 by St. *Odilia, at the foot of the hill topped by her convent of *Mont Sainte-Odile. Gundelinde, niece of the foundress, was its first abbess. A famous relic of the true Cross was venerated at Niedermünster from Carolingian times until the 17th century, when it was transferred to the Jesuits at Molsheim. Niedermünster enjoyed its most brilliant era in the 13th century, but declined in the 14th. The abbey suffered partial destruction during the Peasant's Revolt (1525); it died out completely after a fire in 1542. Important ruins of the church, which had been consecrated in 1180, still remain.

Bibliography: M. BARTH, *Die heilige Odilia, Schutzherrin des Elsass*, 2 v. (Strasbourg 1938); *Handbuch der elsässischen Kirchen im Mittelalter*, 3 v. (Archives de l'Église d'Alsace NS 11–13; Strasbourg 1960–63).

[J. CHOUX]

NIEHEIM (NIEM), DIETRICH OF, chancery official in the Roman Curia, publicist of the *Western Schism; b. Brakel, Westphalia, *c.* 1340; d. Maastricht, Netherlands, end of March 1418. Supported by *William of Ockham, *Marsilius of Padua, and Alexander of Roes, he gave the first comprehensive presentation of *conciliarism in his *Dialogus de schismate* (1410), in which he called for the reunion and reform of the Church. His *Avisamenta* (1414) contains the program for the Council of *Constance. As a representative of the historically conservative approach to the Empire, he stressed the right of the German emperors to call a general *council of the Church. He was an intimate of several Roman popes; in 1395 *Boniface IX tried in vain to bestow upon him the bishopric of Verden (Germany). The Anima, the German hospital in Rome, claims him as its founder.

Bibliography: K. PIVEC and H. HEIMPEL, "Neue Forschungen zu Dietrich von Niem," *Nachrichten der Akademie d. Wissenschaften in Göttingen* (1951) H.4. H. HEIMPEL, *Dietrich von Niem, c. 1340–1418* (Munster 1932); NDB 3:691–692. J. LEUSCHNER, LexThK² 3:386. E. F. JACOB, *Essays in the Conciliar Epoch* (3d ed. Notre Dame, Ind. 1963) 24–43.

[H. WOLFRAM]

NIELSEN, LAURENTIUS, missionary to Sweden; b. Oslo, Norway, 1538; d. Vilnius (Vilna), Lithuania, May 5, 1622. Educated in the Lutheran faith, he received a master of arts degree at Copenhagen and in 1558 began studies for the Lutheran ministry at Louvain. Through contact with the Jesuits there, his interest in Catholicism grew. On Feb. 2, 1564, he was admitted into the Society of Jesus, and he was ordained to the priesthood the next year. He remained at Louvain until chosen for the Swedish mission by the Jesuit General, Everard Mercurian, with the hope that Nielsen's knowledge of the language and his Lutheran background would hasten the conversion of the King, John III. John, partly through the influence of his Catholic wife, the Polish Catherine Jagellon, and partly through consideration of the political advantages of a role as mediator in the religious struggles in Europe, had indicated his interest in reconciliation with Rome. Nielsen arrived at Stockholm (1576), where he taught theology at the new college founded by the King, and defended the King's liturgical innovations, which caused general displeasure in Lutheran Sweden. In 1577 the Jesuit Antonio *Possevino arrived in Stockholm to negotiate the conversion, and in May 1578 absolved John from schism and administered Communion. Nielsen left Sweden in 1580 and taught theology at the colleges at Olmütz (1582), Prague (1587), and Braunseberg (Braniewo). In 1606 he founded a college in Denmark. Among his published writings are *Confessio christiana de via Domini* (Cracow 1604) and *De reformatione religionis christiana* (Cracow 1616).

Bibliography: A. THEINER, *Schweden und seine Stellung zum heiligen Stuhl unter Johann III. Sigismund III. und Karl IX.,* 2 v. (Augsburg 1838–39). I. IPARRAGUIRRE, LexThK² 7:959. Sommervogel 5:1707–09. É. AMANN, DTC 11.1:497–499, with bibliog.

[E. D. MC SHANE]

NIETZSCHE, FRIEDRICH WILHELM

German philosopher and poet; b. Röcken (Prussian Saxony), Oct. 15, 1844; d. Weimar, Germany, Aug. 25, 1900.

Life. The son of a Lutheran pastor, Nietzsche was reared in a strictly religious atmosphere. After his father's death (1849), his mother moved to Naumburg; Nietzsche then attended the humanistic Gymnasium and the renowned Fürstenschule of neighboring Pforta (1858–64). He studied classical philology under F. W. Ritschl at the universities of Bonn and Leipzig (1862–67) and discovered the philosophy of A. *Schopenhauer. Though never endorsing Schopenhauer's metaphysical *pessimism, Nietzsche sensed in the emphasis on the supremacy of will as a universal principle a dynamism that appealed to his thirst for life in its plenitude. To Nietzsche's faltering Christian faith Schopenhauer seemed to offer a possibility of self-redemption.

On Ritschl's recommendation, Nietzsche, aged 24, was appointed professor of classical philology at the University of Basel in Switzerland, a chair he held from 1869 to 1879, when his steadily declining health forced

Friedrich Wilhelm Nietzsche.

his resignation. Of considerable consequence was Nietzsche's meeting and short-lived friendship with Richard *Wagner. Until 1872 Nietzsche's life was actually centered in Wagner's villa near Lucerne. He expected of Wagner's music drama a rebirth of the ancient Greek tragedy of Aeschylus and Sophocles. In defense of Wagner and attacking the "Socratic rationalism" of Euripides, Nietzsche wrote *Die Geburt der Tragödie aus dem Geiste der Musik* (Leipzig 1872). But the ambivalent love-hatred attitude that marked his relationship with Wagner led to disillusionment and eventual total estrangement.

From 1879 to 1889 Nietzsche lived alternately at Sils-Maria in the Swiss Engadine Alps, at Nice, and at Genoa, suffering from multiple physical ailments. His final mental collapse occurred in Turin in January 1889. His remaining 11 years Nietzsche lived in Jena and Weimar under the care of his sister Elisabeth. His mental disease was never accurately diagnosed, and the assumption that Nietzsche was suffering from progressive paralysis induced by syphilis remains unsubstantiated.

Thought. Nietzsche was a *Lebensphilosoph,* castigating the separation of philosophy and science from life. In his sensitive mind the spiritual crisis of the modern age appeared focalized. He was among the first to diagnose *historicism and *scientism as symptoms of decadence and of a nihilism that threatened the foundations of Western civilization. He called for a new beginning and a "transvaluation of all values" in order to stop such threats.

The development of Nietzsche's thought proceeded in three stages. The study of antiquity and the influence of Schopenhauer and Wagner first made Nietzsche experience the "ground of being" as a dialectic of opposites, of "Dionysian" and "Apollonian" life principles. His vision of a synthesis in Greek tragedy and in Wagnerian music was short-lived. The four *Unzeitgemässe Betrachtungen* (Leipzig 1873–76) characterize this period.

Then, after the break with Wagner and the emancipation from Schopenhauer's "pessimism of weakness," Nietzsche applied psychological "experimentalism" to an examination of man and his world, launching a radical attack on traditional theology, metaphysics, and morality. With L. *Feuerbach, Nietzsche saw the idea of God and of absolute Truth as nothing but "projections" of man's most precious qualities into an illusory "beyond"; they must be reclaimed, he argued, for the enrichment of man and his "this-worldly" existence. The "death of God" he solemnly proclaimed and dramatically analyzed in the story of the "madman" in section 125 of *Die fröhliche Wissenschaft* (Chemnitz 1882–86). See also *Menschliches, Allzumenschliches* (Chemnitz 1878–80) and *Morgenröte* (Chemnitz 1881).

Nietzsche finally implemented his early thinking with the "deadly gospel" of biological and social Darwinism. The "world-ground" he now saw as *Wille zur Macht,* a "will-to-power" that by "sublimation" would generate the "Super-Man" (*Übermensch*). Christian "slave morality," born of the *ressentiment* of weaklings, was to be superseded by a "master morality, beyond good and evil." The future "lords of the world" were to rise above brute animality by ascetic self-discipline seasoned by suffering. See *Also sprach Zarathustra* (Chemnitz 1883–84), *Jenseits von Gut und Böse* (Leipzig 1886), *Zur Genealogie der Moral* (Leipzig 1887), *Der Fall Wagner* (Leipzig 1888), *Ecce Homo* (1888; publ. Leipzig 1908), *Der Antichrist* (Leipzig 1888), and *Die Götzendämmerung* (Leipzig 1889). The "vision" that inspired Nietzsche's doctrine of "the eternal recurrence" he interpreted as the revelation of a cosmological law functioning without a divine lawgiver. An eternal cyclical movement of existence was seen as a substitute for the creative activity of a personal Deity. The certainty of the "eternal return" was to justify a joyous affirmation of all existence, signalizing a final victory over nihilism.

Appreciation. The ambivalences and self-contradictory theses in Nietzsche's thinking account for some gross misinterpretations of his philosophy. However, Nietzsche's distorted idea of Christianity bears the imprint of Luther's pessimism regarding the corruption of fallen human nature and of Schopenhauer's Buddhist-tainted view of Christian doctrine. Nietzsche's alleged anti-Semitism and chauvinism—eagerly propagated by the National Socialists—are refuted by his scathing denunciation of racism and his condemnation of the power politics and crude materialism of the German Empire. A distorted Nietzsche image was created also by his sister, who was bigoted and proved unreliable as executrix of Nietzsche's literary remains. But Nietzsche's philosophy did foster the rise of *ir-rationalism, *subjectivism, *voluntarism, and a biologism based on the *élan vital* of a naturalistic *Lebensphilosophie.* Nietzsche's philosophical influence is most conspicuous in secular *humanism and in *existentialism. The hymnal musicality of his prose and poetry also influenced several literary and artistic schools and movements.

See also LIFE PHILOSOPHIES.

Bibliography: Works. *Gesammelte Werke,* 20 v. (Leipzig 1901–1926); *Gesammelte Werke: Musarionausgabe,* 23 v. (Munich 1920–29); *Werke und Briefe: Historisch-kritische Gesamtausgabe* (Munich 1933–), in progress; *The Complete Works,* ed. O. LEVY, 18 v. (London 1909–13); *The Philosophy of Nietzsche* (New York 1937), contains four major works; *The Portable Nietzsche,* comp., ed., and tr. W. KAUFMANN (New York 1954); *The Use and Abuse of History,* tr. A. COLLINS (2d rev. ed. New York 1957); *Joyful Wisdom,* tr. T. COMMON (New York 1960). Literature. F. COPLESTON, *Friedrich Nietzsche: Philosopher of Culture* (London 1942). H. A. REYBURN et al., *Nietzsche:*

The Story of a Human Philosopher (London 1948). W. KAUFMANN, *Nietzsche: Philosopher, Psychologist, Antichrist* (Princeton 1950). F. A. LEA, *The Tragic Philosopher: A Study of Friedrich Nietzsche* (New York 1957). M. HEIDEGGER, *Nietzsche,* 2 v. (Pfullingen 1961). **Illustration credit:** German Information Center, New York City.

[K. F. REINHARDT]

NIEUWLAND, JULIUS ARTHUR, chemist, botanist; b. Hansbeke, Belgium, Feb. 14, 1878; d. Washington, D.C., June 11, 1936. His family moved to South Bend, Ind., in 1880, and Nieuwland received a bachelor's degree from Notre Dame University in 1899. He entered the Congregation of the Holy Cross, was ordained a priest in 1903, and received a Ph.D. degree from The Catholic University of America, Washington, D.C., in 1904. A reference in his doctoral thesis, *Reactions of Acetylene,* to a toxic substance formed from acetylene and arsenic trichloride later led Dr. W. Lee Lewis, working with the Chemical Warfare Service, to the development (1917) of Lewisite, a deadly war gas. From 1904 to 1918, Nieuwland was professor of botany at Notre Dame; during this period he published nearly 100 papers on botanical subjects, founded and edited for 25 years the *Midland Naturalist,* and started the Nieuwland Herbarium. In the course of many excursions in Indiana, Michigan, New Jersey, Alabama, and Oregon, he amassed a large collection of plant specimens. His appointment in 1918 as professor of organic chemistry and Dean of the School of Science at Notre Dame led him to resume studies on acetylene syntheses in the presence of copper catalysts. By 1920 he had succeeded in isolating divinylacetylene and suspected the presence of monovinylacetylene. The vulcanization of the former was achieved by Dr. R. R. Vogt at Notre Dame in 1923. A paper read by Nieuwland to the American Chemical Society at Rochester in 1925 attracted the attention of Du Pont de Nemours & Co. to his work. Studies by the company, with collaboration from Nieuwland, led to the perfection of a new synthetic rubber, neoprene, in

Julius Arthur Nieuwland.

1931. He was awarded the Morehead Medal in 1933 and the Nichols Medal of the American Chemical Society in 1935. As a teacher and scientist he inspired his students and assistants by his infectious enthusiasm for his work.

Bibliography: J. A. NIEUWLAND, "Synthetic Rubber From a Gas," *Scientific American* (Nov. 1935) 262–263. Corning Glass Works, *Famous Names in Chemical History: Father Nieuwland* (Corning, N.Y. 1948). S. LURIÉ, "The Work of Father Nieuwland," *Belgium* 3.9 (1942) 402–406. **Illustration credit:** University of Notre Dame.

[J. O'REILLY]

NIFO, AGOSTINO, Italian Averroist philosopher; b. Sessa (or, possibly, in Calabria), 1473; d. Salerno, 1538 (or 1545–46). He taught first at Naples, then at Padua, where for some time he subscribed to the Averroism of Nicoletto Vernia (1420?–99); after this he occupied chairs at the Universities of Salerno, Pisa, Bologna, and Rome. His writings include *De intellectu et daemonibus* (Padua 1492), *De infinitate primi motoris* (Venice 1504), *Tractatus de immortalitate animae contra Pomponatium* (Venice 1518), *De pulchro et amore* (Rome 1531), and *Opuscula moralia* (2 v. Paris 1645). He composed also numerous commentaries on the works of *Aristotle (14 v. Paris 1654), prepared an edition of the writings of Averroës (Venice 1595–97), and wrote *De regnandi peritia* (Naples 1523), a free translation of the *Principe* of N. *Machiavelli that was circulated in manuscript form as early as 1513. Complete collections of Nifo's writings appeared in the 16th and 17th centuries (Venice 1599; Paris 1645).

Nifo's most important work is undoubtedly his treatise on the immortality of the human soul. In it he attacked the teaching of P. *Pomponazzi, who had maintained it to be absolutely impossible for the soul to subsist or to have any type of activity independent of the body; Nifo accused Pomponazzi of not having taken into account Plato's arguments and of having poorly understood the teachings of Aristotle and Averroës.

See also SOUL, HUMAN, IMMORTALITY OF.

Bibliography: A. GONZALES, EncFil 3:909. L. BAUR, LexThK² 7:1009. E. NOBILE, *L'idea dell'immortalità dell'anima e la sua efficacia sulla civiltà e sull'educazione* (Naples 1951).

[W. A. WALLACE]

NIGEL WIREKER, English satirist; b. probably in the 1130s; d. before 1207. Nigel became a monk of Christ Church, *Canterbury, some time before the martyrdom of Thomas *Becket (1170), of whom he said, "We have seen him with our eyes, our hands have touched him, we have eaten and drunk with him." Not until the work of John Bale in 1557 is there any documentary justification for attaching the name "Wireker" to that of Nigel or Nigellus. In 1189 he was one of the spokesmen at the court of King *Richard I on behalf of the Canterbury monks in their dispute with their archbishop, *Baldwin of Canterbury. Two years later he visited Coventry, where he saw the monastery from which, to his dismay, the monks had been driven by secular canons. From other autobiographical references in his writings it is clear that he spent some time in Normandy, and it is likely that he knew Paris and the routes of English merchants abroad.

In the 14th and 15th centuries Nigel's satires became popular throughout Europe; they were referred to by *Chaucer in the *Nonnes Preestes Tale*. His best-known work, the *Speculum stultorum* (Mirror of Fools), written between 1170 and 1187, is made up of 1,931 elegiac distichs preceded by a prose introduction in which he explains that the central character of the poem, Burnellus, the ass who wants a longer tail, symbolizes the restless monk who is constantly seeking a higher station. Burnellus's adventures in Salerno, Paris, and Rome enable the author to fire sharp shafts of satire at the follies of contemporary monks, priests, bishops, popes, and princes, as well as at the vices of various nations. The

Frontispiece woodcut from an edition of Nigel Wireker's "Speculum stultorum" printed at Cologne in 1499.

William to whom the *Speculum* was addressed is probably the same William, Bishop of Ely and royal chancellor, to whom Nigel addressed his prose treatise, *Contra curiales et officiales clericos* (A Critique of Courtiers and Ecclesiastical Administrators) some 13 years later. This treatise is a straight condemnation of the trafficking in churches indulged in by ecclesiastical and curial families that often resulted in most unsuitable persons being entrusted with the care of souls. It condemns also those who, like the bishop of Ely, try to combine spiritual and secular offices. The same warning note is struck in Nigel's other poem to William of Ely.

Bibliography: R. A. BEALS, *Nigellus Wireker* (Cambridge, Mass. 1927). Manitius 3:809–813. J. H. MOZLEY, "The Unprinted Poems of N. W.," *Speculum* 7 (1932) 398–423. Raby SecLP 2:94–102, 349–350.

[D. NICHOLL]

NIGER, arid, agricultural, and pastoral inland country in west-central *Africa, bordered by *Nigeria, *Dahomey, *Upper Volta, *Mali, *Algeria, and *Libya; 458,997 square miles in area. This former territory of French West Africa became an autonomous state of the French Community in 1958, and an independent republic in 1960. The population in 1960 was estimated at 2.8 million, including 3,000 Europeans. About three-fourths of the inhabitants were Moslems, and the rest pagans, except for a Christian minority totaling less than 1 per cent, including 1,800 Protestants. The first Catholic mission, established in 1831 at Niamey, was entrusted to the Society of African Missions from the Vicariate of Dahomey. In 1942 the Prefecture Apostolic of Niamey was created, with jurisdiction over northern Dahomey. When northern Dahomey was sep-

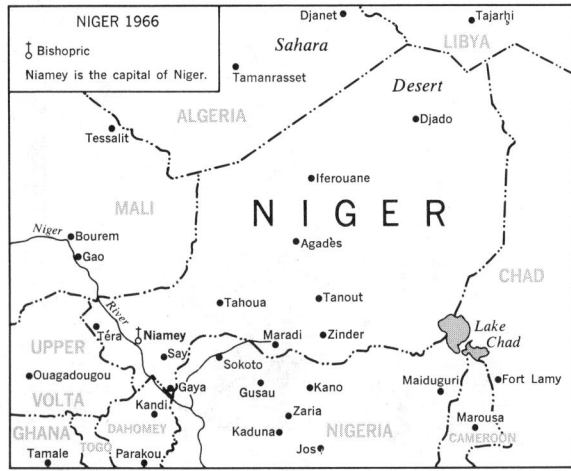

NIGER 1966
☨ Bishopric
Niamey is the capital of Niger.

arated from this prefecture in 1948, Niger, with a portion of Upper Volta, was entrusted to the Redemptorists, but in 1949 the area of the Prefecture of Niamey was restricted to Niger. In 1961 the prefecture became the Diocese of Niamey. In 1964 it had 15,000 Catholics, 1 secular and 17 religious priests, 2 brothers, 33 religious women, and 26 catechists. In 1962 there were 10 Catholic schools with 3,200 students.

Bibliography: *Bilan du Monde* 2:627–629. AnnPont (1965) 301. For additional bibliography, *see* AFRICA.

[J. BOUCHAUD]

NIGERIA

The Federation of Nigeria is a country in West *Africa, 356,700 square miles in area, bordering on the Gulf of Guinea, *Dahomey, *Niger, *Chad, and *Cameroon. This largely agricultural country was created in 1914 out of the British territories of Northern and Southern Nigeria. It received a federal constitution for three autonomous regions (1954) and became an independent dominion in the British Commonwealth (1960). Part of the British Cameroons voted to join Nigeria in 1961. In 1963 Nigeria became a federal republic in the Commonwealth with three regions (northern, eastern, and western) and the federal territory of Lagos. English is the official language. With a population in 1964 of about 40,000,000, Nigeria was the most populous country in Africa. Nearly half of the inhabitants dwelt in the large northern, predominantly Moslem region. Paganism and Islam had about the same number of followers, and together they claimed nearly 90 per cent of the Nigerians. Most of the other inhabitants were Christians, who formed an important minority in the south and west. Protestants totaled about 1,300,000.

In the 15th century the Portuguese introduced Christianity in the coastal area, which was entrusted to the Capuchins in the 17th century. Systematic evangelization did not begin until the 19th century. Both Protestant and Catholic missionaries appeared along the coast *c.* 1840. Nigeria became part of the vast Vicariate Apostolic of the Two Guineas, created in 1842. It was made part of Gabon when this vicariate was created in 1863. Priests from the Society of *African Missions (SMA) arrived in 1861. In 1870 a vicariate was erected for the coast of Benin with jurisdiction extending over Dahomey. Prefectures apostolic were later formed for

Upper Niger (1884) and Lower Niger (1889). The *Holy Ghost Fathers (CSSP) shared the missionary labor with the SMA. The Prefecture of Eastern Nigeria was created in 1911 for the more difficult missions in the north.

In 1950 the hierarchy was established with two ecclesiastical provinces, a third province being added in 1959. In 1964 Nigeria had 3 archdioceses, 15 dioceses, and 4 prefectures. The metropolitan see for western Nigeria was the Archdiocese of *Lagos (entrusted to the SMA), whose suffragan dioceses are Benin City (SMA), Ibadan (SMA), Ondo (SMA), and Oyo (White Fathers). In eastern Nigeria the Archdiocese of *Onitsha (CSSP) had as suffragans the Dioceses of Calabar (*St. Patrick's Missionary Society), Enugu (Nigerian clergy), Ikot Ekpene (Nigerian clergy), Ogoja (St. Patrick's Missionary Society), Owerri (CSSP), Port Harcourt (CSSP), and Umuahia (CSSP). In the north the Archdiocese of *Kaduna (SMA) had as suffragans the Dioceses of Jos (SMA), Makurdi (CSSP), and Yola (Augustinians). There were also the Prefectures Apostolic of Ilorin (SMA), Kabba (CSSP), Maiduguri (Augustinians), and Sokoto (Dominicans). Six of the bishops were Nigerians. There were 2,070,000 Catholics, about 800,000 catechumens, 867 priests (about 70 Nigerians), 117 brothers, 600 sisters, and 11,400 catechists. At the major seminaries in Benin and Enugu there were 211 seminarians. Catholic schools (located primarily in the east) had about 45,000 pupils. There were two Catholic weeklies, the *Catholic Herald* and the *Leader* (*see* CATHOLIC PRESS, WORLD SURVEY, 1). An apostolic delegation for six countries in west-central Africa was created in 1960, with headquarters in Lagos, Nigeria's capital.

Bibliography: *Bilan du Monde* 2:630–638. AnnPont has annual data on all dioceses and prefectures. For additional bibliography, *see* AFRICA.

[J. BOUCHAUD]

NIHILISM

A 19th-century Russian intellectual movement expressed in a party program of revolutionary reform and terrorism. The word is derived from *nihil*, "nothing," and was popularized by Ivan Turgenev's novel *Fathers and Sons* (1862). Russian nihilism has little in common with what is called nihilism in the West. It was born under the czarist absolutism that evoked a powerful revulsion and antagonism in all lovers of freedom and righteousness. A movement for the liberation of human beings from any sort of enslavement found its fullest expression, especially between 1860 and 1870, in nihilism, of which the chief protagonists were Nikolai G. Chernishevsky (1828–89), Nikolai Dobrolyubov (1836–61), and Dmitry I. Pisarev (1841–68). To them the struggle for the complete emancipation of individuality was the highest value. They were extremely hostile toward everything that they termed abstract and refused to grant value to any manifestation that had no social consequences. They waged a rude and relentless war against any kind of social, political, and religious "oppression." In the concrete, they renounced God, spirit, soul, state, church, morality, nationality, and "high" culture. They were earnest in their desire for the creation of a "new man" and the destruction of the old. Their consistency and tenacity in propagating their crude materialist and utilitarian philosophy was

NIGERIA 1966
☩ Archbishopric   ☨ Bishopric
☨ Prefecture Apostolic
Lagos is the capital of Nigeria

comparable with religious endeavor. Many nihilists carried self-sacrifice so far as to volunteer to take the place of revolutionaries under sentence of death, lest the movement should be deprived of its leaders.

Materialism and atheism were at once preconditions and logical consequences of nihilist criticism and negation. The nihilists railed against the "unpractical" rigors of Christian morality. To them all things were lawful as long as they were useful for the individual. Their ethos was expressed in Chernishevsky's novel *What Is To Be Done?* (1863), recognized as the nihilist catechism. It emphasized love of truth; repudiated falsehood, embellishment, and exalted rhetoric; and rejected every sort of felicity that life offers. These principles were consistently followed in personal relationships and, above all, in friendship and in marriage. In nihilist circles friendship was based upon inexorable straightforwardness, and marriage was regarded as the truest of all relationships of life.

Nihilism adopted an attitude of suspicion toward "high" culture created by a privileged class and designed only for this class. Art, as a manifestation of idealism, was absolutely renounced. The nihilists aimed at annihilating aesthetics either in externals or in the forms of social intercourse. They patronized the natural sciences to which they looked for the solution of all problems. In economics they propagated utopian socialism. The negation of higher authority, scientific and artistic individualism, the spirit of absolute independence, the struggle against theological and theocratic

idealism, the extreme radicalism, and, to a large extent, the anarchism of the nihilists anticipated communism in Russia.

Bibliography: T. G. MASARYK, *The Spirit of Russia,* tr. E. and C. PAUL, 2 v. (2d ed. New York 1955). H. KOHN, *The Mind of Modern Russia* (New York 1962). G. A. WETTER, *Dialectical Materialism: A Historical and Systematic Survey of Philosophy in the Soviet Union,* tr. P. HEATH (New York 1959). N. A. BERDÍAEV, *The Russian Idea,* tr. R. M. FRENCH (New York 1948; repr. pa. Boston 1962).

[C. C. GECYS]

NIJMEGEN, ROMAN CATHOLIC UNIVERSITY OF

In the Netherlands, the striving for a Catholic University dates from a time shortly after the legal emancipation of the Catholics (1795). A university became, there as elsewhere, an important part of the program of ultra-Montanism in its struggle against the prevailing temper of liberalism, materialism, and anticlericalism.

Origin. The reestablishment of the Catholic University of Louvain in 1834, and the foundation of a Catholic university in Dublin in 1852, of the Instituts Catholiques in France in 1875, of The Catholic University of America in Washington, D.C., and of a cantonal university with Catholic leanings in Fribourg, Switzerland in 1889, were indicative of the spirit of the age. In the Netherlands, where the total number of Catholics amounted to approximately 40 per cent of the population, this educational tendency manifested itself simultaneously with a similar trend in orthodox

Calvinistic circles, a trend that resulted in the foundation of a Calvinistic institution, the Free Reformed University, at Amsterdam in 1880. When in 1905 the Dutch government granted civil recognition (*effectus civilis*) to all certificates and degrees bestowed by the Free Reformed University, the Catholic episcopacy established the St. Radboud Foundation, whose main purpose was to found a Catholic university. As long as the functions of the projected institute remained mainly polemic and apologetic, the academically trained Catholic laity showed little enthusiasm for the idea. In 1912, however, the philologist and eminent apologist H. W. E. Moller sponsored an educational institute called "Rooms-Katholieke Leergangen," which was destined to develop into a university. Around 1918 the attempt to make Moller's institute a university met with sharp opposition supported by some bishops antagonistic to the idea of putting an exclusively Catholic seal on the new institute. Accordingly, counteraction developed at Nijmegen and resulted in the organization of a working committee whose head was the town clerk and future professor J. H. P. M. van der Grinten. The committee tried to persuade the bishops to accept the idea of a university at Nijmegen, to be called "Keizer Karel Universiteit," not strictly Catholic in its patronage, but rather supervised by a committee appointed partly by the municipal authority of Nijmegen and partly by the St. Radboud Foundation. Although the episcopacy rejected the committee's proposal, they were encouraged by the municipality of Nijmegen's promise of financial support, and decided to found a Roman Catholic university at Nijmegen.

Organization. The University was officially founded on Oct. 17, 1923. It comprised three Faculties: Divinity, Arts, and Law. In accordance with the 1905 act referred to above, the Dutch government at once granted *effectus civilis* to the new university's certificates and degrees. During the first 25 years, the educational program underwent few changes, and the number of students did not increase notably. After World War II, however, there was a period of expansion. In 1947 the Institute for Missiological Studies was created and in 1948, a department of political and social science, from which later developed the Faculty of Social Science and an Institute of Journalism. In 1949 education was added to the curriculum of the Faculty of Arts. In 1951, after a long period of preparation, a Faculty of Medicine was begun, and was followed by a Faculty of Mathematics and Natural Science in 1957. The number of undergraduates increased rapidly also, reaching 1,000 for the first time in 1950. In 1957 more than 2,000 students were registered, and in 1964 the number exceeded 4,000. Keeping pace with the growing number of students, the faculty (*corpus doctum*) increased from 27 professors and 5 senior lecturers in 1923 and a mere 30 professors and 7 senior lecturers in 1946 to more than 100 professors and 16 senior lecturers in 1963. Although a great majority of the undergraduates are Catholics and the environment is pervasively Catholic, the University is open to students and professors of all faiths.

The curriculum is based mainly on the Higher Education Act (1960) and on the Academic Statute that followed it. Entrance and examination requirements are the same as those of state universities, the one exception being the Faculty of Divinity, which is not under state control. Apart from those strictures, the University is free to organize its educational activities and to appoint its own staff.

Administration. From 1923 until 1948 the University was supervised by the St. Radboud Foundation, in which the episcopacy occupied a leading position and held the exclusive right of nomination. The administration of routine affairs was entrusted to a board of governors (*curatoren*), but in 1948 a managing board was chosen from members of the St. Radboud Foundation. Since then the University has been independent of the episcopacy except for the bishops' right of nomination. Following the reorganization of administration, on Sept. 15, 1961, the University created a new society, The Catholic University Foundation, to be administered by a board of governors. The chairman is appointed by the episcopacy, whose official approval is required also for all appointments, although these are generally made in compliance with the recommendations of the Faculty concerned. Both secular and regular clergy and laymen are eligible for all offices including that of vice chancellor (or *rector magnificus*) of the University, a post held for 1 year only. Since before World War II, members of the Faculty of Divinity were numerically superior in the senate; there were only 8 laymen among the 24 vice chancellors during the period from 1923 to 1948. From 1948 to 1964, however, only 4 of the 16 vice chancellors were priests. In 1946 there were 15 priests among the 31 professors; in 1963 there were 29 priests and more than 90 laymen.

Finance. Apart from an annual grant from the municipality of Nijmegen, originally D.Fls. 100,000, or $28,000, and later increased to D.Fls. 200,000, or $56,000, the University was, until 1948, supported solely by revenue accruing from the St. Radboud property, church collections, and voluntary contributions. In 1948, on the recommendation of the Minister of Education, Joseph Gielen, a bill was passed providing state aid for denominational universities; this aid improved the material well-being of the University. Since the Higher Education Act of Dec. 22, 1960, subsidy grants have covered 95 per cent of all net expenses.

Within the sphere of national and international cultural life, the University has only gradually won recognition. An exception is the Faculty of Arts, which from the beginning has counted among its members scholars of worldwide reputation, notably the philologists J. Schrijnen, J. van Ginneken, and C. Mohrmann. With few exceptions, the University has preferred not to publish any periodicals or series of monographs of its own, but rather to concentrate on national and international projects and to engage in academic exchange.

Contemporary Development. Despite its general conformity to national and international traditions, the University is gradually asserting its individuality. The institution of a Chair of the Phenomenology of Protestantism in 1958 and of a Chair of the History and Problems of the Ecumenical Movement in 1961, shows that the University is aware of its role in a nation that is distinctly Christian but not wholly Catholic in outlook. Various members of the Faculty of Divinity have in this spirit interpreted their part in Vatican Council II. The Faculty of Arts has achieved distinction in the study of early Christian Latin and Greek, in its specialization in philosophy, including natural philosophy, and in its pioneer work in psychology; other Dutch universities look to graduates from Nijmegen to head their departments. The Faculty of Medicine since 1961 has had one of the three departments of dental surgery in Holland and is admired for the modern equipment of its laboratories and clinics. The University hospital is the medical center for the southern provinces of Holland. The library, which has a separate medical division and 39 institute libraries, in 1964 housed more than 350,000 volumes. It specializes in *Catholica* and owns one of the world's most important collections of books on the age of Napoleon and the French Revolution.

The University was severely affected by World War II. The resistance it offered to German tyranny under the leadership of Professors Bernard Hermesdorf and Johannes Cornelissen, vice chancellor and secretary to the senate, respectively, led to the total suspension of teaching in 1943. When forced to retreat in September 1944, German troops set fire to the most important university buildings with the result that there was a serious shortage of space immediately after the liberation. The housing problem was satisfactorily solved through various purchases, the most important of which was that of "Heyendael," a property on the southern border of Nijmegen, where a large university town has been growing since 1950. A development program provides for various buildings for the Medical Faculty, and has proposed others for the Faculty of Natural Science. Plans include a new library and buildings to accommodate the Faculties now housed in separate institutes spread throughout the town.

Bibliography: *Annual Reports of the Roman Catholic University at Nijmegen* (1923–). G. B. BROM, *Dies natalis: Stichting van de Katholieke Universiteit* (Nijmegen 1955). J. A. BORNEWASSER, *Vijftig jaar katholieke leergangen* (Tilburg 1962). L. J. ROGIER and N. DE ROOY, *In vrijheid herboren: Katholiek Nederland, 1853–1953* (The Hague 1953).

[L. J. ROGIER]

NIKEL, JOHANNES, Catholic Biblical scholar; b. Sohrau (Upper Silesia), Germany, Oct. 18, 1863; d. Breslau, June 28, 1924. After his courses in theology and Oriental languages at Breslau and Würzburg (1881–86) and his ordination (1886), he was engaged in parochial work (1886–90) and in teaching religion in a high school (1890–97). Thereafter he taught OT exegesis at the University of Breslau, of which he eventually (1923) became the rector. In 1907 he was made a consultor of the *Pontifical Biblical Commission. Both by his personal efforts and by his work as a teacher and writer, he endeavored to strike a balance between the conservative decisions of the Pontifical Biblical Commission under Pius X and the findings of a truly scientific exegesis. Even to a greater degree than in these apologetic endeavors he was successful in making the religious message of the OT meaningful for Christian life. This explains also his participation in the efforts that were being made to solve the social problems of his time.

He was editor of the *Alttestmentliche Abhandlungen* (from 1907) and of the *Exegetisches Handbuch zum AT* (from 1911), as well as the founder and associate editor of the *Biblische Zeitfragen* (from 1908). For a list of his numerous publications, see the articles cited in the bibliography.

Bibliography: N. PETERS, ThGlaube 16 (1924) 449–454. H. HAAG, DBSuppl 6:474–475. H. ERHARTER, LexThK² 7:969.

[A. DEISSLER]

NIKON, PATRIARCH OF MOSCOW, 1652 to 1660; b. Vel'demanovo, near Nizhniĭ Novgorod (Gorkiĭ since 1932), Russia, 1605; d. near Yaroslavl, Aug. 17, 1681. Nikon was the name in religion of Nikita Minin (or Minov), who came of peasant stock. After ordination as a Russian Orthodox priest (1625), he served in a rural parish until 1627, when he went to Moscow. After the death of his children he became a hermit on the island of Anser in the White Sea (1635) and then entered the monastery at Kozheozerskiĭ, where he became abbot (1643). In 1646 he was presented to Czar Alexis I (1645–76), whose influential counselor he became. He was appointed metropolitan of Novgorod (1646) and patriarch of Moscow (1652). Nikon was a zealous pastor, a popular preacher, and a promoter of the evangelization of Siberia. The liturgical reforms he decreed in 1653 brought the Russian liturgy to closer conformity with Greek and Ukrainian customs but suppressed numerous Russian traditional practices. Because of this he incurred the enmity of *Avvakum and other conservatives who formed the ultranationalistic and antigovernment sect of *Raskolniks. Nikon's liturgical innovations paved the way for Moscow's political absorption of the Ukraine (1654–67). Once this was accomplished, Nikon's usefulness to the ambitious Czar was ended. Nikon alienated the Czar by his attempt to make the Church completely independent of the state. He further challenged the Russian tradition of *caesaro-papism by asserting the superiority of the patriarchal dignity over that of the Czar. During the Czar's frequent absences from Moscow, Nikon acted as regent and did so in an authoritarian manner. The combination of religious and civil opposition led to Nikon's deposition (1660). In 1666 a synod in Moscow, attended by some of the Oriental patriarchs, exiled Nikon to the remote monastery of Belozerskiĭ-Ferapontov, but it definitively approved his liturgical reforms. He was granted amnesty by Czar Fёdor III (1676–80), but he died soon after, while journeying to his favorite monastery of Voskresenskiĭ.

Bibliography: W. PALMER, *The Patriarch and the Tsar,* 4 v. (London 1871–76). J. LEDIT, DTC 11.1:646–655; 14.1:292–304. G. OLŠR, EncCatt 8:1880.

[F. L. FADNER]

NILLES, NIKOLAUS, liturgist and canonist; b. Rippweiler, Luxembourg, June 21, 1828; d. Innsbruck, Jan. 31, 1907. After his ordination in 1852 he was appointed a curate at Ansemberg (1853–58). He entered the Jesuits on March 20, 1858. In 1859 he was appointed professor of Canon Law at the University of Innsbruck and held the chair almost to his death; from 1870 to 1896 he was also rector of the seminary. He contributed 57 articles to the *Archiv für katholisches Kirchenrecht* and 94 to the *Zeitschrift für katholische Theologie.* He also published the following works: *Symbolae ad illustrandam historiam ecclesiae orientalis in terris coronae S. Stephani* (2 v. Innsbruck 1885), *De rationibus festorum sacratissimi Cordis Jesu et purissimi Cordis Mariae* (2 v. 5th ed. Innsbruck 1885), *Kalendarium manuale utriusque ecclesiae orientalis et occidentalis* (2 v. 3d ed. Innsbruck 1896–97).

Bibliography: M. BLUM, *Das Collegium Germanicum zu Rom und dessen Zöglinge aus dem Luxemburger Lande* (Luxembourg 1899) 94–109. Hurter Nomencl 5.2:2067–69. H. LECLERCQ, DACL 9.2:1732–34. C. TESTORE, EncCatt 8:1881.

[C. TESTORE]

NILUS OF ANCYRA, ST., 5th-century abbot, ascetic writer; b. probably Ancyra, date unknown; d. Ancyra, c. 430 (feast, Nov. 12). The romantic *Narrationes de caede monachorum in monte Sinae* (PG 79:589–693) purports to be biography, and explains the modern misnomer, Nilus of Sinai. According to this legend Nilus was prefect of Constantinople but left office, wife, and home to become a monk with his son Theodulus on Mt. Sinai. When the monks were attacked by barbarians, Theodulus was captured but later he was set free and reunited with Nilus, who had escaped. Impressed by their piety, the bishop of Eleusa ordained them priests and sent them back to Sinai.

Nilus's own works give more reliable biographical data. At Constantinople he esteemed *John Chrysostom, regarded him as his teacher, and boldly took his side against his foes. Nilus left Constantinople and became abbot of a monastery near Ancyra. His skill as a spiritual counselor is attested by his treatises on moral and ascetic subjects and by more than 1,000 letters addressed mostly to otherwise unknown recipients. Several of these are merely excerpts from his own treatises or the works of others, particularly of John Chrysostom. Many of his writings explain passages of Scripture; in these he follows the literal or historical sense but makes free use of allegorical interpretations. He refutes *Arianism in eight letters to Gainas, general of the Goths. Other topics range from proper uses of mosaics in churches to condemnation of peculiar practices among monks, such as the *stylites. The tracts *De oratione* and *De malignis cogitationibus,* formerly attributed to Nilus, are the work of *Evagrius Ponticus.

Bibliography: PG v.79. K. HEUSSI, *Das Nilusproblem* (Leipzig 1921). G. T. STOKES, DCB 4:43–45. H. C. GRAEF, LexThK² 7:870–871. Quasten Patr 3:496–504. M. T. DISDIER, DTC 11.1:661–674.

[P. W. HARKINS]

NILUS OF ROSSANO, ST., abbot, propagator of Greek monasticism in Italy (known also as Nilus the Younger); b. Rossano, Calabria, Italy, c. 905; d. Abbey of Santa Agata, near Frascati, Italy, Dec. 29, 1005 (feast, Sept. 26 in both Roman and Byzantine calendars). After the sudden death of his wife and daughter and his own recovery from a serious illness, Nilus underwent a profound religious conversion and joined a community of Basilian monks near Mercurion, where the traditions of *Basilian monasticism in Italy had been kept alive in spite of the declining power of the Eastern Empire on the peninsula. He soon left the cloister and led a rigorously ascetic life in a secluded cave, in imitation of the fathers of the desert. But the Saracen invasions forced him c. 950 to found and settle down in the monastery of San Adriano near Rossano, and while abbot there he was offered, but refused, the archbishopric of his native city. Continued Moslem incursions forced his group of Basilian monks to take refuge for a while at *Monte Cassino, the motherhouse of Benedictine monasticism. Nilus's community next settled nearby at Valleluce and 15 years later established its *laura at Serperi near Gaeta. It was here, c. 1000, that Nilus received Emperor *Otto III, who was highly impressed by the abbot's work. Although Nilus had supported Pope *Gregory V against the antipope John XVI, who was supported by the *Crescentii, he pleaded in vain with both Pope and Emperor to show mercy to the usurper when he fell into their hands. Nilus also found time to write a few pieces of liturgical poetry and some letters. In 1004 he received from Gregory, Count of Tusculum, a grant of land on the lower slopes of Monte Cavo, where he made a foundation that remains today the center of Greek monasticism in Italy. Although he died before work was still under way, he is still listed as the first abbot of *Grottaferrata. One of his successors, Bartholomew the Younger (d. c. 1065), wrote a Greek life of Nilus.

Bibliography: Life, ActSS Sept. 7:259–320; PG 120:15–165; and see AnalBoll 61 (1943) 204–206. BHG 1370. G. MINASI, *San Nilo di Calabria* (Naples 1892). A. ROCCHI, *Vita di San Nilo abate* (Rome 1904). J. GAY, *L'Italie méridionale et l'Empire byzantin* (Paris 1904). S. GASSISI IEROMONACO, "I Manoscritti autografi di San Nilo Juniore . . .," OrChr 4 (1904) 308–370; *Poesie di San Nilo Juniore e di Paolo Monaco abati di Grottaferrata,* OrChr 5 (1905) 26–81. Zimmermann KalBen 3:107–108. T. MINISCI, *Santa Maria di Grottaferrata . . .* (Grottaferrata 1955); EncCatt 8:1884. Beck KTLBR 607–608. G. PENCO, *Storia del monachesimo in Italia* (Rome 1961), *passim.*

[B. J. COMASKEY]

NÎMES, town of the Midi and bishopric in the Department of Gard, France. Nîmes, ancient Nemausus, possesses some of the finest ancient monuments of all France. Of Celtic origin, founded near the sacred spring of Nemausus, capital of the *Volcae arecomici* described by Strabo, Nîmes became a Roman ally in 120 B.C. Julius Caesar made it a center of Latin civilization for the Province of Narbonne, and after his Egyptian campaign, Augustus established a colony of Greek veterans with Latin rights, and the city took the name of Colonia Nemaucensis Augusta. The imperial cult was added to that of the sacred fountain and Nîmes became a pilgrimage center.

From the Augustan epoch date the celebrated Square House, originally a Corinthian temple erected to Gaius and Julius Caesar, the sons of Agrippa, and turned into a museum in 1823; the amphitheater (*les arènes*), which seats some 25,000; ruins of the wall surrounding the city, whose Great Tower still stands, and of two city gates, that of Augustus and the Porte de France, as well as of a nymphaeum and the temple of Diana. The famous Pont du Gard and the aqueduct running for 50 kilometers (30 miles) give evidence of the architectural competence of the Romans.

The fatherland of Domitian Afer, master of Quintilian, Nîmes saw its greatest prosperity toward the middle of the 2d century A.D. Hadrian gave it complete rights as a city, and Antoninus Pius, whose grandfather was of Nîmes, added to its prosperity. It replaced Narbonne as capital of the province and was an administrative and commercial center, as well as a pagan shrine.

Christianity entered with difficulty and late. After the religious peace there was a martyr St. Baudilius. St. *Gregory of Tours describes its martyrs (*In glor. mart.* 77). Nîmes has only some inscriptions and sarcophagi attesting to its early Christian history. In 394 an important synod against *Priscillianism was held there. The excavations of 1920 unearthed foundations of a 6th- or 7th-century basilica near the present cathedral that was started in 1096.

Ravaged by the Vandals in 407, Nîmes was occupied by the Visigoths, Franks, Goths, and Saracens who were defeated by Charles Martel in 731. Nîmes had its own Counts, then passed under the control of the Counts of Toulouse, and was reunited to France in 1229. During the Protestant wars, it was the scene of a massacre of Catholics (1567). Louis XIV constructed a citadel there in 1687. Suppressed in 1801, the bishopric was reestablished in 1821. Nîmes is also the fatherland of Nicot, who introduced tobacco to France. The diocese has absorbed those of Uzès and Alès; it has 400 churches and 289 parishes with 373 secular and 54 religious priests for the 310,000 Catholics out of 400,000 inhabitants (1960).

Bibliography: H. LECLERCQ, DACL 12.1:1318–74. E. JOSI, EncCatt, 8:1888–90. O. FELD and J. RATH, LexThK² 7:1005–06. E. ESPÉRANDIEU, *L'Amphithéâtre de Nîmes* (Paris 1934).

[A. DANET]

NINA, LORENZO, cardinal, secretary of state; b. Recanati (Marches), Italy, May 12, 1812; d. Rome, July 25, 1885. After seminary studies at Recanati and Rome, he studied law at the University of Rome and was ordained in 1834. After entering the service of the Roman *Curia, he became successively secretary of the *Rota; then, in the Congregation of the *Council, first auditor to the secretary and later under-secretary. Pius IX named him assessor of the Holy Office and cardinal (March 1877). *Leo XIII appointed him secretary of state (Aug. 9, 1878); ill health forced his retirement (Dec. 16, 1880). Although affable and prudent, he was less a diplomat than a theologian. He favored a settlement with the Kingdom of Italy. He had to deal in Belgium with the "school war" that led to the rupture of diplomatic relations (June 1880) and in France with the hostility of the Third Republic toward religious congregations. In both cases he urged Catholics to moderation. Through the nuncio to Vienna, Ludovico *Jacobini, he negotiated for a settlement of the *Kulturkampf.

Bibliography: E. SODERINI, *Il pontificato di Leone XIII,* 3 v. (Milan 1932–33); tr. B. B. CARTER, v.1 *The Pontificate of Leo XIII* (London 1934), v.2 *Leo XIII, Italy and France* (1935), v.3 not tr.

[J. M. MAYEUR]

NINGUARDA, FELICIANO, Italian Dominican, theologian, writer, and bishop; b. Morbegno (Sondrio), 1524; d. Como, 1595. In 1554 he was appointed vicar-general of the Order, and later professor of theology at the University of Vienna. He was invited by the Archbishop of Salzburg to be his procurator at the third session of the Council of *Trent (1562–63). Then he was entrusted with implementing the reform decrees of Trent in visitations of the religious houses of the mendicant orders in Austria, Bohemia, and Moravia. At the same time, as papal commissioner, he worked toward the reform of the Diocese of Salzburg and convoked a provincial synod in 1569. He was made bishop of Scala (Salerno) in 1577, and shortly after was appointed apostolic nuncio to Bavaria, where he served until 1583. He was transferred to the episcopal See of Santa Agata dei Goti (Benevento) in 1583, and, finally in 1588, to that of Como, his native diocese, where he died. His works include: the *Defensio fidei maiorum nostrorum* (Antwerp 1575); *Manuale parochorum* (Ingolstadt 1582); *Enchiridion de censuris, irregularitate et privilegiis* (Ingolstadt 1583); and the *Manuale visitatorum* (Rome 1589).

Bibliography: Quétif-Échard 2:313–314. K. SCHELLHASS, *Der Dominikaner Feliciano Ninguarda und die Gegenreformation in Süddeutschland und Österreich, 1560–1583* (Rome 1930). A. WALZ, *I Domenicani al Concilio di Trento* (Rome 1961).

[A. L. REDIGONDA]

NINIAN, ST., early 5th-century apostle of Galloway, Scotland (feast, Sept. 16). Ninian, a Briton by birth, educated in the Roman rite and tradition ("regulariter" according to Bede, *Eccl. Hist.* 3.4), preached to the southern Picts and built in Galloway, southwest Scotland, a church of stone, called the *Candida casa,* dedicated to St. Martin of Tours. His "converts among the Picts" were probably the "apostates" referred to in the letters of St. *Patrick (*Epist.* 2, 15). His settlement, renamed Whithorn by the Anglo-Saxons, became a monastic center to which many Irish monks went for religious training in the 6th century. The inscription on his tomb, located at the *Candida casa,* was apparently interpreted in an anti-Celtic sense by Plechtelm, the first Anglo-Saxon bishop of Galloway, so that much of what Bede relates, including the dedication to St. Martin (not earlier than 500 according to P. Grosjean), is untrustworthy.

Bibliography: P. GROSJEAN, "Les Pictes apostats dans l'Épître de S. Patrice," AnalBoll 76 (1958) 354–378. L. BIELER, LexThK² 7:1008. J. MacQUEEN, *St. Nynia* (London 1961). M. ANDERSON, *St. Ninian* (London 1964).

[J. RYAN]

NINIVE (NINEVEH)

Ancient city of Assyria and its capital under the last kings of the Assyrian Empire. Its position on the eastern bank of the Tigris (opposite modern Mosul) where this river is joined by the Khosar River made the site a natural fortress, for water from the latter stream, which ran through the center of the city, could be diverted to fill the moats on the north, east, and

Two Assyrian soldiers in procession to the Temple of Ishtar, fragment of a relief from the Palace of Sennacherib at Ninive, 7th century B.C.

south sides of the city. The massive walls that were erected in the last period of the city's existence (7th century B.C.) enclosed an irregular-shaped area of *c.* 1,800 acres; the wall on the north was *c.* 7,000 feet long, on the east *c.* 3 miles long, on the south *c.* 1,000 feet long, and on the west (along the Tigris) *c.* 2½ miles long. Two large mounds on the western side now stand out over the ruins of the rest of the city: that of Nebi Yūnus (the Prophet Jona), on which is the reputed tomb of Jona, formerly a Nestorian shrine but now Moslem, and that of Quyunjik (little lamb).

The site of Ninive (Akkadian *Ninua* and *Ninâ;* Heb. *nîn°wēh*) was occupied from at least 3800 B.C. until the time of its utter destruction by the Medes and Babylonians in 612 B.C. Although earlier Assyrian kings, who regularly resided at *Assur (Asshur) or Calah (modern Khorsabad), had often used Ninive as a secondary capital, it was only during the most glorious period of Assyrian history under the last three rulers of the Assyrian Empire—*Sennacherib (705–682), *Asarhaddon (681–670), and *Assurbanipal (669– *c.* 633)—that Ninive became the sole capital.

Although the native Arabic-speaking people still call this immense field of ruins Ninawa, as they have apparently done for centuries, the Western world, even in Greco-Roman times, did not know where the famous city lay. The site was first clearly identified and made known to the Western world by C. J. Rich in 1821. The sacred nature of the mound of Nebi Yūnus, which covers the palace of Sennacherib, has prevented extensive excavation from being made there. But the mound of Quyunjik, with its palaces of Asarhaddon and Assurbanipal, has been subjected to repeated excavations. The earlier excavations were merely treasure hunts, which were extremely successful in sensational finds of sculptures and inscriptions; it is only in the 20th century that the site has been scientifically excavated, with careful regard for the archeological strata and the pottery so useful for chronology. Almost all the inscriptions (especially cuneiform tablets), as well as most of the sculptures found at Ninive, are now in the British Museum. The excavations were made here by P. E. Botta (1842), A. H. Layard (1845–47, 1849–51), H. Rawlinson (1853–55), H. Rassam (1854 and 1877–83, when he discovered Assurbanipal's great library of cuneiform tablets), G. A. Smith (1873–74), E. A. Wallis Budge (1888–89), L. W. King (1902). R. Campbell Thomson (1927–28), and the latter with M. Mallowan (1929–32).

In the Bible, Ninive is said to have been built by *Nemrod (Gn 10.11). Sennacherib returned home there after his failure to capture Jerusalem (4 Kgs 19.36; Is 37.37). Sophonia foretold the destruction of Ninive (So 2.12–15), and the whole Book of Nahum is a vivid description of its capture by the Medes and Babylonians. Jona is said to have preached to the people of Ninive, "the great city" (Jon 1.2; 3.1–10; 4.11), and Jesus referred to their repentance as a model for the men of His own time (Mt 12.41; Lk 11.32). Tobit is portrayed as living in this city with his fellow exiles (Tob 1.3; 7.3; 11.1; 14.4, 15).

Bibliography: EncDictBibl 1644–45. M. RUTTEN et al., DB Suppl 6:480–506. R. C. THOMPSON and R. W. HUTCHINSON, *A Century of Exploration at Nineveh* (London 1929). A. PARROT, *Nineveh and the Old Testament,* tr. B. E. HOOKE (Studies in Biblical Archaeology 3; New York 1955; London 1956). S. A. PALLIS, *The Antiquity of Iraq* (Copenhagen 1956). **Illustration credit:** Courtesy of the Trustees of the British Museum.

[L. A. BUSHINSKI]

NIPPUR, ancient Sumero-Babylonian city, located in the southern part of the Mesopotamian plain (*see* MESOPOTAMIA, ANCIENT, 2) between the Euphrates and the Shatt el-Hai, approximately 100 miles southeast of modern Baghdad and 55 miles northwest of *Uruk. The city, at the site of modern Nuffar, was first excavated by a series of four expeditions of the Babylonian Exploration Fund of the University of Pennsylvania (1889–1900), under the leadership of John P. Peters and J. H. Haynes, with the Assyriologists R. F. Harper and H. V. Hilprecht. These expeditions, beset by difficulties caused by the local population, were unfortunately not careful in archeological method and exact in their recording of discoveries. Nevertheless they revealed evidence of continuous occupation from the era of the Sumerian city-states of the mid-3d millennium B.C. to the Parthian period. They also uncovered thousands of cuneiform tablets, of the greatest importance for our knowledge of the literature and the political and economic history of ancient Mesopotamia. Of particular significance are the Sumerian literary texts from the early 2d millennium, because these tablets, though still not completely published, remain the most important source for the knowledge of *Sumerian language and literature. Excavation was resumed after 1948 by a joint expedition of the Oriental Institute of the University of Chicago and the University Museum of the University of Pennsylvania, under Donald E. McCown.

Although Nippur did not exercise political hegemony over Sumer or Mesopotamia at any point during the historical period, but was rather subject to the domination of other city or national states in succession, it remained throughout the period of Akkadian civilization a religious center of the first importance; moreover, it is possible that this religious prominence reflects an earlier period of political power. Nippur's god was Enlil, the storm god, traditionally a central god of the Sumerian-Akkadian pantheon, the executor of divine power and "lord of the lands" who possessed the "tablets of destiny" and appointed human kings to rule. It was in his city of Nippur, according to myth, that the council of the gods was accustomed to meet, and veneration of

Excavations of the temple of Enlil, central deity of the Sumerian-Akkadian pantheon, at Nippur, 1949–52.

the city is historically attested by the fact that Mesopotamian rulers, such as Sargon of Agade, were ceremonially invested with kingship in Ekur, the temple of Enlil in Nippur.

See also MESOPOTAMIA, ANCIENT, 4.

Bibliography: A. PARROT, *Archéologie mésopotamienne,* 2 v. (Paris 1946–53) 1:144–158, bibliog. 167. H. SCHMÖKEL, *Kulturgeschichte des alten Orient* (Stuttgart 1961) *passim.* V. E. CRAWFORD, "Nippur the Holy City," *Archaeology* 12 (1959) 74–83. **Illustration credit:** The University Museum of the University of Pennsylvania.

[R. I. CAPLICE]

NIRVĀNA. The word (in Pāli, *nibbāna*) originally meant extinction as by fire. In *Hīnayāna Buddhism, which denies the existence of God and soul, all beings are transitory. The craving for permanence is the cause of pain and leads to rebirth, whose process can be stopped only by achieving nirvāna. The visible nirvāna (*samditthika nibbāna*), attained in the present life by an *arhat* (Pāli, *arahant*), a being perfected by enlightenment and asceticism, is extinction of lust, hatred, and ignorance producing no seed or nucleus of further rebirth. At death the *arhat* enters the invisible absolute nirvāna (*parinibbāna*), which is variously interpreted as: annihilation of individual personality; liberation from rebirth into an ineffable state; a state of perfect bliss; a populous and blissful heaven where personality abides.

In *Mahāyāna Buddhism, a *bodhisattva,* perfected by enlightened asceticism and moved by compassion, forgoes nirvāna to help others until all have found salvation. In *Amidism, the oldest and most popular school, nirvāna is the Pure Land of Western Paradise that Amitābha, the supreme being of mercy and love, promised all those who invoked his name with faith. For the Mādhyamika school, instead, the universe exists only in the illusion of the percipient. What really exists is emptiness—the absolute truth, being, nirvāna, and the Body of Essence of the Buddha (*dharmakāya*). For the nihilist Vijñānavāda school the universe exists only in the mind of the perceiver, and nirvāna is an absurd notion. In *Vajrayāna (Diamond Vehicle), nirvāna is identical with the final bliss attending the union of the phenomenal Means with the noumenal Wisdom, best symbolized and effected by sexual intercourse. In China and Japan, however, these same tenets were interpreted in a way more consonant with the general belief in the survival of the individual soul and with popular idol worship. *See* BUDDHISM; INDIAN PHILOSOPHY.

Bibliography: L. DE LA VALLÉ POUSSIN, Hastings ERE 9:376–379; *The Way to Nirvāna* (Cambridge, Eng. 1917). T. STCHERBATSKY, *The Conception of Buddhist Nirvana* (Leningrad 1927). V. P. VARMA, "The Philosophy of Nirvana in Early Buddhism: A Critical and Sociological Study," *Journal of the Bihar Research Society* 45 (1959) 226–243. W. T. DE BARY, ed., *Introduction to Oriental civilizations,* 3 v. (Records of Civilization 54–56; New York 1958–60).

[A. S. ROSSO]

NISARD, THÉODORE, musicologist prominent in chant scholarship (real name, Abbé Théodore Elzéar Xavier Normand); b. Quaregnon, Belgium, Jan. 27, 1812; d. Jacqueville, France, Feb. 29, 1888. Nisard, a choirboy in his youth, attended the seminary in Tournai and was ordained in 1835. After a few years as director of a secondary school in Enghien, in 1842 he was named organist at Saint Germain-des-Près in Paris. From then

on he devoted himself to *Gregorian chant research and restoration, publishing many valuable and widely circulated studies (some in collaboration with d'*Ortigue). Among them are his 1847 revision of P. B. de Jumilhac's *La Science et la pratique du plain-chant* (1672); *Études sur la restauration du chant grégorien au XIXe siècle* (1856); *L'Archéologie musicale et le vrai chant grégorien* (1890), which established the importance of historical research in the new chant movement; and many other studies and articles on the antiquity, rhythm, and accompaniment of chant, on the organ, on folk music, and on general questions involving church music. He also investigated the Montpellier Antiphonary discovered by J. L. Danjou (1812–66) and participated in the controversy over St. Gall MS 359.

Bibliography: J. COMBARIEU, *Études de philologie musicale: Théorie du rythme dans la composition moderne* (Paris 1896). F. J. FÉTIS, *Biographie universelle,* 8 v. (2d ed. Paris 1860–65) 6:329–332. W. IRTENKAUF, MusGG 9:1537. Riemann 2:1274. Baker 1164.

[K. G. FELLERER]

NISIBIS, modern Nusaybin, a city in Turkey on the Syrian border, about 130 miles northwest of Mosul, formerly an important military and commercial center, as well as the site of a noted Nestorian theological school. The city, which is situated by the river Yaghyagha (ancient Mygdonius) as it flows through a narrow canyon from the mountains into the plains, was referred to at the beginning of the 1st millennium B.C. in Assyrian inscriptions under the name of Nasibina. In the 3d century B.C. it was the capital of a rich province under the Seleucids, and was called Antiochia Mygdonia by the Greeks. For some time it was also the residence of the kings of Armenia.

Because of its strategic importance and its location on the upper trade route from Mosul to the west, the city has been the scene of warfare until recent times. In 68 B.C. it was captured by Pompey but was retaken by the Persians 15 years later. In A.D. 115 its capture by Emperor Trajan earned him the title of "Parthicus." Once more lost to the Persians, it was restored to Roman rule by Septimius Severus in 297 and served as a frontier fortress. In 338, 346, and 350 it was besieged by the Persian King Shapur II; the sieges are described by St. Ephrem in his *Carmina Nisibena.* In 363 Emperor Jovian was forced to cede the city to Persia, at which time the Christians were allowed to depart. Most of the population, then, including the Christian theological school, settled in Edessa. After being taken by the Arabs in 640, the city continued to prosper well into the 10th century. Ravaged by the Mongols in 1260, Nisibis declined rapidly and by the 14th century was in ruins. In 1965 it was a small town of about 3,000 inhabitants on the main railroad from Baghdad to Alep and into central Turkey.

The beginnings of Christianity in Nisibis are uncertain. According to legend, *Addai and Mari, 2 of the 72 disciples of Christ, are said to have established the church there. The first known bishop, however, was Jacob (290–338). In 410 it appears as a metropolitan see with seven suffragans, ranked immediately after *Seleucia-Ctesiphon and Beth-Lapat. From the second half of the 5th century the bishops were Nestorians, and the school of *Nisibis became the theological center of the Persian Nestorian Church. There exist ruins of an ancient, two-nave church called Mar Yakub, used until very recently by the Jacobites. Today Nisibis is also a Latin titular see.

Bibliography: Le Quien 2:995–998, 1192–1204. C. PREUSSER, *Nordmesopotamische Baudenkmäler,* 2 pts. (Leipzig 1911) 40– .

[G. T. DENNIS]

NISIBIS, SCHOOL OF

About the middle of the 4th century *Nisibis was already known as a center of theological studies, counting among its teachers St. *Ephrem. When the city came under Persian rule in 363, St. Ephrem and the school moved to Edessa within the boundaries of the Roman Empire. After the Council of Ephesus in 431 a large number of Nestorians settled in Edessa and, for a short period, took over control of the theological school. Because of imperial persecution, however, they were forced to seek refuge outside the Empire and moved to Nisibis, where their opposition to the official Roman doctrine and, consequently, to the Roman Emperor earned them the protection of the Persian rulers. The theological school of *Edessa was continued in Nisibis under the patronage of the Nestorian metropolitan Bar Sauma. Its foundation can be dated about 457, the year in which its first great teacher, Narsai (Narses), who had taught in Edessa, arrived and began lecturing on theology, a task that he continued for some 40 years. For 200 years or more the school of Nisibis flourished under a succession of famous teachers, such as Abraham, the nephew of Narsai, Paul, Elias bar Sīnāja, *'Abdisho (Ebedjesus) bar Berīkā, and others. The number of students seems to have been considerable; Abraham de beth Rabban, the second successor of Narsai and rector of the school for 60 years, had over 1,000 students. The graduates of the school filled the episcopal sees throughout the then prosperous Church in Persia, so that the entire Church in that region and in its missionary areas became Nestorian in doctrine. The foundation of another theological school about 541 by Aba Mar in *Seleucia-Ctesiphon was a strong blow to Nisibis, and the establishment of the school of Baghdad about 830 led to its rapid decline.

From the beginning the theological teaching at Nisibis was based on the works of Nestorius, Diodor of Tarsus, and in particular, *Theodore of Mopsuestia. In general, the instructors at Nisibis limited themselves to explaining the doctrine of Theodore, especially his commentaries on Scripture, adding very little of their own. Among the Nestorians Theodore was known as "The Commentator" par excellence. Following the pre-Chalcedonian terminology of Theodore they spoke of two natures and two hypostases with one *prosopon* in Christ. The doctrine was officially accepted by the Persian Church in a synod at Seleucia-Ctesiphon in 486 and again in 612.

The curriculum and the statutes of the school of Nisibis, undoubtedly based upon those of Edessa, have been conserved, and they probably represent the oldest statutes of any Christian theological school that are known to us. The detailed regulations were revised and made stricter in 496 and again in 590. The course of studies lasted 3 years, and instruction was given gratuitously. The school was under the direction of a rector (Rabban) and a master who, aided by a council, was in charge of disciplinary and financial matters. There were two principal professors: the first, referred to as

the Interpreter, explained Scripture according to the commentaries of Theodore of Mopsuestia; the other was known as the Master of the Lessons. The students were obliged to live in community, somewhat similar in organization to a modern seminary. They studied in a common hall where the desks differed according to students' ranks. They were forbidden to enter the Roman (Byzantine) Empire without special permission. The school was practically exempt from episcopal jurisdiction and enjoyed a number of civil privileges as well.

A description of the organization and the spirit of the school is given by a 6th-century teacher: Mar Barhadbešabba 'Arbaya, *Cause de la fondation des écoles* [ed. A. Scher, *Patrologia Orientalis,* 4 (Paris 1908) 317–404, Syriac text with French translation]. A history of the school and an account of the teaching of Narsai and Abraham have been given by the same author [*Patrologia Orientalis* 9 (Paris 1913) 588–631].

Bibliography: R. NELZ, *Die theologischen Schulen der morgenländischen Kirchen* (Bonn 1916) 77–110. A. BAUMSTARK, *Geschichte der syrischen Literatur* (Bonn 1922) 113–115. PatrSyrO 107–111. W. DE VRIES, *Sakramententheologie bei den Nestorianern* (OrChrAnal 133; 1947); *Der Kirchenbegriff der von Rom getrennten Syrer (ibid.* 145; 1955). W. F. MACOMBER, "The Christology of the Synod of Seleucia-Ctesiphon, A.D. 486," OrChrPer 24 (1958) 142–154; "The Theological Synthesis of Cyrus of Edessa, an East Syrian Theologian of the Mid-Sixth Century," *ibid.* 30 (1964) 5–38.

[G. T. DENNIS]

NITERÓI, ARCHDIOCESE OF (NICTHE-ROYENSIS),

located in the state of Rio de Janeiro, Brazil; created a diocese in 1892; raised to an archdiocese in 1960. In 1964 it had three suffragans: Campos (1922), Petrópolis (1946), and Nova Friburgo (1960). Jesuits, Benedictines, Franciscans, and Capuchins did missionary work among the Indians in Niterói in the 16th century, and the first parish was created in 1593. The first seminary was founded in 1747 in Campos by Ângelo de Siqueira. The see of the diocese has been located at various times in Campos, Petrópolis, and finally at Niterói. The proximity of Rio de Janeiro has brought the area in contact with many sects and varied ideas. In the 20th century Protestantism and Spiritism have been growing. In the Diocese of Campos during the episcopacy of Otaviano Pereira de Albuquerque the schism of Dom Maura occurred. The population of the Diocese of Petrópolis is largely made up of German Protestant immigrants. There the Franciscans founded in 1901 the large Catholic publishing house of Vozes, and in 1962, an Intercultural Formation Center. Among the religious orders serving in the province in 1964 were Missionaries of the Sacred Heart, Franciscans, Conventuals, Pallotines, Salesians (whose first Brazilian foundation was

1964 STATISTICS

Area	Population	Parishes	Clergy	
			Sec.	Reg.
Niterói	*623,059	32	58	38
Campos	626,387	26	26	20
Petrópolis	511,429	27	32	56
Nova Friburgo	321,453	32	19	18

* This figure represents Catholics only. All other figures represent total population.

in Niterói in 1883), Redemptorists, Premonstratensians, Vincentians, and Jesuits. A Catholic university was founded in Petrópolis in 1962.

See also BRAZIL.

Bibliography: J. DE S. A. P. E ARAÚJO, *Memórias históricas do Rio de Janeiro*, 9 v. in 4 (Rio de Janeiro 1945–48). A. NÓBREGA, *Dioceses e bispos do Brasil* (Rio de Janeiro 1954).

[O. VAN DER VAT]

NITHARD, Carolingian historian; b. *c.* 800; d. 844–845. He was one of the two natural sons of Bertha, a daughter of Emperor *Charlemagne, and *Angilbert, lay abbot of Saint-Riquier and the court poet whom *Alcuin called the "Homer" of the palace school. Nithard, was thus a cousin of the warring sons of *Louis I the Pious. Inevitably, he was caught up in their fratricidal conflicts; he adhered to the party of *Charles II the Bald, whom he served as counselor. A layman, Nithard actively participated in the struggles, and presumably died either on June 14, 844, in battle against his kinsman Pepin II of Aquitaine, or on May 15, 845, fighting against the Northmen. At Charles the Bald's invitation (841) to write a history of his times, Nithard composed the *Historiarum libri IV,* an account of the strife between the sons of Louis the Pious. The first book is a sketchy description of the reign of Louis (one of the four biographies of the emperor); the other three are a detailed record of contemporary events from 839 to 843. In this plain but valuable work, Nithard preserved the famous Oaths of Strasbourg between Charles the Bald and *Louis the German, the earliest literary specimen of any Romance language, the immediate ancestor of French. Little known in his own age and later —only one early manuscript survives—he has recently been regarded as one of the more successful chroniclers of contemporary events during the Carolingian Age.

Bibliography: Manitius 1:656–660. NITHARD, *Histoire des fils de Louis le Pieux,* ed. and tr. P. LAUER (Paris 1926). L. HALPHEN, *Charlemagne et l'Empire Carolingien* (Paris 1947). Laistner ThLett.

[A. CABANISS]

NITRIAN VALLEY (WADI-NATRÛN), known also as Nitria and the Desert of Scete; a shallow desert valley about 50 miles south of Alexandria in Egypt, the site of the 4th-century beginnings of Christian monasticism. The valley extends diagonally across the extreme northeast tip of the Libyan Desert for some 30 miles. Before the Arab conquests it was called Shiêt (Coptic), Scetis, Scete, Scitium (Latin and Greek). Natrûn and Nitria were used for both the valley and its neighboring mountain only after the 15th century; the name was derived from *natron,* the sodium carbonate found in its numerous small lakes. Its monastic tradition of simplicity and single-minded search for God is effectively set forth in the *Apophthegmata Patrum.* The founder of its monastic settlements (*c.* 320) seems to have been Amon, referred to by St. *Athanasius in his *Life of Antony* and by Palladius, Socrates, and Sozomen. Other important monastic authors wrote of Nitria after residing there: *Rufinus of Aquileia (*c.* 370–377), translator of the *Historia monachorum;* John *Cassian (*c.* 385–392), in his *Institutes* and *Conferences;* and *Palladius (390), in his *Lausiac History.* *Melania the Elder and Aetheria included Nitria in their *pilgrimages. Monastic authors record the names of several of its *Desert Fathers, many of them simple

Coptic peasants. Macarius was one of the earliest and most celebrated.

Archeological remains of the 4th-century Macarian laura have been found on the site of Dêr Abû Makâr, a 9th-century monastery still standing in the valley. Three other 9th-century monasteries remain, two of which were also built on the sites of 4th-century lauras. Important archeological studies were made of Wadi-Natrûn in the 1840s by Tattam, Curzon, and Tischendorf and in the first quarter of the 20th century by Palmer-Jones and Evelyn-White.

Bibliography: H. ROSWEYDE, ed., *Vitae patrum* 2 v. (Antwerp 1628; repr. PL 73–74). H. J. WADDELL, tr., *The Desert Fathers* (New York 1936). J. CASSIAN, *Conlationes,* ed. M. PETSCHENIG (CSEL 13; 1886); *De Institutis,* ed. M. PETSCHENIG (*ibid.* 17; 1888). ATHANASIUS, *The Life of Saint Anthony,* ed. and tr. R. T. MEYER (AncChrWr 10; 1950). SOCRATES, *Hist. eccl.* 4.23, PG 67:509–522. SOZOMEN, *Historia ecclesiastica* 1.14, *ibid.* 917–920. H. G. EVELYN-WHITE, *The Monasteries of the Wadi 'n-Natrûn,* ed. W. HAUSER, 3 v. (New York 1926–33). C. MARTIN, "Les Monastères du Wadi 'n-Natroun," NouvRevTh 62 (1935) 113–134, 238–252. P. DE LABRIOLLE, Fliche-Martin 3:299–369, Eng. tr. E. C. MESSENGER, *The Church in the Christian Roman Empire,* v.2 (New York 1953) 421–512.

[M. C. MC CARTHY]

NIVARD, BL., Cistercian monk; b. Fontaines-les-Dijon (Burgundy), *c.* 1100; d. *c.* 1150 (feast, Feb. 7). Nivard was the youngest brother of *Bernard of Clairvaux. Following his brothers' example, he joined *Cîteaux at an early age and was later transferred to *Clairvaux. By order of Bernard, he participated in the foundation of a number of new Cistercian monasteries in various capacities; further details of his life, including the date and place of death, are unknown. According to unsubstantiated tradition, he was buried at Clairvaux. His cult can be traced to the 16th century but was restricted to certain Cistercian communities.

Bibliography: G. MÜLLER, "Der selige Nivard," CistChron 8 (1896) 43–51. Lenssen HagCist 1:188–189. W. W. WILLIAMS, *Saint Bernard of Clairvaux* (Westminster, Md. 1952) 4–84.

[L. J. LEKAI]

NIVARD OF GHENT, Benedictine of Saint-Pierre-au-Mont-Blandin, Ghent, Belgium; a German by birth, possibly of Cologne; fl. Flanders, *c.* 1148, where he wrote *Ysengrimus,* the famous beast epic. Nivard came under the influence of French learning at the monastic school of Blandigny and at Paris. A man of wide experience, he knew France as the land of polite manners and *haute couture;* he was familiar, moreover, with the Archdiocese of *Reims, the Diocese of Tournai, and the cloisters of *Cluny and *Clairvaux. Nivard was an ecclesiastic with a deep understanding of the duties of the priesthood; in *Ysengrimus* (6,574 lines), he satirized popes, priests, and religious orders. His work consists of a collection of fables with digressions into ecclesiastical satire. In his allegory Nivard disputes with the pope about world domination and inveighs against the bishop of his own diocese and against *Roger of Sicily, *Bernard of Clairvaux, Pope *Eugene III, and other personalities. His attacks on the court and society in general are in measured terms, and Nivard did not take advantage of the fable for moralizing. From the richness of his dealings with men and a degree of poetical inspiration, Nivard fashioned a satirical allegory superior to anything of its kind produced in the Middle Ages up to mid-12th century. For the first time animals appear with the characteristic names of the Reynard epos; the *Ysengrimus* is possibly a source of the *Roman du Renart*.

Bibliography: *Ysengrimus,* ed. E. VOIGT (Halle 1884). *Isengrimus. Das flämische Tierepos aus dem Lateinischen verdeutscht,* tr. into German A. SCHÖNFELDER (Münster 1955). K. LANGOSCH, comp., *Waltharius. Ruodlieb. Märchenepen. Lateinische Epik des Mittelalters mit deutschen Versen* (Basel 1956). Manitius 3:763–769. Ghellinck Essor 2:227–228. M. HÉLIN, *A History of Medieval Latin Literature,* tr. J. C. SNOW (rev. ed. New York 1949). Raby SecLP 2:151–152. P. LEHMANN, *Erforschung des Mittelalters,* 4 v. (2d ed. Stuttgart 1959–61) 3:234, 245–246; 4:184, 220.

[M. J. KISHPAUGH]

NIZA, MARCOS DE, discoverer of Arizona and New Mexico; b. date unknown; d. Mexico City, March 25, 1558. He was most probably a native of Nice, hence a Savoyard and neither French nor Italian. He must have been born around the beginning of the 16th century, for he was already a priest, a member of the Friars Minor of the Regular Observance, and reputed a learned man when, in 1531, he left Europe for New Spain. Nothing is known of his earlier life. While being detained at Hispaniola he heard about Peru, which was then being conquered, and volunteered his services for that region. Once commissioned by the commissary general of the Indies to act in his name, Fray Marcos, as vice-commissary, became the leader of the first Franciscan friars to enter Peru, then comprising Ecuador and the present Peru. He participated in two expeditions there between 1531 and January 1535. His memorandum executed at Santiago del Quito (Riobamba), Aug. 29, 1534, might be regarded as the official proclamation of the existence of the Custody of the Name of Jesus. From April 20, 1535, to at least Sept. 25, 1536, Fray Marcos was in Guatemala, whence he proceeded to Mexico, arriving before April 4, 1537. In 1538 he was commissioned to explore the land north of Mexico; upon his return in August 1539, he submitted a report, his *Relación,* which has provoked much needless controversy and has been subjected to unwarranted attacks. In 1540 he accompanied Coronado on his conquering expedition. From 1540 to 1543 Fray Marcos served also as provincial of the Province of the Holy Gospel in Mexico. Fray Marcos, crippled by paralysis induced by the hardships suffered during the two latter expeditions, was sent to the warmer climate of Jalapa, where *Mendieta met him in 1554. Shortly before his death he asked to be brought back to Mexico City to die.

Bibliography: M. DE NIZA, *Discovery of the Seven Cities of Cíbola,* tr. and ed. P. M. BALDWIN (Historical Society of New Mexico, Publications in History 1; Albuquerque 1926). G. J. UNDREINER, "Fray Marcos de Niza and His Journey to Cíbola," *Americas* 3 (1947) 415–486.

[G. J. UNDREINER]

NIZĀRĪS, a sect of the Ismaʿīlī or "Sevener" Shīʿī division (*see* SHIITES) of Islam, headed by the Agha Khan. At the death of the Ismaʿīlī Fāṭimid Caliph al-Mustanṣir in A.D. 1094, the all-powerful minister al-Afḍal passed over the caliph's eldest son, Nizār, and recognized Nizār's younger brother al-Mustaʿlī as *Imām, or religious leader. The Ismaʿīlīs living outside Fāṭimid territory in Persia, under the leadership of Hasan-i Ṣabbāḥ, master of the fortress of Alamūt, maintained their loyalty to Nizār. They later claimed that their imāms were his descendants, a statement difficult to prove or disprove. Those Ismaʿīlīs who followed

imāms of the line of Mustaʿlī were, after the extinction of the Fāṭimid Caliphate by *Saladin in 1171, confined to the Yemen and the west coast of India, where they became known as Bohras.

Under Hasan-i Ṣabbāḥ's "new preaching" the Nizārī sect, from its strongholds in Persia and Syria, passed to active struggle against the ʿAbbāsid and *Seljuk Sunnī authorities (*see* ʿABBĀSIDS; SUNNITES), seeking to establish its own version of the Islamic state. One of their most common weapons was the careful stalking and assassination of enemies of the sect, by devotees (*fidā'-īyīn*) who usually lost their lives in the act. For this, their enemies gave them the contemptuous name of *Hashshāshīn,* addicts of hashish (intoxicating hemp), thus implying that only drug-crazed men could act so recklessly. The epithet has been europeanized as "assassin," and has become a name for any common murderer by violence. The act of the *fidā'ī* was regarded within the sect as heroic and meritorious.

The crusaders came in contact with a branch of the Nizārīs in Syria, where their local head was known as the Shaykh al-Jabal, the "Old Man of the Mountain." The most vigorous of these leaders, Rashīd al-Dīn Sinān, played an important role in the affairs of 12th-century Syria. In 1256 the strongholds of the sect in Persia were razed by the invading Mongols of Hūlāgū Khan, and the Nizārīs entered a period of voluntary concealment (*taqīya*). In 1817 the Imām of the Nizārīs married a daughter of Fath ʿAlī Shāh of Persia and was given the title of *Āghā Khān,* which his descendants have since used as their secular title. In 1840 the Agha Khan emigrated to India where Nizārī missionaries had converted numbers of Hindus, now known as Khojas, to their doctrine. The Agha Khans of the present day have become international figures, and have done much to reorganize and modernize their community.

Bibliography: M. G. S. HODGSON, *The Order of Assassins* (The Hague 1955). J. N. HOLLISTER, *The Shi'a of India* (London 1953). B. LEWIS, "The Ismaʿīlīs and the Assassins," *The First Hundred Years,* ed. M. W. BALDWIN, v.1 of *A History of the Crusades,* ed. K. M. SETTON (Philadelphia 1955–). J. VON HAMMER-PURGSTALL, *A History of the Assassins,* tr. O. C. WOOD (London 1835).

[J. A. WILLIAMS]

NOAILLES, LOUIS ANTOINE DE

Cardinal archbishop of Paris; b. château of Tessières, near Aurillac, May 27, 1651; d. Paris, May 4, 1729. As the second son of Anne Jules, first Duke of Noailles, he was educated in Paris and received a doctorate in theology at the Sorbonne. In 1679 he was made bishop of Cahors, and in June 1680, archbishop of Châlons, a see that conferred a peerage. In 1682 De Noailles took part in the Assembly of the Clergy that adopted the four Gallican articles (*see* GALLICANISM). Respect for his piety and unblemished life led to his appointment as archbishop of Paris in April 1695, an appointment supported by Mme. de Maintenon. His difficulties then began. At Châlons in 1695 he had approved Pasquier *Quesnel's *Réflexions morales.* But in 1696 he condemned a posthumous publication of the Jansenist Martin de Barcos's *Exposition de la foi.* He was then attacked by an anonymous pamphlet that demanded whether one should follow De Noailles the Archbishop of Châlons in approval of Quesnel, or De Noailles the Archbishop of Paris in condemning the same teachings in De Barcos's book. Despite this involvement in Jansenist controversy, he was made cardinal in 1700. During these same years he condemned several Quietist writings (*see* QUIETISM). In so doing, he supported *Bossuet and became estranged from *Fénelon.

On July 16, 1705, Clement XI published the constitution *Vineam Domini Sabaoth.* This condemned the *Cas de conscience,* a work printed in 1703 and signed by 40 doctors of the Sorbonne, arguing that respectful silence concerning the five propositions of Jansenius should not debar an ecclesiastic from absolution. Thirty-six of the signers subsequently retracted, two died, two were exiled. Cardinal de Noailles then acted, perhaps reluctantly, in support of *Vineam Domini.* Moreover, he neither opposed nor obstructed the suppression of Port-Royal in 1709. On the other hand, he turned more and more against the Jesuits, the most resolute anti-Jansenists. In 1713 he forbade the Jesuits to preach or hear confessions in his diocese. In the same year, when the bull *Unigenitus,* condemning 101 of Quesnel's propositions, was referred to the Assembly of the Clergy, De Noailles opposed it. These actions brought the cardinal openly into disfavor, and Louis XIV forbade his appearance at court. In 1714, with De Noailles still opposing, the *Unigenitus* was registered by royal order. After the death of Louis XIV in 1715, De Noailles was treated more considerately by the Regent, the Duke of Orléans. On April 3, 1717, he appealed against the *Unigenitus* to a future council, although this appeal remained secret until 1718. In August 1718 the Regent ordered acceptance of *Unigenitus* throughout France, all appeals already made being annulled. Cardinal de Noailles only formally withdrew his appeal in August 1720; he did not formally accept *Unigenitus* until October 1728. The cardinal spent generously in repairing and adorning the cathedral of Notre Dame. He was also noted for his charity. He died in 1729, leaving his property to the Hôpital Général, the Hôtel-Dieu, and the Hôpital des Enfants-Trouvés.

Bibliography: É. DE BARTHÉLEMY, *Le Cardinal de Noailles . . .* (Paris 1886). J. CARREYRE, *Le Jansénisme durant la Régence* 2 v. (Louvain 1929–33); DTC 11.1:678–681. L. CROUSLÉ, *Fénelon et Bossuet . . .,* 2 v. (Paris 1894–95). A. LE ROY, *Le Gallicanisme au XVIIIᵉ siècle: La France et Rome de 1700 à 1715 . . .* (Paris 1892). J. F. THOMAS, *La Querelle de l'Unigenitus* (Paris 1950). C. URBAIN and E. LEVESQUE, *Les Dernières années de Boussuet* (Paris 1929).

[D. R. CAMPBELL]

NOAILLES, PIERRE BIENVENU,

founder of the Holy Family Sisters of Bordeaux; b. Bordeaux, France, Oct. 27, 1793; d. there, Feb. 8, 1861. After a very irreligious youth, he suddenly reformed following a visit to the Parisian church of Saint-Sulpice (1813), entered the seminary of Saint-Sulpice, and was ordained (1829). As curate in Bordeaux he took a special interest in the sick, outcasts, orphans, and peasants. To aid them he founded in 1820 the Holy Family Sisters. Until 1903, when the Holy See definitively approved the constitutions, there were seven branches of this institute, each engaged in a different type of apostolate, and bound together only by constitutions common to all of them. Since that time there have been only four branches, engaged in teaching, care of the sick, and social work, and, at one community in Bordeaux, in perpetual adoration of the Blessed Sacrament. Noailles entered into an agreement with Charles Eugène de Mazenod whereby the spiritual direction of the sisters was confided to the Oblates of Mary Immaculate, whose superior general was also the head of the Holy Family Sisters (1858–1903). Since 1903 the sisters have had their own mother general, who resides in Talence, near Bordeaux. Despite numerous difficulties Noailles established 124 houses. In 1961 there were 4,812 sisters, and 294 houses in 15 countries in Europe, Asia, Africa, South America (Brazil), and North America (Canada). In 1944 the cause for Noailles's beatification was introduced in Rome.

Bibliography: J. BAFFIE and P. ORTOLAN, *Vie de bon Père Pierre-Bienvenu Noailles,* 2 v. (Bordeaux 1880–81). Heimbucher 2:516–517. C. SALOTTI, ActApS 36 (1944) 309–312.

[J. DAOUST]

NOBILI, JOHN,

missionary; b. Rome, Italy, April 8, 1812; d. Santa Clara, Calif., March 1, 1856. He entered the Jesuits in Rome on Nov. 14, 1828, and subsequently taught in the Jesuit colleges at Loretto and Fermo in Italy. After ordination in 1843, he volunteered for the missions in the Oregon Country of North America. On Aug. 5, 1844, Nobili with his Jesuit companions, Michael Accolti and Peter De Smet, arrived at Ft. Vancouver. From 1845 to 1848 he worked among the Indians and settlers of New Caledonia (now British Columbia). During these years, Nobili helped to establish chapels in various forts or trading posts of the Hudson's Bay Company, and his successive missionary journeys extended as far as the southern boundary of Alaska. Unexpectedly, he was recalled from his missionary work by his superior, Rev. Joseph Joset. After making his final profession as a Jesuit in May 1849, he was assigned to accompany Accolti to California. Nobili arrived in San Francisco on Dec. 8, 1849, and then assisted Rev. Anthony Langlois in the parish of St. Francis and in the pueblo of San Jose, located 50 miles south of San Francisco. In 1850 the new Bishop of Monterey, Joseph S. Alemany, OP, asked him to administer the Mission Santa Clara, several miles from San Jose, and to establish there a college for young men. Despite the secularization of the mission, Nobili established Santa Clara College, the first Jesuit and Catholic college in California. Although it was not chartered by the state of California until April 28, 1855, instruction began on March 19, 1851. Nobili served as its first president until his premature death.

Bibliography: Garraghan JMUS. J. W. RIORDAN, *The First Half Century of St. Ignatius Church and College* (San Francisco 1905).

[J. B. MC GLOIN]

NOBILI, ROBERTO DE

Missionary in South India and pioneer in the method of missionary *adaptation; b. Rome, September 1577; d. Mylapore, India, Jan. 16, 1656. His parents, Count Pier Francesco de Nobili, a general in the Papal Army, and Clarice Cioli, a Roman lady, were both of noble birth. He was educated at the Roman College and there declared his intention of becoming a Jesuit missionary. On the death of his father (1593), his guardian and cousin Cardinal Francesco Sforza brought pressure to bear to dissuade him from this plan, and Nobili fled from Rome and put himself under the protection of the Duchess of Nocera. He completed his education in the Duchess's house; and, in 1596, with his family's reluctant consent, entered the Jesuit novitiate in Naples. In

Roberto de Nobili.

1600 he returned to Rome for theological study, and he was ordained 3 years later.

Missionary Endeavors. In April 1604 Nobili left for India. He sailed from Lisbon in a Portuguese carrack and, like all non-Portuguese missionaries, was considered a vassal of the King of Portugal, who, by his privilege of ecclesiastical patronage (the Padroado) bore the responsibility for the evangelization of India. After suffering shipwreck near Mozambique, Nobili arrived in Goa on May 20, 1605. He learned Tamil among the Paravas of the Fishery Coast and in November 1606 was sent by his provincial, Alberto Laerzio, to the important inland town of Madura. This was a new departure; before this the Gospel had been preached only to Indians on the coast, where missionaries could be protected by Portuguese naval guns.

Nobili's older companion in Madura was a Portuguese Jesuit, Gonçalo Fernandez, who followed the missionary method used in India throughout the 16th century. Neophytes were required to dress, eat, and behave like the Portuguese colonials. Moreover, they had to take Portuguese surnames. Conversion was, in fact, linked with cultural domination and was therefore strongly resented by the Hindus. Christian converts were, along with the Portuguese, considered as *Parangis* (despised foreigners) and as such were outcastes in Indian society. The *Parangis* were further despised for eating beef, drinking wine, and wearing shoes (leather was considered impure).

Nobili believed this method was mistaken, and decided to adapt himself to native customs, as Matteo *Ricci had done in China. After trying vainly to persuade Fernandez to work within the framework of the caste system rather than to cut across it, Nobili decided

to live separately. He adopted the saffron dress, wooden clogs, and vegetarian diet of a *sannyasi* (holy man). He marked his brow with a rectangular shape of paste to signify that he was a teacher. When the people of Madura learned that he was the son of a count, they identified him with the caste of rulers, or *Rajas*. As a *Raja sannyasi* Nobili was now free to associate with Indians of the higher castes without defiling them.

Conversion of Sivadarma. Nobili's method met with success. In the first 18 months he converted 50 people of Madura, his first convert being a Sivaite schoolteacher whom he christened Albert in honor of his provincial. In 1608 Nobili became friendly with Sivadarma, a Brahmin Sanskrit scholar, who tried to convert Nobili to the system of nondualistic Vedanta professed by most Brahmins in Madura. Through Sivadarma, Nobili became the first European to get firsthand knowledge of Sanskrit, the Vedas, and Vedanta. Meanwhile other Brahmins, jealous of Nobili's successes, tried to have him dubbed a *Parangi* and expelled. At a meeting of 800 Brahmins, Sivadarma defended Nobili and explained that even though his skin was white Nobili was a learned *sannyasi* and quite different from a *Parangi*. Nobili was allowed to remain, and in 1609, he converted Sivadarma. But his baptism raised grave questions. Should Sivadarma have to discard the characteristic Brahmin thread, a triple strand of white cotton worn from the left shoulder across the breast, and the *kudumi,* or single plait of hair? On the coast Brahmin converts had been forced to do so and as a result were treated as outcastes by other Brahmins. After studying the Laws of Manu and the history of the thread and *kudumi,* Nobili drew a distinction between religious and civil signs; the thread and *kudumi* he decided belonged to the latter group. With the approval of his ordinary, Archbishop Ros of Cranganore, Nobili baptized Sivadarma on Whitsunday 1609, allowing him to retain thread and *kudumi.*

Controversy over Adaptation. Fernandez complained about Nobili's methods, including his tolerance of such Indian habits as the marking of the brow with santal and the ceremonial ablutions. In 1610 the newly appointed visitor of the Provinces of Goa and Malabar, Nicolau Pimenta, censured Nobili, who promptly appealed to Rome. Claudius *Acquaviva, the General of the Jesuits, wrote to India suggesting modifications of Nobili's method—notably that Brahmin converts should discard the thread—but adding the "no change should be made which might compromise the existence of the mission." In a brief dated Feb. 18, 1618, Paul V ordered Archbishop de Sa and the inquisitors of Goa to hold a conference at which Nobili was to be present and to write a report on the whole affair. After Nobili had presented his case, the first inquisitor voted against his method, the second in favor of it; of the remaining 20 theologians and Indian priests only four sided with Nobili. However, when the report was forwarded to Europe, both the grand inquisitor of Portugal and the new pope, Gregory XV, in the constitution *Romanae Sedis Antistes* of Jan. 31, 1623, approved Nobili's method and decided that Brahmin converts should be allowed to retain the thread and *kudumi.*

During the years of controversy Nobili was forbidden to baptize, and spent much of his time writing, chiefly in Tamil. His most important book, *Gnanopadesam* (spiritual teaching), is virtually a *Summa theologiae.* In

1623 he was again free to baptize, and thenceforth traveled widely in South India, founding new missions. In 1640, as the result of a Portuguese war against the Nayak of Madura, Nobili and his fellow missionaries were arrested and imprisoned for about a year. In 1654 Nobili, his eyesight failing, was retired from Madura. When he had first arrived, there was not a single Christian in the hinterland of South India. When he left, the number of Christians totaled 4,183.

Nobili spent his last years in a hut outside Mylapore, still wearing his saffron clothes, living on a vegetarian diet, and dictating revised versions of his books.

See also MALABAR RITE.

Bibliography: J. BERTRAND, *La Mission du Maduré d'après des documents inédits,* 4 v. (Paris 1847–54). ROBERT DE NOBILI, *Première apologie,* tr. P. DAHMEN (Paris 1931). V. CRONIN, *A Pearl to India: The Life of Roberto de Nobili* (New York 1959). É. AMANN, DTC 9.2:1704–45. P. M. D'ELIA, "L'abolizione del giuramento contro i riti Malabarici in India," CivCatt 91.2 (1940) 331–340, 424–431. P. DAHMEN, *Robert de Nobili* (Münster 1924); *Un Jésuite Brahme* (Bruges 1924). Streit-Dindinger 5:40–43, 1042. ArchHistSocJesu 22 (1953) 690, no. 135. Pastor 25:358–361; 27:148. Sommervogel 5:1779–80.

[V. CRONIN]

NÓBREGA, MANUEL DA, Jesuit cofounder with the governor general of Portuguese authority in Brazil; b. Portugal, Oct. 18, 1517; d. Rio de Janeiro, Oct. 18, 1570. He received a degree in Canon Law at the University of Coimbra in 1541. He failed to win a competition for a teaching position and entered the Jesuits on Nov. 21, 1544. After serving various apostolic missions in Europe, he was appointed director of the Jesuits in America at the age of 31. He embarked for Brazil with five companions in the company of the first governor general, Tomé de *Sousa. He landed there, according to tradition, carrying a cross, and his first statement to his European companions contains a sentence which is a program: "this land is our enterprise." He helped in the foundation of Salvador, capital of Bahia, and was one of the most efficient advisers of the governor. During the administration of the second governor, at odds with the first bishop, Nóbrega left Bahia for the south. He again became a principal figure in the councils of the third governor, Mem de Sá, who led Brazil for 15 years. He planned the foundation of São Paulo in 1554 and worked toward the foundation of Rio de Janeiro in 1565. He traveled as missionary and observer through all of the captaincies of Brazil, from Pernambuco to São Vicente. He was the first Jesuit superior and the first provincial of Brazil. After turning the province over to Luis da Grã, he remained superior of the southern captaincies of Espírito Santo, Rio de Janeiro, and São Vicente. He founded the Colégio de Rio de Janeiro in 1567 and was its first rector. He was appointed provincial for the second time but died before he could take over the position. He is buried in Bahia in the present cathedral, formerly the Jesuit church, beside Mem de Sá. He was an excellent priest and good administrator, and was called the "Father of the Province." Southey considered him the greatest political figure in colonial Brazil.

Bibliography: S. LEITE, *História da Companhia de Jesús no Brasil,* 10 v. (Lisbon–Rio de Janeiro 1938–50). R. SOUTHEY, *History of Brazil,* 3 v. (London 1817–22).

[A. J. LACOMBE]

NOCK, ARTHUR DARBY, historian of ancient Greek and Roman religion; b. Feb. 21, 1902, Portsmouth, England; d. Jan. 11, 1963, Boston, Mass. He was educated at Trinity College, Cambridge, and attracted early notice for his masterful knowledge of Greek and Latin scholarship. His first major work was an edition of Sallustius, *On the Gods and the Universe* (Cambridge 1926). Its introductory survey of the religious and cultural background of the 4th century A.D. shows that same balance of thoughtful generalization and specific fact which was to make his chapters on Roman religious developments in the *Cambridge Ancient History* small masterpieces of exposition (v.10, 1934; v.12, 1939). In 1930 he became Frothingham Professor of the History of Religion at Harvard University and editor of the *Harvard Theological Review.*

His numerous articles and reviews, often as important as contributions to scholarship as the books he criticized, centered increasingly on ancient magic and religion and on Christian beginnings. His *Conversion: The Old and the New in Religion from Alexander the Great to Augustine of Hippo* (London 1933; repr. 1961) is an indispensable guide to an understanding of the religious experience of the Hellenistic and Roman age and of the coming of Christianity as it may have appeared to pagans. His little book *St. Paul* (London 1938; repr. 1963) was followed by a magisterial four-volume edition in collaboration with A. J. Festugière, OP, of the *Corpus Hermeticum* (Paris 1945–54).

Arthur Darby Nock.

Far more interested in piety and cult than in philosophy and theology, he dwelt upon the practice and the expression of the common man in antiquity, providing a sharp and detailed picture in which the literary and philosophical texts are illustrative rather than central. He had a special interest in Gnosticism, criticizing the view that it was a pre-Christian entity. Nock was awarded three honorary doctorates; he also held membership in national academies and in the American Philosophical Society. An edition of his collected shorter writings, including a list of his publications, was in press in 1965.

[Z. STEWART]

NOE (NOAH)

Hero of Biblical *Deluge story, originator of vineyard cultivation, father of Sem, Ham, and Japheth, and ancestor of all mankind after the Flood. On the meaning of his name (Heb. *nōaḥ,* hence variant English form Noah; Septuagint and NT Νῶε) see page 480.

Noe, the First Vinedresser. According to a tradition preserved in the *Yahwist narrative (Gn 9.20–27), Noe was a farmer and the first to plant a vineyard. The narrative in 9.20–27 appears to know nothing of the Deluge described in 6.9–9.19. Noe's three sons are presented as unmarried and sharing their father's tent, rather than as already married. The tradition in 9.20–27 is concerned not with the whole world, but with the population of Palestine. The original three sons were undoubtedly Sem, Japheth, and Canaan (Chanaan). The words "Ham is the father of Chanaan" (9.18) are a later addition to make this story harmonize with the Table of Nations (ch. 10), according to which all the peoples of the earth are grouped under Sem, Ham, and Japheth, the sons of Noe. (*See* NATIONS, TABLE OF THE.)

The discovery of grapevine cultivation and the subsequent production of wine are probably the "comfort" associated with Noe in 5.29. Noe's drunkenness (9.21) is not blameworthy. As the first to taste wine, he had no way of knowing its ill effects. The action of his son Ham (or Canaan) was not so innocent. He made fun of his father's exposure instead of covering him over to prevent any embarrassment. Noe's curse and blessings explain why the Israelites (Sem) and the Philistines (Japheth) lived together in harmony during the reigns of David and Solomon, while the pre-Israelite population (Canaan) lived in subjection to both groups. As used in the account of the *Primeval Age in the Bible, the story of Canaan's disrespect shows that the Flood did not cure man's sinful nature (see 8.21). The family relationship is fractured once again, and brother is set against brother.

Noe, the Flood Hero and Second Father of Mankind. The Priestly tradition (*see* PRIESTLY WRITERS, PENTATEUCHAL) describes Noe as a righteous man (6.9), implying that God saved him from the Flood for that reason. The Yahwist account simply states that Noe found favor in the eyes of Yahweh (6.8). Something may have been omitted when the two Deluge accounts were combined, or the Yahwist may have presented the choice of Noe as an act of pure grace. In the Priestly account, Noe was told why he should build the ark (6.13–14), while in the Yahwist narrative the command

was a test of obedience. The reason was not given until the ark was complete (7.1, 4).

After the Flood Noe offered sacrifice to Yahweh, who resolved never again to curse the ground on man's account. In the Priestly narrative, God blessed Noe and his sons and renewed the commands given at creation (with two changes: man can now kill animals and eat meat, and the murder of a man will be punished by men). God then bound Himself by covenant [*see* COVENANT (IN THE BIBLE)] with Noe and his descendants never to destroy the earth by flood (9.1–17).

According to both Yahwist and Priestly accounts (10.1–32; 11.10–32), all the nations of the world were descendants of Noe's three sons. These genealogies set a universal frame within which the call of *Abraham can assume its true dimensions.

The Name Noe, its Origin and Meaning. Because of the allusion in 5.29, the name Noe was probably original in the story of the first vineyard. In the long history of the Deluge story in the ancient Near East the hero has borne various names. (*See* GILGAMESH EPIC.) The identification of Noe the vinedresser with the Flood hero was probably made in Israel. Various etymologies have been suggested for the name. Of these, the derivation from the verb "to comfort" (*piel* of *nḥm*) in 5.29 is merely a folk etymology. A name *Naḥman* could be derived from that verb, but *Nōaḥ* should come from the verb "to give rest" (*hiphil* of *nwḥ*), reflected in the Septuagint rendering διαναπαύσει ἡμᾶς, "he will let us rest awhile." An allusion to this root may be found in 8.4: "and the ark rested (*wattānaḥ*) on the mountains of Ararat." While a connection with the Akkadian *nâḥ* (a possibly theophoric element in the names *Nāḥ-ilum* and *Muutnaḥa*) has recently been proposed, the derivation from the root *nwḥ* (meaning "rest") still seems most convincing.

Iconography. In Christian art, especially of the late Middle Ages, Noe is commonly pictured in scenes connected with the Deluge, such as his building of the ark, his entering with his family and the animals, his riding in the ark on the waters of the Flood, his releasing of a raven and a dove, his departure from the ark, and his offering of sacrifice. Some of the elements in these scenes are taken from apocryphal sources. Less frequent are representations of Noe working as a vinedresser or being drunk.

Bibliography: G. VON RAD, *Genesis: A Commentary*, tr. J. H. MARKS (Philadelphia 1961). EncDictBibl 1646–48. Réau IAC 2:104–115. **Illustration credit:** Photo Archives, *Das Münster*.

[K. G. O'CONNELL]

Noe in the Ark, sandstone relief by the German artist Jochem Pechau, 1960, in the Children's Home at Düren Rolsdorf, Germany.

NOËTUS OF SMYRNA, a Monarchian heretic who taught in Smyrna, *c.* 180 to 200. His teachings are known from the antiheretical writings of *Hippolytus of Rome (d. 235). He seems to have been the first to have taught *Patripassianism, i.e., that the Father was born, suffered, and died, since the Father and the Son are only different ways (*modi*) of God's self-revelation. He admitted only an allegorical interpretation of St. John's Gospel, thus rejecting the doctrine of the Logos, and he accused his opponents of ditheism. A synod of the presbyters of Smyrna condemned him *c.* 200. One of his disciples, Epigonus, brought his doctrines to Rome.

Bibliography: HIPPOLYTUS OF ROME, *Contre les hérésies*, ed. and tr. P. NAUTIN (Paris 1949); *Philosophumena*, ed. P. WEND-

LAND (GCS 26; 1916) 9:3–9.3. C. H. TURNER, JThSt 23 (1921–22) 28–35. G. BARDY, DTC 10.2:2193–2209, s.v. Monarchianisme. B. KOTTER, LexThK² 7:1018.

[M. C. MC CARTHY]

NOGARET, GUILLAUME DE, minister of *Philip IV of France; b. near Toulouse, *c.* 1260; d. probably Paris, mid-April 1313. Nogaret, trained as a lawyer, served briefly as a royal judge in the South, but was called to Paris in 1295. As an associate of Pierre *Flotte, he took charge of the dispute with *Boniface VIII when Flotte died. Flotte had merely denied papal power in temporal affairs; Nogaret accused Boniface of heresy and immorality. By propaganda and threats he gained the adhesion of French clergy, nobles, and bourgeois to charges against the Pope. In 1303 Nogaret set out to bring Boniface to France for trial before a general council. With the aid of disgruntled Italians he captured Boniface at Anagni, but a popular uprising forced him to release his captive. The early death of the Pontiff saved Nogaret from immediate condemnation, but in 1304 *Benedict XI excommunicated him. For the next few years Nogaret and his assistant, Guillaume de Plaisian, handled most of the affairs of the Midi, and most of the church business for Philip IV. They probably had some influence on the election of *Clement V and on his decision to remain in France. They certainly led the attack on the *Templars in 1307, and Nogaret was made keeper of the seals so that he could push the condemnation of the order. All during this period Nogaret continued to attack the memory of Boniface VIII, trying to relieve the King of blame and himself of penalties. His shameless writings caused so much scandal that in 1311 Clement V finally declared that the King's motives had been good, and absolved Nogaret. Nogaret remained an important official until his death, though after 1311 *Marigny probably had greater influence.

Bibliography: P. DUPUY, *Histoire du différend* (Paris 1655), contains most of Nogaret's writings. R. HOLTZMANN, *Wilhelm von Nogaret* (Freiburg 1898). J. RIVIÈRE, *Le Problème de l'église et de l'état au temps de Philippe le Bel* (Paris 1926). *See* bibliography under PHILIP IV, KING OF FRANCE.

[J. R. STRAYER]

NOLDE, EMIL, German expressionist who had exceptional mastery of intense color; b. Emil Hansen, at Nolde, North Germany, 1867; d. Seebüll, 1956. Emil Nolde was born near the Baltic coast, where he spent many hours as a working artist under the turbulent skies and on the expansive moors. His art and life became saturated with a pantheistic closeness to nature. It was not until age 30 that Nolde began to devote himself entirely to painting. His preparation was small—only cabinetmaking and a few private lessons—and therefore he sought instruction in Munich, Dachau, Paris, and Copenhagen. He was lonely, poor, and isolated in his rebellion against academic painting until he associated with Die Brücke (the Bridge group) in Dresden (1906–07). Nolde shared with these artists (*Kirchner, Schmidt-Rottluf, etc.) a disturbed vision of life and an interest in primitive art, although his own work went far beyond theirs in brutal character and religiosity. His Bridge association was brief, since he realized that he worked best alone. In 1913 and 1914 Nolde (and his wife) joined a medical expedition to New Guinea in order to search out the primitive and to absorb impressions to be used in later works. The rest of his life was

Emil Nolde, "Scribes," etching and aquatint, 10½ by 11¾ inches, 1911.

spent between Berlin and his cottage in northern Germany. During the period of Nazi control of the arts, Nolde's work was branded immoral and he was forced to work in seclusion, but in the 1940s and 1950s he received his due acclaim as a significant German artist. *See* EXPRESSIONISM (IN ART).

Bibliography: W. HAFTMANN, *Emil Nolde* (Cologne 1958), in Ger., beautiful color reproductions. C. KUHN, *German Expressionism and Abstract Art* (Cambridge, Mass. 1957). E. NOLDE, *Das eigene Leben: Die Zeit der Jugend, 1867–1902* (2d ed. Flensburg 1949); *Jahre der Kämpfe, 1902–1914* (2d ed. Flensburg 1957). P. SELZ, *Emil Nolde* (New York 1963). **Illustration credit:** Collection, The Museum of Modern Art, New York City, Purchase.

[S. L. HENRY]

NOLDIN, HIERONYMUS, Jesuit moral theologian; b. Salurn of the South Tyrol, Austria, Jan. 30, 1838; d. Vienna, Nov. 7, 1922. Ordained in 1861,

Hieronymus Noldin.

Noldin entered the Society of Jesus 4 years later, and after 10 years of study and teaching became rector of the Jesuit theologate at Innsbruck. There, in 1883, he wrote his first book, *Die Andacht zum Heiligsten*

Herzen Jesu (11th German ed. 1923; first English tr. W. K. Kent, OSC, *The Devotion to the Sacred Heart of Jesus*, 1905). From 1886 to 1890 Noldin edited *Zeitschrift für Katholische Theologie* and then taught moral theology for 19 years at the University of Innsbruck. In 1902 he published his major work, *Summa Theologiae Moralis*, a three-volume Latin textbook including sections on the fundamental principles of morality, the Commandments, and the Sacraments, and two appendixes, one on the Sixth Commandment and the use of marriage, and the other on ecclesiastical penalties. This influential textbook was in its 16th edition before the author's death and enjoyed several later editions under the direction of A. Schmitt, also of the University of Innsbruck. The 33d edition appeared in 1961 under the editorship of G. Heinzel. Noldin wrote three other smaller works, including *Decretum de Sponsalibus et matrimonio cum declaratione* (c. 1900) and *De iure matrimoniali iuxta codicem* (1919).

Bibliography: A. SCHMITT, ZKathTh 47 (1923) 11–20. G. HEINZEL, "Hieronymus Noldin und sein Werk," *ibid.* 80 (1958) 200–210.

[J. UPTON]

NOLL, JOHN FRANCIS

Bishop, editor; b. Fort Wayne, Ind., Jan. 25, 1875; d. Huntington, Ind., July 31, 1956. He was the son of John G. and Anna (Ford) Noll. After completing his studies at St. Lawrence College, Mt. Calvary, Wis., he attended Mt. St. Mary's Seminary in Cincinnati, Ohio. He was ordained for the Diocese of Fort Wayne by Bp. Joseph Rademacher, June 4, 1898. After 2 years as curate in various parishes, he became pastor at Kendallville, Ind., in 1900, and of St. Mary's in Huntington, Ind., in July 1910, remaining there until he was named bishop of Fort Wayne. While pastor at Besancon, Ind., Noll's interest in apostolic work among non-Catholics led him to publish a booklet, *Kind Words from Your Pastor,* in 1904. At Hartford City, Ind., in 1908, he began a parish magazine that was later printed for hundreds of parishes as *The Family Digest.* In 1912, in answer to the *Menace* and other anti-Catholic papers, he began to publish a four-page paper, *Our Sunday Visitor.*

John Francis Noll.

Despite his other activities, he never ceased to be a writer and editor. To inform non-Catholics, he produced *Father Smith Instructs Jackson* (1913) and *The Fairest Argument* (1914). In 1925 he founded the magazine *Acolyte,* which in 1945 became the *Priest.* His pamphlets, numbering approximately 150, embraced such titles as *The Catholic Church vs. the Federal Council of the Churches of Christ, A Catechism on Birth Control, Instructing Non-Catholics Before Marriage,* and *The Parochial School, Why?* His longer books included *A Vest Pocket of Catholic Facts* (1927), *The Decline of Nations* (1940), and *Our National Enemy Number One, Education Without Religion* (1942). In 1941 he added a second volume to the *History of the Diocese of Fort Wayne* begun by his predecessor, Bp. Herman J. Alerding, in 1907.

Noll was made domestic prelate in 1923, was named bishop of Fort Wayne May 12, 1925, and was consecrated by Cardinal George W. Mundelein June 30, 1925. To Noll goes credit for introducing into the diocese the Redemptorists (1927), the Capuchins (1928), the Slovak Franciscans (1929), the Oblates of Mary Immaculate (1934), the Society of the Priests of the Sacred Heart (1935), and the Crosier Fathers (1938). He reorganized Central Catholic High School, Fort Wayne, as a coeducational institution in 1938. He opened Bishop Noll High School in Hammond and St. Joseph High School in South Bend, Ind., and established a minor seminary for the diocese at Lake Wawasee under the Crosier Fathers. Nationally, he was one of the founders of the Catholic Press Association. He was one of the original members of the episcopal committee that formed the Legion of Decency to combat immorality in motion pictures, and he acted as the first chairman of the National Organization for Decent Literature. He was a member of the Board of Catholic Missions for more than 25 years. He devoted much time to the National Catholic Welfare Conference (NCWC), especially as a member of the conference's executive committee, chairman of its Department of Catholic Action, and chairman of its Committee of the Department of Lay Organizations. In the latter capacity, he gave aid and direction to the National Council of Catholic Men and the National Council of Catholic Women. Among his other activities and offices was chairmanship of the National Committee on a Religious Census, which sought inclusion of religious affiliations in the Federal census. He raised $125,000, chiefly through *Our Sunday Visitor,* for the erection of a statue of Christ as the Light of the World at the NCWC Building in Washington, D.C. Pius XII made Noll an assistant to the papal throne March 14, 1941, and personal archbishop Sept. 2, 1953.

[T. T. MC AVOY]

NOLLET, JEAN ANTOINE,

French physicist; b. Pimpré, near Noyon, Nov. 19, 1700; d. Paris, April 25, 1770. Nollet first studied at Clermont and Beauvais, later finishing philosophy and theology in Paris. He went back to Noyon as a deacon but decided to join Dufay (1698–1739) in his investigations about electricity, traveling with him through Holland and England. He started a course in Paris in 1735. In 1739 he entered the Academy of Sciences and was appointed by the King of Sardinia as the teacher of the Duke of Savoy. In 1744 he taught physics to the French Dauphin. He obtained the just-created professorship in physics at the College de Navarre in Paris (1753). In 1757 he again taught physics and natural history to the French princes. Finally he was appointed professor at the engineering school of La Fère and Mézières. He wrote several works on the teaching of physics and did much to popularize scientific study.

Bibliography: J. TORLAIS, *L'Abbé Nollet: Un physicien au siècle des lumières (1700–1770)* (Paris 1954).

[E. T. SPAIN]

NOMINALISM

A term deriving from the Latin *nomen,* meaning name, and used to designate a variety of doctrines and movements in philosophy. (1) In an ontological sense, nominalism is a doctrine according to which only individual things exist. In opposition to Platonic *realism, which explains the similarity of individuals by saying that they share a common property or nature, i.e., by assuming the existence of *universals that are not individuals, nominalism holds that if individuals similar to one another may be said to share anything, this can be only a spoken or written name or a mental image, i.e., something itself individual. In the strict sense nominalism is opposed also to *conceptualism, for it does not accept universals that are not individuals even as objects of thought. (2) In a polemical sense, nominalism is frequently used as an epistemological term roughly synonymous with extreme *conventionalism, *empiricism, or *positivism. This is so because ontological nominalism has often led to a skeptical attitude concerning the objective value of intellectual knowledge. It would be wrong, however, to think that the refusal to accept universal essences must of necessity make the use of words entirely arbitrary. Ontological nominalism as such need not deny that individuals are essentially related; it merely rejects the assumption that related individuals have some namable thing that is not an individual in common. (3) Historically, nominalism is a term applied to philosophical and theological movements in early and late *scholasticism whose representatives were called *nominales.* Their doctrines included, among others, ontological nominalism in the broader sense, i.e., not excluding conceptualism.

Greek Origins. Even though the term nominalism appears much later, the doctrine can be found already in antiquity. Thus Antisthenes the Cynic is said to have objected to *Plato: "I see a horse, but I do not see horseness" (Simplicius, *In Arist. Categ.* 208.30). *Aristotle defended an intermediate position between those of the *Cynics and Plato; in his view, although only individual beings with individualized natures exist in physical reality, the intellect is able to form universal concepts of such natures. This view may be referred to as a realistic conceptualism—realistic, in order to distinguish it from an idealistic conceptualism of the Kantian school.

The Stoics, who are often classified as nominalists, accepted the individuals of the material world but in addition, as an ontological foundation for logic, they postulated a special kind of universal, viz, τὸ λεκτόν, "what is said," the meaning of sentences or words. The Stoic position, therefore, amounted to an original form of conceptualism. It resembles the position of the *nominales* of scholasticism, but as yet no line of direct influence has been traced from one school to the other.

Early Scholasticism. The famous scholastic discussion of universals arose in the wake of a renaissance of Aristotelian logic or, more exactly, in connection with an argument concerning logic's place with respect to the other sciences (J. Reiners). The Neoplatonic tradition had assumed that logic was concerned with a special kind of thing, namely, with the *categories and *predicables. *Boethius had distinguished between physics as a science of things (*res*) and logic and grammar as sciences of words (*voces*); he had stated also that the treatise on the categories dealt with words. Then, at the beginning of the 11th century, some writers asserted that predicables too could be considered not only as things but also as names. Toward the end of the century, a controversy arose between those who taught logic in the old way as dealing with things (*in re*) and those who, like John the Sophist, the master of Roscelin, taught logic as concerned with words (*in voce*). Finally, *Roscelin of Compiègne explicitly denied that universals, i.e., the predicables of *genus and *species, could be things. His arguments, known from his disciple Peter *Abelard, were mainly negative, showing how Platonic realism leads to incongruous consequences. An important positive argument appealed to the authority of Aristotle, who defines a universal as "that which can be predicated of many" (*De interp.* 17a 39). Assuming that only words (and not things) could be predicated, it concluded that universals had to be words.

Such nominalism, however, did not exclude a realistic conceptualism (B. Geyer). It seems that Roscelin simply did not consider the problem of the *concept. Abelard, however, explicitly discussed the universality of products of thought (*ficta*) and accepted the objective existence of the meanings (*dicta*) of sentences, as did the Stoics. To stress that words are not merely sounds, Abelard in his later writings preferred to say that universals were *sermones,* i.e., meaningful terms of discourse. He was convinced that there had to be an ontological justification for the use of general names: e.g., although two men do not share some "thing," man (*in homine*), they do share the status of being man (*in esse hominem*). Roscelin and Abelard continued the tradition of the earlier dialecticians by applying logical analysis to theological matters. Roscelin's incautious teachings elicited from St. *Anselm of Canterbury the first-known polemics against nominalism (*De fide trin.* 2), and the nominalists' heretical formulations of the mystery of the Holy Trinity were later condemned by the Church (see Denz 721–739). *See* DIALECTICS IN THE MIDDLE AGES.

High Scholasticism. In high scholasticism the nominalist school disappeared. Everyone now taught logic as a science of meaningful words (*scientia sermocinalis*), and the new logical theories of the *consequentiae* and of the suppositions of terms, initiated by Abelard, were in full elaboration. But leading logicians, such as Peter of Spain (Pope *John XXI), found the acceptance of universals no longer problematical, and they did not hesitate to say that a universal term *in suppositione simplici* stood for a universal thing (*res universalis*). It was rather among Aristotelian theologians, such as St. *Thomas Aquinas, that Abelard's criticism of Platonic realism continued to be developed.

Late Scholasticism. A new school, whose members again were called *nominales,* originated in the 14th century with *William of Ockham at its head. Intending to purify Aristotelian doctrine from Avicennist-Neoplatonist corruptions (see E. A. Moody, *Logic,* 9–11), Ockham rejected the doctrine of formal distinctions proposed by *Duns Scotus, according to which common natures could be distinguished in individual things. For Ockham all distinctions within a thing can be only real distinctions, and all the components distinguished are as individual as the thing itself. Like Abelard, he stressed that universals are only names or terms: two similar individuals do not agree in a common nature but only "in themselves" (*conveniunt se ipsis—In 1 sent.* 2.4EE). By denying the reality of relations he made the separation between individuals even more radical.

Ockham's Nominalism. But again this type of nominalism did not immediately exclude conceptualism. Ockham recognized not only spoken or written terms but also mental terms or concepts. However, in his explanations as to how concepts are to be understood, he was hesitant: whereas in the beginning he tended to consider them as objective products of thought (*ficta*), he later estimated that it might be sufficient to identify them simply with the subjective acts of thinking (*intellectiones*)—see Boehner, "The realistic conceptualism . . . ." Since psychological acts are concrete and individual, the latter interpretation of the concepts amounts, in the terminology explained above, to ontological nominalism in the strict sense.

Ockham defended his ontological viewpoint by revising the logic of the suppositions of terms accordingly. Furthermore, he insisted that science was, properly speaking, of terms and not of things [*Philosophical Writings,* ed. and tr. P. Boehner (Indianapolis 1964) 11], since one knows propositions and these are made up of singular and universal terms. By this he did not mean to deny that one knows about real things, for in the logic of suppositions he explicitly explained how terms stood for things. His peculiar preoccupation with terms, however, explains why Ockhamist nominalists were also called terminists (*terministae*).

The above-mentioned identification of concepts and acts of thinking was in keeping with the famous principle of economy that Ockham often applied in logical analysis: "Plurality is never to be posited without necessity" (*numquam ponenda est pluralitas sine necessitate—In 1 sent.* 27.2K), or "What can be explained by fewer assumptions is vainly explained by more" (*frustra fit per plura quod potest fieri per pauciora—Summa tot.log.* 1.12). This principle, later called "Ockham's razor," can be found already before Ockham, but it characterizes very well the pragmatic aspect of nominalism. Ockham also recognized clearly the connection between ontological assumptions and linguistic formulations. For example, he explained the abstract noun *humanity* nominalistically by the complex phrase "man insofar as he is man" (*Summa tot.log.* 1.8). Such reformulations have gained special prominence in the contemporary discussion of nominalism (see below).

But Ockham was more than a logician. His ontological nominalism was intimately connected with his theological view of a free, all-powerful, and all-merciful God. (Distinctive of late scholastic nominalism is the fact that it included members of both the arts and theology faculties.) For Ockham, the affirmation of a real distinction in things implied that God could create one of its components without the other. In view of God's absolute power (*potentia absoluta*), the coexistence of individuals was entirely contingent; the actual

order of nature and grace, moreover, was necessary only insofar as God in fact directed His power in this way (*potentia ordinata*). As a consequence, arguments depending on man's experience of the *de facto* order could lead only to probable conclusions. For Ockham, God's inner life was entirely beyond the reach of philosophical investigation. Since he admitted only real distinctions, he taught that God's nature could be only of unanalyzable simplicity, rejecting even the existence of exemplary ideas in God's mind. In his view, only theologians could attempt to formulate the mystery of Trinitarian life.

Ockhamist School. The followers of Ockham formed a new school, the *via moderna,* in opposition to the old schools of *Scotism and *Thomism, the *via antiqua.* In England the first Ockhamists were *Robert Holcot and *Adam Wodam. In Paris the extremism of the first admirers of Ockham led in 1339 to a decree of the arts faculty prohibiting the teaching of the new doctrine (ChartUnParis 2:485). Apparently some participants in the scholastic art of disputation had made exaggerated use of Ockham's method of logical analysis, calling some propositions of accepted authorities, and even those of Scripture, "false according to their formulation" (*falsae de virtute sermonis*) or "simply false" (*simpliciter falsae*). The opponents of the nominalists blamed Ockham's doctrine that science was of terms and not of things for these exaggerations; thenceforth they were quick to stress that they were interested primarily in things and not in terms (*nos imus ad res, de terminis non curamus*—see Ehrle, 322).

Yet more dangerous were early accusations of heresy. Two thinkers whose doctrines were related to Ockhamism, *Nicholas of Autrecourt and *John of Mirecourt, were condemned by Pope Clement VI (see Denz 1028–49). But the theological writings of Ockham himself were never condemned by the Church, and later nominalist theologians were careful not to overstep the bounds of orthodoxy.

Growth of Ockhamism. *Ockhamism soon attracted leading personalties such as *John Buridan, *Nicholas of Oresme, *Albert of Saxony, and *Marsilius of Inghen. Although these men did not accept all of Ockham's theses, they did help the nominalist school to gain respectability. It spread to old universities, but especially to newly founded centers of learning throughout Europe. Only a few places, such as Cologne and Louvain, remained devoted exclusively to the *via antiqua.* Unfortunately, the rivalry between *antiqui* and *moderni* meant endless quarreling. Thus in Paris in 1474 the realists succeeded in curbing a strong nominalist party with the help of royal power, although in 1481 the prohibitions were abolished.

In the 14th and 15th centuries the leaders of the conciliar movement, *Peter of Ailly and Jean *Gerson, belonged to the *via moderna.* (Ockham himself had already suggested the establishment of a general council to counterbalance papal power). The nominalist school has thus been characterized as "the late medieval ecumenical movement" (H. Oberman). Its theologians intended to heal the divisions in the Church by returning to the golden age of St. *Bernard of Clairvaux and *Peter Lombard. The quarrels of the *antiqui* about metaphysical distinctions seemed to them "to thin out the food" of true Biblical revelation, and apologetical proofs based on purely philosophical reasons (*remoto*

Christo) were regarded as of little use (Ockham's criticism had made their conclusions already doubtful). The influential theologian and faithful interpreter of Ockham in the late 15th century was Gabriel *Biel.

Reformation and Modern Science. There has been much debate over the relationship between the nominalist school and the Reformation. Protestants used to stress Luther's break with the "corrupted" Catholic tradition of the late Middle Ages, whereas Catholic authors, accustomed to see in Thomism the recommended doctrine of the Church, considered the Reformation to be a consequence of the "decadent" scholasticism of the nominalists. Both views seem to be mistaken. *Luther had been strongly influenced by the theology of Biel, but in his doctrine of justification he rejected the nominalist *semi-Pelagianism, according to which man can do his very best by his natural power and so put himself in the proper disposition for the infusion of grace. It may also be mentioned that other Reformers, such as John *Wyclif, John *Hus, and John *Calvin, were of Scotist origin and that Ulrich *Zwingli had a Thomist background, while Johann *Eck, a foremost defender of the Catholic position, belonged to the nominalist school. During the late Middle Ages nominalism, Scotism, and Thomism were all equally accepted schools of Catholic thought. It is true that, after the Council of Trent, the nominalist semi-Pelagianism came to be antiquated and can no longer be considered compatible with Catholic belief. But, on the other hand, there are reasons to believe that Biel's teachings about Scripture and tradition and his Mariology were forerunners of the Tridentine formulations (see Oberman, 423–428).

Also prevalent is a theory to the effect that modern empirical science was a direct result of Ockham's philosophy. It is true that from his doctrine of the contingency of the world order it follows that the only adequate ground for asserting a causal relation between two phenomena is the empirical observation of regular sequence. But Ockham himself had shown no particular interest in empirical science; and although many 14th-century physicists, such as Buridan and Oresme, were associated with the *via moderna,* it must be stressed that in their physical theories they did not follow Ockham but rather continued the work of their realist predecessors (see Weisheipl).

Modern Empiricism. At Oxford the Ockhamist tradition of grammatical and logical analysis survived until far into the 17th century. T. Hobbes's logic clearly goes back to the nominalist version of the logic of terms, and, continuing up to the "ordinary language" school of philosophy of the 20th century, one finds a steady series of warnings not to be misled by the use of abstract nouns.

What characterized modern philosophy, however, was not *linguistic analysis but *epistemology. Here the empiricist postulate to justify all knowledge by reduction to sense experience necessarily led to a strict ontological nominalism. J. *Locke still accepted general ideas, but G. *Berkeley and D. *Hume made it clear that if an idea was a picture formed by sensation or by the imagination, then it could be the picture only of something individual. There is, for example, no such thing as a picture of a triangle in general that is "neither oblique nor rectangle, neither equilateral, equicrural, nor scalenon, but all and none of these at once" (cf. Berkeley, *Principles,* Introd. 13; Hume, *Treatise* 1.1.7). The use of general names was explained psychologically by saying that a general name evoked, through habitual association, a whole chain of similar individuals. Among positivists and psychologist logicians, such views were frequently discussed throughout the 19th century, e.g., by J. S. *Mill. They were later subjected to a thoroughgoing criticism by E. *Husserl.

Contemporary Discussion. With the rise of mathematical logic, psychological questions were pushed into the background. But the problem of universals has reappeared in the 20th century in a new form, consequent on the development of set theory by *Cantor. In this theory, sets or classes are Platonic universals and are not to be confused with wholes, i.e., with "heaps" or concrete collections of individuals. A sphere, for example, is identical with the whole made up of its two halves or with the whole made up of its quarters, but in set theory the sphere, the set that has the two halves as elements, and the set made up of the quarters are three different entities. With a finite number of atomic individuals, one is able to compose only a finite number of different "heaps"; in set theory, however, the number of sets, sets of sets, etc., that can be formed from these same individuals is infinite. At first the Platonic assumption of higher and higher infinites of sets was generally accepted, and set theory became the basis of all mathematics; numbers were defined as particular sets of sets of individuals. But about 1900 various antinomies were discovered when unrestrained Platonism led to contradictions (*see* ANTINOMY). Up to the present no single way of repairing the Platonic edifice has satisfied all logicians, and some (S. Leśniewski, T. Kotarbiński, N. Goodman, W. V. O. Quine, J. H. Woodger, and R. M. Martin) have come to doubt the meaningfulness of the very notion of set. In other words, nominalism has been again resuscitated.

Yet simply to deny the existence of Platonic entities is no longer sufficient. It has become clear that a limitation of ontological assumptions implies that some logical languages are no longer meaningful. The nominalist has therefore the task of formulating everything in a suitable nominalistic language. This encounters great difficulties, and most logicians accept a limited form of Platonism. Logical positivists, such as R. Carnap, try to escape into their *conventionalism: although unable to do without a Platonic language, they continue to claim that metaphysical questions are meaningless and that the issue is simply a matter of linguistic convention.

See also ANALYTICAL PHILOSOPHY; EMPIRICISM; LOGICAL POSITIVISM; OCKHAMISM; POSITIVISM.

Bibliography: A. CARLINI, EncFil 3:927–931. J. AUER, Lex ThK² 7:1020–23. J. KLEIN, RGG³ 4:1505–08. B. MATES, *Stoic Logic* (Berkeley, Calif. 1953). G. M. A. GRUBE, "Antisthenes Was no Logician," *American Philological Association, Transactions and Proceedings* 81 (1950) 16–27. P. VIGNAUX, DTC 11.1: 717–784; *Nominalisme au XIVᵉ Siècle* (Montreal 1948). J. REINERS, *Der Nominalismus in der Frühscholastik* (BeitrGesch PhilMA 8.5; 1910). E. A. MOODY, *The Logic of William of Ockham* (New York 1936); "Ockham, Buridan and Nicholas of Autrecourt: The Parisian Statutes of 1339 and 1340," *Franc Studies* 7 (1947) 113–146. P. BOEHNER, "The Realistic Conceptualism of William of Ockham," *Traditio* 4 (1946) 307–335. E. HOCHSTETTER, "Nominalismus?" FrancStudies 9 (1949) 370–403. F. EHRLE, *Der Sentenzen Kommentar Peters von Candia des Pisaner Papstes Alexanders V: Ein Beitrag zur Scheidung der Schulen in der Scholastik des vierzehnten Jahrhunderts und zur Geschichte des Wegestreites* (FranzStud Beiheft 9; Munster 1925). G. RITTER, *Studien zur Spätscholastik,* 3 v. (SBHeidel,

Philos.-Hist. Klasse, v.12.4, 13.7, 17.5; 1921–27). H. A. OBER-
MANN, *The Harvest of Medieval Theology: Gabriel Biel and Late
Medieval Nominalism* (Cambridge, Mass. 1963). J. A. WEIS-
HEIPL, *The Development of Physical Theory in the Middle Ages*
(New York 1960). R. I. AARON, *The Theory of Universals* (Ox-
ford 1952). E. C. LUSCHEI, *The Logical Systems of Leśniewski*
(Amsterdam 1962). W. V. O. QUINE, *From a Logical Point of
View* (Cambridge, Mass. 1953). N. GOODMAN, *The Structure
of Appearance* (Cambridge, Mass. 1951); "A World of Indi-
viduals" in *The Problem of Universals: A Symposium* (pa.
Notre Dame, Ind. 1956). R. CARNAP, *Meaning and Necessity:
A Study in Semantics and Modal Logic* (2d ed. Chicago 1956).
T. KOTARBIŃSKI, "Sur l'attitude réiste (ou concrètiste)," *Syn-
thèse* 7 (1948–49) 262–273. E. HUSSERL, *Logische Untersuch-
ungen* (2d ed. Halle 1913–21).

[G. KÜNG]

NOMOCANON, comes from the Greek words
νόμος, meaning law, and κανών, meaning a rule. The
word nomocanon was first used in the 11th century to
indicate canonical collections that were composed of
both ecclesiastical and civil laws dealing with ecclesiastical matters. The word was used later to indicate a
book containing "cases of conscience," which was employed by the monks of Mt. Athos. The most popular
use of the word, however, was in regard to canonical
collections containing both secular and ecclesiastical
laws. This type of canonical collection was proper to
the Oriental Churches from the early Middle Ages
and played an important role in the history of Oriental
Canon Law.

From the 4th century on, an important place was
accorded to ecclesiastical matters in imperial law, such
as in the Theodosian Code, the Justinian collections,
and the Novellae and *Bascilicae*. Already from the
time of Constantine civil rulers had taken on the role
of protectors of the Church. As a result civil rulers
became involved in matters exclusively, or at least
partially, ecclesiastical; and they began to order these
matters with civil laws. Collections of these imperial
laws dealing with ecclesiastical matters were made and
were at first added to strictly canonical collections as
appendices. They were later included in the main body
of canonical collections, alongside strictly ecclesiastical
materials, thus giving rise to a new species of canonical
collection that became known as a collection of
nomocanons. A "rubric" (a brief sentence indicating
the subject matter) was followed by several texts that
were intended to demonstrate and support the particular
norm in question. These texts were drawn from both
civil and ecclesiastical authorities. Frequently only a
summation of the text was given, with an indication
where it could be found in its entirety.

Collections of nomocanons have been among the
principal sources of Oriental Canon Law since the early
Middle Ages. The earliest one is the *Nomocanon L
titulorum,* compiled toward the end of the 6th century.
It has been falsely ascribed to Joannes Scholasticus.
It underwent several revisions and was in use until the
12th century. The most important of all collections of
nomocanons is the *Nomocanon XIV titulorum*. It was
compiled during the reign of Emperor Heraclius,
about the year 629. It is most likely the work of
Enantiophanes, although it has been falsely ascribed
to Photius. It consists of decrees of councils, texts of
letters of the Fathers, and imperial constitutions. It
underwent several revisions: a second revision in 883,
which definitively placed the imperial constitutions on
a par with the ecclesiastical canons; a third revision

in 1198 by the celebrated canonist Theodore *Balsamon. In 928 it had been accepted by a council held
at Constantinople, under the Patriarch Nicholas the
Mystic, as the universal law of the Oriental Church.

Bibliography: R. NAZ, DDC 6:1014. C. DE CLERCQ, *ibid.* 2:
1171–74. Stickler 71–72, 407. Van Hove 1:168–171.

[J. M. BUCKLEY]

NON EXPEDIT

This phrase, "it is not expedient," is of Biblical origin
(1 Cor 10.22) and has long been used by the Roman
Curia to indicate a negative reply for reasons of oppor-
tuneness. Signified here is its most famous application
expressive of the Holy See's policy prohibiting Italian
Catholics from participating in political elections and
most other political activities of the new kingdom,
which unified the peninsula by seizing the *States of
the Church and ending the papal temporal power and
whose attempt to solve the *Roman question by the
Law of *Guarantees (1871) proved unacceptable to
*Pius IX.

Origins. Giacomo *Margotti, a journalist in Turin,
anticipated this policy when he inaugurated a widely
successful propaganda campaign in 1857 urging Catholics to abstain from civil elections and coined the
phrase *nè eletti nè elettori* (neither elected nor electors). Yet in 1866 Pius IX permitted Catholics who were
elected deputies to take the oath of loyalty to the state
provided they added: *salvis legibus divinis et ecclesiasticis* (divine and ecclesiastical laws remaining intact).
The *non expedit* policy first received formal acceptance
in the decree of the Sacred Penitentiary (Sept. 10,
1874). Since numerous Catholics were uncertain
whether the *non expedit* was an absolute prohibition or
a recommendation, Pius IX issued a brief that declared
abstention a duty and reproved attempts to entice
Catholics to the polls (Jan. 29, 1877). *Leo XIII renewed the prohibition on the eve of the 1880 elections,
in a more solemn manner in the encyclical *Immortale
Dei* (Nov. 1, 1885), and again in his approval of the
Holy Office decree (June 30, 1888).

Application. Filippo Meda made the formula *nè eletti
nè elettori* gradually give way to another, *preparazione
nell' astensione* (preparation in abstention), which advocated that Catholics should not be mere abstention-
ists, but should use their civil rights, improve social and
political institutions by instilling in them Christian principles, regain society to Catholicism, and terminate the
hostility between Church and State. The *non expedit*
did not apply to administrative elections and other
forms of civic activity. Catholic participation in administrative elections was always rather sizable, and it was
greeted with satisfaction by the Catholic press not as a
preparation for political elections, but as an act of hostility against the revolution. Especially in the big cities
of Genoa, Turin, and Naples, the administrative elections of 1878, 1879, and 1880 resulted in sensational
Catholic successes; Catholics in Rome joined in the
Unione Romana and gained control of the communal
government (1879–87). In political elections, on the
other hand, the *non expedit* was observed in orderly
fashion by Italian Catholics, thereby causing a very notable electoral absenteeism, which created a deep chasm
between the "legal country," representative of a small
group of citizens who possessed and exercised the right
to vote, and the "real country," constituting the vast

majority, which did not possess, or refused to exercise, this right.

Disappearance. Confronted with the dangerous expansion of parties of the extreme left and with the rupture of diplomatic relations between France and the Holy See, *Pius X(1903–14) edged toward a reconciliation with Italy, whose government, headed by Giovanni Giolitti, proved more conciliatory. On the eve of the political elections of Nov. 13, 1904, *Bonomelli explained to the Pope the risk to the social order involved in Catholic electoral abstention and the consequent victory of the extreme left, and Pius X advised Catholics to follow their consciences. This authorization abrogated the *non expedit* virtually but not formally, because the encyclical *Il fermo proposito* (June 11, 1905) confirmed the generic prohibition against participating in elections, but admitted a dispensation when bishops recognized the necessity of using the ballot for the good of souls and the supreme interests of the Church and society.

When the Universal Council (*Consiglio universale*) was established (1913), Giolitti, president of the Council of Ministers, feared a leftist victory and sought to introduce into the ministerial majority representatives of the Catholics, who were economically potent especially in country districts and who enjoyed the veneration surrounding Catholic religious tradition. This led to the Gentiloni pact inviting Italian Catholic support of candidates who would follow the Catholic Electoral Union's religious and social ideas. With the formation of the Popular party (Jan. 19, 1919), inspired by Don *Sturzo, Italian Catholics finally entered the political life of Italy as an autonomous force. About this time Benedict XV abrogated the *non expedit*.

Bibliography: G. DALLA TORRE, *I cattolici e la vita pubblica italiana,* ed. G. DE ROSA, 2 v. (Rome 1962). G. DE ROSA, *Storia del movimento cattolico in Italia,* 2 v. (Bari 1966). F. OLGIATI, "Per la storia del Non expedit," *Vita e Pensiero* 33 (1950) 364–369; "La politica di S. Pio X e il conservatorismo," *ibid.* 37 (1954) 525–540. A. C. JEMOLO, *Church and State in Italy, 1850–1950,* tr. D. MOORE (Philadelphia 1960). A. VIAN, EncCatt 8:1930–32. For additional bibliography *see* ROMAN QUESTION.

[R. MORI]

NONANTOLA, ABBEY OF, former Benedictine monastery outside Modena, north central Italy; since 1926 an abbey *nullius* perpetually united with the archbishopric of *Modena. It was founded (752) by *Anselm (d. 803), the first abbot, and endowed by the Lombard King *Aistulf, receiving the relics of Pope St. Sylvester I in 756. It soon achieved political and cultural importance, and its possessions extended as far as Constantinople. It was favored and controlled by the emperors until 1083; resident abbots replaced absentee appointees in 1044. *Matilda of Tuscany brought the abbey to the side of the popes in the investiture controversy; the *Liber de honore ecclesiae* by Placidus (1111) defended papal rights. Nonantola was long a center of piety and learning with a famous library and scriptorium; it became an abbey in *commendation (1449). Incorporation by the Cistercians (1514), reform by G. F. Bonhomini (1566), and the building of a seminary in 1567 by St. Charles *Borromeo (a commendatory abbot) did not stop the abbey's decline; and it was suppressed in 1797 by the Revolutionary government. Restored as an abbey *nullius*

The Romanesque portal of the abbey church of Nonantola.

(1815), it was united with Modena (1821), secularized (1866), and again restored (1926). Nonantola now has its own chapter, ordinary, and minor seminary and serves 31 parishes (1964).

Bibliography: G. TIRABOSCHI, *Storia dell'augusta Badia di S. Silvestro di Nonantola,* 2 v. (Modena 1784–85). *Miscellanea di studi nonantolani* (Modena 1953). G. GULLOTTA, *Gli antichi cataloghi e i codici della Abbazia di Nonantola* (Vatican City 1955). J. RUYSSCHAERT, *Les Manuscrits de l'abbaye de Nonantola* (Vatican City 1955). P. GROSSI, *Le abbazie benedettine nell'alto medioevo italiano* (Florence 1957). Chevalier TB 2123. Cottineau 2:2087–88. E. LAVAGNINO, EncCatt 8:1928. A. VASINA, LexThK[2] 7:1025–26. **Illustration credit:** Italian Information Center, New York City.

[L. J. LEKAI]

NONBEING

Nonbeing or, in modern philosophical usage, nothing, is the negation of *being; as such, it is to be distinguished from *evil, which is the privation of being. Nonbeing is a being of reason, i.e., its meaning is constituted through reference to being by way of negation, which is an act of the intellect (*Aristotle, *Meta.* 1003b 10; 1004a 9–12; *Thomas Aquinas, ST 1a, 16.3 ad 2, 5 ad 3, 7 ad 4; *De ver.* 1.5 ad 2). Because being has many senses, nonbeing, the product of its negation, has many senses also (*Meta.* 1089a 16). Thus *Plotinus calls the One as well as matter and evil nonbeing because they are not *essence, which he identifies with being (*Enneads* 1.8.3.1–8; 3.6.7.9–13; 3.8.10.28–32; 5.2.1.1–7; 5.5.6.1–13).

Nonbeing is not independent of being, nor is being constituted by nonbeing, as G. W. F. *Hegel claimed. In its adequating and assimilating grasp of being, the intellect produces—as a by-product, as it were—that which is inadequate or unassimilated to being, viz, non-being. Being is evident to the intellect as not nothing. This "not nothing," however, is not that which causes being to be; rather being is not nothing simply because being *is*.

The theological truth of creation out of nothing deepens the metaphysics of nonbeing. "Out of nothing" does not mean that nothing itself is a kind of matter out of which creatures come to be. Rather, it implies that the being of creatures—as a *participation of, and therefore a nonidentity with, the being of God—is made possible by the divine intellection of that which is simply other than God. But that which is simply other than God, the Subsisting Being, is "pure" nothing. Creatures could not exist as other than God, if before creation God did not know what is simply other than Himself. This "other" in no way measures God's knowledge, but depends upon it. The divine ideas as the exemplars of creatures are the divine essence known as able to be participated. Since participation implies difference, God must know the ways in which creatures differ from His own being (*deficiunt a vero esse;* cf. St. Thomas Aquinas, *C. gent.* 1.54) as well as the ways in which they imitate it. But that which is simply different from, or other than, the subsisting plentitude of being (*esse*) is nothing. Such an explanation avoids *pantheism and explains the diversity in being without supposing matter or possibles independent of creation and without introducing real diversity into God, the source of the diversity of being. Essence, not nothing, is the intrinsic principle of the finitude of beings other than God. Nevertheless, nonbeing is the condition of the possibility of the procession of essence (as the principle limiting the *esse* of creatures) from God.

For *Parmenides and Gorgias, nonbeing is not in any sense whatsoever. In the *Parmenides* (142A; 161E–164B) and the *Sophist* (237A–239E; 257B–259B), *Plato suggests a reality of nonbeing that grounds becoming and multiplicity (cf. Aristotle, *Phys.* 191a 23–191b 34). For Aquinas the first division or opposition is that between being and nonbeing; from this first otherness (*alteritas*) springs the plurality of beings and their difference from each other and from the First Cause (*In Boeth. de Trin.* 4.1). For B. *Pascal, man is the mean between God and nothing, so that nothing is one of the extremes that locate man's being. For H. *Bergson, nothing is a pseudo-idea, resulting from a generalization of the displacement of one being by another. For M. Heidegger, the naught is both the veil and the unveiling of the "to be," because the "to be" is not the totality of "that which is." In dread, the pathos of the naught or of the "no-*thing*-ness" of the "to be," man transcends beings or "that which is" toward the "to be" itself. For J. P. Sartre, man is his own nothing and the being in which nothing comes into the world, because the primordial fluidity and otherness of consciousness is not held by any being-in-itself. (*See* EXISTENTIALISM, 2, 3.)

See also PRIVATION (PHILOSOPHY).

Bibliography: G. KAHL-FURTHMANN, *Das Problem des Nichts* (Berlin 1934). E. PACI, *Il nulla e il problema dell'uomo* (Turin 1950). G. SIEWERTH, *Der Thomismus als Identitätsystem* (2d ed. Frankfurt a. M. 1961). H. BERGSON, *Creative Evolution*, tr. A. MITCHELL (New York 1944). M. HEIDEGGER, *Was ist Metaphysik?* (8th ed. Frankfurt a. M. 1960), tr. in part in *Existence and Being*, introd. W. BROCK (2d ed. London 1957). J. P. SARTRE, *Being and Nothingness*, tr. H. E. BARNES (New York 1956).

[T. PRUFER]

NON-BELIEVERS, SECRETARIATE FOR.

This Secretariate was erected by the Holy See in April 1965 to investigate the problem presented to modern Christianity by the spread of atheism. Rather than attempt actually to bring the message of the gospel to nonbelievers, it seeks instead to delineate clearly the points of contact between Christians and atheists.

The Secretariate is not part of the official organization of Vatican Council II and has no direct connection with the latter's Secretariate for Promoting *Christian Unity. It does not seek to enter at once into dialogue with atheists but is to serve as an information-gathering agency for the bishops of the world in their pastoral mission. It will conduct a continuous historical and doctrinal study of atheism under all its various forms, particularly the form of state-controlled atheism prevalent in a number of countries today. It will study also the sociological and psychological factors that favor the spread of atheism. The direct results of this study are not expected to produce any social or political solutions to the problem but only such as are of a cultural, spiritual, and pastoral nature. It is hoped that through the promotion of initiatives in all these areas the difficulties that give rise to the different forms of atheism will be met and provided for.

The headquarters of this Secretariate are at Rome. The president of the Secretariate, Cardinal Franz König, will retain his position as archbishop of Vienna. The daily operation of the organization will be directed by its secretary, Rev. Vincenzo Miano, SDB, dean of the faculty of philosophy at the Salesian Pontifical University (Salesianum) in Rome. The members of the Secretariate are composed of bishops appointed by the pope; its staff of experts and consultants will be chosen from all over the world and will include both Catholic and non-Catholic Christians. A special commission has been created within the Secretariate for relations between Moslems and Christians, with Rev. Joseph Cuoq, WF, as its undersecretary.

[L. A. VOEGTLE]

NON-CHRISTIANS, SECRETARIATE FOR

The Secretariate for Non-Christians, established by Pope Paul VI in a papal bull dated May 19, 1964, had been in the planning stage since September 1963.

Purpose. Its aim is the extending of the ecumenical movement fostered by the establishment of the Secretariate for Promoting *Christian Unity to all believers, even the nonbaptized. Numerous petitions had come to Vatican Council II from various mission countries suggesting that the dialogue be extended to Moslems, Hindus, Buddhists, and to all religions without exception. The Holy Father was painfully aware that more than a billion and a half souls had not yet been reached by the gospel message.

It was necessary to find a common ground of understanding and union. This could not be represented either by the Bible or by the belief in Jesus Christ, as in the case of Protestants or Jews. It had to be based on the common human nature created by God in His image, the gift of the natural law, which expresses itself in the conscience, the vestiges of revelation, and finally the grace that God never denies to men of good will.

The work of salvation of all nations is thus pursued in the Church according to two parallel plans: wherever the gospel can be openly preached, the missionary shall continue his work as in the past; whenever lack of spiritual readiness makes the preaching of the gospel impossible because of political, racial, or other reasons, the Church shall operate in the midst of the people's culture and religion. It is in effect a twofold manner of looking upon religions of human origin: imperfect and imbued with errors or impurities, they are evil; but in preserving and emphasizing natural law and works of exceptional and selected minds, they assume a providential role of helping worshipers in their search for God. In addition, they represent the expression of a nation's natural tendencies toward the divine, just as logic and aesthetics are the proper means toward truth and art. These religions may be sublimated and purified by enriching them with the principles of the Christian religion, in proportion to their power of assimilation: any progress toward what is good and true is an actual step toward God, and each of these steps prepares the following one.

Therefore the secretariate is not designed exclusively for believers in one God, *qui unum Deum colunt* (apostolic letter, April 30, 1964), but is aimed also at responding "to the spiritual needs of all men" (reply to Cardinal Tisserant, June 23, 1964). In fact, by a decision of the Secretariate of State dated July 7, 1964, almost all monotheists have been entrusted to the care of this secretariate. The Jews were assigned to the Secretariate for Promoting Christian Unity, while a special commission was being organized to include Moslems. The Secretariate for Non-Christians has been instituted for all those who recognize a power above or beyond nature; it does not reject even those who no longer practice their religion and consider themselves unbelievers, but remain nevertheless profoundly impressed, in their way of thinking and feeling, by the belief they have abandoned. Other unbelievers will be entrusted to a particular secretariate, in state of organization at this writing (1965).

Organization. The Secretariate for Non-Christians has its center in Rome (Ospizio Santa Marta, Vatican City). Its task is to plan and coordinate contacts between Christians and non-Christians throughout the world. It is charged also with receiving in Rome transient non-Christians, thus realizing a desire of the Holy Father that "no pilgrim, regardless of how distant his country of origin is, religiously or geographically, be any longer a stranger in Rome . . ." (Pentecost message, May 17, 1964).

This Roman center is connected with the various episcopal conferences of the mission countries inhabited mostly by non-Christians. Each conference must have its commission for non-Christians, and must appoint a correspondent for communications with the center. Other branches are to be established on a diocesan level and in every important center of contact. A bulletin of the secretariate, reserved to ordinaries and their assistants, will facilitate contact and information.

The secretariate is also in touch with those ordinaries and organizations that grant assistance to non-Christians in Europe or America for their work or studies. It directs to them non-Christians who have recourse to the secretariate, but at the same time offers its services for the solution of difficulties they might encounter.

The Secretariate for Non-Christians avoids needlessly duplicating organs already in existence. It does not have missionaries of its own, but works with those that the Church has already sent to each country. Its activity is limited to guiding and directing, while diligent care is used not to undertake any initiative without the consent of the ordinaries, who are directly responsible for the missionaries. It utilizes the same centers of assistance and institutes of research.

It has secured the cooperation of a certain number of experts on particular religions and in other spheres of activity. Those who reside in Rome are consultors; the others are consultor-correspondents; all are appointed by the Holy See. Their role within the secretariate is not research in the strict sense, but rather the study and solution of particular cases presented by the ordinaries and of possible difficulties that may hinder the work of those who seek contacts. In addition, they work for a constant improvement of the organization and activity of the secretariate and for a betterment without delay of its methods of approach with the various religions.

Function. The methods, which vary according to the case, fall more or less within the following program: while carefully avoiding indifferentism and syncretism, one has to examine each religion without prejudice and with sympathy, in order to emphasize the good elements that are found in its doctrine as well as in the manner in which the religion tends toward the divine. All that is good is of God. With reference to the attitude toward God, one sees that here it may be of reverence, and there of gratitude; some insist on sacrifice, others on purification, and still others on simple contemplative union. All these means are excellent, yet there is everything to gain in following the feeling that appears to be inherent in the spirit of a nation. One seems to forget his own religion while striving to improve other creeds, so that one may repeat the words of St. Paul: "To those without the Law, I have made myself one without the Law (though I am not without the law of God) so that I might gain to God those without the Law" (1 Cor 9.21).

For the most part, bishops and priests must play, in their first contacts, a role of direction and formation, but it is particularly the laymen who are called to initiate a dialogue, each in his own way and according to his ability. The action of the laity must begin with their example in private, social, and political life.

This presupposes that Catholics abandon the policy of the ghetto, which they have unfortunately been following in many places. Even where the Catholic religion is looked down upon or persecuted, the duty of the Christian is to enter into public life, adding, to the justice of the accomplished task, what Christian charity alone can inspire. Catholics must remember that their neighbor will judge the Church according to the conduct of each one of them.

To this basic contact are to be added the collective means of information: radio, television, books, and newspapers. Very important also are the works of social service, particularly schools, even if it is not permitted to teach religion. It is necessary that schools be open to all without restriction of creed.

Finally, of primary importance are conferences on religions, which should be conducted without polemics, but simply on positive and constructive terms.

Unlike the Secretariate for Promoting Christian Unity, the Secretariate for Non-Christians remains outside Vatican Council II, by reason of the people who are entrusted to its care. It does not enjoy more authority than a council of bishops, mainly because all the bishops of the mission countries are its first and necessary counselors, and also because the secretariate acts only in strict cooperation with them.

Bibliography: Secretariate for Non-Christians, *Information for the Conciliar Fathers,* report by CARDINAL P. MARELLA (Vatican City 1964). "Il Segretariato per i non-cristiani," OssRom (May 21, 1964) 2. G. A. ZANANIRI, "Le Secrétariat pour les non-Chrétiens," AmiDuCl 74 (July 16, 1964) 460–462.

[P. HUMBERTCLAUDE]

NONCONFORMISTS

English Protestants who refused Anglican uniformity, also called Dissenters. In the 16th century the most important nonconformists were *Congregationalists and Brownists; in the 17th century, *Presbyterians and the Society of *Friends (Quakers); in the 18th and 19th, *Methodists. All nonconformist groups before the Civil War (1638–49) were frequently called *Puritans. Today the term "Free church" is preferred.

Although the name "nonconformist" dates from 1662, actual dissent began when Protestants refused Elizabeth's Act of *Uniformity in 1559, objecting to bishops and Anglican liturgical usages, and advocating a "pure" (Calvinistic) Christianity. They favored local autonomy in church government, and many wished to limit the powers of the monarchy and even separate Church and State. James I therefore regarded them as a danger to the monarchy and in 1604 deprived 300 Puritan divines. Some, the Pilgrim Fathers, fled to the New World. In the reign of Charles I, Archbishop Laud's attempt to eliminate Puritan usages helped bring about the Civil War, during which nonconformist factions quarreled bitterly among themselves, united only in their opposition to Catholicism and the Anglican Establishment. After the Restoration of Charles II in 1660, the Anglican Cavalier Parliament sought to impose religious uniformity by the Clarendon Code. These harsh measures were enforced by justices of the peace eager for revenge for the oppression they had suffered under Puritans in the Civil War, and some 20 per cent of the English clergy came to be deprived. James II sought nonconformist support in 1687–88 by his Declarations of Indulgence, but without success because of nonconformist suspicion of Catholics. James's Calvinist successor, William III, by the Toleration Act of 1689, granted freedom of worship to nonconformists (but not to Roman Catholics or *Unitarians), though still excluding them from public office. Many nonconformists evaded this exclusion by taking the Anglican sacrament once a year. The restrictive legislation of 1660 to 1689 was not formally repealed, however, until 1828, the year of Catholic emancipation. Nonconformity waned during the heyday of 18th-century deism and might have died out save for the great Methodist revival.

Most 17th-century nonconformists came from the middle classes. The Whig party, organized in the 1670s, was for 150 years the champion and stronghold of Dissent. Its descendant, the Liberal party, contained most nonconformist groups of the 19th century. After 1850 nonconformists interested themselves in social questions. The rise of British socialism and the Labor party owes more to the nonconformist conscience than to Karl Marx. Among the important nonconformists were O. Cromwell, J. Milton, G. Fox, J. Bunyan, I. Watts, J. Wesley, C. Wesley, G. Whitefield, C. H. Spurgeon, R. W. Dale, and P. Forsyth.

Bibliography: T. PRICE, *The History of Protestant Nonconformity in England,* 2 v. (London 1836–38). H. S. SKEATS and C. S. MIALL, *History of the Free Churches of England* (London 1894). W. K. JORDAN, *The Development of Religious Toleration in England,* 4 v. (London 1932–40). E. ROUTLEY, *English Religious Dissent* (Cambridge, Eng. 1960). P. SCOTT, RGG³ 2:209. W. F. ADENEY, Hastings ERE 9:381–393.

[B. NORLING]

NONGRADED SCHOOL

A school in which pupils are grouped primarily on the basis of *readiness or achievement rather than on age or grade level. Designed to facilitate continuous pupil progress, the nongraded school represents an attempt by American educators to counteract the weaknesses of the graded system. The graded school, which evolved as an expedient for classifying large numbers of children, was formally introduced into the U.S. in 1848 with the opening of the Quincy Grammar School in Boston, Mass. A few decades later, as school enrollments increased, especially in the cities, grading schools became the accepted practice. Although convenient from the administrative point of view, the graded school, through its inability to provide adequately for individual differences, soon created problematic conditions resulting from nonpromotion. In addition, graded classes frequently did not motivate above-average pupils to perform at their highest level of ability.

In an effort to overcome the inadequacies of the graded structure, various plans for providing for pupil variability were advanced, beginning in 1868 with William T. *Harris's proposal of frequent promotion and reclassification. Other efforts included individualized instruction, departmentalization, a multitrack curriculum, enrichment for the gifted, and grouping pupils within a grade.

Unlike previous attempts to improve instruction, the nongraded school dispenses with grade levels as a necessary condition for adapting instruction to the different needs and capacities of pupils. Its flexible groupings provide for both irregularity in progress and for varying rates of progress, without the disadvantages of retention and acceleration. The nongraded structure, moreover, encourages a longitudinal view of the curriculum that emphasizes the development of concepts and principles rather than the mastery of specific facts. To be effective, a nongraded program requires a wide variety of instructional materials and frequent evaluation of pupil progress.

The development of the nongraded school began with the primary unit, which replaced the traditional first three grades, and sometimes the kindergarten. Most nongraded primaries are essentially continuous growth plans in reading, although some extend the plan to include other subjects. With the removal of grade pressures and grade restrictions, each child is free to progress at his own pace; accordingly, the length of time a child spends in a primary unit depends largely upon his rate of learning.

Nongraded programs at the intermediate and junior high levels present a diversity of structure with regard to grade span, choice of ungraded subjects, method of grouping, and utilization of teachers; yet all aim to enable each child to perform at his own level of achievement. A large-scale experiment that provides for nongraded advancement in mathematics, science, music, and art, in grades three through eight, with specialists as teachers, is described by George D. Stoddard in *The Dual Progress Plan* (New York 1961).

The first nongraded high school in the U.S. was the Melbourne (Fla.) High School, which offers courses in "phases," or ability levels. B. Frank Brown, the principal who introduced the Melbourne program in 1958, gives a detailed explanation of it in his book, *The Nongraded High School* (New York 1963).

Of the hundreds of nongraded programs in operation, the most numerous are nongraded primaries; the oldest is the primary unit of the Milwaukee (Wis.) public schools, begun in 1942 and gradually adopted in 116 other schools. The Appleton (Wis.) school system was the first to introduce nongrading into the intermediate grades in 1951 [A. D. Morse, *Schools of Tomorrow—Today* (New York 1960)].

Among Catholic school systems, the Archdiocese of St. Louis was the first to adopt the nongraded primary (1953); and several years later, to begin nongrading five through eight; by 1964 programs of total nongrading were in effect in 88 St. Louis Catholic schools. The Diocese of Pittsburgh initiated its program of nongrading in 1957. In other dioceses, nongraded programs are in operation in pilot schools, sponsored by either the diocese or a religious community.

Bibliography: J. I. Goodlad and R. H. Anderson, *The Nongraded Elementary School* (rev. ed. New York 1963).

[C. F. Bamberger]

NONIUS MARCELLUS, fl. *c.* A.D. 323 at Thubursicum in Numidia (Algeria); compiled the *De compendiosa doctrina per litteras ad filium,* an alphabetic encyclopedia of 20 books on grammar, lexicography, and antiquities. Because of the many early Latin authors quoted, the work was widely used by later writers. It was a mine of information for Hincmar of Reims, Lupus of Ferrières, John of Salisbury, and for medieval lexicographers and glossarists in general. Isidore of Seville followed Nonius and Gellius in dividing his *Etymologiae* into 20 books.

Bibliography: N. Marcellus, *Nonii Marcelli De compendiosa doctrina libros,* ed. W. M. Lindsay, 3 v. (Leipzig 1903). W. M. Lindsay, *Nonius Marcellus' Dictionary of Republican Latin* (Oxford 1901). W. V. Strzelecki, Pauly-Wiss RE 17.1:882–897. SchHosKrGeschRL 4.1:142–148.

[R. T. Meyer]

NONJURORS, ENGLISH, the name given to 8 bishops and some 400 clergy of the Church of England who refused to take the oath of allegiance to William and Mary after the Glorious Revolution of 1688 out of loyalty to their previous oath to James II (*see* JAMES II, KING OF ENGLAND). Among them was Archbishop Sancroft of Canterbury. They were not notably friendly to the deposed James II and would have accepted William and Mary as regents, but not as king and queen. They were all High Churchmen, believers in passive obedience and the divine right of kings, and regarded James II as their rightful sovereign. Three days after the landing of William, George Hickes, Dean of Worcester, preached a sermon on submission to persecuting princes, citing the early Christians as examples. In February 1690, Parliament deprived the bishops of their sees and benefices and expelled them from the Anglican Church. Though reduced to poverty and persecuted by the government, they held to their claim to represent, and their duty to preserve, the true Anglican succession. They held services in secret. In 1694 the exiled James consented to nominate two new bishops, and G. Hickes and J. Wagstaffe were consecrated in secret. In 1713 Hickes, the only living nonjuring bishop, consecrated three more bishops. After the death of the Young Pretender in 1788, nonjurors largely disintegrated. The last nonjuring bishop was Charles Booth, who died in 1805.

The nonjurors found support in Jacobite families for whom they were chaplains or tutors. Many English regarded them as apostate Anglicans or stalking horses for popery. After some time they had, in London alone, 50 chapels. Through the mediation of Peter the Great in 1716 they entered into discussions for union with four Eastern patriarchs, but by 1725 the efforts had failed. In England they sympathized with and prayed for the exiled Stuarts but were never actively disloyal to the government. In Scotland, however, where most of the Episcopal clergy were nonjurors, they took part, in accord with Episcopal disestablishment in 1689, in Jacobite uprisings in 1715 and 1745. In 1701 on the death of James II, some nonjurors accepted Queen Anne and rejoined the Anglican Church while others held that their oath to James bound them to support his descendants. In 1714 they were split over the oath to George I. They were divided also on points of theology and liturgical usage. Their secession deprived the Church of England of a group of devoted, pious, learned, and experienced churchmen whose small numbers belied their importance. They continued the tradition of the *Caroline Divines and may be regarded as forerunners of the *Oxford Movement. They included T. Brett, T. Carte, J. Collier, T. Deacon, H. Dodwell, T. Hearne, T. Ken, J. Kettlewell, W. *Law, C. Leslie, and R. Nelson.

Bibliography: J. H. Overton, *The Nonjurors* (London 1902). C. Gaskoin, Hastings ERE 9:394–396. N. Sykes, *Church and State in England in the XVIIIth Century* (Cambridge, Eng. 1934). Cross ODCC 963–964. D. Carter, RGG³ 4:1509–10.

[B. Norling]

NONNBERG, ABBEY OF, in *Salzburg, Austria; the oldest abbey of Benedictine nuns in Germany or Austria. It was founded *c.* 700 by St. *Rupert and endowed by Duke Theodo of Bavaria and his wife St. Regintrude. Until 987 Nonnberg was part of the mensal possessions of the archbishop of Salzburg. In 1043 the abbey was rebuilt in honor of St. Erentrude (d. *c.* 718), the first abbess and probably the niece of St. Rupert. The rich abbey was reserved for the nobility until the 18th century. In 1242 Abbess Gertrude of Stein received pontifical privileges, the faldstool, and a golden crown; the abbess sat with prelates in the Landtag. After a fire in 1423 the church was rebuilt (1464–1509). Archbishop Paris Lodron introduced the Tridentine reform (1623). The abbey, which founded or restored several other convents and was never suppressed, has always been a center of learning and education. In 1964 it had 75 nuns and conducted a women's college.

Bibliography: M. Regintrudis von Reichlin-Meldegg, *Stift Nonnberg in Salzburg* (Salzburg 1953). Cottineau 2:2089. Kapsner BenBibl 2:244. F. HERMANN, LexThK² 7:1026–27. H. SCHMIDINGER, DHGE 15:697–698.

[N. BACKMUND]

NONNUS OF PANOPOLIS

NONNUS OF PANOPOLIS, epic poet and Christian exegete; b. Panopolis, Thebaid, Egypt, *c.* 400; d. after 450. Nothing is known of the education or career of Nonnus. He is the author of an epic poem in 48 books called the *Dionysiaca,* which was written at Alexandria and describes the journey of the pagan god Dionysus to India, and he probably wrote a verse *Paraphrase of St. John's Gospel* in hexameters. There is an obvious relationship between the two works on the basis of language, style, and identical phraseology. Although the theme and language of the *Dionysiaca* are definitely pagan, the poem does embody Christian notions, whereas the *Paraphrase* reflects the epic form and uses pagan similes particularly in the names of the gods. The older theory that the author wrote the *Dionysiaca* while a pagan and the *Paraphrase* after conversion has been rejected. He seems to have been steeped in the Egyptian Hellenistic tradition. In the *Paraphrase* he introduced pagan Eons as well as Monophysite theological ideas. He called Mary the *Theotokos* and quoted Origen, Gregory Nazianzus, John Chrysostom, and Cyril of Alexandria.

Bibliography: PG 43:749–1228. A. SCHEINDLER, ed., *Nonni Panopolitani Paraphrasis* (BT; 1881). W. H. D. ROUSE, ed. and tr., *Nonnos Dionysiaca,* 3 v. (LoebClLib; 1940). R. KEYDELL, Pauly-Wiss RE 17.1 (1936) 904–921. É. AMANN, DTC 11.1:793–795. K. KUIPER, *Mnemosyne* NS 46 (1918) 225–270. L. R. LIND, *L'Antiquité classique* 7 (1938) 57–65. P. BERNARDINI MARZOLLA, *Studi italiani di filologia classica* 26 (1952) 191–209. Altaner 327–328. W. BAUER, RGG³ 4:1510. Cross ODCC 964.

[F. X. MURPHY]

NORBERT OF XANTEN, ST.

Founder of the *Premonstratensians and archbishop of Magdeburg; b. Xanten, Duchy of Cleves, Germany, *c.* 1080; d. Magdeburg, Germany, June 6, 1134 (feast, June 6; in the order, June 11). Norbert was a son of the lord of Gennep and was made a canon at nearby Xanten. He served at the courts of Frederick, Archbishop of Cologne (d. 1131), and Emperor *Henry V. Norbert accompanied Henry to Rome; and although he repented of his part in the humiliation of Pope *Paschal II in 1111, he remained with the Emperor. In 1115 a bolt of lightning felled Norbert from his horse; and considering this an invitation to a life of perfection, he retired to a cell near Xanten, where he spent 3 years (1115–18) in a life of penance. Ordained a priest, he unsuccessfully attempted to reform the canons of Xanten, and his occasional preaching journeys brought him the censure of *Rupert of Deutz. Norbert then distributed his possessions to the poor and, barefoot, made a trip to *Saint-Gilles, where Pope *Gelasius II authorized him to preach throughout the universal Church. During 1119 he wandered through northern France, Hainault, and Brabant preaching, by his life of poverty and simplicity as well as by his words, a catechism of Christian morality. On the advice of Pope *Callistus II and with the support of Bartholomew, Bishop of Laon (d. 1157), Norbert established a monastery near Laon in the isolated valley of Prémontré in 1121. In the same year he assisted at the Council of Soissons, which condemned Peter *Abelard. Norbert also traveled to Cologne for relics and on his return journey made a

second foundation at *Floreffe near Namur. Since his itinerant preaching had attracted many followers to Prémontré, a decision on their way of life was necessary, and Norbert decided that they should follow the Rule of St. *Augustine. The life was chiefly contemplative, though the active labor of preaching was not excluded, certainly not for Norbert himself. Many foundations were made over Europe in the next few years, and in 1125 Norbert set out for Rome, where Pope *Honorius II confirmed the order: the trip through Germany was marked by preaching, conversions, and even more new foundations.

King *Lothair III was at that time defending his crown against the Hohenstaufen, and at the Diet of Speyer in 1126, Norbert preached a sermon on loyalty and obedience that won him Lothair's continuing support. At Speyer the canons of the cathedral of Magdeburg were to choose a new archbishop in Lothair's presence, thus following the form established by the Concordat of *Worms. They chose Norbert, whose unwillingness was overcome only by pressure from Lothair and the papal legates. In July 1126, Norbert, still barefoot, entered Magdeburg and was consecrated. He attempted to recover the lands of the Church lost through nepotism or confiscation and also to reform the lives of the clergy, but his efforts tended only to aggravate the discontent and rebellion in his diocese. The Wends under his jurisdiction were alienated by Lothair's expedition of 1127 that subjected them to the crown and to the *tithe, while the order Norbert had left behind also went through a crisis without his leadership. Norbert summoned the Premonstratensian leaders to Magdeburg and asked them to choose as his successor *Hugh of Fosse, who was able to give the order direction and structure, even as the Wends were being won over by the preaching of *Otto of Bamberg. Norbert expected to aid his reform efforts by introducing Premonstratensian canons into Magdeburg, but this resulted only in several assassination attempts and the archbishop's temporary exile.

In the schism of 1130, Norbert supported *Innocent II's claim to the papacy and helped persuade the Emperor to adhere to Innocent's cause. He accompanied Lothair's expedition to Italy (1132–34) against Anacletus II (Peter *Pierleoni) and joined *Bernard of Clairvaux in a vain attempt to win over Anacletus by persuasion. Although his preaching helped strengthen the resistance to imperial attempts to win back the right of *investiture, Norbert continued to serve Lothair after the trip back to Germany, until illness forced him to return to Magdeburg. His fever lasted through Lent of 1134; he died soon after and was buried on June 11 at the Premonstratensian church in Magdeburg. In 1582 *Gregory XIII authorized a liturgical cult for St. Norbert, and his body was moved from Magdeburg to Strahov near Prague in 1627. In 1672 *Clement X extended his feast to the universal Church.

Bibliography: Contemporary lives are the *Vita A,* ed. R. WILMANS, MGS 12:663–706, and *Vita B,* PL 170:1253–1344. G. MADELAINE, *Histoire de saint Norbert,* 2 v. (3d ed. Tongerloo 1928). P. E. VALVEKENS, *Norbert van Gennep* (Bruges 1943). P. LEFÈVRE, "L'Épisode de la conversion de s. Norbert et la tradition hagiographique du *Vita Norberti,*" RHE 56 (1961) 813–826. AnalPraem has many excellent articles on Norbert, esp. 10 (1934); 22–25 (1946–49); 31 (1955); 34–36 (1958–60); 38 (1962). N. BACKMUND, LexThK² 7:1030–31.

[J. R. SOMMERFELDT]

NORFOLK

A line of Catholic earls and dukes whose peerage dates back to the 11th century, when Ralph, a staller or constable of the court of Edward the Confessor (reign 1043–66) and a benefactor of St. Riquier's Abbey, Ponthieu, was confirmed in his lands. The earldom proper was created in 1140 or 1141 for *Hugh Bigod* (d. 1176 or 1177), who ruled East Anglia from Framlingham castle. *Roger,* fifth Bigod earl of Norfolk (1245–1306), died without heirs.

The Mowbray Line. Edward I (reign 1274–1307) revived the earldom for his son, *Thomas of Brotherton* (1300–38), who in turn died leaving no son.

Thomas de Mowbray. First duke of Norfolk; b. 1366?; d. Venice, Sept. 22, 1399. Thomas was the grandson of Thomas of Brotherton's daughter, Margaret (*c.* 1320–1400), and received the revived dukedom in 1397. He had been earl marshal at 20, and had achieved power for revealing to Richard II (reign 1377–99) the plots of the Earls of Arundel and Gloucester. In 1398 he was accused of treasonable words and fled abroad.

John de Mowbray. Second duke of Norfolk; b. 1389; d. Epworth, Isle of Axholme, Oct. 19, 1432. He distinguished himself in the wars with France (1417–21; 1423–24), and was restored to his father's dukedom in 1425. He was marshal at the coronation of Henry VI in 1429.

John de Mowbray. Third duke of Norfolk, hereditary earl marshal of England and fifth earl of Nottingham; b. Sept. 12, 1415; d. Nov. 6, 1461. The son of John, he supported Richard, Duke of York, in the wars for the English succession (War of the Roses, 1455–85), but changed his allegiance to the Lancastrian King Henry VI in 1459. At the second battle of St. Alban's (1461) he fled from Henry VI's camp and fought for the Yorkist Edward IV, who was crowned king of England after his victory over the Lancastrians at Towton (1461).

John de Mowbray. Fourth duke of Norfolk; b. Oct. 18, 1444; d. Framlingham, Jan. 17, 1476. He also supported the Yorkist cause, but at his death the title again lapsed. Upon the marriage of his 5-year-old daughter, Anne, to Richard, Duke of York, second son of Edward IV, on Jan. 15, 1478, the dignity was added to his titles.

The Howard Line. The illustrious house of Howard, which long stood next in blood to the sovereign, traces its lineage to John Howard of Wiggenhall St. Peter, Norfolk, whose son, William, became a judge in 1297. The Howards came to power as Yorkists.

John Howard. First duke of Norfolk; b. 1430?; d. Bosworth Field, Aug. 22, 1485. As John of Stoke Neyland he became treasurer of Edward IV's household in 1468, and was summoned to Parliament as Lord Howard. He served as captain general at sea, and was later appointed lord admiral. On June 28, 1485, 12 days after young Richard, Duke of York and Norfolk, had been sent to the Tower by his uncle Richard III (reign 1483–85), John Howard was granted the vacant dukedom; as constable of the Tower he probably was in league with the prince's murderers. At the battle of Bosworth he commanded Richard's vanguard of archers. The "Jockey of Norfolk" fell while fighting alongside his sovereign.

Thomas Howard, fourth Duke of Norfolk, portrait by an unknown English artist, c. 1558.

Thomas Howard. Second duke of Norfolk; b. 1443; d. May 21, 1524. Like his father, John Howard, he fought for the cause of Richard III at Bosworth, and after defeat spent 4 years in the Tower as prisoner of the new Tudor king, Henry VII (reign 1485–1509). On release he was created earl of Surrey and proved an indispensable servant of the new monarchy as lord treasurer (1501–22) and as military general on the Scottish border. He inflicted the decisive defeat on the Scots at the battle of Flodden Field on Sept. 9, 1513, and for this service was elevated to the dukedom in February 1514, and named lord admiral. He was guardian of the realm while Henry VIII (reign 1509–47) met Francis I, King of France, on the Field of the Cloth of Gold at Calais on June 7, 1520.

Thomas Howard. Third duke of Norfolk; b. 1473; d. Kenninghall, Norfolk, Aug. 25, 1554. He succeeded his father, Thomas, and also became lord treasurer. In 1495 he was married to Anne, daughter of Edward IV. A man of "very great experience in political government," as the Venetian ambassador noted, he clung to office despite the upheavals of the Reformation. He rebuilt Kenninghall Palace in the form of a letter H, and the grandeur of it and his new palace at Norwich outdid the buildings of his rival Cardinal Thomas Wolsey. Like his father he was a fearless soldier and an astute politician. He had led the vanguard at Flodden Field, and was created earl of Surrey in February 1514. At intervals he devastated the Scottish border and raided the French coast. He led the council's attack on Cardinal Wolsey, and at the latter's fall Thomas became Henry VIII's most trusted adviser. His position had been strengthened by the King's marriage to his niece, Anne

Boleyn (1533), and by his daughter's marriage to Henry's natural son, the Duke of Richmond. His enemies hoped that Anne's trial for adultery (1536) would bring down the whole house of Howard, but Norfolk, who presided, acquiesced in her execution, and scotched a rumor that he was to be sent to the Tower by remarking that it were no more likely than "Tottenham shall turn French."

That autumn he was sent to suppress the *Pilgrimage of Grace, the popular rising under Robert *Aske that was provoked by recent religious changes. At first he offered the rebels the choice of battle or submission, but at Doncaster, seeing their numbers so strong, he made a truce while their demands were forwarded to the King. In January under royal instruction he dealt with severity against the rebels, terrifying the north by his executions. In 1539 Norfolk put forward the Act of Six Articles, devised by Stephen *Gardiner, which restated the doctrinal position of the Henrician Reformation. The passing of this act pointed to the decline of Thomas Cromwell's power, and it was Norfolk who in June 1540 arrested Cromwell at the council table and sent him to the Tower. In July, to consolidate his position the Duke promoted the marriage of his niece Catherine Howard with Henry, but the sordid business of her trial and execution in February 1542 brought the house of Howard into disrepute. Thereafter, though far too useful to be cast aside, Norfolk remained outside the inner ring of councilors. In 1544 he defeated the Scots at Solway Moss and as general of the army in France captured Boulogne, though he was soon replaced by Edward Seymour, Earl of Hertford and Duke of Somerset (1506?–52).

As the uncle of Prince Edward, Hertford was bent on becoming regent on the accession (1547), but to achieve this meant the overthrow of the Howards. A dynastic alliance between the families, proposed by Norfolk, foundered and before the end of 1546 he was in the Tower, for his son Henry Howard, Earl of Surrey, poet and soldier of renown, had played into Hertford's hands. Surrey, it was said, had devised a plan for his sister, the widowed duchess of Richmond, to become Henry's mistress. He had designs on the regency himself and was indiscreet enough to quarter the royal arms with his own. There was sufficient evidence to send him to the block on January 19 on a technical charge of treason. Old Norfolk was compromised by his son's indiscretion. On January 29 King Henry appointed commissioners to give assent to the bill of attainder against the Duke, but died during the night, so Norfolk's life was saved, though he remained a prisoner of state throughout Edward VI's reign. On Mary's accession (1553) he at once returned to power, and despite his age, he prepared for the coronation as lord treasurer and earl marshal. He died full of years and honors. Though he had suppressed the Pilgrimage of Grace and shared in the scramble for monastic lands, the third duke was essentially a conservative, and it was for political and dynastic reasons that he abhorred Protestantism and despised the New Learning.

Thomas Howard. Fourth duke of Norfolk; b. March 10, 1538; d. June 2, 1572. He was the son of Henry Howard, Earl of Surrey. After a year in the custody of Sir John Williams he was placed at Reigate (1548) under his aunt, the Duchess of Richmond, who engaged John Foxe (1516–87) as his tutor. Brought to court on Queen Mary's accession (1553) he was placed in the households successively of Bps. Stephen Gardiner and John White, who sought to eradicate the teaching of Foxe. In 1554 he became a gentleman of the chamber of the Infante, Philip of Spain, and that summer succeeded to the dukedom of his grandfather. In 1555 he married Mary Fitzalan, daughter of Henry, Earl of Arundel, but she died in childbirth in June 1557. In the first week of Elizabeth's reign (1558–1603) Thomas married Margaret Audley, widow of Lord Henry Dudley. As premier peer and sole duke he was connected by descent or alliance with most of the nobility. He was the richest landowner and his Liberty of Norfolk was the greatest private franchise in the kingdom. Despite his power as a territorial magnate that enabled him to return East Anglian and Sussex members of Parliament to Westminster, Elizabeth delayed taking him into her confidence. In December 1559 she appointed him lieutenant general in the war against the French in Scotland, which culminated in the treaty of Edinburgh, breaking the "Auld Alliance." There he came close to William Cecil (1520–98) and shared his suspicion of Robert Dudley, Earl of Leicester (1532?–88), Elizabeth's favorite; for 7 years opposition to Dudley remained the basis of Norfolk's political action. On the Queen's recovery from serious illness in October 1562 Dudley was made a privy councilor, and on Cecil's insistence Norfolk entered the council the same day to balance Leicester's power. Cecil, with the Duke's enthusiastic support, began negotiations for Elizabeth's marriage to the Archduke Charles of Austria, which were to founder on the question of his right to a private Catholic chapel. In the Parliament of 1566 Norfolk was spokesman for the lords, insisting that Elizabeth should marry and settle the succession, and he displayed real political courage. As a result the Hapsburg negotiations were resumed, but the Duke was too ill to attend the vital council meetings in the autumn of 1567 that settled the issue, and in his absence Leicester's intrigues for a French match and his stirring Protestant opinion against the Austrian alliance and its begetters wounded Norfolk.

After Margaret Audley's death Norfolk married Elizabeth, widow of Lord Thomas Dacre, in January 1567. She was a devout Catholic. Her death in childbed that autumn brought him low and it was as a widower for the third time that he began to listen to the suggestion that he should marry *Mary, Queen of Scots.

Following Mary's flight to England Norfolk went as principal commissioner to York to investigate the charges brought against her in September 1568. Here William Maitland (1528?–73), Mary's secretary for foreign affairs, whispered his proposal that a match with Mary would at a stroke solve the Scottish problem and the question of the succession in England. The Duke had been openly mentioned as a consort for Mary on two earlier occasions, but now that the Casket Letters had convinced him of Mary's guilt in Lord Darnley's murder (1567) he was noncommittal. Elizabeth suspected that Norfolk was not behaving impartially toward Mary and recalled him from York to an enlarged commission in London. Intrigues and the double dealing of James Stewart, Earl of Moray (1531?–70), here showed the Duke in an unfavorable light and by the end of 1568 he had decided to go forward with the marriage scheme as the only avenue to power. To achieve this he made an uneasy alliance with Leicester and together they planned to get rid of William Cecil, then especially unpopular; but Elizabeth stood by her secretary and his opponents could only pursue their goal by intrigue. Other schemes were devised, such as the design of Henry *Fitzalan, Earl of Arundel; John Lumley; Thomas, Earl of Northumberland; and Charles, Earl of Westmorland, for liberating Mary with Spanish arms and deposing Elizabeth. In all these schemes Norfolk's marriage with Mary was a cardinal feature.

Leicester prevaricated. He had insisted on obtaining Elizabeth's consent to the marriage himself and finally outwitted Norfolk. Elizabeth put Norfolk on his allegiance to deal no more with Mary and fearing for his life he fled from court to London and thence, on September 16, to Kenninghall. Having instructed the northern earls to call off their rising he went to Windsor to submit. The charges against him did not add up to high treason, but in the prevailing political uncertainty the Tower seemed the safest place for him, and the outbreak of the Northern Rebellion made an early release unlikely. In August 1570, after Norfolk had written a full submission, Elizabeth allowed him to go to the Charterhouse under strict supervision, on account of his health. Within weeks Roberto di Ridolfi (1531–1612), the Florentine banker, had him involved in his grand design for a Spanish invasion of England. Norfolk himself never signed the fatal letters to the Duke of Alva, Philip II, and the Pope. With the unravelling of the Ridolfi conspiracy there was ample evidence to send Norfolk for trial on Jan. 16, 1572. Though he protested his innocence, his peers found him guilty. Elizabeth hesitated signing his death warrant but could not hold out indefinitely against the logic of statecraft, and the last duke of medieval creation was executed on June 2, maintaining his innocence and denying he was a Catholic. Though aloof and indecisive he remained a popular figure to the end.

The dukedom did not pass to Thomas' eldest son, Philip *Howard, who lost the favor of Elizabeth I and was imprisoned allegedly for treason. Philip's eldest son, *Thomas* (1586–1646), however, was restored to the earldom of Arundel in 1604. The friend of the antiquaries Sir Robert Cotton and Sir Henry Spelman, he formed the first notable art collection in England. Out of sympathy with the court of Charles I (reign 1625–49), he left England for Italy before the civil war, but contributed £54,000 to the royalist cause, in recognition of which he was created earl of Norfolk on June 6, 1644. His second son, *Henry* (1608–54), a zealous royalist, fought at Edgehill, and upon his return to his estates found that they had passed into the possession of Parliament. By a vote of the House of Commons, he was allowed to compound them for £6,000 in 1648. Henry's son *Thomas* (1627–77), while in exile with his grandfather, developed brain fever from which he never recovered, but at the restoration of Charles II (reign 1660–85) he became the fifth duke of Norfolk by an act of Parliament on Dec. 29, 1660. He died unmarried, and with him the earldom of Arundel descended with the dukedom. His successors for the next century play little part in public affairs: *Henry,* sixth duke (1628–84), brother of Thomas, succeeded in 1677; *Henry,* seventh duke (1655–1701), son of Henry, succeeded in 1684; *Thomas,* eighth duke (1683–1732), nephew of Henry, suceeded in 1701;

Edward, ninth duke (1685–1777), brother of Thomas, succeeded in 1732; *Charles,* tenth duke (1720–86), descendant of the seventh duke, succeeded in 1777.

Charles Howard. Eleventh duke of Norfolk; b. March 5, 1746; d. Norfolk House, London, Dec. 16, 1815. He had been a member of Parliament for Carlisle and turned Protestant during the *Gordon Riots. Described as a hard drinker, he, with the Prince Regent George, set the fashion for late and boisterous dinners. At a political banquet (1798) he gave a toast to "our sovereign's health—the majesty of the people," which offended King George. He was dismissed from his posts. Charles took in hand the rebuilding of Arundel Castle (1791) and lived to see the completion of the new Baron's Hall (1815).

Bernard Edward Howard. Twelfth duke of Norfolk; b. Sheffield, Nov. 21, 1765; d. Norfolk House, London, March 19, 1842. The third cousin of Charles, Bernard was a Catholic and by an act of Parliament, was allowed to retain the hereditary dignity of earl marshal. He was admitted to the House of Lords after the Catholic Relief Bill (1829), and was named a privy councilor in 1830.

Bernard Edward Howard. Twelfth duke of Norfolk; b. London, Aug. 12, 1791; d. Arundel Castle, Feb. 18, 1856. He succeeded his father, Bernard, and became the first avowed Catholic member of Parliament since 1688, being returned as member for Arundel on May 4, 1829, following the passage of Catholic Emancipation. As a supporter of Lord John Russell (1792–1878), he voted for the anti-Catholic Ecclesiastical Titles Bill (1850) and remained little more than Catholic in name until his deathbed reconciliation.

Henry Granville Howard. Fourteenth duke of Norfolk; b. London, Nov. 7, 1815; d. Arundel Castle, Nov. 25, 1860. He changed his surname to Fitzalan-Howard in 1842. He was a Whig member of Parliament for Arundel (1837–50) when he resigned his seat on the enactment of Russell's Ecclesiastical Titles Bill and broke with the Whigs. He was renowned for his zeal as a Catholic and for his charity.

Henry Fitzalan-Howard. Fifteenth duke of Norfolk; b. London, Dec. 27, 1847; d. there, Feb. 11, 1917. He succeeded in 1860 and was the first to play a notable part in public life since the Reformation. Educated under John Henry *Newman at the Oratory School, he became the recognized head of the English Catholic laity, and his influence aided Newman's election to the cardinalate in 1878. He was the first lord mayor of Sheffield and first mayor of Westminster. A Unionist, he resigned the post of postmaster general in 1900 to join the Imperial Yeomanry in South Africa. As earl marshal at the coronations of Edward VII (Aug. 9, 1902) and George V (June 22, 1911) he revised several ancient usages. He built churches at Arundel and at Norwich, the latter as a thank-offering for the birth of an heir to his second wife.

Bernard Marmaduke Fitzalan-Howard. Sixteenth duke of Norfolk; b. Arundel House, May 30, 1908. He officiated as earl marshal at the coronations of George VI (May 12, 1937) and Elizabeth II (June 2, 1953). An experienced landowner, he served as joint parliamentary secretary to the Ministry of Agriculture (1941–45). His interests in sports and the countryside made him a popular figure, and in 1962 and 1963 he was manager of the English Cricket XI on its Australian tour. He also directed the state funeral of Sir Winston Churchill in 1965.

Bibliography: A. COLLINS, *The Peerage of England . . .*, enl. S. E. BRYDGES, 9 v. (London 1812). J. E. DOYLE, *The Official Baronage of England . . . 1066–1885*, 3 v. (London 1885). E. LODGE, *The Peerage and Baronetage of the British Empire as at Present Existing* (70th ed. London 1901). W. DUGDALE, *The Baronage of England . . .*, 2 v. (London 1675–76). C. READ, ed., *Bibliography of British History: Tudor Period, 1485–1603* (2d ed. New York 1959). W. HUNT et al., DNB 10:1–76, J. TAIT, DNB 13:1114–35. Hughes RE. DictEngCath 5:184–187. L. B. SMITH, *A Tudor Tragedy: The Life and Times of Catherine Howard* (New York 1961). N. WILLIAMS, *Thomas Howard, Fourth Duke of Norfolk* (London 1964). **Illustration credit:** National Portrait Gallery, London.

[N. WILLIAMS]

NORIS, HENRY, theologian and historian; b. Verona, Italy, Aug. 29, 1631; d. Rome, Feb. 23?, 1704. He was the son of Alessandro Noris and Caterina Manzoni. After joining the Augustinians at Rimini (1646), he served as regent of studies at Pesaro, Perugia, Florence, and Padua. He then became tutor to the son of the Grand Duke of Tuscany and professor of ecclesiastical history at Pisa (1674–92). Brought to Rome by Innocent XII, he was named custodian of the Vatican Library (1692), consultor to the Holy Office (1694), and cardinal (1695). Noris, one of the leading savants of the 17th century, was the primary figure in the later school of Augustinian theology (*see* AUGUSTINIANISM, THEOLOGICAL SCHOOL OF). He became involved in many controversies, especially by reason of two of his writings, *Historia pelagiana* and *Vindiciae augustinianae* (both published at Padua 1673), which contained his interpretation of the soteriology of St. Augustine, a doctrine that he claimed was wrongly understood by both the Jansenists and their adversaries. Noris was repeatedly accused of Baianism (*see* BAIUS AND BAIANISM) and *Jansenism, but he was cleared of these charges both during his lifetime and after his death (brief of Benedict XIV, July 31, 1748). Of his numerous works (about 19 in print, 14 in MS, and many letters), the best edition is the *Opera omnia* edited by P. and G. *Ballerini (v.1–4 Verona 1729–32; v.5 Mantua 1741).

Bibliography: F. ROJO, "Ensayo bibliográfico de Noris, Bellelli y Berti," *Analecta Augustiniana* 26 (Rome 1963) 294–363. A. ZUMKELLER, LexThK² 7:1036.

[A. J. ENNIS]

NORMALITY

The condition of being in accordance with a norm. A problem relative to normality has arisen in recent times particularly in the life sciences. The difficulty of discovering normal traits has been compounded by an initial unsureness as to the way in which normality should be defined. Negatively, the normal is what is not abnormal, i.e., whatever functions at least sufficiently well to survive and to continue to function without requiring extraordinary assistance. Positively, two different norms have been proposed: the *average* norm, according to which the normal is what is characteristic of the greatest number; and the norm taken from the *best,* according to which the most perfect specimens are considered normal, all others to some extent falling short of normality. While each of the positive norms is easily reconciled with the negative, it is difficult to see how the positive norms are to be reconciled with

one another, and hence to discover whether a given trait, admittedly not the best, should be considered normal or a falling short of the norm.

Types of Solution. Logically, the question of normality can arise only in a context of comparability, which involves in turn a multiplicity of similar things and also a judge to make the comparison. In a Platonic conception of the universe, the Ideas exist as the norms of all things. On any other hypothesis it is necessary to discover the norm. If the mind of the judge is taken as the sole source of the norm, either the norm is purely arbitrary, and hence of no scientific value, or the question recurs as a question about the nature of the mind itself. The source of the norm is therefore to be sought in nature as well as in judgment.

Several recent writers have noted that the question of determining the normality of anything, whether of the member of a species, the function of an organ, the mental state of an individual, or the working of a society, arises only in a context of means and end relationships.

Aristotle's *Physics* (192b 8–200b 9) supplies the elements of a solution to the problem of normality in the doctrine of *causality, particularly *final causality. For Aristotle, *nature in this regard is "the principle and cause of motion and rest to those things, and those things only, in which she inheres primarily, as distinct from incidentally" (192b 21–23). Each natural thing, inasmuch as it has a definite structure, has a definite function possible to it. What is definite in nature is made so by final cause. Parts are parts of a whole that specifies them by constituting their end; organs exist for the sake of the function they perform; actions are defined by the end to which they are directed. Things have definite tendencies, and the definiteness of these tendencies is explainable in terms of their final causality.

What is normal, therefore, is what performs its function well: An organ is normal if it functions in such a way as to serve the whole body; an action is normal if it attains the end such actions are directed to attain. The end may be attained perfectly or imperfectly; but if it is attained, even badly or in an extraordinary way, the function is to that extent normal. Only an act that failed to achieve the end it was directed to could be called altogether abnormal. Thus the majority, over a long period of time, can be said to be normal at least to the extent of having what is necessary for mere survival; and in this way the average is the norm. And since it belongs to the very notion of the *end to be a *good, that which is most perfect, most in possession of its end, can also be said to be the norm. Thus the two norms, the average and the best, can be reconciled in the notion of the end.

Problems with Finality. There remains the difficulty of knowing the final causes of things. Certainly it is possible to infer from structure something of the nature of function; but no one has yet succeeded in defining even so common a natural being as a dog. The difficulty is particularly acute in the case of a human *person, since the person as such is unique and incapable of being defined. Negatively it may be quite clear that a person is functioning inadequately in some respect; but normality in the positive sense would seem to be impossible to determine absolutely in the case of the person. Only on the basis of actual functioning can the person be said to be normal in his personal traits; and since the potentialities of a person can never be known with complete adequacy, it is impossible to say to what extent he is realizing them. Admittedly, the natures of many things are unknown to man; but in many instances one does know what things are for; and to the extent that it is possible to discern means-end relationships, and to that extent alone, is it possible to judge the normality of anything.

Objections against the proposition that the final cause constitutes the norm in natural things are directed principally against the possibility of knowing the final cause. *Descartes considered that on account of God's omnipotence and the weakness of the human intellect, it is impossible for man to know the final causes of natural beings, so that "what are called final causes are of no use at all in Natural Philosophy" (*Meditations*, 4). Evolutionists consider the evolution of new species an obstacle to the doctrine of natures in things. And historicity would replace human nature with history. A different objection, springing from the common confusion of final and *efficient causality, need not be considered here.

The fact of human ignorance of the purposes of many things, and particularly of "external finality" (e.g., of the purpose of a frog), does not invalidate human knowledge of many instances of "internal finality" (e.g., of the purpose of a frog's eye), especially in biology, where the notion of adaptation, or organization for an end, is fundamental. Evolution, which rests upon the chance mutations of genes and selective reproduction, logically presupposes the existence of the "matter" of the new species in the genes of the old and also the basic lawfulness of nature, which Aristotle (195b 30–200b 9) has shown must underlie *chance. The fact that human beings to some extent "make themselves" and make their culture argues for *habit as "second nature" rather than against final cause. Explanation through final cause does not eliminate the usefulness of explanation through material, formal, or efficient cause. It merely makes evident the reason for the efficient cause's forming the matter in such a way as to bring about the desired result. Deficiency on the part of the other three causes, in turn, will result in partial or total interference with the attainment of a result that could be considered in reference to what was to be expected on the basis of the usual behavior of most individuals (the average norm) or on the basis of the behavior of those recognized as the best example of a group.

See also PERSONALITY; ABNORMAL PSYCHOLOGY.

Bibliography: T. PIACENTINI, EncCatt 8:1936–38. A. POMPEI, EncFil 3:937. G. AMBROSETTI and C. NEGRO, *ibid.* 934–937. M. K. O'HARA, "Toward a Norm for Normality," ProcAmCath PhilAs 36 (1962) 83–91. M. JAHODA, *Current Concepts of Positive Mental Health* (New York 1958). C. SMITH, *Contemporary French Philosophy: A Study in Norms and Values* (New York 1964). E. L. FACKENHEIM, *Metaphysics and Historicity* (Milwaukee 1961).

[M. K. O'HARA]

NORMANDY

Ancient province of France, bordered on the north and west by the English Channel, on the northeast by the Bresle River, which separates it from Picardy, and on the south by the region of the Vexin and the Epte River. After the French Revolution, Normandy was

Normandy, view of the 13th-century buildings at Mont-Saint-Michel.

divided into the modern *départements* of Seine-Maritime, Eure, Orne, Calvados, and Manche.

Part of the Roman Empire after its conquest by Julius Caesar, Normandy was occupied by the *Franks in the late 5th century and became a part of the Merovingian Kingdom. In the 4th century St. Mello and St. *Victricius of Rouen had introduced Christianity, which spread throughout the region. By the 6th century Normandy was divided into seven dioceses: *Rouen, *Bayeux, Coutances, Lisieux, Avranches, *Évreux, and Sées. Early Norman abbeys included *Saint-Ouen, *Fontenelle, *Jumièges, and *Mont-Saint-Michel. After falling to the Carolingians in 751, Normandy remained under their rule until the 9th-century attacks of the Vikings (*Normans). By the Treaty of Claire-sur-Epte in 911, the Carolingian Charles the Simple granted Normandy in fief to the Norman leader Rollo, who did homage for it and was baptized a Christian. This marks the beginning of the duchy of Normandy.

Little is known about the Normans before the 11th century except that they adopted Frankish customs and institutions and forged the most powerful feudal state in northern France. During the 11th century adventurous Normans established states in southern Italy and Sicily. In 1066 Duke *William I the Conqueror defeated Harold at Hastings and acquired the Anglo-Saxon kingdom. Upon William's death in 1087, Normandy went to his eldest son, Robert Curthose, and England to his second son, *William II Rufus. *Henry I, acceding to the English crown in 1100, invaded Normandy, and by 1106 it was his. Norman bishops and abbots reformed the English Church after 1066. At that time monastic houses of Normandy included *Bec, *Savigny, *La Trappe, *Saint-Pierre-sur-Dives, *Saint-Évroult, and *Fécamp. Except for a brief period after Henry's death (1135), Normandy was ruled directly by English kings until its loss by King *John in 1204 to the French King *Philip II Augustus. The conquest of Normandy was a significant step in the formation of the French

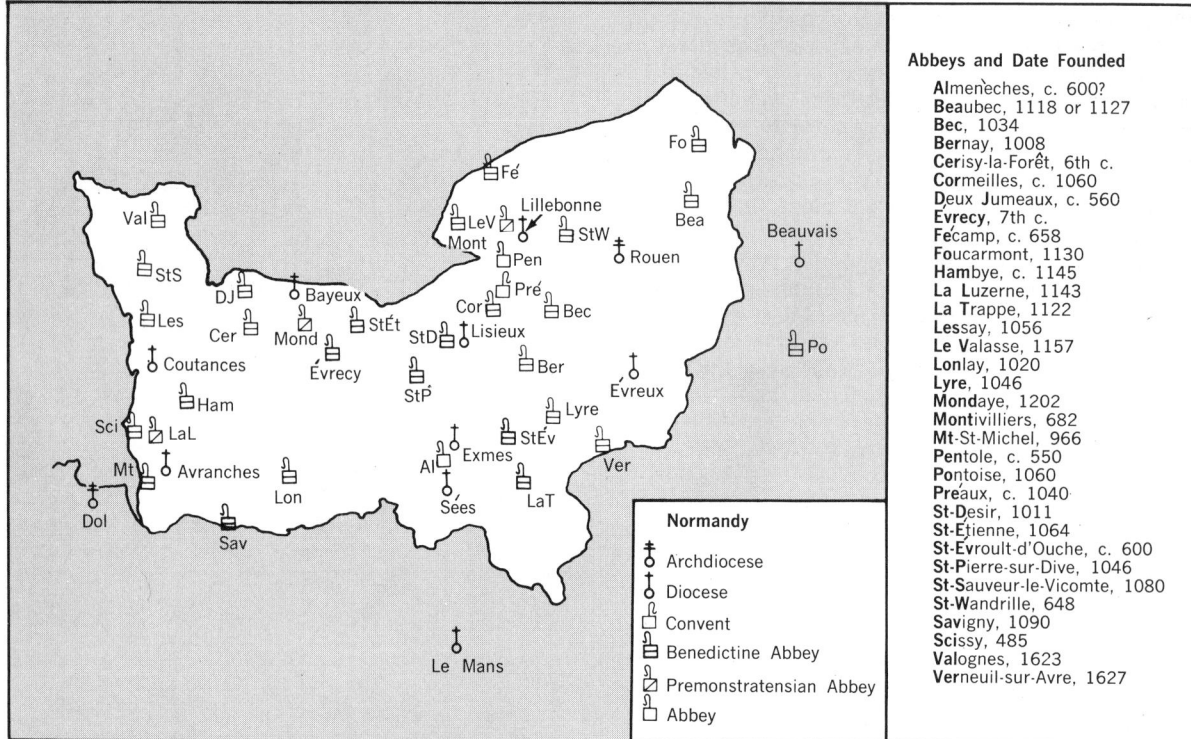

Abbeys and Date Founded

Almenèches, c. 600?
Beaubec, 1118 or 1127
Bec, 1034
Bernay, 1008
Cerisy-la-Forêt, 6th c.
Cormeilles, c. 1060
Deux Jumeaux, c. 560
Évrecy, 7th c.
Fécamp, c. 658
Foucarmont, 1130
Hambye, c. 1145
La Luzerne, 1143
La Trappe, 1122
Lessay, 1056
Le Valasse, 1157
Lonlay, 1020
Lyre, 1046
Mondaye, 1202
Montivilliers, 682
Mt-St-Michel, 966
Pentole, c. 550
Pontoise, 1060
Préaux, c. 1040
St-Désir, 1011
St-Etienne, 1064
St-Evroult-d'Ouche, c. 600
St-Pierre-sur-Dive, 1046
St-Sauveur-le-Vicomte, 1080
St-Wandrille, 648
Savigny, 1090
Scissy, 485
Valognes, 1623
Verneuil-sur-Avre, 1627

Normandy

‡ Archdiocese
† Diocese
Convent
Benedictine Abbey
Premonstratensian Abbey
Abbey

kingdom and enabled the French kings to model their institutions upon the more efficient ones that had developed in Normandy. During the Hundred Years' War, France and England again fought over Normandy. Although conceded to England in 1359, it was returned to France in 1360 by the Treaty of Brétigny. Until the invasion of Henry V in 1415, most of Normandy remained under French rule. But Henry's victories and internal French dissension led to the loss of Normandy, which was formalized by the Treaty of Troyes in 1420. Spurred by the victories and the martyrdom of *Joan of Arc, the French mounted repeated campaigns in the years after 1431. By 1450 the English had been driven from Normandy, and it was again ruled by the French; it has remained so to the present. From the 11th to the 15th century the Archdiocese of Rouen, which included all Normandy, held 14 provincial synods. During the Wars of Religion, Normandy remained Catholic. John *Eudes led the reform of the clergy there in the 17th century. The revolt of the Chouans was one of the factors that prompted the *Concordat of 1801. Since then Normandy has included the Archdiocese of Rouen, with the Dioceses of Bayeux, Coutances, Évreux, and Sées.

Bibliography: C. H. HASKINS, *Normans in European History* (Boston 1915; repr. New York 1959); *Norman Institutions* (Cambridge, Mass. 1918; repr. New York 1960). É. PERROY, *The Hundred Years' War* (New York 1951). M. DE BOÜARD et al., "Le Duché de Normandie," in F. LOT and R. FAWTIER, *Histoire des institutions françaises au moyen âge*, 3 v. (Paris 1957–62) 1:1–33. F. M. POWICKE, *The Loss of Normandy, 1189–1204* (2d ed. Manchester, Eng. 1961). **Illustration credit:** Fig. 1, French Embassy, Press and Information Division, New York City.

[B. LYON]

NORMANS

A generic term used to designate the migrant people who, from the 6th to the 11th century, spread by sea from Scandinavia over the whole western section of the northern hemisphere. Little is known of the Scandinavian populations in the prehistoric age. There are vestiges of the Ertebølle civilization in Denmark called *Kokkenmodings* (kitchen middens or refuse heaps); the Nøstvet civilization left a few remains in Norway and Skåne. Jutland's cultivated fields are similar to those of southern England. Trade with the Roman Empire was established through Pannonia and Poland, native amber being exchanged for bronze and metals. Burial under a mound or *tumulus* (*gravhoje*), figurative inscriptions on rocks, and the first runic alphabet characterized this Nordic civilization. In spite of the semantic kinship between *Got* (*Goths) and Götaland, one must not take literally the adage of *Jordanis, "Scandinavia, the mother of all Germanic peoples," except in the case of the Cimbri, *Vandals, and *Burgundians, who actually were from Jutland.

The Scandinavian people undertook great migratory movements during their development: after the migration of the Heruli (3d to 5th centuries), the first authentically Scandinavian raid was that made on the Frisian coastline by Hygelac, Beowulf's uncle, mentioned by *Gregory of Tours in 520. From this time forward the Vikings become, without interruption, a part of Western history, even though into the 7th century their activity was confined to waters adjoining their homeland. The unification of Sweden (6th to 9th centuries) and the migration of the Danes after the exodus of the Angles and the Jutes gave birth to new raids.

Of the many peoples who comprised the contemporary Scandinavian population it was the *Suiones* or *Svear* who gave their name to Sweden, and the *Dani* or *Dene,* to Denmark. It has long been accepted that the national groups, that is, the Danes, the Swedes, and the Norwegians, each swarmed to a particular sphere. Yet any distinction among the three groups is necessarily arbitrary, and any name or term used must be applied cautiously: e.g., the name *Dani* is commonly used as a synonym for Danes (Danois), but it is, in fact, used also as a generic name comparable to Normans and is often transposed into *Daci* (*see* DACIA). And so, in Dudo of Saint-Quentin one must distinguish between *Daci* or *Northmanni* (subjects of the king of Denmark, including Norwegians) and *Dacigeni* (natives of Denmark) and *Northguegigeni* (natives of Norway).

Vikings and Varangians. The term Vikings, now used to designate all those sea raiders who sailed the Western waters in their *snekkjur,* originally applied to the function, not to the people. (The etymology of the term is still uncertain: *vîkingr,* pirate; *vîk,* bay; *vising,* mariner.) Viking exploits constituted an honorable sport in Scandinavian society: on long winter evenings the skalds would transpose a Viking's narrative into poetic language. If the adventurous Norwegians succeeded the Celts on the great sea routes, it was the more highly developed Danes who undertook expeditions of any real scope. The Norwegians struck out for Arctic lands, while the Danes welded together the islands of the Sound, Jutland, and Skåne; the expansion of this state would propel the Danes in the 9th century to stretch on toward East Anglia and Northumbria in Britain, and into Frisia and the river basins of the Frankish coastline.

To the east—on the Baltic and on the Volga and Dnieper Rivers—the Scandinavian invaders were known under the name of Varangians (probably from the Russian *warjag,* tradesman; *war,* merchandise; *vârar,* pledge, oath). There, organized in merchant companies, they set up trading posts on the Baltic coastline. Thus, the terms Varangian and Viking both designate the men from the North who by different methods—some peaceful, others hostile—came into contact with the populations of the European continent from the 7th to the 10th century. At the beginning of the 9th century, Göttrik, King of Denmark, compelled the local merchants to relinquish the market of Reric on the Baltic to the town of Hedeby (Schleswig) in Jutland, thus establishing, properly speaking, "the era of the Vikings." Around the same time the Varangians reestablished a junction between the Baltic and the Caspian Seas, a step toward achieving their goal of a direct route to Baghdad. The first Varangian route, that of the Volga, united the Baltic seacoast, which was occupied by the Finnish tribe of the Cours (or Kurs), with the shores of the Caspian Sea, then peopled by hostile tribes. But the Danes and the Swedes continued to search for a shorter route back to the west, success crowning the undertaking of the Swedish King Oleph between 854 and 860, when the "great route of the Varangians to the Greeks" was opened, first by way of the Neman and the Dnieper Rivers, and then by way of the Dvina and the Dnieper. The Varangian chief Askold attacked the Khazars, seized Sembat, established the state of Kiev, and launched an assault on Constantinople (860). This Varangian advance into the Ukraine sometime between the departure of the *Avars and the invasion of the Patzinaks resulted in the pact of 874, which authorized the new commercial route opening on the Black Sea. Thus the route served as a hinge in a vast trading network joining the West, by way of the Rhine and the middle Danube, to Samarkand and the Middle East. In spite of the agreements of Emperor *Louis the German with the Danish princes and with Byzantine Emperor *Basil I, however,

any benefit western Europe derived from this route was ephemeral.

The first friction between the Vikings and western Europe dates back to the Frankish penetration into Frisia, Saxony, and Nordalbingia (or Ditmarsh). Yet it was only *c.* 840—the end of the Carolingian apogee, paralleled in England with the death of Kings *Offa of Mercia (d. 896) and *Egbert of Wessex (d. 839)— that the massive raids of the Vikings began. Satisfied at first with booty and tribute, after 865 they aspired to conquer and settle. The "grand army" successively attacked Britain's East Anglia, Northumbria, and Mercia, laying the foundations of the Danelaw; the resistance of the kings of Wessex, Ethelred I and *Alfred the Great, and the victory of Edington over Guthrum near the Danish camp of Chippenham set the southern limit of the Danish sphere of influence along Watling Street. Repeatedly injected with fresh troops, the remainder of the "grand army" moved on to attack western France between the Seine and the Meuse; their capture of prosperous Rouen (885) opened the route to Paris that was defended by Bishop Gozelin and by Odo, Count of Paris. In 886 Emperor Louis the Fat bribed the Vikings to retreat. But at the dawn of the 10th century, a strong detachment of Normans (the *Northmanni*) settled on the lower Seine and threatened the Frankish kingdom more than ever since efforts to Christianize the Scandinavians in the West had so far ended in failure: the mission of *Ansgar in Denmark, inaugurated in 823, retreated to Frisia; the missionary archbishopric of Hamburg (*see* BREMEN-HAMBURG) was sacked (845); the baptism of Guthrum in England brought no subsequent Christian baptisms. Only the state of Kiev was receptive to Christianity.

Norman States. The extraordinary dynamism of the Normans generated new political states, some unstable, but others destined to play a major role in the medieval world. As for *Kiev, the question of the origin of that principality and the ethnic element responsible for its organization has split Soviet and Swedish scholars. Objecting to the *Russian Primary Chronical* of *Nestor, the Soviets claim that Kiev was founded in the time of *Justinian I and ascribe its origin to Slavic tribes whose name (*Rhos, Rus*) was taken from the Ros River. The Swedes, however attribute it to the Varangians, holding that their local name came from the Finnish word *ruotsi,* men from the north, or from the Greek *rousios,* men of ruddy complexion, similar to the Anglo-Norman word *rufus.* Archeological excavations along the rivers and the critical publication of Eastern sources suggest a new interpretation according to which the Rus were a branch of Nordic stock, of the same lineage as the Varangians and the Normans, the last wave of the great Asiatic migration of the first millennium; thus the principality of Kiev had as a rough skeleton a Rus state that incorporated Slavic societies evolving from tribal to political status.

Other Varangian states had been established besides Kiev—those on the banks of the Sea of Azov (tributaries of the Khazars) and those on the banks of Lake Ladoga (the colony of Aldjborg, which eventually was subjugated to Kiev). Under Varangian influence, the word "Russian" soon came to mean a people, a state, a Christian rite, and a civilization essentially Slavic.

In contrast to the Kievan settlements, the Norwegian expansion, undertaken as it was by a small group of explorers followed by warriors, remained anarchical

Normans: (a) One of the three sides of the great carved stone at Jelling, Jutland, erected c. 980 by King Harold II Bluetooth commemorating his heroic deeds. (b) The restored 9th-century Viking boat unearthed near Oseberg, Norway. (c) Duke William of Normandy and four of his knights embark for the invasion of England, detail of the 11th-century "Bayeux Tapestry" preserved in the Musée de Tapisserie at Bayeux, France.

with the exception of a few settlements in bay areas. Their southwestern sea routes opened to them the western archipelagoes (Faeroes, the Hebrides, Sodor, Shetland, the Orkney Islands) and Ireland, although there the resident Gall-Gaidil (Foreign Irish) made a pact with the Celts to push back the Danes, and hence, after the battle of Clontarf in 1014 (*see* BRIAN BORU), Ireland remained a Celtic land except for the so-called "Danish Kingdoms" of the seacoast (i.e., Cork, Waterford, Dublin, and Limerick). After 1171 the Anglo-Norman conquest absorbed any trace of these non-assimilated principalities. The northwestern sea route led some audacious navigators first toward Iceland (*c.* 870), which became the refuge for banished chiefs, whose clans and genealogy were recorded in the *Landnâmabôk* (late 12th century), and then toward Greenland, not yet occupied by the Eskimos (e.g., the expedition of Eric the Red, 985). The Norwegians seem to have reached "Vinland," an assumption strengthened by the discovery (1965) of the "Vinland Map." They were the first Europeans to explore the northern islands; the recent excavations of Helge Ingstad at Lance-aux-Meadows, Labrador, further confirm the tradition of their early "discovery of America"—a tradition preserved in Norwegian lands until the end of the 14th century but not passed along as the common tradition of the West.

In general, every colonization by the Danes took on the aspect of a conquest made legitimate by a pact with the authorities of the country. Thus King Harold II Bluetooth ruled over Skåne, the straits, Jutland, and then a part of Norway. The Danelaw—a name covering the Nordic settlement in Great Britain—reflects Danish sovereignty in its organization, at once military and political; but at the same time it incorporates a *sui generis* society, on whose original features scholars do not agree. Thus, to the traditional thesis holding that the original Anglo-Saxon institutions in the area were destroyed and that the *sokemen* were of Scandinavian origin, R. H. C. Davis and P. H. Sawyer oppose the low number of pagan tombs, which seems to prove that the effective number of conquering *here* was too small to have replaced most of the preexisting institutions with their own. Clinging to the estuaries, the Danes formed unstable states in East Anglia, in Mercia, at York, etc., all of which served as prelude to the brilliant flowering of Norman principalities in the 11th century.

However, Danish hegemony must not be allowed to obscure the basic Viking solidarity or the intermixing of the conquering bands: from Dyflinn (Dublin) to Jorvîk (York), from Ruduborg (Rouen) and Holmgard (Novgorod), there was a never-ceasing interchange of warriors and merchants. In a world ready for expansion, Denmark and later Normandy were the catalysts. Thus it was Rollo, son of Ragnald, Jarl of Möre, a Danish subject of Norwegian blood, who settled at the mouth of the Seine *c.* 906. The pact of Saint-Clair-sur-Epte (911) made the lower Seine a region of Nordic colonization: by its surrender to the pirates, Neustria became *Normandy, defined by 933 as the territory of the second Lyonnaise with the seven cities of Rouen, Bayeux, Évreux, Lisieux, Sées, Coutances, and Avranches.

The unity of the *Anglo-Saxons, reestablished under the royal line of Wessex, was endangered in the period beginning in 990 by the raids of *Olaf I Tryggvessøn and Sweyn I Forkbeard of Denmark; in 1016 all of England fell to Sweyn's son, King *Canute of England and Denmark. This Viking thus became the head of a Danish Empire that extended from the Baltic to Iceland, of which England—up to his death (1035)—was the political, economic, cultural, and religious center. The short-lived domination of his sons, Harold I Harefoot and Hardecanute, and the accession of the Anglo-Norman Prince *Edward the Confessor (1042) prepared the way for the conquest of England in 1066 by the Duke of Normandy, *William the Bastard (the Conquerer), descendant of Rollo and progenitor of the kings of the Norman and Angevin lines.

Christianization of Scandinavia. Conversion to Christianity, inaugurated at the periphery of the Scandinavian world, reached Denmark in the middle of the 10th century (e.g., Harold II Bluetooth, Canute), Iceland *c.* 1000, Norway in the 11th century (King *Olaf II), and Sweden later. For a long time, pagan mores and customs continued alongside the new faith. But William the Conqueror fought at Hastings under the papal *banner, and previously the sons of *Tancred of Hauteville, seigneur of the Cotentin, had gone to southern Italy to fight the Moslems (1038). Once there the Normans served as auxiliaries of the *Lombards against the Byzantines, and then of the Byzantines against the Moors; William Iron Arm and *Robert Guiscard (the Crafty) carved out for themselves a fief in the Apennines and then, moving down to the plains, drove out the Greeks, supported Pope *Leo IX after having previously fought against him, and finally received from *Nicholas II the investiture of the Duchies of Apulia and Calabria (1059). They then moved on to the conquest of Sicily from the Arabs (1061–91). Although Robert Guiscard failed in his attempt to erect a Sicilian-Dalmatian Empire, his brother *Roger I of Sicily organized the new Sicilian state, and his son *Bohemund distinguished himself among the leaders of the First *Crusade (e.g., at the capture of Antioch, 1098). The same Norman line of Tancred of Hauteville ruled, in the 12th century, at Palermo (Roger II of Sicily was crowned king in 1130) and at Antioch. Just as Canute and William the Conqueror had posed as legitimate successors of the Anglo-Saxon kings and preserved in England a number of its ancestral customs, so also the Norman kings of Sicily and the Norman princes of Antioch took on the dress of Byzantium and manifested a remarkable propensity for assimilation. Thus the organizing spirit of a handful of Normans succeeded in uniting the most dissimilar ethnic elements. Everywhere they gave birth to an original and brilliant civilization, be it Anglo-Norman, Sicilio-Norman, or Normano-Syrian.

Bibliography: Sources. DUDO OF SAINT-QUENTIN, *De moribus et actis primorum Normanniae ducum,* ed. J. LAIR (new ed. Caen 1865). WACE, *Roman de Rou,* ed. H. ANDRESEN, 2 v. (Heilbronn 1877–79). WILLIAM OF JUMIÈGES, *Gesta Normannorum ducum,* ed. J. MARX (Rouen-Paris 1914). WILLIAM OF POITIERS, *Histoire de Guillaume le Conquérant,* ed. and tr. R. FOREVILLE (Paris 1952). ORDERICUS VITALIS, *Historia ecclesiastica,* ed. A. LE PRÉVOST, 5 v. (Paris 1838–55). *Anglo-Saxon Chronicle,* ed. and tr. B. THORPE, 2 v. (RollsS 23; 1861); ed. and tr. D. WHITELOCK et al. (London 1961). *Two of the Saxon Chronicles Parallel,* ed. J. EARLE and C. PLUMMER, 2 v. (Oxford 1892–99). *Landnámabók,* ed. F. JÓNSSON (Copenhagen 1900). *Altnordische Saga-Bibliothek,* 18 v. (Halle 1892–1929). H. KOHT, *Saga litteraturen* (Oslo 1938). *L'ystoire de li Normant et la chronique* *de Robert Viscart par Aimé moine du Mont-Cassin,* ed. J. J. CHAMPOLLION-FIGEAC (Paris 1835).

Literature. H. PRENTOUT, *Étude critique sur Dudon de Saint-Quentin* (Paris 1916). T. D. KENDRICK, *A History of the Vikings* (London 1930). L. M. LARSON, "The Political Policies of Cnut as King of England," AmHistRev 15 (1909–10) 720–743; *Canute the Great, 995–1035, and the Rise of Danish Imperialism* (new ed. New York 1931). C. OMAN, "The Danish Kingdom of York," *Archaeological Journal* 91 (1934) 1–21. O. MOBERG, *Olav Haraldsson, Knut den store och Sverige* (Lund 1941). P. NÖRDLUND, "Trelleborg," *Nordiske fortidsminder* 4.1 (Copenhagen 1948). C. G. SCHULTZ, "Aggersborg, Vikingelejren ved Limfjorden," *Fra nationalmuseets arbejdsmark* (1949) 91–108. H. ARBMAN and M. STENBERGER, *Vikingar i västerland* (Stockholm 1935). H. ARBMAN, *Svear i österviking* (Stockholm 1955). A. STENDER-PETERSEN, "Das Problem der ältesten byzantinisch-russisch-nordischen Beziehungen," *Relazioni del X Congresso internazionale di scienze storiche* 3 (Florence 1955) 165–188. E. OXENSTIERNA, *Die Nordgermanen* (Stuttgart 1957). L. MUSSET, "Relations et échanges d'influences dans l'Europe du Nord-Ouest," *Cahiers de civilisation médiévale* 1 (1958) 63–82. A. RUPRECHT, *Die ausgehende Wikingerzeit im Lichte der Runeninschriften* (Göttingen 1958). B. NERMAN, *Grobin-Seeburg: Ausgrabungen und Funde* (Stockholm 1958). D. C. DOUGLAS, "The Earliest Norman Counts," EngHistRev 61 (1946) 129–156; "The Rise of Normandy," *Proceedings of the British Academy* 33 (1947) 101–130; *William the Conqueror* (Berkeley 1964). R. A. SKELTON et al., *The Vinland Map and the Tartar Relation* (New Haven 1965). **Illustration credits:** Fig. 1*a*, The National Museum of Denmark. Fig. 1*b*, Norwegian Embassy Information Service. Fig. 1*c*, From *The Bayeux Tapestry,* edited by Sir Frank Stenton, published by Phaidon Press Ltd.

[R. FOREVILLE]

NORTH AFRICA, EARLY CHURCH IN

The Romans conquered Carthage in 146 B.C. and turned its territory into the *provincia Africana,* roughly northeast Tunisia, to which Tripolitania was later added. In 46 B.C. the Numidian kingdom of Juba was annexed (*Africa nova*) and, with *Africa vetus,* formed *Africa proconsularis.* In the year 40 Mauretania also was annexed, and two provinces were formed: Caesariensis, of which Caesarea was the capital, and Tingitana with Tingis as its capital. Numidia became a separate province in 198. Flourishing cities developed, and Roman civilization reached a high peak in the 2d and 3d centuries, with famed writers, both pagan and Christian. *Diocletian divided Proconsularis into three provinces: Zeugitana, Tripolitania, and Byzacena. Out of eastern Mauretania Caesariensis he carved Sitifensis, making Sitifis the capital. He placed the western part of Africa, Tingitana (today Morocco), under the jurisdiction of the Diocese of Spain. Tingitana depended on the ecclesiastical province of Mauretania Caesariensis, whereas a separate ecclesiastical province corresponded to each of the other six civil provinces by the 4th century, though the civil and ecclesiastical boundaries were not quite the same.

Christianity. Apostolic origin for the African church cannot be proved. Christianity came probably through Carthage, an important harbor, no later than the first half of the 2d century. The earliest dated event occurred on July 17, 180; 12 Christians of Scilli were martyred in Carthage. But as early as 197 *Tertullian (*Ad Scap.* 56) proudly appealed to the general Christian penetration of all ranks of society, which indicates that the evangelization had begun quite some time before. A striking fact is that the bishops were remarkably numerous, a condition explained by the fact that small dioceses were customary. By the year 225 at least 70 bishops were found in Proconsularis and Numidia; by 411, there were 470 Catholic bishoprics, and the number had grown to nearly 600 in 430. For this vast territory no metropolitan existed, except for Proconsularis, where the bishop of Carthage since the 3d century held metropolitan rights for all Africa. In the other provinces, the *primae sedis episcopus* was the bishop who exceeded the others by seniority.

Persecution under Decius. The Church seems to have been left in peace, until in the year 197, and especially in 202, a persecution took place, in which the most famous martyrs were *Perpetua and Felicity, with four companions. The recording of the events of their martyrdom is traceable possibly to Tertullian. Other works

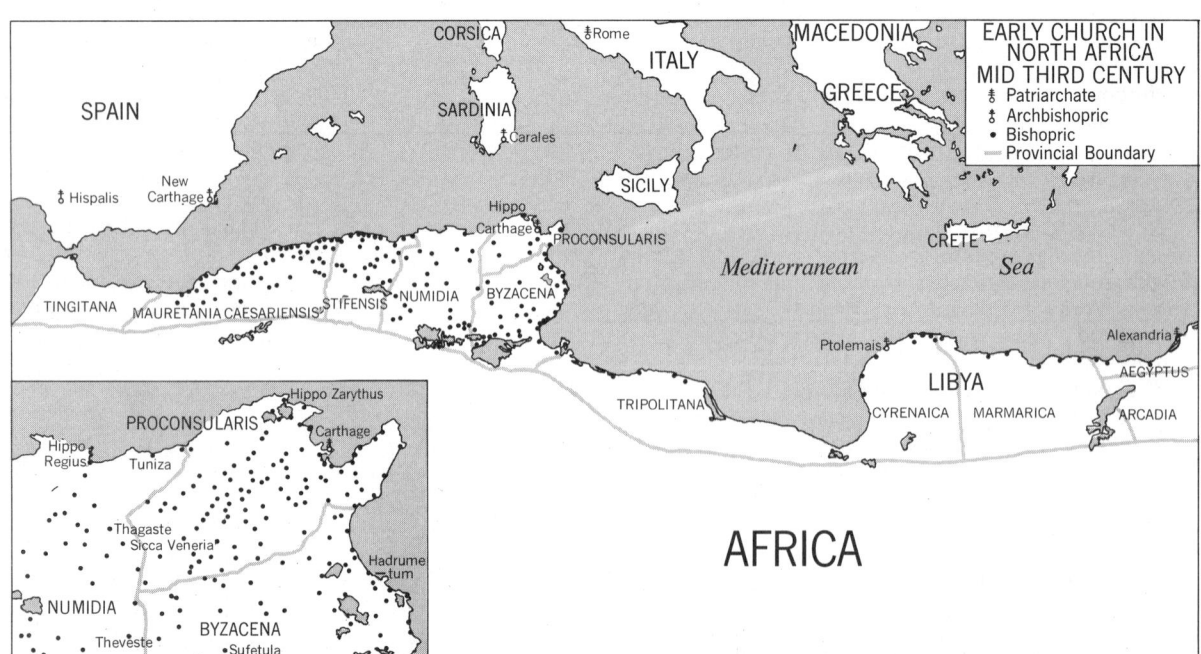

Fig. 1. Map showing the principal churches of North Africa in the early Christian period.

of this writer indicate that another persecution in 211–212 followed. But the greatest trial of the local church came in the persecution of *Decius, who in 249–250 demanded of all inhabitants of the empire a certificate of sacrifice. The bishop of Carthage, *Cyprian (249–258), testified to the large numbers of apostates (*De lapsis* 7–9). Some of these actually offered sacrifice (*sacrificati, thurificati*); others managed to obtain a false certificate to prove their compliance (*libellatici, acta facientes*). Yet, many suffered martyrdom.

After Decius' death in 251, a grave problem arose as to the treatment of the *lapsi.* Some confessors granted *libelli pacis* to the *lapsi,* but Cyprian demanded that the *sacrificati* and *thurificati* perform a lifelong penance. This occasioned a schism at Carthage, headed by the deacon Felicissimus and the priest Novatus.

Persecution under Valerian and Diocletian. St. Cyprian distinguished himself by his charitable work for those who suffered from famine and pestilence (252–254), and convoked various synods (255–256), where the question of the validity of baptism conferred by heretics was treated. Following the opinion of Tertullian (*De bapt.* 15) and many bishops of Asia, especially *Firmilian of Caesarea, Cyprian denied the validity of such baptism, thus setting a precedent for the *Donatists. He withstood Pope *Stephen I, who insisted on the Roman tradition, recognizing the validity of baptism conferred with the intention of doing the will of Christ. Though neither side yielded its viewpoint, no schism occurred, and the persecution of *Valerian (257–259) claimed the Pope and Cyprian as victims, along with many Africans, including those who were later called the *massa candida.*

The Emperor Gallienus restored peace to the Church; but it was rudely interrupted by the persecution of Diocletian in 295, which began in the army with the martyrdom of the young Maximilian at Theveste. Other martyrs were the veteran Typasius, the centurion Marcellus, and the standard-bearer Fabius. When the persecution became general in 303, it claimed victims in Africa, including the 19 women and 30 men of Abitina near Carthage. The peace of 313 was to bring grave problems to the African Church.

Donatism. During the 3d century, heresy in Africa had been represented by *Montanism, to which Tertullian adhered in his later life, and *Manichaeism (not strictly a Christian heresy). A movement arose, however, that united social and religious elements, renewed the errors of Tertullian and Cyprian, and caused havoc in the African church for more than a century. It was known as *Donatism. The Bishop of Carthage, Mensurius, died in 311. The Archdeacon Caecilianus, his successor, had made enemies by his previous severity. These claimed that one of his episcopal consecrators, Felix of Aptungi, had been a *traditor,* that is, guilty of the sin of having given up the sacred books during the persecution, and thus he was incapable of validly administering a Sacrament. The church was for them a society of saints, in which authority and spiritual effectiveness depended on personal sanctity. Catholics were considered *traditores;* on conversion, freely or by force, to Donatism, baptism was repeated, and the other Sacraments given by Catholics, including the Eucharist, were treated with contempt. Donatism spread rapidly, in spite of the Emperor Constantine's persecution of the sect. Donatist doctrine was condemned first by a Roman ecclesiastical sentence in 313, and then by the council at Arles in 314.

Donatus (d. *c.* 355) was the first outstanding schismatic bishop of Carthage; under him the sect spread into other provinces, especially Numidia, which became its stronghold. In 347, a group of nomadic workers from the south, called Circumcellions, was used by Optatus, the Donatist Bishop of Bagai, against the Roman troops who tried to uproot the schism. Later, these workers adopted Donatism as a convenient ally to oppose the Roman Empire, which hindered their desire for absolute freedom from restraint.

*Optatus of Milevis and St. *Augustine narrate sad details of the horrors perpetrated by the Donatists, especially the Circumcellions, against Catholic priests and monks. The sect increased so rapidly that a Donatist council of 336 was attended by 270 bishops. After the death in exile of Donatus, he was succeeded by Parmenianus (d. 391), who not only displayed organizing activity, but wrote anti-Catholic works. Refutations by Optatus of Milevis and Augustine and efficient pastoral opposition under the Catholic Bishop of Carthage, Aurelius (392–430), took effect. The Donatists themselves split into various sects, against whom Augustine sharply pressed their inconsistencies and elaborated his theology of the Sacraments.

The Emperor Honorius aided the Catholic cause, and in 411 a meeting was held at Carthage, at which 286 Catholic and 284 Donatist bishops were in attendance. Bishops from both sides were allowed to present their viewpoints, and after a 3-day discussion, the victory of the Catholics was announced by the imperial representative. In 412 the Emperor ordered the schismatics to return to the Catholic Church, threatening the disobedient with confiscation, corporal punishment, and deportation. After some hesitation Augustine admitted the wisdom of the state's intervention against the destructive activities of the Donatists and Circumcellions; when many returned to the Church, from which fear of the wild fanatics had held them, the schism was greatly weakened. Yet, even Pope *Gregory I complained in the 6th century that the error was not yet completely eradicated in Africa.

St. Augustine and Pelagianism. Augustine, himself a convert from Manichaeism, devoted a series of brilliant works as priest and bishop to a refutation of Donatism when another error called for response, namely, *Pelagianism. With his collaborator Celestius, Pelagius had denied original sin and claimed that man could perform good acts and avoid sin without internal grace. Both came to Carthage in 410, but Pelagius left at once for Palestine. Paulinus of Milan attacked the errors of Celestius, and upon his refusal to retract Celestius was excommunicated by the council of Carthage in 411. Augustine saw the fundamental rejection of Christianity implied in the heresy and brought out the works that earned him the title of "Doctor of Grace." Though Pelagius was declared orthodox by the Council of Diospolis in 415, provincial councils at Carthage and Milevis in 416 renewed the condemnation of Pelagianism, and when Pope Innocent I concurred, Augustine exclaimed: *causa finita est* (*Serm.* 131.10).

Pope *Zosimus (417–418), on receiving professions of orthodoxy from the two heretics, blamed the African bishops for excessive zeal in condemning men who admitted the necessity of grace. The African answer was a general council at Carthage in May 418, inspired by Augustine, in which the errors of the heretics were laid bare. Zosimus then condemned Pelagianism, but the stubborn opposition of *Julian of Eclanum obliged Augustine to write several further tracts dealing with marriage and grace, as well as 12 books *Contra Julianum.* In 426–427 he composed his *De gratia et libero arbitrio* and *De correptione et gratia* for the monks of Hadrumetum who challenged human liberty in relation to predestination and questioned the gift of perseverance. Thus *Semi-Pelagianism met its chief refutation from the African Church.

Monasticism. The monastic movement was introduced into Africa in its cenobitic form by Augustine in 388 on his return from Italy. Previously, individual

Young man holding a Cross, carved and painted grave stele found at Sheykh 'Ibâda (Antinoë) in Egypt, late 4th century, now in a private collection.

monks and virgins, including Donatist sisters, had existed in Africa, but no monastery is recorded before 388. Augustine propagated the movement, as convert, priest, and bishop, living with a group of ascetics. His sister became superior of a convent of nuns at Hippo, and Augustine's monastery provided 10 bishops for other churches, who transplanted the monastic life to their new dioceses.

Even during the period when the *Vandals ruled in Africa (429–534) monasticism flourished in both clerical and lay circles. The life of *Fulgentius of Ruspe (d. *c.* 533) is witness to this, for he followed Augustine's example and practiced a monastic way of life as layman, priest, and bishop. Monasteries are found as far east as Tripolitania and as far west as Mauretania Caesariensis before, during, and after the Vandal occupation. These barbarians had crossed from Spain in 429, besieged Hippo in the last days of St. Augustine, and captured Carthage in 439. By treaty with the Emperor *Valentinian III in 442 they became the recognized masters of Zeugitana, Byzacena, and part of Numidia. After the death of this Emperor in 455 they seized the two Mauretanias, though their control there was nominal, owing to the bellicose nature of the native Mauri.

Of the six Vandal kings, all Arians, who ruled in Africa, Geiseric, Huneric, and Thrasamund persecuted the Church severely, concentrating on the higher clergy. The first two kings nearly succeeded in extirpating the Catholic bishops in favor of the *Arians. Hence in Zeugitana under Geiseric (429–477) the number of Catholic bishops was reduced from 164 to 3. Yet, in his desire to make a favorable treaty with the Emperor *Zeno, Geiseric in 475 allowed the return of the Catholic exiles. His son Huneric (477–484) forced all the Catholic bishops of Africa to come to Carthage in 484 for a discussion with the Arians, after which he sent them into exile, deporting the bishops of Zeugitana to Corsica and others into the African desert. Five hundred clerics of Carthage were scourged and exiled. Later Huneric dispatched some 5,000 Catholics including many clerics to exile among the savage Mauri and tried systematically to destroy monastic life in Africa by ordering that all monasteries of men and women, together with their inhabitants, be given to the Mauri. His death put an end to the persecution, and King Gunthamund (484–496) allowed the exiled bishops to return (494). King Thrasamund (496–523) conducted the most effective persecution. No bishops could be elected, and when this decree was violated in Byzacena, 120 bishops were exiled to Sardinia, from which they returned only after his death, when King Hilderic (523–530) granted a period of peace for the Church. The last king, Gelimer, was conquered by the army of *Justinian I under Belisarius in 534.

Byzantine Influence. Under the Byzantines some of the Church's ancient splendor returned; capable theologians such as Ferrandus of Carthage and *Facundus of Hermiane and frequent councils gave it a part in the affairs of the universal Church. In the dispute over the *Three Chapters, the African bishops refused to subscribe to the condemnation rendered by Justinian and the *Council of Constantinople II, and even excommunicated Pope *Vigilius. African monks and bishops were among those who were exiled for their opposition.

Byzantine occupation, however, did not bring an enduring peace to Africa either internally or externally. The Mauri inflicted many defeats on Byzantine arms, and many Christians, including 70 monks with their abbot Donatus, fled to Europe about the year 570. Internally, the corruption of civil officials went unchecked and revolts were frequent. Yet many Mauri became Christians. In the 7th century the Byzantine emperors favored *Monothelitism, which was rejected by many African monks under the inspiration of St. *Maximus Confessor. When in 638 the Emperor *Heraclius with his *Ecthesis* imposed Monothelitism on the whole Church, most Africans refused to sign the document and in 645 revolted against his successor Constans II.

African ecclesiastical dissension prepared the way for the Arab invasions that began with a first raid in 643. The Arabs captured Carthage in 698, and took the last Byzantine stronghold at Septem, or Ceuta, in 709. The Mohammedans gradually brought about the extinction of Christianity, first by a rapid conversion of the volatile Mauri, then by a process of attrition, reducing the number of bishoprics to three for all Africa in the time of Pope *Gregory VII. They had disappeared entirely by the 13th century.

Bibliography: A. AUDOLLENT, DHGE 1:705–861. G. BARDY, *Catholicisme* 1:186–191. L. DUCHESNE, *L'Église au sixième siècle* (Paris 1925). G. BARDY et al., Fliche-Martin v.3, 4, 5. J. GAUDEMET, *L'Église dans l'Empire Romain* (Paris 1958). G. KRÜGER, LexThK² 1:175–176. C. A. JULIEN and C. COURTOIS, eds., *Histoire de l'Afrique du Nord* (2d ed. Paris 1956). B. H. WARMINGTON, *The North African Provinces from Diocletian to the Vandal Conquest* (Cambridge, Eng. 1954). C. COURTOIS, *Les Vandales et l'Afrique* (Paris 1955). W. H. FREND, Reallex AntChr 4:128–147. J. J. GAVIGAN, *De vita monastica in Africa Septentrionali* (Turin 1962). E. L. GRASMÜCK, *Coercitio: Staat und Kirche im Donatistenstreit* (Bonn 1964). **Illustration credit:** Fig. 2, Gertrud Pappert, courtesy Villa Hügel, Essen, Germany.

[J. J. GAVIGAN]

NORTH AMERICAN COLLEGE

A pontifical institution in Rome, Italy, that serves as a residence, under seminary discipline, for ecclesiastical students training for the diocesan priesthood of the U.S. Only those men specifically designated by their bishops are admitted to its student body.

Foundation and History. Founded on Dec. 8, 1859, by Pope Pius IX, on the recommendation of Abp. Gaetano *Bedini, the College was housed from 1859 to 1953 in a former Visitandine convent at Via dell'Umiltà. A department for graduate students already ordained was established in 1933 in the Casa San Giovanni on the Janiculum Hill. When the College acquired a new home on the Janiculum in 1953, the graduate department moved into the original college, renamed Casa Santa Maria dell'Umiltà. Pius IX had loaned this property to the American bishops in 1859. On July 26, 1948, Pius XII, as an "act of deference" to the American hierarchy, presented it to them outright.

From 1859 to 1932 the undergraduates attended classes at the Urban College of Propaganda Fide. Academic affiliation was transferred in 1932 to the Gregorian University.

For a quarter century after its inauguration, the American College was financially insecure. Nevertheless it quickly became the American Catholic headquarters in Rome, and its rectors assumed a role of increasing influence as spokesmen for the American Church. During Vatican Council I (1869–70), 18 American archbishops and bishops lived and held conferences in the College. On Sept. 20, 1870, papal Rome surrendered to the invading armies of the King of Italy. A few days before the final siege 13 students from the American College proffered their services to the little papal army. Pius IX gratefully refused, reminding them that they were called to a nobler warfare.

Anticlerical policies of the Kingdom of Italy directly affected the North American College in March 1884, when the Italian government moved to confiscate the College buildings, still owned by the Congregation of Propaganda Fide. Informed of this threat, Cardinal John McCloskey, of New York, immediately sought the aid of the U.S. government. President Chester A. Arthur, by his prompt personal intervention, averted the peril.

On Oct. 25, 1884, Pope Leo XIII, by the brief *Ubi Primum,* decreed the long-delayed canonical establishment of the American College, and bestowed on it the rank "pontifical" (i.e., papal). Increased registration obliged the College superiors to add a new wing to the property in 1901. Two years before, the handsome Villa Santa Caterina at Castel Gandolfo had been purchased as a summer home.

World War I vexed but did not impede the College. World War II forced it to close. In May 1940, when it became apparent that Italy would enter the struggle, the students were sent home to finish their studies. During much of the war the College proper and the Villa Santa Caterina harbored exiled children of Italian colonials. In 1943 and 1944 the Villa and the Casa San Giovanni gave shelter to as many as 1,600 refugees and their possessions.

When the College finally reopened on Sept. 4, 1948, the students lived at the Villa Santa Caterina pending the rehabilitation of the Umiltà property. That same year work commenced on a new college near St. Peter's Basilica, in a section of the Janiculum Hill that belongs to Vatican City. Pius XII came in person to dedicate the completed buildings on Oct. 14, 1953. Pius IX had celebrated Mass in the original College on Jan. 29, 1860. Pope John XXIII, participating in the centennial observance of Oct. 11, 1959, became the third pope to visit the American institution.

Administration. The American College is under the double direction of the pope, represented by a cardinal patron, and a board of U.S. bishops. The rector, the resident superior, is chosen by the pope from a list of three priests proposed by the board. The following men have held this post: Bernard Smith, OSB (1859–60, temporary), William George McCloskey (1860–68); Francis Silas Marean Chatard (1868–78); Louis Edward Hostlot, né Hasslocher (1878–84); Augustine Joseph Schulte (1884–85, temporary); Denis Joseph O'Connell (1885–95); William Henry O'Connell (1895–1901); Thomas Francis Kennedy (1901–17); Charles Aloysius O'Hern (1917–25); Eugene Sebastian Burke, Jr. (1925–35); Ralph Leo Hayes (1935–44); James Gerald Kealy (1945–46); Martin John O'Connor (1946–64); and Francis F. Reh (1964–   ).

During its first century the College registered 2,500 undergraduates (of whom over 1,700 were eventually ordained) and 250 graduate priests. Alumni have served in all types of work customary to diocesan clergy. Furthermore, between 1859 and 1959, 116 of them were named bishops. Seven of these have been created cardinals: John M. Farley, William H. O'Connell, Dennis J. Dougherty, Edward Mooney, Samuel A. Stritch, Francis J. Spellman, and Albert G. Meyer.

In continuing to be Rome's chief American Catholic center, the College has played host to many noted guests: innumerable prelates; five U.S. presidents (W. H. Taft, W. Wilson, H. S. Truman, D. Eisenhower, J. F. Kennedy); and many celebrities, including Mark Twain, G. K. Chesterton, Will Rogers, and Alfred E. Smith. It has also had the duty, since 1870, of arranging papal audiences for visitors from the U.S. Its Office for Papal Audiences provides this service for as many as 50,000 travelers each year.

Bibliography: R. F. McNamara, *American College in Rome, 1855–1955* (Rochester, N.Y. 1956).

[R. F. MC NAMARA]

NORTH AMERICAN MARTYRS

The word martyr has a very precise meaning in ecclesiastical literature. Those who bear the name do so only when a rigorous inquiry by the Church has attested to the fact that hatred of the faith motivated those who killed them. North America honors eight martyrs; all were of European and French origin and belonged to the missions of Canada, then called New France. Six of them were priests of the Society of Jesus: Isaac Jogues, Antoine Daniel, Jean de Brébeuf, Gabriel Lalemant, Charles Garnier, and Noël Chabanel. The other two,

Martyrdom of the Jesuits Jean de Brébeuf and Gabriel Lalemant by the Iroquois in Canada, 1649.

René Goupil and Jean de la Lande, were *donnés,* lay assistants, who, without binding themselves by religious vows, worked for the Jesuit missions. Unsalaried, they received food, shelter, and help in case of illness from the fathers. All the martyrs died between Sept. 29, 1642 and Dec. 9, 1649. They were beatified on June 21, 1925, and canonized June 29, 1930; their feast day is September 26. In terms of time and place of martyrdom, they make up two groups.

First Group. This included Goupil, Jogues, and La Lande, who were martyred near Auriesville, N.Y., at Ossernenon, seat of the Mohawk tribe in the U.S.

Goupil. He was born at Anjou, France, May 13, 1608; as a youth he entered the Jesuit novitiate in Paris, but was forced to leave because of deafness. He then studied surgery at the Orléans hospital; in 1640, he arrived in Canada, where he was assigned as *donné* to the Sillery mission near Quebec. As the infirmarian at Sillery and at the Hôtel-Dieu of Quebec, he set out for Huronia. When the flotilla taking him there fell into Iroquois hands, he was captured and underwent the rigors of barbaric torture. An Iroquois killed him with an axe stroke on Sept. 29, 1642, for having made the sign of the cross over a child. The first of this group of martyrs, he is the only one whose life has been told by another martyr, Jogues. The original of this document, which was recently translated into English, is kept in the archives of the College of St. Marie of Montreal. Catholic doctors of the U.S. honor Goupil as the first of their profession to have crossed the Adirondacks.

Jogues and La Lande. Jogues was born in Orléans, France, Jan. 10, 1607. In 1636, after ordination on July 2, he arrived in Quebec and was assigned to the Huron missions. He was taken with Goupil in 1642 as he was returning to the missions after a visit to Quebec, and he was subjected to all the cruelties that the Iroquois perpetrated on their prisoners. During his captivity he baptized 60 children and in midwinter conducted his annual retreat before an outdoor cross. He was ransomed by the Dutch of Fort Orange (Albany) in 1643, and he escaped to New York and thence to France. Urban VIII granted him a dispensation to celebrate Mass, despite his mutilated left hand, saying: "It would be shameful for a martyr of Christ not to drink the blood of Christ." In Canada again in the spring of 1644, Jogues was entrusted with a brief peace mission to the Iroquois. He departed Sept. 24, 1646, for Ossernenon, but a Mohawk war party captured him; on October 18 Jogues was tomahawked and the following day his companion La Lande suffered the same fate. Jogues was known to have desired the grace of martyrdom; so when the news of the double martyrdom reached Quebec in the spring of 1647, his fellow missionaries celebrated a Mass of Thanksgiving rather than one of Requiem for the repose of his soul.

Second Group. This group—composed of Daniel, De Brébeuf, Lalemant, Garnier, and Chabanel—met death within the actual confines of Canada, the first three were killed by the Iroquois, and Chabanel by a Huron apostate.

Daniel. This first martyr of Huronia was born in Dieppe, France, in 1601 and became a Jesuit novice at 20. He arrived at Cape Breton in 1632 and went to Quebec the following year. In 1634 he left for Huronia, where he remained, except for 2 years during which he served as director of the Huron seminary in Quebec. On

Isaac Jogues, martyred by the Mohawks at Auriesville, N.Y., 1646.

July 4, 1648, he had just celebrated Mass when the mission of St. Joseph was overrun by Iroquois. After ministering to the wounded and baptizing some of them, he was struck by arrows and shot; and his trampled and desecrated body was then cast into the fire that consumed the chapel.

De Brébeuf and Lalemant. Brébeuf was born at Condé-sur-Vire, Normandy, France, March 25, 1593, and had already been ordained when he arrived in Canada, June 1625. The English occupation of Quebec in 1629 necessitated his return to France, but he was able to get back to his mission in 1633 and Huronia became his field of apostolate. Lalemant, born in 1610, was the nephew of Revs. Charles and Jerome Lalemant and had long dreamed of the Canadian missions. In 1646 he arrived at Quebec; but because of ill health, it was 2 years before he reached the Huron missions. There on March 16, 1649, an Iroquois band attacked the town of St. Ignace and captured Brébeuf and Lalemant, who were tied to stakes and underwent one of the worst martyrdoms ever recorded in history. Brébeuf suffered for 3 hours before dying; Lalemant died the following morning, March 17. The *Relation* states: "Before their death both their hearts were torn out through an opening made in their chest; these barbarians feasted on them inhumanly, drinking their warm blood which they drew from its source with a sacrilegious hand. While still full of life, pieces of their thighs, calves, and arms were removed by the butchers who roasted them on coals and ate them in their sight."

Garnier. He was born in Paris in 1605 and joined the Society of Jesus at 19; in 1636 he arrived in Canada, where he was assigned to the Huron mission. After devoting himself to it for 13 years, he was sent to St. Jean in 1649, when Fort St. Marie was abandoned. During an Iroquois attack on St. Jean, Garnier exhorted his faithful to flee but to keep the faith. He remained at his post and was first struck down by two bullets. Then, according to the *Relation,* "The Father received shortly thereafter two axe strokes on both temples which penetrated the brain." He died on Dec. 7, 1649.

Chabanel. He was born at Saugues in southern France, Feb. 7, 1613, entered the novitiate in 1630, and arrived in Canada in 1643. By education and temperament, this brilliant professor of rhetoric in France was far removed from the Indian ways of living and acting, and he had no aptitude for the Huron language. But in order to protect his missionary vocation, he made the vow of stability, with his superiors' permission. After serving with Garnier at St. Jean (with the Petuns?), he was on his way to Fort St. Marie II (Christian Island) when he was killed by an apostate Huron near the Nottawasaga River in Ontario, Dec. 8, 1649. He had expressed the desire to be a *martyrem in umbra,* a martyr in obscurity, unknown and forgotten. His death at first appeared to be shrouded in mystery, but in the *Relation* of 1650, Rev. Paul Ragueneau wrote: "We learned from very reliable testimony that Father Noël Chabanel was put to death by the apostate Huron whom we suspected. He himself admitted it and added that he had committed the murder in hatred of the faith, because he saw, in his words, all the evils befalling him and his family since he had embraced the faith."

Cult of the Martyrs. In Canada the belief that these missionaries were martyrs in the strict sense of the word led Rageneau, Jesuit superior at Quebec, to set up a dossier on the subject. This *Manuscript,* or *Mémoire,* of 1652, the original of which is kept at the College of St. Marie in Montreal, contains the text of the *Relations* and the deposition of trustworthy witnesses on the lives and circumstances of death of the martyrs. They were equally known and venerated in Europe, where the *Relations des Jésuites* (1648–49), telling of the death of Brébeuf and Lalemant, was translated into Latin and Flemish. The *Relazione* of Rev. Francesco Bressani (Florence 1653) made them known in Italy. But events such as the society's suppression in 1773, the French Revolution in 1789, and the political changes of the times, in both Canada and the U.S., contributed to the martyrs' oblivion. Eventually, however, the cult of the martyrs, who had always had their devotees in American lands, was revived as a consequence of the Jesuit's return to Canada in 1842; of Edmund B. O'Callaghan's discovery of the *Relations,* a subsequent edition of which was published by the Canadian government in 1858 and later by R. G. Thwaites; and of the historical research of Felix Martin, John Gilmary Shea, Francis Parkman, and others. In 1912, following requests to the Holy See by the hierarchies of Canada and the U.S., the martyrs' cause was introduced; beatification followed in 1925 and canonization in 1930. Annually thousands of pilgrims visit the two sanctuaries erected in their honor: at Auriesville, the Ossernenon of old, where Goupil, Jogues, and La Lande are venerated; and at Midland, Ontario, near the site of old Fort St. Marie of the Hurons, commemorating Daniel, De Brébeuf, Lalemant, Garnier, and Chabanel.

[L. POULIOT]

NORTH CAROLINA

Located in southeastern U.S., one of the 13 original colonies, admitted to the Union in 1789. The state is bounded on the north by Virginia, on the east by the Atlantic Ocean, on the south by South Carolina and Georgia, and on the west by Tennessee.

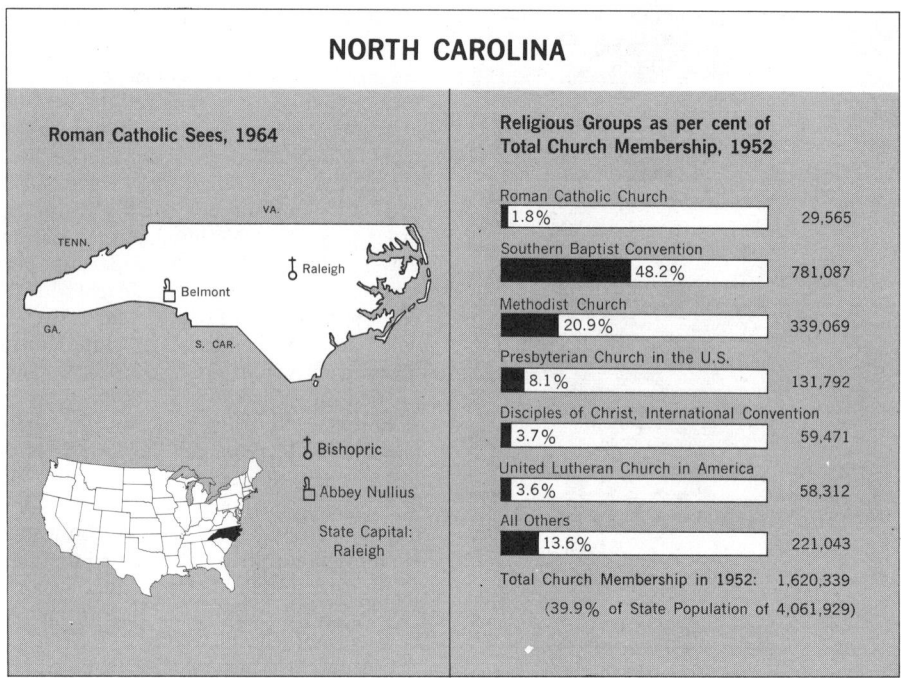

NORTH CAROLINA

Roman Catholic Sees, 1964

Religious Groups as per cent of Total Church Membership, 1952

Roman Catholic Church	1.8%	29,565
Southern Baptist Convention	48.2%	781,087
Methodist Church	20.9%	339,069
Presbyterian Church in the U.S.	8.1%	131,792
Disciples of Christ, International Convention	3.7%	59,471
United Lutheran Church in America	3.6%	58,312
All Others	13.6%	221,043

Total Church Membership in 1952: 1,620,339
(39.9% of State Population of 4,061,929)

† Bishopric
♙ Abbey Nullius
State Capital: Raleigh

Church-membership statistics were compiled by the Bureau of Research and Survey of the National Council of the Churches of Christ in the U.S.A.

History. After several unsuccessful attempts at colonization dating from 1584, a permanent English settlement was planted in North Carolina about 1653. In 1663 the territory was granted to eight lords proprietors, who practiced discrimination against persons not of the Anglican communion. In 1729 North Carolina became a royal colony, whereupon discrimination ceased, except that only Anglican clergymen could witness marriages until 1778 and all who denied the truth of Protestantism were debarred from office until 1835. With the establishment of the Catholic hierarchy in 1789, North Carolina formed part of the Diocese of *Baltimore, Md. Information about Catholics in the state is vague until shortly before this time, when Alexander and Margaret Gaston settled at New Bern, N.C. These early Catholic inhabitants were the parents of William *Gaston, state senator, congressman, and associate justice of the state supreme court, who was chiefly responsible for the enactment of complete religious freedom in 1835. In 1820 North Carolina became a part of the Diocese of *Charleston, S.C., and after 1838 Fayetteville was the residence of the priest who served the entire eastern part of the state. Despite strong and often violent anti-Catholic feeling, churches were erected at Mountain Island (1843) and Charlotte (1851).

On March 3, 1868, Pius IX established the Vicariate Apostolic of North Carolina, with Wilmington as its center. In the territory some 700 Catholics were cared for by three priests. The first vicar, James *Gibbons (later cardinal), gained many converts. In 1869 he brought Sisters of Mercy from Charleston to Wilmington; and in 1876, Benedictine monks from Latrobe, Pa., to Garibaldi (later Belmont). The first three vicars could not devote their exclusive attention to North Carolina. The Abbot of Belmont, Leo Haid, OSB, was named (1887) fourth vicar. In 1892 the motherhouse of the Sisters of Mercy was transferred to Belmont. Father

Thomas Price founded an orphanage at Nazareth and a society of diocesan priests, the Apostolic Band, for missions to non-Catholics. Catholic schools and hospitals were opened. In 1910 Pius X constituted eight counties as the Abbey Nullius of *Belmont. On Dec. 12, 1924, Pius XI erected the vicariate into the Diocese of *Raleigh.

Population. The state population in 1952 was 4,061,-929, of whom Catholics constituted 0.7 per cent; Protestants, 39 per cent; Jews, 0.1 per cent; and all others, 61.2 per cent (*see* CHURCH MEMBERSHIP, U.S.). In 1961 the total population of the state had increased to 4,556,155, with Catholics forming 0.9 per cent.

Education. In 1964 the Catholic educational system in the state embraced *Belmont Abbey College, a 4-year institution, and Sacred Heart Junior College for women, both in Belmont; 11 high schools, caring for 1,295 students; and 55 elementary schools, with a total enrollment of 10,682 pupils. An additional 7,285 students received religious instruction on released-time programs.

Church-State Relations. References to and provisions affecting religion are incorporated in the state constitution and in acts of the legislature and the judiciary.

Constitution. North Carolina is governed by the Constitution of 1868, as amended. The preamble states that the people are "grateful to Almighty God the Sovereign Ruler of nations" and it acknowledges "our dependence upon Him for the continuance of those blessings to us."

"All persons have a natural and inalienable right to worship Almighty God according to the dictates of their own conscience, and no human authority should, in any case whatever, control or interfere with the rights of conscience" (art. 1, sec. 26). Members of the general assembly and the governor must take an oath or affirmation of office (art. 2, sec. 24; art. 3, sec. 4).

Property used for religious purposes and personal property not exceeding $300 in value may be exempt from taxation (art. 5, sec. 5). Every office-holder must take an oath or affirmation that ends with the words, "So help me God" (art. 6, sec. 7). Persons who deny the existence of God are disqualified from holding office (art. 6, sec. 8).

Article 12, sec. 1, states that "all persons who may be averse to bearing arms, from religious scruples, shall be exempt therefrom."

Marriage and Divorce. Marriages of men and women under 16 are forbidden except in certain cases of pregnancy. The consent of parents is needed for persons under 18. A license and blood test are required. Common-law marriages are not recognized.

Marriages are void if either party is bound by a prior subsisting marriage; if parties are related by blood in any degree of the direct line, up to but not including first cousins; if a person is under age, physically impotent, or incapable of contracting from want of will or understanding. Marriages may be annulled on the following grounds: prohibited marriages; nonage; marriage contracted with the belief that the female is pregnant if there is a separation within 45 days and lasting for 1 year and if no child is born within 10 lunar months of separation.

The grounds of absolute divorce are adultery, natural impotency at marriage and after, pregnancy of the wife by another at the time of marriage without the knowledge of her husband, continuous separation for 2 years, separation for 5 or more years without cohabitation by reason of incurable insanity of one spouse, and crimes against nature. There are no restrictions on remarriage after divorce. *See* MARRIAGE, U.S. LAW OF; DIVORCE (U.S. LAW OF).

Abortion, Birth Control, Sterilization. The law forbids *abortion unless it is necessary to preserve the life of the mother. Any person willfully administering to any woman pregnant or quick with child, or prescribing, advising, or helping such woman to use any substance or instrument to destroy the child is guilty of a felony and may be imprisoned from 1 to 10 years and fined. If it is done to produce a miscarriage or to injure the pregnant woman, it is a felony punishable by a 1- to 5-year sentence. Criminal abortion resulting in death is culpable homicide.

There are no references to birth control, contraception, or anovulants in the state code.

The law allows *sterilization in certain cases of the mentally diseased, feebleminded, or epileptics in institutions, if it is conducive to the mental, moral, or physical improvement of the patient or inmate or for the public good. Sterilization of mental defectives not in institutions is allowed also; there are provisions for sterilization as a prerequisite to marriage under certain conditions.

Property and Taxation. Religious societies and charities may incorporate under the Non-Profit Corporation Act; if special legal provisions have been made for the organization of designated classes, they shall be formed under those provisions and not under the nonprofit provisions. When church rule or policy permits, property may be held in trust by the bishop for the use of the congregation.

Real and personal property of religious societies and charities not run for profit is exempt from taxation.

There are no mortmain statutes in the state code.

Statutes regulating solicitation of funds require licensing, and persons or organizations must show proof of authority upon the request of the person being solicited. This does not apply to religious groups where solicitation is wholly within its membership or to certain organizations where solicitation takes place wholly within the city or county.

Prisons and Reformatories. The director of prisons must arrange for the holding of religious services for the prisoners in the state prison and in the state farms and camps on Sunday and at such other times as it is deemed wise. Attendance is voluntary. If possible, the director must provide for the visits of ministers at the hospital to administer to the spiritual wants of the sick. At Caledonia Farm, the state prison, provision must be made for a resident minister of the Gospel.

Holidays and Sunday Observance. Christmas and New Year's Day, Labor Day, general election day, Thanksgiving Day, January 19, February 22, April 12, May 10, July 4, and November 11 are legal holidays. Easter Monday and May 30 are legal holidays for state and national banks only. When a holiday falls on Sunday, the following Monday is a holiday. Notes maturing on a Sunday or holiday are payable on the next business day. The sale of alcoholic beverages is prohibited on Sunday and election day. Hunting is prohibited on Sunday. The sale of enumerated articles is unlawful on Sunday, but many counties are exempt from these provisions.

Morality, Public Health, and Safety. No state condones polygamy. It is a misdemeanor to disturb a religious congregation while people are assembled for worship. Where healing practices are confined to prayer or spiritual means there is no license tax for the art of healing. All children living in North Carolina are required to be immunized against diphtheria, tetanus, and whooping cough before reaching the age of 1 year; they are required to be immunized against smallpox before attending any public, private, or parochial school. The intentional exposure of human beings to contact with reptiles of a venomous nature, when such is essentially dangerous, injurious, and detrimental to public health, safety and welfare, and the indulgence in and inducement to such exposure is deemed a public nuisance and a criminal offense. In *State v. Massey* 51 S.E. (2) 179 (1949) the supreme court of North Carolina held that the city ordinance prohibiting the handling of poisonous reptiles in such manner as to endanger the public health, safety, and welfare was not void and did not infringe on the freedom of religious worship that involves the handling of poisonous reptiles, since the public safety is superior to religious practice.

Bibliography: J. J. O'CONNELL, *Catholicity in the Carolinas and Georgia 1820–1878* (New York 1879). J. T. ELLIS, *The Life of James Cardinal Gibbons,* 2 v. (Milwaukee 1952). *General Statutes of North Carolina, 1943* (reissued Charlottesville, Va. 1953–   ).

[A. G. BIGGS]

NORTH DAKOTA

A Northwestern state bordered on the north by Saskatchewan and Manitoba, Canada; on the east by Minnesota; on the south by South Dakota; and on the west by Montana. In a total area of 70,665 square miles, it contained in 1960 a population of 632,446, ranking

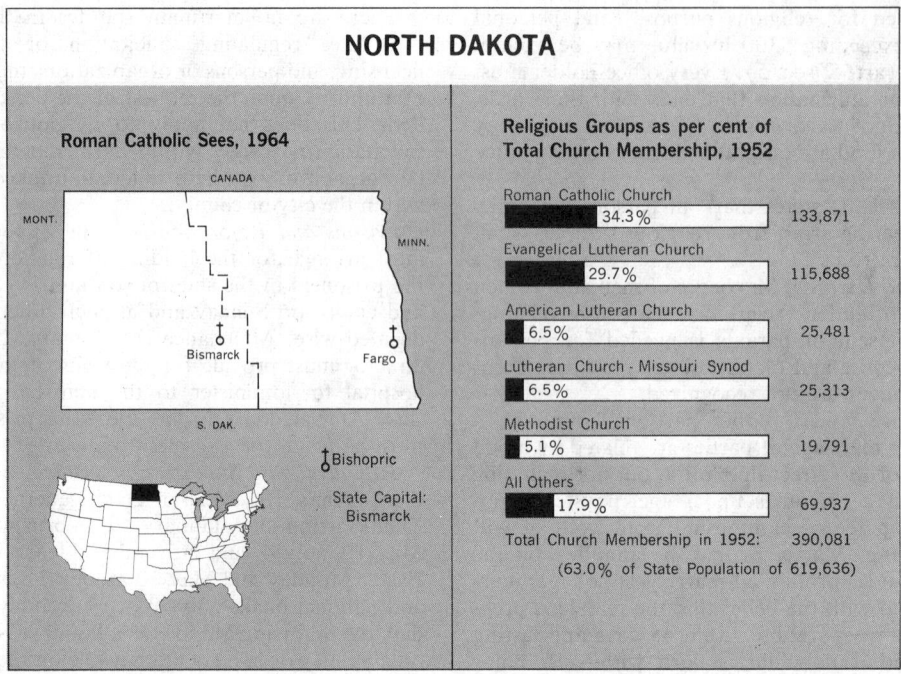

Fig. 1. Church-membership statistics were compiled by the Bureau of Research and Survey of the National Council of the Churches of Christ in the U.S.A.

41st nationally. The state contains no cities with a population of 50,000 or more. In 1960 Fargo, the largest city, had 46,662, while Grand Forks had 34,451 and Bismarck, the capital, had 27,670. The population, chiefly northern European in origin, had declined slightly from its peak of 680,000 in 1930. Slightly less than 75 per cent lived in rural areas, and farming occupied more than 40 per cent of the state's work force. Farms are generally large, averaging more than 875 acres, and wheat, barley, and flaxseed are the major crops. Oil was discovered in the Williston Basin on April 5, 1951, and has since become the second greatest source of income in North Dakota.

Population. Catholics constituted 21.6 per cent of the state's population in 1952, a figure that rose sharply to 27 per cent in 1965. Protestants, among whom Lutherans predominated, made up 41.2 per cent of the population in 1952, with Jews numbering 0.2 per cent and all others 37 per cent (*see* CHURCH MEMBERSHIP, U.S.).

Education. North Dakota law provides for compulsory school attendance between the ages of 7 and 15, or to age 17 when the pupil has failed to complete the eighth grade. In 1956 there were 2,839 public schools with 94,961 elementary students and 30,727 high school pupils. State college and university enrollment amounted to 10,834. In 1960 Catholic grade schools enrolled 15,139 pupils, and there were 3,200 high school students and three small Catholic colleges. Special religion classes were offered for 33,000 Catholic children in the public schools. Religious employed as public school teachers are forbidden to wear religious garb by an initiative measure passed by a close vote on June 29, 1948.

History. The first white men in North Dakota were the Catholic Frenchmen of P. de *La Vérendrye's expedition, which reached the Missouri River in 1738. Fur traders, most of them Catholic, became the earliest residents of the area. The trader Toussaint Charbonneau and his Catholic wife, Sakakawea, the "Bird Woman," became guides for Lewis and Clark in 1804.

Rev. Severe N. Dumoulin founded the Catholic Church in North Dakota in 1818, when he began a 5-year pastorate at Pembina on the Red River, the earliest settlement in the state. After 2 decades as a mission station from Canada, Pembina in 1848 received its second resident pastor, Rev. George A. *Belcourt, noted missionary to the Chippewa. Pierre J. *De Smet, on a dozen trips to and from St. Louis, Mo., between 1840 and 1868, baptized thousands of Indians and métis on the Upper Missouri, and he was planning missions among the Sioux and the Fort Berthold Indians when he died in 1873. His designs were carried out by Abbot Martin *Marty, OSB, who arrived in Dakota Territory in 1876 and became vicar apostolic in 1880. A majority of Catholics in the territory were German-speaking colonists from Russia.

Settlement of Dakota Territory, begun in the 1870s, picked up momentum in the 1880s and reached its peak in the next 2 decades. On Nov. 2, 1889, the territory was divided and North Dakota became the 39th state. The Diocese of Jamestown (now *Fargo), embracing the entire state, was established that same year with John Shanley as first bishop. In 1910 the state was divided into two dioceses, *Bismarck and Fargo, suffragans of the Archdiocese of St. Paul. During these years the state was a center of the Progressive Movement in American politics, adopting the presidential primary (1912), the referendum (1914), and the recall (1920).

Church-State Relations. References to and provisions affecting religion are incorporated in the state constitution and in acts of the legislature and the judiciary.

Constitution. North Dakota is governed by the Constitution of 1889, as amended. The preamble states that the people are ". . . grateful to Almighty God for the blessings of civil and religious liberty. . . ." The constitution provides for religious freedom and freedom of conscience, ". . . but the liberty of conscience hereby secured shall not be so secured as to excuse acts of licentiousness, or justify practices inconsistent with the peace or safety of this state (art. 1, sec. 4). Under the "Compact With the United States" in art. 16, sec. 203, "Perfect toleration of religious sentiment shall be secured, and no inhabitant of this state shall ever be molested in person or property on account of his or her mode of religious worship." No person is incompetent to be a witness or juror because of his religious opinions. Article 12, sec. 188, reads in part: "Persons, whose religious tenets or conscientious scruples forbid them to bear arms shall not be compelled to do so in times of peace, but shall pay an equivalent for a personal service." The constitution also exempts from taxation property used exclusively for religious purposes (art. 11, sec. 176), while money raised for the support of public schools may not be used for sectarian schools (art. 8, sec. 152).

Members of the legislature and judiciary, with certain exceptions, must take an oath or affirmation before entering office, and in the case of an oath it ends with the words ". . . So help me God." Article 14, sec. 195, states that the senate shall try impeachments and "the senators shall be upon oath or affirmation to do justice according to the law and evidence."

Marriage and Divorce. Marriages of men under 18 and women under 15 are forbidden, except in certain cases of pregnancy, and the consent of parents is needed for men under 21 and women under 18. A license and blood test are required. Certain public officials and clergy may perform the ceremony, and common-law marriages are not recognized.

Marriages are void if the parties are related by blood in any degree of the direct line, up to and including first cousins. There are health restrictions that forbid marriage of persons with certain diseases or of a certain mentality. Marriages may be annulled on any of the following grounds: nonage, prior subsisting marriage, unsound mind, force, fraud, continual physical incapacity, and incest. The grounds for absolute divorce are: adultery, extreme cruelty, willful desertion, willful neglect, habitual intemperance, conviction of a felony, or insanity with confinement for 5 years. Neither party can remarry except as specified in the decree. *See* MARRIAGE, U.S. LAW OF; DIVORCE (U.S. LAW OF).

Abortion, Birth Control, Sterilizction. The law forbids *abortion unless it is necessary to preserve the life of the mother. A person who administers, prescribes, advises, or persuades a woman to have a miscarriage may receive from 1 to 3 years in prison. If the mother or quick child dies, the person is guilty of manslaughter in the first degree. A woman soliciting an abortion may be fined or imprisoned.

The law regulates *birth control (*see* CONTRACEPTION; ANOVULANTS). While there is no statute prohibiting the dissemination of contraceptives, North Dakota does prohibit the advertisement of matters concerning venereal disease or reference to person or persons from whom treatment of the disease may be obtained.

The law provides for *sterilization of institutionalized feebleminded, mentally ill, habitual criminals, moral degenerates, or sexual perverts when they are potential producers of offspring who, because of the inheritance of inferior or antisocial traits, would probably become social menaces or wards of the state. The usual safeguards are established. Persons not institutionalized also can be sterilized if there is no likelihood that their condition will improve.

Property and Taxation. Religious and charitable societies may incorporate under the Non-Profit Corporation Act. The property of such congregations, parishes, or missions is held in trust by the bishop for the use and

Fig. 2. Assumption Abbey and College, Richardton, N.Dak., founded in 1899 and maintained by the Benedictines.

Fig. 3. Bell tower and cloister of Annunciation Priory, Bismarck, N.Dak., built 1954–63.

benefit of the respective congregations, parishes, or missions. No corporation or association organized for religious or charitable purposes may acquire or hold real estate of a greater value than $500,000, but this does not apply to the property of corporations or associations actually used for charitable, religious, educational, or hospital purposes. All real estate acquired or held contrary to the provisions of this section may be forfeited and escheat to the state.

The real and personal property of religious societies and charities not run for profit is exempt from taxation. The exemption is limited to two acres for that property of religious organizations upon which there is a building used for religious services or as a residence for a bishop or minister, whether such property consists of one tract or more.

A license is required to solicit for benevolent associations, but this does not apply to sisters of charity, to representatives of the Salvation Army, to deaconesses who wear a distinct garb, or to the taking up of collections in churches for organizations distinctly denominational in character and management.

Prisons and Reformatories. The keeper of each county jail shall provide, at the expense of the county, sufficient copies of the Bible or New Testament for the use of the prisoners in his custody. Any minister of the Gospel desiring to instruct the prisoners in their moral and religious duties shall have access to them at reasonable and proper times. There are no similar statutes concerning the penitentiary.

Holidays and Sunday Observance. Sunday, Christmas, New Year's, Good Friday, Labor Day, Thanksgiving Day, general election days, any day appointed by the president or governor for a public holiday, February 12, February 22, May 30, July 4, October 12, and November 11 are legal holidays. When certain of these days fall on Sunday, the next day is a holiday. Business done on a holiday (except Sunday) is valid. Secular acts appointed to be done, which fall on a holiday, may be done on the next business day. The sale of alcoholic beverages on Sunday or election day is forbidden. Certain work, sports, and public dancing are forbidden on Sunday, as are boxing and wrestling.

Morality, Public Health, and Safety. No state condones polygamy. Any person who willfully disrupts a religious assembly of people gathered for worship, who attempts to prevent another person from performing a religious act, or tries to compel adoption of a religious belief, is guilty of a misdemeanor. The chapter regulating physicians and surgeons exempts from its provisions the practice of Christian Science or other religious tenets, rules, or ceremonies, if the person administering, making use of, assisting in, or prescribing such religious worship, devotion, or healing does not prescribe or administer drugs or medicines, does not perform surgical or physical operations, and does not claim to be a physician or surgeon. Vaccination or innoculation is not required for admission to any school or for the exercise of a right.

Various Constitutional Freedoms. The constitution grants to every man the right to write, speak, and publish his opinion on all subjects, but makes one who abuses the right responsible for such abuse (see *Englund v. Townley* 174 N.W. 755). A statute prohibiting the willful publication and distribution of pamphlets concerning a candidate for the U.S. Senate without disclosing the names of persons responsible for the publication and distribution does not violate the First Amendment to the Federal Constitution. Such a statute is not judged to be unconstitutional because a farmer who publishes such pamphlets operates his farm under governmental regulations and fears possible reprisal.

Bibliography: L. PFALLER, *The Catholic Church in Western North Dakota, 1738–1960* (Mandan, N.Dak. 1960). Federal Writers' Project, *North Dakota: A Guide to the Northern Prairie State* (2d ed. New York 1950). *North Dakota Century Code*, 14 v. (Indianapolis, Ind. 1959–60). *Callaghan's Dakota Digest, 1867 to Date* (Chicago 1930–). **Illustration credit:** Fig. 3. Marcel Breuer and Associates, Architects. Photo by Shin Koyama.

[L. PFALLER]

NORTHWEST ORDINANCE

A decree, issued by the Continental Congress in 1785 and confirmed in 1787, for the government of Western territories ceded to the central government by the states. The Land Ordinance of 1785 drew up the plan of a 6-mile square township to be divided into 36 sections of 640 acres each. In each township, Congress reserved four sections and specifically set aside section 16 for the maintenance of public schools. Ohio was the first state to receive a grant; later states received two or four sections.

While the Ordinance solved the problem of selling the land, it did not provide for its administration, nor did the sales bring the financial returns Congress had expected. When the government finally sold several million acres to private companies, their agents pointed out that the lands were useless unless provision for orderly government existed. In 1780, in fact, Congress had promised that the ceded lands would be formed into states. The method of doing this, however, posed a problem for the central government.

Congress was debating the issue when the Rev. Manasseh Cutler, agent of the Ohio Land Co., appeared with a petition. His prodding resulted in a committee report that delegates from eight states unanimously enacted into the Ordinance of 1787. The first article of this law created the territory northwest of the Ohio, now represented by Illinois, Indiana, Ohio, Michigan, and part of Minnesota, which was to be divided into not less than three or more than five states. The second article provided for government in three stages: (1) the appointment by Congress of a governor, secretary, and three judges to control the area; (2) when the territory had 5,000 male adults, the establishment of a legislature and an assembly selected by the governor and Congress, and the right to send a nonvoting member to Congress; (3) when the territory numbered 60,000 inhabitants, the right to adopt a constitution and petition Congress for admission as a state. The third article provided a bill of rights for the territory. Due largely to Thomas Jefferson, Nathan Dane, and Rufus King, the law declared that "religion, morality and knowledge, being necessary to good government and the happiness of mankind, schools and the means of education [should] forever be encouraged." Congress supported these words by setting aside two townships for the establishment of schools. Although state legislatures were slow to act, the provision itself is significant and eventually led to state action.

Both ordinances show not only the central government's early interest in education, but also emphasize the responsibility of the school in promoting "religion, morality and knowledge." Since the constitution had not yet been adopted, however, both laws must be credited to the government under the Articles of the Confederation, and cannot be construed as Federal aid to education. In fact, attempts to discuss Federal participation in education during the Constitutional Convention came to nought, although the new government continued to operate under the ordinances, and thus supported their provisions.

Bibliography: R. M. ROBBINS, *Our Landed Heritage* (Princeton 1942). F. H. SWIFT, *A History of Public Permanent Common School Funds in the United States, 1795–1905* (New York 1911). H. C. TAYLOR, *The Educational Significance of the Early Federal Land Ordinances* (New York 1922).

[A. J. CLARK]

NORTON, MARY TERESA, member of Congress; b. Jersey City, N.J., March 7, 1875; d. Greenwich, Conn., Aug. 2, 1959. She was the daughter of Thomas and Marie (Shea) Hopkins. After being educated in Jersey City, she married Robert Francis Norton and had one son, Robert Francis. In 1920 she was appointed to represent Hudson County on the Democratic State Committee, of which she became vice chairman (1921–39) and chairman (1939–44). She was selected as delegate-at-large to the Democratic National Convention from 1924 to 1944, when she was elected to the Democratic National Committee. In 1925 she was elected to Congress from the 12th New Jersey district; she served until 1933, when she was elected to represent the 13th District, and then reelected successively until 1949. The first Democratic woman elected to Congress, she was also the first woman to become chairman of a major Congressional committee. She acted as chairman of the District of Columbia Committee (1930–37)

and of the Committee on Labor (1937–47). At the Paris Conference of International Labor Organizations in 1945, she was adviser to the U.S. Government delegation. The College of St. Elizabeth, Convent Station, N.J., conferred on her its first honorary LL.D. degree in 1930; Rider College, Trenton, N.J., in 1937, and St. Bonaventure University, New York, in 1950 also conferred honorary doctorates. She received the Siena medal in 1947 as the outstanding Catholic woman of the year and the achievement award of the Women's National Press Club in 1946. For more than 12 years she was president of the Queen's Daughters' Day Nursery in Jersey City, and was an active member of other civic organizations.

[M. T. ROONEY]

NORWAY

This article summarizes the origin and historical development of the Catholic Church in Norway. This Scandinavian kingdom, 125,031 square miles in area, had a population of 3,680,622 in 1964. In 1905 it regained its independence, lost to *Denmark (1380–1814) and to *Sweden (1814–1905).

Christianity until 1500. Norwegian history begins in the 9th century. Christianity came to the country mainly from England and Ireland during the reign of King Hakon the Good (935–996). It did not, however, gain a real foothold before the reigns of *Olaf I Tryggvessøn (995–1000) and St. Olaf Haraldson (1025–30; see OLAF II, KING OF NORWAY, ST.). Soon after the latter was killed in the battle of Stiklestad (July 29, 1030) he was reverenced as the sainted hero of medieval Norway. His shrine at *Trondheim made the town the capital of the country. The first bishops had been attached to the King's retinue, but St. Olav sent Bishop Grimkell to *Bremen in northern Germany, the former bishopric of St. *Ansgar. Until 1100 Norwegian bishops, like other bishops of Scandinavia, were suffragans of the archbishop of Bremen. In 1104 the See of *Lund (in southern Sweden, but then belonging to Denmark) became the metropolitan see for all the northern regions. Cardinal Nicholas Breakspear, an Englishman, was sent to Norway by the Pope in 1152. In cooperation with the assembly of Norwegian peers he made the See of Trondheim metropolitan for all Norway, including Norway proper, the Orkney Islands, the Faroe Islands, the Hebrides, the Isle of Man, *Iceland, and *Greenland. Dioceses within the country from 1153 included also Bergen, Stavanger, Oslo, and Hamar. Since Breakspear became the next pope, *Adrian IV (1154–59), his ordinances received the highest respect.

As elsewhere in medieval Europe, clashes between king and hierarchy were not infrequent. The struggle of Archbishops Eystein (1161–88) and Eirik (1189–1206) with King Sverre (1177–1202) revolved mainly about royal interference in the designation of bishops and pastors and the collection of ecclesiastical tithes. Eirik went into exile to Denmark, Eystein to England, where he was impressed with the new *Gothic style. On his return, Eystein introduced it into Norway as he expedited the construction of the cathedral at Trondheim. Similar Church-State tensions were finally resolved by the short-lived Union of Tönsberg (1277), by which the King granted the Church freedom in ecclesiastical nominations, while the archbishop renounced rights that the Church had enjoyed in the elections of kings. When the peace-loving Magnus Lagabōter (the Lawmender) died in 1280, both his sons were minors. Thereupon the regents revoked the Union of Tönsberg. Protests from Rome and Trondheim were met by the banishment of Archbishop Jon Raude and Bishops Andrew of Oslo and Torfinn of Hamar. Jon died in Sweden (1282) and Torfinn in Flanders (1285) after visiting Rome to seek help.

When the *Black Death afflicted the country in 1349, it ended the flourishing period of the Church in medieval Norway. Losses were tremendous. Out of 300 priests in the archdiocese, only 40 survived, and only one of the five bishops survived. During the next 2 centuries no churches were built. This was evidence that the Church and the people had lost their strength.

Monastic life was introduced very early by English *Benedictines. *Cistercians, *Dominicans, and *Franciscans followed (see DACIA). These religious orders were likewise decimated by the plague. The typically Scandinavian order of the *Bridgettines appeared in the second half of the 14th century.

Protestant Reformation. *Lutheranism was introduced to Norway from Copenhagen by royal decree in 1537. Since 1380 Norway and Denmark had been ruled by the same kings; in practice Norway had become a Danish province. As a follower of *Luther, King Christian III (1536–59) had to use military force to get the Norwegians to recognize him after his election. In southern Norway he was acknowledged by officeholders who were of Danish origin, but in Trondheim Abp. Olav Engelbrektsson organized resistance in order to defend Norwegian independence as well as the Catholic faith. Since his forces were too small, he withdrew (April 1537) to the Netherlands, where he died at Lier (Feb. 6, 1538). The *Reformation came to the Norwegians from abroad, served only the interests of the Danish king and the magnates, and did not correspond

Fig. 1. God with Adam and Eve, Romanesque painted ceiling (detail) from a stave church, Hallingdal, Norway.

to any desire among the populace. The property of parishes was ordinarily respected, but all possessions of monasteries and dioceses were confiscated by the crown. Lutheran beliefs and practices were introduced with great circumspection. Generally priests were allowed to continue in their posts, but when they died the royal government provided Lutheran successors. Modern historians do not believe that Lutheranism was generally accepted in Norway before 1600. Bishop Mogens of Hamar and Bishop Hoskold of Stavanger opposed the new order; the latter was committed to prison and died at Bergen; the former was brought to Denmark, where he died at Antvortskov (1542). The See of Bergen had been vacant since 1535. Hans Rev of Oslo, born in Denmark, was the only bishop who embraced Lutheranism. He did not ordain any bishop; thus the *apostolic succession was lost in Norway, as it was in Denmark.

Catholic priests were now no longer admitted to the country. About 1600 it became apparent that many young men of the higher classes, even sons of Lutheran ministers, were attending *Jesuit schools abroad. A royal decree of 1604 excluded from any office in school and church all who in the future began or continued to study at these institutions. A few years later several priests of the Lutheran Diocese of Oslo were sentenced to exile at a public trial in Skien (1613) for Catholic sympathies, correspondence with Catholics abroad, and disregard of Lutheran beliefs. The influence of the Norwegian Jesuit Laurentius Nicolai Norvegus was discovered. From 1624 capital punishment threatened any Catholic priest entering the country. Even so, the secular priest John Martini Rhugius visited his native country and stayed at Larvik for three short periods (1637–41) caring for a small number of widely scattered Catholics. Improved commercial relations attracted Jesuits from the Netherlands; they stayed in Bergen for 6 weeks in 1648, but enforcement of the draconian laws forced them to leave. Since 1648, however, despite widely varying situations, one or more Catholic priests have always resided in Copenhagen, the capital and royal residence of the Danish-Norwegian kingdom. In Norway itself, which lacked a court and foreign ambassadors, it was possible for a Catholic priest to dwell only by serving as chaplain to foreign mercenaries in time of war or to foreign artisans in commercial establishments. Thus, foreign mercenaries made it possible for German Jesuits to stay in Fredrikstad (1677–91) as military chaplains to General Cicignon. The royal glassworks, begun after 1740, required skilled workers from the Catholic regions of central Europe. From time to time a priest from Denmark was permitted to visit the factories so that the workers could receive the Sacraments. After 1790 a priest, probably French, stayed some years with the French consul in Christiania. But all these instances were merely temporary arrangements and concerned only foreigners.

Reestablishment of Catholicism. The first regular Catholic parish in modern times was founded in 1843 in Christiania (renamed Oslo in 1925). From 1814 Norway had had the same king as Sweden, Charles-John Bernadotte. The existing draconian legislation against Catholics was not officially changed by the Norwegian Constitution of 1814 (which declared Norway independent), but it was gradually permitted to lapse. Jacob

Fig. 2. Nave and sanctuary of St. Olav's Church, Oslo.

Studach, chaplain to the Catholic Princess Josephine Beauharnais, visited Norway several times. In 1833 Studach was appointed vicar apostolic of Sweden and Norway and resided in Stockholm. When Studach sent the German priest Gotfred Montz to the Norwegian capital to baptize the French consul's child, Montz presented a petition to the King from about 60 Catholics he had met while in the capital. On March 6, 1843, provisional dispensations to celebrate Mass were granted, and on Easter Sunday, April 16, the first official Catholic service was held. The Dissenter Act of 1845 brought definitive regulations whereby religious freedom was granted to all Christians, but Lutheranism remained the official religion of the country. Austrian *Redemptorists were placed in charge of the parish (1849–54) and started the construction of St. Olav's Church (the present cathedral), dedicated in 1856. The next year a small chapel was opened in Bergen, the second largest town in the country, by the Norwegian secular priest Christopher Holfeldt-Houen. In the extreme north another effort was made when the Congregation for the Propagation of the Faith (Propaganda) created (1855) the Prefecture Apostolic of the Arctic Missions (*Poli Arctici*) comprising the northern part of the Scandinavian peninsula, the Russian peninsula of Kola, Iceland, Greenland, the Arctic part of Canada, the Faroes, and from 1860 even the Shetland Islands, the Orkneys, and Caithness in the north of Scotland. The first prefect apostolic was the Russian convert Djunkowski, who in 1863 returned to Russia and to the Orthodox Church. On Norwegian territory, stations were established at Alta (1856) and at Tromsö (1859), where in 1860 a small church, which still exists, was erected. Difficulty of communication in the Prefecture Apostolic of the North and a lack of priests in the south led to entirely new divisions in 1869, when

Rome created a prefecture apostolic for each of the three northern countries: Norway, Sweden, and Denmark. Prefect Bernard Bernard, Djunkowski's successor, administered the entire Norwegian territory, with residence in Christiania (1869–87). Norway constituted a single vicariate apostolic from 1892 until 1932, when the country was divided into three ecclesiastical territories. The one in the south became the Diocese of Oslo in 1953; the one in central Norway has had a vicar apostolic resident in Trondheim since 1953; the one in the north was elevated to a vicariate apostolic in 1955, with its seat in Tromsö. All three bishops depend directly on Propaganda.

The areas of Trondheim and Tromsö are entrusted to religious congregations, northern Norway to the Fathers of the Holy Family, and central Norway to the Fathers of the *Sacred Heart (Picpus Fathers). The Oslo Diocese is administered by secular clergy, assisted by various orders and congregations. In 1964 seven priests were working in each of the vicariates of Trondheim and Tromsö; one was Norwegian. The Diocese of Oslo had 20 secular priests (8 Norwegians) and 24 religious (6 Norwegians) priests. Nearly all the Norwegian priests were converts; five of them were occupied in regular parish work.

In a total population of 3.6 million in 1960, only 7,875 were Catholics; these lived mainly in towns. Because of their small numbers, most Catholics contracted mixed marriages. This, together with the overwhelmingly non-Catholic environment, keeps the number of Catholics practically unchanged in spite of some 60 conversions a year. Since 1950 about 1,400 Catholic refugees from Central and Eastern Europe have entered Norway. Widely scattered as they are and anxious to be assimilated, a considerable number of them may leave the Church. Religious instruction in Lutheranism is compulsory in all elementary and secondary schools; but like other "dissenters" Catholic pupils are exempt from this instruction if they receive regular Catholic instruction elsewhere. The four Catholic schools do not receive any support from the central government, but municipal subsidies have been voted in some cases of recent date. Catholic hospitals exist in nearly every town where a parish has been established and are run by sisters of various congregations. These hospitals enjoy general esteem, and almost all

Fig. 3. Chapel in Tromsö, Norway, built in 1859.

Fig. 4. Norway, showing sites of ecclesiastical interest.

their patients are non-Catholic. The presence of the sisters, who numbered more than 500, is vital to the parishes. Although Catholics are a small minority, the vitality of their Christian life is high.

Bibliography: R. KEYSER, *Den norske Kirkes historie under Katholicismen,* 2 v. (Christiania 1856–58). C. C. A. LANGE, *De norske Klostres historie i Middelalderen* (2d ed. Christiania 1856). T. B. WILSON, *History of the Church and State in Norway* (London 1903). J. METZLER, *Die apostolischen Vikariate des Nordens* (Paderborn 1919). S. UNDSET, *Saga of Saints,* tr. E. C. RAMSDEN (New York 1934). C. JOYS, *Hvad skjedde i Norge i 1537* (Oslo 1937). I. H. KNUDSEN, *De relationibus inter Sanctam Sedem et Norvegiam* (Rome 1946). K. LARSEN, *A History of Norway* (Princeton, N.J. 1948). E. MOLLAND, *Church Life in Norway 1800–1950,* tr. H. KAASA (Minneapolis 1957). H. RIEBER-MOHN, *Catholicism in Norway* (London 1959; repr. from *Month,* Feb. 1959). Latourette Christ19th-20thCent v.2, 4. G. SCHWAIGER, *Die Reformation in dem nordischen Ländern* (Munich 1962). E. D. VOGT, *The Catholic Church in the North* (Bergen 1962), mimeographed. O. GARSTEIN, *Rome and the Counter-Reformation in Scandinavia,* v.1, *1539–83* (New York 1964). L. S. HUNTER, ed., *Scandinavian Churches* (London 1965). *Bilan du Monde* 2:638–643. H. HOLZAPFEL, LexThK² 7:1039–43. E. AMDAHL, RGG³ 4:1522–30. AnnPont (1964) 317. *St. Ansgar's Bulletin* (New York 1963). **Illustration credits:** Fig. 1, Universitetets Oldsaksamling, Oslo. Figs. 2 and 3, Norwegian Embassy Information Service, New York City.

[J. J. DUIN]

NORWEGIAN LITERATURE

The Norwegian language belongs to the North Germanic group of the Indo-European languages. Its development is generally divided into five periods: the primitive Nordic up to A.D. 500; the period of syncopation, *c.* 500–700; the Old Norse period, 700–1370; Middle Norwegian, 1370–1525; Modern Norwegian, subdivided into an older period from 1525 to *c.* 1840–50, and thereafter the recent era.

Development of the Language. For a survey of the literature up to the end of the middle period, *see* OLD NORSE LITERATURE. The Middle Norwegian period is characterized by a growing influence of Danish on the written language. This period was previously considered to have begun *c.* 1350 when so many scholars and writers perished in the *Black Death, but more recent studies indicate that the changes brought about by the writing tradition of imported Danish scribes did not appear until about one generation later. At the same time, political events furthered the use of Danish as the language of administration: the royal chancery moved to Copenhagen, and Danish officials were appointed to offices in Norway. The activities of the German Hansa also caused an influx of loan words mainly connected with commerce.

Diverse currents of linguistic development flowed on into the older phases of Modern Norwegian. During the first years after the Reformation (1536) Danish gained stature as a written language. The Bible was printed in Danish, and when the humanists in Bergen started their literary activity, Danish was introduced as the vehicle for that literature. In the 18th century, with the establishment of elementary schools and growing trade and industry, Danish settled in more securely until nationalistic tendencies urged a claim for a proper Norwegian language. In the final decades of the 18th century a literature in the Norwegian spoken dialects had had a very modest beginning. At the political break with Denmark in 1814, nationalistic groups encouraged the use of vocabulary taken from contemporary dialects. At the same time, a more Norwegian pronunciation became customary not only among the working classes and in the provinces, but among the educated as well.

It was not, however, until the 1840s that the Norwegian language, kept alive in the spoken dialects, became a real challenge to the written language. At that time a linguistic genius, the self-taught Ivar Aasen (1813–96), made up a written language based on his knowledge of Old Norse, but above all on his personal study of the dialects spoken mainly in the Western provinces (the *landsmål,* later called *nynorsk*). From the second half of the 19th century on, the tendency in linguistic policy has been to eliminate the traces of Danish influence on the traditional written language (the *bokmål* or *riksmål*). Knud Knudsen was most intimately connected with this movement in the 19th century. At the same time, more radical nationalists wanted to introduce the *landsmål* as the official language.

In the 20th century the tendency has been to blend the *landsmål* with the traditional *riksmål* into one common language. The orthographic reforms of 1917 eliminated several differences between the two, and another approach was made in 1938. Meanwhile Didrik Arup Seip, after a linguistic analysis of early MSS from the eastern provinces, proved that certain characteristics considered as Danicisms were extant also in the Middle

Norwegian dialects; these, he argued, ought to be considered as genuine Norwegian forms just as the dialects of the western provinces had been. In order to regulate the linguistic reforms, and eventually to blend the two into one language, the National Assembly in 1951 established a linguistic commission, the *Norsk Språknemnd,* as a consultative committee. In 1964 the two official languages coexisted in Norway and were taught in all secondary schools. The *bokmål* is used mostly in the eastern and northern provinces, while the *nynorsk* prevails in the western provinces and in the mountain regions.

The Norwegian Lapps living on the Finnmark plateau speak a northern dialect of the Lapp language that belongs to the Finno-Ugric linguistic group. Lapp has been made a particular field of study at the University of Oslo as well as in certain teachers' colleges, and is taught in Lapp elementary schools. Lapp literature consists mainly of devotional books and hymns in translation. In recent years, Anders Larsen and Isak Saba have written original works in their mother tongue.

Late Medieval Literature. When the writing of literature in Old Norse died out in Norway, literary activity was reduced to the writing of public documents and diplomas, and the oral development of the *folkevise* (ballad). The public documents have mainly a local historical and linguistic interest, while the *folkevise,* introduced into Norway from western European court poetry and changed into a popular folk poetry, is important not only for comparative purposes, but also as proper literature.

The *folkevise* differs in form from the Old Norse poetry in the substitution of simple assonance or end rhyme for the elaborate Old Norse alliteration. Instead of the rich variety of the Old Norse meters, a standard quadruple verse, frequently with an interwoven refrain, emerges. The content may be of epic as well as of lyric character, while the refrain often carries an allusion to the origin of the *folkeviser* as these were used for

*Fig. 1. Ivar
Aasen.*

dancing. Several *folkeviser* are from Germanic, Romance, or even Slavic countries. According to subject they are divided into *troll-viser,* historical *viser* (e.g., the ballad about Charlemagne), religious *viser,* mythical

viser, and knighthood *viser.* The merit of the Norwegian *folkeviser* lies in their dramatic power and lyric sensitivity; the characters are more standardized than in the Danish versions.

One of the most interesting of the approximately 200 extant *folkeviser* is the visionary *Draumkvaedet* (*c.* 1300), a poem connected with the Old Norse tales of the Irish knight Tundal and the English monk Gundelin. For 13 days during the Christmas season the narrator is transferred to the realm of death, and, on his return, gives a powerful description of the punishments of hell, the glory of paradise, and of the Last Judgment. Although the *Draumkvaedet* is of Christian inspiration and is traditionally Catholic in detail, it still carries the marks of pagan mythology. About 1650 the *folkevise* developed a simpler form, the "new rhyme," which was used mostly for popular entertainment. Folk tales also belong to the oral literature of the late Middle Ages. Although the topics in these were frequently imported from the Arabs by the crusaders and merchants or from the Normans in Sicily, the folktale has become a true expression of Norwegian temperament and folk culture.

Revival in the 16th Century. The revival of literary interest in Norway is indicated by the translation by Anders Saebjörnsson of the Old Norse national law (1520–30) and by the translations of the sagas of the kings by Laurids Hanssön and Mats Störsson. Shortly afterward followed an original work, the *Hamarkrönike* (*c.* 1550, The Chronicle from Hamar), a somewhat sentimental farewell by an anonymous canon in Hamar to the era preceding the Reformation. In this period the influence of the Humanist movement reached Norway and stimulated awakening interest in the national culture. The central figures in this development were the rector of the cathedral school in Bergen, Geble Pederssön (*c.* 1490–1557), and his protégé, Absalon Pedersson Beyer (1528–75), a Lutheran minister. Beyer's diary, *Bergens Kapitelbog,* written partly in Latin, partly in Danish-Norwegian, gives interesting glimpses of the cultural life in his contemporary Bergen. He also wrote a topographical work, *Om Norgis Rige* (1567, About the Kingdom of Norway), a work not printed until *c.* 1780.

To the group of humanists in Oslo belonged Jens Nielssön and Halvard Gunnarsson, the latter the author of a famous inquiry on religious knowledge, the *Prestepine,* reprinted several times up to 1870. An outstanding personality of this period was Peder Claussön Friis (1545–1614), a Lutheran minister who acquired some knowledge of Old Norse and whose translations of Snorri's *Heimskringla* influenced the stand of the nationalist party at the end of the Danish-Norwegian union (*see* SNORRI STURLUSON). Also noteworthy is the Danish-born minister, Mikkel Pederssön Escholt, who published his *Geologia Norvegica* in 1657.

Apart from these samples of a scientific literature, the Norwegian contribution of Danish-Norwegian letters was scanty. Dorothea Engelbretsdatter (1634–1716) revealed great sensitivity as a hymn writer, although her sincerity was sometimes disguised under a rather baroque taste. A unique personality from this period was Petter Dass (1647–1707), a vigorous Lutheran minister who combined academic training with popular wit and rustic humor. He expressed his firm religious belief in a series of hymns, and in *Nordlands Trompet* he described in verse the strenuous, colorful life of the fisher folk in the province of Nordland.

The 18th Century. Partly as a consequence of the political union between Denmark and Norway, intellectual life in Norway was not very vigorous. Norway had no university of its own, and promising students went to Copenhagen for academic training. One of the first to leave Norway for these reasons, Ludvig Holberg (1684–1754), traveled in France and England before he settled in Denmark and brought the two Scandinavian countries in contact with the spirit of the *Enlightenment. In Norway, Christian Braunman Tullin (1728–65) combined this spirit with a strong personal predilection for the English romantic movement, as represented in his wedding poem *Maidagen* (A Day in May).

Toward the end of the 18th century, the Norwegians studying in Copenhagen formed a club called *Det Norske Selskab* (The Norwegian Society), which in general adhered to French-English classicism in opposition to the German tendencies in the Danish literature of the time. Its outstanding members were Johan Nordahl Brun (1745–1816), later bishop of Bergen and author of several powerful hymns; Claus Fasting (1746–91); Claus Frimann (1746–1829); Jonas Rein (1760–1821); and Jens Zetlitz (1761–1821). Although their poetry is highly nationalistic, a reader may also find in it discrete descriptions of everyday life back in Norway. The most talented in the group was Johan Herman Wessel (1742–85), whose *Kiaerlighed uden Strömper* (Love without Stockings) is a valuable satire on affected imitations of high tragic drama.

The slow development during this period of a literature written in Norwegian dialects has been noted above. Ordinarily the subject is rural daily life, but one finds also criticisms of artificial urban culture. Among writers on this type of subject are Edvard Storm from Gudbrandsdalen, Hans Hansen, and Thomas Rosing de Stockfleth. Further intellectual activity was stimulated by the founding (1760) of *Det kongelige norske videnskabers selskab i Trondhjem* (The Royal Norwegian Society for Research) by Gerhard Schöning, Johannes Ernst Gunnerus, and the Danish-born Peter Fredrik Suhm. The growing interest in Norwegian dialects led to lexicographical studies and publications: Erich Pontoppidan's *Glossarium Norvegicum,* Knud Leem Laurent's *Hallager,* and the work of Wilhelm Frimann, *Koren Christie,* whose word lists were published as early as 1802 and as late as 1939.

The 19th Century. The isolation of Norway from the Continent during the Napoleonic wars led to an increasing desire for political independence, and the poetry of this period is more notable for its patriotic tendencies than for its literary merit. Two names deserve to be mentioned: Henrik Anker Bjerregaard (1792–1842), who was the first to use Norwegian dialects on the stage in *Fjeldeventyret* (The Adventure in the Mountains), and Mauritz Hansen (1794–1842), who wrote realistic short stories of life in the provinces.

The period following the political break with Denmark in 1814 is dominated by a national struggle for cultural independence. On the extreme left were those who wanted a complete break with Denmark; these were opposed by the more conservative classes who, although equally patriotic, wanted to combine nationalism with foreign cultural influences. The leader of the radical party was Henrik Arnold Wergeland (1808–45), a giant in body and spirit. He fought for national, cultural, and

Fig. 2. Title page, 1st edition, "Skabelsen, Mennesket og Messias" by Wergeland.

social freedom, and his life and writings influenced not only his own generation, but nationalistic authors from *Björnson to Nordahl Grieg. At 22, Wergeland had published his main work, the religious-philosophical epic *Skabelsen, Mennesket og Messias* (The Creation, Man, and Messiah), in which he expressed his unlimited, though undogmatic, confidence in the capacity of the human being to achieve fulfillment through self-development. The poem expressed also revolutionary political ideas based on the ideas of the Enlightenment and was written in his characteristic style; it is rich in metaphors, abrupt associations, and ecstatic emotions.

Wergeland's work soon provoked the bitter opposition of Johan Sebastian Cammermeyer Welhaven (1807–73) and led not only to a literary debate, but to a conflict on the general principles of a national culture. Welhaven, influenced by Danish literary taste and tradition, but a fervent patriot nevertheless, condemned as unrealistic the idea that a free development of national culture could be achieved through a break with Denmark. In a mighty sonnet sequence, *Norges Daemring* (1834, The Dawn of Norway), he challenged his adversary and put forth his own cultural program: national growth enriched by the assimilation of foreign culture. Taking his themes from Norwegian folklore, he expressed his approval of the national heritage in a series of ballads; at the same time his symbolic poems, heavily dependent upon Greek mythology, reflect his respect for classical learning. Welhaven, overshadowed by Wergeland, never achieved the fame or the importance of his adversary; yet his poetry excels in formal beauty and emotional depth and serenity. Wergeland's poetry is visionary and often emotionally uncontrolled. His work is little known outside Scandinavian countries despite the fact that some of his poetry ranks among the best in Norwegian literature.

The Romantic Movement. The philosophical aspects of *Romanticism never aroused any interest in Norway, but the movement had a decisive influence on Norwegian literature. Folklorists started writing down the folk tales and ballads (*folkeviser*) that had been kept alive through oral tradition for almost 400 years. From 1841 to 1844 the *Norske Folke-Eventyr* (The Norwegian Folk Tales) were published by Peter Christen Asbjörnsen (1812–85) and Jörgen Moe (1813–82). Important as this collection was in itself, it also exercised a great influence toward a more oral literary style. A similar collection of *Norske Huldreeventyr og Folkesagn* published by Asbjönsen alone had the same effect. The *folkeviser* were saved for posterity by the minister Magnus Brostrup Landstad (1802–80) of Telemark, a region particularly rich in folklore. In this connection mention should be made of Ludwig Lindeman, who collected the melodies to which the *folkeviser* were sung.

In the field of linguistics the products of this era were those of Ivar Aasen (1813–96): *Det norske Folkesprogs Grammatikk* (1848, A Grammar of the Popular Norwegian Language) and his dictionary of dialect vocabulary, *Ordbog over det norske Folkesprog* (1850). At the same time outstanding scholars such as the historians Peter Andreas Munch (1810–63) and Rudolf Keyser (1803–64), together with the linguist Carl Richard Unger (1817–97), furthered the study of Old Norse by providing texts and translations. Among the original poetry of this period the sentimental descriptions of nature by Andreas Munch (1811–84) should be mentioned, as well as the lyric prose of Bernhard Herre.

The search for historical continuity and background for contemporary Norwegian society was particularly evident in the work of two "national authors," *Ibsen and Björnson. Ibsen's plays from this period are less important dramatically than his later work, the most significant of these early efforts being *Fru Inger til Östraat* (1857, Lady Inger of Östraat), *Haermenderne paa Helgeland* (1858, The Vikings of Helgeland), and *Kongsemnerne* (1864, The Pretenders), in which he combines national themes with personal experiences. The Romantic movement also furnished literary material for Ibsen's *Brand* (1866) and *Peer Gynt* (1867), although the nationalist note in them is muted by their criticism of contemporary society. In the same Romantic spirit Björnson started his idealistic program of alternating historical plays culminating with *Sigurd Slembe* (1862) with tales from contemporary farming society, *En Glad Gut* (1860, A Happy Boy), and *Synnöve Solbakken* (1857).

More realistic in his approach to folk culture was the farmer's son Aasmund Olavsson Vinje (1818–70), who knew the dark side of a backward, isolated society. He abandoned farm life and associated with a group of radicals in Oslo, among them Ibsen, Björnson, and Paul Botten-Hansen, with whom he published the satirical journal *Andhrimner*. His *Ferdaminni fraa Sumaren 1860* (Souvenirs from a Journey in the Summer), written in *landsmål*, is a realistic appreciation of folk customs combined with severe criticism of outmoded traditions. More one-sided in her condemnation of contemporary society was Camilla Collett (1813–95), a sister of Henrik Wergeland. In her most important work, *Amtmandens Döttre* (1855, The Daughters of the County Sheriff), she took up a topic that became one of central interest in the following years: marriage and the degrading role of women compelled to look to it as the only way of earning a livelihood. Adherents of the Romantic movement began to be disillusioned, mainly through critical studies of the actual conditions of rural society (e.g., the work of Eilert Sundt, 1817–

75), and the ideas of the realistic movement began to make themselves known in the 1850–60s.

The Rise of Realism. The final break with Romantic ideas came in the early 1870s, when Ibsen fell under the influence of the Danish critic *Brandes, the apostle of realism in Denmark. From that era Ibsen and Björnson in plays and novels assailed the destructive effect of a stratified society on the free development of personality. Among Ibsen's plays of this period are *Samfundets Stötter* (1879, The Pillars of Society), *Et Dukkehjem* (1879, A Doll's House), *Gengangere* (1881, Ghosts), and *En Folkefiende* (1882, An Enemy of the People). Björnson attacked the educational system and the "double moral" standard for men and women in *En Handske* (1883, The Gauntlet), *Det flager i byen og på havnen* (1884, The Heritage of the Kurts), and *På Guds veje* (1889, In God's Way).

The realistic movement called forth also the talent of Jonas Lie (1833–1908), whose *Livsslaven* (1883, The Convict) is an attack on the social structure and public authority. In *Familjen paa Gilje* (1883, The Family on Gilje), and *Kommandörens Döttre* (1836, The Daughters of the Commander), he joined Camilla Collett, Ibsen, and Björnson in their crusade for women's rights to develop their personality through education and marriage based on love. More sophisticated in his criticism was Alexander L. Kielland (1849–1906), who with aristocratic elegance satirized hypocritical small-town humanitarians [e.g., in *Garman og Worse* (1880), *Skipper Worse* (1882)]. *Arbeidsfolk* (1881, Working People) is a biting satire on bureaucratic inefficiency and *Gift* (1883, Poison) is an attack on old-fashioned education. During this period of realism, Arne Garborg (1857–1924) was prominent. His search for truth led him into deep religious conflict as he opposed the rigid pietistic society of his childhood, as in *Ein Fritenkjar* (1878, An Atheist). In *Bondestudentar* (1883, Students from the Provinces), he reveals his rootlessness as he exchanges life in a farming society for that of the intellectual circles of the city.

From Realism to Naturalism. In the 1880s the realistic movement developed into naturalism (*see* NATURALISM, LITERARY). The subjects of attack were the

Fig. 3. Camilla Collett.

conventions of society in general, and particularly marriage. The naturalist movement was, so to speak, identified with the "Bohemian movement" in Christiania. Hans Jaeger's (1854–1910) *Fra Christianiabohemen* (1885, From the Christiania Bohemians) and Christian Krohg's *Albertine* were both condemned by public censure because of their libertinism. Some of Garborg's later works also belong to this period, *Mannfolk* (1886, Men), and *Hjaa ho Mor* (1890, With Mother). Personal tragedies color Amalie Skram's (1846–1905) strong naturalistic novels of the fishing districts around Bergen (e.g., her 4-volume *Hellemyrsfolket*, 1887–98, The Hellemyr Family).

End of the 19th Century and the 20th Century. By the turn of the century naturalistic literature had outlived itself.

Emergence of Neoromanticism. A tendency toward analysis of hidden emotions and drives had already been perceptible in Ibsen's *Vildanden* (1884, The Wild Duck) and *Gengangere,* but it was *Hamsun's *Sult* (1890, Hunger) that opened the way for neoromanticism. His *Mysterier* (1892, Mysteries) and *Pan* (1894) were written in the diffuse twilight of the subconscious and created an entirely new school of poets. Nils Collett Vogt (1864–1937) praised the strength and ruggedness of the Norwegian landscape; subtle and sensitive Vilhelm Krag (1876–1933) portrayed the idyllic landscape of the south coast; and mystical Sigbjörn Obstfelder (1866–1900) revealed in poems and novels his painful questioning of the purpose of life. To this period belong also Ibsen's symbolic plays, *Rosmersholm* (1886) and *Fruen fra Havet* (1888, Lady from the Sea); Garborg's collection of poetry from his home farm, *Haugtussa* (1895); and Jonas Lie's short stories, *Troll* (1891–92), from the mystical, colorful Nordland. A well-known dramatist of the realistic period, Gunnar Heiberg (1857–1920) abandoned programmatic literature also and produced his main works *Balkonen* (1894, The Balcony) and *Kjaerlighedens tragedie* (1904, The Tragedy of Love), in which he attempted to analyze the problem of love.

Prose authors of this period were Thomas Krag and Tryggve Andersen (1867–1920); the latter was one of the most remarkable stylists of the 20th century. As the neoromantic movement developed, its adherents were gradually attracted by lyric poetry and prose treatment of nature, and about the turn of the century a series of authors became the laureates of different regions. Hans Ernst Kinck (1865–1926) described the steep, isolated valleys along the west coast and their crippling effect on human psychology in *Flaggermusvinger* (1895, The Wings of the Bat) and *Driftekaren* (1908, The Herdsman).

More limited in their scope were Per Sivle (1857–1904), Jens Tvedt (1857–1935), Jacob B. Bull (1853–1930), and Hans Aanrud (1863–1953), whose good-natured sense of humor made him extremely popular as an author of short stories. The south coast is represented by Gabriel Scott, Vilhelm and Thomas Krag, and Olaf Benneche, while the northern provinces have been portrayed by Andreas Haukland, Andreas Markusson, Bernt Lie, Regine Normann, and Cora Sandel. The Trondheim region is introduced by Johan Bojer, Peter Egge, Kristofer Uppdal, and Inge Krokann. Although rooted in the narrow society of a bleak fishing district, Olav Duun (1876–1939) lifted his char-

acters to a universal level as he probed the problem of free will struggling against hereditary characteristics in his 6-volume *Juvikfolket* (1918–23, The Juvik Family). Notable authors from the west coast include Hjalmar Christensen and Kristian Elster the younger.

Social Themes. At the beginning of the 20th century, a tendency toward making the working classes the center of interest took shape. Nevertheless, the literature of this period is far from being programmatic, but is rather a sympathetic description of their life and work. Johan Falkberget (1879–) painted the life of the miners in Röros, their professional pride and traditions, in *Christianus Sextus;* Kristofer Uppdal (1878–) dealt with the transition from a farming to an industrial society, and Oskar Braathen (1881–1939) was the humorous observer of Oslo's East End. The middle classes are the subject of *Undset's novels on contemporary society, although her psychological insight gave them a universal aspect. In her two monumental historical novels, *Kristin Lavransdatter I–III* and *Olav Audunssön I–II,* she combined the religious problem of man's rebellion and guilt with colorful descriptions of 14th-century Norway. She described the motives for her conversion to Catholicism (1925) in the novels *Gymnadenia, Den braendende busk* (The Burning Bush), and *Ida Elisabeth.*

In the years before World War II a number of lyric poets arose—Herman Wildenvey, Olaf Bull, Arnulf Överland, Olav Aukrust, Tore Örjasaeter, Gunnar Reiss-Andersen, and Rudolf Nilsen. Social and political struggle is reflected in the poems and novels of Sigurd Hoel, Nini Roll Anker, and A. Överland. The psychological theories of *Freud and Alfred *Adler are apparent in the novels of Sigurd Christiansen, Tarjei Vesaas, Aksel Sandemose, and Cora Sandel.

Mid-20th Century Developments. During World War II Nordahl Grieg and A. Överland, both in active service, won general recognition for their patriotic poetry. After the war, novelists such as Kåre Holt, Terje Stigen, Jens Björneboe, and Finn Carling were prominent, and the short story had a revival in the work of Torolf Elster, Torborg Nedreaas, and especially Johan Borgen. Mid 20th-century poetry was represented by Tor Jonsson (1916–51), Gunvor Hofmo, Jan-Magnus Bruheim, Paal Brekke, and Erling Christie. Literary criticism was well represented in the reviews *Edda* and *Vinduet.* The most prominent scholars in the field of Norwegian literature in the 1900s were Francis Bull; Fredrik Paasche; Halvdan Koht; Harald Beyer, Sr.; Harald Beyer, Jr.; and Philip Houm. An eminent contemporary Catholic scholar was Daniel Haakonsen.

Bibliography: H. BEYER, *A History of Norwegian Literature,* tr. and ed. E. HAUGEN (New York 1956). F. BULL et al., *Norsk litteraturhistorie,* 6 v. (2d ed. Oslo 1957–). R. ØKSNEVAD, *Norsk litteraturhistorisk bibliografi, 1900–1945* (Oslo 1951), *1946–1955* (Oslo 1958) contains several references to works in English. *Scandinavica* (London and New York 1962–). E. DAL, "Scandinavian Ballad Research Today," *ibid.* 1 (1962) 5–16. E. BREDSDORFF et al., *An Introduction to Scandinavian Literature* (New York 1951). **Illustration credits:** Norwegian Embassy Information Service.

[A. SALVESEN]

NORWICH, ANCIENT SEE OF, founded in 1095, when Herbert Losinga transferred his see there from Thetford, since Norwich had become the most important town in East Anglia. Losinga, one of the

The medieval cathedral at Norwich, planned in 1096.

foremost men of his day, had been prior of *Fécamp and abbot of *Ramsey, and then decided to introduce Benedictines into his cathedral. In 1096 he planned the buildings and dedicated them to the Holy Trinity; much of his work is still visible, so that Norwich remains the most purely Norman cathedral in Britain (*see* CHURCH ARCHITECTURE, 4). Provision was made for a community of 60 monks. The wealth of the community increased during the following centuries mainly because of the appropriation of churches. Income came also from the shrine of St. *William of Norwich, a boy alleged to have been murdered by Jews in 1144. There were frequent disputes with the townsmen over the rights of tolls and commons. After a great affray in 1272, which resulted in the burning of the monastic buildings, the citizens had to contribute 3,000 marks toward the repairs. Bishop Percy built (*c.* 1360) a clerestory and spire to replace ones damaged in a storm, and Bishops Lyhert and Goldwell replaced the timber roof with one of stone. The diocese suffered heavily during the *Black Death; in 1 year Bishop Bateman made over about 800 institutions. In 1370 Henry *Despenser was provided to the see; he was a military bishop, unusual in English history, who took a prominent part in the suppression of the Peasants' Revolt (*see* RICHARD II, KING OF ENGLAND). The diocese was much affected by the *Lollard heresy, and Bishop Alnwick labored hard to control the danger. The most distinguished members of the monastic community were the 14th-century scholar-monks, Thomas Brinton and *Adam Easton, both of whom spent most of their working lives at the papal Curia. The priory was dissolved in 1538, when the prior became dean and the monks were appointed canons of the new chapter.

Bibliography: Dugdale MonAngl 4:1–24. *The Victoria History of the County of Norfolk,* ed. H. A. DOUBLEDAY and W. PAGE, v.2 (Westminster, Eng. 1906). E. H. CARTER, ed., *Studies in Norwich Cathedral History* (Norwich 1935). Knowles MOE; ROE.
Illustration credit: The British Travel Association, New York.

[F. R. JOHNSTON]

NORWICH, DIOCESE OF (NORVICENSIS), suffragan of the metropolitan See of *Hartford, comprising the counties of Middlesex, New London, Tolland, and Windham in eastern Connecticut; and Fishers Island, a portion of Suffolk County, N.Y.; this area of 1,978 square miles was separated from the Diocese of Hartford and established a diocese on Aug. 6, 1953, the same day Hartford was made a metropolitan. The first bishop, Bernard J. Flanagan, former chancellor of the Diocese of Burlington, Vt., was appointed to Norwich on Sept. 1, 1953, and served until his transfer to Worcester, Mass., in 1959. His successor, Vincent J. Hines, former chancellor of the Diocese of Hartford, was named on Nov. 27, 1959, and consecrated in St. Patrick's Cathedral, Norwich, March 17, 1960.

By 1963 the diocese numbered 174,325 Catholics in a total population of 412,319. They were organized in 66 parishes and 17 missions, and were served by 119 diocesan and 88 religious priests, including representatives of the Society of St. Edmund, whose novitiate is located in Mystic, Conn.; the Jesuits, whose tertianship for the New England Province is in Pomfret, Conn.; LaSalette fathers, in Danielson; and Capuchin fathers, in Middletown. The Brothers of the Sacred Heart conduct a preparatory school in Pomfret, and Holy Apostles Seminary for delayed vocations to the priesthood is located in Cromwell. Other communities of religious men working in the diocese include the Oblates of Mary Immaculate, Basilians, Marian fathers, and Brothers of St. Francis Xavier. Annhurst College (1941) in South Woodstock is conducted by the Daughters of the Holy Ghost for young women. There were also 7 high schools and 26 elementary schools caring for a total of about 12,000 students, 2 homes for the aged, 2 retreat houses, and 1 hospital. Among the religious communities of women helping to staff these institutions were the Felicians, Religious of the Cenacle, Franciscan Missionary Sisters, Daughters of the Holy Ghost, Filippini Sisters, and Sisters of Charity, Holy Cross, Holy Family, Mercy, Immaculate Conception, St. Joseph, and Precious Blood.

[J. J. REILLY]

NORWID, CYPRIAN KAMIL, Polish poet, dramatist, critic, and painter; b. Laskowo-Głuchy, Sept. 24, 1821; d. Paris, May 23, 1883. He received a religious and patriotic upbringing in the home of his grandmother, a Sobieski; the home was of modest circumstances yet filled with ancient aristocratic traditions. Educated at Warsaw (1832–37), Norwid began there a study of painting, which he completed in Florence (1843–44). He demonstrated his religious and philosophic attitude and his exceptional gift of observation in such works as *Sieroty* (1840, The Orphans) and *Pióro* (1842, The Pen). His poetry gradually became more profound and elaborate and the difficulties thus posed for the ordinary reader caused a rejection that doomed the poet to both oblivion and poverty.

After a period of travel in Italy, Germany, Belgium, and Greece (1844–48) and the experience of an unhappy love for Maria Kalergis, Norwid settled in Paris, where, except for the years between 1852 and 1854, spent in the U.S. and a brief time in England, he resided for the rest of his life. He lived his last 6 years at St. Casimir's Asylum for poor Poles in Paris. During

Cyprian Kamil Norwid, self-portrait.

his time in Italy Norwid took an active part in the defense of the Vatican against the revolutionaries (1848).

Most of his more valuable work, especially his poems, plays, essays, criticism, and lectures on religious subjects, is moralizing in tone. It includes his Marian poems *Modlitwa: Mario* (1848, Prayer, O Mary), *Czestochowskie Wiersze* (1850, Czestochowa Poems), *Legenda* (1852), *Psalm w Hebronie* (1880, Magnificat), and one of the most beautiful religious lyrics of the 19th century, *Do N.P. Maryi Litania* (1852, Litany to the Most Blessed Virgin).

Many contemporaries considered Norwid a mystic, but he was not one in any theological sense, although he based his philosophic and aesthetic outlook upon the Gospel. His poetic and patriotic program was outlined in *Poezje* (1863, Poetry), *Vademecum* (prepared 1866; pub. 1947), and especially in *Promethidion* (1881) and *Rzecz o wolności słowa* (1869, On the Liberty of Speech). In beautiful, though at times hermetic language, Norwid gave new perspectives to the future of Polish poetry. As a dramatist he returned to Greek and medieval models, e.g., *Krakus* (1863), *Wanda* (1863), and *Kleopatra* (1904). His artistry is best shown in his short poems, such as *Fortepian Szopena* (1865, Chopin's Piano), considered a masterpiece. His rich literary legacy, scattered throughout various periodicals or in MSS, was collected and published by Z. Przesmycki at the beginning of the 20th century.

Bibliography: C. K. NORWID, *Pisma zebrane*, 5 v. (Warsaw 1911–45); *Wszystkie pisma*, 6 v. (Warsaw 1937); *Pisma polityczne i filozoficzne* (London 1957), all ed. Z. PRZESMYCKI. A. KRECHOWIECKI, *O Cypryanie Norwidzie* (Lvov 1909). W. BOROWY, *O Norwidzie* (Warsaw 1960). I. SŁAWIŃSKA, *O Komediach Norwida* (Lublin 1953). T. F. DOMARADZKI, "Le Culte de la Vierge Marie chez C. N.," *Études slaves et est-européennes* 6 (1961) 3–45. J. JARZĘBOWSKI, *Norwid i Zmartwychwstancy* (London 1960). **Illustration credit:** Bibliothèque Polonaise, Paris.

[T. F. DOMARADZKI]

NOTARY (CANON LAW)

A notary can be defined as a person legitimately constituted by ecclesiastical authority to authenticate by his signature ecclesiastical documents. The office of notary is not an ecclesiastical *office in the strict sense, and the term is not defined in the Code of Canon Law.

The function of notary has its roots in the *notarius* who took notes to aid the public scribes (*tabelliones*) in drawing up documents, and in the *tabularius*, who took notes and kept the records of court proceedings in Roman law. This latter official can be found fulfilling the same function in the Church of the 5th century, and by the 12th century he had acquired the name "notary" and the right to authenticate public documents with his signature. The Fourth Lateran Council (1215) prescribed that every ecclesiastical court must have a notary.

Canon Law uses "notary" as a general term (CIC c.373; ClerSanc c.440), "chancellor" as a specific type of notary (CIC c.372; ClerSanc c.439), and "actuary" referring to the notary whose presence and signature are necessary for validity in all trials (CIC c.1585; SollNostr c.56). *See* CHANCELLOR, DIOCESAN (EPARCHIAL).

The general duties of a notary (c.374; ClerSanc c.441) are as follows: to draft acts or documents attesting enactments, orders, commitments, judicial summonses and notifications, decrees, sentences, and similar matters; to record minutes of what transpired in the meetings to which he is accredited, and to sign this record; to give access to records to those who have a right to it; and to furnish authenticated copies of the originals.

The power to authenticate documents is vested in the diocesan chancellor, in those appointed notaries as such, and in those appointed or employed as actuaries or judicial notaries.

The power of the notary may be extended to include the authentication of all ecclesiastical acts, or limited to judicial or processual documents only or to specified acts or occasions. His duties are further limited to the territory in which the one appointing has jurisdiction. Laymen may be appointed, but in criminal trials involving clerics, the notary should be a priest. Although it is not required by law, knowledge of Canon Law is obviously of great value. Removal from office, temporary or permanent, is entirely in the hands of the nominator and his superior and successor.

The duties, appointment, and removal of the notary in the legislation for Oriental Catholics is essentially the same (ClerSanc cc.440–441), but in trials the drawing up of the acts is not demanded for validity. The signature of the judicial notary suffices (SollNostr c.56.1).

Bibliography: R. NAZ, DDC 6:1015–20. G. BARRACLOUGH, *Public Notaries and the Papal Curia* (London 1934). J. C. BROWN, "The Origin and Early History of the Office of Notary," *Juridical Review* 47 (1935) 201–240, 355–417. C. J. DUERR, *The Judicial Notary* (CUA CLS 312; Washington 1951).

[C. J. DUERR]

NOTBURGA, ST.,

maidservant; fl. 9th or 10th century; or, according to a recent version of the legend, b. Rattenberg, Tyrol, *c.* 1265; d. September 14, 1313 (feast, Sept. 14). Most of her life was spent in the service of Count Henry of Rottenburg. Pious, a diligent worker, she was noted for charity to the poor, to whom she gave food and drink. She died at Rottenburg castle, and was buried at Eben. Her relics were exhumed in 1718; ecclesiastical confirmation of her cult was given on March 27, 1862. She is an extremely popular saint among the farmers and peasants of the Tyrol, of Bavaria, Slovenia, Croatia, and Istria, where numerous churches and altars are dedicated to her. Patroness of maidservants and farmers, she is invoked in cases of animal sickness and for successful childbirth. Her symbols include a sickle, a metal jug and a loaf of bread (relating to her care of the poor), and a ring of keys.

Bibliography: ActSS Sept. 4:709–768. *Andenken an die Feier der Heiligsprechung der Jungfrau und Dienstmagd Notburga von Rottenburg* (Brixen-Lienz 1863). H. BACHMANN, "Die historischen Grundlagen der Notburgalegende," *Tiroler Heimat* 24 (1960) 5–49. W. VON PFAUNDLER, *Sankt Notburga: Eine Heilige aus Tirol* (Vienna 1962), complete bibliog. 282–300.

[D. ANDREINI]

NOTES, THEOLOGICAL

Most recent manuals of theology present their doctrine in the form of theses, and to each thesis they regularly assign a "theological note." Thus one thesis may be qualified as "of divine faith," another as "Catholic doctrine" or, again, "theologically certain." The system of theological notes is of considerable value to theologians and to all who are intent on accurate theological knowledge, for such notes indicate what kind of certitude the thesis involves, what kind of assent it demands. This article briefly treats the definition, author, division, and main types of theological notes.

Definition. A theological note is a judgment of the dogmatic or theological value of a proposition according to its relation with the norms of faith. The remote norms of faith are Sacred Scripture and tradition; the proximate norm is the teaching of the magisterium. *See* TRADITION (IN THEOLOGY). A note presenting such an evaluative judgment is called "theological" because it makes known the theological value of a proposition. It is also called a "qualification" or "value" because it manifests the theological quality or value of the proposition.

A "theological censure" (*see* CENSURE, THEOLOGICAL) is a pejorative judgment that indicates a proposition is in some way opposed or harmful to faith or morals. If a thesis is given the theological note "of divine and Catholic faith," then a proposition that directly contradicts this thesis will be given the theological censure of "heresy."

Author. Strictly speaking, a dogmatic or theological evaluation of theses is matter for the ecclesiastical magisterium, since it alone has binding authority in the Church. *See* TEACHING AUTHORITY OF THE CHURCH (MAGISTERIUM). But theologians can be empowered to pronounce sentence in doctrinal matters, and sometimes popes have given this power expressly to faculties of theology. Gradually it has come to be customary for theologians to pass judgment on the theological or dogmatic value of their own theses, though sometimes the Church has restricted their power and forbidden them to censure certain propositions that are still freely discussed among Catholics.

Division. There are many theological notes in use today: "divine faith," "divine and Catholic faith," "defined faith," "ecclesiastical faith," "proximate to faith"; "Catholic doctrine," "theologically certain," "common and certain doctrine"; "probable," "more probable," "common," "more common," and others.

The propositions that are qualified by these theological notes may be grouped into three or four general categories. The first embraces propositions that are in some way "of faith." The second includes propositions that are "not of faith" but are in some way "theologically certain." The third includes propositions that are "not certain" but are more or less "probable." Many authors break the second category into two, so as to distinguish "theologically certain" propositions into those that are "Catholic doctrine" and those that are "not Catholic doctrine." The reasons for this distinction will appear presently.

Main Types. It is now possible to consider the main types of theological notes in greater detail.

Divine and Catholic Faith. The most important theological note is that of "divine and Catholic faith." It is given to truths that are dogmas of the faith and must be believed if one is not to incur the censure of heresy. Such truths demand an absolute assent, based not on intrinsic truth seen with the natural light of reason but on the authority of God revealing, who can neither deceive nor be deceived (Denz 3008).

The meaning of this note is best gathered from a dogmatic constitution of Vatican Council I: "... by divine and Catholic faith everything must be believed that is contained in the written word of God or in tradition, and that is proposed by the Church as a divinely revealed object of belief either in a solemn decree or in her ordinary, universal magisterium" (Denz 3011).

Thus two points must be verified if a proposition is to be "of divine and Catholic faith": it must be divinely revealed and it must be proposed by the Church for belief as divinely revealed. If it is divinely revealed, or, as the Council puts it, is contained in the written word of God or in tradition, then it is "of divine faith." If it is also proposed by the Church as a divinely revealed object of belief, then it is "of divine and Catholic faith."

Such a dogma of the faith can be proposed for belief by the Church in two ways: either by a solemn decree or by her ordinary, universal magisterium. If it is proposed for belief by a solemn decree, that is, if it is solemnly defined, then its theological note is slightly changed by many theologians so as to indicate this. Instead of saying that it is "of divine and Catholic faith," they say that it is "of defined divine faith," or simply "of defined faith."

Such solemn definitions can be made by a pope speaking *ex cathedra, as in the definition of the Immaculate Conception by Pius IX and of the Assumption by Pius XII. Solemn definitions are also issued by ecumenical councils, such as Trent and Vatican I, in their various decrees and dogmatic constitutions.

But not only solemn definitions of the Church receive the note "of divine and Catholic faith." It is also applied to truths proposed by the Church's ordinary, universal magisterium as divinely revealed objects of belief. According to Pius IX, "... that subjection which is to be made by an explicit act of divine faith must not be limited to those things which have been defined in express decrees of ecumenical councils or of Roman pontiffs . . . ; but it must also be extended to those things which, through the ordinary teaching of the whole Church throughout the world, are proposed as divinely revealed and, as a result, by universal and constant consent of Catholic theologians are held to be matters of faith" (Denz 2879). One finds truths of this kind in certain famous symbols, such as the so-called Athanasian Creed (Denz 75) or the Niceno-Constantinopolitan Creed (Denz 150).

There are also some particular councils whose propositions have acquired universal and irreformable value from their confirmation by a Roman pontiff and acceptance by the Church as expressions of her faith. Such are the Council of Carthage (Denz 222) against the Pelagians and the Second Council of Orange (Denz 370) against the Semi-Pelagians. From these, too, we derive propositions that are "of divine and Catholic faith" and whose denial incurs the censure of heresy.

Divine Faith. This note is used by some theologians, and more frequently in the treatise on revelation than in other treatises. They consider a truth to be "of divine faith" if it is found in the written word of God or in tradition so clearly that, even if it were not proposed by the Church for belief as divinely revealed, it would still have to be believed by divine faith. For them such truths are the divinity of Christ and His Resurrection.

Ecclesiastical Faith. This is another note occasionally encountered in manuals of theology. It is a controverted note, maintained by some theologians, rejected by others. When used, it is applied to truths that are revealed only virtually, not formally, but that are proposed by the magisterium of the Church to be held absolutely and universally. These truths are often defined, but not as dogmas of the faith. They require absolute assent because they are backed by the infallible authority of the Church. Hence they are qualified as "of ecclesiastical faith." An instance of such a truth is drawn from the Constitution of Alexander VII: "we declare and define that these five propositions taken from the book of the aforementioned Cornelius Jansen . . . were condemned in the sense intended by that same Cornelius Jansen . . ." (Denz 2012).

Proximate to Faith. This frequently used note is applied to a doctrine that by almost unanimous consent is held to be revealed but is not yet expressly proposed as such by the infallible magisterium. That "God sincerely wills the salvation of all adults" is said to be such a doctrine. This note does not command absolute assent.

Catholic Doctrine. This is a common theological note but an ambiguous one. Some theologians apply it to dogmas of the faith. For others it seems to have the same meaning as "proximate to faith." By still others it is applied to one species of theologically certain propositions. Sometimes it is difficult to determine just what meaning it has.

It applies strictly to propositions that are not dogmas of the faith or strict theological conclusions from revealed truths, but yet are taught expressly and authentically by the magisterium of the Church. Such propositions, based on the authority but not the infallibility of the Church, require of the faithful a truly internal assent from a religious motive of obedience.

"Catholic doctrine" is said to extend to whatever the supreme magisterium wishes to teach expressly, without proposing it for belief, such as the chief ideas of encyclicals, propositions contrary to those that have been condemned, what is contained in the chapters of general councils without being certainly defined or what is easily deduced from these chapters, doctrinal decrees of the Roman pontiff or of Roman Congregations if these have been approved and confirmed by the pope. These latter decrees are not irreformable and are of lesser weight than strictly papal precepts, but they too require an obedient assent.

Theologically Certain. This is another very common but not very satisfactory note. For it is sometimes applied only to strict *theological conclusions, sometimes also to Catholic doctrine, sometimes even more widely to any common and certain doctrine of theologians. Hence "theologically certain" propositions must be carefully examined to determine just what this qualification means in each case.

In its strictest sense a proposition is called "theologically certain" if it is a certain theological conclusion from one premise that is revealed and from another that is not revealed but is naturally certain. Thus the proposition that Christ is capable of laughter is called theologically certain because it is deduced from a revealed premise (Christ is man), and from a naturally certain premise (every man is capable of laughter). *See* ERROR, THEOLOGICAL.

In its widest sense, a "theologically certain" note is applied to propositions that theologians commonly hold as certain but that are neither strict theological conclusions from revelation nor Catholic doctrine. Many theologians qualify such propositions simply as "common and certain."

Probable. Another very common note is "probable," "more probable," etc. A thesis is termed theologically "probable" if it rests on a fallible but sufficiently grave theological motive. The Ecumenical Council of Vienne used this note: "We . . . consider the second opinion which says that in Baptism informing grace and virtues are conferred on children as well as on adults, as more probable . . ." (Denz 904).

In conclusion, one may say it is extremely regrettable that theologians, while they have found these and other theological notes very useful, have not found a way to achieve greater uniformity in the definition and use of them.

See also THEOLOGICAL TERMINOLOGY.

Bibliography: H. QUILLIET, DTC 2:2101–13. S. CARTECHINI, *De valore notarum theologicarum et de criteriis ad eas dignoscendas* (Rome 1951). J. B. FRANZELIN, *Tractatus de divina traditione et Scriptura* (4th ed. Rome 1896). L. DE GRANDMAISON, *Le Dogme chrétien: Sa nature, ses formules, son développement* (Paris 1928). J. SALAVERRI, "De valore et censura propositionum in theologia," *Estudios Ecclesiasticos* 23 (1949) 170–188.

[E. J. FORTMAN]

NOTICIAS SECRETAS DE AMÉRICA, fraudulent title under which the English editor David Barry published in London in 1826 a confidential report submitted to the Spanish crown in 1749 by two Spanish scientists, Jorge Juan and Antonio Ulloa. The report contained their personal observations, made during a trip in America with the Hispanic-French scientific expedition from 1736 to 1744, on the disregard shown the laws of the Spanish government in the vice-

Autograph note of Notker Balbulus, dated Dec. 28, 909. The last words read "Ego Notker infans notavi."

royalty of Peru. The original title of the MS, which did not present a fair description of the situation in the viceroyalty but was merely a list of abuses that needed correction, was *Discurso y reflexiones políticas sobre el estado presente de los reynos del Perú, su gobierno, reximen particular de aquellos avitadores y abusos que se han introducido en uno, y otro. . . ."* Five MSS copies of this document are extant; three belong to the Royal Library of Madrid, one to the National Library of Madrid, and one to the New York Public Library. The five copies are substantially the same, except for variations in syntax and arrangement of the material, and in textual agreement with the London edition. Barry, however, invented the new title and omitted the original preface, substituting another that distorted the aims and the limitations of the report and exaggerating its value as an eyewitness account, in both time and area. Although this work of Juan and Ulloa had widespread acceptance for many years, 20th-century investigations raised serious doubts as to its value. These doubts were based on the youth and prejudices of the authors at the time they collected their data, on the tendency to exaggeration inherent in the literary form of the report, on the limited contact that they had with the various social levels of the population in spite of the years they spent in Peru, and on the scanty evidence of the abuses they described found in other published and unpublished documents of the period.

Bibliography: A. P. WHITAKER, "Antonio de Ulloa," *Hispanic American Historical Review* 15 (1935) 155–194; "Jorge and Antonio de Ulloa's Prologue to Their Secret Report on Peru," *ibid.* 18 (1938) 507–513. L. MERINO, *Las Noticias Secretas de América: Estudio crítico de las acusaciones de Ulloa sobre general relajación del clero colonial, 1720–1765* (Washington 1956).

[L. MERINO]

NOTKER BALBULUS

Poet, chronicler, Sequence writer; b. either in Heiligau (now Elgg, near Zurich) or Jonschwil (near Sankt Gallen), Switzerland, *c.* 840; d. Sankt Gallen Abbey, April 6, 912. Born of a noble Swiss family, Notker entered the Benedictine Abbey of *Sankt Gallen as a child, remained there as a student under such masters as Iso and Moengal (Marcellus) the Irishman, and stayed on to become an admired and beloved teacher, despite the speech defect that won him the sobriquet Balbulus, the "Stammerer." He was appointed librarian of the monastery in 890 and was guest master in 892 and 894, but his reputation is based on his literary activities.

Notker is now almost universally recognized as the *monachus Sangallensis* who *c.* 884 composed the anecdotal and highly imaginative *Gesta Caroli* (MGSrer GermNS 12), based on folk tales and legends and written in colloquial Latin prose. This work, of which only the first part and some of the second are extant, won immediate and lasting popularity in the Middle Ages; its tales of Charlemagne's encounters with his Frankish bishops are chiefly responsible for the emergence of the legendary (as opposed to Einhard's historical) figure of Charlemagne in medieval literature. About 881 Notker wrote the *Breviarium regum Francorum,* a continuation of Erchanbert's chronicle. He is the author of four hymns in honor of St. Stephen and the metrical *Vita s. Galli,* of which only fragments remain; the hymn *Media vita,* ascribed to him by a tradition that can be traced only to 1613, is probably not his. His extant letters reveal a man of spirit and wit.

It is, however, for his role in the development of the *Sequence that Notker is most often remembered (*see* HYMNOLOGY). In the preface of his *Liber hymnorum* [ed. W. von den Steinen (Bern 1960) with melodies], a collection of Sequences dedicated *c.* 884–887 to Liutward, Bishop of Vercelli and chancellor of Charles the Fat, Notker recounts that in 862 a monk from the recently sacked monastery of *Jumièges in France brought to Sankt Gallen an antiphonary in which a text (*prosa*) had been set to parts of the *jubilus* (the melody that prolonged the final *a* of the *Alleluia* following the Gradual of the Mass). Considering this an excellent mnemonic device for committing to memory the difficult *jubilus* melody, Notker composed a text that both imitated and improved upon the French text, the *Laudes Deo concinat.* His master Iso praised his first attempt but suggested making each syllable of the text correspond to a note of the *jubilus;* this Notker did in the *Psallat ecclesia,* a text for the dedication of a church, which won the approval of both Iso and Moengal. Many scholars are not totally satisfied with this account of Notker's, for it only obfuscates the question that they consider crucial to a proper estimate of his traditional role as originator of the Sequence; that is, to what extent was he influenced by the earlier and much simpler French Sequences of the 8th and 9th centuries (AnalHymn 53)? In addition, scholars are not certain how many or, in some instances, which Sequences are to be attributed to Notker. The original manuscript of the *Liber hymnorum* is not extant, and though there are eight MSS dating from not later than the 11th century, no two of them are identical. Nor is *Ekkehard IV's statement in the Sankt Gallen chronicle that Notker composed 50 Sequences of any help, since Ekkehard does not identify them by *incipit.* Whether or not Notker was the originator of the Sequence, there can be no doubt of his influence on German literature. His Sequences, in rhythmical prose and without rhyme, were in frequent use throughout northern Europe until the middle of the 12th century. They are characterized by simplicity and nobility of language and style and by profundity and orthodoxy of theological content. Notker is also called the first musical composer of German stock, for he is known to have composed the music as well as the words of some of his Sequences, thus freeing the text from too great dependence upon an already existing musical composition.

Notker was beatified in 1512. Permission for a commemoration of him on April 8 was granted to the monastery of Sankt Gallen by a papal bull of Dec. 12, 1512, and was extended to the Diocese of Constance in 1513. His relics were brought to the cathedral of Sankt Gallen in 1628. Notker's vita by Ekkehard V (ActSS April 1:579–595) is not altogether reliable.

Bibliography: Julian DictHym 1:812–816. Manitius 1:354–367, for Notker's works. S. SINGER, *Die Dichterschule von St. Gallen* (Leipzig 1922). W. VON DEN STEINEN, *Notker der Dichter und seine geistige Welt,* 2 v. (Bern 1948). Raby ChrLP 211–215, brief but comprehensive survey in Eng. H. F. HAEFELE, "Studien zu Notkers *Gesta Karoli,*" DeutschArch 15 (1959) 358–392. W. KOSCH, *Deutsches Literatur-Lexikon,* ed. B. BERGER (Bern 1963). Szöverffy AnnLatHymn 1:282–299. **Illustration credit:** Stifts-Archiv, Sankt Gallen.

[M. F. MC CARTHY]

NOTKER LABEO, Benedictine scholar, one of the earliest authors to translate Latin works into German, for which he was given the nickname *Teutonicus;* b. Thurgau, Switzerland, *c.* 950; d. Abbey of Sankt Gallen, June 29, 1022. He was one of four nephews of Abbot *Ekkehard I to enter the community at *Sankt Gallen, which he joined as an *oblate. Widely read in all branches of knowledge, he was later chosen to direct the monastic school, where one of his pupils was *Ekkehard IV. In a letter (P. H. Piper, 1:859–61) to Bp. Hugh of Sion (d. 1017) Notker lists his works; of 11 translations, only 5 are extant. His clear poetic style, which made him the earliest master of German prose, appears in his translations of *Boethius's *De consolatione philosophiae,* the two extant books of *Martianus Capella's *De nuptiis Mercurii et philologiae,* the *Categories* and *Hermeneutics* of *Aristotle (from an earlier translation into Latin by Boethius), and in the *Psalter, perhaps Notker's most famous work (an Old High German–Latin interlinear text, MS Sankt Gallen 21, dating from *c.* 1100). No copies have been found of Notker's translations of Boethius's *De trinitate* and *Elements of Arithmetic*(?), Vergil's *Bucolica,* the *Disticha Catonis,* Terence's *Andria,* and the *Homilia in Job* of Pope *Gregory the Great, to which Notker devoted his last days.

Notker wrote an original work in German on music, dealing with, among other things, the measurement of organ pipes. It is the first such work on music known in German. He is the author of a Latin work, the *Computus,* for the determining of dates, especially that of Easter. He is credited also with a Latin textbook, *De arte rhetorica,* composed principally of excerpts from Boethius.

Notker contributed to the development of German orthography; in the letter to Hugh of Sion he recommended accents for German words (acute for short vowels, circumflex for long). His contribution to the German vernacular may be compared to *Alfred the Great's work in making Anglo-Saxon a literary language. Like Alfred, Notker translated the Latin classics to make them available to a wider audience.

Bibliography: Works. *Die Schriften Notkers und seiner Schule,* ed. P. H. PIPER, 3 v. (Freiburg 1895). *Notkers des Deutschen Werke,* ed. E. H. SEHRT and T. STARCK 7 v. (Halle 1933–55). Literature. J. M. CLARK, *The Abbey of St. Gall as a Centre of Literature and Art* (Cambridge, Eng. 1926), *passim.* Manitius 2:694–699. É. AMANN, DTC 11.1:806–807. O. A. DIETER, *The Rhetoric of Notker Labeo* (St. Louis 1940). W. VON DEN STEINEN, *Notker, der Dichter und seine geistige Welt,* 2 v. (Bern 1948). A. K. DOLCH, *Notker-Studien,* 2 v. (Borna-Leipzig 1951–52). I. SCHRÖBLER, *Notker III. von St. Gallen als Übersetzer und Commentator von Boethius . . .* (Tübingen 1953). E. H. SEHRT,

Notker-Wortschatz (Halle 1955). Cross ODCC 967. J. Duft, LexThK² 7:1051.

[B. J. COMASKEY]

NOTKER OF LIÈGE, BL., prince bishop of Liège; b. *c.* 940; d. Liège, April 10, 1008 (feast, April 9 or 10). He came of a noble Swabian family and was a nephew of Emperor Otto I. Although he seems to have been educated at Sankt Gallen, it is unlikely that he was provost there. Made bishop of Liège in 969 and called its "second founder," he directed his energies to strengthening Church discipline, building churches, and improving the schools of his diocese. As a result of his work the *cathedral school of Saint-Lambert, divided into clerical and lay sections, was among the best in the West. He was often in the service of the Emperors Otto II, Otto III, and Henry II; and on one of his four trips to Italy he accompanied back to Germany the body of *Otto III, whose classical notions of the Empire he had enthusiastically supported. He built a cathedral in Liège after the model of Aachen, but it was destroyed by fire in 1185. He was buried in St. John's at Liège, but the present relics there are not genuine.

Bibliography: I. HELLER, ed., *Aegidii Aureaevallensis gesta episcoporum Leodiensium*, MGS 25:57–63. ActSS April 1:58, 847. U. BERLIÈRE, "Une Biographie de l'évêque Notger au XIIe siècle," RevBén 8 (1891) 309–312. G. KURTH, *Notger de Liège et la civilisation au Xe siècle*, 2 v. (Brussels 1905).

[W. E. WILKIE]

NOTKER PHYSICUS, or Notker II, surnamed *Piperis Grannum,* physician and painter; d. Nov. 12, 975. He was educated at *Sankt Gallen by his uncle, *Ekkehard II, and became its most famous physician. He perhaps also assisted in painting the walls of the abbey church after the fire of 937. He became *cellarius* about 956 and *hospitarius* in 965. Notker also achieved some distinction as a painter of miniatures and composer of hymns, and his work was highly praised by the abbot *Ekkehard IV. He may be identical with the Notker Notarius whose medical knowledge was well known in the court of *Otto I, and who, in 940, drew up at Quedlinburg the confirmation of the immunity of Sankt Gallen. He was especially remembered for his observance of the monastic life.

Bibliography: EKKEHARD IV, *Casus Sancti Galli*, ed. G. MEYER VON KNONAU in *Mitteilungen zur vaterländ. Geschichte* (Saint Gallen 1877) x, xxxi, cxxiii, cxlvii. C. BRUNNER, *Über Medizin und Krankenpflege im Mittelalter in Schweizerischen Landen* (Zurich 1922), *passim.* J. M. CLARK, *The Abbey of St. Gall as a Centre of Literature and Art* (Cambridge, Eng. 1926), *passim.*

[T. C. HERNDON]

NOTRE DAME, COLLEGE OF

A 4-year liberal arts college for women, located at Belmont, Calif. Originally known as the Academy of Notre Dame, it began in the mining days of the late 1840s when a small group of Sisters of Notre Dame de Namur, on the advice of Bp. Sadoc *Alemany, established a foundation in Pueblo San José, then capital of the state of California. Although San José settled into a period of slow development, the Academy expanded quickly after its first commencement in 1851. From its earliest years, the school attracted students from California and Central America, and the Belgian-born faculty was increased by English-speaking mem-

bers. It was chartered in 1868 by the state of California as College of Notre Dame. Collegiate courses were introduced into the curriculum, and the equivalent of a junior college diploma was conferred. Notre Dame Music Conservatory, however, carried a complete college course, with universally recognized degrees and standing. With the expansion of the business section of San José, the board of directors found it advisable to seek another campus. In 1923 they purchased the Ralston estate at Belmont, and on this 100-acre campus the new College of Notre Dame took form.

The College of Notre Dame is accredited by the Western Association of Schools and Colleges and by the National Council for Accreditation of Teacher Education. It is empowered by the California State Board of Education to recommend candidates for the elementary teaching credential, and is affiliated with The Catholic University of America. It is a member of the American Association of University Women, Association of American Colleges, National Catholic Educational Association, National Commission on Accrediting, National Education Association, and American Dietetics Association.

The College is governed by a board of regents composed of university administrators, professors, and laymen. Besides the offices of president, dean, dean of students, and registrar, the administration includes a director of evening division and a director of development. In 1964, the faculty numbered 22 sisters, 36 lay professors, and 4 priests, who held 15 doctoral and 23 master's degrees. There were 345 full-time and 69 part-time students in the regular session and 542 in the summer session. Revenue accrues from tuition, grants to faculty and students, scholarships, bequests, and annual gifts by business corporations, the contributed services of the religious community, and a fund drive sponsored by the development and alumnae offices.

The curriculum leading to a B.A. and B.S. in business administration centers around the humanities, natural and social sciences, and community service, which includes education. All courses are integrated in the division of theology and philosophy. Since there is no major in education, teaching candidates enroll in one of the liberal arts majors. Although candidates attend a special campus demonstration school, after graduation they fulfill practice teaching requirements in the public schools of the surrounding districts.

Facilities include the Greenan Library, which in 1963 housed 44,328 volumes and subscribed to 418 periodicals, and a special laboratory for radioisotope experiments, in addition to the usual science laboratories.

The College conducts a large evening division and summer educational workshops for teachers. It also sponsors the Annual Belmont Conference on Literature and a series of cultural lectures by specialists from the University of California at Los Angeles, and Stanford University.

[M. D. MC NAMEE]

NOTRE DAME, SISTERS OF

The congregation of the Sisters of Notre Dame (SND), a pontifical institute, is devoted chiefly to education, including the training of teachers. It was founded in Coesfeld, Germany, in 1850 by two young teachers, Aldegonda Wolbring (Sister Mary Aloysia) and Lisette Kuehling (Sister Mary Ignatia), assisted by their spiritual director, Rev. Theodore Elting. The first members were trained by sisters from the Notre Dame Convent of Amersfoort, Netherlands, who gave them the rule that Bl. Marie Rose Julie *Billiart had adopted for her community. In 1900 the Holy See gave final approbation to this rule as adapted by the new congregation. A revision, undertaken by Mother Mary Antonie, fourth superior general, to incorporate the provisions of the new Code of Canon Law, was approved by Rome in 1935.

The first teacher-training school for the sisters and for other young women was opened, with government approval, in 1853 by Sister Mary Bernarda Perger. Three years later, the Amersfoort sisters returned to their own community and the Coesfeld group elected their first superior general. Growth and expansion characterized the next 20 years until the congregation's further development in Germany was arrested by the anti-Catholic decrees of the *Kulturkampf. In 1874, therefore, Mother Mary Chrysostom, second superior general, welcomed the invitation of Bp. Richard Gilmour, of Cleveland, Ohio, to work in his diocese. She and eight sisters arrived in the U.S. in July 1874 and 2 months later they began to teach in St. Peter and St. Stephen schools in Cleveland, and the Mother of God school in Covington, Ky. Two hundred sisters were transferred to the U.S. during the next 3 years, and Cleveland became the administrative center of the community. In 1884 a few sisters were permitted to resume work in Germany, and when their work prospered the motherhouse was reestablished there in 1888, in Muelhausen. From the Cleveland province, other provinces were organized with headquarters at Covington responsible for home missions in Alabama; the province at Toledo, Ohio, has a foreign mission in New Guinea. There are a province with a central house in Los Angeles, Calif., and a foreign mission with vice-province status in the Diocese of Patna, India. The congregation's two German provinces founded provinces in Brazil, the Netherlands, and Italy, and vice-provinces in England and Indonesia. In 1947 the generalate was transferred to Rome, Italy, by Rev. Mother Mary Vera, fifth superior general, and perpetual daily adoration of the Blessed Sacrament was inaugurated in the motherhouse chapel.

In 1963 there were about 3,550 members and 311 foundations. The 122 U.S. houses, located in Ohio, Kentucky, Indiana, California, Alabama, Virginia, and Washington, D.C., operated a liberal arts college (*Notre Dame, Cleveland); sisters' junior college (Toledo); 5 private high schools; 14 diocesan high schools; 99 elementary schools; the elementary demonstration school of The Catholic University of America, Washington, D.C.; 2 schools for mentally retarded children; 1, for the visually handicapped; 3 children's homes; 2 convalescent homes; 1 hospital; and 1 home for women. Each province conducts a school for aspirants of high school age. In addition the community undertakes the catechetical instruction of thousands of children who do not attend Catholic schools, as well as special religious instruction of the mentally retarded.

[M. M. SMITH]

NOTRE DAME COLLEGE (CLEVELAND, OHIO), a 4-year liberal arts college for women, founded by Mother Mary Cecilia, third superior general of the Sisters of Notre Dame. Under the jurisdiction of

Most Rev. Joseph Schrembs, Archbishop-bishop of Cleveland, the College formally opened in temporary quarters, Sept. 18, 1922, but soon moved to a 50-acre campus in the suburbs of Cleveland. The first unit on the new campus was opened for classes in September 1928. The financial crisis of the 1929 depression, however, checked further progress during the 1930s, as well as other expansion plans during the next 2 decades. In 1955, the College inaugurated Harks Hall (named for Mother Mary Evarista Harks), a residence for 80 residents; in 1961, the completion of the administration building added classroom and laboratory facilities; and in 1962, Providence Hall provided accommodations for 80 additional residents.

Notre Dame College aims to develop Christian women of intellectual maturity. It offers courses leading to a B.A. degree in the humanities, classical and modern languages, fine arts, and sciences. It seeks through the program of theology to bring to every student an adult grasp of divine truth. Recognizing the need to assist its students to become economically independent, it offers courses in medical technology, secretarial arts, and home economics.

In 1922 Notre Dame enrolled 23 students. In 1964 enrollment numbered 502 full-time and 60 part-time students, and the original faculty of 5 professors had increased to 50 members: 3 priests, 32 sisters, and 15 laymen, holding 9 doctoral and 36 master's degrees. From the first graduating class of 14 degree candidates in 1926, the Notre Dame alumnae developed into an association of approximately 1,800 members. A 1959 survey of alumnae activities revealed that Notre Dame College women fill many specialized positions: artists, interior decorators, teachers, supervisors, business executives, attorneys, editors, librarians, dietitians, science researchers, laboratory technicians, engineers, therapists, physicians, psychologists, and social workers.

The College is accredited by the North Central Association of Colleges and Secondary Schools, and is registered for State Teachers' Certificates by the State of Ohio Department of Education. It holds membership in the National Catholic Education Association, American Council on Education, Association of American Colleges, American Association of Colleges for Teacher Education, National Conference of Church Related Colleges, Ohio College Association, Ohio Foundation of Independent Colleges, Inc., and American University Women.

Bibliography: M. VINCENTIA, *Their Quiet Tread* (Milwaukee 1955).

[M. L. ARNTZ]

NOTRE DAME COLLEGE (MANCHESTER, N.H.). The third and youngest college for women in the Diocese of Manchester, N.H., Notre Dame was founded in 1950 by the Sisters of Holy Cross and of the Seven Dolors. A liberal arts college, Notre Dame operates under a charter granted by the legislature of New Hampshire, May 17, 1950. In June 1956, the State Board of Education of New Hampshire approved the teacher-training program of the College. Notre Dame is affiliated with The Catholic University of America, and its credits are recognized by the Registry of Medical Technologists of the American Society of Clinical Pathologists, Muncie, Ind. In 1961 it was affiliated with Notre Dame Hospital School of Medical Technology.

Administration of Notre Dame is through a board of trustees composed of the mother general, the community supervisor of studies, the provincial superior of the New England province, the assistant provincial, and the superior of the College. The bishop of Manchester acts as honorary president. An advisory board consists of 11 laymen. Administrative officers are the president, dean, registrar, treasurer, librarian, and the director of summer sessions, all of whom are members of the Holy Cross community.

In 1964 the 28-member staff was composed of 1 priest, 23 sisters, and 4 laymen, holding 6 doctoral and 15 master's degrees. Enrollment numbered 176 full-time and 105 part-time students in the regular session and 200 in the summer session.

The library contained approximately 12,315 volumes and subscribed to 94 periodicals. Notre Dame College receives financial support through tuition fees, gifts, and the contributed services of the religious community.

The curriculum of the College includes courses leading to the B.A., B.S., B.Mus., and B.S. in education. In addition to theology and philosophy, Notre Dame offers liberal and fine arts, sciences, mathematics, business subjects, education, and sociology. The College conducts annually a 6-week summer session offering a limited number of courses. Lecture and seminar methods are employed.

On the campus are five buildings: the first original foundation or the administration building, housing administration offices, music studios, chapel, cafeteria, and faculty quarters; St. Joseph Hall, including the library and the business department; Holy Cross Hall, housing the auditorium, classrooms, and laboratories; and Vadnais and Assunta Halls, the resident quarters. Long-range building plans were in progress in 1964.

[M. GIROUX]

NOTRE DAME COLLEGE OF STATEN ISLAND

A liberal arts college for women founded in 1931, it was heir to two educational traditions: the first school founded in Montreal in 1657 by the Congrégation de Notre Dame, and Notre Dame Academy established on Staten Island, N.Y., in 1903. By 1928 the academy had established its academic reputation and become an extension center for Fordham University, N.Y. With the cooperation of Fordham, a full-time college program was introduced in 1931, and Notre Dame became Staten Island's first women's college. In May 1933, the University of the State of New York granted the College a charter with power to confer B.A., B.S., and B.S. in Education degrees. It was accredited by the Middle States Association for Colleges and Universities in 1941 and holds membership in national educational associations.

The 18-acre campus includes the original administration building, Lavelle Hall, Mahoney Science Hall, and the Cardinal Spellman Library, dedicated in 1956. In 1964 the library housed 25,000 volumes of its 50,000 capacity and subscribed to 200 periodicals. In the rare-book collection are an incunabulum (*St. Bernard's Sermons*) and a 1515 edition of *The City of God*. Besides the usual science equipment, Mahoney Hall has laboratories for advanced research for undergraduates in chemistry and biology.

The college is administered by a board of trustees composed of a president, six members of the Notre Dame community, and distinguished clergy and laymen. The president is assisted by the dean and the heads of departments. In a faculty of 32 religious, priests, and laymen, 10 hold doctorates and 20 hold master's degrees. The student registration of 400 (1964) is expected to increase as plans for expansion are completed. The teacher-student ratio averages 1 to 14. The college is financed by student tuition and fees; its only endowment is the contributed services of the nonsalaried religious faculty.

A broad liberal arts program is integrated with the study of religion and philosophy, adapted to the individual student and her potentialities. The college offers majors in 10 fields and prepares students for professional schools in law and medicine and for graduate work in the arts and sciences. In the field of science, research in radiation biology and radiochemistry receives special attention. The education curriculum includes training for both elementary and secondary teaching. Among the special methods used are the senior thesis and the honors reading seminar for the superior student, conducted by the faculty with the participation of guest scholars. By invitation of the dean 15 undergraduates take part in the periodic round-table discussions of the classics, modern literature, and contemporary issues.

Both faculty and alumnae have achieved distinction in various fields. The president, Mother St. Egbert, received the medal "Pro Pontifice et Ecclesia," an honorary L.H.D. from Fordham, and was named "Woman of Achievement" for 1962. Writers, scientists, and other outstanding laywomen are among the alumnae. The juniorate for the training of young religious of the American province is located at Notre Dame College.

[V. M. COTTER]

NOTRE DAME DE NAMUR, SISTERS OF

A congregation of religious teachers founded in 1804 at Amiens, France, by Bl. Marie Rose Julie *Billiart. They conduct schools in Belgium, Brazil, the Congo, France, Italy, Japan, the Union of South Africa, the United Kingdom, and the U.S.

Foundation. The beginnings of the congregation were made when Julie Billiart joined a noblewoman, Françoise Blin de Bourbon, in charitable work at Amiens, where Julie had fled from her native Cuvilly, Picardy, during the disturbances of the French Revolution. In 1804 they undertook the formation of a religious community, under the direction of Joseph Désiré d'Ainville *Varin, superior of the Fathers of the Faith, an association of priests who lived in the spirit of St. Ignatius, pending the restoration of the Jesuits. The rule adopted by the Sisters of Notre Dame (SND) differed in three main respects from those usually found in congregations of women. The distinction between choir and lay sisters was eliminated, the educational program was concerned primarily with the needs of the poor, and government of the community was centralized under the authority of a superior general. These innovations occasioned difficulties with the bishop of Amiens and resulted in a transfer of the motherhouse to Namur, Belgium.

Development. In the mind of Julie Billiart, education was a "net to catch souls," and she was determined that it should do so efficiently. Hence the effectiveness of her schools in their secular as well as in their religious administration was a matter of deep concern to the foundress. The actual organization of the community's instructional method she left to the much better educated Mère Blin, later known as Mère St. Joseph. In spite of the Napoleonic Wars and the ensuing period of militantly Protestant Dutch rule in Belgium, the congregation spread rapidly. In 1840 the first U.S. foundation was made at the invitation of Bp. John B. Purcell of Cincinnati, Ohio. Leadership of the U.S. group was early entrusted to Sister Louise *Van der Schrieck, and the work expanded rapidly. In 1846 eight sisters sailed to Oregon with a Jesuit mission led by Pierre *De Smet; 5 years later, however, the sisters' Pacific headquarters were transferred to California. The community's first school in England opened at Penryn, Cornwall, in 1845; in England as in the U.S., Notre Dame educational enterprises grew steadily. By 1963 there were more than 3,000 sisters in the U.S., organized in five provinces, with novitiates in California, Connecticut, Maryland, Massachusetts, and Ohio. The sisters spend a minimum of 5 years in preparation for their religious life and their apostolic work. When the *Sister Formation Movement assumed an important role in the life of the U.S. sisterhoods in the 1950s, the Notre Dame provinces cooperated by setting up a juniorate program to prolong and improve the spiritual and intellectual preparation of the sisters.

Apostolate. The congregation undertook instruction at many levels. The oldest of its U.S. colleges, *Trinity in Washington, D.C., was chartered in 1897, and in 1964 enrolled about 750 young women. *Emmanuel College, with about 1,000 students in 1964, was founded in 1919 in Boston, Mass. In Belmont, Calif., the sisters opened the College of *Notre Dame as an academy (1851) and in Stevenson, Md., Villa Julie as a junior college (1952). Older than any of the Notre Dame colleges in the U.S. are the Notre Dame Training College for teachers (1856) in Liverpool, England, and the Notre Dame College of Education (1894) in Glasgow, Scotland. Two teachers colleges—in Bastogne and in

Notre Dame de Namur convent, Cincinnati, Ohio, first U.S. foundation of the congregation.

Bercham—are conducted by the sisters in Belgium. After World War II, the Massachusetts province of the U.S. established a liberal arts college at Okayama in Japan, which cares for about 650 students. In 1961 a Japanese junior college was established in Hiroshima. A large majority of the sisters in all the provinces are employed in elementary and secondary education. In Liverpool and Glasgow and in the U.S. at Columbus, Ohio, and Washington, D.C., they conduct clinics for exceptional children.

Missions. Several established Notre Dame provinces take responsibility for foundations in mission lands. The Belgian sisters have worked in the Congo since 1894 and have received a number of native vocations. They remained in the country during the disorders of the 1960s that followed Congolese independence. The sisters of the English province opened their first mission school in Southern Rhodesia in 1899. In 1929 the Cincinnati, Ohio, province opened a school in Wuchang, China, that, however, had to be abandoned after the Communist government assumed power. The Massachusetts province undertook Japanese mission work in 1924, and its Japanese pro-province opened a novitiate in Tokyo. In 1931 the order spread to Italy, where under the jurisdiction of the Belgian province the work has expanded, with schools staffed by sisters of various nationalities. The generalate was moved from Namur to Rome in 1957. Total membership in 1963 was about 5,000.

Bibliography: J. CLARE, ed., *The Life of Bl. Julie Billiart* (London 1909). M. HALCANT, *Educational Ideals of Bl. Julie Billiart* (New York 1922). M. F. McMANAMA, *As Gold in a Furnace: The Life of Bl. Julie Billiart* (Milwaukee 1957); *Treasure in a Field: The Life of Ven. Mother St. Joseph* (Milwaukee 1960). M. D. McNAMEE, *Willamette Interlude* (Palo Alto, Calif. 1959). R. PIKE, *Outline History of the Sisters of Notre Dame de Namur* (Washington 1938). A. QUINLAN, *In Harvest Fields by Sunset Shores* (San Francisco 1926).

[J. BLAND]

Sister Louise Van der Schrieck.

NOTRE DAME DU LAC, UNIVERSITY OF

The University was founded in 1842 by a group of French missionaries led by Edward F. *Sorin, CSC, who became its first president. The original site was the mission outpost of Rev. Theodore *Badin, first Catholic priest ordained in the U.S., and for a time his log chapel was the school's only building. On Jan. 15, 1844, the Indiana legislature granted Notre Dame its university charter. Then an obscure school in the northern Indiana wilderness, it had by 1963 expanded to a 1,200-acre campus with 70 buildings providing facilities for instruction and research.

Organization and Development. The University consists of a graduate school, which offers the doctorate in 16 departments and the master's degree in 26; the Notre Dame law school, the oldest Catholic law school in the U.S.; and the undergraduate colleges of arts and letters, science, engineering, and business administration. In 1964 the faculty numbered 500 professors, scientists, and artists, about one-fifth of whom were priests and religious. Of this number, 262 held doctorates from major universities throughout the world. Its 6,982 students represented every state in the Union and 40 foreign countries.

The Notre Dame Administration Building is at the heart of the campus that stretches from the South Bend city limits to the Northern Indiana Toll Road. A new addition to the campus skyline is the 13-story Notre Dame Memorial Library, opened in 1963, the largest college library building in the world. It has a capacity of 2 million volumes and seats half of the undergraduate body at one time. On its facade is Millard Sheets' "Christ the Teacher," a monumental mosaic in granite. On the campus is the Gothic Sacred Heart Church, erected in 1871. It is the setting for major religious events and has the oldest carillon in North America. There also can be seen Ivan Meštrović's "Pietà." Interred in the campus church are the remains of Cardinal John *O'Hara, CSC, president of Notre Dame (1934–39), an outstanding figure in its history, and Orestes *Brownson, the noted philosospher.

Other major campus facilities include the O'Shaughnessy Hall of Liberal and Fine Arts, which houses the University gallery and its collection of 300 paintings; Nieuwland Science Hall, named for Julius A. *Nieuwland, CSC, whose research led to the development of synthetic rubber; the Computing Center and Mathematics Building, whose UNIVAC 1107 expedites research throughout the University; and the Radiation Research Building, erected by the U.S. Atomic Energy Commission. There are 17 student residence halls on the campus, each with its own chapel.

The impressive physical growth of the University through the years has been accompanied by a steady increase in academic development. Total enrollment statistics since the turn of the century give evidence of rapid expansion, i.e., from 438 in 1910 to 6,467 in 1960. Only liberal arts subjects were offered at Notre Dame until 1865 when science courses were introduced. Law and engineering became part of the curriculum in 1869 and 1873, respectively. These four areas of study were designated as separate colleges in 1905, and in 1920 the College of Commerce (now Business Administration) was added. A Freshman Year of Studies, with its own dean, was inaugurated in 1962, and a Sophomore Year of Studies was instituted at Innsbruck, Austria, in 1964.

Research. Notre Dame's Graduate School and the University's extensive research program are intimately linked. Graduate enrollment, which is about 900 during the academic year, triples during the summer session when more than 1,500 sisters, representing a cross section of the Catholic educational system, come to the campus to study for advanced degrees. Graduate education for nuns has grown so at Notre Dame that a residence hall specially designed for the sisters' year-round use was erected on the campus in 1964.

Notre Dame's research dates from before the turn of the century when Dr. Albert *Zahm conducted pioneering experiments in aeronautics and Prof. Jerome Green sent the first wireless message in the U.S. Today, faculty members are engaged in 100 research projects supported by grants totaling more than $3 million annually. Scientists at the University's Lobund Laboratory developed the germ-free animal as a unique tool in biological and medical research. These animals are employed in a variety of projects dealing with cancer, heart disease, nutrition, and germfree human surgery.

The Radiation Laboratory, an organization of scientists representing the chemistry, chemical engineering, biology, and metallurgy departments, is investigating the effects of radiation on matter. Other major areas of research at the University include nuclear physics, international relations, aeronautical and metallurgical engineering, and the social sciences.

Of special note are two current research projects. The University's Center for the Study of Man in Contemporary Society, in conjunction with the National Catholic Educational Association and with the support of the Carnegie Corporation of New York, is conducting a 3-year, nationwide study of Catholic elementary and secondary schools. It marks the first time that the U.S. Catholic educational system has been studied on so comprehensive and intensive a basis. In another major undertaking, Notre Dame's Mediaeval Institute is microfilming 30,000 classical, medieval, and Renaissance manuscripts in the famed Ambrosian Library in Milan. The documents will be available for the first time in this country in the new Notre Dame Memorial Library.

Publications. Learned publications of the University of Notre Dame include the *American Midland Naturalist,* a botanical journal founded by Father Nieuwland; the *Review of Politics,* a periodical survey of philosophical and historical aspects of political realities; the *Journal of Symbolic Logic;* and the *Natural Law Forum,* a Notre Dame Law School publication that evolved from The Natural Law Institute, once held annually on the campus. Aside from these periodicals, the University of Notre Dame Press has published more than 175 titles,

Administration building of Notre Dame du Lac.

The thirteen-story Notre Dame Memorial Library.

the majority in theology, the humanities, and social sciences. About 20 volumes are published annually.

Undergraduate School. The undergraduate student and the development of his intellectual power, professional competence, and moral responsibility are central to Notre Dame's purpose. The University's undergraduates come from approximately 750 high schools throughout the U.S. Forty-five hundred live in campus residence halls. The campus life they share helps generate the Notre Dame spirit, which is particularly evident in football stadiums, on the campus and away, in the fall. The spirit of competition, however, is not restricted to the athletic field. Notre Dame seniors have been prominent in nationwide fellowship competitions conducted by the Woodrow Wilson, Danforth, and National Science Foundations, among others.

In close and cordial association with the nation's defense establishment, Notre Dame maintains Reserve Officer Training Units, with a combined strength of 1,800, in the Army, Navy, and Air Force. During the Civil War, when the University was less than 25 years old, seven Holy Cross priests left the campus to serve as chaplains with the Union troops. The memorable "final absolution" given by Notre Dame's Father William Corby at the Battle of Gettysburg was commemorated with a special Field Mass there in the summer of 1963. During World Wars I and II, thousands of Notre Dame men served in the armed forces, and hundreds of them died in their country's defense. During World War II, the University turned many of its facilities over to the Navy, and 12,000 young men received officer's training on the campus. In the summers of 1961 and 1963, another generation, many of them Notre Dame men, came to the campus for intensive Peace Corps training before embarking for rural Chile.

Administration and Finance. To administer this complex educational institution, with 1,800 full-time employees, the president is assisted by an executive vice president, vice presidents for academic, student, and business affairs, and a vice president for public relations and development. The Graduate School, Law School, and undergraduate colleges have deans to whom the heads of academic departments report. Important units that form a bridge between the University administration and faculty are the Academic Council, the Graduate Council, and the University Research Council.

Through the years, Notre Dame has benefited from the counsel of nationally prominent leaders in business and the professions. Its associate board of lay trustees, created in 1920, has the dual responsibility of investing the University's endowment funds and guiding its long-range development. The University has also created advisory councils for science and engineering, liberal and fine arts, business administration, and law. Wives of the lay trustees and council members have formed a women's advisory council whose members are particularly interested in the University's library, art gallery, and cultural life.

Notre Dame's operating budget for 1963–64 was approximately $24 million. Its endowment of $37 million increased markedly during the 1950s. Because student tuition and fees pay only about two-thirds of educational costs, the University, particularly since World War II, has turned to alumni, friends, corporations, and foundations for financial support. In 1947 the Notre Dame Foundation was created to coordinate the University's public relations and fund-raising programs. During its first 10 years of existence, Notre Dame received more than $27 million in gifts and grants.

In September 1960, Notre Dame was one of the first five private universities selected by The Ford Foundation to participate in its Special Program in Education, whose purpose is "to assist institutions in different regions of the country to reach and sustain a wholly new level of academic excellence, administrative effectiveness and financial support." The Ford Foundation pledged a matching grant of $6 million to Notre Dame if the University would double that amount in gifts by June 30, 1963. The University launched its $18 million Challenge Program with major objectives including the Notre Dame Memorial Library and other buildings, increased resources for faculty development and student aid, and a retirement program for nonacademic employees. In this, its greatest fund-raising effort, it was more than successful, with 23,438 gifts totalling $18,603,157. Eighty per cent of the school's graduates contributed to the development program.

Honors and Awards. Through the years the University has welcomed a distinguished group of honorary alumni into the Notre Dame family. Honorary doctorates have been conferred on noted prelates, statesmen, scientists, and scholars. President Franklin D. Roosevelt came to the campus to accept an honorary doctorate in 1935, and Cardinal Eugenio Pacelli (later Pius XII), was similarly honored at a special convocaton a year later. Perhaps the most memorable event in more recent times took place on June 5, 1960, when Pres. Dwight Eisenhower and Cardinal Giovanni Battista Montini received honorary doctorates. The President delivered the commencement address, and the future Pope Paul VI celebrated the Baccalaureate Mass and spoke briefly.

The highest honor annually conferred upon Catholic laymen in the U.S. is Notre Dame's Laetare Medal. Established in 1883, the Medal honors American men and women who have coupled distinction in their chosen field of endeavor with exemplary private lives. The historian John Gilmary *Shea was the first recipient. The history of the Laetare Medal chronicles the ascent of Catholic leadership in the U.S. In 1961 it was presented to John F. Kennedy, then president. Among other recipients have been Admiral George Anderson,

Chief of Naval Operations; psychiatrist Francis J. Braceland; educator George N. Shuster; diplomats Robert Murphy, Clare Booth Luce, and Jefferson Caffery; Thomas E. Murray, of the U.S. Atomic Energy Commission; George Meany, AFL-CIO president; and business executives Frank Folsom and I. A. O'Shaughnessy.

Notre Dame's President Theodore Hesburgh, CSC, is a member of the National Science Board, the U.S. Commission on Civil Rights, and the U.S. Advisory Commission on International, Educational and Cultural Affairs. Hesburgh is permanent Vatican City representative to the International Atomic Energy Agency, a trustee of The Rockefeller Foundation, and a former president of The Association of American Colleges. In 1963 he was elected president of The International Federation of Catholic Universities, and has been awarded honorary degrees by 13 colleges and universities.

Bibliography: A. J. HOPE, *Notre Dame: One Hundred Years* (Notre Dame, Ind. 1943).

[J. E. MURPHY]

NOTRE DAME OF MARYLAND, COLLEGE OF

A Catholic liberal arts college for women, founded as a school in 1848, became an academy in 1863, a collegiate institute in 1873, and a 4-year college in 1895. It is conducted by the School Sisters of Notre Dame, a religious congregation of European origin established in the U.S. in 1847 by Mother Mary Teresa of Jesus. The school began in Baltimore in 1848. By 1871 registration justified a larger campus, and the school opened at the new site in 1873 with three levels of instruction and 63 students. Known as Notre Dame of Maryland Collegiate Institute for Young Ladies, the school offered courses leading to the degrees of mistress of English literature and mistress of liberal arts that were conferred for the first time by U. S. Grant, President of the U.S. in 1876. In 1895 Notre Dame of Maryland offered the first 4-year college courses intended to prepare for graduate study then opening up to women. In 1896 an act of the Maryland Legislature amended the charter of 1864 to authorize the granting of baccalaureate, master's, and doctoral degrees. At the commencement of 1899 Cardinal James Gibbons, Archbishop of Baltimore, conferred the B.A. degree on four graduates, and the B.Litt. on two. Charles Bonaparte, the speaker, remarked that for the first time in America, a Catholic college for the education of young ladies had bestowed the bachelor's degree.

The curriculum developed with the times, but has never lost its liberal arts character. Since 1895 the College has offered professional training for teachers within the framework of liberal education. With the advent of the elective system in the late 1890s, the prescribed program expanded. In the 1940s and 1950s, the function of theology and philosophy was redefined, and reading lists, seminars, and comprehensive examinations reemphasized. A noncredit adult education program was inaugurated in 1949, while television courses and tutorial and interdisciplinary honors work were introduced in the late 1950s. In 1957 the College took over Sister Formation classes at the Baltimore motherhouse and in 1961 sponsored a branch, since independent, in Connecticut.

Notre Dame of Maryland is an independent corporation governed by a board of directors consisting of five members of the religious community and two laymen. In 1963 the 82-member faculty included 5 priests, 41 sisters, and 36 laymen, holding 22 doctorates and 41 master's degrees. Total enrollment numbered 763 students from 22 states and 12 foreign countries in the regular session and 263 in the summer session. The Fourier library housed 50,000 volumes and received 350 periodicals.

In 1902 the College was registered by the Board of Regents of the University of the State of New York, and in 1920 by the Maryland State Board of Education. It was accredited by the Middle States Association in 1925.

Growth of the College physical plant has accompanied academic expansion. Six buildings, including Gibbons Hall which was rebuilt in 1960 when the academy moved to a separate campus, provide classroom, residence, gymnasium, auditorium, and laboratory facilities. In 1962 the state of Maryland voted a matching grant of $750,000 for a science building to be completed in 1965.

[B. M. ENGELMEYER]

NOUMENA

A term used by philosophers, and mainly by Kantians, to designate objects that cannot be sensibly perceived and can only be mentally apprehended. This article sketches the pre-Kantian usages and then explains and criticizes the place of the term in *Kantianism.

Pre-Kantian Usages. The word noumena (Gr. νοούμενα) is encountered in *Plato in several passages (*Rep.* 508C, 509D; *Parm.* 132C; *Tim.* 30D, 51D) and designates ideas of which it is said explicitly that they can be grasped only mentally and not sensibly (*Rep.* 507B; *Tim.* 51D). The only things accessible to sensible visualization, for Plato, are those that are subject to multiplicity and becoming; these do not exist in the full sense of the word, and form the τόπος ὁρατός (*Rep.* 532D). The Ideas, on the contrary, constitute the τόπος νοητός (*Rep.* 508C) and are the only true being (*Phaedrus* 247C, 249C; *Tim.* 28A), which, as such, is eternal and immutable and can be apprehended only mentally by reminiscence and dialectics. This is especially true of the original source of all ideas, of absolute goodness and absolute beauty—the beautiful and good in every respect that fully encompass all beauty and goodness (*Symp.* 210E–211D; *Rep.* 509B).

In *Aristotle, the term noumena is encountered in one passage only (*Meta.* 1074b 36–1075a 5), where it is used three times; elsewhere, the term νοητά is employed in the same sense (e.g., *Anim.* 431b 20–432a 14). More specifically, Aristotle distinguishes what can be mentally comprehended from what can be sensibly perceived; on actuation, the latter coincides with sense *perception in the same way as the former with simple *apprehension (*Meta.* 1075a 3–5; *Anim.* 431b 22–23). Contrary to Plato, Aristotle holds that what can be apprehended only mentally is not separated from sensible phenomena, but is contained in phenomena and is to be sought in them (*Anim.* 432a 3–5). Thus the mind extracts essences from visible things (*ibid.* 431b 2); the essential forms inherent in such things therefore take the place of Plato's transcending Ideas. The apprehension of the noumena, which is a kind of *intuition in Plato, appears thus as an *abstraction in Aristotle. It is perfected by a reasoning process that ascends to the highest noumena, i.e., the

Divine as eternal, immovable, and separate (*Meta.* 1026a 10–30).

St. *Thomas Aquinas, working through St. *Augustine as an intermediary, effected a synthesis of Plato and Aristotle. The noumena inherent in things (*intelligibilia*) are essences, and, above all, *being; they are grasped by abstraction. Their bases, as transcendental noumena, are the archetypal ideas of the divine intellect, which, in turn, are founded upon the archnoumenon, i.e., upon God as the subsistent being; man ascends to this conclusion by metaphysical discourse.

Kantian Notion. According to I. *Kant, noumena must be distinguished from *phenomena; the latter are called "phenomena, in so far as they are thought as objects according to the unity of the categories" (*Critique of Pure Reason* A 248). In this text, as opposed to ordinary usage, phenomena are distinguished from appearances; the distinction, however, must be correctly understood. When one says: "The senses represent objects as they appear, the understanding as they are, the latter statement" must "be understood in the empirical meaning" (*ibid.* A 258), i.e., as objects-for-man. On the contrary, the term "noumena (*intelligibilia*)" is applied to those things "which are merely objects of understanding, and which, nevertheless, can be perceived as such by intuition, though not by sensible intuition (therefore, *coram intuitu intellectuali*)" (*ibid.* A 249). Man's concepts themselves can never determine an object; for this purpose, an intuition is needed to supplement such concepts, and for man this can only be sensible. Man has no intellectual intuition that would make possible the "transcendental use" of his concepts, i.e., a use that would reach the thing-in-itself "beyond the sphere of possible experience" (*ibid.* A 248). The noumena are ordered to this usage, which is "not contradictory" (*ibid.* A 254), since they are "merely a limiting concept" (*ibid.* A 255); one encounters them not as "intelligible objects" but merely as "a problem" (*ibid.* A 256). But they are not an "arbitrary invention" (*ibid.* A 255); on the contrary, they are "necessary" (*ibid.* A 254), although only of "negative use" (*ibid.* A 255) "in order to impose a limit upon the presumptions of sensibility" (*ibid.*). Here, moreover, one should "prevent sensible intuition from being extended to things in themselves," and one should not claim that "sensibility is the only possible mode of intuition" (*ibid.* A254). As a consequence, "our understanding attains in this way a sort of negative extension, i.e., it is not limited by, but rather limits, sensibility by giving the name of noumena to things, not considered as phenomena, but as things in themselves. But our understanding imposes also limits upon itself, recognizing that it cannot know these noumena by means of the categories; hence, it is compelled to think of them merely as of an unknown something" (*ibid.* A 256).

Beyond this usage lies that of the moral order, which shows man "as a being endowed with internal freedom (*homo noumenon*)" (*Metaphysik der Sitten*, Berlin Academy ed., 6:418), and which can give to his "causality as a noumenon" (*Critique of Practical Reason; ibid.* 5:50) "for the first time objective, although only practical, reality" (*ibid.* 48).

By way of evaluation, it may be said that Kant loses the synthesis characteristic of Aquinas by disregarding the process of abstraction that obtains the noumena, i.e., essences and being, from the phenomena. At the same time, he returns to Plato by assuming that the noumena are accessible to intellectual intuition alone, an accessibility that he justly denies to man.

See also CRITICISM, PHILOSOPHICAL; KNOWLEDGE, THEORIES OF.

Bibliography: I. KANT, *Prolegomena*, §§32–35. Eisler 2:271–273. Copleston 6:267–272. A. CARBINI, EncFil 3:940–942.

[J. B. LOTZ]

NOVATIAN AND NOVATIANISM

Novatian was the first and for a long time the only writer of the Roman Church to use Latin. The little known of his life is dependent on untrustworthy information supplied by his enemies. His name was certainly Novatianus, not Novatus as given by the Greeks. He must have been born about 200, and received a good education in Latin as his language attests; but he was not a Phrygian as Philostorgius asserts (*Hist. Eccl.* 8.15).

Pope Cornelius. In his letter to Bp. Fabius of Antioch Pope *Cornelius furnishes information on the baptism, ordination, and later conduct of Novatian (Eusebius, *Hist. Eccl.* 6.43.6–22) that is at least questionable. It may be true that he received Baptism by sprinkling during a severe sickness, but it is hardly credible that he did not receive confirmation, or that his ordination was performed despite the opposition of the clergy and many of the laity and that he hid himself during a persecution, refusing to give priestly assistance to his suffering fellow Christians. If these contentions are true, it is difficult to understand how he became the mouthpiece of the Roman college of priests after the martyr death of Pope *Fabian (Jan. 20, 250). As such, he wrote letters to the Church throughout the world, of which two to St. *Cyprian of Carthage have been preserved (Cyprian, *Epist.* 30, 36; CSEL 3:2).

Novatian as Bishop. After the election of Cornelius as the new pope in March or April 251, Novatian had himself consecrated a bishop by three south Italian bishops, certainly not merely through foolish ambition as his enemies asserted; otherwise he would not have had the support of many clerics and contemporary confessors (Cyprian, *Epist.* 46; Eusebius, *Hist. Eccl.* 6.43); but rather as a protest against the compliant attitude of the new Pope on the question of penance.

Roman Synod. In an encyclical letter to the other bishops, Novatian announced his consecration (Cyprian, *Epist.* 55; *Ad Novat.* 13). That same year a Roman synod of 60 bishops excommunicated him (Eusebius, *Hist. Eccl.* 6.43.2). The confessors made their peace with Pope Cornelius (Cyprian, *Epist.* 53; CSEL 3), and, after some hesitation, Cyprian and the bishops of Asia Minor unanimously deserted Novatian (Sozomen, *Hist. Eccl.* 3.8). Nevertheless, he was able to propagate his church with his own bishops in every sector of the Christian world.

In the persecution under Gallus and Volusianus (251–253), Novatian had to flee Rome, and under Valerian in 258 he suffered martyrdom (Pacian, *Epist.* 2.7), or at least became a confessor (Socrates, *Hist. Eccl.* 4.28). In 1932 a tombstone was discovered on the Via Tiburtina with the inscription: *Novatiano Beatissimo/ Martyri Gaudentius Diac[onus]/ fec[it]*; however, the relationship is questionable. The *Martyrology of Jerome cites a Roman martyr named Novatianus for June 27 or 29, but without a title.

Writings. Novatian's writings do not merely show him to have been an elegant stylist, but they likewise betray a good theological and philosophical education. Of the nine works listed by Jerome (*De vir. ill.* 70), only two have been preserved: one of them, his chief work, the *De Trinitate,* is basically apologetic in character and brings the teaching on the Trinity down to his time. In it he defends the oneness of Almighty God, and God the Creator, against the Gnostics (*see* GNOSTICISM); Christ as the Son of God the Creator, against Marcion; Christ as true man, against the Docetists; as true God, against the Adoptionists (*see* ADOPTIONISM); and as Second Person to the Father, against Sabellius (*see* SABELLIANISM); and he demonstrates, after a hymn of praise to the Holy Spirit, that despite the Godhood of Christ there is only one God.

There is much here that is imperfect; not only in the fact that the Holy Spirit is not considered a divine Person, but also in that Novatian's Christology furnishes sufficient leads for heretical development. If, however, the purpose of this work is kept in mind, it is obvious that for the most part the fault lies in an insufficient analysis using expressions as yet untroubled by future strife.

His alleged angelology, as well as his supposed teaching on the absorption of Son in the Father, is a misunderstanding. Since he did not distinguish between the substantial attributes of the Godhood and the properties of the Persons, he could only preserve the Oneness of God through a *subordinationism; all the more so, since he sees God not from an ontological viewpoint, but rather in the aspect of His power. Still his work is an improvement over that of Tertullian and Hippolytus.

Opposition To the Church. Novatian's dispute with the Church stemmed from the problem concerning the reception into the Church of those who had fallen in persecution. In his two letters to Cyprian, he praised Cyprian's refusal to grant a pardon to the *lapsi* before the end of the persecution, except in cases involving danger of death. Thus far one could go along with him. But as the sharpness of his first letter had caused some estrangement, so the second went beyond the limit. It betrayed the fact that Novatian saw in Cyprian's temporary solution not merely a cautionary measure but a fundamental challenge. He thus betrayed the rigorism of an earlier period of which, at Rome, Callistus, and, in Africa, Agrippius, had broken through the first barriers. Behind Novatian's attitude there was a different conception of the Church.

If, with Cyprian, one believed that only an unconditional membership in the Church was a guarantee of eternal salvation, one would act differently than if, with Novatian, he believed the Church should be announced as a community of saints who must be kept free of all taint. While Cyprian saw in the refusal to grant pardon a prejudgment involving eternal damnation, Novatian believed that God's judgment could be compromised through pardon, since the way to God's mercy led through penance, compunction, and sorrow.

De Cibis Judaicis. This work, which has been preserved and is mentioned by Jerome, was written to Novatian's community from a distance. Here Novatian shows that the Old Testament prohibitions regarding food are to be understood in a spiritual and not in a literal sense. In particular, it is the vices symbolized by impure animals that should be avoided. The taste of their flesh is not forbidden, but rather the flesh of sacrifice. A particular chapter is directed against the immorality of early morning drinking.

Other writings listed by Jerome are lost. But apparently Novatian is the author of two works that have been preserved under the name of Cyprian. In a *De spectaculis,* the author is dependent on Cyprian and Tertullian for his condemnation of Christian attendance at spectacles and advises his readers to meditate instead on the beauties in nature and on the word of God. In a *De bono pudicitiae,* he praises virginity, continence in marriage, and marital fidelity.

Novatian Churches. Thanks to his animated activity (Cyprian, *Epist.* 55.24) and his rigorism, which later led his followers to deny the forgiveness of all grave sins after Baptism (Socrates, *Hist. Eccl.* 5.22), Novatian won a large following. Marcian of Arles went over to his side; and even in Spain, Rome, and Africa, there were Novatian communities with their own bishops. On their return to the Church, a dispute over Baptism broke out in Africa.

In the East it was above all in Phrygia, where the Montanists had prepared the way, that almost all the greater cities had Novatian bishops; Constantine I invited the Novatian Bishop of Constantinople, Acesius, to attend the Council of Nicaea (Socrates, *Hist. Eccl.* 1.10). Their acceptance of the *homoousios and their good relations with the Catholics won them longstanding sufferance in Constantinople (Socrates, *ibid.* 5.10). Cyril fought against them in Alexandria (Socrates, *ibid.* 7.7), and in Rome, they were opposed by Popes Innocent I and Celestine I.

In the West the Novatians gradually submitted to the Church, and we hear of the return of a bishop with his whole community (Leo I, *Epist.* 12.6). In the East they held out longer. Eulogius of Alexandria directed a large work against them. But cooperation between Church and State forced them to disappear, at first in the cities and then in the country, and by the end of the 7th century the last communities were extinct.

Bibliography: É. AMANN, DTC 11.1:816–849. H. KOCH, Pauly-Wiss RE 17.1 (1936) 1138–56; *Cyprianische Untersuchungen* (Bonn 1926) 403–406. A. D'ALÈS, *Novatien* (Paris 1925). M. SIMONETTI, "Alcune osservazioni sul De Trinitate di Novaziano," *Studi in onore di Angelo Monteverdi,* 2 v. (Modena 1959) 2: 771–783. F. SCHEIDWEILER, ZKirchgesch 55 (1954–55) 126–139. A. FERRUA, "Novatiano beatissimo martyri," CivCatt 95.4 (1944) 232–239. C. MOHRMANN, "Les Origines de la Latinité chrétienne à Rome," VigChr 3 (1949) 67–106, 163–183.

[P. H. WEYER]

NOVEL, THE

As late as the 16th century the word "novel" still referred mainly to lengthy tales or extended short stories, such as those in *Boccaccio's *Decameron* (1348–53), which Italians called *novelle* (plural of *novella*), or those in Marguerite of Navarre's *Heptameron* (1559), which the French called *nouvelles.* The continued use of many synonyms for novel (e.g., *roman* in French and German, *récit,* romance, tale, adventure) suggests that the novel is too varied to define exactly. Understandably, a literary form that includes Daniel Defoe's *Robinson Crusoe* and James *Joyce's *Ulysses,* *Cervantes' *Don Quixote* and *Tolstoi's *War and Peace,* as well as popular varieties, such as the detective story, the mystery, the touched-up autobiography, and the imaginative journal, must be described simply as "a fictitious prose work of considerable length and complexity."

Earliest Prose Fiction. The *Milesiaca* of Aristides (c. 1–2 B.C.) consists of a series of love stories centered about the author's native town of Miletus. Of historical rather than literary importance, the *Milesian Tales* were enjoyed for some time throughout the Greco-Roman Empire, especially in the Latin translation of Sisenna. Later Greek romances show a great advance in technique. The *Ephesian Stories* of Xenophon of Ephesius (c. A.D. 2) are lively accounts of the adventures of Atheia and Abrocomes, whose endurance of separation, shipwrecks, pirate attacks, and pretended deaths results in their happy reunion. Of more lasting importance is the *Aethiopica* of Heliodorus (c. A.D. 3), a prose romance in 10 books that celebrates the love of Theagones, a Thessalian, for the dark-skinned Princess Chariclea of Ethiopia. An apologetic novel, partly designed to justify a rejected race, it shares with *Daphnis and Chloe,* a pastoral romance by Longus (c. A.D. 3), the honor of being imitated by many European authors.

To these already existing elements in the Greek novel the Roman Petronius Arbiter (d. A.D. 66) contributed, in his *Saturae,* the famous "Banquet of Trimalchio," an original vein of caustic wit directed against new millionaires, affected aesthetes, and inflated poets. Another Latin prose writer, Lucius Apuleius (b. A.D. 130), described the adventures of a hero who was magically changed into an ass until restored to humanity by the goddess Isis. His *The Golden Ass* became a source book for Cervantes, Boccaccio, *Rabelais, and other later comic writers. By the end of the 4th century the Greco-Roman novel was an established type of literature with three main branches, the adventure story, the pastoral romance, and the satire.

Although the poets, among them *Chaucer, provided the chief fictional entertainment throughout the Middle Ages, prose fiction was not a lost art. It survived in notable exemplary or cautionary tales, such as those collected by Pedro Alfonso in his *Disciplina Clericalis* (c. 1100) for the use of preachers, and in the anonymous *Aucassin and Nicolette* (c. 1200), the *chantefable,* or combination of song and story, that evoked memories of the old Greek romance. Other kinds of early prose fiction are the Spanish romance of knight-errantry, e.g., *The Knight Cifor* (c. 1301); parables drawn from history, e.g., *Gesta Romanorum* (c. 1340); and countless didactic fictional lives of the saints, such as *James of Voragine's *The Golden Legend* (c. 1385). Fictitious travel books, such as *The Travels of Sir John *Mandeville* (1496; originally composed in French in 1366), were also popular. It was the publication of Sir Thomas *Malory's *Le Morte Darthur* (1485), however, that provided an extended narrative that began to resemble a modern novel; for this late rendering of the Arthurian cycle is not simply a collection of related stories on the various themes of history, romance, and holy quest. Its unity consists, as Eugene Vinaver has remarked, in "a very complex pattern of themes alternating one with another like the strands of a woven fabric." *See* ARTHURIAN AND CAROLINGIAN LEGENDS.

The 16th-Century Novel. The novel in the 16th century, like Chaucer's *Canterbury Tales* in the 14th, incorporated many diverse themes, conventions, and styles. Some were frankly romantic, such as Vasco de Lobeira's *Amadís de Gaul* (1508), a chivalric romance in which the hero, a knight-errant, sought perilous adventures to gain the admiration and to win the hand of Oriana, daughter of King Lisuarte of England (*see* ROMANCE, MEDIEVAL). Others, such as *Celestina* (1501) by Fernando de Rojas, combined the lofty theme and style of Petrarchan love with earthy and at times corrosive realism. Still others, such as François Rabelais's *Gargantua and Pantagruel* (1532–64), included in the satire of human follies all forms of action, thought, and literary expression.

Romantic Tradition. If the 16th-century novel may be judged by its two chief manifestations, the highly idealized romance of the knightly tales and the highly exaggerated comic realism of the picaresque or rogue novel, one may conclude that it had already achieved a twofold direction. Out of the romantic tradition, on the one hand, novelists created rich, ornate, and self-consciously classical stories stressing idealistic love and courtly romances. In that tradition were John Lyly's *Euphues* (1578), Anthony Munday's *Zalanto* (1580), Robert Greene's *Gwydonius* (1584), Thomas Lodge's *Rosalynde* (1590), and Sir Philip *Sidney's *Arcadia* (1590).

Picaresque Development. Out of the picaresque tradition, on the other hand, novelists created vivid, racy descriptions of actual life. This tradition, brilliantly begun in Spanish by Diego Hurtado Mendoza in *Lazarillo de Tormes* (1556), presented the rogue-hero who told in the first person a story of robbing, cheating, and dissembling in the interests of a series of outwardly respectable masters. Its vivid ironies and circumstantial realism attracted a host of imitators. In England Thomas Nashe's *The Unfortunate Traveller* (1594) borrowed many features of the rogue novel, particularly in the gulling incidents. Considerably later, in Henry Fielding's *Jonathan Wild the Great* (1743) and in Tobias Smollett's *Ferdinand, Count Fathom* (1753), the rogue novel reappeared in England. But in the 16th century it flourished more brilliantly in Spain and France. In Spain, Mateo Alemán's *Guzman de Alfarache* (1599), a book decidedly more bitter in its irony than *Lazarillo,* presented an attractive model for many writers, among them Francisco Gómez de *Quevedo y Villegas, whose *Pablos de Segovia* (1626) has been called the most vitriolic book ever written, and Vincente Espinel, whose *Marcos de Obregon* (1618) detailed military as well as criminal adventures. The Spanish picaresque novel, immediately and widely appreciated in France, directly stimulated at least two great novels, Paul Scarron's *Le Roman comique* (1651–57) and Alain René Lesage's *Gil Blas de Santillane* (1715–35), a novel rightly described as more Spanish than that of the Spaniards.

The 17th and 18th Centuries. The tradition of the romance continued to develop. Honoré d'Urfé's *L'Astrée* (1607–27) linked together episodes in the life of the chivalrous Celadon, a courtly soldier, in the course of which the varieties of love, ranging from the platonic sublime to the lusty terrestrial, are defined, classified, and evaluated. A school of writers, known as the *Précieuses,* exploited the kind of romance that enthroned the noble, witty, and almost unattainable lady and dissected the emotions in stories set in exotic places (*see* FRENCH LITERATURE, 3). Mlle. de Scudéry's *Artamène ou le Grand Cyrus* (1649–53), for instance, combined the idealized adventures of the 4th-century

B.C. Persian monarch and his courtship of the princess of the Medes with thinly disguised portraits of Louis XIV's most prominent courtiers. These and countless other novels surfeited the craving for romance and intrigue among English as well as Continental readers.

Cervantes and Mme. de La Fayette. The novel cannot be accounted for, however, simply by tracing the rise of the picaresque and the romance. Two books of literary genius, Cervantes' *Don Quixote* (1605–15) and Mme. de La Fayette's *La Princesse de Clèves* (1677), stand both within and without these two conventions of prose fiction. The first, unquestionably the greatest novel of the Renaissance, began as an exemplary tale designed to show the evil effects of chivalric romances on both human conduct and aesthetic taste. Its actual achievement, however, embraced all forms of literary expression, tragic and comic, epic and lyric, chivalric romance as well as picaresque realism. In exploring the essential ambiguities and paradoxes of human life through the adventures of Don Quixote and Sancho Panza, Cervantes developed the theory that art helps nature to restore the harmony of justice disturbed but not irretrievably lost by error, folly, and vice. Believing that criticism alone could not suffice to restore justice, he added the more persuasive element of mimetic action. Thus the embodiment of true wit, true art, and true entertainment was Cervantes' constructive criticism of folly.

Mme. de La Fayette's *La Princesse de Clèves* can only superficially be identified as a romance in the manner of her contemporaries Mlle. de Scudéry, La Calprenède, or D'Urfé, although it also concerns the conflict between love and duty. Like *Don Quixote,* it is a serious work of a highly intelligent person on an important theme. Unlike *Don Quixote,* its action concentrates on the analysis of one soul. After her husband dies and she is free to marry her lover, the Duc de Nemours, Mme. de Clèves renounces a genuine love in the interests of a highly complex standard of virtue. With a grace and economy of style comparable to that of her contemporary, *Racine, Mme. de La Fayette combined an analysis of the customs and morality of the French court with her exhibition of a heart torn between passion and reason. In her hands the romance became a realistic assessment of human psychology.

The 17th-Century English Novelists. In the 17th century the English novelists produced no work that ranked with the fiction of Cervantes or Mme. de La Fayette. Perhaps all that could be expected was that the English novel managed to survive the rigors of Puritan disfavor, thanks largely to the timely genius of John *Bunyan. His *Pilgrim's Progress* (1678–84) derived its story from the medieval *allegory and the then current *sermon literature. Although it aimed directly at religious improvement rather than at entertainment, it contained abundant evidence of narrative artistry. Bunyan's vivid realistic style, his soaring imagination, and his expert rendering of the agonies of conscience won both respect and respectability for the popular novel. His work prepared the way for Daniel Defoe, the first true novelist in English.

Daniel Defoe (*c.* 1703–31) was, like Bunyan, a dissenter. He wrote for the growing audience of middle-class merchants and manufacturers, and his professed aim was the improvement of society. After a busy career as a journalist, Defoe turned to writing novels. His

Fig. 1. Daniel Defoe, engraving by M. van Der Gucht after a portrait by J. Tavener.

Robinson Crusoe (1719) and its two sequels are travel adventures brilliantly complicated by problems of survival and rescue and deftly unified by a theme that exalts simplicity, naturalness, and belief in God. Defoe reduced Bunyan's religious views from allegory to actuality, spelling out in realistic incident, perhaps too explicitly, his parables of "moral and religious improvement." But whereas Bunyan's realism was either verbal or incidental to a theological generalization, Defoe's resided chiefly in the history of events and the biographies of his characters. Thus his *Memoirs of a Cavalier* (1720) exploits the events of the English civil ports to be an account written by a saddler in 1665. Both works presented their "facts" so authentically that they were long accepted as history. Similarly, *Moll Flanders* (1722) and *Roxana* (1724) are fictitious autobiographies that paralleled the notorious lives of London adventuresses. What Defoe could not have said effectively or agreeably as a pamphleteer, he managed to present as fictitious history or adventure.

Significantly, Defoe's political opponent Jonathan *Swift also turned to fiction as an instrument of satire, instruction, and moral persuasion. Swift's first use of fiction as the vehicle of argument occurred in the mock-heroic prose epic, *The Battle of the Books* (1704), wherein the Bee, symbolic of ancient writers such as Homer, Aristotle, and Plato, struggled with the Spider, symbolic of modern writers such as *Milton, *Dryden, and Hobbes. In *A Tale of a Tub* (pub. 1704), a satire on religious controversy, Swift dramatized the three warring Christian groups in the persons of Peter, Martin, and Jack. For his satire on human nature in general, *Gulliver's Travels* (1726), Swift chose for his narrator a sailor not unlike one of Defoe's heroes and endowed him with his own knowledge of geography, history, and exotic information. He established Gulliver's credibility by making him speak the plain style appropriate to the average man and reflect the normal biases and sensibilities of the middle-class Englishman. As told from Gulliver's point of view, the voyages to Lilliput, Brobdingnag, Laputa, and to the Country of the Houyhnhnms read like burlesques of the tall tales of travel writers. Amusement yields to fascinated horror as Swift's manipulation of ironic tone represents man as unjust, coarse, stupid, and, finally, less admirable than the beasts. Ruthlessly opposed to the "soft" view of human nature set forth in what he considered the obnoxious secular ethic of his day, Swift reminds the reader that though man is not normally rational or religious, he has the capacity to be both.

The 18th-Century English Novelists. Swift's and Defoe's narratives, for all their vivid realism and ironic thrust, were too general or too objective to allow for the rendering of intricate emotions. A reader can know the minds of Lemuel Gulliver and Robinson Crusoe but not their sentiments, sensibilities, or their intense particularities. The task of dealing with these remained for the great novelists of the mid-18th century, Richardson, Fielding, and Smollett. Taken together, they set the course to be followed by the English novel for at least a century; taken singly, each man left his individual stamp on the novel. All were, at least professedly, didactic writers bent on the reform of morals, of manners, or of social conduct. But, whereas Richardson emphasized the subjective elements of the novel and pointed ahead to a new kind of realistic romance, Fielding stressed the comic sense, benevolence, and classic form characteristic of the well-made novel. Smollett, in turn, elevated the picaresque journey to a quest for personal and social adjustment and prepared the ground for the growth of the novel of social criticism.

As Samuel Richardson (1689–1761), a fat and prosperous printer of 50, was composing Letter 135 of his *Familiar Letters,* a manual of form letters, the thought struck him that he might show his readers how to think and act as well as how to write. The result was *Pamela, Or Virtue Rewarded* (1740–41), an epistolary novel detailing the strategies by which Pamela Andrews fended off the advances of Squire B. until that unworthy proposed honorable marriage. Although many critics have protested that Richardson's "prolix fondling of [amatory] episodes was even more indecent than vulgarity would have been," 18th-century society accepted *Pamela* as an attempt to inculcate virtue "at the same time that it agreeably entertains." Dr. Samuel *Johnson, Alexander *Pope, and David Garrick, together with "the chambermaids of all nations," read *Pamela* with fascinated pleasure.

Richardson not only succeeded in touching the sentiments of his readers, but also he raised the analysis of sentiment to a fine art. In his hands the epistolary method of storytelling fostered unity by focusing on a few main characters, conveyed a sense of immediacy by retailing each incident in the present tense, and established credibility by introducing various points of view. Moreover, Richardson's command of this method helped him to avoid the defects of his predecessors, namely, the persistent interference of the author in

the narrative, the inconvenient necessity of accounting for chronology, setting, and historical realities.

In his second novel, *Clarissa: or The History of a Young Lady* (1747–48), consisting of seven volumes containing 547 letters, Richardson introduced a more complicated plot involving a loveless marriage, seduction, attempted escapes, duels, and retribution. *Clarissa* also reveals a rounded sense of character. The heroine, as Richardson observed in his preface, "is not in all respects a perfect character." In accounting for her imperfections, as well as those of Robert Lovelace, Lord M., William Morden, and the Marlowes, Richardson challenged the equivocal moral standards of the upper and middle classes and thus added a social dimension to his study of character. Moreover, *Clarissa* is an early example of the psychologically ambivalent personality. She abides by the law of her family yet revolts against it; she wants to escape *with* Lovelace and *from* him; she is both unforgiving and overforgiving; she is both responsible for her own distress and yet a victim of fate. Finally, *Clarissa* illustrates the beginnings of the stream-of-consciousness novel in those passages where the heroine expresses her feelings of guilt and fear in meaningfully incoherent language.

In *Pamela* and *Clarissa* Richardson represented his principal male characters chiefly as villainous predators of female virtue. In *Sir Charles Grandison* (1753–54) he proposed a perfect Englishman, aristocratic, Protestant, and romantic. This seven-volume work is less concentrated than its predecessors, since the hero is torn between his love for Protestant, middle-class Harriet Byron, whom he has rescued from rakish Sir Har-

Fig. 2. Samuel Richardson, portrait by J. Highmore, 1750.

grave Pollexfen, and Catholic Lady Clementina della Porreta, who, driven mad by his departure from Italy, has a claim upon his honor. Despite interesting passages, the author exerted a too-conscious control over his story and a too-obvious appeal to the prejudices of readers, who saw nothing grotesque in his division of characters into "men, women, and Italians." With all its faults, *Sir Charles Grandison* was widely read and contributed greatly to the popularity (506 examples in England alone from 1740 to 1799) of the epistolary novel.

Like Richardson, Henry Fielding (1707–54) came to the novel indirectly, partly because of the censorship of the stage set up in the Licensing Act of 1737, partly because of his urge to expose the follies of a corrupt society and of some of its representative spokesmen. From 1728, the date of his going up to London, to 1737 Fielding wrote some 26 plays. They were, for the most part, satires, some of them in the manner of Cervantes and *Molière. *Pasquin* (1736) and *The Historical Register for 1736* (1737) were topical gibes at the ministry of Sir Robert Walpole. One play, *The History of Tom Thumb the Great* (1731), was a brilliant parody of contemporary heroic tragedy. After the Licensing Act Fielding turned to the law and pamphleteering. Richardson's *Pamela* offended his aristocratic, classical, and realistic prejudices, and he countered with *Shamela* (1741), a brutal burlesque of Richardson's moralizing postures, and with *Joseph Andrews* (1742), in which Pamela's brother takes on his sister's role and Lady Booby, that of Squire B. *Joseph Andrews,* however, was neither a mere satire based on reversal of roles nor a mere parody of Richardson's style. It introduced several new elements, chief among them a moral sense at once wider, deeper, and more genial than that in Richardson's novel.

Moreover, Fielding elevated corrective comedy to the level of humorous wisdom. In the writing of *Joseph Andrews* Fielding defined the novel as "a comic epic in prose," a theory that he developed with great consistency. From this point on Fielding's development was extraordinarily rapid. In 1743 he published *Jonathan Wild the Great,* a satire on the popular adulation of the amoral "great" soldier and politician. His masterpiece, *Tom Jones,* appeared in 1749. This long, structurally splendid novel aimed, according to Fielding's statements in the preface and in the many interpolated essays, to laugh mankind out of its own weaknesses and to reassert the value of the understanding heart. Its 18 books are divided into three equal parts. The first part, covering Tom Jones's first 20 years, introduces the main characters, develops Tom's quarrel with Squire Allworthy, and establishes the motives for Tom's departure and search for his identity. The second and third parts describe his adventures on the road to London and his career in the city, where all the complications are resolved, the good rewarded, and the evil punished. In the course of the novel virtually every type of character and every class of society are depicted as evil, foolish, or hypocritical. No man is perfect. All, including right-hearted Tom and benevolent Squire Allworthy, require correction of some excess or defect.

Fielding's last novel, *Amelia* (1751), departed from the comic formula of its predecessors in favor of a kind of realistic epic. Captain William Booth, the hero, is an essentially good man who is partly the victim of his own weakness for gambling, and partly the victim of unjust laws, corrupt magistrates, conniving lawyers, and false friends. Amelia, his wife, is an admirable heroine whose benevolence and fidelity sustain her husband throughout two imprisonments and his other trials. Although Fielding has here written an extremely well-made novel, the deft resolutions of the many plots and counterplots are perhaps less memorable than his attacks on injustice, and his delineations of the Christian virtues of Amelia and Dr. Harrison, a wise and kindly curate, and of Captain Booth himself.

Tobias Smollett (1721–71) was, if possible, more fully representative of 18th-century fiction than his two rivals. His novels, taken together, recapitulate the principal developments of prose fiction up to his time. *Roderick Random* (1748), an adventure story of a surgeon's apprentice, follows the autobiographical pattern popularized by Defoe. *Peregrine Pickle* (1751) is a rogue novel whose excellent character portraits more than compensate for its lack of plot. *Ferdinand, Count Fathom* (1753), partly a rogue novel, partly a supernatural horror story, offers a hero-villain not unlike the antihero of later times. Smollett attempted to adapt *Don Quixote* to an improbable 18th-century background in *Sir Launcelot Greaves* (1760–61), and he turned to Swift for the model of his political allegory, *The Adventures of an Atom* (1769). In *Humphrey Clinker* (1771), his last novel and by far his best work, Smollett raised the epistolary tradition popularized by Richardson to the level of great art.

An immediately noticeable innovation is Smollett's use of five principal letter writers, two men and three women, who represent distinctly different points of view and literary styles. There exists, too, among the characters a far more complex set of relationships than Richardson attempted. The subjects of the letters, life in Scotland and England and on the roads in between, include comments on law, medicine, politics, recreation, dress, husbandry, as well as realistic portrayals of human action. A serenely melancholic temper provides the novel with a philosophic tone if not a systematic philosophy of life. Moreover, *Humphrey Clinker* emphasizes growth and change in character. Matthew Bramble's search for health results in a clearer understanding of himself and his times.

To the achievements of Richardson, Fielding, and Smollett should be added those of Laurence Sterne (1713–68), whose *Tristram Shandy* (1759–67) is a potpourri of witty observations, reflections, and parodies; of Samuel Johnson, whose *Rasselas* (1759) is a philosophical narrative depicting the folly of seeking happiness on earth; and of Oliver *Goldsmith, whose *The Vicar of Wakefield* (1766) stresses the value of sentiment, benevolence, and contentment. Thus by the end of the 18th century the novel had emerged as an important literary genre distinguished by a variety of forms and marked by its special concern for personal conduct in the context of a complex society.

The 19th Century. A growing sophistication in both the theory and the practice of fiction evolved. The novelist was more than an entertainer.

France. That his mission was to interpret the age for his readers was already evident in *Goethe's *The Sorrows of Werther* (1774), whose hero symbolized the sentimental world-sorrow characteristic of romanticism, the same *mal de siècle* *Rousseau had treated in *La Nouvelle Héloïse* (1761). By 1804 Étienne de Sénancour's *Obermann* explicitly related melancholy to the post-Revolutionary milieu. *Stendhal's *Le Rouge et le Noir* (1831) and *La Chartreuse de Parme* (1839), for all their historical trappings, were chiefly revelations of a world agitated by revolutionary change. So too, Honoré de *Balzac, in his carefully planned scenes from Private Life, Provincial Life, Parisian Life, and so on, aimed to present "not only a history and criticism of society, but also an analysis of its evils and an exposition of its principles . . .," in short, to make sense of *La Comédie Humaine*. The same awareness is evident in George Sand (1804–76), whose major works embody social and philosophical criticism of her age. Gustave *Flaubert, too, while preeminently the poet of the novel, remained within its main stream of history and criticism by virtue of his penetrating analysis of the effects of contemporary ideals on characters like Emma Bovary, Bouvard, and Pécuchet. Other French writers identified as historians and critics of various aspects of contemporary society were Edmond (1822–96) and Jules (1830–70) Goncourt, Émile *Zola, and, in part, Alphonse Daudet (1840–97).

Russia. As in France, so too in Russia the novel became the vehicle for expressing the growing involvement of prose fiction with society in the process of rapid change. Perhaps because of their more recently discovered national identity and their consequent sense of destiny, Russian novelists explored their own history. In *Dead Souls* (1842) and *The Overcoat* (1842) Nikolaĭ Vasil'evich *Gogol', the first of the great modern Russian writers, combined realism and pathos in an attempt to satirize inefficient bureaucracy and at the same time to evoke pity for its victims. Partly inspired by Gogol', Ivan Turgenev presented in *Fathers and Sons* (1862) and *Smoke* (1867) the classic struggle between a conservative older generation and a new generation dreaming of reform. Fëdor Mikhaĭlovich *Dostoevskiĭ's career began with *Poor Folk* (1846), a book professedly derived from Gogol's *The Overcoat*. From descriptions of human suffering Dostoevskiĭ turned to psychological analysis in *Crime and Punishment* (1866), then to a study of atheistic politics in *The Possessed* (1871–72), and finally to the apocalyptic vision of *The Brothers Karamazov* (1879–80). Despite his frequent concentration on individual obsessions, Dostoevskiĭ always emphasized the close connections of personal action with the weal or woe of the human community. Leo *Tolstoi was even more directly concerned with Russian society and its spiritual destiny. *War and Peace* (1865–69) is a massive chronicle of the Russian nation at war with Napoleon. Impelling for its narrative skill, the novel is also an important study of the meaning of history, of the role of the various classes of society, and, above all, in the characters of Pierre Bezukhov and Prince Andrey, of the personal quest for a sustaining ideal. *Anna Karenina* (1873–77) contrasts the widening gulf between the corruptions of metropolis and aristocracy and the humble, natural life of country and peasant. *Resurrection* (1899), his last and longest novel, explores the crisis of an aristocrat who redeems himself by sharing the punishment of a servant girl whom he has led to degradation.

England. To a large extent the English novel of the 19th century developed patterns similar to those on the Continent. Its first presiding genius was Sir Walter *Scott, who, after a brief career as a poet and man of letters, turned to the historical novel. Of the some 30 novels he wrote between 1814 and 1832, several, like *Waverly* (1814), *The Heart of Midlothian* (1818), and *Quentin Durward* (1823), are masterpieces in a genre that up to his time had been exploited rather than developed by the Gothic novelists in England (*see* GOTHIC REVIVAL) and the early German Romantics (*see* GERMAN LITERATURE, 5). Scott brought to the historical novel a vivid sense of the relevance of the past to the present, a gift for spectacular drama, and the saving grace of humor. Admired by Goethe in Germany, by Balzac and Alexandre *Dumas in France, and by Alessandro *Manzoni in Italy, his generosity of spirit won both respect and respectability for his profession.

Though different in temperament, intellectual interest, and range of experience, Jane Austen (1775–1817) was clearly Scott's equal in the quality of her achievement and his superior in the now admired art of presenting her material from a limited point of view and in just proportions. Her insight into the follies of human nature was balanced by her firm command of moral principles. *Pride and Prejudice* (1813), a brilliant comedy of manners, most fully displays her gift for comic dialogue and ironic wit, while *Emma* (1816) is her most mature and complex study of the various arts of self-delusion.

The appearance of both Scott and Austen at the beginning of the 19th century emphasized the growing variety of the English novel. While English 19th-century novelists inherited the features of their 18th-century forebears, they all exhibited their own unique characteristics. Thus, though William Makepeace Thackeray (1811–63) and Charles *Dickens were both indebted to Fielding, among others, each assimilated Fielding according to his different sensibilities. For all his imputed sentimentalism, Thackeray was temperamentally a satirist with strong classical and aristocratic instincts and establishmentarian standards of behavior. Thus, while *Vanity Fair* (1847–48) appears cynically to criticize human nature in general, at bottom it reflects Thackeray's affection for and belief in the ethos of the 18th century. This tendency is more clearly marked in his *Pendennis* (1848–50), a notably autobiographical novel; in *Henry Esmond* (1852), a book that brilliantly portrays an earlier style of life; and in *The Newcomes* (1855), a long family chronicle that enshrines, in the person of Colonel Newcome, Thackeray's ideal of the humane and chivalrous old-fashioned English gentleman.

Dickens, however, was himself the son of a lower middle-class family that had suffered, through temporary depressions, the bitterness of poverty, and even the degradation of the debtors' prison. Although his robust imagination prompted him to describe some of the miseries and absurdities of day-to-day life with humor, as in his incomparable *The Pickwick Papers* (1836–37), he was haunted by the cruelty of social customs and often enraged by the inequities of the law. Partly a satirist, as in the exposure of inadequate poor laws in *Oliver Twist* (1837–39), he was more often the tragic poet evoking pity for those too poor, too weak, or too fine to survive the 19th-century industrial jungle. After writing *David Copperfield* (1849–50), his long autobiographical novel, Dickens's tone became increasingly mordant and his images more relevant to his themes. He continued to fabricate involved plots, neatly adjusted to the needs of serial publication, but the later novels are memorable chiefly for his extraordinary synthesis of character, setting, and theme. The symbolic fog that introduces *Bleak House* (1852–53), the grime of Coketown in *Hard Times* (1854), the prison scenes of *Little Dorritt* (1855–57), the wine shop of *A Tale of Two Cities* (1859), the graveyard in the marshes and the spectral wedding breakfast of *Great Expectations* (1860–61) all exemplify his unique ability to unify agent, act, and scene. If Dickens did not substantially change the mechanics of fiction, he gave it a new soul, a passion and intensity that relates him to Dostoevskiĭ. Few today praise Dickens exclusively for making his readers weep for Paul Dombey, laugh at Mrs. Gamp, or sneer at Mr. Podsnap. More than the vivacity of his characters, it is chiefly his poetic vision of a world in chains that is enthralling.

Anthony Trollope (1815–82) once described the novel as "a picture of common life enlivened by humor and sweetened by pathos." His more than 60 novels embrace stories about Ireland, clerical life, English politics, and upper-middle-class society. In most of these, despite occasional sharp thrusts of satire and mild gushes of romance, he maintained a genial level that neither lost the reader's attention nor aroused enthusiasm. For this reason, and because his *Autobiography* (1883) revealed an attitude toward writing that eschewed both aesthetic refinements and reforming zeal, he was for a long time regarded merely as a successful professional writer. More recently, however, critics have shown that Trollope's middle course was not the easy path of mediocrity but, in his most successful stories, the achievement of a golden mean. In *The Warden* (1855), *Barchester Towers* (1857), and other chronicles

Fig. 3. Anthony Trollope, portrait by S. Lawrence, 1865.

of Barsetshire, he gave an account of Victorian provincial life that seems to many more accurate, more natural, and more just than comparable novels of Thackeray and Dickens. While his political novels lacked the flair of those of his contemporary Benjamin Disraeli (1804–81), they were more accurate portrayals of the Victorian reality. Trollope's avoidance of strong ideological bias or class conviction freed his "society" novels, *The Way We Live Now* (1875), for example, from partisan bitterness without, however, robbing him of his satirical bite. Where he excelled his great contemporaries was not in his avoiding the defects of their genius but in cultivating his own field of domestic realism. In his hands the usual shone with unusual luster.

With George *Eliot (the pen name of Mary Ann Evans) the English novel reached a kind of watershed. Her earlier novels were homely, realistic tales of provincial rural life based largely on her own observations. *Scenes from Clerical Life* (1858), *Adam Bede* (1859), *The Mill on the Floss* (1860), and *Silas Marner* (1861) were greatly admired by Dickens, Thackeray, and Trollope, possibly because they embodied various aspects of their own art. Thackeray's combination of satire and sentiment, Dickens's power of bringing characters to life, and Trollope's reliance on domestic details to create verisimilitude are all present in these realistic novels. Each of the three might have written her foreword to fiction: "I wish to stir your sympathy with commonplace troubles—to win your tears for real sorrow, sorrow such as may live next door to you. . . ."

Another and deeper George Eliot emerged with the appearance of *Romola* (1863). This novel, a combination of historical fiction and psychological analysis, portrays the turbulent politics of Savonarola's Florence and traces the spiritual degeneration of Tito Melema and the regeneration of the heroine. After *Romola*, Eliot was less concerned with her old admiration for "the faithful pictures of monotonous, homely existence" associated with the Dutch painters, than she was "with the ideals and philosophies that underlie human character." *Felix Holt, Radical* (1866) examined the intellectual and spiritual wellsprings of the reform movement. Her masterpiece, *Middlemarch* (1872), was a brilliant interweaving of individual triumph and tragedy with political, economic, and intellectual history. *Middlemarch* presented not only a persuasive evaluation of the state of England in the 1830s but also a magnificent achievement of organization and style. Despite its complexity of subject and theme, Eliot maintained a strict control of her story without destroying the spontaneity of her characters or exhausting her great verbal energy. Small wonder that the English critic F. R. Leavis places Eliot preeminently in the great tradition of English fiction as one who recapitulates the achievements of the past and prepares the way for the achievements of the future.

Eliot clearly influenced Thomas *Hardy, her immediate successor as England's most important novelist. Like Eliot, Hardy was a master of "Dutch painter" realism. He also tempered his realistic view of life by an intense sympathy for human suffering, and he interpreted tragic situations in the light of philosophic views. Of his 14 novels, *The Return of the Native* (1878), *The Mayor of Casterbridge* (1886), *Tess of the D'Urbervilles* (1891), and *Jude the Obscure* (1895) are outstanding for their plot, characterization, and the poetic use of environment.

The U.S. Novel. As the English novel was moving to the front rank of that nation's literature, a similar situation was unfolding in America. At first dependent on European novels, as in the "Gothic" tales of Charles Brockden Brown (1771–1810), the American novel soon acquired its own distinctive flavor by virtue of its native subject matter, its specific moral concerns, and its characteristic patterns of speech. James Fenimore *Cooper began writing to prove that an American could write a better book than could the conventional British novelist. His actual achievement, measured by his 5 Leatherstocking Tales, 9 sea stories, 11 historical novels, and more than 12 novels of social criticism, far exceeded this modest aim. Though hampered by a prolix style, especially in his dialogue, Cooper succeeded in giving artistic form to American experience and an epic grandeur to its national aspirations. Although much less prolific than Cooper, Nathaniel *Hawthorne wrote 3 masterpieces, *The Scarlet Letter* (1850), *The House of the Seven Gables* (1851), and *The Blithedale Romance* (1852), which, together with his short stories and notebooks, gave permanent and memorable shape to the Puritan themes of guilt and alienation. Herman *Melville pursued similar themes in his whaling epic *Moby Dick* (1851). Here, as in the *novelle* contained in *Piazza Tales* (1856) and *Billy Budd, Foretopman* (published posthumously in 1924), the central problems of good and evil, love and hate, are explored with both psychological realism and imaginative insight.

Mark *Twain and Henry *James presented the American scene from opposite points of view. Twain, a Westerner, was almost purely native in his inspiration. *Tom Sawyer* (1876), *Huckleberry Finn* (1884), and *A Connecticut Yankee at King Arthur's Court* (1889) derive from the observations and attitudes of frontier experience. Episodic, humorous, colloquial, they attack the sins of civilization, its hypocrisies, frauds, feuds, and tyrannies. James, an Easterner, reflected not only the Puritan tradition received from Hawthorne but the European culture he acquired from British and continental writers and from the society of the cultivated classes here and abroad. James's heroic ideal, often symbolized by the central character of his novels and stories, was a man or woman of exquisite perception who knew himself, learned to know others, and aspired to live according to altruistic principles. His major novels, *The American* (1877), *Daisy Miller* (1879), *The Portrait of a Lady* (1881), *The Wings of the Dove* (1902), *The Ambassadors* (1903), and *The Golden Bowl* (1904), involved nobly innocent Americans of refined conscience with the complexities and equivocations of European society. In these and numerous other works James brought the novel to a rare perfection of dramatic form and established it as the dominant genre in our national literature.

The U.S. and English Symbiosis. James's career served, too, to join English and American fiction in a symbiotic life so that today the major novelists of each country belong to the other. As the novel approached the 20th century, it became increasingly difficult to describe in terms of one line of development or one succession of masters. Without losing their identities, national literatures began to commingle under the influence of new modes of communication and the increasingly swift and competent translations. Irish James *Joyce and English D. H. *Lawrence were as widely read and studied in America as in the British Isles, and Americans like Sinclair Lewis, Ernest *Hemingway, John Steinbeck, and William *Faulkner were eagerly read in Britain and on the Continent. Franz *Kafka, an Austrian Jew, had important followers in virtually all the Western countries.

Divisions and Recent Trends. Moreover, the main roads of the historical romance, the realistic novel, and the naturalistic analysis of society divided into several paths. The historical romance became aesthetic in Walter Pater, dramatic in Robert Louis *Stevenson, scholarly in Sigrid *Undset, and philosophic in Thomas *Mann. The realistic novel ranged from the individual-centered observations of Samuel Butler, George Gissing, and George Moore to the social orientation of H. G. Wells, Arnold Bennett, and George *Orwell. Naturalism, particularly in America, produced a rainbow variety suggested by the names of Frank Norris, Stephen Crane, Theodore *Dreiser, Maxwell Anderson, and John Dos Passos. Not unexpectedly, some writers belonged to several traditions simultaneously or at different stages of their career. Graham Greene, for instance, has used romantic adventure, realism, naturalism, and intuitive religious knowledge, notably in *The Power and the Glory* (1940).

Perhaps the most typical current in recent fiction is a pronounced drift toward the novel of psychological analysis. Joseph *Conrad, Dorothy Richardson, James Joyce, and Virginia Woolf in England; Marcel *Proust, André *Gide, and Albert *Camus in France; Thomas Wolfe and William Faulkner in the U.S.; Thomas Mann, Robert *Musil, Hermann *Broch, and Heinrich Böll among German writers—all are explorers of the subconscious mind. Often indebted to Sigmund Freud, Alfred Adler, or Carl Jung, or to the psychological theories of William James, Henri Bergson, or F. H. Bradley, such writers are not their slavish disciples. As a result, the psychological novel varies from the intensely personal focus of Virginia Woolf to the historical and mythic range of Joyce and Mann.

From 1914 to midcentury the experience of 20th-century depressions, wars, cold wars, and drastic social change has been reflected in a series of novels with a strong autobiographical flavor, often with a pessimistic or existentialist tone (*see* EXISTENTIALISM IN LITERATURE). This is no less apparent in sequence novels such as Ford Madox *Ford's *Tietjens* series, Anthony Powell's *Dance to the Music of Time* (1962), Evelyn Waugh's *Brideshead Revisited* (1945) and his World War II trilogy, or C. P. Snow's *Strangers and Brothers* than it is in the readily identifiable self-portraits of Virginia Woolf, D. H. Lawrence, James Joyce, Thomas Wolfe, and Saul Bellow. The autobiographical novel stresses the quest for identity in an alien world either empty of values or, as Holden Caulfield put it in J. D. Salinger's *The Catcher in the Rye* (1951), full of "phony" values. Often, however, as in the work of Georges *Bernanos, François Mauriac, and the American Paul Horgan, autobiographical fiction is directly related to the finding or confirming of religious faith.

Vitality of the Novel. But if the variety of the 20th-century novel precludes any generalization on its theme or form, it also testifies to the extraordinary vitality of prose fiction. Everywhere, in new nations as in old, the novel has become the principal literary form through which writers communicate private perception and passion and public dream or vision. In their crea-

Fig. 4.
Paul Horgan.

tive imitation of how men see, feel, think, and respond to experience, novelists continue to adapt and modify the techniques of fiction and to discover, in the light of man's increasing knowledge of himself, new and exciting ways of communicating an ever-deepening awareness of the gifts of life.

Bibliography: W. E. ALLEN, *The English Novel* (New York 1955; pa. 1957); *The Modern Novel in Britain and the United States* (New York 1964). E. A. BAKER, *History of the English Novel*, 10 v. (London 1924–39). J. W. BEACH, *The Twentieth-century Novel: Studies in Technique* (New York 1932). *The Concise Encyclopedia of Modern World Literature*, ed. G. GRIGSON (New York 1963). A. COWIE, *The Rise of the American Novel* (New York 1948). M. COWLEY, ed., *After the Genteel Tradition* (New York 1937; repr. Glouchester, Mass. 1959). J. C. DUNLOP, *History of Prose Fiction*, ed. H. WILSON, 2 v. (new ed. London 1906). L. EDEL, *The Psychological Novel: 1900–1950* (Philadelphia 1955). E. M. FORSTER, *Aspects of the Novel* (Harvest, New York 1956). F. R. LEAVIS, *The Great Tradition* (New York 1948). P. LUBBOCK, *The Craft of Fiction* (London 1921; repr. New York 1957). W. V. O'CONNOR, ed., *Forms of Modern Fiction* (Minneapolis 1948). M. O'DONOVAN (F. O'Connor), *The Mirror in the Roadway: A Study of the Modern Novel* (New York 1958). S. O'FAOLAIN, *The Vanishing Hero: Studies in Novelists of the Twenties* (Boston 1957). A. H. QUINN, *American Fiction: An Historical and Critical Survey* (New York 1936). H. R. WARFEL, *American Novelists of Today* (New York 1951). **Illustration credits:** Figs. 1–3, National Portrait Gallery, London. Fig. 4, Farrar, Straus & Co., Inc.

[F. X. CONNOLLY]

NOVENA

Nine successive days of prayer, private or public, to obtain special favors or graces. It differs from an octave, or the 8 days of prayerful celebration that follow certain feasts, because the octave has a place in the liturgy that the novena (which generally precedes a feast with which it may be associated) has not. Moreover, the octave is celebrated in a more festal spirit, whereas the novena tends to be marked by a feeling of urgent need and yearning. The novena can be considered a triple *triduum, involving a more prolonged concentration of devotion and spiritual effort.

The nine days that the Apostles spent in Jerusalem at the command of the Lord as they awaited the coming of the Holy Spirit (Lk 24.49; Acts 1.4) has been sug-

gested as a scriptural prototype of the novena, but this devotion was first introduced not as an exercise preparatory to an event of great spiritual significance but as the observance of a period of mourning. The Greeks and the Romans, as well as other peoples of antiquity, were accustomed to observe 9 days of mourning (*novendialia*), with a special feast on the 9th day, after a death or burial. This practice was adopted by Christians, but with Christian rather than pagan forms of observance. Nevertheless, the pagan origin of the custom gave offense to some, and protest eventually led to the substitution of a 7-day mourning period, 7 being the number of the days of the Christian week and therefore considered to have greater religious significance. However, a vestige of the earlier practice remains in the *novendialia,* or Pope's Novena, still observed after the death of a supreme pontiff. In the Middle Ages a like period was often observed after the death of other wealthy or noble individuals, but except for the novenas of Masses and prayers for the departed, this custom has fallen into disuse.

The devotional novena for the purpose of special prayers to gain some needed grace or to prepare for the celebration of some special occasion with greater solemnity made its appearance in the early Middle Ages. It began in France and Spain with a preparation of 9 days for the feast of Christmas, the number 9 representing the months Our Lord had spent in His mother's womb. The *O antiphons that begin on December 17th are probably a vestigial survival in the liturgy of this ancient practice.

Preparatory novenas of this kind came in time to be celebrated in connection with other occasions, especially the feasts of popular saints or of Our Lady, and they were often undertaken publicly and with much external solemnity. Because Our Lady under various titles and the saints were popularly esteemed for their intercessory powers with respect to particular kinds of blessings, novenas came to be times of special supplication in which the devout sought favors such as could be hoped for through the intercession of the saints who were honored. Very often the favor sought was the recovery of health, and in times when medical science had little comfort or hope to offer those afflicted with disease it is understandable that people should turn so readily to heavenly intercessors for healing and protection.

Novenas have been attacked as superstitious, partly because of the peculiar efficacy the practice seems to attach to the number nine, and partly because of the many extraordinary and even miraculous effects with which some novenas have been credited. No doubt the possibility of superstitious abuse exists and it should be guarded against, and no other effectiveness should be attributed to novena prayers as such than is attributable to devout prayer earnestly and perseveringly undertaken in other forms. There is nothing doctrinally objectionable in the idea of a novena; on the contrary, it is a practice that can be most serviceable to true devotion and piety. Perseverance and constancy are qualities of all good prayer, and it is well that some devotional practices should give special emphasis to them by requiring repetition on successive days over a more or less extended period of time, for this manifests and stimulates the worshiper's earnestness and fervor. That one should pray more confidently and hope for special graces by the use of such means is not unreasonable.

The novena grew out of popular piety, and it was not until the 19th century that the Church recommended the practice by the granting of indulgences.

Bibliography: J. HILGERS, CE 11:141–144. G. Löw, EncCatt 12:516–519. F. BERINGER, *Die Ablässe, ihr Wesen und Gebrauch*, 2 v. (Paderborn 1921) 1:638–644. *Enchiridion indulgentiarum* (Rome 1952).

[P. K. MEAGHER]

NOVGOROD

A city on the Volkhov River, north of Lake Ilmen, in the *Union of Soviet Socialist Republics. The Apostle *Andrew is said to have reached the site, which was an important point on the water road between the Baltic and the Black Sea and which later controlled the north end of a trade route with the *Byzantine Empire. The city was seized by Varangians under the legendary Riurik in mid-9th century and one of his descendants, Oleg, seized *Kiev (*c.* 880), which then became the capital of the emerging Russian state; Novgorod (the New City) became an appanage for the prince's sons. *Vladimir ruled in Novgorod before he drove his elder brother from the throne of Kiev. The conversion of Russia to Christianity, begun by Vladimir (989), was accepted in Kiev, but a strong pagan party in Novgorod had to be overcome by force.

The Byzantine bishop, Joachim (d. 1030), transferred from Cherson, was succeeded in Novgorod by a native Russian, Luke Zhidiata (1034–54, 1057–59). Bishops Theodore (1069–77) and Nicholas (1096–1108) are venerated as saints in the Russian Church. Another native Russian, John Papynin (1108–30), was succeeded by Nifont (1131–56), a monk from the Kievan Crypt Monastery, who was personally raised to archiepiscopal rank by the Byzantine Patriarch Nicholas IV (1147–51) because of his resistance to the jurisdictional claims of the metropolitan of Kiev, Clement of Smolensk (1147–54). Under Prince Andrew Bogoliubsky (d. 1175) Novgorod was made a *metropolitan see (1165). The first archbishop, Elias (1163–86), was followed by Gabrial (1187–93) and Mantury (1193–99). With Anthony Dobrynya (1211–19, 1225–28, 1229) the office became the center of a struggle for power, but Spiridonius (1229–49) brought some stability in the troubled period of the Mongol invasions.

Distance, as well as marshes and forests not easily penetrated by cavalry, saved Novgorod from the *Mongols, although the city did pay them tribute. The fall of Kiev (1240) left Novgorod to assume religious, cultural, and political leadership of Russia. Prince *Alexander Nevski (d. 1263) of Novgorod came to terms with the Mongols and defended Russia's western frontiers against Swedes and *Teutonic Knights. The city continued through the late Middle Ages to be a commercial center; St. Peter's Yard in Novgorod was the easternmost depot of the *Hanseatic League, which carried on a rich trade in furs, hides, wax, honey, and tar. The rich trading city of Pskov remained subject to Novgorod until 1348.

The government of the city, in the hands of a merchant aristocracy, resembled more a city state than a medieval principality. The *veche* (assembly), a body that achieved importance only in Novgorod and Pskov after the 11th century, ruled the city and invited or rejected the assistance of *posadniks* (princes), whose chief duty was to command the army. The republic,

which styled itself Lord Novgorod the Great, had the first charter in Russia, issued by Yaroslav the Wise (d. 1054). The churchmen in Novgorod were an influential but not restrictive class, controlling vast estates and often, like the princes, engaging in trade. The hierarchy was frequently elected, or deposed, by the *veche;* the Novgorod chronicle describes the election of Bishop Arkady (1156) and Archbishop Mantury (1193). The archimandrite (abbot of the monastery of St. George) was second in importance only to the archbishop. It was in this city that the *Novgorodskaia pervaia letopis* (Novgorod chronicle), second only to *Nestor as a source for Russian medieval history, was written [ed. U.S.S.R. Academy of Science (Moscow 1950)].

The decline of the Hansa and the disruption of trade by the Mongol incursions into Central Europe brought about a crisis in the economic life of Novgorod in mid-15th century. *Moscow, the seat of the primatial Metropolitanate of Russia from 1459, began to challenge Novgorod for political leadership. In 1478 Ivan III of Moscow had himself recognized as sovereign of the republic, backing his demands with military force. Archbishop Gennadi (1485–1503), who opposed the heresy of the Nonpossessors, was deposed because he resisted Ivan's secularization of church lands (1503). In 1509 Archbishop Ciprion was removed for refusing to submit to the arbitrary acts of the metropolitan of Moscow, backed by Basil III, and the see remained vacant for 17 years. During this period Abbot Philothey of Eleazar Monastery in Pskov, writing to Basil about the vacancy, first mentioned the idea of Moscow as "the third Rome." In 1570 Czar Ivan the Terrible, to break Novgorod's resistance to his efforts to create a centralized state, massacred or deported most of its population. Novgorod never recovered from this blow, although it long was a bone of contention between Russia and an aggressive Polish-Lithuanian kingdom. Its population, estimated at 500,000 in the Middle Ages, has declined to 61,000 today; it is now important chiefly as a communication point between Moscow and *Leningrad (St. Petersburg).

Novgorod was long famous for its fine churches. The cathedral of St. Sophia (1045–52) is a small four-column church on an inscribed cross plan. Its somewhat Romanesque decoration includes frescoes and the 12th-century "Kerson doors," probably made in Magdeburg. The church of St. Nicholas (1113), St. George Monastery church (1119) and the church of the Transfiguration in Volotovo (1352) are also important monuments. A school of icon painting flourished in Novgorod, whose churches were decorated with beautiful frescoes; but after the Moscow fire of 1547 Metropolitan Macarius (1543–64) forcibly moved most of the artists to Moscow to decorate its rebuilt churches. Many of the buildings and paintings in Novgorod were damaged in heavy fighting during World War II.

Bibliography: E. E. GOLUBINSKII, *Istoriia russkoi tserkvi*, 2 v. in 4 (Moscow 1880–1917). G. K. LOUKOMSKY, *L'Architecture religieuse russe du XIᵉ siècle au XVIIᵉ siècle* (Paris 1927). G. VERNADSKY and M. KARPOVICH, *A History of Russia*, 4 v. (New Haven 1943–59). V. N. LAZAREV, *Iskusstvo Novgoroda* (Moscow 1947). A. M. AMMANN, *Storia della Chiesa russa e dei paesi limitrofi* (Turin 1948). S. H. CROSS, *Medieval Russian Churches* (Cambridge, Mass. 1949) 27–46. I. SMOLITSCH, *Russisches Mönchtum* (Würzburg 1953); *Geschichte der russischen Kirche, 1700–1917*, v.1 (Leiden 1964). H. GOMEZ, *Historia eclesiastica*

Bronze doors of the church of St. Sophia at Novgorod, probably cast in Magdeburg, mid-12th century.

de Rusia (Madrid n.d.). A. V. KARTASHEV, *Ocherki po istorii russkoi tserkvi*, 2 v. (Paris 1959). *Bol'shaia sovetskaia entsiklopediia*, ed. S. I. VAVILOV, 51 v. (2d ed. Moscow 1950–58) 30:66–76. G. H. HAMILTON, *The Art and Architecture of Russia* (Pel HArt Z6; 1954). D. S. LIKHACHEV, *Novgorod Veliki* (Leningrad 1945). **Illustration credit:** Marburg-Art Reference Bureau.

[B. J. COMASKEY]

NOVITIATE, CANON LAW OF

The novitiate may be defined as the period of time during which candidates for the religious life study and live the rule of the religious institute they wish to join, and during which the superiors of the institute judge the candidate's suitability for membership. As an institution, the novitiate is as old as the religious life itself. From the time of the Fathers of the Desert, a period of probation has always been required of all aspirants to the states of perfection. (*See* STATES OF PERFECTION, CANONICAL.) It was not until the Council of Trent (1545–63), however, that a full year of novitiate was made an essential requirement for the validity of subsequent religious profession (Sess. 24, cap. 15). (For a detailed history of the development of the novitiate, consult the works listed in the bibliography.) This article will consider the subject under four main headings: establishment of the novitiate, admission to the novitiate, duration of the novitiate, and training of novices.

Establishment of the Novitiate. The validity of the novitiate hinges upon a number of conditions, the first being that it must be made in a religious house established as a novitiate. In the case of religious institutes of papal approbation such establishment requires permission of the Holy See (CIC c.554.1; PostApost c.87.1n2) as well as consent of the local ordinary (CIC c.497.1; PostApost c.19.1). *See* ORDINARIES, ECCLESIASTICAL. In religious institutes that are divided into *provinces, only one novitiate is permitted in each province, unless otherwise allowed by special papal indult (CIC c.554.2; PostApost c.87.1n3). Although the normal rule is that each province shall have its own novitiate, the law does not prohibit a centralized novitiate serving several provinces, or even the entire institute.

Much of the Canon Law concerning the novitiate has in view the more centralized religious institutes, all the houses and provinces of which are subject to a superior general. A special case is found among the older monastic religious orders that have preserved their ancient discipline of having a novitiate in each monastery. The same is true of monasteries of nuns. However, a modern adaptation of this practice among monastic nuns has been introduced by the apostolic constitution *Sponsa Christi* [ActApS (1951) 43:5–24], which urged the federation of independent monasteries of monastic nuns. Where such federation seems advisable, a novitiate common to all the monasteries of the federation could be established.

In all houses of institutes where solemn vows are professed, the law of the papal cloister is to be observed (CIC c.597.1; PostApost c.140.1). *See* CLOISTER, CANONICAL RULES FOR. The cloister must also be observed in the houses of religious congregations where simple vows are pronounced (CIC c.604.1; PostApost c.150.1). Although this is not stated expressly regarding the novices, it is common teaching of canonists that they too are bound by this obligation.

Admission to the Novitiate. Catholics wishing to enter the religious life must be not only rightly intentioned and capable of bearing the burdens of religious life, but also must be free of any canonical impediments (CIC c.538; PostApost c.70). The law enumerates eight impediments to valid admission to the novitiate and six others that would render admission illicit, but valid (CIC c.542; PostApost c.70).

Conditions for Admission. The categories of persons who cannot be admitted validly are: those Catholics who have joined a non-Catholic sect or a sect professing atheism or agnosticism [ActApS (1934) 26:494]; those who have not yet completed their 15th year of age (CIC c.555.1n1; PostApost c.88.1n1); those entering religious life through force or grave fear, or fraudulently, or those admitted by superiors who are influenced by any of these circumstances; married persons, as long as the marriage bond exists; persons who are, or once had been, bound by the vows of religious life; those liable to punishment for a serious crime of which they have been accused or readily can be accused before the civil or ecclesiastical courts; any bishop, even if only designated as such by the pope but not yet consecrated; clerics who by papal requirement have taken a special oath of service to the diocese or mission territory where they are assigned.

The following persons are impeded from being admitted to the novitiate, although a contravention of the law would not render the admission invalid, but merely illicit: clerics in major orders wishing to enter without first consulting their local ordinary, or against the wishes of their ordinary, when departure would be gravely and unavoidably detrimental to the good of souls; debtors incapable of paying their debts; persons obligated to render accounts to others or involved in secular business matters to such a degree that the institute has reason to fear lawsuits and similar annoyances may develop; persons whose parents or grandparents are in such dire need as to require the assistance of the candidate; likewise, parents whose presence is needed for the children's welfare and education; in the case of candidates destined for the priesthood, any irregularity of impediment to Sacred Orders must first be removed (cf. CIC cc.984–991); finally, written permission of the Holy See is needed in the case of Catholics of an Eastern rite wishing to join a Latin-rite institute. This permission is not required if the candidates remain members of their native rite and are simply being trained in a Latin-rite novitiate to be employed eventually in establishing houses and provinces within the Eastern rite [ActApS (1925) 17:583].

Right to Admit. The right of admitting novices to the novitiate belongs to those major superiors designated by the constitutions of the institute. These in turn must consult their advisers, and must investigate the possible presence of any of the above-mentioned impediments. Should an impediment be detected, a dispensation must be obtained, or admission must be refused or at least deferred. Superiors must likewise obtain the record of the candidate's Baptism and Confirmation, as well as the various *testimonial letters required by CIC c.544; PostApost c.76.

Duration of the Novitiate. To be valid the novitiate must be made in the novitiate house for a complete and continuous year (CIC c.555.1; PostApost c.88.1). The novitiate year begins with the reception of the religious habit, or in some other manner prescribed in the constitutions (CIC c.553; PostApost c.85). *See* RELIGIOUS HABIT; RELIGIOUS, CANON LAW OF.

Interruption of the Canonical Year. The required continuity of the novitiate year is not so absolute as to be disrupted altogether by a brief absence from the novitiate. This is clear from the distinction made between a total interruption and a simple suspension of the canonical year (CIC c.556; PostApost c.89). Total interruption means that the time already spent in the novitiate is nullified, and if the novice wishes to continue in his vocation, the year must be begun anew and properly completed before a valid profession of vows may be made. Such an interruption can occur: when a novice, having been dismissed by the competent superior, leaves the novitiate house; when a novice leaves the novitiate without permission of superiors, intending not to return; and when a novice has been absent from the novitiate for more than 30 days, whether this time is continuous or intermittent, regardless of the reason and even though the novice had obtained permission for such absence and intends to return.

In contradistinction to a total interruption of the novitiate, simple suspension occurs if the novice is absent more than 15 days, whether continuous or intermittent, but not more than 30 days, whether with permission of superiors or because of some unforeseen necessity. It is then necessary, but sufficient for the validity of the novitiate, that the days of absence be added to the canonical year. If the absence lasts less than 15 days, the law leaves to the discretion of superiors the decision whether these must be supplied. Superiors are empowered to require that they be supplied, but it is not required for the validity of the novitiate (CIC c.556.2; PostApost c.89.2). However, superiors are cautioned not to allow absences from the novitiate except for grave and equitable reasons (CIC c.556.3; PostApost c.89.3). No total interruption occurs if a novice is transferred by superiors from one novitiate to another of the same institute (CIC c.556.4; PostApost c.89.4). However, the time spent in traveling from one to the other is reckoned as an absence from the novitiate. If this lasts more than 15 days, or in conjunction with other absences totals more than 15 days, the total time of absence must be supplied. If this and other absences total more than 30 days, the entire novitiate year must be begun anew [ActApS (1930) 22: 365].

Second Year of Novitiate. Many institutes demand a longer novitiate than the canonical year required by law (CIC c.555; PostApost c.88). This time is not required for the validity of profession unless the constitutions of a given institute expressly require it (CIC c.555.2; PostApost c.88.2). Nevertheless, the 2d year of the novitiate, where required, constitutes an important stipulation of particular law from which the superiors cannot dispense unless this power has been granted them expressly in the constitutions. Some points of law do not apply so strictly to the 2d year as they do to the canonical year. During the 2d year, for instance, some absences in connection with the training of the novices are permitted. Yet, the spiritual formation of the novices remains the primary objective [ActApS (1921) 13: 539–540].

Termination or Conclusion of the Novitiate. The novitiate can be terminated in three ways: (1) by voluntary departure of the novice, with or without permission of superiors, but with the intention of not returning; (2) by dismissal and actual departure of the novice (CIC c.571.1; PostApost c.105.1); and (3) by

interruption of the novitiate because of an absence of more than 30 days, as explained above.

Canon Law states that at the end of the novitiate the novice is to be admitted to profession, if judged a worthy candidate; dismissed if judged unworthy. If some doubt remains, the major superiors are empowered, but not obliged, to prolong the novitiate up to but not beyond another 6 months (CIC c.571.2; PostApost c.105.2). The law implies that if doubt still remains after this period the novice is to be dismissed.

Training of Novices. The training of novices is committed to the novice master, who alone governs the novitiate and whom the novices must obey. In the exercise of this office he is answerable to higher superiors, but to the local superior only in matters of general discipline, such as the time of meals and religious exercises and permission to leave the house (CIC c.561; PostApost c.94). The object of the novitiate is that, under the care and discipline of the novice master, the novices devote themselves to studying the rules and constitutions and to prayer and meditation. They must learn thoroughly everything pertaining to the vows and virtues, following those spiritual practices calculated to aid in conquering vices, controlling the passions, and acquiring virtue (CIC c.565.1; PostApost c.98.1).

No novice is to engage in the external works of the institute nor pursue formal courses of study. Limited study of courses already completed is permitted. These regulations are directed at achieving the primary objectives of the novitiate: the spiritual and religious formation of the novices and the mutual probation undertaken by the institute and the novice.

Novice masters who are priests cannot hear the confessions of their novices regularly (CIC c.891; PostApost c.100.3), but in all institutes the novice master or mistress should have confidential talks with each novice without bringing any undue pressure upon him to make an intimate *manifestation of conscience (CIC c.530; PostApost c.62). In all novitiates sufficient confessors and opportunity for confession must be provided (*see* CONFESSORS OF RELIGIOUS).

The novices enjoy all the privileges and spiritual favors granted to the institute, but may not be promoted to major or minor orders during the novitiate (CIC c.567; PostApost c.101). *See* HOLY ORDERS, IRREGULARITIES AFFECTING. Any novice in danger of death may be admitted to profession of vows by the competent superior. On recovery the vows cease to bind and the novitiate must be continued and the profession of vows made in the usual manner [ActApS (1912) 4: 589–590; (1923) 15:156–158].

Bibliography: É. JOMBART, DDC 6:1024–36. Abbo 1:542–571. L. FANFANI and K. O'ROURKE, *Canon Law for Religious Women* (Dubuque, Iowa 1961). R. BAKALARCZYK, *De novitiatu* (CUA CLS 36; Washington 1927). J. BROWN, *The Invalidating Effects of Force, Fear, and Fraud upon the Canonical Novitiate* (CUA CLS 311; Washington 1951). J. LOVER, *The Master of Novices* (CUA CLS 254; Washington 1951). L. KOESLER, *Entrance into the Novitiate by Clerics in Major Orders* (CUA CLS 327; Washington 1953). R. BALZER, *The Computation of Time in a Canonical Novitiate* (CUA CLS 212; Washington 1945). Pospishil PersOr 270–281. C. PUJOL, *De religiosis orientalibus* (Rome 1957) 218–277.

[J. F. LOVER]

NOW, in its secondary and common signification, a slice of time near the *present, just gone or immediately impending. It primarily signifies the limit of the timeline or the punctiform divisor distinguishing but linking past and future. Because *indivisible, the now is essentially imperceptible. We conceive it directly but implicitly when we define *time, and by thinking away the divisibility of time, we see that the now is indivisible. A complex proportional resemblance leads to its definition. As time is related to *motion, so the now is related to mobile being. The alternant now, the temporal correlate of mobile being, is formally other in the diverse phases of time: the now is formally alternant qua alternant. A second and similar definition reads: the now is the *number of mobile being; i.e., the alternant now is the formal pluralization of the mobile along the timeline. Because invariant and formal, the now measures time as the arithmetical 1 measures number.

See also INSTANT.

[J. M. QUINN]

NOYES, ALFRED, English poet, critic, and biographer; b. Wolverhampton, Sept. 16, 1880; d. Isle of Wight, June 28, 1958. He was educated at Exeter College, Oxford. He married an American, Garnett Daniels, in 1907; a year after her death (1926) he married Mary Weld-Blundell. His first book of poems, *Loom of Years* (1902), appeared when he was still at Exeter, and its warm reception determined him to devote his life to poetry. He varied this career with lecturing in the U.S. (1913) and teaching at Columbia University and Princeton (1914–23), with the exception of 1916, when he served in the British Foreign Office. For some years before his death he was afflicted with blindness.

Noyes was a conservative in politics and a traditionalist in poetry. His study of English patriotism led him to devote much of his early verse to Drake and other Elizabethans (e.g., in *The Golden Hynde,* 1908), a preoccupation that gave his early work an inevitable anti-Catholic tinge. His thought soon after began to center on the need for a *philosophia perennis* as the basis of civilization, and in his poetic trilogy *Torchbearers* (1925) he showed how this philosophy had been passed along by the great thinkers of every generation. From this originally secular line of thought he came to see that the supreme expression of this philosophy was to be found in the Catholic Church. He became a Catholic in 1927. His *Unknown God* (1934) details his intellectual pilgrimage to Rome. His novel, *No Other Man* (1940), was prophetic in dealing with the holocaust wrought by a secret weapon. From his numerous volumes of poetry, *Tales of the Mermaid Tavern* (1913) and *Poems of the New World* (1943) may be singled out as displaying his earlier and later styles. *Pageant of Letters* (1940), essays on English poets from Chaucer to Alice Meynell, is representative of his best literary criticism.

His biography of Voltaire (1936) was delated to the Holy Office of the Vatican and a correction was demanded; Noyes's critic was under the impression that the atheistic views commonly attributed to Voltaire were condoned by the author. Noyes had no trouble in showing that his intention had been to prove that Voltaire held no such views. His poetry (collected edition, New York 1947) is rather old fashioned in style, but the wide historical perspective he brought to his work marks him as a writer of considerable stature.

Bibliography: D. STANFORD, "Alfred Noyes 1880–1958," *Catholic World* 188 (1959) 297–301. J. E. TOBIN, "Alfred Noyes: A Corrected Bibliography," *Catholic Library World* 15 (March 1944) 181–184, 189.

[C. HOLLIS]

NOYON, city in northern *France and a bishopric (*Noviomensis*), founded in the 5th century, suffragan to *Reims. It was united with Tournai from the time of Bishop St. *Acharius (*c.* 627–664) until 1148, suppressed in 1801, and incorporated into *Amiens; since 1882 it has been incorporated into *Beauvais. In 786 *Charlemagne was crowned king in Noyon; Hugh Capet was elected king there in 987; and John *Calvin was born there in 1509. Bishop Sopronius attended the Council of Orléans in 511. In 531 St. *Médard moved his episcopal residence to Noyon from *Saint-Quentin, where in honor of the 3d-century martyr Bishop St. *Eligius built a monastery that became a pilgrimage shrine. Since the 8th century there has been a cult of Bishop St. Mummolenus (d. *c.* 686; feast, Oct. 16), a monk of *Luxeuil and cofounder of the abbey of *Saint-Bertin. The abbess St. Godeberta (d. *c.* 690) is one of the patrons of Noyon. The former cathedral of Notre-Dame, in early Gothic, which replaced the cathedral burned in 1131 and was badly damaged in World War I and II, has three naves, a polygonal choir, rounded transept, a 12th-century façade and bell tower, and a 13th-century cloister. The Benedictine abbey of Saint-Eloi (Eligius), built on the tomb of its founder, joined the *Maurists in 1631, and was destroyed after its suppression in 1791. Six councils were held in Noyon (814, 831, 1231 or 1233, 1271 or 1272, 1280, and 1344).

Bibliography: R. J. J. PAGEL, *Bibliographie noyonnaise* (Auch, France 1903). Cottineau 2:2107–08. G. ALLEMANG, LexThK² 7:1066.

[E. P. COLBERT]

NUBIA

The section of the Nile Valley from the first cataract to the Sennar parallel. The conversion of Nubia to Christianity occurred in the 6th century, when there were close relations between the Byzantine Empire and the Christian state of Axum to the south. The region of Nubia was controlled by three kingdoms: Nobatia, in lower Nubia; Makuria, or Mukurra, in the Dongola region; and Alwa, or Alodia, with its capital near the present city of Khartoum. The inhabitants spoke Nubian, and seem to have pushed into the Nile Valley from Kordofan and Darfur a few centuries earlier. They were pagans and worshipped the gods of ancient Egypt and Meroe.

Conversion to Christianity. Christianity was brought to Nubia prior to the official conversion of the people by Monophysite refugees from Syria who had settled near Philae after the Council of *Chalcedon (451), and by a few Axumite followers of *Julian of Halicarnassus, who are reported to have been living in Alwa. Most historians agree that the first missions to Nubia, and especially to Nobatia, were directed from Constantinople rather than from Egypt or Ethiopia. According to John, bishop of Ephesus, Nobatia was formally converted to Monophysite Christianity *c.* 543 by a mission led by Theodore, Bishop of Philae, and Julian, a priest sent from Constantinople by Empress *Theodora (1). Although John was a contemporary of these events, he was a Monophysite and is considered biased by some scholars; they prefer the account of Eutychius, Patriarch of Alexandria (933 to 940), who claims that Nobatia was orthodox prior to the 8th century.

According to *John of Biclaro, Makuria was converted to orthodox Christianity in 569, and the same year Longinus, a Monophysite, was invited by the King of Alwa to convert his kingdom. This happened soon after the pagan temples at Philae were closed by *Justinian I at the expiration of a 100-year treaty that left them open for the pagan peoples to the south. The Nubian kings seem to have accepted Christianity in part to promote good relations with Byzantium and Axum, and in part out of admiration for Byzantine culture. Pagan customs seem to have lasted until the 7th century, although Byzantine influence in art, literature, politics, and religion remained strong during the Christian period. Officials bore titles used at the imperial court and Christian names of Byzantine origin were common. Among the educated, Greek appears to have been spoken as late as the 12th century.

Moslem Invasions. In 640 Nobatia repelled a Moslem invasion led by Abdullah ibn Saad, Governor of Egypt, but in 651 an Arab force reached the capital of Makuria. Because of the spirited resistance of the Nubians, the Arabs did not hold the country, but concluded a peace treaty that had important provisions concerning trade. By 710 the kingdoms of Nobatia and Makuria had been united to form a single kingdom with its capital at Old Dongola. The influence of Dongola reached as far west as Darfur, where the ruins of a Christian church appear to exist at Ain Farah.

In the 8th century, the Nubian Church was wholly Monophysite. At that time the Arabs, who preferred Coptic Christianity to the orthodox discipline of Constantinople, interfered with the appointment of new orthodox bishops. However, funerary inscriptions occurring as late as the 12th century are written in Greek and bear prayers from the Byzantine Euchologia. Between 850 and 1100 both Alwa and Dongola apparently prospered. Each country was divided into a number of bishoprics; those south of Aswan had cathedrals at Dakka, Qasr Ibrim, and Faras. Excavations in the cathedral at Faras have brought to light a list of 27 bishops who held office there, as well as a vast number of wall paintings showing kings, bishops, and religious scenes that are in an unparalleled state of preservation. Churches were common throughout the region and many are still standing.

Islamization. For a time the Nubians controlled much of upper Egypt. The presence of Christian refugees and Egyptian priests probably accounts for the prevalence of Coptic as a written language. Religious books were written also in Old Nubian. During this period, Nubians appear to have been free to settle in upper Egypt, while Moslems were free to purchase land in Nubia. By the 10th century Islam was widespread in the northern part of lower Nubia. In the 12th century Egyptian invasions and Bedouin attacks brought an end to Christian culture in most of lower Nubia, and led to the concentration of the population in fortified communities farther south. The architecture of some of the forts is said to reflect crusader influence. Christian power in Dongola was weakened by disputes over the succession to the throne, and in 1315 Kerenbes, the last Christian king, was deposed and removed to Cairo. During the rest of the century, the Beni Kanz,

Hawara, and other Arab tribes rapidly introduced Islam to the Dongola region. The kingdom of Alwa was overrun by Moslems c. 1500 and the Nubian language gave way to Arabic.

Recent discoveries show that the Christian religion persisted for a time in many communities in lower Nubia, as it still does in upper Egypt. A scroll found in a bishop's tomb at Qasr Ibrim records his appointment to that office in 1372. In Ethiopia, Francisco *Alvares heard reports that suggested the survival of Christianity in the Dongola region c. 1525; and a colony of Nubian Christians is said to have been living near Esna, in upper Egypt, in the 1630s. In the last century, the Nubians living at Tafa, near Aswan, took pride in their descent from the Christians of medieval Nubia.

Bibliography: U. MONNERET DE VILLARD, *Storia della Nubia cristiana* (OrChrAnal 118; 1938); *La Nubia Medioevale*, 4 v. (Cairo 1935–57). L. P. KIRWAN, *The Oxford University Excavations at Firka* (Oxford 1939) 49–51. G. S. MILEHAM, *Churches in Lower Nubia* (Philadelphia 1910). The UNESCO Campaign to Save the Monuments of Nubia has produced new information about Christian Nubia that appears in *Kush* (Kharloum 1953–   ), the Journal of the Sudan Antiquities Service, and in the JEgyptArch.

[B. G. TRIGGER]

NUCLEAR ENERGY AND NUCLEAR WEAPONS

The particular reactions used to obtain energy from the interaction of atomic nuclei can be divided into two categories: one in which energy is produced by the splitting, or fissioning, of heavy nuclei, and the other in which energy is produced by the fusion of two light nuclei. (*See* NUCLEUS; RADIOACTIVITY.) Typical reactions of each type can be represented by the following expressions.

Fission: uranium + neutron

$\rightarrow$ 2 fission fragments + neutrons + energy

Fusion: $H^2 + H^2 \rightarrow He^3$ + neutron + energy

In the first reaction a uranium nucleus is struck by a neutron traveling at an appropriate speed, and is fissioned. The fragments resulting are not always the same, but in general, they have masses of about one half the mass of the uranium nucleus. Most of these fission fragments are radioactive, and have half lives of from a few minutes to many years. In addition to the fragments, two to three neutrons are usually emitted when a heavy nucleus is fissioned.

In the second reaction two nuclei of a heavy *isotope of hydrogen, called deuterium, and written H^2, combine to form an isotope of helium, He^3, and a neutron. An important property that these two types of reactions share is that in both of them the mass of the nuclear particles entering the reaction is greater than the mass of the nuclear particles leaving the reaction. Thus, in each type of reaction, part of the mass of the participating nuclei is converted to energy. (*See* EINSTEIN, ALBERT; RELATIVITY.)

The energy released per unit mass of interacting material is much greater for nuclear reactions than for conventional chemical reactions. For example, the complete fission of a pound of uranium would produce as much energy as the explosion of 9,000 tons of TNT. For this reason, nuclear reactions are a very attractive source of energy, and much effort has been directed toward exploiting this source. In this article, methods by which nuclear reactions can be used to produce energy in a controlled manner are first described, and then the uncontrolled release of nuclear energy in weapons is discussed.

CONTROLLED RELEASE OF NUCLEAR ENERGY

If an array of fissionable material can be arranged so that one of the neutrons emitted in each fission produces another fission, the fission reactions are self-sustaining; that is, a chain reaction is established. The device in which a controlled chain reaction can be established is called a nuclear reactor.

Thermal Reactors. The element uranium is the naturally available fissionable material that can be used for fuel in a nuclear reactor. This element consists of two isotopes, U^{235} and U^{238}, and, as found in nature, U^{238} is 140 times as abundant as U^{235}. The probability that a high-speed neutron emitted in fission will produce a second fission of U^{238} is so small that a chain reaction cannot be established in a block of natural uranium (uranium with isotopic abundances as they occur in nature). However, if the speed of the neutrons emitted in fission can be reduced to a very low value, the probability that these slow neutrons will produce a fission of U^{235} becomes large enough so that a chain reaction with natural uranium can be attained. Many reactors include a material, such as water or graphite, that is composed of light elements, for the purpose of reducing the speed of neutrons emitted in fission without absorbing an appreciable number of them. This material is called a moderator, and a reactor containing a moderator is classified as a thermal reactor, since the fissions in a thermal reactor are induced by thermal neutrons, i.e., neutrons having speeds that they attain when they are in thermal equilibrium with the molecules in the moderator.

The rate at which fissions occur in a thermal reactor is regulated by the use of a material, such as boron or cadmium, that readily absorbs thermal neutrons. This material is usually fabricated into units that can be mechanically driven into or withdrawn from the reactor in order to reduce or increase the rate of production of fissions in the reactor.

To summarize, a typical thermal nuclear reactor consists of fuel, a moderator, and control elements. To start the chain reaction, the control elements are withdrawn from the reactor until it is supercritical, i.e., until more neutrons are created in fission than are lost by absorptions or by leakage of neutrons from the reactor. A few neutrons, either from cosmic rays or from some other external source, are introduced into the reactor. Some of these neutrons cause fissions, and their number is multiplied. When the number of neutrons in the reactor reaches the point at which the fission rate, and thus the rate of energy generation, is at a desired level, the control elements are inserted until the neutron density in the reactor becomes constant. At this point, the reactor is said to be just critical. Fissions will then occur at a constant rate, and the energy produced in the fissions will appear as heat. This energy can be removed from the reactor by a coolant, and converted to a useful form, such as electrical energy. In 1962 the largest reactor that had been built for the production of electrical energy was generating about 200,000 kilowatts. The possibility of obtaining nearly one million kilowatts of electrical power from a nuclear reactor has been given serious consideration.

The energy produced in controlled chain reactions

Enrico Fermi (1901–54), Nobel prize-winner in physics (1938) and director of the project that achieved the first sustained and controlled release of nuclear energy (University of Chicago, Dec. 2, 1942).

has been exploited for purposes other than the production of electrical energy. The striking applicability of nuclear reactors to submarine propulsion has been demonstrated by the U.S. Navy. Since a nuclear reactor requires no oxygen to generate energy, a submarine that is powered by a nuclear reactor may travel submerged for indefinite periods.

Besides U^{235}, two other isotopes, U^{233} and Pu^{239} (plutonium), have properties that make them useful as a source of nuclear energy. These isotopes do not occur in nature, but can be manufactured. More than 99 per cent of the uranium in a reactor fueled by natural uranium is the isotope U^{238}. In the ordinary operation of such a reactor many neutrons are captured by this isotope, forming U^{239} according to the following reaction:

$$U^{238} + \text{neutron} \rightarrow U^{239} + \text{radiation}$$

This U^{239} then decays by emission of electrons to Pu^{239}, a material that is readily fissioned by neutrons. Thus, a reactor that has natural uranium for fuel will produce, as a by-product, fissionable material. In some thermal nuclear reactors, as much as 0.8 to 0.9 atoms of new fissionable material are produced for each atom destroyed. The isotope Pu^{239} can be used in nuclear weapons, and during World War II several nuclear reactors were constructed at Hanford, Wash., for the purpose of manufacturing plutonium by the method described above.

The isotope U^{233} can be manufactured in a similar manner from the element thorium, which occurs in abundance in nature. Thorium is introduced into a nuclear reactor, and the following reaction occurs:

$$Th^{232} + \text{neutron} \rightarrow Th^{233} + \text{radiation}$$

The Th^{233} then decays to U^{233} by virtue of the emission of two electrons.

Fast Reactors. Most of the reactors built through 1962 are thermal reactors. However, much effort is being devoted to the problems of construction and operation of so-called fast reactors. This type of reactor does not contain any moderator, and fissions are produced by high-speed neutrons. The fuel for fast reactors is one of the fissionable isotopes, U^{233}, U^{235}, or Pu^{239}. In addition to one of these isotopes, a fast reactor usually contains some thorium or U^{238}. The advantage of a fast reactor over a thermal one is that no neutrons are lost by absorption in a moderator, and losses to other structural materials are minimized. It has been shown that, with careful design, such a reactor can produce more fissionable material, U^{233} or Pu^{239}, from thorium or uranium, than it burns. Such a reactor is sometimes called a breeder reactor.

Because a moderating material, such as water, cannot be used in fast reactors, and also because these reactors are very compact, heat removal problems with fast reactors are difficult. Some type of metal in the liquid state, such as liquid sodium, is usually used as a coolant. Another difficulty encountered in the operation of fast reactors results from the fact that an accident with such a reactor could reach explosive proportions. For these reasons, the development of fast reactors has been slower than that of thermal reactors. However, if all of the uranium and thorium in nature is to be available as nuclear fuel, some of the nuclear reactors in a nuclear power industry must be fast reactors, capable of producing more fissionable material than they consume.

Nuclear reactors present some problems that do not occur in oil- or coal-powered plants. Two of these are the problems of safety and waste disposal. Most of the energy released when a heavy nucleus is fissioned is converted to heat inside the reactor. However, some energy escapes the reactor in the form of nuclear radiation, gamma rays and neutrons, that can produce harmful biological effects. Also, the fuel of a reactor eventually becomes contaminated with radioactive fission fragments, which emit beta and gamma radiation. Ordinarily, operating personnel and the general public are protected from these radiations by a shield, a large mass of material that surrounds the reactor and absorbs the radiations. However, if the reactor should become supercritical and out of control, the possibility exists that the fuel could be melted, and radioactive fission fragments might then be spread over an area in the vicinity of the reactor. Much effort and money is expended to ensure the safe operation of nuclear reactors. In the U.S. the design of a reactor must be approved by a special committee within the Atomic Energy Commission before it can be operated.

As reactors for the generation of power from nuclear fission become widespread, the difficulty of disposal of radioactive wastes will increase. After an extended period of operation a fission reactor contains a large amount of radioactive fission fragments. These fragments can be chemically separated from the fuel elements, but by 1962, no satisfactory method for disposing of these potentially dangerous fission fragments had been agreed upon.

Fusion Reactions. The heavy isotope of hydrogen, deuterium (H^2), which can be used to produce fusion reactions, occurs in abundance in the oceans of the world. The fuel for fusion is virtually inexhaustible.

Further, it is hoped that it will be possible to operate a fusion reactor in such a way as to generate power without producing large quantities of radioactive wastes. For these reasons, controlled fusion reactors potentially provide a source of power that is much more desirable than fission reactors. However, the technical problems to be solved before a practical fusion reactor can be built are much more difficult than those of fission reactors. In 1962 extensive research programs, carried on in countries throughout the world, had not yet yielded solutions to these problems.

In order for two nuclei to fuse, to combine in a nuclear reaction, they must come within approximately a nuclear radius (about 2×10^{-13} cm for deuterium) of one another. However since both nuclei are positively charged, they repel one another according to Coulomb's Law (*see* ELECTRICITY AND MAGNETISM). In order to overcome this mutual repulsion and come together so that a nuclear reaction may occur, the two nuclei must be traveling originally at high speed. The approach to a controlled fusion reactor has been to try to contain a gas of nuclei that can interact by the fusion process, and to heat this gas to a temperature such that the individual nuclei are traveling with a speed that is sufficient to overcome the Coulomb repulsion. (*See* KINETIC THEORY.) For a gas of deuterium, the temperature at which this requirement is fulfilled is approximately 10^8 degrees Kelvin (or Centigrade). For nuclei other than the isotopes of hydrogen, which have greater positive charges than hydrogen, the required temperature is even higher. To contain a gas at such a temperature with material walls is, of course, impossible. Since the particles in the gas are charged, it may be possible to confine them in space by the use of various arrangements of magnetic fields, and this is the direction that research has taken. However, as late as 1962, the day in which fusion reactions would be used in a controlled manner for the production of power still seemed distant.

UNCONTROLLED RELEASE OF NUCLEAR ENERGY

As discussed above, the isotopes U^{233}, U^{235}, and Pu^{239} can be made to sustain a chain reaction and generate nuclear energy. The mass of one of these metals that is just able to sustain a chain reaction is called a critical mass. When a mass greater than the critical mass is assembled, the assembly is supercritical, and more neutrons are produced than are lost. The neutron density in the assembly will increase, and the rate of fissioning, or the rate of generation of energy will increase. If the assembly is very supercritical the rate of energy generation will increase rapidly, doubling many times in a time interval as short as a millionth of a second. Such an assembly will blow itself apart with explosive force. A fission bomb, sometimes called an atomic bomb, is thus a highly supercritical assembly of fissionable material.

Fission Weapons. The first fission weapons, built in the U.S. during World War II, were capable of producing the same amount of energy as the explosion of about 20,000 tons of TNT. Since 1945 several countries have produced nuclear weapons; in 1964, in addition to the U.S., England, the U.S.S.R., China, and France were known to have exploded fission devices. The principal difficulty encountered in building fission weapons is the procurement of fissionable material. Either U^{235} must be separated from natural uranium by physical methods, or U^{233} or Pu^{239} must be produced from thorium or uranium by the method previously described. However, throughout the world, the number of power-generating nuclear reactors that are fueled with natural uranium and produce Pu²³⁹ as a by-product is growing rapidly. It seems likely that many countries will eventually possess enough plutonium to produce fission weapons.

Fusion Weapons. A fusion weapon derives part of its energy from the interaction of light nuclei, such as the various isotopes of hydrogen and lithium. As mentioned above, these nuclei are positively charged and must, therefore, be moving at very high speeds if they are successfully to approach one another and fuse. That is, the temperature of the gas of light nuclei in which the nucleus reactions occur must be very high. For this reason, these reactions are called thermonuclear reactions. The high temperatures required for fusion are much easier to attain in weapons than in a controlled manner in the laboratory. In a fusion weapon, the high temperature is produced by a fission core. A typical thermonuclear weapon might consist of a core, made of fissionable material, surrounded by the light elements that are to be fused. The fissionable material is detonated, creating the high temperatures necessary for the fusion reactions to proceed. Such a combination of fission and fusion has been used to construct weapons with explosive yields equivalent to tens of millions of tons of TNT.

Since fusion reactions produce no radioactive fission fragments, it is possible to minimize the radioactive fallout from a nuclear weapon by designing it so that most of its energy is produced by fusion reactions. Such weapons have been called "clean" weapons. However, as long as a core of fissionable material is used to produce temperatures at which fusion can occur, it will not be possible to construct a nuclear weapon that will not produce radioactive fission fragments. (*See* RADIATION AND SOCIAL ETHICS.)

The yield of nuclear weapons can be increased further by utilizing the high-speed neutrons produced in some of the fusion reactions. For example, the neutron from the deuterium-deuterium reaction discussed earlier has a speed that is high enough so that there is a reasonable probability that it will cause even the abundant isotope of uranium, U²³⁸, to fission. If a fusion weapon consisting of a fissionable core surrounded by light nuclei is enclosed in a shell of inexpensive natural uranium, or U²³⁸, the neutrons produced in the fusion reactions will cause further fissions in the enclosing shell. In this manner, the energy yield of a nuclear weapon can be considerably increased, with only a small increase in cost. Weapons of this type, however, produce an abundance of radioactive fission fragments.

The energy generated by a nuclear weapon is emitted in four forms: a blast, or shock wave; radiant energy, or heat; prompt nuclear radiation composed of neutrons and gamma rays; and residual radiation, from the fission fragments. The damage done by each form of energy depends on many things, such as the altitude at which the weapon is detonated, the terrain in the vicinity of the explosion, and the atmospheric conditions at the time of the explosion. A qualitative idea of the magnitude of the damage from a large nuclear weapon can be formed by considering the damage caused by a thermonuclear weapon with a total energy equivalent to 20 million tons of TNT, and with a fission energy equivalent to about one million tons of TNT, when it is exploded near the surface of the earth.

The central, high-temperature region of such a weapon has a radius of about 2 miles. This region is known as the fireball, and within it, temperatures are high enough to vaporize structural materials. At a distance of about 8 miles from the explosion, buildings and houses may be destroyed by the shock wave, and 25 miles from the explosion, exposed persons could receive third degree burns. Finally, it is possible that the delayed radiation, or fallout, could kill persons 100 to 200 miles downwind from the detonation point. (For a discussion of the moral problems involved, *see* WAR; WAR, MORALITY OF.)

Bibliography: U.S. Atomic Energy Commission, *Effects of Nuclear Weapons* (2d ed. rev. Washington 1962). C. F. BONILLA, ed., *Nuclear Engineering* (New York 1957). H. ETHERINGTON, ed., *Nuclear Engineering Handbook* (New York 1958).

[D. J. DONAHUE]

NUCLEIC ACIDS (DNA, RNA)

Nucleic acids are chemical compounds that play an essential role in the reproduction and growth of cells. Recent discoveries have identified deoxyribonucleic acid (DNA) as the substance of *genes and ribonucleic acid (RNA) as the material necessary for transcribing the genetic code. A discussion of the present knowledge of the composition, structure, and function of these molecules is necessary for a review of current research in the field. It is also pertinent to any speculation regarding the use man may make of future discoveries to control, for good or ill, his heredity and development.

Composition. The nucleic acids were discovered as a result of F. Miescher's investigations of the nuclei of pus cells in 1868. DNA exists in the nuclei of cells as a constituent of the chromosomes and is believed to be the carrier of hereditary characteristics. RNA is present to a small extent in the nucleus and to a greater extent in the cytoplasm. At least three kinds of RNA exist, differing in composition, size, and intracellular location. RNA is intimately associated with protein synthesis. Both nucleic acids are long-chain molecules or polymers, made up of repeating units called "nucleotides." The nucleotides are composed of phosphoric acid, a pentose, or five-carbon sugar, and a purine or pyrimidine base. In DNA the pentose is 2-deoxyribose; in RNA it is ribose. These sugars differ in that the former lacks an oxygen atom attached to the second carbon atom of the molecule. The purine bases, adenine and guanine, and the pyrimidine base cytosine are common to both nucleic acids. In addition, RNA contains uracil, and DNA contains thymine, which is 5-methyluracil. The isolation of other bases from various nucleic acid sources has been reported. For example, 5-methylcytosine occurs as a minor constituent of mammalian DNA's but as a major component of wheat germ DNA.

The base-sugar combination in a nucleotide is called a "nucleoside." If one, two, or three phosphoric acid molecules are attached to a nucleoside, a nucleoside mono-, di-, or triphosphate is formed. The five common bases and their corresponding sugar and phosphate complexes are as follows:

Base	Nucleoside	Nucleotide
Adenine	Adenosine	Adenylic acid
Guanine	Guanosine	Guanylic acid
Cytosine	Cytidine	Cytidylic acid
Uracil	Uridine	Uridylic acid
Thymine	Thymidine	Thymidylic acid

Nucleic acids occur in tissues in combination with proteins and may be separated from them by various procedures such as extraction with hot trichloroacetic acid. DNA and RNA can be identified and assayed quantitatively by specific agents that react with the sugar components of each to give characteristic colors. For example, DNA reacts with the diphenylamine reagent of Dische to give a blue color; RNA gives a green color with the phloroglucinol reagent of Euler and Hahn. The conjugated ring systems of the purines and pyrimidines make possible the absorption of ultraviolet radiation and provide a basis for the qualitative and quantitative analysis of nucleic acids, nucleotides, nucleosides, and their component bases by spectrophotometry.

Determination of molecular weights of DNA samples indicates values of the order of 6 to 12 million. Since a nucleotide has a molecular weight of about 300, a DNA molecule must contain more than 20,000 nucleotide units. Molecular weights for RNA varying from 20,000 to 2 million have been reported and reflect the difference in size between different types of RNA as well as the probable degradation of the molecules in the process of isolation. Physical measurements such as viscosity and light scattering determinations show that the molecules are of a long, fibrous character.

Certain organic catalysts called *enzymes, which are *protein in nature, can break bonds along the nucleic acid chain and produce various smaller molecules such as oligonucleotides, made up of several nucleotide units, or mononucleotides. Such enzymes are nucleases or phosphodiesterases. Other enzymes have been found that can selectively build up the nucleic acid chain from its components.

Since DNA is believed to be the carrier of hereditary characteristics, it is not surprising to find that DNA molecules from different species differ in the relative proportions of their purine and pyrimidine bases. All DNA molecules of a given species, however, have the same base composition. Moreover, Chargaff has shown that in all cases the adenine-thymine ratio is one, as is also the guanine-cystosine ratio.

Structure. The X-ray crystallographic analysis of DNA by Wilkins and others led Watson and Crick to propose that the DNA molecule consists of two chains of nucleotides wound around the same axis in a double helical structure. Each chain consists of repeating sugar-phosphate units and is attached to the other chain by hydrogen bonds between their bases, which lie in a plane perpendicular to the long axis of the helix (Fig. 1). The distance between the chains was found to accommodate one purine and one pyrimidine base. Hydrogen bonds exist between adenine and thymine on opposite chains and likewise between guanine and cytosine. It is now known that London forces and dipole-dipole interactions between the bases are also important in stabilizing the helix. The two strands are complementary: where adenine exists on one chain, thymine exists on the other; guanine and cytosine are related in the same way. RNA molecules are usually single-stranded. However, in some cases a portion of the molecule loops back and forms hydrogen bonds with another part of the same strand (Fig. 2).

The relation between DNA, RNA, and protein synthesis was suggested by T. Caspersson in 1947. Although his original theory has undergone some changes, it is still

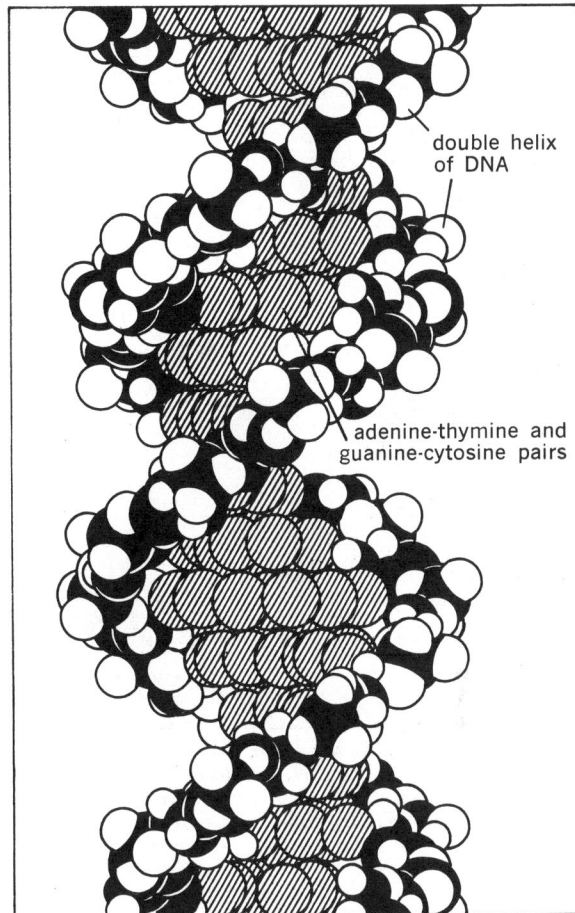

double helix of DNA

adenine-thymine and guanine-cytosine pairs

Fig. 1. The Watson-Crick model of the DNA molecule.

generally believed that the genetic information contained in DNA is transferred to cytoplasmic protein-synthesizing systems through RNA. Experimental evidence identifying DNA as the genetic material came particularly from studies on the "transforming agent" of pneumococci. In 1944 Avery, MacLeod, and McCarty found that if DNA from a capsular (S) type pneumococcus is introduced into a culture of noncapsular (R) type, the R type will be transformed into S type. The new S type will continue to produce S-type progeny. The S-type DNA is thus able to induce specific characteristics and to perpetuate them.

The relationship of RNA to protein synthesis was first reported when it was observed that RNA is especially abundant in cells producing protein for growth or secretion. RNA has since been found to be abundant in rapidly growing cells (for example, tumors and embryos).

Kornberg and his coworkers, in experiments designed to shed light on the chemistry of DNA synthesis and replication, discovered an enzyme system in the microorganism *Escherichia coli* that required a single-stranded DNA as "primer" and built double-stranded DNA on this primer from nucleoside triphosphates. DNA was formed only when nucleoside triphosphates of all four bases, adenine (A), thymine (T), guanine (G), and cytosine (C), were present in the medium. The enzyme responsible for this polymerizing action has been named DNA nucleotidyltransferase. Evidence that the added

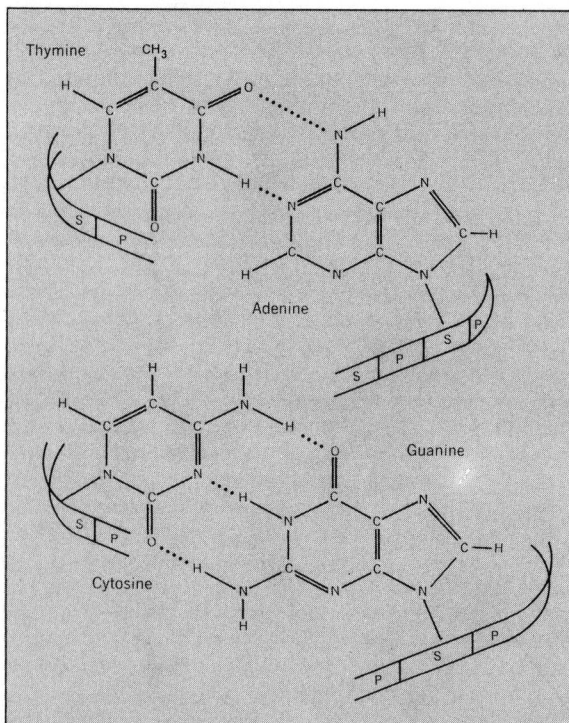

Fig. 2. Base-pairing in the DNA molecule. In hydrogen-bonded portions of the RNA molecule, thymine is replaced by uracil, which has a hydrogen atom (H) in place of the methyl group (CH₃). S represents the sugar 2-deoxyribose. (In RNA the sugar is ribose.) P represents the phosphate group.

DNA served as a primer or template was obtained by using DNA preparations of different base compositions. If the primer contains only A and T, the polynucleotide strand that is synthesized will contain only A and T, even if G and C nucleoside triphosphates are present in the medium.

It has been known for a long time that the DNA content of the cell nucleus doubles shortly before cell division. The experiments of Meselson and Stahl give some indication of how this occurs. These workers grew *Escherichia coli* in a medium in which the only nitrogen available was the isotope of atomic weight 15 (N^{15}). When the DNA of the bacteria had been completely labeled with N^{15}, the cells were transferred to a medium containing N^{14} as the only available nitrogen source. The first generation of offspring contained DNA in which half of the nitrogen was N^{15} and half was N^{14}. The second generation contained an equal number of half N^{15}-N^{14} DNA molecules and all N^{14} DNA molecules. These data are interpreted to mean that in cell division each DNA molecule replicates by separating into two single strands, one of which is incorporated into each daughter cell. On each of the original strands a complementary strand is built by the action of enzymes, the material for the new strands being supplied by the free nucleoside triphosphates in the medium. This is known as a semiconservative mechanism (Fig. 3). Since specific base-pairing imposes the restriction of A-T bonding and G-C bonding between the strands, each new strand is the complement of the one on which it is built, and therefore the newly formed molecules are exact replicas of the original one.

Genetic Code. It is the role of DNA as the carrier of genetic information to determine the nature of each of the cellular proteins synthesized. Some of these are structural proteins; others are the enzymes that regulate metabolic processes. Proteins, like nucleic acids, are polymeric molecules. The units, however, are amino acids, of which 20 different kinds are known. Each particular protein is characterized by the number and arrangement of its constituent amino acids. Since the site of protein synthesis has been found to be the cytoplasm of the cell, the location of DNA in the nucleus raised the question of how DNA directed the synthesis of protein. The answer came from such experiments as those of Furth, Hurwitz, and Goldman, who discovered that the base ratio of the RNA produced in a cell-free system is determined by the base ratio of the DNA used as a primer. In a manner analogous to DNA replication, an enzyme, RNA polymerase, catalyzes the synthesis of RNA on the single-stranded DNA template. Base pairing again takes place, the only difference being that uracil (U) in RNA takes the place of thymine (Fig. 3).

In 1955 Ochoa and Grunberg-Manago had found an enzyme, polyribonucleotide phosphorylase, that forms RNA strands by linking ribonucleotides together. Using this enzyme, Nirenberg and Matthaei produced a strand of RNA having only one base, uracil, along its chain. This compound was called polyuridylic acid. In a cell-free, protein-synthesizing system containing free amino acids, a protein was produced that had only one amino acid in its composition, phenylalanine. This was in-

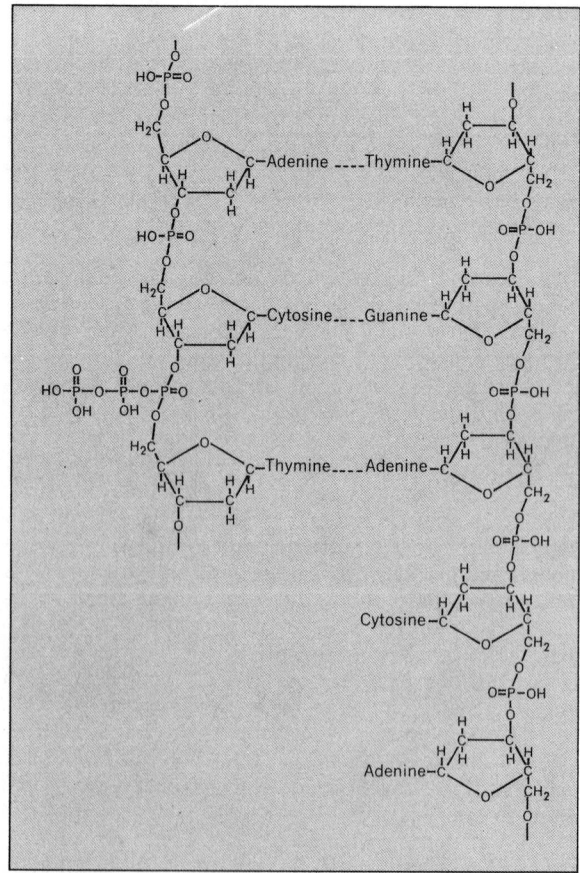

Fig. 3. Replication in DNA.

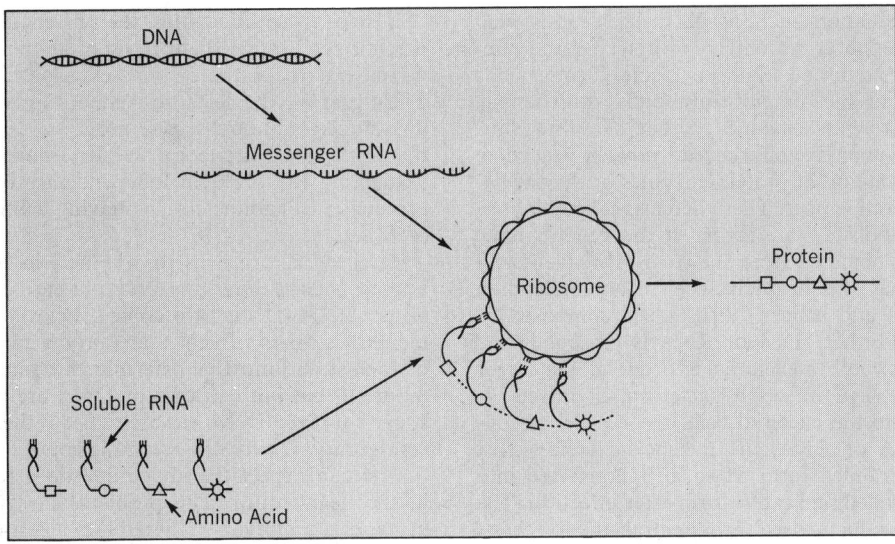

Fig. 4. The mechanism for the coding of a protein.

terpreted to mean that the sequence of bases along the RNA chain determines the type of amino acid that is polymerized into protein. Therefore a sequence of U-U-U, etc., is needed for the synthesis of the amino acid phenylalanine. Ochoa found that when some of the uracil was replaced by adenine along the RNA template chain, a protein was produced that consisted mainly of phenylalanine but contained small amounts of another amino acid, isoleucine. If the ratio of bases in the RNA is known, the "code" for each amino acid can be derived. For example, if poly-AU contains 70 per cent U and 30 per cent A, the probability of the occurrence of the triplet sequence of UUU is equal to $0.7 \times 0.7 \times 0.7$, or 0.34. The probability of the occurrence of the sequence UUA is $0.7 \times 0.7 \times 0.3$, or 0.147. Therefore, randomness in the polymer being assumed, 34 per cent of the triplets will probably be UUU, and 14.7 per cent will be UUA. Again, when more adenine was incorporated into the polyuridylic acid, small amounts of the amino acid asparagine were found in the protein in addition to the phenylalanine and isoleucine. This time the proportion of bases indicated that the code for asparagine was AAU. The 2 to 1 relationship of the base requirement suggested a triplet formation in which three of the four bases, A, G, C, and U, are needed to direct the incorporation of a specific amino acid into a protein.

The mechanism proposed for such a coding is represented schematically in Fig. 4. The double-stranded DNA separates into two single strands. On one or both of these a strand of RNA is built from ribonucleoside triphosphates. This "messenger" or "template" RNA, its base sequence determined by that of the DNA template on which it was formed, peels off the DNA and passes into the cytoplasm, where it attaches itself to a particle called the ribosome. Ribosomes are cytoplasmic particles composed of protein and a specific kind of RNA designated as ribosomal RNA. In at least some systems, protein is synthesized on an aggregate of ribosomes, five or more in number. The messenger RNA now serves as a template for protein synthesis. A third form of RNA, of lower molecular weight than messenger RNA, has been found in the cytoplasm. This "soluble" or "transfer" RNA is believed to form a com-

plex with an amino acid, each particular amino acid being attached to a specific type of soluble RNA. The lining up of the amino acids in correct sequence to form a protein is achieved by the mating of a particular group of bases on the soluble RNA with a complementary group of bases along the messenger RNA on the ribosome. For example, the base sequence UGC on the transfer RNA would form hydrogen bonds with the base sequence ACG on the messenger RNA. When the amino acids have been joined through peptide bonds, the resulting protein breaks off the soluble RNA.

RNA polymers containing all possible combinations of the four bases, A, G, C, and U, have been synthesized and tested. Since there are four bases, there are $4 \times 4 \times 4$ or 64 possible combinations of any three bases. As there are only 20 amino acids, it seems likely that there should be more than one base triplet for each amino acid. Such a code is said to be degenerate. This is indeed the case. Alanine can be coded by RNA polymers containing C, U, and G, or C, A, and G, or C and G. In like manner, 58 of the 64 triplets have been assigned. The triplets are called "code words." (For a complete listing of code words see GENES, CHEMICAL STRUCTURE OF.)

Defects and Mutations. The necessity for correct coding, that is, a correct sequence of bases, in the original DNA is obvious. An error in coding could result in the incorporation of the wrong amino acid into a protein, making it nonfunctional as an enzyme or defective in some other way. This is what is believed to take place in the hereditary disease called sickle-cell anemia. In the hemoglobin of persons suffering from this disease, one of the 300 amino acids of the protein is an abnormal one: valine has been substituted for glutamic acid. This replacement so changes the charge distribution on the molecule as to render it less soluble. Blood corpuscles containing this kind of hemoglobin undergo a change in shape called "sickling," caused by crystallization of reduced hemoglobin. Other cases are known in which the substitution of an amino acid in a protein can be correlated with a change in one of the bases of a code-word triplet.

Some agents known to produce mutations in microorganisms are chemicals such as nitrous acid, or electromagnetic radiation such as X rays. Nitrous acid removes the amino group (NH_2) of cytosine and converts the base to uracil. Since cytosine forms bonds with guanine and since uracil forms bonds with adenine, a mutation is readily explained. Other hereditary diseases, such as phenylketonuria, can now be traced to the lack of formation of protein enzymes or the formation of nonoperative ones. These defects, called "inborn errors of metabolism," are errors in the genetic code.

Information obtained from the study of nucleic acid metabolism may be of assistance in understanding *virus diseases and cancer. Viruses are composed of nucleoprotein. Either DNA or RNA is present in the smaller viruses; both nucleic acids occur in the larger ones. When a virus infects a bacterium, it injects its nucleic acid into the bacterial cell. In viruses that contain only DNA or RNA, the nucleic acid may exist in the single-stranded form. If so, it is converted into the double-stranded replicative form after infection. The virus then reproduces itself by directing the synthesis of virus material from the constituents of the host. It has been established that the infection of *Escherichia coli* with phage MS2 leads to the induction of a new RNA synthesizing enzyme, which has been named RNA synthetase. This enzyme catalyzes the incorporation of ribonucleotides into an RNA with the properties of MS2 RNA.

Cancerous growth seems to be somewhat similar to virus infection in that a cancerous cell has a different enzyme pattern from that of a comparable normal cell. Some cancers, in fact, have been demonstrated to be induced by viruses. In cancer tissue the biochemical machinery of the cell may have been perverted from the production of its usual proteins to those of cancer cells.

Future Research. It is impossible to predict the accomplishments in the fields of medicine and human welfare that may result from further knowledge of nucleic acids and the genetic code. Current prophecies range from the cure of genetic defects to the manipulation of the genes to produce a race of supermen.

The work of Benzer at Purdue University gives some hope that a hereditary defect caused by a single mutation can be corrected. He showed that genes on the chromosome of the T4 virus each consist of several hundred distinct sites arranged in linear order. This is consistent with the view that a gene is a segment containing from 500 to 1,000 bases of the DNA molecule that forms the virus chromosome. Certain mutations in these regions made the genes inactive. Still other mutations were able to suppress the effects of the harmful mutations and restore the functions of the genes. This seems to imply that errors in coding produced by one mutation can be corrected by a further mutation.

An appreciation of the difficulties involved in even such a seemingly simple change can be obtained if one considers that so far only viruses and microorganisms have been subjected to this type of genetic study. To code the formation of a protein having 200 amino acids, a gene must have at least 200 code words. If the code is composed of triplets, this gene corresponds to 600 bases. Although the sequence of amino acids has been determined for a few of the proteins, no one yet knows the base sequence of even one gene. Viruses may contain as many as several hundred genes; bacteria, a thousand; a human cell, a million.

Besides these difficulties, the universality of the code has not been established. It is not known whether code words are the same in viruses, plants, and animals. The order of the letters in code words has not been determined, although some progress is being made in this direction. Nirenberg and Khorana have been investigating the problem independently by synthesizing proteins on oligonucleotides having a known sequence of bases.

A question exists as to whether, in the living cell, both strands of DNA, or only one, are copied by messenger RNA. If two are copied, two different complementary strands of RNA are produced. The function of each strand must be determined. Some workers have reported that both strands of DNA are copied. Others state that if the DNA has a circular rather than a linear configuration, only one strand is copied.

One can expect the above questions to be answered in the near future. The problems of virus infections, of cancer, and even of hereditary diseases seem likely to be solved. It is much less likely, however, that the genetic code can be utilized to direct the body cells to replace a missing organ or limb. To suggest, as some have done, that man may be able to "create" life or to "create" new and different forms of life is to misuse the term "create." Living things are recognized by their ability to grow and reproduce. If man should be able to prepare in the laboratory the nonliving material that has the potential of life, and if the potential is realized, man has not created life. He has achieved on the molecular level a feat not unlike that of the cattle breeder, who does not create the calves he raises. The same can be said of the creation of new and different forms of life.

It is easy to envision ways of manipulating the genetic material that are at variance with God's law. Problems similar to those involved in abortion, contraception, and sterilization will probably arise. The same moral responsibility that is demanded in those areas will be required of human beings who possess the ability to control man's hereditary and development. However, the scientist should not be prevented from seeking for knowledge by the possibility that others may abuse it.

See also CELL DIVISION; CELL PHYSIOLOGY.

Bibliography: I. ASIMOV, *The Genetic Code* (New York 1963). A. WHITE et al., *Principles of Biochemistry* (3d ed. New York 1964). J. N. DAVIDSON, *The Biochemistry of the Nucleic Acids* (4th ed. New York 1960). A. KORNBERG, *Enzymatic Synthesis of DNA* (New York 1961). E. CHARGAFF and J. N. DAVIDSON, eds., *The Nucleic Acids . . .*, 3 v. (New York 1955–60). J. N. DAVIDSON and W. E. COHN, eds., *Progress in Nucleic Acid Research*, 2 v. (New York 1963–64). V. G. DETHIER, "Breaking the Genetic Code," *Catholic World* 195 (1962) 295–301, moral aspects. M. W. NIRENBERG and W. MARSHALL, "The Genetic Code," *Scientific American* 208 (1963) 80–95. T. H. JUKES, "The Genetic Code," *American Scientist* 51 (1963) 227–245. O. T. AVERY et al., "Studies on the Chemical Nature of the Substance Inducing Transformation of Pneumococcal Types," *Journal of Experimental Medicine* 79 (1944) 137–158. J. D. WATSON and F. H. C. CRICK, "A Structure for Deoxyribose Nucleic Acid," *Nature* 171 (1953) 737–738. M. H. F. WILKINS et al., "Helical Structure of Crystalline Deoxypentose Nucleic Acid," *ibid.* 172 (1953) 759–762. M. GRUNBERG-MANAGO et al., "Enzymic Synthesis of Polynucleotids," *Biochimica et biophysica acta* 20 (1956) 269–285. M. MESELSON and F. W. STAHL, "The Replication of DNA in Escherichia Coli," *Proceedings of the National Academy of Sciences* 44 (1958) 671–682. I. R. LEHMAN et al., "Enzymatic Synthesis of Deoxyribonucleic Acid," *Journal of Biological Chemistry* 233 (1958) 163–170.

[M. J. SMITH]

NUCLEUS

As its name suggests, the nucleus is the central part or core of an atom. The constituent particles of nuclei are protons and neutrons, known collectively as nucleons (*see* ELEMENTARY PARTICLES). These two particles, approximately equal in mass, differ principally in that the proton possesses a positive electric charge equal in magnitude to the charge of the electron, while the neutron is electrically neutral. A nucleus is characterized by its atomic number Z, which is equal to the number of protons in the nucleus, and by its mass number A, which is equal to the total number of nucleons present. Since the chemical behavior of an element is governed by the number of electrons present in an atom of the element, and this number is equal to the atomic number (in order that the atom as a whole be electrically neutral), all atoms having nuclei with the same atomic number exhibit the same chemical properties (*see* PERIODIC TABLE). Nuclei possessing the same atomic number but different mass number are referred to as *isotopes of the particular element to which the atomic number corresponds.

All nuclei can be classified as either stable or radioactive. A radioactive nucleus is one that sooner or later spontaneously emits some form of radiation and in so doing becomes transformed into a different nucleus. Stable nuclei, on the other hand, do not spontaneously emit radiations of any kind, and therefore retain their identity indefinitely unless externally disturbed in some way. More than 250 different stable isotopes are found in nature, and several times this number of radioactive isotopes have been produced and studied (*see* RADIOACTIVITY).

Although protons and neutrons are generally treated as the ultimate constituents in discussing the structure of nuclei, high-energy experiments have shown both of these particles to be themselves structured. However, the energies at which the effects of this structure become evident are much greater than those usually encountered in nuclei, so that in discussing nuclear structure, the nucleons are usually treated as simple particles. A complete understanding of nuclear phenomena must take into account the composite nature of the proton and the neutron.

Historical Background. The concept of the atomic nucleus arose during the period from 1909 to 1913 as a result of the work of E. *Rutherford, H. Geiger, and E. Marsden in England. Using the α-particles emitted by radioactive elements, Geiger and Marsden carefully studied the deflection of these particles as they passed through thin metal foils. Rutherford showed that the results of these measurements implied that all of the positive charge and virtually all of the mass of the atom are concentrated in a small region, or nucleus. From these early experiments it was inferred that the size of the nucleus is of the order of 10^{-12} cm, less than a millionth part of a millionth of an inch. Later experiments by Rutherford showed that when certain elements were irradiated with α-particles, besides the deflection or scattering of the particles, protons were occasionally produced. Their production in these instances indicated that nuclear reactions had taken place and suggested that atomic nuclei contain protons. In 1932, J. Cockcroft and E. Walton in England succeeded in inducing nuclear reactions with protons that had been electrically accelerated to high speeds. During the same year J. Chadwick, also working in England, showed that a penetrating radiation that had been found to result from certain nuclear reactions consisted of electrically neutral particles now called neutrons. Subsequent studies resulted in the conclusion that all nuclei are built up of protons and neutrons.

During the years before World War II important progress in the understanding of the nucleus was made by physicists. Prominent among these were N. *Bohr in Denmark, E. *Fermi and his collaborators in Italy, G. Breit and E. Wigner in the U.S., F. Joliot and I. Curie in France, to mention only a few. In 1939 the discovery of nuclear fission was reported by O. Hahn and F. Strassman in Germany. During World War II, as the potential applications of nuclear fission were realized (*see* NUCLEAR ENERGY AND NUCLEAR WEAPONS), considerable effort was directed toward research in nuclear physics, particularly in the U.S.

Nuclear Forces. The fact that stable nuclei do not spontaneously separate into their constituent nucleons and require considerable amounts of energy to be disrupted, indicates that powerful attractive forces are acting between the nucleons to bind them together. These forces are referred to as nuclear forces, to distinguish them from the electromagnetic force, which is responsible for the structure of the atom, or the gravitational force, which exists between all bodies. Though also present in the nucleus, these latter forces are unable to account for nuclear binding. The gravitational force is far too weak, and the electrostatic force in the nucleus acts to repel the protons from each other.

For a given nucleus, the mass is always less than the sum of the masses of the Z protons and the $A - Z$ neutrons that make up the nucleus, indicating that the total energy of the nucleus is less than the energy of its constituent parts when they are not bound together into a nucleus. This difference in energy between a nucleus and its separated nucleons is referred to as the total binding energy of the nucleus. It is equal to the amount of energy that would have to be provided to separate the nucleus into Z free protons and $A - Z$ free neutrons. From the Einstein mass-energy relation the total binding energy can be computed from the formula:

$$\text{TBE} = [ZM_p + (A - Z)M_n - M_{nucleus}]c^2$$

where M_p, M_n, and $M_{nucleus}$ are the masses of the free proton, the free neutron, and the nucleus, respectively, and c is the speed of light (*see* RELATIVITY). If the total binding energy of the nucleus is divided by A (the total number of nucleons), the binding energy per nucleon is obtained. This quantity is remarkably constant throughout most of the range of stable nuclei, and is approximately 8 Mev per nucleon. Because of the approximate constancy of the binding energy per nucleon, it is also approximately equal to the energy required to remove just one nucleon from a given nucleus. By contrast, the energy required to remove one of the outer electrons from an atom is generally about a million times smaller, or around 10 ev. From the constancy of the binding energy per nucleon, it can be concluded that the nuclear forces exhibit the property known as saturation. This means that a given nucleon can at a given time effectively be attracted to only a limited number of other nucleons in the nucleus. As a consequence, the increase in total binding energy is about the same each time a nucleon is added to a nucleus, regardless of the size of the nucleus. If the forces were not saturable this would not be the case, since a nucleon added to a heavy nucleus would interact with many more nucleons than would one added to a light nucleus, and would consequently be bound much more tightly.

As one progresses from the lighter to the heavier elements, the relative magnitude of the proton and neutron numbers, Z and $Z - A$, exhibits a smooth variation. For the light nuclei, the proton and neutron numbers tend to be equal. As the mass number increases, the number of neutrons increases more rapidly than does the number of protons. This trend is illustrated by comparing the most abundant isotopes of a light element, such as carbon, with that of a heavy element, such as uranium. For the former, the most abundant isotope is $_6C^{12}$, with six protons and six neutrons, while for the latter it is $_{92}U^{238}$, with 92 protons and 146 neutrons. This tendency toward a preponderance of neutrons as the nucleus increases in size is a consequence of the repelling electrostatic force acting between the positively charged protons, since the additional neutrons contribute to the total binding energy to compensate for the increased repulsive force among the protons. Even so, for sufficiently large A, the increased binding energy (or lowering of the nuclear mass-energy) brought about by the excess neutrons increases less rapidly with increasing A than the repulsion energy between the protons, so that eventually the latter predominates and the nuclei become unstable against breakup into lighter nuclei.

Among the very light nuclei, where the electrostatic energy is least important, the most abundant stable nuclei tend to be those having equal numbers of protons and neutrons. This tendency for neutrons and protons to be present in equal numbers in stable nuclei is related to the Pauli exclusion principle, which in the case of nucleons has the effect of limiting the number of particles of the same kind that can interact attractively with each other in the nucleus. The addition of a proton and a neutron to a given nucleus will therefore generally produce tighter binding than would the addition of two protons or two neutrons. Furthermore, from the greater stability of isotopes having even numbers of protons or neutrons, it is evident that a pairing effect is present in the nuclear interaction. This effect favors even numbers over odd numbers of a given type of nucleon being present in the nucleus. It has also been observed that exceptional stability is associated with certain numbers of neutrons or protons, such as 20, 28, 50 and 82. These so-called "magic numbers" arise from the closing of groups or shells of nucleons within the nucleus, much in the same way that the extreme stability of the inert gas atoms is associated with the closing of subshells of electrons, which is also a consequence of the exclusion principle mentioned above.

Another implication of the tendency toward equality of proton and neutron numbers in light nuclei is that the forces between like nucleons are almost exactly the same whether they be neutrons or protons. More detailed consideration of the structure of nuclei, combined with the results of scattering experiments involving just two nucleons, has shown this definitely to be the case. In fact, all the evidence indicates that the specifically nuclear force between two nucleons is almost exactly the same, regardless of whether they are two neutrons, two protons, or a neutron and a proton. This is known as the charge independence of nuclear forces and implies a fundamental kinship between protons and neutrons that permits them to be regarded as two different charge states of a single particle.

A variety of experimental evidence, particularly from nucleon-nucleon scattering experiments, has shown that the range, or radius of action, of the nuclear force is extremely short, being of the order of 10^{-13} cm. In this respect also the nuclear force differs fundamentally from the electrostatic and gravitational forces, both of which vary with the inverse square of the distance between the particles involved.

Nuclear Size. Another property of the nucleus that displays systematic behavior is its size. Experimental results show that the nuclear radius increases fairly uniformly with increasing A and is represented reasonably accurately by the formula $R = r_0 A^{\frac{1}{3}}$, where R is the nuclear radius, A the mass number, and r_0 a parameter that has a value close to 1.3×10^{-13} cm. The dependence of the nuclear radius on the cube root of the mass number, together with the fact that nuclear masses are approximately proportional to mass number, means that the nuclear volume is approximately proportional to nuclear mass, i.e., the density of nuclear matter is almost constant.

There are many other nuclear properties that provide important clues to nuclear structure. Among these may be mentioned the nuclear angular momentum and the so-called electric and magnetic moments of nuclei. The former is a mechanical property involving the orbital motion of the nucleons inside the nucleus as well as their intrinsic mechanical momentum, or spin. The latter are electric and magnetic manifestations of the detailed way in which the nucleons move and are distributed within the nucleus. All these properties are of importance in developing any detailed picture of the nucleus.

See also ELEMENTARY PARTICLES.

Bibliography: R. D. EVANS, *The Atomic Nucleus* (New York 1955). J. M. BLATT and V. F. WEISSKOPF, *Theoretical Nuclear Physics* (New York 1952). R. G. SACHS, *Nuclear Theory* (Reading, Mass. 1953). M. A. PRESTON, *Physics of the Nucleus* (Reading, Mass. 1962).

[S. E. DARDEN]

NUDISM

An international movement opposed to the use of clothing, and originating in the early 20th century. Although nudity as such was advocated by a few individuals in earlier times, the beginning of an organized movement in favor of it appears to have had its first articulate support in Germany, where Richard Ungewitter published his *Die Nacktheit* in 1906. In Europe nudism began to be practiced in park areas and was known as Free Body Culture (*Freikörpercultur*). Groups were founded in the U.S. in the early 1930's. The American League for Physical Culture was established in 1932, and in 1937 this became known as the American Sunbathing Association, with headquarters at Mays Landing, New Jersey. There are approximately 25,000 nudists in the U.S. (*Newsweek* 58:73–74) and some 150 parks and clubs for their use. West Germany has about 50,000 members and 80 official beaches (*Time* 80:25). Nudism has an international organization, the International Naturist Foundation, which represents 13 national organizations in four countries.

It is claimed by adherents of the cult that nudism can contribute much to man's physical, psychical, and moral well-being. It is said to be conducive to better physical health, to the greater enjoyment of certain sports, and to the improved performance of certain work. The benefit to physical health would come from direct contact with the elements and from the easing of psychic tensions associated with clothing. The psychic gain would come as a consequence of the fact that the general practice of nudism would teach people that the nude body is not obscene or a necessary cause of erotic stimulation. This, it is maintained, would help greatly in the proper education and development of children. Because morbid curiosity would be lessened, since this is the consequence of covering erogenous areas, sexual aberrations would be minimized. Nudists claim that there is much hypocrisy in current moral and social thinking, for the nude body is considered admirable in art but is rejected in its manifestations in life.

The nudist idea appears so bizarre when considered from the point of view of human comfort or of established aesthetic and moral values that it is difficult to see how anyone can be found to take it seriously. The alleged improvement in health, physical or mental, is founded on no evident fact but is simply a gratuitous supposition, or at most is based on farfetched analogies with life among certain primitive peoples. The protection of clothing is necessary most of the time in almost all inhabited regions of the globe, either because of climatic conditions or as a protection from various forms of physical harm. The arguments for psychic or moral benefits to be expected from the adoption of nudism are generally based on the behavior of primitive peoples and are inapplicable to an advanced culture in which intellectual understanding and moral awareness are better developed. The desirability and fittingness of clothing are recognized by the overwhelming majority of mankind.

From the moral point of view, nudism disregards the problem of concupiscence, and therefore rests on unrealistic premises.

Bibliography: M. F. PARMELEE, *Nudism in Modern Life* (4th ed. Mays Landing, N.J. 1941). H. C. WARREN, "Social Nudism and the Body Taboo," PsychRev 40 (1933) 160–183. R. EGENTER, LexThK² 7:773–774.

[P. J. KELLY]

NUDITY. Even the simplest of the primitives seldom go entirely without clothing. Nakedness among men is found, for example, among some split tribal groups in the Sudan and on the Zambezi River, in both cases as a survival of ancient Negrito practice. Even in these cases women wear an apron of leaves around the middle of their bodies, and not merely at menstruation. Where dress is normal, exhibitionist acts of nakedness often have a magical meaning. In the Norse myth of Loki and in the Japanese myth of Amaterasu, such exposure takes on a cynical aspect and is intended either to cause shock or to arouse joy. The Baubo motif among the Greeks is to be interpreted as a form of fertility magic. In the realm of magic, nakedness wards off a spell or other harmful form of magic, compels love, and gives strength to one's own practice of witchcraft and conjuring. Complete disrobing at the questioning of an oracle, in lustrations, and in temple incubation

was a mark of reverence. Eschatological nakedness [see *Anthropos* 58 (1963) 579] and the ancient Arab practice of offering sacrifice naked, because of the dirt on clothes, is primarily religious in character, while the nakedness of the "air-clothed" Jainist monks is based rather on asceticism. Naked dances are connected with spirits (as in New Guinea) but also with fertility divinities.

Bibliography: A. CLOSS et al., LexThK² 7:772–773, with bibliog. C. A. SCHMITZ, RGG³ 4:1294. EncDictBibl 1602–04. F. PFISTER, "Nacktheit," Pauly-Wiss RE 16.2 (1935) 1541–49. Hastings ERE see "Nudity" in Index. Thompson MotInd, see "Naked, Nakedness, Nude, Nudity," v. 6, Index.

[A. CLOSS]

NUDITY (IN THE BIBLE). In OT history the cult practice of sacred nudity does not appear as part of Israel's religion; rather, it is expressly forbidden, and exposure of one's nakedness is looked upon as shameful. In the NT, nakedness appears most significantly in a metaphorical sense in contexts commanding the Christian to clothe the "naked," i.e., the "ill-clad."

Certain pagan religions of the ancient Near East practiced sacred, ritual nakedness. Professional prophets and dervishes would work themselves into a frenzy at the shrine of a god, slashing their limbs (cf. Dt 14.1), mumbling unintelligible sounds, and whirling their naked bodies before idols in order to induce favors from the gods. There is no indisputable case of Israelite Prophets' presenting themselves stark naked before Yahweh, for the ethical spirit of the OT insisted on the personal decency of the one who was to approach Yahweh (Ex 20.26). The closest Israelite parallel to the sacred nudity of pagan prophets is that of Saul, who "stripped himself also of his garments and prophesied with the rest before Samuel and lay down naked all that day and night" (1 Sm 19.24). It is quite probable that this "nakedness" consisted in wearing only a loincloth; David is spoken of as dancing naked before the ark, even though he was girt with a linen *ephod (2 Sm 6.14, 20). The Israelites with their high regard for personal modesty considered exposure of one's nakedness a disgrace and a shame (Gn 9.22–27), which was inflicted as punishment on prisoners of war (Is 47.3) and women guilty of adultery (Jer 13.26). Various Hebrew words for naked often mean partly clothed (Dt 28.48; Lam 4.21; 2 Chr 28.15; Ez 18.7, 16).

The Greek γυμνός means both completely naked and poorly clothed, and it is also used figuratively in the meaning of bare, exposed, and uncovered. In the episode of the young man fleeing the scene of Jesus' arrest (Mk 14.52), and perhaps in the narrative of Acts in which the evil spirit strips the Jewish exorcists (19.6), the word means "completely naked." When John writes that Peter was "stripped" while fishing (21.7), the meaning is that he was without his outer garment and was merely wearing a sleeveless blouse or smock. The Christian duty of clothing the naked refers to the obligation of helping those who are poorly clothed (Mt 25.36, 38, 43–44; Jas 2.15). In Heb 4.13 "naked" conveys the idea that all things are exposed to the eyes of God. In another sense the soul is said to be naked in the state between death and resurrection, since it is stripped of the body, which is its natural covering (2 Cor 5.3), and the "bare" grain of wheat is naked and unclothed before reaching its full growth (1 Cor 15.37). The words naked in 1 Cor 4.11 and nakedness in Rom 8.35 and 2 Cor 11.27 refer to extreme misery and destitution.

See also DRESS (IN THE BIBLE).

Bibliography: EncDictBibl 1602–04. A. OEPKE, Kittel ThW 1:773–775. H. P. SMITH, *Samuel* (ICC; New York 1904) 182–183, 295–297.

[F. J. MONTALBANO]

NUEVA PAMPLONA, ARCHDIOCESE OF (NEO-PAMPILONENSIS),

located in the department of Norte de Santander, Colombia; created a diocese Sept. 25, 1835; raised to an archdiocese May 29, 1956. In 1963 it had five suffragan dioceses: Barranca Bermeja (1962), Bucaramanga (1952), Cúcuta (1956), Ocaña (1962), and Socorro y San Gil (1895); and the prelature *nullius* Bertrania. Nueva Pamplona was founded in 1549 and was a city from 1555. During the colonial period it was the center of an important mining district and a center for missionaries, particularly Dominicans, who evangelized the area. In the 20th century Nueva Pamplona is largely a rural area, only the capital having more than 30,000 inhabitants. The area belonged first to the Archdiocese of Bogotá until 1783 when it was included in that of Mérida. From 1808 negotiations were undertaken to set up the diocese, but because of the revolutionary uprisings, the court of Madrid dropped the project. President Santander obtained the bull of erection from Gregory XVI after independence was achieved. At first the diocese covered a huge territory with a widely dispersed population, impossible for the few priests to care for. The area was gradually divided as new dioceses were erected. Among the bishops of the diocese have been: José Jorge de Torres Stans (1837–53), José Luis Niño (1856–64); Bonifacio Toscano (1866–73), Indalecio Barreto (1874–75), Ignacio Antonio Parra (1876–1908), Evaristo Blanco (1909–15), Rafael Afanador y Cadena (1916–56), Bernardo Botero, first archbishop (1956–59), and Aníbal Muñoz Duque (1959–   ).

Bibliography: G. PÉREZ RAMÍREZ and I. WUST, *La Iglesia en Colombia* (Bogotá 1961).

[A. M. PINILLA COTE]

NUEVA SEGOVIA, ARCHDIOCESE OF (NOVAE SEGOBIAE),

metropolitan see since 1951, in northern Luzon, *Philippines. In 1963 it had 111 secular and 22 religious priests, 12 men in 1 religious house, 226 women in 13 convents, and 550,000 Catholics in a population of 650,000; it is 1,567 square miles in area. Its two suffragan sees, Laoag (created in 1961) and Tuguegarao (1910), and two suffragan prelatures *nullius,* Bangued (1955) and the Batan and Babuyan Islands (1950), had 100 secular and 94 religious priests, 187 sisters, and 999,000 Catholics in a population of 1,452,000.

The Spanish settlement of Nueva Segovia (1581), made a diocese suffragan to *Manila (1595–1951), has been absorbed by the town of Lal-loc on the Cagayan River 11 miles south of Aparri. The name Nueva Segovia continues only in the see, which moved to Vigan (1758), founded by Juan de Salcedo (1572); Vigan, on the west coast of Luzon, is the most important trade center in north Luzon. The jurisdiction of Nueva Segovia has been diminished to create new jurisdictions: Tuguegarao (1910), *Lingayen (1928), and Mountain Province (1932). Miguel de *Benavides

(1595–1602), Diego *Aduarte (1634–36), and Dennis *Dougherty (1903–10) have been Bishops of Nueva Segovia. Gregorio Aglipay, founder of the *Philippine Independent Church (1902), was born in the Diocese of Nueva Segovia.

Bibliography: *Catholic Directory of the Philippines, 1963* (Manila 1963). AnnPont (1964) 308–309.

[D. ABELLA]

NUGENT, FRANCIS

Capuchin friar, agent of the Counter-Reformation, and founder of the Capuchins in Ireland and Germany; b. Ballebranagh, County Meath, Ireland, 1569; d. Charleville, France, May 18, 1635. His father was Sir Edward Nugent; his mother, Margaret O'Connor, was of the princely O'Connor Faly. At the age of 13 he was sent to the Scots-Irish college at Pont-à-Mousson in Lorraine. Thence he went to Louvain, secured his M.A., and in 1590 was appointed to lecture in philosophy in the University. He joined the Capuchins at Brussels on Oct. 4, 1591, the first Irishman to do so. While he was still a deacon, his preaching at Valenciennes (September 1594) brought him fame; as a result a Capuchin friary was founded there. He became prominent in the pre-Quietist mystical movement in the Low Countries and was delated to Rome. Nugent, twice tried by the Inquisition in Rome, defended himself successfully and earned the commendation of Pope Clement VIII, who presided in August 1600 at the second trial. He served in France for 5 years as guardian and professor of theology—Friar Joseph of Paris (François *Le Clerc du Tremblay) was one of his pupils. He returned to the Low Countries (1605), where he held office continuously as guardian and definitor of the Belgian province. When in Rome as delegate for a general chapter of his order, he secured a papal brief, on May 29, 1608, from Paul V, authorizing a Capuchin mission to "England, Scotland, and Ireland." Before he could realize this project, he was appointed commissary general of the Capuchin mission to the Rhineland, Aug. 28, 1610. Under his guidance the Capuchins became a powerful religious force in Germany, particularly through his Confraternity of Our Lord's Passion. As a result of internal disputes among the Capuchins, he was dismissed from his post, and in March 1615 was given a foundation at Charleville as a center for the mission to Ireland. Nugent also directed the Capuchin missionaries in England and Scotland, but on a minor scale.

During 1623 and 1624 he negotiated with James I of England for religious toleration for English and Irish Catholics. He visited England and Ireland secretly during 1624 and 1625 and went to Rome as agent for the Irish hierarchy. A long, drawn out dispute with the Walloon Capuchins came to a head in 1631 when he opposed a Walloon visitator sent to Charleville by the Capuchin vicar-general. Nugent was deposed from office in January 1632 and lived in retirement at Charleville until his death. Though intellectually powerful, he was primarily a man of action, founding Capuchin houses at Valenciennes (1595), Courtrai (1610), Cologne (1611), Charleville (1615), and Dublin (1624). Courageous, tenacious, and resourceful, he was a leader of men, but often too demanding; he had the defects and virtues of the pioneer.

Bibliography: Most studies have been eulogistic and uncritical. Exceptions are: A. DASSEVILLE, "Francis Nugent," *Round Table*

of Franciscan Research 15 (1950) 103–117. P. HILDEBRAND, "Franciscus Nugent," *Franciscaansch Leven* 11 (1928) 21–28; 21 (1938) 301–312, 339–346; *De Kapucijnen in de Nederlanden en het prinsbisdom Luik,* 4 v. (Antwerp 1945–48) 1:146–151, 274–287; 3:13–29. F. X. MARTIN, "Sources for the History of the Irish Capuchins," CollFran 26 (1956) 67–69; *Friar Nugent* (Rome 1962). A. TEETAERT, DTC 11.1:849–850.

[F. X. MARTIN]

NUMBER

Number is variously defined by modern mathematicians as the class of all classes that can be placed in one-to-one correspondence with one another, or, in the Aristotelian tradition, as a species of discrete *quantity, a plurality measurable by unity (cf. Aristotle, *Meta.* 1057a 3). The notion has undergone so radical a conceptual change with recent developments in mathematics that it is considered here under two aspects. The first part of the article treats number from the viewpoint of mathematical theory, whereas the second presents an analysis of the concept of number from the viewpoint of traditional philosophy.

NUMBER IN MODERN MATHEMATICS

This part of the article concentrates on number as it relates to two other basic notions—that of quantity (the intuitive idea of more or less) and that of computation. In the history of mathematics, these have acted as two poles of attraction for the concept of number, which began as an expression of the quantitative intuition, and ended up as a part of the formalist outlook in modern mathematics, where computational axioms are said to define their objects.

Integers. That the natural numbers 1, 2, 3, . . . are given in experience is not so obvious as one might think; there are primitive tribes for whom "one," "two," and "many" sum up the concept of quantity. Anybody can observe a 2-year old passing through that same primitive degree of awareness, and can notice the child's startling discovery later on that there is no such thing as a "largest" integer; in other words, the sequence of integers can be extended indefinitely. Since this step soon becomes part of the obvious things that form the substratum of mental processes, its boldness and its magnitude are not commonly emphasized; nor is it often realized that it is the first typical case in which mathematics breaks loose from reality, "arbitrarily large" numbers obviously being beyond the grasp of the senses. The assumption that the integers form an infinite sequence may be aesthetically satisfying, because of the beauty and simplicity of its consequences; however it is a fantastic extrapolation from experiment, or, in other words, an a priori axiom in the modern sense of the term.

Fractions and Irrational Numbers. Integers can be used only to evaluate discrete quantities; in most civilizations, there soon arose the need to enlarge the concept of number in order to cope with the very practical problem of *measurement, i.e., the comparison of quantities such as lengths, areas, or weights, which did not appear as a collection of given units. These problems gave rise (independently in the Egyptian, Babylonian, Hindu, and Chinese civilizations) to the concept of fraction (or ratio of two quantities, or, in modern parlance, positive rational numbers a/b, where a and b are natural numbers) and to the extension to these new numbers of the fundamental operations on integers, addition and multiplication. From the purely empirical point of view, this is entirely satisfactory: a sufficiently fine subdivision of a unit of length, e.g., will give a measurement of every length within the reach of man's experimental processes, with all the accuracy one needs for practical purposes, even in the refined physics of today. No wonder, therefore, that all civilizations but one never felt the need for elaboration of the concept of number.

Not so with the Greeks, however. From their studies in musical theory, and also probably for religious or mystical reasons, they had developed an interest for ratios with small terms, such as ⅗ or ⁴⁄₇. Furthermore, like the Egyptians and the Babylonians, they knew that a fraction can usually be simplified, e.g., ⁶⁄₉ = ⅔ by suppression of the factor 3 in both terms; and they had proved that for a given fraction, there is a unique simple form, p/q, such that no further simplification is possible. Finding the simple form of any given ratio was thus one of their problems. This was of no practical importance, and is historically one of the first examples of a mathematical problem that was not introduced in view of practical applications. They found, as others had before them, that if one constructs the square S' having as its side the diagonal of a given square S, S' has twice the area of S; in other words, if a and d are the side and the diagonal of S, one has $d^2 = 2a^2$. What then should be the simple form of d/a? The surprising answer is that there is none. Suppose indeed p/q was that simple form; this implies in particular that p and q are not both even numbers (otherwise one could suppress the factor 2 in both); however, one has $p^2 = 2q^2$. The right-hand side is obviously an even number since it is divisible by two; therefore p^2 is even, and since the square of an odd number cannot be even, p must be even, say $p = 2p'$. But then one has $2q^2 = 4p'^2$, and therefore $q^2 = 2p'^2$; but the same argument then shows q should also be even, and one has reached an impossibility.

Simple as it is, this argument is of such a different type and degree of sophistication from all that is known of human thought before the Greeks, that it can properly be considered as marking the birth of mathematics in the modern sense of the word. With regard to the concept of number, it showed that no satisfactory theory can be obtained unless one admits the existence not only of fractions but also of numbers not expressible as fractions, those now called irrational numbers. The preceding proof shows that $\sqrt{2}$ is an irrational number, and the same is true for all square roots of integers, n, that are not themselves squares of integers. Of course, these are only examples of irrational numbers, and the problem of giving a precise definition of these numbers in general (or, equivalently, a system of axioms characterizing what are now called *real* numbers, i.e., numbers that are either rational or irrational) was not an easy one; it was solved in a masterly way by the Greek mathematician Eudoxus (4th century B.C.), but his solution is too long and involves techniques too complicated to be described here.

Negative and Complex Numbers. The introduction of irrational numbers was effected for computational purposes, i.e., the possibility of extracting square roots. This is still more apparent in the next extensions of the notion of number: the concepts of zero and of the negative numbers, which appear in Hindu mathematics c. A.D. 500, and the complex numbers, a creation of the Italian algebraists of the Renaissance.

There is no natural meaning attached to a difference such as $3 - 5$, and this lack turns out to be a nuisance as soon as one wants to develop algebra. One cannot, for instance, write formulas such as $a - (b - c) = c + (a - b)$ even when the left hand side is meaningful, e.g., for $a = 3$, $b = 5$, $c = 4$. In this example, the formula becomes correct if one agrees to replace $3 - 5$ by the symbol -2 on the right-hand side. In spite (or because?) of their matchless logical training, the Greeks were not prepared for such formal manipulations, and it took more than 1,000 years for these new numbers (variously labeled as "false," "fictive," "absurd," etc., during the Middle Ages) to gain final acceptance in mathematics. Here is a case in which computation is performed on no corresponding quantities; the concept of "directed segments," by which negative numbers are now usually represented, was historically introduced only much later. Even in modern teaching, it is usually quite difficult to give more than plausible reasons for the validity of such formulas as $(-a)(-b) = ab$. In reality, the reason for this formula is the mathematician's desire to keep all the familiar rules of algebra for negative numbers, in particular the distributive law $x(y + z) = xy + xz$. If in that formula 0 is substituted for z, resulting in $xy = xy + x \cdot 0$, this yields $x \cdot 0 = 0$, which implies $0 = x \cdot 0 = x[y + (-y)] = xy + x(-y)$, or equivalently $x(-y) = -xy$, which is the "rule of signs." The rule of signs implies in particular that $(-a)^2 = a^2$ is always a positive number; this seems to preclude the existence of square roots of negative numbers.

The next and boldest step was to enlarge again the concept of number by the adjunction of an imaginary quantity i such that $i^2 = -1$, and subsequent computation with expressions $a + bi$ (with a, b real numbers, positive or negative) according to the usual rules of algebra, but replacing i^2 by -1 whenever possible. These computations went on for 200 years with no interpretation whatsoever of these complex quantities. Only around 1800 was it discovered that, by associating to $a + bi$ the point having a and b as coordinates (with respect to a fixed system of rectangular axes in the plane), one obtains a system of rules of computation on points (or vectors) in a plane, having important connections with geometry (for instance, multiplying a vector by the number i amounts to rotating it around the origin by an angle of $+90$ degrees).

This raises the question whether mathematicians can create at will new entities having any properties they want them to have. The answer, in modern mathematics, is: yes, almost. The only restriction is that the required properties should be consistent; in other words, they should not lead to a contradiction. For instance, it can be shown that it is impossible to define addition and multiplication in three-dimensional space in such a way that the usual properties of these operations be again preserved; more precisely, for any such definition, there will be points x, y, both of which are not 0, and such that their product xy is 0 (a phenomenon that cannot happen for complex numbers, i.e., points in a plane). In four-dimensional space, this can be avoided provided allowance is made for the noncommutativity of multiplication, i.e., the existence of pairs of points x, y such that $xy \neq yx$ (these numbers are called quaternions). In a sense, the extension of the concept of number to the complex numbers is maximal; no further enlarge-

ment is possible while still preserving all its essential properties.

In the last 100 years, mathematicians usually dismiss questions regarding the value of abstract mathematical constructions as irrelevant to what they are doing. Nevertheless, it is perfectly legitimate to ask: (1) whether the system of numbers defined by the mathematicians is well adapted to applications in the external world, and (2) why, since mathematicians can choose among many possible systems, are they interested in any particular one?

The first question is difficult to answer. At the beginning of the 20th century the answer would have been an emphatic yes; but with the advent of modern physics serious doubts have crept in. In the 1960s it is clear to both physicists and mathematicians that there is no such thing as a priori necessity or absolute truth in a particular number system; it would be easy to imagine other systems that would apply just as well (if not better) to the experimental facts. In other words, it is pointless to try to find concrete models of real numbers (except as a very rough first approximation), or to seek to justify the abstract constructions outlined above by some of their applications.

To the second question, however, the answer is easy: real and complex numbers form the cornerstone of mathematical analysis, and of all its applications to various other branches of mathematics, astronomy, and physics. The most remarkable character of the number system on which these are based is that it yields, so to speak, unsuspected bonuses, far beyond the modest algebraic requirements from which it sprang in the first place. For instance, complex numbers were introduced to give meaning to the square root of any real number, which amounts to solving quadratic equations without any restriction. But, in addition, it enables one to solve all algebraic equations with complex coefficients (not, of course, by explicit formulas such as the one solving a quadratic equation). More precisely, it can be proved that any algebraic equation has at least one complex root (theorem of D'Alembert-Gauss).

Notion of Limit. Another, and more important, feature of the solution found by the Greeks to the problem of the irrational numbers, is the existence of limits. To illustrate how this concept has to be introduced the ancient problem of measurement of areas will be discussed. Assuming the unit of length u and the square of side u as a unit of area, one knows that the area of a rectangle of sides a, b is measured by the number ab. How can the area of a circle be computed? There is no obvious way of comparing that area with the area of the unit square, as would be done for the length of a segment by juxtaposition of a certain number of copies of the unit length, or fractions of the same. However, suppose the diameter AB of the circle is divided into n equal parts, and the corresponding rectangles are formed within the circle, as depicted in Fig. 1 (with $n = 8$). As a first approximation to the area one can take the sum S_n of the areas of all these rectangles; and it is quite clear that the larger the n chosen, the closer will be the approximation. However, the numbers S_n will not be the same for all values of n, even if they differ by very small values, and since none of the polygons they measure is identical to the circle, none of these numbers may properly be considered as a measure of the area of the circle. It can however be proved that

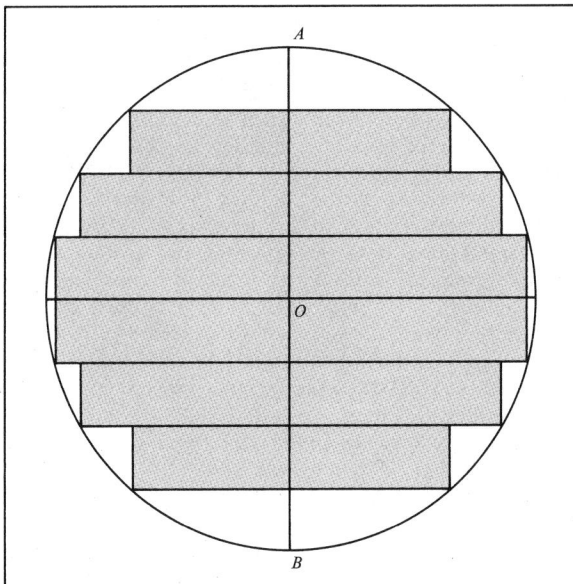

Fig. 1. The area of a circle approximated by rectangles.

the S_n have a definite *limit: this means that there exists a unique number S with the following property: provided n is taken large enough, the difference $S - S_n$ can be made smaller than any given number $\epsilon > 0$ (the choice of n depending of course on ϵ).

This sophisticated notion is far removed from experimental science—the most demanding engineer or physicist will be satisfied with the value of some S_n. The Greeks alone (and after them, all mathematicians) remained adamant in insisting that no matter how close the approximation, none of the members S_n tending to S would ever be equal to it. This insistence is in fact a necessary consequence of the definition of the real numbers, and it is not a coincidence that the exhaustion method for the computation of areas is due to the same Eudoxus who gave the first general definition of these numbers.

The concept of limit has extraordinary range and flexibility. The exhaustion method was successfully used by Eudoxus and his immediate successors to compute many elementary areas and volumes. In the 17th century, it was to blossom into the imposing structure of *calculus, with a far greater range of applications. More recently, it has been realized that the idea of limit (and the related concepts of continuity and proximity) are not concerned exclusively with real or complex numbers, but can be fruitfully applied to a wide variety of mathematical objects, such as curves, surfaces, and functions. Even for rational numbers, it is possible to define and to use with great success notions of limit that are different from the usual one and sometimes strange at first sight: take for instance a prime number p, e.g., $p = 3$; then in p-adic analysis a power p^n of p is not considered very large for large n (as in classical analysis) but very small; and for that new notion of limit, the series $1 + 3 + 3^2 + \cdots + 3^{n+}$ (for $p = 3$) is convergent to the sum $-\frac{1}{2}$! All this has given rise to modern abstract analysis, which includes calculus as one of its branches, but goes far beyond it in the beauty and simplicity of its concepts and in the power of its methods.

The intrinsic difficulty of the concept of limit has been the source of many misunderstandings. For in-

stance, when a sequence $x_1, x_2, \ldots, x_n$ of real numbers $x_n > 0$ has 0 for a limit, one sometimes says that x_n becomes infinitely small. This expression has given rise to the fallacy that infinitely small numbers actually exist. If one tried to give a mathematical meaning to these words, an infinitely small number would be a positive number α, other than 0, such that any other real number $\beta > 0$ would be greater than α. This, however, is ruled out expressly by one of the axioms for real numbers, the so-called axiom of Archimedes. One should observe that this is the only acceptable way, in mathematics, to refute such a fallacy: it is an immediate consequence of the fact that there actually exist systems of mathematical objects, which include the real numbers as a part and obey the same computational rules except for the axiom of Archimedes. Such systems are called non-Archimedean ordered fields.

Some idea of how this is possible may be derived from the consideration of a geometric object that was the source of much speculation among the Greeks, the angle of contact. Consider for instance a circle C touching a line OA at the point O (Fig. 2). For any line OD through O, different from OA, it seems quite natural to say that the curvilinear angle AOC is smaller than the rectilinear angle AOD; hence, although there is no rectilinear angle different from O and smaller than all others (this follows from the axiom of Archimedes), one can conceive of other kinds of objects having these properties. The construction of non-Archimedean fields is a mathematical elaboration of that idea. It should be observed that, in a non-Archimedean field, if $a > 0$ is infinitely small (i.e., smaller than all real numbers $x > 0$), then $1/a$ is infinitely large (i.e., larger than all real numbers). This easily follows from the rules of computation. When, instead of real numbers, one considers rectilinear angles, an infinitely large element would be the curvilinear angle AOE.

Transfinite Numbers. The idea of infinitely large has, however, a very different and less artificial meaning in mathematics. To describe it, discrete quantity will again be considered. Two finite collections of objects, A and A', have the same number of elements, if and only if there is a pairing $a \leftrightarrow a'$ between these two collections, each element a of A being paired to a unique element a' of A', and vice versa. (This is the mathematical description of the process of counting; in mathematics, the

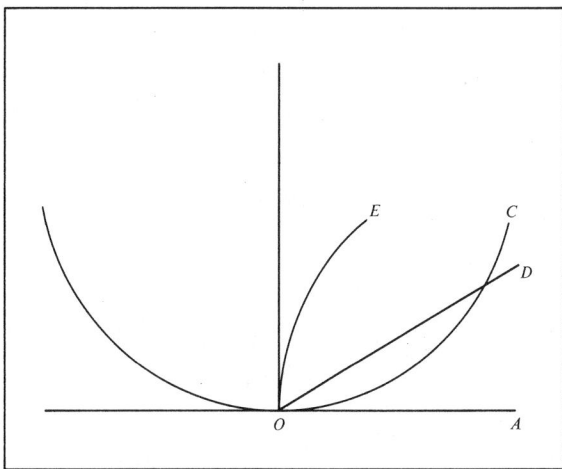

Fig. 2. Comparison of curvilinear and rectilinear angles.

expression one-to-one correspondence is used instead of pairing.) Now, at the beginning of the 17th century, *Galileo observed that if to any integer n, one associates its square n^2, one obtains a one-to-one correspondence between the collection N of all integers and the part N' of N consisting of all squares. This, however, seemed to contradict the traditional axiom that the whole is greater than the part, and so Galileo concluded that infinite collections such as N are illegitimate in mathematics. This of course stems from a misunderstanding (although a very natural one at the time of Galileo) of the nature of a mathematical axiom. What drove Galileo to his inglorious retreat was not an axiom in the precise modern sense of the word; it was merely a vague statement that could be interpreted in various and conflicting ways. The apparent contradiction arose from the confusion between two such interpretations: one in which *greater* simply meant containing, and the other in which, by analogy with finite collections, reference was made to some undefined quantity or number of elements of an infinite collection.

In fact, as G. *Cantor discovered around 1880, such a quantitative notion can actually be defined. It simply consists in considering as equivalent any two collections A, A' between which there is a one-to-one correspondence, and then assigning the same cardinal number to any two equivalent collections. For finite collections, this yields back the usual natural numbers; but there also exist infinite (or transfinite) cardinal numbers, for instance the cardinal number, written $\aleph_0$ (aleph null), of the collection N of all integers; and $\aleph_0$ is actually greater than all integers. (One says that the cardinal number of a collection A is greater than the cardinal number of A' if there is a one-to-one correspondence of A' with a part of A, but not vice versa.)

This definition immediately raised a number of important questions, most of which were answered by Cantor himself. In the first place, Galileo's observation could be generalized to prove that any infinite subcollection of N has the same cardinal number $\aleph_0$. A natural guess was that $\aleph_0$ would in fact be the only infinite cardinal number, but Cantor proved that such was not the case, first by showing that the cardinal number $\mathfrak{C}$ of the collection R of all real numbers is greater than $\aleph_0$, and later by showing how to define infinitely many different infinite cardinal numbers. (In fact, cardinal numbers behave like integers in that there is no largest one among them.)

This development brought a new way of thinking into mathematics, but more startling results were yet to come. One can easily generalize addition and multiplication to arbitrary cardinal numbers by imitating the definition of these operations for integers; however, the rules of computation turn out to be very different from the usual ones. For instance if m is any infinite cardinal number, one has $m + m = m$, and $m^2 = m$. (The last formula yields, as a special case, Cantor's celebrated theorem that there are "as many points" in a square as on one of its sides.) In the 1880s, most people were still convinced that the real or complex numbers were the only objects on which computation could be done. The discovery of such badly behaved new numbers was considered by some mathematicians as almost a personal offense, and this led them to such extremes as to cast doubt on the correctness of Cantor's proofs. All this furor has long since abated, and Cantor's results and ideas are now classical; if his hopes of a new transfinite arithmetic have failed to materialize—due to the fact that infinite cardinal numbers do not obey the rules of computation which, as experience has taught us, seem to be indispensable for any fruitful kind of algebra—his extension of the notion of number has found important applications in mathematics.

One of the first results obtained in this way has to do with the classification of irrational numbers. As noted above, irrational numbers first appeared as square roots of integers; one can, more generally, consider cubic roots, fourth roots, etc. Even more generally, one can say that an irrational number is algebraic if it is a solution of an algebraic equation $a_0 x^n + a_1 x^{n-1} + \cdots + a_n = 0$ whose coefficients $a_0, a_1, \ldots, a_n$ are integers. A natural question then arises: Are all real numbers algebraic? Liouville ($c.$ 1840) said "no" to this; he was able explicitly to define real numbers that he could prove were not algebraic (these are also called transcendental real numbers). Later on, it was proved that the famous number π is also transcendental, settling in the negative the old problem of "squaring the circle"— which precisely meant finding an algebraic equation with integral coefficients, of which π would be a root. However, the existence of transcendental numbers can be much more easily settled by Cantor's methods. Using the rules for infinite cardinal numbers quoted above, it is an easy matter to prove that if A is the subcollection of R consisting of algebraic numbers, then the cardinal number of A is $\aleph_0$; however, the cardinal number of R is greater than $\aleph_0$, and therefore A may not be equal to R. More precisely, this proves that there are as many transcendental numbers as there are real numbers, i.e., infinitely more than algebraic numbers. The construction of Eudoxus, which was to give meaning to the notion of algebraic numbers, introduces in fact many more elements than are needed for that particular purpose; but this superabundance is in fact the boon that makes analysis possible.

See also MATHEMATICS, NATURE OF; AXIOMATIC SYSTEM; FORMALISM.

Bibliography: M. RICHARDSON, *Fundamentals of Mathematics* (rev. ed. New York 1958). L. BRUNSCHVICG, *Les Étapes de la pensée mathématique* (2d ed. Paris 1922). E. LANDAU, *Vorlesungen über Zahlentheorie* (New York 1946); *Foundations of Analysis: The Arithmatic of Whole, Rational, Irrational, and Complex Numbers,* tr. F. STEINHARDT (New York 1957). J. DIEUDONNÉ, *Foundations of Modern Analysis* (New York 1960).

[J. DIEUDONNÉ]

PHILOSOPHICAL ANALYSIS

The following philosophical analysis of number describes various theories concerning the nature of number, and takes into account the notion and use of number by mathematicians and other scientists. It also considers the origin and elaboration of the concept of number, its nature and existence, and the way it is treated in the science of logic.

Theories of Number. The earliest known view of number is the Pythagorean contention that number is the sole inner reality of each thing, e.g., justice is 4, perfection is 10. This theory reappears, with modifications, in J. *Kepler and *Nicholas of Cusa and is implicit in L. E. J. Brouwer's intuitionism. The Pythagoreans may be said to have originated the quantitative study of nature; they also fostered an inclination to number mysticism.

*Plato considers mathematical number as intermediate between the ideal numbers of the world of ideas (philosophical number) and their imperfect realization in sensible things (popular number). His tendency to make number a self-subsistent entity is adopted generally by objective idealists, and a Platonizing tendency is evident in some current views on the foundations of mathematics.

A third view of number that arose with Sextus Empiricus is the inclination to make of number a totally empirical notion with no conceptual counterpart (*see* SKEPTICISM). This attitude toward number is found in *empiricism; it also manifests itself in some current views on mathematics that consider number as a symbol derivable from postulates or conventions as the result of a manipulation of symbols.

The theory of number as a concept deriving from experience—formalized and clarified in mathematical abstraction as the determination of quantity, and reapplicable to nature—is basically Aristotelian. It is generally accepted by medieval scholasticism and in contemporary Thomism.

The theory of number as a purely psychological entity, derived from and based on successive intuitions, is the view proposed by Immanuel *Kant, and, in modified form, by Leopold Kronecker and Brouwer.

That the number of pure mathematics is a logical entity, and that arithmetic and the entire body of mathematics is derivable from logic was proposed by Bertrand *Russell and is held by some advocates of *logicism.

Number in Mathematics and Science. It is evident that mathematical abstraction affords the mathematician a working area within the mind where he need not feel afraid of, nor crowded by, extramathematical considerations. Like all scientists, the mathematician has his own methods, modes of proof, and technical language. Qua mathematician, then, he defines number in the modes indigenous to his subject and to his purposes: operationally, functionally, logically, axiomatically, recursively, and so forth.

In pure mathematics, number is a highly refined and determinate concept related only analogously to the numbers of experience. Numbers arise within mathematics from two principal sources. Algebraically, numbers are the result of operating mathematically on two or more numbers and obtaining another number as a result (i.e., the number system is a closed system); or they may arise from geometric considerations on the assumption that to every point in the line (or in space, generally) there should correspond some number. To the pure mathematician, $\sqrt{-1}$, 0, π, $\aleph_0$, are equally numbers, and, in his modes of classifying numbers, the words "rational," "real," "imaginary," "transcendental," and "transfinite" have lost the impact of their historical origins. In fact, as pure mathematics develops, number grows more abstract, but the appreciation of number grows more clear, precise, and certain. The pure mathematician takes the natural numbers for granted and hopes to express all numbers in terms of these; this goal frequently leads him to such extramathematical considerations as the nature, the origin, and the meaning of number. Like the body of mathematics itself, number too has benefited from the richly symbolic language and highly formalized techniques of the axiomatic method and from the development of formal logic (*see* LOGIC, SYMBOLIC).

In applied mathematics, scientists make extensive use of number and its processes, as they do of other parts of pure mathematics. Number is a way of knowing the quantity, intensity, order, or structure of material reality. With the aid of *statistics and *probability, number affords scientists the opportunity of predicting and controlling countable or measurable things or events with varying degrees of probability and success.

Origin and Elaboration. It is currently held that the notion of class correspondence (from which the concept of cardinal number derives) is more basic in the psychology of number than the notion of sequence (from which the concept of ordinal number derives). There are, however, even more basic concepts that man possesses before he achieves the number concept; among these should be enumerated the notions of unity or singularity, multitude, and measure.

Unity. In order that an object be regarded under the aspect of *unity, it is sufficient that it be seen as distinct, and as identifiable from other objects. This notion of unity is not number, but it is one of the basic principles from which number derives. Now, before the mind grasps this notion of unity, it is first united or fused to what is (being), wherein it sees that one thing is not another (formal division), and that each thing is divided from other things (formal distinction) but undivided in itself (identity, unity). These basic notions are called *transcendentals, since they are concerned with being as such, and they equip the mind to handle the notion of the "one and the many" at any level. It is in this fashion that metaphysicians speak of transcendental one and multitude and conclude that the notion of number is a truly metaphysical and hence an analogous notion applicable, proportionately, to spiritual, material, logical—to any identifiably distinct being(s). This quasi-intuitive sight of the one and many forms the basis for the origin of number as used in daily life, and ultimately, of mathematical number. At this level of sensible experience, one sees likewise that one thing is not the other (material division), and each thing is divided from other things (material distinction) and undivided in itself (a unity that is sense-perceptible). These notions are called predicamental, since they are concerned with beings as classifiable into the 10 predicaments or *categories of being. In order, then, to achieve the concept of "one" as a basis for number, the mind needs to grasp, at least confusedly, the notion of unity or singularity.

Multitude. From the above, it follows that the notion of a *multitude, collection, set, or aggregate of objects—corresponding to the notion of unity—is another insight needed for the understanding of number. This collection is not merely conceived of as a plurality of objects, to each of which the notion of unity is attributed as in the above, but the collection itself is viewed as an object to which unit is ascribed—it is considered a unity or a single whole.

Correspondence. The notion of correspondence or matching between the elements of one group or collection with another permits the comparison of multitudes as having the same (all the chairs in the classroom are filled) or different (there are more chairs than students) collection of things.

Measure. The unity from which number derives (called predicamental as opposed to transcendental) adds the notion of a measure to transcendental unity. To function as a measure, the unity must be some minimum within the required process of counting (in answer to the question, How many?) or of measuring (in answer to the question, How much?). This notion of unity as a minimum and as a measure accounts for the various types of numbers that man has invented.

Order or Sequence. Finally, in order to develop numbers, the notion of order or sequence is required; this gives priority and posteriority to a collection or multitude, so that number signifies a certain position or rank of one thing with respect to another.

Nature and Existence. It is only in the above terms that one can approach the problem of the nature and of the reality of number. But first the concept of number must be distinguished from the numerals that are symbols indicative of number (as, analogously, words are of concepts). In this connection, one cannot properly define number, as has been attempted, if he identifies numbers with numerals, e.g., to identify the number "one" with "1" or the number "two" with "1 + 1." The properties of numerals are not the properties of numbers, and conversely. Numerals may be printed or written, they may be black or blue, but these properties cannot be ascribed to numbers. Likewise, numbers can be odd or even, prime or composite, but these properties are not true of numerals. Moreover, to identify numbers with numerals in this sense would be to deny that the Arabic and Roman numerals basically symbolize the same numbers. All types of numerals, accordingly, are merely symbols or representations of number.

Once number is freed from its symbols, it should also be carefully separated from the objects that are numbered. The number 10, for example, does not refer merely to one, or to any given particular group of 10 things. At the same time, for any given collection of things and some unity that can function as a measure, one can know the number of the collection either by a process of correspondence or of counting.

Number, then, designates a genuine property of a group or a collection of things, such that changing the color or the arrangement of the group would not alter its number. Moreover, number designates the relationship of a group to a unity of human origin and determination—as in a given group of nine ships afloat, one may say there are nine ships, or seven destroyers and two aircraft carriers, and so forth. Number is a concept truly indicative and expressive of the observable distinction between sensible things and, analogously, between beings in general. The numbers of ordinary experience are real in the sense that they are universal (though at this level, vague) concepts representing man's ability to cope with the quantified aspect of things—with their very plurality, their magnitude, and their intensity. Mathematical numbers are real, also, but in a refined and more abstract sense: they are the measure and the means of ordering the parts of the *continuum (as in the odd and even; positive and negative; open, closed, and dense sets, etc.) depending on the basic unity that the mathematician chooses as a measure.

Relation of Number to Logic. There can be no doubt that there is a logic of numbers, for numbers can be viewed as man-made symbols of the liberal arts of mathematics. Like other concepts expressive of reality, numbers are not merely formal signs expressing the predicamental unity native to an object or objects. Numbers also are expressed in conventional symbols that constitute the language of mathematics, characterized by its own formal laws and rules, its own syntax and even rhetoric. This recognition and development of the logic of mathematics is one of the great contributions of symbolic logic.

See also MATHEMATICS, PHILOSOPHY OF; LOGIC; SCIENCES, CLASSIFICATION OF.

Bibliography: E. T. BELL, *The Development of Mathematics* (2d ed. New York 1945). J. PIAGET, *The Child's Conception of Number,* tr. C. GATTEGNO and F. M. HODGSON (London 1952). Thorndike. J. R. NEWMAN, ed., *The World of Mathematics,* 4 v. (New York 1956).

[E. A. MAZIARZ]

NUMBERS, BOOK OF

The fourth book of the Pentateuch bears the Hebrew title *bammidbār,* "in the wilderness," recalling the traditional 40 years of Israelite wandering in the desert between Egypt and the Promised Land. In English Bibles the name is derived ultimately from the title in the Septuagint (LXX), 'Αριθμοί, suggesting the book's interest in the census and other matters calling for arithmetical precision, such as the division of the land. *See* CENSUS (IN THE BIBLE). This article covers the sources and literary form, authorship, and division of the book.

Sources and Literary Form. The Book of Numbers incorporates a mass of legal, statistical, and liturgical material into the historical narrative of events that took place between Sinai and the last days at Moab. Since the thrust of the account is toward the permanent establishment of norms—sanctioned by Mosaic authority—within the community, the book does not convey the absorbing concern with the acts of God in history that are found in the Deuteronomic (*see* DEUTERONOMISTS) and Yahwistic (*see* YAHWIST) traditions.

The merged Yahwistic and Elohistic (*see* ELOHIST) traditions are found in the book, but the principal source is the Priestly Tradition (*see* PRIESTLY WRITERS, PENTATEUCHAL) that has contributed almost three-quarters of the material and has given the final form and spirit to the work.

In assessing the historical value of this heterogeneous assemblage, whose origin is very complex, two extremes should be avoided: It should not be expected that the book give a detailed, purely factual, and documentary description of events; it should not be judged according to the standards and ideals of modern historical writing (*see* LITERARY GENRES, BIBLICAL). On the other hand, to consider the historical events irrelevant would falsify the author's perspective. For him a religious message was important because it implied an impact of God in time and space, the irruption of God into man's history. In addition, historical and archeological studies have enormously enhanced respect for the basic historicity of the Israelite traditions in the Book of Numbers and elsewhere in the OT. *See* ARCHEOLOGY, II (BIBLICAL).

Authorship. The Book of Numbers is a compilation of material from different strata of traditions and has no clearly recognizable unity. Jewish and Christian tradition has ascribed the book to *Moses, but this must be understood only according to contemporary knowledge of what composition and authorship meant in Old Testament times (*see* PENTATEUCH). It may be said that the book was composed in the spirit of Moses and of material that in part goes back to Moses himself. In its final form, the Book of Numbers is post-Exilic.

Division. The absence of any logical and consistent plan in the arrangement of its contents makes it difficult to provide an adequate division of the book. However, selecting the geographical factor as the basis of division, the work may be divided into three parts: The first section covers the last days at Sinai (1.1–10.10). The material is from the Priestly Tradition and is concerned mostly with legal and ecclesiastical affairs. The second division concerns the journey from Sinai to Moab (10.11–22.1). This period includes the sojourn at Cades, as well as the story of Israel's abortive attempt to enter the Promised Land from the south. The last section is concerned with the events on the Plains of Moab (22.2–36.13). The *Balaam cycle dominates this section, which includes also the transfer of leadership to Josue [see JOSUE (JOSHUA), SON OF NUN], directions concerning the occupation of Canaan, and miscellaneous laws from different periods. As the book ends, the Israelites are prepared to cross the Jordan and launch the assault on Canaan.

See also DESERT JOURNEY OF THE ISRAELITES; PHINEES (PHINEHAS); CORE (KORAH), DATHAN AND ABIRAM.

Bibliography: H. CAZELLES, *Les Nombres* (BJ 4; Paris 1952). G. B. GRAY, *Numbers* (ICC; New York 1903). B. D. EARDMANS, "The Composition of Numbers," *Oudtestamentische Studien* 6 (1949) 101–216. S. R. DRIVER, *Introduction to the Literature of the Old Testament* (New York 1905). G. E. WRIGHT and R. H. FULLER, *The Book of the Acts of God* (Garden City, N.Y. 1957). I. FRANSEN, "Du désert à la terre promise. Les plus anciens récits du livre des Nombres," BiblVieChr 5 (1954) 68–84.

[F. L. MORIARTY]

NUMBERS AND NUMBER SYMBOLISM

This article is concerned with the employment of numbers in a symbolic religious, magicoreligious, and philosophical sense. One or the other form of symbolic usage is found almost universally, but the explanation for the choice of some numbers as sacred or magical is not always clear, being lost in the remote past of the cultures involved. In practice, it is often difficult to separate the religious, magical, and philosophical usages, especially in the higher cultures or civilizations. Accordingly, it will be convenient to group the various usages under each number treated. Special attention is given to number symbolism in the ancient Near East and the Greco-Roman world.

Numbers 1 to 6. The number 1 is confined principally to religiophilosophical use. It represents the monad of the Pythagoreans and the One of Plato and the Neoplatonists.

The number 2 pairs or symbolizes opposites that have a clear relation with one another in ancient mythology and religion: right-hand–left-hand, earth-heaven, sun-moon, day-night, Ahura Mazda-Ahriman in Persian religion, *yang-yin* in Chinese thought. Whereas 1 is regarded as a male number, 2 is considered female.

The Number 3. The number 3 is one of the oldest and most widespread of all sacred or symbolical numbers, playing an equally important role in religion, magic, and philosophy. The divine family of father, mother, and child is already represented in the earliest strata of prehistoric Jericho and is well known from the Egyptian group of Osiris, Isis, and Horus. Divine triads—such as Indic Brahma, Vishnu, and Siva; Greek Zeus, Athena, and Apollo; Roman Jupiter, Juno, and Minerva, and Jupiter, Mars, and Quirinus—are common. Lesser divinities are likewise widely found in triads: the three Fates, the three Graces, the three Furies, and similar groups in Teutonic and Finno-Ugric mythology. Three-headed gods are found from ancient Ireland to India. The Babylonians, Greeks, and Hindus all distinguished three worlds—Heaven, Earth, and Lower World, or Heaven, Earth, and Water. In sacrificial ritual the Romans offered a joint sacrifice of a pig, a sheep, and a bull; and in most ancient rituals there were threefold prayers, threefold invocations of the dead, and sacred festivals of 3 days' duration. There was a similar threefold repetition of magic formulas or incantations. The triangle was regarded by the Greeks as a perfect figure and had a central place in Greek mathematics and mystic symbolism. Time was thought of in terms of morning, midday, and evening and of past, present, and future. It should be observed also that there was a close relationship between 3 and 9, and groups of nine things are very often to be explained as a mere tripling of groups of three.

The Number 4. The number 4 was connected very early with the four phases of the moon, the four seasons, the four points of the compass, and the geometrical figure of the square. It was a symbol of completeness and perfection. Among the Greeks, 4 marked the birthdate of Hermes. The Ionic philosophers identified four elements, and Pythagoras adopted 4 as a symbol of justice. Later, four cardinal virtues were stressed by Plato; and Simonides, Plato, and Aristotle spoke of "the four-square man." The Greeks, the post-Vedic literature, and the Zoroastrians all referred to four ages or periods of the world. The Romans used fourfold prayers as well as threefold ones (see Ovid, *Fasti* 4:778). The number 4, especially as embodied in the square, has had an important place in the history of magic.

The Numbers 5 and 6. The number 5 had a natural significance from the five fingers. It was the number of the Babylonian goddess Ishtar, whose symbol, the pentagram, or five-pointed star, was regarded as a magic protection against evils. The Romans offered certain sacrifices at 5-year intervals, and the censor held office for a 5-year term. In Manichaeism there were five Archons and five Aeons. In Chinese tradition 5 is a lucky number. The number 6 represents the macrocosm and is symbolized by the six-pointed star, a combination of two triangles.

Numbers 7 to 10. The number 7 occupies the supreme place in Babylonian religion and astrology. Its use and symbolism were disseminated widely eastward and westward from Mesopotamia. The Babylonians recognized seven planets: Jupiter, Venus, Saturn, Mars, Mercury, the Sun, and the Moon. Each day of their 7-day "week" was sacred to one of these celestial bodies. The four phases of the moon were comprised in a period of 4 × 7 days. The Babylonian underworld had seven divisions, and the temple towers, or ziggurats, had to have seven stories. Among the Greeks, Apollo's birthday was celebrated on the 7th of the month. In Old Persian religion there were seven Amesha Spentas, and the Rigveda speaks of seven regions and seven ponds and of the god Agni (Fire) as having seven tongues and seven wives. The tripling of 7 (21) is very common in Indic literature. In Buddhism 7 is as important as 8. It is to be noted that 7 itself is the sum of the two sacred numbers 3 and 4.

Numbers 8 and 9. The number 8 symbolizes perfection. The Elamites had eight heavens. Of greater importance is the use of 8 in Buddhism to indicate the eightfold path that is central in its teaching. The number 9, so often used as a tripling of groups indicated by 3, was much favored by the Celts, Germans, and Finno-Ugric peoples. The Greeks had nine Muses beside the three Fates and three Graces. The Chinese regarded 9 as a symbol of perfection. The pagoda of nine stories was modeled on the Chinese conception of heaven.

The Number 10. The number 10, the combined total of the fingers, symbolized perfection and wisdom. In Pythagoreanism the all-important $\tau\epsilon\tau\rho\alpha\kappa\tau\acute{\nu}s$ was constituted by the sum of $1 + 2 + 3 + 4$, arranged in a series of dots with the monad forming the apex of an isosceles triangle. The number 10 was significant also in the Hermetic literature. It can be resolved, furthermore, as $7 + 3$, $6 + 4$, and $5 + 5$, with various symbolic meanings attached to such analyses.

Numbers 12, 40, 60, 70, 72, and Others. The number 12 is a great cosmic symbol, made up of 3×4 or $5 + 7$. It is the number of the Zodiac in Babylonia and elsewhere, either under Babylonian influence or independently, for example, in China and in Greece. The Babylonians divided their year into 12 months and their days into 12 hours. The Greeks divided their year in the same way, worshiped a pantheon of 12 Olympian gods, and recorded 12 labors for Hercules. The Gnostics introduced 12 Aeons into their system. The Babylonians assigned the number 13 to their underworld and also to the intercalary month in their lunar calendar. It was considered unlucky because it exceeded the just and fixed number 12. There are some examples of 11's being considered as unlucky for exceeding 10. The number 14, as the double of 7, was regarded as lucky. The number 15 was the sacred number 5, the symbol of Ishtar, in triple form. The numbers 25, 50, and 100 had no special significance apart from being used as round numbers in legends and stories.

The number 40, however, was important. The precise origin of its symbolic use is obscure. The tradition that the Pythagoreans transferred the germination of the bean, which took 40 days, to the human fetus and then reckoned the period of pregnancy as 7×40 (280 days) is more plausible than convincing. At any rate, 40 was used also for a period of years corresponding to a generation and then applied symbolically in various other ways. The number 60 (5×12) was fundamental in the Babylonian sexagesimal system but without special significance for religion. However, 70 (7×10) and 72 (one-fifth of the circle of 360 degrees) were both used symbolically to emphasize size and multiplicity.

The Alphabet in Number Symbolism. The letters of the Greek alphabet were given numerical values at an early date. These letter-numbers served as the foundation for the development of an elaborate system of symbolism and divination based on the addition of the numerical values of the letters in given words and their synonyms or opposites. An example from a late Byzantine treatise (see Dornseiff 96) is sufficient to illustrate the practice:

$\theta\epsilon\acute{o}s$ $(9 + 5 + 70 + 200) = 284$; $\dot{\alpha}\gamma\alpha\theta\acute{o}s$ $(1 + 3 + 1 + 9 + 70 + 200) = 284$; $\ddot{\alpha}\gamma\iota\sigma s$ $(1 + 3 + 10 + 70 + 200) = 284$.

See also ASTROLOGY; DIVINATION; ABRAXAS.

Bibliography: H. J. ROSE, OxClDict 614. N. TURCHI, EncCatt 8:1995–97. A. SCHIMMEL and W. FUNK, RGG³ 6:1861–64, with bibliog. T. DAVIDSON et al., Hastings ERE 9:406–417. R. THURN-WALD, ReallexVorgesch 14:459–479, with bibliog. R. MEHLEIN, "Drei," ReallexAntChr 4:269–310, with bibliog. A. STUIBER, "Dreieck," *ibid.* 310–313. E. T. BELL, *The Magic of Numbers* (London 1952). C. M. EDSMAN, "Alphabet und Buchstabenmystik," RGG³ 1:246. F. DORNSEIFF, *Das Alphabet in Mystik und Magie* (2d ed. Leipzig 1925).

[M. R. P. MC GUIRE]

NUMBERS AND NUMBER SYMBOLISM (IN THE BIBLE)

Numbers may be used as simple expression of numerical values, as rhetorical expressions of the same, or as symbolic expressions of realities in some way related to number.

Simple Enumeration. In all existing Hebrew and Greek MSS of the inspired text, words expressing numbers are spelled out in full. In early times the Israelites may have used strokes or digits of some sort to express numbers, as did the Babylonians and Egyptians (e.g., in the *Elephantine papyri). In later times both Jews and Greeks used the letters of their respective alphabets as numerical signs. The Masoretes (*see* MASORA) indicated divisions of the Biblical text in this manner. The decimal system was basic, but traces of a duodecimal or sexagesimal system exist. *See* WEIGHTS AND MEASURES (IN THE BIBLE). In Hebrew the digits 1 to 9 were represented by the first 9 letters of the alphabet (' to *t*), the decades 10 to 90 by the next 9 (*y* to *ṣ*), and 100 to 400 by the last four (*q* to *t*). All other numbers were expressed as combinations of these. The abbreviation (*yh*) for the sacred name of God, Yahweh, was avoided by writing 15 as 9 plus 6 (*ṭw*) instead of 10 plus 5 (*yh*). The explanation for some apparent errors in textual transmission may lie in the similarity of certain letter numbers, especially in the primitive script; e.g., the confusion of *d* (3) with *z* (7) may explain the discrepancy in the parallel texts of 2 Sm 24.13 and 1 Chr 21.12. Erroneous transmission of the text, however, is not the only explanation of numerical discrepancies in the Bible. Biblical inspiration does not demand that every enumeration in the Bible be a direct revelation from God. Human values that are simply the vehicle for the transmission of divine truth are not made divine absolutes by the fact of inspiration, but are to be judged according to the nature of the human contingencies in which they appear. *See* BIBLE, II (INSPIRATION).

Rhetorical Use of Numbers. Peculiar to Semitic rhetoric was the use of two numbers in sequence in order to emphasize the completeness of the enumeration. The use is frequent in numerical proverbs and oracles (Prv 30.15, 18, 21, 29; Sir 25.7; 26.5, 19; Am 1.3–2.6). Much more general and varied are what one might call round numbers. Certain numbers are used to express an indefinite amount, large or small: 1 for someone, 2 for a couple, 3 for a few, and 1000 for very many (e.g., Os 6.2; Ex 20.6; Is 30.17). An exact number may be given for what is only an approximation. Since the superlative in Hebrew is rendered by triple repetition (Is 6.3), the number 3 signifies a certain completeness. Because of the 4 cosmic directions, the number 4 connotes a certain totality (in every direction). Because of the 5 fingers of the hand, the number 5 may signify a relatively sufficient number. Possibly because of its connection with lunar phases (approximately 7 days between each quarter), the number 7 is especially significant as indicating a complete cycle or series, and multiples of 7 emphasize the extent of the series (Gn 4.15, 24; Prv 24.16; Mt 18.21–22; Mk 16.9). The number of fingers of both hands, 10, may signify all of a kind, i.e., a totality (Ex 34.28; Jb 19.3; Mt 25.1). Since it was associated with the 12 months of the solar year, the number 12 suggests a complete cycle. The number 40 is a very frequent round number and designates a rather long period the exact duration of which is not known, but the general idea is that of reaching full maturity, or perhaps more generally, any large number that could be counted but not quickly or easily (cf. the Persian word "forty-footer" meaning a centipede, and see Nm 14.34; 2 Sm 5.4; Mk 1.13). The numbers 60, 80, and 100 are sometimes found as round numbers, but 1,000 is quite frequent and evokes the idea of a large number. However, there is no real proof that it simply means "group" or "clan" and is not a real number. The rhetoric of "Saul has slain his thousands, and David his ten thousands" (1 Sm 18.7) signifies that David slew a fabulously large number (cf. Lv 26.8). In fact, many large numbers that are given as sums may actually be very rough estimates, or exorbitant exaggerations expressive of a hyperbolical intent rather than an exact summation.

Number Symbolism. While usually classed together, a distinction can be made between symbolic and mystic numbers.

Symbolic Numbers. A symbol is something that represents an idea, sacred or otherwise, by convention or because of some association. What is important are the things symbolized, but the symbol is a rallying point that emphasizes a common aspect. The conventional and rhetorical use of numbers readily leads to symbolism through particular association, but it is often difficult to determine just where the transition begins. Moreover, the same number may have different symbolic connotations. The number 1, for example, is associated with God's uniqueness (Dt 6.4; Sir 1.6; Jn 17.11; Rom 3.30). The superlative, 3, denotes that a thing is entirely what it is said to be (e.g., dead for 3 days, i.e., really dead; God thrice holy, i.e., perfectly holy); it is often associated with the perfection of God's being or action (Gn 18.2). The number of cosmic totality, 4 (e.g., the 4 living creatures in Ez 1.5; Ap 4.6), designates comprehensiveness (4 plagues, Ez 14.21; 4 beatitudes, Lk 6.20–22). The number 6 is associated with the creation of man and his personal efforts (6 days to work), a fullness of human action but lacking the final completeness in God. The number 7 traditionally designates a complete series. Although it can designate a full complement of evil (7 devils of St. *Mary Magdalene) as well as of good, it is particularly associated with sacred objects and with cult (week, *Sabbath, feasts, sacrifices, angels, etc.). From such a concept the apocalyptic speculations of Dn 9.2, 24 about the 70 weeks of years (10 jubilees of 7 times 7 years) lead to the *Day of the Lord independently of any real chronology. In general, as a number of perfection (3 plus 4), 7 and its multiples, and even its half (Dn 7.25), occur frequently as symbolic numbers. As a round number of totality, 10 may have some special symbolism, but it is not well defined (10 plagues of Egypt, 10 commandments). Through its association with the temporal cycle, 12 seems to designate cyclic perfection or the perfection of order and gov-

ernment. Whether or not the division of Israel into 12 tribes arose from the monthly assignment of sanctuary care to a particular tribe cannot be ascertained, but 12 as a symbol of the people of God is found throughout the Bible—12 *Apostles, 12 gates of the new Jerusalem, the number of the saved 144,000, i.e., 12,000 for each of the 12 tribes, etc. (Mt 19.28; Ez 48.30–34; Ap 7.4, 8; 21.12–14). The number 40 acquires also a certain symbolism through association with successive periods in salvation history, periods characterized by the struggle with evil from which man is ultimately saved by the power of God (Gn 7.12, 17; Dt 8.2; 9.9; 3 Kgs 19.8; Mt 4.2). The number 1,000 and its multiples, as a very large round number often without any exact numerical sense, may symbolize the perfect age. (*See* MILLENARIANISM.) The fabulous ages of the antediluvian patriarchs, quite modest alongside their Mesopotamian counterparts, probably have some special signification. However, this is scarcely discernible now (even the textual traditions do not agree on the numbers), except in the case of *Henoch, the just man, who lived 365 years, the perfect number of the solar year. Perhaps there is a similar symbolism for the ages of Israel's ancestors, the census in Numbers ch. 1, the 38 years in Jn 5.5, and the 153 (sum of numbers from 1 to 17) fishes in Jn 21.11. Some numbers may be the result of gematria, the designation of a person or thing by the numerical value of the letters of a word. For example, in Matthew's genealogy of Jesus (Mt 1.1–17), where 3 series of 14 ancestors each are given, there may be gematria based on the name of David (in Hebrew *dwd*, i.e., 14), to show that Jesus is eminently Davidic and messianic. The interpretation of the beast's number, 666, in Ap 13.18 as Nero Caesar (written in Aramaic) is commonly accepted but not certain. Given the symbolism of 6, the triple repetition may simply designate the number of the man who refuses to enter into the designs of God and to advance to the perfection of 7.

Mystic Numbers. As distinct from a symbolic, a mystic number may be defined as a number having some hidden signification or even hidden power that only special knowledge, investigation, or supernatural enlightenment can discover and put to use. The Bible never attributes any special power to numbers, even though it recognizes that God "disposed all things by measure and number and weight" (Wis 11.20). Things are not related simply because they have the same number. Number has no special meaning apart from the thing signified. Moreover, the main purpose of inspiration is revelation, not concealment. The allegorical interpretations given to numbers by some of the Fathers of the Church, e.g., St. Augustine, must be considered as done merely by way of fanciful accommodation. While avoiding the excesses of the Pythagoreans (*see* PYTHAGORAS AND PYTHAGOREANS) and the later Cabalists (*see* CABALA), some Fathers and their audiences were fascinated by numbers and their supposed hidden meanings. See BIBLE, VI (EXEGESIS), 2. The Biblical symbolism of numbers, where it really exists, is quite controlled and secondary to the more important intentions of the Biblical authors.

Bibliography: EncDictBibl 1649–53. W. H. BENNETT, Hastings DB (1963) 701–704. O. RÜHL, Kittel ThW 1:461–464; Eng. 1:461–464. N. TURCHI, EncCatt 8:1995–97. J. SAUER, "Zahlensymbolik," LexThK¹ 10:1025–30. X. LEON-DUFOUR, ed., *Vocabu-*

laire du Théologie Biblique (Paris 1962) 687–691. J. BONSIRVEN, *Vocabulaire Biblique* (Paris 1958) 110.

[H. J. SORENSEN]

NUMISMATICS

Coins of fixed weight, stamped with governmental authority and used as money for exchange of value, and also medals, frequently supply dates, depict styles of weapons, clothing, and art forms, indicate attitudes, or testify to the existence of an institution or administrative procedure otherwise not known from written or archeological sources. They thus have value for both religious and secular history. They are important not only for tracing the evolution of the Roman Empire but also for the history of the Church from antiquity to modern times. After a brief survey of the Roman imperial coinage as background, this article discusses chiefly the coins and medals of direct concern to Church history. Hebrew coinage, and Hellenistic coinage that is pertinent, are covered in other articles.

Roman Coinage from Augustus to Constantine. During the Republic, magistrates called the *tres viri auro, argento, aere flando, feriundo* (the three men for minting and striking [coins] of gold, silver, and bronze) controlled the issue of coinage under the authority of the Senate, which was indicated by the stamp S.C. for *Senatus consulto.* The obverse image gradually changed from the goddess Roma and the Dioscuri on horseback to Jupiter, to the figure of Victory, to Juno of Lanuvium in a chariot, etc., and eventually to the personal history and portraits of the magistrates. In 44 B.C. the head of Julius Caesar appeared on silver coins. Augustus permitted the Senate to coin bronze, but in practice he exercised complete control of the mints, and only the portraits of members of the imperial family were authorized. On the reverse side of the coinage political phrases were employed, such as the *signis receptis* of Augustus commemorating the recovery of the standards lost to the Parthians at the battle of Carrhae. Later Vespasian proclaimed his subjection of the Jews with the legend *Iudaea capta.* Further propaganda purposes were served by the portrayal of civic virtues, such as *Abundantia, Concordia, Pudicitia,* and this continued almost to the end of the empire. The imperial coinage regularly records the titles of the emperors and, until the reign of Alexander Severus (d. 235), the current or last consulship of the given *princeps* and his tribunician year.

Thus the life of the Roman state is depicted on its coins: official acts of the *princeps,* his *liberalitas* in the distribution of money and bread, the arrival of the grain fleet at Ostia, the departure on a military expedition against the barbarians, the *adventus* or salute by the troops to the emperor sitting before them on horseback, the circus games and temple sacrifices, public and family religious cults and ceremonial, the association of members of a dynasty or colleagues in the rule of the empire, and the rise and fall of individual emperors. The establishment of the tetrarchy by Diocletian after 293 is depicted on medals, and the coins of Diocletian demonstrate the gradual growth of the Emperor's religiopolitical consciousness of himself as the protégé of Jupiter (*Iovi conservatori Augusti*); and the coins of Maximian show him as a protégé of Hercules. The emperor gradually assumed a *maiestas divina,* as the *comes* or *numen praesens* of the godhead; he pos-

sessed the divine virtues of *pietas* and *felicitas.* This concept was already portrayed on coins that began with Aurelian's *deo et domino nato.* In solving the difficult historical problems concerned with the chronology of the tetrarchy and the reasons for its dissolution, coins play an essential part.

Constantine and Christian Coinage. In 306 *Constantine I is depicted on the imperial coinage as still a protégé of Hercules in the divinely ordered Diocletian tetrarchy; but in the official speech delivered at Constantine's wedding to Fausta, the daughter of Maximian (spring 307), the latter is compared to the sun god (*Sol invictus*) rather than to the Jupiter of the tetrarchy's political theology. After 310, with the death of Maximian, Constantine's coinage no longer portrays Hercules; instead, *Mars conservator* is depicted as the protective deity accompanying the *Sol invictus.* This is a return to the tradition of Aurelian and Gallienus. Stress is placed too, on the legitimacy of Constantine's rule, which can be traced to his lineage as the son of Constantius Chlorus. Subsequent coinage indicates the steps whereby Constantine gradually achieved full control of the empire, the year 312 being the turning point in both his religious and political thinking.

Silver coins minted at Treves (312–313) portray Constantine as *Victor,* crowned with an ornamented helmet at whose peak is the Christian monogram ☧; and a similar portrait appears on a silver medallion at Ticinum (315) and on coins issued at Siscia (317–318). Coins in 320 carry the Vexillum with the *Monogram of Christ; in 326 the Christian *Labarum appears with the legend *Spes publica.* However, as the empire was still pagan, Constantine did not interfere with the ordinary representations of the civic cult or the pagan portraiture of the emperor, and it took a century before all signs of pagan cult disappeared from the imperial coinage. Under Constantius II, Victory is depicted on a coin in the form of an angel crowning the Emperor, who holds the standard of the cross. The legend reads: *Hoc signo victor eris.* During this period the Christian monogram appears frequently and is often accompanied by the alpha and omega. After a temporary revival of pagan types under Julian the Apostate, Christian-oriented coins predominate.

Byzantine and Medieval Coins. A medallion in gold commemorates the founding of Constantinople in 330 with the turreted statues of the two capitals, Rome and Constantinople, as the subject of equal veneration. After the death of Theodosius I (395) the gradual partition of the empire under Honorius (395–425) and Arcadius (395–408) is pictured on the coinage current at the time of the birth of Byzantium. Byzantine money as such begins under the Emperor *Anastasius I (491–518) with a new copper coinage and also a gold coin modeled on the solidus of Constantine, eventually called the bezant. It was divided into a half (the semissis) and a third (the tremissis). The main silver coin was the miliarensis, along with a small coin, the siliqua or *keration.*

Under Heraclius (610–641) the double miliarensis was first issued. Gradually the effigy of the emperor on the obverse of these coins was changed to that of the basileus in a majestic setting and clothed in hieratic vestments. Christ appears first on the reverse of a coin of A.D. 451, where He is depicted as assisting in the marriage of Marcian and Pulcheria. His next appear-

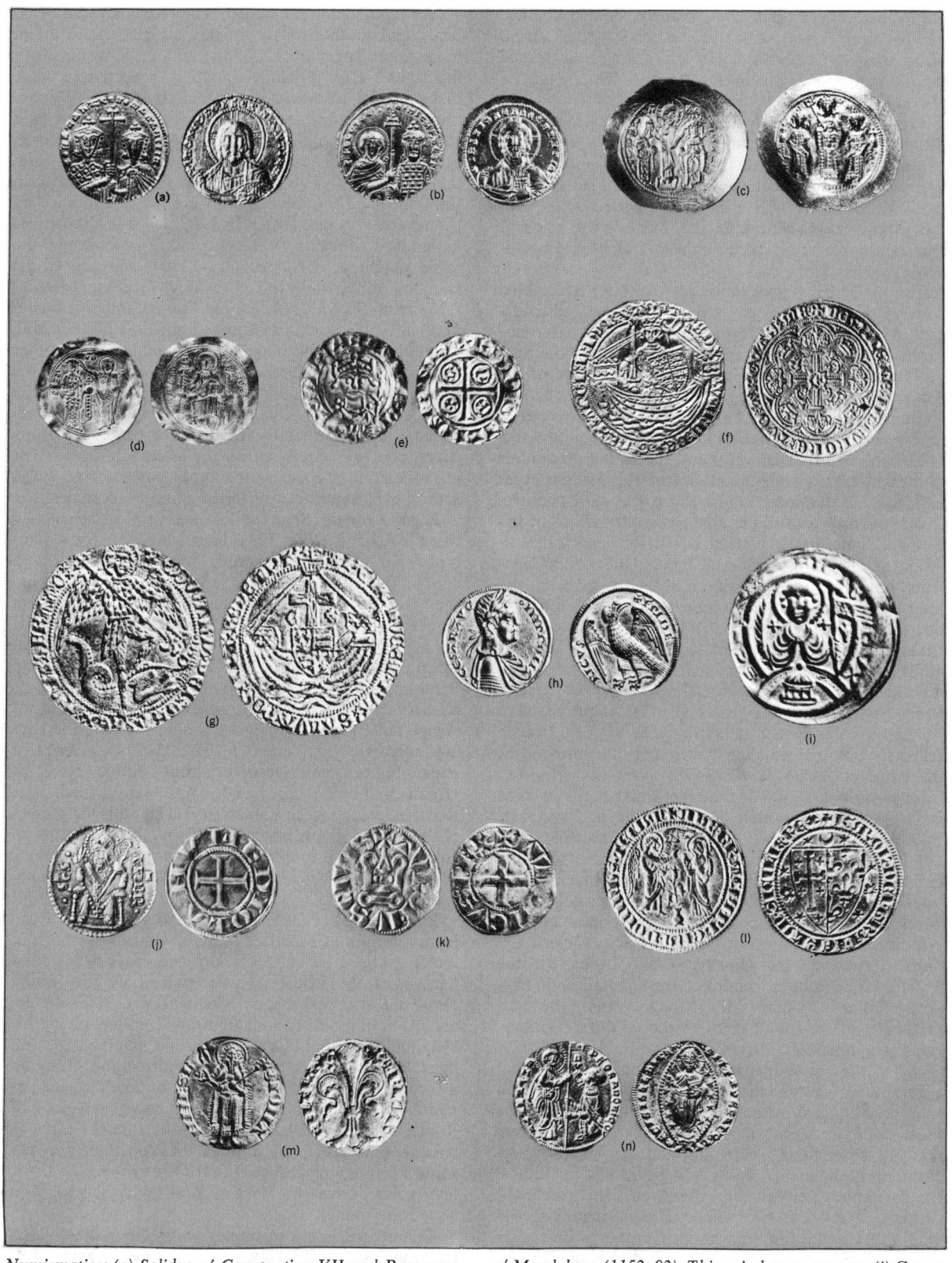

Numismatics: (a) Solidus of Constantine VII and Romanus II (945–959). (b) Nomisma of Nicephorus II (963–969). (c) Nomisma of Romanus IV (1067–71). (d) Nomisma of John II Comnenus (1118–43). (e) Pax of William I (1066–87). (f) Half Noble of Edward III (1327–77). (g) Angel of Edward IV (1461–83). (h) Augustalis of Frederick II, Brindisi (c. 1231). (i) Bracteate or "Moritzpfennig" of the Archdiocese of Magdeburg (1152–92). This coin has no reverse. (j) Groat or "Ambrosino" of Milan, First Republic (1250–1310). (k) Denier Tournois of Louis IX (1226–70). (l) Saluto d'oro of Charles of Anjou (1266–78). (m) Florin d'oro of Florence (1313). (n) Zecchino of Doge Pietro Gradenigo of Venice (1289–1311). All coins are reproduced here at approximately their actual sizes.

ance, however, is much later, namely, on the coinage of Justinian II (685–695). From *c.* 900 the Virgin Mary, and eventually the saints, appear on coins, despite the difficulties over *iconoclasm, whose history can be traced to the coinage of the period.

From the 10th century the Byzantine emperor is usually depicted in the company of a sacred personage; this is particularly true of the cup-shaped *solidi* called the *nummi scyphati,* which appear in the 11th century. In 1261 *Michael VIII Palaeologus issued coins with the Virgin Mary standing in the midst of the walls of Constantinople after its reconquest from the Crusaders.

The principal inscriptions on the later Byzantine coinage refer to the emperor on the obverse and to the city of minting on the reverse, along with a reference to the saint depicted and often a prayer. From the time of *Justinian I profiles give way to the full face of the emperor, and the language of the inscriptions changes from Latin to Latin and Greek under Heraclius and to Greek alone under *Alexius I Comnenus.

Coinage of the Medieval West. The Byzantine solidus or bezant had a widespread use in the Middle Ages and was the dominant gold coin to the 13th century. The Merovingians still imitated the golden triens of the Romans, but Charlemagne struck silver denarii in imitation of the Roman imperial types. Under the Capetians, however, the Byzantine influence is marked; the king is represented as a basileus, seated beneath a canopy, or standing with scepter in hand, or on horseback, or as a knight in battle. The legends have both a religious and a political significance: *Christus vincit, Christus regnat, Christus imperat;* or *Karolus Dei gratia Francorum rex.* Under Henry II of England the *Ave Maria* on coins issued in his name as king of France reflects a political situation that lasted until the end of the Hundred Years' War.

The Arabs first adopted current Persian silver coins in the Orient; Byzantine copper coins in Syria and Palestine; and in Africa, the current gold coinage. Byzantine influence predominates in the Caliphite mints begun at Bashran (A.D. 660) and in the regular coinage established by Abdalmik (A.D. 695), having a gold dinar, silver dirhem, and a copper fels. The inscriptions are in Arabic and are uniformly religious. The various dynasties, such as the Omayyads and Abbasids, the Fatamids and Seljuks, continued the adaptation of Byzantine coinage, whereas the Mongols and Ottomans gradually adapted their coins to those of the Mediterranean commercial powers.

With the development of feudalism, individual suzerains as well as cities and monastic centers issued their own coinage. Although the golden solidus was the ideal coin, its large value gave way before a silver coinage under the Carolingians, and for general usage the denarius or penny of some 24 grains became almost the sole coin in circulation. The Arab silver piece, the dirhem, was worth two denier or denarii and spread with the Carolingian coinage to Germany, Italy, England, Scandinavia, Castile, and Aragon. A continuous depreciation in the value of coinage, which Gresham's (1519–79) law of bad money driving out good money would later explain, brought the denarius so low by the 12th century that it was issued in Germany as a bracteate, stamped on only one side.

Normans and Venetians. The Norman dukes in Sicily and southern Italy quickly adopted the Moslem money, but Roger II (1130–54) struck Latin coins with the legend *Dux Apuliae,* and they accordingly came to be known as ducats. Frederick II (1215–50) continued the Arab coinage but also struck Roman gold solidi and half solidi showing his bust on the obverse, as the Emperor Augustus, and the imperial eagle on the reverse side. The famous gold florin with St. John the Baptist on the obverse and the lily of Florence on the reverse was first struck in 1252 and quickly became a standard of value. Venice struck gold coins of the same weight as the florin (*c.* 1280), showing Christ standing on the obverse and the doge receiving the gonfalon from St. Mark on the reverse. Although it was at first called the ducat, it became known as the zecchino or sequin. This coinage, which was imitated by the other maritime and commercial Italian city-states, caused the Mameluke sultans of Egypt to employ the weight of the florin and sequin for their gold money in commerce between Europe and India. In the 14th century a heavy silver coin appeared called the *denarius grossus,* or groat, and in its successive types can be traced the artistic evolution that was leading into the Renaissance.

Papal Coinage. The popes began to strike money when Adrian I (772–795) issued a gold Beneventan-type coin on which a crude hieratic human figure adorns the obverse, and a cross with an inscription, the reverse. The names of the popes and the Western emperors are associated on papal coins from Leo III (795–816) to Leo IX (1049) in monogrammatic inscriptions. Under John VIII (872–882) the bust of St. Peter appears; it is crowned with a conic miter in coins of Sergius III (904–911), whereas on the coins of Agapetus II (946–955) Peter is depicted with the keys and a cross. With Benedict VI (973–974) a series of papal effigies began. However, from Leo IX (1049) to Urban V (1362) no papal coins were issued. The Roman Senate struck coins after 1188 with the effigies of Peter and Paul crowned with nimbi on ducats of gold and with inscriptions, such as *S. Petrus Senator Mundi, Roma Caput Mundi,* and SPQR (*Senatus Populusque Romanus*).

Boniface VIII (1295–1303) issued a large silver coin from the mint at Ponte della Sorga bearing his portrait under a miter; he carries a key and cross in his right hand, and the whole is accompanied by the legend *Domini Bo(nifaci) Papae.* Clement V (1305–14) depicted the pope in frontal figure with miter, giving his blessing, and John XXII (1316–34) stamped the full figure of the pope on the obverse, mitred and sitting on a throne. Charles of Anjou (King of the Two Sicilies 1266–85), struck gold ducats when he was governor of Rome, and Cola di Rienzi (1347–48) did the same as tribune. Charles's coins imitate the Venetian type and show Peter giving the gonfalon to a kneeling senator; later coins portray the coat of arms of the senator who issued the money.

Some papal issues of money were struck at Avignon between 1342 and 1700, and there were papal mints at Ancona, Bologna, Piacenza, Parma, and Ferrara. On his return to Rome, Urban V (1362–70) claimed the sole right to issue papal money; and from Martin V to Pius IX there was a continuous papal coinage on which the effigy of the popes appears in realistic and

Numismatics: (a) Joachimstaler of the counts of Schlick of Bohemia (1516–26). (b) Large Scudo of the Republic of Genoa (1652). Both coins are reproduced here at approximately their actual sizes.

often highly artistic style. Callistus III (1455–58) struck ducats of gold and an issue of silver *grossi denarii* exhibiting the bark of Peter (or *navicella*) with full rigging surmounted by a cross and the legend *Modice fidei quare dubitetis.* Julius II (1503–13) put both Peter and Paul on the ship with a blown sail and the legend *Non prevalebunt.* This type was continued under later popes. Papal coins were struck also with Biblical scenes, representing Christ, the crib, the ark of Noa, etc., or to commemorate the architectural accomplishments of Renaissance and later popes.

Renaissance and Modern Period. With the issue of the thaler or dollar in Germany in 1518, silver money was widely used all over Europe, but it did not displace the denier since it was issued in various weights and purity by different countries. The ability to represent nature, the human portrait, and other objects had reached the zenith of accomplishment in Renaissance medallions, and the artistic style of medals influenced that of coinage. However, the requirements of rapidly expanding trade soon made the production of coins a commercial interest, and art was all but forgotten. In general trade the denier was the coin of exchange, while the solidus or German shilling was used as a

gauge for money of account, and the system of librae (L), solidi (s), and denarii (d), was adopted; the pound was divided into 12 shillings and 20 pence to the shilling.

French and English Coinage. In France during the Middle Ages the common coin was the denier of the Abbey of St. Martin of Tours (*denier tournois*), while the royal coinage was known as *monnaie parisis.* St. Louis IX (1226–70) introduced the gold sou and the *gros tournois,* and thus began an important reform in the French monetary system. Fourteenth-century French coinage had considerable artistic merit, and French medallions produced during the Renaissance and the Napoleonic period exhibit the same high artistic quality.

Following the example of Pepin, Offa of Mercia (757–796) introduced the silver penny into England. Some types have the king's head or a religious symbol on the obverse and an ornament and inscription on the reverse. This coinage was imitated in the several English kingdoms and prevailed down to the late 10th century. Edward III in 1343 introduced a gold coinage that included the florin and the noble showing the picture of a rose. Edward IV (1461–70) struck a new gold coin, the angel. Henry VII brought in sovereigns worth 20 shillings and the shilling itself; his coins show a marked advance in portraiture.

Several attempts were made to introduce a copper coinage to replace the private tokens in wide, local circulation, but it was only in 1613 that John Harrington obtained a patent to produce copper farthings. The gold sovereign of James I was called a unite from the legend *Faciam eos in gentem unam.* Owing to the scarcity of gold during the civil wars, 20- and 10-shilling silver pieces were issued; but the Oxford mint put out 3-pound pieces, on one of which John Rawlins depicted the king on horseback looking over the town, and on the reverse, the heads of the "Oxford Declaration." In 1672 a true copper coinage of halfpence and farthings was introduced.

Italian and German Coinage. In Sicily and southern Italy the Normans first adopted the Arabic currency; but gradually Robert Guiscard (Duke of Apulia) and Roger I and Roger II of Sicily introduced also gold and silver coins modeled on Latin usage, while the Emperor Frederick II issued the first gold ducats or augustals. Charles of Anjou's gold coinage, already mentioned, quickly spread through the Levant. With Ferdinand I of Aragon the coinage of the Two Sicilies began to display the artistic portraiture that was characteristic of the Italian city-states all during the Renaissance.

In Germany, after Louis IV of Bavaria (1314–47), local coinage in the Low Countries, along the Moselle, and in the Rhinelands and Bavaria predominated over the imperial coinage. The introduction of the groat and the florin late in the 14th century began the modern period. From the 16th century, the thaler—first produced by the Counts of Schlick, in St. Joachimsthal in Bohemia, in 1518—became the dominant silver coin. The counts Palatine, who began coining in 1294, had mints at Heidelberg and Frankfurt. The margraves of Brandenburg minted coins in the late Middle Ages also, continuing the practice after 1701 as the kings of Prussia.

An abundance of gold in the 15th and 16th centuries is evident from the coins of Hungary and Transylvania. Early Polish coinage reflects direct English, German, and Byzantine influence, while the emerging Scandinavian states adopted the Anglo-Saxon types, using the runic alphabet for legends. During the late Middle Ages these lands drew upon the common European inheritance. In the Balkan states, both Byzantine and Venetian influences were predominant, as they employed images and legends that are entirely Christian. In Russia the Byzantine coinage held sway until Peter the Great modernized the currency. Ecclesiastical city-states, such as Cologne, Münster, Treves, Augsburg, Salzburg, and Mainz, issued their own coinage between the 11th and 18th century, as did other independent cities.

Contemporary coinage, while generally reflecting the standards of modern minting skills, suggests the vagaries of political fortunes in the various nations of the world. Moreover, it is dominated by the practical demands of trade and commerce, artistic considerations playing a secondary role. Modern metal coinage has become largely token currency, paper money takes the place of the earlier gold and silver coinages.

Numismatic Study. Collections of coins and medals are known to have existed in antiquity. On the occasion of celebrations, the Emperor Augustus gave rare or valuable coins to his entourage; and the bronze medals issued by the Antonine emperors trace the legendary history of Rome on their reverse; festive gold medals of Constantine Chlorus struck in 302 were discovered in Arras in 1922.

During the Middle Ages a number of medals were issued in commemoration of special events, such as the expulsion of the English from France at the close of the Hundred Years' War, and were distributed as gifts among the civil and ecclesiastical nobility. The main collections of coins and medals were inaugurated by the monasteries, most of which had a treasury for coins connected with the copyrooms and libraries. These monastic collections, seized by modern European governments after the French Revolution, became the foundation of many numismatic displays in public museums.

Petrarch and his circle of savants were among the first to recognize the value of coins for the interpretation and illustration of literary sources. With Cola di Rienzi, Petrarch turned to the study of numismatic evidence in an attempt to resurrect the customs of the ancient Roman republic and suggested that every library be equipped with an archive of numismatic specimens. This suggestion was honored by amateur savants and princes as well as by emerging commercial houses, such as the Fuggers, and by ecclesiastical nobles from prince-bishops to cardinals and popes. In 1553 Guillaume Rouille published a *Promptuarium,* which contained engravings of the Roman emperors obtained from coins and medals; and in 1570 Fulvio Orsini, the protégé of Pope Gregory XIII (1572–85), issued his *Imagines et elogia virorum illustrium et eruditorum.* His predecessors had been interested mainly in the iconography of the Roman rulers, but he extended his study to include a view of the past in all its achievements.

The treatise *De asse et partibus eius* by the great French classical scholar Guillaume Budé (1468–1540) was the first really systematic study on Roman coinage. Despite the increasing interest in coins and medals, the science of numismatics was founded only at the end of the 18th century by the Jesuit J. H. von *Eckhel (1737–98). Since that time the study of coins and medals has been pursued systematically and scientifically throughout the world. Owing to the progress of archeology, furthermore, large numbers of coins and medals not hitherto known are constantly being added to the earlier collections.

Bibliography: P. GRIERSON, *Coins and Medals: A Select Bibliography* (London 1954). J. BABELON, "Numismatique," *L'Histoire et ses méthodes,* ed. C. SAMARAN (Paris 1961) 329–392. H. HOCHENEGG, LexThK² 7:1069–70. G. LANCZKOWSKI and W. JESSE, RGG³ 4:1184–87. R. S. POOLE et al., EncBrit, 11th ed. (1911) 19:869–911. J. ECKHEL, *Doctrina numorum veterum,* 8 v. (Vienna 1792–98), v.9, *Addenda* (Leipzig 1826). J. MAURICE, *Numismatique constantinienne,* 3 v. (Paris 1908–12). P. GARDNER, *A History of Ancient Coinage* (Oxford 1918). C. SUTHERLAND, *Art in Coinage* (London 1955). H. MATTINGLY, *Roman Coins from the Earliest Times to the Fall of the Western Empire* (London 1928; rev. ed. 1960). W. WROTH, *Catalogue of the Imperial Byzantine Coins in the British Museum,* 2 v. (London 1908). B. LAUM, *Über das Wesen des Münzgeldes* (Halle 1930). C. T. SELTMAN, *Greek Coins* (2d ed. London 1955). R. SEDILLOT, *Toutes les monnaies du monde* (Paris 1954). E. BERNAREGGI, *Monete d'oro con ritratto del rinascimento italiano* (Milan 1954). M. BLOCH, *Esquisse d'une histoire monétaire de l'Europe* (Paris 1954). S. L. CESANO, EncCatt 8:1997–2004; 2004–19, papal coinage. C. SERAFINI, in B. APOLLONI-GHETTI et al., eds., *Esplorazioni sotto la confessione di San Pietro in Vaticano*, 2 v. (Vatican City 1951), numismatic appendix. **Illustration credits:** Division of Numismatics, Smithsonian Institution, Washington, D.C.

[F. X. MURPHY]

NUN, a term commonly used to designate any professed religious woman. However, correct legal usage in the Latin Church limits its signification to a religious woman professed of solemn vows or of simple *vows, temporary or perpetual, in a monastery in which solemn vows are actually or should be taken; and in which at least the minor papal cloister is observed (CIC c.488n7; *Sponsa Christi* 1.1, ActApS 43:5; Instruction Cong. Rel. March 25, 1956, n4, ActApS 48:512). Among the Orientals the term is used to designate a professed religious woman who lives according to the ancient Oriental tradition (PostApost c.313.3). By way of apostolic privilege, there are certain communities of women that, although organized as a *congregation, enjoy the title of nun, for example, the congregation of Ursulines of the Roman Union.

The life of the nun is primarily one of contemplation and mortification, and in almost all monasteries there is a distinction made between the choir sisters and the lay sisters. Although both may be professed of solemn vows only the choir nuns are bound to the choral recitation of the *Divine Office, and following their solemn profession they are obliged as well to the private recitation outside of choir (CIC c.610.3). Similar norms regarding the Divine Office govern the nuns of the Oriental Church (PostApost c.157).

Bibliography: Bousc-O'Connor 3:221–248. L. G. FANFANI and K. D. O'ROURKE, *Canon Law for Religious Women* (Dubuque 1961).

[W. B. RYAN]

NUNC DIMITTIS (CANTICLE OF SIMEON), title (in Latin) of the short hymn sung by Simeon on the occasion of the presentation of Jesus in the Temple (Lk 2.29–32). Enlightened by the Holy Spirit, Simeon recognizes in the Infant presented by Mary the long-awaited "Christ of the Lord," that is, the Messiah sent by God (v.26). The Holy Infant is the embodiment of God's salvation; this salvation is universal, that is, destined for all: "prepared before the face of all peoples," Gentiles as well as Jews (v.31; cf. Is 49.6; 60.3). For the former, salvation is described as a light (cf. Is 42.6), which dispels the night of ignorance and error, a light that is revelation of divine truth (v.32). For the Jews ("thy people Israel") the Savior is "glory" (v.32), in that He is from "the Israelites . . . according to the flesh" (Rom 9.5), and brings salvation "to Jew first and then to Greek [Gentile]" (Rom 1.16).

The liturgical use of the *Nunc dimittis* is remarkably appropriate at daily Compline, the official nightprayer of the Church. In the evening of his life, Simeon has at last seen, according to the express promise made him (v.26, 29), "the consolation of Israel," the object of his ardent longing. The salvation of his people is now assured; therefore he can say, "*Nunc dimittis* . . . Now thou dost dismiss . . . ." Serenely Simeon looks forward to a peaceful death whenever it shall please the Lord to "dismiss [him] in peace"; having seen the Christ, he is fully prepared to see death. In like man-

Miniature illustrating the "Nunc dimittis" in the St. Alban Psalter, a 12th-century English manuscript in the treasury of the cathedral at Hildesheim, Germany.

ner, as the Christian prepares to sleep in peace at the end of the day, he repeats the pious Jew's words to express his loving trust in his Savior, looking beyond to his own final dismissal in peace.

See also CANTICLES, BIBLICAL.

Bibliography: U. HOLZMEISTER, "Canticum *Nunc dimittis*," VerbDom 26 (1948) 363–364. **Illustration credit:** Warburg Institute, London.

[A. LE HOULLIER]

NUNES, PEDRO, Portuguese mathematician of Jewish origin (known also as Nunez, Nonius); b. Alcacer do Sol, 1502; d. Coimbra, Aug. 11, 1578. He studied languages, philosophy, and medicine at the University of Lisbon, and shortly after receiving his bachelor's degree, he occupied the chairs of moral philosophy (1529), logic (1530), and metaphysics (1531) at the same institution. He pursued his mathematical studies at the Universities of Lisbon and Salamanca, and from 1544 to 1562 was professor of mathematical sciences at the University of Coimbra. Under the patronage of Don João III, he held the posts of royal cosmographer and tutor to the royal princes. Nearly all his published works were in the fields of cosmography and navigation. Chief among these were the *Tratado da Esphera* (1537); *De Crepusculis* (1542), in which is described the nonius, an instrument for measuring small angles; and *De Arte atque Ratione Navigandi Libri Duo*

(1546), wherein is analyzed the curve known as the loxodrome. His only mathematical work, *Libro de Algebra en Arithmetica y Geometria* (1567), was the most clearly written work of his time on these subjects. An edition of his works was published by the Portuguese Academy of Sciences (Lisbon 1940–60).

Bibliography: *Obras* (rev. ed. Lisbon 1940–   ). R. GUIMARÃES, "Sur la vie et l'oeuvre de Pedro Nunes," *Annaes Scientificos da Academia Polytechnica do Porto* 9 (1914) 54–64, 96–117, 152–167, 210–227; 10 (1915) 20–36. D. E. SMITH, *History of Mathematics.* 2 v. (New York 1958). F. CAJORI, *History of Mathematics* (2d ed. rev. New York 1919).

[M. S. M. VAN RYZIN]

NUNES BARRETO, JOÃO, patriarch of Abyssinia; b. Porto, Portugal, date unknown; d. Goa, India, Dec. 22, 1562. He entered the Society of Jesus as a priest in 1544 and was sent to Morocco, where he labored to redeem and care for Christian slaves. Ten years later he was called to Rome: and at the counsel of St. Ignatius Loyola and King John III of Portugal, he was named patriarch of Abyssinia by Paul IV. With Melchior Carneiro and Andrew Oviedo, chosen to be his coadjutors, he traveled to Lisbon in 1555 and after their consecration there sailed for Goa. King John, like his predecessors, dreamed of establishing communications with the descendants of *Prester John, medieval Christian monarch in Asia whose legend began in the 12th century. He also wished a firm alliance against the Moslems. Nunes sent Bishop Oviedo to win the favor of Negus (Emperor) Claudius (Calāwēdōs) of Abyssinia, but after much hardship the mission was not fruitful. In 1557 Pedro Paez, SJ, converted Negus Susenyos, but by 1633 the Jesuits were expelled through the suspicions of Negus Fasilidas.

Bibliography: Sommervogel 5:1840–41. E. CERULLI, LexThK² 7:1070. P. TACCHI VENTURI, *Storia della Compagnia di Gesù* (2d ed. Rome 1950–   ) 2.2:559–565. C. TESTORE, EncCatt 8:2020. Koch JesLex 1316. S. DELACROIX, ed., *Histoire universelle des missions catholiques,* 4 v. (Paris 1956–59) 1:230–231. Streit-Dindinger v.15.

[E. D. MCSHANE]

NUNRAW, ABBEY OF, to date the only Cistercian monastery built in Scotland since the Reformation. It was founded in 1946 as a daughterhouse of *Roscrea (Ireland) at Haddington, East Lothian, near Edinburgh, and made an abbey in 1948. The site originally belonged to a Cistercian convent (founded 1152–58), which passed into private hands on the death of the last prioress (1563). In 1964 Nunraw had 29 priests, 19 brothers, and several students and novices.

Bibliography: M. SHERRY, *Nunraw* (Edinburgh 1963). *Royal Commission of Ancient and Historical Monuments of Scotland: County of East Lothian* (Edinburgh 1924) xxix, xliv, xlvi, 45. W. F. GRAY and J. H. JAMIESON, *A Short History of Haddington* (Edinburgh 1944) 9, 22, 29–30, 41, 83, 121, 146. *Transactions of the East Lothian Antiquarian Society* 5 (1952) 2–24; 6 (1953) 1–5. *The Catholic Directory for the Clergy and Laity of Scotland, 1964* (Glasgow 1964) 75.

[L. MACFARLANE]

NUREMBERG, city of 460,000 on the Pegnitz River in Bavaria, southeast Germany; in the Archdiocese of *Bamberg. Its importance derives from its position between the Rhine and Danube Valleys; with *Augsburg it was a major medieval center for trade between north Germany and the Levant.

The 16th-century bronze shrine of St. Sebald, by Peter Vischer, in the church of St. Sebald, Nuremberg.

First mentioned in 1050, it received the fair privileges of nearby Fürth (1062) and became a free imperial city (1219–1806). St. Sebald Church (completed in 1379) and St. Lorenz Church (1477), on opposite sides of the Pegnitz, became parishes *c.* 1300; the church of Our Lady, the oldest hall church in Franconia (1355–61), was built on the site of a synagogue. In the Middle Ages the city contained many cloisters, the earliest being the Scottish abbey (*c.* 1140), and the latest the Charterhouse (1380). In 1425 the hermit missionary St. Sebald, patron of Nuremberg, was canonized; he came to Nuremberg *c.* 1000 (in the 8th century according to a 14th-century tradition), and miracles were reported at his tomb as early as 1072. Albrecht *Dürer was but one of Nuremburg's famous artists and craftsmen. Hartmann *Schedel was a noted humanist. The town council had secured from Rome considerable ecclesiastical freedom of the bishop of Bamberg before Nuremberg accepted Lutheranism (1525), which was popularized by the Meistersinger Hans Sachs.

The opening of new routes to the Indies, the development of state economic policies, and the Thirty Years' War caused Nuremberg's decline. When it was incorporated into Bavaria in 1806, its population was 25,200, and it had a large debt. The first Catholic parish was restored in 1810; since 1649 the Teutonic Knights have been allowed the use of St. Elisabeth Church. Catholics, whose religious freedom and rights of citizenship were restored, numbered 1,010 in 1810; in 1905 there were 87,000 Catholics in a population of 291,000. Bombing of the industrialized city during World War II destroyed its picturesque medieval center.

After the war Nuremberg was the scene of the trial and execution of Nazis accused of war crimes (1945–46).

Bibliography: R. Schaffer, *Andreas Stoss, Sohn des Veit Stoss, und seine gegenreformatorische Tätigkeit* (Breslau 1926). H. Gürsching, *Die Unionspolitik der Reichsstadt Nürnberg* (Munich 1932). W. Haas, *Die Geschichte der Entstehung der katholischen Kirchengemeinde in der ehemaligen freien Reichsstadt Nürnberg* (Würzburg 1934). *Mitteilungen des Vereins für Geschichte der Stadt Nürnberg* (1879–). J. Kist, LexThK² 7:1073–74. **Illustration credit:** Marburg-Art Reference Bureau.

[E. P. COLBERT]

NURSES, MORAL OBLIGATIONS OF

Usage in the U.S. gives many and confusing meanings to the term nurse. Here it is taken to signify a man or woman trained to care for sick, injured, or infirm persons receiving active medical care, generally under the supervision of a physician.

Nurses are subject to all the moral obligations incumbent upon human beings generally and, in addition to these, are under obligations peculiar to themselves by reason of their professional commitment. Moreover, their work is such that they are confronted with certain types of moral situations more commonly than are people in other walks of life.

Many of the nurse's obligations involve natural rights, such as those to life, property, truth, and reputation. Others of a contractual nature arise between the nurse on the one hand and the patient, the physician, or the hospital on the other. Sometimes the agreement is explicit and binds both parties to its provisions. Even when there is no formal and explicit understanding, obligations may exist by reason of an implicit, bilateral, conditioned contract: implicit, because it exists in virtue of the nurse's profession and acceptance of a case; bilateral, because the nurse and the patient or those acting for the patient confer on each other certain rights and duties; conditioned, because of its relativity to acceptable standards in a given time and place.

Patients have the right to expect, and the nurse has the obligation to use, such knowledge, skill, attention, and diligence as patients' care reasonably and ordinarily requires. Unless there is a stated condition to the contrary, nurses are not bound to extraordinary measures or committed to unreasonable self-sacrifice. Although a nurse is not obligated to accept any case, once she accepts it, she may not leave the patient as long as leaving might cause harm to him.

Nurses, like other employees, have a right to due compensation and suitable working conditions and can use legitimate means to get them—such as collective bargaining with a hospital. May they go further and *strike? Many hold that such action is unprofessional. But nurses, at least in theory, apparently have the right to invoke this extreme tactic as a last resort, although it may be exercised only if their cause is just and the strike is so organized that it does not jeopardize their patients.

Obligation to the Patient. By reason of their relationship to the patient, nurses are bound in strictest justice to respect his property and private business. Carelessness, waste, and voluntary damage are certainly violations of his property rights. So too are his rights violated—and possibly his family's—when a nurse unjustifiably reveals information acquired in the line of duty. That something thus revealed is true does not excuse *detraction.

Patients have a right also to expect a professional nurse to know whether a physician has made a serious mistake in his orders. When it appears that he has, the nurse must refuse cooperation until the doubt has been resolved. Here *probabilism is not applicable. A more delicate situation arises when the physician is clearly guilty of dangerous malpractice. Even though the nurse's first duty in justice is to the patient, the situation must be carefully considered. Simply to leave the case might be a disservice to the patient, and to charge the physician could get the nurse into serious professional and legal trouble. Since silence would be unjust, the nurse can discreetly suggest the advisability of bringing in a consultant.

The obligations to tell the truth, to avoid lying, and to respect confidential information fall upon everyone, but nurses are charged with a special responsibility in these matters. Indiscriminate truthtelling can be cruelly unjust, uncharitable, and as evil as lying or violating confidences. Unless there are valid reasons to the contrary, the nurse should communicate simply and forthrightly. But when telling a patient the truth might be injurious, an alternative other than *lying must be found. Lying is intrinsically evil and never justified. But intentional falsification, or lying, is different from not telling the truth. Sometimes silence or evasion is the solution. Equivocation and *mental reservation may also be used to maintain secrecy and avoid lying, yet the use of such means is moral only when there is grave reason for concealment, and when the speaker intends not to deceive but to fulfill the obligation of secrecy. Professional secrecy does not bind nurses under all circumstances to withhold confidential information. There can, in fact, be an obligation to reveal it. If the nurse has knowledge, for example, that would help the physician in diagnosing or treating his patient, the nurse must share it with him. Similarly the nurse's own good, or the good of a third party, or the good of society can affect the duty respecting confidences.

By justice and charity the nurse is committed to the patient's total welfare. This means nurturing the health not only of his body but also of his soul. Nurses by their example and advice should do what they can for the spiritual good of the patient, and encourage him to turn to God with faith, love, confidence, and contrition. If the patient is Catholic and seriously ill, the nurse is gravely obligated to take reasonable steps to see that he receives the Sacraments of the sick. This responsibility remains even if those closer to him fail in their duty. There is a similar obligation to have newborn babies baptized when they seem in danger of dying or when there is some possibility that an apparently dead infant may be still alive. Nurses should be alert to the need of ensuring Baptism for any product of human conception as long as it appears living or is not certainly dead. In emergencies, since nurses themselves may have to administer Baptism, they should know when this is lawful and obligatory, how to perform it, and what to do afterward.

When a patient dies, nurses are morally obliged, by implicit contract as well as in charity, to perform the last tokens of service, to dispose of important details, and to do what enlightened sympathy can do to comfort and support the bereaved. It is not the business of the nurse to certify the fact of death but to know what should be done, how to do it, and to do it. Death usually creates a wake of shock, confusion, sorrow, and perhaps rebellion. Nurses, like doctors, must guard against letting familiarity with death make them callous. Their whole demeanor should show reverence and regard for human grief.

Cooperation. Nurses may serve as assistants to the surgeon or physician, but this does not eliminate personal moral responsibility. The plea of obeying orders does not excuse a nurse who either does not have or does not use such knowledge as could rightly be expected. Morally and legally the nurse is not an automaton but, as well as the doctor, is involved in the patient's welfare, and cannot escape the obligation of doing what is right. The nurse sometimes may face the prospect of participating in an immoral procedure (*see* ABORTION; STERILIZATION; ARTIFICIAL INSEMINATION; EUTHANASIA). If cooperation can be avoided, the nurse is bound to abstain. But if, for valid reasons, this cannot be done, cooperation may be lawful if the essential conditions are fulfilled. (*See* SIN, COOPERATION IN; DOUBLE EFFECT, PRINCIPLE OF.)

Obligation to the Physician. Nurses have obligations also to the physician. No more than anyone else may they lie or make unjust revelations injurious to another's good name. The nurse has no duty to inform the public about the relative merits or demerits of physicians. Unless there be good reason to the contrary, nurses should carry out the physician's orders without dispute or argument and, not only in justice to the physician but also because of the patient, avoid adverse criticism. His confidence or lack of it in his doctor can importantly affect his recovery. The nurse is likewise obliged to refrain from usurping the physician's right of diagnosis, from prescribing medicine and therapy, and from changing his orders or discontinuing treatments without his consent. In justice to both physician and patient nurses are bound to be scrupulously honest in their reports and charts.

Bibliography: C. J. MCFADDEN, *Medical Ethics* (5th ed. Philadelphia 1961). J. P. KENNY, *Principles of Medical Ethics* (2d ed. Westminster, Md. 1962). G. A. KELLY, *Medico-Moral Problems* (St. Louis 1958). T. J. O'DONNELL, *Morals in Medicine* (2d ed. Westminster, Md. 1959). J. B. MCALLISTER, *Ethics, with Special Application to the Medical and Nursing Professions* (2d ed. Philadelphia 1955). P. FLOOD, ed., *New Problems in Medical Ethics* (Westminster, Md. 1953–), 4 v. to date. G. HARRISON, *The Nurse and the Law* (2d ed. Philadelphia 1948). C. M. FRANK, *Foundation of Nursing* (2d ed. Philadelphia 1959).

[J. B. MC ALLISTER]

NURSING, CATHOLIC SCHOOLS OF

Educational units approved by state boards of nursing to offer a program in nursing leading to a diploma, associate degree or baccalaureate degree and eligibility to take state examination for licensure as a registered nurse (R.N.). Such educational units may exist in institutions of higher learning within the hospital organization or as independent institutions.

Origin. The first Catholic school of nursing in North America was apparently St. John's Hospital Training School, Springfield, Ill., established in 1886 to prepare Hospital Sisters of St. Francis for nursing. Lay students have been admitted since 1912. In 1889 schools were established at Mercy Hospital, Chicago, Ill., Sisters of Charity Hospital, of Buffalo, N.Y.; and St. Mary's Hospital, Brooklyn, N.Y., a diocesan institution. In the 1890s Catholic hospitals in the U.S. established 54 additional schools of nursing. In 1892 the Sisters of St. Joseph opened the first Catholic school of nursing in Canada at St. Michael's Hospital, Toronto, Ont. St. Boniface Hospital Training School, Winnipeg, Manitoba, opened in 1897 and St. Joseph Hospital Training School, Guelph, Ont., in 1899.

In the early 1900s, religious operated 59 of approximately 393 schools of nursing in the U.S. and 3 of approximately 25 in Canada. About half of these early Catholic schools in the U.S. were established by congregations springing from Mother Seton's Emmitsburg, Md., foundation of Sisters, 21 by the Daughters of Charity, and 7 by three foundations of Sisters of Charity.

In 1900 the preparation of nurses was the concern of hospitals alone; educational institutions were neither invited to participate nor were they interested. The term training school then used was appropriate to the apprenticeship system followed. The programs, usually completed in 2 years, often required students to be on duty more than 10 hours a day, participating in the care of patients. Lectures were arranged after patients' needs were met. Students generally lived in the hospital and were furnished board, room, laundry, uniforms, and a small monthly stipend. Scholastic requirements for admission were practically unknown. One sister was both hospital superintendent and principal of the training school. Until after the establishment of the Catholic Hospital Association (CHA) in Milwaukee, Wis., in 1915, there was little published information about Catholic schools of nursing. Nursing education articles and news items from Catholic schools of nursing appeared in the first issue of *Hospital Progress* in 1920; since 1930 an annual survey of Catholic schools of nursing has been reported in *Hospital Progress;* beginning in 1963, in a separate publication.

Development. Between 1900 and 1918 the number of schools of nursing in the U.S. increased 260 per cent. Comparable data for Catholic schools indicates an increase of at least 350 per cent (see Table 1). With relatively few exceptions, apprenticeship continued through the decade of the 1920s, since the school of nursing was considered essential to a hospital expecting to provide acceptable care for patients. This is evident in the instructions given by the CHA to a committee appointed in 1920. The committee was enjoined to propose a revision of the curriculum that would ensure "a sufficient number of pupil nurses for adequate bedside nursing . . . [and] a sufficient number of . . . registered nurses to meet the public demand for home care of the sick."

Efforts to organize the hospital schools of nursing on an educational basis were more successful in theory than in practice. The suggestion that a board of control be created for the school, with lay citizen participation, was considered incompatible with lines of authority in Catholic institutions. More acceptable was the suggestion that programs be established in institutions of higher education and that hospital schools utilize local educational institutions for assistance in the instructional program. Many institutions of higher

TABLE 1. RELATIONSHIP OF CATHOLIC
SCHOOLS OF NURSING TO TOTAL U.S.
SCHOOLS OF NURSING—SELECTED
YEARS 1900–63*

Year	No. of schools of nursing †		
	Total U.S.	Total Catholic	Per cent Catholic
1900	432	58	13.4
1910	1,129	203	17.9
1918 ‡	1,555	271	17.4
1928	1,884	370	19.6
1931	1,802	403	22.4
1935	1,472	383	26.0
1940	1,311	390	29.7
1945	1,295	380	29.3
1950	1,190	351	29.5
1955	1,125	327	29.1
1956	1,115	322	28.9
1957	1,118	325	29.1
1958	1,126	324	28.8
1959	1,119	323	28.9
1960	1,123	318	28.3
1961	1,118	316	28.3
1962	1,128	313	27.7
1963	1,142	308	26.9

* Years reported 1900–45, inclusive, based on availability of reliable data. † Schools in Hawaii and Puerto Rico included beginning 1955. ‡ 1918 totals include schools in five states not reported in ANA "List of State Accredited Schools of Nursing." sources: U.S. totals. U.S. Department of Interior, Office of Education, "Nurse Training Schools 1917–18," for 1900, 1910, and five states 1918. Lists of state-approved schools of nursing published by: American Nursing Association for 1918, 1928; National League for Nursing Education for 1931, 1950; National League for Nursing for 1955–63. Catholic schools. Estimated from date of establishment of schools listed in 1918 publications, 1900, 1910. Tabulation of Catholic schools included in ANA and NLNE state-approved lists, 1918–31. Catholic Hospital Association, *Annual Directory of Catholic Hospitals and Schools of Nursing*, 1935, 1940–63.

education entered the field of nursing through affiliations requested by the hospital school, often with arrangements for graduates to complete approximately 2 years of academic requirements to obtain a baccalaureate degree. Others responded to the school of nursing faculty's requests for assistance in meeting academic qualifications imposed by the state boards of nursing.

No Catholic college was among the 13 institutions of higher education cited in the Goldmark Report of 1923 as offering courses leading to a diploma and a baccalaureate degree in cooperation with hospital schools. Only Georgetown University Hospital (D.C.), which offered a diploma program, was among state accredited schools in 1924. *St. Louis University (Mo.) appears in the state approved list of 1931, with three hospital school units offering a diploma program and an optional degree program. The *Catholic University of America School of Nursing (D.C.) began offering courses in nursing education for registered nurses (R.N.'s) in the summer of 1932.

*St. Xavier College, Chicago, Ill. (1935), is believed to be the first Catholic college to assume full responsibility for a curriculum leading to the baccalaureate degree and eligibility to write state examinations for licensure as an R.N. Of 77 institutions of higher education that in 1946 offered state-approved baccalaureate degree programs, 19 were Catholic institutions. In 1964 Catholic institutions of higher education offering the baccalaureate program totaled 44. The program that was established in 1958 at the Marillac College Department of Nursing, Normandy, Mo., as a direct result of the *Sister Formation Movement, admits religious women only. Two additional baccalaureate degree programs started at *Marymount College Department of Nursing (Salina, Kans.) in 1964 and at *Marian College of Fond du Lac (Wis.), Division of Nursing in 1964.

Hospital schools continue to utilize facilities of Catholic colleges and universities for assistance in the instructional program, some for single courses such as religion, ethics, or science; others by enrolling students in the college for one or two semesters of required courses. The nursing profession, however, no longer recognizes as fulfilling the nursing subject requirements the development of baccalaureate degree programs based on the acceptance of diploma school subjects.

The 2-year associate degree program, introduced in 1952 as a junior college program, has spread rapidly, reaching a total of 105 in 1963–64, the majority in public junior colleges. *Gwynedd-Mercy College (Gwynedd Valley, Pa.), originally a junior college, in 1959 established the first associate degree nursing program in a Catholic institution. *Mt. Aloysius Junior College (Cresson, Pa.) initated the program in 1963, and *Mt. St. Mary's of Newburgh (N.Y.) and St. Mary's Junior College (Minneapolis, Minn.) introduced the program in 1964.

Recent Status. Among the extensive changes in Catholic schools of nursing occurring since World War II are: (1) Consolidation of nursing education activities in smaller number of schools (see following table). (2) Progress toward the goal of national accreditation for all Catholic schools of nursing, from 34, or 10.7 per cent, of all Catholic schools accredited in 1949 at the beginning of the program to 254, or 82.4 per cent, accredited in January 1964. (3) Experimentation by diploma schools with the academic year as a substitute for the traditional calendar year program of studies and with day school programs. (4) Acceptance by diploma schools of charges for tuition, fees, and board and room in keeping with good education practice. (5) Increase in faculty degrees. In the fall of 1963, 297 of the 308 Catholic schools of nursing reported a total of 3,475 full-time R.N. faculty of whom 80.2 per cent had earned at least a bachelor's and 36.6 per cent, at least a master's degree. Of the 830 religious included in the total, 61 per cent held at least a master's degree.

Catholic schools of nursing have had less tendency to come under the control of educational institutions than has generally been the case with schools of nursing nationally since the 1950s (see Table 2). In part, this can be attributed to the small number of Catholic junior colleges in the U.S. Trends in 1964 seemed to indicate an increasing number of nursing programs in Catholic institutions of higher education and a gradual decrease in the ratio of Catholic schools to all U.S. schools of nursing.

TABLE 2. RELATIONSHIP OF CATHOLIC SCHOOLS OF NURSING TO ALL
SCHOOLS OF NURSING—U.S. AND PUERTO RICO, 1953 AND 1963

Enrollment and graduates (by program)	1953		1963	
	Total U.S. (1,124 schools)	Catholic only (337 schools, 29.9%*)	Total U.S. (1,142 schools)	Catholic only (308 schools, 26.9%*)
Total enrollment	103,019	32,983 (32%*)	124,744	33,262 (26.6%*)
Diploma	85.5%	90.1%	74.8%	83.2%
Associate degree	0.3%		5.1%	0.2%
Baccalaureate degree	14.2%	9.9%	20.1%	16.6%
Total graduates	28,539	9,227 (32.3%*)	32,398	10,071 (31.1%*)
Diploma	90.4%	94.5%	81.6%	89.5%
Associate degree	1.2%		4.6%	0.2%
Baccalaureate degree	8.4%	5.5%	13.8%	10.3%

*Percentage of U.S. total. SOURCES: National League for Nursing, *State Approved Schools of Professional Nursing,* and Catholic Hospital Association, *Directory of Catholic Hospitals and Schools of Nursing,* 1954, 1964.

See also CONFERENCE OF CATHOLIC SCHOOLS OF NURSING.

Bibliography: A. M. SCHWITALLA and M. R. KNEIFL, "The Catholic Schools of Nursing in the United States and Canada at the Beginning of 1935," *Hospital Progress* 16.1 (1935) 1–51. Conference and Catholic Schools of Nursing, *Nursing Education and Catholic Institutions* (St. Louis 1963). M. M. FOLEY, "Catholic Schools of Nursing in 1963," *Catholic Hospital Association 1964 Directory* (St. Louis 1964) 121–126, pub. as a suppl. to *Hospital Progress.*

[M. M. FOLEY]

NURSING, HISTORY OF

Nursing is a direct or indirect service to a person, sick or well, to help him meet those personal health needs that he cannot meet unaided. It is complementary to medical practice and has existed in some measure since earliest times. Until the middle of the 20th century, the primary goal of nursing was physical care of the sick and injured. Contemporary goals include (1) restoration of health, (2) preservation of health, and (3) rehabilitation for normal functioning insofar as possible.

The word nurse as now interpreted had no counterpart in pagan antiquity. Generally, medical and nursing practices were not differentiated. In primitive societies, nursing duties were carried out by persons ranging in status from slaves to physicians. The best nursing procedures of the pre-Christian era existed in Greece, where Hippocrates or a member of his school had written instructions for those who nursed the sick; but even there only the wealthy and others useful to the state were objects of care. The health of the common people was grossly neglected.

EARLY CHRISTIANITY AND NURSING

With the advent of Christianity, care of the sick underwent an important change. Essentially, Christians enlarged nursing service, making it available to all persons in need regardless of creed or social position, distinguished it from medical practice, gave it some organization, and infused into it the virtue of compassion.

In the Early Church. The care of the sick was a primary work of mercy of the infant Church. Motivated by Christian charity and with Christ as their example, the early Christians sought out the afflicted and endeavored to help them. They visited the sick in their own homes and administered to them. Special quarters were provided, usually in the bishop's house, for those who were homeless.

Much of the work, which consisted of many social services in addition to nursing, was done by deacons and deaconesses. Phoebe, mentioned by St. Paul, is honored as both the first deaconess and the first district nurse. Paula (A.D. 347–404), a Roman noblewoman associated with St. Jerome in his Biblical translations, was the first laywoman to teach a distinct art of nursing. She devoted much of her life to the care of the sick in the Holy Land. In 390 *Fabiola, a wealthy penitent, opened the first Roman institution for the care of the sick. She went out into the streets to find the most neglected and personally nursed them.

In late antiquity rising communities and religious associations of men and women took over and expanded the charitable work, including nursing, formerly performed by the deaconesses. Specific mention is made of infirmarians (nurses) in the institutions founded by St. Basil the Great (*c.* 370) in Caesarea and by Cassiodorus (*c.* 490–585) and St. Benedict (480–543) in Italy. The Benedictines, for example, were directed by their rule that "before and above all things, care must be taken of the sick that they be served in very truth as Christ is served." Monks grew herbs for medicinal purposes and studied medicine from the best available sources—the works of the Greek physicians Hippocrates and Galen, which in the West had been translated into Latin. In time, many small hospitals developed in connection with monasteries. As the monks went forward to Christianize Europe, they spread their knowledge and practice of the healing arts.

In the Middle Ages. The isolation of monasteries and manors during the early medieval period checked the development of the widespread epidemics that were later to ravage Europe. But there was an increased need for medical and nursing care because of the many petty wars of the period. Since there were few doctors, medical and nursing practices began to be learned by the ladies and their maids in the manor houses on the feudal estates. Maintaining hygienic surroundings and often performing their work with considerable skill, they added to the store of medical and nursing knowledge already possessed.

Monks and nuns continued to care for the sick as well as performing other charitable works. Often both nursed

Fig. 1. "Visit to a Plague Patient," woodcut by Gentile Bellini, 1493. It has not been determined whether the nurses represented in this print are nuns or laywomen.

the sick in the same institution, caring for patients of their own sex. By the close of the 9th century, confraternities and religious orders devoted primarily to care of the sick began to be established. Such orders multiplied in the next several centuries and helped to make widespread hospital building possible. Among the many *hospitallers and hospital sisters were the Knights Hospitallers of St. John of Jerusalem (and the auxiliary order for women, the Sisters of St. Mary Magdalen), the *Teutonic Knights, the Knights of St. Lazarus, and various orders under the Rule of St. Augustine.

Especially important during the Crusades were the Knights Hospitallers of St. John (*Knights of Malta), a military nursing order. They maintained a hospital staffed with infirmarians near the Holy Sepulcher and provided outstanding medical and nursing care for both pilgrims and soldiers. The Knights of St. Lazarus were devoted to caring for the victims of leprosy (a term that covered a wide variety of diseases), which in the 12th and 13th centuries reached epidemic proportions. Lepers were segregated from society, but generally received no medical treatment. The Knights established large and well-managed leper colonies (lazarettos) for them. Other lazarettos were founded by nuns.

Many nursing orders that staffed hospitals were under the Rule of St. Augustine. The Order of the Holy Ghost, founded as a lay community under that rule in the 12th century, staffed the famous Holy Ghost (city) Hospital in Rome when it was founded in 1204. This institution served as the model for the more than 900 city hospitals subsequently erected throughout continental Europe. The oldest purely nursing order of sisters still in existence is that of the *Augustinian Nuns, who, organized as an order in the 13th century, cared for the sick in the *Hôtel-Dieu de Paris.

Among the great medieval saints, several have been singled out as nursing saints because of their care of the sick. These include *Francis of Assisi, *Elizabeth of Hungary, and *Catherine of Siena. Throughout Europe the only real training for nursing in the Middle Ages was that given to members of religious orders; and, in general, nursing practices were good according to the knowledge of the time. Certainly, there was outstanding devotion to the needs of the sick on the part of those who served them. Outside Europe, others, especially the Moslem Turks, were making other contributions to medical science and nursing; and some of their techniques were absorbed by the West.

Nursing from 1500 to 1850

In the 14th century the Black Death wiped out much of the population of England and continental Europe. Its devastating effect on society, followed by the social, political, economic, and religious upheavals of the next few centuries, plunged nursing into the worst period of its history. The years 1500 to 1850 are thus often termed the "dark ages" of nursing.

Deteriorating Conditions. In England and in many parts of Europe, monasteries and convents were dissolved; charitable organizations, particularly almshouses and hospitals, no longer had the support necessary for their work; and the poor and the sick lived in unrelieved pauperism. With the growth of cities and their attendant slum areas, health conditions grew worse, and further health hazards were introduced by the industrial revolution. The latter part of the 18th and early decades of the 19th century witnessed not only rapid deterioration of the general health, but also the worst nursing standards in nursing history. With the exception of religious nursing orders who did some of the nursing in Catholic countries, nursing was relegated to the illiterate and the lower classes.

The 18th-century reports from hospitals illustrate the low levels of nursing throughout Europe. A report from Milan, Italy, describes terrifying conditions in a lazaretto, where mercenary attendants stole everything they could from patients and spent their time in abuses and revelings.

In England lay nursing attendants were for the most part illiterate, rough, inconsiderate, and alcoholic; there was little, if any, nursing. A London hospital, founded in 1724, reports that "when the hospital first opened, the nurses came to the hospital for the day, and their only uniform was a round tin medal, inscribed with the name of the ward, and the status of the nurse. The Staff hung these around their necks over their own clothes." Extracts from subsequent minutes indicate that "embezzling provisions, pawning patients' clothes, drunken-

ness, admitting disorderly people, and neglect of patients were frequent occurrences. Sisters [a title for lay head nurses], nurses, cooks, porters and keepers of the lunatic house were alike guilty." Charles Dickens immortalized the pseudonurses of this period in *Martin Chuzzlewit* through the characterizations of Betsy Prig, an institutional nurse, and Sairey Gamp, a private duty nurse. Betsy and Sairey, who exemplify types, cheated their employers, tricked their patients, stole their rations and possessions, charged extra for services rendered, and were deliberately cruel and tantalizing to the sick.

Conditions were little better in most of the city hospitals of continental Europe. The standards of the Allgemeines Krankenhaus of Munich, the Moscow Hospital in Russia, and the Hôtel-Dieu de Paris, to name a few, were all in a serious state of deterioration by the 18th century. Poor administrative procedures, untrained nurses, insufficient funds to staff the hospitals adequately, unsanitary conditions, and general apathy on the part of the public, all contributed.

In the New World nursing and hospitals were especially inadequate in that part of North America settled or dominated by the English. Having inherited English health standards at their worst, Americans made few improvements. Health services were unorganized and any community stricken with contagion such as smallpox suffered a major disaster. Isolation and quarantine were employed. Abandoned persons were removed to remote pesthouses with no facilities for care. Medical and nursing care usually consisted of haphazard services by charitable individuals who provided food and bedding. Public health was neglected, and the so-called health educators of the period were mostly charlatans who preyed upon a gullible public. The indigent, the infirm, the sick, the orphan, and the insane were placed in almshouses where all the work was supposed to be done by the inmates. In one of the oldest institutions in the U.S., the situation was a distressing reign of violence, neglect, and cruelty for some 200 years.

There were a few institutions established for the exclusive care of the sick, and these had considerably better standards. Also, following the discoveries of Pasteur and Lister, many eleemosynary institutions became hospitals. However, no real and lasting improvement came in the care of the sick until there were widespread reforms in the selection and preparation of nurses.

Nursing and the Religious Orders in Europe. The religious orders continued to be active in nursing through the dark period in those countries where they were allowed to remain. But they were often hampered in their work by the many restrictions placed on them. The Council of Trent's edict in 1545 that all religious orders of women were to be strictly enclosed; the conflicts in hospital administration that lessened or eliminated the authority of the religious in performing nursing duties; the pervading view that women should not be educated and thus nursing sisters need not learn of advances in medical science; and the hiring, usually by lay authorities, of uneducated, untrained helpers to carry out nursing duties in the hospitals, making the sisters there only figureheads—all contributed to lowering nursing standards in institutions staffed by the religious.

The sisters, being strictly enclosed, could no longer engage in home nursing, a vital service that had been performed since early Christian times. In part to remedy this, *Camillus de Lellis late in the 16th century founded an order of priests in Italy, the Clerics Regular, Servants of the Sick, popularly known as Camillian Fathers, to engage in hospital and home nursing. They had established 16 houses by the time of the founder's death (1614). Still existing today, the Camillians have an exemplary history of service to the sick. Another attempt to fill the need for visiting nurses was not so successful. In 1611 in France a sisterhood of visiting nurses, the Order of the Visitation of Mary, was established by Jane Frances de *Chantal; but objections to noncloistered nuns were so great that within 4 years her order became enclosed.

Daughters of Charity. A friend of St. Jane de Chantal, *Vincent de Paul, did volunteer nursing in La Charité hospital in Paris. Recognizing the needs of the poor and the sick, he began a comprehensive program of charity, laying the foundation for modern social service. To help him in his work, he formed the Association of Charity in 1617 and later the Dames of Charity (*Ladies of Charity). As his work developed, it became apparent that more than volunteer helpers were needed and thus he founded in 1634, together with *Louise de Marillac, the Sisters of Charity of St. Vincent de Paul (*Charity, Daughters of). The order, a modern, nonenclosed sisterhood, grew rapidly. Known for their excellent nursing, these sisters survived the French Revolution although most orders in France were dissolved. The order spread to other countries and still is one of the largest nursing orders in the world, even though the sisters engage also in teaching and various forms of social service.

Other Developments. A contemporary of St. Vincent de Paul, Virginia Bracelli, founded an order modeled on the Sisters of Charity to help the victims of the famine and plague in Genoa. These sisters, the Daughters of Our Lady of Mt. Calvary, later served in many hospitals in Italy and other countries.

The above are but a few examples of the dozens of nursing orders founded during the period 1500 to 1850. And together with the older orders they staffed a great many of the best hospitals in both the Old and New World; many also nursed, often at the cost of their lives, through the plague and other epidemics that ravaged Europe. One order, the Sisters of St. Charles de Nancy, was founded especially for service in epidemics.

The varying conditions of hospitals and nursing in the latter part of the 18th century are vividly portrayed in John Howard's *Prisons and Hospitals* (1784). Howard, an English Calvinist, investigated hospitals, prisons, and lazarettos throughout Europe with a view to bringing about needed reforms; his report was considered the most authentic of its day. He found the medical techniques and quarters for the sick in many hospitals to be shocking and nursing to be of an uneven quality. However, he was on the whole impressed by the nursing sisterhoods and observed that "the great attention of the nuns distinguish the hospitals in the Roman Catholic countries."

Nursing Orders in the New World. Like the English, the Spanish and French colonists brought to the New World the medical and nursing traditions of their homelands. Thus the nursing orders of Europe played an important role in the care of the sick, especially in Latin America and Canada.

In Latin America. About 1524 in Mexico City, Hernando Cortés established the Hospital de la Purísima Concepción (renamed the Hospital de Jesus Nazareno), which is the oldest hospital still in existence in the Western hemisphere. Several different religious orders have made up the nursing staff during its long history.

Throughout Latin America, such institutions multiplied, caring for the rich and poor alike. In Mexico alone, one hospital was provided for each town. The religious were usually in charge of nursing, which generally followed an apprenticeship pattern and was considered part of the religious training.

In Canada. The oldest hospital in Canada still in existence is the Hôtel-Dieu of Quebec, founded in 1639 by the Augustinian Hospitallers of Dieppe. It was called the House of Mercy by the Indians. This house became a haven of refuge for the sick, injured, and poor. With Indian women trained to help them, the sisters served all those in need of care, including both friend and foe in time of war. The Hôtel-Dieu of Quebec and that of Montreal, founded 5 years later, became the two most important centers for care of the sick in Canada. Francis Parkman, the American historian of Canada, writes of the sisters in these two institutions: "It is difficult to conceive a self-abnegation more complete than that of the hospital nuns of Quebec and Montreal. In the almost total absence of trained and skilled physicians the burden of the sick and wounded fell upon them. . . . Nearly every ship from France brought some form of infection and all infection found its way to the Hôtel-Dieu of Quebec. The nuns died, but they never complained." Among those who joined the order and served at the Hôtel-Dieu of Quebec were Françoise Gifford, the first native Canadian nurse, and the Huron Sister Genevieve Agnes of All Saints, the first Indian nurse and nun.

Canada's second oldest hospital, referred to above, is the Hôtel-Dieu of Montreal. It was organized under the direction of Jeanne Mance, a well-born French woman who had nursed the sick poor in Paris as a charitable endeavor. She was the first lay woman in North America to devote full time to nursing. In 1659 she secured the services of the Hospitallers of St. Joseph de la Fleche to help in nursing duties. By the end of the century, there were 30 nursing sisters and the hospital buildings were greatly enlarged.

Among other religious orders whose nursing services were important in the early history of Canada are the *Ursulines, who were significant also in early nursing in French Louisiana; the *Sisters of Charity of Providence, who nursed in the epidemics of typhus and cholera; and

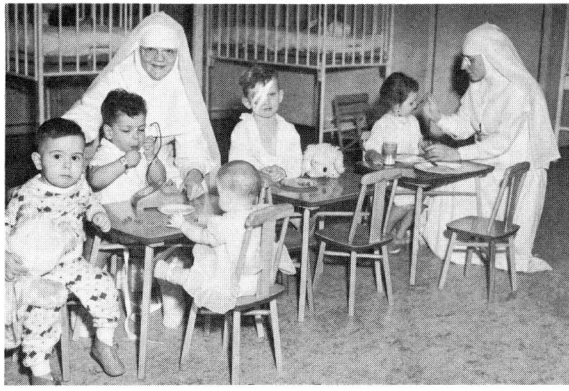

Fig. 2. *Augustinian nursing sisters caring for patients of the pediatrics ward in the Hôtel-Dieu of Quebec, which has functioned as a hospital for 300 years.*

the *Grey Nuns, founded in 1739 by Marguerite d'You-ville, who also engaged in teaching and other social services.

In the United States. The first hospital in the U.S. was probably built by the Dutch at New Amsterdam about 1663. After the English gained control of that territory, a workhouse (prison) was built near the hospital and care of the sick was done by workhouse inmates. This was the beginning of Bellevue Hospital.

The first religious hospital nursing in territory that was later to be part of the continental U.S. was that of the Ursulines in the Military Hospital in New Orleans in 1727. But the largest growth of religious hospital nursing in the U.S. came after 1820. Significant among the religious orders that founded hospitals were the Daughters of Charity of St. Vincent de Paul; the American Sisters of Charity, an order founded by Elizabeth Bayley *Seton in Emmitsburg, Md. in 1809; the Sisters of *Mercy; the *Holy Cross Sisters; the *St. Joseph Sisters; the Sisters of *Charity of Nazareth; and the Ursulines.

Nursing in the Modern Period

The modern period in nursing was ushered in by Florence Nightingale about 1850, and reforms in nursing that she initiated spread throughout the world. Her concept of nursing—that it is a profession, that careful selection and training of candidates are necessary, that there must be prescribed standards, and so forth—was influenced by what she observed in religious nursing rather than the contemporary lay nursing of England.

Among those who anticipated to some degree Florence Nightingale's widespread reforms and in whose work she took great interest were the Anglican nursing

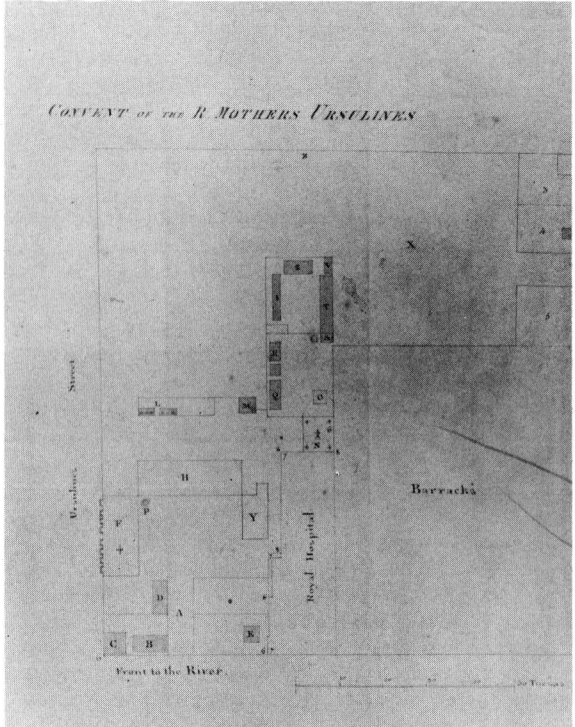

Fig. 3. Plan of the 18th-century Convent of the Ursulines at New Orleans, La., showing the "Royal Hospital" founded upon the arrival of the nuns in 1727.

sisterhoods that were formed in England in the first half of the 19th century; the deaconesses of Kaisers-werth, an Evangelical Protestant group under the direction of Theodor Fliedner (1800–1864), on the Continent; the Daughters of Charity of St. Vincent de Paul in France; and the Sisters of *Charity and the Sisters of *Mercy in Ireland, two Catholic sisterhoods that had begun nursing reform in that country in the 1830s.

Florence Nightingale. Until Florence Nightingale began to manage nursing services in several small English hospitals in the years immediately preceding the Crimean War, the only real nursing standards and training were those of the various religious communities that engaged in nursing. One of Florence Nightingale's essential contributions was to enlarge the "calling" of nursing, making it attractive for qualified lay people. Until her work, secular nurses were almost wholly of the type described earlier, an untrained and illiterate group, working for extremely low wages under discouraging conditions.

Florence Nightingale's interest in nursing and her decision to devote her life to improving nursing standards met with strong opposition from her family. Like the early Christian prototype nurse, she was born of well-to-do parents, was highly gifted intellectually, well-educated, and deeply religious. In her 20s she became conscious of the harder side of life, of pain, suffering, and deprivation. Her first attempts at nursing brought improvement so dramatic and requests for suitable nurses so numerous that it became generally apparent throughout England that some organized system of preparation of qualified candidates for nursing was needed. But before such a project could get under way, England's involvement in the Crimean War and the pressing need for improved care of the injured and sick among the soldiers led to Florence Nightingale's service in the Crimea. Assisted by a staff of Anglican sisters, secular women, and Sisters of Mercy from Ireland, she went to the Crimea in 1854 and brought notable improvement under extremely difficult conditions. Within 6 months of her arrival, the death rate of persons treated went from 42 to 2 per cent. The success of her group's efforts demonstrated that secular women from the middle class could provide excellent nursing service in wartime. It also contributed to the recognition of the need for good nurses as an essential element in promoting the general welfare.

In gratitude for her work, the English people raised a large sum of money and presented it to her. She used this money to found in 1860 a nursing school in St. Thomas' Hospital in London, thereby introducing what became known as "the Nightingale system." The system, which was to spread in modified form to almost all nations, had certain fundamentals including (1) a person in charge of nursing who, though under the hospital board, was supreme in her own field; (2) students in residence under the charge of a nurse; and (3) a required period of training.

By the early 1870s schools of nursing based on the Nightingale system had been organized in other cities of England, Scotland, Australia, Ireland, Canada, Germany, and the U.S. By the 20th century such schools could be found in most parts of the world.

Nursing in the U.S. In the U.S., the need for trained nurses became acute during the Civil War. Prior to that time the Catholic sisterhoods, Anglican nursing orders, and deaconesses trained at Kaiserswerth were the only groups of really trained nurses in the country. However, their numbers were insufficient to meet the great need for nurses, especially in times of epidemics and wars and in periods of swelling immigration. In the Civil War both Catholic and Anglican sisterhoods nursed the wounded and sick on battlefields and in hospitals, as did a number of Protestant women under Dorothea Dix, Superintendent of Nurses for the Union Army. Other nursing was done by volunteers in the various Union and Confederate hospitals. By the end of the War, the medical profession in the U.S. was on record as favoring the training of qualified women for nursing duties.

After 1870 both hospitals and training schools for nurses increased sharply, and the first Nightingale-trained nurses arrived in the U.S. In 1873 there were at least 4 nursing schools, all in the large eastern cities. By 1880 there were 15 such schools with 323 students; in 1900, 432 with more than 11,000 students; and by 1910 almost 1,100 schools with about 30,000 students. Nursing education continued to advance throughout the 20th century. Hospital and nursing school expansion were encouraged, in part, because of the advances in medical knowledge that had revolutionized hospital methods and attracted large numbers of the sick and injured to seek hospital care. (*See* HOSPITALS, MODERN.)

20th Century. The turn of the century marked significant developments in nursing history in the U.S. The Spanish-American War had required many nurses, and nearly 1,600, including about 250 Catholic sisters, had served. Immediately after the war the Army Nurse Corps was formed, soon followed by the Navy Nurse Corps. The Red Cross, which the U.S. had joined in 1882 largely at the instigation of the famous Civil War nurse, Clara Barton, began to be active in nursing; and, at the same time, other types of nursing services were expanding. Particularly significant was the growth of public health nursing and the services performed for the poor through the settlement houses. The most famous of these houses was the Henry Street Settlement House in New York City, founded by nurses Lillian Wald and Mary Brewster. By mid-20th century, public health nurses received a distinct preparation and were employed by a large number of public and private agencies, including insurance firms, industries, and educational systems.

The 20th century also witnessed the growth of nurses' organizations. One of their most important activities at the state level was securing legislation licensing nurses. By 1931 all of the states had some legal control for nurses and had taken steps toward setting minimum standards for training schools. The legal designations are R.N., registered nurse, and L.V.N. or L.P.N., licensed vocational or practical nurse. By mid-century the two major national organizations for nurses were the American Nurses Association, for registered nurses only, and the National League for Nursing, with membership open to nurses, non-nurses, agencies, and schools. On the international level, the important association is the International Council of Nurses, established in 1900, which limits active membership to self-governing national nursing associations.

Among the most important contributions made by American nurses during the 20th century was their service during the two world wars. In World War I the American Red Cross, under nurse Jane A. Delano, re-cruited and assigned about 10,500 nurses to overseas service. During World War II the National Nursing Council coordinated nursing groups to meet both military and civilian nursing needs. Altogether, about 70,500 nurses were assigned to the military. Instrumental in increasing the number of nurses for service in the war was the Cadet Corps Program, passed as Public Law 34, 78th Congress, which made grants-in-aid to qualified institutions for nurse training. In 1947 the Army and Navy Nurses Act established the military nurse corps on a permanent basis and granted commissioned status to female nurses in the armed forces; an amendment in 1955 extended the recognition to male nurses.

Catholic Nurses. Prior to the 1880s in the U.S. Catholic nurses belonged to the various sisterhoods or brotherhoods. After that time, although the nursing orders continued and even expanded, Catholic hospitals began opening schools to train secular nurses. By the 1920s Catholic hospitals operated one-fifth of the nursing schools in the U.S. with about one-fourth of the students. High standards and modern methods—both in Catholic hospitals and in their schools for nurses—were especially prominent after the formation of the *Catholic Hospital Association. The religious orders continued to make important contributions to nursing. In the U.S. about the turn of the century several religious orders devoted to visiting nursing, including the Visiting Sisters of the Sick Poor, the Sister Servants of Relief for Incurable Cancer, the Little Sisters of the Poor, and Sisters of Notre Dame de Bon Secours, began bringing needed health services to the poor, especially in the large cities.

Throughout the 20th century, both Catholic sisters and lay nurses took an active part in nursing organizations and activities at local, state, and national levels; and in 1939 a special organization, the *National Council of Catholic Nurses, was formed. By 1961 there were 350 nursing schools, with 35,894 students, under Catholic auspices.

Continuing Progress. Progress in medicine and nursing since World War II has surpassed the achievements of the previous 100 years. Demands for more health services have necessitated continuing education for nurses at the same time that they must meet service obligations. Increased medical specialization; intricate surgery on vital organs; highly selective drug and radio isotope therapy; changing patterns of patient care utilizing automated and complicated scientific equipment; intensive and progressive care units; out-patient and home care services; and emphasis upon chronic illness, preventive medicine, rehabilitation, epidemiology, and environmental hazards have all required an extension of nursing services and have complicated nursing practice. Thus the need for highly qualified and dedicated nurses continues throughout the world.

Bibliography: C. M. FRANK, *Foundations of Nursing* (2d ed. Philadelphia 1959). J. M. GIBBON and M. S. MATTHEWSON, *Three Centuries of Canadian Nursing* (Toronto 1947). M. A. NUTTING and L. L. DOCK, *A History of Nursing*, 4 v. (New York 1907–12). L. R. SEYMER, *A General History of Nursing* (London 1936). J. J. WALSH, *The History of Nursing* (New York 1929). C. B. WOODHAM-SMITH, *Florence Nightingale, 1820–1910* (London 1954). A. H. WOOLSEY, *A Century of Nursing, 1776–1876* (New York 1950). **Illustration credit:** Fig. 1, Philadelphia Museum of Art, Ars Medica Collection.

[C. M. FRANK]

NUZU (NUZI), an ancient city of the 2d millennium B.C. in northern Mesopotamia. It was unearthed at Yorgan Tepe, about 8 miles southwest of Kirkuk in Iraq, in a series of excavations conducted by American archeologists under the direction of E. Chiera between 1925 and 1931. The archeological campaigns uncovered 12 different strata, disclosing the history of this site back to 4000 B.C. In the 3d millennium B.C. the small but important city of Gasur of the Akkadian empire was situated here. In the 2d millennium it became known as Nuzu (less correctly, Nuzi) and was an important center of the *Hurrians (the Biblical Horrites). This people came into northern Mesopotamia in the second half of the 3d millennium and founded a great empire in the 16th and 15th centuries B.C.

At the Hurrian stratum a wealth of material was uncovered that not only gives us knowledge of the life and culture of Nuzu, but also sheds a great deal of light on the patriarchal narratives of Genesis. At this level 4,000 cuneiform tablets were discovered. These were written by Hurrian scribes in Akkadian with certain Hurrian peculiarities. They exhibit Hurrian customs and laws that are closely paralleled by customs and practices of the Hebrew patriarchs. The many parallels supplied by the Nuzu documents indicate that Abraham and his successors were following the customary practices and laws of their time, and thus imply the antiquity and authenticity of the social customs depicted in Genesis.

Bibliography: Excavation reports. R. F. S. STARR, *Nuzi: Report on the Excavations at Yorgan Tepe near Kirkuk, Iraq, 1927–1931,* 2 v. (Cambridge, Mass. 1937). The Nuzu documents and Genesis. C. H. GORDON, "Biblical Customs and the Nuzu Tablets," BiblArcheol 3 (1940) 1–12. R. T. O'CALLAGHAN, "Historical Parallels to Patriarchal Social Custom," CathBiblQuart 6 (1944) 391–405.

[F. A. PETRU]

NYIRŐ, JÓZSEF, Hungarian novelist; b. Székelyzsombor, Transylvania, 1889; d. Madrid, 1955. The son of peasants, he graduated with honors from the Franciscan Gymnasium at Csiksomlyó. Poverty and the desire to please his pious mother prompted Nyirő to study for the priesthood, but he abandoned this course in 1916. His autobiographical novel, *Isten igájában* (1932, In the Yoke of God), is a moving apology for his apostasy. After the annexation of Transylvania to Rumania he represented the Hungarian minority in the Rumanian Parliament until 1944, when the approaching Russian army compelled the strongly anti-Communist Nyirő to flee to the West. He was reconciled to the Church before his death. Nyirő's novels and short stories, in a most poetic prose, deal with the Transylvanian Hungarian's honesty and religious idealism, which are constantly being tested by the elements of nature and treacheries of men. His most widely read works are: *Jézusfaragó ember* (1925, The Man Who Carves Jesus), *A sibói bölény* (1929, The Bison of Sibo), *Uz Bence* (1933), *Az én népem* (1935, My People), and *Mádéfalvi veszedelem* (1939, The Danger of Madefalva). In exile he wrote *A zöld csillag* (The Green Star) and *Ime, az emberek* (Behold, Men).

Bibliography: N. VÁRKONYI, *Az ujabb magyar irodalom 1880–1940* (Budapest 1942). J. REMÉNYI, *Hungarian Writers and Literature,* ed. A. J. MOLNÁR (New Brunswick 1964).

[O. J. EGRES]

O

O ANTIPHONS

The seven antiphons sung at the Magnificat in the Office on the 7 days before the vigil of Christmas (December 17–23), each antiphon beginning with the interjection "O." During this season the liturgical readings and chants, selected chiefly from Isaia, announce the coming of the Messiah, and the closer the feast of Christmas approaches, the more the liturgy accentuates its call to the Savior with the cry "Come!" (*Veni*). During the Middle Ages the O antiphons enjoyed great popularity. Intonation was assigned in succession to the dignitaries of the monastery or cathedral chapter. Thus the first antiphon, *O Sapientia*, was intoned by the abbot; the next day, *O Adonai*, by the prior; *O Clavis David*, by the cellarer, and so on. The largest bell was rung throughout the singing of the O antiphon and its Magnificat.

Textual Structure and Sources. The O antiphons are all constructed on a plan similar to that of orations: first an invocation to the Messiah with a title inspired by the Old Testament (e.g., "O Emmanuel"); then an amplification stating an attribute of the Messiah and developing the invocation ("our King and our Lawgiver, the one awaited by the nations, their savior"); finally, an appeal commencing always with "Come" and referring to the initial invocation ("Come to redeem us, Lord, our God"). Their sources may be either of scriptural origin or of ecclesiastical composition, the latter being a free manner of juxtaposing scriptural texts from different sources. (1) The texts of the O antiphons are virtually a mosaic of borrowings from the Prophetic and the Sapiential books: *O Sapientia* (Eccl 24.5); *O Adonai* (Ex 6.13); *O Radix Jesse* (Isa 11.10); *O Clavis David* (Ap 3.7; cf. Is 22.22); *O Oriens* (Za 6.12); *O Rex Gentium* (Ag 2.8); *O Emmanuel* (Is 7.14; 8.8). These terms from the Old Testament were very early applied to Christ. Four of them (Sapientia, Rex, Emmanuel, Radix) were already employed by Pope St. Damasus (366–384) in his *Carmen de cognomentis Salvatoris* (PL 103:378). None of the seven invocations, however, can be found in the *De nominibus Christi* of the Gelasian Decretal(s), sometimes attributed to the same Pope [cf. Dobschütz, *Texte und Untersuchungen* 38 1912) fasc. 4:3]. The term *Clavis David* is applied to Christ by St. Ambrose (*De institut. virg.* 9.62, PL 16:321); it was repeated in the *Pontificale romanum* in the admonition *Accipe virgam virtutis* for the consecration of a king. (2) Nonscriptural words are few and are used to link the terms borrowed from Scripture. The two pleas *Veni ad salvandum nos* (from *O Emmanuel*) and *Veni ad liberandum nos* (from *O Radix*) do not seem to be of scriptural origin. The second appears to be taken from a *Responsorium breve* of the Advent liturgy and is a very ancient text, since this appeal for liberation is found in the same words in the Mozarabic antiphonary of Leon and is repeated at the beginning of an oration of the Mozarabic sacramentary (ed. M. Ferotin, col. 162, line 30).

Number and Origin. In inverse order the initials of each invocation (*S*apientia, *A*donai, *R*adix, *C*lavis, *O*riens, *R*ex, *E*mmanuel) constitute the acrostic ERO CRAS. This is interpreted as the response of Christ to the faithful who have called upon Him during the week: "Tomorrow I shall be there." From this acrostic we can draw two conclusions: (1) The primitive order of the antiphons was the same as that preserved today in the Roman Breviary, rather than that indicated by *Amalarius (De ordine antiphonarii, ed. Hanssens, StTes 140:46) or that found in the Ambrosian antiphonary or in many Gregorian MSS. (2) The original number of the antiphons was seven. Other antiphons modeled on these seven (such as *O Thomas Didyme* or *O Virgo virginum*) are not by the same author. They do not enter into the framework of the acrostic; and, above all, they are not addressed to the Messiah. *O Thomas Didyme* was composed for the feast of St. Thomas the Apostle (Dec. 21), always celebrated during the period when the O antiphons are sung. *O Virgo virginum*, in honor of the Virgin Mary, is probably earlier, having been cited by Amalarius, and was sometimes sung on the vigil of Christmas. Amalarius attributes the composition of the O antiphons to some anonymous "cantor" (*De or. antiphonarii*, ch. 13, ed. Hanssens, StTesti 140:44), who probably lived in the 8th century, perhaps even in the 7th. All are adapted to the same melodic theme in the 2d mode. The Magnificat that follows is sung in the solemn tone as on

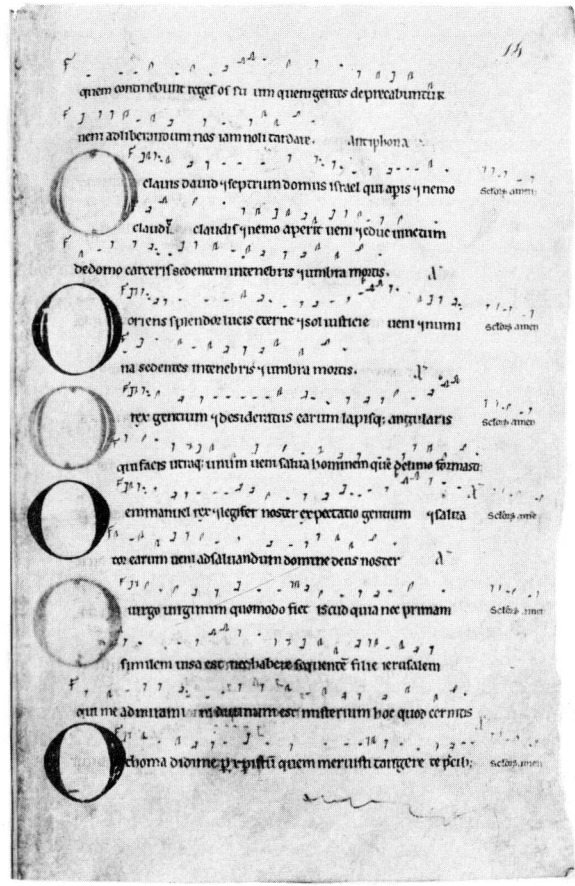

O antiphons in the 12th-century antiphonary of Saint-Denis (Bib. Nat. MS lat. 17296, fol. 14r).

great feasts. Both text and melody were probably composed by one and the same author.

See also ANTIPHON; PSALMODY.

Bibliography: C. CALLEWAERT, "De groote Adventsantifonen O" in his *Sacris erudiri* (Steenbrugge 1940). W. J. MCGARRY, *He Cometh* (New York 1941). "Les Grandes Antiennes," Rev Bén 2 (1885–86) 512–516. Apel GregCh 400. **Illustration credit:** Bibliothèque Nationale, Paris.

[M. HUGLO]

O DEUS EGO AMO TE, a hymn of uncertain authorship, but attributed to St. Francis *Xavier. It is a famous Latin version of *No Me Mueve, Mi Dios,* an anonymous Spanish *soneto* known to have existed for many years before it was first printed in 1628. The sonnet was familiar to *Ignatius of Loyola and to Francis Xavier (d. 1552), who, in his missionary instructions, used Spanish and Portuguese versions of it. In the Latin hymn the five stanzas of irregular rhythm glow with an ardent love for the Crucified Christ. The literal expression of this love has been criticized because it excludes both hope of reward and fear of punishment: *Nec amo Te ut salves me,/ Aut quia non amantes Te/ Aeterno punis igne.* English versions of the hymn are found in numerous hymnals. Another hymn, *O Deus ego amo Te/ Nam prior Tu amasti me,* paraphrases in its five stanzas the familiar prayer ascribed to Ignatius Loyola, the *Suscipe* or "Take, O Lord."

Bibliography: H. A. DANIEL, *Thesaurus hymnologicus,* 5 v. (Halle-Leipzig 1841–56) 2:335; 4:347, for text. Chevalier Rep Hymn 2:12896–98. Julian DictHym 826, 1296. M. BRITT, ed., *The Hymns of the Breviary and Missal* (new ed. New York 1948) 193–194, for a tr. M. C. HUFF, *The Sonnet "No me mueve, mi Dios"* (Washington 1948). J. M. COOPER, "An Aspect of Perfect Love," AmEcclRev 115 (1946) 101–120. F. J. CONNELL, "Unselfish Love of God," *ibid.* 113 (1945) 59–61.

[G. E. CONWAY]

O FILII ET FILIAE, an Easter hymn of 12 three-line stanzas, with a triple Alleluia at the beginning and end of the hymn, and a single Alleluia after each stanza. Each verse has eight syllables and is embellished with end rhyme. The date and authorship are uncertain. Because of its simplicity it was formerly dated in the 12th century, but Julian claims 1650; others ascribe it to the Franciscan, Jean Tisserand (d. 1494). This hymn, which is still sung in many French churches at the solemn salutation of the Blessed Sacrament after *Vespers on Easter Sunday, tells the story of the Resurrection: the coming of the holy women and the disciples, the message of the angel, the doubts of Thomas and his act of faith. The last two stanzas neatly use the versicle and response at the end of Lauds and Vespers:

> In hoc festo sanctissimo
> Sit laus et jubilatio
> *Benedicamus Domino.* Alleluia.
>
> De quibus nos humillimas
> Devotas atque debitas
> *Deo* dicamus *Gratias.* Alleluia.

P. Guéranger calls it the "Joyful Canticle," the insertion of the jubilant Alleluia after each detail in the story of the Resurrection being very effective. There are, besides variations in melody and arrangement, many translations of this hymn, the best known being "Ye Sons and Daughters of the Lord" by E. Caswall.

Bibliography: F. A. MARCH, ed., *Latin Hymns* (New York 1874) 206–208, 312, for text. P. GUÉRANGER, *The Liturgical Year,* tr. L. SHEPHERD, 7 v. in 12 (Dublin 1868–93) 6.1:190–192. Chevalier RepHymn 2:194. Julian DictHym 1:211, 828–829.

[G. E. CONWAY]

O ROMA NOBILIS, an early medieval poem in three monorhymed stanzas discovered in the early 19th century and declared the official hymn of the *Holy Year of 1950. The first stanza praises Christian Rome, the second invokes the aid of St. *Peter, and the third, that of St. *Paul. The text is complete in only one MS (Vat. lat. 3227) from the early 12th century; a second (Monte Cassino 318) from the 11th century carries only the first strophe. The Beneventan script of both MSS suggests an origin in or near the abbey of *Monte Cassino, probably from the late 9th or early 10th century, but *Traube's ascription to Verona is still prevalent. This nonliturgical poem is most frequently described, but without basis, as a medieval pilgrims' song. Its literary fame rests mainly upon the studies of B. G. *Niebuhr (*editio princeps,* 1829) and L. Traube (1891). As early as 1822 the poem was being sung, in Rome and Berlin, in a choral setting by the papal choirmaster G. *Baini, who claimed to have drawn his melody from the not readily intelligible neumes of the Vatican MS. In 1909 at Fribourg, P. *Wagner published the Vatican melody from the exact notation in solmization letters given in the Monte Cassino MS and demonstrated the complete inauthenticity of Baini's transcription. In both text and melody it is the matter

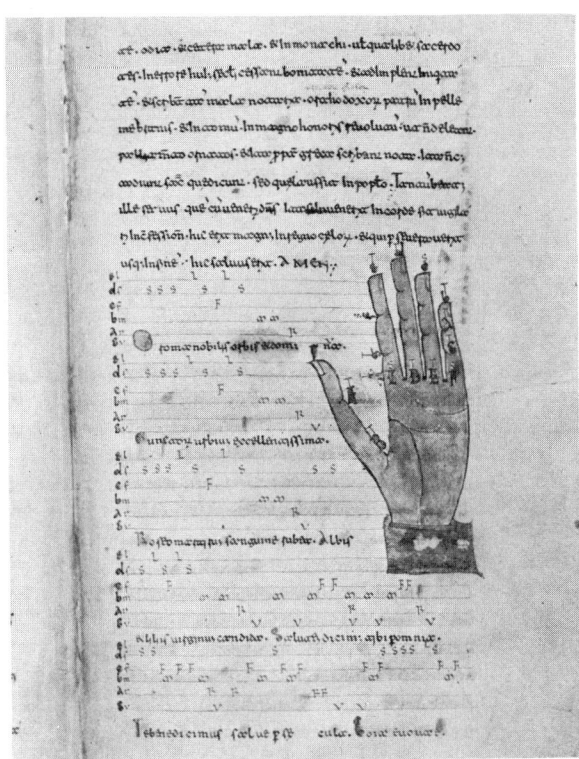

The first strophe of "O Roma nobilis" in the 11th-century Monte Cassino MS (MS 318, fol. 291).

of rhythm that largely occupies scholars today, although they are concerned also with the relation of the authentic melody of this poem to a secular piece, *O admirabile Veneris idolum*. Original settings of *O Roma nobilis* were produced by *Liszt (1879) and L. *Perosi (*c.* 1940). The setting in B. Reiser's *Laudes festivae* [(2d ed. Vatican City 1940) No. 97:306] is of unrecorded and doubtful origin.

Bibliography: F. J. E. Raby, ed., *Oxford Book of Medieval Latin Verse* (Oxford 1959) No. 101, text. Szövérffy AnnLatHymn 1:383–385. Baini's transcription autograph in MS Rome Casanat. 3081. L. Traube, AbhMünchAk 19.2 (1891) 299–309 with facs. of Vat. MS. P. Wagner, in *Kirchenmusikalisches Jahrbuch* 22 (1909) 1–16. B. M. Peebles, AmBenRev 1 (1950) 67–92, and in *Catholic Choirmaster* 36 (1950) 102–104. 143. I. Anglès et al., in *Roma nobilis*, ed. I. Cecchetti (Rome 1953) 1:685–689, 1183–86 (Liszt), 1187–91 (Perosi). NewOxHMus 2: 221. A. Machabey, *Cahiers de civilisation médiévale* 2 (1959) 204. *L'Anno santo 1950 . . . a cura del Comitato centrale A. S.* (Vatican City 1952) 481, 886–887. **Illustration credit:** Archivio di Monte Cassino.

[B. M. PEEBLES]

OAK, SYNOD OF THE, a local council convoked illegally in 403 by Theophilus, Patriarch of Alexandria, in a suburb of Chalcedon called "The Oak," to depose *John Chrysostom from the See of Constantinople. In 401 Theophilus had excommunicated and exiled the *Tall Brothers, and other Nitrian monks who had offended him as Origenists. They appealed to John Chrysostom, who gave them hospitality but withheld ecclesiastical communion pending final settlement of their case. They also appealed to the Emperor Arcadius, and Arcadius summoned Theophilus to appear before a synod of 40 bishops in Constantinople, over which Chrysostom would preside. Chrysostom pro-

tested that, canonically, Theophilus had first to be heard by a synod in his own province.

Theophilus had no such canonical qualms. On his way to the capital, he threatened that he would depose John and, on his arrival (403), connived among court and clergy to achieve that end. His plotting prospered and he moved across the Bosporus to "The Oak," where, although outside his jurisdiction, he convoked a synod of 36 bishops. Of these, at least 29 were his own Egyptian suffragans; the others were John's foes, including some Ephesian bishops whom John had deposed for simony. Two Egyptian bishops were sent to John with a curt command for him to appear before Theophilus and his synod. John refused to appear before a court whose members were at once accusers, judges, and witnesses. Next, two of John's own clergy were told to summon him. John sent back a protest citing the illegality of the synod, and the three bishops who carried this reply were manhandled by the synodal fathers. A final summons, from the Emperor himself, demanded his presence. Sure of his canonical position, John again refused, and was tried *in absentia*. In 46 charges he was accused of a misuse of church funds, tyrannical treatment of his clergy, irregularities in ritual, invasion of jurisdiction, and even high treason. All charges were frivolous, exaggerated, or totally false. Nevertheless, after 14 sessions, the synod condemned and deposed him. The charge of treason was referred to the Emperor, who then ordered Chrysostom into exile.

Bibliography: C. Baur, *John Chrysostom and His Time,* tr. M. Gonzaga, 2 v. (Westminster, Md. 1960–61) 2:237–261. Hefele-Leclercq 2:137–154. E. Venables, DCB 1:526–528. A. Biglmair, Lex ThK² 3:722. Photius, "Bibliotheca, 59," PG 103: 105–114. E. Schwartz, ZNTWiss 36 (1937) 168–181, Theophilus and Chrysostom.

[P. W. HARKINS]

OAKLAND, DIOCESE OF (QUERCOPOLI-TANA), suffragan of the metropolitan See of San Francisco, comprising the Counties of Alameda and Contra Costa, Calif., on the east shore of San Francisco Bay, an area of 1,467 square miles. The auxiliary of

The interior of the Church of St. Louis Bertrand, Oakland.

Cleveland, Ohio, Floyd L. Begin, was named first ordinary and installed in his diocese April 28, 1962. At that time there were an estimated 329,040 Catholics in a population of 1,314,700, served by 74 parishes, 51 elementary schools, and 8 high schools. St. Francis de Sales Church in Oakland was named cathedral.

Part of the Archdiocese of *San Francisco since 1853, Oakland earlier belonged to the See of Monterey and the Diocese of the Two Californias, and presumably Sonora, Mexico, when that see was created by Pius VI on May 7, 1779. The first Mass recorded in the area was that of Father Juan Crespi on March 25, 1772, on the second Fages expedition. On June 11, 1797, Father President Fermin Francisco Lasuen established Mission San Jose de Guadalupe, the first official chapel in the present diocese. From Mission San Jose priests later said Mass in the homes of the Peraltas in the Temescal and Fruitvale areas of Oakland and in 1853 established St. Anthony's chapel, which in 1858 became the parish of St. Mary's, the Immaculate Conception, Oakland. There are records of Masses offered once a month in a store or hall in Martinez by Father Maximiano Agurto in 1851 and 1852. In 1854 both Martinez and Antioch became missions of the Dominican parish in Benicia.

*St. Mary's College, under the direction of the Christian Brothers, established in 1863 by Abp. Joseph Alemany in the old cathedral in San Francisco, moved to Oakland in 1889, and in 1928 was transferred to Moraga. Father Michael King, pastor of St. Mary's, brought the Sisters of the Holy Names of Jesus and Mary to Oakland in 1868 to establish on the shores of Lake Merrit the Academy of the Sacred Heart, chartered in 1880 as College of the *Holy Names. Since 1906 the Berkeley campus of the University of California has been served by the Paulist Fathers in a Newman Center built by Abp. Patrick W. Riordan. There are three seminaries in the diocese: St. Albert's College (Dominican); Holy Redeemer College (Redemptorist); Mt. Mary Immaculate (Oblates of Mary Immaculate). In Mission San Jose are situated the motherhouse of

The chapel at Holy Names College, Oakland, Calif.

the Third Order of St. Dominic, Congregation of the Most Holy Rosary, and the motherhouse of the Sisters of the Holy Family.

Bibliography: W. GLEESON, *History of the Catholic Church in California* (San Francisco 1872). H. M. WOOD, *The History of Alameda County* (Oakland, Calif. 1883). J. E. BAKER, *History of Alameda County* (Chicago 1914). E. W. DEVEER, *The Story of Rancho San Antonio* (Oakland, Calif. 1924). J. N. BOWMAN, "The Peraltas and their Houses," *Calif. Hist. Soc. Quart.* 30 (1951) 217–231. **Illustration credits:** Robert John Wright, photographer.

[J. S. CUMMINS]

OATES PLOT

The Oates Plot (or Popish Plot), named after Titus Oates (1649–1705), the principal informer, provoked the last large-scale persecution of Catholics in England. Between 1678 and 1681 more than 25 Catholics were executed in England, many more died in prison, and many hundreds were imprisoned. In what follows an account is given of (1) the political and religious background, (2) the actual outbreak of the plot, (3) its political consequences and management, and (4) some of the outstanding trials and martyrdoms.

Background. At the Restoration of *Charles II in 1660, a measure of practical toleration had been accorded to Catholics and Dissenters, though fines for recusancy were still levied. The King was obviously well-disposed toward Catholics. Positive legislation in favor of toleration for Catholics was attempted immediately after the Restoration, but this was bedeviled by the rigidity of the King's adviser, Edward Hyde, Earl of Clarendon (1609–74). After the fall of Clarendon in 1667, the question of Catholicism played a part in Charles's negotiations with Louis XIV. By the Secret Treaty of Dover (1670) Charles had agreed publicly to declare himself a Catholic at such time as should appear to him most expedient. The moment never came (till his deathbed), but in 1672, as an earnest of his intentions, Charles proclaimed the Declaration of Indulgence, removing the penal laws against all Nonconformists and recusants and permitting public worship to Dissenters and private worship to recusants. The subsequent Parliament, however, introduced the Test Act, which disabled Catholics from holding public office, and Charles was compelled to reenforce the *Penal Laws.

Royal Succession. The next problem concerned the royal succession of James, Duke of York. Owing to the barrenness of Charles's wife, James was clearly the next in line to the throne, but his refusal in 1673 to take the Sacrament in the Church of England confirmed suspicions of his conversion to Catholicism. Parliament feared a popish successor and an inevitable alliance with France. If Charles could not be induced to divorce his infertile Catholic wife, then means had to be taken to prevent a Catholic successor. On the other hand, Louis XIV wished to stabilize his Continental conquests, to secure English neutrality while he did so, and to prevent an English alliance with the Dutch. In February 1676, therefore, Charles and Louis entered into another secret treaty, whereby, in return for financial aid, Charles promised his neutrality. But to prevent any possible agreement between Charles and Parliament, Louis also intensified his large-scale bribery of members of Parliament through his ambassadors in England. One of the agents for the distribution of parliamentary bribes was a professional newsletter writer, Edward Coleman, secretary to the Duke of York. Coleman was an overenthusiastic convert. He had come into conflict with the authorities because of his infringement of the state monopoly of licensed news, and in 1676 a French apostate, De Luzancy, accused him of dealings with a French Jesuit, Father St. Germain. From December 1676, with the knowledge of Charles II, Coleman's correspondence was being intercepted at the post office by the secretary of state.

In the year prior to the Plot, the King's chief minister, Thomas Osborne, Earl of Danby, was pursuing a difficult policy. By economic reform he was attempting to organize the treasury in such a way that Charles would be as little as possible dependent on either Parliament or Louis for his revenues. At the same time Danby was attempting to maintain a court party in Parliament on a basis of a policy of public nonalignment with France and strong Anglican safeguards for the monarchy and the constitution; but if the worst came to the worst, money from Louis was preferable to concessions to Parliament. The marriage alliance between William of Orange and the Princess Mary, daughter of James, Duke of York, in October 1677 was followed by a treaty of neutrality with the States-General. At the Congress of Nijmegen (1678) negotiations for a general European peace settlement were proceeding.

Early in 1678 the parliamentary opposition, led by the recently disgraced Anthony Ashley Cooper, Earl of Shaftesbury (1621–83), was gaining ground. The strength of the movement toward a Dutch alliance against Louis was growing, and an antipopery scare was started in April. In the early summer Louis seemed to be ready to wreck the negotiations at Nijmegen and to be preparing for a new war. In May 1678 he signed yet another secret treaty of neutrality with Charles, but then on the strength of that Louis signed a separate peace treaty in July with the States-General of Holland. Charles thus got neither the benefit of a French subsidy nor the credit for a Dutch alliance. Danby's policy was in ruins, and he might well expect trouble from Parliament in the autumn of 1678, since he had alienated almost all support there. It is against this background that the emergence of the Popish Plot in the late summer of 1678 must be seen.

Oates and the Outbreak of the Plot. Titus Oates was born in 1649 at Oakham, Rutlandshire, son of Samuel Oates, an Anabaptist weaver. After a highly unsatisfactory career at Merchant Taylors' School, London, and at Cambridge University, he eventually succeeded in 1670 in being ordained in the Church of England. He left two clerical appointments under a cloud and was even unsuccessful as a naval chaplain. By 1676 he had already been found guilty of perjury and was strongly suspected of sodomy. He then made the acquaintance of Matthew Medburne, a Catholic actor, who introduced him into a club at the Pheasant Tavern, Fuller's Rents, London, that served as a meeting place for Catholics and Nonconformists (Richard *Baxter was a member). In 1677 Oates succeeded in being appointed as a Protestant chaplain in the household of the Catholic Duke of Norfolk at Arundel House in the Strand. About the same time he made the acquaintance of Dr. Israel Tonge (1621–80), Rector of St. Michael's, Wood Street, London. Tonge was anti-Royalist and anti-Jesuit, and was a crank. Oates found him

credulous enough and offered to act as a spy on the Jesuits. On Ash Wednesday, March 3, 1677, therefore, Oates had himself received into the Catholic Church by William Berry, alias Hutchinson, a mentally un-

Fig. 1. Titus Oates, by R. White.

balanced priest. In April of the same year Oates obtained an introduction to Richard Strange, Provincial of the Society of Jesus, who arranged for him to go to the English College, Valladolid. Oates arrived there in June; after 4 months he was expelled and returned to England. He next petitioned to be sent to the Jesuit College of Saint-Omer and arrived there in December 1677. During his stay at Saint-Omer he heard that the annual meeting of the officials of the Jesuit English province was being held in London on April 24, 1678. Oates returned to England in June and put his information at the disposal of Tonge; at the same time he attempted to blackmail the London Jesuits.

Tonge, armed with "revelations" of a Jesuit plot to assassinate the King, obtained access to Danby and to Charles. The King took little interest, but Danby saw the possibility of an antipopish "scare" to distract public attention from the failure of his foreign policy. On August 26 Tonge warned Danby that letters concerning the plot had been sent to Rev. Thomas Downes, alias Father Bedingfield, SJ, the Duke of York's confessor at Windsor. Danby hurried to Windsor to intercept them, but Bedingfield had already collected them, had seen them to be forgeries, and had given them to the Duke of York. On September 6 Oates and Tonge approached a London magistrate, Sir Edmund Berry Godfrey, to make an affidavit concerning a deposition of 43 articles concerning a Jesuit plot, though they would not at first allow Godfrey to see the text of the deposition. Godfrey, to the chagrin of Danby, informed the Duke of York, who demanded an investigation by the Privy Council in order to expose the accusations. Oates and Tonge, therefore, with the aid of others unknown, proceeded to draft further depositions. On September 28 Tonge was summoned to attend the Council, but before the Council meeting Oates and Tonge had a plot narrative of 81 articles attested before Godfrey. Both narratives were of course a farrago of nonsense, but the development of the plot between September 6 and 28 is highly interesting. The first depositions centered on the Jesuit "consult" of April and the efforts to assassinate the King. In the later version, more

Fig. 2. Sir Edmund Berry Godfrey, chalk drawing.

names of those in Oates's immediate environment and names of those who could be arrested easily were given. The new depositions included information against Edmund Coleman; Medburne, the actor; Dr. Fogarty, Oates's physician; the Benedictines in the Savoy; and Abp. Peter *Talbot in Ireland. There is every reason for assuming that between September 6 and 28 Oates and Tonge were being guided from another source and that that source was Danby.

The King sat with the Council on the morning of September 28 and made no attempt to disguise his disbelief in Oates, but went off in the afternoon to the races at Newmarket. Nonetheless, Oates's effrontery carried the day, and the Council adjourned in the evening having issued warrants for the arrest of the conspirators. Danby made a special point of having the Council sign a special warrant for the seizure of Coleman's papers, knowing full well the sort of correspondence that Coleman had been maintaining over the past years. Meanwhile, on the same day, Godfrey had warned Coleman of what was afoot; Coleman did not destroy his papers, but surrendered on September 30. Though not by contemporary standards treasonable, Coleman's letters were compromising and indiscreet, and he made it clear in his letters to François de *la Chaize, SJ, Louis XIV's confessor, that he was trying to obtain money from France to influence Parliament in favor of popery. On top of all this, on October 12, Sir Edmund Berry Godfrey disappeared and on October 17 was found strangled, with a sword through his body. Parliament met 4 days later.

If Danby encouraged the Oates Plot in the hopes of making it an instrument of the Anglican-Royalist wing of the court party against the papist Duke of York, there is no doubt that after the reassembly of Parliament the Plot was utilized by Shaftesbury, the leader of the opposition, against the whole court party and the monarchy. Shaftesbury and the Whigs worked up mass hysteria and mob violence as a means of trying to bar the Duke of York from the succession and ultimately to drive Charles from the throne. For 3 years the cry of "No popery" was used constantly for political ends.

Political Consequences. From October 1678 to March 1681 Charles stood virtually alone against Shaftesbury and the Whig opposition. Danby was impeached in December 1678, and the court party was in ruins. Charles has been blamed for not intervening to save those Catholics condemned to death for crimes of which he knew they were innocent. But to expect Charles to have interposed the royal prerogative against the process of the courts at such a juncture is a sentimental misunderstanding of his constitutional position. On two things he stood firm: his personal honor and the succession of his brother. When Oates began to accuse Queen Catherine of treason, Charles made it clear that he would fight back with all the means in his power. Furthermore, he persuaded the unskillful Duke of York to leave the country and then, by prorogation and dissolution, frustrated successive attempts of Parliament to introduce an Exclusion Bill. For the rest he could do nothing but try to ride out the storm. Ultimately, in March 1681, he succeeded in convincing Louis XIV that the only chance for the survival of the English monarchy and the succession of the Duke of York was for the King to rule without Parliament. With a substantial subsidy from Louis in his pocket, Charles summoned his last Parliament at Oxford. On March 21 they met; on March 28 the Commons were beginning to read the Exclusion Bill when the King suddenly dissolved Parliament and for the rest of his reign ruled alone.

The King gradually reasserted his power. In April 1681 Chief Justice William Scroggs, who had conducted most of the Plot trials, was removed from office. In July Shaftesbury was sent to the Tower. In November John Dryden's *Absalom and Achitophel,* a satire on Shaftesbury and the Whigs, appeared; within a year Shaftesbury fled to Holland and died. In June 1683 the "Rye House" Plot was discovered: this was a Whig plot to assassinate Charles on his way to Newmarket. The great Whig magnates who were implicated were prosecuted with the same vigor as the Catholics had been during the Popish Plot. As for Oates, in June 1684 the Duke of York took action against him for *scandalum magnatum,* and damages of £100,000 were given against him. While still in prison, Oates was indicted for perjury and came up for trial in February 1685, but the trial was deferred on account of the death of Charles. In May he was found guilty of perjury and sentenced to be pilloried and whipped annually. In 1688, on the abdication of James and the accession of William III, Oates was released from prison and became once more a government pensioner. He died in 1705.

The Trials. The first trial was obviously designed to instill terror. On Nov. 15, 1678, William Staley, a Cathólic goldsmith, was arrested on the evidence of two obvious rascals and charged with having said that the King was a rogue and that he would stab the King if no one else would. He was brought to trial 6 days later, condemned, and executed on November 26. It was in this atmosphere that the trial of Coleman began on the following day. Seven of the jurors in Staley's case served at Coleman's trial. The most damning evidence against Coleman lay in letters written to François de la Chaize in 1675, but it is significant that the whole of Coleman's captured correspondence was not published until the end of 1680, and Coleman remained remarkably reticent about his political activities. He was condemned and executed on December 3. On Dec 17, 1678, William Ireland, SJ, procurator of the English province; John Grove, a layman employed by the Jesuits; and Thomas Pickering, OSB, a lay brother; together with Thomas Whitebread, SJ, and John Fenwick, SJ, were tried for treason. There was only one witness against Whitebread and Fenwick, but instead of being freed, they were remanded to prison by Lord Chief Justice Scroggs. Ireland and Grove were executed on Jan. 24, 1679; Pickering was respited, probably at the instance of the Queen, but was eventually executed on May 9.

On Feb. 5, 1679, three servants at Somerset House, Robert Green, Henry Berry, and Lawrence Hill, were tried and condemned for the murder of Sir Edmund Berry Godfrey on the perjured testimony of Miles Prance, a Catholic goldsmith, who had originally been arrested as a conspirator but induced to turn king's evidence. Green and Hill were executed on February 21 and Berry, a Protestant, was executed on February 28.

On Feb. 8, 1679, occurred the first acquittal. Samuel Atkins, a Protestant and a clerk of Samuel Pepys, had been arrested in November 1678 for complicity in Godfrey's murder. (The Whigs had hoped that the young man would implicate his master, Pepys, a trusted servant of the Duke of York at the Admiralty.) Fortunately, the efficient Pepys had been able to produce witnesses, all Protestants, to prove an alibi. This was doubtless a setback to the Whig plot managers, and it was not until June 13 that the next batch of major treason trials took place.

First came five Jesuits, Thomas Whitebread, the English Provincial; William Harcourt, Superior of the London district; Anthony Turner; John Fenwick; and John Gavan. Whitebread and Fenwick maintained that they could not be tried twice for the same offense, but this was overruled. Defense witnesses were produced from Saint-Omer who swore that Oates was at Saint-Omer in April 1678 and thus could not possibly have been at the Jesuit "consult" as he had claimed, but to no avail. The following day Richard Langhorne, a Catholic lawyer who had acted for the Jesuits in their business affairs, was also tried and condemned. The five Jesuits were executed on June 20 and Langhorne on July 14.

On July 10 Parliament was dissolved. On July 18 Sir George Wakeman, the Queen's physician; William Marshall, OSB; William Rumley, OSB, a lay brother; and James Corker, OSB, were tried for treason and acquitted. Wakeman and Rumley were released, and retired to the Continent, but Corker and Marshall were remanded to prison to be tried for their priesthood.

Meanwhile a number of priests were put to death in the provinces on account of their priesthood. William *Plessington, secular priest, was executed at Chester on July 19; Philip *Evans, SJ, and John *Lloyd, secular priest, were executed at Cardiff on July 22; Nicholas Postgate, secular priest, at York on August 7; Charles *Mihan (Mahoney), OSF, an Irishman, at Ruthin, North Wales, August 12; John *Wall, OSF, at Worcester August 25; John *Kemble, secular priest, at Hereford, also August 25; and David *Lewis, SJ, at Usk, August 27. It is noteworthy that at Stafford, Andrew Bromwich, a secular priest, though condemned to death for priesthood, was reprieved after taking the Oath of Allegiance and that Charles Carne, a secular priest, who asserted at his trial at Hereford that he had taken the Oaths of Allegiance and Supremacy, was acquitted also.

On Feb. 11, 1680, Sir Thomas Gascoigne, an elderly Yorkshire baronet, was tried for treason on the evidence of two servants and was acquitted. Nevertheless his daughter Lady Tempest was sent for trial at York, together with Sir Miles Stapleton, Mary Pressicks, and a priest, Thomas Thwing. On March 17, at York assizes, they challenged so many jurors that the trial had to be held over until the summer. Eventually they were tried on July 28. Thwing was condemned and executed on October 23; the others were acquitted.

The "Meal Tub" Plot. The so-called Meal Tub Plot brings an element almost of farce into the tragic story. A Catholic midwife, Mrs. Elizabeth Cellier, a woman of extraordinary energy and fortitude, had been bringing what help she could to the Catholics in prison for the plot, and had provided for some of the defense witnesses at the trials. While visiting the jails, she met Thomas Dangerfield, imprisoned for debt, and fell, it seems, a victim to his plausible manners. She paid off his debts, and on his release he acted for her as a spy on the Whigs. He was, however, playing a double game. He gave Mrs. Cellier some papers that he claimed proved the existence of a Presbyterian plot. These Mrs. Cellier hid in a meal tub in her house. Then he made a confession to the authorities, claiming that the papers were forgeries inspired by the Catholics and that the

Fig. 3. William Howard Stafford, miniature after a painting by E. Lutterel.

Earl of Castlemaine, Lady Powis, and Mrs. Cellier had tried to bribe him to kill the King. Lord Castlemaine and Mrs. Cellier were tried for treason in June 1680 and acquitted. Mrs. Cellier then published her own account of her dealings with Dangerfield and of her trial. For this she was fined and condemned to stand in the pillory on September 11.

In November 1680, concurrently with its attempts to push through the Exclusion Bill, the House of Commons resolved to act against the Catholic lords who had been in the Tower since the outbreak of the Plot in 1678. They chose as their first victim William Howard, Viscount Stafford. The trial of Stafford by his peers in the House of Lords took place from November 30 to December 7. If Stafford had had a jury trial, he might have been acquitted. As it was, his fate depended on a public declaration by each individual peer. Fifty-five lords found him guilty and thirty-one declared him not guilty; he was condemned to death. On December 18 Stafford, at his own request, came to the bar of the House of Lords to make a statement. He told of his efforts to obtain toleration for the Catholics at the Restoration by payment of a collective fine and went on to tell of his efforts at the time of the Test Act to secure an alliance between Shaftesbury's party and the Duke of York. At the mention of Shaftesbury he was ordered back to the Tower and was executed on December 29.

The last Plot trial was that of Oliver *Plunkett, Archbishop of Armagh. Plunkett had been arrested and brought as prisoner to Dublin Castle on Dec. 6, 1679. The reason why the Viceroy James Butler, Duke of Ormonde, had delayed so long was that, previous to the Plot, Plunkett had been willing to cooperate with the authorities in the condemnation and extirpation of violence and brigandage. But by the efforts of Henry Jones, Protestant Bishop of Meath and a strong anti-Royalist, who was in close correspondence with Colonel Mansell, one of the English Whig plot managers, it was arranged that Plunkett should be brought to England to stand trial. On Oct. 30, 1680, he was brought to London and committed for trial; a host of Irish informers, mostly apostate priests, were brought over to testify against him. He was not brought to trial until May 3, 1681. By this time, after the dissolution of the Oxford Parliament in March, the Plot was well on the wane. Nevertheless, Plunkett was found guilty of treason and executed on July 1, 1681. What principally told against him at his trial was the fact that the Irish prosecution witnesses were new and had not been discredited as the English informers had been. Though Plunkett was the last to be executed for the Plot, many Catholics sentenced or awaiting trial remained in jail until the end of Charles II's reign.

The savagery and long persistence of the Oates Plot was attributable principally to Shaftesbury and the Whigs; it can also be partly attributed to the general cynicism and dissoluteness of the age. But a great share of the blame must be attributed to the bribery and corruption of the English Parliament by Louis XIV, the Most Christian King.

Bibliography: J. POLLOCK, *The Popish Plot* (London 1903; new ed. Cambridge, Eng. 1944), brilliant pioneer work but unbalanced. J. LANE, *Titus Oates* (London 1949), excellent. F. S. RONALDS, *The Attempted Whig Revolution of 1674–81* (Urbana, Ill. 1937), thorough and detached. J. WARNER, *History of . . . the Presbyterian Plot,* ed. T. A. BIRRELL, tr. J. BLIGH, 2 v. (Cath RecSoc 47, 48; 1953–55), a near contemporary account. D. OGG, *England in the Reign of Charles II,* 2 v. (2d ed. Oxford 1955; repr. pa. London 1963), excellent on political background. Besides bibliog. in the above volumes, see also C. L. GROSE, *A Select Bibliography of British History, 1660–1760* (Chicago 1939), and suppl. in *Journal of Modern History* 12 (1940) 515–534. R. CHALLONER, *Memoirs of Missionary Priests,* ed. J. H. POLLEN (rev. ed. London 1924), invaluable martyrology. J. LINGARD, *The History of England,* 10 v. (Copyright ed. London 1883), relevant ch. are still useful. Special topics: on Coleman, Coventry MSS v.11, Longleat House, Wiltshire and Bulstrode Papers v.12, Carl H. Pforzheimer Library, New York. On Atkins, A. BRYANT, *Samuel Pepys,* 3 v. (2d ed. London 1948–49) v.2, *The Years of Peril.* On Plunkett, A. CURTAYNE, *The Trial of Oliver Plunkett* (New York 1953) and E. CURTIS, *Blessed Oliver Plunkett* (Dublin 1963), popular treatment. **Illustration credits:** National Portrait Gallery, London.

[T. A. BIRRELL]

OATHS

Appeals to God in witness of the truth of statements or of the binding character of promises. The oath has been in use among all peoples; it continues to be regarded as a useful social institution and a formal guarantee of truthfulness necessary in organized society. Some (e.g., the Quakers) have interpreted Mt 5.4 to be an absolute prohibition of oaths, but Christ's words are a condemnation only of the type of trivial or profane oaths that were permitted under pharisaical casuistry (*see* OATHS IN THE BIBLE).

There was some difference of opinion among the Fathers of the Church regarding the licitness of oaths. Chrysostom regarded them as a snare of the devil to be avoided under all circumstances (*Serm. ad pop. Ant.* 15; *In Act. Apost. hom.* 8). Augustine was not concerned about a gospel prohibition, but thought that the oath should be avoided because of the danger of perjury that would arise from the frequent use of it (*In psalm.* 88.4; *De mend.* 28). Others, basing their arguments on NT usage, especially on the example of St. Paul, who frequently expressed himself in language indistinguishable from an oath (e.g., 1 Thes 2.5; 2 Cor 1.23; Gal 1–20; Rom 1.9), thought the taking of oaths was permissible in proper circumstances. This view prevailed in Christian times. Oaths became part of the judicial procedure; and oaths pledging fealty, fidelity, or the faithful performance of the duties of an office were recognized as having a social value. Theologians have generally held that an oath taken under proper conditions is not only licit but is also an act of the virtue of religion inasmuch as it is an expression of homage to the wisdom and power of God (see St. Thomas Aquinas, ST 2a2ae, 81.2).

By reason of the matter with which it is concerned an oath is either assertory (declaratory), that is, it calls upon God to witness that one is speaking the truth; or it is promissory, that is, it calls upon God to guarantee one's pledge to do or not to do something. In mode, an oath is either invocatory or imprecatory. In the former, one calls upon God as a witness; in the latter, one invites God's punishment if what is sworn to is false. An oath may also be either implicit or explicit. In the one, God is mentioned by name; in the other, the formula or gesture used is generally understood to imply the invocation of Him.

To be licit, an oath demands truthfulness, judgment (prudence), and justice (Jer. 4.2). The first of these conditions requires the person who takes the oath to speak truly and, in the case of a promissory oath, to be sincere in his intention to fulfill his promise. Judgment, or prudence, requires sufficient reason for taking the oath. In an assertory oath justice demands that the statement should not be sinful (as would be the case,

bis mdulgrat p sua mianu:claues et mutu cors dus. Itam de tia mea ac unudicaone in sub

The King of France swearing his coronation oath upon the Holy Gospels, miniature in the "Coronation Book of Charles V," c. 1364 (Cotton MS Tiberius B viii, fol. 46v).

for example, if it were defamatory); in a promissory oath, that what is promised should be morally lawful.

In the case of the promissory oath, the object of the promise must be possible and morally good. A promise of what is impossible, evil, or vain dishonors God and has no binding force. Moreover, it is understood that one undertakes to keep the promise only so long as the fulfillment remains morally possible, provided legitimate authority does not forbid it, and provided no notable change occurs in the matter of the promise, and the beneficiary of the promise does not yield his right to the fulfillment.

Because God is called to witness in an oath, the Church, as the official representative of Christ, legislates on the taking of oaths and claims the power of releasing those who are bound by promissory oaths. *See* OATHS (CANON LAW OF).

See also PERJURY.

Bibliography: THOMAS AQUINAS, ST 2a2ae, 89. Davis Mor PastTh 2:44–48. Noldin SumThMor 2:208–223. N. IUNG, DTC 14.2:1940–56. **Illustration credit:** Trustees of the British Museum.

[M. HERRON]

OATHS (IN THE BIBLE)

The custom of swearing, or taking oaths, that is, of putting a curse on oneself if what is asserted is not true or if a promise is not kept, has always been widespread among all people who believe either in the magical power of such self-maledictions or in the avenging justice of a deity who punishes those who swear falsely. This article is concerned with the taking of oaths as mentioned in the Bible. *See* CURSE (IN THE BIBLE).

In the Old Testament. Anthropomorphically, God Himself is often presented in the OT as taking oaths, especially in regard to His covenant. *See* COVENANT (IN THE BIBLE). Thus, "he promised on oath to Abraham, Isaac, and Jacob" (Gn 50.24) to make their descendants a great nation and to give them a special land (Gn 22.16–18; 26.3–4; 35.12). He renewed this sworn promise to Moses (Dt 1.8). And later, "the Lord swore to David a firm promise" [Ps 131(132).11] of an everlasting posterity and rule [Ps 88(89).4–5, 36–37] and an eternal priesthood [Ps 109(110).4]. It is these promises that are reaffirmed by the prophets (Jer 33.21–22; Mi 7.20). Besides these oaths that promise great bless-

ings, there are the oaths that threaten with punishment the Israelites who revolted in the desert (Nm 14.28–35).

Whether men swore by God explicitly (Gn 21.23; Jos 2.12) or implicitly (Gn 42.15; 1 Sm 1.26), an oath was a serious matter (Ex 20.7), for the oath always involved a conditional or contingent curse. Moreover, the oath was ever regarded as a sign of loyalty to God (Dt 6.13; Is 48.1), and therefore a false oath was basically a profanation of God's name (Lv 19.12; Ex 20.7). Oaths were employed both in judicial matters and in a variety of everyday affairs. Thus oaths were taken to certify the truth of an utterance and to pledge fidelity to one's word (1 Sm 14.44; 20.13; 25.22; 2 Sm 3.9; Gn 25.33; 47.31); to ascertain the guilt of a person suspected of a crime, e.g., in the trial by *ordeal (Nm 5.16–28); and to ratify an alliance (Gn 21.24, 26, 31) or a friendship (1 Sm 20.16–17).

In the New Testament. It is only in the NT that the oaths made by God in the OT attain their perfect fulfillment: by sending the Messiah God has been faithful to "the oath that he swore to Abraham our father" (Lk 1.73), His promise to David has been fulfilled by Christ's Resurrection (Acts 2.29–35), and it is God's solemn oath that ratifies Christ's eternal priesthood and guarantees the reality and efficacy of the New Covenant (Heb 7.21, 25).

Respect for oaths seems to have been carefully preserved by the ancient Israelites, but by the time of Christ's coming the Pharisees had distorted this traditional respect through their casuistry. Christ energetically attacked these legalistic abuses, demanding absolute sincerity of his disciples (Mt 23.16–22). He proclaimed a new ideal: "But I say to you not to swear at all" (Mt 5.34). St. James restates this teaching: "Let your yes be yes, your no, no" (Jas 5.12). Yet Christ did not absolutely abolish or condemn the use of the oath; His demand set the Christian ideal, but did not rule out the possibility of an oath on certain occasions. Thus, e.g., St. Paul often employed oath formulas in order to testify to the truth of his assertions (Rom 1.9; 9.1; 2 Cor 1.23; 11.31; Gal 1.20).

Bibliography: EncDictBibl 1656–58. J. PEDERSEN, *Der Eid bei den Semiten* (Leipzig 1914). S. H. BLANK, "The Curse, Blasphemy, the Spell, and the Oath," HebUCAnn 23.1 (1950–51) 73–95. F. HORST, "Der Eid im AT," *Evangelische Theologie* 17 (1957) 366–384.

[J. V. MORRIS]

OATHS (CANON LAW OF). An oath is the invocation of the name of God in witness to the truth. It may be taken only in accordance with the truth, with prudence, and with justice (CIC c. 1316.1). The intention of calling God to witness to the truth of a statement (assertory oath) or a promise (promissory oath) must be sincere and sufficiently manifest to others in words or unmistakable signs. A person is bound by a special and personal obligation of religion to fulfill what he has freely promised by oath to do (CIC c. 1317.1).

An oath extorted by force or grave fear is valid, contrary to the case of vows (CIC c. 1307.3), but it may be relaxed by an ecclesiastical superior (CIC c. 1317.2). This presupposes that there was a genuine intention of taking the oath, despite the force and fear. An oath that is demanded or permitted by Canon Law cannot validly be taken through a proxy. However, apart from such cases, an oath may be taken through a proxy (CIC c. 1316.2).

The obligation of promissory oaths ceases: if it is remitted by the beneficiary; if the thing promised is substantially changed or becomes morally wrong, harmful, useless, or an obstacle to a greater good; or if the final cause or a condition under which the oath was taken ceases (CIC c. 1319).

Those who have the power to annul, dispense, or commute a vow have the same power, under the same conditions, over promissory oaths. However, if the dispensation from an oath should involve injury to others who refuse to remit the obligation, the Holy See alone can grant a dispensation for the necessity or advantage of the Church (CIC c. 1320).

Although no oath as such is reserved, the necessity of annulment may arise from the fact that an oath can be made accessory to a vow by the intention of the one making the oath. In such a case it will follow the nature and conditions of the vow. Hence, in the case of a reserved vow the oath is likewise reserved (CIC c. 1318.1).

In conscience an oath is to be interpreted according to the intention of the person who took it. In the external forum the words used in the oath are interpreted in a strict juridical sense, unless a contrary sense is proved to have been intended (CIC c. 1321).

See also VOW (CANON LAW OF).

Bibliography: Bousc-Ellis 669–672. Abbo, see index.

[J. D. KING]

OATHS, ENGLISH POST-REFORMATION

From the first days of the English Reformation oaths, tests, and formal declarations were used to secure submission to the changes imposed by conformity to the Established Church. Later they were employed to penalize Catholics, and finally, as a condition of relief from legal disabilities.

Oath of Supremacy, 1534 to 1559. The early history of this oath is complicated. The statute (22 Henry VIII ch. 15) of 1530 confirmed *Henry VIII's pardon of the English clergy for unlawfully acknowledging Thomas *Wolsey's legatine authority in return for a grant of £100,000 and the Convocations' recognition (February and March 1530) that he was ". . . of the Church and Clergy of England, [the] especial Protector, single and supreme Lord, and, as far as the law of Christ allows, even Supreme Head." The qualification, "as far as the law of Christ allows," inserted in the Convocations' declaration at the instance of St. John *Fisher, was omitted in a similar acknowledgement made by Parliament after the break with Rome in the Dispensations Act, 1534 (25 Henry VIII ch. 21). Then, the first Act of Succession in 1534 (25 Henry VIII ch. 22), having recited and approved Thomas *Cranmer's annulment of the King's marriage with *Catherine of Aragon and Henry's marriage to Anne Boleyn, enacted that everyone "at their full ages . . . shall make a corporal oath" to keep "the whole effects and contents of this present Act." Refusal was punishable with loss of goods and life imprisonment, but no form for this oath was provided. The text of the oath taken by Lords and Commons (*Lords' Journals*, 1.82) before Parliament was prorogued in March 1534 refers, however, not only to the Act of Succession but to "all other Acts and Statutes made since the beginning of this present Parliament . . . anything therein contained," and thus to the Dispensations Act. This may have been the form of oath that was widely tendered and taken during the summer of 1534, but refused by John Fisher and Thomas *More, among others.

In December 1534 an Act of Supremacy (26 Henry VIII ch. 1) reaffirmed that the "King is the only supreme head on earth of the Church of England called Anglicana Ecclesia," and a second Act of Succession (26 Henry VIII ch. 2) gave a form of oath said to be that intended by the earlier act. It differs from that in the *Lords' Journals* only by omitting the phrase "made since the beginning of this present Parliament," and so equally required an acknowledgement of royal supremacy. Another statute (26 Henry VIII ch. 13) made the denial of any royal title treason, so that refusal of the oath was (after Feb. 1, 1535) treason. It was for this offense that Fisher and More were convicted and executed. In July 1536 an act "For Extinguishing Papal Authority" (28 Henry VIII ch. 10) provided a new oath by which all officeholders (ecclesiastical and lay) and all who held lands of the king or took holy orders or religious vows swore they would "assist and defend" the supremacy. The Act of Succession, 1544 (35 Henry VIII ch. 1), enacted another new and very long oath that involved a profession of faith in the royal supremacy. It was to be taken by all officeholders and by anyone when required.

All legislation inconsistent with papal primacy was repealed in 1554 (1 and 2 Philip and Mary ch. 8) and most of it was revived by the first of Elizabeth I's statutes, the Act of Supremacy, 1559 (1 Elizabeth I ch. 1). This reintroduced what was substantially the 1536 oath, viz, "I, A.B., do utterly testify and declare in my conscience that the Queen's Highness is the only Supreme Governor of the Realm . . . as well in all spiritual or ecclesiastical things or causes as temporal, and that no foreign . . . prelate . . . hath or ought to have any jurisdiction power . . . or authority ecclesiastical or spiritual within this realm . . .." It was to be taken by the clergy and by all holding office under the Crown, and by those taking university degrees; refusal entailed disability from holding office or preferment. It appears in practice not to have been tendered in the universities or to the parochial clergy; an undertaking to use the Book of *Common Prayer was thought sufficient. A statute of 1563 (5 Elizabeth I ch. 1) provided that the oath could be required of schoolmasters, lawyers, and legal officials, and that refusal by anyone should be punished on the first occasion by the penalties of *praemunire (forfeiture of lands and goods, and life imprisonment) and on a second (after the lapse of 3 months), as treason.

Oath of Allegiance (or Obedience), 1606. In response to a royal proclamation of November 1602, distinguishing between Jesuits and the secular clergy, and extending to the latter, in veiled language, hope of some amelioration of the laws against them, 13 secular priests on Jan. 31, 1603, submitted to Elizabeth I a *Protestation of Allegiance* in which they denounced papal sponsored plots of invasion, and bound themselves to disobey any papal decree of excommunication or deposition of the Queen. She was dying, however, and the *Protestation* had no immediate effect. After the *Gunpowder Plot (1605) the persecution of Catholics was intensified, and the first of two severe statutes (3 and 4 James I ch. 4, 5) included (ch. 4 sec. 8, 9, 27) a device to create dissension among the

Catholics. Although there could be no serious doubts as to Catholic loyalty, the *Protestation* and the negotiations preceding it had shown that there were differences of opinion on the pope's deposing power, which was stoutly defended by the Jesuits, among others. The following Oath of Allegiance was therefore drafted to exploit these differences and to cast doubt on that loyalty: "I, A.B., do truly and sincerely acknowledge . . . that our sovereign lord, King James, is lawful and rightful king . . . and that the pope neither of himself nor by any authority of the Church or See of Rome, or by any other means with any other, has any power to depose the king . . . or to authorise any foreign prince to invade him . . . or to give license to any to bear arms, [or] raise tumults . . .. Also I do swear that notwithstanding any sentence of excommunication or deprivation I will bear allegiance and true faith to His Majesty . . .. And I do further swear that I do from my heart abhor, detest, and abjure, as impious and heretical this damnable doctrine and position,—that princes which be excommunicated by the pope may be deposed or murdered by their subjects or by any other whatsoever. And I do believe that the pope has no power to absolve me from this oath. I do swear according to the plain and common sense and understanding of the same words . . .." The oath became law on June 26, 1606. It could be required of anyone convicted or suspected of recusancy (*see* PENAL LAWS, 1), and refusal entailed liability to the penalties of praemunire. After 1610 (7 James I ch. 6) it could be demanded of anyone over 18. Subscription did not, however, relieve Catholics of any of the penalties of the anti-Catholic legislation as the 1603 signatories had hoped.

On Sept. 22, 1606, Paul V condemned the oath "as it contains many things evidently contrary to faith and salvation," though he prudently refrained from enumerating them. James I replied that the oath was not meant to encroach upon anyone's conscience, and among the Catholics, minimizers maintained that the oath might be interpreted by the lawgiver's intention and might, therefore, be taken. But the Church's doctrine has always been that oaths are addressed to God Himself and must be accepted in the precise sense of the words pronounced. If James had made his subjects swear specifically "in the sense by him explained," the oath might perhaps have been endured, but when he made them "swear according to the plain and common sense and understanding of the same words" to what was injurious to Catholic consciences, this could not be tolerated. The most objectionable words were those condemning the deposing power as "impious, heretical, and damnable." The doctrine of the deposing power was, as far as practical politics went, already merely an embarrassment. But it was implied by the current Catholic teaching on the nature of the Church, and until the previous two or three generations it had been generally accepted as a valuable safeguard for liberty, both religious and civil. Many, including Paul V, had not realized that the power would never be in vogue again, even in Catholic countries, and they believed that it could not be denied without seriously impairing the Roman primacy. And while Robert *Bellarmine, Robert *Persons, and several other early opponents of the oath thus went further in condemning it than later theologians have done, it is still difficult to

see how a Catholic could conscientiously swear that a doctrine long maintained by the popes and by many in the Church, albeit not *de fide,* was "impious, heretical, and damnable." On its side, Rome could not allow the state to judge what was heresy or to specify the conditions under which Catholics would disobey the Holy See. Resistance to the oath was not, therefore, chiefly or solely the result of belief in the deposing power as Catholics such as Thomas *Preston (Roger Widdrington), who wrote in its defense, or those with Gallican leanings, such as Charles *Butler or M. A. Tierney, have claimed. (The Sorbonne on June 30, 1681, very shortly before approving the Gallican Articles, censored the oath and found in it very little that was objectionable.) English Catholics like William *Bishop (later made a bishop by Rome) and Leander Jones, President of the English Benedictines, who explicitly rejected the deposing power, nevertheless refused the oath. Bishop was imprisoned for refusing it, while Jones consented only to an oath of his own drafting.

The archpriest George *Blackwell, then head of the English clergy, had at first disapproved of the oath, but then in July 1606, after conferring with some of the leading clergy, allowed it. Later, after the Pope's brief, he disallowed it again, and finally, being imprisoned, he took the oath, relying on James's statement that no encroachment on conscience was intended. In a pastoral letter Blackwell recommended the faithful to do the same. The Pope issued a new brief (Aug. 23, 1607) repeating his prohibition, and on Sept. 28, 1607, Cardinal Bellarmine wrote to Blackwell exhorting him to obey the brief. As this also proved ineffectual, a new archpriest, George Birkhead, was appointed in February 1608, and Blackwell was told that his faculties would be withdrawn if he did not retract within 2 months. This he refused to do, and much to James's satisfaction, continued to defend his opinion for 3 years before he was finally suspended. Meanwhile James himself answered the missives sent to Blackwell in an anonymous tract *Triplici Nodo, Triplex cuneus* ("A triple wedge for a triple knot," i.e., the two briefs and Bellarmine's letter). This was answered by Bellarmine, also anonymously, in *Responsio ad librum: Triplici nodo, triplex cuneus* (1608). James now dropped his anonymity and reprinted his tract with a *Premonition to Christian Princes* and an appendix on his adversaries' supposed mistakes (January 1609). Upon this Bellarmine published under his own name his *Apologia pro responsione ad librum Jacobi I* (1609). James opposed to this a treatise by a learned Scots Catholic, W. Barclay, *De potestate papae* (1609). Barclay was a decided Gallican, and Bellarmine's answer, *Tractatus de potestate summi pontificis in rebus temporalibus* (1610), gave such offense to the Gallican party that it was publicly burned in Paris by a decree of Nov. 26, 1610. A similar fate befell Francisco *Suárez's answer to James, *Defensio Fidei Catholicae adversus Anglicanae sectae errores,* both in Paris and London. At every stage of the contest a host of other combatants joined the fray. On the papal side were Cardinal Du Perron, Leonard Lessius, Jakob Gretser, Thomas Fitzherbert, Martin Becanus, Caspar Scioppius, Robert Persons, N. Coeffeteau, A. Eudaemon Joannes, and Matthew Kellison. On the other side were Bp. Lancelot Andrewes, Isaac Casaubon, Paolo

Sarpi, William Barlow, Robert Burhill, Pierre du Moulin, William Barrett, John Barnes, and especially the Benedictine Thomas Preston writing as Roger Widdrington. Most of the Protestant books written in Latin, together with the works of Preston and Barclay, were put on the Roman Index.

Some idea of the pressures caused by the oath may be gathered from the Acts of the *Martyrs of England and Wales during these years. When William *Laud succeeded to Canterbury, the policy of splitting the English Catholics and driving the Jesuits from England was revived (1634), and in a new attempt to induce Catholics to take the oath another book defending it was produced, it seems by Preston, using (with his consent) the name of William Howard. An answer written in extreme terms by a young Jesuit, Edward Courtney, *vere* Leedes, led to Courtney's imprisonment, and was used to foster the impression that only Jesuit intransigence prevented a settlement between the English government and the Catholics. Courtney was attacked also by Leander Jones who had come to England hoping that he could negotiate a *rapprochement* between Rome and Canterbury, or, failing that, toleration for the English Catholics. Jones unsuccessfully urged that Rome should withdraw its condemnation of the oath if Charles I declared it involved "nothing else but a true and natural civil obedience and loyalty" and was not "a denial of any spiritual authority belonging to His Holiness," and he attempted to devise a formula for the oath that would be acceptable to both sides. Similar proposals were mooted during the Commonwealth and after the Restoration, but none were acceptable to Rome.

Oath of Abjuration, 1643 and 1655. With the success of the Puritans in the civil wars the Oaths of Supremacy and Allegiance naturally fell into desuetude, though they were not repealed until 1650. An act of Aug. 29, 1643, provided that Catholics should forfeit two-thirds of their estates, personal and real, and that everyone should be "adjudged a papist" who refused an oath renouncing papal supremacy, transubstantiation, purgatory, and other doctrines. No Catholic could possibly take this oath. In 1655 the penalties that before 1650 attached to failure to attend the Anglican Church were, by an ordinance, attached to refusal of this oath, which was reissued in an amended (and more objectionable) form. This measure was, however, only sparingly enforced.

Test Oaths, 1672 and 1678. In 1672 after the conversion of James, then Duke of York, a Test Act compelled all holders of office under the Crown to make a short "Declaration against Transubstantiation," viz, to swear that "there is not any transubstantiation in the sacrament of the Lord's Supper . . . at or after the consecration thereof by any person whatsoever" (25 Charles II ch. 2). This test was effective: James resigned his post as Lord High Admiral. After the *Oates Plot (1678) a much longer test was devised with a further clause that "the invocation of the virgin Mary, or any saint and the Sacrifice of the Mass . . . are superstitious and idolatrous . . . and that I make this declaration without any evasion, equivocation, or mental reservation whatsoever, and without any dispensation already granted me by the pope . . ." (30 Charles II st. 2 ch. 1). This formula later became notorious as the "King's Declaration." At the time it was appointed

for officeholders and members of both Houses, except for the Duke of York.

James II largely freed himself from the obstacle to appointing Catholics to office which the Test Act imposed. He did this by exercising the prerogative dispensing power after the judges had held in *Godden v. Hales* (1686; 11 State Trials 1165) that it was contrary to the principles of the constitution to deprive the Crown of the services of any of its subjects when they were needed. After the *Revolution of 1688 the test was more stringently enforced; a clause was even added to the Bill of Rights requiring the sovereign himself to take the declaration (1 William and Mary sess. 2 ch. 2). Since the test was obligatory on all officeholders, the Oaths of Supremacy and Allegiance became otiose, and were therefore cut down to a line or two and joined with the Oath of Fidelity to King William (1 William and Mary sess. 1. ch. 8). This oath could be tendered to anyone by any two justices of the peace at their discretion. Persons refusing the oath were deemed popish recusants and were thereupon liable to all the penalties of the statutes punishing absence from church and were disabled from practicing as lawyers and voting at elections (7 and 8 William and Mary ch. 4; 1 George I st. 2 ch. 13).

The Irish Oath, 1774, to Emancipation, 1829. The first relaxations of the system of penal oaths were due to external pressure: the need to pacify Canada and the military demands of the war of American Independence. The Quebec Act, 1774 (14 George III ch. 83), provided that Catholics resident in the province might freely practice their religion, and should not be obliged to take the Oath of Supremacy under 1 William and Mary sess. 1 ch. 8. A simple oath of allegiance was substituted. In the same year the Irish Parliament similarly authorized an oath of allegiance to King George and rejection of the Stuart Pretender, which involved no rejection of the pope's spiritual authority or any article of faith and which could be taken by Catholic soldiers. The alleged malpractice of "no faith with heretics" was renounced; so was the deposing power, but without the objectionable words, "impious, heretical and damnable." The "temporal and civil jurisdiction of the pope, direct and indirect within the realm" was also renounced, and the promise was given that no dispensation from the oath should be considered valid. This Irish Oath was embodied in the first Catholic Relief Act, 1778 (18 George III ch. 60), which provided that English Catholics on taking it should be freed of the worst penalties of laws passed during the reign of William and Mary (11 and 12 William III ch. 4); the clergy readily took the oath.

In 1788 a committee of lay Catholics with Gallican leanings (who later formed the Cisalpine Club) were negotiating with the government for further relief. To them Lord Stanhope made it clear that if more concessions were required, more assurances should be given. A long *Protest* was accordingly drafted, which not only rejected the alleged malpractices disowned by the Irish Oath, but did so in strong and untheological language. It reintroduced, for instance, the objectionable terms "impious, heretical, and damnable" of the 1606 oath. Nevertheless, the committee insisted (1) that the words would be understood in a broad popular way, and (2) that to obtain the Relief Act, it must be signed at once. For this reason it was freely signed by laity and clergy and by the four vicars apostolic, although two later retracted their names. When the signatures had been obtained, the new Relief Bill was brought forward by the government with an oath founded on the *Protest* (hence called the Protestation oath), which excluded from relief those who would not swear to it and accept the name of "Protesting Catholic Dissenters." This bill would have divided the Catholic community. The successful opposition to it was led by John *Milner, then only a country priest, and the second Relief Act, 1791 (31 George III ch. 32) passed without any significant changes in the previous oath and without changing the name of Catholics. Even though the Emancipation Act, 1829 (10 George IV ch. 7) was eventually carried without any tests, this was not at first foreseen. The Catholic Committee continued its endeavors to disarm Protestant prejudices with proposals (like the Veto) that savored of Gallicanism. So too did the oath annexed to the bill proposed in 1813, which, from its length, was styled the "Theological Oath."

Repeal of the Statutory Oaths, 1867 to 1910. The Relief Acts were generally only measures of relief, leaving the old statutes, oaths, and tests on the statute book. The disused tests and oaths were repealed between 1867 and 1910. In 1867 the declaration was repealed (30 and 31 Victoria ch. 75). After this, the only person bound to pronounce the oath was the king himself at his accession. In 1871 the Promissory Oaths Act removed all the old Oaths of Allegiance (34 and 35 Victoria ch. 48). Between 1891 and 1908 five unsuccessful bills or motions were introduced into Parliament for the abolition of the King's declaration, and it was only in 1910 that this last anti-Catholic declaration was repealed by the Accession Declaration Act (10 Edward VII and 1 George V ch. 29).

Bibliography: *Statutes of the Realm*, ed. A. LUDERS et al., 12 v. (London 1810–28). *Statutes at Large* (London 1762–). *Acts and Ordinances of the Interregnum 1642–60*, ed. C. H. FIRTH and R. S. RAIT, 3 v. (London 1911). C. BUTLER, *Historical Memoirs Respecting the English, Irish, and Scottish Catholics from the Reformation to the Present Time*, 4 v. (London 1819–21). H. TOOTELL, *Dodd's Church History of England*, ed. M. A. TIERNEY, 5 v. (London 1839–43). For particular oaths: Hughes RE v.2. R. G. USHER, *The Reconstruction of the English Church*, 2 v. (New York 1910). C. J. RYAN, "The Jacobean Oath of Allegiance," CathHistRev 28 (1942) 159–183. G. SITWELL, "Leander Jones's Mission to England, 1634–35," *Recusant History* 5 (1959–60) 132–182. T. CLANCY, "English Catholics and the Papal Deposing Power 1570–1640," *ibid.* 6 (1961–62) 114–140, 205–227; 7 (1962–63) 2–10. W. K. L. WEBB, "Thomas Preston OSB, alias Roger Widdrington 1567–1640," *Biographical Studies* 2 (1953–54) 216–268. W. BIRCHLEY, *The Catholiques Plea* (London 1659); *Reflections on the Oaths of Supremacy and Allegiance* (London 1661). H. THURSTON, *Titus Oates' Test* (London 1909). J. MILNER, *Supplementary Memoirs of English Catholics* (London 1820). B. N. WARD, *Dawn of the Catholic Revival in England, 1781–1803*, 2 v. (London 1909); *The Eve of Catholic Emancipation*, 3 v. (London 1911–12).

[P. R. GLAZEBROOK]

OATHS AND AFFIRMATIONS, U.S. LAW OF

The solemn oath is a sworn promise by a witness or affiant to give truthful testimony in a judicial or quasi-judicial proceeding as well as an appeal to God to witness that testimony. An affirmation is an unsworn oath that omits reference to God. Both of these forms are made in the light of criminal, civil, and spiritual sanctions for false testimony. Its judicial character distin-guishes the testimonial oath from a *loyalty oath or oath of public office.

History. A judicial oath is mentioned as early as the Code of Hammurabi (*c.* 2100 B.C.), and was originally a plea to God to curse the swearer if his testimony proved false. By calling upon the supernatural, the swearer gave credence to his words far beyond the weight given them by his reputation in the community. At early *common law a defendant to a "trial by oath" would gather witnesses, called compurgators, to swear to the value of his oath. The defendant was said to "wage his law," and if he could obtain a specified number of swearers, judgment in his favor was assured. The oath, in this instance, was a substitute for evidence rather than a support for evidence already submitted. Use of the testimonial oath for the latter, or modern, purpose is first found in 4th-century Roman law at the time of Constantine. Such an oath is mentioned in the English Yearbook of 1293. As "trial by witness" became the accepted practice, oral testimony and the oath gained in stature.

Since God's witness ensured probity, seemingly those of Judeo-Christian heritage could give testimony, but Lord Coke (d. 1634) had grouped Jews as well as heathens among the class of infidels that were not to be admitted as witnesses. Those Christians, such as Quakers, who refused to swear because of religious scruples were barred from testifying until late in the 17th century. Pennsylvania, in its 1682 Frame of Government (*see* CHARTER OF LIBERTIES AND PRIVILEGES), was the first American colony to allow affirmation of testimony. The Christian prerogative to testify was overturned in 1774 when in *Omychund v. Barker*, I Atk. 21, 26 Eng. Rep. 15, two persons of the Gentoo religion were allowed to testify after swearing an oath to *their* god. The essentially spiritual element of an oath that guaranteed veracity now became a subjective one. The purpose of the oath was no longer to call the attention of God to the swearer, but the attention of the swearer to his god. The privilege of affirmation was later extended to atheists so that today in the U.S. no jurisdiction precludes a person from testifying because of religious belief or nonbelief. Were a state to do otherwise, the constitutionality of this action would be suspect (*Torcaso v. Maryland*, 367 U.S. 488 (1961). *See* RELIGIOUS TEST FOR PUBLIC OFFICE.

By admitting nonbelievers and atheists as witnesses, the American law relies upon a threatened prosecution for perjury rather than spiritual punishment to cajole a witness to truthfulness. The seriousness of the occasion, and the corresponding criminal sanctions may today be called to the witness's attention by an affirmation alone, and the judicial oath is condemned by some as an empty and blasphemous ceremony.

Form. By common law, an oath was required only in a judicial proceeding. Today the oath may be demanded also in hearings before Congressional and state legislative committees, before a grand jury, and in administrative affairs, e.g., application for a marriage license. Affidavits and depositions used in these proceedings must also be sworn to or affirmed. An oath must be administered by a court or its delegate, or by a party authorized by statute. Anyone, regardless of age, who can comprehend the obligation of truthfulness and punishment for false testimony may take an oath and thereby be a witness. It is not necessary that the witness know exactly how he will be punished if he testifies falsely. The form of the oath is immaterial. There is no absolute requirement that a witness raise his right hand or touch a Bible, nor is there a magic word formula [*Atwood v. Mississippi*, 111 S. 865, 51 ALR 840 (1927)]. It is enough that the witness be made to realize the seriousness of the occasion, that his testimony is more than a mere assertion, and that he is obliged by law to tell the truth.

Sanctions. Perjury, once a common law crime and today embodied in statutes, is false testimony willfully given under a valid oath. The prerequisite of a valid oath incorporates in this definition all the elements of the oath: administration, comprehension, proceedings, and the form of testimony. The false testimony must be put forth as more than conjecture or opinion. Many states, by statute, limit perjury to false testimony touching a matter material to the proceedings. Truthfulness and an invalid oath are recognized defenses to a charge of perjury. A statute promising that "no testimony given by a witness shall be offered in evidence against him in any criminal proceeding" is usually held not to give immunity from perjury but only to give immunity from crimes previously committed and testified to.

Civil liability for perjury is rare. On the grounds of privilege, a civil action of *defamation will not be directed against false testimony given in a judicial proceeding, if that testimony is relevant, relevancy being much more broadly defined here than in the law of evidence. But the privilege enjoyed by witnesses in quasi-judicial proceedings is a more qualified one, abrogated by false testimony given in malice, even though relevant. Signing a civil complaint or a criminal warrant does not subject the signer to an action for malicious prosecution unless malice is demonstrated. If the perjury is only a step in a scheme to defraud, however, an action for fraud and deceit may be aimed against a witness giving false testimony [*Morgan v. Graham*, 228 F. 2d 625 (10th Cir. 1956), 54 ALR 2d 1290]. A Maine statute, Maine Rev. St., Ch. 113, Sec. 180, gives a party who has suffered a judgment through the false testimony of a witness a right of action against that witness if he has been convicted of perjury. No scheme to defraud need exist.

Bibliography: H. SILVING, "The Oath," *Yale Law Journal* 68 (1959) 1329–90. T. R. WHITE, *Oaths in Judicial Proceedings* (Philadelphia 1903). *American Jurisprudence*, 58 v. (San Francisco 1936–48) 41–4–45. *Corpus Juris Secundum*, 101 v. (New York 1937–58) 67:4–9.

[M. J. MULLANEY, JR.]

OAXACA, ARCHDIOCESE OF (ANTEQUERENSIS)

Mexican ecclesiastical province in the states of Oaxaca and Chiapas; created a diocese in 1535; raised to an archdiocese in 1891. In 1964 it had three suffragan sees: Chiapas (1539), Tehuantepec (1893), and Tapachula (1957). Among the 3 million people in the area there are several thousand pagans and even more Protestants; however, there are no accurate statistics on religion available. In some areas religious ignorance is so widespread that the territory can be considered mission country.

The Diocese of Antequera, the third oldest in Mexico, and that of Ciudad Real de Chiapas included this extensive area during colonial times. The name

1964 STATISTICS

Area	Catholic population	Parishes	Clergy	
			Sec.	Reg.
Oaxaca	970,000	114	147	16
Chiapas	873,612	32	38	16
Tehuantepec	365,000	25	13	6
Tapachula	469,964	10	14	4

Antequera, given by the conquistadores to the city where they built the cathedral, has fallen into disuse and both the city and archdiocese are now called Oaxaca, the Spanish version of the Indian name Huaxyacac. For several centuries it was the center of evangelization for southeastern New Spain, the center of the ancient Mixtec and Zapotec cultures, populated by hundreds of Indian tribes of different cultural levels and languages. The territory of the Diocese of Chiapas was reduced with the creation of the Diocese of *Yucatán. It was suffragan to Mexico City until Guatemala became an archbishopric in 1743. Since Chiapas was politically a part of the Captaincy of Guatemala, the diocese was then attached to the new archdiocese. After independence, Chiapas was again subordinated to Mexico City (1838), and subsequently to Antequera-Oaxaca (1891).

Antequera, like all primitive dioceses, had its seminary, opened by Bishop Albumquerque (1574) and later completely restored in accordance with the Tridentine norms by Bishop del Puerto (1680). At the time of the wars of the republic, it went into a decline and even closed. Bishop Gillow restored it at the close of the 19th century, endowed it with modern scientific laboratories, and a capable faculty. The revolution of 1914 marked a new era of decadence, and there were years when it was closed. Archbishop Fortino Gómez León made special efforts to restore it to something of its former splendor. In Chiapas, Bishop Bravo de la Serna opened a seminary in 1678 in Ciudad Real (now San Cristóbal de Las Casas). The seminary also deteriorated and even was closed during the revolutionary upheaval. It was reopened in the 20th century.

Among the bishops of Antequera-Oaxaca were Alonso de Cuevas Dávalos (1658–64), who pacified the Indians of Tehuantepec; and Nicolás del *Puerto, a purebred Indian who was a gifted doctor and sacred orator. The first bishop of Chiapas was Bartolomé de *Las Casas. When Mexico became independent, Francisco *Orozco y Jiménez was an outstanding figure. He remained in Chiapas from 1902 to 1912, and was later transferred to Guadalajara. The zealous and cultured Eulogio *Gillow y Zavalza served brilliantly in Oaxaca for many years (1887–1922). He raised the Church from the ruins of the wars of independence, reform, and intervention, and gave great impetus to Christian life, to the seminary, and to the clergy. Leo XIII decided to make him a cardinal, and he would have been the first Mexican so honored if the government had given guarantees that such a high rank would be respected, but Pres. Porfirio *Díaz did not wish to accept that commitment.

The city of Oaxaca, planned by Alonso García Bravo in 1529 (only the sketch and plan of the cathedral remain) has been the focal point of Catholic life in

Tree of Jesse ceiling in the Dominican convent at Oaxaca, Mexico. Probably carved by Pedro Maldonado between 1688 and 1690, it is one of the most splendid monuments of Mexican art of the colonial period.

the whole region. In the 16th century it was the center for the Dominicans, who were entrusted with the work of evangelization in southeastern Mexico. That is the reason for the exceptional importance of their great convent of Santo Domingo, which continues to be the pride of the city and one of the archetypes of neo-Hispanic baroque art (sculptures of renowned Dominicans, the genealogical tree in the vault, and a monumental cloister in the Renaissance style). The cathedral has five naves and a central choir in the baroque style, and the church of Our Lady of La Soledad has a beautiful façade in the form of a folding screen in the typical green stone of the region.

Bibliography: J. BRAVO UGARTE, *Diócesis y obispos de la iglesia mexicana, 1519–1939* (Mexico City 1941). S. MENDEZ ARCEO, *La Santa Sede y la corona de España en la erección de las diócesis de América, 1504–1579* (Rome 1938). **Illustration credit:** C. Arthaud and F. Hebert-Stevens.

[D. OLMEDO]

OBAZINE (AUBAZINE), ABBEY OF, former French abbey, Diocese of Limoges, the present Diocese of Tulle. It was founded in a forest by a group of hermits under *Stephen of Obazine, a follower of the great hermit monk, *Robert of Arbrissel. The *Benedictine Rule was adopted, according to the interpretation of the monks of Dalon, a neighboring community of similar background. Once it was formally organized into an abbey in 1142, it soon founded two other monasteries, La Valette and Bonnaigue, and a convent for nuns, Coyroux. Obazine merged with the *Cistercians in 1147. It founded four more affiliated houses (those of La Garde-Dieu, La Frenade, Grosbos, and Gourdon).

The wars and rule by commendatory abbots led to gradual decline. In 1768 it had only six monks. It was suppressed during the French Revolution. The remodeled early Gothic church (1156–90) survives as a parish church. Other monastic buildings house a community of nuns.

Bibliography: Chevalier TB 2:2165–66. G. Müller, "Der Gründer der Abtei Obazine," CistChron 40 (1928). Cottineau 2:185–186. R. Gazeau, *Catholicisme* 1:1006–07.

[L. J. LEKAI]

OBEDIENCE

The foundation of obedience is *authority. All true authority is ultimately divine. It is either immediately divine or, if vested proximately in men, it is derived from that of God. Authority is ordained to good, common or private. Of a number of possibilities of achieving this good, authority determines and proposes the one that is to be realized. The will of authority is expressed in law, which is the binding rule of human action. Law, moreover, must be understood to include not only that which is written or externally manifest, but also that which the authoritative will of the Creator has implanted in the structure of created being, natural or supernatural. The adaptation of an individual's will to the authoritative will expressed in law is obedience. By its act, the object or content of the legislator's determination is freely adopted by the obedient will and becomes a principle of initiative and action leading to the effect intended by the legislator. The subject who obeys embraces the possibility of action that the will of authority has determined should be realized. He accepts it as commanded, and renounces conflicting possibilities. Thus does he render to authority what is its due, namely, submission. A stable readiness to such submission is the virtue of obedience. This, with respect to certain determined objects, can be confirmed by *vow.

OBEDIENCE IN JUDEO-CHRISTIAN HISTORY

A special value was attributed to obedience in both Old and New Testaments, and in later Christian history this received further emphasis through the development of the concept of religious obedience.

Old Testament. In the Old Testament, obedience to the authority of Yahweh was exercised within terms of the Covenant, whose content was embraced by the formula: "You shall be my people, and I shall be your God" (Jer 11.4; Os 2.25; Jer 7.23; 24.7). Under the Covenant, the people assumed the obligation of fulfilling the Law. This, according to the broader concept of Deuteronomy and the Psalms, was the summit of divine revelation, considered as a norm of life. Thus the Law was the foundation of religion, of ethics, and, because of the theocratic constitution of the people, of civil life in Israel (1 Sm 8.7–9; 10.19). Hence the insistence upon a knowledge of the Law, and upon conformity of life to its demands (Ex 13.8–9; Dt 33.10; Lv 10.11; Os 4.6; Prv 19.16; Sir 19.17; 21.11; Wis 6.18). Psalm 119 is a canticle of praise of the beauty and blessing of the Law, which is no insupportable yoke laid upon the shoulders of men (cf. Acts 15.10), but refreshment to the soul, joy to the heart, and light to the eyes (Ps 19.8–9); it is sweeter than honey (Ps 119.103); it is the theme of the song of the people in their place of exile (*ibid.* v. 54). Just as the lot of the first parents depended upon the command of Yahweh (Gn 2.16–17), so the efficacy of the Covenant and the promises attached to it depended upon the obedience of the people to the Law (Ex 19.5; Jer 11.2–5). For this reason Yahweh watched jealously over its fulfillment (Ex 20.5; Dt 28.15–19; Jer 11.2–5).

Obedience is worth more than sacrifice (1 Sm 15.22; Eccl 4.12).

Obedience to Yahweh included obedience to the civil authority, which derived its power from God (Wis 6.13). The king was chosen by God (Dt 17.14; 1 Sm 8.22; 10.1; 10.24; 16.13; 2 Sm 7.18); he was the son of God (2 Sm 7.14); he was helped by God (2 Sm 7.3); was anointed by Yahweh (1 Sm 24.10; Ps 89.39); was sacrosanct (1 Sm 24.10; 2 Sm 1.14); and was to be feared as Yahweh Himself (Prv 24.21).

New Testament. The Israel of God of the New Testament is the Church-Bride (Gal 6.16), subject to Christ, her Spouse (Eph 5.21–24). Christians here upon earth are pilgrims (Heb 11.13), seeking their own country (*ibid.* v. 14), obedient to the first leader of their journey, Christ (Heb 2.10; 12.2), and to their superiors in the Church (Heb 13.7). The Father, raising Christ from the dead, "put him above every Principality, and Power and Virtue and Domination . . . and all things he made subject under his feet, and him he gave as head over all the Church, which indeed is his body" (Eph 1.20–23). Aggregation to this body is effected by Baptism (1 Cor 12.13; Rom 6.3–11; Col 2.12), by which the Christian is made a "new creation" (Gal 6.15), who ought to walk in a newness of life (Rom 6.4), living in "obedience to faith" (Rom 1.5, 16.26), living not to himself but to God (Rom 5.11, 14.7–8), under the "new covenant" (Mt 26.28; 2 Cor 3.6), under the new commandment of charity (Jn 13.34). As an all-embracing principle, this commandment contains in itself virtually the whole content of the Christian life (Mt 22.40); it includes the fulfillment of the other commandments (Gal 5.14); it sums them up (Rom 13.9); it is the fulfillment of the Law (Rom 13.10). Thus the whole of the New Testament also is, by the commandment of charity, reducible to obedience.

From the very beginning of the New Testament, in its center, which is Christ, it was permeated with obedience by the determination of the Incarnate Word to do the will of the Father (Heb 10.5–7). This purpose, hidden although present from the first instant of the Incarnation, continued through the whole life of Christ. To Him the doing of His Father's will was His food (Jn 4.34); that others might live by the same nourishment He taught them to pray, "Thy will be done" (Mt 6.10), and whoever does this will is His brother and sister and mother (Mt 12.50). This readiness to obey the Father is especially and vividly manifest in His Passion (Lk 22.42). The work of the life of Christ is a work done in obedience to the will of the Father (Jn 17.4). St. Paul expresses the obedience of Christ's life in these words: "He humbled himself, becoming obedient to death, even to death on a cross" (Phil 2.8).

In the New Testament, as well as in the Old, obedience to God includes obedience to human authority, since true human authority is from God. When the Pharisees asked whether it was lawful to give tribute to Caesar, by His answer—"Render to Caesar the things that are Caesar's, and to God the things that are God's" (Mt 22.21)—He acknowledges the rights of civil authority so long as this does not violate the rights of God (cf. Acts 4.19; Dn 3.18). According to His words to Pilate—"Thou wouldst have no power at all over me were it not given thee from above" (Jn 19.11)—God Himself grants civil authority its power, and the lot of Christ depended upon this divine grant. According to

St. Paul, "Let everyone be subject to the higher authorities, for there exists no authority except from God, and those who exist have been appointed by God. Therefore who resists the authority resists the ordinance of God" (Rom 13.1–2). Since the following verses discuss rulers who are a terror not to the good but to the evil, commending the good and as God's ministers carrying the sword to execute wrath on those who do evil, it is evident that St. Paul is speaking of civil authority that does not abuse its rights. To such authority obedience must be rendered not only because of fear of punishment, but also for conscience' sake (*ibid.* v. 5). The same holds true for the relationship of Christians toward the Roman tax-gatherers (vv. 6–7). According to St. Peter, the faithful must subject themselves not only to supreme but to subordinate rulers for the sake of God (1 Pt 2.13–14). If the passages in the Apocalypse concerning the adoration of the beast and its image (13.12–17; 14.9–11; 16.2; 20.4) are understood as referring to the Roman Emperor, they do not express an attitude of hostility toward civil authority as such, but toward the paying of divine honors to the Emperor. The freedom of the children of God was not to be made a pretext for rebellion against civil authority, for this freedom supposes full subjection to the will of God and to those who hold their authority from Him (Gal 5.13; Rom 6.18). Slaves were to obey their masters as they would Christ (Eph 6.5), not only the good and moderate ones, but the severe as well; harsh and unjust treatment they were to endure after the example of Christ (1 Pt 2.18–23). In marriage the woman was to be subject to the authority of the man (1 Cor 11.3; Eph 5.22–23; 1 Pt 3.1) as to that of the Lord (Eph 5.22), or "as is becoming in the Lord" (Col 3.18). The authority of the husband, however, should be exercised without harshness (Col 3.19; Eph 5.25–29). Children were to be subject to the authority of their parents (Col 3.20) in the Lord (Eph 6.1). Obedience to parents is a condition of happiness (Mt 15.4; 19.19) and is acceptable to God (Col 3.20; 1 Tm 5.4). But Christ ought to be loved more than one's parents (Mt 10.37). The authority of parents ought to be used without undue severity (Col 3.21). All human authority, in fact, ought to be exercised after the example of Christ's, who did not come to be served but to serve (Mk 10.45), and He made Himself the servant of His Disciples, although He was their Master and Lord (Jn 13.13–16). In the Christian community authority is not to be distorted into despotism, but to be considered a service (Mk 10.42; Lk 22.25). "Let him who is greatest among you become as the youngest, and him who is chief as the servant" (Lk 22.26; Mk 10.43–45). This principle is true especially for the elders who ought to feed the flock of the Lord not under constraint, but willingly, according to God; nor yet for the sake of base gain, but eagerly; nor yet as lording it over their charges, but as becoming from the heart a pattern to the flock (1 Pt 5.2–3).

Religious Obedience. From ordinary Christian obedience, founded on the doctrine of the New Testament, the idea of religious obedience gradually emerged. The first anchorites were not drawn to their hermitages with any formal intention of subjecting themselves to the yoke of obedience to any human superior, but rather by their desire to seek the sort of annihilation proclaimed in the Gospels and the self-denial demanded by Christ, and to fulfill the obligations undertaken in Baptism to renounce Satan and the world. However, confidence in some outstanding ascetic's experience in the spiritual life inclined many individuals to submit themselves to the direction of such a person. This submission was based less upon a juridically defined authority than upon a kind of spiritual paternity of a more or less charismatic nature. The subjection was freely undertaken, was revocable, was not confirmed by vow, nor did one subject himself for life. Cf. I. Hausherr, *Direction spirituelle en Orient autrefois* (OrChrAnal 144; Rome 1955). Associated with an individual's confidence in the greater experience of another was his distrust of his own disordered will; this made renunciation of this will and submission to the will of a spiritual father seem good. Submission of this kind was esteemed as a great virtue among the anchorites.

However, the solitude of the hermits, though relative, seemed to provide too little opportunity for the exercise of this virtue. It was partly to provide greater scope for it that the cenobitical way of life was introduced with its hierarchical structure. Among the cenobites a new value was found in submission. They aimed at securing the spiritual welfare not only of the individual but of the community as a whole as well. Submission in a monastery meant entering upon a cloistered life under the authority of an abbot whose power was determined by rule or constitutions. Obedience was now not only, not even primarily, based upon confidence in a person but upon a foundation of juridical obligation. Not the person but the office of the religious superior was the primary consideration. Together with humility, the enemy of pride—the original sin of man—obedience took an absolute character. It left no room for questioning or judgment where commands were concerned. Apart from the rule and the will of the superior, nothing was valued as holy or prudent. There was something primitive in this attitude. The concept of obedience needed to be humanized and to be based upon a less pessimistic view of nature. It would be mitigated in time, owing to the demands of the apostolate, by a greater adaptability, a greater respect for initiative, and a more refined sense of the personal dignity of the individual. Meanwhile, the motives underlying primitive asceticism were not without value. The love of Christ, the imitation of His obedience, the practice of humility, are at the heart of all religious life. Cf. M. Olphe-Galliard, *Histoire de l'obéissance religieuse: Des Pères du desert au cénobitisme de saint Basile et de saint Benoît,* in *L'Obéissance et la religieuse d'aujourd'hui* (Paris 1951) 29–30. As early as St. Augustine (*Epist.* 211) and St. Caesarius of Arles (*Regula Sanctarum Virginum,* ed. G. Morin, FlorPatr 34) there was insistence upon the use of discretion in the exercise of authority. "[Let the superior] be to all an example of good works; let her correct the unruly, strengthen the fainthearted, sustain the weak, bearing always in mind that she must render an account to God for them." Even more did St. Benedict in his *Regula Monasteriorum* (ed. B. Linderbauer, FlorPatr 17) strive to make provision against rigid authoritarianism and too great an insistence upon uniformity.

When religious, either as a community or as individuals, undertake missionary or cultural labors in the world, religious obedience must begin to keep in view not only the sanctification of the individual religious and the good of the community but also the demands of the apostolate. With religious engaged in work of this kind, obedience cannot ordinarily consist in doing only that which the rule or the superior commands. It would be unsuited to the apostolate, for the rule cannot make provision for all concrete circumstances, nor can a superior foresee them and by anticipatory commands chart the course to be followed in every particular case. There is frequent need for personal decision by the individual religious in accordance with the spirit of the rule and his general understanding of what his superior would want him to do. See J. Loosen, "Gestaltwandel im religiösen Gehorsamsideal," GeistL 24 (1951) 196–209.

The vow only gradually came to be annexed to the practice of religious obedience. The precise nature of the formula that was signed by the monks in Atripe is not known, for it has not come down to us in its entirety [J. Leipoldt, "Schenute von Atripe und die Entstehung des nationalen agyptischen Christentums," TU 25.1 (1903) 109, 195–196], but it seems to have been a true religious profession, made to God, and probably for the whole time a monk remained in the monastic state or in the monastery. However, there is no evidence in the part of the formula we possess of a vow of religious obedience.

St. Basil seems to have exacted from those seeking admission to the cenobitic life in his monasteries a declaration, at least implicit, of obedience (*Regulae brevius tractatae* 1–2; PG 31:1081–84). The violation of obedience was a "theft and sacrilege" (Basil, *De renunt. saec.* 4; PG 31:633). But there is no proof of the existence of a special vow of obedience. See D. Amand, *L'Ascèse monastique de saint Basile,* (Maredsous, Belg. 1949) 324–335. Without doubt, however, the vow of obedience is contained in St. Benedict's *Regula Monasteriorum:* "Taken to the oratory, before all let him make the promise of stability and of conversion of life and of obedience in the presence of God and his saints" (ch. 58).

Theological Considerations

In Christianity, obedience is the concrete realization of the fundamental commitment to God to which the Christian is obliged by the fact of his Baptism. By Baptism he is, ontologically speaking, holy—or, in other words, consecrated through Christ to God. In correspondence with this ontological state, he ought to live not for himself but for God. But to live for God is to fulfill His will, which is the will of Supreme Authority. The will of God can be known in concrete situations by applying to them the norms of divine positive law and of natural law, and by the actual enlightenment of the Holy Spirit. Just as the whole life of Christ was one of obedience, so also should be the whole life of the Christian, since it is the formal or at least implicit fulfillment of God's authoritative will. This obedience is acceptable to God because it is realized in virtue of the obedience of Christ through the Holy Spirit who shapes the obedience of Christians, whom He moves, to the image of the obedience of Christ.

The principal divine law of Christian life is the commandment of charity. Its fulfillment is, implicitly at least, obedience as well as charity. It is obedient charity. See B. Häring, *Das Heilige und das Gute* (Karilling vor Munchen 1950) 284–290. This obedience is as extensive as charity itself. The commandment, as the ultimate end of the Christian life, is confined by no limits. It can be said that so much love is of precept, and that what exceeds the limits of precept is a matter of counsel. Yet everyone is commanded to love God as much as he can (Thomas Aquinas, *C. retrah. relig. ingress.* 6; cf. ST 2a2ae, 184.3). The power to fulfill this commandment is the theological virtue of charity. To the limitlessness of the command there corresponds a limitlessness in the internal dynamism of the virtue. It is a universal love of benevolence that admits no limits to its desire to do good to the one who is beloved. This desire, by its own inner dynamism, with the universal laws of morality before it, as these are seen with the inner illumination necessary to grasp their relevance to a present situation, seeks to express itself. For this expression, acts are necessary. These, of themselves, may be only of counsel, but they are performed, when they are necessary to the life of charity, as though they were of precept, and this because of the preceptive character of charity itself. This life of obedient charity, although it might at times be explicitly renewed, need not, however, be continuously self-conscious. When the Christian living in the state of grace does not think explicitly of God and does not move toward Him with explicit acts of charity, but conducts himself in accordance with Christian standards, his will, controlling his actions, is perfected and informed by charity, and his charity is activated, implicitly at least, in all his virtuous action. (See Thomas Aquinas, *In 3 sent.* 23.3.1.1.)

Besides the law of charity there are other divine laws, each with its own content. To each there corresponds a proper fulfillment that implicitly or explicitly involves obedience. The chastity of the Christian, for example, is obedient chastity. Obedience does not take anything away from the proper nature of the virtues that it includes, any more than charity—which intrinsically informs obedience and the other virtues included in it—destroys the proper nature of those virtues or the specific distinction between them.

Obedience and Human Law. Since every human law must be included under divine law, and since human authority, whether ecclesiastical or civil, is a participation of divine authority, obedience to human law, if we consider it objectively, is ultimately given to God and in its origin is determined by charity, of which it is an expression. The direct object of the obligation of human law is indicated in the law itself. Indirectly, the law obliges one to use the means necessary for its fulfillment, to procure materials necessary for its observance, to avoid setting up obstacles, without sufficient reason, that would prevent the observance of the law, and to remove such obstacles as have been set up without sufficient reason. Human law, as preceptive, obliges to the act of obedience and to the acts of whatever other virtues may be involved in obedience. The obligation is in proportion to the importance of the object of the law to common or private welfare. The object has importance either on its own account, or dependently upon circumstances or upon the end for the sake of which the law was made. Proper fulfillment of the law supposes true interpretation of it and right application to the particular cases in which it is to be observed. In a concrete case one does not proceed simply in accordance with the words of the law, but rather in accordance with its true meaning, giving the reality of the concrete case due consideration. It belongs to *epikeia, as St. Thomas said, "to moderate . . . the observance of the words of the law" (ST 2a2ae, 120.2 ad 3). And epikeia is the more important part of justice (ST 2a2ae, 120.2 ad 1).

Obedience and Personal Responsibility. True obedience is not a robot-like activity produced entirely by the external impulse coming from the superior. It is a personal act elicited by the subject himself, who in obedience adapts his will to the will of the superior, and it is ultimately the subject who moves himself to act. The possibility that a superior could command something objectively sinful requires the subject, even in his obedience, to keep clearheaded and to remain capable of independent thought. To obey without moral certainty of the lawfulness of what is commanded would be immoral. In his own conscience, the subject remains responsible for whatever he does even when he acts under obedience. The fact that a thing is commanded does not take away responsibility from the subject. His theoretical or speculative judgment regarding the morality of what is commanded is governed per se by the objective light of truth, not by the mind of the superior. A commanded action does not become good because the superior thinks it good, for the superior is not the cause of truth. Acting in accordance with its nature and subjecting itself to truth, the mind of the subject, even when it is in disagreement with the mind of the superior, is obedient: it yields its obedience to Him who created the intellect to act in this way, and who is the Supreme Superior.

When the morality of what is commanded is not evident, reverence, piety, and the supernatural context of the virtue of obedience will incline the speculative judgment of the subject to agreement with his superior. When the speculative judgment of the subject has no cause to see compliance as immoral, the practical judgment, which governs the doing of what is commanded, must submit itself to the command of legitimate authority acting within its proper limits. This is so even when the subject knows, from a speculative point of view, that the situation could be better dealt with otherwise, or even that the superior's command proceeds from malice. (See F. Suárez, *De religione Societatis Iesu,* lib. 4, cap. 15.) Ordinarily no long process of reasoning is required to establish the legitimacy of a command, for the supernatural enlightenment with which God assists the Christian suffices to facilitate judgment and protect him against harmful error. On the other hand, it must not be assumed that the subject's own judgment, as opposed to that of his superior, is something necessarily inordinate or worthy of contempt. The intellect, which judges, is by no means completely corrupt by reason of original sin. Indeed, in spite of the consequences of original sin, it is elevated by faith and may well be aided by the gifts of wisdom, knowledge, and understanding. Caution, however, is necessary, for self-interest or a morbidly hypercritical spirit can dull the intellect's capacity to discern the legitimacy of a concrete command.

Obedience, therefore, does not exist for the purpose of lessening personal activity. Ultimately, even under obedience, a subject must seek the will of the Father by passing judgment upon the lawfulness of a concrete command, by personally accepting and fulfilling it, and in the fulfillment, through his own initiative, determining and realizing the necessary details undefined in the command itself.

From the fact that the superior participates in the authority of God, it does not follow that a subject, faced with a concrete command, must conduct himself as he does in accepting a matter of faith, in which he simply accepts revealed truth, relying only on the authority of God revealing. The subject ought indeed to believe that all legitimate human authority is from God, because this is a revealed truth. But he cannot accept on faith that any concrete command is legitimate, for that is something about which God has revealed nothing. The legitimacy cannot be discerned except by the personal effort of the subject, and only after this is manifest can the subject know that the concrete command expresses the will of God.

Superior and Subject. The superior who commands ought to be himself obedient even while he commands. He owes obedience to God. No one who is in command is only a superior; he is at the same time—and primarily—a subject. The whole end of obedience demands submission on the part of both subject and superior. Moreover, just as there is for the subject, simply because he is a subject, no guarantee of his right fulfillment of commands, so the superior, simply because he has legitimate authority, is not guaranteed the right use of his authority. Before God, superior and subject are redeemed children of the Father, seeking to do His will. It is the superior's duty to seek this by commanding according to the will of God; it is the subject's duty to seek it in fulfilling the legitimate commands according to the will of God. Not only is the subject to see Christ in his superior, but the superior must also see Christ in his subject, for the subject is a member of the Mystical Body of Christ. Because of the fact that the superior's authority is derived from Christ, the subject has additional reason to see Christ in his superior. By the fulfillment of a legitimate command, he ought to minister to the life of the Body of Christ, and in the same way the superior in his exercise of authority should minister to that same life. But it must not be thought that God binds, moves, and illuminates the Christian to the doing of His will only through the commands of a human superior. Such an opinion is contrary to ecclesiastical tradition concerning the immediate guidance of the Holy Spirit, and it contradicts the historical fact that the life of the Church has been influenced again and again by ideas and movements that did not have their origin in obedience to a human superior but that came immediately from God.

Although the end of obedience requires obedience of both subject and superior, and although both are equal as Christians, nevertheless superior and subject, as such, do not stand on the same level. God who leads men not only immediately but also through men, by granting a participation in His authority to the superior, places him over the subject, and He gives to the superior, within the limits of his authority, the office of commanding, and He gives the subject the duty of carrying out the commands of his superior. Every effort to lower the superior within the proper ambit of his authority to the level of the subject is damaging to the essence of obedience. Such efforts cause the idea of authority and hence of true superiority to be lost to sight, and obedience fades into a dialogue that has no real power to bind the subject but leaves him free to determine for himself what he ought and what he ought not to do.

There is a certain dialectical tension between the need of obedience and the need of liberty. The goal of educating in obedience is to effect a synthesis of both elements, or, in other words, a free obedience, which will be a capacity, partly acquired and partly infused, to recognize and understand and to carry out with personal decision and a sense of responsibility the orders given by one in authority.

Orders, commands, or prohibitions that are well chosen develop respect for authority. There should be a progressive unfolding of the meaning and content of the superior's commands so that infantile forms of submission give way to others determined by objective values, particularly by religious values, which can more easily provide a solid basis for ready and free obedience.

Deviations. Distortions of obedience consist of an obsequious submission rooted in a variety of undesirable causes: egoistic ambition; a weakness with regard to the regulation of one's own life, so that obedience becomes a refuge of a person unable to make decisions or unwilling to assume responsibility; a pathological need that a person may have for a hero to admire and worship; or want of courage, or, seen from another point of view, fear of a servile kind. Genuine obedience to the will of the Father carries with it not only the submission of one's will to the command of a superior, but also, when there is abuse of authority, prudent and firm opposition.

See also AUTHORITY; PIETY, FAMILIAL; CIVIL LAW, MORAL OBLIGATION OF; RELIGIOUS LIFE; COUNSELS, EVANGELICAL; FREEDOM; FREEDOM, SPIRITUAL.

Bibliography: J. B. RAUS, *De sacrae obedientiae virtute et voto secundum doctrinam divi Thomae et S. Alphonsi, juxta normas ac codicem juris canonici* (Lyons 1923). F. VALENTINE, *Religious Obedience* (London 1951). R. E. REGAN, "The Exercise of Authority by Religious Superiors in Modern America," *Religious Community Life in the United States,* 2 v. (New York 1952) 1:178–185. P. K. MEAGHER, "The Spirit of Religious Obedience in America," *ibid.* 1:186–199. S. GIET, "Saint Bernard et le troisième degré d'obéissance ou la soumission de jugement," AnnThAug 7 (1946) 192–221. B. HARING, "Freiheit oder Gehorsam?" GeistL 21 (1948) 108–121. K. ESSER, "Gehorsam und Freiheit," *Wissenschaft und Weisheit* 13 (1950) 142–150. H. MOGENET, "L'Obéissance religieuse vertu évangelique et humaine," RevAscMyst 27 (1951) 75–95. *L'Obéissance et la religieuse d'aujourd'hui* (Paris 1951). Congressus Generalis de Statibus Perfectionis, 1950, *Acta et documenta,* 4 v. (Rome 1952) 2:396–429. J. LECLERCQ, *The Religious Vocation* (New York 1955). T. CAMELOT, "Obéissance et liberté," VieSpirit 86 (1952) 154–168. P. PHILIPPE, "La Portée du voeu d'obéissance," *ibid.* 509–524. H. HOLSTEIN, "Le Mystère de l'obéissance," *Études* 278 (1953) 145–157. J. PÉRINELLE, *Les Voies de Dieu* (Paris 1956) 459–518. K. RAHNER, "Reflections on Obedience . . . a Basic Ignatian Concept," *Cross Currents* 10 (1960) 364–374. M. LABOURDETTE, "La Vertu d'obéissance selon saint Thomas," RevThom 57 (1957) 626–656. K. V. TRUHLAR, *Problemata theológica de vita spirituali laicorum et religiosorum* (Collectanea spiritualia 8; Rome 1960) 81–121; VieSpirit Suppl 7 (1953) 249–359; GeistL 29 (1956) 1–56; *Ciencia Tomista* 83 (1956) 219–422. P. LUMBRERAS, "La obediencia dialogada," *ibid.* 82 (1955) 65–84.

[K. V. TRUHLAR]

OBEDIENTIAL POTENCY

A concept originally developed in the theology of miracles, now frequently used in the description of the *natural order's relationship to the *supernatural. In its broadest sense obediential potency means the openness of every creature to the Creator's power to effect in it something beyond the powers of ordinary natural causes; it is the very being of an existing creature as obedient, subject, or as some hold, positively ordered to God's power to act in it. Here the term itself is first examined, then its use regarding miracles and the supernatural.

Term. It derives from two traditions: the first, going back to Ambrose (*Hex.* 1.4.13; 3.1.1) and perhaps to Scripture (Mt 8.27) or Cicero (*De leg.* 3.1.3), spoke of nature's obedience to God in creation and miracles; the second, from Augustine (*Gen. ad litt.* 9.17.32), studied the possibility in the creature of its being miraculously changed (cf. Peter Lombard, 2 *Sent.* 18.6). These traditions united in the late 12th century to produce the concept of obediential potency (Landgraf 1.1:243, fn. 26). The term first appeared in the 13th century as potency of obedience (*potentia obedientiae*), e.g., in the *Summa* said to be Alexander of Hales's (1a2i:231, 469, 491; Quar. ed. 2:288, 632, 686), in Albert the Great (*In 2 sent.* 18.7; *In 4 sent.* 11.4 ad 1), Bonaventure (*In 1 sent.* 42.3 ad 1 neg.; *In 1 sent.* 42.4), in Thomas Aquinas frequently (e.g., *De ver.* 29.3 ad 3). Obediential potency (*potentia obedientialis*) occurred in Albert (*ST* 2.8.31.1.4 sed contra 1; cf. Gillon 304, fn. 3) and in Thomas (*De virt. in com.* 10 ad 13) and gradually became the usual form.

Miracles. If the laws of nature are fixed by God, how can He work a miracle without upsetting these laws and betraying a lack of wisdom? Theologians answer with the concept of obediential potency: although the creature has no positive capacity or exigency to be changed miraculously, its being is subject or obedient to what God wills to do in it beyond the activity of ordinary causes so long as no contradiction occurs. The creature is purely passive; God can do in it whatever is not repugnant to its nature. As author and governor of creatures, God includes in His providence the extraordinary interventions of His power. A miracle is thus possible. This doctrine, taught by Augustine, was formulated in terms of obediential potency by medieval theologians and has remained constant in theology.

The Supernatural. Since for Thomas Aquinas obediential potency implies pure passivity and total indetermination, he finds it inadequate to express the relationship to the supernatural of intellectual creatures; he holds instead that as *image of God they have a capacity for or are apt for *grace, are ordered or habilitated to grace, have a natural *desire to see God, even though the supernatural transcends their nature. Although several medieval theologians did speak of the obediential potency of nature for the supernatural, it was Cajetan who most influenced the modern use of obediential potency for this relationship. Reacting to Scotus's doctrine of man's innate desire for the supernatural and seeking to maintain the gratuity of the supernatural, he said that of itself human nature has only an obediential potency for supernatural elevation in the sense that God's elevating it is possible since this is not repugnant to human nature (*In ST* 1.1.1.7–12; 1.12.1.9–10). *See* ELEVATION OF MAN. His use here of obediential potency, connoting by its origin a passive non-repugnance to miraculous change, was soon imitated by many commentators professing to follow Aquinas; they were urged to this by the need to react against M. Baius's teaching of man's exigency of the supernatural. *See* BAIUS AND BAIANISM. Modern followers of these commentators still retain this use of obediential potency. Some modify this position by distinguishing between the transcendental obediential potency of all things to God's intervention and the specific obediential potency to the supernatural that is proper to intellectual creatures, since they can know universal being and good.

Many theologians today oppose this school of thought. They argue that it gives a view of the supernatural as merely juxtaposed or extrinsic to nature, furthers *secularism's tenet that man can find completion solely in the natural order, makes the supernatural seem adventitious. This reaction was influenced by M. *Blondel's and H. de Lubac's efforts to show the intimate connection and continuity between the intellectual creature and his supernatural destiny and vocation. *See* IMMANENCE APOLOGETICS; DESTINY, SUPERNATURAL; VOCATION TO SUPERNATURAL LIFE. Some, including those studying Aquinas by historical method, would eliminate the use of obediential potency from this area of discussion. Others, while rejecting the pure passivity of nature regarding the supernatural, still describe the relationship in terms of obediential potency but define this as the positive order or direction of nature to its fulfilment in the supernatural. Each seeks in his own way to maintain the Church's teaching that man's supernatural elevation surpasses the powers and exigencies of his nature (Denz 1921, 3005, 3891; Denz³¹ 2103).

Other particular uses of obediential potency include the obediential potency of the human intellect to infused knowledge, prophecy, etc.; of human nature for the hypostatic union; of things and words for sacramental signification and efficacy; of the whole universe to *preternatural perfection under the headship of Christ.

See also ANIMA NATURALITER CHRISTIANA; BEATIFIC VISION; GRACE, ARTICLES ON; MAN, 4, THEOLOGICAL TEACHING; MIRACLES (THEOLOGY OF); SUPERNATURAL EXISTENTIAL; SUPERNATURAL ORDER.

Bibliography: P. DUMONT, DTC 14.2:2665–72, for Suárez's special doctrine of passive and active ob. pot. F. BUUCK, Lex ThK² 8:646–647. P. PARENTE, EncCatt 11:969–979. G. COLOMBO, "Il problema del soprannaturale negli ultimi cinquant'anni," *Problemi e orientamenti di teologia dommatica,* 2 v. (Milan 1957) 2:545–607. A. DARMET, *Les Notions de raison séminale et de puissance obédientielle chez saint Augustin et saint Thomas d'Aquin* (Belley 1934). H. DE LUBAC, *Surnaturel: Études historiques* (Paris 1946); "Saint Thomas, *Compendium theologiae,* c. 104," RechScRel 36 (1949) 300–305. R. GARRIGOU-LAGRANGE, *De revelatione,* 2 v. (5th ed. Rome 1950) 1:345–355. "Die Vorbereitung auf die Rechtfertigung und die Eingiessung der rechtfertigenden Gnade," in Landgraf Doggesch 1.1:238–302. W. R. O'CONNOR, *The Eternal Quest* (New York 1947). K. RAHNER, *Nature and Grace,* tr. D. WHARTON (New York 1964). M. SCHMAUS, *Katholische Dogmatik* (6th ed. Munich 1962) 2.1:115 (pp. 217–235). B. STOECKLE, *Gratia supponit naturam: Geschichte und Analyse eines theologischen Axioms* (StAnselm 49; Rome 1962) 232–263. L. CHARLIER, "Puissance passive et désir naturel selon saint Thomas," EphemThLov 7 (1930) 5–28, 639–662. P. M. DE CONTENSON, "Surnaturel," *Bulletin Thomiste* 8 (1947–53) 794–804, 9 (1954–56) 551–555, 10 (1957–59) 462–468. L. B. GILLON, "Aux origines de la *puissance obédientielle,*" RevThom 47 (1947) 304–310. É. H. GILSON, "Sur la problématique thomiste de la vision béatifique," ArchHistDoctLitMA 31 (1964) 67–68. H. DE LUBAC, *Augustinisme et théologie moderne* (Paris 1965) esp. 242–251; *Le Mystère du surnaturel* (Paris 1965) esp. 87–88, 142, 179–189.

[W. H. PRINCIPE]

OBERMAIER, HUGO, German-Spanish prehistorian; b. Regensburg, Germany, Jan. 9, 1877; d. Fribourg, Switzerland, Nov. 12, 1946. After completing his Gymnasium courses, he entered the Regensburg seminary, and was ordained in 1900. Attracted to research on early man, he studied under Hoernes, Penck, and Toldt at the University of Vienna, obtaining his doctorate in 1904 and receiving an appointment to the staff in 1908. He worked in close collaboration with Henri *Breuil and other noted French prehistorians.

In 1910 he was appointed research professor at the Institut de Paléontologie Humaine, newly founded at Paris by Prince Albert I of Monaco. The outbreak of World War I prompted his move to Spain, where he

Hugo Obermaier.

became a professor at the University of Madrid and a Spanish citizen. At the outbreak of the Spanish Civil War, he was traveling in central Europe, and he took up residence at Fribourg, where he had been offered a professorial appointment at the university. Obermaier's scientific work began with research on the Quaternary period in the Alps and Pyrenees. Taking part in the excavations of the paleolithic loess-stations in the Wachau, Austria, he assisted at the discovery of the famous female statue of Willendorf. While a member of the Paris Institut, he excavated the big cave of Castillo in Spain. After moving to Spain, he started paleolithic research around Madrid, studying glaciation in the peninsula and making pioneer inquiries into the prehistoric cave art of northern Spain, as well as the rock art in the east and in the Iberian megalithic tombs. His extraordinarily precise scientific publications, totalling 166, include many synthesizing works such as *Der Mensch der Vorzeit* (Berlin 1912), *El Hombre Fósil* (Madrid 1916), and *Urgeschichte der Menschheit* (Freiburg 1931). He was coauthor with Breuil, Leo Frobenius, and others, of many monographs on prehistoric art.

Illustration credit: MAS, Barcelona.

[J. MARINGER]

OBJECT, a term derived from the Latin *obiectum,* meaning what is thrown against and signifying anything that confronts another, generally a knowing *subject. Among scholastics, the object is what specifies a knowing power or a science. *See* FACULTIES OF THE SOUL; SCIENCE (SCIENTIA). A distinction is commonly made between the formal object (*obiectum formale*), or the aspect under which the thing is related to the knowing power or *habit, and the material object (*obiectum materiale*), or the *thing itself abstracting from this relation; the formal object is further divided into the *obiectum formale quod,* or the precise aspect that is known, and the *obiectum formale quo,* or the way in which (or the means by which) it is known. In moral science, object is frequently used to designate the goal or purpose of human action; in this meaning it becomes synonymous with *end.

Among modern thinkers, object is opposed more directly to subject and thus takes on a more epistemological connotation; its main use is to designate the content or term of *knowledge. Some employ it to distinguish the content of thought from the act of thinking (L. Lavelle); others make it synonymous with the thing-in-itself as this exists independently of being known (G. Marcel). The main problem of *phenomenology and of some forms of *existentialism is that of bridging the gap between subject and object in the knowing process; realist philosophers provide such a bridge in the notion of *intentionality (see OBJECTIVITY; SUBJECTIVITY).

Objective is a derivative of object and takes on somewhat the same connotations in different philosophical systems. In *idealism, something is objective if it constitutes a proper object of thought; in *realism, and in ordinary linguistic usages, a thing is objective if it is extramental and independent of the conditions imposed by the knower. Knowledge is said to be objective if it is impersonal and universally acceptable, and a person is said to be objective if he abstracts from his particular feelings, tastes, and prejudices and restricts himself to areas of common agreement. Objectivism, when used by philosophers, is opposed to *subjectivism; it may be a synonym for realism or for *positivism, depending on the option of the user.

See also EPISTEMOLOGY; KNOWLEDGE, THEORIES OF.

Bibliography: DictLangPhil 485–490. A. LALANDE, *Vocabulaire technique et critique de la philosophie* (8th ed., rev. and enl. Paris 1960) 695–703. A. GUZZO and V. MATHIEU, EncFil 3:990–1002. U. VIGLINO, EncCatt 9:84–85. J. M. BALDWIN, Hastings ERE 9:440–441; ed., *Dictionary of Philosophy and Psychology*, 3 v. in 4 (New York 1901–05; repr. Gloucester 1949–57) 2:191–193. Eisler 2:275–332.

[B. A. GENDREAU]

OBJECTIVITY

In the *phenomenology of E. *Husserl, the characteristic of an object of awareness by virtue of which it can be grasped as the same by distinct acts of apprehension. Thus not only aspects of physical bodies and essences but also psychological realities such as memories are "objectivities" insofar as they can be thus grasped. The acts of perceiving, thinking, and remembering by which such objects are grasped, on the other hand, are subjective and transient. Husserl customarily distinguishes between *Gegenständlichkeit* and *Objektivität,* the former term referring to the status of things in the physical world, the latter to the meaningful aspects through which these things, as well as all other targets of awareness, are given to man. Thus the second term refers to a realm of objectivities that encompasses both the "interior" and the "exterior" worlds of *epistemology, and for this reason it is more fundamental.

Objective vs. Subjective. As it is commonly used, however, objectivity tends to mean not only a phenomenal (i.e., descriptive) characteristic, but also a principle of value. Objective means whatever is the case, whatever is true for all subjects. In this sense it is understood to be opposed to subjective opinions and preferences, that is, to judgments and evaluations that are distorted by the emotions, stereotypes, biases, etc., of the person. This latter sort of subjective element is called psychological, which in this context is thus a pejorative term for the factors wrongly influencing those judgments and evaluations. An objective judgment or an objective evaluation is therefore one in which the resolution is determined essentially by the object's meaning and value, by "the way things are" rather than by the way one thinks they are or prefers them.

Criteria of Objectivity. One problem here, of course, is how to decide what is true for everyone. Perhaps the first spontaneous criterion that comes to mind is that of common consent, exemplified in language or action. It tends to be assumed that whatever is objectively the case will be independent of an individual's assessment; hence that whatever is spoken of by everyone is not the effect of psychological or cultural predispositions. But reference to unicorns, fairies, phlogiston, and the ether serves to recall the limitations of this criterion. To say that it has limitations, however, is not to say that it is useless when properly confined and controlled. Yet common consent at a given time is clearly not a sufficient ground for concluding to the objective status of what is consented to. It might be thought that it would be at least a necessary condition. But the lack of common consent in matters of morality is remarked on by many philosophers (from Socrates to the present) who nevertheless admit the possibility of objective moral norms.

In the study of nature as well, this criterion has been found insufficient and has been supplemented by that of a controlled method of *verification, a method that attempts to minimize or eliminate the influence of subjective elements. The so-called "scientific method," by reason of its success in promoting consensus among its practitioners and in extending one kind of understanding of nature, has resulted in "scientifically established" becoming nearly a synonym for objective. In fact some schools of philosophy have defended that synonymy, at the price of relegating secondary qualities and values to the realm of the subjective. If the rules for following the scientific method could in fact function as an unambiguous procedure for formulating and testing the truth of a judgment, then it would constitute a necessary if not a sufficient condition for objectivity. But here too the history of scientific innovators such as L. *Pasteur, N. *Copernicus, and G. *Cantor shows in retrospect that (as I. *Kant noted) no system of rules can prescribe the way in which the rules are to be employed. Once again, this is only to note a limitation of a method of verifying objective conditions and not to dismiss a method as worthless.

Phenomenology's Reaction. The fundamental question is whether *whatever* is objective is so in these senses, viz, independent of the individual's attitude and hence in principle accessible to all or establishable by a fixed method. Phenomenology suggests a negative answer to this question, and provides an account of the reasons for the limitations of these criteria. Its fundamental premise is that what is objective is not given in experience without the "cooperation" of the subject. What is disclosed by experience to be the case is essentially related to the noetic attitude or *intentionality taken by the subject with respect to the world. For example, the scientific attitude is a way of understanding the meaning and being of the world that casts some things into relief and others into shadow. But other levels of meaning—the aesthetic, the religious, the social—may be rendered inaccessible by the predominance of this attitude. The aim of phenomenology is, then, the description and correlation of these various intentionalities, all of which are potentially revealing, but some of which are more fundamental than others.

In traditional terms, these observations point toward a difference between *de jure* and *de facto* objectivity, the former virtually accessible to all, the latter actually so accessible, at least to those with the requisite faculties and training. A final question is raised by those who contend that, in some instances, what is the case is accessible only to a unique individual. Gabriel Marcel has argued that one here passes beyond the realm of the publicly verifiable without losing touch with objectivity (*see* EXISTENTIALISM, 4). Such an apparent exception tests the general rule in an important way, because religious affirmations seem to be of this sort.

See also SUBJECTIVITY.

Bibliography: S. STRASSER, *Phenomenology and the Human Sciences* (Pittsburgh 1963). G. MARCEL, *The Mystery of Being*, tr. G. S. FRASER, 2 v. (Chicago 1950–51). M. POLANYI, *Personal Knowledge* (Chicago 1958). Y. SIMON, *Introduction à l'ontologie du connaître* (Paris 1933).

[F. J. CROSSON]

OBLATE SISTERS OF PROVIDENCE (OSP),

a diocesan congregation of religious women founded in 1829 at Baltimore, Md., by the French-born Sulpician Jacques Nicholas Joubert (d. 1843) for the Christian education of Negroes. The original group included Elizabeth Lange, Marie Magdalen Balas, Rosine Boegue, and Almaide Duchemin, the first Negro women in the U.S. to take religious vows. They followed a rule written for them by Joubert and received the approbation of Rome in 1831. Guided by a young Redemptorist, Thaddeus Anwander, who undertook their direction in 1857, the sisters extended their field of labor beyond the confines of Baltimore. By 1900 they were conducting schools and orphanages in rural Maryland, Washington, D.C., Missouri, Kansas, and (until 1961) Cuba. The Oblate mission field was gradually expanded to include Alabama, the Carolinas, Florida, Illinois, Louisiana, Michigan, Minnesota, Mississippi, New Jersey, New York, and Virginia. Although the education of Negro youth constitutes the congregation's special apostolate, the sisters serve wherever needed, staffing elementary and secondary schools, a junior college, and catechetical, retreat, and day-care centers. In 1964 the congregation numbered more than 300 professed members. The motherhouse and novitiate are located in Baltimore.

[M. A. CHINEWORTH]

OBLATE SISTERS OF ST. FRANCIS DE SALES (OSFS),

a congregation with papal approbation (1911), founded in 1866 by Father Louis *Brisson and Mother Francis de Sales Aviat (d. 1914) at Troyes, France, under the inspiration of Mother Maria Salesia *Chappuis. The congregation is devoted to educating youth, providing homes for working girls and students, and assisting the spiritual advancement of girls and women by means of retreats. The sisters profess simple, perpetual vows and are governed by a superior general who is elected at a general chapter that meets every 6 years. Local superiors, who are chosen by the superior general, serve for a term of 3 years and may be reappointed for a second term. The congregation is divided into regions and has houses in France, the Republic of South Africa, Ecuador, Colombia, Switzerland, Italy, Austria, England, Germany, and the U.S. In 1964 there were more than 700 sisters, including 17 in the U.S., where the headquarters and novitiate (1952) are located at Childs, Md. The general motherhouse of the Oblate Sisters of St. Francis de Sales is in Troyes.

Bibliography: K. BURTON, *So Much, So Soon* (New York 1953). P. DUFOUR, *Le Très Révérend Père Louis Brisson* (Paris 1937).

[H. A. PAUL]

OBLATE SISTERS OF THE ASSUMPTION

(OA), a religious congregation founded by Emmanuel d'*Alzon and Mother Emmanuel Marie Correnson in France in 1865. The congregation has no lay sisters, follows the Augustinian Rule, and received papal approval in 1893. At its head is a superior general, elected for a 12-year term, who resides in Paris with her council. Provincial and local superiors are chosen by the superior general and council. In fulfilling their chief aim, Church unity, the Oblate Sisters worked in Turkey and Eastern Europe (Bulgaria, Rumania, and Yugoslavia), where all their houses were confiscated. Moreover, they engage in educational, social, parochial, hospital, and foreign mission work and maintain printing presses. In 1963 there were 677 members in 10 countries. Of the 61 houses, France had 25; the Netherlands and Italy, 9 each; Belgium and the Congo Republic (Léopoldville),

An Oblate Sister of Providence of the Baltimore Province conducting a music lesson.

Oblate Sisters of the Assumption working the printing press at their motherhouse.

5 each; England, 4; and Israel, Turkey, Brazil, and the U.S., 1 house each.

[E. M. LANGLADE]

OBLATE SISTERS OF THE MOST HOLY REDEEMER,

a religious congregation (*Oblatas del Santísimo Redentor,* OSSR) with papal approbation whose motherhouse is in Ciempozuelos (Madrid), Spain. The institute was founded in Madrid in 1864 by Mother Antonia María de Oviedo y Schontal (d. 1898) and José Benito Serra (1810–88), a Benedictine and former missionary in Australia. Their purpose was to establish homes for wayward girls. Later, the sisters took up also other forms of social work, as well as teaching in academies and art schools. The congregation spread from Spain to Portugal, Italy, Argentina, Brazil, Uruguay, and Mexico. Total membership in 1964 consisted of about 1,000 professed sisters and 500 Magdalens. In the U.S. the congregation had 1 foundation in Boston, Mass., with 6 professed sisters.

[A. J. ENNIS]

OBLATES

The word oblate, meaning "one offered" or "made over to God," has had various nuances in the history of the Church.

Children. From the 4th century onward the term was applied to children dedicated to a monastery by their parents. This practice, which is first found in the Eastern Church in the Rule of St. *Basil, was inspired, it appears, by the narrative of the dedication of the child Samuel by his parents (1 Sm 1.25–28): "All the days of his life he shall be lent to the Lord." Its early presence in Western monasticism is attested by the *Benedictine Rule, and by the Rules of *Caesarius and *Aurelian of Arles. St. *Benedict, for example, allowed in his Rule (*c.* 59) for infant oblation by noble parents, stating that the parents should draw up the petition on behalf of the infant, and then wrap the petition and the boy's hand in the altar cloth. For the next 5 centuries and more such parental oblations generally were held to bind oblate children (male and female) irrevocably to the monastic state. Any liberal readings of the prescriptions of St. Benedict's Rule that emerged were more than offset by the rigorous interpretation found in the influential *Liber de oblatione puerorum,* which *Rabanus Maurus, Abbot of Fulda, wrote to defend himself against the decision of a council at Mainz in 829. There he was charged with imposing the monastic habit by force on the later famous Saxon monk *Gottschalk of Orbais, who at a tender age had been made an oblate by his noble father. By the 12th century, however, when in fact the practice of child oblation had almost disappeared, it was the teaching of the legal schools that a valid act of oblation or of profession could not be made before puberty; but there was no general Church legislation on the matter until the Council of Trent fixed 16 years as the minimum age of profession (cf. Session 25, *De Regularibus,* c. 15; ConOecDecr 757).

Adults. From the 7th century the term "oblate" was used also of adults who as *conversi* (lay brothers), *devoti, donati,* or *commissi,* looked after the material interests of monasteries. These oblates were never regarded fully as monks, although in the Cistercian order, unlike other monastic orders, it was recognized that "lay brothers" were committed to a life that was consecrated as that of the monks; the acceptance of lay brothers as an integral part of a religious institute occurred only with the founding of the Dominican Order in the early 13th century.

Secular Oblates. In the 13th century, also, the class known as secular oblates came into being to cover those who, while remaining in the world and retaining the usufruct of their goods, donated their possessions to a monastery and lived according to the monastic rule under the direction of the abbot. Under this heading, perhaps, should be listed the association of noble Roman ladies founded by St. *Frances of Rome in 1425 as the Oblates of Mary and later affiliated to the Olivetan *Benedictines as Oblates Regular of St. Benedict. These Oblates, who now have foundations in Switzerland and the U.S., do not give up their property, nor make vows, but live in a community under a mother president to whom they make revocable vows of obedience.

Congregations of Oblates. The word oblate has also been adopted by certain religious congregations founded since the Council of Trent, the principal of which are:

1. Oblates of SS. Ambrose and Charles (*see* AMBROSIANS), a community of secular priests (originally "of St. Ambrose") founded for pastoral work in Milan in 1578 by St. Charles *Borromeo.
2. *Oblates of Mary Immaculate (OMI), a missionary congregation founded in 1816 at Aix-en-Provence by Eugène de Mazenod (later bishop of Marseilles) for the systematic reevangelization of France.
3. Oblates of the Virgin Mary (OMV), founded at Carignano, near Turin, Italy, in 1815 by Bruno Lanteri and approved in 1826. This congregation in 1964 had some 200 members teaching in Italy, France, and South America.
4. *Oblates of St. Charles Borromeo (of Westminister), a community of secular priests founded at Bayswater, London, in 1857 by Dr. H. E. (later cardinal) *Manning at the instigation of Cardinal *Wiseman and along the lines of the Ambrosians. The community received pontifical approval in 1877.
5. *Oblates of St. Francis de Sales (OSFS), founded at Troyes in 1871 by Abbé Brisson (d. 1908) for the education of the young.
6. *Oblates of St. Joseph (Guiseppini of Asti, OSJ), a congregation for the education of the poor, which Guiseppe Menello (later bishop of Acqui) founded at Asti, Italy, in 1878.
7. Oblates of the Sacred Heart of Jesus and Immaculate Heart of Mary (*see* ST. EDMUND, SOCIETY OF), founded in Burgundy, France, by Ven. M. J. B. *Muard in 1843, with headquarters at the Abbey of *Pontigny, where St. Edmund of Canterbury was buried. Dedicated to education and the foreign missions, the congregation was approved in 1911 and in 1964 included 185 members with houses in France, Canada, England, and the U.S.

See also OBLATES OF ST. BENEDICT.

Bibliography: Sources. BENEDICT, *Regula Monasteriorum,* ed. C. BUTLER (3d ed. Freiburg 1935). RABANUS MAURUS, *Liber de oblatione puerorum contra eos qui repugnant institutis b. p. Benedicti,* PL 107:419–440. Literature. L. OLIGER, "De pueris oblatis in Ordine Minorum," ArchFrancHist 8 (1915) 389–447; 10 (1917) 271–288. A. LENTINI, "Note sull'oblazione dei fanciulli nella Regola di S. Benedetto," StAnselm 18–19 (1947) 195–225. Heimbucher v.1–2. H. LECLERCQ, DACL 12.2:1857–77. A. P. FRUTAZ ET AL., EncCatt 9:22–32. J. BONDUELLE, DDC 4: 562–588. J. MARCHAL, Le 'Droit d'oblat': Essai sur une variété de pensionnés monastiques (Paris 1955). S. HILPISCH et al., LexThK² 7:1083–87.

[L. E. BOYLE]

OBLATES OF MARY IMMACULATE

A congregation of religious men founded at Aix-en-Provence, France, in 1816 by Charles Joseph Eugène de *Mazenod. The members of this society were known first as Missionaries of Provence, then as Oblates of St. Charles (1825). Their success in parochial mission work led to a rapid expansion of the institute, and houses were established in Marseilles (1822) and Nîmes (1825). A rule, written by the founder in 1818, was approved by the first members of the congregation and received episcopal approbation in November 1818. However, by 1823 certain bishops were contesting the validity of the vows pronounced by the missionaries and were threatening to recall their subjects who had joined the society. Further hostility to the group arose when its members opposed Jansenism and showed themselves favorable to papal infallibility and ultramontanism. It became clear that the stability of the society could be ensured only by approbation higher than that of the bishops. Mazenod, therefore, went to Rome and on Feb. 17, 1826, secured the definitive approval of the Holy See for the congregation, henceforth to be known as the Oblates of Mary Immaculate.

Development. Although the first objective of the Oblates was the preaching of missions to the poor of the rural areas, it was not long before their field of work

The first house of the Oblates of Mary Immaculate at Aix-en-Provence, France.

was broadened. In 1824, the congregation accepted the task of improving the clergy by the establishment of seminaries, and 2 years later the Oblates assumed charge of the major seminary at Marseilles. Seminary work was extended to Ajaccio, Corsica; Pittsburgh, Pa.; Buffalo, N.Y.; Frejus, Romans, and Quimper in France; and Ottawa, Canada. After the death of the founder, seminaries were accepted in Asia and Africa.

In 1831, a general chapter of the society voted to take up the work of the foreign missions. The first mission foundations were made in Canada in 1841 and a year later in the U.S. Subsequently, missions were opened in the Oregon territory (1847), Ceylon (1847), Algeria, Northwest Africa (1848–50), Natal, South Africa (1850), Australia, Japan, the Philippines, and Laos. The congregation's efforts began later in Latin America, where foundations were made in Argentina, Brazil, Bolivia, Chile, Haiti, Mexico, Paraguay, Peru, Surinam, and Uruguay.

In addition, the Oblates went to England in 1841 and later spread to Germany, Switzerland, Spain, Belgium, Holland, Italy, and Poland. Teaching was added to the original works because of the need in the mission countries. In 1848, the College of Bytown was founded; it has since become the University of Ottawa, Canada. Establishments of this kind were opened in a great number of countries in the years that followed. Parochial work, originally not considered a part of the congregation's apostolate, was included also, particularly in places like America, Africa, and Ceylon, where parishes were not only accepted but also established by the Oblates.

The development of the congregation is also associated with the care of Marian shrines. The founder accepted nine of them, and this number was increased through the years. The national Marian shrine of Canada, Our Lady of the Cape, Quebec, is under the care of the Oblates. Three shrines in the U.S. are under their jurisdiction: Our Lady of Hope, Essex, N.Y.; Our Lady of the Snows, Belleville, Ill.; and Our Lady of Grace, Colebrook, N.H. Moreover, under the direction of the diocesan clergy the Oblates serve at the National Shrine of the Immaculate Conception in Washington, D.C.

Approximately 150 years after its foundation, the congregation comprised 49 administrative divisions, either provinces or vicariates. It had more than 7,000 members, of whom about 5,000 were priests, including 7 archbishops and 30 bishops. In addition 1,227 scholastics were preparing for the priesthood. It had given to the Church two cardinals, Joseph Hippolyte Guibert (1802–86), Archbishop of Paris, and Jean Mary Rodrigue *Villeneuve (1883–1947), Archbishop of Quebec. Preliminary steps have been taken toward the canonization of the founder, Bp. Eugene Mazenod, as well as of five of his followers.

Canada. When the Oblates arrived in Montreal in December 1841, they lost no time in taking over the care of the Indian Missions, a work that led them to the remotest regions of James Bay and Labrador. In 1845, Alexander Taché, an Oblate seminarian, went to western Canada, where eventually he became successively bishop and archbishop of Saint Boniface. The conquest of western Canada for the Church was accomplished largely by the Oblates. They preached the gospel as far as Alaska, the shores of the Arctic sea, and Hudson Bay.

Ten years after their arrival they had covered the entire expanse of Canada. They were named the first bishops of almost all the episcopal sees of the West: Saint Boniface, Edmonton, Saint Albert, Prince Albert, Gravelbourg, Vancouver, New Westminster, Mackenzie, Yukon, Grouard, and Hudson Bay. They also supplied the first bishop of Ottawa, the vicars apostolic of James Bay and Labrador, bishops to Timmins and Amos, and a cardinal archbishop of Quebec.

United States. From Canada, the Oblates spread to the U.S., where they preached their first mission at Cooperville, N.Y., in 1842. While still under superiors residing in Canada, they established foundations in Pittsburgh, Pa.; Buffalo and Plattsburgh, N.Y.; Burlington, Vt.; Detroit, Mich.; St. Paul, Minn.; and Lowell, Mass. In 1849, a mission was opened in Texas. The first attempt was shortlived, but a permanent foundation was made in 1851. They established a school in Galveston and made a foundation in Brownsville. In 1858 they crossed the Rio Grande into Mexico with foundations at Matamoros, Aqualeguas, and Victoria.

The Oblates in the U.S. were members of the Canadian province until 1883, when they formed a separate American province that included all the Oblate foundations within the U.S. Father James McGrath was named

James McGrath.

first provincial, and a year later the first novitiate was established in the new province at Tewksbury, Mass. Later, other provinces were created: the Eastern, with headquarters located at Boston, Mass.; the Southern, at Houston, Texas; the Central, at St. Paul, Minn.; the Western, at San Fernando, Calif.; and St. John the Baptist province, which is not territorial but was established for the benefit of the French-speaking population, with headquarters at Lowell, Mass. American Oblates staff missions in Brazil, Japan, the Philippines, and Haiti. Some are in apostolic vicariates of the Canadian north as well as in Africa, Ceylon, Laos, Chile, and Brazil. There are American Oblate missionary bishops in the Philippines and Haiti. The American Oblates conduct missions also in Denmark and Greenland; one member was named bishop of Stockholm, Sweden.

In the U.S., the Oblates preach parochial missions, direct retreat houses, conduct high schools, and care for numerous parishes from coast to coast. Without counting those working in foreign fields, American Oblates in 1963 numbered 1,091, of whom 800 were priests, 78, coadjutor brothers, and 213, scholastics.

Rule and Administration. In addition to the three canonical vows of poverty, chastity, and obedience, the Oblates take a vow of perseverance by which they pledge in a particular way to remain in the congregation until death, even in the event that for extrinsic reasons the members should be obliged to disperse.

Supreme authority is found in the general chapter, which is held periodically to examine the major problems of the institute. The ordinary governing authority is in the hands of the superior general, elected for life by the general chapter. He has six assistants and a bursar general. Their mandate is received from and renewed at each general chapter. A procurator to the Holy See, a director general of studies, and a postulator for the causes of canonization are named by the superior general with his council.

The superior general is bound to visit the congregation, either personally or by means of his assistants or other visitors whom he chooses, every 6 years. The congregation is divided into provinces (since 1850) and mission vicariates, with superiors named by the superior general with his council. Within the province or vicariate, each house has its superior. The congregation receives among its members candidates for the priesthood who are trained in its novitiates and scholasticates, and frequently also in its juniorates or minor seminaries. It also receives men who, while not aspiring to the priesthood, wish to devote themselves to the service of the priesthood as brothers.

Bibliography: G. CARRIÈRE, *Histoire documentaire de la Congrégation des Missionaires Oblats de Marie Immaculée dans l'Est du Canada* (Ottawa 1957–63) 5 v. pub. J. E. CHAMPAGNE, *Les Missions catholiques dans l'Ouest canadien, 1818–1875* (Ottawa 1949). K. CRONIN, *Cross in the Wilderness* (Vancouver 1960). B. DOYON, *The Cavalry of Christ on the Rio Grande, 1849–1883* (Milwaukee 1956). *Études Oblatés* (Ottawa 1941–). J. LEFLON, *Eugène de Mazenod, Bishop of Marseilles, Founder of the Oblates of Mary Immaculate,* tr. F. D. FLANAGAN (New York 1961–). *Missions de la Congrégation des Missionaires Oblats de Marie-Immaculée* (Paris 1862–), chronological compilations of official reports and personal letters. T. ORTOLAN, *Cent ans d'apostolat dans les deux hemisphères: Les Oblats de Marie Immaculée durant le premier siècle de leur existence,* 4 v. (Paris 1915–). T. RAMBERT, *Vie de Monseigneur Charles-Joseph-Eugène de Mazenod,* 2 v. (Tours 1883). A. REY, *Histoire de Monseigneur Charles-Joseph-Eugène de Mazenod,* 2 v. (Marseille 1928). G. M. WAGGETT, "The Oblates of Mary Immaculate in the Pacific Northwest of the U.S.A. 1847–1878," *Études Oblatés* 6 (1947) 7–88.

[G. CARRIÈRE]

OBLATES OF ST. BENEDICT

The name given to those men and women who formally affiliate themselves with a Benedictine abbey of monks or nuns in order to consecrate more effectively their Christian life in the world according to the spirit of the *Benedictine Rule, to share in the prayer and work of the monks, and to strengthen their perseverance by means of this membership in a school of the Lord's service.

When the monasteries came near to extinction in the 18th and 19th centuries, their lay oblates suffered the same decline (for their early history, *see* OBLATES). But with the general revival of Benedictine monasticism during the later 19th century, lay people again began to associate themselves with the monasteries as oblates. The revised statutes and rules governing the institute of the oblates for modern times were first approved by the Holy See in 1888; those in use at present were confirmed by the Sacred Congregation of Religious in 1927.

In offering themselves to God, oblates do not take the canonical vows of public religious life—not from any lack of generosity or resolve but because of the circumstances of their lives. The man or woman who applies to a monastery for acceptance as an oblate is usually expected to show seriousness of intention over a preliminary period of some months. Then the candidate begins a year of novitiate under the direction of the monastery by being invested with the scapular of St. Benedict as the symbol of the religious habit, and by receiving the Benedictine medal, which is one of the most richly indulgenced of the Church's sacramentals. During this period the oblate deepens his understanding of the oblate vocation by following its practices and by instruction in its principles. After one year of perseverance, the oblate makes a solemn public promise, in the presence of the abbot of the monastery, pledging the reformation of his life according to the spirit of the Benedictine Rule and the statutes of the oblates. The act of oblation is not a *vow, but it is a firm resolve and public promise made by those called to greater perfection in the Christian life, and it is accepted and confirmed in a sacred rite approved by the Church. Oblates seek growth in their spiritual life through the help of the traditional monastic practices that strengthen them in worship, reverence, humility, stability, and more vital membership in the mystical body of Christ. The main purpose of the act of oblation is not the introduction of numerous additional devotions and practices into the oblates' lives, but the persevering consecration of their daily life of work and prayer, and their ordinary Christian family and social duties.

The reformation of life that the oblate promises according to the spirit of the Benedictine Rule and the statutes of the oblates reaches out toward the perfection of faith, hope, and charity through that conversion of life by which they seek to become men and women of God rather than men and women of the world. The instrumentalities of this conversion include prayer, especially participation in liturgical worship; detachment in the use of material things and generosity toward the poor; chastity according to their own state in life; and regular spiritual reading and study of Sacred Scripture, together with faithful attendance at the regular instructions at their monastery.

Bibliography: St. John's Abbey, *Manual for Oblates of St. Benedict* (Collegeville, Minn. 1953), including a further bibliog.

[A. BOULTWOOD]

OBLATES OF ST. CHARLES (OSC), an English institute of secular priests founded by Henry Edward *Manning in London (1857). The great increase in the Catholic population at that time, because of Irish immigration and conversions resulting from the Oxford Movement, led Cardinal *Wiseman to depute Manning to establish this group. Manning modeled the new institute on the Oblates of Milan, but modified their rule, composed by St. Charles *Borromeo, to suit English conditions. Pius IX approved the rule in 1877. The aim was to have diocesan priests living in communities and engaged in pastoral and domestic mission labors. Under Manning, the first superior, the Oblates established four parishes in the western section of London, built primary and secondary schools, and introduced several sisterhoods into the Westminster archdiocese to aid them. Herbert *Vaughan, while an

Oblate, founded the *Mill Hill Missionaries. In 1964 the Oblates had 18 members in the Archdiocese of Westminster and the Diocese of Brentwood.

Bibliography: E. S. PURCELL, *Life of Cardinal Manning, Archbishop of Westminster*, 2 v. (4th ed. London 1896).

[D. WARD]

OBLATES OF ST. FRANCIS DE SALES

A religious congregation of men begun around 1871 by Rev. Louis *Brisson at Troyes, France. In 1610, when *Francis de Sales and Jane Frances de *Chantal established the Order of the Visitation of Holy Mary at Annecy, France, De Sales was asked to form a society of priests according to the same spirit, but he did not do so. Several centuries elapsed before Brisson, a diocesan priest who was chaplain to the Visitandine convent at Troyes, was influenced by one of its members, Mother Maria Salesia *Chappuis, to found the Oblates of St. Francis de Sales (OSFS).

Early History. The constitutions for the proposed community, completed by 1868, evolved from the correspondence of Brisson with a monk at the Benedictine monastery of Einsiedeln, Switzerland, who adapted the writings of St. Francis de Sales to canonical requirements and to ideas expressed by Brisson. To these was added, with some modification, the "Spiritual Directory," a supplement to the Visitandine Rule consisting of instructions on the spiritual life by St. Francis de Sales. In 1869, Brisson's efforts to save St. Stephen's School in Troyes brought together several priests to help in teaching and administration. Brisson changed the name of the school to St. Bernard's and in 1872 episcopal approval was given to the clerical members of the faculty to organize as a religious community. On Oct. 12, 1873, the first six members were received into the novitiate by the ordinary of the diocese; the first vows were pronounced on Aug. 27, 1876. The decree of praise, officially establishing the congregation and placing it under papal jurisdiction, was received in December 1875. Definitive approval of the constitutions was granted on Dec. 8, 1897.

The aim of the congregation, which comprises both priests and lay brothers, is stated in the constitutions: "Placing themselves under the patronage of St. Francis de Sales, the members of this Institute purpose to practice the virtues of religion and of the priesthood according to their holy patron's spirit and doctrine." The members study the writings of St. Francis de Sales, particularly his "Spiritual Directory," imitate him in their personal lives, and spread his teaching among others. The virtue of charity, which is emphasized in the Salesian system of spirituality, regulates one's attitude toward God and neighbor. It leads to acceptance of the Divine Will and fosters patience and gentleness towards one's fellow men. The apostolate of the Oblates of St. Francis de Sales includes education, foreign missions, and the pastoral ministry.

Expansion. In July 1882 several missionaries were sent from France to Pella, Namaqualand, South Africa. With later territorial additions, this became the Apostolic Vicariate of the Orange River, which was divided in 1908 into what is now known as the Diocese of Keimoes and the Apostolic Vicariate of Keetmanshoop, both of which are entrusted to the Oblates of St. Francis de Sales. The congregation sent two of its members to Brazil in 1885, but because of political unrest and confiscation of church property, their activity was transferred within a short time to Montevideo, Uruguay. However, in 1906 another foundation was made in Brazil, in Rio Grande do Sul. In July 1889 a school was established at Naxos, Greece, followed by another at Athens. By the end of the 19th century, the congregation's activities in Europe had extended to Italy, Austria, and England. Although the Oblates later withdrew from Greece and England, 20th-century European foundations are located in Germany, Switzerland, Holland, and the principality of Monaco.

In 1893 a French priest of the congregation began acting as chaplain to a newly founded group of nuns, the Sisters of the Divine Compassion, at White Plains, N.Y. Three years later, five companions joined him, forming the original community of the congregation in the U.S.; but all were soon recalled to France. In the meantime another priest had been sent as chaplain to the Visitation nuns in Wilmington, Del. Two more Oblate priests, refugees from antireligious legislation in France, joined him in 1903, and together they started a private high school for boys, to which was attached a novitiate. The first provincial of the American province was appointed in 1906, and the novitiate was transferred to Childs, Md. A house of studies for seminarians was opened in 1924 near The Catholic University of America, Washington, D.C.

In 1926, at the invitation of the archbishop of Philadelphia, the community staffed the newly erected Northeast Catholic High School (for boys). Since then foundations have been made in the Archdioceses of New Orleans, La., and Detroit, Mich.; and the Dioceses of Buffalo, N.Y.; Erie, Allentown, and Harrisburg, Pa.; Toledo, Ohio; Richmond, Va.; and Salt Lake City, Utah. In these areas the congregation directs its own seminaries, private and diocesan high schools, colleges, parishes, and boys' camps, while also aiding the local clergy in the work of the ministry. High school teaching engages the largest share of the personnel.

The congregation has its motherhouse in Rome, and is ruled by a superior general, elected for 12 years, and by four councilors general. There are seven provinces: French, Austrian, American, German, Dutch, Swiss, and Italian—each governed by a provincial, who is appointed for 6 years by the superior general and his council. Three elected councilors assist in provincial government. The novitiate is 1 year's duration. Perpetual profession of simple vows follows 3 years of annual vows for clerics, 5 years for lay brothers. In 1964 there were 1,200 members, including more than 300 priests in the U.S.

Bibliography: P. Dufour, Les Oblats de Saint François de Sales (Paris 1938). K. Burton, So Much, So Soon: Father Brisson, Founder of the Oblates of St. Francis de Sales (New York 1953).

[E. J. CARNEY]

OBLATES OF ST. JOSEPH.

The Congregation of the Oblates of St. Joseph (OSJ) was founded in 1878 by Giuseppe Marello (1844–95), Bishop of Acqui, Italy. After surviving its difficult early years, the congregation was given final approval by the Holy See April 11, 1909. The Oblates of St. Joseph are engaged in various apostolic works in parishes, schools, and foreign missions. The founder wished his followers to be humble servants of the Church, ready to serve the bishops in whatever tasks were given to them. The superior general, whose term of office is 6 years, resides at the motherhouse in Rome. Besides the foundations in Italy, the congregation has houses in Belgium, U.S., Mexico, Brazil, Peru, Bolivia, and the Philippine Islands. The Oblates came to the U.S. in 1929 at the request of Thomas C. O'Reilly, Bishop of Scranton, Pa. In 1931 they opened houses in California at Madera, Santa Cruz, Sacramento, and Tomales. The seminaries of the congregation are in Washington, D.C.; West Pittston, Pa.; and Santa Cruz, Cal. The students of theology attend classes either at The Catholic University of America in Washington, D.C., or at the Gregorian University in Rome. In Italy several of the Oblates have been outstanding in theology, music, and religious literature. In the U.S. the congregation is divided into two provinces: the eastern province embraces Pennsylvania, New York, and Washington, D.C.; the western, California. In 1964 the U.S. membership included about 60 professed religious, out of a total number of 430.

[S. CHINI]

OBLIGATION, MORAL

Since Immanuel Kant proposed his theory of duty for duty's sake, based on his doctrine of the categorical imperative, the theme of duty or obligation has become the central one in almost all modern ethical theories. It occupies so important a place in moral reflection that in the history of philosophy moral systems are classed according as they center on the twin notions of duty and obligation or not. Kant's ethical theory, based on the notion of duty (*Pflicht*) for duty's sake, was deeply influenced by his religious background and upbringing (see PIETISM). Much more recently Henri *Bergson, in a truly epoch-making work (*Les deux sources de la morale et de la religion*, 1932), proposed a moral theory built around a double source of moral obligation, namely, social pressure and personal attraction (aspiration) in love and friendship. For both of these eminent thinkers, the notion of duty or obligation is fundamental in moral teaching. And in contemporary thought the English (principally Oxford) moral philosophers have devoted much energy to the semantics of moral theory in general and to the linguistic analysis of obligation in particular (Hare, Nowell-Smith, Ewing, and others). This article, however, is limited to examining the concept of obligation in the Christian ethos, or in the context of the history of salvation (*Heilsgeschichte*).

Semantics and Metaphysics of Obligation. The notion of duty and obligation is found in the sources of revelation and in sacred theology, but in a subordinate or secondary position. This is explainable by the fact that, as against the Kantian conception of things (namely, that an action or way of life is good because it presents itself as a duty or obligation through the categorical imperative), the attitude found in the sources of revelation and in theology (in fact, in most systems of moral philosophy up to the time of Kant) is just the contrary. The attitude may be expressed this way: because an action is good in itself or because it is prescribed in the law of God (see St. Thomas Aquinas, ST 1a2ae, 108.1 ad 2) and as such is a manifestation of His will, it is here and now a *duty* and consequently it *obliges*. It should be carefully noted that "duty" and "obligation," although very closely related terms, are not synonymous. They are, it may be said, the twin facets of one and the same reality—duty indicating the objective reality (to be realized and put into execution) and obligation being the necessity in which one's freedom finds itself when it comes face to face with this reality. Duty is what one is bound to do by moral or legal obligation (see ST 1a2ae, 99.5 and *passim* for the distinction between moral and legal obligation and duty). The very word obligation (from *ob-ligare*) signifies the state of being bound around or enveloped by some constraint or necessity or force limiting the scope of free activity or perhaps orientating and safeguarding it (*see* FREEDOM; see also St. Thomas, *In 3 Sent.* 18.1.2 ad 5; *De ver.* 23.1; *De malo* 16.5; ST 1a, 103.8 in fine c.; *In 1 meta.* 3.58–60). One arrives at much the same notion by examining the word duty, which came into English from the French through Anglo-French (*dû, dueté*) and ultimately from the Latin *debere,* which itself is composed of *de* and *habere* meaning to have something from another, to be in possession of something that in reality belongs to another [see Meillet-Ernout, *Dictionnaire étymologique de la langue latine* (4th ed. Paris 1959–60) s.v. *debeo*].

Going just one step further from this nominal definition of obligation, one gets an insight into the metaphysical roots of obligation. For, supposing the fact of creation [St. Thomas frequently refers to the gift (*beneficium*) of creation: *C. gent.* 3.120; ST 1a2ae, 100.5 ad 2; 2a2ae, 85.2; 122.4; and even once to the *right* of God based on the fact of creation (*ius creationis*): *In 3 Sent.* 9.1.1.1], it follows that all created things, sharing in or participating the being and perfections of God, are by that very fact participated being (*ens per participationem*) and as such belong (ontologically) to the Supreme Being, from whom they receive all they are and have. In this precise sense all creatures must be said to be parts of the Creator; that is, every participated being is, by definition, a part of and belongs to unparticipated, uncreated, uncaused Being, which is God. This is perhaps one of the most brilliant and profound theological insights of St. Thomas, who then proceeds to apply it in many different theological fields. He uses it, for instance, to show that the angels love God by natural love more than themselves, first of all by natural and instinctive inclination and then by conscious and voluntary ordination (cf. ST 1a, 60.5; *In Dion. de div. nom.* 4.9, 10). All created things, then, from the greatest to the smallest, belong to God in their totality, not only as they come from the hands of their Maker and thus enter into being, but also, and perhaps above all, in the fullness of their being and perfection, that is, in the full self-realization brought about by their own free action and life, through which precisely they give full glory to their Creator, whose work they are (cf. ST 1a, 103.2; 1a2ae, 1, 7–8; 1a2ae, 21.4 ad 3; *C. gent.* 3.16–21). This notion is of paramount importance in considering those beings that grow and develop into the perfection or fullness of their being; and above all in considering creatures whose growth into plenitude of being is under their own guidance, as is the case with human beings. Man, endowed with reason and free will, moves or guides himself into the perfection that God, the Creator, has destined for him, whether that perfection is completely proportionate to his connatural powers or corresponds rather to a gratuitous divine call and to gratuitously donated life principles (infused virtues) leading ultimately to consummation in participated divine life in the vision of heaven.

Thus, whether in the order of nature or of supernature, the metaphysical roots of all responsibility and obligation are founded in God's plan for His creation and for its ultimate consummation in and through Christ. In the Book of Sirach it is said that God, having created man from the beginning, committed him into the hands of his own counsel and at the same time gave him His law to guide him (Sirach in the Vulgate 15.14–16; ST 1a, 103.5 ad 2). St. Thomas put the matter this way: just as the ship is committed by the maker or owner to the care of the captain to guide it, care for it and bring it safely to port, so did God commit man to the care and guidance of his reason and will to bring him to the goal set by God, namely, eternal life, beatitude and salvation (cf. ST 1a2ae, 2.5; 2a2ae, 85.2).

From this theonomic notion of obligation and responsibility (based on the interpersonal relationship between the Creator and His creature), it should be immediately manifest that obligation may in no wise be conceived as something imposed from without, hampering freedom and growth, but rather as an exigency of being, and in particular as an exigency of human being in dependence of the divine Being, who wishes that His creatures come to perfection (cf. 1 Thes 4.3) and thus give Him the honor and glory that is His due. In terms of the nominal definition that was the starting point of this analysis, it can be said: man's first and fundamental duty is the perfection appointed him by God and consequently due to God, and his first and fundamental obligation is that of bringing himself to that divinely appointed consummation in being.

Obligation in the Old and New Testament. In the context of the history of salvation, it is evident that God, the Creator and Master of all things, entered into personal contact and dialogue with His creatures, with men, calling them to a special sharing in His life and friendship and entering into a covenant, or alliance, with them and Himself established the conditions of that alliance, setting them down in brief in the Law, in the Decalogue of Sinai. The observance of the Law and the carrying out of all its prescriptions was the one guarantee of retaining the goodwill and friendship of Yahweh. Hence the reverence, devotion, and love with which the chosen people looked upon the Law. The Law and all its prescriptions, that is, the conditions of the alliance, bind or oblige them in all their doings. Of that they are fully conscious. This concentration on and insistence on the Law may in no way be thought of as a kind of legalism, but rather, as a modern exegete has felicitously put it, as true nomocentrism. The voice of God came to Moses on Mt. Sinai: "Thus shall you say to the house of Jacob; tell the Israelites: you have seen for yourselves how I treated the Egyptians and how I bore you up on eagle wings and brought you here to myself. Therefore if you hearken to my voice and keep my covenant, you shall be my special possession, dearer to me than all other people, though all the earth is mine. You shall be to me a kingdom of priests, a holy nation" (Ex 19.3–6). When Moses told the people what the Lord had said and made known to them all the commands He had given, they answered, in the conviction than an obligation was being imposed on them: "Everything the Lord has said, we will do" (Ex 19.7; 24.3); and forthwith Moses committed all to writing (Ex 24.4). The observance of the Law of Yahweh brings blessing and happiness (Ex 23.20–33; Dt 28.1–14);

its breach, maledictions and misfortune (Lv 26.14–43; Dt 28.15–68).

The notion of obligation in the New Law and under the New Alliance remains fundamentally the same; but there are, for all that, important differences, differences not so much of content as of spirit or attitude, caused in men by the teaching and example of Christ and by His efficacious (sacramental) healing and sanctifying influence on those who believe in Him. "God, who at sundry times and in divers manners spoke in times past to the fathers by the prophets last of all in these days has spoken to us by His Son" (Heb 1.1), whom when the time had matured, He sent, in order that we might receive adoption as sons, sending the spirit of His Son into our hearts, so that from being slaves and bondsmen we might, with and in Christ, become sons and heirs by the act of God (cf. Gal 4.4–7). This is the fulfillment of God's promise to enter into a new covenant with His people by transforming their hearts and renewing their spirit (cf. Ez 11.19). However, one must never forget Our Lord's constant and insistent warning that He came not to abolish the Law or the Prophets but to fulfill them down to the minutest detail (Mt 5.17–18) by seeing that they be observed from within, from the spirit of sonship and out of love for the person of the Lawgiver. Another warning of Christ must also be kept in mind, namely, that the sole proof of one's love for Him is the keeping of His Commandments (cf. Jn 14.15, 21; 1 Jn 5.2; 2 Jn 1.6).

In the context, then, of the New Alliance, it is evident that the roots of obligation for the new people of God are visibly and outwardly the Law and the Prophets and, in the inner being of the new creation (2 Cor 5.17), the new spirit of sonship and friendship infused into mens' hearts through and in Christ, together with mens' consciousness of this new nobility and dignity (see CONSCIENCE). Here it is really a question of *noblesse oblige,* and St. Paul, in the parenetic sections of his Epistles, returns to it again and again (see Eph 5.3; Col 3.12; Gal 5.22; Rom 6.22). The *Dogmatic Constitution on the Church* of Vatican Council II (ch. 2.5, 7) insistently recalls the people of God to a recognition and to a renewed consciousness of the dignity of their divine calling and of the obligations that calling imposes, echoing thereby the words of St. Leo: "Recognize, O Christian, your dignity and having become a partaker in the divine nature, do not degrade yourself by returning to your former baseness. Remember the Head and the Body of which you are a member" (*Serm.* 21.3; PL 54:192–193).

Here a point of the greatest importance must be carefully noted. Yahweh did not conclude the alliance with individual members of the chosen people, but with the people as such, making known to them through His Prophets the terms of the alliance laid down by Him and the conditions of its observance. So it was in the course of sacred history; in the designs of divine providence, so it still is in the context of the New Alliance with the new people of God. The conditions of the alliance, it must be confessed, affect and oblige each individual, and the Spirit of God moves the minds and inspires and informs the consciences of the individual faithful (cf. Mt 10.29–33; Lk 12.6–7). But in order to guarantee the genuineness and authenticity of such inspirations (whether in matters of faith or morals), Christ, foreseeing the ever-present danger of error and deception, endowed His Church with an infallible teaching authority vested in its pastors, who receive Christ's injunction to go teach all nations to observe all whatsoever He had commanded them (Mt 28.20), as well as the assurance that whoever listens to them listens to Him (Lk 10.16). This important matter was emphasized in a special way in Vatican Council II (cf. *loc. cit.* 2.12.2).

Obligation and Law. Before termination of the discussion on the notion of obligation in the context of the history of salvation and of the Christian ethos in particular, one final matter must be mentioned. The radical binding force of divine (and natural, which is a direct and immediate participation of divine) law, as the main source and root of obligation in the context of the history of salvation, has been examined above and need not be further expatiated. But the question of the binding force of positive human law—whether civil, ecclesiastical, or religious—must be considered, since there is the ever-present danger of either exaggerating its binding force (*see* RIGORISM) or of so minimizing it that it no longer has any real meaning as law (*see* LAXISM). This question is all the more important in that positive law affects men more tangibly and obviously and, as manmade, appears more readily as an unwarranted curtailment of man's innate freedom. Besides, a wrong conception of things in this domain can and indeed at times must inevitably lead to a falsification of conscience and eventually to *scrupulosity. First, the principle of St. Thomas with regard to the general binding force of positive (human) law should be carefully noted: when there is no evidence of the fact, it is a dangerous thing to lay down categorically what is or is not a mortal sin (*Quodl.* 9.7.2). Second, all positive law, if it be just and prudently made, whether civil or ecclesiastical or religious, binds in conscience and must be observed *ut in pluribus* (see ST 1a2ae, 96.1 ad 3; 1a2ae, 96.6 and *passim*) under pain of sin and corresponding punishment as laid down in the law itself. Third, there is the special case of laws of constitutions that stipulate explicitly that they do not bind under sin, but oblige only to undergo the penalty attaching to their violation. This is the case, for instance, with regard to the 1932 constitutions of the Dominican Order (32.1, dating from the general chapter of Paris, 1236; MonOPraed 3.8) and, following that example, the constitutions and rules of many other orders, congregations, and confraternities. Fourth, it should be noted that therein is the source of much confusion in later moral theology. For such rules and constitutions were (and are) said to bind *sub levi* or *sub gravi,* meaning that they oblige to the acceptance of the light or grave penalty imposed by them, but in no wise insinuating that there is question of sin: quite the contrary. In later times, and especially in post-Reformation theology, the origin of these expressions was overlooked, and they were wrongly given the meaning of obligation under light or grave sin. Hence arose the bitter discussion during the 17th century. The bitterness seems to have disappeared, but the confusion persists and so far shows no sign of being dissipated.

Bibliography: A. MOLIEN, DTC 9.1:871–910. G. ERMECKE, LexThK² 8:426–428. K. E. LØGSTRUP, RGG³ 5:313–317. S. DA ROMALLO, EncCatt 7:1052–59. X. LÉON-DUFOUR et al., *Vocabulaire de théologie biblique* (Paris 1962) 20–29. R. NAZ and C. LEFEBVRE, DDC 6:635–677. J. TONNEAU, "L'Obligation *ad poenam* des constitutions dominicaines," RevScPhilTh 24 (1935) 107–115; "Devoir et morale," *ibid.* 38 (1954) 233–252. W. FARRELL, "The Roots of Obligation," *Thomist* 1 (1939) 14–30. L. B.

GEIGER, *Le Problème de l'amour chez saint Thomas d'Aquin* (Montreal 1952). H. M. BAUMGARTNER, *Die Unbedingtheit des Sittlichen: Eine Auseinandersetzung mit Nicolai Hartmann* (Munich 1962). H. REINER, "Wesen und Grund der sittlichen Verbindlichkeit (obligatio) bei Thomas v. Aquin" in *Sein und Ethos: Untersuchungen zur Grundlegung der Ethik,* ed. P. ENGELHARDT (Mainz 1963) 236–266; "Beatitudo und obligatio bei Thomas von Aquin: Antwort an P. Pinckaers," *ibid.* 306–328. S. PINCKAERS, "Eudämonismus und sittliche Verbindlichkeit in der Ethik des hl. Thomas: Stellungnahme zum Beitrag Hans Reiner," *ibid.* 267–305. CAJETAN, "De obligatione et observatione praeceptorum tam in religione, quam extra" in *Opuscula omnia,* t.1, tract. 25; *Commentarii in ST 1a2ae, 95–96; 2a2ae, 186.9.* BARTHOLOMAEUS DE MEDINA, *Expositio in ST 1a2ae, 96.4.* G. G. MEERSSEMAN, "La Loi purement pénale d'après les statuts de Confréries Médiévales," *Mélanges Joseph de Ghellinck,* 2 v. (Gembloux 1951) 2:975–1002. S. KUTTNER, *Kanonistische Schuldlehre von Gratian bis auf die Dekretalien Gregors IX.* (StTest 64; 1935). R. M. HARE, *The Language of Morals* (Oxford 1952).

[C. WILLIAMS]

OBRECHT, JAKOB, prominent polyphonic composer, also called Hobrecht, Obertus, etc.; b. Bergen-op-Zoom, Holland, Nov. 22, 1452; d. Ferrara, Italy, 1505. He was at the University of Louvain in 1470 and was ordained in 1480. In 1479 he became choir director in his native town, and from 1484 to 1485 he served at Cambrai cathedral; he was then appointed *succentor* at Bruges. On a short leave of absence in 1487 he visited Ferrara at the invitation of Duke Hercules I. From 1492 to 1496 he was a chaplain of Antwerp cathedral, but he spent his last few years at Ferrara, where he died during the plague. Composer of some 30 secular works, he first gained prominence for his Masses, some of which were inspired by (if not based upon) material by Frye, *Busnois, A. *Agricola, and *Okeghem. Mostly scored for four voices, they exhibit some conservative features (rigid *cantus firmus* treatment, little melodic imitation), although harmonically they have strong tonal tendencies. His thematic material derives from a variety of sources: a German song in praise of the Virgin (*Missa Maria zart*), a Marian antiphon and other texts (*Missa Sub tuum praesidium*), an antiphon for Holy Thursday (*Missa Caput*); a secular song (*Missa L'homme armé*), a motet by another composer (*Missa Ave Regina caelorum*); it was the custom to honor past masters by borrowing their melodies, polyphonic textures, and struc-

Jakob Obrecht's "Salve Regina" in a 16th-century MS.

tural ideas, integrating them into new works with entirely different texts. In his motets he sometimes shows an old-fashioned predilection for polytextuality (*Beata es, Maria; Salve crux arbor*), though his treatment of texture usually leans toward the clarity and fluidity of *Desprez. Among his masterpieces are his settings of the *Marian antiphons *Salve Regina, Alma Redemptoris Mater,* and *Ave Regina caelorum.* A motet-Passion long ascribed to him is now known to be the work of Antoine Longueval.

Bibliography: *Werken,* ed. J. WOLF, 30 v. (Amsterdam 1908–21); *Opera Omnia,* ed. A. SMIJERS and M. VAN CREVEL (Amsterdam 1953–). O. J. GOMBOSI, *Jacob Obrecht* (Leipzig 1925). Reese MusR. B. MURRAY, "A New Light on Jacob Obrecht's Development," MusQ 43 (1957) 500–516; "Jacob Obrecht's Connection with the Church of Our Lady in Antwerp," *Revue belge de musicologie* 11 (1957) 125–133. L. FINSCHER, MusGG 9: 1814–22. Baker 1175. **Illustration credit:** Bayerische Staatsbibliothek München.

[D. STEVENS]

OBRECHT, M. EDMOND, fourth abbot of Gethsemani, Ky.; b. Stotzhein, Alsace, Nov. 13, 1852; d. Gethsemani, Jan. 4, 1935. He entered La Grande Trappe, La Trappe, France, at the age of 23, intending to live all his days there in cloistered silence and anonymity. Instead, he traveled all over the globe, was known to four successive popes and many bishops, and was loved by countless people. He was ordained at Seez in 1879 and sent immediately to Rome as secretary to the procurator general of the three Trappist observances. When these amalgamated into an order in 1892, he was commissioned to collect funds in the U.S. for the ancient Abbey of Tre Fontane, Rome, which had become the generalate of the restored order. After 4 years, he returned to Rome, was sent to a struggling abbey in the French Jura, and shortly after appointed provisional superior of Gethsemani. By strong measures he saved this monastery for the U.S. and his order, and was elected its abbot in 1898. Exceptional administrative abilities brought him appointments as visitor to monasteries in Europe, Canada, the U.S., Asia, and Africa. Obrecht was named apostolic administrator of Mariannhill Mission in South Africa; he determined the status of these monks as missioners and not Trappists.

Bibliography: M. AMEDEUS, *Dom Edmund M. Obrecht, OCSO* (Gethsemani, Ky. 1937). M. RAYMOND, *Burnt Out Incense* (New York 1949).

[R. FLANAGAN]

OBREGONIANS (POOR INFIRMARIANS), popular title of the Least Brothers (*Hermanos Minimos*), founded at Madrid in 1568 by Bernardino Obregón; b. near Burgos, Spain, May 20, 1540; d. Madrid, Aug. 6, 1599. Obregón, a young man of noble lineage who had begun his ecclesiastical studies, discontinued them to become an officer in the army of Philip II. Having served in several campaigns, he found himself one day at court, where a sweeper accidentally splattered his uniform with mud. Obregón angrily slapped the humble worker, who instead of retaliating, begged pardon. Heartily impressed, Obregón gave up his military career and began to nurse the sick. Soon he and some companions took over the administration of the general hospital of Madrid and spread their work to Portugal, Belgium, and the colonies. In 1594 Obregón reedited the Constitutions they had been following, and 4 years later his group was permitted to take the vows of religion according to the rule of the Third Order of St. Francis of Paola, adding a fourth vow of free hospitality. Paul V authorized the *Hermanos Minimos* in 1609 to wear a gray habit having a black cross on the left side as monogram. In 1592 Obregón founded in Lisbon an asylum for poor children. He also wrote an early manual on the care of the sick, *Instrucción de enfermos y verdadera practica de como se han de aplicar los remedios que enseñan los medicos* (Madrid 1607). In 1589 Obregón assisted at the deathbed of his former commander, Philip II. The Order of *Hermanos Minimos* disintegrated during the French Revolution.

Bibliography: L. GULLI, EncCatt 9:38. Espasa 39:408–409.

[M. P. TRAUTH]

O'BRIEN, MATTHEW ANTHONY, missionary; b. Nenagh, Ireland, May, 1804; d. Springfield, Ky., Jan. 15, 1871. He was the son of John and Grace (Meagher) O'Brien. In 1826, having received his early education in Ireland, he came to the U.S. and worked his way to Kentucky. He studied and taught at St. Mary's College, Marion County, Ky., from 1829 until he entered the Dominican Order of St. Rose Priory, near Springfield, Ky. O'Brien made his religious profession on Sept. 8, 1837, and was ordained in the summer of 1839 by Bp. Richard P. Miles, OP, of Nashville, Tenn. He completed his studies while serving as assistant novice master at St. Rose and was then transferred to St. Joseph's parish near Somerset, Ohio. There for 8 years he performed missionary and pastoral duties. In 1850 O'Brien was elected provincial of the Dominican province of St. Joseph, which then consisted of only 20 missionary priests in the four states of Kentucky, Ohio, Tennessee, and Wisconsin. During his administration as provincial, he opened St. Joseph's College in Somerset, Ohio, and preached parish missions from the Great Lakes to the Gulf of Mexico and from St. Louis east beyond the Alleghenies. From 1854 to 1857 O'Brien was prior of St. Rose in Kentucky, where he built the parish church and reopened the old College of St. Thomas, which had flourished from 1807 to 1828. In 1857 he resumed his missionary preaching, interrupting it for only 2 years when he was pastor of St. Peter's in London, Ontario, Canada.

Bibliography: V. F. O'DANIEL, *An American Apostle: The Very Reverend Matthew Anthony O'Brien, O.P.* (Washington 1923).

[J. B. WALKER]

O'BRIEN, MORGAN JOSEPH, lawyer, civic reformer; b. New York City, April 28, 1852; d. New York City, June 16, 1937. O'Brien, the son of a merchant who emigrated from Ireland to the U.S. in the 1820s, received in New York City the B.A. degree from St. John's College (1872), the M.A. from the College of St. Francis Xavier (1873), and the LL.B. from Columbia University (1875). He married Rose M. Crimmins in 1880. He was appointed New York City corporation counsel in 1887 and later that year was elected to the state supreme court. In 1896 he was elevated to the appellate division of the court and in 1905 was named presiding judge of that tribunal. He resigned late in 1906 and returned to private practice. In business O'Brien was a trustee of the Equitable Life Assurance Society and the Provident Loan Society, and a director

of the Metropolitan Life Insurance Company and The Bank of Manhattan Trust Company. In civic life he served as a trustee of the New York City public school system, of the New York Public Library, and of the Astor, Lenox, and Tilden foundations. He was among the Catholic laymen who assisted Cardinals John Farley and Patrick Hayes in mobilizing the charitable resources of the New York Archdiocese; his special interest was the Roman Catholic Orphan Asylum. O'Brien's influence in politics began in the 1880s when he became a supporter of Grover Cleveland and an advocate of civil service reform. He continued to serve the Democratic party and was a delegate to the state constitutional convention of 1915. He was a presidential elector on the Democratic ticket on several occasions, and in 1936 he presided over the meeting of the electoral college. O'Brien was also an advocate of municipal reform, and was appointed (1926) chairman of the temporary City Planning and Survey Committee by Mayor James Walker. Thereafter he supported city planning and urban renewal. In 1936 he served as chairman of the Citizens Charter Campaign Committee, which fought for modern governmental organization.

[J. J. HUTHMACHER]

O'BRIEN, TERENCE ALBERT, bishop of Emly and martyr; b. Tower Hill Castle, Cappamore, County Limerick, 1600; d. Balls Bridge, Limerick, Oct. 31, 1651. As the son of Murtagh O'Brien and Catherine Galwey, he was related to many of the public figures of his day. His paternal uncle, Maurice O'Brien, was Protestant bishop of Killaloe (d. 1613); his grandfather, Sir Geoffrey Galwey, was recusant mayor of Limerick in the early 1600s. Terence, educated at St. Peter Martyr Priory in Toledo, Spain, was ordained there c. 1628. After returning to Limerick, he labored in Ireland until 1643, when he was elected provincial of the Irish Dominicans. While attending a general chapter in Rome (1644), he sought assistance for the Irish Confederation, then in revolt against the English. O'Brien, a strong supporter of the Papal Nuncio Giovanni *Rinuccini in the internal and factional struggles within Irish Catholicism, was created bishop of Emly on Rinuccini's recommendation in 1647, and consecrated at Waterford, April 2, 1648. The increasing strength of the Parliamentarians' offensive against the Irish rebels led to his eventual capture after the surrender of Limerick in October 1651. He was condemned to death "as an original incendiary of the rebellion," and executed by the English; he is generally regarded as a martyr.

Bibliography: R. BAGWELL, DNB 14:773–774. M. J. HYNES, *The Mission of Rinuccini . . .* (Dublin 1932). J. O'HEYN and A. COLEMAN, *Irish Dominicans of the 17th Century* (Dundalh 1902).

[P. S. MC GARRY]

O'BRIEN, WILLIAM VINCENT, b. Dublin, Ireland, c. 1740; d. New York City, May 14, 1816. He became a Dominican at S. Clemente, Rome, apparently making his profession there in 1761. He completed at least part of his ecclesiastical training at the Dominican house of studies in Bologna, Italy, where he was ordained. For 17 years he preached in the Dublin area and he became preacher general of the Dominican Order. In 1787 he went to Philadelphia, Pa. While working there and in New Jersey, he supported the prefect apostolic, John *Carroll, against those who opposed the creation of a bishopric at Baltimore, Md. In October 1787 Carroll appointed him pastor of St. Peter's Church, Barclay Street, New York City. He organized and brought peace to that divided parish, and for 20 years he helped to keep order among Catholics in New York State. Under the auspices of Abp. Alfonso Núñez de Haro, O'Brien went to Mexico City, Mexico, about 1790, to raise funds for his church. He returned in 1792 with vestments, paintings, and money enough to install pews and erect a tower and portico. In 1800 he opened at St. Peter's the earliest free school and Catholic educational institution in New York State. During the yellow-fever epidemics of 1795 and 1798, O'Brien ministered to his people. Chronic illness forced his retirement in 1806, but he continued a limited ministry until the end of 1808.

Bibliography: V. F. O'DANIEL, *The Dominican Province of St. Joseph* (New York 1942).

[W. A. HINNEBUSCH]

OBSCENITY, U.S. LAW OF

Laws against obscenity are of ancient origin. The Twelve Tables that stood in the Roman Forum treated the singing of ribald songs as a breach of public order punishable by death [Sohm's *Institutes of Roman Law*, tr. Ledlie (3d ed., 1907) 422]. Less severe laws existed in the American colonies. A 1711 statute of the Province of Massachusetts Bay provided that anyone who should "be convicted of composing, writing, printing or publishing, of any filthy obscene or prophane Song, [or] Pamphlet . . ." was punishable by a fine of £20, or by standing on the pillory with an inscription of his crime in capital letters over his head. After the American Revolution, there was no Federal law on the subject until 1842 when a tariff act authorized customs officers to confiscate "obscene or immoral" prints and to bring court action for their destruction (5 Stat. 548, 566–567). In 1865, the postmaster general became concerned with the great amount of "obscene books and pictures" that was being sent to the Army. He urged, and Congress provided, that "no obscene book, pamphlet, picture, print, or other publication of a vulgar and indecent character" should be admitted to the U.S. mails (13 Stat. 504, 507).

Few American decisions on obscenity predate the Civil War. This is perhaps attributable to a feeling that the problem was not sufficiently important to warrant prosecution, rather than to popular indifference to the propriety of literature, for as innocuous a work as Hawthorne's *Scarlet Letter* was publicly attacked in 1851 as immoral, as degrading to literature, and as encouraging social licentiousness. The few cases that do predate the Civil War followed the precedents of *Commonwealth v. Sharpless*, 2 S. & R. 91 (Pa. 1815) and *Commonwealth v. Holmes*, 17 Mass. 336 (1821). Both held that obscenity was punishable by common law. Later, the financial scandals, the political corruption, and the lax social behavior of the immediate post-Civil War era set the stage for a powerful social reaction. The way was made easy for the social reformer—for Anthony Comstock and his 40-year crusade to purify the reading fare of the American public.

The Comstock Law and the Hicklin Rule. Comstock was 28 years old when he arrived in Washington in 1873 as the lobbyist for the New York YMCA's Committee for the Suppression of Vice. As the self-appointed guardian of the mails, he lobbied through Congress the celebrated "Comstock Law," parts of which were modeled after "Lord Campbell's Act," the English Obscene Publications Act of 1857. The American act banned from the mails "obscene," "lewd," or "lascivious" publications, abortifacients or information about them; and it provided for the fine and imprisonment of any person who "knowingly" mailed or received such items [17 Stat. 598 (1873)]. As a "special agent" for the Post Office Department, Comstock proceeded to establish an astounding record for investigations, confiscations, and convictions.

Neither the English nor the American acts defined the term "obscene," but in 1868 this defect was cured for both England and America in *Queen v. Hicklin,* an English case that arose from the seizure of a pamphlet entitled "The Confessional Unmasked," which was circulated to hamper the election of Roman Catholics to Parliament. Lord Chief Justice Cockburn construed the British act: "I think the test of obscenity is this, whether the tendency of the matter charged as obscenity is to deprave and corrupt those whose minds are open to such immoral influences, and into whose hands a publication of this sort may fall" (3 Q. B. 360, 371). Eleven years later, in *U.S. v. Bennett,* Cockburn's view was described as "very sound" (24 Fed. Cas. 1093, 1104), and before very long it prevailed in both state and Federal courts.

The Hicklin rule permitted isolated passages of a book to be judged out of context, independently of the book as a whole. Whether a particular passage was adjudged obscene depended on the susceptibility of the weakest and the immature to sensuous thoughts and desires. In effect, the basis for the banishment of books and magazines written for adults was their possible impact on the minds of children. Thus, in 1889, in *U.S. v. Clark* the American act was described as "wholesome," designed to protect "the young and immature, the ignorant, and those who were sensually inclined" (38 Fed. 732, 734).

In 1913, Judge Learned Hand expressed his dissatisfaction with the Hicklin rule when he wrote in *U.S. v. Kennerley:* "I question whether in the end men will regard that as obscene which is honestly relevant to the adequate expression of innocent ideas, and whether they will not believe that truth and beauty are too precious to society at large to be mutilated in the interests of those most likely to pervert them to base uses. Indeed, it seems hardly likely that we are even to-day so lukewarm in our interests in letters or serious discussion as to be content to reduce our treatment of sex to the standard of a child's library in the supposed interest of a salacious few, or that shame will for long prevent us from adequate portrayal of some of the most serious and beautiful sides of human nature" (209 Fed. 119, 120, 121). Nevertheless, Judge Hand felt compelled to follow the long-established precedent as he overruled a demurrer to an indictment for sending an allegedly obscene book through the mails.

Trend Away from the Hicklin Rule. By 1930, Judge Hand's prediction had won substantial support as the Hicklin rule was modified by some courts and avoided by others. In addition, the Tariff Act of 1930 permitted the importation, at the discretion of the secretary of the treasury, of classics and books of recognized and established literary or scientific merit even though obscene (46 Stat. 688, §305a). But perhaps the most singular rejection of the "mental sanitation" imposed by the Hicklin standard was Augustus Hand's opinion in 1934 in *U.S. v. One Book Entitled "Ulysses."*

Ulysses, by James Joyce, left little unsaid as it portrayed the "stream of consciousness" of a number of individuals, some of whom were intellectuals and others social outcasts. It was seized for alleged obscenity by customs officials, and proceedings were instituted for its confiscation. When the case reached the Court of Appeals, that court admitted that *Ulysses* contained numerous long passages that were obscene under any fair definition of the word. Nevertheless, the passages were found to be relevant to the purpose of the book, which was to depict the thoughts of the characters and give meaning to the whole rather than to promote or portray lust for its own sake. The erotic passages were said to be submerged so that they had little effect. The question, Judge Hand wrote, was "whether a publication taken as a whole has a libidinous effect," which, he held, *Ulysses* did not have (72 F. 2d 705, 707).

Since *Ulysses,* courts generally have recognized that the word "obscene" is not susceptible of exact definition —that the intangible moral concepts it purports to connote "vary in meaning from one period to another" [*Parmelee v. U.S.,* 113 F. 2d 729, 731 (1940)]. But the problem of obscenity remains and has become intensified with the phenomenal growth of the paperback, comic book, and "slick" magazine industry since World War II. Sex-related material published now is no different from what it has been since man first learned to write, but today it is available for 35 or 50 cents on newsstands, in drug stores, and transportation terminals everywhere. The market is vast—the annual circulation for paperbacks alone now exceeds 300 million—and this has provoked widespread protests by civic, religious, parent-teacher, and fraternal groups. State laws and local ordinances have been adopted to stem the flow but often have done little except promote litigation because the methods of enforcement have been more repressive than corrective. This, in turn, has raised the issue of freedom of the press and the eventual rejection of the Hicklin rule by the U.S. Supreme Court.

The Supreme Court and Obscenity. In 1948, after three oral arguments that extended over a period of 2 years, the U.S. Supreme Court decided *Winters v. New York,* 333 U.S. 507, in which it struck down a New York statute that prohibited publications "principally made up of criminal news, police reports, or accounts of criminal deeds or pictures, or stories of deeds of bloodshed, lust or crime." The law was found to be so indefinite and vague as to violate the due process clause of the 14th Amendment. Also in 1948, in *Doubleday & Co. v. N.Y.,* 335 U.S. 848, the Supreme Court was asked to review a New York Court of Appeals decision that Edmund Wilson's *Memoirs of Hecate County* was obscene. However, the fact that the Court was equally divided prevented the matter from being settled. In 1957, the Supeme Court decided *Butler v. Michigan,* 352 U.S. 380, invalidating the part of the Michigan Penal Code that made it a misdemeanor to sell or make available to the general public any book, magazine, or newspaper "tending to incite minors to violent or depraved or immoral acts, manifestly tending to the corruption of the morals of youth . . ." (§343). The State

insisted that it exercised its power to promote the general welfare when, to shield juvenile innocence, it guaranteed the general reading public protection against books even though these were not too damaging for grown men and women. Justice Felix Frankfurter commented for the Court: "Surely, this is to burn the house to roast the pig" (p. 383). The legislation was found not reasonably restricted to the evil with which it was said to deal and to reduce the adult population of Michigan "to reading only what [was] fit for children"; it so arbitrarily curtailed the liberties of the individual, the Court said, that it violated the due process clause of the 14th Amendment.

Four months after it decided the Butler case, the Supreme Court itself undertook the task of establishing constitutional standards with which to judge obscenity. In *Roth v. United States* and *Alberts v. California,* 354 U.S. 476 (1957), two cases which were decided together, the Court held that obscenity is not within the area of constitutionally protected speech and press. As it upheld the Federal and California obscenity statutes, the Court drew an interesting distinction between obscenity and sex. The former was described as "material which deals with sex in a manner appealing to prurient interest" (p. 487). Of the latter it was said: "Sex, a great and mysterious motive force in human life, has indisputably been a subject of absorbing interest to mankind throughout the ages; it is one of the vital problems of human interest and public concern" (p. 487). The Court then expressly rejected the Hicklin rule as unconstitutionally restrictive of the freedoms of speech and press, and substituted a standard of its own— whether to the average person, applying contemporary community standards, the dominant theme of the material taken as a whole appeals to prurient interest.

Aftermath of the Roth Case. Since the Roth case, the Supreme Court has not had much difficulty in agreeing on opinions or in reaching decisions in cases in which the issue raised has been the validity of the methods by which alleged obscenity is condemned. In these, the question has not been whether or not something in itself has been obscene but rather the validity of the means used to suppress the objectional material. See *Smith v. California,* 361 U.S. 147 (1959); *Marcus v. Search Warrant,* 367 U.S. 717 (1961); and *Bantam Books Inc. v. Sullivan,* 372 U.S. 58 (1963). On the other hand, the Court has had considerable difficulty in agreeing on opinions in cases in which the central issue has been the standards whereby obscenity is judged. More often than not, the Court has been able to reach a judgment, but in its reasoning it has been split in so many directions that in none has there thus far been an "opinion of the Court." See *Manual Enterprises, Inc. v. Day,* 370 U.S. 478 (1962); *Jacobellis v. Ohio,* 378 U.S. 184 (1964); and *Quantity of Copies of Books v. Kansas,* 378 U.S. 205 (1964). How wide the division of opinion has been in the latter-type case can perhaps best be illustrated by the Jacobellis decision in which no less than six separate opinions were written, but with no more than two Justices agreeing on any one. Justice William Brennan announced the judgment of the Court in which a state court conviction for possessing and exhibiting an allegedly obscene film was reversed; he delivered an opinion in which Justice Arthur Goldberg joined; Justice Goldberg then concurred by himself as did Justice Potter Stewart; Justice Hugo Black delivered a concurring opinion in which Justice Wm. Douglas joined; the chief justice, with whom Justice Tom Clark joined, dissented; Justice John Harlan dissented alone. Justice Byron White concurred in the judgment, but without a written opinion.

Chief Justice Earl Warren's dissent is perhaps the most interesting of the six opinions. In it he indicated weariness with the inability of legislatures and courts to evolve a truly satisfactory definition of obscenity. He suggested that the problem be committed to state and lower Federal courts whose judgments would be accepted, with the Supreme Court limiting itself to the sufficiency of evidence upon which a finding of obscenity could be made. He expressed doubt that the "community standard" referred to in *Roth* meant a "national standard." He voiced the opinion that there "is no provable 'national standard,' and perhaps there should be none" (p. 200); he doubted that anyone could define "hard core pornography" with any greater clarity than with the word "obscenity."

The chief justice decried the tendency of law enforcement agencies to take the easy way—simply to seize and destroy books so that courts are often presented with procedurally bad cases. If, he continued, "cases were well prepared and were conducted with the appropriate concern for constitutional safeguards, courts would not hesitate to enforce the laws against obscenity" (p. 202). The chief justice reiterated his acceptance of the rule in *Roth*, but, to his way of thinking, only the application of a "sufficient evidence" standard could obviate the necessity for the Supreme Court to sit as the "Super Censor" of all obscenity purveyed throughout the nation.

Justice Brennan agreed that the chief justice's "sufficient evidence" proposal was appealing—it would lift from the shoulders of the Supreme Court a difficult, recurring, and unpleasant task—but he could not accept it. Such an "abnegation" of judicial supervision would, he wrote, be inconsistent with the Court's duty to uphold constitutional guarantees. In other areas where constitutional rights under the due process clause have been involved, the Court has, he pointed out, consistently recognized its duty to "apply the applicable rules of law upon the basis of an independent review of the facts of each case" (p. 189). He saw no reason why it should be any different with alleged obscenity than it has been with alleged criticism of judges and public officials, advocacy of governmental overthrow, or speech alleged to constitute a breach of the peace.

Justice Brennan also disagreed with the chief justice's version of what constitutes "contemporary standards" as referred to in *Roth*. To him, it was "an incorrect reading of *Roth*" to restrict these standards to the standards of the particular local community from which an obscenity case arose. He noted: "The Court has regularly been compelled, in reviewing criminal convictions challenged under the Due Process Clause of the Fourteenth Amendment, to reconcile the conflicting rights of the local community which brought the prosecution and of the individual defendant. Such a task is admittedly difficult and delicate, but it is inherent in the Court's duty of determining whether a particular conviction worked a deprivation of rights guaranteed by the Federal Constitution. The Court has not shrunk

from discharging that duty in other areas, and we see no reason why it should do so here. . . . It is, after all," he declared, "a national Constitution we are expounding" (p. 194, 195).

On behalf of himself and Justice Douglas, Justice Black restated his belief: "If despite the Constitution . . . this Nation is to embark on the dangerous road of censorship," the Supreme Court "is about the most inappropriate Supreme Board of Censors that could be found" (p. 196).

Justice Stewart expressed his conclusion that as related to obscenity, criminal laws are, under the 1st and 14th Amendments, constitutionally limited to hard-core pornography. He admitted that perhaps he could never intelligibly define "hard-core pornography." "But," he added, "I know it when I see it, and the motion picture involved in this case is not that" (p. 197).

In his separate opinion, Justice Goldberg repeated the language of the Court in *Joseph Burstyn, Inc. v. Wilson,* 343 U.S. 495 (1952)—that the Constitution does not guarantee absolute freedom to exhibit every kind of motion picture at all times and places, and each different method of expression presents its own problems, nevertheless that the basic principles of freedom of speech and press do not vary and that freedom of expression is the rule. In the case at hand, he found the scene objected to in the motion picture so fleeting and fragmentary that there was no justification for making an exception of it.

Justice Harlan based his dissent on the principle that the states are constitutionally permitted greater latitude than is the Federal government in determining what might be banned as obscenity. He would not prohibit the states from banning material which, "taken as a whole, has been reasonably found in state judicial proceedings to treat with sex in a fundamentally offensive manner, under rationally established criteria for judging such material" (p. 204).

In the light of these seemingly irreconcilable views, perhaps the most that can be expected is a continued case-by-case approach out of which some general constitutional standard, more workable than that announced in *Roth,* may evolve. The Court itself tried to show the way in *Freedman v. Maryland,* 380 U.S. 51 (1965), another motion picture case in which a state censorship statute was declared invalid because it failed to provide adequate safeguards against undue inhibition of protected expression. Writing for the Court, Justice Brennan indicated that a model could be found in the New York injunctive procedure designed to prevent the sale of obscene books, which the Court had upheld in *Kingsley Books, Inc. v. Brown,* 354 U.S. 436 (1957). The procedure used there provided for a judicial determination of obscenity after notice and an adversary hearing. The statute required a hearing 1 day after joinder of issue and a decision within 2 days after termination of the hearing. Nevertheless, even if this model should be followed, it is very probable that the process of establishing constitutional standards with which to determine what is or is not obscene will never be complete.

See also FREEDOM OF SPEECH AND PRESS, U.S. LAW OF.

Bibliography: H. CAIRNS, "Freedom of Expression in Literature," AnnalAmAcPolSocSc 200 (Nov. 1938) 76–94. M. L. ERNST, *The First Freedom* (New York 1946). H. KALVEN, "The

Metaphysics of the Law of Obscenity," *1960 Supreme Court Review* 1–45. W. B. LOCKHART and R. C. McCLURE, "Censorship of Obscenity: The Developing Constitutional Standards," *Minnesota Law Review* 45 (1960) 5–121. T. J. MURPHY, *Censorship: Government and Obscenity* (Baltimore 1963). J. C. N. PAUL and M. L. SCHWARTZ, *Federal Censorship: Obscenity in the Mail* (New York 1961). M. C. SLOUGH and P. D. McANANY, "Obscenity and Constitutional Freedom," *St. Louis University Law Review* 8 (1964) 279–315.

[E. G. HUDON]

OBSESSION, a persistent and recurrent fantasy, thought, or judgment that, even when not desired, cannot be controlled or altered by the reason or will of the individual. Obsessions are usually symptomatic of the obsessive-compulsive neuroses and often result from a constant repression of feelings or activities that are considered unacceptable, harmful, or morally wrong. In such cases the individual experiences feelings of guilt, even if the feelings or actions are not objectively wrong in themselves. When the obsession stems from repression of feelings, the type of obsession will be specified by the particular emotion repressed and frequently will be related to the sexual instinct or the drive for self-assertion. As the repression becomes increasingly ineffective, the repressed emotions gradually react from the unconscious level, manifesting themselves by compulsive actions, some of which are not immediately evident as related to the repressed emotion. (*See* COMPULSION; PHOBIA.) Obsessions cannot be cured by reasoning, by simple exertion of one's will power, or by ascetical practices aimed at restricting or curbing the repressed emotions. Obsessive-compulsive neuroses require treatment by psychotherapy, which will instruct the intellect, properly orient the will, and release the repressed emotion so that it can function in accordance with its nature.

Bibliography: A. A. A. TERRUWE, *The Neurosis in the Light of Rational Psychology,* tr. C. W. BAARS, ed. J. AUMANN (New York 1960). A. P. NOYES and L. C. KOLB, *Modern Clinical Psychiatry* (6th ed. Philadelphia 1963). F. J. BRACELAND and M. STOCK, *Modern Psychiatry* (New York 1963).

[C. W. BAARS]

O'CALLAGHAN, EDMUND BAILEY, historian; b. Mallow, County Cork, Ireland, Feb. 28, 1797; d. New York City, May 29, 1880. The youngest of a merchant's six children, he received his early education in Ireland. After medical study in Paris he emigrated to Canada in 1823, completed his studies, and practiced medicine in Quebec. He moved to Montreal in 1830 and entered politics in support of Louis Papineau, who led the French opposition to the English clique that dominated Lower Canada. In 1833 O'Callaghan assumed the editorship of the movement's English organ, the Montreal *Vindicator,* and in 1834 he was elected to the legislative assembly of Quebec. When the offices of the *Vindicator* were wrecked by a mob in 1837, O'Callaghan escaped across the border into the U.S. Although the Canadian government eventually dropped a charge of treason against him, he did not return to Canada or re-enter politics. After settling in Albany, N.Y., he resumed the practice of medicine. In 1841 he remarried, his first wife having died in 1835. He began to publish articles on historical and medical topics in periodicals, notably the Albany industrial journal, *Northern Light,* and the New York *Freeman's Journal.* He became interested in the antirent agitation in New York and studied its historical background. In 1846 he published the first vol-

ume of his *History of New Netherland* and abandoned medicine to devote his life to historical research. He secured a post in the Brooklyn Navy Yard and explored early documents and, in 1848, became editor of New York State's historical records. He returned to Albany, where he remained for more than 2 decades, publishing some 20 books, including the *Documentary History of the State of New York* (1849–51) and *Documents Relating to the Colonial History of the State of New York* (1855–61). He was first to call attention to the historical value of the writings of the early French Jesuits, and he edited and published several *Jesuit Relations* and encouraged John Gilmary Shea to issue his *Cramoisy Series* of the *Jesuit Relations.* In 1870 O'Callaghan became historiographer of New York City. He had edited 15 volumes of the city's early records and had 8 other volumes ready for the press when the Tweed Ring scandal broke. The printed volumes were not published, nor was he paid for his services. He spent his last years in retirement in New York City.

Bibliography: F. S. GUY, *Edmund Bailey O'Callaghan* (CUA StAmChHist 18; Washington 1934). J. J. WALSH, *Studies* 22 (1933) 468–479. O'Callaghan Papers, MS Division, Library of Congress.

[F. X. CURRAN]

O'CALLAGHAN, JEREMIAH, missionary, writer; b. County Kerry, Ireland *c.* 1780; d. Holyoke, Mass., Feb. 23, 1861. He was ordained for the Diocese of Cloyne, Ireland, in 1805. His views on usury and his criticisms of banking alienated him from his bishop. For 11 years he was refused acceptance by various bishops, but in 1830 Bp. Benedict Fenwick of Boston, Mass., accepted him for that diocese. He was sent into Ver-

Jeremiah O'Callaghan.

mont, where he spent most of his remaining days as a missionary to scattered settlements of Catholics. In Burlington, Vt., he was offered 5 acres of land, on which he built St. Mary's Church in 1832. When it was burned to the ground by nativists in 1838, O'Callaghan rebuilt it, dedicating it to St. Peter. In his churches he permitted no pew rent or seat money, but only three voluntary offerings each year. From Vermont he traveled into the western areas of Massachusetts and the eastern regions of New York to say Mass for Catholics and to administer the Sacraments. After 1837 he was aided by Rev. John B. Daly, who divided the state with him and matched his energy and zeal. The priests reported a Catholic population of 5,000 in Vermont in 1840. O'Callaghan served as procurator of the clergy at the first diocesan synod held in Boston, Aug. 21 to 26, 1842. When Burlington was made a diocese in 1853, he returned to Massachusetts and served at Northampton and at Holyoke, where he built a new church. O'Callaghan wrote pamphlets of a polemic nature during these years, explaining Catholicism to Protestants and answering the charges leveled against the Church by non-Catholic pamphlet writers and preachers. The best-known of all his works was his often reprinted *Usury or Interest* (1824), which contained an account of his early years.

Bibliography: R. H. LORD et al., *History of the Archdiocese of Boston . . . 1604–1943,* 3 v. (Boston 1945).

[T. F. CASEY]

O'CALLAGHAN, ROGER, Orientalist, b. New York, N.Y., Oct. 13, 1912; d. near Baghdad, Iraq March 5, 1954. He entered the Society of Jesus in 1929 and, after sacred studies in Toronto and Rome, studied Near Eastern history, archeology, and languages under W. F. Albright in Baltimore from 1942 to 1945. After a final year of studies at the Oriental Institute of the University of Chicago, he taught archeology, Biblical geography, history, and languages at the Pontifical Biblical Institute in Rome. With the assistance of a Fulbright grant, he took part in the American excavations at Nippur (Iraq) in the fall of 1953. He was killed in an automobile accident near Baghdad the following March. Despite Father O'Callaghan's short career, his work was of outstanding significance, particularly his *Aram Naharaim: A Contribution to the History of Upper Mesopotamia in the Second Millennium, B.C.* (Rome 1948). A partial bibliography of his other publications appeared in *Biblica* 35 (1954) 258–259.

Bibliography: F. L. MORIARTY, CathBiblQuart 16 (1954) 328–329.

[J. A. BRINKMAN]

O'CALLAHAN, JOSEPH TIMOTHY, Navy chaplain; b. Boston, Mass., May 14, 1905; d. Worcester, Mass., March 18, 1964. He entered the Society of Jesus (1922), was ordained in 1934, and was educated at Georgetown University, Washington, D.C., where he received his Ph.D. degree and a licentiate in theology. After serving as professor of philosophy and mathematics at Holy Cross College, Worcester, he joined the Navy Chaplain Corps in November 1940. During World War II he served aboard the aircraft carrier *Ranger,* which participated in the North African invasion. He was transferred later to the carrier *Franklin* and served in the Pacific. On March 19, 1945, the *Franklin* was attacked by suicide pilots near Kobe, Japan, but was saved by heroic action. O'Callahan, who was wounded during the attack, was awarded the Congressional Medal of Honor. He told his story in *I Was a Chaplain on the Franklin* (1956), written at Holy Cross College, to which he had returned.

[J. L. MORRISON]

OCAMPO, MELCHOR, Mexican politician and writer, called the Philosopher of the Reform, who played an outstanding role in the development of the Liberal party; b. probably Mexico City, *c.* 1812; d.

Tepeji del Rio, June 3, 1861. He was educated in Morelia and Mexico City, where he prepared for the law but was more interested in agricultural, linguistic, and botanical studies. After traveling in Europe, he became active in politics as a radical Liberal and was governor of Michoacán (1847) and later secretary of the treasury (1850). With Juárez and other Liberals, he was exiled to the U.S. by Santa Anna in 1854. After he returned, Ocampo was active in the constitutional convention of 1856–57. He served under Juárez in various posts and was reputed to have written some of the Reform Laws of 1859, including that on civil marriage. The "Epistle of Ocampo" is still read at all civil marriages in Mexico. Ocampo himself never married, but in his will he acknowledged four natural daughters. On Dec. 14, 1859, he signed the much-debated McLane-Ocampo Treaty with the U.S. minister, but the pact was rejected in the U.S. Senate. He subsequently retired to his ranch in Michoacán, where he was captured by the guerrilla leader Cajigas; he was later executed on the trip to Mexico City. Ocampo refused the Last Sacraments before being shot and then hanged from a tree. Both Gen. Félix Zuloaga and Gen. Leonardo Márquez were accused of his death, but Zuloaga steadfastly denied the charge.

Ocampo's political writings show strong anticlericalism and the influence of the Enlightenment and European liberal doctrines; they were widely read in English and in French. He was a strong proponent of foreign immigration into Mexico. His political career was marked by vacillation and inconsistency in action, as shown by his frequent resignations and retirements to his ranch. He ranks with Juárez and Valentín Gómez Farías as an ideological and political leader.

Bibliography: *Obras completas,* 3 v. (Mexico City 1900–1901). M. MENA, *Melchor Ocampo* (Mexico City 1959). J. ROMERO FLORES, *Don Melchor Ocampo: El filósofo de la reforma* (2d ed. Mexico City 1959). J. C. VALADÉS, *Don Melchor Ocampo: Reformador de México* (Mexico City 1954).

[P. V. MURRAY]

O'CASEY, SEAN

Irish playwright; b. Dublin, March 30, 1880; d. Torquay, England, Sept. 18, 1964. A product of the Dublin tenements, O'Casey was self-educated, and as a boy and young man he worked as messenger, clerk,

Sean O'Casey.

and manual laborer on the Great Northern Railway. Early reading of the works of Marx and Engels determined his lifelong belief that communism held the answers to the economic and social woes of the world.

Many of his leftist tendencies later left their mark on his plays. After several rejections, a play of his was accepted in 1923 by Dublin's Abbey Theatre; it was the two-act drama, *The Shadow of a Gunman*. A great box-office success, it was the first of a series of strongly realistic plays written for the Abbey: plays centered on the Dublin slums, plays that included the fine tragicomedy *Juno and the Paycock* (1924), and *The Plough and the Stars* (1926). In 1928 O'Casey broke with the Abbey Theatre when the directorate rejected his new play, *The Silver Tassie*. Experimenting with dramatic techinques that departed considerably from his earlier realism, O'Casey had turned in *The Silver Tassie* to a broad use of expressionism; and the Abbey directors, notably W. B. *Yeats, found the new approach unacceptable. A bitter exchange of views followed, and O'Casey, then residing in England, remained there in self-imposed exile for the rest of his life. Accordingly his career in the theater after 1928 belongs to the history of the English rather than the Irish stage. He increasingly experimented; his plays betrayed greater evidence of his Marxist leanings and his savage anticlerical attitudes. Although reared in the Church of Ireland (he was never, as so many have believed, a Catholic), he had abandoned adherence to orthodox belief early in life and blamed the Irish Catholic clergy for many of Ireland's political, social, and economic difficulties. His anticlerical bias is most apparent in such plays as *Within the Gates* (1933), *The Bishop's Bonfire* (1955), and *The Drums of Father Ned* (1957). The Marxist line is most in evidence in *The Star Turns Red* (1940).

Critical opinion is generally in agreement that O'Casey was one of the major figures of the 20th-century theater. His three Dublin plays of the 1920s must rate with the most important dramas of our century. A master of dialogue and characterization, he brought to the stage in his early years a freshness and a warmth that had been sadly lacking. There is, however, in his later plays a doctrinaire insistence and a preoccupation with artificial effects that indicate that Yeats was right—realism was O'Casey's real forte. His vast six-volume autobiography, from *I Knock at the Door* (1939) to *Sunset and Evening Star* (1954), is a superb revelation of the man and his times, though marred by some bitterness and ill-founded judgment. A gentle, kindly man, O'Casey was a lover of his fellow men and acutely conscious of the plight of the exploited and the downtrodden. If he chose false solutions for the world's ills, his genuine concern cannot be denied.

Bibliography: S. O'CASEY, *The Collected Plays*, 4 v. (New York 1945–51); *Mirror in My House: The Autobiographies*, 2 v. (New York 1956). D. KRAUSE, *Sean O'Casey: The Man and His Work* (New York 1960). R. G. HOGAN, *The Experiments of Sean O'Casey* (New York 1960). G. FALLON, *Sean O'Casey: The Man I Knew* (Boston 1965). **Illustration credit:** W. Suschitzky, London.

[S. P. RYAN]

OCCASION (*opportunitas agendi*), may be defined as that which affords an opportunity for a free agent to exercise its *causality. The word "free" here does not refer simply to intellectual *freedom, but applies analogously to sensory freedom as well; hence, the actions of a dog, as proceeding from an interior principle and as guided by knowledge, may be termed free in this wider use of the word. An occasion can provide a mere opportunity for a cognitive being to act, or it may serve as a kind of inducement for action. If the latter is the case, the occasion tends to merge with the act's final cause, making it difficult to distinguish one from the other in the concrete situation. Examples of occasions will clarify the definition. If a teacher absents herself from a room of fourth graders, she provides an occasion for her charges to become rowdy. Or again, a beautiful summer day may serve as an occasion for a family picnic.

An occasion does not strictly cause the agent to act, although it does exercise influence upon the agent. It is to be noted also that it is not absolutely necessary that a suitable occasion be present for the agent to act. The agent well may act, even when no formal occasion is presented to it; thus the schoolchildren could become rowdy whether the teacher is present or absent, and a family could go on a picnic regardless of weather conditions. Occasion pertains primarily to the *agent, and should be distinguished from *condition, which pertains primarily to the patient (*see* ACTION AND PASSION).

An exaggerated emphasis has sometimes been given to occasion, particularly in the era of modern philosophy, where it has been used to deny creatural causality. Particularly associated with this movement are the post-Cartesians, A. *Geulincx and N. *Malebranche. *See also* OCCASIONALISM.

Bibliography: J. M. BALDWIN, ed., *Dictionary of Philosophy and Psychology*, 3 v. in 4 (New York 1901–05; repr. Gloucester 1949–57). L. DE RAEYMAEKER, *The Philosophy of Being*, tr. E. H. ZIEGELMEYER (St. Louis 1954). B. GERRITY, *Nature, Knowledge and God* (Milwaukee 1947). T. N. HARPER, *The Metaphysics of the School*, 3 v. (London 1879–84; reprint New York 1940) esp. v.2.

[G. F. KREYCHE]

OCCASIONALISM

A philosophical doctrine with implications in both metaphysics and epistemology. In metaphysics, occasionalism teaches that there is no causal interaction between beings—their contiguity merely serves as the *occasion for the causal influx of God; He is the only true cause. In epistemology, occasionalism teaches that the senses perceive regular sequences of events but that they do not perceive any causal interaction between these events. Thus the intellect, whose truth is measured by the evidence of the senses, can draw the conclusion that event *B* follows event *A*, but not that event *B* is caused by event *A*. One cannot, therefore, say with certitude whether there is present in nature a causal influx among beings. One cannot *know* whether things are causes. A metaphysical occasionalist denies that there *are* true causes; an epistemological occasionalist denies that man can *know* them. It is as a metaphysics that occasionalism is usually treated (*see* CAUSALITY).

History. The main points in the historical development of occasionalism can be discussed in terms of its role in Arabian philosophy and in the teachings of William of Ockham, Nicolas Malebranche, and David Hume.

Arabian Philosophy. When the Moslems were introduced to the philosophy of *Aristotle during the 9th century, there soon arose a conflict between this philosophy and some of their basic religious beliefs (*see* ARABIAN PHILOSOPHY). Aristotle taught that natures are self-contained centers of activity with substantial stability and permanence. This view seemed irreconcilable with the Islamic religious belief in the absolute power and creative activity of God. For the universe of Aristotle was sealed off from the direct, immediate, and all-pervasive power of God. Rejecting Aristotle, some Moslems fashioned a world more in keeping with their religious beliefs. According to these thinkers, known as Mutakallims, the universe is composed of discontinuous atoms; these are indivisible particles devoid of magnitude but completely homogeneous, and they are continuously created by God, who can create or annihilate them at will. No atom endures for two moments of time; each is created at every instant. God's causal efficacy as regards these atoms, and therefore all created things, is both absolute and exclusive. Atoms do nothing. But God wills the regular patterns man observes in the universe. For example, when a white garment is placed in black dye, God creates the corresponding atoms of blackness in the garment. And the same is true of all apparent human activity. Thus when a man is said to move a pen, this is the result of the direct intervention of God who creates four simultaneous accidents: the will-act of the man to move the pen; the power to move it; the movement of the hand; and the actual movement of the pen. The regular sequence of events are merely the willed occasions for God's causality.

Ockham. The occasionalism in the thought of *William of Ockham may be summed up as follows. By the very fact that it is, an individual can be only itself and nothing more. Each existent is absolutely and irreducibly singular. Thus there are no relations among things. For a relation would be something that two things had in common. And since causality, as an objective factor of nature, would be a relation of dependence of one thing upon another, man can never demonstrate that one thing is the cause of another. He has only the empirical presence of sequenced events, and these he calls causes and effects. The only thing that he can affirm with certitude is that, on the occasion of this regular and repetitive sequence, the mind acquires the habit of thinking that one event really causes another. The irreducible singularity and self-identity of Ockham's existent makes any inferential transfer by the intellect to the supreme, uncaused being of God philosophically impossible. (*See* NOMINALISM; OCKHAMISM.)

Malebranche. Like the Moslem Mutakallims before him, it was in defense of religion and the divine power that Nicolas *Malebranche, a Catholic priest and member of the French Oratory, taught that there is only one true cause, and it is God. This fervent and pious philosopher was convinced that the chief cause of idolatry was man's tendency to attribute to natural powers, like the sun or the rivers, the causal source of the life and fertility in the world. Malebranche held that a true cause must know not only what it does but how it does it. When a man moves his hand, he cannot tell how he does it. So he cannot be the true cause of this motion. He is only, says Malebranche, the occasional cause; the true cause, and only true cause, is God.

The occasionalism of Malebranche seems often more nominal than real. In traditional doctrine, God is said to be the first uncaused cause; it is maintained also that all other causes can cause only in actual and continued dependence upon the divine power (*see* CAUSALITY, DIVINE). At times it seems that Malebranche's occasional causes fit the definition of a true finite cause,

in the sense that they are not mere passive occasions. For example, Malebranche will admit that, when one moves one's hand, one does something. This is especially true in his treatment of an act of free choice. The act is personal, and the one placing it is responsible for it; this could not be the case if one were merely a passive occasion for God to make (cause) the choice. But Malebranche's definition of a true cause is unacceptable, as demanding too much. (*See* CARTESIANISM.)

Hume. The doctrine of David *Hume is similar to Ockham's. Ockham denied relations, and hence the relation of being a cause, because of his teaching on the irreducible singularity and self-identity of the existent. Hume denied *causality because it is an unknowable fact. Nothing is in the *intellect unless it is also somehow in the *senses. Hume interpreted this to mean that what a man cannot sense has no meaning for his intellect. All that a man senses is a regular and repetitive sequence of events; he does not sense any causal power effecting these events. Causality is simply the anticipation of this sequence by the mind, an anticipation that has been engendered by habit. Hume was an occasionalist in the sense that he considered sequences of events to be the occasion for the engendering of the habit of anticipating their regularity, which man calls causality. (*See* EMPIRICISM.)

Philosophical Implications. The principal philosophical implications of occasionalism are those relating to the existence of God and the freedom of the human will.

Existence of God. The only valid demonstration in philosophy for the existence of God would be an intellectually seen inference from the beings of man's experience to their causal source. To deny the possibility of man's ever knowing whether causality is an objective truth actually bearing upon the being of things is to deny the possibility of an inference, intellectually grasped, of a causal source. To deny the principle of causality is to cut off any way to demonstrate the knowability of the existence of a First Cause. Occasionalism in epistemology means agnosticism in natural theology.

Freedom of the Will. If one holds in his metaphysics that only God is a true cause and creatures only the occasions on which God exercises His causality, the consequences are logically devastating for created beings. For if creatures do nothing (and what else could a mere occasion mean?), they have no end; they are not *for* anything, and so have no reason for being. In a word, occasionalism makes of a being a contradiction in terms. It also logically destroys *free will; for if a person is not the true cause of his free actions, he can hardly be said to be the cause of why they are free. In a word, causality and being are so closely connected (causality is the *exercise* of being), that to empty creatures of their causality is to empty them of their being.

See also EFFICIENT CAUSALITY; INSTRUMENTAL CAUSALITY; METAPHYSICS, VALIDITY OF; OCCASION; CAUSALITY.

Bibliography: Copleston v.4. Eisler 2:336–338. Ueberweg 3: 261–269, 663–664. J. LATOUR, LexThK² 7:1123–25. A. DEL NOCE, EncFil 3:974–980. M. ELENA REINA, EncCatt 9:42–44. M. FAKHRY, *Islamic Occasionalism and Its Critiques by Averroës and Aquinas* (London 1958). M. GUEROULT, *Malebranche,* v.2.2 *L'Ordre et l'occasionalisme* (Paris 1959).

[M. R. HOLLOWAY]

OCCASIONIST, one who lives in, or places himself in, a situation in which he is drawn to the commission of a specific sin. The situation that leads the occasionist to sin may be free, in that it is self-chosen, or it may be necessary, in that it is imposed upon him. In the first case the occasionist is able to avoid the danger of sinning by getting away from the tempting situation, but he does not do so. Such a person can be said to will the sin by the very fact that he causes or permits the situation to exist. This, in itself, is sinful, and one would be judged to lack a satisfactory *purpose of amendment if he did not will to change a circumstance of that kind. In the second case, the person labors under constraint, physical or moral, that keeps him from getting away from the situation, or at least makes it very difficult for him to get away from it. However, although it may be physically or morally impossible for an individual to avoid a dangerous occasion, he can often lessen its danger—or, as moralists say, make the occasion less proximate—by the use of means such as fervent prayer, reflection, and the reception of Sacraments, which give promise of making his resistance to the temptation more effective.

Moral theologians distinguish between the material and the formal occasionist. On the one hand, the material occasionist is one for whom the occasion is unavoidable, but who is willing to use the appropriate means to control the danger it involves. The formal occasionist, on the other hand, either freely enters or remains in the occasion, or, if it is unavoidable, will not take the steps necessary to render it remote. A penitent who is not determined to avoid proximate occasions of grave sin when this is physically and morally possible, or who is not disposed to take steps necessary to counteract the dangers of occasions he cannot avoid, may not be absolved.

See also SIN, OCCASIONS OF.

Bibliography: Davis MorPasTh 3:290–294. Noldin SumThMor 3:398–401. B. MERKELBACH, *Quaestiones de variis poenitentium categoriis* (3d ed. Liège 1949) 44–51. E. THAMIRY, DTC 11.1: 905–915.

[F. E. KLUEG]

OCCULTISM, a general term employed to designate all those pseudosciences or practices, such as magic, alchemy, astrology, the various forms of divination, clairvoyance, theosophy, or spiritism, which claim to have knowledge of, or even control over, the hidden mysteries or powers of nature. Modern science, and especially psychology, has gradually refuted such claims, although there are occult phenomena and practices in Asia and Africa that still require further investigation and explanation. The pseudomysticism of the devotees or practitioners of occultism should not be confused with genuine mysticism in the Christian sense, nor should occultism be confused with parapsychology or related branches of the science of psychology. The terms occultism and the occult arts are too vague to be satisfactory. Hence they have given way to specific designations, such as magic, alchemy, and astrology.

Bibliography: H. VORGRIMLER, LexThK² 7:1125. G. R. S. MEAD, Hastings ERE 9:444–448. A. KÖBERLE, RGG³ 4:1614–19.

[P. SCHMIDT]

'OCCUPANCY, the act of taking possession of a thing having no owner and thus acquiring title to it. Since in a primary sense, all the world's goods were intended for all the world's people, occupancy is one of the primary means of establishing ownership. The general conditions for occupancy are that the thing truly belong to nobody, that the taking of it be real and not just a desire or an intention, and that there be an intention of making it one's own. The common cases of occupancy today are hunting, fishing, and finding treasure trove or lost articles. In hunting and fishing moralists distinguish between wild and domestic animals. Wild animals and fish belong to the one who captures them. This is true even if hunting and fishing take place on private property. However, the hunter or fisherman may be a trespasser. Animals that are normally wild but escape from captivity are considered as wild. Domestic animals are those that are customarily in the company of men. If they are not in the custody of their owner they are treated like any other lost object. (*See* HUNTING.) Treasure trove refers to goods that have been hidden for so long that their owner has been forgotten. In the U.S. the one who discovers a treasure may keep it, e.g., one who in digging a sewer finds money that was hidden years ago. This is different from finding lost property. In the latter case, although unknown, an owner does exist. A private individual has no obligation in strict justice to take lost property into his custody, but in ordinary circumstances this would be a matter of charity. (For circumstances under which the finder may keep the object found as his own *see* LOST PROPERTY AND OWNERSHIP.)

Bibliography: Prümmer ManThMor 2:39–47. Davis Mor PastTh 283–289.

[J. D. FEARON]

OCEANIA

This collective term refers to the immense number of islands in the central and south Pacific Ocean east of the *Philippines, *Indonesia, and *Australia. It includes Polynesia, the huge triangle formed by Hawaii, New Zealand, and Easter; Melanesia, the island groups south of the equator, north and east of Australia from New Guinea to the Fijis; and Micronesia, stretching northward from the equator to the Marianas and eastward from the Palau to the Gilbert Islands.

Races and Cultures. Generalities concerning the peoples of Oceania are of little use. The Polynesians were the first to have extensive contacts with Europeans; they established relations with the newcomers and were fairly successful in adapting primitive customs to modern ways. Melanesia still exhibits conditions varying from modern to Stone Age, the latter still prevalent in much of the interior of New Guinea. In Micronesia development has been hindered by the multiplicity of small islands scattered over more than 2 million square miles.

Whereas there are about 12 Polynesian and 15 Micronesian tongues, Melanesian languages or dialects number between 500 and 600. This variety presents a formidable obstacle to education, religious instruction, and civilizing influences generally in Melanesia. Before the coming of the missioners, Oceania had no written languages.

Primitive religions still exist in much of Melanesia, where spirits of the dead are credited with an active interest in the welfare of their descendants. This belief has taken fresh shape in the cargo cult and has created difficulties for missions and governments since World War II. For many Melanesians the major problem in life is to keep safe from evil spirits and sorcerers.

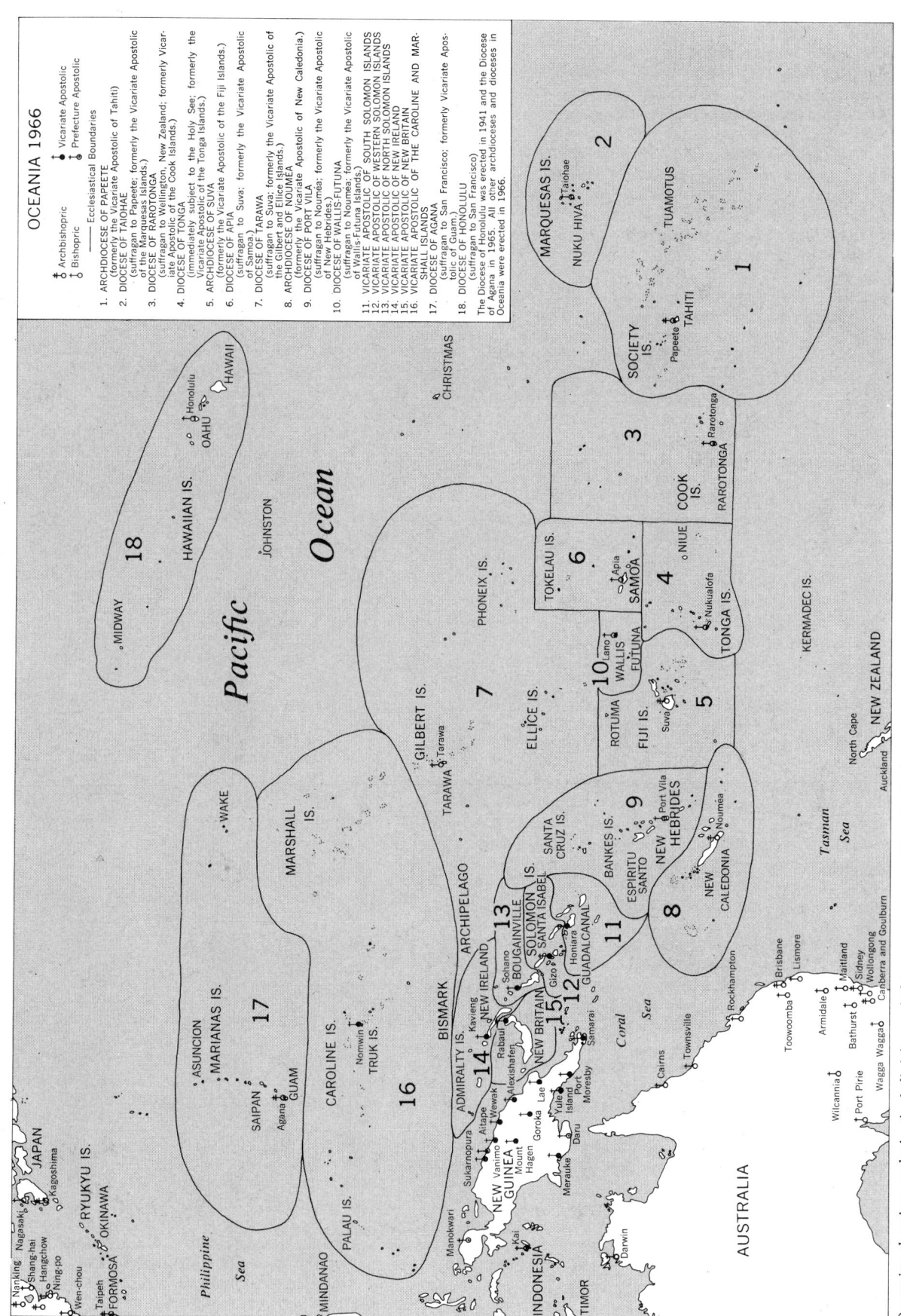

Oceania, showing ecclesiastical divisions of this vast area and the principal centers of mission activity.

OCEANIA 1966

✠ Archbishopric   ✠ Vicariate Apostolic
✠ Bishopric   ⊙ Prefecture Apostolic
—— Ecclesiastical Boundaries

1. ARCHDIOCESE OF PAPEETE
   (formerly the Vicariate Apostolic of Tahiti)
2. DIOCESE OF TAIOHAE
   (suffragan to Papeete; formerly the Vicariate Apostolic of the Marquesas Islands.)
3. DIOCESE OF RAROTONGA
   (suffragan to Wellington, New Zealand; formerly Vicariate Apostolic of the Cook Islands.)
4. DIOCESE OF TONGA
   (immediately subject to the Holy See; formerly the Vicariate Apostolic of the Tonga Islands.)
5. ARCHDIOCESE OF SUVA
   (formerly the Vicariate Apostolic of the Fiji Islands.)
6. DIOCESE OF APIA
   (suffragan to Suva; formerly the Vicariate Apostolic of Samoa.)
7. DIOCESE OF TARAWA
   (suffragan to Suva: formerly the Vicariate Apostolic of the Gilbert and Ellice Islands.)
8. ARCHDIOCESE OF NOUMEA
   (formerly the Vicariate Apostolic of New Caledonia.)
9. DIOCESE OF PORT VILA
   (suffragan to Nouméa; formerly the Vicariate Apostolic of New Hebrides.)
10. DIOCESE OF WALLIS-FUTUNA
    (suffragan to Nouméa; formerly the Vicariate Apostolic of Wallis-Futuna Islands.)
11. VICARIATE APOSTOLIC OF SOUTH SOLOMON ISLANDS
12. VICARIATE APOSTOLIC OF WESTERN SOLOMON ISLANDS
13. VICARIATE APOSTOLIC OF NORTH SOLOMON ISLANDS
14. VICARIATE APOSTOLIC OF NEW IRELAND
15. VICARIATE APOSTOLIC OF NEW BRITAIN
16. VICARIATE APOSTOLIC OF THE CAROLINE AND MARSHALL ISLANDS
17. DIOCESE OF AGANA; formerly Vicariate Apostolic of San Francisco; formerly Vicariate Apostolic of Guam.)
    (suffragan to San Francisco.)
18. DIOCESE OF HONOLULU
    (suffragan to San Francisco)

The Diocese of Honolulu was erected in 1941 and the Diocese of Agana in 1965. All other archdioceses and dioceses in Oceania were erected in 1966.

In some areas a form of *totemism flourishes, sharks, crocodiles, and snakes being worshiped.

Cultural and economic patterns have varied in accordance with the broad divisions of race, the size, nature, flora and fauna of the islands, possibilities of intercommunication, and other factors. Then came contact with Europeans, beginning with sailors, beachcombers and missionaries, and continuing to the accelerated development occasioned by World War II. The economy, a purely subsistence one originally, was modified by the raising of cash crops as European contacts gave rise to new needs and the possibility of satisfying them.

Catholic Missionary Activity. The first priest known to have visited Oceania was the fleet-chaplain of *Magellan in 1521. Natives later met chaplains of the Spanish ships occasionally. A Hawaiian tradition seems to indicate the presence of a priest there for some time, probably in the late 16th century. The names of many islands, e.g., Pentecost, Espiritu Santo, Asuncion, are evidence of the faith of the discoverers. In 1658 Jean Paulmier de Courtonne proposed missions in "the southern land." Nothing came of this. In 1798 the Congregation for the *Propagation of the Faith (Propaganda) entrusted the *Paccanarists with a mission field extending from the Cape of Good Hope to Japan, Australia, and adjacent lands, including part of Oceania. Again there was no result. In 1829, Henri de Solages was appointed prefect apostolic of *Réunion and proposed to extend his mission to Oceania. Propaganda confided to him a prefecture extending from Easter Island to New Zealand, and from the equator to the Tropic of Capricorn. This plan ended with the death of De Solages in Madagascar (1832). An unsuccessful attempt to evangelize Tahiti was made by Spanish Franciscans from Peru (1772–75). The first regular mission was established in the Marianas by Diego de Sanvitores, SJ. (1668); this mission was later staffed by the Augustinian Recollects and since 1907 by the Capuchins.

From about 1800 the Pacific area was visited by a flood of adventurers, whalers, and traders, seeking only profit and pleasure. It is doubtful that the Polynesians would have survived, had it not been for another group who came to save them, in every sense of the word. These were the missionaries, first non-Catholics and then Catholics. Their sometimes bitter differences and petty persecutions are regrettable, but the zeal and spirit of Christian sacrifice displayed by men and women of both groups were noble. The presence of Protestants stimulated later comers and led to an astonishing Catholic expansion.

In 1825 Pierre *Coudrin, founder of the Fathers of the *Sacred Hearts, offered their services to the Holy See just when a request was received by Propaganda for the establishment of a mission in Hawaii. The Prefecture Apostolic of the Sandwich Islands was established in 1825 and the first priests and brothers arrived in 1827. In 1831 the priests were expelled from Hawaii and sought another mission. The Marquesas, Tuamotus, and Society Islands were made into a prefecture (1833) entrusted to them, and together with the Prefecture of the Sandwich Islands, formed the Vicariate Apostolic of Eastern Oceania (1833), extending from the Sandwich, or Hawaiian Islands south to the Society Islands, and westward from Easter Island to the northern Cook Islands.

Western Oceania, a new mission, was accepted by the nascent *Marist Fathers. As a result the Vicariate of Western Oceania was erected (1836) covering Melanesia and the Caroline, Marshall, and Gilbert Islands of Micronesia. The first missionaries, including St. Peter *Chanel, set out the same year. Missions were first established in Wallis and Futuna, New Zealand, and then in Tonga, New Caledonia, Samoa, and elsewhere. The following years saw the painful development of the Church in Oceania. By 1850 the 2 vicariates of Eastern and Western Oceania had been divided into 10 vicariates. In 1841 St. Peter Chanel was martyred at Futuna; Bishop Epalle was killed on Santa Isabel in 1845; Brother Blaise Marmoiton was killed in New Caledonia, and about the same time two priests and a brother were killed and eaten in the Solomons. The Marists lost so many men that they had to withdraw from the Solomons. The Milan Foreign Mission Society, later called the *Pontifical Institute for Foreign Missions, replaced the Marists but in turn withdrew after the murder of Father Mazzuconi in 1855.

Nearly 30 years passed before the Vicariates of Melanesia and Micronesia were confided to the *Sacred Heart Missionaries. They began work in New Britain (1882), establishing a flourishing mission under the direction of Bishop *Couppé. In 1885 they landed in New Guinea, progressing to the Gilbert and Ellice Islands (1888) and to the Marshalls (1891). The Society of the *Divine Word was called upon to take charge of northeastern New Guinea (1896). Very many priests, brothers, and sisters, who were members or associates of these two institutes, died of malaria and other diseases; others were killed by the natives. In western New Guinea, later called West Irian, missions were established from Indonesia. The Caroline Islands mission, begun by *Jesuits (1731), collapsed with the order's expulsion from Spain's colonies (1767), but it began again under Spanish Capuchins when Spain's jurisdiction over the islands was established (1886). Since 1945 the rate of development in Papua-New Guinea has required the added services of Franciscans, Capuchins, Dominicans, Passionists, Montfort Fathers and Marianhill Missionaries to staff newly formed prefectures or vicariates.

Mission Methods and Problems. When missions commenced in Oceania, anthropology and kindred sciences were practically nonexistent. Missionaries had little or no proximate preparation for their task. Languages were not yet reduced to writing. Usually the missionaries had to learn the language and prepare a grammar and dictionary at the same time, a task made more difficult by their failure to appreciate the native culture and way of life. The missionaries had little or no medical training, and very little was known of the causes or treatment for malaria and other tropical diseases, which killed so many, both natives and Europeans. Blunders were made through lack of understanding of native beliefs and customs. The missions have indeed been often blamed for the disintegration of native life and the death of thousands. This disintegration had started with the coming of the whalers, beachcombers, and slavers, and would have been much worse but for the presence and the efforts of the missionaries. Despite inevitable mistakes for which they sometimes paid with their lives, the missionaries were the principal force guiding the native from the Stone Age to the atomic one. They began to educate the native, to reduce his languages to writing, to set up printing presses, to train him in arts and crafts. Most schools in Melanesia remain under mission control, though now aided and supervised by governments. Some missionaries found time to do anthropological and ethnological work of inestimable value.

Catechists have been indispensable in the apostolate. Catholicism was introduced to Samoa, Tonga, Fiji, the Gilberts, and other islands with the help of natives who had been converted elsewhere. When the Solomon Islands missions were begun again (1897–98), Samoan and Fijian catechists accompanied the priests. Catechists, after training, are entrusted with the care of congregations, which can often be visited only at long intervals by the priests; they teach school, conduct daily prayers and Sunday services, baptize in case of necessity, assist the sick, and bury the dead (see CATECHIST, MISSIONARY).

Mission schools have constantly improved, and many vicariates now provide some form of technical education, often under the guidance of brothers. Sisters conduct schools, dispensaries, hospitals, and leprosaria; they have done much to raise the status of women from their former condition of servitude.

World War I impeded the missions principally by interrupting the supply of personnel and income. World War II saw mission stations destroyed and missionaries interned; 128 priests, brothers, and sisters were killed or died of disease and starvation. In New Guinea, New Britain, the Solomons, and Micronesia, stations and staffs were almost annihilated. The interruption of regular instruction plus the demoralizing influence of wartime conditions led to a revival of pagan beliefs and immoral practices in some areas.

In 1847 Propaganda encouraged Bishop *Bataillon to set up a seminary. In 1856 three students from Oceania entered the Propaganda College in Rome. In 1859 a minor seminary started near Sydney, Australia; it closed after some years, then reopened in Wallis (1874) as a major seminary and produced a number of priests for Wallis, Futuna, Tonga, and Samoa. With the opening of the major seminary in New Caledonia (1939) for all the French language vicariates of Oceania, that of Wallis is again a minor seminary. Fiji, Samoa, and Tonga send their students to Australia or New Zealand, while those of the New Guinea Territory and the Solomons go to the seminaries at Rabaul and Madang.

Statistics. In 1964 in the Oceania missions were 872 priests (49 being Oceanians), 451 brothers (124 Oceanians), and 848 Oceanian sisters plus 1,145 from other lands. In addition to the institutes already mentioned, the Vincentians and Columban Fathers share in the work, as do the Marist Brothers, Christian Brothers of Ploermel, Brothers of the Sacred Heart, and many congregations of sisters. Oceania has also a number of diocesan institutes of brothers and sisters. (See CLERGY, INDIGENOUS; MEDICAL MISSIONS; MISSIONARY FORMATION; MISSIONS, CATHOLIC; MISSIONS, SOCIAL ACTION OF; RELIGION IN PRIMITIVE CULTURE.)

Oceania, with about 800,000 Catholics (1.4 million Protestants, the rest pagans) in a population of 3,385,-000, was divided ecclesiastically into 28 apostolic vicariates and 4 apostolic prefectures, exclusive of *Hawaii with one diocese, *Honolulu, for 205,000 Catholics in a population of 650,000, and *New Zealand with 1 archdiocese and 3 suffragan sees for 340,000

Methodists and Catholics on Bougainville in the Solomon Islands competing in a Bible-knowledge "spelling bee."

Catholics in a population of some 2.5 million in 1964.

In 1966 the Holy See established the Archdiocese of Papeete (formerly the Vicariate of *Tahiti) with its suffragan Diocese of Taiohae (*Marquesas Islands); Archdiocese of Suva (*Fiji Islands) with two suffragans—Apia (*Samoa) and Tarawa (*Gilbert and Ellice Islands); Archdiocese of Nouméa (*New Caledonia) with two suffragans—Port Vila (*New Hebrides) and Wallis-Futuna; Diocese of Rarotonga (*Cook Islands), suffragan to Wellington, New Zealand; and Diocese of *Tonga, immediately subject to the Holy See.

See also for Micronesia, CAROLINE AND MARSHALL ISLANDS; GUAM, DIOCESE OF; for Melanesia, NEW BRITAIN; NEW GUINEA; NEW IRELAND; SOLOMON ISLANDS; for Polynesia, WALLIS AND FUTUNA ISLANDS.

Bibliography: Streit-Dindinger 21. J. ROMMERSKIRCHEN and J. DINDINGER, *Bibliografia missionaria* (Rome 1936–), annual. C. R. H. TAYLOR, *A Pacific Bibliography* (2d ed., Wellington, N.Z. 1964). F. M. CAMMACK and SHIRO SAITO, *Pacific Island Bibliography* (New York 1962). H. EMMERICH, *Atlas missionum* (Vatican City 1958), to be used with L. SCHORER's *Data statistica* (Vatican City 1959). MissCattol. Delacroix HistMissCath 3. Latourette v.5, 7. Latourette Christ19th–20thCent 3, 5. J. VERSCHEUREN, "A Growing World: Problems of the Catholic Missions in Oceania," *Carmelus* 7 (1960) 277–330. *Pacific Islands Year Book* (9th ed. Sydney 1963). *Bilan du Monde* 661. AnnPont (1965) 1433–35. *The Official Year Book of the Catholic Church of Australasia* (Sydney 1963–64), annual. **Illustration credit:** Fig. 2, Douglas L. Oliver, "A Solomon Island Society," Harvard University Press.

[S. J. BOURKE]

OCHINO, BERNARDINO, renowned preacher; b. district dell' Oca, Siena (hence his surname), 1487; d. Slavkov, Moravia, c. 1564. He entered the Observant Franciscans (c. 1504), and after broad studies, he rose to be provincial and finally vicar for the Cisalpine province of his order. Craving a yet stricter rule, he transferred in 1534 to the Capuchins, of whom he was vicar-general from 1538–42 (see FRANCISCANS, CAPUCHIN). As a Lenten preacher, the gaunt ascetic of resonant voice and terrifying directness was eagerly sought by competing towns and bishops. In 1536, while in Naples, he had become acquainted with Juan de *Valdés and his circle. Several of his later sermons were popularizations of the works of Valdés, and his understanding of the atonement was Valdesian. In 1539 he delivered at Venice a remarkable course of *Prediche,* showing a Protestant tendency in the doctrine of justification, all under the guise of opposing it.

Suspected and cited to Rome in 1542, Ochino was deterred from presenting himself on the advice of *Peter Martyr Vermigli at Florence. He escaped across the Alps, settling in Geneva, where he was cordially received by Calvin. He married a lady of Tusca who had once heard him as the great Capuchin preacher. From 1542 till 1545 he preached to the Italian congregation and wrote, publishing in 1544 his *Apologhi,* a collection of reminiscences and satirical anecdotes about popes, cardinals, priests, and friars. He served as minister of the Italian Protestant congregation at Augsburg (1545–47). When the city was occupied by the imperial forces, he escaped by way of Basel and Strassburg, to find asylum in England (1547–53). Here he was made a prebendary of Canterbury and preached to the Italians in London, receiving a royal pension. Here also he composed his *Dialogue of the injuste usurped primacie of the Bishop of Rome* and the *Labyrinth,* the latter opposing predestination.

At the accession of Mary Tudor he became pastor of the Italian congregation at Zurich, where he published his *Dialogo del Purgatorio,* in which he upheld the view that the true purgatory is Jesus himself, purifying man of his sins. In his *Syncerae et verae doctrinae de Coena Domini defensio* he described the Lord's Supper in a Zwinglian fashion. His *XXX Dialoghi,* brought together in 1563, occasioned his banishment. His Protestant adversaries maintained that he was weak on the doctrine of the Trinity and that he had justified polygamy under color of a pretended refutation.

He found refuge in Poland under the protection of Prince Nicolas Radziwiłł and preached in Cracow until the edict of August 1564 banished all foreign dissidents. After losing, during his wanderings, three of his children, he found asylum in Slavkov with Niccolò Paruto, an exiled Venetian nobleman who espoused antitrinitarian Anabaptism. He died of the plague.

Bibliography: R. H. BAINTON, *Bernardino Ochino* (Florence 1940). B. NICOLINI, *Il pensiero di Bernardino Ochino* (Naples 1939). F. CALLAEY, EncCatt 9:57–59, with bibliog. G. MÜLLER, RGG³ 4:1555–56.

[G. H. WILLIAMS]

OCKHAMISM

A philosophical and theological system of thought based on the teachings of *William of Ockham that flourished in the universities of Europe during the 14th and 15th centuries.

Characteristics. This philosophical and theological movement has not been adequately characterized by historians, nor has the label "Ockhamist" a completely definite connotation. Even those upon whom the name is imposed exhibit great variety in their theological thinking and are not infrequently opposed to one another. There are, however, general trends that are characteristic of the movement and that have caused it to be referred to as the *via moderna* as opposed to the *via antiqua* of the earlier scholastics.

Conceptualism. The most basic notion is, perhaps, the note of *conceptualism that began to enter into explanations of knowledge. According to this theory, the terms in a proposition signify a *concept that stands for some extramental reality. This concept is a *sign that can refer to one thing or to many. As a sign it is a mental reality and, like any reality, is itself singular and unique. It is universal only insofar as it can stand for many. Hence, its universality is purely functional and does not in any sense refer to a common nature possessed by many things outside the mind. This makes necessary a whole new logic of *supposition, i.e., the manner in which terms stand for things, and gives a new turn to the old Aristotelian logic.

Singulars. Reality itself is a collection of absolute singulars, the distinguishable units of which are things and qualities. All other modifications of things are reduced to the reality of the things themselves. Things are similar, for example, because they are themselves; quantity is indistinguishable from the thing in its magnitude. Such a universe of unique singulars cannot have any necessary connections between the beings that compose it. Furthermore, since singulars depend for their being on the will of God and since the will of God can accomplish anything that does not involve a contradiction, it is always possible to have one given singular without another. Since, for example, an effect is different from its cause, it is possible for God to sustain the effect without its proper cause.

Motion. Another characteristic distinctive of Ockhamism, worth mentioning because it can serve to differentiate this movement from other types of nominalism, is its attitude toward motion. Ockham denied the existence of motion as an entity separate from the moving body, holding that motion was merely a term replacing a series of statements that the body was now here, now there, etc. Others who are commonly referred to as nominalists, such as *John Buridan, *Albert of Saxony, and *Nicholas Oresme, were not only convinced of the reality of motion but, through their attempts to discover its proper cause, contributed to the origin of modern science (see M. Clagett).

Divine Will. The theory of divine omnipotence based on what God can will without contradiction is one of the dominant themes in later Ockhamism. It is basically an attempt to overcome the necessitarianism of Greek philosophy, a necessitarianism that Ockham thought the whole theory of the divine ideas had failed to solve. In place of a universe conceived as an expression of divine intelligibility, there is posited a universe radically contingent upon the divine will, even to the natures of things themselves. The same notion appears in ethics and morality, in which sin comes to be equated with prohibition and good is determined by the will of God instead of by any intrinsic intelligibility. Most of the Ockhamists went so far as to assert that God could command someone to hate Him. And why not, if good and evil are completely determined by what God wills them to be?

Knowledge. The experience one has of such a universe of unique singulars can never be more than a *de facto* association of many such singulars. There is an intuitive grasp of the individual thing sensibly affecting one here and now. All other knowledge is abstract knowledge. Since, in the first place, there is no necessity in such a universe and since relationship is not a reality distinct from the things themselves, there is no hope of establishing the necessity of the causal proposition. As a result, the conclusions of the natural sciences and of the philosophy of nature became at best highly probable propositions. Neither do the traditional arguments for the existence of God based on efficient, formal, and final causality any longer provide a demonstration for such existence. The same can be said about the existence of the human soul and its immortality.

Role of Faith. Hence, many of the conclusions that previous scholastic theologians considered to be capable of rational demonstration were made matters of faith only. The result was an ever widening gap between philosophy and theology, or better, perhaps, the relegation of philosophy to the status of a quasi-science of predictability about the events in nature and a corresponding skepticism about the validity of metaphysics. H. Oberman is probably correct when he questions the retreat to faith as stemming entirely from the low opinion of knowledge prevalent among Ockhamistic thinkers [*The Harvest of Medieval Theology* (Cambridge, Mass. 1963) 35]. But neither are the alternatives he suggests completely satisfactory. There may be other reasons; but granting the Ockhamistic metaphysics and logic, there is little else that can be done except to restrict drastically the range of human reason.

Chief Proponents. The *via moderna* had its influence, and the main themes of the movement appear consistently in the works of such men as *Robert Holcot, *Adam Wodam, *Gregory of Rimini, *Peter of Ailly, and Ockham's commentator, Gabriel *Biel. The two men who seem to represent best the extremes of the position are *John of Mirecourt and *Nicholas of Autrecourt.

John of Mirecourt divides all knowledge into that which is evident and that which is held with fear of error. Evident knowledge in the strictest sense is that which can be reduced to the principle of *contradiction. Experiential knowledge is also evident, but it is never capable of leading to a strict *demonstration. The proofs for God's existence and the causal proposition are classed under the knowledge that is held with fear of error. The theme of the divine omnipotent will shows up strongly also. God can cause any act, including the act of hatred of Himself. John also thought an act could be contrary to the natural law without being demeritorious.

Nicholas of Autrecourt held also that the only certain knowledge was that which could be reduced to the principle of contradiction. Experience provides certain knowledge, but in a universe of individuals the existence of one thing can never be inferred from the existence of another. It is impossible for logic to detect any necessary connections in nature. Nicholas also repeated John of Mirecourt's opinion that God could cause an act of hatred of Himself. In his philosophy of nature, Nicholas returned to the old Greek *atomism, preferring it to the hylomorphic theory of Aristotle. Besides, a universe of disparate atoms with no necessary connections between them was all the more dependent on God.

Others, such as John Buridan, *Marsilius of Inghen, and Nicholas of Oresme, made use of Ockham's logic, although they differed from Ockham in their analyses of the world of nature.

Influence. The University of Paris had issued condemnations against Ockham in 1339 and against John of Mirecourt in 1347. In 1346 the Holy See condemned Nicholas of Autrecourt. Nevertheless, the movement continued to flourish. Terminist logic became prevalent not only at Paris and Oxford, but also at the universities of Heidelberg, Vienna, Erfurt, and Leipzig.

It would be inaccurate to maintain a direct influence of John of Mirecourt or Nicholas of Autrecourt on modern and contemporary *empiricism. Christian theologians such as these were logicians and philosophers only in a secondary way. Nevertheless there are some striking resemblances between the philosophizing of the late Middle Ages and modern empiricists such as J. *Locke and D. *Hume. And the logic of supposition, with its emphasis on functionality, is not too far divorced from the approach of contemporary *linguistic analysis.

Criticism. With its world of absolutely singular entities and its rejection of any necessary connection between them, Ockhamism effectively destroyed any certain knowledge of that world beyond the intuitive grasp of an immediately present sense object. Since all abstract knowledge had nothing to do with existence, such knowledge could be at best a logic of possibilities with only an indirect reference to the real order. These possibilities, moreover, were abstracted from sensible experience. Hence, metaphysics was reduced to a logic of concepts that could not transcend the material world from which such concepts were taken. The causal relationship became a way of thinking about experience, rather than an insight grounded in the actual relationships between things. The rejection of any proof for the existence of God based on efficient or final causality was simply a necessary conclusion from such premises.

There is little reason to be surprised, then, when revelation and faith began more and more to take over conclusions formerly held as rationally demonstrable by the earlier scholastics. Along with this went a corresponding *skepticism about the intellect's ability to achieve any certainty either in natural science or in philosophy. The God who was believed to have created such a world did so with an arbitrariness restricted only by the principle of contradiction. Instead of the divine essence as intelligible being the source and exemplar of the universe, it is the divine will that establishes all things even to their intelligible natures. Instead of right reason being the norm of morality, now the command to act in such a way alone determines moral good and evil. A universe so conceived cannot do without faith. Once that faith was lost, skepticism or a return to reason conceived as sufficient for itself were the only possible answers.

See also NOMINALISM; SCHOLASTICISM.

Bibliography: Copleston v.3. A. A. MAURER, *Medieval Philosophy* (New York 1962). M. CLAGETT, *The Science of Mechanics in the Middle Ages* (Madison, Wis. 1959). K. MICHALSKI, *Les Sources du criticisme et du scepticisme dans la philosophie du XIV*e *siècle* (Cracow 1926). P. VIGNAUX, DTC 2.1:748–784.

[H. R. KLOCKER]

O'CLERY, MICHAEL, Franciscan lay brother, scribe, hagiographer, historian (in Gaelic Mícheál Ó Clérigh); b. Donegal, Ireland, *c.* 1590; d. Louvain, Netherlands, 1643. He studied in Irish schools before going to the Spanish Netherlands some time before 1621. He entered the Franciscan Order in about 1622 at Louvain, where the Irish Franciscans had established the College of St. Anthony in 1607. Many important scholars and writers were attached to the College and it became the center of a movement to provide the Irish people with religious literature in their own language. A printing press, installed at the College in 1611, turned out many books during the next 60 years. At the time of O'Clery's entrance, Fathers Hugh *Ward, Patrick *Fleming, and others connected with Louvain, had formed a plan to publish the lives of the Irish saints. O'Clery was dispatched to Ireland in 1626 to collect hagiographical material and send it to Louvain. He remained in Ireland at this task for 11 years.

In addition to a great amount of transcription, O'Clery compiled works of his own—calendars of saints' feasts, and genealogies of saints and kings—and reedited some early historical documents. In collaboration with three other scholars he produced (1632–36) his greatest work, *The Annals of the Four Masters,* an annalistic compilation from many sources covering the history of Ireland from the earliest times to 1616. In 1637 he returned to Louvain, where he compiled his *Foclóir nó Sanasan Nua* (a glossary of obscure words), which was printed on the college press in the year of his death.

O'Clery's achievement lay in rescuing from destruction many Irish historical records. Some of his material was used by Father John *Colgan, successor to Fathers Ward and Fleming, in his *Acta sanctorum Hiberniae* (1645) and *Triadis thaumaturgae seu divorum Patricii, Columbae, et Brigidae acta* (1647). The plan to publish the Saints' lives fell through after the death (1673) of Colgan's successor, Father Thomas Sheerin, but most of the material in O'Clery's manuscripts was published during the last century.

Bibliography: B. JENNINGS, *Michael Ó Cléirigh, Chief of the Four Masters, and His Associates* (Dublin 1936). T. Ó CLÉIRIGH, *Aodh Mac Aingil agus an Scoil Nua-Ghaedhilge i Lobhain* (Dublin 1936). S. O'BRIEN, ed., *Measgra i gcuimhne Mhichíl Uí Chléirigh: Miscellany of Historical and Linguistic Studies in Honour of Brother Michael Ó Cléirigh* (Dublin 1944).

[G. S. MAC EOIN]

O'CONNELL, ANTHONY, SISTER, Civil War nurse; b. Limerick, Ireland, Aug. 15, 1814; d. Cincinnati, Ohio, Dec. 8, 1897. Mary, the daughter of William and Catherine (Murphy) O'Connell, came to the U.S. as a child and attended the school conducted by the Ursuline Sisters at Charlestown, Mass. Through William Tyler, a convert and priest, she became acquainted with Mother Elizabeth Seton's foundation at Emmitsburg, Md., and joined the Sisters of Charity in 1835. Two years later, as Sister Anthony, she was sent to Cincinnati, Ohio, to care for orphans. During the next 17 years she was active in the administration of hospitals and homes for children, establishing St. John's Hotel for Invalids as the city's first modern medical institution. In 1852 she was one of the seven founders of the Sisters of Charity of Cincinnati, and she served twice as procuratrix-general of the new congregation. In 1861, in response to a government appeal for nurses, Sister Anthony labored in Cincinnati and at various military hospitals. For her work she was praised as "the Florence Nightingale of America." After the war, her congregation was presented with Cincinnati's former Marine Hospital, which was renamed the Good Samaritan. In 1873 St. Joseph's Infant Home, the first hospital for unmarried mothers and abandoned infants in the area, was opened by the congregation. Until 1882 Sister Anthony was administrator of the Good Samaritan Hospital and also of St. Joseph's Home, where she died.

Bibliography: Archives, Sister of Charity, Mount St. Joseph, Ohio. E. R. JOLLY, *Nuns of the Battlefield* (Providence 1927). M. A. McCANN, *History of Mother Seton's Daughters,* 3 v. (New York 1917–23).

[L. C. FEIERTAG]

O'CONNELL, DANIEL

Irish statesman; b. Carhen, Cahirciveen, Co. Kerry, Aug. 6, 1775; d. Genoa, Italy, May 15, 1847. O'Connell was the eldest son of Morgan (1739–1809) and Catherine (O'Mullane) O'Connell. The O'Connells farmed and traded in Kerry, where their ancestors had held military and church offices before the wholesale confiscation of Irish land by Oliver Cromwell. On the advice of an uncle, Count Daniel Charles O'Connell (1745–1833), a distinguished French general, Daniel was sent for education to the Austrian Netherlands— first to the English College at St. Omer (1791) and, the following year, to the Douay English College. Early in 1793, the French overran this area and O'Connell went to London, where he studied law until 1797;

he was called to the Irish bar in 1798. In 1802 he married his cousin Mary, daughter of Dr. Thomas O'Connell of Tralee.

Emancipation Advocate. O'Connell had been an able student. His diary reveals that he had grasped

Daniel O'Connell.

quite clearly the idea of the English common law, and particularly the concept of the rights of the subject. He was one of the first Catholic lawyers permitted to practice in *Ireland after the first anti-Catholic penal laws were modified. O'Connell, one day to be called "the Liberator," was quickly drawn toward the defense of his coreligionists whose political ambitions were being frustrated by the refusal of *emancipation. In 1797 he had been associated with the revolutionary society of United Irishmen and also had joined the volunteer artillery corps of the Dublin lawyers. Yet he took no part in the rebellion of 1798. From 1799 for at least 10 years he was a freemason—the Irish bishops did not implement papal condemnations of *Freemasonry until much later. O'Connell was instrumental in securing the reelection as grand master of Richard Hely-Hutchinson, Lord Donoughmore (1756–1825), a man whose services in the cause of Catholic emancipation he greatly admired. O'Connell probably ended his connection with the freemasons before 1824, and apparently on the advice of Abp. John *Troy (1739–1823).

A highly successful barrister who was earning nearly £8,000 a year by the late 1820s, he was particularly effective in cross-examination, and in defense. His aggressive technique gave courage to Catholics long exploited legally by the Protestant ascendancy. But his method, as in the John Magee case (1814), while it weakened the reputation of opponents, was not always fully effective; the loss of one of his cases could entail the imposition of heavy punishments on his clients. Magee, for example, was imprisoned and fined for publishing criminal libels against the government.

As early as 1800 O'Connell had spoken at a meeting of Dublin Catholics in opposition to the legislative union with Great Britain; his position was contrary to the views of many of the bishops and upperclass laymen. During his 30-year career as a lawyer he gave much time to the successive Catholic organizations that attempted to secure political and social equality. Until 1812 the most important of these was the Irish Catholic Committee on which O'Connell replaced John

Keogh (1740–1817) in the year (1807) when the policy of petitioning Parliament for the abrogation of the penal laws was again taken up systematically. This committee was suppressed by the government in 1812 and was succeeded by the Irish Catholic Board, of which O'Connell was also made a member. In 1813 English members of Parliament, who were pro-Catholic and who believed emancipation could be secured, introduced relief measures. These empowered the government by arrangement with the Holy See to exercise a veto on nominees to bishoprics in Great Britain and Ireland. The proposal was acceptable to the papal secretary of Propaganda G. B. (later Cardinal) Quarantotti, but the bill was abandoned because of the opposition of Bp. John Milner (1752–1826) and of O'Connell, whose views were those of the majority of the board. O'Connell's objection was that if the veto power was thus conceded, the clergy would appear to be civil servants, and in that role would forfeit the people's confidence. For this same reason O'Connell later rejected several relief bills introduced by Henry Grattan (1746–1820). Furthermore, O'Connell had hopes that if Grattan's friends, the Whigs, failed in their purpose, he could secure it through pro-Catholic Tories such as William Conyngham Plunket (1764–1854). For these reasons, also, he avoided committing himself on the subject of parliamentary reform. This issue had become associated with the Whig opposition to the Tory government of Robert Banks Jenkinson, second Earl of Liverpool (1770–1828). At this point of history, however, the pro-Catholic Tories were too weak to be truly effective and, accordingly, on April 25, 1823, O'Connell and Richard Lalor Sheil (1791–1851) started the Catholic Association, which charged membership dues of 1 shilling a year. Within 12 months O'Connell had gained a nationwide support, which had been effectively organized by the diocesan clergy and by the Catholic professional classes.

Alarmed at this development, the government introduced an act to suppress all such societies (1825). O'Connell went to London to promote a Catholic petition; he was persuaded by Plunket and Sir Francis Burdett (1770–1844) to accept a relief bill balanced by provisions for state payment of Catholic clergy and for disfranchisement of 40-shilling freeholders. Despite support by a majority of government ministers in the House of Commons, the proposal was defeated in the House of Lords, a vote largely influenced by a speech of the prime minister Lord Liverpool. In July of the same year, O'Connell organized the New Catholic Association, which in the general election of 1826 achieved spectacular successes and which ended the monopoly of political control of the freeholders in Waterford, Louth, and Monaghan. The government now began to fear that O'Connell would make it impossible for them to win Irish elections.

It was in this atmosphere that Arthur Wellesley, Duke of Wellington (1769–1852), who succeeded as prime minister in 1828, now was obliged to give way on the emancipation issue, for O'Connell had himself defeated the government supporter, William Vesey-FitzGerald (1783–1843), at a by-election for Co. Clare. Since Wellington was in power, the Irish Catholic Association had decided to oppose the reelection of any member accepting office from the government. Although Vesey-FitzGerald had been favorable to

Catholic emancipation, his defeat made it clear that the government risked losing supporters, and that it dare not risk a general election. Such an election in Ireland would almost certainly result in the return of a solid bloc of pro-Catholics hostile to the government's policy.

O'Connell's victory, by a vote of 2057 to 982, was regarded as the death knell of landlord control of freeholders' votes. The clergy had utilized every influence in stimulating their people to believe that the issue was essentially a religious one. Thus, to Wellington, emancipation became a necessary concession in a final effort to insure "that the Irish nobility and gentry would recover their lost influence, the just influence of property." It was the great merit of O'Connell that his efforts helped to build for the Irish masses the growing power that led to eventual control of their elected representatives. The passage of the act of Catholic emancipation, however, was accompanied by the statutory abolition both of the Catholic Association and of the voting rights of the 40-shilling freeholders (1829). Only those Catholics who would take an oath of allegiance to the British king, and thereby deny the temporal power of the pope in the United Kingdom, might thus secure legal exemption from the penal laws. Future members of religious orders need not expect such protection. Even O'Connell himself, without reelection, could not take his seat in Parliament unless he first subscribed to the anti-Catholic oath and declaration made applicable to all members before the Clare election. That no one dared oppose his reelection was some indication that the center of political gravity in Ireland had changed permanently.

Further Political Struggles. For some years after 1829, O'Connell's connections with Catholic issues were peripheral. His attempt to organize a nondenominational movement to repeal the union of the British and Irish parliaments was unsuccessful. He was feared by the dominant Protestant ascendancy, which in any case was not prepared to share its power. Determined to break that power, O'Connell appealed to the parliamentary reformers and to the democracy. In November 1830, Wellington, convinced that he could no longer prevent reform, retired and was succeeded as prime minister by Charles Grey (Viscount Howick and Earl Grey, 1764–1845). With O'Connell's support, this Whig leader secured the passage of the great reform act of 1832, which abolished many unrepresentative boroughs and gave to the upper middle class some share in political power. The Irish act (1833), which maintained many of the unrepresentative bulwarks of Protestant ascendancy, was less satisfactory. Further, social equality was still denied to farming Catholics who now began to refuse to pay tithes to Protestant clergy. The result was that a new form of agrarian revolt, partly countenanced by the Catholic clergy, became common. After 1834, under Grey's successor, William Lamb, Viscount Melbourne (1779–1848), O'Connell made more progress in securing "justice for Ireland" and in particular for the Catholics. A reform administration in Dublin, one particularly influential among the police, abandoned the habit of equating loyalists and Protestants. Catholics were slowly admitted to government offices, but legislative reforms did not go beyond converting tithes into a rent charge upon lands (1838), and abolishing the more indefensi-

ble parliamentary boroughs (1840). Meanwhile, since 1830 the existence of a nondenominational system of elementary education was causing increased Catholic and Protestant resentment particularly on the part of Abp. John *MacHale (1791–1881) of Tuam; his opposition led him to support O'Connell who had revived the repeal of the union question in the Precursor Society in 1838. O'Connell convinced MacHale that the Repeal Association, established in 1839, would prevent the Tory government of Sir Robert Peel (1788–1850), Melbourne's successor (1841), from reestablishing Protestant ascendancy, or, at the least, from permanently obstructing further Catholic emancipation. With renewed clerical support in most parts of the country (Abp. Daniel *Murray of Dublin almost alone held aloof) O'Connell organized an enthusiastic national following. Despite his confident predictions of success for this great moral movement in 1843, Peel secured O'Connell's imprisonment for seditious conspiracy (June 30, 1844). He was released, after a successful appeal, 3 months later. Catholic Ireland treated this event as an occasion for spiritual rejoicing; even Archbishop Murray took part by sanctioning a *Te Deum*. Meanwhile, Peel had endeavored to divert Catholics from the Repeal Association by supporting a more moderate policy, which featured the state endowment of nondenominational higher colleges and a substantially increased subsidization of *St. Patrick's of Maynooth. Through a bequests act, Peel also offered improved facilities for Catholic charities. A simultaneous approach was made to Rome to discourage Irish ecclesiastical involvement in politics. This attempt boomeranged when MacHale insisted on the danger to Catholicism from the colleges and bequests bills. Unfairly, O'Connell argued that the bequests law would be used to bar charities to religious orders. Rome ultimately condemned the legislation for colleges but not the bequests act. Immediately afterward, O'Connell was able to influence the clergy against that more militant group in the Repeal Association, the Young Irelanders, who were opposed to a renewed Irish alliance with the Whigs who had returned to power under Prime Minister Lord John Russell in June 1846. Rather than deny the right to resort to force in any extremity, the Young Irelanders left the Repeal Association.

Thereafter O'Connell desired to persuade the state to take measures to counteract the potato blight, which had first appeared in the autumn of the preceding year. The attempt was unsuccessful; the Whig government proved incapable of arresting the catastrophe, now known as the "Great Famine." Within 10 years, the resultant fever, starvation, and emigration reduced by 25 per cent the population of Ireland, which had once been more than 8 million.

After O'Connell's death from a sudden cerebral illness, suffered at Genoa while he was on a pilgrimage to Rome, his son Daniel was received by Pope Pius IX. Under that Pope's auspices a 2-day funeral oration for O'Connell was delivered by Gioacchino *Ventura di Raulica (1792–1861). The speech glorified the union of religion and liberty.

O'Connell's religious convictions, apparently weakened in his youth, had been reinforced during his maturity, and were quite strong in his last years. Those years were, however, somewhat darkened by what seems to have been almost an obsession with the possibility of his eternal damnation.

O'Connell's Significance. This Irish statesman was the greatest single influence in the emergence of Irish political nationalism. He linked the constitutional movement of Grattan and of the 18th-century Protestant patriots to the emancipated Catholics. In his appeal to the masses he was closer to Theobald Wolfe Tone (1763–98) and to the United Irishmen than to Grattan, though in his mature years he opposed both the use of physical force and of revolutionary methods. His substitution of the clergy for the landlords as the local leaders of the people strengthened their mutual ties even after clerical interference at the end of the career of *Parnell had weakened the Church's relations with the nationalists. A friend to Catholic liberal Europe and a forceful supporter of the advocates of Negro emancipation in America, O'Connell's influence on Irish nationalism helped to shape the 20th-century Republic of Ireland.

Bibliography: R. D. EDWARDS, "The Contribution of Young Ireland to the Development of the National Idea," in *Essays Presented to T. Ua Donnchadha,* ed. S. PENDER (Cork 1947). A. HOUSTON, ed., *D. O'Connell: His Early Life, and Journal, 1795 to 1802* (London 1906). D. O'CONNELL, *A Memoir on Ireland, Native and Saxon* (Dublin 1843; 2d ed. 1844). J. O'CONNELL, ed., *Life and Speeches of D. O'Connell,* 2 v. (Dublin 1846), by his son. W. J. FITZPATRICK, ed., *Correspondence of D. O'Connell,* 2 v. (London 1888). O'Connell MSS in National Library of Ireland, and University College Dublin. J. A. REYNOLDS, *The Catholic Emancipation Crisis in Ireland, 1823–1829* (New Haven 1954). J. F. BRODERICK, *The Holy See and the Irish Movement for the Repeal of the Union with England, 1829–1847* (Rome 1951). C. G. DUFFY, *Young Ireland, 1840–1849,* 2 v. (2d ed. Dublin 1884–87). G. S. LEFEVRE, *Peel and O'Connell, a Review of Irish Policy* (London 1887). **Illustration credit:** Library of Congress.

[R. D. EDWARDS]

O'CONNELL, DENIS JOSEPH

Bishop; b. Donoughmore, County Cork, Ireland, Jan. 28, 1849; d. Richmond, Va., Jan. 1, 1927. He was the son of Michael and Bridget (O'Connell) O'Connell. The family immigrated to the U.S. and settled in South Carolina, where two brothers of Michael, Jeremiah J. and Joseph P., were missionaries. When Bp. James Gibbons was looking for candidates to build up the clergy of his new Vicariate of North Carolina, he met young Denis O'Connell. A close friendship developed between Gibbons and O'Connell that extended over a long lifetime and major national and international issues of Catholicism in the late 19th century. After preliminary studies at St. Charles College, Ellicott City, Md., O'Connell was sent (1871) to the North American College, Rome, for theology courses at the Urban College of the Propagation of the Faith. He was ordained May 26, 1877, and received a Roman doctorate in theology. After returning to Richmond, where Gibbons had been transferred, O'Connell began priestly work as assistant at St. Peter's cathedral there. He was back in Rome within a few months, a postulator for Gibbons's pallium as newly appointed coadjutor archbishop of Baltimore. For the next 5 years he worked in the Diocese of Richmond under the direction of Bp. John J. Keane.

In the fall of 1883 Gibbons called O'Connell to Baltimore to assist in the preliminary arrangements for the Third Plenary Council of *Baltimore, at which he served as one of the four secretaries. After the council he returned to Rome with the American bishops' com-

mittee to secure ratification of the conciliar decrees. In 1885 he was appointed rector of the North American College in Rome, and for the next 18 years he served as liaison man and Roman agent for members of the Amer-

Denis Joseph O'Connell.

ican hierarchy. During his term as rector (1885–95), the student body was enlarged, the physical plant improved, and an honor system established in the college. He served also as a Roman agent for Gibbons, who was elevated to the cardinalate in 1886.

O'Connell, the Roman intermediary, was made a domestic prelate in 1887; he took active part in the Roman aspects of the controversies centered on such questions as the *Knights of Labor, Cahenslyism, The *Catholic University of America, the coming of an apostolic delegate to the U.S., Henry George and the single tax, Abp. John Ireland's *Faribault school plan, and *Americanism. As the lines of difference developed between so-called liberal and conservative members of the American Church of that period, O'Connell became a symbol of the liberal wing's position. He identified himself unqualifiedly with the policies of Gibbons, Ireland, and Keane, and alienated conservative-minded American bishops, who held differing views on the burning issues of the developing Church in the U.S. Criticisms of O'Connell's activities, apart from his rectorship, increased to the point that his resignation from the college was requested on the grounds that he did not have the full confidence of the body of American bishops. From 1895 to 1903 O'Connell served as rector of Cardinal Gibbons's titular church of Santa Maria in Trastevere in Rome.

On Jan. 12, 1903, through the influence of his friends, O'Connell was appointed third rector of The Catholic University of America, Washington, D.C., then badly in need of academic, organizational, promotional, and financial direction. From 1903 to 1910 he worked, with some success, to establish educational improvements at the university. An annual collection was inaugurated that was to be taken up in all the dioceses of the U.S. for the advancement of the pontifical university in Washington. Student enrollment was increased; several prominent and capable professors were engaged; and academic procedures were formalized according to accepted standards in the academic community. The base of the university's educational program was extended to include undergraduate training as well as graduate studies. But O'Connell found it difficult to adjust to the American system of educational operation through a board of trustees and with vital consultation of the faculty. A financial crisis almost destroyed the university in 1904, when the total endowment funds of the institution were endangered by the financial failure of Thomas E. Waggaman, treasurer of the university, who had invested the funds of the university in his enterprises. The university's endowment was reduced by two-thirds of its investment value; confidence in its financial management was severely weakened; and extensive and prolonged revival was slow in developing.

On Dec. 12, 1907, O'Connell was named a titular bishop, a move that advanced his growing desire to be relieved of the rectorship in Washington. After Abp. Patrick W. Riordan of San Francisco, Calif., petitioned Rome for his old friend O'Connell as auxiliary bishop, the appointment was made on Dec. 25, 1908. When O'Connell was transferred to the See of Richmond on Jan. 19, 1912, as a suffragan of Cardinal Gibbons, the old discussions began anew that O'Connell would be appointed coadjutor of Baltimore and succeed to the premier see. But he was too old for such a consideration when Cardinal Gibbons died in 1921, and the bishop of Richmond continued directing the activities of the diocese of his youth until Jan. 15, 1926, when he resigned because of failing health.

[C. J. BARRY]

O'CONNELL, JOHN PATRICK, theologian, editor, actively involved in the liturgical apostolate; b. Chicago, Ill., Jan. 12, 1918; d. Chicago, Feb. 20, 1960. Educated at Quigley Seminary, Chicago, and St. Mary of the Lake Seminary, Mundelein, Ill., where he earned the degrees of M.A. and S.T.D., he was ordained May 1, 1943. After serving as a parish priest and as a teacher at Barat College, Lake Forest, Ill., he was selected by

John P.
O'Connell.

Cardinal Samuel Stritch to be the editor for The Catholic Press, Inc., of Chicago, of the *Holy Bible* (Holy Family edition, 1950, and several subsequent editions); the *Sunday Missal;* the *Prayer Book* and the *Life of Christ,* issued as a set (1954); the *Bible Story* (1959); and *Christ and the Church* (1960). Under his direction, The Catholic Press also published the French *La Sainte Bible* (1956), the Spanish *Sagrada Biblia* (1958), and after delays extending beyond his death, Portuguese and Italian translations of Holy Scripture. O'Connell was a member of the Mariological Society and of the Catholic Biblical Association.

Influenced by his pastor, Joseph P. Morrison, O'Connell became a zealous promoter of the liturgical apostolate. He served the Liturgical Conference as secretary (1946–47); as treasurer (1949–52); as a member of its Board of Directors and Advisory Council; and as editor of the proceedings of the 1946, 1957, 1958, and 1959 Liturgical Weeks. During the last years of his life, he was engaged in the work of programming the annual Liturgical Weeks. O'Connell contributed many articles to publications and addressed many clerical and lay audiences in spreading knowledge of the Church's worship.

At the directive of Cardinal Stritch, Father O'Connell made preliminary surveys with a view to the publication of a new edition of the *Catholic Encyclopedia.* Shortly after he was named a papal chamberlain on Dec. 28, 1959, he fell prey to a fatal disease. Until the day of his untimely death, he continued working to complete many of the projects he had undertaken.

Bibliography: F. R. McMANUS, YrbkLitStud 1 (1960) xi–xiv.
Illustration credit: Fabian Bachrach.

[N. RANDOLPH]

O'CONNELL, WILLIAM HENRY

Cardinal and second archbishop of *Boston; b. Lowell, Mass., Dec. 8, 1859; d. Boston, Mass., April 22, 1944. He was the youngest of 11 children of John and Brigid O'Connell, natives of County Cavan, Ireland. His father died when he was five but family sacrifices enabled him to attend Lowell public schools and then to enter St. Charles College, Ellicott City, Md., to study for the priesthood. However, in 1879 he left the seminary and entered Boston College, from which he graduated in 1881 with first honors in philosophy and physics. He reapplied for the priesthood and was sent by Abp. John J. Williams to the North American College in Rome. Illness terminated O'Connell's studies at Rome before he could obtain a doctorate. He was ordained June 7, 1884, returned to the U.S. in December, and did pastoral work for the next 10 years, first at St. Joseph's in Medford, then at St. Joseph's in Boston's West End.

Early Career. Late in 1895, when a conflict of opinion in the U.S. hierarchy led to the resignation of the rectors of the North American College in Rome and The Catholic University of America, Cardinal James Gibbons named O'Connell rector of the *North American College. During the next 6 years, O'Connell doubled the enrollment of the North American College, rehabilitated its finances, and purchased the Villa Santa Caterina at Castel Gandolfo for summer sessions. He was made a domestic prelate in 1897. His relations with Pope Leo XIII, Papal Secretary of State Cardinal Rampolla, and the future Cardinal Merry del Val were cordial. He also formed friendships in Roman society and diplomatic circles that resulted in the bequest to the North American College of the library of the bibliophile William Heyward, and in the decoration of the college refectory at the expense of the American theater magnate, Benjamin F. Keith. In 1918 O'Connell received from the Keith estate a personal bequest totalling almost $2.5 million. He devoted the entire sum to charities for

Nave and sanctuary of the Basilica of the Assumption of the Blessed
Virgin Mary, Baltimore, Maryland. Designed by the American architect
Benjamin Henry Latrobe for Archbishop John Carroll, the building was
dedicated, as the cathedral of Baltimore, on May 31, 1821.

various Catholic institutions, rendering the final account of these disbursements in 1936.

On May 19, 1901, in the Corsini Chapel of the Basilica of St. John Lateran, O'Connell was consecrated third bishop of Portland, Me., by Cardinal Satolli. Taking possession of his see, which had been vacant for nearly a year, he visited every parish in the state. He redecorated the Cathedral of the Immaculate Conception, introduced a forerunner of the Catholic Youth Organization, and fostered retreats for the clergy. In 1903 he declined the Holy See's appointment to the Archdiocese of Manila in the Philippine Islands, which had recently been acquired by the U.S. Aware of the untrue reports that he had supported the Spanish cause against the U.S. in 1898, O'Connell frankly informed Rome that such gossip would impede his work in the Philippines and recommended that another choice be made.

After the Russo-Japanese War, O'Connell was named special papal envoy to Emperor Mutsuhito, Aug. 31, 1905. He had a personal audience with the Emperor and Empress and was decorated with the Grand Cordon of the Sacred Treasure. He made a thorough survey of the mission field in Japan, reporting to Pius X in Rome in January 1906. His recommendations, all adopted, included the introduction of many religious orders into Japan, the fostering of a native clergy, and the founding of a Catholic university at Tokyo, to be staffed by Jesuits.

Assignment to Boston. On Feb. 21, 1906, Pius X, disregarding the recommendations from the bishops of New England, named O'Connell titular bishop of Constantia, and coadjutor with right of succession to the aged Archbishop Williams of Boston. The news was not favorably received in Boston but O'Connell remained unperturbed. He concluded his affairs in Portland and went to Boston to be installed formally on April 3, 1906. At the death of Williams on Aug. 30, 1907, the 47-year-old O'Connell took up the reins that he would hold firmly for the next 37 years.

A born leader, O'Connell once said: "I have never hesitated to speak as plainly as possible . . . whenever direction was needed." He began at once to reorganize the large archdiocese in which he found many institutions debt ridden and run down. In 1908, when the apostolic constitution of Pius X, *Sapienti consilio,* removed the Church in the U.S. from mission supervision to full national status like that of the Church in older European countries, O'Connell was a leader in establishing diocesan administrative offices. His zeal for the missions, both foreign and home, was shown in his support of the Catholic Missionary Congress held at Chicago in 1908 and at Boston in 1913. He encouraged two Boston priests in the founding of new missionary congregations. James Anthony *Walsh was released from the Boston archdiocese to become a cofounder of the Catholic Foreign Mission Society (*see* MARYKNOLL MISSIONERS); the Vincentian Thomas *Judge, born in Boston, was aided in his work for home missions in founding the *Missionary Servants of the Most Holy Trinity, a community of sisters, the *Missionary Servants of the Most Blessed Trinity, and the *Missionary Cenacle Apostolate. O'Connell also pioneered in supporting (1917) the open-air preaching of the Jewish convert and lay apostle to the man in the street, David *Goldstein.

O'Connell was created the first native cardinal of Boston on Nov. 26, 1911. A group of non-Catholics in Boston presented him with a purse of $25,000, which he used for improving his titular Church of San Clemente in Rome. In the Boston archdiocese he placed institu-

Cardinal William Henry O'Connell.

tions on a sound financial basis, encouraged early and frequent Communion, and introduced retreats for the laity, bringing the Passionists, the Religious of the Cenacle, and the Franciscans to Boston to conduct retreat houses.

Other Contributions. On the national scene, O'Connell's diocese was outstanding in both World Wars in efforts for servicemen. Patriotism was a frequent theme in his sermons. When President Wilson first proposed his Fourteen Points, the Cardinal spoke at Madison Square Garden, Dec. 10, 1918, eloquently urging self-determination for Ireland as well as for other peoples. In 1924, he spoke out publicly against the proposed child labor amendment to the Constitution as infringing on the rights of parents and of the states. He also spoke against birth control and preached against graft in politics. O'Connell helped to convert the National Catholic War Council of World War I into the *National Catholic Welfare Conference. He was prominent in bringing about the change that today enables cardinals from any part of the globe to participate in the election of a new pope. In 1914, and again in 1922, the old rule of convening the conclave 10 days after the death of a pope had frustrated O'Connell's journeys across the Atlantic. He protested so strongly that Pius XI personally promised to extend the time to 18 days. Thus, in 1939, O'Connell was able to reach Rome in time for the election of Pius XII.

Despite his preoccupation with the administration of mundane matters, the cardinal was a man of prayer and a patron of letters. An amateur organist, he composed the music for *The Holy Cross Hymnal* (Boston 1915). His music for the Latin motet *Juravit Dominus,* written in 1882, was sung for many years at first Masses of priests at the North American College in Rome and in the Boston archdiocese. The Universalist Church of the Redemption in Boston, with its fine organ, was bought by the cardinal and was dedicated as St. Clement's Church on Dec. 8, 1935. He served from 1932 to 1936 as a trustee of the Boston Public Library. To encourage Lenten devotions he translated from the Italian *The Passion of Our Lord* by Cardinal Gaetano De Lai (Boston 1923). O'Connell's particular devotion throughout his life was to our Lady of Perpetual Help.

In 1937 he was awarded an honorary degree by Harvard University, the first native Catholic prelate to be so recognized. During his administration parishes in the archdiocese increased from 194 to 322, and clergy from 600 to more than 1,500. Admissions to St. John's Seminary tripled; a score of new religious congregations were introduced into the area; parochial elementary schools were doubled and high schools tripled—taught by a total of more than 3,000 priests, brothers, and sisters. Three colleges for women were founded under his auspices and he aided the establishment of Boston College on its Chestnut Hill campus. In 1908 he purchased as a diocesan organ, the weekly newspaper, the *Pilot;* in 1934 he laid the cornerstone of a diocesan center, a six-story building with presses and offices for the *Pilot,* offices for diocesan bureaus, and a meditation chapel. An archdiocesan residence, the Crehan Library, and the chancery were built; he also enlarged St. John's Seminary, staffing it with diocesan priest-scholars. Active and vigorous in the service of the Church to the last week of his life, O'Connell, at his death, was buried in the mausoleum he had built on the seminary grounds.

Bibliography: W. H. O'Connell, *Reminiscences of Twenty-Five Years* (Boston 1926); *Recollections of Seventy Years* (Boston 1934). R. H. Lord et al., *History of the Archdiocese of Boston . . . 1604 to 1943,* 3 v. (New York 1944). D. G. Wayman, *Cardinal O'Connell of Boston* (New York 1955).

[D. G. Wayman]

O'CONNOR, MARY FLANNERY, novelist and short-story writer; b. Savannah, Ga., March 25, 1925; d. Milledgeville, Ga., Aug. 3, 1964. She was the daughter of Edward Francis and Regina (Cline) O'Connor, of a pioneer Georgia Catholic family. At the age of 12 she moved with her parents to the Cline family home at Milledgeville. There she attended Peabody High School and was graduated (1945) from Georgia State College for Women. She later (1948) studied creative writing at the University of Iowa. The initial attack of an incurable malady brought her home from New York a year later to live with her mother on the farm near Milledgeville, where she spent her remaining years.

Quiet and kind-heartedly humorous, O'Connor was committed to a Christian iconoclasm against the fraudulence and pietism of a secular age. She sought to make "the distortions in modern life" apparent to those "used to seeing them as natural." She did this through an original use of humor, horrendous satire, and violence in two novels and a score of stories. Her work, first meeting with hostility and dismay, won wide literary acclaim in the U.S. and abroad, and within a decade she was accorded front rank and received many recognitions. Her first novel, *Wise Blood* (1952, reissued 1960), is the story of a lunatic-fringe preacher who tries to found a church without Christ. Preaching a progressive nihilism, he backs his way into the Cross. The novel parodies the atheistic existentialism then pervading the literary and philosophical scene. (*See* EXISTENTIALISM IN LITERATURE.) In *A Good Man Is Hard To Find* (1955), a collection of 10 of her stories, O'Connor created a new form of humor to bare "the distortions." She employed it perhaps nowhere with more impact than in the title story. There, what is apparently secular satire on the accidental encounter of a gabbling grandmother and her unlovely family with a psychotic criminal who calls himself the Misfit turns into a religious ordeal that brings the grandmother salvation, along with a bloody slaughter. The story of Jonas (with emphasis on the action at sea) provides the theme of her second novel (*The Violent Bear It Away,* 1960) and, in variation, of a later story, *The Lame Shall Enter First.* These dramas probe deeply the theology of free will (which she viewed as a conflict of wills in the sinner) and freedom (which she called a mystery). Nine of her last stories appeared posthumously in *Everything That Rises Must Converge* (1965), confirming further that the violent themes of her works conceal an apocalypse for her time.

Bibliography: M. F. O'Connor, "The Lame Shall Enter First," *Sewanee Review* 70 (1962) 337–379. *Current Biography* (1958) 317–318. J. F. Farnham, "The Grotesque in the Novels of F. O'C.," *America* 105 (May 13, 1961). **Illustration credit:** Farrar, Straus and Giroux.

[B. Cheney]

O'CONNOR, MICHAEL

First bishop of Pittsburgh, Pa., diocese; b. Queenstown, Ireland, April 27, 1810; d. Woodstock, Md., Oct. 18, 1872. He was the eldest son of Charles and Ellen Kirk O'Connor and brother of Bp. James O'Connor, first bishop of Omaha, Nebr. Michael entered the College of Propaganda, Rome, in 1824, was ordained on June 1, 1833, and received his doctorate in 1834. He then became vice rector of the Irish College and professor of Scripture of the Propaganda College. His mother's death in 1834 led him to refuse the rectorship of St. Charles. Seminary, Philadelphia, and he returned to Ireland to care for his family. While he was preparing for a professorship at the College of St. Patrick, Maynooth, the Philadelphia invitation was renewed in 1838. He accepted and was rector of St. Charles Seminary from 1839 until he went to Pittsburgh as vicar-general of the diocese in 1841. When his appointment as first

Mary Flannery O'Connor with a self-portrait.

bishop of Pittsburgh was pending in 1843, he hastened to Rome to ask permission to become a Jesuit. Pope Gregory XVI's answer was: "You will be a bishop first and a Jesuit afterwards." He was consecrated on Aug. 15, 1843.

During his episcopate the number of priests in Pittsburgh increased fivefold and the number of churches more than doubled. He opened a chapel for Negroes, founded the *Catholic,* a weekly diocesan newspaper, and built a cathedral. A number of religious communities, including the first Sisters of Mercy to establish a convent in the U.S., were invited into the diocese. Two colleges and St. Michael's Seminary were opened. The bishop advocated the right of Catholic education to share in public funds and encouraged development of parish schools. In 1853 the diocese was divided and O'Connor was transferred to Erie, but a year later the Holy See, moved by petitions of the clergy and laity, restored him to Pittsburgh. His health began to fail and he took long trips to Europe, the Near East, and the Caribbean.

He resigned his see in 1860 and entered the Jesuit novitiate at Gorheim, Sigmaringen, Germany. Two years later he made his solemn profession. At first assigned to Boston College in Massachusetts, O'Connor later became assistant to the Jesuit provincial of Maryland. As a Jesuit he was an active preacher, lecturer, and retreat master. In 1870 he went to London to consult physicians about his health and returned to the U.S. on the same ship that carried the future Cardinal Herbert Vaughan and the first Mill Hill missionaries to the Negroes. His last public appearance was at the Negro church of St. Francis Xavier, Baltimore, which he had been instrumental in acquiring. He retired to Woodstock College, Maryland, 6 months before his death in 1872. Although O'Connor excelled in theology and patristic studies, his busy life left little time for writing and he published nothing except some newspaper articles and printed lectures.

Bibliography: A. A. LAMBING, *A History of the Catholic Church in the Dioceses of Pittsburgh and Allegheny* (New York 1880). W. P. PURCELL, *Catholic Pittsburgh's One Hundred Years* (Chicago 1943).

[J. J. HENNESEY]

O'CONNOR, THOMAS FRANCIS, U.S. Catholic Church historian and bibliographer; b. Syracuse, N.Y., Aug. 14, 1899; d. St. Louis, Mo., Sept. 15, 1950. He received his B.A. (1922) from the College of the Holy Cross, Worcester, Mass., and his M.A. (1927) from Syracuse University, N.Y. He taught at Little Rock University, Ark. (1928–30); St. Louis University, Mo. (1931–37, 1948–50); and St. Michael's College, Winooski Park, Vt. (1937–39). He served for a time after 1941 as historiographer of the Diocese of Syracuse and was historiographer of the Archdiocese of New York from 1944 to 1948. Although O'Connor had a vast store of knowledge of the bibliography and history of the Church in the U.S., he left practically no notes. Vollmar's *Catholic Church in America* (2d ed. New York 1963) lists 24 titles published by O'Connor in various historical journals. He was active in various historical societies and was president of the American Catholic Historical Association (1946–47). His early and unexpected death was caused by a hemorrhage resulting from a long-standing tubercular condition.

[E. R. VOLLMAR]

O'CONNOR, THOMAS POWER, Irish politician and journalist; b. Athlone, Ireland, Oct. 5, 1848; d. London, Nov. 18, 1929. He was the son of Thomas Power, a small merchant, and Mary Power and was educated at the College of the Immaculate Conception, Athlone, and at Galway University, where he graduated in classics, June 1866. In 1867 he became a junior reporter on *Saunder's Newsletter,* a Dublin conservative journal. Three years later he joined the staff of the *Daily Telegraph* in London, becoming subeditor. This he relinquished in 1873 for a post in the London office of the *New York Herald.* In 1880 he entered Parliament for Galway, and became prominent in the Parnellite party. Two years later, at Parnell's request, he toured the U.S., lecturing on home rule for Ireland. He was returned for Liverpool in the 1885 election and represented that constituency until his death, becoming "Father of the House of Commons" in 1908. In Parliament he pleaded eloquently and repeatedly for justice for Catholics, especially in the matter of education.

He also founded and edited the *Star* (1888), the *Sun* (1893), *T.P.'s Weekly* (1902), and other journals. When he started the *Star,* one of his staff was George Bernard Shaw, who began at a salary of two guineas weekly. O'Connor was a pioneer in popularizing the periodical press as well as in developing the personal note in weekly publications. Through the same medium he also did much to interest the public in literature. His publications include *Lord Beaconsfield* (London 1879), *Gladstone's House of Commons* (London 1886), *The Parnell Movement* (Sydney 1886), and *Memoirs of an Old Parliamentarian* (London 1929), in addition to numerous essays and articles.

Bibliography: F. LAVERY, comp., *Great Irishmen in War and Politics* (Dublin 1920). H. H. FYFE, *T. P. O'Connor* (London 1934).

[S. O'HANLON]

O'CONOR, CHARLES, lawyer; b. New York, N.Y., Jan. 22, 1804; d. Nantucket, Mass., May 12, 1884. His parents, Thomas and Margaret (O'Connor) O'Conor, were unable to provide many educational opportunities for him, so when his mother died in 1816, he was apprenticed to a tar and lampblack manufacturer. After a year he entered a law office as an errand boy and moved on to several other law offices in the capacity of clerk and law student. He was admitted to the bar in 1824, and with a capital of $25 opened a law office.

O'Conor was a Democrat with political aspirations; he attributed his lack of success in public office to his being a Roman Catholic and the son of an Irish immigrant. In 1846 he was elected as a member of the New York state constitutional convention, and in 1848 he was an unsuccessful candidate for lieutenant governor. In 1853 he was appointed U.S. district attorney for the southern district of New York, and in 1872 he was nominated for the presidency of the U.S. by the "Straight-out" Democrats. For 10 years O'Conor was treasurer of the New York Law Institute, and in 1869 its president; he also served as vice president of the New York Historical Society. He was popular among southern Democrats, because he believed slavery was a "just, benign and beneficent" institution, and because he thought that it was unconstitutional to coerce seceded states. After the Civil War he was senior counsel for

Jefferson Davis when he was under indictment for treason, and with Horace Greeley he provided his bail bond.

In the opinion of all judges before whom he argued and all lawyers against whom he argued O'Conor was "a great lawyer." The cases that brought him the most fame were the Forrest divorce case, the Lispenard will case, the Lemmon slave case, the Parrish will case, the Jumel case, and the W. M. Tweed litigation that ended in the dissolution of this notorious New York City political ring. At the time of the Forrest divorce case, Justice Benjamin R. Curtis said that O'Conor's management of the case was "the most remarkable exhibition of professional skill ever witnessed in this country." In 1854, O'Conor married Cornelia (Livingston) McCracken, the daughter of Francis A. Livingston and the widow of L. H. McCracken. They did not have a happy marriage and agreed to live apart. He wrote *Peculation Triumphant* (1875) on his struggle with Tweed.

Bibliography: H. E. GREGORY, "Charles O'Conor," *Great American Lawyers*, ed. W. D. LEWIS, 8 v. (Philadelphia 1908) 5:83–122. J. BIGELOW, "Some Recollections of Chas. O'Conor," *Century Magazine* 29 (1885) 725–736. J. C. WALSH, "Charles O'Conor," *Journal American Irish Historical Society* 27 (1928) 285–313.

[V. P. DE SANTIS]

O'CONOR, HERBERT ROMULUS, governor, U.S. senator; b. Baltimore, Md., Nov. 17, 1896; d. Baltimore, March 4, 1960. He was the son of James P. A. and Mary Ann (Galvin) O'Conor. After graduating from Loyola College, Baltimore, in 1917, he received his law degree from the University of Maryland Law School, College Park, Md., and was admitted to the bar in 1920. He married Mary Eugenia Byrnes on Nov. 24, 1920.

O'Conor became an assistant state's attorney in 1921, and his handling of the Norris murder trial (1922) won him the post of people's counsel of the Public Service Commission and brought about his election as state's attorney of Baltimore in 1923. He was returned to that office in 1926 and 1930, and elected attorney general in 1934. Following a hard-fought primary contest in 1938, he became the first Catholic of Irish ancestry to win the governorship of Maryland. After completing a second 4-year term in 1946, he was elected to the U.S. Senate where he served until his voluntary retirement in 1953. In nearly 32 years in politics, he never suffered a defeat at the polls. O'Conor made his mark in state politics by restraining government expenses; nationally, he fought organized crime and international Communism. As governor of Maryland, he helped to reform the court system and to lower the bonded indebtedness of the state. As senator, he was responsible for stopping shipments of strategic war materials to the Chinese Communists at the time of the Korean conflict. Shortly after retiring from the Senate, he became chairman of the American Bar Association's Committee on Communist Tactics, Strategy, and Objectives. He served in this capacity until failing health forced him to retire in 1957. Pius XII honored him with the Knighthood of St. Gregory in 1958.

Bibliography: H. W. KIRWIN, *The Inevitable Success: The Biography of Herbert R. O'Conor* (Westminster 1962).

[H. W. KIRWIN]

OCTOECHOS

In Byzantine music the term Octoechos (Gr. ὀκτώ, eight, and ἦχος, mode) has two distinct though closely allied meanings. In general it refers to the system of eight modes that forms the compositional framework of Byzantine ecclesiastical music: four authentic and four plagal modes, as in Western chant. More particularly it designates a collection of proper hymns, chiefly for the Morning and Evening Services, providing an entire set of such pieces for each mode. The collection was designed for performance in cycles of 8 weeks: in the 1st week (beginning after Easter) the hymns of Mode I Authentic would be used, in the second week the hymns of Mode II Authentic, and so on, until after the completion of the modal series the cycle recommenced with Mode I. Thus the Octoechos, taken in conjunction with the hymns of feasts fixed by the calendar, and those of the Lenten and Easter seasons, made provision for music throughout the church year. In its earlier form it comprised pieces for the Sundays only; later additions supplied hymns for the weekdays as well, the whole compilation receiving the name of Great Octoechos (ἡ μεγάλη Ὀκτώηχος) or Parakletike (Παρακλητική).

Origins. The origins of the system, as of the collection based upon it, are obscure. It appears to owe little if anything directly to the classical and Hellenistic Greek tonal system, despite the assignation of classical names to modes of the Octoechos by some medieval Byzantine theorists. Attempts by modern scholars to trace it to the musical vestiges or cosmological beliefs of earlier Near Eastern peoples are speculative at best. Even the time of its appearance in Christian hymnody cannot be determined with any precision. An 11th-century text of the *Plerophoriai* of John of Maiuma (*c.* 515) contains an allusion to "music of the Octoechos," but its authenticity is questionable. Grave doubt attaches also to the oft-repeated assertion that a hymn collection of the same period, the work of the Monophysite Patriarch *Severus of Antioch (512–519), was an Octoechos. The sole surviving MSS of this collection present it in Syriac translation, and the earliest of these MSS, more than a century and a half later than the presumed original, shows no sign of an arrangement according to mode; only in much later copies does such a categorization exist. In any case it seems that the eight-mode system had become established within the Greek liturgical world by the end of the 7th century. To cite one piece of evidence: a papyrus fragment no later than early 8th century gives a modal sign—though no other musical notation—for the hymns it preserves. Byzantine tradition ascribed the composition of the Octoechos, or at least a large part of its Sunday nucleus, to St. *John Damascene (*c.* 750). In its generality the attribution is certainly dubious, but it may contain some element of historical fact. The very earliest musical MSS (10th century) have "John the Monk" as author of the canons of the Octoechos; and the initial letters of another set of Sunday hymns form the word Ἰωάννου (of John)—this sort of acrostic signature is traditional in Byzantine hymnology. But even if the identity of this "John" with the Damascene were assured, whether he was in any sense the composer of the music that the MSS convey would remain doubtful—and this is true generally of the poets to whom hymns are ascribed. In the 9th century, after the resolution of the iconoclastic controversy, the Octoechos was completed by the addition of the weekday hymns, the work of monks of the *Studion monastery in Constantinople—in particular Joseph the Hymnographer (883). The final canon in the series has as its acrostic τῆς Ὀκτωήχου τῆς νέας θεῖον τέλος (the divine conclusion of the New Oktoechos), perhaps the earliest known instance of the term's referring unambiguously to a corpus of hymns. Not until much later does the word occur as heading of a separate MS or section of a MS.

The Modes in Their Technical Aspects. As for the musical system itself, the songs from every particular mode are composed largely from a restricted set of melodic formulas characteristic of that mode. These formulas may be employed in many different combinations and variations; nevertheless, most of the phrases of any given hymn are reducible to one or another of this small number of basic melody-fragments. (For formulas of Mode I as they are exemplified in a selection of phrases from a number of hymns, see Wellesz ByzMus app. V.)

The church music belonging to various peoples, such as the Serbs, the Armenians, the Syrians, and the Copts, as found in our own times, exhibits analogous modal systems, depending in the same fashion on melodic formulae—the specific formulae, of course, differing from one musical culture to another. (No musical documentation from the Byzantine period exists for any of these peoples; there are, e.g., medieval Armenian musical MSS, but their notation is undecipherable.) Study of these modal systems has led some scholars to conclude that, in such a system, each mode is defined simply by its characteristic melody patterns, rather than by some abstract scale pattern: the latter sort of definition was the subsequent rationalization of theorists. Byzantine theory in its full development did provide such a rationalization; and the system thus defined appears to be essentially identical to that of Latin plainchant. This conclusion is suggested by the medieval Latin practice of assigning Greek number names to the Latin modes; it is confirmed by Wellesz' publication of a hymn whose Greek text had been translated into Latin, and whose music appears substantially the same in both kinds of notation. The total range of the system (with rare extensions) covers what is represented in modern transcription as the two-octave white-key gamut *a–a″*. Within this, Mode I Authentic has an approximate range of *d–d′*, with finalis on *a* or *d*; Mode II Authentic, *e–e′*, with finalis on *b′* or *e*; Mode III Authentic, *f–f′*, with finalis on *c′* or *f*; Mode IV Authentic, *g–g′*, with finalis on *d′* or *g*. The plagal modes have ranges lying a fourth below the numerically corresponding authentic; they use only the lower finalis of the two found in the corresponding authentic modes. This diatonic system remained the basis of Byzantine music down to the 17th and 18th centuries, when it disappeared, along with the entire repertory embodying it, under the Turkish influence, leaving only the texts and the modal assignations as they had been in medieval times. For a categorization of the contents of the Octoechos as a musical service-book, see Tillyard.

See also BYZANTINE RITE; BYZANTINE RITE, CHANTS OF; BYZANTINE CIVILIZATION.

Bibliography: Wellesz ByzMus. E. WELLESZ, *Eastern Elements in Western Chant* (*Monumenta Musicae Byzantinae* 1; Oxford 1947); "Die Struktur der servischen Oktoēchos, *Zeitschrift für Musikwissenschaft* 2 (1919) 140–148. H. J. W. TILLYARD, *The Hymns of the Octoechus*, 2 v. (*Monumenta Musicae Byzantinae* 3, 5; Oxford 1940, 1952). J. JEANNIN and J. PUYADE, "L'Octoēchos syrien," OrChr, NS 3 (1913) 82–104, 277–298. A. BAUMSTARK, *Festbrevier und Kirchenjahr der syrischen Jakobiten* (Paderborn 1910). E. W. BROOKS, "The Hymns of Severus," PatrOr 6:1–179; 7:593–803. F. NAU, "Jean Rufus, évêque de Maïouma: *Plérophories*," ibid. 8:1–208. L. TARDO, *L'Ottoeco nei MSS. melurgici* (Grottaferrata 1955). Παρακλητικὴ ἤτοι Ὀκτώηχος ἡ μεγάλη (Rome 1885); Ὀκτώηχος (Rome 1886). O. STRUNK, "The Tonal System of Byzantine Music," MusQ 28 (1942) 190–204; "The Antiphons of the Oktoechos," JAmMus Soc 18 (1960) 50–67.

[I. THOMAS]

O'CULLENAN, GELASIUS (GLAISNE), SOCist, abbot of Boyle, Co. Roscommon, Ireland; b. probably at Mullaghshee near Ballyshannon, Co. Donegal, 1554; d. Dublin, Nov. 21, 1580. He was the eldest of seven sons of whom six became ecclesiastics, five being Cistercians. At an early age Glaisne entered the monastery, completed his novitiate and theological studies at Paris, and eventually became a doctor of the Sorbonne. Having visited Rome, he returned to Ireland, where he was made abbot of the suppressed Abbey of Boyle. There he carried on his sacred ministry until his arrest in 1580 with Eoghan O Maoilchiarain, Premonstratensian abbot of Holy Trinity in Loch Cé. Imprisoned in Dublin Castle, they were tortured and, having refused to conform, were sentenced to death and executed. Glaisne's near-contemporary, the Cistercian Menologist Chrysostomus Henriquez, called O'Cullenan "the ornament of the Cistercian Order, the splendour of our age, and the glory of all Ireland." Glaisne's name is included in the list of Irish martyrs awaiting beatification.

Bibliography: C. HENRIQUEZ, *Menologium Cisterciense* (Antwerp 1630). M. HARTRY, *Triumphalia chronologica Monasterii Sanctae Crucis in Hibernia*, ed. D. MURPHY (Dublin 1895). J. MACENLEAN, "Eoin ó Cuileannáin . . .," *Archivium Hibernicum* 1 (1912) 77–121.

[C. S. ó CONBHUÍ]

O'DALY, DANIEL, priest and diplomat; b. Kilsarkon, County Kerry, Ireland 1595; d. Lisbon, June 30, 1662. His father, Conchubhar, was a bard and soldier of Gerald, Earl of Desmond, his mother an O'Keefe from Duhallow barony. He entered the Dominicans in his youth and because of the persecution in Ireland, he was educated in Spain, studying first in Lugo, then in Burgos, where he was ordained. After further studies he returned to Emly diocese as a "fugitive" priest. He was recalled to Louvain to teach in the newly erected college for Irish Dominicans and he became superior in 1624. While raising funds in Madrid, he obtained Philip IV's consent to begin the college of Corpo Santo at Lisbon, a foundation similar to that of Louvain. He later founded the convent of Bom Sucesso for Irish-born Dominican nuns at Belem in Lisbon, in return for which concession he recruited a body of Irish soldiery for Spanish service in the Low Countries. With the restoration of the Portuguese monarchy (1640) he was appointed confessor to Luiza de Guzman, wife of the new king, John of Braganza. Several diplomatic missions followed: in 1649, to Charles Stuart at Jersey; in 1650 a secret mission to Pope Innocent X concerning the nomination of Portuguese bishops then being blocked by Spain; in 1655 to France first as envoy, then as accredited ambassador to negotiate financial and military help. After King John's death (1656), O'Daly acted as chief adviser to the widow-regent. He also helped to negotiate a matrimonial alliance between Charles II of England and Catherine of Braganza. He refused nomination to the archbishopric of Goa, but was eventually nominated bishop of Coimbra in 1662 by the regent who had previously endowed Corpo Santo when it needed expansion. He died as bishop-elect and was buried in Corpo Santo where a slab bearing his inscription is preserved despite the 1755 earthquake. Both his foundations survive to the present day. His Latin history of the Geraldines was published in 1655, *Initium, incrementum et exitus Geraldinorum*, with an appendix on religious persecution in 17th century Ireland. The work, though slight, has merit and has been translated into French by Abbé Joubert, 1697; and into English by C. P. Meehan, Dublin, 1847.

Bibliography: D. O'DALY, *History of the Geraldines*, tr. C. P. MEEHAN (2d ed. Dublin 1878); MSS in Bom Sucesso Convent, and in National Archives, Lisbon. T. DE BURGO, *Hibernia Dominicana* (Kilkenny 1762). M. A. O'CONNELL, *For Faith and Fatherland* (Dublin 1888). E. PRESTAGE, *The Diplomatic Relations of Portugal with France, England, and Holland from 1640 to 1688* (Watford 1925); *Frei Domingos do Rosário (D. O'Daly) diplomata e politico* (Coimbra 1926).

[M. B. MAC CURTAIN]

O'DANIEL, VICTOR FRANCIS,

educator, historian; b. Cecilville, Ky., Feb. 15, 1868; d. Washington, D.C., June 12, 1960. His parents, Richard Jefferson and Sarah Ann (Hamilton) O'Daniel, sent him to public and parochial schools near Cecilville. He then studied at St. Rose Priory, Springfield, Ky., where he entered the Order of Preachers on March 21, 1886, and at St. Joseph's Priory, Somerset, Ohio. After ordination on June 16, 1891, at Columbus, Ohio, he took further studies in theology (1893–95) at the Dominican house of studies at Louvain, Belgium, and received the lectorate in theology. Upon returning to the U.S., he was professor of theology at St. Rose's and St. Joseph's priories (1895–1901), and at the Dominican houses of study in Benicia, Calif. (1901–06) and Washington, D.C. (1906–13). He held the office of novice master for various periods during his teaching career.

As first archivist of St. Joseph's province, a post he held from 1907 to 1960, O'Daniel organized the Dominican archives in Washington, assembling a valuable collection of materials, much of which would otherwise have been lost. In 1909, when the order awarded him a master's degree in theology, he did extensive research in Europe, especially in the Dominican archives in Rome. He devoted himself exclusively to historical work after 1913. In 1915, with Peter *Guilday, he was cofounder of the *Catholic Historical Review* and was an associate editor from 1921 to 1927. In addition to the historical studies which he wrote for this journal, O'Daniel's works include *The Dominican Province of St. Joseph: Historical-Biographical Studies* (1930), *The Dominicans in Early Florida* (1942), and biographies of such Dominicans as Edward D. Fenwick, Charles H. McKenna, and Richard Pius Miles.

Bibliography: W. ROMIG, ed., *The Book of Catholic Authors* 4th ser. (Grosse Pointe, Mich. 1947). "V. F. O'Daniel," *Dominicana* 26 (1941) 111–112, 237–243; 45 (1960) 283–284.

[W. A. HINNEBUSCH]

ODERISIUS, BL.,

abbot and cardinal; d. Dec. 2, 1104 (feast, Dec. 2 or 4). He was descended from the family of the counts of Marsi, was educated at the Abbey of *Monte Cassino under Abbot Richer (d. 1055), and was made cardinal in 1059. He served as prior of Monte Cassino under Abbot Desiderius, later Pope *Victor III, and succeeded him as abbot in 1087. Oderisius governed Monte Cassino in the same spirit as his predecessor and completed the great buildings that Desiderius had begun. He became involved in Byzantine-German politics, but apparently without prejudice to his primary loyalty to the apostolic see. An author himself, Oderisius was a friend of scholarship and encouraged *Leo Marsicanus to begin his chronicle.

Bibliography: MGS 7:912. L. TOSTI, *Storia della badia di Monte-Cassino*, 3 v. (Rome 1842–43) 2:4–23. Zimmermann KalBen 3:384–385. A. M. ZIMMERMANN, LexThK² 7:1095–96.

[B. D. HILL]

O'DEVANY, CORNELIUS,

bishop of Down and Connor, martyr; b. *c.* 1553; d. Dublin, Feb. 11, 1612. He entered the Franciscan Friary of Donegal (date unknown) and was consecrated bishop of Down and Connor Feb. 1, 1583. In 1587 O'Devany (or Conor) was one of the Irish prelates who met in the Diocese of Clogher, where the decrees of the Council of Trent were promulgated. In 1588 he was arrested and confined in Dublin Castle, but 2 years later he was released by W. Fitzwilliam, the Lord Deputy, since "the law at present does not authorize the execution of the prisoner and the only charge against him is the exercise of spiritual authority." In 1591 he was granted special ecclesiastical faculties by Cardinal William *Allen because of his piety and zeal. He also collected materials on the lives of those who were persecuted for the faith. These were later included in the *Analecta nova et mira* by David Rothe, Bishop of Ossory from 1617 to 1619 (ed. P. Moran, Dublin 1884). In 1605 O'Devany was accused by spies of visiting the Pope and the King of Spain at the request of Hugh *O'Neill, and was again arrested and imprisoned. There he remained until his trial for high treason in 1611. Found guilty, he was sentenced to be hanged, drawn, and quartered. Two heretical ministers accompanied the bishop to the scaffold, offering him bribes if he would renounce his faith. There he was executed together with a secular priest, Patrick O'Loughran (*see* IRISH CONFESSORS AND MARTYRS).

Bibliography: J. T. GILBERT, DNB 14:864–865. D. MURPHY, *Our Martyrs* (Dublin 1896), bibliog.

[L. MCKEOWN]

ODILIA, ST.,

abbess and patroness of Alsace; b. *c.* 660; d. *c.* 720 (feast, Dec. 13). The daughter of Attich (d. *c.* 700), Duke of Alsace, Odilia was first abbess of the convent of Hohenburg (*Mont Sainte-Odile) and foundress of Niedermünster. According to a 10th-century vita of questionable reliability, written probably at Mont Sainte-Odile, she was born blind and taken secretly to a convent, possibly Baume-les-Dames, to escape the wrath of her father. It is reported that she miraculously received her sight when St. *Erhard baptized her, and this extraordinary incident accounts for the portrayal of the saint holding a book on which two eyes are lying. Her cult is very old and widespread; her name was inserted into the Litany of All Saints as early as the 9th century. Odilia is invoked as the patroness of those afflicted with diseases of the eye, and the collect of the Mass for her feast day likewise recalls the saint's cure from blindness and prays that through Odilia's intercession the faithful may turn their eyes from earthly vanity to God.

Bibliography: MGSrerMer 6:24–50. Zimmermann KalBen 3:424–427. Butler Th Attw 4:551–553. M. COENS, AnalBoll 54 (1936) 20, 27; 55 (1937) 68. A. BURG, *Histoire de l'Église d'Alsace* (Colmar 1946). A. SCHÜTTE. *Handbuch der deutschen Heiligen* (Cologne 1941) 272. J. BILLING, *Die Heiligen der Diözese Strassburg* (Colmar 1957) 25–31. Baudot-Chaussin 12: 413–417. L. BIELER, LexThK² 7:1096. Réau IAC 3:999–1003.

[H. DRESSLER]

ODILO OF CLUNY, ST.

Fifth abbot of Cluny; b. Auvergne, 962; d. Abbey of Souvigny, Jan. 1, 1049 (feast April 29). He was a member of the Mercoeur family, who became a cleric at Saint-Julien in Brioude and later requested the monastic habit at *Cluny, which at that time was governed by (St.) *Majolus of Cluny, fourth abbot there. Odilo, chosen by Majolus as coadjutor in 991, was the acting abbot by 994 and showed immediately his outstanding qualities of leadership and organization. His 50 years as abbot (999–1049) were characterized by an ever-growing number of Cluniac daughter houses and properties grouped into an "order" under his firm authority (*see* CLUNIAC REFORM). This formation of an "order" was one of the consequences of *exemption, for Cluny centralized under itself all monasteries that had received the privilege of temporal immunity and exemption from episcopal power granted by Gregory V in 998 or 999, and confirmed by Pope John XIX in 1027. The papacy always upheld the monks of Cluny in any resulting conflicts of jurisdiction, for it recognized clearly the importance of monasticism in strengthening papal authority, in fighting *simony (*see* GREGORIAN REFORM), and in spreading Christianity, e.g., in Spain.

Odilo's diplomatic activity is well known. He received the imperial insignia from Emperor *Henry II, to whom he had been counselor since 1002; Cluny listed Henry in the necrology of the abbey after the Emperor's death in 1024. Odilo was equally loyal to the Capetian monarchy; he was able to be the mediator between Emperor *Conrad II and the King of France, *Robert II, in 1025. Such political activity shows that Cluny and its abbots were not basically opposed to seignorialism, even if relations between Odilo and Emperor *Henry III were less than cordial.

About 1030–31 the abbot established the commemoration of *All Souls' Day for his own monastery and dependent houses. This was later adopted by the universal Church. In 1041 Odilo favored the extension of the Truce of God. He was always concerned with helping the poor, going so far as to sell the holy treasures of the monastery during a famine in 1033. Odilo pursued the building of Cluny to such an extent that his biographer Jotsaldus [ed. F. Ermini, StMed 1 (1928) 401–405] wrote that he had "renewed everything at Cluny except the walls of the church" (*see* CLUNIAC ART AND ARCHITECTURE). About 1042 the abbey was inhabited by about 75 religious. Odilo died after one of

his numerous trips to Italy, and was succeeded by *Hugh of Cluny. He was canonized in 1063. The French Benedictine congregation observes January 1 as his feast day and the rest of the Benedictines, April 29.

His writings include *Vita S. Maioli* (Marrier-Duchesne, 279–290; PL 142:943–962), *Epitaphium Adalheidae* (Marrier-Duchesne, 353–369; MGS 4:633–645), letters (Marrier-Duchesne, 349–354; PL 142: 939–944), sermons (Marrier-Duchesne, 371–408; PL 142:991–1036), and *Medicina spiritualis contra temptationem concupiscentiae carnalis* [ed. G. Morin, RevBén 16 (1899) 477–478]. He wrote also a hymn in honor of St. Majolus, *Maiolus pater inclitus* [ed. G. Morin, Rev Bén 38 (1926) 56–57]. Other hymns are found in PL 142:961–964 and AnalHymn 50 (1907) 297–301; several fragments are in PL 142:1035–38.

Bibliography: Sources. M. MARRIER and A. DUCHESNE, eds., *Bibliotheca cluniacensis* (Paris 1614; repr. Mâcon 1915). A. BRUEL, ed., *Recueil des chartes de l'abbaye de Cluny*, 6 v. (Paris 1876–1903) 3:190–821; 4:1–174, 825–827. Literature. Manitius 2:138–142. B. BLIGNY, *L'Église et les ordres religieux dans le royaume de Bourgogne aux XIᵉ et XIIᵉ siècles* (Grenoble 1960). J. SEMMLER, LexThK² 7:1098. J. HOURLIER, *Saint Odilon, abbé de Cluny* (Louvain 1964).

[R. GRÉGOIRE]

ODIN, JOHN MARY

U.S. missionary bishop; b. Ambierle, France, Feb. 25, 1801; d. there, May 25, 1870. He was the 7th of 10 children born of Jean and Claudine (Seyrol) Odin. After some preliminary schooling with a priest uncle in Nosilly, he pursued studies at the colleges of L'Argentière and Alix. While in the Seminary of Saint-Sulpice in Lyons, he heard of the need for priests in Louisiana from a missionary bishop, Louis William *Dubourg. At 22, as a subdeacon, he came to the

John Mary Odin.

Mississippi Valley, entered the seminary at the Barrens near St. Louis, Mo., and joined the Congregation of the Mission. Having completed his novitiate, he was ordained by Bishop Dubourg on May 4, 1823. The young priest engaged in missionary work in Missouri, Arkansas, and Texas. He also served as professor and president of the Barrens seminary, pastor at Cape Girardeau, and theologian at the Second Provincial Council of Baltimore. At 40, he was appointed vice prefect to Very Rev. John *Timon, CM, in Texas. Odin won the esteem of the Texans; during the first session of the fifth congress of the Texas Republic, the legislature requested him to act as chaplain of the Senate. On April 16, 1841, he received a brief appointing him titular bishop of Claudiopolis and coadjutor-administrator of the American Northwest with see in Detroit. On the advice of Timon, he declined and returned the bulls to Rome. By briefs dated July 16, 1841, Gregory XVI raised Texas from prefecture to vicariate apostolic, confirmed Odin in the See of Claudiopolis, and named him vicar apostolic in Texas. Bishop Antoine Blanc consecrated him in St. Louis Cathedral, New Orleans. Following the Baltimore Council of 1846, the former Republic of Texas became a diocese with Galveston as the see city (see GALVESTON-HOUSTON, DIOCESE OF). Odin, the first bishop, consecrated St. Mary's Cathedral there on Nov. 26, 1848. In 1852 he reported that his diocese had 25 priests serving 30 churches and twice as many mission stations. Nine years later, before leaving for New Orleans, he showed on his inventory 46 churches and 46 priests, including the Oblates of Mary Immaculate whom he had brought to the diocese.

The Mexican War was fought while Odin was ordinary in Texas; the Civil War was raging when he arrived as archbishop in New Orleans (see NEW ORLEANS, ARCHDIOCESE OF). Despite war and Reconstruction, he managed to continue the work of his predecessor, Archbishop Blanc, and to expand it by inviting six communities of men and women to the archdiocese. He was particularly successful in recruiting clerics while he was on a trip to Europe during the height of the Civil War and, despite the blockade of New Orleans, personally escorted nearly 50 priests and seminarians who had volunteered to labor in Louisiana and Texas. Odin had chartered for their transportation a passenger ship, the *Ste. Genevieve*, which was nicknamed "the floating seminary," and which landed at New Orleans on Good Friday, April 3, 1863. Although considerate of his priests in both Texas and Louisiana, he was regarded as a strict disciplinarian. He held synods in the two dioceses over which he presided. From the content of these synodal regulations and from the tenor of his pastoral letters, it is evident that he countenanced no abuses of ecclesiastical discipline and dealt promptly with infractions. During the Civil War, Odin was the Holy Father's contact in the South, as Abp. John Hughes was intermediary in the North. Odin's problems following the war were aggravated by the attitude of priests and people towards the Negroes, who, as slaves, had been admitted to churches and the Sacraments but who, once freed, were made to feel less than welcome at services. The archbishop promptly appealed to various religious communities to assign men and women religious for special ministration to the Negroes and for the education of their children, but antipathy

was so intense that none heeded his request until 1867 when St. Joseph's School in Convent, La., was opened under the auspices of the Religious of the Sacred Heart. Another aftermath of the war was the closing of the diocesan seminary in Faubourg Bouligny because of lack of funds.

Odin accepted the invitation of Pius IX to attend the 18th centenary of the martyrdom of St. Peter in 1867 and in 1869–70 Vatican Council I. Prior to the latter event, the archbishop had asked for a coadjutor and on May 1, 1870, Napoleon Joseph Perché, his vicar-general, was consecrated in St. Louis Cathedral. Less than a month later, having left Rome because of the precarious condition of his health, Odin died.

Bibliography: J. D. G. SHEA, *A History of the Catholic Church within the Limits of the United States,* 4 v. (New York 1886–92) v.4. M. A. FITZMORRIS, *Four Decades of Catholicism in Texas, 1820–1860* (Washington 1926).

[H. C. BEZOU]

ODO OF BAYEUX

ODO OF BAYEUX, bishop; b. Normandy, *c.* 1036; d. Palermo, February 1097. He was a half brother, through his mother Arlette, of William the Conqueror (*see* WILLIAM I, KING OF ENGLAND), who made him bishop of Bayeux in 1049. Always more a feudal baron than bishop, he participated in the Battle of Hastings, and became Earl of Kent (1067) and a powerful minister of William. Between 1077 and 1080 he exercised viceroyal functions in England. In 1082 his lands were forfeited and he was imprisoned, supposedly for recruiting knights for a private expedition to Rome. Restored to his position when William was on his deathbed, he conspired against King William Rufus (*see* WILLIAM II, KING OF ENGLAND), and was forced out of England. He died on the First Crusade. Odo rebuilt the cathedral of Bayeux, patronized scholars, and probably commissioned the *Bayeux tapestry.

Bibliography: GUILLAUME DE POITIERS, *Histoire de Guillaume le Conquérant,* ed. and tr. R. FOREVILLE (Paris 1952). ORDERIC VITALIS, *Historia ecclesiastica,* ed. A. LE PRÉVOST, 5 v. (Paris 1838–55) v.3. EngHistDoc 2. C. L. KINGSFORD, DNB 14:869–871. F. M. STENTON, *Anglo-Saxon England* (2d ed. Oxford 1947). D. C. DOUGLAS, *William the Conqueror* (Berkeley 1964).

[B. W. SCHOLZ]

ODO OF CAMBRAI, BL., or Odo of Tournai, bishop, philosopher, and theologian whose teaching at Toul and Tournai gave a new impetus to realism; b. Orléans, France; d. Abbey of Anchin, near Arras, June 19, 1113 (feast, June 20). He was chosen bishop of Cambrai in 1095. He introduced the *Cluniac Reform into his monastery of *Saint-Martin at Tournai. His principal work, *De peccato originali,* used an exaggerated realism to explain the transmission of original sin. Other extant writings, theological in nature, include a treatise on the Canon of the Mass, a dialogue with a Jew adducing philosophical reasons for Christ's coming, a short treatise on final impenitence, and a Gospel harmony.

Bibliography: F. LABIS, "Le Bx. Odon, évêque de Cambrai . . .," *Revue Catholique de Louvain* 14 (1856) 445–460, 519–526, 574–585. M. DE WULF, *Histoire de la philosophie en Belgique* (Brussels 1910) 24–32. É. AMANN, DTC 11.1:931–935. C. DEREINE, "O. de Tournai et la crise du cénobitisme au XIᵉ siècle," RevMALat 4 (1948) 137–154. T. GREGORY, "La Dottrina del peccato originale e il realismo platonico: O. di T.," *Platonismo medievale: Studi e Richerche* (Rome 1958) 31–51.

[M. I. J. ROUSSEAU]

ODO (ODA) OF CANTERBURY, ST., arch-

bishop of *Canterbury; d. June 2, 958 (feast, formerly June 2; today, July 4). Odo, called "the Good," was born of pagan Danish parents but brought up by a thane of King *Alfred. King Athelstan made him bishop of Ramsbury in 927 and employed him as ambassador to Hugh Capet, Duke of the Franks. In 942 King Edmund offered him the See of Canterbury, which he accepted only after receiving the Benedictine habit from Fleury. As archbishop he restored Elmham as a separate bishopric for East Anglia, ordered his bishops to make annual visitations of their dioceses, and made the building of parish churches part of his church reform. He ordered 10 chapters dealing with morals and ecclesiastical discipline to be drawn up. Although not enacted by a synod, "Oda's *Chapters* are the only 10th-century ordinances of the same category as synodal acts and related sources." The *Chapters* are drawn largely from the Legatine Councils of 786. Odo encouraged Frithegode to write a metrical *Life of St. Wilfrid of York.* Odo's cult was observed at Canterbury, where his name appears in calendars of Christ Church (HBradshSoc 72: 175; 77:73.)

Bibliography: Sources. G. SCHOEBE, "The Chapters of Archbishop Oda (942/6) and the Canons of the Legatine Councils of 786," *Bulletin of the Institute of Historical Research* 35 (1962) 75–83. EADMER OF CANTERBURY, *Vita sancti Odonis,* PL 133: 933–944 (erroneously ascribed to Osbern of Canterbury). "Vita sancti Oswaldi" in *The Historians of the Church of York and Its Archbishops,* ed. J. RAINE (RollsS) 71.1:399–475. WILLIAM OF MALMESBURY, *Gesta pontificum anglorum,* ed. N. E. S. A. HAMILTON (RollsS) 52:20–24, 30, 248. Literature. W. HUNT, DNB 14:866–868. R. R. DARLINGTON, "Ecclesiastical Reform in the Late Old English Period," EngHistRev 51 (1936) 385–428. F. M. STENTON, *Anglo-Saxon England* (2d ed. Oxford 1947) 342, 352–353, 360–362, 431, 442. M. DEANESLY, *The Pre-Conquest Church in England* (New York 1961). R. W. SOUTHERN, *Saint Anselm and His Biographer* (New York 1963).

[B. W. SCHOLZ]

ODO OF CHÂTEAUROUX, French cardinal,

known also as *Odo de Castro Radulphi;* b. Champagne *c.* 1208; d. Orvieto, Jan. 26, 1273. He studied at the University of Paris where he became a master in theology in 1230 and where he undoubtedly taught for some time. In 1234 he was a canon of Paris; in 1238 he was promoted to the chancellorship of the University, but resigned in order to enter the *Cistercians at Grandselve. Innocent IV named him to succeed *Jacques de Vitry as cardinal bishop of Frascati in 1244, and in October 1245 he went to France as papal legate to preach the Sixth *Crusade. While there he condemned John of Brescia's theses on light (Dec. 21, 1247) and the Talmud (May 15, 1248). He was a great friend of King *Louis IX and during the Crusade (1248–54) accompanied him to Egypt and Palestine where Odo was able to pacify the quarrels of the Frankish lords. Back in Italy by 1254 he presided at Anagni (July 1255) over the commission examining the *Liber introductorius in evangelium eternum* written by Gerard de Borgo San Donnino, a work subsequently condemned by Alexander IV. He was sent as legate to Limoges in 1264 but lived most of the rest of his life in Italy. Many sermons and theological works are attributed to Odo. Although it is doubtful that he wrote either a commentary on Jeremia or the *Conciones et homiliae de tempore et de sanctis,* he is credited with a letter written at Cyprus in 1249, which is a kind of journal of the Crusade. Odo's fame derives more from his active life than from his writings.

Bibliography: Sources. ChartUnParis 1:202–211. J. B. PITRA, *Analecta novissima spicilegii Solesmensis,* 2 v. (Paris 1885–88) 2:188–343. F. GRATIEN, "Sermons franciscains . . .," *Études franciscaines* 29 (1913) 171–195, 647–655. A. WALZ, "Odonis de Castro Radulphi . . . sermones sex . . .," AnalOP 17 (1925–26) 174–223. M. M. DAVY, ed., *Les Sermons universitaires . . .* (Paris 1931). J. LECLERCQ, "Le Sermon sur la royauté . . .," ArchHistDoctLitMA 18 (1943) 143–180. Literature. P. C. F. DAUNOU, HistLittFranc 19:228–232. É. AMANN, DTC 11.1:935–936. Glorieux R 1:304–311. M. M. LEBRETON, DictSpirAscMyst 4.2:1675–78.

[É. BROUETTE]

ODO OF CLUNY, ST.

Second abbot of Cluny; b. Aquitaine, *c.* 879; d. Tours, Nov. 18, 942 (feast, April 29). He was the son of Ebbo I, Lord of Déols, who dedicated him to St. *Martin of Tours. Odo received his early education at the court of Duke William of Aquitaine and then studied the liberal arts at Tours and at Paris under *Remigius of Auxerre. After having received the tonsure at 19, Odo lived an austere and industrious life as canon of St. Martin of Tours. Under the direction of Bl. *Berno, he became a monk at Baume, a Cluniac monastery, where he was a master at the age of 30. His humility won the confidence of Berno, first abbot of *Cluny, who had him ordained, and then in 927 elected as his successor as abbot of Cluny. While abbot, Odo received 188 deeds of donation. By March 931 Pope *John XI granted Cluny the privilege of exemption and authorized Odo to reform so many monasteries in Gaul and Italy that the medieval

St. Odo of Cluny, miniature in a 10th-century MS, Austrian National Library, Vienna (Cod. 51, fol. 45 v.).

chronicler *Flodoard of Reims called Odo "the restorer of monasteries and of the Holy Rule." Odo was the initiator of the Cluniac monastic observance, the *ordo cluniacensis* (*see* CLUNIAC REFORM). Struck by the deplorable state of the Church in his day, Odo insisted upon the value of the monastic life to the Church: the "apostolic life" of the monks was a continuation of the renewal and purification begun at Pentecost. Both *Leo VII in 936 and 939, and *Stephen VIII in 941, entrusted him with the peace negotiations in those Italian conflicts that involved the interest of the Roman Church. Odo fell sick in Rome and returned to Tours where he died, having already designated *Aymard as his successor at Cluny. Odo's relics are kept at l'Isle-Jourdain (Gers). The Benedictine Order observes his feast on April 29, but the French Benedictine Congregation has retained the original date of November 18. His literary work includes the *Moralia in Job,* a résumé of the *Moralia* of Gregory I the Great (PL 133:107–152); *Collationes,* conferences or lectures where Odo's patristic and humanistic culture is particularly apparent (PL 133:517–638); *Occupatio,* a poem in seven books, which is a meditation on sacred history (ed. A. Svoboda, Leipzig 1900); *Vita s. Geraldi Auriliacensis comitis* (PL 133:639–704); and the *Vita Gregorii Turonensis episcopi* (PL 133:513–516). He wrote 12 anthems and 4 hymns in honor of St. Martin, as well as the hymn *De corpore Christi* [PL 133:513–516, AnalHymn 50 (1907) 265–270]. The musical works attributed to Odo (PL 133:755–816) are probably apocryphal.

Bibliography: Sources. M. MARRIER and A. DUCHESNE, eds., *Bibliotheca cluniacensis* (Paris 1614; repr. 1915). PL 133:9–816. A. BRUEL, ed., *Recueil des chartes de l'abbaye de Cluny,* 6 v. (Paris 1876–1903) 1:278–530; 5:844–845. Stegmüller RB 4: 6117–20. Literature. J. H. PIGNOT, *Histoire de l'Ordre de Cluny,* 3 v. (Autun 1868) v.1. Manitius 2:20–27. J. LECLERCQ, "L'Idéal monastique de saint O. d'après ses oeuvres," *À Cluny: Congrès scientifique* (Dijon 1950) 227–232. P. THOMAS, "Saint O. de Cluny et son oeuvre musicale," *ibid.* 171–180. J. LAPORTE, "Saint O., disciple de saint Grégoire le Grand," *ibid.* 138–143. JOHN OF SALERNO, *St. O. of Cluny,* tr. and ed. G. SITWELL (New York 1958). J. SEMMLER, LexThK² 7:1100–01. **Illustration credit:** Picture Archives, Austrian National Library.

[R. GRÉGOIRE]

ODO OF KENT

ODO OF KENT, theologian, Benedictine monk, prior of Christ Church, *Canterbury, abbot of *Battle Abbey; d. Jan. 20, 1200. As prior of Christ Church he took a leading part in the negotiations that finally achieved the canonical election of Abp. *Richard of Canterbury to the See of Canterbury in 1173; the monks attempted unsuccessfully to make him archbishop after Richard's death. In 1175 he was elected abbot of Battle. An eloquent and learned man, belonging to the great spiritual tradition of 12th-century monasticism, he put spiritual things first and shared fully in the life of his monks. There is great uncertainty about the authorship of various theological works ascribed to him, and most of his writings must be presumed lost.

Bibliography: *Chronicon monasterii de Bello,* ed. J. S. BREWER (London 1846) 148–163. C. L. KINGSFORD, DNB 14:869–871. Knowles MOE 305–306.

[M. CHIBNALL]

ODO RIGALDUS

ODO RIGALDUS, theologian; b. near Paris (date unknown); d. Rouen, July 2, 1275. He joined the Franciscan Order *c.* 1236, and studied at the University of Paris from 1240–41 to 1245; in this latter year on the death of John de la Rochelle he succeeded him as regent. Rigaldus commented on the *Sentences* of Peter Lombard and on at least 15 disputed theological questions. Only books 1, 2, and 3 of the *Commentary* are authentic, *Bruxelles Bibl. Roy.* 1542 and *Troyes Bibl. Comm.* 1862 being spurious. As a student of theology he had collaborated with Alexander of Hales, John de la Rochelle, and Robert de la Basée on an exposition of the Franciscan Rule, which has become known as the *Expositio Regulae Quatuor Magistrorum.* His other writings remain substantially unedited.

Upon his election to the See of Rouen he was consecrated by Innocent IV at Lyons, April 26, 1248. He was a favorite of Louis, King of France, and was a collaborator on the Treaty with England in 1258. He worked actively with Bonaventure at the Council of Lyons (1274) for the return of the Greeks. An important document, the *Regestrum visitationum,* gives an account of his episcopal activity as metropolitan from July 17, 1248, to Dec. 15, 1269. His intellectual stature has become recognized recently as modern theologians rank him among the superior minds of the mid-13th century.

Bibliography: R. MÉNINDÈS, "Eudes Rigaud, Frère Mineur," *Revue d'histoire Franciscaine* 8 (1931) 157–178. P. ANDRIEU-GUITRANCOURT, *L'Archevêque Eudes Rigaud et la vie de l'Église aux XIIIᵉ siècle, d'après le Regestrum Visitationum* (Paris 1938). F. M. HENGUINET, "Les Manuscrits et l'influence des écrits théologiques d'Eudes Rigaud, O.F.M.," RechThAm 11 (1939) 324–350. K. F. LYNCH, "The Alleged Fourth Book of Odo Rigaud on the Sentences and Related Documents," FrancStudies 9 (1949) 87–145. É. AMANN, DTC 13.2:2703–05. G. GÁL, EncCatt 10:911.

[K. F. LYNCH]

O'DONNELL, EDMUND

O'DONNELL, EDMUND, first Jesuit martyred by the English government; b. Limerick, Ireland, 1542; d. Cork, Oct. 25, 1572. He entered the Society of Jesus at Rome in 1561. After studies at Loreto and Florence he was sent to Flanders for his health. He returned to Limerick in 1564 to teach in the school established by David Woulfe, SJ. The school was dispersed in 1568, and O'Donnell stayed with his family until January 1570, when he left for Madrid to raise funds for Woulfe's release from prison. In 1570 he returned to Ireland with the money but left again for the Iberian Peninsula sometime later. Although his journeys were undertaken in behalf of Woulfe, there is some evidence that he must also have acted as courier in bringing to James Fitzmaurice the bull of Pius V excommunicating Elizabeth. On his last return to Ireland he was arrested on the warrant of Thomas FitzJohn Arthur, a Catholic, and was tried, condemned, and then executed with great barbarity on Oct. 25, 1572. That O'Donnell was in minor orders at the time of his death is clear from the appeal of Arthur to Rome for absolution from the censure he had incurred. Arthur also stated that O'Donnell was unjustly condemned.

Bibliography: Archives, Society of Jesus, Rome. E. HOGAN, *Distinguished Irishmen of the 16th Century* (Dublin 1896). D. MURPHY, *Our Martyrs* (Dublin 1896).

[F. FINEGAN]

O'DONNELL, HUGH ROE

O'DONNELL, HUGH ROE, ruler of the autonomous Irish state of Tír Chonaill and principal ally of Hugh *O'Neill in the Catholic Confederates' War (1594–1603); b. Ballyshannon?, Donegal, Oct. 29,

1572; d. Simancas, Spain, Sept. 10, 1602. He was kidnapped in an English stratagem in October 1587, but escaped from Dublin Castle Jan. 5, 1592, and was inaugurated as "Ó Domhnaill" April 23, 1592. He ejected the English from the Franciscan Abbey of Donegal and maintained almost continual warfare against Elizabeth I. O'Neill joined him openly in 1595. His expeditions into Connacht in 1596–97 opened communications with Western chiefs for conjunction with the Ulster insurgents and facilitated their joint victory of the Yellow Ford, Aug. 14, 1598; this victory encouraged the Southern chiefs to join the Confederation. His victory of the Curlews, Aug. 15, 1599, contributed to the frustration of Lord Deputy Essex's campaign. He preceded O'Neill in marching (November 1601) to support the Spaniards besieged in Kinsale. After the Irish defeat there (December 1601) he sailed to Spain to petition Philip III for reinforcements. Disappointed, he sickened and died at Simancas. His death hastened the end of Irish military resistance; his brother Ruaidhrí submitted in December 1602, O'Neill, on March 23, 1603. However, the lengthy war deferred general persecution of Irish Catholics and allowed time for reinforcements to their clergy from their new continental seminaries.

Bibliography: L. Ó CLÉRIGH, *The Life of Aodh Ruadh Ó Domhnaill,* transcribed by P. WALSH, 2 v. (Irish Texts Society 42, 45; Dublin 1948–57).

[J. HURLEY]

ODORIC OF PORDENONE, BL.

Franciscan missionary; b. Pordenone, Italy, *c.* 1265; d. Udine, Italy, Jan. 14, 1331 (feast, Jan. 12, formerly Jan. 14). He entered the *Franciscan Order at Udine *c.* 1280 and was ordained a priest some 10 years later. In 1296 he began his remarkable career as a world missionary, which lasted about 35 years. For more than a decade and a half he was engaged in missionary work with other Franciscans in the *Mongol khanate of Kipchak in southern Russia and probably also on the Balkan Peninsula. For a short time he returned to Italy, but in 1314 he set sail from Venice for the Near East. During the next 8 years he did missionary work in the three Franciscan custodies of Constantinople, Trebizond (Asia Minor, present Turkey), and Tabriz (Persia, present Iran). From Sultaniyeh in northern Persia he set out in 1322 with an Irish confrere, Friar James, for the Far East in order to join Abp. *John of Monte Corvino in Cathay (northern China). After traveling through southern Persia, northern Arabia, and Chaldea (Iraq), he sailed from Hormuz in the Persian Gulf. At Thana, near Bombay, he recovered the relics of *Thomas of Tolentino and his three companions, who had been martyred there about 2 years earlier. After visiting both the Malabar and the Coromandel coasts of India, he set sail from Quilon and stopped at the islands of Sumatra, Java, and probably Borneo, but by way of Cochin China and Great Nicobar Island. He had to return to Ceylon to get a ship to take him to Canton, China. After arriving there in the latter part of 1324, he traveled overland to the capital in the north. At Zaitun (present Ch'uan-chou in Fukien province) he stayed for a while with Bp. Andrew of Perugia (fl. 1307–26) and his Franciscan confreres, who had two churches in the city. On the northward journey he visited Fu-chou, Hang-chou, Nanking, and Yang-chou, finding at Yang-chou another Franciscan mission center. In 1325 he finally reached Khanbaliq, or Cambaluc, (modern-day Peking), and for 3 years he assisted Abp. John of Monte Corvino and the other Franciscans working in the capital. Shortly before the archbishop's death in 1328, Odoric was commissioned to go back to Europe to recruit new missionaries for China. He made the return journey overland through the vassal kingdom of Tenduk (present provinces Shansi, Shensi, and Kansu), where he found a church at T'o-k'o-t'o, built by King George, a convert of Monte Corvino. Though he mentions Tibet, he did not visit that country but continued through Almalyk, near Kuldja (present-day I-ning) in Sinkiang, the western gateway of China, where seven Franciscans later died (1339) as the first martyrs of China. Then traveling through Chinese Turkestan and central Asia, around the Caspian Sea, to Persia, Iraq, Syria, and probably Palestine, he reached Venice at the end of 1329 or beginning of 1330. He set out for Avignon to see Pope *John XXII, but fell ill at Pisa and returned to Udine by way of Padua, where he dictated his famous journal in May 1330. The journal was one of the most famous travel books of the Middle Ages, and it was plagiarized by the author of *The Travels of Sir John Mandeville.* The cult of Bl. Odoric was approved by *Benedict XIV on July 2, 1775, but his feast, on January 12, is restricted since 1961 to the Conventual Franciscans. Odoric is venerated as the patron of the Chinese missions and also of long-distance travelers. The best edition of his journal is the one published by A. Van den Wyngaert, OFM, in *Sinica Franciscana* (Quaracchi 1929) 1:413–495, and the best account of his life is in the accompanying introduction and notes.

See also MISSIONS, HISTORY OF (MEDIEVAL).

Bibliography: Sources. Eng. tr. of journal in *Cathay and the Way Thither,* ed. and tr. H. YULE, 2 v. (London 1866). Literature. M. GNAUCK, *Odorich von Pordenone, ein Orientreisender des 14. Jahrhunderts* (Leisnig 1895). BHL 6303–16. H. CORDIER, *Les Voyages en Asie, au XIVᵉ siècle, du bienheureux frère O. de Pordenone* (Paris 1891). G. GOLUBOVICH, "Il B. Fr. Odorico da Pordenone, O.F.M.," ArchFrancHist 10 (1917) 17–46. D. SCHILLING, "War der sel. Odorich von Pordenone in Japan?" *ibid.* 35 (1942) 153–176. G. PULLÉ, *Viaggio del beato Odorico da Pordenone* (Milan 1931). Butler Th Attw 1:88–89. I. GIULIANI, Enc Catt 9:77–78. M. A. HABIG, *In Journeyings Often* (St. Bonaventure, N.Y. 1953) 80–108. L. HARDICK, LexThK² 7:1102–03. A. TEETAERT, DTC 11.1:942–947.

[M. A. HABIG]

ODYSSEUS.

Of all the characters created by Homer, Odysseus, or Ulysses, as he is called in the Latin tradition, has had the longest life and the most varied fortunes. From the 6th century B.C. the mental and moral flexibility of Odysseus was viewed unfavorably, and the tradition of Odysseus as a symbol of deceit was established. However, Stoic and Cynic emphasis on his manliness and resourcefulness in overcoming evil forces led to a restoration of his Homeric image and a recognition of his high moral qualities. Vergil reflects the first tradition (*Aeneid,* bk. 2); and Horace, the second (*Epist.* 1.2).

Early Christian writers were inclined to follow the second tradition, being impressed in particular by the story of the meeting of Odysseus and the Phaeacian Princess Nausicaa and, above all, by that of his resistance to the temptations of the Sirens. The voyage of Odysseus became a symbol of the Christian's journey through life; the Sirens, the powers of evil to which he is exposed; his ship, the Church; and its mast, the cross of Christ. In one of the stories of the medieval *Gesta Romanorum* [No. 156, *De subversione Troiae,* ed. H. Oesterley (Berlin 1872)] Paris represents the devil; Helen, the soul or all mankind held captive by the devil; Troy, hell; Ulysses, Christ; Achilles, the Holy Ghost. The temptation of Odysseus by the Sirens has been used as a theme also in Christian art.

See also HOMER.

Bibliography: W. B. STANFORD, *The Ulysses Theme: A Study in the Adaptability of a Traditional Hero* (Oxford 1954); "Studies in the Characterization of Ulysses IV: Ulysses in the Post-Classical Latin Tradition," *Hermathena* 77 (1951) 52–64. H. RAHNER, *Greek Myths and Christian Mystery,* tr. B. BATTERSHAW (New York 1963) esp. ch. VII, "Odysseus at the Mast," 328–386. E. WÜST, "Odysseus," Pauly-Wiss RE 17.2 (1937) 1905–96, esp. 1964–76.

[M. R. P. MC GUIRE]

OECOLAMPADIUS, JOHANNES, originally Husschyn, Hussgen, or Heussgen, theologian and reformer of Basel; b. Weinsberg in the Palatinate, 1482; d. Basel, Nov. 24, 1531. By 1515, when he first came to Basel after years of education at Bologna, Heidelberg, Stuttgart, and Tübingen, his philological erudition in Latin, Greek, and Hebrew was prodigious. As a proofreader for the publisher Froben he worked on Erasmus' editions of the New Testament and St. Jerome, and throughout his life he prepared numerous editions and translations of the Greek fathers. In 1520, weary of his ecclesiastical labors, he abruptly entered a Briggitine monastery in Bavaria, only to withdraw just as abruptly 2 years later. In November 1522 he returned to Basel and was appointed a professor at the university in 1523. Thereafter he ceaselessly promoted the cause of reform in the city through extensive lectures and sermons, in the Minster as well as in St. Martin's Church. Elsewhere in Switzerland he promoted it through his publications, notably in the Eucharistic controversy, and his participation in theological disputations such as those at Baden (1526) and Bern (1528), and the Colloquium at Marburg (1529), where he defended the Eucharistic doctrine of his close friend Huldrych *Zwingli. After the city council on Feb. 8, 1529, ordered the removal of images and the abolition of the Mass, Oecolampadius directed and supervised the reform of the Basel church until his death, employing the monumental reforming ordinance of April 1, which he prepared.

Bibliography: K. R. HAGENBACH, *Johann Oekolampad und Oswald Myconius* (Leben und ausgewählte Schriften der Väter und Begründer der reformirten Kirche 2; Elberfeld 1859) 3–306. E. STAEHELIN, *Das theologische Lebenswerk Johannes Oekolampads* (Quellen und Forschungen zur Reformationsgeschichte 21; Leipzig 1939); ed., *Briefe und Akten zum Leben Oekolampads,* 2 v. (*ibid.* 10, 19; 1927–34); *Oekolampad-Bibliographie* (Nieuwkoop, Neth. 1963). L. CRISTIANI, DTC 11.1:947–951. H. R. GUGGISBERG, RGG[3] 4:1567–68. E. ISERLOH, LexThK[2] 7:1125–26. Cross ODCC 976.

[C. GARSIDE, JR.]

OERTEL, JOHN JAMES MAXIMILIAN, editor; b. Ansbach, Bavaria, Germany, April 27, 1811; d. Jamaica, N.Y., Aug. 21, 1882. He was educated at the University of Erlangen, Germany, before his ordination as a Lutheran minister. Immigrating to New York City in 1837, he led 95 Prussian immigrants to join the Saxon congregations (now Lutheran Church—Missouri Synod) in St. Louis, Mo., in 1839. Denominational quarrels led to his conversion to Catholicism the following year. He served as an instructor in German at St. John's College, Fordham, N.Y., before going to Cincinnati, Ohio, as editor of the *Wahrheitsfreund.* The German-language newspaper *Kirchenzeitung,* which he founded in Baltimore, Md., in 1846, was moved to New York City in 1851 and became the most influential German paper in the U.S. In 1875 Oertel was made a Knight of St. Gregory by Pius IX.

[J. L. MORRISON]

OFFA, KING OF MERCIA, 757 to July 29, 796, the dominating figure in English history during the second half of the 8th century and the greatest English monarch before *Alfred. He succeeded his kinsman Ethelbald after a brief usurpation by a certain Beornred, and his early reign was occupied in reducing the kingdom to order. In 771 he commenced the series of wars that resulted in the establishment of his authority over all the lands south of the Humber. Essex and Kent were reduced to dependency; Wessex was defeated and tied by a dynastic alliance. In the west considerable territory beyond the Severn was conquered from the Welsh, and the annexed lands were secured by a marvelous defensive earthwork—part of which survives—called Offa's Dyke, running along what still remains approximately the boundary of Wales. Offa's supremacy in England was acknowledged by both *Charlemagne and the papacy. With the former he treated as an equal and negotiated (796) "England's first commercial treaty." From Pope *Adrian I he received sanction for a third English archbishopric, Lichfield, a Mercian diocese; this was an astonishing

Johannes Oecolampadius, portrait from the "Bibliotheca Chalcographica," 1650.

if ephemeral (787–803) ecclesiastical innovation. By it Offa aimed at strengthening his control by withdrawing five suffragan bishops from the less friendly jurisdiction of the archbishop of Canterbury. The papacy also approved the consecration as coruler of Offa's son Egfrith, the first known instance (787) of this rite in English history. In this same year Offa committed himself to an annual payment to Rome that seems to be the origin of the famous *Peter's Pence. Offa promulgated a law code that unfortunately is not extant; but the coinage system for which he was responsible—based on the silver penny—remained essentially unchanged for the following 500 years. The death of Offa was followed immediately by a collapse of the Mercian hegemony.

Bibliography. J. EARLE and C. PLUMMER, eds., *Two of the Saxon Chronicles Parallel*, 2 v. (Oxford 1892–99) under years 755–796, *passim*. W. DE G. BIRCH, ed., *Cartularium Saxonicum*, 3 v. (London 1885–93). F. M. STENTON, *Anglo-Saxon England* (2d ed. Oxford 1947) *passim*. R. H. HODGKIN, *A History of the Anglo-Saxons*, 2 v. (3d ed. New York 1952). C. F. FOX, *Offa's Dyke* (London 1955).

[R. D. WARE]

OFFERTORY

The term Offertory (Offerenda or Oblatio) signifies the initial actions of the Mass of the Faithful: from the Offertory Antiphon to the "Per omnia saecula saeculorum. Amen" concluding the Secret. From having been no more at first than the silent setting of the elements on the altar, this traditional rite has gradually been expanded and has taken on liturgical forms and prayers that differ in the West from those in the East. Yet underneath this developed ritual there has remained the same basic structure of the Offertory rite: the setting of the sacred elements on the altar with a view to their Consecration.

History of the Rite. St. Justin is the first to give explicit evidence about the initial actions of the Eucharist. In the first and fuller text of his *Apology* (ch. 65), the account of this simple rite runs as follows: "When the prayers are concluded, we give to each other the kiss of peace. Then there is presented to him who presides over the assembly of the brethren, bread, and a cup of wine with water. He takes them . . .." But *The Apostolic Tradition* of Hippolytus (*c.* 215–218) is the first major liturgical document so far discovered, and in it are two vivid descriptions of the Eucharistic rite. Nothing, however, is added to Justin's account of the Offertory except that the deacons are expressly mentioned as "presenting the oblation" to the bishop who, along with his assisting priests, ritually imposes his hands on it. Though there is no evidence in these texts of any ritual oblation of the bread and wine by the faithful, other indications seem to support Lietzmann when he says that the deacons bring in the bread and wine offered by the faithful [cf. *Messe und Herrenmahl* (Bonn 1926) 175].

Tertullian gives important evidence of usage in Africa in the 3d century. By his time the *Agape was already distinct from the Eucharist. There seems little doubt that it was the custom for the faithful to present the bread and wine for the sacrifice. But there is as yet no indication of the time when these elements were presented. It would seem therefore that the Offertory rite of the 2d and 3d centuries was something almost informal.

By the 4th century there is abundant evidence of an astonishing flowering of the liturgy when peace came to the Church. In the East the faithful provided the oblations, but, except in the Egyptian rite, the exact time of their offering is not known. In this century, in the opinion of most liturgists, the presentation of the gifts at the Offertory died out, if it ever existed [cf. J. M. Hanssens, *Institutiones liturgicae de ritibus orientalibus* (Rome 1932) 3.281]. Clearly it had no place at this moment in the rite of Jerusalem. Strangely enough, evidence about Western practice is meager. In Spain the faithful provided the oblations according to a certain ritual, a custom apparently followed in Milan also.

The 5th century witnessed a widening of the divergence between the rites of East and West. In his *Catecheses* delivered *c.* 410, Theodore of Mopsuestia gave a complete picture of the Antiochene Offertory rite. It had become a "processional" as opposed to an "oblational" rite. In Africa, however, it seems certain from Augustine that the faithful were offering the elements at the Offertory [P. Batiffol, *Leçons sur la Messe* (Paris 1919) 2.151].

Interpretation of Data. But a survey of the rite as practiced in all its variants throughout Christendom shows that in its developed form these initial actions, precisely because they are concerned with the materials of sacrifice, demand six interrelated steps. The East focuses the attention of all on the procession of the elements, while the West stresses their oblation through the hands of the people, ministers, and priest to God. There were (1) the prior presentation by the faithful of the elements either in the Mass or outside of it, (2) their preparation or selection, (3) their transference to the sanctuary, (4) the proximate preparation of the elements, (5) the proximate transference to the altar, (6) the *formal* oblation by the priest, accompanied by ceremonial gestures. The first real Offertory prayer is precisely the Prayer over the Offerings, which later became the Roman Secret. Behind all these actions stands an all-pervading motive, that the Church must provide the elements of the Sacrifice of the Mass. These elements must be transferred to the altar and set thereon. The rest is ritual elaboration that naturally surrounds a constantly repeated act and that a public service of worship of its nature demands.

Fig. 1. The Great Entrance in the Byzantine Liturgy: procession of the clergy at the Offertory.

Among the rites of the West, the Gallican and Spanish show a certain affinity with the East. Though the Gallican rite was brought to an abrupt end in the 8th and 9th centuries, it is in Gaul and Spain that the later Roman Offertory prayers were composed and slowly absorbed into the terse, native rite of Rome. Pius V, in stabilizing the rite of the Roman Offertory, chose such prayers as best expressed the liturgical action. Though perhaps they overload this action with prayers of a personal nature, they are really little more than a natural evolution of the silent private prayer of the priest or bishop in primitive times.

Theology. The relation of the Offertory rite to the sacrifice of the Body and Blood of Christ (i.e., to the Consecration rite) is a point of fundamental agreement among Catholic theologians and liturgists. All agree that the Offertory is the opening of the Mass of the Faithful, and all likewise agree that this opening action is not essential to the sacrifice. There is not the same agreement, however, as to the exact relation of the Offertory to the rest of the Eucharistic liturgy. Confusion has long existed because of two historical assumptions, which modern scholarship has challenged. The first is that the offering of the bread and wine by the people was in fact part of the primitive ritual of the Mass and essential to the Offertory rite. The second is that the Offertory rite was regarded as one in which the part of the people predominated. The fact also that most liturgists have confined their studies to the Roman rite may have caused too biased an interpretation.

Various Proposed Solutions. The strictly theological approach to the Offertory is represented by the theologians who followed the Council of Trent rather than by their scholastic predecessors. Suárez, for example, reduces the Offertory rite to a mere ceremonial preparation instituted by the Church to foster devotion among the faithful. Vasquez, on the other hand, grasped more correctly the nature of the rite: "the bread and wine are offered to God . . . in so far as they are set before Him to be consecrated" (*In Summa Theologica* 3a.83.1, d.222). Pasqualigo, who has exercised considerable influence on modern commentators, considered the Offertory rite a self-contained liturgy in only accidental relation with the main action of sacrifice (*De Sacrificio N. L.,* 1.30.8).

Fig. 2. *Offertory procession in Roman Mass; two sisters present altar breads, wine, and water to the celebrant.*

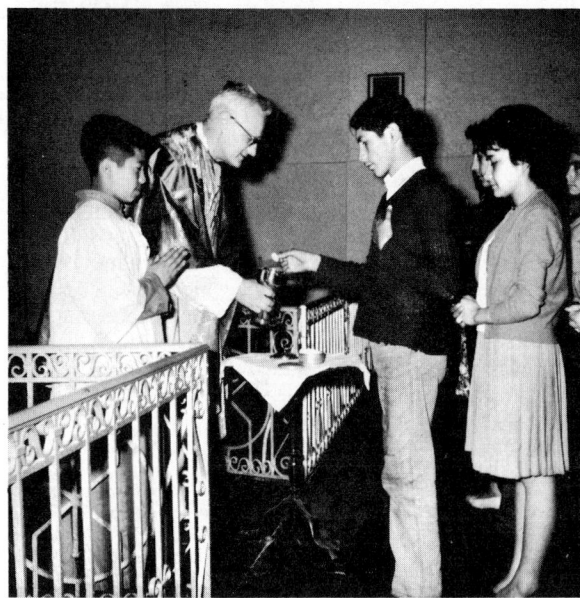

Fig. 3. *Offertory procession in Roman Mass; the entire congregation goes to the sanctuary to present altar breads.*

Several modern writers (e.g., J. Brinktrine, L. Eisenhofer) share this view. J. Jungmann [cf. *The Mass of the Roman Rite* (London 1959) 360–362] rightly asserts that there can be no denying that in the Roman Offertory there is an anticipation of the thought of the Canon. Callewaert, from his study of the Roman Mass, notes that three things are done at the Offertory—the sacrifice is prepared, it is directed to a determinate end, and the offering of the sacrifice is *begun* [cf. "De Offerenda et oblatione in missa," *Periodica* 33 (1944) 61–66].

Nature of Offertory Rite. In spite of the differences of opinion, there is less disagreement than at first sight appears. Once it is seen that the Eucharistic liturgy is one continuous action in which the thought of the offerers is concentrated on the transformation of their gifts into the One Gift that pleases God, the nature of the Offertory rite becomes clearer. There is indeed an anticipation of the thought of the Canon, but this should give little cause for surprise when it is recalled that the elements are brought to the altar precisely so that they may be transformed into the Body and Blood of Christ for the Real Sacrifice. However, the true interpretation of this rite must be obtained not from any preconceived principle (for none exists) but from historical evidence. The nature of the rite can be clearly seen by examining what has been *done* at this point in the Mass throughout the centuries.

Though the moment of the Mass when the elements are brought to the altar differs, all liturgies, in East and West, agree on the moment when these gifts are *formally* set on the altar and by this very action dedicated and offered to God. The majority of liturgies of which there are adequate records show the actual bringing up of the gifts and their setting on the altar at the time of the Offertory. Such rites as place them on the altar beforehand do not *formally* advert to their presence until the Offertory. This is the moment when they are ritually presented to God for transformation into the one sacred Victim of the sacrifice. Though the note of anticipation is there, there is never any suggestion that the Consecration has already taken place or that this Consecration is being symbolically represented. It is clear from the structure of the rite that it centers on the oblations and their destiny. Other thoughts may impose themselves because the Offertory is an action done by men; and although it may concern itself primarily with what is offered, the thought of who are the offerers cannot fail to be present. Hence the note of preparation concerns not so much the gifts as the offerers themselves in both Eastern and Western Offertory prayers. As to other ceremonies that appear in Offertory rites—the Great Entrance, the Oblation of the people, the Kiss of Peace, incense, the Recitation of the Names, the Lavabo, etc.—all have only one term: the fitting oblation of the elements to God for their consecration.

The vindication of the Offertory rite as the beginning of the Mass proper is not a new idea. It is traditional among the medievalists. It is to be seen in St. Thomas (ST 3a, 83.4). It has remained with the Greeks until this day (cf. Hanssens, *op. cit.*, n.1102). One may dare to say that the moment when our gifts are transformed into the Sacrifice of Christ, though carefully celebrated, is of less importance, liturgically, than the great motif of oblation that runs through the whole Eucharistic rite.

Bibliography: F. CABROL, DACL 12.2:1946–62. J. COPPENS, "L'Offrande des fidèles dans la liturgie eucharistique ancienne," *Cours et Conférences de Semaines Liturgiques* 5 (Louvain 1927) 99–123; 6 (1928) 185–196. G. DIX, *The Shape of the Liturgy* (2d ed. London 1945). A. CLARK, "The Function of the Offertory Rite," EphemLiturg 64 (1950) 309–344. Miller FundLit 268–272. E. BISHOP, "Appendix," *The Liturgical Homilies of Narsai*, tr. R. CONNOLLY (Cambridge 1909). **Illustration credits:** Fig. 1, *Byzantine Catholic World*, Pittsburgh, Pa. Fig. 2, Photo Phil Stack, courtesy Marist Mission Center, Waltham, Mass. Fig. 3, Maryknoll Missions.

[A. C. CLARK]

OFFERTORY ANTIPHON

The chant sung at Mass during the offering of the gifts.

Original Responsorial Nature. The Offertory hymn during St. Augustine's time was responsorial in form, i.e., the soloist chanted a Psalm to which the choir responded with a short refrain, or *responsa* (*see* OFFERTORY). It is not known at what period Rome adopted the singing of a Psalm at the Offertory. This form of primitive chant, however, was replaced by a more ornate chant when the "Roman chant" was first formed; the *responsa* became *antiphona ad offerenda* [in the MSS and in *Amalarius's works (Liber officialis* 13: xviii; StTest 139:311) shortened to *offerenda*] or *antiphona ad offertorium*. The verses of the Psalm were then reduced in number to two or three, but the text was ornamented with melismas, the execution of which returned to the specialists of the *schola cantorum*. It is possible, however, to regard this new form of Offertory as a direct issue from the primitive form; in fact, in the Psalter Offertories, which constitute 90 per cent of the repertory, the first verse (and sometimes even the antiphon itself, e.g., *Ad te levavi*) is taken from the first verse of the Psalm. This choice implies that, from the primitive recitation of all the verses of the Psalm, only the first verse or perhaps one or two others were kept.

Melodies of Antiphon and the Repetenda. The Offertory is sung in the following order: (1) Offertory antiphon, (2) first verse, (3) repetition of the last section of the antiphon, (4) second verse, (5) repetition of the last section of the antiphon. This repetition of the last section of the antiphon after the first verse is not prescribed by the oldest MSS. It is called the *repetenda*, or *presa* in Aquitainian MSS; its ending has a conclusive character, for the repetition is linked with the verses (which, of themselves, have only a suspensive cadence) and brings them to a close.

In general, it is in the Offertories and their verses that the Gregorian composition is allowed free rein. True, it does use some forms of classical intonation and cadence, e.g., the interval of the 5th in the Offertory *Jubilate* and *Confitebor tibi*, which is the same as the intonation of the Introit *Gaudeamus;* but they are treated with great reserve and with flexibility. Moreover, the same melody was seldom used for two or more texts (e.g., Offertory *Angelus Domini* and *Posuisti*) at the time Gregorian chant was first composed. This process was used for Offertories composed later [e.g., *Justorum animae* (11th century), adapted in Italy or in Aquitainia in the Offertory *Stetit Angelus; Sacerdotes Dei* for the Feast of Corpus Christi, adapted from *Confirma hoc* of Pentecost]. One may say that almost all the Offertories have their own original melodies. Some are rightly considered masterpieces of Gregorian composition, to such a degree does their expression attain the heights of lyricism (*Jubilate* of the Second Sunday after Epiphany, *Angelus Domini*, *Stetit Angelus*) or, on the contrary, attain dramatic depths (*Eripe me . . . Deus meus, Improperium, Precatus est, Oratio mea*). It must not be forgotten that some of these masterpieces are probably of Gallican origin (*Elegerunt, Erit vobis, Protege*) and have slipped into Gregorian MSS. Their style, however, contrasts with those of properly so-called Gregorian Offertories. It is necessary, finally, to call attention to a procedure proper to the Offertory: the repetition of the initial sentence occurring at the beginning (*Jubilate, Benedictus es, Precatus es*) or sometimes at the end (*Domine in auxilium, De profundis*).

Melody of the Verses. Smits van Waesberghe and Jammers consider the Offertory verses more recent than

Offertory for Thursday of the first week in Lent (from Psalm 33: "The angel of the Lord shall encamp around those who fear Him and shall deliver them; taste and see that the Lord is sweet"), from a Missal written at Ravenna, 11th century (Walters MS 11, fol. 53r, detail).

the rest of the Gregorian repertory. One of the arguments in favor of this opinion is the difference in style between the Offertory verses and the remaining Gregorian repertory. In fact, prolonged vocalises are not rare in the verses, any more than the repetition of the same word to different melodies (especially in the famous *Quoniam, Quoniam* in the Offertory *Vir erat* reproduced by Ferretti, 219) or the melodic progressions, a procedure vainly sought elsewhere in the repertory. It may be said, however, that certain verses are very old, since they have attained the level of an Offertory antiphon in Ambrosian chant (see Heiming), and that certain passages have been centonized in keeping with the classic composition procedure. Their melody remained in use only until the beginning of the 12th century and has been restored, not without error, by K. Ott. The Offertory of the Mass for the Dead (*see* REQUIEM MASS, MUSIC OF) is the only one that has preserved its verse to the present day. As to the Offertory *Recordare* of Our Lady of Sorrows, it is in fact an old verse from the 20th Sunday after Pentecost (Ott, 126), adapted from the 13th-century Offertory for the feasts of Our Lady (see AnalHymn 49:321 on the tropes adapted from the *a nobis* to the end). The verses reserved to soloists require great vocal flexibility because of their extended range. When the antiphon is written in a plagal mode, the verses are often developed in the corresponding authentic mode (see e.g., Offertory and verses of *Anima nostra* and *Scapulis*). The lyrical quality of Gregorian composition is most exuberant in the verses.

Bibliography: P. M. FERRETTI, *Estetica gregoriana* (Rome 1934) 206–220. O. HEIMING, "Offertori romani pregregoriani nella liturgia milanese," *Ambrosius* (1939) 83–88. R. J. HESBERT, *Un antique offertoire de la Pentecôte: Organicae voces* (Amsterdam 1963) 59–69. E. JAMMERS, *Musik in Byzanz, im päpstlichen Rom und im Frankenreich* (Heidelberg 1962) 115, 162. J. A. JUNGMANN, *The Mass of the Roman Rite*, tr. F. A. BRUNNER, 2 v. (New York 1951–55). C. OTT, ed., *Offertoriale sive versus offertoriorum* (Paris 1935). A. SCHARNAGL, MusGG 9:1901–07. H. SIDLER, *Studien zu alten Offertorien mit ihren Versen* (Fribourg 1939), corrections of Ott's ed. Wagner Greg Mel. G. BAROFFIO, *Die Offertorien der ambrosianischen Kirche* (Cologne 1964) 38–53. J. SMITS VAN WAESBERGHE, *Gregorian Chant*, tr. W. A. G. DOYLE-DAVIDSON (Stockholm 1947). Apel GregCh. **Illustration credit:** Courtesy of the Walters Art Gallery, Baltimore.

[M. HUGLO]

OFFICE, ECCLESIASTICAL

In the broad sense an ecclesiastical office is any employment that is exercised for a spiritual purpose, for example, that of sacristan. However, in the strict sense in which it is used here, it is a position permanently established by divine or ecclesiastical law, conferred according to the norms of Canon Law and bearing with it some participation in the power of Orders or of jurisdiction (CIC c.145.1; *see* HOLY ORDERS; JURISDICTION, POWER OF). In the Oriental Code the concept of office is extended to include functions of persons exercising "some other public ecclesiastical power," e.g., a superior general of sisters (PostApost c.305).

THEOLOGY

The definition of ecclesiastical office as found in the Code of Canon Law (c.145.1) includes three elements: (1) a function—an ability or capacity to perform certain actions tending to a spiritual goal; (2) a stable determination of the range and limits of this function through provisions made by Christ or by His Church; (3) a participation of ecclesiastical authority by those who exercise these functions.

First Element. That there must in the nature of things be found some distinction of activities in the Church follows from its constitution by Our Lord as a true society or people [*see* SOCIETY (IN THEOLOGY)]. The Pauline description of the Church as Body of Christ was precisely invoked by him to justify functional differentiations found from the beginning within the community.

> Now there are varieties of gifts, but the same Spirit; and there are varieties of ministries, but the same Lord; and there are varieties of workings, but the same God, who works all things in all. Now the manifestation of the Spirit is given to everyone for profit. . . . For as the body is one and has many members, and all the members of the body, many as they are, form one body, so also is it with Christ. . . . For the body is not one member, but many. . . . Now if they were all one member, where would the body be? But as it is, there are indeed many members, yet but one body. . . . Now you are the body of Christ, member for member. And God indeed has placed some in the Church, first apostles, secondly prophets, thirdly teachers; after that miracles, then gifts of healing, services of help, power of administration, and the speaking of various tongues. [1 Cor 12.4–29; cf. Rom 12.4–8; Gal 3.27–28; Eph 4.11–13.]

Whether society or Body or vine and branches or kingdom or people or family or household, there must be distribution of activities for the good of the whole.

This division of functions is attested in the *Dogmatic Constitution on the Church* promulgated by Vatican II, when the Council states: "As all the members of the human body, though they are many, form one body, so also are the faithful in Christ (cfr. *1 Cor.* 12, 12). So in the building up of Christ's body a diversity of members and functions obtains. There is only one Spirit, who, according to His own richness and the needs of the ministries, gives His different gifts for the welfare of the Church (cfr. *1 Cor.* 12, 1–11)" [7; Act ApS 57 (1965) 10].

Second Element. If the first element found in the definition of ecclesiastical office is well attested by appeal to reason and to the sources of revelation, it is not perhaps clear that the second element is necessarily attested: the stable determination of the range and limits of these functions by permanent and institutionalized provisions emanating directly from Christ or from the Church. Could it not be that Our Lord intended to bestow functions on a quite temporary basis through a transitory energizing of one or other within the community so that he who today speaks in tongues tomorrow interprets, and he who today prophesies tomorrow is endowed with no special function at all? To the Catholic mind this question is answered not so much by an appeal to the unlikelihood or unnaturalness of such a disposition in an enduring group, or to the confusion and disorder that would so easily result, but by an appeal to the evident intention of Christ in creating the original *apostolate. The Catholic view has always been that Christ selected and separated, prepared and instructed the *Twelve to bear His Person and continue His salvific action, not only through their lifetime but until He should come again.

The history of the first age portrays a community in which the permanent apostolic function is of paramount significance. The same Paul who readily enough admits the divine provenance, the legitimacy, of *charisms peremptorily by reason of his apostolic mandate regulates and restrains charismatic functioning:

> What then is to be done, brethren? When you come together each of you has a hymn, has an instruction, has a revelation, has a tongue, has an interpretation. Let all things be done unto edification. If anyone speaks in a tongue, let it be by twos or at most by threes, and let them speak in turn, and let one interpret. But if there is no interpreter let him keep silence in the church, and speak to himself and to God. Of the prophets, let two or three speak at a meeting, and let the rest act as judges. But if anything is revealed to another sitting by, let the first keep silence. . . . Thus I likewise teach in all the churches of the saints. Let women keep silence in the churches, for it is not permitted them to speak, but let them be submissive, as the Law also says. . . . If anyone thinks that he is a prophet or spiritual, let him recognize that the things I am writing to you are the Lord's commandments. If anyone ignores this, he shall be ignored. [1 Cor 14.26–38.]

Paul at least is not unaware that over and above the ephemeral gifts for community sanctification there stands a stable mission entrusted to the Twelve and to him.

So when in the very early days of the community at Jerusalem there arose a practical problem, the *Apostles did not wait for nor seem to expect any charismatic solution but proceeded without delay to set up an institutional arrangement. To meet the complaints of the Hellenist group that their widows were being slighted in the distribution of alms, the Apostles directed the community to present to them seven suitable candidates, "that we [the Apostles] may put them in charge of this work" (Acts 6.3). In the selection and investiture of the seven one can reasonably discern the beginning and the prototype of subordinate ministries with determined functions. Though some special or charismatic endowments may have been expected of those presented as candidates ["select from among you seven men of good reputation, full of the Spirit and of wisdom" (Acts 6.3)], there can be no question that the determination of the function was made by the Apostles as the established representatives and plenipotentiaries of Christ. In the Pauline Churches as time went on there was through prayer and the *imposition of hands designation of those who in a permanent way functioned as bishops or *presbyters (Acts 14.25; 20.28; Phil 1.1; 1 Tm 3.1–7; 5.17–19) and *deacons (Phil 1.1; 1 Tm 3.8–13) of the individual communities.

Third Element. The third and final element in an ecclesiastical office is that of participation of ecclesiastical authority. The determined function is not merely a service, an accommodation to the needs of others, a labor for the benefit of others, as would be the ministrations of a waiter, an usher, a clerk, an attendant, but a ministration that brings life or helps to maintain life, that directs in the way of God. So the one who holds an office does truly serve, does truly benefit others, but as the father or the guardian who stands in the place of the father serves the family. The basis and justification for all this goes back directly to the role of Christ Himself in the economy of salvation. He came not to be the object of ministrations, but as a minister, a servant, to give His life as a ransom for many, without in the least hesitating to accept the designation of Lord and Master ("You call me Master and Lord, and you say well, for so I am. If, therefore, I the Lord and Master have washed your feet, you also ought to wash the feet

of one another"—Jn 13.13–14). In the Christian scheme of things, paradoxical though it may seem, there is no incompatibility between service and power: it is not to "lord it over them" (Mt 20.25) that some are vested with authority in the community, but that they may more effectively serve by standing in His place to whom "all authority in heaven and on earth has been given" (Mt 28.18). From the days of the Apostles and at the level of the apostolic commission given them, those who hold office in virtue of a power received from on high (Acts 1.8) are to exercise a function that connotes a corresponding obligation on the part of the other members to receive this ministration. There is at once power and lowliness, authority and humility, modesty and majesty in one who says in Christ's name: "If I do not wash thee, thou shalt have no part with me" (Jn 13.8).

That offices in the Church connote at once power and service is the repeated teaching of Vatican Council II: "For those ministers, who are endowed with sacred power, serve their brethren in order that all who are of the people of God and therefore enjoy a true Christian dignity, working toward a common goal freely and in an orderly way, may arrive at salvation. . . . That function however which the Lord committed to the shepherds of His people is a true service, which in S. Scripture is significantly called 'diakonia,' or ministry . . . . Bishops govern the particular Churches . . .

Christ washing the feet of St. Peter, detail of a silver crosier designed by the contemporary German artist Hildegard Domizlaff for the bishop of Essen, Germany.

by their authority and sacred power, which they use only for the development of their flock in truth and holiness, remembering that he who is greater should become the lesser and he who is chief become as the servant . . . . A bishop . . . must keep before his eyes the example of the Good Shepherd, who came not to be ministered unto but to minister . . . and to lay down His life for His sheep (cfr. *Io.* 10, 11)" [*Dogmatic Constitution on the Church* 18, 24, 27; ActApS 57 (1965) 21–22, 29, 32–33].

Finally, the existence of offices so described implies no denial of the fact that there will always be room and welcome in the Church for those who without participating in the ordinary, institutional authority of the Church are mysteriously and charismatically called to providential tasks of reformation, renewal, *aggiornamento*. Of these charismatic gifts Vatican Council II remarks, "whether they be the more outstanding or the more simple and widely diffused, they are to be received with thanksgiving and consolation, for they are especially suited to and useful for the needs of the Church. . . . Judgment however as to their genuineness and proper use belongs to those who are leaders of the Church and to whom in particular it belongs not, indeed, to extinguish the Spirit but to test all things and hold fast to that which is good . . . [*Dogmatic Constitution on the Church* 12; ActApS 57 (1965) 16–17].

See also BISHOP (IN THE CHURCH); PRIMACY OF THE POPE; MYSTICAL BODY OF CHRIST; HIERARCHY; AUTHORITY, ECCLESIASTICAL; DISCIPLINE, ECCLESIASTICAL.

Bibliography: R. NAZ, DDC 6:1074–1105. H. ZELLER et al., LexThK² 1:451–457. M. SCHMAUS, *ibid.* 5:386–387. K. MÖRSDORF, *ibid.* 6:188–192. J. COLSON, *Les Fonctions ecclésiales aux deux premiers siècles* (Bruges 1956). H. VON CAMPENHAUSEN, *Kirchliches Amt und geistliche Vollmacht in den ersten drei Jahrhunderten* (Tübingen 1953). W. MICHAELIS, *Das Ältestenamt der christlichen Gemeinde im Licht der Heiligen Schrift* (Bern 1953). H. ASMUSSEN, *Die Kirche und das Amt* (Munich 1939). D. E. HEINTSCHEL, *The Mediaeval Concept of an Ecclesiastical Office* (CUA CLS 363; Washington 1956).

[S. E. DONLON]

CANON LAW

An ecclesiastical office cannot be validly obtained without a canonical provision, i.e., the granting by competent authority according to the norms of Canon Law. The Church enjoys this right independently of any civil authority. Provision of an office is made by free conferral on the part of a legitimate superior or by investiture granted by the superior after the candidate has been presented by a patron or nominated by one enjoying this right. If a candidate has been elected or postulated, the superior confirms the election or admits the postulation (CIC c.148; ClerSanc c.89).

Restrictions. No one may lawfully be granted an office unless he possesses the qualifications required by law. However, such qualifications are not required for the validity of an appointment unless this is explicitly stated in the law (CIC c.153.3; ClerSanc c.95.3). Clerics alone are capable of exercising jurisdiction and Orders in the Church (CIC c.118; ClerSanc c.53). A candidate must therefore be at least tonsured to receive a valid appointment to an office in the Latin Church. Only a person ordained to the priesthood can validly obtain an office that involves the care of souls (CIC c.154; ClerSanc c.96).

An office is fully vacant only when it lacks both a legitimate titular and an actual incumbent. When an incumbent has no legitimate title to an office, the office is said to be vacant in law but not in fact. Provision for an office that is not vacant in law is null and void; the subsequent vacancy of the office does not rectify the invalid conferral. Neither does a promise of an office that is not vacant in law have any juridical effect (CIC c.150; ClerSanc c.91). If an office is vacant in law but not in fact, the letter of appointment must mention that the incumbent is holding the office in an illegitimate manner (CIC c.151; ClerSanc c.92).

No cleric may be given two incompatible offices. Offices are incompatible when, because of the residence requirements or other duties, the incumbent cannot fulfill the obligations of several offices simultaneously (CIC c.156.1, 2; ClerSanc c.98.1, 2). The superior who accepts the resignation of an incumbent or deprives him of an office cannot validly confer the vacant office on his own or the resigning person's relatives by blood or affinity to the second degree inclusively (CIC c.157; ClerSanc c.99.1). Appointment to all offices should be in writing. This requirement does not ordinarily affect the validity of the conferral but may be necessary to prove the incumbent's right to remain in office. Simoniacal conferral of an office renders it invalid, except for the election of the pope (CIC c.729). The Oriental Code provides that appointment to an office made because of unjust and grave fear, fraud, substantial error, or with *simony is automatically void (ClerSanc c.93).

Loss of Office. An office is lost either by a voluntary act on the part of the incumbent or because of some action on the part of the superior who has the power to confer the office. The expiration of the term causes an office to become vacant, as does the death of the incumbent.

A resignation is a free surrender of an office made for a just cause by the incumbent and accepted by the proper superior. If a resignation is made through grave fear unjustly induced, fraud, substantial error, or simony, it is null and void (CIC c.185; ClerSanc c.127). To be valid a resignation must be made in writing or orally before two witnesses (CIC c.186; ClerSanc c.128).

Privation is the forced removal of a cleric from an office for a just cause. It can be effected by the operation of law or by an act of the legitimate superior. The law provides for automatic deprivation of office in certain cases (CIC cc.188, 2266). Deprivation of an office by a superior can result from a penal or administrative action.

Only a superior who has the right to accept the resignation of an incumbent or to remove him from a former office and promote him to another can transfer him from one office to another. If a transfer is made against the will of a cleric, the same procedure must be employed as for the privation of office unless it concerns the transfer of a pastor (CIC cc.193, 2162–67; ClerSanc c.135).

Bibliography: Abbo 1:145–195. J. MANNING, *The Free Conferral of Offices* (CUA CLS 219; Washington 1945). G. V. MCDEVITT, *The Renunciation of an Ecclesiastical Office* (CUA CLS 218; Washington 1946). C. J. THOMPSON, *The Simple Removal from Office* (CUA CLS 285; Washington 1951).

[A. A. REED]

OFFICE CATHOLIQUE INTERNATIONAL DU CINÉMA

The organization (commonly called OCIC) founded at The Hague in 1928, had laborious beginnings, since the intellectual world found it hard to acknowledge the cinema as being culturally important. Further, the OCIC itself suffered from this mistrust of the cinema; and, after a brilliant congress in Munich (1929), its activities slowed down considerably. The OCIC made a new start with "international study days" (Brussels 1933), at which the statutes were revised and a permanent secretariat established. Under the impetus of its president, Canon Brohée, the OCIC made considerable progress, and several new countries became members, especially after the encyclical *Vigilanti cura* (1936) recognized the cultural significance of the cinema and set the tone for the Church's concern with it. The OCIC planned to make *Vigilanti cura* the subject of deep study at a congress in Vienna in 1938, but the Nazi invasion of Austria put an end to this project. Plans to hold meetings in Prague and Warsaw were similarly frustrated, and the OCIC had to cease all activities on the Continent for the duration of the war, maintaining only a weak nucleus in the Americas.

The first postwar meeting took place in Rome, where it was decided to continue the OCIC's idea and publicize it at an international congress in Brussels in 1947 within the framework of the World Festival of the Movies and the Fine Arts.

Since then, the OCIC has grown constantly and operates in Argentina, Austria, Belgium, Bolivia, Brazil, Canada, Chile, Colombia, Congo (Leopoldville), Cuba, Denmark, Dominican Republic, Ecuador, Egypt, France, West Germany, Great Britain, Haiti, Ireland, Italy, Jamaica, Luxembourg, Malta, Mauritius, Mexico, the Netherlands, Nicaragua, Panama, Paraguay, Peru, Philippine Islands, Poland, Portugal, Salvador, Scotland, Senegal, Spain, Switzerland, the U.S., Uruguay, and Venezuela.

Mission and Doctrine. The OCIC is a federation grouping the various National Catholic Offices of the Cinema, for the purpose of helping them in their work and of assuming, with their approval, tasks that reach beyond national frameworks. The OCIC promotes the creation of such national offices where they do not as yet exist; studies possibilities of collaboration among these institutions; and constitutes a center of studies, information, and impetus for Catholic cinematographic work throughout the world. The OCIC respects the autonomy of its sections and does not impose upon them any uniform doctrine or *modus operandi*. However, through the series of its international study days, the OCIC has contributed significantly in formulating the Church's attitude toward the cinema. The OCIC's early years were concerned largely with protection against the evil influences of the cinema. The moral classification of films was a prime concern of member countries; it was the principal, and sometimes the only, mission undertaken by the national offices. Progressively, however, moral evaluation was accompanied by positive recommendations. The national offices initiated cultural movements: groupings of cinema clubs and organization of courses of study and formation. In several countries, the national offices launched movements of film appreciation in teaching, as well as the organization of movie performances for children.

Structure. The member countries of the OCIC are those where there is a National Catholic Office of the Cinema officially approved by its hierarchy. The OCIC's statutes are approved by the Holy See. The OCIC also has a juridical character in Belgium where it has its headquarters and is recognized as an international organization.

The OCIC's organs are the following. The general council, a general assembly of all member nations, is the supreme authority of the OCIC, where each national office has a voice. It nominates administrative organs, approves accounts and budgets, determines congress sites, etc. The directorial committee is composed of 11 members nominated by the general council. This committee is the executive organ, accomplishing the tasks assigned by the general council. The general secretariat (Rue de l'Orme, 8, Brussels 4, Belgium) comprises the president and the general secretary, charged with daily administration of the organization. Because of the multiplicity of activities, the secretariat is assisted by regional secretaries and specialized secretariats, each covering a particular aspect of the problem of the cinema.

Rapid development in Latin America necessitated the formation of the Secretariat for Latin America (Contumaza 1094, Lima, Peru), charged especially with coordinating programs peculiar to Latin America. In 1963, the first Latin American seminar took place in Lima.

From the beginning, the area of the missions was one of the OCIC's main concerns, and as early as 1933 the congress at Brussels gave it much attention. The Missionary Secretariat (Quattre Fontana, 117, Rome) studies the problems of the cinema in developing countries and helps them to set up national offices to develop eventually into full-fledged members in the General Council.

The Secretariat for Youth (Rue de l'Orme, 10, Brussels 4, Belgium) is a specialized secretariat established in 1950.

The Secretariat for Information (Rue du Faubourg Saint-Honoré, 129, Paris 8°, France), handles public relations and edits and publishes the *Revue Internationale du Cinéma*. Within the framework of its relations with the cinema industry, it carries on a film promotion service to organize world campaigns to launch certain films of value, chosen by an international selection committee.

The growing role of the cinema in the development of modern culture demanded the creation in 1962 of the Secretariat of Cultural Issues (Place de l'Abbaye, 10, Saint-Étienne, France) as a meeting place for persons and organizations dealing more specifically with cinema culture and as a center of studies and documentation. The secretariat is aided by a group of international experts.

Activities, Reunions, and Congresses. The OCIC's doctrine has been developed throughout the years by a series of congresses and international study days; in the following listing by years, subjects of discussion are indicated by being set in quotation marks.

1928. The Hague. Congress. Foundation of the OCIC.

1929. Munich. International Catholic Congress of the Cinema. Publication: G. Ernst and B. Marschall, *Film und Rundfunk* (Munich 1929).

1933. Brussels. Study Days.

1947. Brussels. International Congress. Publications: *Les Catholiques parlent du cinéma* (Paris-Brussels 1948); *Orientaciones catolicas del cine* (Madrid 1950).

1948. Venice. General Council. The council decided to replace international congresses of a general nature by days of study on specific themes, to be held in conjunction with the meetings of the general council.

1949. London. OCIC and film professionals. Publications: *Revue Internationale du Cinéma*, No. 3, 1949; *Internationale Film Revue*, No. 3, 1949; *Revista International del Cine*, No. 3, 1949.

1950. Rome. Congress and pilgrimage of film professionals for the Holy Year.

1951. Lucerne. "The Christian cinema critic and his public." Publications: *Revue Internationale du Cinéma*, No. 10, 1951; *Internationale Film Revue*, No. 3, 1951.

1952. Madrid. "Film appreciation." Publications: *Revue Internationale du Cinéma*, No. 13, 1952; *Revista International del Cine*, No. 2, 1952.

1953. Malta. "The cinema in missionary countries." Publication: *Revue Internationale du Cinéma*, No. 17, 1953.

1954. Cologne. "Moral film classification." Publications: *Revue Internationale du Cinéma*, No. 19–20, 1954; *Revista International del Cine*, No. 8, 1954.

1955. Dublin. "Diffusion and influence of moral film classification." Publications: *Revue Internationale du Cinéma*, No. 22, 1955; *Internationale Film Revue*, No. 5–6, 1955; *Revista International del Cine*, No. 17–18, 1955.

1957. Havana. "Promotion of good films and groupings of cinematographic culture." Publications: *Actes des journées d' étude de La Havane* (Brussels 1957); *Revue Internationale du Cinéma*, No. 26, 1957; *Revista International del Cine*, No. 27, 1957, *Internationale Film Revue*, No. 6, 1957.

1958. Paris. "Promotion of good films directed to the general public and professionals." Publications: *Revue Internationale du Cinéma*, No. 30, 1958; *Revista International del Cine*, No. 32, 1958.

1960. Vienna. "Cinema, youth, and public power." Publications: *Elements of a Legislation* (ed. in English, French, Spanish, and German), 1961; L. Lunders, *La Censure des films et l'admission des enfants au cinéma* (Brussels 1961).

1962. Montreal. "Creators of films and of television broadcasts."

1964. Venice. "Film exhibition and its function in regard to spectators."

OCIC Prizes at Festivals. Since 1947 the OCIC has awarded prizes at the great international festivals to films that by their inspiration and artistic qualities have contributed to spiritual progress and the development of human values. The following table lists the place and year of the festival, the title of the prize-winning film, and the director and country of origin of the film.

Brussels 1947	*Vivere in Pace*, L. Zampa (Italy)
Venice 1948	*The Fugitive*, J. Ford (U.S.)
Knokke 1949	*Home of the Brave*, M. Robson (U.S.)
Venice 1949	*Cielo sulla Palude*, A. Genina (Italy)
Venice 1950	*Dieu a besoin des hommes*, J. Delannoy (France)
Punta del Este 1951	*Intruder in the Dust*, C. Brown (U.S.)
Venice 1951	*Journal d'un curé de campagne*, R. Bresson (France)
Cannes 1952	*Due soldi di speranza*, R. Castellani (Italy)
Venice 1952	*The Quiet Man*, J. Ford (U.S.)
Cannes 1953	*Horizons sans fin*, J. Dréville (France)
Venice 1953	*La guerra de Dios*, R. Gil (Spain)
Cannes 1954	*Die Letzte Brücke*, H. Käutner (Austria-Yugoslavia)
Berlin 1954	*La grande speranza*, G. Coletti (Italy)
Venice 1954	*On the Waterfront*, E. Kazan (U.S.)
Punta del Este 1955	*Sinha Moca*, T. Payne (Brazil)
Cannes 1955	*Marty*, D. Mann (U.S.)
Venice 1955	*Amici per la Pelle*, F. Rossi (Italy)
Cannes 1956	*Il Tetto*, V. de Sica (Italy)
Berlin 1956	*Tuntematon Sotilas*, E. Laine (Finland)
Venice 1956	*Calabuch*, L. Garcia Berlanga (Spain)
Cannes 1957	No prize awarded. Honorable mention to *Celui qui doit mourir*, J. Dassin (France); *Le Notti di Cabiria*, F. Fellini (Italy)
Berlin 1957	*Twelve Angry Men*, S. Lumet (U.S.)
San Sebastian 1957	*Ich Suche Dich*, O. W. Fischer (Germany)
Venice 1957	*A Hatful of Rain*, F. Zinnemann (U.S.)
Cannes 1958	No prize awarded
Brussels 1958	*The Old Man and the Sea*, J. Sturges (U.S.)
Berlin 1958	*Do Anklen Barah Haat*, V. Sgantaram (India)
Venice 1958	No prize awarded
Cannes 1959	*Les 400 Coups*, F. Truffaut (France)
Berlin 1959	*Paradies und Feuerofen*, H. Viktor (Germany)
San Sebastian 1959	*Ari No Machi No Maria*, H. Gosho (Japan)
Venice 1959	*Il Generale della Rovere*, R. Rosselini (Italy)
Cannes 1960	*Paw, garçon entre deux mondes*, A. Henning-Jensen (Denmark)
Berlin 1960	*The Angry Silence*, G. Green (England)
San Sebastian 1960	*Robo No Ishi*, S. Hisamatu (Japan)
Venice 1960	*Voyage en ballon*, R. Lamorisse (France)
Cannes 1961	*The Hoodlum Priest*, I. Kerschner (U.S.)
Berlin 1961	*Question 7*, S. Rosenberg (U.S.)
San Sebastian 1961	No prize awarded
Venice 1961	*Il Posto*, E. Olmi (Italy)
Cannes 1962	*Le Procès de Jeanne d'Arc*, R. Bresson (France)
San Sebastian 1962	*The Miracle Worker*, A. Penn (U.S.)
Berlin 1962	*Sasom I en Spegel*, I. Bergman (Sweden)
Venice 1962	*Term of Trial*, P. Glenville (England)
Mar del Plata 1963	*Noche de Verano*, J. Grau (Spain)
Cannes 1963	*I Fidanzati*, E. Olmi (Italy)
San Sebastian 1963	*Days of Wine and Roses*, B. Edwards (U.S.); *Sono Yowa Wasurenai*, K. Yoshimura (Japan)
Berlin 1963	*Lilies of the Field*, R. Nelson (U.S.)
Venice 1963	*Hud*, M. Ritt (U.S.)

The Grand Prix awarded by the OCIC.

Buenos Aires 1964	*I Compagni*, M. Monicelli (Italy)
Cannes 1964	*Les Parapluies de Cherbourg*, J. Demy (France)
San Sebastian 1964	No prize awarded
Berlin 1964	*Kanojo To Kare*, S. Hani (Japan)
Venice 1964	*Il Vangelo secondo S. Matteo*, P. P. Pasolini (Italy)
Mar del Plata 1965	*Dialogos de la Paz*, J. Felin and J. M. Fant Espina (Spain)

OCIC Grands Prix. Since 1955 the OCIC has also awarded a *grand prix* to a film chosen from 10 or 12 that have won prizes at festivals or to a film that has been proposed by national offices of the OCIC.

1955	*On the Waterfront*, E. Kazan (U.S.)
1956	*The Prisoner*, P. Glenville (England)
1957	*Un Condamné a mort s'est échappé*, R. Bresson (France)
1958	*The Old Man and the Sea*, J. Sturges (U.S.)
1959	*The Diary of Anne Frank*, G. Stevens (U.S.)
1960	*Dialogue des Carmélites*, Agostini and Bruckberger (France)
1961	*Question 7*, S. Rosenberg (U.S.)
1962	*Judgement at Nuremburg*, S. Kramer (U.S.)
1963	*To Kill a Mockingbird*, R. Mulligan (U.S.); *Nattvardsgasterna*, I. Bergman (Sweden)
1964	*Il Vangelo secondo, S. Matteo*, P. P. Pasolini (Italy)

Publications. The OCIC publishes the *Revue Internationale du Cinéma*. Begun in 1949 as a quarterly in English, French, and Spanish, it appeared later as a monthly in French. *Informaciones* is a bimonthly bulletin published in Spanish by the secretariat for Latin America. The *International Exchange Service on Information on the New Films* is a multilingual monthly bulletin on the moral value of movies as given by producing countries. *Filmis,* a quarterly bulletin in English and French, is issued by the missionary secretariat.

Outside Relations. The OCIC, as part of the *Conference of International Catholic Organizations (OIC), participates regularly in its meetings and has several times held a position in its Continuity Committee. In 1954 the OCIC obtained a consultative status at UNESCO. It is also the cofounder (with UNESCO) of the International Film and Television Council (IFTC). Since the reclassification of Non-Governmental Organizations (NGO) with a consultative status, the OCIC has an A status, through the IFTC. The OCIC was again a cofounder (with UNESCO) in 1954 of the International Center of Films for Children. The OCIC delegate is a member of the administrative council of the center by reason of its being a delegate of the NGO of a cultural nature. Since 1963 the OCIC has represented the Holy See on the Committee of Film Experts of the Council of Cultural Cooperation of the Council of Europe. The OCIC is also a member of the Union of International Associations and of the Federation of International Associations established in Belgium.

[L. LUNDERS]

OFFICE OF THE DEAD, one of the oldest special Offices in the Roman Breviary. It goes back at least to the 7th century and may even antedate Gregory the Great (d. 604), for this Office is purely Roman in the arrangement of its Psalms and bears no trace of monastic and Gallican elements, such as introductory prayers and hymns. Its schema is similar to the Office of the last 3 days of Holy Week and these are known to be very primitive. Its original form had only Matins, Lauds, and Vespers. Pius X (d. 1914) added the Little Hours. During the Middle Ages this Office was frequently recited in addition to the Divine Office. Although Pius V (d. 1572) did away with all obligation in the matter, he did leave a twofold Office for the Feast of All Souls. Pius X removed this duplication by making the Office of the Dead the sole Office for November 2. The 1960 Code of Rubrics deleted the Vespers of the Dead formerly added to All Saints' Vespers. In addition to its use on All Souls, the Office of the Dead as a suffrage is prayed in whole or in part by most religious communities as part of the funeral services for a deceased member. The same is done for members of the major ranks of the clergy. In recent years the practice of praying a portion of the Office in the vernacular at wakes for lay people has been introduced and is becoming more and more common.

Bibliography: Eisenhofer Lit 474–475. Miller FundLit 344. Righetti 2:218–219. H. LECLERCQ, DACL 12.2:2006–09. C. CALLEWAERT, *Sacris erudiri* (Steenbrugge 1940) 169–177.

[G. E. SCHIDEL]

OFFICIALIS (JUDICIAL VICAR)

In the canonical system the highest judicial power is vested in the Supreme Pontiff, who has the right to reserve to himself certain particular cases (CIC c.1557.1; SollNostr c.15n1). In a diocese, the natural judge is the local ordinary (CIC c.1572.1; SollNostr c.37.1), who constitutes one tribunal with his officialis, or chief judge, of his court (CIC c.1573.2; SollNostr c.40.2).

History. The idea of the officialis has deep historical roots. In the very early days of the Church it was common for the bishop to use priests for the spiritual ministry, or ministry of the power of orders, and deacons for the direction of temporalities. From the middle of the 4th century the archdeacon occupied a very important position in Church administration. His was the duty of finding clerics, educating them, approving them, and presenting them to the bishop for ordination. Moreover, he took care of the treasures and income of the church. At times he was commissioned to make visitations of the diocese for the bishop. From the 6th century on we find he even had jurisdiction in criminal cases. In the 11th century most of the larger dioceses were divided into districts with an archdeacon in charge of each. The most important of these was the archdeacon of Rome. Gradually the jurisdictional power of archdeacons was recognized as ordinary and not too dependent upon the authority or jurisdiction of the bishop.

They held synods, conducted courts, named and invested pastors, and established penalties against clerics. Appeals were made from their tribunals to the tribunal of the bishop.

In the 12th century bishops had to curb the power of the archdeacons; they did so by establishing the institution of rural deans or vicars. In Rome a vicar-general or officialis was named. He had voluntary and noncriminal jurisdiction along with the jurisdiction of the archdeacon. In many regions of Germany, Spain, and France only voluntary jurisdiction would be given to this new office of vicar-general. Jurisdiction in noncriminal cases was given to another who was named the officialis. The power and juridical figure of the archdeacon gradually fell into desuetude. The Council of Trent reduced the office to practically nothing (sess. 24, cap. 3, 20; sess. 25, cap. 14).

What grew up from particular law in certain places was made universal and an obligation of common law by the Code of Canon Law in 1918, namely, that jurisdiction for noncriminal cases, separate and apart from that of the vicar-general, would be committed to a new office, that of officialis.

Appointment, Qualifications, and Jurisdiction. Canon Law directs the ordinary of a place or the ruling bishop of the diocese to select an officialis who will enjoy ordinary authority for making judgments. He is to be an individual other than the vicar-general, unless the smallness of the diocese or the lack of cases persuades the bishop that this office can be assigned to the vicar-general.

The officialis constitutes one tribunal with the bishop of the place; he cannot judge cases that the bishop reserves to himself. He must be a priest no younger than 30 years of age, of good character, and if he is not a doctor of Canon Law he must at least be advanced in that science. He is removable at the will of the bishop. His office does not cease but perdures during the vacancy of a see. Upon the arrival of a new ordinary, he must be reconfirmed in his office. The jurisdiction of the officialis is ordinary—a description that was given in previous times to the noncriminal jurisdiction of the vicar-general. Since he constitutes one and the same tribunal with the bishop of the place, there is no appeal from his sentence or decision to the bishop; the appeal must be made to the authority to which the bishop himself would appeal. However, even though the officialis has ordinary jurisdiction to judge cases brought before the diocesan tribunal, this jurisdiction is secondary and subordinate to the principal jurisdiction of the bishop.

Functions. Since practically all the cases before a diocesan tribunal today are marriage cases, the work of the officialis is to prepare, study, and judge pleas for nullity brought before the court on any of the grounds described in Church law for such a nullity plea. The formal cases, or those involving baptized people who have been married in what appears to be a valid marriage, must be heard and tried before a panel of three judges. The officialis or one of his associates, a vice-officialis, usually presides at such a panel.

In the Eastern-rite groups there is the same historical background for the development of the office of officialis. Until very recent times the vicar-general conducted the tribunal and held the authority of the officialis; today the judicial authority is separate and inheres in the office of judicial vicar. His role is identical with that of the officialis of the Latin rite.

Bibliography: R. NAZ, DDC 6:1105–11. Abbo 2:759–760. E. FOURNIER, *L'origine du vicaire-général et des autres membres de la curie diocésaine* (Paris 1940). M. LEGA and V. BARTOCETTI, *Commentarius in iudicia ecclesiastica iuxta Codicem iuris canonici*, 3 v. (Rome 1950) 1:112. A. COUSSA, *Epitome praelectionum de iure ecclesiastico orientali*, 2 v. (Grottaferrata 1948) 1:320–327.

[J. S. QUINN]

O'FIHELY, MAURICE, also known as Mauritius de Portu Fildaeo, Scotist Franciscan Conventual; b. Baltimore or Clonfert, Ireland, *c.* 1460; d. Galway, March 25, 1513. He studied at Oxford, became regent of studies at the Franciscan friary in Milan by 1488 and regent at the Padua friary in 1491. Shortly thereafter he held the chair of Scotistic theology in the university. Julius II consecrated him archbishop of Tuam, Ireland, on June 26, 1506. In 1513, having attended the first two sessions of the Fifth Lateran Council, he left Italy to take possession of his diocese, but died on the way. The leading Scotist of his day, he is still one of the best interpreters of John *Duns Scotus, many of whose works he edited. A number of his own theological and metaphysical works were included in the Wadding edition of Scotus's *Opera omnia*. To his contemporaries he was known as *Flos mundi*.

Bibliography: Sbaralea 2:242–243. A. G. LITTLE, *The Grey Friars in Oxford* (Oxford 1892) 267–268. Eubel HierCath 3:340. E. LONGPRÉ, DTC 10.1:404–405.

[P. FEHLNER]

OGDENSBURG, DIOCESE OF (OGDENSBURGENSIS)

Suffragan of the metropolitan See of New York, embracing the northeastern section of the state, an area of 12,036 square miles. The diocese was erected on Feb. 15, 1872; in 1963 it numbered more than 165,000 Catholics in a total population of about 385,700.

In 1749 the first settlement was made by the Sulpician missionary François Picquet, who established a fort and mission on the site of the present city of Ogdensburg. Bishop Henri Marie Dubreuil de Pontbriand of Quebec, Canada, journeyed to the mission in 1752 to baptize and confirm Indian converts. The settlement, called Fort Oswegatchie, was under the British from 1760 to 1796. In 1792, before the evacuation of British troops, the land was purchased by Samuel Ogden, from whom the city, and eventually the diocese, received its name. Since the members of the new settlement were mostly Protestants, there were only 20 Catholic families in Ogdensburg in 1827, when Bp. John Dubois of New York made his visitation. The area of the future diocese was successively under the Dioceses of *New York (1808–47) and *Albany (1847–72).

St. James in Carthage, where Count James LeRay de Chaumont brought Irish and German settlers in 1818, was the first parish in the area to be legally incorporated (1825). About 30 years later Carthage became the center of controversy over *trusteeism, and the parish was placed under interdict by Bp. (later Cardinal) John McCloskey. When Pius IX established the Diocese of Ogdensburg in 1872, Edgar P. *Wadhams, a native of Essex County, N.Y., and a convert from the Episcopal church, was named first bishop and served the diocese until his death in 1891. His successors included Belgian-born Henry Gabriels, professor at Troy, N.Y., seminary, who was consecrated for Ogdensburg on May 5, 1892, and governed the see until his death, April 23, 1921. The third ordinary, Joseph H. Conroy, was consecrated titular bishop of Arindela and auxiliary of Ogdensburg on May 1, 1912, and succeeded to the see, Nov. 21, 1921. Under his direction the diocesan minor seminary, Wadhams Hall, was established in 1924. When Conroy died on March 20, 1939, his coadjutor, Francis Joseph Monaghan, who had been consecrated in 1936, succeeded to the see and ruled until his death, Nov. 13, 1942. Bryan J. McEntegart was appointed fifth bishop and consecrated on Aug. 3, 1943. Before his transfer in 1953 to the rectorship of The Catholic University of America, Washington, D.C., he supervised the construction of St. Mary's Cathedral. The sixth bishop, Walter P. Kellenberg, who was appointed, Jan. 19, 1954, was transferred to the Diocese of Rockville Centre, N.Y., on April 16, 1957. The auxiliary of Raleigh, N.C., James J. Navagh, succeeded Kellenberg, May 8, 1957, but was transferred to Paterson, N.J., Feb. 12, 1963. Leo R. Smith, auxiliary of Boston, whose brief episcopate in Ogdensburg began Feb. 12, 1963, died suddenly in Rome 7 months later while he was attending Vatican Council II. Ogdensburg's ninth bishop, Thomas A. Donnellan, rector of St. Joseph's Seminary, Yonkers, N.Y., was consecrated by Cardinal Francis Spellman in St. Patrick's Cathedral on April 9, 1964. His diocese then numbered 269 priests, 56 brothers, and 623 sisters, serving 117 parishes, 1 college for women (*Mater Dei), 14 high and 38 elementary schools, 4 hospitals, 3 schools for nurses, 1 orphanage, and 4 homes for the aged.

Bibliography: J. T. SMITH, *History of the Diocese of Ogdensburg* (New York 1885); *The Catholic Church in New York*, 2 v. (New York 1908).

[J. G. BAILEY]

OGILVIE, JOHN, BL., Jesuit, the only officially recognized martyr in post-Reformation Scotland; b. Scotland, 1579 or 1580; d. Glasgow Cross, March 10 (N.S.), 1615 (feast, March 10; Jesuits, Feb. 20). In his deposition (Oct. 15, 1614) after his capture he gave his father's name as "Walter Ogilvie of Drum." As a Jesuit novice he had described himself as "Strathilensis," "of Strathisla." His family may thus have been associated with Drum-na-Keith, in Strathisla, Banffshire. In the deposition he also noted his absence from Scotland for 22 years, i.e., from 1591 or 1592. One of his name matriculated at Helmstedt, Aug. 19, 1592. Ogilvie was at the Scots College, Louvain (later established at Douai), in 1596; it was there that he, a Calvinist in his youth, became a Catholic. Because of the poverty of the college he was sent in 1598 to Regensburg; he moved to Olmutz, still a lay student. Finally, he became a Jesuit novice at Brno in 1599. He took his vows at the Jesuit College at Graz, Dec. 26, 1601. His 5 years there were later commemorated in a biography [in *Undeni Graecenses Academici*, by M. Bonbardi, SJ (Graz 1727)]. After an interval of teaching he began theology at Olmutz. In 1610 he moved to Paris, where he was afterward ordained. He was afterward stationed at Rouen, but kept importuning the superior general to send him to Scotland. At last his request was granted. In 1613 he began his short missionary career in Scotland, working mostly in Edinburgh, Renfrewshire, and Glasgow. He was betrayed in Glasgow, Oct.

Bl. John Ogilvie, drawing after the "Roman" portrait.

14 (N.S.), 1614, and remained thereafter in captivity. His own account of his imprisonment was smuggled out of prison. He suffered extreme torture, but showed great courage and skill in defending the spiritual supremacy of the pope. He was ultimately sentenced to death, hanged at Glasgow Cross, and buried in the criminals' plot of an unidentified burial ground outside the city. No relic of his body remains. His cause was introduced under the rules drawn up by Urban VIII in 1625. The first process opened at Würzburg in May 1628; the following January a similar process began in Rome. Nearly 3 centuries later the Apostolic Process opened in Glasgow, July 12, 1927. The beatification, by Pope Pius XI, took place on Dec. 22, 1929. Since then, two vice postulators have been appointed: Father James Quinn (in 1960) and Father Thomas Reilly (in 1963), parish priest of Bl. John Ogilvie's, Easterhouse, Glasgow. Other centers of devotion exist at St. Thomas's, Keith, Banffshire; St. Aloysius's, Garnethill, Glasgow; Sacred Heart, Edinburgh; and Craighead House, Bothwell. Each year the martyrdom is commemorated at Glasgow Cross on the Sunday nearest to March 10th. There are two main portraits: the "Douai" portrait, now at the church of S. Gilles, Pecquincourt, Nord, France; and the "Roman" portrait, now at the Gesù, Rome. An illustration (unrelated to either) is given in Bonbardi's *Undeni Graecenses Academici*.

Bibliography: W. E. BROWN, *John Ogilvie . . .* (London 1925). T. COLLINS, *Martyr in Scotland . . .* (London 1955). Butler Th Attw 1:552–556. L. MACFARLANE, LexThK² 7:1121. C. TESTORE, EncCatt 9:85–86. G. G. SMITH, DNB 14:912–914.

[J. QUINN]

O'GORMAN, THOMAS

Bishop, educator; b. Boston, Mass., May 1, 1843; d. Sioux Falls, S.Dak., Sept. 18, 1921. He was the first of four children born to John and Margaret (O'Keefe)

O'Gorman. The family moved west to Chicago, Ill. (1848); with John O'Gorman's childhood friend Richard Ireland and his family, among whom was the future Abp. John *Ireland, they resumed their westward trek

Thomas O'Gorman.

to St. Paul, Minn. (1852). That same year Thomas O'Gorman and John Ireland enrolled among the first students of Bp. Joseph Cretin's Latin School on the upper floor of the frontier Cathedral of St. Paul—the first seminarians of the diocese. When O'Gorman was 10 years old and Ireland 15, they were sent to the minor seminary of the Marists at Meximieux, France, and subsequently to the major seminary at Montbel. O'Gorman returned to St. Paul and was ordained by Bp. Thomas Grace on Nov. 5, 1865. He was first assigned to Rochester, Minn., where he built St. John's church and became known as a preacher and organizer. In 1877 he resigned to join the Society of St. Paul, continuing his preaching in the New York area and converting the financier Thomas Fortune *Ryan to the Catholic Church. He was recalled (1882) to St. Paul by his friend, now Bp. John Ireland, and assigned to Faribault as pastor, and later (1885) as first rector of the newly established St. Paul Seminary and president of St. Thomas College there. After 2 years he resigned to teach dogmatic theology, English, and French in the college. During these years he wrote several articles and deepened his knowledge of ecclesiastical history. In 1890 he was appointed professor of church history in The Catholic University of America, Washington, D.C., where he actively supported the liberal policies of the Americanists during the several controversies of the late 19th century in American Catholicism (*see* AMERICANISM). He wrote *A History of the Roman Catholic Church in the United States* (1895), a summary of the original research of John Gilmary *Shea.

On Jan. 24, 1896, O'Gorman was appointed bishop of Sioux Falls, a suffragan see of the Province of St. Paul, where his friend John Ireland was the first archbishop. The new bishop was consecrated by Abp. Francesco Satolli, first Apostolic Delegate to the U.S., in St. Patrick's Church, Washington, D.C., on April 19, 1896, and installed in the procathedral of his see on May 2, 1896. At that time the diocese had 51 diocesan and 14 regular clergy, 50 churches with resident priests, 61 missions with churches, 100 stations, 10 chapels, 14

parochial schools, 61 Indian schools, 2 orphanages, and 1 hospital. There were 3 communities of religious men and 6 of women in the diocese; and the total Catholic population, both Indian and white, was estimated at 30,000.

O'Gorman, who began his active pastoral apostolate with energy, wrote to his friend Denis O'Connell from "Avignon": "I fear I must resign myself to being the routine Bishop of an unknown Western diocese, and I assure you I find enough work to do as such." New hospitals were opened at Yankton and Pierre (1897), Aberdeen (1901), Sioux Falls (1910), and Mitchell and Milbank (1921). The vast extent of the diocese and growth in population encouraged an east-west division in South Dakota in 1902 between Sioux Falls and Lead (changed to Rapid City in 1930). During his administration in Sioux Falls, O'Gorman continued his Roman contacts and visits and was appointed (1902), through the offices of Archbishop Ireland, to the Taft Commission to deal with Rome regarding the friars' land problem in the Philippine Islands. St. Joseph's Cathedral in Sioux Falls was completed in 1919, and Columbus College was begun in 1909, first in Chamberlain and after 1921 in Sioux Falls, and continued until it was closed in 1939 because of financial difficulties. At the close of O'Gorman's 26 years as bishop of Sioux Falls, the Catholic population had doubled to 69,164 and there were 127 diocesan and 13 religious priests serving 114 churches and 83 missions in his jurisdiction.

[C. BARRY]

O'HANLON, JOHN, Irish hagiographer; b. Stradbally, County Laoighis, April 30, 1821; d. Sandymount, Dublin, May 15, 1905. Educated in the seminary at Carlow, he accompanied his parents to the U.S. (1842) and was ordained for the Diocese of St. Louis (1847). He worked among Irish immigrants and wrote a guide for them (1851). Poor health caused his return to Ireland (1853), where he became assistant chaplain of the South Dublin Union (1854–59) and then curate at St. Michael's and St. John's parish (1859–80). He was appointed pastor of Sandymount (1880) and made a canon (1886). O'Hanlon wrote extensively for the Irish and Irish-American press on the Church history, hagiography, and folklore of Ireland. While a curate, he did extensive research on Irish history in archives and libraries on the Continent, in England, and in Ireland. Concerning the Irish in America he wrote *Life and Scenery in Missouri* (1890), a book of reminiscences, and an *Irish American History of the United States* (1903). His best known work was his *Lives of Irish Saints* (1875–1905). He began work on it by 1856 and completed 9 of the projected 12 volumes. He published also lives of St. Lawrence O'Toole (1857), St. Malachy (1859), St. Dympna (1863), St. Aengus the Culdee (1868), St. David of Menevia (1869), and St. Grellen (1881). O'Hanlon's hagiography was popular. Much of it has become dated, but his *Lives of Irish Saints* still retains value.

Bibliography: D. J. O'DONAGHUE, DNB (1901–11) 3:41–42. E. A. D'ALTON, CE 11:224.

[T. P. JOYCE]

O'HARA, EDWIN VINCENT

Bishop, sociologist; b. Lanesboro, Minn., Sept. 6, 1881; d. Milan, Italy, Sept. 11, 1956. His parents, Owen and Margaret (Nugent) O'Hara, sent him to public schools for his early education. Later he entered St. Thomas College and the Seminary of St. Paul, St. Paul, Minn. He was accepted for the Archdiocese of Oregon City (later Portland), Ore., and was ordained June 10, 1905, in St. Paul. His first assignment by Abp. Alexander Christie was as assistant at the cathedral in Portland. In 1907 he formed the Summer Institute for Teachers and the Catholic Education Association of Oregon. Following a period of ill health in 1910, he spent a year of advanced study at The Catholic University of America, Washington, D.C. Upon returning to Portland, he demonstrated a practical concern for social rights characteristic of the Progressive Movement of that period. His initial interest was in the struggle for minimum wages for women and a general minimum-wage law. Supported by the National Consumers League, he led a committee whose report was instrumental in the enactment in 1913 of the Oregon minimum-wage law, which was to be tested in the courts in the case of *Stettler v. O'Hara.* O'Hara's role in the making of this legislation was indicated when Gov. Oswald West named him chairman of the new State Industrial Welfare Commission.

Apart from such achievements, however, it was in the area of rural sociology that O'Hara was to attain his greatest reputation. After his return from service as chaplain with the U.S. Army in France in 1918, he began to promote Catholic education in rural districts. In 1920 at the *National Catholic Welfare Conference (NCWC) he proposed the establishment of the Rural Life Bureau and became its first chairman. After obtaining a transfer to the rural parish of Eugene, Ore., he devoted himself to the problems of country life, publishing *A Program of Catholic Rural Action* (1922) and *The Church and the Country Community* (1927) and convening the first *National Catholic Rural Life Conference in St. Louis, Mo., in 1923. O'Hara's interest in rural welfare was combined with concern for education. In 1922 he had organized the first Catholic Religious Vacation School and, when the Oregon School Bill requiring compulsory attendance at public schools was proposed, he led the fight against it with the aid of many noted jurists. As archdiocesan superintendent of schools, he conducted litigation in state courts and the U.S. Supreme Court that resulted in the Oregon law being declared unconstitutional. From 1929 to 1930 O'Hara was directly engaged in teaching, offering courses in parish sociology at The Catholic University of America and, during the summer, at the University of Notre Dame, Ind.

On Nov. 5, 1930, O'Hara was consecrated as bishop of Great Falls, Mont. From the start of his episcopacy he sought to advance the Confraternity of Christian Doctrine. After establishing the Confraternity in his diocese on Dec. 17, 1930, he helped to form a Rocky Mountain and Pacific Coast Confraternity and to establish national headquarters for the Confraternity at The Catholic University of America. He secured the appointment of a committee of the hierarchy to study the question, and was instrumental in obtaining a letter from the Congregation of the Council on Jan. 12, 1933, requiring the establishment of the Confraternity in each diocese. Thereafter a national center for the Confraternity was located at NCWC headquarters in Washington, D.C., and on Oct. 31, 1935, the first Congress of the Confraternity was held in Rochester, N.Y. Catechetical reform and Biblical translation received attention also from Bishop O'Hara. He headed a committee of bishops who prepared a revision of the Baltimore Catechism, which had not been changed since its adoption by the Third Plenary Council, 1884. The revision was published June 21, 1941, under the auspices of the Confraternity. In January 1936 O'Hara organized a committee of theologians and Scripture scholars to discuss a revised English translation of the Scriptures. Subsequently, the Catholic Biblical Association of America was formed on Oct. 3, 1936, and the *Catholic Biblical Quarterly* began publication in 1938. In 1952, the anniversary of the invention of printing and of the publication of the Gutenberg Bible, the Confraternity of Christian Doctrine published its first volume of the revised version of the Old Testament, containing eight historical books. At this time O'Hara received a special letter of commendation from Pius XII.

On April 16, 1939, O'Hara was appointed to the See of Kansas City, Mo. (changed on Aug. 29, 1956, to Kansas City–St. Joseph). There he earned the title of "the building Bishop," adding, within 10 years, 42 churches, 14 convents, 16 grade schools, 6 high schools, and 2 colleges. In September 1954 O'Hara was made personal archbishop. He died while on his way to the International Congress of the Restored Liturgy in Assisi, Italy.

Bibliography: J. G. SHAW, *Edwin Vincent O'Hara, American Prelate* (New York 1957).

[T. T. MC AVOY]

O'HARA, JOHN FRANCIS

Cardinal; b. Ann Arbor, Mich., May 1, 1888; d. Philadelphia, Pa., Aug. 28, 1960. As the son of John and Eleanor (Thornton) O'Hara, he received his early education in the parochial grade school and public high school of Peru, Ind., where his father was a practicing lawyer. Later he studied at the Collegio de Sagrada Corazon in Montevideo, Uruguay, where his father served as American consul. On returning to the U.S., he entered the University of Notre Dame, Ind., where he taught Spanish while earning his bachelor of philosophy degree. He entered the novitiate of the Congregation of Holy Cross, Aug. 15, 1912, made his first profession Sept. 14, 1914, and was ordained in Indianapolis, Ind., on Sept. 9, 1916, by Bp. Joseph Chartrand. He spent the 1st year of his priesthood in historical studies at The Catholic University of America, Washington, D.C., followed by a summer at the Wharton School of Commerce at the University of Pennsylvania, Philadelphia. In September 1917 he returned to Notre Dame University and established a department of commerce in response to the increased enrollment of prospective businessmen in the university. With O'Hara as dean, this became the College of Commerce in 1920.

In his priestly activities, O'Hara began to manifest the same zeal in administering the Sacraments that he had shown as a builder of the business school. While acting as a counselor to the students, he urged them to take advantage of the possibility of frequent and even daily Holy Communion, which had been revived by the decrees of Pius X. He was made prefect of religion and gave up his deanship to devote his time to this work and to teaching some classes in religion. Despite the increasing enrollment in the university after World War I, he literally became acquainted with nearly every one of the 2,000 or more students. To reach them, he began to post and later to distribute a one-page religious

Cardinal John Francis O'Hara.

bulletin in which he combined criticism of student weaknesses with strong inspiration. In 1933, when Rev. Charles O'Donnell, CSC, President of Notre Dame University, became fatally ill, O'Hara was appointed acting president. He was elected president the following year. His presidency was signalized by the increase and advancement of the faculty, the erection of new buildings, and the expansion of undergraduate work. On Dec. 11, 1939, Pius XII named him titular bishop of Milasa and military delegate to Abp. (later Cardinal) Francis Spellman of New York, Military Vicar of the Armed Forces of the U.S. O'Hara was consecrated Jan. 15, 1940, at Notre Dame by Spellman; he established headquarters in New York, where he was joined by Bp. William T. McCarty, CSSR.

Because of the draft law and the expansion of the army and navy after World War II began in Europe, the office of military delegate acquired a great importance that was increased when the U.S. entered the war in December 1941. O'Hara not only administered the central office in New York, but visited personally the camps and offices of the chaplains, administering the Sacrament of Confirmation and looking into the spiritual welfare of soldiers and sailors. He reorganized the military ordinariate, setting up eight military vicar delegates, and during the war he supervised nearly 5,000 priests who attended to the religious needs of Catholics in the Armed Forces.

On March 10, 1945, O'Hara was transferred to the See of Buffalo, N.Y., where he was installed by Spellman on May 8, 1945. During his episcopate, he renovated the cathedral church, established new parishes,

introduced new religious communities, and held a National Eucharistic Congress in 1947. O'Hara was appointed to the See of Philadelphia, vacated by the death of Cardinal Dennis Dougherty on Dec. 28, 1951, and he was installed by Abp. Amleto Cicognani, Apostolic Delegate, on Jan. 9, 1952. O'Hara brought to his new position the same zeal for Catholic education and for frequent reception of the Sacraments that had characterized his work as chaplain at Notre Dame University, as military delegate, and as bishop of Buffalo. He established 55 new parishes and 14 new Catholic high schools, and reorganized the administration of the archdiocesan charities. He continued his efforts to have personal contact with both clergy and laity. John XXIII made him a member of the College of Cardinals Dec. 15, 1958. Already his active career as priest and administrator had begun to weaken his health. Although frequently hampered by arthritis and other infirmities, the cardinal endeavored to meet all his commitments. He died in Philadelphia, and his body was returned to Sacred Heart Church at Notre Dame for burial.

Bibliography: Articles by T. T. MCAVOY et al., in RecAmCHS Phila 64.1 (1953) 3–56. **Illustration credit:** American Catholic Historical Collections, St. Charles Seminary, Philadelphia.

[T. T. MC AVOY]

O'HELY, PATRICK, Irish bishop of Mayo, martyr; b. west Ireland, probably Connacht (formerly Connaught), date unknown; d. Kilmallock, County Limerick, 1579. Little is known with certainty of his early career beyond his education in Spain and Italy by the Franciscans, his ordination, and his consecration as bishop of Mayo c. 1576. In this period of Irish history the Celtic clergy, and especially the hierarchy on the continent, were barred from relieving Irish Catholics at home of their shortage of priests and the Tudor government kept a constant vigil on all Irish harbors to prevent European-ordained clerics from returning. But Bishop O'Hely, with a number of clerical companions, slipped into Ireland by following a round-about course through Dingle Bay into Kerry not far from Tralee. Although he eluded the royal guards who were assigned to search ships, he was turned over to the royal authorities by an informer a few weeks after his arrival. Following his arrest he was summoned before Sir William Drury, the king's representative at Kilmallock in County Limerick. O'Hely refused to deny his faith or recognize Queen Elizabeth I as head of the church. He and his close companion Father Cornelius O'Rorke (O'Rourke) were tortured, placed on the rack, their legs and arms broken with hammers, and sharp instruments wedged into the nails of their fingers and toes. After several days of torment both were hanged and their bodies suspended on the gallows for more than 2 weeks.

Bibliography: W. M. BRADY, *The Episcopal Succession in England, Scotland, and Ireland, A. D. 1400 to 1875,* 3 v. (Rome 1876–77). J. S. CRONE, *Concise Dictionary of Irish Biography* (rev. ed. Dublin 1937). M. W. P. O'REILLY, *Memorials of Those Who Suffered for the Faith in Ireland* (London 1868). A. J. WEBB, *Compendium of Irish Biography* (Dublin 1878). A. F. POLLARD, DNB 14:959.

[E. J. MURRAY]

O'HIGGINS, BERNARDO, Chilean political and military leader; b. Chillán, Chile, Aug. 20, 1778; d. Lima, Peru, Oct. 23, 1842. He received his early education in Chillán from the Franciscans and continued his studies in Lima and London. In England he met the Venezuelan Francisco de Miranda, who introduced him to the ideals of American independence. On his return to Chile in 1802 O'Higgins promoted the idea of independence among his friends. Napoleon's invasion of Spain 6 years later brought the opportunity for action. In 1811, as a deputy to the first Chilean Congress, O'Higgins stood out because of his reformist spirit. In 1812 he was a member of the junta, but soon retired to attend to his agricultural business. In 1813, when the viceroy of Peru sent an expedition to suppress the Chilean revolution, O'Higgins came out of retirement. With the rank of colonel, he fought in San Carlos, Chillán, and El Roble, and his integrity and his proverbial battle cry, "Let us live in honor or die in glory," saved the patriotic troops from defeat. Shortly afterward he was appointed commander in chief. In view of the adverse turn in the war he had to sign an agreement to negotiate with the Spaniards in Lircay on May 3, 1814. However, the refusal of the viceroy of Peru to accept any solution that did not involve the unconditional surrender of the patriots and José Miguel Carrera's overthrow of the government that had sanctioned the agreement of Lircay set off the war anew. O'Higgins, although he repudiated Carrera's action, joined him to fight the common enemy. In the fruitless resistance at Rancagua on Oct. 1 and 2, 1814, his exit on horseback from the beseiged square, opening a path with some soldiers through the barricades, was one of the most heroic episodes of his life. Until 1817 he lived in exile in Mendoza, where he collaborated with José de *San Martín in organizing the Army of the Andes. At the head of one of its divisions, he crossed the Andes and defeated the Spaniards in Chacabuco on Feb. 12, 1817. An assembly in Santiago elected him Supreme Director. As such, he stimulated education, created a navy, and with San Martín prepared the liberating expedition to Peru in 1820. He dictated two political constitutions intended to strengthen his authority. Although he exiled the bishop of Santiago for being a royalist, he recognized Catholicism as the official religion, sent a diplomatic representative to the Pope, and gave public evidence of religious faith. Pressured by those who wanted a more liberal regime, he left the government in January 1823 and retired to a hacienda in Peru. He was buried in the Franciscan habit.

Bibliography: *Archivo de don Bernardo O'Higgins* (Santiago de Chile 1946–), 29 v. pub. to 1965. J. EYZAGUIRRE, *O'Higgins* (6th ed. Santiago de Chile 1965); *La actitud religiosa de don Bernardo O'Higgins* (Santiago de Chile 1961).

[J. EYZAGUIRRE]

OHIO

Located in the Great Lakes region of the Middle West, admitted (1803) to the Union as the 17th state. The Ohio River, from which the state takes its name, flows along its southern and southeastern borders, separating it from Kentucky and West Virginia, respectively; the state is bounded by Indiana on the west, Michigan and Lake Erie on the north, and by Pennsylvania on the northeast. Columbus is the capital (since 1816); Cleveland, Cincinnati, and Toledo are among its largest cities.

History. Earthen mounds are the only remains of the earliest settlers, probably ancestors of the American Indians who are referred to as Mound Builders. The Eries, probably the only native Indian tribe, were driven west (1655) by the Iroquois, who claimed the area as their hunting ground until other Indians moved in about 1700. Numbering about 15,000 in 1750, the Indians prevented the settlement of the area by the white man until after the Treaty of Greenville in 1795. The first white men were French explorers, traders, and missionaries from Canada. Robert C. de La Salle sailed down

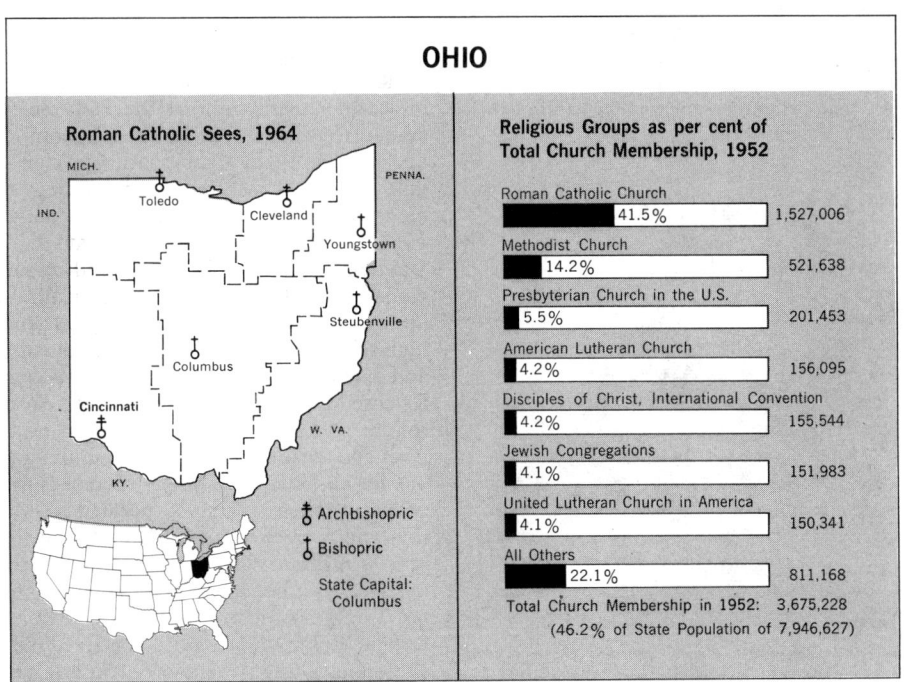

Church-membership statistics were compiled by the Bureau of Research and Survey of the National Council of the Churches of Christ in the U.S.A.

the Ohio (1669); Céleron de Blainville, accompanied by Joseph de Bonnechamps, SJ, led an exploration into the country (1749) to reassert the French claims after a group of Virginians had formed the Ohio Company to trade with the Indians and to cut the French line of communication between Canada and Louisiana. The Treaty of Paris (1763) gave the territory to the English, who placed it under the jurisdiction of Quebec (1764). It was ceded to the U.S. by the treaty of Paris (1783), George Rogers Clark having defended it during the Revolution. The Indians resisted American settlers and were supported by the British until the latter were forced to withdraw under the terms of Jay's Treaty (1796). Congress provided for the survey of the territory with the Land Ordinance of 1785; by 1786 most of the claims of individual states to the area had been turned over to the Federal government. The Northwest Ordinance of 1787 granted territorial government to the Northwest Territory and set the approximate boundaries of the future state of Ohio. The first permanent settlement under the Ordinance was made at Marietta by the Ohio Company (1788). The Symmes Purchase (1794) in the Cincinnati area and the settlement of the Connecticut Western Reserve in 1796 in the Cleveland area established the sites of what later became two of the state's largest cities.

Jesuit missionaries worked among the Ohio Indians in the Sandusky area, where Armand de la Richardie, SJ, built a chapel (1751). In 1795 Rev. Edmund Burke of Quebec ministered to the Indians and to the British garrisons in the same area, which shortly after became the responsibility of Bp. John Carroll of Baltimore, Md. Priests from Kentucky, especially the Dominicans, next served the area where the first chapel was erected near Somerset on Dec. 6, 1818. The Diocese of *Cincinnati was created on June 19, 1821, with Edward Fenwick as its first bishop. After northern Ohio developed with the building of the canals, an influx of Irish and Germans led to the creation of the Diocese of *Cleveland on April 23, 1847; and 3 years later Cincinnati became an archdiocese. Subsequently the southeastern section of Ohio was separated from Cincinnati and the Diocese of *Columbus was created (1868); in northern Ohio, the

St. Joseph's Church, Somerset, Ohio, second church on the site of the first Catholic worship in Ohio. A log chapel, dedicated by Bishop Fenwick, was dedicated there on Dec. 6, 1818.

Diocese of *Toledo was established (1910); the Diocese of *Youngstown was created in the northeastern part of the state (1943); and in 1944 the Diocese of *Steubenville was separated from Columbus, the latter receiving some territory from Cincinnati in exchange.

During the formative years of the Church in Ohio, every effort was made to increase the clergy, resist nativism, further Catholic education, absorb the immigrants, meet the language problems of the non-English-speaking immigrants, and care for the poor and orphaned. Provincial councils were held in Cincinnati in 1855, 1858, 1861, 1882, and 1889. Diocesan synods legislated on matters of local interest. Bishops from Ohio participated in the three Plenary Councils of *Baltimore; Bp. J. B. *Purcell contributed notably to the first two, and Bp. R. *Gilmour of Cleveland played a very important part in the third. The Catholic press also was important in Ohio. The *Catholic Telegraph* was first printed in Cincinnati on Oct. 22, 1831; the *Wahreitsfreund,* the first German-American Catholic periodical, was published from 1837 to 1907; the *Catholic Universe,* later the *Catholic Universe Bulletin,* has been published in the Cleveland diocese since 1874.

Population. In 1821, when Ohio had a population of 581,295, only about 6,000 of them were Catholics. In 1952 the state population stood at 7,946,627, of whom Catholics constituted 19.2 per cent; Protestants, 25.2 per cent; Jews, 1.9 per cent; and all others, 53.7 per cent (*see* CHURCH MEMBERSHIP, U.S.). In 1961 Ohio's total population had increased to more than 9,600,000 and the Catholic proportion to about 21 per cent.

Education. School attendance is compulsory for children between the ages of 6 and 18, although individual cases may be decided by the superintendent of the school district. The legislature has empowered the state board of education to set standards of teacher certification, supervise the curriculum, determine the length of the school day and the school year for private and public schools, to charter all high schools, and to initiate legal processes to close schools that do not observe standards. Ohio's Catholic school system includes the Pontifical College Josephinum, a seminary directly under the jurisdiction of the Holy See; it trains diocesan priests who receive their appointments from the apostolic delegate. Cincinnati, Cleveland, and Steubenville have major diocesan seminaries, and these three along with Columbus have minor seminary facilities. In 1964 there were 2,686 seminarians in 28 institutions. Dayton, John Carroll (Cleveland), and Xavier (Cincinnati) are the largest of the 13 Catholic colleges that in 1964 enrolled more than 24,000 students. Catholic high school enrollment in 127 schools was about 74,300, and elementary enrollment in 630 schools was 306,575. Released-time programs provided religious instruction for an additional 102,873 children on the elementary level and for the same number on the high school level.

Church-State Relations. References to and provisions affecting religion are incorporated in the state constitution and in acts of the legislature and the judiciary.

Constitution. Ohio is governed by the Constitution of 1851, as amended. The preamble states that the people are "grateful to Almighty God for our freedom." Article 1, sec. 7, provides for freedom of conscience. Preferences to any religion or interferences with rights of conscience are forbidden. No religious test may be required for holding office, nor may a person be judged incompetent as a witness because of religious beliefs; however, "nothing herein shall be construed to dispense with oaths or affirmation."

The senate tries impeachments and at such time its members must be under oath or affirmation (art. 2, sec. 23). General laws may be passed to exempt from taxation houses used exclusively for public worship (art. 12, sec. 2).

"Every person chosen or appointed to any office under this state, before entering upon the discharge of its duties, shall take an oath or affirmation, to support the Constitution of the United States, and of this state, and also an oath of office" (art. 15, sec. 7).

Marriage and Divorce. Marriages of men under 18 and women under 16 are forbidden except in certain cases of emergency. The consent of parents is needed for persons under 21. A license and blood test are required. Certain public officials and clergy may perform the ceremony. Common-law marriages are recognized. Marriages are void if the parties are related by blood in any degree of the direct line, and up to and including first cousins; if one of the parties is a habitual drunkard, epileptic, imbecile, or insane person. Marriages may be annulled on the following grounds: prior subsisting marriage, nonage, mental incompetency, fraud, force, nonconsumation of marriage.

The grounds for absolute divorce are: prior subsisting marriage, willful absence for 1 year, adultery, impotency, extreme cruelty, fraudulent contract, gross neglect of duty, habitual drunkenness, imprisonment, and when a divorce is granted in another state to one party and the obligations remain on the plaintiff in Ohio. There are no restrictions on the remarriage of divorced persons. *See* MARRIAGE, U.S. LAW OF; DIVORCE (U.S. LAW OF).

Abortion, Birth Control, Sterilization. The law forbids *abortion unless two physicians advise it as necessary to save the woman's life. Attempts to procure miscarriages are forbidden; if the woman miscarries or dies as a result of such an attempt, the offender may be imprisoned for not less than 1 or more than 7 years.

The law restricts *birth control. No person may sell, give away, or keep for sale or gratuitous distribution, a secret drug or nostrum purporting to be exclusively for the use of females or for preventing conception (*see* CONTRACEPTION; ANOVULANTS). An exception is made for physicians and pharmacists, and advertising in legitimate medical magazines is allowed.

Although the law does not provide for *sterilization by statute, the Ohio probate court was the first court of record to have a mental defective sterilized without express legislative authority [v. 180, North Eastern Reports (second), 206].

Property and Taxation. Religious societies and charities may incorporate under the Non-Profit Corporation Law. In most cases church property belonging to archdioceses and dioceses is held in trust by the respective ordinaries for the use and benefit of the congregation. Real and personal property of religious societies not run for profit is exempt from taxation. Land and tenements conveyed in trust to religious societies for a meeting house, burial ground, or residence for a preacher's house, have perpetual succession, if not in excess of 20 acres. If a testator dies leaving issue, an adopted child or lineal descendants of either, and if the will of such testator gives, devises, or bequeaths his estate or a part thereof for any benevolent, religious, educational, or charitable purpose, or to the state or county or branches thereof, such gift, devise, or bequeath is invalid unless executed at least 1 year prior to the death of the testator. Professional fund raisers and solicitors must register. The regulations concerning the soliciting of funds do not apply to religious organizations.

Prisons and Reformatories. Each administrative board having control of a county jail must provide for the holding of religious services by such persons and at such times as the probate judge directs. They must provide for religious services each Sunday in city prisons or workhouses and may employ a clergyman or religious organization to conduct such services.

The warden of the state penitentiary must furnish each convict of the penitentiary with a Bible and, as often as such warden thinks proper, permit regular ministers of the Gospel to preach to the convicts.

Holidays and Sunday Observance. Christmas and New Year's Day, Labor Day, any days appointed or recommended by the president or governor as days of Thanksgiving, February 12, February 22, May 30, July 4, and October 12 are legal holidays. If any one of these days falls on a Sunday, the next secular or business day is a holiday. Written contracts entered into on Sunday and other holidays are valid if not prohibited by statute. Hunting, fishing, and certain forms of labor or entertainment are forbidden on Sunday. Beer sales are forbidden in certain cases set up by statute.

Morality, Public Health, and Safety. No state condones polygamy. No person may willfully interrupt or disturb a lawful assemblage of persons or a person while he is at or about the place where such assemblage is being held or is to be or has been held. The treatment of human ills through prayer alone by a practitioner of the Christian Science Church, in accordance with the tenets and creed of such church, may not be regarded as the practice of medicine. In *Kraus v. City of Cleveland* 121 N.E. (2) 311 (1954) the Ohio Court of Appeals held that Cleveland ordinances providing for fluoridation of city water were constitutional as their object was to protect health. The state's police power contains anything reasonable and necessary to secure the peace, safety, health, morale, and best interest of the public.

Various Constitutional Freedoms. The right of freedom of speech embraces the right to distribute and receive literature, and a city ordinance making it unlawful for any person distributing handbills or other advertising matter to ring door bells or otherwise summon inmates of the residence to the door for the purpose of receiving such matter violates constitutional rights of freedom of speech (*Mantin v. City of Struthers,* Ohio 63 Supreme Court 862).

An ordinance prohibiting solicitors from going uninvited to private residences for the purpose of soliciting orders for the sale of goods or to sell goods was found unconstitutional as a denial of freedom of speech and press as applied to Jehovah's Witnesses engaged in house to house distribution of printed matter and of oral and written opinion (*Zimmerman v. Village of London* 38 F. Supp 582).

Bibliography: G. F. HOUCK and M. W. CARR, *A History of Catholicity in Northern Ohio and in the Diocese of Cleveland from 1749 to 1900,* 2 v. (Cleveland 1903). M. J. HYNES, *History* *of the Diocese of Cleveland . . . 1847–1952* (Cleveland 1953). J. H. LAMOTT, *History of the Archdiocese of Cincinnati, 1821–1921* (New York 1921). C. F. WITTKE, ed., *The History of the State of Ohio*, 6 v. (Columbus, Ohio 1941–44). E. H. ROSEBOOM and F. P. WEISENBURGER, *A History of Ohio* (New York 1934). *Martindale-Hubbell Law Directory, 1962*, 4 v. (Summit, N.J. 1962). *Page's Ohio Revised Code, Annotated*, ed. C. L. MEIER, 19 v. (Cincinnati 1953–).

[W. M. COSGROVE]

OHOLA AND OHOLIBA, symbolic names given in Ezechiel ch. 23 to two sisters who played the harlot; the elder sister Ohola has already been punished for her wickedness, and equal chastisement awaits the younger sister Oholiba. Although the words in verse 4 are a later gloss on the original text, they are certainly correct: "As for their names, Samaria is Ohola, and Jerusalem is Oholiba." This is clear, not only from the whole context, but also from the direct statement of Ezechiel in the similar parable of ch. 16, where the Prophet says to Yahweh's faithless spouse Jerusalem, "Your elder sister was Samaria" (Ez 16.46). The imagery of adultery or harlotry to depict Israel's infidelity to Yahweh is common in the writings of the OT Prophets.

The symbolic names are commonly and no doubt correctly explained that Ohola (Heb. *'ohŏlāh*) means "her own tent" and Oholiba (Heb. *'ohŏlîbāh*) "my tent [*'ohŏlî*] is in her [*bāh*]," the allusion being to the schismatic sanctuary ("tent") of Samaria and Yahweh's legitimate sanctuary of Jerusalem; cf. Is 62.4, where Yahweh names His repentant spouse Jerusalem "My-delight-is-in-her" (Heb. *ḥepṣi-bāh*). Most likely it is purely accidental that in Hebrew the number of consonants in Ohola (*'hlh*) and Samaria (*šmrn*) are the same, as they also are in Oholiba (*'hlybh*) and Jerusalem (*yrwšlm*), for it is doubtful whether the later devices of *Cabala were known to Ezechiel.

See also EZECHIEL (EZEKIEL), BOOK OF.

Bibliography: EncDictBibl 1662–63. See commentaries on Ezechiel ch. 23.

[L. F. HARTMAN]

O'HURLEY, DERMOT, archbishop, listed among Irish martyrs proposed for canonization; b. Lycadoon, Limerick, 1519; d. Dublin, June 30, 1584. After graduating at Louvain in 1551, he taught philosophy there and subsequently Canon and civil law at Reims. He was consecrated in Rome in 1581, and appointed archbishop of Cashel September 11, receiving the pallium November 27. Landing near Dublin in September 1583, he escaped capture in Drogheda and Slane and proceeded to his own province. Because of the Government's threats to his host in Slane, he surrendered at Carrick-on-Suir and was imprisoned in Dublin Castle October 7. He was examined repeatedly by Lord Justices Loftus and Wallop and, on instructions of Elizabeth's secretary Walsingham, was tortured. Denying charges of treason but refusing religious conformity, he was, on Elizabeth's mandate, hanged after being condemned by martial law, there being no evidence for conviction by civil courts. According to tradition, he was buried in St. Kevin's churchyard, Dublin.

Bibliography: S. Ó MURTHUILE, *A Martyred Archbishop of Cashel* (Dublin 1935).

[J. HURLEY]

OJETTI, BENEDETTO, Jesuit canonist and moral theologian; b. Rome, April 5, 1862; d. there, Sept. 30, 1932. He entered the Society of Jesus Nov. 12, 1878, and was solemnly professed Aug. 15, 1896. He devoted his life to the study of ecclesiastical jurisprudence. In 1896 he began to teach Canon Law at the Gregorian University in Rome, and in 1898 he was transferred to the faculty of theology there. In 1913 he returned to the Canon Law faculty, where he taught until his death. His principal works are: *In jus antepianum et pianum ex decreto "Ne Temere"* (Rome 1908) and *Synopsis rerum moralium et juris pontificii* (4 v. Rome 1899–1904).

Bibliography: C. TESTORE, EncCatt 9:90–91. A. GOMMENGINGER, LexThK² 7:1123. Greg 13 (1932) 482–483, obituary.

[P. F. MULHERN]

OKEGHEM, JAN VAN, great Renaissance composer of the Flemish school (also Ockeghem, Okenghem); b. Hainaut?; Flanders, *c*. 1420; d. Tours, France, *c*. 1495. He began his musical career as a member of the polyphonic section of the Antwerp cathedral choir. In 1446 he joined the chapel of the Duke of Bourbon and 7 years later transferred to the Royal Chapel, where he successively served as chaplain and composer to three French Kings, Charles VII, Louis XI, and Charles VIII. He was appointed treasurer of the Abbey of St. Martin, of which French monarchs were titular abbots. Fellow

Jan van Okeghem with his chapel singers, miniature in a manuscript c. 1530 (MS Fr. 1537, fol. 58 v.).

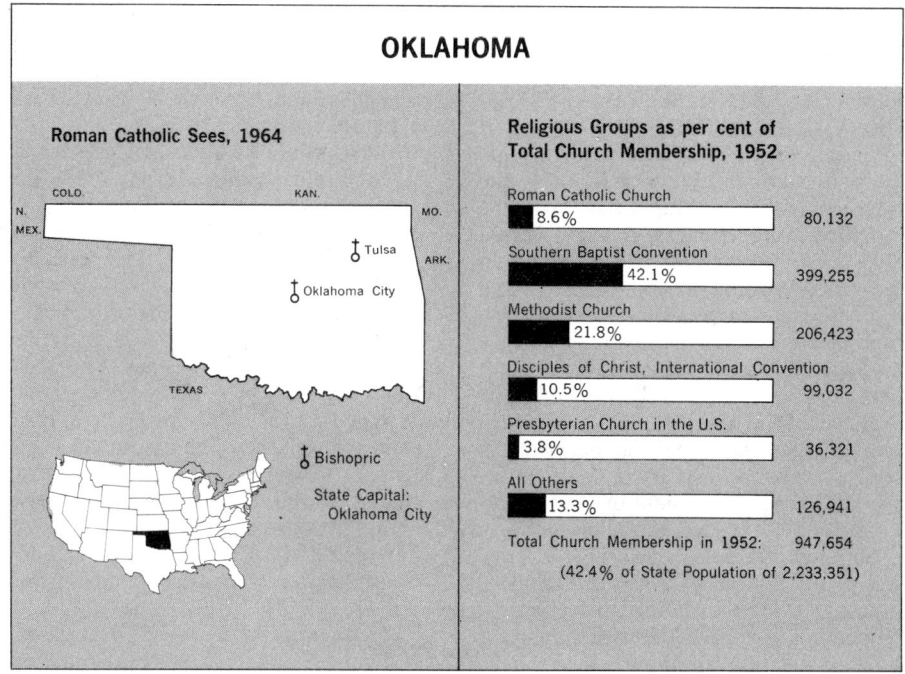

OKLAHOMA

Roman Catholic Sees, 1964

COLO.   KAN.

N.
MEX.   MO.

☩ Tulsa   ARK.

☦ Oklahoma City

TEXAS

☩ Bishopric

☦ State Capital:
Oklahoma City

**Religious Groups as per cent of
Total Church Membership, 1952**

Roman Catholic Church

8.6%   80,132

Southern Baptist Convention

42.1%   399,255

Methodist Church

21.8%   206,423

Disciples of Christ, International Convention

10.5%   99,032

Presbyterian Church in the U.S.

3.8%   36,321

All Others

13.3%   126,941

Total Church Membership in 1952:   947,654

(42.4% of State Population of 2,233,351)

Fig. 1. Church-membership statistics were compiled by the Bureau of Research and Survey of the National Council of the Churches of Christ in the U.S.A.

musicians wrote motets in his honor during his lifetime and elegies at his death. His stature and influence during the later 15th century were considerable, for his style both links and separates the era of *Dufay and that of *Desprez.

Although he wrote some secular music, Okeghem's church music forms by far the larger and more important part of his output. Plainsong is used either as a *cantus firmus* or by way of paraphrase in several of his motets, which include magnificent settings of the antiphons *Ave Maria, *Salve Regina, and *Alma Redemptoris Mater. The responsory for Vespers of the Purification, *Gaude Maria,* is also a work of impressive proportions and noble polyphonic textures. Of his Masses, 11 survive in complete form. He was one of many composers who successfully transmuted the secular character of the *L'homme armé* melody into a contrapuntal mosaic of intensely religious fervor, and (like Dufay and J. *Obrecht) he employed the flowing final melisma of a Maundy Thursday antiphon in a notable *Missa Caput.* In the *Missa Fors seulement* he draws upon a rondeau of his own composition for highly diversified melodic material. Of his four-part Masses, the *Missa Mi-Mi* (so called for its bass voice motto) provides ready proof of his ability to write a straightforward and classical style. Both the *Missa Cuiusvis toni* and the *Missa Prolationum* are feats of almost unrivaled musical technique, the latter providing a veritable "art of canon" comparable to J. S. *Bach's great *Art of Fugue.* The impressive Requiem qualifies as the earliest extant polyphonic setting of the *Missa pro Defunctis.*

See also MUSIC, SACRED, HISTORY OF, 4.

Bibliography: *Collected Works,* ed. D. PLAMENAC (2d ed. Philadelphia 1959–   ). D. PLAMENAC, MusGG 9:1826–38. Reese MusR. **Illustration credit:** Bibliothèque Nationale, Paris.

[D. STEVENS]

OKLAHOMA

A state in southwestern U.S. admitted to the Union (1907) as the 46th state. It is bounded on the north by Kansas, on the east by Missouri and Arkansas, on the south by the Red River and Texas, and on the west by New Mexico and Colorado. Oklahoma City is the capital, and Tulsa is another large city.

History. The area, traversed by Coronado in the 16th century and explored by the Spanish and French in the 17th and 18th centuries, became the property of the U.S. by the Louisiana Purchase of 1803. Federal Indian policy very early designated it as a permanent home for the resettlement of various Indian tribes, and the five civilized tribes of southeastern U.S. were moved there (1830–45). Virtually the whole area was originally apportioned to them, but their districts were later reduced, partially because of the Indians' support of the Confederacy during the Civil War. Many other tribes were then relocated within what became known as Indian Territory. One unassigned portion near the center, Oklahoma Territory, was opened to white settlement by the famous run of 1889, with additional areas added between 1889 and 1901. Meanwhile the U.S. directed the Indians to give up their so-called excess lands and to take allotments. Although ranking first among the states in Indian population in the 1960s, Oklahoma had no open reservation of the traditional type found in other states.

Of the many tribes there during the 19th century, only two were predominantly Catholic, the Osage and Pottawatomi. Nominally under the bishop of St. Louis, Mo., from 1826 but transferred to the bishop of Little Rock, Ark., in 1843, this vast country was visited occasionally by priests who ministered to the army camps and Indian tribes. The first Catholic church in Indian

Territory was built (1872) at Atoka, Choctaw Nation, by Rev. M. Smyth of Ft. Smith, Ark., who attended it irregularly. Permanent missionary activity began in 1875 with the arrival of French Benedictines. From the Abbey of Pierre-que-Vire, Dom Isidore *Robot, briefly taking up residence in Atoka, was appointed the first prefect apostolic of the Indian Territory in 1876, the year in which he concluded an arrangement with the Pottawatomi to settle among them. He founded Sacred Heart Mission, termed "the cradle of Catholicity in Oklahoma," and built boarding schools for boys and girls, the latter in the care of Sisters of Mercy from Macon, Ill. The prefecture under Dom Robot and his successor, Dom Ignatius Jean, OSB, continued until 1891, when the first vicar apostolic, Theophile Meerschaert, took over the rule of the twin territories. With no boundary change since that time, the vicariate became the Diocese of *Oklahoma City–Tulsa (1905).

Population. In Oklahoma, stronghold of white Protestant culture, residents of foreign birth have always been few. The Southern Baptists constitute the most numerous church group; the Methodists, Presbyterians, Church of Christ, and Disciples of Christ have sizable memberships. Numerous evangelical sects are very active, but the Jewish population is minimal. In the 1952 state population of 2,233,351, Catholics constituted 3.5 per cent; Protestants, 38.7 per cent; Jews, 0.2 per cent; and all others, 57.6 per cent (*see* CHURCH MEMBERSHIP, U.S.). In 1963 Catholics numbered 105,338, or about 4.4 per cent of the total population of the state.

Education. Catholic school enrollment in 1964 included 13,093 students in elementary schools, 3,317 in high schools, and 291 in college. Transportation of parochial school children on public school buses, previously permitted in a few districts, was outlawed by a 1941 supreme court decision (*Gurney et al. v. Ferguson et al.* 29753 *Oklahoma Reports,* 254), decreeing that such services to "sectarian institutions" were uncon-

Fig. 2. A procession at Sacred Heart Mission, Pottawatomie County, Okla., photograph made shortly after the founding of the mission in 1876.

stitutional. In *Board of Education for Ind. Sch. Dist. No. 52 v. Antone* (*Oklahoma Reports,* 911), the court reaffirmed the 1941 doctrine, denying application of the principles enunciated in a New Jersey case (*see* EVERSON V. SCHOOL BOARD).

Church-State Relations. References to and provisions affecting religion are incorporated in the state constitution and in acts of the legislature and the judiciary.

Constitution. Oklahoma is governed by the Constitution of 1907, as amended. The preamble reads that the people invoke "the guidance of Almighty God."

Article 1, sec. 2, provides for religious liberty. The use of public monies for any sect, church, religion, or preacher, minister, or teacher of such is forbidden (art. 2, sec. 5).

"When the Senate is sitting as a Court of Impeachment, the senators shall be on oath, or affirmation, impartially to try the party impeached" (art. 8, sec. 4). Property used exclusively for religious purposes is exempt from taxation (art. 10, sec. 6). Senators and representatives of all judicial, state, and county officers must take an oath or affirmation before assuming office (art. 15, sec. 1).

Marriage and Divorce. Marriages of men under 18 and women under 15 are prohibited except in certain cases of pregnancy. The consent of parents is needed for men under 21 and women under 18. Certain public officials and clergy may perform the ceremony. Common-law marriages are recognized. Marriages according to Indian customs are recognized.

Marriages are void if either party is bound by a prior subsisting marriage, if the parties are related by blood in any degree of the direct line and up to and including second cousins, and between persons of African descent and persons not of such descent. Marriages may be annulled because of nonage and mental incapacity.

The grounds for absolute divorce are: adultery; impotency; abandonment for 1 year; pregnancy of the wife at marriage by one other than the husband; extreme cruelty; fraudulent contract; incompatibility; habitual drunkenness; gross neglect of duty; imprisonment; a divorce granted to the defendant in another state that does not release the plaintiff from the obligations of marriage in Oklahoma; insanity, with confinement for 5 years. There are some restrictions on remarriage. *See* MARRIAGE, U.S. LAW OF; DIVORCE (U.S. LAW OF).

Abortion, Birth Control, Sterilization. The law forbids *abortion unless it is necessary to preserve the life of the mother. A person administering to a woman pregnant with a quick child, with the intent to destroy the child, is guilty of manslaughter in the first degree if either dies. Persons intending to procure an abortion may be punished by imprisonment for up to 3 years.

There are no references to birth control, contraception, or anovulants in the state code.

The law permits *sterilization on patients in institutions when the man is under 65 and the woman is under 47 and they are about to be released from the institution and are likely to be a public charge or dependent on charity. Persons afflicted with hereditary forms or recurrent insanity, idiocy, imbecility, feeblemindedness, or epilepsy, and habitual criminals may be sterilized on their release.

Property and Taxation. Religious and charitable associations may incorporate under ch. 14 of title 18 of the nonprofit corporation statute. Three to 41 elected trust-

Fig. 3. *The first pupils of St. Mary's Boarding School, Sacred Heart Mission. The school was established in 1880 and Sisters of Mercy from Macon, Ill., took charge of it in 1884.*

ees hold property in trust; the amount of real property held must be reasonably necessary for the objects of the corporation. Trustees of the Roman Catholic Church are chosen according to the customs and usages of the Church. Real and personal property used exclusively by religious and charitable societies not run for profit is exempt from taxation.

There are no mortmain provisions.

An act, "Oklahoma Solicitation of Charitable Contribution Acts" (effective in 1959), covers a variety of situations and, among other things, exempts from its coverage "organizations incorporated for religious purposes and actually engaged in bona-fide religious programs, and other organizations directly operated, supervised, or controlled by and in connection with a religious organization."

Prisons and Reformatories. The keeper of each prison must provide at the expense of the county or state, as the case may be, a copy of the Bible or New Testament for each prisoner under his charge who is able and desires to read, to be used by such prisoner during his confinement; any minister of the gospel, disposed to aid in reforming the prisoners and instructing them in their moral and religious duties, must be permitted access to them at reasonable and proper times.

Holidays and Sunday Observance. Sunday, Christmas and New Year's Day, Labor Day, Thanksgiving Day, May 30, July 4, and November 11 are legal holidays. If a holiday falls on Sunday, the next day is a holiday. Any acts permitted, authorized, or required to be performed on the above days may be performed on the next succeeding business day. The Sunday sale of beer of 3.2 per cent alcoholic content is optional. Acts constituting Sabbath breaking include certain servile labors; all shooting, horse racing, or gaming; and the selling of certain public commodities.

Morality, Public Health, and Safety. No state condones polygamy. A person who willfully disturbs any assemblage of people gathered for religious worship is guilty of a misdemeanor. The section on practicing medicine may not be construed so as to interfere in any way with the practice of those who endeavor to prevent or cure disease by spiritual means or prayer. The section on the care of the eyes of the newborn may not be construed to compel conformity by persons or parents who have religious beliefs contrary to the use of med-

icines. The same exemption applies to tests for syphilis in pregnant women. In *Dowell v. City of Tulsa,* 273 P (2) 859 (1954), the state supreme court upheld a city ordinance authorizing the fluoridation of the city water supply, finding that it constituted a valid exercise of the police power delegated to cities by the state constitution to promulgate statutes to promote and protect public health. In *Beck v. State,* 233 Pac. 495 (1925), the parent of an 11-year-old boy who had suffered intense and prolonged pain from lockjaw was found guilty of violating a statute by failing or refusing to provide medical treatment for the relief or cure of the child, even though the parent appeared to be influenced by religious belief.

Various Constitutional Freedoms. During Prohibition (1918) in *De Hasque v. Atchison,* T. & S. F. Ry. Co. (9694 *Oklahoma Reports,* 183), the state supreme court upheld, under the constitutional guarantees of religious liberty, the Catholic Church's right to sacramental wine.

An ordinance prohibiting persons in public streets from distributing circulars, handbills, and reading matter to those willing to receive them was found invalid as infringing the constitutional rights of freedom of speech and press secured against state invasion by the 14th amendment to the Federal Constitution [121 P (2) 312].

An ordinance prohibiting the distribution of literature on city streets, when applied to members of Jehovah Witnesses, was found unconstitutional as a denial of freedom of speech, press, and religion [*Ex parte Winnett.* 121 P (2) 312].

Bibliography: G. FOREMAN, *A History of Oklahoma* (Norman, Okla. 1942). R. GITTINGER, *The Formation of the State of Oklahoma, 1803–1906* (Norman, Okla. 1939). E. C. McREYNOLDS, *A History of the Sooner State* (Norman, Okla. 1954). M. H. WRIGHT, *A Guide to the Indian Tribes of Oklahoma* (Norman, Okla. 1951). M. U. THOMAS, *The Catholic Church on the Oklahoma Frontier* (Doctoral diss. St. Louis U.; microfilm 1940). *Oklahoma Statutes, 1961,* 3 v. (St. Paul 1961). *Oklahoma Digest, 1890 to Date* (St. Paul 1934–   ). **Illustration credits:** Figs. 2, and 3, Oklahoma Historical Society.

[J. F. MURPHY]

OKLAHOMA CITY–TULSA, DIOCESE OF (OKLAHOMAPOLITANA-TULSENSIS)

Suffragan of the Archdiocese of San Antonio, Tex., it was erected on Aug. 17, 1905, as the Diocese of Oklahoma; the name was officially changed on Nov. 14, 1930. Embracing the entire state of Oklahoma, an area of 69,919 square miles, the diocese in 1963 had 103,390 Catholics in a total population of 2,328,284, the heaviest Catholic concentrations occurring in the urban areas.

Early History. The area's Catholic history began probably when the expedition of Francisco Vasquez de Coronado, with the Franciscan Juan de *Padilla, crossed the western sector in 1541. Permanent Catholic missionary work in the old Indian Territory, now Oklahoma, began in the 19th century with the periodic visits of the Jesuits from the Osage Mission, St. Paul, Kans. When the Diocese of Little Rock, Ark., was erected (1843) and when Oklahoma was included within its original boundaries, priests from Fort Smith, Ark., made protracted and regular missionary tours through the western extension of the diocese. In 1872, through the efforts of Father Michael Smyth, the first Catholic Church in Oklahoma was built at Atoka, then the terminus of the Missouri, Kansas, and Texas railroad.

Fig. 1. One of the first classes of the boys' school at Sacred Heart Mission, with Bishop Meerschaert (center) and Father Robot (bearded priest at the bishop's left).

Three years later, Bp. Edward Fitzgerald of Little Rock assigned the whole Indian Territory to the Benedictine Isidore *Robot, the first priest to take up permanent residence in Oklahoma. On July 9, 1876, Piux IX established the Territory as a prefecture apostolic and named Robot first prefect, a position he held until his resignation in 1886. With other Benedictines, he established a monastery at Sacred Heart (later transferred to Shawnee, Okla., and named St. Gregory's); the first school for boys was opened there in 1878, and the first Catholic school for girls in 1880. Father Ignatius Jean, OSB, succeeded Robot, until his resignation in 1890.

Diocesan Development. After the opening of a large portion of the area to white settlers, the Holy See, on May 29, 1891, raised Oklahoma to the status of a vicariate apostolic and appointed Theophile Meerschaert, then vicar-general of the Diocese of Natchez, Miss., vicar apostolic with episcopal rank. He was consecrated on Sept. 8, 1891, and 10 days later arrived in Guthrie, the center of Church administration until the establishment of the diocese. Under Meerschaert there was a rapid growth in the number of churches and missions, and a large increase in priests and sisters. The vicariate

Fig. 2. Founders of Sacred Heart Monastery, at the original site at Sacred Heart, Indian Territory. Later moved to Shawnee, Okla., as St. Gregory's.

was raised to a diocese in 1905, and the place of residence of the bishop was transferred to Oklahoma City, which less than 3 years later became the capital of the new state. By the time of the first bishop's death, Feb. 21, 1924, there were 106 priests, 449 religious men and women, and the number of Catholics had grown to 57,587.

On June 25, 1924, Francis C. *Kelley, the founder of the *Catholic Church Extension Society, was appointed the second bishop of Oklahoma. Kelley's deep interest in the missionary areas of the country was an excellent qualification for his work in this missionary diocese. Building on the foundations already established, he added more than 60 churches during his administration. His gifts as lecturer and writer did much to win respect and honor for the Church in Oklahoma. Kelley's failing health led the Holy See, on Nov. 11, 1944, to appoint Eugene J. McGuinness as his coadjutor with right of succession. A close friend of Kelley and his coworker in the Extension Society, McGuinness had been consecrated on Dec. 21, 1937, and had served for nearly 8 years as bishop of the Diocese of Raleigh, N.C. He succeeded to the See of Oklahoma at the death of Kelley on Feb. 1, 1948.

Fig. 3. Mass in St. Patrick's Church, Oklahoma City.

McGuinness's administration was marked by an almost incredible expansion of the Church in Oklahoma during which more than 100 new churches and 150 buildings of other kinds, including 46 new schools and 6 hospitals, were constructed. Even more significant was the increase in the number of priests and seminarians: during this time the clergy increased by 69, and the young men studying for the secular priesthood by more than 100.

On Dec. 5, 1957, Msgr. Victor J. Reed, rector of Holy Family Cathedral, Tulsa, was appointed titular bishop of Limisa and auxiliary to Bishop McGuinness. Plans for his consecration by McGuinness were well under way when the latter's unexpected death occurred on Dec. 27, 1957. Reed was named fourth bishop of the diocese on Jan. 21, 1958, and consecrated at Holy Family Cathedral on March 5. His administration has included the formal dedication of a new diocesan seminary, St. Francis de Sales, at Oklahoma City, begun during the administration of McGuinness; the dedication of the new St. Francis Hospital in Tulsa; and the expansion of high school facilities in Oklahoma City and

Tulsa. Additional buildings have been erected at St. Gregory's Abbey, Shawnee, for an anticipated increase in enrollment of high school and junior college students, and a number of catechetical centers have been established in the mission areas of the state, staffed both by religious and lay women.

In 1963 the diocese was served by approximately 300 priests and 35 brothers, including representatives of 14 religious communities of men, and more than 750 sisters. Motherhouses for women religious are located at Tulsa (Benedictines), Ponca City (Felicians), and Oklahoma City (Third Order of Mt. Carmel). Since World War II, Catholic population has shown a steady growth, the material facilities of the Church in Oklahoma have been greatly expanded, and there has been a rapid increase in vocations to the priesthood and in lay participation in the liturgy and the apostolate.

Bibliography: M. U. THOMAS, *The Catholic Church on the Oklahoma Frontier, 1824–1907* (St. Louis 1938; Univ. microfilms 1940). **Illustration credits:** Fig. 1, Oklahoma Historical Society. Fig. 3, Murray-Jones-Murray Architects, Oklahoma.

[W. C. GARTHOEFFNER]

OLAF I TRYGGVESSØN, KING OF NORWAY,

995 to Sept. 9 (or 10), 1000; b. *c.* 968; d. Swold. Olaf (Tryggvasøn) was brought up in Novgorod and spent his youth as a Viking. From *c.* 991 he lived in the British Isles, where he was baptized. Only in 995 did he return to Norway, which he had left with his mother soon after his birth. He was the great-grandson of Harold Finehair, and thus the chieftains recognized him as the sovereign ruler of Norway without any serious opposition. Olaf was an ardent Christian who was determined to introduce Christianity throughout his country, and this led to minor struggles with the strong pagan chieftains. Christianity was legally introduced in Iceland *c.* 1000 at the instigation of Olaf. His methods of conversion were hardhanded and not very subtle. He is remembered as the apostle of Norway and Iceland, and is the hero of several sagas of a hagiographic cast. He died in the naval battle of Swold, where he was fighting against an alliance of the Danish and Swedish Kings and an exiled Norwegian chieftain.

Bibliography: B. AĐALBJARNARSON, *Om de norske kongers sagaer* (Oslo 1937), with bibliog. S. UNDSET, *Saga of Saints,* tr. E. C. RAMSDEN (New York 1934). H. KOHT, *Norsk biografisk leksikon* (Oslo 1921–) 10:413–419. G. TURVILLE-PETRE, *The Heroic Age of Scandinavia* (London 1951) 130–139. H. HOLZAPFEL, LexThK² 7:1138.

[H. BEKKER-NIELSEN]

OLAF II, KING OF NORWAY, ST.,

reigned 1015 to July 29, 1030; b. Oplandet, Norway, 995; d. Stiklestad, Norway (feast, July 29). His father was a chieftain descended from Harold Finehair. Olaf Haraldsson's early career is not known in detail, but it seems that he was a Viking from his 12th year, the events of his youth being recorded in scaldic verse. Having been baptized in Rouen in 1014, he returned to Norway in 1015 to assert his royal claims. His rebellion against Danish and Swedish overlords in Norway had a strong popular appeal. Olaf was an ardent Christian and tried by every means to uproot the last traces of paganism in Norway; in this he was quite successful. When King *Canute the Great was proclaimed King of all Norway in 1028, Olaf fled the country and went

St. Olaf of Norway, from a 15th-century Icelandic MS (AM. 160, 4°-fol. 1v), Arnamagnean Institute, Copenhagen.

into exile in Russia. In the spring of 1030 he returned to Norway, leaving his bastard son, the future King Magnus the Good at the Russian court. He met his opponents in the battle of Stiklestad, where he was killed. Very soon after his death even his enemies came to recognize that they had killed a saint; his intercession was invoked and miracles were recorded. His body was translated to Trondheim, which became the center of the Olaf cultus. He was the patron saint of Norway and was venerated also in England, Denmark, Sweden, Finland, and Iceland. He was the subject of medieval Scandinavian iconography, and his life is recorded in several legends, or sagas, both in Latin and in the vernacular.

Bibliography: BHL 2:6322–26; Suppl. 240. O. WIDDING et al., "The Lives of the Saints in Old Norse Prose: A Handlist," MedSt 25 (1963) 294–337, esp. 327–328. S. UNDSET, *Saga of Saints,* tr. E. C. RAMSDEN (New York 1934). A. W. BRØGGER, *Norsk biografisk leksikon* (Oslo 1923–) 10:374–390. G. TURVILLE-PETRE, *The Heroic Age of Scandinavia* (New York 1951) 140–164. H. HOLZAPFEL, LexThK² 7:1138.

[H. BEKKER-NIELSEN]

OLÁH, MIKLÓS (OLAHUS),

archbishop of Gran (Esztergom), Primate of Hungary, humanist; b. Hermanstadt (Nagyszeben), Hungary, Jan. 10, 1493; d. Pressburg, Hungary (now Bratislava, Czechoslovakia), Jan. 14, 1568. Oláh, of Wallachian descent, was educated at the Chapter School of Varad and as a page at the court of Vladislav II. After ordination in 1516, he served as secretary to George Szatmáry, Chancellor, and later Archbishop, of Gran. He was also secretary to King Louis II, and continued in this position after Louis's death at the battle of Mohács (1526), serving Queen Mary of Hungary. When Mary was appointed Regent of the Netherlands by Charles V, Oláh accompanied her (1531), and engaged in diplomatic missions and humanistic studies until 1542, when he returned to Hungary. Oláh also won the friendship of Erasmus. As an official at the court of Ferdinand I, he became royal chancellor and bishop of Agram (1544), bishop of Erlau (1548), and eventually, archbishop of Gran (1553). Oláh, as primate of Hungary, vigorously encouraged Church reform and opposed Protestant encroachments in Hungary. By frequent visitations, provincial synods, and administrative decrees, Catholicism was strengthened and advanced. Catholic schools and the Jesuits, invited into Hungary (1561), were the principal means of inculcating Catholic beliefs. The decrees of Trent were also employed to revive devotion and zeal. An author of several theological and historical works including the *Ordo et Ritus Ecclesiae Strigoniensis* (1560) and *Hungaria et Attila* (1562), Oláh combined religious conviction and humanist teachings.

Bibliography: T. VON BOGYAY, LexThK² 7:1137–38. D. SINOR, *History of Hungary* (New York 1959).

[P. S. MC GARRY]

OLAVIDE Y JAUREGUI, PABLO DE, Peruvian scholar and Catholic apologist; b. Lima, 1725; d. Baeza, Spain, 1803. He was a symbol of the century of the Enlightenment, a leader in the movement against traditionalism, and one of those who prepared Spain to adjust to the modern world and come closer to the European intellectual current. In 1752 he went to Spain, occupying there a high position, owing to his intellectual compatibility with the Enlightened ministers of Charles III. Between 1757 and 1764 he spent long periods of time in France and Italy. In 1767 he was unexpectedly appointed chief officer of justice of Seville, intendant of Andalucía, and later superintendent of the colonization of Sierra Morena, an ambitious project for the conversion of vast desert areas into arable lands inhabited by a model rural society. In those positions Olavide's work had two facets: (1) the reform of the cultural regulations of the University of Seville through changing its scholastic orientation and secularizing the teaching system and (2) the reform of the economic order through agrarian reform. These ideas aroused great opposition. In 1776 he became involved in an inquisitorial trial because of his imprudence in religious matters. In 1780 he escaped to France, where he remained for 18 years.

As a friend of the Encyclopedists (he translated various dramatic works, among them, Voltaire's *Zayre*), he was well received there, especially by Marmontel and by Diderot, who wrote a biographical sketch of him. While in exile he recovered his lost faith and piety after having survived Jacobine imprisonment. He became an apologist of the Catholic faith against the secular Enlightenment. He returned to Spain (1798) and remained there until his death. His most important work is *El evangelio en triunfo o historia de un filósofo desengañado* (1798). Autobiographical in nature, it reports the psychological drama in the conversion of an unbeliever and defends the divinity of Jesus and the authenticity of the sacred books. According to *Menén-dez y Pelayo, it was a precursor of *Le génie du christianisme* of *Chateaubriand.

Bibliography: M. DEFOURNEAUX, *Pablo de Olavide ou l'Afrancesado* (Paris 1959).

[G. LOHMANN VILLENA]

OLD CATHOLICS

A loosely associated group of schismatical, autonomous communities brought together in the Union of Utrecht (1889) under the presidency of the archbishop of Utrecht. The term Old Catholic implies that *Vatican Council I introduced into the Roman Catholic Church innovations that left Old Catholicism as the repository of traditional Catholic beliefs. The Old Catholic Church has been colored by many Protestant influences, but it is not a Protestant body. All the Old Catholic Churches are national churches and, with the possible exception of the Little Church of Utrecht (OBC), are strongly influenced by 19th-century nationalism; but none of them is an established state church. These communities totaled less than 250,000 communicants in 1965.

History. The Schism of *Utrecht, which began early in the 18th century, anteceded the Old Catholic movement, which it later joined. Its following was very small by 1870, when a considerable number of Catholic priests and laymen in Germany refused to accept the definitions of Vatican Council I on papal infallibility and primacy. *Febronianism and *Josephinism, particularly as it was expounded by Ignaz von *Wessenburg, greatly influenced the thinking of these men. Ignaz von *Döllinger, Johann *Friedrich, Franz *Reusch, Johann von *Schulte, and other scholars who opposed the Vatican Council's decrees on the papacy exerted still greater influence. Many laymen in these groups belonged to the upper middle class and were strongly influenced also by secularism and nationalism. In September 1871 at Munich 300 representatives met to organize the Old Catholic movement; a similar congress gathered in Cologne in 1872. Episcopal leadership was lacking because the entire Catholic hierarchy subscribed to the Vatican Council's decrees. To obtain a validly consecrated bishop the Old Catholics chose Joseph Reinkens as bishop (June 1873). He was then consecrated by Bp. Heykamp of Deventer in the Netherlands, who belonged to the OBC. Döllinger, whose relations with the Old Catholics were always ambiguous, refused to become involved in organized schism and eventually broke completely with the movement because of its innovations. The leaders of the *Kulturkampf supported the Old Catholics. In Prussia and Baden the government granted them a subsidy and a share of Catholic Church property. In Switzerland the schismatics called themselves *Christkatholiken*; they were more influenced by secularism and theological liberalism than their associates in Germany, but they failed to gain a wide following. Austria likewise produced an inconsiderable number of Old Catholics.

Cultural xenophobia and Polish nationalism gave rise to the *Polish National Catholic Church, which admits intercommunion with Old Catholics and Anglicans and subscribes to the Declaration of Utrecht. Inability to accomodate to a non-Polish priesthood and quarrels over education and the administration of church property led in 1897 to the establishment of a schismatic church in Scranton, Pa., that absorbed earlier Polish dissident groups and created a diocese under the jurisdiction of Francis Hodur. Hodur was consecrated bishop in 1907 by bishops of the OBC. National messianism, secular humanism, and inventive eccentricity mark the doctrines and liturgy of the Polish National Catholic Church.

In Poland the mystical sect of *Mariavites began in 1906 and spread rapidly. At the Old Catholic Congress in Vienna (1909), General Kiréev, a Russian religious enthusiast, presented three Mariavite priests. One of them, John Kowalski, was consecrated bishop in Utrecht by Old Catholic bishops. But after Kowalski began propounding eccentric notions about mystical marriage and after the sect became notorious for gross immorality, the Old Catholics excluded Mariavites from the Union of Utrecht. The sect was rent by intrigues and factions and has almost disappeared.

Yugoslavia has a small Old Catholic community dating from 1924, but its numbers and influence have lessened because of dissensions and the immorality of its first bishop.

Doctrine and Discipline. The autonomous episcopates constituting the Old Catholic community have as a common doctrinal basis the Declaration of Utrecht (1889). However, the Polish National Church and the Swiss *Christkatholisch* Church maintain beliefs out of harmony with this declaration. In accordance with this document Old Catholics accept the decrees of the first eight ecumenical councils. (Until 1889 some Old Catholics considered themselves bound by the Tridentine decrees). They admit Sacred Scripture and tradition as sources of revelation; but they do not place the deuterocanonical books of the Old Testament on a parity with the others, and their notion of tradition differs from the Roman Catholic one. The bishop of Rome is recognized as having merely a primacy of honor, but not a primacy of jurisdiction or infallibility as defined in Vatican Council I. Old Catholics reject the treasury of merits, indulgences, veneration of saints, images, and relics and Mary's Immaculate Conception, Assumption, and position as mediatrix of all graces. They admit seven sacraments and recognize the apostolic succession. They admit the Real Presence in the Eucharist but deny transubstantiation; forbid private Masses, and permit the reception of the Eucharist under one or both species. Auricular confession is not obligatory; sins may be confessed before the congregation or a priest. Clerical celibacy, pilgrimages, processions, the rosary, and scapular have been abolished. Mixed marriages and cremation are permissible. The liturgy resembles the Roman one and is celebrated in the vernacular. Liturgical vestments are the same as the Roman ones.

Each bishopric is autonomous and is governed by a bishop, who in turn must abide by the canons enacted by clerical and lay members of synods, the highest authority. Synods also elect bishops. Since 1889 the Old Catholic archbishop of Utrecht has been president of the International Old Catholic Congress. As a result of an agreement reached in Bonn (1931), intercommunion with the Anglicans has since existed. Each group recognizes the catholicity and independence of the other and admits members of the other communion to participate in its sacraments. The Orthodox Churches view Old Catholicism as a schism within the heretical Roman Church and have rejected Old Catholic overtures for intercommunion.

Bibliography: K. ALGERMISSEN, LexThK² 1:398–402. C. B. Moss, *The Old Catholic Movement: Its Origins and History* (2d ed. London 1964), by an Anglican. L. CRISTIANI, DTC 15.2: 2980–88. J. GRÜNDLER, *Lexikon der christlichen Kirchen und Sekten,* 2 v. (Vienna 1961) 1:82–89, a survey of the present constitution and membership of the Old Catholic communities. J. F. VON SCHULTE, *Der Altkatholizismus* (Giessen 1887), by an Old Catholic. J. TROXLER, *Die neuere Entwicklung des Altkatholizismus* (Cologne 1908). V. CONZEMIUS, "Aspects ecclésiologiques de l'évolution de Döllinger et du vieux Catholicisme," Rev ScRel 34 (1960) 247–279. P. GSCHWIND, *Geschichte der Entstehung der christkatholischen Kirche der Schweiz,* 2 v. (Bern 1904–10). W. H. DE VOIL and H. D. WYNNE-BENNETT, *Old Catholic Eucharistic Worship* (New York 1936). The Old Catholics have published a quarterly journal, *Revue internationale de théologie* (Bern 1893–1910), with changed title, *Internationale kirchliche Zeitschrift* (1911–).

[S. J. TONSOR]

OLD CHAPTER, a body of the English clergy; it was originated by William *Bishop, Bishop of Chalcedon, who in 1623, as part of his plan to reorganize the missionary church in England, instituted a chapter consisting of a dean and canons. Its functions, as he conceived them, were threefold: to act as an advisory body to the bishop; to preserve continuity of jurisdiction *sede vacante;* and when the bishop died, to submit to Rome nominations for his successor. Its author took this step, however, without prior reference to Rome, which refused to accord the chapter any official recognition, maintaining that Bishop had acted beyond his jurisdiction. Nevertheless, Rome refrained from any act of censure, chiefly, it seems, from fear of creating scandal. After the death of Richard *Smith, Bishop of Chalcedon in 1655, the chapter made a somewhat exaggerated claim that it had the unofficial approval of both Innocent X and Alexander VII for assuming jurisdiction over the church in England and issuing faculties *sede vacante.* Rome eventually decided to appoint another bishop, insisting that the chapter should cease to attempt to exercise jurisdiction: both Philip Howard, who was to have been appointed in 1672 if political circumstances had not prevented it, and John Leyburn, who was appointed in 1685, were made to promise to enforce this. Though after 1685 it never again tried to exercise jurisdiction, the chapter continued to claim canonical status and to perpetuate itself until the hierarchy was restored in 1850; its members then disbanded and reformed themselves into the Old Brotherhood of the Secular Clergy. This society still exists. It meets twice a year and distributes funds to various charities.

Bibliography: Archives of the Old Brotherhood, partly catalogued in 1876 (HMC. 5th Report. Appendix: 463–470.). Many documents were removed to Westminster Cathedral Archives (ser. A, v.17ff.; ser. B, v.25ff.). The rest remain with the Old Brotherhood. H. TOOTELL, *Dodd's Church History of England,* ed. M. A. TIERNEY, 5 v. (London 1839–43). E. H. BURTON, *Life and Times of Bishop Challoner, 1691–1781,* 2 v. (London 1909). B. HEMPHILL (pseud. for B. WHELAN), *The Early Vicars Apostolic of England, 1685–1750* (London 1954) *passim.* J. SERGEANT, *An Account of the Chapter . . .* ed. W. TURNBULL (London 1853), based on Ward's MS history in the Old Brotherhood Archives. J. A. WILLIAMS, "The Old Chapter and the Secular Clergy," *Catholic Recusancy in Wiltshire* (in progress). G. V. ANSTRUTHER, *Cardinal of Norfolk* (in progress), ch.4, 5. T. A. BIRRELL, "English Catholics without a Bishop," *Recusant History* 4.4 (1957–58). A. F. ALLISON, "Richard Smith, Richelieu and the French Marriage," *ibid.* 7.4 (1963–64).

[A. F. ALLISON]

OLD DELUDER SATAN ACT. The name given the Massachusetts school ordinance of 1647, derived from its preamble, which begins, "It being one of the chief projects of that old deluder Satan to keep men from the knowledge of the Scriptures . . . ." The legislation proper required that townships of 50 families or more appoint a common schoolmaster to teach reading and writing, his wages to be paid by either the parents or the town. Townships of 100 families were to establish a grammar school to prepare students for the university. Townships failing to comply with these demands were to pay a yearly fine of £5 to the nearest school until the order be carried out.

This ordinance is often quoted both as a measure to restrict Anglican and Catholic influence through the imposition of Puritan belief, and as the first Colonial legislative approval of the Calvinist principle of union of Church and State in education with the latter given the authority to promote education as a public service. The preamble, however, seems rather an expression of religious belief offered as motivation to fulfill an obligation that had educational, social, and religious ramifications: the training of citizens who would be of service to Church and State rather than a charge upon the community.

Although schools had been established by free initiative before the 1647 ordinance, they were few and not widely effective. The ordinance of 1642, the first Massachusetts educational legislation, had placed the responsibility for the literacy of children and indentured servants upon the heads of families. Since this legislation had proved insufficient, the 1647 ordinance required the establishment of an educational system and offered religious motivation and monetary sanctions to ensure its organization.

Bibliography: S. E. MORISON, *The Intellectual Life of Colonial New England* (2d ed. New York 1956).

[F. F. BURCH]

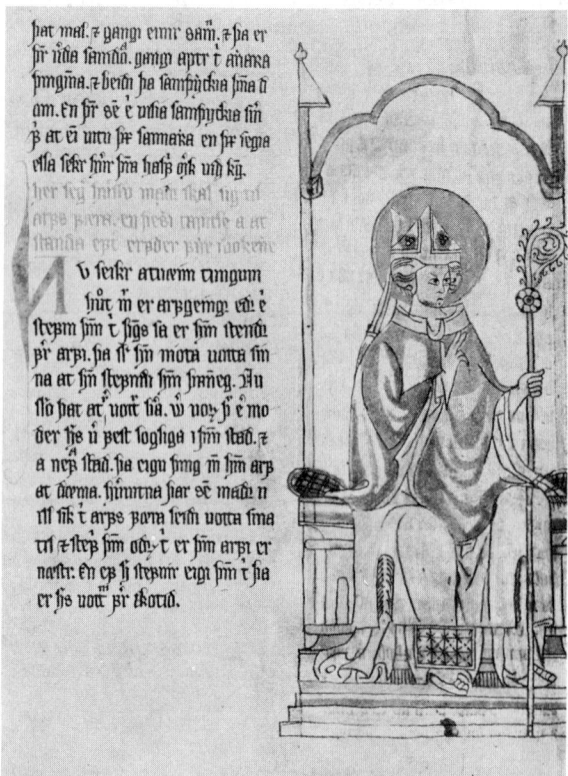

An Old Norse legal manuscript, 14th century, with a miniature depicting a bishop saint (MS AM 135, quarto, fol. 74 v.).

OLD NORSE LITERATURE

Old Norse literature was written in the vernaculars of Norway (until *c.* 1370) and Iceland (down to 1540). It used to be the custom to emphasize the pre-Christian origin of much Old Norse literature, but the oldest extant MSS (*c.* 1150 onward) were composed when Christianity was the established religion of both Norway and Iceland. Christianity had been formally introduced into Iceland in A.D. 1000, and from 1153 the two countries (with some of the island nations in the Atlantic) constituted the Archdiocese of Nidaros (Trondheim). There are growing tendencies among scholars to regard the growth of Old Norse literature as a parallel to and partly a result of the development of a formal ecclesiastical education; most of the literature in the oldest MSS is also of clearly Christian character. It is often quite impossible to demonstrate beyond dispute whether a given work originated in Norway or in Iceland, but the greater part of Old Norse literature is preserved in Icelandic MSS.

Poetry. The *Poetic Edda* (also called by the late and fictitious name of *Saemundar Edda*) is a collection of mythological, didactic, and heroic poems in the famous *Codex Regius,* written in Iceland *c.* 1270, and a few later and less important MSS. Since the poems of the Edda are the chief source of our knowledge of Scandinavian mythology, it is regrettable that neither their provenance inside the Old Norse area, nor the date of their composition is known. Some of the poems may have sprung from an antiquarian interest of the 12th or 13th century, but others seem to have survived (possibly in part through oral tradition) from an older period, e.g., *Völuspá* (The Sibyl's Prophesy), tentatively dated *c.* 1000. Modern scholars find it difficult to believe that the Edda should represent pure paganism totally unmellowed by Christian influence.

Eddic poetry is written in simple alliterative meters (*fornyrðislag, ljóðaháttr, málaháttr*), whereas scaldic poetry makes use of quite elaborate ones: the common *dróttkvætt, hrynhent,* and several others; *runhent* combines alliteration with rhyme. This genre, which probably originated as court poetry, comprises formal eulogies, epitaphs (*erfidrápa, erfiflokkr, erfikvæði*), and other laudatory poems, with a great number of smaller (often less formal and more personal) occasional poems, *lausavísur.* The *Snorri Edda* is a textbook of poetics with a metrical key and chapters on kennings, etc., written by *Snorri Sturlson. While Eddic poetry is anonymous, a fair number of scaldic poems have known authors. Most sacred poetry in Old Norse belongs to scaldic poetry in a wider sense. Religious poems are the *Geisli* (The Sunbeam), composed in honor of St. Olaf II, King of Norway by Einarr Skúlason, an Icelandic scald; the *Plácítusdrápa,* a poetic version of the legend of St. Eustace; and the *Harmsól* (Sun of Sorrow); all are from the 12th century. The *Sólarljóð* (Song of the Sun) from *c.* 1200, and *Líknarbraut* (Path of Mercy) show to what an astonishing degree common European religious feeling had already pervaded Old Norse literature. A translation of *Veni Creator Spiritus* is found in *Heilags anda vísur* (13th century). *Lilja* (The *Lily,* 14th century) is generally conceded to be the greatest religious poem in Old Norse. Later tradition has it that Eysteinn (Ásgrímsson ?), a cleric, was the author. A considerable number of poems dedicated to the Blessed

*Thirteenth-century carved wooden door panel illustrating scenes from the Old Norse saga
"The Rider and the Lion."*

Virgin are known, some of them written on the eve of
the Reformation (introduced in Iceland in 1550). The
last great religious scald in Iceland in the medieval tradition, Jón Arason (1484–1550), was the last Catholic
bishop of Hólar, and a martyr. The Icelandic *rímur,*
epic poems of late medieval origin, constitute a genre
of their own.

Prose. The earliest extant MSS of Old Norse prose are
homilies, sermons, and saints' lives, together with
learned treatises on astronomy, computation, grammar,
and legal writings (civil and ecclesiastical laws). Most
of the early writings are translations, or at least adap-
tions of foreign (chiefly Latin) sources. Apart from their
intrinsic value, they afforded excellent training in the
handling of the vernacular for literary purposes. Note
should be taken of the fact that during this period there
was a beginning of scientific writing in Latin in such
works as the *Profectio Danorum in Terram Sanctam,
Historia Norvegiae,* and Theodoricus the Monk's *Historia de antiquitate regum Norvagiensium.*

The writings of the early, formative years of Old
Norse letters are penetrated by a universal Christian
spirit. Such writings were in turn to influence style and
diction of the more original works in Old Norse prose.

The monasteries, especially in Iceland, had a prominent
place in the formation of literature in the vernacular,
and most early writings are attributable to the clergy.
Hagiographic literature afforded the pattern for the
native bishops' sagas, and for some of the kings' sagas,
not all of them noteworthy for their historicity. *Ari
Thorgilsson, often called the father of Icelandic history,
belonged to another school, usually regarded as more
reliable: in the *Íslendingabók* (Book of the Icelanders)
he wrote the early history of his country, showing extraordinary ability in his firm handling of chronology.
The *Landnámabók* (Book of Settlements), another
cornerstone of historical lore and learning in medieval
Iceland, has also been connected with Ari.

Of the kings' sagas, the great corpus *Heimskringla*
is the best known; in this work Snorri Sturluson copied,
reedited, and rewrote diverse material from older
sources. It has been suggested that Snorri also wrote
the *Egils saga,* one of the finest of the *Icelanders' sagas.*
Other sagas of this class are *Njáls saga* (hailed as the
greatest and most mature), *Laxdæla saga, Gísla saga,
Gunnlaugs saga,* and *Hrafnkels saga.* The *Völsunga
saga,* one of the so-called *Fornaldar sögur* (Sagas of
antiquity), covers the same ground as the heroic Eddic

poems. Contemporary sagas are found in the compilation *Sturlunga saga* and some of the best of the bishops' sagas.

The Norwegian court illustrates the importance of the audience for the creation of literature. A special court style developed in romantic sagas, such as *Karlamagnús saga, Tristrams saga,* and *Erex saga,* based on foreign romances, and in further sagas of Barlaam and Josaphat, and of Dietrich of Bern, the latter derived from German traditions. The Icelandic *Riddara sögur* (Sagas of Chivalry) provides a parallel to the romantic sagas composed in Norway. In *Alexanders saga, Rómverja sögur,* and *Trójumanna saga,* classical antiquity was introduced into Old Norse literature, and Geoffrey of Monmouth was translated in *Breta sögur. Stjórn,* a translation of parts of the Bible with commentaries, and *Konungs Skuggsjá (Speculum Regale),* a didactic dialogue of real merit, are outstanding examples of medieval Norwegian literature.

Although they do not belong to literature proper, the great codes of Norwegian and Icelandic law must be mentioned. There exists in the *Maríu saga* and the collections of miracles a vast Marian literature that was still highly popular down to the Reformation, as was hagiographic literature on the whole. The publication of the Icelandic translation of the New Testament (1540) falls well beyond the Old Norse period (*see* BIBLE IV, 40).

See also ICELANDIC LITERATURE; NORWEGIAN LITERATURE; SAGA.

Bibliography: S. EINARSSON, *History of Icelandic Literature* (Baltimore 1958), with bibliog. G. TURVILLE-PETRE, *Origins of Icelandic Literature* (Oxford 1953). *Islandica* (Ithaca, N.Y. 1908–). **Illustration credit:** Fig. 1, The Arnamagnean Institute, Copenhagen. Fig. 2, The Icelandic National Museum.

[H. BEKKER-NIELSEN]

OLD TESTAMENT LITERATURE

This general article on OT literature will discuss the contents and arrangement of the books as found in the Hebrew and Catholic Bible and will survey briefly the growth of OT literature.

Formation and Division of OT Canon. The books in both the Hebrew and the Catholic Bibles are called canonical, i.e., conforming to a norm. The Hebrew collection comprises the books of the Palestinian canon or protocanon; the Catholic Bible follows chiefly the Greek or Alexandrian canon, the books as listed among the Jews of the *Diaspora. The distinction is accurate, but it unfortunately suggests that the formation of a definitive listing was a direct concern to the Jews and that their efforts resulted in two rival collections. No predetermined rules judged canonicity; rather, after the ancient oral traditions were written down, they were slowly gathered into a collection enjoying special prestige. It is impossible to trace in detail the process by which certain writings came to be regarded as authoritative; no direct pronouncement concerning canonicity was made until the Jewish Synod of Jamnia in A.D. 90. The decision to limit the official list may have been made because of the plethora of apocalyptic books threatening the purity of ancient Jewish faith. The listing may also be in part the result of an increased respect for the written word, a characteristic of rigid postexilic Judaism. In any case, the books were recognized as being specially sacred because they were the vehicle of

God's revelation, and as such they became canonical.

The Palestinian Collection. The 24 books of the Palestinian collection have been changed into 39 books by dividing the books of Samuel, Kings, and Chronicles into two books each, by separating Ezra and Nehemia (originally only one book), and by reckoning the originally single "Book of the Twelve" as 12 separate books of the *Minor Prophets. The books of the Hebrew Bible are grouped in three main divisions: The Law (Torah), the Prophets (Nebi'im), and the Writings (Kethuvim). Some of these divisions appear arbitrary: the Law contains much besides legislation; the Prophets include historical literature; and the Writings show a great variety of literary forms. The Law refers to the five books of Moses: Genesis, Exodus, Leviticus, Numbers, and Deuteronomy. In the prophetic writings long usage has established a twofold division of the Former Prophets (Josue, Judges, Samuel, and Kings) and the Latter Prophets, the Prophets properly so called. These are in turn divided into the Major Prophets (Isaia, Jeremia, and Ezechiel) and the 12 Minor Prophets. The books of the Writings, in the order of the Hebrew Bible, are: Psalms, Job, Proverbs, Ruth, Canticle of Canticles, Ecclesiastes, Lamentations, Esther, Daniel, Ezra, Nehemia, and 1 and 2 Chronicles.

The Law was the first portion of the collection to receive normative authority; after the Exile these writings grew in prestige as they became the great unifying force of the Jewish community. The prophetic books, most of which did not reach their present form until after the Exile, became a recognized part of Jewish Scripture sometime after Malachia, last of the Minor Prophets (probably 4th century B.C.). The Writings were the last works to acquire canonical status; the prologue to Sirach (*c.* 130 B.C.) refers to "the Law, the Prophets, and the later authors," seeming to indicate that the threefold division was already established.

The Alexandrian Collection. For the benefit of the Jews of the Diaspora the Scriptures were translated into Greek. Undoubtedly the sections used in liturgical worship were translated first, but eventually the entire Hebrew canon was available in Greek. In addition to the writings accepted by the Palestinian Jews, the Greek translation, the Septuagint [*see* BIBLE, IV (TEXTS AND VERSIONS), 5], contained other books as well, some of them composed in Greek, others translated from Hebrew or Aramaic. A satisfactory explanation why the books were accepted in the Greek listing and not in the Hebrew collection has yet to be made, although many conjectures have been offered. That the Jews of the Diaspora could accept books considered canonical in Palestine and at the same time make additions of their own serves to emphasize that the concept of a canon as a settled, definitive listing was unknown. The fact is that the Jews outside Palestine included with books of the Hebrew collection certain writings not accepted by Palestinian Jews: Tobit, Judith, Wisdom, Sirach, Baruch, 1 and 2 Machabees, and some parts of Esther and Daniel, as well as certain apocryphal writings.

Certain Church Fathers, especially in the East, favored the retention of the Hebrew canon; nevertheless, the Church finally adopted most of the Septuagint OT writings. Hence, the Catholic Bible is richer by seven books than the Hebrew (and Protestant) canon. These additional books are called by Catholics deuterocanonical, i.e., belonging to the second canon; Jews and Protestants refer to them as apocryphal, a term that in Catholic usage refers to all noncanonical writings. (For noncanonical writings other than the deuterocanonical books, Jews and Protestants use the term "pseudoepigrapha.") No universally binding dogmatic declaration on the canon was made until the Council of Trent (1546), which included the seven additional books found in the Septuagint in the official OT of the Roman Church. The decree of Trent was repeated at Vatican Council I (1870).

The Growth of OT Literature. The OT is a collection of documents compiled in the course of more than a millennium. The presence of very ancient traditions side by side with postexilic materials indicates a protracted process of growth and expansion of original traditions. The stages of development to their present form cannot be exactly determined. Many motives, among them literary and cultic ones, were at work in the composition and preservation of the writings. The use of Israel's sacred traditions in liturgical service doubtless furnished an impetus to writing them down, so that, according to some critics, the life-setting for much of Scripture is to be found in Hebrew cultic observances.

The Law. The growth and amalgamation of traditions is best shown in the structure of the Pentateuch, which reveals four chief strands: J, E, D, and P. The J tradition was written down in the 10th or 9th century B.C.; the E material, slightly later. The combined JE traditions were subsequently joined to D, probably composed in the 7th century. With the addition of the P material after the Exile, the *Pentateuch assumed its definitive form. The solemn promulgation of the Mosaic Code during the reforms of Ezra and Nehemia climaxed a long developmental process.

The Prophets. The Former Prophets (called also the Deuteronomic histories) relate events in Israel from Josue to the Exile, combining oral and written narratives, chronicles, biographies, etc. These books came to be grouped with the Latter Prophets, because they were believed to have been written by prophets; and indeed, as a highly theologized account of Israel and its relations to God, they assert the principles of Yahwism no less than the Prophets do. Although the books were considerably reworked, assuming their present form only in the 6th or 5th century B.C., critics agree that they preserve very ancient traditions. The story of Davidic succession in 2 Samuel, ch. 9 to 20, for instance, is regarded as contemporaneous with the events it describes. The final forms of all the books show the influence of the *Deuteronomists.

The Latter Prophets, Prophets in the strict sense, are the authentic spokesmen of God who made His will known to men. The phenomenon of prophecy flourished in Israel from about the time of Samuel (11th century) to the 5th or 4th century B.C. Some of the Prophets were writers, but for the most part their oracles were orally preserved by disciples. Only later were they written down and implemented by heirs of the prophetic tradition, who were eager to preserve the works of the masters. Since books were frequently compiled from separate collections of oracles, it is sometimes difficult to establish chronology within a book; indeed, it is possible for a single book (e.g., Isaia) to combine oracles from Prophets living at different times.

The Writings. None of the books included in the Writings appeared in their present form until after the Exile, although some of them contain material as old as the ancient monarchy. The Psalms, the most esteemed portion of the collection, have in most instances a cultic life-setting. The definitive Psalter, a combination of smaller collections written over a long period from monarchical to postexilic days, was established by about 200 B.C. Particular esteem was also accorded the Megilloth (scrolls), five books used for the chief Jewish feasts: Ruth, Canticle of Canticles, Lamentations, Ecclesiastes, and Esther. There is little agreement about the exact postexilic dates to be assigned these works. Sapiential writings like Proverbs and Ecclesiastes developed from smaller collections of aphorisms expressing the practical wisdom of the Hebrews. The Writings also include problem literature, such as Job (*c.* 500 B.C.), and apocalyptic writing, such as Daniel (*c.* 150 B.C.). The historical books of 1 and 2 Chronicles, Ezra, and Nehemia were also attached to the Writings, indicating perhaps that the Former Prophets were already established as canonical by the time (*c.* 300 B.C.) these later histories were written.

See also BIBLE, III (CANON); LITERARY GENRES, BIBLICAL.

Bibliography: L. VENARD, DBSuppl 4:7–32. A. ROBERT, *ibid.* 5:405–421. Robert-Feuillet 1:2–68. Robert-Tricot 1²:66–103, 475–514. H. H. ROWLEY, *The Growth of the Old Testament* (New York 1950). A. WEISER, *The Old Testament: Its Formation and Development,* tr. D. BRANDON (4th ed. New York 1961). O. EISSFELDT, *Einleitung in das Alte Testament* (3d ed. Tübingen 1964).

[A. SUELZER]

OLDCASTLE, SIR JOHN, foremost Lollard knight and heretic; b. *c.* 1378; d. London, Dec. 14, 1417. Oldcastle succeeded to his father's Herefordshire estates before 1400, and was a member of Parliament, county sheriff, and an experienced military commander who enjoyed the royal favor of Henry IV and Henry V. Arrested in 1413 as a suspect *Lollard, he was tried for heresy and imprisoned in the Tower of London, from which he escaped. His attempts to organize a Lollard rising in 1414 ended in disaster, in which his motley army of chaplains, weavers, tailors, and artisans was easily routed by royalist forces. Oldcastle escaped but was finally captured in December 1417. A sincere and convinced Lollard, he refused to abjure his beliefs and was accordingly hanged and burned.

Bibliography: W. T. WAUGH, "Sir John Oldcastle," EngHist Rev 20 (1905) 434–456, 637–658. K. B. MCFARLANE, *John Wycliffe and the Beginnings of English Nonconformity* (New York 1953) 160–185.

[L. MACFARLANE]

OLDEGAR, ST., political counselor, crusader, refounder of Tarragona metropolitate; b. Barcelona, 1060; d. there, March 1, 1137 (feast, March 6). A child canon of Barcelona, where he became deacon (1089), dean (1094), and later priest, Oldegar (or Oleguer) retired to Saint-Adrian in Provence, where he became prior (1099), and then to its motherhouse, Saint-Ruf in Avignon, where he became abbot (1113). In 1116 he was elected bishop of *Barcelona, at that time the central see for the autonomous Count of Barcelona-Provence. In 1118 the Pope and the Count made him metropolitan in exile as well, with the task of restoring the metropolitanate of *Tarragona, a step psychologically important to crusading Catalonia. Oldegar traveled to Rome and Palestine, to reform councils at *Toulouse (1119) and *Reims (1119), to the first *Lateran Council (1123), and to Clermont (1130). As crusade legate in *Spain, especially during the Tortosa and Lérida campaigns, Oldegar—in his position of peacemaker—helped remove Castilian armies from Aragon, thus preparing the way for the later union of Aragon and Catalonia.

Bibliography: Flórez EspSagr 29:472–499, biog. Butler Th Attw 1:503–504. F. SOLDEVILA, *Història de Catalunya,* 3 v. (Barcelona 1962). For additional bibliog., *see* BARCELONA; TARRAGONA.

[R. I. BURNS]

OLDERADUS DE LAUDE, professor of Roman and civil law; b. Lodi, Italy, date unknown; d. Avignon, 1335. He taught civil law at Pavia, Siena, Montpellier, and Bologna (or Perugia). He was also an auditor and consistorial advocate of the Rota. He is known to have written at least one important work, namely, his *Quaestiones,* which treats of various questions of law (printed in Venice 1571).

Bibliography: Van Hove 1:464. Schulte 2:232–233. Savigny 6:55–59.

[J. M. BUCKLEY]

OLDHAM, HUGH, bishop of Exeter; b. Lancashire, England, late 15th century; d. Exeter, England, June 25, 1519. Hugh was educated in the household of the Earl of Derby and later at the University of *Oxford, where he took 4 years of arts and 4 more of Civil and Canon Law. He continued his law studies at the University of *Cambridge, possibly Queen's College, after 1493. He gained considerable ecclesiastical preferment, chiefly with the help of Lady Margaret *Beaufort, Countess of Richmond and Derby (d. 1509), whose chaplain he became in 1503. He was present at the laying of the foundation stone of the chapel of *Henry VII, Lady Margaret's son, at *Westminster Abbey. Having been created bishop of Exeter on Nov. 27, 1504, he founded the Manchester Grammar School in 1515. As bishop he was engaged in disputes with the Abbey of Tavistock over his right of episcopal *visitation, but the question was decided by *Leo X in favor of the abbot in 1517. He also had difficulty with Archbishop *Warham over the probate of wills. To the foundation (1516) and his friend, Bp. Richard *Foxe of Winchester, of Corpus Christi College, Oxford, he contributed 6,000 marks. He is buried in St. Saviour's chapel, Exeter cathedral, and the diocesan registry preserves his Register.

Bibliography: T. FOWLER, *Corpus Christi* (London 1898) 13–15. *The Victoria History of the County of Lancaster,* ed. W. FARRER and J. BROWNBILL, 8 v. (London 1906–14) 2:579. Emden 1396–97. A. A. MUMFORD, *Hugh Oldham . . .* (London 1936).

[V. I. J. FLINT]

OLDMEADOW, ERNEST JAMES, journalist and novelist; b. Chester, England, Oct. 31, 1867; d. London, Sept. 11, 1949. He was the son of Wesleyan parents and he embarked on the ministry in Nova Scotia. He was converted to Catholicism in 1897 and

shortly after was appointed editor of the London *Musical Times.* Cardinal Francis *Bourne offered him the editorship of the *Tablet* on the death of James Milburn (1860–1923) who had served the paper for many years, the last 3 as editor. Oldmeadow accepted and was, from Bourne's point of view, a good choice: they agreed that the journal's primary purpose was to defend the Church against the Church of England. In his 13 years as editor Oldmeadow conducted the controversy with unremitting zest; he had a vigorous, pugnacious style, which he kept fresh, he said, by writing standing up and wearing a hat. After World War I, however, there was not the same public for the old controversy in the old way. Bourne expected to draw, as his predecessors had done, a substantial income for the archdiocese from two-thirds of the profits of the paper; the other portion went to Cardinal Herbert Vaughan's foundation for the *Mill Hill Missionaries. When the paper's circulation fell to less than 3,000, Cardinal Arthur *Hinsley, Bourne's successor, soon sold it and thus Oldmeadow's editorship was terminated (1936) in a manner he resented. But the paper had never absorbed all his interests. He had founded a wine business (1912) under the name Francis Downman, and had made some mark as a novelist of the romantic Edwardian school. He was versatile and warmly convivial, and his apparently belligerent manner did him less than justice. In 1933 Bourne made him, together with H. Belloc and G. K. Chesterton, a Knight Commander of St. Gregory. Oldmeadow remained vigorous until he was more than 80, but after leaving the *Tablet* he took little part in Catholic life beyond writing the two-volume *Francis Cardinal Bourne* (1940–44), and novels, among them *Susan* (1907) and *The Scoundrel: A Romance* (1907), and *Antonio* (1909), the best-known of a long list that began with *Lady Lohengrin* in 1896. He wrote also studies of Schumann, Chopin, and Mozart.

See also CATHOLIC PRESS, WORLD SURVEY, 9.

[D. WOODRUFF]

OLDOINI, AGOSTINO, historian and bibliographer; b. La Spezia, Jan. 6, 1612; d. Perugia, March 23, 1683. He entered the Jesuit novitiate at Naples Feb. 4, 1628. Before taking up historical studies, he taught the classics and moral theology in Jesuit colleges at Naples, Rome, and Perugia. His literary works began with a treatise on grammar, continued through studies in the history of the papacy, and ended with bibliographies of the academies of Rome, Liguria, and Perugia. His chief work was the revised edition of Alphonso Cicacconio's *Vitae et res gestae pontificum romanorum,* first published in 1630. Oldoini brought the work to the pontificate of Clement IX (1667–69). It was published as *Vitae et res gestae Pontificum Romanorum et S.R.E. Cardinalium* (4 v., Rome 1670–77).

Bibliography: Sommervogel 5:1880–81. É. AMANN, DTC 11.1:962. Koch JesLex 1322.

[J. V. MENTAG]

O'LEARY, HENRY JOSEPH, second archbishop of Edmonton, Alberta, Canada; b. Richibucto, New Brunswick, Canada, March 13, 1879; d. Victoria, British Columbia, Canada, March 5, 1938. He was ordained Sept. 1, 1901, and after a brief period of parish and chancery work, he was named bishop of Charlottetown, Prince Edward Island, and consecrated at Bathhurst, New Brunswick, May 22, 1913. Zealous in promoting priestly and religious vocations, the young bishop proved himself also a capable administrator, undertaking a vast program of church and school develop-

Henry Joseph O'Leary.

ment. On Sept. 7, 1920, he was transferred to the Edmonton archdiocese, where he continued his pastoral efforts, particularly in the field of education. Schools, churches, and hospitals were the special object of his solicitude. In spite of illness in his later years, O'Leary indefatigably strove to pave the way for the sound future development of the Edmonton archdiocese.

Bibliography: Archives, Archdiocese of Edmonton.

[C. DOZOIS]

OLGA, ST., called also Helga, Princess of Kiev; b. Pskov, Russia, *c.* 890; d. Kiev, Russia, July 11, 969 (feast, July 11). Probably of Slavic descent, Olga married Igor, the Varangian Prince of Kiev in 903, and after his death on campaign in 945 she acted as regent for their son Svyatoslav (d. 972). Her revenge against the Drevlianians for her husband's death is described at

St. Olga of Kiev being received at Constantinople in 957, miniature in a manuscript written c. 1300.

length by *Nestor in the *Primary Chronicle,* and the monastic historian has high praise for her courage and ability as a ruler. She instituted administrative and fiscal reforms throughout the realm and hastened its recovery from the destructive wars of Igor. Late in 957 she visited Constantinople; and although the Russian sources describe her Baptism there, it appears from a careful reading of the Greek accounts that Olga had already been a Christian for several years when she visited the court of Emperor *Constantine Porphyrogenitus. Although she might well have been received into the Latin rite in Kiev *c.* 955, the princess, in an effort to gain autonomy for the Russian Church, was prepared to enter into relations with either Rome or Byzantium, and her visit to Constantine was followed by a letter to *Otto I asking that missionaries be sent to her people. Her Baptism was not followed by the conversion of the whole nation, for the pagan party rallied around her son Svyatoslav, who resisted all efforts of his mother to instruct him in the faith. After her son had come of age in 964, Olga again served as regent in Kiev while he was engaged in wars against the *Bulgars, and on her death he gave her a Christian burial in that city. Olga was early recognized as a saint and is honored in the Russian and Ukrainian Churches, along with her grandson *Vladimir, who effected the Christianization of his people *c.* 988.

Bibliography: *The Russian Primary Chronicle,* ed. and tr. S. H. CROSS and O. P. SHERBOWITZ-WETZOR (Cambridge, Mass. 1953) 64–87, 111. CONSTANTINE PORPHYROGENITUS, *De cerimoniis . . .,* bk. 2, ch. 15 in PG 112:1107–12. E. GOLUBINSKY, *Istoriia russkoi tserkvi,* (2d ed. Moscow 1900–01) 1.1:74–104, 241–242. G. LAEHR, *Die Anfänge des russischen Reiches* (Berlin 1930) 103–106. G. VERNADSKY, *Kievan Russia* (New Haven 1948) 32–47. Butler Th Attw 3:72. **Illustration credit:** Biblioteca Nacional, Madrid.

[B. J. COMASKEY]

OLIER, JEAN JACQUES, founder of the Seminary and the Society of Saint-Sulpice; b. Paris, Sept. 20, 1608; d. Issy, April 2, 1657. Olier was baptized in the church of St. Paul, Paris, on the day of his birth; he spent his childhood in Lyons, where his father had been assigned as administrator of justice. There he completed his classical education with the Jesuits. His philosophical studies he took at the College of Harcourt, Paris. After his theology at the Sorbonne, he undertook further Hebrew study in Rome. Having returned to France in 1631 on the occasion of his father's death, Olier placed himself under the spiritual direction of (St.) *Vincent de Paul and was subsequently ordained May 21, 1633, by Bp. Étienne Puget, auxiliary bishop of Metz. Although remaining a lifelong friend of (St.) Vincent, Olier came under the guidance of Père Charles de *Condren, the superior of the Oratory, who had dedicated himself to the renovation of priestly life in France. When Olier was offered a bishopric, which his family urged him to accept, it was De Condren who prevailed upon him to refuse it. Before he died (Jan. 7, 1641), De Condren divulged his plans for implementing the Tridentine decrees concerning the preparation of candidates for the priesthood.

On Dec. 29, 1642, Olier and two priests rented a small house in Vaugirard, a suburb of Paris, not to initiate a religious community but to establish a favorable environment for the training of priests. The experiment attracted attention, and soon six priests and eight seminarians shared a common schedule of work and prayer. On Aug. 10, 1642, Olier assumed charge of the parish church of Saint-Sulpice, Paris, and the community of Vaugirard joined him there. In 1643 Olier requested the government's approval for his society of priests. In November 1645, this petition was granted. In 1652 Olier relinquished his pastoral charge of the parish of Saint-Sulpice and devoted the rest of his

Jean Jacques Olier.

life primarily to seminary work. He had the happiness of assigning priests of his community to four other seminaries: Nantes (1649), Viviers (1650), Le Puy (1652), and Clement (1653). The last 5 years of his life were marked by great suffering and physical hardship, caused by his intense labors. Olier is a leader of the "French School of Spirituality," and his writings have had a worldwide influence to the 20th century. Although he did not produce a systematic or scientific corpus of ascetical theology, his works show him to be a master of the spiritual life (*see* SULPICIANS; SULPICIAN METHOD IN CATECHETICS).

Bibliography: *Oeuvres complètes*, ed. J. P. MIGNE (Paris 1857). E. M. FAILLON, *Vie de M. Olier*, 2 v. (4th ed. Paris 1873). P. POURRAT, *Father Olier, Founder of St. Sulpice*, tr. W. S. REILLY (Baltimore 1932). P. BOISARD, *La Compagnie de St. Sulpice, trois siècles d'histoire*, 2 v. (multigraphed; Paris 1962). E. A. WALSH, *The Priesthood in the Writings of the French School: Berulle, De Condren, Olier* (Washington 1949). F. MONIER, *Vie de Jean Jacques Olier, curé de la paroisse et fondateur du séminaire de Saint-Sulpice* (Paris 1914). E. LEVESQUE, DTC 11.1:963–982.

[C. J. NOONAN]

OLIGER, LIVARIUS, Franciscan historian; b. Schorbach (Diocese of Metz), France (Germany), Feb. 17, 1875; d. Rome, Jan. 29, 1951. He entered the *Franciscan Order in 1892, was ordained in 1900, and from 1906 to 1950 held the chair of Franciscan history at the Antonianum in Rome. From 1911 to 1915, however, he served as associate editor of the *Archivum Franciscanum historicum* at Quaracchi (near Florence) and during World War I (1915–18) returned to Germany, where he taught at St. Anna in Munich. Oliger held the post of professor of hagiography (from 1931) and historical method (from 1941) at the University of the Lateran and was cofounder of the Franciscan journal *Antonianum* (Rome 1926–   ). His writings—including critical editions and commentaries;

pioneer work on the Franciscan *Spirituals, *Fraticelli, and *Brethren of the Free Spirit; mission history; biography; and hagiographical studies—were crowned by his *Expositio quattuor magistrorum super regulam fratrum minorum, 1241–1242* (Rome 1950).

Bibliography: *Miscellanea historica p. L. Oliger . . . oblata* (*Antonianum* 20; Rome 1945) with bibliog. L. SPÄTLING, Franz Stud 32 (1950) 362–381, with bibliog. since 1945; *Antonianum* 26 (1951) 210–214.

[O. J. BLUM]

OLINDA-RECIFE, ARCHDIOCESE OF (OLIDENSIS ET RECIFENSIS)

Located in the state of Pernambuco, Brazil; created a diocese in 1676; raised to an archdiocese in 1910. In 1964 it had eight suffragan sees: Pesqueira (1910), Nazaré (1918), Garanhuns (1918), Petrolina (1923), Caruaru (1948), Afogados da Ingàzeira (1956), Palmares (1962), and Floresta (1964). The parish of Olinda dates from 1534, but soon a number of other churches were built. In 1552 the Jesuits arrived and founded a college. Other religious orders followed: the Franciscans in 1585, the Carmelites in 1588, and the Benedictines in 1592. The Jesuits and the Franciscans were the principal missionaries among the Indians. In 1614 an ecclesiastical administration was created independent of the Diocese of Bahia, but it was abolished in 1624 and replaced by a vicar-general. During the Dutch occupation (1630–54) the Church declined in spite of the tolerant attitude of Maurice of Nassau. The French Capuchins were permitted to enter the area, but a number of clergymen were imprisoned, executed, or exiled. The clergy took an active part in the wars for liberation against the Dutch. Afterward religious life was reorganized, churches and convents were restored. The Oratory of S. Philip Neri was founded in 1662. Finally the diocese was created for the area of all northeastern Brazil. The first bishop was Estevão Brioso de Figueiredo.

The Church Beleaguered. During the 18th century the bishops were intimately involved with the civil administration of the province. Manuel Álvares da Costa (1706–15) served provisionally as the civil government of Pernambuco. He vacillated in the war between the two rival cities of Olinda and Recife so much that he finally formed a "holy battalion" of more than 100 armed clerics for his own defense. Recife won the struggle and became the capital. The bishop was exiled. Bishop Luis de S. Teresa was an active defender of the rights of the Church and also was exiled. The Brazilian Bishop Tomás da Encarnação Costa e Lima (1774–84) was an active supporter of the policies of Pombal. At the end of the century José J. da Cunha Azeredo Coutinho (1796–1802) introduced a number of administrative reforms when he was in charge of the civil government. Though he was not a Mason as has been claimed, he organized the seminary that he founded in Olinda in a modern, but not liberal and revolutionary, fashion. In the middle of the 18th century in Olinda alone there were 45 secular and 149 regular priests in a population of 3,272. In the entire diocese there were 43 parishes, 470 chapels, 3 Jesuit colleges for philosophy and theology, 2 Benedictine monasteries, 13 Carmelite convents, 8 Franciscan convents, and 2 Oratorian, and one Capuchin. The diocese had 25 Indian missions. However, the frequent periods in which no bishop was in the see contributed to a lack of religious discipline.

The 19th century was a restless period in the diocese. Bishop Antônio de S. José Bastos (1815–19) was prevented from governing because of the "Revolution of the Fathers" of 1817. The cathedral chapter irregularly took upon itself the government of the diocese, which then consisted of 121 parishes and 600 churches and chapels. A start was made on reform in the 1860s by Bishop Manuel do Rego Medeiros, who reorganized the seminary with the help of Italian Jesuits and sent 12 seminarians to study in Rome. Bishop Vital María *Gonçalves de Oliveira (1872–78) fought the influence of Masonry among the clergy and the religious brotherhoods and was one of the important figures in the famous Religious Question (*see* BRAZIL). At his trial in 1874 Dom Vital was accompanied by the bishop of Rio de Janeiro and by John Miege, SJ, apostolic vicar of Kansas, who was traveling in South America at the time. During this same period Father Villemin, CM, founded Vincentian conferences in Olinda. At the end of the century the great lay apostle Carlos A. de Meneses founded the Workingmen's Federation and other social organizations. The Jesuit Bartolomeu Taddei started the Apostolate of Prayer, and there was a general resurgence of the religious orders in the diocese with friars and monks coming from Europe to fill the convents of the old orders and with new orders and congregations establishing houses.

The Church as an Active Social Force. In the 20th century the Church expanded its activities. Bishop Luis R. da Silva (1901–15), who became the first archbishop, founded the Catholic Workers' Center and con-

The church of São Pedro dos Clericos, Recife, Brazil.

1963 STATISTICS

Area	Population	Parishes	Clergy Sec.	Clergy Reg.
Olinda-Recife	1,428,843	61	97	231
Pesqueira	258,727	18	16	7
Nazaré	673,440	22	28	12
Garanhuns	476,522	16	17	22
Petrolina	230,372	12	15	—
Caruaru	423,849	20	19	3
Afogados da Ingàzeira	218,809	9	8	5
Palmares	300,800	11	9	14
Floresta	125,438	6	5	2

voked the first diocesan synod (1908). Sebastião *Leme da Silveira Cintra (1916–21), known as the catechizing bishop, received the Jesuits who had been expelled from Portugal. They founded a school in Recife. That city for all practical purposes became the seat of the archbishopric with the elevation in 1918 of one of the churches there to a *concatedral*. Miguel de Lima Valverde (1922–51) inaugurated the Brazilian Catholic Action movement. Antônio de Almeida Morais Junior (1951–60) organized a general mission in the diocese to revitalize religious life. Carlos Gouvêa Coelho (1960–64) began the construction of the regional seminary of the northeast with contributions from North American Catholics and reorganized and centralized diocesan projects. He acquired a radio station and initiated the Rural Syndicate Movement, bringing together thousands of farmers, to counterbalance the Ligas Camponesas, of Communist inspiration. His successor was Helder Pessoa Camara (1964–), who had been auxiliary bishop of Rio de Janeiro, bishop of the poor and of the *favelas*. Bishop Antônio Campelo de Aragão of Petrolina (1956–) has also founded rural cooperatives.

The Church has begun to use radio for missionary work with stations for educational broadcasts in Olinda, Nazaré, and Afogados da Ingàzeira. It operates a press in Caruaru and two movie houses in Pesqueira, four in Nazaré, and one in Afogados da Ingàzeira. The Jesuit Catholic University of the archdiocese was opened in 1951 and includes an Institute of Religious Science for laymen and another for nuns. There is also a school of philosophy, a school of social service, and in Garahuns a professional technical school. Among the religious orders serving in the provinces in 1964 were Jesuits, Benedictines, Vincentians, Redemptorists, Franciscans, Capuchins, Carmelites, Paulists, Salesians, Marists, Fathers of the Sacred Heart, and Missionaries of the Holy Family.

See also BRAZIL.

Bibliography: C. J. DO CARMO BARATTA, *História ecclesiástica de Pernambuco* (Recife 1922). P. F. DA SILVEIRA CAMARGO, *História eclesiástica do Brasil* (Petrópolis 1955). B. MUELLER, *Olinda e suas igrejas* (Recife 1945). V. WILLEKE, "The Mission of São Miguel de Una in Pernambuco," *Americas* 13 (1956–57) 69–74. E. GUERRA, *A questão religiosa do segundo império brasileiro* (Rio de Janeiro 1952). R. DE OLIVEIRA, *O conflito maçônico-religioso de 1872* (Petrópolis 1952). **Illustration credit:** Brazilian Information Bureau, New York.

[O. VAN DER VAT]

OLIVA, ABBEY OF, Cistercian monastery near Danzig, founded in 1174 by Subislaus I, a Prince of Pomerania, colonized in 1186 from the abbey of Kol-

West façade of the baroque church of the Abbey of Oliva.

batz. It became the center of the *Cistercian mission in Prussia. In 1224 pagan Prussians demolished the monastery, and it was after this that a three-aisled Romanesque basilica, based on the second plan of *Clairvaux (*see* CISTERCIAN ART AND ARCHITECTURE), was built. When this church was destroyed by fire in 1350, it was rebuilt in its present dimensions (more than 300 feet long) with the addition of a polygonal gallery choir. The star vaulting, built from 1577 to 1582, was patterned on English models. In the 18th century the church was remodeled along extravagant baroque lines; among other innovations, a famous organ with 3 manuals and 83 stops was installed. The abbey was secularized in 1831; the abbey church, converted into a parish church in 1835, became the cathedral of the newly established Diocese of *Danzig in 1925. Since 1945 Oliva has been a Polish Cistercian priory.

Bibliography: *Die ältere Chronik und die Schrifttafeln von Oliva,* ed. T. HIRSCH in *Scriptores rerum Prussicarum,* 5 v. (Leipzig 1861–74) v.1. *Fontes Olivenses,* ed. W. KETRZYŃSKI in *Monumenta Poloniae historica,* 6 v. (Cracow 1864–93) 6:257–382. *Annales Olivenses aetate posteriores* (Thorn 1916–18). T. HIRSCH, *Das Kloster Oliva* (Danzig 1850). H. J. SLEUMER, *Die ursprüngliche Gestalt der Zisterzienser Abteikirche Oliva* (Heidelberg 1909). F. J. WOTHE, "Die Kirchen der Diözese Danzig," *Festgabe für Bischof Carl M. Splett* (Hildesheim 1963) 14–22. **Illustration credit:** German Information Center, New York City.

[A. SCHNEIDER]

OLIVAINT, PIERRE, Jesuit priest; b. Paris, Feb. 22, 1816; d. there, May 26, 1871. After studies at the Collège Charlemagne and the École normale, Olivaint gained an *agrégé* in history, taught in Paris and Grenoble, and then tutored the son of the Duc de Rochefoucauld-Liancourt. Although religiously indifferent as a youth, he entered the *Jesuits (1845). After ordination (1850), he taught history (1852–57) in the newly opened Collège de Vaugirard in Paris. During his term there as rector (1857–65), the college became the leading private school in the capital. Olivaint was then named superior of the Jesuit Parisian residence at rue de Sèvres (1865–71). He was absorbed in retreat and sodality work until the outbreak of the Franco-Prussian War (1870). When his residence was designated an auxiliary hospital during the war, he showed an equal devotion to the wounded.

When the Commune revolted against Versailles, he sent his community from Paris but remained there himself with a priest and two brothers. He and Father Caubert were arrested (April 4, 1871), and sent to the Conciergerie prison where they found three other Jesuit priests, Ducoudray, Clerc, and de Bengy. Next day the Commune declared the prisoners "hostages of the people of Paris." By April 13 more than 200 hostages had been gathered in the prison of Mazas. When the government reoccupied all Paris except the 11th *arrondissement,* the Commune ordered their execution, and had them transferred to the Rouquette prison. Six hostages, including two Jesuits, were shot on May 24. Two days later, 47 prisoners, including Olivaint and his fellow religious, were ordered to leave the Rouquette. Guarded by communards, they walked to Belleville through jeering crowds until, at 83 rue Haxo, the mob massacred them and threw their bodies into a cesspool. After the fall of the Commune (May 28), the remains of Olivaint and his Jesuit companions were returned to the rue de Sèvres. Their beatification process was introduced in Rome in 1937.

Bibliography: A. DE PONLEVOY, *Actes de la captivité et de la mort des RR. PP. P. Olivaint . . .* (Paris 1871; 17th ed. 1907). C. CLAIR, *Pierre Olivaint* (Paris 1878). LECANUET ÉglFrance 1: 99–126. Koch JesLex 1324–25.

[R. J. SEALY]

OLIVÉTAN, PIERRE ROBERT, reformer and Biblical scholar; b. Noyon, *c.* 1506; d. Ferrara, 1538. Olivétan was a relative of John Calvin, with whom he was associated at the University of Paris and in the publication of his French version of the Bible. A reformer, he fled from Paris to Orléans and in May 1528 was studying Greek and Hebrew in Strassburg. He may have preceded Guillaume *Farel in teaching Reform doctrines in Geneva, but was soon expelled (1532). At Neuchâtel he was employed by the sect of the *Waldenses in the Piedmont valley, for whom he prepared a French translation of the Bible. The work *La Bible qui est toute la Saint Escriture* appeared at Neuchâtel in June 1535, with a preface by Calvin and a notable introduction by "the humble little translator," who lays the book at the feet of Christ's body, the Church. Calvin credits Olivétan with a lively and penetrating mind; E. Doumergue calls him for his eloquence and humor "un Rabelais évangelique"; H. Kunze pronounces him "a rationalist philologian." He used Jacques Lefèvre d'Étaples's earlier translation with scholarly discretion.

Bibliography: É. DOUMERGUE, *Jean Calvin,* 7 v. (Lausanne 1899–1927) 1:117–125. H. KUNZE, *Die Bibelübersetzungen von Lefèvre d'Étaples und von P. R. Olivétan* (Leipzig 1935). J. COURVOISIER, RGG³ 4:1627.

[J. T. MC NEILL]

OLLÉ-LAPRUNE, LÉON, French philosopher, b. Paris, July 25, 1839; d. there, Dec. 13, 1898. He came of a deeply Christian family. Ollé-Laprune studied at the Lycée Condorcet and the École Normale (1858). He was honored with the degree *agrégé des lettres* (1861), and taught successively at the *lycées* of Nice (1861), Douai (1864), Versailles (1868), and Henry IV in Paris (1871). From 1875 to his death he lectured at the École Normale.

Ollé-Laprune was a fervent Catholic; the example of his life as well as the sublimity of his thought had great influence on his students, especially at the École Normale. The essential characteristic of his teaching was the inauguration of a living philosophy whose duty it was to seek concrete certitude, at once solidly moral and intellectual. The true philosopher, he would say, thinks with his whole being, and is always "attached to God as principle, support, light and rule of all thought." Some of his many works are: *La Philosophie de Malebranche* (1870), *De la Certitude morale* (1880), *Le Prix de la vie* (1894), *La Vitalité chrétienne* (1901), and *La Raison et le rationalisme* (1906). Ollé-Laprune's greatest contribution was the inspiration he gave to a brilliant disciple, M. *Blondel. In his thesis on *L'Action* (1893), the pupil undertook to develop in a systematic manner the message of his master—a message calling for the establishment of an "integral realism" in thought, in action, and in being.

Bibliography: R. CRIPPA, EncFil 3:1010–13.

[R. JOLIVET]

OLMEDO, JOSÉ JOAQUÍN DE, patriot and neoclassical poet of the independence movement; b. Guayaquil, Ecuador, 1780; d. there, 1847. Educated in Quito and Lima, he served as a deputy to the Cortes of Cádiz in 1812 and there gave his celebrated address against the *mita* system of Indian labor. When he returned to Ecuador, Spanish America was fighting for liberty, and he became the leader in Guayaquil when independence was declared there in 1820. From then on he played an active role in the revolutionary movement as governor, legislator, and diplomat. Under the leadership of Simón Bolívar the struggle for independence in South America was ended with the victories of Junín and Ayacucho, which vanquished the last of the Spanish forces. Olmedo, fired by the jubilation over victory, wrote a triumphal ode on the battle of Junín. Before it was finished the battle of Ayacucho occurred and he united the two victories in his poem, *Canto a Junín*. The poem was widely read throughout the Americas, and brought fame to the author. He also wrote other poems, such as the one on the triumph of Miñarica in the civil war, which is perhaps better as a poem; but the *Canto a Junín* alone has endured as an integral part of the independence struggle and a focus for patriotic fervor for later generations. Its value lay in its timeliness, bringing echoes of Pindar and Horace into the Spanish American independence movement. Olmedo's writings were not extensive; the Jesuit Espinosa Pólit has piously collected the fragments.

[I. J. BARRERA]

OLMOS, ANDRÉS DE, Franciscan missionary and linguist, early investigator of Indian lore in New Spain; b. near Oña, Burgos, Spain, *c*. 1491; d. Tampico, New Spain, buried there, August 1570 (not Oct. 8, 1571,

as some sources state). He spent some years in Olmos, near Valladolid, whence came the name he used. He studied at the University of Valladolid and at 20 entered the Franciscan Order at Abrojo. When his su-

Andrés de Olmos.

perior, Juan de *Zumárraga, was named bishop of Mexico, he took Andrés de Olmos to New Spain with him in 1528. According to the chronicler Vázquez he was in Guatemala from 1529 to the middle of 1530, but it is probable that he was there after 1543. He spent some time in Tecamachalco, where he was superior in 1543; in Tlalmanalco; in Cuernavaca; and in Tlaxcala. In 1544 he tried to go to Florida and was at least instrumental in getting the expedition under way. He was chiefly responsible for spreading Christianity among the Huastec, Totonac, Tepehua, and Chichimec tribes, often with great sacrifice. From Hueytlalpan he evangelized the surrounding area and in the process learned Totonac and Tepehua. There, to assist in the work of conversion he wrote his *Arte de la lengua mexicana* (1547) and prepared grammars in Totonac and Huastec. In 1557, or shortly thereafter, he penetrated the interior north of Tamaholipa and sought help in colonizing the area of the three rivers of Palmas (today Soto la Marina), Bravo, and Achiuse (today the Mississippi).

[J. MEADE]

OLOMOUC, ARCHDIOCESE OF (OLOMUCENSIS)

Metropolitan see since 1777, in Moravia, Czechoslovakia. Formerly Olmütz, the see was established in 1063. In 1963 it had an area of 5,830 square miles and a population of 1,950,000; religious statistics (1949?) give 1,500,000 Catholics in 651 parishes with 536 secular priests. Religious houses were suppressed in 1950. The only suffragan see, Brno, was created in 1777.

The Christian origins of Olomouc are obscure. German missionaries from *Salzburg and Passau had penetrated the area before SS. *Cyril and Methodius arrived from Byzantium in 863. Rome *c*. 900 sent an Archbishop John and Bishops Benedict and Daniel into Great Moravia, which the Magyars destroyed *c*. 905. In 973 Moravia was incorporated into the See of *Prague, but a Moravian bishop was mentioned in a synod of Mainz in 976. In 1063 Duke Vratislav II appointed a Benedictine, John, as bishop of Moravia, and Emperor Henry IV invested him in the see. In 1085 Prague again incorporated Moravia into its diocese, but Gregory VII restored its autonomy. Under Bp. Henry Zdík (1126–50) the newly built church of St. Wenceslas (restored in the 14th and early 20th centuries) became the Cathedral of Olomouc. Innocent III confirmed the privilege of the chapter of canons to elect the bishop (1207), and the Golden Bull gave the Czech king the right of investiture (1212). The bishops became ecclesiastical princes with their own courts under Bishop Robert and especially under Bp. Bruno of Schaumburg (1245–81), a supporter of Přemysl Otakar II in the colonizing of Moravia with German settlers.

In 1344 Olomouc became suffragan to the new Archdiocese of Prague, both sees having been suffragan to *Mainz since 1063. The first cardinal of Olomouc, John Zelezny (1418–30), was the principal accuser of John Hus at the Council of Constance. Bp. Stanislaus Thurzo (1497–1540) made Olomouc a center of humanism; Vilém Prusinovsky (1565–72) called the Jesuits to Olomouc, and the college he founded in 1566 became under them a university. (In the early 19th century this became a theological college, which in 1945 was united with Palacký University; the theological college, in Prague in 1950, moved to Leitmeritz in 1953.) In 1599 the Bishops of Olomouc received the right to coin money. Cardinal Franz Dietrichstein (1599–1636) brought Moravia back to Catholicism after the important work of his predecessor, Stanislaus Pavlovsky (1579–98). Charles of Liechtenstein-Kastlelkorn (1664–95) restored the Church after the Thirty Years' War and gave support to ecclesiastical art.

The first Archbishop of Olomouc was Cardinal A. T. Colloredo (1777–1811); when Olomouc became an archdiocese, many Evangelicals entered the Church. Emperor *Joseph II suppressed 83 monasteries in the see. After World War I under the Czechoslovak Republic the Church was challenged by the *Los-von-Rom movement, but the saintly Abp. A. C. Stojan (1921–23) founded the Apostolate of SS. Cyril and Methodius and promoted the union of Orthodox Slavs with Rome. Administrative difficulties during and after World War II were followed by Communist persecution in 1949. Archbishop Josef Matocha (1948–61) was restricted to his residence after 1949. The religious focuses of the diocese have been the pilgrimage centers Velehrad, Svatý Hostýn, Svatý Kopeček in Olomouc, and St. Anthony at Blatnica. The influence of the state-appointed vicar-general, who assumed the jurisdiction of the archbishop, and of "patriotic priests" has not yet been estimated.

Bibliography: L. Nemec, *Episcopal and Vatican Reaction to the Persecution of the Catholic Church in Czechoslovakia* (Washington 1953). M. Gordillo, *Velehrad e i suoi Congressi Unionistici, 1907–1957* (Rome 1957). Z. R. Dittrich, *Christianity in Great-Moravia* (Groningen 1960). AnnPont (1964) 313, 1410.

[L. Nemec]

OLSSON, ERIK (OLAI),

theologian, historian; b. Sweden, c. 1422; d. Uppsala, Sweden, Dec. 24, 1486. Educated in Rostock, where he was *magister artium* in 1452, he became a canon in Uppsala as indicated by a document of 1459, and was a *magister in sacra theo-*

logia of Siena in 1475. From 1477 to his death he was professor of theology in the University of *Uppsala (founded 1477). Though he was a learned theologian and a writer of hymns, he is principally remembered as "the father of Swedish historiography." His chief work, *Chronica regni Gothorum* (*Chronica Erici Olai*), is a chronicle with a fine patriotic spirit and a somewhat strong feeling of hatred toward Denmark. It was written probably in the late 1460s and the early 1470s, and compiled from a vast collection of sources, both in Latin and in the vernacular, among them the rhymed chronicles.

Bibliography: *Chronica Erici Olai* in *Scriptores rerum Svecicarum medii aevi*, 3 v. (Uppsala 1818–76) 2:1–165. H. Östlund in *Svenska män och kvinnor*, v.2 (Stockholm 1944) 438–439. E. Nygren, *in Svenskt biografiskt lexikon*, v.14 (Stockholm 1953) 216–242, with bibliog.; *Kulturhistorisk leksikon for nordisk middelalder*, v.2 (Copenhagen 1957) 603–604. H. Jägerstad, LexThK² 3:992–993.

[H. Bekker-Nielsen]

OLYMPIAS, ST.,

early Christian widow, deaconess, devoted friend of St. *John Chrysostom; b. Constantinople, c. 361; d. Nicomedia, July 25, 408 (feast, Dec. 17; in Greek Church, July 24, 25, and 26). Heiress to a fabulous fortune, Olympias was reared by her uncle, Procopius, an intimate friend of *Gregory of Nazianzus. For her marriage to Nebridius, Prefect of Constantinople (384), Gregory composed a poem, the earliest Christian Mirror for Women (PG 37:1541–50). After 2 unhappy years of marriage she was left a childless widow and devoted herself to God's service and a life of charity. She refused offers of remarriage and rejected a kinsman of Emperor Theodosius, who curtailed her association with ecclesiastics and impounded her property for 5 years. She devoted her time and wealth to charitable works and encouraged Gregory of Nyssa in his Scripture commentaries; and Bishop Nectarius made her a deaconess. When John Chrysostom succeeded Nectarius as patriarch in 398, she placed herself under his spiritual direction and founded a convent adjoining the cathedral. During the tragic events that led to Chrysostom's illegal deposition, she stood by him and refused to enter into communion with his unlawful successor. This led to her own persecution and exile, during which Chrysostom exhorted and consoled her in 17 letters written between 404 and 407, the year before her death. Under *Justinian I her body was returned to Constantinople and buried in the convent that she had founded and that the Emperor had rebuilt.

Bibliography: AnalBoll 15 (1896) 400–423; 16 (1897) 44–51, *Vita*. Tillemont 11:416–440, 629–631. E. Venables, DCB 4:73–75. H. Leclercq, DACL 12.2:2064–71. John Chrysostom, *Lettres à Olympias*, ed. and tr. A. M. Malingrey (SourcesChr 13; 1947). C. Butler, ed., *The Lausiac History of Palladius*, 2 v. (Cambridge, Eng. 1898–1904) ch. 56.

[P. W. Harkins]

OMAHA, ARCHDIOCESE OF (OMAHENSIS)

Metropolitan see comprising 23 counties in northeastern Nebraska, an area of 14,051 square miles. Erected as a vicariate apostolic on Jan. 9, 1857, it became a diocese Oct. 2, 1885, and an archdiocese Aug. 7, 1945, with suffragan sees at Grand Island and Lincoln, Nebr. In 1963 there were about 174,500 Catholics in a total population estimated at 630,890.

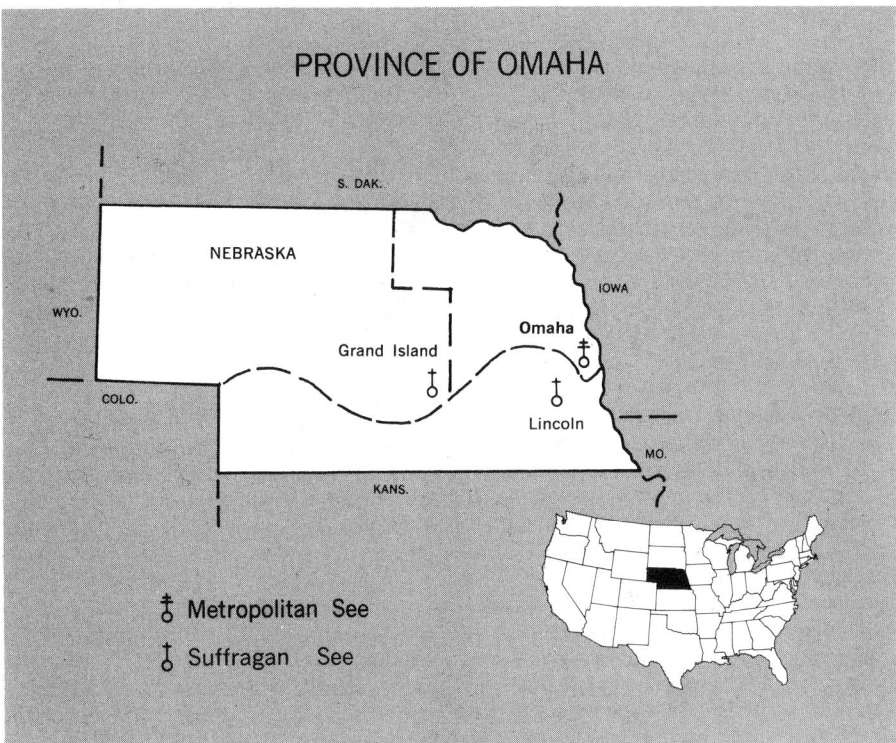

Fig. 1. Province of Omaha, comprising the archdiocese, known as the metropolitan see, and two dioceses called suffragan sees. The archbishop has metropolitan jurisdiction over the province.

Early History. A Catholic settlement, made at St. John's City in Dakota County in 1856 by Rev. Jeremiah F. *Trecy of Dubuque, Iowa, lasted only 4 years. When, on June 3, 1859, the first vicar apostolic, James M. O'Gorman, prior of the Trappist monastery at New Melleray, Iowa, arrived in Nebraska, he found several hundred Catholic families, principally in Omaha and along the Missouri River. O'Gorman brought the Sisters of Mercy (1864) and the Benedictine Sisters (1865), laying the foundations for a continuous history of Catholic education. He built a modest cathedral with money collected in the East and from workers then constructing the Union Pacific and Burlington railroads. When he died in 1874, in addition to the Benedictines who had been laboring in southeastern Nebraska, O'Gorman had admitted approximately 30 secular priests, of whom about 18 continued to serve with some degree of permanence in the vicariate.

Two years later James O'Connor, of Pittsburgh, Pa., was appointed second vicar apostolic and consecrated on Aug. 20, 1876. He continued O'Gorman's work, launching the Sisters of Mercy on a program of secondary education and entrusting *Creighton College (later University), built with a gift from Edward Creighton's estate, to the Jesuits. The bishop also introduced the Poor Clares to Omaha, where, with financial assistance from John A. Creighton, they built their first permanent foundation in the U.S.; invited the Religious of the Sacred Heart to establish an academy, the present *Duchesne College; and requested the Poor Sisters of St. Francis Seraph to inaugurate their extensive system of hospitals. Moreover, O'Gorman personally supervised extensive Catholic colonization in the state,

notably the Irish in Greeley County in the 1880s. His solicitude for other national groups, which were similarly attracted by cheap farmland or railroad employment, was apparent in his bringing into the vicariate the Franciscans and a group of Jesuits from Central Europe to work among the Bohemians and Poles. In addition, he directed the proliferation of parishes and schools that followed the heavy immigration.

Diocese. Montana was detached from the vicariate in 1868, but responsibility for administering the Church there continued until 1883. The Dakotas were separated in 1879. When the Diocese of Omaha was erected in 1885, O'Connor was appointed its first bishop. In 1887 the diocese was further reduced when all of Nebraska south of the Platte River was established as the Diocese of Lincoln, and Wyoming, with its see at Cheyenne, was erected as a distinct diocese. O'Connor died in 1890 and was succeeded by Bp. Richard Scannell, who was transferred to Omaha from Concordia, Kans., on Jan. 30, 1891.

By temperament a scholarly recluse, Scannell nevertheless carried forward the work of building new churches and schools. The House of the Good Shepherd opened its protectory for girls in Omaha. In 1907, following Scannell's decision to raze the old cathedral, the cornerstone was laid for a new edifice in Spanish Renaissance style, which took more than 50 years to complete. St. Cecelia's Cathedral was consecrated in 1959; it contains an array of liturgical art, including Albin Polasek's bronze *Crucifixus* on the high altar, his bronze stations of the cross, and wood sculptures. In 1912 the central and western counties of the state lying north of the Platte River were erected into a distinct diocese; the see, originally at Kearney, was transferred in 1917 to Grand Island.

After Scannell's death in 1916, Jeremiah J. *Harty of St. Louis, Mo., former archbishop of Manila, Philippine Islands, succeeded to the See of Omaha. Ill health marked the greater part of his 11 years there, preventing any aggressive program of accomplishments. Nevertheless, he did introduce new organization, diocesan in scope, and it was during his administration and with his encouragement that the world renowned institution of Boys Town was started by Rev. Edward *Flanagan. On May 29, 1928, Joseph Rummel, a New York priest, was consecrated to succeed Harty, who died Oct. 29, 1927. Unfortunately the depression nullified much of Rummel's work in Omaha. The funds from a successful campaign in 1930 to finance diocesan expansion ultimately were used, in large part, for relief work among the faithful. When Rummel was transferred to the Archdiocese of New Orleans, La., in 1935, his place was taken by Bp. James Hugh *Ryan, Rector of The Catholic University of America, Washington, D.C. World War II similarly neutralized much of Ryan's efforts.

Archdiocese. Under Ryan, the growth of the Church in Nebraska was recognized when, in 1945, Omaha was raised to an archdiocese. Ryan died in 1947 and his place was taken by Gerald T. Bergan of Des Moines, Iowa, under whom the archdiocese experienced phenomenal development. By 1963 more than $60 million had been spent on construction, including that of a home for the aged and a minor seminary. Twenty-three religious orders of women with a total of 805 sisters, assisted by 562 lay teachers, were engaged in elementary and secondary teaching. In the decade 1950 to 1960, the number enrolled in Catholic elementary schools almost doubled, and the number enrolled in secondary schools grew by approximately 50 per cent. In addition to the College of *St. Mary and Duchesne College, Omaha, with a combined enrollment of almost 1,000, Creighton University's seven schools and colleges, all coeducational, numbered almost 3,000 collegiate and professional students. Catholic hospitals in the archdiocese have a bed capacity of 2,200. Father Flanagan's Boys Home, with excellent physical facilities, attracts sightseers from all quarters of the globe. In addition to 202 secular priests active in the archdiocese, the Augus-

Fig. 3. Aerial view of Boys Town.

tinians, Benedictines, Columbans, Franciscans, Jesuits, and Redemptorists have 151 priests serving in parochial or teaching assignments.

Bibliography: Archives, Archdiocese of Omaha. H. W. CASPER, *History of the Catholic Church in Nebraska* (Milwaukee 1960–) v.1 *The Church on the Northern Plains, 1838–1874.*

[H. W. CASPER]

OMAN, JOHN WOOD, Presbyterian theologian; b. Orkney, Scotland, July 23, 1860; d. Cambridge, England, May 1939. After taking first-class honors in philosophy at Edinburgh University (1877–82), Oman studied divinity in Scotland at the Theological College of the United Presbyterian Church and abroad at Erlangen, Heidelberg, and Neuchâtel. After serving as minister in the English Presbyterian Church at Alnwick, Northumberland (1899–1907), he acted as professor of systematic theology and apologetics, and also as principal from 1922, at Westminster College, Cambridge, until his retirement (1935). He was moderator of the Presbyterian General Assembly in 1931. Oman was noted for his learning and originality. His doctrine of man and his relation to God were strongly personalistic, and avoided the Calvinistic outlook. He ascribed to man a freedom that must accept all the risks inherent in freedom and must be respected by God. Oman, who was influenced by *Schleiermacher, claimed that man has a direct awareness of the supernatural, which may lead to a fuller knowledge of God in proportion as man lives in loyalty to those sacred values that God discloses. The most important of his many books are *The Problem of Faith and Freedom* (1906), *Grace and Personality* (1917), and *The Natural and the Supernatural* (1931).

Bibliography: H. H. FARMER, DNB (1931–40) 657–659. Cross ODCC 983.

[W. HANNAH]

OMAN AND MUSQAT, called in Arabic 'Umân wa-Musqaṭ, a coastal independent sultanate of approximately 82,000 square miles, bounded by the Trucial Oman (composed of seven sheikhdoms under British protection) and the Gulf of Oman on the north, the Gulf of Oman and the Arabian Sea on the east, the Arabian Sea on the south, and the Aden Protectorates, the Empty Quarter, and Trucial Oman on the west. It comprises also the peninsula of Musandam, northeast of Trucial Oman. The capital Musqat (of about 7,000 inhabitants) is the principal seaport of the Gulf of Oman. Other important cities are Maṭraḥ (commercial

Fig. 2. St. Cecilia's Cathedral, Omaha.

center of about 15,000 inhabitants, 3 miles northwest of Musqat) and Ṣûr (of about 11,000 inhabitants, some 95 miles southeast of Musqat). The long, semicircular mountain range of al-'Aḥdar protects the fertile and principal coastal plain of al-Bâṭinah, about 150 miles long and from 2 to 30 miles wide, with the seaport of Ṣuḥâr at its center. Oman and Musqat's population of about 830,000 is mostly Moslem. The economy is based on the sea trade and also on the export of dates, for which Oman was renowned in ancient times; vines are cultivated in the mountains; the petroleum industry is still in prospect. Musqat and the hinterland were a Portuguese possession from 1506 until about 1648. Relations with Great Britain began in 1798, and Oman has been under British protection since 1913. The dynasty presently reigning has been in power since 1741; the rulers were called *Imāms until 1793, when Oman became a sultanate.

Bibliography: *Bilan du Monde* (Paris 1964) 2:602. B. THOMAS, *Arab Rule under the Al Bu Sa'id Dynasty of Oman, 1741–1937* (London 1938).

[A. JAMME]

OMAR KHAYYĀM, Persian poet, astronomer, mathematician; b. near Nīshāpūr, Persia, in the latter half of the 11th century; d. Nīshāpūr *c.* 1132. His full name was Abūl-Fath 'Omar ibn-Ibrāhīm. The epithet Khayyām (tent maker) signifies his family's trade. The oldest account of him is in Nīzāmī-e-'Arūẓī's *Chahār Maqāleh (Four Discourses)* in the section on astronomers. Other references to his life and works can be found in Najm-ud-dīn Rāzī's *Mirṣād-ul-'ibād,* which represents him as "an unhappy philosopher, atheist, and materialist"; in Al-Qifti's *Ta'rīkh-ul-ḥukamā,* which introduces him as "a champion of Greek learning . . . without an equal in astronomy and philosophy"; and in Nizām-ul-mulk's *Wasiyat,* which relates his life story. According to this last, partly legendary account, Omar learned theology and the "seven readings of the Koran" under Imām Mowaffaq. His former schoolfellow Nizām-ul-mulk, Alb Arslan's vizier, in keeping with a solemn promise, offered Omar a court office. But the latter contented himself with an annual stipend to enable him to devote his time to the studies of mathematics and astronomy. Omar proved his gratitude by publishing a scientific work classifying equations of the first degree and considering cubes from the standpoint of the general equation. Subsequently, he joined with others in publishing a Zīj or astronomical tables reforming the Moslem calendar (a task comparable to the revision of the Julian Calendar that took place under Pope Gregory XIII).

Omar's Eastern scientific fame, however, is eclipsed by his Western poetical renown. Though a third-rate poet in Iran, he is very well known in almost all parts of the world because of his *rubā'iyāt* (quatrains), which owe their popularity to Edward Fitzgerald's paraphrase (1859). Each *rubā'ī* consists of four lines, the first, second, and fourth of which have the same rhyme, while the third usually remains rhymeless. External and internal evidences fail to give information as to how many of the extant 500 quatrains ascribed to Omar are really his. These quatrains all represent the same humble yet reproachful, hopeful yet fatalistic, rebellious yet acquiescent character before God. Most of them are the musings of a freethinker who protests against the bigotry and narrowness of the clergy as well as the eccentricity and hypocrisy of the Ṣufis of his day (*see* SUFISM), revealing at the same time sympathy with human suffering. Because of these Omar has been called the Voltaire of the East, though Voltaire never wrote fascinating rhapsodies in praise of wine, love, and earthly joys (which some schools interpret symbolically) as a last resort from the inability to resolve questions of the ultimate purpose in life.

Bibliography: *Edward Fitzgerald's Rubâ'iyyat of Omar Khayyâm with Their Original Persian Sources,* tr. E. HERON-ALLEN (London 1899); *L'Algèbre,* ed. and tr. F. WOEPCKE (Paris 1851), preface; Eng. *The Algebra,* tr. D. S. KASIN (New York 1931). V. ZHUKOVSKI, " 'Umar Khayyām, and the 'Wandering' Quatrains," tr. E. D. Ross, JRoyAsSoc 30 (1898) 349–366. E. G. BROWNE, *A Literary History of Persia,* 4 v. (2d ed. Cambridge, Eng. 1929) v.2. For further bibliog. see N. H. Dole's multivariorum edition (Boston 1898), app. xlix. **Illustration credit:** Press Counselor, Embassy of Iran.

[P. KUJOORY]

OMER OF THÉROUANNE, ST., bishop; b. Orval (*Aurea Vallis*), near Coutances, France; d. Thérouanne, Sept. 1, *c.* 670 (feast, Sept. 9). Omer (or Otmar, whence the Latin, *Audomarus*) and his father Friulph, who were perhaps of Saxon origin, entered the Columban Abbey of *Luxeuil after the death of Omer's mother, Domitta. When named bishop of Thérouanne between 635 and 640, Omer took the suggestion of *Acharius of Noyon and sent for three other Luxeuil monks, Momelinus, *Bertinus, and Ebertramnus, to help him in his work of completing the conversion of the peoples of his diocese. Momelinus governed the original abbey they built near Sithiu until 660, when he was elevated to the episcopacy of Noyon-Tournai. Then Bertinus succeeded as abbot. Having received several properties from a certain Adroald, Omer gave Bertinus the island of Sithiu in the River Aa, as a new site for the abbey (later *Saint-Bertin) and also the church of Sainte-Marie, which he had built on a neighboring hill. Omer was buried in this church, after granting Sithiu a privilege of immunity. The city of Saint-Omer was later built on the slopes of the hill between these two shrines.

Bibliography: ActSS Sept. 3:384–417. MGSrerMer 5:729–764. O. BLED, "Les Reliques . . . de St. Omer," *Mémoires de la Société des Antiquaires de la Morinie* 32 (1914–20) 1–112. G.

Tomb of Omar Khayyām at Nīshāpūr, Iran.

COOLEN, "Saint Colomban et Saint Omer," *Mélanges colombaniens* (Paris 1950) 361–375. Butler Th Attw 3:516–517.

[G. COOLEN]

OMISSION, the nonperformance of some action; it is of concern to the moralist only when a person could and should do what he leaves undone. The omission of an act when its performance is impossible or is in no way a matter of obligation is of no moral significance. Similarly, if a person fails to do something through inculpable ignorance of or inadvertence to his obligation to act, the omission is not morally imputable, because if he is unconscious of an obligation to act, it cannot be said that he should, or ought to, act. When there is an obligation to act, the failure to perform the required act can be due either to simple nonchoice or to deliberate choice. It is due to nonchoice, and is negatively or indirectly voluntary, when a person, though conscious of an obligation to act, simply does not act or occupies himself with something incompatible with the fulfillment of his duty, but without reaching a positive decision not to do what he should. It is due to deliberate choice when a person reaches an explicit decision to omit what he should do (St. Thomas Aquinas, ST 1a2ae, 71.5).

In all cases of voluntary omission, whether due to nonchoice or deliberate choice, one is responsible for his failure to act, and the morality of the omission is determined in accord with the same norms that are applied to a positive choice to do something. If there is advertence to the obligation to do something, the omission of the performance of the act is equatable with a positive sinful choice, and the result is a grave or venial sin as the gravity of the obligation and the circumstances of the case demand. It is to be noted, however, that choices of nonperformance are qualified by the same influences that affect choices to act. Accordingly, such subjective elements as fear and passion can, under certain conditions, lessen personal imputability.

Bibliography: THOMAS AQUINAS, ST 1a2ae, 6.3. Prümmer Man ThMor 1:360. Merkelbach SumThMor 1:60. Noldin SumThMor 1:92, 292–293.

[A. BURROUGHS]

OMNI DIE DIC MARIAE, the second section of a lengthy Marian hymn, or *Mariale,* whose first section begins with *Ut jucundas cervas undas.* The *Omni die,* shortest of all the parts, has 19 stanzas whose verse form is alternate acatalectic and catalectic trochaic dimeter with internal rhyme in the first and third verses (aa/b,cc/b). The meter and rhyme scheme are so intricate that their competent use in a lengthy poem demanded talent in Latin verse composition. It has been ascribed variously to *Bernard of Clairvaux (d. 1153), *Anselm of Canterbury (d. 1109), *Casimir of Poland (d. 1484), and others. But it is ascribed also to *Bernard of Cluny (fl. 1150), who in his *De contemptu mundi,* a 3,000-line poem of similar difficulty, proved his ability to use such a meter. And since no manuscript yet discovered precedes his time, the weight of greater probability leads Julian and others to name him as the author. The text, together with a number of other stanzas found in various MSS, is given in AnalHymn 50:423–482.

Bibliography: Chevalier RepHymn 2:14070. Julian DictHym 1200–02. Ghellinck Essor 2:223–226. Raby ChrLP 318–319.

[G. E. CONWAY]

OMNIBONUS (OMNEBENE), bishop and canonist; d. Verona, Oct. 22, 1185. Little is known of Omnibonus's early life other than that he was a student of Gratian. He taught Canon Law at Bologna during the pontificate of Pope Eugene III, and also later at Verona. In 1157 he became bishop of Verona, in which post he remained until his death. As a canonist, he was one of the early members of the group later known as the *decretists (i.e., those whose main concern was to comment on the *Decretum* of *Gratian). He is very likely the author of the *Abbreviatio Decreti,* a reordered version of Gratian's *Decretum.* Omnibonus's *Abbreviatio* is divided into two parts, 26 distinctions and 37 *causae.* It was glossated upon by later canonists, but it does not appear to have played a very important role in the history of Canon Law. He is also most likely the same person as Omnibonus, the author of a theological treatise from about the same period. The theological treatise of Omnibonus shows the influence of the school of Abelard, Hugh of Saint-Victor, Roland, and, of course, Gratian.

Bibliography: Van Hove 1:441–442. R. CHABANNE, DDC 6:1111–12.

[J. M. BUCKLEY]

OMNIPOTENCE

From the Latin *omnis* (all) and *potens* (capable of making or producing). Divine omnipotence is a divine operative attribute, an active *potency, or power, for acting *ad extra.* As an active potency it is distinguished from a passive potency, or capacity for receiving *act, which would be opposed to God's perfection. By this power God has dominion over all things outside Himself, which He has brought into existence and which He holds in existence.

Omnipotence extends, however, only to beings that have the inherent possibility of existence—that is, that do not include a contradiction. Thus, God cannot make a square circle or an infinite created being since the essential notes here cancel each other out. (For this reason it is impossible for God to commit a sin—that is, act in a way contrary to His own intrinsic goodness.) These hypothetical beings lie beyond God's power, not because God's power is limited, but because of the inherent limitation in the idea of the thing itself.

Similarly, God's power cannot reverse His own eternal decrees, for this implies change of intention or new knowledge, both of which are impossible in a perfect God.

Some actions are called impossible for God even though they themselves can exist, yet cannot coexist with God's other decrees. Thus, it is true to say that man's immortal soul could be destroyed by God's power, if one considers His power in itself. Yet granting God's design in making man's soul immortal by nature, it is not possible that He act against His own plan. Thus one may say that destroying man's soul is beyond God's ordered power (*potentia ordinata*—considering His power in conjunction with His divine decrees), but not beyond His absolute power (*potentia absoluta*—considering in itself His power over man's soul). The usefulness, however, and even the validity, of this distinction is generally called into question.

Omnipotence has been considered the attribute most proper to a deity by men of all times and places. The Bible in particular voices continually the theme of God's power in comparison with the limited power of alien gods or of temporal rulers of Egypt or Babylonia. God is always able to save His people from these enemies. If at times He chooses not to, it is only because His people have not observed His laws.

Most of the Biblical names of God imply power to act or make, though the exact meaning of these terms is often under dispute. Abraham worships *'ēl šaddai* (God the Almighty) in Gn 17.1 and *'ēl 'elyôn* (Most High God or God Eternal) in Gn 14.18; *'ēl* [*see* EL (GOD) Gn 46.3], and as found in *'ĕlōhîm* (*see* ELOHIM) throughout the Old Testament, means the Strong God. God is also called "the Mighty One of Jacob" (Gn 49.24), "the creator of the heavens . . . the designer and maker of the earth" (Is 45.18), and "the Lord of the whole earth" (Jos 3.11, 13). This notion of omnipotent Lordship is intimately linked with Jesus' divinity throughout the Gospel of St. Mark.

Somewhat mysterious in meaning is the most proper name of God, *Yahweh* (*see* YAHWEH), probably originally meaning "He who causes all things to be," rather than the later, more common, rendering, "I am who am" (Ex 3.14).

In addition, many metaphors refer to Yahweh's hand or arm as symbolic of God's power to rule or guide or punish (cf. Jos 4.24; Ezr 7.28; Ex 15.16).

Omnipotence is not of merely speculative interest to Israel, for this attribute fosters faith's vision of the *mirabilia Dei:* the salvation acts of God for His people [cf. Dt 3.24; Ps 105(106).2]. It invites the believer to prayer of gratitude or petition; it is one of the motives held out to Israel to sanctify itself.

The doctrine that all things depend upon God appears in the opening chapters of Genesis, where God unfolds His plan of creation. (For treatment of the question whether or not creation out of nothing is to be found here, *see* CREATION, 1; CREATION ACCOUNT.) By God's simple utterance things came to be, and as He wants them to be. Moon and sun, often worshiped by pagans, are here merely creatures. In Exodus, God's power is made manifest publicly before Egypt and its Pharaoh (cf. also Is 19.1). In such a way God has power over all nations (Nm 21.3; 1 Sm 14.12). The more marvelous is the work of God's omnipotence in that He selects an unworthy nation for His favors. Even evil is fitted into God's plan; Israel is often purified by it.

The culmination of God's power is found in the Incarnation (cf. Rom 1.4). Jesus redeems man and even the physical world by becoming man, performing miracles, dying, and rising again. In the last times He will return, the Son of Man (Dn ch. 7), coming to judge all things as Lord and master.

These Biblical teachings have been interpreted by the magisterium of the Church (see Denz, Index syst. Blbc).

Scholastic theology considers a number of questions in this area. Omnipotence follows upon God's essence as *pure act, having within Himself His own fullness of actuality. Since one thing is able to cause another insofar as it is itself in act, God alone is capable of giving existence to created things. Of course, God's omnipotence is in reality completely identified with His essence, distinguished only by a virtual minor distinction. Other problems dealt with in systematic theology are God's freedom in creating (Denz 3002) and man's freedom

under God's causality (*see* OMNISCIENCE; PREDESTINATION, ARTICLES ON).

See also GOD, ARTICLES ON.

Bibliography: DTC, Tables générales 1:975–993. C. SPICQ, LexThK² 1:353–355. THOMAS AQUINAS, ST 1a, 25; *C. gent.* 2.7. F. SUÁREZ, *De Deo* 3.9. J. D. COLLINS, *God in Modern Philosophy* (Chicago 1959). R. GARRIGOU-LAGRANGE, *The One God,* tr. B. ROSE (St. Louis 1943). P. HEINISCH, *Theology of the Old Testament,* tr. W. G. HEIDT (Collegeville, Minn. 1950).

[G. ROXBURGH]

OMNIPRESENCE. The infinite and omnipotent God is in all things everywhere. Such, briefly, is the teaching of Scripture and tradition. Omnipresence is an attribute of God, the infinite and first cause of all, who is actually present in all existing places and things. This presence is not to be interpreted as dimensional or spatial, since God is utterly simple and infinite and thus free of all spatial limitations. Rather He is present as an agent to His effects. So God is everywhere, for He is the source of the being and action in all places and things. Moreover, since in God power and action are one, He is substantially present in all existing things through His power and operation.

God's omnipresence has a relationship to divine immensity of actuality to aptitude. For immensity is the infinite plenitude of subsistent being that is free from all spatial limitations and, thus, is able to be present in all things. Immensity implies the power to be everywhere. Omnipresence is the actual exercise of the power to be everywhere. Whereas immensity is an essential, absolute, and eternal attribute in God, omnipresence is relative to created being.

Omnipresence is implicit in those scriptural texts that speak of God's immensity. But Scripture is explicit also. In earlier books the notion of omnipresence remains undefined, although God's presence is known not to be confined to one place (Gn 12.4–9; 14.20). Later, the idea of God's omnipresence is more definitely expressed: God is everywhere by His nature, for He transcends and permeates all things (Dt 4.39; Wis 8.1) and sees them as they are [Ps 112(113).5–9; 101(102).20–21; Prv 5.21; 15.3]; no one can escape His presence [Ps 138(139).7–12; Am 9.2; Is 43.2]. Christ calls attention to the presence of the "Father, who sees in secret" (Mt 6.6) and who is present in heaven and on earth (Mt 6.9–13; 5.35). God is everywhere, as St. Paul explains to the Athenians (Acts 17.24–28; cf. Eph. 4.6).

Patristic teaching distinguishes God's omnipresence from His immensity (e.g., St. Cyril of Alex., *In Jn.* 1.9) and explicitly states that God is everywhere and wholly everywhere (e.g., St. Hilary, *De Trin.* 2.6). Theologians maintain this patristic doctrine and commonly distinguish how God is present in all things: He is present to them by His essence and power, and all things are open to His knowledge; while in the just, God is present in a special way through His grace (St. Thomas, ST 1a, 8.3). The immensity of God is a defined dogma (Denz 3001).

See also INDWELLING, DIVINE; JESUS CHRIST, III, 11.

Bibliography: E. MANGENOT, DTC 4.1:948–1023. X. LE BACHELET, *ibid.* 1023–1152. M. CHOSSAT, *ibid.* 1152–1243. J. M. DALMAU, SacTheolSumma BAC 2.1:126–134. Y. M. J. CONGAR, *The Mystery of the Temple,* tr. R. F. TREVETT (Westminster, Md. 1962). J. DANIÉLOU, *The Presence of God,* tr. W. ROBERTS (Baltimore 1960). L. REYPENS, DictSpirAscMyst 3:883–929.

[M. F. MORRY]

OMNISCIENCE

The term divine science might also be used here. It brings into focus the heated, lengthy, and continuing theological controversy on the relationship between the certitude of God's knowledge and human freedom. Taken from this standpoint, the attribution of divine science to God signifies that He possesses infinitely perfect science or certain knowledge of Himself. He also knows perfectly all that has existed, exists, or will exist in both the physical and moral order. This divine science extends to every free act, but this foreknowledge implies no necessity. The Catholic Church defined at the First Vatican Council that God is infinite in all His perfections and possessed of intellect and will (Denz 3001). The Council also stated that this knowledge whereby "all things are naked and open to his eyes" (Heb 4.13) is the foundation of the providential governance of all things, "even the future free actions of creatures" (Denz 3003; *see* FREE WILL AND PROVIDENCE).

Historical Considerations. Viewing historically man's understanding of God's omniscience is a useful prelude to the systematic treatment.

Old Testament. In Biblical theology the existence of knowledge in God is a necessary consequence of the fact that for Biblical revelation God is a personal God. In general, therefore, this divine knowledge as personal is at heart a knowledge of God's people (*see* PEOPLE OF GOD). And, frequently, God's knowledge designates acts of care, help, and succor [see Jb 31.6; Ps 1.6; 72 (73).11; 102(103).14; 143(144).3]. It is also this highly personalist note that gives to the Biblical affirmations of the divine knowledge their strongly religious character. There is no shadow of doubt in the Old Testament that God knows all things, but the fundamental note is that He knows all that takes place on earth. All human existence is lived out in His sight and is known to Him. It is this fact that gives dramatic perspective to Job's sorrow (Jb 28.24). God knows the just and the unjust to the very roots of their being [Ps 10(11).4; 32(33).15; Prv 15.11; 16.2]. Knowing men, God knows their thoughts, their intentions, their most secret actions [Ps 93(94).1–2; Psalm 138(139)]. It is this conviction that informs the moral dimension of the religious activity of God's people.

It is, moreover, the conviction of God's perfect knowledge of all things that engenders Israel's confidence in God's providential designs. The deeply personal character of God's knowledge is also emphasized by the fact that it is concrete and experiential. God knows His people as the husband his wife. All things that exist are the work of His hand. The Psalmist proclaims that God knows all that He has created and that He who made the eye does indeed see [Ps 93(94).9].

While this personal note is characteristic of the Biblical affirmation, there is another note that is peculiarly proper to the teaching on divine knowledge. For what gives to the OT teaching on God's knowledge an originality beyond merely natural theology is the note of wisdom. Not only does God know but He understands all these things. What is clear in the OT development is that the sapiential authors move from the idea of wisdom as a largely practical thing to the idea of wisdom being a kind of subsistent reality in God. It

finally becomes a personal characteristic of such cosmic status that it is personified as the agent of God's creation and providential ordering of the universe (e.g., Prv 8.22–31).

It is also from this standpoint of wisdom that the OT conception of God's knowledge has some areas of equivalence to the scholastic concept of divine science; for it is something beyond all human knowing and quite proper to God (e.g., Is 28.29; 40.13). To the sages of Israel God's wisdom in terms of the knowledge of good and evil is far beyond man's—God alone is truly wise (Jb 28.12–28; Is 40.13). It is this approach that makes of wisdom "an aura of the might of God and a pure effusion of the glory of the Almighty" (Wis 7.25). What is of note in the whole sapiential approach in the OT is that only by implication does it involve itself with the great prophetic themes of covenant, election, and salvation [*see* WISDOM (IN THE BIBLE)].

New Testament. It is in the NT that the whole notion of God's knowledge and wisdom is synthesized with His saving work. The personal character of wisdom is revealed in Christ to correspond to a Person distinct from the Father—the *Word (John ch. 1). It is this transcendent and creative wisdom that is incarnated in Jesus Christ (Col 1.15–20). In Jesus Christ, the only Son of the Father, is revealed God's love for the world (Jn 3.16). Wisdom as divine understanding is seen to subsist in the Son: ". . . no one knows the Son except the Father; nor does anyone know the Father except the Son, and him to whom the Son chooses to reveal him" (Mt 11.27). It is the knowledge that God has of Himself that the Son reveals: "No one has at any time seen God. The only-begotten Son, who is in the bosom of the Father, he has revealed him" (Jn 1.18). St. Paul, writing to the Corinthians, tells them that the deep things of God known only by the Spirit (1 Cor 2.11–12) are the wisdom that is manifested in Christ: "From him you are in Christ Jesus, who has become for us God-given wisdom, and justice, and sanctification, and redemption" (1 Cor 1.30). The concern of the NT, like that of the OT, is not a natural theology but God's saving activity. Accordingly the divine knowledge to which they testify is essentially that which looks to *salvation. Yet all these affirmations suppose and rest upon the fact: God truly knows.

Patristic Teaching. When one turns to the actual teaching of the gospel, he finds a new dimension with a radically new note not found in the Biblical affirmations. This dimension arises from the rational tradition that is so much a part of the Greco-Roman culture. Hence, from the beginning, the Greek Christian writers were called upon to make use of a variety of philosophical sources and elements in order to explain and defend the Christian revelation (*see* THEOLOGY, INFLUENCE OF GREEK PHILOSOPHY ON). Thus, along with an extensive use of symbolism to explain the meaning of Christian revelation there is a consistent effort to establish a Christian philosophical notion of God and His actions. It is therefore in this context that the patristic teaching on God's knowledge must be set. For these Christian writers sought to establish and safeguard the spiritual nature, the holiness, and, above all, the supremacy of God through concepts appropriate to men trained in the schools of Greek philosophy.

The first note stressed in this teaching, which in turn forms the foundation for the divine knowledge, is what might be called the total supernaturality of God. G. L. Prestige thinks that "philosophically, this idea was expressed by the [Greek] word ὑπεροχή, which may fairly be translated transcendence" [*God in Patristic Thought* (London 1952) 25]. He points out that the word occurs in Irenaeus (*Adv. haer.* 5.2.3; PG 7:1127) but that its use is best illustrated in the *Clementine Homilies*: "He who would worship God ought before all else to know what is peculiar to the nature of God alone, which cannot pertain to another . . .. This is peculiar to God, that He alone is, as the maker of all, so also the best of all. That which makes is indeed superior in power to that which is made; that which is boundless is superior in magnitude to that which is bounded; in respect of beauty, that which is comeliest; in respect of happiness, that which is most blessed; in respect of understanding, that which is most perfect. And in like manner in other respects He incomparably possesses transcendence" (*Hom. clem.* 10.9; cf. Prestige, 25–26). This serves to illustrate the fundamental emphasis on the transcendent character of God's understanding and affirms the incomparable superiority of God over all that He has made.

The other general note in Greek Christian thought directly related to God's knowledge is the very heavy emphasis on His providence. For, while insisting on the divine transcendence, revelation also makes it clear that God is not remote from man but enters personally into his history. His nature, however, is revealed through His works and His providence (e.g., see Theophilus of Antioch, *Ad Autol.* 1.5; PG 6:1030–31). In the explanation of this providential ordering there is strong emphasis on the notion of planning or designing. It is in this connection that the Greek word οἰκονομία (economy) plays a somewhat striking role. It undergoes in the Christian writers a gradual transformation from the simple meaning of administering or overseeing to planning or designing (cf. Prestige, 57–62). Thus God economizes the affairs of the world, so that the man who realizes that God's providence rules the world knows that events come out for the best under the economy of the ruler (cf. *Hom. clem.* 2.36, PG 2:102; Clement of Alexandria, *Strom.* 3.17; PG 8:1205–08). In general, God's providence or economy involves His action in the world of nature, of human history, of salvation (*see* ECONOMY, DIVINE). It finds its supreme expression in the *Incarnation, "for which, the word 'oekonomia,' without any verbal qualification, is the regular patristic term from the third century onwards" (Prestige, 67). Here can be seen how closely the notion of God's knowledge corresponds to the NT teaching.

Specifically, with regard to the divine knowledge, the basic Biblical teaching is constantly affirmed. God knows all that is and will be, and the whole measure and order of things is disposed in accord with His wisdom (see, e.g., Irenaeus, *Adv. haer.* 2.26.3, PG 7: 801–802; 2.30.9, PG 7:821–823; Origen, *Contra Celsum* 2.30, PG 11:850–851; Cyril of Jerusalem, *Catech.* 4.5, PG 33:459). However, in so affirming this, the Christian teachers were faced almost from the beginning by a problematic raised by the Gnostics. Some of the Gnostics would maintain that men are divided into different categories so that by their nature the spiritual will necessarily be saved, the earthly will necessarily be reprobated, and the psychic, who alone are unnecessitated, are alone free. Marcion, who wrote within the

Christian framework itself, maintained that the God of the OT was distinct from the God revealed in the NT. On this basis Marcion held that the God of the Mosaic dispensation was arbitrary and unjust in His treatment of men, taking no account of their merits. Celsus, whose thought is the object of a major work by Origen, taught that if God has certain knowledge of man's future acts, then human freedom is not possible (cf. H. D. Simonin, OP, "La Prédestination d'après les pères grecs," DTC 12.2:2815–32).

In the face of the issues raised by these heretical positions, there is found in the Fathers a constant defense both of God's foreknowledge of all human activity and of human freedom. Irenaeus sums up the basic problem: "But that which He said, 'how often have I desired to gather your sons and you would not,' demonstrates the ancient law of liberty, because God made man free from the beginning, having his own power even as his own soul to accept God's commands freely and not by compulsion" (*Adv. haer.* 4.37.1; PG 7:1099). Scriptural texts in particular are interpreted to bring out this point. For example, Eusebius of Caesarea insists that the fact that God foreknew Judas would be a traitor does not force him to be such (*Praep. evang.* 6.11; PG 21:491). John Chrysostom, interpreting the texts from Mt 18.7 and Lk 17.1 that it is necessary that scandals come, goes on to say that this does not take away free choice or liberty or subject life to necessity. For the fact that scandal is predicted is not what causes it to occur (see *In Matt. hom.* 59.1; PG 58: 573–575). Augustine, dealing with predestination when he is writing against the Pelagians and Semi-Pelagians, is forced to take up this point on a number of occasions. He affirms in general as well as in specific cases that what God foresees will be the future does not force that particular action to be done (*Lib. arb.* 3.4.11; PL 32:1276). In the case of Adam and Eve the cause of their fall is not the divine foreknowledge but their evil will (*Gen. ad lit.* 11.9.12; PL 34:434). God foresees, too, what is in our wills, but He does not take away free choice (*Civ.* 5.10.2; PL 41:153).

Carolingian Era. The whole question raised by Augustine comes to a head in the Carolingian era with the issues raised by Gottschalk (cf. É. Amman, *L'Époque carolingienne*, Fliche-Martin 6:320–344). In an age when Augustine is the teacher par excellence, Gottschalk takes his ideas on predestination and presents them without their author's nuances or flexibility. It is also true that the Augustinian conceptions have already begun to be harshened under the influence of Isidore of Seville, but they now become the focus of a major conflict in the Carolingian world [cf. H. Rondet, *Gratia Christi* (Paris 1948) 170–179]. For Gottschalk simply it is a fact that God predestines some to eternal life and they will not perish, and those not predestined to eternal life will perish; no question of merit or demerit or liberty appears to enter into his position.

In the controversy that follows upon this, all the great names of Carolingian theology are involved—Hincmar, Rabanus Maurus, John Scotus Erigena, Florus of Lyons, and many others. Two councils are held, one under Hincmar at the royal residence at Quiercy and the other at Valence. The statements of these councils on the issue have a large role in the theological tradition that develops after them; in fact, for a good many modern theologians they have been looked upon as normative. One statement from the Council of Valence is particularly notable. It is largely a quotation from Florus of Lyons: "[We faithfully hold that] God foresees and has foreseen eternally both the good works that the good would do and the evil works that the evil would do . . . He has foreseen that the good would be good entirely through His grace and would receive their reward through that grace, so also that the evil would be evil by their own malice and would be condemned by His justice to eternal punishment. . . . But the foreknowledge of God has not placed on any evildoer a necessity whereby he could not be otherwise, but he was going to be by his own will just as God . . . has foreseen in His omnipotent and unchangeable majesty" (Denz 626–627; cf. B. Lavaud, "La controverse sur la prédestination av XII⁰ siècle," DTC 12.2:2901–35). This statement may be taken as summing up the patristic response to the problematic that is so central to the whole matter of God's knowledge.

Systematic Theology. Revelation clearly affirms the fact that God knows. The task of systematic theology is to determine as far as it can what is to be understood by this revealed fact. It does this by bringing to bear on the revealed affirmation the psychological resources of a man who himself is able to know. It also employs the philosophic intelligence of the Church, since any treatment of knowledge and understanding implies a philosophic position. In the matter of divine knowledge, it should also be noted that the task is complex. For theology must show that God truly knows, but, in using man's knowledge as a resource in understanding, theology must not blur the explanation by excessive anthropomorphism [see ANTHROPOMORPHISM (IN THEOLOGY)]. Ultimately the act of divine knowledge must be reducible to the pure act of being.

Man's Knowing. Beginning with man's own experience of knowing, what stands out is the fact that in some way man as knower enters into a special relationship with objects other than himself. For the fact is that the *knowledge of an object is the presence of the object in thought. The act of knowing appears to grasp the very nature of the object without modifying that object in its own actuality. Yet, in comprehending the object thought does not cease to be thought. Intelligence grasps the idea of a tree or a stone but does not itself become a tree or stone in actuality. Moreover, while the object known and the concept and judgments about it determine the content of knowledge, they are not the only element of knowledge. For there are operations of the central reality that is intelligence itself in action. Thus there is the reflexive consciousness of this knowledge, whereby the knower understands that it is knowledge and is conscious of this central operation of understanding; hence the capacity to reflect upon what he knows and relate it to the rest of what he knows. Finally, this act of knowledge is immanent in the one knowing since it takes place only in the subject, for the act by which the object exists in his thought is the very act by which he knows—the understanding in act is the intelligible in act.

The root of this capacity to know is immateriality. In material things the coming of a new form means the disappearance of the previous form. It is the very possibility of this kind of change that is called matter, since change here means a loss of integrity. To know, on the other hand, means to be another in some way,

yet retain integrity of being. St. Thomas, as the general scholastic tradition, explains this capacity by the use of the term species, which has been translated modernly as "knowledge-likeness" [cf. *Summa theologica*, v.4, *Knowledge in God*, tr. T. Gornall, SJ (New York 1964) 17]. This means that the object is present in thought "intentionally," that is, by reason of its form (that which makes it to be what it is) and with nothing of materiality. To know, therefore, means that the object known exists intentionally (as in contradistinction to actually) in the mind of the knower, or in an intelligible mode of existence. This is possible because intelligibility is present in all things; in the common Christian philosophical and theological tradition this follows from the very fact of creation. Because God has created all things, then the universe in its every part is a participation in God the supreme intelligible.

God's Knowing. It is in the light of this conception of knowledge that the general Catholic theological tradition stemming from St. Thomas has treated of the divine knowledge. It recognizes that in the created way in which man is knower and knows there is the knower not only in act but also in potency. It is also evident that the thing known is in potency as well as in act. Yet, it is maintained that this distinction arises not from the nature of knowing but because the act of knowing takes place in a creature, man. Knowing of itself is essentially act or perfection, and potency is not necessary to knowing. The more perfectly actualized, therefore, the more perfectly intelligible. The more potency is negated, the more closely identified are understanding and the thing understood. In God, as totally perfect and pure actuality, there is no potency; hence essence, intellect, understanding are all one and the same. "Since, therefore, God has no potentiality but is pure actuality, in Him intellect and what is known must be identical in every way" (ST 1a, 14.2). Further, since there is no form in God distinct from His existence, then it follows that His essence is the very way in which God knows. Necessarily, then, God's act of knowing is His essence and His very being ("ipsum eius intelligere sit eius essentia et eius esse"—ST la, 14.4). In sum, what is argued is that God is an infinite, eternal, and substantial act of understanding [cf. B. Lonergan, SJ, "The Concept of Verbum in the Writings of St. Thomas Aquinas," ThSt 10 (1949) 359–393].

Objects of Divine Knowledge. What traditionally have been called the secondary objects of divine knowledge may now be considered. By reason of the fact that God knows Himself perfectly (since His very being is His act of knowledge), then He knows His own power perfectly. This divine power, in turn, extends to other things by the very fact that it is the first efficient cause of all things. God, accordingly, knows things other than Himself, and He knows them immediately and specifically, not successively and generically. God also knows evil. While evil is a privation, an absence of good, yet because God knows all goods perfectly He knows that some of them will suffer corruption because of evils. So, through the very fact of knowing good, God also knows evil. God also knows individuals, and this again stems from His causality. For God's knowledge is coextensive with His causality. "He knows other things through His essence insofar as [His essence] is the likeness of all things as their productive principle; therefore, his essence must be the sufficient principle for knowing all things made through it not only in their universal nature but in their individuality" (ST 1a, 14. 11). Finally God can know not only those things that actually exist or have existed but all that can be produced either by Himself or by creatures. Traditionally this is called the science of simple intelligence (*scientia simplicis intelligentiae*), i.e., the certain knowledge of all possible participations of the divine essence. Once again this is a consequence of the proposition that the divine essence, through which the divine intellect knows, is the adequate likeness of everything that is or can be, both with regard to common principles and what is proper to each individual.

Divine Knowledge of the Future. A distinct place has been given to this matter of God's knowledge of the future because of the extensive theological controversy that has centered on it since the 16th century. As was seen above, the Christian Fathers were quite conscious of the problem of God's knowledge of the future, predestination, and human liberty. By way of a solution, basically, they had simply insisted that there was no incompatibility. In the 16th century, however, as a result of the Calvinist preaching, the question of predestination and God's foreknowledge becomes a central issue. For what is involved is man's free participation in God's salutary activity. This Calvinist preaching is made particularly acute by the teaching of *Baius (cf. H. Rondet, 287–293). The polemical exigencies, in the end, make inescapable the Catholic theological controversy. Any study of this Catholic controversy makes it clear that there is no question that God knows all future events. What is in question is the mode of knowing future contingents, and, in particular, future contingents that are dependent on the exercise of free choice by man. As the controversy originates, both sides rest their case on the interpretation of St. Thomas. The basic article (ST la, 14.13) looks to showing that the divine knowledge of the future contingents is quite different from man's. Man can only foresee these conjecturally because he only knows them in their causes. God, on the other hand, knows these future contingents not only in their causes but in their existence. Hence, while contingents come into existence for men successively, God, who transcends time, knows them at once because His knowledge is measured by eternity. "All things that are in time are eternally present to God . . . because He eternally surveys all things as they are in their presence to Him" (ST la, 14.13).

The problematic of the divine knowledge of the future as it came to the fore in the 16th century was in part the necessary consequence of a more immediate problem. The actual issue, as raised by the reformed preaching (and given immediacy by the teaching of Baius), was the relationship of divine *grace and human liberty. Faced with this issue, the Dominican tradition had tended to respond by giving primacy to the omnipotence of the divine will. Contrariwise, directly confronted with the Calvinist preachers and the followers of Baius, the Jesuits had tended to stress human liberty.

It is these two basically related emphases that are brought into controversial confrontation by the ascendancy of Domingo Báñez to the leadership of the Dominican tradition at Salamanca in 1577. Basically, and at the risk of oversimplification, one may say that Báñez and the Thomistic tradition he gives rise to understand St. Thomas as teaching that God knows all

future contingents in their causes inasmuch as they are determined by Himself, the first cause [cf. D. Báñez, *Scholastica commentaria in primam partem Summae Theologiae s. Thomae* (Madrid 1934) 351]. It is in the light of this principle that the subsequent Bañezian interpretation would seek to interpret the key statement of St. Thomas: "The divine knowledge must be regarded as the cause of things when taken in conjunction with His will" (ST 1a, 14.8). In this statement Bañezians would see St. Thomas as maintaining that the divine will must intervene if the purely possible is, in any sense, to become a future. So viewed, there can be no science of vision, no knowledge of what will be or might be unless the divine will decrees it to be. This decree cannot be a mere matter of execution; it must be a matter of determination—i.e., a predetermining decree (*see* PREDETERMINATION). Only in this way can the merely possible become the future in any sense. In this framework liberty is preserved by making it have its source in man's judgment—the choice of means. The actuality or the efficacy of the act, however, must come from God; this is the physical *premotion. In this view, the unchangeable design of God does not bear on man's judgment and so does not destroy his liberty (*see* BÁÑEZ AND BAÑEZIANISM).

This basic position as formulated by Báñez very quickly was brought into direct confrontation with the Jesuit teaching in Spain. The first confrontation was at a public disputation in Valladolid in 1582. From this point on debates took place all over Spain. Louvain was involved, the Inquisition in both Portugal and Spain was called on, and finally the controversy was brought to Rome (cf. E. Vansteenberghe, "Molinisme," DTC 10.2: 2094–2101; 2154–66). In the midst of this theological turmoil the *Concordia* of Luis de *Molina appeared after much opposition, particularly by Báñez. As a result, it contained an extensive appendix defending the author's work against the critique of Báñez.

Molina had been assigned to comment on the first part of St. Thomas's *Summa.* In this task he had concentrated on the endeavor to reconcile human liberty, divine foreknowledge, providence, and predestination. The key to his whole conception is what he calls middle science (**scientia media*). As does every Catholic theologian, Molina accepts as indisputable the fact that the *futurible (the hypothetical future) is an object of the divine knowledge. In the Bañezian conception these futuribles are a highly secondary issue to the future contingent. Molina, however, makes them a central element in his solution of the question since they are the object of the middle science. The question is: how are such hypothetical futures to be known by God? Molina is convinced that if these futuribles and future free contingents depend from a divine decree then human liberty is inconceivable. Consequently, he looks for another way, and this way is precisely signified by the term middle science. For Molina and those who follow him the divine knowledge of future contingents has, as it were, three stages, or moments. First, by natural science, or the science of simple intelligence, God knows all possibles. So He knows all that a given free agent placed in any possible condition will do. Second, by middle science God knows what any free agent would do if set in such and such a situation with such and such assistance, in a determined set of circumstances. These are the futuribles, the hypothetical futures. Finally, God decides to actualize a particular order of things. In this order are verified the circumstances and conditions already foreseen through the middle science. And so since God knows what this free agent would do, if placed in these circumstances, and then by a simple executive decree He actualizes a particular order, He knows infallibly what the free agent will do. This is free knowledge, or the science of vision. It is the contention of those who uphold this basic position that it preserves God's causal primacy since nothing in fact exists until God decrees it. Yet liberty is also safeguarded since the decree does not bear on man's free determination but only on the realization of a particular order and circumstances (*see* MOLINISM).

The length of this article allows only for a bare statement of each position. It forbids any lengthy discussion of the very rigorous criticism that has been leveled by each side in the controversy, as well as the vigorous, if sometimes violent, defenses that have been undertaken by the proponents of the positions. For a bibliography one may consult E. Vansteenberghe's article on Molinism noted above. To be noted also is the fact that within the general Bañezian and Molinistic positions there are divergences and many carefully nuanced variations. So, for example, Suárez does not accept a number of the conclusions put forth by Molina. Accepting the middle science, Suárez nonetheless differs very strongly on the presentiality of future contingents. He also demands much more of determination with regard to the future contingents than Molina allows and is sharply critical of Molina in this regard (cf. *Opuscula* 2.7.3). Within the Bañezian tradition divergences can also be found, as well as efforts, in the general Thomistic tradition, to reconcile—in such theologians as L. Billot and J. Van der Meersch in their tracts on the one God [J. Van der Meersch, *De Deo uno et trino* (2d ed. Bruges 1928); L. Billot, *De Deo uno et trino* (7th ed. Rome 1926)].

Contemporarily there has been a good deal of dissatisfaction with the focus of the controversy and its results. There is a tendency to judge the elements of the controversy as sifting down from too rigid an approach and the controversy itself as having been conducted on too narrow and too unhistoric a level. The genetic study of the thought of St. Thomas set in its actual historical context has given rise to a critical reevaluation of both the issues and the answers traditionally formulated. And so, B. Lonergan, SJ, believes that the Bañezian system runs counter to a whole body of doctrine and texts in St. Thomas [cf. "St. Thomas's Theory of Operation," ThSt 3 (1942) 387–389; "St. Thomas's Thought on *Gratia operans*," *ibid.* 565]. Lonergan would also maintain that the synthesis of St. Thomas himself demands instrumental cooperation rather than predetermination. He argues ". . . the Molinist lacks the speculative acumen to make his grace leave the will instrumentally subordinate to divine activity. But the Bañezian has exactly the same speculative blind-spot: because he cannot grasp that the will is truly an instrument by the mere fact that God causes the will of the end . . ." (*ibid.* 577). As Lonergan sees it, there is a failure on both sides to understand properly the position of St. Thomas on the divine transcendence (cf. *ibid.* 578). It is criticisms such

as this that have inclined a number of others to restudy the whole question and to reduce its proportionate importance in the theological study of the divine nature [e.g., J. Farrelly, OSB, *Predestination, Grace and Free Will* (Westminster Md. 1964); W. G. Most, *Novum tentamen ad solutionem de gratia et praedestinatione* (Rome 1963)].

For the believing Christian divine knowledge also implies Trinitarian doctrine and theology. Only through revelation is it possible to see that while much of the fact of God's knowledge can be formulated in the natural light of reason, some understanding of the full meaning and depth of this knowledge requires a knowledge of the Trinity. Here, it is affirmed that while God is an eternal subsistent act of understanding and each of the Divine Persons is the same act of understanding, yet only the Father understands as uttering the Word, His only begotten Son (cf. ST 1a, 34.1 ad 3; 34.2 ad 4).

See also CONGREGATIO DE AUXILIIS; FREE WILL; FREE WILL AND GRACE; GRACE, ARTICLES ON; GRACE, CONTROVERSIES ON; PREDESTINATION, ARTICLES ON; PROVIDENCE OF GOD (THEOLOGY OF); PROVIDENCE, ARTICLES ON; WILL OF GOD.

Bibliography: A. MICHEL, DTC 14.2:1598–1620. O. SEMMELROTH, LexThK² 1:356–358. P. DESCOQS, *Praelectiones theologiae naturalis*, 2 v. (Paris 1932–38). W. F. DEWAN, *The One God* (Englewood Cliffs, N.J. 1963). P. DUMONT, *Liberté humaine concours divin d'après Suárez* (Paris 1936). R. GARRIGOU-LAGRANGE, *The One God*, tr. B. ROSE (St. Louis 1943); *Providence*, tr. B. ROSE (St. Louis 1937); *Predestination*, tr. B. ROSE (St. Louis 1939). F. GENUYT, *Le Mystère de Dieu* (Paris 1963). JOHN OF ST. THOMAS, *Cursus theologicus II* (Quebec 1948) 419–684. R. JOLIVET, *The God of Reason*, tr. M. PONTIFEX (New York 1958). B. G. MURCHLAND, ed. and tr., *God Among Men* (Notre Dame, Ind. 1960).

[E. M. BURKE]

OMONT, HENRI AUGUSTE, French scholar; b. Evreux, Sept. 15, 1857; d. Paris, Dec. 9, 1940. After receiving his diploma from the École des Chartes in 1881, he came under the influence of Léopold *Delisle and A. *Giry. In 1879 he had started working for the Bibliothèque Nationale in Paris and 2 years later he transferred to the Department of Manuscripts, where he became *conservateur* in 1903. From 1905 until his retirement in 1935 he was simultaneously inspector-general of the libraries of France. Director of the *Catalogue des manuscrits des Bibliothèques publiques*, he edited several volumes himself; this Greek paleographer edited also the catalogues of the Moreau collection, and of the Greek MSS found in the British Museum, Brussels, Switzerland, the Netherlands, Verona, and the Hanse Towns. As the author of many scholarly studies, such as a work on Stephen of Rouen and an edition of the *Historia Francorum* of Gregory of Tours, he was one of the most noble men of contemporary French historical science. His contributions gave to the Department of Manuscripts of the Bibliothèque Nationale of Paris an unequaled prestige. He became a member of the Académie des Inscriptions et des Belles-Lettres in 1900.

Bibliography: M. ROQUES, in *Comptes rendus des séances de l'Académie des Inscriptions et des Belles-Lettres* (1940) 486–500, memorial. G. BRUNEL in *Bibliothèque de l'École des Chartes* 102 (1941) 371–378. A. DAIN, *Lettres d'humanité* 2 (1943) 194–200.

[É. BROUETTE]

OÑA, PEDRO DE, one of the foremost poets of colonial America and author of the first book of poetry published in America (1596); b. Angol, Chile, 1570; d. place and date unknown. He was the son of Gregorio

Pedro de Oña.

de Oña and Isabel de Acurcio. Nothing is known of his early schooling, but in 1596 he stated that he knew the "phrases, language, and character" of the Araucanians. In 1590 he was in the San Martín School of Lima and a student of the first course of arts in the University of San Marcos. In 1592 he entered the college of San Felipe and San Marcos on a scholarship. At the beginning of 1596 he had already obtained the title *licenciado* and had completed his *Arauco Domado,* which was published in Lima by Antonio Ricardo. The last known date for Pedro de Oña is the year 1635, when he signed *El Vasauro* in Cuzco. He wrote three major poems, the *Arauco Domado* (1596), the *Ignacio de Cantabria* (1639), and *El Vasauro* (which appeared in print for the first time in its entirety in 1941); a short poem, *El temblor de Lima de 1609* (1609); six laudatory sonnets; and three *canciones reales.* Of the *canción real* of 1630 paying homage to St. Francis Solano, Dinamarca said: "That alone would suffice to enshrine him as a good poet." His youthful work, *Arauco Domado,* which has brought him the most renown, was reissued in Madrid in 1605 and has had four editions since that time (two in Chile, Valparaíso 1849 and Santiago 1917), and an English translation (Albuquerque, N.Mex., 1948).

Bibliography: J. T. Medina, *Historia de la literatura colonial de Chile,* 3 v. (Santiago de Chile 1878) 1:133–238. E. Matta Vial, *El licenciado Pedro de Oña* (Santiago de Chile 1924). R. Oroz, Introduction to *El Vasauro* (Santiago de Chile 1941). **Illustration credit:** Library of Congress.

[A. M. ESCUDERO]

ONAHAN, WILLIAM JAMES, businessman, civic leader; b. Leighlin Bridge, County Carlow, Ireland, Nov. 24, 1836; d. Chicago, Ill., Jan. 12, 1919. As the son of John and Johanna Onahan, he lived for a time in Liverpool, England, immigrated to New York in 1851, and joined his family in Chicago in 1854. From office boy and shipping clerk he rose through a flour commission brokerage to high status in the business and political life of Chicago. Onahan was actively interested in political affairs and supported Stephen A. Douglas's presidential aspirations. After marrying Margaret Duffy in 1860, he served during the Civil War as civilian secretary of the Irish Brigade, recruited for the Union Army, and subsequently supported the peace movement and engaged in Democratic ward politics. Business and politics did not preclude Church activities, and he performed countless services for Bp. James Duggan of Chicago, aided the Jesuits in purchasing real estate, assisted several sisters' orders, and engaged in debating at the Catholic Institute and Catholic Lyceum. He was a director of the Catholic Asylum and Reformatory, organized the St. Patrick's Society, and served Abp. John Ireland in promoting Irish Catholic colonization projects in Minnesota and Nebraska. Personal advancement came with his appointment as a member of the Chicago Board of Education in 1863, reform work as city collector, and service as city comptroller and as president of the public library and the Home Savings Bank. In opposing Chicago's socialists, arbitrating strikes, campaigning for temperance, and resisting immigration restrictionists, Onahan performed many civic and religious tasks; for these he received the Laetare medal from the University of Notre Dame, Ind., and was made honorary private chamberlain by Leo XIII in 1895.

Onahan was Chicago correspondent of the New York *Freeman's Journal* and author of articles in the *Catholic World, Illinois Catholic Historical Review, American Catholic Historical Researches,* and other journals. He also published in 1895 some of his lectures on the Jesuits, having previously (1891) published *The Religious Crisis in France, Our Rights and Duties as Catholics and Citizens, Our Faith and Our Flag,* and *The Influence of the Catholic Layman.* He was for 4 decades a corresponding member of the Chicago Historical Society and ended his career as president of the Illinois Catholic Historical Society and honorary vice president of the Illinois State Historical Society. Onahan was considered by many the outstanding layman of the late 19th century, and was chosen to organize the Catholic Lay Congress in Baltimore, Md., in 1889. He proposed an international lay congress in Chicago in conjunction with the World's Fair, and also served as organizing chairman of the Columbian Catholic Congress, which met with the Parliament of Religions in 1893.

Bibliography: M. S. Pahorezki, *The Social and Political Activities of William James Onahan* (Washington 1942).

[J. R. BETTS]

ONAN, second son of *Juda and his Canaanite wife, the daughter of Sue (Heb. *'ônān,* "vigorous"). When Onan's elder brother Her died childless (Gn 38.6–7), Juda ordered Onan to take his brother's widow Thamar in marriage. This was done in accordance with the *levirate marriage custom so that the deceased brother's name might not be blotted out in Israel (Dt 25.6). Onan resented that the children of this union would be legally his brother's and that the eldest male would be his brother's heir. Since he had no concern for the preservation of his brother's name, whenever he had intercourse with Thamar, Onan wasted his seed, spilling it upon the ground "in order not to raise up descendants for his brother" (Gn 38.9). What Onan did has given his name to that type of contraception which is called "onanism."

Since the following verse states, "What he did was evil in the sight of the Lord and He killed him . . .," some conclude that it was precisely for the sin of contraception that he was slain by God. However, it should be noted that the main interest of the passage is to inculcate the binding force of the levirate marriage custom. Furthermore, it is Onan's total action that is condemned. He, for selfish motives, refused to fulfill the prescriptions of the levirate custom and used contraception to that end. It would seem correct to conclude that he was condemned because of his lack of charity toward his deceased brother as well as for the sin of contraception. Hence this passage should not be used as a clear-cut scriptural proof of the gravity of the moral evil of onanism.

See also LEVIRITE MARRIAGE.

Bibliography: C. F. DeVine, "The Sin of Onan: Gen. 38:8–10," CathBiblQuart 4 (1942) 323–340. J. B. Schaumberger, "Propter quale peccatum morte punitus sit Onan?" *Biblica* 8 (1927) 209–212.

[J. A. Pierce]

ONANISM, in common usage often taken to mean improperly completed intercourse or even masturbation. The word is taken from the story of Onan in the Book of Genesis (38.1–10). Onan was commanded by his father, Juda, to take Thamar, the widow of his brother, Her, who had been slain by the Lord, and to perform his duty as brother-in-law and raise up descendants for his brother. This was in accordance with the custom of *levirate marriage. Onan, however, to avoid raising up descendants for his brother, "wasted his seed upon the ground" whenever he had relations with Thamar. Because what he did was evil in the sight of the Lord, Onan was slain. Popular usage of the term onanism is based on the assumption that the evil for which the Lord took Onan's life was his unchastity. This, however, is by no means clear from the text, in which his refusal to conform to the prescribed marriage custom can be seen as the wickedness that brought vengeance upon him. Consequently, no certain argument can be based upon this text to prove the sinful character of either improperly completed intercourse or *masturbation. Evidence for this must be sought elsewhere.

See also CONTRACEPTION; MARRIAGE, USE OF.

Bibliography: Prümmer ManThMor 3:699–704.

[J. D. Fearon]

O'NEILL, EUGENE GLADSTONE

Dramatist; b. New York City, Oct. 16, 1888; d. Boston, Nov. 27, 1953. His parents were James O'Neill, a popular matinee idol, and Ella Quinlan. O'Neill attended a boarding school conducted by the Sisters of Charity in Riverdale, N.Y., and the De la Salle Institute of the Christian Brothers in Manhattan. Both his parents were Catholic, and Eugene made his First Communion but refused to go to Mass after his 15th year and there is no record of his ever again practicing his religion. In 1902 he entered the nonsectarian Betts Academy in Stamford, Conn., and was later graduated with grades adequate to secure his admission to Princeton University in 1906. He was dismissed the following year for poor scholarship and received no further formal education until 1914, when he enrolled in G. P. Baker's 47 Workshop in drama at Harvard, where he spent a year studying playwriting.

Between 1907 and 1913 O'Neill lived a dissolute life in New York's Greenwich Village, toured with his father's production of *The Count of Monte Cristo,* shipped out as a seaman, went on a mining expedition

Eugene O'Neill.

to Honduras, and worked as a newspaper reporter. Sometime during the same period he began to think of writing plays, and he developed the pursuit during his convalescence from tuberculosis. *Thirst,* his first play, was produced at the Wharf Theatre in Provincetown, Mass. (1916). He emerged as a major talent with the production of *Beyond the Horizon* at New York's Morosco Theatre, Feb. 2, 1920. The play, a Pulitzer prize winner, is marked by the crude power, the psychological probing, and the dogged observation of human behavior that runs through all his work. For the next 23 years he produced a body of dramatic literature—45 plays in all—unequaled previously in American drama. He was awarded the Pulitzer prize four times and won the Nobel prize in 1936.

O'Neill's plays cover a wide range of themes and styles. *The Emperor Jones* (1920), an expressionistic character study of a Pullman porter destroyed by atavistic fears and his own thirst for power, employs repeated drumbeats to symbolize fear and build suspense in a notable piece of stagecraft. In *The Hairy Ape* (1922) and *Dynamo* (1929) he deals with the dehumanization of man in the modern world. O'Neill was fond of technical experiment: in *The Great God Brown* (1926) he uses masks; in *Strange Interlude* (1928) he revives the aside to convey interior monologue; *Mourning Becomes Electra* (1931) transfers a Greek legend to New England. In *All God's Chillun Got Wings* he combined a bold theme for 1924—miscegenation—with a symbolic use of scenery. His best plays, however, are written in a stark naturalistic manner. One of his most controversial plays was *The Iceman Cometh* (1946).

O'Neill's two great artistic gifts were his ability to create situations in which driven characters are pitted openly against one another, and his power to write of his own experience with absolute honesty. He labored under two difficulties: his language, in spite of pretentious attempts to correct the fault, lacks eloquence; again, his intense preoccupation with the personal narrows his perspective so that he rarely achieves that double vision that enables the greatest artists to see inside and outside a subject at the same time. As a consequence of this myopia, his best plays are tragedies of circumstance in which his heroes are able to do little except cry in anguish. He declared that his effort was "to see the transfiguring nobility of tragedy, in as near the Greek sense as one can grasp it, in seemingly the most ignoble, debased lives. . . ." What he said of *Anna Christie* (1921) is perhaps true of all his plays: ". . . the play has no ending. Three characters have been revealed in all their intrinsic verity, under the acid test of a fateful crisis in their lives." He bears less resemblance to Aeschylus or Sophocles than to Euripides, who might be said also to scar without healing and burn without purifying.

The degree to which O'Neill's early Catholicism affected his work is debatable; his awareness of sin and guilt is Jansenistic rather than Catholic. One of his characters says: "Man is born broken. He lives by mending. The grace of God is glue." But the plays depict the break, not the mending. Although it is reasonable to believe that he was haunted by the loss of Catholicism, his attitudes appear to have been shaped by Nietzsche and by *Strindberg, whose play *The Father* is similar in mood to much of O'Neill's work. The critic Robert Benchley (1889–1945) pointed out that O'Neill's sense of scene was the result of his familiarity with his father's romantic productions, which he professed to hate; and it may be that he was affected, in spite of himself, by both the dramaturgy and the religion he consciously spurned.

Long Day's Journey into Night (1956) is as representative as a single play can be of a body of work. It is autobiographical in origin, shatteringly intense, verbose and repetitious, merciless in its characterization, unrelieved in its power, and stunning in its theatricality. At his death *Time* magazine commented: "Before O'Neill, the U.S. had theatre; after him, it had drama."

Bibliography: B. CLARK, *Eugene O'Neill: The Man and His Plays* (rev. ed. New York 1947). A. and B. GELB, *O'Neill* (New York 1962). E. D. SKINNER, *Eugene O'Neill: A Poet's Quest* (New York 1935). S. K. WINTHER, *Eugene O'Neill: A Critical Study* (New York 1934). O. CARGILL et al., eds., *O'Neill and His Plays: Four Decades of Criticism* (New York 1961). The best ed. of his plays, 3 v. (New York 1954–55) is incomplete. **Illustration credit:** Library of Congress, Alice Boughton Collection.

[L. BRADY]

O'NEILL, HUGH, second earl of Tyrone, called "The Great Earl"; b. Ulster, 1550; d. Rome, 1616. He was the son of Matthew O'Neill, illegitimate son of Conn, first Earl of Tyrone. In 1562 Hugh succeeded his older brother Brian as Baron of Dungannon. Hugh, educated in Ireland and England, acted more like an English noble than an Irish chieftain. Unlike his kinsman Shane *O'Neill, Hugh avoided violence and war, preferring peaceful cooperation with the English whenever possible. He helped the English in their conquest of the rebel Clandeboy O'Neills (1574), the Earl of Desmond and the Geraldines (1580), and the Antrim Scots of Ulster (1586). Queen Elizabeth I rewarded his loyalty by confirming his title as Earl of Tyrone (1587) originally conferred by the Dublin Parliament (1585). The succeeding years, however, were not always peaceful, as friction grew between O'Neill and the English.

In 1593 Hugh claimed the title of "The O'Neill," a title really forbidden by law. A year later, when Hugh Roe O'Donnell and Hugh Maguire organized an armed rebellion, O'Neill was suspected of sympathy with the rebels. Hugh, accused of treason by Sir Henry Bagenal, his brother-in-law, finally joined the revolt in 1595. His leadership and skill marked O'Neill as a born statesman and soldier. He commanded a well trained and well equipped army. His cautious planning and strategy provided the Irish cause with its greatest leader. Hugh also appealed to Scotland and Spain for aid. A series of pardons and truces interrupted the war until 1596, when the Irish embarked on a campaign that culminated in the great Irish victory at Yellow Ford (Aug. 15, 1598). O'Neill, awaiting Spanish assistance, moved deliberately. The Earl's cautious policies brought Robert Devereux, 2d Earl of Essex, to terms (1599). Sir Charles Blount, Lord Mountjoy, the new English commander, skillfully deployed his excellent army, thereby containing O'Neill and his troops in Kinsale. There Hugh, following the rash advice of Hugh Roe O'Donnell, attacked the English and met defeat. O'Neill continued the war until 1603, when James I pardoned him and confirmed his honors and estates. Years of English interference finally led to the "flight of the earls" on Sept. 14, 1607, when O'Neill and Rory O'Donnell, Earl of Tyrconnel, accompanied by their families and some retainers, fled to the Continent. Hugh was attainted by the Irish Parliament in 1613. His last years (1608–16) were spent in Rome as a pensioner of the pope and Phillip III of Spain. His leadership and exploits entitle him even more than Shane O'Neill to the title, the "Great O'Neill."

Bibliography: R. DUNLOP, DNB 14:1082–90. C. B. FALLS, *Elizabeth's Irish Wars* (London 1950). S. O'FAOLÁIN, *The Great O'Neill* (New York 1942). O. C. E. CURTIS, *History of Ireland* (6th ed. London 1950). J. K. GRAHAM, "The Birth-Date of Hugh O'Neill, Second Earl of Tyrone," *Irish Historical Studies* 1 (1938) 58–59.

[P. S. MC GARRY]

O'NEILL, OWEN ROE, Irish soldier and patriot; b. Ulster, 1582; d. Cavan, Nov. 6, 1649. Owen Roe was the nephew of Hugh *O'Neill, Earl of Tyrone. Owen left Ireland in 1603 at the time of his uncle's surrender to the English. He served in the army of the Spanish Hapsburgs in the Netherlands for more than 30 years. His defense of Arras (1640) won him great distinction even though he was forced to surrender to the French. O'Neill returned to Ireland (1642) after the outbreak of the Irish rebellion (1641). He became rebel commander in chief for Ulster. Owen became the leader of the Old Irish faction of the rebels that favored independence as opposed to the Anglo-Irish rebel faction that favored Irish self-government under the English crown. This division among the rebels was exacerbated by the arrival of Giovanni Battista *Rinuccini, Nuncio of Innocent X (1645). Rinuccini supported O'Neill and independence. O'Neill refused to cooperate with the Anglo-Irish efforts to arrange a treaty with James Butler, Marquis of Ormond, Lord Lieutenant of Ireland.

This treaty would have allied royalists and rebels in an antiparliamentary coalition. O'Neill defeated the English-Scottish army at Benburb (1646) thus strengthening the independence faction. By 1648, however, the Anglo-Irish faction took command and Rinuccini was forced to leave Ireland (February 1649). Ormond unsuccessfully offered terms to O'Neill on the basis of freedom of religion and restoration of lands. In August Oliver Cromwell invaded Ireland; but before O'Neill could mobilize his forces, he fell ill and died, thus depriving Ireland of the services of probably the only Irish commander who could have fought Cromwell with a chance of winning.

Bibliography: S. R. GARDINER, DNB 14:1095–98. E. CURTIS, *History of Ireland* (6th ed. London 1950). T. L. COONAN, *The Irish Catholic Confederacy and the Puritan Revolution* (New York 1954).

[P. S. MC GARRY]

O'NEILL, SARA BENEDICTA, lay apostle; b. Chicago, Ill., March 17, 1869; d. Chicago, Jan. 11, 1954. She studied romance languages at Northwestern University in Evanston, Ill., and, much later, library science at the University of Chicago. She taught for 35 years at Tilden Public High School in Chicago. Through her friendship with Ellen Gates Starr, a convert and a coworker of Jane Addams of Hull House, she acquired an admiration for the Benedictines and the contributions they had made through their libraries. During her life she made five trips to the Benedictine monastery of Monte Cassino in Italy and also visited the monasteries of Maria Laach and Beuron in Germany.

She was professed as an Oblate of St. Benedict at Monte Cassino, Aug. 4, 1902. At that time she conceived the idea of a library that would serve the cultural, religious, and intellectual interests of people in the Loop of Chicago. She spent the next 25 years interesting her friends and associates in the project. The St. Benedict Library, finally established on Oct. 30, 1931, became a rendezvous for writers and intellectuals and afforded them an opportunity to meet informally. She was also known as an apostle of the liturgical movement when the phrase was hardly known to most lay Catholics.

[E. V. CARDINAL]

O'NEILL, SHANE, Irish chieftain and soldier; b. Ulster, 1530; d. Cushendun, Antrim, June 2, 1567. Shane, the son of Conn, first Earl of Tyrone, broke with his father over Conn's acceptance of an English title from Henry VIII. King Henry also designated Conn's illegitimate son Matthew as heir to Conn's estates despite Shane's superior claim. After the death of Matthew (1558) and Conn (1559), Queen Elizabeth I recognized Shane, who was generally accepted as chief of the clan O'Neill and commanded three whole counties in Ulster as well as the vassalage of Maguire, O'Reilly, and other chiefs. Elizabeth eventually withdrew her support and recognized Brian O'Neill, son of the slain Matthew. Shane's stout resistance and the ensuing struggle finally led Elizabeth to summon Shane to London (1562). Elizabeth seems to have admired the "Great O'Neill," and she once again recognized his rights and titles. Shane, returning to Ireland (May 1562), soon became its most powerful figure. He was ready to acknowledge the Queen as sovereign but opposed the introduction of English law into Ulster. Shane was determined to exalt the O'Neill kingship and to remove all threats to his power. He fought the O'Donnells and MacDonnells, who opposed his rule. After his defeat by the O'Donnells at Farsetmore (1567),

Shane sought refuge with the MacDonnells of Antrim, who murdered him.

Bibliography: E. CURTIS, *History of Ireland* (6th ed. rev. London 1950). R. DUNLOP, DNB 14:1102–07. R. BAGWELL, *Ireland under the Tudors,* 3 v. (London 1885–90).

[P. S. MC GARRY]

ONESIMUS, a former slave of Philemon of *Colossae. He had escaped after defrauding his master in some way. After he was converted by the imprisoned Paul, he returned to Colossae with Tychicus, who was taking a letter from Paul to the Christian community there (Col 4.7–9; *see* COLOSSIANS, EPISTLE TO THE). They had also a short letter of the Apostle to Philemon (*see* PHILEMON, EPISTLE TO). In it Paul recommended Philemon should receive his former slave as a brother and even set him free and suggested that he send him back to Paul, who had found him "useful" in his work (Phlm 11; a play on Onesimus's name Ὀνήσιμος, which means "useful" in Greek). Onesimus is identified by many with the man of the same name who was the bishop of Ephesus mentioned in the early 2d-century letter of Ignatius of Antioch to the Church of Ephesus, and by some few with the Onesiphorus of 2 Tm 1.16–18; 4.19.

Bibliography: J. SCHMID, LexThK² 7:1158. T. DA CASTEL SAN PIETRO, EncCatt 9:131–132. EncDictBibl 1669. P. R. COLEMAN-NORTON, "The Apostle Paul and the Roman Law of Slavery," *Studies in Roman Economic and Social History, in Honor of A. C. Johnson,* ed. P. R. COLEMAN-NORTON (Princeton 1951) 155–177. For additional bibliography, *see* PHILEMON, EPISTLE TO.

[E. H. MALY]

ONIAS III, Jewish high priest mainly during the reign of the Syrian King Seleucus IV (187–175 B.C.). When the latter attempted to confiscate the treasury of the Jerusalem Temple, he was foiled by Onias's objections and the supernatural intervention described in 2 Mc 3.24–28. Onias, "a good and virtuous man" (2 Mc 15.12), went to Antioch to plead the cause of Judaism before Seleucus; but after the latter's death, Onias's brother Jason, a champion of Hellenism, bought the high priesthood from *Antiochus IV Epiphanes (175–164 B.C.) and began the Hellenization of Jerusalem. Onias remained safe in Antioch until 171 B.C., when Menelaus, another usurper of Onias's rights, had him treacherously murdered. He is most likely to be identified with the "anointed" in the apocalyptic passage of Dn 9.26. His son, Onias IV, when driven from the Temple of Jerusalem by Alcimus, built a Jewish temple at Leontopolis in the Egyptian Delta. The Romans closed this temple in A.D. 73 (Josephus, *Ant.* 12.9.7; 13.3.1–3; *B.J.* 7.10).

Bibliography: EncDictBibl 1669–70.

[J. J. DOUGHERTY]

ONITSHA, ARCHDIOCESE OF (ONIT-SHAËNSIS), metropolitan see since 1950, in southeast *Nigeria, west central Africa. In 1963 it had 16 secular and 56 religious priests, 21 sisters in 5 convents, and 236,000 Catholics in a population of 820,000; it is 1,197 square miles in area. Its eight suffragan sees, 28,731 square miles in area, had 400 priests, 237 sisters, and 1,159,000 Catholics in a population of 8 million; they were Calabar (created in 1950), Enugu (1962), Ikot Ekpene (1963), Kabba (1964), Ogoja (1955), Owerri (1950), Port Harcourt (1961), and Umuahia (1958). Onitsha, with a population of 77,000 (mostly

Ibos), is on the left bank of the Niger River at its confluence with the Anambra. Holy Ghost Fathers from *Gabon came to Onitsha in 1885. From the Vicariate of the Two Guineas (1842) was detached the Prefecture of Lower Niger (1889), which became the Vicariate of South Nigeria (1920), called Onitsha-Owerri (1934). Onitsha and Owerri became separate vicariates (1948–50). The suffragans were detached from Onitsha and Owerri. The University of Nigeria (1960) is in Nsukka (near Enugu, capital of Eastern Nigeria).

Bibliography: MissCattol 118–119. C. CORVO, EncCatt 9:133. AnnPont (1965) 314.

[E. P. COLBERT]

ONLY-BEGOTTEN ONE, the English equivalent of the Greek μονογενής, used of human relationships in Lk 7.12; 8.42; 9.38; Heb 11.17, but referring exclusively to Jesus in the Johannine writings (Jn 1.14, 18; 3.16, 18; 1 Jn 4.9). The term expresses Our Lord's divine sonship, emphasizing its unique character. In Jn 3.16; 1 Jn 4.9, where the thought of the Father's love is predominant, the term, though retaining its basic meaning of "only," "unique," takes on the nuance of ἀγαπητός (dearly beloved), which together with μονογενής, is used in the Septuagint to render the Hebrew yāḥîd (solitary, alone) in texts where it refers to an only child.

According to John, God's only Son Jesus is Himself God (Jn 1.18, reading with the best MSS, μονογενὴς θεός, only-begotten God). He lives with His Father in the most intimate relationship, and the Father shares His knowledge and power with Him. For this reason the Son alone fully reveals the Father whom no man has seen (Jn 1.18); He alone, in perfect unity with the Father, exercises the divine prerogatives of giving life and of judging (Jn 3.16, 18; 5.27); His being sent into this world is the greatest proof of God's love for men (1 Jn 4.9).

That the only Son (υἱός) is "born of God" in an infinitely deeper sense than are the many children (τέκνα) of God is certainly John's conviction (cf. Jn 1.13; 11.52; 1 Jn 5.18). However, μονογενής refers directly not to the mode of the preexistent Son's generation, as the translation "only-begotten" suggests, but to the incarnate and risen Christ whose glory the disciples beheld (Jn 1.14). While John clearly regards Jesus as a preexisting Being who becomes incarnate, his Gospel is chiefly concerned with showing how Jesus reveals Himself to men as Son of God in His earthly ministry and especially in His Passion and Resurrection. Returning to His Father, He receives the glory that was His before the creation of the world and is proclaimed Son of God. Therefore, though insisting upon the divine and unique character of Christ's sonship, John is silent about the manner in which the Son is generated by the Father.

Bibliography: F. BÜCHSEL, "Μονογενής," Kittel ThW 4:745–750. EncDictBibl 1670–72. R. GYLLENBERG, RGG³ 2:376–377.

[S. MAKAREWICZ]

ONTOLOGICAL ARGUMENT

The phrase "ontological argument" is generally understood by historians of philosophy to refer to an argument for the existence of *God. The term ontological was used by Immanuel *Kant to describe Descartes's version of the argument. Later historians, however, have applied the term to every form of the argument, but especially to that formulated by St. *Anselm of Canterbury in his *Monologion* and *Proslogion*. The effect of such diversity of usage has tended to obscure essential differences in the assumptions on which various forms of the argument rest, as well as to ignore the different purposes for which the argument was employed.

St. Anselm and Descartes. The ontological argument has been used in both theological and philosophical contexts. The texts of St. Anselm and *Descartes are the primary examples of these two uses. According to St. Anselm, the purpose of the argument is to help to understand "in some degree Thy truth which my heart believes and loves." In contrast, Descartes's philosophical use of the argument is concerned with establishing an intellectual sanction for true judgments concerning "the essence of material things."

The direct consequence of locating the argument for the existence of God within a theological context is to see the argument as unique and applicable in only one instance. But Descartes, in formulating his version of the argument, says that he intends to show that the existence of God "would pass with me for a truth at least as certain as I ever judged any truth of mathematics to be . . . ." (*Meditation* 5). For him, mathematical proofs are the paradigms for all proofs concerned with material things. Consequently he regards the ontological argument as a most general and paradigmatic kind of proof.

The failure to distinguish between the ontological argument as a model for other arguments and as a unique argument has had unfortunate consequences in evaluating the argument, especially the version of St. Anselm. Post-Kantian and contemporary criticism have generally relied on criteria of proof that are indeed relevant to any argument serving as a paradigm for other proofs, but irrelevant to an argument intended to hold in only one instance. A summary of St. Anselm's arguments supports this notion.

Argument in the Monologion. St. Anselm describes the *Monologion* as a soliloquy, i.e., as "a meditation on the grounds of faith." He cautions the reader first to "read diligently Augustine's books on the Trinity, and then judge my treatise in the light of those" (*Monologion*, pref.). The subject of the meditation is the "essence of divinity" and includes the many things that we "necessarily believe regarding God and his creatures" (ch. 1). The stated purpose of the argument is to show by reason alone how far one can come toward an understanding of the truths of belief, even if one does not believe. St. Anselm adds one most important condition regarding the strength of his argument: The conclusions drawn should be understood as having a qualified, or quasi, necessity and not an absolute *necessity.

The term necessity, as St. Anselm uses it, means "always either compulsion or restraint" (*Cur Deus Homo*, ch. 17). Moreover, necessity refers to the actions and operations of creatures, but is not predicable of the divine nature itself. For "when we say with regard to God that anything is necessary or not necessary, we do not mean that, as far as He is concerned, there is any necessity either coercive or prohibitory, but we mean that there is a necessity in everything else, restraining or driving them in a particular way" (*ibid.*).

Premises and Conclusion. Since the meditation is about God and His creation, St. Anselm proceeds from assumptions that he regards as most evident regarding creatures. All men seek to enjoy only those things that they consider *good. It is clear that every man sometime reflects on the cause of that phenomenon. St. Anselm's meditation on this resulted in the following argument, which he says has quasi-necessity: Every object of desire is regarded or conceived as good, where good is understood as either a useful or a noble object. Sense experience and intellectual reflection show that there are innumerable objects that vary in goodness and intensity of desirability. This multiplicity demands a single unifying *principle of explanation, which also serves as the principle of order among the degrees of goodness. Such a principle cannot have the same generic characteristics as do other objects of desire. Consequently, the good that is to be the principle of all goods that admit of a variation in degree of goodness must itself not admit of any variation in degree. Hence, the principle of order and explanation of the multiplicity of goods must be a supreme good. For any good that can be thought or perceived to vary in degree can be neither self-ordering nor self-explanatory.

The notion of a supreme good means that it is good in itself rather than by *participation in or by comparison with any other good. Since all other goods are good because of the supreme good, the supreme good must also be the most noble or mighty good (see GOOD, THE SUPREME).

The objects of desire have natures that themselves vary in degree of worth or dignity. Hence, the supreme good too must have a nature or essence that is supreme. It follows that the supreme nature is the ordering principle of all other essences or natures. But the supreme nature, being the principle of all other natures, cannot itself have an ordering principle. Hence, the supreme nature is unqualifiedly autonomous or self-subsistent. As a corollary it follows that all other natures or essences proceed from the supreme nature. St. Anselm observes finally that the meaning of self-subsistence can be expressed only analogically, or more properly, through figurative speech, but this in no way vitiates the truth of what is understood.

Summary of the Reasoning. The argument of the *Monologion* can be reduced to four propositions: (1) Men desire objects they think to be good—objects that vary in degree of goodness. (2) Because the variance in degree is intelligible, there must exist an invariable principle of order, i.e., a supreme good that is the source of all goodness. (3) The objects of desire have natures that vary in worth and dignity. (St. Anselm says that whoever doubts this cannot be called a man.) (4) Because the worth of natures varies in degree there must exist a supreme nature that is invariable and does not admit of comparison, i.e., a self-subsistent nature that is the originative principle of all variable natures.

Argument in the Proslogion. Most commentators do not usually regard the argument of the *Monologion* as a version of the ontological argument, reserving that title to the proof in the *Proslogion.* One commonly held reason for making such a distinction is that the argument of the *Monologion* assumes causal principles and is analogous to the "fourth way" of St Thomas (see GOD, PROOFS FOR THE EXISTENCE OF). St. Anselm, however, seems to see the difference between the two to be in the number of arguments rather than in method or procedure. Whereas in his preface to the *Proslogion* he describes the *Monologion* as bound together by a number of arguments, he aspires in the *Proslogion* to formulate a single argument that would prove the existence of God.

Difference in Intent. A possible explanation for the difference in the number of arguments may be found in the difference in aspect and intention between the two works. The *Monologion* treats of God and His creation, while the *Proslogion* reflects on God and His attributes. The *Monologion* begins with assumptions concerning the actions and nature of creatures that are evidently multiple, but the *Proslogion* begins with a single assumption about the meaning of the term God. Moreover, St. Anselm states that the *Proslogion* differs from the *Monologion* in being a discourse rather than a soliloquy; yet it is a discourse of the soul with itself, rather than a dialogue or scientific treatise on *theology. In the *Proslogion,* St. Anselm advises the reader to "Enter the inner chamber of thy mind; shut out all thoughts save that of God, and such as can aid thee in seeking Him; close thy door and seek Him" (ch. 1). The *Proslogion* is a matter of "faith seeking understanding" (see FAITH AND REASON).

The argument of the *Proslogion* has two distinct concerns. St. Anselm says: "And so, Lord, do Thou, who dost give understanding to faith, give me, so far as Thou knowest it to be profitable, to understand that Thou art as we believe; and that Thou art that which we believe" (ch. 2). The argument for the existence of God is restricted to the first of these concerns, i.e., understanding "that Thou art as we believe."

St. Anselm takes on faith that God is "a being than which nothing greater can be conceived" (*ibid.*). This verbal formula of the belief, he says, is understood by everyone who hears the words. But what is at issue is not that one understand the words, but that what the words signify does exist apart from the understanding of the hearer. St. Anselm argues that there is a difference between something existing both in fact and in the understanding, and something existing in the understanding only. He adds that to exist in both ways "is greater" than to exist in the understanding only. Consequently, he concludes that by understanding the meaning of the term God, one must also understand that God exists apart from the understanding. The corollary to the argument is that it is impossible both to understand the meaning of the term God and to conceive that God does not exist apart from the understanding. St. Anselm does say it is, of course, possible to articulate sentences that assert the nonexistence of God, for understanding in no way coerces the use of *language. But this understanding does prohibit one from conceiving as true the assertion that God does not exist, even if one is unwilling to believe that God does exist.

Synopsis of the Argument. A paraphrase of the argument shows the extent of its claim and implicitly reveals the grounds of the continuing controversy about its validity. In effect St. Anselm says: (1) I hold on faith that God exists. (2) I hold on faith that He is "that than which nothing greater can be conceived." (3) I rationally examine the content of the concepts given by faith. (4) It is impossible that the *understanding* of those concepts totally encompasses, comprehends, or contains the meaning of "that than which nothing greater can be conceived." (5) Hence, the understanding can now truly affirm what was already held on faith, i.e., that God exists extramentally, and is that that we believe. (6)

Given the meaning of God on faith, it is impossible for reason to conceive that He does not exist.

Evaluations of the Argument. St. Anselm's argument was first challenged by a monk named Gaunilon, whose first critical objection was that St. Anselm had begged the question by assuming the definition of God, and then constructing a proof based on the hypothetical character of the definition. St. Anselm in reply calls "on [his] faith and conscience" to deny the arbitrariness of the definition (Anselm, *Apologetic,* ch. 1). The second objection of Gaunilon was that St. Anselm's argument is invalid because it moves without warrant from ideas to realities; he cites as an example the concept of a perfect island, and argues that on St. Anselm's grounds such an island ought to exist. The charge is denied by asserting that the argument holds only in the case of God, and, hence, is incapable of refutation by a counter-example that does not depend on a movement from faith to reason, but only on *reasoning.

Later scholastics are divided on the merits of the argument. St. *Thomas Aquinas and *Richard of Middleton reject the argument. St. Thomas's rejection of the argument invariably turns on the question, "Whether the existence of God is self-evident?" His reply is that St. Anselm's argument does not succeed in showing that the existence of God is self-evident to us (ST 1a, 2.1. ad 2). Other scholastics such as *Alexander of Hales, St. *Bonaventure and *Duns Scotus accepted St. Anselm's argument with modification. Scotus was concerned to show that there is no contradiction in asserting that an infinite being is comprehensible to a finite mind. As part of his proof, Scotus says he will "touch up" St. Anselm's argument: "His description must be understood thus: 'God is a being than which'—when thought of without a contradiction—'a greater cannot be thought of' without a contradiction." The effect of that qualification is reflected in the conclusion Scotus draws: "It follows that there exists in reality such a highest thinkable as mentioned, through which God is described" (*De primo principio,* concl. 9).

After Descartes's use of the ontological argument for strictly philosophical purposes, new criteria of evaluation were introduced. Admitting his indebtedness to Duns Scotus and distinguishing between a priori and a posteriori proofs, *Leibniz argued that if God is possible, He exists. A version of the argument was used also by *Spinoza to show that God necessarily exists, while *Locke rejected the argument for roughly the same reasons as those of St. Thomas. Kant's famous dictum that existence is not a predicate led him to attack Descartes's version of the argument—a rejection that was seconded by *Hegel, but only on the ground that St. Anselm's statement was faulty in form.

Recent discussion of the argument has been led by Norman Malcolm, who construes one form of St. Anselm's argument to conclude that God has necessary existence, a conclusion that Malcolm asserts follows from a valid argument. Critics of Malcolm's position have either found his use of the term necessity ambiguous, or have argued on formal logical grounds that the argument as presented is invalid.

The preponderance of contemporary secular scholarly opinion regards both the Anselmian and the Cartesian view of the ontological argument as logically invalid and metaphysically suspect. There is no consensus among Christian scholars about the proper interpretation and evaluation of St. Anselm's argument. Interpretations vary from seeing the argument as rigorously demonstrative to finding in it an adequate mystical theology, or regarding it as a rough but solid beginning of a systematic natural theology. Judgments concerning the validity of the argument are as varied as are the interpretations.

The position taken here is that the ontological argument of St. Anselm has nothing significant in common with the later versions of Descartes, *et al.* Because St. Anselm's argument is absolutely unique, it cannot be evaluated in the light of later criteria nor can it be criticized for its failure to accomplish purposes for which it was not intended. St. Anselm did not intend to make a formal proof for the existence of God. He was not concerned with making a scientific demonstration for the existence of a necessary being, or for the possibility of a necessary being, or for the non-contradictoriness of the existence of a necessary being. Instead, St. Anselm intended his argument to exemplify a method through which the understanding can find an expression for the certitude of *faith or through which reason can find a way to articulate the "reasonable solidity of Truth." From this perspective the argument can be regarded as valid.

Bibliography: ANSELM OF CANTERBURY, *Proslogium; Monologium; An Appendix in Behalf of the Fool by Gaunilon; and Cur Deus Homo,* tr. S. N. DEAN (La Salle, Ill. 1954); *Opera Omnia,* ed. F. S. SCHMITT, 6 v. (Edinburgh 1946–) critical text. N. MALCOLM, "Anselm's Ontological Arguments," *Philosophical Review* 69 (1960) 41–62; articles in reply, *Philosophical Review* 70 (1961) 56–111. A. DANIELS, "Quellen, Beiträge und Untersuchungen zur Geschichte der Gottesbeweise im Dreizehnten Jahrhundert," BeitrGeschPhilMA 8.1–2 (1909). M. CAPPUYNS, "L'Argument de saint Anselme," RechThAm 6 (1934) 313–330. K. BARTH, *La Preuve de l'existence de Dieu d'après Anselme de Cantorbéry,* tr. J. CARRÈRE (Neuchâtel 1958). R. G. MILLER, "The Ontological Argument in St. Anselm and Descartes," ModSchoolm 32 (1955) 341–349; 33 (1955) 31–38. C. HARTSHORNE, "Logic of the Ontological Argument," *Journal of Philosophy* 58 (1961) 471–473.

[A. NEMETZ]

ONTOLOGISM

Essentially the affirmation that the idea of *being, which is immediately and intuitively present to the human intellect, is God Himself. This description will be borne out and will serve as a general guide in the following historical, theological, and philosophical examination of ontologism.

Ontologism Viewed Historically. The word ontologism as a term generally used to describe a philosophic system is of 19th-century origin. It indicates one element of the basic tenet of the teaching in question, namely, that man has being (ὄν ὄντος, being) as the object of his intellect. From this fact, which ontologists take as axiomatic, another essential element of their theory is deduced: the being that is the object of the intellect is Being, God Himself. The principal defenders of this proposition in the 19th century were V. *Gioberti in Italy, G. Ubaghs in Belgium, and, to a lesser extent, O. *Brownson in the U.S. Brownson, for example, castigates "the Christian peripatetics" for not admitting "that the universal, the necessary, the eternal, the immutable without the intuition of which the contingent and the particular are inconceivable, and no syllogism is possible, are identically the divine being, the *ens necessarium et reale,* or God himself" [*Boston Quarterly Review,* 2d New York series (Oct. 1860) 436]. A. *Rosmini-Serbati, although often called an ontologist, states explicitly: "That which is shown to our mind when it sees being and nothing else is not the living and acting God, and consequently cannot receive in any way the personal denomination of God" [*Del divino nella natura*, v.4 of *Teosophia* (5 v. Turin 1859–74) 11].

Although ontologism was formulated under a specific title only in the 19th century, the theory had been favored for centuries preceding. In France its great master was N. *Malebranche, ably expounded by H. Gerdil, who quotes also from Thomassin and Marcilio Ficino with approval. "Only He [God] can throw light upon the [human] spirit by His own substance . . . it is He who rules over our spirit, according to St. Augustine, without the mediation of any creature . . .. One cannot conceive that the infinite can be represented by anything created . . . it must be said that one knows God through Himself, although the knowledge one has of Him in this life is very imperfect" [Gerdil (quoting Malebranche), 170]. In other words, the knowledge one has of God, even on a natural plane, is dependent upon an immediate, although obscure, intuition of Him.

Malebranche's appeal to St. Augustine indicates sufficiently that the upholders of ontologistic teaching did not consider their theory as new. For them, its roots were deep in history, and, consequently, it drew its nourishment from the instinctive movement of the human spirit as expressed in the great minds of the ages. On a historical plane they appealed to Plato, to St. Augustine, and to St. Thomas Aquinas.

For St. Augustine "the forms—now ideas in the divine mind—yield their eternal truth to the mind in the light of a divine illumination in the mind. This is an exact replica of Plato's image of the sun: for Augustine, too, God is to the mind what the sun is to the things visible to the eye" [A. H. Armstrong and R. H. Markus, *Christian Faith and Greek Philosophy* (London 1960)]. From considerations of this kind, whose truth cannot be denied, ontologists went on to conclude that their teaching was based on that of the masters of antiquity. They found further support in St. Thomas Aquinas: ". . . we are said to see all things in God and to make our judgments according to Him, insofar as through a participation of His light we know and judge all things; for the natural light itself of reason is a certain participation of the divine light" (ST 1a, 12.11 ad 3). Although St. Thomas himself explicitly denies that the purely natural man sees God, ontologists maintain that this cannot follow from his dicta about man's participation in the divine light. According to them, being seen by the mind is either the Creator or a creature. If it is the divine light, it cannot be a creature. Therefore, it must be the Creator [cf. V. Gioberti, *Degli errori di Antonio Rosmini* (Brussels 1841) 37–38].

Ontologism Viewed Theologically. Among the propositions condemned by the Holy Office in 1861 as unsafe for teaching (*tuto tradi non possunt*) was the statement: "At least an habitual, immediate knowledge of God is essential to the human intellect in such a way that, without it, it cannot know anything: for it is the intellectual light itself" (Denz 2841). From a theological point of view this condemnation was the culmination of a controversy that had raged during the previous years between "traditionalists" who main-

tained in various ways that even a purely natural man has an essential need of revelation, and the extremists among those who upheld the natural autonomy of human reason. Although the particular reasons for the dangers inherent in ontologism were not expressed in the condemnatory decree, they may fairly be summarized under two headings of Catholic doctrine: the distinction between the Creator and the creature, and the distinction between nature and grace.

If, as Gioberti maintains, ideas are the real things themselves, there would seem to be no place for a distinction between God and His creatures. Basically, Gioberti's principle leaves no room for a distinction between act and potency or, consequently, between essence and existence. It follows that the essence of all beings is to exist. The way is thus open for the final step to pantheism: if the essence of all beings is to exist, there must be only one Being that embraces all existence.

There is an equal danger of confusing the natural with the *supernatural in the ontologistic way of regarding the nature of the object of man's natural intellect. If by nature, without reference to supernature, man is granted a direct, even if obscure, glimpse of God's reality, it is difficult to see how any grace given to him can differ in kind from the light of reason he receives in his natural creation. Moreover, if his human nature essentially demands the vision of God it would seem that the notion of grace as an altogether gratuitous gift of God to man is to be rejected. Brownson, for example, while avoiding the Scylla of pantheism, seems to be in danger from the Charybdis of naturalism. "Nothing remains [in order to avoid pantheism] but to admit that the soul has, by one and the same act, an intuition of God and itself . . . the Creator presents himself, in the act of creation, to the created spirit as the object of its activity" [*Boston Quarterly Review* (Jan. 1860) 49].

Ontologism Viewed Philosophically. Philosophically, ontologism takes its stand upon a fact open to observation, that is, the knowledge of being in general is that alone which enables man to know particular beings. Ontologists accept wholeheartedly St. Thomas's *ens communissimum* as the first thing known to the intellect. In order to say "the thing is something" (e.g., "the table is large"), one must first know what "is" means. Then they add: but "is" is the name of God. Therefore, one must know God to affirm anything of anything.

It is implicit in this argument that the fundamental knowledge of the human intellect cannot be abstracted from knowledge of material things or spring from the human spirit. It cannot be abstracted from material things because it is the prerequisite by which they are known, and also because being as such is not to be found in them. They are only the effects of being. Just as God precedes the creation, so knowledge of God precedes knowledge of His creatures.

It cannot spring from the human spirit because the spirit itself is created and cannot produce the infinite. According to the ontologists, consideration of material things and of the human spirit can only lead to the conclusion that the knowledge of Being, God Himself, is given to the spirit by the Creator at the first moment of its existence.

Ontologists saw their system as the only answer to the sensism of Locke and the subjectivism common to

Kant and Descartes. Malebranche, by showing that the light of reason cannot itself come from the senses, intended to oppose the materialistic interpretation imparted by Locke to the adage: "Nihil est in intellectu quod non prius fuerit in sensu"; Gioberti, by upholding the reality of the object given to the spirit from outside itself, set himself against German idealism and French psychologism, both essentially subjective.

Philosophical objections to ontologism are not hard to find. The chief difficulty springs from observation. While it is true that one must know being in general as a condition for knowing anything at all (for of anything known it must at least be said: "it *is* something"), experience shows that this being is not Being (God, the infinite reality). If it were, what need would there be to know any finite reality?

The key to the right understanding of the relationship between the limitless being known by man's intellect and the infinite reality is best found in St. Thomas's illustration, not in the ontologistic explanation. Just as one can see the light of the sun without seeing the sun itself, so the light of reason, which is immutable truth, can be seen by the intellect without its seeing God Himself (cf. ST 1a, 12.11; *C. gent.* 3.47). Ignoring this distinction means opting for ontologism.

See also BEATIFIC VISION; GOD, INTUITION OF; ILLUMINISM; KNOWLEDGE, THEORIES OF; LIGHT OF GLORY.

Bibliography: Sources. N. MALEBRANCHE, *De la recherche de la verité*, 2 v. (Paris 1674). H. S. GERDIL, *Défense du sentiment du P. Malebranche* . . . (Turin 1748). G. C. UBAGHS, *Du Problème ontologique des universaux* (Liège 1845). V. GIOBERTI, *Introduzione allo studio della filosofia* (Brussels 1844). Studies. A. FONCK, DTC 11.1:1000–61, the most complete study available. L. LATOUR, LexThK² 7:1161–64. P. BURGELIN, RGG³ 4:1635–36. L. PELLOUX, EncCatt 9:146–149. L. FOUCHER, *La Philosophie catholique en France au XIXᵉ siècle* . . . (Paris 1955). J. HENRY, *Le Traditionalisme et l'ontologisme à l'université de Louvain (1835–65)* (Louvain 1922). L. STEFANINI, *Gioberti* (Milan 1947).

[D. CLEARY]

ONTOLOGY, from the Greek ὄντος and λόγος, meaning the science of being, was first used by J. Clauberg (1647), who called "ontology that science which does not deal with this and that being, . . . but with being in general"; the term occurs also in an undated fragment of *Leibniz, and by 1729 appears as the title, *Ontologia*, of a treatise by Christian *Wolff. Constructing his metaphysics rationally and relying particularly on the notion of possible being, Wolff distinguished between general metaphysics, or ontology, and special metaphysics, comprising *cosmology, *psychology, and natural *theology. His general metaphysics deals with notions concerning all things (e.g., substance, order, truth, perfection, necessity and contingency, the possible and the impossible). As a science of being, it is called ontology; as presenting first principles and notions used in reasoning, it is called first philosophy. The Wolffian influence and tradition survive in modern philosophical usage and serve to explain the order of many scholastic manuals in which ontology is placed after *logic and before the tracts on special metaphysics.

See also METAPHYSICS; PHILOSOPHY; BEING.

[J. V. BURNS]

OPEN SHOP, a term used in the literature of industrial relations to designate an establishment that may hire workers and retain them in employment without regard to their membership or nonmembership in a labor organization. It is contrasted with the union shop where the collective bargaining agreement permits an employer to hire employees who are not members of the union but requires these newly hired men to join the union within a stated period of time, usually 30 days, and with the closed shop where membership in a labor organization is a prerequisite both for the hiring of an employee and his continuance in employment. The Taft-Hartley Act of 1947 (National Labor Relations Act) authorized the States to enact legislation outlawing union membership as a condition of employment. In 1965 nineteen states had such statutes, sometimes erroneously labeled "right to work laws," which virtually enforce the open shop within their borders. As a practical matter, a union operating under an open-shop arrangement enjoys only that minimum of exclusive bargaining rights that is guaranteed by law to all unions that win certification in an election conducted by the National Labor Relations Board.

The true open shop should be distinguished from the expression as it was used in the 1920s when employers pushed the "American Plan," a drive to exclude union members from employment. That effort was supported by individual, so-called "yellow-dog contracts," under which the worker agreed as a condition of employment not to join a union. The Norris-LaGuardia Act of 1932 virtually eliminated such contracts from industry by making them unenforceable.

See CLOSED SHOP; COLLECTIVE BARGAINING (U.S.); UNION SHOP.

[D. J. WHITE]

OPERATIONALISM

A method of defining concepts, mainly those of modern science, in terms of the measuring techniques and other operations associated with their use. It refers also to the doctrine that the meaning of a statement or symbol is synonymous with a set of operations that enable an observer to decide whether or not the statement is true or the symbol is correctly applied. Where no such set of operations can be specified, the statement or symbol in question is said to be meaningless.

Basic Notions. Operationalism was first enunciated by the American physicist, P. W. Bridgman, and in its subsequent development is sometimes called operationism. It is a variation of *positivism, which received its earliest systematic expression in the *Cours de philosophie positive* (Paris 1830–42) of Auguste *Comte. The key thesis of positivism, then as now, is that natural science should limit its concern to what is given in sense experience. Thus, definitions and theories in science should avoid reference to entities or causes whose existence is not experimentally verifiable. Bridgman, in broad agreement with this rule and with the later positivist principle that the meaning of a statement is expressed in the method by which it is verified, attempted a further analysis of verification procedures in terms of particular kinds of operation (*see* LOGICAL POSITIVISM; VERIFICATION).

As a proposal to purify the language of science, operationalism recommends that the terms used in natural science be defined by reference to the human actions associated with their use. For example, an operational definition of length in the context of measuring a straight metal bar might read: "the number obtained by placing one end of a yardstick at one end of the bar and then reading the numeral at the point where the yardstick meets the other end." In the field of thermodynamics Bridgman is celebrated for his efforts to define operationally such concepts as heat and temperature.

Critique. Many theorists in the social and behavioral sciences maintain that operational definitions give precision to their terminologies. However, considered as a blanket proposal for restyling all definitions in science, operationalism has met with criticism. One objection concerns the inclusiveness of the concept of operation. If operation includes everything done with deliberation in the furtherance of scientific inquiries, the term applies to such behavior as waiting for a chemical reaction to complete itself, looking for indications of handwork on a piece of flint, and keeping records of the various strata from which prehistoric relics are excavated. Since such behavior is closely interwoven with the uses of scientific terms, and is in fact learned along with those uses, the wholesale adoption of operational definitions would amount in most cases to spelling out what is already known to scientists and is inseparable from sound scientific practice. Related to this is the criticism that operationalism would multiply rather than clarify scientific concepts by requiring a different symbol for each set of operations associated with a concept. Distance, for example, would splinter into as many separate concepts as there are techniques for measuring distances in optics, astronomy, geodesy, and so on.

It is possible to advocate the use of operational definitions in science without accepting the narrowed conception of meaning woven into Bridgman's discussions. There he sets limits to significant discourse by requiring that the operations needed for verifying a statement be specifiable; otherwise the statement must be counted meaningless. Objections of two types have dogged Bridgman's position from the start. The first points out that the declared synonymity between "knowing the meaning of a statement S" and "knowing what operations would lead to the verification of S" is stipulated by Bridgman himself, and does not sum up what the term meaning conveys in the language from which he borrowed it. Those who appreciate the force of this objection take a relaxed view of the apparent threat posed by operationalism against the meaningfulness of ethical and metaphysical statements. A second objection proceeds in large part from critics who, though in sympathy with Bridgman's *empiricism, argue that his criterion of meaningfulness needlessly puts in question a number of useful and trouble-free types of scientific proposition, such as contrary-to-fact conditional statements and those dealing with the remote past.

See also SEMANTICS; ANALYTICAL PHILOSOPHY.

Bibliography: P. W. BRIDGMAN, *The Logic of Modern Physics* (New York 1927); *The Nature of Some of Our Physical Concepts* (New York 1952). C. C. PRATT, *The Logic of Modern Psychology* (New York 1939; reprint 1948). R. B. LINDSAY, "A Critique of Operationalism in Physics," *Philosophy of Science* 4 (1937) 456–470. C. G. HEMPEL, "A Logical Appraisal of Operationism," *The Validation of Scientific Theories*, ed. P. FRANK (Boston 1956) 52–58.

[H. A. NIELSEN]

OPHEL, word used several times in the OT to designate a fortified hill, especially the earliest section of *Jerusalem. The Hebrew word (*'ōpel*) means, basically, a swelling; applied to topographical features, it des-

Hill of Ophel, site of the ancient City of David, looking northeast. The clump of trees to the right of the city wall (upper right) is Gethsemani, which lies beyond the Cedron Valley. Ophel is the spur on the viewer's side of this valley, sloping down from the city walls, above the Tyropoeon Valley.

ignates a low hill, especially a fortified one. It is used in this sense in 4 Kgs 5.24 and in the *Mesha inscription. Usually, however, the term designates the Jebusite fortress taken by David, the oldest part of Jerusalem, the major part of the City of David (cf. 2 Chr 27.3; 33.14; Neh 3.26; Is 32.14; Mi 4.8). Since this side of the city was the usual point of attack, the walls (which are now completely destroyed) were frequently in need of repairs, as the texts cited above indicate.

The Ophel of Jerusalem lies just southeast of the present walls of the city. It juts out like a rocky spur between the *Cedron Valley and the Tyropoeon Valley. Due north is the Dung Gate leading into what was formerly the Jewish quarter, now under Arab control.

Bibliography: EncDictBibl 1673. L. H. VINCENT, DBSuppl 4:906–920. L. H. GROLLENBERG, *Atlas of the Bible*, tr. J. M. REID and H. H. ROWLEY (New York 1956) pl. 192, 381. **Illustration credit:** Matson Photo Service, Los Angeles.

[W. F. CUMMINGS]

OPHIR, a term used first in Gn 10.29 (see also 1 Chr 1.23) to designate a descendant of Sem, son of Jectan. As a geographical term, however, it designates a locality remarkable for natural products such as gold and silver. Solomon's fleet of Tharsis ships went to Ophir and brought back gold and other commodities (3 Kgs 9.27–28; 10.11, 22; 2 Chr 9.10). Josaphat built ships at *Asiongaber (Eziongeber) to go to Ophir (3 Kgs 22.49). David made an offering of 3,000 talents "of gold of the gold of Ophir" for the Temple (1 Chr 29.4). Job is told that if he repents God will restore his former glory and "the fine gold of Ophir [will be] as pebbles from the brook" (Jb 22.24–25). According to Jb 28.16, wisdom is so precious that it cannot be bought with gold of Ophir. In the famous nuptial Psalm [44(45).10] the queen is said to be adorned with "gold of Ophir." In the oracle against Babylon, Isaia prophesies its destruction will be so great that men will be more rare than gold of Ophir (13.12). An *ostracon of the 8th century B.C. found at Tell Qasîleh near Tel Aviv mentions "gold of Ophir for Beth-horon."

Whether or not the term Ophir applies in general to all territories rich in natural resources or to a specific locality remains in doubt. Speculation as to possible precise places has not been wanting. Among those that merit attention are the eastern coast of Africa, especially Somalia, and Arabia's southern and western areas, especially the site of modern Yemen.

Bibliography: EncDictBibl 1673. O. SAUERMANN, LexThK² 7:1177–78. G. RINALDI, EncCatt 9:167–168. R. BACH, RGG³ 4:1658–59.

[G. H. GUYOT]

OPINION

A state of mind that assents to a *judgment, all the while realizing that its contradictory may be true. It is opposed to *certitude, which means an objectively well-founded and firm assent. Opinion, seeing the judgment as more or less likely to be true, may vary all the way from mere surmise to the settled conviction of some prudential judgment, commonly found in the conduct of the practical affairs of life. In this sense opinion is equivalent to a practical certitude that never loses sight of the possibility of error. Since opinion involves the making of a judgment, however probable, it differs from *doubt, which is defined as the suspension of judgment.

Kinds of Opinion. While differences between the kinds of opinion are not too marked, one can distinguish various degrees. Suspicion or surmise means an opinion that is held on very low probability, since there is little evidence to rely upon. *Hypothesis means a conjecture, or a tentative explanation of a fact or situation, used as a norm in making observations and experiments. Not purely arbitrary, it is a reasonably entertained general opinion (often of an expert in some field) proposed with the expectation of its being later proved true or false, adequate or inadequate, by the testing of predictions derived from the hypothesis.

Theory. The term *theory has many meanings, but in all of them it remains outside the pale of certitude and is so classed as opinion. In one sense, it can mean any hypothesis, unverified or more or less verified. In another, it can be limited to those hypotheses that have been somewhat confirmed and are generally accepted in some particular field (as theory of heat, electromagnetic theory). In this sense a theory is the educated opinion of a learned man. In a given area (e.g., psychology) there may be, and often are, rival theories—depending on the selection of initial principles of explanation.

Public Opinion. This is a sort of collective judgment rendered by a given society relative to some fact or tenet. The term, coined at the end of the 18th century, is reminiscent of the *vox populi* of the Romans. Public opinion may assent to something false (e.g., polytheism in a pagan society), or to something true (e.g., monotheism), or to one side of some proposition that is only probable. Some members (even a majority) may have certitude on the view expressed; others may not. In a democracy this can give rise to crucial questions on the freedom of expression in morality, religion, politics, and education.

Opinion and Knowledge. Despite varying views on the nature and object of *knowledge, philosophers have generally maintained a distinction between knowledge and opinion. For them the opposite of true knowledge is *error and so is untenable; whereas the opposite of an opinion may reasonably be held. Thus, for *Plato the objects of knowledge are the immutable and intelligible forms; for *Aristotle, the essential and the necessary; for *Hume, the relations between ideas that can be proved; for *Kant, sensible presentations informed by the categories; for *Hegel, all of reality as one with Absolute Spirit. On the other hand, for Plato the objects of opinion are sensible things, which are always becoming and never truly are; for Aristotle, the accidental and contingent; for Hume, matters of fact; for Kant, the nonsensible, such as human freedom or the existence of God.

In each case the basic distinction seems to be consistent with what Plato and Aristotle held: the man who knows not only asserts something to be true, but has adequate reasons for doing so; but the man who has opinion, even if it should happen to be true, cannot explain his stand, and so is insecure. Furthermore, in knowledge the object itself compels the mind to assent; in opinion, some factor other than the object does this, for example, the will (Pascal, Thomas Aquinas, Hobbes), or sentiment or instinct (Hume).

Opinion and Dialectical Inquiry. In the *Topics* Aristotle clearly distinguishes between *demonstration, which results in scientific knowledge, and dialectical reasoning, which results in opinion and *probability. The dialectical process proceeds by way of drawing conclusions, "certain things being laid down" (*Topica* 100a 25). In this sense, from the opinions of experts (in science or philosophy) one draws conclusions. Or it may proceed by *induction, "a passage from individuals to universals" (*Topica* 105a 13). In either case one arrives only at probability. So, as viewed by Aristotle, this sort of reasoning serves as a source for new opinions only, and it is midway between *rhetoric and demonstration. *Dialectics, at first meaning the art of dialogue or discussion, has taken on many usages from Zeno to the present day; it is most closely linked with opinion in the Aristotelian usage.

See also DIALECTICS; CERTITUDE; EPISTEMOLOGY; METHODOLOGY (PHILOSOPHY).

Bibliography: L. M. RÉGIS, *Epistemology* (New York 1959); *L'Opinion selon Aristote* (Ottawa 1935). J. OESTERLE, *Logic* (new ed., New York 1963). F. M. CORNFORD, tr., *Plato's Theory of Knowledge: The "Theaetetus" and the "Sophist"* (New York 1952).

[R. F. O'NEILL]

OPPENHEIM, PHILIPP, liturgical scholar; b. at Olpe-Sauerland, Germany, Jan. 7, 1899; d. at Gerleve, Aug. 8, 1949. He became a Benedictine at Gerleve in 1919 and received his doctorate in theology at Breslau in 1928, having studied under F. J. Dölger (1879–1940). He lived in Rome from 1928, lecturing in patrology and liturgy at San Anselmo and was named professor of liturgy there in 1932. He became professor of liturgy at the Lateran University in 1945 and at the Propaganda in 1946. In 1942 he became censor for the Pontifical Academy of Liturgy and in 1947 was named consultor on the Congregation of Rites and a member of its Liturgical Commission. His most famous works are: *Symbolik und religiöse Wertung des Mönchskleides im christlichen Altertum* (Münster 1932); *Die Consecratio Virginum als geistesgeschichtliches Problem: Eine Studie zu ihrem Aufbau, ihrem Wert und ihrer Geschichte* (Rome 1943); and the *Institutiones Syste-*

matico-Historicae in Sacram Liturgiam (Rome 1937–), of which 11 volumes have appeared.

Bibliography: H. ENGBERDING, EphemLiturg 64 (1950) 81–82.

[A. ROTH]

OPPOSITION

The formal relations between pairs of propositions having the same subjects and predicates but varying in quality or quantity are called species of opposition. The four propositions so constituted are: the universal affirmative, called *A*; the particular affirmative, called *I*; the universal negative, called *E*; the particular negative, called *O*. Of these, *A* and *O* are evidently contradictories, for *A*, affirming a predicate of everything subsumed under a subject, and *O*, denying the predicate of at least one instance of that subject, cannot both be true and cannot both be false. So also *I*, affirming the predicate of some instance of the subject, and *E*, denying it of everything the subject denotes, are contradictories. These relations hold, regardless of the existential import ascribed to categorical propositions.

Subalternation and Superalternation. Respecting existential import, one school understands particular propositions as asserting the *existence of what their subjects signify, and understands universals as leaving the question of existence open. On this interpretation, there are no other relations between these propositions: *A* and *E*, *A* and *I*, *E* and *O*, are independent of each other. Another school, however, interprets the affirmatives as existential, so that they are false whenever nothing corresponding to their subjects exists, their contradictories being therefore true. On this interpretation, another relation between these propositions comes to light: universals imply particulars of like quality. This relation, commonly called subalternation, is really twofold; unlike contradiction, it is not symmetrical. The truth of either contradictory implies the falsity of the other. By contrast, the truth of the universal implies the truth of the particular, but not vice versa. For precision's sake, therefore, it is well to call the relation of the universal to the particular superalternation; that of the particular to the universal, subalternation. The universal is the superaltern; the particular, the subaltern.

Contrariety and Subcontrariety. Logicians have long employed the so-called "square of opposition" to illustrate these relations and others derived from them (see illustration).

At the upper corners of this square are the symbols for the universals, at the lower corners, those for the particulars. Each is connected by a diagonal with its contradictory. From the relations described, two others are deduced. Since *A* implies the falsity of *O*, and the falsity of *O* implies that of *E*, by the principle that implication is transitive, one infers that *A* implies that *E* is false, that is, that either *A* or *E* is false. The falsity of *A*, however, implies nothing about *E*, nor does the falsity of *E* imply anything about *A*. For from the falsity of *A* nothing follows but the truth of *O*, which implies nothing with regard to *E*; and the falsity of *E* implies only the truth of *I*, which implies nothing about *A*. This relation, represented by the upper horizontal line, according to which either *A* or *E* or both are false, is called contrariety.

The relation between particulars is shown in a similar manner. The falsity of *I* implies the truth of *E*, which implies that of *O*. Again, since implication is transitive, one concludes that either *I* or *O* is true. But the truth of *I* implies only that *E* is false, from which fact nothing follows as regards *O*; and *O* implies nothing but the falsity of *A*, which determines nothing about *I*. Thus particulars may be both true, or one may be true while the other is false, but they cannot both be false. This relation, represented by the lower horizontal line, is called subcontrariety.

Implied Relationships. On the interpretation of categorical propositions first mentioned, there is no square of opposition for propositions of this kind, but only a "cross of contradiction," representing the relations of *A* and *O*, and of *I* and *E*. Nevertheless, the square is not without significance for the illustration of the relations between propositions of whatever kind; the principles of contradiction and of implication, which are its basis, are of universal validity. For example, if a proposition, *p*, implying another, *q*, replaces *A*, while *q*, not-*p*, and not-*q*, replace *I*, *O*, and *E*, respectively, the following conclusions result: not-*q* implies not-*p*; *p* and not-*q* are contraries; and *q* and not-*p* are subcontraries. Similar relations could be deduced on the supposition that *p* and *q* were contraries, or that they were subcontraries. Aristotle's discussion of the contraries, "Socrates is well" and "Socrates is ill," may be illustrated by this device (*Cat.* 13b 26–35). The square shows that "Socrates is well" implies its obverse, as does "Socrates is ill," but that neither is implied by its obverse; and that either "Socrates is not well" or "Socrates is not ill" must be true.

See also PROPOSITION; LOGIC.

Bibliography: M. GHIO, EncFil 3:1055–56. J. A. OESTERLE, *Logic: The Art of Defining and Reasoning* (2d ed. Englewood Cliffs, N.J. 1963). E. D. SIMMONS, *The Scientific Art of Logic* (Milwaukee 1961). V. E. SMITH, *The Elements of Logic* (Milwaukee 1957). J. J. DOYLE, "The Square of Opposition in Action," NewSchol 35 (1961) 41–75.

[J. J. DOYLE]

OPTATUS OF MILEVIS, ST.

Fourth-century bishop and polemicist; d. *c.* 400 (feast, June 4). Optatus is known primarily as author of a document written between 363 and 376 against Parmenian the Donatist bishop of Carthage. The original title is lost and the work is now known as *Contra Parmenianum Donatistam*. The MS tradition indicates changes and additions in the original document to which Optatus added an incomplete seventh book in 385. Optatus sets himself to ease the return of the Donatists to the Catholic Church by a conciliatory presentation of the causes of the schism, which he shows to be no longer

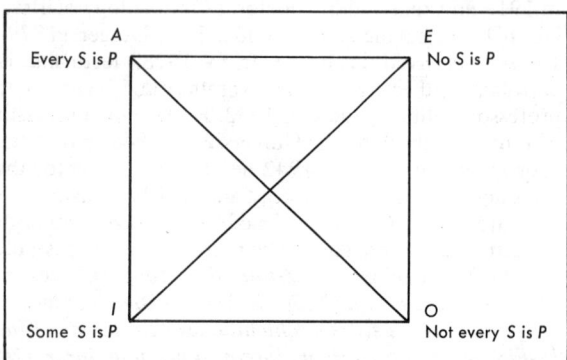

The square of opposition.

consequential in the actual problems under dispute. He calls the Donatists schismatics, not heretics (1:11–12), and refutes the objections of Parmenian with doctrinal and historical considerations, giving the history of the schism wherein the Donatists alone are responsible (b. 1); the Catholic Church is the only true Church of Christ in unity with the Cathedra Petri and spread throughout the world (b. 2). He contends that the Donatists are wrong in proclaiming themselves a martyr church and in accusing Catholics as persecutors. The Catholics did not enlist the civil power, which, however, Optatus defends as just (b. 3). He rejects the Donatist use of Is 66.3 and Ps 140.5 against Catholics and their Sacraments (b. 4), and condemns the Donatist rebaptism since the Sacraments are valid independently of the instrument (b. 5). He objects to the cruelty of the Donatists, and particularly the Circumcellions, against the Catholics (b. 6), and finally tries to judge the *traditores* of the Diocletian persecution as mildly as possible (b. 7).

For his historical argumentation, Optatus used a collection of acts that had been assembled as early as 330 and 347 in defense of Bishops Caecilianus and Felix. This collection is represented by a 10-piece appendix preserved in only one MS tradition, but it is generally recognized as authentic. G. Morin and A. Wilmart also credit him with five sermons of which only the Christmas sermon is genuine.

The theological doctrine of Optatus is particularly weighty, and Augustine, after 400, used much of it for his teaching on the Church and the Sacraments. Optatus distinguishes between person and office. The Sacraments are of themselves sanctifying agents, since the confectors are not the masters but the servants of the Sacraments (5.4, 7). Salvation brings with it faith and the Trinity (5.1). The unity of the visible Church is guaranteed by the bishop's office and the Sacraments; and the Cathedra Petri in Rome is the link of unity for the worldwide Church (2.2–4).

In contradistinction to the Donatists, Optatus is outspokenly friendly to the Emperor, and defends the imperial Church system prevailing since *Constantine I. The Church can live securely in the Roman Empire and not among the barbarians. Above the Emperor there is only God, hence loyalty is due to him particularly as a Christian ruler (3.3, with proof adduced from 1 Tm 2.2).

Bibliography: *Libri VII (Contra Parmenianum) and Acta,* ed. C. ZIWSA (CSEL 26; 1893); *Sermones* PL Suppl 1:288–300; *The Work of Saint Optatus against the Donatists,* ed. and tr. O. R. VASSALL-PHILLIPS (London 1917). Dekkers CPL 244–249. É. AMANN, DTC 11.1:1077–84. P. MONCEAUX, *Histoire littéraire de l'Afrique chrétienne,* 7 v. (Paris 1901–23) 5:241–306. Bardenhewer 3:491–495. E. DINKLER, Pauly-Wiss RE 18.1 (1939) 765–771. A. C. DE VEER, "À propos de l'authenticité du livre VII d'Optat de Milev," RevÉtAug 7 (1961) 389–391. T. ŠAGI-BUNIĆ, "Controversia de Baptismate," *Laurentianum* 3 (1962) 167–209. E. L. GRASMÜCK, *Coercitio: Staat und Kirche im Donatistenstreit* (Bonn 1964).

[A. STUIBER]

OPTIMISM

Optimism may be understood either as a general feeling and attitude of mind or as a philosophical system. The former is a habitual tendency to see the world, and all that happens in it, from the bright side and to look hopefully to the future. The latter teaches that the present world is essentially good and in practice assumes two forms, one absolute, the other relative. Absolute optimism holds that this is the best possible world, that it is either absolutely perfect or as perfect as it can be. Relative optimism admits that the world could be better, but maintains that the good it contains is of such value that its existence is preferable to its nonexistence.

The term optimism is often taken in a broader sense, as in evolutional optimism or sociological optimism, or as in its cognate, meliorism. Evolutional optimism affirms that there is a slow but constant progress in the evolution of the universe (J. G. *Fichte, P. *Teilhard de Chardin); sociological optimism expects a solution to the social question sometime in the future; and meliorism asserts that life possesses a real value, which man can increase by his personal efforts.

Forms of Optimism. All great religions are optimistic. They assure man that the evil that makes him suffer in the present life has no absolute power over him. Even *Buddhism presents its faithful with a method by which they can escape the sorrows of life and the deceptive illusions of existence. Zoroastrianism similarly assures man that the malignant divinity responsible for evil in the world will be finally defeated by the supreme Good Principle (*see* ZOROASTER). *Manichaeism, a synthesis of Zoroastrian, Gnostic, and Christian notions, maintains that man's final salvation can be easily accomplished by belief in Mani as the prophesied Paraclete and by leading an ascetic life. The Gnostics promise their faithful a happy immortality, provided that they adopt the teaching of psychic intermediaries (aeons) between God and man, and cultivate their spiritual and intuitive powers.

Greek philosophy is decidedly optimistic. For *Plato, the world is a product of God's providence, and therefore it is the most beautiful and the best (*Tim.* 30A). According to *Aristotle, nature as well as God does nothing in vain; it foresees the future and implants in all things something divine (cf. *Cael.* 271a 33; *Eth. Nic.* 1153b 32). The fundamental principle of Stoic philosophy is that man can be happy regardless of his position in the world, for happiness is within and is obtained by mastering one's appetites and passions. According to *Plotinus, the objects of intellectual knowledge are the Ideas in the Nous, and its climax is a mystical union with the One, itself the ultimate good.

Such thought exercised a notable influence on philosophers in the Middle Ages and in the Renaissance; in fact, the absolute optimism of *Nicholas of Cusa and Giordano *Bruno is clearly dependent upon Plotinus, as is the later optimism of B. *Spinoza. Pantheistic optimism, such as Spinoza's, starts from a gratuitously asserted identity of God with the world and terminates in a negation of evil in the world that is itself untenable.

More interesting and authentic is the optimism of G. W. *Leibniz. [In fact, the term optimism, used for the first time by the Jesuits (1737), designated Leibniz's theory that the world created by God is the best possible (Lat. *optimus,* best). The term was popularized by Voltaire in his novel *Candide ou l'Optimisme* (1759).] Attacking the Manichaean dualism of P. *Bayle, Leibniz strove to demonstrate his thesis. He argued that if the slightest evil that exists in the world were missing, it would no longer be this world, because, taking all things into consideration, this was judged best by the Creator who chose it. As there is an infinity of possible worlds in the divine ideas, and since only one can exist, there must be a sufficient reason for God's choice. This reason can only be found in the degrees of perfection these worlds contain, since each possibility can claim existence only in the measure of the perfection it possesses (cf. *Monadologie*, ch. 53–54).

Absolute optimism was taught also by N. *Malebranche, who had some influence on Leibniz. "God, discovering in the infinite treasures of His Wisdom an infinity of possible worlds," he writes, "decided to create the one which could come to be and maintain itself in existence by the simplest laws." Such a world bears "to the highest degree the marks, the stamp, of His attributes," and glorifies Him best (*Traité de la nature et de la grâce*, 1.13).

Evaluation. Some maintain that optimism entails the negation of God's *omnipotence, and consequently of God Himself, because if the present world is the best of all possible worlds, God cannot produce anything better. This argument is of doubtful value. Just as no one can make a square circle, so no one (not even God) can create something better than the best.

Again, the notion of the best possible world is fictitious. It applies to a world whose perfection cannot be surpassed by any other world; consequently, a world that constitutes the last term in the series of possible worlds. Yet the series of possible worlds is infinite, and the last term in such a series is as unintelligible as, for example, a square circle. Moreover, no matter how perfect one imagines a world to be, its perfection will always be finite. Consequently an infinite chasm will always exist between it and absolute perfection. And so it will always be possible to interpolate other worlds that are more and more perfect.

Absolute Optimism. According to optimists such as Leibniz and Malebranche, the best world means a world that manifests the divine perfections to a degree that no other world could equal. How does one know that it is precisely this present world that manifests God's perfections in this way? Certainly not by experience. Here the optimists appeal to a priori considerations. Malebranche says that God "acts exactly according to what He is, and according to all He is" (*Entretiens* 9, ch. 11). Now in doing so, how could He fail to give all possible perfection to the world? Malebranche here confounds the divine action in its source with the divine action in its term. The former, being identical with God's essence, is the most perfect. But the latter essentially depends upon the free will of God, and for this very reason can be limited in different ways.

According to Leibniz, God's will always chooses the greatest good. Any theory that would claim the contrary, "would clash with the supreme principle of sufficient reason" (*Théodicée* 2, ch. 175). If one admits this reasoning, one must say that God's action is subject to necessity, that the present world emerged from competition with all possible worlds. Such absolute optimism, under pretension of exalting God, degrades Him. It is incompatible with true Christian belief.

Relative Optimism. For the Christian, the present world cannot be essentially evil. But the Catholic can go further and maintain, with the Fathers of the Church, scholastic philosophers, and many other thinkers, a moderate or relative optimism. Two features are discernible in the present world: (1) the beings that actually exist in it and (2) the relations that unite these beings to each other and produce in this way the admirable order existing in nature. Hypothetically, the present world could contain more perfect things than it does because God could create more perfect things, e.g., new species of living beings. But this would be a different world, not the present world, and thus the hypothesis involves a hidden contradiction. To the objection that things could be better ordered, it suffices to note that the order of this world is not the effect of *chance or of external *necessity. It is founded on the laws of *nature, and the laws of nature have their basis in the natures of things (*see* PHYSICAL LAWS). It must therefore be concluded that the present world cannot be better ordered; and, to this extent, it gives reason for entertaining a moderate or relative optimism.

See also PESSIMISM; UNIVERSE, ORDER OF; GOOD; EVIL.

Bibliography: P. FAGGIOTTO, EncFil 3:1094–96. É. H. GILSON, *The Spirit of Medieval Philosophy*, tr. A. H. C. DOWNES (New York 1940) 108–127. L. STEFANINI, "Ottimismo tomistico e pessimismo esistenzialistico," *Sapientia Aquinatis*, Congressus Thomisticus Internationalis, 4th (Bibliotheca Pontificiae Academiae Romanae S. Thom. Aquinatis 1; Rome 1955) 562–572. L. NUTRIMENTO, *La definizione del bene in relazione al problema dell'ottimismo* (Padua 1936). P. SIWEK, *The Philosophy of Evil* (New York 1950).

[P. SIWEK]

OPTIMISM (THEOLOGICAL ASPECT)

The Christian message supposes the existence, but also the contingency, of *evil in the world: evil is present, but it would not be (at least in its actual extent) without mankind's free choice. Therefore, one can speak of an *optimism in theology only in the sense that evil is not total (the various beings remain essentially good) and does not take the upperhand over good (evil will not only be subordinate to good, but has even now a function in the triumph of good).

Revelation shows the value not only of the spirit but also of matter (cosmological optimism). Christian faith is not compatible with that absolute dualism that makes matter the principle of evil (Plotinism, Gnosticism, Manichaeism, Catharism). The good God has created the whole world and found it good (Genesis ch. 1–2): the world is the work of the divine wisdom (Proverbs ch. 8) and reflects the perfection of its author (Wisdom ch. 13; Romans ch. 1). This teaching was developed by Irenaeus against Gnosticism, by Tertullian against Marcion, and by Augustine against the Manichaeans. The goodness of the material world was also reaffirmed by the magisterium of the Church against Priscillianism (Denz 199, 207, 456, 458, 462) and against medieval Catharism (Denz 790, 800, 1333, 1336).

In opposition to the exaggerated optimism of the Pelagians, the Church teaches that man by *original sin was changed for the worse in body and soul (Denz 371, 1511). He cannot on his own observe the natural law for long (Denz 1541, 1572). To be converted he needs the assistance gratuitously given by God (Denz 374, 376, 1525, 1553). At the beginning, however, he was not in this state, and the corruption introduced by sin does not totally destroy his natural goodness (anthropological optimism). Human reason, by means of creatures, can arrive at the knowledge of God, the principle and end of the world (Wisdom ch. 13; Rom 1.20; Denz 3004, 3026). The human will is capable of good acts, even without any supernatural help, and, above all, maintains its liberty, with which it can consent to the invitation of grace (Denz 1521, 1555). This is denied to no one, not even to the infidel (Denz 2305, 2426, 2439). Sacred Scripture in fact invites sinners to be converted and holds them responsible for not being converted (Mt 23.37; Rom 10.16; Acts 7.51–53).

Although there are individual creatures irremediably hostile to God who ensnare men (the fallen angels), these are not such by their nature, but, having been created good, they became evil through their free individual choice. This doctrine (which has a Biblical foundation in 2 Pt 2.4; Jude 6) was inculcated by Irenaeus, Justin, Athenagoras, Clement of Alexandria, Tertullian, Cyprian, etc. against the various kinds of absolute dualism and was defined by the Fourth Lateran Council (Denz 800). Not even the snares of the fallen angels constitute a completely negative aspect of the universe: diabolical temptation can never overcome the resistance of man assisted by grace (1 Cor 10.13) and is useful for the good of the elect (Rom 8.28). The end of time will mark the definite defeat of the rebel angels (Ap 20.9) and of those who have freely chosen to imitate them (angelological optimism).

See also HAPPINESS; JUSTICE OF MEN; MAN, 4; PROGRESS; TEMPORAL VALUES, THEOLOGY OF; WELTANSCHAUUNG.

Bibliography: On the problem of evil. C. JOURNET, *The Meaning of Evil,* tr. M. BARRY (New York 1963). J. MARITAIN, *Saint Thomas and the Problem of Evil,* tr. M. L. ANDISON (Milwaukee 1942). A. G. SERTILLANGES, *Le Problème du mal,* 2 v. (Paris 1948–51). On the world. S. PÉTREMENT, *Le Dualisme chez Platon, les gnostiques et les manichéens* (Paris 1947). J. H. WRIGHT, *The Order of the Universe in the Theology of St. Thomas Aquinas* (Rome 1957). *Il mondo nelle prospettive cosmologica, assiologica, religiosa* (Atti del XIV convegno di studi filosofici cristiani di Gallarate 1959; Brescia 1960). On man. J. MOUROUX, *The Meaning of Man,* tr. A. H. G. DOWNES (New York 1948). M. FLICK and Z. ALSZEGHY, *Il vangelo della grazia* (Florence 1964). On eschatology. T. F. GLASSON, *The Second Advent* (London 1945). R. W. GLEASON, *The World to Come* (New York 1958). E. C. RUST, *The Christian Understanding of History* (London 1947). J. H. WRIGHT, "The Consummation of the Universe in Christ," Greg 39 (1958) 285–294. On angelology. J. D. COLLINS, *The Thomistic Philosophy of the Angels* (Washington 1947).

[Z. ALSZEGHY]

OPUS DEI

Societas Sacerdotalis Sanctae Crucis (Opus Dei), an association of the faithful, whose members dedicate themselves entirely to the apostolate and to the practice of an intense spiritual life in the world without abandoning their own social environment or the exercise of their profession or secular occupation. The purpose of Opus Dei is to spread the life of sanctity among people of all walks of life, especially among those of intellectual pursuits.

Persons from every profession and occupation belong to Opus Dei. After admission, all remain laymen; they are not religious and hence do not take religious vows, wear a habit, or live a community life. Members of Opus Dei, like all other Catholic members of associations of the faithful, enjoy complete freedom in their professions and secular activities (social, political, financial, artistic, etc.), with no restriction other than those which Catholic faith and morality impose on all the faithful. Therefore, Opus Dei is not responsible for the purely secular activities of its members and does not profess or impose any doctrine of its own concerning these matters.

José María Escrivá de Balaguer.

Opus Dei comprises two branches, one for men and the other for women, each so independent in its government and specific apostolates that in fact they form two different associations, united only in the person of the president general. The general council, with headquarters in Rome, is composed of persons of different countries and assists the president general in governing the association.

Priests also belong to Opus Dei. Some have been trained by Opus Dei itself to give spiritual assistance to the other members; others ask to be admitted after ordination without losing their diocesan status and dependence on their bishop. Married persons, too, belong to Opus Dei, committing themselves to seek Christian perfection in a way compatible with their state in life. Cooperators, although not members of the association, help it in its apostolic activities.

Opus Dei was founded in Madrid on Oct. 2, 1928, by Msgr. José María Escrivá de Balaguer, who became its president general. The women's branch was founded on Feb. 14, 1930. The Holy See issued the *Decretum Laudis* on Feb. 24, 1947, and the final approval on June 16, 1950. Within a few years, the association was established in almost every country of Europe and America and in regions of Africa, Asia, and the South Pacific.

The apostolic works of Opus Dei include educational institutions like the Catholic University of Navarre, Pamplona, Spain; Strathmore College of Arts and Sciences, Nairobi, Kenya; Seido Language Institute, Osaka, Japan; and Instituto Chapultepec, Culiacan, Mexico. It also directs more than 200 residences for students throughout the world, some of them international in character, and maintains conference centers, centers for the technical training of workers and farmers, clinics and nursing schools, and charitable centers in underdeveloped areas. The Holy See has entrusted to Opus Dei the prelature of Yauyos, Peru. Numerous non-

Catholics cooperate with the works of Opus Dei. Steps toward beatification of two members, the Argentinian engineer Isidoro Zorzano (1902–43) and the Spanish girl Montserrat Grases (1941–59), have been initiated.

Bibliography: J. ESCRIVÁ DE BALAGUER, *La Constitución apóstolica "Provida Mater Ecclesia" y el Opus Dei* (Madrid 1949). A. DEL PORTILLO, EncCatt 11:869–870. J. HERRANZ, "What Is the Opus Dei?" HomPastRev 62:336–344.

[I. GRAMUNT]

ORACLE

In addition to that of Delphi, the most famous of Greek oracles (*see* DELPHI, ORACLE OF), a number of other oracles, especially those of Zeus and Apollo, enjoyed a wide reputation in the Greek world.

Oracles of Zeus. At Dodona, Zeus replaced a pre-Greek divinity. The priests, who followed an archaic manner of life, employed as oracular devices the rustling of ancient oaks and the murmurs of a spring in the sacred grove; a device attested for the 4th century B.C. was a noise made by a brazen kettle when it was struck by a little chain hanging beside it, after it had been set in motion by a wind blowing in the proper direction. The oracle was at its zenith in the age of Pindar (518–438 B.C.), but had practically ceased to function by the beginning of the Christian Era.

The oracle of Zeus at the oasis of Siwa was really an oracle of the Egyptian god Ammon. It was already consulted by Greek statesmen in the 5th century B.C., but its reputation was enhanced by that of Alexander the Great, who was greeted by the priest of the shrine as the son of Ammon. Just how the oracle was delivered to Alexander is unknown. Ordinarily, the responses of Zeus Ammon were given in the Egyptian manner, i.e., by the manipulation of a statue of Ammon carried in procession. At Olympia, the cult of Zeus probably took the place of the earlier cult of the goddess Gea. The location of the oracle was a large altar, which was formed from the ashes of the sacrificed animals and was sprinkled with water from the river Alpheus. The response of Zeus was sought by means of haruspicy and empyromancy.

Oracles of Apollo. The most important oracle after Delphi, and probably the oldest, was that of Didyma near Miletus. A pre-Greek divinity of the place was gradually equated with Apollo. For a long period the oracle was under the control of the priestly family of the Branchidae. It possessed the right of asylum, and this right was reconfirmed by the Roman Emperor Tiberius. The responses were given by a priestess after preparation by fasting and prayer and after taking a foot bath in the spring, which bubbled beside the temple. The priestess sat on a tripod, and like the priestess of Delphi, she was probably in a state of ecstasy (Iamblichus, *De myst.* 3.2). The oracle lost its importance in the 2d century A.D. One of its last responses was heavy in consequences, for it led Diocletian to decide on his persecution of the Christians (Lactantius, *De morte pers.* 10).

The oracle of Apollo at Claros, near Colophon, was hardly less famous, and likewise possessed the right of asylum. The consultants assembled in a waiting-room and gave their names. The oracle·chamber may originally have been a grotto in the mountainside, but later it was situated nearer the valley. The priest descended into the grotto, drank from the water of a spring, and

then, without relying on orally expressed questions, but on telepathy, he gave his responses in verse (Tacitus, *Ann.* 2.54). From the 1st century A.D., questions could be presented also in writing. Even "speaking" statues of the god, which were sent into various regions, could be questioned directly. There is evidence that in the later imperial age, questions were presented at the oracle itself from places as far distant as northern Britain.

The island of Delos, the reputed birthplace of Apollo, also had an oracle. The voice of the god sounded from the fissures in Mt. Cynthus (Vergil, *Aen.* 3.90). In the age of the Seleucids, an oracle of Apollo, that of Daphne, was established near Antioch, and its procedure was modeled probably on that of Delphi.

Other Oracles. Oracles were often given through *temple incubation. The healing hero-god Asclepius played a role in this kind of divination at his chief center, Epidaurus, and also in his temples at Athens, Rome, and elsewhere. Healing hero-gods, like Trophonius, delivered their oracles in the manner of oracles at Delphi or Claros. *Necromancy was practiced for the sake of obtaining oracles, especially in those places that were regarded as entrances into the lower world—grottoes or subterranean passages, from which in many cases poisonous vapors were emitted. Such places and their vapors were thought of as means for receiving oracles. Among the best-known sites of this kind were Phigalia in Arcadia, and especially Cumae near Naples, the seat of the Cumaean sibyl, the most famous of all the sibyls.

Bibliography: J. E. FONTENROSE, OxClDict 624, with cross ref. and bibliog. K. LATTE, "Orakel," Pauly-Wiss RE 18.1 (1942) 829–866. P. MONCEAUX, "Oraculum," DarSag 4:214–223. A. BOUCHÉ-LECLERCQ, *Histoire de la divination dans l'Antiquité,* 3 v. (Paris 1879–82) old, but still basic.

[K. PRÜMM]

ORACLE (IN THE BIBLE). The Israelites, like other ancient peoples, asked (Heb. *šā'al:* Nm 27.21; Jgs 1.1; 20.22; 1 Sm 10.22; 23.2; 30.8; 2 Sm 2.1; 5.19; or *dāraš:* Gn 25.22–23; 1 Sm 9.9; 3 Kgs 22.8, 14–23; 4 Kgs 22.18–19) their God for information about imminent matters of personal or national importance or about future events. Yahweh answered in most cases through officially recognized persons (priests, seers, prophets, etc.) and in different oracular ways that were dignified and worthy of His nature and revelation. He condemned practices that were too base or humanistic, or that placed Him as one among equals or even as the chief one of many gods.

One of the principal functions of the priests was to utter oracles (Dt 33.8), and this type of oracle was called *tōrāh,* "instruction law" (Jer 18.18). Thus, Moses was often approached to inquire of God for the people and make known His decisions (Ex 18.15–16; 33.7–11). The high priest through the *Urim and Thummim (Ex 28.30; Lv 8.8) or the *ephod (1 Sm 23.6–12; 30.7–8) gave divine answers. The Levite priest of Micha was consulted by the Danites for a divine decision (Jgs 18.5–6). Levitical priests were to try difficult cases at God's chosen sanctuary, and disobedience to their decisions carried the death penalty (Dt 17.8–12). There was also a common custom of casting lots, and this was regarded at times as indicating the divine will (1 Sm 14.38–42; Acts 1.26).

The seer (Heb. *rō'eh*) and the prophet (Heb. *nābî'*) also were consulted for divine decisions; e.g., the seer Samuel (1 Sm 9.9; 11.18–20), and the Prophets Nathan (2 Sm 7.17), Elia (3 Kgs 18.36–39), Elisae (4 Kgs 8.7–15), Isaia (Is 38.1–6), and Michea, son of Jemla (3 Kgs 22.7–28). Even without its being requested, their pronouncements and writings were regarded as words or oracles of Yahweh. The technical term for an oracle of a prophet is *n^e'ūm yhwh,* literally "pronouncement of Yahweh." It occurs 361 times in the Hebrew OT, mostly in the books of the "writing" Prophets, where it generally stands at the end of a short oracle given in Yahweh's name, traditionally rendered in English as "Thus says the Lord." It serves as a sort of signature guaranteeing the authenticity of the oracle.

See also DREAMS (IN THE BIBLE); THERAPHIM (TERAPHIM).

Bibliography: A. BARUCQ DB Suppl 6:775–787. EncDictBibl 1673–76. DeVaux AncIsr 349–353.

[J. E. STEINMUELLER]

O'RAHILLY, EGAN,

Irish poet (Gaelic name, Aodhagán Ó Rathaile); b. near Killarney, County Kerry, *c.* 1670; d. probably at Killarney, *c.* 1728. His poems are almost the only source of reliable information about his life, but folklore has preserved many anecdotes that show him as a master of repartee. He seems to have spent his life in his native district, and his poems reflect his reactions to the changes of ownership of the old MacCarthy estates at Killarney about the turn of the 18th century. His family seems to have owned land in his youth, but he suffered from poverty in his later years. He was the first and one of the most powerful Irish poets of the 18th century. He preserved little of the tradition of the bardic schools except their pride, and typifies the downtrodden literati of Ireland at that time. His poems are mostly political allegories or occasional pieces for patrons. He was voluble in praise, biting in satire, and in the formulation of the aisling (*see* IRISH LITERATURE) set a fashion that every Munster poet for 100 years felt obliged to follow.

Bibliography: E. O'RAHILLY, *Dánta Aodhagáin Ui Rathaille: Poems,* ed. P. S. DINEEN (Irish Texts Soc. 3; London 1900); ed. P. S. DINEEN and T. O'DONOGHUE (2d ed. London 1911), both editions include prose translations. J. STEPHENS, *Reincarnations* (New York 1918). M. O'DONOVAN, *Kings, Lords, and Commons* (New York 1959) 102–107.

[G. S. MAC EOIN]

ORANGE

An ancient city in southern France, 13 miles north of Avignon. Originally named Arausio, Orange was the capital of the Cavari, an ancient people of Gaul Narbonensis. A Roman army was defeated by the Cimbri and the Teutons there in 105 B.C., and Augustus founded a colony called *Colonia Julia Secundorum Arausio* for veterans of the second legion. The city flourished and was adorned with splendid monuments, of which a few still remain: the magnificent arch of triumph, third in size among those existing in Europe; a vast theater capable of accommodating 7,000 spectators but now two-thirds demolished; and a gymnasium of gigantic dimensions.

By the late 3d century Orange had an episcopal see with a cathedral built by the prefect of Gaul. At the Council of Arles (314) the priest Faustinus represented the diocese of Orange as did Bishop Constantius at

The ancient Roman arch of triumph at Orange, France.

the Councils of Aquileia (381) and Milan (390). On recovery from the ravages of the *Alamanni and the *Visigoths in 412, Orange was the scene of a provincial council (441), presided over by *Hilary of Arles. A second council at Orange was held in 529, presided over by *Caesarius of Arles. In 1228 another council was held in Orange against the Albigenses.

In the 8th century Orange was besieged by the Saracens, who destroyed many of its Roman and religious monuments. Charlemagne reconquered the city, which then became the center of a county and later of a principality. Four families are known for certain to have successively reigned over the principality of Orange: the Giraud-Adémar; from 1173, the Des Baux; later, from 1393, the De Chalon; finally, from 1530 until its annexation by France, the De Nassau. In the 11th and 12th centuries the cathedral destroyed by the barbarians was rebuilt, and Bishop Eutropius erected a basilica, in which he was buried. *Charles IV established a university at Orange in 1364.

The religious wars of the 16th century spoiled many of the medieval monuments of Orange, particularly its cathedral; and several churches were sacked by the Huguenots in 1561. At the beginning of the 17th century Maurice de Nassau transformed Orange into a fortress to resist Louis XIV and used the remains of the ancient monuments including the Roman theater for his ramparts. Louis conquered Orange, however, and destroyed its fortress in 1673, and the territory was incorporated in France and united to the Dauphiné. The treaty of Ryswick (1697) recognized the title of Prince of Orange for William III, King of England, a member of the De Nassau family. In 1713, at the Peace of Utrecht, Orange was recovered by France from the king of Prussia, and Louis XIV gave the family De Nassau the opportunity to transfer its title to a part of the Netherlands.

The French Revolution suppressed the University of Orange and the diocese, whose bishop was then Mgr. G. L. de Tillet (1774–90). Pius VII reestablished the diocese in 1817 and appointed as bishop P. Astos, but immediately after, it was suppressed again and united to the diocese of Avignon. In 1794, 32 sisters were martyred on the public square of Orange; they were beatified by Pius XI in 1925. The city today, though a chief city of the Department of Vaucluse, has only

14,000 inhabitants (1964); it is a market for beet sugar and footwear.

Bibliography: E. Josi, EncCatt 9:178. S. Ribaille-Rogier, Enc Brit (1965) 16:1020. H. Leclercq, DACL 12.2:2273–91. J. Bastet, *Histoire de la ville et de la principauté d'Orange* (Orange 1856). *Larousse du XXᵉ siècle*, ed. P. Augé, 6 v. (Paris 1928–33) 5:227. **Illustration credit:** Archives Photographiques, Paris.

[J. BEAUDRY]

ORANGE, COUNCILS OF

Two synods (441 and 529) held at *Orange (Arausio), in what is now southern France (Dept. Vaucluse).

*Hilary of Arles presided over the first, which 16 bishops attended. There 30 canons were enacted dealing with disciplinary matters.

Orange II was held under the presidency of *Caesarius of Arles. *Augustine's theology of grace, though wholeheartedly adopted by Rome, was held in suspicion by *Lérins, a great intellectual and monastic center near Marseilles. Profoundly influenced by John *Cassian, Lérins was also Semi-Pelagian. Cassian taught that there was some natural sanctity in man before Baptism; he distinguished two modes of action in grace: salvific and tutelary. In the latter mode God only seconds and crowns man's efforts. *Vincent of Lérins distorted Augustine, quoting him out of context to discredit him. *Prosper of Aquitaine emerged as Augustine's indefatigable champion, and Rome itself defended the memory of the illustrious theologian (Denz 237). *Faustus of Riez (abbot of Lérins, 433–462; bishop of Riez, 462–485?), one of the greatest ecclesiastical figures of 5th-century Gaul, in his struggle against Lucidus, a predestinarian, wrote a treatise on grace, which, while it categorically rejected Pelagianism, offered no satisfactory metaphysical alternative, thus emphasizing the fact that Augustinian metaphysics on the topic were hard to replace.

Meantime Caesarius of Arles, a splendid example of the second generation of Lérins (490–497?), was consecrated bishop of Arles (503). In the continuing struggle against Semi-Pelagianism, Caesarius was the champion of pure Augustinian doctrine in regard to ". . . prevenient and liberating grace as an absolute condition of the reintegration of the human will in its supernatural faculties and ends" (Fliche-Martin 4:416). Nineteen *capitula* to this effect were submitted by him to Rome (*c.* 528) but were rejected as too subtle. Maxims gathered by Prosper of Aquitaine from Augustine's writings were substituted by Felix IV. On July 3, 529, at the dedication in Orange of a church built by Liberius, the praetorian prefect, Caesarius submitted to 13 bishops a declaration on grace and free will, which all signed and sent to Rome. Boniface II, successor to Felix IV, approved them on Jan. 25, 531 (Denz 398–400).

The statement of Caesarius has three parts: (1) *prooemium* (Denz 370); (2) 25 canons, 8 on original sin (Denz 371–372) and grace (Denz 373–378) and 17 *capitula* taken from Prosper's digest of Augustine (Denz 379–395); and (3) the conclusion of Caesarius of Arles, which is really the heart of the declaration. In it he corrects the erroneous theories of Cassian and Faustus, emphasizes the need for grace, and condemns predestination to evil. Baptism restores man and strengthens the will. The declaration at Orange, a model of charity, condemns theories not persons.

Orange II enjoyed great prestige; its canons, together with those of *Carthage (418), contributed to the theology of grace and were used by the Council of Trent. Orange II ended the Semi-Pelagian controversy in southern Gaul.

See also SEMI-PELAGIANISM; GRACE, CONTROVERSIES ON; FAITH, BEGINNING OF; FREE WILL AND GRACE; GRACE, ARTICLES ON.

Bibliography: Sources. Mansi 6:433–452; 8:711–724. PL 51: 723–730. Literature. Hefele-Leclercq 2.1:430–454; 2.2:1085–1110. L. Duchesne, *L'Église au VIᵉ siècle* (Paris 1925). F. H. Woods, ed. and tr., *Canons of the Second Council of Orange* (Oxford 1882). M. Cappuyns, "L'Origine des *Capitula* d'Orange 529," RechThAMéd 6 (1934) 121–142. G. de Plinval, DHGE 12:186–196. G. Fritz, DTC 11.1:1087–1103. Fliche-Martin 4: 397–419. P. Fransen, LexThK² 7:1188–89.

[C. M. AHERNE]

ORANGE, MARTYRS OF, a group of 32 beatified religious women martyred at Orange, France, during the *French Revolution between July 6 and July 26, 1794 (feast July 9). Two were *Cistercian nuns from Avignon; the others were from Bollène, near Avignon, and included 16 *Ursulines, 13 *Sacramentine nuns, and 1 Benedictine nun. For refusing to take the oath *Liberté Égalité,* the nuns of Bollène were expelled from their convents (Oct. 13, 1793), arrested, and held in La Cure prison in Orange. There these and other nuns formed a kind of religious community, chose a superior, and spent several hours daily in prayer and pious exercises until condemned for fanaticism and superstition. The first to die by guillotine was the Benedictine Suzanne Deloye (July 6). On July 7 Marie Suzanne de Gaillard, a Sacramentine, followed. The Ursulines Marie Anne de Guilhermier, Marie Anne de Rocher, Marie Gertrude de Ripert d'Alauzier, and Sylvie Agnès de Romillon died on July 9 and 10; and on July 11, three Sacramentines, Rosalie Clotilde Bès, Marie Elisabeth Pélissier, and Marie Claire Blanc, who were joined at the guillotine by Marie Marguerite d'Albarède, an Ursuline. Two more Sacramentines, Madeleine Talieu and Marie Cluse, died on July 12 with Marguerite de Justamond, a Cistercian, and Jeanne de Romillon, an Ursuline. The Ursulines Marie Anastasie de Roquard, Marie Anne Lambert, and Marie Anne Depeyre and the Sacramentines Elisabeth Verchière, Thérèse Faurie, and Anne Minutte suffered on July 13. On July 16 the guillotine claimed Marie Rose de Gordon, Marguerite Charransol, and Marie Anne Beguin-Royal, Sacramentines; Marie Anne Doux, Marie Rose Laye, and Dorothée de Justamont, Ursulines; and the Cistercian Madeleine de Justamont. On July 26 Marie-Madeleine de Justamont, Anne Cartier, Marie Claire du Bac, and Elisabeth Consolin, Ursulines, and Marie Marguerite Bonnet, a Sacramentine, died. The 32 were beatified on May 10, 1925.

Bibliography: H. Leclercq, *Les Martyrs,* 15 v. (Paris 1902–27) v.12. Baudot-Chaussin 7:209–215.

[M. LAWLOR]

ORANS, the figure of a person with arms extended and the palms of the hands open in a prayerful attitude prevalent in ancient pagan and early Christian art. This motif is found in bas-reliefs and sculpture in pagan cemeteries and on coins with the legend *pietas,* particularly of the Roman imperial period. It is seen in funerary monuments such as the late Egyptian stele

Orans: (a) Coptic grave stele from the Delta of Egypt, 4th century A.D., now in the Kelsey Museum of Archaeology, University of Michigan. The jackal and falcon, symbols of the gods Anubis and Horus, indicate its pagan origins. (b) Detail of a Christian fresco, the beginning of the 4th century, in the Catacomb of St. Callistus at Rome.

representing the deceased. In the primitive Christian catacombs the earliest *orantes* are purely representational figures; but in the 2d century, they depict individuals marked with names or richly clothed, with or without an imprecatory legend, e.g., *Zoë in pace; In Deo vivas.* The 3d-century *orantes* are accompanied by petitions for the beholder, e.g., *In pace et pete pro nobis.* That they were considered related to the future life is seen in depictions with the Good Shepherd or with animals and plants being vivified by the Water of life. In the 2d century OT figures such as Abraham, Noe, Isaac, and Susanna were likewise depicted as *orantes* and later, martyrs such as Mennas, Januarius, Thecla, Cecilia, and Agnes. In early Byzantine art Mary is pictured as an *orans;* this mode continued in the

East, but the tradition disappeared in the West with the catacombs.

Considerable study has been devoted to deciphering the exact significance of the *orans* from G. B. de *Rossi's conjecture of the Ecclesia Militans to Styger's symbol of heavenly glory and *Wilpert's prayer for those still on earth. The gesture is still used by priests in the celebration of Mass and sacred functions of the liturgy.

Bibliography: H. LECLERCQ, DACL 1.1:1488–97; 12.2:2291–2322. E. JOSI, EncCatt 9:179–181. T. KLAUSER, JbAntChr 2 (1959) 115–145; 3 (1960) 112–133. F. ZOEPFL, LexThK² 7:1189–91. **Illustration credits:** Fig. 1*a,* Gertrud Pappert, Courtesy Villa Hugel, Essen. Fig. 1*b,* Pontificia Commissione di Archeologia Sacra.

[J. BEAUDRY]

ORATIO SUPER POPULUM,

ORATIO SUPER POPULUM, the prayer of blessing that follows the Postcommunion on the ferial days of Lent. It is introduced by the words *Humiliate capita vestra Deo* (Bow your heads before God). As the Leonine Sacramentary testifies, the *Oratio super populum* is a survival these days only of a blessing given at the close of every Mass. It is evident from the contents of many of these prayers that this is primarily a blessing given to all. Little by little it was restricted until St. Gregory I confined it to the ferial days of Lent. It is usually explained as a special prayer for the penitents, but many of these prayers contain no reference to penance. The *Oratio super populum* was finally supplanted (outside of Lent) by a general blessing at the end of Mass.

Bibliography: Eisenhofer Lit 180–181. J. A. JUNGMANN, *The Mass of the Roman Rite,* tr. F. A. BRUNNER (rev. ed. New York 1959) 531–535. A. G. MARTIMORT, ed., *L'Église en prière* (Tournai 1961) 431–432.

[W. J. O'SHEA]

ORATORIANS

The Institute of the Oratory of St. Philip Neri (CO) was founded in 1575 at Rome, Italy, by Philip *Neri; it was approved by the Holy See in 1612 and confederated and reapproved in 1942. The members live in common without vows and seek their own sanctification by following the evangelical counsels, community life, prayer, and the priestly ministry.

General Organization. Each congregation of the Oratory, composed of priests and lay brothers, is completely autonomous. There is no central government in the Oratory, although in 1942, when the constitutions were reapproved, all Oratories were confederated into "The Institute of the Oratory of St. Philip Neri," with a procurator-general at Rome. His duty is to represent the individual congregations of the Oratory to the Holy See and to assist them when requested. He may also vindicate the rights of Oratories, revive defunct congregations, and aid those in crisis. In 1958 the Holy See provided a new office in the institute, that of visitor of the Oratory. This visitor represents the Holy See to the individual congregations. There also exists in the institute the office of postulator general. Every 10 years delegates of the individual congregations assemble in Rome at the tomb of St. Philip to hold a congress. This is not a legislative group; the continuance of its business is handled between congresses by a board of elected permanent deputies.

It is, however, the individual congregations that constitute the institute, and their form of life is unique in the Church. These congregations are composed of priests and brothers who freely practice the evangelical counsels. Oaths, vows, or promises that would bind one to the congregation are forbidden by the constitution. No congregation may have a second house or assume the task of ruling another congregation. The spirit of the Oratory is democratic and adapted to secular priests living in common. Besides novices there are two categories of priests: triennial fathers, who have only a consultative vote, and the decennial fathers, who have a decisive vote. The superior of the Oratory, who is called provost and "The Father," is elected triennially by the 10-year fathers who have been admitted to active vote. This superior may be reelected every third year according to an ancient privilege and he is a major superior. He is assisted in the government of the congregation by four elected deputies. Without the consent of these deputies he may not make appointments or changes of officials. The provost and the deputies constitute the deputy congregation, which meets weekly to decide community affairs.

The general congregation is composed of all the fathers who have at least attained triennial status, and without the consent of this congregation no general law or regulation binding all the members may be made, nor may any business be initiated with the Holy See. The constitutions provide many checks and balances on the authority of its superiors and officials. Each congregation is commonly known by the name of the city wherein it is located. It is forbidden for two congregations to be located in the same city. The constitution admits of exceptions on this point for large modern cities. The lay brothers are supported by the congregation, but the priests contribute to their own support, either by paying a predetermined board and lodging charge, or by voluntary offerings made to the congregation according to their ability to pay. The system of support for the members and for the congregation varies in each house in view of the circumstances of the times and the place in which a particular congregation is located. The principle is that Oratorians should, as much as possible, serve at their own expense and abstain from community funds.

Admission and Status. New congregations may come into existence either by being established from already existing Oratories, or, more commonly, by the mandate of ordinaries who wish a congregation in their diocese. A newly established Oratory must remain a diocesan congregation until all the elements required by the constitutions are fulfilled. At that time it is admitted by the Holy See to the Institute of The Oratory of St. Philip Neri as a congregation of pontifical right; only then does it become a genuine congregation of the Oratory. The autonomy of each congregation is complete, embracing apostolate, form of life, community exercises, finances, and education of its students. The constitutions and general statutes are observed by all congregations, but their nonpreceptive directives are left to further determination by particular statutes of the individual congregations and to decisions or decrees of the deputy or general congregations. There is no superior general or anyone, other than the Holy See, who may issue directives or rules for the autonomous houses.

The clerical members of each Oratory are generally ordained by their proper ordinary, or with his dimissorial letters, and are incardinated into his diocese. Their usual canonical title of ordination is that of the service of the diocese. The general statutes provide for ordination on the title of common table by authority of the dimissorial letters of the provost. In this case a priest may not depart from the congregation until he has found a bishop to receive him. This canonical title of ordination is not commonly used by Oratorians although it is on the increase. The congregations of the Oratory are closely and fraternally linked to the clergy of their diocese. They are subject to the local ordinary except in those matters that are expressly excluded by force of law, i.e., in matters pertaining to their own institute and its constitutions and general statutes, internal government and discipline, economic administration, and episcopal visitation. Their close union with, and cooperation in, the program of the local ordinary flows from the nature of the congregation as a society of priests of the secular clergy. They cooperate in the bishop's labors and work for souls in their field, according to the command and program of the local ordinary. They do not enjoy the privilege of exemption from the jurisdiction of the local ordinary except in the four above-mentioned areas.

Foundations. Congregations of the Oratory of St. Philip Neri exist in the U.S. in Rock Hill, S.C., in the Diocese of Charleston; and at Yarnell, Ariz., in the Diocese of Gallup. Two congregations exist in England at Birmingham and London. The congregation at Birmingham was established by John Henry (Cardinal) *Newman. The London house was founded by Frederick W. *Faber. There are congregations in Italy, Mexico, El Salvador, Nicaragua, Guatemala, Colombia, Spain, Poland, and Germany. The growth of the Oratory in Germany has been rapid and solid. A great contribution is being made by these congregations in the field of liturgy and catechetics.

The individual congregations of the institute of the Oratory are bound to each other by a bond of fraternal charity and by common constitutions and general statutes. They give to one another needed assistance, advice, labor, and materials and even lend members or transfer them when possible and necessary, although one's vocation is always to a specific congregation. They receive one another with fraternal hospitality into their houses and exchange information among houses. Beyond this they have a strong affection and respect for the autonomy of each house.

Bibliography: L. PONNELLE and L. BORDET, *St. Philip Neri and the Roman Society of His Times*, tr. R. F. KERR (New York 1933). A. CAPECELATRO, *The Life of Saint Philip Neri*, tr. T. A. POPE (new ed. New York 1926). V. J. MATTHEWS, *St. Philip Neri* (London 1934). M. JOUHANDEAU, *St. Philip Neri*, tr. G. LAMB (New York 1960).

[E. V. WAHL]

ORATORIES, CANON LAW OF

An oratory is a place designed for divine services, but not specifically for use by all the faithful for public worship (CIC c.1188.1). This definition establishes the essential difference between an oratory and a church: an oratory is intended primarily for the use of certain specified persons, whereas a church is intended for the use of all the faithful (CIC c.1161). The divine services referred to in this definition include especially the celebration of Mass; a mere prayer room or a room for private devotions is not an oratory in the sense of this canon.

The Three Types. A public oratory is an oratory erected principally for the convenience of a moral person or even of private individuals, but in such a manner that all the faithful who have the legitimately established right may frequent it at least at the time of divine services (CIC c.1188.2n1). Ultimately, the only conclusive proof of a legitimately established right, and of the oratory's being public, is an authentic document of declaration of the local ordinary to that effect. It is obvious that until the faithful are disturbed in their use of the public oratory, no legal proof need be afforded to enable them to use it.

A semipublic oratory is one erected for the convenience of a certain community or group of faithful who assemble there, but to which the other faithful have not the right of free access (CIC c.1188.2n2). The element stressed in this definition is that the community or group of faithful in whose behalf the oratory is erected has the exclusive right to its use. If others are admitted, it is a mere favor that can be withdrawn at will.

A domestic or private oratory is one erected in a private home for the convenience of some family or of a private person (CIC c.1188.2n3). Strictly speaking, domestic oratories are those erected in private homes, whereas private oratories may be erected in a public place, e.g., in a cemetery (cf. CIC c.1190). The two terms, however, are often used synonymously.

Public Oratories. Public oratories are governed by the same laws as churches (CIC c.1191.1). Provided that a public oratory has been perpetually dedicated by the authority of the ordinary to the public worship of God by consecration or constitutive blessing (according to CIC cc.1155, 1156), all sacred functions may be celebrated there, unless there are contrary prescriptions in the rubrics (CIC c.1191.2). Concerning this paragraph, note that: (1) the public oratory must be consecrated or given a constitutive blessing, for it is to be a sacred place (CIC c.1154); (2) the contrary prescriptions of the rubrics here mentioned refer especially to the sacred functions of the last 3 days of Holy Week, which are permitted only in those oratories in which the Blessed Sacrament is reserved.

Semipublic Oratories. A semipublic oratory cannot be erected without the permission of the ordinary (CIC c.1192.1). The ordinary shall not give this permission without having first visited the oratory, either personally or through some other ecclesiastic, and found it properly equipped (CIC c.1192.2).

Once the permission has been given, the oratory cannot be reduced to profane use without the permission of the same ordinary who authorized its erection (CIC c.1192.3).

In legitimately erected semipublic oratories, all divine services and ecclesiastical functions may be celebrated unless the rubrics provide otherwise or the ordinary excludes them (CIC c.1193). The exceptions and limitations upon public oratories made by the CIC or by the rubrics apply a fortiori to semipublic oratories, in addition to whatever additional restrictions the ordinary may make. Especially in institutions where many priests are resident, besides the principal oratory (public or semipublic), other semipublic oratories are erected to enable them to offer Mass. These lesser oratories often

are restricted by the ordinary to the celebration of low Masses only.

Private Oratories. The oratories of cardinals and of bishops, whether residential or titular, although they are private, nevertheless enjoy all the rights and privileges of semipublic oratories (CIC c.1189). These oratories constitute a distinct species of private oratories so far as: (1) they are not erected in private homes, for the residences of these dignitaries canonically are not private homes; (2) they enjoy all the rights and privileges of semipublic oratories.

Oratories in cemeteries erected by private persons or families for their own burial are private oratories (CIC c.1190). Such cemetery chapels are possessed by many royal or noble families in Europe but are practically nonexistent in the U.S. Though these oratories are private, they differ from domestic oratories in that they are not erected in a private home but in a public place and also so far as CIC c.1194 authorizes the local ordinary to permit several Masses to be celebrated there even regularly. The single chapel that is found in many of the cemeteries in the U.S. is a public oratory in the strict sense.

In domestic oratories granted by apostolic indult, unless other provisions are expressly made in the indult itself, one low Mass only may be celebrated daily, but not on the more solemn feasts; other ecclesiastical functions are not to be held there. For just and reasonable causes, other than those on account of which the indult was granted, the ordinary can permit in individual cases the celebration of Mass also on the more solemn feasts (CIC c.1195.1,2). Concerning this canon, note the following: (1) The petition for a private oratory is to be sent through the local ordinary and with his recommendation to the Congregation of the Sacraments. The apostolic delegate has the faculty of granting the indult to aged or infirm priests. (2) A plurality of Masses is lawful only if the indult expressly grants this or if a second Mass would be necessary to obtain Viaticum for the dying. (3) The more solemn feasts that exclude Mass in a private oratory often are explicitly enumerated in the indult. However, indults in favor of aged or infirm priests usually exclude only the last 3 days of Holy Week and the Christmas midnight Mass. (4) Besides the daily low Mass no other ecclesiastical functions are permitted, except the distribution of Holy Communion. (5) The obligation of hearing Mass can be fulfilled in a domestic oratory only by those specified in the indult. These usually are the celebrant, the server, the grantee himself, his relatives who live with him as members of the family, guests, and servants. (6) Lastly, unlike churches and public or semipublic oratories, private oratories cannot be consecrated or given a constitutive blessing; they may, however, be given an invocative blessing (CIC c.1196.1). Whether an oratory is consecrated, given a constitutive or invocative blessing, or even not blessed at all, it must be reserved for divine services alone and not used for domestic purposes (CIC c.1196.2).

Bibliography: DDC 6:1114–17. Abbo 2:456–463. A. H. FELD-HAUS, *Oratories* (CUA CLS 42; Washington 1927). T. ZIOLKOWSKI, *The Consecration and Blessing of Churches* (CUA CLS 187; Washington 1943). J. GUINIVEN, *The Precept of Hearing Mass* (CUA CLS 158; Washington 1942).

[A. H. FELDHAUS]

ORATORIO

In its general sense, a musical setting of a sacred text, with soloists, chorus, and instrumental accompaniment, but without action or scenery. There are also oratorios with secular texts, but these are a later development evolving from the sacred oratorio. While the principles of the oratorio form developed in the 17th century, they have not always been adhered to in subsequent works called oratorios. The name "oratorio," which came into use c. 1640, apparently derives, as does that of the Congregation of the Oratory (*see* ORATORIANS), from the oratories of Roman churches where their performance first took place.

Origins. From its beginnings the sacred oratorio has followed two different but parallel and concurrent paths: that of the *oratorio latino* (with a Biblical Latin text) and that of the *oratorio volgare* (with a vernacular text). The *oratorio latino* developed from a number of sources: dramatic *motet settings, medieval *liturgical drama, the dialogue *laude,* and the traditional chanting of the Passion of the four Evangelists during Holy Week at the Colosseum in Rome.

The *oratorio volgare,* on the other hand, had its roots in the *laude,* which were simple vernacular settings of sacred texts sung by the faithful during their devotions and processions, and especially during the immensely popular "exercises" conducted by St. Philip *Neri, founder of the Oratorians, in S. Girolamo della Carità and then in the rebuilt Sta. Maria in Vallicella (Chiesa Nuova) from 1563 to 1600. These exercises originally consisted of informal half-hour sessions (discourse, spiritual reading, and prayer), interspersed with uncomplicated three- and four-voiced settings (many by his penitents *Palestrina and *Animuccia) of poems usually composed by himself. In his original rule, St. Philip had provided "that the fathers together with the faithful should rouse themselves to the contemplation of heavenly things by means of musical harmony."

At first these musical interludes were of an improvised nature but gradually they became more formal, and a dialogue style emerged. The voice narrating the action was called the *testo;* the dialogues themselves were known as *historiae.* Among the finest examples of early *historiae* are those included in G. F. *Anerio's collection, *Teatro armonico spirituale di Madrigali* (Rome 1619). These pieces, much more dramatic than the earlier Oratorian *historiae,* contain solo monodic as well as polyphonic passages, a formula that was to become standard in all oratorios. Recitative style was reserved for the narration, expressive monodic style for the dialogues, and polyphony for the other sections. There was no orchestra as such, but there is occasional mention of instruments other than organ. The performances were well attended and attracted the attention of a number of visitors in Rome. One such, André Maugars, a French musician, reported that at the Oratory of Sta. Maria in Vallicella was performed a "story from the Old Testament in the form of a spiritual play" in which "each of the characters was represented by a singer" (*Réponse faite à un curieux . . . écrite à Rome, 1639*). When Pietro della Valle called his two *historiae* (*Esther* in Latin and *La purificazione* in Italian: 1640–41) oratorios, he was the first to use the term for this form. (E. de' Cavalieri's *Rappresentazione di anima e di corpo,* performed at Sta. Maria in Vallicella in 1600, is more a *sacra rappresentazione* than an oratorio, since it has a non-Biblical plot.)

Classic Oratorio. The mid-17th century was the golden period of Roman oratorio. Balducci, one of the most important early librettists, wrote a number of vernacular texts between 1630 and 1642. One of these, *La fede,* was designed to be performed in two parts, one before and one after the sermon. This bipartite division, which was to become almost universal in *oratorio volgare,* became more and more dramatic, and some works in this form seemed more appropriate to the stage than to the church. The librettist A. Spagna, who prepared texts for more than 30 oratorios between 1656 and 1716, was responsible for the dictum that an oratorio should be a "perfect spiritual musical drama," with the consequence that melodramatic elements dominated the oratorio during the second half of the 18th century. Oratorio thus became a succession of alternating recitatives and arias, while the chorus steadily decreased in importance. It was this type that the Oratorians carried throughout Italy.

The Latin oratorio blossomed under the hands of *Carissimi (1605–74), the leading oratorio composer of the 17th century. Of his many Latin works, some are entitled *Historia* and some *Oratorium.* The distinction, however, has no connection with the inner structure of his works. The narrator, or *historicus,* is sung by solo voices, as in *Jonas, Jephta,* and the *Judicium Salomonis.* The music of the solo parts is dramatic in that it makes use of the recitative style so common in the opera of the time. The choruses, important elements in these works, are generally homophonic and play an integral part in the action of the drama.

Classical Roman oratorio reached its apogee during the pontificate of Clement IX (1667–69), after which there was a continuous deterioration in musical and poetic quality. During this period of decadence the texts became sentimental and even erotic. Bible stories such as those of Esther, Susanna, and Judith were set time and again. The music became more and more aligned with current fashions in opera, and the *bravura* aria was as much at home in the sacred oratorio as it was on the stage. By the turn of the 18th century the lives of saints had ceased to be used as texts, and the Old Testament stories mentioned above had completely supplanted them. Carissimi's French pupil M. A. *Charpentier (1636?–1704) carried the Latin oratorio with him to France. Charpentier himself wrote 24 *historiae,* which were performed, along with those by Carissimi, in Paris at the Jesuit church where he was *maître de chapelle.*

Early German Oratorio. In Germany the oratorio was slow to develop. Italian oratorios were introduced into Catholic courts such as that of Vienna during the last third of the 17th century and remained popular there throughout the 18th century. True German oratorio, however, came into being in the Protestant areas. There are early records of school performances of sacred dramas in which music played only an incidental part, but these can hardly be classified as true oratorio. The *dialogue* and the *historia* with continuo accompaniment are the two types of German music that most approached the Italian conception of oratorio during the 17th century. In Heinrich *Schütz's larger works, such as the *Historia der Geburt Jesu Christi* (1664), he demonstrates a command of the monodic style and a

Holograph MS of Handel's "The Messiah." Note at bottom, "Fine dell oratorio. G. F. Handel. Septemb. 12, 1741."

feeling for drama rightly identified (by Schering) with true oratorio style. Here the narrator sings in recitative style, and the choruses, accompanied by larger groups of instruments, answer in a more dramatic manner.

By the mid-17th century, German oratorio-like works, as well as settings of the New Testament Passions (*see* PASSION OF CHRIST, MUSIC OF THE), began to include chorale settings interspersed among the recitative and choral passages. This practice remained peculiar to German oratorio composition until the end of the 18th century. *Buxtehude's *Juengstes Gericht* (1683) in five sections also approaches the oratorio. It contains recitative, strophic arias, and choruses, as with J. S. *Bach's great six-part *Weihnachtsoratorium* (Christmas Oratorio, 1734). There is, however, no dramatic plot, for it is composed of a series of smaller church *cantatas strung together. This preoccupation with the small nondramatic cantata rather than the long, more dramatic oratorio seems always to have characterized the German Protestant composers.

In the 18th Century. In the early 18th century German taste in the oratorio was still contingent upon the religious affiliation of the court: in the Catholic courts

the Italian oratorio prevailed; in the Protestant courts the German *historia* and church cantata reached the height of their development. Meanwhile the Italian oratorio text was passing through a period of reform, greatly influenced by the operatic reforms of the poets Zeno and *Metastasio. Although as late as 1706 Spagna had called for reform by omitting the *testo* altogether, the ideas of Zeno and Metastasio were farther-reaching. Oratorio in their sphere of influence (the Viennese court) became more standardized; it was divided into two parts; the versification became more formal; Old Testament stories were favored as librettos; and the role of Christ seldom appeared except in settings of the Passion. The principles of the Zeno-Metastasio oratorio reform lasted throughout the century (e.g., *Mozart, in *Betulia liberata,* set a Metastasio text).

In Italy the opera dictated completely the musical style of the oratorio. The chorus was absent from many Italian works, although A. *Scarlatti's later oratorios introduced more choruses and orchestrally accompanied arias. All the opera composers of the 18th century created oratorios in the style of opera, with histrionic recitatives, many continuo arias, few choruses (in homophonic style), and only occasional contrapuntal sections. This operatic oratorio reached its climax in works such as *Rossini's *Mosè in Egitto* (1818), a "sacred-tragic representation" staged as an opera.

Outside Italy, particularly in Vienna, the oratorio left the churches and went to the concert halls. Though J. J. *Fux's (1660–1741) oratorios were written to be performed in church, those of his younger contemporaries, G. Porsile and A. *Caldara, were often given in concert performance. North German oratorio in the mid-18th century also tended to follow operatic patterns, although with more emphasis on the chorus. Telemann's four-part concert oratorio *Der Tag des Gerichts* (1762), e.g., is much more dramatic than Buxtehude's works, for it makes use of operatic recitative and aria. Again, C. H. Graun's *Der Tod Jesu* (1755), the most renowned oratorio of its day, is operatic but has many choruses. The libretto is filled with the pietistic sentimentalities that afflicted so much of German literature at this time. By the end of the 18th century the concert oratorio was prevalent in both Protestant and Catholic courts.

Haydn's Oratorios. With F. J. *Haydn came at once the fulfillment of the German oratorio and the introduction of new forward-looking characteristics that were unknown in the 18th-century oratorio. *The Creation* (1798) is epic rather than dramatic; there is no trace of the old *testo* and only the recitatives of Adam and Eve have any suggestion of drama. The traditional arias, recitatives, and homophonic and fugal choruses are present, but they are handled in a freer manner and often make use of bolder harmonies than were provided by Viennese classical style. *The Seasons* (1801) goes even farther. It is purely secular in its evocation of scenes from nature, and the soloists sing not as individual characters, but rather as elements of the narrative itself. These great oratorios, whose librettos, not limited by the bonds of a specific story, concern themselves with basic concepts of man and nature, set a pattern that was imitated extensively in German 19th-century oratorio.

Handel and England. During the 18th century England produced a special kind of oratorio, the creation of one towering genius, G. F. *Handel. In 1732, Handel revised an earlier secular masque and planned to stage it as a "sacred drama" entitled *Esther*. When the bishop of London forbade its stage performance, Handel mounted it in concert form. This was the first Handelian oratorio. Handel's oratorios draw their stories from Old Testament, Jewish, and even ancient Greek history. They reveal a range of musical styles from operatic recitative and aria to huge choruses in the spirit of festival anthems. Choruses are important in most of Handel's works (e.g., *Israel in Egypt,* 1739, which consists chiefly of choruses); they either take part directly in the action, as in *Belshazzar* (1745), or function in the manner of the chorus in Greek tragedy, as in *Saul* (1739) and *Hercules* (1745).

Because of the great success of Handel's oratorios, he had few competitors during his lifetime. These few concentrated on adapting the operatic style of Italian oratorios to English taste. After Handel's death, principally because of the shattering influence of his oratorios, English composers ceased to be interested in this form, but early 19th-century works by *Spohr and *Mendelssohn (*St. Paul,* 1836; *Elijah,* 1946) were popular with the English public. Later in the century, with the growth in popularity of choir festivals, oratorio composition once again attracted English composers. The works of Hubert Parry and Charles Villiers Stanford, the best of this group, are, however, but pale imitations of Mendelssohn and Handel. It was not until *The Dream of Gerontius* (1900) by Edward *Elgar that a major oratorio was again written by an Englishman. Elgar's oratorio makes use of Wagnerian leitmotiv techniques and is distinguished for its subtleties of orchestration and its rich harmonies. In his later works (*The Apostles,* 1903, and *The Kingdom,* 1906) Elgar's style became increasingly operatic. Twentieth-century English composers, notably Ralph *Vaughan Williams, William Walton, Michael Tippett, and Benjamin Britten (despite its title, his *War Requiem,* 1962, is similar to oratorio) have demonstrated interest in oratorio composition.

The 19th Century and After. In 19th-century Germany the oratorio ceased to be an important means of musical expression. With the exception of Mendelssohn, who in his *St. Paul* and *Elijah* reintroduced chorales in the Bach manner, German composers of this period have left little to be remembered in the field. In France, however, almost all important composers in the later decades wrote oratorios (e.g., *Saint-Säens, *Franck, *Fauré).

During this century Italian oratorio was completely dominated by the operatic style. The revival of interest in older music in Germany (see CAECILIAN MOVEMENT) had its effects in Italy, however, and students began to restudy the glories of Italian 17th-century oratorio. The 19th-century Italian oratorios became stiff and academic, using on one hand operatic techniques and, on the other, uninspired, academic counterpoint. This situation was recognized by Leo XIII, who in 1884 issued a *regolomento* for sacred music that aimed at reforming the methods of oratorio composition. This was followed in 1903 by Pius X's famous motu proprio and the establishment of the Pontifical Institute of Sacred Music in Rome. The composer L. *Perosi essayed 12 oratorios in its spirit. They follow closely the pattern of Carissimi: a Latin text, often a two-part format, and a *storico* (*testo*) narrating the events; but Perosi was an eclectic who freely adapted vocal stylistic devices from Bach and Handel and orchestral techniques from Wagner. Few present-day Italian composers concern themselves with the oratorio, and nothing of appreciable merit has yet appeared.

American composers of the 20th-century have produced a great amount of choral music, but largely limited to small-scale forms. Oratorios and oratorio-like works such as Horatio Parker's *Hora Novissima* (1893) Howard Hanson's *Lament for Beowulf* (1944), Wallingford Riegger's *The Passion* (1944), Lukas Foss's *A Parable of Death* (1952), and Robert Palmer's *Nabuchodonosor* (1963) represent a small but impressive segment of their composer's artistic production.

During the 20th century there has been a marked increase in composition of what may be labeled opera-*cum*-oratorio (both sacred and secular). Such works as Arthur Honegger's *King David* (1921) and *Jeanne d'Arc au bûcher* (1935; text by Paul *Claudel), Igor Stravinsky's *Oedipus Rex* (1927), and *Schoenberg's *Moses and Aaron* (1954; as an opera, 1957) are commonly classified as operatic, while making use of compositional techniques heretofore identified with ora-

A scene from the New York City Opera production (autumn 1963) of Honegger's "Jeanne d'Arc au bûcher."

torio. Their texts are similar in that they involve subject matter of more epic proportions than has been common in the field of opera. Texts of this type lend themselves to a less dramatic musical setting and at the same time to the expanded use of the chorus. What this synthesis of operatic and oratorio techniques may lead to is not yet possible to conjecture.

See also MUSIC, SACRED, HISTORY OF, 5, 6, 7, 8.

Bibliography: D. ALALEONA, *Studi sulla storia dell' oratorio musicale in Italia* (2d ed. Milan 1945). W. B. DEAN, *Handel's Dramatic Oratorios and Masques* (London 1959); EncBrit (1965) 16:1031–34. A. SCHERING, *Geschichte des Oratoriums* (Leipzig 1911). E. WALKER, Grove DMM 6:247–262. P. DAMILANO et al., MusGG 10:120–168. D. F. TOVEY, *The Forms of Music: Musical Articles from the Encyclopaedia Britannica* (London 1957). Young ChorTrad. **Illustration credits:** Fig. 1, Courtesy of the Trustees of the British Museum. Fig. 2, Fred Fehl, New York.

[W. C. HOLMES]

ORDEAL

A method of determining the guilt or innocence of a suspected or accused person by subjecting him to dangerous physical tests, the results of which are regarded as manifestations of divine judgment. It is essentially a form of divination. The practice is very old and has almost a universal distribution. It was widespread among the ancient Semitic and Indo-European peoples, especially among the Germans and the Slavs, and is found also in India, China, the Pacific islands, Australia, and Africa. While attested for the Americas, the practice is confined largely to Chile and Mexico.

Forms of the Ordeal. Among the numerous forms of the ordeal, several main types may be distinguished: ordeals by poison, by water, by hot iron, by fire, and by combat.

The poison ordeal is found principally among the peoples of West Africa. The accused must drink a concoction that produces vomiting or narcotic effects. If immediate vomiting results, and the accused suffers no ill effects, he is judged to be innocent. On the other hand, if he becomes dizzy and loses control of his faculties, he is thought to be guilty. Witch doctors play an important role in the poison ordeal, and the accused person often betrays his guilt through a fear

that is heightened by the superstitious beliefs of his environment.

Ordeal by water is already mentioned in the Code of Hammurabi (Nos. 2, 132), and was widely practiced among the peoples of Europe. The accused person—often a woman accused of adultery—was required to plunge into deep water, preferably running water. If the person sank at once and did not rise immediately to the surface, he was adjudged to be innocent. If, however, he did not sink at once, or arose quickly to the surface and floated, it was thought that the water rejected him and that he was therefore guilty. Boiling water and boiling oil also were used in ordeals. The accused was required to plunge his hand and forearm into the hot liquid and his guilt or innocence was determined at once, or after 3 days, according to the greater or less degree of injury suffered by his hand or arm.

The hot iron ordeal was common among the ancient peoples of Europe and Asia and is still found in certain primitive cultures. The accused was required to grasp a heated ploughshare or to carry a piece of heated iron a prescribed number of steps. He was judged guilty or innocent either immediately, or after 3 days, according to the extent of injury suffered in this trial. An Irish ordeal requiring an accused woman to run her tongue across a red-hot adze is mentioned, but this practice does not seem to have been common.

The fire ordeal is found to have been practiced especially in Asia among the Hindus and other peoples within the orbit of their influence. The accused person was required to walk over burning charcoal or other material and, if unharmed, was judged to be innocent on the ground that the fire, a living force, refrained from injuring him.

Bibliography: A. E. CRAWLEY et al., Hastings ERE 9:507–533, a comprehensive world survey. L. LEITMAYER, LexThK² 4:1130–32. R. THURNWALD, "Gottesurteil," ReallexVorgesch 4.2:441–448.

[M. R. P. MC GUIRE]

In the Bible. The bitter-water ordeal of Nm 5.11–31 is the only clear example of an ordeal in the Bible. The text appears to be a conflation of two separate but complementary forms of the ordeal ritual: that of the execratory oath [*see* OATHS (IN THE BIBLE)] and that of the drinking of the "bitter water." The results of both were interpreted as judgments of God. Although the latter aspect smacked somewhat of magic, its purpose was sacred: to appeal to God for a decision on the guilt or innocence of the accused. A woman accused of adultery, holding in her hand a cereal offering (without oil or frankincense), was presented to a priest. He then sprinkled some dust from the floor of the tent over a vessel of water and had her take an oath of execration (Nm 5.21). After washing down the solution of ink in which the accompanying curses were written, the priest poured it into the now "bitter water," then waved a part of the cereal offering before the Lord, and had the woman drink the mixture. If the woman was innocent, no harm befell her and she remained fruitful. If she was guilty, the dreaded consequences of the curse took place, usually in the form of frequent miscarriages. If guilty, a woman would apparently prefer to confess and take her chances on a lesser punishment than to suffer the dire consequences of the oath. Even if the bitter-water ritual is ultimately traceable to pagan practices and betrays magical overtones, the Biblical writer has deliberately placed it into a sacral context by attributing its effectiveness to the powerful hand of God (Nm 5.21). It is at least more humane than the corresponding prescription in the Code of Hammurabi.

One aspect of the golden calf episode in Ex 32.1–24 also reflects the bitter-water ordeal; the idolatrous image is ground into powder and given to the Israelites to be drunk (20).

The ordeal was present to some extent also in the custom of seeking decisions by lot, as when Achan's offense was discovered (Jos 7.13–26) and Jonathan's breach of the *ḥērem* (1 Sm 14.36–45) was revealed. For this reason the high priest's breastplate containing the deciding lots *Urim and Thummim was called the "breastplate of judgment" (Ex 28.15). Memory of the ordeal may also have influenced the Prophets to speak of "poisoned waters" of sinfulness contaminating the people of Israel (Jer 8.14; 9.15; 23.14; Ez 23.31–34).

Bibliography: EncDictBibl 1676. E. KUTSCH, RGG³ 2:1808–09. R. PRESS, "Das Ordal im alten Israel," ZATWiss 51 (1933) 121–140. P. VAN IMSCHOOT, *Théologie de l'Ancien Testament*, 2 v. (Tournai 1954–56) 2:263–265.

[E. J. CIUBA]

The Medieval Ordeal. The ordeal in medieval Europe was a form of judicial trial whereby the innocence or guilt of accused persons was made to depend upon some feat of physical endurance. The result was regarded as definitive proof and as a judgment of God. Most forms of ordeal had the favor of the Church until 1215, and were preceded by certain religious acts.

Kinds of Ordeal. In general, medieval ordeals were bilateral or unilateral. In the former, the contending parties to a duel or single combat might be represented on occasion by proxies, for example, by one or more "champions." Thus in 1179, when the people of Rosny claimed not to be serfs of the Abbey of Sainte-Geneviève in Paris, the case was decided "forever" in favor of the abbey by a judicial duel ordered by King Louis VII in which, on the day appointed, the men of Rosny failed in fact to accept the "repeated challenge" of the Abbot, *Stephan of Tournai [A. Luchaire, *Études sur les Actes de Louis VII* (Paris 1885) 2:323]. The unilateral ordeal, on the other hand, tested an accused person as such, who, to prove his innocence, was required to carry a ball of hot iron in his hand for a certain distance, to plunge his arm to the wrist or elbow in a caldron of boiling water, to be submerged in cold water, to walk blindfolded between red-hot ploughshares, or to walk barefoot on glowing coals.

Church Attitudes. The attitude of secular and ecclesiastical authorities to ordeals varied. Although Constantine successfully prohibited gladiatorial combats (CorpIurCivCod 11.44.1), King Liutprand in 731 complained that he was powerless to abolish duels since they were part of Lombard tradition. And whereas Popes Gregory the Great (590–604) and Martin I (649–653) confirmed for the monastery of St. Peter at Rouen the right of holding "secular trials of cold water and the like" (Browe 2:3–4), Pope Nicholas I (858–867), in the famous case of King *Lothair II and Queen Theutberga, averred that a duel at least had "no divine sanction whatsoever" (CorpIurCan C.2 q.5 c.22); but in the same context, Hincmar of Reims defended hot and cold water ordeals. A celebrated prec-

edent was set by Pope Stephan V (886–889) when, in reply to a query whether parents whose children had been smothered while sleeping with them should be made to prove by ordeal that death was accidental, he declared that ordeals of hot iron and cold water "had no canonical basis" (CorIurCan C.2 q.5 c.20; Browe 1:14).

On the whole the canonists were hostile to the idea, from *Ivo of Chartres (1099) and *Gratian (*c.* 1140) to *Huguccio (*c.* 1190), who regarded the practice as utterly unjustifiable and a form of "tempting God"; the aforementioned canonist-theologian Stephan of Tournai was somewhat confused; *Sicardus of Cremona (*c.* 1180) would allow it in cases involving the lower classes (Browe 2:88–104). With the notable exception of *Peter Cantor (d. *c.* 1196), who attacked it resoundingly, theologians of the period generally refrained from discussing it. However, possibly as a result of the opposition of Huguccio and Peter Cantor, the Fourth *Lateran Council in 1215 under Innocent III (who personally had allowed ordeals in civil though not ecclesiastical trials: Browe 1:30–36) prohibited the clergy from blessing or consecrating trials by ordeal (c.18; ConOecDecr 220; CorpIurCan X 3.50.9). Although it did not specifically disallow the use of ordeals in administering secular justice, this canon was a turning point in the disappearance of these customary practices (*purgationes vulgares,* as the canonists called them) from European law. England, Normandy, and Denmark at once followed the Council's lead, and justices in eyre were instructed in England in January 1219 to adopt other evidentiary procedures in the future. Trial by ordeal was further nullified by the development of merchant law, of inquest in ecclesiastical and secular law, and of juries in English law. That ordeals, particularly judicial duels, did not go out of vogue completely is evidenced by repeated papal prohibitions (Browe 1:38–47) and by writers such as Raymond of Peñafort, Thomas Aquinas, Dante, Suárez, and De Liguori. A celebrated survival of bilateral ordeal by fire was the proposal by a Franciscan that it be used by *Savonarola to test his prophecies. Savonarola rejected the proposal.

Bibliography: A. MICHEL, DTC 11.1:1139–52. P. BROWE, ed., *De ordaliis,* 2 v. (Rome 1932–33). H. LECLERCQ, DACL 12.2: 2377–90. C. LEITMAIER, *Die Kirche und die Gottesurteile* (Vienna 1953). H. NOTTARP, *Gottesurteilstudien* (Munich 1956). J. W. BALDWIN, "The Intellectual Preparation for the Canon of 1215 against Ordeals," *Speculum* 36 (1961) 613–636.

[L. E. BOYLE]

ORDER

Few notions have both so rich a heritage of meaning and so clear an application to all fields of knowledge as does order. There are many myths of cosmic order and its polar opposite, *chaos, and there is no great religion without some *principle of order. If men do not worship the transcendent God of Genesis, who imposes arrangement, then they have an immanent principle of law and of right relation of *thing to thing and *person to person (ṛta in Sanskrit, *dhamma* in Pali, *tao* in Chinese, as well as the more familiar Greek notions associated with κόσμος, δίκη, μοῖρα, θέμις, and νοῦς). Until comparatively recent times order is not only always regularly associated with deity ("Order is Heaven's first law," A. Pope, *Essay on Man*, Ep. 4.49) but also always a virtue in man (according to W. Jaeger, cosmos "originally signifies right order in a state or other community"). As preserved in the expression "law and order," the orderly is the right way to behave, the disorderly is the wrong way. Order applies, then, not only to the lawful universe but to right action of man; order is also regularly associated with intelligibility. To order may mean to act regularly, or with system, i.e., to arrange acts by method. In the last meaning, to order is to strive toward a goal, and those things that serve to achieve a goal are said to be ordered to it. Aristotle's favorite example of an order is an army, but St. *Thomas Aquinas uses an example of another kind of order, a heap of stones. Stones can scarcely be said to be led, or to be under a leader; nevertheless, even when placed by chance, there is a gradation from the topmost to the lowermost (*In 5 meta.* 13.939). Order, then, has many senses, and things ordered in one way may yet not be ordered in another.

Formal Analysis. Exact definition of order seems only to have been achieved by scholastic philosophy, and the recent elaboration by symbolic logic, largely in the 20th century, has served to reduce the ambiguity of the term (*see* LOGIC, SYMBOLIC). The primitive notion, itself indefinable, is *relation. Since relation is between things (in the most general sense, including terms of thought), order presupposes a plurality of things. A theorem common to both St. Thomas and such moderns as J. *Royce, A. N. *Whitehead, and B. *Russell is that one thing cannot be ordered. The most general definition of order is to be related in some definite way. One definite way in which things are related is a series; that is, one thing is prior to another. In spite of the many senses in which "this" may be prior to "that," it follows immediately that "that" is posterior to "this." Logicians say of two symbols that they are well ordered when it makes a difference which is to the right of the other. "Before" and "after" are of this type. St. Thomas's defining statement is:

The terms "before" and "after" are attributed according to the relation of some principle. Now order includes some mode of the "before" and "after." Hence, wherever there is a principle, it is necessary that there be also an order of some kind. [ST 2a2ae, 26.1.]

Order, then, is not meant absolutely, but always in some respect, or as Whitehead put it: " 'Order' is a mere generic term: there can only be some definite specific 'order,' not merely 'order' in the vague" [*Process and Reality* (New York 1929) 128].

St. Thomas seems first to have made explicit what is shared by all serial orders and what differentiates one from another:

... the notion of order includes the notion of the prior and the posterior. Thus there can be said to be an order of things according to all those modes, spatial, temporal and all like others, according to which a thing can be said to be before another. [*In 1 sent.* 20.1.3.1.]

The modern way of expressing such a relation is to call it asymmetrical. That is, if A is larger than B, then B cannot be larger than A, etc. In a familiar symbol, if $A > B$, then immediately it follows, $B < A$ (in the example B is smaller than A). There are also symmetrical relations, in which the relation, r, is such that ArB implies BrA. The most obvious example of a symmetrical relation is equality. It makes no difference whether it is said that $A = B$ or $B = A$, for one follows necessarily from the other.

"The notion of order includes the notion of the prior and the posterior," said St. Thomas. The modern says that asymmetry is necessary to an ordering relationship, but that it is not sufficient. For in a series, say the stones piled one atop the other, there is the same relation "on top of" holding between the top and the middle, and between the middle and the bottom stone. The relationship is called transitive when there are three things so related that when ArB and BrC, then ArC. This is certainly the case for "earlier than in time," or "to the right of in space," or "larger than in quantity," etc. Now although, as has been seen, serial relations are transitive and asymmetrical, there are also relations that are transitive and symmetrical. To use the former example of equality, it is obvious that when $A = B$ and $B = C$, then it must follow that $A = C$. The common notion of Euclid is that things equal to the same thing are equal to each other. Those who have developed the theory of order here being expounded consider the principle of ordering relations no less fundamental in human thought. Consider such a relation as "heavier than," says William *James, and symbolizing the relation $>$, when $a > b > c > d$, then $a > d$. Evidently three terms are the minimal number for transitivity, and since there can be no maximum number of terms, the formal types of order are infinite.

The principle of mediate comparison is only one form of a law which holds in many series of homogeneously related terms, the law that *skipping intermediary terms leaves relations the same.* This AXIOM OF SKIPPED INTERMEDIATES or of TRANSFERRED RELATIONS occurs, as we soon shall see, in logic as the fundamental principle of inference, in arithmetic as the fundamental property of the number-series, in geometry as that of the straight line, the plane and the parallel. *It seems to be on the whole the broadest and deepest law of man's thought.* [James, *Principles of Psychology* (New York 1890, 1950) 2:646.]

Asymmetry and transitivity are not sufficient to define serial order. A third important factor to be made explicit, whether in the case of St. Thomas's rocks one atop another or James's objects of different weights, is that if any two are chosen, there is the relation "above" or the relation "heavier than," and either it or its opposite holds. Since by virtue of this property one can form a single system of the items, it is called connexity. It is found in the case of musical notes, where, because of the relation "higher than in pitch," one can construct scales. The beauty of this is obvious to anyone who reflects upon how he uses numbers, whether whole numbers or fractions. Of any two (different numbers, not equal one to the other), one is greater than the other, and occupies a unique place in the series called the order of magnitude.

The foregoing analyzes a common intuitive concept of order that is learned in the nursery: a place for everything and everything in its place. It would be false to argue that this is the only formal definition of order. One might, for example, define order as a relation that is aliorelative (or nonreflexive, i.e., not related to itself but to another), transitive, and connected, and deduce asymmetry [A. N. Whitehead, "Mathematics," Enc Brit, 11th ed.; also in *Essays in Science and Philosophy* (London and New York 1948) 197]. It would be false to argue also that this definition fits all kinds of order. It applies only to series that are open, i.e., in which the same term does not recur. There are not only asymmetrical relations that are called orderly, but also all symmetrical relations, such as the many forms of balance in which an axis divides matching or balanced sides.

Historical Survey. The concrete kinds of order (as distinguished from the formal types of order) may best be sketched in terms of their exemplification in the history of thought.

To a great extent the Egyptians viewed their kingdom as an expression of an eternal and unchanging order. For the Babylonians there was a struggle to maintain order in the universe and in human affairs, and an element of risk. One way of reading history as reflected in men's concepts is to regard *society itself, and man's arts and sciences, as efforts to overcome confusion, to respond to the threat of chaos. Since 20th-century man lives in a period of vast uncertainty, he tends to smile at the complacency of the Egyptians and to feel sympathetically the anxiety of the Babylonians. The facts seem to be that there are periods when questioning the eternal order, or its goodness, rises to prominence. In contrast to the serenity of *Aristotle is the restlessness of St. *Augustine (in the *Confessions*). In contrast to the serenity of St. Thomas and *Dante is the uncertainty of *William of Ockham and his followers. Some of the Elizabethans express confidence in the hierarchical ordering, somewhat as conceived by St. Augustine in *The City of God* (*Civ.* 19.13), but the rise of mechanical science in the early 17th century is associated with the unrest of John *Donne (" 'Tis all in peeces, all cohaerance gone"). Yet the mechanical order became itself the ground of confidence:

> All nature is but art unknown to thee;
> All chance direction, which thou canst not see;
> All discord, harmony not understood;
> All partial evil, universal good.
> [A. Pope, *Essay on Man*, Ep. 1.10.]

In contrast to the serenity of the post-Newtonian men of the Enlightenment is the emphasis on the arbitrary and willful ways of individual genius in the Romantic period. Man is most recently being deeply affected by the existentialists—S. A. *Kierkegaard, F. W. *Nietzsche, F. M. *Dostoevskiĭ, and their followers—who tend not only to question any knowledge of a divine order but also to belittle knowledge of an order of nature, to scoff at the law of human institutions, even to exalt chaos above order.

To trace the history of order is to go to the heart of Greco-Roman, medieval, and modern thought. It is also to discover those experiments that, in both their successes and failures, are most valuable in framing an adequate philosophy.

Greek Thought. The Greek achievement is fourfold. To the pre-Socratics man is indebted for the discovery that he inhabits a cosmos. The Ionian naturalists tend to stress mechanical order; particularly *Democritus (and later *Epicurus and *Lucretius) would account for all qualitative differences by changes in spatial order (τάξις). *Anaxagoras counts this a failure to explain the "why" of order: the "how" alone lacks the purpose of intelligence (νοῦς). *Pythagoras and the Pythagoreans stress an intelligible order of forms to account for the sensuous harmony, especially as musical instruments produce sounds by simple proportions of the lengths of strings or vibrating columns of air. *Plato and Aristotle, however differing in their theories of form, both

account for the *good and the beautiful as illustrations of order (*see* BEAUTY). Thus is born the concept of good order (εὐταξία) that the Stoics stress, and a problem is set for St. Augustine: if everything that is has an order, and some things are bad, how can there be bad order? (*See* EVIL.) Plato and Aristotle achieve concepts of the ordering of men in society and of the succession of the orders of constitutions.

Medieval Thought. The Christian achievement of a philosophy of order is best studied by St. Augustine, particularly in his brilliant dialogue *De ordine*. The plurality of orders is illustrated in nature, in the arts, in language, and above all in the moral life, seen in the light of divine providence. Christian philosophy surpasses its pagan predecessors in richness; problems of great depth are explored and solved, and without these achievements the modern world cannot be imagined. One is the conception of all peoples as part of an evolving pattern in time. History is a succession of orders: a concept developed centuries later by G. *Vico and, most recently, by E. Voegelin's *Order and History* (Baton Rouge, La. 1956–   ). The second problem is that of the ultimate good of man. Salvation belongs to what is commonly called "the order of grace," and Christian philosophies of order stress a sharp break between the methods by which one knows the natural order and the supernatural order. No modern philosopher of order has stated this better than B. *Pascal in his fragmentary *Pensées,* which are worth reading on the three orders, any one irreducible to any other (history is neither nature, nor supernature, and is studied in a unique fashion).

Modern Thought. A great modern achievement is the understanding of the world of nature as a unitary order. How the new science was made possible by the medieval theological framework, which itself grew out of the ancient movements, is shown by Whitehead in *Science and the Modern World* (New York 1925): "There can be no living science unless there is a widespread instinctive conviction in the existence of an *Order of Things,* and, in particular, of an *Order of Nature*"(5). The world ruled by power that is all-extensive, down to the least detail, yet in principle intelligible, is the living faith of Christianity. This was lacking, Whitehead argues, in those regions where science did not arise. Order is coupled by the founders of modern philosophy with method, that is, regular procedure in investigating nature. A crucial question, particularly for modern empiricists (D. *Hume and his followers), is whether science can proceed without knowledge of an order of things and whether method is sufficient without metaphysical grounding. Modern metaphysics of order have been most various; doctrines of two orders ("order dualism"), an order of knowing and an order of being (R. *Descartes); or reduction of all orders to one logical order ("order monism" of B. *Spinoza). There are other forms of "order monism": one mechanical order (T. *Hobbes); one divine order (N. *Malebranche); one order of the mind, without a real material order (G. *Berkeley). There is also the view of mind imposing categorial order on otherwise chaotic sensations (I. *Kant), which might be called "order subjectivism." The later phases have stressed a recognition of change in species and *chance as a factor in their development (C. R. *Darwin). Thus, as argued by A. O. Lovejoy in *The Great Chain of Being* (Cambridge,

Mass. 1936), the hierarchical order persisting from the ancients into the schemes of the Enlightenment has been displaced, and a temporal and dynamic ordering prevails.

The present crisis was prepared by H. *Bergson and the pragmatists, such as James. Bergson denied any real chaos: disorder was merely frustration in not finding the order one had expected (*Creative Evolution,* tr. A. Mitchell, New York 1911). James came to doubt any real order: the world has any order one chooses to recognize in it: it is as beans spilled on the table: a person can see whatever patterns are of interest to him (*Varieties of Religious Experience,* New York 1902, 1963, etc.).

Contemporary Thought. Contemporary philosophies of order—not only pragmatist but also existentialist, positivist, and Marxist—are all reacting against *Hegelianism. The phrase that expresses "order-monism" in Royce is "one true Order of things" (*The World and the Individual,* New York 1900). Contemporary protests often take the form of extreme "order-dualism" or "order-pluralism." Philosophers who voice such protests assert confidently that there is no one final and eternal order; this ideal of one final order is mocked by L. *Wittgenstein as the search for a "crystal palace." The existentialists, following Dostoevskiĭ, who protested against cosmic order in the name of radical human freedom, tend toward acosmism: they tend to say that man alone is the only principle of order, and each individual man from moment to moment as his interests and tasks shift.

The great hope of some contemporaries (G. G. Grisez, I. Jenkins, and P. G. Kuntz, all somewhat close to Paul Weiss, *Modes of Being,* Carbondale, Ill. 1958) is that a new systematic understanding can be developed. The errors of the past have been the fallacious reduction of the cosmos to one mode of being or, on the other hand, the overstress on the discontinuity of orders. Stated positively, there are several modes of order. If the hope of these new systems is fulfilled, the universe can be understood as many orders together.

See also UNIVERSE, ORDER OF; RELATION.

Bibliography: Syntopicon, see index. G. GIANNINI, EncFil 3: 1062–67. Pauly-Wiss RE 18.1 (1931) 930–936. J. ROYCE, Hastings ERE 9:533–540. ProcAmCathPhilAs 17 (1941) 1–52. E. CASSIRER, *Logos, Dike, Kosmos in der Entwicklung der griechischen Philosophie* (Göteborg 1941). W. W. JAEGER, *Paideia: The Ideals of Greek Culture,* tr. G. HIGHET, v.1 (2d ed. New York 1945). H. KRINGS, *Ordo: Philosophische-historische Grundlegung einer abendländischen Idee* (Halle 1941). AUGUSTINE, *Ordine,* ed. and tr. R. P. RUSSELL as *Divine Providence and the Problem of Evil* (New York 1942), also in *Writings of St. Augustine* (FathCh 1; 1948) 239–332. L. R. WARD, *God and World Order* (St. Louis 1961). J. M. RAMIREZ, *De ordine Placita quaedam Thomistica* (Salamanca 1963). H. MEYER, *Thomas von Aquinas: Sein System und seine geistesgeschichtliche Stellung* (2d ed. Paderborn 1961). B. COFFEY, "The Notion of Order according to St. Thomas Aquinas," ModSchoolm 27 (1949) 1–18. E. A. PACE, "The Concept of Order in the Philosophy of St. Thomas," NewSchol 2 (1928) 51–72. H. A. ROMMEN, *The Natural Law: A Study in Legal and Social History,* tr. T. A. HANLEY (St. Louis 1947). C. I. LEWIS, *Mind and the World Order* (New York 1929; pa. 1956). W. D. OLIVER, *Theory of Order* (Yellow Springs, Ohio 1951). J. D. WILD, *Human Freedom and Social Order: An Essay in Christian Philosophy* (Durham, N.C. 1959). C. J. SCHNEER, *The Search for Order* (New York 1960). A. D. RITCHIE, *Studies in the History and Methods of the Sciences* (Edinburgh 1958). E. HEIMANN, *Freedom and Order* (New York 1947). H. KUHN, "Le Concept de l'ordre," *Greg* 43 (1962) 254–267. G. G. GRISEZ, "Sketch of a Future Metaphysics," NewSchol 37 (1964) 310–340. I. JENKINS, "The Matrix of Positive Law," *Natural Law Forum* 6 (1961) 1–50. P. G. KUNTZ, "Modes of Order," *Review of Metaphysics* 16 (1962–63) 316–345; "Mythical, Cosmic, and Personal Order," *ibid.* 718–748; "Order in Language, Phenomena, and Reality: Notes on Linguistic Analysis, Phenomenology, and Metaphysics," *Monist* 49 (1965) 107–136.

[P. G. KUNTZ]

ORDER OF CHRIST, a military order established March 14, 1319, by John XXII, at the request of King Diniz of Portugal. The order received all the Portuguese properties of the suppressed Order of the *Templars. Its chief seat was originally at Castro Marim, and later at *Thomar. The Order of Christ was bound to the observance of the customs of the Castilian Order of *Calatrava and was subject to the visitation of the Cistercian abbot of Alcobaça. The pope appointed the first master, requiring him and his successors to take an oath of loyalty to the Holy See. In the future the abbot of Alcobaça was to preside at the election of the master. The Cistercian general chapter of 1320 consented to these arrangements and the first chapter of the Order of Christ was held at Lisbon in 1321. Until the 15th century the order was governed by a succession of masters; afterward princes of the royal family administered it. The most famous of these, *Henry the Navigator (d. 1460), reformed the order and secured for it spiritual jurisdiction in the Atlantic islands and African regions, which were explored and colonized through his efforts. In 1542 Paul III revoked the right of the abbot of Alcobaça to visit the order. Nine years later Julius III annexed the mastership to the crown in perpetuity. (For illus., see following page.)

Bibliography: *Definições e estatutos dos cavalleiros e freires da Ordem de Nosso Senhor Jesu Christo* (Lisbon 1628, 1671, 1717, 1746). J. VIEIRA DA SILVA GUIMARÃES, *A Ordem de Christo* (Lisbon 1901). A. JANN, LexThK² 2:1183. **Illustration credit:** Leonard Von Matt.

[J. F. O'CALLAGHAN]

ORDER OF THE SWAN, a sodality whose goal was to further devotion to the Virgin Mary and to promote charity; originally membership was confined to princely, knightly, and noble personages. Founded by Elector Frederick II of Brandenburg on Sept. 29, 1440, the order had its seat at Sankt Marien monastery on the Harlunger Berg, near Brandenburg, Germany. The brothers of the Order of the Swan vowed to say seven Our Fathers and seven Hail Marys daily—or to give seven pennies to the poor instead. Furthermore, they pledged to fast on the vigils of all feasts of the Virgin and to celebrate the feasts themselves with the greatest possible dignity. No adulterer, fornicator, traitor, robber, or drunkard could belong to the brotherhood. Members were obligated to make considerable contributions to the order, in return for which they gained all the spiritual benefits it earned. Membership in the order carried considerable prestige, not only in Germany, but elsewhere in Europe; it was originally restricted to 30 men (who had to furnish proofs of nobility) and 7 women. The Elector Frederick II changed the statutes on Aug. 25, 1452, admitting commoners to the sodality. The badge of the order consisted of a gold or silver collar (called "The Society"), from which was suspended a medallion showing the Virgin and Child supported by a crescent bearing the motto of the order, *Ave Mundi Domina.* Hanging

The gold and enamel badge and collar of the Order of Christ.

from this medallion was an image of a swan, the proper titular of the order. The Reformation spelled the end of the order. It was, however, revived by King Frederick William IV of Prussia on Dec. 24, 1843, as a free association of men and women of all social classes, whose purpose was social welfare.

Bibliography: R. M. B. VON STILLFRIED-RATTONITZ, *Der Schwanenorden* (2d ed. Halle 1845). S. HÄNLE, *Urkunden und Nachweise zur Geschichte des Schwanen-Ordens* (Ansbach 1876). R. M. B. VON STILLFRIED-RATTONITZ and S. HÄNLE, *Das Buch vom Schwanenorden* (Berlin 1881). C. MEYER, *Schwanen-ordens-Ritterkapelle* (Ansbach 1909). E. A. PRINZ ZUR LIPPE, *Orden und Auszeichnungen in Geschichte und Gegenwart* (Heidelberg-Munich 1958) 158.

[G. GROSSCHMID]

ORDERICUS VITALIS, Benedictine, the leading historian of France in the 12th century; b. Attingham, England, Feb. 16, 1075; d. Saint-Evroult, Normandy, Feb. 3, 1142. In 1085 he became an oblate in the abbey of *Saint-Evroult-d'Ouche in Normandy, where he received an excellent liberal education under John of Reims. He was ordained in 1108. In 1109 he adapted and enlarged the *Gesta Normannorum ducum* of *William of Jumièges; in 1123, at the request of his abbot, Roger du Sap, he began his most important work, the *Historia ecclesiastica* in 13 books, completed in 1141. An especially important source for the period from 1125 to 1140, the *Historia* was originally planned as a history of his monastery. It soon grew into a universal history of the period, treating of persons and trends in the history of the Church; giving lists of popes, abbots, and rectors of churches; and recounting the history of the *Normans in England, Southern Italy, *Normandy, and the *Crusader States. As an enthusiastic chronicler of the *Crusades, Ordericus represents the best tradition of monastic *historiography, interested in events both religious and profane. Ordericus, little known in the Middle Ages, is appreciated today for his broad interest and accuracy in detail. His principal sources, carefully noted by him, were mainly oral. Among his informants were those who happened through the monastic guest-house: clerics, monks, pilgrims, knights, jongleurs, and merchants. Among earlier historians known to Orderi-cus were Pompeius Trogus, *Gregory of Tours, and *Bede. He also consulted monastic archives and the contemporary chronicles of Dudo of Saint-Quentin, William of Jumièges, and *Fulcher of Chartres.

Bibliography: Editions. *Historia ecclesiastica,* ed. A. Le Prévost, 5 v. (Paris 1838–55); PL 188; *The Ecclesiastical History of England and Normandy,* tr. T. Forester, 4 v. (London 1853–56). Literature. Manitius 3:441–448, 522–528. H. Wolter, *Ordericus Vitalis: Ein Beitrag zur kluniazensischen Geschichts-schreibung* (Wiesbaden 1955).

[B. Lacroix]

ORDINALS, ROMAN

Medieval service books that described the customary (*consuetudines*) ordering (*Ordines, ordinarium*), or sequence of ceremonies in a liturgical function. Here will be treated the purpose and history of the books, the *Caeremoniale Episcoporum,* and various editions of ordinals.

Purpose. Liturgical services are hierarchical actions —a feature pointedly brought out in the ancient Church's practice of having each minister perform only his part of the function (*see* LITURGICAL MINISTERS). In fact, for each minister there was usually a special book containing only those texts pertaining to his role (*see* LITURGICAL BOOKS OF ROMAN RITE). To coordinate the activities of the various ministers and to ensure a smoothly organized service, someone comparable to a *master of ceremonies was required. He had his own book, the ordinal. The first ordinals were very likely succinct personal notes of such a master, compiled by himself or the sacristan for local use. Written ordinals and their wide distribution filled a historical need; namely, that which arose when a local liturgy moved outside its own confines or when strangers replaced a native minister. The need for this type of book today is satisfied by such modern compilations as the Missal, Ritual, Breviary, and Pontifical, which incorporate rubrical directions alongside the liturgical texts. There are also special official rubrical collections: the *Ordo* (*see* ORDO, ROMAN), designating the liturgical texts to be used for each day of the year, and the *Caeremoniale Episcoporum,* containing all the rubrics concerning episcopal functions.

History. The emergence of Carolingian Europe from chaos is in large part due to a program of borrowings from Rome (in organization and institutions, in culture and religion) which was in progress under Charlemagne. Having borrowed sacramentaries, lectionaries, graduals, etc., he needed also Roman ordinals. Members of monastic scriptoria copied prodigious numbers of MSS. Pure Roman manuscripts quickly acquired local elements, unintentional misreadings by copyists, or deliberate modifications by liturgical editors. Not only were collections of pure and altered ordinals amassed as reference works for libraries, but other collections, meant to supply actual norms for the living liturgy, were kept up to date and continuously developed. Still other ordinals were joined to didactic material for the theological training of the clerics. Key monastic centers throughout the Continent and the islands assured the survival of the ordinals.

Editions. Many had edited ordinals, for instance, Morin, Martène, Hittorp, Tommasi, De Rossi, Duchesne, and especially Mabillon, but none had worked on them critically until Michel *Andrieu. Andrieu offers a highly scientific edition, and in texts that he has in common with other scholars, Andrieu must have preference. His lifetime work made available the pure Roman ordinals and their Gallican offspring. Andrieu culled 50 such ordinals from the manuscript libraries of Europe; by tedious line-by-line comparisons of myriad manuscripts, he retraced the genealogy of varied copies to their family homes, carefully dated them, and in the process revealed the slow evolution of the rites of Rome with the admixture of Gallican modifications that was to end in the 10th-century Romano-German pontifical. The liturgy embodied in this new ordinal entered Rome with Otto I (912–973), spread anew from the Lateran, and ultimately dominated the Western world.

In volume 1 Andrieu lists individually the titles of ordinals and under each gives reference to available editions and the known manuscripts in which they are found. Following this is a description of each manuscript consulted. A third section gives a history, and a valuable index ends the 631-page volume. Volume 2, after an introduction, takes up the text of the first 13 ordinals, each preceded by a chapter on the manuscript traditions, date and place of origin, and brilliant essays commenting on the text. A critical text with copious notes closes Andrieu's plan of work. Volume 3 covers ordinals 14–34; volume 4 ordinals 35–49; volume 5,

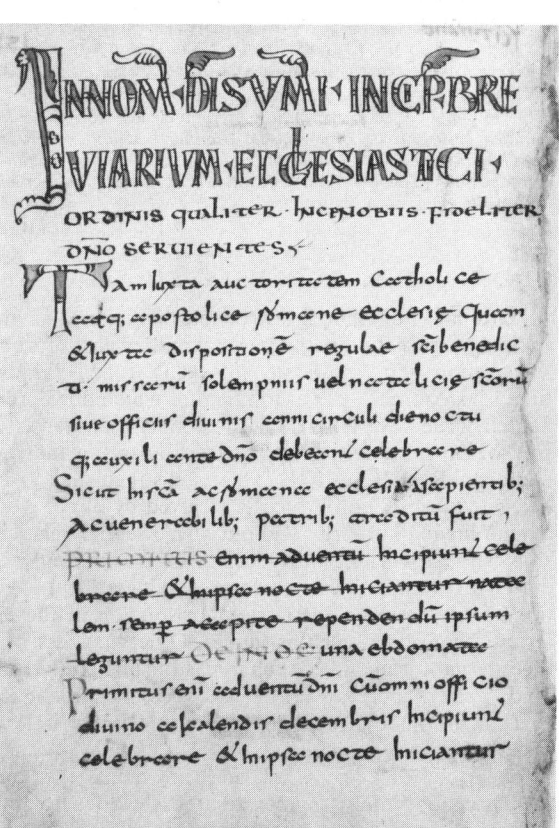

Roman Ordinal XVII, 9th century (Bib. Vat. Cod. Pal. Lat. 574, fol. 152v), describing the recital of the monastic Office; in a 9th-century manuscript.

the famed ordinal 50, covers Hittorp's *Ordo Romanus Antiquus.* This last tome is the work of Andrieu, but his untimely death left to A. van Roey and A. H. Thomas the task of preparing it for the press. In general ordinals 1–10 deal with the Mass; 12–19, the office; 20–33, principal functions of the liturgical year; 34–40, ordinations in their ember day setting; 41–44, dedication of churches and honors paid to relics; 45–48, the crowning of the emperor; 49, obsequies; and 50 deals with the liturgy of the whole liturgical year in 55 chapters. Along with these 50 ordinals, Andrieu points out the original Roman practice.

Caeremoniale Episcoporum. A logical outcome of the ordinal-pontifical evolution is a ceremonial for bishops. The *Caeremoniale Episcoporum,* promulgated by Clement VIII, July 14, 1600, was not a new creation. Such a ceremonial guide found its immediate sources in the compilations of the masters of ceremonies of the papal household. Several of their works have been edited, notably ordinal 14 of Mabillon, compiled by Cardinal Stefaneschi. Such papal custom books eventually end in the *Caeremoniale Romanum* prepared by Patrizzi in 1488, edited in 1516 by Marcellus, and re-edited with a famous commentary by Catalani in 1750. Paris de Grassi, master of ceremonies in Bologna and Rome, edited a book in 1564 intended for bishops in their own sees, but only after vehemently opposing others who earlier had made papal ceremonies available to bishops. The present *Caeremoniale* is basically the work of De Grassi and is still law throughout three typical editions (the last under Leo XIII) all practically without change. The Holy Week section was rendered obsolete by Pius XII's Pontifical of 1957.

Bibliography: R. LESAGE, *Catholicisme* 2:830. J. BAUDOT, DACL 2.2:3296–97. Eisenhofer Lit 29–35. A. HÄNGGI, LexThK² 7:1224–25. F. WASNER, LexThK² 2:939–940. J. NABUCO, "La Liturgie papale et les origines du Cérémoniel des évêques," *Miscellanea Liturgica in Honorem L. Cuniberti Mohlberg* (Rome 1948) 1:283–300; *Ius pontificalium: Introductio in caeremoniale episcoporum* (Tournai 1956). Andrieu OR. **Illustration credit:** Biblioteca Apostolica Vaticana.

[R. T. CALLAHAN]

ORDINARIES, ECCLESIASTICAL

"Ordinary" in Church law denotes any cleric having ordinary jurisdiction in the internal and external forum. Jurisdiction is the power to rule (CIC c.196) as distinguished from the power to sanctify, which flows from Sacred Orders. Ordinary jurisdiction is that power to rule which flows automatically from an office that the cleric holds (CIC c.197). This is distinguished from delegated jurisdiction, which is received by direct grant of one having authority without any essential relationship with an ecclesiastical office. "In the internal and external forum" indicates a certain fullness of jurisdiction. Some possess ecclesiastical jurisdiction in the external forum only, such as judges. Others possess it in the internal forum alone, such as pastors and confessors. And, finally, there are those who possess jurisdiction in both the internal and external forum, such as local bishops and all ordinaries.

The Code of Canon Law does not define the term ordinary but simply enumerates those who are to be considered such. In short, all residential bishops and all provincials of exempt clerical religious are ordinaries. The Code of Canon Law in canon 198 lists the following as ordinaries: (1) the Roman pontiff; (2) residential bishops; (3) abbots *nullius* and prelates *nullius,* i.e., those abbots or prelates who have some territorial jurisdiction; (4) the vicars-general of those enumerated in (2) and (3); (5) apostolic administrators; (6) vicars apostolic and prefects apostolic; (7) all those who legally succeed the above numbers (1), (2), (3), (5), and (6), when their offices become vacant or are impeded. This includes pro-vicars and pro-prefects apostolic, the vicar-general of an apostolic administrator, and, during the vacancy of a diocese, the diocesan consultors or the cathedral chapter until they elect a diocesan administrator or a vicar capitular, and these latter two until a new bishop takes possession of his see.

Canon 198 includes an eighth category of ordinaries: major superiors in exempt clerical religious groups. Canon 488.8 of the CIC designates the following as major superiors: the abbot primate; the abbot superior of a monastic congregation; the abbot of an independent monastery, even though it belongs to a monastic congregation; the supreme superior of a religious society; the provincial superior; the vicars of all those above mentioned; and finally, all those with provincial authority, such as provincial vicars and visitators. The Congregation for Religious, in a rescript dated June 6 and Nov. 25, 1922, declared that cloistral priors in the Benedictine confederation are not to be considered as major superiors. Conventual priors, however, of independent monasteries are major superiors and ordinaries.

Canon 198 makes the distinction between local ordinaries (those in groups 1 to 7 above) and personal or religious ordinaries (major superiors of exempt clerical religious). The local ordinary's jurisdiction extends over all those who are in the territory that he governs. The jurisdiction of the religious ordinary is restricted to his own subjects.

In the Oriental Code the legislation on ordinaries is substantially the same as that in the Latin Code, although the term "ordinary" is not used. The same jurisdiction that local ordinaries enjoy in the Latin Church is recognized as the prerogative of their patriarchs and local bishops. These offices are usually conferred in a patriarchal synod of bishops. As for religious superiors or exarchs of all exempt clerical religious or of monasteries, they have over their own subjects jurisdiction that is the same as that of a local bishop (PostApost c.26; ClerSanc cc.216, 240, 399, 432, 464, 467).

Bibliography: Beste 212–216, 312. M. J. KEENE, *Religious Ordinaries and Canon 198* (CUA CLS 135; Washington 1942).

[M. J. KEENE]

ORDINATION, TITLE OF

The title of ordination, or canonical title, refers to the juridical bond of material support that is assured a cleric with the reception of Sacred Orders.

From the 5th century, churches were referred to as *tituli,* the sign by which they were designated or identified. The title was frequently the name of the martyr to whom the church was dedicated, less often the name of the founder or its location. According to an ancient practice, deacons and priests were ordained and bishops consecrated for a particular church with which they were associated throughout their life. This assured sufficient clergy to serve the needs of the community and precluded the undisciplined wanderings of vagrant clerics [cf. I Council of Nicaea (325), c. 15]. The bond was so intense and personal that it was likened to the bond of marriage. Much of this discipline is now provided by the law on incardination (CIC cc. 111–117).

The practice also provided the cleric with sufficient material support to compensate for his service. Commerce and certain occupations were closed to the clergy, and the work of the ministry required an undivided effort. The resources of the titular church he served became a guarantee that he would not be reduced to beggary or forced to forgo the apostolate while he endeavored to support himself. This assurance soon predominated as the principal motive for the canonically required title for ordination.

The legal requisite of a title was recognized by the Council of Chalcedon (c. 6) and later by those of III Lateran (c. 5) and Trent (sess 23, de ref., c. 16). Papal decrees further modified and expanded the legislation that, in effect, sought to assure the support of the cleric even though he was not assigned to parish work. The CIC treats of the title of ordination in cc. 979–982. The term has now almost entirely lost its primitive association with a particular church and is understood as the guaranteed support itself (CIC c. 979.2).

At the present time secular clerics may be ordained with the canonical title of a benefice, patrimony, pension, the service of the diocese, or the service of the mission. In the U.S., the service of the diocese is most commonly used. Before receiving the subdiaconate, the candidate binds himself by a special oath to serve in the diocese for which he is being ordained, and he can expect from the bishop an assignment that will furnish adequate support. Even in the case of permanent disability or old age, this support must be provided. Occasionally, when private means of support are available, the title of patrimony or pension is used. If for any reason the canonical title ceases, as may happen in the loss of the patrimony, the cleric must arrange for another in its place. This is rarely difficult.

A religious in earlier times was ordained to serve in his monastery, and his membership in that institute was itself a guarantee of material support. Regulars still retain as title their profession of solemn vows, more commonly called the title of poverty. Religious in perpetual vows use the title stated in their constitutions, as that of the common table. Other religious follow the same law as secular clerics.

The canonical title is now required of all candidates for the subdiaconate. As each ordinand is called to present himself before the ordaining bishop, the canonical title is announced together with the name. Severe canonical penalties would be imposed should a prelate ordain a candidate who lacks a canonical title (CIC c. 2373).

Bibliography: S. MANY, Praelectiones de sacra ordinatione (Paris 1905) 130–152. P. HANNAN, The Canonical Concept of 'congrua sustentatio' for the Secular Clergy (CUA CLS 302; Washington 1950). M. J. DLOUHY, The Ordination of Exempt Religious (CUA CLS 271; Washington 1955).

[M. J. DLOUHY]

ORDINATION TO OLD TESTAMENT PRIESTHOOD, rites and ceremonies by which the hereditary Israelite priests were consecrated (set aside, made holy) and so entered into their priestly duties. The principal texts in which the rite of installation is described in detail are Ex 29.1–37 and Lv 8.1–36. The rite comprises several parts: washing, clothing with priestly garments, *anointing with oil (see also Lv 10.7;

21.10), sacrifices for those being ordained, consecration by anointing with the blood of one of the sacrificed animals [see BLOOD, RELIGIOUS SIGNIFICANCE OF (IN THE BIBLE)], *wave offering by the newly ordained, sprinkling of oil and blood upon the priestly garments, and a communion meal. Although the ceremony is placed in the ambit of the desert and the *Tent of Meeting, the Pentateuchal *priestly writers are probably describing the rite practiced in the postexilic Temple of Jerusalem. See TEMPLES (IN THE BIBLE). The anointing with oil, especially, seems to date from a time when there is no longer an active kingship and when royal prerogatives have been transferred to the priesthood that exercised authority in the community; other elements, however, may well be much older.

More ancient texts (Jgs 17.12; Ex 32.29; and 3 Kgs 13.33) speak of "filling the hand" when a priest enters office. The priestly authors understand the phrase of the offerings placed in the hands of the new priests (Ex 29.22–34; Lv 8.22–33), but this may be a late guess. Others suggest that it originally referred either to the salary given the priest or to the right he obtained to sanctuary revenues.

See also HIGH PRIEST; PRIEST AND PRIESTHOOD, ISRAELITE.

Bibliography: EncDictBibl 933. De Vaux AncIsr 346–348.

[J. E. STEINMUELLER]

ORDINATIONS IN THE ROMAN RITE

The object of this article is to treat of the particular form the Sacrament of Holy Orders has taken in the Roman rite. In order to do this it will be necessary to discuss the meaning of terms and then to investigate the historical evolution of each ordination ritual.

MEANING OF TERMS

Like many of the words used in the Roman liturgical books, ordinatio and ordo have a civil origin, going back even to pre-Christian times.

Ordinatio. This was the technical term used at Rome for the act of appointing civil functionaries to office. It was natural enough that the Roman Christians should borrow a familiar word to signify the selection of a man to fill ecclesiastical functions, of which the highest and most important are the liturgical functions or rites. So in time the word was limited to describe the rite of consecration to liturgical office or the sacred ministry.

"Ordination" is used by St. Jerome at the beginning of the 5th century as the Latin synonym for the Greek cheirotonia, the laying on of hands (Commentarium in Isaiam 16.58.10; PL 24:569); in time the word came to embrace all ordinations—even those not conferred by the laying on of hands, such as the minor orders. Nowadays the term simply means to ordain or promote to any order, whether major or minor. At first ordinatio was used to refer to the consecration of bishops as well as to promotion to priesthood and deaconship; the Roman Martyrology still speaks of "Ordinatio Sti Ambrosii Episcopi," for example. The Pontifical has substituted Consecratio for ordinatio in this case, but since the episcopate is the summit of Holy Orders and its source, we must include episcopal consecration in this study.

Ordo. Order is likewise a term that originally belonged to the Roman civil vocabulary, where it was used to designate a definite social body distinct from the plebs, or people—such as the Senate (ordo claris-

simus), or the knights (*ordo equestrianus*), or the group that made up the governing body in any city (*ordo civicus*). Since the word had no pagan religious associations, Christians did not hesitate to adopt it to express the special place the clergy had within the people of God. Thus Tertullian uses it to describe the body of the clergy as set apart from the people (*De exhortatione castitatis* 7; PL 2:922); the Theodosian code made it official by speaking of the *ordo ecclesiasticus* (*Cod. Theodosianus* 16.5.26).

The first step in the adaptation of the word to ecclesiastical use was to make it designate the whole body of the clergy. From that to using it to designate the different degrees into which the clergy was divided was a natural step. So we have the *ordo presbyterii* and the *ordo episcoporum*.

It is important that the word always had a collective sense in the usage of the ancient Church; a man did not so much receive an order as he was received into it and entered into it, as we say today that a man enters into the Society of Jesus, or is received into the Franciscan Order.

HISTORY OF RITUAL

In studying ordinations in the Roman rite different approaches are possible. The best seems to be to trace the historical origin and development and see how it took the form it has today, for the modern rite is the product of a long development in which a multiplicity of rites and formulas have accumulated around the original simple liturgical action. To look into the history of this development is to make the meaning of the essential rite stand out in higher relief.

The modern ritual for the conferring of the Sacrament of Holy Orders is contained in the first volume of the *Pontificale Romanum*. Until the 9th century the prayers and formulas to be used in conferring Holy Orders were found in the Sacramentaries, which contained the celebrant's prayers for Mass and the other Sacraments and sacred rites. The ceremonies or actions that together with the words made up the sacred rites were contained in another book called the Ordinal. During the 9th and 10th centuries someone conceived the idea of putting both prayers and actions together in the one volume for greater convenience. The first compilation of this kind, or at any rate the most successful, originated at Mainz between 950 and 982. It became known as the *Pontificalis ordinis liber* because of its content and the Romano-Germanic Pontifical because of its origin. This book, with an ordination ritual already more developed than that in the Sacramentaries that preceded it, was accepted before the year 1000 at Rome, where it was adapted to the use of the Roman court during the following centuries. William *Duranti the Elder (d. 1296), a civil lawyer who had become bishop of Mende, recast it and adapted it still more for his own use. This Pontifical was revised and approved for use at Rome in 1486; after further revision it was imposed on the Latin Church in 1596. The rite of ordination we use today is substantially the same as that produced by Duranti.

Consecration of a Bishop. Since the episcopate is the fullness of the priesthood, we begin with it; then treat the other major orders—priesthood, diaconate, and subdiaconate; and finally the minor orders.

Fig. 1. Consecration of a bishop, miniature in MS of the works of St. Gregory Nazianzen written for the Emperor Basil I (867–886), now in the Bibliothèque Nationale at Paris (MS grec. 510). The miniature shows the ceremony of the imposition of the Gospel Book on the head of the bishop-elect.

Ancient Roman Ritual: 3d to 5th Century. The ancient Roman rite of episcopal consecration in first described in the *Apostolic Tradition* of Hippolytus drawn up about the year 215 (2–4; Botte LFQ 4–16). The rite is simplicity itself. The neighboring bishops assemble with the local clergy and people on a Sunday. With the consent of those present these bishops impose their hands on the elect, while all pray silently, invoking the Holy Spirit. Then one of the bishops is asked to place his hands on the head of the elect and recite the consecratory prayer. There are, therefore, two distinct *impositions of hands: one in silence and one accompanied by the consecratory prayer. The prayer calls down the Holy Spirit upon the elect that he may shepherd the flock and fulfill the office of priesthood (*sacerdotium*) in a blameless manner, offering sacrifice, and forgiving sins. After the prayer all exchange the kiss of peace with him and "salute him who has been made worthy." The deacons then place the offerings upon the altar and the newly ordained bishop celebrates the Eucharist at once.

This ritual described by Hippolytus has been maintained in the East with slight modifications; but at Rome it fell into disuse, and another more elaborate form was adopted perhaps as early as the middle of the 5th century. At any rate we encounter the main prayers of the present rite in slightly modified form in the Leonine Sacramentary (946, 947; Mohlberg 119).

Consecration at Rome: 6th to 9th Centuries. Two forms of episcopal consecration are described by the Roman Ordinal and they differ considerably from one another. One is the form for the consecration of the bishop of Rome, the pope, by the bishops of the neighboring sees, the other is that conferred by the pope himself upon those chosen for these neighboring sees. The man chosen to be bishop of Rome in these early centuries was often not a bishop at the time of his election. He was therefore consecrated at St. Peter's, and his ordination was the joint action of the suburbicarian bishops; the bishop of Albano says the first prayer (the Collect *Adesto*), the bishop of Porto the second (*Propitiare*). Then the deacons hold the open book of the Gospels on his head while the bishop of Ostia says the prayer of consecration. The archdeacon places the pallium upon the new bishop, who then ascends his throne, gives the kiss of peace to the priests, and intones the *Gloria* (*Ord. Romanus* 40A and 40B; Andrieu OR 4:297, 307–308).

However, when the pope consecrated bishops for one of the dioceses of central Italy, he conferred the episcopate alone without the assistance of coconsecrators. The reason for this seems to be that the pope as chief bishop is considered to embody the *ordo episcopalis,* which in ordinary consecrations is symbolized by the presence of three bishops.

On the eve of his consecration the candidate for the episcopal office is examined by the pope in the presence of all the clergy. The consecration itself takes place on Sunday. During the Gradual of the Mass the elect goes to the sacristy, where he is vested in dalmatic, chasuble, and sandals by the archdeacon, the acolytes, and subdeacons. They then escort him back to the church, where the pope presents him to the people and invites all to join in prayer for the elect. The Litany of the Saints is sung while the pope, the bishop-elect, and clergy lie prostrate before the altar. "When the Litany is completed," Ordo 34 says, "let them arise and let him [the pope] bless him" (40; Andrieu OR 4:613). The blessing consists of the pope placing his hands on the elect and reciting the prayer of consecration given in the Sacramentaries. This prayer is already much longer than the one given in the *Apostolic Tradition* and completely different from it. Then the consecrator gives the kiss of peace to the new bishop, who in turn gives it to the other bishops and to the priests. When that is over, the pope seats him in the first rank of the bishops. At the Communion of the Mass he receives the manual of episcopal functions from the consecrator. The new bishop communicates by receiving a portion of the consecrated bread and at the same time sets aside enough for 40 days so that he may receive Communion during that time from the bread consecrated during the ordination Mass. By order of the pope he then gives Communion to the people.

Romano-Gallican Ritual: 9th to 15th Centuries. Between the ancient Roman rite of episcopal ordination, even in the somewhat developed form just described, and the modern episcopal consecration there is a vast difference. This is the result of the elaboration made by the Romano-Gallican ritual, an elaboration completed by the innovations of Duranti (Andrieu Pont 3:311–320). The ritual of consecration underwent considerable development and addition both in the formularies used and in the individual rites that go to make up the whole. First of all the name was changed from *ordinatio episcopi* to *consecratio electi in episcopatum.* It is beyond doubt that in time this contributed to thinking of the ordination of a bishop as in another class from that of a priest, instead of what it really is, the crowning and culmination of Holy Orders. An examination of the bishop-elect was introduced into the rite after the Collect and the ancient Roman consecration prayer expanded. In fact the Romano-Germanic Pontifical transforms the ancient ordination prayer of the Roman rite into a consecratory Preface after the model of the Preface of the Mass, even to the dialogue at the beginning (*ibid.* 1:147).

The most striking innovation made in the Romano-Gallican ritual was the introduction of the anointings. While the old Roman rite was content to ask that God sanctify the elect with the dew of heaven by anointing, the new rite from beyond the Alps has the consecrator interrupt the prayer at this point to pour sacred chrism on the head of the elect, with the formula "ungetur et consacretur caput tuum . . . ." This was obviously an attempt in true Gallican style to give visible expression to the words of the prayer (it was probably influenced by the contemporary practice of anointing the head of the king at his coronation). After the Preface the new ritual also added the anointing of the thumbs; the 13th-century papal Pontifical extended this to the whole hand (*ibid.* 2:361). At first this anointing of the hands was done only when a man went directly from the diaconate to the episcopate; it was not repeated if the candidate was already a priest.

According to the ancient Roman tradition the bishop-elect presented himself for ordination already invested in the insignia of his office. But outside of Rome the procedure was different; Isidore of Seville (d. 636) attests to the practice of giving the new bishop his ring and staff as symbols of his jurisdiction and his spiritual powers during the ceremony (*De ecclesiasticis officiis* 2.5.12; PL 83:783–784). The 12th-century papal Pontifical introduced the custom of handing the Gospel Book with the admonition to go and preach to the people committed to his care (Andrieu Pont 1:150).

Duranti in his turn added the words *Accipe Spiritum Sanctum* to the imposition of hands, the singing of the *Veni Sancte Spiritus* during the anointing of the hands, the blessing and putting-on of miter and gloves, the enthronement of the bishop, and finally the singing of the *Te Deum* at the end of the rite (*ibid.* 3:382, 383, 389–391).

The ceremony of the placing of the opened Gospel Book upon the head of the bishop-elect makes its appearance for the first time in a 6th-century Ordinal (*Ordo Rom.* 40 A. 5; Andrieu OR 4:297). At first this was confined to the episcopal consecration of the pope, but in the Gallican lands it was extended to all consecrations. The custom itself is quite ancient; it came from the East, where it is mentioned in the ritual of the 4th-century *Apostolic Constitutions* (8.4.6; Funk DidConst 1:473).

Ordination of Priests and Deacons. The essential part of this ceremony, the imposition of hands accompanied by a variable but appropriate consecratory formula, has been a liturgical constant throughout history. However, the surrounding ceremonial has passed through three

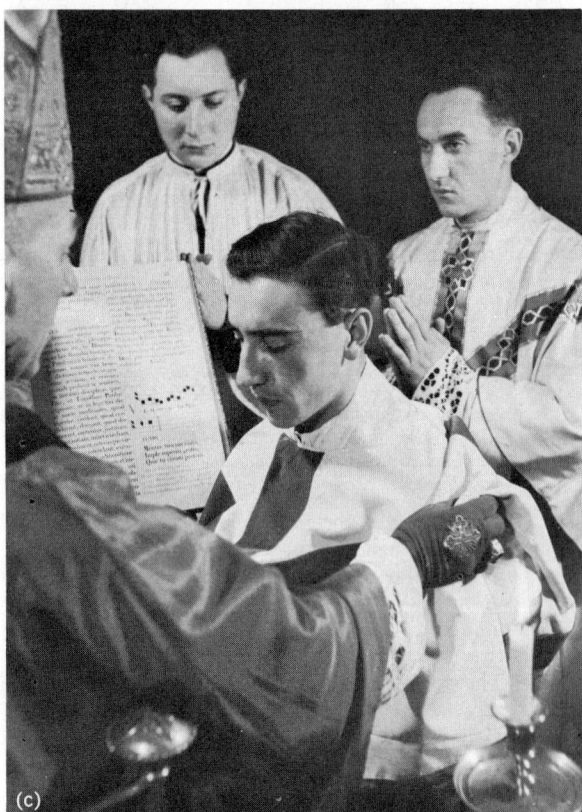

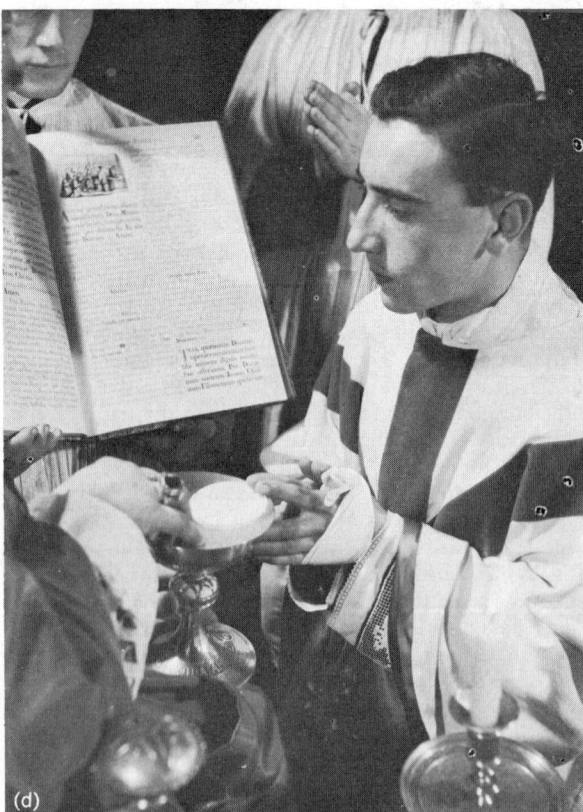

Fig. 2. Ordination of a Priest: (a) Imposition of the bishop's hands on the head of the ordinand; the essential rite in the ordination of a priest. (b) The bishop sings the Consecratory Preface; the essential formula in the ordination of a priest. (c) The newly ordained priest is vested with stole and chasuble. (d) A chalice containing wine and a paten with a host delivered into the hands of the newly ordained priest showing he has the power to offer Mass.

stages of development just as the ritual for the consecration of bishops.

First Stage: the Primitive Roman Ritual. This is also contained in the *Apostolic Tradition* (7–8; Botte LQF 20–26). The ordination takes place in the presence of the presbyterium and the assembly of the faithful, during the Sunday celebration of the Eucharist. It follows the Prayer of the Faithful. For both priests and deacons ordination consists of two elements: (1) the laying on of hands and (2) the prayer of consecration.

The bishop and all the priests present lay hands on the man who is to be ordained to the priesthood. The bishop prays that God may impart the Holy Spirit to him so that he may help and govern God's people with a pure heart. Only the bishop lays hands on the candidates for deaconship because, as Hippolytus says, he is ordained not for the priestly office but to assist the bishop in a special way. The prayer said over the ordinand asks that God will give him the Holy Spirit "of grace, solicitude and industry" so that he may serve the Church and minister at the altar in such a way that he may deserve to be promoted to a higher rank, the priesthood. The bishop is still allowed considerable freedom in the formulas to be used. He may follow the given text or use another "so long as the prayer is correct and orthodox."

Second Stage: 6th to 9th Centuries. The rite described in the 7th-century Sacramentaries and Ordinals took form during the 6th century. The sources for this second stage are the earlier Sacramentaries and the *Ordo Romanus* 34 (Andrieu OR 3:603–613).

First of all came the election of the ordinands by the clergy and the ratification of this choice by the people. Then on Monday in the Ember Week of December those to be ordained were called together by the pope; in his presence they swore an oath that they had not committed any of the crimes that would exclude them from ordination. On Wednesday they attended the pope's Mass. During the Mass a lector read the names of the candidates for priesthood and deaconship and then said the words still found substantially in the Roman Pontifical at the beginning of the ordination, only today they are spoken by the ordaining prelate: "If anyone has anything against these men, let him speak up" (*Ordo Rom.* 36.9; Andrieu OR 4:196). The same proclamation was made again on Friday.

The ordination began Saturday afternoon at St. Peter's. After the Gradual the pope called the ordinands to his throne and designated the church each priest and deacon was to serve. Then those to be ordained deacons, already dressed in the dalmatic, the sign of their future rank, stood with bowed heads before the pope; he invited all to prayer, and while the Litany of the Saints was sung, the ordinands prostrated on the floor. When the litany was finished, the pope placed his hand on the head of each one and blessed him (*Ordo Rom.* 36:18; Andrieu OR 4:198). This blessing included the prayer *Exaudi Domine* and the consecratory prayer *Deus honorum dator.* Then he vested the ordinands with the chasuble over the dalmatic and gave them the kiss of peace, which they in turn gave the others and then took their place beside him.

The ordination to the priesthood followed the same pattern except that the ordinands already wore the chasuble. The blessing was of course proper to the ordination to priesthood. When the pope ordained he

Fig. 3. Investiture of newly ordained deacon with stole.

alone imposed hands; if any other bishop ordained, the other priests present came forth and imposed hands after him. The new priests took their places in the first rank of the priests. At Communion they received the Eucharist first and, like the new bishops, had to set aside enough for 40 days' Communion.

What is immediately striking here is the extreme simplicity of the ancient Roman rite of ordinations, even though there has been some development over that recorded in Hippolytus. There is a minimum of signs (actions and words), and those are extremely clear and well defined.

The Romano-Gallican Ordination Rite: 9th to 15th Centuries. The third and final stage represents a complete transformation from the ancient simplicity to an extreme complexity. This transformation was the result of the fusing of the Roman ritual with that of the Gallican ritual of ordination, a fusion reached in the 10th-century Mainz Romano-Germanic Pontifical. This new composite rite reached Rome about the year 1000 and in the course of the 13th century was further modified by the additions of Duranti. What we have today is therefore the Romano-Gallican ritual as amended by Duranti.

In the new ritual for the ordination of priests the bishop first enquired about the fitness of the candidate and tested his willingness to receive the priesthood and remain in it and to obey the bishop. After the prayer of consecration, *Emitte quaesumus,* the new priest was clothed in priestly vestments (stole and chasuble) with appropriate formulas. The prayer *Deus sanctificationum* was added to the ancient Roman prayers. Some scholars believe that this added prayer was the essential formula of the older Gallican ritual before it was fused with the Roman rite. The new priest's hands were anointed with

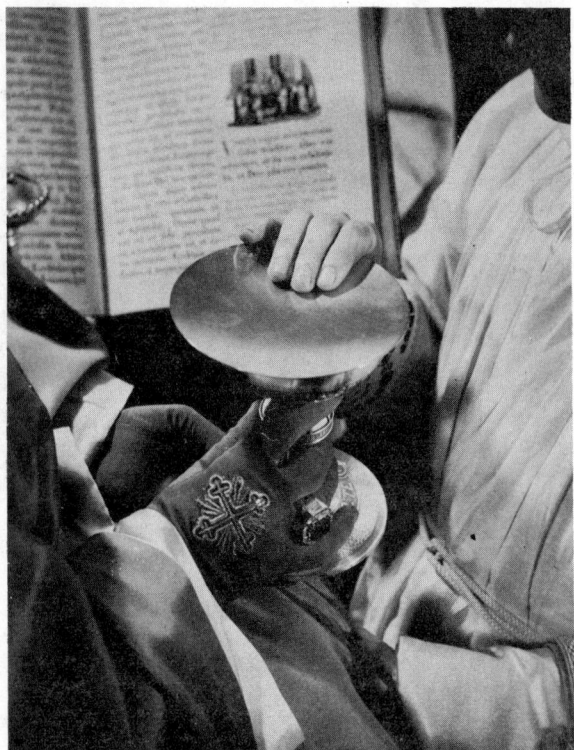

Fig. 4. Presentation of an empty chalice and paten to a subdeacon, deputing him to assist the priest at Mass.

holy oil and he was presented with the chalice and paten containing the wine and the bread. The words *Accipe potestatem* accompanied this *traditio instrumentorum.* The ordination concluded with the special blessing *Ut sitis benedicti in ordine sacerdotali* now given at the end of Mass.

There is a different emphasis in this new rite. While the ancient Roman ordination prayer emphasized the fact that the newly ordained entered the *presbyterium* and became the coworker of the bishop, the new additions underscore the doctrine of the sacrificing priesthood and see the priest primarily as celebrant of the Mass. While something could be said in favor of these innovations taken singly, the general effect in the eyes of discriminating people was to burden heavily a rite that had already departed considerably from the simplicity and sobriety of the ancient Roman ritual.

All these additions had entered into the Frankish service books in the course of the 9th century from various sources. The anointing of the hands, for example, appeared for the first time in the *Missale Francorum* (6th-7th century) that originated in Poitiers (8.33; Mohlberg 10). Since Irish influence was strong in that city, scholars argue from this that the anointing of the hands is Irish in origin. At first chrism was used for this anointing, but by the 13th century the oil of the catechumens had replaced the chrism, at least in Rome. The present custom was definitively fixed by Duranti. The presentation of chalice and paten containing unconsecrated bread and wine, which caused so much discussion among theologians in later times, arose during the 9th century in Gallican lands. It was accepted by the Mainz Pontifical in 950 and from that passed into all subsequent Roman books.

From Duranti come most of the rites added at the end of the present ordination Mass: the antiphon *Jam non dico vos,* the recitation of the Apostles' Creed, the final imposition of hands with *Accipe Spiritum Sanctum; quorum peccata retinueris . . .,* the unfolding of the chasuble, the promise of reverence and obedience, and the final admonition *Quia res quam tracturi estis.* Concelebration by the newly ordained with the bishop comes from the 13th century. Although Duranti spoke only of a silent optional concelebration, the present practice was already established in the 13th-century Pontifical of the Roman Curia.

The ordination to the diaconate underwent a parallel development to that of the priesthood in the medieval Romano-Gallican ritual. Like the priests, deacons were clothed in the vestments of their office after the prayer of consecration; they received the book of the Gospels as the symbol of their office as heralds of the Gospel. The ordination ended with the prayer *Domine sancte spei fidei . . .,* which is found originally in the *Missale Francorum* (7.26; Mohlberg 7); it may have been the consecration prayer of the old Gallican ordination rite.

In the modern ritual of ordination of deaconship is found once again the influence of Duranti. He added to what was in the Romano-Gallican ritual, modified it, and changed it in many details. He added the opening instruction on the duties of the deacon. He made the already existing prayer of consecration into a preface like the Preface at Mass, with introductory dialogue and *Vere dignum.* Moreover, he introduced the formula *Accipe spiritum sanctum.*

Subdiaconate. Here again we have a rite that from original simplicity has reached great elaborateness. Until the later part of the 12th century, in fact, the subdiaconate was considered a minor order, and so the ritual for the ordination of subdeacons was almost like that for minor orders. Thus, according to the *Apostolic Tradition* (13; Botte LQF 32) he received no imposition of hands but was simply nominated to assist the deacon. In the 6th century we find that there was a ritual for his ordination consisting of the delivery of an empty chalice (John the Deacon, *Epist. ad Senarium* 10; PL 59:405). Then the 8th-century Roman Ordinal 34 says that he first took an oath that he had not committed any crime that would bar him from orders. Upon this he received the chalice and the same blessing that was given to the acolytes (Andrieu OR 3:604).

Like the other ordination rituals, that for subdeacons was more fully developed in the Gallican lands. There the 6th-century apocryphal document known as the *Statuta Ecclesiae Antiqua* inspired the Frankish Sacramentaries and their ordination rituals. We find that in the Gallican rite the archdeacon presents the subdeacon with a cruet of water and the towel, in addition to the chalice presented by the bishop. The *Missale Francorum* (6.17; Mohlberg 5) is the first to provide a formula to go with the giving of the chalice; it is much longer than the modern form, though it begins with the same words *Vide cujus ministerium tibi traditur . . ..* The Romano-Germanic Pontifical has a developed rite similar to that for the ordination to minor orders.

The changes in the rite made during the 13th century had as their obvious purpose to give more dignity to the subdiaconate, which by the 12th century had ac-

Fig. 5. Delivery of the Sacred Scriptures to a lector at his ordination.

quired the status of a major order. Again most of these changes were the work of Duranti, who either invented or popularized the investiture with amice, tunic, and maniple; composed the instruction about the liturgical duties of the subdeacon; and inserted the delivery of the Epistle book. What is more, he advanced the singing of the Litany of the Saints so that it would include the candidates for subdeaconship as well as for deaconship and priesthood.

The effect of all this was to make the ordination of the subdeacon superficially similar to the ordination of priests and deacons. But a closer look at the rite reveals the absence of the imposition of hands and the consecratory preface, which, of course, is what really makes the difference. Strangely enough, Duranti did not include the admonition to observe celibacy. This was added only in the 15th-century Roman Pontifical, long after his time.

Minor Orders. The modern ritual for each of the minor orders is very simple in comparison with that of the major orders: (1) an admonition concerning the duties of the office, (2) the presentation of the instruments proper to each order together with a formula indicating the power thus conferred, and (3) a concluding prayer begging God's blessing. Nevertheless this ceremonial is a development of the original rite.

While the third of the Solemn Prayers on Good Friday gives the full list of minor orders as we know them today (with the addition of subdeaconship, which was considered a minor order until the 12th century), the Roman Ordinals speak only of the ordination of lectors, acolytes, and subdeacons—an indication that the other minor orders had by that time fallen into disuse.

Lectors were usually young boys. If a father wanted

to offer one of his sons to be a lector, he had to instruct the lad in reading and then propose him to the pope as a candidate. On a prearranged day he was tested by being made to read a selection at the night vigil. If he passed the test he was then and there ordained a lector by what is surely the shortest ordination formula on record. The pope blessed him with the words "With Blessed Peter the Apostle the Blessed Paul the chosen vessel interceding for you, may the Lord save and protect you and bestow a learned tongue upon you" (*Ordo Rom.* 35.4; Andrieu OR 4.33).

Acolytes were ordained during Mass while bishops and priests were distributing Communion to the people. Since their principal function was to carry the Eucharist to the absent and present the consecrated bread to the priests for the fraction of the Host during Mass, the presentation of the *sacculum,* or little bag to carry the Eucharist, was an important part of the ordination rite. The candidate was first vested in chasuble and stole, then presented to the pope who gave him the *sacculum.* He received this in his hands, which were covered with the folds of the chasuble. Then he prostrated before the pope, who said the blessing over him (*Ordo Rom.* 35.8; Andrieu OR 4:34).

This ritual for the minor orders was much developed by the Romano-Germanic Pontifical, which also revived the other minor orders that had fallen into disuse, porter and exorcist. Already there was a tradition in the Frankish lands of such ordinations as in the *Missale Francorum* (2–5; Mohlberg 4). This Gallican ritual was in turn derived ultimately from the famous apocryphal work the *Statuta ecclesiae antiqua* (Andrieu OR 3:615–619), which originated in southern France at the begin-

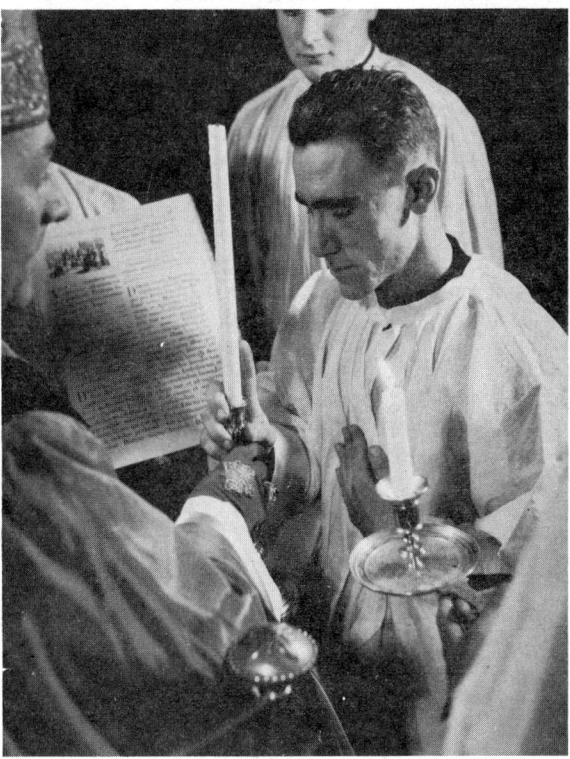

Fig. 6. Presentation of a candle to the ordinand as part of the rite of ordination of an acolyte.

ning of the 6th century. These Gallican practices found their way into the Romano-Germanic Pontifical and from that into the Roman Pontificals of the Middle Ages. Duranti's only contribution was to enlarge the admonition given at the beginning of the ordination to each order.

See also ACOLYTE; BISHOP (SACRAMENTAL THEOLOGY OF); DEACON; DEACONESS; EXORCIST; LECTOR; PORTER; PRIEST AND PRIESTHOOD, CHRISTIAN; SUBDEACON; TONSURE.

Bibliography: M. ANDRIEU, "Les Ordres mineurs dans l'ancien rit romain," RevScRel 5 (1925) 232–274. B. KLEINHEYER, *Die Priesterweihe im römischen Ritus* (Trier 1962). G. ELLARD, *Ordination Anointings in the Western Church before 1000 A.D.* (Cambridge, Mass. 1933). Miller FundLit 475–495. A. G. MARTIMORT, ed., *L'Église en prière* (Tournai 1961) 477–513. Righetti 4:204–270. Eisenhofer Lit 386–404. **Illustration credits:** Fig. 1, Photo Archives-Maria Laach. Figs. 2 to 6, Photo Jean Fortier, Paris.

[W. J. O'SHEA]

ORDINES JUDICIARII

A type of legal literature that flourished from the 12th to the 16th century. The *ordines* were treatises that described procedure in courts. Although some dealt exclusively with procedure in ecclesiastical courts, it was more common, at least from the 13th century, for them to treat also of civil procedure, according to Roman law and Canon Law. The similarities between the two procedures were more significant than the differences.

Purpose. The *ordines* were practical in purpose and design. They described, sometimes in extraordinary detail, judicial procedure step by step, from initial citation to final sentence and appeal. Some *ordines* treated only specific parts of judicial procedure (e.g., the examination of witnesses). The medieval *ordines* varied considerably in length, from just a single folio to a large folio volume. The distinction between the *ordines* and other similar works, namely formularies and *consuetudines,* was not precise (*see* FORMULARIES, MEDIEVAL). Generally speaking, formularies were collections of forms of instruments used in a legal action. Yet many formularies arranged the forms according to the steps followed in court and, in addition, introduced the forms with rubrics; this made them not wholly unlike many *ordines* which contained examples of forms. The formularies, however, were of greatest utility to notaries; the *ordines,* to practicing lawyers. The *consuetudines* described the procedural practice actually in use in a specific court without references to laws, canons, and authors; the *ordines,* on the other hand, stated general procedural principles with the usual references, besides including frequent references to regional and local laws and customs.

Important Examples. The earliest extant *ordo* is probably the very short *Excerpta legum edita a Bulgarino causidico,* composed before 1140. The Anglo-Norman school of canonists in their notable production of canonical works of great variety during the 12th century was responsible for many *ordines* (e.g., Ulpianus, Otto of Paris). An anonymous *ordo* called *Ordo iudiciarius Causa II, quaestio I* was completed in 1171, probably at Amiens or Reims; and before the end of the same century there appeared the *Ordo iudiciarius Bambergensis* (c. 1182–85), the *Rhetorica ecclesiastica* (c. 1190), and other *ordines* by such canonists as Peter

Blois, William Longchamp, Peter de Cadorna, Eilbertus of Bremen, and Ricardus Anglicus. The treatise *Actor et reus,* a procedural dialogue, was composed in England in the early years of Innocent III's pontificate. Another important and popular *ordo* was that of *Tancred (c. 1214–16). It underwent many redactions, was translated into French and German, and became the model for subsequent *ordines.*

Those *ordines* composed after 1234 took account of the procedural titles in the Decretals of *Gregory IX. Among the extant treatises from this period are those by Gratia of Arezzo (after 1234), Peter Penerchio (*Scientiam, c.* 1235–40), *William of Drogheda (*Summa aurea,* 1239), Master Arnulph (*Summa minorum, c.* 1250–54), and the lay canonist *Giles of Foscarari (*c.* 1263–66).

This type of canonical treatise reached its highest peak with the *Speculum iudiciale* of William *Duranti the Elder, in 1272, which underwent redactions, acquired additions, and became the standard procedural treatise for the late Middle Ages. It exercised a commanding influence on the treatises written by John Urbach and John Berberius in the 15th century and by Ulrich Tenngler in the early 16th century.

Bibliography: *Tractatus universi juris duce et auspice Gregorio XIII,* 18 v. (Venice 1584–86). L. WAHRMUND, ed., *Quellen zur Geschichte des römisch-kanonischen Processes im Mittelalter,* 5 v. (Innsbruck-Heidelberg 1905–31). H. KANTOROWICZ and W. W. BUCKLAND, *Studies in the Glossators of the Roman Law* (Cambridge, Eng. 1938). Kuttner. S. KUTTNER and E. RATHBONE, "Anglo-Norman Canonists of the 12th Century," *Traditio* 7 (1949–51) 279–358. Schulte. Van Hove, v.1. A. M. STICKLER, DDC 6:1132–43.

[F. D. LOGAN]

ORDO, ROMAN, basically a calendar needed for the daily celebration of the proper Mass and Office in use throughout the Roman rite. In a ready, abbreviated format, it reduces to practice the many rubrical laws and customs that dictate the rank and content of the liturgical offices. It not only regulates the annual interplay of the temporal and sanctoral cycles, the fixed and moveable feasts, but it also notes any peculiar rubrics and gives seasonal pastoral reminders the faithful will need. Because of special liturgical offices, local churches and monastic groups may vary from the Roman Ordo. The modern Ordo is but the development of local calendars and priests' rubrical and pastoral directories; it became a necessity after Trent decreed a uniform liturgy.

[R. T. CALLAHAN]

ORÉ, LUIS GERÓNIMO DE

Franciscan linguist and bishop; b. Ayacucho, Peru, 1554; d. Concepción, Chile, Jan. 30, 1630. He was one of 11 children (4 of the boys became Franciscan priests, 5 of the girls became Poor Clares, and 1 son became a diocesan priest), who were educated at home with special instruction in music, both instrumental and vocal. He grew up speaking Spanish, Quechua, and Aymará. After being ordained in Lima on Dec. 31, 1582, Oré labored first in Lima, preaching on Sundays and holydays to the Indians gathered in the plaza before the cathedral. He also helped to translate into Quechua the catechism of the Third Council of Lima. He spent the years 1584 to 1598 as a missionary among the Collaguas Indians of southern Peru. This experience enabled him to write *Símbolo cathólico indiano* (Lima 1598), a synthesis of the material taught to the Indians together with many hymns translated or composed by Oré. Many of these are sung today. In 1598 he was appointed vicar of the convent of Lima, and he taught courses in the Indian languages Quechua and Aymará. This work was interrupted by an invitation from Antonio de Raya, Bishop of Cuzco, to supervise the instruction of the Indians in his diocese. Other bishops soon gave him similar powers in Arequipa, La Paz, and Charcas. In 1604 he went to Rome to present the *ad limina* report of Bishop Raya to the Pope. While in Rome he printed in Latin *Conciones per annum* (1606), a work that he had prepared earlier in Quechua and Aymará but had not received royal permission to print in those languages. He published also *Tratado de indulgentiis* (1606) and, perhaps his greatest work, *Rituale seu manuale peruanum* (Naples 1607). This was intended primarily for the missionary in Peru with a special catechism for confession and Communion. It was printed in Latin, Spanish, Quechua, Aymará, Mochica, Puquina, Guaraní, and Brazilian. The Puquina sections are probably the largest fragments of that language still extant. In Spain on his way home, when news of the death of Francis Solano (1610) arrived, Oré was charged with the task of collecting information in Spain for his cause. By 1613 the task was finished and was published as *Relación de la vida y milagros del Venerable P. Fray Francisco Solano* (Madrid 1614). It remains the best source on the life of Francis before he left Spain.

In 1614 Oré led a group of Franciscan missionaries to Florida to inspect the Franciscan missions there and in Cuba. He organized the Franciscan province of Florida and moved the provincial's residence and the novitiate from St. Augustine to Havana. This novitiate was probably the first institution of its kind within the present limits of the United States. On his return to Spain in 1618, Oré published *Relación de los mártires de la Florida*. Shortly thereafter the King named him bishop of Concepción (formerly La Imperial), Chile. He was consecrated in Lima in 1621, and arrived in his see the next year. His diocese was in a deplorable condition: it had been vacant for 14 years, and Indian rebels had dominated the region of Osorno and Valdivia for 20 years, cutting communications between the northern and southern parts of the diocese. Oré visited his diocese three times, began a seminary, and energetically promoted the conversion of the Indians while protecting their rights through laws drawn up in a diocesan synod. He willed his fine library to the Franciscan friary in Concepción.

Bibliography: L. G. DE ORÉ, *The Martyrs of Florida, 1513–1616*, ed. and tr. J. M. GEIGER (New York 1937), also in Franc Studies 18 (1936), whole issue.

[A. S. TIBESAR]

OREGON

A state in northwest U.S. admitted (1859) to the Union as the 33d state. Oregon is bounded on the north by Washington, from which it is separated by the Columbia River; on the east by Idaho and the Snake River; on the south by Nevada and California; and on the west by the Pacific Ocean. Salem is the capital, and Portland is a major center of population on the Willamette River near its junction with the Columbia.

History. During the period that the Oregon Country was jointly occupied by Great Britain and the U.S. (1818–46), it was the home of explorers and fur traders. Gradually the Hudson's Bay Company, under the guidance of Dr. John *McLoughlin at Fort Vancouver, dominated the territory. The first resident priests in the area included two from Quebec, Francis Norbert Blanchet and Modeste Demers, who began (1838) their missionary activities among the French-Canadians and native Indians. The first Mass (1839) was offered in the small log church built (1836) by the pioneers at French-Prairie; it was blessed under the title of St. Paul the Apostle and became Blanchet's headquarters in the early years. In 1840 Pierre J. *De Smet, SJ, visited the Indians in the far eastern part of the Oregon Country; 2 years later he visited Blanchet and Demers at Vancouver to plan for the future development of the Church in Oregon. The advent of large numbers of Americans after 1843 brought trouble with the British. One of the slogans of the 1844 election in the U.S. was "54°40' or fight," but diplomacy prevailed and in 1846 the boundary line was set at 49° north latitude. Somewhat prematurely the Holy See in 1846 established the Archdiocese of Oregon City and two suffragan sees at Walla Walla and Vancouver Island. Blanchet, named archbishop, sought funds and personnel in Europe for his new see and returned in 1847 with 21 missionaries, including 8 priests and 7 sisters. Unfortunately, however, Oregon City failed to develop, and in 1862 Blanchet transferred his episcopal residence to *Portland, which in 1928 officially became the seat of the archdiocese. Meanwhile the territory east of the Cascade Mountains was established (1903) as the Diocese of *Baker City. By 1926 the Catholic population had reached 61,036 in the state's total of about 900,000. In the total state population of 1,521,-341 in 1952 Catholics constituted 7.3 per cent; Protestants, 19.9 per cent; Jews, 0.5 per cent; and all others, 72.3 per cent (*see* CHURCH MEMBERSHIP, U.S.). In 1965 Catholics numbered 222,672 in the state total of 1,901,-989.

Education. A state law of 1922, designed to force all children up to the age of 16 to attend public schools, was declared unconstitutional (1925) by the U.S. Supreme Court in the famous *Oregon School Case. Among Oregon's institutions of higher education are the University of Oregon, at Eugene; Oregon State University, at Corvallis; Lewis and Clark College and Reed College, at Portland; Willamette University, at Salem; and three Catholic institutions: the University of Portland, under the Holy Cross Fathers; Marylhurst College for women, under the Sisters of the Holy Names; and Mt. Angel College, operated by the Benedictine sisters. Public elementary school enrollment in the 1960s exceeded 272,000, and public high schools, 128,000. There were (1965) under Catholic auspices 86 elementary schools (24,497 students) and 17 high schools (5,655 students), with approximately 26,000 additional students receiving religious instruction in released-time programs.

Church-State Relations. References to and provisions affecting religion are incorporated in the state constitution and in acts of the legislature and the judiciary.

Constitution. Oregon is governed by the Constitution of 1859, as amended. "All men shall be secure in the natural right to worship Almighty God according to the dictates of their own conscience" (art. 1, sec. 2).

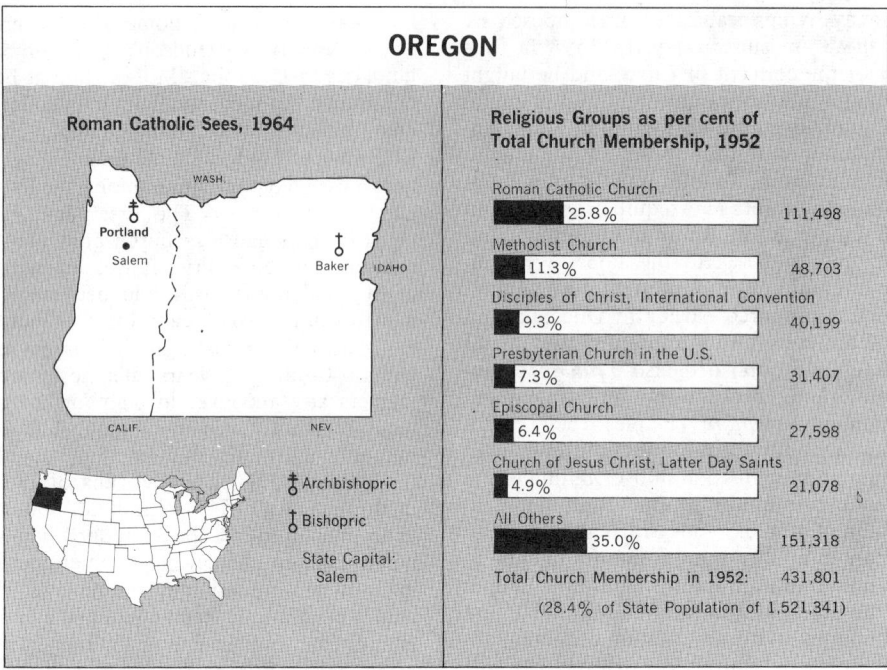

OREGON

Roman Catholic Sees, 1964

WASH.

Portland
● Salem

Baker   IDAHO

CALIF.   NEV.

✚ Archbishopric
○

✝ Bishopric
○

State Capital:
Salem

Religious Groups as per cent of Total Church Membership, 1952

Roman Catholic Church
25.8%   111,498

Methodist Church
11.3%   48,703

Disciples of Christ, International Convention
9.3%   40,199

Presbyterian Church in the U.S.
7.3%   31,407

Episcopal Church
6.4%   27,598

Church of Jesus Christ, Latter Day Saints
4.9%   21,078

All Others
35.0%   151,318

Total Church Membership in 1952:   431,801
(28.4% of State Population of 1,521,341)

Church-membership statistics were compiled by the Bureau of Research and Survey of the National Council of the Churches of Christ in the U.S.A.

"No law shall in any case whatever control the free exercise and enjoyment of religious opinions, or interfere with the rights of conscience" (art. 1, sec. 3). "No religious test shall be required as a qualification for any office of trust or profit" (art. 1, sec. 4). No public money may be used for religion (art. 1, sec. 5). There shall be no religious test for witnesses or jurors (art. 1, sec. 6).

"The mode of administering an oath or affirmation shall be such as may be most consistent with, and binding upon, the conscience of the person to whom such oath or affirmation may be administered" (art. 1, sec. 7).

Article 7 (amended), sec. 7, states that judges of the supreme court must take an oath or affirmation before entering office.

Persons whose religious tenets or conscientious scruples forbid them to bear arms shall not be compelled to do so (art. 10, sec. 2).

"Every person elected or appointed to any office under this constitution shall, before entering on the duties thereof, take an oath or affirmation to support the Constitution of the United States, and of this state, and also an oath of office" (art. 15, sec. 3).

Marriage and Divorce. Marriages of men under 18 and women under 15 are forbidden. The consent of parents is needed for men under 21 and women under 18. A license and blood test are required. Certain public officials and members of the clergy are authorized to perform the ceremony. Common-law marriages are not recognized.

Marriages are void if either spouse is bound by a prior subsisting marriage; if the parties are related by blood in any degree of the direct line and up to and including first cousins. Marriages may be annulled on the grounds of nonage, mental incapacity, force, and fraud.

The grounds for absolute divorce are: impotency at the time of marriage and continuing to the start of the suit; adultery; conviction of a felony; drunkenness that was contracted after marriage and is habitual, gross, and continuing for 1 year prior to bringing the suit; willful desertion for 1 year; cruelty or indignities rendering life burdensome; permanent insanity when it was legally adjudicated as such 3 years before the suit and there has been confinement for the major portion of the 3 years. Neither party may remarry for 6 months from the time of decree or if an appeal is taken, until it is disposed of. *See* MARRIAGE, U.S. LAW OF; DIVORCE (U.S. LAW OF).

Abortion, Birth Control, Sterilization. The law forbids *abortion unless it is necessary to preserve the mother's life. If any person administers to any pregnant woman any medicine, drug, or substance whatever, or uses or employs any instrument or other means with intent thereby to destroy the child, he is guilty of manslaughter if the mother or child dies.

The law restricts *birth control. A license is required for the advertising and dispensing or sale of contraceptives, except in cases of physicians, medical practitioners, or periodicals substantially limited to physicians or the drug trade. No contraceptive may be sold, offered for sale, or given away through the medium of any vending machine or by house to house solicitation (*see* ANOVULANTS; CONTRACEPTION).

The law permits *sterilization in cases of persons who are insane, feebleminded, habitual criminals, incurable syphilitics, moral degenerates, or sexual perverts and who are or are likely to become a menace to society or would produce children likely to have these traits. Certain safeguards are set up to protect the rights of the patient.

Property and Taxation. Religious and charitable institutions may incorporate under the Non-Profit Corporation Statutes. A religious society may be formed as a corporation sole in which property is vested and the bishop and his successors act as the corporation sole.

Real and personal property of religious and charitable societies not run for profit and used exclusively for their intended purposes is exempt from taxation.

There is no mortmain statute.

There are certain restrictions on fund raising; these do not apply to religious or charitable organizations soliciting funds from their own members.

Prisons and Reformatories. The board of control shall ensure that adequate chaplaincy services, including but not limited to Protestant and Roman Catholic, are available at all state institutions administered by the board. The chaplains shall provide for and attend to the prisoners' spiritual needs, visit them for the purpose of giving religious and moral instruction, and participate in the rehabilitation programs for them.

Holidays and Sunday Observance. Sunday, Christmas and New Year's Day, the first Monday in September, Thanksgiving Day, general election day, days appointed by the president or governor, February 12, February 22, May 30, July 4, October 12, and November 11 are legal holidays. When a holiday falls on Sunday, the next day is a holiday. Holiday transactions are valid. No person may carry on the business of barbering or pawnbroking on Sunday. No license may be granted for horse racing; boxing matches or exhibitions may not be held on Sunday.

Morality, Public Health, and Safety. No state condones polygamy. Any person who willfully disturbs an assembly of people gathered for religious worship may be punished by imprisonment from 1 to 6 months or by a fine of $10 to $200. Nothing in the administra-

tion of health laws may interfere with the practices of any person or institution whose religion treats or administers to the sick or suffering by purely spiritual means, but sanitary laws and regulations must be complied with. The slaughter of certain livestock in accordance with the ritual requirements of any religious faith is allowed if done in the humane manner set forth by statute. The statutes on Health Professions generally do not affect or prevent the practice of the religion of persons who endeavor to prevent or cure disease or suffering by prayer or other spiritual means, in accordance with the tenets of any church. In *Baer v. City of Bend,* 229 P (2) 134 (1956), the Oregon supreme court held that a city fluoridation ordinance was not offensive to constitutional guarantees of religious liberty.

Various Constitutional Freedoms. A city ordinance forbidding boys under 10 and girls under 18 to sell periodicals in the streets and penalizing parents or guardians who permit such minors to do so was found not unconstitutional as denying freedom of worship when applied to a member of a religious sect who furnished religious periodicals to her daughter under 18 and permitted the girl to sell these in the streets [*City of Portland v. Thornton,* 149 P (2) 972].

Religious bigotry or intolerance is not a *mala in se* (wrong in and of itself) until actions motivated by intolerant extremes of bigotry contravene the positive law or invade the boundaries of established public policy. The law will then repress such illegal excesses and in proper cases levy tolls on offenders as reparation to those who have been offended [*U.S. Nat. Bank of Portland v. Snodgrass,* 275 P (2) 860].

Reasonable regulations of time and place for the exercise of freedom of religion or speech are valid

Church of St. Thomas More near Portland, Ore.; designed in 1938 by P. Belluschi, built entirely of native wood.

[*Milwaukee Co. of Jehovah's Witnesses v. Mullen*, 330 P (2) 5].

Bibliography: G. W. FULLER, *A History of the Pacific Northwest* (New York 1931). D. O. JOHANSEN and C. M. GATES, *Empire of the Columbia: A History of the Pacific Northwest* (New York 1957). *Oregon Statutes*, Revised, 6 v. (Salem, Ore. 1953-to date). *Oregon Compiled Laws, Annotated 1939* (San Francisco, Calif. 1940). *New Oregon Digest*, 23 v. (San Francisco, Calif. 1961). **Illustration credit:** Fig. 2, Condit Studio.

[M. P. CARTHY]

OREGON SCHOOL CASE

The Oregon School case (*Pierce v. Society of Sisters*, 268 U.S. 510), handed down in 1925 by the U.S. Supreme Court, upheld the right of parents to control the education of their children, when it declared unconstitutional a law that would have made attendance at public schools mandatory.

Background of the Oregon Law. The attempt to divest parents of their right to control the education of their children grew out of the May 1920 resolution of the Masons of the Scottish rite of the southern jurisdiction advocating ". . . the free and compulsory education of the children of our nation in public primary schools. . . ." The procedural plan adopted by the proponents of this move bypassed legislative action. It was decided to have a direct vote of the people on the measure through use of the initiative procedure. Accordingly, in a spectacular 1-day campaign under the direction of the Scottish-rite Masons of Oregon, sufficient signatures were obtained to place on the ballot for the general election in November 1922 an initiative measure to compel children between the ages of 8 and 16 to attend the public schools of Oregon.

Any doubt concerning the sponsorship of the initiative measure was dispelled by an advertisement in Oregon newspapers by P. S. Malcolm, Inspector General of Oregon Scottish-rite Masons, stating that the anti-private school measure was sponsored by the supreme council, Scottish rite for the southern jurisdiction of the U.S., the grand lodge of Oregon, and the imperial council of the nobles of the mystic shrine (*Catholic Sentinel*, Aug. 3, 1922).

Arguments against passage of the initiative measure were filed with the secretary of state by Catholic organizations, Seventh-day Adventists, Episcopalians, Lutherans, Presbyterians, principals of private schools, and a citizen taxpayer association. The lone argument in behalf of the measure was filed by the Scottish-rite Masons.

Those opposing the measure argued that: (1) The title was deceptive to the extent that the measure is described as a compulsory education law. Compulsory education was already a part of the law of the state together with the regulation of private schools. (2) The proposal would deprive the schools and teachers of their property rights under the 14th Amendment to the Federal Constitution. (3) Parents would be deprived of religious liberty, that is, the right to rear and educate their children in accordance with the dictates of conscience.

The Masonic argument was based on the following propositions: (1) "Our nation supports the public school for the sole purpose of self-preservation." (2) "The assimilation and education of our foreign-born citizens in the principles of our government, the hopes and inspiration of our people, are best secured by and through attendance of all children in our public schools." (3) "We must now halt those coming to our country from forming groups, establishing schools, and thereby bringing up their children in an environment often antagonistic to the principles of our government." (4) "Mix the children of the foreign-born with the native-born, and the rich with the poor. Mix those with prejudices in the public school melting pot for a few years while their minds are plastic, and finally bring out the finished product—a true American." (5) "The permanency of this nation rests in the education of its youth in our public schools, where they will be correctly instructed in the history of our country and the aims of our government, and in those fundamental principles of freedom and democracy, reverence and righteousness, where all shall stand upon one common level." (6) "When every parent in our land has a child in our public schools, then and only then will there be united interest in the growth and higher efficiency of our public schools." (7) "Our children must not under any pretext, be it based upon money, creed or social status, be divided into antagonistic groups, there to absorb the narrow views of life as they are taught. If they are so divided, we will find our citizenship composed and made up of cliques, cults and factions each striving, not for the good of the whole, but for the supremacy of themselves. A divided school can no more succeed than a divided nation."

This attack on private schools was not limited to the state of Oregon. Similar legislation was pending in Michigan and California and threatened in Washington, Indiana, Nebraska, and several other states. Throughout the country, newspaper editorials alerted the people to the widespread nature of the proposed legislation.

In Oregon a bitter campaign ensued. Newspaper headlines shouted the divided and bitter feelings of the people. The *New York Post* underscored an important element in this controversy, namely, that the *Ku Klux Klan was actively supporting the initiative measure.

The combination of forces opposed to parochial schools was sufficient to give the proposal a 15,000 plurality and it became law. By its terms it would become operative in 1926.

Struggle in the Courts. Opponents of compulsory attendance in public schools turned to the courts for redress. At this juncture the bishops of the U.S. entered the contest through the recently formed *National Catholic Welfare Conference. The *St. Louis Progress* reported that the Bishops' Committee met in Chicago and the "outstanding result of the gathering was the unanimous decision to get behind a test of the Oregon school law in both State and Federal Courts with all of the moral, spiritual and financial aid necessary, and to use every legitimate means to secure the law's repeal" (Jan. 25, 1923).

In addition to financial aid, the NCWC, through its press department, gave wide coverage to all aspects of the Oregon law and created a national awareness of its implications. The education department and other departments of the NCWC prepared a series of pamphlets on the law, the rights of parents in the education of their children, and the traditional understanding of the Constitution. This material not only aroused the country but, in the words of Father John Burke, General Secretary of the NCWC, "intelligently guided it."

In 1923 legal action was initiated in the Federal District Court to test the constitutionality of the Oregon law. In the same year the Supreme Court rendered a decision in the case of *Meyer v. Nebraska* (262 U.S. 390), which had a very important bearing on the Oregon school law litigation. The Meyer case was an important precedent for the decision in the Pierce case.

Meyer v. Nebraska Precedent. The Nebraska statute provided that no foreign language could be taught in the nonpublic schools of the state. It was enacted in an atmosphere of hostility to private schools—the same legislature having come within one vote of adopting a law that would have forced all children to attend public schools. The Supreme Court of Nebraska upheld the constitutionality of the law, and an appeal was taken to the Supreme Court of the U.S.

In the course of the oral argument an interesting colloquy took place between Mr. Arthur Mullen, attorney for the plaintiff, and Mr. Justice McReynolds. Mr. Mullen argued very forcefully that the Nebraska legislation involved more than a denial of the property right of the teachers. He indicated that in the last analysis the legislation was directed at the right of the parents to send their children to private schools. At this point Mr. Justice McReynolds interposed, saying: "How did they abolish private schools? Did the State prohibit private schools?" Replying, Mr. Mullen observed: "I say, your Honor, that they could no more abolish private schools than they could—" Mr. Justice McReynolds broke in: "I just wanted to see what you claim. What about the power of the State to require the children to attend the public schools? . . . You will admit that, will you not?" Mr. Mullen's reply was clear and definitive: "I do not admit that. *I deny that a State can, by a majority of the legislature, require me to send my child to the public schools.*"

He then proceeded to develop the proposition that the parental right is within the liberty guaranteed by the 14th Amendment. In conjunction with this argument, Mr. Mullen observed that there was a close connection between the exercise of the parental right and freedom of religion. In a colloquy with Chief Justice Taft, he argued that the liberty that is guaranteed by the 14th Amendment includes religious freedom. Mr. Mullen, in taking this position, laid the basis for the eventual argument that the right to send children to a parochial school rests not only on *parental right* but also upon *religious freedom.*

Paradoxically, the Justice who intimated that the state had a right to ban all private schools wrote the opinion for the court invalidating the Nebraska statute. In the course of his opinion, he stated: "[Plaintiff's] right . . . to teach and the right of parents to engage him so to instruct their children, we think, are within the liberty of the [14th] Amendment."

He observed collaterally that, among other rights, the 14th Amendment includes the right to the free exercise of one's religion. Admittedly, this was not the primary basis for the decision. It rested on the property right of the teacher and the right of parents whose children attended the schools in question. Nevertheless, this was the first time in the history of the Supreme Court that the parental right to educate was even obliquely associated with religious freedom. It was a decision that broke new ground and provided a fertile field for the growth of principles establishing the right to educate.

The Court's recognition of the parental right and its association of religious liberty with this right represented a tremendous victory, for at the time of this decision private education had its back to the wall. Many states had adopted legislation similar to the Nebraska law. Others were considering or, as in the case of Oregon, had passed laws banning all private schools, and these laws were not originating in legislatures. Through initiatives and referendums the people themselves were waging a war against private schools. The decision of the Supreme Court in the Nebraska case was the beginning of the end of this movement. The Nebraska case had an immediate impact on the Oregon School case by establishing persuasive precedents for the legal arguments of the plaintiffs.

The Federal District Court. Judge John Kavanaugh, appearing for the Sisters of the Holy Names, called the Federal District Court's attention to the Nebraska case and said: "It leaves nothing, your Honors, to be said upon the question. They have recognized the private school, they have upheld its rights." In addition to developing the institution's rights, Judge Kavanaugh commented extensively on the parental right. For example, in his oral argument to the Court, he stated:

> Now people in this country have certain natural and inherent rights. Those rights existed before constitutions were made, and those rights will exist after constitutions are dissolved. They are not created by the constitution, but they are secured by the constitution; and among these rights are the inherent and the natural right of a parent to direct the education of his own child in a private school that conforms to all of the regulations of the state.

The attorney who appeared as the representative of the Scottish-rite bodies, and Governor Walter M. Pierce, argued that the Oregon law was well within the police power of the state, since the state had the right to control education. He also contended that the corporations that brought the action could not rely on asserted rights of parents.

The Federal District Court ruled that the Oregon law was unconstitutional. In so holding it declared: "The absolute right of these schools to teach in the grammar grades, . . . and the right of the parents to engage them to instruct their children, we think, is within the liberty of the Fourteenth Amendment." And on the institutional right the court asserted:

> Compulsory education being the paramount policy of the state, can it be said, with reason and justice, that the right and privilege of parochial and private schools to teach in the common school grades is inimical or detrimental to, or destructive of, that policy? Such schools and their patrons have the same interest in fostering primary education as the state, and appropriate regulation will place them under supervision of school authorities.

Governor Pierce of Oregon announced that the state would appeal from the decision to the U.S. Supreme Court. The issue thereupon became a national one.

The U.S. Supreme Court. In order to ensure the best possible representation before the court the services of William Guthrie were retained. Associated with him in the defense of the parochial and private school interests were Judge Kavanaugh of Portland, Ore., and Garret McEnerney of San Francisco, Calif. In addition to the briefs filed by these attorneys, briefs *amicus curiae* were filed by the Episcopal Church, the Seventh-day Adventists, and the American Jewish Committee, all of whom argued that the Oregon law was unconstitutional. The general tenor of these briefs is reflected in the following excerpt from the brief of the Seventh-day Adventists: "These natural rights [of parents] have been protected by every Bill of Rights declared in any government at any time and are always spoken of as existing, but never as bestowed by government."

The brief of Mr. Guthrie effectively demonstrated that the issues at stake were the maintenance of religious liberty, the inviolability of the parental right against state encroachment, and the institutional right to the protection of its property. A strong brief emphasizing the property rights of private schools was filed by Mr. John C. Veatch on behalf of the Hill Military Academy, one of the plaintiffs in the action.

The attorneys for the state showed a keen appreciation of the arguments predicated on the parental right. An attempt was made to demonstrate that the rights of parents were not violated but that the law merely represented a harmonization of the respective interests of the state and parents. However, in the conclusion of the state's brief, its basic position was stated in the following words: "The necessity for any other kind of school than that provided by the state has ceased to exist. The public school is everywhere recognized as being an institution vital to the welfare of the individual citizen, and to that of the state and nation" (*Oregon School Cases, Complete Record*, p. 200).

At the outset of the oral argument before the Court, Mr. Justice McReynolds put the main issue in focus when he stated to the Attorney General, Mr. Willis S. Moore: "You understand that the sharp issue presented here is whether the State can require a child to go to the public school." Mr. Moore agreed that this was the critical question and then proceeded to argue that the people have the right, in the exercise of the police power, to enact laws requiring all children to attend public schools and that the "limitations of the power are primarily with the people." At this point the Chief Justice suggested that this power is subject to the limitations of the Constitution. The attorney general replied that, since education was a power reserved to the states under the 10th Amendment, the limits of law rest primarily with the people.

Guthrie, in his oral argument, stated that of all the interests invaded, "First and foremost, the law involves the sacred right of parents in the discharge of their duty to educate their children." He then proceeded to point out that manner in which rights of the children, the teachers, and the institutions were violated. All these issues, he stated, involved the maintenance of basic liberties to such an extent that if these rights were denied, the day would come when men would no longer be able to enjoy those "sacred rights which free men cherish and free governments are established to maintain and secure."

Judge Kavanaugh, in the concluding argument, demonstrated that the private schools had complied with all state regulations and that this law was not in the nature of regulation but of destruction. He emphasized that it deprived the institutions of valuable property rights without due process of law.

Within 3 months the Supreme Court rendered its decision, unanimously holding that the Oregon law was unconstitutional. Mr. Justice McReynolds, writing for the court, stated on June 1, 1925:

Under the doctrine of *Meyer v. Nebraska*, 262 U.S. 390, we think it entirely plain that the act of 1922 unreasonably interferes with the liberty of parents and guardians to direct the upbringing and education of children under their control. As often heretofore pointed out, rights guaranteed by the Constitution may not be abridged by legislation which has no reasonable relation to some purpose within the competency of the state. The fundamental theory of liberty upon which all governments in this Union repose excludes any general power of the state to standardize its children by forcing them to accept instruction from public teachers only. The child is not the mere creature of the state; those who nurture him and direct his destiny have the right coupled with the high duty, to recognize and prepare him for additional obligations. [268 U.S. 534.]

Continuing, he pointed out that the schools had been deprived of their property without due process of law. In this connection, Mr. Justice McReynolds observed that the appellee corporations ". . . have business and property for which they claim protection. These are threatened with destruction through the unwarranted compulsion which appellants are exercising over present and prospective patrons of their schools. And this Court has gone very far to protect against loss threatened by such action" (268 U.S. 535).

It is significant to observe that the Supreme Court's decision rested not merely on the property right of the plaintiff corporations. The most important aspect of this decision is the recognition and application of the right of parents to control the education of their children. From the beginning of the controversy to the final decision, this was the predominant argument of those opposing the Oregon school law. From the first arguments filed with the secretary of the state of Oregon challenging the initiative measure, up to and including the final oral argument, reference was constantly made to the proposition that the fundamental freedom at stake was the inalienable right of parents to oversee their children's education.

Reaction and Influence. Within a few days, 490 major editorials were published in 44 states commenting favorably on the decision. Nor was this attitude sectional. The attitude of the press in the South, where the Klan had its origin and where Masonry was strong, was uniformly laudatory.

The articulation of the principle of the parental right in education has had a strong influence on the growth of the nonpublic school system in this country and has been cited in many countries throughout the world in defense of educational freedom. Pius XI in the encyclical *Christian Education of Youth* gave explicit approval to the Supreme Court's decision. It had more than a little influence on the formulation of Article 26(3) of the United Nations' Declaration of Human Rights providing that: "Parents have a prior right to choose the kind of education that shall be given to their children."

See also EDUCATE, LAW OF RIGHT TO (U.S.).

Bibliography: *Oregon School Cases: Complete Record* (Baltimore 1925). N. G. McCLUSKEY, *Catholic Viewpoint on Education* (Garden City 1959). J. T. TINNELLY, "The Right to Educate: The Role of Parents, Church, State," *National Catholic Education Association Bulletin* 55 (1958) 35–46. L. PFEFFER, *Church, State and Freedom* (Boston 1953) 510–519. P. G. KAUPER, *Civil Liberties and the Constitution* (Ann Arbor 1962). J. C. BRUNNER, *A Critical Analysis of the Development of Arguments Against Nonpublic Schools from the Oregon School Case to 1960* (Washington 1960). C. F. ZOLLMANN, *American Church Law* (St. Paul 1933).

[G. E. REED]

O'REILLY, BERNARD, second bishop of Hartford, Conn.; b. Columkille, County Longford, Ireland, 1803; d. at sea, Jan. 23, 1856. He studied at Grand Seminaire, Montreal, Canada, and St. Mary's College, Baltimore, Md., before his ordination in October 1831. He did parish work in Brooklyn and Rochester, N.Y., until 1847, when he became vicar-general of the new Diocese of Buffalo, N.Y. In 1850 he was named to succeed William Tyler as bishop of Hartford. After his consecration at Rochester on November 10, the new bishop concentrated his efforts on obtaining more clergy for a territory served by only seven priests and five churches. In 1851 he brought the Sisters of Mercy into his diocese and courageously protected them from attack by a Know-Nothing mob. He went to Dublin, Ireland, the following year and brought back a number of priests. During his episcopate, he provided the diocese with 34 new churches, 14 new schools, 3 orphan asylums, and St. Mary's Seminary, Providence, R.I., which he founded in 1851. It was on a trip to Europe to seek the help of the Brothers of the Christian Schools that O'Reilly was drowned, when his ship, the "Pacific," sank with all aboard.

[J. L. MORRISON]

O'REILLY, EDMUND, archbishop of Armagh; b. Dublin, 1606; d. Saumur, France, March 1669. O'Reilly was educated and ordained (1629) in Dublin, where he also did parish work. In 1633 he went to the Louvain, where he studied under the Jesuits and Franciscans before his appointment as prefect of Irish secular priests and seminarians resident at the Louvain. O'Reilly returned to Ireland in 1641. He supported the Irish rebellion, serving as governor of Wicklow (1642). Archbishop Thomas Fleming of Dublin appointed him vicar-general and apostolic administrator (1642–48) while Fleming was at Kilkenny, seat of the Catholic Confederation. O'Reilly's sympathies were with the independence faction of the rebels, and he opposed any truce with the royalist James Butler, Marquis of Ormond, who sought Irish aid against the English parliamentary forces. Fleming replaced O'Reilly as vicar-general in 1649 but restored him in 1650. In 1653 O'Reilly was arrested, imprisoned, and charged with a murder that had occurred while he was governor of Wicklow. He was tried (Sept. 6–7, 1654), found guilty, and pardoned; finally, he left Ireland. O'Reilly fled to Lille, where he received his appointment as archbishop of Armagh, although he did not receive the pallium until 1657. He attempted to return to Ireland by way of London, but fearing possible arrest in England, O'Reilly returned to France. It was not until 1659 that he reached Ireland, where he remained until the Stuart restoration (1661). The Spanish ambassador in London accused O'Reilly of anti-Stuart activities, and for this Pope Alexander VII recalled the primate to Rome (1661–65), where he appears to have vindicated himself. In 1665 O'Reilly visited Ireland and attended the national synod held in Dublin (1666). His opposition to the pro-English activities and remonstrance of Father Peter *Walsh angered Ormond, who imprisoned the primate for 3 months. O'Reilly, exiled once again, went to France, where he died.

Bibliography: A. F. POLLARD, DNB 14:1140–41. R. BELLINGS, *History of the Irish Confederation and the War in Ireland, 1641–1649,* ed. J. T. GILBERT, 7 v. (Dublin 1882–91). E. CURTIS, *A History of Ireland* (6th ed. New York 1951). R. BAGWELL, *Ireland under the Stuarts,* 3 v. (London 1909–16).

[P. S. MC GARRY]

O'REILLY, JOHN BOYLE, soldier, editor, author; b. Drogheda, Ireland, June 28, 1844; d. Boston, Mass., Aug. 10, 1890. He was the son of William and Eliza Boyle O'Reilly. After apprenticeship on the Drogheda newspaper *Argus,* he went to Preston, England, to work on the *Guardian.* He served in the British army, returned to Ireland (1863), and joined the revolutionary Fenian movement; he was convicted (1866) of rebellion. After imprisonment in Ireland and England, he was sentenced to 20 years in the penal colony in Western Australia. He escaped and after an odyssey of 9 months, arrived in the U.S. in November 1869, and settled in Boston. In 1870, a few months after joining the Boston *Pilot,* he was appointed editor.

For the next 20 years the *Pilot* was practically O'Reilly's voice, counseling, admonishing, and directing Irish-Americans in their cultural assimilation. With John Joseph *Williams, Archbishop of Boston, O'Reilly became joint-owner of the *Pilot* in 1876. Under the moderating influence of such men as Williams, Patrick *Donahoe, and Patrick Collins, the erstwhile revolutionary O'Reilly became a leader of a conservative, constructive (although at times violent) program of Irish-American acculturation, and independence from England.

O'Reilly's first publications appeared in the *Emerald* (New York), the *Pilot* (Boston), the New York *Tribune,* and the *Dark Blue* (Oxford University). These were soon followed by *Songs from the Southern Seas* (1873), a book of verse. He also published in the *Atlantic Monthly* and *Scribner's Monthly.* Then followed *Songs, Legends and Ballads* (1878), *Statues in the Block* (1881), and his most popular book of verse, *In Bohemia* (1886). His novel *Moondye Joe* (1879) was only moderately successful.

O'Reilly openly campaigned for Democratic party candidates in the *Pilot,* and his incisive observations on the current industrial scene marked him as a leading social reformer. He was prominent in the activities of the Catholic Union of Boston, the *Irish Catholic Colonization Association of the U.S., and several charitable organizations. He was an outspoken proponent of Catholic education; and two universities, Georgetown, Washington, D.C., and Notre Dame, Ind., honored him with the LL.D.

See also IRISH IN THE U.S.; CATHOLIC PRESS, WORLD SURVEY, 27.

Bibliography: F. G. MCMANAMIN, "John Boyle O'Reilly," *Mid America* 43 (Jan. 1961) 36–54; *The American Years of John Boyle O'Reilly, 1870–1890* (Washington 1959). W. G. SCHOFIELD, *Seek for a Hero: The Story of John Boyle O'Reilly* (New York 1956). M. A. FRAWLEY, *Patrick Donahoe* (Washington 1946).

[F. G. MC MANAMIN]

O'REILLY, POTAMIAN, BROTHER, educator, scientist; b. Baillieborough, County Cavan, Ireland, Sept. 29, 1847; d. New York City, Jan. 20, 1917. He was born Michael Francis O'Reilly. With his parents, James and Julia (Finnegan) O'Reilly, he immigrated to New York City. He attended St. Brigid's elementary school, where contact with the Brothers of the Christian Schools inspired his vocation. In 1859 he entered the Montreal, Canada, novitiate. As Brother Potamian he spent the next 57 years educating young men in

Canada, England, Ireland, and the U.S. At St. Joseph's College, London, (1870–93), as professor and then as president, he prepared students for the public examinations and was commended by Cardinals John Henry Newman and Henry Edward Manning. Meanwhile, he became the first Catholic to earn the degree of Doctor of Science from the University of London (1883). In specializing in electricity and magnetism, he was closely associated with Oliver Lodge, Lord Kelvin, James Thompson, and John Fleming. Three months after Roentgen's theoretical paper on the X ray, Brother Potamian, who had been transferred to De La Salle Normal School, Waterford, Ireland, made the first medical use of the X ray in Ireland. His chief scientific contribution, however, was to the history of electrical science. At Manhattan College, N.Y. (1896–1917), where he was professor of physics and first dean of engineering, he contributed to the *Catholic World, Electrical World, Engineering,* and *Popular Science Review.* Among his publications were: *Essays on Electrical Experimenters and Experiments* (1893); *Makers of Electricity* (1909), with J. J. Walsh; and his monumental *Catalogue of the Wheeler Gift of Books, Pamphlets and Periodicals in the Library of the American Institute of Electrical Engineers* (1909), an annotated guide to what was then the most complete electrical library in the world. He contributed to *Electric Illumination* (1882–85) and to the old *Catholic Encyclopedia,* and was a popular lecturer at the Catholic Summer School at Plattsburg, N.Y. Fordham University, N.Y., and Villanova University, Villanova, Pa., awarded him honorary degrees.

Bibliography: W. J. Battersby, *Brother Potamian* (London 1953).

[B. R. Weitekamp]

OREMUS, a Latin word meaning "Let us pray." In the Roman rite it is commonly used by the officiating minister to invite the attention of the faithful to certain prayers of the Mass (Collect, Postcommunion, Pater Noster), the Divine Office, and other liturgical functions. Ordinarily in the Roman rite, the prayer of the officiating minister follows immediately upon the *Oremus;* and this rule is prescribed by the earlier Roman ordinals, such as the *Ordo Romanus I* (ed. M. Andrieu, no.53). On Good Friday, however, the celebrant adds to the *Oremus* a clause specifying the intention for which he invites prayer. On other occasions, such as Ember days and ordinations, the *Oremus* is followed by *Flectamus genua* (Let us kneel) and a period of silent prayer. *Levate* (Rise) is then pronounced, and the celebrant recites his prayer in the name of all. These latter expanded forms of the *Oremus* represent the earlier practice of the Church. In the Eastern rites, the invitation to prayer is usually expressed by the deacon and, commonly, in less succinct fashion than in the Roman rite. In the other Western rites, the *Oremus* is infrequent.

Bibliography: J. A. Jungmann, *The Mass of the Roman Rite,* tr. F. Brunner, 2 v. (New York 1951–55) 1:366–370. P. Siffrin, EncCatt 9:271–272. A. Fortescue, *The Mass* (New York 1912) 247–248.

[E. J. Gratsch]

ORGAN

The name given to a musical instrument consisting of one or more sets of pipes, called ranks, each pipe activated by wind and producing an individual tone.

Fig. 1. Monk playing an organ while another works the bellows, miniature in an antiphonary from Beaupré, France, 1290 (Walters MS 761, fol. 270v, detail).

The wind is mechanically produced and controlled by a keyboard through various types of playing mechanisms that allow the performer, at will, to direct the wind from a common supply to the pipe or pipes of his choice.

Elements of the Organ. In its simplest form the organ consists of one keyboard and one rank of pipes, the number of pipes corresponding to the number of keys. A rank of pipes producing a pitch corresponding to the norm for other keyboard instruments, e.g., the piano, is said to be at 8-foot pitch, since the normal open pipe for the low C key would be approximately 8 feet long. It is impossible to alter the timbre, intensity, or pitch of a pipe in performance; once these have been established in its construction, dynamic and color control is achieved through the use of supplemental ranks of pipes arranged either to give pitches other than that of the unison rank or to yield tones of contrasting color through different modes of pipe construction. The characteristic ensemble sound of the organ is produced primarily by sounding simultaneously a number of ranks of pipes speaking at various octave and fifth pitches. To enable the organist to add and subtract ranks as required, each rank of pipes is fitted with a control device operated by a knob or tablet placed conveniently near the keyboard. Since this device stops the flow of air to the rank it controls, it has come to be called a stop, as has also, for reasons much less clear, the rank of pipes it controls.

Wind-chest and Console. All the pipes controlled by one keyboard typically stand together in rows, hence the term rank, on top of a large table or box called a wind-chest. The wind-chest serves as a storage area for the wind supply and also contains the valves operated from the keyboard and the stop control mechanism.

To broaden further the scope of the instrument and to increase its flexibility in musical performance, the organ is typically furnished with more than one keyboard, each additional keyboard having its own stops standing on separate wind-chests. Therefore, as commonly constructed, the organ may be said to be composed of two or more separate organs or divisions with keyboards and stop controls brought together so that the various parts may be controlled by one performer. In addition, there is usually a separate division of the organ operated from a special keyboard designed to be manipulated by the feet of the performer. The playing desk that contains the manuals (the hand-operated keyboards), pedalboard (the foot-operated keyboard), and stop controls, all arranged as conveniently as possible, is called the console. The console also contains a set of devices called couplers making it possible to operate the various keyboards together or to couple the manuals to the pedal. All of this may be done at either unison or octave pitches, although the trend of improvements in modern tonal design tends to make octave couplers of much less use today than previously.

Action. There are three modes of action in common use today for connecting the console to the wind-chest mechanism. The most common is that known as electropneumatic action in which the keys and stop controls in the console merely operate a complex of electric contacts that are connected by cables to electromagnets in the wind-chests. The electromagnets serve to actuate small valves, which in turn operate a series of pneumatic devices that eventually open valves directly below the pipes in the wind-chest, allowing the wind to pass into the pipe. Another form of action that is rather common, though not widely accepted, is known as direct electric action. This differs from electropneumatic action in that the armature of the electromagnet in the wind-chest is connected directly to the pipe valve. In direct mechanical action, popularly known in England and America as tracker action, the keys and stop controls are directly connected through a series of levers and linkages to the key valves and stop control mechanism in the wind-chest. Although out of vogue for more than a half-century, tracker action is now preferred in Europe and is currently enjoying a revival in North America because of its simplicity and musical superiority.

The various divisions of the organ have acquired traditional names that are more or less descriptive of their musical function, structural relations, or historical origin. Thus we have in English: great organ, swell organ, positive organ, choir organ, pedal organ; in French: grand orgue, positif, récit, écho, bombarde; and in German: Hauptwerk, Brustwerk, Oberwerk, Rückpositiv. The tonal resources of the organ have varied greatly depending upon the particular concept evolved in a given locale.

Pipes. All organ pipes fall into two main classes according to their mode of construction and principle of tone production. These are flue pipes and reed pipes. Flue pipes are constructed of metal or wood and are identical in principle of tone production to the Blockflöte or recorder, although they may vary in size from a pipe 32 feet in length and 15 to 18 inches in diameter

to a pipe only three-fourths of an inch long and one-eighth of an inch in diameter. They may be of either open or stopped construction. A stopped pipe, one having its upper end closed by a tightly fitting cap, produces a tone one octave lower than an open pipe of the same physical length, and has a characteristic tone in which the odd-numbered harmonics are suppressed. The diameter of a pipe considered with respect to its length is called the scale of the pipe. Pipes having relatively large scales produce broad or flutey tones, and pipes of small scale produce bright or stringy tones. Most characteristic of the organ is the tone of the principals, a family of stops composed of open pipes of moderate scale.

The tone-producing part of a reed pipe is a thin tongue of curved spring brass that vibrates against the face of an opening in the side of a long narrow tube, the shallot. The upper end of the shallot communicates directly to the body of the pipe, which is a resonator of appropriate size and shape for the tone desired. Most typical of the reed stops are those with funnel-shaped resonators comprising the trumpet family.

History of the Organ. While ancient writers clearly indicate that the organ played an important part in the ceremonial life of the people of the ancient world, little is known about the early form of the organ prior to the instrument known as the hydraulus, generally attributed to the Greek engineer Ctesibius, active in Alexandria *c.* 250 B.C. The organ pipe itself and a primitive

Fig. 2. The "Bach" or "Dance of Death" organ in the Marienkirche at Lübeck, Germany. The upper case was built in 1516–18; the lower in the 18th century. The organ was destroyed in a World War II bombing raid.

Fig. 3. Baroque organ played by Johann Sebastian Bach, in St. John's Church, Lüneburg, Germany.

form of wind-chest, in which the flow of air from the common supply to the pipes was controlled by a system of wooden slides, was known much earlier; the unique feature of the hydraulus was the system of maintaining steady wind through the use of hydraulic pressure. For its time the hydraulus was an ingenious and almost perfect device. Complete details of its construction are given by *Vitruvius (A.D. 60) and Hero of Alexandria (A.D. 120). Although the organ continued to increase in size during the first few centuries of the Christian era, we know very little else about the organ of this period except that its outstanding feature seems to have been its loudness. St. *Jerome (400) mentions an organ in Jerusalem so loud that it could be heard nearly a mile away at the Mt. of Olives. By the 4th century, wind was being supplied by bellows. In 951 a very large organ was built for Bishop Elphege in the cathedral at *Winchester. With its 400 pipes of bronze, 26 bellows, and 2 sets of 20 keys, each key controlling 10 pipes, it is reputed to have taken 70 men to maintain the wind supply and 2 organists to play it.

In the Middle Ages and Renaissance. Technical progress was very slow until the last years of the 12th century. Until then the playing was done by pulling and pushing slides, but this became more difficult physically as organs increased in size. By the 13th century, however, there had evolved a type of keyboard consisting of a series of levers that operated the slides. These "keys" were so large as to require the whole hand or fist of the performer to depress them. While some or-

gans had many pipes per key, all of the pipes assigned to a given key spoke together, there being no way to separate them. In 1361 a large and important instrument was completed at Halbertstadt. This instrument had three chromatic keyboards, the first controlling the full ensemble; the second controlling the unison pipes standing in the façade of the instrument (the use of the term "principal" to refer to the main unison rank seems to date from this time); and the third controlling the large bass pipes, which sounded three octaves below the unison. While organs with more than one keyboard were built prior to this, there is little evidence to indicate that the second keyboard did not ordinarily control tonal resources identical to those of the first.

By 1400 there were keyboards that could actually be played with the fingers, and by 1500 many of the characteristics now associated with the pipe organ were developed. Progress continued rapidly throughout the 16th century including the development of the individual stop control, the evolution of many different types of pipe construction and their characteristic tonalities, and the introduction of reed stops. We can say that the modern organ actually dates from *c.* 1600. By that year the influence of the two distinct schools of organ building that had evolved a century earlier in Brabant had spread throughout northern Germany and France, the north Brabant or Dutch school affecting the course of north German organ building, the south Brabant or Flemish school emerging into the unique and highly characteristic French style.

The Golden Age. The 17th century was a period of deepening refinement rather than intensive development or startling innovations. By the beginning of the 18th century the organ reached the peak of its development, and the ensuing period is referred to as the organ's "golden age," which reached artistic culmination in the north German and Dutch instruments by Arp *Schnitger and his school. The spread of Protestantism and the growing popularity of congregational singing undoubtedly encouraged the production of the many fine organs during this period. The clear, transparent texture of the baroque organ made it a vehicle especially well suited to the rich, contrapuntal texture of the keyboard style of that time as exemplified in the works of J. S. *Bach. These instruments were always placed in free-standing, elevated positions, usually in the west end of the nave, where they spoke freely into the main body of the church.

In France development paralleled that in north Germany, although tonal design progressed along different lines. The finest examples of the French tonal concept were probably those of Alexandre Thierry and Robert Clicquot (end of the 17th century). The essential style in France did not change throughout the 18th century, although its purity became muddled by excessive duplication of similar-sounding ranks throughout the divisions. Nevertheless, it was the practice of the builders of the end of the 18th century with which we are most familiar, through the monumental work, which was entitled *L'Art du Facteur d'Orgues,* by Dom *Bedos de Celles.

Decline. In Germany by the middle of the 18th century, a decline in the tonal design and the musical effectiveness of the instrument could be noted even in the work of the finest builders. Typical is the work of Gottfried *Silbermann, whose organs, though beauti-

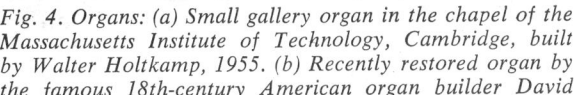

Fig. 4. Organs: (a) Small gallery organ in the chapel of the Massachusetts Institute of Technology, Cambridge, built by Walter Holtkamp, 1955. (b) Recently restored organ by the famous 18th-century American organ builder David Tannenberg in the Brothers House at Salem, North Carolina. It was originally built in 1798. (c) Gallery organ by the Moller Organ Company, installed in 1965 at the Shrine of the Immaculate Conception, Washington, D.C.

fully built and voiced, showed strong traces of the Italian influences brought to Germany by Eugen Casparini. Romanticist influences in the tonal design of the organ continued until, by the middle of the 19th century, organ builders were much preoccupied with experimenting with mechanical devices and organ pipe designs in futile attempts to emulate the sonorities and expressiveness of the symphony orchestra, which by this time had become the chief interest of the finest composers and the listening public. By the end of the 19th century, there were several large "symphonic organs," particularly in France, and it is these instruments that inspired the only worthwhile organ music of the period. The beginning of the 20th century found the state of organ building in complete decadence, especially in England and America, where, by the early 1920s, the organ was used extensively as an instrument for public entertainment in theaters and movie houses. These influences also found their way into the design and construction of organs for church use.

Reform and Revival. In 1926 a reform movement was initiated in Germany with the purpose of bringing back to the art of organ building the techniques required to produce modern instruments that could again present the polyphonic literature that the founders of the movement believed to be the most important body of music written for the organ (*see* CAECILIAN MOVEMENT). The music of Bach, his predecessors, and his contemporaries had more clarity and meaning when performed on the few old baroque instruments that were still in playable condition; and with this music and these instruments as guides, the *Deutsche Orgelbewegung,* as the movement was called, reestablished the fundamental classical principles of organ placement, construction, and voicing.

During the early 1930s an independent renaissance in the U.S. attempted to readapt what was essentially a romanticist concept of the organ by stripping it of its overt orchestralism and introducing classically inspired modifications in the proportioning and voicing of the pipework. Since World War II, however, the general trend, especially among those who have studied in Europe, is toward an essentially classical instrument based on traditional principles. This is often modified to include certain of the more useful features of the romanticist organ where it seems wise to broaden the scope of the instrument. Thus it is possible to have an instrument that reproduces the basic polyphonic literature extremely well, while also having enough scope to cope with some of the more worthy literature of the romanticist period.

Liturgical Use of the Organ. Although it is not known exactly when the organ was first used for religious purposes, the writings of St. Julian of Toledo, a Spanish bishop, indicate that it was in common use in the churches of Spain by the year 450. We know that in the 7th century Pope St. Vitalian (666) introduced the organ in Rome in order to improve the singing of the congregation. As an aid to the introduction of Roman rite into the churches of France, *Pepin (714–768), the father of Charlemagne, ordered an organ from the Byzantine emperor Constantine Copronymus and had it installed in the church of St. Corneille at Compiègne (757). *Charlemagne also received a similar instrument from the Eastern Emperor in the year 812, and a copy of the instrument at Compiègne placed at Aix-la-

Fig. 5. Organ built by Casavant Frères, Sainte-Hyacinthe, Quebec, installed in 1965 in the Basilica of Notre-Dame du Cap, Cap-de-la-Madeleine, Quebec, Canada.

Chapelle *c.* 811 is reputed to have been the first organ in Germany. Apparently the art of making and using organs developed rapidly in Germany in the latter half of the 9th century, for in the year 880 Pope *John VIII requested Anno, Bishop of Friesingen, to send him a good organ and, along with it, a competent player to instruct Romans in the art.

Although the organ has never been prescribed for use in the Roman Catholic Church by Church law, it has apparently been used in the Church consistently since the 9th century. By the 13th century the organ was certainly in general use throughout the Latin Church and thus was deeply involved in the development of the musical and liturgical tradition of the Church. Many of the important liturgical books refer to the organ frequently, and the fact that, though never specifically prescribed, it is assumed to be present and an important aid to the liturgy is seen by the frequent instructions of the Church that direct that it shall be played at specific times (*see* MUSIC, SACRED, LEGISLATION ON). The organ is used for the accompaniment of choir and congregation, and, in most churches, its use in this capacity is absolutely essential. As current instructions indicate a deepening of congregational participation, the importance of the accompanimental role will undoubtedly continue to grow. But the use of the organ alone at appropriate places is also the clear intention of the Church. The high esteem in which the Church holds the organ is perhaps best summarized in the following excerpt from Vatican Council II: "The pipe organ adds a wonderful splendor to the Church's ceremonies, and powerfully lifts up men's mind to God and to higher things."

See also MUSIC, SACRED, LEGISLATION ON; MUSIC, SACRED, HISTORY OF, 4, 5, 6, 7; ORGAN MUSIC.

Bibliography: M. PRAETORIUS, *Syntagma musicum*, 3 v. (v.1 Wittenberg 1614–15; v.2, 3 Wolfenbüttel 1619), fac. ed. by W. Gurlitt (Kassel 1959–). M. MERSENNE, *Harmonie universelle*, 2 v. in 3 (Paris 1636–37), Eng. tr. R. E. CHAPMAN (The Hague 1957) v.3. F. BÉDOS DE CELLES, *L'Art du facteur d'orgues*, 4 pts. in 2 v. (Paris 1766–78) fac. ed. by C. MAHRENHOLZ, 4 v. (Kassel 1934–36). W. ELLERHORST, *Handbuch der Orgelkunde* (Einsiedeln 1936). W. L. SUMMER, *The Organ: Its Evolution, Principles of Construction and Use* (3d ed. London 1962). W. H. BARNES, *The Contemporary American Organ* (7th ed. Glen Rock, N.J. 1959). S. IRWIN, *Dictionary of Pipe Organ Stops* (New York 1962). C. SACHS, *The History of Musical Instruments* (New York 1940). Reese MusMA. Reese MusR. Buk MusB. L. I. PHELPS, "Perspective," *Organ Institute Quarterly* 4.1 (Winter 1954) 21–61; "The Designing of a 2-Manual Organ," *The Diapason* 52 (Sept. 1961) 9, 40. D. J. TARRANT et al., eds., *Proceedings: Symposium Liturgy and Architecture* (Clarke College, Dubuque, Iowa 1964). Congregation of Rites, "De musica sacra et sacra liturgia," (Instruction, Sept. 3, 1958) ActApS 50 (1958) 630–663, Eng. tr. B. AVERY and G. DIEKMANN in *Worship* 32.10 (1958) 590–626. J. E. BLANTON, *The Organ in Church Design* (Albany, Tex. 1957); *The Revival of the Organ Case* (Albany, Tex. 1965). **Illustration credits:** Fig. 1, Courtesy of the Walters Art Gallery, Baltimore. Figs. 2 and 3, German Information Center. Fig. 4*a*, M.I.T. Photo. Fig. 4*b*, Courtesy of Old Salem, Inc., and the Moravian Music Foundation, Inc. Fig. 4*c*, Reni Newsphoto Service.

[L. I. PHELPS]

ORGAN MUSIC

This article is a survey of organ literature from the beginnings of intabulated scores through the succeeding styles of Western music history (*See* MUSIC, SACRED, HISTORY OF, 3–8). Historically the *organ is the instrument par excellence of Christian liturgical service. Some form of organ has been known in the West since the 4th century. Long before it boasted a notation or independent repertory, the organ was used to help in the observance of Mass and the Divine Office, either maintaining the pitch or supporting the chanting or, indeed, sustaining a voice of its own in *organum* and later in the organ Mass, an important liturgical form in which it actually alternated antiphonally with the choir in chant settings of the Ordinary. Only with the appearance of keyboard tablatures in the 14th century, however, does the history of organ music leave the realm of conjecture and yield to scientific treatment. "Tablature" means any of a variety of notation systems for instruments, including the organ, in which letters, numerals, and other symbols are used in place of, or along with, notes to indicate pitch intervals and rhythm; it also designates MSS and books inscribed in such notation.

EARLY KEYBOARD TABLATURES

The earliest preserved music for a keyboard instrument is found in the Robertsbridge Codex of the early 14th century. This MS, possibly of French origin, includes complete transcriptions of two motets from the *Roman de Fauvel* (1316) and two dances known as *estampies*. The notation resembles the later German organ tablature, with notes for the upper part and letters for the lower part or parts. The earliest sources of German organ music, the Sagen MS (*c.* 1425) and the Winsem MS (*c.* 1430), include fragments of organ Masses. The Illeborgh MS (1448) is notable for its five *preambles* (preludes) and the first indication of use of a pedal keyboard. The *Fundamentum organisandi* (1452) by the blind organist Conrad Paumann (1410–

73) contains musical examples for instruction in composition, preludes, and a number of pieces based on German songs. The *Buxheimer Orgelbuch* (*c.* 1460), the most comprehensive of the 15th-century tablatures, contains more than 250 pieces, including a few preludes and arrangements of many secular vocal pieces. The earliest collection of Italian keyboard music is the Faenza Codex, an early 15th-century MS. This extensive collection contains ornamented keyboard transcriptions of vocal pieces by French and Italian composers of the 14th and early 15th centuries and parts of organ Masses.

The organ keyboard had been reduced to playable proportions by the 12th century; stops had been added during the 12th and 13th centuries; by the 15th century the organ was beginning to assert its individuality as an instrument distinct from other keyboard instruments. The major physical problems of construction and manipulation had been solved in favor of emerging concerns of style and expression, and the ranking artists of the organ were mixing tone colors on their own palettes. Henceforth registration would be an increasingly important element in organ composition.

Germany and Poland. The high point of early German Renaissance organ music was the *Tabulaturen etlicher Lobgesang und lidlein uff die Orgeln und Lauten* (1512, Tablatures of Some Songs of Praise and Little Songs for the Organ and Lute) by the blind organist Arnolt Schlick (*c.* 1460–after 1517). It is the first printed collection of keyboard music, and includes 14 organ pieces; some of them, notably *Maria zart* (Gentle Mary), marked the beginning of the organ chorale in Germany. Paul Hofhaimer (1459–1537) was one of the celebrated organists of his time, but only a few of his keyboard pieces have been preserved. His disciples, however, left a large quantity of music in German organ tablature MSS, the most important being collections by Hans Buchner (1483–1538), Hans Kotter (*c.* 1485–1541), Fridolin Sicher (1490–1546), and Leonhard

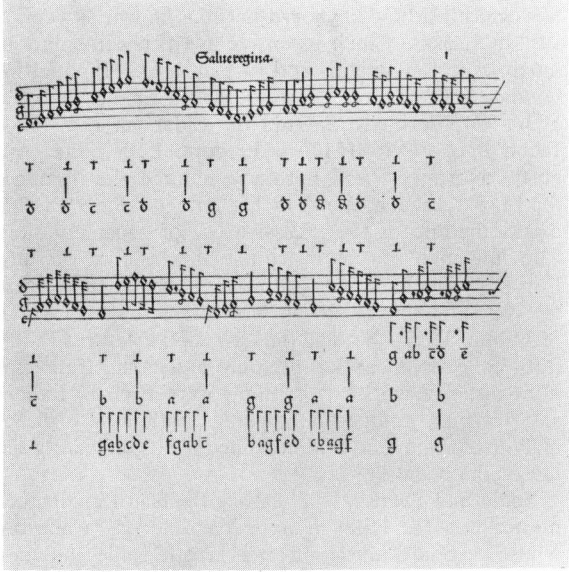

Fig. 1. "Salve Regina" for organ by Arnolt Schlick (c. 1460–after 1517) from "Tabulaturen etlicher Lobgesang," 1512, the first collection of pieces printed in German organ tablature.

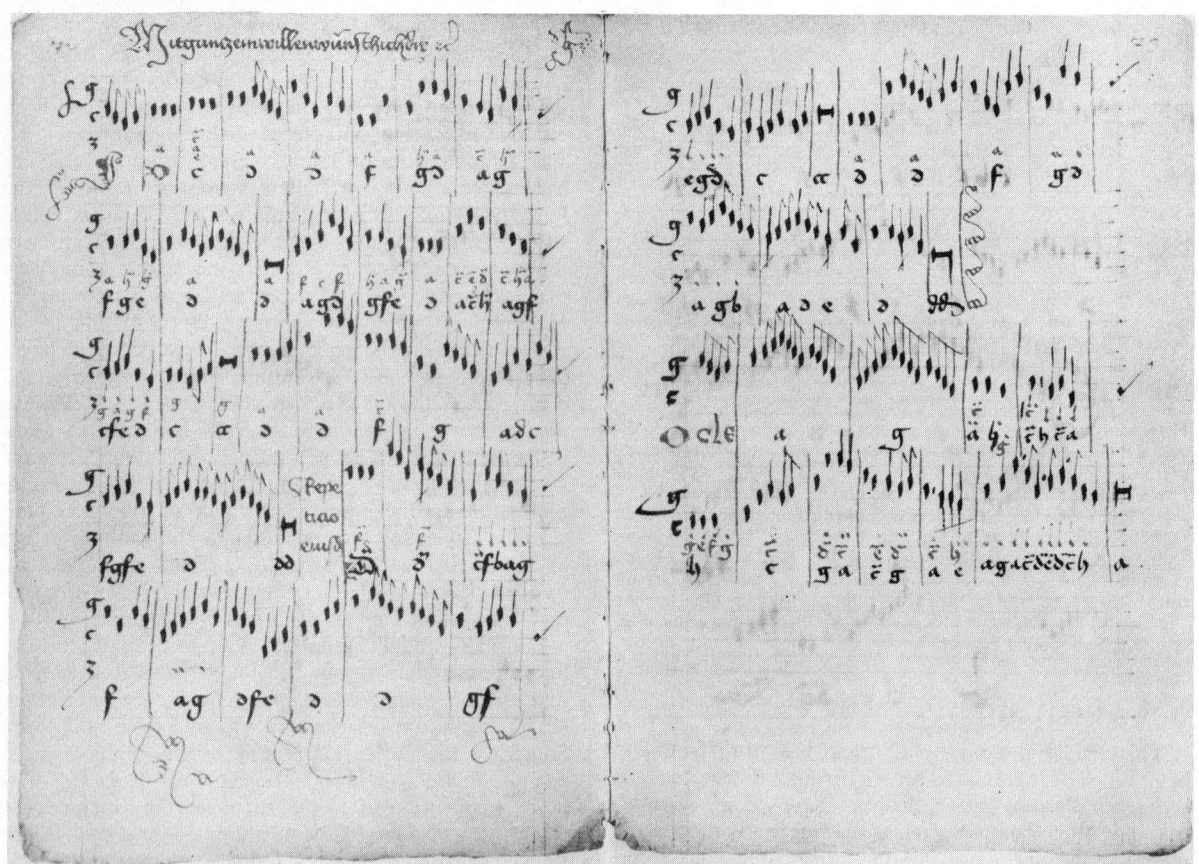

Fig. 2. "O Clemens" by C. Paumann (1410–73), in a German MS, the "Fundamentum organisandi," 1452.

Kleber (*c.* 1490–1556). All these tablatures include settings of plainsong melodies and, except for Buchner, transcriptions of vocal pieces. Kotter and Kleber developed a true keyboard style in their preludes and fantasies.

During the second half of the 16th century arrangers of vocal music for keyboard became known as "colorists" by reason of their extensive use of ornamentation, much of it meaningless and in bad taste. Principal intabulators of the period were E. N. Ammerbach (*c.* 1530–97), Bernhard Schmid the Elder (*c.* 1520–96), Jacob Paix (1556–1617), Christoph Löffelholtz, Augustus Nörmiger, and Bernhard Schmid the Younger (b. 1548). Johann Woltz in his *Tablatur-Buch* (1617) marks the end of the excessive use of ornamentation. The influence of the instrumental music of western Europe, particularly of Germany, is found in two extensive 16th-century Polish tablatures: the MS of Jan of Lublin (1537–48), and the Cracow Tablature (1548). Both collections contain preludes and organ transcriptions of vocal works by contemporary French, Italian, and German composers, together with a few pieces of Polish origin, and both include a piece indicating the use of the pedal keyboard.

Spain and France. The leading Spanish Renaissance master was the blind organist Antonio de *Cabezón, whose keyboard music, of great artistic value, included short contrapuntal settings of psalm tones (*versillos*), fantasias (*tientos*), elaborate arrangements of vocal works (*glosas*), and variations (*diferencias*), these last being the first important keyboard music in this form

and his most interesting and valuable contribution to organ literature. A similar collection by Luis Venegas de Henestrosa appeared in 1557. Other keyboard compositions of 16th-century Spain are found in treatises devoted chiefly to instrumental technique by Fray Juan *Bermudo and Fray *Tomás de Santa María.

The first collection of French keyboard music for "organs, spinets, and clavichords" is found in seven books printed by Pierre Attaignant in 1531. Three of these contain chiefly liturgical compositions (organ Masses, settings of the *Te Deum* and *Magnificat*), transcribed motets, and three preludes. A scant century later (1623) a collection of organ hymns was published by Jean *Titelouze, considered the founder of the French organ school. In their contrapuntal texture and use of dissonance these hymns represent the final flowering of Renaissance organ style in France. They are written for an organ of two manuals and pedalboard, and each hymn melody has a number of different settings, intended for alternation with the sung chant, thus forming a series of variations. A later collection (1626) contains settings of the *Magnificat*.

Italy. The earliest-known printed organ music is Andrea Antico's 26 *frottole* transcriptions (1517) and a small collection of *ricercari* and vocal transcriptions by M. A. *Cavazzoni. Girolamo *Cavazzoni, his son and a genuine master, published two keyboard collections consisting of *ricercari, canzoni,* hymns, music for the *Magnificat,* and three complete organ Masses (1542–43). The *ricercari* of Cavazzoni resembled the vocal motet; his later works in this form were often more thematic. The illustrious organists of San Marco in Venice—Andrea and Giovanni *Gabrieli and Claudio *Merulo—composed *ricercari* and *canzoni;* the latter two also wrote toccatas and fantasias. Luzzasco Luzzaschi (d. 1607), the teacher of *Frescobaldi, and Girolamo Diruta (1557–1612) also composed keyboard *ricercari,* toccatas, and *canzoni;* and eight *ricercari* are attributed to *Palestrina.

England. For the century following the Robertsbridge MS (*c.* 1325) no English MSS containing keyboard pieces are known, although organs were in general use. At first there was little difference between organ and virginal styles, and the vast sources of English virginal music preserved chiefly in 16th-century MSS include many works suitable for organ. The *Mulliner Book* (*c.* 1545–*c.* 1585), one of the oldest and richest sources for English organ music, includes settings of psalm tunes and plainsong melodies, transcriptions of secular songs and anthems, and dances. Among the composers represented are John Redford (*c.* 1486–*c.* 1545), Thomas *Tallis, and William Blitheman. The *Fitzwilliam Virginal Book* (*c.* 1562–*c.* 1612) includes music by William *Byrd, John Bull (1563–1624), and Orlando Gibbons (1583–1625), among many others. Besides the usual keyboard hymn settings of plainsong melodies, Redford developed a type of setting known as "faburden," based on a tenor (faburden) derived from plainsong. An anonymous MS of *c.* 1550 also contains faburden hymn settings, together with the first surviving organ Mass in England and the two earliest keyboard duets. The keyboard music of Tallis, Byrd, Gibbons, Bull, and other important English musicians includes a number of pieces suitable for organ. Bull's fantasia on the Dutch melody set to the sacred text *Laet ons met herten reyne* ("Let us with pure heart") is the oldest known composition with directions for organ registration.

THE BAROQUE

The development of the organ from the instrument of the Renaissance to that of the Baroque era was one of augmented dynamic resources through the introduction of new tone colors and an increase in size. Its function in the church was important, but it became a solo instrument as well as an accompanimental one. A wide variety of abstract forms of composition appeared along with organ settings for the Catholic Mass and the Protestant chorale.

England. In his *Ode for St. Cecilia's Day,* Henry *Purcell, the musical light of the Restoration, extols the "wondrous machine"; yet English organ music in the baroque did not reach the high level of Renaissance achievement. Liturgical stimulus was absent, and organs were small and without pedalboard well into the 18th century. During the early baroque the two chief forms in English organ repertory were the verset and voluntary; both are short, imitative forms, the verset based on a liturgical plainsong theme, the voluntary (first found in the 16th-century *Mulliner Book*) free and nonliturgical. During the 17th and 18th centuries the voluntary incorporated other forms, developing into a sectional work with slow introduction (often imitative) followed by a toccata-like movement. Composers of the period include, besides Purcell, Orlando Gibbons's son Christopher (1615–76), Benjamin Rogers (1614–98), Matthew Locke (*c.* 1630–77), John Blow (1649–

1708), Jeremiah Clarke (*c.* 1674–1707), William Croft (1678–1757), Thomas Roseingrave (1690–1766), and Maurice Greene (*c.* 1695–1755). The only Purcell compositions known to have been indicated for organ are the *Voluntary on the Old Hundreth, Voluntary for a Double Organ,* and *Voluntary for Cornet and Trumpet Stops.*

The culminating figure, G. F. *Handel, whom Germany shares with England, composed no solo organ music except the Six Fugues or Voluntaries for the Organ or Harpsichord (1735) and six fughettas of doubtful authenticity. He did, however, compose or arrange three sets of six concertos for organ or harpsichord and orchestra of strings and oboes (1738, 1740, and 1760). These concertos, a mixture of sonata and dance movements in Italian *concerto grosso* form, were an innovation of Handel's and were intended for performance between the acts of his oratorios. Later composers of voluntaries, concertos, and preludes were Thomas Arne (1710–78), William Boyce (1710–79), John Stanley (1713–86), and William Walond (1725–70).

Italy. The earliest Italian baroque composers for organ were the Neapolitans G. M. Trabaci (*c.* 1580–1647) and Ascanio Mayone (*c.* 1580–?), whose first published collections (1603) included chiefly versets, monothematic *ricercari,* variation *canzoni,* and a new type of toccata. Frescobaldi was the greatest Italian organ composer, and the culminating figure of Italian baroque organ music. His pupils and followers, among them M. Rossi (fl. 1625–50), G. B. Fasolo (fl. 1645), and Domenico Zipoli (1688–1726), were unable to continue at his high level, and Italian organ music declined after him. The real heir and propagator of his art was J. J. *Froberger, his pupil from 1637 to 1641.

Spain and Portugal. Spanish organists following Cabezón were S. A. de Heredia (1570–?), F. Correa de Araujo (*c.* 1581–1663), and J. B. J. *Cabanilles, the greatest organist of the Spanish baroque. Their favorite form was the *tiento,* an imitative composition similar to the *ricercare;* they were also, like Cabezón, masters of the variation form, and the use of chromatic alterations (*falsas*) was a characteristic feature of their music. Correa de Araujo's *Facultad orgánica* (1626), the most representative collection of early Spanish baroque organ music, contains more than 50 *tientos,* many revealing the influence of Cabezón and *Sweelinck. The principal Portuguese organ composer of the time was Padre Manoel Rodrigues Coelho (1583–*c.* 1623), author of *Flores de Musica* (1620), the earliest instrumental music printed in Portugal, a collection including *tentos* in imitative style, pieces based on plainsong, and *glosas.*

The Low Countries. At the start of the 17th century J. P. Sweelinck, "master of organists," was Europe's most influential organ virtuoso, composer, and teacher. Through his own great art and the work of his pupils he furthered the fusion of national styles from English virginal techniques to Venetian polychoral fantasias. His keyboard music marks the beginning of baroque style; his variations on chorale melodies foreshadow the German organ chorale, and his monothematic fantasias led to the baroque fugue. Among his compatriots were Pieter Cornet (*c.* 1593–1626), associated with the Brussels (Catholic) court, whose works for organ include fantasias, toccatas, and versets on the *Salve*

Regina; Anthony van Noordt (d. 1675), whose *Tabulatuur Boeck* of psalms and fantasias (1659) was the first Dutch keyboard collection to appear in print; and Abraham van den Kerckhoven (1627–73), whose works presage the North German school of *Buxtehude.

Germany. German organ music developed steadily from Paumann to J. S. Bach. During the 17th century the earlier imitative *ricercare,* fantasia, capriccio, and verset forms evolved into the fugue; elaborations of a theme flowered in the passacaglia, chaconne, chorale, theme and variations; free improvisations—toccatas, preludes, fantasias—became virtuoso achievements.

North, Central, and South German Schools. Brilliant large-scale projects characterized the North German school, represented chiefly by Samuel Scheidt (1587–1654), George Böhm (1661–1733), Franz Tunder (1614–67), and Buxtehude. Scheidt's *Tabulatura Nova* (1624) was a comprehensive collection of settings of chorales and plainsong melodies, extended fantasias, variations on secular songs, and fugues. The Central German school, whose constituents favored smaller forms, such as the organ chorale and chorale variations, claimed Johann Pachelbel (1653–1706), whose works embrace toccatas, fantasias, *ricercari,* versets (*Magnificat*), and organ chorales; Michael *Praetorius (who belongs partly to the Renaissance); Henrich Bach (1615–92); Johann Christoph Bach (1642–1703); Johann Michael Bach (1648–94); Johann Kuhnau (1660–1722); F. W. Zachow (1663–1712); J. G. Walther (1684–1748); and other productive musicians. Composers of the predominantly Catholic South German school worked in the traditions of the late 16th-century colorist school of Ammerbach and of the Italians Gabrieli, Merulo, and, notably, Frescobaldi, creating in the forms of variation, *canzona, ricercare,* verset, chaconne, passacaglia, toccata, fantasia, capriccio, and fugue—in fact, in every favored baroque form except the chorale. Prominent among them were Froberger, Georg Muffat (1645–1704), whose *Apparatus Musico-Organisticus* (1690) was a high point in South German composition, Hans Leo *Hassler, Christian Erbach (1570–1635), J. U. Steigleder (1593–1635), W. Ebner (1612–65), J. E. Kinderman (1616–55), J. K. *Kerll, F. X. Murchhauser (1633–1738), and J. K. F. *Fischer.

Bach. The music of Johann Sebastian Bach climaxes the German baroque; his organ music particularly marks the complete synthesis and fusion of the Italian, French, and German influences in his own highly personal style. His incomparable mastery of counterpoint and harmony, richness of invention, and monumental architectural structure are reflected throughout his works. The chorales, varying in style from short, simple settings of the melodies to extensive and often elaborate projections, in particular reveal his extraordinary expressiveness and realistic symbolism. His chief organ compositions, besides the organ chorales, are the preludes, fugues, fantasias, toccatas, six trio sonatas, the towering Passacaglia and Fugue in C Minor, arrangements of three concertos by *Vivaldi and two by Duke Johann Ernst of Weimar. Three collections of his organ music were published during his lifetime: the Catechism Chorales (*Clavierübung* III, 1739; 21 organ chorales and the Prelude and Fugue in E Flat, the "St. Anne"); Schübler Chorales (1746; six transcriptions of cantata movements); and five canonic variations on

Fig. 3. Opening page of the autograph MS of Johann Sebastian Bach's "Prelude and Fugue in B Minor."

the chorale *Vom Himmel hoch* (1746). There were also two organ chorale volumes, the *Orgelbüchlein* (*c.* 1717; 45 chorales) and the Eighteen Leipzig Chorales (1747–49).

France. Composers of the early 17th century, such as Charles Racquet and François Roberday, followed the lead of Titelouze in their emphasis on contrapuntal music, much of it for liturgical purposes. Secular music, however, was becoming increasingly influential, and a "less learned," sometimes grandiose, style emerged. Preludes, duos, trios, antiphonal "dialogues" and "echos" were added to liturgical hymns, versets, and *Magnificats,* and there was increased incidence of ornamentation (*agréments*), stylized dance rhythms, *récits* for solo stops, and colorful combinations of stops. Representative composers of the later 17th century, most of whom published collections, were Henri du Mont (1610–84), Etienne Richard (d. 1669), Louis Couperin (1626–61), G. G. Nivers (1617–1703), N. A. Lebègue (1630–1702), Nicolas Gigault (*c.* 1624–1707), J. H. d'Anglebert (1635–91), André *Raison, Gilles Jullien (*c.* 1650–*c.* 1703), Jacques Boyvin (1650–1706), and the two great masters François *Couperin (*le Grand*) and Nicolas de Grigny (1672–1703), whose *Livre d'Orgue* (1699), a volume owned by J. S. Bach, contains two organ Masses, five hymn settings, and a *Point d'orgue* (a piece written above a pedal point). Variations on Christmas melodies (Noëls), unusually popular during the early 18th century, were published by Lebègue, Gigault, Raison, Jean François *Dandrieu and his uncle Pierre, L. A. Dornel (*c.* 1695–1755), and the "king of Noëlists," L. C. *Daquin. During this period a gradual decline set in, particularly after Louis *Marchand, Pierre du Mage (c. 1676–1751), and L. N. *Clérambault, all of whom retained some of the polyphonic and liturgical traditions of earlier composers.

THE CLASSIC PERIOD

The classic period coincided with the emergence of the symphony orchestra; hence its major music makers contributed very little to the organ repertory—unless the musical or organ clock (Flötenuhr, "flute-clock"), a quaint contraption comprised of a set of small organ pipes with bellows operated by a clock mechanism, is considered a true member of the organ family. For this instrument F. J. *Haydn composed 30 short, unpretentious pieces, many of which have been arranged for organ, and for organ or harpsichord, two early concertos in C Major. *Mozart produced three Fantasias in F Minor (K. 594 and K. 608) and an Andante in F Major (K. 616)—all in his most mature vein—for the organ clock; they are, however more familiar in solo piano, four-hand piano, and organ arrangements. He turned out also 17 brief "Epistle" or church sonatas for organ and instruments (usually two violins and bass but in some instances wind and brasses), probably intended for the interval between Epistle and Gospel during Mass at Salzburg's cathedral. *Beethoven in his early years also composed three pieces for the musical clock, together with a two-part Fugue in D Major for organ, and Two Preludes, Opus 39, for organ or piano.

THE ROMANTICIST PERIOD

The orchestral orientation of the classic period became the preoccupation of the romanticist composers, and organ composition suffered accordingly—at least until such masters as Mendelssohn and Liszt explored the organ's potentialities.

Germany. Organ music in Germany, as in other countries, reached its lowest point during the century following Bach's death (1750). Even in the liturgical services, where it had been supreme, the organ now took a position secondary to orchestral instruments. Many of Bach's disciples, such as J. G. Vogler, Homilius, Krebs, Kittel, and J. Schneider, are almost forgotten today, as are many other competent musicians once active in the organ field, e.g., J. G. *Albrechtsberger, G. J. (Abbé) *Vogler, J. C. H. Rinck (1770–1846), and J. C. F. Schneider (1786–1853). Felix *Mendelssohn-Bartholdy created the first organ music of artistic value in the 19th century, his chief works for that instrument being the Three Preludes and Fugues, Opus 37 (1837), and Six Sonatas, Opus 65 (1845). The sonatas (originally called voluntaries) bear little relation to the classical sonata form, since they include chorales and fugues as well as free movements in romanticist style. Robert *Schumann essayed a few pieces for "pedal piano," or organ, among them the Six Fugues on B-A-C-H, Opus 60 (1845), and two groups in lighter vein, Six Canons, Opus 56, and Four Sketches, Opus 58.

Franz *Liszt occupies a significant position in the history of organ music, and his innovations in form, harmony, orchestral effects, and colorful registration initiated a new style in organ composition. Among his three major works in the new spirit, one is the well-known "Prelude and Fugue on B-A-C-H" (1855); he

also composed an organ Mass, a Requiem, and hymn settings. His pupil Julius Reubke (1834–58) wrote only one organ work, the monumental Sonata on the 94th Psalm. Some of the finest music for organ during the romanticist period is found in Johannes *Brahms's Eleven Chorale Preludes Opus 122, his final musical utterance and expressive of the spirit and style of the organ chorales of Bach and the other baroque masters. Joseph *Rheinberger was the most famous organ teacher and composer of his day. He composed 20 sonatas and many shorter works as well as two concertos; his style is dignified, his mastery of form and counterpoint, complete. Gustav Merkel (1827–85), a lesser contemporary, produced nine organ sonatas and several shorter works. Max *Reger was most successful in his Chorale Preludes, Opus 67 (1903), and other relatively brief works appropriate for the church service. On a monumental scale, his fantasias on chorale melodies and his extended Fantasie and Fugue on the Name B-A-C-H, Opus 46, are probably the best known. Sigfrid Karg-Elert (1877–1933), who succeeded Reger as professor of composition at the Leipzig Conservatory in 1916, composed first for harmonium but was induced by Reger to write for organ. His first important work, the Sixty-six Choral Improvisations, Opus 65 (1908–10), display wide variety in treatment of the chorale melody. He created also in impressionistic style, an innovation in organ repertory, as well as in classical forms and extended chorale settings.

France. Except for the efforts of A. F. Boëly (1785–1858), serious organ composition had been virtually at a standstill from the mid-18th century to the emergence of Belgian-born César *Franck. Intervening were Louis Lefébure-Wély (1817–69) and A. E. Batiste (1820–76), mediocre composers of showy, sentimental music. Franck's early organ works were short, easy, derivative pieces for liturgical use; his first significant achievements date from the six Pièces of 1862. The three Pièces of 1878 mark development toward the masterpieces of his maturity, the three Chorals (1890)—free fantasias, not chorale preludes, with many characteristics of the variation form, and largely appropriate for church use. Camille *Saint-Saëns was influenced by neoclassic forms, but, like Théodore Salomé (1834–96) and Théodore *Dubois, he created as well in the currently popular style. The Belgian organist-composer J. N. *Lemmens influenced the French school through his pupils Alexandre *Guilmant and C. M. *Widor. Guilmant himself was a composer, virtuoso, editor of monumental editions of early organ music, and teacher of many distinguished organists of his time. Among his organ works are eight sonatas and numerous single pieces, some for liturgical use. Eugène Gigout (1844–1925) initiated a trend toward liturgical organ composition with his pieces based on plainsong themes. Among others in the field, Henri Dallier (1849–1934), Léon Boëllman (1862–97), Guy Ropartz (1864–1955), and M. J. Erb (1860–1944), reveal variously a neoclassic discipline, a lighter, colorful disposition, and occasionally a liturgical drift. The Italian Enrico *Bossi elected the popular style of some of his French contemporaries.

The "organ symphonies" of Widor and Louis *Vierne (the outstanding French organ composers succeeding Franck) are unique in organ literature. These symphonies, 10 by Widor from 1876 to 1900 and 6 by Vierne from 1899 to 1931, are suites in form, bearing little resemblance to the classic symphony form and consisting of up to seven contrasting movements, some on an extended scale. Although they are essentially recital works, many of the individual movements are suited to church use, and Widor's last two—and major—symphonies introduce plainsong themes: the *Gothique* (1895), embodying the Christmas chant *Puer natus est;* the *Romane* (1900), with the Easter chant *Haec Dies.* Charles *Tournemire, a Franck pupil, restored the organ to the service of the church with his monumental *L'Orgue mystique,* a cycle of 51 suites for the liturgical year, each suite with few exceptions including a prelude on the Introit, Offertory, Elevation, Communion, and Finale (*Sortie*). All the movements are based on appropriate plainchant melodies, adorned and freely paraphrased in a colorful and often impressionistic style. Other eminent virtuoso-composers of the period were Jean Huré (1877–1930), Henri Mulet (1878–1945), and Joseph *Bonnet. Darius Milhaud (b. 1892), one of *Les Six,* wrote a number of colorful pieces; and J. J. Roger-Ducasse (1873–1954), a nonorganist, composed a *Pastorale* (1909) that stands alone in organ literature as an impressionistic tone picture of symphonic proportions.

THE 20TH CENTURY

Just as Bach had sounded the ultimate depths of the baroque organ's resources so that organ composition had no way to go but into desuetude after his death, so by the turn of the 20th century had the possibilities of the Wagnerian orchestra been exhausted. It was that fact, together with the organ's reinstatement (thanks to the *Caecilian movement) as the official liturgical instrument, the vast technical improvement in the instrument itself, and the solid production of the late 19th-century organ composers, that reversed the trend and generated new interest in the organ as an instrument for both liturgical and concert performance.

France. In France particularly this revival of interest in the organ was continued and promoted by its 20th-century composers. Most of these artists have composed for the church, using Gregorian melodies in various ways as a prime source of inspiration. Dupré has had a profound influence on organ repertory and performance in his roles as composer, virtuoso, improviser, and teacher. His works include both concert pieces and such sacred works as the *Symphonie-Passion,* with its plainsong themes. Maurice Duruflé (b. 1902), a disciple of Tournemire, has contributed notable works based on plainsong (e.g., *Veni Creator*), as well as a number of concert works. Langlais (b. 1907) is interested in the modern adaptation of French baroque music and also in Gregorian chant (*Trois paraphrases grégoriennes, Suite médiaévale*). Oliver Messiaen (b. 1908) has introduced many new ideas in his organ compositions, notably, in rhythm, harmony, and the use of bird song. Most of his organ music is inspired by religious or liturgical themes, often projected in the form of suites, such as *L'Ascension, La Nativité, Les Corps Glorieux, Messe de la Pentecôte.* The music of Jehan *Alain, who died in combat during World War II, combines free rhythms, oriental colors, plainsong themes, and original forms growing out of content. Jacques Charpentier (b. 1933) writes in a modern idiom somewhat reminiscent of Messiaen. Other contemporaries who have produced liturgical organ music are Henri Nibelle (b. 1883),

Fig. 4. Opening page of "Consécration (Le don de Sagesse)" from "Messe de la Pentecôte" for organ by Oliver Messiaen.

Dom Paul Benoît, Daniel-Lesur (b. 1908), Gaston Litaize (b. 1909), J. J. Grunenwald (b. 1911), Roland Falcinelli (b. 1920), and Jeanne Demessieux (b. 1921).

Germany and Austria. The early decades of the 20th century saw the emergence of a neoclassic movement in Germany. Features derived from the baroque masters were incorporated in a contemporary compositional style; the characteristic sound of the baroque organ became the ideal of the new organ school; and the classical forms of toccata, prelude and fugue, passacaglia, sonata, and above all the organ chorale were resurrected. Among composers of this persuasion were Heinrich Kaminski (1886–1946), Johannes Weyrauch (b. 1897), Ernst Pepping (b. 1901), H. F. Micheelsen (b. 1902), Günter Raphael (1903–60), Joseph Ahrens (b. 1904), Hermann Schroeder (b. 1904), Helmut Walcha (b. 1907), Helmut Bornefeld (b. 1906), Karl Höller (b. 1907), Hugo Distler (1908–42), Siegfried Reda (b. 1916), Johannes Driessler (b. 1921), and the Austrians J. N. David (b. 1895) and Anton Heiller (b. 1923). Significant contributions to organ literature have been made also by Paul *Hindemith, Arnold *Schoenberg, and Ernst Křenek (b. 1900)—all of whom have resided in America.

Belgium, Holland, and Other Countries. Organ composers of 20th-century Belgium display a diversity of styles from the Franckian evocations of Joseph Jongen (1873–1953) onward. Paul de Maleingreau (1887–1956) composed much liturgical music and made good use of plainsong themes, particularly in his *Symphonie de Noël* and *Symphonie de la Passion.* Flor Peeters (b. 1903), an internationally respected representative of contemporary organ music, has composed concert organ works (many of symphonic proportions), chorales, and practical chant-based liturgical Masses.

Auguste de Boeck (1865–1937) and the neoimpressionist Marinus de Jong (b. 1891) also have composed for the organ. Among their many Dutch contemporaries are Jan Zwart (1878–1937), Hendrik Andriessen (b. 1892), Marius Monnikendam (b. 1896), A. van der Horst (1899–1965), Cor Kee (b. 1900), Herman Strategier (b. 1912), Henk Badings (b. 1907), A. de Klerk (b. 1917), Piet Post (b. 1919), and Piet Kee (b. 1927). Swiss composers include Arthur Honegger (1892–1955) and Frank Martin (b. 1890), both familiar to American listeners, together with Willy Burkhard (1900–55), Henri Gagnebin (b. 1886), and Paul Müller (b. 1898).

Scandinavian composers have written in the liturgical vein as well as producing important concert works in extended forms. Among the Danes are Otto Malling (1848–1915), known for his descriptive pieces on religious subjects; the romanticist Carl Nielsen (1865–1931), composer of the monumental *Commotio;* Kai Senstius (b. 1889); Svendove Møller (1903–49); N. V. Bentzon (b. 1919); Leif Kayser (b. 1919); and Leif Thybo (b. 1922). Sweden's late 19th-century composers worked in the romantic-nationalist spirit, but early in the 20th century neoclassicism became strong, and under the influence of Schoenberg and *Webern the younger composers turned to modern techniques. Representative modern composers for organ are Valdemar Söderholm (b. 1909), Sven-Eric Johanson (b. 1919), Torsten Nilsson (b. 1920), and Bengt Hambraeus (b. 1928), one of the *avant-gardists*. While retaining their national heritage of folk song (in common with other Scandinavian peoples), Norwegian musicians have been variously influenced by French, German, Austrian, and even American styles. Organ composers include Arild Sandvold (b. 1895), Conrad Baden (b. 1908), Leif Solberg (b. 1914), Knut Nystedt (b. 1915), and Egil Hovland (b. 1918).

Czechoslovakia (Bohemia) and Russia. Because the Bohemian composers of old had so great a part in stabilizing the forms perfected in the classic period, their musical expression—in organ composition as elsewhere—revealed a strong classic discipline until the emergence of a national school in the 19th century. Bohuslav Czernohorsky (1684–1742), Joseph Seeger (1716–82), J. K. Kuchar (1751–1829), and Antonin Rejcha (1770–1836) were pioneers in the history of organ music in Bohemia. Leoš *Janáček inspired the modern Czech school of organ composition, and B. A. Wiedermann (1883–1951) and Peter Eben (b. 1929) have carried it on. The organ is not used in Russian Orthodox services, but a number of Russians have written concert music for organ, among them Alexander Glazunov (1865–1936), Alexander Gedeke (1877–1957), Jossas Karossas (b. 1890), Alfred Karindy (b. 1901), Eugen Kapp (b. 1908), and Edgard Arro (b. 1911).

England. During the 19th century the growth of English organ literature was inhibited by the same circumstances that plagued all creative musical activity—a complacent, somewhat sanctimonious Victorian mentality coupled with the public's infatuation with imported romanticist products. Toward the turn of the century, however, organ composition revived with the publication of sonatas and smaller works by C. V. Stanford (1852–1924), Basil Harwood (1859–1949), Edward Bairstow (1874–1946), and Sir Edward *Elgar, the first English composer after Purcell to achieve international recognition. Concert pieces, some of the salon type, were composed by Alfred Hollins (1865–1942), William Wolstenholme (1865–1931), and Edwin Lemare (1865–1942). New settings of ancient hymn tunes and service music were written by Sir Hubert Parry (1848–1918), Charles Wood (1866–1926), Harold Darke (b. 1888), Alec Rowley (b. 1892), Herbert Howells (b. 1892), Percy Whitlock (1903–46), and eminently by Ralph *Vaughan Williams. Among English composers who have used plainsong themes in their compositions are Harvey Grace (1874–1944), George Oldroyd (1886–1951), and the influential Healey Willan, who since 1913 has lived, taught, and composed in Canada. Contemporary English composers writing concert pieces as well as music for church use include Guy Weitz, born (1883) in Belgium, Richard Arnel (b. 1917), and Malcolm Williamson (b. 1931). Michael Tippet (b. 1905) and Benjamin Britten (b. 1913) have also shown an interest in writing for organ.

The U.S. Serious organ composition began only during the second half of the 19th century with the New England composers Arthur Foote (1853–1937) and Horatio Parker (1863–1919). The 20th century has produced a flourishing school of composers who have written preludes based on hymn tunes and other melodies, as well as concert pieces in many forms and styles. Among the more prominent are Seth Bingham (b. 1882), English-born Tertius Noble (1867–1953), Herman Berlinski (b. 1910), and Leo Sowerby (b. 1895). Liturgical organ music based on plainsong has been composed by Philip Kreckel (1886–1963), Joseph J. McGrath (b. 1889), Camil van Hulze (b. 1897), Everett Titcomb (b. 1910), A. C. Peloquin (b. 1918), and Rev. Russell Woollen (b. 1923). The list of Americans who have written a few works for organ while concentrating on works for other instruments and orchestra would include the whole galaxy of contemporary composers, among them Walter Piston (b. 1894), Douglas Moore (b. 1893), Roger Sessions (b. 1896), Virgil Thomson (b. 1896), Henry Cowell (1897–1965), Aaron Copland (b. 1900), Paul Creston (b. 1906), Samuel Barber (b. 1910), Vincent Persichetti (b. 1915), E. B. Kohs (b. 1916), and Ulysses Kay (b. 1917). A Canadian repertory was developed in the mid-20th century along parallel lines.

Bibliography: Books. G. S. BEDBROOK, *Keyboard Music from the Middle Ages to the Beginnings of the Baroque* (London 1949). N. DUFOURCQ, *La Musique d'orgue française de Jehan Titelouze à Jehan Alain* (2d ed. Paris 1949). K. G. FELLERER, *Orgel und Orgelmusik* (Augsburg 1929). G. FROTSCHER, *Geschichte des Orgelspiels und der Orgelkomposition*, 2 v. (2d ed. Berlin 1959). H. GRACE, *French Organ Music Past and Present* (New York 1919). V. LUKAS, *Orgelmusikführer* (Stuttgart 1963). C. F. WATERS, *The Growth of Organ Music* (London 1957). Periodicals. W. APEL, "Early German Keyboard Music," MusQ 23 (1937) 210–237; "Early Spanish Music for Lute and Keyboard Instruments," *ibid.* 20 (1934) 289–301; "Neapolitan Links between Cabezon and Frescobaldi," *ibid.* 24 (1938) 419–437. W. MELLERS, "John Bull and English Keyboard Music," *ibid.* 40 (1954) 364–383, 548–571. F. RAUGEL, "The Ancient French Organ School," *ibid.* 11 (1925) 560–571. L. SCHRADE, "The Organ in the Mass of the 15th Century," *ibid.* 28 (1942) 329–336, 467–487. Collections of Renaissance and baroque organ music. J. BONNET, ed., *Anthology of Early French Organ Music* (New York 1942); comp., *Historical Organ Recitals*, 6 v. (New York 1940) v.2, 6. W. E. BUSZIN, *Chorale Preludes by Masters of the XVII and XVIII Centuries* (St. Louis 1948). N. DUFOURCQ, *L'Orgue parisien* (Copenhagen 1956); ed., *Les Grandes heures de l'orgue* (Paris), a series. N. DUFOURCQ et al., eds., *Orgue et liturgie* (Paris), a series. M. H. GLYN, ed., *Early English Organ Music* (London 1939–). A. F. GUILMANT, ed., *Archives des* *maîtres de l'orgue des XVIe, XVIIe et XVIIIe siècles,* 10 v. (Paris 1898–1910). E. KALLER, ed., *Liber Organi* (New York 1931–). J. MUSET, *Early Spanish Organ Music* (New York 1948–). F. PEETERS, *Oudnederlandsche Meesters* (Paris 1938–). G. PHILLIPS, *Tallis to Wesley* (New York), a series. M. S. KASTNER, *Cravistas portuguezês,* 2 v. (New York 1935–50). K. STRAUBE, ed., *Alte Meister des Orgelspiels* NS, 2 v. (Leipzig 1929). **Illustration credits:** Fig. 3, Courtesy of Frau Gisella Selden-Goth, Florence. Fig. 4, Copyright by Alphonse Leduc & Co. (1951), 175 rue Saint-Honoré-Paris Ier. Owners and Publishers.

[C. CROZIER; H. GLEASON]

ORGANIC ARTICLES

This term refers to the law enacted by the French legislature on the same day (April 8, 1802) it accepted the *Concordat of 1801. The law was called organic because such a law is one whose aim is to organize an institution. The Organic Articles sought to reorganize in detail the Church in *France, more so than the concordat, whose provisions were phrased in broader fashion. Only after *Pius VII had ratified the concordat did Napoleon, without informing the Holy See, present to the legislature both the Organic Articles and the concordat (*see* NAPOLEON I). Once enacted, the Organic Articles were promulgated along with the concordat as if part of it. Both acts acquired and retained equal legal status in French law.

Napoleon tried to justify his action by citing article 1 of the concordat, which permitted the government to establish such police regulations concerning public worship as might be judged necessary for public tranquillity. According to him, the Organic Articles did not exceed this scope; actually they went far beyond it and reintroduced into religious legislation measures based on the principles of *Gallicanism that had been dropped at the Holy See's insistence during the long negotiations preceding the concordat. In part Napoleon was motivated by a desire to facilitate the concordat's passage through legislative assemblies that viewed it with slight favor; but his main purpose was to retract the concessions in the concordat and to subject the Church to the State.

The 77 articles (gathered under four titles) in the Organic Articles were well designed to achieve Napoleon's goals. Title 1 submitted to the *placet* all Roman acts, decrees, and briefs, and all synodal decrees, even those of ecumenical councils (*see* EXEQUATUR AND PLACET). Title 1 also required government authorization for the holding of national, metropolitan, and diocesan synods. Papal nuncios, legates, and vicars apostolic were forbidden to exercise their functions on French soil or to do so anywhere else on matters relative to the Gallican Church without government permission. The *appeal as from an abuse (*appel comme d'abus*) also was reintroduced by granting recourse to the Council of State.

Title 2, dealing with the clergy, ended exemptions from episcopal jurisdiction and permitted bishops, with government authorization, to establish cathedral chapters and seminaries, but it suppressed other ecclesiastical establishments. Bishops were forbidden to leave their dioceses, even to go to Rome, without the first consul's consent. Seminary professors were required to subscribe to the *Declaration of the French Clergy (1682) and to teach the doctrines contained in this classic exposition of Gallicanism. Other articles regulated priestly

ordinations and revenues, the administration of vacant sees, and many other details of clerical life.

Title 3 concerned worship. It required the adoption of a single catechism and a single liturgy for the entire country (*see* CATECHISM, IMPERIAL). Besides regulating preaching, the establishment of domestic chapels and private oratories, and even the ringing of church bells, it forbade the introduction of religious feasts without government permission. Nuptial blessings could not be bestowed on couples who had not previously contracted marriage before a civil official. At parish Masses pastors were required to pray for the prosperity of the republic and of the consuls. Title 4 dealt with the number and size of dioceses and parishes, the reimbursement of the clergy, pious foundations, and ecclesiastical properties.

Pius VII protested against these unilateral regulations in his consistorial allocution of May 24, 1802, and again in 1804 on the occasion of his visit to Paris for the imperial coronation. Cardinal *Caprara, the papal legate, also decried the promulgation of this ecclesiastical code without the Holy See's concurrence and the detailed regulations that affected the clergy and their relations with Rome but prescinded from papal authority. Above all Caprara objected to the intimation, especially in articles 1 and 3, that the spiritual power is inferior to the temporal. Despite the many conflicts to which the Organic Articles gave rise and the many attempts to have them abolished, they remained on the statute books until the abrogation of the concordat in 1905, although several of their provisions had fallen meanwhile into disuse. In Alsace-Lorraine, however, the Organic Articles remained in effect after 1905, along with the concordat.

Bibliography: F. MOURRET, *A History of the Catholic Church,* tr. N. THOMPSON, v.7 (St. Louis 1955) 565–574 has Eng. text of the law. C. CONSTANTIN, DTC 3.1:760–770. R. NAZ, DDC 1: 1064–72. S. DELACROIX, *La Réorganisation de l'Église de France après la Révolution, 1801–1809* (Paris 1962–), in course of publication.

[J. LEFLON]

ORGANIC TRANSPLANTS

The transplantation of an organ involves its removal, in whole or in part, from a body (living or dead, man or animal) and the engrafting of it in the body of another living being, of whose organism it then becomes a part. This article is concerned with the morality of such a procedure when the transplant is made: (1) from a dead to a living person; (2) from a living person to another when the organ removed is either harmful or at least useless to the donor; (3) from one living person to another when the organ is healthy and normally fulfills its function; and (4) from an animal to a human being.

From a Dead to a Living Person. This kind of organic transplant presents little moral difficulty provided the donor has given consent before death, or provided that those who are the legal custodians of the corpse give their consent. Speaking of this problem in his allocution of May 14, 1956, Pius XII added this further caution: "It would not be fair that the bodies of poor patients in public clinics and hospitals be officially deputed to the service of medicine and surgery, while those of richer patients would not be so deputed. Wealth and social status should not intervene when it is a matter of dealing with such delicate human sentiments."

Pius XII also raised two complementary questions that are relevant to every lawful organic transplantation. Ordinarily one should not say that the grant of the cornea or any other organ is a duty or an obligatory act of charity. Furthermore, it would undoubtedly always be nobler for the donor to refuse financial compensation, but it is not necessarily immoral to accept or demand such compensation.

From a Living Donor When the Organ Is Harmful or Useless to Him. Removing a pathological organ that harms the whole organism of one living person but can be useful to another person is not immoral in itself. In such a case the mutilation serves the interests of the whole being of the donor himself before those of the person receiving the graft. The difficulties that can be raised with regard to the engrafting of ovarian tissue or even transplanting a whole ovary do not seem decisively important to some authorities.

Moreover, it is not immoral to remove an organ, or part of an organ that, without being harmful, does not perform its function in the body of the donor, as, for example, the cornea of a blind man; this does not involve the suppression of a function since the function does not exist. It is true that some authors are opposed to such a graft because of the principle, to be discussed later, that all mutilation is unlawful if it is not ordered to the good of the whole being. However, it seems that theologians generally do not condemn this practice.

From a Living Donor When the Organ Is Healthy and Functioning. This case involves greater difficulty. In 1944 Bert J. Cunningham published a thesis wherein, on grounds of the unity of the human race and the Mystical Body, he maintained that organic transplants are lawful under the same title as blood transfusions and for the same charitable motive. Citing the commonly admitted teaching that the indirect taking of a life can be justified by the application of the principle of the *double effect, he concluded that charity should be able to authorize what is less than the taking of a life, namely, mutilation. He also stated as a principle that whatever a person can reasonably do for himself in this matter he can do also for his neighbor. He nevertheless declared that the procedure would not be licit except under two conditions; namely, that the removal of the organ does not endanger the donor's life and that the intervention does not induce sterility.

A number of articles appeared attacking this position, and much debate has not yet completely clarified the problem. Many theologians hold that such a transplantation of a healthy organ is unlawful, although some concede that the contrary opinion is truly probable. Several moralists have distinguished between mutilations that damage the substantial integrity of the human body, i.e., completely suppress an important function, and mutilations that do not produce such an injury because they suppress a function only partially, as in the case of the removal for the purpose of transplantation of one of doubled or paired organs, such as eyes, ovaries, or kidneys. In the opinion of these theologians, mutilations of the former type would be illicit, whereas those of the latter type could be permitted if the beneficiary stands to gain an advantage proportionate to the loss suffered by the donor. Some theologians who take this view, however, think that even in the case of paired or-

gans the greater or lesser harm to the function in the remaining organ ought to be taken into consideration. Thus they would oppose the transplant of a cornea but not of a kidney.

Those who deny the lawfulness of organic transplants from one living person to another base their position primarily upon the traditionally admitted principle that a mutilation is permitted only if it is ordered to the good of the whole being. Most of these theologians justify this principle in this way: Man is not the proprietor of his life and the organs constituting his physical integrity, but is only the usufructuary and administrator of these goods, of which God retains the ownership; man, then, cannot dispose of them as he likes. L. Bender, OP, prefers that terms signifying right (such as property and administration) should not be used in speaking about life and the integrity of various organic functions. According to him organic transplants are immoral because they are contrary to the finality proper to each being in its tendency to its own perfection.

Adhering to the principle that every mutilation not ordered to the good of the whole being of the person mutilated is immoral, the supporters of this opinion claim that their opponents try to justify by the extrinsic aim of charity an action that is evil in itself. They accuse their opponents also of making an unwarranted inference from the lawfulness and occasionally, as in the famous case of Father Kolbe, the high moral value of an indirect taking of life to the lawfulness of direct mutilation. As regards the argument drawn from blood transfusions and skin grafts, they argue that the comparison is invalid since blood plasma builds itself up again and skin mends itself and hence, in these cases, there is no mutilation in the strict sense of the term.

Those holding this opinion rely especially upon the texts of Pius XI and Pius XII, as well as upon the 1940 document in which the Holy Office condemned direct sterilization. In his encyclical on Christian Marriage, Dec. 31, 1930, Pius XI said: "Individuals have no power over the members of their bodies other than that which pertains to their natural ends; they are not free, then, to destroy or mutilate their members, or in any other way make themselves unfit for their natural functions, except when no other provision can be made for the good of the whole body. This is the solid teaching of Christian doctrine and the certain conclusion furnished by the light of reason." Pius XII took up the same idea, almost in the same terms, in his allocution of Oct. 19, 1953. In that of May 14, 1956, he said: "To show that the extirpation of organs needed for transplantation from one living person to another is in conformity with nature and lawful, some have put it on the same basis as that of a definite physical organ done with concern for a whole physical organism . . .. The end intended through this argumentation, namely, remedying the misfortune of another or at least mitigating it, is comprehensible and praiseworthy, but the proposed method and the proof supporting it are erroneous." Interpreting "the proposed method" to be the transplantation itself and "the proof" to be the principle of totality upon which those holding its licitness rely, some have concluded, on the basis of both points, that Pius XII condemned these types of transplants.

These arguments, however, do not seem absolutely convincing. In the citation from Pius XI, which deals also with sterilization, the Pope does not mention the problem about organic transplants. Moreover, in his allocution of May 14, 1956, Pius XII explicitly said that he did not want to take up the questions about transplants from one living person to another; he stated that, to justify these transplants, one cannot appeal to the principle of *totality, but he refrained from approving or condemning the transplants themselves. The "proposed method" could be taken to mean the method of argumentation, that is, drawing a false parallel between the relations of an organ to the physical whole that is the human body, and relations of a member of society to the whole that is society. "The proof" could be understood as indicating every attempt to justify this parallelism.

However, although one cannot speak about a subordination in the strict sense, such as in the case of a physical whole, does not the unity of the human race and the unity of the Mystical Body produce true bonds among men founded upon charity? It is this that justifies blood transfusions and skin grafts, which, in comparison with transplants, admits a difference not of nature but of degree. Charity, too, justifies certain hysterectomies needed for the success of Caesarian operations; and these hysterectomies are really mutilations ordered to another's good.

In this discussion one cannot simply take it for granted that every mutilation is intrinsically evil if it is not ordered to the good of the whole being, since that is precisely what must be proved. The fact that men are not the proprietors but only the administrators of their bodies does not make it necessary for one to conclude that charity could not justify any transplant whatsoever. At most this fact places limits upon what charity permits one to sacrifice for his neighbor. Furthermore, it is true that every being should tend toward its perfection; but charity itself is a personal value pertinent to a higher order, and the perfection of the human being should not be understood only in reference to his physical integrity. Moreover, while admitting a difference between the indirect taking of life and direct mutilation, cannot one say that charity, capable of justifying the former, can also justify the latter, since in the concrete order of purely physical values organic integrity is still less than life?

Two opinions, then, are still maintained, one condemning these transplants, and the other admitting them or at least holding that it has not been proved as yet that they are unlawful, since they do not suppress an important function. The second of these opinions appears to be winning more adherents. In any event, the opinion seems probable enough to be admitted in practice until such time as its opponents build a stronger case.

From Animal to Human Being. Organic transplants from an animal to a human being are not necessarily unlawful, since infrahuman creation is immediately ordered to man. These transplants are permitted as long as they are truly to man's advantage.

However, in his allocution of May 14, 1956, Pius XII rejected the transplant of sex glands from an animal to a man as being immoral. The reason (not given by Pius XII) is that it seems such a transplant cannot be accomplished without serious modifications of a physical and psychic order. However, as far as can be judged, the Pope's condemnation seems not to apply to a partial graft of an animal sex gland if and to the extent that such a graft does not entail any disturbance but, on the contrary, is to a man's genuine advantage. In this domain, as in many others, what is good medically, that is, in keeping with medicine that is truly for the service of the human person, is also good morally.

Bibliography: Pius XII, "Vous Nous avez demandé," (Address, May 14, 1956) ActApS 48 (1956) 459–467, Eng. AmEcclRev 135 (1956) 159–166. B. J. Cunningham, *The Morality of Organic Transplantation* (Washington 1944). G. Kelly, "Pope Pius XII and the Principle of Totality," ThSt 16 (1955) 391–396; "The Morality of Mutilation: Towards a Revision of the Treatise," *ibid.* 17 (1956) 333, 341–344.

[J. PAQUIN]

ORGANICISM

In general, organicism refers to the theory that everything is essentially organic, vital, dynamic, or processlike in character. More specifically, in medicine, organicism suggests that each bodily organ has its own dynamic unity, and consequently every disease is associated with a structural lesion of the organ. In biology, organicism states that the individual dynamic system running through the entire organ is equivalent to the life principle. The organicistic theory is meant to serve as a mediator between *vitalism on one hand and *mechanism on the other. Defenders of organicism insist that *life in general and all the specific life processes are manifestations of a basic function or operation made possible only because of the autonomous organization of the whole system. Negatively expressed, the individual components of the living system cannot explain life.

In social thought, organicism suggests that it is most fruitful to interpret societies, large and small, as individual, living, grouplike entities. Again the most significant feature of these organic groups is their dynamic, vital, processlike structure. A social group must be viewed as an intermingling process of ideas, beliefs, goals, drives, and wants. Like every other living being, a society goes through the processes of birth, growth, death, and decay. Each social entity has its own peculiar moods, patterns, likes, dislikes, passions, and attitudes.

Concerning theological matters, the organicists argue that all religious truths and beliefs must be seen as living, changing, and relative to the problems of the time. That is, while religious convictions grow and change, the more important ideas remain only relatively stable and of greater or lesser importance depending on the needs of the people and the entire social situation.

In contemporary philosophy, the theory of organicism has undergone rigid development and detailed application in the writings of A. N. *Whitehead. The impact of this concept on Whitehead's thinking can be seen in the fact that the word process plays a key role in the title and the development of his work *Process and Reality*, in which he sets out to explain the "philosophy of organicism." Many of the basic terms in his philosophy, such as experience, creativity, actual entity, concrescence, prehension, event, and ingression are indicative of the importance that the concept of organic process has in his philosophy.

Whitehead argues that an organicistic interpretation will give a clearer understanding of God, man, and the universe in general and will aid in repudiating some of the more serious contemporary philosophic inadequacies. Specifically, a philosophy of organicism will rekindle trust in speculative philosophy, help question the belief that language is an adequate expression of thought, enable man to see the errors in faculty psychology, encourage criticism of the subject-predicate form of expression, and aid in repudiating sensationalism as well as the Kantian idea that the world is a construct.

Bibliography: A. N. WHITEHEAD, *Process and Reality* (New York 1929).

[M. J. FAIRBANKS]

ORGANISM

The term organism applies, in the strict sense, to living corporeal creatures; these are said to be organic, in contradistinction to nonliving or inorganic entities. Named from the Greek ὄργανον, meaning instrument or tool, organisms are understood to be made up of different parts (or organs) that are instruments, or tools, of the whole.

Philosophical Analysis. Because all its parts and their respective functions are subordinated to, or ordered to, the good of the whole, an organism is structurally and functionally a *unity. Its structural unity is manifest to anyone attempting to remove one of its parts; this entails not only physical severance from the organism, but also does violence to the whole, particularly when a necessary or vital part is involved. Thus excising the heart of a frog kills the animal. The organism is also a functional unity, since the parts are subordinated to, and act for the good of, the whole. Each organ has a unique structure and a consequent proportionate function, but apart from this there is an interdependence of parts and of functions. This interdependence is of such import that I. *Kant used it to define organism. An organism, for him, is an organized natural product in which every part owes its presence to the agency of all the remaining parts, and also exists for the sake of the others and of the whole (*Critique of Judgment,* 65). It thus differs from a machine.

Aristotelian View. In defining organism, *Aristotle first distinguished natural bodies into two categories: those having *life and those not having it. "By life," he said, "we mean self-nutrition and growth" (*Anim.* 412a 15). A mature organism that is not mutilated, he observed also, has the power of reproduction (*ibid.* 415a 25–30). Thus he conceived the organism as an entity with distinctive powers enabling it to perform functions not found in the inanimate.

Aristotle considered attributing the operation of living things to their material parts. But he knew from observing an animal's death that the power by which it runs, sees, feels, and chooses its mate, departs all at once (*Part. animal.* 641a 18–21). Furthermore, he recognized the fundamental unity of his own nature, including all of his operations (*Anim.* 414a 13–14). From such observations he concluded that the organism has a life principle—an animate *form, *soul, or *entelechy—that distinguishes it from the nonliving (*ibid.* 414a 27–28, 413a 20–21). This form is manifest also in the natural power of adapting to varying external situations, which Aristotle said distinguished an organism from a machine (*Motu animal.* 701b 1–15).

Cartesian Dualism. The climate of opinion created by Aristotle endured to the time of W. *Harvey, when it underwent a marked change under the influence of R. *Descartes. Biology has not yet recovered from the *dualism of Cartesian and Newtonian thought that characterized the 17th and later centuries. The earlier notion of an organism's being the resultant of organized matter that is disposed for, and informed by, a proper and proportionate form quickly became unacceptable. Such a form had no place in Descartes's conception of organism, although he did see that it was applicable to man. Every other organism, for him, is the product of mechanical forces and is itself a machine. For Descartes the "laws of Mechanics are identical with those of Nature" (*Discourse on Method,* 5). See MIND-BODY PROBLEM.

Scientific Theories. The intervening period between Descartes and the present has been one of wide proliferation of philosophical views; these run the gamut from seeing organisms as manifestations of *spirit to regarding them as mere epiphenomena of *matter. At the same time, scientists were formulating their own theories of organism along empirical lines, while interpreting their data within the framework of existing philosophies. This accounts for a corresponding diversity of scientific viewpoint on the nature of organism, some scientists advocating a mechanical theory, others a cell theory, still others various theories based on the chemico-physical bases of life, homeostasis, different levels of organic function, and the organismic concept itself.

Mechanical Theory. With some notable exceptions (J. S. Haldane, J. H. Woodger, W. E. Ritter, E. S. Russell, L. H. Hyman, and J. Oppenheimer, among others), 20th-century biologists adopt the Newtonian outlook of their predecessors in the 18th and 19th centuries. In the spirit of mechanism and Cartesian dualism, they investigate and interpret the organism in terms of its constituent parts, much as a mechanic examines the parts of a machine to explain its operation. The heuristic value of such an approach is evident in the triumphs of modern medicine and surgery. Transplantation of corneas and arteries, the use of mechanical heart and lung machines, the reattachment of severed limbs, delicate heart surgery, and injections of organ-regulating hormones are some of the achievements of modern medicine that result from concentrating on the mechanics of the organism. In light of such results, it seems that the organism can best be understood in terms of mechanical models.

Cell Theory. But biologists have not limited themselves solely to the study of organs and systems within organisms. While C. R. *Darwin was working at his great synthesis, interrelating all organisms through time and space, investigators found other ways of viewing the organism. The cell theory, formalized through the writings of M. J. Schleiden and Theodor *Schwann (c. 1840), actually stemmed from the work of 17th-century microscopists, and has proved to be a major generalization in biology. The "unit of life" or cell, of which all animals and plants were seen to be constituted, became comparable to the chemists' molecule. In the cell theory, the organism is itself a vast symphony of separate units with different forms and functions; these coalesce to make up the composite.

Since the mid-19th century the cell has won increasing recognition among biologists as the unit of life. Study of the functions of higher organisms has been largely replaced by investigations of similar functions in unicellular organisms. The advent of the electron microscope and high-speed centrifuges in the 20th century has resulted in increased concentration on the composition and function of subcellular units, such as the ribosomes, mitochondria, endoplasmic reticulum, and lysosomes.

Chemicophysical Basis. When Friedrich Wöhler synthesized urea artificially in 1828, he broke down a long-established basis for distinction between organic and inorganic compounds. Some biologists used this development to justify a theory of organism that went beyond the mechanical. Then, in the mid-19th century, Félix Dujardin, Max Schultze, and T. H. *Huxley proposed the concept of *protoplasm as "the physical basis of life." Claude *Bernard, Louis *Pasteur, and Justis Liebig helped lay the groundwork for this concept, as for the implied theory of the biochemical continuity of living things, both of which have been intensively studied and extensively documented during the 20th century.

Protoplasm is a gelatinous, colloidal substance composed largely of water and of important classes of organic substances, viz, *proteins, fats, sugars, salts, and more elaborate molecules. These organic substances are in turn composed chiefly of carbon, hydrogen, nitrogen, phosphorus, and sulfur. All these elements are found in inorganic matter as well, but in the cell they seemed to be organized into highly specialized molecular configurations; accordingly, scientists began searching for macromolecules peculiar to living things. Since proteins and nucleic acids are found universally in living things (even in the *virus, whose status as an organism has not yet been established), intensive studies in protein and *nucleic acid chemistry followed. In 1926, after J. B. Sumner had prepared the enzyme urease in a pure form and identified it chemically, biologists and biochemists decided that enzymes were sufficiently complex to account for the functions of living things. But, as mounting evidence showed that the hereditary material for bacteria and viruses is a nucleic acid (deoxyribonucleic acid or DNA) rather than a protein, interest shifted away from proteins toward nucleic acids.

Nobel prizes were awarded to three teams of scientists in the years 1958 to 1962 for work on DNA. The model of DNA, as constructed on the Watson-Crick plan, itself symbolizes the 20th-century advance in biology and medicine. Biology has come to be labeled molecular biology, diseases are classified as genetic, molecular, or metabolic disorders, and the organism is regarded as the resultant of instructions given by DNA to the cell constituents and its metabolites.

Homeostasis. Another central biological concept born in the 19th century brought scientists back into the mainstream of Aristotelian thought of organismic unity. Bernard saw the constancy of the internal environment of an organism, which is maintained through special substances secreted by the organs, as the condition for a free and independent life. W. B. Cannon extended these studies and gave the name homeostasis to the process by which the organism maintains its body fluids and temperature constant. The "second wind" of the athlete and the uniformity of sugar content in human blood are examples of homeostasis. In such cases, physiological unity transcends molecular structure and cell boundaries, and furnishes evidence that some operations in the organism exceed the potential of its parts, whether these be cells or molecules.

Multilevel Approach. The state of research in the 1960s indicates that only a multilevel attack on the problems posed by man's attempt to understand the nature of an organism can yield valid results. Contractile enzymes do not adequately explain muscle contraction, nor do pontifical chemical organizers account for embryonic development. Isolated cells or colonies of cells of themselves have not yet produced differentiated cells or tissues, much less an organism.

Experiments rather indicate that the cell, while an active worker in the organization, is subordinate both to other tissues and to the whole. When cells are grown in tissue culture, *metabolism and growth proceed independently of the organism from which the cells came; yet such cells rapidly lose their capacity to maintain the functioning distinctive of the organs from which they are taken. Thus thyroid cells in tissue culture do not continue to produce thyroxin. Cells growing in vitro are much influenced in their chemical makeup, number of chromosomes, and to some extent in structure, by the media in which they are grown. Usually, cells of unlike type are necessary to initiate structural and functional changes in cells in vitro. Experimental embryologists have found that each level of differentiation in the embryo is, in some measure, a necessary prerequisite for the next higher level. However, Alan Haber at Oak Ridge has shown that concurrent growth of plants is not dependent on cell division. Irradiated wheat seeds in which cell division is blocked have germinated and grown into seedlings without cell division, DNA synthesis, or mitosis.

It is evident, then, that the structure and function of all the parts of the organism must be studied in their interrelationhip with other parts and with the whole. This multilevel approach cannot stop even at the stratum of the organism, for the organism is itself conditioned by its environment and its relationship with other members of the biological community of which it is a part. Thus ecological and populational studies emerge as important areas of study in 20th-century biology.

Organismic Theory. Biophysics, biochemistry, molecular biology, cell biology, organismic biology, and populational biology have all made important contributions to the study of organisms. The organismic viewpoint is the oldest approach to this study, with outstanding adherents in every age. Aristotle, *Galen, Harvey, Bernard, Pasteur, and in the 20th century, Ritter, Haldane, Russell, Woodger, Hyman, Oppenheimer, Otto Loewi, Hans Selye, and G. S. Simpson may be listed as organismic biologists. They hold that nature's primary natural biological unit is the organism. It is true that cells in tissue culture metabolize, grow, and reproduce—all characteristics of living things—but only an organism, whether uni- or multicellular, exhibits the full range of specialized structures and functions of which living things are capable. Moreover, an organism alone has a proper internal principle that can repair or replace parts, or adjust one part to meet the needs of another or of the whole. Again, only in an organism is there a gradual emergence of more complex forms from embryo to adult. The end of such organic activity is obviously the good of the organism. Even the coordination of its many parts for an act such as the digestion of food is an indication that the organism is in command of its parts, which it calls upon to make partial surrender of their autonomy for the good of the whole. (*See* TELEOLOGY.)

Evaluation. The concept of organism is changing with, and may well account for, the revolution biology is presently undergoing. H. *Bergson, A. N. *Whitehead, and P. *Teilhard de Chardin are among leading philosophers of science who have rejected mechanical explanations of the organism and have urged that the fundamental laws of nature be sought instead in living things. In substituting a philosophy of organism for the mechanical laws of Descartes, they lend support to the reinstatement of the organism as one of nature's primary units, and to the reinterpretation of much of reality in the likeness of this primary unit. Even Darwin's theory of evolution, though often used to substantiate a mechanistic view of nature, furnishes a valid foundation for views that recognize the fundamental unity of the organism. Again, an increasing number of scientists point out the limitations of a reductionist view in biology that resolves an organism into its component parts and, at the same time, reduces biology to a department of chemistry and physics. Impressed by this tendency, L. L. Whyte, in his *Accent on Form* (New York 1954), predicts that the science of the future will take on a more organismal character, that interest in science will shift from the 18th- and 19th-century accent on matter to an accent on form.

The accumulated evidence of archeologists and paleontologists shows that organisms similar to those found in nature have existed on earth for some 500 million years. Thus a great number and diversity of forms of animals and plants preceded the coming of man, the machine-designing organism. Just as the presence of worked tools in fossil beds is taken as an indication of man's presence, so the multiplicity of parts of an organism integrated through a unifying principle can be seen as the evident handwork of a Master Artisan.

See also ORGANICISM; MECHANISM; MECHANISM, BIOLOGICAL; VITALISM.

Bibliography: W. E. RITTER, *The Unity of the Organism* (Boston 1919). L. VON BERTALANFFY, *Modern Theories of Development,* tr. and ed. J. H. WOODGER (New York 1962). B. H. WILLIER et al., eds., *Analysis of Development* (Philadelphia 1955). E. S. RUSSELL, *The Directiveness of Organic Activities* (Cambridge, Eng. 1945); *The Interpretation of Development and Heredity* (Oxford 1930). J. H. WOODGER, *Biological Principles* (New York 1929). L. H. HYMAN, *The Invertebrates* (New York 1940–). K. GOLDSTEIN, *The Organism* (New York 1939). C. S. SHERRINGTON, *Man on His Nature* (2d ed. Garden City, N.Y. 1953). A. N. WHITEHEAD, *Science and the Modern World* (New York 1925). W. B. CANNON, *The Wisdom of the Body* (New York 1939). L. E. R. PICKEN, *The Organization of Cells and Other Organisms* (Oxford 1960). A. C. HILDEBRANDT et al., *Plant Tissue Culture and Morphogenesis,* ed. J. C. O'KELLY (New York 1963). A. M. HOFSTETTER, "Viruses: Are They Alive?" NewSchol 31 (1957) 297–316. J. H. RANDALL, "The Changing Impact of Darwin on Philosophy," JHistIdeas 22 (1961) 435–462.

[A. M. HOFSTETTER]

ORGANIZATION OF AMERICAN STATES

A regional system of international cooperation with roots deep in the history of the Western Hemisphere. No sooner had independence been won by the states of Central and South America than they were invited by the Great Liberator, Simón *Bolívar, to meet at Panama in 1826. Although the Treaty of Perpetual Union that he proposed failed to come into being, it remained an inspiration for plans of union until, in 1889, the first International Conference of American States met in Washington at the invitation of Secretary of State James G. Blaine.

Successive conferences followed, each widening the scope of mutual interests. The Commercial Bureau, established in 1890, became by 1910 the Pan American Union, and plans of arbitration and practical measures of economic cooperation, regulation of customs duties, protection of copyrights and patents, and codification of international law appeared on the agenda of the conferences. It was not, however, until the special Conference for the Maintenance of Peace at Buenos Aires in 1936 that the significant step was taken of providing for common consultation in the event of threats to the peace.

For some 30 years there had been strong opposition in Latin America to the interpretation of the Monroe Doctrine by Pres. Theodore Roosevelt in 1904. Under this interpretation, the U.S. justified its exercise of what Roosevelt described as an "international police power" as necessary to keep European powers from occupying the ports of delinquent American states. To Latin America it was the doctrine of the "big stick," and it created a resistance to intervention that dominated all other policies until, in 1936, the U.S. accepted the principle of nonintervention in return for the assumption by the Latin-American states of a collective obligation to meet threats to peace.

By 1940, with the possibility that a victory of the Axis Powers might lead to annexations in the Caribbean, the procedure of consultation took on the more specific character of a resolution declaring that an attack upon one would be an attack upon all. Thus was established a regional security system for the 21 American states. Five years later, when plans for a new international organization to replace the League of Nations were under discussion, the American states met 2 months in advance of the Conference at San Francisco and insisted that the *United Nations should not absorb their regional system but should make provision for the settlement of regional disputes by regional procedures. Further, distrusting the power assigned to the Security Council, they secured a provision in the Charter that allowed them, in the event of an armed attack, to retain the inherent right of self-defense, individual or collective, until such time as the Council should take the necessary measures to maintain the peace.

On the basis of the agreements reached at San Francisco, the American states met at Rio de Janeiro in 1947 and signed the Treaty of Reciprocal Assistance, providing for mutual defense in the event of an armed attack or in the event of an act of aggression of a grave character affecting the territorial integrity or the political independence of an American state. Then, with regional security established, the American states met in Conference at Bogotá in 1948 and signed the Charter of the Organization of American States. The signing of the Charter provided a sort of constitutional structure to the agencies and procedures under which they had been functioning since 1890.

Delegates to the first International Conference of American States, held in Washington, D.C., 1889–90.

The succeeding years have proved the value of the regional organization both as an agency of peace and security and as an effective procedure for the promotion of the common welfare. Controversies that might have resulted in hostilities have been settled by the application of the procedures of the Rio Treaty. Notable among these was the boundary controversy between Honduras and Nicaragua, which in response to a meeting of consultation was referred to the International Court of Justice. Hostilities between Venezuela and the Dominican Republic were averted when the dictator Trujillo was found to have conspired in the attempted assassination of President Betancourt of Venezuela. Only in the case of Cuba was the inter-American regional system ineffective, because the situation involved the intervention of international communism. The government of Cuba was, however, excluded from participation in the inter-American system, and when on Oct. 22, 1962, the President of the U.S. demanded the removal of Soviet missile bases, the Organ of Consultation of the American States supported the demand with a resolution calling upon members to prevent Cuba from receiving military material from the Sino-Soviet powers.

Supplementing its regional security system, or rather building upon it, the Organization of American States has extended its activities into the field of economic and social welfare. Cooperation has, to a degree, succeeded competition; progress has been made in the regulation of prices and markets; the Inter-American Development Bank has offered financial assistance to promote new enterprises; and problems of transportation and communication have been solved in the interest of the community as a whole.

But the most significant feature of recent economic development is to be found in the social objective of improvement in standards of living. In response to an address of the President of the U.S., the Alliance for Progress was established in 1961 as "a vast effort to bring a better life to all the peoples of the Continent." Economic measures, reform of taxation, industrialization, investments, and agrarian reform are indicated as means to raise average income and secure fair wages, better working conditions, health and sanitation, and elimination of illiteracy. The U.S. has undertaken to provide a major part of the $20 billion or more required by Latin America to supplement its own efforts during a 10-year period.

Closely associated with the Organization of American States are a number of specialized organizations established by multilateral agreements and having specific functions with respect to technical matters of common interest. Among them are the Pan American Health Organization, the Inter-American Institute of Agricultural Sciences, and the Inter-American Commission of Women. Outstanding among other intergovernmental agencies is the Inter-American Peace Committee, which seeks to prevent controversies from reaching a critical stage, and the Special Consultative Committee on Security, created in 1962, which studies the subversive activities of international communism and makes recommendations to the governments.

Bibliography: C. G. FENWICK, *The Organization of American States* (Washington 1963). A. VAN W. and A. J. THOMAS, *Organization of American States* (Dallas 1963). J. L. MECHAM, *The United States and Inter-American Security, 1889–1960* (Austin 1961). **Illustration credit:** Pan American Union.

[C. G. FENWICK]

ORGANUM. A generic term used from the 9th to the mid-14th century to describe various methods of adding two-, three-, or four-voice parts to a chant melody. Isolated communities, notably in Germany, were still using organum as late as the 15th century, and the term as well as the style has occasionally been revived in modern times, especially by composers influenced by the resurgence of interest in medieval music. Organum (also called diaphony) is first defined and discussed in a 9th-century musical treatise, *Musica Enchiriadis,* and in the slightly later commentary on it, *Scholia Enchiriadis* (*see* MUSIC, SACRED, HISTORY OF, 3). Both indicate the basic two-voice structure as consisting of a given plainsong (*vox principalis*), which may be doubled at the octave below, or the fifth below, or the fourth below. Similar techniques may be found in primitive, non-Western, and medieval secular music. The additional third or fourth voice parts were permitted to double the *vox principalis* or the second voice (*vox organalis*) at the octave above, thus increasing the solemnity and sonority of the composition, which by its own nature and according to the theorists, was performed in a resonant building and at a moderate, steady

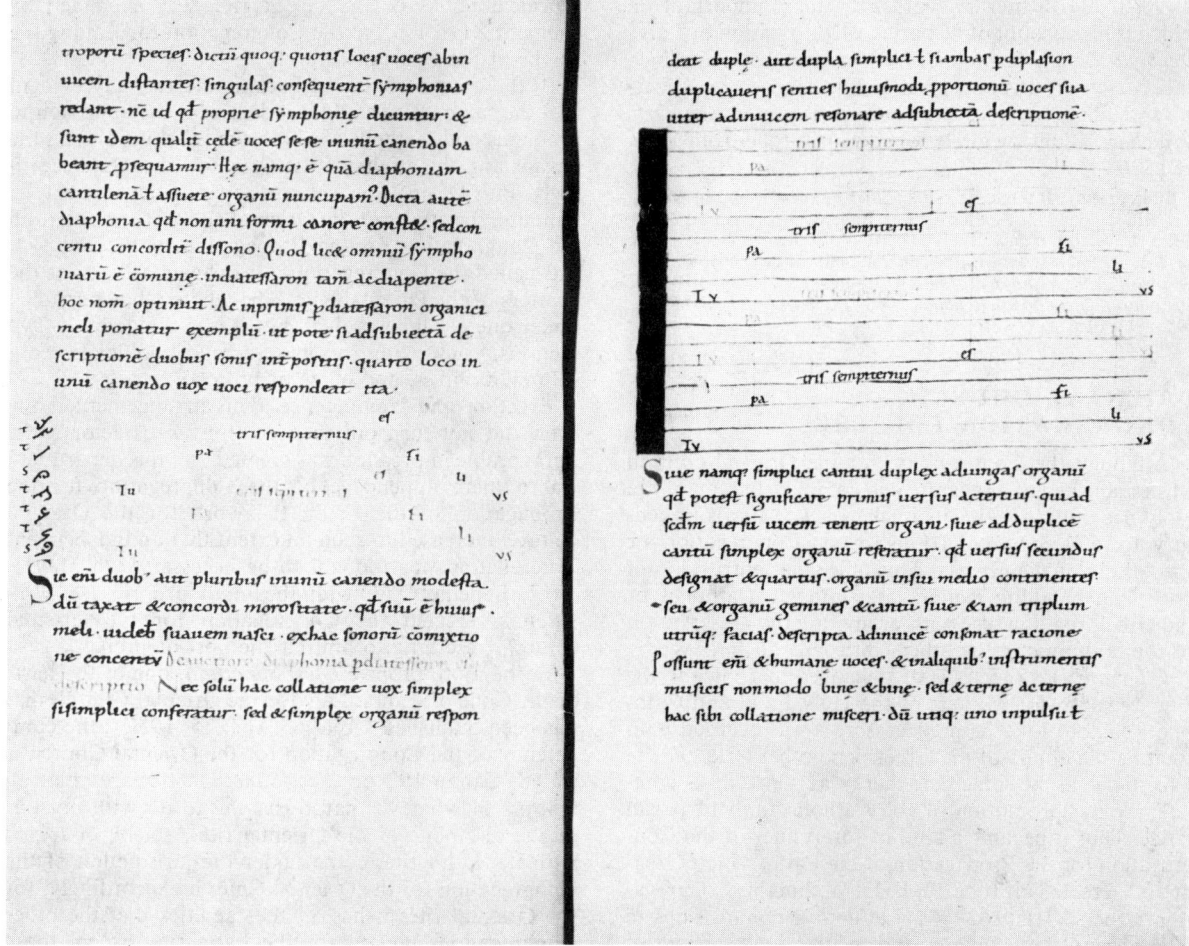

Discussion of organum in an 11th-century MS of the "Musica Enchiriadis" (Vatican Library, Cod. Pal. Lat. 1342).

pace. Like the later *fauxbourdon,* organum was essentially a simple and functional means of harmonization, meant to be sung from the chant books in accordance with rules known to the singers. Written examples are therefore rarely found outside the treatises.

In its earliest forms, organum is said to be parallel or strict when the intervals between any two melodic lines remain constant. In free organum, already recognized as the norm by *Guido of Arezzo in his *Micrologus* (c. 1040), there is considerable use of oblique motion, whereby one voice moves and another remains stationary, sometimes for the duration of a short phrase. Free organum greatly influenced the development of melismatic organum, in which one single note of the chant was long sustained so that the added voice or voices might move rapidly above it in complex and rhapsodic patterns at first unmeasured but later measured. The earliest and most extensive repertory of organa for the Mass and Office is found in the Cambridge MS of the Winchester Troper (11th century). The perfection of melismatic organum, although in some senses a communal effort of continental Europe, is associated particularly with the Abbey of Saint-Martial, *Limoges, and the Cathedral of Notre Dame in Paris, where, in the 12th century, *Léonin, and after him *Pérotin, continued to honor organal style while encouraging newer compositional techniques. *Franco of Cologne in his *Ars cantus mensurabilis* (c. 1260) provides brief examples of organum as it was practiced in his day, but by c. 1335 the *Speculum musicae* of Jacques de Liège mentions the various kinds of organum as almost extinct.

Bibliography: G. ARETINUS, *Micrologus,* ed. J. S. VAN WAESBERGHE (Nijmegen 1955). Reese MusMA 249–330. A. HUGHES, Grove DMM 6:361–362. Apel HDMus 539–541.

[D. STEVENS]

ORICELLARIUS, BERNARD (RUCELLAI),

Renaissance historian and politician; b. probably Florence, Aug. 11, 1448; d. Oct. 7, 1514. Son of Giovanni Rucellai and Iacoba Strozza, Bernard came from a family enriched by the wool industry since the 13th century and politically important in the 15th century. His father commissioned Leone *Alberti to build the family palace and the façade of S. Maria Novella. In 1466 Bernard married Nannina, sister of Lorenzo de' *Medici. He became *gonfaloniere* of justice in 1480, Florentine ambassador to Milan from 1482 to 1485, to Geneva in 1484, and to Naples 1486–87 and 1494–95. Because of his opposition to the absolutism of Piero II de' Medici (1492–95), Bernard was later (1512) chosen a member of the Committee of Twenty authorized to reorganize the government of Florence. Rucellai devoted himself

(1498–1511) to literary works, the most important of which is his account of *Charles VIII's invasion of Italy, *De bello italico* (London 1733), where the term "balance of power" first appears in political literature. Rucellai and his sons were the leading figures in the *Orti Oricellari,* a literary circle famous in Europe from 1502 to 1506.

Bibliography: B. ORICELLARIUS, *Liber de urbe Roma* in Muratori RIS 2:765–782. É. PICOT, "Les Italiens en France au XVIᵉ siècle," *Bulletin italien* 2 (1902) 108–147. A. PANELLA, EncIt 30:211. R. PALMAROCCHI, EncCatt 10:1430. F. GILBERT, *Journal of the Warburg and Courtauld Institutes* 12 (1949) 101–131. *Dizionario enciclopedico italiano,* ed. U. BOSCO, 12 v. (Rome 1955–61) 10:613.

[M. G. MC NEIL]

ORIENTAL CHURCH, CONGREGATION FOR THE

Although the Congregation for the Oriental Church was established as a separate and complete bureau of the Holy See only in 1917, its nucleus lies in the 16th century. In 1573 Gregory XIII instituted a Congregation for the Affairs of the Greeks. This office was entrusted not only with handling matters pertaining to Catholics of the Greek rite, but also with promoting the preservation of the faith among the other Christians of the East.

Clement VIII (1592–1605) changed this office to the Congregation for Matters of the Holy Faith and Catholic Religion. Like its predecessor, it was charged with treating the affairs of the Greeks and other Oriental-rite Christians; at the same time there was added to its competency the promotion of the Catholic faith in pagan lands. Thus it became a kind of forerunner of the Congregation for the Propagation of the Faith, which Gregory XV erected on June 22, 1622. Within this Congregation Urban VIII (1623–44) set up two commissions to administer Oriental affairs: the one treating questions of the Oriental rite; the other, charged with editing the liturgical books of the Greek rite, was expanded by Clement XI in 1719 to the Congregation for Editing the Books of the Oriental Church.

In the course of time it became increasingly evident that the same office could not deal with the approach to problems and methods for both the missions among the pagans and the affairs of the Oriental Church. Accordingly, Pius IX, in 1862, set up a separate department for handling the affairs of the Oriental-rite Christians within the Congregation for the Propagation of the Faith. It was called the Congregatio de Propaganda Fide for the Matters of the Oriental Rite. The whole office remained under one cardinal prefect, but it was divided into two sections, each with its own secretary, officials, consultors, archives, and office of protocol.

Erection and Competence. This arrangement, however, did not turn out to be entirely satisfactory: the unfavorable impression was created that this department was a mere appendage of the Congregation for the Propagation of the Faith; the work for the Oriental Church increased to such an extent that an independent congregation was thought to be necessary. On May 1, 1917, Benedict XV, with the motu proprio *Dei Providentis,* erected the Congregation for the Oriental Church, reserving to himself the post of prefect.

In the motu proprio *Cleri Sanctitati,* one of the parts of the Code of Canon Law for the Oriental Church that has been published (ActApS Aug. 15, 1957), the competency of the Congregation for the Oriental Church is stated. Canon 195 of *Cleri Sanctitati* declares that all matters of whatever nature having to do with persons or the discipline of the Oriental rites, solely, or mixed with the Latin rite, come under the jurisdiction of the Congregation for the Oriental Church. Accordingly, for the Oriental rites it has all the faculties that the other Congregations possess for the Latin rite, except those that are reserved to the Holy Office (ClerSanc c.193),

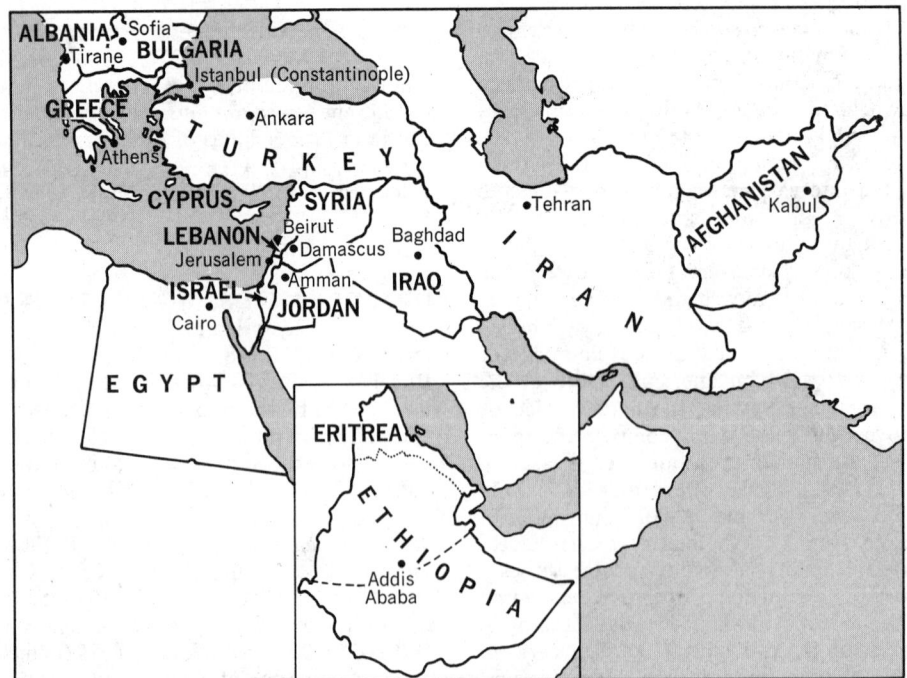

Map showing the areas in which the Congregation for the Oriental Church has complete and exclusive jurisdiction over all Churches in union with Rome.

to the Congregation of Rites with regard to the canonization of saints, to the Congregation for Extraordinary Affairs in treating with civil governments, to the Congregation of Seminaries and Universities for higher institutions of learning, and to the Sacred Penitentiary for the internal forum and indulgences.

The Congregation for the Oriental Church is qualified to approve the liturgical books of the Oriental rites as well as to resolve doubts regarding their texts and translations. It also oversees and regulates the rubrics and the ceremonies of the Divine Liturgy, the Sacraments, the sacramentals, and the Divine Office (Cler Sanc c.195.2). These faculties, however, are not exercised in prejudice to the rights of Patriarchs in such matters.

In those territories in which this Congregation has complete and exclusive jurisdiction its faculties embrace the hierarchy, the faithful, the institutions, and the religious organizations of the Latin rite. There are exceptions for those matters that are reserved to the Holy Office, the Congregation of the Discipline of the Sacraments, the Congregation of Universities and Seminaries, and the Sacred Penitentiary (ClerSanc c.195.3). Members of Latin-rite religious communities considered as missionaries, whether individually or as a group, are subject to the Congregation for the Oriental Church in Oriental territories; but as religious, whether singly or as a whole, they are under the Congregation of Religious (ClerSanc c.195.4).

The Congregation for the Oriental Church decides controversies submitted to it in a disciplinary manner. It has full judicial powers for questions that are customarily treated judicially; it may set up its own tribunal. It may also refer cases submitted to it to the ordinary tribunals of the Holy See (ClerSanc c.195.2).

Jurisdiction. The territories in which the Congregation has complete and exclusive jurisdiction are: Egypt and the Sinai Peninsula, Eritrea and northern Ethiopia, southern Albania, Bulgaria, Cyprus, Greece, the Dodecanese, Iran, Iraq, Lebanon, Palestine, Syria, Jordan, Turkey and that part of Thrace that is subject to Turkey, and Afghanistan.

Outside of these regions, the Congregation has jurisdiction over the followers of the Oriental rites in whatever part of the world they happen to be. In the U.S. there are approximately 800,000 Catholics belonging to various Oriental rites and more than 2,500,000 separated Oriental-rite Christians.

The Congregation for the Oriental Church stands, as it were, at the gateway of history in relation to the many Oriental-rite Christians in the Slav countries. It is not easy to find statistics on matters of a religious nature in the Soviet Union. After World War II, however, it was found that there were more than 3,800,000 Catholics of the Byzantine rite in the Soviet Union, and in 1961 the Orthodox Patriarch of Moscow of the Byzantine Russian rite claimed 50 million faithful in his patriarchate.

The Congregation has no territorial jurisdiction in India. It is worthy of note, however, that Indian Catholics of the Oriental rite form a significant part of the Church there. Catholics as a whole constitute only slightly more than 1 per cent of the entire population of India, and half of them are concentrated in the state of Kerala, where most of them are of the Syro-Malabar and the Syro-Malankara rites. Since the Church in India is constrained to depend largely on natives for vocations to the priesthood and the sisterhood, these two flourishing communities of Eastern-rite Catholics offer a solid hope for the future of Catholicism in India.

The Congregation is assisted in its sponsorship of mission works by four organizations: *L'Oeuvre d'Orient,* with its main office in Paris, France; the *Catholica Unio,* operating from Fribourg, Switzerland; the Dutch society, *Apostolaat der Hereniging;* and the *Catholic Near East Welfare Association, with headquarters in New York.

In his decree for erecting the Congregation for the Oriental Church, Benedict XV called for a return to the splendor and the sanctity of the ancient Eastern Church. The Pontiff wrote, "Would that, by divine favor, there might be restored to our beloved Oriental children the possession of their pristine prosperity and glory!" This is the spirit in which the Congregation for the Oriental Church operates.

Bibliography: Congregatio pro Ecclesia Orientali, *Oriente cattolico, cenni storici e statistiche* (Vatican City 1962). Abbo 2:257. Pospishil PersOr 104.

[R. ETTELDORF]

ORIENTAL CODES (CANON LAW)

The need of a collection and codification of the Canon Law of the Eastern Catholic Churches was mentioned at Vatican Council I (1869–70). After the promulgation of the Code of Canon Law (CIC) for the Western or Latin-rite Church (1917), the call for an Oriental code was repeated and resulted in the circular letter of the Congregation for the *Oriental Church (Jan. 5, 1929), directing all Eastern-rite ordinaries to submit suggestions and proposals to this end. Pius XI appointed a commission of cardinals for the preparation of such a code (July 13, 1929), under the presidency of Cardinal Pietro Gasparri (d. 1935), who had headed the codification of CIC. His major collaborator as secretary of the commission was the canonist Amleto Giovanni Cicognani. He was replaced by Acacius Coussa, a Basilian monk of the Melkite patriarchate, later assessor and secretary of the same congregation.

Delegates from all rites began their work in 1930. In 183 meetings they prepared the *schemata,* which were submitted to the Oriental ordinaries for their suggestions. On July 17, 1935, Pius XI established the Pontifical Commission for the Redaction of the Code of Oriental Canon Law (CICO), which began with the work of the determination of the actual text of the canons. The entire material was divided into 21 parts, forming 2,666 canons.

Since 1949 four parts of the future CICO have been promulgated in the form of motu proprios, having the same relationship to the CICO as such decrees as *Ne temere* had to the CIC. With the preparations for Vatican Council II, promulgation of other parts ceased. The fruit of this council will be a total revision of the Latin-rite CIC, and also of the published and unpublished Oriental codification. Certain decrees of Vatican Council II, such as *Orientalium ecclesiarum* on the Eastern Catholic Church (Nov. 21, 1964), have already introduced changes in the Canon Law of the Oriental Churches as it is contained in the four motu proprios described below.

Crebrae Allatae. The first motu proprio, publishing parts of the future CICO, was *Crebrae allatae* (Creb

Allat). It was promulgated Feb. 22, 1949 (ActApS 41:89–119), beginning its legal force May 2, 1949. It contains the marriage law of the Eastern Catholic Churches, which in some countries has legal force in the civil forum also. This Oriental marriage law follows closely the Latin-rite CIC for several reasons: divine law norms, especially those forbidding complete divorce, are common to all Catholics; the legal tradition of the Catholic Orientals followed for several centuries that in the Latin-rite Church; if their marriage law was uniform with that of the Western Church, they could make use of the same commentaries, textbooks, legal definitions, terminology, and judicial precedents, etc. CrebAllat also replaced with their Oriental counterparts certain legal terms loaned from the Latin rite; for example, *eparchy* for diocese, *hierarch* for ordinary, *syncellus* for vicar general, *major* and *minor profession* for solemn and simple profession.

Of the 131 canons of CrebAllat, 101 are identical to the canons of the Code of Canon Law (CIC cc.1012–1143), or differ solely in terminology. The major differences in the remaining 30 canons are:

Marriage banns are required only if particular law demands them (CrebAllat c.12). The impedient impediments of the CIC, which did not impede marriage, are now called prohibitive (CrebAllat c.26.1). Local ordinaries receive ordinary power to dispense from certain impediments (CrebAllat c.32.1), whereas Latin-rite ordinaries received such power by quinquennial faculties. Patriarchs and major archbishops have even more extensive dispensative power (CrebAllat c.32.2–3). The ordinary of the groom is competent to grant dispensations when the parties belong to different Catholic rites (CrebAllat c.32.5). The vicar cooperator (assistant pastor) enjoys the same power of dispensation as the pastor in cases of urgency and when there is a possibility of death (CrebAllat c.34.1). The ordinary shall be considered legally unavailable if he can be reached only by telegraph or telephone (CrebAllat c.34.2). The ordinary can dispense from the marriage form itself if higher authorities cannot be reached without danger arising from delay (CrebAllat c.35.4). Depending on civil law, guardianship might constitute a canonical impediment, either prohibitive (CrebAllat c.49), or diriment (CrebAllat c.71).

Whereas in CIC c.1070.1 all Western non-Catholics, i.e., Protestants, are exempt from the diriment impediment of disparity of worship when marrying unbaptized persons, CrebAllat c.60 establishes it as a diriment impediment if one party is a Catholic or non-Catholic Eastern-rite Christian.

Bishops must be celibate or freed from bonds of marriage, but married men can be ordained to all orders, including the presbyterate, if particular law of that rite permits it (CrebAllat c.71). The ordination to the subdiaconate, although remaining a minor order, constitutes the diriment impediment of holy orders (CrebAllat c.72).

Degrees of *consanguinity and *affinity are reckoned according to the Roman computation, once used also in the Latin-rite Church; this leads to forbidden degrees that are not impediments in CIC c.66.4. In particular law, affinity as a matrimonal impediment can exist also between blood relations of the husband and blood relations of the wife (*ex digeneia*), and between blood relations of one spouse and persons who are related by

affinity to the other spouse (*ex trigeneia*) (CrebAllat c.66.2–3). Spiritual relationship is an impediment between the godparents and the godchild and his parents (CrebAllat c.70) but not between the baptized and the baptizing person, as in CIC c.1078.

Fear that invalidates the marriage contract is defined (CrebAllat c. 78.1) as that which is brought to bear upon a person with the intention to induce him to give marriage consent (*metus consultus*), while CIC c.1087.1 considers only the effect produced in the person.

Marriage by proxy can be entered solely with permission of the ordinary (CrebAllat c.80), making it thereby an extraordinary measure, not available at the will of the parties as it is in CIC c.1089. Marriage cannot be contracted on condition (CrebAllat c.83); Latin-rite marriage law (CIC c.1092) does not allow it expressly but speaks of the legal consequences should it have taken place.

Marriage assistance by the priest includes as an essential element, in addition to the exchange of consent, a religious blessing to be imparted by the priest (CrebAllat c.85.1). A pastor assists invalidly, even within his territory, at a marriage of persons of a rite different from his own. Territorial jurisdiction for assistance at marriages is suspended in places such as churches, rectories, convents, etc., that are under the exclusive jurisdiction of another rite (CrebAllat c.86.1n2).

The vicar cooperator, delegated to assist at marriage, can subdelegate in single cases (CrebAllat c.87.1n2). General faculty of assistance can be given also to a priest in charge of Eastern-rite Catholics in a diocese lacking Oriental-rite pastors (CrebAllat c.87.5). In mixed-rite marriages the pastor of the rite of the bridegroom is competent for the wedding (CrebAllat c.88.3). Marriages with non-Catholics are to be celebrated with the liturgical rite and in church (CrebAllat c.91).

CrebAllat also clarified a number of provisions that were doubtful in the CIC, by changes introduced in the text of the corresponding canons, thus interpreting also the marriage law of CIC.

Sollicitudinem Nostram. The second motu proprio that promulgated parts of a future Oriental CIC was *Sollicitudinem nostram* (SollNostr). It was issued Jan. 6, 1950 (ActApS 42:5–120) and received legal force from Jan. 6, 1951. It is the law of procedure for the Oriental Church. Its appearance was desired by the Eastern-rite Catholics in the Near East for their daily use, since the decisions of their tribunals in family relationships had exclusive application also in civil law.

The contents correspond to book 4 of CIC, but without the 2d and 3d parts, i.e., the procedure for canonization and some administrative procedures. SollNostr treats the same material in 567 canons, 120 more than the CIC. Specific differences from the Latin-rite CIC are the following:

The procedure on arbitration (SollNostr cc.98–122), for which the CIC has only 4 canons (CIC cc.1929–32); criminal procedure in 69 canons (SollNostr cc.507–75), compared to the 27 of the CIC (CIC cc.1933–59), and the section in SollNostr on the civil procedure before one judge is new (SollNostr cc.453–467). The *officialis* of the CIC is called *vicarius judicialis* in SollNostr.

Peculiar to Oriental rites are certain tribunals in the patriarchates. The permanent synod is composed of the patriarch and four bishops. In addition to making administrative decisions, it constitutes also a court of minor criminal proceedings against bishops (SollNostr cc.86–91). The patriarchal tribunal (SollNostr c.85) is a court of higher appeals. As a court of first instance it decides matters pertaining to minor ordinaries (ex-archs, *syncelli* or vicar generals, and patriarchal delegates), physical and moral persons subject to the patriarch, religious institutes of papal and patriarchal status, etc. Metropolitan tribunals are courts of first appeal. Eparchial tribunals must exist in every eparchy or exarchy. A regional tribunal replaces tribunals of several dioceses (SollNostr c.38). Interritual tribunals are common to eparchies of several rites (SollNostr c.39).

Postquam Apostolicis. The third part of the Oriental code to be enacted into law was *Postquam apostolicis* (PostApost). It was promulgated Feb. 9, 1952 (ActApS 44:65–152), with the legal force from Nov. 21, 1952. It contains three unequal parts: the law on the religious (PostApost cc.1–231); on the temporal property of the Church (PostApost cc.232–301); and a number of definitions of legal terms (PostApost cc.302–325), *De verborum significatione*.

The law on religious had to take cognizance of the fact that the majority of Eastern Catholic religious institutes have characteristics adopted from the Latin-rite Canon Law, e.g., instead of one monastic state, there exist orders and congregations, separated from each other; appointment of superiors for a specified time only; and the taking of temporal vows before perpetual profession. PostApost legislates for both kinds of religious, those living according to Latin-rite constitutions and those following Eastern monastic traditions.

Oriental religious institutes can be divided according to the degree of autonomy they enjoy in respect to the hierarchy: those with (1) papal exemption; of (2) papal right but without exemption; (3) patriarchal right; (4) eparchial right (PostApost c.312.2); and (5) stauropegial monasteries, subject directly to the patriarch (PostApost c.313.2n2).

The appearance of the new motu proprio gave each institute the opportunity to decide whether to retain the Latin-rite canonical organization or return to the original form of Western and Eastern religious life, the monastic institute. Only a few chose to become monastic institutes, of which the major features are these:

There is no division of the religious into different orders or congregations, but only one monastic state, to which all monks and nuns belong. Federations of monasteries and federations of monastic federations are known (PostApost c.16). The organizational unit is the independent monastery, a self-contained unit with its own novitiate and house of studies and a superior governing with a council of monks. Members of a monastery may be permitted to lead the life of anchorites or hermits, remaining under the authority of the superior (PostApost c.313.4; c.4). The superior of an independent monastery is elected for life, receives a constitutive blessing, and confers on his subjects the minor orders (PostApost c.174).

The monastic state is not a clerical or lay institute. All members are equal except in matters in which the possession of Holy Orders is required. All participate in the recitation of the monastic Office, the liturgical language being usually an older form of the vernacular.

Choir duty obliges the monastery as such and not the individual members and is carried out by those whom the superior assigns; there is no obligation to recite the Office privately (PostApost c.157).

The novitiate lasts 3 years, and it is not preceded by any specified period of trial (PostApost c.74). After the novitiate perpetual vows are taken by those who are 21 or older (PostApost c.88.1n2; c.108). Profession, which is always solemn in the meaning of Latin-rite Canon Law, is divided into major and minor or simple profession. There are degrees in profession (PostApost c.109): *rasophorate; microscheme* (little habit); and *macroscheme* (grand, angelic habit). Most monks or nuns belong in the category of *microscheme*.

Monasteries are, as a rule, subject to the local ordinary (PostApost c.162), while the opposite, exemption from his jurisdiction, is true for the Latin-rite religious with solemn vows (CIC c.615). A monastery might receive the *stauropegium* from the patriarch, by which it becomes exempt from the local ordinary and exclusively subject to the patriarch (PostApost c.164).

The second part of the motu proprio (PostApost cc.232–301) is a nearly exact copy of the corresponding canons of CIC cc.1495–1555 on the temporal property of the Church.

The third part gives the meaning of certain new legal terms. Oriental regions are those parts of the world where the Eastern rites have been observed since antiquity, as in the Near East, India, and the Ukraine; Oriental territories are areas where a hierarchical organization has been set up for Eastern Catholics (eparchy, exarchy). Five rites are especially mentioned: Alexandrian, Antiochian, Constantinopolitan, Chaldean, and Armenian; but others also are admitted, i.e., those that were recognized as such tacitly or expressly by the Church (PostApost c.303.1n1).

Cleri Sanctitati. The fourth part of the future CICO was *Cleri sanctitati* (ClerSanc), promulgated June 2, 1957 (ActApS 433–603), with legal force from March 25, 1958. After an introductory section on how the Eastern rites are acquired and changed (ClerSanc cc.1–15), this motu proprio presents the general norms concerning physical and moral persons (ClerSanc cc.16–37), the laws on clerics in general and in particular, i.e., the hierarchical organization (ClerSanc cc.38–526), and those on the laity (ClerSanc cc.53–558). The number of canons (558), larger in comparison with the number in the CIC (442), was necessitated by the insertion of three chapters on the patriarchs, major archbishops, and their synods (136).

Canons 16–158 of ClerSanc contain general principles affecting legal age (majority is reached at 18 years), domicile, consanguinity, and affinity; moral and physical persons; clerics in general (incardination is called ascription); permission for permanent stay in diaconate or lower orders; celibacy, which is not a general law for the clergy but is to be observed in accordance with particular law; the obligation of private recitation of the Divine Office (Breviary).

The institute of the patriarchs is treated in 99 canons (ClerSanc cc.216–314). The patriarch is the father and head of his Church or rite and has ordinary power over metropolitans, bishops, clergy, and faithful of his patriarchate (ClerSanc c.216). Wherever a hierarch of any rite is appointed outside the territorial limits of the patriarchate, he remains attached to the hierarchy of the patriarchate of that rite, in accordance with the norm of law (*Orientalium ecclesiarum* 7). But the patriarch has jurisdiction over such a hierarch only in those cases specifically mentioned in law. The patriarch is elected by his bishops (ClerSanc cc.221–239). He can enact laws with the patriarchal synod; communicate decisions of the Roman pontiff to his patriarchate; address encyclical letters to all his churches; make visitations of the entire patriarchate; call conferences of bishops together; with the patriarchal synod, erect, change, and suppress provinces and dioceses; transfer metropolitans and bishops; assign coadjutors and auxiliaries to bishops; appoint administrators for vacant eparchies; preside at the election of bishops by the patriarchal synod; ordain and install metropolitans; appoint up to three titular bishops as his personal aides; supervise bishops and clergy; send visitators to the faithful outside the patriarchate; confer the *stauropegium* (privilege of exemption) on independent monasteries, churches, or ecclesiastical institutions; order extraordinary holy days or days of abstinence; grant dispensations from impediments to sacred orders, fast and abstinence, censures and vindicative punishments; grant sanctions in marriage cases and invalid judicial acts; request financial support from the patriarchate; appoint preachers and confessors for the entire patriarchate; exercise the civil prerogatives granted in personal statutes; be commemorated in divine services by all bishops, clergy, and religious (ClerSanc cc.240–272).

The following duties of the patriarch are mentioned: subjection to the Roman pontiff, whom he commemorates in divine services; forwarding every 5 years a report to him and making a visit *ad limina;* residence at the seat of the patriarchate; offering the divine liturgy for his people; supervising the bishops; directing the liturgical life in the patriarchate, especially the edition of liturgical books; supervising the administration of all ecclesiastical property; entering into treaties and pacts with the civil authority; carrying out the duties as bishop of his patriarchal eparchy (ClerSanc cc.273–282).

The privileges of the patriarch are similar to those of cardinals in the CIC. He receives the pallium from the pope. Specific Oriental tradition is shown in these: the use of special formulas for blessing, which includes calling his see apostolic if it is proper; the use of patriarchal insignia outside the patriarchate; the title of Beatitude; the appointment of procurators and delegates (*apocrisiars*) to represent his person; the conferring of Baptism and Confirmation everywhere and assistance at marriages; and if particular law decrees so, the employment of the white *supracamelaucium* and blessing of the holy chrism for all the dioceses of his patriarchate (ClerSanc cc.273–285).

The patriarch has a curia, of which the permanent synod is the most important part, consisting of the patriarch and four bishops; there is also a patriarchal tribunal, an econome or manager of all property, a chancellor, a liturgical commission, consultors in matters theological and canonical, etc. (ClerSanc cc.286–305).

The present Catholic patriarchates are too small in the number of the faithful to warrant subdivision into ecclesiastical provinces and they therefore have only titular metropolitans. Metropolitans outside of patriarchates have more ample power in presiding over their coprovincial bishops, and they receive a pallium from the pope. Otherwise, their position is the same as that of the metropolitans in the Latin rite (ClerSanc cc.306–323).

A peculiarity of the Oriental Canon Law is the major archbishop, who has metropolitans with bishops under his quasi-patriarchal jurisdiction. In 1965 there was only one: the Byzantine-rite Ukrainian Metropolitan-Archbishop of Lwiw (Ukraine), Cardinal Joseph Slipy. A similar legal position is accorded to the catholicus and the maphrian, delegates of certain patriarchs (Cler Sanc cc.324–337).

Precedence among the bishops is regulated according to the same norms as in the Latin rite with one exception: metropolitans who are heads of ecclesiastical provinces precede titular metropolitans and (minor) archbishops (ClerSanc cc.338–339).

The various synods—patriarchal or archiepiscopal, provincial, and interritual—are treated in ClerSanc cc.340–351; administrators apostolic are treated in Cler Sanc cc.352–361. The abbot *nullius* of the CIC is represented by the exarch who governs his own territory outside the patriarchate (ClerSanc cc.362–365); vicars and prefects apostolic have as counterparts papal (apostolic) and patriarchal exarchs (ClerSanc cc.366–391).

Concerning bishops, their rights and duties, and the diocesan administration, ClerSanc does not differ from the corresponding canons of the CIC, except in a few particulars: the *syncellus* (vicar general) must be a celibate priest (ClerSanc c.433), while a bishop could be a widower; the eparchial synod is called a *conventus* (ClerSanc cc.422–428), because the term synod was in the East reserved to gatherings of bishops; there is an obligatory eparchial econome in charge of the management and supervision of temporal property (ClerSanc c.438); chapters of canons are tolerated where they were introduced under Western influence (ClerSanc cc.465–466), their place otherwise being taken by eparchial consultors (ClerSanc cc.458–464), appointed not for 3 but for 10 years; the dean (*vicarius foraneus*) is called protopresbyter (ClerSanc cc.483–488).

The parish and the pastoral clergy are treated in Cler Sanc cc.489–518, with these differences from the Latin-rite CIC: moral persons cannot be so-called habitual pastors, and the priest in charge of a parish united with a religious house is always called pastor. Pastors can administer Confirmation together with Baptism, but not separately without the consent of the bishop; they are entitled to 40 days of vacation; the *vicarius oeconomus* is called *vicarius administrator*.

The canons on the laity and their associations (Cler Sanc cc.527–558) parallel nearly all the respective canons of CIC (CIC cc.682–751), with a few additional references to the patriarchs and their authority over such associations.

Bibliography: Crebrae allatae. A. Coussa, *Epitome praelectionum de iure ecclesiastico orientali,* 3 v. (Grottaferrata-Rome 1941–50; suppl. 1958) v.3. F. Galtier, *Le Mariage: Discipline orientale et occidentale* (Beirut 1950). Pospishil LawMarr. C. de Clercq, "Le Nouveau droit canonique oriental," RevDrCan 2 (1952) 195–239. A. Herman, "Adnotationes ad motu proprio *Crebrae allatae sunt,*" PeriodicaMorCanLiturg 38 (1949) 93–125. C. Pujol, "El Motu Proprio 'Crebrae allatae sunt' de disciplina Sacramenti Matrimonii pro Ecclesia Orientali," *Estudios eclesiasticos* 23 (1949) 307–330. J. Rezac, "De nova legislatione matrimoniali orientali," OrChrPer 20 (1954) 371–405. A. Wuyts, "Le nouveau droit matrimonial des Orientaux," NouvRevTh 71 (1949) 829–839.

Sollucitudinem nostram. F. Galtier, *La Procédure judicaire en droit oriental* (Beirut 1954). V. Bartocetti, "Motu Proprio De iudiciis pro Ecclesia Orientali," *Apollinaris* 24 (1951) 5–101. A. Herman, "De novissima lege processuali Ecclesiae Orientalis edita Motu Proprio *De iudiciis*," *Monitor Ecclesiasticus* 75 (1950) 599–620. T. J. Tobin, "Trials, Eastern and Latin," *Jurist* 12 (1952) 66–91, 190–231.

Postquam Apostolicis. A. Coussa, *Epitome praelectionum de iure ecclesiastico orientali, op. cit.,* v.2. C. Pujol, *De religiosis orientalibus ad normam vigentis iuris* (Rome 1957). Pospishil PersOr. A. Wuyts, "De monachis ceterisque religiosis in Motu Proprio *Postquam apostolicis litteris*," PeriodicaMorCanLiturg 42 (1953) 5–23.

Cleri sanctitati. A. Coussa, *Epitome praelectionum de iure ecclesiastico orientali, op. cit.,* v.1 and suppl. K. Mörsdorf, "Streiflichter zum neuen Verfassungsrecht der Ostkirche," Münch ThZ 8 (1957) 235–254. Pospishil PersOr. M. M. Wojnar, "The Code of Oriental Canon Law *De ritibus orientalibus* and *De personis*," *Jurist* 19 (1959) 212–245, 277–299, 413–464. A. Wuyts, "Il diritto delle persone nella nuova legislazione per Chiesa orientale," OrChrPer 24 (1958) 175–201. OrientCatt 35–61.

[V. J. POSPISHIL]

ORIENTATION OF CHURCHES.

The long-standing tradition of orientation in the building of Christian churches has its origins in the cosmic orientation of Greco-Roman temples (toward the east) rather than in the geographic orientation of Jewish synagogues (toward the Temple of Jerusalem). With rare exceptions, due usually to restrictions of site, early Christian churches were oriented on an east-west axis. The earliest churches, the great Constantinian basilicas of the 4th century, generally pointed west, with entrances on the east end. By the 5th century, however, this arrangement gave way to the opposite plan, with the entrances on the west and the apse on the east, a plan that became standard in the medieval church.

Though without scriptural warrant, the orientation of churches assumed an eschatological significance. Christ coming in glory is described as returning from the east (Mt 24.27). Hence in private prayer as well as in public, the Christian became accustomed to turn to the east, and in the great early basilicas a large mosaic cross in the apse, the "Sign of the Son of Man," gave focus to their prayer. In the East, orientation became mandatory in liturgical prayer very early. The church faces east, Pseudo-Germanus of Constantinople explains, because Christ is our sun and from the east He will restore the paradise we lost (PG 98:391–392). In the Western liturgy, orientation became the rule in Carolingian times, when not only the east, but all the directions of the compass were assigned allegorical and spiritual interpretations. The Gospel is read toward the north side, Honorius of Autun explained, because the north represents the power of the devil, who is being driven out (PL 172:551).

In actual practice, of course, the east-west axis was rarely laid out with exactitude. Yet only recently has it become customary to build churches without any reference to the compass. Perhaps modern man finds the symbolism of orientation too remote and the price of city land too dear to justify reestablishing the tradition. *See* SYNAGOGUE; BASILICA.

Bibliography: F. J. Dölger, *Sol salutis: Gebet und Gesang im christlichen Altertum* (2d ed. Münster 1925). E. Weigand, "Die Ostung in der frühchristlichen Architektur," *Fest-Schrift Sebastian Merkle,* ed. W. Schellberg (Düsseldorf 1922) 370–385. J. Wagner, *Die räumliche Disposition der Eucharistiefeier in den Kirchen des Westens* (Trier 1960). L. Voelkl, " 'Orientierung' im Weltbild der ersten christlichen Jahrhunderte," RivArchCrist 25 (1949) 155–170. C. Vogel, "Versus ad orientem," *Maison-Dieu* 70 (1962) 67–99. E. Peterson, "La croce e la preghiera verso Oriente," EphemLiturg 59 (1945) 52–68. O. Nussbaum, *Der Standort des Liturgen am Christlichen Altar von dem Jahre 1000,* 2 v. (Bonn 1965).

[C. VOGEL]

ORIGEN AND ORIGENISM

A distinction must be made between the life and teachings of Origen himself and the teachings, in part not strictly his, ascribed to him by later followers and opponents. Hence the first part of this article deals with Origen himself and the second with the influence of his teachings and of doctrines ascribed to him in the centuries following his death.

ORIGEN

Surnamed Adamantius (man of steel or diamond), Origen was the principal theologian of the early Greek Church; b. probably Alexandria, 184 or 185; d. probably Tyre, 253 or 254.

Life. The main details of Origen's life are preserved in a panegyric by St. Gregory Thaumaturgus, in Eusebius of Caesarea (*Hist. eccl.* 6), and in several writings of St. Jerome. Of a Christian family, the oldest of seven children, Origen was taught profane and sacred literature by his father, *Leonides, and may have been a student under *Clement of Alexandria. Under Septimius Severus in 202 Leonides was decapitated as a martyr, but Origen, despite his desire for martyrdom, continued his studies; at 18 he opened a school of grammar to support his family. Demetrius, Bishop of Alexandria, entrusted him with the instruction of catechumens, and he courageously assisted many of his students who were martyred. He gave up his grammar school to concentrate on *catechesis and devoted himself to an austere life. With more zeal than wisdom he took Mt 19.12 literally and mutilated himself.

Entrusting his colleague Heraclas with the catechumens, Origen gradually gave his main attention to the Christian formation of the more advanced group; and in order to answer the objections of learned pagans and heretics, as well as for direction in the study of the Scriptures, he followed courses in philosophy given by Ammonius Saccas, the father of *Neoplatonism. Porphyry witnesses this in his *Contra Christianos,* cited by Eusebius. But there is still some doubt whether it is the Christian Origen whom Porphyry calls a disciple of Ammonius Saccas in his *Life of Plotinus* and whom Proclus cites.

Origen did acquire a considerable philosophical education, which he utilized in his teaching. He began to write between 215 and 220, aided by a rich convert named Ambrose, who furnished him with secretaries and copyists; the *Peri Archon* was one of his first books. He also journeyed to Rome and to Arabia (Jordan) at the invitation of the governor. He left Alexandria in 215 during the reprisals visited on the city by Emperor Caracalla and apparently spent 2 years in hiding at *Caesarea in Cappadocia, living at the expense of the virgin Juliana (Palladius, *Hist. Laus.* 64); he then visited Palestine, where Bps. Theoctistus of Caesarea and Alexander of Jerusalem invited him to preach, though he was still a layman. This action elicited the protest of his own bishop, *Demetrius of Alexandria. Mammaea, the mother of the Emperor, had him sojourn in Antioch *c.* 224 to inform her about the Christian religion. Called to Greece in 230 for a discussion with heretics, he passed through Palestine and was ordained a priest by Bishop Theoctistus. On his return to Alexandria he was banished by Bishop Demetrius, who called two synods to censure his ordination as illicit.

Leaving his catechetical school to Heraclas, Origen began to teach at the school of *Caesarea in Palestine (231 to 233), where one of his disciples was *Gregory Thaumaturgus, who spent 5 years with him and wrote a panegyric (*On Gratitude to Origen*) in which he described Origen's program and pedagogical method. Origen preached frequently, and only toward the end of his life his homilies were, with his permission, taken down by stenographers and published. He also composed commentaries on the Scriptures and wrote his *Contra Celsum.* He journeyed to Arabia to bring Bp. *Beryllus of Bostra back to orthodoxy and to combat the Thnetopsychites, the sect that proclaimed the mortality of the soul before the Resurrection. It was probably there that he engaged in a *Dialogue with Heraclides,* who was accused of *modalism, the verbatim report of which was discovered in Egypt in 1941. He spent some time in Cappadocia with his disciple *Firmilian of Caesarea, stopped at Nicomedia and wrote a *Response* to *Julius Africanus, and was in Athens for several months in 240. The persecution of *Decius put an end to his multifarious activities in 250, when he was imprisoned and tortured; but he confessed the faith with fortitude. He was cruelly kept alive in the hope that he could be forced to apostatize, but on the death of the Emperor he was set free. His health was broken, however, and he died at 69. His grave was still visible in the cathedral of Tyre during the 13th century.

Writings. A man of virtue and genius with prodigious capacity for work, Origen left a large corpus of writings of which only part has been preserved in Greek or in the Latin versions by *Rufinus of Aquileia, *Jerome, and others. The question of the exactitude of the translations, the authenticity of numerous fragments preserved in exegetical *catenae, and citations in later writers have given rise to many literary problems. The most trustworthy quotations are preserved in the *Apologia* of *Pamphilus of Caesarea and the *Philocalia of Origen,* the latter a selection of his thoughts published by SS. *Basil and *Gregory of Nazianzus.

Scriptural Exegesis. Origen's ambition was to be an interpreter of the Scriptures. The majority of his works are exegetical, and the Bible holds a principal place in all his writings. To furnish Christians with a valid text of the Scriptures in their discussions with the Jews, he constructed his *Hexapla* of the Old Testament, a work composed in six columns containing the Hebrew text both in Hebrew and in Greek characters and the Greek versions of Aquila, Symmachus, the *Septuagint, and Theodotion, in which he uses diacritical marks to indicate divergences in readings. For certain OT books he added three further translations and, in his *Tetrapla,* probably edited four versions without the Hebrew. Only fragments of this gigantic labor remain. In his letter to Julius Africanus he discusses the canonicity of the story of Susanna.

Kinds of Exegetical Works. Origen's exegetical works are of three kinds. (1) Scientific commentaries, of which four have been partially preserved: on John

Page from a 6th- or 7th-century MS of Origen's homily on Genesis (MS Nouvelle Acqu. lat. 1591, fol. 1r).

(in Greek), Matthew (in Greek, and an anonymous Latin version), the Canticle of Canticles, and the Epistle to the Romans (in Latin by Rufinus). Numerous fragments of his on Genesis, the Psalms, Lamentations, the Major and Minor Prophets, and the Pauline Epistles also have survived. (2) His homilies preached at Caesarea, Jerusalem, Athens, and elsewhere include those on Genesis, Exodus, Leviticus, Numbers, Josua, Judges, and 1 Samuel (in the Latin version by Rufinus); on the Canticle of Canticles, Isaia, Jeremia, Ezechiel, and St. Luke (in Jerome's translation); a homily in Greek on the Pythoness of Endor; 20 homilies in Greek on Jeremia, the majority translated by Jerome; and numerous fragments. (3) Finally, the scholia, or short exegetical notes, now lost in the mass of fragments. The most complete list of his works, without being exhaustive, however, was made by Jerome in his *Letter to Paula* (*Epist.* 33), which was omitted in many manuscripts and was unknown to earlier editors of Jerome's letters. It was rediscovered *c.* 1845.

Method of Exegesis. Origen's literary, critical, grammatical, and historical explanations of scriptural passages are innumerable, but the literal sense of a text is the basis for his spiritual interpretation; he believed in the historicity of a pericope even when he gave it an allegorical interpretation. Sometimes, however, he admitted that a "corporeal" meaning was nonexistent. At times Origen dealt with figurative or anthropomorphic passages and referred to the "materiality" of a metaphor as the literal meaning, in contradistinction to the modern practice of considering the literal meaning to be the sense intended by the original author. Sometimes he dealt with passages that were incoherent in the Greek text or that posed difficult exegetical problems of which he was fully aware but did not always have the means of resolving. Occasionally he failed to consider the literal, literary, psychological, or historical context or displayed an exaggerated subtlety; but these instances are rare in relation to the whole of his works.

The literal sense, according to Origen, was not the reason for which the Holy Spirit had given the Scriptures to the Christians. The juridical and ceremonial prescriptions of the Law had been abolished by Christ, and the historical narratives in themselves are worthless for the spiritual director and pastor. The true sense willed by the Holy Spirit is the spiritual sense, which Origen found in the New Testament and earlier tradition and of which he is the great proponent.

Christ is the center of history. The Old Testament is revelation only insofar as it is a prophecy related to Christ. In each of the OT characters, narratives, and prescriptions, the interpreter will find the image of Christ or of the Church, the realities of the New Covenant, and particularly the Sacraments. The first coming of Christ still retains its prophetic character; it brought about an eschatological accomplishment that is as yet only incompletely possessed, "as in a mirror or an enigma," but the desire to possess it completely is felt by the Christian. The "gospel in time" is identical in substance (hypostasis) with the "eternal gospel" of beatitude; it only differs by reason of epinoia, or the imperfect manner in which men contemplate and possess it.

It is thus that Origen expresses the essential fact of Christian sacramentalism. The spiritual sense, then, foreshadows future blessings and determines for the faithful their comportment in the interval between the two parousiai, or comings, of Christ and brings them celestial gifts according to the measure of their spiritual ascension or development. In this vision of the world on two planes—that of symbol and that of mystery, which he borrowed from Platonism—Origen describes the sacramentalism of the New Covenant and the symbolism essential to any true knowledge of God.

Hardly understood by historians between the Renaissance and modern times, this type of exegesis is, except for certain bizarre developments and doubtful procedures, an essential element of Christian teaching. But Origen, along with the majority of Fathers, may be criticized on two points. Although they were correct in concluding that the Holy Spirit is the author of Scripture, they did not pay sufficient attention to the human author; accordingly, they could not resolve the difficulties arising on this score, although Origen himself was fully aware of them. In his opinion it did not become the Divine Dignity to have dictated even one useless word; hence under the most insignificant detail or pleonasm some intention of the Holy Spirit had to be discovered. It is thus that the artificiality of certain particular interpretations arose, despite the profundity or beauty of a commentary as a whole. They are frequently introduced by an etymology or an arithmetic symbolism, a procedure that is Biblical as well as Hellenic in origin. Origen's spiritual exegesis forms a complex whole; but from the schema outlined above, one can see that other influences—rabbinical, apocalyptic, Philonian, Hellenic, and Gnostic—were operative.

Spirituality. Origen's spiritual teaching, everywhere present in his exegesis, makes him the creator of a spiritual theology. Mystical theology occupies a large place in his commentaries on John and on the Canticle of Canticles; but in his later works, written as a priest, he was more attentive to the practical aspects of the Christian life than he was in those written in Alexandria. The Exhortation to Martyrdom, addressed to Ambrosius during the persecution of Emperor Maximinus the Thracian, betrays one of the constants in the life of Origen, the spirituality of martyrdom. The Treatise on Prayer, which is preserved in Greek, contains, among other things, the first methodical explanation of the Our Father.

The moral and ascetical doctrine of Origen is worthy of careful study, for it can render service in the attempt to clarify the origins of *monasticism. A thesis regarding spiritual combat pervades his *anthropology and his *angelology: the soul, the seat of free will and of the personality, is fought over by the spirit (pneuma, spiritus, including grace and participation of the Holy Spirit) and the flesh. The soul is divided into a superior part, the organ of contemplation and virtue, which is called intelligence (nous, mens) or the dominant faculty (hēgemonikon, principale cordis), and an inferior part, which corresponds in a certain measure to concupiscence. In this battle man is solicited by both good and evil angels to follow Christ or Satan.

On many points Origen possessed an integral doctrine, which is not outlined in systematic fashion but is dispersed at the hazard of his exegesis: on martyrdom, virginity and chastity, mortification, etc. Virtues are the names (epinoiai) given to Christ and identified with him as pertaining to His very substance. He who possesses them participates in the divine nature. But human beings only receive them through the humanity of Christ, which is His "Shadow"; here below man has only the "shadows" of virtue.

Mysticism and Mystery. Many of the great themes of mystical literature go back to Origen. In his commentary on the Canticle of Canticles, instead of the traditional, ecclesial interpretation given to this allegory, he sees the soul of the Christian as the spouse of Christ and closely relates the individual with the collectivity of Christ's body, the Church. The Ascent of the Mountain prefigures a spiritual ascension through prayer and virtue: as on Mt. Thabor the divinity of Christ appeared more and more in His transfigured humanity.

In order for the Incarnation to produce its effects in an individual, Jesus has to be born in him by Baptism and grow there, as He will if the subject gives Him the opportunity by leading a virtuous life. Among those making progress five spiritual senses develop: sight, which uncovers divine realities; hearing, which lets the words of God be heard when He reveals the meaning of the Scriptures interiorly to the soul; touch, which allows one to examine the flesh of the Word; smell and taste, which express the delicacies of knowledge—a connaturality that increases with the ascension of a soul dedicated to perfecting its immediate knowledge of the divine. Such is the object of the charism of Wisdom, of which one effect is the *discernment of spirits. The source of this connaturality is in the creation of the soul according to the *Image of God, who is the Word; only the similar can know the similar.

The object of this knowledge is Mystery: the mysteries of visible and invisible realities, or of the relations in the Trinity, all of which are recapitulated in the person of the Son, the Image of the Father, containing the intelligible world, insofar as wisdom is concerned, the ideas and reasons for all things. Perceived in this light, which the divine Persons freely communicate, mystery is a nourishment, transforming the soul to the true nature of mystery, which is supernatural; it is a wine rejoicing in a "sober drunkenness," which exalts conscience and liberty. For understanding, which is an encounter of two liberties, includes at once passivity and activity: divine grace does not lay hold to man despite himself, in an ecstasy that would be a kind of divine folly; inconscience or lack of understanding is a sign of diabolic possession.

Knowledge is given in meditation on Scripture and requires the renouncement of sin and the world, as well as purity of heart. Faith is its necessary principle; but with faith the object becomes present; it is seen and touched without an intermediary: to comprehend and to love are confounded in union. The "esotericism" with which Origen is often reproached is common to all the mystics: it is not necessary to give someone something he can comprehend; otherwise revelation will be useless to him and could even prove to be an evil. To accuse him of spiritual snobbishness, one would have to ignore the continual exhortations contained in his homilies urging all Christians to make progress in their spiritual knowledge. It is necessary to call attention likewise to the profoundly affective devotion Origen has for the person of Christ, which is so similar to that of St. *Bernard of Clairvaux. Evidence of his own personal mystical experience is rare, for Origen speaks little of himself; but it is sufficiently explicit.

Speculative Theology. Origen's speculation, like his spiritual doctrine, is inseparable from his exegesis. He ignores distinctions into branches or categories in the knowledge of God. For this his commentaries and homilies are the sources, particularly his masterpiece, the *Commentary on John;* then the tract *On the Resurrection,* and the *Stromateis,* of which we have but fragments; the *Treatise on First Principles (Peri Archon)*; and finally his last work, which is entirely preserved in Greek, the *Contra Celsum,* a vast, apologetic tract that refutes step by step the *True Discourse* of the philosopher Celsus. This discourse of Celsus was the most serious attack in the intellectual realm that Christianity had ever experienced; it was considered still pertinent by the freethinkers of the 19th century who discovered in it so many of their anti-Christian arguments. In Origen's rebuttal the essential proof for the divinity of Christianity is the profundity and multitude of the moral conversions it brought about.

Fidelity. The fidelity of Origen to the rule of faith as known in his day cannot be doubted; and if he is occasionally mistaken in his pursuits, it is on points that were clarified only later. But his work gives a handle to incomprehensions or obtuseness, for it is scarcely systematic, not even in the *Peri Archon.* Docile most frequently to the scriptural text on which he is commenting, he tries to attain the unknowable mystery by many different approaches, some of them antithetic. This is why he should not be studied except in the totality of his work; one cannot draw a definite conclusion from a text isolated from the rest of his writings. His is a theology of research, modestly making use of hypotheses, suppositions, attempted explanations; and one is not fair to Origen if he transforms these into affirmations of dogmas of the faith.

Origen can be explained by the heresies he combats. Facing the Marcionites he sustains both the goodness of God the Creator, who is one with the Father of Jesus, and the agreement of the two Testaments, as well as the value of the Old Testament. Against the Valentinians he defends *free will and personal responsibility, the refusal of recognition of a *predestination by nature. Against the Modalists he defends the personality of the *Logos; and against the Adoptionists, His eternal *generation. Against the Docetists, he defends the true humanity of Christ as a condition for the Redemption. Against anthropomorphic tendencies, *Chiliasm, and the literalists in the Church he defends the spirituality of God, the soul, and final beatitude, as well as the abolition of the Jewish law by Christ. One cannot reproach him for not having foreseen later heresies, as his detractors try to do; or for employing with an orthodox intention—as can be proved from other passages in his works—formulas that later came to have a heterodox sense.

The philosophy of Origen underlying his doctrines and his vocabulary is Middle *Platonism, a mystical Platonism mixed with much *Stoicism and some *Aristotelianism. He makes use of it as a theologian, using it largely with a Christian end in view. Its defects have often been exaggerated in unconscious imitation of Protestant tendencies or a too scholastic mentality.

Origen's Theology. Theology, in almost all its divisions, made considerable progress with Origen, even if the results were not always perfect. His conception of the Trinity sought to safeguard the divine "monarchy" and to avoid modalist and adoptionist solutions. Thus in God he insists on a hierarchy of origin and speaks of the Father, because He is Father, as the source of divinity; hence He is the source of the divine nature that He shares with the other two Persons without diminution.

Origen refuses to consider the *probolē (prolatio)* of the Valentinians, who suppose a division of the divine substance similar to the process of human and animal generation; the Son and the Holy Spirit do not come forth from the bosom of the Father. The Trinitarian vocabulary was as yet not precise, and Origen did not always clearly distinguish the hierarchy of origin from the hierarchy of power; thence arose a *subordinationism that betrays a theological insufficiency and not a dogmatic position.

The Son. Engendered from all eternity, mediator between God and the world, the Son possesses multiple *epinoiai* or names: His diverse scriptural titles that the Valentinians dissected into different Eons but that connote for Origen the relations of the Son with the world and with men. They have a real foundation in the simplicity of His hypostasis. The principal of these is Wisdom, who embraces the intelligible world of the principles of all beings (and here, Platonic "forms" are confounded with Stoic "reasons"), and is the model for creation. Then comes the Word (*Logos*), who gives expression to this Wisdom and is the agent of Creation; then a great number of others, viz, virtues and diverse functions of the Son in the Redemption and in man's spiritual progress.

The union of the Son with human nature is anterior to the Incarnation. According to the Origenian hypothesis, His soul had been created with the preexistent intelligences. Finding itself "under the form of God" by its union with the Word, His soul was the spouse of the preexistent Church, that is to say, of the collectivity of intelligent being. It alone escaped the cosmic fall. The Son, agent of the theophanies of the Old Testament, appears in His soul, which has retained its primitive angelico-human state; thus He is an angel among angels, a man among men. For love of his fallen spouse, the soul of Christ took flesh in Mary, and the Word followed it in the *Kenosis, remaining mysteriously in the bosom of the Father, His proper "place." He revealed the divine to man, expressing it in a human being.

On the cross Christ was delivered to diabolic powers as a ransom according to the scriptural image of the Redemption that Origen exploits with many other images. He descended into hell to deliver the captive souls whom He carried with Him in the Ascension. The lack of a precise concept of person saves this doctrine from *Nestorianism, for in many of his other passages Origen affirms the equivalent of the *hypostatic union and the *communication of idioms. Against the Gnostics, Origen defended the reality of the flesh of Jesus, who, according to quite clear statements, "subsists in glory."

The Holy Spirit. The Holy Spirit proceeds from the Father through the Son, who communicates to Him His *epinoiai.* He is the Sanctifier and constitutes the "material" of the charisms which corresponds to our "actual graces." But His role as inspirer of Scripture is not clearly distinguished from that of the Son.

Spirits and Man. Origen's angelology and demonology are strongly developed: good and evil angels are guardians of nations, provinces, dioceses, individuals; they are appointed to diverse parts of nature, to virtues or to vices. The stars, animated and intelligent, are not agents of man's destiny, which depends on grace and free will, but constitute the signs that the angels alone can read. The heavens are the Bible of the angels.

Man, like the angels, has been created according to the image of God, the Word. This participation in the existence and divinity of the Father and in the filiation and rationality of the Son, understood in a supernatural (sanctifying grace) rather than in a natural sense, to employ modern distinctions, is not destroyed by sin but obscured by diabolic and bestial images that the Redeemer alone can remove.

Origen often speculates on the nature of the risen body according to 1 Cor 15.35–44; a material substance, always fluent, cannot determine the identity of the body, made stable by a corporeal form (Platonism) or a seminal reason (Stoicism), the latter, present in the earthly body, germinating to endow the body with glory.

Mary, the Church, and the Sacraments. Describing Mary as the *Theotokos, according to the testimony of Socrates (*Hist. eccl.* 7.32), Origen is the first theologian to affirm clearly her perpetual virginity. Even though he did not believe her to be without fault, he sees in her a great spiritual type. He is very attentive to the mystical aspects of the Church rather than to its visible aspects, without, however, losing sight of them. He possessed a doctrine for Baptism, the Eucharist, Penance, Orders, and Matrimony. His Platonic and realistic notion of symbolism expresses very well the identity in substance between the "temporal" gospel and the "eternal gospel" mentioned above. But the essential "sacrament" for him is Scripture, an incarnation of the Logos in the written word, analogous to the flesh, preparing or announcing the unique Incarnation.

ORIGENISM

The current of thought called Origenism is far from representing the complete heritage of the master: it comes from certain of his speculations separated from the whole, deprived of their hypothetical and antithetical character, and made into a system by posterity. The substance of Origen's theology nourished the Fathers of the 4th century and has become through them the anonymous common good of Christian thought.

The Peri Archon. These speculations are found particularly in the *Peri Archon,* or *Treatise on the First Principles,* one of his earliest works, written at Alexandria, and the cause of his posthumous difficulties. This book seems to be composed of two tracts placed end to end, following the same plan: Trinity, rational creatures, and the world; then, of an appendix on Scripture and a résumé. He desires to oppose to the "principles" of *Marcion those of the Church. It seems to have originated in the oral teaching of Origen, which Gregory Thaumaturgus describes as following the Socratic manner: a discussion of opposing opinions and manners of research rather than a *summa theologica.* It is difficult to gauge how far Origen is involved in the opinions he discusses, which are in themselves at times contradictory.

The preface sets out the various matters that form part of the rule of faith; beyond them, the author engages in research with its risks and perils, making use of Scripture, reason, and his philosophic erudition. Of this work the only sections now available in Greek are the chapters on free will and on Scripture that are published in the *Philocalia.* The whole treatise is preserved in a Latin version made by Rufinus; but his adaptations are the subject of diverse judgments on the part of critics who consider them according to their evaluation of Origen. A number of Greek and Latin fragments are available, coming for the most part from decided adversaries of Origen, such as Jerome and Justinian. P. Koetschau, in his edition for the Berlin Corpus (GCS), has added to the confusion by inserting in the text of Rufinus, as if he had consciously omitted them, the *Testimonia* that were collected in relation to Origenism or to the heresies that have no indisputable connection with Origen. Thus this edition must be used with caution.

The Preexistence of Souls. The preexistence of souls, including that of Christ, is a favorite hypothesis of Origen: in the beginning God created pure intelligences (*noes*), all equal, which were vested with ethereal bodies, since the Trinity alone is incorporeal; these spent their being in contemplation of God. All except that of Christ grew cold in their fervor and became souls (*psyche,* or soul; the word is derived by Origen from *psychos,* cold). The degree of their fall differentiated them into angels, men, and demons, categories that do not seem to be separated by impassable limits. God then created the sensible world and the grosser bodies to furnish men with a means for redemption. This Platonic doctrine offered Origen too easy a means of answering the Valentinian theory concerning the nature of souls and the Marcionite accusation of injustice on the part of the Creator by attributing the diversity of conditions among angels, men, and devils to free will and an original choice.

The Apocatastasis. It is not possible to prove that Origen's doctrine concerning the *apocatastasis or universal restoration at the end of time is heretical. It was drawn from Pauline texts and is not pantheistic. It does not entail the destruction of individual personalities, as the reproaches made by Origen to the Stoic final conflagration demonstrate. No precise text of his holds the salvation of the devil; in fact he expressly protested against this idea in a letter to friends in Alexandria that is mentioned by both Jerome and Rufinus; and his speculations are susceptible of two interpretations. He certainly preferred to speak of purgatory, of a baptism of eschatological fire, of which he is one of the earliest proponents, rather than of the eternity of punishment. His reserve manifested a certain constraint, but one can affirm no more, and the rule of faith at the time did not yet have defined limits.

A categorical assertion of Origen regarding the *apocatastasis* would contradict his hypothesis of the perpetual return of things, which at times he presupposes, even when he criticizes the idea among the Stoics. It is certainly irreconcilable with one of his master ideas, namely, free will. It was no more than a great hope on his part.

Other Errors. Other errors imputed to Origen are contradicted by indisputable citations of his authentic works. His speculations concerning the divine *henad* have been exaggerated in a pantheistic sense, being unmindful of the Christian context that modifies them. Jerome thought he discovered in the *Peri Archon* the final disappearance of the "risen" bodies that were absorbed in this *henad* or unity. But this notion is not in the Greek texts or in Rufinus's translations; nor is it attested by *Methodius of Olympus, who read this book and described Origen's conception of the glorious bodies, which he attacked vehemently.

According to *Epiphanius of Constantia, Origen said that the Son does not see the Father; and this would underline His inferiority in the Godhead. Actually Origen was intent on affirming merely His incorporeality; and there are any number of citations that affirm that the Son knows the Father. Methodius mentions a text from the *Peri Archon* according to which God is the creator from all eternity; but the text is not concerned with the creation of intelligent being, in spite of Methodius, for Origen shows that these have had their beginning. He has reference to Platonic ideas or Stoic "reasons," which are the principles of being, created in the eternal generation of the Word or Wisdom that contains them.

*Jerome and *Justinian I attribute to Origen the notion of *metempsychosis, which certain Greek texts treat as absurdity, foreign to the thought of the Church. According to Jerome, again Origen held that in heaven there would be a renewal of the sacrifice of Christ for the demons; but in his *Commentary on John* (1.35) Origen affirms the unicity of Christ's sacrifice. Jerome did not comprehend Origen's insistence on the universal effect of the drama of the cross.

Certain misunderstandings come as a result of a later particularization of the Christian vocabulary. Origen seems to have made the Word and the Spirit creatures, because following Prv 8.22 and Col 1.15 he speaks of the first as *ktisma* (the created), reserving for the word *poiēma* (something made) the meaning of a creature; in this he is followed by Pope *Dionysius and he treats of both as *genētoi*, not distinguishing, as was later done, between this word in the sense of created and *gennētoi* (begotten).

Justinian said Origen thought the risen bodies were spherical in shape. The probable source of this absurdity is in the tract *On Prayer* (31.3), where Origen means the stars and not risen bodies when he speaks of "celestial bodies." Origen certainly uses expressions that are depreciatory in relation to the earthly body in keeping with his Platonic ideas and for an ascetical purpose; but the opposite is not lacking; and the whole complex of his ideas taken together show great equilibrium.

In brief, although statements that have given rise to Origenism are to be found in the works of Origen, all the arguments which serve for the refutation of Origenism can likewise be found there.

Later Origenism. The *Kephalaia gnostica* of *Evagrius Ponticus (345–399), of which an unexpurgated Syrian version has recently been discovered, and a letter of Evagrius to *Melania the Elder give us information regarding the opinions of a group of monks in Egypt and Palestine, admirers of Origen in the second half of the 4th century: Evagrius, Isidore of Pelusium, Palladius, Ammonius, and the three other *Tall Brothers. Melania, Rufinus, and *Didymus the Blind were in relation with them. The ocean of Origenistic ideas, tumultuous, ever in flux and reflux, had become a river flowing down through banks that had been wisely reenforced. The different theses described above were developed in a grandiose system, cleared of all that was contradictory. While the master's synthesis, purified from its too bold speculations by theological progress and the experience of heresies, was anonymously preserved in the orthodox tradition, the heterodox character of these speculations, separated from their counterparts, was accentuated in this system.

Evagrius, who is above all a great spiritual author, underwent a systematization similar to the spiritual doctrine of Origen, an increasing of the Platonic and Gnostic elements and a taking of them over into a monastic context of pure contemplation; but in so doing he did not run counter to orthodoxy.

This doctrine brought about the first Origenistic crisis at the end of the 4th century. Origen was criticized; but he was read only onesidedly, in accordance with the interpretation provided by his so-called disciples. The crisis passed, and it was Evagrius who was read rather than Origen.

The Origenist monks of the 6th century, whose turbulence provoked the second Origenistic quarrel, were divided into two factions. The moderates desired to preserve in Christ as man, distinguished from the Word, a certain superiority over other intelligent beings; but they thus brought the whole system into question. These were the Protoctists, called such because they saw in Christ as man the first created. Their adversaries accused them of introducing a fourth person into the Trinity, whence their nickname of Tetradites.

On the contrary, the Isochristes, faithful to Evagrius it would seem, made of Christ an intelligent being like others, whose sole superiority was temporary and consisted in having remained united to the Word when all the others fell; but in the end they too will become the "equals of Christ" in the reconstituted *henad* or unity.

If the "impious" Origen was spurned by the Syrians —and none of his works are preserved in that language—they paradoxically attested a great admiration for the "holy father" Evagrius, whom they knew through expurgated texts, such as the first Syrian version of the *Kephalaia gnostica*. But the second version, which was discovered recently, shows that the real Evagrius was not completely unknown. His thought has been found, reinforced with Gnostic influences, in *Stephen bar-Ṣūdhailē, who was in Palestine during the second Origenistic quarrel. In the *Book of Hierotheus*, which is attributed to Stephen, this thought of Evagrius, mixed with *Pseudo-Dionysian ideas, takes on a pantheistic aspect that Evagrius had wanted to avoid.

Origenistic Controversies. During his lifetime, Origen experienced contradictions. It is not certain that doctrinal difficulties were involved in his troubles with Bishop Demetrius, but it is not improbable (*Comm. in Jn* 5; *Epist. ad Fabianum.*). But he had the reputation of a defender of the faith, as his *Dialogue with Heraclides* indicates. During 150 years his admirers prevailed over his detractors. At the time of his death many of his disciples and friends occupied important episcopal sees and safeguarded his memory: Dionysius the Great at Alexandria, Theoctistus, then Theotecnus at Caesarea in Palestine, Firmilian in Caesarea of Cappadocia, Gregory Thaumaturgus, and his brother Athenodorus in Pontus. The processes against *Paul of Samosata, Bishop of Antioch, were in good part their doing.

Supporters. The schools of *Alexandria (with Theognostus and Pierius) and of *Caesarea remained faithful to the doctrine of the master. In the latter, Pamphilus, aided by Eusebius, composed an *Apology for Origen*, refuting his accusers by citing his texts. His opponents were, above all: *Methodius of Olympus, who, although dependent on Origen, fought against his ideas on the glorious bodies and the creation *ab aeterno*; *Peter of Alexandria, on subordinationism, preexistence, and the glorious bodies; and *Eustathius of Antioch, on the interpretation of the *Pythoness of Endor*.

The opposition between the Antiochians and Alexandrians in scriptural exegesis continued. But the great doctors of the 4th century read his works assiduously, and their own writings attest to this fact. They had reservations about his ideas but still considered him as "the stone which sharpens all of us" (Gregory of Nazianzus) and "the second master of the Church after the Apostle" (Didymus the Blind, followed by Jerome).

*Athanasius of Alexandria used his Trinitarian texts in the Arian controversy; Basil and Gregory of Nazianzus composed the *Philocalia* of Origen; *Gregory of Nyssa is the most representative inheritor of his mysticism and accepted his *apocatastasis;* Eusebius of Caesarea gave him a most important place in his *Ecclesiastical History;* and Didymus wrote a commentary on the *Peri Archon.*

*Ambrose of Milan and other Latin Fathers used him constantly; *Eusebius of Vercelli and *Hilary of Poitiers translated some of his writings and were imitated by Rufinus of Aquileia and Jerome, still full of enthusiasm for him. Having an intimate knowledge of his writings, which would be much less read subsequently in the Orient, these 4th-century Fathers were capable of judging his boldnesses in relation to the whole of his thought.

Opponents. The Arians, however, took refuge behind him, and his Egyptian disciples compromised him. Epiphanius of Constantia denounced him in his *Ancoratus* and *Panarion* (ch. 64) and attacked *John of Jerusalem in 392 as a protector of the Origenists. He won over Jerome, who started a pamphlet war against his old friend Rufinus because the latter remained true to his master; their subsequent quarrel scandalized Augustine. Rufinus defended Origen and asserted that the *Peri Archon* had been interpolated by heretics (*De adult. librorum Origenis*). *Theophilus of Alexandria, who had read Origen, changed camps in the interest of his patriarchal politics, chased Isidore and the Tall Brothers from Egypt, and was able to depose *John Chrysostom from the Patriarchate of Constantinople for having sheltered them. He condemned Origen in a synodal letter (400) and in three paschal letters (401, 402, 404), which were immediately translated into Latin by Jerome; and Pope *Anastasius I confirmed the condemnation in letters to Simplicianus and Venerius of Milan.

This was the first Origenistic crisis; it came to a close in 402 with the silence of Rufinus, whose death in 411 did not disarm his adversary, St. Jerome. (The questions that were raised in the course of the controversy have been discussed above.) He was reproached with having allegorized the scriptural narratives of Creation and of paradise. To the interpretations made by contemporary Origenists, Jerome and Theophilus did not hesitate to add their own conclusions. Epiphanius in particular, making use of a supposititious apostasy of Origen, widely spread unbelievable gossip, which weighed long and heavily on his reputation (see H. de Lubac, *Exégèse médiévale* 1:257–274).

6th Century. In the first half of the 6th century Origenistic monks provoked trouble in the Great Laura of St. *Sabas and in the New Laura near Jerusalem. In 543 an edict of Justinian I appeared, which had been provoked by the papal apocrisiarius Pelagius (later pope), in the form of the *Liber adv. Origenem* or the *Letter to Mennas,* the patriarch of Constantinople (Mansi 9:487–534). It was approved apparently by the Pope and the four patriarchs. The text of this decree does not manifest a direct knowledge of Origen's writings; the accusation that he placed the image of God in the body of man confounds Origen with the Anthropomorphites, his constant adversaries, and directly contradicts all his teaching. The citations and the fragments of the *Peri Archon* that accompany it come from a dossier sent to Pelagius by the anti-Origenists of Palestine. The ten anathemas adjoined (Denz 203–211) are aimed at Origen and reproduce the complaints raised in the first controversy, concerning subordinationism and "the spherical-shaped glorious bodies."

But these troubles did not cease. On the death of their leader, Nonnus, the Origenists divided into two camps, and the Protoctists allied themselves with the anti-Origenists. The complicated history of the Council of *Constantinople II in its relation to Origenism has been narrated by F. Diekamp. The council had been retarded by the resistance of Pope *Vigilius, and during the interval Justinian had addressed a letter to the bishops (preserved by Georgius Monachus and by Cedrenus; Mansi 9:533–538) to which correspond the 15 anathemas, discovered by P. Lambeck in 1679, but which do not appear in the official acts of the council. They expressly concern the Origenistic monks. A. Guillaumont has shown that they reproduce the Christology of Evagrius.

Justinian opened the council without the agreement of Vigilius; and in its discussions little attention was paid to Origen, except to put his name in the list of heretics condemned in canon 11. He was not mentioned in the Emperor's opening discourse, which is the source of the council's anathemas, nor in the letter of Vigilius approving the council after the fact (Mansi 9:413–420). But later councils have repeated the condemnation. Following ordinary norms of interpretation, however, there is no question of holding that Origen was a formal heretic—the bishops were persuaded that he was a heretic through the belief of Epiphanius; nor is it necessary to admit that the errors with which he was charged are really his. Unfortunately, this condemnation occasioned the loss of the greater part of his works in their original language.

Present. The West continued to read Origen and to appreciate him as exegete and spiritual director until the end of the 12th century (Bernard of Clairvaux, William of St.-Thierry); but the rise of Aristotelianism caused his star to recede. Brought back to honor during the Renaissance (Pico de la Mirandola, Erasmus), he has been a sign of contradiction among his numerous historians ever since. At the end of the 19th and beginning of the 20th century he was considered more a Greek philosopher than a Christian theologian: he was accused of having preached Plato all during his life thinking he was preaching Christ. But in 1931 W. Völker raised his spiritual doctrine to its proper honor, and in 1950 H. de Lubac rediscovered the technique for understanding his exegesis. Despite variations in appreciation, modern critics can no longer ignore these two aspects of his teaching.

Bibliography: Works. PG v.11–17, with *Hexapla*, ed. P. L. B. DRACH, v.15–16; GCS (1899–1955); *Entretien avec Héraclide*, ed. J. SCHERER (Cairo 1949; 2d ed. SourcesChr 67; 1960); *Commentary on St. John's Gospel*, ed. A. E. BROOKE, 2 v. (Cambridge, Eng. 1896); *Hexapla*, ed. F. FIELD, 2 v. (Oxford 1867–75); *Philocalia*, ed. J. A. ROBINSON (Cambridge, Eng. 1893), Eng. tr. G. LEWIS (Edinburgh 1911); *Prayer, Exhortation to Martyrdom*, tr. J. J. O'MEARA (AncChrWr 19; 1954); *The Song of Songs*, tr. R. P. LAWSON (ibid. 26; 1957); *Origen on First Principles*, tr. G. W. BUTTERWORTH (SPCK; 1936), Eng. tr. of *De Principiis; Contra Celsum*, tr. H. CHADWICK (Cambridge, Eng. 1953); *Selections from the Commentaries and Homilies*, tr. R. B. TOLLINGTON (SPCK; 1929). J. E. L. OULTON and H. CHADWICK, eds. and trs., *Alexandrian Christianity* (Philadelphia 1954), includes selections from Origen.
Literature. R. CADIOU, *Origen: His Life at Alexandria*, tr. J. A. SOUTHWELL (St. Louis 1944). J. DANIÉLOU, *Origen*, tr. W. MITCHELL (New York 1955). E. DE FAYE, *Origen and His Work*, tr. F. ROTHWELL (London 1926). W. VÖLKER, *Das Vollkommenheitsideal des Origenes* (Tübingen 1931). R. GÖGLER, *Zur Theologie des biblischen Wortes bei Origenes* (Düsseldorf 1963). R. M. GRANT, *The Earliest Lives of Jesus* (SPCK; 1961). R. P. C. HANSON, *Allegory and Event* (Richmond, Va. 1959); *Origen's Doctrine of Tradition* (SPCK; 1954). H. DE LUBAC, *Histoire et espirit* (Paris 1950); *Exégèse médiévale*, 2 v. in 4 (Paris 1959–64) v.1. M. F. WILES, *The Spiritual Gospel* (Cambridge, Eng. 1960). F. BERTRAND, *Mystique de Jésus chez Origène* (Paris 1951). S. BETTENCOURT, *Doctrina ascetica Origenis* (St Anselm 16; 1945). H. CROUZEL, *Théologie de l'image de Dieu chez Origène* (Paris 1956); *Origène et la "connaissance mystique"* (Paris 1961); *Origène et la philosophie* (Paris 1962); *Vir-

ginité et mariage selon Origène (Bruges 1963). G. GRUBER, *Zōe. Wesen, Stufen, und Mitteilung des wahren Lebens bei Origenes* (Munich 1962). M. MARTINEZ, *Teologia de la luz en Origenes* (Comillas 1963). G. TEICHTWEIER, *Die Sündenlehre des Origenes* (Regensburg 1958). H. T. KERR, *The First Systematic Theologian: Origen of Alexandria* (Princeton 1958). P. NEMESHEGYI, *La Paternité de Dieu chez Origène* (Paris 1960). F. DIEKAMP, *Die origenistischen Streitigkeiten im 6. Jahrhundert* (Münster 1899). G. FRITZ, DTC 11.2:1565–88. A. GUILLAUMONT, *Les "Kephalaia gnostica" d'Évagre le Pontique* (Paris 1963). Quasten Patr 2:37–101. **Illustration credit:** Bibliothèque Nationale, Paris.

[H. CROUZEL]

ORIGINAL JUSTICE

In the present study two questions will be posed. The first and more important asks what the faith is that Catholics profess relative to original justice. The second is not dogmatic in the strict sense. It is rather theological, and inquires how and in what way this truth—like other *mysteries—can be understood by man after divine revelation.

Dogmatic. By way of introduction, it may be of assistance to present in diagram form what is under consideration here. If one were to attempt to plot out on a time line the various states that form the religious-moral history of humanity in relation to God, the first, for Catholicism, would be innocence, or original justice.

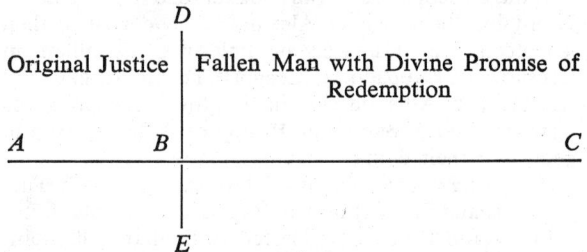

The dividing line *DBE* is that of *original sin. The period or duration signified by the segment *AB* is discussed subsequently. [Dogmatically it is possible that points *B* and *A* coincide with the first moment of humanity's conscious life.]

There is another way to consider the same phenomenon. In the life of the Christian on earth (falling into the segment *BC* above), there are two stages.

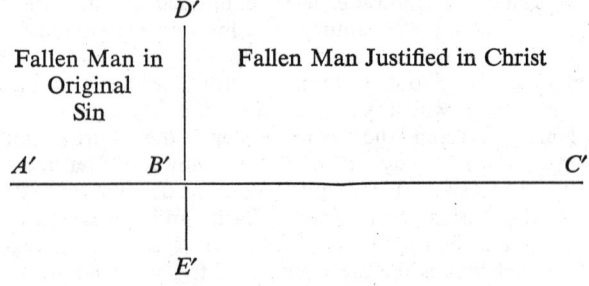

The segment *A'B'* is his original religious-moral condition as he enters the world. This is designated as original sin and means the individual is debilitated with regard to leading a life that is worthy of a human being —let alone a son of God. Though this weakness affects his mind and will, he did not personally cause it. Baptism for the child (together with personal conversion in the adult) effects a transformation known as *justification. Christ's merits renew in fallen man the image of his Maker. That renewal, the result of divine initiative, involves at least a partial restoration of the individual to mankind's original condition, or state. In a true sense, the justified man today relives, or recapitulates, in himself the religious-moral history of the race—only in reverse order, as the above diagrams indicate. All of this has further implications.

The first thing one must keep in mind is this. The justified man by God's *grace through Christ is internally proportioned to living out a life as a son of God. He is not thus constituted when he first comes into the world. Even then, however, he is still absolutely called to do so despite his condition of personal inability to respond without Christ's assistance—which is from the first moment divinely assured him in view of his need and God's goodness. His state at birth or conception is that of Adam in ch. 3 of Genesis rather than of Adam in ch. 1 or 2—fallen but with divinely inspired hope of salvation already begun and already affecting him. The justified man, however, is in many, if by no means all, respects like humanity itself in its primordial religious-moral condition. Positive scientific method may not disclose a difference between the baptized and unbaptized, the justified and unjustified. This does not, however, exclude the fact that a difference is there, one perceptible only through divine revelation and its acceptance in faith. Similarly it may be that neither science nor secular history finds any traces of a change in humanity now in a fallen state though once in a condition of original justice. That change, or difference, is no less real and impresses itself on man only as a result of God's interpretation of human religious history.

Even in divine revelation, however, the state of original justice is not in itself an object of direct, extended consideration. This does not imply that it is without foundation in the written word of God. It is there but somewhat in the background. Even in the Old Testament Genesis ch. 2 does not seem to have been written to spell out in detail what man was like before and without the sin and injustice only too evident to Israel beholding itself and other peoples. Together with the third chapter, it forms a divinely inspired account of the origin of evil—tracing it to man and not to God, whose works are just, who made all things good, and who walked in peace, harmony, and friendship with man. Still it is the fact that man caused the central disharmony and injustice in the world that makes him unlike what he was before or what he would have been had he acted otherwise.

A pivotal theme of the New Testament is that God has called sinful man to sonship through Jesus Christ in Baptism. Through the latter man is restored, renewed, and reformed in the image of his Maker (Eph 4.23–24; Col 3.10; Ti 3.4–5). The life that was once in the world before sin and death gained entrance is restored to men through Jesus Christ, the second Adam (Rom 5.10–21; 1 Cor 15.21–22). The precondition for this is man's existence in a similar state at one point of his religious-moral history.

The same phenomenon manifests itself in the teaching of the Church. It is not as if the Church were directly concerned with Adam's original condition. Its real mission to preach and teach is directed to fallen and redeemed man. Humanity in its state of innocence is relevant as a factor required for a less inadequate grasp of what Jesus Christ has done for historical, guilty man. To restore is to give back what was lost; to restore justice and holiness implies man's possession of both at one time.

In view of this, it is not surprising that the teaching Church prescinded from defining certain questions regarding original justice. One of these was whether man was created immediately in this condition or in one where by divine assistance he was to dispose himself for the latter. Another was whether man in justice and holiness possessed sanctifying grace prior to the Fall. It is dogmatically tenable as well to hold that man was faced with a choice in the first moment of his existence (his response being negative—original sin). In this way original justice is a real, historical divine offer, one with definite effects in man, effects proposed immediately for man's acceptance or rejection. Even in this conception of things, it is still a gratuitous gesture on the part of a loving God, whose generosity does not leave humanity unaffected. Implied is an irrevocable invitation to a rational creature to share in the fellowship or life of the Trinity. Acceptance would have signified man's willingness to be thus transformed, elevated, supernaturalized—in a word, deified but without losing his human condition. But there were other gifts as well. One was immortality, the promise of life with immunity from the necessity of undergoing the death man now experiences. Another was integrity; effective commitment to the truly good was not to be accompanied by the difficulty man now feels because of internal conflict within himself.

The Church taught, especially at the Council of Trent (Denz 1511), that Adam was constituted by God in holiness and justice. The latter signified a condition in which man was destined for personal union with God in the *beatific vision. This involved as well provision of whatever man needs to live a life ordered to such a union. It is interesting, however, to note that the Biblical expression with which St. Paul described the Christian was applied in retrospect to man in his original condition as related to God.

In reference to the above state, the term historical is rightly taken to mean real, factual, but not necessarily verifiable or detectable by positive scientific method. Consequently the prehistorian's inability to discover evidence from such a period in no way stands at odds with Catholic dogma. Catholic theologians can maintain that the condition, state, or period in question was momentary and no more. Thus the lack of any traces left behind would not be unintelligible, especially since science would find it even more difficult to deal with this religious-moral condition of primitive man than with many other factors of greater permanence in his existence. Why then has there been such insistence on such a state or condition?

The reason is that the Church considers it necessary to make faith in the redemptive act of Jesus Christ more integral (and, hence, also more intelligible). It fills in important details, gives nuances to what is otherwise a blunt fact. There is much to the Redemption-justification of man that transcends his power to understand. Only God could attest—since only He can make just—that the death of Jesus Christ, His Son, is redemptive for the latter's brothers and sisters. Only He could relate to man precisely to what extent humanity needed to be saved and redeemed, what the salvation brought by His Son entailed in terms of restoration. The Church, especially by reading and reflecting on His word, came under the inspiration of the Spirit to understand Redemption-justification as restoration to a prior state, at least under certain aspects; hence original justice in its profession of faith.

Theological. Further questions have arisen in the course of time regarding the intelligibility of this dogmatic truth. One of the foremost is the extent to which the details of Genesis ch. 2 are to be taken as a description of factual conditions realized in the state of original justice. Recognition that the history there related is of a very special type—accompanied by and embellished with many symbols—has helped considerably. Thus the degree of cultural attainment realized in Adam of Genesis appears less as a direct object of scriptural affirmation than as antithesis to the assertion that man's present state of ignorance, strife, etc., is humanly caused, consequent upon a misuse of freedom. The world is different for man in Genesis ch. 2 and 3; many theologians are beginning to regard this as a way of asserting that man's change for the worse in relation to God sets him in disaccord with the rest of nature as well. Such an interpretation has the obvious advantage of posing fewer difficulties in a confrontation with positive science, which finds only a primitive degree of development in men in their earliest states.

There was once a type of speculation current in Catholic theology that was often introduced with the question: What if Adam had not sinned? The exact, concrete details of a universe with man abiding in a state of original justice were not directly revealed by God. The fact—however long or short a period was entailed—is one thing; all the implications are another. The first is necessary to grasp the meaning of Christ's redemptive act. The latter is not. A fortiori one can only conjecture about the concrete mode of realization of what might have been. More and more Catholic theologians have come to wonder whether such a line of inquiry is likely to be conducive to further insights and truth. The proper and direct object of theology is rather the divinely revealed word of what the Triune God has done, does, and will do for man in salvation history—not the even more abstruse area of concrete detail in the realm of what He might have done.

This is not to say what might have been is always irrelevant to what is or has been. The scriptural description of original justice involves an intimacy between God and man surpassing but not destroying that of Creator-creature. The dogmatic way of putting this is that in its original state humanity was deified, or endowed with gifts belonging properly to God alone or Divine Persons. Because of this, it is necessary to conclude that God could have produced man without this relation of sonship and merely with that of creaturehood. In this case, the "what might have been" is quite relevant to the gratuity of "what is." But "what might have been" had original justice been preserved casts little light on what has been through divine intervention in Jesus Christ for restoration.

A final question has concerned Catholic theologians as well. That deals with the relation between sanctifying grace and original justice. In terms of causal theory, it has been asked whether the former acts as formal or efficient cause of the latter.

See also CONCUPISCENCE; DESTINY, SUPERNATURAL; ELEVATION OF MAN; FALL OF MAN; JUSTICE OF MEN; MAN, 4; OBEDIENTIAL POTENCY; PRETERNATURAL; RECONCILIATION WITH GOD; REDEMPTION, ARTICLES ON; SUPERNATURAL; SUPERNATURAL EXISTENTIAL; VOCATION TO SUPERNATURAL LIFE.

Bibliography: A. MICHEL, DTC 8.2:2038–42. K. RAHNER, Lex ThK² 8:72. A. M. DUBARLE, *The Biblical Doctrine of Original Sin,* tr. E. M. STEWART (New York 1965). M. FLICK and Z. ALSZEGHY, *Il creatore: L'inizio della salvezza* (2d ed. Florence 1961). J. DE FRAINE, *The Bible and the Origin of Man* (New York 1962), tr. from Dutch (Antwerp 1956). J. B. KORS, *La Justice primitive et le péché originel d'après s. Thomas* (Le Saulchoir, Kain 1922). H. DE LUBAC, *Le Mystère du surnaturel* (Paris 1965). S. LYONNET, *De peccato originali* (Rome 1960). H. RENCKENS, *Israel's Concept of the Beginning,* tr. C. NAPIER (New York 1964). W. A. VAN ROO, *Grace and Original Justice according to St. Thomas* (AnalGreg 75; 1955). H. U. VON BALTHASAR and E. GUTWENGER, "Der Begriff der Natur in der Theologie," ZKathTh 75 (1953) 452–464. J. BITTREMIEUX, "La Distinction entre justice originelle et la grâce sanctifiante d'apres s. Thomas d'Aquin," RevThom 26 (1921) 121–150. P. J. DONNELLY, "The Gratuity of the Beatific Vision and the Possibility of a Natural Destiny," ThSt 11 (1950) 374–404. C. J. PETER, "The Position of Karl Rahner regarding the Supernatural: A Comparative Study of Nature and Grace," CathThSoc 20 (1965). L. RENWART, "La Nature pure à la lumière de l'encyclique *Humani generis,*" NouvRevTh 74 (1952) 337–354. A. HULSBOSCH, *God in Creation and Evolution,* tr. M. VERSFELD (New York 1965). P. SCHOONENBERG, *Man and Sin,* tr. from the Dutch J. DONCEEL (Notre Dame, Ind. 1965). R. FRANCOEUR, *Perspectives in Evolution* (Baltimore 1965).

[C. J. PETER]

ORIGINAL SIN

The hereditary sin incurred at conception by every human being as a result of the original sinful choice of the first man, *Adam. Before treating theologically of original sin, this article considers the Biblical data.

IN THE BIBLE

First the possible evidence for original sin in the OT is considered, then the NT teaching.

Possible Evidence in the Old Testament. The OT makes no explicit or formal statement regarding the transmission of hereditary guilt from the first man to the entire human race; but such a doctrine harmonizes with the general atmosphere of the OT and is hinted at in some passages. Thus, the story of the *fall of man in Genesis ch. 3 explains the human condition, and this is marked by a universal tendency toward sin. Chapter 4 of Genesis (from the *Yahwist tradition, like ch. 3) illustrates, by a series of anecdotes, how sin has invaded mankind. Chapter 5 (of the Pentateuchal *priestly writers) may show the same thing through its reduction of life spans (see also Gn 11.10–26, also of the priestly tradition), even though this would be a more subtle method. In Gn 6.5 a strong indictment is presented against man's universal inclination to sin, and the "justice" of Noe (Noah) is qualified by 8.21—a kind of divine resignation to man's sinfulness. Solomon's prayer (3 Kgs 8.46) implies the same, and Ecclesiastes is aware of some evil having entered into mankind (Eccl 7.20). The words of Ps 50(51).7 may be no more than a personal outcry, but many good scholars have seen a universal condition reflected in its words. Of dubious value is Jb 14.4 in the Masoretic Text, even if the Vulgate, perhaps through Christian influence, is most expressive. However, Wis 2.24 is significant: "By the envy of the devil death entered into the world." In strict exegesis one may not call the doctrine of original sin, as defined by the Council of Trent, a teaching of the OT; but the foundations for it are there, strong and undeniable.

Teaching of the New Testament. It should be remarked that the NT seldom, if ever, formulates theological definitions such as are currently used. Its doctrine is set forth mostly in a descriptive manner. While one may gather, here and there in the NT, hints at the universality of sin, it is only St. Paul, in Eph 2.3 ("We were by nature children of wrath even as the rest") and especially in Rom 5.12–19, who forcefully brings out the doctrine. Through an extended series of contrasts Paul's doctrine gains great power: sin and death have entered into all men (Rom 5.12); in the transgression of the one, the rest died (5.15); consequent upon the judgment passed on one man, all men were condemned (5.18); and through the disobedience of one man the rest were constituted sinners (5.19). Only one inclined to quibble could deny Paul's general thought. Still it is true that Paul does not explicitly say all that will be said by the Council of Trent. This, of course, is quite a normal phenomenon in the development of doctrine. Paul lays a strong foundation from which details may be drawn harmoniously and legitimately.

Bibliography: J. BLINZLER, LexThK² 3:965–967. F. SPADAFORA, EncCatt 9:1027–31. EncDictBibl 1677–78. A. M. DUBARLE, *Le Péché originel dans l'écriture* (Paris 1958). T. BARROSSE, "Death and Sin in St. Paul's Epistle to the Romans," CathBiblQuart 15 (1953) 438–458. S. LYONNET, "Le Péché originel en Rom 5,12: L'Exégèse des pères grecs et les décrets du concile de Trente," *Biblica* 41 (1960) 325–355; "Le Péché originel et l'exégèse de Rom 5,12–14," RevScRel 44 (1956) 63–84; "Le Sens de ἐφ' ᾧ en Rom 5,12 . . .," *Biblica* 36 (1955) 436–456. A. HULSBOSCH, *God in Creation and Evolution,* tr. M. VERSFELD (New York 1965) ch.2. A. VANNESTE, "La Préhistoire du décret du Concile de Trente sur le péché originel," NouvRevTh 86 (1964) 355–368, 490–510.

[I. HUNT]

In Catholic Faith and Theology

The term original sin designates a number of things. One is a condition of *guilt, weakness, or debility found in human beings historically (or in which they are personally situated), prior to their own free option for good or evil (*peccatum originale originatum*). This is a state of being rather than a human act or its consequence. The other meaning has to deal with the origin of that state: its cause or source (*peccatum originale originans*). In what follows, both meanings will be treated from a dogmatic and from a strictly theological point of view.

Dogmatic: Sin of Adam. It is first of all imperative to understand the motivation behind the Church's concern with this issue. The Church saw it closely connected with something very central to the Christian's profession of faith: that the Father has sent His Son Jesus as Savior. This was present in the earliest apostolic preaching and creeds (Acts 2.38–40; 3.26; 4.12; Denz 1, 3, 4, 40, 42). Similarities notwithstanding, it was not just another human confrontation with the problem of evil or a purely philosophical stand relative to the same issue. Faith in Jesus as redeemer implied that God had offered a solution of His own. If man was in a state of real need, it was one his Creator took into account and sought to remedy. To the adults who heard Peter on Pentecost, the need of salvation was not one that required a great deal of elaboration. They might inquire about ways and

means, but they accepted the fact itself without undue question (Acts 2.36–41). Then and later the preaching-believing Church radiated the conviction that through divine condescension in Christ, man could reach God's own interpretation-solution of the evil present in the human situation.

It is not surprising, however, that questions soon arose concerning the further implications of that evil. These had a significance at once soteriological and sacramental. To what extent is Christ really the savior of all men—only after their personal sins, or even before? To what degree is Baptism conducive to the forgiveness of sins—only for those who have offended God on their own initiative?

These questions led to an explicitation of the Church's faith and understanding of man's need for Christ in terms of sin and death. A scriptural basis for such a development existed (Eph 2.10; Rom 5.12–21; 1 Cor 15.22). It is quite another matter, however, to ask whether the Church in this matter proceeded from the Bible by making use of purely scientific, positive criteria to determine its meaning. There is no indication that it did; the Church relied on the Spirit of Truth who guides its faith throughout the ages (cf. Denz 1514 relative to Rom 5.12). This is not to say that its interpretations, authentically formulated, have been contrary to sound exegetical determination of the literal sense. It is only to assert that the believer contends the Church had other aids as well in expressing the latent significance of God's written word.

Question of Origins. One of the Church's earliest confrontations with problems of this nature dealt with the question of origins. The Marcionists and Manichaeans tended to see in human history a struggle between the good God—father of Jesus Christ and author of the New Testament—and the evil god, who manifested his severity and justice in the Old. Equivalently the question was, when did God begin to save. The Church asserted the strict unity of the redeeming God, the maker of all things who directs all to man's salvation from the earliest beginnings to culmination in His Son, Jesus.

This is an element that is often overlooked, though it is of considerable significance in the *Nicene Creed. There Jesus the Savior in time is said to have preexisted in the realm of invisible realities before becoming incarnate. He is begotten but not made; this by the Father, who is, however, the maker of all other realities, visible and invisible (Denz 125–126). This distinction between the Son as invisible though not made and other invisible realities that are made by the Father through the same Son has soteriological as well as strictly Christological import. As Son and Savior, He stands related to the Father in a manner different from that of other invisible realities, which are made. Although the Holy Spirit was not directly taken into account in this context at Nicaea I, the twofold distinction just enumerated was expanded at the First Council of Constantinople and later (Denz 75, 150, 800, 1300). As proceeding, the Holy Spirit is neither Father nor Son; as Lord and life-giver, He shares their creative-salvific work. God three-in-one is thus presented as distinct from all other realities, both visible and invisible.

Satan and Adam. The same invisible world became again the object of concern in the Middle Ages at the instance of the Albigenses. What was at issue was not philosophical dualism as such or even a mere denial of universal divine providence, or government, of human affairs. Again the question was intimately related to a central Christian truth, though the technical terms in which it was answered might at first seem to indicate otherwise.

The Jewish people had once asked themselves: When did Yahweh begin His saving action in history—at the Exodus or before, with the Patriarchs or earlier? The Christian, who professed belief in the same saving God, had a similar difficulty. The God who so commended His love for man in the work of His only Son Jesus, how much did He love? How strong was His love? St. Paul had written that neither death nor life nor any creature could separate the Christian from the love of God in Jesus Christ (Rom 8.31–39). What then of the principle hostile to man's salvation?

In the Fourth Lateran Council, the Church proclaimed more than the universal origin of all realities from the same good God. It went further and pronounced that the principle opposed to man in working out his salvation is not only dependent on that God but was originally created good and chose evil personally. It was at his instigation that man gave sin and death admission to the world (Denz 800). Thus the origin of the evil situation in which the world is found came not from God but from man himself at the instigation of a created, invisible power. Dualism in salvation history is therefore different from the philosophical dualism encountered elsewhere. For an interpretation that makes the decree *Firmiter* of this Council at once more symbolic and philosophical, see Peter Schoonenberg, *God's World in the Making* (Duquesne Studies, Theological Series 2; Pittsburgh 1964) 8–9.

Monogenism. Even though it is treated in a separate encyclopedia article, mention must be made of *monogenism in this context. In *Humani generis* Pius XII warned:

> For Christ's faithful cannot embrace that opinion which maintains either that after Adam there existed on this earth true men who did not take their origin through natural generation from him as from the first parent of all, or that Adam represents a certain number of first parents; since it is in no way apparent how such an opinion can be reconciled with that which the sources of revealed truth and the documents of the teaching authority of the Church propose with regard to original sin, which proceeds from a sin actually committed by an individual Adam and which through generation is passed on to all and is in everyone as his own. [Denz 3897.]

It is well to note the intentional precision with which this was expressed. Monogenism is not described as an article of faith or even unequivocally as a theological conclusion following necessarily from the dogma of Adam's sin. Still the question of polygenism, at least in certain forms, is proposed as one affecting original sin as the faith of the Church professes it. According to the document carefully interpreted, certain polygenistic hypotheses *appear* to offer insoluble difficulties with regard to the dogma of original sin as proceeding from one Adam, but this does not rule out the possibility that the incompatibility may be seen in the future to have been only apparent. It must be added that *Humani generis* does not offer positive justification for the hope of any who may think this will be the case. For a further discussion of the question, e.g., from the

point of view of the possibility of preadamites, see K. Rahner, *Theological Investigations,* v.1, tr. C. Ernst (Baltimore 1961) 231–239.

Fact. The precise nature of the sin of Adam in Genesis ch. 3, as well as the time and circumstances of its commission, have not been the objects of explicit definition by the Church. As is the case with original justice, it is more the fact than the details surrounding it that has concerned the Church in teaching (Denz 3514, 3862–64).

Dogmatic: Consequences in Progeny. First of all the Church professes belief that Adam of Genesis by his sin brought about a change of religious-moral condition in relation to God not only for himself (*see* ORIGINAL JUSTICE) but also for subsequent men. This the Catholic episcopate expressed most clearly in the Council of Trent. The change in question is there described as involving loss of justice and holiness, incurrence of divine wrath, death of soul as well as of body (Denz 1512). Men may and do imitate Adam in his sin; they may personally set up obstacles to a state of *friendship with God. Even prior to so doing, however, they are, for the reason that they are human beings descended historically from him, affected by the sin and guilt he brought into the world—a condition or state at least in its most extended ramifications their more immediate ancestors may have aggravated or

Pennsylvania German fraktur of the early 19th century with an apple, symbol of the fall of man.

helped to perpetuate through personal sins (Denz 1513). Exaggerated humanism at the time of the Renaissance had particular difficulty in accepting the fact that one's religious-moral state could be so affected by something prior to his own free choice. A similar tendency at the time of Pelagius and St. Augustine had occasioned a much earlier determination of Adam's influence on his progeny (cf. Denz 222–224, 231, 237, 239, 371–372, 398–400). In both instances the Church reacted by seeing in the assertion of man's autonomy in self-determination, both for good and for evil, a direct challenge to the saviorship of Jesus Christ.

Capacity for Good. If, on the one hand, there has been insistence that man in his religious-moral life depends on Christ, that without Christ he has no religious-moral significance (cf. Council of Orange; Denz 392), still another truth has been present in the Church's teaching as well. Affected though he is by the sin of Adam, man is nevertheless a being possessed of the capacity for good; he has free will. This does not mean that he will ever exercise that power without Christ, or even that his possession of it to begin with is without Christ, in whom all things are created. This simply means that historical man, affected by Adam's sin, is not so corrupted as to be without a radical power for choosing good (Denz 1555).

At this point it may be well to note the fact that insistence on a humanity that remains truly human though affected by original sin is by no means out of accord with the Scriptures. The New Testament speaks of the community of Christ and other men, His brothers, in humanity despite humanity's sinfulness in them and sinlessness in Him (Heb 4.15; 7.26–27). An observation similar to this has been made by Karl Barth (*Kirchliche Dogmatik* 4.1:480–481).

Role of Christ. The Church has forcefully asserted Adam's evil influence on his progeny and has simultaneously taught that Christ exerts a contrary and superior influence for good. To speak solely and exclusively of man as under the sway of sin and evil caused by the first human sin is therefore to make use of an abstraction. It is a useful one and corresponds to a portion of a complex reality. Man in his relations with God is historically subjected to the most varied influences. From the start he is created in Jesus Christ, called to God through the latter, and aided in attaining such union; but he is affected also by the evil introduced into the world by the first Adam. An age that has come to recognize the major influence of heredity and environment on man may not find it difficult to understand that man, even from a religious-moral point of view, can be affected both adversely by human evil that he did not perpetrate and favorably by good for which he was not ultimately responsible. The Church itself has tried to make clear that for all its insistence on the reality of the adverse moral condition that man is born into because of Adam, still it is not the same as a situation of personal sin (recall the distinction made in this regard at the Councils of Lyons II and Florence, and in later ecclesiastical documents; Denz 858, 1306, 1946–48, 2003).

Specifically, Catholic faith includes the assertion that because of man's first offense against God, human beings now enter this world in special need of the redeeming assistance-grace of Jesus Christ. Called to live as a son of God, man cannot do so without special

The fraktur with the apple lifted showing the Redeemer.

reliance on the natural Son—this due to the original ingratitude of the first human beings to whom adopted sonship was offered. As to death, this much is likewise certain from the teaching of the Church: the death that man now dies he undergoes because of the sin of Adam. [For disputed interpretations of the implications this has, see further M. Flick and Z. Alszeghy, *Il Creatore: L'Inizio della salvezza* (2d ed. Florence 1961) 319; R. Troisfontaines, *I Do Not Die,* tr. F. E. Albert (New York 1963); K. Rahner, *On the Theology of Death,* tr. C. H. Henkey (Quaestiones Disputatae 2; New York 1962) 54–57.] What is more, the difficulty man now experiences in applying himself effectively to accomplishing real, religious good is there because of Adam historically. For all the natural character of *concupiscence, it is not what God intended or what He offered man in his original religious-moral condition. As a result, according to Catholic teaching, the lack of justice-holiness, immortality, and integrity in historical man is a real privation and not a mere absence. The reasoning leading to this is that because their restoration through Jesus Christ (at least in its state of consummation) is a real deification of sinful man, it follows that justice-holiness, etc., were a deification in relation to innocent man as well, there by divine offer and intent but absent subsequently (save through Jesus Christ), because of human sin, which sets man in discord with himself, the world, and God.

Theological. In what follows, it is proposed to give special attention to the theological hypotheses proposed to understand, within the limits open to man after revelation, the mystery involved in *peccatum originale originatum*. There can be no question that the nexus between a personal sin of a remote ancestor and a condition of guilt in a descendant has received different nuances of understanding in the history of Christian thought. St. Augustine was hesitant when it came to deciding whether parents passed on merely a body or a body and soul both directly affected by Adam's sin (*C. Iulian.* 5.4.17; PL 44:794). Nevertheless, the connection between original sin in offspring and concupiscence in parents is something he asserted as well (*C. Iulian. op. imperf.* 2.45, PL 45:1161; cf. *Nupt. et concup.* 1.24.27, PL 44:429). One can hold with Trent for transmission "generatione, non imitatione" without being constrained to accept such a view of marital relations. The assertion that the sin of Adam affects man before his own personal sin is by no means coincident with stating that he contracts it by a sin his parents commit at his generation or by some result of sin present therein though his parents may not actually be guilty.

Theories concerning Transmission. In this precise area a number of theories have been put forward by Catholic theologians. They attempt to explain how a truly guilty condition can affect man historically prior to his own choice and due to a misuse of liberty on the part of previously deceased humanity. One of these theories accords Adam a type of moral or juridical headship over the human race. In this conception of the matter, God by an inscrutable decree established Adam of Genesis as the legal representative of all Humanity, which would descend from him. His exercise of free choice would be taken as theirs; he would act in their name, for better or worse. The consequence of his conduct would affect all. As a matter of fact he rejected God's offer of friendship and passed on to his descendants a heritage of enmity with God. All men can be said to have acted in him and through him because of the fact that he was their head, so constituted not by them but by their Creator in His good pleasure. This theory has at least the advantage of appealing directly to the free choice of God. Cardinal Juan de Lugo (1583–1660) expounded it at some length; for this reason it is often associated with his name (see *De poenitentia* 7.7; *De incarnatione* 7.3–4). What remains extremely difficult to understand in the explanation is the analogy made between the sinfulness of a state in subsequent men and an act of choice in Adam. Still it has proponents, at least in its mitigated form, among Catholic theologians today (see J. F. Sagues, *De Deo creante et elevante*, SacTheolSumma BAC 2.2).

Since the theory of Adam's moral headship involves the problem of understanding how each man's will can be presumed (even by God) to have coincided with that of Adam, certain Catholics proposed an alternative theory according to which Adam is to be considered as the physical, not the moral, head of the human race. This was the position, for example of Cardinal L. Billot [*De peccato originali* (Rome 1912)].

Their assumption is that Adam could pass on his humanity only as he possessed it. Having rejected divine friendship, he found that humanity affected by sin in himself, and he generated children similarly disposed.

His descendants come from him in this condition: they are deprived of the wherewithal to live out their ineradicable call to divine sonship, save through Jesus as head in a redemptive as well as a creative order.

One major difficulty with this theory is that it has often in the past looked as if man received from Adam a humanity that in its own line was fully intact. One must try to see this in comparison with the tradition that man was, if not corrupted, nevertheless really wounded even in his humanity. When original justice and the gifts it involved are conceived as an accident affecting human nature, it is only too simple to imagine its loss with the nature remaining not only intact but in equilibrium in its own right. Still the Church maintains that man historically without Christ (a state he never totally experiences but one that merits consideration to see the primacy and necessity of Christ) is incapable of living an entire life worthy of a human being and much less of a son of God. How is it that because of Adam, even if he does pass on a humanity that is deprived of the wherewithal to live as son, man cannot even live as long as befits a human being? How can the lack of what in themselves were gifts cause anything even approximating a condition of sin or guilt, particularly in those whose wills have not yet ratified the act that caused the loss?

Other attempts to formulate theories have been made with questions such as these in mind. An aspect of physical headship has been retained: Adam as progenitor did pass on his humanity as he possessed it after his sin, that is, in a truly weakened condition. How? The divine offer of friendship entailed as well a possibility of living without the difficulty injected into life by concupiscence. With concupiscence, selfishness is an obstacle to leading a truly human life. To do so requires at times a recognition and acceptance of the fact that sacrifice of personal convenience and preference is required for the glory of God and the good of man. To love God above all else and to love all creatures as He loves them are imperative for man; selflessness often is required to achieve this. Whatever there is to be said for the possibility of other orders in which man might have been, there is no reason to hold or even think tenable that man in this present order can make that option other than through Jesus Christ. His aid is always at least remotely ordered to man's living as a son and not as a mere human being. And even so, the value found in the old theological distinction between *gratia sanans* and *elevans* may still be recognized. To pass on a humanity subject to concupiscence, in an order where purely natural aids against concupiscence are not offered, is to pass on a humanity that is in a weakened condition morally even before it acts. Prior to its option for good or evil, it is so disposed that without aid in the order of humanity itself it is going to fall freely. But to avoid failure requires divine assistance, an assistance that is given only in ultimate relation to living a life worthy of a son of God. For an extended treatment of this opinion, see M. Flick and Z. Alszeghy, 455–470.

Related Questions. There are many other questions that are raised by the dogma of original sin. Some of these are connected with a particular conception of the state from which Adam fell. Some presuppose more than divine revelation has offered in telling man about that state and what would have been had it lasted or been initially accepted by Adam. Others are peculiarly modern and ask, for example, just what the implications are for the doctrine of original sin in the evolutionist assumption that the present human race did have more than one pair of ultimate ancestors in the remote past.

Whatever answer is offered to such a question, the defectibility that follows necessarily as a consequence of creaturehood is not sufficient to explain the present evil in the human situation. Philosophy might well conclude with probability to the opposite; empirical sciences similarly. The Church, starting with its experience of Christ as redeemer and revealer, has concluded that He offered gifts that were at once a restoration and a deification. As a restoration, they were at least really available to man previously through God's goodness; as a deification, their loss involved more than the exercise of liberty that is present and a necessary condition of defectibility in every creature that is human. One cannot, in the light of revelation, start with the assumption that original sin has been satisfactorily accounted for if an explanation is given of how each of a number of remote ancestors sinned as men. That would indeed explain evil, but not the evil God Himself has indicated to be present in the world. Misuse of human liberty is one thing; it is involved in original sin. But the misuse revealed is one that brings with it a privation of godliness, which is not identical with defective creaturehood. A truly superhuman, or God-like, condition was present in humanity originally, at least by divine offer; it was lost, possibly in the first moment of truly human existence, only to be reoffered in restoration to all men by Christ.

See also DEATH (THEOLOGY OF); DESTINY, SUPERNATURAL; ELEVATION OF MAN; GRACE, ARTICLES ON; IMMACULATE CONCEPTION; JUSTIFICATION; MAN, 4; NATURAL ORDER; OPTIMISM (THEOLOGICAL ASPECT); POLYGENISM; PRETERNATURAL; REDEMPTION, ARTICLES ON; SALVATION; SUPERNATURAL; SUPERNATURAL ORDER; VOCATION TO SUPERNATURAL LIFE.

Bibliography: A. GAUDEL, DTC 12.1:275–606. J. BLINZLER et al., LexThK² 3:965–973. S. LYONNET, DBSuppl 7:481–567; *De peccato originali* (Rome 1960). A. M. DUBARLE, *The Biblical Doctrine of Original Sin*, tr. E. M. STEWART (New York 1965). J. DE FRAINE, *The Bible and the Origin of Man* (New York 1962), tr. from Dutch. V. J. PETER, *The Doctrine of Ruard Tapper regarding Original Sin and Justification* (Rome 1965). H. RENCKENS, *Israel's Concept of the Beginning*, tr. C. NAPIER (New York 1964). M. SECKLER, *Instinkt und Glaubenswille nach Thomas von Aquino* (Mainz 1961). M. FLICK, "Lo stato di peccato originale," Greg 38 (1957) 299–309; "Problemi teologici sull' 'ominazione,'" *ibid*. 44 (1963) 62–70. R. J. PENDERGAST, "The Supernatural Existential, Human Generation, and Original Sin," DownRev 82 (1964) 1–24. C. J. PETER, "The Position of Karl Rahner regarding the Supernatural: A Comparative Study of Nature and Grace," CathThSoc 20 (1965). E. SCHILLEBEECKX, "L'Instinct de la foi selon s. Thomas d'Aquin," RevScPhilTh 48 (1964) 377–408. J. DE FRAINE, *Adam and the Family of Man*, tr. D. RAIBLE (New York 1965). A. HULSBOSCH, *God in Creation and Evolution*, tr. M. VERSFELD (New York 1965). H. DE LUBAC, *La Pensée religieuse du Père Teilhard de Chardin* (Paris 1962). P. SMULDERS, *La Vision de Teilhard de Chardin*, tr. from the Dutch C. D'ARMAGNAC (Paris 1964). P. SCHOONENBERG, *Man and Sin* (Notre Dame, Ind. 1965). For additional bibliography, *see* ORIGINAL JUSTICE. **Illustration credit:** Rare Books Department, Free Library of Philadelphia.

[C. J. PETER]

ORIOL, JOSEPH, ST., miracle-worker; b. Vich (Barcelona), Nov. 23, 1650; d. Barcelona, March 23, 1702 (feast, March 23). His father died when he was a child and his mother worked hard to bring up her family. With the help of friends, he was able to reach ordination and obtain a doctorate in theology. He lived humbly, did penance, and adhered strictly to the demands of his priestly life. He was not an extraordinary preacher, but his evangelical simplicity inspired his hearers. Impelled by a strong desire to go to the foreign missions, he journeyed to Rome but fell ill and Our Lady, in a vision, directed him to return to Barcelona. He predicted the day and hour of his death, and distributed his few possessions to the poor without revealing the reason. He was beatified in 1806 and canonized by Pius X, May 20, 1909.

Bibliography: ActApS 1 (1909) 605–621. J. BALLESTER DE CLARAMUNT, *Vida de San José Oriol* (Barcelona 1909). *Enciclopedia de la Religión Católica*, 7 v. (Barcelona 1951–56) 4.2: 838–840.

[S. A. JANTO]

ORIONE, LUIGI, founder of the Piccola Opera della Divina Providenza; b. Pontecurone (Alessandria), Italy, June 23, 1872; d. San Remo (Imperia), Italy, March 12, 1940. He joined the Franciscans at an early age but left because of poor health. St. John *Bosco then accepted him into the Salesian Oratory in Turin. In 1890 Orione returned to his native diocese and entered the seminary in Tortona. As a seminarian he served as sacristan in the cathedral and began what was to be his main work in life by welcoming poor boys to his small room in the bell tower. After ordination (1895) he opened a lodging house for needy seminarians. As the work expanded he accepted orphans

Luigi Orione.

and elderly and needy persons. His Little Work of Divine Providence (Piccola Opera della Divina Providenza) was modeled on the foundation of St. Giuseppe *Cottolengo. To attain the goals of the Piccola Opera, Orione founded the *Sons of Divine Providence; the *Little Missionary Sisters of Charity; the Hermits of Divine Providence; the Brothers of Divine Providence, who wear lay dress, but follow a common rule of life; and the blind Sacramentine Sisters, who dedicate themselves to prayer. By 1964 Orione's disciples in these related institutes numbered about 4,000 and were found in all five continents. The earthquake of 1908 brought Orione to Sicily, where his skill in directing recovery operations moved the archbishop of Messina to appoint him temporarily vicar-general of the see. In 1921 and 1934 he visited his followers in Latin America. His remains repose in Tortona. The *Decretum super scripta* in his beatification cause was issued in 1956.

Bibliography: D. HYDE, *God's Bandit* (Westminster, Md. 1957). **Illustration credit:** Reprinted with permission of the Newman Press, Westminster, Md.

[T. F. CASEY]

ORISTANO, ARCHDIOCESE OF (ARBO-RENSIS), metropolitan see since 1296, on the Gulf of Oristano, in *Sardinia, Italy. In 1963 it had 134 secular and 32 religious priests, 42 men in 8 religious houses, 400 women in 73 convents, and 150,000 Catholics; it is 1,202 square miles in area. The major seminary at Cuglieri has 46 students; the minor seminary in Oristano, 115 students. Its one suffragan, which had 88 secular and 4 religious priests, 93 sisters, and 100,-000 Catholics, was Ales-Terralba (Ales, created before the 6th century, Terralba in the 13th, were united in 1503). The city of Oristano, founded in defense against Saracen coastal raids (1070), was the seat of Arborea, one of four medieval civil jurisdictions on Sardinia, and became a marquisate in 1476. The diocese, established at the same time as the city, was united with S. Giusta (1515) and the monastery of S. Michele (1803). The cathedral of Oristano, begun by Archbishop Torgorius (1228) and restored (18th–19th centuries), has 13th-century illuminated antiphonaries and precious vestments. The wooden crucifix (c. 1350) in the Gothic S. Francesco (13th century) is famous. The former cathedral in nearby S. Giusta is in Pisan Romanesque with Lombard influence (12th century). Noteworthy synods were held in Oristano (1646, 1649, 1680, 1708, and 1756).

Bibliography: R. CIASCA, *Bibliografia sarda*, 5 v. (Rome 1931–34). D. FILIA, *La Sardegna cristiana*, 3 v. (Sassari 1909–29). D. SCANO, *Codice diplomatico delle relazioni fra la S. Sede e la Sardegna*, 2 v. (Cagliari 1940–41). M. MANCONI, "La cattedrale di Oristano," *Studi sardi* 12–13 (1952–54) 33–69. R. BONU, *Serie cronologica degli arcivescovi di Oristano* (Sassari 1959). E. JOSI, EncCatt 9:352–353. AnnPont (1965) 316, 1065, 1415.

[F. RAFFAELE]

ORLANDO DE' MEDICI, ST., hermit (called also Roland de' Medici); d. Borgone, near Parma, Italy, Sept. 15, 1386 (feast, Sept. 15). He seems to have come from *Milan and was therefore probably not a member of the famous *Medici family of *Florence. He spent some 26 years leading a solitary existence in the small monastery of Borgone, in the village of Salsmaggiore near Parma, devoting himself to meditation and self-denial. After his death his relics were translated to the church of S. Bartholomeo in Busseto, near Cremona, and numerous miracles were reported as owing to his intercession. His cult has been popular in the area since the end of the 14th century.

Bibliography: ActSS Sept. 5:117–122. I. AFFÒ, *Vita del beato Orlando de'Medici* (Parma 1784). BHL 7291–92. Baudot-Chaussin 9:307–308. Mercati-Pelzer DE 2:1238. G. LUCCHESI, LexThK² 8:1367.

[H. MAC KINNON]

ORLÉANS

The Gallo-Roman *Cenabum* or *Civitas Aureliani* in *Lugdunensis IV,* the medieval *Orlhiens,* at the edge of the chalk plateau of Beauce on the right bank of the Loire River at its northernmost bend, in central France, has always been on a north-south thoroughfare and an east-west river route. It was taken by Julius Caesar in 52 B.C. Orléans's Bishop St. *Anianus, patron of the see, helped defeat the Huns at the "Catalaunian Fields" (451), and St. *Joan of Arc's first and most definite victory was the deliverance of Orléans from the English on May 8, 1429. Bishop Felix *Dupanloup defended the city against the Germans (1870), and the 1915 invasion of France came to a halt at Orléans. A Merovingian capital (561–613) and a Capetian county, Orléans became a royal duchy in 1344. The Abbey of *Saint-Benoit-sur-Loire near Orléans was an intellectual center for thousands of students from the early Middle Ages; and the university (1309–1790) founded by Philip IV had a faculty of law that rivaled that of *Bologna and attracted many German and other European students. The university is being restored.

The Diocese of Orléans (*Aurelianensis*), suffragan of *Sens until 1622, since then of *Paris, in 1963 had 334 parishes, 372 secular and 32 religious priests, 65 men in 4 religious houses, 800 women in 68 convents, and 360,000 Catholics; it is 2,630 square miles in area. Christianity came to Orléans very early but not in Apostolic times. St. Euvertus, elected bishop by the people, attended the councils of *Valence (374). Six Merovingian national councils were held in Orléans (511–549). The first, attended by 33 bishops, enacted 31 disciplinary canons (after those of Agde in 506) and transferred the right of asylum from pagan temples to Christian churches. The other five councils, also important for the organization of the Church in Gaul and for social and charitable work, organized the Christian cult, regulated clerical celibacy, passed laws for the emancipation of slaves, and put lepers in the care of

The five-nave Gothic cathedral of Saint-Croix, Orléans.

the bishops. King Robert convoked a council in 1022 against Neo-Manichees and Cathars. Orléans's bishops include *Eucherius (d. 738), *Theodulf (d. 821), *Jonas (d. 843), Theodoric II (d. 1022), Cardinal Reginald of Chartres (1439–49), A. Sanguin (1535–50), later archbishop of Toulouse, Pierre du Cambout Coislin (1666–1706), E. A. *Bernier (1802–06), and S. X. A. Touchet (1894–1926).

Orléans's monuments, frequently destroyed and restored, suffered from Norman raids (865), the Hundred Years War, the Wars of Religion between Catholics and Huguenots, the French Revolution, and World War II. The five-nave Gothic Saint-Croix cathedral (1288), destroyed by Huguenots (1567), was restored (1601–1790) and damaged in World War II. Saint-Aignan, rebuilt c. 1500 and partly destroyed in the 16th century, has an 11th-century crypt. Saint-Euverte (12th and 14th century), Notre-Dame-de-Recouvrance (16th), the elegant Hotel de Ville (16th), and the rue Royale, with its bridge from the time of Louis XV attest the city's past.

The cult of Our Lady of Miracles, a pilgrimage from the 5th century, is preserved in Orléans; the modern shrine, in an annex to Saint-Paul Church, miraculously escaped a fire that ravaged the church in 1940. The city venerates especially St. Joan of Arc, since the 17th century known as "The Maid of Orléans." On the annual holiday (May 8) an elaborate and impressive ceremony of religious and military significance takes place in her honor.

A 1959 survey in Orléans (population 85,000) and the suburbs (15,000), indicated that 85 per cent of the boys and girls took catechism lessons and made their first Communion, while 10 per cent of the men and 17 per cent of the women regularly practiced their faith. Except among worker groups, youths are more religious than their elders. The survey, carried out under the bishop, is permitting the clergy slowly to contact areas previously beyond their reach.

Bibliography: E. DUCHATEAU, *Histoire du diocèse d'Orléans* (Orléans 1888). G. CHENESSEAU, *Orléans* (Paris 1941). L. D'ILLIERS, *L'Histoire d'Orléans* (2d ed. Orléans 1954). P. GUILLAUME, *Essai sur la vie religieuse dans l'Orléanais du XVIᵉ au XIXᵉ siècles,* 3 v. (Orléans 1958–62); LexThK² 7:1237–38. G. LEFREBVRE, *Études orléanaises,* 2 v. (Paris 1962–63). H. LECLERCQ, DACL 12.2:2678–2719. **Illustration credit:** French Embassy, Press and Information Division, New York City.

[P. GUILLAUME]

ORLÉANS-LONGUEVILLE, ANTOINETTE D',

foundress of the Benedictines of Notre-Dame du Calvaire; b. Trie, near Rouen, 1572; d. Poitiers, April 25, 1618. Having been married in 1588 and widowed in 1596, she entered the Feuillantines of Toulouse in 1599 and became prioress in 1604. In 1605 her aunt Éléonore de Bourbon, Abbess of *Fontevrault, used papal and royal influence to bring the unwilling Antoinette to be her vicar for reform of the abbey and its priories. In this post, the Pope first allowed her to remain a Feuillantine, but in 1607 made her assume the habit and rule of Fontevrault. Meeting constant resistance to her reforms, she sought, and in 1609 obtained, permission to resign; this she did in 1611 after her aunt's death. Guided always by Father Joseph *Le Clerc du Tremblay, she went to Lencloître, a priory of the order, and successfully reformed it, but interference by the jealous new abbess of Fontevrault led her to get permission in 1617 to found the independent community of Notre-Dame du Calvaire. For this Antoinette established primitive Benedictine observance in a new monastery at Poitiers, where she died. Papal approbation in 1622 assured the future of the still-flourishing congregation.

Bibliography: *La Fondatrice de la Congrégation des Bénédictines de Notre-Dame du Calvaire, Madame Antoinette d'Orléans-Longueville,* by a nun of Notre-Dame du Calvaire (Poitiers 1932). T. CIVRAYS, DHGE 3:826–829. J. CHAUSSEY, *Catholicisme* 1:674–675.

[W. H. PRINCIPE]

OROSIUS, ancient Church historian; b. Spain, c. 390; d. after 418, place unknown. Paul Orosius first appeared in history at Hippo, Africa, in 414 as a young priest consulting *Augustine about a book on the origin of the human soul, *Commonitorium de errore Priscillianistarum et Origenistarum.* Augustine gave him his written opinion in 415; but meanwhile he had instructed Orosius about the new and dangerous heresy of Pelagianism, and sent him to the Holy Land, where Pelagius himself was residing (*see* PELAGIUS AND PELAGIANISM). Orosius and Pelagius met at Jerusalem in July 415, before a synod of the bishops of Palestine. After listening to both sides, Bishop *John of Jerusalem referred the matter to Rome and insinuated that Orosius's teaching was not entirely orthodox. In his *Liber apologeticus* Orosius indignantly refuted this accusation and explained why the bishops should have condemned Pelagius. Upon Orosius's return to Hippo in 416, Augustine requested him to write a book proving that greater calamities had occurred in pagan than in Christian times. This would serve as a historical supplement to his own monumental *City of God.*

Orosius completed this task in 2 years (418) and disappeared from history. He had divided the history of mankind from the creation to his own day into seven distinct periods. His work, called *Historiarum adversus paganos libri VII,* is dependent for its information on previous writers, except for the events from 377 to 417 about which he provides contemporary information. Orosius proved conclusively what Augustine had asked him to do, and *Dante therefore called him "the advocate of the Christian centuries" (*Paradiso* 10.119).

This first history of the world by a Christian writer enjoyed an immense prestige for many centuries, and over 200 MSS have been found in the medieval libraries. *Bossuet in his *Universal History* is indebted to Orosius. Modern historians regard it as one-sided and superficial; but even they admire the author's literary style, his appreciation of what *Romania*—his favorite word for Roman culture—meant to the world, his hope of a better civilization from a commingling of the Roman and Germanic people, and his sublime faith that a wise, omnipotent, and merciful God governs the affairs of men.

Bibliography: OROSIUS, *Historiarum adversum paganos libri VII,* ed. C. ZANGEMEISTER (CSEL 5; 1882), Eng. *Seven Books of History Against the Pagans,* tr. and ed. I. W. RAYMOND (New York 1936). É. AMANN, DTC 11.2:1602–11. P. GUILDAY, ed., *Church Historians* (New York 1926). G. DE PLINVAL, Fliche-Martin 4:96–97. J. MARTIN, LexThK² 7:1238–39.

[S. J. MC KENNA]

O'ROURKE, JOHN JOSEPH, Scripture professor and rector of the *Pontifical Biblical Institute; b. New York, N.Y., June 16, 1875; d. there, March 27, 1958. Having entered the Society of Jesus in 1895, he studied in Stoneyhurst, Oxford, and St. Louis, and was ordained in 1910. After having taught the humanities, he was called to Rome in 1913 to lecture on Biblical Greek and papyrology at the Biblical Institute; there he gave courses also in NT exegesis from 1916 to 1918 and from 1921 to 1926. As rector (1924–30), he increased the number of professors, added Egyptian, Sanskrit, Iranian, Armenian, and Georgic to the curriculum, founded a subsidiary house in Jerusalem in 1927, obtained in 1928 the faculty for granting the doctorate in Sacred Scripture, and arranged for the archeological excavations at Teleilât Ghassûl under A. *Mallon in 1930. He continued to teach Greek and Biblical geography until 1937, when he returned to New York, where he held various educational posts. After another year in Rome, he was appointed superior of the Jerusalem house (1947–49) during the Arab-Israeli war. Finally, he returned to New York, where he acted as spiritual director for the remaining years of his life.

Bibliography: E. Vogt, *Biblica* 39 (1958) 397–399.

[P. J. CALDERONE]

OROZCO, ALFONSO DE, BL., Augustinian ascetical writer; b. Oropesa (Toledo), Oct. 17, 1500; d. Madrid, Sept. 19, 1591. He studied first at home, then at Salamanca, and followed the lead of his elder brother Francis by entering the Augustinians in 1521. From 1530 to 1554 he was superior, successively, at Soria, Medina, Seville, Granada, and Valladolid. He was appointed court preacher and counselor to Charles V in 1554. Later he was adviser to Philip II, son of Charles. His intense apostolate merited him the good will of all. King and people alike were edified by his zeal, penitential life, and works of charity. He was beatified by Leo XIII on Oct. 1, 1881. Orozco wrote and edited many spiritual and apologetical works. His first and most important work was *Vergel de oración y monte de contemplación* (Seville 1544). He wrote also *Desposorio espiritual* (Seville 1551); *Regimiento del alma* (Valladolid 1551); *Las siete palabras de la Virgen* (Valladolid 1556); *Victoria de mundo* (Valladolid 1565); *Arte de amar a Dios y al projimo* (Valladolid 1568); *De la suavidad de Dios* (Valladolid 1588); *Bonum certamen* (Valladolid 1562); and *Regalis institutio* (Alcalá 1565).

Bibliography: LEO XIII, "Quod Paulus Apostolus aiebat" (Apostolic letter, Oct. 1, 1881) *Leonis XIII Acta,* 23 v. (Rome 1881–1905) 2:374–384. T. J. CÁMARA Y CASTRO, *Life of Bl. Alphonsus Orozco, O.S.A.,* ed. and tr. W. A. JONES (Philadelphia 1895). D. GUTIÉRREZ, EncCatt 9:368–369. F. LANG, DictSpirAscMyst 1:392–395.

[B. CAVANAUGH]

OROZCO, JOSÉ CLEMENTE, social-protest painter whose frescoes ushered in the Mexican mural renaissance of the 1920s; b. Zapotlan, Jalisco, Mexico, Nov. 23, 1883; d. Mexico City, Sept. 7, 1949. After graduating in agricultural engineering, and training in architecture, he turned to art, studying at San Carlos Academy of Fine Arts. Unable to bear arms because of a childhood accident in which he had lost his left hand, he was active as a political cartoonist during the 1910 revolution and followed President Carranza into exile in Vera Cruz. In return, Carranza commissioned his monumental painting, "The Last Spanish Troops on Mexican Soil Surrender at San Juan de Ulua," which

José Clemente Orozco, "The Martyrdom of St. Stephen," oil on canvas.

initiated the mural revival (*see* FRESCO). From 1922, when he began his decorations at the National Preparatory School, Mexico City, he never lacked commissions, most of them on a gigantic scale. In the U.S., 1927–32, he produced much-discussed murals at Dartmouth College, Hanover, N.H.; Pomona College, Claremont, Calif.; and the New School for Social Research, New York City.

While his strongly dynamic style may suggest superficial affinities with German *expressionism, his cartooning experience accounts sufficiently for the boldness of his distortions. An avowed freethinker opposed to all established order, and preoccupied with Marxist social goals, he never stopped to please either political friends or aesthetic foes. His frescoes in praise of St. Francis of Assisi were painted on public walls and paid for by a government actively engaged in persecuting the Church, and his Golgothas and Martyrdoms equal those of the Catholic *Rouault in spiritual content.

See also LATIN AMERICA, ART AND ARCHITECTURE IN.

Bibliography: J. C. OROZCO, *An Autobiography,* tr. R. C. STEPHENSON (Austin, Tex. 1962). A. REED, *Orozco* (New York 1956). L. CARDOZA Y ARAGON, *Orozco* (Mexico City 1959).

[J. CHARLOT]

OROZCO Y JIMÉNEZ, FRANCISCO, Mexican archbishop and educator; b. Zamora, Michoacán, Nov. 19, 1864; d. Guadalajara, Feb. 18, 1936. After entering the seminary in Mexico, he was sent to the *South American College in Rome, an institution for which he had great affection and whose benefactor he remained all his life. He studied in the Gregorian University, from which he received the licentiate in theology and the doctorate in philosophy. Years later he earned another doctorate in the newly restored Pontifical University in Mexico. On his return from Rome he became professor and then vice rector of the College of Arts in Zamora, held the same post in the Clerical College of Tacuba, and again in the Seminary of Mexico. Consecrated bishop of Chiapas (1902), he devoted himself to caring for the hitherto neglected flock. Among his achievements in the diocese were the following: he founded five schools for girls and one for boys staffed with professors trained in Europe; he brought electricity to San Cristóbal de las Casas; and he helped to pacify the warring Chamulas Indians and to lead them to a peaceful Christian existence. He became archbishop of Guadalajara in 1913, just as the years of persecution and social and political upheaval were beginning in Mexico. By 1914 he had to go into hiding, living disguised for many months, as he again had to do under President Calles in 1925. Three times he was forced into exile because of the desperate conditions. Nevertheless, Archbishop Orozco managed to increase the number of schools and bring about social improvements among his flock. Orozco y Jiménez was a great admirer of the Society of Jesus and helped it in many ways, even with financial aid during the years of persecution and exile. To him the Jesuits owed the construction of the Colegio of Ysleta where their novices and scholastics were trained from 1925 to 1951. The archbishop favored giving the Jesuits charge of the projected Montezuma Seminary. He was responsible for the publishing of various collections of documents on the history of the Church in Chiapas and Guadalajara and even paid personally for the publication of important historical works.

Bibliography: J. I. DÁVILA GARIBI, *Serie cronológica de los prelados que a través de cuatro siglos ha tenido la antigua diócesis, hoy arquidiócesis de Guadalajara, 1548–1948* (Mexico City 1948); *Labor científica y literaria del Excmo y Rvo. Sr. Dr. y Mtr. D. Francisco Orozco y Jiménez* (Guadalajara 1937). E. VALVERDE TÉLLEZ, *Bio-bibliografía eclesiástica mexicana, 1821–1943*, 3 v. (Mexico City 1949).

[D. OLMEDO]

ORPHAN (IN THE EARLY CHURCH). In the primitive Church, the local Christian community took into its care any child who had lost one or both parents. This attitude set the Church clearly apart from the pagan world, which was "without affection." Actually, except in Athens, where the law said that the state must educate the children of citizens killed in war until age 18, orphans among the pagans could count on no other assistance except that of their near relatives or the rare individual who was moved by their misery.

From the Jews of the OT the Christians inherited the conviction that God is the Father of orphans (Ps 67.6) and that the surplus of the harvests granted by God accrue by right to the orphan (Dt 24.21). But it was chiefly their "faith which works through charity" (Gal 5.6) that provided Christians with the bases and motives for their attitude toward orphans.

At Rome in the 2d century *Justin Martyr declared explicitly that every Sunday, at the end of the apostolic assembly, "those who have in abundance . . . give freely, each as he wills, and what is collected is given over to him who presides, and he aids the orphans and widows" (*Apol.* 67). In 197 at Carthage, Tertullian wrote in the same vein and said that Christians had a common treasury into which each placed his contribution freely according to his means "to aid the boys and girls who have neither fortune nor parents" (*Apol.* 39). In the more important communities the deacons kept up-to-date books of the persons assisted, and the Christian orphans were officially inscribed in these. Even though the non-Christian orphans were not listed here, they were not discriminated against in the distribution of alms. The Church especially urged the faithful to adopt orphans or to give the girls dowries so that they could marry and to set the boys up as apprentices (*Const. Apost.* 4.1–2).

Only after the official recognition of the Church (*c.* 313), when the emperor aided charitable institutions by according them legal protection and financial assistance, did the Church inaugurate a new form of aid to orphans by founding, especially in the East and later in the West, homes for orphans, called *orphanotrophia*. St. Ephrem, St. Basil, and St. John Chrysostom distinguished themselves especially by such foundations. These houses were built not only in the shadow of the cathedrals together with other hospices, but also close to monasteries when they began to spread. Steps were taken simultaneously to educate and instruct orphan children and to use their talents for chant and liturgical ceremonies, bringing about an identification of the *orphanotrophion* and the *schola cantorum;* in some cases priests and monks were recruited from among them. About the end of the 6th century such recruitment gave rise in Rome to a type of junior seminary that provided the Church in the 7th century with four popes: Deusdedit, Leo II, Benedict II, and Sergius II.

Bibliography: L. LALLEMAND, *Histoire des enfants abandonnés* (Paris 1885); *Histoire de la charité*, 4 v. in 5 (Paris 1902–12). R. HERRMANN, *La Charité de l'Église* (Mulhouse 1961) 19–53. H. LECLERCQ, DACL 1.1:1301–06.

[J. BEAUDRY]

ORPHISM

A modern term for the complex of beliefs and religious practices associated with the name of Orpheus, the legendary "sweet singer" of Thrace. Contemporary scholarship is by no means in accord on the content and nature of Orphism, or even, in any meaningful

Orpheus taming the animals, mosaic dating from the Roman period, Sparta.

sense, on its existence. Some scholars admit as evidence virtually all that is atypical of Greek religion (e.g., the so-called "Orphic" grave tablets and the Pindaric passages on metempsychosis); others reject whatever is not specifically designated as Orphic.

Classical Greece recognized Orpheus not only as a poet but as the culture hero who first instituted in Greece mystery cults and rites ($\tau\epsilon\lambda\epsilon\tau\alpha\acute{\iota}$). Any and all mysteries, therefore, including the Eleusinian, might be called "Orphic." In addition, Athens in the 5th and 4th centuries B.C. knew of sectarian groups who called themselves Orphics, regarded Orpheus as their "lord," reverenced sacred books, and lived an "Orphic life," in which vegetarianism and a taboo on the use of wool were conspicuous features. There were also Orphic practitioners who preyed on men's superstitious fears of the afterlife, professed the ability to perform salutary rites of purification, and even dabbled in magic. There is little archeological or literary evidence to suggest that these groups represented a stable and continuing movement.

In support of the claim that Orphism was possessed of a lofty spiritual content, it is customary to cite the myth of the Titans, who dismembered the infant Dionysus and were then blasted by the thunderbolt of Zeus. From their ashes or soot man was created. Thus, in the alleged Orphic interpretation, man's nature is primarily Titanic and evil, but also, since the Titans had tasted the god's flesh, it contains a divine element. The corollary is that man should so live as to free his divine soul from the "tomb" or "prison" of the body, and so realize his potential immortality.

The primary purpose of the myth was evidently to account for the $\sigma\pi\alpha\rho\alpha\gamma\mu\acute{o}s$, the rending ritual of the Dionysiac cult; it enjoyed a certain currency, and with or without the sequel of man's creation appears in several of variant forms. Some of these may have been "Orphic," in the sense that speculative theological writings were often sealed with his name. Yet if this was the "cardinal myth" of historic Orphism, it is strange that the inference as to man's divine nature was explicitly drawn only once, by the late Neoplatonist, Olympiodorus (fl. 6th century A.D.). Pending proof that the doctrine was specifically Orphic and early, the precise nature and influence of Orphism must remain problematical.

Bibliography: NILSSON, GeschGrRel 1:678–699; 2:246–431. W. K. C. GUTHRIE, RGG³ 4:1703–05, with bibliog. K. PRÜMM, DBSuppl 6:55–86; "Die Orphik im Spiegel der neueren Forschung," ZKath Th 78 (1956) 1–40. **Illustration credit:** Photo: R. Schoder, SJ.

[F. R. WALTON]

ORSI, GIUSEPPE AGOSTINO, Dominican theologian and cardinal; b. Florence, Italy, May 9, 1692; d. Rome, Italy, June 12, 1761. He taught philosophy and theology first in the convent of San Marco, *Florence, where he was also prior, and then after 1732 at the Casanatense Library in Rome. In 1738 he was appointed secretary to the Congregation of the *Index; in 1749, master of the Sacred Palace; and in 1759, cardinal priest with the title of San Sisto. A man of wide learning and deep piety, he was a controversialist, theologian, and historian of high merit. His chief work is the *Istoria ecclesiastica* in 21 volumes (Rome 1749–62, the last volume, posthumously), which he wrote to counteract the obvious tendencies toward *Gallicanism in Claude *Fleury's *Histoire ecclési-

astique* (Paris 1691–1723). His work goes only as far as the end of the 7th century, but it was continued up to 1529 by Filippo Becchetti, OP, and several times republished. One of the best editions is that of Venice in 1822, which with its continuation runs to 42 volumes. Noteworthy among his other numerous works is the *De irreformabili Romani pontificis in definiendis fidei controversiis iudicio* (Rome 1739) in three volumes, written in defense of the papacy against Gallican theories.

Bibliography: G. G. BOTTARI, who edited the posthumous ed. of v.21 of the *Istoria,* wrote a life of Orsi as an introd. to be found in all eds. of the work. A. FABRONI, *Vitae Italorum doctrina excellentium,* 18 v. (Pisa 1778–99) 11:6–36. M. M. GORCE, DTC 11.2:1612–19. Moroni 49:144–145. A. D'AMATO, EncCatt 9:369–370.

[S. OLIVIERI]

ORSINI

Important noble family of Rome, leader of the Guelfs, the supporters of the papacy in the long struggle against the Empire and the Ghibellines from the 12th to the 16th century. The Orsini, Colonna, *Savelli, and Conti were among the oldest Roman families. These four had the greatest prestige in the centuries after 1100; the Orsini and Colonna gradually became the leaders and outlived the Savelli and Conti. All depended on legends and tradition to some extent for their early history. One Orsini legend told of a widow in Flanders whose son was nursed by a domestic bear; this boy, *Orso* (bear), who gave the family its name, arrived in Rome c. 425 and was given land in Umbria. The Orsini claimed relationship with 2 medieval popes, *Stephen II and St. *Paul I, and with 17 other saints and blessed persons who lived between 222 and 1330, among them the brothers SS. *John and Paul, martyred in 362, St. *Benedict, and his sister St. Scholastica.

Bl. *John Orsini,* b. Rome, 1032; d. Trogir (Yugoslavia), 1110–11 (feast, Nov. 14). Before 1073 he was sent with others by Pope Alexander II to prevent a schism in Trogir. Orsini became bishop there in 1100 and kept the see united with Rome. His interest in both the spiritual and civic welfare of the city was recognized by his being declared its patron.

Anti-Ghibelline Activity. The years from c. 1100 to 1562 were of high importance for the papacy-Orsini alliance. Pitted against them were the Empire and the *Colonna. Often the cries resounded in Rome: "Orsi and Holy Church," "The People and Colonna" (*see* GUELFS AND GHIBELLINES). From 1144 to 1280 the prestige of the Orsini increased and was higher than that of the Colonna. The first of the Orsini cardinals became Pope *Celestine III* (1191–98), and he rewarded the family with fiefs for their assistance in defeating the Colonna. From a few villages the possessions of both families had grown to a dozen or more in the 13th century, requiring the maintenance of more retainers. Then in 1241 Senator *Matteo Rosso Orsini* (d. 1246) inflicted a severe defeat on the Colonna. Their houses were destroyed and their fortified mausoleum of Augustus was captured, and Matteo remained powerful in Rome (1241–43). One of his sons, *Giovani Gaetano,* became cardinal and later Pope *Nicholas III* (1277–80). But between 1288 and 1431 the Orsini during three periods were forced to play a secondary role while their rivals dominated the city. First, Pope *Nicholas IV* (1288–92), who had been bishop of Palestrina, the principal Colonna possession, favored the Colonna. They exercised great influence over him; then having become bolder, they dared to challenge Pope *Boniface VIII. The Orsini assisted Boniface in capturing Palestrina, and several Colonna fled to France; but the triumph of the Orsini lasted only until 1303, when Sciarra and Stefano Colonna returned to Rome and were powers there for about 25 years. They made a truce with the Orsini in 1306, but fighting broke out again, and the Orsini achieved no important gains except for a brief interval after Sciarra left Rome in 1328. However, the family did not lose prestige. During the *Avignon papacy and the *Western Schism (1305–1417) eight members were created cardinals. In the 14th century the Orsini added to their holdings Bracciano, a most valued possession for 300 years and the seat of the major branch of the family until it became extinct. With the election of a Colonna as Pope *Martin V (1417–31), the Colonna family again became powerful. Alarmed by the position of their rival, the Orsini persuaded Martin's successor, Pope *Eugene IV, to curb the Colonna and helped to destroy Palestrina. Again in the pontificate of *Sixtus IV, the Orsini family assisted papal troops in defeating the Colonna (1481–84). There were other evidences of the importance of the Orsini: they contracted marriages in 1444 and 1487 with two future kings of Naples, Ferdinand of Aragon and Frederick of Aragon; in 1469, with Lorenzo de' *Medici; and in 1488, with his son Piero. During these years the Orsini built the great castle at Bracciano.

Cesare *Borgia's defeat of the Colonna seemed a victory for the Orsini; then he turned on them, and they too lost possessions. Pope *Julius II (1503–13) restored properties to both families and brought about a brief reconciliation between them. There were times between 1523 and 1557 when the Orsini were overshadowed or defeated by the Colonna, and the Guelf cause seemed lost. The Ghibellines did not succeed, however, in overthrowing or limiting the temporal power of the papacy. The Orsini and other Guelfs were on the winning side, and were rewarded for their support. In 1560 Pius IV promoted the Bracciano branch to the rank of Duke and bestowed the honor of being one of the two princes in attendance at the papal throne. The Colonna was the other. Another service of the Orsini to the Church was the governing of the *States of the Church, Orsini bishops and laymen performing the required duties.

Orsini Cardinals. A study of the Orsini cardinals is another way of measuring the importance of the family to the Church. It was natural for the popes to reward their ally; accordingly, the Orsini had more cardinals than the Colonna during the centuries of conflict; between 1144 and 1562, there were 22 Orsini and only 11 Colonna cardinals. Several times there were two or three Orsini in the college of cardinals at the same time; only twice were there two Colonna. The Orsini had a pope and three cardinals before the first Colonna was created cardinal in 1192 or 1193, and even then the Colonna had to share his honor with an Orsini simultaneously created cardinal. During the Avignon papacy and the Western Schism, eight Orsini and only four Colonna became cardinals. None of the Orsini cardinals was ever so independent as Cardinals Giacomo and Pietro Colonna in Pope Boniface VIII's

pontificate, or so aggressive as Cardinal Pompeo Colonna in Pope Clement VII's. There were two Orsini popes before a Colonna was elected pope, and *Martin V proved to be the only Colonna ever to achieve that honor. After the Guelf-Ghibelline conflict became passé c. 1562 and before 1789, another Orsini became Pope *Benedict XIII; twelve Colonna but only five Orsini became cardinals. The Orsini cardinals (the first date indicates appointment) included Giacinto, 1144, who later became Pope Celestine III; Giordano, 1145 (d. 1165); Pietro, 1181 (d. 1181); Bobone, 1182 (d. 1189); perhaps another Bobone, 1192 or 1193; Giovanni Gaetano, 1244, later Pope Nicholas III; Matteo Rosso, 1261–63? (d. 1305); Giordano, 1278 (d. 1287), brother of Nicholas III; Latino Frangipane Malabranca, 1278 (d. 1294), nephew of Nicholas III; Napoleone, 1288 (d. 1342), another nephew of Nicholas III. Matteo Rosso was the grandson of Senator Matteo Rosso; he participated in 13 election conclaves, including the one that elected his uncle, Pope Nicholas III. He supported Pope Boniface VIII and opposed the French influence that lured the papacy to *Avignon. Latino was a student in Paris and prior of the Dominican friary in Rome. Popes Martin IV, Honorius IV, and Nicholas IV consulted him on important questions; Dominican writers call him blessed. Napoleone also studied in Paris. He restored Orvieto and Gubbio to papal obedience under Boniface VIII. In contrast with his cousin, Cardinal Matteo Rosso, he worked for the election of Pope *Clement V, the first pope in Avignon. Philip IV of France gave him a pension.

The 14th century numbered other Orsini cardinals, including Francesco, 1295 (d. 1312); Gian Gaetano, or Giovanni, 1316 (d. 1335), a legate in several provinces, opposed the Ghibellines who invited Emperor *Louis IV the Bavarian to Rome, withdrew from Rome, and then brought Rome back to papal obedience after Louis's departure—Pope *John XXII did not approve of the cardinal's war against the Colonna and ordered him to return to Tuscany. Matteo, 1327 (d. 1340), a nephew of Cardinal Gian Gaetano, a Dominican who taught in Florence, Rome, and Paris (Dominicans call him blessed); Rinaldo, 1350 (d. 1374); Giacomo, or Jacopo, 1371 (d. 1379); Poncello, 1378 (d. 1395); Tommaso, 1379? (d. 1390); and Raimondello, 1381, marked the latter half of the turbulent century. Giordano, 1405 (d. 1438), attended the Councils of *Pisa and *Constance; served as legate in France, England, Hungary-Bohemia for Pope Martin V; visited churches and religious houses in Rome to reform abuses; and as legate at *Basel supported Pope Eugene IV. Latino, 1448 (d. 1477), was pious and well educated in law; in 1472 he commanded the fleet against the Turks; during an illness Pope Sixtus IV and the college of cardinals visited him; he established a library that was destroyed in the sacking of Rome, 1527. Giambattista, 1483 (d. 1503); Franciotto, 1517 (d. 1533?); and Flavio, 1565 (d. 1581), spanned the 16th century. Alessandro, 1615 (d. 1626), spent his youth in Florence at the court of Ferdinand I, his maternal grandfather; served as legate in Ravenna, where he relieved distress during a time of poor harvests and paid peasants for their losses during the delay of court procedures; in Rome he was the patron of G. *Galilei, engaged in many charitable works, and led an ascetical life. Virginio, 1641 (d. 1676), who gave up his right of in-

Virginio Orsini, one of the commanders of the papal troops of Sixtus IV, detail, fresco, Sistine Chapel.

heritance as the firstborn son in order to be a religious, became a *Knight of Malta and won reknown in war against the Turks. *Vincenzo Maria* (his name in the Dominican Order), 1672, later became Pope Benedict XIII. *Domenico,* 1743 (d. 1789), a great nephew of Benedict XIII, was made a grandee of Spain by Charles III and served as Ferdinand IV's ambassador from Naples to Rome.

Conclusion. A present-day map of Rome reflects the importance of the family in four place names, three of them streets. One of the streets refers to a palace on Monte Giordano, the site of the Taverna palace today. A few years after the Savelli family became extinct, the Orsini purchased their palace (1717) at the theater of Marcellus. Later it was sold, but it is still called the Orsini palace. In 1834 Pope Gregory XVI confirmed the honor of being princes in attendance at papal functions as the exclusive right of the Orsini and Colonna families. (Special circumstances have on occasion modified this declaration.) It has been exercised by both families into the 20th century.

Bibliography: P. Litta et al., *Famiglie celebri italiane,* 14 v. (Milan 1819–1923) v.10. Moroni 27:147; 49:145–172; 55:233–243. Pastor 1:293–297; 4:379–384; 5:247–248; 6:125–127, 218; 9:275–276. L. Càllari, *I palazzi di Roma* (3d ed. Rome 1944). P. Paschini, EncCatt 9:371–376. G. B. Colonna, *Gli Orsini* (Milan 1955). F. Bock, LexThK² 7:1241–44. **Illustration credit:** Alinari-Art Reference Bureau.

[M. L. SHAY]

ORTEGA Y GASSET, JOSÉ

Spanish philosopher; b. Madrid, May 9, 1883, d. there, Oct. 18, 1955. Ortega obtained his doctorate in philosophy and letters at the Central University, Madrid (1904), and subsequently attended the universities of Leipzig, Berlin, and Marburg. From 1910 to 1936 he was professor of metaphysics at the University of Madrid. He was a prolific writer; his complete works, including those published posthumously, fill nine volumes.

From his first writings Ortega preferred the vitalistic philosophy of the turn of the century to the *idealism of his professors at Marburg, and focused his attention on the individual within a concrete "circumstance." The influence of F. W. *Nietzsche and W. *Dilthey is apparent in Ortega's writings, although he defends the originality and superiority of his philosophy over the empiricist thought of Dilthey. Several of his themes on human existence are also found in M. Heidegger, but Ortega is careful to point out the priority of his own publications.

In interpreting Ortega's thought, the chronology of his works (especially those published posthumously) must be kept in mind. The main ideas of his "metaphysics" and epistemology, substantially unchanged since about 1932, are the following. The radical reality is life, "my life." All other realities are rooted, in the sense that they must appear in one way or another, in my life. Life can be described as what "I" do with the "circumstance," or as the effort for "my" realization within a given "circumstance." The "I" or the ego is a project, a program. "Circumstance" means everything else, including my body and soul. Independently of my interpretations, the circumstance (i.e., things) consists in mere facilities and difficulties.

The "instrument" by which one can capture radical reality is the vital reason that, in the last analysis, is identical with life itself. My life, a continuous making and not something already made, must constantly consider and weigh the facilities and difficulties of the situation; it must choose—"we are necessarily free"—between the different possibilities or alternatives, and it must reason. This is the meaning of vital reason, and since life is essentially time or history, vital reason is also historical reason. Its method is narration. It does not use Eleatic, universal, and identical concepts, but concrete and "occasional" concepts of variable content.

Since every individual is a project, the circumstance or the facilities and difficulties each one faces are different. Hence each man is a different point of view vis-à-vis the universe. What one sees, another cannot see; what is true for one may not be true for another. All points of view are necessary for seeing the whole truth. The truth of ideas, as distinct from truth as authenticity, consists in their correspondence with one's idea of reality; it is "a matter of internal policy."

In spite of his perspectivism and his definition of truth, Ortega rejects *relativism in the traditional sense of the term. A few texts in Ortega's earlier writings explicitly affirm the existence of a transcendent, absolute reality, whereas later expressions seem to preclude its truly transcendent and absolute character. The later position, which can hardly be interpreted from a purely phenomenological point of view, seems more in harmony with his final philosophy. Ortega wrote also, with genial insights, on philosophy of history, psychology, literature, art, sports, technology, and above all on social and political philosophy.

Ortega contributed immensely to the philosophical awakening of his countrymen; his writings, encompassing in masterful style all realms of culture, and the *Re-*

vista de Occidente, which he founded and edited, introduced their readers to the whole of European and world thought. His own philosophy has influenced, in greater or less degree, contemporary Spanish laymen and thinkers in other lands. The deficiencies of his philosophy stem from his deessentialized ideas concerning the "I" and life; his idealistic and, in spite of his protests, relativistic concept of truth; the inability of his vitalistic conception to reach transcendence; his radical historicism; and the exclusion of universal moral norms.

See also SPANISH PHILOSOPHY; LIFE PHILOSOPHIES.

Bibliography: *Obras completas,* 9 v. (4th ed. Madrid 1957–63). J. MARÍAS AGUILERA, *Ortega y la idea de la razón vital* (2d ed. Madrid 1948); *La escuela de Madrid* (Buenos Aires 1959). J. FERRATER MORA, *Ortega y Gasset: An Outline of His Philosophy* (New Haven 1957). S. M. RAMÍREZ, *La filosofía de Ortega y Gasset* (Barcelona 1958). F. ALLUNTIS, "The Vital and Historical Reason of José Ortega y Gasset," FrancStudies 15 (1955) 60–78.

[F. ALLUNTIS]

ORTHODOX CHURCHES

The term is employed here in its conventional historical sense to designate those Churches that accepted and have maintained the teachings of the Council of Chalcedon, but which, beginning in the 11th century, became estranged from Rome, refusing to acknowledge the juridical primacy of the pope. The term is used also in a broader sense, but improperly, to include the Monophysite and Nestorian Churches (*see* EASTERN CHURCHES).

History of the Name. The word Orthodox is derived from the Greek words ὀρθός (right) and δόξα (teaching). Before the 5th century, there was predominantly only one Catholic, Apostolic Church made up of various nationalities each possessing its own language and liturgical expression of the essential unity of doctrine, Sacraments, and hierarchical magisterium. But in 431 Nestorius was condemned for his doctrine that would thereafter bear his name, *Nestorianism, and would remove the East Syrian Church from the unity of the whole Church. Twenty years later, at the Council of *Chalcedon (451), *Monophysitism was condemned, and the Churches of *Armenia, *Syria (Jacobites), *Egypt (Coptic Church), *Ethiopia, and *India broke away from those that accepted the doctrinal teachings of Chalcedon. The Churches of *Constantinople (Byzantine rite) and of Rome (Roman rite) remained faithful to the teachings of the Councils of *Ephesus and Chalcedon and hence called themselves "the Orthodox," i.e., those holding the true, correct teaching of the early Christian Church, as promulgated in these two councils. In the 9th century under *Photius, Patriarch of Constantinople, and in the 11th century under Patriarch *Michael Cerularius, an estrangement began, which in the course of the next 3 centuries culminated in a formal division between the Eastern Churches that employed the Byzantine rite and the Church of the West that followed the Latin rite and acknowledged the primacy of the Roman pontiff. The Eastern Churches in this sense included the Greek, Rumanian, and much of the Slavic-speaking world. They continued to call themselves Orthodox, insisting on their fidelity to the "right teachings" of the first seven ecumenical councils. Thus the term Orthodox is commonly employed in modern times, as indicated above, to designate the Eastern Churches of the Byz-

antine rite that do not recognize the primacy of the Roman pontiff, yet preserve an essential unity in doctrine under an apostolic hierarchical magisterium that existed in their Churches before the 11th century. They thus are to be distinguished from their Eastern Catholic brethren of the Byzantine rite who, either through corporate or individual reconciliations, have recognized the pope as the head of the universal Church.

The Orthodox collectively call themselves by various titles. Sometimes the terms Oriental Church, Greek Church, and Greco-Slav Church are used, but these are not correct for there are many other Oriental Churches other than Orthodox, e.g., Eastern Catholics, Nestorians, Monophysites, and there are many Orthodox who are not Greek or Slavic. Usually, however, the Orthodox refer to themselves as the Eastern Orthodox Church, the Orthodox Catholic Church, the Orthodox Catholic Church of the East, the Church of the seven Ecumenical Councils, or describe themselves in similar fashion.

Divisions of the Orthodox Churches. The Orthodox Churches form a group of self-governing Churches, with no centralized organization of the whole body. The Patriarchates of *Constantinople, *Alexandria, *Antioch, and *Jerusalem have the first places of honor, owing to their ties with the venerable apostolic see that they represent. Four other patriarchates have been formed in the course of history: the Bulgarian (formed in 917), Serbian (1346), Russian (1589), and Rumanian (1925). The Georgian Church is ruled by a catholicos, a title less exalted than that of patriarch, and the Church is called a catholicate. There are six other Churches, fully independent in their self-government from any other Orthodox Church, namely the autocephalous Churches of Cyprus (formed in 431), Sinai (1575), Greece (1830), Poland (1924), Albania (1937), and Czechoslovakia (1951). Other Orthodox Churches enjoying some degree of self-government are still canonically attached to one of the larger patriarchates and hence are called autonomous, but are not autocephalous. They comprise the Churches of Finland, Estonia, Latvia, Hungary, China, Japan, Macedonia, and the three autonomous Russian Churches outside Russia, along with those of the Ukrainians and Ruthenians abroad.

Individual Orthodox Churches. Fuller information on the individual Churches can be found in the articles dealing with the particular rite or country. A brief treatment is given here, however, so that the reader can obtain a comprehensive view of the principal Orthodox Churches in the 1960s.

Patriarchate of Constantinople. The patriarch of Constantinople is called the "Ecumenical Patriarch." Since the break between the East and the West, he has enjoyed a position of special honor among the Orthodox communities. From a small suffragan see of Heraclea in Thrace, Byzantium was transformed into the imperial capital of Constantine and his successors and assumed, as the "New Rome," a special importance ecclesiastically as well as politically. The jurisdiction of the patriarch of Constantinople extended to the far limits of the Byzantine Empire and was ratified solemnly in the Councils of Constantinople (381), Ephesus (431), and Chalcedon (451). In 1054, when the formal rupture of relations with ancient Rome took place under Patriarch Michael Cerularius, the jurisdiction of this patriarchate extended over all Christians using the Byzantine rite in North Africa, South Italy and Sicily, Syria, Palestine, Asia Minor, the Balkan States, and throughout all of the Slav countries as far as the northern Baltic Sea. In the 11th century more than 600 episcopal sees were under the jurisdiction of the patriarch of Constantinople. But with the sacking of Constantinople by the Latin Crusaders in 1204 and its complete capitulation under the Turks in 1453, the patriarch was reduced to the status of servant of the Moslem caliphs.

In modern times this patriarchate has been greatly reduced in actual numbers and jurisdiction. In 1928 it lost 49 dioceses that were given over to the Synodal Church of Greece, while other dioceses, lost in lands surrendered to Turkey in 1912, were subsequently given to Yugoslavia and Bulgaria. By the Treaty of Lausanne (1923), Greeks were forced to leave Asia Minor. Today the patriarch is forced to reside in the Phanar, a section of the modern city of Istanbul in Turkey, and has immediate jurisdiction over about 80,000 faithful in Istanbul and on the neighboring islands making up the Dioceses of Constantinople, Chalcedon, Derkos, Imbros, and Prinkipos. He rules also over the four dioceses of the Dodecanese Islands (numbering about 170,000 faithful), chief among which is Rhodes. The small theocratic peninsula of Mount Athos in northern Greece with approximately 2,000 monks is also under his jurisdiction. Theoretically he claims jurisdiction over all Orthodox, apart from the accepted autocephalous Churches, in accordance with a canon of the Council of Chalcedon giving him the rights *inter barbaros*. In fact, it extends in the 1960s to the adherents of the Greek Church in North and South America (about 1,200,000 faithful), Western Europe, and Australia. Small autonomous splinter groups among the Slav Orthodox in the New World recognize his jurisdiction; e.g., the American Carpatho-Russian Orthodox Church. Thus, the total number of faithful under the jurisdiction of the patriarch of Constantinople in the early 1960s was about 1,500,-000. (*See* CONSTANTINOPLE, PATRIARCHATE OF.)

Patriarchate of Alexandria. Before the rise of imperial Constantinople the Patriarchate of Alexandria enjoyed first place after that of Rome, with jurisdiction over 100 dioceses. But its unity was split by the Monophysite (*See* MONOPHYSITISM) heresy that was condemned in the Council of Chalcedon (451). From 457 there existed two parallel hierarchies claiming the See of Alexandria: the one favoring politically the Byzantine emperor and ecclesiastically the patriarch of Constantinople; the other desiring an Egypt freed from the Byzantine Empire and the establishment of an independent Patriarchate of Alexandria. The second group evolved into the Monophysite Coptic Church. The Orthodox of the Patriarchate of Alexandria are the descendants of those who favored political and ecclesiastical ties with Constantinople (*see* MELCHITE RITE). They were supported mainly by immigration of Greeks to Egypt, but since the rise (1952–) of Gamal Abdil Nasser this influx has been stopped. Many Greek Orthodox have emigrated from Egypt owing to religious and political pressures placed on them, so that the Orthodox in Egypt under the jurisdiction of the patriarch of Alexandria in the early 1960s numbered approximately 35,000. Three-fourths of these are of Greek origin, and

one-fourth of Syrian origin, a fact that causes serious internal strife. The patriarch resides in Alexandria. He has jurisdiction over all of Africa, which is divided into 11 dioceses: 4 in Egypt and 1 each in Ethiopia, Sudan, Tunisia, Congo, Cameroon, Kenya, and the Republic of South Africa. (*See* ALEXANDRIA, PATRIARCHATE OF.)

Patriarchate of Antioch. This ancient apostolic patriarchate was split into two parts in the 5th century. The first part embraced the Monophysite heresy, while the second, which remained faithful to the teaching of the Council of Chalcedon (451), came to be called Melchite Orthodox. Owing to the close relationship between the Antiochene and Constantinople Patriarchates, the second group accepted the Byzantine rite from Constantinople in the 12th century. The city of Antioch suffered greatly under the Mameluk Turks, and in 1366 the Orthodox patriarch moved his see to Damascus. There are 18 dioceses under the jurisdiction of the Orthodox Patriarchate of Antioch: 6 in Syria, 6 in Lebanon, 1 in Iraq, 2 in the U.S., 2 in Brazil, and 1 in Argentina. The faithful, mostly Arab-speaking (originally at least), number about 300,000. (*See* ANTIOCH, PATRIARCHATE OF.)

Patriarchate of Jerusalem. At the Council of Chalcedon (451) Bishop Juvenal obtained the recognition of Jerusalem as an autonomous patriarchate, occupying the fifth place of honor after the Patriarchates of Rome, Constantinople, Alexandria, and Antioch. As the Holy Land, it flourished under the early Byzantine emperors and was dotted with shrines and chapels. However, as a result of the Persian and Arab invasions of the 7th century and the rise of the Crusaders' States in the 12th and 13th centuries, Jerusalem lost much of its religious authority and significance in the East. The patriarch came under the influence of the patriarch of Constantinople, but, into the 19th century, tried to regain autonomous control over his ancient patriarchate. In the 20th century a struggle within the patriarchate developed between the Greek hierarchy and the Arab clergy. The patriarch in the 1960s is reduced to poverty and, because of continued tensions between the Jews and the Arabs, the problem of Greek-Arab cooperation among the Orthodox in the Patriarchate of Jerusalem remains unresolved. The Orthodox total about 75,000, with about 15,000 found in Israel and 60,000 in Jordan. The patriarch resides in Jerusalem (Jordan) and has jurisdiction over three dioceses: Jerusalem, Nazareth, and St. John of Acre. (*See* JERUSALEM, PATRIARCHATE OF.)

Bulgarian Patriarchate. Czar Boris (853–889), after vacillating between Byzantium and Rome, chose to accept Christianity under the form of the Byzantine rite. The autocephalous Bulgarian Patriarchate was set up in 1017 under Czar Simeon, but was suppressed in 1019 by the great Byzantine Emperor Basil II Bulgaroctonos. A second patriarchate was established at Trnovo in 1186, only to be suppressed by the Ottoman Turks in 1393. In 1870 the Bulgar Orthodox obtained from the Turkish Sultan Abdul Aziz the right to reestablish their national patriarchate, independent of Constantinople. This, however, the patriarch of Constantinople would not accept, and hence from 1872 until 1945 the Orthodox Church of Constantinople held the Bulgarian Church in excommunication, while the other Slav Orthodox remained in communion with the Bulgars.

Finally, in 1961, the Bulgarian Patriarchate was officially recognized as independent by the patriarch of Constantinople. Out of an estimated total of 8 million inhabitants, 6½ million may be regarded as Orthodox, but since the beginning of the Communist regime accurate religious statistics are not available. The patriarch resides at Sophia and governs 10 dioceses in Bulgaria. There is one autonomous Bulgarian Orthodox diocese in the U.S. (*See* BULGARIA; BULGARIAN RITE.)

Serbian Patriarchate. In Serbia (now Yugoslavia) Western and Eastern Christianity met, because from A.D. 395 the boundary line between the eastern and western halves of the Roman Empire was formed by the Sava, Drina, and Zeta Rivers. The organizer of the Church in Serbia was St. Sava, son of Prince Stephen Nemanja (*c.* 1167–96). Sava in 1219 was consecrated archbishop of Serbia by the patriarch of Constantinople and established 10 dioceses. The first Serbian Patriarchate was proclaimed by Czar Dusan the Great in 1346, but was suppressed by the Turks in 1458. A second patriarchate, with its center at Pec, lasted from 1557 to 1766, when it too was abolished by the Turks. The third and present patriarchate was established in 1920. In the 1960s it comprised the five autonomous Serbian Churches of Belgrade, Karlovci, Sarajevo, Cetinje, and Dalmatia. The patriarch resides in Belgrade and governs 27 dioceses, 3 of which are in the U.S. and 1 in Hungary. The faithful number about 7 million Orthodox. (*See* YUGOSLAVIA; SERBIAN RITE.)

Russian Patriarchate. The Patriarchate of Moscow and of All Russia, to employ its official title, embraces the Russian, Ukrainian, White Russian, and all other Orthodox found within the U.S.S.R. except the Georgians of the Byzantine rite. The patriarchate was established only in 1589, and was subsequently suppressed by Peter the Great (1672–1725), who replaced it by the Holy Synod. It was restored in 1917, but the Orthodox Church was almost immediately subjected to heavy persecutions by the new Communist regime. When Patriarch *Tikhon died in 1925, the election of another patriarch was impeded until 1943, the see thus remaining vacant for 18 years. Finally, to gain the support of the Orthodox Church during World War II, Stalin permitted the election of a patriarch. In 1948 an attempt was made to gain greater influence among other Orthodox Churches by calling a pan-Orthodox synod in Moscow, but this move received bitter criticism from the Patriarchate of Constantinople. In 1961 the Russian Orthodox Church of Moscow became a member of the *World Council of Churches. In the early 1960s there were 73 Orthodox dioceses in Russia under the jurisdiction of the patriarch. Accurate statistics of clergy and faithful are unavailable, but an estimated 14,000 priests serve 11,000 churches, with a total of 50 to 55 million faithful. (*See* UNION OF SOVIET SOCIALIST REPUBLICS; RUSSIAN RITE. For the Russian Orthodox Church abroad and in the U.S., see below.)

Rumanian Patriarchate. The principalities of Vallachia, Moldavia, Transylvania, and Bukovina were united in 1881 to form modern Rumania. In 1885 independence of the Rumanian Orthodox Church from the Constantinople Patriarchate was recognized. In 1925, through a fusion of five autonomous metropolitan Churches—Vallachia, Moldavia, Transylvania,

Fig. 1. Orthodox Church life in Russia: (a) The Liturgy at the Laura of the Trinity at St. Sergius. (b) The feast of St. Sergius at the monastery of Zagorsk. (c) Blessing of Easter foods in Yelokhov Cathedral, Moscow.

Fig. 2. Orthodox Church life: (a) Greek Orthodox priest casts a cross into the harbor at Piraeus, Greece, on Orthodox Christmas day, symbolically blessing waters and fleets. (b) Woman venerating a wall icon at the Russian Orthodox monastery of Zagorsk, near Moscow. (c) First veneration of the icon of Nektarios Kefalas, a Greek saint of the 20th century. (d) A venerable icon from Mount Athos carried in procession at Athens, Greece.

Bukovina, and Bessarabia—there was formed the Rumanian Patriarchate. Until the 17th century the language used in the Byzantine liturgy of this area was Old Slavonic, but since the formation of the patriarchate the modern vernacular—a Romance tongue—has been employed. After World War II Bessarabia and the northern part of Bukovina were incorporated into the Moscow Patriarchate with a resulting reduction of the Rumanian Orthodox by more than 3 million members. The Communist regime, however, liquidated the growing Rumanian Catholic Church of the Byzantine rite, which numbered 1,572,000 adherents and incorporated its property and members into the Rumanian Orthodox Church. There are 12 dioceses in the patriarchate and one in the U.S. with an estimated total membership of 16,300,000. It is one of the more vibrant Orthodox Churches, owing especially to the high intellectual formation of its clergy. The desire among Orthodox for reunion with the Catholics has been perhaps strongest among the Rumanians. (*See* RUMANIA; RUMANIAN RITE.)

Georgian Catholicate. The Church of Georgia is one of the most ancient. Christianity penetrated its western part by the 3d century, and its central area during the 4th century. In the beginning it was influenced by the Churches of Constantinople, Armenia, and Antioch, but gradually the Byzantine influence dominated. It received its autonomy as an independent Church in the 8th century, but from 1811 to 1917 its autocephaly was suppressed. However, its autonomy was restored in 1918 and recognized by the other Orthodox Churches in 1944. As in the case of the Russian Church, it is difficult to estimate the number of Orthodox in Georgia, but it is probably near 2 million faithful. (*See* GEORGIAN RITE; GEORGIA, CHURCH IN ANCIENT.)

Church of Cyprus. The Council of Ephesus (431) declared this Church autocephalous because of its apostolic origin (evangelized by SS. Paul and Barnabas). The archbishop, who is the head of this Church, resides in Nicosia. In the eyes of the Greek Orthodox he holds the fifth place of honor among the heads of the Orthodox Churches, but the Slavs, especially the Russians, refuse to give him this position. The Orthodox, who constitute three quarters of the total population, have long desired political union with Greece, and Cypriote ecclesiastics have been the leaders in *enosis* or the reunion movement. There are 350,000 Orthodox faithful. (*See* CYPRUS.)

Church of Mount Sinai. The autocephalous Church of Mount Sinai with some 100 members is the smallest Orthodox independent Church. Originally belonging to the Patriarchate of Jerusalem, it received its independence in 1575. The superior of the monastery of St. Catherine is an archbishop who rules over this Church.

Synodal Church of Greece. A synod of Greek bishops declared autocephaly for their Church in 1833, but the patriarch of Constantinople recognized this action only in 1850. The Church is administered by a synod headed by the king of Greece. The archbishop of Athens is leader of the hierarchy, which numbers 67 residential bishops, all having the title of metropolitan. Religious organizations such as *Anaplasis and Zoi*, founded in 1887 and 1907, respectively, have done much to make the Orthodox faith more dynamic than it had traditionally been in the lives of the majority.

Orthodoxy is the official religion of the state, and the faithful number about 8 million. (*See* GREEK RITE.)

Church of Poland. This Orthodox Church was formed after World War I of White Russians, Russians, and Ukrainians who found themselves living in newly annexed Polish territory. Autocephaly was granted by Constantinople in 1924. After the partition of Poland following World War II, only about 400,000 Orthodox faithful were still in Polish territory. The hierarchy was forced to come under the jurisdiction of the patriarch of Moscow, who in 1948 granted a new autocephaly to the Polish Orthodox Church, but with a Russian metropolitan as its head. (*See* POLAND.)

Church of Albania. The Christian faith penetrated into *Albania from two directions, from the Roman West and the Byzantine East. The Byzantine rite was accepted in the southern part, in the ancient province of Epirus. The Turks occupied this area from 1468 until 1912, and the majority of the people accepted Islam. After 1912 the Orthodox Albanians, under the leadership of the priest Fan Noli, started a movement for an autocephalous Church, which was established on their own initiative in 1922. The patriarch of Constantinople excommunicated all those involved but finally in 1937 recognized the autocephaly of the Albanian Orthodox Church. The faithful number about 300,000, approximately 20 per cent of the total population. (*See* ALBANIA.)

Church of Czechoslovakia. This Orthodox Church was formed from various small splinter groups. A small core of Orthodox existed in Prague from 1870, and to this was added a part of the Czechoslovakian National Church, which accepted Orthodoxy in 1920 under the guidance of Bp. Gorazd Pavlik. Another group in 1945 returned to Czechoslovakia from Volynia in the Ukraine, where they had accepted Orthodoxy. Finally, the Orthodox Church was augmented by the forced "conversion" of the Catholic Ruthenians of the Diocese of Presov in 1950. The faithful number about 50,000, with a metropolitan residing in Prague. The Moscow Patriarchate granted autocephaly in 1951. (*See* CZECHOSLOVAKIA.)

Autonomous Orthodox Churches. Besides these 15 autocephalous Churches, either patriarchates or independent metropolitan Churches, there are several smaller Orthodox Churches, not autocephalous but "autonomous," namely, those of Finland, Japan, China, Estonia and Latvia, Hungary, and Macedonia. These enjoy a restricted independence, being, ordinarily, united juridically with a mother patriarchal Church.

Church of Finland. The Orthodox Church of Finland numbered 60,000 in the 1960s. When in 1918 Finland received its independence from Russia, the Orthodox Church opted for independence from the Moscow Patriarchate. In 1923 the patriarch of Constantinople recognized its status as an autonomous Church, but under his general jurisdiction, a situation not accepted by the Russian Church until 1957. There are the two Orthodox Dioceses of Kuopio and Helsinki. (*See* FINLAND.)

Church of Japan. This Church grew out of the Russian mission started in Japan in 1860. In the early 1960s the Japanese Orthodox numbered 35,000, under the jurisdiction of the autocephalous American-Russian metropolis of New York. (*See* JAPAN; JAPANESE RELIGION.)

Church of China. After the 1917 revolution in Russia, many thousands of Orthodox immigrated into China, but with the rise of Chinese communism these same Russians fled to the free West. Hence the Orthodox Church of China may be described strictly as that group of indigenous Chinese who embraced the Orthodox faith through the Russian mission among the Chinese started in 1858. By the 1950s there were 20,000 Chinese Orthodox. From 1957 the Church has been autonomous under the Moscow Patriarchate, with two Chinese bishops residing in Peking and Shanghai. (*See* CHINA.)

Orthodox Churches of Estonia and Latvia. Only a small part of predominantly Protestant Estonia is Orthodox, perhaps a total of 100,000. Its Orthodox Church received its autonomy from Constantinople in 1923, but after World War II it was incorporated as autonomous under the Moscow Patriarchate. In Latvia the Orthodox numbered about 185,000, of whom 130,-000 were Russians or other nationalities, and only 55,000 were native Latvians. The Latvian Church received its autonomy from Constantinople in 1923, but on being taken over by the Russian Communists after World War II, it too was forcibly placed under the jurisdiction of the Moscow Patriarchate. Since 1929 the Latvians have been using their vernacular language in the liturgy. (*See* LATVIA; ESTONIA.)

Hungarian Orthodox Church. In the early 1960s Orthodox numbered about 40,000 and were composed of Orthodox immigrant groups of Rumanian, Ruthenian, and Serbian origin. After the Soviets took control this autonomous Church came under the Moscow Patriarchate. (*See* HUNGARY.)

Church of Macedonia. This autonomous Church depends on the Serbian Patriarchate. The metropolitan resides in Skoplje and has reassumed the ancient title of archbishop of Ochrid. In 1960 the faithful numbered about 175,000. (*See* SERBIAN RITE.)

The autocephalous or autonomous emigrant Churches will be treated below in dealing with Orthodoxy in the Americas.

Orthodox of the Western Rite. Special attention must be called to a recent phenomenon in non-Orthodox countries, namely, development of Orthodox Churches employing the Roman rite in contradistinction to the traditional Orthodox usage of the Byzantine rite.

Approval for a Western rite within Orthodoxy was given by the Holy Synod of Russia in 1870, and the first parish was canonically established in France in 1936 by Louis-Charles Winnaert. The Western rite parishes of Europe are attached either to the Moscow Patriarchate or to the emigré Russian Synodal Church of New York. The Western rite of Orthodoxy started in the U.S. in 1958 under the Syrian Orthodox Church headed by Metropolitan Antony Bashir. The Russian Patriarchal Exarchate under Moscow also has several Western rite parishes. The total membership of these various Churches using the Western rite but belonging to various Orthodox jurisdictions is difficult to ascertain, but in the early 1960s was approximately 4,000, the adherents being largely former Anglicans or Roman Catholics.

Characteristic Features of the Orthodox Churches. The Orthodox Churches in general lack a central authority with effective juridical power and emphasize traditionalism and liturgy rather than formal dogma in the Western sense.

Organization of Churches. Centralization of Church government was never developed in the East; therefore the stress has been on the autonomous action of each local bishop in his diocese, guided by the concerted actions of a Holy Synod or collegiality type of government. In all the Orthodox Churches, the bishop of the capital city, whether he is a patriarch, metropolitan, or archbishop, is considered the chief among all the other bishops of that given nation, but he has no jurisdiction in the strict sense over other bishops. All Church decisions are made by the episcopal council or synod at which the chief prelate presides, but as an equal among equals. Not only is there a supreme synod gathered around the chief prelate, but there are also lesser synods and councils for each diocese and parish. Ordinarily there are two such councils: one, an ecclesiastical tribunal, passes judgments on marriage cases, dispensations, and the granting of divorces; the other deals with the financial administration of ecclesiastical property.

Weakness Resulting from Lack of Central Authority. One of the great weaknesses of the Orthodox Churches has been the lack of a central voice of authority enjoying authentic jurisdiction. Historically, through their strong reaction to the papal claims of primacy and through centuries of domination by Moslems, Mongols, and other foreign powers, the Orthodox have developed into national Churches that have in practice become completely autonomous in their relations to one another. They have reacted vehemently when any leading outside patriarch has tried to interfere in the government of the given national Church. The relations among the various autonomous Churches consist mostly in the sending of irenic letters announcing the election of a new patriarch or archbishop as titular head of a specific Church. Some Churches exchange the holy chrism, but throughout the centuries this has caused friction, so that in recent times Alexandria, Jerusalem, Cyprus, and Greece obtain theirs from Constantinople, and the Bulgarians get theirs from Rumania, while the others individually bless their own chrism.

Several attempts have been made to call a pan-Orthodox synod, but with very little real success. The first one in recent times was called in 1923 at Istanbul, but not all the Churches sent representatives. A commission met on Mount Athos in 1930 to prepare for a pan-Orthodox council to be held in 1931, but all preparations were postponed. In 1948, when the patriarch of Moscow called a synod that he hoped would have been a pan-Orthodox meeting, the patriarch of Constantinople and the other Greek-speaking Orthodox Churches refused to send any representatives. Finally, in 1961 the first preparatory pan-Orthodox prosynod was held in Rhodes, and a preliminary schema of topics eventually to be discussed in a future pansynod was drawn up. Two other meetings were held in 1963 and 1964 to discuss chiefly the Orthodox rapport with Roman Catholics, but concrete proposals were delayed until the termination of Vatican Council II.

Theological Sources of Revelation. All Orthodox hold Sacred Scripture and tradition as the two fonts of Christian revelation. These two sources are presented to the faithful mainly in a setting of strongly liturgical emphasis and conservative traditionalism. For the Orthodox the divine liturgy is not so much an expression of defined dogma as emphasized in the West, but dogma follows the liturgy, seeking to protect and conserve it. Orthodox traditionalism is revealed in its scrupulous fidelity to the teachings of the first seven ecumenical councils and the writings of the early Fathers. (*See* BYZANTINE THEOLOGY, I (TO 1500); RUSSIAN THEOLOGY.)

Differences between Orthodoxy and Catholicism. The differences are treated here in brief form. Each point is covered in detail in a number of pertinent separate articles: *see* CANON, BIBLICAL; TRADITION (IN THEOLOGY); ECCLESIOLOGY; FILIOQUE; MARIOLOGY; SACRAMENTAL THEOLOGY; ESCHATOLOGY (THEOLOGICAL TREATMENT).

Canon of Holy Scripture. All Orthodox regard Scripture as a source of revelation, but there are various opinions concerning the canon of inspired books. Under Protestant influence, F. *Prokopovitch and many other Russian theologians have denied canonical authority to the Deuterocanonical books of the OT, while the Greek Orthodox continue to consider these books as canonical. This problem came up in the first pansynod of Rhodes (1961) preparatory to a pan-Orthodox council, and an attempt to obtain unanimity on this problem was being made.

Authority of Tradition. Tradition admits of various sources and degrees of authority. For most Orthodox an ecumenical council is the sole means of proposing new truths as objects of faith for all. First only Prokopovitch denied its authority, then *Khomîakov; they placed ultimate infallibility either in Holy Scripture alone or in the people of God accepting the decrees of a council, thus making it truly ecumenical. Certain ancient local synods also are accepted as ecumenical, such as those of Ancyra, Neo-Caesarea, Gangra, Antioch, Laodicea, Sardica, Carthage, and Alexandria, all approved in the Second Canon of the Council of Trullo (691–692). Many Orthodox add this council as a complement to the fifth and sixth ecumenical councils of Constantinople II (553) and Constantinople III (680–681). Many symbols of faith are accepted with varying degrees of unanimity and infallibility; the only one unanimously accepted by all Orthodox being that of Nicaea-Constantinople.

Dogmas of faith are to be interpreted according to the thought and testimony of Christian antiquity, expressed either in the decrees of councils or the writings of the Fathers. Except for Leo the Great, Gregory the Great, and St. Ambrose, the Latin Fathers are rarely cited. Among the national groups certain Fathers are favored as constituting an integral part of the given nation's theological and spiritual heritage. A bridge to more modern formulations of the Orthodox faith is provided by the Books of Symbols. These also vary in importance with each national group. Some are accepted with greater authority among the Slavs, while the same formulation may be rejected by others. The best known confessions of faith are: The *Confession* of Peter *Moghila, written originally in Latin but revised by Meletius Syrigos in his Greek translation, the version accepted by the Greeks (1642); the *Confession* of Dositheus, Patriarch of Jerusalem, (1672); the *Catechism* of Philaret, Metropolitan of Moscow (1839); and the *Confession* of Gennasius, Patriarch of Constanti-

nople (1460). Other documents of lesser authority are: the *Replies* of Jeremias II to the Lutheran theologians of Tübingen (1573–81); the *Reply of the Orthodox Patriarchs* to Pope Pius IX (1848); and the *Reply of the Synod of Constantinople* to Pope Leo XIII (1895).

Canon Law also forms an essential part of tradition. Canons deal with the temporalities of the Church and with changing situations. Hence their values vary from century to century, from national Church to national Church. Very little attention was given in the past by the West to the study of the Canon Law of the Orthodox Church, with the result that Orthodoxy is regarded as an organization that spurns any juridical organizational structure. Theodore Balsamon, John Zonaras, and other Byzantine canonists codified canons from ecumenical and local synods that represented a universal disciplinary procedure among all Orthodox Churches. Nicodemus of Mount Athos published in 1800 the well-known Greek commentary called the *Pedalion* (Rudder). It must be pointed out, however, that one of the major problems facing the Orthodox Churches in the 1960s was precisely the revision of their Canon Law, since many of the ancient canons are impossible to apply or have fallen into disuse.

Ecclesiology. In the Orthodox concept of the constitution of the Church is found the greatest difference separating Catholics and Orthodox. For the latter, all agree unanimously in refusing to recognize the juridical primacy of the Roman pontiff. Christ is the sole head of the Church, and, though many Orthodox, in keeping with the early ecumenical councils, accept the primacy of the bishop of Rome, this primacy is only one of honor, "primus inter pares," since, they hold, neither Peter nor his successors have been given special prerogatives that had not been given by Christ to the other Apostles and their successors, the other bishops. Traditionalists maintain that there is a special teaching hierarchy, distinct by its commission given it by Christ from the one given to the other members of the Church. A second group of theologians, following Alekseĭ Khomîakov, place no distinction between the people of God and the bishops; they seek to lessen the institutional authority by assigning the traditional hierarchical powers to the people of God, who then transfer these powers to the episcopal body for practical direction.

Filioque. From the time of *Photius until the decree of Vatican Council I on papal infallibility the chief theological obstacle between Orthodox and Catholics was the question of the filioque. (*See* BYZANTINE THEOLOGY.) The Greek Fathers had taught that the Holy Spirit proceeded from the Father, through the Son (διὰ τὸν Υἱόν). In the West, beginning in Spain in the 7th and 8th centuries, then moving to Gaul, Germany, and Italy, the doctrine was held that the Holy Spirit proceeded both from the Father and the Son (filioque). This remained largely a liturgical question until Patriarch Photius in the 9th century began to interpret the writings of the early Greek Fathers as teaching that the Holy Spirit proceeds *only* from the Father; he maintained that the patristic meaning of the Greek preposition διά was not *through* but *after* the Son. Many theologians, including some leading Orthodox, tend to dismiss the whole question as one of semantics, while others cling tenaciously to their traditional view as constituting the basis of an orthodox Trinitarian theology.

Mariology. The Orthodox reverence the Blessed Virgin Mary as the most exalted among God's creatures, "more honorable than the cherubim and incomparably more glorious than the seraphim." She is highly honored as the Mother of God, especially in the divine liturgy and through the numerous Marian liturgical feasts and icons in her honor. The two Roman Catholic defined Marian dogmas, however, her Immaculate Conception (1854) and her Assumption (1950), are commonly rejected by the Orthodox, not because of the doctrinal content, which is found confirmed in the Byzantine liturgical texts of the Marian feasts and in the homilies composed by the great Eastern Fathers, but because the pope of Rome has personally confirmed these as infallible dogmas defined and approved by an ecumenical council.

Sacraments. All Orthodox hold seven Sacraments, but some Orthodox theologians would be ready to admit a larger number. The indelible character conferred by the Sacraments of Baptism, Confirmation, and Holy Orders is denied by many Orthodox from a juridical point of view, yet they have difficulty explaining why these Sacraments are generally not repeated. There is no universal agreement among the Orthodox respecting the validity of Catholic Sacraments. Russian Orthodox normally do not rebaptize or reordain Catholics; the Greeks usually deny the validity of Catholic Sacraments, but through their theory of *economia* the Orthodox Church has the power to render an invalid Sacrament valid or can confer a valid Sacrament without any external sign.

Baptism is administered by a triple immersion, yet in special cases the Latin method of pouring water over the forehead is allowed. Confirmation, administered by the local priest, follows immediately after Baptism. The child usually receives Holy Communion at the same time. The Eucharistic dispute about the use of azymes (nonleavened) bread by Catholics of the Roman rite is generally regarded as a liturgical question only. Formerly the Orthodox made much of the difference of giving Communion under one or two species but they themselves in the case of Viaticum to the sick or Communion to babies admit the validity of giving only one species. Penance imposed by the priest is purely medicinal and has, for the Orthodox, no expiatory power, and especially carries with it no remission of temporal punishment. Indulgences are dismissed as a legalistic abuse.

The Anointing of the Sick is given among the Greeks also to those not sick, as a preparation for the larger liturgical feasts. The indissolubility of marriage is denied in theory and in practice. Through centuries of interpreting the texts of Mt 5.32 and 19.9 as exceptive clauses, true divorce on grounds of adultery may be obtained by the Orthodox. Other grave reasons have been added in the course of centuries, varying with the respective national Orthodox Church. The usual additional reasons are attempted murder of one of the parties, permanent insanity, or a 3-year absence of one party. Married laymen may be ordained deacons and priests, but married priests may not remarry. Bishops must be celibates—they may be either monks or widowers.

Eschatology. There are marked discrepancies in Orthodox teaching. Usually the Catholic doctrine of purgatory is denied, so that before the universal judgment the just enjoy an inferior type of happiness while sinners are consigned immediately to the fires of hell. But souls cannot expiate in any intermediate state for their own sins. Perfect retribution takes place only in the universal judgment. Yet all Orthodox admit that it is wholesome to pray for the dead because the prayer of the Church can change the lot of the damned. Some hold that prayers serve to liberate the souls whose salvation has been belated. Although the *Confessions* of Peter *Moghila and *Dositheus hold a doctrine similar to purgatory, today the majority of Orthodox reject this idea, at least in the form of souls enduring the pains of fire to expiate for sins. For those who would hold some suffering of the faithful departed, it would be medicinal or purificatory, but not expiatory. If a man dies in God's grace, his sins are forgiven, for Christ is the only atonement and satisfaction. Other Orthodox tend to leave the eschatological questions open, insisting that God has not deemed it necessary for man to know all the details for the afterlife.

Ecumenical Rapport with Rome. The Orthodox recognize that they have more in common with Roman Catholics as regards doctrine, the Sacraments, and an Apostolic teaching hierarchy than with any other Christian group. Yet, in practice, since the Reformation they have had more intimate contact with the Anglicans and Old Catholics and recently, as members of the World Council of Churches, with the whole Protestant world. Yet under the mutual inspiration of Popes John XXIII and Paul VI and Ecumenical Patriarch Athenagoras I there has been created an entirely new atmosphere of ecumenical rapport between Catholic and Orthodox. When Pope Paul VI embraced Patriarch Athenagoras in January 1963 in Jerusalem, the cradle of Christianity, a new impetus for serious dialogue was given. At all of the sessions of Vatican Council II, Orthodox observers were present, and the Catholics profited from their comments. At the third pan-Orthodox conference (1964) on the island of Rhodes, the 14 autocephalous Orthodox Churches unanimously agreed to launch a serious, ecumenical dialogue on the theological differences with Rome following the close of Vatican Council II.

New Attitude of Mutual Good Will. This initial good will marked the beginning of a new attitude on the part of both the Roman Catholic Church and the Orthodox toward each other. The Vatican Secretariate for Promoting Christian Unity established an undersecretariate to deal with Orthodox *rapprochement.* Solid scholarship and personal contacts with the Orthodox have been a part of the important work launched in 1926 by the Benedictine monastery of Union at Chevetogne in Belgium. This monastery is divided into monks who worship according to the Roman and the Byzantine rites. Their scholarly journal, *Irenikon,* is read by many Orthodox, and often Orthodox are the chief contributors. *Istina,* published by the Dominican Fathers of Paris under the direction of Father Christopher Dumont, OP, is another scholarly periodical that has tried to carry on the dialogue between Catholics and Orthodox on a high, theological plane. In the U.S. the John XXIII Center for Eastern Christian Studies of Fordham University, through lectures, published works, and informal discussions with the Orthodox of America, has tried in similar fashion to initiate the ecumenical dialogue in the New World.

Fig. 3. *Patriarch Athenagoras of Constantinople and Pope Paul VI embrace on the Mount of Olives, Jerusalem, Jan. 6, 1964. Their meeting was the first between an Orthodox patriarch and a pope since the 15th century.*

Obstacles. Among the Orthodox, as well as among the Catholics, the psychological barriers are the strongest, usually stemming from inherited prejudices. Besides those inherited from the past, the Orthodox still have a sense of misgiving toward Roman Catholicism, especially in its expression of papal prerogatives. Roman theologians in Vatican Council II became aware of the necessity of supplementing the one-sided definitions of Vatican I with a teaching on the prerogatives of the bishops in terms of collegiality rather than in those of juridical monarchism. The Orthodox also are beginning to see that there exists an obligation in charity on their part to reexamine their ecclesiology in the light of their early traditions that once granted more than a primacy of honor to the bishop of Rome. Reunion between the Orthodox and Roman Catholics will not be an easy task, but a dialogue has begun. Patriarch Athenagoras I outlined in 1963 the program of the future: "The problem of full dogmatic union is a long-term prospect and must be preceded by a clean sweep of the evil past . . .. This will require time. And it can be achieved only through constant contact and discussion . . .. A basic prerequisite for successful conversations on unity is a knowledge and understanding of the theology of the sister-Church. Only in this way can the formulas be found which will do justice to the different concepts."

Rapport with Anglicans and Protestants. Many Anglicans, appealing to the early tradition common to all Christian bodies before any schism had occurred, namely, that found in the early ecumenical councils and the writings of the Fathers, have revered the antiquity and traditionalism found in Orthodoxy. This has caused pioneers in Anglican-Orthodox relationships, such as William Palmer (d. 1879, received into the Catholic Church in 1855), J. M. Neale (d. 1866), and W. J. Birkbeck (d. 1916), to lay the foundations for a solid dialogue that has unfolded steadily during the 20th century. Various official meetings have taken place. The first of importance was that of the Lambeth Conference in London (1930), where representatives of 10 autocephalous Orthodox Churches met with Anglican leaders to discuss their theological differences. A joint conference was held in 1935 in Bucharest that gave a sense of euphoria to both Churches but was over-optimistic. After World War II more serious and realistic attempts to discuss differences in the context of a wider background took place, as at the conference held in Moscow in 1956. At the third pan-Orthodox conference of Rhodes in 1964 the 14 autocephalous Orthodox Churches agreed to renew their theological discussions with the Anglicans.

Obstacles to Reunion with the Anglicans. The main obstacles to reunion stem from the ambiguity of Anglican doctrinal formulations and the wide variety of interpretations given by different sections of the Anglican Church. One of the practical difficulties has been the inconsistent attitude of the Orthodox concerning the validity of Anglican orders. The Greek-speaking Orthodox Churches—Constantinople, Jerusalem, Cyprus, Alexandria, Greece, and Rumania—have made various declarations (between 1922 and 1939) that would seem to recognize Anglican orders as valid. The Russians have almost unanimously denied this validity, as in the Moscow Synod of 1948. Those who, on the other hand, seem to recognize validity in theory deny it in practice by reordaining all Anglican ministers. This apparent inconsistency is explained by the Greek theory of *economia* as explained above.

Besides official Church discussions, more personal contacts have been made through various societies for Anglo-Orthodox reunion. The chief leaders in this field have been the Anglican and Eastern Churches Association and the Fellowship of St. Alban and St. Sergius. The Fellowship edits a biannual periodical called *Sobornost* (Unity).

The Orthodox and the World Council of Churches. Many Orthodox, especially among the Greek theologians, have studied in Protestant universities, often in Germany. Thus initial contacts were made on a serious plane to discuss theological differences. But the World Council of Churches remains the most extensive organ of contact between the Orthodox Churches and those of the various Protestant denominations. Orthodox participation has been varied and gradual in the official discussions of the World Council conferences. The Patriarchate of Constantinople has given full participation from the very beginning of the Faith and Order Movement at Lausanne in 1927. At the opening of the first World Council of Churches in Amsterdam in 1948, Constantinople, Greece, and the Rumanian Church in America were the only Orthodox represented. The other Orthodox Churches felt membership compromised their claim to be the only true Church. The Russian Church of Moscow in 1948 condemned all participation in the World Council. But, encouraged by the Soviet government, the Moscow patriarch applied in 1961 for official membership and was accepted. This paved the way for the other autocephalous Churches under communism to accept membership also. The Synod of the Russian Church in Exile still

Fig. 4. Reconstruction of the 1812 Russian Orthodox church built at Fort Ross, California, by Russian traders.

withholds any cooperation in the World Council of Churches as full members.

Orthodox in North America. The history of the Orthodox Churches in North America began with the formation of a Russian Orthodox mission in Alaska in 1794. In 1812 a part of this Alaskan mission moved to California and a Russian church was built near San Francisco as part of a Russian military fort; today the shrine, called Fort Ross, is a national monument, the first Orthodox church in the U.S. The episcopal see was transferred from Sitka, Alaska, to San Francisco in 1872.

Prior to this, the Greek Orthodox established the first Greek parish in the New World, in New Orleans, in 1864. The first great period of growth took place toward the end of the 19th century with the wave of emigration from eastern and southern European and Near East countries. From 1880 until World War I nearly 1 million Eastern Christians immigrated to the U.S., half of whom were Orthodox, with Russians, Greeks, Melchites, and Serbs predominating. However, all the Orthodox, who had left their own hierarchy behind in their native land, recognized the jurisdiction of the Russian episcopate on the basis of canon 2 of the Council of Carthage, which conferred jurisdiction on the Church that had initiated missionary work in a new land.

After World War I. But shortly after 1918 other Orthodox bishops arrived and began to create autonomous Churches. In the 1920s two Syrian bishops developed different jurisdictional missions, separating themselves from the one Russian original mission episcopate. Greece sent a bishop in 1918, and in 1926 the first Serbian bishop was consecrated for the U.S. Thus, in less than a decade a new situation for Orthodoxy had developed and had been accepted as an established fact, namely, various episcopates with independent jurisdictions in the same geographical area. At the end of the 1930s, four jurisdictions set up Orthodox seminaries to form their future priests, thus admitting an independence of the motherland for their clergy.

After World War II. The Orthodox, on being made more aware of their minority groups by World War II, attempted to band together in an effort to secure proper religious ministrations for their faithful in the armed forces. Up to that time Orthodoxy had no official standing either in the military or in the legal statutes of most states. Today the larger Orthodox Churches are recognized in many of the states, and a bill was introduced in 1961 by Sen. Clifford Case of New Jersey to recognize Orthodoxy as one of the major religions. The years after World War II brought many new immigrants who bolstered the membership of the Churches and strengthened ties with the mother country and tongue. By the early 1960s a ferment to create better inter-Orthodox relations was in evidence. In 1960 a dozen Orthodox bishops formed the Standing Conference of Canonical Orthodox Bishops in an attempt to foster cooperation among the various jurisdictions and to establish a norm of relations with non-Orthodox groups. The Russian and Syrian Orthodox groups are emerging as the leaders in fostering an American Orthodox Church under one single jurisdiction by promoting intensive programs of high educational standards, modern catechetical techniques, choir director training programs, the use of English in the liturgical services, and in general by adapting traditional Orthodoxy to an American way of life. The Greeks tend to stress the Hellenic culture, language, and orientation and thus make it more difficult for their people to transcend the ties that bind them still to a national Church of Greece.

In the early 1960s there were 26 autonomous Orthodox Churches or groups in the U.S. Some of these Churches are not recognized by all Orthodox groups as truly canonically Orthodox, that is, having a hierarchy with true apostolic succession. This constitutes the principal problem of the Orthodox in America, the splitting up into many Churches or jurisdictions, a situation that has led in the past to bitter quarrels among themselves. But the many new multinational parishes, a new generation of priests born and educated in America, with many priests being assigned to parishes of a different national background from their own, have all been leading factors in breaking down division and in promoting greater unity.

Summary. The Orthodox are split into 10 jurisdictions that are in communion with world Orthodoxy and three splinter groups that are independent of any communion with the other Orthodox Churches of the world. The approved Orthodox jurisdictions in America, with their affiliated autonomous Churches, are: Albanian; Bulgarian; Greek, with a second Albanian church, Carpatho-Russian; Ukrainian; and White-Russian under the Greek jurisdiction as autonomous affiliated Churches; the Russian-American *metropoleis,* with the Japanese Orthodox Church, a Rumanian jurisdiction, and the Carpatho-Russian Church under its tutelage; the Russian Patriarchal Exarchate, with the splintered Greek Old Calendar Orthodox and a Western rite group founded by Rev. William Henry Francis as autonomous Churches under its protection; Syrian Orthodox with an associated Western rite group founded by Rev. Alexander T. Turner; another Syrian jurisdiction of Toledo that broke from the Syrian main church of New York; the Rumanian jurisdiction under the Patriarchate of Rumania; Serbian and Estonian. The three jurisdictions not in communion with the other Orthodox branches are: the Russian Orthodox Church Outside Russia (Synodal) with the affiliated Western Hemisphere Rumanian Orthodox Missionary Episcopate of Canada; the Ukrainian Orthodox Church of the U.S.A. under Metropolitan John Theodorovich; and, finally, the Ukrainian Autocephalous Jurisdiction.

ORTHODOX IN NORTH AMERICA

Ethnic group	Faithful	Jurisdictions	Parishes
Albanians	15,000	2	22
Bulgarians	80,000	1	22
Estonians	2,000	1	3
Greeks	1,206,000	2	384
Melchite (Syrian Antiochene)	115,000	1	81
Rumanians	125,000	3	74
Russians	830,000	3	471
Ruthenians	100,000	2	67
Serbians	250,000	2	73
Ukrainians	259,000	5	246
White Russians	20,000	3	17
Western rite	4,000	2	6

Fig. 5. Map showing the four Orthodox Patriarchates and the autocephalous churches in communion with them.

The Greek Orthodox in North America number about 1 million and are by far the best organized Orthodox Church. The clergy, at least most of the younger members, have been born or raised in America, but the bishops and professors of the Greek Theological School of the Holy Cross near Boston are usually from Greece. The Russians, split as they are into various jurisdictions, have four theological seminaries in America. St. Vladimir's in New York City and St. Tikhon's in South Canaan, Pa., serve the American *metropoleis;* Holy Trinity at Jordanville, N.Y., is the seminary and chief monastery of the Synodal Russian Church in Exile; Christ the Savior Seminary in Johnstown, Pa., supplies clerical training for the Carpatho-Russian Diocese.

For one not a member of an Orthodox Church the situation of the Orthodox Churches in America presents a picture of confusion resulting from the national divisions, the various liturgical practices, different usages of languages and calendars (Julian or Gregorian), and the many jurisdictional lines, which at times create nonintercommunion among certain groups, all calling themselves Orthodox. But within the Orthodox Churches of America there is a gradual awareness of apparent inconsistencies among themselves that are being dissolved slowly as native-born American Orthodox priests strike at the root of most of these inconsistencies, namely, nationalism, in their efforts to bring about a single, autocephalous American Orthodox Church.

See also BYZANTINE CHURCH, HISTORY OF; BYZANTINE THEOLOGY, II (FROM 1500 TO PRESENT).

Bibliography: D. ATTWATER, *The Christian Churches of the East,* v.2 *The Churches Not in Communion with Rome* (rev. ed. Milwaukee 1962). E. BENZ, *The Eastern Orthodox Church, Its Thought and Life,* tr. R. and C. WINSTON (New York 1963). S. N. BULGAKOV, *The Orthodox Church,* ed. D. A. LEWIS, tr. E. S. GRAM (London 1935). F. DVORNIK, *The Slavs in European History and Civilization* (New Brunswick, N.J. 1962). C. C. ENGLERT, *Catholics and Orthodox: Can They Unite?* (New York 1961). R. M. FRENCH, *The Eastern Orthodox Church* (New York 1951). G. FLOROVSKY, "The Eastern Orthodox Church and the Ecumenical Movement," *Theology Today* 7 (1950) 68–79. A. FORTESCUE, *The Orthodox Eastern Church* (London 1907). F. GAVIN, *Some Aspects of Contemporary Greek Orthodox Thought* (Milwaukee 1923). P. HAMMOND, *The Waters of Marah: The Present State of the Greek Church* (New York 1956). J. KARMIRIS, *The Orthodox Catholic Church and Her Relations with the Other Churches and with the World Council of Churches* (Geneva 1949). A. KELLIHER, "United States Orthodox-Western Rites," *Unitas* 15 (1963) 275–284. J. MEYENDORFF, *The Orthodox Church: Its Past and Its Role in the World Today,* tr. J. CHAPIN (New York 1962). A. PALMIERI, *Theologia dogmatica orthodoxa,* 2 v. (Florence 1911–13). A. J. PHILIPPOU, ed., *The Historical Appeal of Orthodoxy* (London 1965). A. SCHMEMANN, *Byzantine Theocracy and the Orthodox Church* (Geneva 1948); *The Historical Road of Eastern Orthodoxy,* tr. L. W. KESICH (New York 1963). P. SHERRARD, *The Greek East and the Latin West* (New York 1960). T. WARE, *The Orthodox Church* (Penguin Bks. Baltimore 1963). Statistics on Orthodox membership. *World Christian Handbook,* ed. W. COXHILL and K. GRUBB (London 1962) 234–236. F. S. MEAD, *Handbook of Denominations in the United States* (2d rev. ed. Nashville 1961). *Parishes and Clergy of the Orthodox and Other Eastern Churches in North America, together with the Parishes and Clergy of the Polish National Catholic Church* (Buffalo 1962). "The Orthodox Churches throughout the World," *Herder-Korrespondenz* 19 (1964), statistical suppl. for Sept., with tables and bibliog. OrientCatt. **Illustration credits:** Figs. 1, 2*a*, 2*c*, 2*d*, and 4, Religious New Service. Fig. 2*b*, Wide World Photos. Fig. 3, Copyright, Ernst Herb.

[G. A. MALONEY]

ORTHODOXY

The word orthodoxy, derived from the Greek, means primarily right belief. As such it is one of the characteristics of the Church of Christ, since this Church is indefectible and so will always preserve intact the message of Christ (*see* INFALLIBILITY; INDEFECTIBILITY). As St. Paul tells Timothy (2.1), it is the Church's task to hand on faithfully what it has received; any departure from this would be a betrayal of Christ. And so orthodox teaching is traditional, *apostolic, and *Catholic teaching. It is the teaching of Christ free from human error that has been given men for their sanctification. This right belief is to be found not only in official pronouncements of the Church, such as those of councils, but also in the *faithful, since both the teaching Church and the Church that is taught are protected by the Holy Spirit from error. The use of such a term as orthodoxy indicates that it is possible to discern what is true from what is false; it implies an absolute standard and the existence of some authority that can anathematize certain teachings as either false or heretical.

However, historical circumstances have meant that this word is most commonly used in connection with those churches of the East that followed the church of Constantinople into schism from Rome in the 11th century. Just as the word catholic is often used in a sectarian sense, so too the word orthodox. These Eastern churches claim to be orthodox in that they not only preserve true belief about God and Christ but also preserve right worship; they glorify God in the true way in the liturgy. This extension of the term orthodoxy to embrace not only right belief (ortho-dogma) but also right glory (ortho-doxa) indicates the importance of the Church as a worshiping community and the fundamentally liturgical and practical approach of the Eastern Christians. The Catholic admits the validity of their worship but does not allow these churches to be considered fully orthodox since they are out of communion with Rome. One of the marks of the true faith is the union of bishops under the successor of St. Peter. However, there are very many truths that Catholics and Orthodox possess in common.

The title itself is an old one and was not used by the Orthodox to express their position in reference to Rome so much as to indicate their fidelity to the first seven general councils. Unlike the Nestorian and Monophysite communities of the East, these churches stand by the teaching of these Eastern councils and so their Christology is sound. But unfortunately the dynamism of true orthodoxy has lost some of its force in these communities. The existence of autocephalous churches and the lack of a supreme authority has meant a certain amount of stagnation. Although their traditions are for the most part unaffected by the controversies of the age of the Reformation, they have been isolated from the development of Christian thought that has gone on in the West. Circumstances are such that it hardly seems likely that the Orthodox could consider the immediate possibility of a new council on the lines of the first seven.

See also MIND OF THE CHURCH; RULE OF FAITH; TEACHING AUTHORITY OF THE CHURCH (MAGISTERIUM); THINKING WITH THE CHURCH, RULES FOR; BYZANTINE

THEOLOGY, I; BYZANTINE THEOLOGY, II; ORTHODOX CHURCHES.

Bibliography: P. Joannou and B. Schultze, LexThK² 7:1246–56. J. Chrysostomus, Fries HbThGrdbgr 2:256–266. T. Ware, *The Orthodox Church* (pa. Baltimore 1963). N. Zernov, *Eastern Christendom* (New York 1961).

[M. E. Williams]

ORTIGUE, JOSEPH LOUIS D', music scholar influential in French church-music reform; b. Cavaillon, France, May 22, 1802; d. Paris, Nov. 20, 1866. Ortigue was educated in both music and law, and served as a judge while active as a music teacher and critic. He contributed to *La Quotidienne* for 40 years and also to *Gazette Musicale;* in 1863 he succeeded *Berlioz on *Journal des Débats.* Berlioz was his lifelong friend; and Ortigue's *De l'École musicale italienne et de l'Académie royale de musique* (1839) was a defense of the composer's *Benvenuto Cellini.* From 1840 Ortigue was dedicated to revitalizing church music, specifically to a revival of *Gregorian chant. He provided the initiative for the Congress of Arezzo in 1860. In collaboration with L. de Niedermeyer (1802–61), who had reorganized *Choron's church-music institute, he founded the periodical *La Maîtrise,* whose purpose was the betterment of church music. His own historical publications were also directed toward this goal. Most important among them were the *Dictionnaire de plain-chant* (1853), which stimulated chant research and performance; *Traité theorique et pratique de l'accompagnement du plain chant* (1857); *La Musique à l'église* (1861); and several essays on the organ.

Bibliography: M. Barber, "J. d'Ortigue," *Mémoires de l'Académie de Vaucluse* (Avignon 1918). B. Bardet, MusGG 10:421–422. G. Chouquet, Grove DMM 6:454–455. Riemann 2:1319. Roland-Manuel v.2.

[K. G. Fellerer]

ORTIZ, DIEGO, composer and pioneer teacher of the art of variation for bowed instruments; b. Toledo, Spain, c. 1510; d. Naples?, 1570. While music master of the Naples viceroyal chapel he published in Rome (1553) simultaneous Spanish and Italian editions of his epoch-making *Trattado de Glosas sobre Clausulas y otros generos de puntos en la Musica de Violones* (treatise on how to ornament cadences and other passages in viol music). The easy availability and the attractiveness of his arrangements (four ricercatas on *Arcadelt's madrigal *O felici occhi miei* and four on Sandrin's chanson *Douce memoire*) have diverted attention from the original sacred compositions in his *Musices Liber primus* (1565), which contains Magnificats in each of the 8 tones, 9 psalms, 13 motets, 34 hymns, and other pieces for Vespers and Compline. According to *Cerone's *El melopeo y maestro* [(Naples 1613) 144], Ortiz modeled his sacred style on *Morales. In the Latin foreword Ortiz learnedly defends the practice of using instruments in musical arrangements for sacred ceremonies.

Bibliography: K. Proske, ed., *Musica divina,* 4 v. in 7 (Regensburg 1853–63), 8 motets from *Musices Liber primus.* R. J. Borrowdale, *The Musices liber primus of Diego Ortiz,* 3 v. (Doctoral diss. unpub. U. of Southern Calif. 1952). J. Subirá, *La música en la Casa de Alba* (Madrid 1927). R. Stevenson, *Spanish Cathedral Music in the Golden Age* (Berkeley 1961). I. Horsley, MusGG 10:422–423. Reese MusR. G. Pannain, ed.,

L'Oratorio dei Filippini, v.5 of *Istituzioni e monumenti dell'arte musicale italiana* (Milan 1934) xv.

[R. Stevenson]

ORTIZ DE ZÁRATE, PEDRO, VEN., Argentine martyr; b. Jujuy, 1622; d. in the Chaco, Oct. 27, 1683. He was the grandson of one of the founders of the early settlements in Jujuy and inherited a fortune in land and money. In 1644 he married Petronila de Ibarra, a member of another of the founding families; they had two sons. After the death of his wife in 1653, Ortiz de Zárate studied with the Jesuits; he was ordained in 1659. He was then appointed pastor in Jujuy. However, his great ambition was to convert the Indians of the Chaco and to civilize them through preaching the gospel. He sought permission from the royal authorities and from the bishop of Tucumán to organize a missionary expedition into the region with two Jesuits. They left Jujuy Oct. 18, 1682, with Ortiz de Zárate paying all the expenses of the expedition. Within the forests of the Chaco he founded two settlements: Santa María and San Rafael. The Indians gave the appearance of being friendly but the next year they killed Ortiz de Zárate and the Jesuit Father Salinas. All the existing documents that refer to Ortiz de Zárate assert that he led a holy life of mortification. His reputation for saintliness has grown since his death. A bone from his arm is preserved in the House of the Good Shepherd in Jujuy.

Bibliography: M. A. Vergara, *Estudios sobre historia ecclesiástica de Jujuy* (Tucumán, Argen. 1942).

[M. A. Vergara]

ORTLIBARII

A strongly ascetic movement, known also as Ortlibenses, that owed its name to Ortlieb of Strasbourg (c. 1200). An example of lay protest against institutional religion, they are mentioned in 13th-century documents with the *Cathari and *Waldenses, and lesser sects as well, thus underscoring the confusion about their teaching in the minds of their contemporaries. For example, a constitution issued by Emperor *Frederick II on May 14, 1238, proscribed the *Ortolevos* with a number of other heresies (MGL 4: Const. 2:284–285). According to *Albert the Great's judgment of the heretics of the Swabian district of Ries (Diocese of Augsburg) c. 1270, the Ortlibarii had been condemned by Innocent III for holding "that man must abstain from externals and follow the spirit that is in him." They were reminiscent, on the one hand, of the pantheism of the *Amalricians centered in Paris (according to Jundt, Preger), and on the other, of the dualism of the widespread Gnostic-Manichaean stream (Haupt). However, significant differences set them apart from these movements as well as from the Waldenses with whom Müller was anxious to establish a relationship. The Ortlibarii espoused a cause that not only aimed to dissolve the visible Church but sought also to undermine essential tenets of the Christian tradition. The principal source for their teachings is the so-called Passau Anonymus (*Pseudo-Rainer*), begun c. 1260. The sect did not accept divine creation of the world, which they considered eternal. Its members reopened the Christological question with an attack on Trinitarian doctrine. Turning to the Sacraments, they rejected the

Eucharist and adjudged infant Baptism useless since conscious adherence to their movement alone was efficacious. To the Catholic hierarchy they opposed their own Perfect Ones who, they claimed, could bind and loose. They recognized no obligation to pay *tithes, asserting that the clergy ought to earn its livelihood by manual labor. The papacy was identified with the harlot of the Apocalypse. Once the pope and emperor were converted to the sect, the Last Judgment would be imminent. Failure to be numbered among the sectaries merited damnation. Although they denied the resurrection of the body, they assumed the perfection of the spirit. Of particular interest to civil government was their rejection of oaths and capital punishment. While unlike the Cathari they countenanced marriage, they enjoined continence. The Ortlibarii did not survive the 13th century; presumably they were absorbed by the *Brothers and Sisters of the Free Spirit of the 14th century.

Bibliography: S. M. DEUTSCH, Herzog-Hauck PRE 14:498–501. W. PREGER, Geschichte der deutschen Mystik im Mittelalter, 3 v. (1874–93) 1:191–196. A. JUNDT, Histoire du panthéisme populaire au moyen âge et au seizième siècle (Strasburg 1875) 36–41. H. HAUPT, "Waldensia," ZKirchgesch 10 (1888) 316–328. K. MÜLLER, Die Waldenser und ihre einzelnen Gruppen (Gotha 1886) 130–132, 169–171. H. GRUNDMANN, Religiöse Bewegungen im Mittelalter (2d ed. Hildesheim 1961). J. J. I. VON DÖLLINGER, Beiträge zur Sektengeschichte des Mittelalters, 2 v. in 1 (Munich 1890; repr. New York 1960) 2:299, 301, 317, 330, 400, 703.

[E. W. MC DONNELL]

ORTOLANA (HORTULANA), BL., mother of Clare of Assisi; d. before 1238 (feast, Jan. 2). A descendant of the noble Fiumi family, she grew up to be a very devout young woman. She made several pilgrimages to Monte Gargano and to Rome, and c. 1192 she undertook the hazardous journey to the Holy Land. On her return she married Count Favarone di Offreduccio of Assisi. She was the mother of four children, including St. *Clare of Assisi and St. *Agnes of Assisi. After the death of her husband, who had at first strongly opposed the religious vocation of their children, Ortolana joined the *Poor Clares at the convent of San Damiano at Monticelli near Florence, where her third daughter, Beatrice, was also a nun. She was buried close to her daughters in the church of St. Clare at Assisi, and she is honored by the *Franciscans with the title of blessed.

Bibliography: CIRO DA PESARO, La beata Ortolana d'Assisi (Rome 1904). Z. LAZZERI, "Il processo di canonizazione di S. Chiara d'Assisi," ArchFrancHist 13 (1920) 403–507. A. FORTINI, "Nuove notizie intorno a S. Chiara di Assisi," ibid. 46 (1953) 3–43. L. BRACALONI, S. Chiara d'Assisi (2d ed. Milan 1949), passim. Englebert-Brady-Brown.

[B. J. COMASKEY]

ORTON, WILLIAM AYLOTT, philosopher, economist; b. Bromley, England, Feb. 9, 1889; d. Northampton, Mass., Aug. 13, 1952. He was the son of William Amor and Emma (Aylott) Orton. During World War I he served in the British army at Gallipoli, and in Egypt and France. He was wounded at the Battle of the Somme and later joined the intelligence staff of the British War Office. In 1917 he married Olmen Marlais Moment. Orton received the B.A. degree from Cambridge University, England, in 1919, and then entered the industrial relations department of the Ministry of Labour. Later, while studying at the University of London, he won the London Athenaeum's essay contest and published essays and articles in the Westminster Review and the New Age. After receiving the M.A. degree from Cambridge University, he went to the U.S. to join the faculty of Smith College, Northampton, Mass.; Bryn Mawr College, Bryn Mawr, Pa.; and the University of California at Berkeley. He was awarded honorary degrees by the University of London; Boston College, Boston, Mass.; and Georgetown University, Washington, D.C. He published articles in popular magazines, and in the American Journal of Sociology, International Journal of Ethics, American Economic Review, and Encyclopaedia of the Social Sciences. Among his books were America in Search of Culture (1933), Prelude to Economics (1933), The Economic Role of the State (1949), and The Liberal Tradition (1945). In his writings Orton often referred to Catholic history and to classic literature. In his public lectures he frequently urged the people of the U.S. to accept the role of leadership in the modern world. Although aware of the value of conservative philosophy, he believed that the liberal viewpoint alone assumed responsibility for the future and was based on the confident outlook of Christianity.

[J. R. BETTS]

ORVAL, ABBEY OF, a Cistercian abbey in Luxembourg Province, Belgium, founded in 1070 by Count Arnulf II of Chiny for some Benedictine monks from Calabria. Orval (Aureavallis, Güldenthal) passed into the possession of the Clerks Regular in 1110 and eventually was taken over by Cistercians from the Abbey of *Tre Fontane in 1132. The first Cistercian abbot was Constantine (d. 1145), a disciple of St. Bernard of Clairvaux, who was noted for holiness. In 1251 or 1252 Orval was burned, and the monks dispersed. Under succeeding abbots it flourished and was well governed except during the decline following the Reformation in the Netherlands in the 16th century. Its spirit was restored by Abbot Bernard de Montgaillard (d. 1628), but the buildings were again destroyed by Huguenots in 1637. Abbot Carl von Benzeradt (d. 1707) drew up new statutes of strict observance for Orval. During the rule of Abbot E. Henrion (d. 1729), it was a focal point of Jansenism, but in 1750 those monks infected with the heresy were removed. Orval prospered and in 1750 it owned 300 towns, from which it derived a rich income. It fell victim to the French Revolutionists and was suppressed in 1796. In 1926 Trappists from the Abbey of *Sept-Fons built a priory upon its ruins.

Bibliography: Cottineau 2:2148–49. N. TILLIÈRE, Histoire de l'abbaye d'Orval (6th ed. Gembloux 1958). C. GRÉGOIRE, Lex ThK² 7:1258.

[E. D. MC SHANE]

ORWELL, GEORGE, English novelist and essayist; b. Motihari, Bengal, India, 1903; d. London, Jan. 23, 1950. His real name was Eric Blair, and he was the son of a customs official. He was educated at Eton and, after leaving school, joined the Indian Imperial Police in Burma. He was dissatisfied with the imperialistic regime he was there called upon to serve and resigned in 1927. His first novel, Burmese Days (1934), recounts those times. In order to purge his soul he felt the necessity of identifying himself with the lowest of the oppressed and he lived for a time as a tramp in Paris and London, later describing this experience in *Down and Out in Paris and London* (1933). Adopting more conventional left-wing habits, he spent some time among the unemployed in Lancashire and wrote about them in *Road to Wigan Pier* (1937). He joined the Republicans in the Spanish Civil War only to discover that the Communists, while pretending to support the Republican forces, were in fact sabotaging them for their own purposes; this disillusionment is the burden of *Homage to Catalonia* (1946).

This experience taught Orwell that in the essential battle for freedom there are enemies on both the left and the right, and thereafter his enmity to Nazism and Communism alike was unrelenting. Unhappy over the alliance with the Communists in World War II, he wrote *Animal Farm* (1945) to warn free people against the dangers from the Communist menace in the postwar world. This superb satire, which has been judged the peer of *Gulliver's Travels,* appeared immediately after the war, when Western leaders were beginning to realize the extent of Red tyranny behind the Iron Curtain. Whereas all of Orwell's earlier books had had only a limited circulation, *Animal Farm* met with a spectacular success. In the closing months of his life, *1984* appeared (1949); it is a stark portrayal of life under Communist tyranny, which Orwell foresaw for a mankind that in his judgment was fast losing all courage in devotion to freedom. A volume of critical essays, largely political, appeared in 1946.

Bibliography: N. Braybrooke, "George Orwell," *Catholic World* 178 (Dec. 1953) 178–184. C. S. Lewis in *Time and Tide* 36 (1955) 43–44. C. Hollis, *A Study of George Orwell* (Chicago 1956).

[C. HOLLIS]

OSBALD, KING OF NORTHUMBRIA, abbot, reigned 27 days in 796; d. 799. When King Ethelred of Northumbria was dethroned in 779, Osbald and another Northumbrian nobleman, Athelheard, gathered together a force and burned the house of Bearn, the son of the new king, Aelfwald (779–788). In 793 *Alcuin wrote to Ethelred (restored to the throne in 789), Osbald, and Osbert, pressing them to give up their disruptive lives and to practice Christian virtues. Then on April 20, 796, King Ethelred was murdered. Osbald was chosen his successor, but after a reign of only 27 days his followers abandoned him, and he was forced to take refuge at *Lindisfarne. He was probably still at Lindisfarne when he received a second letter from Alcuin, who suspected that Osbald had murdered Ethelred, urging him once again to abandon his warlike living, to refrain from any attempts to regain the throne, and to take the monastic habit for the sake of his soul. Soon after this Osbald sailed north to the land of the Picts, where he eventually became an abbot. He was buried at *York.

Bibliography: Simeon of Durham, *Symeonis monachi opera omnia,* ed. T. Arnold, 2 v. (RollsS 75; 1882–85) 2:47, 57, 62. Alcuin's letters in *Monumenta Alcuiniana,* ed. W. Wattenbach and E. Dümmler (*Bibliotheca rerum Germanicarum,* ed. P. Jaffé, v.6; Berlin 1873) 184–190, 305–306. W. Hunt, DNB 14:1167–68. F. M. Stenton, *Anglo-Saxon England* (2d ed. Oxford 1947) 89–90, 93. E. S. Duckett, *Alcuin, Friend of Charlemagne: His World and His Work* (New York 1951) 165, 168–169.

[M. J. HAMILTON]

OSBERN OF GLOUCESTER, lexicographer, exegete; fl. *c.* 1150. Little is known about his life beyond the fact that he was born probably in the township of Pinnock in Gloucestershire, England, that he was a Benedictine at Gloucester under Abbot Hamelin (1148–79), and that he dedicated his commentary on Judges to Gilbert *Foliot, who was then bishop of Hereford (1148–63). Although Osbern also wrote commentaries on Genesis, Exodus, Deuteronomy, and Numbers and treatises on the Incarnation, Nativity, Passion, and Resurrection (none published), his most influential work remained his *Liber derivationum* (sometimes called *Panormia*), which is to be assigned to the third quarter of the 12th century when Osbern was an old man. Set in an allegorical framework and arranged alphabetically with two sections to each letter, this dictionary of derivations, well equipped with *testimonia* from both ancient and medieval writers, entered the main stream of European learning, appearing in Bavaria and Austria before the end of the 12th century and becoming the main source for the glossary of *Huguccio of Pisa (d. 1210).

Bibliography: Works. *Liber derivationum,* ed. A. Mai, in *Classicorum auctorum e Vaticanis codicibus editorum,* 10 v. (Rome 1828–38), v.8. G. Loewe, *Corpus Glossariorum latinorum,* ed. G. Goetz, 7 v. (Leipzig 1888–1923) 1:196–215, for description of work and reproduction of preface. Preface also in R. W. Hunt, "The 'Lost' Preface to the *Liber derivationum* of Osbern of Gloucester," MedRenSt 4 (1958) 267–282. British Museum MS Bibl. Reg. 6DIX, for exegetical works.
Biography. W. Meyer, "Ueber Mai's Thesaurus novus latinitatis," *Rheinisches Museum für Philologie* 29 (1874) 179–183. G. Goetz, "Beiträge zur Geschichte der lateinischen Studien im Mittelalter," *Berichte über die Verhandlungen der Königlich-Sächsischen Gesellschaft der Wissenschaften zu Leipzig, Philologisch-Historische Klasse* 55 (1903) 121–154. Manitius 3:187–190. É. Pellegrin, "Un Manuscrit des *Derivationes* d'Osbern de Gloucester annoté par Pétrarque (Paris BN cod. lat. 7492)," *Italia medioevale e umanistica* 3 (1960) 263–266.

[R. B. PALMER]

OSBERT OF CLARE, English author and poet; fl. 1136 to 1160. Though hardly a major literary figure, Osbert, who was prior of Westminster from *c.* 1136, gained a certain reputation among his contemporary writers. Two Latin hymns on St. Anne (AnalHymn 15:186 and 33:36) are ascribed to him. These works, for which he used a two-syllable rhyming system, indicate a personal devotion to the saint. Besides his devotional pieces he wrote a Latin poem in rhyming hexameter couplets to follow a letter to Geoffrey, Abbot of Saint Albans Abbey, as well as a poem in Latin to Prince Henry, the future King *Henry II of England. This piece in eight-syllable trochaics, in rhyming-couplet form, looks to Henry as a hope for liberation and betterment of government. In his plea for Henry's patronage, he likened the prince to Augustus and would see himself treated as Vergil. Osbert prepared a collection of letters that provide valuable insights for the period; his life of St. *Edward the Confessor in rhymed prose was quickly superseded by the biography written by *Aelred of Rievaulx. Osbert was a strong promoter of the Feast of the Immaculate Conception.

Bibliography: "La Vie de S. Édouard le Confesseur par O. de C.," ed. M. Bloch, AnalBoll 41 (1923) 5–131; *The Letters of Osbert of Clare, Prior of Westminster,* ed. E. W. Williamson (London 1929), with a biog. by J. A. Robinson. H. Bradley, DNB 4:386–388. Raby ChrLP 344. Raby SecLP 2:139–140. Knowles MOE 510–513.

[W. C. KORFMACHER]

OSEE (HOSEA), BOOK OF

Osee (Hosea), whose name is an abbreviated form meaning "Yahweh is salvation," was one of the two Prophets from the Northern Kingdom who left us writings of their ministry.

The Prophet. Unlike Amos, his precedessor from the South, Osee was probably an Ephraimite, for he frequently refers to this tribe and to sites in this geographical area. He possessed a perceptive mind and refined sensitivity and, like Jeremia a century later, had to endure the personal agony of announcing the visitation of divine retribution upon his native land. Because of the many images drawn from agriculture and nature, it is likely that he came from a rural rather than an urban background. There is no evidence that he belonged to one of the prophetic guilds or was of priestly descent, though he is acquainted with both offices as well as with the political realities of his time. The opening verse places his ministry during the reigns of Jeroboam II (786–746 B.C.) to Ezechia (715–687 B.C.), but this is a later Judean addition to the work intended to make Osee a contemporary of Isaia (Is 1.1). Internal evidence points to the last years of Jeroboam II as the beginning of his ministry, thus, *c.* 750 B.C. The turbulent years of the dynastic upheavals from 746–732 B.C. are alluded to (5.8–10; 7.3–7; 8.4), but the end of his ministry is a matter of conjecture. Since the fall of Samaria (721 B.C.) is nowhere mentioned, it is probable that Osee did not live to see it. (For the social conditions and the political situation of this period, *see* ISRAEL, 3.)

Characteristics of the Book. Osee stands at the head of the canon of the "Twelve Prophets" in the Hebrew and Greek Bibles. From a literary point of view, the work is a mélange of terse, originally independent oracles that contain warnings, threats, pleas for conversion, and a number of Messianic passages of hope for a happier future. Characteristic of the book is the abrupt alternation between the words of Yahweh and those of the prophet (4.10–15; 12.1–15). This is best explained as a conscious use of the disputation form (*rîb*) common in litigation before the elders at the gate of the city. The prophecy is rich in imagery redolent with the language of love; parallelism, play on words, alliteration, and repetition of a key idea are devices employed by Osee to seize the attention of his hearers. Osee's fragmented style, due in part to the poor condition of the text, raises many problems about the original order and sequence of his preaching. Various statements about Juda, at times interrupting the harmony of thought, are signs of a Judean redaction after the death of the Prophet (1.7; 5.5; 6.11; 12.1). These were probably interpolated to make the prophecy pertinent to readers of the South. There are also some other additions and glosses (e.g., 14.10) but the present form was perhaps fixed by the year 700 B.C. Scholars are generally agreed today upon the substantial genuineness of the work and attribute it to Osee himself, though much was recorded and compiled by his disciples.

Contents. The prophecy falls into two unequal divisions: ch. 1–3 treat of the marriage of Osee; ch. 4–14 are a collection of oracles that evince little logical organization or chronological continuity.

The celebrated marriage of the Prophet to Gomer is presented in an unusual fashion: in ch. 1 the episode is related biographically; in ch. 3 the Prophet speaks of it in a firsthand account; ch. 2 contains in oracular speech the divinely intended significance of the event. The juxtaposition of these forms in one literary unity is almost certainly artificial and the result of editing.

From the patristic age to modern times an allegorical interpretation of the marriage was in vogue. Since the 19th century, however, exegetes have tended to view the marriage as an historical reality that had symbolic meaning. An attempt at reconstruction is as follows: At the bidding of God, Osee took to wife Gomer, who is called a harlot (1.2). After bearing Osee several children, who by divine command received the ominous names: "Jezrael," "Unpitied," and "Not my People," she abandoned her husband and gave herself up to a life of adultery. The outraged anger of the Prophet is vanquished by the still more ardent love he feels for his perfidious spouse. At this point the seer is instructed to reclaim his erring wife; symbolism demands that the unnamed woman of ch. 3 be Gomer. Osee ransomed her for the price of a slave and then imposed upon her a time of salutary chastisement before restoring her to full marital union. Aided by revelation Osee understands that his unrequited love for Gomer and her wayward conduct are but a reflection of what Yahweh has experienced from faithless Israel (2.4–15).

In the second part of his prophecy (ch. 4–14), Osee applies this symbolism to the concrete reality of his society in a series of severe denunciations of the immorality of the priests (4) and the princes (5) who bear a major share of guilt for the apostasy of the nation. He deplores Ephraim's ephemeral conversions to the Lord, which are likened to the passing of the morning dew (6). He warns of the folly of political alliances with Assyria and Egypt (7–8), as if these could deliver the land from the "day of the Lord" (9). Idolatry, a syncretism of Baalistic practices with the worship of Yahweh, is the crime of Ephraim (9), which merits utter destruction of king and people alike (10). Yet for all this, God's love for His son endures, and in ch. 11 Osee rises to one of the most sublime expressions of Yahweh's tender concern for the chosen people. To this, Israel continually responds with rebelliousness (12–13). The prophecy closes with an impassioned plea for a sincere return to God with the assurance of His pardon and favor (14).

Theology. The prophet's chief complaint is the lack of knowledge of God in the land (4.1,6; 5.4; 6.6), which is practically synonymous with faithful obedience to the religion of Moses. No other prophet insists so poignantly upon the loyal devotedness (*hesed*) that binds Yahweh and Israel and that should inspire the Israelites in their dealings with each other. Osee in his portrait of Yahweh as a God of love (2.21–25; 11.1–4) approaches as close as anyone in the OT to the conception of the fourth Evangelist. The idolatrous Baal ritual he terms the whoredom of Israel. While the overall tone of the message is one of despair of salvaging the ancient alliance, there appear passages of hope for a new covenant (2.20–22) to be based on right, justice, love, and loyalty, which will bring about the reunion of all of the chosen people (2.2; 3.5). Osee's grasp of Israel's past as a history of salvation, his insistence upon purity of worship and a morality in accord with the postulates of the Law certainly influenced the Deuteronomical writers. He was the first to conceive of the marriage image to describe the relation of Yahweh and his people, which became a classical figure in the writings of Isaia, Jeremia, Ezechiel, and St. Paul.

Bibliography: Commentaries A. VAN HOONACKER, *Les Douze Petits Prophètes* (ÉtBibl; Paris 1908). W. R. HARPER, *Critical and Exegetical Commentary on Amos and Hosea* (ICC; New York 1905). H. W. WOLFF, *Dodekapropheton I: Hosea* (Biblischer Kommentar: Altes Testament 14; Neukirchen 1961). G. RINALDI, *I Profeti Minori II: Osea-Giole-Abia-Giona* (Turin 1960). A. DEISSLER, *Les Petits prophètes* (Osée; Bible Pirot-Clamer, 8.1; Paris 1961). Studies. A. GELIN, "Osée (Livre D')," DBSuppl 6:926–940. H. H. ROWLEY, "Marriage of Hosea," Bull JRylLibr 39 (1956) 200–233. N. H. SNAITH, *Mercy and Sacrifice* (London 1953). J. L. McKENZIE, "Divine Passion in Osee," CathBiblQuart 17 (1955) 287–299; "Knowledge of God in Hosea," JBiblLit 74 (1955) 22–27. E. H. MALY, "Messianism in Osee," CathBiblQuart 19 (1957) 213–225. B. VAWTER, *Conscience of Israel* (New York 1961).

[J. K. SOLARI]

OSEE (HOSHEA), KING OF ISRAEL, *c.* 732

to 724 B.C., son of Ela, last king of the northern kingdom of Israel. When Phacee (*c.* 737–732), in league with Damascus and other Syrian states, revolted against *Tiglath-Pileser III of Assyria (744–727) and was crushingly defeated, Osee, engineering a *coup d'état* in which Phacee was killed, seized the throne for himself. His kingdom, however, included only Ephraim and Manasse west of the Jordan, all the rest having been incorporated into the Assyrian empire. During most of his reign he was a faithful vassal of Assyria, but after the death of Tiglath-Pileser III he allowed himself to be persuaded by the King of Sais in the Egyptian Delta [see H. Goedicke, "The End of 'So, King of Egypt,'" BullAmSchOrRes 171 (1963) 64–66] to revolt against *Salmanasar V of Assyria (726–722 B.C.). For refusing to pay the annual tribute he was arrested and imprisoned. His capital of Samaria was beseiged but held out for 3 years before it was taken and destroyed (4 Kgs 17.1–6). The judgment of the Deuteronomistic editor of Kings on his reign is somewhat kinder than usual: "He did evil before the Lord, but not as the kings of Israel who had been before him" (4 Kgs 17.2). For the text from the Annals of Tiglath-Pileser III regarding his accession, *see* PHACEE (PEKAH), KING OF ISRAEL.

Bibliography: EncDictBibl 1680. J. GAMBERONI, LexThK² 7:1261.

[B. MC GRATH]

O'SHAUGHNESSY, NELSON JARVIS, dip-

lomat; b. New York City, Feb. 12, 1876; d. Vienna, Austria, July 25, 1932. As the only son of James Francis and Lucy (Waterbury) O'Shaughnessy, he was educated by private tutors and attended Georgetown University, Washington, D.C. He received his B.A. from St. John's College, Oxford, and then studied international law in London at the Middle Temple. In April 1901 he married Elizabeth Louis Coues in Rome. After language study in Europe, he entered the foreign service in 1904. By 1911 he was secretary of legation in Mexico City under Minister Henry Lane Wilson. When left in charge of the legation after Pres. Woodrow Wilson recalled Minister Wilson, O'Shaughnessy achieved good personal relations with the new dictator, Victoriano Huerta. But President Wilson disliked the Mexican dictator, who was accused of having murdered his predecessor, Francisco Madero. When O'Shaughnessy was accused of being too friendly with Huerta by

President Wilson's special agent, John Lind, his usefulness as an American representative in Mexico was impaired. He was unable to negotiate a settlement of the Tampico incident of April 10, 1914, and was given his passports after U.S. Marines occupied Vera Cruz. Except for a short mission to Vienna in 1914, he was given no more assignments by the State Department, and in September 1916 he resigned. In testimony before a Senate subcommittee in 1920, O'Shaughnessy sharply criticized Wilson's Mexican policy. During World War I, O'Shaughnessy was employed in South America by the Western Union Telegraph Company, which was seeking to break the British monopoly of communication facilities. In the 1920s he represented a bondholders' group in Yugoslavia. Fordham University, New York, awarded him an LL.D. in 1922.

Bibliography: A. S. LINK, *Woodrow Wilson and the Progressive Era, 1910–1917* (New York 1954). E. L. O'SHAUGHNESSY, *A Diplomat's Wife in Mexico* (New York 1916).

[J. T. FARRELL]

OSIANDER, ANDREAS, Nuremberg reformer;

b. Gunzenhausen in Frankish Brandenburg, Dec. 19, 1498; d. Königsberg, Oct. 17, 1552. He was a classical student at Leipzig, Altenburg, and Ingolstadt, and became an accomplished linguist, but did not obtain a degree. He was ordained in 1520; taught Hebrew in the Augustinian Cloister at Nuremberg; and was later identified with Lazarus Spengler (1479–1534), Wenceslaus Linck (1483–1547), and Willibald *Pirkheimer as a Nuremberg reformer. In 1522 he published his *Biblia sacra,* a version of the Vulgate based on original texts. As a Lutheran, he married in 1525, and he later opposed Zwingli's view of the Lord's Supper. He was invited to the Marburg Colloquy (1529) and to Augsburg (1530). He assisted in church visitations in lands of Markgrave George of Brandenburg-Ansbach and, with Johann *Brenz, drafted the Brandenburg-Nuremberg Church Ordinance (1532). He was a discussant at Schmalkalden (1537); Hagenau; Worms (1540); and Regensburg (1541), where his criticism of Melanchthon brought about his recall. Though he was unusually gifted, Osiander's haughty, overbearing, disputatious, and unrestrained manner irritated his enemies and alienated his friends. Although adept at pointing out error, he rarely contributed constructive solutions. He could not forego polemics. When asked by Rhäticus (Georg Joachim von Lauchen 1514–76) to edit and publish Copernicus's *De revolutionibus orbium coelestium* (1543), Osiander added his own preface, in which he claimed the work was based on hypotheses. Although Copernicus's adherents were furious, the claim kept the book off the Index until the 17th century. Although he was nominally Lutheran, Osiander's teachings, because of certain mystical assumptions, had a strange twist on sin, grace, and, particularly, justification, which he regarded not as a forensic act, as did Luther, but a gradual process resulting from Christ's indwelling in the sinner. He differed also with Luther's teaching on church discipline and private confession.

After his abrupt departure from Nuremberg (1548), Osiander remained in Königsberg in the service of Duke Albert of Prussia, first as pastor of the *Altstädtische Kirche,* and later, as professor *primarius* at Königsberg. His lack of academic degrees aroused the jealousy of older professors, and his dissident views caused friction with the orthodox younger men who had studied under Luther and Melanchthon. Particularly divisive was Osiander's strange view of justification, an argument in which Melanchthon and Flacius were eventually embroiled; but Duke Albert continued his confidence in Osiander and even elevated him in 1551 to president of the bishopric of Samland. At Osiander's death the Duke honored him with a royal funeral.

See also JUSTIFICATION, 3. IN PROTESTANT THEOLOGY.

Bibliography: W. MÖLLER, *Andreas Osianders Leben und ausgewählte Schriften* (*Väter und Begründer der Lutherischen Kirche* 5; Elberfeld 1870); ADB 24:473–483. W. MÖLLER and P. TSCHACKERT, Herzog-Hauck PRE 14:501–509. E. BIZER, RGG³ 4:1730–31. P. MEINHOLD, LexThK² 7:1261–63.

[E. G. SCHWIEBERT]

OSMUND OF SALISBURY, ST.,

bishop, chancellor; d. Dec. 3–4, 1099 (feast, Dec. 4). Osmund, or Osmer, was a Norman noble who went to England with his uncle, *William I the Conqueror, for whom he served as chaplain and then chancellor (c. 1072–78). He was consecrated bishop of *Salisbury in 1078. Prominent in civil as well as ecclesiastical affairs of the realm, he is believed to have directed a large portion of the *Domesday survey. As bishop he completed the cathedral of Old Sarum (not the present cathedral of Salisbury) and established there a *cathedral chapter of secular canons. Emulation of this example gradually brought the English cathedral system into conformity with Continental practice. He also organized the liturgical services for his diocese and the compilation provided the basis of the later "Sarum Use" that was widely adopted throughout the British Isles (*see* RITES, ENGLISH MEDIEVAL; SARUM RITE). He was canonized by Pope Callistus III, Jan. 1, 1457, the last canonization of a saint from England until that of Sir Thomas *More in 1935. On July 23, 1457, his remains were translated from Old Sarum to the Lady Chapel in Salisbury.

Bibliography: WILLIAM OF MALMESBURY, *Gesta pontificum Anglorum,* ed. N. E. S. A. HAMILTON (RollsS 52; 1870) 183–184, 424–431. *The Register of S. Osmund,* ed. W. H. R. JONES, 2 v. (*ibid.* 78; 1883–84). *The Canonization of Saint Osmund,* ed. A. R. MALDEN (Salisbury, Eng. 1901). C. L. KINGSFORD, DNB 14:1207–09.

[R. D. WARE]

OSNABRÜCK

City on the left bank of the Hase River, northwest Germany. It was ruled by bishops until 1803, became part of Hanover, and was made subject to Prussia in 1866. With a population of 143,000 (59,500 Catholics and 77,400 Lutherans), the city had 66 secular and 11 religious priests and 319 sisters in 1963. The diocese, suffragan to *Cologne, is the largest German see in area (17,682 square miles). Its two sections are separated by the Diocese of *Hildesheim. In 1963 the See of Osnabrück had 727 secular and 139 religious priests, 194 men in 26 religious houses, 2,737 women in 259 convents, and 892,500 Catholics in a population of 7,167,400. The present see comprises parts of 14 medieval sees.

Made a mission by Charlemagne (780), Osnabrück became a diocese under Bishop St. Wiho (d. 804). Viking raids (852–890) did not prevent it from growing as a city and becoming the capital of a principality.

A struggle between the see and the Abbeys of *Corvey and Herford began under Bishop Egilmar (d. 918), the first historian of Osnabrück, and continued until the time of Philip von Katzenellnbogen (1141–73). The talented *Benno II (1068–88) played a role in the investiture controversy. St. Adolf of Tecklenburg (1216–24) and Conrad III of Diepholz (1455–82) were reform bishops. In 1543 Bp. Franz von Waldeck (1533–53) introduced the Reformation through the Lutheran theologian Hermann Bonnus (1504–48); but it did not succeed because of the opposition of the cathedral chapter and the imperial defeat of the *Schmalkaldic League (1548). Until 1623 the bishops favored Protestantism. Eitel Friedrich von Hohenzollern (1623–25) and Franz Wilhelm von *Wartenberg (1625–61) promoted the reforms of Trent, but their labors were undone by the Swedish invasion (1633–51).

By the Peace of *Westphalia (*Instrumentum pacis Osnabrugense,* 1643–48), Osnabrück had Catholic and Lutheran bishops alternately until 1803—Lutherans 1661–98, 1715–21, and 1761–1803. Bishop Carl Clemens von Gruben (1795–1827) administered the see through its secularization and occupation by Hanover (1803). Paulus *Melchers (1858–65) and Wilhelm Berning (1914–55) developed religious life. The Prussian Concordat of 1929 gave Osnabrück its present boundaries and status, as well as responsibility for the Vicariate of North German Missions, which it had in fact cared for from the 17th century. Reestablishment of the hierarchy in Scandinavian lands (1953–55) ended the dependence of these areas as missionary fields of north German bishoprics and vicariates, which they had been from the time of the Reformation.

Detail of the 13th-century reliquary of SS. Crispin and Crispinian in the cathedral at Osnabrück.

The Romanesque cathedral-basilica and the Gothic hall churches of St. Johann, St. Marien, and St. Katharinen are noteworthy, as are the Gothic town hall and the Renaissance episcopal chancery, castle, and houses. Osnabrück had more cloisters than any other city in Westphalia. In the city were Franciscans (1233), Dominicans (1295), Augustinians (1287), Augustinian nuns (1445), and Jesuits (1625). Outside the city were Benedictines (Iburg), Brethren of the Cross (Osterberg), and Benedictine (Gertrudenberg) and Cistercian (Rulle) nuns. Beside the Carolinum cathedral school and Dominican and Augustinian schools arose the Catholic university (1628–33), brought to an end by the Swedish invasion.

Artwork includes the chapter cross (c. 1050), a bronze baptismal font (1225), masterpieces of Osnabrück goldsmiths (the reliquary of SS. *Crispin and Crispinian, 1240–50; and the chalices in the cathedral treasure), a triumphal cross (c. 1240), the splendid *Codex Gisle* (c. 1330), bells, and many works of the "Master of Osnabrück," especially carved altars and Madonnas (c. 1500–30). There are four charitable institutions in the city: Holy Spirit Hospital, St. Elizabeth, St. Jürgen, and 11,000 Virgins. Despite bombing damage of World War II, most of historical Osnabrück has been preserved or restored.

Bibliography: *Mitteilungen des Historischen Verein zu Osnabrück* (Osnabrück 1848–), superseded by *Mitteilungen des Vereins für Geschichte u. Landeskunde von Osnabrück* (1882–), superseded by *Osnabrücker Mitteilungen* (1952–), 72 v. to date. *Osnabrücker Geschichts-Quellen*, 5 v. (1891–1935). *Osnabrücker Urkunden-Buch*, ed. F. PHILIPPI and M. BÄR, 4 v. (1892–1904). *Das Bistum Osnabrück*, ed. J. VINCKE (1939–), 4 v. to date. F. WITTE, *Der Domschatz zu Osnabrück* (Berlin 1925). L. SCHIRMEYER, *Osnabrück und das Osnabrücker Land* (Osnabrück 1948). H. THÜMMLER, *Der Dom zu Osnabrück* (Munich 1954). H. POPPE-MARQUARD, *Osnabrück: Schöne alte Stadt* (3d ed. Osnabrück 1964), text also in Eng. L. NIEHUS, *Geschichte des Bistums Osnabrück* (2d ed. Hildesheim 1962); LexThK² 7: 1265–67. W. RAHE, RGG³ 4:1733–34. AnnPont (1965) 318.

[L. NIEHUS]

OSRHOENE, a region between the Euphrates and Tigris rivers whose capital was *Edessa. During the first 2 Christian centuries it was a small kingdom under the dynasty of Abgar. In 216 the Emperor Caracalla incorporated it into the Roman Empire as a province. Christianity had been introduced into Osrhoene early, most probably from Antioch by Jewish Christians. There is no historical foundation for the legends of *Abgar, King of Osrhoene, recorded by Eusebius (*Hist. eccl.* 1.12–13) to the effect that the king begged Jesus to come and heal his daughter. To this request Jesus was alleged to have sent a written reply saying that he was going to send his disciple, Thaddeus (Thaddai), to heal the girl and preach the Gospel. However, according to trustworthy sources, there were Christians in Osrhoene as early as the latter half of the 2d century.

The Epitaph of *Abercius and information in Eusebius (*Hist. eccl.* 5.24) witness to the fact that counsel was sought from the Diocese of Osrhoene in the matter of the fixing of the date for Easter. At the beginning of the 3d century *Julius Africanus found the heretic *Bardesanes in the court of King Abgar IX. There is no conclusive evidence for A. von *Harnack's contention that this King embraced Christianity and that Osrhoene was the first Christian kingdom. The Chris-

tians of Osrhoene wrote in Syriac; their greatest glory was St. *Ephrem.

Bibliography: J. P. MARTIN, *Les Origines de l'Église d'Édesse et des églises syriennes* (Paris 1889). I. ORTIZ DE URBINA, "Le origini del cristianesimo in Edessa," Greg 15 (1934) 82–91.

[I. ORTIZ DE URBINA]

OSSAT, ARNAUD D', French diplomat, bishop, cardinal; b. Larroque-en-Magnoac, c. 1537; d. Rome, 1604. In 1572 he became an aide of the diplomat Paul de Foix, archbishop-elect of Toulouse. After De Foix's death in 1584, Ossat served in Rome as secretary to the successive Cardinal Protectors of France, Louis d'Este and François Joyeuse. Ossat refused an offer to be Henry III's minister of foreign affairs in 1588, and in the following year he became the Roman representative of Henry's widow. Ossat used his position to further the cause of *Henry IV, serving as negotiator with Pope Clement VIII to gain the Pope's acceptance of Henry's conversion. In 1595 Ossat, in cooperation with Cardinal *Duperron, finally gained absolution for Henry IV and regularized his relationships with Rome. Ossat continued to represent Henry's interests on a number of occasions thereafter. Though he remained in Rome, he was consecrated bishop of Rennes in 1596, made a cardinal in 1599, and given the See of Bayeux in 1600. Ossat's letters long served as a model for diplomatic correspondence.

Bibliography: A. N. AMELOT DE HOUSSAYE, *Lettres du cardinal d'Ossat*, 5 v. (Amsterdam 1708). P. TAMIZEY DE LARROQUE, *Lettres inédites du cardinal d'Ossat* (Paris 1872). A. DEGERT, *Le Cardinal d'Ossat* (Paris 1894). Fliche-Martin 18.1:383. P. SANNAZZARO, EncCatt 9:421–422. P. LARCADE, *Le Cardinal d'Ossat* (Tarbes 1937).

[J. M. HAYDEN]

OSSERVATORE ROMANO

Daily newspaper owned by the Holy See and published in Vatican City. Under the prompting of the substitute Minister of the Interior, Marcantonio Pacelli (grandfather of Pius XII), the lawyer Nicola Zanchini of Forlì, and the journalist Giuseppe Bastia of Bologna, the journal began on July 1, 1861. These three men were also its first directors. It carried as subtitle "Political-Moral Newspaper," later replaced by the present one, "Daily Political-Religious Newspaper." The phrases *Unicuique suum* and *Non praevalebunt* were added to the masthead in 1862, and the papal tiara in 1873. In 1929 the newspaper's offices were moved into Vatican City.

The *Osservatore Romano* publishes the official text and authorized Italian translation of the encyclicals and other papal documents, the pope's speeches, the appointments of bishops, the announcements of consistories, and various acts of the congregations. Completely official notices are published, according to time-honored custom, without a headline. Although the *Osservatore Romano* is not the official organ of the Holy See (*see* ACTA APOSTOLICAE SEDIS), the articles by its editors are generally considered to present correct views and interpretations of Vatican thinking. As for other contributors to the paper, they are on their own responsibility.

The newspaper had special significance in the pontificate of Leo XIII (1878–1903) when, even while being published under the scrutiny of the Italian government, it progressively emphasized its character as the editorial voice of the Holy See. Its significance grew under Pius XI (1922–39) with the controversies following the *Lateran pacts; under Pius XII (1939–58) for illustrating that Pontiff's thinking on war and peace (particularly in the *Acta diurna* of Guido Gonella); and then with the timely defense of Christian thought and human rights in the last Fascist period and during the Nazi occupation, especially through the pen of Count Giuseppe Dalla Torre, who was its editor from 1920 to 1961.

The paper is accountable to the second section (for Ordinary Affairs) of the Papal Secretariate of State. The editor and subeditors are appointed by papal order but (through an unexplained anomaly) they are not named in any way in the *Annuario Pontificio.*

The *Osservatore Romano* provides a press relations service that is the daily, authorized link between the Secretariate of State and the Italian press, both religious and secular.

Bibliography: *Osservatore Romano.* Special issues 1937 (for the 75th anniversary) and 1961 (for the centenary). *Annuario Unione Cattolica della stampa italiana* (Rome 1963). G. DALLA TORRE, *I Cattolici e la vita pubblica italiana,* ed. G. DE ROSA, 2 v. (Rome 1962). G. GONELLA, *Presupposti di un ordine internazionale: Note ai messaggi di S. S. Pio XII* (2d ed. Vatican City 1943).

[E. LUCATELLO]

OSSUARIES, rectangular containers of limestone, baked clay, or wood, used to store the bones of bodies deposited in the *loculi* (*see* BURIAL, I) of tombs or caves, to make room there for new burials. Several hundred ossuaries, some plain, many decorated on one side with matching rosettes in a paneled framework, have been found near Jerusalem, Nablus, and other places in Palestine. Their size (20-to-32 by 12-to-20 by 10-to-16 inches) was dictated by the measurements of skull and femur bone. The lids, often fitted in grooves, were flat, rounded, or gabled. The chief interest of these caskets lies in the *graffiti found on many of them; written, probably by the one who transferred the bones, in Aramaic, Greek, or both, they give, usually, only the name of the person whose bones the box contained. Many of the names are known from the Bible, Josephus, or the Murabba'āt finds; some are new. The Aramaic inscription *yhwš' br ywsp* (Jesus son of Joseph) on a 1st-century ossuary has no bearing on the Resurrection; both names were very common among Jews of the period. Cross marks, not certainly of Christian origin, on the

lids or sides of ossuaries, may have been inspired by Ez 9.4–6 or placed there to ward off demonic influence.

Bibliography: R. MOTTE, DBSuppl 6:940–948. R. NORTH, LexThK² 7:1270–71. EncDictBibl 1683–84. E. L. SUKENIK, "The Earliest Records of Christianity," AmJArch 51 (1947) 351–365. N. AVIGAD, "A Depository of Inscribed Ossuaries in the Kidron Valley," IsrExplorJ 12 (1962) 1–12. D. FISHWICK, "The Talpioth Ossuaries Again," NTSt 10 (1963–64) 49–61. B. BAGATTI and J. MILIK, *Gli Scavi del 'Dominus Flevit,'* v.1 (Jerusalem 1958). C. H. KRAELING, "Christian Burial Urns?" BiblArchaeol 9 (1946) 16–20. **Illustration credit:** Pontifical Biblical Institute.

[M. A. HOFER]

OSTIA, suburbicarian see, 28 kilometers from Rome on the Mediterranean, with important archeological excavations. The most ancient nucleus of Ostia goes back to 330 B.C., when a port was constructed on the left bank of the Tiber where it empties into the sea (*ostium* means mouth). During the second Punic War (218–202) Ostia was a naval base and a depot for the importation of grain and was connected with Rome by one of the oldest consular roads, the Via Ostiense. Destroyed during the civil war between Marius and Sulla (87 B.C.), it did not lose its importance as a city when Claudius (A.D. 41–54) founded the town of Porto as the new port; but with the transfer of the imperial capital from Rome to the Orient in the 4th century the value of Ostia as a commercial center decreased, and Constantine I transferred its municipal rights to Porto. Decadence had set in by 414, and when Pope Gregory IV in 827 began important military fortifications at the mouth of the Tiber, the old city of Ostia was in ruins. Nicholas I (858–867) further fortified the region, and Julius II (d. 1513), while still cardinal, built a castle designed by B. Pontelli.

The first known bishop was St. Quiriacus, or Cyriacus, whose sarcophagus (3d century) has been unearthed. He died a martyr in 230. Bishop Maximus consecrated Pope *Dionysius (259–268), and this function became a prerogative of the bishops of Ostia. In 336 the Bishop of Ostia received the pallium and always took precedence over the suburbicarian sees. St. *Augustine experienced his famous vision at Ostia, and St. *Monica died there.

Pope Eugene III in 1150 united the See of Ostia to Velletri and the title of the bishop became "Episcopus Ostiensis et Veliternensis." In May 1914, with the motu proprio *Edita a nobis,* the modern city of Ostia was

Decorated stone ossuaries of the Judeo-Christian style, seen at the excavation site.

Fragment of the epitaph of St. Monica in the Museo di Antichità at Ostia, Italy.

separated from Velletri and made the possession of the cardinal dean (can. 236.4). Pope John XXIII gave a new status to the suburbicarian sees, including Ostia (motu proprios of March 10, 1961, and April 11, 1962), which gives them an auxiliary bishop with ordinary powers and permits the pope to appoint the cardinals as bishops at will instead of by precedence.

The site of ancient Ostia, which is now some 6 kilometers inland from the modern city, contains one of the most important archeological excavations in Italy, particularly for its Roman *edilizia,* or buildings of the imperial age. It has many vestiges of early Christianity including a 5th- or 6th-century oratory, and a vast basilica of uncertain date. Near the basilica of St. Aurea, restored by Popes Sergius I and Leo III, the fragment of an epitaph was found with partial text from 408 composed for the tomb of St. Monica, which had been known through 12 ancient MSS. This makes it appear that the remains of St. Augustine's mother were not transported to Africa.

A quickly expanding vacation resort, the modern city has 4,000 regular inhabitants in one parish, with one diocesan and three religious priests in residence in 1964.

Bibliography: E. JOSI and R. CALZA, EncCatt 9:431–435. D. GIRGENSOHN, LexThK² 7:1286. R. CALZA and E. NASH, *Ostia* (Florence 1959). R. MEIGGS, *Roman Ostia* (Oxford 1960). Ann Pont (1964) 318–319.

[G. ORLANDI]

OSTRACON, an inscribed potsherd. Since papyrus or leather often proved expensive for ordinary writing chores such as memoranda, letters, and receipts or even at times for official communications, the ancients resorted to potsherds as a writing material. Such material was readily available, required no preparation, and could be reused if necessary. The writing was sometimes scratched on the surface but was normally inscribed with pen and ink. Such a surface, however, was not practical for writing in cuneiform (*see* WRITING, AN-CIENT SYSTEMS OF). Some inscribed potsherds (ostraca) have been found in Palestine and have thrown light on the Biblical period. The most famous are the *Lachis Letters and the Samarian ostraca (*see* EPIGRAPHY, HE-BREW).

Illustration credit: Palestine Archaeological Museum.

[T. H. WEBER]

An ostracon of the 6th century B.C., *one of the Lachis Letters (No. IV, the reverse).*

O'SULLIVAN-BEARE, PHILIP, Irish historian; b. Ireland, 1590?; d. Madrid, 1660? Philip, the son of Dermot O'Sullivan, was sent to Spain in 1602 by his uncle, Donal O'Sullivan-Beare, Lord of Dunboy, a leading Irish patriot. After studying at Compostella, his early years were spent as a Spanish soldier. Abandoning military affairs for literature, he wrote and published *Historiae Catholicae Iberniae Compendium* (Lisbon 1621). The section dealing with the Elizabethan wars is based largely on oral descriptions and writings of participants, and amounts to an eyewitness account. Vivid, partisan, and inaccurate, it is a work of dubious merit. O'Sullivan's other works included history, a life of St. Patrick, *Patriciana Decas* (1629), polemical attacks on Irish Protestants, and many lives of the saints. The *Bollandists made use of O'Sullivan's historical skills. The last 30 years of his life were devoted to writing. The Beare in his name referred to the district in County Cork in which the O'Sullivans originated.

Bibliography: J. K. LAUGHTON, DNB 14:1214–15; T. D. Mc-GEE, *Irish Writers of the 17th Century* (Dublin 1846).

[P. S. MC GARRY]

OSWALD, KING OF NORTHUMBRIA, ST., martyr; b. 604; d. Aug. 5, 642 (feast, Aug. 5). The son of King Aethelfrith, he lived in exile after his father's death in 616, and was brought up in the monastery of *Iona. His cousin, King *Edwin of Northumbria, was slain in battle in 633 fighting against *Penda, the heathen King of Mercia, and Cadwallon, Penda's British ally. A year later Oswald attacked Cadwallon at Heavenfield, near Hexham, and won a great victory. The wooden cross Oswald erected before the battle long enjoyed fame for its miraculous powers. After Edwin's death Northumbria had lapsed into heathenism, but Oswald, with the help of *Aidan of Lindisfarne, sent as bishop from Iona at his request, set about its reconversion. He often accompanied Aidan on evangelizing tours from his see in *Lindisfarne, sometimes acting as interpreter since Aidan spoke but little English. So Christianity, in its Celtic form, was restored.

*Bede recounted many tales about the King's humility and generosity. For some time he was overlord of all the English kingdoms, but in 642 he was killed fighting against Penda. His last words, "May God have mercy on their souls," a prayer for his soldiers, later became a proverb. Bede is the source for several stories about cures that took place on the spot where Oswald fell. His body was later discovered and brought by his niece, Queen Osthryth, to a monastery at Bardney in Mercia; but the brethren were unwilling to receive the bones of a former foe. At length the monks were convinced by a column of light above the bier that these were the relics of a saint and gladly received them. From then on the monastery doors were kept continually open. Oswald's head was placed in the coffin of St. *Cuthbert of Lindisfarne and is still in Durham. The arms, long incorrupt, were deposited at Bamborough. The body was translated to Gloucester when Bardney was destroyed in 909 by the Danes; later *Willibrord took some of the relics to Frisia, and many continental churches still claim them. He is venerated as a martyr, and churches were dedicated to him in France, Belgium, Switzerland, Germany, and northern Italy.

Bibliography: BEDE, *Hist. eccl.* 2.5, 20; 3.1–3, 5, 6, 9, 11–13; 5.24. ActSS Aug. 2:83–103. W. HUNT, DNB 14:1215–17. A. H.

SS. Oswald and Aidan, illumination from the "Berthold Missal" (1200–32) of the Abbey of Weingarten in Swabia (Morgan MS 710, fol. 101v).

THOMPSON, ed., *Bede, His Life, Times, and Writings* (Oxford 1935) 217–220. J. OSWALD, LexThK² 7:1296. **Illustration credit:** The Pierpont Morgan Library, New York City.

[B. COLGRAVE]

OSWALD OF YORK, ST., archbishop; d. Worcester, Feb. 29, 992 (feast, Feb. 28). As bishop of Worcester (961) and archbishop of York (972), Oswald shared with *Dunstan and *Ethelwold the glory of establishing the 10th-century Anglo-Saxon monastic revival. A Dane by birth, he was brought up by his uncle, Archbishop *Odo of Canterbury. Ordained deacon and priest at *Fleury, he introduced its reformed practices into England, founding a small Benedictine monastery at Westbury (*c.* 962), an influential house at *Ramsey (*c.* 971), and communities at Winchcombe, Pershore, and perhaps Deerhurst, Ripon, and Evesham. Unlike Ethelwold, Oswald avoided violent reform, monasticizing the See of *Worcester gradually and by example (*c.* 974–977). With Dunstan, he helped to crown Kings *Edgar, *Edward the Martyr, and Ethelred II. The sources for his life include the *Vita sancti Oswaldi auctore anonymo* (ed. J. Raine, *Historians . . . York,* RollsS), *Eadmer's *Vita sancti Oswaldi,* as well as the *Chronicon abbatiae Rameseiensis,* and the works of *Florence of Worcester and *William of Malmesbury.

Bibliography: ActSS Feb. 3:755–762. W. HUNT, DNB 14: 1217–19. J. A. ROBINSON, *The Times of Saint Dunstan* (Oxford 1923). E. S. DUCKETT, *Saint Dunstan of Canterbury* (New York 1955). E. JOHN, "St. Oswald and the Tenth Century Reformation," JEcclHist 9 (1958) 159–172. Knowles MOE.

[W. A. CHANEY]

OTHLO OF SANKT EMMERAM, Benedictine scholar; b. near Freising, Germany *c.* 1010; d. Sankt Emmeram Abbey, Regensburg, Nov. 23, *c.* 1070. A precocious child, Othlo received his early education at *Tegernsee and *Hersfeld Abbeys. Finding the secular clerical life unsatisfactory, he entered *Sankt Emmeram in 1032. A sensitive, gifted, and imaginative monk, Othlo experienced various spiritual trials and worried especially about his enthusiasm for classical literature. Such concern reveals the early influence of those *Cluniac reform ideals that led him into serious patristic and scriptural studies. At Sankt Emmeram, where he taught *William of Hirsau, he was encouraged to write. His first major composition, the *De doctrina spirituali,* was a long poetic exhortation to virtue, with criticism of pagan classical studies. His *Dialogus de tribus quaestionibus* (*c.* 1053) expounds various theological themes: it rests on St. Augustine and attacks the new dialectical approach to theology.

Because of disagreements that he had with the bishop of Regensburg, Othlo left Sankt Emmeram and lived at *Fulda (1062–66), where he composed a biography of St. *Boniface and probably the life of St. *Wolfgang of Regensburg, the *Liber visionum,* describing divine manifestations including some he himself received, and the *Libellus manualis,* a powerful harangue to clergy and laity to reform and return to proper respect for religion—a realistic commentary on the age. At Fulda he also began the *Proverbia* (ed. C. G. Korfmacher, Chicago 1936), an extensive collection of memorable sayings culled for pedagogical purposes from Christian and classical sources. Leaving Fulda, Othlo visited Amorbach Abbey, where he wrote the *Quomodo legendum sit in rebus visibilibus,* on Christian education. Having returned to Sankt Emmeram (*c.* 1068) and feeling the weight of years, Othlo composed the *De cursu spirituali,* a homiletic work using St. Paul's figure of speech. It displays a thorough familiarity with Scripture and skill in the allegorical method of exegesis. His final work, the *Libellus de suis temptationibus, varia fortuna et scriptis,* is autobiographical. Among Othlo's minor works, difficult to date, are lives of SS. *Alto, Nicholas, and Magnus, some religious poetry, sermons, and his puzzling *Translatio s. Dionysii.* He also produced counterfeit charters on behalf of Sankt Emmeram.

Bibliography: Works. PL 146:9–434. MGS 4:521–542; 11: 376–393; 15.2:843–846; 30.2:823–837. MGSrerGerm 53:111–217. ActSS Nov. 2:565–597. Literature. Manitius 2:83–103. G. MISCH, *Geschichte der Autobiographie* (3d ed. Bern 1949–) 3.1:57–107. B. BISCHOFF, Stammler 3:658–670; 5:831; LexThK² 7:1298–99.

[R. H. SCHMANDT]

OTHMAR, ST., abbot; b. *c.* 689; d. Werd near Stein am Rhein, Switzerland, Nov. 16, 759 (feast, Nov. 16). Othmar (Otmar, Audemar, Audomar) was educated for the priesthood at the imperial court. In 719 he was invited to assume the direction of a colony of monks who had settled near the grave of St. *Gall. Othmar built them a monastery to be governed by the *Benedictine Rule. Later, in his defense of the autonomy of the Abbey of *Sankt Gallen, he suffered imprisonment and exile. He also established the first house for lepers in Switzerland. In 769 his remains were returned to Sankt Gallen, and in 867 they were buried in the church named for him. He is represented in art as an abbot with a staff, sometimes with a small cask for the refreshment of pilgrims.

Bibliography: MGS 2:41–47. J. DUFT, ed., *St. Otmar: Die Quellen zu seinem Leben* (Zurich 1959). Réau IAC 3.2:1014–15. J. M. CLARK, *The Abbey of St. Gall as a Centre of Literature and Art* (Cambridge, Eng. 1926). Zimmermann KalBen 3:312–315. G. HEER, LexThK² 7:1299–1300.

[B. D. HILL]

O'TOOLE, GEORGE BARRY, educator, author, cofounder of the Catholic University of Peking, China; b. Toledo, Ohio, Dec. 11, 1886; d. Washington, D.C., March 26, 1944. He studied at St. John's University, Toledo, and received doctorates in philosophy and theology from the Urban University, Rome. After ordination in Rome (Nov. 1, 1911), he served as secretary to Joseph Schrembs, Bishop of Toledo (1912–15); diocesan canonist (1913–15); pastor of St. Aloysius, Bowling Green, Ohio (1915–17); professor of philosophy, St. Vincent Seminary, Latrobe, Pa. (1917–18); U.S. Army chaplain (1918–19); professor of philosophy (1919–20) and dogmatic theology (1923–24) again at St. Vincent's; professor of animal biology, Seton Hill College, Greensburg, Pa. (1919–20, 1923–24); rector of the Catholic University of Peking (1925–33); professor and head of department of philosophy, Duquesne University, Pittsburgh, Pa. (1934–37), professor of philosophy, The Catholic University of America, Washington, D.C. (1937–44); and editor in chief of the *China Monthly* (1939–44). With Archabbot Aurelius Stehle, OSB, he established the Catholic (*Fu Jen*) University of Peking (relocated at Taipei, Formosa, 1962); at the time of his departure from China in 1933, it included schools of arts, sciences, and education, with approximately 100 faculty members and 1,100 students. O'Toole was made a domestic prelate in 1934. A detailed list of his writings is included in D. D. Runes, ed., *Who's Who in Philosophy* (New York 1942) 348.

Bibliography: Archives, The Catholic University of America, unpub. biog. of Rt. Rev. Msgr. George Barry O'Toole. M. HOEHN, ed., *Catholic Authors: Contemporary biographical sketches, 1930–47* (Newark 1948) 603–605.

[J. F. WIPPEL]

OTRANTO, ARCHDIOCESE OF (HYDRUNTINUS), metropolitan see since the 11th century, in Apulia, on the heel of Italy. In 1963 the archdiocese had 179,508 Catholics (almost the entire population), 113 secular and 30 religious priests, 45 men in 8 religious houses, and 265 women in 47 convents; it is 475 square miles in area. Its two suffragans, which had 118,000 Catholics, 123 priests, and 179 sisters, were: Gallipoli (established in the 6th century), which followed the Greek rite from *c.* 1100 to 1513; and Ugento-S. Maria di Leuca, whose first known bishop appears in 1254. The former suffragan of Lecce (1057) has been immediately subject to the Holy See since 1960. Castro was united with Otranto in 1818.

The first known bishop of Otranto, Peter, was appointed by Gregory the Great in 595 as papal visitor to the vacant Sees of *Brindisi, Lecce, and Gallipoli. In the 9th century Otranto sided against Rome with Constantinople, which recognized it as a metropolitan in the 10th century; in the late 11th century it returned to Rome, retaining its status as metropolitan. The city declined rapidly after the Turks massacred 800 men

and the bishop in the cathedral in 1480; Otranto has the relics of 560 of these martyrs. Bp. V. M. Morelli (1792–1812) has been declared Venerable. The cathedral of three naves, consecrated under the Normans (1088), and redone in baroque (1674–1764), has recently been restored; its 12th-century crypt shows Byzantine influence. The priest Pantaleone (1163–66) laid a bizarre mosaic on the cathedral floor portraying classical and allegorical themes, and scenes of the Bible and King Arthur's Round Table. The 15th-century Church of S. Pietro, built in a Greek cross, has Romanesque frescoes.

Bibliography: Gams. Eubel HierCath. P. TESTINI, EncCatt 9:446–448. A. ANTONACI, *Hydruntum, Otranto* (Galatina 1954); *I processi nella causa di beatificazione dei martire di Otranto, 1539–1771* (Galatina 1960). AnnPont (1964) 319, 1414.

[G. A. PAPA]

OTT, MICHAEL, abbot; b. Neustad am Main, Bavaria, March 18, 1870; d. Crookston, Minn., Feb. 15, 1948. He took his classical studies at St. John's University, Collegeville, Minn., and there joined the Benedictine Order in 1889. He was sent to the International College of Sant' Anselmo in Rome, where he received his doctorate in philosophy and was ordained, June 29, 1894. Upon returning to St. John's University, he taught commercial subjects and supervised the student publication, the library, and the print shop. He was secretary of the university's board of administration and subprior of the abbey when he was elected abbot of St. Peter's Abbey, Muenster, Saskatchewan, Canada. The abbatial blessing took place in St. Peter's Church at Muenster, Oct. 28, 1919. Two years later St. Peter's Abbey became an abbey *nullius,* subject directly to the Holy See, and Ott was designated as the first abbot ordinary (*see* ABBOT NULLIUS). One of his first decisions after becoming abbot was to establish a secondary school at Muenster. In 1921 a new building was completed and classes began in St. Peter's College, which was soon recognized as a junior college affiliated with the University of Saskatchewan at Saskatoon. From 1931 until his death in 1948, he served as chaplain to the Benedictine convent in Crookston, Minn.

[J. WEBER]

OTTAWA, ARCHDIOCESE OF (OTTAVIENSIS)

Metropolitan see comprising the counties of Carleton, Prescott, Russell, and part of Lanark in the Province of Ontario, Canada. It was erected as a diocese June 25, 1847, and became an archdiocese June 8, 1886. Its suffragans include the Dioceses of Timmins (1915), Mont Laurier (1913), Pembroke (1898), Hearst (1938), Hull (1963), and the Vicariate Apostolic of James Bay (1938). In 1963 the archdiocese numbered about 210,-500 Catholics.

The Ottawa area was visited quite early by explorers and missionaries. Samuel de *Champlain was there at least by June 1613, followed in 1615 by the friar Joseph Le Caron. At that time the Ottawa River provided a natural route for the exploration of the regions to the north and west. In 1800 Philemon Wright of Woburn, Mass., immigrated to Canada, set up an establishment opposite the present site of Ottawa, and built up a lumber business, an industry that became very important throughout the entire area. At the time of American Independence there was concern for the

Province of Ottawa, comprising the Archdiocese of Ottawa, called the metropolitan see, and six suffragans. The archbishop exercises metropolitan jurisdiction over the province.

safety of the English settlement in Canada, and one of the military defense measures proposed was the canalization of the Rideau River, which flows through the city. In 1826 Col. John By was appointed engineer for this project and gave his name to Bytown, which became Ottawa in 1855. The first Catholic church, a wooden building, was opened during 1832. Father Haran, of Richmond, who had been making regular visits to Bytown, seems to have established himself there in 1827.

Bishop Ignace *Bourget of Montreal, who considered Bytown excellent headquarters for the evangelization of that area and the North, induced the bishop of Kingston to appeal to the Oblates of Mary Immaculate to minister to the city, the timber yards, and the Indian missions. The Oblates reached Ottawa in 1844 and found no need more pressing than that of providing suitable charitable and educational institutions. In 1845, therefore, they obtained the assistance of the Sisters of Charity of Montreal (Grey Nuns) in establishing a hospital and a school. Bourget soon conceived the idea of having a diocese established with Bytown as the diocesan center. With the concurrence of his colleagues in the episcopacy, the diocese was erected in 1847, and Joseph Eugene Bruno Guigues, OMI, was appointed first ordinary and consecrated July 30, 1848. Under his direction the new diocese grew rapidly. He organized the ministry on a bilingual basis (French and English); founded a seminary; opened a college, which later became the University of *Ottawa (1848); extended colonization, Indian missions, and aid to the employees of the lumber industry; and greatly increased the number of missions and parishes. After his death Feb. 8, 1874, the diocese continued its progress under his successors: Joseph Thomas Duhamel (1874–1909), Charles Hugh Gauthier (1910–22), Joseph Médard Emard (1922–27), Guillaume Forbes (1928–40), Alexandre Vachon (1940–53), and Marie Joseph Lemieux, OP,

who was appointed June 20, 1953, and enthroned in Ottawa Sept. 17, 1953. In 1961 he was named an assistant to the pontifical throne.

In 1963 the archdiocese had 93 churches, 199 secular priests, 374 religious priests, including the Oblates of Mary Immaculate, Capuchins, Augustinians, Basilians, Dominicans, Franciscans, Jesuits, Redemptorists, Servites, White Fathers, and Fathers of the Company of Mary, Sacred Heart, and St. Vincent de Paul. Among the religious communities of women were the Grey Nuns, Sisters of Notre Dame, Precious Blood, Good Shepherd, Sacred Heart, Visitation, Holy Cross, St. Martha, Assumption, St. Mary, St. Joseph, Jesus and Mary, Little Sisters of the Holy Family, Sisters of Service, and Missionary Sisters of Our Lady of Africa. In Ottawa the Oblates of Mary Immaculate operate a coeducational college, St. Patrick's (1928). In 1965 control of the University of Ottawa was transferred from the Oblates to a lay board of governors; the university was entitled to state support. St. Paul's University (ecclesiastical faculties) was opened under the direction of the Oblates.

Bibliography: A. DE BARBÉZIEUX, *Histoire de la province ecclésiastique d'Ottawa*, 2 v. (Ottawa 1897). L. BRAULT, *Ottawa, Old and New* (Ottawa 1946).

[G. CARRIÈRE]

OTTAWA, UNIVERSITY OF

A pontifical university founded in 1848 as the College of Bytown by the Oblate Fathers of Mary Immaculate. The institution received its civil charter as a university in 1866 and was canonically erected on Feb. 5, 1889, by decree of Pope Leo XIII. In 1903 the University buildings were destroyed by fire. In 1933 a revised charter was approved by the Ontario legislature and the pontifical charter amended according to the requirements of the constitution *Deus Scientiarum Dominus*. The charter was given a new approval by Rome in 1934.

The University of Ottawa comprises the Faculties of Arts; Pure and Applied Science; Law; Medicine; Social Sciences; Canon Law; and Philosophy, Theology. It also maintains a teachers' college, and Schools of Psychology and Education, Library Science, Hospital Administration, Physical Education, Nursing, and Social Welfare, operated at St. Patrick's College, Ottawa, a constituent college of the University.

The Art Faculty includes departments, schools, and institutes of geography, home economics, commerce, mathematics, general science, liberal arts, philosophy, and Slavic studies. Within the faculty of medicine are 15 departments, including those in general medical studies, otorhinolaryngology, preventive medicine, psychiatry, neurology, radiology, and pharmacology. The Science Faculty contains departments in natural sciences and mathematics, and chemical and electrical engineering. Ten colleges are affiliated with the University: Collège de Cornwall, Ont.; St. John's College, Edmonton, Alta.; the Collège Mathieu de Gravelbourg; Sacred Heart Scholasticate, Lebret; St. Thomas College, North Battleford; and Notre Dame College, Wilcox, Sask.; Bruyère College, Ottawa; a major and a minor seminary, and St. Pius X Preparatory Seminary, Ottawa.

In academic affairs authority rests with the senate, made up of the chancellor, rector, deans and directors of faculties and schools, and members of the council of administration. Administrative powers of the

University are vested in the council of administration, a board composed of seven members of the Oblate Order. This board is advised by the senate on academic matters and, in financial matters, by a board of regents composed of laymen prominent in fields of industry, finance, trade, merchandising, journalism, and politics. The University is financed through student fees, the contributed services of the religious, government grants, a small endowment, and from miscellaneous sources (including services to outside organizations), and sponsored or assisted research.

In 1964 the teaching staff comprised approximately 626 members. In 1964 full-time regular students totaled 4,156, in addition to 1,573 evening students, 1,516 in correspondence courses, 3,273 in the summer program, and 636 in its affiliated colleges. According to a 1962 survey conducted by the National Conference of Canadian Universities and Colleges, the University's library holdings, numbering 382,000 volumes, were Canada's most outstanding in philosophy and religious history.

The University is bilingual. In most faculties students may choose to follow courses in either French or English, and if competent, in both. The University has no restrictions of color, race, or creed, and both students and staff are drawn from all five continents. Since emphasis is on graduate study and research, in 1963 one of every six students was in graduate school. In 1961 the University ranked third in Canada in number of doctoral theses accepted and sixth in total graduate theses accepted. All faculties offer honors programs.

The University of Ottawa Press, founded in 1937, by 1961 had published more than 100 volumes by staff members and graduates of the University. Regular University publications include the bilingual *University of Ottawa Quarterly;* the quarterly *Medical Journal; Publications Sériées; Inscape,* a quarterly review of literature; and the students' *The Fulcrum* and *La Rotonde.*

An adult education unit of the University, known as The Catholic Centre, publishes several correspondence courses and three liturgical publications and in 1961 had a combined weekly circulation of 286,900. The Catholic Centre's best-known works are courses in fundamentals in marriage and in marriage preparation; the latter are published in English, French, Spanish, Portuguese, German, Dutch, and Italian. In 1963 editions were in preparation for Basutoland in the Sesotho dialect and for Hong Kong in a Chinese dialect.

Alumni are organized into 16 regional chapters and 4 faculty or school groupings of medicine, law, psychology, and physical education. In 1962 the active alumni numbered 7,816 French-speaking and 2,480 English-speaking members.

In 1963 the University, located in 27 buildings on 42 acres, announced plans to develop an integrated 82-acre campus providing space for 8,000 full-time students by 1970.

[R. LA BERGE]

OTTERBEIN, PHILIP WILLIAM, cofounder and first bishop of the Church of the *United Brethren in Christ; b. Dillenburg, Germany, June 3, 1726; d. Baltimore, Md., Nov. 17, 1813. He studied for the ministry at Herborn and was ordained (1749) a minister of the German Reformed Church. In 1753, Rev. Michael Schlatter encouraged him to immigrate to America. Otterbein was the pastor of Reformed churches in York and Lancaster, Pa., and Frederick, Md., before accepting a call to Baltimore in 1774. The origin of the Church of the United Brethren is traced to his meeting with the Mennonite preacher Martin *Boehm in 1767. Although Otterbein commissioned lay preachers and held the first conference of the Brethren in 1789, he continued to attend the Reformed synods until 1800. The consecration of Methodist Bishop Francis Asbury took place in 1785 in Otterbein's Baltimore church, and he maintained close ties with other early Methodist leaders.

Bibliography: A. W. DRURY, *The Life of Rev. Philip William Otterbein* (Dayton 1894). F. ASBURY, *Journal and Letters,* ed. E. T. CLARK et al., 3 v. (Nashville 1958).

[R. K. MAC MASTER]

OTTO I, ROMAN EMPEROR

Reigned 936 to May 7, 973; son of Henry I and Matilda, descendant of *Widukind, Duke of Saxony; b. Oct. 23, 912; d. Memleben (buried in the cathedral of Magdeburg).

Early Career—The German Kingdom. His first marriage in 929 to the Anglo-Saxon Princess Edith (d. 946), sister of King Athelstan, brought him into close kinship with the West Frankish Carolingians, making him the brother-in-law of King Charles the Simple of France and of Hugh, Duke of the French. In 936 at the Erfurt Assembly of Princes Otto's father designated him his successor. Otto was the eldest son of Henry's second marriage and, in designating him successor, Henry passed over the rights of Thankmar, his first-

Otto I, 13th-century statue on a portal of Magdeburg cathedral.

born by a marriage that had not been recognized by the Church. Nominated by the Saxons and Franks, Otto was elected King at Aachen (Aug. 7, 936) by the incumbents of the five duchies. Wearing Frankish clothes, he received their homage, which was followed by the enthroning, commendation, and swearing of the oath of fealty. Next came the consecration in the Aachen cathedral, with the delivery of the royal insignia, the anointing and coronation, and the enthronement on the chair of Charlemagne by the archbishops of Mainz and Cologne, amid loud acclamations of the people. At the coronation banquet, the incumbents of the Duchies of Lorraine, Franconia, Swabia, and Bavaria served as chamberlain, steward, cupbearer, and marshal. With this solemn act the German Kingdom, which had come into being in a long process of development out of the realm of the Frankish Carolingians, attained its definite form.

Internal Problems. Like every historical innovation, Otto's kingdom was greeted with hostility, due in part to personal opposition by the King's brothers, Thankmar and the younger Henry who had been born during his father's reign and who, in Byzantine eyes, had special prerogatives. It encouraged the political enmity of Bavaria and Swabia and was attacked by bordering peoples, the Danes, the Slavs on the Elbe, and the inhabitants of Bohemia. Even in Saxony considerable opposition was triggered by the cession of two newly founded marches on the Elbe to Counts Hermann Billung and Gero, two loyal supporters of the King. In 939 there were stiff battles with Duke Giselbert in Lorraine and with Henry on the Rhine. Both tried to link with the Carolingians in France and were given assistance by Duke Eberhard of Franconia and Abp. *Frederick of Mainz. While the King was besieging Breisach, his opponents risked a bold thrust into Saxony. However, in October 939 the King's army won a decisive victory near Andernach on the Rhine; Eberhard and Giselbert were killed. For the King this success opened the road to Burgundy and France via Lorraine. Once again Henry took up the battle against his brother, planning, with the support of the Saxon nobility, to murder Otto at Easter 941 in Quedlinberg. But the plan was betrayed and Henry made prisoner. At Christmas he begged pardon of Otto, to whom he then pledged fealty.

So well had Otto's position been consolidated that the West Frankish King was likewise inclined to reconciliation and, at a meeting at Visé on the Meuse in November 942, he gave up his claims to Lorraine and parts of the Kingdom of Burgundy. As an ally of King Louis IV, Otto again campaigned in France, supporting Louis in his struggle with Duke Hugh of the French; a great synod was convoked at Ingelheim in 948 to settle this dispute, but only in 950 did Hugh give up the fight against King Louis.

During this period of unrest, Otto continued to expand the northern border defenses against the Danes in Jutland and simultaneously pursued missionary work among them with the support of Margrave Hermann Billung and Abp. *Adaldag of Hamburg-*Bremen. The Dioceses of Schleswig, Ribe, and Aarhus were erected and made suffragans of Hamburg-Bremen. Adjacent to them were the three Slavic dioceses on the Elbe, Oldenburg, Havelberg, and Brandenburg, which were assigned to the Archdiocese of *Mainz.

Otto in Italy. The extension of his power and influence over West Franconia and Burgundy led Otto to devote special attention also to the confused situation in North Italy. He was here following the example of his father who had planned a march on Rome and had induced King Rudolph II in 935 to bequeath to him the *holy lance of St. Maurice, the victory-bringing talisman for pilgrimages to Rome and for the fight against the infidels. The insignium was kept at the Abbey of *Sankt Emmeram near Regensburg. In 951 Otto undertook the first Italian campaign of the German Kingdom. At this juncture an appeal for help reached him from the rightful sovereign of the Italian Kingdom, St. Adelaide, a daughter of King Rudolph II of Burgundy, who had been married in 947 to King Lothair of Italy, a son of Count Hugh of Provence. Lothair died 3 years later, in 950, and Adelaide was exposed to the pitiless attacks of Berengar II, Margrave of Ivrea, who had himself and his son elected and crowned King of the Lombards. Berengar held Adelaide in close confinement in the castle of Garda. Her supporters appealed to Otto for help. Otto was willing to intervene in the Italian disorders since Berengar showed no inclination to keep the oath of vassalage he had sworn earlier and since the domination of North Italy was the necessary preliminary to the restoration of the Empire of Charlemagne in the West. Otto had been a widower since the death of his first wife in 946 and he then proposed to Adelaide, who had meanwhile escaped from confinement and fled. The marriage, celebrated in the autumn of 951, gave the German King a legal claim to North Italy, the principal area of the Lombard Kingdom. But his attempt to achieve imperial coronation in Rome was unsuccessful, because of the resistance of the consul, Alberic, and of Pope *Agapetus II. A settlement with Berengar was reached only in 952 at the Diet of Augsburg; Berengar was forced to recognize the overlordship of Otto and to surrender the marches of Verona and Friuli, together with Istria, which was necessary for securing communications with Rome.

Civil War. After the 1st decade of his reign Otto had hoped to strengthen royal power in Germany by giving the German duchies to his nearest relatives and thus securing himself against new shocks, but it soon became evident that because of his marriage the make-up of his family was to be the cause of new unrest. His eldest son, Liudolf, Duke of Swabia, his son-in-law Conrad the Red, Duke of Lorraine, and Abp. Frederick of Mainz allied themselves to overthrow Otto. A civil war broke out, directed this time against Duke Henry of Bavaria, Otto's brother. In vain Otto laid siege to Mainz for 2 months, and the efforts of Otto's youngest brother, *Bruno, Archbishop of Cologne, were likewise fruitless. But it was of paramount importance that in 953 the King gave Bruno the Duchy of Lorraine, taken from Conrad the Red, and simultaneously transferred to him the vice-regency of the kingdom. This gifted and erudite prince of the Church, the "Archduke," succeeded in effecting a political and cultural penetration of the area west of the Rhine and its annexation to Germany. Another firm bulwark was *Ulric, Bishop of Augsburg; but the Bavarian bishops, led by Archbishop Herold of Salzburg, were enemies of the King.

The struggle took a tragic turn in 954 through the Magyar invasion; Liudolf and Conrad had not actually invited the incursion of the Hungarians into Germany, but once the invaders had entered, the two dukes formed an alliance with them. This fact cost Liudolf and Conrad much of their support, and they had to abandon the fight. Archbishop Frederick of Mainz died in 954 and was succeeded by William, Otto's illegitimate son by a Slavic noblewoman; Liudolf and Conrad the Red lost their duchies at the Diet of Arnstadt at the end of 954.

Magyar Invasion. Scarcely had this dangerous civil war ended, when the Magyars again invaded (summer, 955) and in early August besieged Augsburg, which was gallantly defended by Bishop Ulric. In eight army groups made up of Bavarians, Franks, Saxons, Swabians, and Bohemians, the German troops advanced on Lechfeld where the decisive battle was fought on St. Lawrence Day, Aug. 10, 955. The King was in the midst of his troops with the holy lance and won a brilliant victory. Conrad the Red died bravely in the battle.

The importance of the success at Lechfeld cannot be overestimated; it was the decisive victory of Christendom over paganism penetrating from the East. The Magyars were then compelled to abandon their fearful plundering raids, extending far into Western Europe, and were forced to settle down and adopt a stable political organization. Otto's prestige had risen enormously; he was now the accepted leader of the West. The same year (Oct. 16, 955), at the Recknitz River, Otto decisively defeated the rebellious Slavs of the region of the Elbe.

On the day of the Battle of Lechfeld, the King had sworn to erect a diocese in Merseburg in honor of St. Lawrence. This was the beginning of his great missionary plans, centered round the erection of the Archdiocese of Magdeburg, which took over a decade (until 968) to accomplish. In 955 construction was begun on the cathedral.

The Liudolf uprising had effected a revolution in the internal structure of the Kingdom. Otto then sought his support from the Church in Germany, from the princes of the Church, the bishoprics and royal abbeys, which, according to German proprietary church law, were under the supreme authority of the King. By granting secular authority to the prelates, Otto sought to create a counterbalance to the dukes. The court chapel, closely related to the royal chancery, assumed special importance, and from it the majority of the court clergy and bishops were created.

The Empire. The last decades of Otto's reign, apart from this transformation in Germany, were filled with problems connected with his involvement in imperial policy, and which brought him into contact even with the world of Islam. For several years, reports of the drastic decline of the papacy and of the factional struggles of the Roman nobility had been coming from Rome. Berengar, who had again shored up his position, hoped to seize the Papal State and the Lombard Duchy of Spoleto as a result of these disorders, and this drive caused Pope *John XII in 961 to appeal for aid to the German King. Otto was well aware of the great difficulties and dangers involved in a second march on Rome. He took precautions against the period of his absence, provided for the election of his 15-year-old son, *Otto II, as his successor in May 961, and for his coronation as King a few days later in Aachen. The management of the Empire was entrusted to Bruno, Archbishop of Cologne, whose loyalty and capabilities Otto had already tested.

In August 961, Otto with his wife Adelaide marched from Augsburg through the Brenner Pass to Pavia and on Feb. 2, 962, in solemn procession, entered Rome; there the royal couple were crowned and anointed. At the Coronation Synod (Feb. 12, 962), Pope and synod gave permission for the erection of the new Archdiocese of Magdeburg and for the Emperor's missionary plans in the country of the *Slavs. On the following day the Pope received the *Ottonianum,* the solemn confirmation of the Donation of Pepin, which had erected the *States of the Church in 754; Otto effected the confirmation in his own name and that of his young son. Then Otto set out for Pavia, to finish the campaign against Berengar.

The Pope's dissolute life and hostile attitude caused Otto to march on Rome once again. This time the Romans were compelled to swear never to elect a pope without the consent of Otto and his son. At a synod held in St. Peter's (Dec. 4, 963), John XII was deposed, and a papal official of irreproachable life, after receiving all clerical orders, was elevated as his successor and took the name *Leo VIII. Despite their oath, however, the Romans elected an antipope (Benedict V), whom the Emperor refused to recognize; he was handed over to Abp. Adaldag of Hamburg-Bremen to keep under surveillance.

At the beginning of 965, the Emperor returned to Germany, and at the end of May, in Cologne, he brought together his entire family at an Imperial Diet. But soon the report of new unrest in the Lombard Kingdom and in Rome forced the Emperor to return to Italy. This last 6-year stay of the Emperor in Italy was filled by his efforts to strengthen his position in North Italy by administrative measures, primarily by granting secular rights (*districtus*) to the bishops in their diocesan estates. Otto also tried to secure the Lombard principalities of Salerno, Capua, and Benevento in South Italy. In 967, his supporters assembled in a great imperial and ecclesiastical congress in Ravenna. At this synod, the Pope raised the Magdeburg church to the dignity of an archdiocese and for the moment put the Dioceses of Brandenburg and Havelberg under its jurisdiction; later Merseburg, Zeiz, Meissen, and the Polish Diocese of Posen were also subordinated to Magdeburg. The importance of the city of Ravenna for the Emperor's position on the Adriatic coast is attested by the erection of an imperial castle at Caesarea outside the gates of the city; this fortress thenceforth served the Ottos as residence, law court, and troop rendezvous.

During this period, Otto sought to achieve closer ties with the Byzantine Empire. He conceived the plan of cementing these ties by a marriage of his son Otto, who was crowned Emperor in Rome (Christmas 967), with a princess of the Byzantine imperial family. But the proposals of his emissary, Bishop *Liutprand of Cremona, met with a rude rebuff in Byzantium, and Otto's wish was fulfilled only when a change of sovereigns brought *John I Tzimisces to the throne after the murder of the Emperor, *Nicephorus Phocas, Dec. 11, 969. Otto's ambassadors returned to Rome with the Princess Theophano; she was not the bride Otto had hoped to obtain for his son, but she did possess beauty, wisdom, and diplomatic skill, and on April 14, 972, the marriage and the coronation of Theophand as Empress were celebrated.

The same year, Otto returned to Germany with his son and the two Empresses and proceeded to Quedlinburg to devote himself again to problems in the East. At Easter, March 23, 973, the Emperor held a brilliant court to which came representatives of all the peoples of the then-known world, including the Saracens, Fatimids from Africa and Sicily, Russians, Hungarians and Bulgarians, Romans and Greeks, Danes, Bohemians, and Poles. A few weeks later, the Emperor succumbed to a sudden illness in his castle in Memleben.

Bibliography: Sources. MGD 1 (1879–84) 80–638. J. F. BÖHMER, *Regesta Imperii* 2.1, ed. E. VON OTTENTHAL (new ed. Innsbruck 1893). Dahlmann-Waitz 5922ff., 5963ff., 6010–35. Wattenbach-Holtzmann 1.1–2. Literature. R. KÖPKE and E. DÜMMLER, *Kaiser Otto der Grosse* (Leipzig 1876). R. HOLTZMANN, *Geschichte der sächsischen Kaiserzeit* (4th ed. Munich 1961). H. GÜNTER, *Kaiser Otto der Grosse* (2d ed. Stuttgart 1943). G. TELLENBACH, *Die grossen Deutschen*, v.1 (Berlin 1956) 35–51. K. JORDAN, *Handbuch der deutschen Geschichte*, ed. L. JUST, v.1. (Constance 1957) 14–30, 65. F. ERNST in Gebhardt-Grundmann 1:174–191. H. NEUMANN, *Deutsche Geschichte im Überblick*, ed. P. RASSOW (2d ed. Stuttgart 1962). Hauck 3. H. ZIMMERMANN, "Papstabsetzungen des Mittelalters," MitteilIÖG 69 (1961) 241–291. H. BEUMANN and H. BÜTTNER, *Das Kaisertum Ottos des Grossen* (Munich 1962). P. E. SCHRAMM, *Kaiser, Rom und Renovatio* (2d ed. Darmstadt 1957). M. UHLIRZ, "Die italienische Kirchenpolitik der Ottonen," MitteilIÖG 48 (1934) 201–231; "Die Restitution des Exarchates Ravenna durch die Ottonen," *ibid.* 50 (1936) 1–34. W. OHNSORGE, "Die Anerkennung des Kaisertums Ottos I. durch Byzanz," ByzZ 54 (1961) 28–52; *Abendland und Byzanz* (Darmstadt 1958). H. AUBIN, *Otto der Grosse und die Erneuerung des abendländischen Kaisertums im Jahre 962* (Göttingen 1962). H. BEUMANN, "Das Kaisertum Ottos des Grossen," HistZ 195 (1962) 529–573. H. GRUNDMANN, "Betrachtungen zur Kaiserkrönung Ottos I," SBMünch 2 (1962) 1–19. *Festbericht über der Jahrtausendfeier der Kaiserkrönung Ottos des Grossen 962–1962*, MitteilIÖG 20 (Vienna 1962), suppl. **Illustration credit:** Marburg-Art Reference Bureau.

[M. UHLIRZ]

OTTO II, ROMAN EMPEROR

Reigned May 7, 973, to Dec. 7, 983; b. to *Otto I and *Adelaide, early 955; d. Rome (buried in St. Peter's). His education was entrusted to his relatives Abps. *Bruno of Cologne and William of Mainz. When scarcely 6 years old, he was elected king, before his father's march on Rome, and was crowned in Aachen May 26, 961. To further secure the succession, Otto I brought the boy to Rome and crowned him emperor (Dec. 24, 967). On that occasion he was given those areas and states that were later to occupy so much of his energy as Emperor; namely, the Lombard duchies of Spoleto and Benevento and Salerno, Capua, Naples, Gaeta, and Amalfi as well. Byzantium had maintained only a shadowy dominance in southern Italy, and by the mid-9th century the Saracens, who had conquered Sicily and founded the Dominion of the Fatimids in North Africa, appeared on the scene. Also by his father's provision, Otto was married to the Byzantine Princess Theophano in St. Peter's, Rome (April 14, 972).

Upon his father's death (May 7, 973) the court returned to Germany, and Otto began his independent rule. Although Otto had initially been influenced by his mother, Adelaide, and his cousin Henry the Wrangler of Bavaria, the Empress Theophano managed gradually to win a position of importance. But the peace of the Empire was threatened by unrest among the nobility in Lorraine, which was followed by similar turmoil in Bavaria, where Duke Henry allied himself with Boleslav II of Bohemia and Mieszko of Poland to op-

pose the Emperor. But Otto succeeded in overcoming his coalition, and Henry was imprisoned in Ingelheim (974). A campaign against the Danish King Harald Bluetooth also was successful, and the border fortress of Danewirk was taken. In the following year the Emperor campaigned against Boleslav, and in his capital the newly founded See of Prague was filled by the appointment of the Saxon *Thietmar (976).

Henry the Wrangler fled his prison in Ingelheim and again took up the fight against Otto, who besieged him in Regensburg in the summer of 976 and once more forced him to flee to Bohemia. In 977 the Bavarian Duke, in alliance with Bp. Henry of Augsburg and Duke Henry of Carinthia, yet again opposed the Emperor (War of the Three Henrys). The sharpest battles were fought around Passau, but the Emperor managed to defeat his opponents; Henry the Wrangler was condemned to prison and handed over to Bp. Folkmar of Utrecht, and Henry of Carinthia lost his duchy.

These campaigns had prevented the Emperor from intervening in the west, where King Lothair of France, reconciled with Duke Hugh of the French, marched on Lorraine (June 978) and fell upon the Emperor at Aachen. Otto and his consort were almost taken prisoner. An Imperial Diet in Dortmund resolved on the creation of a larger army, with which Otto marched on Paris to revenge the Aachen raid. But he could not take the city, and with the onset of winter he abandoned the siege and retreated. Before departing, he sang an Alleluia on Montmartre. In May 980 peace was concluded between the Emperor and Lothair in a meeting at Margut-sur-Chiers, and Lothair abandoned his claim to Lower Lorraine. A few weeks later Theophano gave birth to the long-awaited successor to the throne, Otto III.

Late in the year the imperial couple left for Rome. In Pavia the Emperor met his mother, Empress Adelaide, who had been estranged from him because of her annoyance at his anti-French policy. In the Emperor's entourage were *Adalbero of Reims, Gerbert of Aurillac (*Sylvester II), and Ohtrich, former head of the Magdeburg cathedral school. Because of his lively interest in such questions, the Emperor staged at his court in Ravenna (end of 980) the famous debate on the divisions of philosophy, reported by Richer of Saint-Remi [R. Latouche, *Histoire de France* (Paris 1937) 2:57–64]. Soon after, Gerbert was appointed to head the abbey of *Bobbio, and the imperial abbeys of *Farfa and *Nonantola were given to other supporters. Otto celebrated Easter in Rome, where Duke Hugh Capet (*see* CAPETIAN DYNASTY) had also arrived and had sworn amity with the Emperor. In Germany Abp. Adalbert of Magdeburg had died (June 20, 981), and the intelligent but unscrupulous Bp. Giseler of Merseburg succeeded in having his own See of Merseburg suppressed at the Synod in Rome (Sept. 10, 981) and himself entrusted with the Archdiocese of Magdeburg.

About this time the Emperor had decided to intervene in the difficult situation in south Italy, where the Saracens had penetrated from Sicily into Salerno and Benevento. He took Apulia, assembled the advancing German troops at Taranto, and marched against the Saracens (June 982). On July 15 at the bloody battle of Cape Colonne, south of Crotone, he was defeated and the flower of his army, destroyed.

The news of the costly defeat of the imperial army caused great shock in northern Italy and in Germany, and the German princes pressed for a consultation and the return of the Emperor. In June 983 at Verona an Imperial Diet of German and Italian princes was held; there German imperial business was dispatched with Italian princes taking part. The central point of the negotiations was the election of *Otto III as King of Germany and Italy. The incumbency of the duchies was regulated anew. The Emperor returned from Verona to Rome, but fell ill of malaria and died.

Bibliography: Sources. MGD v.2. J. F. Böhmer, *Die Regesten des Kaiserreiches unter Otto II,* ed. H. L. Mikoletzky (Regesta imperii 2.2; Graz 1950). Dahlmann-Waitz 6036–43. Wattenbach-Holtzmann 1.1–2. Literature. K. and M. Uhlirz, *Jahrbücher des Deutschen Reiches unter Otto II. und Otto III.,* v.1 (Leipzig 1902). R. Holtzmann, *Geschichte der sächsischen Kaiserzeit, 900–1024* (4th ed. Munich 1961). P. E. Schramm, *Kaiser, Rom und Renovatio* (2d ed. Darmstadt 1957). M. Hellmann, "Die Ostpolitik Kaiser Ottos II.," *Syntagma Friburgense* (Lindau 1956) 49–67.

[M. UHLIRZ]

OTTO III, ROMAN EMPEROR

Reigned, as king from 983; as Emperor, May 21, 996, to Jan. 23–24, 1002; b. the son of *Otto II and the Byzantine Princess Theophano, in Ketil Forest near Cleves, end of June 980; d. Paterno, near Rome. He was elected King of Germany and Italy at the Imperial Diet in Verona (June 983), and was crowned in Aachen on Christmas Day by Abps. *Willigis of Mainz and *John of Ravenna. During the celebration, the assembly was notified of the death of Otto II. At once an uprising broke out in Germany. Henry the Wrangler escaped from his confinement in Utrecht, and seized the imperial insignia and the royal child, who was in the custody of Abp. Warin of Cologne. Henry then attempted to assemble his supporters for an invasion of Lorraine. As cousin of the deceased Emperor, he had the right of wardship over Otto, but it soon became evident that he was aiming at the throne. At the outset, no one offered serious resistance. But by early 984 an alliance was formed against Henry; it was led by Abp. Willigis of Mainz and joined by the South German princes and the prelates of Lorraine. Henry's hopes were dashed both in Saxony, where he lost the fortress of Ala with valuable treasures, and in Bavaria. At an assembly in Bürstadt near Worms (mid-May 984) Henry had to promise to hand over the young King, who was still in his power, to the Empress Theophano at a meeting in Rara (Rohr near Meiningen) on June 29.

The Regency. The two Empresses (St. Adelaide, widow of Otto III's grandfather, and Theophano), who had been staying at the castle in Pavia, were then invited by Archbishop Willigis to come to Germany. They appeared at Rara with a large entourage that included King Conrad of Burgundy and many princes of Germany and Italy. Henry fulfilled his promise on June 29 and brought the 4-year–old King, who was restored to his mother. The decision on the juridical form of Theophano's rule may have been taken in the autumn of 984, when the head of the chancery, Willigis of Mainz, and the chancellor, Hildibald of Worms, assumed their duties; these were the bulwark of Theophano's regency. Only at the end of June 985 was a complete reconciliation effected with Henry the Wrangler, who was again given the Dukedom of Bavaria at the diet in Frankfurt; Henry did homage to the royal child and swore fealty. This oath he kept until his death in 995.

In the period of struggle for the throne there had been violent clashes also in Lorraine, in which King Lothair of France was deeply involved. Twice he succeeded in taking Verdun (May-June 984 and January 985), but had to retreat before the solid opposition of Otto's supporters, who were on intimate terms with Archbishop Willigis and the Saxon nobility. The brunt of these campaigns was borne by Godfrey, Count of Verdun, by Duchess Beatrice of Upper Lorraine with her son Duke Theodoric, by Bishops *Notker of Liège and *Gerard of Toul, and especially by Abp. *Adalbero of Reims and Gerbert of Aurillac (*Sylvester II), who had left his Abbey of *Bobbio and had been sent by Theophano on a political mission to Reims. The extant letters of Gerbert dating from this period are priceless but somewhat enigmatic sources of information.

When the struggle for the throne was over, Empress Adelaide returned to Italy, while Theophano began a tour of the Empire with the young King; Henry the Wrangler joined the party as a palpable sign of his submission. This tour ended in Bamberg, where the two Henrys (of Bavaria and of Carinthia) were installed in their ducal office (*Modus de Heinrico*). Easter 986 was celebrated in Quedlinburg with a solemn coronation of Otto, which the German princes and Boleslav of Bohemia and Mieszko of Poland attended.

The death of King Lothair of France (March 2, 986) caused the situation in Lorraine to deteriorate. The Dowager Queen Emma, a daughter of Adelaide by her first marriage, initially ruled as regent for Lothair's successor, Louis V; but Adelaide soon had to beg Theophano for help in Emma's name. Theophano proceeded to Cologne and declared herself willing to arbitrate a peaceful settlement. Again Gerbert proved himself a skillful mediator. Louis's attack was directed primarily against Adalbero of Reims, whose brother, Godfrey of Verdun, was still in French captivity. Reims was besieged and the archbishop was at the point of being forced to justify himself before a court in Compiègne, when the unexpected death of Louis V changed the political situation. The heir of the Carolingian house was then Charles, Duke of Lower Lorraine, who with his sons then took up the struggle against Hugh Capet (*see* CAPETIANS), but Charles was subdued by his powerful foe. On June 1, 986, Hugh Capet was proclaimed King, and he was crowned by Archbishop Adalbero in Reims (July 3). Theophano had remained in the West during the period of unrest and had assembled a formidable army. Hugh declared himself ready for peace and fulfilled the first condition, evacuation of Verdun.

By this time Otto had begun his thorough education, principally under the direction of *Bernward of Hildesheim. The boy grew up in a circle of happy youngsters, mainly of Saxon and Lorraine lineage; he owed his excellent education to the solicitude of his highly cultured mother, who, after undertaking one last journey to Rome in 990, died suddenly June 15, 991. The Empress Adelaide then assumed the regency and continued in that office until the young King was recognized as capable of bearing arms by the Imperial Diet in Sohlingen, September 994. Otto's first important governmental act was to summon Abbot Heribert of

Otto III enthroned between two clerics and two warriors, illumination in a late 10th-century Gospel Book from Reichenau preserved in the Bavarian State Library, Munich (Clm. 4453, fol. 24r). The figure of the Emperor is an idealized rather than an actual portrait.

Brogne as chancellor for Italy. Heribert had been trained in the spirit of the reform ideas emanating from *Gorze. He was close to Otto as his chaplain and presumably also as his teacher, and henceforth was Otto's influential adviser in all political matters.

Imperial Coronation and Reign. Preparations were begun early in 996 for Otto's first journey to Rome. The *holy lance was fetched from the abbey of *Sankt Emmeram in Regensburg, where Abbot Ramwald was able to fill his young sovereign with enthusiasm for this imminent adventure. The expedition crossed the Brenner, where it was met by the ambassadors of Doge *Peter Orseolo of Venice. A quarrel with the bishops of Treviso and Belluno was settled in favor of Venice and the son of the Doge was sent to Verona where he received the Sacrament of Confirmation with the King standing patron. This cemented a bond of spiritual kinship between Otto and the Doge. In Pavia, the magnates of Italy did homage to the King and renewed their oath of fealty. On the road to Ravenna, the train of the King was met by ambassadors from Rome where Pope *John XV had died; they begged Otto to name a successor. Otto selected a member of his chapel, his

kinsman Bruno of Carinthia, who was elevated to the papal throne as *Gregory V and who crowned Otto emperor, May 21 in Rome. A great Coronation Synod was held (May 24–26), at which many German prelates gained privileges for their sees and the affairs of the dioceses of Reims and Prague were discussed. Bishop *Adalbert of Prague had relinquished his see and retired to a monastery. On this occasion, Otto came into intimate contact with Gerbert and Bishop Adalbert, whose profound piety captured his imagination. Both men exerted great influence on Otto's political plans, and Adalbert confirmed his enthusiasm for missionary activity on the Eastern frontier.

It was probably Adalbert who in Cologne (Christmas 996) baptized Waik, the son of the Hungarian prince Geisa; Waik was given the baptismal name of *Stephen (of Hungary) and commissioned to Christianize the Magyars. The next year, Adalbert went to Poland to convert the pagan Prussians, and suffered a martyr's death in the vicinity of Danzig. The news of the loss of this friend was a profound shock to Otto, and to honor his memory he built several churches and assisted in the composition of commemorative verse.

In Germany, under the young Emperor's command, there were almost annual clashes with the Lusatians in the region of the Elbe. In Rome, meanwhile, fresh disorders had broken out: the hostile nobility of the city, led by the *Crescentii, had seized power, driven Gregory V out of the city, and installed an antipope, John Philagathos (John XVI), Otto's former teacher. The Emperor assembled a large army in 998, stormed the *Castel Sant' Angelo, and captured Crescentius and his antipope. Although *Nilus of Rossano came to Rome and begged for clemency, a frightful sentence was pronounced and executed upon the two rebels.

At Gregory's death the next year, the Emperor installed Gerbert of Aurillac, then archbishop of Ravenna, as Sylvester II. Supported by his chancellor Heribert, now archbishop of Cologne, and by Bp. *Leo of Vercelli, Otto attempted to harness German missionary zeal to promote the *Renovatio imperii Romanorum,* a renewal of the Roman Empire in a Christian sense. Emperor and Pope were to rule jointly this new Christian world empire to which Otto hoped to annex Poland and the Slavic peoples, even those beyond the Adriatic, together with Venice and Hungary. As the *Servus Christi,* he succeeded in convincing the Duke of Poland to Christianize his people; this success was scored during Otto's visit to Adalbert's grave in Gnesen in 1000. He also had considerable success in Hungary, where Stephan was crowned, probably in August 1001, and permitted to organize the Church. By these moves, Otto inhibited the influence of the *Byzantine Empire in both countries. The attitude of Venice remained uncertain, despite the Emperor's treaty with Orseolo and his secret visit to the Doge (Pentecost 1001). A new Roman uprising was a severe blow to the Emperor, forcing him in February 1001 to retreat to Ravenna. While awaiting the arrival of German troops in the fortress of Paterno, north of Rome, Otto succumbed to malaria. At his request, his body was carried to Aachen and interred at the side of Charlemagne.

Bibliography: J. E. BÖHMER, *Regesta imperii* 2.3, ed. M. UHLIRZ (new ed. Graz-Cologne 1956). Dahlmann-Waitz 6044–61. Wattenbach-Holtzmann 1.1–2. Hauck v.3. R. HOLTZMANN, *Geschichte der sächsischen Kaiserzeit (900–1024)* (4th ed. Munich 1961). P. E. SCHRAMM, *Kaiser, Rom und Renovatio* (2d ed. Darmstadt 1957). F. DÖLGER, "Die Ottonenkaiser und Byzanz," *Festschrift Dölger* (Ettal 1961). W. OHNSORGE, *Abendland und Byzanz* (Darmstadt 1958). K. and M. UHLIRZ, *Jahrbücher des Deutschen Reiches unter Otto II. und Otto III.,* v.2 (Berlin 1954). H. ZIMMERMANN, "Papstabsetzungen des Mittelalters" MitteilIÖG 69 (1961) 270– . M. UHLIRZ, "Die italienische Kirchenpolitik der Ottonen," *ibid.* 48 (1934) 201–321; "Die Restitution des Exarchates Ravenna durch die Ottonen," *ibid.* 50 (1936) 1–34; "Studien über Theophano," DeutschArch 6 (1943); 9 (1951) 122–135; 13 (1957) 369–393; "Die staatsrechtliche Stellung Venedigs zur Zeit Kaiser Ottos III.," ZSavRGGerm 76 (1959) 82–110; "Der Adriaraum in der Südostpolitik der ottonischen Kaiser," *Südost-Forschungen* 22 (1963) 118–125; "Venezia nella politica di Ottone III.," *Venezia del mille* (Florence 1931–43) 31–43. Gebhart-Grundmann 1:196–209. **Illustration credit:** Hirmer Verlag München.

[M. UHLIRZ]

OTTO IV, HOLY ROMAN EMPEROR, opponent of Philip of Swabia in the civil war for the disputed German imperial title; b. Germany, probably 1175 or 1176 (or Argentan, Normandy, 1182); d. Castle Harzburg, Germany, May 19, 1218. The son of *Henry the Lion and Matilda, daughter of *Henry II of England, Otto was reared chiefly at the English court in England itself, in Normandy, or in Aquitaine. In 1196 he was

Otto IV, Holy Roman Emperor, obverse of the gold seal on his diploma issued at Speyer on March 22, 1209, recognizing the papal "recuperationes."

enfeoffed with the county of Poitou by his uncle, King *Richard I, who hoped to secure for his nephew the imperial throne as an instrument of diplomacy against his rival, the French King *Philip II. Supported by the English crown, Otto was elected on June 9 and crowned king of the Germans at Aachen on July 12, 1198, by Archbishop Adolph of Cologne. He opposed the Hohenstaufen Philip, who had been crowned at Mainz the previous March. After the death of Emperor *Henry VI (Sept. 28, 1197), Pope *Innocent III at first remained neutral in the contest for the German throne; but in 1201, after judging the pleas of the electors from both parties, he recognized Otto, who in the Convention of Neuss (June 8, 1201), surrendered the German imperial position south of the Alps and accepted the claims of the Pope to the states of central Italy. Philip's cause continued to advance, however, and by 1207 Innocent was prepared to abandon Otto in his favor. But Philip's murder (June 21, 1208) cleared the way for his rival, who was then generally accepted by the German princes in a new election, Nov. 11, 1208. If he had been serious about his previous promises to the Pope, Otto now began to hedge his commitment, but from Speyer (March 22, 1209) issued a diploma recognizing the papal *recuperationes* and on Oct. 4, 1209, was crowned emperor by Innocent in St. Peter's in Rome. Fresh from his coronation, Otto suddenly attacked southern Italy and Sicily, the papal fiefs of *Frederick II; after a warning Innocent excommunicated the Emperor on Nov. 18, 1210. Promoted by the Pope, young Frederick was elected emperor at Nuremberg in September 1211, and with his appearance in Germany in the spring of 1212, Otto's support evaporated. His old alliance with England was his final undoing, for at the French victory over King *John and his allies at the Battle of Bouvines (July 27, 1214) Otto's cause was lost, and he died a deserted man.

Bibliography: G. BARRACLOUGH, *The Origins of Modern Germany* (2d ed. Oxford 1957), *passim.* INNOCENT III, *Regestum* *super negotio Romani imperii,* ed. F. KEMPF (Miscellanea historiae pontificiae 12; Rome 1947). F. KEMPF, *Papsttum und Kaisertum bei Innocenz III* (Rome 1954). A. L. POOLE, CMedH 6:44–79. Gebhardt-Grundmann 1:341–356. **Illustration credit:** Archivio Segreto Vaticano.

[O. J. BLUM]

OTTO OF BAMBERG, ST.,

bishop, Apostle of Pomerania; b. 1060–62; d. Bamberg, June 30, 1139 (feast in the Diocese of Bamberg, Sept. 30; in Pomerania, Oct 1; in *Martyrologium Romanum,* July 2). Born of a noble family in Swabia, Otto received a thorough education. In 1088 he was appointed chaplain to the court of Duchess Judith of Poland, the sister of Emperor *Henry IV. He was sent on diplomatic missions to the court of the Emperor and was given the task of supervising the construction of the cathedral of *Speyer. Early in 1102 he was made chancellor of Henry IV, and on Dec. 25, 1102, was appointed bishop of *Bamberg. Because of controversies between Henry IV, *Henry V, and the metropolitans of Mainz, Otto was not consecrated bishop until May 13, 1106, at Anagni by Pope *Paschal II. He prudently avoided taking sides in the continuing political and ecclesiastical conflicts in the Empire and tried to act as mediator between the groups. When Henry V went to Rome to be crowned emperor in 1110–11, Otto accompanied him and received the *pallium on April 15, 1111, probably because of his success as a mediator. He also took an essential part in preparing the Concordat of Worms (1122). *See* WORMS, CONCORDAT OF. For many years he directed a great number of activities in his diocese: he rebuilt the cathedral, which had been destroyed by fire; he improved the cathedral school, founded new parishes, and built many churches and hospitals. In a well-balanced policy he fortified the territory of the Diocese of Bamberg (by building castles) and enlarged it through new acquisitions. He especially favored monasticism, founding or renovating about 30 monasteries and giving them to Benedictines of the *Hirsau Congregation, to *Premonstratensians, and to *Cistercians.

He limited the power of the district rulers. Otto's two missions to Pomerania (1124–25 and 1128), where he established and organized the Church, won for him the title of Apostle of the Pomeranians. He is buried in the abbey of Michelsberg near Bamberg. Canonized in 1189 by Pope *Clement III, he is venerated especially in the territory and monasteries of the Diocese of Bamberg.

Bibliography: E. VON GUTTENBERG, ed., *Das Bistum Bamberg,* v. 1.1 of *Die Bistümer der Kirchenprovinz Mainz* (Germania Sacra 2; Berlin 1937) 115–138. J. BRAUN, *Tracht und Attribute der Heiligen in der deutschen Kunst* (Stuttgart 1943). J. KIST, *Fürst- und Erzbistum Bamberg* (Bamberg 1962). H. CHRIST in *900 Jahre Speyerer Dom* (Speyer 1961) 110–122. J. PETERSOHN, *Baltische Studien* NF 49 (1962–63) 19–38. D. ANDERNACHT, *Die Biographien Ottos von Bamberg* (Unpub. diss., Frankfurt a. M. 1950. F. J. SCHMALE, LexThK² 7:1302–03. W. DZIEWULSKI, "Stasunek Ottona Bamberskiego . . .," in *Zapiski historyczne* 23 (Toruń) 119–140. **Illustration credit:** Allgemeines Staatsarchiv München.

[F. DRESSLER]

OTTO OF CAPPENBERG, BL.,

Premonstratensian; d. Feb. 23, 1171. The sons of Godfrey, Count of Cappenberg, and of Beatrice, Otto and his brother Bl. Godfrey of Cappenberg (feast, Jan. 13), a devout layman, gave their ancestral lands to *Norbert of Xanten for the foundation of the first abbey of *Premonstratensian canons in Germany in 1122. Otto entered the community and served as the fourth prior of Cappenberg Abbey from 1156 to his death. Godfrey died (1127) at Ilbenstadt Abbey, which he had founded, and Otto had some of his relics brought back to Cappenberg.

Bibliography: Life of Godfrey, MGS 12:513–530. M. ERENS, DHGE 11:917–927. Backmund MonPraem 1:101, 158. S. SCHNEIDER, *Cappenberg* (Münster 1949). H. GRUNDMANN, *Der Cappenberger Barbarossakopf . . . Stiftes Cappenberg* (Cologne 1959).

[C. DAVIS]

OTTO OF FREISING

Bishop, historian; b. Neuburg? near Vienna *c.* 1111–12; d. Morimond, Sept. 22, 1158. Otto, the son of Margrave *Leopold III of Austria and Agnes, daughter of Emperor *Henry IV, studied at Paris, perhaps under Abelard, Gilbert de la Porrée, and Hugh of St. Victor. He entered the Cistercians at the Abbey of *Morimond, was elected abbot (1137), and shortly after, was made bishop of the Bavarian See of Freising. Under his stepbrother, Emperor *Conrad III, he joined the Second Crusade as a military commander. Otto served as political adviser and diplomat at the German court under Conrad and his successor, the Emperor Frederick I Barbarossa.

Otto's great interest in the intellectual pursuits of his time led him to be the first to acquaint his countrymen with the New Logic of Aristotle. His main historical work, the *Historia de duabus civitatibus,* a world chronicle in eight books, is the most noteworthy attempt at a philosophical interpretation of world history in the Middle Ages. Unlike earlier and contemporary world chroniclers Otto selected his facts in accordance with certain leading ideas that he discussed at length in the prefaces. He was influenced especially by St. Augustine's *City of God* and fully endorsed the saint's concept of the *Civitas Dei* as the community of all saints living and dead (*see* HISTORY, THEOLOGY OF). Otto began his ac-

Seal of St. Otto of Bamberg, obverse, 12th century.

Otto of Freising, stained glass window, probably 12th century, in the abbey of Heiligenkreuz near Vienna.

count with man. Like Augustine, he saw one city deriving from Cain, the other from Abel. Unlike Augustine, Otto did not tend to identify completely the pagan empires or *regna* with the City of Satan, but rather saw them as a sphere where his "two cities" met and intermingled. Otto believed that by God's providence the Roman Empire was selected to be the world organization that would prepare mankind for the coming of the City of God. At first, this task fell on the Church of the early Christians. But under Constantine and still more completely under Charlemagne, Emperor and Pope, those "two persons in the Church," each acting as a vicar of Christ in his own sphere, achieved that unity and peace on earth that paved the way to the City of God in a transcendental future. Insight into the ever deepening conflict between *regnum* and *sacerdotium* that marked the history of the West after the collapse of the Carolingian Empire (*see* CAROLINGIAN DYNASTY) —a conflict in which Otto hesitated to take sides— tinged his account with a deep pessimism. This was especially apparent in the seventh book, which described contemporary events. To Otto history had become the story of human misery. As his hope for the realization of the City of God on earth faded, he turned, in the last chapters of the seventh book, to the Cistercians, which in turn led to the description of the eschatological events that would herald the appearance

of the Heavenly Jerusalem after history, *post praesentem vitam* (book 8). Otto finished his chronicle in 1146, in the midst of the confusions and wars of the reign of Conrad III.

When Otto's nephew, Frederick Barbarossa, ascended the German throne (1152) a new era of peace and good government seemed to augur well for a renewal of the empire. Otto began another historical work, the *Gesta Friderici imperatoris* or *Deeds of Frederick Barbarossa*, in a more optimistic vein. Otto died after finishing only the two first books. His clerk, *Rahewin of Freising, continued the work.

Bibliography: Editions. *Ottonis episcopi Frisingensis chronica sive historia de duabus civitatibus*, ed. A. HOFMEISTER, MGSrer Germ; *Ottonis et Rahewini gesta Friderici imperatoris*, ed. G. WAITZ, MGSrerGerm; *The Two Cities*, tr. C. C. MIEROW (New York 1928); *The Deeds of Frederick Barbarossa*, tr. C. C. MIEROW (New York 1953). Literature. Wattenbach 2:271–279. J. HASHAGEN, *Otto von Freising als Geschichtsphilosoph und Kirchenpolitiker* (Leipzig 1900). Hauck 4:476–485. A. HOFMEISTER, "Studien über Otto von Freising," NeuesArch "37 (1912) 99–161, 633–768. Manitius 3:376–388. F. FELLNER, "The Two Cities of Otto of Freising," CathHistRev 20 (1934–35) 154–174. J. SPÖRL, LexThK² 7:1307–09; *Grundformen hochmittelalterlicher Geschichtsanschauung* (Munich 1935) 31–50. P. BREZZI, "Ottone di Frisinga," *Bullettino dell'Istituto storico Italiano* 54 (1939) 129–328. *Otto von Freising: Gedenkgabe zu seinem 800. Todesjahr,* ed. J. A. FISCHER (Freising 1958).

[H. WIERUSZOWSKI]

OTTO, RUDOLF, Protestant theologian and scholar; b. Peine, Germany, Sept. 25, 1869; d. Marburg an der Lahn, March 6, 1937. He was a professor at Göttingen (1897–1914), at Breslau (1914–1917), and at Marburg (1917–1929). Otto was influenced especially by Kant, J. F. Fries, (1773–1843), and F. D. E. *Schleiermacher, and became prominent as a philosopher of religion. As opposed to Neo-Kantian ideas, he developed his concept of "the Holy," as a religious a priori, in his own independent attitude toward the good, the true, the beautiful. His book, *Das Heilige* (The Holy) appeared (Breslau 1917) at the so-called "turning point in the philosophy of religion" in Germany that is associated especially with the name of M. *Scheler (1874–1928). The latter was one of the first to recognize the importance of Otto's work. In his analysis, which now has a permanent place in the science of religion, Otto defined the Holy as "the Numinous," which expresses itself in feeling or consciousness as the "contrasting harmony" of the *fascinans* (the attracting element) and the *tremendum* (the awe-inspiring element). On the epistemological side, however, he was not able ultimately to win conviction for his position.

His chief works are *Das Heilige* (Breslau 1917; 35th ed. Munich 1963); English translation, *The Idea of the Holy,* tr. J. W. Harvey (New York 1958); *Aufsätze, das Numinose betreffend* (Stuttgart 1923; 4th ed. 1929); *West-Oestliche Mystik* (Gotha 1926); *Die Gnadenreligion Indiens und das Christentum* (Gotha 1930); and *Das Gefühl des Ueberweltlichen* (Munich 1932).

See also SACRED AND PROFANE.

Bibliography: G. WÜNSCH, RGG³ 4:1749–50 with bibliog. J. HESSEN, *Religionsphilosophie,* 2 v. (2d ed. Munich 1955) 1:269–297. R. F. DAVIDSON, *Rudolf Otto's Interpretation of Religion* (Princeton 1947). F. K. FEIGEL, *Das Heilige: Kritische Abhandlung über Rudolf Ottos gleichnamiges Buch* (2d ed. Tübingen 1948).

[A. HOLL]

General view of the Benedictine Abbey of Ottobeuren, in Allgäu, near Memmingen.

OTTOBEUREN, ABBEY OF, Benedictine monastery in the Diocese of *Augsburg, Germany. Founded perhaps in 764, it became important under Abbot *Rupert I (1102–45), who introduced the *Hirsau *Consuetudines,* reformed Irsee and *Ellwangen, founded *Marienberg and one of the abbey's convents, completed the building of Ottobeuren's abbey and church, and instituted a scriptorium that flourished under his successor Isingrim. After a gradual decline until 1477, the abbey revived with reform from *Melk. Prior N. *Ellenbog (d. 1543) roused an interest in scholarship, and Abbot L. Wiedemann (1508–46) instituted a printing press in 1509. In 1617 Ottobeuren furnished almost the whole staff of professors (six priests) for the new University of *Salzburg. Priests from Ottobeuren later taught in Rottweil, Freising, and Fulda, and in the abbey's own school. Abbot Rupert II Ness (1710–40) completely rebuilt the church and cloister in a masterpiece of south German baroque. Of the 19 out of 45 priests who maintained the monastic life after the secularization of 1802, only one lived to see the restoration in 1834. Ottobeuren then remained a priory under St. Stephen in Augsburg until it again became an independent abbey (July 2, 1918). The Bavarian Concordat of 1817 gave permission for educational and pastoral work to the house; the abbey, which cares for the parish of Ottobeuren, has maintained a boys' boarding school since 1855, an agricultural school (1920–36), and a Gymnasium for liberal arts (1922–38 and since 1946). After 1,200 years of uninterrupted Benedictine tradition, Ottobeuren in 1964 had 19 priests, 3 clerics, and 20 lay brothers.

Bibliography: *Ottobeuren: Festschrift zur 120-Jahrfeier der Abtei* (Augsburg 1964). *Ottobeuren 764–1964: Beiträge zur Geschichte der Abtei* (Augsburg 1964), special issue of *Studien und Mitteilungen zur Geschichte des Benediktinerordens und seiner Zweige,* v.73 (1962). B. Kuen, LexThK² 7:1310–11. **Illustration credit:** German Information Center, New York City.

[B. KUEN]

OTTOMAN TURKS

A militant dynasty of Anatolian Turks who created an Islamic state in the Balkans, the Near East, and North Africa, threatening western Europe and assuming leadership of the Moslem world. This empire, which arose in the later Middle Ages, survived until modern times, when it disintegrated into nation states.

Rise to Power. The Ottoman state, founded in Bithynia *c.* 1299, was one of many petty principalities that sprang up in the ruin of the Seljuk Sultanate of Konya after that state was forced to become a vassal of the Mongol Il-Khans (*see* SELJUKS). Weakened by the Turcoman invasions of Asia Minor and by the Fourth Crusade (1202–04), the Byzantine Empire could not prevent the Islamic expansion westward. The Ottoman state was created by warriors, who refused to become peaceful citizens, on the Byzantine-Islamic frontier. Its location and the vigor of its ruling family helped the principality to grow rapidly at Byzantine expense, and by 1353 it had reached the European side of the Hellespont. In 1389 the power of Serbia was broken at the battle of Kosovo, and in 1396 Western Europe's attempt to meet the swiftly growing threat failed with the ill-fated Crusade of Nicopolis. The fortress city of Constantinople on the Bosphorus became a free enclave in the Ottoman state. At the same time, by marriage and political pressure, the Anatolian Turkish principalities were being absorbed. Reasons for this astonishing expansion must be sought in the comparative weakness of the Balkan Byzantine successor-states, the military and political efficiency of the Ottomans, and the post-Crusade hostility of the Greeks and Slavs to the Franks and the Latin Church. Given a choice of domination by Western Europe or the *sultan, popular sentiment favored the sultan.

Ottoman Sultan Mohammed II, portrait by Gentile Bellini, 1479, now in the Layard Collection at Venice. Bellini had gone to Constantinople upon the recommendation of the Signory of Venice, who had friendly contact with the Sultan.

Ottoman civilization, which arose on the frontier between Byzantine civilization and the Persian-Islamic Seljuk culture, borrowed freely from both in its formative stage and took its final form only around the beginning of the 16th century A.D. The defeat of Sultan Bayazid by *Timur (Tamerlane) in 1402 was only a temporary setback to Ottoman expansion. In 1453 Constantinople was taken after a heroic defense, to become the Ottoman capital.

Subject Peoples. While the ruling class were Moslems, Eastern Orthodox Christians were governed through their bishops and clergy subject to the patriarch of Constantinople, appointed by the sultan. The Greek clergy thus had far more real power than they had had in the Byzantine period, particularly over the Slavs in Ottoman territory. Jews and Armenians also were governed as separate communities through their own clergy, and this arrangement (see DHIMMI) seems to have been highly acceptable to the subject peoples until the 18th and 19th centuries, when internal Ottoman decline brought oppressive fiscality and interference.

Religious practice at the folk level in Anatolia and the Balkans, among Christians and Moslems, was strikingly similar, and equally distant from either orthodox Christianity or orthodox Islam; this situation together with the tax benefits of conversion explains why many subjects became Moslems despite the absence of forced conversion.

The talents of the subject peoples were channeled into the ruling class by the peculiar system of *devshirme.* Promising Balkan Christian boys were taken in levies, nominally converted to Islam, and educated as the sultan's private property. The ablest of them could rise to the highest offices of the state, frequently benefiting their Christian relatives, and forming an elite dependent on neither birth nor wealth. The rest were enrolled in the Janissaries, the sultan's private army. The Moslems opposed their own exclusion from the fruits of power, hence the *devshirme* was discontinued c. 1700.

Consolidation and Decline. State theory depended on an absolute autocracy, hereditary in the male Ottoman line, and the first 10 sultans were long-lived, able soldier-statesmen. The last of these, Süleyman I, "The Magnificent," (1520–66) took Hungary, invaded Austria, and besieged imperial Vienna. Since each Ottoman prince was a candidate for the throne, state security demanded that the successful candidate put his brothers to death. In theory the sultan was subject to the Law of Islam, but since he controlled the conditions by which it was interpreted he was bound only insofar as he chose.

With the rise of the dynasty of the *Safavids in Western Iran in 1502, its theocratic Islamic heresy, preached by the Safavi brotherhood (*Shiites) had a deep appeal for the Turcomans of Anatolia. Largely in self-defense, the Ottomans became officially, militantly, *Sunnites. This was intensified after 1517, when the kingdom of the *Mamelukes in Syria and Egypt was annexed. Soon North Africa, except for Morocco, came under Ottoman rule. Without continuing the shadowy *'Abbāsid caliphate of Cairo, the sultans could truly claim to be the leaders of Sunnite Islam. Western Christendom, torn by wars and heresies, was kept from being overrun only by the fact that the Ottomans were also at war with Persia.

The internal decline of the Ottomans coincided with the growth and transformation of Europe; but, blinded largely by its own early military success, the still medieval Ottoman state found no reason to transform itself as Europe was doing. With a more formidable West in the 17th century and several defeats from Western armies, together with an aggressively expanding Russia entertaining Balkan ambitions in the 18th, xenophobia and anti-Christian fanaticism grew in Ottoman society, estranging the subject peoples. The sultans sought alliances with Europe against Russia, but had to pay a heavy price in concessions and capitulations, chiefly to England and France. Whereas it had been once the terror and fascination of Europe, the empire became the "sick man" of Europe.

The spread of nationalist ideologies among the Balkan peoples in the 19th century, abetted by foreign powers, led to continual losses of territory; in World War I even the predominantly Moslem Arabs rebelled. Tardy and inconclusive efforts at internal modernization from 1839 to 1922 led to no lasting gains. Finally, in a rejection of the whole imperial system, a revolt headed by Kamal Ataturk in 1922 put an end to the Ottoman state and set up a national Turkish republic in Anatolia.

See also TURKEY.

Bibliography: P. WITTEK, *The Rise of the Ottoman Empire* (London 1938). G. J. S.-L. EVERSLEY and V. CHIROL, *The Turkish Empire (1288–1922)* (London 1923). H. A. R. GIBB and H. BOWEN, *Islamic Society and the West* (New York 1950). B. LEWIS, *The Emergence of Modern Turkey* (London 1961). J. H. KRAMERS et al., EncIslam[1] 3:965–1024. **Illustration credit:** Alinari-Art Reference Bureau.

[J. A. WILLIAMS]

OTTONIAN ART

German art may be said to have had its beginning in the 10th century under the rule of the Ottos. It was then that German influence extended into Italy as far as Rome and, mindful of his great predecessor *Charlemagne, *Otto I had himself crowned at Rome in 962. In 972 his son *Otto II married Theophano, a Byzantine princess, thus establishing contacts with the more sumptuous East. Their son, *Otto III, died in 1002 at only 23 years of age, and during some 8 years of his reign his mother had served as regent. Otto III was well educated, since he came under the influence of the best Latin scholars in Italy, of *Bernward of Hildesheim, and of Gerbert of Aurillac, who later became Pope *Sylvester II. The cultural emphasis of the Ottonian era found expression in the monasteries and towns of Germany and persisted into the third quarter of the 11th century.

The island of *Reichenau in the Lake of Constance, a halting place for the emperors on their journeys to Rome, became a prominent center for the new style. The church of Saint George at Oberzell on the island was decorated with mural paintings that derive from early Christian examples in Rome. They were probably executed under the abbacy of Witigowo (985–997), for he is known to have lavished huge sums on the adornment of the monastery. From the scriptorium at Reichenau went books and artists to other centers, *Trier, *Regensburg, *Fulda, *Echternach, and Bamberg. Of these, the Codex Egberti of 980, now at Trier, is outstanding. Here one is aware of the source in classical models, but the illustrations of New Testament scenes done with haunting pathos and powerful gestures are highly original. Three years later Egbert commis-

(a)

(b)

(c)

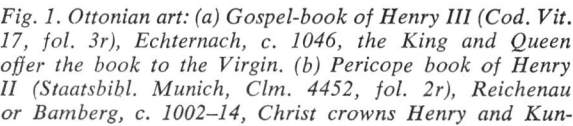

(d)

Fig. 1. Ottonian art: (a) Gospel-book of Henry III (Cod. Vit. 17, fol. 3r), Echternach, c. 1046, the King and Queen offer the book to the Virgin. (b) Pericope book of Henry II (Staatsbibl. Munich, Clm. 4452, fol. 2r), Reichenau or Bamberg, c. 1002–14, Christ crowns Henry and Kunigunde. (c) Gospel-book of Otto III (Staatsbibl. Munich, Clm. 4453, fol. 139v), Reichenau, c. 1000, the Evangelist Luke. (d) Gospel-book of the Abbess Uota of Niedermünster (Staatsbibl. Munich, Clm. 13601, fol. 2r), Regensburg, c. 1002–25; the abbess kneels before the Virgin and Child.

Fig. 2. "The Doubting of Thomas," ivory panel by the "Master of Echternach," late 10th century.

sioned for Trier Cathedral the Registrum Gregorii. One leaf of this Registrum preserved at Chantilly represents Otto II, regally enthroned, surrounded by personifications of the provinces, Germania, Francia, Italia, Alemania. The most sumptuous manuscript of the Reichenau school is the Gospels of Otto III, now at the Staatsbibliothek in Munich. Here on a double page the provinces Slavinia, Germania, Gallia, and Roma bear gifts to the Emperor. The evangelist portraits

are magnificent. The style reached maturity in several books now in Munich, executed for Henry II and given by him to the cathedral at Bamberg.

Probably the Codex Aureus of the Landesbibliothek, Gotha, was written at Echternach just before 991, for it shows Otto III and Theophano on the cover with patrons of Echternach. A decorated full page imitating Sassanid-Byzantine textiles bespeaks fresh Byzantine influence. The finest manuscript written at Echternach is the Gospels from Speyer, now preserved in the *Escorial. On one page Henry III and Agnes kneel before the Virgin surmounted by a rendering of the cathedral of Speyer, which had been built by a grant from Conrad II. Henry no doubt offered the manuscript as a memorial to his parents between 1043 and 1046.

By far the most complex manuscript of the period is the Munich Evangeliary written for the Abbess Uota of Niedermünster (1002–25). The Virgin wears a jeweled crown suggesting the Madonna of Essen. The Crucifixion page shows the Church and Synagogue and legends that contain a cosmic symbolism.

In the more tangible forms of art the Ottonian period was equally creative. Especially fine as sculpture is the gold antependium from Basel, now in the Cluny Museum in Paris. Its source is not known, but it was presented to the cathedral at Basel by Henry II (1002–24) and his wife, Kunigunda. Even in the 10th century the German tendency towards a greater expressiveness is apparent in the ivories done by the Master of Echternach.

To Bp. Bernward of Hildesheim (993–1022) we owe the achievement of the great doors now in the cathedral. The Old Testament scenes were probably inspired from some earlier illustrated Bible, but they take on an expressiveness in the high relief and forceful drawing that is indigenous to the German spirit. Another forceful bronze is the Crucifix of Werden. It is about two-thirds life size and must date around 1065. Brutal realism tempered by religious zeal, characteristic of the first flowering of German art, has here run its course.

See also ROMANESQUE ART; CHURCH ARCHITECTURE, 4. ROMANESQUE.

Bibliography: M. BURG, *Ottonische Plastik* (Leipzig 1922). S. BEISSEL, *Der heilige Bernward von Hildesheim als Künstler und Förderer der deutschen Kunst* (Hildesheim 1895). A. BOECKLER, "Die Reichenauer Buchmalerei," *Die Kultur der Abtei Reichenau,* 2 v. (Munich 1925) 2:956–998; *Das Goldene Evangelienbuch Heinrichs III.* (Berlin 1933). E. W. BRAUN, "Beiträge zur Geschichte der Trierer Buchmalerei im frühen Mittelalter," *Westdeutsche Zeitschrift für Geschichte und Kunst,* v.9 (Trier 1895) 1–120. H. EHL, *Die Ottonische Kölner Buchmalerei* (Bonn 1922). A. GOLDSCHMIDT, *Ottonian Period,* v.2 of his *German Illumination,* 2 v. (New York 1928); *Die Elfenbeinskulpturen aus der Zeit der Karolingischen und Sächsischen Kaiser,* 4 v. (Berlin 1914–26); *Die deutschen Bronzetüren des frühen Mittelalters* (Marburg 1926). L. GRODECKI, *L'Architecture ottonienne* (Paris 1958). W. KÖHLER, "Die Tradition der Adagruppe und die Anfänge des Ottonischen Stiles in der Buchmalerei, *Festschrift zum 60. Geburtstag von Paul Clemen* (Bonn 1926) 255–272. G. LEIDINGER, ed., *Miniaturen aus Handschriften der Kgl. Hof- und Staatsbibliothek in München,* 9 v. (Munich 1912–28) v.1, 5, 6. H. W. PICTON, *Early German Art and Its Origins* (London 1939). H. V. SAUERLAND and A. E. G. HASELOFF, eds., *Der Psalter Erzbischof Egberts von Trier, Codex Gertrudianus* (Trier 1901). H. SCHIEL, ed., *Codex Egberti der Stadtbibliothek Trier,* 2 v. (Basel 1960). A. SCHMIDT, ed., *Die Miniaturen des Gerocodex* (Leipzig 1924). G. SWARZENSKI, *Denkmäler der süddeutschen Malerei des frühen Mittelalters,* 3 v. (Leipzig 1901–13) v.1, 2. W. VÖGE, "Eine deutsche Malerschule um die Wende des 1. Jahrtausends," *Westdeutsche Zeitschrift für Geschichte und Kunst,* v.7 (Trier 1891) 1–389. H. WÖLFFLIN, ed., *Die Bamberger Apocalypse* (2d

Fig. 3. Full-page illumination of the Church in procession to Christ, who sits enthroned among the choirs of angels, in a MS written at Reichenau in the late 10th century (Bamberg, Staatl. Bibl., Cod. bibl. 22, fol. 5r).

ed. Munich 1921). E. H. ZIMMERMANN, *Die Fuldaer Buchmalerei in Karolingischer und Ottonischer Zeit* (Halle 1910). C. R. MOREY, *Medieval Art* (New York 1942). **Illustration credits:** Fig. 1a, El Escorial, Madrid. Figs. 1b, 1c, 3, Hirmer Verlag München. Fig. 1d, Bayerische Staatsbibliothek, München. Fig. 2, Stiftung Preussischer Kulturbesitz, Berlin.

[W. R. HOVEY]

OTTONIAN RENAISSANCE

The popular name for the cultural surge experienced throughout the *Holy Roman Empire under the Roman emperors *Otto I the Great, *Otto II, and *Otto III, that is, during the years 936 to 1002. If this renaissance is to be understood, it must be linked with the intellectual movement initiated by *Charlemagne and his successors, the so-called *Carolingian Renaissance, when scholars tried to preserve and revitalize the culture of the late classical and early Christian period. The most distinctive characteristic of the Ottonian as opposed to the earlier Carolingian Renaissance was the greater part played by indigenous northern and eastern European influences in the cultural flowering of the 10th century.

Furthermore, the Ottonian Renaissance profited from the increased trade and communication with the older and more cultivated areas to the south, such as the Lombard kingdom, Venice, and Córdoba, and from its continued relations with Byzantium. Although the Ottonian, like the Carolingian, Renaissance attempted essentially to revive classical antiquity, it was able to imbue its work with a more personal touch and greater depth. Especially effective in creating the new intellectual atmosphere were the currents emanating from the imperial court of the Ottos, especially from such men as Abp. *Bruno of Cologne, *Notker of Liège, and *Adaldag of Bremen. This new intellectualism spread as the missionary efforts of the Archdiocese of *Salzburg and the Dioceses of Freising, Passau, and Regensburg were directed southeastward; the cathedral school in Magdeburg, directed by Ohtric, one of the most famous scholars of his time, became both recipient and disseminator of the new Christian learning. Monasteries, reinvigorated by the *Cluniac reform and the "strict observance" movement initiated at *Gorze (*Brogne), roused themselves to special spiritual and intellectual endeavors. Works of historical importance and literary worth were written in both Italy and Germany (*Liutprand of Cremona, *Widukind of Corvey, and *Roswitha of Gandersheim)—works outstanding both for the knowledge of classical culture they displayed and for their rhetorical skill. Works of architecture, such as the abbey church of the nuns of Gernrode, the narthex and crypt of Oberzell monastery at Reichenau date from the period.

The Ottonian renaissance is sometimes designated as a renaissance of Carolingian culture; but, in continuing the work of the Carolingians, it produced much that was peculiar to itself. It undoubtedly reached its peak under Otto III (983–1002), both in its cultural efforts and in its maturity of religious thought; it was an era marked by the desire to evangelize peoples still heathen (an endeavor that entirely consumed Otto III) and by enthusiasm for the arts and learning. While there are only meager remains of this artistic and intellectual activity, it is known to have been the developmental period of guilds of builders and artisans. It is clear also that the Emperor himself attempted with some success to write poetry. There is well-documented evidence to his collaborations in more than one literary venture, e.g., when his friend Bp. *Adalbert of Prague was martyred, he personally took part in the composition of a poetic life and paean in honor of his martyrdom. Contemporaries saw the Emperor, even while he was still very young, as the center of the intellectual and artistic life of his era. His almost impassioned participation in such endeavors increased considerably in his mature years, and through his tutors, who were also the most brilliant men at court, viz, Gerbert of Aurillac, the future Pope *Sylvester II, whom the Emperor personally invited to his service, accompanying the summons with a poem, and Archchancellor *Heribert of Cologne, he provided the empire with effective intellectual leadership.

In view of Otto III's commanding personality, it is understandable that during his reign sculpture, miniatures, and book illuminations all served the glorification of the ruler. An example is found in those pages produced by the *Reichenau school of art after the imperial coronation on May 21, 996, including the famous double page of the Otto III Gospel Book (in Munich), the undisputed masterpiece, as well as similar pages in the Musée Condé in Chantilly, and in the Bamberg Josephus MS. These illuminated pages, which undoubtedly were produced after the coronation and which seem to have been products of competition among the most distinguished master miniaturists of the day (K. and M. Uhlirz, *Jahrbücher . . . Otto III*), show the influence of lands to the east (Sclavinia, that is, southern Slav and Polish territories, Hungary, and the Balkans). In charming contrast to these artistically arranged representations in which every detail (the color of hair, the stance, the weapons, etc.) is expressive in its political significance, is the simple work of a cleric from Ivrea who naïvely represented the Emperor in his ordinary winter clothes, receiving from the hands of the Blessed Virgin a crown that has pediments like the crown of St. Stephen. Although sculptured likenesses of the Emperor are rare, he is represented by a carving on the ivory holy-water font in Aachen and on the fountain at St. Bartholomew-in-the-Island, Rome, which shows the likeness of St. Adalbert on the reverse side of the column. It may be expected that future archeological discoveries will extend the knowledge of the Ottonian period.

See also MEDIEVAL LATIN LITERATURE; OTTONIAN ART.

Bibliography: Ghellinck Litt 2:9–43. P. E. SCHRAM, *Kaiser, Rom und Renovatio* (2d ed. Darmstadt 1957). E. R. CURTIUS, *European Literature and the Latin Middle Ages*, tr. W. R. TRASK (New York 1953). Raby SecLP 1:252–306. Raby ChrLP 202–229. K. and M. UHLIRZ, *Jahrbücher des Deutschen Reiches unter Otto III* (Berlin 1954). J. F. BÖHMER, *Die Regesten des Kaiserreiches unter Otto III, 980–1002*, ed. M. UHLIRZ (*Regesta imperii* 2.3; Graz-Cologne 1956–57). M. UHLIRZ, "Das deutsche Gefolge Ottos III in Italien," *Gesamtdeutsche Vergangenheit: Festgabe für H. v. Srbik* (Munich 1938) 21–38; "Aus dem Kunstleben der Zeit Ottos III," *Festschrift Schramm* (Weisbaden 1964) 51–56.

[M. UHLIRZ]

OTTUMWA HEIGHTS COLLEGE

A resident and nonresident 2-year college for laywomen and religious in Ottumwa, Iowa. Ottumwa Heights is conducted by the Congregation of the Humility of Mary, a pontifical institute with motherhouse and novitiate on the College campus. The College, organized in 1925 as St. Joseph Junior College, is a development of the former St. Joseph Academy, a girls' resident and day school, established in Ottumwa in 1890. In 1957 fire destroyed the five-story building housing the motherhouse, novitiate, and college. For 3 years Ottumwa Heights operated in three renovated buildings of a former Navy airbase outside Ottumwa. Colleges and universities throughout the country contributed books and equipment to help restore the College. The new Ottumwa Heights, a 10-unit complex constructed on the original 140-acre campus, was opened in 1960. The College occupies four buildings and shares two others with the motherhouse and novitiate.

The College is governed by a board of trustees composed of the superior general, general councilors, and general secretary of the congregation. Officers of administration are the dean, registrar, director of admissions, librarian, guidance director, and treasurer. They are assisted by committees on educational policies, admissions, student affairs, library, and finance. In 1964 the 32-member faculty consisted of 1 priest, 29 sisters, and 2 laywomen, holding among them 18 master's degrees. The total enrollment of 291 included 141 resident students from 12 states and 5 foreign countries; 55 nonresident students; 56 student sisters; and 39 student nurses. The library housed 19,408 volumes and subscribed to 130 periodicals.

For lay students Ottumwa Heights offers 10 programs, which may be either terminal or preparatory. All are fully accredited and are so arranged that graduates may transfer to a 4-year college or university. Students may follow a basic liberal arts course or a liberal arts and professional program in secretarial science, medical-secretarial science, home economics, prenursing, library science, art, music, medical records, medical technology, and teacher-education.

For religious, Ottumwa Heights provides the first 3 years of a 5-year program in philosophy, theology, the arts and sciences, and professional subjects. The final 2 years of the program are completed at *Marycrest College, Davenport, Iowa, a 4-year college conducted by the Congregation.

To accommodate student nurses, Ottumwa Heights cooperates with the St. Joseph Hospital School of Nursing, Ottumwa, in offering an academic program of English, biology, anatomy and physiology, psychology, and sociology.

As a service to the Ottumwa community, the College sponsors public lectures, exhibits, and plays and opens its facilities to local organizations for meetings and programs. Each year the College conducts an annual educational tour of cultural and scenic centers in the U.S. or Canada.

Ottumwa Heights is accredited by the North Central Association of Colleges and Secondary Schools, the Intercollegiate Standing Committee of Iowa, and the Iowa State Board of Educational Examiners. It holds membership in the National Catholic Educational Association and in the American Association of Junior Colleges.

[M. M. REIDY]

OUAGADOUGOU, ARCHDIOCESE OF (UAGADUGUENSIS), metropolitan see since 1955, whose seat is the capital of Upper Volta, west Africa. In 1963 it had 25 secular and 43 religious priests,

34 men in 5 religious houses, 124 women in 17 convents, and 39,000 Catholics in a population of 833,000; it is 20,927 square miles in area. The six suffragan sees were Bobo-Dioulasso (created in 1955), Fada N'Gourma (1964), Koudougou (1955), Koupéla (1956), Nouna (1955), and Ouahigouya (1958); they had 208 priests, 238 sisters, and 125,000 Catholics in a population of 3,300,000. The population is mostly pagan, with a large Moslem element. Originally part of the Prefecture of the Sahara and the Sudan, which was detached in 1868 from the Vicariate of Central Africa, Ouagadougou in 1901 was a mission and in 1921 became a vicariate on the division of the Sahara and the Sudan. Several ecclesiastical territories have since been detached from it. The see has 20 African priests, 76 African sisters, and 14 African brothers, a minor seminary, and two Benedictine monasteries (for men and for women). The laity, especially the youth, is organized in several active groups. Paul Zoungrana, a White Father and a native African, became archbishop in 1960 and cardinal in 1965.

See also UPPER VOLTA.

Bibliography: MissCattol 100–101. S. PAVENTI, EncCatt 9: 474–475. AnnPont (1965) 319.

[J. R. DE BENOIST]

OUEN OF ROUEN, ST., bishop; b. near Soissons, France; d. Clichy, Aug. 24, 684 (feast, Aug. 24). Ouen, also known as Owen, Audoin, Dado, or Audoi(e)nus, came from a wealthy family and was the longest-lived of several distinguished men educated at the court of Chlothar II (d. 629), who served Dagobert I (629–639) and ultimately became bishops. While referendary (chancellor) to Dagobert, he founded the monastery of Rebais near Meaux and obtained for it a famous privilege (635). Consecrated bishop of Rouen (May 13, 641), he promoted monasticism (notably at *Fontenelle) and built many churches. His support of the palace mayor Ebroïn illustrates a continued interest in public affairs. Late in life he undertook a pilgrimage to Rome. His remains were translated to Rouen and accorded a public cult (May 7, 685).

Bibliography: DESIDERIUS CADURCENSIS, *Epistulae* 1:9–10; 2: 6; MGEp 3:198–199, 206. *Vita Audoini,* ed. W. LEVISON, MG SrerMer 5:536–567. E. VACANDARD, *Vie de saint Ouen, évêque de Rouen* (Paris 1902); also in RevQuestHist 63 (1898) 5–50; 69 (1901) 5–58; 71 (1902) 5–71. F. BEYERLE, "Das Formelbuch des westfränkischen Mönchs Markulf und Dagoberts Urkunde für Rebais, a. 635," DeutschArch 9 (1952) 43–58.

[W. GOFFART]

OUR FATHER, THE

The model prayer, named from its first words, which, because it was taught by Jesus to His disciples, is also known as the Lord's Prayer. From its first words in Latin it is commonly called the Pater Noster. It is treated here according to its form, its contents, and its use in the liturgy.

Form. The Our Father is found in Mt 6.9b–13 and in Lk 11.2b–4, but in different contexts and with considerable variations.

In Matthew. In the first Gospel the Our Father is part of the *Sermon on the Mount, following an instruction on prayer and introduced by the words of Jesus, "In this manner therefore shall you pray" (Mt 6.9a). It is composed of an address and six petitions. The verse numbers are included in parentheses.

Address: Our Father who art in heaven (9b),
Petitions: 1. hallowed be thy name (9c).
2. Thy kingdom come (10a),
3. thy will be done on earth,
as it is in heaven (10b).
4. Give us this day our daily
bread (11).
5. And forgive us our debts,
as we also forgive our
debtors (12).
6. And lead us not into temptation, but deliver us from
evil (13).

Many manuscripts, but not the best nor the oldest, add the words, in variant forms, "For thine is the kingdom and the power and the glory. Amen." This doxology was used by the Jews at the time of Christ. In a more elaborate form it already occurs in 1 Chr 29.11–13. The Christians in the East added it to the Our Father when they said this prayer at divine service, as can be seen in the *Didache* (8.2) version of the Lord's Prayer. The Greek scribes, accustomed to this liturgical use of the prayer, gradually introduced it into the text of Matthew's Gospel. It is certain, however, that it is not a part of the Gospel text. It is not in the Vulgate, Douay Version, or Confraternity Version. English-speaking Protestants know it from the Authorized Version. But the Revised Standard Version relegated this doxology to a footnote.

In Luke. In the third Gospel the setting of the Our Father is the prayer of Jesus Himself (11.1). After seeing Jesus in prayer, the disciples ask Him to teach them also how to pray. The Lucan version has an address and five petitions. The verse numbers are shown in parentheses.

Address: Father (2b),
Petitions: 1. hallowed be thy name (2b).
2. Thy kingdom come! (2c)
[3 not in Lk.]
4. Give us this day our daily bread (3),
5. And forgive us our sins,
for we also forgive everyone
who is indebted to us (4a).
6. And lead us not into temptation (4b).

In his smaller number of phrases Luke may be closer to the original Aramaic than Matthew, who may have added other words of Jesus: for "who art in heaven," cf. Mt 6.1; 6.14; etc.; for "thy will be done," cf. Mt 26.42; for "deliver us from evil," cf. Jn 17.15. In some of his wording, however, Luke may be further from the original, for he shows signs of adaptation to a later Gentile audience: in petition (5) he uses "sins" instead of the more Semitic "debts"; in petition (4) he uses the Greek present imperative δίδου, "keep on giving," instead of Matthew's aorist δός, "give (once and for all)." This may show a later emphasis on the present rather than the eschatological needs of the church.

Contents. While the Our Father contains words used by Jesus Himself in prayer, the plural forms indicate that it had already become the liturgical prayer of the Christian community in the 1st century. Although many of the phrases of the prayer may be found in the Jewish liturgy, there is a new spirit that pervades it. For the Jews God had provided a "way" by manifesting Himself to their fathers; but for the Church, Jesus Himself was now the new way. Through the gift of His Spirit, they could now pray to the Father in the same manner He did (Rom 8.15; Gal 4.6). Jesus, however, was not

Initial letter of the Pater Noster from the 12th-century St. Alban Psalter in the treasury of the cathedral, Hildesheim, Germany.

only the way, but the end of the way, the object of hope. So the early Christian community looked forward to his speedy return from heaven. This eschatological atmosphere must be kept in mind for a full understanding of the Our Father. Lending itself to this interpretation is Matthew's use of the Greek aorist tense with its "once and for all" meaning.

Address. The direct "Father" in Luke translates the original Aramaic *abba* of Jesus. This was His own distinctive and intimate way of speaking with His Father, now shared by Christians (Rom 8.15). The "our" in Matthew shows that the Pater Noster has already become a Christian community prayer, since Jesus nowhere addresses God in this manner. "Who art in heaven" (Mt) distinguishes Him from any earthly father and may indicate the absence of any localization such as the temple.

Petitions. The first petition is literally, "may your name be sanctified." However, the passive Greek forms in the first two petitions really represent Semitic reflexives, with the *name of God standing for God Himself, so that the sense is: "May God Himself sanctify His Name." The name in Semitic usage indicates the person as he makes himself known to others. God makes Himself known through the communication of His Spirit. The Greek aorist and the eschatological atmosphere of the prayer point to the last times: that God may sanctify all mankind through the Holy Spirit. The Jewish *Kaddish has a similar prayer: "May His great Name be magnified and sanctified. . . ."

Second petition. Understanding the passive Greek form as above, the sense would be, "May God establish His kingdom" (*see* KINGDOM OF GOD); Jesus came on earth to establish God's rule (Jn 18.36–37). By obeying the Son's word men can enter the kingdom of the Father. But the final stage of the kingdom can come only at Jesus' return, when He crushes the power of Satan (2 Thes 2.8). So the early Church prayed for the definitive establishment of God's kingdom at the end of time. The wording resembles the verse of the Jewish Kaddish following the one quoted above: "May He establish His kingdom during your life. . . ."

Third Petition. Parallel to the second petition, the Church prays that God may accomplish His salvific will, which is to redeem all mankind by making them subject to His Son (Eph 1.5–12; Jn 6.39–40). "On earth as in heaven": the Hebrew expression, "heaven and earth," means the whole universe. Hence the petition refers to the redemption of all the universe through Christ (Col 1.20).

Fourth Petition. Literally, in Matthew, "Give us this day our future (?) bread"; in Luke, "Keep on giving us each day our future (?) bread." The word, ἐπιούσιον (modifier of bread), has no proved parallel in Greek writings. Etymology offers two possibilities: (1) ἐπί (on) plus εἶναι (to be), which could give us "daily" or "for existence," i.e., the bread that is needed; (2) ἐπί plus ἰέναι (to go, come), which could give us "the bread of tomorrow" or "the future bread." The Bohairic and Sahidic versions as well as Marcion have the latter reading, and St. Jerome writes that he saw the reading *māḥār* or "of tomorrow" in the Gospel of the Hebrews [*see* BIBLE, III (CANON), 5]. The reading "bread of the future," or "tomorrow," would link with other Gospel references to the coming eschatological banquet (Lk 14.15; Mt 8.11). Words very similar to the petition are found in a Eucharistic context in John 6, particularly 6.31–35. This would also indicate a Eucharistic interpretation in this petition of the Our Father. Luke has the present imperative δίδου, "keep on giving," and καθ᾽ ἡμέραν, "each day," in place of Matthew's δός, "give" (once and for all), and σήμερον, "today." He thus draws more attention to that daily nourishment which anticipates the eschatological bread.

Fifth Petition. Literally, in Matthew it is, "and forgive us our debts as we have forgiven our debtors"; in Luke, "and forgive us our sins, for we also forgive our debtors." The perfect tense in Matthew, "as we have forgiven," is the attitude of the Christian awaiting a proximate judgment. He begs his Father's forgiveness while disposing himself by a generous forgiving of his brothers' debts, knowing that if he does not, the words of Mt 18.35 apply to him: "So also my heavenly Father will do to you, if you do not each forgive your brothers from your hearts." Luke, with his present tense, "as we also forgive," emphasizes forgiveness for the sins of each day as a preparation for the future judgment.

Sixth Petition. Literally, in Matthew and Luke it is, "and lead us not into trial," to which Matthew adds, "but deliver us from the evil one." Before the final judgment, the early Church expected a great time of trial, a final terrible onslaught of the devil (2 Thes 2.1–8). The Christian asks to be delivered from this test, for he knows that no human power could withstand such a trial (Mt 24.21–22). Only the power of God can accomplish this (Ap 3.10). This final battle is the same basic struggle that Jesus faced by prayer in Gethsemane, where He asked His disciples to pray they might be spared the same trial (Mt 26.41). "But deliver us from the evil one" (Mt): the Greek phrase ἀπὸ τοῦ πονηροῦ means either "from evil" or "from the evil one." In Jn 17.15 Jesus prays, "[I ask] that you keep them from the evil one." Parallels such as this, and the meaning of the first half of the petition, incline us to the second translation, "the evil one." A reference to daily trials and temptations is not eliminated, for these prepare the way for the final test.

Use in the Liturgy. The early use of the Pater Noster in the baptismal liturgy is witnessed by a variant reading of Luke's second petition as quoted by several Fathers: "May your Holy Spirit come upon us and cleanse us." The *Didache* (8.2–3) has the Matthaean form of the Our Father where it follows the baptism ceremony and precedes the Eucharist. Christians are to recite it thrice daily (8.3). In the ancient disciplines of the catechumenate there was a *traditio* or explanation of the Pater Noster before Baptism. The Our Father is sung or recited before Communion in the Eucharistic liturgy of every rite, and it is still recited in the baptismal ceremony.

Bibliography: H. VAN DEN BUSSCHE, *Understanding the Lord's Prayer,* tr. C. SCHALDENBRAND (New York 1963). R. E. BROWN, "The Pater Noster as an Eschatological Prayer," ThSt 22 (1961) 175–208. M. DROUZEY, "Le 'Pater,' prière du Christ," VieSpirit 93 (1955) 115–134. M. E. JACQUEMIN, "La Portée de la troisième demande du 'Pater,' " EphemThLov 25 (1949) 61–76. J. ROCHE, "Que ta volonté soit faite," VieSpirit 93 (1955) 249–268. J. B. BAUER, "Libera nos a malo," VerbDom 34 (1956) 12–15. G. WALTHER, "Untersuchungen zur Geschichte der griechischen Vaterunser-Exegese," TU 40.3 (1914). P. J. VAN KASTEREN, *Was Jesus predigte: Eine Erklärung des Vaterunsers,* tr. J. SPENDEL (Freiburg 1920). **Illustration credit:** Warburg Institute, London.

[J. A. GRASSI]

OUR LADY MOTHER OF MERCY, BROTHERS OF, popularly known as the Brothers of Tilburg, *Congregatio Fratrum Beatae Mariae Virginis, Matris Misericordiae* (CFMM), founded in 1844 by Joannes Zwijsen (1794–1877), then a parish priest in Tilburg, and from 1854 archbishop of Utrecht. Its principal purpose is teaching. Members included priests and brothers until 1916. Since then all members have been brothers, because of the limited scope for priestly activities and the extension of educational work. In its modified form the institute received papal approval in 1927. Brothers take perpetual vows. The congregation is governed by a superior general and a council of four assistants general, who reside in Tilburg, Netherlands. By 1864 the congregation had many primary schools in the Netherlands and some boarding schools, notably St. Henricus Institute for blind boys at Grave. A school for deaf mute boys was opened in Maaseik, Belgium, in 1851. In the 1880s the brothers erected schools in the West Indies. After World War I they started schools in Indonesia. The most important recent foundation in Belgium is a school for deaf mute boys in Hasselt. Since 1939 houses have been established in Africa and South America. The congregation in 1963 had 1,002 members, 57 houses, 2 residences, and 43,682 pupils in primary schools, high schools, commercial and technical schools, orphanages, and institutes for blind, deaf, mute, and destitute children. The 741 brothers in the Netherlands cared for 25,892 children. Belgium had 66 brothers and 2,614 pupils; Indonesia, 32 brothers and

4,323 pupils; Africa, 36 brothers and 1,096 pupils; Brazil, 9 brothers and 275 pupils; Surinam (Dutch Guiana), 33 brothers and 3,787 pupils; the Antilles, 74 brothers and 5,695 pupils. Ireland had 1 residence with

Archbishop Joannes Zwijsen.

6 brothers. Oxnard, Calif., had a residence, opened in 1963, with 5 brothers.

Bibliography: T. HORSTEN, *De Fraters van Tilburg, 1844–1944,* 3 v. (Tilburg 1946–52). *In de voortuin der Congregatie der Fraters van O. L. Vrouw Moeder van Barmhartigheid* (Tilburg 1950). *Ontmoetingen,* 17 v. (1957–64).

[P. N. BROEDERS]

OUR LADY OF CHARITY OF REFUGE, SISTERS OF

SISTERS OF (OLCR), a congregation of religious women founded in Caen, France (1641), by St. John *Eudes. They follow the Rule of St. *Augustine and the constitutions of the Visitation nuns, modified to suit the work of the order. Preliminary papal approbation was granted Jan. 2, 1666, and complete approval in 1741. The seven Houses of Refuge in existence at the time of the French Revolution were dispersed, but the work was resumed again at Tours and spread through France as circumstances permitted. The first American foundation was established in 1855 at Buffalo, N.Y., by Mother Mary of St. Jerome, from Rennes, France. Although each house of the order is autonomous, the U.S. communities established a federation in 1944 for the purpose of strengthening the contemplative and apostolic life of the sisters. Similar federations were organized in France, England, and Ireland. In addition, houses were opened in Spain, Portugal, Italy, Canada, Mexico, and Kenya, Africa.

The original purpose of the congregation was to provide a shelter for women of dissolute behavior, but it was later modified to include the care and training of neglected, dependent teenage girls. When numbers of these desired to remain in the Refuge, secondary communities of the order were established, known variously as Sister Auxiliaries, Consecrates, and Oblates. These groups assist in the work for girls and lead a life of prayer, penance, and manual labor. In the 19th century

a separate branch developed as the Sisters of Our Lady of Charity of the *Good Shepherd. Combining the contemplative and active apostolates, the Sisters of Charity of Our Lady of Refuge lead a semicloistered life; in addition to the three simple vows of obedience, chastity, and poverty, they take a vow of zeal for souls. In 1964 the congregation numbered more than 270 professed sisters, with monasteries in Buffalo and Rochester, N.Y.; Pittsburgh, Erie, and Coraopolis, Pa.; Wheeling, W.Va.; Green Bay, Wis.; Hot Springs, Ark.; and Dallas, El Paso, San Antonio, and San Benito, Tex.

[M. GRABIAK]

OUR LADY OF CINCINNATI COLLEGE

A 4-year liberal arts college for women founded in Cincinnati, Ohio, in 1935 by the Religious Sisters of Mercy at the request of John T. McNicholas, Archbishop of Cincinnati. The College was chartered in 1935 with power to grant degrees. It is accredited by the North Central Association of Colleges and Secondary Schools, the Ohio College Association, and the Ohio Department of Public Instruction for teacher certification. It is affiliated with The Catholic University of America and holds membership in the American Council on Education, American Dietetics Association, American Association of University Women, North Central Study on Liberal Arts, and other professional organizations.

General control of the College is vested in the board of trustees and members of the provincial council, which approves policies and bears legal responsibility for all aspects of the institution. Officers of administration are the president, academic dean, vice president for financial affairs, registrar, director of admissions, dean of women, and librarian. In 1964 the 83-member faculty was composed of 11 priests, 34 sisters, and 38 laymen, holding 20 doctoral and 50 master's degrees from universities in the U.S. and abroad. Enrollment numbered 702 full-time and 320 part-time students in the regular session and 443 in the summer session. The Brennan Memorial Library housed 27,250 volumes and received 300 periodicals. A curriculum library of approximately 1,500 volumes is available to prospective teachers.

The College is financed by tuition and fees, and by the contributed services of the Religious Sisters of Mercy. It is a member of the Ohio Foundation of Independent Colleges, and receives assistance through contributions of the alumnae, fathers club, and mothers club. Grants have been awarded by the Ford Foundation for salary increment; Kellogg Foundation for library holdings for teacher education; and U.S. Department of Health, Education, and Welfare and National Science Foundation for scientific research and equipment. A government loan was approved for the construction of the dormitory. Funds have been contributed for competitive scholarships, and assistance to students is available through the National Defense Student Loan Program.

The curriculum is divided into lower and upper 2-year periods devoted respectively to general education and specialization. Majors in the principal disciplines of the liberal arts lead to the B.A. degree; in elementary education, home economics, and medical technology, to the B.S. degree. The foods and nutrition program meets the standards of the American Dietetic Association. The medical technology program includes clinical practice at approved hospitals. Other methods employed are lectures, student-participation, seminars, independent study, experimentation, and language laboratory experience.

The Edgecliff Academy of Fine Arts, founded in 1961 to raise the standards of collegiate endeavor in this field, integrates the art, drama, and music departments of the College. The year's program consists of dramatic presentations, notably Shakespeare, a music series, and exhibits of contemporary artists. Opportunity is offered students to observe and work with resident artists and actors of professional status. In addition to affording students a laboratory and steppingstone to active participation, Edgecliff Academy is recognized as one of Cincinnati's cultural centers.

Besides Grace Hall of Science, completed in 1962, which provides science and language laboratories, an audio-visual room, and roof-top observatory, the College's master plan includes more extensive building expansion.

Bibliography: M. E. Evans, *The Spirit Is Mercy* (Westminster, Md. 1959).

[M. R. A. GRESSEL]

OUR LADY OF GOOD COUNSEL

The church that enshrines the original fresco of Our Lady of Good Counsel is located in the small town of Genazzano about 30 miles southeast of Rome in the Diocese of Palestrina. According to the still current legend, this church stood unfinished and roofless when, on April 25, 1467, the image of the Madonna was miraculously transported there from its former home in Scutari, Albania. Coming to rest precariously on a narrow stone ledge in the wall inside the church, the legend continues, the picture has remained in that position to the present day.

Careful investigations undertaken between 1957 and 1959 for the purpose of restoration have revealed something of the true origin of the fresco. The image of the Madonna—about 12 inches wide and 17 inches high—that the viewer sees encased in its elaborate glass,

Our Lady of Good Counsel, fresco, Genazzano, Italy.

metal, and marble framework, is part of a larger fresco that once covered a portion of the wall now hidden by the baroque shrine altar. Art experts consulted during the restoration suggest that the fresco, and therefore the Madonna as well, is the work of the early 15th-century artist, *Gentile da Fabriano. On the site of the present church once stood a small chapel within which Gentile painted his fresco around the time of Martin V (1417–31). At some subsequent date, but before 1467, the fresco, so it is surmised on the basis of the evidence, was covered over with plaster, and on the wall was hung a terra cotta Madonna, which was known as Our Lady of Good Counsel.

In 1467 the *Augustinians (in whose custody the shrine still remains) undertook to build a church on the site, enclosing within the structure the wall on which the then covered fresco was painted. This work was sponsored by a widow named Petruccia, who exhausted her means on the project and was unable to continue the construction. At that point the image of the Madonna appeared and was taken to be a token of divine favor. The unexpected appearance was perhaps brought about by the construction work in this way: when the stone ledge referred to above was being inserted into the wall, the plaster covering cracked and separated from the wall, revealing the fresco beneath. The image was immediately hailed as the Madonna of Paradise, an allusion to its apparently heavenly origin; but soon it came to be known by the former title of the shrine, Madonna of Good Counsel. One striking aspect of the fresco, which has lent a certain credence to the legends surrounding it, is that the upper portion of the image is separated from the wall and leans slightly forward. The fresco, nothing more than a thin layer of plaster, has survived for centuries in this precarious state, even through the aerial bombardment of Genazzano during World War II. Because of this condition, the restoration undertaken in 1957 was a delicate task.

The unfinished church was completed soon after the event of April 1467 and became the center of continuous pilgrimage. The numerous cures recorded as having occurred since then have caused the Madonna to be called miraculous. Many honors have been granted to the shrine by the Holy See, especially in more recent times. The initial approval of the devotion to Our Lady of Good Counsel was apparently given by Paul II. Although the record of his approval is not extant, there is abundant evidence of recognition by later popes: Sixtus IV, Alexander VI, Pius V, Gregory XIII, and Urban VIII. In 1682 Innocent XI approved the placing of a golden crown over the image, and in 1753 Benedict XIV established the Pious Union of Our Lady of Good Counsel, a spiritual society to which many indulgences were attached. Pius VI granted to the Augustinian Order, in 1779, a proper Mass and Office for the feast day. Pius IX had a personal devotion to the Mother of God under this title; he made a pilgrimage to Genazzano in 1864.

More than any other pope, Leo XIII was deeply attached to this devotion, which had associations with his childhood in Carpineto, a town not far from Genazzano. He instituted the white scapular of Good Counsel, inserted the title Mother of Good Counsel into the Litany of Loreto, declared the shrine a minor basilica, and installed a copy of the image over the altar in the Pauline chapel in the Vatican. Pius XII dedicated his reign to the Madonna of Good Counsel, and John XXIII made a visit to her shrine on Aug. 25, 1959. The present church, which replaced the former one about 1628, has been renovated in recent years, and elaborate mosaics have been added to the facade. A noteworthy 19th-century pastor of this church, Bl. Stefano *Bellesini, is buried beneath the main altar. The feast day of Our Lady of Good Counsel is celebrated on April 26.

Bibliography: *Acta ordinis e. S. Augustini: Commentarium officiale* (1961) 25–33. A. F. ADDEO, "Apparitionis imaginis B.V.M. a Bono Consilio documenta," *Analecta augustiniana* 20 (1946) 3–140.

[A. J. ENNIS]

OUR LADY OF PERPETUAL HELP (SUCCOUR)

A title given to the Blessed Virgin Mary, emphasizing her unfailing eagerness to pray for the welfare of human beings, especially those who seek her intercession. The original picture of Mary under this title is venerated in the Redemptorist church of Sant'Alfonso in Rome.

History. This picture, painted by an unknown artist in Crete in the 14th or 15th century, was brought to Rome *c.* 1495 by a merchant who apparently had stolen it from some church in Crete. In Rome he contracted a mortal illness, but before his death consigned the painting to the friend in whose house he had been lodging, with the request that it be placed in some church, as a form of restitution. The friend promised, but later changed his mind at the request of his wife who wished to keep the picture. Then Mary herself was seen in a vision by the little daughter of the family, and commanded that her picture be placed in a church dedicated to St. Matthew between the basilicas of St. Mary Major

Our Lady of Perpetual Help, original icon preserved in the Redemptorist church of Sant'Alfonso in Rome.

and St. John Lateran. To this child Our Lady also revealed herself as "Holy Mary of Perpetual Help."

Accordingly, on March 27, 1499, the picture of Our Lady of Perpetual Help was solemnly enthroned on the high altar of St. Matthew's church, cared for by the Augustinians. A tablet narrating the history of the painting was affixed nearby. For the next 3 centuries Our Lady of Perpetual Help was venerated there, and many miracles were ascribed to her intercession. However, in 1798 the French army seized Rome and led Pius VI into captivity. Shortly afterward, the church of St. Matthew, together with 30 other churches of Rome, was leveled to the ground at the order of the French commander. The picture of Our Lady of Perpetual Help was removed by the Augustinians from the church before its destruction and after being kept for a short while in the church of St. Eusebius, was transferred to the private chapel of the Irish Augustinians at their monastery of Santa Maria in Posterula, on the left side of the Tiber, where it remained in comparative obscurity for many years.

In 1863 Francis Blosi, SJ, preaching at the church of the Gesù on the Roman shrines of Mary, related the history of Our Lady of Perpetual Help at St. Matthew's and expressed the desire that the picture be found and again placed in a church between St. Mary Major's and St. John Lateran's. This came to the attention of Michael Marchi, a Redemptorist, who knew the whereabouts of the picture, because as a boy he had served Mass in the private chapel of the Augustinians. In 1855 the Redemptorists had purchased land for their motherhouse and a church on the Via Merulana, including the site on which St. Matthew's had stood. When Pius IX heard the story, he commanded that the picture be given to the Redemptorists for their church, since it fulfilled the condition laid down in the vision—"between the basilicas of St. Mary Major and St. John Lateran." The superior general of the Redemptorists was told to give the Augustinians another picture in compensation.

The picture of Our Lady of Perpetual Help was exposed for public veneration above the high altar of the church of Sant'Alfonso on April 26, 1866. The feast of Mary under the title of Perpetual Help (though restricted to certain churches and not in the calendar of the universal Church) is June 27.

Devotion to Our Lady of Perpetual Help, especially in the form of weekly services, prevails throughout the entire Catholic world. In the Redemptorist church at Baclaran in the Philippines between 80,000 and 100,000 attend the novena of Our Lady of Perpetual Help every Wednesday. In the U.S. thousands of churches have these devotions every week and many more have a picture of Mary under this title. A beautiful altar with a mosaic of Our Lady of Perpetual Help, a gift of the Redemptorists of the U.S. and their friends, adorns the National Shrine of the Immaculate Conception in Washington, D.C.

Iconography. The original picture of Our Lady of Perpetual Help is painted on wood, and is about 17 by 21 inches. It is distinctly Byzantine in style, and many similar portrayals of Our Lady are found throughout the East and in Russia. This manner of portraying Mary is a further development of the famous Hodegetria, an icon of Mary (painted by St. Luke, according to some) venerated for centuries in Constantinople but destroyed in 1453 when that city fell to the Turks.

In addition to Mary, the picture represents her divine Son as a child of 2 or 3, seated on his Mother's left hand, with his hands clasping her right hand. On either side are the angels Michael and Gabriel, bearing the instruments of the Passion. In Greek characters the abbreviated names of the four figures are added. The artist wished to depict the mental anguish of Christ as He gazes at the cross, and with a touching stroke painted the left sandal falling off His foot as He winces in terror. This portrayal of the Passion of Christ in an image of Mary classifies the picture as a "Passion Madonna." Such pictures are found today in many Orthodox churches, such as the cathedral of Rethymnon on the island of Crete.

The title "Our Lady of Perpetual Help," originally derived from Mary's own apparition to the little girl, is also most appropriately symbolized by this picture. For, although the sufferings awaiting her Son are so vividly portrayed, Mary's face is turned, not to Him but to those who gaze on the picture. Though she is indeed saddened by the vision of the instruments of the Passion, her sympathy goes out primarily to the children of men.

Bibliography: C. M. Henze, *Mater de Perpetuo Succurso* (Bonn 1926), first scientific monograph, extract; *Our Lady of Perpetual Help*, tr. F. J. Connell (New York 1940). J. F. Byrne, *The Glories of Mary in Boston* (Boston 1921).

[C. Henze]

OUR LADY OF THE ELMS, COLLEGE OF

A liberal arts residence and day college for women founded in 1928 in Chicopee, Mass., by the Sisters of St. Joseph of the Springfield Diocese. The sisters had been teaching in the parochial schools in Flushing, N.Y., until 1880 when they were invited by P. T. O'Reilly, first Bishop of Springfield, to open schools in Chicopee Falls and Webster. While conducting an academy and normal school in Chicopee, they recognized the need for a 4-year college program and under guidance of the Bishop of Springfield, Thomas M. O'Leary, who served as first president of the College, founded the only Catholic college for women in western Massachusetts. In February 1928 the Massachusetts Legislature granted a charter; in June 1932 the College conferred its first academic degrees upon 24 graduates.

Since administrative reorganization in 1958 the chancellor is the ordinary of the diocese and the president, a member of the religious community. In 1963 the administrative and teaching staff, both full and part time, included 12 priests, 25 sisters, and 12 laymen, holding 12 doctoral, 3 professional, and 25 master's degrees. Enrollment in the regular session totaled 800 students, of whom 614 were full-time; the summer session registered 283. The College library housed 25,000 volumes and received 225 periodicals.

The College is accredited by the New England Association of Colleges and Secondary Schools, the Connecticut State Department of Education, the Board of Regents of the University of the State of New York, and the Massachusetts State Department of Education. It is affiliated with The Catholic University of America and holds membership in the Association of American Colleges, American Association of University Women, American Alumni Council, American Council on Education, American Association of Deans of Women, American Association of Collegiate Registrars and Admissions Officers, National Commission on Christian Higher Education of the Association of American Colleges, National Commission on Accrediting, American Library Association, American Catholic Historical Association, and Association for the Advancement of Catholic Cultural Affairs.

Our Lady of the Elms offers courses leading to the B.A. and B.S. degrees with majors in philosophy and liberal arts, natural sciences, mathematics, modern language, teacher education, medical technology, secretarial science, and sociology. Preprofessional training is provided in medicine. Both the summer session, inaugurated in 1942 for members of the religious community, and the evening session, begun in 1953, have been coeducational since 1953. In addition to undergraduate courses, summer and evening sessions include graduate study in education.

Graduates of Our Lady of the Elms have entered fields of teaching, social work, homemaking, medical technology, medicine, law, research, business, and industry. Graduates teach on elementary, secondary, and college levels throughout the U.S. and in Europe.

In 1964, anticipating the enrollment of 1,000 students, the College engaged in the first phase of a development program to provide a 3-story dormitory, campus center, chapel, library, and residence hall for religious.

[J. M. Foley]

OUR LADY OF THE GARDEN, DAUGHTERS OF,

known also as the *Gianelline,* or *Hortus conclusus,* are a religious congregation founded by St. Anthony *Gianelli, Jan. 12, 1829, at Chiavari, in Liguria, Italy, with the collaboration of Sister Caterina Podestà, who succeeded Gianelli upon his death in 1846 as superior general, and gave a vigorous impulse to the institute. It is a papally approved congregation having simple vows. Sister Podestà went to Rome (1864) to obtain papal approval of the institute and of the rules (1882). The residence of the superior general, transferred by her to Rome, is at Via dei Quattro Cantoni, 45. At the head of the institute is a superior general whose term of office is 10 years. She is aided by four assistants.

Daughters of Our Lady of the Garden motherhouse in Rome, with 13th-century tower of the Capocci.

The institute's purpose is "the sanctification of the members, eternal salvation, and the corporal service of the neighbor" (Rule I, 1), in simplicity and poverty, wedding the active and contemplative lives. During the plague in Liguria (1835–37) the Daughters became distinguished for such heroic charity that they were awarded medals of merit by King Charles Albert. The impulse of social charity has directed their activities to hospitals, schools for girls, homes for the aged, and orphanages. In 1856 the first members went to South America and undertook hospital work in Montevideo. From there they spread to Argentina (1859), Brazil (1908), Chile (1929), and Paraguay (1945). They also began work in Jordan (1901), Spain (1949), and the U.S. (1962). In 1964 there were 7 provinces, 172 houses, and about 2,000 members.

Bibliography: L. RODINO, *Istoria del religioso istituto delle Figlie di Maria SS. dell'Orto* (Genoa 1889).

[A. FERRAIRONI]

OUR LADY OF THE LAKE COLLEGE

A 4-year liberal arts college with two professional schools, it is under the jurisdiction of the Congregation of Sisters of Divine Providence. The 115-acre campus, bordering on Elmendorf Lake, is located in the western section of San Antonio, Tex.

In line with the pattern of American educational development in the early 20th century, the College grew out of the normal school established in the 1870s by the Congregation for the teacher-training of its members. In 1883 the state granted the Congregation a charter empowering it to grant diplomas and degrees; this charter was amended in 1910 to include a liberal arts college. In 1911 a 2-year college program was opened to lay and religious students. In 1913 the College was affiliated with The Catholic University of America; in 1919 the Texas Association of Colleges recognized Our Lady of the Lake as a 4-year college; in 1923, the College was accredited by the Southern Association of Colleges and Secondary Schools; and in 1927, it was approved by the Association of American Universities. In 1954 the Council on Social Work Education approved the 2-year graduate program for the Worden School of Social Service, established in 1942. In 1958 the graduate department of education, inaugurated in 1950 with courses leading to the M.Ed. degree, was approved by the National Council for Accreditation of Teacher Education, which in 1961 approved the expansion of the program to the M.A. in education degree with areas of specialization in English, history, and speech.

The administration of the College consists of a board of directors, which determines the major policies of the institution and is formed of five religious and two lay members, one of whom is president of the College. The board is assisted by an advisory board of lay trustees working through three committees: finance, scholarships, and plant development. The president, chief executive of the College, is assisted by administrative officers. In 1964 the faculty was composed of 5 priests, 62 sisters, and 31 laymen holding 23 doctoral, 2 professional, and 49 master's degrees. Enrollment numbered 623 full-time and 478 part-time students in the regular session and 1,638 in the summer session.

Financial resources for the College come primarily from the contributed services of the religious community who serve on the staff and on the faculty. Other sources are tuition, fees, grants, and gifts. In 1923 the Congregation began to build a cash endowment, which was greatly augmented by Ford Foundation grants in 1956 and 1957.

The College offers programs leading to the bachelor degrees in one of 15 departments covering general education and specialization: humanities; the natural, social, and political sciences; classical and modern languages; and education. An undergraduate may obtain certification for teaching in elementary or high school through additional summer school courses. Because of the general educational background developed through fields of specialization in liberal arts, students achieve a liberal arts education even when specializing in a professional field. There are preprofessional courses in law, medicine, and nursing, and a 2-year program in social work.

Besides the traditional classroom procedures of lecture, seminars, and discussion, the College has introduced educational closed-circuit TV and a workshop in human relations.

The plant consists of 15 buildings whose architecture is the prototype of the cultural pattern of the College: the older buildings in Gothic exemplify the past, with roots in European traditions; the recent ones in modern American, suggest progress into the future. One of the most recent, the $220,000 Harry Jersig Speech and Hearing Center, provides a distinctive community service to San Antonio.

Bibliography: Administration and Faculty, *A Report on the Self-Study of Our Lady of the Lake College, San Antonio, 1962.* M. G. CALLAHAN, *The History of the Sisters of Divine Providence, San Antonio, Texas* (Milwaukee 1955).

[M. G. CALLAHAN]

OUR LADY OF THE MISSIONS, SISTERS OF,

religious congregation founded in 1861 at Lyons, France, by Mother Mary of the Heart of Jesus (Euphrasie Barbier, 1829–93), whose cause for beatification was introduced in Rome in 1960. The institute, established primarily for educational work in mission lands, received papal approval in 1906. Members take simple, perpetual vows and are governed by a superior-general who is elected for a 6-year term and resides at the motherhouse in Hastings, England. Each mission country constitutes a separate province. By 1890, houses existed on three continents. Administrative difficulties led to the closing of one Australian foundation in 1870. The houses in Oceania closed in 1877 after a domestic crisis. In 1920 the congregation reopened its French houses, which had been suppressed in 1902 by the laic laws. In 1964 the 1,238 members worked in 12 countries on 4 continents and operated 9 dispensaries, 2 workrooms, 3 nurseries, 5 hostels, 1 institute for the blind, 33 boarding schools, and 191 other schools with 33,410 students.

Bibliography: A. COULOMB, *Life of the Very Reverend Mother Marie du Coeur de Jésus* (Mechlin 1914). R. RIOS, *A Heroine of the Mission Field* (London 1944). *Teaching Nations 100 Years* (Regina, Can. 1961).

[I. ROSS]

OUR LADY OF THE SACRED HEART, DAUGHTERS OF

(FDNSC), a congregation of religious women founded in 1882 at Issoudun, France, by Jules *Chevalier and Marie Louise Hartzer (1837–1908). The institute developed from a small group that

Father Chevalier united into a congregation in 1874, but that languished until the arrival of Madam Hartzer, a widow born in Wissembourg (now in the Bas-Rhin department) in northeastern France. Following the Franco-Prussian War she came to France with her father and two sons, settled in Issoudun after her sons joined the Sacred Heart Missionaries, and became associated with Chevalier's followers. Under her leadership, the Daughters grew into the present congregation. The Holy See granted its decree of praise in 1908 and approved the constitutions in 1928. Members take simple vows, which are at first temporary, then perpetual. Governing the congregation is a superior general, aided by four assistant generals. All are elected for 6-year terms. The original two classes of members have been reduced to one. A special aim of the institute is to offer to the Sacred Heart homage, love, and reparation in imitation of the Blessed Virgin, who is honored as Our Lady of the Sacred Heart. In their apostolate the Daughters engage in educational and hospital work, mostly in the mission fields of Oceania, Indonesia, and Africa. The congregation spread first to Australia (1884), then to Belgium, Switzerland, Netherlands, Brazil, Italy, Ireland, England, and Spain. In 1955 it entered the U.S., in the Diocese of Camden, N.J., where 21 professed sisters labored in 1964. In 1961 there were 1,863 members in 196 houses. The motherhouse is in Rome.

Bibliography: F. and L. HARTZER, *La Réverende Mère Marie-Louise Hartzer* (Paris 1913).

[L. F. PETIT]

OUR LADY OF THE SNOW. The legend that gives this name to the feast (Aug. 5th, also called the Dedication of the Basilica of St. Mary Major) is that in the pontificate of Liberius (352–366) a childless Roman couple promised their wealth to the Virgin Mother of God. Her approval of their vow was indicated by a miraculous midsummer snowfall on the Esquiline Hill; by her appearance the same night in a dream to the patrician John and his wife, instructing them to build a church on the site; and by her confirmation of these instructions in the dream of Pope Liberius. The church was built, and later rebuilt during the pontificate of St. Sixtus III (432–440). It has been called by various titles and is now known as the Basilica of St. Mary Major.

No mention of the legend is found before the 10th century, and the prevailing attitude toward it is one of disbelief. It has been noted, for example, that in tracing the site for the church the snowfall untraditionally oriented the basilica to the west rather than the east. The congregation that Benedict XIV appointed in 1741 to reform the Breviary recommended that the lessons proper to the feast be omitted, on the grounds that it seemed unlikely that such an extraordinary occurrence would have gone unmentioned for so long. However, the feast had been extended to the universal Church during the pontificate of St. Pius V (1566–72), who is buried in the basilica, and the feast remains in the liturgical calendar.

Bibliography: Duchesne LP 1:207–208, 232. H. GRISAR, *History of Rome and the Popes in the Middle Ages,* ed. L. CAPPADELTA, 3 v. (London 1911–12) 1:140. para 2. H. LECLERCQ, DALC 10.2:2091–2119. E. JOSI, EncCatt 10:1228–31.

[M. S. CONLAN]

OUR LADY OF THE WAY, SOCIETY OF, a secular institute of women of pontifical right founded in 1936. The members vow to follow the evangelical counsels of chastity, poverty, and obedience; but they remain integrated in their social and occupational groups. They follow various occupations, live wherever appropriate for their apostolate, and do not wear a distinctive garb. The society does not have works of its own; its apostolate is accomplished by penetration, frequently where no other arm of the Church can reach, but first of all in the occupational fields of its members. The spirit of the society and its constitution stem from the *Spiritual Exercises* of St. Ignatius: to work for the glory of God; to develop an alert conscience and a strong sense of responsibility; to be ready for self-sacrifice; and to be aware of the call to apostolic service in each and all encounters. Advanced religious education and close contact among members are stressed. The society has members in Austria, Belgium, Germany, India, Ireland, Italy, Japan, the Philippines, Puerto Rico, Switzerland, the U.S., and the West Indies. The central house is in Vienna, Austria; there are several regional houses, one in Los Angeles, Calif.

[A. EMERY]

OUR LADY OF VICTORY MISSIONARY SISTERS, (OLVM), a pontifical institute of religious women founded in 1922 at Chicago, Ill., by Rev. John J. Sigstein; its members devote themselves to religious education and social work. Bp. John F. Noll, of Fort Wayne, Ind., built Victory Noll, the congregation's motherhouse and novitiate, at Huntington, Ind. Our Lady of Victory Missionary Sisters, commonly known as Victory Noll sisters, teach religion on the elementary and secondary levels for Catholic children who attend public schools. Catechetical centers are located throughout the U.S. and training programs are offered for Confraternity of Christian Doctrine personnel. The congregation also conducts parish visitations, staffs clinics, and is engaged in the Newman apostolate. The sisters take first vows after making a year's postulancy and 2 years of novitiate; final profession is made after 5 years. They wear a modern, dark blue habit with white collar and cuffs, a simple dark blue veil with a small white band, and a medal and chain of Our Lady of Victory. In 1964 the congregation had 81 mission convents and about 400 professed sisters.

[E. A. CLIFFORD]

OVALLE, ALONSO DE, Chilean Jesuit priest and historian; b. Santiago, Chile, 1601; d. Lima, Peru, March 16, 1651. He entered the Jesuits in 1618 and studied at Córdoba de Tucumán. In 1625 he returned to Chile, where he became famous as a preacher. He taught philosophy and theology and was rector of San Francisco Javier Seminary. In 1640 he was elected procurator for Rome and Madrid. He went to Europe via Lima and Panama and arrived at Cádiz at the beginning of 1642. While in Madrid he persuaded the King and the Council of the Indies to finance a large Jesuit expedition to accompany him upon his return. He also obtained tax exemptions and other benefits for the many victims of the earthquake of Santiago in 1647. He spent 2 or 3 months with the Chilean missionary Luis de *Valdivia in Valladolid, and their conversations contributed to his historical publications of those years. At the end of 1643 he arrived in Rome. After consulting, among others, the General of the order, Muzio Vitelleschi, he wrote *Histórica relación del reino de Chile* (Rome 1646, in two editions, Spanish and Italian), which has been reprinted many times and translated into the principal European languages. This work is the basis of Ovalle's reputation. Because of its sound historical information and its elegant classical diction, it is considered the outstanding literary monument of colonial Chile.

[F. MATEOS]

OVARIOTOMY, which literally means the cutting of an ovary, is a term often used loosely to signify the removal of one or both ovaries of a female (ovariectomy). Oophorectomy is considered by many a preferable term for this procedure. Its morality is discussed in the article CASTRATION.

[T. J. O'DONNELL]

OVERBERG, BERNARD, educator; b. Höckel bei Voltlage, northwest of Osnabrück, May 1, 1754; d. Münster, Nov. 9, 1826. He began studies for the priesthood in 1774 and was ordained at Rheine on Dec. 20, 1779. He was chaplain in Everswinkel (1780–83), director of the Münster normal school (1783), synodal examiner (1786), rector of the diocesan seminary and dean of Liebfrauenkirche (1809), Konsistorialrat (1816), honorary canon (1823) and Oberkonsistorialrat (1826).

In 1783 Franz von *Fürstenberg, the vicar-general, entrusted Overberg with the direction of the newly organized normal school in Münster. Overberg completely transformed the Catholic educational system in Münster, bringing it to a high degree of excellence. His pedagogical system was based on religious and moral education stressed equally with the development of teaching skills and complete mastery of subject matter. Foreseeing difficulties for the teaching religious orders in Germany, he encouraged the education of laywomen, inspiring them to regard the vocation of teaching as a true apostolate. When appointed rector of the seminary in Münster, he concerned himself especially with the moral formation of the clergy, at the same time continuing to exercise a strong influence on diocesan education through books and lectures, notably in the field of Christian doctrine.

Overberg was also a successful confessor and spiritual guide. He won the confidence of Amalia *Gallitzin and was instrumental in her return to the Church, remaining her lifelong friend and advisor. He also guided the priestly career of her son, Demetrius Augustine *Gallitzin. He influenced many contemporaries, including the convert Graf Friedrich Leopold von *Stolberg; the stigmatized mystic Anna Katharina *Emmerich; foundresses of religious institutes: Clara *Fey, Franziska *Schervier, Pauline von *Mallinckrodt; and the poets Luisa Hensel and Annette Elisabeth von *Droste-Hülshoff.

Overberg's most important work is his *Anweisung zum zweckmässigen Schulunterricht für die Schullehrer im Fürstentum Münster* (Münster 1793, 1835; Joseph Esterhues, ed, Paderborn 1957), in which he sets forth his pedagogical aims, methods, and principles. He also wrote *Die Geschichte des alten und neuen Testamentes* (Münster 1799, 1889), *Christkatholisches Religions-Handbuch* (Münster 1804, 1827), *Katechismus der christkatholischen Lehre zum Gebrauche der grösseren Schüler* (Münster 1804, 1852), *Katechismus der christkatholischen Lehre zum Gebrauche der kleineren Schüler* (Münster 1804–48), and *Kleiner Haussegen* (Münster 1807, 1836).

Bibliography: B. OVERBERG, *Aus dem Tagebuche einer grossen Seele: Die Tagebücher Bernard Overbergs,* ed. P. KRÜGER (Kavelaer 1937). R. STAPPER, *Bernard Overberg als pädagogischer Führer seiner Zeit* (Münster 1926). H. M. HEUVELDOP, *Leben und Wirken Overbergs* (Münster 1933). H. HOFFMANN, *Bernard Overberg* (2d ed. Augsburg 1949). W. SAHNER, *Overberg als Pädagoge und Katechet und das Arbeitsschulprinzip* (Gelsenkirchen 1949). S. SUDHOF, LexThK² 7:1319.

[M. F. LAUGHLIN]

OVID IN CHRISTIAN CULTURE

Publius Ovidius Naso (43 B.C.–A.D. 17), one of the most gifted of Roman poets, exercised an influence on Christian and secular poetry in the Middle Ages and the Renaissance second only to that of Vergil. Within a few years of his death his *Metamorphoses* became the standard work of reference for Greek and Roman mythology and legend, a position it has never lost. For painters, poets, and preachers, it became the greatest single source of myth, although the *Heroides* and *Fasti* were much used also. Similarly, Ovid's treatment of love is the most significant single literary formulation of erotic experience in the Latin tradition. When Augustine (*Conf.* 3.1) says, "I was not yet in love, but in love with loving" (*nondum amabam sed amare amabam*), he uses the word "love" (*amare*) with just that shade of meaning given it by Ovid. In the tradition before Ovid, love was usually treated as an aberration, madness, or sickness (*furor, uesania, morbus,* etc.) affecting the individual lover. Ovid extended and deepened this conception to emphasize his view that love is essentially a mutual experience between two persons who are equally involved. His Pyramus and Thisbe, Ceyx and Halcyone, Philemon and Baucis, and many others become typical examples for the Latin tradition after him. One always thinks of these lovers in pairs, whereas the typical lover of Greek epigram, the new comedy, or earlier Latin elegy is usually thought of by himself.

In technical matters, such as metrics, prosody, and poetic diction, Ovid's usage became the classical standard. Later writers admired Vergil but wrote in the language of Ovid. Ovid's influence became so dominant in the 12th and 13th centuries, especially as the patron of the wandering scholars, that the great medievalist L. Traube called this period the *Aetas Ovidiana* in Latin poetry. In the Middle Ages Ovid was widely interpreted in an allegorical manner and so ingeniously construed as to be found an authority on moral conduct. His works were an important source of the tradition of courtly love. E. K. Rand says that Chaucer owed to him "a greater debt than to any other poet, old or new." He was much used by Dante and Boccaccio and had a great vogue in Neo-Latin poetry in general.

Poets tend like other craftsmen to learn their trade from earlier masters; in this sense Ovid has been one of the great masters, not only in the Latin tradition, but in modern European languages also. The English authors Dryden, Pope, and Milton, among many others, were his pupils. The Romantic revolt in poetry may be understood as a rebellion against the too dominant and restrictive influence of those standards of classicism that Ovid seems best to represent.

Bibliography: SchHosKrüg GeschRL 2:206–264. E. K. RAND, *Ovid and His Influence* (Boston 1925). R. R. BOLGAR, *The Classical Heritage and Its Beneficiaries* (Cambridge, Eng. 1954). H. F. FRÄNKEL, *Ovid: A Poet between Two Worlds* (Berkeley 1945). F. MUNARI, *Ovid im Mittelalter* (Zürich 1960). Manitius, v.1–3, indexes s.v. Ovidius. L. K. BORN, "O. and Allegory," *Speculum* 9 (1934) 362–379. J. SEZNEC, *The Survival of the Pagan Gods: The Mythological Tradition and Its Place in Renaissance Humanism and Art,* tr. B. F. SESSIONS (New York 1953).

[M. P. CUNNINGHAM]

OVIEDO, FRANCISCO DE,

Jesuit theologian; b. Madrid, 1601; d. there, Feb. 9, 1651. He entered the Society of Jesus in 1618 and became a professor of theology at the universities of Madrid and Alcalá. His most important works are *Integer cursus philosophicus ad unum redactus* (2 v. Lyons 1640; new ed. 1651, 1653); *Tractatus theologici, scholastici et morales respondentes 2a2ae D. Thomae* (Lyons 1646); and *Tractatus de virtutibus fide, spe, et charitate* (Lyons 1651).

Bibliography: É. AMANN, DTC 11.2:1674–75. N. PALMARINI, Mercati-Pelzer DE 2:1260. Sommervogel 6:42–43. Hurter Nomencl³ 3:921.

[P. F. MULHERN]

OVIEDO, ARCHDIOCESE OF (OVETENSIS)

Metropolitan see since 1954, in northwest Spain. In 1963 it had 779 parishes, 792 secular and 223 religious priests, 325 men in 33 religious houses, 1,657 women in 139 convents, and 1,011,000 Catholics; it is 4,079 square miles in area. Its three suffragans, which had 1,979 parishes, 2,266 priests, 1,780 sisters, and 1,184,850 Catholics, were: *León, *Santander, and Astorga (created *c.* 250 and a religious center after the Arab invasion of Spain in 711).

The See of Oviedo was founded before 812 by Alfonso II, who wished to make his capital the heir of Visigothic Toledo in Church and State. Claims that refugee bishops at the royal court elected Oviedo a metropolitan in councils of 821 and 876 are open to dispute. When Oviedo gave way to León as the northern capital *c.* 924, it became a bishopric, made exempt by Pascal II (1105).

In 1134 Bishop Gutierre obtained the County of Noreña, a title held by the bishops to 1951. Bishop *Pelayo (d. 1153) forged documents to prove that Oviedo was a metropolitan see. Oviedo's bishops include Rodrigo Sánchez de *Arévalo (1457–67); Diego de Muros, who founded the College of Oviedo in Salamanca and contested his authority with the town of Oviedo; Jeronimo de Velasco, who attended the Council of Trent; and Juan Álvarez de Caldes, who introduced Tridentine reforms (1606). The concordat of 1851 made Oviedo suffragan to *Santiago de Compostela.

The university, endowed by Bp. Fernando de *Valdés (1532–39), opened in 1608 with chairs of theology and canon and civil law. The theologian Benito Feijóo (1676–1764), the regalist jurist and historian Pedro Rodríguez Conde de Campomanes (1723–1802), and the statesman Gaspar Melchor de Jovellanos (1744–1811) came from the university, which lost its theology faculty in 1840 and came under the state. Until Bp.

The Gothic cathedral at Oviedo, completed 1556.

Ignacio Diaz Caneja founded the seminary in 1854, clerics were educated in the university and in the Colleges of San Pedro de los Verdes (1593) and of San José (1662).

The cathedral built by Alfonso II (792–842) was the center of a complex, of which the Camara santa and other elements remain. Additions of the 11th and 12th centuries appear in the old tower and the cloister. The present cathedral was built over the old nucleus in flamboyant Gothic (early 14th century to 1556). The churches of Santullano (with murals), Santa Maria de Naranco, San Miguel de Liño, Santa Cristina de Lena, and Valdedios are 9th-century examples of the rich and sedate Romanesque "Asturian" art, which was spread by monks, who, after San Vicente (761), built hundreds of monasteries, first under Spanish rules (*Fructuosus of Braga and *Isidore of Seville), then under Benedictine (10th) and Cistercian (13th century) rules. Few traces of these monasteries remain, however. Today the main shrine is Covadonga, where, thanks to miracles, a small band of Christians held out against hordes of Arabs. But from the 11th century it was the Camara santa that drew pilgrims on the northern route to Santiago, with the famous casket of relics brought from Toledo in the Arab invasion, the precious crosses of the Angels (1808) and of Victory (908), and the casket of chalcedonies (10th century).

Oviedo, three-fourths destroyed by fire in 1521, was sacked by the French in 1808. Today it is a growing center of the munitions and chemical industries and is dealing with problems of urbanization by suburban settlements.

Bibliography: Flórez EspSagr, v.37–39. L. BARRAU-DIHIGO, in *Revue hispanique* 52 (1921) 1–360. S. GARCÍA LARRAGUETA, *Sancta Ovetensis* (Madrid 1962). A. FLORIANO, *Estudios de Historia de Asturias* (Oviedo 1962). F. CANELLA SECADES, *Historia de la Universidad de Oviedo*, 2 v. (2d ed. Oviedo 1903). A. VIÑAYO, *El arzobispado de Oviedo* (Oviedo 1955). A. LAMBERT, DHGE 4:1199–1226. **Illustration credit:** MAS, Barcelona.

[G. NOVALIN]

OWEN, NICHOLAS, BL., called "Little John," English martyr and Jesuit lay brother; b. place and date unknown; d. London, March 2, 1606 (feast, March 12). He probably was the son of Walter Owen of Oxford, and the brother of Henry, a Catholic printer, and Walter and John, priests. Nicholas first appears in Catholic history as a prisoner in London in 1582. He was the open champion of the innocence of Edmund *Campion, whose servant he is said to have been. Soon after the arrival of Henry *Garnet in England (July 1586) Owen, then at liberty, entered his service, in which he remained for the next 18 years. He was employed principally in the construction of hiding places in Catholic centers established by his master, since he was a superb carpenter, mason, and architect. A few authentic examples survive, e.g., at Sawston Hall near Cambridge; Huddington Court, Worcestershire; Coughton Hall, Warwickshire; which point to his limitless ingenuity. The fullest contemporary appreciation of his character and work was written by John *Gerard: "I verily think no man can be said to have done more good of all those that laboured in the English vineyard. For first, he was

Hiding hole at Sawston Hall, made by Bl. Nicholas Owen. It is one of few unaltered surviving examples.

the immediate occasion of saving many hundreds of persons, both ecclesiastical and secular, and of the estates also of these seculars, which had been lost and forfeited many times over if the priests had been taken in their houses." Since he knew the hiding places of most priests in England, he was certain to receive very severe treatment if captured. He was finally taken at Hinlip Hall, near Worcester, on Jan. 23, 1605. With Ralph Ashley he was forced out of hiding by starvation, and tried to pass himself off as a priest to save Garnet. The ruse failed. Taken to London, Owen was mercilessly tortured in the Tower. As a result of a fall from a horse he had a rupture, which legally exempted him from racking, but this was ignored by the Council. When he gave no information injurious to any Catholic, the torture became more violent. On March 2 while Owen was on the rack, his entrails burst out. He survived some hours in agony. On his death the Council gave out that he had committed suicide but few believed it. He was beatified by Pius XI on Dec. 15, 1929 (*see* MARTYRS OF ENGLAND AND WALES).

Bibliography: Butler Th Attw 1:579–581. H. FOLEY, ed., *Records of the English Province of the Society of Jesus*, 7 v. (London 1877–82) 4.1:245–267. J. GERARD, *The Autobiography of a Hunted Priest*, tr. P. CARAMAN (New York 1952); *The Condition of Catholics under James I. Fr. Gerard's Narrative of the Gunpowder Plot*, ed. J. MORRIS (2d ed. London 1872). DictEngCath 5:224. M. WAUGH, *Blessed Nicholas Owen* (Postulation pamphlet; London 1961). **Illustration credit:** Copyright, Country Life.

[G. FITZHERBERT]

OWENSBORO, DIOCESE OF (OWENSBURGENSIS), suffragan of the metropolitan See of *Louisville, Ky., comprising 32 counties in western Kentucky, an area of 12,502 square miles. The diocese was established Dec. 9, 1937, from territory taken from Louisville, which became a metropolitan see at that time. Owensboro's first bishop, Francis R. Cotton (1895–1960), was consecrated Feb. 24, 1938, and installed March 8. He made early preparations for a diocesan synod, which in its final session in February 1943 adopted 114 statutes, later approved by Rome and promulgated. Aid for priestless counties was obtained from the *Glenmary Home Missioners (1942), and an offer from the Benedictines of Collegeville, Minn., resulted in the establishment of St. Maur's Priory and Seminary, South Union. Contemplative Passionist nuns from Scranton, Pa., were welcomed to Owensboro (1946), where they founded St. Joseph's Monastery. Care of the sick under Catholic auspices was undertaken when Mercy sisters of Cincinnati, Ohio, staffed a hospital at Morganfield (1945) and opened another in Owensboro (1948); Franciscan sisters of Tiffin, Ohio, took over the city hospital at Paducah (1959). Care of the aged was provided by Carmelite sisters of Milwaukee, Wis., who established Carmel Home, Owensboro (1952). Sisters of the Lamb of God, Brest, France, accepted the invitation to do social work, and opened their first convent in the U.S. at Owensboro (1958). In education the original communities—Charity of Nazareth, Dominican, Mercy, and Ursuline sisters—increased their diocesan labors, and were augmented by Franciscans (1941) and by the Glenmary and Loretto sisters (1947). Ursulines opened *Brescia College, Owensboro; in September 1946.

The second bishop, Henry J. Soenneker (1907–   ), was consecrated April 26, 1961, and installed May 9.

In 1964 his diocese numbered about 39,450 Catholics in a total population of 650,000. There were 67 parishes and 84 priests, including 19 religious. Also serving the diocese were 11 brothers and nearly 300 sisters, helping to staff the diocese's 44 elementary and 14 high schools, 1 college, 3 general hospitals, and 1 home for the aged.

Bibliography: *The First Synod* (Owensboro, Ky. 1943). *First Review & Year Book* (Owensboro, Ky. 1952).

[M. E. NAHSTOLL]

OWL AND THE NIGHTINGALE, THE.

A 12th-century poem generally regarded as one of the outstanding works in Middle English. It takes the form of a debate between the two birds, as to which excels the other. The birds are well trained in the medieval *débat* tradition, and as their arguments develop, they range over many of the central intellectual questions of the century. The author never forgets, however, that the antagonists are birds, and they speak in character as they attack each other's personal habits, singing ability, and nest-building skill, as well as philosophical and moral outlooks. The poem is as, noted for its liveliness and wit as for its rhetorical accomplishment.

It is clear, however, that the owl and the nightingale are more than mere representatives of two species of birds. Though scholars disagree upon any specific interpretation of their characters, or of their debate, the nightingale clearly stands for a joyous, the owl for a sober, approach to life. Among the most important of their topics is man's attitude toward his religion: should it be penitential or celebratory?

The birds are unable to convince one another, and agree to take their quarrel to one Nicholas of Guilford, who, we are told, is preeminent for both learning and able judgment. But the reader is left simply with the debate: the author appears to suggest that either view of life alone is partial, that both the sober owl on its stump and the playful nightingale on its branch have important things to say and make mistakes, which need correction, and that a proper tension of their attitudes contributes balance to life; resolution of the argument is less important than practical truth.

The author and the exact provenance of the 2,000-line, octosyllabic poem are unknown. It is not now generally supposed that Nicholas was the author, or that the poem was written at Guilford. The dialect is that of the southwestern part of England, and the work has importance as a philological document, as well as for its literary qualities.

Bibliography: *The Owl and the Nightingale,* ed. E. G. STANLEY (London 1960), the best text, with excellent introd. and nn. R. M. WILSON, *Early Middle English Literature* (London 1939) ch. 7. H. HÄSSLER, *"The Owl and the Nightingale" und die literarischen Bestrebungen des 12. und 13. Jahrhunderts* (Frankfurt a. M. 1942). H. WALTHER, *Das Streitgedicht in der lateinischen Literatur des Mittelalters* (Quellen und Untersuchungen zur lateinischen Philologie des Mittelalters 5.2; Munich 1920), the standard work on the Medieval Debate.

[N. D. HINTON]

OWNERSHIP

Ownership is the juridical power or faculty of disposing of something as one freely desires. Hence an owner is one who can give away, sell, destroy, or use something that is his own, and all this within the bounds set by legitimate authority. Ultimately, this power finds its source in God as the Supreme Lawgiver; it is also part of the natural law inasmuch as it constitutes the most reasonable solution to man's problem in regard to his duty, both as an individual and as a member of society, to strive after his final end. This right of man to dispose freely of his goods is not absolute, but conditioned by the many limitations necessarily set by right reason and the common good. In regard to the latter, the legitimate authority of any given society rightfully exercises a certain power (*dominium altum*) over the individual's right and the exercise of ownership (*dominium humile*) in order to insure the good of all within the society. Of necessity, then, all are required in conscience to observe the regulations set down by the civil authority when these are in keeping with right reason and are strictly necessary for the common good.

In general there are two kinds of ownership, perfect and imperfect. Perfect ownership is the strict right to the total substance of a thing and all benefits connected with it. One who enjoys perfect ownership in regard to some object can freely dispose of it, use it, or allow others to use and profit from it. Imperfect ownership, however, is the right only to the substance of the thing (radical dominion) or the right to derive some benefit from the thing without touching its substance in any way. This latter kind of imperfect ownership is the right to derive either use or usufruct or service from the thing. Since these are strict rights in themselves, they cannot be arbitrarily revoked by the owner of the substance.

All those things of which man can be the owner are called "goods." Goods in this sense can be of three general kinds: internal, external, and those sharing the qualities of both, namely, mixed goods. Internal goods that are not distinct from the man himself (as, for example, his limbs, his health, and his very life) do not and cannot fall within the area of man's perfect ownership, nor does he possess them even radically, for he is not his own, but God's possession. Instead, man possesses only a partial or utilitarian right over his body and his other internal endowments. However, any man not legitimately impeded in his right to own, can possess and exercise all the rights of perfect ownership over external goods, as long as these are not incapable of being privately owned, as is the case for example with such things as churches, cemeteries, public highways, and other facilities; and the gifts of nature that men enjoy in common, such as air and light. Mixed goods, such as fame and honor, also constitute possible objects of perfect ownership to the extent to which they are the fruits of one's own industry.

The right of ownership can belong to any human person, physical or moral. The physical person, an individual human being, enjoys this right because his rational nature is inherently capable of possessing and disposing of whatever goods are necessary for him to attain his end. Seen in this light, infants not yet born, as well as those permanently deprived of their reason, enjoy this right radically, even though they are incapable of its exercise. After death, however, this right ceases in regard to all former objects of ownership save that of personal reputation, an exception due to the fact that this good is radically incapable of transfer to another.

Moral persons, that is, societies of individual human beings joined together for an honest purpose, enjoy the right of ownership since they possess the right to acquire whatever is necessary for them in the pursuit of their legitimate objectives. Bodies of this kind can be either ecclesiastical or secular in nature. The latter class includes the state itself, provinces, cities, colleges, universities, and a host of other minor societies; the former includes the Universal Church (which is by natural and divine law absolutely independent of the civil power in this regard), dioceses, parishes, seminaries, hospitals, religious societies, etc.

Ownership, whether perfect (full) or imperfect (partial), can be acquired in six general ways: occupancy, finding, increase, *labor, prescription, and contract. Occupancy means taking possession of something that does not belong to any one, with the intention of keeping it as one's own. Finding is a species of occupancy in which the ownership of whatever is found depends on whether the object is entirely without a past or present owner, abandoned, or merely lost; in the latter case, there may be an obligation of finding its owner and of restoring it to him (see LOST PROPERTY AND OWNERSHIP). Increase is to be understood as accretion or increment added to one's property but without previous contract or donation. Labor also is a legitimate way of acquiring ownership, since it is only just that man should benefit from his efforts. Prescription is another means recognized by law of acquiring something as one's own or of wiping out a debt. It consists in the possession of something for a continuous length of time and in the manner defined by law. Perhaps the most frequent way one acquires ownership in modern society is by way of contract. Although there are several different kinds, a contract can be defined simply as consent between two or more persons about transferring the rights of ownership.

See also PROPERTY, PRIVATE.

Bibliography: Davis MorPastTh 2:259–295. J. TONNEAU, DTC 13.1:757–846. T. PIACENTINI, EncCatt 10:138–145.

[J. T. O'CONNOR]

OXFORD, UNIVERSITY OF

One of two ancient English universities, in Oxford, the county seat of Oxfordshire, England.

City of Oxford. Situated between the upper Thames and the Cherwell, this ancient "ford of oxen" was fortified against the Danes in 912 by Edward the Elder, King of the West Saxons. By 1000, Oxenford was one of the principal towns of the country. After the Conquest, Norman earls built a massive castle, city walls, and many churches. In the 12th century the ancient nunnery of St. Frideswide was given to the Austin Canons. The growth of the University in the 13th century brought Dominicans (1221), Franciscans (1224), Carmelites (1256), Friars of the Sack (c. 1262), Cistercians (1280), Benedictines (1283), Trinitarians (1293), and other religious orders. From the 13th to the 16th century the privileged position of the University repressed growth of the town, particularly after the riots of St. Scholastica's day, 1355. Formerly a township in the Diocese of Lincoln, it became a cathedral city under Henry VIII. During the Reformation religious houses were suppressed or turned into secular colleges. National divisions of sympathy were reflected in the perennial feud between city and University, which was not reconciled until the visit of George III in 1785. The 20th century has brought great growth and change (1960

Carfax Tower, the hub of the university town of Oxford.

population 104,500). Many ancient religious orders have returned, and some newer congregations share in the activity of the city and the University. Since the reestablishment of the Catholic hierarchy, Oxford has been in the Diocese of Birmingham.

University. The origin of this oldest university in England is lost in obscurity, even after all legend has been discounted. Individual masters, like Theobald of Étampes, are known to have taught clerks (clerics) in Oxford before 1117; around 1150 some masters held their own schools there. It was not until Henry II checked the flow of English scholars to Paris, however, that English masters and students flocked to Oxford. By 1180 "a large number of scholars" from different faculties resided there (*Gerard of Cambrai), but probably without much formal organization until the legatine ordinance of 1214. *Robert Grosseteste was appointed chancellor (c. 1215–21), representing the bishop of Lincoln; curricula in theology, law, medicine, and arts were modeled on University of *Paris practice. The arrival of mendicant orders proved beneficial. In 1254 Innocent IV confirmed all immunities, liberties, and customs of the University and as at Paris, no clerk could enroll in theology unless he had first been a regent master in arts. The congregation of regents and nonregents of all faculties (*congregatio magna*), later called the convocation, was the supreme governing body; the congregation of all regent masters of all faculties (*congregatio minor*) governed ordinary affairs. To govern the arts faculty, regent masters in arts formed their own congregation (*congregatio nigra*), presided over by two proctors, one *Australis* and the other *Borealis,* who were the original University executives. Lectures were always given in the schools, and scholars lived wherever they could. Riots and disorders between "town and gown" induced Bp. Walter de Merton in 1264 to found a residence for secular students of theology, mainly his relatives, similar to the college founded by Robert de *Sorbon in Paris. Two earlier residential halls, University College (1249) and Balliol (1263), were soon reorganized to conform to Merton's statutes. Originally these colleges merely provided good lodging and company for a select group of fellows. Only later did the colleges become the self-contained, autonomous units that, grouped together, make up the University of Oxford as it exists today.

As a corporate body, the University dates only from the reign of Elizabeth I, when an act of Parliament, passed in 1571, incorporated "the chancellor, masters and scholars" of Oxford, and imposed the oath of supremacy and the 39 Articles. In 1634 the ancient, scattered statutes of the University were codified by Abp. William Laud and ratified by royal charter. The Laudian Code is still the basis of the existing statutes, although many modern provisions have been added. In 1850 the first royal commission was appointed to reform and modernize the University. Since 1854 continued organizational reform has been accompanied by the introduction of modern subjects: natural science, economics, modern and Oriental languages, social studies, fine arts, agriculture and forestry. In 1920 women were admitted to full membership in the University.

Organization. The chancellor, masters, and scholars form a corporate body within which the colleges are individual corporations. The highest officer is the chancellor, usually a man of distinction, elected by convocation. In practice the head is the vice-chancellor, a head of one of the colleges, who is nominated annually by the chancellor for a total of 3 years. Two proctors are appointed annually by two of the colleges in rotation. University business is initiated by the Hebdomadal council and decided upon by the congregation (all resident M.A.'s). The council consists of 5 ex officio members (chancellor, vice-chancellor, 2 proctors, and either the outgoing or incoming vice-chancellor) and 18 M.A.'s elected by the congregation. Since 1926 the power of convocation (resident and nonresident M.A.'s) has become nominal. The administrative work is delegated to academic bodies, supervised by the general board of faculties, and nonacademic bodies, such as curators.

No one can study for a degree or be a member of the University unless he is a member of one of the 26 colleges for men: University (founded 1249), Balliol (1263), Merton (1264), St. Edmund's Hall (c.1278), Exeter (1314), Oriel (1326), Queen's (1340), New College (1379), Lincoln (1427), All Souls (1438, no undergraduates), Magdalen (1458), Brasenose (1509), Corpus Christi (1517), Christ Church (1546), Trinity (1554, formerly Benedictine, Durham), St. John's (1555, formerly Cistercian, St. Bernard), Jesus (1571), Wadham (1612), Pembroke (1624), Worcester (1714, formerly OSB, Gloucester), Keble (1870, only for Anglicans), Hertford (1874), St. Antony's (1951), Nuffield (1958, for doctorate candidates), St. Catherine's (1868, reorganized 1962), and St. Peter's (1929, reorganized 1962); or the 5 colleges for women: Lady Margaret Hall (1878), Somerville (1879), St. Hugh's (1886), St. Hilda's (1893), and St. Anne's (1952). Besides innumerable authorized lodgings, there are five permanent private halls: Mansfield College, Campion Hall (Jesuit), St. Benet's Hall (Benedictine), Regent's Park College, and Greyfriars (Franciscan). Since 1954

Queen Elizabeth House has been a center for commonwealth studies.

Studies for degrees are of three kinds: (1) the normal undergraduate studies for the B.A. in any set subject; (2) undergraduate studies in one of the higher faculties, normally taken after the B.A., for the B.D., in theology, B.C.L. in law, the B.M. and B.Ch. (Surgery) in medicine, and B.Mus. in music; (3) original research under a supervisor for the degrees of B.Litt., B.Sc., B.Phil., and D.Phil. Higher doctorates are awarded for published work containing an original contribution to the advancement of learning.

There are 16 faculties and 1 department in which one may study: theology, law, medicine, litterae humaniores ("greats," the ancient arts faculty), modern history, English, modern European languages, Oriental studies, physical science (including mathematics), biological sciences, social studies (philosophy, politics, and economics, or "modern greats"), anthropology and geography, music, agriculture and forestry, psychology, fine arts, and a department of education.

Examinations for the B.A., the basic Oxford degree, are: (1) responsions—entrance examination taken before coming up to the University or its equivalent; (2) first public examination, which may be an honors examination (moderations), taken between the 3d and 6th term after matriculation, in Greek and Latin, mathematics, natural science or law, or a pass examination designed as a preliminary to one of the final honor schools; (3) final schools examination, generally an honors examination, in a single subject or in two or three closely related subjects, taken between the 8th and 12th term after matriculation. Having passed the final schools examination, a B.A. graduate may retain his name on the books of his college for a total of 21 terms (7 years) and supplicate for the degree of M.A. without any further examination, and thus become a member of the convocation.

Oxford uses two educational systems: the university lecture system, which centers on the lecturer's current interest or university needs, and the tutorial system, which centers on the needs of the undergraduate. The undergraduate is not obliged to attend any lectures, but he usually attends those pertinent to the final schools

High Street, Oxford; Queen's College on the right; University College on the left; the spires of St. Mary's in the background.

examination or those recommended by his tutor. The tutorial system, perfected in the 19th century, is the basic educational technique at Oxford. A freshman on his arrival at the beginning of his first term is introduced to the college tutor in charge of the subject that he intends to study. This college tutor determines the immediate needs of the individual and assigns one or more tutors who will be responsible for the intellectual development of the undergraduate. The precise form of the tutorial, or weekly session with the tutor, varies with the subject. Basically it is the presentation of some exercise, essay, or experiment, read or performed, singly or in small groups, for the tutor to criticize, query, or explain. The weekly tutorial is based on a heavy reading course, including the list published by the board of faculty concerned. The tutor's primary function is to instruct and to develop the critical abilities of the undergraduate.

The academic year at Oxford consists of three full terms of 8 weeks each, fixed by the Hebdomadal council: Michaelmas, beginning on the second Sunday in October; Hilary, beginning on the first Sunday after January 14; and Trinity, beginning on the last or next to last Sunday in April, depending on the date of Easter. Specified terms of residence, usually nine and never less than six, are a condition of admission to any degree. These terms, each of which must be at least 42 days long, must be kept by residence within the walls of a college, hall, or in licensed lodgings. During the two short vacations of 6 weeks each and during the long summer vacation the student is expected to complete the heavy reading program set by the board of faculty and his tutor.

Strictly speaking, Oxford offers no graduate courses. Since 1895, however, certain faculties have established research degrees, particularly for graduates of other universities. The first research degree established was the B.Litt. The candidate must be accepted by a college or society, and through the college by the appropriate board of faculty for the area of research. The subject proposed for a thesis must be approved and a supervisor appointed. The examination for the degree is based solely on the written dissertation, which can be submitted after 1 year (if he is a graduate of Oxford) or 2 years of research, but not later than the third.

Application for admission as an advanced student in the technical sense for the D.Phil. degree is similar to the B.Litt. and B.Phil. However, much more is expected and a longer time is allowed (between 2 and 5 years, with possible extensions). A successful dissertation for the D.Phil. degree is "an original contribution to knowledge set forth in such a manner as to be fit for publication." When the original statute establishing the degree of D.Phil. was passed in 1917, advanced studies at Oxford secured a definite position subject to systematic control by the University.

In recent decades, through the work of the royal commission the University has come to assume a greater responsibility in the advancement of learning. Nuffield College, founded in 1937, was unique in being a University institution and not an independent corporation. It is a postgraduate college intended "to encourage research especially but not exclusively in the field of social studies." St. Catherine's was reconstituted as a full college in 1962 to promote study of the technological sciences. The University museum, the University labora-

tory of physical chemistry, erected in 1939–40, the Clarendon laboratory, completed in 1940, and more recent science buildings are under the direct control of the University and not of any particular college, although many of the colleges have their own laboratories.

Oxford is particularly blessed with good libraries. Besides college libraries, there is a central University library consisting of more than six separate collections in various buildings. The most famous is the Bodleian, founded in 1602 by Thomas Bodley, and its extensions, the Radcliffe Camera and the New Library, opened in 1946 to hold 4 million volumes. The Bodleian is particularly rich in manuscripts (approximately 40,000) and books (2¼ million). The Radcliffe science library contains the scientific section of the University library. The library of Rhodes House specializes in African and colonial history; the Indian Institute contains books dealing with India and Pakistan; Taylor Institute specializes in modern European languages and literature; and the Ashmolean Museum contains a number of specialist libraries in fine arts, archeology, antiquities, classics, and papyrology. Besides these there are smaller faculty libraries specializing in English, modern history, China and Chinese books, geography, and mathematics.

After World War II the University grew at an unusual pace. In 1964 the University had 9,022 students, double the enrollment of 1935, and about 900 teachers, including 108 professors in the various faculties.

Details of the various fees, grants, prizes, and scholarships, notably the Rhodes scholarship, are given in *Handbook to the University of Oxford,* published and revised periodically by the Oxford University Press. The Rhodes scholarships, established under the last will (1899–1901) of the South African statesman, Cecil Rhodes, are for students from the British Empire, the U.S., and Germany. The great majority of American Oxonians have been Rhodes scholars.

Bibliography: A. G. LITTLE, *The Grey Friars in Oxford* (Oxford 1892). C. E. MALLET, *A History of the University of Oxford,* 3 v. (London 1924–27). J. WELLS, *Oxford and Its Colleges* (9th ed. London 1910). S. GIBSON, ed., *Statuta antiqua universitatis Oxoniensis* (Oxford 1931). A. G. LITTLE and F. PELSTER, *Oxford Theology and Theologians, c. A.D. 1282–1302* (Oxford 1935). H. RASHDALL, *The Universities of Europe in the Middle Ages,* ed. F. M. POWICKE and A. B. EMDEN, 3 v. (new ed. Oxford 1936). D. A. CALLUS, "Introduction of Aristotelian Learning to Oxford," *Proceedings of the British Academy* 29 (1943) 229–281. W. A. HINNEBUSCH, *The Early English Friars Preachers* (Rome 1951). E. CRASTER, *History of the Bodleian Library, 1845–1945* (Oxford 1952). Emden. M. H. CURTIS, *Oxford and Cambridge in Transition, 1558–1642* (Oxford 1959). F. PELSTER and D. A. CALLUS, LexThK² 7:1320–23. Publications. *Oxford University Calendar* (1810–) yearly. *University of Oxford Examination Statutes* (1883–) yearly. *Oxford University Gazette* (1870–), regularly. *Oxford Historical Society Publications* (1884–1936; N.S. 1939–). *Handbook to the University of Oxford* (1932–) esp. 1962 and periodic revisions. *Oxford Studies Presented to Daniel Callus* (Oxford 1960). **Illustration credits:** British Travel Association, N.Y.C.

[J. A. WEISHEIPL]

OXFORD MOVEMENT

An effort by Anglican clergymen of Oxford University between 1833 and 1845 to renew the Church of England by a revival of Catholic doctrine and practice. The following phases of the movement are discernible: (1) rise and progress (1833–39), (2) crisis (1839–41), (3) Tract 90 and its aftermath (1841–45), and (4) the period after Newman.

Background. The Church of England (*see* ANGLI-CANISM) had emerged from the Reformation as an amalgamation of Catholic and Protestant doctrine and practice. These two disparate elements were welded together in the interest of national unity, mainly during the reign of Elizabeth I. The Catholic tradition, or *High Church element, triumphed over the Protestant element during the period of such famous Anglo-Catholic divines as Lancelot *Andrewes and William *Laud. But the *Revolution of 1688 enabled the Protestant party to gain the ascendancy. *Latitudinarianism, which minimized doctrine, represented a third party.

By 1800 the English Church greatly needed reform. With its deep internal divisions, worldly prelates, and ineffectual clergy, however, it was hardly prepared to undertake this task itself. Hence it was faced with the prospect of having unwelcome reforms imposed on it by secularist and liberal members of Parliament. The first such reform occurred in 1833 when 10 Anglican bishoprics were suppressed in Ireland. To many loyal churchmen this was an omen of more drastic changes, perhaps even of disestablishment.

Rise and Progress (1833–39). A fear of such drastic moves motivated John *Keble in a sermon entitled "National Apostasy" (July 14, 1833), which John Henry *Newman considered the beginning of the Oxford Movement. The sermon was followed by a meeting held from July 25 to July 29 at Hadleigh, Suffolk, attended by a number of prominent clergymen, including Hugh Rose, William Palmer, and Richard Hurrell *Froude. They decided to organize a defense of the Church through the formation of committees and the issuance of joint manifestoes.

Newman, Keble, and Froude, however, believed that the only true remedy for the evil condition of the Church lay in a theological and spiritual renewal. They held that the Catholic heritage of the Book of *Common Prayer and of the 17th-century divines had to be recovered. The English Church had to reaffirm her commitment to the almost forgotten Catholic truths, namely, that she held divine authority as part of God's visible kingdom; that her sacraments were indispensable channels of grace; and that her bishops were successors of the Apostles. This message they decided to communicate to the clergy in brief pamphlets, subsequently named *Tracts for the Times*, an expedient originated by Newman, who wrote the first one (*see* TRACTARIANISM).

Keble, "the true and primary author" of the movement according to Newman, was a gentle poet and scholarly pastor who had imbibed the Catholic tradition in his father's rectory. Froude, an ardent disciple of Keble, burned with an impatient zeal to restore the Church of England to its medieval spiritual power. Newman, a bold, searching thinker, was a patristic scholar who had moved from an Evangelical to a Catholic position through his reading and his personal contacts at Oxford, especially his friendship with Froude and Keble.

One of the first important conquests of the movement occurred at the end of 1833 when Edward B. *Pusey signed his initials to *Tract 18*. Regius professor of Hebrew, canon of Christ Church, and an aristocrat with friends in high places, he already enjoyed a reputation for great learning and holiness. His adherence to the cause was of invaluable assistance in establishing the movement as a serious contender for influence in the Church.

Newman, with his natural gifts, his acute, sensitive mind, his great capacity for friendship, and his insight into the minds of others, was destined to be the movement's natural leader. It was a leadership he exercised in many ways. His sermons at St. Mary's, Oxford, where he was vicar, were a powerful means of attracting many to the movement's ideals. Published as *Parochial and Plain Sermons* (1834–42), they reveal the essence of the Oxford reformation, its unworldliness, uncompromising quest for holiness, and unflinching asceticism. The sermons' psychological penetration, scriptural wisdom, and matchless beauty of language have made them enduring masterpieces.

Newman also did most to establish a theoretical basis for the movement. This was the object of a series of lectures delivered between 1834 and 1836 and published as *The Prophetical Office of the Church* (1837). Drawing on the 17th-century Anglican divines, he argued that the Church of England held an intermediate position, a *via media* between the extremes of Roman infallibility and Protestant private judgment. Her rule of faith was simple fidelity to the teaching of the Fathers. He confessed, however, that Anglo-Catholicism was still merely a religion on paper. There was a great need of theological investigation of the Anglican tradition to make it one, intelligible, and consistent. To this end Newman, Keble, and Pusey began to edit the 45-volume *Library of the Fathers* (1838–88), a series of English translations of patristic writings, and the 83-volume *Library of Anglo-Catholic Theology* (1841–63).

In his *Apologia* Newman revealed that the *via media* was based on three fundamental principles—dogma, the sacramental system, and anti-Romanism. The chief opponents of dogma, he said, were the Liberals, who viewed religion as a mere matter of opinion. His anti-Romanism at the time was evident in his reference to the pope as anti-Christ and in his accusations against Rome of corrupting the Gospel truths.

Valuable recruits were soon gained, especially among the younger fellows of Oriel and Trinity. Such talented scholars as Charles Marriott, Robert Wilberforce, Frederick Rogers, Richard W. Church, and Isaac Williams rallied to the reform banner. As Newman remarked (*Apologia*, 76) "the Anglo-Catholic party suddenly became a power in the National Church and an object of alarm to her rulers and friends."

Latent hostility erupted with the publication in 1838 of the private papers of Froude, who died in 1836. These *Remains* offended great numbers by their strong anti-Protestant character and confirmed a growing suspicion that the movement was pro-Roman.

Crisis (1839–41). Newman considered the year 1839 as the zenith of the movement. The revival of Catholicism seemed to answer definite spiritual needs of many members of the Church of England. Several developments, however, marked this year as the beginning of a crisis. There was, first, the formation of a new party of eager, acute, resolute minds with definite sympathies for Rome. Such men as William G. *Ward, Frederick Oakeley, F. W. *Faber, and J. D. *Dalgairns "cut into the original movement at an angle, fell across its line of thought, and then set about turning that line in its own direction" (*Apologia*, 164).

A more fateful development occurred when doubts suddenly arose in Newman's mind about his *via media*. He found in his study of early history that *Monophysitism had upheld a *via media* similar to the Anglican one. At the same time he saw in St. Augustine's phrase *"securus judicat orbis terrarum"* a rule of faith that seemed to invalidate the Anglo-Catholic's rule of fidelity to the Fathers. As he put it, "the deliberate judgment in which the whole Church at length rests and acquiesces, is an infallible prescription . . . against such portions of it as protest and secede." (*See* PRESCRIPTION, THEOLOGICAL USE OF.) Catholicity, or communion with the whole Church, was the essential mark of the true Church, not fidelity to antiquity.

> While the history of St. Leo showed me that the deliberate and eventual consent of the great body of the Church ratified a doctrinal decision as a part of revealed truth, it also showed that the rule of Antiquity was not infringed, though a doctrine had not been publicly recognized as so revealed till centuries after the time of the Apostles. Thus, whereas the Creeds tell us that the Church is One, Holy, Catholic, and Apostolic, I could not prove that the Anglican communion was an integral part of the One Church, on the ground of its teaching being Apostolic or Catholic, without reasoning in favour of what are commonly called the Roman corruptions; and I could not defend our separation from Rome and her faith without using arguments prejudicial to these great doctrines concerning our Lord, which are the very foundation of the Christian religion. The Via Media was an impossible idea! [*Apologia*, 149.]

Still Newman tried to meet his own difficulty in an article in the *British Critic* (January 1840), in which he argued that jurisdictional or other forms of visible intercommunion were not necessary between the parts of the one visible Church. The English Church, although separated from Rome, was still the Catholic Church in England since it was still in possession of "the Succession, the Episcopal form, the Apostolic faith, and the use of the Sacraments" (*Essays Critical and Historical*, 20).

Tract 90 and Aftermath. But Ward and others in the party leaning toward Rome cited the *Thirty-nine articles to disprove Newman's contention that the Anglican Church held a common faith with Rome. The Articles were drawn up to exclude Roman doctrines from the English Church, they said. In reply Newman undertook a commentary on the Articles in *Tract 90*, which he published in February 1841. It was a crucial experiment, he recognized. He tried to prove that the Articles implied a distinction between Catholic teaching and Roman dogma; that they definitely did not condemn the former and did not even condemn the latter entirely. Rather the historical circumstances of their composition show that they were deliberately made general and vague in order to pacify those in the national Church with Catholic tendencies as well as those with Protestant ones. Thus, although Article 21 simply states that "General Councils . . . forasmuch as they be an Assembly of men may err . . .," Newman claimed that this did not rule out their inerrancy "when they are a thing of heaven." Despite the extreme subtlety of some of his distinctions, subsequent study has verified Newman's main contention.

But the tract was not answered with argument. Panic and wrath ensued at this denial of the Protestant character of the Articles. All the resentment stored up against the "Oxford Malignants" now burst out in full fury. The heads of houses at Oxford, notorious for their ignorance of theology, publicly censured *Tract 90* as an evasion. Newman's bishop demanded the cessation of the tracts.

Newman retreated to a mission church he had built at Littlemore, his position in the established Church seriously compromised. Then three more blows fell, all but destroying his belief in the Anglican Church. A further study of *Arianism showed him again the existence of another heretical *via media* in early Church history, i.e., Semi-Arianism. Second, the bishops one by one disowned Newman's interpretation of the Articles. Finally, the establishment of an Anglican bishopric in Jerusalem embracing Lutherans and other Protestants indicated a formal recognition of Protestant doctrines. This was the ultimate condemnation of the *via media* for Newman.

Meanwhile Pusey was suspended from preaching for 2 years after delivering a moderate Tractarian sermon on the Holy Eucharist. Then Ward entered the conflict. With remorseless logic he defended the thesis that since Rome alone fulfilled "the ideal of a Christian Church" (the title of his book), the Anglican Church must humbly sue for readmission to her communion. Official Oxford was outraged. His book was censured, and he was deprived of his master's degree in the Oxford convocation (Feb. 13, 1845).

Newman despaired of the Anglican Church and withdrew into lay communion after preaching his last sermon, "The Parting of Friends" (Sept. 25, 1843). He was kept back from Rome for 2 years by difficulties over Tridentine doctrines, transubstantiation, and Catholic devotion to the Blessed Mother and the saints. Further study led him to favor the view that a principle of development was at work in the Church from earlier times. After writing his *Essay on Development* (1845) to prove this point to his own satisfaction, he made his profession of Catholic faith to Father Dominic *Barberi (Oct. 9, 1845).

After Newman. Ward, Faber, Oakeley, Dalgairns, and many others left Anglicanism with Newman. Pusey and Keble assumed leadership of the faltering party. Oxford ceased to be its headquarters. Pastoral and liturgical matters overshadowed doctrinal ones.

Another wave of secessions to Rome occurred in 1851 over the case of Rev. George C. Gorham. The bishop of Exeter had refused a parish to Gorham because of his questionable views on Baptismal regeneration. The bishop's decision, however, was reversed by the Privy Council in an unprecedented intervention in doctrinal matters. The impotence of the teaching authority of the Church appeared manifest to a number of clergymen, including Henry *Manning (later cardinal), who thereupon made their submission to Rome.

A long struggle was waged within the Church of England by Pusey, Keble, and their associates to revive the Catholic Sacraments, particularly the Eucharist and Penance. Puseyites were condemned by the archbishop of Canterbury and were brought to court for advocating the Catholic doctrinal interpretation of these Sacraments. But their patience and perseverance gradually won partial acceptance of this doctrine in the Church of England.

The revival of Catholic ceremonial, the use of altar lights, Eucharistic vestments, etc., was another result of work by Pusey and his friends. Although these practices were sanctioned by the Prayer Book, their advocates had to contend with furious mobs that wrecked churches where the reforms were introduced and with hostile bishops who condemned them as popish innovations. The revival of religious orders in the Church of England was another outcome of the Oxford Movement. Pusey's foundation of a sisterhood in 1845 was followed by the foundation of other communities of men or women. *See* RELIGIOUS ORDERS (COMMUNITIES), PROTESTANT.

The Oxford Movement failed to revive Catholic orthodoxy or to check the rising Liberalism in the Church of England. Its successful revival of Anglo-Catholic sacramental and liturgical practice, however, has greatly influenced the spirit and form of contemporary Anglican worship (*see* ANGLO-CATHOLICS).

Bibliography: R. W. CHURCH, *The Oxford Movement: Twelve Years* (London 1891). P. THUREAU-DANGIN, *La Renaissance catholique en Angleterre au XIXᵉ siècle*, 3 v. (Paris 1899–1906). I. MARCHAL, DTC 11.2:1675–1704. S. L. OLLARD, *A Short History of the Oxford Movement* (London 1915). C. DAWSON, *The Spirit of the Oxford Movement* (New York 1933). H. FRIES and W. BECKER, eds., *Newman Studien* (Nürnberg 1948–). E. FAIRWEATHER, ed., *The Oxford Movement* (New York 1964). W. H. HUTTON, CambHistEnglLit 12:280–308. S. L. OLLARD, *ibid.* 496–508. J. H. NEWMAN, *Apologia pro vita sua* (1st ed. London 1864). H. P. LIDDON, *Life of Edward Bouverie Pusey*, ed. J. O. JOHNSTON and R. J. WILSON, 4 v. (London 1893–97).

[T. S. BOKENKOTTER]

OXNAM, GARFIELD BROMLEY, U.S. Methodist bishop; b. Sonora, Calif., Aug. 14, 1891; d. White Plains, N.Y., March 12, 1963. He received his B.A. (1913) from the University of Southern California, Los Angeles, and his S.T.B. (1915) from Boston University, Mass. After ordination as a Methodist minister in 1916, he held several pastorates and teaching positions before being named president of De Pauw University, Greencastle, Ind. He held this post until his election as bishop in 1936. During the next 24 years he served as bishop of Omaha, Nebr. (1936–39), Boston, Mass. (1939–44), New York, N.Y. (1944–52), and Washington, D.C. (1952–60). He was one of the first presidents of the *World Council of Churches (1948–54) and headed (1947) the anti-Catholic organization, *Protestants and Other Americans United for Separation of Church and State (P.O.A.U.). He was known as a liberal in civil liberties and was frequently associated with liberal causes. In 1953 he appeared before the House Un-American Activities Committee (HUAC) to defend liberal Protestant clergymen charged with Communist leanings. He was accused by one member of HUAC of "serving God on Sunday and the communist front for the rest of the week," but his testimony cleared his own record and brought the investigations to a close. Among his books are *Labor and Tomorrow's World* (1945), *The Church and Contemporary Change* (1950), *On This Rock* (1951), and *I Protest* (1954).

[E. DELANEY]

OXYRHYNCHUS, a provincial capital (Coptic, Pemdjie) about 200 kilometers south of Cairo, which became a large and important city during the Hellenistic period. In about A.D. 380 it was listed as a diocese with at least 10 churches, in addition to many monasteries in the surrounding region. During the Byzantine period it was the metropolis and commercial center of the province of Arcadia, but it gradually declined under Moslem rule and is now in ruins. Its chief importance lies in the immense collection of papyri discovered there, beginning with the excavations of B. Grenfell and A. Hunt (1897–1907), W. F. Petrie (1922) and Breccia (1927–28). They unearthed thousands of unknown and very important pagan and Christian documents: fragments of classical literature, gospels, apocrypha, Greek and Hebrew hymns, patristic texts, calendars and inventories of churches, as well as civil and commercial items.

Bibliography: B. P. GRENFELL et al., eds., *The Oxyrhynchus Papyri* (London 1898–). K. PREISENDANZ, *Papyrusfunde und Papyrusforschung* (Leipzig 1933). H. GERSTINGER, LexThK² 7:1324–35. A. CALDERINI, EncCatt 9:428–429. H. DELEHAYE, AnalBoll 42 (1924) 83–99.

[G. T. DENNIS]

OZANAM, ANTOINE FRÉDÉRIC

French historian and literary scholar, founder of the Society of St. Vincent de Paul; b. Milan, April 23, 1813; d. Marseilles, Sept. 8, 1853. A tradition of the Ozanam family traced its descent from a 7th-century Jew, Samuel Hosannam, converted by St. Didier, whom he sheltered from persecution. Frédéric was brought up and educated in Lyons. In 1829 he underwent a "crisis of doubt," which he overcame with the assistance of his teacher, Abbé Noirot. This experience consolidated the intellectual basis of his faith and also imbued him with deep charity in controversy with unbelievers.

In 1831 he published his first work, a refutation of the socialistic theories of the Saint-Simonians. In the same year he went to Paris to study law and made the acquaintance of the leaders of the Catholic revival—Chateaubriand, Montalembert, Lacordaire, Ballanche, Ampère, and others. He was concerned to refute the attacks on Catholicism which were widespread in the Sorbonne. It was in May 1833 that he and a few fellow students formed a "Conference of Charity" to undertake practical work among the poor. This is accepted as the foundation date of the Society of St. Vincent de Paul, although its formal title and rules were not adopted until 1835. Ozanam insisted that the Society should not

Antoine Frédéric Ozanam.

restrict its charity to Catholics and that countries should assist each other; thus, the Paris Society aided Dublin during the Irish famine and Dublin reciprocated during the Revolution of 1848.

Ozanam completed his first degree in law in 1834, and was called to the bar in Lyons. However, his true bent was for literature and history. He returned to Paris, where he took his first degree in literature in 1835, his doctorate in law in 1836, and his doctorate in literature in 1839. During this period he was active in the Society of St. Vincent de Paul, the Society for the Propagation of the Faith, Catholic journalism, and many Catholic causes. He was instrumental in bringing about the first of Lacordaire's famous series of Lenten sermons in Notre Dame.

Ozanam became the first to hold a chair as professor of commercial law at Lyons in 1839, but returned to Paris the following year to teach foreign literature at the Sorbonne. He was elected professor in 1844. His studies of Dante, beginning with his doctoral thesis, revolutionized critical work on the poet. Although Ozanam is a neglected figure in 19th-century historiography, his research in the development of Christian Latin, literature, and art showed an acquaintance with the original texts and contemporary critical research in the major European languages which was remarkable in the French scholarship of his day.

Ozanam advocated that Catholics should play their part in the evolution of the democratic state and unsuccessfully stood for election to the National Assembly in 1848. He denounced economic liberalism and any form of socialism. Lecture 24 in his course of commercial law is a brilliant exposition of Catholic social doctrine, foreshadowing *Rerum novarum and antedating the Communist Manifesto in its attention to the social question. Ozanam's personal visitations to the poor and his reports of the St. Vincent de Paul Society antedated even Villermé's pioneer social investigation published in 1840. Ozanam may justly be regarded as an exemplar of the lay apostolate in family, social, and intellectual life. His cause for beatification was introduced in 1923.

See also ST. VINCENT DE PAUL, SOCIETY OF.

Bibliography: *Oeuvres complètes,* 11 v. (Paris 1859–65). C. A. OZANAM, *Vie de Frédéric Ozanam* (Paris 1879). G. GOYAU, *Frédéric Ozanam* (Paris 1925); et al., *Ozanam: Livre du centenaire* (Paris 1913), contains complete bibliography of Ozanam's writings and studies of him at that date. L. BAUNARD, *Ozanam d'après sa correspondance* (Paris 1912), a standard work published by the Catholic Truth Society of Ireland as *Ozanam in his Correspondence,* without the name of tr. F. MÉJECAZE, *Fr. Ozanam et l'église catholique* (Paris 1932). E. RENNER, *The Historical Thought of Frédéric Ozanam* (Washington 1959).

[F. MACMILLAN]

P

PACCA, BARTOLOMEO

Cardinal, papal diplomat; b. Benevento (Campania), Italy, Dec. 25, 1756; d. Rome, April 19, 1844. Of noble birth, he studied in Naples under the Jesuits and in Rome at the Collegio Clementino and the Accademia dei Nobili Ecclesiastici. In 1785 he received minor and major orders, becoming titular archbishop of Damietta and nuncio to Cologne, where he met the opposition of the bishop-electors of Mainz and Cologne, who were incensed against the Holy See because of the erection of the nunciature at Munich. These bishops, who were hostile to interventions in spiritual matters by nuncios, were impregnated with *Febronianism, and were defenders of the Congress of *Ems. The repercussions of the French Revolution did more to improve the situation than did Pacca's firmness and ability. He was named nuncio extraordinary to Louis XVI, whose flight Pius VI believed successful, but the king's capture at Varenne made Pacca's mission pointless. As nuncio to Lisbon (1794–1801), he had to struggle against the regalianism inherited from *Pombal and upheld at the University of Coimbra. Created cardinal (1801), Pacca became one of the most influential *zelanti*. He opposed the French *Concordat of 1801 and remained in contact with the bishops of the Ancien Régime who refused submission to it. His nomination as prosecretary of state (June 18, 1808), after the occupation of Rome by Miollis and the expulsion of Cardinals Consalvi and Giulio Gabrielli by the French, indicated *Pius VII's will to resist. For impeding Pacca's arrest, the Pope was also seized and carried off from Rome (July 1809). Pacca was imprisoned in the stronghold of San Carlo di Fenestrelle in Piedmont from July 1809 until the *Concordat of Fontainebleau (February 1813), after which he was permitted to rejoin Pius VII.

Contrary to what Pacca wrote in his memoirs (*Memorie storiche del Ministero*), neither he nor the cardinals around the Holy Father were responsible for the Pope's decision to withdraw the concessions to Napoleon I in this so-called concordat, only the basis of a definite arrangement. On January 28 Pius VII made his own decision and annulled these agreements in a secret declaration. Pacca's role consisted in counseling the best procedure to minimize the consequences of the Pope's act. For this, Pacca incurred Napoleon's wrath and was deported to Uzès in southern France. He reentered Rome with Pius VII (May 24, 1814). During the Hundred Days he fled with the Pope to Genoa to escape *Murat, who invaded the States of the Church (March 1815).

As prosecretary of state (May 19, 1814–July 2, 1815), during the sojourn of the secretary of state *Consalvi at Paris and the Congress of Vienna, Pacca practiced a policy of restoring the old order, contrary to Consalvi's broader views. During the latter part of Pius VII's pontificate, Pacca allied with the *zelanti* and ceaselessly opposed the reforms judged necessary by the Pope. At the conclave in 1823 Pacca actively participated in the reaction which resulted in Consalvi's disgrace. Pacca became bishop successively of Frascati (1818), Porto and Santa Rufina (1821), and Ostia and Velletri (1829). Under Leo XII, Pius VIII, and Gregory XVI he was prodatary and a member of important congregations in the Curia.

Pacca was a true churchman, solidly pious, courageous in upholding the Church's rights, cultured, a patron of artists, and promoter of the first archeological excavations at Ostia; but his outlook was that of the Ancien Régime and lacked open-mindness. He failed to understand Pius VII and Consalvi and passed severe judgments on them. His volumes of memoirs, published under various titles, are valuable historical sources, but they must be utilized with caution, because later he substantially altered the section concerning Pius VII's captivity. To know his real sentiments it is necessary to recur to the original text. (For illustration, see following page.)

Bibliography: G. BRIGANTE COLONNA, *Bartolomeo Pacca, 1756–1844* (Bologna 1931). A. DURANTE, *Tre papi e un cardinale* (Rome 1940). J. LEFLON and C. PERRAT, "Les Suppressions et édulcorations qu'a fait subir à ses *Mémoires* le cardinal P.," *Chiesa e stato nell'ottocento: Miscellanea in onore di P. Pirri,* ed. R. AUBERT et al., 2 v. (Padua 1962) 2:355–381. L. PASZTOR, "Per la storia del *Concordato* di Fontainebleau," *ibid.* 597–606. V. E. GIUNTELLA, EncCatt 9:494.

[J. LEFLON]

PACCANARISTS,

popular title of the Society of the Faith of Jesus, a religious institute that followed the rule of the *Jesuits, dedicated itself to carry on their work, and above all sought the restoration of this order, suppressed in 1773. Its founder, Niccolò Paccanari (1773–?), was an enthusiastic and eloquent Italian, born at Valsugana near Trent; he was, however, deficient in formal education, humility, and prudence.

Bartolomeo Pacca, papal diplomat.

Business and soldiery occupied him until a serious illness (1795) followed by the influence of a pious Roman confraternity called the Oratory of Caravita, and 14 months of prayerful retirement, led him to establish in Rome a religious congregation (Aug. 15, 1797). His four companions, one a former Jesuit priest, chose him superior although he had only the tonsure. Members took the three vows of religion, plus a fourth vow of special obedience to the pope, whose formulation proved a stumbling block to many former Jesuits. The garb was that once worn by Italian Jesuits. Pius VI early in 1798 approved the new institute, selected its name, permitted it to recite the Breviary with Jesuit supplements, and to admit former Jesuits.

With papal encouragement Paccanari arranged a union with the Society of the *Sacred Heart of Jesus (April 18, 1799), almost identical in rule and purpose with his own institute. Paccanari, not a priest until 1800, became superior of the merged groups, which bore the title of his original foundation, although this had but 19 members, whereas the other had 50, far superior in caliber, education, influence, and material resources.

For a few years the society increased rapidly in numbers as it spread from Italy and Austria into Germany, Switzerland, France, Holland, and England. It gained a good reputation for varied pastoral and educational activities. When Pius VII confirmed the Jesuits in White Russia (1801) and in parts of Italy (1804) and allowed them to accept recruits from elsewhere, many Paccanarists joined them. Paccanari discontented his subjects by his worldly outlook, ambition to retain authority, and disinclination to restore the Society of Jesus or to affiliate with it. All the 70 or so members in France won the nuncio's approval to form an independent body. After a papal investigation Paccanari received a 10-year prison sentence (August 1808). Released by the French (1809), he returned to prison for another offense (1810). No further reliable record of him exists. When the Jesuits were completely restored (1814), most of the few remaining Paccanarists joined them.

Bibliography: O. PFÜLF, *Die Anfänge der deutschen Provinz der neu erstandenen Gesellschaft Jesu* (Freiburg 1922). J. BURNICHON, *La Compagnie de Jésus en France, 1814–1914* (Paris 1914–) v.1. A. GUIDÉE, *Vie du R. P. Joseph Varin* (2d ed. Paris 1860). H. CHADWICK, "Paccanarists in England," Arch HistSocJesu 20 (1951) 143–166. A. RAYEZ, "Clorivière et les Pères de la Foi," *ibid*. 21 (1952) 300–328. Koch JesLex 1763–64. L. DERIÈS, *Les Congregations religieuses au temps de Napoléon* (Paris 1929).

[J. F. BRODERICK]

PACE, EDWARD ALOYSIUS

Educator, author; b. Starke, Fla., July 3, 1861; d. Washington, D.C., April 26, 1938. As the son of George Edward and Margaret (Kelly) Pace, he was descended on his father's side from 17th-century English colonists in Virginia; his maternal grandfather was Owen Kelly, comptroller of ports of Halifax, Nova Scotia. He attended public school in Starke, and Duval high school, Jacksonville, before studying for the priesthood at St. Charles College, Ellicott City, Md. (1876–80), and the North American College (with classes at the Propaganda University), Rome, where he was ordained on May 30, 1885.

After being awarded the S.T.D. degree in 1886, he returned to the Diocese of St. Augustine, Fla., and served for 2 years as rector of the cathedral and chancellor. In 1888, following his selection for the faculty of the projected Catholic University of America, Washington, D.C., he returned to Europe for graduate studies in psychology. After a year at Louvain and Paris, he transferred to Leipzig, where he studied under Wilhelm *Wundt, and received the Ph.D. *magna cum laude* in 1891. Thereafter he served at The Catholic University of America as professor of psychology (1891–94) and of philosophy (1894–1935), dean of the School of Philosophy (1895–99; 1906–14; 1934–35), general secretary (1917–25), vice rector (1925–36), and founder (1899) and first director of the Institute of Pedagogy, which developed into the department of education. In 1936 he was named vice rector emeritus and professor of philosophy emeritus. The psychological laboratory that he established in 1891 was the second in America and the first in a Catholic university. As an editor of the *Catholic Encyclopedia* (1907–14), Pace took a leading part in planning and bringing it to a successful conclusion. At the international Congress of Arts and Sciences held in St. Louis, Mo., in 1904, Pace, a pioneer in experimental psychology, served as chairman

Edward Aloysius Pace.

of the section of experimental psychology. He became first editor of *Studies in Psychology and Psychiatry* (1926), and with Thomas Edward *Shields he founded and edited the *Catholic Educational Review* (1911).

He was founder and first president of the American Catholic Philosophical Association, which was established at The Catholic University of America in 1926, and with James Hugh *Ryan he first edited its journal, *New Scholasticism*. In 1925 he was elected president of the American Council on Education and in 1929 was appointed by Pres. Herbert Hoover to the National Advisory Committee on Education. He received the medal *Pro Ecclesia et Pontifice* (1914), was named a prothonotary apostolic (1920), and received various honorary degrees.

Pace's publications include his doctoral dissertation, *Das Relativitaets-prinzip in Herbert Spencer's psychologischer Entwicklungslehre;* many articles in philosophy, religion, and education; and *The Mass for Every Day in the Year* (1916), one of the first modern translations of the Missal, which he prepared with John J. Wynne, SJ. A pioneer in experimental psychology, Pace's teaching and writing were characterized by depth and originality of thought, careful reasoning, and clarity of expression. In 1919, the American bishops commissioned him to compose a national pastoral letter; his notable document analyzing issues then facing the Church and the nation was signed by Cardinal James Gibbons "in his own name and in the name of the hierarchy."

Bibliography: Pace Papers, The Catholic University of America Archives, Washington, D.C. J. K. RYAN, "In Memory of Edward Aloysius Pace," NewSchol 35 (1961) 141–151. H. MISIAK and V. M. STAUDT, *Catholics in Psychology: A Historical Survey* (New York 1954). C. A. HART, ed., *Aspects of the New Scholastic Philosophy* (New York 1932), Festschrift.

[J. K. RYAN]

PACE, RICHARD, English humanist, diplomat, dean of St. Paul's; b. Winchester, 1482?; d. London, July 1536. Pace, a student at Winchester, served as secretary to Thomas Langton, Bishop of Winchester (1493–1500). By 1510 he had studied at Oxford and had been ordained; he had also toured the Continent. Pace accompanied Cardinal Bainbridge of York to Italy (1509–15) where the young priest was scandalized by Roman worldliness. While secretary to Henry VIII, Pace served also Cardinal Wolsey as a diplomat in France, Switzerland, and Germany. Weary and ill, he was awarded the deanery of St. Paul's (1519), succeeding John Colet. King Henry conferred many ecclesiastical honors and benefices on Pace. At one time in his life, he held posts and prebends in York, Dorset, Colchester, Leeds, and Bangor as well as deaneries in Exeter and Salisbury. As a friend and ardent correspondent of Erasmus, Pace was instrumental in establishing Greek chairs at Oxford and Cambridge. Despite his academic and ecclesiastical interests, Pace served also on further diplomatic missions. He was present at the Field of the Cloth of Gold (1520) and at Venice furthered Wolsey's papal ambitions and English policy (1521–25). When recalled to England, he seems to have suffered a physical and mental breakdown from which he only slowly recovered. The last 10 years of his life were spent in relative obscurity. An advocate of the new learning, Pace was a friend of Thomas More and John Fisher, and like them, he wrote a number of Latin commentaries.

Bibliography: J. H. LUPTON, DNB 15:22–24. H. M. SMITH, *Pre-Reformation England* (London 1938).

[P. S. MC GARRY]

PACEM IN TERRIS

Eighth encyclical of John XXIII, issued April 11, 1963. Although widely hailed as an encyclical on international peace, in the narrow sense, its scope covers the whole range of order in human affairs, for it identifies peace with that unity of order that is based on respect for the law of God. To this end it expounds, in a more comprehensive manner than any previous papal document, the order that should prevail between man and man, between man and the community, and between communities *inter se* and the world community.

Because of the immense scope of the encyclical, it is not surprising that different interests welcomed it for different reasons. In one respect it appealed to all, namely, in its sincere desire for brotherhood between men. Western newspapers welcomed the encyclical for its humanitarian vision and boundless confidence in man's capacity for peace. Soviet news agencies gave it the favor of relatively extensive summary. In certain respects its welcome was selective. Some socialist sources praised it vaguely for positions already advocated by socialists, particularly internationalism, while the Communist press headlined its plea for disarmament to the extent that Radio Vatican felt it necessary to issue a reminder that insistence on human freedom and dignity rather than advocacy of *disarmament was at the core of the document.

The first part of *Pacem in terris* is built on the truth that order between individual men must be founded on the fact that man is a *person. Such order consists essentially in respect for rights and duties that pertain to man entirely in virtue of his personality. The encyclical is a veritable charter of *human rights, which it lists in specific detail, and is in a way reminiscent of the UN Universal Declaration of Human Rights.

In its second part the encyclical presents the relationship between the individual and the *state as basically one of subjection to *authority—not, however, as an authority rooted simply in physical force, but rather one representing the coercive power of a moral entity. For this reason the ordinances of human authority must be in accordance with the order of God's law. The encyclical launches into an important exposition of the philosophy of *law that is diametrically opposed to all forms of legal positivism.

In its third part the encyclical argues that states, just as individuals, are the subjects of rights and duties. These rights and duties are translated into practical action by the persons who govern the state, for through these alone can the state be subjected to the moral law. Among the many things that this entails is a practical recognition of the equality of all states in dignity, whatever their racial backgrounds or their political or cultural stages of development. Recognition of solidarity implies in the concrete, not only that individual states should pursue their ends without hurting one another, but also that they should join forces whenever the efforts of an individual government cannot achieve its desired goals. The encyclical insists that trust rather than fear should be the vivifying factor in relationships between states. In place of the law of fear, which has prevailed for so long, the law of love should be substituted. Here there is a direct reference to *war and peace, in the form of a plea that the arms race cease, that the stockpiles that exist be reduced equally and

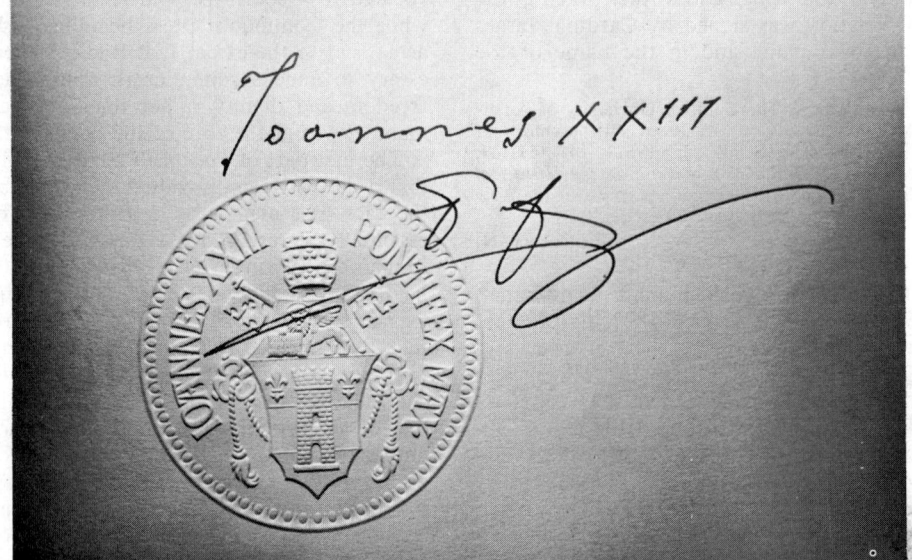

— 49 —

inter se fraterno more complectantur, in iisque semper floreat semperque dominetur optatissima pax.

Extremum id ominantes, Venerabiles Fratres, ut eiusmodi pax ad greges prorepat vobis commissos, per commodum maxime tenuissimorum hominum, qui peculiari egeant adiumento et tutela, Apostolicam Benedictionem vobismetipsis, sacerdotibus ex utroque clero, religiosis viris virginibusque Deo devotis, et christifidelibus omnibus, sed iis nominatim, qui Nostris hisce hortationibus magno animo parebunt, peramanter in Domino impertimus. Universis vero bonae voluntatis hominibus, ad quos etiam hae Litterae Nostrae pertinent, salutem et prosperitatem a summo Deo imploramus.

Datum Romae, apud S. Petrum, in Cena D. N. I. C., die XI mensis Aprilis anno MDCCCCLXIII, Pontificatus Nostri quinto.

Signature of Pope John XXIII on one of the three autographed copies of "Pacem in terris." This copy, willed to Pres. John F. Kennedy, is preserved in the Kennedy Memorial Library, Boston, Mass.

simultaneously by the countries concerned, and that nuclear weapons be banned and eventually a general disarmament reached.

The fourth part of the encyclical urges the importance of interdependence between states. Greater today than ever before, the collaboration that such interdependence stimulates puts an end to former ideas about absolute sovereignty and absolute national self-determination. The conclusion of the encyclical is devoted to pastoral exhortations. Catholics are urged to cooperate both individually and corporately with non-Catholics and even non-Christians for the advancement of praiseworthy social and political ends.

See also INTERNATIONAL LAW; INTERNATIONAL ORGANIZATION; INTERNATIONAL RELATIONS; PEACE, INTERNATIONAL.

Bibliography: John XXIII PacTerr gives the official Latin text. J. NEWMAN, *Principles of Peace* (New York 1964). P. RIGA, *Peace on Earth* (New York 1964). **Illustration credit:** Thomas M. Atkins, The White House.

[J. NEWMAN]

PACHER, MICHAEL, the leading Late Gothic painter and woodcarver in the Tyrol; b. near Brixen, *c.* 1435; d. Bruneck?, 1498. Pacher's workshop in Bruneck was on an important Alpine road, and Pacher himself seems to have traveled to northern Italy, first as a young painter in the 1450s and again about 1475. His art shows a synthesis between the north Italian style of Mantegna's frescoes in the Eremitani church, Padua, and the widespread early Netherlandish style of Rogier van der Weyden. Pacher's most important work is the "St. Wolfgang Altarpiece" (1471–81, St. Wolfgang, Austria), which has a carved wooden shrine with life-size colored figures in a "Coronation of the Virgin" and a predella forming the center for two pairs of double-

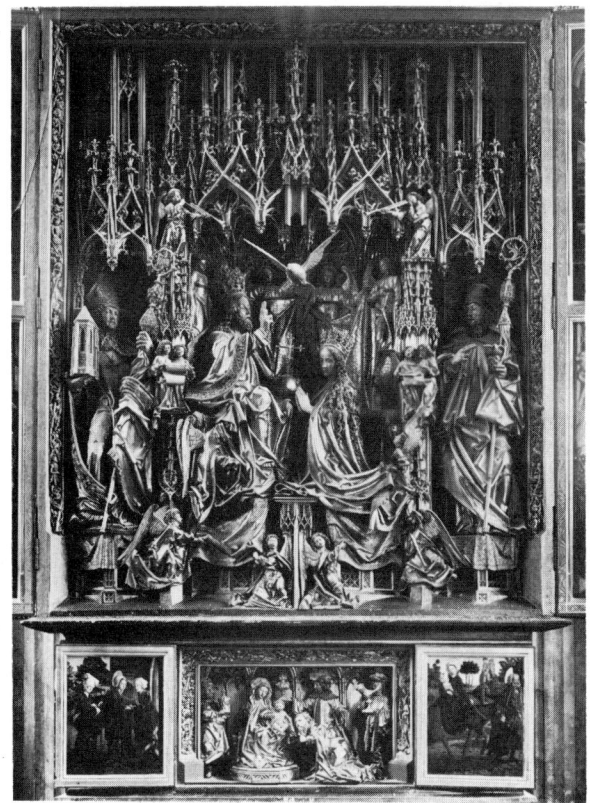

Michael Pacher, the "St. Wolfgang Altarpiece."

tiered painted wings. The spiky, carved pinnacles of the frame contain painted and gilded wooden figures; the sharp, angular folds of their drapery can be paralleled in Pacher's paintings. Scenes from the life of Christ and of the Virgin are depicted with detailed realism in spatially roomy surroundings in which the "worm's-eye view" perspective has been derived from Mantegna. His "Altarpiece of the Four Latin Fathers" (c. 1483, Pinakothek, Munich) shows a further development. Instead of a series of independent pictures, there is a central perspective construction for the four panels, and the elaborately carved frame of the "St. Wolfgang Altarpiece" is here painted illusionistically. The monumental figures under ornate painted canopies carry on a lively dialogue with their foreshortened symbols.

Bibliography: E. HEMPEL, *Das Werk Michael Pachers* (4th ed. Vienna 1941). **Illustration credit:** Austrian Information Service, New York.

[M. M. SCHAEFER]

PACHOMIUS, ST.

Founder of *cenobitism, one of the greatest of the monastic fathers; b. Esneh, Egypt, c. 290; d. Egypt, 346 (feast, May 14; Coptic Church, May 9). Pachomius founded nine monasteries for men and two for women in the *Thebaïd, of which he was a native, and gave them a written rule that is still extant. Born and raised a pagan, he met some Christians in his youth, while he was serving in the army. Their charity so edified him that he became a Christian and, eventually, a solitary (c. 314) at Schenesit under the direction of the hermit Palemon. About 6 years later he moved a short distance away to *Tabennisi and there began to develop

what later became the first *coenobium* or monastery of the full communal life. His contemporaries, as well as present-day scholars, viewed him as a man of vision and purpose who from the beginning of monasticism saw the need for a development that would provide against the spiritual and physical hazards of the solitary life, by centering the movement on the communal charity inherent in Christianity from its start. He began with a few monks, who promised to obey him and to share in common the fruits of the employment that they had secured for themselves.

As the number of his disciples increased, Pachomius gradually developed a concept of mortification based on total obedience to superiors and subordinate officers, under whom all work was organized, and complete common ownership of goods and the fruits of labor. By the time he died, his monasteries formed a great and closely knit congregation, in which thousands of monks were organized for work in many trades and for common morning and evening prayer and meals. Throughout his lifetime Pachomius presided as superior general. He established Pebou, his second foundation, as his motherhouse and held there at Easter and in August of each year a general gathering of his superiors. The style and contents of his rule indicate that it was composed over a long period of time and not dictated by an angel according to the legend recorded by *Palladius (*Hist. Laus. 32.1*). Its achievement was to provide an adequate economic and spiritual basis for the common life, legislating with discretion for what was of common obligation and allowing freedom for greater austerity on the part of the individual monk.

Six biographies of Pachomius by contemporaries survive; and also several of his instructions to his monks and the instructions and letters of his two great successors, Horsiesi (d. 380) and Theodore (d. 368). The two ruled jointly after a schism threatened the congregation in 350. Their writings, especially Horsiesi's *De doctrina institutione monachorum*, reveal a deep understanding and development of the Pachomian ideal. Within Horsiesi's lifetime the influence of Pachomius's rule had extended beyond the Pachomian monasteries and affected the cenobitic foundations and Rule of *Basil of Caesarea.

In 404 *Jerome responded to a request to provide a Latin translation of the rule for the Latins who were entering the Pachomian monasteries. This text is the only one that has survived; it was the means by which Pachomian influence advanced in the West. The *Regula Vigilii* (or *Regula Orientalis*) written in Gaul c. 420 depends much on Pachomius's rule, borrowing about a quarter of its text. The 6th- or 7th-century *Regula Tarnatensis* also shows significant dependence. The Rule of St. *Benedict (c. 540), and the rules of *Caesarius of Arles and of his successor Aurelian (written c. 512–550) show less but unmistakable dependence. *Benedict of Aniane (d. 821) includes the Latin version of Pachomius's rule in his collection of rules and refers to it frequently in his *Concordia regularum*. Besides the direct influence of his rule, Pachomius's influence must be estimated to some extent in terms of the total influence of cenobitism as the prevailing form of monasticism in Christian civilization.

Bibliography: Quasten Patr 3:154–160. *Vitae.* Gr. ed. F. HALKIN (SubsidHag 19; 1932). Syriac. P. BEDJAN, ed., *Acta martyrum et sanctorum*, 7 v. (Paris 1890–97) 5:122–176. Arabic.

E. Amélineau, ed., *Histoire de S. Pakhôme et de ses communautés* (Annales de Musée Guimet 17; Paris 1889) 337–711. L. T. Lefort, tr., *Les Vies coptes de S. Pachôme et de ses premiers successeurs* (Louvain 1943); ed. and tr., *Oeuvres de S. Pachôme et de ses disciples,* 2 v. (CSCO 159–160, Scriptores Coptici 23–24; 1956). A. Boon and L. T. Lefort, eds., *Pachomiana latina* (Louvain 1932). E. A. T. Budge, *Coptic Apocrypha in the Dialect of Upper Egypt* (London 1913) 352–382. P. Ladeuze, *Étude sur le cénobitisme pakhomien* (Louvain 1898). H. Bacht, "L'Importance de l'idéal monastique de S. P. pour l'histoire du monachisme chrétien," RevAscMyst 26 (1950) 308–326; in *Antonius Magnus Eremita,* ed. B. Steidle (StAnselm 38; 1956) 66–107. C. de Clercq, *Mélanges L. Halphen* (Paris 1951) 169–176. A. J. Festugière, *Les moines d'Orient,* v. 4 (Paris 1964).

[M. C. McCarthy]

PACHYMERES, GEORGE,

Byzantine historian; b. Nicaea, 1242; d. Constantinople, *c.* 1310. In 1261 he moved to Constantinople, where he held high positions in both state and Church. He was well educated, and his interests and writings covered a wide range of topics; but his most important work is his Συγγραφικαὶ ἱστορίαι, or history of the reigns of the Emperors *Michael VIII Palaeologus and *Andronicus II Palaeologus (1261–1308), since he was an eyewitness of many of the events he narrates. He is noted for his impartiality, even when writing of Michael's policy of ecclesiastical union with Rome, to which he was strongly opposed. He enters into detail on doctrinal matters, and his style is often difficult because of his fondness for archaisms. He also composed a short treatise on the Procession of the Holy Spirit, in which he accepted the Damascene formula, "through the Son," some works on *Aristotle and several others on Dionysius and Areopagite (*see* PSEUDO-DIONYSIUS).

Bibliography: G. Pachymeres, *De Michaele et Andronico Palaeologis libri XIII,* ed. I. Bekker, 2 v. (Bonn 1835), repr. PG v.143–144; *Quadrivium,* ed. P. Tannery, rev. E. Stephanou (StTest 94; 1940). G. Moravcsik, *Byzantinoturcica,* 2 v. (2d ed. Berlin 1958) 1:280–282. V. Laurent, DTC 11.2:1713–18. F. Dölger, LexThK² 7:1332. Beck KTLBR 679.

[G. T. Dennis]

PACIAN OF BARCELONA, ST.,

bishop; b. Spain, *c.* 310; d. Barcelona, before 392 (feast, March 9). Though married, and the father of the praetorian prefect, Dexter, Pacian became bishop of Barcelona and was praised by *Jerome for his learning, sanctity, and pastoral zeal (*De vir. illus.* 106). Of his writings, only three works are certainly authentic: *De Baptismo* or sermon to catechumens, which speaks of the spiritual renewal and purification effected by Baptism and describes the effects of *original sin with a clarity that was rare before the time of Augustine; a *Contra Novatianos,* in three letters to Sympronian, a rigorist propagating the condemned doctrines of *Novatian; and a *Paraenesis sive exhortatorius libellus,* an earnest plea in favor of penance, and a stern reminder of the far more severe punishments awaiting those who die without having fulfilled the penances imposed on them. This work presents invaluable source material for the study of the penitential system then in vogue throughout Spain. Pacian's other writings have disappeared, and the treatises attributed to him by Dom G. *Morin are of doubtful authenticity.

Pacian's doctrine on penance elaborated the teaching of Scripture and tradition—particularly as set forth by *Tertullian and *Cyprian—to assert that the Church has the power from God to forgive all sins committed after Baptism. In his first letter to Sympronian occurs the famous phrase "My name is Christian; but my surname, Catholic." By Catholic he meant the worldwide expansion of the Church, the unity of faith among all its members, and their submission to one supreme head.

Bibliography: *Obras,* tr. and ed. L. Rubio Fernández (Barcelona 1958). Altaner (Span. ed. 1949) appendix. K. Baus, LexThK² 7:1332–33. É. Amann, DTC 11.2:1718–21. G. Morin, "Traité inédit de Pacien de Barcelone," RevBén 29 (1912) 1–28; "Un nouvel opuscule de Saint Pacien" *ibid.* 30 (1913) 286–293; RHE 38 (1942) 414–417.

[S. J. McKenna]

PACIFICO OF SAN SEVERINO, ST.,

Franciscan administrator and mystic; b. San Severino in the Marches, March 1, 1653; d. there, Sept. 24, 1721 (feast, Sept. 24). A member of the distinguished family of the Divini, he was orphaned at an early age and brought up by an uncle who treated him very harshly. He entered the Observant Franciscans at Forano when he was 17 and was ordained to the priesthood in 1678. He taught philosophy for 2 years before beginning his preaching career. For 8 years he worked with marked success among the poor inhabitants of the Apennine villages. When he was 35, he contracted an illness that left him deaf, blind, and crippled. These infirmities, which he bore with resignation for more than 30 years, did not prevent him from ably performing the duties of vicar and guardian at the Friary of Our Lady of Grace in San Severino, where he resided continuously after 1705. He frequently experienced prolonged ecstasies while celebrating Mass, on several occasions displayed the gift of prophecy, and many times miraculously cured the sick. He was beatified by Pope Pius VI in 1786 and canonized by Pope Gregory XVI in 1839.

Bibliography: Léon de Clary, *Lives of the Saints and Blessed of the Three Orders of St. Francis,* 4 v. (Taunton, Eng. 1885–87) 3:224–229. S. Melchiorri, *Vita di San Pacifico da San Severino* (Rome 1839). C. Ortolani, *San Pacificio da San Severino* (Rome 1929).

[C. J. Lynch]

PACIFICUS OF NOVARA, BL.,

known also as Pacific of Cerano (Ceredano), Franciscan Observant preacher; b. Ceredano, province of Novara, Italy, *c.* 1420; d. Sassari, Sardinia, June 4, 1482 (feast, June 9; in the order, June 8). After the death of his parents he was educated by *Benedictines in his native city. In 1445 he joined the *Franciscan Order and from 1452 to 1471 was engaged in preaching popular missions in most of the provinces of Italy. Appointed apostolic nuncio to Sardinia, he preached the crusade, announced by *Sixtus IV, against Mohammed II (1480). Shortly after, at the instance of the general chapter of the Observants in Ferrara (1481), he conducted the *visitation of the Sardinian friars. In 1473 he prepared a *Somma morale,* a casuistic manual for confessors, known also as the *Somma Pacifica;* it was printed at Milan in 1479 and frequently thereafter. His cult was confirmed in 1745.

Bibliography: ActSS June 1:406–407. Wadding Ann 14:190, 306, 375–376. M. Cazzola, *Il b. Pacifico Ramati* (Novara 1882). Sbaralea 2:302. Butler Th Attw 2:506. A. Ghinato, EncCatt 9:506. E. Grau, LexThK² 7:1333.

[O. J. Blum]

PACIFISM

This term admits of no single definition. It can denote a political movement that seeks to eliminate war by inducing all nations to settle their disputes peacefully, but more commonly nowadays it denotes an ideology based on a personal conviction that war is morally unjustifiable. Absolute or doctrinal pacifism condemns all war as immoral; relative or practical pacifism limits its objection to particular wars or forms of war.

Pre-Christian Attitude. The ancient pagan world seems to have regarded war as a natural phenomenon or necessary evil entailed by the struggle for existence, and military service as a duty of citizenship or a burden owed to the sovereign that might bring gain or glory. Buddhism was exceptional among pagan religions in preaching a creed of nonviolence. The historical books of the OT echo with the clash of battles fought in the conquest or defense of the Promised Land, always with the conviction that they were a sacred duty willed by the God of Israel, Lord of Hosts. Jeremia (27–29) might condemn particular wars, and Isaia (11.1–9) foretell the reign of the Prince of Peace, but none of the prophets condemned all war as such. The *Essenes, an ascetical Jewish sect dating probably from the 2d century B.C., are said to have repudiated violence, but they were unrepresentative of Israel and are not mentioned in the Bible.

New Testament. The NT message is fundamentally one of peace among men of good will (Lk 2.14), based on brotherhood in Christ and sonship of His Father. Christ indeed warned His disciples that His Gospel would set men at variance: "I have come to bring a sword, not peace" (Mt 10.34); but He Himself blessed the peacemakers, rejected the *lex talionis* of an eye for an eye, and urged His followers not to resist evildoers, but to turn the other cheek, love their enemies, do good to them that hated them, and pray for them that persecuted and calumniated them (Mt 5.9, 38–39, 44).

That He did not condemn all use of physical force is clear from His use of a whip in driving the merchants from the Temple (Jn 2.14–16). Nor, to judge from his warm commendation of the faith of the centurion (Lk 3.14), did He regard the military profession as an impediment to discipleship. Nevertheless, though He had warned His disciples that they would need swords (Lk 22.36), He would not let them be used to save Him from arrest, and He ordered Peter to sheath the sword with which he had struck the High Priest's servant, "for all those who take the sword will perish by the sword" (Mt 26.52).

The subsequent attitude of the Apostles to the use of force was similarly qualified. St. Paul wrote: "If it be possible, as far as in you lies, be at peace with all men" (Rom 12.18); yet he acknowledged the right and duty of rulers to wield the sword, as God's ministers, in defense of the public good (Rom 13.4). So too St. Peter preached peace (1 Pt 3.8–11), but he baptized the centurion Cornelius without apparently requiring him to seek another profession (Acts 10.47).

Early Christian Position. For the first 3 centuries of the Christian era, the general exclusion of Christians from public life removed the moral problem of war from the area of their immediate responsibility and con-cern. Only in regard to service in the imperial forces did a practical case of conscience arise. Many converts continued in fact to serve, and those who left the army seem to have done so in order to avoid being involved in idolatrous practices, or to devote themselves more directly to the service of God, rather than from any conscientious objection to war as such. The problem was never officially solved. Some, like St. Hippolytus (c. 170–c. 236), condemned voluntary military service by Christians (F. Funk, *Didascalia et Constitutiones Apostolorum,* Paderborn 1905, 2:97); and, a century later, after the Emperor Licinius had imposed idolatry on all his forces, canon 12 of the First Council of Nicea (325) enacted a severe penalty against Christians who reenlisted in the imperial army; but only Tertullian, writing as a Montanist c. 202 A.D. (*De Idololatria,* 19), and Lactantius (*Divinae Institutiones* 6.20) condemned military service outright. None of the accepted Fathers of the Church ever adopted this extreme position; and although the episcopate generally discouraged the military career while it involved religious and moral dangers, it ceased to do so after the conversion of Constantine, when these religious and moral dangers were largely removed.

Post-Constantine Tradition. What eventually became the accepted Christian attitude toward war was first established by St. Augustine. His doctrine, as contained in *Civ.* (19.7, 12, 13, 15), can be summarized as follows: peace is a supreme social good, indispensable to the proper development of man and human institutions; true peace consists, however, not in the mere absence of war, but in the tranquillity of order. It presupposes a just, equitable, and harmonious order of things like and unlike that secures to everyone and everything its due place. War cannot be justified except as a necessary means to the establishment or restoration of this order and of the peace that is its fruit; but it can so be justified because just men may be forced into war by the injustice of others. Nevertheless, war is so monstrous a means to just order that no public authority has the right to undertake it, even for a just cause, unless all peaceful means to an equitable settlement have first been tried in vain.

The conclusion that war can be justified was accepted by subsequent Christian writers of the early Middle Ages, notably by St. Isidore of Seville (*Etymologiae,* 18.1; PL 82:639) and by Gratian (*Decretum,* 23, 1–3); St. Thomas Aquinas was himself content merely to enumerate and to analyse the necessary conditions, viz, legitimate authority, just cause, and right intention (ST 2a2ae, 40.1). The outstanding Catholic authorities of later days, Francisco de Vitoria, OP (c. 1485–1546), Francisco de Suárez, SJ (1548–1617), and Louis Taparelli d'Azeglio (1793–1862), underlined or developed certain aspects of this traditional doctrine, but kept its substance intact. Vitoria, by arguing that the right of princes to make war on unjust aggressors was necessary to world order (*Relectiones Theologicae* 6; *De Iure Belli* 19; Lyons 1587, 234), implicitly made the exercise of the right dependent on the interests of world order. Taparelli enlarged on this point and drew the conclusion that the right of war of individual states would cease if and when an international society capable of imposing justice came into being (*Saggio Teoretico di Diritto Naturale,* Prato 1883, 2:198). Suárez rejected the notion that princes have the right to punish injustice anywhere in the universe (*De Charitate* 13.4.3; *Opera Omnia* 12, Paris 1858, 744). The point to note is that none of these representative Catholic authors denied the right of war itself.

Pacifist Sects. Denial of the right of war was indeed limited in effect to a few heretical sects of relatively later date and minor influence. The *Waldenses, who originated in the 12th century, initially condemned all war or taking of human life, but eventually fought in their own self-defense. Certain groups of the 16th century Anabaptist sect, notably the Swiss Brethren and the *Mennonites, likewise advocated pacifism and nonresistance. John Smyth, from whom the English Baptists derive, came under Mennonite influence, but not a few of his religious descendants fought in Cromwell's army. More consistent in their religious opposition to war and military service were and are the Quakers, founded by George Fox in 1668 and established in Pennsylvania by William Penn in 1682. Most of these sects, like the later Plymouth Brethren and Christadelphians, were inspired primarily by the desire to return to what they believed to have been the primitive and true form of Christianity, or else to withdraw from a world which they believed to be irretrievably bad; pacifism was a consequence of their religious creed rather than one of its basic tenets.

Modern Developments. Modern pacifism is less closely associated with religious belief. Its adherents are to be found in all the major religious denominations and may belong to none. Some, like Tolstoy (1820–1910), base their philosophy of absolute pacifism on the Sermon on the Mount but without necessarily accepting the divinity of Christ. Others have been inspired by the success of Gandhi's policy of nonviolent resistance in India. With others, pacifism is a matter merely of personal conviction, either in regard to the will of God or in regard to the futility of war as a means to justice. Others see it as a practical policy, either in the form of nonviolence, which will convert aggressors by benevolence, or in the form of passive resistance, which will finally break their will. Others still, whom few would discourage, are pacifist only in the sense that they work unceasingly for an international order in which war will be replaced by arbitration, judicial decision, or, failing these, by international police action. Fruits of their activity may be seen in the international peace congresses that led up to the Hague Convention (1899), the Hague Court (1907), or even the Kellogg Pact (1928), by which the signatory nations formally renounced war as a means of settling international differences.

Modern Catholic pacifists are almost all of the relative kind. They admit that a war of national defense against unjust aggression could be justified if the traditionally required conditions were fulfilled, but deny that they can in fact be fulfilled now, because war has become so violent and indiscriminate that its evil consequences, moral and physical, are bound to outweigh the intended good. One of the best-known defenders of this position is the German Dominican, F. Stratmann (*The Church and War*, New York 1928; *War and Christianity Today*, Westminster, Md. 1956). Many more adherents have been won to it with the growing realization of the awful possibilities of nuclear war. Their views can be found in collections of essays, such as *Nuclear Weapons: A Catholic Response* (ed. W. Stein, New York 1961) and *Morals and Missiles* (ed. C. S. Thompson, London 1959). Cardinal Ottaviani, Secretary of the Holy Office, writing in his private capacity, has come close to accepting this position, when he insists that not even a defensive war may be waged unless the responsible authority is *sure* of victory and even more sure that the good accruing to the nation outweighs the monstrous evils that will result for itself and the world (*Institutiones Iuris Publici Ecclesiastici,* Rome 1947, 1.86).

Moral Appraisal. It is clear from what has been said that absolute pacifism is irreconcilable with traditional Catholic doctrine. Catholic exegetes likewise commonly reject the pacifist interpretation of Christ's teaching. His pronouncement on nonresistance to evil is taken as a counsel rather than as a precept, and for private individuals rather than for public authorities, since these latter would fail in an essential duty were they to offer no forceful resistance to violent aggressors from within or without. His warning to those who "take the sword" is commonly understood, as by St. Augustine (*Contra Faustum* 22.70), to refer to those who usurp the function of rulers, for rulers alone bear the sword as God's ministers (Rom 13.14). Nor is there any intrinsic contradiction between a just war and Christ's command that we love our enemies. A just war expresses hatred of the evil deed rather than of the evildoer.

On the other hand, the chief contention of relative pacifism is deduced from accepted Catholic principles. It is the logic of the conclusion that is disputed. No one can deny that the fulfillment of one of the essential conditions of just war (that the intended good shall outweigh the evil entailed) becomes less likely with every increase in the violence and indiscriminate destruction of modern war. Indeed, it is almost impossible to conceive of any merely temporal good that could outweigh the evil consequences of a total nuclear war; and though experience since 1945 has shown that not every modern war need be either total or nuclear, such a conflict remains a serious possibility. It was this consideration that led Pius XII to declare that nothing less than the absolute necessity of self-defense against an unjust aggression threatening the very life or integrity of a state or the essential and inalienable rights of its members can nowadays provide a just cause for war (address, Sept. 30, 1954, ActApS 46:589). The same consideration drew from John XXIII the remark that "in this age of ours which glories in its atomic might, war cannot any longer be reasonably regarded as an apt means of repairing violated rights" (*Pacem in terris,* ActApS 55:291). But Pius XII was equally insistent that "the right to stand on the defensive cannot be denied to any State even today" (address Oct. 3, 1953, ActApS 45:733) and that a situation can arise in which it can legitimately be exercised even against nuclear attack (Christmas message 1956, ActApS 49:19). Catholics are certainly free to form their own opinion whether the conditions required for justification are likely to be fulfilled in any future war, but the authentic Catholic position is that a war of self-defense can still be justified, in practice as well as principle. The immense evils liable to result from it are not demonstrably greater than those that would afflict mankind if force could no longer be used to repel the armed aggression even of a godless tyranny.

See also WAR, MORALITY OF; CONSCIENTIOUS OBJECTORS; EPIKEIA.

Bibliography: In addition to the works already cited, R. COSTE, *Le problème du droit de guerre dans la pensée de Pie XII* (Paris 1962). M. F. SCHELER, *L'Idée de paix et le pacifisme* (Paris 1953). J. NEWMAN, *Studies in Political Morality* (Chicago 1963) 69–118. W. J. NAGLE, ed., *Morality and Modern Warfare* (Baltimore 1960) contains an article by a practical pacifist, GORDON C. ZAHN, and an excellent bibliography by W. J. BROWN. C. J. CADOUX, *The Early Christian Attitude to War* (London 1940) non-Catholic pacifist. J. LEWIS, *The Case Against Pacifism* (London 1940). E. A. RYAN, "Rejection of Military Service by the Early Christians," ThSt 13 (1952) 1–32. H. LECLERCQ, DACL 11.1:1110–81.

[L. L. MC REAVY]

PACIOLI, LUCA, mathematician, Franciscan friar, the great teacher of mathematics in the courts and universities of Renaissance Italy; b. Borgo San Sepolcro, Tuscany, 1445; d. after 1514. His education was provided by the Franciscan Friars, and his writings show that his life was shaped by the reading of his early years. The force and influence of the Humanistic movement also are apparent in his works, into which he introduced theological moralizing, literary reminiscences, scholarly anecdotes, and practical hints. He brought the mathematics of the universities into close relation with that of artists and architects. Pacioli's great contribution to civilization consisted in unearthing old material on mathematics and systematizing and formulating it with reference to the discovery of general truths and the operation of general laws.

The *Summa de arithmetica, geometrica, proportioni et proportionalita* (Venice 1494) is the first known published book of Pacioli. The *Summa* was influenced in a great measure by the *Liber Abaci* of Leonard of Pisa (1202) and is an extension of the works of *Jordanus de Nemore (1236) and *John de Sacrobosco (1256). The *Divina Proportione* (Venice 1509) was written in collaboration with *Leonardo da Vinci, and is of interest to both artist and mathematician.

Bibliography: R. E. TAYLOR, *No Royal Road: Luca Pacioli and His Times* (Chapel Hill, N.C. 1942), with extensive bibliographical data. **Illustration credit:** Anderson-Art Reference Bureau.

[M. C. ZELLER]

Fra Luca Pacioli explaining a theory to a young man, painting by Jacopo de Barbari in the Museo Nazionale at Naples. The figure of the young man may be the artist.

PADERBORN, ARCHDIOCESE OF (PADERBORNENSIS)

Metropolitan see since 1930, in central *Germany, with the suffragans *Fulda and *Hildesheim. In 1963 it had 1,519 secular and 392 religious priests, 601 men in 34 religious houses, 6,659 women in 414 convents, and 2,206,000 Catholics in a population of 9,155,000; it is 14,658 square miles in area.

With a good water supply, Paderborn was settled early but intermittently. Charlemagne occupied the Saxon settlement of the 7th-8th century and built a palace there (excavated 1963–64). Imperial assemblies with synods were held in 777, 785, and 799 (when Charlemagne received Leo III), and Paderborn became a mission center under the bishop of *Würzburg. The Saxon Hathumar was the first bishop (806–807 to 815) of the small diocese, suffragan to *Mainz. The first Saxon cloister (815) moved to *Corvey (822) and became a famous imperial cloister. Badurad (815–862), who completed the episcopal organization, built a new cathedral and translated the relics of St. Liborius (d. 397?) from *Le Mans (836), with which Paderborn still has a close bond. St. *Kunigunde was crowned queen under Rethar (1002). *Meinwerk, made bishop by Henry II (1009), built a new cathedral and an episcopal palace (excavated in 1963) and founded *Abdinghof and Busdorf (church after the Holy Sepulcher in Jerusalem, consecrated in 1036). His great-nephew Imad (1051–76) rivaled him as a patron of the arts (Imad Madonna) and supporter of the cathedral school. Archbishop Dietrich of Cologne, administrator of Paderborn (1415–63), had Paderborn united to his own see (1429–44).

The Reformation entered (1529–32) and became dominant under Bp. Heinrich von Lauenburg (1577–85). The Jesuits, called to Paderborn by the chapter in 1580, and *Prince-Bishop Dietrich von Fürstenberg (1585–1618) preserved or won back the heart of the see for Catholicism. The university which opened under Dietrich (1616) and in which Friedrich von *Spee taught and Athanasius *Kircher studied, was suppressed in 1818; but it has survived as a philosophical-theological academy where Gottfried *Hoberg, the exegete Joseph Feldmann (1866–1944), Bernhard *Bartmann, and Norbert *Peters have taught. Bishops Dietrich Adolf von der Reck (1650–61) and the scholarly Ferdinand von Fürstenberg (1661–83) worked to restore the diocese after the Thirty Years War. Bishop Franz Egon von Fürstenberg (1789–1825) lost the episcopal domain in the secularization of 1802 but preserved the bishopric.

In the ecclesiastical reorganization of Germany (1821) Paderborn, suffragan to *Cologne, gained territory in Westphalia and Saxony; much of the see was diaspora. After freedom of domicile was introduced, the Bonifatius Association was established in Paderborn to care for the diaspora (1849). The Commissariat of Magdeburg, under Paderborn from 1821, has an auxiliary bishop (1949), who has been vicar general since 1951. Part of Paderborn went to the new See of Essen in 1958.

Paderborn's prelates include Konrad *Martin (1856–79); the scholar Hubertus Simar (1891–99), Archbishop of Cologne (1899–1902) and a founder of the *Görres-Gesellschaft; the theologian Wilhelm Schnei-

The Cathedral of Paderborn.

der (1900–09); Karl Joseph Schulte (1910–20), Archbishop of Cologne (1920–41); K. Klein (1920–41); and Lorenz Jaeger (1941–   ), cardinal in 1965.

Bibliography: *Realschematismus: Westfälischer Anteil* (Paderborn 1961). G. J. BESSEN, *Geschichte des Bisthums Paderborn,* 2 v. (Paderborn 1820). *Westfälisches Urkundenbuch,* v.1, 2, 4, 5 (Münster-Regensberg 1847–94). *Westfälische Zeitschrift,* v.1-114 (Münster-Regensberg 1834–1964). E. STAKEMEIER, *Liborius, Geschichte und Legende* (Paderborn 1952); *Alte und neue Kunst im Erzbistum Paderborn* (Paderborn 1950–63). K. HONSELMANN, LexThK² 7:1343–45. AnnPont (1965) 321–322.

[K. HONSELMANN]

PADEREWSKI, IGNACY JAN, foremost pianist of his time, composer, premier of Poland (1919–20), signer of the Versailles Treaty (1919); b. Kury-

Ignacy Jan Paderewski.

lówka, Poland, Nov. 6, 1860; d. New York City, June 29, 1941. Both his parents, Jan Paderewski, estate administrator, and Polixena (Nowicka) Paderewska, had musical backgrounds. His first wife, Antonia Korsak, died in childbirth, leaving him with an invalid son, Alfred. He married Mme. Helena de Rosen Gorska in 1899. He studied piano and composition privately, at the Warsaw Conservatory (1872–78), and in Berlin, and piano with Leschetizky in Vienna. His pianistic debuts were in Vienna (1887) and in the U.S. (1891) at Carnegie Hall with the New York Symphony Orchestra under Walter Damrosch. He was noted for his performance of music by his compatriot *Chopin, whose works he was editing before his death. His compositions include 2 operas, a symphony, a cantata, 3 works for solo instrument and orchestra, a violin and piano sonata, 22 songs, and more than 54 piano pieces.

Paderewski donated generously to Polish relief during World War I, and was an architect of Poland's independence at the war's end. After its reenslavement by Hitler he vowed never to return until Poland was again free. In life he was honored by many nations and universities; at his death his body lay in state in St. Patrick's Cathedral, New York, and was interred in Arlington National Cemetery, a temporary haven granted by President Roosevelt. A bronze marker was placed at the site in 1963 at the instance of President Kennedy.

Bibliography: R. LANDAU, *Ignace Paderewski: Musician and Statesman* (New York 1934). A. STRAKACZ, *Paderewski As I Knew Him,* tr. H. CHYBOWSKA (New Brunswick, N.J. 1949). C. R. HALSKI, Grove DMM 6:482–484. **Illustration credit:** Paderewski Foundation, New York City.

[H. E. MEYERS]

PADILLA, DIEGO FRANCISCO, Colombian priest, patriot, and pamphleteer; b. Bogotá, Colombia, *c.* 1754; d. Bojacá, Colombia, April 9, 1829. His parents were Alejo Padilla and Juana Francisca Rico. Diego, who joined the Augustinians about 1770, had two brothers in the same order, in addition to four other brothers and three sisters who entered the religious life. Of the 10, Diego was the most gifted; he gained a reputation for erudition, eloquence, and literary skill. A contemporary reported that by 1809 Padilla had published 49 pamphlets (the majority of them anonymous) in defense of religion and of the movement for independence in New Granada. In 1810 he was one of the leading spokesmen for independence and he became a member of the first junta of the revolutionary government. With Manuel Bernardo Álvarez he published a weekly political journal, *El aviso al público,* that lasted for 5 months beginning on Sept. 19, 1810. He also founded a similar publication called *El sabatino.* In 1816, convicted of revolutionary activity by the Spanish authorities, Padilla was sent into exile in Spain. Pardoned on Jan. 15, 1820, he was released from prison and, some months later, at his request, granted permission to return to Colombia. His remaining years were spent in Bojacá where he had previously served as pastor.

Bibliography: M. G. ROMERO, "Participación del clero en la lucha por la independencia," *Boletín de historia y antigüedades* 49 (1962) 325–344. L. MONROY, "Los Agustinos en el pueblo de Bojacá, Colombia," *Archivo agustiniano* 56 (1962) 348–397.

[A. J. ENNIS]

PADILLA, JUAN DE, martyr, missionary; b. Andalusia, Spain, *c.* 1500; d. probably at Herington, Kans., *c.* 1542. He arrived in Mexico in 1528. Little is known of his background, but he had reportedly been a soldier in his youth and had joined the Order of Friars Minor in Spain. He accompanied the expedition of Nuño de Guzmán to New Galicia in 1529 and 1530. He went to Tehuantepec in 1533 to join an expedition that Hernando Cortez planned to send to the Orient. When the expedition did not materialize, he served in the Indian missions of Poncitlan and Tuchpán and founded the Franciscan friaries of Zapotlan and Tamazula. He also was superior at Tulantzingo. In 1540 Padilla joined Francisco Vázquez de Coronado's expedition to New Mexico. On the way north he was in the vanguard of the expedition with the exploratory groups. He went with Capt. Pedro de Tovar to the Hopi pueblos in July and August 1540; with Capt. Pedro de Alvarado across western New Mexico to the Rio Grande pueblos in August and September 1540; with Don Lope de Urrea to Pecos in the summer of 1541; and with Coronado's select team in the final dash to Quivira. When Coronado returned to Mexico in 1542, Padilla stayed behind to work among the Indians. In the spring of 1542 he set out for Quivira, accompanied by two Indian assistants, a Portuguese named Andrés do Campo, a few personal servants, and some Wichita braves from Quivira. He was well received among the Quivirans, but during a visit to another tribe he was attacked and killed by strange Indians. Do Campo and the two Indian assistants escaped and, after several years of wandering, reached Mexico to tell their story. The first priest to be martyred on what became U.S. soil, Padilla is commemorated on November 30.

[F. WARREN]

PADILLA Y ESTRADA, IGNACIO DE, Augustinian bishop; b. Mexico City, 1695; d. Mérida, Yucatán, July 20, 1760. His family held high social position; his grandparents were the Oidor Juan de Padilla Guardiola y Guzmán and Jerónima Cisneros; his parents, Juan Ildefonso Padilla Cisneros and Micaela Gregoria Estrada. Apparently he used various combinations of these names during his lifetime. After joining the Augustinians, he dedicated his life to study and preparation for an ascetic life. He received the doctorate in theology at the University of Mexico, then taught philosophy and theology at the Colegio of San Pablo, where he soon became rector. He held a number of offices: secretary of the province, visitor of the convents of Guadalajara and Havana, and prior of the convent in Mexico City. He was sent to Rome as a representative of the province, and was in Spain in 1743 on his way back to America when he was nominated archbishop of Santo Domingo. After consecration in Madrid, he arrived in Santo Domingo in 1745, where he undertook the reformation of the clergy and the rebuilding of churches, restoring the cathedral and opposing the destruction of the Jesuit college. He refused the bishopric of Guatemala in 1751 and that of Popayán in 1752, but finally accepted that of Mérida, Yucatán, in 1753. There he reformed the seminary, providing it with a new constitution and with an enlarged building; he endowed three chairs and brought in professors from Mexico to fill them; at his own expense he set up 10 scholarships in the seminary for children of the poor and of the Indians. He stressed the welfare of the Indians in many ways and supported, with his interest and his money, hospitals for them.

[E. RODRÍGUEZ-DEMORIZI]

PADUA

City of ancient origin in northeast Italy, 25 miles west of Venice. It received Roman citizenship (49 B.C.) and under Augustus was, with Cadiz (Spain), second in wealth only to Rome in the empire, but it then declined. Destroyed by the Lombards (568–602), it revived in the late 10th century. During the investiture struggle the bishops sided with either the papacy or the empire; but the free commune of Padua took part in the *Lombard league against the Empire (1087). Ruled by the tyrant Ezzelino da Romano (1237–56) and the Carrara family (1320–1406), Padua succumbed to Venice (1406–1797) and belonged to Austria (1797–1866), except when part of the French kingdom of Italy (1805–15), before it became part of the kingdom of Italy. Livy was from Padua; Dante, Petrarch, and Tasso studied at the university. The Diocese of Padua (*Patavinus*) was suffragan to *Aquileia to 1752, to *Udine to 1818, and since then to *Venice. In 1963 it had 936 secular and 380 religious priests, 508 men in 48 religious houses, 4,268 women in 456 convents, and 850,000 Catholics; it is 1,133 square miles in area.

The Christian origins of Padua are obscure. The 12th-century vita of St. Prosdocimus, first bishop and patron of Padua and supposedly a disciple of St. Peter, is legendary. St. Justina was martyred c. 305 (feast, Oct. 7), and the first historically known bishop, Crispin, lived c. 350. To the 10th century the decline of Padua is reflected in the fragmentary episcopal list. In the 7th and 8th centuries the bishops, in exile and involved in the *Three Chapters Schism, lost most of their jurisdiction to the bishops of *Vicenza, Treviso, and *Verona and to Benedictines at S. Giustina Basilica in Padua.

By the 12th century, feudal rights and privileges had made the bishop the leading authority in West Veneto. Rorigo (861–874) built a new cathedral (866), a castle-palace, and other sacred edifices. Peter II (897–904) was slain in the Hungarian invasion. Ursus (992–1013) rebuilt the city and organized parishes. Uldericus (1064–83), a famous theologian in the Eucharistic controversy and papal legate in Germany, supported Gregory VII. Sinibaldus (1106), patron of city

Padua, relief of Bp. St. Prosdocimus in the martyrium of the Basilica of S. Giustina (5th–6th century).

institutions, restored Church unity after a 20-year schism and reformed morals. St. Bellinus (1128–47), defender of Church rights, protector of the oppressed, promotor of the Gregorian reform, restorer of religious authority, and mediator in civil conflicts, was slain by hired assassins. Conrad (1229–39) supported Dominicans and Franciscans, as well as the reform work of St. *Anthony (d. 1231), Bl. Forzatè (d. 1248), and Bl. Arnaldus (d. 1254). Hildebrandinus dei Conti (1319–52), patron of art and culture, reformed monasteries, the cathedral chapter, and the clergy (constitution of 1333 and synod of 1339).

Many later bishops came from Venice. Marcellus (1409–28) fostered an institute to aid the poor. Pietro Barbo (1459–60) became Pope Paul II. Pietro Barozzi (1487–1507) sponsored the *Monte dei pegni* (pawn shop) in 1491 and defended the rights of the oppressed poor. St. Gregory *Barbarigo (1664–97) greatly expanded the seminary established by Nicolò Ormaneto (1571), founded a college for nobles at Tresto, promoted catechesis and pastoral care in accord with the Council of Trent, and supported the union of the Greek Church with Rome. Carlo Rezzonico (1743–58) became Pope Clement XIII. Francesco Scipione Dondi dall'Orologio (1807–19) was a victim of Napoleonic secularization and a strong opponent of *Josephinism. Giuseppi Callegari (1882–1906) promoted the union for social studies and the Catholic movement.

The Italo-Byzantine Martyrium of St. Prosdocimus (*c*. 500) under S. Giustina Basilica, in a Greek cross, has chapels of the relics of the two saints. S. Sofia (9th–10th century) in its present form has a Byzantine-style apse of Romanesque construction, reproducing 12th-century features. S. Antonio Basilica (13th century), in Franciscan Romanesque-Gothic with Byzantine-Arabic elements, contains famous paintings and sculpture, as does the cathedral (9th century), redone after plans by Michelangelo, in a Latin cross. In the 12th-century Romanesque baptistery is the master painting of Giusto dei Menabuoi (1376–78); Giotto's masterpiece is in the 15th-century Scrovegni Chapel; Mantegna's cycle of painting in the Eremitani church was destroyed in a bombardment (March 1944). The vast

"Deposition," fresco by Giotto, Scrovegni Chapel, Padua.

16th-century Romanesque-Gothic S. Giustina, in a Latin cross with three naves, has 14 precious altars and 8 cupolas.

The cult of the miracle worker St. Anthony has grown since the translation of his body to S. Antonio Basilica (1263) and has given rise to the theological studium and to such charitable works as the distribution of bread to the poor and orphanages. The Benedictine S. Giustina monastery (7th-8th century), a medieval spiritual and economic center, became a center of Benedictine reform through the work of Lodovico Barbo in the 15th century. Some 15 men's and women's monasteries in ruin are now used by the state for public buildings.

Bibliography: F. LANZONI, *Le diocesi d'Italia,* 2 v. (Faenza 1927). Gams 797–799. Kehr ItalPont 7.1:152–211. F. UGHELLI, *Italia sacra,* 2d ed. N. COLETI, 10 v. (Venice 1717–22) 5:386. Cottineau 2:2167–71. F. S. DONDI DALL'OROLOGIO, *Dissertazioni sopra l'istoria ecclesiastica di Padova,* 9 v. (Padua 1802–17). M. CHECCHI et al., *Padova* (Venice 1961), bibliog. P. PASCHINI, Enc Catt 9:517–523. *Annuario delle diocesi d'Italia* (Rome 1951). *Annuario Cattolico d'Italia, 1963–1964* (Rome 1964). *Annuario della diocesi di Padova, 1964* (Padua 1964). AnnPont (1965) 322. J. HYDE, *Padua in the Age of Dante: A Social History of an Italian City-State* (New York 1966). **Illustration credit:** Fig. 2, Alinari-Art Reference Bureau.

[A. GAMBASIN]

PADUA, UNIVERSITY OF

An Italian state institution of medieval origin, enjoying administrative autonomy.

Early History. The establishment of the University of Padua can be traced to 1222, although a law school and a school of arts, annexed to the cathedral, existed even before this date. The first university group is said to have been composed of law students and masters who migrated from Bologna during a period of political unrest to seek a more peaceful climate of learning in Padua. The nucleus of the University was the *collegium iuristarum,* made up of doctors of law, and the *universitas iuristarum,* composed of cisalpine and transalpine students who, like those at the University of *Bologna, elected their own rector and professors. They were later joined by the *universitas artistarum* with its masters of arts and medicine. The University was under the jurisdiction of the archbishop of Padua, who was chancellor ex officio and conferred the doctoral degrees. On Jan. 2, 1264, Pope Urban IV approved the University statutes and confirmed its privileges.

The University of Padua did not assume its own character and authority until after the Carrara arbitration in 1339, which marked the separation of the *universitas iuristarum* from the *universitas artistarum.* The former was essentially a *universitas scholariorum,* or student university, in which each Faculty had its own rector elected by the student body. The students assembled in the *universitas scholariorum;* the professors in the colleges of jurists or artists, which were under the presidency of a prior of one of the religious orders in Padua. On April 15, 1363, Pope Urban V established the Faculty of Theology and empowered the University to confer the doctorate in theology. This resulted in the amalgamation with the University of the various schools of theology operated by Dominicans, Franciscans, and Augustinians. Degrees were awarded after three tests: the license, the private examination, and the public examination held in the cathedral. The teachers belonged to two categories—ordinary, or doctors (full-time professors), who taught during the day, and extraordinary, or masters (instructors), who taught in the evening session. Both had to submit to a reciprocal competitive examination.

Student influence in the University gradually diminished during the Carrara rule and finally ceased under the Venetian republic (1405), although the students retained the usual University privileges. During this time the students took up residence in the vicinity of the Faculties, which had added grammar, rhetoric, and medicine to civil and Canon Law, and divided into nations according to their origin. Outstanding among students of the 14th century was Albertino Mussato; among teachers, Pietro d'Abano, Guido da Suzzara, Giovanni da Ravenna, Pier Paolo *Vergerio, and the Franciscan Antonio *Trombetta, who was a famous Scotist.

Later Development. In the 15th century the students could appeal to their Faculties to settle disputes. Law schools were to be found on the Piazza del Santo [Antonio], at Ca di Dio, opposite San Biagio, and in the Santa Margherita road; schools for the art students were established near the church of S. Catherina, and numerous hostels (*colleges) were located in the vicinity.

When the Carrara regime collapsed in 1405, the Venetian republic took care to make the best possible use of the University of Padua, which became the only university in the Venetian state. At the University of Padua was forged that select class of Venetian scholars which includes Francesco and Ermolao Barbaro, Dandalo, Foscari, and Foscarini. At first, during the Venetian rule, the local magistrature was in control of the *studium,* for which it was financially responsible. Later the state took over the direction and administration, reserving to itself the right to appoint professors and assuming financial responsibility. In 1421, of a total of 32 chairs, the university of jurists had 15: 6 in Canon Law, 7 in civil law, 1 for the reading of the Code of Canon Law, and 1 for notary law. The other 17 were destined for the artists and divided among medicine, surgery, logic, rhetoric, astrology, and mathematics.

In 1493 the University began to erect its own buildings and established its headquarters in the *Hospitium Bovis,* where it became the bulwark of Aristotelianism and Averroism with Pietro Pomponazzi and *Savonarola. In 1543 the University expanded its program with the establishment of a clinical school; a botanical garden, the first in Europe, was added in 1545, and the anatomical theater of Acquapendente in 1594. During this time the influence of the nations decreased; the authority of the professors was increased, and the need for a *studium generale* as a directive center was recognized. It was at the University of Padua that Galileo, who taught there from 1592 to 1608, invented the telescope.

During the early 17th century the University declined, but later recovered its pristine vigor. In 1738 the division of the students into nations was discontinued, the conferring of degrees was entrusted to the masters, the rectors were elected by the professors, the division into two Faculties was confirmed, and the departments of physics, geometry, chemistry, hygiene, and obstetrics were expanded. A school of veterinary science, the first in Italy, was established in 1773.

After the fall of the Venetian republic (1797), the French government united the Faculties into one, abolished the colleges, and appointed a single rector. Under the Austrian government (1814) the Faculty of Theology was transferred to the seminary, and the Faculties were separated into schools. Under Italian rule (1866) the University was divided into four Faculties—Theology; Government and Law; Medicine, Surgery and Pharmacy; and Philosophy and Mathematics—the colleges were restored, the rector was appointed by election, the administration was subordinated to the state, and the Schools of Pharmacy and Applied Engineering were established.

Development in the 20th Century. In 1923 the Faculty of Political Science was established with several graduate departments. It was followed by the Faculties of Education and Agriculture. In 1965 the University was composed of the Faculties of Law; Medicine and Surgery; Mathematics, Physics, and Natural Sciences; Pharmacy; Engineering; Agriculture; Political Science; and Economics and Business (with separate headquarters in Verona). Every Faculty has a president elected by the Faculty council composed of full-time professors. The rector and the deans of the Faculties constitute the academic senate together with the administrative director of the University, who is also president of the Faculties and confers the doctorates. The Faculties are divided into seminars and institutes over which a director presides. The Paduan Academy of Science, Letters, and Arts and the Medical-Surgical Society are cultural institutions affiliated with the University.

The students have at their disposal the libraries of all the seminars, institutes, and Faculties besides the various other libraries: university, municipal, Antonine, cathedral, American, and that of the episcopal seminary. They may also avail themselves of the student center and the university youth center in Bolzano, where courses have been established for foreigners, besides numerous other university organizations, laboratories, and a modern medical clinic. The institution is constantly faced with the problem of scientific progress and building expansion in order to maintain the University at the level of its long tradition of academic excellence and to meet the demands of the students who are continually increasing in number. In 1965 enrollment numbered 16,000 students with a teaching staff of approximately 1,200 members. The University library housed more than 320,000 volumes, 2,468 manuscripts, and 1,529 incunabula; the Pinali library had 40,000 volumes, and the engineering library, 25,000.

The University grants the laureate and doctoral degress in law, political science, arts, literature, philosophy, education, physics, mathematics, natural sciences, biology, geology, pharmacy, agriculture (4 years), chemistry, industrial chemistry, engineering (5 years), and medicine (6 years).

Bibliography: A. Riccoboni, *De Gymnasio Patavino* (Padua 1598). J. F. Tomasini, *Gymnasium Patavinum* (Udine 1654). N. C. Papadopoli, *Historia Gymnasii Patavini,* 2 v. in 1 (Venice 1726). J. Facciolati, *Fasti gymnasii Patavini,* (Padua 1757). F. M. Colle, *Storia scientifico-letteraria dello Studio di Padova,* ed. G. Vedova, 4 v. in 2 (Padua 1824–25). A. Gloria, *Monumenti della Università di Padova 1318–1405,* 2 v. (Padua 1888), basic work. A. Favaro and R. Cessi, *L'Università di Padova* (Padua 1946), historical survey. L. Rossetti and E. Grossato, *Guido dello studente* (Padua 1963–64), student guide.

[M. BLASON-BERTON]

PAGAN, a term now used in a religious sense to designate a person who is not a Christian, Jew, or Mohammedan. How the Latin word *paganus,* from which it comes, acquired the meaning of non-Christian is still not entirely settled. In profane Latin of the 1st century A.D., *paganus* was used in two senses: first, in the meaning of "rural" to describe the inhabitant of a *pagus,* or country district; second, in the sense of "civil" or "civilian," in contrast to the "military." It was long assumed that the Christians eventually adopted the term *paganus* to designate a non-Christian, either because the inhabitants of country districts resisted conversion to Christianity or because the Christian was a *miles Christi,* "a soldier of Christ," and therefore to be distinguished in a religious sense from the non-Christian civilian. It is significant, however, that the Christians did not adopt the term *paganus* in the meaning of non-Christian before the age of Constantine. They commonly employed the terms of Scriptural origin—*nationes, gentilis,* and *ethnicus.* With paganism still so strong in urban centers, especially in the West, there was no reason for making a sharp distinction between urban and rural conditions and for adopting a term for non-Christian that would apply primarily, if not exclusively, to rural areas. But when, in the course of the 4th century, Christians became more numerous and increasingly conscious of their own solidarity and social and religious prestige, the analogy of the contrast between *paganus* and *militaris* undoubtedly suggested the employment of the word as an appropriate designation, but not necessarily a derogatory one, for non-Christians as profane persons, outsiders, not members of the Christian community. The term, incidentally, seems to have had a history of popular usage before it was given literary and official sanction, for St. Augustine speaks of *"gentiles vel iam vulgo usitato vocabulo paganos"* (*Epist.* 184 *bis* 3,5). It is first employed officially in a rescript of Valentinian I of the year A.D. 370 (CodTheod 14.2.18).

Bibliography: J. ZEILLER, *Paganus: Étude de terminologie historique* (Paris 1917); "Paganus: Sur l'origine de l'acceptation religieuse du mot," *Comptes rendus de l'Acad. des Insc. et Belles Lettres* (Paris 1940) 526–543. C. MOHRMANN, "Encore une fois: 'Paganus,'" VigChr 6 (1952) 109–121, the best treatment, and with pertinent bibliography. E. BICKEL, " 'Pagani': Kaiseranbeter in den Laren-Kapellen der 'pagi urbani' im Rom Neros und des Apostels Petrus," *Rheinisches Museum für Philologie* 97 (1954) 1–47.

[M. R. P. MC GUIRE]

PAGI

Antoine, church historian; b. Rognes, March 31, 1624; d. Aix, June 5, 1699. He studied with the Jesuits at Aix, then entered the Conventual Franciscan Order at Arles and made solemn profession, Jan. 31, 1641. His early interest was in preaching and the study of the sermons of St. Anthony, but soon he turned to history. Though he was elected provincial at 29, and was reelected four times, he found time to devote to history. After he found mistakes in the *Annales ecclesiastici* of Baronius, Pagi labored the rest of his life in correcting and clarifying this great work. The first volume was published in Paris in 1689 while Pagi was living; the rest remained in manuscript until edited by his nephew in 1705 as the *Critica historico-chronologica in universos annales ecclesiasticos cardinalis Baronii.* It was included later by G. Mansi in his edition of the *Annales.* Among Pagi's other historical treatises are the *Dissertatio*

hypatica seu de consulibus caesareis and *Dissertatio de die et anno mortis S. Martini episcopi Turonensis.* He also edited the sermons of St. Anthony of Padua in 1685.

François, church historian, nephew of Antoine; b. Lambesc, Provence, Sept. 7, 1654; d. Orange, Jan. 21, 1721. He studied with the Oratorians at Toulon and then joined the Conventual Franciscans. Three times he was elected provincial. François helped his uncle on the works of Baronius and wrote a history of the popes from the beginning until 1447, *Breviarium historico-chronologico-criticum illustriora pontificum romanorum gesta* (Antwerp 1719–27). This history was later continued by his nephew, Antoine Pagi, the younger.

Bibliography: Wadding Ann 30:88, 383. Hurter Nomencl 4: 506–508, 1190–91. Sbaralea 4.3:185–226. A. TEETAERT, DTC 11.2:1729–30.

[R. BARTMAN]

PAGNINI, SANTES, also known as Pagninus or Pagnino, philologist and Biblical scholar; b. Lucca, Tuscany, Oct. 18, 1470; d. Lyons, France, Aug. 24, 1536. He entered the Dominican Order, Feb. 16, 1487, at Fiesole (near Florence), where one of his early masters was Girolamo *Savanarola. Florence at that time was a center for Oriental studies, and Pagnini displayed a facility in this field. He was elected prior several times (e.g., at Pistoia 1502, Florence 1504, Lucca 1508), and gained a reputation for sanctity as well as for learning. Called to Rome by Leo X, he taught Oriental studies there until 1521. Adrian VI named him apostolic preacher and master of sacred theology. In 1524 he went to Lyons, where he fought successfully against the Waldensian and Lutheran heresies, and where appeared the most important of his several publications, the *Veteris et Novi Testamenti nova translatio* (1528), a Latin translation of the Bible from the original texts. The fruit of 25 years of labor, it was the first Latin translation of the Hebrew Bible since that of St. Jerome and the first Bible in which all the verses were numbered, chapter by chapter, a notation still in use in modern Bibles. Whatever the translation's defects, all admit its faithfulness in rendering the original idiom, and many concede that it influenced the English versions of the OT through the use made of it by the early Protestants.

Bibliography: J. D. GAUTHIER, "Santes Pagninus, O.P.," CathBiblQuart 7 (1945) 175–190. EncCatt 9:557. DB 4.2: 1949–50.

[A. SMITH]

PAIDEIA, CHRISTIAN

The system of education in the faith that the early Christians created through a combination of the Biblical revelation and the cultural patterns suggested by Hellenistic literature and philosophy. It had as its objective the achieving of the wisdom of God, through a spiritual formation under the divine Pedagogue, the Logos, or the Word of God. The paideia looked to the formation of character and appreciation of values as much as it did to imparting knowledge or information. Its final aim was the true Gnosis, or Christian philosophy, whose end was the imitation of Christ.

Development to Clement of Alexandria. The early Church provided detailed instruction for catechumens

Sarcophagus of the first third of the 3d century in the church of Santa Maria Antiqua, Rome. The seated man in the center represents a Christian teacher or scholar reading from a religious text. The woman is undoubtedly his wife, who is listening to the reading in a reverent manner. Framing the central figures are representations of Jonah cast up by the whale under the gourd vine (left) and (right) the Good Shepherd and the Baptism of Christ.

and clergy but did not think of creating a separate educational system for children. In the secular schools the Christian child pursued the *enkyklios paideia,* the all-round culture of Hellenism that the Romans called *humanitas* and studied in the *trivium* and *quadrivium.* Religious development was provided, outside this classical training, mainly in the family circle and in the Church.

The expression Christian paideia was first used in the Epistle of *Clement I of Rome (*1 Cor.* 21.6, 8; cf. 16.5; 35.8; 56.2, 16). Like St. Paul, the author stressed that the young should be subject to parental formation and discipline. *Polycarp bade husbands teach their wives "to train their children in the knowledge and fear of God" (*Ad Phil.* 4.2). The Shepherd of *Hermas also insisted on family sanctification through discipline and training (*Vis.* 1.3.1–2; 2.3.1).

Since Homer and pagan mythology formed the basis of secular paideia, it presented dangers to the faith of Christians. But to shun the schools was impossible, as even Tertullian admitted: "How can we reject profane studies, without which religious studies are impossible?" (*De idol.* 10.4). But he banned Christians from teaching in the schools, and his basic opposition to Hellenism was expressed in his frequently quoted: "What has Athens to do with Jerusalem; the Academy with the Church?" (*Praescrip.* 7). *Tatian, the Syrian, was even more uncompromising in regard to pagan learning. For him the grammarians were idle prattlers (*Orat.* 26), and he turned his back on Greek paideia to become a professor of the philosophy of the barbarians. He found the Scriptures unpretentious in their language but too old and divine to be compared with the erroneous opinions of the Greeks (*Orat.* 29). Tatian had been a pupil of the more liberal *Justin Martyr at the latter's school in Rome, where Christianity was offered as the true philosophy.

By the end of the 2d century the catechumenal schools seem to have taken final form. Here the bishop or his delegate gave elaborate instructions preceding Baptism; examples of these courses of instruction survive in the *Great Catechism* of *Gregory of Nyssa, the *Catecheses* of *Cyril of Jerusalem and of *Theodore of Mopsuestia, and in the *De catechizandis rudibus* of

St. *Augustine. These schools contributed to the intellectual formation of candidates for Baptism, but their main function was to impart doctrinal, ascetical, and liturgical training, with the Scriptures as the basic text.

The catechetical schools offered more advanced instruction in the *Christian way of life; provided protection against the immorality and persecutional attacks of pagan adversaries; and deepened the knowledge of the faith for the neophytes. The most famous of these was the school of Alexandria. While Pantaenus and Clement of Alexandria evidently lectured on the Christian doctrines, it is only with *Origen that the school acquired its official, ecclesiastical standing. Its pupils were adults in the process of conversion; and under Origen's direction the elementary catechesis came to be delegated to Heraclas, and Origen devoted himself to advanced philosophy and exegesis.

The Major Roles of Clement and Origen. For *Clement of Alexandria (*c.* 200), paideia was the most excellent and perfect possession in life, a useful propaedeutic for the appreciation of the word of the Lord (*Paid.* 1.5.16; *Strom.* 1.5). His indebtedness to Greek classical authors, poets, and philosophers is obvious on every page. He had a decided predilection for Plato but was actually eclectic, regarding all of Greek philosophy as a guide to Christ, the best of educators (*Strom.* 2.2). His *Paidagogos* is the first complete educational treatise that combines pagan learning and cultural patterns with Christian theological thought and the sacramental way of life. It gives a minute description of the Christian's day, beginning with the main meal in the evening, and discusses every phase of his life.

Origen urged *Gregory Thaumaturgus "to extract from the philosophy of the Greeks what may serve as a course of study or a preparation for Christianity, and even from geometry and astronomy what would serve to explain the Sacred Scriptures, in order that all that the sons of philosophy are wont to say about geometry and music, grammar, rhetoric, and astronomy, as fellow helpers of philosophy, may be said about philosophy itself in relation to Christianity." Thus he regarded all secular subjects as "ladders to reach the sky"; and his students were expected to be familiar with every aspect of Hellenic knowledge as a preparation for their study of Scripture. Origen taught at Alexandria from 212 to 231 and thereafter at Caesarea until his death. During the 4th century the Church Fathers in the various areas where the Church was well established used their secular education as a background for developing the Church's understanding of divine revelation.

The Golden Age of Christian Paideia in the East. The Cappadocian Fathers made important contributions. *Gregory of Nazianzus, in his *Panegyric on Basil,* spoke for both of them when he said: "As we have compounded healthful drugs from reptiles, so from secular literature we have received principles of inquiry and speculation, while we have rejected their idolatry, terror, and pit of destruction." *Basil of Caesarea, a friend of the pagan orator Libanius and an impeccable Greek stylist, elaborated on the utility of Greek literature properly used for the educated Christian in his *To Young Men, on How They Might Profit from Pagan Literature.* His *Monastic Rules* also was important in shaping an erudite monasticism. Gregory of Nazianzus in his *Invective Orations against Julian* [the Apostate] severely castigated that Emperor for his efforts to exclude Christians from higher education. In virtue of a decree of Julian on June 17, 362 (*CodTheod* 13.3.5), Christian teachers had either to abandon Christianity and return to belief in the pagan gods or cease to teach. *Marius Victorinus had to quit his professorship of rhetoric at Rome, and many grammarians, rhetors, and even professors of medicine were affected; but the decree was rescinded by Julian's successor (364).

*John Chrysostom is the outstanding writer on pedagogy among the Fathers. Of especial importance is his *De inani gloria et de educandis liberis,* which deplores the lack of religious and moral training in an age that devoted so much energy to training in the arts, in literature, and in rhetoric. He reminded parents that they were bringing up "a philosopher, and a champion, and a citizen of Heaven."

Christian Paideia in the West. In the West the study of Greek declined in the 4th century; but the great Christian writers, such as *Lactantius, *Hilary of Poitiers, *Ambrose, *Jerome, and Augustine, were masters of the rhetorical culture of their time. They derived their knowledge of Greek philosophy mainly from Latin sources, especially Cicero. *Ausonius, however, spoke of "Greek grammarians" in his native Bordeaux, who used Homer as the first text (5.46) in their instruction.

Jerome studied under the famed *grammaticus* Donatus, and he himself expounded Vergil, the comedians, lyric poets, and historians during his sojourn in Bethlehem. Two of his letters (*Epist.* 107, 128) deal with the education of girls dedicated to God's service. Letter 22 gives an account of his famous dream in which he heard the Judge's condemnation, *Ciceronianus es, non Christianus,* and he asked rhetorically, *Quid facit cum psalterio Horatius? Cum evangeliis Maro? Cum apostolo Cicero?* But it is clear from his subsequent writings that his studies of the sacred writers did not exclude a continued interest in the classical.

According to St. Augustine, the Christian writer should despoil pagan literature as the Jews despoiled the Egyptians when they were leaving Egypt; the gold and silver in the writings of pagans are not their own but are dug out of the mines of God's providence and more properly belong to the follower of Christ when he has abandoned paganism. The arts in secular learning are a help in understanding the Scriptures (*Doct. Christ.* 2.16.28). His *De beata vita* ushered in the birth of Western Christian philosophy and a renewal of paideia under Christian auspices. Among later writers, Boethius, with his *Consolation of Philosophy,* integrated a wealth of classical learning and pagan philosophy with an apparently orthodox Christianity; *Cassiodorus's *Institutes* was devoted to an encyclopedic treatment of sacred and profane knowledge; *Gregory I the Great scorned literary niceties and endorsed monastic education and a new, specifically Christian education that rejected the classical and emphasized home training and moral formation; *Martianus Capella and *Isidore of Seville handed on the tradition of paideia to the Middle Ages.

Bibliography: H. FUCHS, ReallexAntChr 2:350–362, with bibliog. F. X. PORTMANN, *Die göttliche Paidagogia bei Gregor von Nazianz* (St. Ottilien 1954). P. PETIT, *Les Étudiants de Libanius* (Paris 1956). H. HAGENDAHL, *Latin Fathers and the Classics* (Göteborg 1958). M. L. W. LAISTNER, *Christianity and Pagan Culture in the Later Roman Empire* (Ithaca, N.Y. 1951). M. TESTARD, *Saint Augustin et Cicéron,* 2 v. (Paris 1958). A. J. FESTUGIÈRE, *Antioch païenne et chrétienne* (Paris 1959). J. FONTAINE, *Isidore de Séville et la culture classique dans l'Espagne wisigothique,* 2 v. (Paris 1959). E. L. FORTIN, *Christianisme et culture philosophique au Vᵉ siècle* (Paris 1959). H. I. MARROU, *A History of Education in Antiquity,* tr. G. LAMB from 3d Fr. ed. (New York 1956); ed. and tr., *Clément d'Alexandrie: Le Pédagogue,* v.1 (SourcesChr 70; 1960). W. BARCLAY, *Educational Ideals in the Ancient World* (London 1959). W. W. JAEGER, *Early Christianity and Greek Paideia* (Cambridge, Mass. 1961). P. RICHÉ, *Éducation et culture dans l'Occident barbare, VIᵉ–VIIIᵉ siècles* (Paris 1962). E. KEVANE, *Augustine the Educator* (Westminster, Md. 1964). **Illustration credit:** Hirmer Verlag München.

[T. P. HALTON]

PAIN

Both the Latin and Greek derivatives of the word "pain" have the basic meaning of penalty or punishment. This meaning is obsolete in modern usage, and the word is now employed to convey the meaning of physical or mental discomfort. There is a wide spectrum of pain, since discomfort can vary both in intensity and in character.

Types. Pain is readily classified into two major types: physical and psychological. This artificial distinction arises from the nature of pain in man. It is artificial since physical pain is always associated in some way with psychological discomfort, and psychological pain often possesses a correlative, physical experience of pain.

Physical pain varies greatly in type and in intensity. One can learn from his own experience significant differences between various kinds of physical pain. It is difficult to verbalize this difference in quality, scope, and intensity, but the difference one can call to mind between such a painful experience as an abrasion and a headache can help to crystallize it. In the less commonly experienced forms of pain there are marked variations in intensity. Certain forms of malignancy, renal colic, and intestinal obstruction are notorious for the intensity of the pain they produce.

Psychological pain also is of great variety. *Fear, *anxiety, *guilt, depression, and grief are a few of the many types of psychological pain. These painful affective states are of varied intensity; e.g., anxiety ranges from a mild apprehension to stark terror or panic.

Subjectivity. Clinical experience repeatedly illustrates a remarkable subjectivity in the experience of both mental and physical pain. Reactions can vary from the stoic tolerance of severe pain to the unusual phenomenon of getting pleasure from pain. This latter phenomenon, called masochism, certainly complicates the understanding of pain and is a remarkable example of the subjectivity of pain. It also illustrates the effect of the mind on the experience of pain. Another dramatic illustration of this is in *hypnosis. Extremely painful major operations have been performed under hypnosis during which the patient has had no subjective experience of pain. Hypnosis is also used extensively to alleviate certain kinds of mental pain, such as specific anxieties or *phobias.

This subjectivity is also important with regard to psychological pain. One of the critical factors in the genesis of emotional illness is the capacity of the individual to bear psychological pain. As psychological development proceeds, any individual is confronted with recurrent experiences that are painful. From infancy on humans must learn to endure the pain of frustration of many differents kinds of emotional needs. Bearing this pain of frustration and developing specific ways to deal with it is a critical learning experience. Some are taught well how to bear painful basic emotional experiences, while others are thrown back on their own immature helplessness. As development goes on and psychological pain recurs or is intensified, the struggle of the individual in dealing with it may result in extremely abnormal personality reactions and serious *mental disorder.

Chronic *alcoholism is an example of how some adults deal with what is basically psychological pain. Ever-increasing amounts and almost constant use of alcohol are the means by which the pain of anxiety is made tolerable by many alcoholics.

Physical Pain of Psychological Origin. An important notion about certain forms of pain that mimic physical pain but have no organic basis is that subjectively there is essentially no difference. There has been a prevailing misconception about this. Patients often receive extensive medical evaluation to determine the origin of certain painful physical symptoms, e.g., abdominal pain. When all available examinations and tests have been made and no cause can be found for the pain, it is often implied that the pain is "imaginary" or "in the patient's mind." In actuality the pain is the same as if the patient had a serious physical illness, such as an ulcer. It is just the cause that is different. In a sense the pain is in the patient's "mind," but the subjective discomfort is the same. (*See* PSYCHOSOMATIC ILLNESS.)

Physical pain that is psychogenic or psychological in origin is produced in one of two basic ways. People can experience severe pain as a result of conversion symptoms or of psychophysiologic disorders. In conversion symptoms the pain is a result of the symbolic translation of instinctive impulses into somatic symptoms. Abdominal pain as a conversion symptom is the individual's way of getting some instinctual gratification. The unique subjective mechanism of this is part of the adaptive technique of the individual, and working out the individual mystery of the production of this pain is the combined work of the doctor and patient in psychiatric treatment.

In psychophysiologic disorders the pain is a result of the exaggerated physiologic function of some organ system. This can lead to pain in the same way that a physical illness affecting the organ system would. Abdominal pain as a psychophysiologic symptom can be due to actual bowel inflammation with hemorrhage as seen in ulcerative colitis. The bowel as an organ is reacting in an exaggerated way to emotional stimuli. The physical condition of the bowel is the same as if the patient had a severe bowel infection, and the pain is exactly the same.

The phenomenon of *malingering is often associated with the complaint of pain. Individuals with certain characterological problems often learn that pain can result in their being treated in a way that is rewarding to them. They then actually mimic pain in such a way to be so treated to gain the desired reward. This is a fully conscious phenomenon, and there is no pain whatsoever experienced by the individual. Many reported cases illustrate the incredible extent to which such persons can mimic the actual clinical picture of a pain syndrome, characteristic of a physical illness.

Treatment. The treatment of pain must be oriented to the basic element of subjectivity, which is an essential part of any painful experience. The treatment must always be rendered in light of an appreciation of the total person and the particular situation. No two pain experiences are alike because they exist in the subjective world of a unique person. The correlative psychological and physical elements in any painful experience must be assessed. There is always a dualistic phenomenon present.

The anatomical and physiological aspects of pain production have been the subject of extensive monographs. As scientific knowledge has advanced, more has been discovered about the exact mechanisms by which stress on the human mind or body produces the discomfort called pain. The acquisition of this knowledge has enabled progressive development of more refined techniques to deal with pain.

There are highly specific neurosurgical procedures designed to alleviate pain not previously understood. There are also an ever-increasing number of tranquilizing drugs aimed more and more specifically at forms of mental pain.

The treatment of physical pain proceeds from the basic principle of understanding the cause of such pain before any treatment is begun. Failure to do this could lead to disastrous consequences in many instances. There are many forms of headache, chest pain, and abdominal pain, as well as many others, that if merely alleviated by pain-killing drugs could disguise serious and treatable physical illness.

The attempt to understand the cause of pain is also of the utmost importance in the treatment of psychological pain. An understanding of the cause of anxiety, guilt, and depression is an integral part of the process of psychotherapy.

In trying to comprehend the pain of another it is important to reaffirm just how variable pain can be. Because one has a personal knowledge of pain is no guarantee that one has a foolproof yardstick to evaluate pain in others. This is true in regard to both physical and mental pain.

The appreciation of psychological pain is undeniably a universal human experience. The appreciation, however, of the psychological pain of another calls for a faculty of man that is developed to a far greater degree in some and which is of the utmost importance in the helping of one's fellow man. Some individuals who have felt great psychological pain have a capacity to appreciate this experience in others and a capacity to communicate that this pain is tolerable and manageable. They are in a position to be of great assistance because of their personal encounter with similar pain.

Pain has classically been regarded as a warning signal of danger or threat to the organism. In this context one must assess every human experience of pain. A person with intractable physical pain from progressive cancer is receiving a signal about his severe ill-health. The therapy here is clearly to minimize this intense subjective discomfort and allow as painless a course as possible.

But there are many other forms of pain in which a clear course of therapy is not obvious. The pain may be a signal of danger, but the danger might be quite subtle and complex and demand extensive evaluation. In the realm of psychological pain the question will arise as to whether to treat the pain as a symptom or to attempt to increase understanding, which in itself can then be therapeutic.

To comprehend and treat pain is indeed an endless challenge. The task of doing it must proceed, under the guidance of a deep understanding of the scientific and philosophical knowledge available to man.

Bibliography: R. J. BEHAN, *Pain, its Origin, Conduction, Perception and Diagnostic Significance* (New York 1920). C. H. BEST and N. B. TAYLOR, *The Physiological Basis of Medical Practice* (6th ed. Baltimore 1955). J. J. BONICA, *Management of Pain* (Philadelphia 1953). W. B. CANNON, *Bodily Changes in Pain, Hunger, Fear and Rage* (2d ed. New York 1929). P. CHODOFF and H. LYONS, "Hysteria, the Hysterical Personality and Hysterical Conversion," AmJPsych 114 (1958) 734–740. Ciba Foundation Study Group No. 1. *Pain and Itch: Nervous Mechanisms,* ed. G. E. W. WOLSTENHOLME and M. O'CONNOR (Boston 1959). M. C. D'ARCY, *The Pain of This World and the Providence of God* (New York 1952), first pub. (Milwaukee 1935) *Pain and the Providence of God.* H. F. DUNBAR, *Emotions and Bodily Changes* (New York 1954). O. FENICHEL, *The Psychoanalytic Theory of Neurosis* (New York 1945). B. E. FINNESON, *Diagnosis and Management of Pain Syndromes* (Philadelphia 1962). S. FREUD, *Three Essays on the Theory of Sexuality* (1905), v.7 of *The Standard Edition of the Complete Psychological Works,* ed. J. STRACHEY, 24 v. (London 1953–). J. D. HARDY et al., *Pain, Sensations and Reactions* (Baltimore 1952). H. A. LIEF et al., eds., *The Psychological Basis of Medical Practice* (New York 1963). W. K. LIVINGSTON, *Pain Mechanisms, a Physysiologic Interpretation of Causalgia and its Related States* (New York 1943). J. C. WHITE and W. H. SWEET, *Pain, its Mechanisms and Neurosurgical Control* (Springfield, Ill. 1955). T. S. SZASZ, *Pain and Pleasure: A Study of Bodily Feelings* (New York 1957). H. G. WOLFF, *Pain* (Springfield, Ill. 1958).

[E. J. CONLEY]

PAINE, JOHN, BL., English martyr; b. Peterborough, date unknown; d. Chelmsford, Essex, April 2, 1582 (feast, April 2). His family was probably Protestant, but the time and circumstances of his conversion are unchronicled. He entered Douai College in 1574 to study for the priesthood and was for a time made bursar of the college; this indicates that he had some experience in stewardship, probably as a servant of the Shelley family at Stondon Hall in Essex. While he was at Douai, he saw a vision of the figure of Christ rising from the Sacra-

ment during the Elevation. This vision was the subject of the Bosworth Burse now in Leicester Museum. On April 7, 1576, John Paine was ordained, and a few days later he set out for England with (Bl.) Cuthbert

Bl. John Paine.

*Mayne. Paine made his way to Ingatestone Hall in Essex, where the old, widowed Lady Petre lived, an uncompromising Catholic. Here he remained in the guise of a steward until about February 1577 or earlier, when he was arrested and, for a brief time, imprisoned. After a visit to Douai he returned to Ingatestone some time before June 1578. He continued to work there until the middle of July 1581, when he was betrayed into the hands of George (Judas) Elliot, Edmund *Campion's captor, at Haddon in Oxfordshire. He was examined before Walsingham at Greenwich, then sent to the Tower and racked several times. In March 1582 he was taken to the dungeons of Colchester castle to await trial. He was charged with conspiracy against the Queen, and was sentenced to be hanged, drawn, and quartered. When offered his liberty if he would change his religion, he told the officials "to stop their foolish babbling." The sentence was carried out at Chelmsford on April 2, 1582. After praying, he protested that "his feet did never tread, his hands did never write, nor did his wit ever invent any treason against her majesty." Since he was so well known and loved in the district, the crowd would not allow the hangman to cut him down and disembowel him until he was dead. He was beatified by Leo XIII on Dec. 29, 1886 (*see* MARTYRS OF ENGLAND AND WALES).

Bibliography: W. ALLEN, *A Briefe Historie of the Glorious Martyrdom of Twelve Reverend Priests,* ed. J. H. POLLEN, 2 v. (St. Louis 1908). B. C. FOLEY, *Blessed John Paine* (Postulation pamphlet; London 1961). Butler Th Attw 2:16–17. B. CAMM, *Lives of the English Martyrs,* 2 v. (New York 1904–05).

[G. FITZ HERBERT]

PAINE, THOMAS

Journalist and pamphleteer, whose political writings influenced American opinion in favor of independence and whose popular tracts on Deism attacked organized religion; b. Thetford, Norfolk, England, Jan. 29, 1737; d. New York City, June 8, 1809. His early religious training was in his mother's Anglican faith; his father was a Quaker artisan, and young Paine served his apprenticeship in his shop. He was later employed as a staymaker, opened his own shop (1759), and became a customs officer (1764). Paine found his true calling in 1772, when he wrote *The Case of the Officers of*

Excise, a plea for higher wages printed for distribution to Parliament by a subscription raised among his fellow customs officers. Discharged from his post, he immigrated to Philadelphia, Pa., in 1774; there he edited the *Pennsylvania Magazine,* contributing articles to its columns. He published a plea for the abolition of the slave trade and joined an antislavery society (1775), but his political views did not find expression until *Common Sense* (1776) issued a spirited demand for independence from Great Britain. Although the ideas he expressed were in no sense original, the influence of *Common Sense* in shaping public opinion was immense. Unlike earlier pamphleteers, Paine did not argue abstract truths but struck at George III and the whole British constitution. Paine's Hobbesian view of government was modified by a Lockean approach to society, but his isolationist view of America's role in world affairs owed little to literary sources. He served briefly as brigade major with Gen. G. Washington's army and began to write *The American Crisis* on a drumhead during the retreat across New Jersey. *The Crisis* appeared in 13 numbered pamphlets issued between 1776 and 1783.

In 1781 he visited France as secretary to an American mission and in 1782 was formally hired as a publicist for the Continental Congress; he later served the French embassy in the same capacity. Always interested in practical science, Paine invented an improved bridge and visited France again in 1787 to promote it. The French foreign office subsidized his *Prospects on the Rubicon* (1787) on Anglo-French relations, while he divided his time between London and Paris. As a reply to Edmund Burke's *Reflections on the French Revolution,* he issued *The Rights of Man,* rejecting the-

ories of rule by a priesthood or an aristocracy as based on superstition or force and arguing in favor of democracy with its basis in reason and the free consent of individual citizens. Any theory looking to the past is to be rejected, since every generation must act for itself and has no power to bind posterity. His positive suggestions for reform appeared in the second part of *The Rights of Man* (1792).

The French Assembly made him an honorary citizen in 1792 and shortly thereafter he was elected to the Convention. He took his seat, but his opposition to the execution of Louis XVI and his association with the Girondists led to his arrest and imprisonment in 1793. With the help of James Monroe he was released in 1794 and restored to his post as a deputy. *The Age of Reason* was still in manuscript at Paine's arrest; it appeared in 1794, offering the classic explanation of Deism and attacking the Bible and Christianity. Stating his belief in God and humanity, he argued that Christ did not found a religion, but called men to the practice of moral virtues and belief in one God; thus for him Christianity was the invention of myth-makers. Large segments of the work dealt with rather pedestrian scriptural criticism. Bishop Richard Watson of Llandaff wrote a refutation in 1796, and Paine was engaged in writing a lengthy reply until shortly before his return to America in 1802. He was closely associated with Elihu Palmer in promoting Deism and wrote articles for Palmer's monthly, the *Prospect* (1804–05). In 1807 he published a critical pamphlet on the New Testament.

Bibliography: *Complete Writings,* ed. P. S. FONER, 2 v. (New York 1945), with biog. essay. G. VALE, *The Life of Thomas Paine* (New York 1841). M. D. CONWAY, *Life of Thomas Paine,* 2 v. (New York 1892). A. O. ALDRIDGE, *Man of Reason* (Philadelphia 1959). H. M. MORAIS, *Deism in 18th Century America* (New York 1960). G. A. KOCH, *Republican Religion: The American Revolution and the Cult of Reason* (New York 1933). **Illustration credit:** National Portrait Gallery, London.

[R. K. MAC MASTER]

PAINTING, ARTICLES ON

This *Encyclopedia* contains articles on the techniques of painting and allied arts, as well as on the history of painting, famous painters, modern art movements, and common subjects of Christian art.

Techniques. For the techniques of painting and related arts, *see* FRESCO; MANUSCRIPT ILLUMINATION; GRAPHIC ART; MOSAICS; STAINED GLASS; BOOK, THE PRINTED; PHOTOGRAPHY, THE ART OF.

History of Painting. For the earliest manifestations of painting in human history, *see* ART, PREHISTORIC. For discussions of the painting of non-Christian peoples, *see* ISLAMIC ART; JEWISH ART; DURA-EUROPOS. The historical development of painting is treated in a series of systematic period surveys that include, along with sculpture and the minor arts, a discussion of painting, less important in the earlier periods but of increasing importance in succeeding periods. *See* ART, EARLY CHRISTIAN; BYZANTINE ART; CAROLINGIAN ART; OTTONIAN ART; ROMANESQUE ART; GOTHIC ART; RENAISSANCE ART; MANNERISM; BAROQUE ART; ROCOCO ART; NEOCLASSICISM (IN ART). The article ART, MODERN EUROPEAN begins with the 18th century and concludes in the mid-1960s of the 20th century.

The historical period surveys tend to concentrate on artistic development in Western Europe; for painting in areas peripheral to this development, see the

Thomas Paine, painting by A. Millière after an engraving by George Romney.

more specialized articles: ARMENIAN ART; BULGARIAN ART; COPTIC ART; CZECHOSLOVAKIAN ART; GEORGIAN LITERATURE AND ART; HUNGARIAN ART; IRISH ART; POLISH ART; YUGOSLAVIAN ART.

In the course of history, painters have banded together for a common aesthetic or religious aim, or have been considered as a group; *see* NAZARENES (BROTHERHOOD OF ST. LUKE); BEURONESE ART; FAUVES; NABIS. Outstanding works of art in the field of painting and places particularly rich in the production of painting are discussed in individual articles; *see* SISTINE CHAPEL; KELLS, BOOK OF; LINDISFARNE GOSPELS; ASSISI; FLORENCE; ASSY, NOTRE-DAME-DE-TOUTE-GRÂCE.

Special kinds of painting are discussed in the articles FOLK ART and PRIMITIVIST ART.

Biographies of Painters. Important painters, including modern artists whose work has indirectly influenced the modern renewal in religious art, are discussed in biographical articles or in articles of broader scope (see index volume). Biographical articles give the scope and character of each painter's work, with important dates in his career and the museums or sites where his works may be viewed. *See,* e.g., GIOTTO DI BONDONE; LEONARDO DA VINCI; MICHELANGELO BUONARROTI; RAPHAEL SANZIO; TITIAN (TIZIANO VECELLI); TINTORETTO (JACOPO ROBUSTI); CARAVAGGIO, MICHELANGELO MERISI DA; TIEPOLO, GIOVANNI BATTISTA; DÜRER, ALBRECHT; HOLBEIN, HANS (THE YOUNGER); RUBENS, SIR PETER PAUL; REMBRANDT HERMANSZOON VAN RIJN; POUSSIN, NICOLAS; CHARDIN, JEAN BAPTISTE SIMÉON; DELACROIX, FERDINAND VICTOR EUGÈNE; COURBET, GUSTAVE; MANET, ÉDOUARD; GAUGUIN, PAUL; GOGH, VINCENT VAN; KANDINSKY, WASSILY; MATISSE, HENRI; LÉGER, FERNAND. Articles on painters active in the renewal of Christian art in the 19th and 20th centuries include: REDON, ODILON; PUVIS DE CHAVANNES, PIERRE; DENIS, MAURICE; DESVALLIÈRES, GEORGES; ROUAULT, GEORGES.

Modern Art Movements. The styles and movements of modern art have been covered in a variety of articles; *see,* e.g., EXPRESSIONISM (IN ART); ABSTRACT EXPRESSIONISM; IMPRESSIONISM; CUBISM; FUTURISM; DADA; SURREALISM; POP ART; ABSTRACT ART. Modern schools of painting have been important not only in their own right but for their relation to and their influence on developments in modern religious art; *see* ABSTRACT ART AND THE CHURCH.

Content of Painting. For an introduction to the history of development and the methods of research in the subject matter of painting, *see* ICONOLOGY AND ICONOGRAPHY. Articles on motifs and subjects of particular relevance in Christian art are found under names' or categories of persons, theological subjects, and narrative or descriptive subjects; *see* APOCALYPSE, ICONOGRAPHY OF; APOCRYPHA, ICONOGRAPHY OF THE; APOSTLES, ICONOGRAPHY OF; BIBLE CYCLES IN ART; BIBLE MORALISÉE; CHURCH, SYMBOLS OF; CRUCIFIXION (IN ART); ECCE HOMO; EVANGELISTS, ICONOGRAPHY OF; GOD THE FATHER, ICONOGRAPHY OF; DESCENT OF CHRIST INTO HELL; HOLY NAME, ICONOGRAPHY OF; HOLY SPIRIT, ICONOGRAPHY OF; ICON; JESUS CHRIST, ICONOGRAPHY OF; JOHN THE BAPTIST, ST., ICONOGRAPHY OF; LAST SUPPER, ICONOGRAPHY OF; MARY, BLESSED VIRGIN, ICONOGRAPHY OF; PENTECOST, ICONOGRAPHY OF; SACRAMENTS, ICONOGRAPHY OF; SACRED HEART, ICONOGRAPHY OF; SAINTS, ICONOGRAPHY OF; TRINITY, HOLY, ICONOGRAPHY OF; VIRTUES AND VICES, ICONOGRAPHY OF.

[L. P. SIGER]

PAINTINGS, CONSERVATION OF

The science of preserving and restoring painted works of art. While a painting is the unique expression of an artist and his time, it is fashioned out of matter and subject to the same altering forces as any other form of matter. A painting is a three-dimensional, laminated structure, and each organic or inorganic material in its layers has its own properties and characteristic behavior. Below the visible varnish covering and painted surface are other paint layers, priming, size, support, even auxiliary supports, all of which are subject to various kinds of deterioration; alteration in these unseen parts can change the entire aesthetic character of a painting. From the moment a picture is finished, it begins to change chemically and physically. It is affected by the atmosphere, cycles of the seasons, sun, light, oxygen, moisture, heat, air-borne pollution, and damages by man. If attempts had not been made to take care of them, there would be few ancient pictures extant today.

The history of restoration has never been compiled, but fragmentary records and internal evidence indicate efforts to consolidate decaying structures, along with such devastating procedures as scraping with knives, scrubbing with spirits, and drenching with boiled oils. The term "restoration" itself fell into disrepute because too often the ravaged paintings were repainted into falsifications by inept artists. In the 19th century, isolated artists and scientists, distressed over the extreme state of some masterpieces, began a search for methods to preserve them. With the advent of the 20th century, the technical laboratory, where paintings could be studied in depth, came into existence. Today, all over the world, centers exist to study paintings, to analyze their structure and the causes of their deterioration, and to explore sound methods for their preservation.

As in the medical world, professional conservators use multiform materials, natural and synthetic, and a variety of methods, by mechanical means and by hand, sharing their research in a constant effort to improve preservation of the painting's integrity. Conservators use X ray to study the skeleton of a picture; ultraviolet to reveal changes in the surface films; infrared to hunt for forms just beneath the surface; the binocular microscope to magnify detail; chemical and spectroscopic analysis to identify materials in the structure; and photography to record all evidence for the future. Conservation has become a joint undertaking by trained technicians, art historians, and curators to present the public with an accurate and lasting pictorial heritage.

Bibliography: International Museum Office, *Manual on the Conservation of Paintings* (Paris 1940). H. J. PLENDERLEITH, *The Conservation of Antiquities and Works of Art* (New York 1956). "The Care of Paintings," *Museum* 3 (1950) 109–251. C. K. KECK, *How To Take Care of Your Pictures* (New York 1954). S. KECK, "The Technical Examination of Paintings," *Brooklyn Museum Journal* (1941) 71–82.

[C. K. KECK]

PAISIELLO, GIOVANNI, church and opera composer of early classical style; b. Taranto, Italy, May 9, 1740; d. Naples, June 5, 1816. As a youth he studied at the conservatory of S. Onofrio in Naples; he then taught there while composing his first music. At first he wrote only sacred music, but later he became extremely successful in opera, composing more than 100 works in this form. He spent 8 years (1776–84) at the court of Catherine II at St. Petersburg, Russia, pro-

Giovanni Paisiello, engraving by L. Bridi.

ducing there his most famous opera, *The Barber of Seville* (1782). He later held the post of *maestro di cappella* at the court of Naples until he left in 1799 for political reasons. He was Napoleon's favorite composer and became his *maître de chapelle* in Paris 1802; but after an unsuccessful struggle to please the Paris public, he resumed his position at Naples under Joseph Bonaparte a year later. His sacred music includes, among other works, 30 Masses with orchestra; several Masses for varying combinations; a Requiem scored for two choruses, orchestra, and organ; 40 motets; a Miserere; a Magnificat; and an oratorio on the Passion. Like his operas, these have the florid arias and grandiose choruses of the period, but also reveal the natural melodic beauty that characterizes his best work.

See also MUSIC, SACRED, HISTORY OF, 6.

Bibliography: A. LOEWENBERG, "Paisiello's and Rossini's Barbiere di Siviglia," MusLett 10 (1939) 157–167. H. V. F. SOMERSET, "Giovanni Paisiello," *ibid.* 18 (1937) 20–35. A. MONDOLFI, MusGG 10:639–647. **Illustration credit:** Museo Teatrale alla Scala.

[W. C. HOLMES]

PAKISTAN, an Islamic republic, which attained independence on Aug. 14, 1947, after being carved out of the predominantly Moslem areas of British *India. It consists of two widely separated provinces, West Pakistan, 310,403 square miles in area, and East Pakistan, 55,126 square miles. It became a republic in 1956 within the British Commonwealth with the acceptance of a constitution. In October 1958 this constitution was abrogated by the revolutionary government. A new system of government, called basic democracy, began in 1960. A new constitution was introduced in 1962, which guaranteed religious freedom. Rawalpindi, the capital, had 343,000 inhabitants in 1961. The name Pakistan is a neologism, meaning land of the pure, formed from Urdu (the official language) *pak* (pure) and *stan* (land). In a total

population of 93,700,000 (1962), Moslems numbered 82,500,000, Catholics 330,000, and all other Christians 388,000.

By the 5th century there were Christians among the Roman traders to this region, as attested by the discovery of a statuette of St. Peter at Charsadda. In the 16th century the Jesuits had a mission to the Mogul court of Akbar at Lahore, and Augustinians and Dominicans began work in Bengal. A century later, Carmelites and Augustinians labored in Sind. Their work included the spiritual care of the foreign personnel at the trading posts established in the country. Evangelization of the native populace started in mid-19th century. In 1886 the Dioceses of Lahore and Dacca were created.

When the hierarchy was established in Pakistan (1950), *Karachi became the metropolitan see for West Pakistan with Lahore (created in 1886), Rawalpindi (1887), and Multan (1939) as suffragans. Hyderabad became a suffragan in 1958 and Lyallpur in 1960. In East Pakistan, *Dacca was made the metropolitan see with Chittagong (1927) and Dinajpur (1927) as suffragans, to which was added Khulna (1952). Diplomatic relations were established with the Holy See in 1951.

In 1962 there were 11 bishops (2 Pakistanis), 391 priests (88 Pakistanis), and about 900 religious women belonging to 25 congregations. Five native congregations of sisters had more than 300 members in 1965. The 460 Catholic primary and secondary schools had 69,875 students in 1960. Catholics had also 58 dispensaries, 25 hospitals, 34 orphanages, and 1 leprosarium. A growing suspicion among the masses concerning missionary evangelization has brought to a close the period of mass conversions. The higher classes, however, regard Catholic churches and institutions with respect.

For map, see following page.

Bibliography: P. THOMAS, *Christians and Christianity in India and Pakistan* (London 1954).

[L. MASCARENHAS]

PALACE SCHOOLS

A name applied to education given in the courts of kings and emperors at the end of the Merovingian and all through the Carolingian periods.

Historical Development. When Charlemagne reorganized education, which had been sorely neglected during the long period of military campaigns, churches and monasteries were in almost exclusive control of schools. Palace schools (*schola palatii*), however, which Charlemagne, taking advantage of an ancient tradition of royal patronage, had established for members of the court, boy lectors at the royal chapel, children of the nobility, and laymen, were an exception.

In fact, although there were no schools properly so-called in the Merovingian palaces, many young nobles and future bishops spent some years in the *contubernium* (residence) of the prince, often after having previously attended some school, as we see in the 7th century in the case of St. Ermenland, if we can believe his biographers, who was "withdrawn from school to be placed in a royal palace." Even at the time of the early Carolingians, where, as among the Merovingians, the term *schola palatii* is found, this *schola* does not seem to be a school, as the word is

INDIA AND PAKISTAN
⚓ **Archbishopric** ⚓ **Bishopric**
● **Prefecture Apostolic**
—·—·— **International Border**
—·—·— **Internal Civil Boundary**

generally understood, but rather a group of clergy and laymen who surrounded the king in his palace; for example, Benoît d'Arlane, who, though ranked *inter scholares,* was appointed cup-bearer, a duty that seems incompatible with the pursuit of serious literary studies. Nevertheless, constant association with palace officials did not fail to afford the young people some insight into state affairs, which explains the passage from *Vita Adalardi:* "Adalard, Charlemagne's cousin, was instructed at the palace in the *prudentia* (wisdom) of the world by the same teachers as the prince of the land." This prince of the land was Charlemagne whose early education was incidental and who, only in later years when he came into power, received any formal intellectual training.

Organization. Whatever doubt may exist about the Merovingian school, it is certain that Charlemagne's palace was an active center of serious study. Charlemagne took a personal interest in the restoration of arts and letters. In 774, on his return from the cam-

paign in Italy that established the papal state, he brought back with him the grammarian Pierre de Pise and Paul Warnefield, also called Paul the Deacon; and in 776 he called in Pauline d'Aquilée. Charlemagne's truly great teacher, however, the head of the palace school, was the renowned Alcuin, former pupil at the episcopal school at York, who after several short visits to the court, established his residence there in 793. Even though Alcuin later withdrew to Tours, he never lost interest in his first mission where he continued to wield a strong influence. The Irish monk Dungal and Theodulf d'Orléans were among other famous teachers at the court for short periods. The school continued its activity under Charlemagne's successors, when from 845 to his death in 875, John the Scot (Joannes Scotus) was one of its most representative masters.

At the end of the 9th century, the most renowned palace school was that established by Alfred the Great, considered in English literature as the first translator. Having heard of the great learning and virtue of *Grimbald, abbot of Saint-Bertin in France, Alfred invited him to Great Britain to restore the teaching of letters. Like the Carolingians, he gathered at his court the children of high birth to teach them to read both Latin and their native tongue, Anglo-Saxon.

Objectives. Education in the palace school was intended first of all for the emperor and his court who formed, it seems, an academy, since Alcuin in a letter to Charlemagne referred to his academicians. The women of the Carolingian family also took part—reading poetry, solving problems, discussing theological and grammatical questions, and the like. The academicians took assumed names: Charlemagne called himself David; Angilbert, Homer; Eginhard, an artist, Beseleel; and the Abbess Gisela, Charlemagne's sister, Lucy. Mingled with these scholars were children who followed more elementary and no doubt more formative courses. The monk St. Gall, in his *Gestis Caroli Magni,* tells us that the children were entrusted to the special care of the Irishman Clement.

Curriculum. It would be a mistake to place the academicians of either Charlemagne's or Alfred the Great's palace school and the children of the *schola* on the same plane as that of the students in the later medieval universities. The subject matter taught was, in comparison, very elementary, based on German common sense and subtlety and adapted to minds barely familiar with the most rudimentary notions of early science.

The education given at the Carolingian palace school has come down to us through the works left by Alcuin. Like Cassiodorus, 6th-century Roman monk, author, and educator, he divided the courses among the seven *liberal arts: the *trivium*—grammar, rhetoric, and logic, which constituted the first step—and the *quadrivium*—arithmetic, geometry, music, and astronomy, which made up the second step. On each of the subjects Alcuin wrote a small tract summarizing his teaching methods in which the oral exchange (dialogue) between teacher and student played an important part. Although Alcuin compared the seven liberal arts to the seven pillars of the house of wisdom, his teaching seems to have been elementary and not devoid of mistakes; for example, in his pamphlet on spelling he gives *hippocrita* (*hypocrita*), synonym for *simulator,* as a derivative of *hippo-falsum,* and *chrisis-judicium.*

Educational Influence. It is evident that the educational influence of the *scholae palatii* was not so extensive as the vast program drawn up by Alcuin and theoretically adopted by his successors. This rather tenuous influence was felt principally on the grammatical plane since all the schools, from the end of the 11th century, devoted more time to grammar, considered the most necessary of all the arts. The palace school also contributed to the development of oratory. Charlemagne in Alcuin's *Rhetorica* remarks that since this art was of major importance in civil affairs, it would be absurd "to ignore the precepts of the art in which they are constantly involved." A prominent place was also given to logic, which, wrote Rabanus Maurus, "is the discipline of disciplines that teaches how to teach, and to learn how to learn; and in which reason discovers and shows what it is, what it wishes, what it sees." The four other liberal arts, on the contrary, seem to have been somewhat neglected and wielded little educational influence.

Finally, while other schools founded by Charlemagne and Alfred were devoted to the education of priests only, the palace schools contributed considerably to the literary and administrative formation of great laymen. At a time when culture was at its lowest ebb, the palace schools restored ancient disciplines—the liberal arts—and kept alive the legacy of classical antiquity, particularly by the interpretation of Sacred Scripture and the use of commentaries made by the Fathers of the Church. This dependence on ancient learning, both pagan and Christian, deeply influenced curricular orientation until the end of the 12th century.

Bibliography: J. B. Weiss, *Geschichte Alfreds des Grossen* (Schaffhausen 1852). Sandys. C. Plummer, *The Life and Time of Alfred the Great* (Oxford 1902). L. Maître, *Les Écoles épiscopales et monastiques en Occident avant les universités* (2d ed. Paris 1924). Laistner ThLett. P. Riché, *Éducation et culture dans l'Occident barbare, VIᵉ–VIIIᵉ siècles* (Paris 1962). H. Leclercq, DACL 4.2:1805–13, 1872–76.

[J. IMBERT]

PALACIOS, MANUEL ANTONIO, Paraguayan bishop, executed for his supposed involvement in a conspiracy against the republic; b. Luque, near Asunción, July 1824; d. Lomas Valentinas, Dec. 21, 1868. He attended the literary academy where he was a brilliant student. In September 1848 he was ordained by Bishop López. When he was curate of Villeta, he was proposed, on Nov. 20, 1862, as auxiliary bishop by the president of the republic, Francisco Solano *López. He was consecrated in the Cathedral of Asunción on Aug. 30, 1863, by Bishop Urbieta, whom he succeeded on Jan. 29, 1865. From the beginning of the Paraguayan War, he served as first chaplain of the army, accompanying Marshal López as friend and confidant. However, by order of López, he was taken prisoner in San Fernando, along with several other persons accused of treason to Paraguay and its government. In 1868 he was condemned to death in a summary judgment at Lomas Valentinas and was executed by firing squad in company with Benigno López, the marshal's brother; Gen. Vicente Barrios, the marshal's brother-in-law; José Berjes, Minister of Foreign Affairs; Eugenio Bogado, Vicar General; José María Leite Pereira, Consul of Portugal; Capt. Simón Fidanza of the Italian Navy in the service of Paraguay; Col. Paulino Alem, former commandant of Humaitá; Juan Bautista Zalduondo, nephew of Palacios; and three distinguished ladies from Asunción.

The cause and manner of Palacios's death have given an unhappy fame to his episcopate, although the truth of the San Fernando conspiracy has been much discussed. The prosecutor himself, a relative of Palacios, later referred to it as a "supposed" plot. Further, the accused were denied the right of defense; the trials were secret; and the confessions were extracted by whippings, by an old form of military punishment known as "cepo," and by crushing the fingers with a hammer. Scholars now believe that the plot never existed, that the sentencing and execution of a group of prominent men was simply a desperate attempt by Marshal López to maintain the morale of a decimated population whose total destruction was increasingly imminent. According to the most reliable documents and the statements of some survivors, it had become clear that the Paraguayan cause in the war was definitely lost when Paraguayan resistance on the southern frontier was broken with the fall of Humaitá. Two opposing factions resulted: those who believed it preferable to risk total destruction of their country rather than see it submit to an iniquitous tyranny and become the victim of injustice; and those who believed that such an extreme position was inhuman and useless, that no people should be obliged to sacrifice itself completely. Bishop Palacios and the others who were executed held the second opinion, as the statements of the prosecutor of the trial indicated.

Bibliography: S. Gaona, *El clero en la guerra del 70* (2d ed. Asunción 1961).

[A. N. Acha Duarte]

PALAFOX Y MENDOZA, JUAN DE, VEN.

Spanish bishop of Puebla, Mexico; b. Fitero, Navarre, Spain, 1600; d. Osma, Spain, 1659. Even in recent times Palafox has been a subject of controversy and heated discussion. The illegitimate son of Jaime Palafox, Marquesa of Ariza, he studied in Salamanca and was ordained after having served as fiscal to the Councils of War and the Indies. As chaplain he accompanied Empress María to Germany. In 1610 he arrived in Mexico, in the same group that included the new Viceroy López Pacheco, Duke of Escalona, to assume his duties as bishop of Puebla de los Angeles. Along with his appointment as bishop, Palafox had been designated Visitor of the *audiencia* and of the University of Mexico. The viceroy, a first cousin of the Duke of Braganza in Portugal, became suspect during the war for Portuguese independence and was recalled to Spain. Palafox, who had also suspected López of sympathy for the Portuguese cause, took over the post of viceroy for a few months but later, recognizing the viceroy's loyalty to the King, returned to his diocese.

The bishop's ecclesiastical policies brought him into conflict with several religious orders, particularly the Jesuits, with whom he had a famous lawsuit that originated when Palafox denied the Jesuits the right to hear confessions and preach. The dispute lasted several years and was eventually settled in favor of the bishop. A cultured and enthusiastic person, Palafox worked zealously. He supported education, enlarging the existing institutions such as the Tridentine College, and founding new ones, such as a girls' school and a literary academy to which he gave a library of 6,000 volumes, known today as the Biblioteca Palafoxiana de Puebla. In 1644 he inspected the University of Mexico and the next year drafted a new constitution for it. It was not well received by some members of the faculty, especially the religious, who had been excluded from the rectorship. At their request the viceroy suspended the constitution. It was not confirmed by the King until 1649, after Innocent X settled the case between Bishop Palafox and the Jesuits, and through a series of complications it did not become effective until 1671.

On his return to Spain in 1649, Palafox was minister of the Council of Aragon and later became bishop of Osma. His fame as a holy man brought the introduction of his cause for beatification. In 1767 the Pope confirmed his "reputation for sanctity, virtue, and miracles *in genere*." Palafox wrote many works—canonical, religious, moral, political, historical, and literary—which were published in 15 volumes after his death. His political writings reflect a great concern for the decline of Spanish power, and in *Juicio político de los daños y reparos de cualquiera monarquía* he analyzed the foreign and national policies that contributed to the decline. Although he was essentially a Hispanist, Palafox was able to see the importance of the various nations, that is, of the multiple nationality of the monarchy. He pleaded for the recognition of the individuality of each group and its equality with Castile and decried the distrust that prevented the full use of the monarchy's resources and energy.

Bibliography: G. García, *Don Juan Palafox y Mendoza, obispo de Puebla y Osma, visitador y virrey de la Nueva España* (Mexico City 1918). J. L. Becerra López, *La organización de los estudios en la Nueva España* (Mexico City 1963).

[H. Pereña]

PALAMAS, GREGORY

Byzantine mystical theologian, and defender of *Hesychasm, bishop and saint in the Orthodox Church; b. Constantinople, *c.* 1296; d. Thessalonica, Nov. 14, 1359. Of a well-to-do family from Asia Minor, Gregory received a liberal education at the imperial university, came under the influence of the mystically-minded metropolitan of Philadelphia, Theolytus, and at 22 entered a monastery on Mt. Athos with his two younger brothers. When the Turkish invasions of 1325 threatened the monastic life there, Palamas migrated to Thessalonica, where in 1326 he was ordained a priest and with 10 companions retired to a hermitage on a mountain near Beroea. For 5 years he lived the life of the Hesychastic monk: 5 days of solitude and silence; then, on Saturday and Sunday, meeting with the others to celebrate the Eucharist and engage in spiritual conversation. He returned to Mt. Athos in 1331, fleeing Serbian incursions, and lived in the hermitage of St. Sabas, where he followed the same regime as at Beroea. In 1335 or 1336 he was appointed hegumen (abbot) of the Grand Laura, but he returned after a short while to St. Sabas.

Controversy with Barlaam. At St. Sabas Palamas became acquainted with the theology of *Barlaam, a Greek Orthodox monk from Calabria who was employing the syllogistic method in his attempt to refute the doctrine of the Latin Church regarding the procession of the Holy Spirit. Palamas wrote two letters to Barlaam (1332–33) in which he defended the position that apodictic arguments were possible in theology and rejected the agnosticism implied in the extreme apophatic, or negative, theology of Barlaam.

Barlaam, meanwhile, had begun to criticize the Hesychastic monks. He sarcastically impugned their psychophysical prayer practices, calling the monks *omphalopsychoi* (men-with-their-soul-in-their-navel) because of the prayer posture adopted by the monk, who was to focus his eyes on a spot below his chest for concentration (*see* Jesus prayer). Barlaam attacked in particular the explanation of the monks' goal of meditative contemplation (*hesychia*). The Hesychasts claimed that the saints as "the pure of heart" have the vision of God promised them in this life (Mt 5.8). They can see within themselves the working of the Holy Spirit as an uncreated grace. The Spirit is seen as a white light, the same light that shone about the Lord during the Transfiguration on Mt. Tabor. Barlaam accused the monks of Messalianism, a 4th-century dualistic heresy apparently adopted by the *Paulicians in their claim that God was visible to human eyes. Barlaam prepared a work against this Hesychastic doctrine; but before its publication, Isidore, the future Patriarch of Constantinople, called Palamas from Mt. Athos to aid in the refutation of Barlaam's charges (1338). Palamas prepared a threefold work (Triad) on the Hesychasts. He followed this with a second Triad, in which he described his famous distinction between God's being and His energy or operation. This became a distinctive characteristic of his theology. Later he defended the bodily prayer practices of the monks by insisting on the unity of the engraced man and rejected an extreme Platonic division of body and soul that would not see grace influencing and elevating the body of man to actual participation in the divine life of grace.

Elaboration of Palamas's Theology. In defending the presence of the Holy Spirit as uncreated grace within the saints, Palamas rejected Western explanations based on the idea of grace as created *and* supernatural. Such a concept of grace, Palamas argued, did not sufficiently explain the deification of the engraced man. A created entity is not the divinity, and man must somehow be deified by grace and thus participate in the very divinity. Only uncreated grace, the Spirit of God, can truly elevate the Christian to the divine life.

Palamas further sought to justify the Athonite monks and maintained that the action of God within the soul is a visible light, although not visible in the Messalian, heretical way, but visible to eyes elevated by grace. This light is the same as the light of the Transfiguration, which was not, as Barlaam claimed, a material light, but rather the divinity of the Lord, a divine energy. However, Palamas admitted that the Apostles did not see the essence or the nature of the divinity, which is invisible and incomprehensible, but rather this divine "energy" or activity. So too the saint sees a divine energy and not the essence of the Godhead. Even in the eternal life the blessed will not see the essence of God, which is incomprehensible, but rather the divine energy. The Holy Spirit, who sanctifies the saint, is seen as an uncreated divine energy present in the saint and deifying him. Barlaam rejected Palamas' explanations as unsatisfactory because they divided the Godhead into nature and energies. In 1341 Palamas accepted the theology of the *Hagiorite Tome* of *Philotheus Coccinus which became a fundamental manual for the monks of Mt. Athos.

Continued Controversy and Last Years. At a synod held in the Hagia Sophia in Constantinople (June 10, 1341) his position was examined; but despite Barlaam's representations, the theological question was left open, and both monks were forbidden to engage in further polemic. A former student of Palamas, *Gregorius Akindynos (d. 1349), led an opposition party of anti-Palamites who unsuccessfully attempted to have the *Tome* of 1341 repudiated. In August, however, a second synod was held without the patriarch; and *John VI Cantacuzenus, who was eventually to seize the imperial throne, upheld the Palamite theology. However, Palamas was banished to Heraclea a short while later. In 1344 the anti-Palamite party led by Akindynos had Palamas condemned and excommunicated; but this action was colored by a mixture of motives that were both political and ecclesiastical in nature.

In 1347 Cantacuzenus overthrew the Emperor and

Gregory Palamas, Greek icon of the 15th or 16th century, in the collection of the Byzantine Museum, Athens.

selected the former monk Isidore as patriarch. He set about the vindication of Palamas, who was named archbishop of Thessalonica but could not take possession of his see until 1350 when the city came under the control of the new Emperor. In July 1351 at a new synod in Constantinople Palamas's doctrines were declared orthodox, while Akindynos and Barlaam were condemned and Nicephorus Gregoras was banished. The *Tome* published by this synod was signed by the Patriarch Callistus, and the actions of the synod established Palamas as a teacher of orthodoxy. In a journey between Constantinople and Thessalonica, Palamas was captured by the Turks and was released only after several years upon the payment of a ransom. Meanwhile, in 1354 John V Palaeologus had regained the throne. He arranged a confrontation between Palamas and

Nicephorus Gregoras, but was so badly impressed by the two disputants that he lost all interest in their quarrel. Palamas spent his last years as archbishop of Thessalonica, engaged mainly in refuting the charges of Gregoras and composing mystical treatises. He died of an intestinal paralysis, and was canonized in 1368 by the synod under the Patriarch Philotheus Coccinus of Constantinople. He has a special commemoration on the second Sunday in Lent.

Critical Evaluation. Several Western theologians, such as D. Pétau, M. Jugie, and E. Candal, have regarded the teachings of Palamas as at variance with the doctrines of the Western Church, particularly his distinction between the divine nature and the divine operation, which they maintain destroys the simplicity of God's nature. The teaching of Palamas that the blessed in heaven do not see the divine nature but a divine energy seems to be in contradiction with the teaching of Pope *Benedict XII (Denz 1000) that the blessed enjoy a face-to-face vision of the divine essence.

Palamite doctrine on the divine nature of the light of Mt. Tabor and the visible presence of uncreated grace in the pure of heart has been an obstacle for Western theologians in accepting Palamas as a teacher of orthodoxy. On the other hand, Palamas's insistence that the whole man is engraced, body and soul, and the stress that he placed on the role of the body in prayer has been adopted in the West by recent theologians, such as I. Hausherr.

The majority of Palamas's literary productions were devoted to defending his Hesychast doctrine by using a combination of Platonic and Aristotelian philosophy as foundation. Besides 9 tracts in defense of the Hesychasm of the monks, 10 treatises against Akindynos and 5 against Gregoras, he wrote small tracts, letters, and a poem of 618 iambic verses. He published six writings against the Latin theology, two of which (in 1355 and 1356) were directed against a papal legation in Constantinople, and a third, against *John XI Beccus. He wrote also apologetic tracts on his captivity in Islam; 150 chapters on spiritual practices, ethics, and theology; prayers; sermons, of which a homiliarium with 63 pieces was published soon after his death; and a commentary on the Ten Commandments.

Bibliography: PG v.150–151. Beck KTLBR 364–368, 712–715. J. MEYENDORFF, *A Study of Gregory Palamas,* tr. G. LAWRENCE (London 1964); Θεολογία 25 (1954) 602–613; ed. and tr., *Défense de saints hésychastes,* 2 v. (SpicSacLov; 1959). R. JANIN, LexThK² 4:1214. M. JUGIE, DTC 11.2:1735–76. E. CANDAL, EncCatt 9:563–565. I. HAUSHERR, "L'Hésychasme," OrChrPer 22 (1956) 5–40, 241–285. B. KRIVOSHEIN, EChurchQ 3 (1938–39) 26–33, 71–84, 138–156, 193–214. V. LOSSKY, *The Vision of God,* tr. A. MOORHOUSE (London 1963). G. G. ARNAKIS, *Speculum* 26 (1951) 104–118; *Byzantion* 22 (1952) 305–312. P. WITTEK, *ibid.* 21 (1951) 421–423.

[H. D. HUNTER]

PALEOGRAPHY, GREEK

The philological discipline dealing with Greek writings on papyrus, parchment, and paper from the 4th century B.C. to the 16th century A.D.

The Epigraphical Style of the Papyri and the Formation of the Ptolemaic Literary and Documentary Hands. Before the copious finds of papyri in the second half of the 19th century, inscriptions were almost the sole evidence for the form of Greek writing before the 4th century A.D. (*see* PAPYROLOGY). The earliest Greek papyri from the second half of the 4th century B.C.,

such as the Vienna Papyrus, the *Curse of Artemisia,* the Berlin papyrus containing the *Persians* of Timotheus, and the Orphic text on a charred papyrus found in a Hellenistic grave near Thessalonica in 1962 and not yet published, all exhibit in their writing close connections with inscriptions incised on stone. It is surprising to note that there are no ligatures in these earliest examples of Greek handwriting. The letters follow each other without connection, and word and sentence divisions are absent. Round forms are avoided, Epsilon and Sigma are written in angular form as in inscriptions, and Phi shows a triangle in place of a circle or ellipse. This form of writing, which may be called the "Epigraphical style" (Hunger), falls regularly within the space of two lines (majuscule writing) with only individual letters (e.g., Epsilon, Rho, or Nu) rising above or going below these boundaries.

On the basis of the few examples so far known from this early period, it appears that the Greeks did not have a cursive hand before the Hellenistic Age. The investigation of early Ptolemaic papyri has shown that both the literary hand, i.e., the calligraphic script employed for literary texts and books, and the documentary hand, i.e., the cursive or common form of writing, of the last centuries B.C., developed from the epigraphical style (*see* EPIGRAPHY, CHRISTIAN). While the literary hand in principle avoids ligatures, the cursive tries constantly to combine two, three, or more letters, and often employs numerous time and space saving abbreviations, without, however, obscuring the meaning of the text for the addressee familiar with the circumstances or allusions. The literary hand always remained essentially a majuscule script running between two lines. The cursive, on the contrary, soon broke through the two-line system and, from the Late Empire, became a typical four-line form of writing.

Development of the Greek Literary Hand to the End of the Uncial. During the more than 1,000 years during which the Greek literary hand flourished in a majuscule form, few stylistic tendencies can be noted, and they are limited to a few centuries. In the 1st century B.C. and the 1st century A.D. the so-called "Hook style" was in vogue, but its antecedents are to be traced to a much earlier period. The most famous example of this type of writing is the Florentine papyrus containing the *Lock of Berenice* of Callimachus (*Papiri greci e latini* 1092). The rounded forms predominate not only in the case of Epsilon and Sigma, but also in that of Alpha, Mu, and Pi. In the way of ornament many letters standing on the line are furnished with little horizontal hooks or serifs—so Eta, Iota, Mu, Nu, Pi, Rho, Upsilon, and Phi. Occasionally such hooks are found on the upper line as well. The two-line system is strictly maintained, and there are no ligatures. The famous rolls of Herculaneum, which were already discovered in the 18th century, fall largely within this stylistic category.

Many papyri of the 2d and 3d centuries A.D. exhibit another stylistic form that, since W. Schubart, is called the "Strict style." Marked regularity in the composition of the individual letters and of the whole line gives the script an aesthetically pleasing character. While some papyri of the Strict style observe regularly the vertical position in their letters, and others admit a slight slope to the right, all show in common a contrast between unusually broad and especially small let-

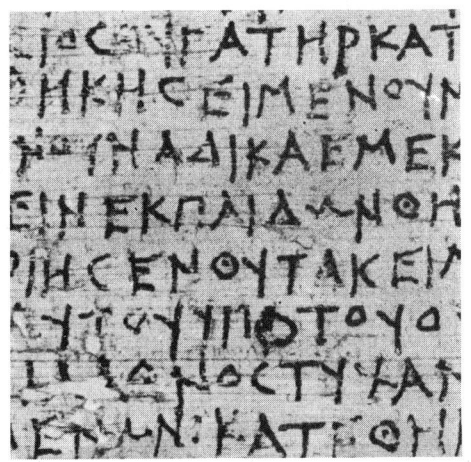

Fig. 1. Epigraphical style: "Curse of Artemisia," 4th century B.C. (Austrian National Library, Pap. Gr. 1).

Fig. 2. Hook style: Fragment of Callimachus, 1st century B.C. (Società Italiana Pap. 1092).

GREEK PALEOGRAPHY

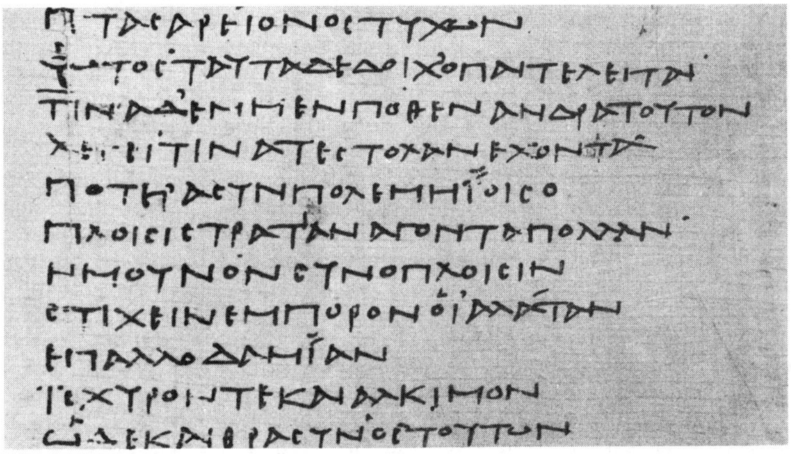

Fig. 3. Strict style: Bacchylides Papyrus 3d century A.D. (Brit. Mus. Pap. 733).

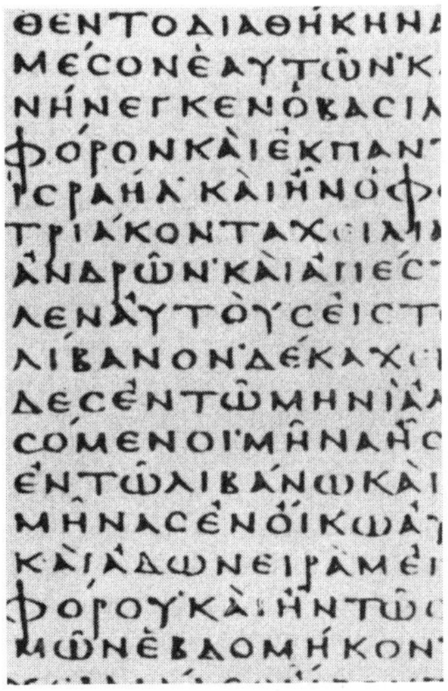

Fig. 4. Biblical style: Bible (Codex Vaticanus), 4th century A.D. (Cod. Vat. Gr. 1209, fol. 405r, detail).

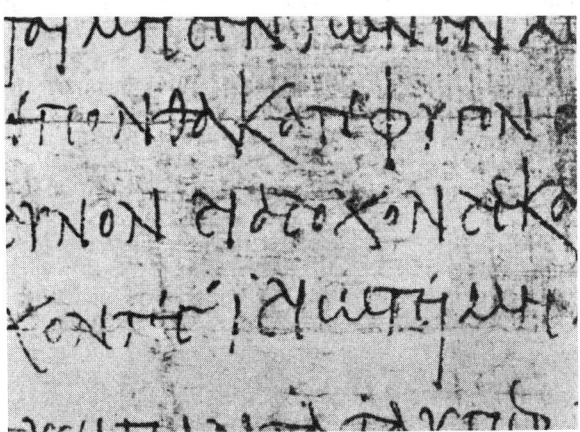

Fig. 5. Chancery style: Document, A.D. 325 (Aust. Nat. Lib., Pap. Gr. 19799/19800, detail).

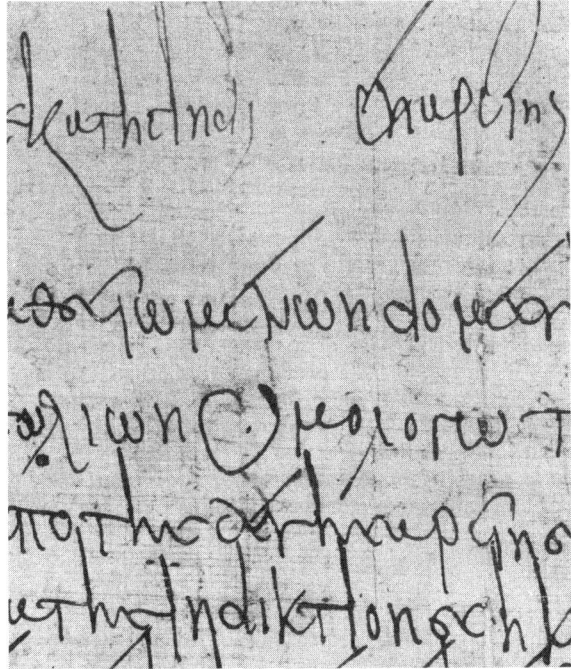

Fig. 6. Byzantine cursive: Document, A.D. 487 (Aust. Nat. Lib., Pap. Gr. 2127, detail).

ters. Eta, Mu, Nu, Pi, and Omega are broadened to a marked degree, and Delta, Kappa, Lambda, and Chi are flattened. On the other hand, letters such as Beta, Theta, Epsilon, and Sigma are kept extremely small. Omicron, Sigma, and Omega are frequently written in such small and cramped form that they cannot fill the interval between the two lines, which in other cases is well occupied. True letter connections (ligatures) are lacking. However, through the writing of two letters close together (juxtaposition) there are frequent examples of apparent ligatures. As reading aids, accents, apostrophes, and punctuation marks are found in papyri of the Strict style, especially in those containing poetic texts. They are to be explained by the contemporary interest in the theory and use of accents (see Herodian, Καθολικὴ προσῳδία, 2d century A.D.). Subsequently, this usage declined until a full accentual system was developed in the Middle Byzantine minuscule. Characteristic representatives of the Strict style are the Bacchylides Papyrus (British Museum), the Alcaeus Papyrus (Oxyrhynchus Papyri 1234), the Vienna Xenophon (G.24568), and the Phaedrus Papyrus (Oxyr. Pap. 1016).

The "Biblical style" developed out of the Strict style in the course of the 3d century A.D. It takes its name from the famous Biblical MSS of the 4th and 5th centuries, namely, the *Codex Sinaiticus* (London), *Codex Vaticanus* (Vat. Gr. 1209), and *Codex Alexandrinus* (London). The conventional designation "uncial" for this stylistic form is rightly questioned, but, in any case, to avoid misunderstandings the term should not be used for other types of writing. To the early precursors of the Biblical style in the 2d and 3d century A.D., a London Homer Papyrus (Pap. Lit. Lond. 7) and a Berlin Homer Papyrus (Pap. Berol. 7499), must now be added the earliest witness for the Gospel of St. John, known only since 1956 (Pap.[66] = Pap. Bodmer II). The most important characteristic feature of the Biblical style is the tendency to equalize the divergent sizes of small and broad letters. In this style most letters can be reduced to a basic square form or inscribed in a square. Iota, Rho, Phi, and Omega are the only exceptions. Full, rounded forms dominate, and the two-line system is strictly observed. Narrow or "emaciated" letters are avoided except at the ends of lines.

After the century of the great Biblical MSS this style developed only very gradually. The uncials of the famous Dioscorides MS at Vienna, which was written *c.* 512, exhibit thickenings at the extremities of Epsilon and Sigma, heavy dots on the top of the upper line in the case of Kappa, Pi, and Tau, and knoblike feet on the extended base of the Delta. Kappa frequently appears in two parts, a phenomenon that leads to popular confusion of EK and EIC. The length of the lower parts of Phi, Rho, and Upsilon is marked. Besides the uncial MSS showing vertical letters, others are found with a significant slope. This slope, however, should not be employed as a criterion for dating. In the Middle Byzantine period the uncial was used beside the newly introduced minuscule, especially in liturgical texts, well into the 12th century. Characteristic features of this late and so-called liturgical uncial are pointed oval forms of the earlier round letters, long trunnions on the crossbars of the Gamma, Delta, Theta, Pi, and Tau, and a marked contrast between light up-strokes and heavy down-strokes.

A special development of the uncial in the 6th to the 10th centuries has recently been called the "Coptic style" (by J. Irigoin). The Copts adopted the Greek uncial as the literary hand for committing their own literature to written form, but they stylized it probably under the influence of the chancery of the Alexandrian Patriarchate—in the direction of the chancery hand. The Coptic style exhibits unusually large individual letters, a small Alpha, and a deep-saddle form of Mu. Good examples are the Papyrus Codex of *Cyril of Alexandria in Dublin, Paris, and Vienna, and the *Paschal Letter* from Alexandria of 719, now in Berlin. The Biblical Style, as an ornamental script for superscriptions, colophons, lemmata, and marginalia lived on for centuries in the form of a small uncial influenced by the chancery hand.

The Cursive from the Early Empire to the Arab Domination in Egypt. The Greek cursive of the Imperial Age developed without marked transitional features from the Ptolemaic documentary hand. The papyrus documents of the Early Empire are often written in a small, narrow script that consciously ignores stylization and constantly permits interchange in the *ductus* of its letters. The same letters are often written by the same hand in two or three different ways. The possibilities of confusion between various letters, as between Mu and Nu, Eta and Upsilon, multiply. In the 2d and 3d centuries, Beta usually rests on a broad horizontal base, and the bipartite Epsilon rises above the upper line. In the 3d century the lower extremities of letters increase in length to such a degree that they extend into the next line or even beyond it. The neglect of style, *ductus,* and alignment, and the deterioration of regular letter forms in documents written in this script increased steadily from the 4th century. As opposed to this kind of writing, the chanceries of high officials clung to their markedly characteristic style (the Chancery style). The vertical is emphasized, and the letters are regularly formed, but they are always taller than they are broad, so that the script reminds one of a trellis or lattice ("Lattice Script"). Individual "emaciated" forms (Alpha, Omicron, and also Delta and Omega), marked lower extensions, and ornamental hooks at the foot of many letters distinguish the Chancery style.

After the establishment of *Constantinople as the new imperial residence and the foundation of the Byzantine Empire, the field belonged to the so-called Byzantine cursive, which is preserved in many thousands of papyrus documents and letters of the 4th to the 7th century. This new script of everyday use was strongly influenced by the Chancery style. Through numerous extensions of its letters upward and downward it became, toward the end of the 4th century, a true four-line system of writing. The most striking upward extensions are shown by Beta, Epsilon, Eta, Iota, and Kappa, and by Delta also in the shape of the Latin D. Extensions downward appear in Beta, Gamma, Iota, Rho, Phi, Chi, Psi, and especially in Lambda, which sinks completely below the line. Large and small letters are set off clearly from one another. The Byzantine cursive, with its many gradations and its frequent baroque ostentation, is the living image of the Byzantine spirit and outlook, characterized by its predilection for orders of rank and ceremonial in all phases of life.

Following the Arab conquest of Egypt (641) the Byzantine cursive deteriorated, and the difference between large and small letters increased even more. However, in a parallel development, there should be noted the gradual consolidation of letter forms that later—from the second half of the 8th century—were to constitute the elements of the new Byzantine minuscule. Hence many documents of the 7th and 8th centuries exhibit side by side in their colophons uncial and half-cursive letter forms that point to the coming of the minuscule.

The Byzantine Minuscule from Its Beginning to the 16th Century. The greater number of some 60,000 extant Greek MSS from the Byzantine period are written in the consciously created script that is customarily called book minuscule, calligraphic minuscule, or simply minuscule. The beginnings of this script, which developed out of the Byzantine cursive, may be traced back to *c.* 800. Clearly an attempt was made to combine the beauty and clarity of the uncial with the fluidity and practical utility of the cursive. The so-called *Codex Uspensky,* an *evangeliarium* written in 835, is the oldest dated MS to show pure minuscule. The transfer of the extant works of ancient literature from uncial MSS to MSS written in the new minuscule was a process of decisive importance for the history of the transmission of texts. It was carried out in the age of the Macedonian Dynasty (9th and 10th centuries).

The minuscule, like the Byzantine cursive, is a four-line system of writing: the elements of many letters rise above or sink below the lines. It exhibits a tendency to combine 2 to 10, or even more, letters into a continuous unit—often without regard for separation of words. The following features are valuable for dating in the first centuries of the minuscule: writing above the line—the letters standing on the pre-drawn or impressed line (mostly in the 9th century); a slight slope to the left (likewise in the 9th century); and the form of the rough breathing—a half-Eta in the 9th and 10th centuries, an angular form in the 10th and 11th centuries, and a round form predominating from the late 10th century and gaining ground steadily in subsequent centuries. The entrance of uncial letter forms into later MSS (from the 10th century) can also be observed, but not everywhere with the same regularity.

The older division of minuscule MSS into three or four periods has been abandoned. It seems preferable to make only two major divisions: (1) the period from the 9th to the 12th century, characterized by a predominantly conservative script retaining symmetrical forms and exhibiting gradual introduction of changes; (2) the period from the end of the 12th century, characterized by marked changes in the form of writing and a pronounced deterioration of order or regularity in *ductus.*

From the 9th to the 12th Century. In general, the minuscule MSS of the 9th and 10th centuries present a fairly symmetrical aspect, with an austere to reserved character that results from a certain angularity of forms. In the 11th century the scribes in the scriptoria of the capital overcame this harshness or primness by using regular round forms, avoiding points and angles, and eliminating uncial letters and abbreviations. Because of the resemblance of many groups of letters in which the elements of this script, especially the circular Omicron and the fanlike round Upsilon similar to a string of pearls, predominate, this form of writing has been christened "Pearl script" (Hunger).

The changes in the aspect of writing that appear in many MSS of the 12th century resulted from the enlargement and cruder formation of many letters, new ligatures and abbreviations, and from the piling up of letters on one another. The circumflex is extended in use and spans three or more letters, and the boundaries of the writing area are broken by lines running into the margin, or by letters with excessively large upper and lower extremities in beginning and closing lines. A glance at the originals of imperial documents of the 10th and 11th centuries shows that the script of the imperial chancery reveals in especially pronounced forms the characteristic features mentioned above. In all probability, therefore, the chancery may have exercised its influence on the minuscule.

From the End of the 12th to the 16th Century. The majority of minuscule MSS experienced marked changes in the course of the 13th century. The phenomena noted above increased in a much more extensive manner. The ligatures Epsilon-Rho and Epsilon-Xi pass from the pointed to the rounded form. The syllable $\mu\epsilon\nu$ is written in a single character with a high, drawn-out and hooklike Epsilon. The prepositions ἐπὶ and μετὰ appear in cursive abbreviation, and Iota subscript and the modern Epsilon (sloping to the left) are frequent. Accents are connected not only with abbreviations, but also with letters and tachygraphic signs. Neglect of alignment and *ductus,* and abandonment of aesthetic considerations, often transform the calligraphic minuscule into a purely utilitarian hand.

The influence of political events is closely connected with the history of writing. The establishment of the *Latin Empire by the Venetians and the Crusaders (1204) forced many Byzantines to leave Constantinople. From new centers (Nicaea and Epirus) they planned restoration of the Byzantine state. During this period, following the dissolution of the Byzantine imperial chancery in the capital, it was possible to employ the large ornamental letters and flourishes and the extended extremities of letter forms that had hitherto been restricted to the imperial chancery. It should not be overlooked, however, that in addition to such degenerate and undisciplined hands of the 13th century, there were others that, in a consciously archaizing tendency, attempted to continue an approximation of the "Pearl script" of the 11th century. In most such cases there is question of Biblical texts or liturgical MSS. A closer examination indicates that the archaizing scribes from the 13th to the 15th centuries sooner or later betrayed themselves by the use of modern elements in their writing.

In the late 13th and in the first half of the 14th century two further styles of Greek writing may be noted. Many MSS from the period 1275 to 1325 are characterized by the fact that some of their rounded letters, such as Omicron, Sigma, Omega, Alpha, and the ligature Epsilon-Iota are written especially large. These closed, round forms float over the jumble of the rest of the script after the manner of blobs of fat in a soup (the "Blob style").

The imperial chancery under *Andronicus II (1282–1328) and his grandson, *Andronicus III (1328–41), employed another distinctive style. Archaizing and calligraphic elements were used to create a new and aesthetically satisfying minuscule that, to its advantage, turned away from the examples of the unpretentious

Fig. 7. Coptic style: Easter letter from Alexandria, A.D. 719, detail (Staatliche Museen, Berlin).

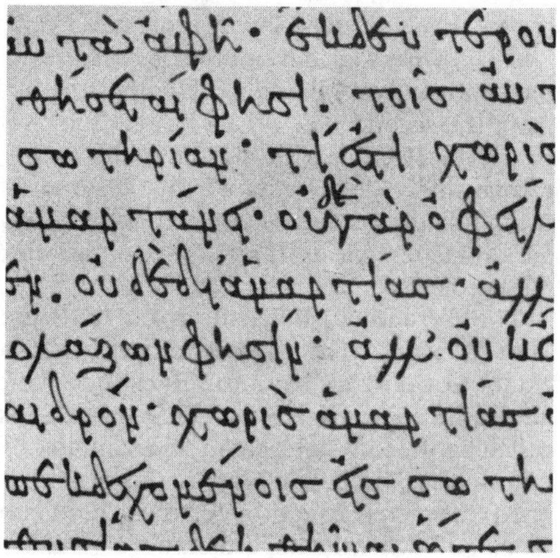

Fig. 8. Byzantine minuscule: 10th century A.D. (Aust. Nat. Lib., Cod. Theol. Gr. 108, fol. 155v, detail).

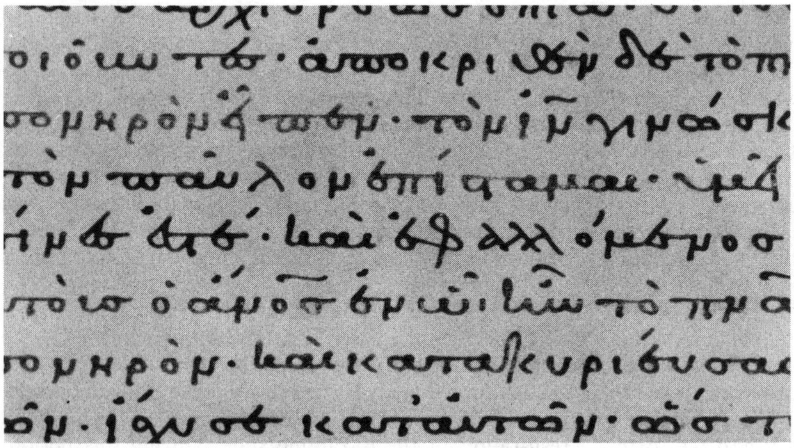

Fig. 9. Pearl style: 11th century A.D. (Aust. Nat. Lib., Cod. Theol. Gr. 302, fol. 72v, detail).

GREEK PALEOGRAPHY

Fig. 10. Blob style: A.D. 1290 (Aust. Nat. Lib., Cod. Theol. Gr. 149, fol. 75v, detail).

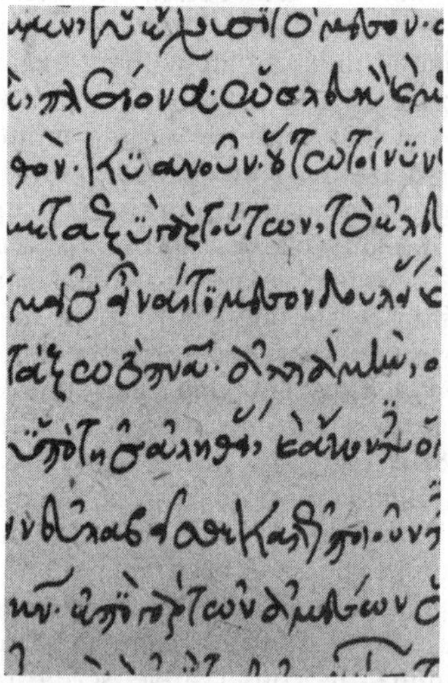

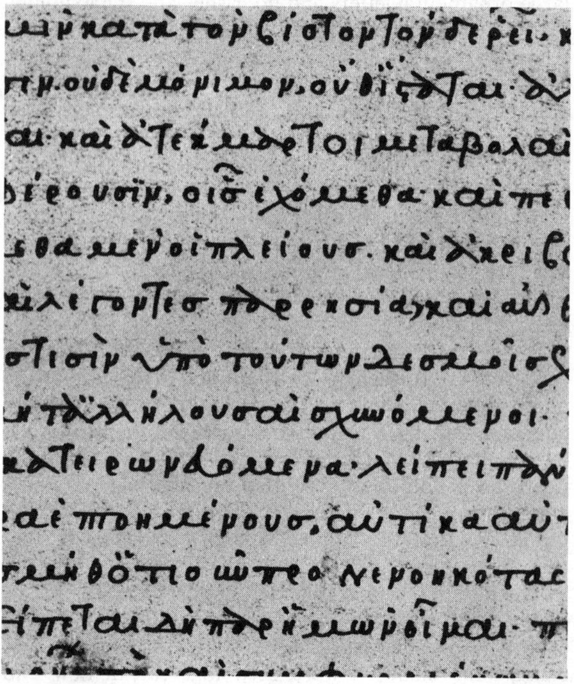

Fig. 11. Metochites style: 14th century A.D. (Aust. Nat. Lib., Cod. Phil. Gr. 95, fol. 193v, detail).

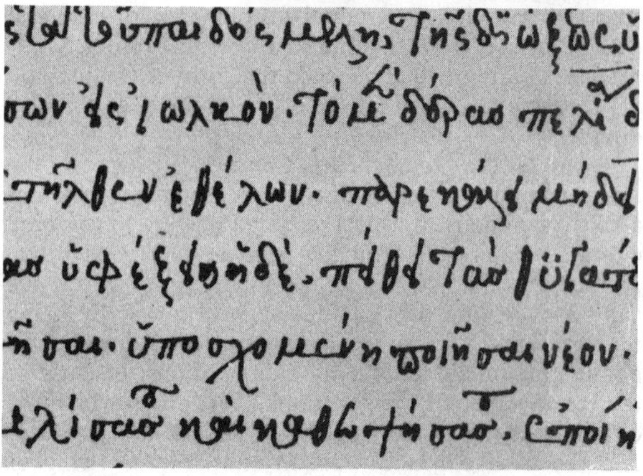

Fig. 12. Press minuscule: c. A.D. 1490 (Aust. Nat. Lib., Cod. Phil. Gr. 284, fol. 30r, detail).

common script described above. Its limited use of abbreviations and large letters with long upper and lower extremities, its reduction of the large accent marks to small form, and its moderation in the employment of ligatures, all bear witness to the work of disciplined scribes. Since this style, in addition to its use in imperial documents of the age, appears especially in MSS containing the works of Theodore Metochites, Grand Logothete and friend of Andronicus II, it may be called the "Metochites style" (Hunger). It is found—in somewhat modified form—until the end of the 14th century.

In the early 15th century the Byzantines, in an effort that parallels that of the Western humanists in Italy, attempted to go back to the minuscule forms of the 9th to the 12th centuries, thus improving the contemporary script and putting a brake on further deterioration. By the use of separation of letters and words, punctuation, and free standing accents, the MSS written in the revised style—often containing classical authors —were made much more legible.

Following the invention of printing by Johannes *Gutenberg, the first book set wholly in Greek type, namely, the *Greek Grammar* of Constantine *Lascaris, was published at Milan in 1476. The cutting of Greek type fonts, difficult as it was at first, reached its maturity by the 1490s at the presses of Zacharias *Calliergis, but especially in the outstanding productions of Aldus *Manutius. At this time, and far into the 16th century, a reciprocal influence may be noted in MSS and printed books. Many letter forms of the "Press Minuscule" betray their origin by a certain rigidity and lack of adaptability. The single-stroke Tau with handlelike crossbar, the elongated Gamma with a similar handle, the ugly, squashed majuscule Theta, and the angular Phi, all characterize the "Press Minuscule."

Much more research remains to be done in Greek paleography. The refinement of methods of dating, which at this stage are not to be compared with the achievements in Latin *paleography, is not the only concern. The investigation of the training schools of Greek scribes and of style traditions in writing, despite welcome beginnings, is still a desideratum.

Bibliography: B. A. VAN GRONINGEN, *Short Manual of Greek Palaeography* (3d ed. Leiden 1963). E. M. THOMPSON, *An Introduction to Greek and Latin Palaeography* (Oxford 1912). A. DAIN, *Les Manuscrits* (rev. ed. Paris 1964). W. SCHUBART, *Griechische Paläographie* (Munich 1925). R. DEVREESSE, *Introduction à l'étude des manuscrits grecs* (Paris 1954). A. SIGALAS, Ἰστορία τῆς Ἑλληνικῆς Γραφῆς (Salonika 1934). V. GARDT-HAUSEN, *Griechische Paläographie*, 2 v. (2d ed. Leipzig 1911–13). H. HUNGER, *Studien zur griechischen Paläographie* (Vienna 1954); "Antikes und mittelalterliches Buch- und Schriftwesen," in *Geschichte der Textüberlieferung der antiken und mittelalterlichen Literatur*, ed. H. HUNGER et al. (Zurich 1961–   ) 1:25–147, esp. 72–107. J. IRIGOIN, "Pour une étude des centres de copie byzantins," *Scriptorium* 12 (1958) 208–227; 13 (1959) 177–209; "L'Onciale grecque de type copte," *Jahrbuch der österreichischen byzantinischen Gesellschaft* 8 (1959) 29–51. C. H. ROBERTS, *Greek Literary Hands, 350 B.C.–A.D. 400* (Oxford 1956). K. and S. LAKE, eds., *Monumenta palaeographica vetera. First Series: Dated Greek Minuscule Manuscripts to the Year 1200*, 10 v. (Boston 1934–39), indexes to v.1–10 (1945).

[H. HUNGER]

PALEOGRAPHY, LATIN

The object of Latin paleography is the study of the various forms of handwriting in which Latin texts were written and of the forms of writing derived from them. Like all alphabets used in ancient Italy, the Latin al-

phabet represents a Western type of Greek alphabet, that is, an alphabet in which the Γ, Δ, Λ, Π, Ρ, Σ, and Υ of the Eastern and classical Greek alphabet have forms that are quite similar to C, D, L, P, R, S, and V (U), but in which the Χ was pronounced *ks* and not *kh,* the Η indicated aspiration, and the Ϝ (Digamma) and Q (Koppa) were still in use. The Latins, however, did not borrow their alphabet directly from the Greeks but took it from the Etruscans. This would explain why their C had the value of a voiceless guttural, which gave it the same value as K and Q, and why there was no symbol to denote the voiced guttural (ModE G). Their G was created only in 312 B.C. by modifying the letter C.

Rise and Spread of Latin Writing. The oldest Latin text is that engraved on the mutilated stele found in 1899 on the site of the old *Forum Romanum.* It dates from either the end of the 7th century B.C. or the beginning of the 6th. Latin writing was used by Roman soldiers, merchants, and officials throughout the empire. In the East, however, as well as in other areas where Greek was used as a means of communication, neither the Latin language nor the Latin hand took root. In the Eastern areas of the empire various native linguistic groups, such as the Copts, the Goths, and later the Slavs, used alphabets derived essentially from the Greek alphabet. As a result, after the fall of the empire, Latin writing, like the Latin language, survived only in the West.

After the 3d century, Latin writing became that of the Roman Church, and from the 6th to the 12th century, in the course of the Christianization of the pagan peoples of northern Europe, it became the writing of Ireland, Germany, Norway, and Sweden. At various times Latin writing was adopted by the vernacular languages (even by the non–Indo-European): by Celtic in the 1st century; in the 8th century by Welsh, English, and German; by French in the 9th century; by Provençal, Catalan, Spanish, Portuguese, Norwegian, and Icelandic in the 12th century; by Italian, Hungarian, Czech, Danish, and Swedish in the 13th century; by Old Prussian in the 14th century and by Polish and Croatian in the 15th century. Basque, Breton, Lithuanian, Lettish, Estonian, and Finnish adopted Latin writing in the 16th century; Albanian and Romanian, in the 19th century.

Through the influence of printing, Latin writing became widely disseminated and received a fixed form during the 15th century, and it has since become the writing of Western civilization. During the 19th century, Catholic and Protestant missionaries adapted the Latin alphabet to many native languages, among others, those of Vietnam and Madagascar. Today nationalistic and revolutionary movements are in progress that, in an attempt to fight illiteracy and to promote modernization, have abandoned traditional writing in favor of the Latin form of writing. Even though the U.S.S.R. itself retains its Cyrillic alphabet, other nations have recently adopted the Latin hand. Since 1926 it has been used by the Islamic-Turkish republic of the U.S.S.R.; and since 1928, by Turkey. China officially adopted the Latin alphabet in 1958 but is faced with a tremendous task of adjustment, which it has hardly begun.

The Science of Paleography. The first scientific treatise on Latin paleography is found in the last four chapters of the *De re diplomatica* (1681) by Dom Jean

Fig. 1. The oldest known Latin text, fragment of an inscribed stele, c. 7th century B.C., Roman Forum.

*Mabillon. A contemporary of the first naturalists, among them J. P. de *Tournefort, whose Éléments de Botanique (1694) contained the first modern classification of plants, Mabillon attempted to classify the scripts known to him on the basis of their distinctive characteristics. He thus distinguished three types of Roman script—the uncial, or capital; the minuta, or minuscule; and the minuta forensis—as well as four types of national hands that he believed to be original creations, Gothic, Lombard, Frankish, and Anglo-Saxon.

This classification was refuted and rejected by Scipione *Maffei in his Istoria diplomatica (1727). Maffei was the first to advance the thesis of the original unity of Latin writing. He maintained that the so-called national hands were only "degenerate" forms of Roman writing.

The six-volume Nouveau traité de diplomatique by R. P. Tassin and C. F. Toustain (1750–65), Benedictines of the congregation of Saint-Maur (see MAURISTS), is the masterpiece of the "Nomenclature School," or, as their members would be called today by the naturalists, the "taxonomists." To some extent the Nouveau traité is to the De re diplomatica of Mabillon what the Systema naturae (1735) of C. *Linnaeus is to the Éléments de botanique of Tournefort. The paleographic section of the Nouveau traité is an "abecedarian history" in which the authors strove to teach the "art of

determining the age and the country of origin of the letters by studying the variety of their forms and characteristics, acquired between their origin and the 16th century" (2.2). One can only admire the work of the two Maurists. Unfortunately, however, their classifications were not based on such obvious and fundamental characteristics as those selected by the genius of Linnaeus. Script is neither a living organism, the product of natural growth, nor even a system of self-developing forms. The ordering of hands on the basis of external characteristics can lead only to arbitrary and extremely complicated classifications. In fact, the classification of the Maurists is recognized today as completely inadequate, and frequently incomprehensible.

Toward the end of the 19th century, W. Wattenbach in his Anleitung zur lateinischen Paläographie (1866) and Léopold *Delisle in his works after 1875 found a new and more fruitful approach. Both Wattenbach and Delisle studied the letters in relation to their formation in writing. Botanists might describe their approach as that of the "geneticists," for they tried to reconstitute the ductus, i.e., the movement of the pen in forming the letter, and to establish a genealogy of writing based on the historical development of its forms. The latter approach resembled that of their contemporaries the comparative philologists, who sought to establish families of languages. Delisle and Wattenbach succeeded in separating paleography from *diplomatics and in definitively making paleography an autonomous discipline. At the same time L. *Traube assigned paleography its true place among the historical sciences by viewing it as the expression or reflection of a civilization.

Latin Writing from the 1st to the 6th Century. Since the late 1920s paleography has further defined its scope and its method. Although in principle the "science of handwriting" does not need to concern itself with the material on which the letters are written, the very fact that scholars turned their attention to the *ductus* led them to neglect the fixed forms of writing, which are characteristic of engraved letters. Latin inscriptions on stone and bronze were, even as late as 1850, almost the only known specimens of Roman writing and the only "documents" preserved—as opposed to narrative sources and juridical codifications. The study of these inscriptions was established as an autonomous discipline under the name of *epigraphy. Paleography, accordingly, abandoned inscriptions to devote itself solely to the study of official documents and books written by hand and in ink. Since the oldest MSS then known could be dated no earlier than the 4th or 5th century, paleographers ignored the preceding centuries. Epigraphists, however, showed little or no interest in the form of the letters. As a result, scholars began the history of Latin writing only with the 5th century. So complete was the ignorance of earlier scripts that Natalis de Wailly attempted to prove that the wax tablets found in 1841 in the gold mines of Transylvania, and dated between A.D. 139 and 162, were forgeries. In 1889 M. Prou expressed the same opinion in the first edition of his *Manuel de paléographie* (24).

Meanwhile, the excavations at Pompeii had revealed the cursive Latin hand of the 1st century. The first graffiti were discovered in 1765 but were not published until 1792 and 1793 in Nuremberg (cf. R. Garucci, *Graffiti de Pompei*, 2 ed. Paris 1856). Their publication was barely noticed, and it was not until 1837 that the *Inscriptiones Pompeianae* of J. Wordsworth brought them to the attention of the scholarly world. In 1849 the first edition of the *Graffiti* of Garucci contained a thoroughly satisfactory study of cursive writing, but it too was scarcely noticed by paleographers. Finally, some slight interest was shown in the publication of C. Zangemeister's *Inscriptiones parietariae Pompeianae* (CIL 4; Berlin 1871).

Four years after Zangemeister's publication, the tables of the banker Jucundus were discovered at Pompeii, but they did not become common knowledge until Zangemeister in 1898 devoted the *Supplementi pars prior* of CIL v.4 to their publication. The first-known Latin papyrus, the *Carmen de bello Actiaco,* had been found during the excavations at Herculaneum in 1730 and was reproduced as an engraving in 1793 in the first volume of the *Herculanensium voluminum quae supersunt* (*see* PAPYROLOGY). Zangemeister and Wattenbach in their *Exempla codicum latinorum litteris maiusculis scriptorum* (Heidelberg 1876) plates 1, 2, 3, reproduced two others in part. From 1895 Egypt began to furnish literary as well as documentary papyri but in very small numbers—approximately 200 between 1895 and 1914—of which only half were published at the time; and only about 50 were reproduced by 1915. A young American papyrologist, H. B. Van Hoesen,

Fig. 2. Classic capitals: Inscription from the aqueduct of Trajan, Rome, A.D. 109.

Fig. 3. Painted inscriptions at Pompeii, before A.D. 79.

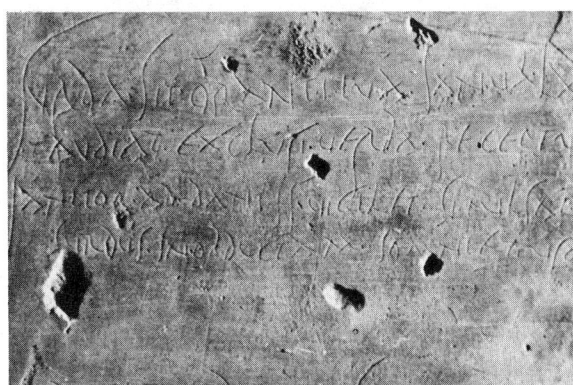

Fig. 4. Graffiti at Pompeii, before A.D. 79.

Fig. 5. Latin capital bookhand: Fragment of Palaemon, "De grammatica," end of the 2d century A.D. (BM pap. 2723).

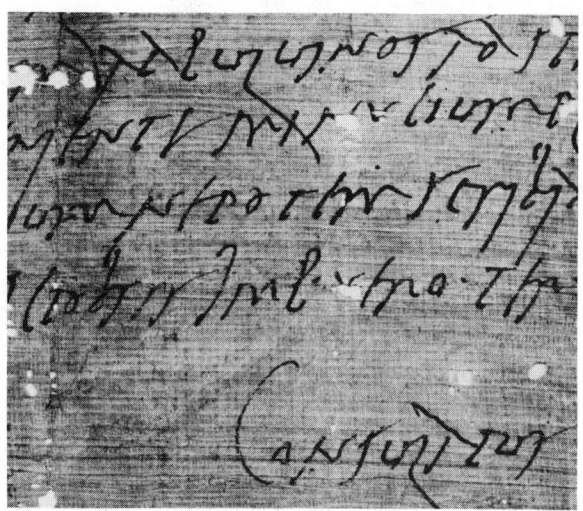

Fig. 6. Ancient cursive: Receipt, Oct. 7, A.D. 167 (Brit. Mus. Pap. 730, detail).

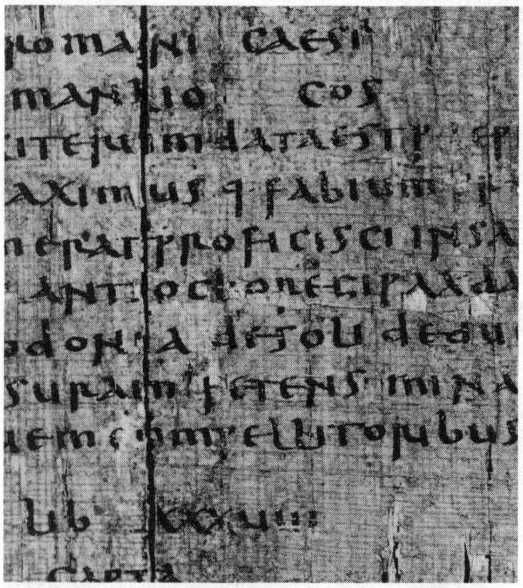

LATIN PALEOGRAPHY

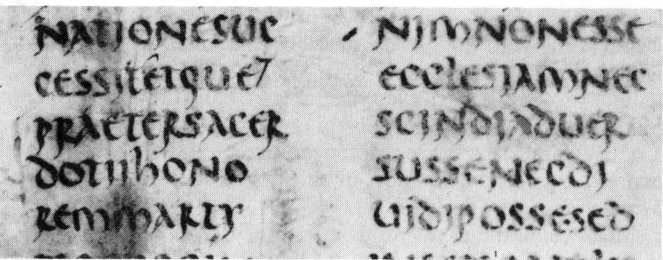

Fig. 8. Uncial: Fragment of St. Cyprian, "Letters," end of 4th century A.D. (Brit. Mus. Add. MS 40165, detail).

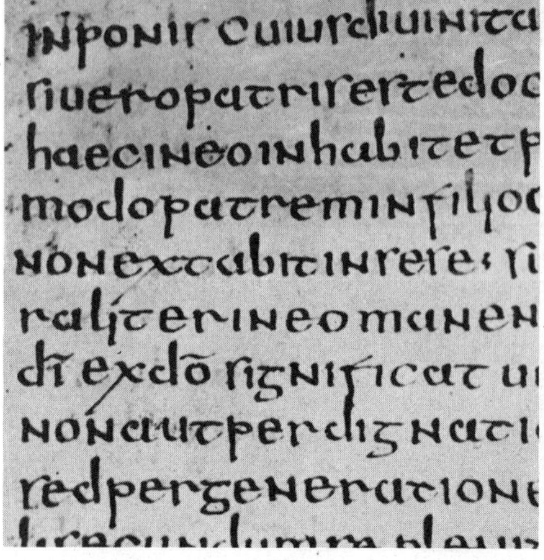

Fig. 7. Primitive minuscule: Fragment of Livy, "Epitome," end of 3d century (BM pap. 1532).

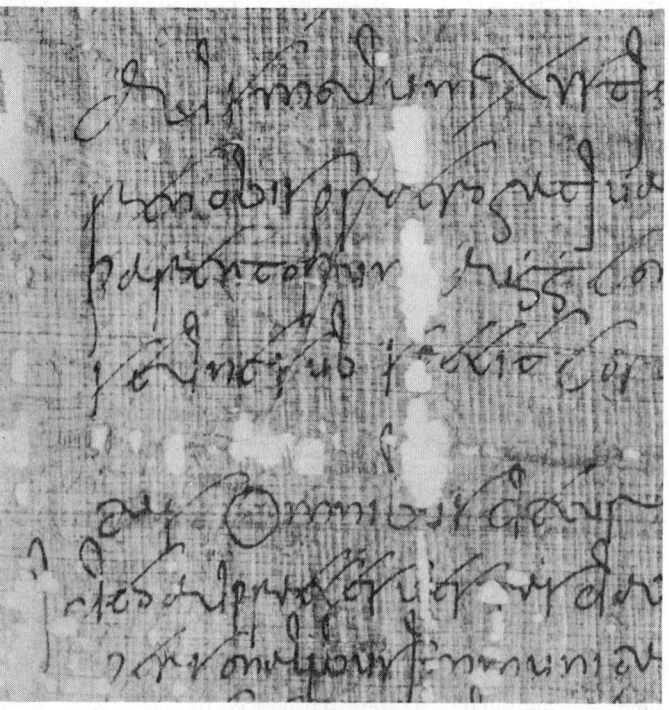

Fig. 9. Half uncial: St. Hilary, "De Trinitate," before A.D. 510 (St. Peter's Basilica, MS D.182).

Fig. 10. Recent cursive: Rescript of Diocletian and Maximian, mid-4th century (Leipzig Pap. 530, detail).

studied their script (*Roman Cursive Writing,* Princeton 1915) and traced the history of the Roman cursive hand from the 1st to the 6th century. But the study of all forms of writing used prior to the 5th century was not definitively included in Latin paleography until the publication in 1921 of Luigi Schiaparelli's *Scrittura latina nell'eta romana.*

All the above-mentioned works were remarkable; yet they were not as perfect and precise as their authors might have made them had the available documentation been less rudimentary.

The Use of Photography and Photoengraving. Photography was first introduced into paleography in 1858 by T. von Sickel, who later used photoengraving as well in his *Monumenta graphica medii aevi ex archivis et bibliothecis imperii Austriaci collecta* (10 fasc. 1858–82). Paleographers were rather slow in recognizing the potential role of photomechanical reproduction. The imperfections of the first processes, the high cost of the stereotype plates, and the unsatisfactory lighting apparatus were no doubt the cause of their slowness. In 1871 Zangemeister failed in his attempts to reproduce photographically the graffiti (CIL 4:11.39), and E. Hübner decided against employing photoengraving in his *Exempla scripturae epigraphicae latinae* (Berlin 1885). In fact, even today, the photography of graffiti and inscriptions presents particular difficulties (cf. J. S. and A. E. Gordon, *Contributions to the Paleography of Latin Inscriptions,* Berkeley 1957). The most adequate process for photographing graffiti and wax tablets involves the use of sodium lamps, but this is extremely difficult outside a well-organized laboratory. The paleographical study of inscriptions is therefore still in its infancy, and the history of the Latin calligraphy of the first 4 centuries has hardly begun. Even in 1953 there were barely three or four photographs of the *graffiti of Pompeii, and scholars were content to use copies. The first photographs of the Latin papyri of Herculaneum were published by E. A. Lowe in *Codices latini antiquiores* (v.3 Oxford 1938, Nos. 385–387).

There have been numerous reproductions of medieval MSS, and since 1875 several large collections have appeared in which the photography leaves nothing to be desired. These collections, however, had no preestablished design and were arranged by chance, depending on findings and research. As a result they contribute only a fragmentary documentation on which no exhaustive study can be based. The prodigious development of microfilm technique has partially remedied these insufficiencies.

In 1934 E. A. Lowe first conceived and energetically carried on the idea of a systematic inventory of Latin MSS. His *Codices latini antiquiores* (v.10, the second-last volume, Oxford 1963) contains a reproduction of several lines of all MSS falling in the period before 800. Since 1954 A. Bruckner and R. Marichal have followed his example, *mutatis mutandis.* Their *Chartae latinae antiquiores,* when complete, will contain a full facsimile edition of all official documents prior to 800. To date, three volumes have been published. Marichal will reproduce also in their entirety the Latin papyri of Herculaneum and a large number of graffiti in the *Archivio paleografico italiano.* The publication of the wax tablets will complete the project. Thus, within a few years, paleographers will be able to study at home all documents written in the Latin form of writing prior

to the 9th century, with the exception of scattered inscriptions, the publication of which will remain the task of the epigraphers.

While it has been feasible to reproduce the less than 2,000 extant MSS written prior to 800, it is, of course, impossible to do the same for the several hundred thousand MSS written after that date. It has, therefore, been agreed to limit their reproduction to only those MSS that can be dated and to give only a skeletal outline of Latin paleography. An international conference held in Paris in 1953 under the presidency of C. Samaran decided to undertake this publication. Under the charge of an international committee, two volumes have already appeared. The catalog will end with the period in which the codex was definitely supplanted by the printed book, i.e., in France c. 1530. An analogous project for the publication of documents (charters, etc.) down to modern times has yet to be undertaken. When this is completed—one can only hope that it will be reasonably soon—the composition of a truly comprehensive history of Latin writing in all its aspects will be possible.

Modern Trends in Paleography. In England and in Austria at the beginning of the 20th century the two calligraphers Edward Johnston and Rudolph von Larisch, as a result of their researches in Latin MSS, began to study the writing technique and the shape and holding of the pen best adapted for forming the ancient letters (see E. Johnston, *Writing and Illuminating and Lettering,* London 1906); and the work of a student of Larisch, Otto Hurm, *Schriftform im Schreibwerkzeug,* Vienna 1928). In France, Jean Mallon and R. Marichal sought to find in the technical modifications of ancient writing the origin of the considerable changes that Latin writing had undergone during the first 4 centuries of the Christian era. Their research was independent of that of Johnston and Larisch but led to similar conclusions. In Germany many scholars working in fields touching paleography tried, with considerable temerity, to explain the variations of script in the light of similar changes in architecture and the other arts; at the same time others applied graphology to the history of writing (see H. Fichtenau, *Mensch und Schrift im Mittelalter,* Vienna 1946). As paleography became conscious of its true object, it was more able to clarify its relationship to neighboring disciplines. The study of book scripts was no longer isolated from that of the book itself; and, in fact, a new name, "codicology," was invented for this specialized discipline. This new tendency, advocated particularly in Belgium by M. Masai, led in 1946 to the creation in Brussels of the review *Scriptorium* and in 1957 to the founding of the Centre Belge d'Archéologie et d'Histoire du Livre.

Finally, greater knowledge of the Latin papyri of Egypt has given greater urgency to the question of the relationship between Greek and Latin writing, and J. Mallon would even wish to establish a distinct field of "Greco-Roman" paleography. The result of these various developments has been a rather profound change in theory regarding the history of Latin script. Originally the Greek, Etruscan, and Latin alphabets consisted of "capitals," i.e., generally their form was similar to the letters that are still used in the titles of most books and signs; hence their name. Over a long period the capital, more or less carelessly employed, had been the only form of Latin writing, and at the beginning of the

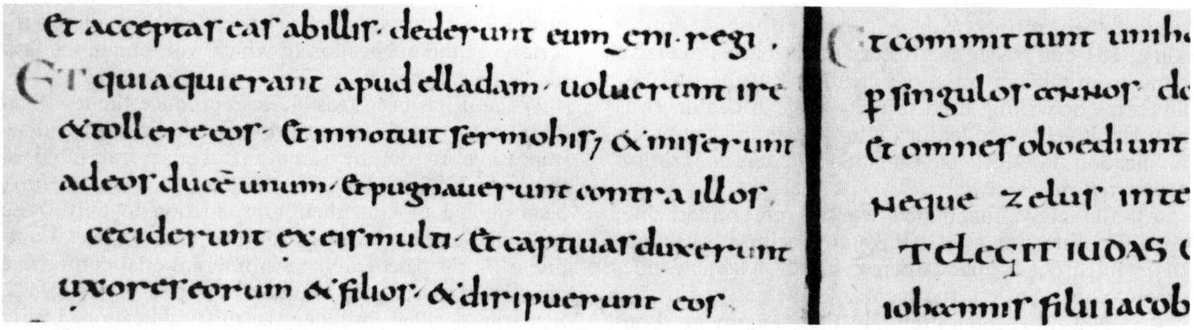

Fig. 11. Carolingian miniscule: fragment of Old Testament, before A.D. 781 (Amiens, Municipal Library MS 11, detail).

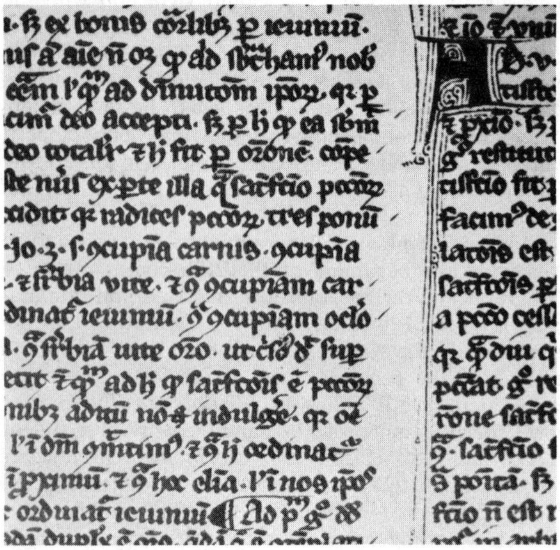

Fig. 12. Gothic miniscule: Thomas Aquinas, "Commentary," France, A.D. 1286 (Brussels, Royal Library MS II, 943, fol. 1r, detail).

Fig. 14. Humanistic round hand: Cicero, Italy, A.D. 1410 (Vatican Cod. Pal. lat. 1496, fol. 1r, detail).

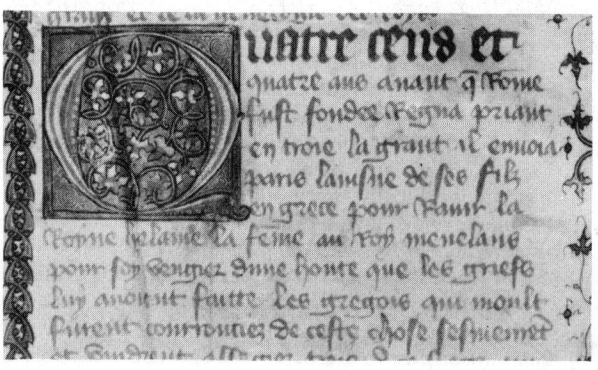

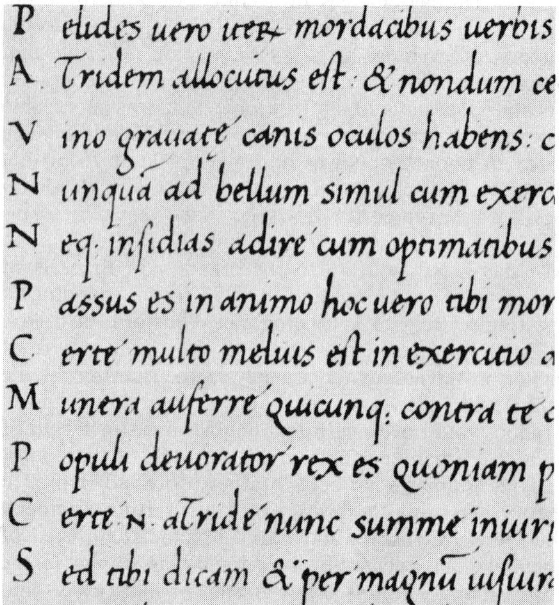

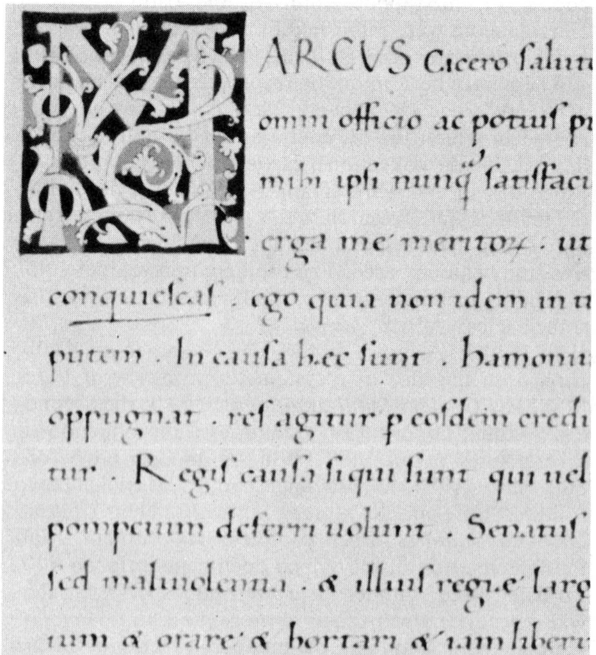

Fig. 13. Gothic bastard: "Chronicles of the Kings of France," France, end of the 16th century (Paris, Bibl. de l'Arsenal MS 5223, fol. 2r, detail).

LATIN PALEOGRAPHY

Fig. 15. Humanistic cursive: manuscript written at Rome, 1477 (Vatican, Cod. gr. 1626, fol. 8r, detail).

Christian era it was still the only bookscript. The script that became the printed type of today, the minuscule, was the humanist round hand that had been copied at the beginning of the 15th century by the humanists of Florence from the Caroline minuscule of the *Carolingian renaissance. To be sure, the Caroline minuscule underwent many changes between the 9th and the 15th centuries. Toward the end of the 12th century the Carolingian book hand assumed angular forms that the humanists disdainfully called "Gothic." As writing developed, the Caroline minuscule was debased into various cursive forms, which during the 16th century became extremely difficult to read. These cursive hands continued to be used throughout the 17th century especially by notaries, bailiffs, and lawyers. But at Florence, as early as the 15th century, a humanist cursive hand known as "Italic" had been created, paralleling the humanist round hand and influenced by it. The Italic hand had its beginning in the chanceries. Meanwhile in France the normal Gothic cursive hand, known as bastard Gothic, became the book hand, particularly for books written in the vernacular. Modern forms of handwriting were born of both the Italic and the bastard hands, and even the German *Fraktur* is merely a special form of the humanist cursive hand. Therefore, since the 14th century at the latest, all Latin forms of writing have been derived from the Caroline minuscule.

The origin of the Caroline minuscule was once sought in the so-called national hands, which were chronologically the closest to it. Previously scholars had known only the hands that dated from the 5th century, namely, the capital, the uncial, the half-uncial, the cursive minuscule (known also as the new cursive), and the national scripts, Merovingian, Visigothic, Beneventan, Irish, and Anglo-Saxon. Since the time of Maffei scarcely anyone doubted that the first three national hands were derived from the cursive minuscule or that the Irish and Anglo-Saxon hands came from the uncial and the half-uncial. Now that more is known about the forms of writing used during the first 5 centuries A.D., it is held, especially in France, that the Caroline minuscule is basically the same as the half-uncial. Consequently the fundamental problem is no longer the origin of the Caroline minuscule but of the half-uncial, or rather of its immediate ancestor, the so-called primitive minuscule. This brings the problem to the 3d and not to the 8th century.

Generally speaking, this new theory has been fairly well accepted. In their carefully prepared books the Romans always used the capital script. In less formal writing, however, the capitals were debased into cursive scripts, two of which appear in the wax tablets and papyri. One of these, the old, or majuscule cursive, was used until the end of the 3d century, and its evolution from the capital is fairly easy to follow. The other script, the new cursive, made a sudden appearance toward the end of the 3d century, and several of its letters, for example the *b,* could not possibly have been derived from the old cursive. About the same time the primitive minuscule appeared in the book script, and its relationship to the new cursive is quite obvious. Apparently, therefore, during the 3d century a form of revolution occurred in Roman writing. Some scholars believe that the break between the old and the new cursives is only an illusion. They maintain that the differences resulted from the fact that we are better

acquainted with the old cursive, which had remained stable since the 1st century because of the bureaucratic tradition. The new cursive, they insist, appeared only in the 4th century in official writings, although it had been used by individuals and had undergone progressive changes since the 1st century. According to this theory the minuscule book script derived from the new cursive. Yet another theory claims that the transformation took place in the book hands. Both theories are forced to invent the existence of an unknown script. It is unfortunate that the 3d century is one of the periods from which documents have been poorly preserved. It is nevertheless a fact—and historically speaking this is essential—that the new scripts appeared after the crisis of the 3d century, which for some marks the beginning of the Middle Ages.

To the paleographer the great lines in the development of Latin writing appear, at last, to have been surely drawn: they follow closely the outline of the intellectual evolution of Western civilization. Yet one tremendous task remains, and it is a special challenge: to determine —with greater or lesser certainty, depending on the degree to which the various types of scripts have been "canonized"—the geographical and chronological characteristics of the last 3 centuries of the Middle Ages, which will permit localizing and dating all documents of that period. With this achievement paleography will have made a valuable contribution to the history of culture and to the history of the diffusion of ideas, which it alone can supply.

Bibliography: G. CENCETTI, *Lineamenti di storia della scrittura latina* (Bologna 1954). H. P. FOERSTER, *Abriss der lateinischen Paläographie* (2d ed. Stuttgart 1963). E. M. THOMPSON, *An Introduction to Greek and Latin Paleography* (Oxford 1912), out of print and old; progressively replaced by the *Oxford Palaeographical Handbooks.* Of this series, the only v. on Latin paleography pub. to date is C. E. WRIGHT, *English Vernacular Hands* (Oxford 1960). G. BATTELLI, *Lezioni di paleografia latina* (3d ed. Vatican City 1949). Current bibliog. in the *Bulletin codicologique,* in *Scriptorium* (Brussels 1959–). B. BISCHOFF et al., *Nomenclature des écritures livresques du IXe au XVIe siècle* (Paris 1954). C. PERRAT, "Paléographie romaine," B. BISCHOFF, "Paläographie der abendländischen Buchschriften vom 5. bis zum 12. Jahrhundert," and J. POST, "A General Report: Suggestions for Future Studies in Late Medieval and Renaissance Latin Paleography," in *Relazioni del X Congresso internazionale di scienze storiche* (Florence 1955) 345–422. R. BLOCH, "Etrusques et Romains," in *L'Écriture et la psychologie des peuples* (Paris 1963) 183–198. R. MARICHAL, "L'Écriture latine et la civilization occidentale du Ier au XVIe siècle," *ibid.* 199–247. M. COHEN, "Les Écritures latines, extensions passées et récentes," *ibid.* 313–323. J. MALLON, *Paleographie romaine* (Madrid 1952). **Illustration credits:** Fig. 1, Alinari-Art Reference Bureau. Fig. 2, Anderson-Art Reference Bureau. Figs. 3 and 4, R. Marichal.

[R. MARICHAL]

PALEOGRAPHY, MUSICAL

The first MSS written to contain Gregorian chant with musical notation date from the 9th century. Among these early sources, several different kinds of notation may be observed. They may be divided into three groups: (1) notation consisting principally of dots that are painstakingly aligned horizontally and vertically (as in Aquitanian notation); (2) notation apparently evolved from the grammatical acute and grave accents (French and St. Gall notation); and (3) notation in which elements of the other types are mixed (Messine, Paleofrankish, and Breton notation).

Although examples of Paleofrankish notation have been known for many years, only recently has the

MUSICAL

PALEOGRAPHY

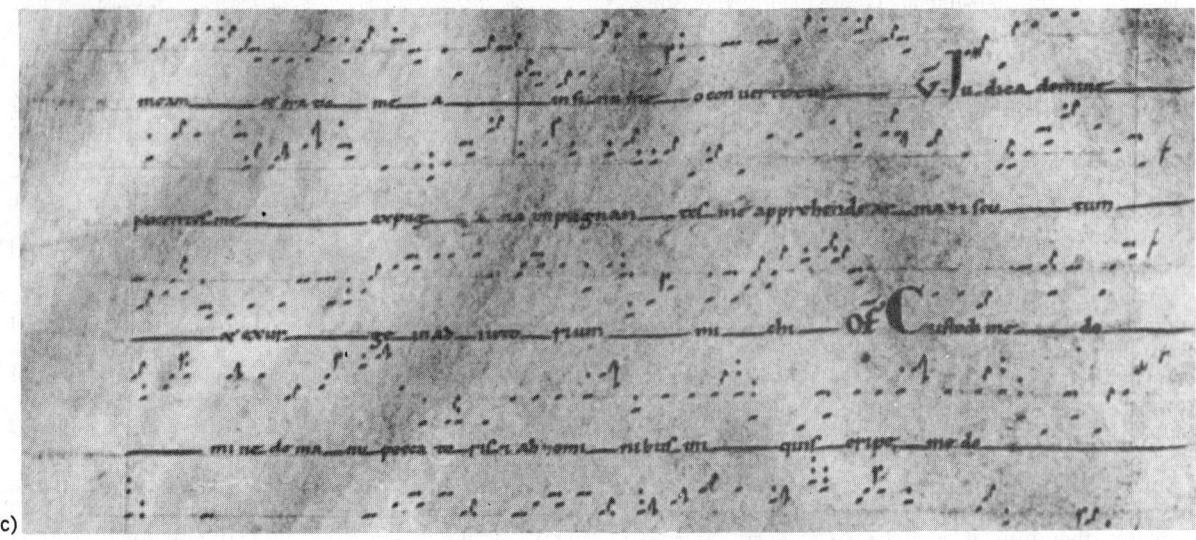

Fig. 1(a) St. Gall notation: 9th century (St. Gall, Stiftsbibliothek, MS 359, fol. 74–94, detail). Examples are from the Gradual "Ego autem." (b) Messine or Lorraine notation: *10th or 11th century (Laon, Bibliothèque, MS 239, fol. 47v, detail). (c) Aquitanian notation: 11th century (Paris, Bibliothèque Nationale, MS lat. 903, fol. 63v, detail).*

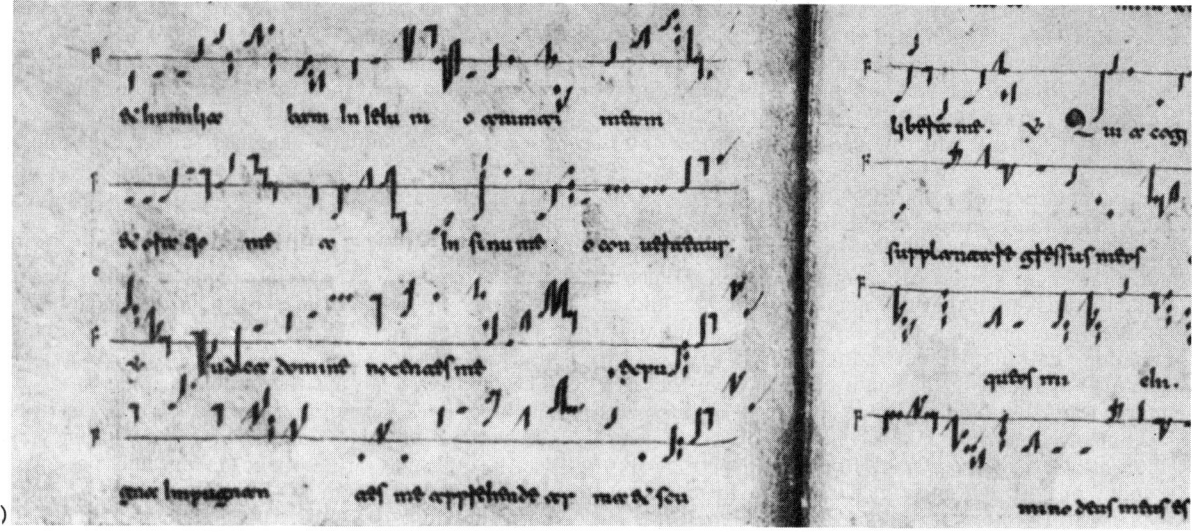

Fig. 2(a) French notation: 11th century (Montpellier, Bibliothèque de la Faculté de Médecine, MS H 159, fol. 84r, detail). (b) Nonantolan notation: 12th century (Monza, Biblio-
teca capitolare, MS B. I. 41, guard leaf, detail). (c) Beneventan notation: 11th or 12th century (Benevento, Bibl capitolare, MS VI, 34, fol. 112v, detail).

claim of its unique importance as the oldest of all notations been advanced. In other theories it is only one more type of notation, contemporaneous with, or perhaps even somewhat later than the others. A number of questions about this notation are still unanswered.

How and when neumes were invented is not known. As noted above, some neumes may be considered modifications of grammatical accents: the grave, tipped slightly to the horizontal and shortened, becomes the punctum or tractulus of St. Gall and related notations; the acute becomes the virga. The two signs are combined to form other neumes: grave followed by acute becomes the podatus, to indicate two notes ascending; acute followed by grave becomes the clivis, and so on.

Systems of Notation. The evidence of the earliest sources is clear that the various notations are more or less distinct from each other, and though there are common elements that suggest the possibility of a common ancestor, none of the notations now preserved shows certain traces of having been derived from any of the others. In the 9th century great effort was put forth to spread and standardize the use of chant. To this end, notation, as a way of fixing on parchment the hand movements of the person who directed singing, appears to have been devised in various localities from various elements—points or dots, accent signs, punctuation marks, cheironomic gestures, ekphonetic symbols.

Geographic Distribution. The various kinds of notation are found in specific areas. One group of MSS that has attracted attention is from the monastery of St. Gall (*Sankt Gallen) and its environs. Four volumes of chant in St. Gall notation have been reproduced in facsimile in PalMus: v.1 St. Gall 339, a 10th-century collection of Proper chants of the Mass; v.4 Einsiedeln 121, from the same period with similar contents; ser. 2, v.1 St. Gall 390–391, a collection of 10th-century Office chants; and ser. 2, v.2 St. Gall 359, a 9th-century volume containing only Graduals and Alleluias fully notated. In France the areas for each of the regional notations seem coterminous with the boundaries of the ecclesiastical provinces as they were between 840 and 911. One notation, called Messine, has relatively few connections with the celebrated school of Metz; the term "Lorraine" notation might be more appropriate. It is represented in MS Laon 239 (PalMus v.10), a 10th- or 11th-century collection of Proper Mass chants.

The notation found in MS Chartres 47 (10th century, containing Proper chants of the Mass; PalMus v.11) is used in relatively few of the preserved chant MSS; all these sources are Breton in origin. Hence it has been suggested that this notation should be known as Breton, rather than Chartres, notation. Aquitanian notation (PalMus v.13, a Gradual from St. Yrieix, 11th century) is found in the south of France, in the area marked off by Nantes, Châteauroux, Moulins, and Vienne. Manuscripts in French notation come from the northwest and center of France and part of Burgundy; one of the most celebrated of them, Montpellier MS H 159, is reproduced in PalMus v.8; it is an 11th-century source containing Proper chants of the Mass. This particular MS, discovered in 1847 by Danjou, and containing letter notation in addition to

neumes, was an important aid in early chant research. In Italy various types of notation are found, among them Nonantolan (from Nonantola, near Modena, site of a Benedictine abbey) and Beneventan (associated with the south of Italy, particularly with the Archabbey of *Monte Cassino). An 11th-century Beneventan Gradual is reproduced in PalMus v.14.

Variations. Virtually all the early notations named above are richer in forms than modern chant notation. For example, in Paleofrankish notation there are six different ways of writing the progression of notes represented in modern chant books by the torculus. Hence any discussion of neumes that selects forms in use since the 13th century as its point of departure will fall short in explaining the distinctive characteristics of various systems of notation. This approach, however, has the advantage of emphasizing elements common to the various systems, which is an important aspect of this subject.

The Note Shapes. The two signs used for the single note, virga and punctum, appear in St. Gall and French notation, among others, and in them the virga, apparently deriving from the acute accent, is used for a note of relatively higher pitch; the punctum, coming from the grave accent, for a pitch the same as or lower than the preceding. The two-note neumes are the podatus or pes (ascending) and the clivis (descending); the three-note neumes are scandicus (ascending) and climacus (descending); other neumes are torculus (up and down) and porrectus (down and up). In St. Gall notation these forms may all be traced to the combining of grave and acute accent signs; in other notations, such as Aquitanian, the placement of dots or dashes, connected or not, presents no great problems of interpretation. The neumes mentioned above may be linked to form compound neumes, but the basic shapes remain the same. They are modified, and certain of their elements may be replaced by new symbols, for either of two reasons: to indicate some special method of performing a particular note or to indicate rhythm. Thus, the scandicus may have its middle element replaced by a special form; in this case the neume is called the salicus. In several notations the special form used to replace the middle element is known as the oriscus, and it is found replacing an ordinary note when the pitch it represents is the same as the preceding or one step above or below. Thus the oriscus is used for the middle element in another neume, the pressus. The oriscus is rarely approached by leap; it is not known exactly what method of performance is hinted at by the distinctive shape of this note in the early MSS.

Quilisma. Another special note shape is the quilisma. Although St. Gall and Messine notations have different symbols for this note, both may be traced to symbols used as question marks in 8th-century literary MSS. The quilisma is always the middle member in a group of three notes ascending stepwise. Despite the striking appearance of this symbol and the consistency with which quilismas are notated in specific passages in MSS in different kinds of notation, the manner of performing the quilisma is still unknown. Among other special symbols for which there are no distinctive signs in notation since the 13th century are the trigon (often transcribed as a pressus), the apostropha (not found alone, but with two or three, sometimes more, for a single syllable of text, usually represented as repeated notes and performed as a prolongation). Sometimes in the tristropha the first note is lower than the two following.

Liquescent Neumes. At times the shape of a neume is modified to indicate a special mode of performance. This is the case with the liquescent neumes. The shape of the clivis is still recognizable in the cephalicus, that of the podatus in the epiphonus. The use of these forms appears to be determined by the sound of the spoken text—specifically the sound with which the syllable ends, though there is not perfect consistency in this. From the appearance of the neumes and their frequent if not universal relation to the text, it seems probable that some diminishment of the sound and quality of the main vowel is indicated.

Rhythm Signs. The notation in some early chant MSS is accompanied by signs that seem most probably intended to show rhythm. These signs are of two types: letters conveying tempo indications and additions to or modifications of the neumes. The variety of these signs and the complex and sophisticated ways in which they are combined in various MSS have constituted the greatest obstacle to the general acceptance of any transcription of the rhythm of chants—even the rhythm presented in only one chant MS—into modern notation. The letters used to indicate tempo may apply to a single note or a small group. The most common ones are *c* (*celeriter,* fast) and *t* (*tarde,* slow). In St. Gall notation these indications are called "Romanian" letters, after the monk Romanus, who, according to the chronicle of Sankt Gallen, brought Roman chant to the abbey. Similar letters are used in other rhythmic notations, particularly the Messine notation of Laon 239.

In St. Gall notation, small horizontal lines known as episemas are added across the tops of some virgas. Episemas may be found added to the clivis and to the highest note of the climacus. These signs are thought to indicate lengthening. Other neumes may be given signs of length by being modified; the lower notes of the climacus, normally represented by dots, may be indicated by dashes. In Messine notation, lengthening is indicated by splitting a neume and indicating each of its elements by a separate sign, with or without the letter *a* (*augete,* broaden). A special problem is presented by the notation of the punctum, used either singly or in a brief series. In both St. Gall and Messine notation the normal form of the punctum forming part of a neume, as in the climacus, is a dot. When it is used as a single note to set a syllable of text, the form used most frequently is the "long" form, the dash—which would indicate lengthening if it were used in the climacus. On the other hand, on the rare occasions when the point is used alone to set a syllable, it is usually accompanied by the letter *c,* indicating a fast performance. Whether this reveals an intrinsic difference between the values of the individual notes in the climacus and individual punctums is one of the many problems of Gregorian rhythm.

Present Scholarly Problems. Studies in the notation of chant have revealed that in general there is close agreement among the MSS in regard to the melodies, and much agreement in regard to rhythm. Neverthe-

less, differences persist. The question raised by these differences is fundamental, and it must be considered before efforts to produce a definitive edition of Gregorian chant can bear fruit:

> Is there one archetype from which all the medieval local chant traditions sprang? If so, is it a unified oral tradition that was written down for the first time in various localities at the end of the 9th century—each region having evolved a written system of its own; or is it a single *written* archetype, reflecting perhaps but one local tradition, that served as the model for other traditions? [Weakland, 62–63.]

Within each neume all of the early notations agree in placing the symbols for high notes higher on the page than those for low notes. Most of these notations, however, cannot be accurately transcribed with regard to pitch because it is impossible to tell whether an ascent, for example, is a second, third, or fourth. The placement of succeeding neumes is determined by convenience, not by relative pitch; in passages of single notes—punctums or virgas, or a combination of the two—the notes are written for the most part on the same level. The virgas represent relatively high notes, but there is no way of telling just how much higher they were. The idea of lining up notes on a series of levels, each of which is identified with one particular pitch, revolutionized musical notation and led directly to the invention of the staff, even though early efforts in this direction used no actual lines at all. In the Aquitanian MS from St. Yrieix (PalMus v.13), a single line has been scratched into the parchment; by measuring carefully above and below this line one can transcribe the music with reasonable ease and accuracy. It is necessary to determine what pitch is indicated by the scratched line, since this varies from one chant to the next. Ultimately a number of horizontal lines were drawn; but the decisive step of identifying the lines with pitches a third apart and specifying which pitch one or two of the lines identified is attributed to *Guido of Arezzo.

The notation used in modern publications of chant is in general modeled on that of chant MSS from the 13th and succeeding centuries. A four-line staff is used, and the notes have sharply defined square or diamond forms. In these manuscripts, the number of symbols is reduced—the oriscus and the quilisma, for example, are written as ordinary notes; and rhythmic signs, such as episemas and rhythmic letters, are omitted. This notation became standard over a large part of Europe, and it is exemplified in PalMus v.12, a 13th-century antiphonary from Worcester. In Germany a different kind of notation was used; the distinctive shapes of its notes have given it the name "horseshoe-nail notation" (*Hufnagelschrift*). The gain in accuracy of the notation of melodies brought by the invention of the staff was accompanied by a reduction in the richness and variety of the information conveyed by musical notation.

Bibliography: PalMus, valuable commentaries as well as facsimiles. G. Suñol, *Introduction à la paléographie musicale grégorienne* (Tournai 1935). J. Hourlier, *La Notation musicale des chants liturgiques latins* (Solesmes 1963). J. Hourlier and M. Huglo, "Notation paléofranque," *Études grégoriennes* 2 (1957) 212–219. S. Corbin, "Les notations neumatiques en France à l'époque carolingienne," *RevHistÉglFrance* 38 (1952) 225–232. R. G. Weakland, Music Library Assoc. *Notes* 19 (1961–62) 62–64, review of *Études grégoriennes* v.2, and *Le Graduel romain,* ed. Monks of Solesmes, v.2 (Solesmes 1957).

[R. Steiner]

PALERMO, ARCHDIOCESE OF (PANORMITANUS)

Metropolitan see since the 11th century, in northwest *Sicily, Italy. In 1963 it had 267 secular and 359 religious priests, 277 men in 48 religious houses, 2,143 women in 149 convents, and 799,500 Catholics; it is 541 square miles in area. Its three suffragans, which had 491 priests, 1,000 sisters, and 554,000 Catholics, were: *Cefalù (8th-century Byzantine bishop, restored in 1131), Mazara del Vallo (created in 1093), and Trapani (1844). The city of Palermo, capital of Sicily, in 1962 had a population of 595,000.

History. Phoenician in origin (c. 700 B.C.), Palermo was a Carthaginian naval base against Greek colonies in Sicily. Rome occupied it in the First Punic War and made it a free city c. 254 B.C. After domination by Vandals and Goths (476–535), it was taken by Byzantium. Under the Saracens (831–1071) it was the capital of the Emirate of Sicily and flourished in agriculture and commerce. Roger I conquered it (1072) and reorganized it ecclesiastically under Rome, Palermo having had several Greek bishops and archbishops during Saracen rule. Urban II made Roger papal legate for Sicily (1098), and antipope Anacletus II gave the title of king to Roger II, who was crowned in Palermo's cathedral (1130). See ROGER OF SICILY. Palermo was the capital of Norman Sicily (including the mainland) until the advent of the House of *Anjou (1266), which preferred *Naples. The Normans built beautiful monuments and made Palermo a center of Mediterranean trade. Under the Hohenstaufen *Frederick II (1198–1250) it was also a center of Arab, Byzantine, and Latin culture. The *Sicilian Vespers uprising against the Angevins (1282) broke out in Palermo, which thereafter was ruled by Aragon and Spain until the 18th century.

The Aragonese resided in *Catania, and Palermo declined. A Latin party posing as champions of independence, headed by the powerful Chiaramonte family, struggled against a party defending Aragon. In 1409 Sicily was united to the Crown of Aragon; and, although Palermo was the usual seat of the viceroy, it

Palermo church of the Holy Spirit, site of the Sicilian Vespers uprising of 1282.

continued to decline in competition with Catania and *Messina. Its bad state was manifested in the sociopolitical uprising led by Giovanni Alessio (1647), contemporary with that of Masaniello in Naples. After the War of the Spanish Succession, Palermo went to Amadeo II of Savoy (1713), who was crowned in Palermo. In 1718 it passed to Austria, and in 1735 to Charles III of Bourbon, King of Naples (1734–59), who established an independent dynasty. When Ferdinand IV fled Naples for Palermo (1799, 1806), the city revived somewhat. In 1812 Sicily was given a constitution modeled on English lines; but in 1815 it was abolished, and Palermo became just another provincial city. Discontent spread, and anti-Bourbon feelings for independence, which caused the revolutions of 1820 and 1848, facilitated *Garibaldi's expedition and the unification with Italy (1860).

Art. There are no Phoenician or Carthaginian and few Roman or early Christian ruins (traces of catacombs at S. Michele and Porta d'Ossuna). Nothing survives from the Byzantines, and very little from the Saracens. The most significant monuments are Norman. From Roger II (1101–54) dates the Palatine Chapel, with a cupola, three small naves and apses, Byzantine mosaics, and an Arabic stalactite ceiling. S. Giovanni degli Eremiti, in the form of a cross with small cupolas, has a small cloister and portico adjoining. The Martorana, in a Greek cross with a central cupola, has a bell tower and mosaics, one depicting Roger II crowned by Christ. S. Cataldo has three small cupolas. The cathedral, which dates from William II (1166–89), has been restored through the centuries; its portico (15th century), cupola (18th century), and interior are noteworthy, and it houses the tombs of Roger II, Henry VI (d. 1197), the Empress Constance (d. 1198), and Frederick II. Halls with mosaics in the royal palace, and the royal villas La Zisa and La Cuba are from the same period.

The portal of S. Agostino and the Chiaramonte and Sclafani palaces were built in the 14th-century. S. Maria della Catena and the Aiutamicristo palace are 15th-century; S. Maria dei Miracoli, 16th-century; and S. Guiseppe, Casaprofessa, and the oratories of S. Cita, S. Lorenzo, and Rosario, with sculpture by Giacomo Serpotta (1656–1732), are 17th-century. On Monte Pellegrino to the west is the shrine of St. *Rosalia, patroness of Palermo since the 17th century. In the museum is a Greek collection that includes metope of the temple of Selinunte (6th century B.C.). The university (1805) is the continuation of a Jesuit college (1550), which succeeded a Dominican school where lectures had been given since 1469.

The Diocese. The Christian community is of early origin, but the first known bishop is Mamilianus, deported by the Vandals in 439. Silanus, a deacon of Palermo, carried a letter of Pope Leo I to Bishop Pascasinus of Lilibeo. Pope Gregory I, who made Palermo the administrative center for the goods of the Church in west Sicily, wrote to Bishop Victor (591–602) not to molest the Jews and gave the pallium to John (603). In the *iconoclastic controversy of the 8th century, Palermo came under the jurisdiction of the Patriarch of Constantinople. At the time of the Norman Conquest, Nicodemus had the title of archbishop. Gregory VII in 1083 confirmed metropolitan rights and gave the pallium to Acherius (1083–99). Ludovico Bonito (1383–

92) held a provincial council in 1388. The canonist Nicolaus de *Tudeschis (1434–45) took part in the Council of Basel and was made a cardinal by antipope Felix V. Bl. *Peter Geremia of Palermo attended the Council of Florence. *Cajetan (Tommaso De Vio) was appointed archbishop but resigned in the face of opposition (1518). Cesare Marulli founded the seminary (1578). Cardinal Giannettino Doria (1609–42), several times viceroy of Sicily, held diocesan synods in 1615, 1622, and 1633. Cardinal Ferdinand Pignatelli (1839) was general of the Theatines. The proceedings of eleven diocesan synods that were held at Palermo have been published.

Bibliography: R. Pirri, *Sicilia Sacra*, 4 v. (Palermo 1633–1734), v.1. L. Biagi, *Palermo* (Bergamo 1929). F. de Stefano, *Storia della Sicilia dal secolo XI al XIX* (Bari 1948). B. Pace, *Arte e civiltà della Sicilia antica*, v.4 *Barbari e Bizantini* (Rome 1949). O. Demus, *The Mosaics of Norman Sicily* (London 1950). G. Agnello, *L'architettura bizantina in Sicilia* (Florence 1952). A. Zanca, *La cattedrale di Palermo*, (Palermo 1952). P. Toesca, *La cappella palatina di Palermo* (Milan 1955). G. Giacomazzi, *Il palazzo che fu dei re. Divagazioni storico-artistiche sul Palazzo dei Normanni* (Palermo 1959). J. Deér, *The Dynastic Porphyry Tombs of the Norman Period in Sicily*, tr. G. A. Gillhoff (Cambridge, Mass. 1959). G. Spatrisano, *Architettura del Cinquecento in Palermo* (Palermo 1961). Ann Pont (1965) 323. **Illustration credit:** Alinari-Art Reference Bureau.

[F. RAFFAELE]

PALESTINE

This article treats of Palestine under the following headings: (1) The Name, (2) Geology, (3) Physical Geography, (4) Political Geography, (5) Economic-Cultural Geography, (6) Natural History, (7) Archeology, (8) Pre-Israelite Ethnology, and (9) Holy Places.

1. THE NAME

The term Palestine is derived from the *Philistines who invaded and settled the central and southern coastal area of the Holy Land about the same time that the Israelites were invading the central highlands from the eastern and southern deserts (*c.* 1200 B.C.). In early Christian terminology Palestine included the territory that extended from the foothills of the Lebanon Mountains in the north to the edge of the desert, the *Negeb, in the south, and from the Mediterranean Sea eastward to the Transjordan Plateau, a usage derived from the Roman designation *Syria Palaestina* for this area, the southern section of the Roman province of Syria. This usage prevails today.

Biblical Names for Palestine. The writers of the *Pentateuch called this territory *Canaan and its inhabitants Canaanites (Gn 12.5; Ex 15.15). The Hebrews, after their gradual conquest of it during the 12th and 11th centuries B.C., called it the land of Israel, the name that they used to refer to their confederation of 12 tribes descended from the patriarch Israel (Jacob). They considered it to be the land promised them by God as part of His covenant blessing (Heb 11.9; Gn 12.6–7; Ex 12.25). After the Exile, Zacharia termed it the Holy Land, the land of Yahweh's holy people, ruled by Him as their King (Za 2.16; 2 Mc 1.7; Ex 19.5–8). In Hellenistic and Roman times it was known as Judea from *Juda, the tribe that dwelt in the hill country from *Jerusalem south to *Bersabee (Beersheba). To this greatly reduced territory the Jewish exiles returned from Babylon and there established an ethnarchy that became the Hasmonaean Kingdom.

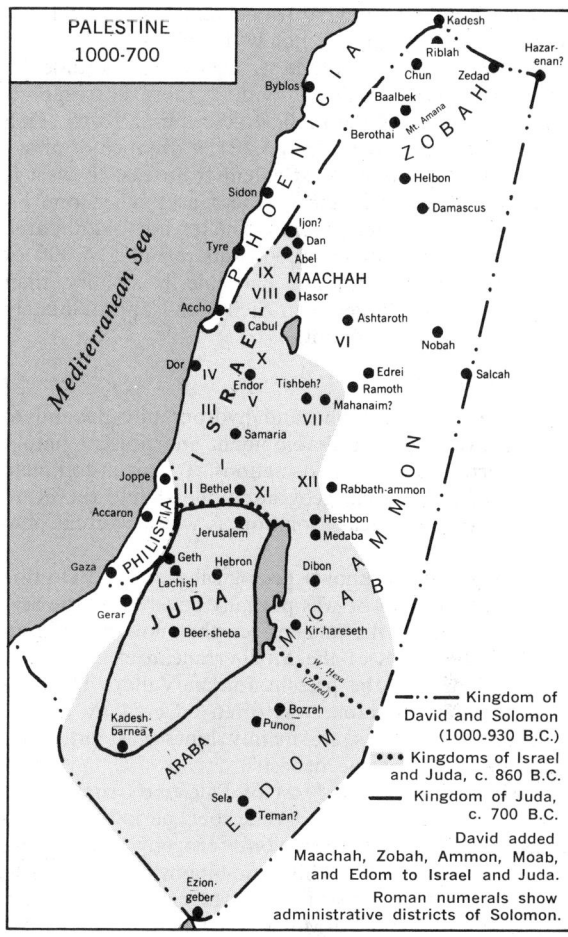

Fig. 1. Ancient Palestine, with the regions where the 12 tribes of Israel were settled (Josue ch. 13–19).

More generally, localities that were frequently mentioned or that played an important part in the Bible have been given the name Lands of the Bible. These extended much beyond the confines of Israel at the time of its greatest expansion in the reigns of David and Solomon (10th century B.C.). The OT Bible Lands included what is known today as the Fertile Crescent going from *Ur, an ancient city of Sumer, near the Persian Gulf, through the fertile lands of Mesopotamia, North Syria, Lebanon, and Palestine, to the lands made fruitful by the Nile River. They also included, in late books of the OT, Persia, Asia Minor, Greece and its islands, and Rome. In the NT the geographical outlook spread with the carrying of the gospel "to the ends of the earth" (Acts 1.8) and became centered more to the west, on Asia Minor, Greece, and Italy, mainly because of the Pauline literature and the Acts. This general area is of interest to all serious Biblical students, but this article restricts itself to the much smaller territory known as Palestine.

The Area of Modern Palestine. Today the Hashemite Kingdom of *Jordan and the Zionist State of Israel (*see* ISRAEL, 4) occupy most of the area traditionally called Palestine, although Egypt possesses the so-called Gaza strip, and Syria the plateau region east and north of the Sea of *Galilee. Palestine thus lies between the Arabian Desert and the Great Sea, the Mediterranean, as east and west boundaries; its north and south limits are the Lebanon and Anti-Lebanon massif and the southern desert, approximately from the 33d to the 29th degree north latitude (roughly the latitude of Alabama). This north to south expanse corresponds generally to that of the Biblical description, from *Dan to Bersabee (Jgs 20.1; 1 Sm 3.20), a distance of about 145 air miles. The greatest extent from east to west is close to 100 miles in the southern area when one includes the Transjordan region. The territory's total area therefore is only about 10,000 square miles, 4,000 of them east of the Jordan. Palestine is smaller than Belgium, hardly larger than Sicily, and approximately the same size as Vermont.

2. GEOLOGY

Palestine's topography and hydrography depend to a great extent on the development and present nature of its terrain and rock formations. To get a complete picture of its physical geography one should therefore examine its geological evolution as well as actual phenomena.

Throughout the known geological periods, Palestine either bordered on or was partially covered by the sea. The shoreline of the ancient sea that now has diminished to the limits of the Mediterranean extended for long periods into the present Jordan Valley. The Cisjordan region therefore was often covered by it, and as a result its rocks are mainly limestone and chalk resulting from marine deposits.

Early Development. Most of Palestine's rock strata were formed during the Cretaceous period that preceded the surrounding region's orogeny terminating in the emergence of the high mountains in Turkey and Iran. The great pressure that formed the Taurus, Armenian, and Zagros Mountains was separated from Palestine by the expanse of Syria and caused there only a relatively gentle rock folding.

Transjordanian Palestine is the western edge of the great solid block of Nubian sandstone that composed the ancient platform of the Arabian Peninsula. A vast crystalline mass, very hard and resistant, it was not subject to folding, but the strain on it was so great that it developed longitudinal cracks and faults. Some parts of the block broke off and were heaved up out of the Tertiary diluvial waters, 5,000 to 6,000 feet. Other segments broke off and dropped below sea level. The most striking result was the depression of a wide segment (14 miles at Jericho) now famous as the world's lowest valley, the great rift or trough of the Jordan Valley cleaving the Holy Land from north to south. This valley and the Wadi *Araba south of the *Dead Sea form part of an immense system of rift valleys that extend south through the Red Sea all the way to Lake Nyasa in East Africa. The sinking of the Jordan rift even cut some of Palestine's streams in half. The *Cison (Kishon), for example, was apparently part of the Tertiary *Jaboc (Jabbok) Valley. The faulting on each side of the Jordan rift was very complicated and included several smaller rifts entering into the main one, such as the valley leading down from *Jezrael.

On the western side of the Rift Valley, on top of the hard sandstone, a thick layer of Cenomanian limestone followed by a layer of soft chalk and then more Eocene limestone were deposited by the ancient incursions of the sea. The upwarping, folding, and faulting connected with the far-northern mountain formation produced the limestone hills of the highlands of Judea; Samaria, with its extension northwestward along the headland of Mt. *Carmel; and Lower and Upper Galilee. Volcanic activity caused the formation of basalt in the region around the Sea of Galilee. Then the torrential rains of the pluvial periods eroded the hills and formed the deep river valleys cut through the various layers of rock by the waters rushing either to the sea or the Jordan rift.

Later Development. Pliocene sands were then heaped on the maritime plain, and the Pleistocene epoch left after it a thin thread of low hills that now lie a short distance inland from the coast and hinder drainage. The coastal plain is a strip of alluvial soil covered in its southern reaches around *Gaza by loess. Except where sand dunes make it sterile, this land is quite fertile when properly drained and irrigated.

The central highland, *Galilee, and the rolling hills rising from the coast, called the Shephelah, are thus composed mostly of a limestone that affords good building material. The two layers of limestone readily soaked in the water that formed the subterranean channels and hollow caves with which the land is honeycombed. The intermediate layer of chalk was easily washed away; where it was prevalent, valleys that give access to the hill country are formed, such as the valley of *Aialon (Ajalon), the main gateway to the Judean highlands. The erosion of this chalk was the cause also of the narrow moat east of the Shephelah, a further protection for the highlands. The arid and barren slopes that fall off steeply to the Jordan rift east of the highland ridge, called the wilderness of Juda in its southern section, are also composed mainly of this chalkstone. Thus, the Judean wilderness is "badlands" country, a burned out, deeply seamed region, inhospitable to vegetation. In this area, close to the Dead Sea, Biblical scrolls have recently been uncovered after having lain hidden for about 2,000 years. Their preservation was due mainly to the region's extreme aridity.

Sandstone found on the eastern edge of the Jordan Valley contains copper and justifies the description of Palestine in Dt 8.9. The copper and iron ores of the Araba south of the Dead Sea were exploited during the period of the Israelite monarchy, from the 10th to the 6th centuries B.C. The oldest rock in Palestine is the granite of the southern Araba that has been forced up from below the sandstone where it was formed in the Pre-Cambrian Archean era.

Volcanic basalt around the Sea of Galilee and in the northern Transjordan area known in the Bible as *Basan (Bashan) contributes to the fertility of this region. Farther to the east lies a curious region, the Trachonitis district (Lk 3.1), covered with cinder cones, plugs of volcanos, and 350 square miles of lava. Remnants of the ancient volcanic activity that threw bars of volcanic rock across the Jordan Valley and formed Lake Huleh are found in the present hot springs in the valley of the *Yarmuk River in Transjordan and at *Tiberias.

Palestine was an unstable region throughout the Biblical period and remains so today. Earthquakes are noted in 1 Sm 14.15; Am 1.1; and Za 14.5. In modern times serious earthquakes occur about every 50 years, but smaller tremors are much more frequent.

3. PHYSICAL GEOGRAPHY

Palestine's position on a land bridge between the ancient civilizations of the Tigris-Euphrates and Nile Valleys gave it a special importance as a highway for caravans and rival armies. It also was the only easy land passage from Egypt to the Phoenician coast and on to Asia Minor; the Transjordan route to the Red Sea and southern Arabia ran along its eastern boundary. By its physical surroundings, therefore, it was one of the main crossroads of the Near East. Israel's economic, political, and cultural life was always greatly influenced by this fact.

Topography of Palestine. Three of the four main regions of Palestine are mentioned in Nm 13.29: the highlands, the seacoast, and the Jordan Valley. Add to these the Transjordan Plateau, and one obtains four zones, running north and south, parallel to the sea, which may be considered separately in their physical and topographical characteristics. Here only three will be described, the coastal plain, the hill country, and Transjordan (see JORDAN, THE; NEGEB; SINAI, MOUNT).

The Coastal Plain. Most of Palestine's littoral is flat and without natural shelter except for the smallest boats. The eastbound currents that run along the north coast of Africa have banked the shores with sand as far north as Mt. Carmel, leaving a straight coastline without natural harbors. In fact, the two seaports that had any importance, *Jaffa (Joppe) and *Caesarea, were mainly artificial. North of Palestine the irregular coast of Phoenicia provided many harbors suitable for ancient ships, the most important being *Tyre and *Sidon whence ships sailed southwest to Egypt and Carthage and northwest to the Aegean and Italy. The best harbor along Palestine's coast was *Accho (Acre), the Greek Ptolemais (Acts 21.7), and St. Jean d'Acre of the Crusaders, a port that remained throughout the Biblical period in other than Israelite possession. Accho's function as a port has now passed to Haifa at the foot of Mt. Carmel, southward across the Bay of Accho.

The limestone hills of Upper Galilee reach all the way to the coast a short distance south of Tyre and form a headland separating the Phoenician plain from that of Accho or *Aser, thus protecting the southern approach to Tyre. Southward, beyond the Plain of Aser (very fertile, except for the sand dunes along the shore) and the interruption of Mt. Carmel projecting its head into the sea, the narrow plain of Dor (Jos 12.23; 1 Mc 15.11–14) widens into the marshy, luxuriant plain of Saron (Sharon), in Biblical times thickly covered with an oak forest (Is 33.9; 35.2) and now famous for its citrus groves. The plain of Saron extends to the valley of Aialon, which joins the Brook of Cana to enter the sea a little north of Jaffa. The rich plain of Philistia, the ancient land of the Philistines, lies to the south of this main entrance into the hill country of Judea and Ephraim, occupying a section of the coast that is likewise very fertile except for the sand dunes along the shore. The area's fertility was exploited by Palestinian Arabs who cultivated extensive citrus groves there, now the possession of the Israelis. Farther south the annual rainfall diminishes rapidly and the plain gradually becomes desert in the western reaches of the Negeb. The width of the coastal plain varies from 5 miles at Accho, and 2 miles around Dor, to the maximum of 20 miles inland from Gaza.

This coastland provided the main route northward from Egypt, "the way of the Philistines' land" (Ex 13.17). It terminated its desert journey across the base of the Sinai triangle at Gaza, where it met the road leading east to Bersabee. The next main junction was just outside *Ascalon where it crossed the road going inland to Lachis [see LACHIS (LACHISH) LETTERS], thence to Jerusalem and *Jericho. It then passed before the walls of *Azotus (Ashdod) at the confluence of three valleys coming down from the east, then on to Jabnia (Jamnia), crossing the road to Jerusalem through the Valley of Sorec. Farther north it met at Beth-Dagon the main road between Jaffa and *Lydda (Lod) that continued eastward to Aialon, the Beth-Horons, and *Rama. A caravan having business in the western Plain of Saron, Caesarea, Dor, Accho, and the Phoenician coast would have veered west to Jaffa here and then north along the coast, but one whose destination was Damascus or the Plain of Esdraelon with its many important cities would have continued directly north until it came to the western end of the pass of *Mageddo (Megiddo), whence it would veer northeastward toward the Sea of Galilee, passing many junctions with east-west roads. The coastal plain was therefore a funnel for almost all traffic toward Egypt. The only other route was the more difficult Road to Sur from Bersabee southwestward through the Negeb and the Desert of Sur to Lake Timsah, a way that the Israelites would have had to follow whenever enemies occupied the Philistine Plain.

The Hill Country. East of the coastal plain the highland ridge of Judea and Ephraim does not begin immediately, but some foothills of more recent formation interpose a barrier to direct entrance to the hill country. Along this minor ridge important frontier cities were placed, such as Aialon, Gazer, Lachis, and Dabir, guarding the various valleys leading farther inland. This region was called the Shephelah, the foothills of Dt 1.7. To its east and forming another natural barrier lay a narrow chalkstone valley or moat sometimes referred to as the Moat of Juda. One easily sees why the Israelites and the Philistines were continually vying to control this territory.

The central highlands of Palestine are the backbone of the country, formed by the ridge of Juda and Ephraim that, with only the interruption of the Plain of Esdraelon, runs from the Negeb to join, through Lower and Upper Galilee, the Lebanon ranges. The Lebanons rise 6,000 feet above the sea level, while in the Anti-Lebanon range Mt. *Hermon towers at 9,232 feet. Palestine's highest peak is Mt. Jarmak in Upper Galilee at almost 4,000 feet. Compared to these heights Mt. *Thabor (Tabor), 5 miles east of *Nazareth in Lower Galilee, is not much more than a prominent hill rising out of the Esdraelon Plain to less than 2,000 feet.

Upper Galilee is a lofty plateau, rugged and wild, forming the foothills of the Lebanons, with Safad as its principal modern town. The waters of Merom (Jos 11.5, 7) were probably those of the Wadi Meiron east of Safad. The ancient Hyksos and Canaanite city of *Hasor (Jos 11.10; 3 Kgs 9.15) and its plain lie on the eastern slope of the central ridge, a short distance southwest of Lake Huleh.

Lower Galilee is a series of transverse, east-to-west ridges alternating with enclosed valleys and picturesque wooded defiles. This was the more populated and cultivated part of northern Palestine, the "District of the Gentiles" and "the seaward road," i.e., the main trunk route past the Sea of Galilee and Hasor to Damascus (Is 8.23; see also Mt 4.15). Bethsaida, the home town of the Apostles Peter, Andrew and Philip, at the northern end of the Sea of Galilee, *Capharnaum, the headquarters of Jesus during the first part of His public ministry (Mt 4.13), and Tiberias, built in honor of the Roman Emperor Tiberius by *Herod Antipas during the life of Jesus, were really in the Jordan Valley but can be considered as Galilean cities. Sepphoris was the capital of Herod's tetrarchy of Galilee (Lk 3.1) before he built Tiberias. Some other important cities of Galilee were Arbela (1 Mc 9.2), *Cana (Jn 2.1), *Endor (1 Sm 28.7–8), *Nain (Lk 7.11–17), and *Sunem (Shunem; 4 Kgs 4.8). Gabaath-Hammore (Jgs 7.1), an ancient volcano a few miles south of Thabor, is responsible for the fertility of the surrounding valleys and was called at one time "Little Hermon." Nazareth is a pleasant spot nestling on the side of a steep hill a few miles south of Sepphoris. The Horns of Hattin, a pass along the main trunk route as it descended to the Sea of Galilee, was a strategic spot and the site of many battles, including *Saladin's victory over the Crusaders in 1187.

The plains of Mageddo and Jezrael form an important break in the central highlands and an easy passage from the Mediterranean to the Jordan Valley. The water parting near Jezrael marks the division between the two valleys. The Plain of Megeddo, "the great plain" (1 Mc 12.49), and the coastal Plain of Accho are drained to the west by the Cison (Kishon) River, which in the rainy season becomes a torrent (Jgs 5.21). In the Hellenistic period the Plain of Mageddo was called the Plain of *Esdraelon, from the Greek name for Jezrael, a town guarding its eastern boundary. From Jezrael a more narrow plain drops off quickly eastward to below sea level and merges into the plain of *Beth-San (Beth-shan), part of the Jordan Valley. These plains formed a zone of great agricultural wealth and strategic importance, as is clear from the many fortified cities guarding their gates, from west to east, Jecnaam (Jokneam), Mageddo, *Thaanach, Jeblaam (Ibleam), Jezrael, and Beth-San. Mageddo, already occupied in the 4th millennium B.C., was where King Josia was killed in battle while trying to stop the northward march of the Egyptian army under *Nechao (4 Kgs 23.29). Since so many battles were fought at this pass, it became in the Apocalypse (16.14–16), under the form *Armageddon, the scene of the last great battle between the forces of good and evil. Beth-San (1 Sm 31.10) was known in the Hellenistic period as Scythopolis (2 Mc 12.29–30), a city of the *Decapolis. Mt. *Gelboe, just west of Beth-San and the site of Saul's death (2 Sm 1.21), forms the northeast end of the mountain ridge of Ephraim.

The highlands of Ephraim or Samaria, rising to the maximum height of 3,332 feet at Baalhasor just northeast of Bethel (2 Sm 13.23), have several fertile valleys and small plains, those of Dothain, *Sichem (Shechem), and Lebona. The Judean section of the range is more uniformly hill country and less fertile, although adequate for olive groves and vineyards. No well-defined geographical feature, however, marks the boundary between the regions of Ephraim and Juda.

Ascending from the plain of Esdraelon, the highland road passed the cities of Dothain, *Samaria, and Sichem, which controlled the important defile between Mt. *Garizim (Gerizim) and Mt. Ebal, the mounts of cursing and blessing (Dt 27.11–13). Farther south the road followed the water parting most of the time, passing near Lebona, *Silo (Shiloh), *Bethel, *Maspha (Mizpeh), Machmas, *Gabaa (Gibeah), Jerusalem, *Bethlehem, and reaching its highest point just north of *Hebron, whence it descended to Bersabee. At Hebron another road branched off to the southeast, passing Carmel of Juda, Maon, Arad, and joining the road from Bersabee that led to the Araba and the mining and smelting area of *Asiongaber (Eziongeber).

East of the divide the land falls rapidly to the Jordan Valley, forming an eroded wilderness that is much more desolate in the southern Judean section. From Sichem a road along the Wadi Fara leads gradually down to the Jordan Valley and was possibly the way used by Abraham and his family to ascend to Sichem (Gn 12.6). More arduous canyon roads link Bethel and Jerusalem with Jericho. South of Jerusalem the paths leading down to the Dead Sea along canyon walls were used only by shepherds or fugitives, for they terminated in the wilderness of Juda, useful only for winter grazing and seclusion from the inhabited lands.

The central and southern hill country of Palestine has the aspect of a pocket cut off from the surrounding regions by the narrowness of its transverse valleys and canyons. Although it was close to the main trunk route of the Middle East, it was not astride it, as was the Plain of the Philistines and the Esdraelon Valley. It looked down upon the crossroads of the world and the caravans laden with treasures from Egypt and Mesopotamia, but it was by its physical nature aloof in its heights. Passing armies could ignore it on their way to Egypt or to Syria and Iraq and would slash back at it only when it provoked or hindered them in their main purpose. This physical aloofness has always been an important factor in the hill country's history.

Transjordan. The great plateau east of the Jordan Valley, with its lofty and precipitous bluffs facing toward the west and its gradual merging with the Arabian Desert to the east, is commonly known as the *Transjordan. The lowest level on the plateau is 1,500 feet, but to the south in Edom it rises to 5,000 feet. Its principal peaks in the central region range in height from 3,500 to 4,000 feet.

Four important river valleys, the *Yarmuk, the Jaboc, the *Arnon, and the *Zared cut this tableland in a westerly direction and form boundaries of well-known regions. North and east of the Yarmuk lay *Basan (Bashan) and the plain of Hauran. *Galaad (Gilead) with its fertile highland valley lay between the Yarmuk and the Arnon, and at the eastern headwaters of the Jaboc the kingdom of Ammon flourished. Sihon's Amorrite kingdom once possessed all of the region from the Arnon to the Jaboc but was conquered by the Israelites and surrendered its territory to the tribes of Gad and Ruben. Moab (*see* MOABITES) was originally situated between the Arnon and the Zared (Nm 21.13) but later extended its territory northward to include the eastern bank of the Jordan River just north of the Dead Sea, thus giving its name to this region, the Plains of Moab. South of the Zared lay Edom in the highest part of the Transjordan. Farther

Fig. 2. (a) Site of Bethsaida, birthplace of Apostles Peter, Andrew, and Philip, north end of the Sea of Galilee. (b) The Herodium in the wilderness of Judea, 3 miles southeast of Bethlehem and 12 miles west of the Dead Sea.

south the *Madianites, a seminomadic people, dwelt along the shores of the Gulf of Aqaba.

The King's Highway (Nm 20.17) was the main route running north and south along this plateau from Damascus to Aqaba. In Roman times it was Trajan's Road, and under Turkish rule, the Sultan's Highway. By it the Damascus market had access to the exotic products of South Arabia. Some of the most important towns along the route were Theman, *Sela (Petra), and Bosra in Edom; Kir-hareseth (the capital), Aroer, and *Dibon in Moab; *Medaba (Madeba) and Hesebon in land constantly contested between Moabites and Israelites; Rabba, the capital of Ammon (see AMMON-ITES), conquered by Joab and David (Philadelphia, now Amman, the capital of the Hashemite Kingdom of Jordan); *Gerasa, a city of Galaad, captured by Alexander Jannaeus, one of the *Hasmonaeans, in 83 B.C.; *Ramoth in Galaad, Arbela (Beth-Arbel); and finally, in Basan, Ashtaroth and Carnaim (Gn 14.5; Am 6.13).

The fertile region of Transjordan was much wider in the north (in Basan and Hauran) than in the south. Galaad was also very fertile, producing oil, wine, and grain, the staples of the Near East, and was famous for its timber.

Hydrography of Palestine. In Dt 8.7 Palestine is described as a land highly favored by water courses and springs, and other texts mention numerous wells. A land's water resources depend on its climate, especially its rainfall, and on its geological nature.

Climate. In no such small area of the world are there such differences in rainfall and climate as are found in Palestine. This is due to a complex of causes: its situation between the southeastern angle of the Mediterranean and the vast Arabian Desert, its hill country immediately falling off to the world's lowest and hottest valley, and its high plateau in the Transjordan. Whatever the causes, the effects are startling.

The climate's main feature is its two seasons: the long completely dry summer, and the comparatively short rainy season when cyclonic storms come blowing off the sea. The rainy season has a quite variable beginning and ending, the early and late rains of the Bible (Dt 11.14), both of great importance. The early rains are necessary for plowing and planting, the late rains, for bringing the grain to full ear. The early rains should begin in late October, and when they are delayed until late November or even early January the crops suffer from a tardy germination, and man suffers even more from the prolonged dryness and anxious expectation. The heaviest rains arrive in January, February, and early March, not the steady, soaking rain of more northern regions, but heavy showers, continuous on the first day of the storm, followed by intermittent showers for 2 or 3 days. Once the storm has passed, the atmosphere becomes extremely clear, and one may look from Jerusalem and see to the east every crag of the mountains of Moab more than 30 miles away. This is the time for collecting as much water as possible in pools and cisterns for the long dry season ahead. The late rains, ripening the harvest, occur in late March and early April, but when they come much later and are violent hail storms, the crops and the frail blossoms on the fruit trees may suffer irreparable damage.

May and early June on the one hand and late September and October on the other are transitional periods during which the dry, scorching desert wind, the sirocco, may descend on Palestine without warning and with dire results for all living things. The heat and dryness are oppressive; verdure quickly withers; the air becomes opaque with fine sand that magnifies the sun's heat; and man and beast grow irritable. Fortunately, the sirocco usually last for no more than 2 or 3 days—in autumn, blown away by the rain-burdened westerly winds, and in June, by the summer westerlies that become a constant feature of every day when the land heat of late morning grows intense enough to draw them from the sea.

From mid-June to mid-September the weather pattern remains the same, the heat of the late morning gives way to the cooling sea breeze of the afternoon, which gradually moves inland, reaching the edge of Transjordan by about 4 P.M. Along the coast the humidity is higher; the breeze, less refreshing; and the discomfort of the day, prolonged into the night. In the hill country the nights are cool and the shade during the day is always refreshing compared to the coast's humid shade. In the Jordan Rift even the sea air rushing down its steep slopes is so heated that it becomes only an afternoon annoyance. The wind's effect on the eastern plateau is refreshing, but it arrives too late to lower the day's heat very much.

The amount of rainfall diminishes greatly from north to south, from west to east, and from higher to lower altitudes. The annual rainfall of Jerusalem is almost 24 inches, while only 5 miles to the east it decreases rapidly; and in Jericho, 17 miles away, it measures only about 5 inches. At Bersabee, 50 miles south of Jerusalem, the annual rainfall measures only 8 to 9 inches, but at the same altitude and distance to the north it measures more than 20. In the highlands of Upper Galilee it reaches more than 35 inches; on the summit of Mt. Hermon, the source of the Jordan River's water, the annual precipitation is more than 60 inches. The coastal region, because of its low altitude, receives less rain than the hills; thus Transjordan, higher than the central ridge, sometimes receives more rainfall than Jerusalem, although it is much farther from the sea. One must remember that Palestine's annual rainfall is crowded into a 5-month period, a fact that is important in understanding its reliance on springs, wells, and cisterns, and the formation of its wadis or torrent canyons.

Springs and Wells. The absorbent limestone structure of Palestine's rock bed provides storage for the heavy winter rains. The sources of the subterranean water occur sporadically throughout most of the land and afford places for human habitation. The main towns usually were built near an important spring or well, and intricate subterranean passages were devised to bring the well's water within the city walls so that in times of siege a supply would always be available. Such a tunnel to the fountain of Gihon in Jerusalem was repaired and extended by Ezechia in preparation for the onslaught of the Assyrians (4 Kgs 20.20). Similar constructions have been found at Mageddo, Lachis, *Gabaon (Gibeon), etc. The spring at Jericho is one of the main reasons why this is the site of the oldest-known town in the world.

Where well water was insufficient, or simply to supply a greater abundance of water, cisterns were built to store the winter rains. Samaria, built by Israel's King *Amri (Omri), had no natural spring and depended solely on its vast cisterns.

Rivers and Wadis. The only copious perennial watercourse in Palestine that merits comparison with even a minor American river is the Jordan. The few perennial rivers are rushing torrents during the rainy season, quickly draining the highlands and causing marshes in the low-lying plains, but, as summer advances, they become quiet rivulets whose courses may be discovered only by the vegetation along their narrow banks. Most of the watercourses, however, flow only during the rainy season, becoming dry beds or washes soon after its end.

The wadis of Palestine have scarred the domelike hill country with deep canyons, especially on the eastern and western slopes of the Jordan rift. One of the most impressive wadis is the canyon of the River Arnon, which rivals the rugged beauty of the canyons of southwestern U.S. Though they are beautiful, these torrents have been the main source of erosion of the hill country. They also are impediments to travelers and the cause of many a tortuous road.

Bibliography: Abel GéogrPal. L. H. GROLLENBERG, *Atlas of the Bible,* tr. J. M. REID and H. H. ROWLEY (New York 1956). M. DU BUIT, *Géographie de la Terre Sainte* (Paris 1958). *Oxford Bible Atlas,* ed. H. G. MAY et al. (New York 1962). D. BALY, *The Geography of the Bible* (New York 1957); *Geographical Companion to the Bible* (New York 1963). For an excellent detailed map of the Holy Land today, see *National Geographic Magazine* atlas plate (December 1963) 52. **Illustration credits:** Fig. 2 The Matson Photo Service, Los Angeles, Calif.

[E. LUSSIER]

4. POLITICAL GEOGRAPHY

"This is a list of the kings whom Josue and the Israelites conquered west of the Jordan . . . thirty-one kings in all" (Jos 12.7–24). A statement such as this gives a good indication of conditions in Palestine prior to the Israelite invasion. It was a land divided, a country of mixed population and independent city-states. (For the pre-Israelite ethnology of the country, *see* section 8, below.) However, this feature is characteristic of Palestine throughout its long history. Rarely was there ever one single united country, and when, on occasion, such a union was achieved, it was of relatively short duration.

Period of Josue and the Judges. A picture of the division of the land among the twelve tribes of Israel is given in Josue ch. 13–21. *See* JOSUE (JOSHUA), BOOK OF. Despite the apparent details that are presented, it is, nevertheless, difficult to determine the precise boundaries of each of the tribal allotments. East of the Jordan, half of the tribe of *Manasse (specifically, the clan of Machir) occupied the districts of *Basan (Bashan) and part of *Galaad (Gilead; Jos 13.8–14); *Gad, the rest of Galaad between the *Jaboc (Jabbok) and Hesebon (Heshbon; 13.24–28); and *Ruben (Reuben), the land between Hesebon and the *Arnon (13.15–23). West of the Jordan, *Juda received the greatest portion —from the Valley of Hennom (*see* GEHENNA) at Jerusalem to Cadesbarne (Kadeshbarnea) and the Wadi of Egypt in the *Negeb (15.1–63). Part of this territory was alloted to *Simeon—cities in the general vicinity of *Bersabee (Beersheba; 19.1–9). North of Juda were the smaller possessions of *Benjamin (18.11–28) and *Dan (19.40–48). Central Palestine was occupied by *Ephraim (16.4–10) and the other half of Manasse (17.1–13). In the district of *Galilee, *Nephthali (Naphtali; 19.32–39) was in the north, *Zabulon (19.10–16) and *Issachar (19.17–23) in the south, and *Aser (Asher; 19.24–31) along the coast.

The division of the land is presented as the outcome of the Israelite conquest under the leadership of *Josue (Joshua), son of Nun. But the Book of *Judges gives a different story (Jgs 1.1–36). The two accounts seem to be but two aspects of a much more complicated history. Probably some of the tribes had been there since the time of Jacob and were already in possession of land. In the course of time these tribes made attempts to increase their territorial possessions. With the coming of Josue and the tribes under his command, the conquest reached its full proportions. The complete picture, therefore, would be one of occupation and settlement in different stages over a long period of time culminating in the invasion led by Josue. The land thus became the possession of tribes who were related by common ancestry and eventually united by the bond of a religious *covenant with *Yahweh, the God of their fathers, Abraham, Isaac, and Jacob, the God who had brought deliverance to those Israelites who had been enslaved in Egypt. But this bond was a very loose one, and there was little lasting unity. It was only when a common danger, the extension of *Philistine power, threatened all the tribes that unity was achieved by the establishment of the monarchy (1 Sm 4.2–10.27). But even this would turn out to be of relatively short duration.

Period of the Monarchy. With the establishment of the monarchy the tribes in fact gained control of the land to which they had laid claim. Israel's first king, *Saul, began the offensive and began well, but in the end was far from successful (1 Sm 11.1–15.9; 31.1–6).

It was up to *David to lead a united Israel to victory. This warrior king began by reducing the Philistines to subjection, so that they were never again troublesome to Israel (2 Sm 5.17–25; 8.1). He continued the conquest by subduing the Canaanite city-states of the land and taking Jerusalem, making it the political and religious capital of the kingdom (5.6–10). His dominion eventually included the *Aramaeans in the north and the *Ammonites, *Moabites, and *Edomites in the east and southeast (8.2–14; 10.6–19; 12.26–31). Thus the kingdom reached its greatest limits, the extent of which was never again to be seen by any subsequent king of Israel. From the frontier of *Hamath in the north to the Gulf of Aqabah in the south, from the Mediterranean Sea to the desert—all the land was subject to Jerusalem.

This was the inheritance of *Solomon, a kingdom of peace and prosperity. His task was to keep it intact. It was, indeed, the golden age. However, while the royal court grew in size and splendor, the condition of the people grew worse. To maintain his court Solomon divided the country into 12 administrative districts (3 Kgs 4.7–19), the boundaries of which ignored the old tribal divisions. Moreover, in all of this, Juda seemed to have enjoyed a privileged position. The result was a widespread dissatisfaction that eventually, after the death of the King, brought about the dissolution of the empire and the division of the kingdom.

Two independent kingdoms emerged: Israel in the north and Juda in the south, with the border between the two of them in the tribal territory of Benjamin. During their joint existence they were sometimes hostile, sometimes friendly, and at times even allied in a common cause. But whatever the internal problems, the greatest dangers were from without.

Israel remained in existence a little more than 200 years before the power of Assyria brought about its destruction. An initial Assyrian conquest (734–732 B.C.) resulted only in a reduction of territory to central Palestine; the districts of Dor, Mageddo and Galaad became provinces of Assyria (4 Kgs 15.29). However, 10 years later (722 B.C.) Samaria was invested and annexed to the Assyrian kingdom as a province, and Israel ceased to exist.

Juda alone remained, by choice, a vassal of Assyria. With the rise of Babylonian power, the might of Assyria was crushed, and the end of the southern kingdom was near. The first Babylonian capture of Jerusalem (597 B.C.) was accompanied by deportations (4 Kgs 24.10–16), but the kingdom was permitted to survive. A second onslaught (587 B.C.), however, ended it; and a governor was put in charge of the territory (4 Kgs 25.1–22).

From the Exilic to the Roman Period. Little is known about events during the exilic period. In the 6th century the *Nabataeans occupied the land of Edom, forcing the Edomites to move into the Negeb, subsequently known as Idumea. From there they caused trouble for the people remaining in the land of Juda and left bitter memories of these years. In Babylon the exiles cherished the hope of returning, a hope that was fulfilled with the rise of Persian power.

The Persian conquest freed the exiles and permitted them to return to their own land (538 B.C.; Ezr 1.1–4). It also saw the organization of the empire into satrapies. Palestine was in the fifth satrapy, called Abar Nahara (Beyond the River, i.e., west of the Euphrates). It was composed of various provinces, each under the jurisdiction of a local governor. The province of Juda was called Yehud, and its people Yehudim (Jews). The other provinces of Palestine were: Idumea, to the south of Juda; Samaria, Galilee, Dor, and Ashdod (*Azotus), to the north and along the coast; Galaad, Ammon, and Moab in *Transjordan.

The conquest by *Alexander the Great (333 B.C.) brought Palestine under his dominion. But after his death, it changed hands five times during the struggle of the Diadochi (323–301 B.C.). Eventually the kingdom of the *Ptolemies in Egypt and that of the *Seleucid dynasty comprising Asia Minor, Syria, and Babylonia were established. Palestine at first fell to the Ptolemies, but in fact it remained a bone of contention and the cause of conflicts for a century (301–198 B.C.). In the end it fell to the Seleucids.

Seleucid policy of Hellenization caused the Machabean uprising (166–135 B.C.), resulting in independence for Palestine [see MACHABEES (MACCABEES), HISTORY OF THE]. A kingdom came into existence, ruled by the descendants of the Machabees, the *Hasmonaeans. The extent of this kingdom reached proportions almost as great as that of the time of David; it included Idumea, Juda, Samaria, Galilee, and Transjordan. But internal affairs brought its downfall, and in 63 B.C., Pompey, who had already annexed Syria as a Roman province, intervened and annexed most of Palestine in

the same way, Juda, Galilee, Perea, and Idumea alone remaining semi-independent vassal states.

For a brief period Palestine was reunited under *Herod the Great (40–4 B.C.). At his death it was divided among his sons. *Archelaus received Judea, Samaria, and Idumea; *Herod Antipas, Galilee and *Perea; and *Philip the Tetrarch, the northern districts of Transjordan. In A.D. 6 the territory of Archelaus was added to the imperial province of Syria and a procurator was put in charge; in A.D. 34 the same fate befell the territory of Philip. In A.D. 37 Herod *Agrippa I was given the territory of Philip. To this was added the territory of Herod Antipas in A.D. 40, and shortly thereafter, Judea, Samaria, and Idumea—initiating another short period of unity until A.D. 44, when Palestine once more became a Roman province under a procurator. Northern Transjordan and parts of Galilee and Perea formed the kingdom of Herod *Agrippa II. But after the turbulent uprising of A.D. 70, which saw the destruction of Jerusalem, all of Palestine passed under Roman rule, to remain so for more than half a millennium. During this time Palestine enjoyed a period of relative peace and prosperity, undisturbed by outside aggression. Internally the revolt of *Bar Kokhba (132–135) caused some disturbance, but it was quickly suppressed by the Romans with widespread destruction. Jerusalem was rebuilt as a Roman provincial city by the emperor Hadrian, who called it Aelia Capitolina. Then in 313 *Constantine I, the Great, having embraced Christianity, proclaimed its liberty, and his mother, *Helena, converted it into a Christian city and restored its name.

From the Byzantine Period to Modern Times. With the division of the Roman Empire into West (Rome) and East (Constantinople) toward the end of the 4th century, the welfare of Palestine was bound to Byzantine rule. It was a time for pilgrimages, and the years that followed were tranquil.

This period of internal development was shattered in 611 when the Persians under Chosroes swept through Palestine, wrought havoc, and established themselves there for about 15 years. Byzantine rule came to a definitive end with the coming of the followers of Mohammed in 636. By 640 the Arab conquest was complete (see ARABS, HISTORY OF THE). Palestine was divided into two provinces: Al-Urdunn in the north and Filistin in the south. It was ruled successively by the *Umayyad, *'Abbāsid, and Fatimid Caliphs.

The devastation caused in the Holy Land by the *Seljuk Turks in 1071 was followed by the turbulent era of the *Crusades beginning in 1099. Under Crusader rule, Palestine became the Kingdom of Jerusalem, and the country was divided into various baronies. The Crusaders were followed by the *Mamelukes of Egypt in 1250. Then, in 1517, the conquest of Palestine by the *Ottoman Turks brought it under Turkish rule until the 20th century.

The beginning of the 20th century saw the growth of Arab nationalism, the rise of *Zionism, and World War I. When the allied troops led by General Allenby entered Palestine in 1917, Turkish rule came to an end, and Palestine was under British mandate until 1948. It was indeed the modern period, but the events were only a repetition of past history. It was a time of warfare and territorial division, hardly a new occurrence for the land

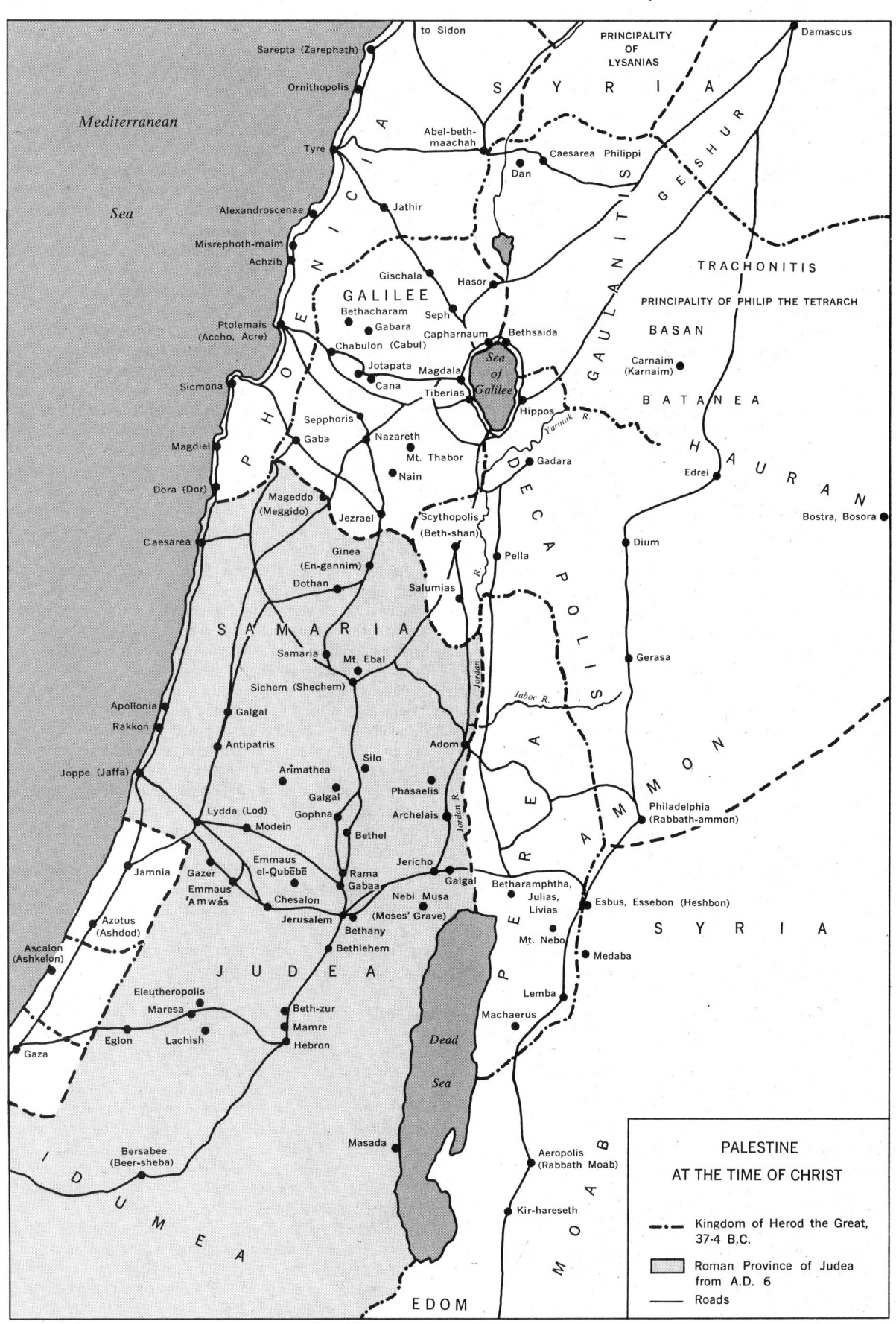

Fig. 3. Palestine in the time of Christ, showing the principal towns of the area.

of Palestine. For the modern period, *see* ISRAEL, 4; JORDAN, HASHEMITE KINGDOM OF.

Bibliography: H. HAAG, LexThK² 7:1362–63. D. BALDI, EncCatt 9:611–618. G. E. WRIGHT and F. V. FILSON, eds., *The Westminster Historical Atlas to the Bible* (rev. ed. Philadelphia 1956). J. BRIGHT, *A History of Israel* (Philadelphia 1959), good bibliog. J. W. PARKES, *A History of Palestine from 135 A.D. to Modern Times* (New York 1949), excellent bibliog. S. RUNCIMAN, *A History of the Crusades*, 3 v. (Cambridge, Eng. 1951–54), excellent bibliog.

[F. SEPER]

5. ECONOMIC-CULTURAL GEOGRAPHY

Physical geography plays an important role in the economic conditions of a country, particularly when its inhabitants are an agricultural and pastoral people. Palestine is, for the greater part, a land of hills and mountains; plains and wide valleys are relatively few. The soil is rocky. There are only two seasons: a cool rainy season from October to April and a warm dry season from May to September. In the transition period between the two, the hot dry wind from the desert, the khamsin (similar to the sirocco of Italy), can produce devastating effects. A prolonged drought can be disastrous.

Yet despite this, Palestine in Biblical times was a land in which grain, vines, and olive trees were the chief concern of its inhabitants. It was a land that produced figs, dates, and pomegranates; where lentils, beans, peas, cucumbers, onions, leeks, garlic, and melons were raised. And in certain regions there were cattle and grazing animals. In the words of the Bible, "The Lord your God is bringing you into a good land, a land of brooks of water, of fountains and springs, flowing forth in valleys and hills, a land of wheat and barley, of vines and fig trees and pomegranates, a land of olive trees and honey, a land in which you will eat bread without scarcity, in which you will lack nothing, a land whose stones are iron, and out of whose hills you can dig copper. And you shall eat and be full, and you shall bless the Lord your God for the good land he has given you" (Dt 8.7–10).

Regional. Agriculture was practiced throughout all of Palestine, yet the nature of the terrain made some regions more suitable than others. Of the different districts, lower *Galilee was the most fertile and productive. Its valleys and plains were covered with good rich soil. Rainfall was adequate, and springs, streams, and rivers supplied water in all seasons. Grain could be grown in abundance, especially on the large plain of *Esdraelon when it was properly drained; so too could olives and grapes. The region was suited also for cattle, sheep, and goats.

*Samaria was another of the productive districts of the country. Grain grew on the plains, and olives and grapes on the slopes of the hills.

*Juda was more pastoral in aspect and less fertile than the other territories. Yet some grain was grown in the valleys, as well as olives, grapes, and figs. The plateau from Jerusalem south to Hebron was one of the best grape-growing regions of Palestine.

To the west, the Shephelah was the buffer zone between the coastal plains and the hill country of Juda. But, in addition to its strategic importance, it was one of the most fertile regions of Palestine. In its valleys grain, olives, grapes, and sycamore figs could be found in great abundance. Moreover, the grass-covered valleys permitted the pasturing of considerable herds of cattle and other grazing animals.

In the districts across the Jordan, *Basan (Bashan) was known for its wheat and cattle. The well watered highlands of *Galaad (Gilead) were suited for cattle, grapes, and olives. The balms and ointments of Galaad were proverbial to the Israelite (Jer 8.22). Moab was famous for its sheep, but grain also was grown in this area. Edom was partly agricultural but was better known for its iron and copper mines and its caravan trade.

Main Agricultural Produce. The chief products of Palestine were grain, olives, and grapes. Wheat, barley, and spelt were the grains that were produced. They were sown in November and December, at the beginning of the rainy season; they grew throughout the winter and were harvested in the months of April, May, and June. Wheat was the most important of all the grains. The ears were eaten fresh or roasted, and could serve as food for travel. Chiefly, however, the grain was made into flour for bread. At harvest time, reaping was done with a sickle, and the ears of grain were cut off close to the stalk. These were then threshed on a hard floor by dragging a threshing sled of boards over it. The grain was then winnowed by throwing it up into the air so that the chaff would be blown away by the wind. It was then usually stored away and ground into flour as it was needed for bread.

Barley was the ordinary food of the poor and was used also as food for animals. Less expensive than wheat, it was at times planted as a protective border around the wheat fields, as well as on poorer ground. Spelt, a coarse, inferior type of wheat, was used for flour for bread (Is 28.25; Ez 4.9).

Olive trees were to be found in all parts of Palestine. Their cultivation is a relatively easy matter, even though it takes a number of years until good olives are produced. The trees require little care and a small amount of water to grow, and therefore they are well suited for the rocky soil of Palestine. Once it reaches the proper age, an olive tree will continue to produce for hundreds of years. Though its wood could be used for fuel or for the manufacture of ornaments, the importance of the olive tree is in the fruit that it produces. Olives ripen in September. They were usually knocked from the trees with sticks and then gathered. Both unripe (green) or ripe (black) olives were gathered for eating. However, their chief value came from the oil that was pressed from them. The finest oil came from the crushed olives that were simply left to drop, before being taken and put into presses for the extraction of every possible drop of oil. The oil was used for cooking, for liturgical ceremonies, for fuel in lamps, and for medications and ointments.

Sufficient warmth and rainfall made Palestine a suitable country for the cultivation of grapevines. Though cultivated on the lowlands, vines were frequently planted on the sides of hills. Rocks had to be removed from the soil prior to planting. The vineyard itself was surrounded by a stone wall as protection against animals, and a watchtower was erected. The wine press and vat were also part of the vineyard. The vines themselves had to be cared for by pruning, loosening of the soil, and weeding. Ordinarily they were allowed to grow and spread out upon the ground; the clusters were propped up by means of forked sticks. The harvest time occurred in September and October. Grapes were eaten in their natural state or dried for raisins and raisin cakes. Most commonly, however, they were pressed and the juice extracted. This was taken in its natural state, boiled into a thick syrup, or fermented into wine. Naturally wine varied in quality, depending on the quality of the grapes used to make it. Wine was consumed in full strength or mixed with water. A strong intoxicating beverage could be made of wine mixed with spices. Wine served also for medicinal purposes and as a drug, mixed with myrrh.

Other Agriculture and Animal Husbandry. While grain, olives, and grapes were the main products of Palestinian agriculture, other important products also were grown. There were figs, dates, pomegranates, and vegetables.

Figs were of two kinds: the ordinary, commonly known fig and the sycamore fig. The ordinary fig tree is mentioned in the Bible as a symbol of prosperity and security: "every man under his vine and his fig tree" (3 Kgs 5.5; Mi 4.4; etc.). Its fruits are eaten ripe or else dried and pressed into cakes. Sycamore figs, though little esteemed in modern times, were very important in Biblical times. Planted on the lowlands and the plains to escape the dangers of frost, they apparently grew in great abundance. The sycamore fig required special care, since the fruit would spoil if the fig were not punctured to let the insect that is found inside it escape; the Prophet Amos was "a dresser of sycamores" (Am 7.14). This tree was often planted along the roadside for shade (cf. Lk 19.4).

Dates are never mentioned by name in the Bible, but the frequent references to the palm tree, which bears fruit only in the subtropical climate of the Jordan Valley, make it clear that this too formed part of the Israelite diet. Dates were eaten in their natural state and were also used for making wine. The pomegranate, an orangelike fruit filled with seeds, was much cultivated. It served mainly for its juice and for the making of wine.

Pastoral activities were concerned with the raising of cattle, sheep, and goats. Although the daily diet of the Israelite consisted primarily of agricultural products, meat was not totally lacking. In addition, such important necessities of life as clothing, milk, butter, and cheese were supplied by these animals. At times some of the animals were used as pack and draft animals. Cows, goats, and especially sheep played an important part in the liturgical rites of Israel. The main areas in which they were to be found were in northern Transjordan, Moab, Judea, and the northern part of the *Negeb.

Commerce. As far as trade is concerned, most of it was internal rather than external and international. To be sure, more grain, wine, and oil was produced than was needed, and these served as important items of trade. They were exchanged with Tyre and the Phoenicians for manufactured articles, tools, and textiles. Within the country itself, the market was a common affair. Markets were to be found at the city gates, where all transactions of importance were carried out. Transactions involved locally produced food stuffs and manufactured articles, such as tools, items of luxury, household utensils, pottery, and ornaments.

The products of the land therefore served as sustenance for the people and as items of trade. The natives, as an agricultural and pastoral people, knew the value of what they possessed and its importance for their daily existence. But above all, these things had also a religious significance. The Israelites saw in the products of the land the blessings and gifts of God.

Bibliography: A. C. BOUQUET, *Every Day Life in N.T. Times* (New York 1954). E. W. HEATON, *Every Day Life in O.T. Times* (New York 1956). D. BALY, *The Geography of the Bible* (New York 1957), esp. 83–108. G. CORNFELD, ed., *Pictorial Biblical Encyclopedia* (New York 1964) 17–30, 687–691.

[F. SEPER]

6. NATURAL HISTORY

The study of the natural history of Palestine is limited here to botany and zoology of the Holy Land, therefore, to a description and classification of its flora (or plant life) and its fauna (or animal life).

FLORA

After a description of the plant life of the Holy Land in the Biblical period, tables are given of the plants and their products that are mentioned in the Hebrew OT and the Greek NT, followed by an account of the flora of modern Palestine according to its phytogeographic areas.

Plant Life in the Biblical Period. It is accepted by most modern scholars that no radical change has occurred in the climate of the Holy Land since the beginnings of recorded history. This conclusion is based upon evidence from many sources. In the literary realm, the descriptions of the land found in the Bible, the *Mishnah, and the *Talmud show that the seasons and agricultural variations were identical then with those of the present day.

Forests. Contrary to the commonly accepted theory, studies have shown that the forest was not an important factor in the Biblical landscape. Even before the conquest by *Josue (Joshua), son of Nun, the land was settled in noticeable density, and the major portion of the regions suitable for agriculture was seeded or planted and cultivated intensively. These conditions precluded the existence of forests. In the rocky mountainous regions there were, indeed, woods, but these were not protected from man or beast. In the Biblical and Talmudic descriptions of the land there is very little mention of forests. Individual trees that served cultic purposes or had been associated with important events are noted. Yet, since the Bible mentions the existence of wild animals, it can be deduced that the land of Israel was forested to some extent. These animals inhabited the deserts, the Jordan Valley, and the forests of *Basan (Bashan) and Mt. *Hermon, and from these regions they came out to the settlements. Widespread forests existed principally in Basan and in *Lebanon, and these regions supplied lumber for palaces, temples, and other large buildings. Extensive woods called the Forest of Ephraim existed in *Galaad (Gilead), where the war between David and Absalom took place (2 Sm 18.8). Perhaps this was the forest referred to by Josue when he advised the landless sons of Joseph to clear the forest and settle there (Jos 17.15). The accepted interpretation, however, is that the reference is to the forest on the mountains of Ephraim in Samaria.

The development of a forest in a region of sufficient rainfall usually follows the destruction of agriculture there. This idea is expressed several times in the Scriptures (e.g., Os 2.14; Mi 3.12; Jer 26.18), and actually, during all the periods of settlement on the land, there was continual struggle between the sown and cultivated tracts on the one hand and the forest and wasteland on

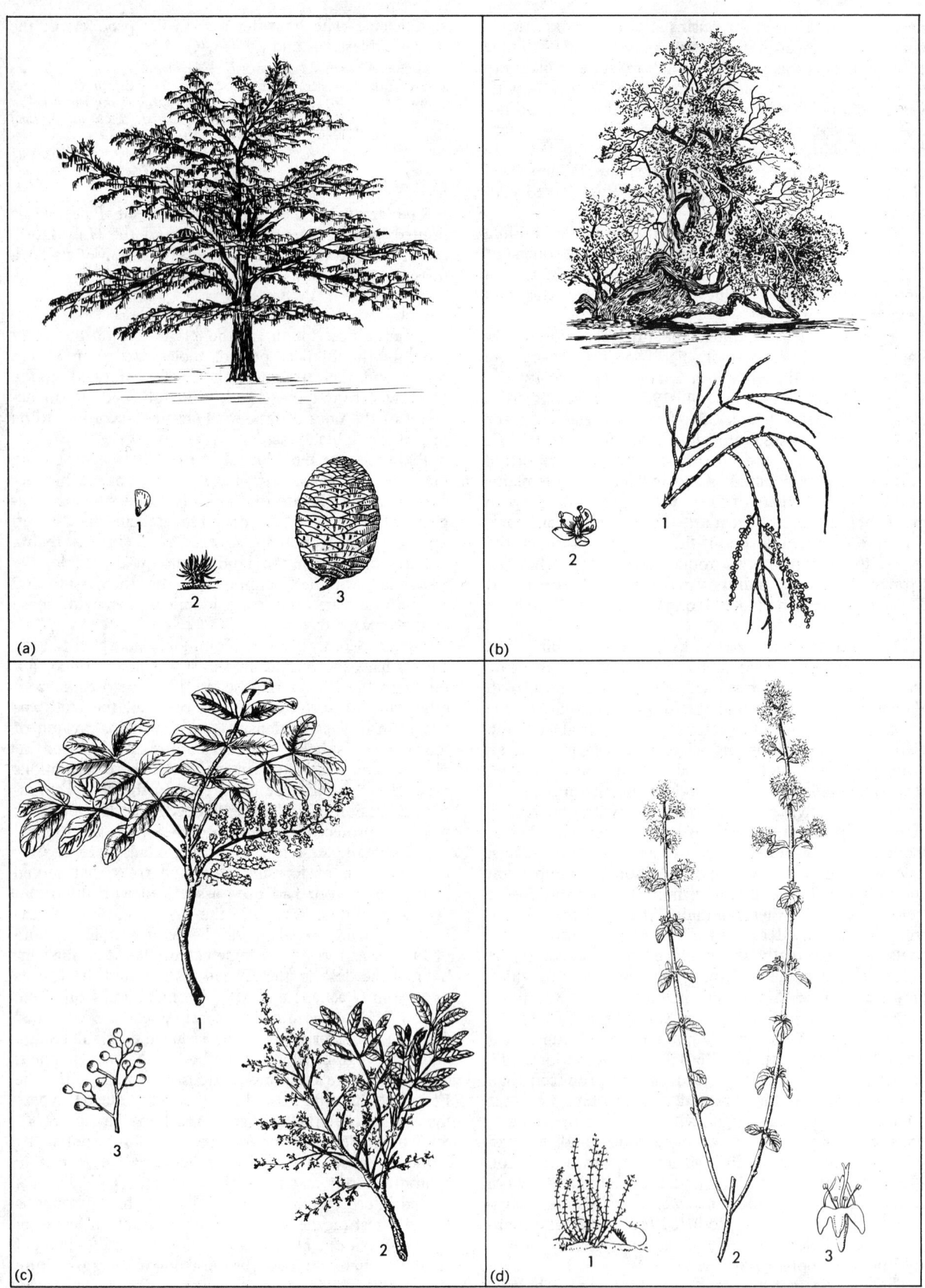

Fig. 4. Palestine flora: (a) Cedar (Cedrus libani), (1) seed, (2) spiny leaves, (3) cone. (b) Tamarisk (Tamarix articulata), (1) flowering twig, (2) flower. (c) Terebinth (Pistacia at-lantica), (1) twig with stamen flowers, (2) twig with pistil flowers, (3) fruits. (d) Syrian marjoram (Majorana syriaca), (1) whole plant, (2) twig, (3) flower.

the other. During periods of war and postwar destruction the cultivated areas were deserted, and wild grasses, bushes, and trees thrived; but in peacetime these areas were reclaimed by agricultural settlement.

Grazing Lands. Following Josue's conquest of Canaan and during the period of the early Judges, the cultivation of the terraced hills was destroyed, and in its place the wild flora flourished, as the Bible had warned (Dt 7.22; see also Is 17.9), and as a result of the destruction of agriculture, the grazing lands were extended (see also Is 7.28). This process recurred repeatedly during the various periods of peace and war in Biblical times. The major wealth of the Holy Lands consisted of fruits and grains. Although it was described as a "land of milk and honey," one cannot assume from this that the pasture land ("milk") exceeded in extent the land used for cultivation. From the Scriptures it is evident that, while extensive pasture lands existed on the east side of the Jordan and in Basan, on the west side of the Jordan livestock-raising existed only on a small scale, and the herds were fed mostly from the stubble of the grainfields.

Dependence on Rainfall. The agriculture of the Holy Land depended on natural rainfall; this fact is emphasized in the Bible by the comparing of the land of Israel, (at the south of Mt. Hermon), of the Yarkon (at Aphec, which "drinks in rain from the heavens,") with Egypt, which is completely dependent on irrigation (Dt 11.10–12). In this connection came the warning regarding the withholding of rain as a consequence of sin (Dt 11.17). Years of famine caused by lack of rain are often noted in the Bible. One verse describes Israel as a "land of streams of water, with springs and fountains welling up in the hills and valleys" (Dt 8.7). From this some might conclude that there have been changes in the land since those days, but there is no basis for such a conclusion. There are still many springs there (about 800 of them having been counted), but most of them have a very limited flow. Only the sources of the Dan Rās el-'Ain), and of the Na'aman (at 'Ayūn el-Baṣṣ 7 miles southeast of Accho) supply in normal years more than a cubic meter of water a second. Some 40 others supply between 100 to 1,000 liters per second (the majority of them being in the Huleh and in the Beisan Valley); all the others are minor. The author of the Letter of *Aristeas exaggerates in evaluating the Jordan as the most important factor in the agriculture of the Land of Israel. Flavius Josephus heaps praise on the irrigation of Jericho (*Bell.Jud.* 4.8.3) and the Plain of Genasar (*ibid.* 3.10.6), but he is correct in his conclusion that the most fertile part of the land of Israel is the "land of thirst [for rain] according to its nature" (*ibid.* 3.3.4). Indeed, farming that depends on rainfall has to a large extent determined the landscape of Israel.

The cultivated areas in ancient times were not different from those of today. The deserts described in the Bible include in their boundaries the areas of desert and wasteland of the present day. The *Negeb was a grazing land, though in rainy years its northern parts could be seeded (Gn 26.12). Here and there in the Bible is mentioned the growth of certain wild trees in specific localities: sycamore trees in the foothills (3 Kgs 10.27); willows along the brooks (Is 44.4); tamarisks in the desert (Jer 17.6); wild jujubes in swampy jungles (Jb 40.21); etc. Of forest trees, mention is made especially of the oak, the terebinth, and the storax. The conifers grew especially in Basan and Lebanon; cedar, juniper, pine, and cypress are mentioned in Isaia as species that will bloom in the desert and wasteland in the time to come (Is 41.19; 60.13).

The praise of Israel in Dt 8.8 refers to its seven basic farm products: it is a "land of wheat and barley, of vines and fig trees and pomegranates, of olive oil and of honey." Three groups are included: of the grains are wheat and barley, of the fruits are grapes, figs, and pomegranates, and of important produce from trees are oil from olives and honey (i.e., syrup) from dates.

Plants of the Bible. The Bible mentions about 100 names of plants, most of which grew in Israel, and it is relatively easy to identify almost all of them by studying the descriptions of them as given in the Scriptures, the Mishnah, and the Talmud, as well as by philology, etymology, and a comparison with the flora of modern Palestine. There are names of flora in the Bible that identify whole groups, *šāmîr wešayit* (thorn bushes of all kinds: Is 5.6; 9.17) and *qôṣ wedardar* (thistles of all kinds: Gn 3.18; Os 10.8). The Bible mentions mainly plants that either have economic importance or that suitably illustrate a parable. Doubtless there were other important plants and trees that the Bible had no occasion to mention, such as the carob, which is referred to only in Lk 15.16. The accompanying table of plants lists the plants of the Bible and their scientific identification.

PLANTS AND PRODUCTS OF PLANTS MENTIONED IN THE BIBLE

English name	Scientific name	Hebrew and Greek names	Reference in the Bible
		Old Testament	
Acacia	*Acacia albida*	*šiṭṭâ*	Ex 26.15; Is 41.19; etc.
Almond	*Prunus amygdalus*	*lûz*	Gn 30.37
		šāqēd	Nm 17.23; Jer 1.11; etc.
Aloeswood	*Aquilaria agallocha*	*'ahālîm*	Nm 24.6; Prv 7.17
		'ahālôt	Ps 44(45).9; Ct 4.14
		'algummîm	2 Chr 2.7; 9.10–11
		'almuggîm	3 Kgs 10.11–12
Apple	*Pirus malus*	*tappûaḥ*	Jl 1.12; Ct 2.3; etc.
Balm	*Commiphora opobalsamum*	*bōśem*	Ct 2.1; 5.1; etc.
		nāṭāp	Ex 30.34
		ṣŏrî	Gn 37.25; 43.11; etc.

PLANTS AND PRODUCTS OF PLANTS MENTIONED IN THE BIBLE—*Continued*

English name	Scientific name	Hebrew and Greek names	Reference in the Bible
			Old Testament
Barley	*Hordeum sativum*	*śeʿôrâ*	Ex 9.31; Dt 8.8; etc.
Barley, Two-rowed	*Hordeum distichum*	*śôrâ*	Is 28.25
Bdellium	*Commiphora africana*	*beḏōlaḥ*	Gn 2.12; Nm 11.7
Bean, Broad	*Vicia faba*	*pôl*	2 Sm 17.28; Ez 4.9
Boxthorn	*Lycium europaeum*	*ʾāṭāḏ*	Gn 50.10–11; Jgs 9.14–15; etc.
Broom Plant, *Retama*	*Retama roetam*	*rōtem*	3 Kgs 19.4–5; Jb 30.4; etc.
Calamus, Indian Sweet	*Cymbopogon martini*	⎰ *qāneh haṭṭôb* ⎰ *qenēh-bōśem* ⎱ *qāneh*	Jer 6.20 / Ex 30.23 / Is 43.24; Ct 4.14; etc.
Cane, Biflorate	*Saccharum biflorum*	*ʾagmôn*	Is 9.13; 58.5; etc.
Caper Berry	*Capparis spinosa*	*ʾăḇiyyônâ*	Eccl 12.5
Castor-oil Plant	*Ricinus communis*	*qîqāyôn*	Jon 4.6–10
Cattail	*Typha angustata*	*sûp*	Ex 2.3, 5; Is 19.6; etc.
Cedar	*Cedrus libani*	*ʾerez*	Is 2.13; Am 2.9; etc.
Chick-pea	*Cicer arietinum*	*ḥāmîṣ*	Is 30.24
Cinnamon, Ceylonese	*Cinnamon zeylanicum*	*qinnāmôn*	Ex 30.23; Prv 7.17; etc.
Cinnamon, Chinese	*Cinnamon cassia*	*qiddâ*	Ex 30.24; Ez 27.19
Cinnamon, Indo-Chinese	*Cinnamon laurei*	*qeṣîʿâ*	Ps 44(45).9
Citron	*Citrus medica*	*ʿēṣ hāḏār*	Lv 23.40
Coriander	*Coriandrum sativum*	*gaḏ*	Ex 16.31; Nm 11.7
Cotton	*Gossypium herbaceum*	*karpas*	Est 1.6
Crocus, Saffron	*Crocus sativus*	*karkôm*	Ct 4.14
Cucumber, Bitter	*Citrullus colocynthis*	*paqqūʿâ*	4 Kgs 4.39
Cumin	*Cuminum cyminum*	*kammôn*	Is 28.25, 27
Cypress	*Cupressus sempervirens*	⎰ *gōper* ⎱ *teʾaššûr*	Gn 6.14 / Is 41.19; 60.13; etc.
Daffodil, Sea	*Pancratium maritimum*	*ḥăḇaṣṣelet*	Is 35.1; Ct 2.1
Durra	*Sorghum cernuum*	*dōḥan*	Ez 4.9
Ebony	*Diospyros ebenaster*	*hobnîm*	Ez 27.15
Emmer	*Triticum dicoccum*	*kussemet*	Ex 9.32; Is 28.25; etc.
Fennelflower	*Nigella sativa*	*qeṣaḥ*	Is 28.25, 27
Fig	*Ficus carica*	*teʾēnâ*	Nm 20.5; Dt 8.8; etc.
Fig, Sycamore	*Ficus sycomorus*	*šiqmâ*	3 Kgs 10.27; Is 9.9; etc.
Flax	*Linum usitatissimum*	⎰ *pēšet* ⎱ *pištâ*	Jos 2.6; Os 2.7, 11; etc. / Ex 9.31; Is 42.3; etc.
Frankincense	*Boswellia carteri*	*leḇōnâ*	Ex 30.34; Is 60.6; etc.
Galbanum	*Ferula galbaniflua*	*ḥelbenâ*	Ex 30.34
Garlic	*Allium sativum*	*šûm*	Nm 11.5
Grapevine	*Vitis vinifera*	*gepen*	Gn 40.9–10; Nm 20.5; etc.
Hemlock, Poison	*Conium maculatum*	*rōʾš*	Dt 29.17; Os 10.4
Henna	*Lawsonia alba*	*kōper*	Ct 1.14; 4.13; etc.
Jujube, Wild	*Zizyphus spina-Christi*	*ṣeʾělîm*	Jb 40.21–22
Juniper, ⎰ Savin ⎱ High	*Juniperus sabina* ⎱ *Juniperus excelsa*	*berôš* ⎱ *berôt*	Is 14.8; 37.24; etc. / Ct 1.17
Labdanum	⎰ *Cistus creticus* ⎱ *Cistus ladanum*	*lōṭ*	Gn 37.25; 43.11
Laurel	*Laurus nobilis*	*ʾōren*	Is 44.14
Leek	*Allium porrum*	*ḥāṣîr*	Nm 11.5
Lentils	*Lens esculenta*	*ʿăḏāšîm*	Gn 25.34; 2 Sm 17.28; etc.
Lily, Madonna	*Lilium candidum*	*šôšannâ*	Os 14.6; Ct 6.2–3; etc.
Mallow	*Malva* sp.	*ḥallāmût*	Jb 6.6
Mandrake	*Mandragora officinarum*	*dûḏāʾîm*	Gn 30.14–16; Ct 7.14
Maple(?; or Pine?)	*Acer*(?; or *Pinus*?)	*tiḏhār*	Is 41.19; 60.13
Marjoram, Syrian	*Mojorana syriaca*	*ʾēzôḇ*	Ex 12.22; Lv 14.4,6; etc.
Mastic	*Pistacia lentiscus*	*bākāʾ*	2 Sm 5.23–24; Ps 83(84).7
Muskmelon, Chate	*Cucumis melo Chate*	*qiššūʾâ*	Nm 11.5
Myrrh	⎰ *Commiphora schimperi* ⎱ *Commiphora abyssinica*	*mōr*	Ex 30.23; Ct 1.13; etc.
Myrtle	*Myrtus communis*	⎰ *hăḏas* ⎱ *ʿēṣ ʿāḇôt*	Is 41.19; 55.13; etc. / Lv 23.40; Neh 8.15; etc.

PLANTS AND PRODUCTS OF PLANTS MENTIONED IN THE BIBLE—*Continued*

English name	Scientific name	Hebrew and Greek names	Reference in the Bible
Old Testament			
Narcissus	*Narcissus tazetta*	šôšannat hā'amāqîm	Ct 2.1
Nard (Spikenard)	*Nardostachys jatamansi*	nērd	Ct 1.12; 4.13–14; etc.
Nettle	*Urtica* sp.	sirpad	Is 55.13
Oak	{ *Quercus ithaburensis* { *Quercus calliprinos* }	'allôn	Gn 35.8; Is 2.13; etc.
Olive	*Olea europea*	zait	Dt 6.11; 8.8; etc.
Onion	*Allium cepa*	bāṣāl	Nm 11.5
Palm, Date	*Phoenix dactylifera*	tāmār	Ex 15.27; Nm 33.9; etc.
Papyrus	*Cyperus papyrus*	gōme'	Ex 2.3; Is 18.2; etc.
Pine, Aleppo	*Pinus halepensis*	'ēṣ šemen	3 Kgs 6.23; Is 41.19; etc.
Pine, Stone(?)	*Pinus pinea*(?)	tirzâ	Is 44.14
Pistachio	*Pistacia vera*	boṭnîm	Gn 43.11
Plane, Oriental	*Platanus orientalis*	'ermôn, 'armôn	Gn 30.37; Ez 31.8
Pomegranate	*Punica granatum*	rimmôn	Nm 20.5; Dt 8.8; etc.
Poplar	*Populus euphratica*	ṣapṣāpâ	Ez 17.5
Raspberry, Wild	*Rubus sanctus*	sᵉneh	Ex 3.2–4; Dt 33.16
Reed, Ditch	*Phragmites communis*	qāneh	Is 19.6; 35.7; etc.
Rocket, Garden	*Eruca sativa*	'ōrōt	4 Kgs 4.39
Saltbush	*Atriplex halimus*	mallûaḥ	Jb 30.4
Storax	*Styrax officinalis*	libneh	Gn 30.37; Ct 4.11; etc.
Tamarisk	{ *Tamarix* sp.	'ar'ār	Jer 17.6
	{ *Tamarix articulata* { *Tamarix jordanis* }	'ēšel	Gn 21.33; 1 Sm 22.6; 31.13
Terebinth	{ *Pistacia palaestina* { *Pistacia atlantica* }	'ēlâ	Gn 35.4; Os 4.13; etc.
Thistle	*Centaurea* sp.	dardar	Gn 3.18; Os 10.8
Thistle, Golden	*Scolymus maculatus*	ḥôaḥ	Os 9.6; Prv 26.9; etc.
Thistle, Silybum	*Silybum marianum*	qimmôš	Is 34.13; Os 9.6; etc.
Thistle, Sow	*Sonchus oleraceus*	mᵉrōrîm	Ex 12.8; Lam 3.15; etc.
Thorn	*Calycotome villosa*	ḥārûl	So 2.9; Jb 30.7; etc.
Thorn, Camel	*Alhagi maurorum*	na'ăṣûṣ	Is 7.19; 55.13
Thorn, Gundelia	*Gundelia tournefortii*	galgal	Is 17.13; Ps 82(83).14
Thorn, Poterium	*Poterium spinosum*	sîrîm	Is 34.13; Os 2.8; etc.
Thorn, Prosopis	*Prosopis farcata*	nahălōlîm	Is 7.19
Tragacanth	{ *Astragalus gummifer* { *Astragalus tragacantha* }	nᵉkō't	Gn 37.25; 43.11
Walnut	*Juglans regia*	'ĕgôz	Ct 6.11
Watermelon	*Citrullus vulgaris*	'abaṭṭîaḥ	Nm 11.5
Weed, Ridolfia	*Ridolfia segetum*	bo'šâ	Jb 31.40
Wheat	{ *Triticum durum* { *Triticum vulgare* { *Triticum turgidum* }	ḥiṭṭâ	Ex 9.32; Dt 8.8; etc.
Willow	*Salix* sp.	'ărābâ	Lv 23.40; Ps 136(137).2; etc.
Wormwood	*Artemisia* sp.	la'ănâ	Dt 29.17; Jer 9.14; etc.
New Testament			
Amomum	*Amomum subulatum*	ἄμωμον	Ap 18.13
Carob	*Ceratonia siliqua*	κεράτιον	Lk 15.16 (pod)
Cinnamon	*Cinnamon zeylanicum*	κιννάμωμον	Ap 18.13
Citronwood	*Callitris quadrivalvis*	ξύλον θύϊνον	Ap 18.12
Cumin	*Cuminum cyminum*	κύμινον	Mt 23.23
Darnel	*Lolium temulentum*	ζιζάνιον	Mt 13.25–30, 38–40
Dill	*Anethum graveolens*	ἄνηθον	Mt 23.23
Fig	*Ficus carica*	συκῆ	Mt 24.32; Jn 1.48; etc.
Fig, Sycamore	*Ficus sycomorus*	συκομορέα	Lk 19.4
Frankincense	*Boswellia carteri*	λίβανος	Mt 2.11
Mint	*Mentha*	ἡδύοσμον	Mt 23.23; Lk 11.42
Mulberry, Black	*Morus nigra*	συκάμινος	Lk 17.6

PLANTS AND PRODUCTS OF PLANTS MENTIONED IN THE BIBLE—*Continued*

English name	Scientific name	Hebrew and Greek names	Reference in the Bible
New Testament			
Mustard	{*Brassica nigra* / *Sinapis alba*}	σίναπι	Mt 13.31; 17.20
Myrrh	*Commiphora*	σμύρνα	Mt 2.11
Nard (Spikenard)	*Nardostachys jatamansi*	νάρδος	Mk 14.3; Jn 12.3
Rue	{*Ruta bracteosa* / *Ruta graveolens*}	πήγανον	Lk 11.42
Thistle	*Centaurea* sp.	τρίβολος	Mt 7.16; Heb 6.8
Thorn	*Alhagi; Poterium;* etc.	ἄκανθα	Mt 7.16; 27.29; etc.

Flora of Modern Israel according to Phytogeographic Areas. Israel is very rich in plant species, their number reaching to more than 2,000. The abundance of species is due to several causes: the variegated history of the flora, dating back to early geologic periods, the variation in topography, and, above all, the fact that the country provides a meeting ground for three vegetation belts—the Mediterranean, the Irano-Turanic, and the Saharo-Sindic.

Mediterranean Vegetation. Included are areas on both sides of the Jordan, where the amount of rainfall is more than 350 millimeters (13.8 inches), which makes cultivation of the land possible either summer or winter. In this zone the flora of the mountain areas differs from that of the seashore.

The mountain area was the most important for ancient agriculture. Cultivation of the land pushed back the forests that had abounded there in prehistoric times. At present (1965) there still remain forests and groves containing such trees as the Aleppo pine (*Pinus halepensis*) and its oft-associated species, the common oak (*Quercus calliprinos*), and the Palestine terebinth (*Pistacia palaestina*), several other species of trees, as well as many bushes and shrubs. This type of forest is still widespread in Galaad, and its traces remain in Upper Galilee, the Carmel Range, Samaria, and Juda. Such forests develop well on soil developed from Cenomanian and Eocene limestone.

Another type of Mediterranean forest is that of the Thabor oak (*Quercus ithaburensis*), with which is associated the Atlantic terebinth (*Pistacia atlantica*). This type is found in the western part of Lower Galilee, in Golan, and in the Huleh Valley. Such a forest was formerly in Sharon, but it was destroyed to make way for agriculture and pasture land.

Most of the groves in the land consist of the common oak (*Quercus calliprinos*) and the Palestine terebinth (*Pistacia palaestina*). As a result of the cutting of timber and the gnawing of goats, the trees are in the form of bushes. Such woods are spread on the mountains at an altitude of 1,000 to 4,000 feet.

On the foothills at the west range of the mountains of Galilee and on Mt. Carmel are spread the carob (*Ceratonia siliqua*) and the mastic (*Pistacia lentiscus*). Occasionally this type of flora is found on the sandy limestone hills near Caesarea and on the sands near Netanya. All these types of flora are accompanied by many types of bushes, perennial and annual. Another type of flora is that of the so-called garigue, scrubland with bushes not above the height of a man. Here the *Calycotome* thorn bush and various species of rockroses (*Cistus*) and salvia predominate.

On the unforested Mediterranean shore is found a distinctive group of low plants, wooded or grassy. Very prevalent is the Poterium thorn bush (*Poterium spinosum*), which is important in the prevention of soil erosion on the slopes of the hills. In the places where this flora has been destroyed, the land has been swept away by the winds and the rain.

Along the Mediterranean shore are sandy soil, mixtures of sandy clay and sandy chalk. Such soils are not favorable to plant development because of their poor organic composition and meager ability to hold rain water. Here grow deep-rooted plants, those of the steppe and the desert that can thrive on a small amount of water, as well as annuals that have a short period of growth. These plants are in constant danger of being covered by shifting dunes or undercut by winds. But there are species here that have developed means of defense against the force of the wind, particularly the *Retama* broom plant (*Retama roetam*) and the Gallic tamarisk (*Tamarix gallica*) Here grow species that are not sensitive to the salty spray of the sea or to the saline sand. There are also tropical trees such as the sycamore fig (*Ficus sycomorus*) and the wild jujube (*Zizyphus spina-Christi*).

Irano-Turanic Vegetation. This is centered in the northern Negeb, the Judean Desert, and the highlands of Transjordan. The climate is dry and the amount of rainfall 200 to 300 millimeters (8–12 inches), within the limits for stable growth. In this area there are almost no natural woodlands. Its soils are semiarid or loess. One finds sparse groups of trees or bushes; the common type is wormwood (*Artemisia herba-alba*).

Saharo-Sindic Vegetation. This type covers the largest territory, but it is poorest in species. It includes the southern Negeb, the Araba, and the desert regions of Edom and Moab. The amount of rainfall is less than 200 millimeters (8 inches) and is usually far below this level. The rains are concentrated in a very short winter. The soil is not fertile. It is comprised mainly of gravel and rocks; trees are found only in the bottom of the wadies, and the plant cover is very sparse, the typical type being the *Zygophyllum dumosum* bush. In the sandy regions plants are more plentiful, with species of *Haloxylon* and *Retama* predominating. In this area there are large salt deposits, especially in the lower Jordan Valley and in the Araba. There are dense growths of saline flora, including species of *Atriplex* and *Salicornia*. Near fresh-water springs are oases where a tropical flora thrives, of which acacia and wild jujube are typical.

Hydrophilic Vegetation. Throughout the country plants are found that grow alongside bodies of water, swamps, river banks, and springs. Among the trees in this category are the poplar (*Populus euphratica*), tamarisk (*Tamarix jordanis*), Oriental plane (*Platanus orientalis*), and willow. At the side of every body of water are reeds and cattails, and in the Huleh swamps (which have now been drained) the papyrus was formerly common.

Cultivated Plants and Associated Species. In modern times essentially the same crops are being raised as in the ancient era; but in fruits the emphasis has moved away from the sweet fruits that are rich in calories, such as figs and dates, which were highly valued in ancient times, to the juicy fruits, especially the fruit trees of the *Rosaceae* family, such as the apple, pear, plum, and peach. Hundreds of new species, such as the orange, have been brought in; many of them originated in the New World. Especially numerous are the kinds of ornamental flora that have been brought to the land from countries all over the world.

Hundreds of species of weeds are associated with the cultivated plants. These are more closely connected with the plants that they accompany than to any specific locale. Among them are species established in the country from antiquity, whose seeds are found in archeological excavations along with the seeds of cultivated plants, and others that have been introduced in recent times along with the new plants.

FAUNA

After a brief description of the Palestinian fauna in the prehistoric period, lists of the Biblical fauna are given; the changes in the Holy Land from Biblical to modern times are then discussed, with an account of the zoogeography of modern Palestine, and finally a few words are said on the domestic animals of ancient Israel.

Palestinian Fauna in the Prehistoric Period. The natural history of Israel reaches far back in time. The most important and dynamic period was the Pleistocene era, when changes appeared in the fauna of the area,

especially as a result of invasions from other areas. This fauna was similar to that which is now found on the savannas of East Africa. Bones of the wart hog, hippopotamus, rhinoceros, striped hyena, and many different species of gazelles other than those currently found in Palestine have been discovered. Bones also of elephants and mastodons have been found in the Lower Pleistocene. Later there occurred a migration of animals from India and Central Asia, among which were wild cattle, wild horses, wild asses, gazelles, wolves, and badgers. There was only limited migration of northern animals following the Ice Age in Europe. During the Upper Pleistocene a tropical climate prevailed in Palestine. After this there occurred a period of drought, which brought about the disappearance of the tropical fauna. By the end of the Stone Age, the Holy Land was already the habitat of the fauna that is described in the Bible and has persisted to recent times. This is supporting evidence for the theory that since the Stone Age there have not been radical climatic changes in the country.

Biblical Fauna. About 120 animal names appear in the Bible (not including synonyms). They may be grouped systematically as follows. Mammals (39 names) may be subdivided according to cloven-hoofed and ruminating (13), cloven-hoofed nonruminating (3), single-hoofed (4), carnivora (8), rodents (4), and other orders (7). Birds (38 names) may be divided according to ritually clean fowl (9), birds of prey (diurnal) (5), vulturine birds (4), birds of prey (nocturnal) (11), and birds of other orders (9). Other fauna includes reptiles and similar creatures (13) and insects and other small creatures (20).

From this list it can be seen that mammals, birds, and reptiles are the most adequately represented in the Bible. Of the 75 species of mammals in modern Palestine (including domestic cattle), about half are mentioned. Of the 350 species of birds, 38 are mentioned, and of the 80 species of reptiles, 12 are mentioned in the Bible. It must be stressed that the references to these animals (as also to the flora) are incidental, and they are cited to illustrate laws of ritual cleanliness or are used symbolically or allegorically. The occurrence of so many names demonstrates the highly developed perception of the scriptural writers in their understanding of the phenomena of nature. It is thought possible in the following table to identify in a majority of cases the names of the Biblical fauna with established species.

ANIMALS OF THE BIBLE

English name	Scientific name	Biblical Hebrew name	Reference
		Mammals	
Addax	*Addax nasomaculatus*	dîšôn	Dt 14.5
Ass	*Equus asinus*	ḥămôr (male)	Gn 12.16; 24.35; etc.
		'ātôn (female)	Gn 12.16; 32.16; etc.
		'ayir	Gn 32.16; Jgs 10.4; etc.
Ass, Arabian Wild	*Equus hemionus onager*	'ārôd	Jb 39.5; Jer 48.6
Ass, Syrian Wild	*Equus hemionus hemihippus*	pere'	Jer 14.6; Jb 6.5; etc.
Bat	*Chiroptera*	'ăṭallēp	Lv 11.19; Is 2.20; etc.
Bear, Syrian	*Ursus arctus syriacus*	dōb	1 Sm 17.34–37; Os 13.8; etc.

ANIMALS OF THE BIBLE—*Continued*

English name	Scientific name	Biblical Hebrew name	Reference
Mammals			
Bison, European	*Bison bonasus*	t^e'ô	Dt 14.5
		tô'	Is 51.20
Boar, Wild	*Sus scrofa*	ḥăzîr miyya'ar	Ps 79(80).14
Buffalo, Water	*Bos bubalus*	m^erî'	2 Sm 6.13; Is 1.11; etc.
Camel	*Camelus dromedarius*	gāmāl	Lv 11.4; Jgs 6.5; etc.
		beker (young male)	Is 60.6
		bikrâ (young female)	Jer 2.23
Cattle, Bovine	*Bos taurus*	bāqār	Gn 13.5; 18.7; etc.
		šôr	Gn 32.6; Ex 20.17; etc.
		'ălāpîm (oxen)	Dt 7.13; 28.4; etc.
		'abbîr (bull)	Is 34.7; Jer 46.17; etc.
		par (steer)	Gn 32.16; Jgs 6.25; etc.
		pārâ (cow)	Gn 32.16; etc.
		'ēgel (young male)	Lv 9.2; Is 11.6; etc.
		'eglâ (young female)	Gn 15.9; Jgs 14.18; etc.
Coney, Syrian	*Procavia syriaca*	šāpān	Lv 11.5; Prv 30.26; etc.
Deer, Fallow	*Cervus dama*	yaḥmûr	Dt 14.5; 3 Kgs 5.3
Deer, Roe	*Cervus capreolus*	'ayyāl	Dt 12.5; Ct 2.9; etc.
		'ayyālâ (female)	Jer 14.5; Ct 2.7; etc.
Dog	*Canis familiaris*	keleb	Ex 22.30; Jgs 7.5; etc.
Fox	*Vulpes vulpes*	šû'āl (see also jackal)	Jgs 15.4; Ez 13.4; etc.
Gazelle	*Gazella* sp.	ṣ^{e}bî	Dt 12.15; Ct 2.9; etc.
		ṣ^{e}biyyâ (female)	Ct 4.5; 7.4
Goat	*Capra hircus*	'ēz	Lv 7.23; Ct 4.1; etc.
		śā'îr (male)	Gn 37.31; Lv 4.23; etc.
		ś^e'îrâ (female)	Lv 4.28; 5.6
		tayiš (male)	Gn 30.35; Prv 30.31; etc.
		'attûdîm (mature male)	Gn 31.10; Jer 50.8; etc.
		g^{e}dî (kid)	Gn 38.17; Jgs 6.19; etc.
Goat, Wild	*Capra aegagrus*	'aqqô	Dt 14.5
Hare	*Lepus* sp.	'arnebet	Lv 11.6; Dt 14.7
Hippopotamus	*Hippopotamus amphibius*	b^{e}hēmôt	Jb 40.15–23
Horse	*Equus caballus orientalis*	sûs	Gn 47.17; Ex 9.3; etc.
		pārāš	Ez 27.14; Na 3.3; etc.
Hyena	*Hyena hyena*	ṣābûa'	Jer 12.9; Sir 13.18; etc.
Ibex	*Capra nubiana*	yā'ēl	Jb 39.1; Ps 103(104).18
		ya'ălâ	Prv 5.19
Jackal	*Canis aureus*	'iyyîm (see also fox)	Is 13.22; 34.14
Leopard	*Felis pardus tullianus*	nāmēr	Is 11.6; Jer 13.23; etc.
Lion	*Felis leo*	'ărî	Is 38.13; Am 3.12; etc.
		'aryeh	Mi 5.7; Jb 4.10; etc.
		lābî'	Is 5.29; Os 13.8; etc.
		layiš	Jb 4.11; Prv 30.30; etc.
		k^{e}pîr (young lion)	Ez 19.3; Jb 4.10; etc.
		šaḥal (young lion)	Os 5.14; Jb 4.10; etc.
		gûr (lion cub)	Ez 19.2; Na 2.12; etc.
Mole Rat	*Spalax ehrenbergi*	ḥăparpārôt	Is 2.20
Monkey	*Simia*	qôpîm	3 Kgs 10.22; 2 Chr 9.21
Mouse	*Microtus guenthri* *Mus musculus*	'akbār	Lv 11.29; Is 66.17; etc.
Mule	*Equus asinus mulus*	pered	Is 66.20; 4 Kgs 5.17; etc.
		pirdâ (female)	3 Kgs 33.38, 44
		rekes (?)	Mi 1.13; Est 8.10; etc.
Oryx	*Oryx leucoryx*	zemer	Dt 14.5
Ox, Wild	*Bos primigenius*	r^e'ēm	Nm 23.22; Is 34.7; etc.
		rêm	Jb 39.9–10
Rat	*Rattus rattus*	ḥōled	Lv 11.29

ANIMALS OF THE BIBLE—*Continued*

English name	Scientific name	Biblical Hebrew name	Reference
		Mammals	
Sheep	*Ovis vignei platyura*	ṣō'n	Gn 4.2; 1 Sm 25.2; etc.
		śeh	Ex 21.37; Lv 22.19; etc.
		'ayil (ram)	Gn 22.13; 31.38; etc.
		rāḥēl (ewe)	Gn 32.15; Is 53.7; etc.
		kebeś (male lamb)	Ex 12.5; Lv 9.3; etc.
		keśeb (male lamb)	Lv 3.7; Nm 18.17; etc.
		kibśâ (female lamb)	Lv 14.10; Nm 6.14; etc.
		kiśbâ (female lamb)	Lv 5.6
		ṭāleh (new-born lamb)	1 Sm 7.9; Is 65.25
		tᵉlî (new-born lamb)	Is 40.7
Swine	*Sus domestica*	ḥăzîr	Lv 11.7; Prv 11.22; etc.
Thahas (Tachash)	*Dugong* (?); *Giraffa* (?)	taḥaš	Ex 26.14; Nm 4.6; etc.
Whale	*Balenoptera; Physeter*	liwyātān	Ps 103(104).26
Wolf	*Canis lupus*	zᵉ'ēb	Is 11.6; Jer 5.6; etc.
		Birds	
Buzzard	*Buteo* sp.	'ayyâ	Lv 11.14; Jb 28.7; etc.
Chicken (?)	*Gallus gallus domesticus* (?)	śekwî	Jb 38.36
		zarzîr	Prv 30.31
Crane	*Grus grus*	'āgûr	Jer 8.7
Dove	*Columba* sp.	yônâ	Gn 8.8–12; Is 38.14; etc.
		gôzāl	Gn 15.9
Eagle	*Aquila* sp.	'ayiṭ	Gn 15.11; Is 18.6; etc.
Goose	*Anser anser domesticus*	barbūr	3 Kgs 5.3
Gull	*Larus* sp.	šaḥap	Lv 11.6; Dt 14.15
Hawk	*Accipiter nissus*	nēṣ	Lv 11.16; Jb 39.26; etc.
Heron	*Egreta; Ardea*	'ănāpâ	Lv 11.19; Dt 14.8
Hoopoe	*Upupa epops*	dûkîpat	Lv 11.19; Dt 14.18
Kestrel	*Falco tinnunculus*	taḥmās	Lv 11.19; Dt 14.13
Kite	*Milvus* sp.	dā'â	Lv 11.14; Dt 14.13
		dayyâ	Is 34.15
Nightingale (?)	*Luscinia megarhynchos* (?)	zāmîr	Ct 2.12
Ostrich	*Struthio camelus*	yā'ēn	Lam 4.3; Jb 39.13
Owl, Barn	*Tyto alba*	tinšemet	Lv 11.18; Dt 14.16
Owl, Dark Desert Eagle	*Bubo bubo ascalaphus*	bat-ya'ănâ	Lv 11.16; Is 34.13; etc.
Owl, Dark Little	*Athene noctua glaux*	kôs	Lv 11.17; Ps 101(102).7; etc.
Owl, Desert Little	*Athene noctua saharae*	qā'at	Lv 11.18; Is 34.11; etc.
Owl, Eagle	*Bubo bubo aharonii*	'ōaḥ	Is 13.21
Owl, Fish	*Ketupa zeylonensis*	šālāk	Lv 11.17; Dt 14.17
Owl, Long-eared	*Asio otus*	yanšûp	Lv 11.17; Is 34.11; etc.
Owl, Pale Desert Eagle	*Bubo bubo desertorum*	tannîm	Is 34.13; Mal 1.3; etc.
Owl, Scops Screech	*Otus scops*	śā'îr	Is 13.21; 34.14
Owl, Short-eared	*Asio flammeus*	qippōd	Is 14.23; So 2.14; etc.
		qippôz	Is 34.15
Owl, Tawny	*Strix aluco*	lîlît	Is 34.14
Partridge, Chuckar	*Alectoris graeca*	ḥoglâ (woman's name)	Nm 26.33; 27.1; etc.
Partridge, See-see	*Ammoperdix heyi*	qōrē'	1 Sm 26.20; Jer 17.11
Peacock	*Pavo cristatus*	tukkî	3 Kgs 10.22; 2 Chr 9.21
Quail	*Coturnix coturnix*	śᵉlāw	Ex 16.13; Nm 11.31; etc.
Raven	*Corvus* sp.	'ōrēb	Gn 8.7; Lv 11.15; etc.
Sparrow	*Passer domesticus biblicus*	ṣippôr	Lv 14.14; Ps 83(84).4; etc.
Stork	*Ciconia ciconia*	ḥăsîdâ	Lv 11.19; Jer 8.7; etc.
Swift	*Apus* sp.	sîs	Is 38.14; Jer 8.7
Turtledove	*Streptopelia turtur*	tôr	Jer 8.7; Ct 2.12; etc.
Vulture, Bearded	*Gypaetus barbatus*	peres	Lv 11.13; Dt 14.12
Vulture, Black	*Aegypius monachus*	'ozniyyâ	Lv 11.13; Dt 14.12
Vulture, Egyptian	*Neophron percopterus*	rāḥām	Lv 11.18
		raḥāmā	Dt 14.18
Vulture, Griffon	*Gyps fulvus*	nešer	Lv 11.13; Dt 32.11; etc.

ANIMALS OF THE BIBLE—*Continued*

English name	Scientific name	Biblical Hebrew name	Reference
		Reptiles and similar creatures	
Chameleon	*Chameleon vulgaris*	*tinšemet*	Lv 11.30
Cobra	*Naja haje*	{ *peten* *śārāp*	Dt 32.30; Is 11.8; etc. Nm 21.6; Is 14.29; etc.
Crocodile	*Crocodilus vulgaris*	{ *tannîn* *liwyātān*	Ex 7.9; Dt 32.33; etc. Jb 40.25–41.26
Frog	*Rana esculenta*	*ṣ⁽e⁾pardēa*	Ex 7.27–8.9; Ps 77(78).45; etc.
Gecko	*Hemidacylus; Ptyodactylus*	{ *ʾănāqâ* *ś⁽e⁾māmît*	Lv 11.30 Prv 30.28
Lizard	*Lacerta* sp.	*l⁽e⁾ṭāʾâ*	Lv 11.30
Lizard, Dab	*Uromastix aegyptius*	*ṣāb*	Lv 11.29
Lizard, Monitor	*Veranus* { *griseus* *niloticus*	*kōaḥ*	Lv 11.30
Skink	*Eumeces; Chalcides*	*hōmeṭ*	Lv 11.30
Snake	*Ophidia*	*nāhāš*	Gn 3.1; Am 5.19; etc.
Viper, Carpet	*Echis* { *colorata* *carinata*	*ʾepʿeh*	Is 30.6; Jb 20.16; etc.
Viper, Horned	*Cerastes* { *cerastes* *vipera*	*š⁽e⁾pîpôn*	Gn 49.17
Viper, Palestinian	*Vipera palaestina*	{ *ṣepaʿ* *ṣipʿōnî*	Is 14.29 Is 11.8; Jer 8.17; etc.
		Fish	
Fish	*Pisces*	{ *dāg* (individual) *dāgâ* (collective)	Jon 2.1; Gn 9.2; etc. Gn 1.26; Ex 7.18; etc.
		Insects and other small creatures	
Ant	*Messor semirufus*	*n⁽e⁾mālâ*	Prv 6.6; 30.25
Bee	*Apis mellifica*	*d⁽e⁾bôrâ*	Dt 1.44; Jgs 14.8; etc.
Beetle	*Cerambyx*	*tôlaʿat*	Dt 28.39; Jon 4.7; etc.
Centipede	{ *Scolopendra;* *Eraphidostrephus*	*marbēh raglaim*	Lv 11.42
Cricket, Mole	*Gryllotalpa gryllotalpa*	*ṣ⁽e⁾lāṣal*	Is 2.20
Earthworm	*Lubricus*	*tôlaʿat*	Is 14.11; Jb 25.6; etc.
Flea	*Pulex irritans*	*parʿōš*	1 Sm 24.15; 26.20
Fly	*Musca domestica*	*z⁽e⁾bûb*	Is 7.18; Eccl 10.1
Gnat	*Culex; Anopheles*	*ʿārōb*	Ex 8.17–27; etc.
Grasshopper, Long-horned	*Tettigonidae*	*hargōl*	Lv 11.22
Grasshopper, Short-horned	*Acrididae*	{ *ḥāgāb* *solʿām*	Nm 13.33; Is 40.22; etc. Lv 11.22
Leech	*Hirundo; Limnatus*	*ʾălûqâ*	Prv 30.15
Locust	*Schistocerca gregaria*	{ *ʾarbeh* *yeleq* *ḥasîl* *gāzām* *gōbai*	Ex 10.4–19; Dt 28.38; etc. Jer 51.14; Jl 1.4; etc. Is 33.4; Jl 1.4; etc. Am 4.9; Jl 1.4; 2.25 Am 7.1; Na 3.17
Louse	*Anoplura*	{ *kēn* *kinnām* (collective)	Is 51.6; Ex 8.12 Ex 8.13–14; etc.
Maggot	*Lucilia; Drosophila*	*rimmâ*	Ex 16.24; Jb 7.5; etc.
Moth, Carpenter	*Cossidae*	*sās*	Is 51.8
Moth, Clothes	*Microlepidoptera*	*ʿāš*	Is 50.9; Jb 13.28; etc.
Scorpion	*Scorpio; Buthus*	*ʿaqrāb*	Dt 8.15; Ez 2.6
Spider	*Aranaida; Solifugae*	{ *ʿakkābîš* *ʿakšûb*	Is 59.5; Jb 8.14 Ps 139(140).4
Wasp	*Vespa orientalis*	*ṣirʿâ*	Ex 23.28; Dt 7.20; etc.
		Material produced by animals	
Corals	*Coralium rubrum*	*p⁽e⁾nînîm*	Lam 4.7; Prv 8.11; etc.
Crimson Dye	*Kermes biblicus*	{ *tôlaʿat šānî* *karmîl*	Ex 25.4; Nm 4.8; etc. 2 Chr 2.6, 13; 3.14

ANIMALS OF THE BIBLE—*Continued*

English name	Scientific name	Biblical Hebrew name	Reference
Material produced by animals			
Ivory	*Elephas africanus*	$\{$ *šenhabbîm*	3 Kgs 10.22; 2 Chr 9.21
		šēn	Ez 27.6; Am 3.15; etc.
Onycha	*Onguis odoratus*	*šᵉḥēlet*	Ex 30.34; Sir 24.15
Purple Dye	*Murex* sp.	$\{$ *tᵉkēlet*	Ex 25.4; Jer 10.9; etc.
		'argāmān	Prv 31.22; Ez 27.7; etc.
		'argᵉwān	2 Chr 2.6

Changes in Fauna from Biblical to Modern Times. Although no great changes have transpired in the fauna of the Holy Land since Biblical times, the last few generations have witnessed the disappearance from the country and the surrounding regions of some of the animals that are mentioned in the Bible. The depredations have been especially severe in the case of the ruminants and cloven-hoofed, for of the 10 mentioned in the Bible, only the gazelle and the Nubian ibex are left today. The wild ox (*Bos primigenius*) had already disappeared from the region at a rather early period. The others continued to inhabit the country or region up to the beginning of the 20th century. As previously noted, this does not imply a change in climate or plant cover. The main reason for the disappearance of these animals, whose flesh is eaten, is the improvement of hunting weapons. To the gun must be ascribed, as well, the destruction of the large predators, such as the lion, the bear, the leopard, and the cheetah in the confines of the country. Some think that the existence of these predatory animals in the Holy Land in the time of the Bible is proof that the land was sparsely settled at that time. But these animals inhabited the country in the Roman and Byzantine periods, when the land was, undoubtedly, densely populated. We may infer from the Scriptures that even in Biblical times these beasts of prey did not inhabit the cis-Jordanian area; their habitat was the thickets of the Jordan (Jer 49.19), the forests of Basan (Dt 33.22), and the mountains of Lebanon and Hermon (Ct 4.5). From these places they invaded settled areas, and in times of destruction and famine they would remain there for awhile.

The lion was still found in the Negeb during the Crusades. The Syrian bear ranged down to the northern borders of Palestine until the beginning of the 20th century, and scattered traces of it have recently come to light in the mountains of Lebanon. The leopard still reaches Upper Galilee from Lebanon occasionally. Until only a generation ago the cheetah (*Acinonyx jubata*) still survived in the Negeb, and some of its traces have recently been found at Yotvata in the Araba. Of the big animals that are now completely extinct in the country, the hippopotamus (*hippopotamus amphibius*)—the behemoth of Jb 40.15–24—may be mentioned. The crocodile—called the *tannîn* [the "dragon" of Ps 90(91).13; Is 27.1; etc.] and the Leviathan (Jb 40.25–41.26)—inhabited the western streams of Palestine until the end of the 19th century. The ostrich (*Struthio camelus*)—mentioned in Lam 4.3; Jb 39.13—disappeared from the area in the 19th century. At the end of the 19th century the last survivors of the Syrian wild ass (*Equus hemionus hemihip-*

pus) and the Arabian wild ass (*Equus hemionus onager*) were exterminated in the Syrian desert.

The expansion of Jewish settlement in the country, especially modern agricultural settlement, has altered the populations of various animals. There has been an increase in those species that have been able to adapt themselves to the new conditions. The increased number of fishponds has brought an increase in waterfowl. Also the swamp cat (*Catolynx chaus chrysomelo notis*) is spreading. All the means employed against the jackals have not deterred them from multiplying. The poisonous bait laid out to exterminate the jackals and rodents have caused the destruction of the vulturine birds that have eaten the poisoned carrion. Thus, for example, of the griffon vulture (*Gyps fulvus*), which ranged over the country until a generation ago and is often mentioned in the Bible as the *nešer* (commonly mistranslated as "eagle"), only a few pairs still survive. Laws for the protection of wildlife that were recently enacted in the state of Israel have prevented the annihilation of certain creatures that had been in danger of complete extinction. The gazelle has noticeably increased throughout the country, and the Nubian ibex, too, has spread into the hills of Ein Gedi and Eilat.

The Zoogeography of Modern Palestine. The animal ranges coincide with the vegetation zones in Palestine (see above). To the Mediterranean group belong the hare, the chuckar partridge, the swallow, the agama, and others. To the Saharo-Sindic group belong various species of desert mice, the desert lark, the sandgrouse, the gecko, the cobra, and many other species. To the Irano-Turanic group belong the creatures that inhabit the northern Negeb and the desert of Juda, for instance, the tiger weasel (*Vormela*), the bustard, the *isolepis* agama, and others. To the Sudano-Decanic group belong the creatures that inhabit the lower Jordan Valley, especially the oasis areas of the desert and the vicinity of the Dead Sea. To the tropical groups belong the cheetah, the honey badger, the tropical cuckoo, the carpet viper, and others. To the holarctic group belong the northern creatures, for instance, the shrew, and the meadow pipit.

Palestine, at the juncture of three continents, is a meeting place of creatures of many different regions, and it has a rich variety of species. Currently known are 68 species of mammals, about 350 species of birds, about 80 species of reptiles, about 40 species of freshwater fishes, and 8 species of amphibia. According to F. S. Bodenheimer, the number of recognized insect species is about 8,000 and, in his opinion the total reaches about 22,000. According to this scholar, the Arthropoda number about 900 known species and pos-

Fig. 5. Some of the representative Palestine fauna: (a) Syrian coney (Procavia syriaca). (b) Gecko (Hemi- dacylus turcicus). (c) Kestrel (Falco tinnunculus). (d) Griffon vulture (Gyps fulvus).

sibly total about 2,000. As for the invertebrates, there are about 300 recognized species, with the possible total of about 2,750.

Domestic Animals. Domestication of animals began at a very early period in Palestine. On the rocks of Kilwa in Transjordan prehistoric carvings of camels and cattle have been found. Jericho has yielded clay statues of a herd of goats, lambs, and pigs from c. 5000 B.C. Inside an Egyptian temple at Beisan figurines of cats have been found. (Cats are not mentioned in the Bible.) There have been found in the Holy Land paintings of dogs of at least four different breeds. The cattle are of uncertain breed. In paintings of the Roman and Byzantine period, hunchback cattle, such as the zebu, are depicted. The black long-eared goat was a very early inhabitant, and it is pictured as early as 1500 B.C. This is also the case in regard to the broad-tailed sheep. The horse was not an important domestic animal; more important were the ass and the mule. In addition to the dove, chickens were raised as early as the period of the Israelite monarchy; a cock is depicted on a seal found at Tell en-Nasbeh, probable site of ancient *Maspha (Mizpeh). To the royal courts were brought

decorative tropical birds, such as the peacock; and the courts received monkeys also (3 Kgs 10.22).

Bibliography: Flora. H. BALFOUR, *The Plants of the Bible* (new ed. London 1885). O. CELSIUS, *Hierobotanicon*, 2 v. (Amsterdam 1748). P. CULTRERA, *Flora Biblica* (Palermo 1861). G. H. DAL- MAN, *Arbeit und Sitte in Palästina*, 7 v. in 8 (Gütersloh 1928–42). I. LÖW, *Die Flora der Juden*, 4 v. in 5 (Vienna-Leipzig 1924–34). H. N. and A. L. MOLDENKE, *Plants of the Bible* (Waltham, Mass. 1952). In Hebrew. B. CHIZIK, *Otsar ha-Tsemahim* (Herzlia 1952). M. ZOHARY, *Olam ha-Tsemahim* (Tel Aviv 1954); *Geo- botanikah* (Merhavya 1955). J. FELIKS, *Olam ha-Tsomeah ha- Mikrai* (Tel Aviv 1957); *Ha-Haklaut be-Eretz Yisrael bi-tekufat ha-Mishnah veha-Talmud* (Jerusalem 1963). Fauna. F. HASSEL- QUIST, *Iter palaestinum*, ed. C. VON LINNÉ (Stockholm 1757). H. B. TRISTAM, *The Fauna and Flora of Palestine* (London 1884); *Natural History of the Bible* (10th ed. New York 1911). L. LEWYSOHN, *Die Zoologie des Talmuds* (Frankfurt 1858). F. S. BODENHEIMER, *Tierwelt Palästinas*, 2 v. (Leipzig 1920); *Pro- dromus faunae palaestinae* (Cairo 1937); *Animal and Man in Bible Lands* (Leiden 1960). J. FELIKS, *The Animal World of the Bible*, tr. P. IRSAI (Tel Aviv 1962). In Hebrew. I. AHARONI, *Torat ha-Hai*, 3 v. (Tel Aviv 1927–49); *Zikhronot Zoolog Ivri* (Tel Aviv 1942–43). Y. MARGOLIN, *Zoologia* (Tel Aviv 1959). F. S. BODENHEIMER, *Ha-Hai be-Artsot ha-Mikra*, 2 v. (Jerusalem 1949–56); *Ha-Hai be-Eretz Yisrael* (Tel Aviv 1953). J. FELIKS, *Ha-Hai shel ha-Tanakh* (Tel Aviv 1954). **Illustration credit:** Figs. 4 and 5, Drawings courtesy of J. Feliks.

[J. FELIKS]

7. ARCHEOLOGY

Palestine, as used here, embraces the lands not only to the west but also to the east of the River Jordan. After World War I both territories were under British mandate. Under the mandatory power a Department of Antiquities was organized to protect and promote the study of the antiquities of the country. According to the norms of this Department an antiquity is "an object which has been constructed, shaped, inscribed, erected, excavated or otherwise produced or modified by human agency earlier than the year 1700 A.D." To preserve the movable antiquities, John D. Rockefeller, Jr., provided funds for the construction of an appropriate museum in Jerusalem (currently in the Arab city); it was opened to the public in 1938. The Department of Antiquities established its headquarters here also. At that time the files of the Department contained records of about 4,000 archeological sites [see R. W. Hamilton, "Schedule of Historical Monuments and Sites," *Palestine Gazette Extraordinary* 1375, suppl. 2 (Nov. 24, 1944)] and about 40,000 objects, all of which were made accessible to scholars. Typical objects of all periods have been arranged in chronological order in the visitors' galleries. The *Palestine Archaeological Museum Gallery Book* (hereafter *PAMGB*) aids the visitor in studying those objects and gives him a good survey of all the periods. The Department published its own periodical *Quarterly of the Department of Antiquities in Palestine* (hereafter *QDAP*) and a number of books and pamphlets on special places and themes. Since the termination of the Mandate in 1948 the museum has been administered by an international board of trustees, under whose direction it has become the center for the study of the so-called Dead Sea Scrolls. The museum continues to be a valuable aid for study, although now both Jordan and Israel have their own Departments of Antiquities with their own museums and publications.

Both before and after 1948 the Departments of Antiquities have been assisted in their work by numerous foreign individuals, schools, and organizations. Thus, for example, N. Glueck alone, in his surface surveys, has added more than 1,400 names of archeological sites to the registers, and numerous excavations by others have greatly augmented the number of objects in the museums.

Summaries of the results achieved have been published by such scholars as C. Watzinger, W. F. Albright, Miss K. Kenyon, and G. E. Wright. These have followed an ascending chronological order which will be followed also in the present article.

The earliest periods are named for the most effective materials available for tools, thus Stone, Bronze, and Iron Ages. Later periods are named for the political rulers of the area—the Persians, Greeks, Romans, Byzantines, Arabs, Crusaders, and Turks. Each such period is subdivided by archeologists using chronological (early, middle, late) or stratigraphical terms (lower, middle, upper); these are then often reduced to numbers or subdivided (e.g., Late Bronze III). Great strides have been made in refining the methods used, but much still remains vague and uncertain.

STONE AGE

Palestine is remarkable for the profusion of informative evidences that it has provided bearing on human existence in all phases of this long, essentially prehistoric period from *c.* 500,000 to *c.* 3100 B.C. After a long Early Stone Age (Paleolithic) period, rapid development in the Mesolithic and following (Neolithic, Chalcolithic, Proto-Urban) periods leads up to the historical times.

Paleolithic or Early Stone Age. This period extends from *c.* 500,000 B.C. to *c.* 10,000 B.C. The names of its subdivisions have been derived from similar cultures discovered in European countries: Chellean, Tayacian, Acheulean, Levalloiso-Mousterian, and Aurignacian. Animal remains suggest that the people of this entire period were primarily hunters and fishers. Such remains have turned up both in open-air sites and in caves.

Open-air Sites. The principal stations of this sort known until now are in the neighborhood of Jerusalem and near the lakes in the north. The oldest of these sites is near the southern end of the Sea of Tiberias at a place called Afiqim. It was discovered in 1960. Regarding it, M. Stekelis [*Israel Exploration Journal* (hereafter *IEJ*) 10 (1960) 118] reports: "The finds prove that the site was inhabited by men in the Lower Pleistocene Age, half a million years ago. These finds include few human remains: two fragments of a human skull, four times as thick as that of modern man, and one incisor tooth, the most ancient human remains ever discovered in the Near East. . . . Fossil bones of some forty different species of animals, most of them now extinct, were found . . . . Other finds consisted of flint tools and chopping instruments belonging to what is known as the 'pebble culture.'" The relation of this find to other Lower Paleolithic levels in Galilee and Lebanon is discussed by E. de Vaumas ["Chronologie des dépôts paléolithiques stratifiés . . .," *IEJ* 13 (1963) 195–207, with bibliography].

Caves. Near the northwestern shore of the Sea of Tiberias, near Nazareth, south of Mount Carmel, and in the Judean Desert, caves containing Early Stone Age deposits were excavated by F. Turville-Petre, R. Neuville, M. Stekelis, D. A. E. Garrod, and others. As a result of the work carried out in these caves, D. A. E. Garrod writes: "In the caves of Wady el-Mughara, for the first time, the Stone Age industries hitherto known only from isolated deposits, or as part of a very incomplete series, were found in place in a long and apparently continuous sequence extending from the Tayacian to the end of the Mesolithic" [D. A. E. Garrod and D. M. A. Bate, *The Stone Age of Mount Carmel: Excavations at the Wady el-Mughara* (hereafter *SAMC*) v.1 (Oxford 1937) 114]. The oldest industry found in the caves, the Tayacian, is characterized by small irregular flakes (see *SAMC* 114). The Acheulean level comes next; its flint industry is highly developed and consists chiefly of flakes. In this period human beings seem first to have been buried in or near caves. The minimum date suggested for such burials is about 50,000 years ago. The Galilee Skull, the first of these human remains in caves to be found, was excavated in 1925 by F. Turville-Petre in Mugharet ez-Zuttiyeh, northwest of the Sea of Galilee [see F. Turville-Petre et al., *Researches in Prehistoric Galilee 1925–1926* (London 1927) 15–106]. It is now on exhibit in the Palestine Archaeological Museum. According to *PAMGB* No. 33, "the skull belongs to a type of man closely related to the Neanderthal race," which is "distinguished by strongly protruding eye-brow ridges, and by a low, receding forehead which indicates incomplete development of the brain." See also Bibl Archaeol 26 (1963) 73–91.

The Lower Aurignacian industry marks an advanced flint culture; the hand axes disappear completely. It is followed by the Middle Aurignacian, the Athlitian and the Kebaran, the latest Palaeolithic industry. This industry belongs to a society of food-gatherers, leaving no buildings. See *SAMC* 116–117; *IEJ* 10 (1960) 259.

Mesolithic Period. During this time people lived in caves, near caves, or in structures out in the open. The first cave in which this culture was found was the Shukba cave in Wadi Natūf, northwest of Jerusalem. The excavations were made in 1928 by Garrod, who named the industry Natufian (see *SAMC* 114). Later, in her work in the Wadi el-Mughara, she found two layers of this industry in the Mugharet el-Wad: the lower (B 2) she called Lower Natufian; the upper (B 1) Upper Natufian. The former was also found by F. Turville-Petre in layer B of el-Kebara; it was particularly rich in worked and carved bone (*SAMC* 113, 117). R. Neuville found the same culture in various caves of the Judean Desert [R. Neuville et al., *Le Paléolithique et le Mésolithique du Désert de Judée* (hereafter *PMDJ*) (Paris 1951)]. The upper Natufian was found at Khiam on a terrace out in the open [see *SAMC* 113; *PMDJ* 135, 155; RevBibl 70 (1963) 106–110].

Typical of the Mesolithic Period are blades and tools of minute size, called pygmy flints or microliths. Harpoons and fishhooks suggest that the people were fishers; sickles may indicate the beginning of agriculture; heads of animals carved on bone handles mark the beginnings of art; a carving of a human head is the oldest representation of a human being hitherto discovered in Palestine; and figures of deer or gazelles carved on or out of stone or bone illustrate high artistic skill. Pendants worn as charms or amulets suggest religious views [see *PAMGB* No. 150–249; *Eretz Israel* 6 (1956) 21–24, 27]. The shrine found beneath the tell near the spring of Jericho also suggests that the people were religious [see K. Kenyon, *Archaeology of the Holy Land* (hereafter *AHL*) 41–42]. This shrine preserved wood that made a carbon-14 test possible, and for the first time yielded an absolute date near the 9th millennium B.C. for this period. Other objects associated with this shrine made it possible to link it with the Lower Natufian of Mugharet el-Wad and thus fix the absolute chronology of that well-stratified site.

Mesolithic remains outside of caves have been found both at Eynan and Oren. They consist at present of stone foundations of both dwellings and tombs, close together. The dwellings are supposed to represent the first colony living outside of caves known in Palestine. The burial of the dead near their habitations continues an older custom. See *IEJ* 10 (1960) 14–22; *Antiquity and Survival* 2:2–3, 91–110; *IEJ* 7 (1957) 125, 8 (1958) 131, 10 (1960) 118–119; BiblArchaeol 26 (1963) 76–77; *PAMGB* No. 249.

Neolithic Period. Between the Mesolithic and the Neolithic periods at *Jericho there were transitional settlements, which K. Kenyon called Proto-Neolithic; they produced 13 vertical feet of deposit without any substantial structure. The deposit was made up of innumerable floors bounded by slight humps, which were all that remained of slight hutlike structures. The same flint and bone industry, allied to the Lower Natufian of

Mount Carmel, extended through the transitional Proto-Neolithic state to the large-scale settlement that followed. Jericho has, therefore, provided evidence of the transition from man as a hunter to man as a member of a settled community (see *AHL* 42–43).

Prepottery-Neolithic Period. This period is represented in the next two stages in the development of Jericho. In the earlier of these stages (Prepottery Neolithic A) Jericho had a solid, free-standing, stone town wall. A great stone tower was built against the inside of the western sector of the wall. Against the wall and its tower, curvilinear houses were built. The third series, successively constructed, of these houses produced charcoal timbers that gave a carbon-14 dating of 6850 B.C. plus or minus 210. The walls and tower were older (see *AHL* 43–47). According to Miss D. Kirkbride [PalExplQ (1960) 117–119] the flint instruments of this period resembled the Natufian flints of the two preceding periods.

The Prepottery-Neolithic B stage at Jericho had a flint industry that is called Tahunian and is considered the classic Neolithic industry of Palestine. It is not certain whether it developed from the Natufian or was superimposed on it; the latter seems to have been the case at Jericho, where there are new city walls and rectangular buildings, several of which were places of worship. The floors were covered with plaster, beneath which were found human burials. The heads were separated from the bodies and covered with plaster; the life-size clay figures found by J. *Garstang and later by K. Kenyon most probably came from this stage. Carbon-14 tests gave the following dates: 6250 B.C. plus or minus 200; 5850 B.C. plus or minus 160 (see *AHL* 47–57).

Evidence of this same period was discovered by Miss Kirkbride in excavations carried out by her in 1956, 1958, 1959, and 1961 at Seyl Aqlat, in Beida, north of ancient *Petra. Carbon-14 tests yielded dates in the 7th millennium B.C. [see PalExplQ (1960) 136–145].

Pottery-Neolithic A and B Periods. These two periods are distinguished from all the preceding periods by the presence of fired-clay vessels. In the A stage some of the ware is coarse, other ware is fine and decorated. The chief difference is the finish. The finer ware has a comparatively smooth surface and is covered as a rule by a cream-colored slip. This slip in turn is partially covered by a red slip, so that the reserve portions of the cream slip form a pattern, usually in some combinations of chevrons or triangles. To heighten the contrast, the red slip is finely burnished with a beautifully lustrous finish. Altogether, it is a most attractive ware and contrasts strongly with the coarse pottery (see *AHL* 61, 62, and Fig. 4 in that source).

The Pottery-Neolithic-A material was discovered by Garstang in a level at Jericho that is known as Jericho IX and by Kenyon in numerous pits that served as habitations all over the site; in the next level there is a slight improvement in the habitations, as in the objects used in them.

In the B stage many of the vessels are covered with a deep-red slip, sometimes burnished, sometimes matte. The most characteristic decoration, found on both jars and bowls, is bands of herringbone incisions. The bands are usually delineated by grooves, and very often they are covered by a band of cream slip, with the rest of the vessel covered by a red slip (see *AHL* 65).

J. Kaplan ["The Neolithic Pottery of Palestine," Bull AmSchOrRes 156 (Dec. 1959) 15–22] asserts that Miss Kenyon's B stage is mixed, consisting of both Neolithic and Chalcolithic wares; the former he calls Yarmukian, the latter Jericho VIII or Ghassulian. In both phases the herringbone bands occur, but they differ from one another: "in the Yarmukian phase the pattern is part of the filling between the lines which create the zigzag band, whereas at Jericho VIII or Ghassul it is independent ornamentation surrounding the vessel in a band or bands and not in a zigzag pattern." Kaplan's conclusions are that only two main Neolithic phases have become known in the pottery of Palestine up to now: the "Yarmukian" and the older Jericho IX; the latter can be subdivided into two secondary phases based on a related site, Batashi IVa (upper) and Batashi IVb (lower). He asserts that Jericho VIII should not be combined with the Yarmukian Neolithic, nor is the Wadi Rabah material to be so combined, as seems to have occurred at Byblos in Lebanon (Byblos A). "Jericho VIII" and "Wadi Rabah" constitute distinct Chalcolithic phases.

Jericho was the first site in which the earliest pottery of Palestine was found in a stratified context. In 1959 Kaplan knew of seven such sites: besides Jericho, also Abu Usba', Sha'ar ha-Golan, Tell-Aviv, Teluliyot Batashi in the Vale of Sorek, Khirbet Sheikh 'Ali in the Jordan Valley south of Tiberias, and Kfar Gil'adi in the extreme north of Palestine. More recent explorations are rapidly increasing the number of sites in which this period is represented. The Pottery Neolithic Periods fall in the 5th millennium B.C.

Chalcolithic Period. In Palestine, this period, roughly the 4th millennium B.C., is characterized by the manufacture and use of copper objects, while stone implements continued to be used. It first became known through the work that the *Pontifical Biblical Institute carried out from 1929 to 1938 at Tulaylat el-Ghassūl, a site east of the Jordan and a little north of the Dead Sea. Since that time this culture has been noted in many other places throughout Palestine. Details are given by R. North in *Ghassul 1960, Excavation Report* [Anal Bibl 14 (1961)]. As a result of his own work at Ghassul (1959–60), North confirmed the existence of four levels or strata there, but he was not able to detect any change in culture in those strata. The same is said regarding the Chalcolithic sites explored in the neighborhood of Beersheba (see S. Yeivin, 13–19). The houses at Ghassul were rectangular and their interiors were often painted; in the Beersheba region the inhabitants lived partly underground, partly in pits sunk beneath the surface, and partly in rectangular buildings above ground. Ossuaries in the form of buildings, animals, or jars, found especially at Hedera, Azor, and Bne Beraq in the plain adjacent to the Mediterranean, suggest the form of the houses in that region.

At Ein Gedi, near the Dead Sea, a sacred enclosure of this period was found high up a mountain above the spring there. It consists of a wide open court, with a high place and three houses in the center; one, of the "broad house" type, was certainly used for ritual purposes; it is very well preserved, with a fireplace and benches inside [see *Christian News from Israel* (hereafter *CNI*) 14 (1963) 2:16; RevBibl 70 (1963) 575–576, Pl. 23a]. In a cave in the Judean Desert a hoard of

Fig. 6. Chalcolithic "apse house" at Meser near entrance of Wadi 'Ara, northeastern end of the Plain of Sharon.

bronze and ivory cult objects of this period was discovered [see *IEJ* 11 (1961) 78–79, 12 (1962) 156].

According to J. A. Callaway [BiblArchaeol 26 (1963) 78–82], the first intimations of *Sheol (the abode of the dead) go back to this period, when the dead began to be buried away from the habitations of the living. The chronological relations of the different phases of this culture are not yet clear. This holds true especially with reference to the gray burnished ware first found in Esdraelon sites. Carbon-14 tests yield dates toward the end of the 4th millennium for this culture (see *AHL* 82).

Proto-Urban Period. This is a new term invented by Miss K. Kenyon (explained in *AHL* 84–100). It deals with three groups of pottery in use at about the same time and interlocking. These point to three different groups of people who are known principally from their tombs, not from their towns; they do not seem to have had any fortified towns, but seem to have been mere villagers living in poor dwellings. Some of the sites on which they lived were subsequently abandoned and remained so for a long time; such are Tell en-Nasbeh, a little north of Jerusalem, and Samaria; others were later to develop into towns, such as *Mageddo (Megiddo), Jericho, *Beth-San (Beth-shan), and Tell Far'ah (northeast of Nablus). The tombs are peculiar; they are the earliest to be cut into rock and to contain multiple burials. Their date has been fixed in the latter part of the 4th millennium. A central point has been fixed by a carbon-14 test made on material from Jericho; it is around 3200 B.C. and is confirmed by sealings on jars. Originally some of these finds were assigned to the latter part of the Chalcolithic Period (the gray burnished ware, generally known as Esdraelon ware) and others (red painted ware) to the Early Bronze Age. Most scholars still retain these terms. But Miss Kenyon's suggestions have stirred up discussion that will undoubtedly prepare the way for a better sequence in the future.

BRONZE AGE

In Palestine, as in other areas of ancient occupation, the term Bronze Age was intended originally as a designation of the period between the earliest use of nonprecious metals and the spread of iron tools. Today, the name is largely conventional, and includes three well-known periods (Early, Middle, and Late Bronze) extending from c. 3100 to c. 1200 B.C.

Early Bronze Age. This age (EB) is characterized by the development of villages into towns or cities that were protected by walls, of which good examples have been found at various places. At Jericho the walls were built of unbaked bricks made in molds. On the western side of the city 17 phases of building and rebuilding of the walls were traced. The walls were protected by round and rectangular towers and by an external ditch. The defenses of Tell el-Far'ah (northeast of Nablus) date from the fourth phase of its existence at the beginning of EB II; at the north they are of stone protected by a glacis of beaten earth; on the west they are of brick; this brick section collapsed at the end of the fifth period of occupation, before the beginning of EB III. The massive wall found at Mageddo was considered a city wall by the excavators, but Miss Kenyon considers it a terrace wall because of the houses built against its exterior. The fortifications of Khirbet Kerak were built of brick either in EB I or in EB II. Those of *Hai (Ai) were constructed of stone, and consist of either three or two lines at various points; their date, however, remains uncertain. The so-called citadel was still in use in EB III. The town wall of Ras el-'Ain may go back to EB I.

Buildings inside the fortifications show a marked change in the course of this period. The earliest houses are the best; some have rounded ends; others are completely round. Timber was common. Associated with the houses are brick-built silos. From Tell el-Far'ah there is evidence that a new type of pottery kiln was introduced during the period; it continued in use down to the Roman Period. A conical stone altar with steps originated in EB III at Mageddo. V. M. Seton-Williams [*Iraq* 11 (1949) 79–83] distinguishes two types of temples in the EB Age, each with its distinctive ground plan. One is a single-chambered type, as at Jericho VII; the other is a more complex structure that contains at least three rooms, as at Hai. The sanctuary at Tell el-Far'ah has two rooms [see RevBibl 68 (1961) Pl. 33, No. 671]. A remarkable building at Khirbet Kerak may have been either a shrine or a granary. The tombs were large rock-cut chambers with multiple burials. The pottery is characterized by a burnished slip, usually red, but occasionally black; it forms the basis for distinguishing three phases known as EB I, II, and III, beginning *c.* 3100 and ending *c.* 2300 B.C. The period is conventionally known as the EB Age, but in fact there is no certain evidence that bronze was used, and even copper was not very common (see *AHL* 101–134).

Fig. 7. Round altar base of unhewn stones, with steps; Mageddo (Megiddo), Early Bronze Age (c. 2700 B.C.).

The Middle Bronze Age. This period (MB) begins with a subperiod characterized as intermediate (EB/MB) by Miss Kenyon [*AHL* 135–161; K. Kenyon, *Excavation at Jericho I: The Tombs Excavated in 1952–54* (Jerusalem 1960) 180–262, hereafter *EJ I*]. Others insist on calling it MB I, which term is retained in this article.

Middle Bronze Age I. In this period (2250–1850/1800 B.C.) the inhabited places were without walls and the houses were few in number. The three temples of stratum 15 at Mageddo probably belong to it. Tombs are numerous and characterized by individual burials. Much of the pottery is peculiar; R. Amiran endeavored to arrange it in three groups which she called A, B, and C [see *IEJ* 10 (1960) 204–225]. Albright, however, prefers a different sequence; he thinks that Mrs. Amiran's A should come after C [BullAmSchOrRes 168 (1962) 36–42]. Both Albright and Glueck think that this is the period during which Abraham came to Palestine [see BullAmSchOrRes 163 (1961) 38–40; Glueck, *Rivers in the Desert,* 60–105].

Middle Bronze Age II. In this period (*c.* 1850/1800–1550/1500 B.C.) the cities were defended by walls. All those that have been excavated reveal a number of phases and can be illustrated by the walls of Jericho. In the earlier stages the single-wall type was used; this was replaced in the later phases by massive ramparts that consisted of three or four sections: an enormous fill, revetted below by a stone wall and crowned on top by the actual defensive wall. It is doubtful whether there was a ditch. All or some of these elements (the ditch, the revetment, the bank, and the wall) have been found at Tell ed-Duweir (Lachis), Tell Jeriseh, Tell el-'Ajjūl, Tell Far'ah (Beth-pelet), Tell Beit Mirsim, Mageddo, *Hasor (Hazor), and *Sichem (Shechem). At several places the gateways also were preserved; they consisted of a passage with three pairs of buttresses between which the actual gates were probably placed; this was the case at Mageddo X, Sichem, Tell Beit Mirsim, and Tell Far'ah (in the south).

The eastern side of the mound of Jericho reveals several streets and the houses flanking them. On the lower floor there were shops and storage places; on the upper floor habitations. In one group of chambers J. Garstang [*The Story of Jericho* (London 1940) 97–98] found vases of such fine quality that they seemed to represent temple offerings and furniture. One vase was decorated with a molded snake, "a terrestrial emblem of the Mother-goddess, symbolizing Life within the earth." Modeled serpents on cult objects of this period are very numerous (see *PAMGB* No. 773 and *passim*). Temples and cult objects of this period are known from Nahariya [see *QDAP* 14 (1950) 1–41; *IEJ* 6 (1956) 14–25]; from Sichem [see BullAmSchOrRes 169 (Feb. 1963) 5–32; BiblArchaeol 16 (1963) 129–130], both a temenos (1800–1650) and a fortress-temple (1650–1550); probably from Mageddo VIII; and from Tell el-Far'ah in the north [see RevBibl 64 (1957) 559–567].

The tombs of Jericho in this period are noteworthy because they preserved till modern excavation not only the usual objects of clay and metal, but also objects of wood. The clay vessels found at Jericho provided Miss Kenyon with a basis for distinguishing five phases of MB II, for which, however, she has not yet fixed accurate chronological limits. Regarding the MB II Period, see *AHL* 170–194; *EJ I* 263–518.

Late Bronze Age. Archeology reveals that in the Late Bronze (LB) period (16th–13th centuries B.C.) numerous cities were destroyed; good examples are Jericho, which fell twice, and Tell Beit Mirsim, both of which were restored only after long intervals. From those that survived or were rebuilt there is evidence that the art of fortification changed but little; both vertical and battered city walls remained in use. The city gates at Mageddo and *Beth-Sames (Beth-shemesh) were a continuation or a development of the type in use in the MB Period. The better houses consisted of rooms built around a courtyard. The palace near the gate at Mageddo contained a large number of ivories; an inscription dated one ivory object to the time of Ramses III (1175–1144 B.C.). For further information, *see* IVORIES OF PALESTINE.

The discoveries of temples and objects used in them have been reported from Mageddo, Sichem, Tell Abu Hawam near Haifa, Beth-San (Beth-shan), Hasor, and Tell ed-Duweir. A stele of the god Mekal was found in the 14th-century temple at Beth-San; it contained also a panel representing a struggle between a lion and a dog. In one of several temples at Hasor was found a stele with two hands raised in prayer, along with many other stelae without representations. For the burial of prominent persons shaft tombs continued in use. For the first time in history plastered cisterns began to be used; this made it possible to build homes and towns at places where there was no natural water supply.

Fig. 8. Lion-and-dog fights, stele from 14th-century B.C. *stratum at Beth-San, now in Palestine Archaeological Museum, Jerusalem, Jordan.*

Written sources from Palestine are now quite numerous. From Beth-San come royal and private stelae dating from the 14th and 13th centuries; their inscriptions are in Egyptian hieroglyphs and reveal something about the political and religious conditions in Palestine at that time. A fragment of another stele of Thutmose III or Amenophis II was discovered at Tell el-'Oreimeh near the northwestern part of the Sea of Tiberias. Inscribed statues of Ramses III (1175–1144 B.C.) were found at Beth-San and Mageddo. At Tell el-Amarna in Egypt were found more than 350 cuneiform tablets, mostly official letters sent from Palestine between 1364 and 1347 B.C. Other cuneiform tablets turned up in Palestine itself at Taanach (12 tablets), Tell el-Hesi, Sichem, Lachis, and Beth-Sames. The art of the period is illustrated by stelae, statues, figurines, ivories, etc. Peculiar to this period are bichrome ware, base ring ware, and stirrup vessels. The first group is characteristic of the beginning of the period, the second of the whole period, and the third of the end of the period. The first is a local product; the other two come from Cyprus and Mycenae, respectively. They indicate the country's extensive trade contacts with the Mediterranean. See *AHL* 195–220; Albright, *Archaeology of Palestine* (hereafter *AP*) 96–109.

BIBLICAL PERIOD AND LATER

The Israelite settlement in Palestine coincides roughly with the beginning of the Iron Age (*c.* 1200 B.C.); later periods are identified by archeologists with the name of the occupying power of the moment, beginning with the Persians.

Iron Age. Towns and fortresses of the Iron Age (12th to 6th centuries B.C.) were protected by casemate walls, though solid walls with projections and recesses also are found, for example, at Mageddo. Their gates continued older traditions with slight modifications. The use of Proto-Aeolic capitals is now known from Jerusalem, Ramet Rachel, Samaria, Mageddo, and Hasor. Tunnels supplied water to Jerusalem, Gabaon, Mageddo, and Saidiyeh. Temples are reported from Beth-San, Mageddo, Hasor, Arad, *Azotus (Ashdod), etc. Palaces, storerooms, and vast stables are reported from Mageddo and elsewhere. For the burial of the dead divan-shaped tombs were used; coffins made of clay have been recovered at Tell el-Far'ah in the Negeb, at Beth-San, and at Sahab; they have anthropoidal lids (see Galling BR 448–449). At Tell el-Kheleifeh, ancient *Asiongaber (Eziongeber), a copper refinery has been excavated (see N. Glueck, *The Other Side of the Jordan*, 89–113).

Inscriptions are numerous. D. Diringer in *Le iscrizioni antico-ebraiche palestinesi* (Florence 1934) and S. Moscati in *L'epigraphia ebraica antica* (Rome 1951) have collected most of the Hebrew inscriptions known up to 1951. To these we may now add a Canaanite tablet of the 12th century B.C. from Taanach [Bibl Archaeol 26 (1963) 125]; new material from the 7th century B.C. [BullAmSchOrRes 165 (Feb. 1962) 34–46]; numerous inscriptions from Arad since 1961; stamped jar handles from Jib; the *Lachis (Lachish) Letters, etc. Ivories, especially from Samaria [see J. W. and G. M. Crowfoot, *Samaria-Sebaste, II: Early Ivories from Samaria* (London 1938)] illustrate the art of the period. Religious practices are illustrated by numerous Astarte figurines and stands for burning incense or making offerings; they are often decorated with human figures or with animals such as doves and snakes (see *AHL* 221–297; *AP* 112–142).

Persian Period. In this period (6th to 4th centuries B.C.) administrative buildings existed principally at Lachis, Tell Jemmeh, and Ramet Rachel. Tombs of the shaft type are reported from Tell el-Far'ah in the Negeb, from Gezer, and from 'Athlit. Coins put in their appearance for the first time in the Persian period [*see* COINAGE, ANCIENT (IN PALESTINE)]. Astarte figurines, numerous in earlier periods, still continued to be in use, though their style was already influenced by Greek art (see *PAMGB* No. 710). From Lachis alone over 150 crude incense altars are reported [see O. Tufnell et al., *Lachish III: The Iron Age* (London, New York, and Toronto 1953) 226; *PAMGB*, No. 720, 721]. Glass began to be used for seals (see *PAMGB* No. 766). Amulets had representations of Egyptian gods. Inscriptions occur on many small objects. Most interesting, however, are the papyri found in 1962 and 1963; they come from Samaria, and deal with legal and administrative matters; they are written in Aramaic and date from the time between Artaxerxes III (358–338) and 335 B.C. [see Bibl Archaeol 26 (1963) 110–121; BullAmSchOrRes 171 (1963) 2].

Greek Period. This period (4th to 1st centuries B.C.) is also commonly referred to as the Hellenistic period. Greek culture had been introduced into Palestine long before Alexander the Great had conquered it (332 B.C.) and subjected it to his rule and that of his successors, the Ptolemies of Egypt (down to 198 B.C.) and the Seleucids of Syria. For a description of the round towers and the fort of the Greek period at Samaria, see J. W. Crowfoot et al., *Samaria-Sebaste, I: The Buildings of Samaria* (London 1942) 24–31 (hereafter *SS I*); the fortifications and buildings of Tell Sandahannah are treated by F. J. Bliss and R. A. S. Macalister, *Excavations in Palestine 1898–1900* (London 1902) 52–57. In Tell Sandahannah are the earliest tombs of the *kôkîm* (oven-shaped) type found in Palestine; the walls are painted and have numerous inscriptions [see J. P. Peters and H. Thiersch, *Painted Tombs in the Necropolis of Marissa* (London 1905)]. Rhodian jar handles with stamped inscriptions characterize this period. Moreover, coins are now a very important means for dating the monuments. The discovery of the Samaria papyri has convinced F. M. Cross that his dates of "the old Exodus manuscript from Cave 4, Qumran (*c.* 250 B.C.) and the archaic Samuel manuscript (*c.* 225 B.C.) now appear to be minimal, and it is clear in turn that the so-called Hasmonean hands of Qumran cannot be reduced in date" [BiblArchaeol 26 (1963) 120]. New light has been shed on this period by work at 'Araq el-Emir [see BullAmSchOrRes 171 (Oct. 1963) 8–55; see also C. Watzinger, *Denkmäler Palästina II* (hereafter *DP II*) 10–30; *AP* 146–154].

Roman Period. Jerash in Transjordan (*see* GERASA) and Samaria west of the Jordan (see *SS I*, 31–37) were typical Roman cities of this period (1st century B.C. to 4th Christian century). Walls, gates, columned streets, forums, stadia, theaters, nymphaea, baths, and temples were some of their chief features; the palaces were noteworthy for their architecture, paintings, mosaics, and baths. As places of worship the pagans had their temples, dedicated to many deities, and also Semitic-style high places; the Jews had not only their famous temple in Jerusalem but also numerous synagogues, especially in Galilee. For burial purposes there were mausoleums built of stone containing sarcophagi; rock-cut chambers with graves in the form of *kôkîm* or arcosolia also contained sarcophagi or ossuaries, often with decorations and inscriptions carved on them; in a few cases the chambers were painted [see Annual of the Department of Antiquities of Jordan (hereafter *ADAJ*) 4–5 (1960) 116]. Most of the Qumran manuscripts and those which have been and are being found more to the south belong to this period (*see* DEAD SEA SCROLLS). For more details regarding this period one can consult *AP* 154–176; *DP II* 31–116. The excavations at Herodium, *Liber Annuus Studii Biblici Franciscani* (hereafter *LA*) 13 (1963) 219–277; Masada, *IEJ* 7 (1957) 1–65; Caesarea, *CNI* 14:3–4 (1963) 20–24; Jerash, *ADAJ* 4–5 (1960) 123–127; Petra, *ADAJ* 5–6 (1960) 119–122; 6–7 (1962) 13–54, and other sites, are constantly shedding new light on this period.

Byzantine Period. This period (4th to 7th century A.D.) was characterized by the public use of the cross on churches, monasteries, private homes, and burial places. All these monuments were generally quite plain on their exteriors, but inside they were beautified by the extensive use of marble, mosaics, and paintings. The decorative elements now took on a Christian character; their inspiration was generally derived from the Scriptures and the liturgy. The same holds true regarding the numerous inscriptions, which, however, contain much historical information as well. The dead continued to be buried in rock-cut tombs like those of earlier periods, especially the arcosolia type; a new practice was that of interment in shaft tombs inside churches and monasteries or in nearby cemeteries [see *DP II*, 117–164; B. Bagatti, *L'Archeologia Cristiana in Palestina* (Florence 1962)]. *Synagogues of this period closely resembled churches in their form and decorations, though their distinctive character was generally indicated by candelabra and inscriptions. See *LA* 4 (1954) 219–246.

First Arab Period. At the beginning of this period (7th–11th centuries), i.e., up to about the middle of the 8th century, synagogues, churches and mosques, as well as new palaces, flourished; after that almost all began to be neglected and to fall into ruins. The palaces at Khirbet el-Minyeh, at the northwestern part of the Sea of Tiberias (see *IEJ* 10 (1960) 226–243), and at Khirbat al Mafjar, north of Jericho [see *QDAP* 5–14; D. C. Baramki, *Guide to the Umayyad Palace at Khirbat Mafjar* (Jerusalem 1947); R. W. Hamilton and O. Grabar, *Khirbat al Mafjar: An Arabian Mansion in the Jordan Valley* (Oxford 1959)] have been excavated. The latter consisted not only of a royal palace, but also of baths, mosques, colonnaded courtyards, pools, gardens, groves, etc. For some of the floors, beautiful mosaics were used; for the walls and ceilings, geometrical motifs, human beings, and animals were executed in stucco. All is being repaired; the same is planned for the palaces at Amman and in the deserts east of Amman. See also *A Short Account of Early Muslim Architecture* (Pelican Bks. Baltimore 1958); K. A. C. Creswell, *Early Muslim Architecture: Umayyads, Early Abbasids and Tulunids* (Oxford 1932).

Period of the Crusades and After. Palestine is still dotted with the castles, churches, and monasteries built by the Crusaders (11th and 12th centuries); some are well preserved. The location of these monuments is indicated on a map published by the Palestine Government in 1937 (*Palestine of the Crusaders: A Map of the Country*); an accompanying text was prepared by C. N. Johns, who himself carried on work at the castle at 'Athlit (see *QDAP* 1–4). On pages 20–21 of the brochure he indicates other sources dealing with these monuments. In the period after the Crusades (late 12th to 16th centuries) Saladin and his successors generally adapted older buildings to their purposes and repaired them. See R. W. Hamilton, *The Structural History of the Aqsa Mosque* (Jerusalem 1949); H. Luke and E. Keith-Roach, *The Handbook of Palestine and Transjordan* (London 1934) 85–89.

Bibliography: W. F. ALBRIGHT, *The Archaeology of Palestine* (Pelican Bks. Baltimore 1960). K. M. KENYON, *Archaeology in the Holy Land* (New York 1960). G. E. WRIGHT, *Biblical Archaeology* (rev. ed. Philadelphia 1963). S. YEIVIN, *A Decade of Archaeology in Israel 1948–1958* (Istanbul 1960). C. WATZINGER, *Denkmäler Palästinas*, 2 v. (Leipzig 1933–35). H. C. J. LUKE and E. KEITH-ROACH, eds., *The Handbook of Palestine and Transjordan* (3d ed. London 1934). N. GLUECK, *Rivers in the Desert* (New York 1959); *The River Jordan* (Philadelphia 1946); *The Other Side of the Jordan* (New Haven 1940). *The Holy Land: New Light on the Prehistory and Early History of Israel* (Antiquity and Survival 2.2–3; The Hague 1957). **Illustration credits:** Pontifical Biblical Institute.

[S. J. SALLER]

8. PRE-ISRAELITE ETHNOLOGY

References to the pre-Israelite population of Palestine are far from lacking in the Bible. They are to be found in the lists of peoples dispossessed by the invading tribes of Israel and in incidental statements about the earlier inhabitants of the land or of particular localities. About some of these people very little is known. They have left little more than their names on the pages of the Bible. Such, for example, are the so-called giants of the land: the Emim who are said to have dwelt in Moab (Dt 2.10–11); the *Enacim (Anakim), found in the vicinity of Hebron (Nm 13.22, 32–33; Dt 2.10, 21); and the *Raphaim (Rephaim), inhabitants of Basan (Bashan) and the environs of Jerusalem (Gn 14.5; Dt 3.13; 2 Sm 21.16, 18). Other enigmatic names are those of the Avvim who lived in villages near Gaza (Dt 2.22); the Zuzim (Gn 14.5) in Galaad (Gilead); and the Zomzommim (Zamzummim), found in Ammon (Dt 2.20). Gergesites (Girgashites) are named without any locality (Gn 10.16; 15.21; Dt 7.1). The *Amalecites (Amalekites) were a primitive people of the Negeb (Ex 17.8–16; Nm 13.29).

Other groups, however, have left their mark on the pages of history. They are known, not only from Biblical references, but can be found in extra-Biblical literature as well—in such texts as those coming from *Mari, Amarna (*see* AMARNA LETTERS), etc. First and foremost are the two Semitic groups, the Canaanites and the Amorrites. In addition, the non-Semitic elements are represented by the Hurrians, Hittites, Hevites (Hivites), Jebusites, and Pherezites (Perizzites).

Canaanites and Amorrites. Canaanites (Channanites) occupied the whole area west of the Jordan (*see* CANAAN AND CANAANITES). The land of Canaan, later known in part as Phoenicia (*see* PHOENICIANS), is the oldest designation for the land of Palestine. Historically the Canaanites were apparently in Palestine as early as the 4th millennium B.C. Biblically this term has both a geographical and an ethnic meaning. Geographically it can refer to any and all the inhabitants of the territory west of the Jordan, whatever their ethnic origin may be.

More precisely, however, it is used to refer to that ethnic group of peoples who were dispossessed by the Israelites (Ex 3.8, 17; 13.5; 33.2) and who are said to have inhabited the coastal regions and the plains (Nm 13.29).

*Amorrites appear in northern Syria, the land of Amurru, toward the beginning of the 2d millennium B.C. Thence they spread out through the fertile crescent, founding such dynasties as those of Mari and Babylon. Biblically they are found on both sides of the Jordan and are said to have preferred the mountainous regions (Nm 13.29). They dwelt particularly in Juda (Jos 10.5) and in the areas of Basan (Nm 21.33–34) and Hesebon (Heshbon: Nm 21.26). As a geographic term Amorrite is used to refer to the pre-Israelite population of Palestine in general, regardless of ethnic affiliation (Am 2.9–10).

Hurrians and Hittites. Of the non-Semitic population, Hurrians, Hittites, and Hevites deserve special considerations. The *Hurrians were a non-Indo-European Armenoid people who settled especially in northern Mesopotamia, particularly in the land subsequently known as *Mitanni, and in eastern Mesopotamia, e.g., at Nuzi. They were among the *Hyksos who invaded Egypt. According to the Bible, where they are called *Horrites (Horites), the Hurrians were among the ancient inhabitants of central Palestine [Gn 34.2 (Septuagint)] and Seir (Edom: Gn 14.6; Dt 2.12, 22). Ethnically, it would seem that the *Jebusites, the early inhabitants of Jerusalem, belonged to Hurrian stock (Ez 16.45). Despite the prominence of Hurrians in extra-Biblical literature they receive only scant attention in the Bible.

On the other hand *Hevites (Hivites) are found at Sichem (Shechem: Gn 34.2), Gabaon (Gibeon: Jos 9.7), Mt. Lebanon (Jgs 3.3), Mt. Hermon (Jos 11.3), and in the vicinity of Sidon (2 Sm 24.7), but they receive no mention whatever in any of the extra-Biblical literature. It has been suggested that Hevite is a local name for Hurrian. Another attractive theory is that the Hurrians of Seir (Edom) were really Hevites and that the Hevites mentioned in the Biblical narratives were in fact Hurrians.

More enigmatic still are the references to the Hittites of the Bible, where they are called *Hethites. Historically three groups called *Hittites are known: the Proto-Hittites or Hattians, the Hittites of the 2d millennium B.C. or Nesians who used mostly cuneiform for their writings, and the Hittites of the 1st millennium B.C. whose inscriptions are in hieroglyphics. Who the Hittites of Palestine might have been remains a historical problem. They are said to have dwelt in the vicinity of Hebron (Gn 23.2–4; 25.10) and Bersabee (Beersheba) and in the hill country of southern Palestine (Gn 26.34). It is possible, though not probable, that Hurrian should be substituted for Hittite in the Biblical narratives. All three of these terms—Hurrian, Hevite, Hittite—differ only in the middle letter in the Hebrew consonantal text: *ḥry*, *ḥwy*, and *ḥty*. Confusion, therefore, could easily have resulted in the transmission of the text.

Receiving frequent mention, usually in conjunction with other dispossessed peoples, are the Pherezites (Perizzites). They are found at Bethel, at Sichem, and in the hill country of Juda (Gn 15.20; Ex 3.8, 17; Dt 7.1; Jos 17.15; etc.). However, not much can be said about them. Judging from the above name alone, the Pherezites could have been of Hurrian origin. Names ending in "-izzi" are known from extra-Biblical Hurrian references. Whatever the case may be, they were a distinct ethnic group in the pre-Israelite population of Palestine.

For the peoples who invaded Transjordan shortly before the Israelites, *see* AMMONITES; EDOMITES; MOABITES.

Bibliography: J. BRIGHT, *A History of Israel* (Philadelphia 1959) 106–107. J. C. L. GIBSON, "Observations on Some Important Ethnic Terms in the Pentateuch," JNEastSt 20 (1961) 217–238.

[F. SEPER]

9. HOLY PLACES

For Christians the term holy places of Palestine designates the sites in the Holy Land that have been made sacred by the presence of Jesus or His blessed Mother or the Apostles. From the viewpoint of relative importance, the holy places are either primary or secondary. In the former class are the cave where Jesus was born, the tomb in which He was buried, etc.; in the latter class are the Pool of Siloe, the place where St. Stephen was stoned, etc. The holy places may be connected either with private houses, as the home of Mary at Nazareth, the Cenacle, etc., or with sites in the open, such as the Mount of the Beatitudes, the place at the Jordan where Jesus was baptized, the Garden of Gethsemani, etc. On the basis of scholarly certitude the holy places may be regarded either as authentic or as based on pious legend. To the former class belong the site of the Annunciation, the cave of Christ's Nativity, the tomb of Lazarus at Bethany, etc.; to the latter belong the stations of the *Way of the Cross, the site where Mary and Joseph found Jesus in the Temple, etc.

Nature. Shrines or sanctuaries were erected at the holy places at different times. The reasons for building them were various: to honor the place as a king is honored by giving him a crown, to preserve them from profanation, and especially to have a proper edifice for the celebration of the sacred liturgy. Bad weather or, in certain periods of history, the interference of unbelievers would have prevented Christians from celebrating the Eucharist there in peace, and since the Eucharist was considered the best means of being united with Christ at these venerated sites, sacred edifices were erected there.

In regard to the architectural form, at the holy places the churches are or have been of five naves (the basilica at Bethlehem and the former basilica at Calvary), of three naves (at Gethsemani, Thabor, Bethany, etc.), and of one nave (the ancient chapel of the Multiplication of the Loaves and of the *Beatitudes at et-Tabga), or churches with the ground plan of a Greek cross (formerly at Jacob's Well), or of a circle (the rotunda of the Ascension), or octagonal (over the house of Peter at Capharnaum). The present owners are either Moslems (the church of the Ascension), or Israeli (the Cenacle), or Latin-rite Catholics (Thabor, Nazareth, Capharnaum, Ain Karem, etc.), or Greek Orthodox (Jacob's Well, Jebel Quarantal, i.e., the site of our Lord's 40-day fast), or the three communities jointly of Latin Catholics, Greek Orthodox, and Armenians (the Holy Sepulcher and the Basilica of Bethlehem, in both places the *status quo* going back to 1852, when a Turkish decree ordained that these three Christian communities should henceforth retain what rights they had there as of that year).

From a liturgical aspect, the holy places under the control of Catholics are either of the first class or of the second class. In the former places, plenary indulgences may be gained and proper votive Masses may be celebrated on almost any day; at the latter places partial indulgences may be gained, and votive Masses under certain limitations may be celebrated. Churches with liturgical first-class privileges are those of the Annunciation, the Holy Sepulcher, the Flagellation, etc.; of liturgical second-class privileges are those of Dominus Flevit (where "the Lord wept" on the Mount of Olives), *Cana of Galilee, Bethphage, etc.

History. The sanctuaries at the holy places date almost exclusively from the 4th century, when Christians of Gentile origin first came in numbers to the Holy Land. At first the Judeo-Christians of Palestine regarded the holy places as memorials, and they left most of them in their pristine state. Such were the tombs of Jesus, of the Blessed Virgin, of St. Joseph, and of *Lazarus. But a few of the holy places they adapted, in simple fashion, for Christian worship, such as the house of the Holy Family at Nazareth and the upper room on "Christian Sion." The first important period for the building of Christian sanctuaries at the holy places in Palestine was that of the 4th and 5th centuries, when construction proceeded chiefly under the patronage of the Byzantine emperors. The second such period was in the 12th century, when the crusaders had control of the Holy Land, and the third was from the middle of the 19th century to the present. Between these periods of construction there were periods of destruction: in 614, when Palestine was devastated by the Persians; from 638 to 1099, during which time the Moslems on several occasions destroyed certain Christian sanctuaries, and from 1187 to the present, when the Moslems, though not actively destructive, have often interfered with Christian worship at the holy places.

Authenticity. To evaluate the authenticity of any of the holy places of Palestine, two main conditions must be fulfilled if the site is to be considered authentic: its localization must not contradict the data of the Bible, and the tradition connected with it must go back to Apostolic times. If either of these requirements is missing, the place must be regarded as having merely devotional value. Thus, the localization of *Emmaus at modern Amwas has, in its favor, a tradition going back at least to Byzantine times; but the site does not seem to agree with the Gospel data, since its distance from Jerusalem is much greater than the 60 stadia given in the best manuscripts of Lk 24.13. The location of Emmaus at modern el-Qubeibeh agrees with the Gospel data of 60 stadia, but the tradition connected with this site does not seem to be older than crusader times.

Since almost all the sanctuaries in the Holy Land date from the 4th and later centuries, and consequently the earliest descriptions left by pilgrims date from these centuries, one may wonder how it is possible to show that there is any tradition in regard to them going back to the time of the Apostles. However, for a certain group of the holy places it is possible to suppose that throughout the early centuries of Christianity there were Judeo-Christians in these places who would have been as interested in these sacred sites as modern Christians are. Until not long ago such continuous presence of Judeo-Christians in the Holy Land was not suspected. But recent discoveries at *Nazareth and at Dominus Flevit, as well as a more careful study of the Talmudic sources, of certain statements of the Fathers, and of the sparse data collected by Eusebius, have shown that during the first few Christian centuries a certain number of Judeo-Christians continued to live in Palestine, especially in its mountain regions.

Judeo-Christian Traditions. To mention a few cases in particular, it is known, for instance, that "the brethren [relatives] of the Lord" lived at Nazareth at least until 250 as leaders of the local Christian community, and precisely at the present traditional site of the Annunciation, archeological excavations have brought to light a religious edifice resembling a synagogue that was built not later than the 3d century, together with certain caves that were venerated at even an earlier date. Many graffiti here with the words "holy place" or with such an invocation as X[AIP]E MAPIA ("Hail, Mary!") show, not only the continuous veneration of the place, but also the Judeo-Christian character of its possessors and visitors, which had already been surmised from the literary sources.

The presence of *Mînîm* (Judeo-Christians) at Capharnaum during the early Christian centuries is well known from the Talmud. The tradition locating the *Cenacle on Christian Sion is witnessed to by a retrospective passage in Epiphanius and especially by the so-called "Tomb of David" there, which is to be related with the Christian synagogues at Nazareth. The tomb of the blessed Virgin at *Jerusalem, which is mentioned in Judeo-Christian sources, was held to be connected with "very ancient" tradition when the sanctuary there was erected by Gentile Christians. At the cave of *Gethsemani there was preserved, even after the Constantinian peace, the remembrance of a sacred supper that had been held there formerly by the Judeo-Christians. The cave of the Eleona (ἐλαιών, olive grove) on the *Mount of Olives, regarded as the site where Jesus taught His disciples the *Our Father, is mentioned in the apocryphal sources and is spoken of as a venerated site by Eusebius 5 years before Constantine began his program of building sanctuaries in the Holy Land. The same is true of the tomb of Lazarus and the cave of the Nativity at *Bethlehem. The latter site was known also to Origen and even St. Justin. When the site of the Holy *Sepulcher was recovered in 326, the Gentile Christians took pains to verify its authenticity by establishing its agreement with the Gospel data, such as the earthquake fissure in the rock of *Calvary and the single burial niche in the tomb chamber there, so that the tradition that had been maintained by the Judeo-Christians for this site was relegated to a subordinate position.

The Evangelists did not think it opportune to refer to everything that concerned the holy places. But other points of information were transmitted by the apocryphal Gospels; thus, the Gospel of the Hebrews places the fasting of Jesus on Mount *Thabor, and the Proto-Evangelium of James has the beginning of the Annunciation take place at the fountain in Nazareth. This does not mean that such extraevangelical traditions are always historical. Rather, they give evidence of a difference, going back to a very early period, between Galilean traditions and Judean ones, e.g., regarding the place of the 40-day fast of Jesus after His Baptism. (*See also* TEMPTATIONS OF JESUS.)

Despite the many vicissitudes that Palestine has suffered in the course of its long history, most of the place names throughout the country have been preserved from remote antiquity to the present with remarkable fidelity. Therefore, there is no reason to doubt the local traditions that preserved the Biblical names, not only of such villages as Nazareth and *Nain, but also also of such localities as Gethsemani and Siloe.

From the examples just cited, as well as from others that could be given, it can be seen that, in order to establish the authenticity of the holy places, it is necessary to study each case by itself, against its historical background. To reject all of them as spurious or to accept all of them as authentic without further ado is an easy way out, but it does not lead to the truth.

Exegetical Value. The scientific study of the holy places can contribute much to general Biblical studies, whether this confirms the authenticity of the places or whether it establishes their value more precisely. Thus, for instance, the excavation and study of the Pool of *Bethesda both confirm and explain the statement in Jn 5.2 that this pool had "five porticoes"; the location of the Garden of Gethsemani shows how far from Jerusalem Jesus was when arrested (Mt 26.36, 47); *Jacob's Well at Sichem shows what the Samaritan woman meant when she told Jesus that "the well is deep" (Jn 4.6.11); the sanctuary of the Nativity at Bethlehem shows that the manger in which the infant Jesus was bedded was in a cave that was used for a stable, as many caves still are so used in Palestine (Lk 2.7); the rustic character of Nazareth at the time of Christ, as shown by the archeological excavations there, throws light on Nathanael's question, "Can anything good come out of Nazareth?" (Jn 1.46).

Bibliography: C. KOPP, *The Holy Places of the Gospels,* tr. R. WALLS (New York 1963). E. HOADE, *Guide to the Holy Land* (Jerusalem 1942 and later eds.); *Marian Shrines in Mary's Land* (Ottawa 1958). B. BAGATTI, *L'archeologia cristiana in Palestina* (Florence 1962). D. BALDI, *Enchiridion locorum sanctorum* (2d ed. Jerusalem 1955). G. PERELLA, *I Luoghi Santi* (Piacenza 1936). A. OLIVAN, *Maria nella sua terra* (Milan 1958).
Authenticity of the Holy Places. B. BAGATTI, "Sguardo storico (ai giudeo-cristiani)," *Il simbolismo dei giudeo-cristiani,* ed. E. TESTA (Jerusalem 1962) 19–33; "Sainte Sion," *Saint Jacques le Mineur* (Jerusalem 1962) 13–22; "Le origini della 'tomba della Vergine' in Getsemani," *Revista Biblica Italiana* 11 (1963) 38–52; "Autenticità del S. Sepolcro," *La Terra Santa* 38 (1962) 299–302; "Origine dei Luoghi santi di Palestina," *Liber Annuus* 14 (1963–64) 32–64. E. TESTA, "Le Grotte dei misteri giudeo-cristiane," *ibid.* 65–144. B. BAGATTI, *L'Église de la circoncision* (Jerusalem 1965) 93–113.

[B. BAGATTI]

PALESTINE, EARLY CHURCH IN

Since the time of Diocletian, it was customary to distinguish: (1) Palestina prima, or the middle section of West Jordania, with Caesarea as capital; (2) Palestina secunda, or Galilee and Peraea, with its capital at Scythopolis; (3) Palestina tertia, or salutaris, the southern part of Judaea and Peraea, with capital at Petra.

Early Palestinian Christianity. With the Palestinian revolt against Rome in 66, the Christian community left Jerusalem for Pella in Transjordan. Their bishop was Simeon, relative of Jesus and successor of James. By this gesture the Jewish Christians separated themselves from the Temple, which was destroyed in 70 by Titus. Some Christians returned from Pella, and Eusebius (*Hist. eccl.* 4.5) states that 15 bishops succeeded one another at Jerusalem up to the revolt under Hadrian, all of Hebrew descent. This large number probably includes the *presbyteroi,* one of whom was chosen as bishop. The Christians of Jerusalem adhered to Jewish practices, and the Epistle of Jude and the Apocryphal Gospel of James seem to come from this group. They were not favored by the Jews, and *Bar Kokhba persecuted them during his revolt of 132 to 135. Suppressed by Hadrian, Jerusalem was rebuilt as Aelia Capitolina, and only a few Christians returned. Others migrated to Kokaba in Transjordania, to Nazareth, and to Aleppo. In Jerusalem itself, pagan statues were erected on the site of the Temple, and on Golgotha, the mount of the Crucifixion, a temple was erected to the Capitoline Triad.

Palestinian Bishoprics. Christian missionaries were sent from Palestine to the churches of Egypt, Osrhoene, and Adiabene. Though it was the land where Christianity originated, Palestine was not the scene of its most rapid diffusion and remained considerably behind the Greek-speaking cities of Syria. Palestinian towns with bishops before 325 were, besides Jerusalem and Caesarea (which had a bishop *c.* 190): Maximianopolis; Scythopolis; Sebaste; Flavia Neapolis; Ascalon; Diospolis, or Lydda; Nicopolis; Gadara; Azotus; Ascalon; Eleutheropolis; Jericho; Capitolias; Aila; and Gaza. Jaffa became an episcopal see after the time of Constantine. Pella seems to have become a permanent episcopal see only in the 5th century.

Silver ampulla from Palestine, c. 600, in the Treasury of the cathedral at Monza, Italy. The inscription around the edge reads "Oil from the wood of life, from the holy places of Christ" and shows the piece to be a souvenir of a pilgrimage to the Holy Land.

As early as the reign of Domitian, Gnostic tendencies appeared among the Palestinian Christians. As Vespasian before him, Domitian sought out relatives of Jesus, fearing a renewed Messianism. When Christians were martyred under Trajan, Simeon, bishop of Jerusalem and son of Cleophas, was among them. Lucian's satire in his *Life of Peregrinus* gives a garbled picture of a Palestinian community of the 2d century. When synods were held under Pope Victor concerning the date of Easter, the assembled bishops of Palestine (*c.* 190) wrote a letter acknowledging agreement with the Western usage. Two Palestinian bishops are known to have attended this synod: Theophilus of Caesarea and Narcissus of Jerusalem. Bishops of Syria also were present, a fact that indicates that they did not belong to distinct ecclesiastical provinces at this time. Under Marcus Aurelius, Jerusalem had bishops of gentile descent, e.g., Narcissus and Alexander. Little by little, this community adapted itself to the universal Church, while a minority tended to sectarianism. Virginity was highly honored, and there are indications of a renewed Christian messianism, contemporary with a similar Jewish movement that inspired Septimius Severus, during a journey through Palestine in 202, to forbid further proselytism.

Origen at Caesarea. In 231, Theoctistus, Bishop of Caesarea, ordained *Origen a priest, and made him head of the school which achieved considerable renown. Origen was active as lecturer and preacher, so that the city became an intellectual center for the Christians. The persecution of Valerian produced martyrs in Palestine in 257–258, but in spite of the Emperor's hostility the majority of the region had been Christianized by the end of the 3d century.

As early as 260, Theotecnus, a student of Origen, was bishop of Caesarea, and under his successor the school was directed by *Pamphilus who continued the tradition established by Origen and developed the famous library, which contained many Christian texts, including the Hexapla. Its intellectual direction reflected Alexandrian rather than Antiochene thought. When Arius was condemned, however, he took refuge with *Eusebius of Caesarea, and was declared innocent by a local council in Palestine, even though the bishop of Jerusalem, Macarius, opposed him. A certain number of Palestinian bishops, including Maximus and St. *Cyril of Jerusalem, agreed with the condemnation of Arius at Nicaea, but Eusebius of Caesarea led the attack against the Nicaean bishops that culminated in the council of Tyre-Jerusalem of 335. This assembly deposed Athanasius and repudiated the term *homoousios. The successor of Eusebius, Acacius of Caesarea, became the head of the homoean faction and with imperial help in 360 reversed ecclesiastical power in the East. But even the support of the Emperor Valens (364–378) could not prevent the victory of orthodoxy. In 379, 153 Eastern bishops expressed their agreement with Rome.

Palestinian Monasticism. Monasticism began in Palestine during the first years of the 4th century with Hilarion of Gaza, who settled near Maiuma and whose fame attracted disciples. The Laura of Pharan on the Dead Sea was founded by St. Chariton of Iconium about 320, and the coenobitic form of monastic life flourished. Other foundations were those of St. *Epiphanius of Constantia (*c.* 335) at Besanduk near Eleutheropolis; of SS. *Euthymius and Theoctistus near

Jericho; of St. *Gerasimus on the Jordan; and of St. *Theodosius near Bethlehem. Particularly important and lasting to our own times is the Great Laura founded near Jerusalem by St. *Sabas (d. 532). Latin monks were located at Bethlehem under St. *Jerome (386), while nuns dwelt nearby under Paula. *Melania the Elder and *Rufinus of Aquileia founded a double monastery on Mt. Olivet in Jerusalem (c. 376). *Melania the Younger took up her abode there early in the 5th century and erected two monasteries, as she had previously done at Tagaste in Africa.

In the 4th century Jerusalem entered into dispute with Caesarea over possession of the metropolitan see. The Council of Nicaea (c. 7) admitted a special position of honor for Jerusalem. But its bishops, particularly John (386–417) desired metropolitan status, and in 451 the Council of *Chalcedon declared Juvenal (421–458) patriarch and head of the three provinces of Palestine at the expense of Antioch.

Jerusalem further owed its growing importance to pilgrimages, which became progressively popular in the 4th century. *Constantine I and *Helena erected several magnificent buildings in Jerusalem and Bethlehem. The liturgy of Jerusalem, described by Aetheria, exercised a great influence in the whole church, by reason of the pilgrims who witnessed it (see ITINERARIA).

Monophysitism and Origenism. Palestine had a strong anti-Chalcedonian party, though weaker than in Syria and Egypt. Juvenal, the patriarch, was ejected and replaced by an opponent of the council of Chalcedon and was not restored until the Byzantine army had defeated hordes of fanatical monks in 453. Though the monks generally favored orthodoxy, especially under Euthymius and Sabas, the Monophysite leaders, and particularly the intruder Theodosius, installed anti-Chalcedonians in many sees, and the opposition was kept alive especially from the monastery of Maiuma. In 513 the monk Severus succeeded in having Elias, the patriarch of Jerusalem, exiled even though he was defended by the great abbots, Theodosius and Sabas. The Patriarch John (d. 524) was hostile to the Monophysites, so that Jerusalem was the only patriarchate not in the hands of the Monophysites when Justin became emperor in 519. Since Jerusalem relied upon the powerful patriarchate of Constantinople for protection against its rivals, Antioch and Alexandria, it was involved on the side of this see in the *Acacian Schism. In the 6th century, it was considered to hold fourth place among the patriarchates of the East, after Constantinople, Alexandria, and Antioch.

*Pelagianism was dealt with by a provincial council at Diospolis (or Lydda) in 415, which was misinformed by Pelagius and declared him innocent. A dispute over Origenism lead to a heated controversy at the end of the 4th century between Bp. John of Jerusalem and Rufinus on the one side, and SS. Jerome and Epiphanius on the other. The problem became acute in the 6th century when the monks of the New Laura of Thecue defended Origen's orthodoxy, whereas the outstanding monk of Palestine, St. Sabas, head of the old or Great Laura, led his opponents. When two Origenist monks, Domitian and *Theodore Ascidas, were named bishops by Justinian and enlisted the support of *Theodora (1) in their cause, a strong anti-Origenist movement was begun by the Patriarch Peter of Jerusalem. This led to a Synod at Gaza (539) and an edict of Justinian in 542

condemning nine propositions of Origen. Several Palestinian monks, headed by Theodore Ascidas, in the desire to avenge themselves and to avoid further persecution, persuaded Justinian to devote himself to another problem, that of the *Three Chapters.

In addition to the earliest Judeo-Christian writers of Palestine, several early apologists and propagandists are considered Palestinian by birth or activity: Ariston of Pella, *Justin Martyr, *Julius Africanus, Pamphilus and Eusebius of Caesarea, Cyril of Jerusalem, Epiphanius of Constantia, and *Cyril of Scythopolis. The end of the 6th and the beginning of the 7th centuries constituted a period of prosperity, but the Persian invasion of 614 proved catastrophic: thousands of Christians were slaughtered, many churches and monasteries were destroyed or damaged, and the patriarch Zacharias was exiled. At this time the true cross was captured. Even though the victory of the Emperor *Heraclius forced the Persians to restore the cross, the dispute over *Monothelitism brought new troubles, and the Patriarch St. *Sophronius (634–638) sharply attacked this heresy. But he was forced to arrange the surrender of Jerusalem to the Arabs under the Caliph Omar in 637; and although Christianity survived under Moslem rule, the distrust of the Arabs for the orthodox patriarchs made it impossible to give him a successor for 68 years.

Bibliography: Le Quien. F. M. ABEL, *Histoire de la Palestine,* 2 v. (Paris 1952). A. VON HARNACK, *The Mission and Expansion of Christianity in the First Three Centuries,* tr. and ed. J. MOFFATT, 2 v. (2d ed. New York 1908). Jedin HbKirchgesch v.1. Daniélou-Marrou ChrCent. J. A. FITZMEYER, "The Bar Cochba Period," in *The Bible in Current Catholic Thought,* ed. J. L. McKenzie (New York 1962) 133–168. F. VAN DER MEER and C. MOHRMANN, *Atlas of the Early Christian World,* ed. and tr. M. F. HEDLUND and H. H. ROWLEY (New York 1958). L. DUCHESNE, *L'Église au VIᵉ siècle* (Paris 1925). Fliche-Martin v.1–4. Stein-Palanque HistBEmp v.1–2. **Illustration credit:** Hirmer Verlag München.

[J. J. GAVIGAN]

PALESTRINA, GIOVANNI PIERLUIGI DA

Foremost composer of Renaissance vocal polyphony of the Roman school; b. Palestrina, Italy (whence the name by which he has been known ever since), probably at the end of 1525; d. Rome, Feb. 2, 1594. He may have been a chorister of the Palestrina cathedral, for after its bishop, Cardinal della Valle, had been made archpriest of the basilica of St. Mary Major, Rome (1534), the young boy was transferred to that choir and was singing as a full member in 1537. He returned home when his voice changed in 1539 but began his higher musical education in Rome in 1540. At that time the new St. Peter's was being built, and the city was full of great Renaissance artists, architects, and sculptors—a stimulating environment for the rising musician. In 1544, his training finished, he was appointed *organista e maestro di canto* of the cathedral of Palestrina, a post that lasted 7 years, during which time he married a fairly wealthy girl. When the reigning bishop of Palestrina, Cardinal del Monte, became Pope Julius III (1551), the young composer returned to Rome, this time as master of the Julian choir.

The Early Phase of His Work. His first volume of Masses, dedicated to Julius and containing the famous engraving of the Pope receiving the music from Palestrina's hands, was published in 1554. Four of these Masses are earlier compositions, but the fifth, *Ecce*

Giovanni Pierluigi da Palestrina, 16th-century portrait in the convent of the Fathers of the Oratory at Rome.

Sacerdos Magnus, was a new work in the Pope's honor. Julius' ill-advised reward was to appoint him to the pontifical choir, an exclusive and proud body of singers, who were not pleased to have the newcomer forced upon them. This appointment, moreover, meant that Palestrina had to give up his Julian choirmastership. Even more unluckily, Julius III died within 3 months, and his successor, Marcellus, within 23 days of election. The next pope, Paul IV, a reformer, soon found two reasons to dismiss Palestrina from his new position: he was married, and he had recently published a book of madrigals—both were against the rules for Church musicians. The young man, however, had the perspicacity to obtain a papal pension that was to last for the rest of his life, even though he had been a member of the choir for only a few months.

The music at the Lateran Basilica had deteriorated since the departure of *Lasso for Antwerp in 1555, and in October of the same year Palestrina easily obtained this post (his impressive *Lamentations* setting was composed there; *see* TENEBRAE). Although the pay was small, he had his pension and also a wine-selling business. Indeed, so sure was he of his financial position that he could afford to leave the Lateran over a monetary squabble concerning his eldest son; he did not accept another position until March 1561, when he became choirmaster at St. Mary Major, the basilica of his childhood. But a few years later restlessness overtook him, and an opportunity to direct the music in the fabulous Villa d'Este during the summer of 1564 turned his thoughts to court employment. Also, the new Roman seminary had offered him the directorship

of music with free living, education for his family, and leisure to pursue his courtly career; it is not surprising, therefore, that he relinquished the position at St. Mary Major. These years, however, remained indecisive, and after an offer from Emperor Maximilian of Vienna had been lost through Palestrina's own cupidity, he turned his attention to ecclesiastical work. The one friend in all these courtly contacts was the Duke of Mantua, to whom he sent many compositions during 20 years. In 1571 he again accepted the mastership of the Julian choir, and from this time on he was exclusively a church musician. His good fortune, however, was darkened by a series of personal sorrows. The ever-present Roman plagues and pestilences killed his son Rodolfo in 1572, his brother Silla a year later, his second son Angelo in 1575, and finally (1580), the wife whom he had deeply loved.

During this long, checkered period, Palestrina had published several collections: the first book of motets in 1563, the second book of Masses (which included the *Missa di Papa Marcello*), in 1567, and more motets in 1569.

The Later Phase. His style changed notably at this time: the number of vocal parts began to increase. In 1572 the number in the motets rose from the usual four and five to from five to seven, and in 1575 to eight. The style of composition, too, rapidly matured. The early canonic writing which featured Netherlandish technique gave way to a more serene style where contrapuntal and homophonic writing were integrated into a unique fluency, and the madrigalism of the earlier works almost disappeared. His sorrows had enabled him to produce some of his more poignant works, such as the *Improperia* and some of the *Lamentations* as well as many of the larger motets. From 1577 he was engaged partly in an abortive effort to revise the Gradual, whose plainsong had become so full of errors that it was impossible to construct a unified liturgy. This herculean task was abandoned after a few years, and nothing more was done about it for another 4 decades. The Medicean edition, as it was called when finally published, had little or no connection with Palestrina's work (*see* CHANT BOOKS, PRINTED EDITIONS OF).

Depressed by his losses of both family and fortune, Palestrina turned to religion and offered himself for the priesthood. He received the tonsure and even a benefice, but within a few months he was quietly married to a rich widow who brought with her a prosperous furrier's business. Palestrina, ever a resourceful businessman, switched comfortably from the wine trade to furs, and life began afresh. Whereas publication of his works had been sporadic between 1563 and 1575, three volumes were produced in the year 1581 and another in 1582. Indeed, these last 13 years saw the publication of 16 different collections, comprising more than 400 compositions. After his death, his son Iginio published many volumes of Masses and motets, but some of the finest works, because of changing musical fashion, remained in manuscript. Glorious Masses like *Assumpta Est Maria* and *Ecce Ego Joannes,* and motets, such as *Salve Regina* and *O Sacrum Convivium,* had to wait for 3 centuries before gaining wide currency.

Evaluation. Palestrina's position at the end of his century was rather like that of Bach after his death. Both composers used a conservative technique, a style virtually reflecting a past age, although in a strikingly individual and compelling manner. But the new music was already emerging, and it is small wonder that their music was abandoned as being old-fashioned. There is no doubt that Palestrina deliberately adopted a restrained manner of composing in order to produce a more remote and less modern style than that of his contemporaries. Even the madrigals, both secular and spiritual, are restrained to a point where they may be compared unfavorably with those of lesser contemporaries, although they contain much good music. Some of the early church music is a little unsure and derivative, but the works of his middle period, and certainly his later compositions are ideal for liturgical use. They possess those qualities of serenity and impersonality that are essential for divine worship.

Palestrina's coffin bore the title *Princeps Musicae.* It could be argued that composers such as *Morales, Lasso, and *Victoria were perhaps more adventurous, and that Lasso and many others were more effective in the secular field. No one, however, would seriously deny Palestrina the title *Princeps Musicae Sacrae.*

See also MUSIC, SACRED, HISTORY OF, 4.

Bibliography: *Opera omnia,* ed. F. X. HABERL, 33 v. (Leipzig 1862–1903), see pref. by Haberl; *Le Opere complete,* ed. R. CASIMIRI et al. (Rome 1939–), there are innumerable performing editions of his most popular items.

Biography: G. BAINI, *Memorie Storico-critiche della vita e delle opere . . .,* 2 v. (Rome 1828), a curiosity. M. BOBILLIER, *Palestrina,* 2 v. in 1 (Paris 1906). F. RAUGEL, *Palestrina* (Paris 1930). H. COATES, *Palestrina* (New York 1938; repr. 1949), best biog.

Technical. A. CAMETTI, "Le case di G. P. da Palestrina in Roma," *Rivista musicale italiana* 28 (1921) 419–432; "Rubino Mallapert, maestro di G. P. da Palestrina," *ibid.* 29 (1922) 335–347; "G. P. da Palestrina e le sue alleanze matrimoniali," *ibid.* 30 (1923) 489–510. R. CASIMIRI, *Giovanni Pierluigi da Palestrina Nuovi documenti biografici,* 2 pts. (Rome 1918–22), pamphlet; *Il codice 59 del'archivio musicale lateranense, autografo di inedite e dieci tavole fototipiche* (Rome 1919), pamphlet. H. K. ANDREWS, *An Introduction to the Technique of Palestine* (London 1958), the only complete study of Palestrina's technique of composition. K. G. FELLERER, *Palestrina* (Regensburg 1930). K. JEPPESEN, *The Style of Palestrina and the Dissonance,* tr. M. W. HAMERIK (New York 1927). Reese MusR. Láng MusWC. **Illustration credit:** Giraudon.

[P. E. PEACOCK]

PALEY, FREDERICK, A.,

English classical scholar; b. Easingwold, near York, Jan. 14, 1815; d. Bournemouth, Dec. 9, 1888. His father and grandfather were Anglican clergymen. After completing his secondary education at Shrewsbury School, he matriculated at St. John's College, Cambridge, and received his B.A. degree in 1838. He continued his studies there until 1846, when he was expelled from residence at St. John's on the charge that he had encouraged one of his students to become a Catholic. He became a Catholic himself in the same year. He supported himself as a tutor in prominent Catholic families until 1860, when he was permitted to return to Cambridge, remaining there until 1874. He then accepted the post of professor of classical literature in the short-lived Catholic University College at Kensington (1873–77). He was classical examiner to the University of London from 1875 to 1880, and then spent his last years in semiretirement at Bournemouth in Hampshire. A man of versatile talent and interests, he published studies in ecclesiastical architecture as well as in classics and contributed to a wide range of journals, including the *American Catholic Quarterly.* Of his voluminous output in the classical field, only his edition of Aeschylus (1844–51) and his prefaces to editions of certain authors, especially to that of Euripides (1857), have lasting value. He enjoyed a great vogue in his own period, particularly as the editor of school texts, but he was not familiar with the contemporary German classical scholarship in Greek and Latin and made no significant scholarly contributions beyond those mentioned.

Bibliography: E. C. MARCHANT, DNB 15:99–101, with a listing of 52 publications by title. Sandys 3:409–410.

[M. R. P. MC GUIRE]

PALEY, WILLIAM,

English divine and philosopher; b. Peterborough, July 1743; d. Lincoln, May 25, 1805. Educated at Christ's College, Cambridge, he served there as a successful lecturer and tutor until 1776, when he became rector of Musgrave in Westmorland. In 1782 he was made archdeacon of Carlisle. *The Principles of Moral and Political Philosophy* (London 1785), based on his lectures at Cambridge, went through 15 editions in his lifetime and was used at Cambridge as a standard textbook. His most original work, *Horae Paulinae, or the Truth of the Scripture History of St. Paul evinced by a Comparison of the Epistles which bear his Name and the Acts of the Apostles and with one another,* appeared in 1790. The most famous of his books are *A View of the Evidences of Christianity* (2 v. London 1794), and *Natural Theology, or Evidences of the Existence and Attributes of the Deity collected from the Appearances of Nature* (London 1802), in which he set forth his fully developed argument from design for the existence of God. He changed the ground of the argument from astronomy to anatomy in order to argue to God from the evidences of design in animal and human organisms. One of the most successful apologists of his time, Paley was a guiding light of the "evidential school" of rationalist theologians who were very influential in the Church of England, especially at Oxford, during the early 19th century, and against whose ideas the leaders of the Oxford Movement reacted.

Bibliography: *Works,* ed. E. PALEY, 7 v. (London 1825). Copleston 5:195–199. L. STEPHEN, DNB 15:101–107; *History of English Thought in the Eighteenth Century,* 2 v. (London 1927).

[E. SILLEM]

PALI CANON

The main body of the Buddhist canonical texts developed in the period between Buddha's death (483 B.C.) and Asoka's reign (273–231 B.C.), though its oral tradition was committed to writing in the Pāli language only in the reign of Vattāgamani Abhaya (29–17 B.C.), in Ceylon. The *Tipiṭaka* (Skt. *Tripiṭaka*), The Three Baskets of Theravāda tradition, consists of three main divisions.

The first is the *Vinaya Piṭaka,* The Basket of Rules for the orders of monks, nuns, and lay people, subdivided into three collections: (1) *Suttavibhaṅga,* under 15 headings grouping the rules for individual discipline and the disciplinary action required in case of infringement; (2) *Khandhaka,* in 22 chapters outlining the norms for the organization of the orders; (3) *Parivāra,* containing 19 supplementary sections on the foundation of the order of nuns and the sacred councils, which were convoked at Rājagṛha and Vaiśālī.

The second is the *Sutta Piṭaka,* The Basket of Discourses, attributed to Buddha, divided into five sections (*nikāya*): (1) *Dīgha Nikāya,* a series of 34 long lectures on points of doctrine (reward of asceticism, attitude to caste, points of contact and contrast with Brahmanism), including the *Mahāparinibbānasuttanta* (The Great Chapter of Complete Nirvāṇa), an account of the last days of Buddha; (2) *Majjhima Nikāya,* a series of 152 medium-length sermons and dialogues on points of Buddhist religion; (3) *Saṃyutta Nikāya,* a series of more than 2,700 short statements on related topics, including the *Dhammacakkapavattanavagga,* the so-called Sermon of Benares on setting in motion the wheel of the law; (4) *Aṅguttara Nikāya,* a progressive series of 11 sections arranged according to the number of topics expounded in each; (5) *Khuddaka Nikāya,* "minor series" of 15 works including the exquisite and ancient stanzas of the *Dhammapada* (Way of the Law), the *Theragāthā,* and *Therīgāthā,* psalms for choir recitation, and the *Jātaka* containing 547 stories of former lives of Buddha, along with the *Nidānakathā,* the oldest connected biography of Buddha in three parts.

The third is the *Abhidhamma Piṭaka,* The Basket of Supplementary Doctrines, treating in systematic fashion doctrinal questions evidently raised at a later epoch in debates among rival schools and comprising seven works: *Puggalapaññatti; Dhātukathāpakarana; Dhammasaṃgani; Vibhaṅga; Patthānapakarana; Yamaka;* and *Kathāvatthu.*

See also BUDDHISM.

Bibliography: B. C. LAW, *A History of Pāli Literature,* 2 v. (London 1933). M. WINTERNITZ, *A History of Indian Literature,* tr. S. KATKAR, 2 v. (London 1927–34) v.2. G. BORSANI, *Prospetti e Indice del Tipiṭaka* (Milan 1942). A. S. ROSSO, "Buddhism in India, Ceylon and Burma," *Worldmission* 3 (1952) 62–82. A. BAREAU, *Les Premiers conciles bouddhiques* (Paris 1956). W. RAHULA, *The History of Buddhism in Ceylon: The Anuradhapura Period, 3d Century, B.C. - 10th Century A.D.* (Colombo, Ceylon 1956). W. T. DE BARY et al., comps., *Sources of Indian Tradition* (Records of Civilization 56; New York 1958). G. F. ALLEN, ed. and tr., *The Buddha's Philosophy: Selections from the Pāli Canon and an Introductory Essay* (New York 1959). A. B. GOVINDA, *The Psychological Attitude of Early Buddhist Philosophy and its Systematic Representation according to Abhidhamma Tradition* (London 1961). C. H. PHILIPS, ed., *Historians of India, Pakistan and Ceylon* (New York 1961).

[A. S. ROSSO]

PALIMPSEST, a technical term of paleography, used to designate a MS of leather or parchment that was used more than once. Since such materials were scarce and expensive, the writing was often erased from an old codex by washing and/or scraping, so that the surface could be used again. The term refers only to leather or parchment MSS, since papyrus and paper would not permit such rough treatment. If the MS was erased twice, it was called a double palimpsest. The original writing was seldom completely destroyed and can frequently be read, at least in part. As a result, some palimpsests have great value for the scholar. Chemical agents such as ammonium hydrosulfide once proved useful in making the text readable, but today ultraviolet lamps and especially infrared photography aid in deciphering a text. The most famous palimpsests of the Bible are the Codex Ephraemi Rescriptus (C), Codex Nitriensis (R), and Codex Syrus-Sinaiticus.

Illustration credit: Bibliothèque Nationale, Paris.

[T. H. WEBER]

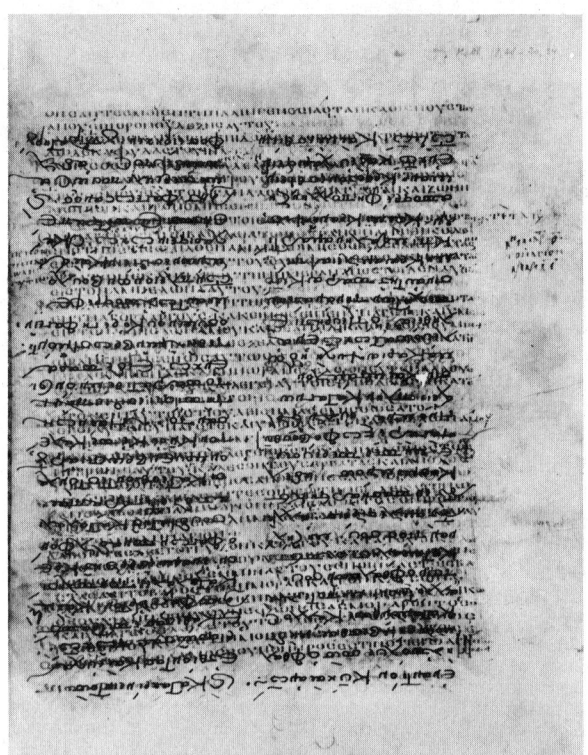

Palimpsest folio from Codex Ephraemi Rescriptus (Cod. gr. 9, fol. 60v). Two lines of the original uncial text show clearly at the top of the page. The cursive Greek text (here inverted) was the later addition.

PALLADINO, LAWRENCE BENEDICT, missionary; b. Tiglieto, Italy, Aug. 15, 1837; d. Missoula, Montana, Aug. 19, 1927. Lawrence was the youngest boy of Giulio and Maddalena (Rizzi) Palladino's seven children. After attending Genoa's minor seminary, he became a Jesuit novice at Querciuoli in the Duchy of Modena, Italy, Nov. 18, 1855. The anti-

Lawrence Benedict Palladino.

clericalism of Italian nationalists explains his training in Austria and France before he was ordained on May 30, 1863, at Nice, France. Early in 1864 he went to California, where he studied and taught at St. Ignatius

College, San Francisco, until 1867. He then began missionary service in the Pacific Northwest. During the next 60 years he worked among settlers and Indians in Washington, Idaho, and Montana. He is usually associated with Montana where he spent 44 years (at St. Ignatius Mission, at Helena, and at Missoula). He purchased property in Helena that was later transferred to John B. Brondel, first Bishop of Helena, when the see was established in 1884. Palladino served at different times as the new bishop's secretary, counselor, director of education, and vicar-general. He spent many years, also, as pastor of St. Francis Xavier's Church, Missoula. His civic activities during Montana's formative years and his role as regional historian gave his works lasting value. Because of the disappearance of many of the materials he used, his *Indian and White in the Northwest: A History of Catholicity in Montana* (1894) became a primary source for Montana history.

Bibliography: W. N. BISCHOFF, *The Jesuits in Old Oregon* (Caldwell, Idaho 1945). W. P. SCHOENBERG, *Jesuits in Montana, 1840–1960* (Portland, Ore. 1960). **Illustration credit:** Montana Historical Society.

[W. N. BISCHOFF]

PALLADIO, ANDREA, greatest architect of the later 16th century in Italy; b. Padua, 1508; d. Vicenza, 1580. Palladio was a humanist and theorist as well as a practicing architect. He wrote two small but influential guidebooks to Roman antiquities and the *Quattro*

Architectural elevation, engraving in Andrea Palladio's "Quattro libri dell'architettura," Venice, 1570.

libri dell'architettura (1570). To an unusual degree Palladio's buildings were constructed in accordance with his theories, derived from *Alberti and *Vitruvius and from careful study of classical monuments. He is best known for his palaces and villas built near Vicenza, e.g., the Villa Rotunda (begun 1550), which follows his typical plan of a hall on the central axis flanked by rooms arranged symmetrically on either side. The square central portion is surmounted by a dome; a temple portico on each side serves as a porch. The extreme complication in ground plan and architectural detail of the Palazzo Valmarana (1566) is influenced by Michelangelo's Capitoline palaces and antique architecture. Palladio's individualistic late style may be seen in the Loggia del Capitanio (1571) and three Venetian churches. In S. Giorgio Maggiore (1566–1610) the superimposition of a high temple front on a lower one reflects the varying heights of nave and aisles. Palladio's work can best be understood within Venetian architectural tradition.

Bibliography: R. WITTKOWER, *Architectural Principles in the Age of Humanism* (3d ed. London 1962). **Illustration credit:** Harvard College Library.

[M. M. SCHAEFER]

PALLADIUS, ST., 5th-century bishop of Ireland; d. probably in Brittany, after 432 (feast, July 6). According to the *Chronicon* of *Prosper of Aquitaine, Pope *Celestine I sent Palladius, a Roman deacon "ad Scottos in Christum credentes," to the Christians of Ireland, where he labored to combat Pelagianism and reorganize the Church. His history is complicated by the legends that accompany the diverse lives of St. *Patrick. Palladius seems to have settled near a Christian center (the port of Inber De, south of Dublin?) and he had to battle against *Pelagianism. The details concerning his departure from Ireland in 432 and the possible lack of success that caused it, as well as his death in Britain, are not certain. On learning of the death of Palladius, Patrick, then in Gaul, is supposed to have received permission from *Germanus of Auxerre to continue the work of Palladius in Ireland. The *Chronicon* of Prosper of Aquitaine alleges that Palladius was still in Ireland in 433 or 434, but this interpretation is not widely held.

Bibliography: ActSS July 2:286–290. L. GOUGAUD, *Christianity in Celtic Lands,* tr. M. JOYNT (London 1932). J. L. G. MEISSNER, *Proceedings of the Royal Irish Academy* 40 (1931–32) 371. P. GROSJEAN, AnalBoll 63 (1945) 73–86, 112–119. J. CARNEY, *The Problem of St. Patrick* (Dublin 1961).

[P. ROCHE]

PALLADIUS OF HELENOPOLIS

Fourth-century monk, bishop, and writer; b. Galatia, 363 or 364; d. probably Aspuna, before 431. At 23, a pupil of *Evagrius Ponticus, he embraced the monastic life on the Mount of Olives in Jerusalem. Later he became acquainted with the Egyptian ascetics, spent some time in Alexandria, and retired to the Nitrian Desert about 390. He remained there for 9 years, became ill, and at the advice of an Alexandrian physician returned to Palestine (399). The next year he journeyed to Bithynia and was consecrated bishop of Helenopolis by (St.) *John Chrysostom.

When sent to Ephesus to investigate charges brought against Bp. Antoninus by Eusebius of Valentinopolis,

Palladius appeared with John Chrysostom at the Synod of the *Oak near Chalcedon in 403. The Synod banished John, and Palladius went to Rome to lay the case before Pope *Innocent I (405). The Western Emperor *Honorius sent him to Constantinople with a decision in favor of John, but the Eastern Emperor Arcadius exiled him to Egypt, where, at Syene (406–408), he wrote his *Dialogus de vita Sancti Joannis Chrysostomi,* a principal source for the life of John Chrysostom.

Palladius spent 4 years in the Thebaid of Egypt at Antinoë and returned to his diocese only after opposition to John Chrysostom ceased in 412. In Galatia he lived with a priest named Philoramus, and in 417 he was transferred to the Diocese of Aspuna, where he wrote the *Lausiac History* (419–420). The *Epistola de Indicis gentibus et de Bragmannibus* attributed to Palladius suggests a trip to India; but is actually a report he seems to have received from a Theban advocate. The Palladian authorship is suggested by similarities in style and diction with his other works.

The writings of Palladius have a moral purpose. His *Dialogus* seeks to edify by the example of a saintly bishop and shows how John Chrysostom's enemies fell victims to greed and pride in planning his downfall. In the *Historia Lausiaca* he portrays the life of good monks but does not develop a theory of ascetical theology. He used the example of those who had fallen from grace to show how temptations to pride and vainglory must be expelled. The *Epistola* describes the gymnosophists of India as dedicated to an ascetical ideal. This work was read and copied frequently during the Middle Ages.

The Palladian authorship of these works has been contested. In antiquity, however, there was no doubt that the interlocutors in the *Dialogus* are Palladius and Bishop John. The exordium is strongly reminiscent of the opening passage in Plato's *Republic*.

The *Lausiac History* of Palladius is a work of the highest importance for the history of early monasticism. In the 19th century his veracity was questioned; but today the work is accepted as reliable in the sections where Palladius had spoken to the people involved or had seen the events he describes. His account falters when he depends upon hearsay.

The *Epistola de Indicis* was known in Europe during the Middle Ages in a garbled Latin translation as the *Commonitorium Palladii* supposedly translated by St. Ambrose. Actually only the first part of the work belongs to Palladius; and thus far no satisfactory proof has been offered against his authorship.

Bibliography: PALLADIUS OF HELENOPOLIS, *Dialogus de vita S. Joannis Chrysostomi,* ed. P. R. COLEMAN-NORTON (Cambridge, Eng. 1928); Eng. tr. H. MOORE (London 1921); *The Lausiac History,* ed. C. BUTLER, 2 v. (Cambridge, Eng. 1898–1904); ed. and tr. R. T. MEYER (AncChrWr; 1965). H. RAHNER, LexThK² 8:6. H. LECLERCQ, DACL 13.1:912–930. A. KURFESS, Pauly-Wiss RE 18.3 (1949) 203–207. Quasten Patr 3:176–180. J. D. M. DERRETT, "The History of *Palladius on the Races of India and the Brahmans,*" *Classica et Mediaevalia* 21 (1960) 64–99. E. SCHWARTZ, "Palladiana," ZNTWiss 36 (1937) 161–204. F. X. MURPHY, *Rufinus of Aquileia* (Washington 1945) 175–179. R. DRAGUET, RHE 41 (1946) 321–364; 42 (1947) 5–49.

[R. T. MEYER]

PALLAVICINO, PIETRO SFORZA,

cardinal, historian, theologian; b. Rome, Nov. 28, 1607; d. Rome, June 5, 1667. Although he was a descendant of the Parma line of the noble Pallavicini family, he renounced his rights as first-born to become a cleric. He studied letters, philosophy, and theology at the Roman College, and law at the Sapienza. He became a doctor of theology (1628), and on June 21, 1637, he entered the Society of Jesus, becoming a professor of philosophy and then of theology at the Roman College. In the spring of 1652 he took up his greatest work, the history of the Council of Trent. His friend Alexander VII proclaimed him a cardinal on Nov. 10, 1659. In his earlier years he was strongly inclined toward purely literary pursuits, publishing works on literary style and a tragedy, *Ermenegildo martire.* In his later theological writings, *Del bene* (4 v. Rome 1644), *Assertiones theologicae* (Rome 1649–52), and *Disputationes in primam secundae D. Thomas* (Rome 1653), he was a faithful disciple of Cardinal Juan de Lugo and not an original thinker. Pallavicino proved his loyalty to his order by his *Vindicationes Societatis Jesus* (Rome 1649) and his last published work *Arte della perfezione cristiana* (Rome 1665). On his historical works rests his greatest fame. His *Vita di Alessandro VII,* which remained in manuscript till 1839, is a careful work of high value. Since the appearance of the antipapal *Historia del Concilio Tridentino* by Paolo *Sarpi in 1619 there had been need for a refutation based on a thorough study of available documents. Terenzio Alciati, SJ, who had been gathering materials for such a work for 25 years, died in 1651. Pallavicino was given the task and the work appeared during 1656 and 1657 and in further improved editions. For centuries it was a reliable source, though heavy with polemical tone.

Bibliography: I. AFFÒ, *Memorie della vita e degli studi del Cardinale Sforza Pallavicino* (Faenza 1792). Sommervogel 6: 120–143. J. DUHR, DTC 11.2:1831–34. Koch JesLex 1362–63. H. JEDIN, *Der Quellenapparat der Konzilsgeschichte Pallavicinos* (Rome 1940). Jedin Trent. I. MACCHIA, *Relazioni fra il padre gesuita Sforza Pallavicino e Fabio Chigi* (Turin 1907).

[A. C. WAND]

PALLEN, CONDÉ BENOIST,

editor; b. St. Louis, Mo., Dec. 5, 1858; d. New York City, May 26, 1929. His parents were Montrose A., a physician and

Condé Benoist Pallen.

teacher of medicine, and Anne (Benoist) Pallen, daughter of a St. Louis banker and a descendant of the Chevalier Benoist who served with Montcalm in the French and Indian War. After graduating from Georgetown University, Washington, D.C., Pallen received a doctorate (1885) from St. Louis University, Mo., and taught there briefly before continuing his studies in Rome. After his return to St. Louis he was editor of *Church Progress* (1887–97) and served as Catholic revisory editor for two general encyclopedias. He joined a small group of scholars to project the first comprehensive Catholic encyclopedia in the English language, serving as an organizer of the board of editors (1904–05) and as managing editor (1905–13); *The Catholic Encyclopedia* (16 v., 1907–14; supplement, 1922) became the authoritative international work of reference on the constitution, discipline, and history of the Catholic Church. As president of the Encyclopedia Press, Inc. (1913–20), he was later associated with other publishing ventures, including the *New Catholic Dictionary* (1929).

Pallen was an advocate of conservative economic and social views and served as chairman of the department of subversive movements of the National Civic Federation. Leo XIII honored him with the medal *pro ecclesia et pontifice* and Pius XI named him a Knight of St. Gregory. His published works include numerous articles and *The Philosophy of Literature* (1897), *New Rubaiyat* (1898), *Epochs of Literature* (1898), *The Feast of Thalarchus* (1901), *Death of Sir Launcelot and Other Poems* (1902), *The Meaning of the Idylls of the King* (1904), *Collected Poems* (1915), *Education of Boys* (1916), *The Story of Literature* (1917), *Crucible Island* (1919), *As Man to Man: The Adventures of a Commuter* (1927), *Ghost House* (1928), and *The King's Coil* (1928).

[F. X. GERRITY]

PALLIUM

The pallium is a circular band about 2 inches wide, made of white wool, and worn over the chasuble about the neck, breast, and shoulders. It has two pendants, one hanging down in front, the other in back. It is set with six black crosses of silk, one each on the breast and back, one on each shoulder, and one on each of the pendants.

In the Oriental Churches the pallium is a longer and wider cloth, marked by four red crosses and given by the Oriental patriarchs to their metropolitans and other distinguished bishops, once the patriarchs have themselves received the Latin pallium from the Roman pontiff.

The pallium is made (at least partially) from the wool of two lambs—suggesting Christ, the Lamb of God and the Good Shepherd—blessed each year in Rome (on Jan. 21, the feast of St. Agnes, in her basilica on Via Nomentana), presented to the pope, and sent to the Benedictine Sisters of St. Cecilia in Trastevere. There they are cared for and shorn and the wool is used for weaving the pallia, which are blessed by the pope in the Vatican basilica on June 28, the eve of the feast of SS. Peter and Paul. Then the prefect of pontifical ceremonies places them in a silver urn, enclosed in a cabinet under the Altar of the Confession and over the tomb of St. Peter in the Vatican basilica. The same prefect, to whom the keys of the cabinet are entrusted, takes the pallia, as needed (usually on the occasion of a consistory), and places them at the disposal of the cardinal protodeacon or whoever is entitled or delegated to proceed to their imposition.

Fig. 1. Archbishop Maximinianus wearing the pallium, from the mosaic in S. Vitale, Ravenna, c. 547.

Origin and Symbolism. The pallium began to be worn in the 4th century by bishops of the Eastern Churches and by the Bishop of Rome to emphasize the episcopal dignity and pastoral office. One cannot say definitely whence it derived. In the 6th century, the pallium was conferred by the pope on bishops of the Latin Church, especially metropolitans, until it gradually became the symbol of the metropolitan office. In the 9th century, John VIII commanded all metropolitans to petition the pope for the pallium within 3 months of their appointment or confirmation. Since then the pallium has been the symbol of the super-episcopal jurisdiction given metropolitans by the Roman pontiff and it signifies a certain participation in the pope's supreme pastoral office. It also represents their close union with the See of Rome. When worn by the pope, the pallium signifies the fullness of pontifical power.

Petition and Use. In the Latin Church, a metropolitan is obliged, either in person or by proxy, to ask the Roman pontiff (*instanter, instantius, instantissime*) for the pallium within 3 months of his consecration or, if already consecrated, of his canonical promotion in the consistory (CIC c.275). So necessary is the pallium that any act of jurisdiction belonging to his office as metropolitan or any act of the episcopal order for which the liturgical norms require the use of the pallium, would, before its imposition, be illicitly (though not invalidly) performed by him. Some such acts are the ordination of clerics, the consecration of bishops, the convocation of a provincial council, the confection of chrism, the dedi-

Fig. 2. A contemporary pallium.

cation of a church (CIC c.276). In the Oriental Churches, the metropolitan outside a patriarchate is bound to ask the Roman pontiff, either in person or by proxy, for the pallium within 3 months of his episcopal ordination or, if already ordained, from the date of his canonical appointment in the consistory (ClerSanc cc.321.1, 321.2). The pallium may be imposed in Rome, by the pope himself (on cardinals) or by the senior cardinal deacon (on other prelates, CIC c.239.3; ClerSanc c.185.3) or in the cathedral church or any other more convenient church of the metropolitan's own diocese or province by an archbishop or bishop. The ceremony always follows Mass and the taking of an oath of allegiance to the pope.

The pope may use the pallium at any time. A metropolitan (in the Latin Church) may use the pallium in every church of his province in the solemn ceremonies of the Mass on the days mentioned in the Roman Pontifical and on others through special concession, but not outside his province even with the consent of the local ordinary (CIC c.277). The same rule is binding on a metropolitan of the Eastern Churches (ClerSanc c.231.3). If a metropolitan loses his pallium or is transferred to another metropolitan see, he must obtain another pallium (CIC c.278). The pallium can neither be lent, nor given away, nor bequeathed to anyone at death, but all pallia received by a metropolitan are to be buried with him (CIC c.279): the last pallium placed over the chasuble of the deceased metropolitan, the others, folded, under his head.

Honorary Pallium. At times, archbishops who are not metropolitans and bishops are given the pallium by the pope. An episcopal see may even be given the pallium in perpetuity. In all such cases, unless it is ruled otherwise, the pallium, which is given merely as an honor and a token of benevolence, does not carry with it the archiepiscopal title or the metropolitan jurisdiction (Cler Sanc c.322).

Bibliography: H. LECLERCQ, DACL 13.1:931–940. L. TROMBETTA, *De pallio archiepiscopali: Elucubratio canonico-liturgico-historica* (Sorrento 1923). Wernz-Vidal 2:530–531. R. LESAGE, *Vestments and Church Furniture,* tr. F. MURPHY (New York 1960) 139–142. F. J. WEBER, "The Sacred Pallium and Its History," *Liturgical Arts* 30 (1962) 91. 106. **Illustration credits:** Fig. 1, Hirmer Verlag München; Fig. 3, Alinari-Art Reference Bureau.

[J. A. ABBO]

Fig. 3. St. Peter conferring the pallium upon Pope St. Leo III and giving the royal standard to Charlemagne; from a mosaic of the 8th century in the Triclinio Lateranense in Rome—a graphic representation of the medieval idea that both spiritual and temporal power came through the Church.

PALLOTTA, MARIA ASSUNTA, BL., missionary; b. Force, in the Marches of Ancona, Italy, Aug. 20, 1878; d. Tong-Eul-Koo, China, April 7, 1905 (feast April 7). From her early years she worked to help support her poor family. She acquired only enough formal schooling to read and write. In 1898 she joined in Rome the Franciscan Missionaries of Mary (*see* FRANCISCANS—SISTERS). During the next few years she dwelt in the congregation's convents in Rome, Grottaferrata, and Florence, working about the house and in the garden and infirmary, and teaching catechism. She sailed for China (1904), and there in the orphanage at Tong-Eul-Koo, she continued her humble tasks. While caring for the plague-stricken during a typhus epidemic she fell victim to the disease. Humility, kindness, obedience, and prayerfulness distinguished her life. Her remains, which were incorrupt when exhumed in 1913, are in China. She was beatified Nov. 7, 1954.

Bibliography: E. FEDERICI, *Bienheureuse Maria Assunta* (Rome 1954). ActSSed 47 (1955) 28–33. Baudot-Chaussin 13:205–208.

[M. F. S. CONDON]

PALLOTTI, VINCENT, ST., religious founder; b. Rome, April 21, 1795; d. there, Jan. 22, 1850 (feast, Jan. 22). He was the son of a prosperous grocer. From

St. Vincent Pallotti with his reliquary, portrait painted c. 1850, probably by Dominic Cassaretti.

St. Vincent Pallotti's reliquary with painting on cover representing the Mother of Divine Love.

his early years he developed a special devotion to the Blessed Virgin and an intense compassion for the poor. After studying in Rome at the Roman College and at the Sapienza, he was ordained (1818). He taught theology at the Sapienza for 10 years before he devoted himself completely to spiritual guidance and preaching. In 1827 he became spiritual director at the Roman College and often acted as confessor at various national colleges for future priests. He was intimately acquainted with St. Gaspare del *Bufalo and Nicholas *Wiseman. As rector of the church of Santo Spirito dei Neapolitani, he suffered for more than a decade from slanders by the other priests there, who were jealous of his promotion and resentful of his zeal. Vincent interested himself also in projects to revive artisan guilds and to establish schools for young workers and farm boys. During the cholera epidemic of 1837 he organized relief for the plague-stricken. His spiritual and charitable ministrations so impressed the Romans that they referred to him as a second St. Philip *Neri. In 1835 he founded the *Pallottines, and later, the Sisters of the Catholic Apostolate, from whom developed the *Pallottine Missionary Sisters. Vincent shared Rome's hopes for the conversion of England arising out of the *Oxford Movement and sent priests to assist Frederick William *Faber. His inspiration was instrumental in the founding of the *Mill Hill Missionaries and of several mission colleges. His fame for sanctity was increased by his reputation as a thaumaturge and prophet. Pius XI called him a forerunner of *Catholic Action. His body lies incorrupt in the church of San Salvatore in Onda, Rome. Vincent Pallotti was beatified on Jan. 22, 1950, by

Pope Pius XII, and he was canonized on Jan. 20, 1963, by Pope John XXIII.

Bibliography: E. WEBER, *Vincent Pallotti: Apostle and Mystic,* tr. from the Ger. (New York 1964). J. FRANK, *Vincenz Pallotti,* 2 v. (Friedberg 1952–63), index to be pub. later. **Illustration credits:** Pallottiner Limburg.

[H. E. SCHAAK]

PALLOTTINE MISSIONARY SISTERS, a congregation founded in Rome, Italy, in 1843, by St. Vincent *Pallotti, to care for children, especially orphans. When, in 1890, the Pallottine Fathers began a mission in the German colony in the Cameroons, Africa, the help of sisters also was required. Since the Italian sisters were not interested in mission work, it was decided to invite candidates from Germany to enter the novitiate in Rome. Those who answered this call were trained there and sent to Africa. When it became evident that the Pallottine Missionary Sisters should have their own motherhouse in Germany, a plan that was realized in 1895, a new branch of the Pallottine family came into existence. From Limburg, Germany, these sisters spread to England, Switzerland, Central America, Poland, South Africa, and in 1912 to the U.S. Their headquarters are at St. Mary's Hospital and Convent, Huntington, W.Va. Of the 800 professed members in the community (1964), 145 are active in the U.S. as teachers in elementary and high schools and a school of nursing, and as nursing sisters and supervisors in hospitals. Though mainly in West Virginia, the sisters have houses also in Maryland and Michigan.

When papal approval was granted to the congregation in 1964, its official title was established as Missionary Sisters of the Catholic Apostolate.

[M. B. KURTH]

PALLOTTINE SISTERS OF THE CATHOLIC APOSTOLATE,

a pontifical institute founded in 1843 by St. Vincent *Pallotti in Rome, Italy, to care for children orphaned by the cholera plague. Benedetta Gabrielli was the first sister to receive the habit at the Pia Casa di Carità, Rome. The first general chapter, held in 1886, elected Mother Raphael Castellani as superior general. Mother Raphael sent five sisters to the U.S. in 1889 to work among the Italian immigrants. In 1911 the congregation was approved by the Holy See, and in 1933 missions were begun in South America, in Brazil and Argentina.

The spirit of the Pallottine Sisters of the Catholic Apostolate (CSAC) prompts them to engage in any work that corresponds to the needs of the places where they serve; the sisters conduct hospitals, day nurseries, orphanages, parochial schools, catechetical classes, and academies. For the training of their young religious at the U.S. motherhouse in Harriman, N.Y., a sister formation institute, Queen of the Apostles College, was established in 1956 with the approval of the New York State Board of Regents. In 1964 the number of professed sisters was more than 1,000, of whom some 230 were in the U.S. in 32 missions.

[M. E. ZIEGLER]

PALLOTTINES

The Society of the Catholic Apostolate (SAC and SCA), popularly known as Pallottine Fathers, was founded by St. Vincent *Pallotti in 1835 at Rome, Italy. Under his direction, a group of clerics and lay people formed the Pious Union of the Catholic Apostolate, which received formal approbation in 1835. Its objective was to revive faith and charity in all Catholics and to diffuse these virtues throughout the entire world by prayers, labors, or other contributions.

As the membership increased and activities expanded, Pallotti saw the need for a group of priests who would devote their energies entirely to the work. Those who with him assumed this task, soon evolved into a society entitled Congregation of the Catholic Apostolate; it was to function as a connecting bond between the secular and religious priests, both of whom Pallotti desired to see labor side by side in all apostolic activities. Thus the society assumed a secular and a religious character: the secular was expressed by the absence of vows; the religious, by the observance of common life and promises. At first Pallotti did not favor constitutions or rules other than the Gospels, but he was constrained by experience to introduce them.

Despite papal approval, Pallotti's work was seriously threatened. The Lyons Society for the Propagation of the Faith claimed that Pallotti's work was merely duplicating its own program on behalf of foreign missions and had his society suppressed in 1838. When Pallotti clarified the situation for Gregory XVI, the decree of suppression was revoked. The words Catholic Apostolate raised objection from some who believed that the apostolate was reserved to the hierarchy. Four years after Pallotti's death the controversy was settled by a decree (1854) that changed the name to Pious Society of Missions. The original title was restored in 1947, when the concept of the universal apostolate was better understood.

Because of the Roman Revolution, Pallotti's death in 1850, and the change in title that obscured its nature, the society's development was slow until 1880. However, by the turn of the century there were 30 houses in 8 countries. In 1890 the Pallottines accepted a request to evangelize the African Cameroons, where by 1914 they had baptized 25,000 converts and were instructing 40,000 catechumens. By 1909 the society had over 500 members and was divided into 4 provinces. After World War I, it continued to flourish, and created in Germany the Schoenstatt movement, a Marian apostolic movement that implements Pallotti's program (*see* SCHOENSTATT SISTERS OF MARY).

The first Pallottines arrived in the U.S. to minister to New York's Italians; this was the beginning of the Immaculate Conception Province of the eastern states. The foundations for a midwestern province, the Mother of God Province, were laid when, in 1921, a house was established in Milwaukee, Wis. Two other provinces, the Irish and the Italian, have members serving in the U.S., as does the French region. In 1963 there were more than 160 Pallottines engaged in the lay apostolate, retreats, Indian missions, hospitals, immigrant care, schools, parishes, home missions, and publications in the U.S.

In 1963 the society, with its generalate in Rome, was divided into 18 provinces and regions, and had more than 2,200 members active in 21 countries. The Pallottines are an exempt society of clerics and lay brothers, without vows, leading a common life. After a 2-year novitiate they promise poverty, chastity, and obedience, and also perserverance and perfect common life; in addition, clerics promise not to aspire after ecclesiastical dignities. Before final profession, promises are renewed annually for 3 years by clerics, and for 5 years by brothers. In harmony with their objective, the Pallottines concern themselves in a special way with home and foreign missions, retreats, publications, and the spiritual care of immigrants, besides engaging in other works of the ministry.

Bibliography: J. GAYNOR, *Life of St. Vincent Pallotti* (Rome 1963). E. WEBER, *Vincent Pallotti: Apostle and Mystic* (New York 1964).

[H. E. SCHAAK]

PALLU, FRANÇOIS, vicar apostolic in southwest China and a founder of the Paris Foreign Mission Society; b. Tours, France, Aug. 30, 1626; d. Moyang, China, Oct. 29, 1684. His father was a lawyer and mayor. During his youth, Pallu was made a canon of St. Martin's. In Paris, he met Father De Rhodes, SJ, who was coming from Tongking to obtain from Rome the appointment of native bishops in the Far East. Pallu and his friends agreed to support De Rhodes and went to Rome, aided by the Assembly of the Clergy and the Company of the Blessed Sacrament. In 1658 Pallu was appointed titular bishop of Heliopolis, and vicar apostolic of Tongking, Laos, and southwest China. He wanted helpers and money, and this led him to start a society of priests without vows who would go to the missions. With the help of Pierre *Lambert de la Motte, his first fellow-worker, he wrote instructions for the benefit of missioners. Throughout his life he traveled

Christ's entry into Jerusalem, detail from sarcophagus of Adelphia (c. 340–345), in National Museum of Syracuse.

from the East to Rome to further mission work and to obtain the approval and help of the Holy See. He had to struggle against the governments of Spain and Portugal, and a number of religious who were opposed to the setting up of native churches. He is recognized as the main founder of the *Paris Foreign Mission Society. Pallu was a man of great gifts, kindly, and with sound judgment and strong willpower. He gave himself zealously to spread the Church in the Far East.

Bibliography: F. PALLU, *Lettres,* ed. A. LAUNAY, 2 v. (Angoulême 1905). A. LAUNAY, *Histoire générale de la Société des Missions Étrangères,* 3 v. (Paris 1894). L. BAUDIMENT, *François Pallu* (Paris 1934). J. GUENNOU, *Les Missions Étrangères* (Paris 1963). A. ANOGE, EncCatt 9:649–650. J. GLAZIK, LexThK² 8:11.
[H. PROUVOST]

PALM

A branch of the palm tree, in Greek φοῖνιξ, in Latin, *dactylifera,* or date-bearing palm. The palm tree was considered in Biblical times as a princely tree and was used as a symbol of victory and well-being and also as temple decoration. Because of the tree's height and graceful trunk, with its crown of serrated branches and shade-providing leaves, it served as a shelter and provided food in desert borderlands and was highly prized among Egyptians, Babylonians, Assyrians, and Jews. The palm tree was considered holy in Babylon and later was sacred to the Greek god Apollo at Delos. Several cities were referred to specifically as the Palm City: Thamar (Ez 47.19), Jericho (Dt 34.3), and En-Gedi

(Pliny, *Hist. nat.* 5.17). The palm tree supplied figures and similes for poets (Ps 92.13) and was used as a name for girls (Gn 38.6; 2 Sm 13.1). It provided decor for the ornamentation of temples among the Phoenicians, Assyrians, and Egyptians (1 Kgs 6.29; Ez 40.16, 22).

Among both the Romans and the Jews it was carried in joyful or triumphant processions. In 293 B.C. victorious Roman soldiers bore palm branches when parading in Rome; and the palm was given as a victory emblem at public games. Of earlier date was its usage among the Israelites; people carried palm branches during the Feast of Tabernacles (Lv 23.40; Neh 8.15); and it was part of the bouquet, or *lulab,* offered on festive occasions as a sign of homage or to celebrate a victory (1 Mc 13.37; Jn 12.13).

Christ's triumphal entry into Jerusalem, when the people strew palm branches in his path and greeted him with Hosannas (Jn 12.12–13), became a liturgical function on *Palm Sunday in the 4th century. But already in the New Testament the palm was connected with martyrdom (Apoc 7.9) and was used to decorate gravemarkers and tombs in the catacombs as a sign of the triumphal death of the martyr (Paul. of Nola, *Epist.,* 32.10). On mosaics and on sarcophagi it usually stands for paradise, and Christ is frequently portrayed amid palms in heaven. So also in ancient church decorations the Lamb of God and the Apostles are depicted amid palms. In the Middle Ages palms served as a symbol of Sunday; and in the Renaissance, under hu-

Modern Palm Sunday procession on the Mt. of Olives following Christ's route into Jerusalem.

manist influence, they came to stand for virtues or an augury for a good marriage and length of years.

The palm blessed at Mass on Palm Sunday is carried home by the faithful as a sacramental and symbol of Christ's presence among them. It is usually placed over the bed, entwined on a crucifix, or displayed near some holy picture or statue. Often it is decorated with ribbons or worked into an artistic pattern, such as a cross. In Western countries this has been the custom since at least the 11th century, and both palm and olive tree branches are so employed. In sections of Switzerland the branch of a specific pine tree is used and is decorated with leaves and fruit; in other countries different trees, such as boxwoods, are used. Blessed palm is also placed on tombstones and graves in cemeteries among certain peoples. Before Ash Wednesday the blessed palm is burned, and its residue is used in the distribution of ashes as a symbol of penance during Lent.

In St. Peter's in the Vatican the privilege of presenting the pope with palm was given to the Brescia family of San Remo on the Riviera by Pope Sixtus V (1585–90). For this purpose 300 choice palm branches are selected and bound into five fascicles. The actual branch that the pope carries in procession is in the form of a trophy and has been presented to him by the Camaldolese monks since the time of Pope Leo XII (1829).

Bibliography: H. LECLERCQ, DACL 13.1:947–961. A. STEIER, Pauly-Wiss RE 20.1 (1941) 386–404. H. I. MARROU, *Mélanges d'archéologie et d'histoire* 58 (1941–46) 109–113. V. HAMP and O. FELD, LexThK² 8:12–13. P. SIFFRIN and P. TOSCHI, EncCatt 9:654–657. J. E. HARRISON, *Prolegomena to the Study of Greek Religion* (3d ed. Cambridge, Eng. 1922) 78–82.

[F. X. MURPHY]

PALM SUNDAY

Since 1955 the official name of the Sunday before Easter is the "Second Sunday of the Passion or Palm Sunday," thereby reviving the original Roman name (Second Sunday of the Passion), which was given because the Passion was read in the Mass on that day. But the title "Palm Sunday" appears as early as the Gelasian and Gregorian Sacramentaries, even though the procession of the palms apparently was introduced into Rome only in the 12th century. It seems therefore that the title was a mere reference to the day's original historical event. (See illustration on preceding page.)

The procession gives this Sunday its distinctive char-

acter. The aim of Pius XII's Holy Week Ordinal was to bring this procession into greater prominence as the triumph of Christ, the risen King of glory. Like all the Holy Week rites, it is not a mere commemoration, but a mysterium in which not only the historical event is recalled to mind but Christ's own victory is reenacted in the Church. We celebrate this event only by living it. Hence all are invited to take part in it by carrying palms and singing the acclamations to the King. Because of the festive nature of the procession the priest and the sacred ministers wear red—the royal color, the color of victory—instead of the penitential purple; and the cross, the standard of victory, is carried unveiled.

The annual procession of the palms originated in Jerusalem as a commemoration of the entry of Christ into the Holy City to consummate the great work of the Redemption. Sometime in the 4th century, if not earlier, the people of Jerusalem were led to reenact this event at the spot where it had actually happened. The faithful of Jerusalem gathered around their bishop on the Mt. of Olives. There they sang hymns and listened to readings from the Old Testament and to the Gospel account of our Savior's entry. Then at five o'clock they set out carrying olive or palm branches in their hands, accompanying the bishop, who was seated on a mule, to the Church of the Resurrection. During this procession they sang psalms and hymns with the constant refrain: "Blessed is He who comes in the Name of the Lord." Upon arriving at the church they sang Vespers.

From Jerusalem this custom made its way to the churches of the Gallican rite in the West. In turn, the entire rite came to Rome from the Gallican lands through the Romano-Germanic Pontifical of the 10th century.

By the Middle Ages the rite of the palms had acquired a distinctly dramatic form. The procession would go from one church to another, usually one outside the city walls. The presence of Christ was symbolized in various ways: in some parts of France by the gospel book, in northern Italy by a large cross decorated with green foliage, in Germany by an image of Christ borne on the back of a wooden donkey, in England and Normandy by the Blessed Sacrament itself. Upon returning to the gate of the city or to the door of the principal church, the faithful would cast their garments and their palm or olive branches before the symbol of Christ and repeat the same acclamations the Jews had used to greet the coming of the Messiah King. There too the hymn *Gloria Laus* was sung, a choir within the gates alternating with those outside. Then one of the clerics knocked at the door and all entered singing the antiphon *Ingrediente Domino in Sanctam Civitatem.*

In the beginning there was no blessing provided for the palms. The earliest blessing is found in the *Liber Ordinum* of the Mozarabic Rite (6th century). By the end of the Middle Ages this had become a very elaborate ceremonial, amounting to a *Missa sicca* (*see* MASS, DRY).

Such emphasis was laid upon the blessing and upon the palm itself as a sacramental that the real purpose of the whole ceremony was obscured. In time the procession became secondary, and often was not observed at all. That is why Pius XII's Holy Week Ordinal simplified the blessing; the *Missa sicca* disappeared. Thus the triumphal procession in honor of Christ the King once more occupies the central place that belongs to it. The new rite encourages having the blessing outside the church or even in another building so that a real procession can be had. The prayer for the blessing shows the meaning of the palms and the olive branches: the palm is the emblem of victory and so recalls Christ's triumph over death and hell achieved by His Passion; the olive branch is the emblem of peace with God and so of the reconciliation brought about by the cross. The prayer asks that we may share in this victory of Christ.

With the beginning of Mass the whole mood of the celebration changes and is in striking contrast to the triumphant procession preceding it. The royal red vestments give way to penitential purple; the chants become somber and even sad. The Mass is penetrated with the thought of the redeeming Passion of the Son of God.

Originally the Passion was sung by the deacon, and this practice was retained until as late as the 14th century. But in the northern lands the dramatic possibilities of the singing of the Passion were exploited by having three deacons take various parts in the singing; this practice continues to this day.

Bibliography: Miller FundLit 373–376. W. J. O'SHEA, *The Meaning of Holy Week* (Collegeville, Minn. 1958). Eisenhofer Lit 186–189. Cross ODCC. **Illustration credits:** Fig. 1, Hirmer Verlag, München. Fig. 2, Wolfe World-Wide Films.

[W. J. O'SHEA]

PALMA, RICARDO, Peruvian literary figure; b. Lima, Feb. 7, 1833; d. there, Oct. 6, 1919. He studied at the Convictorio de San Carlos and began an early association with writers and poets. In 1860 he was sent into exile in Chile, where he became involved in journalism. In Valparaíso he edited *Revista de Sur América* and wrote many of the articles in it. He also began publishing poetry, e.g., *Armonías, libro de un desterrado* (Paris 1865). He traveled widely in Europe and in South America, often as a political exile. He was recalled to Peru in 1884, and from then until 1912 he served as director of the National Library. It had been almost destroyed during the war with Chile, and he

Ricardo Palma.

set to work restoring it. His most famous work is a collection of volumes published from 1872 to 1910 called *Tradiciones Peruanas.* It is a classic of its kind and one of the most popular works in Spanish American litera-

ture. It consists of short sketches that blend history, anecdote, and satire, popular tales that embroider upon tradition. Many of the *Tradiciones* deal with the foibles of the clergy and religious. Palma's treatment of them is humorous and gently sarcastic, clearly differentiating his writing from that of his contemporaries such as *González Prada.

Bibliography: R. PALMA, *The Knights of the Cape,* ed. and tr. H. DE ONIS (New York 1945). L. A. SÁNCHEZ, *Don Ricardo Palma y Lima* (Lima 1927). C. MIRÓ, *Don Ricardo Palma: El patriarca de las Tradiciones* (Buenos Aires 1953). **Illustration credit:** Library of Congress.

[J. HERRICK]

PALMER, WILLIAM, theologian and archeologist; b. Mixbury, Oxfordshire, England, 1811; d. Rome, 1879. Palmer was educated at Rugby School and Oxford University, and was ordained deacon in the Church of England in 1832. From 1834 to 1843 he was tutor at Durham University and then classical examiner and tutor at Oxford, where he had been elected a fellow of his college, Magdalen. He was a high churchman, and in 1840 and again in 1842 went to Russia to learn about the Orthodox Church there and investigate the possibility of intercommunion between it and the Anglicans. This led to his best-known written work, *Notes on a Visit to the Russian Church,* edited by Cardinal Newman and published in 1882. Palmer was disturbed by certain aspects of the Church of England and for a time seriously considered joining the Orthodox, but in 1855 he was received into the Catholic Church and spent the rest of his life in Rome studying archeology. Among his other published writings on ecclesiastical and archeological topics were a *Harmony of Anglican Doctrine with the Doctrine of the Eastern Church* (1846) and an *Introduction to Early Christian Symbolism* (1859). In his later years he wrote, in Latin, a commentary on the book of Daniel (1874) and translated from the Russian *The Patriarch Nicon and the Tsar,* 6 v. (1871–76). His learning was highly respected by Newman, Perrone, and Dölinger.

He must be distinguished from his contemporary, another William Palmer (1803–85), an Anglican theologian of repute who in 1846 published a reply to Newman's *Essay on the Development of Christian Doctrine.*

Bibliography: DNB 15:167–168. DictEngCath 5:240–242. Cross ODCC 1009.

[D. ATTWATER]

PALMIERI, AURELIO, Italian Orientalist; b. Savona, May 4, 1870; d. Rome, Oct. 18, 1926. After joining the *Augustinians (1885) he transferred to the *Assumptionists (1890) and then returned to the Augustinians (1902). Because of his private conduct and erroneous ideas he fell into difficulties with ecclesiastical authorities and was laicized. During 2 decades devoted to Oriental, especially Byzantine, studies, he published 15 scholarly books, notably *Die Polemik des Islam* (Salzburg 1902), *La Chiesa Russa* (Florence 1908), *Dositeo patriarcha greco di Gerusalemme, 1647–1707* (Florence 1909), and *Theologia dogmatica orthodoxa* (2 v. Florence 1911–13). Besides editing *Bessarione,* the Italian journal devoted to Byzantine studies, he wrote 130 articles for it between 1896 and 1923. Together with his writings for other Italian and foreign periodicals and for the DTC, the total of his articles exceeded 300. During his last years he headed the Institute for Eastern Europe.

Bibliography: *Studi Bizantini* 1 (1925) 261–269, list all Palmieri's writings. E. Lo Gatto, *"Bibliografia essenziale degli scritti di A. P.,"* *L'Europe orientale* 6 (1926) 519–532. D. A. Perini, *Bibliographia Augustiniana,* v.3 (Florence 1935) 45–48.

[G. A. MALONEY]

PALMIERI, DOMENICO,

Jesuit philosopher, theologian; b. Piacenza, Italy, July 4, 1829; d. Rome, May 29, 1909. He was ordained and entered the Society of Jesus in 1852. After teaching philosophy, theology, and Scripture for a period at the seminary of Fermo and the college at Spoleto, he became professor of philosophy (1861–67) and of dogma (1867–78) at the Gregorian University. He espoused a kind of dynamism, claiming that hylomorphism was incompatible with the findings of natural science. His position in Rome became precarious during the Thomistic revival under Leo XIII. After transfer to Maastricht in Holland in 1878, he taught exegesis there until 1894. In that year he returned to Rome as theologian to the Sacred Penitentiary and consultor to the Holy Office. He was later on the Commission for the Code of Canon Law. He was among the first to attack the Modernist error of Loisy. The publication of his works extends from 1874 to 1910. Noteworthy are his *Institutiones Philosophiae,* his reedition of Gury's and Ballerini's moral works, and his commentary on Dante's *Divina Comedia.*

Bibliography: P. Dezza, EncCatt 9:660–661.

[J. FLYNN]

PALMYRA

Ancient and modern caravan center of the Syrian Desert between Damascus (150 miles) or Homs (100 miles) to the west and Deir ez-Zor (130 miles) to the east. The name is apparently a Latinized form of the Semitic word for date palm (Heb. *tāmār;* Aramaic *tamrā';* Arabic *tamrun*) that survives in the modern name Tadmor. But it is scarcely *Solomon's Tadmor that is mentioned in 2 Chr 8.4, where the reading should be Tamar (Thamar), a town in southern Juda (Ez 47.9; 48.28), as in 3 Kgs 9.18 [see J. Starcky, DBSuppl 5:1068; for the other view, see E. Vogt, VerbDom 16 (1936) 222]. The only other mention of a pre-Hellenistic city here may be in the *Mari documents (*c.* 1750 B.C.) or in the inscriptions of Tiglath-Pileser I (1116–1078 B.C.); see P. Dhorme, RevBibl 53 (1924) 106. The far-flung surviving ruins, cleared by T. Wiegand's German expedition, come from a period beginning *c.* 200 B.C., but they owe their chief magnificence to Hadrian's visit (A.D. 129)—especially the major temple of Bel (*Baal), distinct from a smaller temple of Bel-šamin (Baal-šamayim); see A. Collart, *Annales aréhéologiques de Syrie* 7 (1957) 67–94. Several hundred of the original 750 sandstone columns are still erect, stretching 1,240 yards from a monumental gateway (now partly reconstructed) past a theater (built *c.* A.D. 140) in the heart of the city—unlike most Roman-Syrian parallels; see E. Frezouls, *Syria* 36 (1959) 202.

Palmyra's most characteristic contribution to world culture is its funerary sculpture [see H. Ingholt, *Studier* (Copenhagen 1928)], showing the whole family of the deceased reunited around a festive banquet table, framed by rows of busts of near relatives that seal their respective burials. These sculptured burials are arranged either

Temple of Baal at Palmyra, pillars of its peristyle.

in several stories of a tower, of which a good number survive, notably those of Elahbel (A.D. 103) and Jamblichus (A.D. 80)—see E. Will, *Syria* 26 (1949) 87–116, 258–312; cf. 34 (1957) 262–277—or in underground chambers, most of which have been transferred to museums, especially Yarhai's (A.D. 108), reconstructed in Damascus [see R. Amy and H. Seyrig, *Syria* 17 (1936) 229; *Annales archéologique de Syrie* 1 (1951) 32–40]. Some of the tombs contain inscriptions in the Palmyrene language (see bibliog.), closely related to Nabataean (*see* NABATAEANS) and the Aramaic of the *Dead Sea Scrolls (*see* ARAMAIC LANGUAGE, 1).

Rome built up Palmyra's strength to a maximum under the local ruler Odeinat; but after his death (A.D. 268) his widow Zenobia declared her independence and successfully resisted sporadic attacks by the Roman legions until a strong army was sent against her. She was captured and made to grace Aurelian's triumph and end her days in a villa at Tivoli.

The desert ruins of Palmyra are now dominated by a castle named for Ibn Ma'an but really built by *Fakhr-al-Dīn II al-Ma'nī (*c.* A.D. 1600).

See also ARABIA, 3.

Bibliography: J. Starcky, *Palmyre* (Paris 1952); DBSuppl 6:1066–1103. T. Wiegand, ed., *Palmyra: Ergebnisse der Expedition von 1902–1917,* 2 v. (Berlin 1932). M. I. Rostovtsev, *Caravan Cities,* tr. D. and T. Talbot Rice (Oxford 1932) 91–152. O. Feld, LexThK² 8:14–15. S. Moscati and G. Furlani, EncCatt 9:661–664. EncDictBibl 1702–03. Palmyrene language: J. Cantineau, *Grammaire du palmyrénien épigraphique* (Cairo 1935). F. Rosenthal, *Die Sprache der palmyrenischen Inschriften . . .* (Leipzig 1936). **Illustration credit:** Matson Photo Service, Los Angeles, Calif.

[R. NORTH]

PALOMAR, JOHN OF,

Spanish theologian; fl. 1431–43. Although he was one of the leading figures at the Council of *Basel, very little is known of his early life. He served successively as archdeacon of Barcelona, chaplain to Pope *Eugene IV, and auditor of the Sacred Palace. With John of *Ragusa he presided briefly over the Council of Basel from July 1431 until the return of Cardinal *Cesarini from Bohemia. After 1433 Palomar was engaged in debate with the *Hussites at the council over the Church's right to possess goods and temporal jurisdiction. He was also one of a small group led by Cesarini who defended the principle of papal supremacy against the proponents of *conciliarism, defending the basic dictum that the See of Peter may be judged by no one. His *Scriptum contra Basileense concilium* (MS Paris, B.N. lat. 1442) was a bitter rejection of the council's decrees and claims to superiority.

Bibliography: Mansi 29:1105–68. J. J. I. VON DÖLLINGER, *Beiträge zur Politischen, Kirchlichen und Kulturgeschichte . . .,* 3 v. (Regensburg 1862–82) 2:414–441. N. VALOIS, *Le Pape et le concile, 1418–50,* 2 v. (Paris 1909) 1:116–129; 2:53–56. É. AMANN, DTC 8.1:796–797. EncRelCat 4:895.

[D. S. BUCZEK]

PALÓU, FRANCISCO

PALÓU, FRANCISCO, missionary; b. Palma, Majorca, Jan. 22, 1723; d. Querétaro, Mexico, April 6, 1789. He entered the Franciscan Order in 1739 and studied under Junípero *Serra. Palóu was ordained in 1747, and 2 years later went to Mexico as a missionary. He and Serra were assigned to the missionary Apostolic College of San Fernando, Mexico City. From 1750 to 1760 he served in the Indian missions of the Sierra Gorda, north of Querétaro. In 1767 he went to Lower California to work in the missions left vacant by the expulsion of the Jesuits, and he eventually became missionary president of that area. Palóu remained in charge of the missions of the Lower California Peninsula until the region was transferred to the Dominicans in 1773. In that year he went to the newly opened mission field of Upper California, where he became temporary superior because of Serra's absence in Mexico. During this period he began his *Noticias de la Nueva California* (1874), a

Francisco Palóu administering Viaticum to Junípero Serra. Painting by Mariannus Guerrero, 1785, in the Castillo de Chapultepec at Mexico City.

history of the first years of California's colonization. He also accompanied two expeditions to the San Francisco Bay area, acting as diarist. In 1776 Palóu founded Mission San Francisco, where he served during most of his years in California. He assisted the dying Serra at the latter's Mission San Carlos in 1784. Upon the president's death, Palóu again assumed temporary charge of the Upper California area and began his classic biography of Serra, the *Relación Histórica de la Vida y Apostólicas Tareas del Venerable Padre Fray Junípero Serra* (1787). Recalled to San Fernando College in 1785, he was elected superior in 1786 and held office until he died.

Bibliography: F. PALÓU, *Life of Fray Junípero Serra,* tr. and annot. M. J. GEIGER (Washington 1955). H. E. BOLTON, *Palóu and His Writings* (Berkeley 1926). **Illustration credit:** Archivo Fotografico del Instituto Nacional de Antropologia e Historia.

[E. D. BURNETT]

PAMMACHIUS, ST.

PAMMACHIUS, ST., Roman senator; b. *c.* 340 of the Furian family; d. Rome, 409 or 410 (feast, Aug. 30). He was a friend and fellow student of St. *Jerome in their youth, and Jerome's extant correspondence of later years includes a number of letters addressed to Pammachius, who was intensely interested in theological controversy, as well as one (*Ep.* 83) addressed to Jerome from Pammachius and Oceanus. Pammachius was married to Paulina, the second daughter of St. Paula of Rome. After Paulina's death, near the end of the 4th century, Pammachius turned to the religious life and used his wealth for the care of the poor. In conjunction with Fabiola he founded a hospice at Ostia, and he may have been a founder of the church of SS. John and Paul on the Caelius in Rome. He was termed *ecclesiae munerarius* by Paulinus of Nola (*Ep.* 13). St. Augustine's *Ep.* 58 is addressed to Pammachius.

Bibliography: *Sancti Eusebii Hieronymi epistulae,* ed. I. HILBERG, 3 v. (CSEL 54–56; 1910–18) 48, 49, 57, 66, 83, 84, 97. ActSS Aug. 6:555–563. F. CAVALLERA, *Saint Jérôme,* 2 v. (Spic SacLov 1, 2; 1922).

[T. C. LAWLER]

PAMPHILUS

PAMPHILUS, 3d-century saint and martyr; b. Berytus (modern Beirut); d. Caesarea in Palestine, Feb. 16, 310 (feast, June 1). The two early biographies, one written by his master Pierius, according to Philip of Side, and the other by his disciple *Eusebius of Caesarea, have been lost. Eusebius took his name (Eusebius Pamphili) to display the spiritual filiation between them and speaks of him with admiration in his *Ecclesiastical History* and in his *On the Martyrs of Palestine,* where he gives a résumé of his career, imprisonment, and martyrdom (ch. 11.1).

Pamphilus, of a noble family of Berytus, received a careful education and exercised public office there, then became, at the Didaskaleion of Alexandria (Photius, *Bibliotheca* 118–119), a student of Pierius, head of the school under Bishop Theonas after 281 (Jerome, *De vir. ill.* 76). Pierius was called Origen the Younger because of his talents and the admiration he had for that great theologian; he communicated this conviction to Pamphilus, who later reopened the School of *Caesarea founded by Origen. Ordained by Bishop Agapius (*c.* 290), Pamphilus was renowned for his asceticism and charity as well as for his knowledge.

Speaking of his disciples, the brothers Apphianus and Aedesius, Eusebius described the spiritual and scriptural orientation of the teaching of Pamphilus (*De mart. Palest.* 4.6; 5.2). He reorganized the Christian library attached to the school at Caesarea and employed a band of copyists. Arrested in 307, he was held in prison for 2 years and then decapitated during the persecution of Maximinus Daia.

The only known writing of Pamphilus is his *Apology for Origen,* composed while in prison with the assistance of Eusebius of Caesarea, who was the author of the work's sixth book (Eusebius, *Hist. eccl.* 6.33, 36; Photius, *Bibl.* 118). Jerome testifies to Pamphilus's authorship (*De vir. ill.* 75). But after Jerome became an anti-Origenist, he attributed the *Apology* to Eusebius, whom he described as a semi-Arian to discredit the work. Only book 1 in the translation of *Rufinus of Aquileia exists. It begins with a letter to the Palestinian confessors condemned to the mines and indicates the proper manner of judging the difficulties in *Origen's thought: the hypothetical and doubtful character of his speculations, which are not dogmatic affirmations and frequently are self-contradictory. Pamphilus bears witness to Origen's fidelity to orthodoxy. By numerous citations of Origen's works, some of which are otherwise unknown, he refutes the accusations made against Origen's doctrine on the Trinity, the Incarnation, the historicity of the Scriptures, the Resurrection, the soul, metempsychosis, and eternal damnation.

Bibliography: PG 17:541–616. E. VENABLES, DCB 4:178–179. G. BARDY, DTC 11.2:1839–41. Quasten Patr 2:144–146. F. X. MURPHY, *Rufinus of Aquileia* (Washington 1945).

[H. CROUZEL]

PAMPLONA, FRANCIS OF,

PAMPLONA, FRANCIS OF, Capuchin lay brother and missionary; b. Pamplona, Spain, Aug. 11, 1597; d. La Guaira, Venezuela, Aug. 31, 1651. He was born Tiburcio de Redin, of a noble family, and first followed a career in the military, holding high offices and distinguishing himself for his skill and courage. In 1637, however, he was converted to a life of penance as a Capuchin and dedicated his efforts to the foreign missions. He joined Bonaventure of Allesano in founding a Capuchin mission in the Congo in 1645. Returning to Europe he solicited support for the missions in London, Rome, and Madrid. After 1647 he went to the missions in Spanish America, where he spent his remaining years laboring in Panama and Venezuela.

Bibliography: C. DA TERZORIO, *Le missioni dei Minori Cappuccini,* v.10 (Rome 1938) 370–398. *Documentos históricos: Fray Francisco de Pamplona,* v.3 (1948) 67–73. I. DA MILANO, Enc Catt 5:1597.

[J. C. WILLKE]

PAMPLONA, ARCHDIOCESE OF (PAMPILONENSIS)

Metropolitan see since 1956, covering the province of Navarre and part of Guipuzcoa in north Spain. In 1961 it had in 3,495 square miles 381,217 Catholics in 610 parishes, 1,065 secular and 458 religious priests, 1,087 men in 61 religious houses and 1,156 women in 201 convents. Its three suffragans, with 753 parishes, 1,962 priests, 4,693 sisters, and 795,526 Catholics, were: Calahorra and La Calzada-Logroño (first-known bishop in 457, suppressed under the Moors c. 711–1045); Jaca (residence of bishops of Huesca 1063–96, independent in 1571); and San Sebastián (established in 1949).

Interior of the cathedral of Santa María at Pamplona.

Pamplona was suffragan to *Tarragona in Visigothic days, to *Auch in the early Middle Ages, to Tarragona from 1118, to *Saragossa from 1318, to *Burgos from 1574, and to Saragossa again by the 1851 concordat. It lost control of the liberated Tudela church by royal intervention (1143), acquired the administration of it as a codiocese (1787), absorbed it (1851), lost it to Tarazona (1889), and in 1955 reacquired its administration (9 parishes, 66 priests, 191 sisters, 28,327 Catholics in 1961).

Pompey rebuilt Pamplona (68 B.C.); the Visigothic Euric held it briefly (466), as did the Merovingian Franks (542). Charlemagne reconquered it from the Moslems, apparently three times (778, 806, 812); it seems to be the "Noples" of the Song of Roland. Acquiring independence during the 9th-century turmoils and Reconquest, it emerged as the focal city of the Kingdom of Navarre (839, 852). When Sancho III the Great (970–1033) subdued the neighboring Christian states of north Spain, Pamplona shone briefly as the center of a small empire. It continued as center of a diminished Navarre and later as a provincial capital.

Early diocesan history is obscure. According to legend SS. Saturninus and *Firmin preached there in Apostolic times. The Christian community with its bishop Liliolus first appears in history in 589. Liliolus and several successors attended the Toledo councils. Opilanus (829) is the first bishop known after what may have been a Moslem occupation. Bishop Wiliesindus consecrated the monastery of Santa María, a royal foundation (848). King Sancho Garcés broke up this Navarre-Aragon diocese of Pamplona (922), creating additional dioceses of Tobia, Nájera (later Calahorra), and Sasabe (soon Aragon, then Jaca).

Pamplona bishops governed from nearby San Salvador of Leyre, a 6th-century Visigothic monastery restored and fortified (Cluniac from 1090, with a Cistercian interlude 1269). Sancho the Great, educated at Leyre, convoked a synod there (1022) and at Pamplona (1023), formally restoring the See "of Pamplona and Leyre" or "of Navarre," the bishops to be drawn from the monastery. Later in the century the bishops moved into Pamplona, Leyre continuing as royal pantheon. The bishops were secular lords of Pamplona and presidents of the national parliament. Sancho VII gave them his palace and properties in Pamplona (1198).

The Romanesque cathedral of Santa María (1100–1240), consecrated in 1127, was rebuilt in Gothic by Charles the Noble from 1390. The Pamplona canons of Our Lady of Roncesvalles conducted a famous hospice from the 9th century. Notable shrines include the basilica built (1694) where St. Ignatius Loyola fell wounded and St. Francis Xavier's castle home. Pamplona's church architecture reflects its Franco-Spanish border situation. King Thibaut II and Pope Alexander IV projected a university in Pamplona (1259); the Navarre cortes founded one (1608). The present Estudio General de Navarra (1959) is a pontifical university (1960).

Bibliography: G. Fernández Pérez, *Historia de la iglesia y obispado de Pamplona* (Pamplona 1920). J. Gavira Martín, *Estudios sobre la iglesia española medieval: Episcopologios de sedes navarro-aragonesas durante los siglos xi y xii* (Madrid 1929). J. Zunzunegui, *El reino de Navarra y su obispado de Pamplona durante la primera época del cisma de occidente* (San Sebastián 1942). J. Pérez de Urbel, *Sancho el Mayor de Navarra* (Madrid 1950). S. A. García Larragueta, *El gran priorato de Navarra de la orden de San Juan de Jerusalén, siglos xii–xiii,* 2 v.

(Pamplona 1957). J. Goñi Gaztambide, *Príncipe de Viana* 18 (1957) 41–240; *ibid.* 23 (1962) 5–194, on medieval bishops. **Illustration credit:** MAS, Barcelona.

[R. I. Burns]

PANAMA

The Republic of Panama is, geographically, the narrowest part of Central America and unites North and South America. Christopher Columbus, on his fourth voyage to the New World, discovered the largest portion of the territory in 1502. One year before, however, Rodrigo de Bastidas had traveled over the eastern part of it on an exploratory trip from east to west. Neither explorer perceived that it was an isthmus. This was noted only by Vasco Núñez de Balboa, who crossed it from one ocean to the other in 1513, determining precisely its geographic constitution.

Area and Population. Panama is situated between the Republics of Colombia on the east and of Costa Rica on the west. On the north is the Atlantic and on the south the Pacific. Since the territory is an isthmus, the interoceanic canal was constructed at its narrowest point, 47 miles wide. It was begun by the French in 1882; when they suspended work, it was continued by the North Americans, who finished it in 1914, the year in which the canal was placed at the service of worldwide maritime trade. The area of the republic is 28,576 square miles, and in 1963 its population totaled 1,075,541. The Canal Zone, not included in the above figures, has an area of 553 square miles, and its 1963 population totaled approximately 42,000. This territory, although governed by the United States under the authorization of the Republic of Panama, belongs to the

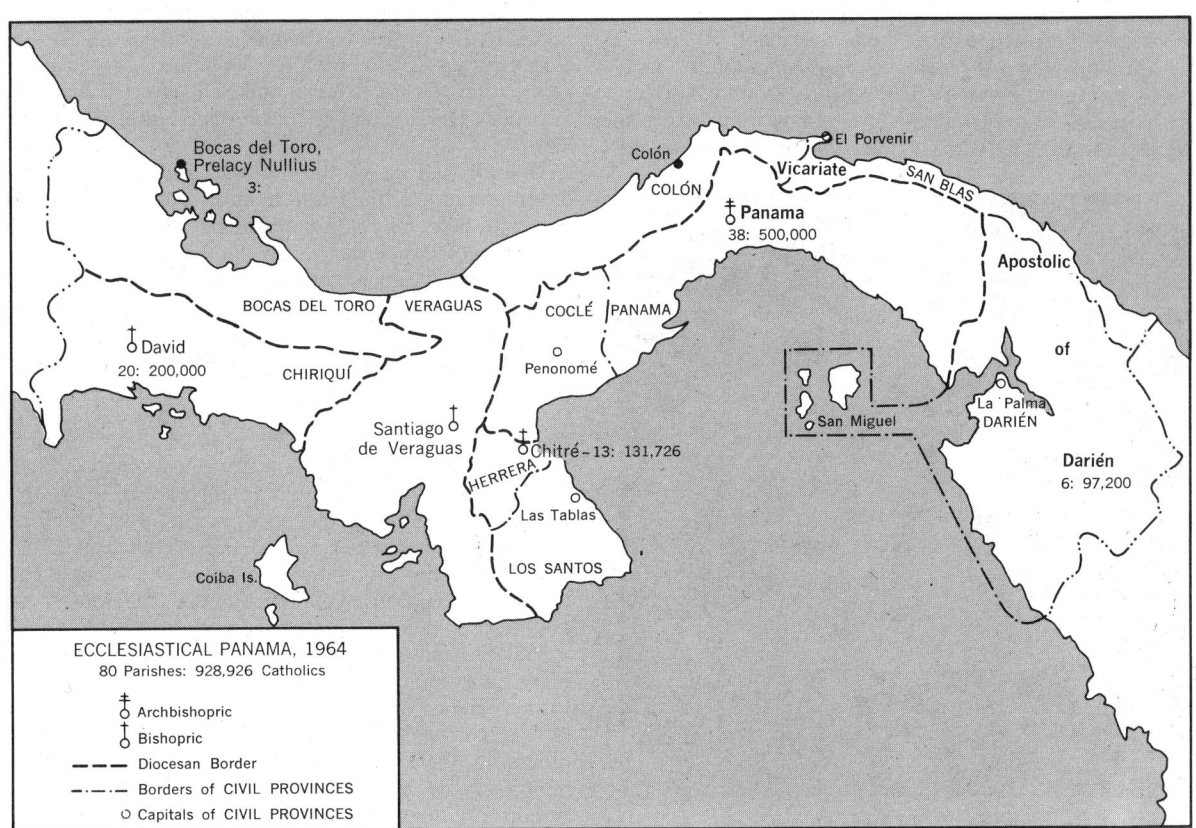

Fig. 1. The ecclesiastical and civil provinces in the modern Republic of Panama for the period 1964–65.

latter, which retains exclusive titular sovereignty over it. The national capital is the city of Panama with 294,359 inhabitants, followed in importance by the cities of Colón, David, Chorrera, and Chitré.

The dominant race in the republic is mestizo, a mixture of whites with Indians, Negroes, and Asiatics, all of which have contributed substantial numbers to make up the general population. Nevertheless, autochthonous Indians and whites descended from the Spaniards who conquered and colonized the country, still maintain separate groups: the first as inhabitants of the mountainous zones and the latter concentrated in the centers of greatest population, in which they form the governing wealthy class.

Early Christianization. The first missionaries brought to the country at the beginning of the 16th century to preach the gospel to the Indians were Franciscans and Dominicans. The former began their work in 1514, when they came in the company of Bp. Juan de *Quevedo, who belonged to that order, and the latter in 1520, when they accompanied the second bishop, the Dominican Vicente Peraza. To them was given the task of beginning the catechizing of the natives of Darién. Years later, the Jesuits joined them in this work. The early missionaries staked out settlements in the mountains, valleys, and plains, founding them with the support and cooperation of the royal government. The majority of these towns still exist, and some have been transformed into true cities, focal points of wealth and culture that are the pride of Panama. Christianity became so deeply rooted in the inhabitants of Panama that, in spite of modern ideological currents that reached the people more readily than in other countries because of the geographic position of the isthmus, the majority continue to be Catholics by conviction and confess their creed without embarrassment.

The most famous person in the history of the missions in Panama was the Dominican General Adriano Ufelde de Santo Tomás, whose name is cited with veneration in colonial chronicles for his effective evan-

gelical work. His written works, several of them published, provide a valuable source of historical information.

The Jesuits began their residence in the isthmus in the middle of the 16th century, and, in addition to missionary work, embraced the function of teaching the youth. Attracted by the example of their teachers and prompted by religious vocations, some of the students entered the Society of Jesus and became notable figures: Pedro Ignacio de Cáceres, distinguished theologian and preacher; Juan Antonio Giraldo, an educator who became rector of the Real y Pontificia Universidad de San Javier de Panama; Agustín Hurtado, a zealous missionary who was martyred (1677) by the savages to whom he was preaching the gospel; Esteban Ferriol, called the "Apostle of Darién," who preached to the natives for 27 consecutive years; and Hernando de la Cruz, theologian (because of humility, he did not choose to receive Holy Orders), poet, and noted painter, who left evidence of his artistic talent in the Jesuit church in Quito.

Diocesan Organization. The Holy See, by petition of the Catholic King Ferdinand, created in 1513 the bishopric of Darién, the fourth in the New World. Juan de Quevedo, assumed his functions in 1514 and initiated the series of 45 bishops who in continued succession have ruled the Panamanian Church. The Diocese of Panama is for that reason the oldest on the American continent. The Panamanian curia was suffragan of the Archdiocese of Seville till 1546, of Lima till 1836, of Bogotá till 1901, and finally of Cartagena de Indias till 1925, at which time, by disposition of Pius XI, the Republic of Panama became an archdiocese. It has since been divided into three suffragan bishoprics, an apostolic vicariate, and a *nullius* prelature. In 1963 three of the bishops and the archbishop were natives of Panama. The bishoprics are, in order of creation, David, Chitré, and Santiago; the apostolic vicariate, Darién; and the *nullius* prelature, Bocas del Toro.

Historical Role of the Church. If one studies the development of the Church in Panama through the apostolic labor of its prelates during the course of 4½ centuries of existence of the Panamanian curia, one will become aware of the beneficial influence exercised by it on the civic and cultural life of the country. This work is revealed in the creation of the first university, the University of St. Xavier (1749–67), by a native priest, Francisco Javier de Luna Victoria, later elevated to the episcopate; in the active participation of the national clergy, with Bp. José Higinio Durán at the head, in the movement for emancipation from Spanish rule in 1821; in the zeal of Bp. Juan José Cabarcas in teaching the poor; in the erection of cathedrals and churches, in the present as well as the past; and in the foundation and maintenance of highly reputed educational plants by the religious communities.

Panamanian Prelates. The Panamanian nation has made an estimable contribution to the Catholic Church in the persons of its prelates born in Panama. Several of them served their apostolate in foreign dioceses, others in their homeland. Several reached the high honor of the episcopate: Francisco Javier de Luna bishop of Chuquisaca, Bolivia, in 1777 but died before taking office; Manuel Moreno y Ollo, Bishop of Pan-

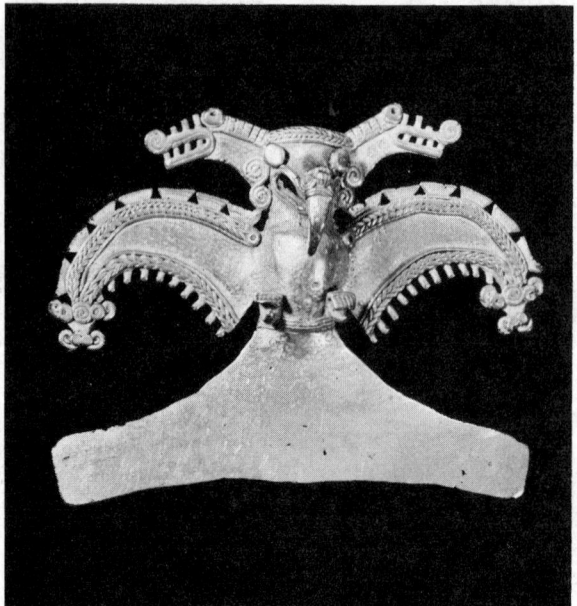

Fig. 2. Eagle pendant of cast gold, in the Veraguas style of Panamanian pre-Columbian art, c. A.D. 800–1540.

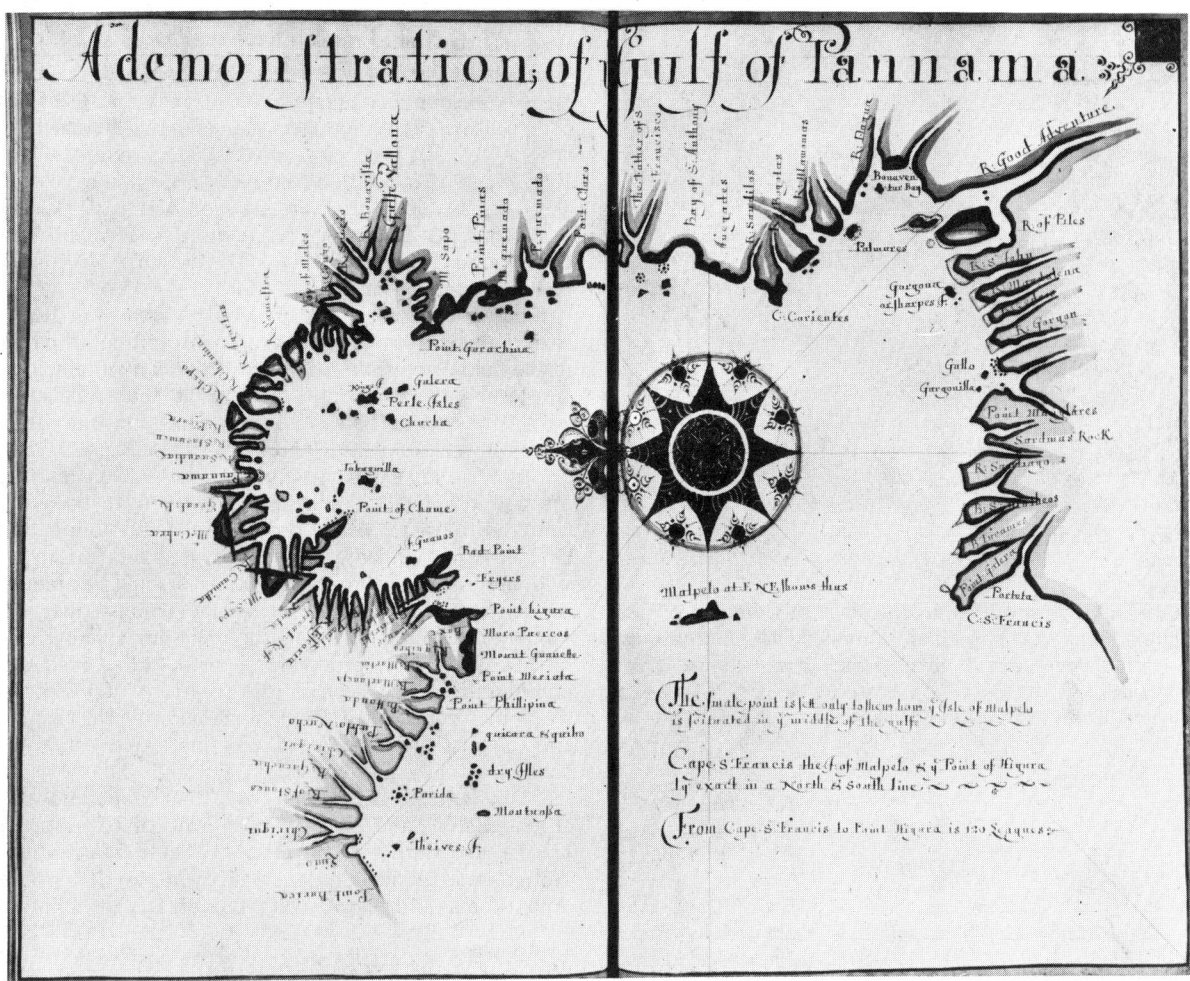

Fig. 3. *The Gulf of Panama as shown in a manuscript atlas, "Waggoner of the South Seas," written and illuminated by* William Hack *on order of the pirate Bartholomew Sharp in 1683 for presentation to King Charles II of England.*

ama (1763–69) and of Guamanga, Peru (1770–80); José Luis de Lila, Bishop of Guamanga, Peru (1764–69); Agustín de Gorrichategui, Bishop of Cuzco, Peru (1770–78); José Andrés de Achurra y Núñez de Arco, Bishop of Trujillo, Peru (1788–91); Manuel Joaquín González de Acuña y Sanz Merino, Bishop of Panama (1797–1813); Rafael Lasso de la Vega, Bishop of Mérida, Venezuela (1815–28) and of Quito, Ecuador (1829–31); Tomás Alberto Clavel Méndez, Bishop of David, Panama (1955–64), Archbishop of Panama in 1964; Marcos Gregorio McGrath, Titular Bishop of Ceciri and auxiliary of the archbishop of Panama (1961–63), Capitular Vicar (1963–64), Bishop of Santiago, Panama, in 1964; José Maria Carrizo Villarreal, Bishop of Chitré, Panama, in 1963; Daniel Núñez, Bishop of David in 1964; and Carlos A. Lewis, Titular Bishop of Nova Terra and Auxiliary Bishop of Panama in 1965.

The Church Today. In the middle of the 20th century the number of priests is insufficient to attend to the existing parishes. Although national vocations are increasing, they have had to be supplemented, primarily by Spanish clergy. There is only one seminary for training native priests in the city of Panama. Vocations are more plentiful among women, and there are more Panamanian nuns than priests.

Religious Communities. Of the 26 communities in Panama, half maintain schools; viz: Jesuits, Recollect Augustinians, Paulists, Salesians, Christian Brothers, Benedictines and Crusading Brothers of St. John the Evangelist, the Slaves of the Sacred Heart, Bethlehemites, Sisters of Charity, Maryknoll, and Auxiliary Mothers of Mary. Others are dedicated to charity, to preaching, to missions, and other social work. They are: the Clarists, Discalced Carmelites, Franciscans, Dominicans, Sisters of the Good Shepherd, Missionary Catechists (a Panamanian foundation), Elizabethans, Mercedarians, Servants of Mary, Visitation Nuns, Capuchin Tertiaries, Sisters of the Presentation, and Missionaries of the Catholic Press.

Relations between Church and State. In Panama the Catholic Church enjoys absolute liberty, separate from the civil government, with which it enjoys cordial relations. In the middle of the 19th century, freedom of religion was established by law, and respect exists toward the practice of other religions. Most of the Protestant groups are foreigners. The constitution of the republic recognizes, however, that the Catholic religion is the major one and gives it special protection. The government cooperates with the Church in financing the missions, gives subsidies for the construction of churches and the development of charitable

Fig. 4. Crucifixion on an appliquéd blouse panel by the Indians of the San Blas Islands of Panama, 20th century.

foundations, especially in the field of education, and scholarships for parochial schools. The Church has no other properties or income except donations.

Bibliography: E. J. CASTILLERO REYES, *Historia de Panamá* (6th ed. Panama 1959). **Illustration credits:** Fig. 2, Courtesy of the Dumbarton Oaks Collections. Fig. 3, Rare Book Department, Free Library of Philadelphia. Fig. 4, Collection of Monroe H. Fabian, Washington, D.C.

[E. J. CASTILLERO R.]

PANAMA, ARCHDIOCESE OF (PANAMENSIS)

The Archdiocese of Panama was created by Pope Pius XI on Sept. 14, 1925. In 1963 it had three suffragan sees, a vicariate apostolic, and a prelature *nullius*. The territory under the jurisdiction of the archbishop consisted of three political provinces and the Canal Zone, with a total population of 637,234. Pius XI initiated the vicariate apostolic on Nov. 29, 1925. The Diocese of David with only one province and 188,450 people was established May 6, 1955, by Pius XII. John XXIII on July 21, 1962, created the diocese of Chitré with two provinces and a population of 125,131; and on October 17 of the same year, the prelature *nullius* of Bocas del Toro in the province of the same name, having 32,600 inhabitants. Santiago, consisting of the province of Veraguas, was declared a diocese by Paul VI, July 13, 1963; it had a population of 130,930.

Thirty-eight centers of Catholic teaching were directed by members of the clergy, with faculties of 308 religious and 344 lay professors and 14,763 students. There were 71 parishes with 37 secular priests and 39 members of the regular clergy. In 1950 Bp. Francisco Beckmann reestablished the minor seminary, closed for many years, for the education of a national clergy. There were 34 students in it in 1963, in addition to 19 seminarians being educated in major seminaries in Rome, the United States, Costa Rica, and Colombia.

In 1963 the religious orders present, in the numbers indicated were: Recollect Augustinians (ORSA), 26; Discalced Carmelites (OCD), 7; Claretians (CMF), 29; Franciscans (OFM), 8; Jesuits, 21; Vincentians (CM), 35; Salesians (SDB), 22; Dominicans (OP), 2; Benedictines (OSB), 4; Christian Brothers (FSC), 27; Brothers of St. John the Evangelist, 4; Bethlemite Sisters (SCIF), 29; Sisters of the Good Shepherd, 7; Catechical Missionary Sisters (Panamanian foundation by Archbishop Beckmann), 22; Franciscan Sisters of St. Elizabeth, 7; Handmaids of the Sacred Heart of Jesus (ACI), 30; Franciscan Sisters, 78; Sisters of Charity, 38; Mercedarian Sisters, 11; Maryknoll Sisters, 18; Salesian Sisters, 12; Servants of Mary, 29; Visitation Nuns, 32; Sisters of Presentation, 4; Capuchin Sisters of the Third Order (RTC), 16; and Missionary Sisters of the Catholic Press, 5.

Since 1950 the clergy has been an important factor in national cultural development, contributing primarily in the field of education through schools maintained by the Jesuits, the Christian Brothers, the Vincentians, the Augustinians, the Salesians, the Franciscan and Bethlemite Sisters, and the Handmaids of the Sacred Heart of Jesus. Many beautiful churches have been built in the country. Outstanding in this work have been the Claretian Fathers, whose order built the Gothic cathedral in Cólon and other churches, and the Carmelites and Salesians, who have both erected attractive churches. The catechizing of the indigenous tribes, begun by the Missionary Sons of the Immaculate Heart of Mary (CMF), progressed satisfactorily. Religious communities have been in the forefront of all social work that contributed to the well-being of the people, and they assisted with zeal the philanthropic establishments that the state undertook. Through the efforts of the Augustinian friars, and with the cooperation of other religious and lay people desirous of backing the project, the Catholic University of Santa María de la Antigua was founded in Panama City in May 1965, with Abp. Tomás Alberto Clavel Méndez as chancellor.

Bibliography: C. RUIZ CAJAR, *Historia de las misiones en Panama en el siglo XVI* (Madrid 1957–58). G. ROJAS Y ARRIETA, *History of the Bishops of Panama*, ed. and tr. T. J. McDONALD (Panama 1929). **Illustration credit:** Pan American Airways.

[E. J. CASTILLERO]

The residential area of Panama City, Panama. The church at the right is Our Lady of Mount Carmel.

PANBABYLONISM

A theory of interpretation of history advanced in Germany at the beginning of the 20th century that claimed to find traces of an essential Babylonian influence in all the cultures and religions of the world. The theory was proposed in several forms, the most notable being those of Hugo Winckler, *Himmels- und Weltenbild der Babylonier als Grundlage der Weltanschauung und Mythologie aller Völker* (1903), and Alfred Jeremias, *Die Panbabylonisten* (1907). These men observed that the cosmogonies of the various nations were permeated with astral motifs and concluded that this worldwide similarity in mythological types argued for a common cultural heritage that had its roots in Babylonia, the birthplace of both astronomy and astrological religion. Some of the ramifications of their theory were to picture Israelite history and tradition as a shadowy borrowing from Mesopotamia and to portray Christ as a fictional reincarnation of the Babylonian god, Bel-Marduk. Another variety of Panbabylonism was exemplified in P. Jensen's *Das Gilgamesch-Epos in der Weltliteratur* (1906), which found that Babylonian hero under different guises in the literature of almost all nations and viewed Christ as a solar-myth figure modeled on Gilgamesh. The extravagant claims of the school were effectively dismissed from serious consideration after the scientific investigations of the astronomer-Assyriologist F. X. *Kugler in his *Auf den Trümmern des Panbabylonismus* (1909) and *Im Bannkreis Babels* (1910).

Bibliography: A. DEIMEL, *Pantheon Babylonicum* (Rome 1914) 35–39. C. M. EDSMAN, RGG³ 5:35–36. A. JEREMIAS, RGG² 4:879–881. P. SCHEBESTA, *König Christus* 1:548–550. F. M. TH. DE LIAGRE BÖHL, *König Christus* 2:447–448. F. KÖNIG, *König Christus* 3:745–746.

[J. A. BRINKMAN]

PANDULF

PANDULF, subdeacon and papal legate to England during the critical years before and after *Magna Carta; b. probably Rome; d. Rome, Sept. 16, 1226. His negotiations with King *John, who was excommunicated and whose kingdom was under an *interdict owing to the quarrel over the election of *Stephen Langton as archbishop of Canterbury, led to the King's submission in May 1213. Pandulf absolved John from excommunication, lifted the interdict, and received England as a fief, which he granted back to John to hold of the pope. Pandulf supported the King during the baronial rebellion and at one point suspended Langton for refusing to excommunicate the barons who extracted the Magna Carta from John. For his service he was rewarded by election to the See of *Norwich. After John's death Pandulf's role was minimal until 1218, when he returned to England to become a dominant member of the regency during the minority of *Henry III. His efficient administration made more enemies than friends, and in 1221 Langton and Hubert de Burgh persuaded the Pope to recall him to Rome, where he died. He was buried in Norwich cathedral.

Bibliography: M. PARIS, *Chronica majora*, ed. H. R. LUARD, 7 v. (RollsS 57; 1872–83) v.2–3. Annals of Burton in *Annales monastici*, ed. H. R. LUARD, 5 v. (*ibid.* 36; 1864–69) v.1 *passim*. T. F. TOUT, DNB 15:174–179. F. M. POWICKE, *King Henry III and the Lord Edward*, 2 v. (Oxford 1947).

[R. S. HOYT]

PANEGYPTIANISM

PANEGYPTIANISM, term used by the Catholic historian Christopher Dawson in his criticism of the theory of G. E. Smith and W. H. Perry of the worldwide diffusion of the Egyptian civilization.

The theory is not entirely new. The ancient authors, including Herodotus, Plato, and Plutarch, impressed by the age and magnificence of Egyptian monuments, ascribed an Egyptian origin to their own gods and cultural traditions. The Egyptian campaign of Napoleon stirred up the new interest in Egyptian antiquities. In the 19th century John Taylor and C. Piazzi Smyth developed a preposterous theory of the Great Pyramid, attributing both scientific (mathematical and astronomical) and enigmatic significance to its shape and dimensions. The inner passages of Cheops' pyramid were interpreted as a graphic image of prophetic world history. In spite of repeated exposures of Egyptologists, who demonstrated the absurdity of such views, the so-called religion of the Great Pyramid spread all over Europe and America, and the alleged prophecy of the Great Pyramid gained new currency during World Wars I and II.

In the first quarter of the 20th century two prominent British anthropologists, G. E. Smith and W. H. Perry, developed the diffusionist theory, ascribing an Egyptian origin to the sun cult, megalithic architecture, mummification, and many other aspects of religion and social structure of prehistoric Europe, Asia, and America. The theory of unilateral diffusion of civilization from a single area, as presented by Smith and Perry, found no support either in anthropological or in Egyptological literature. In view of archeological discoveries, Egypt lost its unique position as the center of the earliest civilization. The historical value of the Sothic date, 4241 B.C., has rightly been questioned, and the long chronology, placing Menes, the first historical king, in the 5th millennium B.C., has been abandoned in favor of much more condensed systems. Archeological evidence has been offered for Mesopotamian influence (or "inspiration") at the very beginning of the Egyptian urban civilization.

Bibliography: The theory of the Great Pyramid. J. TAYLOR, *The Great Pyramid: Why Was It Built and Who Built It?* (2d ed. London 1864). C. P. SMYTH, *Our Inheritance in the Great Pyramid* (London 1864); *Life and Work at the Great Pyramid*, 3 v. (London 1867). For criticism, see J. P. LAUER, *Le Problème des pyramides d'Égypte* (Paris 1948). The diffusionist theory. G. E. SMITH, *The Ancient Egyptians and the Origin of Civilization* (rev. ed. New York 1923); *Human History* (New York 1929). W. J. PERRY, *The Children of the Sun, a Study of the Early History of Civilization* (2d ed. London 1927). For criticism of the theory, see A. J. TOYNBEE, *A Study of History*, 12 v. (New York 1948–61) 1:424–426. C. H. DAWSON, *Dynamics of World History*, ed. J. J. MULLOY (New York 1956; Mentor Omega Bk. 1962) 175–176. For the generally accepted view on the origin of the Egyptian civilization, see H. FRANKFORT, *The Birth of Civilization in the Near East* (Bloomington, Ind. 1951).

[B. MARCZUK]

PANENTHEISM

Panentheism (Gr. παν, all; εν, in; θεος, God) views all things as being in God without exhausting the infinity of the divine nature. In metaphysics, it utilizes a real distinction between the essence of God and His existence, or considers God as having accidents really distinct from His nature. Panentheism stands as a kind of surrelativism holding for a real convertible relation of dependence between God and the world—not only is the world dependent upon God, but He is dependent upon the world. It regards the world as an actual fulfillment of God's creative possibility.

The term panentheism seems to have been introduced by Karl C. F. Krause (1781–1832) to distinguish his doctrine from contemporary forms of *pantheism and *emanationism. The term was used also by Friedrich *Jacobi and by a few members of the theological faculty at Tübingen, though not so pointedly. Today it describes the views of those who introduce a polarity in the notion of God as both eternal and temporal and as including yet transcending the world.

Panentheism is rooted in a conviction that the world as possible in the mind of God becomes actualized and thereby adds to God's actuality. It opposes the Thomistic view of God as *Pure Act. Panentheists give special importance to what they call a logic of polarity, which has a close affinity to Hegelian dialectics, as the only means of escaping ultimate dilemmas arising from the use of categories.

Historical Survey. In one sense, the present forms of panentheism can be traced to *Plato, who discussed both being and becoming in a manner that could imply a bipolar view of ultimate reality. His "One" seems to have contained individual beings even as it remained indivisible.

Medieval Thought. *John Scotus Erigena viewed creation as the production of Ideas in the Word, and designated a stage of completion for such productivity in quite the same manner as do present-day panentheists. Moreover, his distinction of God as Creator and God as the End of all things implies fulfillment, and reads much like Whitehead's primordial and consequent natures of God.

Rāmānuja (1017–1137) tempered the impersonal Hindu pantheism of his day with a personalistic notion of *Brahman as cause of all things, but he also maintained that all the things of this world formed the body of Brahma. His doctrine of nonduality with differences (vishiṣṭādvaita) seems more in line with modern polaristic views than with either pantheistic *monism or theistic *dualism.

Although John *Duns Scotus insisted on freedom in the act of creation, traces of panentheism may be seen in his view of God as being necessitated to will the ideas of things, and in his doctrine of the univocity of being. Further, his ideas on infinity and his insistence upon the limitations of metaphysics imply a polarity.

Meister *Eckhart emphasized the transcendence of God and maintained that one could not affirm anything of God in such a way as to rule out its opposite—an idea similar to the later notion of polarity.

Renaissance and Modern Thinkers. *Nicholas of Cusa leaned even farther toward panentheism. He held that the world is explication of what is implication in God and conceived of the infinite as including and reconciling all opposites. Such ideas not only established ground for the bipolar logic, but also emphasized the theme of fulfillment that was presented by later panentheists.

Friedrich *Schelling described the *Absolute as the identity of all differences. For Schelling, God will "be" only when the Absolute has fully revealed itself. His God is in process in somewhat the same manner as Whitehead's consequent God.

The triadic doctrine of the Absolute Spirit proposed by *Hegel considers nature as an externalization of the Absolute, and portrays the Absolute itself as a never-ending process that implies eternity and temporality.

Two Russian thinkers, Vladimir *Solov'ev and Nikolaï *Berdïaev, have emphasized the incarnational aspect of panentheism. Solov'ev presents God as polarized and developed through the notions of man-Godhood and God-manhood. Berdïaev looked to a transfigured world as the ultimate expression of God.

Contemporary Directions. Alfred N. *Whitehead offers a dipolar God by distinguishing between the so-called primordial and consequent aspects of the divine nature: the primordial aspect is God considered as the first cause of all things; the consequent aspect is God as the end of all things. Arguing from the relativity of all things, he holds for a reaction of the world upon God to the extent that the whole of the created order stands as a fulfillment of God's concrete being, though not of His conceptual nature.

Muhammud Iqbal (1875–1938) described God's creative life as an organic whole existing as an open possibility, so that God is ever being completed by the world without changing His essential nature.

The interpretation of participated being given by Pierre *Teilhard de Chardin seems to have concluded with the placement of all things in God by what he calls a unitive transformation. While insisting that this fusion of the one and the many does not add anything essential to God, he implies that it does add something accidental to the divine being.

Paul Tillich's approach to ultimate reality through symbolization uses the notion of polarity to overcome the tendency to impose limitations upon God. It fits in well with the basic approach of panentheism.

Sarvepalli Radhakrishnan (b. 1888) makes a distinction between divine being and divine action in rejecting the idea of confining the illimitable to a single form or perfection. He holds that abstract possibility and concrete realization are both contained in the one reality, which he identifies as the Absolute-God. Although he says that this distinction is only logical, he seems to use it as a real distinction; thus it gives his thought a panentheistic polarity.

Charles Hartshorne has done most to give panentheism formal expression as a view of God. His philosophical approach to the existence and nature of God involves a notion of causality that includes a convertible relation of dependence between cause and effect, so that a cause depends upon its effects and effects upon their cause. For him, God is the supreme stream of causation rather than the first cause, and He has yet to be fully realized.

Critical Evaluation. Panentheism rests upon a principle of polarity that holds that contraries may both be true without one excluding the other. In Aristotelian logic both contraries cannot be true, although both can be false; again, when a middle position is accepted as true, both contraries become false (*see* OPPOSITION). But panentheists seem to look upon one of a set of contraries as always implying the possibility of the other.

In applying the notion of polarity to *causality, panentheists place a real reciprocal relation of dependence between cause and effect. If such interdependence is granted, it would seem to do away with the meaning of causality as such. While lower orders of causes are more involved with their effects through the principle of reaction, such involvements exist by reason of the limitations of these causes—causality as such does not demand such reciprocity. This is especially the case with God. Speaking of God as the first cause does not limit Him to a mode of action found in secondary causes; rather it affirms His transcendental perfection.

A further inadequacy evidenced in panentheism involves the notion of *analogy. Panentheists seem convinced that the only way to escape the limiting univocity of the categories is to introduce apparent contradictions, and to explain their copredication in terms of changing meaning of the terms; this results, however, in equivocity [see EQUIVOCATION (LOGIC)]. The antepredicamental role of analogy seems to be what panentheists are seeking here. Only through analogy can one predicate perfections of being that are simply different, yet somewhat the same. Only through analogy can reality be presented as both one and many, without the oversimplification of either monism or pluralism.

Bibliography: C. HARTSHORNE and W. L. REESE, eds., *Philosophers Speak of God* (Chicago 1953). F. H. PARKER, "Head, Heart and God," *Review of Metaphysics* 14 (1960–61) 328–352. F. J. THONNARD, *Short History of Philosophy,* tr. E. A. MAZIARZ (New York 1955). E. H. GILSON, *Being and Some Philosophers* (Toronto 1949). Gilson HistChrPhil. S. N. DASGUPTA, *A History of Indian Philosophy,* 5 v. (Cambridge, Eng. 1922–55). J. D. COLLINS, *God in Modern Philosophy* (Chicago 1959). V. S. SOLOVIEV, *Lectures on Godmanhood* (London 1948). N. A. BERDIÁEV, *The Russian Idea,* tr. R. M. FRENCH (New York 1948; repr. pa. Boston 1962). A. N. WHITEHEAD, *Process and Reality* (New York 1929). P. WEISS, *Modes of Being* (Carbondale, Ill. 1958). P. TEILHARD DE CHARDIN, *The Divine Milieu* (New York 1960). P. A. SCHILPP, ed., *The Philosophy of Sarvepalli Radhakrishnan* (New York 1952).

[E. R. NAUGHTON]

PANGE LINGUA GLORIOSI, the opening words of two liturgical hymns. (1) *Pange lingua gloriosi lauream certaminis,* a hymn of the holy cross by Venantius *Fortunatus, written *c.* 569 for the reception of a relic of the cross, sent by Emperor *Justin II to Queen *Radegunda, in *Poitiers (*see* CROSS, FINDING OF THE HOLY). One of the most famous Passiontide hymns of all times, it has been used in the *Good Friday ceremony of the veneration of the cross since the 9th century and later at *Matins and *Lauds of Passiontide, as well as for the Feast of the Exaltation of the Cross (September 14). The original text (modified under *Urban VIII and reestablished under *Pius X) consists of 10 stanzas, each having three lines in trochaic tetrameter, a form once used in marching songs of the Roman soldiers. The hymn briefly recounts Christ's earthly life, embedded in the history of the Redemption, beginning with man's fall, and makes passing allusions to the instruments of the Passion. Christ's cross appears as the tree of life, especially selected for the glorious task of bearing Christ. This holy cross hymn later became the model for many compositions, among them the not less famous Eucharistic hymn, (2) *Pange lingua gloriosi corporis mysterium,* sung at Vespers and during procession on *Corpus Christi and *Holy Thursday. It has five three-line stanzas and a doxology, in catalectic and accentual trochaic tetrameter. This masterpiece of medieval poetry was written probably by St. *Thomas Aquinas (or by someone in his entourage) *c.* 1264. Written to a preexisting melody (that of the holy cross Sequence *Laudes crucis attollamus),* by the *Goliardic poet Hugh Primas of Orléans, it contains many echoes and reminiscences from earlier

hymns; still it is an original piece of work, with highly poetic inspiration and doctrinal exactitude. Many later hymns imitated it and borrowed from its contents. Its fifth stanza, *Tantum ergo,* is sung (to various melodies) at *Benediction of the Blessed Sacrament.

Bibliography: Connelly Hymns 118–120, the Eucharistic Sequence, 82–84, the holy cross, etc., hymn. AnalHymn 50:71, 585–586. Szövérffy AnnLatHymn 1:129–135; 2:251–252. Raby ChrLP 90, Venatius Fortunatus; 408, Thomas Aquinas. B. FISCHER, LexThK² 8:21, cf. H. VANDERHOVEN, *Paroisse et Liturgie* 33 (1951) 168–173.

[J. SZÖVÉRFFY]

PANIGAROLA, FRANCESCO, Franciscan Observant preacher and theologian; b. Milan, June 6, 1548; d. Asti, May 31, 1594. He was born of the noble Panigarola family and baptized Jerome. He began his studies at Pavia in 1561 and continued them later at Bologna. He led a very dissipated life, but was suddenly converted and entered the Friars Minor Observant in Florence on May 15, 1567. There he took the name Francesco to distinguish himself from an uncle Jerome, a member of the same province. He made his regular ecclesiastical studies at Padua and Pisa. It was said of him that he became as devout in religion as he had been dissipated in the world.

After his ordination, he began to preach in the large cities of Italy and gained great renown. St. Pius V was so impressed by his eloquence that he sent him to Paris for 2 years to study the Fathers.

In 1579 Panigarola refused the generalate of his order, but was elected a general definitor and was appointed visitator for all the Italian provinces. In 1583 he was commissioned by St. Charles Borromeo to preach against Lutheranism and Calvinism, which were gaining a foothold in the Tyrol. He became celebrated as a controversialist and is credited with saving the Rhaetian provinces from the Reformation. His sermons on Calvinism, *Lettioni sopra dogmi dette calviniche* (Milan 1582), were translated into several languages and were many times reprinted.

In 1586 Sixtus V named him bishop of Grisopolis and the next year transferred him to Asti, where Calvinism was active. In 1587 he was sent by Sixtus V as part of a diplomatic mission to Paris; he did not return to his diocese until 1590. In Asti he spent his few remaining years in energetic action, especially preaching and combatting the doctrines of the Reformation.

Panigarola's published works number 33, and there are as many more in manuscript form. Most of his writings are in the field of sacred eloquence, and include especially his philosophical and theological polemics against the teachings of Luther and Calvin. Notable among his printed works are *Rhetorica ecclesiastica* (Cologne 1605) and *Conciones 100 supra Christi passionem coram D. Carlo Borromeo recitatae* (Venice 1585).

Bibliography: E. BOTTASSO, EncCatt 9:680–681. A. TEETAERT, DTC 11.2:1850–53. O. BONMANN, LexThK² 8:22. Hurter Nomencl³ 3:249.

[P. F. MULHERN]

PANNETON, PHILIPPE, French-Canadian physician and novelist who wrote under the pseudonym of Ringuet; b. Trois-Rivières, Province of Quebec, April 30, 1895; d. Lisbon, Portugal, Dec. 29, 1960. The independence of mind and the violent dislike for conformism to which he was to give expression in his literary work asserted themselves early. As a youth he went to one college after another, unwilling to submit himself to discipline. After graduating from the school of medicine at the University of Montreal (1920), he did postgraduate work in Paris for 3 years. Upon returning to Canada, he distinguished himself as a medical practitioner, member of the medical staff of the University of Montreal, and head of the department at that institution and at the Hôpital Notre-Dame.

His first literary venture, *Litteratures . . . à la manière de nos auteurs* (1924, with Louis Francoeur), was a collection of pastiches after the fashion of the French writers Paul Reboux and Charles Muller. His second book, *Trente Arpents* (1938), was a novel dealing with contemporary rural life in French Canada; an immediate success, it won four literary prizes—two in France and two in Canada—and was translated into English, German, and Dutch. Its theme is the disintegration of a peasant family brought about by the blind attachment of a father to a way of life being rapidly undermined by industrialization. The story's realism shocked many Canadian readers and critics, used to traditionally lyrical descriptions of French-Canadian country life. Ringuet's keen psychological analysis and his skillful handling of dialogue and narrative have nonetheless won for *Trente Arpents* recognition as one of the masterpieces of French-Canadian fiction.

Ringuet never wrote an equal work. *Le Poids du jour* (1949) a penetrating study of the mores and aspirations of urban society in French Canada, is distinguished, but fails in quality of style and organization. Ringuet wrote a third novel, *Fausse monnaie* (1947); a collection of short stories, *L'Héritage et autres contes* (1946); and two historical sketches, *Un Monde était leur empire* (1943) and *L'Amiral et le Facteur: Ou Comment l'Amérique ne fut pas découverte* (1954). At his death, he was Canadian ambassador to Portugal, a post to which he had been appointed in 1956.

Bibliography: P. ANGERS in *Profils littéraires* (Cahiers de l'Académie canadienne-française 7; Montreal 1963). G. TOUGAS, *Histoire de la littérature canadienne-française* (2d ed. Paris 1964).

[J. M. CARRIÈRE]

PANNONHALMA, ABBEY OF, archabbey and center of the Hungarian *Benedictines (Mártonhegy, Martinsberg, *Mons sacer Pannoniae*). The foundation, near Györ (Raab), was initiated by Duke Géza in 996 and completed in 1101 under King St. *Stephen by monks from Brevnov in Bohemia. An abbey *nullius* with all the privileges of *Monte Cassino, it was the chief agent of Hungary's conversion to Christianity and throughout the Middle Ages was a center of learning and culture, as well as the scene of political events. After organizing the Hungarian Benedictine Congregation in 1512 and becoming an archabbey in 1514, it was for a century a bastion that resisted the Turkish invasion. *Joseph II secularized it (1786) but Francis I restored it (1802). From then until World War II it was engaged in secondary education and headed the Congregation, which, incorporating the abbeys of Bakonybél, Tihany, Dömölk, and Zalavár and administering 25 parishes and 8 gymnasia, had about 300 priest monks. In 1948 the Communist government secularized the possessions of the Congregation. Since 1950 Pannonhalma has been the only Benedictine monastery in Hungary. The mon-

astery has a valuable library and is rich in cultural monuments. Hungarian Benedictines have settled in Brazil and California.

Bibliography: L. ERDÉLYI, *A Pannonhalmi Szent-Benedek-rend története*, 14 v. (Budapest 1902–16). T. VON BOGYAY, LexThK² 7:125.

[L. J. LEKAI]

PANPSYCHISM

From the Greek $\pi\tilde{\alpha}\nu$ meaning all, and $\psi\nu\chi\dot{\eta}$ meaning soul, a philosophical theory that all reality, including inorganic matter, is animated and possesses a psychic nature similar to that of the human soul. It is to be distinguished from *hylozoism, the doctrine that all matter is endowed with life but possesses no psychic element.

Old Forms. Panpsychism can be traced back to early Greek philosophers, such as *Heraclitus and *Empedocles, but it is only in the Renaissance that it assumed a concrete and systematic form. Thus in his *Nova de universis philosophia* (Venice 1593), Francesco *Patrizi (1529–97) developed the Neoplatonic theme of an eternal divine light pervading the whole universe, and described knowledge in terms that indicated a similarity of nature between knower and object known. Likewise, Geronimo *Cardano (1501–76) defended the doctrine of a *world soul informing the universe as a psychic principle, and Giordano *Bruno (1548–1600) stated even more clearly that the world soul is "the formal constitutive principle of the universe and all that is contained in it" [*De la causa, principio et uno,* Venice (London): 1584]. The doctrine of a world soul was defended also by Tommaso *Campanella (1568–1639), who accepted the theory of universal sensation propounded by Bernardino *Telesio, and developed it into a metaphysical theory that being is essentially composed of power, knowledge, and love.

Modern Forms. In modern times panpsychism has found supporters among philosophers of different trends of thought, principally in Germany, but also in England, the U.S., Italy, and France.

Germany. The theory of G. W. *Leibniz that all reality is made up of monads considered as conscious units reflecting the entire universe is clearly of a panpsychic nature. More recently G. T. *Fechner (1801–87) revived the Renaissance theme of an animated universe, which he held to be a unitary system penetrated by the spirit of God and including all other minor "systems" as sentient subjects. Among such systems he classed not only animals, but plants, the earth, and the heavenly bodies. Rudolph *Lotze (1817–81) restated Leibniz's theory of unextended and conscious monads, and Friedrich Paulsen (1846–1908) presented physical reality as a manifestation of a supreme psychic unit, God, conceived essentially as Will, a doctrine that has many elements in common with the systems of A. *Schopenhauer and W. *Wundt. This monistic conception of reality was shared also by Ernst *Haeckel (1834–1919), for whom God was the sum total of the infinite psychic realities that compose the universe.

England and the U.S. Like Haeckel in Germany, William K. Clifford (1845–79) in England arrived at panpsychism from his theory of evolution. If man evolves from inorganic matter, matter must contain the elements of consciousness as this is known to exist in man. Hence the entire universe consists of "mind stuff." Another British philosopher whose conception of reality was impregnated with panpsychic motives was Alfred N. *Whitehead (1861–1947), who, with Leibniz, is believed to be "one of two great artificers of the panpsychic philosophy in its present form" (C. Hartshorne, 450). He pictured the world as a process of events rather than of things. Each event contains within itself its own past, anticipates its future, and represents all other events by their effects on it. Thus an event is the synthetic unity of the universe comprehended as oneness, as well as the mirror of the entire universe. It is also an organism in which each part affects the whole and, in turn, is determined by the whole as to its role within it.

In the U.S. also panpsychism had a few followers. Charles S. *Peirce (1839–1914) maintained that mind and matter are but different aspects of a single feeling process. When something is considered in its relations and reactions, it is regarded as matter; when understood as feeling, it appears as consciousness. Josiah *Royce (1855–1916) shared Fechner's basic view of the psychic aspect of all beings. However he defended the peculiar theory that in addition to individual animals, each species of animal as a whole is a single conscious unit. A more recent American exponent of the panpsychic doctrine was Charles A. Strong (1862–1940), whose attempt to solve the problem of interaction between body and mind led to the denial of their essential difference and to the conception of matter as a psychic reality. (See MIND-BODY PROBLEM.)

Italy and France. In Italy and France panpsychism was found chiefly among philosophers of spiritualistic tendencies. Thus, in Italy, Vincenzo *Gioberti (1801–52) not only held the doctrine of an animated universe but also claimed that the principle of animation is of an intellectual nature. In France the spiritualistic movement started by *Maine de Biran and developed by J. G. F. Ravaisson (1813–1900) reached its climax in the theory of vital impulse (*élan vital*) as the immanent principle directive of all organic evolution, a doctrine proposed by H. *Bergson. By P. *Teilhard de Chardin (1881–1955) the process of integral evolution was conceived to extend from elemental matter to reflex consciousness and to attain to its final stage in the "Omega Point." (See SPIRIT, MODERN PHILOSOPHIES OF.)

Evaluation. Panpsychism is untenable both as a scientific theory and as a philosophical doctrine. Living beings differ from inanimate matter because of their structural organization and their activities. They are composed of cells or combination of cells forming organs, and they are characterized by metabolism, growth, reproduction, and internal power of adaptation to environment. This distinction becomes even more evident in animals, which, in addition to vegetative powers, have the capacity for sensation, and in man, who alone among all corporeal creatures is endowed with the power of reasoning. By attributing to matter vital and psychic forces that are proper to plants and animals respectively, panpsychists fail to take into account the essential distinction that separates one order of being from another.

See also LIFE; SOUL; SOUL, HUMAN; SPIRIT.

Bibliography: C. HARTSHORNE, "Panpsychism," *A History of Philosophical Systems,* ed. V. T. A. FERM (New York 1950). G. MARTANO, EncFil 3:1127–29. Eisler 2:372–374. P. TEILHARD DE CHARDIN, *The Phenomenon of Man,* tr. B. WALL (New York 1959). C. A. STRONG, *Essays on the Natural Origin of the Mind* (London 1930).

[B. M. BONANSEA]

PANTAENUS, ST., 2d-century Christian author (feast, July 7; Coptic Church, June 22). The scanty knowledge about Pantaenus comes primarily from Eusebius, who stated (*Hist. Eccl.* 5.10) that he had been trained in the Stoic philosophy and was head of a private school of philosophy at Alexandria about 180. Previously although Eusebius reported this only as tradition, he had been a zealous missionary and had reached India (i.e., probably South Arabia), where he had found Christians who knew the Gospel of St. Matthew in Hebrew (Aramaic) which they had received from St. Bartholomew. He was still alive in 194 (Eusebius, *Chron.* 2210) and died probably in that decade, being succeeded by *Clement of Alexandria.

In the *Hypotyposes,* Clement mentioned Pantaenus as his teacher and quoted "his opinions and traditions" (*Hist. Eccl.* 6.13). Eusebius thought that he also alluded to him in the *Stromateis* (1.11.2; particularly quoted *Hist. Eccl.* 5.11), where after mentioning certain unnamed teachers Clement concluded: "I found rest when I came upon the last (he was the first in power), after tracking him to where he was in Egypt. He the true Sicilian bee, gathering the flowers of the prophetic and apostolic meadow, engendered in the soul of his hearers an unfading element of knowledge."

Possibly Pantaenus came originally from Sicily. He seems to have promoted liberal studies, for Origen (*Hist. Eccl.* 6.14) defended his own study of philosophy by reference to his example. He also wrote scriptural commentaries that were extant in Jerome's time (*De vir. ill.* 36), but nothing has survived. His importance lies in his contribution to the scholarly tradition of Alexandrian Christianity.

Bibliography: J. A. FISCHER, LexThK² 8:24. E. PETERSON, EncCatt 9:693–694. Quasten Patr 2:4–5. J. MUNCK, *Untersuchungen über Klemens von Alexandria* (Stuttgart 1933) 151–204. G. BARDY, RechScRel 27 (1937) 65–90, school. M. HORNSCHUH, ZKirchgesch 71 (1960) 1–5, 19–25. H. I. MARROU, ed. and tr., *À Diognète* (SourcesChr 33; 1951) 266–268.

[M. WHITTAKER]

PANTHEISM

Pantheism, from παν, all, and θεός, god, is a view of reality that tends to identify the world with God or God with the world. Pantheism is not so much a doctrine as it is the implication of views expressed in terms of the world, *God, the *Absolute, or *infinity. It generally emphasizes the *immanence of God in the world and deemphasizes, or ignores, His *transcendence over the world. Since no one has as yet failed to make some distinction between transcendent and immanent aspects of infinite being, there never has been a complete and utter pantheism.

Scholastics tend to reduce pantheism to a form of *atheism on the ground that identification of God with the world implies the denial of Him as transcendent and really distinct from the world—a view fundamental to all forms of *theism. However, the majority of those who are labelled pantheists manifest a strong religious commitment to God in one way or another; in fact, many of them are properly classified as religious thinkers. Again, views of reality termed pantheistic usually embody some limitation that effectively negates complete identification between God and the world. One such limitation now identifies itself as *panentheism and claims many earlier thinkers as proponents. Beyond this, a more general element of restriction is found in *monism, which distinguishes between absolute and *finite being, but reduces one to an illusion or appearance of the other. Interpretations of such reductions, of course, differ widely.

Origins in the East. Throughout ancient Indian philosophy, with its direction toward self, themes occur that are clearly pantheistic. The general current of Vedic literature conveys the notion of a purely immanent deity (Purusa), frequently described as the whole of reality (*see* VEDAS). In the *Upanishads, the notions of *Brahman and Ātman are proposed as manifestations of the Absolute, Brahma being the objective evolutionary manifestation and Ātman the conscious or subjective manifestation. In idealistic interpretations of Upanishadic literature, the world is appearance or illusion (*see* MAYA RELIGION). In materialistic interpretations, the world is the reality, deity is impersonal, mythical, a manifestation of the world. Even the lofty Bhagavadgītā presents the Absolute as equally present in all things. Since *Jainism and *Buddhism fully identify the Absolute with the world, their pantheism is at root atheistic.

In ancient Chinese thought, *Taoism, especially in doctrines of *Lao-tzŭ, reflects a certain pantheism in that the Tao is said to have produced all things out of itself.

Greek and Roman Thought. Among the ancient Greeks, Xenophanes denounced the polytheism of his day but made God the totality of being. *Parmenides extended this pantheism to an extreme monism expressed in terms of being and paralleling some of the ancient Hindu notions of the Absolute. This doctrine of Parmenides was developed by Melissus to include the notion of infinity. For these monists, changing reality was an illusion, much as it was for the idealistic interpreters of the Upanishads. On the other hand, *Heraclitus offered a monism in which permanence was the illusion and change the only reality. He called his primal fire Zeus, Logos, or Deity, and developed a doctrine similar to the almost contemporary Buddhist theory of "momentariness" (Kṣaṇabhaṅgavāda). [*See* GREEK PHILOSOPHY (RELIGIOUS ASPECTS).]

Both Platonism and *Neoplatonism evidence tendencies toward pantheism that derive from foundations in Plato's thought. The relation between the doctrine of the One and that of Ideas suggests a similarity to the Hindu doctrine of Maya, where the only reality is God and everything else is merely an appearance. Centuries later, *Plotinus reinforced this Platonic implication of pantheism with his own doctrine of *emanationism, which gave inspiration to many later pantheists.

The *Stoicism of Greece and Rome tried to overcome polytheism but seems have fallen short of theism and to have settled for pantheism. The Stoics maintained that the material alone was real, yet they looked upon God as the author of the world. For most of them God was the *world soul, and they described Him as fire, ether, air, mind, or combinations of these; in this sense the Stoic God was part of this world.

Non-Christian Medievals. Among the Hindus of the Middle Ages, Shankara (788–820) tried to maintain the transcendence as well as the immanence of God, but his doctrines imply a limited variety of pantheism (panentheism) that accepts the Upanishadic notion of God as the lower Brahma (Īshvara) and immanent in the world. In the 12th century, Ramanuja also perceived the inadequacy of pure pantheism, identified Brahma as

God and individual, but then regarded God as qualified by matter with souls constituting His body. A limiting factor in Ramanuja's thought is his notion that identity includes difference and unity includes diversity, much as this was later proposed by Hegel.

The Islamic philosopher *Alfarabi, under the influence of the Neoplatonic *Theologia Aristotelis* and *Liber de Causis,* combined the Aristotelian spheres with emanationism to maintain the existence of a supreme agent intellect from which all substantial forms were derived. No Arabian philosopher went further than Alfarabi, and most of them, including *Avicenna and *Averroës, were saved from the pantheistic implications of their views by their concern for religious truth and the transcendence of God. (*See* ARABIAN PHILOSOPHY.)

While relatively little pantheism is found in Jewish thinkers of the time, one man stands out for his leanings in this direction, viz, *Avicebron (ibn-Gabirol). He seems to have identified the matter of this world with God and to have reduced the doctrine of *creation to a theory of emanation. Yet his attempt to unite the world and God in terms of Divine Wisdom or the Divine Word led many European scholars to regard him as a Christian. Avicebron exerted a strong influence also on the cabalists, a 13th-century group of mystics (*see* CABALA).

Christian Thinkers. Four distinct tendencies are apparent among the Christians of the Middle Ages. First there is that of the controversial *John Scotus Erigena, the 9th-century Neoplatonist. In his *Division of Nature,* he made what seems to be a real distinction between God as the Creator and God as the end of all things— a distinction similar to Whitehead's antecedent and consequent God. For Erigena, creation was a "theophany," a manifestation of God. Although this strongly resembles the Hindu doctrine of Maya, Erigena clearly accepted the reality of both God and the world, and his pantheism (a matter of prolonged controversy) may be more a consequence of inadequate language than an attempt to identify the world with God.

Then, at the beginning of the 13th century, *Amalric of Bène made God the formal principle in all things by his notion that the Holy Spirit was the soul of the world, while *David of Dinant presented a monistic and materialistic view of the world by identifying primary matter, mind, and God in the ancient Hindu tradition.

Thirdly, the thought of Meister *Eckhart shows the influence of Neoplatonism on the highest levels of religious thought. For Eckhart, God transcends all concepts, even that of being, so that strictly He cannot be called a being. Yet Eckhart held that being flows eternally from God, and this led him to identify being with the Holy Spirit. Thus he tended to confuse ideas in the mind of God with the world itself, much as did Erigena.

Finally *Nicholas of Cusa, the leading Platonist of his day and a staunch believer in the orthodoxy of both Erigena and Eckhart, held that the world is explication of what is implication in God; God is infinitely one so that, in Him, all opposites are reconciled or overcome. Although Nicholas does mark God off from the world, his expressions have implications similiar to the views of the ancient Hindus on the Absolute and of Plotinus on the One.

Renaissance and Reformation. Giordano *Bruno anticipated Spinoza in his monistic concept of substance: God is substantial nature. For him, God (*natura naturans*) is transcendent and beyond our knowledge;

yet the world (*natura naturata*) is that into which the Infinite divides itself and is likewise infinite. Consequently there is a recurrent identification of God, as Nature, with the world, with God being the immanent principle as well as external cause of the universe.

In the 17th century, the Protestant mystic Jakob *Böhme exerted wide influence, especially on later German and Russian *mysticism. While his doctrine of external dualism suggests panentheism more than pure pantheism, Böhme viewed God as an evolutionary figure, sometimes nothing more than a divinity in man or his spiritual force.

Later in the same century, *Spinoza formulated his pantheism. His monistic approach to the notion of substance made the world attributes or modes of God. While he did use the term creation, he also spoke of *natura naturans* and *natura naturata* in the same way as Bruno, with the same suggestion of emanationism. Thus, while Spinoza looked upon God as the cause of the world, immanent cause and nature are for him one in essence and identical with God.

It was during the 18th-century debate over religion that Toland actually introduced the terms pantheism and pantheist. Toland's final view seems to have reduced God to the material universe and to have made Him little more than a mechanistic law of nature.

Transcendentalism and Idealism. Although *Kant was not a pantheist, his idealistic *immanentism did occasion in many of his followers a tendency toward pantheism. An interesting aspect of this development of transcendental *idealism was the great outpouring of ideas about God in the end of the 18th and beginning of the 19th centuries (*see* KANTIANISM; NEO-KANTIANISM).

Within the 19th century, *Schopenhauer distinctively and consciously took direction from Indian thinkers, principally from Buddhism. Although his philosophy tends toward atheistic Buddhism, Schopenhauer makes the world and man momentary reflections of a transcendent Will. His views of this absolute Will imply something more personal than mere force, even though he considered his pantheism as an atheism. Later *Fechner held that God is the totality of things as the infinite consciousness of the universe and a kind of world soul.

The transcendental *egoism of *Fichte reduced God to moral order and an expression of the self. *Schelling developed a bipolar approach like that used later by Whitehead and identified both the real and the ideal in the Absolute in a manner reflecting Böhme's influence and the Upanishadic approach. While Hegelian monism—qualified by dialectical logic—seems more panentheistic than pantheistic, *Hegel regarded the Absolute as totally immanent to, and constantly developing in, human consciousness. Later *Feuerbach reduced the Absolute to a mere abstraction in his atheistic philosophy. The Russian mystic *Solov'ev reflected the influence of Spinoza, Schopenhauer, and Buddhism; he proposed a spiritualistic personalism that drifted toward pantheism through its emphasis on the unity of all beings with the Divinity and its relatively uncritical notion of Godmanhood.

Recent Directions. Among significant contemporary thinkers, *Spencer viewed God as some kind of physical force and the ground of evolution. *Haeckel, while attempting to find some middle position between making

God either extrinsic or intrinsic to the world, identified God with nature. For E. von *Hartmann, the Absolute was the Unconscious but also the principle of vitality in all things. H. Höffding offered a critical monism in which reality was one; yet for him the One is immanent in the many, although it transcends the many. Although *Peirce admits a doctrine of creation, he seems to have looked upon God as a primordial element of the universe, an evolutionary principle within the world. William *James described his position as a kind of pantheism, not absolute and monistic, but rather a "finite pluralism" that provided for God's being in the world but not as the only existing substance. For F. H. *Bradley, the Absolute was the reality of things in their psychical existence. Josiah *Royce considered God the absolute experience of which our minds were fragments; this absolute was infinite and all comprehensive.

Although *Bergson denied any suggestions of pantheism in his ideas, his doctrine of creative evolution is open to such implications. Samuel *Alexander identifies Deity as a quality of the world and goes on to consider the world as God's body and Deity as God's mind in much the same way as Upanishadic Hinduism. Because *Whitehead deliberately limited his pantheism through the instrumentality of Hegelian dialectics, he is more properly classified as a panentheist. *Brightman tried to limit his own tendency toward pantheism by negating absolute unity in God and by having God achieve his goals gradually. Weiss presents God as one of his modes of being; yet, in offering four coordinate and irreducible modes of being, he insists that each mode enters as part of the others.

Catholic Doctrine. Catholic teaching has always opposed the basic notions of pantheism. A personalistic religion, Catholicism upholds metaphysical reality of the individual, the spirituality but finitude of the human *soul, and personal fulfillment through immortal union with God as an infinite and distinct personal being. All such ideas are suppressed or negated by pantheism.

From the Middle Ages to the present, the Church has concerned itself with pantheistic implications in the writings of individual thinkers such as Erigena, Eckhart, and Bruno. Yet a formal condemnation of pantheism as such was not made until *Pius IX condemned pantheism by a decree of the Holy Office (1861), in his allocation *Maxima quidem* (1862), and in his "Syllabus of Errors" (1864) [Denz 2843, 2845, 2846, 2901]. Vatican Council I condemned it formally also (Denz 3023–25). Under *Leo XIII, the Holy Office again condemned such ideas as those implied in the works of *Rosmini-Serbati (Denz 3206, 3209, 3212–15). *Pius X, in his encyclical *Pascendi,* further warned against the implications of pantheism (Denz 3477, 3486).

The fact that pantheistic leanings are found primarily among Catholic thinkers who are more mystical than doctrinal, and whose religious sincerity can hardly be questioned, may serve to explain why other views with pantheistic overtones have never been formally condemned.

Critical Evaluation. In criticizing pantheism, one should first acknowledge the religious fervor manifested in the works of most pantheists, their dislike of distinctions and abstract analysis, and a basic difficulty in their subject matter, viz, that it is impossible for finite minds to comprehend the infinity of God.

As a general criticism, pantheism negates or limits the excellence of God to the point where He does not seem to be a special and distinct being. The confusing element is that all pantheists use special terms, usually capitalized, such as God, the Absolute, the One, or the Infinite, and seemingly intend to denote a special being or, at least, a special mode of being that transcends other beings. Nevertheless, atheistic implications are almost always present, if only because the thinkers involved, in their religious enthusiasm, do not concern themselves with the theoretical implications of their statements.

Pantheists further fail to distinguish between cause and effect. They often speak of God as the cause of the world, but not as the efficient, extrinsic cause; rather they tend to reduce God to some kind of a material source of the universe. Such thinkers frequently substitute a doctrine of emanationism for creation, ignoring the notion of *efficient causality—itself basic to our understanding of the world.

Ignoring fundamental metaphysical distinctions, pantheists approach or discuss reality in a univocal, rather than an analogical, manner that does not take into account difference as well as sameness (*see* ANALOGY). In this respect, pantheism is too limited in its treatment of ultimate values. This limitation of viewpoint is reflected in the monism that is either explicit or implicit in pantheism. Where *dualism seems to be accepted, one aspect is actually reduced to the other, considered as a mere manifestation of the other, or treated as an illusion.

Another confusion arises from the notion of transcendence, reduced by some pantheists to the potentiality of the world or of man. This view seems to contradict itself by establishing transcendence, which stands for perfection, as a mere extension of this world or finite beings in this world: both notions involve imperfection. Other pantheists look upon transcendence as the negation of all finite being to the degree that all perfections of finite being, such as *personality, immortality, and *freedom, become ultimately meaningless. Such reductions of transcendence to either superimmanence or negation cannot be accepted as reasonable.

Lastly, pantheism does not seem to grant the infinite positive value except as a mere quantitative inclusion of all things. It makes no distinction between actual infinity, which must be looked upon as pure perfection, and potential infinity, which involves incompleteness or imperfection. Reason demands that a superlative being—and the Infinite is presented by pantheists as superlative—be judged as actually and absolutely infinite.

Bibliography: C. N. BITTLE, *God and His Creatures* (Milwaukee 1953). F. J. THONNARD, *A Short History of Philosophy,* tr. E. A. MAZIARZ (rev. and correc. New York 1955). J. F. ANDERSON, *The Bond of Being* (St. Louis 1949). J. D. COLLINS, *God in Modern Philosophy* (Chicago 1959). C. SHARMA, *A Critical Survey of Indian Philosophy* (London 1960). E. H. GILSON, *Being and Some Philosophers* (Toronto 1949). N. A. BERDÍAEV, *The Russian Idea;* tr. R. M. FRENCH (New York 1948; repr. pa. Boston 1962). C. HARTSHORNE and W. L. REESE, eds. *Philosophers Speak of God* (Chicago 1953). F. CLARK, "Pantheism and Analogy," IrTheolQ 20 (1953) 24–38. J. BAYART, "Hindu Pantheism," *Clergy Monthly Supplement* 3 (1956) 102–108. E. A. PACE, CE 11:447–450. F. A. SCHALCK, DTC 11.2:1855–74.

[E. R. NAUGHTON]

PANVINIO, ONOFRIO

"The first outstanding historian of Christian antiquity" and "the father of modern church history"; b. Verona, Italy, Feb. 24, 1530; d. Palermo, April 7, 1568.

Onofrio Panvinio, OSA, portrait from life by Titian, in the Galleria Colonna at Rome.

At the age of 12, he entered the Augustinian order and began his study of history. The Prior General Jerome *Seripando recognized his talents and called Onofrio to Rome where Cardinals Alexander Farnese and Marcellus Cervini, the protector of the order and future Pope *Marcellus II, became his patrons. Pope *Pius IV gave Onofrio a position as reviser in the Vatican Library. Through constant research he gained a vast knowledge of historical sources. His research brought him into contact with such learned men in his field as Antonio Augustin, Ottavio Pantagota, Peter Veltori, Achille Maffei, Gentile *Delfino, Annibal Caro, Guglielmo *Sirleto, and Latino Latini. Panvinio wanted to rewrite by himself the whole history of Roman and Christian antiquity, basing it on the most reliable sources. For this purpose he collected a tremendous amount of material, and within 19 years had filled over 68 volumes, only a few of which were published during his lifetime. Archives and libraries of Italy opened their treasures to him; Emperor Ferdinand I gave him a letter of recommendation for all transalpine libraries. His research was quick, but even close study reveals his superior knowledge of the sources.

His works, which excel in rich illustration, may be divided into four categories: (1) 23 volumes on the history of the Roman Empire and its religions, including an especially valuable collection of 3,000 inscriptions; (2) 17 volumes on the history of the popes and cardinals, including a valuable collection of papal portraits made for Jacob Fugger, now in the Staatsbibliothek of Munich, also an edition of the *Lives of the Popes* by *Platina; (3) 10 volumes on the origin of liturgy, including copies of ancient rituals; and (4) 6 volumes on the history of leading Roman families and Verona.

His transcript of Bukard's *Diary* is the only complete and reliable copy. His *Chronicon* of the Augustinian order, an early work, lacks depth. The complete edition of his works contemplated by Pope *Sixtus V was not realized. Many of his unpublished collections are in the Vatican Library and the Staatsbibliothek of Munich. There is no competent evaluation of his works, although the criticism by Pastor (7.676–687) of his life of Pius IV is significant.

There is a monument to Panvinio at St. Agostino, Rome; Titian painted his picture; Peter Canisius judged him capable of answering the *Centuriators of Magdeburg.

Bibliography: D. A. Perini, *Onofrio Panvinio e le sue opere* (Rome 1899); *Bibliographia Augustiniana,* 4 v. (Florence 1929–38) 3:53–65. *Concilium Tridentinum: Diariorum* . . . (Freiburg 1913–30) v.2. P. Lauer, *Le Palais de Latran* (Paris 1911). O. Hartig, "Des Onuphrius Panvinius Sammlung von Papstbildnissen in der Bibliothek Johann Jakob Fuggers," HistJb 38 (1917) 284–314. G. de Libero, "Panvinio Onofrio," *Roma* 21 (1943) 98–111. G. Ferretto, *Note storico-bibliografiche di archeologia cristiana* (Vatican City 1942) 91–99. A. Mercati, "Documenti dall'Archivio Segreto Vaticano," *Miscellanea Pio Paschini,* 2 v. (Rome 1948–49) 2:1–37. G. Ladner, "I mosaici e gli affreschi ecclesiastico-politici nell'antico Palazzo Lateranense," RivArchCrist 12 (1935) 265–292. P. Paschini, EncCatt 9:694–695. H. Jedin, LexThK² 8:31. **Illustration credit:** Alinari-Art Reference Bureau.

[F. ROTH]

PANZANI, GREGORIO

Secret papal agent in England (1634–36), Bishop of Mileto; b. date unknown; d. Mileto, Italy,. 1662. When Henrietta Maria married Charles I in 1625, her godfather, previously nuncio in Paris, had become Pope Urban VIII. Urban sent a personal emissary to Henrietta, primarily, to assess the papist situation in England. For this delicate mission, the Pope's nephew and Secretary of State Francesco Barberini, who was also Cardinal Protector of England, chose Panzani, a former Oratorian. Panzani's instructions were to try to settle sharp differences among the English Catholics, particularly between the secular and regular clergy (most of all, the Jesuits) on the need or expediency of having a bishop and on the lawfulness of taking the Oath of Allegiance to the King. Panzani was to look for signs, at Court and among the Anglican clergy, of good will towards Rome. With this in mind he formed a close friendship with Sir Francis Windebank, Secretary of State and a Crypto-Catholic enthusiastic for reunion. Both worked to establish an official exchange of agents between Pope and Queen. The latter's first two candidates, Sir Robert Douglas and Sir Arthur Brett, both Catholics and approved by King Charles, died before taking up their appointments. Eventually, Sir William Hamilton, a distant relative of the King, was sent to Rome (June 1636). A month later George *Con, a Scot long resident in Rome, arrived in London as Pope Urban's agent to the Queen. He was well received by Charles I and at once became popular in court and clerical circles. Panzani, who remained with him for 6 months, had meanwhile been sending fortnightly dispatches to Cardinal Barberini, reporting every sign of friendliness: the general esteem in which Pope Urban was held, particularly by the King; sermons preached by Anglican clergy attacking the Puritans or deploring the break with the Holy See; reunion talks with the Bishop of Chichester, who expressed his readiness to acknowledge the Pope as Vicar of Christ; and suggestions for discussions in France between "moderate" Catholics and Anglicans. Panzani also sent Barberini a dossier on the 2 archbishops and 25 bishops of the Church of England, classifying the theological and personal attitude of each. Con's dispatches after Panzani's departure show that the Church of England would never reunite with the Holy See except on a basis of parity of rights, which Con at once made clear could never be. On his return to Rome early in 1637, Panzani was made a canon of San Lorenzo in Damaso and a court judge. In August 1640, he became bishop of Mileto, where he remained until his death in 1662.

Bibliography: G. Panzani, *Memoirs,* tr. J. Berington (Birmingham, Eng. 1793). G. Albion, *Charles I and the Court of Rome* (London 1935).

[G. ALBION]

PAPACY

This article treats of the development of the papacy (*papatus*) and the office of *pope in four historical divisions: (1) the early period, to 590, (2) the medieval period, (3) the Renaissance and early modern period, and (4) the modern period (1789–1965).

1. EARLY PERIOD

At the earliest stage of the papacy's development, two elements will be discussed: its Biblical foundations and its juristic complexion.

Biblical Foundations. The title deed of the papacy as an institution in its claim to universality in the spiritual sphere of government is found in two crucial passages of the New Testament. The one is the text of St. Matthew (Mt 16.18–19), which traditional exegesis understands to have been a promise made by Christ to St. Peter; the other is the fulfillment of the promise contained in Christ's words to Peter: "Feed my sheep" (Jn 21.17). Both passages gave rise to the claim of two kinds of *primacy (*primatus*) in the Roman Church: a magisterial and a jurisdictional primacy; the former is concerned with the final definition of doctrine and teaching (*see* TEACHING AUTHORITY OF THE CHURCH; INFALLIBILITY); the latter, with government in the sense of a final decision.

This article deals mainly with the jurisdictional aspect of the Roman Church, for it is in this function that the popes themselves saw the true nature and character of the papacy, and from the outset they considered that it was part of their duty to direct the path of organized Christianity.

The essential point, which was invariably stressed by the papacy, was that in the Biblical passages, notably in the Matthean verses, Christ founded a new society, namely, the Church, and provided a government for the Church by conferring on Peter a fullness of power. It was a unique, creative act of Christ Himself. Further, since the Church was never, from the papal point of view, a merely spiritual or sacramental body, but an organized, visible, juristic, and corporate society that needed constant guidance for the realization of its aims, the conferment of governmental powers on Peter implicitly and necessarily contained the provision for a succession into these powers, specifically bestowed as they were on the Prince of the Apostles. In the consideration, therefore, of the governmental work of the papacy, the character of the body over which govern-

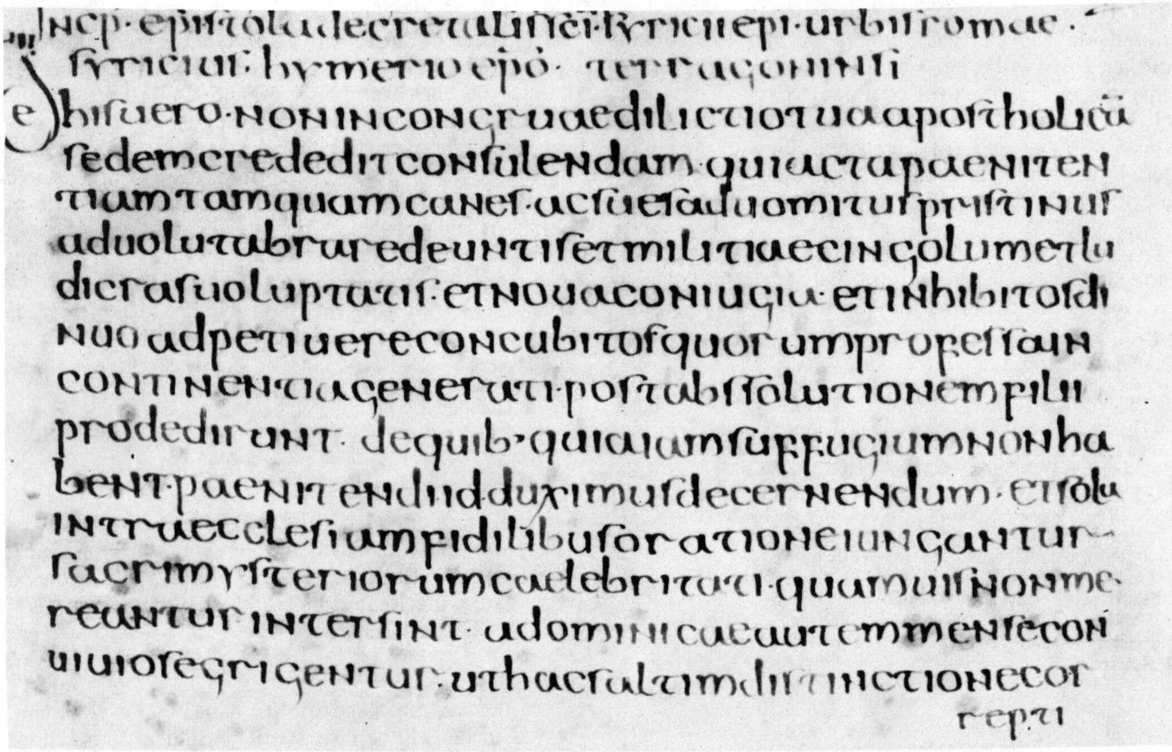
Incp· epistola decretalis siricii epi· urbis romae·
Siricius himerio epō· terraconensi
(e)his uero· non incongrue dilectio tua apostholicam
sedem credidit consulendam qui acta paenitentiam
tiam tamquam canes ac sues ad uomitum pristinum
ad uolutabra redeunt et militiae cingolum et lu
dicras uoluptates et noua coniugia et inhibitos de
nuo adpetiuere concubitos quorum professam
continentiam generati post absolutionem filii
prodedirunt· de quib· quia iam suffugium non ha
bent paenitendi id duximus decernendum· ut sola
intra ecclesiam fidelibus oratione iungantur
sacri mysteriorum caelebritati quamuis non me
reantur intersint· a dominicae autem mensae con
uiuio segregentur· ut hac saltim districtione cor
repti

Fig. 1. The beginning of Pope Siricius' letter to Bishop Himerius of Tarragona, A.D. 385, in a manuscript "Collectio canonum" written between 590 and 604, preserved in the treasury of the cathedral at Cologne, Germany (MS 212, fol. 77r, det.). This letter is the earliest known extant example of a papal decretal.

ment was to be exercised and the divine establishment of that government must always be given due attention.

Juristic Complexion. That in the primitive Christian period the Roman Church was credited with an authority superior to that of any other *patriarchal see, can be gathered from the letter written by Pope *Clement I (*c.* 92) to the Corinthians in which he made important statements concerning the nature of the Church and laid down principles that in embryonic form contained maxims of government. That in view of its location, the Roman Church was in actual fact credited with preeminence over other sees is a matter of history. Perhaps the most telling witness to this preeminence is *Irenaeus (*c.* 180), who clearly stated that the Roman Church possessed *potentior principalitas* and that special importance attaches to the apostolicity of that Church. Numerous testimonies could be cited to prove the factual preeminence of the Roman Church. It is similarly a matter of history that in the early centuries of the Christian era there was no doctrinal elaboration of the jurisdictional position of the Roman Church. Its function as the supreme jurisdictional authority, though operative, did not become the subject of reflective thought before the end of the 4th century; at least there is no evidence to suggest the contrary. Actual proof of the function of the Roman Church as the institution charged with making Christian doctrine part of the social fabric is contained in the first extant decretal letter of a pope—that of *Siricius, dispatched in 385 to Spain—which is an important legal document. It may be said that the period between Siricius and *Leo I (440–461) was the period of gestation in the conceptual development of the Roman primacy.

The juristic complexion of the papacy as an institution of government similarly finds a ready explanation in the location of the Roman Church. The form in which government was exercised was Roman, i.e., the Roman law and constitution served as models on which to formulate governmental principles and to transact governmental affairs. The matter was Biblical, i.e., the substance of the papal government principles and measures was derived from the Bible. It is therefore noteworthy that at exactly the time when *Jerome took on the enormous task of rendering the Hebrew text of the Bible into Latin, the Roman Church had begun the process of entering fully into the life of contemporary society. Moreover, it was the legislation of *Theodosius the Great that made *Christianity the official religion of the Roman Empire. There was a steady accumulation of papal decrees in the early 5th century; there was also a rapid development of concept and actions that, under Leo I, gave shape to a system culminating in the properly juristic function of the pope as successor of Peter. Nor should one underestimate in this historical process the factual, primatial position of the Roman Church, endorsed by the Roman synod of 380, which clearly stated the "double apostolicity" of this Church, i.e., the one Church that had been founded by the two Apostles, Peter and Paul. The Councils of *Ephesus and *Chalcedon confirmed this development.

Leo I's supreme mastery of Roman law enabled him to construct the thesis of Peter's function, and therefore that of the pope, in so satisfactory a way that it stood the test of time. The Roman Church had by right the primacy (*principatus*) because, according to Leo, the head of this Church was, though personally unworthy, the heir of St. Peter (*indignus haeres beati Petri*). In these two terms, coined by Leo, the whole papal program is epitomized. It was the merit of Peter, the Prince of the Apostles, to have recognized Christ at Caesarea Philippi, and because of this recognition Christ had distinguished him by conferring plenary powers on him. This was a special merit that belonged to Peter, personally, which meant that it could not be transmitted or conveyed to anyone else. But the functions, i.e., the powers given by Christ, were purely objective, and could be transmitted.

To explain this theme Leo utilized the Roman law of inheritance according to which the heir inherits all the deceased person's assets and liabilities, though not his personal qualifications, distinctions, and merits. The powers given by Christ to Peter constituted an office that was indeed capable of being inherited. Hence, although the *pope was heir to the full Petrine powers—the office of Peter as builder of the Church—he was unworthy as a person to wield the powers contained in that office. Leo's doctrine therefore clearly distinguished between the person of the pope and the office itself—a distinction with far-reaching consequences. What mattered for purposes of government was the office, and not the personal character of the individual pope. He may personally have been a saint, a mediocrity, or even a scoundrel; all this was of no interest, as many popes pointed out. The essential point was that the pope succeeded into the powers of Peter, and the totality of powers constituted, according to Leo, a fullness of power—*plenitudo potestatis*. Consequently, there was, as far as the scope and extent of powers went, identity between Peter and the pope. This identity placed a great burden of responsibility upon the pope, because his verdicts, judgments, and pronouncements took effect in this world as well as in the next; hence the frequently stated *gravissimum pondus* of responsibility upon papal shoulders. The so-called automatism of papal plenitude of power, as conceived by Leo, was to be a hallmark of papal thought throughout the Middle Ages. There was no tribunal and no higher court that could subject papal rulings to a revision; nor did an appeal lie from a papal decision to any other authority or court. This explains the later emergence of the view that the decrees of general *councils acquire their validity through papal sanction, either in the convocation of the council or in posterior approval. It explains also why in the Middle Ages an appeal from the papacy's judgment to a general council was branded as a sign of heresy. In short, the pope was the point of intersection between heaven and earth. There is no intermediary between pope and Peter: no pope *qua* pope succeeds his predecessor, but succeeds Peter directly, again a principle of the papacy that has stood the test of time.

The Leonine thesis brings into clear relief the properly conceived monarchic institution of the papacy according to which the sum total of powers is in the hands of the pope. Therefore, one can speak of a vertical or descending concept of government, because whatever power is found in the Church, in the congregation of the faithful, is conceptually derived from the pope: hence the early pictorial representation of the Roman Church as the source of a river. This theme has particular relevance for episcopal power, which only later was formally held to have been dependent on the pope for its exercise of jurisdiction. In other words, the bishop was called upon to participate in the papal solicitude for all Christians, but not in the papal plenitude of power. The *principatus Romanae ecclesiae* was the usual designation for this monarchic conception. The exercise of this papal *principatus* had, however, exclusive reference to government, i.e., to jurisdiction, the final verdict arrived at by the law and exhibiting effects solely by means of the law. Correctly understood, the pope as monarchic governor (*gubernator*), and in his function as pope, stands outside and above the Church that was entrusted to him, and this idea was expressed by the maxim *papa a nemine judicatur*. Although this statement was made at the beginning of the 6th century in a spurious document, the idea itself was considerably older, as is proved by a similar statement of Pope *Zosimus. In modern terminology this concept is called absolute sovereignty (*superioritas*), a notion that can likewise be found in the medieval concept of kingship. Further, because the pope in his official capacity is identical with Peter, the principle of the infallibility of certain papal pronouncements finds its ready explanation. As heir to Petrine powers, a pope cannot pronounce erroneously in matters of faith and morals. Therefore, no pope could or did say that any of his predecessors had erred in doctrine, because the consequence would have been that Peter himself had been the victim of error. A further consequence of the fundamental Leonine position was that the pope claimed, by virtue of his function, to be endowed with an *auctoritas sacrata,* i.e., a supreme and final authority, in which concept a number of charismatic qualities are discernible. The secular power, on the other hand, possessed a regal power (*potestas regalis*). As a result of the spread of Christianity amongst the barbarian nations, the papacy thus became the primary instrument in propagating the idea that civilized government could be conducted solely by means of law. In other words, the papacy, itself the heir of the ancient Roman principle of the superiority of law, utilized this idea in the interests of the whole Christian community while pursuing its evangelical mission. In this lies one of the great historic achievements of the papacy.

In order to understand the full import of the terms *auctoritas* and *potestas,* adapted to ecclesiastical usage by Leo I, then by *Gelasius I, one should realize that the second half of the 5th century witnessed an acceleration of the monarchic program by the imperial government at *Constantinople. At the same time the papacy, as a result of Leo's clear exposition of the Petrine function of the pope, acquired the means, i.e., the legal principles with which to combat the ever-increasing claims of the imperial government. The papacy was now faced with the necessity of challenging the validity and legality of imperial measures that, in its opinion, fell outside the scope of imperial functions. In so doing, the papacy was forced to declare itself on certain vital governmental points; and throughout its long and checkered history in the Middle Ages it never deviated from them. The imperial government had gone so far as to decree the faith and doctrine of Christians and to intervene drastically in the ecclesiastical organism by appointing and dismissing prelates. Armed with the primatial doctrine of Leo, the papacy issued its serious challenge to the imperial government and raised the question whether the emperor was suitably qualified to direct the body under his control in the manner in which he did, and by what authority he did so. Although the emperors acted in the belief that it was their duty as divinely appointed rulers to direct the Empire in all its vital aspects, the papacy maintained that the direction of the body of Christians, i.e., the Church, must be in the hands of those who were specially qualified to carry out this function: the definition of dogma, fixing the purpose and aim of Christian life, and the organization of the Church were the right and duty of the papacy, and not of the imperial government. The papal position, arrived at in the late 5th century and adhered to throughout subsequent centuries, was that the overall direction, the final authority in matters that affected the vital interests and the structural fabric of the Church—in short the *auctoritas sacrata*—belonged by virtue of his function solely to the pope. He was instituted as the "builder of the Church" and had to lead the faithful to their end, and the means to this was the law. The emperor, though clearly also instituted by God, had different functions in Christian society, and as a Christian actually belonged to the body entrusted by Christ to Peter's successor. He had a *potestas regalis,* i.e., power to act within the framework of his divine trust, or as *Gelasius I said, the emperor's duty was to learn (*discere*), not to teach (*docere*), in the religious sphere. What the papacy here laid down was nothing less than the principle of division of labor and of respective spheres of power. This Leonine-Gelasian program received precision in the subsequent development, notably through *Isidore of Seville and above all through *Gregory VII, according to whom the *potestas regalis* existed to supplement the word of the *sacerdotium* by regal power so as to eradicate evil. But since evil (sin) was prompted by the devil, God Himself had instituted secular government for the purpose of exterminating evil. It is thus clear that from the 5th century onward the papacy adhered to a teleologically conceived system of government.

The firm stand taken by *Felix III and Gelasius I in the matter of the imperially imposed *Henoticon, dealing with a doctrinal matter, led to the first serious *schism between East and West (*see* ACACIAN SCHISM), lasting some 30 years. A settlement was reached between the Emperor *Justin I and Pope *Hormisdas in 519.

Subsequent development was to show that the theory of government in Constantinople culminated in the concept of the emperor as priest and king, the former admittedly only in an external sense, yet in a manner that seriously infringed the exercise of papal primatial rights. This was especially true during the reign of *Justinian I, which brought so-called *caesaropapism to its apogee. The position of the papacy was difficult: the city of Rome and the whole of Italy were parts of the Empire and the popes themselves civil subjects of the emperor. Though fundamentally Constantinople recognized the primacy of the pope, the imperial government left no doubt about the final direction of the Christian body politic. The dilemma was most serious: if the popes remonstrated against the regal-sacerdotal decrees of the imperial government and insisted upon the exercise of Roman primacy, they ran the risk of committing the *crimen laesae majestatis* against the emperor; if they acquiesced, they became unfaithful to their own vocation and duty. (In this connection *see* VIGILIUS I, POPE.) It is at this juncture in the late 6th century that the truly historic significance of *Gregory I emerges.

2. MEDIEVAL PERIOD

The medieval papacy logically built on the premises inherited from its immediate past.

Gregory I to Gregory VII. Gregory I had been papal representative (*apocrisiarius*) to the imperial court for a number of years before his election to the papacy. While at Constantinople he reached the conclusion that the regal-sacerdotal idea of government was so firmly entrenched there that, however regrettable this state of affairs, it would be futile and dangerous to press the Roman primatial claim against the East. As long as the popes were subjects of the Empire, they were exposed to serious charges if they insisted upon the exercise of their primatial rights because in their civil capacity they were under the emperor. But if they were to act as popes in regions where the imperial writ did not run, they could press the primatial claim to its fullest extent. In this realization lies Gregory I's historic importance: he never acquiesced in or approved of the imperial theory, but accepted reality and, with the history of the 6th century before his eyes, logically concluded that the future held no promise for the papacy in the East. Gregory I opened up the West to the papacy by his missions to Gaul and *England. In these areas, from the outset, papal jurisdiction was exercised without reference to Constantinople. It was, in actual fact, from the farthest corner of medieval Europe, the British Isles, that the historic conversion of the Germans took place; and it was Anglo-Saxon missionaries who not only established close relations between England and the papacy but also were instrumental in forging the strong links between the *Franks and the papacy, links that were to give medieval Europe its specific character. It cannot be said that the papacy in the 7th century inherited Gregory's vision and appreciation of a historical situation for it was difficult for the popes in this century to break with established traditions. Of these none was stronger than the fact that Rome was Roman, the papacy was Roman, and the Empire was Roman. And yet the imperial government advanced more and more on the road that had so alarmed the papacy. The period was indeed a heroic age of the papacy, which suffered for its principles in the face of imperial encroachment upon religious and ecclesiastical policy. When after the turn of the century the imperial government promoted *iconoclasm by legislation, *Gregory II openly challenged Constantinople. Indeed, if the papacy wished to live up to its vocation, two alternatives were open. The pope would have to remove himself physically from Rome and reside among "the barbarians"; or the city of Rome with its surrounding districts would have to be withdrawn from imperial control. The first alternative was certainly in the mind of Gregory II when he issued in 729 his challenge to the Emperor *Leo III. But it was abandoned for excellent reasons. As later events were to show, the papacy, deprived of its historic and natural surroundings, would become the pawn of contending territorial factions. There remained the other alternative that was adopted by *Stephen II. When Rome was threatened by the Lombards, he appealed to *Pepin, King of the Franks. The background of this crucial step was the sanction given by Pope *Zachary to the deposition of the last Merovingian king, *Childeric III. The papal sanction was based on the principle that only he should be effective king who was useful—and about the uselessness of Childeric there was no doubt. Later *Gregory VII was to utilize this principle fully. Stephen's appeal culminated in his journey to Ponthion in Gaul (Epiphany 754) where he made clear to Pepin that the Lombards had conquered and stolen territory that by right belonged to St. Peter and hence to the pope. The document that was to support this papal claim of ownership was the *Donation of Constantine. Although the ostensible reason for this appeal was the restitution of stolen property, a real motive was the establishment of a territorial entity in central Italy, independent of Constantinople. In two campaigns (754 and 756) Pepin drove the Lombards out and made over the territories to the pope. The document was deposited at the Confession of St. Peter and established the *States of the Church (*Patrimonium beati Petri*), which were to last until 1870. A most powerful link was forged between the new and virile Frankish dynasty and the papacy, a link that was to endure through the Middle Ages and beyond. The emergence of the papacy as an independent entity gave rise to a number of institutional changes: the regulation of papal elections (769), confining this function to the Roman clergy; notice of the elections was no longer to be sent to Constantinople, but to the Frankish court; papal coins were now struck; and the popes abandoned the dating of their documents according to imperial years.

The papacy had won freedom of action and was, so to speak, master in its house. The last chapter in the direct relations between Constantinople and the papacy in the 8th century was the coronation of Pepin's son, *Charlemagne, upon whom Pope *Leo III conferred the imperial crown, making him thereby emperor of the Romans. This coronation had far-reaching results. It set a precedent for the papacy insofar as no pope had ever crowned an emperor in Rome; the title deed for the pope's action was at least implied in the Donation of Constantine. And as there could not be two emperors of the Romans, the Eastern emperor was degraded to a mere "king of the Greeks" whose orthodoxy was in any case rather suspect; the Roman imperial crown was where the pope wished it to be. Although Charlemagne himself had reservations regarding this papal notion, it subsequently came to be accepted in the West, though never in the East. What is remarkable and what explains the eventual victory of the papacy is the dynamic initiative that the papacy in the earlier Middle Ages had firmly kept in its hands. Throughout the 9th century small but significant elements were added, e.g., the combination of coronation and *anointing in one ceremony when *Stephen IV crowned *Louis I emperor of the Romans at Reims in 816; and the subsequent coronation in 823, which was performed in St. Peter's basilica, henceforth the rightful place for imperial coronations, and at which for the first time a sword was conferred on the emperor as part of the coronation ceremonial. It was in the 9th century that the pope appeared as the constituent organ of Roman emperorship, a function that enormously added to the prestige of the papacy. Other factors not of its own making, but nevertheless potently assisting the papacy in its growth, were the troubles of succession during Louis I's reign, the *false decretals, the brisk conciliar activity in the Frankish domains, and the general unrest in the Frankish

empire—all of which likewise served to make the papacy the rallying point of Christian civilization in the 9th century. The papacy was in a position to state or to restate and define its fundamental principles in numerous letters and decrees, notably those of *Nicholas I and *John VIII. The papacy's relations with the East, especially as a result of *Photius' attitude, worsened considerably when Nicholas I had opportunity to elaborate the primatial function of the papacy vis-à-vis the recalcitrant Eastern patriarch. But precisely because the papacy had established closest links with the Frankish dynasty, the collapse of that power had repercussions on the papal institution itself. The history of the papacy in the 10th century proves that it was still partly in the hands of the Roman nobility and partly in the hands of the newly risen Saxon dynasty in Germany. *Otto I, though humbly supplicating for the imperial crown, treated the Roman Church as if it were a German *proprietary church. The essence of this system was lay patronage exercised to a degree that violated basic principles of Church government, above all, those relating to the conferment of the ecclesiastical office itself. Otto I applied this even to the papacy itself in his so-called *Ottonianum* (963) and imposed severe restrictions on the freedom of the papal electors, with equal severity circumscribing the governmental activity of the papacy. At the same time, however, the personalities and lives of the popes in the 10th century inspired little reverence and still less respect for the successors of Peter. Nevertheless, the papacy, despite the low moral standard of individual popes, kept the program alive. In this period the coronation rites were greatly improved and embodied the traditional papal theme of the emperor as the organ of government specifically created on a universal scale and charged with specific tasks mentioned in the ceremony. However low the virtues of the popes were, the papacy as an institution was none the worse for it; it continued to develop internally and to promote its principles, at least programmatically. Perhaps at no other time in its long history has the papacy so much profited from the Leonine distinction between person and office.

Hildebrandine Era. The overbearing power of the Saxon and early Salian emperors had prevented the papacy from translating its principles into reality. During this period popes were made and unmade by the emperors, who, inspired as they were by the *Cluniac reform, certainly were convinced that they acted in the interests of Christendom and of the papacy. The premature death of *Henry III (1056) and the minority of his son, *Henry IV, provided the papacy with the long-sought opportunity for implementing basic principles of government. The Papal *Curia was assisted in this process by the influx of a number of outstanding men from beyond the Alps, who were mainly responsible for the cosmopolitan outlook characteristic of the papacy in the 11th century. Perhaps nothing reflects better the new attitude of the papacy than the numerous institutional measures initiated, developed, or modified in the second half of the 11th century. One of the first measures was the passing of the *papal election decree in April 1059. The significance of this decree lies partly in its adoption and refinement of the procedure envisaged in 769 and partly in the abolition of the obnoxious *Ottonianum*. With this decree the college of *cardinals came into being as the advisory body of the pope. The same year witnessed the first coronation of the pope (*Nicholas II), which, though not an essential element in his assumption of power, was nevertheless a symbolic means of presenting the pope in his monarchic status, and was readily understood by contemporaries. The wide-flung policy of the pre-Gregorian papacy necessitated the institution of the legatine system, for only by the prolonged arms of the pope, the *legates, could the papacy be in constant touch with faraway bishops, princes, and governments. The legates were also a guarantee that papal instructions were carried out. Because of the papacy's wide European connections a number of new departments came into being, and old ones were adapted to the exigencies of the time. Of these departments, none was more important than the *chancery, which became the very nerve center of the Christian body politic. The residence of the pope, the *Lateran, was reconstituted and here a number of new departments came to be greatly developed, especially the financial and judicial (see FINANCE, ECCLESIASTICAL; TRIALS, ECCLESIASTICAL). From this time onward the papacy also began to harness *feudalism to its governmental scheme, and the enfeoffment of the *Normans in 1059 started the long line of papal feudal contracts, so that by the end of the following century the Papal Curia had more feudal vassals than any other European court. In strictest theory the feudal lord was not the pope, but St. Peter himself, on whose behalf the pope acted. Some of the feudal services could be rendered by money payment (feodum censuale) in the place of the usual military service. The governmental scheme of the papacy was above all in need of a law. Hitherto there was no single law of the Church, and it was the acute realization of Gregory VII, when he was still Archdeacon Hildebrand, that the Roman Church as a governmental institution needed a legal code that was specifically related to the papacy. His impetuous demand to some of his colleagues in the Curia resulted in a spate of *canonical collections of which the common feature was the emphasis on the primatial position of the Roman Church. This was the beginning of the legal development that culminated in the Decretum of *Gratian in the 12th century. It should be pointed out, however, that all these collections of Canon Law were private efforts and did not receive official papal sanction.

The pontificate of Gregory VII demonstrated for the first time the practical application of papal principles of government: the papacy had now entered upon the path of effective rulership by means of the law. Although there was at first not much tangible success for the papacy, a number of important principles were clearly reformulated and restated and came to be subsequently the pillars of the papal government: the exaction of the episcopal oath of obedience, the enforcement of episcopal visits to Rome (visitatio liminum apostolorum), stern prohibition of *simony and lay *investiture, the enforcement of *celibacy, and appeals to the Roman Curia. In the exercise of its governmental functions the papacy made known and acted upon the principle that the life of a Christian on earth determined his life in the other world, i.e., obedience to papal law was an indispensable condition for salvation, and that the material things of this world had merely auxiliary value insofar as they assisted the realization of the Christian's true aim—salvation. Resting upon this basic

principle, amply supported as it was by the Bible, patristic lore, and earlier papal doctrine, the papacy could not and did not attribute inherent value to matter (the temporal) as such, but merely recognized its function as a means to an end. From this arose the claim, again pursued and acted upon by the papacy, that the end determined the use of material things—from the Christian teleological standpoint a perfectly understandable thesis. Precisely because the papacy was the divinely instituted government of the Christian world, its opponents, especially kings and emperors, could make little headway against it; they had little with which to answer the papal arguments of governing a Christian world. For the papal principles of government were basically rooted in the concept of the Church as the congregation of the faithful, entrusted by Christ to the pope through St. Peter and ruled by Peter's successor. Its end was otherworldly, and none other than the holder of the keys of the kingdom of heaven knew by virtue of his special qualification how to achieve this end. Kings and emperors were indubitably members of the Church and as such were subject to papal jurisdiction. They had, moreover, as their title "king by the grace of God made clear," received their kingdom as a trust from God for the sake of actualizing Christian principles, and who else but the pope was the proper organ to watch over the discharge of this trust? From the medieval-historical point of view these papal principles of government exhibited extraordinary consistency and logical coherence. Nonetheless, censorious criticism has often been directed against both the principles themselves and their application by contemporaries as well as by modern critics. Their observations culminate in the assertion that the papacy, by dealing with temporal matters, became oblivious of its primary function as a spiritual organ. The point, however, to which insufficient attention and importance is attached by the critics of the papal government at work, is that the Church was an earthly society held together by faith in Christ as well as a society that by virtue of the same faith pursued otherworldly aims. This dual nature of the Church—an organic, visible, and juristic body, as well as a sacramental society—makes understandable the exercise of governing powers by the papacy. But there is no statement or action by any medieval pope that justified papal jurisdiction solely on grounds that were or could be considered purely temporal. What the medieval papacy at all times insisted upon was the application of the teleological principle. No criterion has ever been formulated according to which the spiritual could be separated from the temporal. Indeed, in a Christocentric society this separation could not conceptually come about: the categorization of human activities into religious, moral, or political is of postmedieval origin, while in the Middle Ages the Christian was viewed from no other standpoint than that of Christianity.

The schism between East and West (see EASTERN SCHISM) had already moved Gregory VII to issue an appeal for a crusade. *Urban II succeeded in bringing about the *crusade, in itself a major undertaking, which released the first large-scale mass movement in the Middle Ages. The resistance to *Islam and the liberation of the holy places from *Seljuk oppressions were most pressing and urgent motives. Meanwhile the problem of lay investiture by king or emperor was settled on a somewhat pragmatic basis, first in France, shortly followed by the compromise reached with England, and lastly with the German Emperor in the Concordat of *Worms (1122). The principles for which Gregory VII had fought gradually received recognition: the subsequent period saw the highest ascendancy of the medieval papacy. The so-called First *Lateran Council of 1123 is counted as the first general council of the Middle Ages, soon to be followed by the second in 1139 and the third in 1179. Each was held under the presidency of the pope and issued numerous and fundamental decrees regulating virtually all aspects of public and social life. Now that canonistic scholarship also had come into being at the University of *Bologna, the papacy was in a position to call upon well-trained jurists for all its essential departments, and with *Alexander III the long and distinguished line of jurist-popes began. The outstanding features of the 12th-century papacy were its considerable legal output in the shape of *decretals and its successful fight against the new and overbearing Staufen dynasty in Germany as well as against other kings, notably *Henry II of England who resisted the full implementation of papal principles of government. Another feature of the 12th century was the stand taken against emerging *heresies, notably those of the *Waldenses and the *Cathari, who showed a keen spirit of resistance to papal law and order. These successes of the papacy are all the more remarkable as a considerable period of Alexander III's pontificate was marred by a pernicious schism, engineered and sustained by the Staufen *Frederick I. The work of the papacy in the 12th century also entailed institutional changes: the systematization of the legatine machinery, the chancery, and appellate jurisdiction; the emergence of new papal documents to cope with the increased output; the regulation of the papal election procedure and the introduction of the two-thirds majority for a valid election; the introduction of regular meetings of pope and cardinals (the *consistory) in which fundamental questions were discussed and decided; the reorganization of the financial departments of the Curia by outstanding chamberlains.

Zenith of the Medieval Papacy. With the accession of *Innocent III in 1198, the papacy entered upon its most splendid period. A man of great learning and vision, a first-class jurist with an enormous working capacity, he reconstituted the papal state and clarified the vital relations between the papacy and *Sicily. His dealings with the disputed succession in Germany are a model of astute diplomacy; he made kingdoms (such as Bulgaria, England, and Portugal) fiefs of the papacy; he was highly successful in bringing back to the fold a number of heretical sects; he witnessed the fall of *Constantinople in 1204 and became instrumental in establishing a Latin ecclesiastical organization in the Near East; in the regular consistory meetings his legal acumen shone forth; he prevented tension between the episcopacy and the papacy from deteriorating into rebellion. Almost all the *papal registers of his pontificate have been preserved. The Fourth *Lateran Council in 1215 under his presidency marked the zenith of papal power in the Middle Ages. More than 1,200 participants attended this assembly, and its legislation was to exercise an influence beyond the medieval period. During this pontificate, the first official collection of *Canon Law

Fig. 2. A portion of "The Line of Popes," a series of woodcut figures from the borders of the pages of the "World Chronicle" of Hartmann Schedel, printed at Nuremberg by Anton Koberger in 1493.

was published by Innocent himself (1209). In short, the papacy had reached the status of a universal power, not only in name but also in fact, taking an active part in every department of public life.

In many respects the history of the papacy in the 13th century is an appendix to the Innocentian pontificate. Under *Honorius III the new *mendicant orders were established and emerged as great civilizing and pastoral agencies in medieval Europe and beyond. In this pontificate the Staufen king, *Frederick II, was crowned emperor (November 1220), and on this occasion Frederick issued a number of laws dealing with the menace of heresy. Throughout the 13th century the papacy refined and expanded its principles and institutions. New institutions developed in this period had a significant bearing upon the making of modern international law, e.g., the protection of legates and their safe conduct; the sanctity of treaties; proper treatment of hostages, prisoners, and exiles. As a universal power the papacy was in a position to command kings and other secular princes to take steps against heretics, to allot territory to a victorious belligerent party, to depose rulers and establish others in their place, and to take (especially in Eastern Europe) effective steps in organizing diocesan structures. The papacy, now ruled by some of its ablest lawyer-popes, such as *Innocent IV, had to face the full rigor of the conflict with Frederick II. In the First Council of *Lyons (1245) Innocent excommunicated and deposed the emperor; this step resulted in an anarchic interregnum in Germany, lasting some 30 years. The same Council also promulgated disciplinary decrees that remained in force until 1918. The Second Council of *Lyons (1274) under *Gregory X witnessed the temporary union between the Eastern and the Latin Churches (see ECUMENICAL MOVEMENT), and among other decrees issued an important one on papal elections: the practice hitherto observed in holding elections in *conclave was turned into law. Among the institutional measures developed in the 13th century were those concerned with papal *provisions, reservations, *expectancies, collations, and the regularization of papal taxation. In its attempt to combat heresy, the papacy under *Gregory IX instituted the *Inquisition, a special tribunal directly subordinated to the pope. There are many explanations for the increase of heresy throughout Europe, but as far as the papacy itself was concerned, one measure that seems to have engendered most opposition was the ready exercise of papal plenitude of power through ecclesiastical *censures, which, though not misused nor abused, was certainly over used and thus became blunted. The theme of papal plenitude of power was not a problem of theology or law, but one concerned with handling power wisely and prudently.

The papacy was at all times, if not the begetter, at any rate a strong supporter of the universities. *Toulouse and *Rome saw the establishment of seats of learning by the papacy, which had always entertained amicable relations with the older universities, such as *Bologna and *Paris, and with the more recent foundations as well. Nevertheless, the spirit of inquiry promoted in the universities released forces that in their full maturity contributed to the diminution of papal authority in the following decades. Above all, the rediscovery of *Aristotle and of his corpus of thought and the awakening of a national spirit in the individual kingdoms, notably in France, brought about a considerable estrangement between the papacy and the faithful in general. By virtue of its commanding governing position in Europe, the papacy had perforce to deal with a number of issues that were not always properly explained nor adequately understood by the faithful. Unwittingly thereby the papacy aroused antagonism and resistance in quarters that were basically by no means antipapal. Moreover, in the conflict between the papacy under *Boniface VIII and the French king, *Philip IV, the former had failed to realize the strength and influence of the new forces. Instead, he relied for his arguments almost exclusively on traditional (Roman) doctrine which was largely conceived within the framework of the imperial government, but which made little impression on national kingdoms, such as France. That the papacy suffered defeat in this conflict was not the fault of Boniface VIII (who brought forth no argument that had not been advanced before), but arose partly from the loss of dynamic initiative by the papacy throughout the second half of the 13th century and partly from its underestimating the power and strength of "mere" kings. Precisely because the papacy concentrated so much on the Empire, European kings had been able to strengthen their position, virtually unimpeded by the papacy. It would be erroneous, nevertheless, to say that the papacy after Boniface became virtually a French satellite because it took up residence at *Avignon for the following 70 years (see AVIGNON PAPACY). That the papacy under *Clement V assisted in the suppression of the *Templars in France was due to papal timidity and to a number of circumstances over which the papacy had no control.

Decline of Papal Authority. It is worth pointing out that by the middle of the 13th century the papacy had reached its apogee of authority, influence, and prestige in Europe. There can be no doubt that the secret of its success had been an unyielding adherence to its program and the pursuit of dynamic and constructive policies that contributed to the welding of Europe into one more or less coherent whole. Apart from the factors already mentioned as contributing to the papacy's decline, there were others, such as opportunism; the *ad hoc* adjustment of some vital principles to emerging situations; the frequently questionable conferment of *benefices by way of reservation, collation, and postulation; the incidence of very high taxation; the underestimation of new forces; and the blunting of papal censures through overuse. More and more Europe disintegrated into its national component parts, and the role of the papacy as a supraregal governmental organ was considerably modified: what came to count more and more was the law of the national kingdoms and less and less the law of the papacy. The development of political thought proper—one of the byproducts of the renewed study of Aristotle and of the revival of Roman law—also must be reckoned as a contributory factor in the decline of papal authority. For this development led to the conceptual elaboration of a dualism of public bodies, i.e., the State as a product of nature and the Church as a supranatural product. This dualism found its reflection in the view—advocated particularly by *Marsilius of Padua—that only the laws of the State were true, enforceable laws, while the laws of the Church were not, strictly speaking, laws, but statements to which a merely persuasive force could be attributed. Law was, according to this thesis, the expression of the

Fig. 3. The Coronation of Pope Martin V at the Council of Constance, 1417; woodcut from the "Concilium Book" of Ulrich von Reichenthal, printed at Augsburg in 1483.

will of the people, and because the pope was said to be the head of a divinely instituted society, his decrees could assume the character of law only if the people (or the State) so willed it. The Avignon papacy was very much overshadowed by these and similar doctrines, which to some extent influenced even the Curia itself; the monarchic function of the pope came to be questioned, with the consequence that the college of *cardinals assumed greater powers. Electoral *capitulations were a clear symptom of the tension between pope and cardinals. Similarly, the *Western Schism was a symptom of unresolved constitutional conflicts resulting in the emergence of *conciliarism, which saw its victory in the Council of *Constance.

Eve of the Reformation. The election of *Martin V meant not only the end of the schism, but also the beginning of an era in which the papacy was to recoup a good deal of its lost prestige. The reestablishment of the papal state, which had sunk into anarchy, was taken in hand, and so was the fight against the *Hussites. As all traces of conciliarism had not been wiped out, Martin, in implementing the decrees of Constance, convoked a new synod at Pavia for April 1423, but shortly afterward transferred it to Siena. This council produced none of the necessary reform decrees, and a new council was summoned to *Basel in 1431. Meanwhile the new pope, *Eugene IV, showed little taste for bowing to conciliarism. The much desired *reformatio in capite* as

well as the reforms of the clergy, of papal taxation, elections, reservations, etc., brought about such serious tension that an open breach resulted. One part of the council was transferred to Ferrara in 1437, while the other remained at Basel. The Council of Ferrara was recognized as the legitimate continuation of the original Council of Basel and counts as the 17th general council of the Church. Its great success, however temporary, was the union between the Latin and Greek Churches, eventually achieved at *Florence in 1439. The papacy also provided a great stimulus to the revival of Greek studies and thus in a way assisted in the birth of the *Renaissance. A great preoccupation of the 15th-century papacy was the threat to the West by the advance of the Turks, who, since the fall of *Constantinople in 1453, were justifiably considered a menace to Christianity. In the second half of the century, the papacy became very active in the promotion of a crusade against Islam, though circumstances were no longer propitious for its execution. A further notable achievement was the arrangement of *concordats with secular governments; in fact, since the 15th century, this form of treaty came to be the *modus* by which the relations between the papacy and states were regulated on an international scale. A good part of the city of Rome was rebuilt during this century under the aegis of the papacy, and above all, plans of rebuilding St. Peter's, the papal library, and the *Vatican were actively taken in hand, though the moving spirit behind these plans, *Nicholas V, did not live to see the fruit of his planning. The vision of the papacy had nevertheless become restricted: it was Rome and to a certain extent Italy that almost exclusively preoccupied papal interest, and far less the universal tasks in which the papacy traditionally saw its foremost mission. Moreover, the personal character of some of these popes was far from approaching the customary bearing of St. Peter's successors, and it is understandable that the institution of the papacy should have suffered from them, although the cataclysm into which Europe was thrown after the turn of the century was due only to a very small degree, if at all, to the personal bearing of these popes. What they made abundantly clear on an objective level was that the office of the supreme pontiff must be separated from his personality, as indeed Leo I had proclaimed exactly a millennium earlier. It was on this distinction between office and person that the papacy had actively entered the historic scene in that age, and it was on that distinction that the papacy as an institution successfully recovered from the depth into which it had been plunged by the popes of the late 15th century.

Bibliography: H. VON SCHUBERT, *Geschichte der christlichen Kirche im Frühmittelalter* (Tübingen 1921). L. NINA, *Le finanze pontificie nel medioevo*, 3 v. (Milan 1929–32). Mann. Caspar. W. E. LUNT, ed. and tr., *Papal Revenues in the Middle Ages*, 2 v. (New York 1934). H. LECLERCQ, DACL 13.1:1111–1345. V. MARTIN, DTC 11.2:1877–1944. G. GLEZ, ibid. 13.1:247–344. E. EICHMANN, *Die Kaiserkrönung im Abendland*, 2 v. (Würzburg 1942); *Weihe und Krönung des Papstes im Mittelalter* (Munich 1951). Haller. M. MACCARRONE, *Vicarius Christi* (Rome 1952). Seppelt. J. GAUDEMET, *La Formation du droit séculier et du droit de l'église aux IV e et V e siècles* (Paris 1957). H. RAHNER, *Kirche und Staat im frühen Christentum: Dokumente aus acht Jahrhunderten und ihre Deutung* (Munich 1961). D. KNOWLES et al., *Encyclopaedia Britannica* (1961) 17:194–215. J. LORTZ, *Geschichte der Kirche in ideengeschichtlicher Betrachtung* (21st ed. Münster 1962–) v.1. W. ULLMANN, *Principles of Government and Politics in the Middle Ages* (New York 1961); *The Growth of Papal Government in the Middle*

Ages (2d ed. New York 1962). K. BIHLMEYER, *Church History,* ed. H. TÜCHLE, tr. V. E. MILLS and F. J. MULLER from 13th German ed. (Westminster, Md. 1958–) v.1–2. Jedin Hb Kirchgesch v.1. H. BARION, RGG³ 5:44–47. K. ALAND et al., *ibid.* 5:51–71. G. SCHWAIGER and K. RAHNER, LexThK² 8:36–48. H. E. A. FEINE, *Kirchliche Rechtsgeschichte* (4th ed. Cologne 1964–). **Illustration credit:** Fig. 3, Library of Congress.

[W. ULLMANN]

3. RENAISSANCE AND EARLY MODERN PERIOD

This section of the history of the papacy extends from the period of cultural transition known as the *Renaissance (c. 1450) to the great political, social, and religious upheaval of the *French Revolution (1789).

The Renaissance Papacy. The bitter conciliar quarrels of the 14th and 15th centuries had shown that the most dangerous crisis of the Church of the late Middle Ages was a constitutional one: its background was the impassioned demand for a reform *"in capite et membris."* Attempts for a stronger democratization of the Church had failed with the fateful ending of the Council of *Basel, though the conciliar ideas reaffirmed there remained powerful for centuries. After the experience of Constance and Basel, the strengthened papacy resisted the summoning of a general council, thereby abandoning its most powerful court for proposing reform measures. As the needed self-reform did not come about, the multicolored "autumn of the Middle Ages" was the forerunner of a religious revolution in the Church. With the highly cultured *Nicholas V (1447–55), under whom the last antipope, Felix V, resigned, there began that close connection between the papacy, *humanism, and the Renaissance which would endure well into the 16th century. After the evident decline of the political power of the Holy See, Nicholas and many of his successors aimed at regaining esteem for the papacy and Church by making them the leading centers of culture. Rome of the Renaissance became a focal point of arts and sciences, while at the same time the religious character of the papacy declined. With a few exceptions, the Renaissance popes became deeply involved in secular affairs, wars, money-making, nepotism, and sensual passion. Nicholas V, the first and most high-minded pope of this epoch, concluded with the German King Frederick III, as ruler of the realm, the Vienna Concordat, which remained in force till the end of the Holy Roman Empire in 1803. But since the "gravamina of the German nation" were not heeded, the anticurial opposition in the Empire grew. In 1452 Frederick III was crowned emperor in St. Peter's; it was to be the last imperial coronation ceremony in Rome. In 1453 Constantinople fell to the Turks—not without the fault of the popes and of the Occident, neither of whom had given efficient aid.

The pontificates of the Spaniard *Callistus III (1455–58) and of the cultured humanist Enea Silvio Piccolomini, *Pius II (1458–64), were dominated by the thought of a crusade against the Turks. But everywhere in Europe national interest prevailed, so that notwithstanding all papal efforts, a common undertaking did not come about. The sense of spiritual responsibility receded more and more during the pontificate of *Sixtus IV (1471–84), under whom the Spanish Inquisition was expanded; Innocent VIII (1484–92), who issued the fateful "Witches' Bull" (*Summis*

desiderantes, Dec. 5, 1484), was gravely compromised by his role of guardian of the Turkish Prince Dschem; finally, under the impetuous *Borgia (Borja), *Alexander VI (1492–1503), the papacy further declined. Unrestricted nepotism and unscrupulous money-making involved the popes more and more in unseemly political quarrels. While Alexander VI showed political foresight in drawing a demarcation line between the Spanish and Portuguese empires of the New World, his anti-French policy in Italy and his plans for making the papal state a permanent fief of the Borgias came to naught. His successor was the high-minded *Pius III (1503), whose reign lasted less than a month. The bitter foe of the Borgias, *Julius II (1503–13), physically and intellectually a powerful character ("il terrible"), was one of the most capable popes, though far more an Italian Renaissance prince and general than a priest. With all diplomatic and military means he sought to establish a strong, independent papacy in an Italy free from foreign domination; the League of Cambrai (1509) and the Holy League (1511) were formed to serve this purpose. A schism in France was prevented only with difficulty when King *Louis XII reinforced the *Pragmatic Sanction and, with the aid of several cardinals, caused a general Church council to convene at Pisa in 1511. Julius II countered this move by calling together the Fifth Lateran Council (1512–17). Under his princely protection, Rome became the center of the Italian High Renaissance, where Bramante, Michelangelo, and Rafael created masterpieces to the glorification of Church and papacy. His successor of the house of *Medici, *Leo X (1513–21), greatly disappointed the expectations of all friends of reform. His secular, extravagant mode of life, as well as his whole manner of Church government, indicated a lack of spiritual responsibility.

With the inglorious end of the Fifth Lateran Council vanished the last possibility of an internal reform (*see* LATERAN COUNCILS). Thus, when, in 1517, Martin *Luther made his open challenge, a catastrophe for papacy and Church was at hand. The occasion was given by the promulgation of an indulgence stipulating a money offering in connection with the building of the new basilica of St. Peter. Neither Pope nor Curia was aware of the religious motives of Luther, nor did they foresee the weighty consequences of his action. They underestimated also the anti-Roman state of mind of the whole of Europe. Thus, in a short time large sections of central and eastern Europe, as well as the whole Germanic North (England, Scotland, Scandinavia), went over to *Protestantism. From 1520 on, Luther looked more and more upon the pope as Antichrist; against the papacy he cast disrespectful insults. A still deeper chasm between Luther and the papacy was opened by John *Calvin. The Protestant Reformation of the 16th century was indeed an attempt to restore the purity of an original Christianity, but the resultant split in Christendom became the greatest misfortune in Church history.

In 1516 Leo X and Francis I of France signed a concordat in which, in exchange for the abolition of the Pragmatic Sanction, the Pope had to recognize a nearly complete supremacy of State over Church. The pious and moral Netherlander *Adrian VI (1522–23), the last German and last non-Italian pope, initiated against powerful opposition the reform of the Church

Fig. 4. "Pope Leo X and the College of Cardinals," fresco by Giorgio Vasari, Palazzo Vecchio, Florence.

Fig. 6. "Pope Urban VIII Visiting the Church of the Gesù," painting by Andrea Sacchi (1599–1661) in the Museo di Roma.

Fig. 5. "Pope Paul III and the Cardinals Setting Out for Trent," painting by Sebastiano Ricci (1659–1734).

in capite. At the Imperial Diet at Nuremberg (1522) he had his legate Francesco *Chieregati pronounce the papal acknowledgment of guilt and assert the Pope's firm intention to achieve Church reform. The Pope's early death ended these great hopes. The Medici Pope *Clement VII (1523–34) followed more the old ways. Besides, he allowed himself to come into fateful opposition to Emperor *Charles V (1519–56), whose lifelong efforts to restore the unity of faith were rather hindered than supported by papal policy. Under Clement VII the great defection from papacy and Church advanced rapidly, especially in Germany and in the Nordic kingdoms. England separated from the papacy following the marriage scandals of King *Henry VIII. And from the 1530s on, a rigidly organized fighting Calvinism spread from Geneva to France, the Netherlands, Scotland, Hungary, and Poland, and became with *Lutheranism and *Anglicanism the third main branch of a reformed Christendom (*see* REFORMED CHURCHES).

Catholic Reform and Counter Reformation. The Protestant Reformation of the 16th century definitely ended the worldwide power of the papacy. Yet, the immense shock at last caused the Curia to join the movement of reform that had been growing for decades in Spain and in small circles of Italy. After the early failure of Adrian VI, the pontificate of *Paul III (1534–49) signified a turn of events. Though his way of life still followed wholly the traditions of the Renaissance popes, his wide education and political sense convinced him that the real strength of papal policy lay in following spiritual and ecclesiastical principles. But he seems to have had no clear ideas about the extent of necessary measures, and since he shrank from radical steps, his pontificate is characterized by hesitation. Of great importance for the Catholic reform was the thorough renewal of the college of cardinals, the appointment of the commission for the reform in 1536 (*Consilium de emendanda ecclesia*), the promotion of new orders (*Theatines, *Barnabites, *Somaschi, Capuchin *Franciscans), especially the approval of the Society of Jesus in 1540, the renewal of the Roman Inquisition (*Sanctum Officium*, 1542), and most of all the Council of *Trent, in session with interruptions from 1545 to 1563. The council could not indeed restore the lost unity of faith, but it laid the broad basis for a thorough internal renewal by determining the most important articles of faith and issuing sweeping decrees of reform. Notwithstanding considerable temporary episcopalian tendencies, especially from the Spaniards and French, the popes remained masters of the council. Although showing serious weaknesses, *Julius III (1550–55) had a pronounced sense of his spiritual office. *Paul IV (1555–59) tried with passionate energy to hurry the reform without the council, thereby involving himself in a series of catastrophes through political ineptitude and uncompromising severity. Under *Pius IV (1559–65) the Council of Trent completed its labors, having successfully overcome several threatening crises. A whole series of unfinished topics (the Roman Catechism, Missal, and Breviary, the edition of the Vulgate) were expressly entrusted to the Pope. The new edition of liturgical books, appearing for the most part under *Pius V (1566–72), resulted in the acceptance of the Roman rite by nearly the whole Church. The Council of Trent and active new religious orders, such as the *Jesuits, were two of the most important factors in strengthening the Church.

Since the defection of nearly all the Germanic nations, post-Tridentine Catholicism has been characterized by a preponderance of Romanic nations. The radical attacks on the papacy by Protestant reformers made the Catholic reaction stress the importance of the priestly office in the Church, especially the office of the pope. Their pitiless judgments, however, also made even well-meaning and necessary criticism in the Church difficult. All attempts at reunion with Protestants, the aim of some of the most generous minds on both sides, remained without tangible success. The most difficult problem, then as now, proved to be the position of the pope in the Church. Although the mentality and character of some post-Tridentine popes showed serious defects, there can be no further question of "unworthy" popes. The great Popes Pius V, *Gregory XIII (1572–85), and *Sixtus V (1585–90) energetically and successfully seized the leadership in Catholic reform. In 1570 Pius V declared *Elizabeth I of England excommunicated and deposed—the last and unsuccessful papal deposition of an important ruler. The naval victory at *Lepanto over the Turks (1571) also was due to his efforts. Gregory XIII everywhere supported Counter-Reformation forces, especially in Germany, France, England, Poland, and Sweden, though these were sometimes ill-advised. Existing diplomatic representation of the Holy See at Vienna, Paris, Madrid, and Lisbon were expanded by permanent nunciatures at Lucerne in Switzerland, at Graz in Inner Austria, at Cologne for Lower Germany, and at Brussels. These nunciatures assumed an important ecclesiastical and political role in preventing innovations, giving effect to the Tridentine reform, supervising bishops and the whole Church organization, and promoting Counter-Reformation forces.

Conflicts with state power and with individual metropolitans and bishops developed, especially in the 18th century. The Jesuits, besides gaining leadership in a rapidly developing new educational system, became the most important helpers of a strengthened papacy. Sixtus V, combining a tremendous capacity for work with political wisdom, continued the reconstruction of the Church. His reorganization of the Curia and of the general government of the Church by setting up 15 Cardinal Congregations in 1588 and limiting the number of cardinals to 70 remained unchanged until the 20th century. He made Rome a baroque city and—less felicitously—ordered a new edition of the Vulgate. *See* BIBLE, IV (TEXTS AND VERSIONS) 13. This period shows clearly the trend toward greater centralization in Church government around papacy and Curia. It also reveals that the restrengthened papacy's most significant Protestant adversary was well-organized Calvinism, while Lutheranism and Anglicanism had noticeably declined as foes, the former by splitting up into numerous national churches, the latter through its isolation.

Catholic reform and the reconquest of lost ground, once started, were continued by *Clement VIII (1592–1605), *Paul V (1605–21), *Gregory XV (1621–23), and, to a lesser degree, *Urban VIII (1623–44). They found the strongest political backing for their plans, though not without differences, from the Spanish and Austrian *Hapsburgs and the Bavarian Wittelsbachs. France at last came to rest when, after the end of the destructive wars with the *Huguenots, the Bourbon King *Henry IV turned Roman Catholic in 1593 (*see*

WARS OF RELIGION; ST. BARTHOLOMEW'S DAY, MASSACRE OF; NANTES, EDICT OF). In the 17th century France rapidly advanced to the position of a great European power, thanks to the statesmanship of *Richelieu. Paul V, impressed with the lofty position of the papacy, attempted to revive medieval claims of supremacy of the Church in political matters, although everywhere, even in the Catholic national states, a tendency toward national churches was acquiring new strength, especially in the *Gallicanism expressed by Edmond *Richer. His policy led to serious political conflicts and failures, in particular with the mighty republic of Venice (1605–07, excommunication of the Senate, interdict over the Republic) and with England (prohibition of the loyalty oath of Catholics to the king after the *Gunpowder Plot of 1605). In the *Thirty Years' War Paul V and Gregory XV supported with large subsidies Emperor *Ferdinand II and the Catholic League under *Maximilian I of Bavaria. The reintroduction of Catholicism into Bohemia after the victory of 1620 and in the Upper Palatinate was greeted in Rome with joy. The transfer of the electoral office to Maximilian of Bavaria was vigorously supported by papal diplomacy in order to safeguard the election of a Catholic emperor.

The establishment of the Congregation of the Propagation of the Faith in 1622 showed that the papacy definitely intended to take over the leadership of the expanding world missionary movement. Under the *Barberini Pope Urban VIII, a patron of arts, stately baroque buildings were erected in Rome; as in the Renaissance period, this building was accompanied by the destruction of many monuments of antiquity and the Middle Ages. Nepotism, never quite extinct, flared up again in Urban's pontificate. The Pope, deceived by Richelieu, leaned toward the French side during the Thirty Years' War, thereby harming indirectly the Catholic party in Germany, though he strove sincerely for peace. The Peace of *Westphalia, which caused great damage to the Catholic Church, was concluded in 1648 under *Innocent X (1644–55) after long negotiations. During the war and at the time of the peace the political weakness of the papacy had become painfully apparent. It was seen that more and more often political thought and action were determined by simple reasons of state rather than by religious and ethical principles.

From the Peace of Westphalia to the French Revolution. In this period princely absolutism became firmly established in nearly all European states. The progressive secularization of the West forced the papacy, now internally strengthened and of high moral caliber, to accept not only the increasing loss of its political influence but even the control of its internal affairs. It had to fight absolutism, an Enlightenment that too often was antipapal and antiecclesiastical, *Jansenism, Gallicanism in France, Episcopalianism (*Febronianism) in Germany, and *Josephinism in the Hapsburg lands. All these phenomena were evident to a greater or lesser degree in all Catholic countries. Probably wishing to avoid political conflicts, the cardinals in this period elected honest but undistinguished popes; none were strong personalities, with the exception of Innocent XI and Benedict XIV.

The greatest political difficulties for the Holy See arose from France. Through the labors of Cardinals Richelieu and *Mazarin and during the long reign of *Louis XIV (1643–1715) that country had its "great century" when it stood at the top of its political power and spread its cultural influence over the whole Europeanized world. After a painful confrontation during the pontificate of the peaceable and restrained *Alexander VII (1655–67), the incorruptible and deeply religious *Innocent XI (1676–89) lived to see bitter quarrels with the unscrupulous absolutism of Louis XIV regarding the *régale,* rights of diplomatic immunity of the French ambassador in Rome, and papal condemnation of the four Gallican articles of 1682 (see REGALIA; ASSEMBLIES OF FRENCH CLERGY). An open schism was prevented probably only by the intervention of François *Fénelon and the change of government in England brought on by the Glorious *Revolution of 1688.

In international politics, also, Innocent XI found the King of France always his bitterest opponent, a fact especially fateful in view of the mortal Turkish danger. Considerable aid from the Pope made possible the decisive victory at Vienna in 1683 that relieved Europe from Turkish pressure on its Eastern boundaries. Purity of aims and means gained Innocent XI high repute even with non-Catholics. Under *Innocent XII (1691–1700) the quarrel with France could finally be settled in view of the imminent extinction of the Spanish Hapsburgs because of the death on Nov. 1, 1700, of Charles II, King of Spain, without a son. A long war for the rich Spanish inheritance was not settled until the Treaty of Utrecht (1713) recognized Philip of Anjou as Philip V of Spain. Fearing a Hapsburg preponderance, *Clement XI (1700–21) took the side of the French Bourbons, which led to a short war with Emperor Joseph I in 1708.

The teachings of Luther, Calvin, and their followers on grace and justification brought Catholic theologians to a renewed attention to the doctrine of the original state of man in paradise, to the Fall, and to the relation of divine grace and man's freedom. This was more necessary since the Protestant reformers in developing their theology appealed to the rigorous view of St. Augustine concerning sin, grace, and predestination. The Council of Trent had left the central problem of cooperation of grace and free will undecided. As in late antiquity, this gave rise to long and violent debates, in which the papacy had to interfere again and again. The old distinction between the theological schools of Thomists and Scotists emerged vividly in a modern form. In 1567 Pius V rejected 79 theses of Michel de Bay, professor at Louvain, and his adherents (see BAIUS AND BAIANISM). The aftermath of this quarrel was seen in the discussion about the doctrine of grace of the Jesuit Leonard *Lessius. Sixtus V forbade both parties to censure each other. At the end of the 16th century another severe conflict broke out between Dominicans and Jesuits (Domingo *Báñez, OP; Luis de *Molina, SJ). After long deliberations of the papal commission of inquiry (see CONGREGATIO DE AUXILIIS), neither Clement VIII nor Paul V gave a decision. A similar situation existed in the 200-year dispute over systems of moral theology. Both extremes were condemned: *laxism by *Alexander VII (1665–66) and *Innocent XI (1679), *rigorism by *Alexander VIII (1690). Theological contention came to a pitch in the century-long quarrel over the interpretation of the *Augustinus,* written by the high-minded bishop Cornelius *Jansen and printed posthumously (1640). Jansenism, which started in

Fig. 7. Clement XIV announcing dissolution of the Society of Jesus to the Ambassador of Spain, 18th-century engraving.

Louvain, soon took hold of France and came to infect all Catholic lands of Europe. Jansenistic doctrines were first condemned by Urban VIII (1642), later by Innocent X (1653); after the interference of Alexander VII (1664), the charitable Clement IX brought about a temporary truce in 1669 (Clementine peace). The hostile activity of Louis XIV made the quarrel in France flare up again *c.* 1700 and occasioned Clement XI's two great bulls of condemnation, *Vineam Domini* (1705) and *Unigenitus* (1715). In the end the bishops of France submitted, but not so in the Netherlands, where Utrecht became the seat of schism (1723). The papal condemnation of Jansenism made the latter movement often an ally of the opponents of Roman centralization, as in the Gallican and Josephinist movements and the Synod of *Pistoia (1786). Quietism also received papal condemnation, first by Innocent XI, who after long hesitation proscribed propositions found in the *Guía espiritual* of Miguel de *Molinos (1687), then by Innocent XII, who was pressured by the French crown to censure the *Explication des Maximes des Saints . . .* of Fénelon (1699).

The period of *Enlightenment brought a great turning away from the acknowledgment of Christianity as revealed religion. The Catholic Church and the papacy especially were mercilessly attacked by many enlightened philosophers in France, Portugal, Spain, and Naples-Sicily. Increasing difficulties were overcome for the time being by the capable and learned *Benedict XIV (1740–58), whose measures for internal reform of the Church and whose wise and timely policy of compromise in external affairs testify to his deliberate moderation, prudent compliance, and sincere love of peace, without surrender of essential rights of the Church. The pontificates of *Clement XIII (1758–69) and *Clement XIV (1769–74) were completely overshadowed by discussion about the dissolution of the Society of Jesus. Long demanded vehemently by the Bourbon states, which unilaterally had already effected it in their respective dominions, the suppresion of the order was decreed in 1773 by Clement XIV, after deep reflection. The long antecedents of this affair, the brutal execution of the decree, especially in the Bourbon states, and also the unsuccessful petitionary journey of *Pius VI (1775–99) to Emperor Joseph II in Vienna (1782), showed to the whole world the political impotence of the papacy in the period of Enlightenment. The end of the 18th century witnessed the deepest humiliation of the modern papacy in the wake of the French Revolution.

Bibliography: For extensive sources and literature see: Pastor. Seppelt v.4–5. Bihlmeyer-Tüchle. Fliche-Martin. P. Paschini and V. Monachino, eds., *I papi nella storia,* 2 v. (Rome 1961). F. X. Seppelt and G. Schwaiger, *Papstgeschichte von den Anfängen bis zur Gegenwart* (Munich 1964). G. Schwaiger, Lex ThK² 8:36–44. **Illustration credits:** Fig. 4, Alinari-Art Reference Bureau. Fig. 5, Museo Civico, Piacenza. Figs. 6 and 7, Gabinetto Fotografico Nazionale, Rome.

[G. SCHWAIGER]

4. Modern Period (1789–1965)

The main lines of historical development in the institution of the papacy during the period 1789 to 1965 are clear-cut. The quarter century between the outbreak of the French Revolution and Napoleon's downfall witnessed determined and violent assaults against the papal spiritual and temporal power that seriously menaced the very existence of the office; yet it also registered gains of long-term significance. Then followed a reversal of fortune almost unparalleled in suddenness and importance. Since 1815 the prestige and effective spiritual powers of succeeding popes have continued to mount, even after 1870. More than ever Rome became the vital center of the Church throughout the world. Particularly since mid-19th century, ecclesiastical administration has been centralized in the Eternal City to an unprecedented degree. Clergy and laity have become accustomed to turn to the popes for doctrinal and pastoral guidance regularly, not merely in periods of crisis; and they have entertained for recent pontiffs a personal reverence that earlier centuries rarely knew. Papal temporal power nevertheless suffered mounting difficulties from its restoration in 1815 to its disappearance in 1870; its revival in 1929 was on a much more limited scale.

From 1789 to 1815. Events in France gave direction to the history of the Church and of the papacy during these years.

Losses. From the beginning of his pontificate, *Pius VI (1775–99), like his predecessors, had to contend with Catholic governments imbued with the tenets of monarchical absolutism and regalism that viewed with suspicion or hostility any exercise of papal authority within their borders and defied or disregarded Rome save when it suited their interests to do otherwise. These states utilized the *exequatur and placet, the *appeal as from an abuse, and the menace of schism as standard devices to maintain as much national spiritual autonomy as possible within a universal Church. *Gallicanism, allied with *Jansenism, continued to oppose the full hierarchical supremacy of the papacy. In Germanic lands *Febronianism and *Josephinism, with similar aims, reached their peak during this pontificate. All four of these antipapal tendencies converged close to Rome at the Synod of *Pistoia (1784), convoked by Bp. Scipione de' *Ricci, whose decrees merited the solemn papal condemnation, *Auctorem fidei* (1794). Protestant rulers preserved their antipapal traditions and displayed more intolerance toward Rome than toward their Catholic subjects. After engineering the suppression of the Jesuits in 1773, the more radical champions of the *Enlightenment looked forward to the abolition of the papal office. Their confidence did not lack foundation.

As the *French Revolution (1789–99) progressed, leaders intent on de-Christianizing France gained control. Their antipapal predispositions were intensified by Pius VI's evident distaste for the principles of 1789, and still more by his condemnation of the *Civil Con-

stitution of the Clergy and the oaths of civil obedience demanded of the clergy, and by his aversion to the whole body of ecclesiastical legislation of the French Assembly. When the Pope participated in the first coalition of European powers to help destroy a movement that he considered essentially evil, the French revolutionaries retaliated by annexing papal territories in southern France, invading Italy, seizing the *States of the Church, and establishing a republic in Rome. After stripping Pius VI of his temporal power, the French deprived him of his liberty. His death while a prisoner marked a low point in papal fortunes not plumbed for centuries and gave rise to a prophecy that the apostolic succession had come to a close with the demise of "Pius the Last."

The next Pope's humiliations surpassed those of his predecessor. After election at a conclave forced to convene in Venice, *Pius VII (1800–23) quickly revealed his characteristic independence despite weakness by spurning Austrian enticements to reside in Vienna and by returning to his own capital. The first part of his pontificate was linked with the career of *Napoleon I. As Bonaparte's military prowess extended his political sway and religious system over most of western Europe, including Italy, danger mounted that the Holy See would become a French vassal, the Pope an imperial chaplain, and Paris the center of the Church. Pius VII could not decline an invitation to attend the coronation in Paris, where he sat among the onlookers as Napoleon crowned himself emperor (1804). The Pope then retraced his steps homeward with very slight advantages to show for his journey. When he refused a demand to league with France in the Continental Blockade, Napoleon seized Rome, deprived Pius VII of all temporal power, and held him prisoner in Savona and Fontainebleau (1809–14). So close was the Pope's confinement that he could scarcely function even in his spiritual capacity.

Gains. An audit confined to adversities would be incomplete and misleading. The revolutionary era brought gains for the papacy that at least balanced the losses and prepared the way unwittingly for still greater advances. Badly as the two popes fared, their traditional foes fared worse. In the collapse of the monarchy and the *ancien régime,* Gallicanism, particularly Political Gallicanism, received a serious wound from which it never fully recovered. *Parlement, long a stronghold of Gallicanism, did not survive the Revolution. Although the Civil Constitution of the Clergy started a schism in France, it caused also a noticeable rift in the façade of Ecclesiastical Gallicanism. After the Constituent Assembly, without consulting the Church, passed (July 12, 1790) and promulgated this law (Aug. 24), it prevented the French hierarchy from meeting in a national synod to chart a course through the crisis. Thereupon 30 of the 32 bishops among the Assembly's delegates drew up an *Exposition des principes sur la Constitution civile* (October 30) and with the almost unanimous approval of their fellow bishops submitted it to Pius VI and asked his guidance in applying the Civil Constitution. In the *Exposition* the Gallican bishops referred to the "successor of St. Peter, placed in the center of Catholic unity, who must be the interpreter and organ of the will of the universal Church." Pius VI delayed his formal condemnation of the law until the following March.

The *Concordat of 1801, arranged between Napoleon and Pius VII without the concurrence of the French hierarchy, dealt a blow to Ecclesiastical Gallicanism. It was a recognition by the First Consul that the Pope held the key to restoring religious peace to France. In redrawing the ecclesiastical map of France and reducing the number of dioceses from 85 to 60, the Concordat permitted an unprecedented exercise of papal power by requiring that the entire French hierarchy, whether Constitutional prelates or ordinaries in office previous to 1789, resign their sees. The 45 bishops who refused to resign were summarily removed from office. Twelve Constitutional bishops were named to the new sees, but they had to sign a submission to papal decisions concerning French religious affairs. Thereby they implicitly retracted their adherence to the Civil Constitution.

Napoleon's secularization of ecclesiastical principalities in *Germany and bestowals of them on lay princes who were often Protestants impoverished a group of wealthy, powerful, traditionally anti-Roman Rhenish bishops, weakened their Febronianism, and forced them and German Catholics in general to look more and more to Rome for support.

From 1815 to 1878. Waterloo proved a very memorable victory for the noncombatant papacy. After Napoleon's downfall it became a principal beneficiary of the widespread disillusionment with the bloodshed and political and social upheaval in France, where democracy had quickly given way to military dictatorship. The statesmen who assembled at the Congress of *Vienna (1814–15) sought a restoration of the *ancien régime* as far as possible. In their plans to stabilize a conservative, monarchical, legitimist system of law and order throughout Europe, they recognized the altar as the sturdiest support of thrones. The allied powers that had displayed slight concern for the Pope's welfare when he was despoiled of his territories and his liberty, returned to him the States of the Church, save for the land in France. For the future of the papacy it was significant that no other ecclesiastic regained his confiscated principality. Governments that had expelled the Jesuits in the third quarter of the previous century and browbeaten the popes until the order was completely suppressed did not object when in 1814 Pius VII restored throughout the world the Society of Jesus, which soon provided strong upholders of the papacy as it had previous to 1773.

Reorganization of the Church. The second part of Pius VII's pontificate was in marked contrast with the first. Events since 1789 had disorganized religious as well as secular society throughout Europe. Pius VII utilized his newly won influence and assumed leadership in rebuilding the Church. States that in the previous century had insisted on controlling internal religious affairs were eager to cooperate in arranging with Rome concordats or less formal agreements. The Holy See's policy in Germany took advantage of the fact that this region emerged from the Congress of Vienna as a loose confederation of political units. *Dalberg, *Wessenberg, and others favored a single German concordat in the hope of unifying the Church there with minimal dependence on Rome. Pius VII forestalled them by making separate arrangements with individual rulers, notably the Protestant king of Prussia, who found this an advantageous way of keeping formerly independent

prelates civilly obedient. Succeeding decades witnessed the *Cologne mixed marriage dispute and other Church-State disagreements that caused extended vacancies in several German sees, placed Catholics on the defensive, and nurtured the growth of *ultramontanism.

New Political Trends. Changes in society at large and the utilization of them by Roman pontiffs account in good part for the papacy's widely varying spiritual and temporal fortunes across the centuries, even though its hierarchical position is founded on revealed doctrines. These developments served to weaken the papacy after the Counter Reformation; but in the 19th century they had the opposite effect, at least in regard to the papal spiritual power. Since the French Revolution the trend has been toward constitutional governments, secular in aim, officially indifferent or hostile toward religion, unwilling to favor one creed over another or to help any creed. Many states have followed the U.S. in separating Church and State. The material support, privileges, social and political status that the clergy enjoyed under the *ancien régime* greatly diminished or disappeared. The ties that once bound the clergy so closely to the civil power and kept alive Gallicanism and other forms of ecclesiastical particularism no longer held. Political factors were very important in diverting the clergy en masse toward Rome as the one source willing and able to help them. The best example is France, particularly after 1830. What had long been the main center of Catholic opposition to the papacy assumed the lead in ultramontanism. Secular nationalism swelled to excessive proportions throughout the world during the 19th century, but ecclesiastical nationalism greatly declined.

The increasing menace of secularism, laicism, anticlericalism, materialism, and communism on an international scale also impelled Catholics to solidify their own ranks under the common leadership that Rome alone could provide.

Effects of Technological Progress. The papacy has profited greatly from the tremendous improvements in communication that began in the 19th century. Their effect has been to remove practical barriers that used to prevent regular papal action on a universal scale. Travel has become much faster, more pleasant, and more common with the introduction of the steamship, railroad, automobile, and airship. Ad limina visits to Rome and the dispatch of papal representatives to all corners of the world have ceased to be onerous. Pilgrims descend on the Eternal City in such vast numbers that audiences with visitors are nowadays almost a daily routine for popes. No longer are Roman pontiffs the remote figures they once were for dwellers north of the Alps. With the telegraph, wireless, telephone, radio, and greatly improved postal service, the Holy See can keep in close touch with clergy and faithful everywhere. The living voice of the popes has been heard by millions. The camera and television have made the features of recent popes among the most recognizable of mankind. The press has at times been hostile to Rome, but its immense growth has been more helpful than harmful. Newspapers and radio have rendered obsolete the measures that governments once took to prevent the dissemination of Roman decrees.

Ultramontanism. Doctrinal and, even more, practical considerations promoted a remarkable growth of ultramontanism, which began early in the 19th century and developed into a well-organized, aggressive, and irresistible movement by mid-century. Ultramontanism was a complex movement, but in general it favored an authoritarian, highly centralized ecclesiastical government with the pope exerting his primacy of jurisdiction in all domains of the entire Church. This, the ultramontanes were convinced, was essential for the effectiveness of the Church and even for the salvation of society. Ultramontanism advocated also freeing the Church from all State tutelage and unifying liturgy, discipline, devotion, and customs according to the Roman model. Like most important movements in the life of the Church, this one grew from humble origins and won wide popular support among the lower clergy and laity. Purely local influences kept urging it until midcentury. Until then the popes remained somewhat aloof from it, partly because of its connection with Hugues Félicité de *Lamennais and partly from a papal dislike of alienating the French government. Pius IX favored it strongly and placed himself at its head. The three most prominent literary champions of ultramontanism were not theologians but publicists and apologists: Joseph de *Maistre, Lamennais, and Louis *Veuillot. Ultramontanism won followers in many countries, but chiefly in France, Germany, and Belgium. It proved a major force in preparing the way for the solemn definition of papal prerogatives in 1870 and in undermining the vestiges of Gallicanism, Febronianism, and Josephinism. Some ultramontanes allowed their enthusiastic adulation for the papacy to carry them to theologically unsound extremes, but this was not characteristic of the movement as a whole.

Action by Popes (1823–46). *Leo XII (1823–29) and *Pius VIII (1829–30) continued the centralizing tendencies of Pius VII. Much more important was *Gregory XVI (1831–46). As pope he retained his previous keen interest in theology and in the missions. His principal theological work, *Il trionfo della Santa Sede e della Chiesa* (1799), strongly upheld the Church's independence of the civil power and papal primacy and infallibility and foretold the ultimate triumph of the Holy See and the Church. Gregory XVI put his teachings into effect by withstanding the secularizing aims of several governments and their encroachments on the spiritual power in Prussia and elsewhere. He was insistent of Rome's right to name bishops, particularly in Latin America, where he conflicted with some of the newly independent republics (*see* LATIN AMERICA, CHURCH AND INDEPENDENCE IN, 1). Despite growing unrest in the States of the Church, he determined to retain his temporal power. As a teacher he took the lead in condemning the doctrines of Lamennais and *Hermes.

Complete papal control of Catholic missions throughout the world dates from this pontificate. Civil rulers, with little counsel from Rome, had often been responsible for spreading Christianity during the Middle Ages. The great missionary expansion of the 16th and 17th centuries after the era of geographical discoveries was accomplished largely by the Spanish and Portuguese governments, which interpreted the *patronato real* and *padroado* in such a way as to monopolize control of the missions in their far-flung colonies. A combination of factors made the 18th century one of such precipitous decline that scarcely 300 missionaries were active

by 1800. Penury of personnel and other reasons did not allow this situation to improve much during the following 3 decades. Circumstances became more favorable under Gregory XVI, whose preoccupation with evangelization won him a reputation as the great mission pope of his century. Since Spain and Portugal had by then ceased to be major powers and were unable to supply their former material support, they could not effectively resume their old *patronato* and *padroado* pretensions. Gradually Rome gained exclusive control. The Congregation for the *Propagation of the Faith (Propaganda), which Napoleon I had abolished in 1808, was reorganized in 1817. Bartolomeo Capellari acted as its prefect from 1826 until his election as Pope Gregory XVI in 1831. Propaganda soon played the important role designed for it at its foundation in 1622. Its jurisdiction included Asia, Africa, Oceania, Australia, and the entire Western Hemisphere, as well as Prussia, Scandinavia, the Netherlands, and the British Isles. Acting through the Congregation, Gregory XVI assigned mission territories to religious institutes, decided the status of all missions, and appointed, promoted, and transferred the vicars and prefects who headed them. The Pope worked out the guiding principles and methods for the missioners. Gregory XVI and his successors took the lead in trying to eliminate colonialism and nationalism, particularly European nationalism, from the missions and in developing native clergies. Gone were the interminable negotiations among Propaganda, the *patronato* powers, and religious orders with a quasi-monopoly in certain areas. Save for very limited territories remaining under the *patronato real* and *padroado,* all missions depended directly on Propaganda, except for those under the Congregation for the Oriental Church since 1917 and the few subjected to the Consistorial Congregation.

The extraordinary mission development since 1831 has received slight financial support from governments. Gregory XVI and later popes have promoted the organizations to raise by private charity the huge sums needed; they have exhorted the faithful to contribute and in the 20th century brought the headquarters of many of these societies to Rome.

The peoples whom these missions have converted have proved very loyal to the Holy See and remained singularly untouched by European particularist traditions. This has been characteristic of the native clergies and native hierarchies, whose development has been so much favored by Rome. At the same time the Holy See's multiplication of apostolic delegations in mission lands demonstrates its intent to keep them under its personal direction and to obtain firsthand information about them.

Loyalty, obedience, and affection have characterized also the relations between the papacy and Catholics in the U.S., Canada, Australia, New Zealand, and other lands where the Church has grown since the 19th century largely as a result of emigration from Europe.

Pius IX (1846–78). In the development of the papacy the most important pontificate in modern times is that of Pius IX. He was the first pope to assume active leadership of ultramontanism, which he helped build almost into a "party." To undermine Gallicanism still further, the Pope placed several well-known works on the Index. Some of them had been textbooks in French seminaries, and one of them, by Louis Bailly, had been taught at Maynooth. Pius IX promoted also liturgical unification by substituting Roman practices for a variety of local liturgies, particularly French ones. A concentrated effort was made to standardize ecclesiastical usages according to norms established in Rome. Centralization of authority and administration made such strides, even before 1870, that it stands out as one of the most notable features of this pontificate. The Roman *Curia became more and more the Church's administrative nerve center. Its functionaries served the Pope in the ever more effective exercise of his jurisdictional primacy throughout the world. Accompanying this growth in the Roman Congregations was a marked improvement in the spiritual earnestness, intellectual caliber, professional competence, and industry of their staffs; but not always a thorough grasp of contemporary needs and trends. Although the Curial cardinals were of high quality, Pius IX reduced their spiritual and temporal influence and consulted them rarely on broader issues, save for *Antonelli and a few others.

Individual bishops came into more direct contact with papal authority. More so than his predecessors, Pius IX named bishops himself, regardless of local preferences, and in doing so showed his own preference for ultramontanes. (By 1869 only 81 bishops chosen by Gregory XVI remained in a total of 739). Papal initiative was responsible for an increasing number of national seminaries in Rome, where promising future priests and bishops received ultramontane training and a preference for Roman usages. *Ad limina visits became more frequent. Refractory bishops were beckoned to Rome. Appeals to the Curia from diocesan decisions, even in minor matters, were countenanced. The Holy See frowned on national synods but approved provincial councils. The large number of these provincial gatherings between 1846 and 1869 demonstrated the progress of ultramontanism among the bishops. The same trend was evident in the large episcopal assemblages in Rome in 1854, 1862, and 1867. Papal nuncios were more active than before in the internal affairs of local churches; they intervened regularly between Rome and bishops and between bishops and local clergy. Fornari in Paris was the most memorable example of a nuncio utilizing every circumstance to promote ultramontanism.

As a teacher for the entire Church Pius IX was more active than his predecessor. It is especially noteworthy in the present context that the solemn definition of the *Immaculate Conception, pronounced by Pius IX (Dec. 8, 1854) in the presence of a great international gathering of bishops, made no mention of episcopal approbation, although this had been sought and received. The manner of defining this doctrine was intended as a practical demonstration of papal infallibility. The bishops attended the ceremony as spectators.

It was during this pontificate above all that the Catholic world developed a strong personal devotion to each incumbent in the chair of St. Peter. Pius IX's winning personality and his conduct during very troubled years won him immense popularity, unequaled perhaps by any of his predecessors.

*Vatican Council I climaxed this pontificate with a solemn definition of papal *infallibility and *primacy of jurisdiction. It brought to completion centuries of doctrinal development and removed permanently from serious consideration conciliarist or episcopalist arguments about the pope's position in the Church. When the final decision came, there was no energetic opposition from governments. Within the Council the minority based its case mainly on the inopportuneness of defining these matters at this time. The Catholic world as a whole immediately rejoiced in the definitions and has never ceased to do so. Those irreconcilables who started the schism of the *Old Catholics failed to attract more than an insignificant minority.

Temporal Power. If alterations in society benefited the papal spiritual position, they weakened and finally destroyed the *temporal power. Economic backwardness made the States of the Church a financial burden instead of a source of income for the Holy See. As the forces unleashed by the French Revolution permeated Italy, the Papal States ceased to provide independence for the popes, who were compelled to rely on military aid from France and Austria to restrain domestic unrest fomented by the drive to unify the Italian peninsula politically. Almost simultaneously in 1870 Vatican Council I established the pope permanently at the pinnacle of spiritual power, and an invading Italian army ended the papal temporal power. Rome feared that loss of the States of the Church would eventually entail the sacrifice of papal spiritual independence; but matters turned out otherwise. Pius IX and his successors until Pius XI retired behind the walls of the Vatican as voluntary prisoners protesting against the seizure of their state and against the Law of *Guarantees and awaited the solution of the *Roman Question. Meanwhile their international diplomatic standing remained intact and their spiritual power continued to increase.

Since 1878. *Leo XIII (1878–1903), *Pius X (1903–14), *Benedict XV (1914–22), *Pius XI (1922–39), *Pius XII (1939–58), *John XXIII (1958–63), and *Paul VI (1963–   ) have all been zealous men of high spiritual and intellectual caliber. In wide circles outside the Church they have been esteemed and influential, particularly John XXIII. In 1917 the promulgation by Benedict XV of the *Code of Canon Law terminated a long process of growth in ecclesiastical law and exalted the position of the papacy in the Church's legal structure, just as Vatican Council I did in a doctrinal way. To Heiler the Code marked "the victory of papalism, the completion of centralization, the conclusion of centuries of development of the primacy of jurisdiction." Never has the papal magisterial power been more in evidence than since 1878. As teachers in matters of faith and morals these seven popes have been prodigiously active. Heterodox doctrines have been rare in Catholic ranks recently; but when they have appeared, they have served to reveal the enormous influence of the papal magisterium. Thus *Modernism subsided quickly after Pius X's condemnation. Pius XII's *Humani generis* nipped in the bud several novel doctrines. The contrast is striking between the effectiveness of those pronouncements and those issued by 17th- and 18th-century popes during the Jansenist disputes. For topical variety and volume of teachings, the writings, allocutions, and broadcasts of Pius XII surpass anything in papal history. This extremely conscientious and industrious supreme pontiff kept in the closest possible touch with all sections of the Church, familiarized himself with current prob-

Fig. 8. Interior of the Sistine Chapel immediately after the election of Pope John XXIII. The baldachino over the seat of the newly elected Pope signifies his selection, those of the other cardinals having been lowered.

Fig. 9. Dean of the college of cardinals kisses Pope John XXIII's ring at ceremonies on the day of coronation.

lems, and considered it his duty to provide solutions for all of them. It is doubtful that any pope made more extensive use of his position as spiritual monarch. After Cardinal Maglione's death in 1944, for example, Pius XII dispensed with even a secretary of state. Since 1929 the popes have also possessed temporal power. The State of *Vatican City, created by the *Lateran Pacts, is very small in area, but it is a sovereign entity, and in it the pope rules as absolute monarch without legislature or voters.

Administrative centralization in Rome has continued to increase, although this is not a necessary corollary of the definitions in 1870. Primacy of jurisdiction does not require limitless centralization of administration any more than it compels the absorption of all episcopal jurisdiction. The Church is not a replica of a highly unified civil state in which the head of the government delegates to subordinates such authority as he wishes; but neither is it a federation whose bishops constitute semiautonomous dynasties joined to the pope as president. Burgeoning bureaucracy and its effects have roused criticisms in the ranks of the hierarchy and elsewhere. Doctrinally the popes have remained within their rights. In the practical order each pope must endeavor to conciliate his powers and obligations with those of the bishops, according to changing circumstances. The tendency toward centralization and uniformity has not been the same everywhere. Thus the Eastern Churches in union with Rome long enjoyed autonomy in choosing their patriarchs and bishops and in regulating their liturgy, law, and discipline. In recent times, especially since Pius IX, this autonomy has been considerably reduced, notably in disciplinary matters, but not to the same extent as in the West.

Papal relations with bishops have been harmonious and close. Detailed quinquennial reports, which must be sent to Rome from all dioceses, enable 20th-century popes to maintain over all episcopal administrations careful surveillance and methodical control. Vatican Council I did not pronounce on the relationship between the pope and the bishops, but *Vatican Council II devoted the third chapter of its dogmatic constitution on the Church to the Church's hierarchical structure. It taught that the bishops are by divine institution the successors of the Apostles, that they govern the Church together with the Vicar of Christ and form with him a college, just as did St. Peter and the other Apostles. It further declared that the college of bishops has no authority without the Roman pontiff at its head and that the papal primacy over all, pastors and people, remains whole and intact. In virtue of his office the pope has full, supreme, and universal power over the Church and he is always free to exercise it. The college of bishops is also the subject of supreme and full power over the universal Church, but only when it is united to the pope; and it can exercise this power only with the consent of the Roman pontiff.

At the opening of the fourth session of Vatican Council II (Sept. 14, 1965), Paul VI announced that, in response to the Council's wish, he would set up a synod of bishops to collaborate with him in an advisory capacity and at times in a deliberative one. According to his motu proprio *Apostolica sollicitudo* (Sept. 15, 1965), members are to be chosen for the most part by national episcopal conferences, subject to papal approval, but the pope may appoint up to 15 per cent of the members himself. The pope will convene sessions when for the general good of the Church it seems to him opportune; he will preside over meetings in person or by deputy, and approve or disapprove synodal decisions.

Bibliography: F. VIGENER, "Gallikanismus und episcopalistische Strömungen im deutschen Katholizismus zwischen Tridentinum und Vatikanum," HistZ 111 (1913) 495–581. Y. DE LA BRIÈRE, et al., DictApolFoiCath 3:1333–1534. V. MARTIN, DTC 11.2:1877–1944. G. GLEZ, DTC 12.2:2670–2772; 13.1.247–344. F. HEILER, *Altkirchliche Autonomie und päpstlicher Zentralismus* (Munich 1941). H. MARC-BONNET, *La Papauté contemporaine, 1878–1945* (Paris 1946). Delacroix HistMissCath 3:18–20, 27–162. P. BREZZI, *The Papacy: Its Origins and Historical Evolution,* tr. H. J. YANNONE (Westminster, Md. 1958). Latourette Christ19th–20thCent v.1, 4. R. AUBERT, *Le Pontificat de Pie IX* (Fliche-Martin 21; 2d ed. 1964). M. D. KNOWLES et al., EncBrit (1965) 17:194–228. B. G. THILS, *Primauté pontificale et prerogatives épiscopales* (Louvain 1961). G. SCHWAIGER, LexThK² 8:37–44. W. DE VRIES, *Rom und die Patriarchate des Ostens* (Freiburg 1963). W. BERTRAMS, *The Papacy, the Episcopacy, and Collegiality,* tr. P. T. BRANNAN (Westminster, Md. 1964). **Illustration credits:** Figs. 8 and 9, Leonard Von Matt.

[J. F. BRODERICK]

PAPADOPOULOS, CHRYSOSTOMOS, Orthodox archbishop, ecclesiastical historian; b. Madytos, eastern Thrace, July 1, 1868; d. Athens, Oct. 28, 1938. After earlier training at Constantinople, Jerusalem, and Smyrna, he studied theology at the University of Athens (1889–91) and at the ecclesiastical academies of Kiev (1891–93) and St. Petersburg (1893–95). From 1895 until 1909 he taught at the theological School of the Cross in Jerusalem, where he was ordained and was made an archimandrite (1900). After 2 years spent in parish work in Alexandria (1909–11), he acted as director of the Rizarion Seminary in Athens (1911–23) and also as professor of ecclesiastical history at the University (1914–23). The Holy Synod elected him archbishop of Athens and of all Greece (1923). Papadopoulos published numerous articles on ecclesiastical history, his principal scholarly interest, and also many on ethics. He wrote also a history of the Oriental patriarchates and a history of the Greek and Slavic Orthodox Churches. He influenced deeply the cultural and political life of Greece between World Wars I and II. He favored the ecumenical movement, but showed slight sympathy for Catholics of the Greek rite.

Bibliography: Biography and complete list of his works in *Enaisima* (Miscellanea in his honor), ed. G. PAPAMICHAIL (Athens 1931); and in *Theologia* 16 (1938) 369–408; 17 (1939) 257–272. H. PIERRE, "L'Union de l'Orient avec Rome," *Orientalia Christiana* 18.1 (1930) 5–165, correspondence between P. Ch. and the Catholic exarch of Greece, George Calavassy. J. SALAVILLE, *Catholicisme* 2:1116–17. M. GORDILLO, EncCatt 9:778.

[J. KRAJCAR]

PAPAL ARBITRATION

International arbitration, of which papal arbitration is an aspect, evoked a vast literature between 1870 and 1920. These writings mirrored quite perfectly the assumption of civilized society that rational juridical forms might be substituted for irrational military methods to resolve conflicting claims of sovereign states. Since 1929 and the abandonment of the assumption that *ratio* can control *vis,* arbitration as a juridical form has its greatest utility in cases of private law and labor negotiations and is scarcely noticed in international legal literature save in its historical aspects. Arbitration, a method of adjudication developed in classical Greece and refined by Roman usage and jurisprudence, depends on several assumptions common to the contenders and the arbitrator. Some of these assumptions are good faith, equality, and a belief in some kind of punitive sanction. The contenders assume, first, that the losses incurred in arbitration are substantially less than would occur were they to resort to a trial of strength and, second, that the arbitrator is as much concerned with equity, as they understand the term, as are they themselves.

Medieval Development. Papal arbitration was one aspect of that subtle process by which the Roman Catholic Church in the West became in the Middle Ages the veritable heir of the Roman Empire. The process had already begun in the NT period, when Church members were exhorted to settle their differences without recourse to pagan courts (1 Cor 6.1–9). Among the privileges extended to bishops by the Constantinian peace was imperial recognition (CodTheod 1:27.1) of the validity of decisions rendered by the bishop in his capacity either of *iudex* (judge) or *arbiter* (arbitrator), and the obligation of the state to enforce the decisions rendered by an ecclesiastical person. As the internal cohesion of the Empire dissolved especially in the 5th and 6th centuries, not only did all bishops assume greater administrative and judicial responsibility, but the bishops of the patriarchical sees, except Constantinople, became shadowy proconsuls.

From the time of the Lombard invasions into Italy, the bishops of Rome became steadily the sole Roman, political, and judicial power of the West. After freeing itself first from Byzantine and, later, Carolingian domination, the papacy of the 11th century rose to a position of leadership based solidly on written law in contrast with Germanic contention for headship based on custom of relatively brief duration. The great popes of the 12th and 13th centuries, many of them former professors of law—both Canon and Roman—appointed Roman law forms of arbitration for many classes of difficulties arising between two juridical persons. "It is in the collection of *Gregory IX (1234) that one must seek out the Canon Law doctrine on arbitration and its codification. This doctrine is taken from Roman law, which it reproduced almost completely and without change, except in those areas peculiarly inspired by Christian ideas or which the dictates of practice necessitated. The doctrine remained without notable change up to the Code of Canon Law of 1917" (Amanieu).

However, as the feudal monarchs of the 13th century developed greater awareness of their own juridical personalities (*Rex est imperator in regno suo*), the popes, who became more deeply involved in European power politics and were recognized for this reason to be of the same power stature as the secular monarchs, were more and more often called upon to act as arbitrators. *Boniface VIII arbitrating the dispute between King *Philip IV the Fair and *Edward I of England (1297); *Alexander VI, between Portugal and Spain (1493); and *Gregory XIII, between Poland and Russia (1572–83), exemplified successful papal adjudication of international disputes. Whereas textbooks often refer to popes as arbitrators, they seldom note that the Holy See itself not infrequently employed the method of arbitration to resolve its own political differences with Italian states and combinations of states, a fact that underscores the grave responsibilities which devolved on the pope as a territorial sovereign.

Modern Era. The religious and political upheavals of the 16th and 17th centuries diminished the possibility of arbitration but by no means ended the need for it. With J. *Bodin's definition of sovereignty and the growth of the modern state with its large and absolute authority, the peacelovers of the civilized nations began to seek juridical mechanisms for the promotion of peace; and in the early writers, such as Hugo *Grotius, one finds recourse to the Roman law doctrine of arbitration. The congress system of making and maintaining peace, begun in the 18th century and developed in the years that followed, recognized arbitration and finally set up at The Hague a panel of jurists to be employed for arbitration of disputed claims. But only rarely did secular rulers employ the good offices of the Holy See in arbitration. In 1885 Pope *Leo XIII was selected to arbitrate the claims of the German Empire and Spain in the Caroline Islands. The overtures of *Benedict XV (July 28, 1915, and especially Aug. 1, 1917) to serve as mediator between the belligerents in World War I met with no success. More cautiously, *Pius XII fashioned his public reactions during World War II to the prospective role of peacemaker—to which, however, he was not invited. In his first encyclical, *Ecclesiam suam,* *Paul VI, by offering his services in the cause of peace, maintained the traditional attitude of the papacy toward international arbitration.

It may be concluded that the prevailing ethical standard of European society has been gauged by its view of papal arbitration. The Church preserved the Roman law of arbitration and the great legist popes of the

Middle Ages disseminated that equitable form. Since secular governments began to replace Romano-canonical methods, they have sought, particularly from the 17th century, to devise universally acceptable systems of arbitration. But lacking a common ethic and a common religious orientation, modern nations can act in concert only *ad hoc* and on the basis of the balance of power, best described by St. Augustine as a *latrocinium*, or robbers' treaty.

Bibliography: J. H. Ralston, *International Arbitration from Athens to Locarno* (Palo Alto 1929). J. Eppstein, *The Catholic Tradition of the Law of Nations* (London 1935). A. Amanieu, DDC 1:862–895. G. Balladore Pallieri and G. Vismara, *Acta pontificia juris gentium* (Milan 1946). C. Pharr et al., eds. and trs., *The Theodosian Code and Novels* (Princeton 1952). A. Berger, *Encyclopedic Dictionary of Roman Law* (Transactions of the American Philosophical Society NS 43.2; Philadelphia 1953).

[S. WILLIAMS]

PAPAL CEREMONY AND VESTURE

As supreme head of the universal Church, the pope can officiate in any existing rite, Eastern or Western. However, as bishop of Rome, he regularly celebrates according to the rubrics of the Roman rite.

Ceremonial. While the ritual he observes is that followed by all archbishops, there are nonetheless many ceremonies special to the pope.

The Papal Pontifical Mass. When pontificating, the pope wears several vestments, as explained below; the college of cardinals and bishops or abbots attending Mass are vested in cope or chasuble (the cardinal deacons in dalmatics), and all wear the white miter (cardinals, of silk, bishops and abbots, of linen). The first part of the service is the solemn entry of the pope, carried on the *sedes gestatoria* and wearing his great mantle and the *tiara. The second part is the chanting of Terce and the vesting of the pope, cardinals, and bishops for Mass. The third part of the office is the Mass of the Catechumens at the throne, which follows closely the rite of a bishop's pontifical Mass in his own cathedral. The special rite in this part of the Mass is the singing of the Epistle and Gospel in Latin and Greek. The fourth part is the celebration of the Mass of the faithful at the altar; the pope leaves his throne after the chant of the *Credo*. During the pope's Mass,

The dean of the cardinal deacons placing the tiara on the head of Pope Paul VI, June 30, 1963.

The Communion of the Pope at his throne during a papal pontifical Mass. The Pontiff is receiving the Sacred Species through a silver straw.

there is one very particular rite, which has never been allowed in any other diocese or rite, that is, the pope's Communion at his throne.

Coronation. In the ceremony of coronation, three times during the procession to the altar for the celebration of pontifical Mass, a cleric sets fire to a ball of coarse material atop the silver cane he holds and, facing the pope, sings "Pater sancte, sic transit gloria mundi" (Holy Father, thus passes the glory of the world). After Mass the pope is led to the loggia above the main door of St. Peter's Basilica to be crowned before the people standing in the square below. As the pope is seated on the throne erected for the occasion, the choir sings the antiphon *Corona aurea super caput eius*. After the pope's miter is removed, the dean of the cardinal deacons places the tiara on his head, saying: "Receive the tiara adorned with three crowns and know that you are the father of princes and kings, ruler of the earth, and earthly vicar of our Savior Jesus Christ, to whom is honor and glory forever. Amen." The pope then gives his blessing, and the cardinal deacon announces the plenary indulgence granted by the Holy Father.

Canonization. Until the time of Pius XII the ceremony was quite long. The *Ave Maris Stella* was sung during the procession into St. Peter's Basilica behind the banner of the servant of God. Upon arrival before the papal throne, the postulator of the cause knelt before the pontiff and asked *instanter* (urgently) the canonization; the Litany of the Saints followed. Again the postulator approached the throne and requested *instantius* (more urgently) for the glorification of the servant of God; the *Veni Creator* was then sung. For a third time the postulator went to the pope and begged *instantissime* (most urgently). At this the pontiff read the declaration of canonization. The *Te Deum* concluded this part of the rite.

However, in order to abbreviate the ceremony Pius XII had the Litany of the Saints chanted during the procession into the basilica; the three petitions were joined into one followed by the *Veni Creator* and the declaration. In the Mass that follows there is a solemn procession with offerings of candles, wine, bread, and doves. The first report of such an offertory procession comes from the canonization of St. Bridget of Sweden, which took place in 1391.

Other Rites. The pope also reserves to himself the opening and closing of ecumenical councils, the opening of the Holy Doors in *jubilee years, the blessing of the archbishop's pallium, the blessing of the *Golden Rose that he offers from time to time as a gift to some personality or sanctuary.

Vesture. The pope has two kinds of vesture: the prelatial, or nonliturgical, and liturgical.

Prelatial Dress. This is very simple. In his daily life he wears a white cassock or simar, with the small humeral cape and oversleeves that go with it; a white silk sash; and a zucchetto to match. In cold weather the pope wears a long cloak of red wool, called a *mantello,* and a red hat with gold trimmings. His stockings are white and his shoes are of red velvet, with a cross embroidered on them. For receptions the pope wears a long linen rochet, usually ornamented with lace, and over it the mozzetta or humeral cape, which, in summer is of red satin, and in winter of red velvet, with ermine trimmings. During Eastertide the mozzetta and shoes are of white satin. With the red velvet mozzetta the pope wears, instead of the white skull cap, a papal biretta, called *camauro,* made to match the mozzetta. For solemn receptions, especially when preceded by the papal cross, and when carried on the *sedes gestatoria,* he wears a large red stole, not as a liturgical garment, but as a sign of his universal jurisdiction in the whole Church. According to the best traditions, when wearing the mozzetta, the pope wears the pectoral cross under it and over the rochet. Although the use of a white cassock goes back many centuries, the papal color is red and that is the reason mozzetta, *camauro,* shoes, *mantello,* and hat are always red, except during Eastertide.

Liturgical Vestments. Besides the pontifical vestments worn by all archbishops, the pope has two vestments that are proper, or reserved, to him, viz, the *fanon and the *subcinctorium* (below the girdle).

The *subcinctorium* takes the form of a maniple of the same width from top to bottom and is ornamented with an *Agnus Dei* at the lower end. It is attached to a special girdle and hangs on the pope's right side. The *subcinctorium* has now no practical meaning. Up to the 13th century it was commonly worn by all bishops, and St. Charles Borromeo tried to reintroduce its use in the Milanese rite as a pontifical vestment. The *subcinctorium* is closely related also to the Greek epigonation: a lozenge-shaped piece of stiff, embroidered material attached to the girdle and worn as part of pontifical dress. Both the vestments were originally related to the *maniple, which was a towel or handkerchief, usually attached to the waist of the garment, and of hygienic use.

The falda, worn by some popes, is not a vestment but a white flowing robe with a train that falls around the feet. When used, it is placed over the rochet. Since the falda is so long, it must be lifted by assistants whenever he walks during ceremonies. The diaries of Alexander VI (d. 1503) speak of it as a papal ornament, but there is no agreement regarding its origin or significance.

The pope's cope or great mantle is like any other cope, except that it is about 15 inches wider than the ordinary one, and is either white or red. He wears the cope at solemn entries, before he vests for Mass, and when he is present, vested, at his throne. When

attending a solemn Requiem Mass, he wears the red cope with a violet stole, since, according to custom, he should not wear black vestments. The tiara, though worn at solemn papal entrances, it not a liturgical insigne. (*See* EPISCOPAL CEREMONY AND VESTURE.)

Bibliography: P. SIFFRIN and E. DANTE, EncCatt 6:1779–82. J. LÖW, *ibid.* 3:569–607. E. DANTE, *ibid.* 5:962. P. SIFFRIN, *ibid.* 11:1478–79. P. SALMON, *Étude sur les insignes du pontife dans le rit romain* (Rome 1955). R. LESAGE, *Vestments and Church Furniture,* tr. F. MURPHY (New York 1960). T. KLAUSER, *Der Ursprung der bischöflichen Insignien und Ehrenrechte* (2d ed. Krefeld 1953). **Illustration credits:** Felici, Rome.

[J. NABUCO]

PAPAL CHAMBERLAIN. Named by means of a *biglietto* of the secretariate of state, papal chamberlains are divided into secret chamberlains of his holiness and chamberlains in violet habit.

The first category consists (1) of a few participating secret chamberlains (right reverend monsignori), the first three of whom are respectively styled *pincerna, vestiarius,* and *nuntius,* who daily attend his holiness, and (2) of several thousands of supernumerary secret chamberlains (very reverend monsignori), whose dignity, although merely honorary, also allows them to do occasional service in the apostolic palace. They possess no liturgical privileges, but they outrank *simplices sacerdotes,* though not abbots or canons in chapter.

The secondary category, chamberlains in violet habit (very reverend monsignori) is similar to the preceding, although the service these chamberlains perform in the apostolic palace is limited to the throne room, and they are preceded by the first category.

All wear a violet cassock with *mantellone* for choir dress (over which they may wear a surplice when administering the Sacraments) or violet-buttoned and violet-lined cassock with black *ferraiolone* as *piano* (i.e., nonliturgical) dress. Papal chamberlains cease to exist as such at the tumulation of the pope who created them, but on request they are normally reconfirmed by the succeeding pontiff. Among the requisites for eligibility is, normally, at least 5 years in the priesthood. Their coat of arms is surmounted by a black prelatial hat with six violet tassels pending on each side of the crest.

See also PAPAL HOUSEHOLD.

[P. C. VAN LIERDE]

PAPAL ELECTION DECREE (1059)

A judgment issued by the Roman Synod in April 1059, under the presidency of Pope *Nicholas II, to regularize the procedure of papal elections.

Background. Earlier attempts had been made to avert uncanonical accession and the civil disorders that normally attended elections: the synodal decree of 816, the oath that *Louis the Pious and *Lothair I required of the Romans (824), and the cession of Pope *Leo VIII to *Otto I (963). All had tried to ensure orderly and canonical accessions by guaranteeing the emperor's role as arbiter in the elections. The decree of 1059, however, was the first effort to establish administrative machinery within the Church for that purpose. Prepared for by the development of the college of cardinals under the reformed papacy, the burden of the decree was anticipated early in 1059 when Nicholas II became the liege lord of *Robert Guiscard, Duke of Apulia and Calabria, receiving Robert's promise in future to assist the "better" cardinals, the clergy, and the laity of Rome in electing and consecrating suitable men as popes.

Content. The framers of the decree began by recalling that the Roman Church had been endangered by *simony after the death of *Stephen IX and stating their hope that the subsequent provisions would provide against the recurrence of such peril. They specified that on the death of a bishop of Rome the cardinal bishops should consider the succession among themselves, then admit the cardinal priests to their deliberations, and finally take counsel with the rest of the Roman clergy and with the Roman laity. Scholars interpret these rules to mean that the cardinal bishops were to nominate a candidate, that the lesser cardinal clergy were to approve him, and that the other clergy and the people were formally to accept him. The decree then quotes a passage from the letter of Pope *Leo I to Rusticus saying that no one could be truly a bishop unless he were elected by the clergy of his church, accepted by his people, and consecrated by the bishops of his province on the approval of their metropolitan. It adds that, since the Roman Church had no metropolitan superior, the cardinal bishops discharged the office of the metropolitan in the case of papal elections.

In accord with a decree of *Stephen III, the 1059 decree required that the pope be elected from the Roman Church itself, and that to *Henry IV of Germany and his successors must be reserved the "honor" (i.e., the formal privileges) that Rome had already granted Henry in accepting him as emperor-designate, which his successors must personally request of the apostolic see. This provision is commonly understood to refer to the right of approval that Byzantine emperors from *Justinian I onward had demanded in papal elections and that the earlier regulations about accessions to the Roman See had guaranteed. The decree added that if civil conditions in Rome were too disturbed to allow the immediate enthronement of the bishop-elect, he might exercise the full authority of the papacy even before his formal installation, and it concluded by cursing those who would work to subvert its provisions and blessing those who observed them. The subscriptions of witnesses, led by the signature of Nicholas II, ended the text.

Significance. The appraisal of the decree's intent and importance is one of the most vexed problems of medieval history, and it has been complicated by the presence of a deliberately corrupted version of the decree written within 40 years after the issuance of the original. The earliest students of the problem distinguished the original as the "papal" version and the corrupted reading as the "imperial" and tended to judge the two documents outside their historical context. Scholars at the end of the 19th and the beginning of the 20th century generally accepted the distinction of "papal" and "imperial"; but they argued that the original decree was the first major effort of the *Gregorian reform to free papal elections from lay influence, especially from imperial intervention, and that, to achieve their goal, its authors ascribed the effectual act of election to the cardinals, leaving only ceremonial rights to the German king.

The decree was, scholars judged, the true cause of the repudiation of Nicholas II by German bishops

in 1061 and of the schism that followed. In 1936 A. *Michel brought this interpretation into doubt, setting the decree into the ecclesiological context of the Gregorian reform rather than into the conventional setting of the struggle between the Church and the temporal power; and H. G. Krause has recently developed and convincingly modified Michel's thought. Michel argued on textual grounds, and Krause has since confirmed, that the distinctions of "papal" and "imperial" were erroneous, and that the corrupt reading came not from the imperial chancery but from among the schismatic cardinals who abandoned *Gregory VII in 1084. Michel dated the false version for 1084, but Krause assigned it generally to the period 1085–1100. They both pointed out that the later version is much the same as the original and that such changes as it contains enhance, on balance, the powers of the lesser cardinal clergy, rather than those of the German king. This version, however, had only slight effect. Krause particularly contested the view that the original decree was designed to free papal elections from imperial control. He suggested rather that the authors of the decree intended to free the papacy from the schism and local conflict that attended Nicholas's accession in 1058 by confirming precisely those powers of arbitration that the earlier enactments on papal elections had described and that *Henry III had vigorously exercised. In this way they hoped to subject local interests to the superior juridical competence of the Empire and to give the earlier process canonical force through synodal approval. Krause further maintained that the repudiation of Nicholas II by the German bishops and the schism of 1061 resulted, not from displeasure at the curtailment of imperial prerogatives by the decree, but from the quite unrelated animosity of Abp. *Anno of Cologne toward Nicholas. In addition to its critical importance in polemical works of the *investiture struggle, the decree has significance as the basis of modern procedure in papal elections.

Bibliography: Editions. MGConst 1:537–551. H. G. KRAUSE, *Das Papstwahldekret von 1059 und seine Rolle im Investitursteit* (StGreg 7; 1960). Literature. A. MICHEL, *Papstwahl und Königsrecht oder das Papstwahl-Konkordat von 1059* (Munich 1936); "Das Papstwahlpaktum von 1059," HistJ 59 (1939) 291–351. R. HOLTZMANN, "Zum Papstwahldekret von 1059," ZSavRG Kan 27 (1938) 135–153. B. SCHMEIDLER, "Zum Wahldekret Papst Nikolaus II. vom Jahre 1059," *Historische Vierteljahrschrift* 31 (1937–39) 554–560.

[K. F. MORRISON]

PAPAL HOUSEHOLD

This term signifies the papal court in its proper, restricted sense. The papal household consists of the ecclesiastics and laymen who have a recognized function by protocol in the papal residence. This function can be merely honorific, or, as is frequently the case, associated with a determined function. The papal household (*Famiglia pontificia*) is distinguished from the papal chapel (*Capella pontificia*), which includes all those who have a right to participate in the liturgical functions celebrated solemnly by the supreme pontiff and who are listed in the *Annuario Pontificio* (1964, pp. 983–1000). The papal household and chapel together constitute the papal court in the broader sense of the word. This court in turn is distinct from the Roman *Curia, the totality of congregations, tribunals, and other organisms that serve the pope in the government of the universal Church. Many individuals who are members of the Curia belong also to the court.

Both the papal court and the Roman Curia find their justification in the functions pertaining to the pope as head of the Catholic Church. Independently of the sovereignty exercised by him until 1870 over the *States of the Church, and since 1929 over *Vatican City, the pope has always been considered a sovereign as head of the Church possessing universal jurisdictional and teaching authority. Before 1870 the relations of the *Holy See with other states were based on the pope's temporal sovereignty and his more important sovereignty as head of the Church. After the former ceased, no one questioned the latter, as is demonstrated by the continued accreditation of diplomats to the Holy See, the right of legations exercised by these, and the concluding of concordats and other international agreements. Since 1929 the pope has again been sovereign in two senses, even though Vatican City is territorially small. The temporal sovereignty has been restored above all to guarantee the liberty and independence of the Holy See.

History. The first dependable notices of the existence of a papal household date from the Carolingian period. During the Avignon papacy (1306–76) the household developed greatly and took its precise form during the Renaissance. Considering that in all the life of the Church tradition is important, it is not surprising that the papal court has remained faithful, perhaps more than any other institution, to the customs and even the names of the past. Even in the 1960s it is substantially an Italian court of Renaissance days, influenced by that religious element which was the first characteristic of the sovereign of Rome.

The norms regulating the activity of the papal household and its privileges are to be sought in papal documents of past centuries. The present Code of Canon Law (canon 328) has not legislated on the subject; and so the earlier documents preserve their validity in great part. Some change has, however, occurred. The term "court" is no longer in common use, nor is it found in the *Annuario Pontificio*. The last mention of it in official documents was in the Lateran Treaty of 1929 (article 10) and in the protocol signed Sept. 6, 1932, between the Holy See and Italy containing a list of major offices composing the court.

The papal household contains many non-Italians, especially among the lay chamberlains of sword and cape, the clerical domestic prelates, and supernumerary privy chamberlains. Paul VI alluded (Jan. 14, 1964) to the advantage of changing some external forms in the relations of the nobility to the Holy See.

Composition of the Papal Household. The diverse groups are listed below in the order of precedence. Only a few perform regular, effective services; these are said to be *de numero*. The others are called supernumeraries and hold purely honorific titles; they render services only in conjunction with the former. The chief characteristics and actual functions of the various groups are noted where necessary, but not their historical development.

Palatine Cardinals. These prelates are so named because they are assigned to the personal service of the pope in the apostolic palace (*palatium*). Their number has varied during the centuries, but for some decades it has included only the cardinals in charge of the apostolic datary and the cardinal secretary of state.

Noble Privy Antechamber. This group, the *Camera secreta SS'mi Domini Papae,* comprises several different officials. First among them are the *palatine prelates,* the most immediate and intimate members of the household:

1. Majordomo of His Holiness (*praefectus palatii apostolici*), foremost among the prelates. At one time he had important jurisdictional and administrative functions in the apostolic palaces, but in recent times his duties have been to distribute invitations to papal ceremonies and to make known the pope's whereabouts.
2. Master of the chamber (*praefectus cubiculi secreti Pontificis*), next in rank after the majordomo; he presides in the papal antechamber, regulates papal audiences, and accompanies the pope always. He stands at the pope's left, the majordomo at the right. Both reside in the Vatican and have the title "Excellency."
3. Auditor of His Holiness, a title held since the time of Benedict XV (1914–21) by the secretary *pro tempore* of the apostolic *signatura.
4. Master of the sacred palace, the pope's trusted theologian. Formerly, he granted the *imprimatur* to books published in Rome. Dominicans have held the post since its inauguration in the 13th century. Lodging in the Vatican is reserved for this official.

Next in the noble privy antechamber come the *participating privy chamberlains* (*cubicularii,* or *camerieri segreti partecipanti*), whose name derives from the fact that they formerly partook of meals at the papal table. Their offices cease with the death of a pope. In order of preference they are:

1. Privy almoner (*eleemosinarius secretus*), an archbishop who supervises papal beneficences and who participates in papal functions.
2. Secretary of letters to princes (*pro litteris in forma brevi ad principes secretarius*), he composes the Latin form of letters signed by the pope to heads of state, as well as encyclicals, apostolic letters, consistorial allocutions, and homilies for canonizations and beatifications.
3. Secretary of the code (*notarius arcanarum Sancti Patris vulgo cifrarum secretarius*), once the depository of messages in code, now combines his work with that of the substitute secretary of state.
4. Under-datary of His Holiness, an official immediately under the cardinal datary.
5. Secretary for Latin letters (*litterarum latinarum scriba seu secretarius*), composes in Latin the letters and other documents confided to him directly by the pope.

The following three personages (6, 7, 8) work in weekly rotation in the pontifical antechamber. They are generally called participating privy chamberlains and not by the names of their original offices, which have practically ceased to exist.

6. Cupbearer (*pincerna*), replaces the master of the chamber in his absence, and holds the pope's candle and palm during liturgical functions.
7. Secretary of embassies (*nuntius*), presents papal homages and gifts to distinguished persons in Rome.

8. Keeper of the wardrobe (*vestiarius*), brings the red hats to new cardinals.

9. Sacristan of His Holiness (*praefectus sacrarii apostolici*), by custom since 1352 always an Augustinian; an archbishop in rank, who dwells in the Vatican, has the right to participate in conclaves, and stands near the papal throne during ceremonies. Since the time of Pius XI, he has also been the pope's vicar-general for the Vatican City.

Also in the noble privy antechamber is the grand master of the sacred hospice (*magister sacri hospitii*), the sole layman in the group. He receives and assists heads of state during their official visits to the pope, and replaces absent princes at the papal throne. The office has been hereditary for more than 2 centuries in the Ruspoli family.

Participating Privy Chamberlains of Sword and Cape. Each of these laymen (*cubicularii intimi ab ense et lacerna*) has a title that has been made hereditary in Roman patrician families by centuries-old privileges. The costume worn is the traditional dress of the Spanish court. In order of precedence these officials are:

1. Quartermaster general of the sacred palaces (*forerius major*), takes part in the procession when the pope solemnly leaves his private apartments; he was formerly in charge of construction, equipment, and the waterworks in the apostolic palace.

2. Master of the horse (*praefectus stabuli*), once supervised the grooms in the apostolic palace. The office remains in the Serlupi Crescenzi family.

3. Postmaster general (*praefectus tabellariorum*), formerly in charge of couriers and the postal service, as well as having other duties. The office is hereditary in the princely Massimo family.

4. Bearer of the *Golden Rose.

5. Secretary of embassies, a layman whose title dates from June 30, 1948; the office is distinct from the above-mentioned ecclesiastical one.

6. Captain commander, lieutenants (*tenenti*), and colonels (*esenti*) of the papal noble guard—all of these officers are participating chamberlains of sword and cape.

7. Colonel of the *Swiss Guard.

Domestic Prelates. This category includes those bearing the title of prelate in virtue of an office, or by direct concession of the pope. Members carry the title of right reverend monsignor.

Papal Noble Guard. This body, chosen from among the noble families of the former States of the Church, originated in 1801.

Privy Chamberlains. These personages compose the college of masters of papal ceremonies.

Supernumerary Privy Chamberlains. These ecclesiastics bear the title of very reverend monsignor.

Privy Chamberlains of Sword and Cape of His Holiness. These are lower in rank than the participating privy chamberlains of the same title, and higher than the honorary ones noted below.

Honorary Chamberlains in Purple Attire. These chamberlains (*in abito paonazzo*) have the same insignia and privileges as privy chamberlains, carry the title of monsignor, and accompany the pope to St. Peter's Basilica for sacred functions.

Honorary Chamberlains Outside the City. Instituted by Pope Pius VI (1775–99), these chamberlains (*extra Urbem*) serve the pope outside Rome. They bear the same title and privileges as the preceding group.

Honorary Chamberlains of Sword and Cape of His Holiness. These are laymen who serve in the throne room and at certain ceremonies. All are supernumeraries except four who are *de numero.*

Staff and Higher Officials of the Papal Armed Guards. In order of precedence, these are the Swiss Guards, the Palatine Guard of Honor, and the Papal Gendarmes. The colonel of the Swiss Guard is a member of the noble privy antechamber, as noted above.

Privy Chaplains. These ecclesiastics assist the Holy Father during sacred functions.

Honorary Privy Chaplains. The office of these ecclesiastics was instituted by Pope Clement XII (1730–40).

Honorary Privy Chaplains Extra Urbem. All of the members of this group and of the two preceding groups are monsignors; their garb is identical, and all of them lose their title with the death of the pope. Their office was established by Pius VII (1800–23).

Privy Clerics. Ecclesiastics assigned to the private chapel of the pope.

Common Papal Chaplains. These clerics form a college and hold office for life. There are two classes, participating and supernumerary; all wear the same dress. Their name derives probably from the public or common services they perform in ordinary public functions.

Apostolic Preacher. This title (*pontificiae aulae orator*) was reserved by Benedict XIV (1740–58) to Capuchins, and is given to the preacher assigned to deliver sermons during Lent and Advent in the presence of the pope, the cardinals, and the prelates of the Curia.

Confessor of the Papal Household. This office has been held by Servites since 1762.

Papal Physician. The personal physician to the Holy Father (*archiatra*).

Assistant of the Chamber. This personage serves, in a sense, as the pope's private chamberlain.

Privy Steward. This functionary (*scalco segreto*) supervises the pope's private table and solemn meals. Since 1923 the office has been vacant, because the supreme pontiffs have preferred the services of religious women.

Dean of the Hall. This official (*magister palafrenariae*) is in charge of the grooms and the bearers of the *sedia gestatoria.*

Doorkeepers. These are laymen, known as *bussolanti,* who assist visitors to the papal antechamber and examine invitations to papal audiences. Twelve of them are classified as participating, the others as supernumeraries.

Bibliography: H. SCHARP, *How the Catholic Church is Governed,* tr. A. DERRICK (New York 1960). T. ORTOLAN, DTC 3.2: 1931–83. G. FELICI, EncCatt 5:999–1008. P. TORQUEBIAU, DDC 4:726–729. AnnPont (1964) 1001–10 (composition of Papal Household), 1120–1299 (names of members), 1589–1601 (historical notes). R. RUFFO DELLA SCALETTA, "La famiglia pontificia," *Vaticano,* ed. G. FALLONI and M. ESCOBAR (Florence 1946) 159–190.

[A. GIOVANNETTI]

PAPAL LINE OF DEMARCATION. Portugal began exploring the west coast of Africa in 1418. Spain recognized Portuguese control of the Cape Verde Islands in the Treaty of Alcaçovas (1479), and Portugal

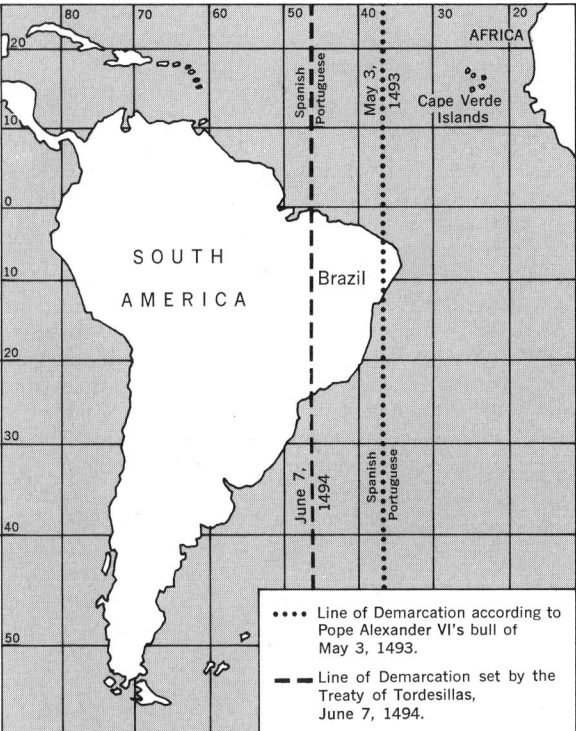

AFRICA

SOUTH AMERICA

Brazil

Cape Verde Islands

Spanish | Portuguese

May 3, 1493

June 7, 1494

Spanish | Portuguese

•••• Line of Demarcation according to Pope Alexander VI's bull of May 3, 1493.

━━ Line of Demarcation set by the Treaty of Tordesillas, June 7, 1494.

acknowledged Spanish ownership of the Canaries. Pope *Sixtus IV extended the blessings given Portugal in five earlier bulls and confirmed the treaty (1481). Forced into Lisbon by bad weather while returning from his first voyage, *Columbus explained his discoveries to King John II (March 9, 1493). John asserted exclusive rights south of the Canaries and west of Africa in the Atlantic. Before Columbus reached the court at Barcelona, the Spanish sovereigns reported to the new Pope, *Alexander VI, and a bull of May 3, 1493, confirmed Spanish title to lands newly discovered or to be discovered, provided they had never been in the possession of any Christian prince. Rights previously granted to Portugal were reserved, and the two governments were treated as equals.

But King *Ferdinand V demanded more. A second bull, predated May 3, was more emphatic than the first. A third bull, predated May 4, contained the Line of Demarcation between the spheres of influence of Spain and Portugal. Columbus suggested a line 100 leagues west of the Azores, believing he found there "a great change in the sky, the stars, the air temperature, and in the ocean. . . ." A fourth bull (Sept. 26, 1493) unfairly revoked earlier papal grants that seem to have given Portugal title to lands not in her possession on Christmas Day 1492. Serious diplomatic discussions opened (Aug. 18, 1493) after John began obvious preparations for war. Ferdinand and Isabella wrote to Columbus (September 5) concerning modification of the Demarcation Line. Spain and Portugal agreed on a line 370 leagues west of the Cape Verde Islands, longitude 46° 30′ west, in the Treaty of Tordesillas (June 7, 1494).

Earlier bulls, as well as that of 1481, recognized Portugal's exploring efforts, gave papal blessings to the declared intention of Christianizing natives, and attempted to preserve peace by asking observance of Portugal's commercial laws. The first two bulls of Alexander VI followed these precedents. The idea of the

Line of Demarcation was a logical definition of spheres of influence, and not an attempt to divide the world between two nations. The great colonial expansion of Portugal and Spain was carried on with remarkably little friction. It is clear, however, that Ferdinand of Aragon applied pressures to obtain the unreasonable fourth bull. He "used the Pope" as other statesmen have done before and since.

See also ALEXANDRINE BULLS.

Bibliography: F. G. DAVENPORT, ed., *European Treaties Bearing on the History of the U.S. and Its Dependencies,* 4 v. (Washington 1917–37) 1:33–100, texts and Eng. trs. of the treaties and bulls. H. VANDER LINDEN, "Alexander VI and the Demarcation of the Maritime and Colonial Domains of Spain and Portugal," AmHistRev 22 (1916–17) 1–20. D. J. HILL, *A History of Diplomacy in the International Development of Europe,* 3 v. (New York 1905–14). G. ZELLER, *Les Temps modernes,* 2 v. (Paris 1953–55) v.1.

[J. B. HEFFERNAN]

PAPAL REGISTERS

Papal registers (*regesta, regestra, registra*) are bound volumes containing copies of official papal letters and documents, today preserved in the *Vatican Archives (with a few exceptions). They represent a fairly continuous series from *Innocent III (1198–1216) onward, but there is evidence that registers were kept as early as the 4th century, and probably earlier. They followed the Roman imperial model of the *commentarii,* and were the work of the papal notaries, whose office eventually became the chancery by the 11th century (*see* CHANCERY, APOSTOLIC). Such records were essential, for the Roman pontiff ruled largely by promulgation and written acts and decrees. However, apart from the reconstructed register of *Gregory I (590–604), based on 9th-century and later materials, a late excerpt of *John VIII (872–882), the first contemporary register of *Gregory VII (1073–85), and some partial transcripts of the 12th century, e.g., of the antipope Anacletus II (1030–38; *see* PIERLEONI), none of the early registers have survived. We deduce their existence from various *canonical collections, e.g., the *Dionysiana, *Quesnelliana,* and *Britannica,* and the testimony of such canonists as Deusdedit (*see* DEUSDEDIT, COLLECTION OF) and *Anselm of Lucca. The order of registration was generally chronological (by indictions, and from Gregory VII onward by pontifical years). No attempt was made to classify matter until the 13th century, when, e.g., Innocent III ordered a *Regestum super negotio Romani imperii.* With the growth of papal administration and the problems created by the *Avignon papacy and the *Western Schism came an increasingly complicated system of registers.

There are three main series of papal registers. (1) Vatican Registers are the oldest and the most important. There are 2,042 items, mostly on parchment, opening properly with Innocent III (Reg. Vat. 4) in 1198 and extending to *Clement VIII (1592–1605). (2) Avignonese Registers were compiled at Avignon between 1316 and 1415, and remained there until the 18th century. There are 349 volumes on paper. The majority were transcribed into the Vatican Registers. They contain *Litterae communes* and *Litterae secretae.* (3) Lateran Registers constitute 2,467 volumes, kept in the *Lateran Palace until 1892. They cover the period between 1389 and 1897, but their contents concern only ecclesiastical and administrative matters, i.e., copies of *Litterae communes* (favor and justice). Many volumes are missing, especially as a result of the Napoleonic Wars.

The opening of the Vatican Archives to the scholarly world in 1881 fulfilled a long-felt need. The Archives constitute a major source for European history, especially that of the Middle Ages. The registers themselves are not easy to use, e.g., the chronological arrangement of the early registers makes it difficult to deal with problems that call for an arrangement by subject or place. Although the work of scholars such as P. *Jaffé, A. *Potthast, P. F. *Kehr, W. *Holtzmann, and others has helped to overcome this difficulty, much remains to be done. Nor are all the registers complete; fire, war, and forced sale took their toll. On the whole the Vatican Registers are the most useful. Some documents are of outstanding importance. Thus Gregory VII Reg. 2.55a (Caspar 202–208) is the famous *Dictatus Papae and 3.10a (Caspar 270–271) is the deposition of the Emperor *Henry IV. Finally, there is a continuing discussion among historians as to the method and form of compiling the registers, e.g., whether the corrected draft or the finished letter was the model, and also how far the registers are themselves original or merely transcripts of the original Chancery Registers. The likely solution is that no single system prevailed throughout.

Bibliography: For detailed studies, consult the numerous articles that have appeared in QuellForschItalArchBibl. P. RABI-KAUSKAS, LexThK² 8:59–60. R. L. POOLE, Lectures on the History of the Papal Chancery (Cambridge, Eng. 1915). Stickler. R. MORGHEN, "Ricerche sulla formazione del Registro di Gregorio VII," Annali di storia del diritto 3–4 (1959–60) 35–63. G. MOLLAT, DDC 7:536–538. "Bulletin of the Institute of Research and Study in Medieval Canon Law," Traditio 17 (1961) 551–552; 19 (1963) 551 contains bibliographical details of Studien und Vorarbeiten zur Edition der Register Papst Innozenz III, ed. L. SANTIFALLER.

[J. GILCHRIST]

PAPAL VOLUNTEERS FOR LATIN AMERICA (PAVLA)

are lay Catholics who offer themselves to the Church in Latin America for short-term service, normally for 3 years. Teams of candidates are enlisted as requested by Latin American bishops. Volunteers must be between 21 and 45 and have a spiritual motivation.

The Pontifical Commission for Latin America (CAL) approved PAVLA on April 20, 1960. The program in the United States is under the Bishops' Committee for Latin America and is administered through the NCWC Latin America Bureau, with a national secretariat in Chicago. More than 100 U.S. bishops have named PAVLA diocesan directors of recruitment programs. In addition to these diocesan units, lay volunteers for Latin America are recruited also by Catholic educational institutions, mission-sending societies of priests and sisters, and lay-sending societies such as the *Association for International Development, *Grail, *International Catholic Auxiliaries, and *Lay Mission Helpers Association.

Two independent training schools provide formation for candidates. The Center for Intercultural Formation administered by Fordham University conducts a Spanish-language institute at Cuernavaca, Mexico, and a Portuguese-language affiliate at Petropolis, Brazil. The Catholic University of Puerto Rico at Ponce conducts an Institute for Intercultural Communication.

As of September 1963 there were 245 Papal Volunteers in Latin America, serving in 12 countries and engaged primarily in teaching, medicine, social work, community development, and credit unions.

See also LAY MISSIONARIES.

[J. J. CONSIDINE]

PAPCZYŃSKI, STANISLAUS,

founder of the Marian Fathers; b. Podegrodzie, near Stary Sacz, Poland, May 18, 1631; d. Góra Kalwaria, Sept. 17, 1701. His baptismal name was John Baptist. He studied in the Piarist college in Podoliniec (Spicz) and in Jesuit colleges in Lvov and in Rawa Mazowiecka. In 1654 he entered the Piarist novitiate in Podoliniec, receiving the religious name Stanislaus of Jesus-Mary. In 1656, in Warsaw, at the close of his second novitiate combined with a theology course, he took his simple vows and became a subdeacon. In 1661 he was ordained at the Piarist college of Rzeszów. Transferred to Warsaw in 1663, he became renowned as a teacher of eloquence, a preacher, and confessor. In 1669 he was secularized, but in the act of his release from vows and the oath of perseverance in the Piarist Institute, Dec. 2, 1670, he solemnly promised God to continue in the religious life through the "Society of the Marian Clerics of the Immaculate Conception," which he planned to found. This new Marian Congregation received its first ecclesiastical approval in 1673, and he was appointed superior of a small hermitage at Korabiew (Puscza Mariańska), near Zyradów. In 1677 he fixed his residence in Nowa Jerozolima (Góra Kalwaria) near Warsaw and devoted the rest of his life to the government and canonical establishment of the Marians in the strict observance of the Norma Vitae, the consitutions he had written for them. Upon the approval of the Marians by the Holy See in 1701, Papczyński made his solemn profession, and he died a few months later. His body rests in the "Cenacle" Chapel of Góra Kalwaria. His beatification process, begun in 1769, was interrupted in 1775 and resumed in 1953. His principal writings are: Prodromus Reginae Artium (Cracow 1669), Templum Dei Mysticum (Cracow 1675), and Norma Vitae (Warsaw 1687).

Bibliography: G. A. NAVIKEVIČIUS, Stanislao di Gesù Maria Papczyński 1631–1701 (Doctoral diss. Gregorian U. Rome 1960). C. KRZYŻANOWSKI, Stanislaus a Jesu Maria Papczyński, . . . Magister studii perfectionis (Rome 1963).

[M. RZESZUTEK]

PAPERBACKS

The colloquial designation of paper-covered books of 100 pages or more (as distinguished from pamphlets), distributed in the U.S. through bookstores and the mass-market media of newsstands, drugstores, and grocery chains. Before the 1840s European printer-publishers customarily issued books without hard covers until edition binding was adopted in Great Britain, the U.S., and German-speaking countries; the Romance-language countries still prefer paper-covered editions.

After the U.S. Civil War, the development of wood-pulp papers, the inventions of linotype and electrotype, the wider use of stereotype, the proliferation of periodicals, and a nationwide system of rail transportation (and consequently of distribution) led to many reprint "libraries" such as Lovell's (New York 1882–90), which totaled almost 1,500 titles by 1890. The 1891 International Copyright Act acted as a deterrent to further expansion. During World War II the Armed Services Editions published 1,324 titles; their financial success encouraged Robert de Graff to establish Pocket Books, Inc., in June 1939, followed within 2 months in the U.S. by Penguin Books Inc., already successfully launched in England in 1935. Several hundred firms now issue paperbacks.

Since paperback sales depend heavily on visual appeal as well as price, lurid illustrations have often stressed sex, sadism, and smoking guns in cover art and contents, against which criticism has been primarily directed. The mode of mass-market distributions through outlets patronized by children and adolescents has often stirred group action against such ready availability. To counter harmful social effects, various U.S. state legislatures have passed restrictive measures while so-called "extralegal" action has been taken by various private groups, notably the National Organization for Decent Literature (now the *National Office for Decent Literature) founded by the U.S. hierarchy in December 1938. Community and group pressure campaigns have engendered much opposition from the American Book Publishers Association, the American Civil Liberties Union, and *Publishers' Weekly;* this phase is well summarized in Gardiner (see bibliography). *See* CENSORSHIP.

Although several Catholic publishers, such as the Catechetical Guild, P. J. Kenedy & Sons, the Paulist Press, and Sheed & Ward, had developed several relatively small series of paperbacks, the major breakthrough occurred in 1954 with the Image Book series (Doubleday & Co.), which has since issued 16 to 20 titles annually. Other firms (e.g., the Daughters of St. Paul, Fides Publishers, the University of Notre Dame Press) have published exclusively Catholic series while some general firms (e.g., All Saints Press, Harper and Row, Dell Publishing Co., New American Library, and Penguin Books) have had strong Catholic categories within a larger subject context. The annual *Catalog of Catholic Paperback Books* provides an index to more than 2,000 in-print titles. An ever-expanding trend toward reprints of more scholarly works began in 1953 with Doubleday's Anchor Books series. Paperbacks on this level have been beneficial in educational circles and have encouraged the formation of personal libraries.

Bibliography: F. LEWIS, "Paper-Bound Books in America," *Bowker Lectures on Book Publishing* (collected ed. New York 1957). F. L. SCHICK, *The Paperbound Book in America* (New York 1958). H. C. GARDINER, *Catholic Viewpoint on Censorship* (rev. ed. Image Books; New York 1961). E. P. WILLGING, *Catalog of Catholic Paperback Books* (New York 1959–). *Catholic Book Merchandiser* (New York 1958–). *Paperbound Books in Print* (New York 1955–). Moral evaluations appear monthly in *Best Sellers* (Scranton, Pa. 1941–).

[E. P. WILLGING]

PAPHNUTIUS, the name of many monks in the Egyptian desert, among whom the more important were:

St. Paphnutius, a bishop of the Upper *Thebaid who attended the Council of Nicaea, 325, and the Synod of Tyre, 335 (feast, Sept. 11). His left knee had been mutilated and his right eye torn out in the persecution of Maximinus. He was esteemed by *Constantine I and by the prelates at Nicaea. It was perhaps due to his influence that the Council left the question of continence to the discretion of those clergy who hade been married before ordination. If this Paphnutius is the

"confessor and monk" to whom a miracle is attributed in the *Vita Antonii* (58; see R. Meyer, tr., ACW 10:69, 122, n. 198), he may also be the "anchorite . . . of the desert about Heracleos . . . in the Thebaid" mentioned in the *Historia Monachorum* (16).

Paphnutius, the Buffalo, anchorite and priest of the desert of Scete. He was 90 years old when visited by John *Cassian in 395, and was the only monastic leader in Scete to hold a public reading of the letter of the Patriarch *Theophilus of Alexandria condemning anthropomorphism (397).

St. Paphnutius, anchorite who suffered martyrdom under Diocletian, according to the Roman Martyrology (feast, Sept. 24).

Bibliography: H. DELEHAYE, ed., "Passio," AnalBoll 40 (1922) 328–343, Gr. ActSS Sept. 6:681–688, Lat. SOCRATES, *Hist. eccl.* 1:11 in PG 67:102–106. SOZOMEN, *Hist. eccl.* 1:23 in PG 67:925–926. Hefele-Leclercq v.1.1. J. CASSIAN, *Conlationes,* ed. M. PETSCHENIG (CSEL 13; 1886) 3:4.1, 10.2–3, Paphnutius the Buffalo. H. LECLERCQ, DACL 13.1:1358–61.

[M. C. MC CARTHY]

PAPIAS OF HIERAPOLIS, bishop and chronicler of primitive Christianity; b. *c.* A.D. 60 or 70; d. *c.* 125. Information on Papias is supplied by *Eusebius of Caesarea (*Hist. Eccl.* 2.15.2, 3.39.13) and *Irenaeus of Lyons (*Adv. haer.* 5.33.4). Irenaeus testifies that Papias heard the Apostle John preach and was acquainted with Polycarp; Eusebius makes mention of his *Explanation of the Sayings of the Lord* (in 5 bks.). In the preface to this work, Papias asserts that his main endeavor is to record the truth, that he had made a collection of the *logia* (sayings that included both words and deeds) of the Apostles that were reported to him by a presbyter. Irenaeus took this to mean that Papias was quoting the Evangelist John, whereas Eusebius maintains that Papias spoke of two Johns, indicating the Evangelist as one, and the other as the companion of Aristion, one of the presbyters, or elders, of the primitive Church (*Hist. Eccl.* 3.39.7). Eusebius further believed that the second John was the author of the Apocalypse and accused Papias of transmitting the heretical doctrine of *Chiliasm to Irenaeus and other early churchmen (*ibid.* 3.39.12–13).

Papias stated that Mark the Evangelist was the interpreter of Peter, that Mark had never heard Christ, but that he had carefully recorded everything he remembered from Peter's preaching (*ibid.* 3.39.15). Of Matthew, Papias maintained that he "wrote down the *logia* of the Savior in the Hebrew *dialektikos* [language or dialect], and each one interpreted them as best he could" (3.39.16). Irenaeus took this to refer to the Hebraisms that appear frequently in Matthew's Gospel. Origen, however, thought it meant that Matthew had originally written his Gospel in Hebrew. Papias also witnessed to the existence of the apocryphal Gospel according to the Hebrews, out of which he reported a story of the woman taken in adultery that differs from the disputed pericope in John's Gospel (7.53–8.11). Papias refers to the daughters of the Apostle Philip, who told him of a miracle concerning a certain Justus Barsabbas, as well as, in Eusebius's judgment, several bizarre parables attributed to the Savior (*Hist. Eccl.* 3.39.9–13).

Papias's exegesis was used not merely by Irenaeus but by Origen and Western theologians down to *Victorinus of Pettau. His testimony, however, has raised many problems in regard to the formation of the Gospel texts, an Aramaic version of Matthew, the identity of the two Johns, and other problems in the history of the primitive Church. According to a late legend he died a martyr.

Bibliography: Quasten Patr 1:82–85. G. BARDY, DTC 11.2: 1944–47. M. JOURJON, DBSuppl 6:1104–1109. J. KÜRZINGER, LexThK² 8:34–36. E. PREUSCHEN, ed. and tr., *Antilegomena* (2d ed. Giessen 1905) 91–99, 195–202. K. BIHLMEYER, ed., *Die Apostolischen Väter* (2d ed. Tübingen 1956–) 133–140. F. WOTKE, Pauly-Wiss RE 18.2 (1949) 966–976. J. F. BLIGH, ThSt 13 (1952) 234–240. J. MUNCK, HarvThRev 52 (1959) 223–243; *Neotestamentica et Patristica* (Leiden 1962) 249–260. K. BEYSCHLAG, *Studia patristica*, v.4 (TU 79; 1961) 268–280.

[F. X. MURPHY]

PAPIAS THE LOMBARD, lexicographer; fl. northern Italy, possibly Pavia, *c.* 1050. Probably a married cleric, he was the father of two sons, to whom he dedicated his works. In addition to a Latin grammar (still in MS), he is credited with an alphabetic glossary, the *Elementarium doctrinae rudimentum* (*c.* 1053), which served for centuries as an encyclopedic manual of reference. A work of compilation, it depended on the 8th-century *Liber glossarum;* on Isidore of Seville, Boethius, Priscian, and other grammarians; on the *Physiologus;* and on Remigius of Auxerre. Frequently cited without credit by later authors, the work of Papias was significant for the development of medieval *lexicography. The *Elementarium* has survived in more than 90 MSS and was first printed in Milan (1476).

Bibliography: G. GOETZ, "Papias und seine Quellen," SB Münch, Phil.-hist. Abt. (1903) 267–286. Manitius 2:717–724; 3:191, 192, 790. A. FINGERLE, LexThK² 8:36. C. VASOLI, EncFil 3:1146.

[O. J. BLUM]

PAPINEAU, LOUIS JOSEPH, Canadian politician; b. Montreal, Canada, Oct. 7, 1786; d. Monte Bello, Quebec, Canada, Sept. 23, 1871. After his studies at the Seminary of Quebec, Papineau served as deputy from Kent County (Chambly) from 1808 to 1811, becoming a lawyer in Lower Canada in 1810. He was an officer in the Canadian militia during the War of 1812 and took part in the capture of Detroit, Mich. As elected representative (1814) of Montreal West in the legislative assembly of Lower Canada, he was chosen speaker (1815), and he fulfilled these duties without interruption until the outbreak of the rebellion of 1837–38.

Papineau was the head of the French-Canadian reformers, or *Patriotes,* and was their main spokesman. He opposed the bill for uniting the provinces and went to England in 1822 to protest against it. The soul of the nationalist movement, he became the implacable foe of the British government in Canada. Although he was opposed to violence and recommended constitutional resistance in Parliament, his policies, labeled by Bp. J. J. Lartigue of Montreal as outrageous and fraught with danger, led to revolution. When the Association of the Sons of Liberty was founded in Montreal (1837) and set itself up as an armed corps, Papineau recognized the danger and recommended constitutional resistance and an embargo on British goods. Although he took no part in the armed revolution, he encouraged the insurgents by his presence at meetings. Forced to take refuge at Albany, N.Y., shortly after the outbreak of hostilities,

Papineau spent 2 years in exile and was unsuccessful in enlisting American intervention. He then left for France, where he lived in Paris until the Canadian government granted him an amnesty in 1844. Returning to Canada, he became a member of the legislative assembly (1848–54), after which he retired from public life to his manorhouse of Monte Bello. Papineau followed, rather than led, public opinion; and his vacillation during the rebellion of 1837 greatly discredited him. He is important chiefly for his sponsorship of the Red (Liberal) party. His religious convictions were shaken during his stay in France, and he died impenitent.

Bibliography: A. D. DE CELLES, *Papineau, 1786–1871* (Montreal 1905); *Louis Joseph Papineau* (Toronto 1911); *Papineau, Cartier* (New York 1926). R. RUMILLY, *Papineau* (Paris 1934).

[G. CARRIÈRE]

PAPINI, GIOVANNI

Italian novelist, poet, critic; b. Florence, Jan. 9, 1881; d. there, July 8, 1956. He was largely self-taught, but had a wide range of intellectual interests. He began writing at 14 and produced no less than 65 volumes of fiction, poetry, philosophy, literary criticism, theology, and history.

Up to the time of his conversion to Christianity in 1921, he had ventured all sorts of intellectual experiment, becoming ever more pessimistic, but at the same time more eager to find meaning and unity in life. Dissatisfied with the social and cultural conditions of his age, he founded, with G. Prezzolini, the review *Il Leonardo* (1903), whose program was to demolish *positivism in philosophy and academicism and tradition in literature, and to modernize Italian culture by opening it to European thought, mainly Bergsonianism and Anglo-American pragmatism (*see* BERGSON, HENRI; PRAGMATISM). He was particularly attracted to pragmatism; in the "will to believe," Papini thought to find the key to liberation from the entanglements of systematic doctrines and the promise of unlimited power that satisfied his extreme individualism. In 1907 *Il Leonardo* ceased publication, but Papini continued his campaign against positivism in *La Voce,* founded in 1908. His *Il Crepuscolo dei filosofi* (1906), *Ventiquattro cervelli* (1912), and *Pragmatismo* (1913) are characteristic of his intellectual quest.

Unable to reconstruct after demolishing, and yearning for the absolute although he was too critical to believe in it, Papini felt, during this period of *Sturm und Drang,* the futility of searching for eternal values through philosophy and science. *Un Uomo Finito* (1912) is a pathetic assessment of his intellectual failure. In 1913 he joined the futurist group of the review *Lacerba,* finding a temporary affinity with their program of total rejection of traditional culture, and in its pages he conducted an inflammatory campaign for Italian intervention in World War I. When he was rejected for war service, he sought consolation for his restless mind in literary creation and criticism—*Cento pagine di poesia* (1915), *Stroncature* (1916), *L'Uomo Carducci* (1918), and *L'Esperienza futurista* (1920).

The disillusionment of the war, the social and moral corruption of the immediate postwar period, and the never satisfied desire for absolute certitude turned Papini to the study of the Gospels, in which he saw the only doctrine capable of regenerating the world. The fruit of this study and meditation was *La Storia di Cristo* (1921), a work neither theological nor scientific in nature, but one impregnated with love and hope. Although the sincerity of Papini's conversion was questioned, his *Storia di Cristo* was notably successful. There were 35 editions in Italian and 25 in other languages.

From 1921 to the end of his life, Papini was a staunch defender of Christian thought and a critic of contemporary society, constantly concerned with deepening his faith. While always showing deference to the authority of the Church in theological matters, he maintained a certain intellectual independence which he considered vital to Catholic thought. The list of his works attests to his relentless activity—notable are: *Gli Operai della vigna* (1929), portraits of saints and artists who imitated God's work; *Sant'Agostino* (1930); *Gog* (1931), a bitter satire on modern society; *Dante vivo* (1933); *Vita di Michelangelo* (1949); *Lettere agli uomini di Papa Celestino Sesto* (1946), focusing on man's great dilemma — be Christianized or die. But the most astonishing book of the later period of his life was *Il Diavolo* (1953), which shocked the Catholic world and was placed on the Index. In *Le Pazzie del poeta* (1950), he had shown a certain reluctance to accept the dogma of eternal punishment; in *Il Diavolo* he expressed his ardent hope that God's mercy might prevail over His justice and that in the end the cursed angel would be restored to his celestial seat. This paradoxical plea for final reconciliation and the end of universal antithesis was the last notable manifestation of a tormented mind whose mistaken generosity carried him beyond the Christian concept of charity.

Bibliography: *Tutte le opere di Giovanni Papini* (Milan 1958–). E. PALMIERI, *Giovanni Papini* (Florence 1927). A. VIVIANI, *Gianfalco: Storia e vita* (Florence 1934). R. RIDOLFI, *Vita di Giovanni Papini* (Milan 1957).

[G. GULLACE]

PAPINI TARTAGNI, NICCOLÒ, historian, b. San Giovanni Valdarno, Italy, 1751; d. Terni, Dec. 16, 1834. He served as minister general of the *Franciscan Conventuals (1803–09). He was a contemporary and successor of Giovanni Giacinto *Sbaraglia in the historical research on the *Franciscans, and his published works are all in the area of Franciscan history. These include *Etruria francescana* (part 1ª, Siena 1787; part 2ª, unpublished), *Notizie sicure della morte, sepoltura, canonizzazione e traslazione di s. Francesco e del ritrovamento del di lui corpo* (Florence 1822; Foligno 1824), *Storia del Perdono di Assisi* (Florence 1824), *Storia di s. Francesco d' Assisi* (2 v. Foligno 1825–27, 3d unedited) and "Index Fratrum Minorum Conventualium qui scientias et artes, conducti, publice tradiderunt," *Miscellanea Francescana* 31 (1931); 32 (1932). His unpublished bibliographical works can be found in the archives of the general Curia of the Franciscan Conventuals in Rome. They are in a folio volume, Cod.c. 128, *Appendix ad supplementum scriptorum Franciscanorum P. M. Hyacinthi Sbaraglii; Scriptores ordinis Minorum Conventualium ab anno 1650 ad annum 1820,* which also includes a supplementary appendix and a second essay continuing the list to the year 1830. A MS, *I et II Index onomasticus scriptorum universae Franciscanae familiae seu trium ordinum S. Francisci ab origine usque ad annum MCDL,* dated

1828, is in the collections of the National Library of Florence, No. II ii, 181.

Bibliography: D. SPARACIO, "Gli studi di storia e i minori conventuali," *Miscellanea Francescana* 20 (1919) 56–64. G. ABATE, EncCatt 9:782–783.

[J. J. SMITH]

PAPYROLOGY

The study of ancient documents written on papyri (plural of papyrus). Papyrus [Greek ὁ or ἡ πάπυρος, ἡ βίβλος (*see* BIBLE, I); Latin *papyrus;* as writing material also Greek ὁ χάρτης, Latin *charta*] was the name given to a certain plant (*Cyperus papyrus* L.) and to a writing material made from it in antiquity. The papyrus plant, which was cultivated especially in the delta of the Nile, was put to various practical uses, e.g., for the making of rafts and boats in Egypt.

Writing Material. The most important use of papyrus, however, was in the manufacture of a writing material that was employed by the Egyptians from the 3d millennium B.C., by the Greeks from the 6th century B.C., and by the Romans from the 3d century B.C. until well into the Middle Ages, when it was supplanted by paper. (Although the word paper is derived from the word papyrus, paper is made by an entirely different process.) On the ancient use of papyrus, see Herodotus, *Hist.* 2.92; Theophrastes, *Hist. plant.* 4.8, 3; Pliny, *Hist. nat.* 13.11(68)–12(83); S. N. Lewis, *L'Industrie du papyrus dans l'Égypte Greco-Romaine* (Paris 1934). According to Pliny [*ibid.* 13.12(74)], for the making of the writing material the pith of papyrus stalks was sliced into thin strips (called σχίζαι in Greek and *scissurae* or *philyrae* in Latin), a number of the strips were laid vertically side by side, over these a number of strips were laid horizontally side by side, and the two layers were pressed together, dried out, and rubbed smooth, to form oblong leaves. The finished leaves were called σελίδες in Greek and *plagulae* in Latin. Several such leaves (20 of them according to Pliny, *ibid.*) were then pasted side by side (hence the word κόλλημα, literally "a glueing," came to mean page or column) in such a way that the sides of the leaves with the horizontal fibers were all kept on the same (upper or recto) side of the long sheet. Sheets were made in different lengths and heights. A finished sheet was rolled around a narrow cyclinder (*scapus*) with the recto on the inside, and so it was offered for sale. The sheet itself was often called a *scapus* ("roll" of papyrus). The long sheet either served as a *scroll (volumen)* on which lengthy documents, especially literary works, were written, or the individual pages were cut from it for the writing of short documents, letters, etc. Writing was put ordinarily only on the recto with its horizontal fibers, seldom on the back or verso with its vertical fibers. A papyrus written on the verso was called an ὀπισθόγραφον.

The earliest instrument used for writing on papyrus was a sedge stalk cut off at an angle at one end or frayed at the end into a sort of small brush. After the 3d century B.C. a thin reed (κάλαμος, *calamus*) sharpened to a point and split at one end was used as a pen. The ordinary ink used for writing was black (μέλαν, *atramentum*), made from soot; but other colors, such as brown (sepia) and crimson (ἔγκαυστον, *encaustum*) were employed. Pictorial additions were in cinnabar (vermillion) or other colors.

Papyrus fragment, 4th century (Brit. Mus. Pap. 1532v) with the text of Heb 12.1–11.

In pharaonic times the Egyptian manufacture of papyrus was a monopoly of the individual temples and their priests; in Ptolemaic times it was a state monopoly. In the Byzantine and Arabic periods the first leaf (πρωτόκολλον, whence the word protocol) of a papyrus roll was impressed with a government stamp stating where and when the roll was made. According to its quality there were various kinds of papyrus, from the fine *charta hieratica* or *regia* (*Augusta, Livia*) down to ordinary wrapping material (*charta emporetica*); see Pliny, *Hist. Nat.* 13.74–79; Isidorus, *Orig.* 6.9. Writing was done on other material also, such as potsherds (*see* OSTRACON), wax tablets, and *parchment. In the early imperial period literary texts began, apparently in Christian circles, to be written on separate leaves that were bound in a codex (modern book form). Parchment was more suitable for this purpose and soon was the only material used for codices. Smaller documents, however, continued to be written on papyrus for many centuries, e.g., in the papal chancery until the 11th century.

Papyrus Manuscripts, Papyri. Outside of Egypt, where the climate was kind to them, ancient and medieval papyrus MSS have almost entirely fallen victims to the destructive forces of time. Only by accident have a few Latin papyrus codices or fragments of them and some papyrus documents been preserved in European libraries and archives. Thus in papyrus there are a codex of Josephus's *Jewish Antiquities* in Milan; a codex of some of St. Hilary's works in Vienna; individual leaves of a codex containing some sermons and letters of St. Augustine in Paris, Geneva, and Leningrad; a codex containing extracts from St. Isidore's *Synonyma* and a homily of St. Eucherius in St. Gall, Switzerland; and a codex containing some of the writings of St. Avitus of Vienne in Paris. Some of the other preserved papyrus documents are a few dozen papal bulls in French, Italian, German, and Spanish archives, in addition to

some 800 mostly Greeks scrolls containing philosophical works recovered in 1572 from the ruins of the city of Herculaneum that was covered with lava from Mt. Vesuvius in A.D. 79. A few papyrus documents have been found also at *Dura-Europos on the Euphrates, at Nessana in the *Negeb of Palestine, and at some other places (see Preisendanz, *Papyrusfunde* 18–66; *Handbuch* 166–170).

Papyri from Egypt. Large masses of papyrus MSS written in ancient Egyptian, Coptic, Arabic, Persian, Aramaic, Hebrew, Latin, and especially Greek have been found only in the sand-covered graves, ruins, and rubbish piles of the ancient settlements of the native land of the papyrus plant, rain-poor Egypt. As early as the end of the 18th century and the beginning of the 19th the learned world became aware of Egyptian papyri through accidental finds. But it was only in 1877 that the interests of scholars was fully aroused by the discovery of an immense amount of papyrus MSS at El Faiyûm (site of the ancient city of Arsinoë), and impetus was thereby given to organized excavations by European and American scholars, especially in the ruins of the Faiyûm regions (at Arsinoë, Soknopaiu Nēsos, Theadelphia, Tebtynis, and Philadelphia) and in Heracleopolis Magna, Oxyrhynchus, Hermopolis Magna, El Ḥiba, *Thebes (No-Amon), Panopolis, *Syene, *Elephantine, and other places. (For the location of these places on a map, *see* EGYPT.)

Some of the papyri that were discovered in these excavations have been kept in Egyptian museums (in Alexandria and Cairo). But most of the papyri entered public or private collections in Europe or America, especially in England (London, Oxford, and Manchester), Ireland (Dublin), France (Paris, Lille, and Strasbourg), Italy (Milan, Turin, Florence, and Naples), Germany (Berlin, Munich, Heidelberg, Giessen, Marburg, Jena, and Würzburg), Holland (Leiden), Norway, Denmark,

Russia (Tiflis), Switzerland (Basel, Geneva, and Zurich), and the U.S. (Ann Arbor, Chicago, Princeton, New York, Berkeley, and other cities). In these collections the papyri, which were usually found in a damaged and soiled condition, have been restored, preserved, and scientifically studied by specialists in papyrology, a discipline that has been developed for this purpose. By the 1960s about 7,000 papyri had been published, and the number of those still unedited in the collections and still hidden in the sands of Egypt is no doubt several times that amount.

Contents. The papyri have thrown lasting light on all branches of the study of antiquity: not only *Egyptology and Arabic studies, but especially classic philology and the history of Greek and Roman law, economics, sociology, and religion. Classical philology has been enriched by the discovery of many literary papyri, mostly from the 1st to the 3d century, containing fragmentary or even complete classical works that previously had either been preserved in much more recent parchment MSS or been considered entirely lost, e.g., Aristotle's Ἀθηναίων Πολιτεία (*Constitution of Athens*), Sophocles' Ἰχνευταί (*The Investigators*), Herondas's *Mimes,* Bacchylides' *Choral Odes,* and Menander's Δύσκολος (*The Discontented Man*), and other comedies. However, not only classical studies but other disciplines also have been greatly benefited by the many thousands of papyrus MSS that have been discovered, such as official edicts and decrees, business documents, financial accounts, invoices, receipts, last wills, contracts (for sales, rents, loans, hiring, teaching, and marriage), and letters. Such papyri give a faithful and impressive picture of all public and private life in Egypt until the Arabic period.

The study of the script and language of these records has made it possible to obtain for the first time an accurate knowledge of the development both of Greek handwriting from the 4th century B.C. to the 10th Christian century and of the colloquial Greek language (Κοινή) throughout the same period, so that the Biblical *Greek language, which previously had been a rather isolated phenomenon, can now be assigned its rightful place in this development.

Biblical and Christian Papyri. The papyri are of immense importance for all branches of theological studies, but especially for Biblical studies, since many of the papyri contain fragments of OT and NT books (such as some in the Chester Beatty Papyri, the Freer Collection, the Bodmer Collection, and others) that go back, at least in part (e.g., P⁶² of the Fourth Gospel from A.D. 125), to the 2d century. They are therefore much older than the oldest parchment MSS and consequently of inestimable value for Biblical textual criticism. *See* BIBLE, V (TEXTUAL CRITICISM). At least fragments of every book of the NT except 1 and 2 Timothy and 2 and 3 John are preserved in the papyri.

Of scarcely less value are the Greek and Coptic papyri that contain liturgical or patristic texts, e.g., those of the 1941 find at Tura of writings of Origen and Didymus, the menologies (liturgical calendars), the *libelli* (documents certifying that the persons named in them have offered sacrifice to the gods) from the Decian persecution (middle of the 3d century), certain Gnostic apocrypha (as the *Gospel of Thomas* and the *Gospel of Truth* found at Nag' Hammâdi) and other heretical writings, and last but not least, numerous incantation

and other magical texts. All these religious texts, together with the secular documents, bring to life for modern man the world in which the gospel was first preached and offer him a vivid picture of Egypt's early Christian life, of its flourishing monasticism, of the turbulence of its religious quarrels and schisms, and even of the continuance, in the Christian era, of its ancient pagan superstitions, concepts, and customs.

Bibliography: Manuals and introductions. L. MITTEIS and U. WILCKEN, *Grundzüge und Chrestomathie der Papyruskunde,* 4 v. (Leipzig-Berlin 1912). W. SCHUBART, *Einführung in die Papyruskunde* (Berlin 1918). A. CALDERINI, *Papyri: Guida allo studio della papirologia antica Greca e Romana* (Milan 1944). W. PEREMANS and V. VERGOTE, *Papyrologisch Handboek* (Louvain 1942). F. G. KENYON, *Books and Readers in Ancient Greece and Rome* (2d ed. Oxford 1951). K. PREISENDANZ, *Papyrusfunde und Papyrusforschung* (Leipzig 1933); "Papyruskunde," *Handbuch der Bibliothekswissenschaft,* ed. G. LEYH, v.1 (2d ed. Wiesbaden 1952) 163–248, extensive history of the discoveries and collections, with bibliog. of the whole pertinent literature. A. BATAILLE, *Les Papyrus* (Paris 1955), with extensive bibliog. also for the language and script and a list of the *religionsgeschichtlich* papyrus literature, 58–66. H. HUNGER et al., eds., *Geschichte der Textüberlieferung der antiken und mittelalterlichen Literatur,* v.1 (Zurich 1961) 29–50, 72–113, 168–170. H. METZGER, *Wege und Probleme der Papyrusforschung,* v.2 *Die frühchristliche Welt im Lichte der Papyri* (Schweizer Beiträge zur Allgemeinen Geschichte 10; 1952) 199–208. C. H. ROBERTS, *Greek Literary Hands, 350 B.C.–A.D. 400* (Oxford 1956).

Encyclopedia articles. H. LECLERCQ, DACL 13.1:1370–1520, with extensive bibliog. and many illustrations. E. LEVESQUE and F. PRAT, DB 4:2079–94. B. BOTTE, DBSuppl 6:1109–20. EncBibl 5:3556–63. A. CALDERINI, EncCatt 9:783–787. H. GERSTINGER, LexThK² 8:63–65. A. DEISSMANN, Herzog-Hauck PRE 14:667–675. K. TREU, RGG³ 5:91–93. EncDictBibl 1704–13.

Publications of papyri. These are listed in most of the works mentioned above under Manuals and introductions, esp. those of Preisendanz and Bataille; current pubs. are given in the period. mentioned below under Periods., with current reports and bibliogs.; among the more recent pubs. are the following. J. O. TJAEDER, *Die nichtliterarischen lateinischen Papyri Italiens aus der Zeit 445–700* (Lund 1955). R. CAVENAILE, ed., *Corpus papyrorum latinorum* (Vienna 1956–). V. A. TCHERIKOVER et al., eds., *Corpus papyrorum Judaicorum,* 3 v. (Cambridge, Mass. 1957–64).

Selections and special eds. E. J. GOODSPEED and E. C. COLWELL, *A Greek Papyrus Reader* (Chicago 1935). A. S. HUNT et al., *Select Papyri,* 3 v. (New York 1932–50). W. SCHUBART, *Ein Jahrtausend am Nil: Briefe aus dem Altertum verdeutscht und erklärt* (2d ed. Berlin 1923). J. G. WINTER, *Life and Letters in the Papyri* (Ann Arbor 1933). H. THIERFELDER, *Unbekannte antike Welt: Eine Darstellung nach Papyrusurkunden* (Gütersloh 1963). A. DEISSMANN, *Light from the Ancient East,* tr. L. R. M. STRACHAN (rev. ed. New York 1927). G. GHEDINI, *Lettere cristiane dai papiri greci del III e IV secolo* (Milan 1923). C. DEL GRANDE, ed., *Liturgiae, preces, hymni christianorum e papyris collecti* (Naples 1938). R. KNIPFING, "The Libelli of the Decian Persecution," HarvThRev 16 (1923) 345–390. A. BLUDAU, "Die ägyptischen Libelli und die Christenverfolgungen des Kaiser Decius," RömQuartalsch 27 (1913), suppl. K. PREISENDANZ, et al., eds., *Papyri graecae magicae,* 2 v. (Leipzig 1928–31).

Periodicals, with current reports and bibliogs. *Aegyptus: Revista italiana di egittologia e papirologia* (Milan 1920–). *Archiv für Papyrusforschung und verwandte Gebiete* (Leipzig 1900–). *Chronique d'Égypte* (Brussels 1925–). *Études de papyrologie* (Cairo 1932–). *The Journal of Egyptian Archaeology* (London 1914–). *The Journal of Juristic Papyrology* (New York 1946–). *Mizraim: Journal of Papyrology* (Philadelphia 1933–). *Revue des études grecques* (Paris 1888–). *Recherches de papyrologie: Travaux de l'Institut de papyrologie de Paris* (Paris 1961–). *Studia papyrologica: Revista española de papirología* (Barcelona 1962–).

Lists of published papyri. R. A. PACK, *The Greek and Latin Literary Texts from Greco-Roman Egypt* (2d ed. Ann Arbor 1965). Biblical papyri. A. RAHLFS, *Verzeichnis der griechischen Handschriften des AT* (Berlin 1914). M. M. PARVIS and A. P. WIKGREN, eds., *NT Manuscript Studies* (Chicago 1950). G. MALDFELD and B. M. METZGER, "Detailed List of the Greek Papyri of the NT," JBiblLit 68 (1949) 359–370. G. MALDFELD, "Die griechischen Handschriften des NT auf Papyrus," ZNT

Wiss 42 (1949) 228–253; 43 (1950–51) 260–261. F. G. KENYON, *Our Bible and the Ancient Manuscripts*, 5th ed. rev. A. W. ADAMS (New York 1958) 113–119, 185–190. W. C. VAN UNNIK, *Evangelien aus dem Nilsand* (Frankfurt 1960). O. PARET, *Die Bibel: Ihre Überlieferung in Druck und Schrift* (Stuttgart 1949) 50–52. **Illustration credit:** Courtesy of the Trustees of the British Museum.

[H. GERSTINGER]

PARABLES OF JESUS

Before undertaking to describe the characteristics of Jesus' parables, this article discusses the nature of a parable and reviews the history of parable exegesis; a final section is devoted to special problems.

Nature of Parable. The English word parable is from the Greek παραβολή, whose root connotation involves the placing of things side by side for the sake of comparison; it was a technical term for a figure of speech in ancient oratory. Since many studies of the parables of Jesus approach the subject from the background of this technical usage, some relevant points about figures of speech must be set forth.

The most basic forms of illustration are the simile and the metaphor. In a simile one thing is likened or compared to another thing of a different kind for illustrative purposes (often with the words "like" or "as"); for example, "Woe to you, scribes and Pharisees, hypocrites! because you are like whitewashed tombs" (Mt 23.27). This colorful method of description is common in ordinary speech. A metaphor is a compressed simile in which one thing is identified or equated with another, or the qualities of one thing are directly ascribed to another; for example, "You are the salt of the earth" (Mt 5.13); "Beware of the leaven of the Pharisees" (Mk 8.15). This figure is more literary than the simile and is frequent in poetry.

The more elaborate forms of illustration, the parable and the allegory, are really expansions of the basic figures. A parable is a developed simile in which the story, while fictitious, is true to life. The latter feature differentiates a parable from a fable. Parables are frequently used today in speeches and sermons in which the speaker tells a story whose moral or punch line illustrates his topic. An *allegory is a developed metaphor prolonged into continuous narrative. Ideally, in the technical and classical usage, the parable is distinct from allegory. In the parable the details and characters have no hidden meaning; the important thing is the lesson of the story. Details serve only to bring out the principal point. Another mark of differentiation is that the parable, like the simile, is a popular and less literary figure of speech. But in practice the traits of allegory are often present in a parable. The story may have one principal point (parable), but some of the characters may have a significance of their own. Already Quintilian, the 1st-century Latin authority on oratory, recognized such intermingling.

History of Parable Exegesis. The importance of understanding these figures of speech is illustrated in the history of the interpretation of the Gospel parables. In the exegesis of the Church Fathers the parables of Jesus were treated as allegories, and the Fathers were greatly concerned with the significance of all the details of the parables. In this treatment, they indulged in an exegesis that is rather fanciful for our taste today, although beneath this allegorizing the Fathers often came to a valid basic interpretation of the parable involved.

It is in modern times that a violent reaction to the long centuries of allegorizing the parables is encountered. The German Protestant scholar A. *Jülicher, in *Die Gleichnisreden Jesu* (2 v. Freiburg 1888–89) rejected 18 centuries of allegorizing and insisted that the parables of Jesus were simple, moralizing stories. The parables had one point, and no one should seek hidden meaning in the details or characters of the parables; allegory is a literary figure, and Jesus was a simple preacher.

The wide implications of this popular position are very serious. As they are reported in the Gospels, some of the parables of Jesus have obvious allegorical characteristics, e.g., the parable of the Tenants in the Vineyard (Mk 12.1–11), where the characters are identifiable. If one were to follow Jülicher's principle strictly, the allegorical features would indicate that the parable could not be attributed to Jesus but would have to be regarded as a literary creation of the early Church. Again, three parables receive an explanation in the Gospels: the Sower (Mk 4.13–20), the Weeds (Mt 13.36–43), and the Fish Net (Mt 13.49–50). These explanations are somewhat allegorical, for they interpret the individual details and characters. Here too, according to Jülicher's principle, the explanation of these parables could not be attributed to Jesus. (For the allegorical parables in John see below.)

Scholars are now beginning to challenge Jülicher's principle and to recognize that, like most revolutionaries, he was too doctrinaire. It is clear that, while the parables have one principal point, many of them are not free from allegorical features. This is evident if one approaches the parables of Jesus from a Semitic viewpoint rather than from the technical distinctions of classical oratory. Hebrew has one word for these figures of speech, *māšāl,* which covers all the Greek divisions and more. Under *māšāl* are grouped, in the OT and the rabbinical writings, proverbs, maxims, symbols, riddles, parables, allegories, and fables. The παραβολή of the Greek NT is the equivalent of *māšāl.* Subsumed under it are proverbs (Lk 4.23), maxims (Lk 14.7–11), riddles (Mk 7.15–17), examples (Lk 12.15–21), figurative speech (Mk 4.33), similes (Mt 13.33), metaphors (Mt 5.14), and, finally, parables, and parables with simple allegorical characteristics. Thus, "parable" can cover a range from a single-line metaphor or simile to a long narrative. The distinctions that underlie Jülicher's theory would have been strange to Jesus and cannot be used mechanically to interpret His parables. Finally, it should be noted that the word παραβολή does not occur in the Fourth Gospel; there, as a synonym, another Greek word, παροιμία, is used, which also covers a range of figurative speech (16.25).

Characteristics of Jesus' Parables. Jesus took illustrations from daily life that attracted the hearers' attention by vividness and narrative color. While these illustrations enabled the hearers to understand His message better, they often had a strange or novel twist that left enough doubt to challenge the hearers into active thought and inquiry. These characteristics are worthy of detailed study.

Illustrations from Daily Life. Jesus was familiar with a rural Galilean milieu: outdoor scenes of farming and

Parable of the Laborers in the Vineyard, full-page illumination in the "Codex Aureus" from Echternach, written at Trier c. 983–991, and now preserved in the Stiftung für Kunst und Wissenschaft, Coburg, Germany.

shepherding, and domestic scenes in a simple one-room house (Lk 11.5–8). The homes of the rich were seen only through the kitchen door—the view of servants and slaves. The farming was hill-country farming, done in small patches with stone fences and briars (Mk 4.5–7), not in the broad lowland plains. There were donkeys, sheep, wolves, and birds; seeds, wheat, and harvest; lilies of the field and fruit trees; patches and wineskins and lamps; children in the market place, laborers and merchants. Now, even for those readers who know something of rural life the ancient techniques described in the Gospels are somewhat puzzling, and special knowledge is required. For instance, the care-

less broadcasting of seed in the parable of the Sower is explained by the fact that in Palestinian farming sowing sometimes took place before plowing.

Storytelling Techniques. Among the Gospel parables are found vivid narratives employing all the techniques of storytelling. One of these would be the rule of three, namely, that in popular stories it is customary to have three characters with the point of illustration lying in the third. Thus, in the parables, three servants are entrusted with the talents, and three men pass the man who fell among robbers. Another technique of storytelling is direct discourse: rarely is it told in the third person what a character is thinking. Rather, the characters talk aloud to themselves so that the hearer may find out what is in their minds, e.g., in the parable of the Pharisee and the Publican (Lk 18.9–14) and in that of the Rich Fool (Lk 12.16–21). Only one conversation can hold the stage at a time; and consequently, when three characters are involved, as in the Talents, the direct confrontation is repeated three times (Mt 25.14–28). Thinking of the parables as stories will also help to make understandable the peculiarities and inconsistencies that appear in them. "That is for the sake of the story" is the answer to many a difficulty that arises if one is too logical, e.g., why a dishonest steward should be allowed to make an inventory (Lk 16.1), or why workers should be paid in inverse order (Mt 20.8).

Novel Twists and Challenging Points. In the stories told by Jesus there is often a novel twist that must have made his hearers take notice. Who would have expected the scapegrace prodigal son to emerge as a more sympathetic character than the elder son who stayed at home? At times, as one may suspect from the similarity of Jesus' parables to those of the rabbis, Jesus may have used well-known stories or characters and have supplied new endings. The priest, the Levite, and the layman may have been stock characters in religious tales; but in Jesus' story, the third character was a hated Samaritan, and it was he who was the most sympathetic of the three.

Frequently there was a challenge in the parables of Jesus, the challenge of the kingdom of God. In evaluating the parables as moral lessons Jülicher made the mistake, so common in the liberal theology of the late 19th century, of reducing Jesus to a preacher of good morals. Some of the parables, such as that of the Good Samaritan, were a blistering attack on the established religious policy of the time. Others, such as the parable of the Tenants in the Vineyard and that of the Talents, were threats of imminent judgment on the leaders of Judaism. Still others, such as the Sower and the Mustard Seed, were an apologia for the slowness and insignificance of the results of His own ministry in Galilee. Jesus sought constantly to involve His hearers personally in the challenge of the parables. Many times He asked them, "What do you think?" (see Mt 21.31; Lk 7.42) and made them pass judgment on the outcome of the parabolic story. The Matthean version of the parable of the Tenants in the Vineyard has the audience itself pass judgment on the Jewish leaders who rejected Jesus (Mt 21.41; but cf. Mk 12.9). Throughout the Gospel is heard the personal appeal of Jesus: "He who has ears to hear, let him hear."

Purpose of the Parables. The fact that some of the parables had to be explained by Jesus to the disciples who had not understood them (Mk 4.10, 34; Mt 13.36; Jn 16.29) raises the question of the purpose of the parables. The overwhelming evidence of the Gospels is that the parables made Jesus' message intelligible. Yet in a passage that separates the parable of the Sower from its explanation (Mk 4.11–12) the disciples are told: ". . . to those outside, all things are treated in parables, that 'Seeing they may see but not perceive; and hearing they may hear but not understand.' " Was the purpose of the parables, then, to confuse and obfuscate?

Today many authors recognize that this passage is really a summation, not of the purpose, but of the

Two episodes from the parable of the Prodigal Son, Pennsylvania German "fraktur" by Friedrich Krebs, 1st decade of the 19th century.

result of preaching the kingdom of God in parables. The challenge of the parables was rejected by the majority of hearers who saw and heard but refused to perceive and understand. The parables were a sword of judgment. The passage cited above as part of Mark ch. 4 is an adaptation of Is 6.10, which is quoted several times in the NT and became the standard Christian explanation of why Jesus' ministry had not been received by Israel (Jn 12.37–41; Acts 28.26–27).

Therefore, if the parables blinded men's minds and hearts, it was more because men refused their piercing challenge than because men could not intellectually understand them. This does not mean that the parables were always clear to all. Jesus' picture of the kingdom of God was quite different from that of the political kingdom of David that was popularly expected, and so his parabolic exposition of the kingdom often had to be explained. Also, Jesus was chary of detailed descriptions of the future action of God in definitively establishing the kingdom (Mt 24.36; Acts 1.6–7). The parables could unfold the true nature and destiny of the kingdom without arousing vain speculation about the future. Thus, the vagueness, which is of the nature of symbolic language, served Jesus' purpose. Well does Mark say of the parable: "And in many such parables he spoke the word to them according as they were able to understand it" (Mk 4.33).

Problems. In approaching the parables of the Synoptic Gospels we must remember that no one of the three Evangelists, Mark, Luke, or the final author of Matthew, was an eyewitness of what he recounts. (The Fourth Gospel is not as important to our considerations because it contains so few parables, but even here there seems to be a final editor other than the eyewitness Apostle.) This fact accounts for a great deal of the diversity of sequence and localization that we find in the Gospels when they are compared among themselves. This does not mean, of course, that the material reported in the Gospels is unreliable, but it does mean that with stories such as the parables, where there are no accompanying indications of time and place, the Evangelists could not be sure where or when they were spoken by Jesus. Each Evangelist had to use his own judgment about where he could best insert a particular parable into the narrative sequence of the Gospel.

Evaluation of Setting. The first problem to be dealt with is the evaluation of the settings in which the parables are found in the Gospels. As an example of the same parable being found in different settings, compare Matthew's placing of the parable of the Marriage Feast (Mt 22.1–10) in Jerusalem and Luke's placing of the parable of the Banquet (Lk 14.15–24), which originally was probably the same parable, on the journey to Jerusalem. Some parables that Matthew places in the Sermon on the Mount, Luke places elsewhere (Mt. 5.13; Lk 14.34–35).

The audience to whom the parable was originally directed is part of this same problem. Many of the parables must have been hurled at Jesus' enemies, in particular the Pharisees; but as the parables were preached in the Church, the importance of the Pharisees naturally decreased. What now mattered was the value of the parables for the Christians and their lives. Therefore, in the Gospels, which reflect the Church's use of the parables, we find these stories directed to the disciples. The parable of the Lost Sheep is an example of such a redirection: the parable as it is found in Lk 15.3–7 is an attack on the scribes and Pharisees who despised the outcasts with whom Jesus associated (Lk 15.2); the parable as given in Mt 18.12–14 is part of a sermon directed to the disciples (Mt 18.1), so that the parable now inculcates the duties of Church authorities toward erring Christians.

Because of the possibility of different settings and audiences, it often happens that the same parable can have a different meaning in the different Gospels. The words of Jesus had a wealth of meaning, and each Evangelist seizes on the nuance most suitable for the people of his time and place. The parable of the Lamp seems to have one meaning in Mk 4.21, another in Mt 5.14–16, and still another in Lk 11.33. In such cases it is not always easy to decide which was the original meaning of the parable as it was spoken by Jesus. Of course, it is not impossible that Jesus told the same parable several times, but we cannot honestly resort to such an explanation to account for all the differences of context found in the Gospel parables. If, then, a certain freedom of interpretation in the parables as they are passed down from Jesus to the Evangelist must be admitted, it must also be remembered that in the Gospels is found an inspired interpretation of the parable according to the mind of Jesus and an application of the parable to the needs of the Christian.

Grouping of Parables. Jesus seems at times to have narrated His parables in groups, or at least in pairs. This is seen particularly in the "twin parables," e.g., the new patch on the old garment and the new wine in the old wineskins (Mk 2.21–22); the man building a tower and the king going to war (Lk 14.28–32). The Evangelists, because of Jesus' example and because of the reasons given at the beginning of this section, tend to insert parables as groups into the sequence of the ministry. Very often they place all the parables dealing with the same topic together. A collection of three parables about seed is given in Mk 4.1–34. Other significant groupings are a collection of seven parables all referring to the kingdom of heaven in Mt 13.3–50, seven parables dealing with the Parousia in Mt 24.32–25.46, three banquet parables in Lk 14.7–24, three parables on regaining what was lost in Lk 15.1–32, and a series of parables on using wealth correctly in Lk 16.1–31.

Such grouping of parables has some interesting and disconcerting side effects. At times originally separate parables have become fused into one. For instance, comparing the parable of the Marriage Feast (Mt 22.1–14) with the parable of the Banquet (Lk 14.16–24) makes scholars think that two additional parables have been interwoven into the Matthean account: that of the king who destroyed the city (Mt 22.2, 7–8) and that of the man without the wedding garment (22.11–14). To attempt to make one consistent story of such fused parables leads to difficulty. Again comparing the parable of the Pounds (Lk 19.11–27) and the parable of the Talents (Mt 25.14–30) makes one think that an additional parable about a man being crowned king has been interwoven into the Lucan account (vv. 12, 14, 27).

Appended Maxims. Just as parables have been fused in the Gospels, so too wise maxims spoken by Jesus have been appended to the parables because of a similarity of topic or vocabulary. Sometimes we find the same maxim appended to different parables, occasionally even to a parable to which it does not really apply. "Everyone who exalts himself shall be humbled" is found at Mt 23.12; Lk 14.11; Lk 18.14. This maxim does not fit the last reference, the parable of the Pharisee and the Publican, because the Pharisee is actually not humbled. The maxim, "The last will be first and the first last," is found in Mt 19.30 (= Mk 10.31; Lk 13.30) and again in Mt 20.16, where it is appended to the parable of the Laborers in the Vineyard. It has been attached to the latter parable simply because the laborers hired last were paid first, and is not a real interpretation of the parable. Nor does the maxim, "Many are called but few are chosen," really fit the parable of the Wedding Garment (Mt 22.14), for only one person is rejected in this parable. Probably the most famous example of appended maxims is the parable of the Dishonest Steward. To the basic parable (Lk 16.1–8) has been added a series of maxims (vv. 9, 10, 11–12, 13) dealing with topics mentioned in the parable. These collected maxims do not interpret the parable.

Introductory Formulas. Another problem concerns the introductory formulas that accompany many parables: in particular, "The kingdom of heaven is like . . ."—a formula that is frequent in Matthew, where there are ten kingdom-of-heaven parables as compared to two each for Mark and Luke. The real object of comparison often does not follow the word "like." In Mt 13.47 the phrase is "The kingdom of heaven is like a net"; yet the comparison is not actually to the net, but to the catch of fish and the separation of the good and the bad. In Mt 13.24 the comparison of the kingdom of heaven is not actually to the man who sowed the seed, but to the whole situation of the weeds and grain growing together until harvest. This difficulty can be solved by using a translation of the introductory formula, which allows a broader comparison. The meaning of the formula is "The kingdom of heaven is like the case of . . . ," where the object of comparison is the whole situation.

Variation in Detail. There is a problem in the variation of detail that appears sometimes when the same parable is narrated by different Evangelists. If it is remembered that the Evangelists are recording stories that have been handed down through years of oral tradition, it will not be surprising to find that details have varied in a process of simplification and polishing. The parable of the Tenants in the Vineyard is presented in the same general circumstances in all three Synoptic Gospels (Mk 12.1–11; Mt 21.33–43; Lk 20.9–18); yet there is a variation in details concerning the servants (single servant or groups, the same servant three times, or three different servants) and the number of times they are sent.

Sometimes the variant details are so striking that one cannot be sure that the same version of the parable is reported in each case. Jesus could have told a parable in different ways at different times. Scholars find it difficult to decide whether the differences apparent in the parable of the Pounds (Lk 19.12–27) and the parable of the Talents (Mt 25.14–30) stem from two different narrations by Jesus or from one narration that has undergone variation in the course of oral transmission. The same question may be raised about the parable of the Banquet (Lk 14.16–24) and the parable of the Wedding Feast (Mt 22.1–10). In this case the latter solution seems preferable (see above).

Parables in the Fourth Gospel. John differs markedly from the Synoptics in the use of figurative language. However, if one recalls the scope of the term *māšāl* and that in the Biblical mentality there is no emphatic distinction between the various types of figurative language, then what is found in John can certainly come under the designation παραβολή (as the equivalent of *māšāl*), even though John does not use that word.

Jesus is found citing proverbs in Jn 4.35, 37. More often Johannine figurative language is applied to Jesus Himself, e.g., metaphors wherein Jesus is the bread of life (6.35), the source of living water (7.38), the light of the world (8.12). In the Synoptics, figurative language is frequently used for the kingdom of God, a term which does not loom large in Johannine thought. Actually, the emphasis that the Synoptics put on the coming and acceptance of the kingdom of God, John puts on the sending of Jesus by the Father. The challenge to men presented in the Synoptic tradition by the kingdom of God is presented in John (e.g., 3.16–21) by the person of Jesus. The uses of figurative language in the two traditions are quite analogous, then, to their theological emphases. (*See* JOHN, GOSPEL ACCORDING TO ST.; SYNOPTIC PROBLEM.)

There are more elaborate instances of figurative language in John that border on allegory. On the basis of Jülicher's theory, some use Johannine allegory as an indication of the lateness of the Gospel and its lack of authentic tradition (*see* ALLEGORY IN THE BIBLE). Jesus, however, was just as capable of speaking in simple allegories as were the rabbis of his time. Moreover, the

proposed Johannine allegories must be analyzed. Taking the figure of the shepherd and the sheep in Jn 10.1–13 as an example, one may suggest that in 10.1–3a and 3b–5 there really are two short parables. Then, in 10.6 there is a failure to understand the parables, just as there is in Mk 4.10; and in 10.7–13 there is a somewhat allegorical explanation of the parables, just as in Mk 4.13–20. Again, an analysis of the simple allegory of the vine and branches in Jn 15.1–8 would show OT and Synoptic parallels (*see* VINE, SYMBOLISM OF THE). Thus, the Johannine tradition in relation to parables is not as startlingly different as it might seem at first sight.

Bibliography: D. BUZY, *Les Paraboles* (Paris 1948). C. H. DODD, *The Parables of the Kingdom* (rev. ed. New York 1961). B. T. D. SMITH, *The Parables of the Synoptic Gospels* (New York 1937). M. HERMANIUK, *La Parabole Évangélique* (Paris 1947). J. JEREMIAS, *The Parables of Jesus* (rev. ed. New York 1963). W. MICHAELIS, *Die Gleichnisse Jesu* (3d ed. Hamburg 1956). A. GEORGE, DBSuppl 6:1149–77. E. F. SIEGMAN, "Teaching in Parables," CathBiblQuart 23 (1961) 161–181. R. E. BROWN, "Parable and Allegory Reconsidered," NovTest 5 (1962) 36–45. **Illustration credits:** Fig. 1, Hirmer Verlag München. Fig. 2, Rare Book Department, Free Library of Philadelphia.

[R. E. BROWN]

PARACELSUS, PHILIPPUS AUREOLUS, alias for Philippus Theophrastus Bombastus von Hohenheim, German physician and theologian who directed chemistry toward making medicines; b. near Einsiedeln (Switzerland), Nov. 10, 1493?; d. Salzburg, Sept. 24, 1541. His father, illegitimate child of a nobleman, was a naturalist and alchemist. From Villach, where his father worked at a mining school, Paracelsus began his wanderings in 1507, studying at several uni-

Philippus Aureolus Paracelsus, shown holding a sword upon the handle of which appear the letters AZOTH, the alchemical name for the element mercury. After an etching by Balthazar Jenichen, 1550.

versities, especially Padua and Ferrara. He became an army surgeon in Italy, then in Denmark, probably also in Moscow and Constantinople. From Strassburg, where he settled in 1526, he was called to Basel as municipal doctor. He was not admitted as professor at the university, but lectured off-campus, until feuds with the authorities forced him to leave. He worked in mining laboratories and came to Nuremberg, where his treatises on the French disease (syphilis) were published in 1530. His *Opus Paramirum* was dated St. Gall 1530; the *Great Surgery Book,* 1535; the *Philosophia Sagax,* 1537. Royally received in Vienna, he again alienated his friends and found his last asylum in Salzburg (1540).

Always healing, working in improvised laboratories, writing, teaching, and preaching, he stressed the study of nature and belittled the school traditions. The art of healing rests on four pillars; philosophy, astronomy, alchemy, and virtue. The correspondence of the universe with the microcosmic organism guides the physician to the proper remedies. To the four elements of *Aristotle, he added the three elements sulfur, mercury, and salt, as well as several principles of action, like the archeus, an occult vital force. In his philosophy and theology he was greatly influenced by Duns Scotus. Most of his writings, including those on the diseases of the mind, were published posthumously and had wide and lasting influence.

What Paracelsus contributed to the development of medicine and chemistry emerged out of a combination of experience with alchemical and gnostic ideas; his arrogant manner did as much to alienate his contemporaries as did his unorthodox views.

Bibliography: *Sämtliche Werke,* ed. K. SUDHOFF and W. MATTHIESSEN, 15 v. (Munich 1923–33). C. G. JUNG, *Paracelsica* (Zurich 1942). W. PAGEL, *Paracelsus: An Introduction to Philosophical Medicine in the Era of the Renaissance* (New York 1958). R. P. MULTHAUF, "Paracelsus," in *Great Chemists,* ed. E. FARBER (New York 1961) 47–63. W. PAGEL, LexThK² 8:65–67. K. GOLDAMMER, RGG³ 5:93–94. **Illustration credit:** Philadelphia Museum of Art, Ars Medica Collection.

[E. FARBER]

PARACLETE

The word Paraclete, peculiar in the Bible to the Gospel of St. John, directly denotes the role of the Holy Spirit as intercessor, consoler, teacher, and defender of Christ's disciples; yet implicit in the fourth Gospel (Jn 14.26) is the fundamental thought that Jesus Himself is the primary Paraclete, a thought that John clearly enunciates elsewhere (1 Jn 1.2).

Extra-Biblical Use of the Term. The English word Paraclete comes, through the Latin *Paracletus,* from the Greek Παράκλητος. The verb παρακαλεῖν means "to call to one's side"; hence it has various derived meanings depending on the function for which one is called, such as to defend, to intercede, to console. Morphologically, as a verbal adjective ending in -τος, the word Παράκλητος would normally have a passive meaning, "one called to another"; yet in usage, the meaning derives primarily from the function of the one called, so that the few examples of this word in extra-Biblical Greek show rather the active meaning, "helper, defender, mediator, consoler." In Jb 16.2 the Hebrew active (hiph'îl) participle mᵉnaḥămîm, "comforters," was translated as παράκλητοι by Aquila and Theodotion. The term appears also in Philo in an active sense, "helper" or "mediator" (*De Specialibus Legibus* 1.237;

De Opificio Mundi 23). In rabbinical Judaism this Greek term was taken over into Mishnaic Hebrew as a transliterated loanword, pᵉraqlîṭ. As such, it was used for both human and angelic mediators or intercessors, and especially for the "advocate" (the one called) who pleads the cause of another in a judicial process.

Johannine Usage. The word Paraclete occurs only five times in the Bible, and all five occurrences are in the writings of St. John: 1 Jn 2.1; Jn 14.16, 26; 15.26; 16.7.

Christ, the Paraclete. In 1 Jn 2.1 it is Jesus Christ who is termed the paraclete. The active sense of the word is clear in this case; Jesus is our defender, our intercessor before the Father. If Christians commit sin, they should not despair; they have Christ, who is Himself "just" (i.e., innocent), as their advocate to plead their case before God's supreme tribunal. This concept of Jesus Christ as the heavenly Paraclete, or Advocate, leads naturally to the use of the term in the *farewell discourse of Jesus at the *Last Supper (Jn 14–16).

The Holy Spirit, the Paraclete-Advocate. In His discourse at the Last Supper Jesus announces His imminent departure from this earth (Jn 13.33; 14.2; 16.5), but He also tells His disciples of a return that is to follow very shortly after this absence (14.18, 28). This return is then explained in terms of the abiding presence of the Spirit of the glorified Lord who will be sent from the Father and the Son after the Son's glorification (16.7–11; see also 7.39). When the *Holy Spirit is first mentioned in this context, He is described as "another Paraclete" (14.16). Jesus is the primary and, in a certain sense, even the unique Paraclete; the Holy Spirit is "another" only in the sense that through Him Jesus will remain forever present with the Apostles and with all who through them come to believe in Him. They and their spiritual descendants in the Church will not be left like defenseless orphans to become the prey of an evil world; they will have a permanent advocate to plead their cause before the just tribunal of God against all the evil tribunals of this world (14.16–18). The usage of the term here is similar to, but broader than, that in 1 Jn 2.1. The Paraclete who is the Spirit of the glorified Christ, in defending the Church, must condemn the world that has wrongfully accused it. Here the defender is also a prosecutor. But this activity of the Spirit-Paraclete can be perceived only by faith; even though this divine Advocate is the very "Spirit of truth" (14.16; 15.26; 16.13), the world will not listen to Him (14.17).

The Holy Spirit, the Paraclete-Defender. The next passage where the Spirit-Paraclete appears is Jn 14.26. This time only one aspect of His dual role as defender-prosecutor is stressed. He must keep the Apostles ever mindful of all that Jesus has taught them and make plain to them what they have not yet fully understood (see also 16.12–15), for only insofar as they remain faithful to His teaching can their divine Advocate prove them blameless before the judgment seat of God against all the accusations of this world (16.1–4). In these two Paraclete passages in John ch. 14, the Spirit appears primarily as the Advocate defending the Apostles and the Church.

The Spirit-Paraclete, Witness of the Truth. In Jn 15. 1–8 the absolute need of the Apostles to remain united with Jesus is described under the symbolism of the *vine. Then in 15.18–25 the Apostles are warned that they, in their union with Christ, will share in the world's hatred and persecution of Him. Therefore, the Spirit-Paraclete will also have to come to the defense of Christ; He will bear witness to the truth of what Jesus did and said and was (15.26). It is in the Spirit's defense of the mission of Jesus that the truth of the Apostles' mission is guaranteed (15.27; see also Mk 13.11; Mt 10.20; Lk 12.12).

Judicial Role of the Spirit-Paraclete. The exact meaning of Jn 15.26 is made clearer in the final and climatic use of the term Paraclete in Jn 16.7. Once again Jesus reiterates that His departure is but the condition and prelude to His return in the Spirit (16.5–6). Moreover, when the Spirit-Paraclete of Jesus comes, He will do three things: first, He will prove that the world is guilty of sin because it acted unjustly in refusing to believe in Jesus, as well as in condemning Him "without cause" (15.25) to death before its human tribunal; secondly, He will prove that Jesus was "just," i.e., innocent, by bearing witness to the fact that His death was not a defeat but a glorious return to the Father; thirdly, having established both the guilt of the world and the innocence of Jesus, He will pass sentence of condemnation on "the prince of this world," i.e., Satan. Human tribunals may condemn Jesus and His followers (15.18–25; 16.1–4; 17.16), but before the solemn tribunal of God, the Paraclete overturns and reverses these judgments—on Jesus (15.26; 16.7) and on those who are faithful to Him (14.16, 26).

Bibliography: EncDictBibl 1717–20. J. BEHM, Kittel ThW 5: 798–812. X. LÉON-DUFOUR, ed., *Vocabulaire de théologie biblique* (Paris 1962). L. J. LUTKEMEYER, "The Role of the Paraclete (Jn. 16:7–15)," CathBiblQuart 8 (1946) 220–229. O. BETZ, *Der Paraklet: Fürsprecher im häretischen Spätjudentum, im Johannes-Evangelium und in neu gefundenen gnostischen Schriften* (Leiden 1963).

[D. M. CROSSAN]

PARACLETE, SERVANTS OF THE HOLY.
The Servants of the Holy Paraclete (SP), a clerical congregation of diocesan right, was founded by Gerald M. C. Fitzgerald at Jemez Springs, New Mexico, in January 1947. Father Fitzgerald considered Cardinal Francis Spellman, of New York; Abp. Edwin V. Byrne, of Santa Fe; and Abp. William D. O'Brien, of the Extension Society, as cofounders because of their vital interest and support. The specific purpose of the congregation is the care of priests, especially those on temporary retirement from active duty. At Jemez Springs, where the first monastery, Via Coeli, was opened in what had formerly been a mountain inn, priests quickly gave support to the work in a spirit epitomized by the motto of the congregation: "For Christ in His priests." There are, besides the four retreat houses at Jemez Springs, houses in Santa Fe and Albuquerque, New Mexico; Nevis, Minn.; Canton, Ohio; Randolph, Vt.; Chicago, Ill.; and Brownshill, in the Diocese of Clifton in England. Other foundations are located in the Dioceses of Rome and Sabina in Italy, and in the Bolivian Diocese of Santa Cruz de la Sierra.

The Paracletes and their retreatants live a common life. They carry on an intense devotion to the Eucharist under the aspects of both Sacrament and Sacrifice. Where numbers permit, daily Exposition of the Blessed Sacrament is the rule; at the motherhouse in Jemez Springs a perpetual guard of honor is maintained night and day in the Adoration Chapel. A unique privilege of the congregation, enjoyed at the motherhouse, is that of Mass around the clock, from midnight to midnight, on the first Friday of each month. The constitutions were approved in May of 1952, and the congregation was formally erected by Archbishop Byrne on June 1, 1952. Favored by the blessings and personal interest of Popes Pius XII and John XXIII, as well as by most of the members of the hierarchy in the U.S., the work has continued to flourish. In 1964 there were more than 50 professed priests and clerics in perpetual simple vows.

[G. FITZGERALD]

PARADISE

Place or state of bliss and immortality. This concept has its roots in the description and conditions of the Garden of Eden in Genesis, but appears in other places in the OT and the NT and in extra-Biblical writings, in all of which it has undergone considerable development. This article will discuss first the terminology and then the concept of paradise as related to the primeval age, the eschatological age, and the present age.

Terminology. The word paradise comes to us through the Greek παράδεισος, which in turn derives from the ancient Persian *pairi-daēza,* meaning an enclosure wall, the space enclosed, and finally a park. This Persian term was taken over by late Hebrew in the form of *pardēs* and is found in Neh 2.8; Eccl 2.5; and Ct 4.12. The Septuagint uses παράδεισος to translate both *pardēs* and the more classical Hebrew word for garden, *gan,* whether there be reference to a garden in the ordinary sense (e.g., Nm 24.6; Is 1.30; Jer 29.5) or to the Garden of *Eden (Gn 2.8–3.24 passim; Jl 2.3), which is elsewhere called the Garden of God (e.g., Gn 13.10; Is 51.3; Ez 28.13; 31.8–9) or simply Eden (e.g., Ez 31.9, 16, 18; Sir 40.27). In later Jewish writings and in the NT, Paradise takes on a special and at times intricate religious significance.

Paradise of Primeval Age. The Yahwist narrative of Gn 2.4b–3.24 states that after creation man was placed in a garden (*gan*) where trees of all kinds grew (including the *Tree of Life and the *Tree of Knowledge), where there was copious water and a wide assortment of natural life. References to the Garden of Eden or the Garden of God are found in Gn 13.10; Is 51.3; Ez 31.8–9; 36.35; Jl 2.3; Sir 40.27, with slightly varying terminology being used. The enigmatic Ez 28.13–19 not only speaks of Eden, the Garden of God, but also gives a kind of parallel and variant tradition of the Fall; in this text there is reference to a richly clad royal figure, a mountain, a cherub, and a fall from pristine innocence through trafficking and haughtiness (to mention some obvious features that differentiate it from the Genesis account).

In Genesis one may note several discordant features within the account, e.g., the probable reference to a kind of artesian well in 2.6 stands in contrast with the river system in 2.10–14, from both of which the ground or earth (Heb. '*ădāmâ*) is watered (the '*ădāmâ* being understood for the moment as outside the Garden). In 2.9 the reference to the Tree of Knowledge seems to be added to the verse, and 3.3 bears out the suggestion. In 3.22–23 only the man is spoken of as being driven out of the Garden, although the narrative has involved the woman very intimately. These examples point to various elements having been brought together from different sources with clever, but not perfect, literary skill.

From these and other disharmonies, it appears that there are various teachings in this account. One teaching is sin's influence on the earth's poverty (3.17–19), although one is free to suggest that the real cause is man's lack of industry and resourcefulness in his fallen condition. The Garden, too, is depicted as a place of blessedness and of closeness to God. One may note here, as in the case of Utnapishtim's dwelling in the *Gilgamesh epic, the idea of remoteness: "far away at the mouth of the rivers" (Pritchard ANET² 95b). Thus Gn 2.8 speaks of the Garden "out in the steppe" ("Eden" presupposing the Sumerian e d i n, via the Akkadian *edinu,* which means steppe), "off towards the East"—the terms that are both vague and somewhat mysterious. The Hebrew *'ēden* (delight) is a clever and significant wordplay. The parallel use of terms in Is 51.3 brings out the same idea.

The possible location of Paradise has long intrigued men, especially those of fundamentalist outlook who have little knowledge of and concern for literary forms. Since two of the four rivers in 2.10–14 can be identified, the *p⁵rāt* and the *ḥiddeqel* being the Euphrates and the Tigris respectively, while the other two remain difficult to identify, many have thought of some location near the headwaters of the above named rivers. It is, however, extremely doubtful that the Yahwist had scientific geography in mind. He more likely borrowed famous names out of the past, thus adding to the luster of the Garden—which was not the site where earliest man actually lived. The emphasis is on man's primitive state and his lost opportunity for immortality. The number four elicits a note of universality (cf. "four corners of the earth" in Is 11.12 and the "four winds" in Mt 24.31).

Paradise in the Eschatological Age. In the writings of the OT Prophets man's future happiness—vaguely situated in the "latter times"—is often depicted in terms reminiscent of Paradise. The peace and ideal justice to be procured by the messianic king will be like those of Paradise in Is 11.6–11. The same image is found in Os 2.20, where peace in the animal kingdom and cessation of war are depicted. References to Eden are found in descriptions of the Promised Land in Is 51.3 and Ez 36.35, while the promise of longevity reminiscent of the immortality proffered to man in Eden is found in Is 65.17–25.

According to the Apocrypha [*see* BIBLE, III (CANON), 4] and some rabbinical writings, Paradise will be the place of reward and bliss following upon judgment (e.g., Enoch 61.1–13; Testament of Levi 18.10–14; Apocalypse of Baruch 4). In these descriptions one finds the most varied ideas, e.g., Paradise is to be established in Jerusalem; the Tree of Life will flourish once more. The eschatological Paradise is often identified with the primeval Paradise. The Testament of Levi 18.10 tells how the high priest of the messianic age will open the gates of Paradise and remove the flaming sword mentioned in Gn 3.24. On the other hand, Paradise was described by some rabbis as close to *gehenna or as associated with *sheol, the latter term now being taken as one form of reference to future bliss [for many references, see R. H. Charles, *The Apocrypha and Pseudepigrapha of the OT* (Oxford 1913) 1:861 s.v. "Paradise"].

In the NT Paradise is described with more restraint, and only three times by name. Of these references only Ap 2.7 is of interest. In this text the conquerors are promised the fruit of the Tree of Life that is in the Paradise of God. This fruit, symbolizing a very real spiritual value, is already available. Such a notion is common to NT thought, where union with Christ anticipates eschatological benefits. Apocalypse ch. 22 is filled with imagery drawn from Genesis ch. 2 and 3, although Paradise is not specifically named.

Paradise in the Present Age. If one makes the identification of the primeval Paradise with that to come, one might presuppose that Paradise has never ceased to exist. Such a notion could be derived from Gn 3.23–24, understood in a crassly literal sense. On the other hand, as the doctrine on *retribution after death developed, and a separate lot for the good and the wicked was postulated, speculation regarding entrance into Paradise quite normally increased. Some of the apocryphal writings state that after death and prior to resurrection the elect (and especially the Patriarchs) will be placed in Paradise (see Jubilees 4.23). The location of Paradise was likewise discussed. Some situated it, with Gn 2.8, in the East (e.g., Jubilees 8.16); others placed it in the North (Enoch 61.1–4; cf. 77.3; see also Is 14.13); and still others placed it in the West (reported by Josephus as Essene doctrine in *Bell. Jud.* 2.155–158; see also 4 Esdras 14.9). Still others assumed, seemingly, that after the *Fall of man, Paradise was removed from the earth and taken up to heaven with God (Life of Adam and Eve 25.3; Apocalypse of Baruch 4.6; 4 Esdras 4.7–8) and is, more precisely, in the "third heaven" (Apocalypse of Moses 37.5; Slavonic Enoch 8.1).

In the NT in Lk 23.43 Our Lord refers to the then already existing temporary abode of the just after their death. The notion is linked to that of *Abraham's Bosom, mentioned in Lk 16.23. In 2 Cor 12.2–4 Paradise is situated in the "third heaven" (an identification found in Slavonic Enoch 8.1), God's abode being the "seventh heaven." Underlying the "great chasm" of Lk 16.26 is the same notion of temporary beatitude, opposed in this instance to *Hades. With our present knowledge of the universe it is impossible to point toward Paradise, i.e., heaven, as a distinctive place, though it would seem preferable to conceive of it as a place distinct from the earth.

See also AFTERLIFE, 2.

Bibliography: C. COTHENET, DBSuppl 6:1177–1220. EncDict Bibl 1720–25. P. HOFFMANN, LexThK² 8:69–72. A. ROMEO, Enc Catt 9:791–792. A. JEPSEN and F. HESSE, RGG³ 5:96–100. J. JEREMIAS, Kittel ThW 5:763–771. J. L. McKENZIE, "The Literary Characteristics of Gn 2–3," ThSt 15 (1954) 541–572. H. RENCKENS, *Israel's Concept of the Beginning,* tr. C. NAPIER (New York 1964) 204–213. J. DANIÉLOU, *From Shadows to Reality,* tr. W. HIBBERD (Westminster, Md. 1960) 11–65. J. WEISENGOFF, "Paradise and St. Luke 23:43," AmEcclRev 103 (1940) 163–167.
[I. HUNT]

PARADOX, a statement that seems at first to defy ordinary understanding, even to the point of self-contradiction, but that may, on closer examination, prove to be well founded. The term has been applied to certain religious teachings, e.g., God at one time took on the identity of a particular man, and to antithetical sayings found in Scripture, such as St. Paul's description of the ministers of God, "As sorrowful yet always rejoicing; as poor yet enriching many; as having nothing yet possessing all things" (2 Cor 6.10). For paradoxical constructions arising in sciences such as metaphysics, logic, and mathematics, *see* ANTINOMY.

[H. A. NIELSEN]

PARAGUAY

Inland country in the heart of South America, joined to the sea by the great Paraguay and Paraná Rivers. It has an area of 157,000 square miles and, in 1965, a population of about 2 million, of which 82 per cent are mestizo; 10 per cent, Creole; 5 per cent, unassimilated Indians; and 3 per cent, foreigners. The area was originally inhabited by the Cario Indians and was discovered by Alejo García in 1524. Conquest and colonization was begun in 1536. Paraguay has been an independent republic since May 14, 1811. According to its constitution, its form of government is unitary, democratic, and representative. It has been involved in two bloody international wars: that of the Triple Alliance against Brazil, Argentina, and Uruguay (1864–70) and the War of the Chaco against Bolivia (1932–35). It is an agricultural and cattle-raising country, with industrial centers in the capital, Asunción, and in Pilar, Pinasco, Casado, Concepción, Ypacaraí, Capiatá, Itaguá, Itá, Areguá, San Bernardino, Yegros, Yturbe, Vallemí, Villarrica, Tebicuary, and Colonia Independencia.

Early Missionary Activity. Franciscans arrived in Paraguay in 1537. From Asunción they carried on missions in interior regions. Among the early missionaries were Alonso Lebrón, Alonso de San Buenaventura, Luis de *Bolaños, Bernardo de Armenta, the Indians Gabriel de la Anunciación and Francisco de Guzmán, Pedro Fernández de la Torre (first bishop to arrive in Paraguay), and Martín Ignacio de Loyola. At the same time came Mercedarians, Hieronymites, and Dominicans. The last to arrive in Paraguay were the Jesuits. Each one of these orders had its schools and convents, and the famous *reductions are owed to the Franciscans and Jesuits. The most famous Jesuits in colonial Paraguay were Manuel de Lorenzana, Antonio *Ruíz de Montoya, Nicolás del *Techo, Pedro *Lozano, Francisco Xavier de Charlevoix, Nicolás Yapuguai (Indian), José Guevara, Simón Bandini, José *Cardiel, José Insaurralde (Indian), Diego de Boroa, Manuel Paramás, Nicolás Mastrilli, Alonso Barzana, Martin *Dobrizhoffer, Pablo Restivo, José Sánchez Labrador, Pedro Montenegro, Roque Gonzáles de Santa Cruz, Domingo Muriel, and José Quiroga. The principal obstacles for the propagation of the faith were learning of languages, the nomadic character of the native population, the ravages of the Portuguese *bandeirantes,* and the conflicts between political and religious authorities. The first missionaries used music and gifts to attract the natives. After they had learned the native languages, they tried to persuade the Indians through songs and prayers to come to the *doctrinas* and oratories, the foundations of the reductions that were centers of learning and work. Success was real and fertile.

Diocesan Organization. The Church of Asunción was the first erected as a cathedral in South America (bull of Paul II, July 1, 1547). The canonical founder of the episcopal See of Paraguay was the Spaniard Juan de Barrios (Jan. 10, 1548). He never reached his bishopric. The first person to occupy the see was Pedro Fernández de la Torre (1556–72). During the 417 years of its existence, from its creation to 1964, the see has been governed for only 243 years. It was vacant or abandoned for 174 years. Of the first 40 bishops, only 20 came to Paraguay. The ecclesiastical Province of Paraguay was erected by a bull of Pius XI, May 1, 1929. The most important synods or councils held in the country were Asunción 1603, organized by Martín Ignacio de Loyola; Asunción 1631, organized and presided over by Bp. Cristóbal de Arestí; Concepción 1936, 1946; and Villarrica 1949. The episcopate meets regularly each year and more than once it has met in extraordinary session. The episcopate and the clergy meet in national study workshops every 3 years.

Clergy and Religious Orders. From its earliest history Paraguay made no distinctions between European, American, and Indian priests and nuns. During the colonial period Spain had provided an ample number of priests for the area and had protected the religious orders in order to evangelize the Indians and multiply the subjects of the Crown. There was no lack of priests until the War of the Triple Alliance. After that conflict the clergy diminished considerably and the Church was leaderless for 11 years. The first postwar priests were ordained in 1886 by Bp. Pedro Juan Aponte. They included Juan Sinforiano *Bogarín, who later became the first archbishop of Asunción. The principal center for the formation of priests is the Seminario Conciliar de la Asunción, and there are other seminaries, in Concepción, Villarrica, San Juan Bautista de las Misiones, Encarnación, Colonia Obligado, Caacupé, Mariscal, Estigarribia (Chaco), Ycaparaí, Areguá, and Eusebio Ayala. In 1964, 12 male religious orders and 20 female orders were carrying out missions in Paraguay. These groups dedicate themselves to the propagation of the faith, teaching at all levels, and charitable works. They assist in hospitals, missions established in distant regions in the interior of the country, boarding schools, and all centers of social assistance. Their funds come from the foreign mission bureaus of each order and the contributions of the faithful. Their work supplements the social work of the state. There were 187 Catholic charitable organizations in 1964.

Relations between Church and State. During the independence period the Church was sympathetic toward the revolution and some priests worked for its success. No major reform touched the Church as a result of independence, but relations between Church and State were always relatively tense because of the right of patronage that the new state assumed and that influenced the election of bishops. During the colonial period the Paraguayan Church was very rich; it held ranches on government lands. In 1822 the dictator José Gaspar de *Francia confiscated all its properties and transformed its convents into barracks. During the War of the Triple Alliance the most serious crisis occurred between Church and State as a result of the execution of Bp. Manuel Antonio *Palacios (1868). In 1964 the Church was under the protection of the state and was supported by the contributions of the faithful. Absolute divorce is not recognized in Paraguay; only physical and financial separation is legal.

Education. The most important institute founded in Asunción during the colonial period was the Colegio

PARAGUAY, 1964
172 Parishes: 1,686,300 Catholics
✠ **Archbishopric**   ✝ **Bishopric**
● Vicariate Apostolic and Prelacy nullius
CIVIL DEPARTMENT and Capital.

The capital of Paraguay is Asunción.
Ipacaraí is the capital of CENTRAL
DEPARTMENT.

Seminario Conciliar de San Carlos, which was inaugurated April 12, 1783. It educated almost all the leaders of the independence movement. The Universidad Católica Nuestra Señora de la Asunción, made up of five faculties and having four branches, was founded by the Paraguayan episcopal conference Feb. 13, 1960. Both rich and poor study there. In 1964 there were 1,343 students and 165 professors. It is the first private university officially recognized by the Paraguayan government. In addition there are a great number of primary and secondary schools for men and women conducted by religious throughout the republic. In 1964 these schools had 63,172 students and 2,872 teachers. In spite of these schools, the influence of Catholic teaching in the country has not been great.

The Modern Church. The situation of the Church is improving. It is making a spiritual, moral, and cultural contribution to the nation, even though just maintaining itself and making some modest extensions is arduous. Catholic Action has begun to have a positive influence on the morality of the people and of their political leaders. While the missions of the colonial period have not been continued, others have been established more in harmony with 20th-century needs. The Church has maintained the presses of the colonial

period—San Ignacio Guasú, Santa María la Mayor, and San Javier—and has established two more in the 20th century—Los Principios and Talleres Gráficos Asunción. It publishes a number of periodicals, such as *Primicias* (1915), *Revista Diocesana* (1921), *Alborada* (1935), *Veritas* (1937), *Resonancias* (1939), *La Estrella* (1943), *Salesianito* (1948), and *Alas* (1957).

The principal center for pilgrimages in Paraguay is the Sanctuary of the Virgin of the Miracles in Caacupé, 50 kilometers from Asunción. This image has a legendary origin and its sentimental influence is great. In December 1963, 180,000 faithful went to the Sanctuary. Protestant activity has grown in Paraguay, and its influence has spread through the country.

Outstanding Paraguayans. Important figures in the Church were Pedro Fernández de la Torre, Alonso de Guerra, Martín Ignacio de Loyola, José de Palos, Pedro García de Panés, and Bp. Marco Antonio Maíz, as well as such contemporary figures as Juan Sinforiano Bogarín; Hermenegildo Roa, writer and effective collaborator in Church-State relations; Manuel Gamarra, poet and orator, who propagated the faith with word and deed; Isidro Gavilán, reorganizer of the Church after the War of the Triple Alliance; Bernabé Colmán,

La Trinidad Church, suburbs of Asunción, Paraguay.

builder of the largest and most opulent church in Asunción; Tomás Aveiro, author of *Índice del Clero Paraguayo;* Fidel Maíz, writer and orator, and a man of a restless strange life; Ernesto Pérez Acosta; Pantaleón García; Secundino Núñez; Felipe Santiago Benítez; Julio B. Laschi González; Agustín Rodríguez; Emilio Sosa Gaona; Anibal Maricevich Fleitas; Juan Moleón; Bartolomé Adorno; Mariano Celso Pedrozo; Juan C. Prieto; Gilberto Giménez; Antonio Rojas; Angel Achá Duarte; Ramón Bogarín Argaña; Juan Escalante; Ismael Rolón; and others. Among the outstanding political figures, who are numerous, were Carlos Antonio *López, who, as president of the country, collaborated in the reconstruction of the Paraguayan Church after the long dictatorship of José Gaspar de Francia, during which the loss of hegemony reduced the clergy to an extraordinarily poor condition in spiritual and material matters, and Pres. José Patricio Guggiari, during whose term the ecclesiastical Province of Paraguay was created.

Sèe also, ASUNCIÓN, ARCHDIOCESE OF.

Bibliography: A. N. ACHÁ DUARTE, *Anuario eclesiástico del Paraguay* (Asunción 1963). *Registro oficial de la República del Paraguay* (1869). H. FERREIRA GUBETICH, *Geografía del Paraguay* (4th ed. Asunción 1960). G. FURLONG CÁRDIFF, *Misiones y sus pueblos guaraníes* (Buenos Aires 1956). C. R. CENTURIÓN, *Historia de las letras paraguayas,* 3 v. (Buenos Aires 1947–51); *Historia de la cultura paraguaya,* 2 v. (2d ed. Buenos Aires 1961). **Illustration credit:** Pan American Union, Washington, D.C.

[C. R. CENTURIÓN]

PARALIPOMENON (CHRONICLES), BOOKS OF

or, 1st and 2d Paralipomenon, are the names given to the two books, originally one, that recount the history of the chosen people from a postexilic viewpoint, tracing it from Adam to the Edict of Cyrus in 538 B.C., but concentrating mostly on the history of the Judean monarchy. Palestinian Jews (and Hebrew printed Bibles) called these books (*sēper*) *dibrê hayyāmîm,* a title idiomatically equivalent to "annals" or "happenings of the times." Greek-speaking Jews in their Septuagint (followed by the Vulgate and some modern editions) referred to these books by the name παραλειπόμενα, which the Fathers of the Church understood as designating the books' content, "things omitted" (from previous Biblical histories). Some scholars, however, prefer to translate παραλειπόμενα as "things trans-

mitted." St. Jerome, in his *Prologus galeatus,* says that these books are a "chronicle of the whole of divine history," with which phrase the modern appellation of these books, Chronicles, agrees. For these books themselves, *see* CHRONICLER, BIBLICAL.

[N. J. MCELENEY]

PARANÁ, ARCHDIOCESE OF (PARANENSIS).

The Diocese of Paraná was created on June 13, 1859, by Pope Pius IX from territory belonging to the Diocese of Buenos Aires. It had jurisdiction over the provinces of Entre Ríos, Corrientes, Santa Fé, and the three northern territories of Chaco, Formosa, and Misiones, until Pope Leo XIII established the Diocese of Santa Fé on Feb. 25, 1897, to include the provinces of Santa Fé, Chaco, and Formosa. Paraná was a suffragan see of the Archdiocese of Buenos Aires until 1934 when it was elevated to an archdiocese that included the entire province of Entre Ríos; its suffragans are Concordia (1961) in the north and Gualeguaychú (1957) in the south. The following bishops governed the diocese: Luis Gabriel Segura y Cubas (1859–62), José María Gelabert (1865–97), Rosendo de la Lastra (1898–1909), Abel Bazán y Bustos (1910–26), and Julián P. Martínez (1927–34). As an archdiocese, it has been governed by Zenobio Guilland (1935–62) and Adolfo Tortolo, who succeeded to the see in 1963. In 1960 there were 190 priests for the 50 parishes and 14 parish missions of the archdiocese, 74 of whom were members of religious orders. The 9 congregations of men maintained 16 houses; the 27 religious communities of women had 51 convents. Boys' schools numbered only 1 secondary and 3 primary schools. There were 16 secondary and 37 grade schools for girls. The sisters staffed 16 hospitals and sanitariums. In 1960 there were 115 seminarians.

See also ARGENTINA.

[G. FURLONG]

PARAPSYCHOLOGY

The scientific study of physical and psychological events that cannot be explained by the principles or laws of the physical sciences. The term parapsychology was first applied to this study by German and American scientists; the equivalent terms "psychical research" and "metapsychics" are used in England and France, respectively.

Occurrences that are beyond the ordinary level of man's experience are usually referred to as paranormal phenomena. This focuses attention on their being extraordinary or unusual, without implying that these phenomena have as their only source supernatural or occult forces. Among paranormal events some are further classified as psychical phenomena because they seem to be attributable to the activity of the human mind, the psyche. Psychical events, or psi-phenomena, are the proper subject matter of the science of parapsychology.

Early History. For many centuries paranormal phenomena were considered the work of some dismembered ghost or supernatural force working through a "crossed" human agent. In recent times, however, this facile explanation came to be questioned; eventually scientists began to examine these occurrences and suspect that at least some paranormal phenomena had a human cause. In the 20th century the embryonic science gradually disassociated itself from *spiritism and other occult practices; by mid-century parapsychology had come to be recognized generally as a science concerned with experimental proofs for the existence of psychical events, although not all were agreed on the interpretation of its findings.

Historic references to paranormal phenomena are to be found in the Bible. A strict dichotomy determined their validity: they were acts of the Lord or they were futile pagan imitations. In no case were these actions seen as the result of psychic powers of mere humans. Either the phenomena were miraculous confirmations of God's prophets or they were blasphemous pagan superstitions. *See* DIVINATION; MAGIC (IN THE BIBLE); NECROMANCY; ORACLE; ORACLE (IN THE BIBLE); SIBYLLINE ORACLES.

In the Middle Ages, particularly after the *Crusades to the Middle East, black *magic and *cabala, *astrology, and the *ordeal found willing practitioners. St. *Thomas Aquinas classified superstitious practices that seemed to produce paranormal phenomena into three classes: (1) invocation of the devil, e.g., necromancy; (2) prediction through the observation of natural objects, e.g., omens; and (3) casting lots to decide actions or solve problems (ST 2a2ae, 95.1–8). He concluded that all phenomena attributable to the devil were to be prohibited, but noted that those that result merely from natural causes offer only vain or useless information.

During the Renaissance, as scholars began to study anew the classical pagan cultures, the popularity of occult practices grew. However, those who adopted the attitude of "methodical doubt" viewed the problem in a new light: either paranormal phenomena were the products of supernatural forces beyond man's power to know, or they were illusions. Others refused to ignore the subject and applied the methods of physical science to its study with the intention of either dismissing, once and for all, paranormal occurrences or establishing their reality in definitive fashion.

Beginnings in Europe. The study of the reactions of mesmerized patients led some to suspect that not all paranormal events were supernatural or illusory; attention was therefore directed to the psychical aspect. Sir William Crookes (1832–1919), the English scientist, reported that his study of necromantic mediums proved the reality of some occurrences unexplainable by the sciences. This information interested other scientists to join in the study of psychic phenomena. For this reason, the Society for Psychical Research was founded in 1882; it enumerated among its members Henry Sidgwick (1838–1900) and other professors of Cambridge University. A similar group, the American Society for Psychical Research, was founded in the U.S. in 1884. Both bodies are still in existence and are influential in fostering the study of parapsychology.

The early years of serious study were spent investigating and reporting various phenomena and their possible causes. The first areas of study were séances, mediums, and purported instances of the unusual. Since investigators often were not able to obtain firsthand information, the task of investigation in most instances was reduced to a search for authentic phenomena. Nonetheless, a new science was growing, criteria were discovered, and techniques were refined.

In France Charles Richet (1850–1935) collected whatever evidence he could verify concerning psychic phenomena. In his report on this work [*Thirty Years of Psychical Research,* tr. S. De Brath (New York 1923)], Richet attempted to give a firm foundation for future psychical study. He wished so to define the new science of parapsychology as to bar from it any occult presuppositions; the duty of the scientist, as he conceived it, was to examine those phenomena that demand an intelligent cause—whether this intelligence be human or superhuman. Richet could not advance any explanatory theories; the science was too immature for that. But it was to be protected from the invasion of spiritism, the pseudoreligion of the occult.

Richet's work led others in Europe to follow his lead. The International Metapsychical Institute was founded in 1919, and the French Association for Parapsychological Studies appeared in 1941. Meanwhile, work was begun in a laboratory in the University of Groningen, Netherlands. A Belgian committee was formed in 1948 to study "objectively and scientifically" all paranormal phenomena wherever they were to be found. This left a door open for occultists and spiritists; it exposed the whole science to the suspicion with which such practitioners were viewed. Parapsychologists had only one recourse: to divorce themselves completely from the suspect areas and conduct an impartial study of paranormal events. To do this, objective experiments were necessary.

Objective Tests. Although he did not originate the objective test, J. B. Rhine (1895–) restricted himself to the method on which this was based; he was also most influential in introducing statistical analysis into psychical research. In 1927 William *McDougall of Oxford, then head of the psychology department of Duke University, invited Rhine to join him and initiate a program of research in the paranormal field. By 1934 the Parapsychology Laboratory was founded at Duke; Rhine and his colleagues there set out to prove the objective existence of psi-phenomena and to search for their causes.

The procedure of an objective test was slowly refined as faults were discovered. Basically, two persons, a sender and receiver, attempted to transmit information by means other than the normal methods of communication. A particular bit of information was determined by the experimenter, lest the skeptic attribute success to inference or generalization. The type of information was changed from a series of numbers to a group of symbols to eliminate the possibility that the receiver be influenced by a subconscious preference for any particular number. This is the form of the general extrasensory perception (GESP) experiment.

The parapsychologist can evaluate such a test by one of two methods: qualitative or quantitative. The qualitative method is the more complex, but it can help to reveal factors or qualities that characterize psychic phenomena. Using this method, the technician examines all the factors present in the particular experiment and tries to determine the significance of each in the production of the event. The interpretation here involved, however, exposes conclusions to the accusation of prejudgment on the part of the evaluator. Although the qualitative test is a valuable tool for analyzing the nature of psychic events, it is incapable, for this reason, of proving the existence of psi-phenomena.

In the quantitative method, the GESP test and similar experiments are used. A number of tests are determined, conducted, and scored using the mathematics of probability. Thus, if a set of Zener cards—25 cards, 5 cards each having 1 of 5 different symbols—is used, the level of chance guessing is 1 over 5 for each symbol or 5 over 25 for the complete deck. Although any one test can admit of a chance score higher than 5 over 25, such a possibility disappears as the number of tests conducted increases. The results of millions of such tests, at Duke and at laboratories throughout the world, seem to prove the existence of psychic abilities. Success patterns above chance have been obtained for many types of psychic phenomena; such tests, in fact, enable scientists to classify the various types of psychic phenomena.

Types of Psi-Phenomena. Psi-phenomena were immediately and universally divided into those that display either a physical or a psychological character. Of those phenomena that can be experimentally reproduced in a laboratory, the psychological psi-abilities are generally termed *extrasensory perception (ESP): specifically, they are telepathy, clairvoyance, and precognition (*premonition). The physical psi-ability that can be empirically observed is called *psychokinesis (PK).

In 1919 H. Brugmans (1884–) conducted tests at the University of Groningen to prove the existence of *telepathy, i.e., the power to transfer mental content from one mind to another by paranormal means. A subject sat blindfolded near a board with numbers and letters printed in 48 squares. Two experimenters were in a room above, one attempting to send a letter or number telepathically, while the other noted through a viewing apparatus the subject's answers. G. H. Estabrooks (1895–) also ran telepathy experiments at Harvard in 1921. He used a set of 20 playing cards, recording the successful calls of color and suit. The results of both tests, it is alleged, prove the reality of telepathy.

Rhine believed that there was evidence for another power of ESP, namely, clairvoyance, the ability to know the outcome of some action unknown to anyone else. J. G. Pratt (1910–) recorded the order of shuffled pack of Zener cards only after dealing, unobserved and face down, at a predetermined rate of speed. A Mr. Hubert Pearce recorded his calls, often from a post in another building, at the same rate of speed. Neither knew the results of the other's recording. Rhine then compared the results. The conclusions of the Pearce-Pratt tests have convinced many of the reality of clairvoyance.

S. G. Soal and colleagues devised experiments for the Society for Psychical Research in London to test the existence of precognition, i.e., the noninferred knowledge of some future event or action. In these tests the subject was asked to write down the order of cards to be determined and dealt later. Many different methods were used to determine the ordering of the cards. These and later tests have been interpreted as proofs of the existence of some measure of precognition.

L. A. Dale conducted experiments for the American Society for Psychical Research to study psychokinesis, the power of the mind to act directly on physical actions or events. These tests, together with those run by R. A. McConnell at the University of Pittsburgh, generally support the conclusion obtained at the Parapsychology Laboratory that PK exists. Reports of these tests and others can be found in the journals of the laboratories and the proceedings of the societies.

Characteristics. The phenomena that can be experimentally reproduced in laboratories with a variety of subjects display similar characteristics. (1) Although some are more successful than others, all subjects seem to share to some extent in psychic abilities. (2) There is a decline in efficiency with most subjects over an extended test period; flagging interest and attention seem to account for a decrease in successful calls. This is reinforced by the fact that success can be noticeably affected by giving the subject stimulants or depressants. (3) Patterns have been detected in test results. Success most often falls within the first half of an experiment; chance results would hardly display such regularity. Often a subject seems to show a regular pattern of calling a particular symbol one place before or after the actual order. Or he may repeatedly call a symbol before *and* after its actual place in the order. Chance guessing could not explain such a repeated "displacement effect," as this phenomenon is called.

These few characteristics are detected in all clinically observed phenomena, both of ESP and of PK. This seems to indicate that the abilities producing the various psi-phenomena are parts of one psi-function of the human mind. That these characteristics and this function are nonphysical also seems to confirm that psi-phenomena result from the operation of man's mind.

Other Phenomena. Many other psychic phenomena come within the scope and interest of parapsychology. Scientific studies of such phenomena have not yet been undertaken, largely because it is difficult to apply proper controls to them or to reproduce them in laboratories. Psychical researchers presently fill the role of objective observers when studying events such as séances, poltergeists, dowsing, apparitions, automatic writing, and other forms of divination. The tendency is to classify all such phenomena under one of three headings: (1) ESP phenomena—although automatic writing, ouija boards, or dowsing with rods involve muscular reactions, they are basically forms of paranormal knowledge; (2) PK phenomena—séance noises and poltergeist disturbances reflect intelligent direction and would be studied as psychokinetic effects, if conditions permitted; and (3) problems concerning the soul. The major conclusion of psychical research is that some part of man is immaterial or spiritual. Apparitions of persons, immediately prior to or after their death, concern the human *spirit; as psychical events they are proper subject matter for the science of parapsychology.

The phenomena associated with *mysticism, though most extraordinary, are too infrequent to draw much attention from scientists. The mystic is one who lives in extremely close union with God; as a result of that union he enjoys special knowledge and love of God. Such intense internal activities can produce the external reactions of ecstasy, visions, revelations, stigmatization, levitation, and even bilocation. Theologians insist that such phenomena are purely secondary and nonessential to mystical union with God: pseudomystics can perform parallel feats. The impartial scientist attributes these phenomena either to a human cause or to a force beyond his realm of investigation.

Appreciation. The acceptance or rejection of parapsychology too often depends on associations or prejudices. Those who reject psychic phenomena as illusory usually do so on the basis of a previous rejection of the occult. Those who accept the reality of psi-phenomena explain their reality in terms of either scientific naturalism or animism. For the scientific naturalist, the universe of reality is completely natural; there is neither need nor evidence of the supernatural or the spiritual. All things are physical and deterministic. Paranormal phenomena are natural events with physical causes that as yet remain undiscovered. For the animist, on the other hand, souls exist and have equal reality with material beings. Paranormal phenomena, in his view, are the product of a psi-function of the rational soul.

The reaction of the Church to psi-phenomena is one of reservation. Her first concern is to determine whether or not such events are supernatural operations. If not, the study of such phenomena pertains to the scientist, and his findings are to be judged on their own merit and objectivity. Religion has nothing to fear from an explanation that is truly scientific. The proper study of parapsychology can only increase man's knowledge and appreciation of God's universe.

See also EXTRASENSORY PERCEPTION; POLTERGEIST; PREMONITION; PSYCHOKINESIS; TELEPATHY.

Bibliography: R. OMEZ, *Psychical Phenomena,* tr. R. HAYNES (New York 1958). A. NIEDERMEYER, *Compendium of Pastoral Medicine,* tr. F. BUONANNO (New York 1960). J. G. PRATT, *Parapsychology: An Insider's View of ESP* (New York 1964). J. B. RHINE, *New World of the Mind* (New York 1953).

[C. P. SVOBODA]

PARAVICINO Y ARTEAGA, HORTENSIO FÉLIX, Trinitarian preacher, theologian, and poet of Spain's golden age of letters; b. Madrid, 1580; d. there, 1633. He was a literary child prodigy, educated at the

Fray Hortensio Félix Paravicino y Arteaga, by El Greco.

The 12th-century Basilica of the Sacred Heart at Paray-le-Monial, France.

Jesuit college at Ocaña. He entered the Trinitarians at Madrid (1600), studying further at the universities of Alcalá and Salamanca, where his oratory impressed the visiting King Philip III (1605). About this time he transferred briefly to the Discalced Trinitarians, returning to the calced branch in which he afterward held various prelatures. Paravicino was the unrivaled orator of the age and as such became court preacher to Philip III (1617) and Philip IV (1621), and was dubbed "preacher of kings and king of preachers." His elaborate style was hailed by Calderón as "succulent," and after the manner of the Roman orator Quintus Hortensius. In 1853 his collected sermons were still considered classics by the Royal Academy. He wrote also *Gridonia o cielo de amor vengado,* a picaresque mythological comedy. Paravicino's literary reputation rests on several lyrics including *The Divine Passion, To Our Lady of Guadalupe, Sonnet on the Tomb of the Painter Who Was "El Greco" of Toledo.* But it is as the subject of two of El Greco's finest portraits (in the Boston Museum of Fine Arts and at Madrid, both dated 1609) that he is immortalized.

Bibliography: ANTONINO DE LA ASUNCIÓN, *Diccionario de escritores trinitarios de España y Portugal,* 2 v. (Rome 1898–99) v.2. EncRelCat 5:1247–48. Espasa 41:1407. **Illustration credit:** Courtesy, Museum of Fine Arts, Boston.

[E. BEARDSLEY]

PARAY-LE-MONIAL, city in Saône-et-Loire department, Diocese of *Autun, Burgundy, east central France. Next to *Lourdes, it is the most popular pilgrimage center in France (since 1865). The rural parish

Paray became le-Monial when *Cluniac monks were sent there by St. *Majolus at the request of Count Lambert of Chalon (973), who endowed the foundation and gave a charter to the people. As the population increased, the monastery became a priory under Cluny and continued so, the prior being lord of the town, until 1789. The monastery church, dedicated to Our Lady in 977 and consecrated in 1004 by Bp. Hugh of *Auxerre, Lambert's son, was replaced c. 1100 by the present model of Burgundian Romanesque (with a semicircular choir beneath an octagonal tower 184 feet high and a 14th-century fresco of Christ Pantocrator, discovered in 1935). In 1794 the city purchased the church, which revolutionaries were about to destroy. Following the revelations of the Sacred Heart to St. Margaret Mary *Alacoque (1673–75), the church became the Basilica of the Sacred Heart (1875). The shrine of the revelations and the saint's relics are in the Visitation monastery founded through the efforts of Jesuits (1626), who had established a mission in Paray to combat Calvinism (1619). The relics of Bl. Claude de *la Colombière were translated from the monastery to the Jesuit chapel (1930). The hospital of Paray, originally under Benedictines, is now staffed by Sisters of St. Marthe. Other monuments in Paray include the Chapel of Notre Dame de Romay, the tower of St. Nicholas, the hôtel de ville, and Hiéron (a Eucharistic museum founded in 1893).

Bibliography: Lecanuet EglFrance, v.1. A. GAUDILLIÈRE, *Lumières de Paray* (St. Léger-Vauban 1955). J. VIREY, *Paray-le-Monial et les églises du Brionnais* (new ed. Paris 1962).

[M. L. LYNN]

PARCHMENT, an ancient writing material. According to tradition it was invented and developed by King Eumenes II (197–158 B.C.) of Pergamum in Asia Minor. Though few would accept the story in view of the discovery of a Greek parchment document dated c. 195 B.C. at *Dura-Europos, it does reflect the fact that such material became popular as a substitute for leather in the early 2d century B.C. The story undoubtedly explains why, since the 3d Christian century, the material has been called *charta pergamena,* from which the word parchment is derived. Earlier it had been known as *membrana* or διφθέρα, the usual word for leather prepared for writing.

Parchment is distinguished from leather in that it is made of hide not subjected to the tanning process that produces leather. The hide of an animal is soaked in lime, and the hair and flesh are removed by scraping and washing. The skin is then treated with a powdered chalk, stretched on a frame, and dried. After this process has been completed, the hide is rubbed with pumice until smooth. The skin is then ready for writing, which may be done on either side. Because of its durability and the fact that both sides could easily be used, parchment was more suitable for the codex form of book, which eventually replaced the *scroll.

Strictly speaking, one may distinguish parchment from vellum, a fine quality parchment. Vellum is produced usually from the skins of embryos—calves, kids, or lambs—whereas ordinary parchment was made from the hides of full-grown sheep and goats. In practice, however, quite frequently no distinction is made, and the two terms are used interchangeably.

The only mention of parchment in the Bible is the reference in 2 Tm 4.13. Paul asks Timothy to bring his cloak and "the books, especially the parchments." The author distinguishes between ordinary scrolls, which were made probably of papyrus rather than of leather, and the more expensive parchment scrolls, which presumably contained some important writing, judging from the material used.

Bibliography: EncDictBibl 1726. H. GERSTINGER, LexThK² 8:273. R. FRATTAROLO, EncCatt 9:1176–77. R. WÜNSCH, Pauly-Wiss RE 5:1157–58; 15:596–601.

[T. H. WEBER]

PARDO BAZÁN, EMILIA, Countess, Spanish realistic novelist and theorist; b. La Coruña (Galicia), Sept. 11, 1851; d. Madrid, 1921. As a deeply committed Catholic and one of the more important novelists of Spain's realistic period (see SPANISH LITERATURE, 4), she was also concerned with problems of aesthetics and made notable contributions to the contemporary debate on that subject. Her outlook, like that of *Pérez Galdós, was cosmopolitan; her father had been in the Cortes; she herself was widely traveled and well-read, and had lectured at the University of Madrid. Among her literary interests were the Russian novel and the work of the Spanish mystics. A realist in both art and life, she was devoted to the spirit of the 18th-century Benedictine, Padre Feijóo, who did so much to lay at rest the medieval ghosts, the memories of which still haunt a chamber of the Spanish mind.

Pardo Bazán's important novels, *Los Pazos de Ulloa* (1886) and *La Madre Naturaleza* (1887), abound in descriptions of her native place. But she uses such natural description as the stage upon which she deftly probes the psychological motivation of her characters as revealed through their actions. Her realistic temper does not flinch from portrayal of the ugly, when artistic need demands such portrayal.

Like most of her contemporaries, she is in the tradition of Spanish prose that is rooted in the *Siglo de Oro* and the "ready-made" realism of *Cervantes, *Tirso, and Lope de *Vega. In her controversial treatise *La*

Emilia Pardo Bazán, portrait by Joaquín Sorolla y Bastida (1863–1923).

Questión Palpitante (1883) she examines the aesthetic problem posed by realism in the light of the ascendant school of French realism and the subsequent naturalism of Émile *Zola. She rejects those developments of the movement that led to determinism, materialism, and utilitarianism. The effect of this widely discussed essay upon the ultimate development of Spanish realism is problematical.

A certain practical, almost masculine cast of her mind has caused her to be compared with St. *Teresa of Avila; yet her work, especially in such novels as *Viaje de Novios* (1881), reflects also the kind of tender, graceful spirit often associated with Gabriela *Mistral. Some even sense echoes of the romantic in her work.

Although she was never admitted to the Academia Real, Pardo Bazán has left behind an important achievement; her firm prose, her evocative descriptive power, her searching and impressive psychological probing make her novels a clear testament to the power of realism and to her literary talent. Her essays, especially those of literary theory, add further dignity to her solid place in modern Spanish literature.

Bibliography: *Obras completas*, ed. F. C. SÁNIZ DE ROBLES, 2 v. (Madrid 1947). E. GONZÁLEZ LÓPEZ, *Emilia Pardo Bazán, novelista de Galicia* (New York 1944). D. F. BROWN, *The Catholic Naturalism of Pardo Bazán* (Chapel Hill 1957). B. ERSKINE, "Emilia Pardo Bazán," *Contemporary Review* 120 (1921) 240–244. R. HILTON, "Emilia Pardo-Bazán's Concept of Spain," *Hispania* 34 (1951) 327–342. C. BRAVO-VILLASANTE, *Vida y obra de Emilia Pardo Bazán* (Madrid 1962). **Illustration credit:** Courtesy of the Hispanic Society of America, New York.

[J. DEVLIN]

PARDOW, WILLIAM O'BRIEN, preacher; b. New York City, June 13, 1847; d. New York City, Jan. 23, 1909. He was one of five children of Robert and Augusta (O'Brien) Pardow. He was educated at the College of St. Francis Xavier, New York City, and joined the Society of Jesus upon graduation in 1864. After early training in French Canada and at Woodstock College, Woodstock, Md., he taught at St. Francis Xavier (1871–75), and then went to France for theological studies. He was ordained in 1877. In 1880 when the Third Republic suppressed the Jesuit Order, he was expelled from France. Pardow held a number of offices in the Maryland–New York province of the Jesuits: *socius* (assistant) to the provincial (1884–88); rector of the College of St. Francis Xavier (1891–93); and pastor of St. Ignatius Loyola Church, New York (1901–03, 1907–09). As provincial (1893–97), he established in Jamaica, British West Indies, the first foreign mission of the U.S. Jesuits. Twice (1888–91, 1903–06) he held the office of master of tertians (Jesuits in their 3d year of probation). He was in constant demand as a speaker throughout the Eastern U.S., and gave many retreats to priests, religious, and laity. Pneumonia, which he contracted in 1909 while traveling to fulfill a preaching engagement, proved fatal.

Bibliography: J. WARD, *William Pardow* (New York 1914).

[F. X. CURRAN]

PARÉ, AMBROISE, great French surgeon of the Renaissance and an important figure in the history of surgery; b. in a village near Laval, 1510; d. Paris, Dec. 20, 1590. Following a brief apprenticeship to a provincial barber-surgeon, Paré served for 3 years at the Hôtel Dieu, the large public hospital in Paris. The rich experience there provided the basis for his further development. He then entered military service, and for the rest of his life alternated between army duty and civilian practice. His skill, courage, and dedication brought him

Ambroise Paré, woodcut in his "Opera Chirurgica," 1594.

great esteem, and he became royal counselor and chief surgeon to four successive kings of France. Paré wrote widely of his experiences and made numerous innovations in treatment. Defying tradition, he wrote in the vernacular instead of Latin, and he successfully challenged the authority of the powerful Paris Faculty of Medicine. His books went through numerous editions and translations, and still rank among the classics in surgery. Although he was thought to be a Protestant by some, Paré was a faithful Catholic. He publicly refuted rumors to the contrary, and denounced those who persecuted him for his stand. A man of high moral stature, he possessed deep compassion and modesty. He frequently wrote of his surgical successes, "I dressed him, God cured him."

Bibliography: A. PARÉ, *The Workes of That Famous Chirurgion, A. Parey,* tr. T. JOHNSON (London 1649); *Textes choisis,* ed. L. DELARUELLE and M. SENDRAIL (Paris 1953); *The Apologie and Treatise,* ed. G. KEYNES (Chicago 1952). L. M. ZIMMERMAN and I. VEITH, *Great Ideas in the History of Surgery* (Baltimore 1961). G. A. L. SARTON, *Six Wings: Men of Science in the Renaissance* (Bloomington, Ind. 1957). J. DOE, *Bibliography of the Works of Ambroise Paré* (Chicago 1937). **Illustration credit:** Philadelphia Museum of Art, Ars Medica Collection.

[L. M. ZIMMERMAN]

PAREDES Y FLORES, MARIANA DE JESÚS, ST., the "Lily of Ecuador"; b. Quito, Ecuador, Oct. 31, 1618; d. there, May 26, 1645. The eighth child of Jerónimo Zenel Paredes y Flores and Mariana Jaramillo de Granobles, Mariana upon her parents' death was left to the care of her sister Jerónima and brother-in-law Cosme de Caso. Since the child had already begun her life of prayer, fasting, and penance, her guardians found a religious adviser for her in the

Jesuit priest Juan Camacho. She had a series of Jesuit confessors but her most influential spiritual adviser was the Jesuit lay brother Hernando de la Cruz. As models for her spiritual life she chose St. *Catherine of Siena, St. *Rose of Lima, and St. Teresa of Jesús. Mariana did not enter a convent but spent most of her time in an austerely furnished upper room in her sister's house. She wore a black garment modeled on the Jesuit cassock. Tradition holds that she joined the Third Order of St. Francis at 21 and wore its cord; though she never wore the habit while she was alive, she was buried with it over her black "Jesuit dress." While continuing her life of personal mortification, she encouraged the poor, hungry, and ill to come to her for help. In her sister's house she developed a kind of free clinic and a schoolroom in which she taught Indian children. A number of times she predicted that the house would eventually become a Carmelite convent. In 1645, when Lima was visited with a number of calamaties—earthquakes, epidemics, volcanic eruptions—Mariana publicly offered her life for the benefit of the city. Within the generation after her death the process for beatification was begun but it was beset with mishaps to the documents and the sponsors. She was finally canonized by Pius XII July 9, 1950. Her feast is celebrated in Ecuador on May 26.

Bibliography: F. P. KEYES, *The Rose and the Lily* (New York 1961). A. ESPINOSA PÓLIT, *Santa Mariana de Jesús hija de la Compañía de Jesús* (Quito 1957).

[J. M. VARGAS]

PAREJA, FRANCISCO, Mercedarian chronicler; place and date of birth unknown; d. Sept. 9, 1688. Nothing is known of his early years, not even his parents' names. He probably studied at the Mercedarian convent in Mexico City. In 1652 he was in Spain. He was the first rector of the San Ramón Nonato College in Mexico City (1654); professor of theology at the University of Mexico (1656); provincial twice (1655 and 1668); and provincial chronicler (1671). His main literary work was *Crónica de la provincia de la Visitación de Ntra. Sra. de la Merced redención de cautivos, de Nueva España,* which was completed Nov. 4, 1687. It remained unedited for 2 centuries. Cristobal de Aldana published a compendium of it about 1770; this edition was poorly printed and lacked a press signature. Juan Rodríguez Puebla (1798–1848), Mexican educator, made a manuscript copy of Pareja's *Crónica.* This copy was taken to Europe in 1869 and sold to a London bookseller, but was not published. The original manuscript, signed by Pareja, was discovered in Mexico and then published in two volumes in 1882–83. The unsigned preface contains historical information on Pareja and the vicissitudes the manuscript had gone through. The *Crónica* has three distinct parts: the first is an account of the Mercedarian pioneers in Mexico; the second is concerned with the Mercedarians who came to Mexico in 1576 to found a permanent community and carries the history to 1687; the third part is a collection of documents, added by editors, bringing the history of the order up to 1844. Pareja's purpose was to support his claim that the Mercedarians came to Mexico before the Franciscans, Dominicans, or Augustinians. The *Crónica* is very useful for the history of the Mercedarian Order. Two copies are extant: one in the library of the Museo de Antropología e Historia

in Mexico City; the other in the Library of Congress, Washington, D.C.

[E. GÓMEZ TAGLE]

PAREJA, FRANCISCO DE, Franciscan missionary in Florida; dates of birth and death unknown. He was a native of Auñon, Spain, and joined the Franciscan Order in the Province of Castile. Pareja went to Florida as an Indian missionary in 1595 and served at San Juan del Puerto (in the area of modern Jacksonville) until 1616. He was then elected provincial of the Province of Santa Elena, which comprised Cuba, Florida, and Georgia. According to Fray Luis Gerónimo de Oré, Visitor General to Florida in 1616, Pareja was a missionary of great sanctity and incredible zeal; he had expert knowledge of the Timucuan language. He wrote valuable mission reports and made frequent trips into the interior. Pareja composed the following works, all of which were printed in Mexico: *Cathecismo en lengua castellana y timuquana* (1612), *Cathecismo y breve exposición de la doctrina christiana* (1612), *Confessionario en lengua castellana y timuquana* (1613), *Arte y pronunciación en lengua timuquana y castellana* (1614), and *Cathecismo y examen para los que comulgan en lengua castellana y timuquana* (1627).

Bibliography: L. J. DE ORÉ, *Relación histórica de la Florida, escrita en el siglo XVII;* ed. A. LÓPEZ, 2 v. (Madrid 1931–33); *The Martyrs of Florida (1513–1616),* tr. M. J. GEIGER (Franc Studies 18; New York 1936). M. J. GEIGER, *The Franciscan Conquest of Florida (1573–1618)* (Washington 1937).

[M. GEIGER]

PARENT AND CHILD, U.S. LAW OF

Legal recognition of the parent-child relationship takes the form of prescribing various rights and duties attached to the reciprocal statuses. The law provides also the criteria for determining when the natural relationship is to be deemed legitimate.

Legitimacy. Only the birth of a legitimate child gives rise to all the usual legal incidents of the parent-child relationship. Generally a child is legitimate if it is born during the marriage of its mother to its father, and there is a very strong presumption in the law that a child born to a wife during marriage is her husband's. The presumption prevails unless the contrary fact is clearly established. The presumption is applicable although conception has occurred before the marriage. In addition, at common law and in many states today, both spouses are incompetent to testify to matters that would tend to show that the husband could not be the father. This disability to so testify has been abolished in some jurisdictions, and its effect has been greatly mitigated in many others that permit the use of blood tests to determine paternity. Although the presumption in favor of legitimacy is still initially applicable, a negative finding of paternity based on a blood test is usually made conclusive in rebutting the presumption.

The legal incidence of illegitimacy has been much reduced in recent times by a variety of ameliorating statutes, the most common of which provides that a subsequent marriage of the natural father and mother will legitimate children born before the marriage. In some states there must be in addition a written acknowledgement of paternity by the father, and in other states acknowledgement alone will legitimate the child.

Two states have simply abolished the status of illegitimacy by providing that all children are the legitimate children of their natural parents whether or not they are married to one another. Of course there is still the problem of establishing the father's identity when it is not admitted. Many states legitimate the children born during a marriage that is later annulled for original invalidity.

At the present time under traditional rules governing legitimacy a number of cases have held that children conceived by means of artificial insemination and reliance upon a third party donor are illegitimate. It has been suggested that this result should be modified by legislation in the light of present-day public attitudes toward this procedure. *See* ARTIFICIAL INSEMINATION (U.S. LAW OF).

According to early common law not even the mother was legally obliged to support an illegitimate child. This was later changed by statute in England, and today all states impose such a duty upon both natural parents. Aside from what may be serious personal and social problems involved in illegitimacy, the most significant legal detriment to the bastard child has been its ineligibility to inherit from either parent. Again, most states today by statute permit the illegitimate child to inherit from the mother and often from the mother's kindred, and these relatives may be given the right to inherit from the child. Sometimes the child is given the right to inherit from the father, and perhaps his kindred, if he has acknowledged the child as his or if the identity has been established in paternity proceedings.

A very interesting recent case has considered for the first time the claim of an illegitimate child against its father for the wrong committed by causing it to be born an adulterine bastard. The court recognized the wrong committed as a tort, but refused relief on the grounds that the legal consequences in allowing the action would be so sweeping that any redress should be provided by the legislature only after a thoughtful and thorough study. (*See* ILLEGITIMACY, U.S. LAW OF.)

Adoption. Adoption is the legal procedure for establishing the parent-child relationship between persons not so related by birth. Although it was widely accepted in ancient civilizations as a means of continuing the adopter's family, adoption was never recognized by common law for fear of detracting from the tradition that property devolution should follow blood lineage. In this country adoption statutes date from about 1850 and have been enacted by all states. When the statutory procedure is followed, the relationship between the adopted child and the adoptive parents becomes substantially equivalent in law to the natural parent-child relationship.

Apart from custody and guardianship, which are transferred to the adoptive parents exclusively, the extent to which legal incidents may continue to subsist between the child and its natural parents has varied depending on the wording and construction given other laws, especially those of intestate succession. In some states the adopted child has been held entitled to inherit from both the natural parents and the adoptive parents, although there is no valid reason to so prefer an adopted child. Moreover the basic purpose of adoption is best served by the effecting of a complete substitution of the adoptive family for the natural family and the placing of the adopted child on the same footing as a natural child. Under more recent adoption legislation the trend has been to terminate all legal incidents of the natural parent-child relationship. Of course there remains the physical fact of consanguinity, which may be relevant under other laws.

While the primary object of adoption statutes is to improve the lot of illegitimate, abandoned, or orphaned children, most states permit the adoption also of adults, sometimes providing that the person adopting must be older that the person adopted. This use of adoption is often resorted to in situations that depend upon the existence of a child heir to bring about a desired result under decedents' estate laws.

Adoption statutes usually provide that the adoptive parents be of a certain minimum age and, frequently, that when a petition for adoption is made by one spouse alone, the other spouse must give consent.

Generally the natural parents must consent to the adoption, but in the case of an illegitimate child the consent of the natural mother alone is usually sufficient. If the child to be adopted is of sufficient discretion to understand the proceedings, its consent is essential.

Closely related to the matter of consent in adoption is the procedure for termination of parental rights. By their consent to adoption the rights of the natural parents are permanently terminated with the final decree approving the adoption. However, most statutes provide that when it is judicially determined that the natural parents have abandoned the child, are guilty of gross and persistent neglect in providing for its care, or are seriously and culpably unfit to exercise the parental guardianship, their consent to the adoption is not necessary. The case must be clear to warrant such drastic sanctions. With increasing frequency adoption statutes require that an investigation be made and reported to the court by an appropriate state office of public welfare to determine the fitness of adopting parents. Such a procedure provides an objective appraisal upon which to determine the best interests of the child privately or independently placed for adoption without intervention of a licensed child-care agency. A further trend in recent legislation is the requirement that all placements be made by a state-approved intermediary unless the child is adopted by natural relatives.

The statutes often prescribe that "when practical" or "whenever possible" the adopting parents shall be of the same religious faith as the child. Although the prescription is not phrased as an absolute requirement, the cases in which the issue has been raised indicate that the statutory direction ordinarily must be followed. In the exceptional case where a child's different religious affiliation may not have been determined until after strong affective ties have been developed in the prospective adoptive home, it has sometimes been held that the welfare of the child will be best served by permitting the adoption.

In the last analysis the courts are uniform in adhering to the maxim that the ultimate test in determining the merits of an adoption petition is the welfare and best interest of the child, taking into account all relevant circumstances. (*See* ADOPTION, U.S. LAW OF.)

Care and Support. While the child is a minor and unemancipated, the legal incidents of the parent-child relationship relate largely to the duty of parents to provide the child with care, support, protection, training, and education according to their circumstances in life. The parents are entitled to the services and earnings of the child. The obligation to support is primarily that of the father, and various statutory procedures in aid of neglected dependents are available to enforce the obligation. In addition, the father may be charged, for the reasonable value of necessaries furnished a child by other persons. (Necessaries are those essential items needed by the child for material wellbeing and not supplied by the father.) Under modern family expense statutes both parents may be liable for all expenses incurred by members of their family, including a child.

With respect to training of children, parents may administer reasonable corporal punishment as necessary to teach discipline without incurring civil or criminal liability. In this connection there seems to be an alarming growth in the incidence of the severe beating of children by parents of small children and even infants. As a result a number of states have recently enacted legislation providing for mandatory reporting to an appropriate public authority by doctors and hospitals of all cases in which a child's injuries are suspected of being nonaccidental. Under some laws child abuse is defined as a crime. Most such laws prescribe an immediate investigation, usually by a public welfare agency, and the providing of protective social services to prevent further abuse. Removal of a child from its home is undertaken only as a last resort.

Taken together, the duties owed by parents to minor children are denominated a guardianship by nature, which is imposed by law for the protection of the young. *See* GUARDIANS, U.S. LAW OF.

Custody. Ordinarily parents are entitled without question to the custody of their minor children. Custody is essentially the right to the control of the person of the child concomitant with the exercise of the parental duties of guardian. The right to custody is surrendered when a parent consents to a child's adoption, and it may be determined as between parents by agreement at the time of separation. Public authority may seek removal of custody from parents even against their will if they are guilty of gross neglect in fulfilling their duties to the serious detriment of the child's welfare. Such steps have been taken also against parents who, on the basis of religious beliefs, have refused to provide usual and necessary medical treatment or have failed to send their children to school as required by law. Apart from these cases, the most frequent legal contests involving the natural right of parents to custody occur when parents are divorced or when a parent seeks the return of a child from a third party, often a relative, who has been raising it.

Under common law between parents the primary right to custody belonged to the father without much regard to what might be best for the child. Today custody courts apply the "best interests of the child" test, and it is usual to prefer the mother if the child is very young. When the child is of sufficient age to exercise some discretion, his own preference is accorded weight. Generally the outcome of a divorce action is material only as it bears clearly on the personal fitness of a parent to have custody. When one parent is awarded custody, the other may be entitled to visitation rights. One very difficult question from the Catholic point of view arises when an antenuptial agreement to raise children as Catholics, required by the Church for obtaining permission for a mixed marriage, is sought to be enforced. If subsequent to such an agreement a civil divorce or separation takes place, the question of the children's religious rearing may be raised in the legal proceeding for determining custody.

Since the custody of a child of tender years is almost always awarded to the mother unless she is shown to be unfit, the antenuptial agreement is usually not a factor in that instance. In other cases the courts are committed to a policy of awarding custody based on an objective evaluation of what is best for the child. They refuse to be bound by prior agreements between the parents in reaching such a determination. In this perspective it becomes a question of whether one religion or another will best serve the child's welfare rather than whether one parent should be required to observe a prior agreement with the other concerning the child's religion. On this question the majority of courts have been unwilling to pass any judgment, with the result that these agreements are given little or no weight in awarding custody. Should custody once be awarded to the non-Catholic parent who only later refuses to observe the agreement, a court is faced with other problems. It may be difficult to enforce compliance with the agreement without a change in custody. Compliance may be contrary to the presently held religious beliefs of the non-Catholic parent. Moreover the order of enforcement might be charged with placing the authority of the court as an agent of state government in support of a particular religion in violation of federal and state constitutions. The majority of such cases have refused to order enforcement of the agreement. For the most part these agreements must rely on the willingness and good faith of the parties for observance.

In a contest over child custody between parents and third persons the courts again apply the "best interests" test but they also display varying degrees of preference in favor of the natural parent who is not shown to be unfit.

Generally the last surviving parent may by will direct the appointment of a guardian who, subject to court approval, will assume the custody of minor children upon the parent's death.

With regard to property, although parents are entitled to the earnings of an unemancipated child, they have no rights to the child's separate property otherwise acquired.

For the child's part, prior to emancipation he is subject to parental control reasonably exercised. Legal enforcement of this authority can rely only upon procedures available for declaring a child wayward or incorrigible and thereby subject in some instances to commitment to a public training school.

Under decedents' estate laws parents and children are given rights of inheritance in the estate of a child or parent, as the case may be, who dies intestate. In most jurisdictions the child's right may be defeated by a will of the parent. The parents' rights are not so vulnerable during the child's minority when he is incapable of making a will.

Emancipation. Emancipation may occur by agreement, express or implied, between the parent and child.

In such an instance it is understood that the child shall be substantially independent of parental custody, control, and support and entitled to retain its own earnings. Emancipation with the same effect of severing the filial tie may occur by operation of law when, under various circumstances, parental control and support is in fact terminated and the child thereafter maintains itself. Marriage of a minor ordinarily emancipates him, as does enlistment in the armed forces. If emancipation has not previously occurred, the parental rights and duties will normally terminate when the child reaches its majority, usually at 21 years of age. This might not be the case, however, should a child not by then have completed its education, provision for which in the circumstances of the parents could reasonably be expected to continue beyond minority. The duty to provide care and support for an incompetent child continues without regard to age.

After emancipation, apart from a statutory duty to support indigent parents, which is frequently imposed upon self-supporting children, the only remaining legal incident of the parent-child relationship is the right of inheritance.

Suits may be brought between parents and unemancipated children in cases involving contracts or property torts. The rule is generally otherwise in the case of personal injury torts. This is explained principally on the theory that these actions would tend to foster domestic strife and to interfere with the exercise and performance of parental rights and duties. Nonetheless, a number of courts have made an exception to the rule, permitting the action where the injury is willfully inflicted or where the parent is acting in a business or vocational capacity and is insured for such liability. In these cases courts have reasoned that the wrongful conduct may be viewed as falling outside the normal parent-child relationship so that relief should not be barred by a policy of insulating the family against disruption. Generally a parent is not indirectly liable for the liability incurred by a child for its tortious conduct toward others. However, a parent may be liable on a general theory of negligence for failure to exercise reasonable parental restraint over a child's conduct where the failure results in foreseeable injury to another. In addition, many states now have antivandalism statutes, which impose vicarious liability upon parents for the malicious or willful destruction of the property of others by their minor children.

In an action against another for tortious injury to the person of an unemancipated child, a parent is entitled to damages for loss of the child's services and earnings, in addition to the cost of medical treatment for the child.

See also ABORTION, IV (U.S. LAW OF); BIRTH CONTROL, U.S. LAW OF; STERILIZATION, U.S. LAW OF.

Bibliography: C. G. VERNIER, *American Family Laws,* 5 v. (Stanford 1931–38). A. C. JACOBS and J. GOEBEL, eds., *Cases and Other Materials on Domestic Relations* (4th ed. New York 1961), pt. 4. P. A. RYAN and D. GRANFIELD, *Domestic Relations* (New York 1963), ch. 7. W. E. McCURDY, "Torts between Parent and Child," *Villanova Law Review* 5 (1960) 521–560.

[J. J. CLEARY]

PARINI, GIUSEPPE

Italian writer; b. Brianza (Bosisio), May 23, 1729; d. Milan, Aug. 15, 1799. A poor boy, he studied for the priesthood at Milan, inspired by the example of an uncle

and helped by a small legacy from a great-aunt. The transition to city life entailed financial difficulties, and after ordination he sought relief as tutor in aristocratic families. Here he developed the habit of observation

Giuseppe Parini.

that was to make him "the leading painter of lordly manners." After the anonymous publication of *Mattino* (1763) and *Mezzogiorno* (1765), the first two parts of *Giorno,* his writing and tutoring brought him further financial security. When the French replaced the Austrians (1796) and set up a democratic government, Parini was assigned a post in public administration, from which, because of an uncompromising attitude, he was soon dismissed.

Heir to a moralism that for centuries had animated the still meager Lombard portion of Italian literature, *Giorno* pretends to train a young lord in the ways of the social world. In *Mattino,* a reader observes the lord from his awakening to the time he leaves home; *Mezzogiorno* pictures him at dinner with his lady; in *Vespro* (1801), the lord accompanies her on social calls; finally, in *Notte* (1801), the theater, the evening party, and the game of chance are depicted. This apparently pedestrian material is treated in mock-epic style, and not without traces of Boileau and Pope. Yet with a controlled moral disdain and a highly original inventiveness Parini condemns the entire ruling class, so removed in circumstances and attitude from their plain, industrious forefathers. These ancestors were the cultural parents of the contemporary laboring people, from whose ranks Parini himself had come and for whom his sympathy was clear and deep. *Mattino,* focused entirely on the protagonist, is a bitter satire; *Mezzogiorno* is more cunningly directed against the beliefs and attitudes of aristocratic society itself. In *Vespro* and *Notte,* both published posthumously, the poet's animus is muted, his anger mollified; he is somewhat amused by the absurdities of Italian aristocracy but now views them with detachment. The whole is a triumph of a sort of translucent Mozartian magic.

The moral design and stylistic perfection he seeks for his poetic, analyzed and expounded in *Principi fondamentali e generali di belle lettere applicati alle belle arti* (1773–75), are clearly followed in the *Odi* (19 of them composed between 1757 and 1796). Moving away from the Arcadian theme of *Alcune poesie di Ripano Eupilino* (1752), he substitutes for its idyllic aim the practical goals of the common good. The laborious work of the fields, public health menaced by the plague-ridden air of the city, the necessity for smallpox vaccination, the need for female education, the danger of politics, the thoughtless dismissal of the massacres of the French Revolution: these are the themes that guide him first to harsh warning, then to cold disdain. Slowly his poetry moves toward the noble affirmation of individual worth (*La caduta*, 1785), to a freer animation of the natural and human world (*Il messagio*, 1793; *Alla Musa*, 1796). The poet's old age is marked by well-bred tolerance of a society in which Christianity has been reduced to pleasant broadmindedness. In *Dono* (1790), he has abandoned the tragic note that was to reappear in the poetry of Vittorio *Alfieri, harbinger of a new age.

Bibliography: *Opere*, ed. E. BELLORINI, 4 v. (Bari 1913–29); *Tutte le opere edite e inedite*, ed. G. MAZZONI (Florence 1925); *Poesie e prose: Con appendice di poeti satirici e didascalici del Settecento*, ed. L. CARETTI (Milan 1951). A. CHIARI, *Sulle "Odi" di G. Parini* (Milan 1943). G. GIUSTI, "Della vita e delle opere di G. Parini," intro. to G. PARINI, *Versi e prose* (Florence 1846). C. CANTÙ, *L'abate Parini e la Lombardia nel secolo passato* (Milan 1854). F. DE SANCTIS, *Nuovi saggi critici* (Naples 1879), includes his essay of 1871. G. CARDUCCI, *Studi su Giuseppe Parini*, v.16–17 of *Edizione nazionale delle opere*, 30 v. (Bologna 1935–40); *Storia del "Giorno" di G. Parini* (Bologna 1892). G. DE ROBERTIS, "Il regno del Parini," *Saggi* (Florence 1939). D. PETRINI, *La poesia e l'arte di G. Parini* (Bari 1930). R. SPONGANO, *La poetica del sensimo e la poesia di Parini* (Milan 1933). M. FUBINI, *Dal Muratori al Baretti* (Bari 1946). W. BINNI, "La sintesi pariniana," *Preromanticismo italiano* (Naples 1948). G. NATALI, EncIt 26:357–363.

[M. APOLLONIO]

PARIS

Capital of *France, on both banks of the Seine River and on the Île de la Cité. The city (40 square miles) coincides with the Seine department. Since 1622 Paris has been the seat of a metropolitan see of 1,850 square miles.

City. The first settlement of the Gallic *Parisii* was on the Île de la Cité. After the Roman conquest the town (*Lutetia Parisiorum*) expanded to the south, on the left bank, where the remains of arenas, baths, and other monuments still exist. Christianity was introduced by St. *Denis (d. 258) and his companions, all later martyred; after the emperors became Christian, persecution ceased (313). *Julian the Apostate, a Roman general, was proclaimed emperor in Paris by his troops (360). In the 5th century Paris frequently fought off invasions, and St. *Geneviève rallied forces who were successful against Attila (451). Franks settled in the area; and after defeating the Visigoths at Vouillé (507), *Clovis, with his queen *Clotilde, made Paris the capital. His *Merovingian and *Carolingian successors, however, somewhat neglected Paris until the days of Bishop Gozlin and Count Odo, who defended it against Normans (884–886). Odo (887) and his nephew Hugh Capet (987–996) became kings. *Philip II Augustus enclosed Paris with walls (1180). Paris then had three parts: the merchant *ville* on the right bank; the *cité* on the Île, political and religious center of the capital, with the royal palace, the cathedral, and the episcopal residence; and the *université* on the left bank, the Latin Quarter. In the 13th century Paris had about 100,000 people.

Political Strife and Expansion. Despite troubles in the 14th and 15th centuries, Paris continued to expand. The rich merchant Étienne Marcel and the Estates General (1356–58) forced the King out of the capital. Charles V built the fortress of the Louvre and a new wall (1370), well beyond that of Philip II, anchored to the east by the fortress of the Bastille. Besieged by Burgundians, the Duke of Bedford, and *Joan of Arc (1430), Paris was reconquered by Charles VII (1437).

Paris probably had 400,000 people when trouble and devastation returned with the *Wars of Religion. It was the center of the *St. Bartholomew's Day massacre (1572) and of resistance to Henry of Navarre. Peace and order were restored only when *Henry IV abjured Protestantism at Saint-Denis (1593).

The Fronde and other political troubles of the 17th century did not keep Paris from reaching 500,000 people by 1700. New quarters arose, especially to the west (Saint-Honoré, Saint-Germain). After the *French Revolution, *Napoleon I began to replan the city in grandiose style. At the time of the revolution of 1848, which was directed against the monarchy only, Paris had 1 million people.

Fig. 1. *Paris in the 15th century, miniature by Pol de Limbourg in the "Très Riches Heures" of the Duc du Berry, in the Musée Condé, Chantilly, France. In the right background can be seen the Sainte-Chapelle.*

After serious insurrections *Napoleon III seized power from the Second Republic. In 1860 Paris annexed some of the suburbs, doubling its area and bringing its population to nearly 2 million. The prefect Baron Haussmann built wide avenues and transformed the city for Napoleon III.

New destruction came with the commune revolt after the fall of the empire in 1871, but peace returned under the Third Republic. Paris, with 3 million people, soon had more people in its suburbs than in the city itself. It is still an economic and intellectual capital, despite World Wars I and II.

Intellectual Life. From the 11th century Paris was not only an economic center, but intellectual life flourished in the schools of Notre-Dame, Saint-Victor, and Sainte-Geneviève, all of which had banded together by 1215 to form the university (see below). Colleges opened to lodge students from all western Europe; the College of Constantinople (1204) for students from the East was the first with academic goals. Learned men from many countries taught in Paris: e.g., *Thomas Aquinas, *Albert the Great, *Bonaventure, John *Duns Scotus. In 1480 Louis XI founded the Bibliothèque Royale. Printing gave new impetus to intellectual life, as did the founding of the *Collège de France (1532). While scholasticism declined at the Sorbonne, the humanities and sciences progressed, especially in Jesuit colleges, such as the College of Clermont (later called Collège Louis-le-Grand).

Besides the major seminary of Saint-Sulpice, which attracted students from all France and even from abroad, Paris has a minor seminary at Conflans and many Catholic colleges. Apart from the state university, higher education is represented by the Catholic Institute (1875), with several faculties and specialized schools, such as the Higher School of Economic and Commercial Sciences.

Churches. The first churches were built *c.* 400; St-Marcellus, on the left bank, on the tomb of Bishop St. Marcellus (d. *c.* 436); the cathedral, on the Île; and St-Martin, on the right bank, dedicated to the famous bishop of *Tours.

On Mount Saint-Geneviève, site of the Panthéon, Clovis founded the basilica of the Holy Apostles, where he was buried. King Childebert, who probably rebuilt Notre-Dame on the Île, built the church of the Holy Cross and St. Vincent (543); the latter became the Abbey of *Saint-Germain-des-Prés (754). Other religious edifices followed, and parishes were organized. Monasteries were founded that exploited vast domains, attracting important populations, such as that around Saint-Germain-des-Prés. Parts of several Romanesque buildings of this period remain: Saint-Germain-des-Prés, Saint-Martin-des-Champs (since 1794 the National Conservatory of Arts and Trades), Saint-Pierre in Montmartre. Bishop Maurice de Sully laid the first stone of a new Gothic cathedral (1163–1246), for which *Pérotin revised (*c.* 1200) *Léonin's book of organ music.

Shrines. There are several popular shrines: St-Étienne-du-Mont with the tomb of St. Geneviève, patroness of Paris; Sacré-Coeur; Notre-Dame-des-Victoires, seat of the archconfraternity of the Immaculate Heart of Mary; the chapel of the Sisters of St. Vincent de Paul, called the Chapel of the *Miraculous Medal,

where the Blessed Virgin appeared to St. Catherine *Labouré (1830).

Monasteries. The oldest monastery is the abbey of *Saint-Denis, north of Paris. The basilica built by St. Geneviève was rebuilt by King Dagobert I (d. 639) and by Abbot *Suger (*c.* 1135). Occupied by Benedictines from 656 to the Revolution, it was important in the 9th and reached its peak in the 12th century. Until 1789 it was the burial place of *Capetian kings.

Saint-Germain-des-Prés (558), originally dedicated to the Spanish martyr St. Vincent, in 754 took the name of the Paris bishop who had consecrated it. Benedictine, it was in the Middle Ages the center of a distinct community that came to be attached to Paris. In the 17th and 18th centuries, as the motherhouse of the *Maurists, it was the residence of learned Benedictines: Jean Luc d'*Achéry, Edmond Martène (1654–1739), Jean *Mabillon, and Bernard de *Montfaucon.

Also Benedictine were the abbeys of Blancs-Manteaux and Saint-Martin-des-Champs, and the College of Cluny in the Latin Quarter. The College of Bernardines and the Monastery of Feuillants (17th century) were Cistercian. Carthusians had a monastery near Luxembourg.

Canons regular in 1108 founded Saint-Victor, famous for the theologians *Hugh and *Richard and the poet *Adam. Sainte-Geneviève was the center of their congregation in France. There were also convents of Augustinians on the left bank quai, reformed Augustinians (Little Fathers) at Notre-Dame-des-Victoires, and Discalced Augustinians (Little Augustinians) at what is today the École des Beaux-Arts.

Mendicant orders of the 13th century had many houses in Paris (Dominicans, Franciscan Observantines, Capuchins, Carmelites), as did orders founded after 1500 (Jesuits, Oratorians, Lazarists, Sulpicians, Foreign Missions, Holy Ghost Fathers). Among the many women's convents were Saint-Martial (founded by St. *Eligius, d. 660), Franciscans at Longchamp (founded by Bl. *Isabelle, sister of Louis IX), *Port-Royal (a Jansenist center in the 17th century), and the abbeys of Val-de-Grâce and *Montmartre.

All these houses were suppressed in the Revolution; new ones have been gradually established since. Of note today are the Benedictine Sainte-Marie Abbey, Benedictine nuns of rue Tournefort, Dominicans of rue du Faubourg-St-Honoré, Franciscans of rue Marie-Rose, Capuchins of rue Boissonade, and many houses of modern congregations.

Architecture. The ogival style of architecture that developed at this time was the style of Paris and the Île-de-France. Notre-Dame was a model for Gothic churches. *Louis IX's Sainte-Chapelle (1243–48), built to house relics of the Passion sent him by the Latin Emperor of Constantinople, was Gothic, as were St-Séverin, St-Médard, St-Merri, the abbey church of Saint-Denis near Paris, and other churches. Several churches were built or modified in the new Gothic style (St-Laurent, St-Nicholas-des-Champs, St-Germain-l'Auxerrois), as were several *hôtels* (those of Sens and of the abbots of Cluny near the Sorbonne). A new art, inspired by the Italian Renaissance, appeared in the churches of Saint-Étienne-du-Mont (1517–1626) and in secular buildings (Louvre, Tuileries, and many *hôtels* in the Marais quarter to the

*Fig. 2. Detail of the 13th-century main portal of the ca-
thedral of Notre-Dame de Paris. In the tympanum over the
door, elaborately decorated with ironwork, are sculpted
scenes from the life of the Blessed Virgin.*

east). With absolute monarchy came classical art: large secular buildings (Luxembourg; Richelieu's Palais Cardinal, later Palais Royal) and churches (Notre-Dame-des-Victoires, St-Roch, St-Sulpice, St-Nicholas-du-Chardonnet, SS. Paul-et-Louis, the Oratory). Façades were adorned with columns and frontons, and cupolas marked the centers of transepts (Carmelites, Sorbonne, Val-de-Grâce, Palais Mazarin). Religious art illustrated Paris's Catholic renaissance. The colonnade of the Louvre and Invalides, whose dome (1675–1706) is the most noteworthy in Paris, characterized the age of *Louis XIV. The church of Sainte-Geneviève (1759–90; the modern Panthéon), modeled on Greek art, and St-Philippe-du-Roule, modeled on early Christian basilicas, were masterpieces of religious art. The Madeleine (1806–42; originally the Temple of Glory) and the churches of St-Pierre-du-Gros-Caillou, Notre-Dame of Loretto, and St-Vincent-de-Paul were neoclassical religious monuments. The old churches that were unfortunately destroyed were replaced by imitation Gothic (St-Clotilde), Romanesque, and Renaissance (St-Honoré of Eylau, St-François-Xavier, Trinité, and St-Augustin).

Probably no other city in the world has such a variety of laboratories, museums, and schools. But until recently religious art produced nothing. Montmartre's Sacré-Coeur (1875–1919), dominating the city with its mass, is but an imitation of Roman-Byzantine basilicas. A new religious art appears in St-Espirit and Ste-Odile. The Eiffel Tower was built in 1879.

For many years Paris has been a center of international organizations. World's Fairs have been held there since 1855. Its many institutions include the National Observatory (1667); École Polytechnique (1794); École Normale Supérieure (1794); École Supérieure des Mines (1783); and the Institute National de France (1795), which comprises the Académie Française (1635), Académie des Inscriptions et Belles Lettres (1663), Académie des Sciences (1663), Académie des Beaux-Arts (1795), and Académie des Sciences Morales et Politiques (1795).

Archdiocese. Paris's first bishop was St. Denis, according to Gregory of Tours (d. 593) one of seven bishops sent to Gaul by Rome in 250. He was martyred with the priest Eleutherius and the deacon Rusticus (c. 258). St. Geneviève built a church on his tomb (475). In the 9th century he was wrongly identified as *Pseudo-Dionysius (the Areopagite), and to the history of his martyrdom was added the legend that, decapitated, he carried his head in his hands to his place of burial. The Diocese of Paris, which was organized later, included all the former civitas Parisiorum and was for more than 1,000 years suffragan to *Sens. In Merovingian times it had sainted bishops: *Marcellus, *Germain of Paris, and *Landry. In Carolingian times the intellectual influence of the Abbey of Saint-Denis was strong.

In Capetian times bishops were associated with the university as famous theologians and canonists: *Peter Lombard (1157–60), *Maurice of Sully (1160–96), Odo of Sully (1196–1228), *William of Auvergne (1228–49), and Étienne *Tempier (1268–79). The episcopacy was less distinguished in the 14th and 15th centuries, when the university (Chancellors *Peter of Ailly and Jean *Gerson) represented the Church of Paris. The university retained its brilliance in the 16th

century, despite the Wars of Religion, with such students as *Ignatius of Loyola and *Francis de Sales. Paris's bishops were dealing more with political and diplomatic affairs than with pastoral duties: Étienne de Poncher (1503–19), Jean du Bellay (1532–51), and Pierre de Gondi (1569–97).

On the request of *Louis XIII in 1622, Gregory XV made Paris an archbishopric with the suffragans Chartres, Meaux, Orléans, and Blois (when created in 1697). The left bank became a quarter of mysticism; Pierre de *Bérulle, Charles de *Condren, and Jean Jacques *Olier represented a spirituality that attracted many. A Catholic renaissance was marked by flourishing religious orders: Cardinal de Bérulle founded the Oratory and, with Bl. Marie of the Incarnation, the first Carmelite convent of Paris; Jean Jacques Olier founded the seminary and the *Sulpicians. St. *Vincent de Paul founded the Congregation of the Missions (Lazarists) and with St. *Louise de Marillac, the Daughters of Charity. The lay apostolate had the *Compagnie du Saint-Sacrement. *Jansenism and *Gallicanism made headway, more or less supported by certain archbishops (e.g., Cardinal Louis Antoine de *Noailles, 1695–1729); but Abp. Christophe de Beaumont (1746–81) combatted Gallicanism and agnostic philosophes, and defended the Jesuits.

Under the old regime the archbishop of Paris was duke of Saint-Cloud, a title and land held by the bishops since the 6th century and made a peerage duchy by Louis XIV in 1690. His income in 1789 was more than 250,000 livres. With an enclave (Champeaux deanery) in the Diocese of Sens, the See of Paris was larger than at present. It had the two archpresbyteries of Madeleine (parishes on the Île and the right bank) and St-Séverin (left bank); and the three archdeaconries of Paris in the north (Chelles and Montmorency deaneries), Josas in the west and south (Chateaufort and Montlhéry), and Brie in the east (Lagny and Vieux Corbeil). Some 500 parishes had more than 1 million people in 1789. The archbishop governed with eight vicars-general and a chapter of canons at Notre-Dame. There were chapters also at Ste-Chapelle, St-Marcel, St-Merry, and elsewhere.

The religious feeling that gave rise to mass movements c. 1730 with regard to "miracles" of the deacon Paris in Saint-Médard cemetery was later seriously harmed by philosophes' attacks.

In the uprising and vandalism of the *French Revolution, churches were disfigured and destroyed; and for several years religious life was clandestine at best. From a religious viewpoint the Revolution was marked by the closing of churches for several years and the massacres (Sept. 2 and 3, 1792) in the Carmelite convent and other places where many priests and religious were imprisoned and martyred (see below). The constitutional bishop J. B. *Gobel died on the scaffold, and his successor, J. S. *Maury, was not recognized by Pius VII. Bonaparte's *Concordat of 1801 restored religion officially. The alliance of throne and altar under the restoration (1814–30) provoked a revolution (1830) that turned against the clergy and devastated the diocese. Despite the more liberal regime of the July monarchy of *Louis Philippe (1830–48), the mobbing of St-Germain-l'Auxerrois in 1831 was very anticlerical. Thanks to diverse influences, however, religious feeling improved afterward. The Concordat of 1801 provided for too few parishes and churches. After 1830 religious life revived with devotion to the Miraculous Medal and *Lacordaire's preaching. Religious orders gradually recovered, and free education developed, especially after the *Falloux law (1850). The revival was furthered by the zeal of Abps. H. L. de *Quelen (1821–39); D. A. *Affre (1840–48), who died in the barricades of the June days; M. D. A. Sibour (1848–57), who was stabbed to death by an apostate priest; and Georges *Darboy (1863–71), who was shot during the revolutionary commune.

During the episcopacies of Cardinals J. H. Guibert (1871–86) and F. M. B. *Richard de la Vergne (1886–1908) the Church suffered from the political persecution of Jules *Ferry, P. M. R. *Waldeck-Rousseau, and especially J. L. E. *Combes. World War I restored the "sacred union" fostered by Cardinals L. A. *Amette (1908–20) and L. E. *Dubois (1920–29). Diplomatic ties with the Holy See, broken in 1904, were restored in 1921. Youth movements began. A Catholic movement appeared in the state university, and Catholic writers helped raise the intellectual prestige of the Church. Cardinal J. Verdier (1929–40) founded some 100 new places of worship. Cardinal E. C. *Suhard (1940–49), concerned with the evangelization of the masses, began the Mission de France and the Mission de Paris. When Catholic socialists came to power after World War II, the government took measures favorable to the Church, such as the Barangé (1951) and Debré (1960) laws favoring free education.

In 1963 the Archdiocese of Paris had 262 parishes, 1,854 secular and 490 religious priests, 1,216 men in 11 religious houses, 8,480 women in 564 convents, and 3,800,000 Catholics in a population of 5,700,000. Its five suffragans, which had 2,203 parishes, 2,151 secular

and 345 religious priests, 5,781 sisters, and 3,128,000 Catholics, were: Blois, Chartres, Meaux (first known bishop in 549), Orléans, and Versailles (created in 1801). Religious practice is better in the city than in the suburbs, but evangelization is hindered by the large population. Many people belong to groups of *Catholic Action, and the *Chantiers du Cardinal* multiply places of worship. In 1963 deaneries were created to regroup parishes. Paris also has an auxiliary bishop for foreigners.

Councils and Synods. The statutes of the synods of Paris, annual since the Fourth Lateran Council (1215), have had an importance extending beyond the diocese. The first statutes, deriving from Odo of Sully (after 1200, it seems), were used in the East: they offer a systematic teaching on the Sacraments and deal with the banns of marriage and the elevation of the Host at Mass. The next statutes are from William of Auvergne and a third (anonymous) set from after 1311. Bishops Étienne de Poncher (1503–19) and Eustache du Bellay (1551–64) contributed to the statutes, which were edited by J. de Harlay (Paris 1674) and C. de Beaumont (Paris 1777). Sources for the statutes of Paris were the statutes of ecumenical councils and of provincial councils, especially those of Sens until 1622 and notably c. 1250.

Interprovincial councils met in Paris (360–829), as did national councils (557–1811). The council of 360 under St. *Hilary of Poitiers confirmed the decrees of *Nicaea I. Among Merovingian councils (552–653), that of 557 dealt with marriage, episcopal elections, and other matters. In 825 the *iconoclasm controversy was the subject of interest. A council of 829 dealt with the life of the clergy and laity and with civil power (rights and duties of king and subjects). In 1051 the

Fig. 3. View from the Place de la Concorde toward the 19th-century classic revival church of the Madeleine.

Fig. 4. View of a street in Montmartre with the domes of the church of the Sacré Coeur in the background.

errors of *Berengarius and *John Scotus Erigena on the Eucharist were condemned. In 1147 a council under Pope Eugene IV examined the teachings of *Gilbert de la Porrée on the Trinity. Philip II Augustus convoked councils in 1185 and 1188 for the Third Crusade. In 1212 reforms for secular and religious clergy were legislated. A council convoked by *Philip IV the Fair suppressed the *Templars (1310). Councils supported by the university (1395–98) figured in the Western Schism. A provincial council condemned Luther's teachings (1528). *Napoleon I convoked a national council in 1811, under Cardinal J. *Fesch, to put pressure on Pius VII with regard to the investiture of bishops by archbishops; but it yielded to the decision of the Pope. No councils have met since, apart from reunions of the provincial and, recently, the national hierarchy.

Bibliography: G. D'AVENEL, *Les Évêques et archevêques de Paris,* 2 v. (Tournai 1878). J. RUPP, *Histoire de l'Église de Paris* (Paris 1948). P. PISANI, *L'Église de Paris et la Révolution,* 4 v. (Paris 1908–11). A. GARREAU, *Le Pèlerin de Paris* (Paris 1936). J. DE LA MONNERAYE et al., *Visages de Paris* (Paris 1946). A. FRIEDMANN, *Paris, ses rues, ses paroisses* (Paris 1959). G. LE BRAS, "Paris, seconde capitale de la Chrétienté" RevHistÉgl France 37 (1951) 5–17. Y. DANIEL, *Aspects de la pratique religieuse à Paris* (Paris 1952). R. BARROUX, *Paris des origines à nos jours et son rôle dans l'histoire de la civilisation* (Paris 1950). *Annuaire statistique de la ville de Paris* (Paris 1880–   ). A. H. BRODRICK, ed., *Greater Paris and the Ile-de-France* (London 1952). P. MICHAUD-QUANTIN et al., LexThK² 8:93–101. H. LECLERCQ, DACL 13.2:1696–2160. G. RUPP et al., EncCatt 9:825–837. **Illustration credits:** Fig. 1, Giraudon. Fig. 2, Leonard Von Matt. Figs. 3 and 4, Pan American Airways.

[R. LIMOUZIN-LAMOTHE]

PARIS, INSTITUT CATHOLIQUE DE

An institution of higher learning, the Catholic university of Paris.

History. In 1845 Denis Auguste Affre, Archbishop of Paris, opened an ecclesiastical school of higher learning in a former Carmelite convent. It was an old building situated in a large park where, in the 17th century, the Carmelites, desirous of introducing St. Teresa's reform into France, had established residence. It was in this house and park that in September 1792 the priests and bishops (240 in number) imprisoned in the convent were massacred. Their remains were buried in the crypt of the church. J. B. *Lacordaire, OP, lived in the same house for several years and F. *Ozanam is interred there (1853).

In 1875 the French parliament passed a law granting freedom to higher education and permitting the establishment of private universities. That same year 22 bishops meeting in Paris decided to found a Catholic university in the capital. The three Faculties of Law, Letters, and Science were thereupon established and the Catholic University of Paris inaugurated July 16, 1876. It lacked only a Faculty of Theology, which was difficult to found since there already existed a state Faculty of Theology at the Sorbonne. This, however, was discounted in 1886 and another one established at the Catholic University in 1889.

In the meantime, the law of 1880 curtailed freedom of higher education by denying private institutions the power to grant degrees and the right to use the title university. Thenceforth the Catholic University of Paris had to be satisfied with the title Catholic Institute of Paris, which it still bears.

The years 1893 to 1910 were very trying ones for the Catholic Institute, which had to cope with serious financial difficulties (1893–95) and problems arising from what was later known as Modernism, a movement precipitated by the venturesome theories on the inspiration of Sacred Scripture and its historical value, proposed by Alfred *Loisy, whom Maurice d'*Hulst, the rector, and Louis *Duchesne had appointed to the Catholic Institute in 1893. Following the Modernist crisis, the Faculty of Theology was reorganized and the major chairs of dogma, apologetics, and moral philosophy were entrusted to the Society of Jesus. In 1906, acting on the law of separation, the state confiscated the property and buildings of the Catholic Institute. They were not bought back until 1923. The importance of the canonical Faculties (Theology, Philosophy, and Canon Law) was established in 1935 when the Catholic Institute, having adopted the constitution *Deus scientiarum Dominus,* was named a pontifical university.

Development. The Catholic Institute has continued to grow, especially since World War I. New buildings have been erected; the number of students has increased; and the seminary adjoining the canonical Faculty has considerably developed. Above all, it has witnessed the multiplication of affiliated institutes and schools which, because of their specialization, have succeeded in eliminating the rigid programs imposed in the Faculties and in opening up its instruction to the new problems of science and to those of ecclesiastical import: e.g., the praiseworthy Institute of Electronics and the Institutes of Catechetics, Liturgy, and Social Sciences.

Organization. This concords with the French laws of 1875 (private universities) and 1880 (associations); the recognition of public utility granted by the law of June 18, 1941; and the statutes approved by the Holy See, June 7, 1936.

The Catholic Institute is governed by the association of 31 archbishops and bishops whose dioceses constitute the territorial boundaries. The archbishop of Paris is the chancellor ex officio. A permanent commission of 11 archbishops and bishops, a 5-member administrative council, and a board of regents make up the regular administrative offices. The bishops' assembly delegates the direction of the Institute to the rector, who is appointed by the Holy See and assisted by a vice rector.

The Institute is composed of three Faculties of Religious Science (Theology, Canon Law, and Philosophy) and three of profane sciences (Law, Letters, and Natural Sciences); schools of Oriental languages, social studies, liturgy, education, educational psychology, economic and social science, library science, organic and mineral chemistry, and applied biology; institutes of general studies (law, literature, and science) and Christian Greek and Latin; higher institutes of interpretation and translation, electronics, geology, French language and culture (for foreigners), and agriculture (at Beauvais); the Cluny School at Madrid; and a center of studies in Rome. A summer school for foreigners is open during August.

Each Faculty, Institute, or School has its own program, examinations, and diplomas, the most common of which are the licentiate and the doctorate. Each has its own dean (Faculties), director, or president (Schools and Institutes), assisted by a council that determines internal affairs and elects the professors. The decisions of these councils are approved by the rectoral council.

Faculties, Schools, and Institutes all enjoy administrative but not financial autonomy; the recruitment and titles of professors vary according to each Faculty, School, or Institute. Chaplains are responsible for the students' religious instruction and formation. Representatives chosen by the students assure rapport between teachers and pupils. The latter have their own autonomous organizations.

In 1964–65 the teaching staff was composed of 560 members holding higher degrees. Enrollment numbered 10,800 students, including 245 in theology, 20 in Canon Law, 244 in philosophy, 682 in law, 1,782 in letters, 457 in science, and the remainder in affiliated Schools and Institutes. The library housed 500,000 bound volumes and subscribed to 300 periodicals.

Prominent Rectors and Professors. Among the most outstanding rectors are: Maurice d'Hulst (1881–1903); P. L. Péchenard (1903–07), later bishop of Soissons; Bp. (later Cardinal) H. *Baudrillart (1907–42); Bp. J. Calvet, prorector (1942–46); and Emile Blanchet (1946–   ). Well-known professors include Bp. J. Arquillière (church history), L. Bouyer, COR (theology), E. *Branly (physics), A. T. de *Broglie (apologetics), G. de Broglie, SJ (theology), J. Carrière (history of the Church in France), E. Colin (science), A. Dain (classics), J. Daniélou, SJ (theology and patrology), L. J. Dalaporte (ancient history), L. M. Duchesne (ancient church history), P. *Gasparri, later cardinal secretary of state (Canon Law), G. *Goyau (history of the missions), L. de *Grandmaison, SJ (theology), M. d'Harcourt (German language and

civilization), Y. de La Brière, SJ (international problems), A. A. de *Lapparent (geology), A. F. Loisy (exegesis), F. *Prat, SJ (positive theology), P. J. Rousselot, SJ (experimental phonetics), and A. G. *Sertillanges, OP (apologetics and philosophy).

Bibliography: *Annuaire de l'Institut catholique de Paris. Nouvelles de l'Institut catholique,* periodical. A. BAUDRILLART, *Vie de Monseigneur d'Hulst,* 2 v. (Paris 1912–14); *L'Institut catholique* (Paris 1930); *Vingt-cinq ans de rectorat: L'Institut catholique de Paris (1907–1932)* (Paris 1932). J. BRUGERETTE, *Le Prêtre français et la société contemporaine,* 3 v. (Paris 1933–38) v.2 *Vers la séparation.* J. CALVET, "L'Institut catholique de Paris" in L. HALPHEN et al., *Aspects de l'Université de Paris* (Paris 1949) 251–266.

[E. JARRY]

PARIS, MARTYRS OF

This term refers to a group of 191 men who were beatified after being put to death in various Parisian prisons during the *French Revolution (feast, Sept. 2 or 4). They are sometimes called the September Martyrs because their execution occurred on Sept. 2 or 3, 1792, as part of the September massacres during the first Reign of Terror. The catalogue of beatified martyrs includes 2 archbishops, 1 bishop, 176 priests, 1 lay brother, 5 deacons, 1 tonsured cleric, and 5 laymen. The martyrdoms occurred in 4 places: 95 being executed in the Carmelite convent, 72 in the Vincentian seminary of St. Firmin, 21 in the Abbey of *Saint-Germain-des-Prés, and 3 in the prison of La Force.

The Circumstances. Two sets of circumstances led up to the massacres. The first was the strong opposition of a large part of the French clergy to the *Civil Constitution of the Clergy, resulting in their refusal to take the required oath to support it. The second was the critical situation that developed from the military reverses of the revolutionary armies and that permitted bitterly antireligious groups to operate freely. Following the manifesto (July 11, 1792) of the Duke of Brunswick, leader of the Prussian forces, threatening vengeance on the French for mistreating their rulers, the Parisian mob stormed the Tuileries (August 10), massacred the Swiss guards, and imprisoned King Louis XVI and the Queen in the Temple. Effective power in the capital passed from the Legislative Assembly to the Commune and the Jacobin clubs. Municipalities received authorization (August 11) to arrest suspects, including nonjuring priests. Most priests in the provinces went into exile following the decree of August 11 that banished them. In Paris ecclesiastics and other suspects were herded into Bicêtre, Châtelet, the Conciergerie, La Force, and other prisons, or into the jails improvised in the Carmelite convent, St. Firmin, and Saint-Germain-des-Prés. Panic spread as fears of invasion grew. When false rumors circulated (September 2) that Verdun had surrendered and that the prisoners were preparing an uprising, mobs invaded the prisons and executed hundreds after summary trials. About three-fourths of the victims, totaling between 1,100 and 1,400, were criminals. Some were political prisoners, but the clerics had been incarcerated for religious reasons. Beatification occurred only in cases where it was proved that death was inflicted for reasons of faith. Almost all the beatified martyrs were massacred for their refusal to support by oath the Civil Constitution. In 1926 the Congregation of Rites deferred action on 22 other persons who were put to death in the last three of the above-named prisons. None of those who were put to death in other prisons during the September massacres have been beatified.

The Martyrs. The list of beatified martyrs follows (with year of birth noted when known).

At the Carmelite convent perished Jean Marie du Lau d'Alleman (b. 1738), Archbishop of Arles; François Joseph de *La Rochefoucauld Maumont (1736), Bishop of Beauvais; and his brother Pierre Louis de la Rouchefoucauld Bayers (1744), Bishop of Saintes.

Most of the martyred priests belonged to the Archdiocese of *Paris. Several of them, who came from other French dioceses, were residing in the capital. About one-third of the secular priests had been stationed in one or another of 26 dioceses throughout the country. Their occupations were diversified. The majority were engaged in pastoral work as pastors, curates, or chaplains; several served in seminaries as superiors, professors, or librarians; and some were vicars general of dioceses or held other equally important administrative posts.

The following were secular priests: Vincent Abraham (1740), André Alricy (1712), Daniel André Des Pommerayes (1756), André Angar, Jean Aubert, Pierre Balzac (1750), Jean Bangue (1744), Louis Barret (1753), Joseph Bécavin (1767), Louis Remi Benoist (1740), his brother Louis Remi Nicolas Benoist (1755), Michel Binard (1742), Robert le Bis (1719), Nicolas Bize (1737), Pierre Bonsé (1719), Jean Bottex (1749), Jean Bousquet (1751), Antoine du Bouzet (1739), Pierre Briquet, Pierre Brisse (1733), Jean Capeau, Charles Carnus (1749), Jean Caron (1730), Bertrand de Caupenne (1753), Armand Chapt de Rastignac (1727), Claude Chaudet, Antoine Boucharenc de Chaumeils (1738), Nicolas Clairet (1726), Claude Colin (1728), Nicolas Colin (1750), Louis le Danois (1741), François Dardan (1733), Mathurin Deruelle, Gabriel Desprez de Roche (1751, vicar general of the Archdiocese of Paris), Thomas Dubuisson (1737), Jacques Dufour, François Dumasrambaud de Calandelle (1754), Denis Duval (1740), Henri Ermès, Joseph Falcoz (1726), Gilbert Fautrel (1730), Claude Fontaine (1749), Armand de Foucauld de Pontbriand (1751), Philibert Fougères (1742), Michel de la Gardette (1744), Pierre Garrigues (1725), Nicolas Gaudreau (1744), Louis Gaultier (1717), Pierre Gervais (1753), Étienne Gillet (1758), Georges Girous (1765), Jean Goizet (1742), André Grasset de Saint-Sauveur (born in Canada 1758), Joseph Gros (1742), Jean Guilleminet (1738), Yves Guillon de Keranrum (1748, vice chancellor of the University of Paris), Julien Hédouin (1760), Pierre Hénocq (1749), Saintin Huré (1765), Jean Jannin (1754), Pierre Joret (1761), Jean Le Laisant (1753) and his brother Julien (1761), Gilbert Lanchon (1754), Jacques de la Lande (1735), Pierre Landry (1762), Jean Lanier (1753), Laurent, Jean de Lavèze Belay (1742), Michel Leber (1731), Jean Lecan, Pierre Leclerq (or Clerq, 1744), Olivier Lefebvre (1728), Jean Legrand (1745), Jacques Lejardinier des Landes (1750), Jean Lemaitre (1767), Jean Leroy (1738), François Londiveau (1764), Louis Longuet (1757), Martin Loublier (1733), Jacques de Lubersac (1729), Louis Mauduit (1763), Gaspard Maignien (1752), Jean Marchand (1765), Claude Marmotant (1748), Claude Mayneaud de Bisefranc (1750), François Méallet de Fargues (1764), Jacques Menuret (1734), Jacques Le Meunier (1747), Henri Millet (1760), François Monnier (1763), Thomas Monsaint (1725), Marie François Mouffle (1754), Jean Baptiste Nativelle (1743) and his brother René (1751), Mathias Nogier (1764), Joseph Oviefve (1748), Joseph Pazery de Thorame (1751), his brother Jules (1763) and uncle Pierre (1735), François Pey (1759), Jean Philippot (1743), Pierre Ploquin (1762), René Poret (1732), Julien Poulain de Launay (1744), Jean Quéneau (1758), Jacques Rabé (1750), Jean Rateau (1758), Pierre Régnet (1755), Yves Rey de Kervisic (1761), Nicholas Roussel (1730), Marc Royer (1720), Jean de Saint Clair (1734), Pierre Saint James (1742), Urbain Salin de Niart (1760), Henri Samson (1754), Jacques Schmid (1752), Jean Séguin (1754), Jean Simon, Pierre de Turmenyes (1744), René Urvoy (1766), Pierre Verrier (1722), and Pierre Vitalis (1759).

Priests belonging to the regular clergy included three Maurists: Louis Barreau de La Touche (1758), René Massey (1732), and Ambroise Chevreux (1728), the superior general. Jean Bonnel de Pradal (1738) and Claude Ponse (1729) belonged to the Canons Regular of St. Genevieve; Jean Bernard (1759), to the Canons Regular of St. Victor. Jean Burté (1740) was a Conventual Franciscan; Jean Morel (Père Apollinaire, 1739), a Capuchin; and Georges Girault (Père Severin, 1728), a Third Order Franciscan. Charles Hurtrel (1760) was a Minim. Claude Bochot (1720) and Eustache Félix (1735) were Doctrinarians. François Hébert (1735), Pierre Pottier (1743), and François Lefranc (1739), assistant to the superior general, were Eudists. Urbain Lefebvre (1725) was a member of the Paris Foreign Mission Society. The Vincentians numbered Jean Gruyer (1734) and Louis François (1751), head of the Parisian seminary of St. Firmin.

The Sulpicians supplied 12 martyred priests: Bernard Cucsac (1728), Thomas Dubray, Jacques Galais (1754), Pierre Gaugain (1725), Pierre Guérin (1759), Jacques Hourrier (1751), Henri Luzeau de la Mulonnière (1762), Jean Pontus, Pierre Psalmon (1749), Claude Rousseau (1751), Jean Savine (1760), and Jean Tessier. Six of them had been in charge of seminaries.

Twenty-three priests had been *Jesuits until the suppression of the order. They were: René Andrieux (1742), François Balmain (1733), Jean Benoît (1731), Charles Béraud du Pérou (1737), Jacques Bonnaud (1740), Claude Cayx-Dumas (1724), Jean Charton de Millou (1736), Guillaume Delfaut (1733), Jacques Friteyre-Durvé (1725), Claude Cagnières des Granges (1722), Charles Le Gué (1724), Pierre Guérin du Rocher (1759) and his brother Robert (1736), Éloy Herque du Roule (1741), Anne Alexandre Lanfant (1726), Claude Laporte (1734), François Le Livec de Tresurin (1726), Thomas Loup (called Bonnotte, 1719), Vincent le Rousseau (1726), Jean Seconds (1734), François Vareilhe-Duteil (1734), Nicolas Verron (1740), and Mathurin de la Villecrohain le Bous de Villeneuve (1731).

Louis Boubert (1766), Louis Hurtrel (brother of Bl. Charles Hurtrel, the Minim), Jacques Robert de Lezardière (1768), Étienne de Ravinel (1769), and Charles Veret (1763) were seminarians who had received the deaconate. Nezel, a tonsured cleric, was a professor at the Sulpician seminary in Issy, near Paris. Guillaume Nicolas Leclercq (Brother Solomon, 1745) was general secretary of the Christian Brothers.

Five laymen complete the catalogue. Sebastien Desbrielles (1739) and Jean Duval had been teachers, and Louis Rigot (1751), a sacristan. Jean de Villette (1731) and Charles Régis de la Calmette, Count of Valfons, were former army officers.

The entire group was beatified Oct. 17, 1926.

Bibliography: ActApS 18 (1926) 415–425, 439–447. G. LEN-ÔTRE, *Les Massacres de Septembre* (Paris 1907); *La Maison des Carmes* (Paris 1933). H. WELSCHINGER, *Les Martyrs de Septembre* (Paris 1927). P. CARON, *Les Massacres de Septembre* (Paris 1935). J. HÉRISSAY, *Les Journées de Septembre* (Paris 1946). H. FOUQUERAY, *Un Groupe des Martyrs de Septembre 1792: Vingt-trois anciens Jésuites* (Paris 1926). W. J. BATTERSBY, *Brother Solomon, Martyr of the French Revolution* (New York 1960). Baudot-Chaussin 9:53–71, good bibliog.

[W. J. BATTERSBY]

PARIS, UNIVERSITY OF

One of the oldest and most influential universities of Europe, founded as a voluntary association of teaching masters in the 13th century.

ORIGIN AND EARLY DEVELOPMENT BEFORE 1500

At the turn of the 12th century, such masters as Anselm of Laon, William of Champeaux, Peter Abelard, William of Conches, Adam du Petit Pont, Gilbert de la Porrée, Alan of Lille, and Richard and Hugh of Saint-Victor had attracted to Paris large numbers of masters and students from all parts of Europe. As a result of the influx, many of the teaching masters, especially those attached to the School of Notre Dame Cathedral, found it necessary to teach outside the cathedral cloister. They lectured in the open streets, particularly in the Rue du Fouarre, in the schools of the Abbey of Mont Ste. Geneviève; on the Petit Pont, and, in the vicinity of Saint Germain-des-Prés, on the left bank of the Seine, henceforth known as the Latin quarter. The masters thus removed from the immediate control of the cathedral organized themselves, in accord with the contemporary guild movement, into a corporate association bound together by oath.

The masters' association was formally approved in 1200 when King Philip Augustus accorded the masters the charter of privileges that guaranteed them exemptions and immunity from the civil and criminal jurisdiction of the local provost and his magistrates, and recognized that as clerics they were subject to their own elected officials and to the bishop of Paris. Between 1208 and 1215 the University obtained papal sanction as a corporate association with the right to representation at the papal court, to have a seal of its own, and to regulate the dress, method of teaching, and the funerals of its deceased masters. It also affirmed the University's independence from the jurisdiction and control of the cathedral chancellor. Although the chancellor retained the power to confer the license to teach (*licentia docendi*), he could not withhold it from anyone judged competent or qualified by a majority of the teaching masters. As a result of another revolt against local authorities, Gregory IX reinforced the University's autonomous rights in the bull *Parens scientiarum* (April 13, 1231), often referred to as the Magna Carta of the University. The provisions of this bull reaffirmed the University's right to make its own rules and regulations regarding the curriculum, the individual members of the association, and the rents of hospices, and to call a cessation of lectures whenever any of these rights were violated or abrogated.

Organization. By the early 13th century the teaching masters were differentiated into four Faculties: Arts, Medicine, Canon Law, and Theology.

Nations. The Faculty of Arts, the most numerous of the Faculties and the stepping stone to the others, was at an early period divided into four nations: French, Picard, Norman, and English (English-German). These nations, representing primarily geographical regions rather than states or localities, were probably based on an earlier voluntary grouping of the masters and students according to the land from which they had come or in which they were born. Masters in the French nation came not only from France but also from southern and eastern Europe and from Asia Minor: in the Picard, from Flanders and the Walloon country; in the Norman, from Normandy and Brittany; and in the English (English-German), from the British Isles, Holland, the Germanies, and Scandinavia, as well as from Hungary and the Slavic lands. Each nation had its own elected officers: a proctor who headed the nation, a treasurer or receptor, and its own bedels and messengers to serve the nation and its members; its own chapel, patron saint and feast days, places of assembly, and revenues. Moreover, each nation drew up its own rules and regulations in the assemblies called by the proctors. The four nations, through their proctors and other officers, also maintained matriculation rolls, looked after the schools in which masters of the nations taught, and took care of members who fell ill or died. The proctors or other delegates of the nations elected the rector, who served as head of the Faculty of Arts and eventually as head of the University association as a whole.

Each of the four Faculties had its own similar officers, statutes, and schools: in the Faculty of Arts the executive officer was the rector; in the three Faculties of Medicine, Canon Law, and Theology, a dean was chosen by the members of his Faculty. The deans, like the rector, presided over the Faculty congregations that discussed and drew up measures relating to the Faculty as a whole: curriculum, qualifications for matriculation and for obtaining the baccalaureate or other degrees, and the rules governing the determination or defense of the thesis by candidates for the degree or license to teach.

University Council. The other administrative agencies of the University were the council and the general University congregation. The council, which met at stated intervals and was made up of the rector, the three deans, and the four proctors of the nations, examined and acted upon matters relating to the University association and its members. It was at the University congregation, however, to which were summoned all the teaching masters, that measures affecting the teaching, the relations of the University to the outer world, and other matters, were drawn up, debated, and voted upon. At these congregations, and in accordance with specified rules, other officers elected to assist the rector in carrying out University measures were the bedels, treasurer, messengers, *peciarii* (supervisors of texts), parchment dealers, booksellers, and copyists or scribes.

Colleges. Since the University of Paris was a masters' association, the students were attached to it only through the masters and therefore at first lacked discipline and supervision outside the schools. To fill this need, as well as to provide for the basic necessities of food, lodging, and a small stipend for poor scholars, from an early date philanthropists and other benefactors endowed hostels or *colleges. Provision was thus made for poor scholars and for those coming from specified localities. Examples of the former are the College of Eighteen (Collège des dix-huits); the College of the Good Children of St. Honoré, founded by Étienne Belot and his wife; and Ave Maria College. Illustrative of the latter are the Colleges of Bayeux and Narbonne, France, and of Linkoping and Skara, Sweden. The Collège de Sorbonne was founded by Robert de *Sorbon to accommodate poor scholars who were already masters of arts but who were studying in the Faculty of Theology. In time several colleges became places of instruction as well as of lodging.

Curriculum. The curriculum of the University was administered under the four Faculties. In the Faculty of Arts, instruction was based on the *liberal arts, the mastery of which was to serve as the foundation and stepping stone for higher Faculties. The course of study in medicine comprised lectures on the Latin translations of the works of the Greek physicians Hippocrates and Galen, of the Arabic physicians Rasis and Avicenna, and of some Latin authors, with practical experience under the direction of a doctor of medicine for 6 months in Paris and for 1 year outside the city. In Canon Law the principal texts studied were the Decretum of Gratian, together with several additions, namely, the Decretals of Gregory IX, the Liber Sextus of Boniface VIII, the Constitutions of Clement V, and the Extravagantes or collection of papal laws. In theology instruction was centered upon the Bible, the works of the Church Fathers, Peter Lombard's *Sentences,* and compilations of Thomas Aquinas's *Questiones* and *Summae,* as well as upon some works of other medieval authors.

Method of Instruction. In general use was the lecture or commentary and gloss on a specific text, followed by the repetition or review and the *collatio* or discussion and conference. The lectures were usually divided into the ordinary, those given in the morning by the members of the Faculty, and the extraordinary or cursory, usually given in the late afternoons or on feast days by guest lecturers or bachelors in the Faculty. In addition, there were disputations that applied the rational method of inquiry in the presentation, explanation, and proving of a specific proposition and the answering of objections raised against it. Frequent references were made to the Bible, the Fathers, Aristotle, and other standard authors. There were also the *Quodlibeta* disputations and the disputed questions. In the former, at a public session, the professor in charge was asked questions at random from the leading topics of the day. A bachelor closely associated with the professor then gave tentative replies; at a later session the professor made a formal reply in the form of a disputation. In the disputed questions, the professor set his own question and then proceeded in the form of the disputation.

Examinations: Determination and Inception. At Paris, after following a prescribed course of studies, the candidate for a degree or license to teach underwent a series of examinations: (1) a private interrogation or *responsion* conducted by his own professor to ascertain

whether he was ready for the examination for the determination; (2) after a careful scrutiny of the candidate's qualifications and fitness, the examination for determination, conducted by a committee of professors chosen for the purpose; (3) the determination, consisting of a series of disputations carried on for several weeks by the candidate himself. If judged successful, he was accorded the license to teach anywhere (*Licentia ubique docendi*). The final step was the initiation or inception (*inceptio*) into the Faculty.

Rights, Privileges, Immunities. The University of Paris and its members, through the grants and support of the French monarchs and the papacy, held a highly privileged position. It enjoyed, among other exemptions, immunity from the civil and criminal jurisdiction of the local magistrates, from the disciplinary ban of excommunication by the local bishop, from all tolls and taxes as well as from military and other levies except under very unusual circumstances, and freedom from the obligation to respond to summons to civil or ecclesiastical courts outside the city of Paris except under the direct will of the pope. The University had the right to make and enforce rules and regulations for its own members; to set up courses and examinations; to regulate the time, content, and method of teaching; and to determine the rent of houses occupied by its members. University members also enjoyed the right to be named to vacant benefices, to be preferred to all others for appointment whenever such vacancies occurred, and to enjoy the returns of their benefices while they were studying at Paris for a period of from 5 to 7 years. In the 13th century, moreover, they could call a cessation of lectures whenever their rights were violated. The provost of Paris served as the conservator of royal privileges; one of the bishops outside Paris, but in its vicinity, acted as the conservator of apostolic privileges.

Influence. The fame and importance of the University of Paris between the 13th and 15th centuries attracted many famous European scholars and theologians: Roger Bacon, *Alexander of Hales, *Albert the Great, *Thomas Aquinas, *Bonaventure, *Duns Scotus, Jean Buridan, *William of Ockham, Nicole Oresme,

Seal of the University of Paris, a medieval impression in the Bibliothèque Nationale, Paris.

Jean *Gerson, *Peter d'Ailly, and others. The University's influence was far-reaching. Not only did it provide a model for the universities of northern Europe founded before 1500; but through its professors and graduates, bound to it in perpetuity by an oath, it made a strong impression upon contemporary thought and action. Many of its graduates were leaders in affairs of church and state: Innocent III, Gregory IX, Urban IV, and other popes as well as bishops, archbishops, and others who served as royal and ecclesiastical judges, counselors, and administrators. Doctors on the Medical Faculty, moreover, served as royal and papal physicians; other members of the University gave aid and counsel to the French monarchs, participated in the theological and doctrinal discussions of the time, served in the peace commissions during the Hundred Years' War, and played an important role in the Council of Constance, which healed the papal schism.

Bibliography: H. RASHDALL, *The Universities of Europe in the Middle Ages,* ed. F. M. POWICKE and A. B. EMDEN, 3 v. (new ed. Oxford 1936). L. J. DALY, *The Medieval University, 1200–1400* (New York 1961). P. KIBRE, *The Nations in the Mediaeval Universities* (Cambridge, Mass. 1948); *Scholarly Privileges in the Middle Ages* (Cambridge, Mass. 1962). L. HALPHEN et al., *Aspects de l'Université de Paris* (Paris 1949). J. BONNEROT, *L'Université de Paris du moyen âge à nos jours* (Paris 1933). A. L. GABRIEL, *Student Life in Ave Maria College, Mediaeval Paris* (Notre Dame, Ind. 1955); *Skara House at the Mediaeval University of Paris* (Notre Dame, Ind. 1960); "The College System in the Fourteenth Century Universities," *The Forward Movement of the Fourteenth Century,* ed. F. L. UTLEY (Columbus, Ohio 1961). P. GLORIEUX, *Les Origines du Collège de Sorbonne* (Notre Dame, Ind. 1959).

[P. KIBRE]

LATER HISTORY

Although the University's prestige was not enhanced throughout the 14th century, its numbers increased regularly (almost 800 master regents in the Faculty of Arts alone in 1408). It was "Milady the University, daughter of the king of France," and its members were conscious of its importance. The intellectual vigor of the 13th century, however, was lacking during the 14th and 15th centuries when minds went astray in subtile and often futile discussions. In 1400 Gerson said of his colleagues: "The theologians are the laughing stock of the other Faculties."

The *Western Schism, in which the University took sides, dealt it a heavy blow. It not only turned certain students away, but what was still more serious, it provoked the departure of certain masters for Prague, Vienna, Cologne, or Heidelberg. Finally, the English conquest and occupation of Paris, to which the University rallied, and the establishment in the 15th century of several universities in France (Caen, Poitiers, Bordeaux) dimmed its radiance. Its renown was sustained, nevertheless, by such masters as Pierre d'Ailly (1350–1420) and Gerson (1363–1420).

The University, moreover, greatly impaired its intellectual prestige by allowing itself to become deeply involved in the Western Schism. After having rallied under pressure from Charles V of France to the French antipope, Clement VII (Robert of Geneva), the University decided in an assembly of the four Faculties to submit the matter of allegiance to the council (1381), thus following the teaching of its two illustrious masters, Conrad of Gelnhausen and Henry of Langenstein. It henceforth adhered to the resolution of the council,

from which it did not swerve except when obliged by force to propose the abdication of the rival popes (1394) or the withdrawal of obedience (1398 and 1406–08). At the Council of Constance (1415–18), it was the Parisian masters Pierre d'Ailly, Guillaume Fillastre, and Gerson who were the leading spokesmen.

The University was no less engaged in political controversy than in religious disputes. In 1413 it condemned the theories justifying tyrannicide; but in 1418 the Duke of Burgundy forced it to reverse its decision. Likewise, in February 1413, the University joined the people of Paris in asking the King for reforms; in May it took part in the preparation of the *ordonnances cabochiennes* that prescribed the reforms.

Soon overcome by popular violence (of which Gerson was personally a victim), the University broke with the Cabochians and by its presence approved the session of the Parlement in which the King dissolved the *ordonnances cabochiennes* (September 1413).

These political entanglements and the reversal of loyalty that often accompanied them could not enhance the authority of the University. The deterioration of scholastic methods also dimmed its scientific brilliance. Faced with growing humanism, the University of Paris could not recover its pristine vigor. When it became evident that a new body of teaching was necessary, the crown created it outside the aged body of the University, which had fought against registration of the concordat of 1516 in the name of Gallican liberty and thereby opposed both pope and king. In 1530 Francis I established royal lectors to answer the intellectual needs of the new age; the lectors later separated from the University to become the *Collège de France (built in 1610 on its present site). During the religious crises of the 16th century, the Faculty of Theology aligned itself against the reformers, while the University as a whole opposed the admission of Jesuits into France.

In 1598 Henry IV (whom the University had recognized the day following his entry into Paris) reformed the University, determining the discipline, the living arrangements of the students, and the curriculum. For the first time, University regulations were established without the intervention of ecclesiastical authority.

Development in the 17th and 18th Centuries. The University continued its educational function of training lawyers, physicians, and jurists. Just as it had been untouched by the spirit of the Renaissance, it remained insensitive to the great philosophical currents and the first signs of a modern scientific spirit.

At the beginning of the 17th century the Sorbonne became the center of the Faculty of Theology not only because of the quality of its teachers but also because of the number of its students. Cardinal Armand Jean du Plessis Richelieu, elected headmaster of the Sorbonne in 1622, restored and enlarged its buildings. Since then the Sorbonne has been the center of theological activity and of Parisian university life. By its approval or disapproval, it exercises a kind of spiritual magistracy that reaches beyond the limits of the Ile-de-France.

The Edict of April 1679 reformed all French universities into four Faculties: Theology, Décret (which in 1679, with the reintroduction of Roman law in Paris, became the Faculty of Law), Medicine, and Arts (which gave access to the other three). The rector, elected by the proctors of the four nations of the Faculty of Arts, administered the entire corporate body. He was admitted to the Parlement of Paris and to the king's council whenever the interests of the University were in question. Each Faculty was headed by a dean, elected by the regent doctors. The master and student personnel was increased by the addition of registrars, collectors, lawyers, and attorneys who defended the University's interests in Parlement and at the *Chatelet* (law court) of Paris; and by bedels, booksellers, illustrators, and writers. Mendicant monks (Franciscans, Carmelites, Augustinians), as well as Dominicans, regular canons of St. Victor, Trinitarians, and monks of Cluny and of Saint Germain-des-Prés were also affiliated with the University. All enjoyed important privileges (tax exemption, jurisdictional privileges, etc.).

As in the preceding period, the concerns of the University extended beyond the strict framework of teaching. Several times the Sorbonne interfered in political debates under pretext of juridical or theological questions (e.g., condemnation in 1616 of the theses of the Jesuit Anton Santarelli, who taught that the pope could remove incompetent princes; the attack on ecclesiastical competence in the matter of marriage apropos the annulment of Gaston of Orléan's marriage in 1634).

These political involvements were proof of the University's prestige without, however, increasing its influence. Concerned mainly with professional preparation, the University left new research to the academies. In the period following the expulsion of the Jesuits (1762) and the closing of their colleges, diverse projects were published on national education (La Chalotais in 1763, and also others in Parlement) that contained requests for the introduction of subjects ignored by the University: modern languages, modern history, geography, physics, etc. Renewing the heritage of the dissolved Jesuit colleges, the University changed the Collège Louis le Grand into a training school for teachers. The enterprise, however, was not successful. On the eve of the Revolution, the Faculty of Theology had 10 professors; Law had 7 in addition to 12 doctors; Medicine had 152 doctors, of whom 7 were teachers; Arts combined the principals and regents of the colleges; there were 5,000 students. A doctoral examination for recruiting teachers for the Faculty of Arts was inaugurated in 1766.

From 1789 to 1896. The University of Paris disappeared together with the other universities during the revolutionary years, without being formally dissolved. The law of the 3 Brumaire year IV, instituting central schools reestablished an outline for higher education. Medical schools were founded in the year XI (1804). The term university reappeared with the law of May 10, 1806, establishing a national university for the whole empire. In fact, an Imperial University was organized by the decree of March 17, 1808. Within this University, and according to territorial distribution, were Faculties of Catholic Theology, Law, Medicine, Sciences, and Literature. The entire organization was subject to strict control by the emperor. Isolated one from the other, these Faculties were not federated into universities. It was not until the laws of April 28, 1893 (art. 71) and July 10, 1896 (art. 1) that Faculties were regrouped into universities. Juridically the University of Paris was reborn (the system of French universities is actually ruled by the decree of July 31, 1920).

In fact, the Faculties of Paris had resumed work as early as 1808. In 1821 Theology (suppressed in March 1885), Sciences, and Literature had set themselves up in the "old house of the Sorbonne." The Faculty of Law remained in the buildings that were planned by J. Soufflot and constructed for it between 1764 and 1772; they were still the center of its activities in 1964.

Contemporary Developments. The University of Paris is composed of the five Faculties—Law and Economics, Medicine, Sciences, Literature and Human Sciences, and Pharmacy. The higher normal schools for boys and girls, 37 university institutes, diverse educational and research organizations, and libraries are connected with the University by various legal ties. Administration is vested in a University council composed of the rector, who is the presiding officer, five Faculty deans, directors and subdirectors of the two higher normal schools, ten elected professors (two for each Faculty), and four persons chosen by the council. Each Faculty has its own administration and financial autonomy. After World War II, the University of Paris continued the expansion begun at the turn of the century. On Dec. 1, 1962, the number of students was 90,756, of whom 5,000 were foreign students. Provisional estimates for 1963–64 surpassed 91,000 (literature 30,000; science 25,000; law 23,000; medicine 13,000). If one were to include students in the *grandes écoles* and the various scientific establishments that, without being part of the University, constitute essential elements of Parisian intellectual life, the number would go beyond 100,000 students. This increase in enrollment had been accompanied by the multiplication of new educational subjects and the ever-broadening horizons in exact and human sciences, in all of which the University has shown great interest. To meet these needs, the number of professors has increased annually (e.g., Faculty of Law, 18 professors in 1841; 42 in 1915; about 60 in 1950; 96 in 1963, still an insufficient number). In 1964 the teaching staff numbered about 750 (270 in medicine, 220 in sciences, 128 in literature and human sciences, and 27 in pharmacy).

The influx of students and educational developments necessitated additional space for new laboratories, amphitheaters, libraries, and study halls. In a saturated city where one university alone must meet the needs of 8 million inhabitants, it was necessary to consider a dispersion of educational and research centers toward the suburbs. By the 1960s the Faculty of Sciences had already acquired a very important center at Orsay, and other constructions to the west and north of Paris were under way in 1964.

Bibliography: P. GLORIEUX, "La Faculté de théologie de Paris et ses principaux docteurs au XIIIᵉ siècle," RevHistÉglFrance 32 (1946) 241–264. L. HALPHEN and P. GLORIEUX, *L'Université de Paris au XIIIᵉ siècle* (Paris 1949). A. LUCHAIRE, *L'Université de Paris sous Philippe-Auguste* (Paris 1899). P. MICHAUD-QUANTIN, "Le Droit universitaire dans le conflit parisien de 1252–1257," *Studia Gratiana* 8 (1962) 579–599. G. POST, "Parisian Masters as a Corporation, 1200–1246," *Speculum* 9 (1934) 421–445. M. TOULOUSE, *La Nation anglaise-allemande de l'Université de Paris, des origines a la fin du XVᵉ siècle* (Paris 1939). A. DOUARCHE, *L'Université de Paris et les Jésuites (XVIᵉ et XVIIᵉ siècles)* (Paris 1888). C. M. JOURDAIN, *Histoire de l'Université de Paris aux XVIIᵉ et XVIIIᵉ siècles*, 2 v. (Paris 1888). A. J. M. LEFRANCE, *Histoire du Collège de France, depuis ses origines jusqu'à la fin du premier Empire* (Paris 1893). **Illustration credit:** Bibliothèque Nationale, Paris.

[J. GAUDEMET]

PARIS FOREIGN MISSION SOCIETY

A religious institute of secular priests, the first one devoted exclusively to foreign missions (Société des Missions Etrangères de Paris, Societas Parisiensis Missionum ad exteras gentes, MEP).

It began *c.* 1660 as a result of the following conjunction of circumstances: (1) the French clergy and laity, especially the members of a pious apostolic association called the *Compagnie du Saint-Sacrement, were eager to participate in missions hitherto reserved to religious; (2) some missionaries, notably Alexandre de *Rhodes, SJ, wished to form a native clergy in the Far East; (3) the Congregation for the *Propagation of the Faith (Propaganda), founded in 1622, wanted to gain effective control of missions up to then dominated by the Spanish and Portuguese governments with their claims of *patronato real* and *padroado*. The efforts of the Compagnie du Saint-Sacrement, begun in 1646, led to the naming in various missions of a *vicar apostolic dependent on Propaganda and charged with the formation of a native clergy in Tonkin, Cochinchina, and China. Before departing for the East, Bps. François *Pallu, Pierre *Lambert de la Motte, and Ignace Cotolendi ordered their procurators to establish a seminary. King Louis XIV and the local ordinary approved the Paris Mission Seminary in 1663; the Holy See approved it in 1664.

One hundred missionaries, including many laymen, embarked for Asia between 1660 and 1700; but only 62 went between 1700 and 1822, for the 18th century lacked fervor, and the seminary, closed by the French

Msgr. Pierre Lambert de la Motte, one of the founders of the Paris Mission Seminary, portrait in the possession of his grandnephew the Marquis de Frondeville.

Revolution in 1792, was unable to open until the fall of Napoleon I (1815). Between 1822 and 1963 there were 3,816 departures for the missions. Bishop François *Laval confided to the MEP his seminary in Quebec and the missions dependent on him, in Acadia, Ill., and elsewhere. This situation lasted from 1665 to the Treaty of Paris (1763). From its start the society centered its activities in the Far East, and labored in Tonkin, Cochinchina, Siam, and western China. In 1776 it assumed responsibility for evangelizing southern India, until the Jesuits took over part of this region (1836). As MEP missioners became more numerous, Propaganda assigned them new territories: Japan and Korea (1831); Manchuria (1838); Tibet (1846); the Chinese provinces of Koang-Tong, Koang-Si, the Hainan (1848); Burma (1855); and Malaysia, detached from the mission of Siam (1899). By 1920 the society had relinquished three of these fields, but its 1,139 members, aided by 1,109 native priests, were still entrusted with regions populated by 250 millions. Since 1920 the society has ceded 30 mission fields to various religious congregations, and 41 to native clergies formed by it. After the closing of China to missionaries, the MEP was assigned Hwalien in Taiwan (1952); Madagascar, for work among the Chinese (1953); and the mission of Mananjary (1961).

To develop a native clergy the society founded a general seminary in Siam (1665), which has since been transferred to Penang, Malaysia. Other seminaries were opened in Cochinchina (1665), Tonkin (1666), and China (1703). The original Chinese one lasted only a short time, but reopened in Su-Tchuen (1777). In Asia the society operated 19 seminaries in 1845; 41 in 1900, and 75 in 1939. In 1909 membership reached its highest total, with 38 bishops, 1,377 priests, and 6 lay auxiliaries or brothers. There were also 187 aspirants, or seminarians, who are not counted as members, and 783 native priests in MEP mission fields.

Of its 4,137 members during 3 centuries, 163 have sacrificed their lives for the faith, apart from victims of wars, brigands, natural disasters, etc. Sixteen martyrs have been beatified. (*See* CHINA, MARTYRS OF; KOREA, MARTYRS OF; TONKIN, MARTYRS OF.) Bl. John *Moyë was beatified in 1955 as a confessor. The beatification process of eight martyrs in Korea (1866) is in an advanced stage.

In its government the MEP followed a collegiate form until 1921. Since then it has had a superior general, who since 1950 has been elected by a decennial general assembly for a 10-year term, as are his four assistants. All of these reside at 128 rue du Bac, Paris, location of the original seminary of foreign missions. The procurator general, also elected decennially, resides in Rome. Members do not take religious vows, but promise to serve for life in the missions while receiving temporal support from the MEP. Candidates are normally under 35, and must know French, but need not be Frenchmen. The thousands of native priests who have been educated by the MEP or worked in its missions have not joined the society, but have been ordinarily incardinated in their native dioceses. In 1963 the total membership of 880 included 24 bishops, 849 priests, and 7 brothers; aspirants numbered 97. MEP directed 11 dioceses and served 21 native bishops.

Bibliography: J. GUENNOU, *Les Missions étrangères* (Paris 1963). G. GOYAU, *Les Prêtres des Missions Étrangères* (Paris

1932). A. LAUNAY, *La Société des missions étrangères, 1658–1913*, 2 v. (Paris 1912–16); *Histoire générale de la Société des Missions Étrangères*, 3 v. (Paris 1894). Heimbucher 2:600–606.

[J. GUENNOU]

PARISH

A portion of a diocese under the authority of a priest known as the pastor or parish priest who is charged with the care of the souls (*cura animarum*) of the congregation officially entrusted to him. This article is concerned with the derivation of the term, the history of the institution, and the theology underlying the concept.

Etymology and Early Usage. In the OT παροικία means a stay or sojourn in a foreign country, without civil or domestic rights. Among the Israelites the πάροικος was generally an acceptable foreigner standing in close relation to Israel. Later the term was applied to the nation of Israel itself in its Egyptian exile. Finally, the entire earthly life of Israel in this world is conceived as a stay in a foreign country. "For we are sojourners before thee, and strangers, as were all our fathers" (1 Par 29.15).

The NT and early Christianity adopted this understanding of the concept of παροικία. It signified the present existence of the Christian community whose true country and citizenship is in heaven. St. Peter admonished the faithful to conduct themselves with fear in the time of their sojourning (1 Pt 1.17).

After A.D. 150 παροικία was used as an ecclesiastical term denoting the individual community, the *ecclesia* here and now. But with the expansion of the Church in the period after Constantine παροικία dropped from use as a term signifying a municipal Christian community ruled by a bishop, and thereafter was employed only to designate smaller communities with an ordinary priest as pastor (see J. Hohmeyer, "The Renewal of the Parish," in H. Rahner, *The Parish*, 122–123).

History. In apostolic times the parish as it is known in modern times did not exist. The diocese was the sole unit of pastoral care with the bishop as pastor. The local presbyterium assisted the bishop and had no territorial area of endeavor as such. Sunday Mass celebrated by priests other than the bishop must have existed as early as the beginning of the 2d century when Christianity had spread from the cities to rural areas. In Rome a number of homes were used for community worship by the end of the 2d century. The groups that assembled for worship in these places did not look upon themselves as constituting independent, geographical entities, but were intimately united to the bishop, as both Ignatius of Antioch and the practice of the Eucharistic *fermentum testify. The priests who presided at the *tituli* or rural stations where Mass was celebrated were sent by the bishop for that purpose, and when their work was done they returned forthwith to the bishop's house. It was not until the 4th century that the practice of stationing priests at such places was introduced. It was this development that led to the beginnings of the parish as it has come to be known. By the time of Pope Zosimus (417–418) and Leo the Great (440–461) the parish was acquiring boundaries and thus becoming a geographical entity. But the union of the parish and the bishop was strong from the beginning. Only the ordinary could ordain and he had the right to visit rural churches and hold synods. Only the

bishop could absolve solemnly and thereby effect the reconciliation of a sinner with the Church. One-third of the parish income went to the bishop, who in turn maintained the parishes and administered church property.

After the Baptism of Chlodwig (496) and the conversion of the Germanic tribes the work of rebuilding the parishes destroyed in the barbarian invasions fell to the secular as well as to the ecclesiastical powers. A noble who built a church on his land became the owner of it and administered it as he saw fit. The income was his and the priest was a person of his choosing whose position was that of a servant. His spiritual duties were likely to be minimal, and in addition he might have other functions such as that of stable boy, etc. His superior was the landowner rather than a bishop. Although in urban areas some form of seminary or cathedral school was possible, this was not true of the rural places where priests lived isolated from one another and could hardly be called pastors in the modern sense of the term.

As a partial solution to problems arising from this arrangement, bishops sought to build as many churches as possible on land belonging to themselves. The right to perform Baptisms was conferred exclusively on the priests of the bishop's churches, and on greater feast days the celebration of Masses in private oratories was forbidden. Thus the faithful were obliged to attend Mass in a church controlled by the bishop at least on those occasions. The obligation of belonging to a specific parish was also introduced. The parishes as opposed to the private churches were few in number and in consequence bishops were sometimes forced to choose a few private churches and establish them as parishes with some dependence on a mother parish of the districts in which they were located. As a rule, the right to baptize and bury remained with the mother parish, which was also entitled to a definite part of the income of the auxiliary parish.

This trend was abruptly halted by the secularization of church property that began mainly with Charles Martel, who ruled from 714 to 741 and who forced the bishops to turn all church possessions over to him. This was known as the *precario verbo regis*. In this way even the episcopal or parish churches became private, with the rights of protection and administration taken from the bishops. Here and there efforts were made by ecclesiastical authorities to improve the situation, but even if their demands had been fully met, the basic problem would have remained. In 743, for instance, the Consilium Germanicum convoked by St. Boniface, stipulated that during Lent every priest had to render an account of his ministry to the bishop, that he must procure the holy chrism from the episcopal see, and that he must be prepared to receive the bishop in visitation.

In 826 Eugene II gave official recognition to the private church, and this recognition was confirmed by Leo IV in 853. With parishes thus afflicted by the evils of lay investiture and prized as sources of revenue, true pastoral endeavor was all but impossible.

Under Alexander III (1159–81) the right of patronage was introduced but the landowner was supposed to have only the right of administration. However, a landowner could acquire as many patronages as he desired. Monasteries, which were also patronages, were eager to incorporate parishes to themselves and thus obtain greater income.

It was not until the Council of Trent (1545–63) that a real beginning was made in the reorganization of the parochial structure of the Church in such a way as to make it possible for the parish apostolate to flourish. The council insisted upon the following basic reforms. (1) The bishop was declared to be pastor, i.e., shepherd, of his diocese. It was his duty to rule personally and to reside with his flock. He must preach, conduct visitations, and see to the education of the clergy of his diocese. It was his responsibility to see that God's word was preached correctly in every community. New regulations were drawn up for candidates for Holy Orders, and no one was to be ordained unless his livelihood was assured. (2) The parish priest was to be primarily responsible for the care of the souls of those within his parish. He, too, must reside with his flock, preach, and care for the religious education of the young. (3) The parish must have determined boundaries. They must not be too large. Where they were needed, the pastor should have assistants. Parishes should be established in areas where they did not exist. (4) The relationship between diocesan and regular clergy was determined and regulated. Although priests belonging to religious orders were not forbidden to do pastoral work, they were to come to an understanding with the local bishop and were to help with the education of the younger clergy.

The movement toward reform was given considerable impetus by these regulations. They led to the development of better apostolic methods and the parish, organized now as it had never been before, became a true center of apostolic activity. This became in time the parish as it is known today, answering to the description of CIC c.216.

Theology of the Parish. The Church, founded by Christ for the salvation of all men, is a perfect society. It was established as an organization with a hierarchy of offices and powers and with many members who become and remain so by fulfilling certain conditions. The Church would continue to exist even though it were not acting through any of its powers, or in or through any of its members. But when it acts—when it teaches, confesses the faith, prays, celebrates the Sacrifice of Christ—the Church reaches a higher degree of actuality than it would achieve simply by continuing in existence.

Without denying its social constitution, the reality of tradition and apostolic succession, or a divinely appointed law, it can be said that the Church, to become its richer self, has need to become "event" over and over again at definite spatio-temporal points, and to pass from a certain potentiality to a particular actuality. Indeed the whole enduring essence of the Church is ordered toward such events. The Church, moreover, becomes an actual "event" with spatio-temporal tangibility in the highest degree when it becomes event as the communion of saints, i.e., when it appears as a plurality of men bound together by a visible occurrence and united by grace.

When does this occur? Because essentially the Church is the historically continuing presence in the world of the Incarnate Word of God and of the salvific will of God as revealed in history, it is most tangibly and intensively "event" when Christ Himself is present in His own congregation as the crucified and risen author of salvation, when redemption becomes in a manner sensible to the congregation by becoming sacramentally visible, where the New and Eternal Testament that Christ founded on the cross is palpably and actually present in the holy memorial of its first institution. For this reason the celebration of the Eucharist is the most intensive event of the Church. Moreover, by this celebration not only is Christ present in the Church's liturgical solemnity as the Redeemer of His body, as the salvation and Lord of the Church, but the union of the faithful with Christ and with one another is also most externally apparent and most interiorly realized in the Eucharist. The sacramental of the heavenly marriage banquet, the final eternal form of the community of saints, shines forth in the celebration of the Eucharist.

Localization. It is essential to the Eucharistic celebration as a sacramental rite that it be localized, for all the Sacraments are bound up essentially with the corporeal. The Eucharist must be celebrated by one congregation in one place. Thus the Church, without prejudice to its social constitution, permanency, universality, or relation to all men, is by its nature orientated to local concretization and actualization. The Eucharist as event not only takes place in the Church, but the Church itself becomes event in the fullest sense only in the local celebration of the Eucharist. Scripture applies to individual local communities the same name—*ecclesia*—that is applied to the unity of believers all over the world.

As the Eucharist exists because the Church exists, so, in a true sense, the Church exists because the Eucharist exists. The Church remains as a whole because it is continually being actualized by the one all-embracing event in the Eucharist. And because this event is essentially localized at one point of time and space in one local community, the local Church is not only an agency of the universal Church, but is the event itself of this universal Church.

The parish thus enjoys the chief place among the local communities by which the Church is materialized as the locus of event. Among the various bases for the division of the faithful into communities, the principle of locality is of prime importance. "If one asks why the liturgical celebration unfolds itself in a certain locality and in a certain community, the answer will simply be: because it is a parochial community and because the Christians of this community live in the same locality to which they are bound" [K. Rahner, *Esquisse d'une théologie de la paroisse* (Paris 1961) 40].

The Christians of a parish are in a true sense neighbors. This is in accord with man's natural needs—his need of a place of residence and of other men with whom to associate himself. Apart from his ties with his immediate family, his strongest bond of association in the supernatural as well as in the natural order is that which links him with those who live in close proximity to himself (*ibid.* 43, 45). In the parish as in no other religious community, locality is the exclusive principle of association. In other situations this is not the case; e.g., in Eucharistic celebrations of a monastery, or those that take place at some congress or convention, the locality does not constitute the exclusive principle of association. Besides locality and vicinity there may be other principles by which communities are formed. But it is the fact of the local community that puts the territorial parish in a privileged position.

The fact that the parish is not the only form of local church in which the Church as a whole becomes event deserves some emphasis, for this is realized in every legitimate Mass (K. Rahner, "Theology of the Parish," in H. Rahner, *The Parish,* 32–34). "The parish in which placeness is the sole form of religious societalization need not be the only form of community which becomes a real local community in the celebration of the Eucharist" (*ibid.*).

Moreover, the territorial consideration should not be urged without qualification, and it seems an exaggeration to see territorial proximity as necessarily involving a close connection of persons. In modern times geographical mobility has caused some decline of communities based on the idea of neighborhood alone. The neighborhood is no longer in many places the main arena of social life, and men are often linked with others in different groupings based on such considerations as work, recreation, education, and social life, and pursue their various activities in different places and in different groups. Urban renewal may do something to reverse this trend, but it seems improbable that it will greatly diminish the choice people have of fulfilling their social needs outside their neighborhood.

Liturgical and Apostolic Consequences. The individual Christian in Baptism becomes a member of a priestly people that is called to offer spiritual sacrifices to God through Christ. "The Eucharist is for all time the true gathering place of God's people" (J. A. Jungmann, "Liturgy in the Parish," in H. Rahner, *The Parish,* 67–68) with whom the Church identifies itself in the prayers of the Mass. This is not accomplished in a cloudy and ideal way, but concretely and visibly when the faithful, gathered together in their parish church, come to the same table and eat of the same Bread, which is the Body of the Lord. Thus in the Eucharist the Church is realized, but always and necessarily in a spatially limited manner. The parish, the assembled local community, with its pastor, constitutes the immediate and ideal framework for the celebration of the Eucharist and the realization of the Church. Sunday's liturgical celebration is the climax in which all parish work culminates and is brought to its final significance.

The parish of its very nature is a dynamic entity because it is Christ working in a given area through the instrumentality of men to achieve in time and space the purpose of the Incarnation. But Christ, as Savior of all, commanded His followers to preach the gospel to every creature. The parish is therefore missionary in the first place because all men within its area of jurisdiction are called to belong to it and its mission is to effect this as best it can. The missionary vitality of the parish is the vitality of Christ whose instrument it is. The parish would not be identified with Christ if it were otherwise. Every renewal of the Church necessarily implies a rededication to this purpose, which is intrinsic to the nature and form of the parish and which is also Christ's salvific will.

The laity together with the pastor and his assistants comprise the parish, that is, the assembly of those in and through whom Christ lives and works in a given area. A parish is people and what the parish does or does not do is not something apart from what the people do or do not do. The role of the laity in the parish is therefore to function in a manner consonant with the apostolic demands of their Baptism and Confirmation in which they were commissioned to worship God and charged with the spreading of His kingdom. Since the laity are the Church in a given locality, they are responsible under the pastor's guidance for the Church in that area. The apostolic endeavors of the laity within the parish may either be individual or organized. In either case the lay person's charge to witness what he believes is a function intrinsic to his calling. He is to be perfect himself and to let his light so shine before men that they may see his good works and glorify the Father who is in heaven (Mt 5.16).

Bibliography: H. RAHNER, ed., *The Parish,* tr. R. KRESS (Westminster, Md. 1958). J. HAMER, "A Basis for a Pastoral Theology of the Parish," in *Apostolic Renewal in the Seminary in Light of Vatican II,* ed. J. KELLER and R. ARMSTRONG (New York 1965). Y. M. J. CONGAR, *Mission de la paroisse* (Lille 1948). M. RAHNER, *Esquisse d'une théologie de la paroisse* (Paris 1961). P. IMBERT DE LA TOUR, *Les Paroisses rurales dans l'ancienne France du IVᵉ au XIᵉ siècle* (Paris 1898). U. BERLIÈRE, "L'Exercise du ministère paroissal par les moines dans le haut moyen-âge," Rev Bén 39 (1927) 227–250. Y. DANIEL and G. LE MOUEL, *Paroisses d'hier, paroisses de demain* (Paris 1958). C. FLORISTAN SEMANES, *The Parish, Eucharistic Community,* tr. J. F. BYRNE (Notre Dame, Ind. 1964). P. BAILBY, *Le Curé et sa paroisse* (Paris 1961).

[C. RIEPE]

PARISH, SOCIOLOGY OF THE

The identification of the Catholic *parish as a setting for sociological research developed in Europe during the 1930s and in the U.S. and Latin America after World War II. With very few exceptions, research studies of the period were inspired by what were perceived to be the practical apostolic and pastoral values of reliable empirical information. Typically, they were sociographic or demographic surveys designed with technical skill but without reference to hypotheses or concepts relevant to the main body of sociological theory (*see* SOCIOLOGY).

European Research. In Europe the pioneer work was carried out in France and Belgium. It was stimulated by a growing sense of crisis within French Catholicism and by the need for data that might serve as a basis for programs of rechristianization. The research conducted or directed by Gabriel LeBras, professor of the history of Canon Law at the Sorbonne; Ferdinand Boulard, editor of *Les cahiers du clergé rural;* and Joseph Lebret, OP, and the Dominicans of Économie et Humanisme aroused considerable ecclesiastical as well as public interest. Historical studies and questionnaire surveys of parishes and dioceses not only described the religious practices of French Catholics but correlated data concerning these practices with such variables as sex, age, region, occupation, educational attainment, and social class. The sociographic profiles thus produced were promptly utilized pastorally for the redistricting of parishes, the adjustment of clergy-laity ratios, the development of new action programs, and the design and testing of experimental types of parish organizations.

Similar studies in Belgium, the Netherlands, Germany, and Italy also served pastoral values and attracted the interest of an increasing number of young Catholic sociologists trained at the Sorbonne, Louvain, the Gregorian University, or in American graduate schools. These empirically oriented religious and lay sociologists contributed a more sophisticated methodology to the sociographic type of parish study. François Houtart's study of the parishes of Brussels, a survey of parish life in Lyon by Émile Pin, SJ, and Conor K. Ward's survey in England exemplify the scientific advances. Perhaps the more important contribution of the professional sociologists, however, was their enlargement of the sphere of parish research and their more theoretically sensitive analyses of parish problems. These developments are still embryonic; but Pin's study of the priesthood, the pilot investigations of Houtart and his staff at Louvain's Centre de Recherches Socio-Religeuse, and the activities of the *International Conference on the Sociology of Religion and the *International Federation of Institutes of Social and Socio-Religious Research (FERES) are portents of a promising development. Their promise is enhanced by the fact that in Continental Europe and, more recently, in Latin America the pastoral values of such studies have received widespread official approbation. As they extend beyond the sociographic stage, these investigations may provide inductive bases for theological and ecclesiological developments.

Parish Research in the U.S. The situation has been quite different in the U.S. On the positive side, sociological studies of American Catholic parishes have been less sociographic and more systematically sociological than those in Europe. This advantage has been offset by the fact that they have been fewer in number and less highly appreciated in ecclesiastical circles. The differences are in part attributable to the lesser sense of religious crisis within American Catholicism; but they reflect, too, sponsorship of studies by professional rather than pastoral interest groups. Although the cooperation of bishops and pastors has been encouraged by the practical values of sociological investigations, design and interpretation usually have been guided by more formally sociological concepts and hypotheses. Thus, in a symposium in the field edited by C. Joseph Nuesse and Thomas J. Harte, CSSR, the parish was defined not simply as an area for sociographic study but as a partial social system amenable to analysis in structural and functional terms. This focus on the group structure of the parish did not ignore the usefulness of sociographic study but identified in addition the values, attitudes, and interactive behavior associated with the roles of pastors, curates, religious, or lay members as the vital center of the sociology of the parish. There has been, however, little empirical investigation of the interpersonal relations of priests and parishioners in the parish setting.

Except for a few doctoral dissertations and a socioreligious survey by Joseph B. Schuyler, SJ, the sociology of the Catholic parish in the U.S. is mainly identified with the research of Joseph A. Fichter, SJ, of Loyola University of the South (New Orleans). He initiated large-scale research in the field with a comprehensive and highly detailed sociological survey published in 1951 as the first of the projected four volumes. Unfortunately, the ensuing ecclesiastical furor prevented publication of the remaining volumes and increased pastoral resistance to research along these lines. In later works Fichter described types of parishioners, the roles of the parish priest, the social origins of priests and seminarians, the structure and style of a parish school, and critical evaluations of priests regarding their own

roles as well as evaluations of these roles by lay friends of priests. The explicitly sociological frame of reference of these studies no less than their foci distinguish them from European research and represent significant theoretical as well as methodological advances. Realization of their sociological and pastoral value, however, requires replication in order to widen the base of the findings and to neutralize distortion potentially present in studies of limited cases and samples.

Parish research has been pursued at The Catholic University of America, Fordham University, and the University of Notre Dame; and some diocesan surveys have been directed by trained sociologists. For an increasing number of American Catholic sociologists, the focus on the parish has been replaced by concern with the whole subculture of American Catholicism. There has been especially significant sociological research in the areas of Catholic education and of the values and attitudes of priests and laity. These investigations have at least indirect implications for the sociology of the parish.

The decline of the sociology of the parish in the U.S. is a significant recognition of the fact that the ideal of the parish as a communal social organization is seldom capable of realization in a highly urbanized society. For a significant proportion of the highly mobile urban population, the parish structure and the interrelationships among priests and parishioners are not central in socioreligious life. Contemporary liturgical reforms have recognized and seek to change this fact. Among other difficulties, social realities render the geographical boundaries of the parish partial and inadequate for the definition of meaningful socioreligious interaction. Extraparochial social and religious structures are more significant centers of influence and interaction. Some of the traditional functions of the parish and some of the traditional roles played by priests and parishioners have been preempted by other structures and other roles. The parish still fulfills important functions for the Church but in sociological terms it is perhaps less fruitful than other areas for the investment of research effort.

See also LEAKAGE (IN CHURCH MEMBERSHIP); PARISH CENSUS; RELIGION, SOCIOLOGY OF.

Bibliography: C. J. NUESSE and T. J. HARTE, eds., *The Sociology of the Parish* (Milwaukee 1951). AmCathSocRev 15.2 (1954), special issue ed. T. J. HARTE. G. LEBRAS, *Introduction à l'histoire de la pratique religieuse en France*, 2 v. (Paris 1942–45). F. BOULARD, *Introduction to Religious Sociology*, tr. M. J. JACKSON (London 1960). F. BOULARD and G. LEBRAS, *Carte religieuse de la France rurale* (2d ed. Paris 1952). F. HOUTART, "Les Paroisses de Bruxelles, 1803–1951," *Bulletin de l'Institut recherches économiques et sociales de l'Université de Louvain* 19 (1953). J. H. FICHTER, *Southern Parish* (Chicago 1951); *Parochial School: A Sociological Study* (Notre Dame 1958); *Priest and People* (New York 1965). É. PIN, *Pratique religieuse et classes sociales dans une paroisse urbaine, Saint-Pothin à Lyon* (Paris 1956). J. B. SCHUYLER, *Northern Parish: A Sociological and Pastoral Study* (Chicago 1960). C. K. WARD, *Priests and People: A Study in the Sociology of Religion* (Liverpool 1961).

[J. D. DONOVAN]

PARISH CENSUS

Canon Law prescribes that in addition to keeping registers of baptisms, confirmations, marriages, and deaths, each pastor must also "compile as accurately as possible a register of the spiritual condition of the members of his parish" (c.470). The possibility of fulfilling this law by a mere enumeration of individuals or families living within parish boundaries is excluded by the reference of the text to the *status animarum* (literally, the state of souls). The purpose of the parish census is pastoral, and this purpose—with all that it implies, for example, in the use of confidential matter—takes precedence over other ends, such as those of religious research, that may be served incidentally.

In the Old Testament King David was blamed for bringing a plague upon Israel when, to swell his royal pride, he ordered a census of the people [*see* CENSUS (IN THE BIBLE)]. Superstitious interpretations of the event brought census-taking into disrepute, so that even as late as the 18th century a member of the English House of Commons expressed the fear that an enumeration of His Majesty's subjects might be followed by some "epidemical distemper." Of course, Rome's imperial census assisted the fulfillment of the Messianic prophecies when Jesus was born in Bethlehem after Mary had accompanied Joseph on the journey from Nazareth in order to be enumerated in his ancestral city. The growth of the Church led eventually to the keeping of records, but uniformity of practice was not imposed until the Council of Trent prescribed parochial registers of baptisms and marriages. Sixtus V (1585–90) made it the duty of all bishops to send to Rome periodic comprehensive reports of their dioceses. The modern requirements of parish registers, including the *Liber status animarum,* were incorporated into the Code of Canon Law that became effective in 1918.

Scope. The Roman ritual prescribes that the *Liber status animarum* should enumerate all the families of each parish, including the family name, given name, and age of each member and of any persons living with the family as guests or servants. Notations are to be made for those who have received their first Communion and Confirmation. The record is to be kept up-to-date to inform the pastor concerning the state of the parish. Actually, there is great variation in the degree to which the requirement is observed and in the kinds of information sought through the parish census. In general, family record cards are preferred to individual record cards, and the following items are considered to provide the minimum information needed: (1) definite identification, including name, address, and date of birth for each individual; (2) the occupation of the head of the family; and (3) questions concerning religious duties, i.e., Baptism, first Holy Communion, Confirmation, valid marriage, fulfillment of the Easter duty, and attendance at Mass. The latter questions are central to the census interview. The question on occupation is asked to provide an indication of the family's economic status; more specific questions on this point are probably unnecessary for pastoral purposes and are often unfavorably received.

Purpose. According to the most commonly accepted interpretation of the canonical requirement, the purpose of the parish census is therapeutic. In addressing the National Conference of Catholic Charities in 1934, Mother Mary Teresa Tallon (1868–1954), founder of the *Parish Visitors of Mary Immaculate, described the census visitation of families as "not only a systematic study of parish conditions but a veritable missionary crusade of Catholic Action," through which "the wayward are instructed and reclaimed to the Church; faithful Catholics are exhorted to become fervent and apostolic . . . [and] all are urged to con-tribute personal interest and service to the upbuilding of the Catholic cause" [*Proceedings* (Washington, D.C. 1934) 214]. The rectification of invalid marriages, the return of lax Catholics to sacramental participation in the Church, the instruction of the uninstructed, and other salutary effects of a therapeutic census are outstanding. The taking of the census is an opportunity for fruitful dialogue not only with lapsed Catholics but also with persons having no church affiliation.

The therapeutic purpose is evident particularly in a letter of June 12, 1941, addressed to all bishops of the U.S. by the apostolic delegate, then Abp. Amleto Cicognani, reminding the bishops, in order "to make the pastoral ministry by this means even more fruitful," of their obligation for the *Liber status animarum.* "The observance of this law," the apostolic delegate wrote, "will form every priest on the model of the Good Shepherd." Emphasizing that the pastor and his assistants are the proper census workers, he remarked that "the taking of the census by others than priests is but a preparation for the visit of the pastor or his assistant and can never take its place." Nevertheless, zealous helpers "can prepare the faithful to attach greater importance to the visit of the parish priest; they can oftentimes smooth the way in difficult circumstances, so that parishioners will welcome the priest and profit spiritually by his visit." The desire to conform to the apostolic delegate's directive was reflected in the statutes of diocesan synods. For example, the eighth synod of the Archidocese of St. Louis decreed in 1950 that "the *Status animarum,* or census, of the parish is to be kept accurately by pastoral visitation of each family. This visitation should be continuous." This statute was repeated substantially by the ninth synod in 1960.

Census-Taking. Although it is the mind of the Church that the parish census should be the personal concern of the pastor, since it is so positively directed to the

A Parish Visitor of Mary Immaculate conducting a census interview.

point of orientation of all pastoral responsibility, it is not practical to demand of priests in large urban parishes that they personally execute the detailed and time-consuming task of door-to-door visitation. Communities of religious women have been found to be particularly well suited to offer "spiritual first-aid," and brothers and seminarians are also frequently assigned to the task. Personal counseling is readily developed in the dialogue that follows census questions. Calling at every home provides opportunities not only for interviews with marginal or lapsed Catholics but also for ecumenical dialogue, since persons of varied religious convictions or none are encountered.

It may be noted also that the increasing participation of the laity in the work of the Church releases parish priests from tasks that are less pastoral than the census. For example, a well organized *Confraternity of Christian Doctrine relieves a pastor of many burdens and thus releases his time for home visitation. Lay persons, e.g., members of the *Legion of Mary, as well as religious, are used for census-taking. Laymen are used particularly in the "blitz" technique that became popular in several parts of the U.S. during the 1940s and 1950s. A large area or a diocese can be covered in a few days by a well-organized corps of lay volunteers who visit all homes, inform residents of inquiry classes, invite them to "open-house" activities of Catholic churches, and distribute literature. This type of census is coordinated with evangelization.

Use in Research. The "blitz" census has provided material for some surveys that have placed in relief the value of census data that are accurate, up-to-date, and available for immediate study. The use of computers for the analysis of census findings on the parish level may not be practical, and their advantages on the diocesan level have not been thoroughly tested. But the practical questions that would be involved in a nationwide Catholic census are under examination, and the study of the possibilities of such an undertaking is a logical development of the Church's interest in the use of the census for statistical and research purposes as well as for therapeutic purposes.

Social scientists and others have suggested that the adoption of a standardized parish census form might be a first step toward the establishment of a national Catholic statistical bureau. The desirability of such a development is indicated by the individual studies of parishes or dioceses that have been made from time to time. A therapeutic census tends to be a slow, painstaking task, and it does not usually provide data that can be used for research on such questions as Catholic fertility, the social correlates of mixed marriage, or other aspects of religious practice. This kind of research is of both scientific interest and practical consequence.

The two outstanding practical obstacles to further progress in the use of the parish census are (1) the lack of trained personnel to conduct therapeutic censuses and (2) the lack of funds to support statistical and research studies. The purposes of the therapeutic census and of statistical or scientific investigations are not antithetical. Their simultaneous pursuit would be advanced by a deeper consciousness of the value of the parish census to the pastoral ministry and to the Church as a whole. For pastoral purposes, of course,

nothing can take the place of home visitation by the priest or of the preparation for his visit by persons whose total commitment to Christ is evident.

See also LEAKAGE (IN CHURCH MEMBERSHIP); PARISH, SOCIOLOGY OF THE; STATISTICS, ECCLESIASTICAL.

Bibliography: G. A. KELLY, "The Parish Census," in *The Sociology of the Parish,* ed. C. J. NUESSE and T. J. HARTE (Milwaukee 1951) 234–260. M. T. TALLON, "A Systematic Study of Parish Conditions," *Parish Visitor* 10 (Dec. 1934) 20–36. J. B. SCHUYLER, "Parish Census," *Catholic Management Journal* 1 (1958) 5–9. J. E. ROSS, "A National Catholic Statistical Bureau," *AmEcclRev* 86 (1932) 29–41. F. GRONER, "The Office of Ecclesiastical Statistics for Catholic Germany," LumV 6 (1951) 242–250. J. F. SCHEUER and F. A. SANTOPOLO, "Why Not an Adequate Parish Census?" *Priest* 16 (1960) 280–284. M. LOYOLA, "Your Parish Is a Mission," *Ave Maria* 85 (Jan. 12, 1957) 16–19. M. LUDIVINE, "Census for Souls," *America* 97 (Sept. 21, 1957) 646–648. **Illustration credit:** Ted Rozumalski, Milwaukee.

[M. L. WHITTY]

PARISH VISITORS OF MARY IMMACULATE

(PVMI), a contemplative missionary congregation of women under simple vows, founded in New York City on Aug. 15, 1920, by Mother Mary Teresa Tallon with the approval of Archbishop (later Cardinal) Patrick Hayes. The congregation was canonically erected on April 25, 1927. At a time when Christian family life was rapidly declining, the foundress conceived the idea of sisters engaging in family visitation to restore the spirit of the Holy Family to the home. The chief means used by the sisters to reach families and individuals is a census, or spiritual survey, made in urban and rural parishes at the request of pastors. Parish Visitors also help to establish the Confraternity of Christian Doctrine in parishes, prepare lay teachers, and teach public school children. The sisters conduct no institutions, but visit families, orphanages, jails, and institutions for the aged and for the physically and mentally ill. In 1963 they were serving in nine archdioceses and dioceses of the U.S. The motherhouse is at Monroe, N.Y.

[M. L. COONEY]

PARISIS, PIERRE LOUIS,

French bishop; b. Orléans, Aug. 12, 1795; d. Arras, March 5, 1866. He was ordained in 1819 and was bishop of Langres (1834–51) and then of Arras (1851–66). Soon after ordination he gained fame as a preacher. At Langres he was one of the most prominent members of the French hierarchy, especially because of his writings in the struggle to obtain for the Church freedom of education and other liberties. He was among the first in the episcopate to support *Montalembert and in 1844 published a famous letter to him concerning the role of the laity in the Church's struggle for educational freedom. In his *Cas de conscience* (1847) he upheld, with some reservations, the liberalism professed by Hugues Félicité de *Lamennais. During his terms (1848–51) as an elected member of the national legislature, he opposed the *Falloux law on education, considering it a compromise. At Arras he concentrated on diocesan administration and engaged little in public affairs. Detaching himself from Montalembert and the Catholic liberals, he upheld the *ultramontanism of Louis *Veuillot and *L'Univers.* He supported *Napoleon III until events in Italy changed his opinion of the Emperor. In his *Cas de conscience sur les libertés publique* (1865),

Parisis conformed to the principles of the *Syllabus of Errors (1864).

Bibliography: C. GUILLEMANT, *Pierre Louis Parisis,* 3 v. (Paris 1916–21). C. CONSTANTIN, DTC 11.2:2039–40.

[L. P. MAHONEY]

PARK (LE PARC), MONASTERY OF,

Premonstratensian abbey at Heverlee, Louvain, Belgium, Diocese of Mechelen, circary (province) of Brabant. It was founded as a double monastery c. 1128 by Duke Godfrey I of Lorraine, and itself founded in 1137 the Abbey of Ninove on the Dendre (suppressed in 1796). The nuns of Park soon transferred, probably to the Augustinian Parc-les-Dames (Cistercian 1215–1796). The nuns of Gempe and 19 churches were under the rule of the abbot of Park, which became a flourishing monastery. The *Annales Parchenses* (1148–1458) were compiled in the abbey. Abbot T. van Tuldel, mitred in 1462, resisted the commendary system energetically. In the 17th century Park was a center of Tridentine reform in the order. Abbots J. Druys and J. Maes in 1630 drew up new statutes and the *ordinarius* of the order. Suppressed in 1789–90 by *Joseph II and in 1797 by the French, Park was restored in 1836 and became an abbey again in 1872. In 1896 it undertook a mission in Montes Claros, Brazil. Until 1914 it published the scientific periodical *Analectes de l'ordre de Prémontré.* The abbey, one of the most charming in Belgium, had about 60 members in 1964. The Romanesque church was extensively remodeled in the 17th and 18th centuries; the style of the monastery is Renaissance and baroque. Park has always been a center of learning; its monks included the historian R. van Wafelghem and the Vatican expert in Coptic sciences F. A. van Lantschoot. Its archives are extensive and valuable.

Bibliography: Hugo OrdPraemAn v.2. J. E. JANSEN, *L'Abbaye norbertine de Parc-le Duc* (Malines 1929). Backmund Mon Praem 2:317–322.

[N. BACKMUND]

PARKER, FRANCIS

American educator whom John Dewey called the "father of progressive education"; b. Bedford, N.H., Oct. 9, 1837; d. Chicago, Ill., March 2, 1902. A New Englander by birth, temperament, and education, from the age of 16 Parker taught school until the outbreak of the Civil War in 1861. Retiring from the army in 1865 with the rank of colonel, he returned to the schools, where he served as principal in Manchester, N.H., and then as instructor in the Dayton (Ohio) normal school. Unhappy with what he found in the classroom, he decided to visit European schools seeded with the ideas of J. *Pestalozzi, F. *Fröbel, H. *Spencer, and J. *Herbart. Parker accordingly sailed for Europe in 1872 and spent the next 3 years attending university lectures in Berlin and visiting schools throughout western Europe.

In 1875, shortly after his return from Europe, Parker was appointed superintendent of schools in Quincy, Mass., where within 5 years he had sprung to national prominence with the introduction of European educational thought to America. His "Quincy method," embodying much of what he had acquired abroad, can be considered a forerunner of the *progressive movement in education. The 3 following years (1880–83),

when he served as assistant superintendent of schools in Boston, were merely an interlude before his move to Chicago, Ill., and to the principalship of the Cook County normal school. Here between 1883 and 1889 Parker propounded his philosophy of democratic education and in large measure transformed teaching in the Midwest.

He introduced the best Pestalozzian techniques, particularly in geography (*see* PESTALOZZIANISM). He stressed the primacy of method over content because the child was the true center of the educational process. He urged the generations of teachers that came under his dynamic influence to liberate the child's spontaneous tendencies, which he styled "the records of inborn divinity." He systematized the "self-expression" of Fröbel by creating outlets through the arts and crafts. During his Chicago years manual training, physical education, and science became more common in the elementary school curriculum, and Fröbel's kindergarten movement came into its own.

He insisted above all that the school was to channel the child's personal happiness (arrived at through self-expression) into social outlets. "The sole function of the teacher," he declared, "is the organization of sound community life, the development of public opinion." He anticipated Dewey in describing the school as "a model home, a complete community, an embryonic democracy."

Like other emancipated Puritan sons whose energies helped power the public school movement, Parker left to the schools a legacy of moral and spiritual values, which has practically become the religion of American public education. His optimistic faith in the natural goodness of man and in the power of natural education to resolve all social ills, is an amalgam of J. J. Rousseau and R. W. Emerson. His belief in progress and the role of divinity in man's life stemmed from German idealism that the impact of Darwinian scientism shattered. Yet as a synthesizer and popularizer, Parker remains an important figure in an important chapter of American education.

Bibliography: F. W. PARKER, *Talks on Teaching* (New York 1903); *Talks on Pedagogics* (New York 1894). M. E. CURTI, *The Social Ideas of American Educators* (rev. ed. Paterson, N.J. 1959). L. A. CREMIN, *The Transformation of the School* (New York 1961). W. S. MONROE, *History of the Pestalozzian Movement in the United States* (New York 1907). I. C. HEFFRON, *Francis Wayland Parker* (Los Angeles 1934).

[N. G. MC CLUSKEY]

PARKER, MATTHEW,

scholar and archbishop of Canterbury who helped shape the Elizabethan religious settlement; b. Norwich, Aug. 6, 1504; d. London, May 17, 1575. Parker entered Corpus Christi College, Cambridge, in 1522 and took his B.A. degree in 1525. In 1527 he was ordained and in 1528 became associated with the Cambridge Reformers, a student group with Lutheran sympathies. When Anne Boleyn became queen, Parker was made her chaplain, and in 1537 chaplain to Henry VIII. In 1544, on the King's recommendation, he became master of his old college and in 1545, vice chancellor of Cambridge. At the accession of Edward VI in 1547 Parker married Margaret Harlestone of Norfolk. Parker's Protestant sympathies were avowed with increasing openness as the successive regencies of Somerset and Northumberland drew

England steadily in a Protestant direction. Upon Edward's death in 1553 Parker espoused the cause of Northumberland's unfortunate pawn, Lady Jane Grey. For this and for his marriage he was deprived of his offices by Catholic Queen Mary. Having no taste for martyrdom, he spent the 5 years of her reign in hiding, devoting his time to translating the Psalms and writing in defense of the marriage of priests.

Following the accession of Elizabeth I, Parker was elected Archbishop of Canterbury in 1559, and was consecrated by four Henrician and Edwardian bishops. Since the Ordinal employed had been repealed in the reign of Mary, the consecration was valid only if royal supremacy is also accepted. Parker's consecration thus became a key problem in the later controversy over *Anglican Orders. The most important among Archbishop Parker's hundreds of appointments were to 10 sees that Mary and Cardinal Pole had left vacant. He furthered the English Reformation by filling them with Protestants.

Parker, a modest, pious, reserved man, was always a moderate. In 1545 he saved Cambridge's colleges from dissolution during the Henrician confiscations. Years later he strove to limit further spoliation of the church by Elizabethan courtiers. Always interested in scholarship and antiquities, Parker tried to revive the Saxon language, founded the Society of Antiquaries, and collected ancient manuscripts at a time when learning was being plundered. His magnificent manuscript collection was the most important of many gifts he bequeathed to Cambridge. As archbishop, Parker sought a middle way between Catholics and Puritans. Significantly, the worst Elizabethan persecution of Catholics commenced only after his death. With the Puritans

Parker ordered an end to "prophesyings" and enforced a compromise between the Queen's desire for elaborate vestments and the Puritans' insistence upon none at all, depriving those Puritans who refused to comply.

Bibliography: J. STRYPE, *The Life and Acts of Matthew Parker,* 3 v. (Oxford 1821). H. GEE, *The Elizabethan Clergy and the Settlement of Religion, 1558–1564* (Oxford 1898). H. N. BIRT, *The Elizabethan Religious Settlement* (London 1907). B. M. H. THOMPSON, *The Consecration of Archbishop Parker* (London 1934). J. B. MULLINGER, DNB 15:254–264. V. J. K. BROOK, *A Life of Archbishop Parker* (Oxford 1962). E. W. PERRY, *Under Four Tudors* (London 1940). Hughes RE.

[B. NORLING]

PARKER, THEODORE, Unitarian minister; b. Lexington, Mass., Aug. 24, 1810; d. Florence, Italy, May 10, 1860. Parker was a child prodigy, but poverty prevented his receiving any formal education. He taught school for some years to finance his studies at Harvard Divinity School; he was ordained in 1837 as pastor at West Roxbury, Mass. He stressed the immanence of God in nature and the human mind, and rejected many traditional Christian teachings. Parker became the center of controversy with the publication of *The Transient and Permanent in Christianity* (1841) and *Discourse of Matters Pertaining to Religion* (1842). After resigning his pastorate, he organized his own Boston, Mass., congregation in 1845. Parker was active in reform movements, particularly the antislavery cause. He wrote abolitionist tracts and participated in the rescue of fugitive slaves.

Bibliography: *Collected Works . . .,* ed. F. P. COBBE, 14 v. (London 1863–71). H. S. COMMAGER, *Theodore Parker* (Boston 1936). J. E. DIRKS, *Critical Theology of Theodore Parker* (New York 1948).

[R. K. MAC MASTER]

PARKINSON, ANTHONY, English Franciscan historian; b. Cuthbert, Lancashire, England, 1667; d. East Hendred, Berkshire, Jan. 30, 1728. Professed as a Franciscan at Douai, he was appointed philosophy professor at the Franciscan college there in 1692. After being assigned to the English mission 2 years later, he served as superior of the Franciscans at Warwick (1698–1701) and at Birmingham (1701–10), as guardian at Oxford (1710–13), and as provincial (1713–16, 1722–25). In this last post, he participated in the Franciscan general chapter at Rome in 1723. His principal work is the *Collectanea Anglo-Minoritica, or a Collection of the Antiquities of the English Franciscans or Friars Minors Commonly Called Gray Friars* (London 1726). He spent his remaining years as guardian of Coventry and as chaplain to the Eyston family of Berkshire.

Bibliography: FATHER THADDEUS, *The Franciscans in England 1600–1850* (London 1898). T. COOPER, DNB 15:312. DictEng Cath 5:243–244.

[P. S. MC GARRY]

PARKMINSTER, St. Hugh's Charterhouse, Partridge Green, Horsham, Sussex, England; Southwark diocese. This *Carthusian monastery was founded in 1873 from La Grande Chartreuse as a refuge in anticipation of the possible expulsion of religious orders from France. This need coincided with the desire of the English Catholic hierarchy to restore the Carthusians to England, and a property in Sussex called Parknowle (changed to Parkminster) was chosen. Building commenced in 1876, using local and Bath

Matthew Parker, Archbishop of Canterbury. Portrait in the "Bibliotheca Chalcographica," 1650.

Parkminster, St. Hugh's Charterhouse, Sussex, England.

stone and paving stones from Belgium for the cloisters. More than 600 workmen of different nationalities were employed, and the foundation stone was laid in October 1877. In 1883, the first prior was appointed, the novitiate opened, and the church consecrated. The spire has become a well-known landmark. There are cells for 36 choir monks and 50 lay brothers (called *conversi*), and 4,000 feet of cloisters, the main garth being one of the largest of its kind in the world. A fine library houses 30,000 volumes, including valuable MSS dating from the earliest days of the order. Parkminster is the only charterhouse in England today and continues the tradition of the nine English charterhouses (from *Witham to *Sheen) prior to the Reformation.

Bibliography: A Monk of Parkminster, "The Return of the Carthusians to England," *The Southwark Record* (Sept.–Oct. 1939). *St. Hugh's Charterhouse* (Marseille 1963), guidebook. **Illustration credit:** Aerofilms and Aero Pictorial Limited, London.

[A. GRAY]

PARLEMENT

In France before 1789 a *parlement* was a court of appeal endowed with political and administrative prerogatives, whose jurisdiction extended over a defined territory. The *parlement* of Paris excelled in antiquity and prestige; but the French *parlements* as a group formed an original institution that is not to be compared with the English parliament of the same epoch or with the French legislative *parlement* of the 19th and 20th centuries.

Establishment. The possibility of appealing from a decision rendered by royal justice gave rise to *parlements,* or occasional assemblies, held here and there by men of the law pertaining to the *Curia regis* (court of the king), in which prelates ordinarily took part. At the beginning of the 14th century a stable tribunal was organized with its seat on the island of the city of Paris (Palace of Justice); it sat continuously from November 12 until July or August. Bishops and abbots ceased to act as judges by 1319, but numerous clerics continued in this function. The ecclesiastical and lay peers of France had the right to sit in the *parlement* of Paris, which became the court of peers. When the king came there to preside and communicated his wishes by the voice of his chancellor, the session was called a "bed of justice" (*lit de justice*). *Parlements* were established also at Toulouse (1420), Grenoble (1456), Bordeaux (1462), Dijon (1477), Rouen (1499), Aix-en-Provence (1501), Rennes (1553), Pau (1620), Metz (1633), Douai (1668), Besançon (1676), and Nancy (1775). Without bearing the title of *parlement,* four sovereign councils exercised these functions at Arras, Bastia, Colmar, and Perpignan.

Membership and Powers. Until about 1515 the *parlements* were mixed tribunals in which ecclesiastical judges were as numerous as lay judges and sometimes more numerous. New members were chosen by cooptation by those already in office. Under Francis I (1515–47) the number of ecclesiastics among the judges declined because judicial offices were offered for sale, and exemptions were made to facilitate the replacing of clerics by laymen. The makeup of a *parlement* depended on the extent of its jurisdiction. In 1789 there were more than 200 magistrates in Paris, 80 in Rouen, and 40 in Douai. Each *parlement* had a first president (named by the king), presidents, counselors, a public minister, a procurator general, and advocates general. It had also a Great Chamber, open to the oldest counselors, that handled the chief appeal cases, the *appeals as from an abuse (appels comme d'abus)*, and in Paris matters relative to the right of *regalia. Each parlement* had one or more chambers of inquiry that judged most appeals; it had also a chamber of requests that acted as a court of first instance to settle those questions concerning privileges that were provided with royal letters, called *Committimus* or *garde gardienne* (for chapters, abbeys, or religious communities). New laws (ordinances, edicts, declarations) and letters patent (for papal bulls and rescripts and for approvals and favors accorded to communities) had to be presented, verified, and registered before these assembled chambers in order to fall under the competence of a *parlement. Parlement* could defer registration by using its right of remonstrance. In other ways, too, it could pronounce judgments, as when the *parlement* of Paris forbade the "refusal of the Sacraments" (Aug. 18, 1752).

Qualities and Defects of Parlements. Members of the *parlements* were noted for their dignity and zeal for the common welfare; they formed an elite that furnished bishops to the Church and ministers to the state. There were exceptions, to be sure, but the defects of some were less important than the *esprit de corps* that animated *parlements* as a whole. The magistrates soon came to liken themselves to Roman senators, and to consider themselves fathers of their country and tutors of their king. Their Catholicism was, like their patriotism, a jealous one; it always dreaded any excessive exercise of papal power. Members of the *parlements* were traditionally imbued with *Gallicanism, but most of them did not adhere to *Jansenism. They were rich and held offices involving serious obligations; yet they liked to appear as representatives of the people, especially in the 18th century, in their remonstrances, which were neither moderate nor secret, as custom prescribed. Their excesses destroyed them in 1790, during the French Revolution, when they were legislated out of existence.

Parlements and the Church. The first conflicts between the *parlement* of Paris and ecclesiastical officials were less battles of laymen against clerics than rivalries among clerics who were not free from seeking material benefits and prestige, as was to be expected in a new organization. Thus the members of the *parlements* claimed the right to handle inheritances and wills, certain types of matrimonial cases (separation of husband and wife, separate maintenance), and cases concerning benefices. In the name of the liberties of the Gallican Church, *parlements* sought to maintain the practice of electing bishops. In 1518 they registered the concordat of 1516 only under duress. They refused obstinately to receive the decrees of the Council of *Trent and waged ceaseless battle against the papal bull *Unigenitus.* Almost all the *parlements* voted the suppression of the *Jesuits. In 1763 the president of the *parlement* of Toulouse prophesied: "You are giving a bad example of suppressions, gentlemen; you will be suppressed in turn yourself."

Bibliography: H. DE BASTARD D'ESTANG, *Les Parlements de France.* 2 v. (Paris 1857). M. MARION, *Dictionnaire des institutions de la France aux 17e et 18e siècles* (Paris 1923) 287, 422–433. R. DOUCET, *Les Institutions de la France au 16e siècle,* 2 v. (Paris 1948) 1:167–188. L. MIROT, *Manuel de géographie historique de la France.* ed. A. MIROT, 2 v. (2d ed. Paris 1947–50) 2:375–380. F. LOT and R. FAWTIER, eds., *Histoire des institutions françaises au moyen âge,* v.2 *Institutions royales* (Paris 1958) 332–508. F. BLUCHE, *Les Magistrats du Parlement de Paris au 18e siècle (1715–71)* (Paris 1961). J. ÉGRET, "Note d'orientation de recherches sur les Cours souveraines," *Comité des travaux historiques et scientifiques* 5 (1964) 45–53.

[C. BERTHELOT DU CHESNAY]

PARMA

City of 141,000 population on both banks of the Parma River, at the foot of the Apennines south of the Po, in Emilia-Romagna, north central Italy. The Diocese of Parma (*Parmensis*), immediately subject to the Holy See since 1875, in 1963 had 348 secular and 172 religious priests, 366 men in 15 religious houses, 882 women in 90 convents, and 299,000 Catholics; it is 811 square miles in area.

Terramara culture attests to Parma's antiquity. Probably Etruscan in name, the city was overrun by Celts (4th century B.C.) and became a colony of Rome (183 B.C.). A decline that began *c.* A.D. 387 ended under *Theodoric the Great (493–526). Byzantine rule (553–568) was followed by Lombard conquest; Charlemagne made the Lombard duchy a county (774). In 1035 Conrad II made Bishop Hiepo count, a position occupied by the bishops until 1106, when Parma became a free commune. During the 14th century the city was ruled by outside *signori,* ending with the *Visconti of Milan (1346–1447). Parma then came under the *Sforzas (1449–1500) and France (1500–12) before it was incorporated into the *States of the Church (1512–45). Pope Paul III, who had resigned the episcopacy of Parma in favor of his nephew, made his son, Pierluigi Farnese, Duke of Parma and *Piacenza (1545–47). *Farnese rule, which lasted to 1731, was a golden age for Parma. Bourbon rule (1732–1859) was interrupted by Austrian rule (1738–48) and the Napoleonic Empire (1802–14), which was followed by the reign of Maria Louisa of Austria (1815–47). In 1860 Parma became part of independent Italy.

The evangelization of Parma, attributed to SS. Apollinaris, Barnabus, and Lucian of Beauvais, probably came from *Milan, to which Parma was suffragan until the early 5th century, when it came under *Ravenna. Bishop Urbanus, who attended the Council of *Rimimi (359), was condemned for his support of antipope Ursicinus (372), but was still bishop in 378. According to the *Liber pontificalis, Parma was part of the Donation of *Pepin; but actually it seems to have belonged to the kings of Italy. Bishop Vigbodus was counselor of Charles the Fat (880) and archchaplain of Guido (888); Elbungus, Aicardus, Sigfredus, and Adeodatus served kings of Italy; Hubert was in the service of Otto I and II; Henry was chancellor of Henry II. The count-bishops sided with the Emperor in the *investiture controversy. Cadalus, who built the cathedral, became antipope Honorius II (1061–64); and Guibert, supported by Bishop Eberardus, opposed Pope Gregory VII as antipope Clement III (1084–1100).

The appointment of St. *Bernard degli Uberti as bishop (1106–33), under whom Parma ceased for a while to be suffragan to Ravenna, improved the situation of the Church. Aicardus, a partisan of Frederick I, was deposed (1167). Pope Innocent IV (1243–54) regained Parma to the papal side. Thereafter the episcopal history is not remarkable. Parma became suffragan to *Bologna (1583–1875).

Parma's cultural history dates from Roman times. There are no Lombard or Carolingian remains. The cathedral of the Assumption existed as early as 877, when Carloman, son of Louis the German, made a donation to the chapter of canons. It was rebuilt after fires in 923 and 1058 and an earthquake in 1117. The present Romanesque structure has a façade with three rows of arches; the brick tower (1284–94) is Romanesque and Gothic; chapels and a sacristy were added in the 13th and 14th centuries. The Romanesque baptistery (1196–1281), an irregular octagon in red marble, was designed by Benedetto *Antelami. *Correggio,

Parma, Romanesque cathedral with 13th-century campanile.

who worked in Parma (1518–30), did the fresco of the Assumption in the octagonal cupola of the cathedral. Parma has other notable Romanesque churches and a few notable Gothic churches.

The University of Parma grew from the 11th-century school of liberal arts. Medicine and law were added in the 12th century; and from the 13th century, when logic was added, the school was regarded as a university. Ranuccio I Farnese in particular favored it. Closed for political reasons (1831–54), it reopened but was reduced to faculties of literature and theology (1862). Since 1923 it has had faculties of law and medicine only.

Bibliography: J. Affò, *Storia della città di Parma*, 4 v. (Parma 1792–95), continued by A. Pezzana, 5 v. (1837–39). EncItal 26:382–388. G. Del Monte, *Il collegio dei teologi dell'Università di Parma* (Parma 1948). G. Bertuzzi, EncCatt 9:846–850. I. Dall'Aglio, *I seminari di Parma* (Parma 1958). D. Girghenohn and K. Noehles, LexThK² 8:108–109. AnnPont (1965) 328. **Illustration credit:** Alinari-Art Reference Bureau.

[C. M. AHERNE]

PARMENIDES

Parmenides of Elea inaugurated Western metaphysical thinking; b. probably in the middle of the latter half of the 6th century B.C. He is reported to have been introduced to philosophy by a Pythagorean named Ameinias, and his cultural background at Elea, a Phocaean colony on the west coast of Italy, was Ionian. His philosophy was expressed in a poem of which considerable fragments, as quoted by ancient writers, survive.

Content of the Poem. Although this was composed as a literary unit, it is divided by commentators into three parts: a proem or apocalyptic introduction, a section on truth, and a section on opinion (δόξα) or things as they appear. Textual difficulties and ambiguities in key passages, as well as the poetic form, often leave the meaning highly controversial.

Introduction. In the proem, in imagery found to a large extent in Hesiod (*Theog.* 744–761), Parmenides is borne from the dwellings of night aloft toward light on a chariot guided by sun maidens. Beyond the portals of the ways of night and day he is ushered into the presence of an unnamed goddess, there to be instructed in the knowledge of all things, first of the convincing truth, then of the unreliable "opinions of mortals," in the sense of being shown how things had to appear as they do (Diels FrgVorsokr 28B 1).

Truth. The way of inquiry following upon truth asserts that there is being—for there not to be is not possible. The directly opposite way, namely, that there is no being and cannot be any, cannot even be entered by human thought (*Frg.* 2). But Parmenides is also barred by the goddess from another way, the way actually traveled by mortals. This is two-headed, reverberating, perplexed, unseeing, undiscerning; for it gives nonbeing the same status as being and yet distinguishes them, setting up for everything a way that goes simultaneously in opposite directions. It is the way of sense perception and hearsay, and has to be superseded by difficult reasoning. The signposts identifying the legitimate way are: being cannot become or perish, it is a whole, without motion or change, without end, without past or future, all together, indivisible, continuous, finite, lacking nothing, perfectly self-identical, entirely homogeneous, and unique—for, since there is no nonbeing, there is nothing that could in any way come to be or cease to

be, or divide or multiply being, or cause defect or difference in it. All apparent changes in the cosmos, and distinctions between being and nonbeing, are but conventional names for the one all-embracing reality.

Opinion. From the goddess, Parmenides then learns why things appear to mortals differently from the way they are. By custom mortals set up two basic and opposite forms, light and night, one of which it is not legitimate to posit. Each is entirely self-identical and in no way the same as the other. Given equal status by human cognition, they fill everything and differentiate things from one another according to their relative predominance in each thing (*Frgs.* 6–9). Even individual cognition, with all conscious identity in a man, is but an ever-varying combination of the two basic forms, light and darkness (*Frg.* 16). In this framework cosmogony is taught Parmenides by the goddess (*Frgs.* 10–15; 17–19). Complete predominance of darkness in an individual's constitution is death (*Frg.* A 46), while full predominance of light, as the proem makes clear, allowed Parmenides during special inspiration to see things solely under the aspect of being.

Influence and Interpretation. Parmenides's teaching had wide influence in *Greek philosophy. His formal (in contrast to existential) notion of being, passed on through Aristotle and Neoplatonism, deeply impregnated scholastic, classical, and neoscholastic metaphysics, with the notable exception of that of St. Thomas Aquinas.

Interpreters differ widely over Parmenides. His doctrine of being, isolated from its poetic setting, is variously regarded as an abstract dialectic, a mystical experience, a philosophical monotone, or a sediment from preceding philosophies. His way of seeming, likewise isolated, has been viewed as a report of teachings rejected by him, or as tenets impossible to reconcile with his doctrine of being. Yet the contrast between light and night in the proem seems explained in terms of being and then carried through to the concluding section. No rational link between the sections is possible. In this cast the whole poem gives a consistent and penetrating account of both the way things are and the way they appear. Aristotle (*Meta.* 986b 31–33; 1010a 2–3) is almost certainly right in reporting that for Parmenides beings meant sensible things only, and that the same reality known as one by reason appears multiple through sensation.

Bibliography: K. Reinhardt, *Parmenides und die Geschichte der griechischen Philosophie* (2d ed. Frankfurt a.M. 1959). W. J. Verdenius, *Parmenides: Some Comments on His Poem* (Groningen 1942). G. Vlastos, "Parmenides' Theory of Knowledge," American Philological Association, *Transactions and Proceedings* 77 (1946) 66–77. J. H. M. Loenen, *Parmenides, Melissus, Gorgias* (Assen 1959).

[J. OWENS]

PARMIGIANINO (PARMIGIANO),

whose real name was Girolamo Francesco Maria Mazzola, or Mazzuoli, Italian painter and graphic artist, usually classified among the mannerists; b. Parma, Jan. 11, 1503; d. Casalmaggiore, Cremona, Aug. 24, 1540. On the death of his father, his education was entrusted to his uncles, who were artists, and from whom he may have received his first instructions in painting. His early works show the influence of the art of *Correggio with its accompanying illusionism (frescoes at San Giovanni Evangelista, Parma, 1522). As a result of a sojourn

Parmigianino, self-portrait in a convex mirror, 1524.

in Rome (1524–27), where he had the opportunity of studying the paintings of *Raphael, he underwent the influence of that master's later Michelangelesque style without, however, entirely emancipating himself of Correggio's manner ("Vision of St. Jerome," 1526–27, National Gallery, London). From these various elements Parmigianino evolved a style of rhythmic beauty and elegance, in which cool colors are habitually employed; elongated figures are endowed in their contours with sinuous grace and occupy most of the pictorial space ("Madonna dal Collo Lungo," *c.* 1535, Pitti, Florence; "Antea," 1535–37, Pinacoteca del Museo Nazionale, Naples).

Bibliography: Vasari. L. Fröhlich-Bum, *Parmigianino und der Manierismus* (Vienna 1921). A. Venturi, *Storia dell'arte italiana,* 9.2 (Milan 1926) 623–691. G. Copertini, *Il Parmigianino* (Parma 1932). A. O. Quintavalle, *Il Parmigianino* (Milan 1948). S. J. Freedberg, *Parmigianino: His Works in Painting* (Cambridge, Mass. 1950). A. E. Popham, *The Drawings of Parmigianino* (London 1953). **Illustration credit:** Kunsthistorisches Museum, Vienna.

[L. A. Leite]

PARNASSIANISM.

A movement in 19th-century French poetry that protested the effusiveness and sentimentality of such older Romantics as *Hugo, *Musset, *Lamartine, and their many imitators. Whereas the Romantics were subjective and exhibitionary, the Parnassians sought impersonality and impassibility, frequently writing in the third person to achieve Parnassian calm and objectivity.

Taking their cues from pivotal poets such as Théophile Gautier, Leconte de Lisle, and Théodore de Banville, the Parnassians professed an aesthetic of *l'art pour l'art,* free of social protest or utilitarian concerns. They wrote in "imagist" or pictorial style, finding their themes in antiquity or primitivism: in Hellenism, fable, and folklore. They sought in *echos sonores* (sonorous tones and rich rhythms) to create a "pure poetry," as frozen and accurate as photographs.

Their appearance was associated with three anthologies of verse, *Le Parnasse contemporain* (1866, 1870, 1876), launched by the poets Catulle Mendès and Xavier de Ricart, and the publisher Lemerre. The first issue provided, in the poetry of Leconte de Lisle, Banville, and José Maria de Heredia, models that were to degenerate into lifeless formulas in the last two issues. Protosymbolists such as *Baudelaire, *Verlaine, and *Mallarmé also appeared in this series.

Despite their disenchantment with Romanticism, and their supposed alliances with scientism, positivism, and realism, the Parnassians were in truth residual Romantics, some of whose theories bore fruit in the far more important movement of *symbolisme.*

See also ROMANTICISM, LITERARY; SYMBOLISM, LITERARY.

Bibliography: M. Gilman, *The Idea of Poetry in France: From Houdar de La Motte to Baudelaire* (Cambridge, Mass. 1958). K. Cornell, *The Symbolist Movement* (New Haven, Conn. 1951). M. Z. Shroder, *Icarus: The Image of the Artist in French Romanticism* (Harvard Study in Romance Languages 27; Cambridge, Mass. 1961).

[A. J. Montesi]

PARNELL, CHARLES STEWART

Irish nationalist leader; b. Rathdrum, Wicklow, Ireland, June 27, 1846; d. Brighton, England, Oct. 6, 1891. The son of John Henry and Delia (Stewart) Parnell, he was sympathetic to the cause of Irish parliamentary independence despite his Protestant background, his education in England, and his wealth as a large landholder. In 1875 he was elected to represent Meath in the United Kingdom House of Commons as a member of the Irish Home Rule party led by Isaac Butt. When Butt's gentler methods failed to win conservative or liberal support for Home Rule, Parnell headed a small group and embarked upon an obstructionist course using parliamentary filibusters.

In the wake of an economic crisis and an agricultural failure that made famine and evictions imminent, Parnell organized the National Land League in 1879, with Irish-American assistance and the sympathy of Archbishop *Croke of Cashel. Parnell's pressure compelled the government of *Gladstone to pass (1881) a land act protecting farmers from arbitrary evictions and rack rents. When Land League methods were represented to Rome as revolutionary, Leo XIII disapproved of them. Pressure from suffering Catholic tenants and dislike of conservative intrigues at Rome led a majority of the bishops to favor Parnell's policies and to side with Archbishop Croke and Abp. William *Walsh of Dublin, the successor of Edward McCabe, who had been an opponent of the Land League.

Previously, comments in the London *Tablet* critical of the Irish clergy's national sentiments and the activities of George Errington and other English Catholics at Rome had promoted an informal attempt to prevent Walsh's appointment to Dublin. Objections against Walsh ceased when several Irish bishops accepted the views of Cardinal *Manning and Joseph Chamberlain on a Home Rule plan that would exclude a separate parliament. The policy of Cardinal *Cullen was reversed and the Catholic clergy became a substantial force in the first well-disciplined and tightly organized Irish political party. Parnell's balance-of-power politics effected Gladstone's conversion to Home Rule. After the first Home Rule bill was defeated (1886), a minority of liberals combined with Conservatives to form the Unionist party. Under the leadership of Salisbury and Balfour, this party controlled the government during most of the next 2 decades. It continued to protest informally at the Vatican against clerical support of nationalist movements. After the visit of Monsignor Persico to Ireland (1887), Rome condemned the Irish party's Plan of Campaign to compel landlords to reduce rack rents. The Duke of Norfolk was generally considered the English Catholic most responsible for this action. Walsh had been asked to supply a memorandum on the land question, but action was taken shortly before the memorandum was submitted.

The London *Times* accused Parnell of complicity with the Invincibles, a revolutionary secret society that arranged the assassination of Chief Secretary Lord Frederick Cavendish and Undersecretary Thomas Henry Burke in 1882, but Parnell contested the charge and successfully disproved it (1890). With Walsh's help, Parnell demonstrated that the charge depended upon letters forged by Richard Pigott. Parnell's involvement as corespondent in an uncontested divorce suit by William O'Shea against his wife, Katharine (1889–90), effectively impeded his continuance as party leader.

Although Parnell endeavored to focus on English encroachment on the Irish party, he lost a series of by-elections (1891) in which the clergy played a prominent role in opposing his candidates. In this last campaign he advanced a program that went far beyond the one favored by Gladstone and that gained radical nationalist support. John Redmond succeeded Parnell; eventually the anti-Parnellite majority accepted Redmond's leadership. Catholics continued to support Home Rule, while Protestants favored Unionism.

Only Daniel *O'Connell surpassed Parnell as the outstanding Irish political leader in the 19th century. Parnell was instrumental in bringing about an agrarian revolution in Ireland and in winning most of the Irish Catholic clergy and British Liberal party to the cause of self-government for *Ireland.

Bibliography: R. B. O'BRIEN, *The Life of Charles Stewart Parnell* 2 v. (New York 1898). H. HARRISON, *Parnell Vindicated: The Lifting of the Veil* (New York 1931). J. L. HAMMOND, *Gladstone and the Irish Nation* (New York 1938). C. C. O'BRIEN, *Parnell and His Party* (Oxford 1957). F. S. L. LYONS, *The Fall of Parnell* (London 1960). R. D. EDWARDS, "The Fall of Parnell: Seventy Years After," *Studia Hibernica* 1 (1961). E. LARKIN, "The Roman Catholic Hierarchy and the Fall of Parnell," *Victorian Studies* 4 (1961) 315–336. **Illustration credit:** National Portrait Gallery, London.

[R. D. EDWARDS]

PAROCHIAL SCHOOLS, CATHOLIC ELEMENTARY

Educational institutions under diocesan control serving children who live within the boundaries of particular parishes of the Roman Catholic Church. This type of parochial school, distinct from free schools or private academies, and more common in the U.S. than in other parts of the world, is maintained through parishioners' voluntary contributions, supplemented in some instances by special fees or tuition paid by students' parents, and through the contributed services of religious teachers, and professional services of lay teachers.

A study of the Catholic elementary parochial school includes consideration of its historical development, its aims and objectives, administration and staff, organizational pattern, curriculum, methods and materials of instruction, school services, and its present status, together with current issues and trends that affect its existence.

Historical Development. Although Catholic schools existed in colonial America, they were few in number, widely scattered, and seriously hampered by English penal laws [*see* NEWTOWN MANOR SCHOOL; NEW YORK LATIN SCHOOL; BOHEMIA MANOR; ST. MARY'S SCHOOL (PHILADELPHIA, PA.)]. After Congress ratified the Bill of Rights in 1791, however, Bp. John *Carroll of Baltimore hoped that a plan would be evolved whereby Catholics could work together with their fellow Americans of other creeds in providing equal educational opportunities for all children. When it became apparent that this was a vain hope, the Church established separate schools. In 1801 the Carmelites from Antwerp, Belgium, opened a small school in Georgetown, the first sisters' school in the U.S., though not a permanent one. On Feb. 22, 1810, at St. Joseph's parish in Emmitsburg, Md., Mother Seton started a free school for boys and girls staffed by religious teachers. The definite order to erect a parochial school near every parish church came from the Third Plenary Council of Baltimore in 1884 and has been in effect ever since.

Aims and Objectives. The main purposes of Catholic elementary education are both ultimate and proximate. Cooperating with the family, the Church, and the state, the school seeks to form the true and perfect Christian who will so fulfill his destiny in time as to attain his destiny of union with God for eternity. This formation calls for the total development of the whole person,

Charles Stewart Parnell, drawn c. 1888 by S. P. Hall.

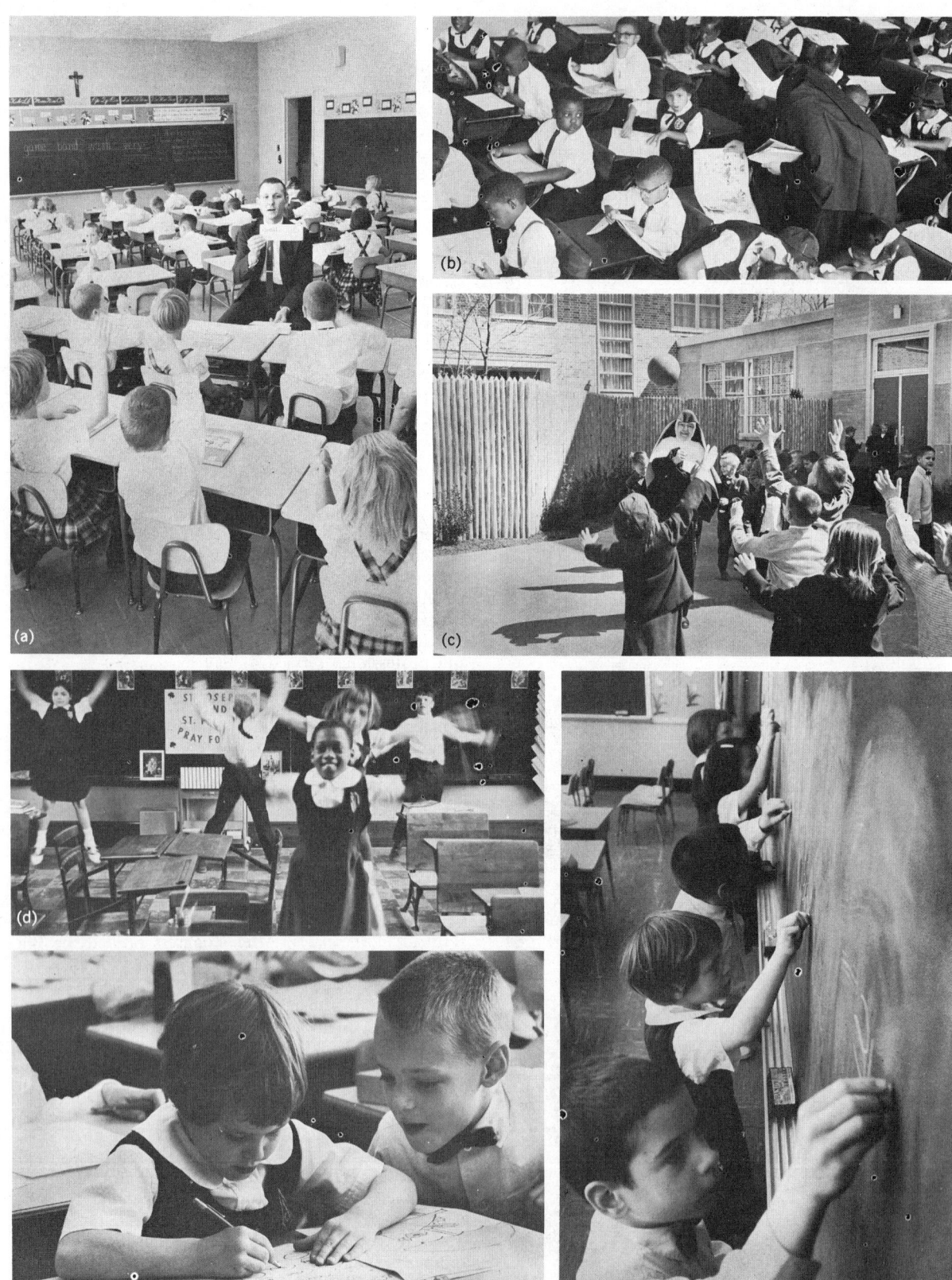

Class activities in Baltimore, Md., school system: (a) special developmental reading group in regular class setting; (b) special class in basic three R's; (c) playtime in the school compound; (d) setting-up exercises to start the day for the emotionally disturbed; (e) creative art with an appreciative audience; (f) solving arithmetic problems on the blackboard.

spiritual and physical; mental, moral, and emotional; individual and social [see EDUCATION II (PHILOSOPHY OF) 1]. The proximate objectives of Catholic elementary education seek to provide experiences that will result in the acquisition of knowledge, attitudes, and habits that will contribute to growth in Christian social living befitting the age, abilities, and aptitudes of each individual child [see EDUCATION III (PSYCHOLOGY OF)].

Administration and Staff. Catholic elementary parochial schools are organized within a diocesan system. The administrative head of the school system is the bishop, chief pastor of his diocese. He, in turn, delegates authority to pastors in their respective parishes and to a diocesan superintendent, who represents him as educational leader. The diocesan superintendent usually serves as secretary of the diocesan school board, a policy-making body for the schools of the dioceses. Following the organization of the parochial school system in the last quarter of the 19th century, until the 20th century, these boards were composed mainly of members of the diocesan clergy. Since the 1950s, however, bishops have more and more frequently included representatives of religious communities of men and women teaching in the dioceses and laymen.

Immediate responsibility for the daily operation of the parochial school rests with the pastor and the principal, who cooperate with the parents and responsible educational authorities of church and state in the school program. Although the pastor is the head of the parish school, except in some isolated areas of the U.S., the duties of principal are delegated to a member of the religious community that staffs the school.

In colonial times and the early years of the Republic, *Jesuits and later (1790) *Sulpicians, as well as lay men and women, conducted Catholic schools. As the system expanded and native religious teaching institutions were founded between 1808 and 1840, members of religious communities of women staffed these schools, with religious teaching brothers and lay teachers sharing in the elementary school apostolate only to a limited degree. The marked Protestant orientation of the public schools and their increasing secularization after the 1840s fostered the growth of parochial schools. Their development was further stimulated by European religious teaching orders of men and women who established centers in the U.S. and staffed both parochial and private schools. The rapid expansion of the parochial school system after World War II resulted in a marked increase in the number of lay teachers. The Notre Dame Study of Catholic Schools reported a ratio of 1 lay teacher to 2.24 religious in elementary schools in 1962.

Organization. The most common organizational pattern in Catholic elementary schools has been grades 1 to 8. Efforts to improve educational opportunities have stimulated experimentation with nongraded primary and *nongraded elementary schools, and in rare instances with Montessori nursery schools within the framework of the Catholic elementary parochial school (see MONTESSORI METHOD). Where finances and personnel are available, kindergartens are included as a part of the school (see KINDERGARTEN, DEVELOPMENT OF). Shortages of teachers and funds have been largely responsible for experiments with a variety of organizational patterns, such as grades 1 to 6, 1 to 9, 2 to 8, 4 to 8 and junior high school (see JUNIOR HIGH SCHOOL MOVEMENT). Statistics for October 1963 show that since 1959

of 10,544 schools in 133 dioceses reporting this item, 170 schools had dropped some grade or grades other than kindergarten.

Curriculum. As partial implementation of a 1938 directive of Pope Pius XI to The Catholic University of America to "draw up for the people of our country a constructive social program based on Christian principles," Rt. Rev. Msgr. George *Johnson planned and constructed a curriculum for Catholic elementary schools, intended not only to provide a plan for learning activities but also and primarily to guide the child's living "in the light of Christian principles."

The guided experiences that constitute the curriculum under the direction of the school were considerably different in 1964 from what they were when the Baltimore Council decreed the establishment of parochial schools in 1884. Yet basic to this curriculum at all times have been instruction in the truths of faith and formation of American Catholics who will be prepared to live intelligent, productive lives in recognition of their relationships to God, to fellowman, to nature, and to self. The reading, writing, arithmetic, and religion of colonial times have been expanded to include the social studies of history and geography, science, health and safety, literature, music, art, speech, drama, and physical education, with foreign language instruction offered in 1 out of every 5 Catholic elementary schools in the 1960s.

Methods. To bring the child and the curriculum together the teacher uses a variety of methods. While the traditional method of assignment, study, and recitation may still predominate in some classrooms, teachers more frequently adapt methods to the objectives of instruction, the needs of the students, and the particular curricular experience (see INDIVIDUAL DIFFERENCES). Recitation, drill, memorization, socialized recitation, group discussion, field trips, and individual and group projects are accepted methodology at some time or other in any area of the curriculum, from religion to physical education. Methodology is affected by new organizational patterns and teaching techniques and likewise by technological developments. Large and small group instruction, *team teaching, educational *television, *programmed instruction, departmentalization, ability grouping, and programs for the gifted, the underachiever, and the culturally deprived are among influences reflected in teaching methods in Catholic elementary parochial schools of the second half of the 20th century.

Textbooks and materials of instruction also influence the quality of education. Instead of the single textbook for every child, multiple texts and references materials, including maps, charts, and globes, are found in the typical Catholic elementary school classroom. Since Catholic educators are concerned that no undercurrent of materialistic and secularistic philosophy may penetrate the curriculum, special textbooks for Catholic schools are used in such curricular areas as religion, literature, social studies, and science. In earlier periods of American history an unfortunate trend to overemphasize the integration of religion in all instructional materials brought justified criticism, no longer applicable to most instructional materials used in Catholic schools (see CURRICULUM, PHILOSOPHY OF; EDUCATIONAL METHODS, PHILOSOPHY OF).

Ideally, Catholic elementary parochial school administrators provide school and/or classroom libraries as centers for instructional materials. Some schools have excellent library facilities and qualified librarians; some are not well equipped. Public library services, however, such as book loans, bookmobiles, itinerant librarians, provided for nonpublic as well as public schools, may supplement existing facilities.

School Services. Personnel and guidance services are reaching down into the modern Catholic elementary parochial school. Clinics for speech correction and for *remedial reading are sponsored by some diocesan school systems, cooperating with clinical psychologists and psychiatrists in an effort to prevent, as well as to remedy, emotional and educational problems (*see* SPEECH AND HEARING EDUCATION). Where the school or school system does not offer guidance services, referrals are made to a variety of clinics and centers where specialized service may be obtained.

Through sharing facilities and teachers for released-time and Saturday classes and for summer vacation schools, Catholic elementary parochial schools participate in the continuing efforts of the Confraternity of Christian Doctrine to provide more adequate religious formation for students from the parish in attendance at public schools.

Status, Current Issues, and Trends. Statistics on Catholic elementary parochial schools show that for every 10 children in these schools in 1950 there were 17 in 1960. At the beginning of the 1963–64 school year there were 141 dioceses in the 50 states, each with its own school organization ranging in size from a system consisting of 2 schools in the Diocese of Juneau, Alaska, to one of 440 schools in the Archdiocese of Chicago, Ill. Diocesan officials and religious superiors indicate that many additional schools would have been opened, especially since the 1950s, if more religious and lay teachers had been available to staff them.

The accompanying table, compiled by Miss Emma Kammerer, a statistician in the Department of Education, National Catholic Welfare Conference, shows the growth of Catholic elementary parochial schools over a period of 40 years.

GROWTH OF CATHOLIC ELEMENTARY PAROCHIAL SCHOOLS (1922–64)

Type	1922–24	1953–54	1963–64
Schools	7,198	9,279	10,775
Priests	151	190	580
Sisters	46,765	66,146	75,867
Brothers	906	1,141	666
Lay teachers	5,623	9,356	38,355
Pupils	2,036,569	3,235,251	4,534,336

The social revolution in American society during the 1960s and Vatican Council II were making an impact on the development of Catholic elementary parochial schools. The Notre Dame Study of Catholic Schools and the National Opinion Research Center (Chicago) investigation of the outcomes of Catholic education also have significance. The U.S. Supreme Court decision of 1954 ordering desegregation of public schools and the passage of the Civil Rights Bill in 1964 are affecting the teaching apostolate to the Negroes, especially in the Southern states (*see* CIVIL RIGHTS, U.S. LAW OF). Over

and above all this, expanding enrollments, financial pressures, and imbalance between teacher supply and demand continue to be the most significant problems facing Catholic elementary parochial schools, problems that history proves to have been inseparable from Catholic elementary parochial schools from their foundation.

Bibliography: C. H. BOFFA, *Canonical Provisions for Catholic Schools* (CUA CLS 117; Washington 1939). J. A. BURNS, *The Growth and Development of the Catholic School System in the United States* (New York 1912). J. A. BURNS and B. J. KOHLBRENNER, *A History of Catholic Education in the United States* (New York 1937). S. E. DEAN, *Elementary School Administration and Organization: National Survey of Practices and Policies* (Washington 1960). F. G. HOCHWALT, *Spotlight Catholic Education U.S.A.* (Washington 1964), pamphlet. R. M. HUBER, ed., *Our Bishops Speak* (Milwaukee 1952). J. M. HUGHES, *Education in America* (Evanston, Ill. 1960). L. KAISER, *The Development of the Concept and Function of the Catholic Elementary School in the American Parish* (Washington 1955), bibliog. 126–144. *The Official Catholic Directory* (New York 1923). R. KOURY, *Elementary School Organization . . . What Direction Shall It Take?* (Washington 1960). NCWC Department of Education, *Summary of Catholic Education: 1962 and 1963* (Washington 1964), pamphlet. M. J. SMITH and M. N. MCGREAL, *Guiding Growth in Christian Social Living*, 3 v. (Washington 1952–59). M. R. QUIRK, *Catholic Elementary Schools, U.S.A.* (Washington 1960), pamphlet; *What's New in Significant Research and Experimentation in Catholic Elementary Education* (Washington 1964). **Illustration credit:** The Barton-Gillet Co., Baltimore.

[M. R. QUIRK]

PAROUSIA

The coming of the glorified Christ as the climax of *salvation history. This article treats first of the Biblical data on the Parousia and then of the Parousia from a theological viewpoint.

1. IN THE BIBLE

For a better understanding of the NT data on the Parousia it is well to begin by considering the general questions of the terminology, the meaning of the doctrine, and the time of the Parousia, particularly as presented in the writings of St. Paul. The doctrine as contained in the individual books of the NT is then examined, and the NT solution of the problem of the delay of the Parousia is briefly considered.

Terminology. The term Parousia is a transliteration of the Greek word παρουσία. In classical Greek the word had the meaning of "presence" or "arrival." St. Paul used the word to speak of his own presence among the Corinthians (2 Cor 10.10) and the Philippians (Phil 2.12), of the presence of Stephanas, Fortunatus, and Achaicus among the Corinthians (1 Cor 16.17), of his future arrival at Philippi (Phil 1.26), and of the arrival of Titus at Corinth (2 Cor 7.6–7). In Hellenistic Greek παρουσία had acquired two technical meanings: (1) the public arrival of officials, which was accompanied by appropriate ceremony; and (2) the presence of the gods, manifested in acts of power, or assumed to be an invisible reality in the cult. Before A.D. 51, the approximate date of 1 Thessalonians, the Church borrowed this technical usage to express its doctrine of the presence of the risen Christ to conclude salvation history. After NT times the doctrine came to be known as the Coming (*adventus*) or the Second Coming of Christ. The word παρουσία in the sense of the presence of the risen Christ at the conclusion of history is found in 1 Thes 2.19; 3.13; 4.15; 5.23; 2 Thes

2.1, 8; Jas 5.7–8; 2 Pt 1.16; 3.4, 12; 1 Jn 2.28. An exceptional usage occurs in 2 Thes 2.9, where παρουσία refers to the presence of "the lawless one," the Pauline opponent of Christ at the end of history.

The primitive Church understood the Parousia event as the time of God's final judgment upon all men (1 Thes 1.10). For this reason NT authors made use of the term "the day of the Lord" in reference to the Parousia. In the OT the *day of the Lord (Yahweh) is a technical term for God's saving acts in history. Before the time of Amos the day of Yahweh was understood as a time of blessings and happiness; but Amos taught that the day of Yahweh was also a time of punishment. The term and its meaning were borrowed by NT writers, who substituted Christ's title *Lord for the name *Yahweh. Clear examples of the usage of "the day" or "the day of the Lord" to designate the Parousia as the time of the final judgment to be rendered by Christ on mankind are in Rom 2.16; 13.12; 1 Cor 1.8; 3.13; 5.5; Eph 4.30; Phil 1.6; 1 Thes 5.2, 4; 2 Thes 1.10; 2.2; 2 Tm 1.12; 4.8; 2 Pt 3.10; Acts 17.31. *See* JUDGMENT, DIVINE (IN THE BIBLE).

In the Pastoral Epistles ἐπιφάνεια (*epiphany, manifestation) is the term used for the Parousia (1 Tm 6.14; 2 Tm 4.1, 8; Ti 2.13). Some authors consider ἐπιφάνεια to be synonymous with παρουσία, but this opinion may be questioned. It is certainly not true for 2 Tm 1.10, where ἐπιφάνεια is used of the Incarnation. In 2 Thes 2.8 Paul combines the two terms: ". . . by the manifestation [ἐπιφάνεια] of his coming [παρουσία]." While some scholars consider this phrase to be a pleonasm, i.e., the repetition of the same idea in different terms, it is probable that Paul intends a particular nuance of meaning here (indicated below). Although the word ἐπιφάνεια is employed in classical Greek in the meaning of outward appearance, only in later Greek is it used to mean the visible (not necessarily corporeal) manifestation of a hidden divinity. Finally, the NT designates the παρουσία with the word ἀποκάλυψις (1 Cor 1.7; 2 Thes 1.7; 1 Pt 1.7, 13; 4.13). In ordinary Greek ἀποκάλυψις meant the uncovering of something hidden. In the Greek of late Judaism and the Jewish apocalyptic literature the word meant the revelation of divine secrets.

The Meaning of the Doctrine. In the NT Parousia is an eschatological concept, i.e., it expresses faith in a final act of God that is to occur when human history has reached its divinely determined goal. This act of God will usher in a life in which all humanity is completely under the rule of God. The doctrine presupposes the *resurrection of the dead (1 Thes 4.16), whose eternal condition and new existence (1 Cor 15.51) are under the direction and dominion of the risen Christ, mysteriously present to effect and to govern the lot of humanity (in His παρουσία). The initial effect of the presence of the risen Christ, with which all humanity will be confronted, is the final judgment rendered by Christ (the day of the Lord). The just are to be "with the Lord" (1 Thes 4.17), while the unjust are to be banished from Him (2 Thes 1.9). Thus the Parousia will make known the significance of Christ for all humanity (ἐπιφάνεια), and at the same time it will disclose God's design for the eternal destiny of mankind (ἀποκάλυψις). The language in which Paul describes the Parousia event in 1 Thes 4.16–17 and 2 Thes 2.3–10 is taken mainly from Jewish *apocalyptic. It is not to

be understood as a literal historical description. The NT does not indicate how the presence of the risen Christ is to occur at the end of history or how this presence will be recognized by mankind.

Time of the Parousia. Once the doctrine of the Parousia is presented to faith, the question naturally arises regarding the time when the event is to occur. The teaching of Christ and of St. Paul on the time of the Parousia is one of the most celebrated questions in the field of NT scholarship. Many scholars have argued that in the teaching of Jesus the Parousia is certainly proximate, i.e., it is to occur within the lifetime of the *Twelve or within a single generation. Other scholars have attributed a similar teaching to St. Paul. Some Catholic scholars have believed that Paul was personally convinced of a proximate Parousia, which he himself would live to witness, though he did not actually teach this personal opinion as a certitude of faith. At an opposite extreme are the opinions of those scholars who attempt to prove that there was no thought at all of a proximate Parousia in the Church of NT times, and a fortiori in the teaching of Jesus. The NT Church anticipated the imminent destruction of the Temple, prophesied by Jesus, and a union with Him through personal death. The Parousia was expected only in the remote future.

In 1 and 2 Thessalonians. The study of NT thought on the time of the Parousia has its natural point of departure in the Epistles to the *Thessalonians, which are certainly among the earliest and probably the earliest of the Pauline Epistles (written *c.* A.D. 51). These Epistles and 2 Pt 3.3–14 are the only documents in the NT to speak expressly (and not simply by allusion) of the doctrine of the Parousia. In 1 Thes 4.12–18, Paul addresses himself to the question of mourning for the Christian dead in Thessalonica. He considers that some among the Thessalonians are guilty of an undesirable manifestation of grief over their dead (v. 13). His response is to stress (1) the certainty from faith of the resurrection of these dead (v. 14), and (2) the time of their resurrection as an occurrence before the Parousia (v. 16), so that (3) death itself will not place these believers in Christ at a disadvantage when the Parousia occurs (v. 15). Paul's main doctrinal objective in this passage is quite clear. He wishes to state the chronological relationship between the Parousia and the resurrection of the dead: first the resurrection, then the Parousia. The Thessalonians, therefore, are not justified in understanding the doctrine of the Parousia to imply that death deprives the Christian of the joys to be anticipated from the event itself. Paul concludes his remarks with the observation that the Thessalonians should "comfort one another with these words" (v. 18), i.e., with the doctrine he has presented to them: resurrection first, then the Parousia. Here he envisions the possibility of further deaths among these Christians. On these occasions, the living should remind the bereaved of the doctrine he has here taught.

This concluding advice of Paul was of practical relevance only on the supposition that the Thessalonian Christians made a direct connection between their faith in Christ as Savior and the Parousia of Christ; they considered it undesirable that death should intervene between the time of their conversion to Christ and the Parousia of Christ. This sentiment indicates that they were in anticipation of a proximate Parousia, i.e., the presence of Christ as the concluding event of salvation history within their own lifetimes. In framing his doctrine so as to point up the chronology—resurrection first, then the Parousia—Paul wrote to them exactly in terms of this proximate expectancy: ". . . we who live, who survive until the coming of the Lord . . ." (v. 15). Thereby he included himself in their hope of escaping death because of an early occurrence of the Parousia. Analysis of 1 Thes 4.12–18 makes it impossible to avoid the conclusion that both Paul and the Thessalonians had in view a proximate Parousia. The Apostle felt bound to write as if the Parousia-event were, at the least, a real possibility within the lifetime of the Thessalonians and himself. Further, he ascribed his teaching that the resurrection precedes the Parousia to the "word of the Lord," i.e., the teaching of Jesus. Mindful as he was of the "word of the Lord," he did not appeal to it to disabuse the Thessalonians of their expectancy of a proximate Parousia. Instead, he wrote from this very standpoint. This fact suggests that Paul knew of nothing in the teaching of Jesus that required him to fix the Parousia in the distant future.

In 2 Thes 2.1–12 (2 Thessalonians was written about 6 months after 1 Thessalonians) Paul again concerned himself with the Thessalonians' expectancy of the Parousia. On this occasion, however, he rejected an idea being spread among them: that the "day of the Lord is already here" (v. 2), i.e., that the time of the final judgment by Christ has actually arrived. Paul flatly denied that such is the case, characterizing this opinion as a deception (v. 3). He reminded them of his previous teaching concerning the occurrence of a religious apostasy and the appearance of a "man of lawlessness" before the Parousia (v. 3–5). Since in his judgment there was no evidence that these events were occurring, he declared that the day of the Lord was not a process that had begun. In effect, he denied that the Parousia was imminent, i.e., an event to be anticipated from day to day; but he said nothing in this passage in 2 Thessalonians to modify the position on the proximity of the Parousia that he had taken in 1 Thessalonians. In 2 Thessalonians he stated categorically that the Parousia was not about to occur; but in neither Epistle did he state categorically that the Parousia would not occur within the lifetime of some of the Thessalonian Christians.

In Other Epistles. There is no evidence in the NT that other Christian communities underwent similar crises of faith over the doctrine of the Parousia as occurred in Thessalonica. There is abundant testimony, however, that Christian communities in general entertained the same proximate expectancy as the Thessalonians. In Jas 5.7–8 (the Epistle of St. *James may have been written as early as the mid-40s or as late as 90–100) the hope of the Parousia is held out as a motive for patience in trials. In 1 Jn 2.28 (probably to be dated before 98) the possibility of the occurrence of the Parousia in the near future is still left open (see also 1 Jn 2.18). In 1 Pt 1.7, 13 (probably in the early 60s, but possibly 90–95), as in James, the thought of the Parousia is presented as a consolation in the midst of persecutions. The passage in Jude 14–24 (datable from the early 60s to 100) also seems to have been composed in a thought context of the proximate Parousia. In 1 Cor 1.7–8 Paul can appeal to the Corinthians' expectancy of the revelation (ἀποκάλυψις) of Christ for which

the gifts of Christ have prepared them. In 1 Cor 4.5 he warns them against rendering condemnatory judgments "until the Lord comes," when judgment will be rendered by Christ. In 1 Cor 6.1–7, he criticizes them for appealing against one another to pagan lawcourts, and he asks why they are not willing to accept injustice. The latter question appears a plausible one only in view of the proximate Parousia, a possibility that, in the view of Paul, depresses the importance of the things of this world.

Paul's observations on marriage in 1 Cor 7.28–31 are couched in the framework of the proximate Parousia, to which he expressly alludes in the phrase "the time is short" (v. 29). He reminds the Corinthian Christians, lately converted from paganism, that preparation for the final judgment is the main factor that should influence their decision on marriage. He recommends virginity as a more desirable state than marriage, provided this choice is motivated by the desire to prepare for the judgment of Christ at the Parousia (1 Cor 7.32–35) and provided it is freely made by those Christians who see in virginity the opportunity for a fuller dedication to the Christian life (1 Cor 7.36–38). *See* CORINTHIANS, EPISTLES TO THE.

The Parousia in the Books of the New Testament. The teaching of St. Paul on the Parousia has been considered above. Other NT literature is here discussed on the basis of the commonly accepted chronology, Mark (A.D. 65–70), Luke (*c.* 75), Matthew (75–85), 2 Peter (probably 80–100). The Johannine writings and Apocalypse are discussed separately.

In Mark. Although actual data on the Parousia is slight in Mark's Gospel, the conception is undeniably present (Mk 8.38; 13.26; 14.62). Its setting in the discourse on the destruction of the Temple (Mk 13.26) has provoked extensive discussion among scholars on the origin of the discourse as a whole and in particular on the authenticity of Mk 13.24–27, a series of verses apocalyptic in style. It is generally agreed that Mark ch. 13 is a composition that incorporates words spoken by Jesus on different occasions into a unit centering on the theme of the destruction of the Temple. All that is said in the discourse on this point is stated to be proximate in time (13.28–31), i.e., it is to occur within the period of the first Christian generation. It is this clear assertion that has produced the question concerning the authenticity of Mk 13.24–27, since these verses can be understood to forecast the occurrence of the Parousia immediately upon the destruction of the Temple.

Beginning with the work of Timothée Colani (1824–88), *Jésus Christ et les croyances messianiques de son temps* (1864), many scholars (including the Catholic M. J. *Lagrange) have sided with Colani in judging Mk 13.24–27 to be of Judaeo-Christian origin rather than a record of the teaching of Jesus. Two arguments are advanced for this opinion, namely, that Jesus was not guilty of error and that He never spoke in apocalyptic language. Recent scholars, however, have recognized the arbitrary character of the opinion that Jesus never employed apocalyptic language. There is in fact nothing in Mk 13.24–27 that could not have been uttered by Jesus Himself. Apart from the problem of attributing error to Him when Mk 13.24–27 is understood in the sense of chronological time, it is necessary to question the assumption that the passage is concerned solely with chronological time. Like all Biblical writers, Mark proposes salvation history, i.e., the salvific acts of God within history. When Mk 13.24–27 is interpreted from this standpoint, the Evangelist must be understood to say that after the fulfillment of Jesus' prophecy on the destruction of the Temple, Christians are not to anticipate another messianic intervention into history until the Parousia. Mark's passage, to be sure, does not exclude the possibility of the Parousia in the chronological sense as an immediate occurrence after the destruction; the Evangelist leaves this possibility distinctly open. But his position on the proximity of the Parousia is no stronger than that of St. Paul in 1 Thes 4.12–18. The evidence of the Pauline Epistles, outlined above, shows clearly enough that the Church of NT times commonly entertained the possibility of a proximate Parousia. The Gospel of Mark remains within this tradition. Whereas St. Paul had occasion to inculcate the time sequence—resurrection first and then the Parousia—Mark advances the sequence—the destruction first, and then, as the next messianic intervention of God, the (possibly proximate) Parousia. (For further consideration of the position of Mark, see below on the teaching of Jesus and the Parousia). *See* MARK, GOSPEL ACCORDING TO ST.

In Luke. Luke's eschatological discourse (Luke ch. 21) closely parallels Mark ch. 13 both in material content and in sequence of thought. Nonetheless, it contains certain ideas that show that Luke was in a position to offer some degree of clarification to the Church of his time on the relationship between the destruction of the Temple and the Parousia. As in Mark, the Lucan discourse answers two questions raised by the prophecy of Christ concerning the destruction of the Temple: the first question inquires when the destruction is to occur; and the second requests the sign by which the imminence of the event will be recognizable (cf. Lk 21.5–7 with Mk 13.1–4). The Lucan answer to the question on the sign (Lk 21.20–24) differs from Mark's (Mk 13.14–20) in four significant respects: (1) the sign itself, a siege by armies, is on the historical level in contrast to the indeterminate Biblical phrase of Mark-Matthew, "the *abomination of desolation" (Dn 9.27); (2) the destruction of Jerusalem, not simply that of the Temple, is the point at issue; (3) the destruction is presented as a divine judgment against the Holy City, a conception that follows the OT understanding of Israel's catastrophes (3 Kgs 9.6–9; Os 9.7; Jer 5.29); (4) a period of time is envisioned after the destruction, described by Luke as "the times of the nations," during which the teachings of Christ are to be offered to the Gentiles.

Luke's counterpart (Lk 21.25–28) to the apocalyptic passage in Mk 13.24–27, expanding upon the Parousia, is set in the context of "the times of the nations" instead of the context of the destruction, as in Mark. Amid distress and fear upon the earth, the Parousia of the Son of Man occurs. During this period the Christian is not to be disturbed; rather he is to reflect that the fullness of the Redemption awaits him with the Parousia. Luke thus removes the possible relationship in time between the destruction and the Parousia that is so conspicuous in Mark. Although it is perhaps too much to say with some modern scholars that Luke eliminates the proximity of the Parousia altogether, he does disassociate it in time from the destruction of Jerusalem.

In accordance with his chronological disassociation of the destruction and the Parousia, Luke, by comparison to Mark, modifies the response of Jesus to the question on the time of the destruction (cf. Lk 21.29–33 with Mk 13.28–31). Although "all things" prophesied by Jesus are to occur before His generation has passed away (Lk 21.32), the fulfillment of the prophecies in Luke consists in the knowledge that the reign of God is near (Lk 21.31). Thus in Luke the destruction of Jerusalem is understood as a sign of the Parousia of Christ: the fulfillment of His prophecy on the doom of Jerusalem indicates the fulfillment of His prophecy on the Parousia. Those who witness the fulfillment of the first prophecy should look to the fulfillment of the second (Lk 21.32–36). In this sense of the gradual revelation in history of God's salvific plan, Jesus' words are fulfilled within a single generation. *See* LUKE, GOSPEL ACCORDING TO ST.

In Matthew. Matthew's is the only one of the four Gospels to use the term παρουσία (Mt 24.3, 27, 37, 39). His use of it gives his discourse on the destruction of the Temple (Matthew ch. 24) a different orientation of thought from its parallels in Mark ch. 13 and Luke ch. 21. In Mark and Luke Jesus is asked concerning the time of the destruction and for a sign by which the imminence of the event will be recognizable. In Matthew the question on the time of the destruction remains. However, the request of the disciples for a sign pertains, not to the destruction, but to "your Parousia and the end of the age [τοῦ αἰῶνος, *aeon]" (Mt 24.3b). Unlike the discourse in Mark ch. 13 and Luke ch. 21, Matthew ch. 24 treats explicitly of a question that is only implicit in Mark and Luke: whether or not the proximity of the Parousia, and therefore of the end of natural human history, is to be recognized by a sign.

Although the question of the time of the end is the main one for Matthew ch. 24, the Evangelist has retained the traditional question on the time of the destruction of the Temple (Mt 24.3a) as well as the traditional material that responds to it (Mt 24.4–26). This material has substantially the same meaning as in Mk 13.5–23: it pertains to the destruction of the Temple, warning against false messiahs and false signs, forecasting persecution, demanding perseverance, and advising flight upon the appearance of the "abomination of desolation." However, to the Marcan warnings against false messiahs and false prophets (cf. Mk 13.21–23 with Mt 24.23–26), Matthew adds two sayings of Jesus (Mt 24.27–28) to the effect that the Parousia will be unannounced (v. 27) and will be inevitably recognized by all men (v. 28). He thereby strengthens the teaching of Mk 13.21–23 that after the destruction no messianic intervention other than the Parousia is to be expected.

Matthew's apocalyptic passage (Mt 24.29–31) parallel to Mk 13.24–27, elaborating upon the Parousia, is introduced by the word εὐθέως (immediately). As in Mark, the Evangelist's thought is best comprehended in terms of salvation history: in the divine, salvific plan the Parousia is the only messianic intervention to be anticipated as following upon the destruction. The entire human race is to recognize the presence of the Son of Man, and the last judgment is to occur.

Up to this point in the discourse (Mt 24.4–31), Matthew, as Mark, asserts the destruction of the Temple and the Parousia, but does not address himself to the questions concerning the time of the destruction and the sign of the Parousia. He now does so (Mt 24.32–36), utilizing, however, traditional material, found also in Mk 13.28–32: as the fig tree in bloom indicates the nearness of summer, so the fulfillment in history of the prophecies of Jesus (Mt 24.33) is "the sign of [His] parousia and of the end of the age" (Mt 24.3b). The fulfillment in history can only refer to the destruction of the Temple, since the day and the hour of the Parousia itself is a secret held by the Father alone (Mt 24.36). For Matthew the destruction of the Temple is the theological sign of the Parousia, but not its chronological sign. The time of the Parousia is a divine secret that the Father did not reveal even to the Son. Whereas in Mark the Parousia is left in possible chronological proximity to the destruction of the Temple, and whereas in Luke it is chronologically separated from the destruction of Jerusalem, in Matthew the stress is on the mystery enshrouding the time of the event. *See* MATTHEW, GOSPEL ACCORDING TO ST.

In the Historical Teaching of Jesus. Scholars of the Gospels are not in agreement that Jesus actually taught the Parousia during His lifetime. Numerous passages in the Gospels attribute sayings to Him concerning "the coming [ἔρχομαι]" of the Son of Man (Mk 8.38; 13.26; 14.26; Lk 9.26; 12.40; 18.8; 21.27; Mt 10.23; 16.27; 24.30, 44; 25.31; 26.64). The interpretation of these sayings is rendered difficult by the fact that the Gospel tradition has not always conserved their original historical context. Either the Evangelists or the tradition before them have, to a degree, reinterpreted some of these sayings in the light of the NT Church's fuller understanding of Jesus' mission. From the critical standpoint two sound points of departure for the interpretation of these sayings can be indicated: (1) in 1 Thes 4.15 St. Paul asserts that he bases his statements about the Parousia on "the word of the Lord," i.e., on the historical teaching of Jesus; (2) the passages indicated in the parenthesis above have in common the doctrine of the "coming [ἔρχομαι]" of the Son of Man. These facts reveal that there is no ground to deny a priori that the Parousia originated in the historical teaching of Jesus. On the other hand, one must ascertain carefully whether Jesus taught this doctrine explicitly or merely contented Himself with providing a foundation for the Church's later comprehension of it.

The most significant passage for the understanding of Jesus' historical teaching on the Parousia is the statement He made at His trial before the Sanhedrin as quoted in Mk 14.62 (see also Mt 26.64): ". . . You will see the Son of Man seated at the right hand of the Power and coming with the clouds of heaven." Although scholars of the Gospels concede that the saying is substantially historical, they are not in accord on the meaning Jesus intended to convey. For some scholars Jesus here declared not only His Resurrection, but also His Parousia. For others He simply affirmed that He would be vindicated by being brought to God upon His execution. Interpretation of the saying must take into consideration its prophetic character. Prophecy is frequently obscure in its content at the time it is uttered. Only through the development of events and the evaluation of the prophecy in the light of other religious doctrines is its true significance comprehended. Thus the *Resurrection and *Ascension of Jesus Christ (cf. the *exaltation of Jesus in Phil 2.9), as well as

His headship of the new messianic community (cf. Acts 2.36), provide a fuller comprehension of His saying in Mk 14.62 than was possible when He made the statement historically. St. Paul's allusion in 1 Thes 4.15 to the historical teaching of Jesus on the Parousia finds its minimal justification in the fact that Jesus spoke of the "coming" of the Son of Man that would have future and final relevance, not only to His own disciples, but also to the entire world. The recollection of such sayings is embodied in Mk 8.38 and Mt 25.31–32.

Jesus' historical teaching insisted upon vigilance in preparation for "that day" (Mk 13.33–37; Mt 24.42–51; Lk 21.34–36), i.e., the time of final judgment, and He declared His own ignorance of the time of the event (cf. Mk 13.32 with Mt 24.36). St. Paul sets forth the same doctrine (1 Thes 5.1–2) as well known to the Thessalonians. It would seem, then, that the historical teaching of Jesus Himself compelled the NT Church to entertain the possibility of an imminent Parousia, since nothing in the Lord's teaching excluded this possibility. Such an orientation of thought in the primitive Church forced it to focus its attention on the person of Jesus and His teaching, and to a considerable degree it was responsible for the development of the material on Jesus and His teaching that made possible the composition of the four Gospels. *See* JESUS CHRIST, IPSISSIMA VERBA OF.

In the Johannine Literature and the Apocalypse. The only explicit reference to the Parousia in the Johannine literature (1, 2, 3 John and John) lies in 1 Jn 2.28, which expresses a Christian hope concerning the presence of Christ as judge not unsimilar to 1 Thes 2.10. Elsewhere in 1 John the doctrine of the Parousia seems clearly to be assumed (1 Jn 3.2) or can be inferred from statements about the *Antichrist (2.18; 4.3). No mention is made of the doctrine in 2 and 3 John, but 2 John does speak of the Antichrist (2 Jn 7). *See* JOHN, EPISTLES OF ST.

The Fourth Gospel does not employ the term παρουσία. Neither does it utilize the figure of the Son of Man to depict a presence of the risen Christ in history that will terminate the course of human events. The Gospel begins and ends by placing its central figure, "the Anointed One, the Son of God" (Jn 20.31), within the Godhead. The prologue (1.1–18) names Him the *Logos, eternally preexistent, who entered the world by becoming Incarnate (1.14). The remainder of the Gospel conceives His life as a passage through suffering, death, and Resurrection to the realm of the Father (12.32; 20.17). The significance of the divine origin, earthly career, and final glorification of Jesus for Christians is not spelled out in the Fourth Gospel in terms of the Parousia, but rather in terms of a union with Christ that has its beginning in the Christian's earthly existence (3.3; 4.10; 6.53; 15.1) and its terminus in a life that will transcend the bonds of human mortality (3.15; 4.14; 6.54; 14.2). This presentation of Christian faith as a supernatural union with Christ, the Son of God, that begins in mortal human existence and ends in a superterrestrial sharing in the divine life draws out the ultimate significance of the doctrine of the Parousia. The Parousia is the logical presupposition of such Johannine statements as the following: "The Father loves the Son and has handed all things over to him. Whoever believes in the Son has life eternal.

Whoever disobeys the Son will not see life, but must endure God's wrath" (3.35–36); "I solemnly assure you, an hour is coming and is now here when the dead shall hear the voice of God's Son, and those who have listened shall live" (Jn 5.25); ". . . And when I do go and prepare a place for you, I am coming back to take you along with me so that where I am, you may also be" (Jn 14.3). In these passages the Christian life is conceived as an anticipation of the Parousia. *See* JOHN, GOSPEL ACCORDING TO ST.

The Apocalypse, like the Fourth Gospel, rather presupposes the doctrine of the Parousia than inculcates it. At the outset of the work the risen and ascended Jesus is described symbolically as existing within the Godhead (Ap 1.13–16). From this position He addresses messages to the seven churches (2.1–3.22), in the course of which perseverance in the Christian faith is urged until His coming (2.25). The coming is directed especially against persecutors of Christians (6.10) and is described in 6.15–17 in terms reminiscent of Lk 23.30. The coming on behalf of the just is taken up from Ap 19.11 to the conclusion of the work. Here the Parousia is explicitly announced as part of the divine irrevocable plan: "And behold, I am coming quickly" (22.7). This assertion is repeated at the end of the book, together with the author's prayer affirming his firm conviction of the coming and requesting that it take place in accordance with God's design: "Amen. Come, Lord Jesus" (22.20). The Apocalypse is clearly the product of the persecutions experienced by the early Church, especially under Nero (A.D. 54–68) and Domitian (A.D. 81–96). Its author, writing probably during the reign of Domitian, utilized the Church's doctrine of the Parousia to encourage the faith of Christians in these dire circumstances. *See* APOCALYPSE, BOOK OF.

Delay of the Parousia. Criticism of the Christian doctrine of the Parousia is reflected in 2 Pt 3.3–10, a late Epistle dating probably after A.D. 80. *See* PETER, EPISTLES OF ST. The criticism consists in ridicule of the doctrine on the ground that the Parousia has not materialized (3.4). The objection presupposes a Christian expectancy of an early Parousia. However, neither the source of the criticism nor the concrete circumstances of it is ascertainable. The author of the Epistle responds by invoking the creative power of the word of God (3.5), the punitive power of His word (3.6), and the difference between the human conception of time and the working out of God's design in history (3.7–8). He reassures his Christian readers that the nonoccurrence of the Parousia is not evidence against the truth of the doctrine but rather an indication of the divine mercy still bent on the repentance of mankind (3.9). Finally, he reasserts the doctrine, stressing that the occurrence of the Parousia will be unanticipated because of its suddenness and that this event will terminate human history as men have known it (3.10).

Some scholars have urged that the Gospel of Luke also is preoccupied with the question of the so-called delay of the Parousia. They appeal to such passages as Lk 12.45, which speaks of a delay in the return of a householder, and 19.12, which describes a man embarking upon a long journey (see also 20.9). It remains possible that the Gospel of Luke anticipated a problem that arose among some early Christians when the Parousia failed to materialize; but these passages can be understood also as parabolic detail that has no intentional reference to the Christian expectancy of a proximate Parousia.

See also ESCHATOLOGY (IN THE BIBLE).

Bibliography: A. FEUILLET, DBSuppl 6:1331–1419. A. ROMEO, EncCatt 9:875–882. H. CONZELMANN, RGG³ 5:130–132. Enc DictBibl 1728–39. G. R. BEASLEY-MURRAY, *Jesus and the Future* (New York 1954), with extensive bibliog.; *A Commentary on Mark Thirteen* (London 1957). H. CONZELMANN, *Theology of St. Luke,* tr. G. BUSWELL (New York 1960). A. CORELL, *Consummatum est: Eschatology and Church in the Gospel of St. John* (New York 1958). T. F. GLASSON, *The Second Advent* (3d ed. London 1963). W. G. KÜMMEL, *Promise and Fulfillment,* tr. D. M. BARTON (Naperville, Ill. 1957). B. RIGAUX, *Saint Paul: Les Épîtres aux Thessaloniciens* (ÉtBibl; 1956). J. A. T. ROBINSON, *Jesus and His Coming* (Nashville 1958).

[C. P. CEROKE]

2. IN THEOLOGY

Early symbols professing the great Christian mysteries place the Second Coming (always an essential truth of faith) side by side with the Incarnation, death and Resurrection of Christ [see the apostolic, Athanasian, Nicene, and Nicene-Constantinopolitan creedal formulations (Denz 11, 30, 41, 76, 125–126, 150)]. The patristic tradition witnessing to the centrality of the Parousia in the Christian mind is clear and constant. The writings of the Apostolic Fathers, reflecting a lingering Jewish apocalyptic spirit, as well as the teaching of Christ on the seeming imminence of His eschatological predictions, are strongly eschatological. Clement of Rome, in his letter to the Corinthians (96–97), affirms the proximity of the Parousia and reproves the skeptical (23.3–5). The Didache concludes facing the Parousia and the duties of Christians arising from its approach (16.1). Widespread yearning for the return of Christ in glory attests to an intense parousial faith in the early Church. Any misunderstanding of the proximity of the Second Coming was born of obscurity inherent in the prophetico-apocalyptic message of Christ and Paul.

Millenarianism. Many in the first 2 centuries interpreted 2 Pt 3.8–9 and Ap 20.4–5 literally and looked to a future messianic kingdom prior to the Parousia. Thus *Millenarianism was born. A residue of Jewish speculation on the duration of the intermediary messianic reign was probably at work here [cf. J. Bonsirven, *Le Judaïsme palestinien au temps de Jésus-Christ, sa théologie* (Paris 1934–35) 427]. Papias of Hierapolis in the 2d century paints a vivid picture of the millenial era (PG 7:1213–15). Among its early adherents Millenarianism numbered Pseudo-Barnabas, Irenaeus, Justin, Tertullian, Lactantius, and Hippolytus. Never universally held as part of apostolic tradition, chiliasm did tend to replace in the 2d century what previously had been the expectation of an imminent Parousia. Such excess indicates the force of eschatological hope in the early Church. An unfortunately inept way of affirming that history is the expectation of Christ, chiliastic dreams revive from time to time [cf. decree of Holy Office, ActApS 36 (1944) 212 (Denz 3839)].

Kingdom and Empire. As the Church expanded through the Roman world in the 3d and 4th centuries and won state recognition, Millenarianism waned. Persecution lessened; the present time seemed less provisory; the Parousia less imminent. Wed to Rome, many considered the messianic kingdom as realized in the spread of the empire (see, e.g., Eusebius, *Hist. eccl.* 10.4). Others, by solitude and virginity, renounced identification of the eschatological kingdom with the world and saw the establishment of the true kingdom in the Parousia (see, e.g., tracts on virginity by Methodius, Ambrose, Basil of Ancyra, Gregory of Nyssa). It was Augustine who dealt the death blow to both the chiliasts and those identifying Christ's reign with temporal society (*Civ.* 20.6–13). The fall of Rome in 410 further stifled such deviations. Like men in every other age, faced with the fragility and radical impermanence of the world's institutions, many saw the empire's demise as presaging the end.

Particular Judgment, Purgatory, Beatific Vision. The vivacity of early belief in the Parousia left its stamp on patristic theologizing about the particular judgment, purgatory, and the beatific vision. At the outset it was thought that departed souls lived in a state of parousial expectancy. The evident delay of the Second Coming gradually gave rise to closer study of the lot of the soul after death, and a marked doctrinal development evolved. It was only in the 4th century that particular judgment was generally received into the mainstream of patristic thought, without, however, usurping the primacy of the parousial judgment. Similarly, since retribution immediately after death hinges upon particular judgment, patristic teaching on purgatory developed slowly and was first conceived in function of the Parousia. For Origen and others, purification of the just commences with the Parousia (see A. Michel, "Purgatoire," DTC 13.1:1193–96). The Greek Fathers of the 4th century fell heir to Origen's thought and with but rare exception viewed the dead as awaiting definitive parousial judgment and purgation in the final conflagration. In the 9th century this parousial orientation perdured in Photius (*Ad Amphil* 6.15) and survived to the beginning of the 15th century and the Council of Florence. In the West it was Augustine especially who insisted on purification immediately after death (*Civ.* 21.46). In the ante-Nicene period beatitude was likewise so closely bound up with the return of Christ that it was generally considered delayed until the parousial resurrection. From the 4th to the 9th century the lot of the elect was gradually though not wholly separated from the Parousia. Following the 9th-century cleavage between East and West, enjoyment of the beatific vision by the elect immediately after death was common doctrine in the West, whose tradition culminated in 1336 with the constitution *Benedictus Deus* of Benedict XII (Denz 1000–02). Though the doctrine was not yet in possession in the East, it had numerous and weighty partisans there.

Perspective. Doctrinal development concerning retribution was slow and faltering precisely because patristic theologians, like the New Testament itself, focused primarily on the perfection of creation, history and humanity redeemed in Christ and glorified with Him at the term of this earthly economy, and only secondarily on the fate of the individual. Recall the New Testament images of the meal, the wedding, the holy city. In this perspective all converges upon the Parousia: judgment, retribution, consummation of life inaugurated by Christ's Resurrection, definitive constitution of His kingdom. Though time corroded the urgency of parousial hope, the Parousia always remained a key mystery [see the conciliar teaching of Lateran IV, 1215 (Denz 801), Lyons II, 1274 (Denz 852), Florence, 1442 (Denz 1338), the Tridentine profession of faith, 1564 (Denz 1862)]. The impact of the doctrine in the medieval period, an age not of printed word but of artistic image, is felt in the painting and sculpture of the era, as well as in the popular preaching. With time joyous hope for the return of Christ was colored with pessimistic desire for the last day, when Christ's justice would pronounce vengeful judgment on this world's injustice. With the rise of rationalistic theology and the decline of historical sensitivity, the Parousia lost much of its larger significance and became little more than doomsday.

In the rediscovery of eschatology by contemporary theology the Parousia is restored to its rightful place as final event of *salvation history. The glorious return of Christ and the ensemble of eschatological events He will then effect mark the consummation of God's redemptive plan. As such the Parousia is certain and promised, yet a reality already at the heart of the present world. Salvation is now present, though not yet unveiled in full cosmic dimension (Rom 8.17–23). While the *kingdom of God is essentially a kingdom to come, it is presently realized in those who share by grace in the redemptive work of Christ (Jn 12.31; 2 Cor 5.17; 6.2; Col 1.22; 1 Jn 1.7). The present is the future anticipated. For in this realized Redemption are sewn new promises. The Parousia will harvest in final, perfect form what already is (1 Jn 3.2). Dead with Christ by Baptism and already risen to a new life (Rom 6.1–11), through adhesion to Christ Christians anticipate final judgment (Jn 3.17; 5.24). This in no way implies that the Parousia brings with it nothing new. Christ's emergence from His secret presence in His Church, His resurrection of the dead, His definitive judgment and situation of each person within the divine plan, His transfiguration of nonrational creation, His enthronement as center of creation, all are new events giving the personal *eschata,* death and particular judgment, their full significance. Yet these final events now exist hiddenly in Christ's *kingdom, as Christ Himself lives hiddenly in glory to be manifested only at His return (Col 3.1–4). Hence the Parousia is not simply another item in an array of last things. As God's final loving intervention it is the plenitude of Redemption, the crowning triumph of Christ as *savior.

The central, decisive event of history is neither at the beginning nor at the end; it is the Resurrection of Christ. What preceded was preparation; what follows is the "end time" (cf. 1 Cor 10.11), the time of the Church in and through which Christ incorporates into Himself all comprised in His eternal decree, communicates to them divine life, and reveals His power to bring to its ultimate state the kingdom predestined. The appearance of Christ at the end of ages will close this period of growth. Then He will present to the Father His kingdom finally established as the perfect, unfailing realization of divine wisdom, power, and love (1 Cor 15.20–28). The glory of Christ will be extended by Him to the members of His kingdom who by faith and baptismal *rebirth are associated to His paschal mystery (1 Thes 4.14–18; 2 Thes 1.10; Phil 3.20–21). The root of the parousial mystery is men's solidarity with Christ (1 Jn 2.28). Thus Redemption is actualized in history now hastening to fulfillment in the parousial theophany wherein the ultimate defeat of Satan will be realized in the completion of the Trinity's saving work.

Sacraments. It is not difficult to see why the early Church did not fear the end of time but yearned for it, as Tertullian says, as the farmer for the harvest, the soldier for the definitive end of struggle (*De orat.* 5). The Christian is turned to the future with tranquil assurance that the Parousia will perfect and manifest what has already been wrought in him inchoatively and is possessed in pledge (2 Cor 1.22; 5.5). In the present stage of the redemptive process, intermediary between the two comings of Christ, creation possesses in the obscurity of faith the glory now perfectly possessed by the "Firstborn" (Col 1.15) and awaits the definitive reality in the final stage ushered in by the Parousia. Meanwhile it is especially in its Sacraments that the Church meets in veiled contact the Christ to come. Each Sacrament mysteriously renders accessible the mystery of Christ and associates the Christian to Him. Commemorating the past, introducing the Christian presently to an ultratemporal and ultraterrestrial life, the Sacraments are pregnant with future reality and announce the return of Christ to reveal and crown His victory now hidden in Himself and those united to Him. Parousial dimension is found above all in the Eucharist, the food of immortality (Jn 6.54), which heralds the death of Christ "until He come" (1 Cor 11.26) and is a foretaste of the heavenly banquet (Mt 8.11). By sacramental insertion into the mystery of Christ the Christian knows a double-track existence: he lives now in the era of the Parousia, yet remains in the era of history.

For schools of Protestant theology holding a "consequent" and wholly supratemporal eschatology, no eschatological transformation has penetrated history. Hiddenly accomplished only in Christ, it is extrinsically appropriated to the Christian by faith. The kingdom is present only insofar as Christ, who brings it, is present. Wholly future, the kingdom has not begun its realization in us. The Parousia, far from being the maturation and culmination that Catholic theology views it to be, will be a commencement.

Expectation of Parousia. If anything is clearly affirmed by Christ, it is that we remain ignorant to the end concerning the day of the Parousia (cf., e.g., Mt 24.36; Lk 12.40). Theologians follow the healthy skepticism of Aquinas (ST 3a, suppl., 73) relative to any literal interpretation of scriptural signs. Perturbations in nature and society are foretold not to date the Parousia but to kindle men's hope and orientate them. The definitive theophany cannot be determined by any cosmic catastrophe or by human *progress. What is relevant for Christians, living now in the paratemporal, is the theological rather than the chronological imminence of Christ's return. This parousial hope gives meaning and consistency to history and manifests God's immanence to its linear development. If Redemption works in and through historical evolution, only when the redemptive decree of God has run its divinely plotted course will Christ come forth from His abiding presence in His Church. The expectancy of the Church, however, is not directed merely to history's term but to encounter with the Bridegroom, who will show time to have been a history of salvation, and subject all

things to Himself. Through the Word all things were made at the beginning (Col 1.16); through the Word Incarnate all things will be remade at the end. The seed of glory in man will be brought to fruition; the universe, far from being annihilated, will be gloriously transfigured into a suitable habitat for glorified man and a luminous reflection of Christ's glory (Rom 8.19–23; 2 Pt 3.7–13). Aside from the fact of transformation, Scripture and patristic tradition provide little detail on the extent and mode of this re-creation. Linked with man in sin, the cosmos will be linked to him in Redemption (*C. gent.* 4.97; *Comp. theol.* 169–171). The new Adam will create a new Eden where the cosmic integrity destroyed by sin will be restored and God will be "all in all" (1 Cor 15.28).

See also BURIAL WITH CHRIST; DEATH (THEOLOGY OF); END OF THE WORLD; ESCHATOLOGISM; ESCHATOLOGY (THEOLOGICAL TREATMENT); ESCHATOLOGY, ARTICLES ON; FIRE OF JUDGMENT; INCORPORATION IN CHRIST; JESUS CHRIST, III (SPECIAL QUESTIONS), 11, 12; JUDGMENT, DIVINE (IN THEOLOGY); JUDGMENT, DIVINE (IN THE BIBLE); MYSTERY THEOLOGY; PURGATORY; RESURRECTION OF CHRIST, 2; RESURRECTION OF THE DEAD, 2.

Bibliography: E. PAX and K. RAHNER, LexThK² 8:120–124. A. WINKLHOFER, Fries HbThGrdbgr 1:327–336; *The Coming of His Kingdom*, tr. A. V. LITTLEDALE (New York 1963). J. GALOT, "Eschatologie," DictSpirAscMyst 4:1020–59. A. FEUILLET, DB Suppl 6:1331–1419. L. BILLOT, *La Parousie* (Paris 1920). O. CULLMANN, *Le Retour du Christ* (Neuchâtel 1943); *Christ and Time*, tr. F. V. FILSON (rev. ed. Philadelphia 1964). R. SCHNACKENBURG, *God's Rule and Kingdom*, tr. J. MURRAY (New York 1963. H. U. VON BALTHASAR, "Eschatology," in *Theology Today: Renewal in Dogma*, v.1, ed. J. FEINER et al., tr. P. WHITE and R. H. KELLY (Milwaukee 1965) 222–244. L. BEAUDUIN, "Ciel et résurrection," in H. M. FÉRET, ed., *Le Mystère de la mort et sa célébration* (Lex orandi 12; Paris 1956). A. M. HENRY, ed., "The Return of Christ," *The Historical and Mystical Christ*, tr. A. BOUCHARD (Theology Library 5; Chicago 1958). P. HUMBERT et al., "La Fin du monde," LumetVie 11 (Sept. 1953), whole issue. A. JANSSENS, "La Signification sotériologique de la parousie," DivThomP 36 (1933) 25–38. A. MICHEL, "La Doctrine de la parousie et son incidence dans le dogme et la théologie," *Divinitas* 3 (1959) 397–437. M. SCHMAUS, "Das Eschatologische im Christentum," in *Aus der Theologie der Zeit*, ed. G. SÖHNGEN (Regensburg 1948). J. WRIGHT, "The Consummation of the Universe in Christ," Greg 39 (1958) 285–294. J. A. T. ROBINSON, *Jesus and His Coming* (Nashville 1958). O. CULLMANN, *Immortality of the Soul or Resurrection of the Dead?* (New York 1958). J. P. MARTIN, *Last Judgment in Protestant Theology from Orthodoxy to Ritschl* (Grand Rapids 1963). J. DANIÉLOU, "Christologie et Eschatologie," Grill-Bacht Konz 3:269–286.

[S. J. DUFFY]

PARRAS, PEDRO JOSÉ, Franciscan missionary and writer; b. Pancrudo, near Teruel, Spain, *c.* 1710; d. Córdoba, Argentina, Sept. 7, 1784. Parras joined the Franciscan Order in Aragon and was being trained to teach when he volunteered for the missions of Río de la Plata. In 1748 his expedition was in Cádiz at the same time as that of Junípero *Serra. After arriving in Buenos Aires, Parras traveled to Paraguay as visitator of the Franciscan province. His learning and moderate tendencies were valued by Manuel Antonio de la Torre, Bishop of Paraguay, who chose him as his adviser on his official visit to the Jesuit Reductions in 1759, and also by Pedro de Cevallos, the governor of Paraguay. Parras was not a member of the anti-Jesuit group, and his attitude was reflected in the objective position of Cevallos. Both Cevallos and Parras returned to Spain in 1766, where Parras attended the General Chapter of the Order (Valencia 1768) as delegate of the Argentine Province and remained to become guardian of the Franciscan house in Zaragoza. When the Portuguese threat again increased in La Plata, Cevallos was sent back, and he requested Parras to accompany him. Grateful for his services, Cevallos frequently recommended him for a bishopric, but this was opposed by the Commissary General of the Indies, Manuel de Vega. Parras was named rector of the University of Córdoba, Argentina, in 1778, a post that he filled with great success and tact until his death. He published two works of permanent merit: *Diario y derrotero de sus viajes* (1749–52), a delightful travel account of his trip from Valencia to Paraguay, together with an appendix of his report on the Jesuit Reductions in 1759; and *Gobierno de los regulares de la América* (2 v. Madrid 1783), a masterful account of the legal position of religious in Spanish America at that time; it is clear, reasonable, and often marked by a touch of humor.

Bibliography: P. J. Parras, *Fray Pedro José de Parras: Diario y derrotero de sus viajes, 1749–1753* (Buenos Aires 1943). P. Pastells, ed., *Historia de la Compañía de Jesús en la provincia del Paraguay,* 8 v. in 9 (Madrid 1912–49).

[L. G. CANEDO]

PARRENIN, DOMINIQUE, missionary and sinologist; b. Russey, near Besançon, France, Sept. 1, 1665; d. Peking, Sept. 29, 1741. He was admitted into the Society of Jesus on Sept. 1, 1685, and left for the China mission in 1697. At the court of Peking he pleased Emperor K'ang-hi with his extensive knowledge and his familiarity with the Chinese and Tatar-Manchu languages. With this advantage he discussed physics, history, and the place of Christianity in producing the culture of the West. His great service to China was in making maps, especially the great map of China. His popularity at court was greatly responsible for preventing the total destruction of the Christian mission during the hostile reign of Yong-tsching (1723–35), son of K'ang-hi. Many of his letters have been published by J. B. du Halde in *Lettres édifiantes et curieuses* (Paris 1711) and *Description de la Chine et de la Tartarie chinoise* (Paris 1735, Eng. tr. E. Cave, 2 v. London 1738–41). Others are found in the Bibliothèque Nationale, Paris.

Bibliography: Sommervogel 6:284–290. Koch JesLex 1383–84. Delacroix HistMissCath 2:177, 360. B. H. Willeke, LexThK² 8:110.

[J. S. SCHWARZ]

PARSCH, PIUS, leading Austrian liturgist and Biblicist; b. Olmütz, Moravia, May 18, 1884; d. Klosterneuburg, Austria, March 11, 1954. He became a Canon of St. Augustine at Klosterneuburg in 1904, and studied there until his ordination in 1909. He taught pastoral theology for a while and then served as a military chaplain during World War I.

Upon entering the Order he took the name Pius in honor of Pius X, with whom he shared a great love of Holy Scripture. Parsch not only taught Scripture but also devoted to it his doctoral dissertation and his best efforts after World War II, especially in the periodical he founded, *Bibel und Liturgie.* He also shared Pius X's concern for bringing the liturgy to the people and making it understood by them. To this purpose he devoted

the many editions of liturgical texts and numerous published explanations of the liturgy that made his monastery a liturgical center of Austria, indeed of all the German-speaking lands.

Pius Parsch.

The name he gave his work, "Popular Liturgical Apostolate," is noteworthy. It pinpointed his main concern; it was not for research, neither for monastic or academic liturgical forms, much less for liturgical reform. His energy was spent in an apostolate for the Christian people, to bring them to both interior and exterior participation in the liturgy. He aimed at vanquishing liberalism in Austria by unfolding the mysteries of faith and grace. These goals he sought by means of an ideal form of worship celebrated daily in the little Church of St. Gertrude in Klosterneuburg. Because he concentrated on the popular aspects of the liturgical revival, he occasionally risked superficiality in his explanations, which in part have been brought up to date by later research. Parsch was a pioneer in his insistence on an intimate connection between liturgy and Scripture. He came upon this not only through his own scriptural training and teaching, but also through his realization that the people can be brought to an understanding of the liturgy only by a knowledge of Scripture. His spirit and work have been a major influence in the popular liturgical movement throughout the world. Chief among his works are: *The Church's Year of Grace* (Collegeville, Minn. 1953–58; first in German in 1929); *The Liturgy of the Mass* (St. Louis 1936; rev. ed. 1957); *The Breviary Explained* (St. Louis 1952; first in German in 1940); *Seasons of Grace* (New York 1963); and *Volksliturgie* (Klosterneuburg 1940).

Bibliography: EphemLiturg 68 (1954) 256–257. T. Warnung and T. Schnitzler, "In memoriam Pii Parsch," LiturgJb 4 (1954) 230–236. G. Zunini, "Apostolato liturgico in azione; le conquiste del P. Parsch," *Ambrosius* 5 (1929) 26–32. **Illustration credit:** Maria Laach.

[T. SCHNITZLER]

PARSEES, as their name indicates, are descendants of Persian immigrants who settled in Bombay and its vicinity and who brought their Iranian religion with them. To the 130,000 who now live in India should be added about 20,000 "cousins" who remain in Iran, in the regions of Kerman and Yazd. The Parsees of India have adopted the Gujerati language of the Bombay area. All claim allegiance to the god Mazda or Ormazd and to his prophet Zardusht or Zoroaster. However, under the influence of Hinduism, Islam, and Christianity, their religion has lost much of its original dualism. Ahriman has for the most part been reduced to a symbol of man's evil tendencies.

The most striking features of the Parsees' religion are fire worship and the exposure of corpses in "Towers of Silence." During their fire worship, which is carried out in fire temples, the priest, holding a ritual staff, covers his mouth with a veil which is intended to protect the fire from any possible impurity. The ceremony is completed by a continuous reading of a large portion of the Avesta. The Parsees are not a caste, but they remain a closed community. They never marry outside their group and they make no attempt to convert non-Parsees to their religion. They are antiascetic and have little interest in astrology and mysticism. They are conspicuous for their generosity and interest in education as well as for their wealth, their desire to alleviate misery without distinction of race or religion, and their founding of hospitals, orphanages, and schools. Under Western influence they have changed their dress and abolished infant marriage.

Bibliography: D. MENANT, Hastings ERE 9:640–650. J. DUCHESNE-GUILLEMIN, *La Religion de l'Iran ancien* (Paris 1962).

[J. DUCHESNE-GUILLEMIN]

PARSONS, WILFRID,

editor, author, educator; b. Philadelphia, Pa., March 17, 1887; d. Washington, D.C., Oct. 28, 1958. He was the son of Paul Julian and Alice (Avery) Parsons. After attending high school in New York, he entered the Society of Jesus in 1903. He studied at the Jesuit seminary in Louvain, Belgium (1907–09), and at Woodstock, Md., where he obtained his Ph.D. (1910) and was ordained (1918). He went to Rome, received a doctorate in theology from the Gregorian University (1921), and then returned to Woodstock as professor of theology (1922–24). From 1925 to 1936 he served as editor of the Jesuit weekly, *America,* tending to support New Deal reforms and to oppose Republican economic policies; he was also a sharp critic of Rev. Charles E. Coughlin (1891–   ), a bitter opponent of F. D. Roosevelt's administration. After 1936 Parsons was engaged in teaching political science at Georgetown University (1936–37, 1948–50, 1954–58) and The Catholic University of America (1938–47), both in Washington, D.C. He contributed articles to several Catholic journals, including *Thought,* which he founded in 1926. His books include *The Pope and Italy* (1929), *Mexican Martyrdom* (1936), *Early Catholic Americana* (1939), *Which Way Democracy?* (1939), and *The First Freedom* (1948).

[J. L. MORRISON]

PART

A part is related to a *whole as something into which a whole is divisible and of which it is constituted. Thus a whole is prior to its parts in the order of being and of understanding, but in the order of becoming the parts are prior to the whole that is made from them by process of change.

Quantitative and Integral Parts. In the clearest case, a part is something into which a *quantity is divisible. A quantitative part is smaller in comparison with the larger whole of which it is a part when both whole and part are finite and actual. A part that can measure the whole without remainder is called an aliquot part, as two is of four or three of nine. A continuous quantity is always divisible into parts that in turn are also divisibles, not indivisibles. A quantitative point can be the beginning or end of a line or of a segment of a line, but it is indivisible and so is not a part of a line. A whole or cardinal number is a discrete quantity composed of units. The unit is both part and measure of numbers, but in the order of discrete quantity it is without parts and is indivisible. The parts of which a quantity is composed or integrated and into which it is divisible are called integral parts. A natural body has integral parts that exhibit qualitative differences and are called heterogeneous parts, as the various organs of plant or animal and the parts of molecules or atoms. Integral parts that are required for the whole to be, without which it cannot be, or that are regularly present in the whole, are called proper parts, as the head or hand in man.

Physical, Entitative, and Virtual Parts. In a sensible thing composed of matter and form, both the matter and the form are called physical parts. The wood of which a chair is made is part of the chair, namely, the *matter, and the figure of a statue is part of the statue, namely, the *form. When both matter and form are extended or quantified, they are likewise divisible into parts, as this or that part of the wood or part of the figure. The primary principles, or natures, of which natural bodies are made and composed are also called physical parts, as the material nature, or proper matter, of a chemical compound or of an organism and its formal nature, or specifying form. The parts of which any created being, as such, is composed are called entitative parts, namely essence and existence.

Parts that do not include the full perfection of the whole, as the vegetative and sensitive parts of the animal, are said to be virtual, or potential. Such parts are distinguishable by human reason even though they are not distinct in the whole, which is one and undivided in itself, and when made distinct by mental precising they include the whole but not wholly. Thus the animal is an organism; moreover, it is a sensitive organism.

Logical Parts. The parts signified by terms expressed in a definition are called logical parts, because they express man's understanding of an essence, or essential nature. In a *definition composed of terms that signify the *genus and the specific difference, the genus is part of the *species, because the species expresses the whole essence, whereas the genus expresses the virtual part that is determinable by the difference. Thus if man is defined as a tool-making animal, the term animal signifies the determinable part of the essence, or essential nature, of man, and the term tool-making, understood radically, signifies the determining part, or specific difference in man. However, the species that are included in a genus are parts of the genus, called subjective parts, because the genus is the whole that includes the species, whether these are actual or merely in potency.

See DISTINCTION, KINDS OF; DIVISION (LOGIC); ELEMENT; ATOMISM.

Bibliography: ARISTOTLE, Meta. 1023b 12–25. THOMAS AQUINAS, *C. gent.* 2.72. V. MATHIEU, EncFil 3:1171–72.

[W. H. KANE]

PARTICIPATION

In the Platonic tradition, where the notion was first systematically developed, participation (μέθεξις) signifies the derivation of temporal diversity from eternal unity, and the structural dependence of the many on the One. In Christian thought it means the complete dependence of creatures on the Creator in the order of efficient, exemplary, and final causality. Not only was the word commonly used by the Fathers and schoolmen, but the notion is fundamental to their entire thought.

Various Usages. In ordinary usage the word signifies a sharing or taking part in a common effort, glory, nature, or movement; thus in every order of causality one may "share" or "take part" in some whole (*pars,* part; and *capere,* take). As a transitive verb, it signifies the act of giving or communicating something to others, as when we say that God shares or participates His life, goodness, and truth with creatures. Ordinarily it is used in the intransitive sense of a subject "having a part" or "taking part" in some reality (physical, moral, or spiritual), as though a whole were somehow divided among many. In this sense it is said that Christ "deigned to become partaker of our humanity" (*Sacram. Leon.,* 159). The postclassical abstract noun designates the active and passive reality of sharing or communicating. In grammar the adjective form of a verb called a participle similarly signifies a subject sharing some quality or situation (cf. Isidore, *Etymol.* 1.21.11; PL 82:88).

In philosophical usage the word is analogical, always involving a reference of many to one or one to many. "To participate is to take a *quasi* part; thus when something receives a part of what belongs to another fully, it is said 'to share' it, just as man is said to share animality because he does not have the whole of animality exclusively; for the same reason Socrates shares humanity; similarly even a subject shares accidents, and matter shares form, because substantial or accidental form, which of its very nature is common, is limited to this or that subject; likewise an effect is said to participate in its cause, particularly when it does not equal the cause, as when we say that the air shares the light of the sun, because it does not receive light with the same brilliance that exists in the sun" (St. Thomas, *In Boeth. de hebdom.* 2.24).

Origins with the Greeks. The philosophical notion of participation was used by *Plato to explain the relation between the contingent, individual forms and the eternal, unchangeable Ideas. *Aristotle attributes the origin of this doctrine to the Pythagoreans, who taught that all things exist by imitation (μίμησις) of numbers; for him, Plato simply introduced the new term participation (μέθεξις) and said that all things exist by participation, changing only the name. According to Aristotle, both the Pythagoreans and Plato left undecided what this participation or imitation of Forms could be (*Meta.* 987b 10–14). It is true that the doctrine of participation in the writings of Plato is undeveloped and includes all types of being involving any kind of dependence, likeness, coexistence, and the like.

HISTORY OF THE CONCEPT

Already in the *Phaedo* things are said "to participate" (μετάσχεσις: 100C, 101C), "to receive" (μετάληψις: 102B), to be what they are by a "presence or communion" (παρουσία, κοινωνία: 100D; also *Rep.* 437E; *Soph.*

247A, 248C, E) or even by an "appertaining" (ἐπεῖναι, παραγίγνεσθαι: 103D, 105C; cf. *Symp.* 211B) of the "model" in which many participate (*Phaedo* 78D; cf. *Rep.* 476A, D; 496A; 507B). In this doctrine Plato saw the answer to Zeno's problem: if many things exist, they must simultaneously be similar and dissimilar, one and many, in motion and in rest (*Parm.* 127E); Plato's answer is that the "Ideas" do not combine with sensible things but exist per se "apart" (καθ'αὑτά: *Phaedo* 129D–130A).

Plato and Aristotle. According to Aristotle, who apparently is reporting the oral teaching of the master, between sensible things and separated Forms Plato placed mathematical beings, "which occupy an intermediate position, differing from sensible things in being eternal and unchangeable, from Forms in that there are many alike, while the Form itself is in each case unique" (*Meta.* 987b 15–18). For Plato the object of wisdom is the Idea as Exemplar (παράδειγμα), the Idea as "that which completely is" (το παντελῶς ὄν) and therefore "perfectly knowable" (το παντελῶς γνωστόν) as "the One among many" (τὸ ἓν ἐπὶ τῶν πολλῶν), thus permitting knowledge transcending the perception of transitory and corruptible things (τὸ νοεῖν τι φθαρίνοτς: *Soph.* 248E). In the *Dialogues* of his maturity Plato presents two orders of participation: that of sensible objects in ideal Forms, and that of Forms among themselves. This extension of the notion of participation to the ideal Forms themselves was important for the later development of philosophy, for it allows for various kinds of participation [μετέχειν δὲ πολλῶν οὐδὲν κωλύει: *Parm.* 161A; cf. P. Natorp, *Platos Ideenlehre* (2d ed., Leipzig 1921) 231, 469–470].

One of the major difficulties inherent in the Platonic notion of participation, based as it is on the logico-mathematical relation of the universal to the particular, is the famous problem of the "third man" (τρίτος ἄνθρωπος) discussed by Plato (*Parm.* 132A, B) and urged by Aristotle (*Meta.* 990b 17 and 1059b 8): If similarity among many individuals presupposed a "form in itself," then the similarity of the many to the one presupposes another form, and so on (see the detailed argument in Alexander of Aphrodisia, *In meta.* 990a 15, ed. Hayduck, 83–85). For this and other reasons, Aristotle firmly and contemptuously rejected Platonic participation: "To say that they are patterns and that other things share them is to use empty words (κενολογεῖν) and poetical metaphors" (μεταφορὰς λέγειν ποιητικάς: *Meta.* 991a 20; cf. 1079a 4–13, 1079b 24–26).

In opposition to the Platonic imitation of a transcendent ideal, Aristotle insisted on the *immanence of concrete forms and on the true *causality of particular causes on particular effects. Aristotle did not deny the existence of spiritual substances, intelligences, or souls in celestial bodies (*Cael.* 285a 29–30), but his insistence on physical causality distinguished his doctrine from Platonic participation. The apparent impasse was solved in two ways. Pure Aristotelians such as Alexander of Aphrodisias explained participation by means of causality, while Neoplatonists admitted the necessity of causality within the framework of participation. This latter approach was more influential in Christian thought.

Neoplatonic Teaching. The distinctive aim of *Neoplatonism was to show the basic harmony between Plato and Aristotle, blaming Aristotle's critique on Plato's faulty expression through "poetic metaphors," "myths," etc. For pagan Neoplatonists it was important to demonstrate the overall harmony between the two outstanding Greek philosophers in order to defend the Greek ideal of wisdom against what they regarded as a barbaric religion founded on expiation for sin by the Crucifixion of Christ.

While faithful to the basic principle of Platonic participation, Neoplatonism transformed it in such a way as to make Aristotle's critique and principles its own. This harmony between Plato and Aristotle was already proclaimed by Ammonius, the teacher of Plotinus, who transcended apparent differences by his "intensive method" (Photius, *Bibl.* cod. 214; PG 103: 701A–708B). For the Latin West *Boethius proclaimed this same harmony (*In Arist. de interp.* 2, prol.; PL 64:433). In Arabic Neoplatonism the theme of agreement pervaded the whole of philosophy; for *Alfarabi the difference between the two philosophers was simply one of method—Plato chose analysis, Aristotle synthesis—and Aristotle was seen as "the follower and perfecter, the help and consultor of Plato" [F. Dieterici, *Alfarabis philosophische Abhandlungen* (Leiden 1892) 3, 17–21].

Plotinus. *Plotinus, the most eminent representative of Neoplatonism, clearly absorbs Aristotelian notions in his Platonic synthesis. In his celebrated doctrine of the three Hypostases (Mind, Soul, Life), Plotinus tried desperately to reduce the distance between transcendence and immanence. For him the νοῦς of Aristotle coincided with the ὄντως ὄν of Plato since the Mind, the supreme principle of the world, cogitates a multiplicity of Ideas, which are the eternal exemplars of all reality and true knowledge. This multiplicity of Ideas cannot be derived from the sensible world, but from Mind itself. Thus Plato's world of Ideas is localized by Plotinus in the νοῦς of Aristotle. The crucial problem of causality is solved by the doctrine of emanation (πρόοδος) by means of the *world soul, which fashions the world and everything in it according to the separated Ideas in Mind. Since for Plotinus the separated Ideas are endowed with specific quantities, qualities, movements, and rest, all sensible realities depend on the Ideas and derive from them their individual movements and appropriate changes of quantity and quality [cf. A. Covotti, *Da Aristotele ai Bizantini* (Naples 1935) 226–228]. *See* EMANATIONISM.

Proclus. More profoundly, the syncretist, Neoplatonic notion of participation revived the pre-Socratic notion of "dialectical method," which reached its widest application in *Proclus. The novelty of this dialectic, explicitly introduced into the doctrine of participation, is the importance given to negation as the momentum of change, and consequently as the foundation of dialectics itself [cf. G. W. F. Hegel, *Geschichte der Philosphie,* ed. Michelet (Berlin 1833) 2.66]. These negations (ἀποφάσεις) were not considered privations of being, but productions of opposite determinations, as sketched in Plato's *Parmenides.* Proclus maintained that "the method of negations (τρέπος τῶν ἀποφάσεων) has an unusual character; it conforms to the dignity of the One; its function is primary; it far transcends all things in the unknowable and ineffable excellence of simplicity" (*Theologia Platonis,* 2.10). The work of Proclus marks the high point in the speculative syn-

thesis of Plato and Aristotle, replacing the negative attitude of Alexander (see the explicit statement of Simplicius, *In 3 de caelo,* 7.306a 1).

In general it can be said that Arabic Neoplatonism and *Augustinianism developed the common, intuitive notion of participation ascending toward the One; it stemmed from the traditions of Plotinus and Porphyry. The Thomistic notion of participation, on the other hand, is directly inspired by the more rigorous dialectical method, which stemmed from *Iamblichus and Proclus through *Pseudo-Dionysius and the small Arabic work entitled *Liber de causis.*

THOMISTIC NOTION

From the beginning St. *Thomas Aquinas appreciated the radical difference between Platonic and Aristotelian principles. Rejecting the Neoplatonic concordism prevalent in medieval Augustinianism and Arabic writers, he developed a precise notion of participation based upon a new concept of *esse* as the *actus essendi,* not to be confused with the *existentia* of Augustinianism and *rationalism. It is from the concept of *esse* as the ultimate act that St. Thomas developed his notion of participation and his entire metaphysics (*see* EXISTENCE).

Basic Elements. The most important elements in the Thomistic notion of participation include the concepts of act, of the unicity of the substantial form, of the personal individuality of the human soul, and of the real distinction between essence and *esse,* or act of being, in creatures.

Concept of Act. Aquinas's starting point is the Aristotelian concept of *act as perfection *in se* and *per se.* Thus by its very nature act is prior to *potency, whether it is understood as activity or as *form. St. Thomas accepted this "primacy of act" without reservation, and rejected the attempt of *Avicebron to reduce everything to potency instead of to act. Because of this new concept of act as perfection, the affirmation of *being, there arose a new and wider concept of potency as capacity to receive perfection, i.e., negation as *privation. Two important consequences follow from this for St. Thomas: (1) Potency is not a univocal concept signifying prime matter alone, but an analogical concept embracing all the ways a thing can be a subject of act: "Being a subject is not peculiar to the matter that is part of substance, but is a universal property of all potentiality" (*De subs. sep.* 8). (2) Prime matter, being exclusively a "subject," can have no act whatever of its own; all its actuality stems from form so that not even God can make matter exist without form (*Quodl.* 3.1.1). *See* MATTER AND FORM.

Unicity of Substantial Form. The second element in the Thomistic metaphysics of participation follows from this new concept of act and potency: the unicity of substantial form in all bodies, living and nonliving. In man this unique substantial form is his intellectual soul. For St. Thomas a "plurality of forms," even hierarchically ordered from lowest (*forma corporeitatis*) to the highest (*forma intellectiva*), would destroy the essential unity of act in man; all acts after the first could be nothing but accidental forms. This view was fiercely contested during St. Thomas's lifetime, because it seemed to deny that Christ's dead body continued to be divine when separated from a permanent form; but for St. Thomas divinity and identity were due not to form, but to the

Person of the Word who continued to be united hypo-statically to both body and soul (*Quodl.* 2.2.1 and ad 1). In St. Thomas's view the single form in man is responsible not only for the spiritual functions of thinking and willing, but also for the lower functions of sensation, nutrition, and natural motions (ST 1a, 76.3–5). Thus the higher form is said to contain the lower forms virtually. (*See* FORMS, UNICITY AND PLURALITY OF.)

Individuality of the Soul. The third element in the Thomistic metaphysics of participation is the personal individuality of the human *soul and its functions. This rejection of the principal Averroist tenet is developed under two aspects: (1) Phenomenologically, one's consciousness, thoughts, aspirations, desires, and loves are seen to be personal functions, belonging to a concrete, individual person. (2) Metaphysically, the ground of this phenomenon is seen to be none other than the personal intellectual soul (first act), which is the root of human activity (second act). The immateriality of certain personal functions, such as thinking and aspiring, indicates that the personal soul has an immaterial *esse* proper to it and inseparable from it: "*Esse* properly belongs to the form, which is act. . . . But it is impossible that a form be separated from itself; therefore it is impossible that a subsistent form should cease to be" (ST 1a, 75.6; 50.5).

Essence and Esse. The fourth element in the Thomistic metaphysics of participation is the real distinction in all created things between essence and the act of being (*esse*). This fundamental Thomistic insight, originally derived from Boethius and *Avicenna, was eventually seen as a consequence of the primacy of act in participation. This is seen in two stages: (1) Being (*esse*) is the first perfection and the act of all acts (ST 1a, 4.1 ad 3, 2); pure perfection (*perfectio separata*) cannot be anything but unique; subsisting being must be one, namely God, whose essence is to be. (2) All creatures, whose essence is not to be, must participate or share existence as a gift; thus all creatures are beings (*entia*) by participation. In this view essence is a subject, a potentiality for *esse,* which is the sublime reality shared by many as a gift from God. With this view of participation, St. Thomas could reject Augustinianism, which made matter essential for creatures, and Averroism, which made immaterial substances (intelligences) independent of God's creative and sustaining act. Finally, this participation is the basis for the Thomistic doctrine of *analogy between God and creatures, for just as God is being by essence (*per essentiam*), so creatures are being by participation (*per participationem:* see ST 1a, 4.3 ad 3). In St. Thomas's conception, *esse* is no longer an accident, as Avicenna thought, but the immanent act of substance, and the proper effect of God alone (*Quodl.* 12.5.1).

Kinds of Participation. Some Thomists (e.g., L. B. Geiger) believe that St. Thomas developed two notions of participation, each distinct: (1) Participation by similitude (*secundum similitudinem*), in which participated beings diversely reflect, mirror, or symbolize the reality participated. (2) Participation by composition (*secundum compositionem*), in which a subject shares, or has, the participated characteristic, e.g., *esse.* In this view creatures not only participate in *esse* by composition, but the very composite is a "similitude" reflecting God.

Static Structure of Being. Other Thomists, rejecting this interpretation of the Thomistic synthesis, prefer to see in St. Thomas's doctrine of participation a complete dissolution (the Hegelian *Aufhebung*) of the Platonic-Aristotelian tension. For these, *esse* as the act of all acts must be distinguished not only from essence, but also from existence in the Kantian sense. In order to preserve the theory of *actus essendi,* they prefer to divide participation initially into transcendental and predicamental: the first type concerns *esse* and its transcendental attributes; the second concerns univocal formalities of *genus with respect to *species, and species with respect to individuals. Transcendental participation of *esse* has already been mentioned; it is the second that needs special consideration because of its Aristotelian roots. It is true, as Aristotle says, that genera and species are predicated of subjects essentially (*per essentiam*) and not by participation (*per participationem*). However, a genus is differently realized and actualized in the various species according to different degrees of participated perfection (cf. Fabro, *La nozione metafisica di participazione,* 161). Thus while genera and species may be logically predicated as univocal and essential attributes, in the physical order they must be considered as potestative wholes, capable of being shared unequally according to different degrees of perfection. Predicamentally even individual men participate in human nature (see text of *In Boeth. de hebdom.* 2.24, quoted above). St. Thomas speaks about predicamental participation when he says, "Just as this individual man participates in human nature, so every created being participates, if I may say so, in the nature of being (*naturam essendi*), since only God is His *esse*" (ST 1a, 45.5 ad 1; cf. *C. gent.* 1.32; *Quodl.* 2.2.1). Thus in a static or structural consideration of beings, transcendental participation is the real composition of subject and *esse;* while predicamental participation is the real composition of matter and form in essence, and substance and accident in general.

Causal Participation. Parallel to this static consideration of being, one must consider the dynamic or causal order. Causal participation is likewise twofold: transcendental and predicamental. Causal transcendental participation is the production of the common *esse* of all creatures by creation (*De pot.* 3.5 ad 1–2; *De ver.* 21.5 ad 5–6). *Esse* is the proper effect of divine *causality (*creation and divine *conservation), and it is in virtue of this direct production of *esse* that God works immediately on every created cause. Causality as predicamental participation, on the other hand, is concerned with *fieri* or *becoming in the order of genera and species. Here the pertinent principle is "form gives *esse*" (*forma dat esse*), which seems to invert the causal relationship discovered in the transcendental order. However, the principle has two meanings: (1) substantial form bestows formal and constitutive *esse,* inasmuch as it confers a specific kind of being; (2) substantial form as formal act of the essence is the true subject of the *actus essendi* (*C. gent.* 2.54). Thus form is the predicamental mediator between God and the existing finite being (cf. Fabro, *Participation et causalité,* 344–362). From this it follows that in all the actions of creatures, even the free actions of men, God intimately operates in all things as the universal First Cause of all being and all activity. Creatures, however, participate in this causality only on condition that they likewise remain true and responsible causes of action.

Extension of Participation. To the extent that participation allows one to conceive the universe as a reflection of divine ideas or exemplars, one may speak of participation by similitude. The *exemplary causality of immaterial forms on material forms is expressed by Boethius (*De trin.* 2), while Pseudo-Dionysius refers to the exemplars of all existing things as preexisting in the mind of God (*De div. nom.* 5.8; PG 3:824). But here again participation by similitude must be considered in both the transcendental and the predicamental orders. Transcendentally this similitude exists in the relation of dependence of *finite being on the Infinite (*see* INFINITY). In the predicamental order this similitude can be seen in the universal affinity all beings have for each other. Thus lower beings tend to approach the more perfect as though they participated in their perfections. This ontological affinity, which orders the entire cosmos, can be expressed as the principle of the metaphysical continuity of beings, which St. Thomas borrows directly from Pseudo-Dionysius: "Divine wisdom joins the highest of the lower to the lowest of the higher" (*De div. nom.* 7.3; PG 3:872; cf. Proclus, *Elem. theol.,* prop. 147, ed. Dodds, 128).

In view of this principle all created knowledge can be seen in terms of participation. Thus angelic intuitive knowledge of itself resembles (by participation) divine intuition, while through infused species it participates in all other things (ST 1a, 56.2; *De subs. sep.* 13). Similarly, human intuitive knowledge of *first principles resembles angelic "intellection," while man's more characteristic knowledge is *reasoning, whereby he reaches out to all other reality. Even the highest of the sense faculties, the *cogitative power, participates in rationality and in a certain freedom (ST 1a, 78.4 ad 5; *In 3 anim.* 13.397). Likewise, sense appetites participate in rationality and freedom when they obey the order of right reason (*In 3 sent.* 35.1.1.4; ST 2a2ae, 47.5 ad 1); this participation is realized through moral *virtue.

From this principle of the metaphysical continuity of all being emerges also a conception of the world as an orderly solidarity of all things (*De ver.* 16.1). This continuity, imperfectly realized in the static structure of being, reaches its fullness when beings reach their ultimate goals through activity. For man this ultimate goal is the dynamic, supernatural union with God that is possible only through *grace, which is a participation in the life and powers of God as He is in Himself. "Only a rational creature is capable of God (*capax Dei*) in this way, because he alone can know and love God explicitly" (*De ver.* 22.2 ad 5); for this reason "only rational creatures have an immediate directedness to God" (ST 2a2ae, 2.3). Consequently because man's spirit is infinitely receptive, he cannot find complete happiness in anything that is good only by participation, but can find it only in Him who is goodness *per essentiam* (ST 1a2ae, 3.7). This is eternal beatitude. The highest and most sublime participation ever willed by God is the personal union of the Word with human nature in Christ. As "a partaker of our human nature" God not only renewed the whole human race (ἀνακεφαλαίωσις), but He also gave men the power to become partakers of divinity through the grace of Christ.

Participation and Analogy. The Platonic theory of vertical imitation and the Aristotelian theory of horizontal causality of universals on particulars tend to emphasize formal univocity, while the true language of participation is necessarily that of *analogy. The Thomistic notion of participation, founded in *esse* as supreme intensive act, makes it possible to pass from finite to Infinite Being through analogical discourse. Since the foundation of all analogical language is participation, the three basic types of analogy are discussed here in terms of participation.

Analogy of Proportionality. Basically this analogy, whether proper or metaphorical, is a proportion of two or more proportions, e.g., accidents are to their being proportionately what substance is to its being. Despite the radical difference between *substance and *accident, there is a certain proportional similarity that allows us to use one predicate of both analogically. The basis of this proportional similarity is the fact that all accidents participate in the being (*esse*) of substance. Thus while the formal, logical structure of this kind of analogy is simply relations of *similarity, its root is actual dependence and participation. In the wider, transcendental order, all creatures have their *esse* by participation from God, *Ipsum Esse Subsistens.* Consequently the analogical proportionality between the goodness of God and the goodness of creatures, the wisdom of God and the wisdom of creatures, etc., is based on the fact of transcendental participation, which is the basis also for predicamental participation (composition of substance and accidents, matter and form). It is this static analogy of proportionality that is expressed in the tension of similarity-dissimilarity according to the Platonic view of the vertical "fall" of beings. Moreover, it is precisely through this static analogy of proportionality that beings obtain the proper consistency of *esse,* each in its own way, since each being is actuated by the proper act of participated *esse.* For St. Thomas—in keeping with the demands of Heidegger—the difference between to be and to exist is founded on being, as intensive emergent act, that is diversely shared by each being.

Analogy of Attribution. In contrast to static analogy of proportions, analogy of intrinsic attribution is dynamic in that it is based on causality and dependency. In analogy of attribution, a term that properly belongs to one subject, e.g., healthy in body, is attributed to other subjects because of some causal dependence, e.g., healthy apples, healthy medicine, etc. In the analogy of being, *esse* properly belongs to God alone, but it is predicated of creatures because God creates and conserves the *esse* of each creature. This analogy is called intrinsic attribution because each creature really does have being intrinsically, even though it is from another. Analogy of attribution emphasizes the "otherness" of the characteristic participated. Thus creatures are being only by participation (*ens per participationem*), and accidents are being only by participation. In this way analogy of proportionality presupposes analogy of attribution in the existential order. For this reason analogy of attribution culminates metaphysical investigation in resolving the many to the One, the diverse to the All. While *pantheism denies the *transcendence of God, either by reducing God to creatures or by identifying creatures with God, the metaphysics of St. Thomas maintains the transcendence of God above all creatures and at the same time recognizes His *immanence in participated being. In fact, only a doctrine of participation can maintain both His transcendence and His immanence.

Analogy of Inequality. The analogy of inequality within genera and species, as has been explained, is founded on predicamental participation. While the logician considers genera and species to be univocal abstractions, the realist sees that a genus is differently realized in the various species; that is, the perfection of the genus is unequally shared by the various species within a given genus. This inequality of participation is the indispensable condition for multiplicity of species, just as the indispensable condition for multiplicity of individuals is the divisibility of matter. Thus from the formal point of view, a generic definition is univocally predicated of various subjects, but from the existential point of view, these subjects participate unequally in the full perfection (cf. ST 1a2ae, 88.1 ad 1; *C. gent.* 1.32).

See also BEING; EXISTENCE; EMANATIONISM; IMMANENCE; TRANSCENDENCE; ACT; CAUSALITY; ANALOGY.

Bibliography: C. FABRO, *La nozione metafisica di partecipazione secondo S. Tomaso d'Aquino* (3d ed. rev. and enl. Turin 1964); *Participation et causalité selon S. Thomas d'Aquin* (Louvain 1961). L. B. GEIGER, *La Participation dans la philosophie de S. Thomas d'Aquin* (Paris 1942). R. J. HENLE, *Saint Thomas and Platonism* (The Hague 1956). *De Thomistische Participatienleeren* (Nijmegen 1944). J. DE FINANCE, *Être et agir dans la philosophie de saint Thomas* (Paris 1945). P. KLUBERTANZ, *St. Thomas Aquinas on Analogy* (Chicago 1960). J. MUNDHENK, *Die Begriffe der "Teilhabe" und des "Lichts" in der Psychologie und Erkenntnislehre des Thomas von Aquin* (Würzburg 1935). G. SÖHNGEN, "Thomas von Aquin über Teilhabe durch Berührung," *Die Einheit in der Theologie* (Munich 1952). K. KRENN, *Vermittlung und Differenz?* (Rome 1962). F. ULRICH, *Homo Abyssus* (Einsiedeln 1961). L. OEING-HANHOFF, *Ens et unum convertuntur* (Münster 1953). A. HAYEN, *L'Intentionnel dans la philosophie de saint Thomas* (Brussels 1942). G. SIEWERTH, *Der Thomismus als Identitätsystem* (2d ed. Frankfurt 1961). E. J. SCHELLER, *Das Priestertum Christi im Anschluss an den hl. Thomas von Aquin* (Paderborn 1934).

[C. FABRO]

PARUTA, PAOLO, historian and political theorist; b. Venice, May 14, 1540; d. there, Dec. 6, 1598. He was educated at Padua, where he showed interest in the study of history, literature, and politics. He served the Venetian Republic in several offices, including director of the *Camera dei Prestiti* (public loans, 1580), Governor of Brescia (1590–92), ambassador to Rome (1592–95), and procurator of St. Mark's (1596). His historical works are *Storia della guerra di Cipro* (1605) and *Istoria Veneziana* (1605), which is a continuation of Pietro *Bembo's *Rerum Veneticarum libri 12* (1551). His fame rests principally on the *Della perfectione della vita politica* (1579), which in dialogue form extols the active life over the contemplative, especially for the welfare of Venice, and the *Discorsi politici* (1599), a discussion of the causes of the greatness and fall of ancient Rome, as well as an apology for the modern type of government in Venice, built upon his policy of equilibrium of power among the states of Italy. The *Lettere inedite* (1885) and the *La legazione di Roma* (3 v. 1886–87), reveal, besides his affection for Venice, a great ability as diplomat and politician, and a shrewd understanding of Roman affairs.

Bibliography: T. BOZZA, *Scrittori politici italiani dal 1550 al 1650* (Rome 1949). E. ZANNONI, *Paolo Paruta nella vita e nelle opere* (Livorno 1904). M. PETROCCHI, EncCatt 9:882–883, with bibliog.

[E. D. MCSHANE]

PASCAL, BLAISE

Mathematician, Christian apologist; b. Clermont-en-Auvergne, June 19, 1623; d. Paris, Aug. 19, 1662. Despite his brief life and incomplete work, Pascal was one of the most universal geniuses of modern France and a singularly novel and profound interpreter of the Christian conscience. In him life and thought were intimately commingled: the witness of the man is no less significant than the message of his work.

Pascal's life can be thought of as a drama in which three principles confront each other: science, the world, and God. His genius first became apparent through science. Deprived of maternal care at the age of 3, he was brought up with admirable devotion and competence by his father, Etienne, a mathematician of genuine ability, who, in order to devote himself more fully to the education of this son and two daughters, Gilberte and Jacqueline, gave up his post as magistrate of Clermont-Ferrand to move to Paris in 1631. In the capital, Blaise, whose mathematical genius manifested itself at an early age, was soon able to take part in the discussions of those savants who gathered around Father *Mersenne. In 1639 Pascal wrote his *Essai pour les coniques,* a widely acclaimed treatise in which he demonstrated a remarkable new property of conic sections.

From 1640 to 1647 Pascal lived at Rouen, where Richelieu had appointed his father administrator. Here Pascal invented his famous arithmetical machine, the first known mechanical calculator, an achievement by

Blaise Pascal, marble bust, French, 17th century.

which he showed himself as competent in technical matters as he was in pure science. His machine enjoyed considerable success, not only among the savants, but with the general public as well, and made him famous.

First Conversion. From his father Blaise had received a thorough, though not very fervent, religious education. In 1646 the young man was exposed to the revelation of a much more demanding Christianity. Several disciples of Jean du Vergier, Abbé of Saint Cyran (d. 1643), lived in the vicinity of Rouen, and Pascal became acquainted with their austere doctrine which advocated, primarily, the necessity of "conversion"—an abandonment of the world and submission to God. He accepted this demand enthusiastically, became a convert himself, and won his family over to his point of view. He woke to the fact that he genuinely relished one of the most dangerous of worldly enticements, fame, and resolved forthwith to abandon the sciences, the means by which he had won renown.

This resolution, however, was not immediately reduced to practice. Pascal continued his research and plunged into physics in an effort to interpret the famous experiment of *Torricelli. Through some original, most ingenious experiments, he demonstrated the existence of the vacuum and the weight of air. At the same time he advanced the principles of a truly modern scientific philosophy based on primary reliance on the experiment; through him came the final break between true science and metaphysics.

Meanwhile, stricken by a serious illness, the young savant returned to Paris in 1647. His doctors had recommended diversions—advice which was, indirectly, the cause of some relaxation of his religious discipline. Worldliness again gained ground in his mind, and he began again to frequent the "world." He attached himself principally to a nobleman, the Duc de Roannez, through whom he made the acquaintance of two very charming men, the Chevalier de Méré and Mitton. They became the models for his "emancipated freethinker" of the *Pensées,* and though he turned away from them, they had taught him much—they made him taste of *Montaigne, and they convinced him that the science of man was of far greater importance than the science of things.

During this time Pascal continued his scientific labors and established the foundations of the *calculus of probabilities. But neither science nor the world could satisfy this soul so enamored of the absolute. In 1654 his sister Jacqueline, who had become a religious in the Convent at *Port-Royal, privately heard him confess his confusion and understood immediately that, for the second time, he had become a convert. The famous and brilliantly written *Mémorial* recalls the intense religious experience that resulted, during the night of Nov. 23, 1654, in the revelation of the living God.

Second Conversion and Port-Royal. Through this second conversion Pascal found himself intimately linked with the theologians and recluses of Port-Royal. He traveled there repeatedly for retreats, and the one of January 1655 gave rise to the *Entretien avec M. de Sacy sur Epictète et Montaigne.* A similar period of prayer the following year made him decide to embark on *Les Provinciales* (*Lettres écrites par Louis de Montalte à un provincial*), the masterpiece of the great mass of pamphlet literature brought out by the Jansenist controversies. (*See* JANSENISM.) At the same time Pascal re-

mained in touch with his fashionable friends, trying to win them over to his views. He succeeded in the case of the Duc de Roannez, and addressed some remarkable letters to the duke's sister, Mlle. de Roannez (1656). It was in thinking about Méré and Mitton that Pascal conceived his project of an apologetic for the Christian religion, to be directed toward the unbelievers, for which the *Pensées* form the rough draft.

Although he had given up the sciences on his conversion in 1654, Pascal returned to them in 1658 at the urgent request of friends who persuaded him that publication of a worthwhile discovery would add weight to the arguments of his apologetic. Thus it was that he published (1658) some investigations on the curve called *roulette,* or cycloid, that provided the foundations for differential and integral calculus. But this episode was unique; following it Pascal withdraw from all lay activity. His illness, which returned in 1659 and from which he would never again be free, prohibited from that moment on any mental effort. His only writing of this period, a "Prayer asking God to make good use of his illness," expresses an ardent desire for a conversion still more perfect. In his last years Pascal accomplished one final spiritual ascension, which, reaching its culmination during the course of a terrible agony, brought him to a sort of sainthood.

Significance of his Work. He left a diversified life's work touching on the sciences, philosophy, theology, and spirituality, but at the same time extending beyond them because it was the work of neither a savant nor a specialist, but of a man gifted with a winning personality and a mind of profound insight. He owed to science his rigorous regard for truth, based on geometric reasoning or the experimental method, but he had come quickly to the conclusion that science was powerless to discern the condition of humanity, to fix the objectives of human life—in a word, powerless to attain those truths essential to man. One may properly say that the two fundamental traits of Pascal's mind were the strict demands of the absolute and the need of a living truth.

It is not surprising that he fervently embraced the Christian message, especially in the form in which it was made known to him. A devout Catholic, Pascal at the same time adhered to the thought of Port-Royal that one need not be too rigid in the formulation of theological propositions, and as a fervent Augustinian, he believed that in the domain of religion knowledge is inseparable from love. The certainties of faith are not grasped through reason, but through the heart, the mainspring of love, which submits to revealed truth and fosters its manifestation. (*See* AUGUSTINIANISM.)

From this conviction springs the deep feeling of the *Provinciales.* If Pascal grappled with the "casuistry" of the Jesuits, it was not because he was ignorant of certain difficulties and the necessity of resolving them, but because he wished to use only the light of revelation and not that of a reason corrupted by the Fall, which tends, understandably, to define duty as a function of self-interest. He was hostile to any compromise between humanism and Christianity, and refused to place any faith in a human nature sustained only by its own strength.

The impotence of man's reason is no less clearly set forth in the *Pensées.* Granted that impotence, how can the verities of Christianity be demonstrated? As a matter of fact, Pascal does not propose a rational demonstration. If the reason is too weak to achieve the absolute, it is at least strong enough to prove "that there are an infinite number of things which surpass it." It can realize the contradiction of man—his weakness and his nobility—but it cannot explain them; only revelation can resolve the problems imposed by the reason. In addition, reason can grasp revelation as a historical fact surrounded by certain wonderful events that guarantee its supernatural character. The method of the physician, who from some facts arrives at an explanatory hypothesis, is equally applicable to apologetics. (*See* FAITH AND REASON.)

Through his sensitivity to the human drama, and the exalted ideal he propounded of a religion that rejects any compromise with worldly standards of value, Pascal impregnated his work with a ferment whose power is far from being exhausted.

Bibliography: *Oeuvres complètes,* ed. L. BRUNSCHVICG and P. L. BOUTROUX, 14 v. (Paris 1904–14); *Pensées,* ed. L. LAFUMA, 3 v. (Paris 1951). J. MESNARD, *Pascal: His Life and Works,* tr. G. S. FRASER (London 1952). M. L. HUBERT, *Pascal's Unfinished Apology: A Study of His Plan* (New Haven 1952). A. MAIRE, *Bibliographie générale des oeuvres de Blaise Pascal,* 5 v. (Paris 1925–27). **Illustration credit:** Archives Photographiques, Paris.

[J. MESNARD]

PASCENDI, encyclical letter of *Pius X (Sept. 8, 1907), which, along with the Holy Office's decree *Lamentabili* and the Oath against Modernism (*see* MODERNISM, OATH AGAINST), forms the basis of the Church's condemnation of *Modernism. Presenting a logical synthesis, not found wholly in any one Modernist's work, *Pascendi* emphasized root tendencies and principles. Successively it considered various roles of the Modernist. As philosopher he proposed an agnosticism that limited all knowledge to phenomena and a vital immanence that made religion, revelation, and faith simply a sense springing from the collective subconscious and the Church its product apart from historical events. As believer he resorted to an intuition of the heart to find the divine reality. *Dogma he considered a series of secondary symbolic formulas that must be continually adjusted to the religious sense. As theologian he postulated an *immanence that often savored of *pantheism. As historical critic he based his work on a concealed philosophy of vital immanence. *Pascendi* termed Modernism "the synthesis of all heresies." The encyclical concluded with a list of disciplinary measures to be taken in the training of priests and in the censoring of written works.

The various statements of the encyclical should be interpreted in the context of its major preoccupation, which is to condemn (1) agnosticism, both in natural theology and in the symbolic, nonobjective approach to dogmatic content; (2) vital immanence, an exclusive immanence of the divine and a consequent natural, vital evolution of revelation; (3) total emancipation of exegesis from dogma and of political-religious movements from ecclesiastical authority. The encyclical is not of itself clearly infallible; yet some of its ideas had already been defined, and it has the solemn authority of a major papal pronouncement written on the occasion of an acute religious crisis.

Bibliography: PIUS X, "Pascendi dominici gregis" (encyclical, Sept. 8, 1907) ActSSed 40 (1907) 593–650, Eng. *All Things in Christ,* ed. V. A. YZERMANS (Westminster, Md. 1954). J. RIVIÈRE, *Le Modernisme dans l'Église* (Paris 1929). A. FARGES and J. LEBRETON, DictApolFoiCath 3:637–695. H. STIRNIMANN, LexThK² 8:126–127.

[J. J. HEANEY]

PASCHAL I, POPE, ST., Jan. 26, 817, to Feb. 11, 824; b. Rome (feast, May 14). Paschal, of nonnoble origin, was educated at the papal court. He became a priest and served as an official in the Curia before he succeeded *Stephen IV as Pope. Paschal's pontificate was highlighted by continued efforts to define the relationship between the *papacy and the newly established Frankish Empire. Shortly after his consecration, Paschal asked Emperor *Louis the Pious to reconfirm all privileges conceded to the papacy by *Pepin III and *Charlemagne. In 817, Louis, being more inclined to respect the independence of the Church than Charlemagne, issued the *Pactum Ludovicianum* (MGCap 1:352–355). This document clearly affirmed the principle of papal sovereignty over papal territories (*see* CHURCH AND STATE) and of freedom of papal elections (*see* POPES, ELECTION OF). This arrangement worked well throughout most of Paschal's pontificate. Louis called on Paschal to confirm the division of his empire arranged in 817. When Paschal decided to send Abp. *Ebbo of Reims to convert the Danes, Louis sent him to Rome to receive papal blessing. In 823 Paschal crowned Louis's son, *Lothair I, as coemperor. In the meantime Paschal ruled the *States of the Church without Frankish interference. However, trouble eventually arose. A plot against Paschal ended in the execution of two curial officials. When their partisans appealed to Louis, who sent his legates to investigate, Paschal, like *Leo III, was compelled to clear himself of charges that he was responsible for the executions by taking an oath of purgation. The affair convinced the imperial court to establish closer control over Rome, but Paschal died before this reform was instituted.

Bibliography: Duchesne LP 2:52–68; 3:343. *Epistolae,* MGEp 5.1:68–71. Jaffé E 1:318–320. L. M. O. DUCHESNE, *The Beginnings of the Temporal Sovereignty of the Popes, A.D. 754–1073,* tr. A. H. MATHEW (London 1908). Mann 2:122–155. É. AMANN, DTC 11.2:2054–57. Fliche-Martin 6:205–208. O. BERTOLINI,

Pope Paschal I, the figure at the extreme left, mosaic of the 9th century in the apse of the church of S. Prassede in Rome. The Pope was the donor of the mosaic and the restorer of the church, which dates from the 5th century.

"Osservazioni sulla *Constitutio Romana . . .* dell' 824," *Studi medievali in onore di Antonino De Stefano* (Palermo 1956) 43–78. Seppelt 2:203–212. W. ULLMANN, *The Growth of Papal Government in the Middle Ages* (2d ed. London 1962). **Illustration credit:** Alinari-Art Reference Bureau.

[R. E. SULLIVAN]

PASCHAL II, POPE

Pontificate, Aug. 13, 1099, to Jan. 21, 1118; Benedictine; b. Rainerius, at Bieda, in central Italy. He entered a monastery as a boy (not Cluny as commonly supposed, but probably a dependent house of Vallombrosa), became cardinal priest of San Clemente under *Gregory VII, served as legate in Spain under *Urban II, and was subsequently abbot of *St. Paul-Outside-the-Walls. His personal sanctity helped determine his election to succeed Urban II. His pontificate did not prove an easy one. The main problems he faced were (1) the existence of antipopes; (2) the conflict with the secular powers, especially in Germany, France, and England; (3) the need to further the reform of the Church. Underlying them all was one theme—the struggle for control of episcopal elections.

His reign opened well. Emperor *Henry IV, after the death of *Guibert of Ravenna (Clement III) in 1100, withdrew support from subsequent antipopes, Theodoric (1100–02), Albert (1102), and Sylvester IV (1105–11); these no longer proved a serious threat to Paschal. Both Henry and the Pope hoped to settle their differences, but neither of them would give way on the investiture issue. Paschal renewed the ban against Henry and prohibited lay investiture at the Roman synod in 1102. Subsequently he favored the revolt of Henry's son (1105). The son made a large number of promises, but as *Henry V he proved just as determined to retain control over investiture.

Despite meetings with the royal legates in 1106, 1107, and 1110, Paschal was disillusioned, and he condemned Henry V at the Synods of Guastalla (1106), Troyes (1107), Benevento (1108), and the Lateran (1110). Polemic literature on both sides aggravated the dispute. Henry finally marched on Rome, for he was determined to obtain imperial coronation and the right of investiture. The outcome was the fiercely debated concordat at Sutri (Feb. 9, 1111), by which, in return for free elections, Paschal granted church property in the Empire to Henry and agreed to crown him as emperor.

Both papal and imperial supporters condemned the agreement. Henry then took Paschal prisoner and forced him to recognize lay investiture (Privilege of Ponte Mammolo, April 12, 1111). These actions seriously damaged the unity of the papal party. Ultimately Paschal repudiated the privilege (1112) and explicitly condemned lay investiture in 1116. He finally left Rome and returned only on Jan. 14, 1118, to die there a few days later. During this long struggle with Henry V, Paschal had also intervened to settle the dispute of *Anselm, Archbishop of Canterbury, with *Henry I of England (1107). The interest of that settlement lies in its departure from the strict principles of the *Gregorian reform, thus providing a basis for subsequent settlements with France (also in 1107) and with Henry V (Concordat of *Worms, 1122).

Paschal has generally been criticized for his failure, and little has been said of his work for the Church in other regions, e.g., in the Latin Kingdom of *Jerusalem.

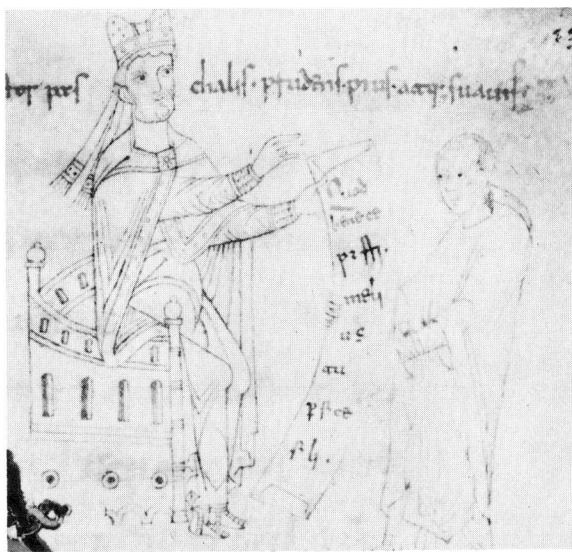

Pope Paschal II invites the monk John to continue the "Chronicon Vulturnense," drawing in a 12th-century copy of the work (MS Vat. Barb. Lat. 2724, fol. 13v).

Even his contemporaries—enemies and friends alike—condemned his actions (see the *Liber de honore ecclesiae* of Placidus of Nonantula, MGLibLit 2:568). He did not solve the conflict with the Empire; but if success be the guiding principle, it may be asked how much he differed from the example of his more able predecessors? His attitude toward temporal possessions was ideally the right one. He certainly contributed toward depriving the *regalia* of their sacramental character, making the concordat of 1122 possible. His pontificate was one more step in the direction of sharply distinguishing lay and clerical powers and offices.

See also INVESTITURE STRUGGLE.

Bibliography: Seppelt 3:134–151. C. MARCORA, *Storia dei papi* (Milan 1961–) 2:346–358. A. STACPOOLE, "Hildebrand, Cluny and the Papacy," DownRev 81 (1963) 142–164, 254–272. J. G. ROWE, "Paschal II and the Relation Between the Spiritual and Temporal Powers in the Kingdom of Jerusalem," *Speculum* 32 (1957) 470–501. Jaffé L 1:702–772. MGConst 1:134–152, 564–574. Fliche-Martin 8:338–375. **Illustration credit:** Biblioteca Apostolica Vaticana.

[J. GILCHRIST]

PASCHAL BAYLON, ST.,

b. Torre-Hermosa, Aragon, May 24, 1540; d. Villareal in Castellon, May 15, 1592 (feast, May 17). He was a shepherd, the son of Martin Baylon and Elizabeth Jubeira, peasants of lowly origins, and he taught himself to read and write. In 1564 he was received into the Alcantarine Franciscans at Monteforte. His superiors urged him to study for the priesthood, but he chose to become a lay brother. During most of his religious life he served as porter. In this office he showed remarkable kindness to the poor who came to the friary door. His personal austerities surpassed the severe demands of the Alcantarine constitutions. He was granted marvelous insights into the mysteries of religion, and his counsel was sought by learned and saintly persons. But it was his devotion to the Eucharist that emerged as the dominant theme of his life. In this connection numerous miracles are reported by his early biographers, but it is not always easy to distinguish fact from legend.

St. Paschal Baylon Adoring the Eucharist, detail of a painting by Giovanni Battista Tiepolo in the Prado at Madrid.

His writings consist of two books of prayers and reflections that he jotted down on scraps of paper. One of these volumes was edited by Jaime Sala and published at Toledo in 1911 under the title *Opúsculos de San Pascual Bailón.* Because of the number of cures worked through his intercession, Pope Paul V beatified Paschal in 1618, 26 years after the saint's death. He was canonized by Pope Alexander VIII in 1690, and, in 1897 Pope Leo XIII designated him patron of all Eucharistic congresses and societies.

Bibliography: ActSS May 4:48–131. O. ENGLEBERT, *Saint Pascal Baylon* (Paris 1942). V. FACCHINETTI, *Pasquale Baylon, frate minore: Il santo dell'Eucaristia* (Milan 1922). A. GROETEKEN, *Paschalis Baylon: Ein Heiligenbild aus Spaniens Goldenem Jahrhundert* (Cincinnati 1912). L. GUIM CASTRO, *San Pascual Bailón: Celestial patrono de los Congresos Eucarísticos* (Vich, Spain 1953). L. A. PORRENTRUY, *The Saint of the Eucharist,* tr. O. STANIFORTH (San Francisco 1905). J. XIMENEZ, *Chrónica del beato Fr. Pascual Bailón* (Valencia 1601). **Illustration credit:** Photo MAS, Barcelona.

[C. J. LYNCH]

PASCHASIUS RADBERTUS, ST., abbot, theologian of the Eucharist; b. Soisson *c.* 785; d. *c.* 860 (feast, April 26). He entered the Benedictine abbey of *Corbie under Abbot *Adalard the Elder (814–821) whose life he was to write (PL 120:1507-56). Though only a deacon, he was elected abbot of Corbie *c.* 843 but later resigned (before 853) because of opposition to his plans for reform. In 831, Paschasius wrote his treatise *Concerning the Lord's Body and Blood* (PL 120:1267-1351), the first monograph ever written on the Eucharist. Revised by Paschasius in 844, it was severely criticized by *Ratramnus and *Rabanus Maurus. Toward the end of his life Paschasius answered his critics in his famous letter to Frudegard (PL 120:1351-66). In addition to commentaries on Psalms 44, Jeremias, and Matthew (PL 120:31-1256), he wrote works dealing with the three theological virtues (PL 120:1387-90), the Virginal Birth (PL 120: 1367-86), the martyrdom of Rufinus and Valerius (PL 120:1489-1508), the life of Abbot *Wala (PL 120:1559-1650), and a number of poems and letters. His letter on the Assumption of the Blessed Virgin, formerly attributed to St. Jerome (PL 30:122-142), was often cited in Christological treatises of the Middle Ages. Paschasius is known to have attended the synods of Paris (847) and Quierzy (849), but the date of his death is uncertain.

Concerning the Eucharist, Paschasius taught that "the substance of bread and wine is changed into Christ's Body and Blood" (*De Corp.* 8.2). In dealing with the Real Presence of Christ in the Eucharist he described it as the very flesh of Mary, which had suffered on the Cross, was buried, and rose again (*De Corp.* 4.3 and 7.2). He held that by the omnipotence of God it is miraculously created or multiplied daily at each Consecration (*De Corp.* 4.1 and 12.1). His opponents rejected this doctrinal presentation as too crude and materialistic. In his letter to Frudegard Paschasius reaffirmed his view and tried to show that it was in complete accord with the teaching of the Fathers. Modern historians of theology agree that Paschasius overstressed the identity of the historical and the Eucharistic Body and that the manner in which he had recourse to legends was not commendable. Paschasius's great influence was partly due to the fact that at the end of the 11th century a number of passages copied from his work began to be circulated under the name of St. Augustine.

Bibliography: Works. Collection of his works ed. J. SIRMOND (Paris 1618), MABILLON (Paris 1677), and MARTÈNE (Paris 1733) reprinted in PL 120; *Poems,* ed. L. TRAUBE, MGPoetae 3.1:38–53; *Letters,* ed. E. DUEMMLER, MGEp 6.1:133–149, critical eds. A. RIPBERGER, *Der Pseudo-Hieronymus-Brief IX "Cogitis me"* (Spicilegium Friburgense 9: Fribourg 1962), with bibliog. Literature. E. CHOISY, *Paschase Radbert* (Geneva 1888). D. STONE, *A History of the Doctrine of the Holy Eucharist,* 2 v. (New York 1909) 1:216–220. J. GEISELMANN, *Die Eucharistielehre der Vorscholastik* (Paderborn 1926). H. PELTIER, *Pascase Radbert* (Amiens 1938). K. VIELHABER, LexThK² 8:130–131.

[N. M. HARING]

PASCHINI, PIO, historian, rector of the Pontifical University of the Vatican; b. Tolmezzo, Italy, March 2, 1878; d. Rome, Dec. 14, 1962. The eldest of 11 children, he studied at the seminaries of Treviso (1887) and then Udine (1895). In 1898 he went to Rome, and in 1900 he received a degree in Canon Law and was ordained there. From 1900 to 1913 he taught Latin and Italian literature and Greek in the seminary at Udine, where an attempt to remove him and Giuseppe Ellero (d. 1925) on charges of *Modernism failed (1906–08). In 1913 he became professor of Church history in the Ateneo Lateranense in Rome. He had already published in Udine (1911), and with the libraries and archival facilities of Rome available, he produced scholarly works for the rest of his life. He was rector of the Ateneo from the time it became a university (1932) until 1957. In 1962 he was consecrated titular bishop of Eudossiade. He is buried in the cemetery del Verano.

His writings are numerous: many articles in the *Dictionnaire d'histoire et de géographie Ecclésiastiques, Enciclopedia Italiana,* and *Enciclopedia cattolica,* and articles, brief notices, and book reviews in periodicals. He refounded the *Rivista di storia della chiesa in Italia* in 1947 and began the *Enciclopedia cattolica* (EncCatt) in 1948. He specialized in two fields: his native Friuli and Aquileia, and Italy in the 16th century. His method, a detailed exposition of data that speaks for itself, replaced the apologetical presentation of Church history in Italy.

Bibliography: P. PASCHINI, *Storia del Friuli,* 3 v. (Udine 1934–36); *Notizie storiche della Carnia* (2d ed. Udine 1960); "Su Mons. Lanzoni," Riv StorChIt 17 (1963) 248–258. R. AUBERT, RHE 58 (1963) 1119. A. P. FRUTAZ, *Studi romani* 11 (1963) 63–65. M. MACCARRONE, *S. E. Mons. Paschini* (Rome 1962); RivStorChIt 17 (1963) 181–221; "Bibliografia degli scritti di P.P.," *ibid.* 259–304. C. G. MOR, "P. e la *Storia del Friuli*," *ibid.* 222–233. G. ALBERIGO, "Il cinquecento religioso italiano nell' opera storica di P.P.," *ibid.* 234–247.

[E. P. COLBERT]

PASCOLI, GIOVANNI

Italian poet; b. San Mauro, Romagna, Dec. 31, 1855; d. Bologna, April 6, 1912. He was a pupil of *Carducci, and was awarded the Litt.D. in 1882. He taught Latin and Greek in several *lycées* and at the Universities of Messina and Pisa. In 1907, after Carducci's death, he succeeded to the chair of Italian literature at the University of Bologna. Pascoli's early adolescence was darkened by family tragedies: his father was killed in 1867 and the murderer was never found. Soon thereafter his oldest sister, his mother, and two brothers also died. These events left an indelible mark on him, and in his poetry death became a recurring symbol of ruthless destruction. He dwelt also on the mystery of life and fate, on the vastness and motion of the cosmos, and on a world man senses but cannot explain.

Pascoli's first book, *Myricae* (1892), remains fundamental. In it he treats the humble elements of everyday living and the feelings they evoke. He already reveals his characteristic intensity and emerges as an instinctive, perhaps unconscious, symbolist. The continuation of *Myricae, Canti di Castelvecchio* (1903), represents—particularly in the group "Ritorno a San Mauro"—the peak of his work. During the intervening years he had written the *Poemetti* (1897), subsequently split into *Primi Poemetti* and *Nuovi Poemetti,* in which he treats mostly georgic subjects in a symbolistic key, and the *Poemi Conviviali* (1904). His later volumes, such as *Odi e Inni* (1906), and *Poemi Italici* (1911), are somewhat artificial.

Pascoli presented his own poetics in an essay called *Il fanciullino,* where he states that the poet sees things as if for the first time, marvels while he observes, and spontaneously finds the most unusual analogies for the expression of his vision. This is precisely what may be said of Pascoli himself. He used all kinds of technical devices, including coenesthesia, which he did not consider new but as inherited from the classics. He enlarged the Italian poetic vocabulary beyond traditional limitations, and enriched Italian poetry with innumerable new and daring images and analogies. His influence on subsequent writers has been such that the large body of distinguished Italian poetry produced during the 20th century would have been far less imposing without his example and leadership.

Pascoli was as well versed in Latin as in Italian. His *Carmina* (1914), which have been judged the best Latin poems since the age of Vergil and Horace, recreate chiefly the people and events in Rome during the early Christian period. Yet his *Carmina* are informed by the poetic sensibility of a modern man, and the images and tone are peculiarly Pascoli's. His Latin works, therefore, belong in the same category as his Italian poems.

He also published some critical interpretations, including three volumes on Dante, but they are more interesting as a means of understanding Pascoli than as a guide to the poets he attempts to interpret.

Bibliography: *Opere,* 5 v. (Milan 1939–52); *Poems,* tr. E. STEIN (New Haven 1923); *Poems,* selected and tr. A. M. ABOTT (New York 1927). F. FELCINI, *Bibliografia della critica pascoliana, 1887–1954* (Florence 1957). E. CECCHI, *La poesia di Giovanni Pascoli* (Naples 1912). R. VIOLA, *Pascoli* (2d ed. Padua 1949). G. CECCHETTI, *La poesia del Pascoli* (Pisa 1954). Società di studi romagnoli, Comitato di onoranze a G. Pascoli, *Studi pascoliani* (Faenza 1958). F. FLORA, *La poesia di Giovanni Pascoli* (Bologna 1959).

[G. CECCHETTI]

PASSAGLIA, CARLO

PASSAGLIA, CARLO, theologian; b. Pieve S. Carlo, Lucca, Italy, May 2, 1812; d. Turin, March 12, 1887. In 1827 he became a Jesuit. From 1840 to 1844 he was prefect of studies at the Germanicum in Rome, and in 1844, professor of dogma at the Roman College. He became professor at the papal Sapienza University in Rome in 1858, left the Jesuits in 1859, and in 1860 was named a member of the papal commission for the theological investigation of the *Causa italica.* In 1860 he wrote *Il Pontifice ed il Principe.* He was Cavour's mediator, and in 1861 he published, anonymously, *Pro causa italica ad episcopos catholicos,* which was placed on the Index. He fled Rome in October of the same year and accepted a professorship in moral philosophy at the state university of Turin. In 1862 he directed to Pius IX a petition on behalf of about 9,000 Italian priests and was suspended. He was the editor of the weekly *Il Mediatore* (1862–66), the daily *La Pace* (1863–64), and *Il Gerdil* (1864). In 1863 and 1864, he was a member of Parliament. He had been seeking reconciliation with the Church since 1868, and on March 8, 1887, a few days before his death, he obtained it.

Passaglia was a patristically oriented theologian with strong leanings toward Petavius and Thomassin. He published the first book of Petavius's *Dogmatics* in 1857. He showed a mastery of theology, and together with G. *Perrone and his two disciples, K. *Schrader and J. B. *Franzelin, he renewed the study of it at the Roman College. There he was the teacher of renowned German theologians, including H. J. *Denzinger, F. *Hettinger, B. *Jungmann, H. von *Hurter, and M. *Scheeben. Passaglia took part in the preparatory work that led to the definition of the Immaculate Conception of Mary, and to the wording of the bull *Ineffabilis Deus.* Yet at Vatican I, Passaglia's view of the mediate papal power of jurisdiction was rejected. His theological works are of lasting value, for example: *Commentarium theologicorum,* 3 v. (Rome 1850–51), *De Ecclesia Christi,* 2 v. (Regensburg 1853–56), *De Immaculata Deiparae semper Virginis Conceptu,* 3 v. (Rome 1854, Naples 1855). From his unpublished material H. Schauf edited *De Conciliis Oecumenicis, Theses C. Passaglia* (Rome 1961).

Bibliography: Sommervogel 6:332–336. C. BOYER, DTC 11.2: 2207–10. Hurter Nomencl 5.2:1499–1500. C. TESTORE, EncCatt

9:908–909. L. BIGINELLI, *Biografia del Sac. Prof. Carlo Passaglia con documenti* (Turin 1887). P. D'ERCOLE, *Carlo Passaglia: cenno biobibliografico e ricordo* (Turin 1888). C. G. AREVALO, *Some Aspects of the Theology of the Mystical Body of Christ in the Ecclesiology of G. Perrone, C. Passaglia and Cl. Schrader* (Rome 1959). W. KASPER, *Die Lehre von der Tradition in der Römischen Schule* (Freiburg 1962).

[H. SCHAUF]

PASSAIC, EPARCHY OF (BYZANTINE RITE),

ecclesiastical jurisdiction embracing all Byzantine Catholics of Ruthenian, Hungarian, and Croatian nationalities and their descendants on the Eastern Seaboard of the U.S. and in eastern Pennsylvania as far west as Harrisburg. The eparchy (diocese), created from the former Apostolic Exarchate of Pittsburgh, Pa., by Paul VI on July 31, 1963, was canonically erected on Sept. 10, 1963, with Bp. Stephen J. Kocisko, former auxiliary of the Exarchate of Pittsburgh as first bishop. The new eparchy had a total of 95,000 Catholics; there were 74 parishes, 13 parochial schools, 82 secular priests, 16 religious priests, 54 religious sisters, and 51 seminarians studying in three seminaries. The Franciscan fathers had monasteries in New Canaan, Conn., and Sybertsville, Pa. Religious communities of women included the Daughters of Divine Charity, Sister Servants of Mary Immaculate, Sisters of the Order of St. Basil the Great, and Sisters of Christ the Teacher.

[S. J. KOCISKO]

PASSERINI, PIETRO MARIA;

b. Cremona, 1597; d. Rome, 1677. Passerini, a canonist, became procurator general of the Dominican Order. For 20 years he was a professor at the Sapienza in Rome and was renowned for his work on the Roman Curia. His principal writings are the *De electione canonica tractatus* (Rome 1661), *De hominum statibus et officiis* (1665), and the *Regulare Tribunale* (1677).

Bibliography: M. M. GORCE, DTC 11.2:2210–11. R. NAZ, DDC 6:1253. Hurter Nomencl 4:253–254.

[L. R. KOZLOWSKI]

PASSIO,

originally the account of suffering of a martyr written by Christians and based on the testimony of eyewitnesses. In the earliest type of *passio*, the miraculous element plays a restricted part, as in the accounts of the martyrdoms of St. *Polycarp and SS. *Perpetua and Felicity, or in the *passio* of the Scillitan Martyrs (c. 180). Later authors embellished this type of narrative with fanciful and miraculous happenings to edify, or to satisfy, popular tastes. This was done in the case of the *passiones* of SS. *Hippolytus, *Sebastian, *Cecilia, *Agnes, and the *Four Crowned Martyrs, making the task of discovering the authentic ones difficult for modern hagiographers. Another type of *passio* that became popular from the 5th century onward was a completely legendary account of a martyr's or saint's life and death, which usually had nothing more than a name and possibly a location as foundation. The *passio* of St. *Catherine of Alexandria and that of St. *George are without historical foundation. The *passio* even in its most authentic form is to be distinguished from an authentic Act of the martyrdom, which is the official shorthand report of the trial and death of a martyr. Only a few of these have survived. (*See* ACTS OF THE MARTYRS.)

The *passio* was used by the *apologists as a subsidiary proof of the divine origin of the Christian religion; but its specific purpose was to encourage Christians to honor and imitate the martyrs. In theology the *passio* as an account of the sufferings of a martyr points to the relevance of the faith as an absolute factor in the life of the early Church. The martyr was challenged to forswear his faith or die for it. Likewise the confessions of faith frequently put into the mouth of the martyr, whether authentic or not, witness to belief in a living, triune God, the Resurrection of Christ, and Christian belief in final glory.

Bibliography: A. HAMMAN, LexThK² 7:133–134; ThGlaube 45 (1955) 35–43. G. LAZZATI, *Gli sviluppi della letteratura sui martiri nei primi quattro secoli* (Turin 1956). ActSS, AnalBoll, BHL, BHG. R. AIGRAIN, *L'Hagiographie* (Paris 1953). H. DELEHAYE, *Les Passions des martyrs et les genres littéraires* (Brussels 1921).

[F. X. MURPHY]

PASSION,

from the Latin *passio* (Gr. πάθος), meaning something suffered or undergone, has a variety of significations. In its etymological sense it refers to physical suffering, particularly that associated with the martyrdom of early Christians (*see* PASSIO). In a broader philosophical meaning, as opposed to action it signifies the reception of the activity of some extrinsic agent or mover, and as such is enumerated among the *categories of being (*see* ACTION AND PASSION). It is used also to designate the species of *quality according to which there can be alteration (*see* MOTION), and, by extension, to signify any attribute, affection, or *property of a subject. In psychology, Cartesian usage identifies passions with states of the soul resulting from the action of "animal spirits"; Aristotelian and scholastic usage, on the other hand, refers to all types of emotional activity as passions (*see* EMOTION). More commonly accepted usages refer to any violent or intense emotion, particularly an ardent affection for one of the opposite sex, as passion (*see* LOVE; SEX). Among Christians, the word is frequently used to indicate the sufferings of Christ (*see* PASSION OF CHRIST, I, II, III).

[W. A. WALLACE]

PASSION OF CHRIST, I (IN THE BIBLE)

This article, concerned primarily with the story of Christ's Passion and death as told in the four Gospels, is composed of four main sections: the ancient, common basis of a Passion narrative prior to the four written Gospels; the development of the Gospel tradition about the Passion; characteristics of the four canonical Passion narratives; the use of the OT in the Passion accounts. A specific treatment of the Resurrection is not included in this article, although the realization of the unity of the one redemptive mystery, Passion-death-Exaltation, is basic to the discussion (*see* RESURRECTION OF CHRIST, 1). For the theological significance of Christ's Passion, *see* EXPIATION (IN THE BIBLE); REDEMPTION (IN THE BIBLE); SALVATION.

Pre-Gospel Passion Narrative. The Passion narratives in the present Gospels (Mark ch. 14–15; Matthew ch. 26–27; Luke ch. 22–23; John ch. 18–19) differ from the rest of the Gospel material in that they seem not to have been compiled from individual, self-contained units or stories, but present a unified, sequential account of the final events in Jesus' life and ministry. Recognizing the very different character of these stories as continuous narratives, the adherents of the form-critical school have acknowledged the very ancient tradition upon which they are based. Modern Biblical scholarship agrees that there was a primitive narrative; but there are divergent opinions on the genre, content, and milieu of the formation of that narrative. Only as a whole could the story answer the question, "How could Jesus have been brought to the cross by the people who were blessed by His signs and wonders?" To counter this scandal of the cross, individual incidents from the Passion would not do; the entire purposeful narrative, giving exact geographical and temporal data, was seen to be necessary. (*See* FORM CRITICISM, BIBLICAL.)

Several arguments from literary criticism support the hypothesis of such a primitive narrative. More than any other part of the Gospels, this section has the nature of a connected historical account. Although the first 10 chapters of Mark, for example, comprise separate blocks of material loosely connected and without continuous chronological or topographical coherence, with the beginning of the Passion story, we find a definitely sequential account. Among all four Gospels there is substantial agreement regarding the course of events of the Passion. Although chronological arrangements in earlier parts of the Gospels reflect more freely the particular interests of the writers, the events of Holy Week seem to have been so fixed in the tradition and so respected as the record of the climax of Jesus' life that the order could not be freely changed; it might be abridged, expanded, or supplemented, but its general order was retained. J. Jeremias observes that John's Gospel rarely shows parallels to Mark's account in the description of Jesus' ministry, but beginning with the entrance into Jerusalem, the Johannine narrative agrees with the Marcan rather broadly until the arrest, and then quite strictly after that. These parallels are striking, for the substance of the narrative is the same, even though details and wording may differ and even though religious and doctrinal interests are more obviously present in John than in Mark. This similarity of structure in the Passion accounts of all four Gospels has a natural explanation if there was such a basic narrative, traditional before the written Gospels.

At present critics do not express complete agreement about what the pre-Gospel narrative comprised, but most include the following incidents, which can be distinguished more easily in Mark: the plot of the priests (Mk 14.1–2); *Judas' treason (14.10–11); the *Last Supper (14.17–25); the arrest of Jesus (14.43–52); the trial before the *chief priests (14.53–72—not admitted by all as part of the primitive narrative) and before *Pilate (15.1–15); the *Crucifixion with some of its concomitant events (15.21–41); and the burial (15.42–47). These episodes are the ones referred to in Christ's own prophecies of the Passion (Mk 8.31; 9.29–30; 10.33) and in the earliest apostolic preaching (e.g., Acts 3.13–16; 13.27–31). From an analysis of Semitic expressions in Mark, V. Taylor proposes that Mark utilized the Greek Passion narrative current in Rome and that he expanded this with certain personal reminiscences of Peter. X. Léon-Dufour, however, maintains that an examination of Semitisms in Matthew indicates that the first Gospel also witnesses to an older, more primitive narrative, of which Matthew and Mark would represent two recensions, the one Semitic (Matthew), the other Roman (Mark).

Development of the Gospel Tradition. While there is essential agreement among the four Gospels on the important events of the Passion, each of the accounts is a unique composition with its own literary characteristics and theological viewpoint. Even Mark's presentation, though barely more than an outline, has singular features and theological interests. Present-day understanding of the NT emphasizes the benefits to be gained by appreciating the differences for what they are: signs of the individual view of the Evangelist, the needs of the particular audience addressed, and the literary style of the author. The passion narratives can best be understood as *salvation history (*Heilsgeschichte*), i.e., history with a theological intent. In order to appreciate the narratives fully, one must be alert to the theological, missionary, and liturgical factors that influenced their formation.

In Acts and in the Pauline Epistles evidence is found of the focus on Jesus' death and Resurrection in the early preaching and doctrinal development. Christ's death on the cross determined the conception not only of messianic salvation, but also of God's entire revelation through the OT. In Paul's early Epistles it can be seen how the first missionaries overcame the tremendous stumbling block of the cross by their Christological interpretation of the OT. The apologetic necessity of answering objections to a crucified Messiah led them to seek and achieve profound religious and theological insights into the meaning of the event. From saying that Jesus was Messiah despite the Crucifixion (Acts 2.23, 36; 3.13–15, 17–18; etc.), they came to say that He was Messiah in virtue of the Crucifixion because this was the fulfillment of the will of God (Gal 3.10–13; 6.14; Rom 4.25). Liturgical influences on the Passion narratives include the celebration of the Eucharist, the administration of the Sacraments, and what may be called the "liturgy of the word."

While the kerygma (preaching) is the core of the apostolic preaching, the Passion narrative based on it is chiefly didache (instruction); that is, it is an illustration and an elucidation of the basic proclamation of salvation (*see* KERYGMA). To retain all the many deeds and sayings of Jesus was not possible (Jn 21.25); so the primitive community and the Evangelists preserved certain ones by a selective operation. Evidence of this is seen in the preservation of incidents from the Passion that prove that Jesus, Messiah and God's Son, foreknew His Passion and freely chose to suffer for our Redemption. The three Synoptic writers stress Christ's prophecies of the Passion, and John underlines the same truth in the parable of the Good Shepherd (Jn 10.11–18). To stress the innocence of Jesus, the tradition emphasizes the guilt of the Jews, while in comparison it seems to mitigate the responsibility of Pilate. The Evangelists achieve this emphasis, however, only by leaving out some things that would tend to exonerate the Jews and not by inventing anti-Jewish stories; at the same time, they present the Passion as the fulfillment of God's will, so that both the Jews and Pilate are but instruments in God's redemptive design (Lk 24.45–47).

Particular Characteristics of the Gospel Narratives. A study of similarities and differences among the four Gospel Passion narratives deepens appreciation of their significance and also reveals much about the way in which the early Christian community and the Evangelists understood them. Mark may be taken as the basis

Two scenes from the Passion, "The Agony in the Garden," and "The Betrayal of Christ," tempera on panels by the Sienese painter Sassetta (1392–1450), 19¼ inches by 25¼ inches and 14⅞ inches by 23⅜ inches, respectively.

for comparison because it is simplest and earliest. Mark presents a historical view of Jesus' ministry and emphasizes the themes of hiddenness, secrecy, and lack of understanding about Jesus and His mission. The narrative of the Passion itself makes up a substantial part, approximately one-fifth, of the entire Gospel. For this reason, some critics have described Mark's Gospel as simply a Passion narrative with an introduction. Its purpose is more comprehensive than this, however; it seeks to elucidate the doctrine of Jesus Christ as Redeemer and Son of God. This basic theme is highlighted in three key places: in the opening statement (1.1); at Caesarea Philippi, the turning point of the Gospel (8.29); and at Jesus' death (15.39). The Passion narrative is an integral part of this total plan; as Peter's confession prepares the way for the narrative of the Passion, so the words of the pagan centurion (15.39) provide the final comment on it. Immediately after Peter's confession (8.29), Jesus' new teaching on the necessity of suffering is introduced.

In their account of the trial of Jesus, the Synoptic writers imply what John states explicitly: that the issue for which Jesus is condemned by the *Sanhedrin is His teaching of His divinity (Mk 14.61–62; Mt 26.63–64; Lk 22.66–71; Jn 18.19–21). Before Pilate, however, the Sanhedrin attempts to indict Jesus on political charges, knowing well that blasphemy is not a charge that will win a death sentence from the Roman governor. The religious issue central to the trial is evident when the Jews insist: "We have a Law, and according to that Law he must die, because he has made himself Son of God" (Jn 19.7). Under pressure from the chief priests and the mob, Pilate fears an insurrection, so he delivers Jesus to be crucified (Mk 15.15). The connotation of παραδιδόναι (to deliver, to hand over), so frequently used in the accounts, is that ultimately it is God's will that is being fulfilled, the human agents being but instruments (cf. Rom 8.32; Acts 2.23; Is 53.4). Significant of the restraint of the Gospel accounts is the fact that the cruel torture of the scourging is described with a single Greek word (Mk 15.15).

Like John, both Mark and Matthew associate a mocking and spitting scene with that of the scourging (Mk 15.15–19; Mt 27.26–30); and like the fourth Evangelist, also, they emphasize the royal caricature of the "King of the Jews." Luke, on the other hand, in a scene proper to his Gospel, separates the mocking and scourging; he attributes the mocking to the court of *Herod Antipas, where Jesus is treated with contempt because of His claim to royalty (Lk 23.11). In the third Gospel the scourging alternative proposed by Pilate follows closely upon this scene at Herod's court. Luke's special source has apparently given him information about the dealings between Herod and Pilate, for the other Evangelists do not seem to know of Jesus' appearance before the Tetrarch of Galilee (see also Acts 4.24–30). As the mercenaries of Pilate took their cue from the official accusations at the trial and mocked Jesus as a political pretender, so also earlier, the attendants at the court of the Sanhedrin had taken their cue from the charges of that court, ridiculing and maltreating Jesus as a religious pretender, taunting Him to exercise now His powers of prophecy (Mk 14.65). John associates maltreatment of Jesus with the questioning before *Caiphas (Jn 18.22–23); indeed, this unofficial hearing is more likely than the official meeting of the Sanhedrin.

Mark, followed by Matthew and Luke, tells of Simon of Cyrene's part in carrying the cross. For John's theological purpose, the incident of Simon's help seems unimportant, and he chooses instead to emphasize that Jesus goes freely to His death carrying the cross Himself and fully in charge of His destiny (Jn 19.17). In keeping with the Roman custom, the plaque announcing the deed for which He was being executed was posted on the cross above Jesus' head. All four accounts report this, but in four slightly different wordings, an interesting example of the way in which the primitive tradition preserved the substance, but not necessarily the exact details, of the events.

Old Testament in Passion Narratives. In Jesus' own teaching regarding His Passion, one of the most striking elements is His use of OT allusions and His interpretation of the Scriptures in function of His own person and mission: in God's salvific plan, He is the climax toward which all of Israel's history has been moving. His doctrine is so firmly rooted in scriptural thought that one can have little understanding of it unless one knows the significance of the OT references made. Especially in the *Servant of the Lord oracles in Deutero-Isaia and in Psalms 21(22) and 68(69), the early Church and the Evangelists saw delineated clearly the prefiguring of the Just One who suffered vicariously for His people (Mk 15.23, 34, 36; Mt 27.42–43; Lk 23.34, 35–37; Jn 19.24, 28, 29). Jesus Himself had consistently taught that He was the fulfillment of the Scriptures and had identified Himself with the Isaian Servant. The Apostles and first Christians, meditating upon these passages, were impressed with the great similarities between the sufferings of the Isaian Servant and of Christ. Their desire to stress prophetic fulfillment was an important influence upon the formation, selection of events, and manner of narration of the Passion story. In the tradition we find preserved especially those things that show the fulfillment of prophecy, while more profane information may be omitted. Not merely the Passion as a whole, but also many individual happenings are seen as the fulfillment of Scripture and God's foreordained will, e.g., the betrayal by Judas, the arrest of Jesus, the flight of His disciples, His being raised up on the wood of the cross, and His shameful death as a criminal. The use of the OT by each of the Evangelists provides some unique insights into the meaning of the Passion.

Mark. The chief OT theme developed by Mark is that of Christ as Suffering Servant (cf. Is 52.13–53.12). In Mk 14.21 the Gospel points out that Jesus, the Son of Man, "goes his way" to death "as it is written." Mark seems to allude to Is 53.7 in his description of Jesus' silence before the high priest and before Pilate (Mk 14.61; 15.5). The description of the mistreatment of Jesus before the Sanhedrin (Mk 14.65) recalls the language of Is 50.6. On Calvary, Jesus' Crucifixion between the two thieves (Mk 15.27) recalls a passage from Isaia (53.12).

Matthew. The account in Matthew likewise emphasizes Jesus' role as Servant of Yahweh, but it reveals a particular interest in showing a literal accomplishment of prophecy. The language of Matthew is noticeably Biblical, e.g., in 26.3–5, 14–16, describing the plot of the Jewish council against Jesus and perhaps recalling Ps 30(31).14 and Ps 2.1–2. His account of Judas' betrayal of Jesus for 30 pieces of silver recalls Za 11.12–13, which he later cites explicitly in telling of Judas' fate

"The Procession to Calvary," tempera on panel by the 15th-century Sienese artist Sassetta, 19¼ by 25 inches.

(Mt 27.9–10). The derision by those standing about the cross recalls the words of Ps 21(22).9, and their resemblance to the words of Wis 2.12–20 is even more striking.

Luke. For his Passion narrative, Luke uses not only the Mark-Matthew tradition, but other sources as well. He includes incidents and OT allusions that contribute to the themes of his Gospel, including Jesus as the Chosen One of God, the Messiah (Lk 23.35). Luke's stress upon Jesus' fulfillment of the Servant prophecy is apparent, for he includes the allusions of the other Synoptics; and he makes a special point of emphasizing the realization of Is 53.12, "And he was counted among the wicked," by alluding to it in three different verses (Lk 22.37; 23.32–33). On Calvary Jesus' last words as recorded in Luke express the filial obedience of the Redeemer, the Chosen One, as He cries in the words of Ps 30(31).6, "Father, into thy hands I commend my spirit" (Lk 23.46).

John. In his use of OT allusions, the fourth Evangelist presents a developed, refined theology of Jesus' redemptive death. John omits many of the Synoptic details (e.g., Simon of Cyrene, the weeping women, the jeering of the onlookers, the darkness, the tearing of the Temple veil) and selects other incidents in which he sees special significance. Deep reflection on the meaning of Jesus' life and mission enabled John to see profound and sometimes subtle symbolism in the circumstances of the Passion. He conceives of Jesus' Passion as the beginning of His Exaltation, the supreme revelation to the world of His universal kingship and His divinity. John alone mentions the seamless tunic; his intention here may be to stress that Jesus dies as high priest of the New Covenant; for according to the Jewish historian Josephus, the robe of the Jewish high priest was a seamless one, described by Ben Sirach as a "glorious robe" (Sir 50.11). John concludes the description with another citation of Psalm 21(22); here is an interesting example of the personal way in which John employs data from the apostolic tradition. Matthew and Mark cite the opening words of this Psalm in their description of the Crucifixion; John, however, sees Jesus' Passion primarily as the beginning of His glory, so he omits this seeming cry of desperation and prefers to point out (Jn 19.24) the fulfillment of those other words in the same Psalm: "They divided up my garments among them, and for my vesture they cast lots" [Ps 21(22).19].

The typology of the Paschal Lamb is paramount in John's account. John stresses that Jesus' sacrifice takes place at the same time as that of the paschal lambs in the Temple (Jn 13.1; 18.28; 19.14, 31). When the sacrifice has been accomplished, and the Divine Lamb hangs dead upon the cross, John points out the significance of the piercing of His side (19.34–37). The meaning of this event is explained by two texts of Scripture: the blood attests to the reality of the sacrifice, and the water, symbol of the Spirit (Jn 7.39), its spiritual fecundity.

Many Fathers of the Church, with accurate insight into John's teaching, have seen in the water the symbol of Baptism, in the blood that of the Eucharist, and thus in the two Sacraments, the sign of the Church, the New Eve being born from the side of the New Adam. John's citation (19.36), "Not a bone of him shall you break," presents a composite picture of the Savior as Servant of Yahweh and Paschal Lamb [cf. Ex 12.46; Ps 33(34).21]. Thus John sees the consummation of Jesus' Exaltation realized even at His death. He applies the citation of Za 12.10, "They shall look on him whom they have pierced," not only to the piercing there on Calvary but also to the compelling, attracting power of the crucified, exalted Jesus (Jn 19.37; see also 3.14; 8.28; 12.32). His sacrifice accomplished, Jesus, the Paschal Lamb whose sacrifice wins universal redemption, draws all men to Himself so that with Him and through Him, all return to the Father.

See also TRIAL OF JESUS.

Bibliography: X. LÉON-DUFOUR, DBSuppl 6:1419–92, with detailed bibliog.; "Mt et Mc dans le récit de la Passion," *Biblica* 40 (1959) 684–696; "Autour des récits de la Passion," RechScRel 48 (1960) 489–507. K. H. SCHELKLE, *Die Passion Jesu in der Verkündigung des N.T.: Ein Beitrag zur Formgeschichte und zur Theologie des N.T.* (Heidelberg 1949). A. M. RAMSEY, *The Narratives of the Passion* (Contemporary Studies in Theology 1; London 1962). V. TAYLOR, "The Narrative of the Crucifixion," NTSt 8 (1961–62) 333–334. M. JUDGE, *The Passion Narratives in the College Sacred Doctrine Courses* (Doctoral diss. microfilm; CUA 1963), bibliog. 267–280. **Illustration credits:** Courtesy of the Detroit Institute of Arts.

[M. JUDGE]

PASSION OF CHRIST, II (THEOLOGY OF)

The Passion of Christ is a term applied preeminently to those redemptive sufferings endured by Jesus from the *agony in the garden of Gethsemane until His death on Calvary. Strictly speaking, any receptive experience felt in Christ's body, soul, external senses, or internal faculties can be rightly called a *passion (ST 3a, 15.4). His very ability to be so receptive of painful experience is a human endowment enveloped in mystery and marvel. Yet God-man though He was, Christ could and did suffer. This article touches briefly on three areas of theological interest: (1) apparent hindrances to Christ's ability to suffer, (2) factual experience of suffering in Jesus, and (3) experiences incompatible with His holiness that are still to be "filled up" in His members (cf. Col 1.24).

Apparent Hindrances. Jesus Christ walked through this world as a pilgrim, yet all the while, as man, had the abiding delight of being already at home with His Father (ST 3a, 15.10). His human mind was beatified with a vision proper to heaven just as soon as Jesus was conceived in the womb of Mary. *See* JESUS CHRIST, III (SPECIAL QUESTIONS), 1.

As head of the redeemed human race His beatific knowledge extended into the inner secrets and intimate destiny of every man and woman in history (ST 3a, 10.2). He could never be unwittingly victimized by treachery or deceit. He could anticipate each word, scheme, and movement of His enemies. The very perfection of His knowledge ruled out such sufferings as fear of the unexpected or dread of failure (ST 3a, 15.7).

Rooted in holiness, His flesh was perfectly submissive to the reign of His mind (ST 3a, 15.2). No movement of uncontrolled passion could blur His vision of reality (*Comp. theol.* 232). The redundant overflow of His glorified soul should normally have inundated His still passible flesh with a glory of its own (*ibid.* 231). Such an overflow was forestalled by the divine will, whose design was that Christ should be a victim (ST 3a, 14.1 ad 2).

His human consciousness could never lose sight of that design. While capable of preoccupation with temporal affairs involving pain, this human consciousness of Jesus was still plunged in the beatifying and changeless truth of God. The Divine Person of Jesus, sole possessor of this human consciousness, was mysteriously both delighting in joy and suffering pain at the same time (*Quod.* 7.2.1).

Factual Experience. The Gospel narrative records the facts of Christ's bodily suffering: He sweated blood, was scourged, was crowned with thorns, and was crucified. The very delicacy of His flesh, its exquisite sensitivity to pain, predisposed Him for this role of victimhood. With vivid imagination and infused knowledge this role was lovingly embraced by Him even during the years of His infancy and boyhood.

In Gethsemane His internal sufferings were real enough to cause anguish issuing in a bloody sweat. Components of His agony included such human experiences as fear at the ensuing loss of beauty, honor, power, and well-being; instinctive dread of death; sorrow at the disloyalty of friends; sadness over the rejection of His own chosen people; and loathing at His sense of solidarity with a guilt-laden human race, which became in some mysterious oneness His own body (ST 3a, 46.6 and ad 4).

By bent of nature His human reason and human will recoiled from these contacts with redemptive pain. But His human will, informed by well-counseled judgment, produced in Him by His Father's gift of grace, made Him joyful in accepting the cup prepared for Him by the Father's love (ST 3a, 18.5). This divinely willed conflict between Christ's spontaneous judgment of natural instinct and His well-counseled judgment of sacrificial love was poignant enough to make Him naturally sorrowful even unto death (ST 3a, 18.6 and ad 3).

Experiences Incompatible with Christ's Holiness. There were some kinds of suffering that Jesus Christ could never experience personally (ST 3a, 14.4). Such suffering would be that which was simply incompatible with His perfection of knowledge, love, and grace. Although He could experience hunger, thirst, fatigue, and a certain amount of inner tension between flesh and spirit, He could never know the oppressiveness of sickness. He was never tortured by the humiliation of finding unruly passion in His own members. He could never be harassed by doubts about being pleasing to His Father. He could never be inordinately cast down over weaknesses in those whom He loved. Throughout His whole career Jesus never knew the gnawing anguish of indecision. His soul could never be racked by scruples. He was never asked to walk in the darkness of faith, plagued by uncertainty about His future. Jesus never had to struggle through a mist of vagueness to come to a clear idea or to solve a complex problem.

Yet all these sufferings, inseparable from ordinary human living, belong somehow to the sacrificial cup of Christ. All of them are meant to be imbued with the

Scenes from Christ's Passion in prints by Rem-   *People," etching, first state, 1655. (b) "The*
brandt van Rijn: (a) "Christ Presented to the   *Three Crosses," etching, fourth state, 1653.*

sacrificial love of the crucified Man-God. In Him and with Him and through Him they become the prolonged Passion of one mystic Christ who will love the Father from a cross until the end of time.

See also EXPIATION (IN THEOLOGY); JESUS CHRIST, III (SPECIAL QUESTIONS), 8; SACRIFICE OF THE CROSS; SATISFACTION OF CHRIST; REDEMPTION, ARTICLES ON.

Bibliography: DTC, Tables générales 2:2587–90, 2613–15, 2624, 2630–32, 2638. K. H. SCHELKLE, LexThK² 8:144–146. I. SOLANO, SacTheolSumma 3.1:581–750. THOMAS AQUINAS, ST 3a, 46–52. L. CHARDON, *The Cross of Jesus,* tr. R. T. MURPHY and J. THORNTON, 2 v. (St. Louis 1957–59). P. GALTIER, *L'Unité du Christ* (2d ed. Paris 1939). R. GUARDINI, *The Humanity of Christ,* tr. R. WALLS (New York 1964). P. R. RÉGAMEY, *The Cross and the Christian,* tr. A. BOUCHARD (St. Louis 1954). **Illustration credit:** National Gallery of Art, Washington, D.C., Rosenwald Collection.

[A. P. HENNESSY]

PASSION OF CHRIST, III (DEVOTION TO)

In the strict sense *devotion is an act of the will giving oneself with fervor to the service of God or divine cult. The Passion is the suffering both interior and exterior endured by Jesus Christ from the Last Supper until His death on the cross. Further, the earliest Latin use of the term *passio* refers to the entirety of the paschal mystery, and this includes the Resurrection and the Ascension, as well as the sufferings of Good Friday.

From apostolic times these events have been looked on as an integrated action on the part of the Savior of mankind and, aside from the actual NT Passion narratives, are generally mentioned as a whole in the writings of the early Church. Thus are they referred to in the Acts of the Apostles (1.3), where St. Luke wrote of Christ alive "after His Passion." St. Paul, using the same unification, preferred the personification in "Christ Crucified" (1 Cor 1.23) or the instrumentality in "the Cross" (Gal 6.14). St. Peter referred to the totality of His "sufferings" (1 Pt 2.21, 23) and exhorted his hearers to follow in Christ's steps. In the carrying out of this exhortation the lives and the martyrdom of the Apostles show the intensity of their devotion to to the service of God and His Son. But from the early Church, in a period close to the Passion, when the Second Coming was thought of as imminent, there is little literature specifically concerned with devotion to Christ's Passion, but rather a group of human, individual, joyous passions patterned on Christ's action and reported sometimes by the sufferers, sometimes by their pagan onlookers.

Moreover, there is also the hypothesis that the emphasis on the Resurrection rather than the suffering came about through the desire on the part of the Church to combat misunderstandings of the two natures of Christ that overemphasized His humanity. Special attention to the Passion sufferings may have been deliberately avoided in order to prevent adding to the imbalance.

From the East there came, on the one hand, most of the early heresies concerning Christ's nature, and on the other hand, outstanding devotion to Christ's Passion.

The Syrian Church, although lacking Rome's influence, had a certain aura because it was centered in the Holy Land and possessed the relics of the Passion, which

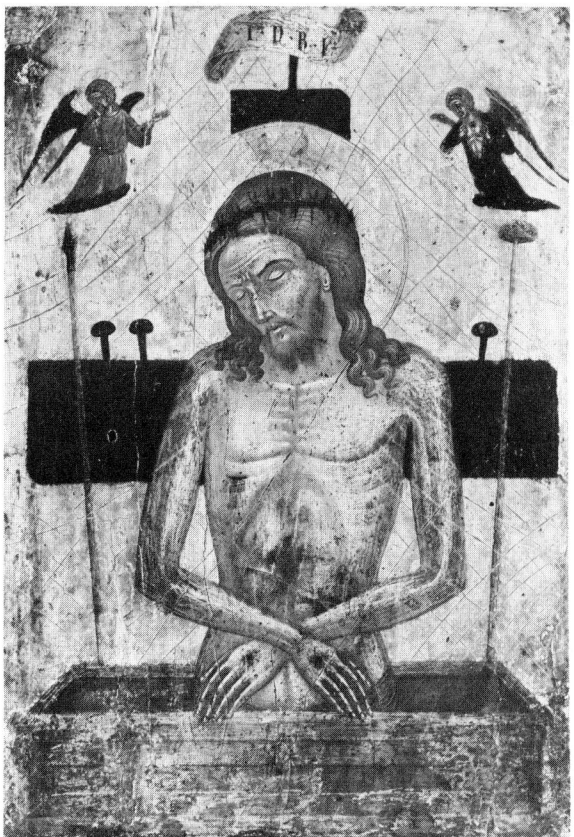

"The Mystical Sufferings of Christ," devotional picture of the Passion by a follower of the 14th-century Venetian artist Maestro Paolo.

it concealed and revealed in turn. The personalized and intense devotion to Christ's Passion that the Syrian Church nurtured was typified by St. Ignatius of Antioch, who, on his way to Rome to his own martyrdom, wrote in glowing terms of the triumph of Christ's Passion and Resurrection, "Him I seek who died on our behalf; Him I desire who rose again for our sake. . .. Permit me to be an imitator of the Passion of my God" (*Epist. ad Rom.* 4, 9).

St. Melito of Sardis (2d century), in a homily on the Passion, referred to the "Passover" and Christ in His mission to the world and His Resurrection, ending: "Listen while you tremble! He that suspended the earth was hanged up; He that fixed the heavens was fixed with nails; He that supported the earth was supported upon a tree; the Lord was exposed to ignominy with a naked body; God put to death!" [W. Cureton, *Spicilegium Syriacum* (London 1861) 55]. St. Ephraem—who used to interrupt his own sermons from time to time to exclaim, "Glory be to Him, how much He suffered!"—gives this vignette: "Let the heavens and earth stand awestruck to behold Him who swayeth the rod of fire, Himself smitten with scourges, to behold Him who spread over the earth the veil of the skies and who set fast the foundations of the mountains, who poised the earth over the waters and sent down the blazing lightning-flash, now beaten by wretches over a stone pillar that His own word had created" [T. J. Lamy, *S. Ephraemi Syri Hymni et Sermones* (4 v. Louvain 1882–1902) 1.511].

It was in Jerusalem, part of the Syrian Church, that the relics of the Passion were rediscovered; and in the 4th century the pilgrim Aetheria reported the veneration of the true cross on Good Friday and the reading of the Gospel of the Agony in Gethsemane during Holy Week. The veneration of the true cross was the precursor of adoration of the wood in the Good Friday liturgy.

Development in the West. In the period of the expansion of the Church from the 5th century, there are the teachings of the Fathers regarding the Passion. St. Augustine, bearing in mind Christ's tremendous sacrifice and the men for whom He died, prayed, "Look, O loving Father, on thy most loving Son suffering so many outrages for me: See, most loving Ruler, who it is that suffers and remember to be kind to him for whom He suffered. . .. Note His innocent hands dripping with holy blood and being placated forgive the sins which my hands have done" [*Meditationes S. Augustini* (pseudo.) ch. 6]. St. Anselm wrote: "I, myself am the wound of your sorrow, I am to blame for your murder. I have merited that you should die, I am the scourge of vengeance upon you. I am the real malice in your Passion, the real suffering in your Crucifixion" (*Meditations* 7). St. Bernard advised: "As much as we can,

let us love our wounded Lord, let us give love for love, and embrace Him whose hands and feet and side wicked ploughmen have furrowed" (*Omnia Opera S. Bern.* 3:3). These three quotations span 5 centuries. The Church passed from an age of persecution into one of missionary zeal and from a time of adult Baptism into one when infant Baptism was general. The necessity of replacing the catechesis of those who learned, accepted, and were baptized with one for those who were baptized and then learned and had to be led to acceptance produced a new emphasis on compassion, the actual feeling with the suffering of Christ. The development of a concept of sin as something that man must put off anew every day after baptism also contributed to the idea of a personal wounding of Christ by each man's sin.

St. Francis of Assisi introduced a new element into devotion to the Passion. Through the use of crib scenes and crucifixes, he began to bring to the people a human Christ with whom to suffer. Francis bore the signs of his own devotion to the Passion in the *stigmata, the wounds of Christ in man's flesh, of which Francis is the first known example. From Francis we have the invocation "We adore The, O Christ, and we bless The, because by Thy Holy Cross Thou hast redeemed the

"Meditation on the Passion," Christ of the Passion with St. Jerome and Job, tempera by Vittore Carpaccio, c. 1455.

world." St. Thomas Aquinas and St. Bonaventure excelled in their teachings concerning the dignity and effects of devotion to the Passion. All of this devotion was strengthened among the laity by the practices the Crusaders brought back from the Holy Land and by the instructive devices that mendicant preachers had developed, such as the *Way of the Cross, miracle plays, Passion tropes, hymns, prayers, and Books of Hours, replete with Passion references.

The Devotio Moderna, which is crystallized in the *Imitation of Christ,* and in a similar way the *Spiritual Exercises* of St. Ignatius of Loyola, stressed the Passion as a means of daily perfection, the support of every virtue, and the means to endure every affliction.

Among the outstanding missionary preachers who moved the masses by their emphasis on the Passion of Our Lord were SS. Vincent de Paul, John Eudes, Alphonsus Liguori, Paul of the Cross (who founded the Passionists), and Leonard of Port Maurice (who preached the Way of the Cross). The love of the crucified Christ was promoted by such pulpit orators of the 18th and 19th centuries as Bossuet, Bourdaloue, Fénelon, and Lacordaire. Through these periods there was a steady increase in the number and type of devotion accorded not only the Passion itself but also the individual phases and even the instruments of Christ's suffering. Among these subsidary devotions are numbered the cult of Holy Relics, reaffirmed by Vatican Council II, devotion to the Holy Infancy, the Holy Face, the Precious Blood, and the instruments of the Passion, as well as to the Sacred Hearts of Jesus and Mary and the Sorrows of Mary. Passion feasts and Offices also have developed, and the practices of the Holy Hour, the Three Hours Agony, and the Forty Hours devotion have become common.

The Mass and the Sacraments. St. Francis of Assisi was followed in the stigmata by many mystics of the Passion, and every age has produced new writers to develop the theme of Christ's Passion in ways pertinent to that age. In every age, however, it is the Mass that is the major source and the prime mover of devotion to the Passion. The Mass, as the perfect reenactment of all the events of Christ's Passion, His suffering, death, and Resurrection, forever present to man, is also the perfect act of devotion to those events for man. All the Sacraments commemorate the Passion, most especially, of course, the Holy Eucharist, but in Baptism man is called upon to be baptized "into Christ Jesus . . . into His death. For we were buried with Him by means of Baptism into death, in order that, just as Christ has risen from the dead . . . so we also may walk in newness of life" (Rom 6.3–5). In Confirmation we have become "the temple of the Holy Spirit . . . for you have been bought at a great price. Glorify God and bear Him in your body" (1 Cor 6.19–20). And in the other four Sacraments there are equal reminders that it is in Christ and His Church through the Passion in all its fullness that we receive the abundance of God's life. In a like manner the sacramentals of the Church, and in a special way the Sign of the Cross, draw efficacy from Christ's Passion. But it is the restored rites of Holy Week that have brought the Passion into prominence so that Christians may appreciate the words of Pope St. Leo I: "Our Lord's Passion is being continually reenacted until the end of the world; for just as, in the person of His saints, it is Christ Himself who is honored, it is Christ

Himself who is loved; just as in the person of His poor, it is Christ Himself who is fed and clothed, so, in the person of all who suffer wrongs for justice' sake, it is Christ Himself who suffers" (*Sermo* 7.5).

Bibliography: P. POURRAT, *Christian Spirituality,* tr. W. H. MITCHELL et al., 4 v. (New York 1922–27; Westminster, Md. 1953–55). M. J. OLLIVIER, *The Passion,* tr. E. LEAHY (Boston 1901). R. PLUS, *Folly of the Cross* (New York 1927). J. MEAD, *Hours of the Passion* (Milwaukee 1956). C. MARMION, *Christ in His Mysteries* (St. Louis 1926). J. DANIÉLOU, *The Bible and the Liturgy* (Notre Dame, Ind. 1956). F. X. DURRWELL, *The Resurrection: A Biblical Study,* tr. R. SHEED (New York 1960). W. F. HOGAN, *Christ's Redemptive Sacrifice* (Englewood Cliffs, N.J. 1963). J. A. JUNGMANN, *Pastoral Liturgy* (New York 1962). **Illustration credits:** Fig. 1, National Gallery of Ireland, Dublin. Fig. 2, The Metropolitan Museum of Art, Kennedy Fund, 1911.

[J. MEAD]

PASSION OF CHRIST, MUSIC OF, the chants used for singing the Passion—St. Matthew's on Palm (Second Passion) Sunday, St. Mark's on Tuesday in Holy Week, St. Luke's on Wednesday, and St. John's on Good Friday. They can be assigned to no particular mode, since they derive from early formulas for liturgical recitative, such as the simple tone for the Gospel. It was the custom, until the 15th century, to assign the chanting of the Passion to one singer, who used a middle register and moderate speed for the words of the Evangelist (narrator); a higher range and speed for the words of the Jews and other Gospel characters; and a lower, steadier voice for the words of Christ. MSS of the 9th century use the letters *t* (*tarde,* slowly) and *c* (*celeriter,* quickly) to distinguish the words of Christ from those of the Evangelist and *turba* (crowd); later sources add the letter *s* (*sursum*) to mark off the *turba* sections. A further development of these signs caused the transformation of *t* into a cross (†), while *s* stood for *synagoga* (*turba*) and *C* for *chronista*. Yet other MSS employ the musical abbreviations *a, t,* and *b,* for alto, tenor, and bass, showing that the chant was then divided among three voices of those ranges, a dramatic touch due partly to Franciscan influence.

The earliest mention of a polyphonic setting of the Passion is at Douai in 1438; *Binchois was commissioned to write *Des Passions en nouvelles manières.* These appear to be lost, although there are settings of the *turba* sections of a St. Matthew and a St. Luke Passion, both anonymous, in a MS written about 1440 (British Museum, Egerton 3307). This "new manner" of providing part of the Passion with harmonized music spread to France, Germany, Italy, and Spain. Sermisy, Walther, Asola, and Victoria wrote settings that long remained standard in their respective countries. Less familiar but of high artistic order are settings by Byrd, Davy, Guerrero, Villanueva, and Lasso. In many of these, the Passion tones are used as the tenor *cantus firmus,* and this is true also of the contemporaneous development of the so-called "motet-Passion," a polyphonic setting of the entire text. An early example by Longaval was for many years attributed to J. Obrecht; later settings include those by Maistre Jhan of Ferrara, Cipriano de Rore, Jacob Händl, and Lechner.

German composers of the baroque era, notably Schütz, Selle, Flor, and Theile, added instruments, extra texts, arioso, and chorus passages, so creating a new type of Passion, the "Passion-Oratorio." Eventually the Biblical texts were paraphrased in lyrical and often sentimental poetry (this had happened, too, in 16th-

Opening section of a three-part Passion according to St. Luke written in England at the middle of the 15th century (British Museum, MS Egerton 3307, fol. 20r).

century Italy) and set to music by Telemann, Mattheson, *Handel, and their lesser contemporaries. Bach's dignified and expressive Passions (St. John, St. Matthew) rely on the Biblical texts mainly, although arias and some choruses make use of poetry. Later paraphrases of the Passion were composed by Graun, Haydn, Beethoven, Spohr, Jommelli, Perosi, Dubois, and others.

Bibliography: B. SMALLMAN, *The Background of Passion Music* (London 1957). Reese MusR. Apel HDMus.

[D. STEVENS]

PASSION PLAYS

The Passion play was a genre of medieval religious drama, of relatively late and slow development, which concentrated on the suffering, death, and Resurrection of Christ, and was thus distinguished from the Corpus Christi cycles narrating the entire Biblical story from Creation to Judgment (*see* DRAMA, MEDIEVAL, 1).

Origins. A survey of the origins and primitive forms of Passion drama will reveal the liturgical background and the lyrical character of these cautious and tentative experiments and will disclose the pattern of the more elaborate plays staged in Germany and France during the late Middle Ages. The absence of any dramatic representation of Christ's death until the early 13th century, when all other types of liturgical play had long been performed, may very well mean a reluctance to imitate in a fictive manner the awesome mystery of Christ's sacrifice, especially since the Mass as the central act of the liturgy was itself the actual continuation of that sacrifice.

During the 12th century, however, the custom of chanting a long, lyrical *planctus,* or lament, of the

Blessed Virgin became attached to the Good Friday veneration of the cross. The latter ceremony already included the choral singing of the Savior's reproaches (the **Improperia*) and the uncovering of a veiled crucifix with the words "Ecce lignum crucis." A cleric would then stand before this cross and sing the lament of the Sorrowful Mother in stanzas of Latin verse marked by the literary and musical artistry characteristic of the great Sequences and hymns (*see* SEQUENCE). Some texts contained lines of reply in the voice of Christ or of St. John, and, as impersonation of these voices probably accompanied the chanting, real drama was present. Rubrics calling for solemn, stylized gestures eventually appeared (e.g., in the text from Cividale, Italy). Karl Young regarded such activity as genuine Passion drama. When incidents from Christ's trial, journey to Calvary, and Crucifixion were included in the plays of the 13th century, the *planctus* of Mary was structured into the complex design, the texts often using the two best known of the earlier lyrical compositions, the "Planctus ante nescia" and the "Flete, fideles animae."

Further Influences. Other formative influences on these plays have been suggested. One was the dramatic homily on the Passion, in which the preacher often came close to impersonation of characters through quoted speech and imitated gesture. Important, too, was the long narrative poem on the death of Christ, the most important being the so-called *Passion des jongleurs,* written *c.* 1200, which is said to underlie a whole group of Burgundian dramas of about a century later. The only extant texts of Passion plays in Latin, however, are the two in the Benediktbeuern MS from the 13th century, and their form suggests a development rather than by accretion to dramatic lyric, sermon, or narrative poem.

The first of these Benediktbeuern plays, the *Ludus breviter de Passione,* was meant to be followed by a Resurrection scene, as the rubric directs, and therefore can be regarded as a prologue to the Easter play. It covers the events from the Last Supper to the burial of Christ, but much of its action was left to be performed in pantomime, e.g., the nailing to the cross. Hardin Craig, who regards this short text as an expansion backward of an Easter play, believes also that the longer Passion dramatization in the same MS was built around an already existing and highly embellished play of Mary Magdalene and her brother Lazarus. Such a hypothesis about the origin of the Passion play in earlier liturgical drama rather than in any extrinsic source is supported by the difference in literary maturity between the prose of the Passion incidents (which often reads like mere stage direction) and the mature poetry of the Magdalene performance, some of it in Latin and some in German. Both of these Benediktbeuern plays reveal lyrical association, however, for they contain the *planctus Mariae,* the shorter text using the "Planctus ante nescia" and the longer one the "Flete, fideles animae." Although these texts from Germany are the only surviving ones, records of nonextant plays of the same nature are to be found in Siena, Padua, and Sulmona in Italy.

Vernacular Palys. The early vernacular Passion plays belong to the turn of the 14th century in both Germany and France. It is clear that this stage of development for the dramas on the death of Christ was reached more slowly than the parallel elaboration of the Christmas plays, which had probably achieved cyclic proportions in the 13th century. In any case, it is important to regard the Passion play as an integral unit separate from the Christmas plays and also from the Corpus Christi plays. The typical plan of the vernacular Passion drama is a threefold design: the Fall (of the angels and of man), the suffering of Christ, and finally the Resurrection. This plan omits virtually all of the Old Testament history except the original sin of Adam and Eve and ordinarily does not include the Nativity of the Savior. The life of Christ may be taken up at the beginning of His public ministry or at His triumphal entry into Jerusalem.

German Plays. The oldest surviving German Passion play is found in a St. Gall MS, undated but probably of the early 14th century. Its span of sacred history extends from the marriage feast of Cana to the Resurrection. Of comparable date is the Vienna play, which adds to the St. Gall pattern the narrative of Adam's Fall, thus presenting for the first time the triptych effect of the usual Passion play. Perhaps the most notable feature of the St. Gall text is the presence of a prologue in the voice of St. Augustine, a trace thus appearing of the famous Prophet plays, in which the Church Father summoned a procession of witnesses to the Messiah. This prophetic prologue was a common feature of the Christmas plays, but Creizenach regards the abridged form of it in the St. Gall text as an indication that it fulfilled the same function for the Passion plays. Au-

A page from the MS of the oldest surviving German Passion play (St. Gallen Codex 919, fol. 205v). The text includes the scene of the washing of the Apostles' feet.

gustine serves also as a commentator here, at times interrupting to give a brief outline of coming action and at other times to give a little homily based on a scene just concluded. After Christ washes the feet of the Disciples, for example, Augustine gives an exhortation to humility, and after the Crucifixion he offers a meditation on the sorrows of Mary.

The flowering of German Passion plays occurred in the 15th and 16th centuries, which witnessed the expansion of the texts to many thousands of lines and thus to an action requiring 3 days for performance. Among those surviving, two groups of plays call for special mention, the Frankfurt and the Tyrol texts.

The nucleus of the first group of plays is the so-called Frankfurt *Dirigierrolle*, that is, an outline or register of the characters, incidents, and cues for a Passion play. It reveals in skeletal form a very extensive undertaking, from a Prophet play to an Ascension scene, with an epilogue debate between the allegorical figures Ecclesia and Synagoga. This is a director's manual, but it is rich enough in detail to reveal indebtedness to a long narrative poem on the Redemption entitled *Die Erlösung* and to simpler plays of the St. Gall type. In its turn it has served as a point of departure for other Passion plays performed in the same general area, of which the best known are the Alsfeld and the Heidelberg texts. These come to us in MSS written shortly after 1500, and the latter in its present form is really a library version rather than an actors' copy. The great length of the scenes is due to the loquacity of the characters, which has grown immeasurably from the cryptic speeches in the early plays, and also to the lavish use of comic motifs.

The presence of buffoonery is quite marked in these southwestern German plays, notably in the scenes of merry devils, of Mary Magdalene's worldly life, and even of the counting out and quarreling over Judas's 30 silver coins. Allegory also is used, sparingly but effectively, e.g., in the Heidelberg personification of Death as summoner of Lazarus; Death boasts ironically of his unlimited power and then suffers humiliation in his defeat by Christ's miracle at Lazarus's tomb (Jn 11.1–46). Also noteworthy in this text is the juxtaposition of prefigurative scenes from the Old Testament immediately before the corresponding events of the New Testament related typologically to them. Thus the acquittal of Susanna by Daniel (Daniel ch. 13) is staged as a prelude to Christ's encounter with the woman taken in adultery (Jn 8.1–11). This method of structuring type and antitype in sacred history is not widespread in drama. The much later Oberammergau play has something akin to this arrangement in a series of *tableaux vivants* from prefigurative Old Testament events preceding each New Testament scene.

The Tyrol Passion plays from the eastern Alpine region are, like the Frankfurt group, related one to another and are presumed to have a common original. They are distinguished from other German specimens by a greater selectivity of incident and by a uniformly elevated tone. Omitting Old Testament material, they begin late in the life of the Redeemer, with the council of the Jews plotting His death. They cover a 3-day division of performance: the arrest and trials of Christ, the Crucifixion, and the Resurrection. On the first 2 days comic intrusion into the solemn scenes is virtually absent, but on the 3d day there is a notable amount of it. It is therefore highly probable that the first and second divisions were actually performed on Holy Thursday and Good Friday, when the buffoonery would have been regarded as unacceptable; the 3d day's action, given on Easter or shortly afterward, would have a context of returning joy capable of supporting the comic dimension.

French Plays. Passion plays on French soil reveal much the same history as do those in Germany. The early vernacular texts are of Burgundian provenance and are all related ultimately to the nondramatic narrative poem *Passion des jongleurs,* mentioned above. The oldest play in this group is called *La Passion du Palatinus.* Although it has many dramatic and interesting touches—such as the forging of the nails for the Crucifixion by the wife of the blacksmith, who himself refuses the odious task—this play is still clumsy and awkward in many ways. G. Cohen has even expressed doubt that it was actually performed, since it lacks rubrics that can be regarded as stage directions. There is a closely related *Passion d'Autun,* existing in two versions; and a much later and more elaborate *Passion de Semur* also is associated with the Burgundian area.

The really great French Passion plays are those of Eustache Mercadé and Arnoul Greban, both 15th-century dramatists, whose gigantic plays were subjected to revision and adaptation by later writers, most skilfully by Jean Michel. These French *mystères* show divergence from the standard German design; although they omit most of the Old Testament narrative, they do include the Nativity and early life of Christ. Moreover, they envelop the titanic serial narrative in a unifying framework known as the *Procès de Paradis,* quite different from the German forms of prophetic prologue and Augustinian commentary. The *Procès* is a dramatization of the debate among Righteousness, Mercy, Truth, and Peace at the throne of God, allegorizing the conflict between His justice and His mercy. The allegorized virtues, known in homiletic literature as the Four Daughters of God, are reconciled only when the Second Person of the Trinity undertakes to expiate man's sin; they reappear at intervals in the long cycle, most notably at the return of Christ to heaven, when Justice (Righteousness) at first sulks in a corner, but then in a dramatic and thrilling capitulation accepts the satisfaction made by the Redeemer.

Mercadé's *Passion d'Arras,* as it is called, surpasses Greban's in the theological profundity of its material but is in turn excelled by the latter's skill in poetry and music. The position held by Greban as organist and choirmaster at Notre Dame Cathedral in Paris developed in him the technical mastery that he displayed in versification, dialogue, lyric forms, and musical pieces. His *Passion* has been well termed a melodrama, not in the modern sense but in the original concept of a play rich in musical melody. Closely associated with this technical achievement and inseparable from it is Greban's mastery of emotional language, especially that of tenderness and pity. He could thus express in moving fashion the anguish of Christ in the Garden and His plea to the Father; above all he could imaginatively represent the role of the Sorrowful Mother pleading with her Son to evade the Passion and cross and then lamenting in her traditional *planctus Mariae* the actualization of her worst fears for His welfare.

Theater at Oberammergau during a performance of the Passion play; the scene is Christ's entry into Jerusalem.

Modern Survival. Performances of Passion plays continued long into modern times. One of the German dramas is still flourishing in a regular presentation at Oberammergau every 10th year. The origin of this custom is a well-known series of events related to the Thirty Years' War of the early 17th century. During the devastation of the Bavarian countryside by Swedish troops in 1632, a severe outbreak of the plague occurred, first in the lowlands, spreading gradually to the upland villages, including Oberammergau. After months of such disaster, the town council of this devout Catholic village decided upon a vow: they would sacrifice a year in every decade to the presentation of a Passion play. This promise was made by all the villagers for themselves and their descendants, as an act of penance and petition for deliverance; it is the Oberammergau tradition that no one died of the plague after this solemn religious act. The most famous actors to play the role of the "Christus" in the 20th century have been members of the Lang family, Anton and a distant relative, Alois.

From the 12th-century *planctus Mariae* and the simple Latin plays of the Benediktbeuern MS to the gigantic spectacles of the German and French cycles, the Pasison play has been a paraliturgical expression of popular devotion to the suffering of the Redeemer and has engaged the talents of innumerable craftsmen, poets, musicians, and actors, who have coveted an opportunity to take part in it by designing its scenes, singing in its chorus, or being chosen to act in the great role of the "Christus."

Bibliography: G. Cohen, *Le Théâtre en France au moyen âge* (rev. ed. Paris 1948). H. Craig, *English Religious Drama of the Middle Ages* (Oxford 1955). W. M. A. Creizenach, *Geschichte des neueren Dramas,* 5 v. (Halle 1893–1916; v.2, rev. ed. 1918). G. Frank, *The Medieval French Drama* (Oxford 1954). C. J. Stratman, *Bibliography of the Medieval Drama* (Berkeley 1954). K. Young, *The Drama of the Medieval Church,* 2 v. (Oxford 1933). E. H. Corathiel, *Oberammergau and Its Passion Play* (Westminster, Md. 1960). R. Froning, ed., *Das Drama des Mittelalters,* 3 v. (Stuttgart 1891–92). F. Mone, ed., *Schauspiele des Mittelalters* (Karlsruhe 1846). *Le Mystère de la Passion d'Arnoul Greban,* ed. G. Paris and G. Raynaud (Paris 1878). E. Roy, *Le Mystère de la Passion en France du XIVe au XVIe siècle,* 2 v. (Dijon 1903–04), still a classic, but corrected by later studies. J. E. Wackernell, *Altdeutsche Passionsspiele aus Tirol* (Graz 1897). **Illustration credits:** Fig. 1, Stiftsbibliothek, St. Gallen. Fig. 2, German Information Center, New York.

[E. C. DUNN]

PASSIONEI, DOMENICO

Cardinal, statesman, and man of letters; b. Fossombrone, Italy, Dec. 4, 1682; d. Camaldoli di Frascati, Italy, July 5, 1761. When 13 years old he attended the Clementine College at Rome, conducted by the *Somaschi. Under the guidance of his uncle Msgr. Guido Passionei he completed his studies with distinction and won the friendship of the scholars Antonio *Magliabechi and Giusto Fontanini and the Cardinals Henry *Noris and Tommaso Ferrari. Through them he was introduced to the *Maurists and the highest cultural circles. Family tradition more than vocation (so he writes in a letter to Cardinal Neri Corsini) initiated him into an ecclesiastical career, and he studied dogmatic theology and Church history under the direction of Giuseppe *Tommasi. Clement XI commissioned him to take the cardinal's hat to Ludovico Gualtieri, nuncio to France; Passionei remained in France from 1706 to 1708.

From his friends Jean *Mabillon, Bernard de *Montfaucon, Eusèbe Renaudot, and Cardinals Cesar d'Estrées and Louis Antoine de *Noailles, he learned a great love of books and with them he frequented the Abbey of Saint-Germain-des-Prés, which had become the meeting place of French intellectuals. His initiative and desire to excel annoyed Msgr. Agostino Cusani, the new nuncio to France. He was ordered to leave, and with resentment went first to Brussels, then to Holland, where he remained from 1708 to 1713. As the representative of Clement XI, he showed diplomatic skill at the Treaty of Utrecht (1713–14) and the Congress of Baden (1714), which ended the conflict between France and Spain over the Spanish succession. At Solette he presided at the renewal of the alliance between France and the Catholic Swiss cantons, and in 1715 he returned to Fossombrone.

Passionei became secretary of the Propagation of the Faith in 1720 and played a notable role in the conversion to Catholicism of the Protestant historian Johann Georg von Eckart. He was made bishop of Ephesus in partibus by Innocent XIII (1721) and sent to Switzerland as nuncio. Transferred to the nunciature of Vienna (1730), he became the friend of Eugene of Savoy; Prince Ludwig von Würtenburg, whom he converted to Catholicism; and the Venetian ambassador, Marco Foscarini. Later, in Rome, Foscarini stole from him the MSS Arcana Papatus of Paolo Sarpi and a dossier of Sarpi's letters. At Vienna Passionei tutored the daughters of Charles VI; he also blessed the marriage of Francis of Lorraine with Archduchess Maria Theresa of Austria. In 1738 he was appointed to the secretariate of briefs by Clement XII and created cardinal, first of S. Bernardo alle Terme and later of S. Lorenzo in Lucina. In 1755 Benedict XIV named him prefect of the Vatican Library. In the palace of the Consulta on the Quirinal Passionei amassed a rich private library of 40,000 volumes. After his death this library was bought by the Augustinians, and later added to the Angelica Library in Rome, except for about 6,000 volumes that made up the first nucleus of the Civic Library of Fossombrone (April 19, 1784). Among his writings are Universae philosophiae studia (Rome 1701) and Acta legationis helveticae ab anno 1723 ad annum 1729 (Zug 1729; 2d ed. Rome 1738).

Passionei remains a figure of controversy. He has been considered an enemy of the Jesuits because he rejected Molinism and probabilism; and because he opposed the beatification of Robert Bellarmine, but voted for that of Juan de Palafox. This antipathy is alleged as the chief cause of his failure to win the papal election in the conclave of 1758. He is also censured as a Roman Jansenist because of his association with scholars, themselves suspected of Jansenistic sympathies, who gathered at the "Hermitage" at Camaldoli da Frascati. Here he presided, seated beneath a portrait of Antoine Arnauld and holding the Lettres provinciales of Blaise Pascal. G. V. Vella calls him a bibliophile with "library kleptomania," who used his position as papal nuncio to visit monasteries with the intent of finding and receiving as gifts precious MSS and rare books. His critics seem in agreement, however, on his skills in his various diplomatic posts. Regarding his alleged Jansenistic sympathies, it can be said that Passionei shared the anti-Jesuitism of the transalpine Jansenists, but remained substantially orthodox in his theology and loyalty to Rome.

Bibliography: M. RIOLLET, Correspondance, 1724–1727 de Valbonnais avec Mgr. Passionei (Grenoble 1933). P. L. GALLETTI, Memorie per servir alla storia della vita del Card. Domenico Passionei (Rome 1762). F. M. TORRICELLI, comp., Antologia, 4 v. (Fossombrone, Italy 1842–46). A. VERNARECCI, Fossombrone dai tempi antichissimi ai nostri, 2 v. (Fossombrone 1907–14). E. ROSA, "La causa del ven. card. Bellarmino e l'opozione del card. Passionei," CivCatt 69 (1918) 2:336–346; "Carteggio inedito del card. de Tencin a Benedetto XIV intorno al ven. card. Bellarmino" ibid. 4:48–55; "Le Memorie della città di Fossombrone e il card. Domenico Passionei," ibid. 2: 254–261. M. COSTELBARCO-ALBANI, Della Somaglia, un grande bibliofilo del secolo XVIII (Florence 1937). E. DAMMIG, Il movimento giansenista a Roma nella seconda metà del secolo XVIII (Vatican City 1945). A. MERCATI, Note per la storia di alcune biblioteche romane nei secoli XVI–XIX (Vatican City 1952). G. V. VELLA, "L'abate Domenico Passionei e le sue missioni diplomatiche dal 1708–1716," Nuova Rivista Storica 33 (1949) 302–341; 34 (1950) 197–234; Il Passionei e la politica di Clemente XI, 1708–1716 (Biblioteca della Nuova Rivista Storica 19; Rome 1953). E. SGRECCIA, Il fondo card. Passionei della Biblioteca civica di Fossombrone (Fano, Italy 1963), extract from Studia Picena, v.31. B. MATTEUCCI, EncCatt 9:922–924.

[R. BELVEDERI]

PASSIONIST NUNS, Nuns of the Most Holy Cross and Passion of Our Lord Jesus Christ (CP), founded by St. *Paul of the Cross. The Saint wished to establish, along with the congregation he founded for men, an institute for religious women in a purely contemplative life centering on devotion to the Passion of Christ. It was the Costantini family of Corneto (now Tarquinia), Italy, who enabled Paul to realize his desires. Two brothers in that family offered to build the convent for the new institute, and one of their sisters, Faustina Gertrude, eventually became the first superior (1771–87) as Mother Mary of Jesus Crucified. The principal difficulty in the project lay in securing the approval of Rome. Not until 1770 did Clement XIV, a friend of Paul, approve the rule for nuns. The convent of Corneto, established May 3, 1771, was the only foundation during the first 100 years of the institute. In 1872 the second convent was founded at Mamers, France. Growth since then has been slow but steady. In 1964 there were 24 convents in Europe, South America, the U.S., and Japan, numbering more than 500 professed members. Pittsburgh, Pa., was the first U.S. foundation

(1910). Stemming directly or indirectly from the Pittsburgh foundation are convents at Scranton, Pa. (1926); Owensboro (1946) and Erlanger (1947) in Kentucky; Ellisville, Mo. (1947); and Hyogo-Ken, near Osaka, Japan (1957). The institute is of papal right and enjoys papal cloister. Each convent is independent and elects its own superiors, but is subject to the local ordinary as external superior. The religious are either choir nuns or lay sisters. Besides the three customary vows, they also take a fourth vow, to promote in the hearts of the faithful devotion to the Passion (a vow that gives its proper form to their life), and a fifth vow of strict enclosure. The schedule embraces work, recreation, mental prayer, and the Divine Office, part of which is said during the night hours. Fridays are set apart for meditation on the Passion. Women wishing to make retreats are admitted within the cloister. With the growth of the retreat movement such retreats have become a regular practice of the American convents of this congregation.

Bibliography: Gaétan du St. Nom de Marie, *St. Paul de la Croix et la fondation des Religieuses Passionistes* (Tirlemont, Belg. 1936).

[M. GOHMANN]

PASSIONIST SISTERS (CP), known also as Sisters of the Most Holy Cross and Passion of Our Lord Jesus Christ, a branch of the Passionist Congregation founded in 1720 by St. *Paul of the Cross. They were established in 1852 in Lancashire, England, by Gaudentius Rossi, CP, and Mother Mary Joseph Prout, CP. They adopted the Passionist Rule and made the conversion of England their special mission. A pontifical institute since 1875, the community has houses in England, Scotland, Ireland, Wales, Bulgaria, Chile, Africa, Argentina, Spain, and the U.S. There were more than 1,500 members in 1963, conducting hostels, schools, colleges, retreat houses, and hospitals and engaging in parish visitation and social work.

The foundations of the American province were laid in 1924 in the Diocese of Providence, R.I., by Mother Gonzaga. By 1963 the province had more than 100 professed sisters staffing the motherhouse and Mt. St. Joseph novitiate at Wakefield, R.I., as well as 1 high school, 5 junior high schools, 7 grammar schools, 2 kindergartens, 2 houses of retreat, 1 summer camp, and several catechetical centers throughout Rhode Island, Connecticut, New York, and Maryland.

Bibliography: Sister of the Cross and Passion, *Sisters of the Cross and Passion* (Dublin 1960).

[M. G. O'GRADY]

PASSIONISTS

An exempt clerical religious order professing simple perpetual vows and officially entitled the Congregation of the Discalced Clerics of the Most Holy Cross and Passion of Our Lord Jesus Christ (CP). Their habit is a black tunic and mantle with a leather belt and rosary. The heart-shaped emblem of the order, bearing the inscription *Jesu XPI Passio,* is worn on the tunic and mantle.

Origin. The Passionists were founded in Italy in 1720 by Paul Francis Danei (now St. *Paul of the Cross), who, at the age of 26, after a retreat of 40 days, wrote the rule and constitution of his order. The following year he took a vow to promote devotion to the Sacred Passion; this vow accounts for the order's distinct spirituality and its specific apostolate. In 1725 Benedict XIII permitted Danei to recruit members, but it was not until 1737 that the first foundation was completed on Monte Argentaro near Orbetello.

Papal approval was granted for the rule in 1741 and again in 1769, following two revisions to reduce some of the more extreme austerities. Then on Nov. 16, 1769, Clement XIV's bull *Supremi Apostolatus* lauded and sanctioned the Passionist congregation. Soon after, the pope entrusted to the perpetual custody of the Passionists the ancient Basilica of SS. John and Paul on the Coelian Hill in Rome, together with the monastery and extensive gardens, which became the motherhouse of the order. By the time of his death, Oct. 18, 1775, Paul of the Cross had established 12 houses, all in Italy. His followers numbered 114 priests and 62 brothers.

Spirituality. The spirituality of the institute is identical with that of its founder. The Cross dominated Paul's life; he desired to participate as intimately and absolutely as possible in the sufferings and death of the Redeemer to effect the complete transformation of his soul in God. The establishment of an institute whose members would perpetually carry out this program and bring its fruits to countless souls was the single object of all his labors. The rule and the way of life he bequeathed his followers aimed at removing every obstacle to this supreme participation in Christ's Passion and at providing every means to render it efficacious. Hence the spirit of the congregation, repeatedly emphasized in its official documents, is one of prayer, penance, and solitude.

Rule. The Rule of St. Paul of the Cross has had only two revisions in about 200 years. In 1917 a minor revision was occasioned by the new Code of Canon Law. The second was completed in 1958 after a study carried out according to the desires and norms of the Holy See. The rule and constitution were again given papal approval by John XXIII, in the brief *Salutiferos Cruciatus.*

The first chapter of the rule states:

> This Congregation has the same object in view which every Christian and more particularly every cleric ought to have, namely, to fulfill exactly the precepts of the divine law and in so far as his strength may permit and his particular state in life require, the evangelical counsels. . . . Since however one of the chief objects of our Congregation is not only to devote ourselves to prayer that we may be united to God by charity but also to lead others to do the same, instructing them in the best and easiest manner possible, those members who may be considered fit for so great a work should, as well during apostolic missions as other pious exercises, teach the people by word of mouth to meditate devoutly on the mysteries, suffering and death of our Lord Jesus Christ, from whom, as from a fountain, all our good proceeds.

Subsequent chapters treat of admission into the congregation, the manner of fulfilling the vows and promoting devotion to the Passion, the monastic life, the fulfilling of offices, and the government of the congregation. The importance of apostolic missionary life also is clearly delineated and emphasized.

The entire Divine Office is chanted daily. The night office (the chanting of Matins and Lauds after midnight) is required in the novitiate and in the houses of greater solitude. In the others, particularly in the houses of formal study, the night office is prescribed weekly and on certain specified feasts. Spiritual reading is made in common after Vespers; spiritual conferences are held weekly; each night before Compline the superior delivers any necessary corrections and admonishes the members to fulfill perfectly the duties of their state. The religious are required to fast and abstain every Wednesday, Friday, and Saturday. The discipline is taken thrice weekly and on certain other fixed days.

The order comprises postulants, novices, cleric students, brothers, and priests. The brothers receive special training extending from 5 to 7 years. They are responsible for the full maintenance of the monastery and are prepared for duty on the foreign missions. A unique aspect of the order is the status of the brothers, who share the common life on the same level as the professed priests. The vow of obedience is taken in the first place to the pope; then to the general, who exercises supreme command in the congregation; and then to the proper superiors of one's province. Only the major superiors are elected: the general for 12 years, the provincials for 6, their consultors for 6 and 3 years, respectively. Other superiors are appointed.

Apostolate. The decrees of the 36th general chapter (1952) clearly distinguish the two fields of apostolic work proper to the congregation. In Catholic regions the specific apostolate, which is primary and essential to the end of the institute, is the preaching of missions and retreats. Allied to it, but of secondary rank, are other works of the ministry such as devotional sermons and catechetical instructions, which may be engaged in only when the primary work suffers no detriment. They are to be carried out in such a manner as to cultivate devotion to the Sacred Passion and to turn souls away from sin. In infidel regions the conducting of foreign missions in the proper sense of the term is an apostolic activity proper to the order. Activities opposed to the end of the institute are those that would habitually interfere with the fulfillment of the regular monastic life and observance or prevent the accomplishment of the primary work.

History. For the first 35 years after the death of its founder, the order progressed slowly but steadily, with emphasis on the contemplative and penitential aspects of the life. The first crisis occurred in 1810, when for 4 years the congregation was forced underground by the Napoleonic suppression of religious corporations. Reestablished by Pius VII in 1814, it required several years to regain its vitality before considering any further expansion. Thus, before 1840 the order was restricted to Italy, where it had two provinces. The 60 following years, however, were years of expansion and growth during which houses were founded in 13 countries in Europe and America; 10 new provinces were formed; the mission in Bulgaria was expanded; and a mission to the Australian aborigines was undertaken. The membership rose from 371 in 1840 to 1,475 in 1905. The man credited for this new growth, Anthony Testa, was well prepared to direct the progress of the order. After 12 years as provincial of the important north Italian province, he reluctantly accepted the burdens of supreme moderator. As general he governed for 23 years (1839–62), and is regarded as the second founder. Bernard Silvestrelli guided the institute from 1875 until his death in 1911. His reputation for holiness and the favors obtained through his intercession led to the introduction

of his cause before the Holy See. In 1963 the total membership of the Passionists was about 4,100; there were 207 foundations, 19 provinces, 2 vice provinces, and one commissariate. Seventeen foreign missions were also under the direction of the order.

Bernard Mary Silvestrelli.

Outstanding Members. Besides St. Paul of the Cross two other members of the congregation have been canonized: St. Gabriel of the Sorrowful Virgin in 1920 and St. Vincent *Strambi in 1950. Fourteen other causes are in various degrees of advancement before the Holy See. Most notable are Ven. John Baptist Danei (d. 1765), brother of the founder; Ven. Dominic Barberi (d. 1849), who received John Henry Newman into the Church; Father Charles Houban of Mount Argus (d. 1893), Dublin, Ireland; Confrater Galileo Nicolini (d. 1897), a novice from northern Italy; Brother Isidore DeLoor (d. 1916), from the Holland province; Father Niceforo and the 27 martyrs of the Spanish Civil War (d. 1934). About 50 other religious were listed in the postulation archives by 1964, although their causes were not yet introduced. In England and Ireland, respectively, Paul Mary Pakenham (d. 1873) and George Ignatius Spencer (d. 1864) were both members of nobility; in Holland Leo Kierkels (d. 1958) was a former general and apostolic nuncio to India; in the U.S. James Kent *Stone (d. 1921) did outstanding work in the retreat movement.

Work in U.S. The Passionists established the first house of their order in the U.S. at Pittsburgh, Pa., in 1852 at the invitation of Bp. Michael O'Connor. In 1963 they had 29 monasteries in the U.S. and 1 in

Canada, numbering about 925 religious in 2 provinces: the eastern with the motherhouse at Union City, N.J., and the western with headquarters in Chicago, Ill. Among the foremost preachers in the country, Passion-

John Dominic Tarlattini, first provincial and associate founder of the Passionists in the U.S.

ists have pioneered in the retreat movement; they conduct retreats for priests and laity at all their monasteries. Until forced out by the Communists, they maintained a very large and prosperous mission in central China. They are engaged in Japan, the Philippines, and the West Indies, as well as among the Negroes in the southern U.S. They publish the *Sign,* a monthly magazine of national interest (1964 circulation 410,000), and produce a weekly radio program "The Hour of the Crucified."

Bibliography: F. Ward, *The Passionists* (New York 1923). E. Zoffoli, *I Passionisti, spiritualità-apostolato* (Rome 1955).
[C. J. Yuhaus]

PASSOVER, FEAST OF

From later Biblical times the Passover, formerly sometimes called the Pasch (Heb. *happesaḥ,* Gr. τὸ πάσχα), celebrated on the night of the 14th to the 15th of Nisan (March or April), has been the principal feast of the Jewish calendar. In the Bible it is combined with the Feast of Unleavened Bread, which is kept from the 15th to the 21st of Nisan. Passover commemorates the Israelites' *Exodus from Egypt and is observed with great solemnity as well as rejoicing. From the many Biblical references to it, both legislative and historical, no completely clear picture of its origin and evolution is apparent, but there is a widespread consensus of scholarly opinion.

The Sources. The OT texts that contain laws for the observance of the Passover are the passages in the ancient festival calendars of Ex 23.15; 34.18 (see also 34.25); Dt 16.1–8; Lv 23.5–8; Nm 28.16–25 (see also 9.9–14), besides Exodus ch. 12, which gives the feast a historical setting. Celebrations of the Passover are described or referred to in Nm 9.1–14; Jos 5.10–12; 4 Kgs 23.21–23 (see also 2 Chr 35.1–19); 2 Chr 30.1–27; Ezr 6.19–22. In addition to the principal OT texts, important witnesses to the antiquity of the feast are

found in a papyrus and two ostraca of the 5th century B.C. from the Jewish settlement at *Elephantine in Egypt. In the NT, the Passion narratives of all four Gospels mention details of the Passover. Moreover, the intertestamental *Book of Jubilees,* the writings of Philo Judaeus and Flavius Josephus, and other ancient works describe the feast. The Mishnah tractate *Pesaḥim* contains details of the later mode of observance.

Name. The OT derives the name *pesaḥ* from a Hebrew verb meaning to limp or to jump and hence to jump over or to pass over (e.g., Ex 12.27), referring to Yahweh's "passing over" the houses of the Israelites during the 10th *plague of Egypt. But this historical explanation is secondary, and it is not clear that the etymology in it is the original one. Attempts to derive the word from Akkadian or Egyptian roots have not won general acceptance.

In this article the name Passover will be understood to refer to the combined Feast of Passover and Unleavened Bread except where otherwise indicated.

Origin. The oldest Biblical allusions to the festival (Ex 23.15; 34.18) do not mention the name Passover but enjoin the keeping of the Feast of Unleavened Bread for 7 days in the spring month of Abib (the old name for Nisan). Since in the later texts this observance forms part of the Passover festival, it is generally held that two originally distinct feasts were combined into one. Probable origins of both can be reconstructed.

The Feast of Unleavened Bread or Feast of Azymes (Heb. *ḥag hammaṣṣôt,* Gr. ἡ ἑορτὴ τῶν ἀζύμων) was one of the three great agricultural pilgrimage feasts, along with the Hebrew Feasts of *Pentecost and *Booths (Tabernacles), that the Israelites, after their entry into the Promised Land, adopted from the Canaanites. It was celebrated at the beginning of the barley harvest but at no fixed date; the fact that it extended from Sabbath to Sabbath may have been an Israelite innovation. The avoidance of leaven was probably a symbol of the new beginning being made with the new harvest; nothing from the old year was to be retained when the new season began. Though the calendars give as the reason for the feast, "For in the month of Abib you came out of Egypt," this theme was not original; the Feast of Unleavened Bread, like the other *ḥaggîm,* or pilgrimage feasts, was originally a harvest festival. *See* UNLEAVENED BREAD (IN THE BIBLE).

Passover in the restricted sense appears in the oldest allusions as a sacrifice and sacrificial meal of quite different significance and background. A lamb was sacrificed on the evening of the full moon in the month later called Nisan, and its blood was spread around the doorframes of homes. The meat was roasted and consumed that night with bitter herbs and unleavened bread. Apparently the rite was conducted privately by families or small groups at home, although one cannot exclude the possibility that at some early epoch whole tribes gathered for it at local sanctuaries. In any event, it appears to be very ancient in the history of Israel, even though the oldest festival calendars do not mention it, perhaps because it was not at the time a public celebration.

Passover seems to be the spring festival of nomadic peoples when they sacrificed one of the firstlings of the flock in petition for an ensuing year of prosperity. Analogies for it have been pointed out among ancient and modern Arab tribes, and all of its details can be accounted for among the customs of a shepherd people. For example, the bitter herbs were a natural seasoning, the unleavened bread the normal fare of nomads, and the blood upon the doorframes an apotropaic rite, i.e., one performed to ward off evil spirits. The "destroyer" mentioned in Ex 12.23 is regarded as a trace of this last element. The Israelites had been seminomads prior to their settlement in Canaan, and they may have celebrated this feast even in Egypt before the Exodus. But sometime after that event they altered its meaning radically.

Evolution. The description of the "first Passover" in Exodus ch. 12 (a late text embodying several traditions) relates the familiar story of the slaughter of the firstborn of Egypt and the destroying angel's "passing over" of the Israelites as they feasted within their homes. Moses enjoins observing the feast and explains all its rites as growing out of and commemorating the events of that historic night. In this passage, the 7 days of Unleavened Bread are said to commemorate the going out of Egypt, and all references to either feast in the festival calendars make the same association. It is not a natural association, however, and the very probable origin of the feasts lies elsewhere. What is found in these texts is evidence of the process of historicizing by which the three great pilgrimage festivals of the Israelite year were invested with a role in reliving the drama of *salvation history. In the case of Unleavened Bread this process took place earlier than for Pentecost and Booths, since it is only for Unleavened Bread that the earliest calendars (i.e., those of the *Yahwist and the *Elohist) mention the historical connotation. How early the nomadic Passover was cast in the historical mold of Exodus ch. 12 it is impossible to say, but it is not unlikely that it happened in the time of Moses himself. The intervention in Israel's history portrayed as the Exodus may in fact have occurred at the spring sacrificial celebration.

One can be somewhat more precise in estimating the time when the feasts of Passover and Unleavened Bread were combined into one festival. This event is connected with the centralization of the Israelite cult under *Josia, King of Juda (c. 640–609 B.C.), that is reflected in the Deuteronomic tradition of the Pentateuch. Josia's Passover (4 Kgs 23.21–23; 2 Chr 35.1–19) is described as unique since the most ancient times, and the Deuteronomic ordinances (Dt 16.1–8) insist that the feast must be celebrated at the Jerusalem Temple. Josia had made the shepherd Passover a pilgrimage festival as well, and since it nearly coincided in time with the Feast of Unleavened Bread—and also in its connotations, the latter recalling the hardships of the Israelites' flight—the two were eventually held to be parts of one festival. Unleavened Bread thus received a specific date (Nisan 15–21), and although it could no longer be observed from Sabbath to Sabbath, the first and last days were still kept as days of rest from work.

That this combining of the feasts was preexilic is confirmed by the fact that they are joined in Ezechiel's ideal festival calendar (Ez 45.21). Several texts seem to suggest that the combining took place even earlier, but the evidence of the calendars must be preferred. The Passover of Josue (Jos 5.10–11) does not clearly mention the eating of unleavened bread as a festival rite; the account of King Ezechia's Passover (2 Chron-

icles ch. 30), purportedly celebrated at the Temple in the 2d month because it had not been done properly in Nisan, is probably not historical, at least in its details. The "Passover Papyrus" from Elephantine, which may be dated 419 B.C., confirms the union of the two feasts.

Ancient Rites. It is the passages of the Priestly tradition (see PRIESTLY WRITERS, PENTATEUCHAL), especially Ex 12.1–20, 43–49; Nm 28.16–25, that provide the most detailed picture of the Passover celebration. The rites began on the 10th day of the 1st month (with the year reckoned as beginning in spring) when the sacrificial victim was chosen, a spotless male lamb, 1-year old, for each family or group of families. In the early evening of the 14th day of the month the people assembled at the Temple, and the lambs were slaughtered; previously this had taken place privately at home or at local shrines. Immediately afterward, the blood of the *Passover lamb was daubed upon the doorposts and lintel of the house where the meal was to be consumed, in memory of the sign used to protect the Israelites in Egypt. The lamb was then roasted and had to be consumed that night, along with bitter herbs and unleavened bread, which recalled the haste and the rigors of the flight from Egypt. No bone of the sacrificial victim could be broken and no leftovers kept; all remains had to be burned by the next morning.

The participants were to eat the Passover meal "in haste," with loins girded, sandals on, and staff in hand, i.e., dressed for traveling in remembrance of the suddenness of Israel's departure from Egypt. All the members of the household participated in the meal, even slaves and strangers, provided they were circumcised. The observance was of obligation for all, and ritual uncleanness in certain circumstances or the fact of being on a journey did not excuse from it (Nm 9.9–13), although in general, later texts imply the need for ritual purity (e.g., Ezr 6.20–21).

For the following 7 days all were required to eat only unleavened bread and to be certain that no leaven was found in the home under penalty of being "cut off from Israel." The strictness of this obligation seems more a consequence of the agricultural origin of the custom than of the symbolic meaning attached to it. On the 1st and 7th days (i.e., the 15th and the 21st of Nisan) there was to be rest from work, an assembly at the Temple, and special sacrifices. In Lv 23.9–14 it was prescribed that "on the day after the sabbath" (an ambiguous dating that was to be the subject of controversy in later Judaism) a sheaf of the first fruits of the harvest should be waved before Yahweh (i.e., offered as a quasi sacrifice of the new harvest). Special sacrifices accompanied this ceremony, and from this day were calculated the 7 weeks to Pentecost.

At the time of the NT, Passover was observed according to the general lines of the Priestly tradition, with strict adherence to the Deuteronomic insistence that the sacrifice itself take place at the Temple; people brought their lambs to be killed and then returned home or to some nearby house to eat the ritual meal. The atmosphere of familial joy surrounding the feast had by that time been considerably heightened. In the Gospels themselves the Passover plays an important role, historically and symbolically, but the Synoptics and the Fourth Gospel disagree about whether or not the Last Supper was a paschal meal.

There is some evidence that the *Qumran community observed the feast, perhaps even quite independently of the Temple ritual and following their own calendar, which assigned the Passover annually to the same day of the week, Tuesday. After the destruction of the Temple at the fall of Jerusalem (A.D. 70), the sacrifice of the paschal lamb disappeared, along with all Temple rites, from the festival observance, and the rite for the Passover meal was embellished to preserve the symbolism of the feast. It is disputed whether this rite, to be described below, may not have come into existence even before the destruction of the Temple.

The slaughter of the Passover lamb survives even today in the practice of the Samaritan community centered about Nablus in the Hashemite Kingdom of Jordan. It is sometimes argued that, since the destruction of their temple on Mt. *Garizim (129 B.C.) did not destroy this ritual, the ritual must have been performed privately in a family festival and not merely as a temple sacrifice. Indeed, many aspects of the Samaritan Passover celebration recall what it must have been like in the time of the Israelite kingdom. In Samaritan usage, for example, the feasts of Passover and of Unleavened Bread are still regarded as separate.

Modern Passover Meal. The ritual paschal meal, held privately in the home and sometimes conducted for groups, especially of travelers away from home, is commonly called the Seder (Heb. *sēder,* order, arrangement). The present-day Seder is substantially the same as the ceremony outlined in the Mishnah (*Pes.* 10). The narrative text followed during the meal is called the Passover *Haggadah (story), and both terms Seder and Haggadah are used to designate the booklet containing text and ceremonies.

Two preliminary rites are closely linked with the Seder. One is the formal searching of the home on the night before Passover for any form of leaven or leavened food, which is set aside and later destroyed or given away. No leaven may remain in the home during the festival, and utensils used for leavened foods must be replaced or purified. The other preliminary ceremony is the so-called Fast of the Firstborn observed prior to the Passover meal.

A table set for the Seder contains the following special items: three cakes of unleavened bread (*maṣṣôt,*

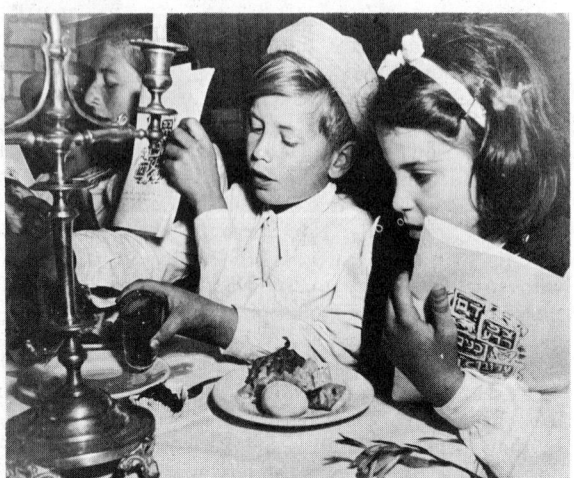

Jewish children celebrating the Passover Seder at a co-operative settlement in the State of Israel.

matzos) placed on a Seder dish and covered, a roasted shank bone symbolizing the paschal lamb, a roasted egg as an offering for the feast, bitter herbs (*mārôr,* usually horseradish), some parsley and salted water, a mixture of nuts and fruit (*ḥărōset*) used to sweeten the bitter herbs, enough wine for four cups each, and a cup at each place with an extra one for Elia (Elijah), who is expected to announce the redemption on Passover night.

The ceremony begins with the blessing (*qiddûš*) over the first cup of wine. Parsley dipped in water is eaten in memory of the hardships of the Israelites' life in Egypt. The master of the house breaks the middle cake of *maṣṣâ* and conceals half of it to be eaten at the end of the meal (the *'ăpîqômān*). Then the youngest one present asks the dramatic question, "Why is this night different from other nights?" There follow four specific questions regarding the unleavened bread, the bitter herbs, reclining on cushions, and eating parsley. In answer, the master of the house reads the main narrative of the Haggadah, recounting the events of the Exodus (fulfilling the command of Ex 13.8 to teach the children on Passover night). There are also several rabbinic explanations, including a commentary on Dt 26.5–8, "A wandering Aramean was my father . . .." The Hallel is then begun [Psalms 112(113)–113A(114)], the second cup is drunk with a blessing, and all wash their hands in preparation for the meal. This begins with handing around and eating first *maṣṣôt,* then bitter herbs dipped in *ḥărōset,* and these again served on pieces of unleavened bread. Then the main body of the meal is taken, and the *'ăpîqômān* is eaten last to retain the taste of *maṣṣâ.* Grace is said, and the third cup is drunk. Finally the Hallel is completed [Psalms 113B(115)–117(118)], the Great Hallel [Psalm 135(136)] sung, and the last cup taken with a blessing.

At various times and in various regions additions have been made to this basic structure. The most familiar of these is the addition in the Ashkenazic (German-Jewish rite) Seder of five medieval folk songs or poems at the end of the meal, including the *'Eḥād mî yôdēa'* (Who knows one?) and the *Ḥad gadyā'* (An only kid).

Bibliography: EncDictBibl 1746–51. H. HAAG, LexThK² 8: 133–137; DBSuppl 6:1120–49. S. ZEDDA, EncCatt 9:894–898. De Vaux AncIsr 484–493. E. G. HIRSCH, JewishEnc 9:548–556. T. H. GASTER, *Passover, Its History and Traditions* (New York 1949). J. B. SEGAL, *The Hebrew Passover from the Earliest Times to A.D 70* (London Oriental Series 12; London 1963), review in CathBiblQuart 26 (1964) 123–126. P. GRELOT, "Études sur le 'Papyrus Pascal' d'Éléphantine," VetTest 4 (1954) 349–384. C. W. ATKINSON, "The Ordinances of Passover-Unleavened Bread," AngThRev 44 (1962) 70–85. N. FÜGLISTER, *Die Heilsbedeutung des Pascha* (Studien zum Alten und Neuen Testament 8; Munich 1963). J. JEREMIAS, *Die Passahfeier der Samaritaner,* ZATWiss Beiheft 59 (Giessen 1932). "Pesahim," *The Mishnah,* tr. H. DANBY (Oxford 1933) 136–151. *The Haggadah,* tr. C. ROTH (London 1934). L. N. DEMBITZ, JewishEnc 11:142–147. A. Z. IDELSOHN, *Jewish Liturgy and Its Development* (New York 1932) 173–187.

[G. W. MAC RAE]

PASSOVER LAMB, the animal sacrificed annually at Passover and consumed in the ritual meal.

In the OT, the ancient Priestly law of Ex 12.3–10 probably reflects an earlier custom of sacrifice among shepherd peoples. The victim, taken from the flock, could be either a lamb or a kid, male, unblemished, and born within the preceding year, hence the first fruits representing the whole flock. It was to be separated from the flock in advance to mark it as a sacred victim set apart for the divinity. The animal was immolated by having its throat cut at twilight, then roasted whole over an open fire. None of its bones could be broken (Ex 12.46). Its flesh was consumed in a ritual *Passover meal during the night. Since Passover was a family feast, the sacrificial slaying was originally performed by the father of the family.

The Deuteronomic law, which transformed the Feast of *Passover into a pilgrimage feast, permitted the use of the young of oxen as well as of smaller animals (Dt 16.2), an updating resulting from the change from a pastoral to an agrarian economy. The ritual sacrifice thenceforth had to be performed at the Jerusalem Temple and was eventually assimilated to the regulations of Leviticus ch. 3 for communion sacrifices: the immolation could be performed only by priests, and the fat pieces were burned on the altar (2 Chr 35.10–14). The immolation was performed at sunset.

In NT times, the evening sacrifice was anticipated by an hour to provide time for the immolation of the lambs, which had to be completed by sunset. The owner of the lamb slew it himself, but the priests dashed the blood at the foot of the altar and burned the fat, to the sound of trumpets and the singing of the Hallel. Then each Israelite took his lamb home and roasted it whole on a spit made of pomegranate wood (Pesaḥim 5.1–7). Since the destruction of the Temple, the Jews celebrate Passover without the lamb; only the Samaritans retain the ancient usage.

The comparison of Jesus to the Passover lamb is the result of the reflection of the early Christian community upon the circumstances of His death at Passover. Paul is the first to express it, in 1 Cor 5.7: as the sacrifice of the lamb is a memorial of the deliverance from Egypt and in later times was regarded as expiatory, so Christ's sacrificial death at Passover has redeemed mankind from the slavery of sin. The theme occurs also in Jn 19.36, where the prohibition against breaking a bone is applied to Jesus on the cross, and also in the Johannine chronology, which places the Crucifixion on the *Preparation Day, when the lambs were sacrificed in the Temple.

See also LAMB OF GOD.

Bibliography: EncDictBibl 1751. J. BLINZLER, LexThK² 8:137. G. WALTHER, *Jesus, das Passalamm des Neuen Bundes* (Gütersloh 1950).

[C. J. PEIFER]

PASSOVER MEAL, ritual meal in which the *Passover lamb was consumed; celebrated annually in memory of the deliverance from Egypt.

In the Old Testament. Although part of the Priestly tradition, the legislation of Ex 12.1–14 is very ancient. After the ritual immolation, the victim was roasted whole and its flesh eaten by the members of the household, together with unleavened bread and bitter herbs, nothing remaining over until morning. The Israelites ate standing, with loins girded, wearing sandals, and with staff in hand. These customs, typical of nomadic sacrificial meals, were probably of pre-Mosaic origin; in the service of the Yahwist religion, they became a symbolic memorial of the deliverance from Egypt. The law of Dt 16.1–8 transformed Passover into a pilgrimage feast: the victims were slaughtered at the Temple, but the meal was still a family rite, and apparently re-

mained such during the postexilic period in spite of the emphasis upon its national character.

In New Testament Times. The principal source for the later Jewish Passover rite is the Mishnaic treatise *Pesaḥim;* but it must be used with caution, as the antiquity of its prescriptions cannot be determined with certainty. The lamb was immolated at the temple in the afternoon. Natural families were often replaced by artificial groupings, usually of 10 to 20 persons, though there could be as many as 100. The ancient custom of standing was abandoned in favor of the Hellenistic practice of reclining. The meal began with the first cup of wine, accompanied by two blessings, one for the feast and one for the cup. Then came the herbs and unleavened bread, dipped with the fingers into a sauce called *ḥărōset.* After the lamb was brought in, the symbolism of the rite was explained (Haggadah), the first part of the Hallel was sung [Ps 112–113A(113–114)], and the second cup drunk. Then the lamb was eaten with herbs and unleavened bread, and sometimes other dishes, and a third cup drunk, with thanksgiving to God for the meal. The rite ended with a fourth cup of wine and the singing of the rest of the Hallel [Ps 113B–117(115–118)].

The Synoptics represent the *Last Supper as a paschal meal; the disciples "prepare the Passover" (Mk 14.12–16; Mt 28.17–19; Lk 22.7–13), and in Lk 22.15 the Supper is explicitly called a Passover meal, though none of the Evangelists mentions the lamb. However, John places the Supper on the evening before the *Preparation Day, i.e., 24 hours before the Jews ate the Passover (Jn 13.1, 29; 18.28; 19.14, 31). This problem has received no completely satisfactory solution. Since it is now known that the *Qumran community had a different calendar, it is possible that Jesus celebrated the

Twentieth-century Samaritans eating the Passover meal on Mount Garizim in Palestine.

Passover on a different day than the official Jewish usage. He may have performed the paschal rite without using a lamb that had been ritually immolated in the Temple.

See also PASSOVER, FEAST OF.

Bibliography: EncDictBibl 1752. H. HAAG, LexThK² 8:133–137; DBSuppl 6:1120–49. Bonsirven TR 811–879. **Illustration credit:** Matson Photo Service, Los Angeles, Calif.

[C. J. PEIFER]

PASTERNAK, BORIS LEONIDOVICH

Russian poet; b. Moscow, Feb. 10, 1890; d. Peredelkino, a village near Moscow, May 30, 1960. Pasternak's father was a noted painter and an intimate friend of *Tolstoi; his mother was a talented concert pianist. He first studied music, then philosophy, at the University of Moscow and in Germany (1912–14), but finally turned to literature as a career. His first collection of poems (1914) was followed by *Sestra moĩa zhizn'* (1922, *My Sister, Life*), *Spektorsky* (1926), and *Vtoroe rozhdenie* (1932, *Second Birth*). Political hostility under Stalin forced him, an exile in his own country, to turn to translations, especially of Shakespeare, until 1943, when he published *Na rannikh poezdakh* (*On Early Trains*), followed by *Zemnoĭ prostor* (1945, *The Terrestrial Expanse*).

Pasternak unexpectedly received world attention and sympathy when his novel *Doctor Zhivago,* banned in the Soviet Union in 1956, was published without authorization in Italy (1957), the U.S. (1958), and soon after in other countries. Foreign reaction was one of surprise and critical acclaim. In October 1958, Pasternak was awarded the Nobel prize for literature. Soviet

Boris Leonidovich Pasternak.

literary officials immediately launched a campaign of vituperation and pressure against him: he was expelled from the Union of Soviet Writers and compelled to decline the honor, to give a public accounting of his behavior, to beg Premier Khrushchev for permission to live out his days in his beloved homeland, and again to remain silent. The Pasternak affair thus displayed before the world the harsh control exercised by the Soviet government over its art and artists. Pasternak became another Zhivago. (*See* SOCIALIST REALISM.)

Largely autobiographical, *Doctor Zhivago* is a total rejection on Christian and humanistic grounds of all systems, the Soviet system in particular, which degrade the free individual by a demand for unconditional conformity. Speaking through his characters, Pasternak maintains that the 1917 Bolshevik Revolution and the social system that grew out of it were tragic mistakes, because they violated the basic Christian principle of the primacy and inviolability of the person. He asserts that the central and highest point of history was the Incarnation of Christ, who revealed man's individual and immortal dignity that transcends the fates of nations, states, and systems. Inspired by the Gospels and the Byzantine liturgy, Pasternak uses them as symbols to unfold the meaning of man's passage through time. The dialectic of life-death-resurrection recurs symbolically throughout the novel. The story of Christ is the story of Zhivago and of everyman. The hero's poems, which form an appendix, are a legacy of pure religious inspiration.

Bibliography: *Sochinenia,* ed. G. STRUVE and B. FILIPOFF, 3 v. (Ann Arbor 1961); *The Poetry of Boris Pasternak, 1917–1959,* ed. and tr. G. REAVY (New York 1959); *Poems,* tr. E. M. KAYDEN (Ann Arbor 1959). R. CONQUEST, *The Pasternak Affair: Courage of Genius* (Philadelphia 1962). **Illustration credit:** Pantheon Books, Inc., New York City.

[W. J. MCBREARTY]

PASTERWITZ, GEORG VON, church composer, mathematics and physics professor; b. Bierhütten (near Passau), Germany, June 7, 1730 (baptized Robert); d. Kremsmünster, Austria, Jan. 26, 1803. He was the son of Andreas and Theresia (Mohr von Seneca und Mohrenberg) Pasterwitz. After receiving elementary schooling at the Benedictine abbey in Niederaltaich, Bavaria, he studied from 1745 at Kremsmünster Abbey in Austria. He was already composing quartets, trios, and songs; and when, after his Benedictine profession in 1750, he took further work in theology, law, mathematics, and languages at the University of Salzburg, he also studied music with J. E. *Eberlin. After ordination in 1755 he taught at the abbey school and from 1767 to 1783 directed the abbey's music, while creating an immense quantity of church music. When the abbey was dissolved as a consequence of *Josephinism, he was able to prevent liquidation of the school, but its musical activities were terminated, and Pasterwitz took parish work at Buchkirchen. After 10 years (1785–95) in Vienna, representing the interests of his abbey and teaching (F. X. Süssmayr, who completed Mozart's Requiem, was a pupil here), he returned to Kremsmünster as dean of the school. His compositions, numbering more than 300, include unpublished Masses, Requiems, motets, oratorios, Office settings, and school dramas, together with published fugues and organ interludes. His style is deeply influenced by that of *Palestrina, by Neapolitan vocal art, and after 1785, by Viennese classicism.

Bibliography: W. HAAS, *Georg Pasterwitz als Kirchenmusiker* (Doctoral diss. Vienna 1925). I. KOLLPACHER, MusGG 10:936–937. Riemann 2:1353. Eitner QuellLex 7:332–333. K. G. FELLERER, *Der Palestrinastil und seine Bedeutung in der vokalen Kirchenmusik* (Cologne 1928). A. KELLNER, *Musikgeschichte des Stiftes Kremsmünster* (Kassel 1956).

[F. HABERL]

PASTEUR, LOUIS

Father of bacteriology; b. Dôle, France, Dec. 27, 1822; d. near Saint-Cloud, Sept. 28, 1895. His father, a tanner, moved his young family to Arbois. There Louis received his primary and secondary education. He earned his *bachelier ès lettres* (1840) from the Royal College of Besançon, where he assisted in mathematics and physical science. Steady performance rather than brilliance characterized his student efforts. Pasteur's prime academic objective was admission to École Normale. Unimpressive examination scores, however, deterred him at first and he undertook additional preparation. While attending Dumas's lectures in chemistry at the Sorbonne, he became fascinated by the field and the teacher, thereby entering upon a lifelong attachment to both. In 1843 he gained admission to the École Normale and submerged himself in study. He became an ardent laboratory assistant to A. J. Balard. In 1848, for his doctoral dissertation, he presented a significant discovery, showing, on the basis of light rotation during transmission through its crystals, that racemic acid was made up of a mixture of two tartaric acids.

Successive stages in his academic career took Pasteur steadily upward: to Dijon as professor of physics (1848); to Strasbourg as professor of chemistry (1849); to Lille as professor and dean of the faculty of sciences (1854). Here he offered students what was to become his own success formula: "Live in the serene peace of laboratories and libraries." In 1859 he accepted the directorship of studies at the École Normale.

Pasteur married Mlle. Laurent, daughter of the rector of the University of Strasbourg. Pasteur was an indefatigable investigator, who, despite a partial paralysis suffered at the age of 46 (1868), continued his productive research until shortly before his death. He was politically conservative, devoted to the French Empire, and faithful to the Catholic religion. He maintained complete faith in his work and ideas, but became intellectually belligerent when challenged. His opponents were met by his meticulously performed experiments, planned and arranged on a base of irrefutable logic. Because of inherent and subtle anomalies, the outcome of battles, which sometimes went on for years, often rested upon the validity of techniques; he always won.

Fermentation and Silkworms. About 1854, at the request of Napoleon III, he investigated the failings of wine and vinegar processing. He soon identified microorganisms as the cause of fermentation, proved that different microbes produced diverse products, and showed that the qualities of wine and vinegar depend upon the metabolic activities of microbes. He further insisted that these microbes are transmitted through the atmosphere. Opposition to these principles led to much-publicized quarrels over spontaneous generation and involved such respected chemists as A. Pouchet and J. von Liebig. Pasteur declared against spontaneous generation in 1864 and executed sophisticated experiments to prove his thesis. Even after such prestigious figures as Claude *Bernard were convinced, certain other scientists retreated slowly and fought tenaciously for every traditional point. The Englishman J. Lister, seizing upon the idea of ubiquitous microbes, developed antiseptic surgery by utilizing carbolic acid. On several occasions he acknowledged his debt to Pasteur.

Louis Pasteur, after a painting by Albert Edelfelt, 1885.

The insistence of Dumas, as well as patriotic considerations, persuaded Pasteur to investigate the ravaging silkworm disease. France was losing her silk industry because something was sickening the silk moth's larvae. This unique and difficult problem was solved (1868) by the discovery and control of the offending protozoan, *Nosema*. Pasteur had again restored a segment of France's economy. During these and subsequent years honors poured in upon the dynamic genius. Industries, villages, agricultural districts, governments, scientific societies, and universities offered him praise and glory unusual in the lifetime of a scientist. In 1874 the French National Assembly voted him a life pension. The passing of time has not altered his position as one of the greatest scientists of the 19th century.

Theory of Immunization. His paralysis, endured for about 25 years, made one arm useless and impeded walking; but he completed several important research programs, any one of which would have immortalized him. After solving the silkworm problem, he returned to Paris (1868) and resumed the work on fermentation that was eventually to be worth millions of dollars to his country, but that, by his own choice, yielded him no monetary advantage. The War of 1870 made nationalism and its attendant economic competition even more acute. These considerations precipitated his classic paper on fermentation because of the international economic importance of wine and beer.

In 1877 he encountered another threat to France's security and honor—anthrax in sheep. By 1879 he had worked out its bacterial cause and in 1880 its preventive vaccine (from the Latin *vacca,* cow). Pasteur coined the word to honor Edward Jenner, who earlier had injected cowpox material to prevent smallpox. He dramatically defended his theories in an open-field demonstration. In the same year he determined the cause of chicken cholera. By attenuation, or weakening, of germs he made them instruments of prevention: pathogens, too weak to infect when introduced into a body, caused that body to resist deadly strains of the same species. He then turned to rabies, an invariably fatal disease. He located the causative agent in spinal tissue of the infected dog. After drying and storing the tissue (attenuation), he made an effective inoculant from it, and first employed it on a boy on July 6, 1885. World gratitude created, by public subscription, the Pasteur Institute—originally for the control and treatment of rabies. From 1889, until shortly before his death, Pasteur devoted his full time to directing it.

His complete works have been published in seven volumes (Paris, Masson). Some important works are: *Étude sur le vin* (Paris 1868) and *Études sur le vinaigre* (Paris 1866).

Bibliography: S. J. HOLMES, Louis Pasteur (Dover, New York 1961). R. VALLERY-RADOT, *The Life of Pasteur,* tr. R. L. DEVONSHIRE (New York 1937). **Illustration credit:** Courtesy of the National Library of Medicine.

[L. P. COONEN]

PASTOR, LUDWIG VON

Historian; b. Aachen, Jan. 31, 1854; d. Innsbruck, Sept. 30, 1928. Pastor is known as the "Historian of the Popes" and is remembered for his monumental history of the papacy from Martin V (1417) to Pius VI (1799). His use of the Vatican archives, in an age when methods of scientific research were greatly influencing historical exposition, made his study the first thoroughly documented history of the papacy, surpassing the works of Leopold von *Ranke and Mandell *Creighton. Born to a Lutheran father and a Catholic mother, Pastor was converted to Catholicism after his father's death (1864). Johannes *Janssen, famed Catholic historian, influenced Pastor in his youth, and he pursued his natural inclination for historical studies. As Janssen's protégé and friend, he received a solid education, graduating from a Gymnasium (1875) and studying at the universities of Louvain, Bonn, Berlin, and Vienna. He earned his

Ludwig von Pastor.

doctorate in history at the University of Graz (1878). Interested in Church history, he investigated various archives in Italy, and sought permission to inspect the secret papal archives, which had been open to scholars only on a limited basis before 1870 and closed thereafter. Pastor, determined to gain access to the undisclosed treasure of Vatican documents, wrote petitions and appealed to high-ranking churchmen. His persistence was rewarded (1879) with the granting of limited privileges. In 1883, however, Pope *Leo XIII unexpectedly removed all research restrictions for all scholars. At a special audience of historians, Leo XIII stated: "True history must be written from the original sources. . . . We have nothing to fear from the publication of these documents." To Pastor personally, who was then engaged in research on the papacy, the Pontiff said: "Owing to this decree [*Saepenumero considerantes*] you have a good advantage over Ranke. . . . The fact that many of these writings have never been used and some not even known, must increase the value of your work considerably. Naturally it will spread your fame as an historian." Pastor is generally credited with influencing this new Vatican policy.

He spent his remaining years engaged in research, writing, and teaching. As professor at the University of Innsbruck (1881–1901) Pastor became a popular teacher with an enthusiastic student following. He received numerous honorary degrees and decorations and was eventually raised to the rank of hereditary nobility by the Austrian Emperor. He was appointed director of the Austrian Historical Institute in Rome (1901) and Austrian ambassador to the Holy See (1920). Pastor died 8 weeks after the death of the other renowned Catholic historian of the popes, Msgr. Horace K. *Mann.

Pastor was a prolific writer of books and articles; his principal work was *History of the Popes from the Close of the Middle Ages* (16 v. 1886–1933; Eng. ed. 40 v. 1891–1953). This massive study aims at describing the forces of the Reformation era as reflected in the history of 55 popes. Pastor skillfully blended the inner life of the papacy with political and cultural tendencies. Certain interpretations and his criteria for selecting documents have been questioned by historians. Pastor's belief that only a Catholic can adequately understand and interpret the papacy has also been challenged. In general, however, the tone of his magnum opus is moderate and far from apologetic. That he provides a wealth of unused sources and presents an erudite, comprehensive account of the popes of the 15th through 18th centuries makes this study indispensable. His other major work is J. Janssen and L. Pastor, *Geschichte des deutschen Volkes* (8 v. 1893–1926), a cultural history of Germany during the Reformation begun by Janssen and completed by Pastor who wrote the last two volumes after his friend's death. Pastor also wrote a biography, *Johannes Janssen, ein Lebensbild* (1892), as well as biographies of others, e.g., August Reichensperger, Max von Gagern, and Viktor Dankl. Among his Church histories are *Die Korrespondenz des Kardinals Contarini während seiner deutschen Legation 1541* (1880), *Allgemeine Dekrete der Römischen Inquisition aus den Jahren 1555–1597* (1912), and *Katholische Reformatoren* (1924).

Bibliography: L. VON PASTOR, *Tagebücher, Briefe, Erinnerungen,* ed. W. WÜHR (Heidelberg 1950); autobiography in *Die Geschichtswissenschaft der Gegenwart in Selbstdarstellungen,* ed. S. STEINBERG, 2 v. (Leipzig 1925–26) 2:169–198. F. FELLNER, "Ludwig von Pastor," *Church Historians,* ed. P. GUILDAY (New York 1926) 373–415. J. W. THOMPSON and B. J. HOLM, *History of Historical Writing,* 2 v. (New York 1942) 2:546–549. **Illustration credit:** Bildarchiv Herder, Freiburg.

[J. T. COVERT]

PASTOR

The term "pastor" is defined in the Code of Canon Law as a priest or a moral person to whom there has been granted in title a parish with the care of souls that is to be exercised under the authority of the local ordinary (CIC c.451.1; ClerSanc c.489.1). When the pastor is a moral person (for example, a religious community), the law requires that a vicar, with all the rights and obligations of a personal pastor, be appointed for the actual ministration of the parish (CIC c.471). *See* PERSON, JURIDICAL (CANON LAW). This article, however, will treat only of the priest who is a pastor in his own name, since he is the one commonly designated by the term pastor.

History. In the first centuries of the Church, the bishop took direct charge of all the faithful committed to his care, and he personally presided over all sacred functions. As the numbers of the faithful increased, however, it became necessary for the bishop to share his responsibility with other members of the clergy. Conciliar legislation of the 4th century indicates that by that time chapels and oratories erected in rural areas had begun to enjoy a certain independence. Some of these chapels became known as baptismal churches because the priest in charge had the right to administer solemn Baptism. Thus for the first time there was established a relationship between the faithful in a definite locality and an individual church that was presided over by a priest. But it was not until the Council of Trent (1545–63) that the division of dioceses into distinct parishes with proper pastors was made universal (Sess. 24 de ref. c.13). The term "proper pastor" further adds to the notion of pastor the element of a stable, juridic relationship existing between the pastor and the faithful living within his parish. The basis of the relationship is the domicile or quasi-domicile of the parishioner within the parish limits (CIC c.94.1; ClerSanc c.22.1). *See* DOMICILE (CANON LAW).

Qualifications. Only a priest may be validly appointed pastor. The requisite qualities for the office are good moral character, learning, zeal, prudence, and all other qualifications which may be prescribed by the CIC or by particular law, especially diocesan regulations (CIC c.453; ClerSanc c.493). In order to act as pastor, a juridic act of investiture or taking possession of the parish is required. The manner in which this is done is left to diocesan law or custom. With regard to stability in office, a pastor may enjoy either removable or irremovable tenure. Irremovable tenure imports greater stability, but even this does not prevent removal from office under certain conditions (CIC c.454; ClerSanc c.494).

Functions. By virtue of his office, the pastor possesses ordinary jurisdiction. *See* JURISDICTION (CANON LAW). But he can exercise it fully only in the internal forum, that is, the area which concerns the private relations of the faithful with God. He cannot therefore make laws, pronounce judicial sentences, or punish with ecclesiastical penalties. However, he does enjoy a very limited jurisdiction in the external forum, that is, the area of public actions which have juridic effects. Thus, he can dispense from certain matrimonial impediments in case of emergency and from the laws regarding the observance of feast days and days of fast and abstinence (CIC cc.1044, 1045, 1245.1; ClerSanc cc.34,35).

In caring for the souls committed to him, the pastor also possesses what is called domestic power, that is, a certain disciplinary and administrative power by virtue of which he watches over his subjects as a good father and ministers to their spiritual and temporal needs. Specifically, he must celebrate the divine services (Mass, Vespers, Benediction of the Blessed Sacrament, etc.), administer the Sacraments as often as he is reasonably asked to do so, know his parishioners, correct the erring, show paternal charity to the poor and distressed, and instruct the young in Christian doctrine (CIC c.467.1; ClerSanc c.508.1). Sundays and feast days of obligation, at an hour which he judges best for good attendance, the pastor must also explain the catechism to the adults in language suited to their intelligence (CIC c.1332). On these same days he must also preach the customary homily to the faithful (CIC c.1344.1). *See* PREACHING, IV (CANON LAW OF).

As the shepherd of his flock, the pastor must exercise vigilance lest anything harmful to faith and morals be introduced into his parish; and he must promote works of charity, faith, and piety (CIC c.469; ClerSanc c.510). Non-Catholics in the parish are also commended to his care, and he has a general duty to strive for their conversion (CIC c.1350.1).

It is required by law that the pastor reside in the parish residence, which should be in the vicinity of the church. In the event of his absence, the needs of the parish must always be provided for by a priest substitute (CIC c.465; ClerSanc c.506).

From the very beginning of the parochial system pastors have been accorded by law special prerogatives in connection with their office. Certain parochial functions concerning the administration of the Sacraments and liturgical actions have become so reserved to the pastor that he has the exclusive right to perform them in his parish; no other priest may do so without his permission. Unless other provision is made by law, the functions so reserved to the pastor are the following:

1. To administer solemn Baptism
2. To carry the Blessed Sacrament publicly to the sick within his own parish
3. To carry the Blessed Sacrament as Viaticum, publicly or privately, to the sick, and to administer Extreme Unction to those in danger of death
4. To announce sacred ordinations and nuptial banns; to assist at marriages and to impart the nuptial blessing
5. To perform funeral services in accordance with canon 1216 (*see* FUNERAL)
6. To bless homes in accordance with the liturgical books on Holy Saturday or another day according to local custom
7. To bless the *baptismal font on Holy Saturday; to lead public processions outside the church; to bestow solemn blessings outside the church, unless the parish church is also a capitular church and the cathedral or collegiate chapter performs these functions (CIC c.462)

By general indult pastors also have the power to administer Confirmation to all persons, even infants, in their territory who are in danger of death from illness, if no bishop is available [S.C. Sacr. Decretum, ActApS (1946) 349–358].

The pastor also has the serious duty of keeping parish records. He is obliged to keep records of Baptisms, Confirmations, marriages, deaths, and the parish census. Copies of all these records, except the census, must be sent to the diocesan chancery at the end of each year. The pastor must also make use of a parish seal, maintain archives of the parish records, and preserve those letters of the bishop or other documents that are necessary or useful (CIC c.470; ClerSanc c.511).

Oriental Pastors. Pastors of the Oriental rites are governed by the provisions of the Code of Oriental Canon Law, especially the fourth part, which was promulgated by the motu proprio *Cleri sanctitati* (ActApS 49:433–603). In general, the rights and duties of pastors of the Oriental rite are similar to those of the Latin rite with certain minor differences. In Oriental Canon Law, there is no possibility of a moral person's being the pastor; only a physical person may be appointed a pastor (ClerSanc c.489). Among the functions reserved to pastors of Oriental rites, the following differ from those mentioned in canon 462 of the CIC: to confer Confirmation together with Baptism; to perform the solemn blessing of water on Epiphany or on another day, determined according to law; and to give other blessings or recite other prayers in accordance with the customs of the proper rite (ClerSanc c.503).

Bibliography: F. CLAEYS BOUUAERT, DDC 4:900–941. C. A. BACHOFEN, *The Pastor According to the New Code of Canon Law* (St. Louis 1924). J. J. COADY, *The Appointment of Pastors* (CUA CLS 52; Washington 1929). B. F. DEUTSCH, *Jurisdiction of Pastors in the External Forum* (CUA CLS 378; Washington 1957). L. G. FANFANI, *De iure parochorum ad normam Codicis iuris canonici* (Rome 1924). F. W. FREKING, *The Canonical Installation of Pastors* (CUA CLS 273; Washington 1948). J. F. HALE, *The Pastor of Burial* (CUA CLS 234; Washington 1949). B. M. KELLY, *The Functions Reserved to Pastors* (CUA CLS 250; Washington 1947). C. J. KOUDELKA, *Pastors: Their Rights and Duties According to the New Code of Canon Law* (CUA CLS 11; Washington 1921). M. WOJNAR, "The Code of Oriental Canon Law," *Jurist* 19 (1959) 458–461.

[B. M. KELLY]

PASTORAL EPISTLES

Three Pauline Epistles, 1 and 2 Timothy and Titus, that are commonly known by this term because they consist largely of instructions on Church government and discipline.

General Nature and Contents. In general, the two Epistles to Timothy and the one to Titus are directed, according to the Muratorian fragment, toward the "ordering of ecclesiastical discipline." These letters are, in fact, basically a series of practical directives for the proper pastoral care of the Christian communities at Ephesus and Crete. If one assumes that they were written by St. Paul (see below), it seems that the Apostle had entrusted the Church of Ephesus for a time to Timothy and had given temporary direction of the Christian community at Crete to Titus. Since these disciples of his faced serious problems, Paul instructed them concerning their struggle against certain false teachers, who were a danger to the Churches, and concerning the proper ecclesiastical *hierarchy. The Pastoral Epistles were not merely personal letters, but letters whose public reading was intended to teach the communities of Ephesus and Crete and to strengthen the position of Timothy and Titus as Paul's legates in the eyes of these Churches. These three letters form a natural unit, quite distinct from the other Pauline writings. They are united by form, language, and style, as well as by content and historical circumstances.

According to tradition, Paul was released from his Roman imprisonment of 61 to 63 [where the end of Acts (28.30–31) leaves him]. Thereafter, during a missionary journey in the East, Paul would have assigned Timothy and Titus their temporary posts at Ephesus and Crete respectively. The ecclesiastical conditions seen in the Pastoral Epistles would have required such a chronology. The letters presume a Church development more advanced than that of the so-called *Captivity Epistles, which are commonly believed to have been written by Paul during his Roman imprisonment of 61 to 63. Second Timothy was written apparently while Paul was a prisoner in Rome for the second time (2 Tm 1.8, 17). The difficult conditions of this confinement (2 Tm 2.9) prove that this was not the house arrest of 61 to 63 (Acts 28.30–31). Since Paul was convinced that death was near, the letter must have been composed about the year 67, the traditional date of his death, and was thus the last of the three Pastoral Epistles to be written. The other two Pastoral Epistles were written perhaps between 64 and 66 in Macedonia (1 Tm 1.3; Ti 3.12). The Pastoral Epistles develop principally two themes: the struggle against heresies and the organization of the Church. Apparently, the faithful of Ephesus and Crete are being troubled by false teachers, Christians of Jewish origin (1 Tm 1.3–7; Ti 1.10–14). The teachings of these men represent a Gnosticizing Judaism of the 1st century. An earlier letter of Paul to the *Colossians testifies to a similar Gnosis (Col 2.16; see GNOSIS, CHRISTIAN). In view of the dangers involved, Paul orders Timothy and Titus to combat these false teachers.

Paul also discusses in detail the organization of the Church. The community is still under his leadership. He directs it through his temporary legates, Timothy and Titus, who possess true episcopal power (1 Tm 5.22). Locally there is a council of priests, who receive power through the imposition of hands to rule and teach the Church (1 Tm 5.17–22). These men are helped in their work by *deacons (1 Tm 3.8–13), probably also by deaconesses (1 Tm 3.11), and by an ecclesiastical institution of widows (1 Tm 5.3–16). Paul lists the qualifications that must be demanded of these various classes.

Pauline Authorship. The principal question connected with the Pastoral Epistles is that of their authenticity. The letters explicitly claim to be the work of Paul. With one or two relatively insignificant exceptions, these letters were universally accepted as Paul's until the beginning of the 19th century. Since that time doubts and denials have continued to grow. Today many non-Catholic scholars take it as a fact that the Pastoral Epistles are spurious. Although some admit the presence of genuine fragments, the majority of non-Catholic scholars reject explicitly the authenticity of these letters for several reasons. First, their Pauline authorship is denied because more than one-third of the Epistles' words (305 out of 848) are not found elsewhere in Paul's works. This line of reasoning is questionable, since Romans, for instance, has almost the same proportion of *hapax legomena*—so that it is no longer a serious objection today against the Epistles' authenticity. Much more to the point is the fact that many typical expressions of Paul are absent from the Pastoral Epistles, e.g., the justice of God. On the other hand, words and phrases characteristic of the Pastoral Epistles are not found in Paul's other works; e.g., the word ἐπιφάνεια

St. Paul handing the Gospel to a youth, representing possibly either Titus or Timothy, miniature from a 14th-century manuscript, probably illuminated at Paris.

(coming) is preferred in the Pastoral Epistles to the usual Pauline παρουσία (coming). These letters show also a greater Hellenistic influence than Paul's earlier writings. Finally, their slow and smooth, yet often disconnected, style is far from Paul's usually vehement, vigorous manner. This argument based on language and style presents a serious problem for Pauline authorship, but not an insurmountable one. The Pastoral Epistles are unique in contents, and thus call for a different style and vocabulary. They are the notes of a pastor, giving practical directives to fellow pastors, who are involved in new problems. There is also the possibility that Paul used a scribe to whom he gave considerable freedom. Finally, the Greek Fathers, who discussed the authenticity of Hebrews because it differed in language and style from Paul's other works, never questioned the Pauline authorship of the Pastoral Epistles.

Second, the Church organization of the Pastoral Epistles is supposedly too developed for the time of Paul. The monarchical episcopate of these letters is that seen in the 2d-century writings of St. Ignatius of Antioch. A study of the letters, however, reveals that both Timothy and Titus, the only true bishops, possess neither permanence nor independence, two essential characteristics of the monarchical episcopate. This intermediate stage of development accords perfectly with the time of the Pastoral Letters. Appointment of bishops to represent the Apostle prepares for the monarchical bishop in the postapostolic era. Furthermore, the words *presbyter (priest) and *bishop in the Pastoral Epistles are still synonymous. Finally, the attention Paul gives to these offices indicates that they have not been long established at Ephesus and Crete.

Third, their Pauline authorship is denied since the errors attacked by Paul are said to belong to the 2d century. These may be, however, errors of Jewish *Gnosticism of the 1st century. Even earlier, similar errors were found at *Colossae in Asia Minor.

Fourth, the Pastoral Epistles supposedly lack Paul's originality. There is a non-Pauline emphasis on fixed doctrine, on good works. The circumstances of composition best answer this objection to Pauline authorship.

Recognizing that the Church is in serious danger because of innovators, Paul strongly stresses the traditional teaching, the deposit of faith, as the surest safeguard for the Church. Besides, a careful reading of the letters reveals typically Pauline doctrines, e.g., salvation by faith, not works (Ti 3.5), although the practical nature of these Epistles often put stress on good works. According to a decision of the *Pontifical Biblical Commission (June 12, 1913; EnchBibl⁴ 407–410), none of the arguments advanced are strong enough to overthrow the Christian tradition of the Pauline authorship of the Pastoral Epistles.

Occasion and Contents. The First Epistle to Timothy was written after Paul had left him at Ephesus to combat false teachers and to organize the Church. Paul wrote this letter because his own contemplated visit might be delayed (3.14; 4.13). Timothy, therefore, had the task of opposing the false teachers and of regulating Church discipline and organization (1.3–3.16); after Paul advised him how to combat doctrinal errors, he instructed him on discharging properly his duties toward various classes of persons in the Church (4.1–6.2); finally, he concluded with a warning against avarice and certain final counsels for Timothy (6.3–21).

The Epistle to Titus was written after Paul had left him at Crete to complete the organization of the Church (Ti 1.5). Writing from Macedonia, Paul told him to rejoin him at Nicopolis (3.12), where he hoped to spend the winter. After the introductory greeting, in which Paul discussed the dignity and authority of the apostolate, he advised Titus on the selection of worthy ministers and on the refutation of false teachers by sound doctrine (1.5–16); instructions were then provided on the duties of the different classes in the Church (2.1–3.8); Paul concluded with another warning against doctrinal errors (3.8–11), together with some personal advice to Titus (3.12–15).

In 2 Timothy, Paul appears as a lonely prisoner in Rome, expecting to be executed soon; he writes Timothy to join him quickly (4.9). This inspiring letter exhorts and encourages Timothy to sacrifice himself fearlessly for the gospel (1.1–2.13); advice is given on dealing with the false teachers (2.14–4.8); the letter concludes with Paul's urgent request that Timothy and Mark should come to Rome (4.9–22).

Bibliography: C. SPICQ, *Les Épîtres pastorales de saint Paul* (ÉtBibl; 1947). J. JEREMIAS, *Die Briefe an Timotheus und Titus* (Das N.T. Deutsch 9; 7th ed. Göttingen 1956). M. DIBELIUS, *Die Pastoralbriefe* (Hanbuch zum N.T. 13; 3d ed. H. CONZELMANN, Tübingen 1955). P. DORNIER, *Les Épîtres de saint Paul à Timothée et à Tite* (BJ; 2d ed. 1958). P. N. HARRISON, *The Problem of the Pastoral Epistles* (London 1921). Wikenhauser NTIntro 437–452. EncDictBibl 1753–58. J. SCHMID, LexThK² 8:155–158. W. SCHMITHALS and W. WERBECK, RGG³ 5:144–148. **Illustration credit:** Rare Book Department, Free Library of Philadelphia.

[R. KUEHNER]

PASTORAL LETTERS

Formal letters, doctrinal, devotional, or disciplinary in their purpose, written by a bishop for the faithful of his diocese. There are two types of pastoral letters—the individual pastoral, written by a bishop for his own diocese, and the group pastoral, written by several bishops together and intended for all their dioceses. Such are national pastorals issued occasionally by the bishops of an individual country. These latter should be distinguished from statements issued by national *episcopal conferences. Since they do not take the form of letters, such statements would not seem to be pastorals properly so-called.

Because the bishop within his diocese has governing powers analogous to those possessed by the pope over the entire Church, it is not surprising that he should exercise them in a similar manner. Thus it is that ordinaries exercise their pastoral ministry of teaching in many ways—individual sermons, outlines of sermon instructions, radio and television addresses, and the like. But perhaps the most solemn of all these forms is the pastoral letter. For it is in the pastoral that the bishop most fully exercises his function as "true shepherd," asserted by Vatican Council I (Denz 3061) and reasserted more amply by Vatican Council II [e.g., in the *Dogmatic Constitution on the Church* 18–20; Act ApS 57 (1965) 21–24], and as "true doctor or teacher," affirmed by canon 1326 of the Code of Canon Law.

Indeed, just as *encyclicals are today a common expression of the pope's ordinary magisterium, so too pastoral letters are the most common expression of the ordinary magisterium of the bishops throughout the world. Thus, pastorals are similar to encyclicals insofar as they are per se an expression of the Church's ordinary teaching authority. But they differ from encyclicals in several ways. First, they are ordinarily composed by bishops as directives for their own dioceses, whereas an encyclical, composed by the pope, is intended for the entire Church. Second, whereas an encyclical demands per se a true internal assent of the mind to doctrine proposed therein, an individual pastoral does not seem to impose such an obligation, even on all the faithful of the dioceses concerned. Of course, where it is clear that the ordinary is using the letter as a means of promulgating a precept for his diocese, the pastoral would demand obedience in disciplinary matters pertaining to the bishop's competence. But it remains to be said that even aside from the more general topic of episcopal collegiality discussed and affirmed during the Second Vatican Council, much remains to be written concerning the precise scope of the bishop's teaching authority within his own individual diocese.

See also BISHOP (IN THE CHURCH); TEACHING AUTHORITY OF THE CHURCH (MAGISTERIUM).

Bibliography: DTC, Tables générales 1:1199. L. HOFMANN, LexThK² 5:387–388. A. DE BOVIS, *What Is the Church?* tr. R. F. TREVETT (New York 1961). P. K. GUILDAY, ed., *The National Pastorals of the American Hierarchy, 1792–1919* (Washington 1923). K. RAHNER and J. RATZINGER, *The Episcopate and the Primacy*, tr. K. BARKER et al. (New York 1962).

[G. K. MALONE]

PASTORAL PSYCHOLOGY

Pastoral psychology presents the essential psychological data that underlie pastoral care and contribute to its effective practice. This article gives the definition of pastoral psychology, its relation to *pastoral theology, its subject matter, its techniques, and its goals.

Definition. Pastoral psychology is a branch of practical or applied psychology. The latter consists in the application of psychological data, methodology, and techniques to a particular group of people with a view to modifying their behavior in the direction of some accepted goal. In pastoral psychology, the group comprises those who come under the pastoral care of the priest, and the goal is to help them achieve a more adequate and mature spiritual life. Applied psychology is a scientific discipline that employs the experimental method in its approach to human behavior. Thus, in gathering its data, it relies upon empirical observation, controlled conditions, replication of findings, the use of representative samples, and a determination of the margin of error inherent in its procedures. In its service functions, it adopts a problem-solving attitude, developing a succession of tentative hypotheses, each hypothesis in turn being confirmed or disproved by the facts as they unfold in a specific case (see Anastasi).

Relation to Pastoral Theology. Pastoral theology consists in the application of dogmatic and moral theology to pastoral problems. It is a practical science concerned with the care of souls. This care is primarily of a spiritual nature and is exercised through the spiritual ministration of the priest. The duties of this office have been traditionally divided into those of teacher, of minister of the sacred mysteries, and of shepherd or pastor. The data gathered and the techniques developed by psychology are capable of making a contribution to pastoral care in each of these principal areas. Pastoral psychology is thus an ancillary discipline serving to provide more efficient and more effective pastoral care.

The contributions of pastoral psychology to the care of souls are twofold: increased understanding and techniques for helping. The emphasis is on understanding, so that an appropriate motto for pastoral psychology, after the model of the Good Shepherd, would be ". . . and I know mine . . .." (Jn 10.14).

Pastoral psychology emphasizes the personal nature of the relationship between the priest and his people, and applies to this relationship the extensive data that psychology has gathered with respect to human psychological development, the dynamics of human behavior, and the conscious aspirations and the less conscious motivations of men. These data combine to give the priest an increased understanding of the people entrusted to his spiritual care. The more fully he understands them, the more effectively he can minister to them: in his preaching, in his administration of the Sacraments (particularly the Sacrament of Penance), and in his individual spiritual guidance.

The increased understanding of people that psychology provides is a valuable asset to the priest in all areas of his pastoral ministry. It is essential if the priest is to help the psychologically troubled and disturbed parishioner, a certain number of whom are realistically to be expected in every parish. These are the cases that elude, and baffle, and frustrate the psychologically unenlightened pastor. One of the chief contributions of pastoral psychology is to offer at least a basic understanding of these conditions.

The second principal contribution of pastoral psychology to the care of souls is in terms of the techniques of helping which it provides. The help that pastoral psychology is competent to give is psychological help. Such help is in keeping with the personal relationship between the priest and the parishioner, which pastoral psychology emphasizes, and consists principally in guidance and counseling.

Subject Matter. Pastoral psychology does not have an independently developed body of scientific data. Rather it relies on the data accumulated in other areas of psychology to the extent to which these findings are relevant to pastoral care. For this reason, there are no clearly defined limits, nor is there any precise agreement as to what areas of psychology furnish relevant data for pastoral care. It is clear, however, that pastoral psychology draws on the psychology of the normal person on the one hand, and on abnormal psychology on the other.

The psychological data accumulated from the scientific study of the normal person furnish the principles that underlie the pastoral care of the ordinary individual. Here the contributions of a number of areas of psychology are pertinent. Foremost perhaps are the data provided by *developmental psychology. This branch of psychology deals with the characteristic behavior found at various ages or stages of development, and with the general principles that describe the course of development. It includes the psychologies of infancy, childhood, adolescence, maturity, and old age (see Geoghegan, et al.). Special consideration attaches to *personality development, and the data furnished in support of personality theories are often relevant to pastoral care (see McLaughlin). Hardly less pertinent to pastoral care are the data derived from a study of the dynamics of human behavior and *motivation (see Devlin). Finally, the findings of religious psychology, including the relationship between religion and personality, are pertinent to pastoral psychology (see Van Kaam).

*Abnormal psychology contributes data on behavior deviations (the neuroses and psychoses) and behavior deficiencies (character disorders, psychopathic personalities, and mental retardation). The pastor of souls must be able to recognize psychological disorder when he encounters it, because mental confusion, instability, and disorder interfere with spiritual well-being and religious practice, and are impervious to spiritual remedies (see Van der Veldt and Odenwald).

Techniques. It is of value for a priest to show an understanding of human personality in his sermons and to employ a psychological approach in his preaching. It is, however, particularly in his contact with his parishioners on an individual basis that the techniques provided by pastoral psychology are of assistance.

The help which pastoral psychology provides is in the form of techniques, developed largely by clinical, personnel, and counseling psychology, but appropriate for pastoral use. Two of these techniques, namely, interviewing and guidance, are appropriate for all individual contacts with parishioners, the other two, *counseling and referral, have relevance principally to the psychologically troubled parishioner.

Interviewing. The interview, which is "conversation with a purpose," is an important tool in implementing the personal nature of the relationship between the pastor and his people. This is undoubtedly the most extensively used technique in individual pastoral care. There are empirically developed principles of effective interviewing (see Bingham, Moore, and Gustad), and it is evident that these findings are relevant to the use of the interview in pastoral work.

Teaching is one of the chief functions of the priest, and guidance is an extension of this function to individual circumstances. It is individualized instruction. It is part of the responsibility of the priest as a spiritual guide to advise those under his care. Part of this duty he discharges in the confessional, the rest when his parishioners come to him for advice on an individual basis. This is one of the traditional functions of the priest as pastor of souls, and a role that his seminary training predisposes him to fulfill. The priest is an expert in religious and spritual matters, and when people come to him for help in these areas, it is natural that he should respond to their appeal for assistance by advising them as to the most appropriate course of action. If the advice given is based on an understanding of the individual and his problems, and if the individual accepts and follows the advice given, the pastor has succeeded in helping him. The wise and sympathetic pastor has helped his people greatly by functioning in this traditional way as a spiritual guide. Sometimes, however, those most in need of advice are least able to accept it, a fact which suggests that the priest must take another approach if he is to become effective in his efforts to help them. These are the people who need counseling rather than guidance, self-understanding rather than advice.

Counseling. Counseling derives from psychology and emphasizes the development of understanding rather than the imparting of information as does guidance. The understanding sought in counseling is self-understanding, or insight on the part of the counselee, which the priest uses counseling techniques to develop. It is evident that counseling is a more subtle, sophisticated, time-consuming process than is the imparting of advice. It is essential, however, if certain members of the flock of Christ are to be helped (see Cavanagh).

Pastoral counseling lies at the heart of pastoral psychology and represents the most extensive effort on the part of the pastor of souls to use psychological means in his pastoral work. As soon as the pastor refrains from offering solutions to the problems brought to him by his parishioners and renounces the imparting of advice in favor of an attempt to bring people to understand themselves, he begins to adopt what is essentially a counseling approach. This attitude and this approach can be recommended to all pastors of souls. If, however, the priest becomes a formal counselor, he enters upon a field in which some fundamental training is necessary, because counseling is both a science and an art. Considerable research has gone into the study of the techniques of counseling (see Harms; Tyler), and the priest who would employ counseling in his pastoral work should have a good acquaintance with these principles and have supervised training in the development of these techniques.

The pastoral counselor should limit himself to the problems of normal people, who are not obviously neurotic, much less psychotic, but who yet have problems which require a psychological approach for their alleviation. Emotional problems that are realistically related to the circumstances of life, such as illness, the death of a loved one, adolescent problems, marital adjustment, and the like, are the domain of the pastoral counselor, especially when they have religious overtones. The pastoral counselor, applying counseling as an adjunct to his pastoral work, always remains a counselor, and does not attempt to function as a psychotherapist.

*Psychotherapy is the general method of treating *mental disorders employed by *psychiatry. It is, therefore, the domain of the psychiatrist and to a lesser extent that of the clinical psychologist, and by no means that of the pastoral counselor. When the pastor of souls encounters a parishioner in need of psychotherapy he refrains from trying to help him directly, because such help is beyond his technical competence, but he helps him indirectly by referring him to a suitable psychotherapist. This indeed is help, and it may be help which only the priest can give, because only he can persuade the troubled parishioner to accept the psychotherapy he needs.

Goals. Even though pastoral psychology does not have an independently gathered body of scientific data or independently developed techniques, it does have goals which are specifically its own, and different from those of any other branch of psychology. The goals of pastoral psychology are the same as those of pastoral theology, namely, to aid the individual in attaining his eternal salvation.

The goals of pastoral psychology in general may be illustrated by the specific example of the goals of pastoral counseling. The latter combines counseling with pastoral aims, so that two goals may be distinguished, a proximate and an ultimate goal. Its proximate goal, which is psychological, pastoral counseling shares in common with other types of counseling, namely, by relieving the counselee of his conflicts and inhibitions to make it possible for him to live his life in a free, mature, and responsible manner. The ultimate goal, which is spiritual, is to bring the individual in this way closer to God and to the attainment of his eternal salvation. The proximate goal is the only one which pastoral psychology is able directly to contribute, but this goal, once attained, facilitates the attainment of the ultimate goal. The actual attainment of the ultimate goal (eternal salvation) rests, however, with the individual who remains free to accept God's plan for his life and eternal destiny or to reject it. What pastoral psychology does is to render man more capable of freely making this fundamental life decision.

See also DIRECTION, SPIRITUAL; SPIRITUAL LIFE AND MENTAL HEALTH.

Bibliography: A. ANASTASI, *Fields of Applied Psychology* (New York 1964). B. GEOGHEGAN et al., *Developmental Psychology* (Milwaukee 1963). B. MCLAUGHLIN, *Nature, Grace and Religious Development* (Westminster, Md. 1964). W. J. DEVLIN, *Psycho-dynamics of Personality Development* (New York 1965). A. L. VAN KAAM, *Religion and Personality* (Englewood Cliffs, N.J. 1964). J. H. VAN DER VELDT and R. P. ODENWALD, *Psychiatry and Catholicism* (2d ed. New York 1957). W. V. D. BINGHAM et al., *How to Interview* (4th rev. ed. New York 1959). J. R. CAVANAGH, *Fundamental Pastoral Counseling* (Milwaukee 1962). E. HARMS and P. SCHREIBER, eds., *Handbook of Counseling Techniques* (New York 1963). L. E. TYLER, *The Work of the Counselor* (2d ed. New York 1961). E. E. BRUDER, *Ministering to Deeply Troubled People* (Englewood Cliffs, N.J. 1963). R. L. DICKS, *Principles and Practices of Pastoral Care* (Englewood Cliffs, N.J. 1963). A. GODIN, *The Pastor as Counselor*, tr. B. PHILLIPS (New York 1965). G. HAGMAIER and R. W. GLEASON, *Counseling the Catholic: Modern Techniques and Emotional Conflicts* (New York 1959). R. HOSTIE, *Le Dialogue Pastoral* (Bruges 1963). W. E. OATES, *An Introduction to Pastoral Counseling* (Nashville 1959). A. SNOECK, *Confession and Pastoral Psychology*, tr. T. ZUYDWIJK (Westminster, Md. 1961). Pastoral Psychology Ser. ed. W. C. BIER (Fordham U. Press) 4 v. to 1965. *Pastoral Psychology* (Great Neck, N.Y. 1950–).

[W. C. BIER]

PASTORAL THEOLOGY

The general designation for the science of the care of souls. The subject is treated here under these headings: notion, necessity and importance, history, sources, and content.

Notion. The term pastoral derives from the Latin *pastor,* meaning shepherd, and thus suggests the work of a shepherd with his sheep. Hence pastoral theology is defined as a science that discusses the duties, obligations, and opportunities of the priest in care of souls and proposes the means of success in his work. Like moral and ascetical theology, it is a practical science as distinct from purely speculative theology. Still it includes in some measure all theological sciences insofar as all have for their ultimate purpose the salvation of souls and all aim to make priests fit "servants of Christ and stewards of the mysteries of God" (1 Cor 4.1). The object of pastoral theology is to demonstrate how the various sacred sciences and related subjects may be used efficaciously for the salvation of souls. Its immediate end is to assure that "the man of God may be perfect and equipped for every good work" (2 Tm 3.17); its ultimate end is to direct souls to eternal salvation. Its more immediate purpose is to state and explain principles that direct the priest in discharging the duties of pastoral life and to offer guide lines for the successful fulfillment of his office. It provides techniques calculated to make abstract and theoretical principles productive of spiritual good.

Pastoral theology presupposes and borrows from other sacred sciences; yet it is not identified with any. It includes all, yet is distinct from all; what other branches of theology speculatively teach about the threefold function of teaching, ruling, and sanctifying pastoral applies concretely and effectively to the daily ministry of the priest. Dogma establishes and discusses scientifically the doctrinal basis of Catholic faith in God; pastoral establishes a new dimension of application and action called for by revealed truth. *Moral theology explains moral precepts and establishes duties; pastoral emphasizes their pertinence to daily life. Canon Law is concerned with duties and obligations insofar as they are enforceable in the external forum; pastoral teaches not merely what must be done but what can be done and indicates the means of doing it. *Liturgy discusses the theory and practice of public worship; pastoral suggests methods of making it more effective and more sanctifying. *Casuistry determines what is to be done or left undone and the existence and extent of guilt; pastoral goes beyond the limits of *probabilism to define not only what is obligatory but what is becoming to the true follower of Christ, and seeks to persuade people to live a truly Christlike life, to give more than the required minimum. Pastoral, though distinct from *spiritual theology, the science of Christian perfection, employs ascetical principles to exhort and direct those who are capable of the higher reaches of the spiritual life.

Necessity and Importance. From the notion of pastoral its necessity and importance are obvious. *Ars artium regimen animarum* (St. Gregory the Great, *De Cura Past.*, 1.1). The Code of Canon Law prescribes that lectures on pastoral theology shall also be given in the seminary with practical exercises on the method of teaching catechism to children and others, hearing confessions, visiting the sick, and assisting the dying (CIC c.1365). Pope Pius XII added to this prescription the injunction that pastoral theology "must be emphasized" in the seminary because it deals directly with souls. To this end he prescribed a year of pastoral apprenticeship under the care of skilled teachers and ordered that the philosophical and theological courses be properly geared to pastoral work. This "pastoral year" is obligatory among religious institutes (apostolic constitution *Sedes sapientiae;* ActApS 48:354). An apostolic constitution of June 3, 1958 (ActApS 50: 460), established the Pontifical Pastoral Institute at the Lateran Athenaeum in Rome and declared that its program of study was to be recognized as contributory to academic degrees, including the doctorate in sacred theology.

The method of studying and teaching pastoral theology is both formal and informal. It is formally taught and learned as a distinct science in the seminary curriculum; usually it is reserved for the last year, when the student has already had most of the speculative principles. Informally it is learned and taught in the study of the other theological subjects, most of which are pastorally oriented and in which theoretical doctrine ends with a practical application to life. It is stressed in books of spiritual reading, in spiritual lectures, and in meditation books as used by priests. In many seminaries the study is supplemented by practical exercises in teaching catechism, visiting the sick, preaching, and census taking.

History. Pastoral theology began with the establishment of the Church and its redemptive mission. Christ imparted definite pastoral instructions to His disciples: "Those twelve Jesus sent forth having instructed them thus . . ." (Mt 10.5). "Now after this the Lord appointed seventy-two others and he sent them before him, two by two, into every town and place where he himself was about to come" (Lk 10.1). "And he instructed them" (Mk 6.8). St. Paul in his Pastoral Epistles traces out detailed lines to guide Timothy, Titus, and their coworkers in ruling and sanctifying their Christian converts.

Patristic Period. As the Church grew and spread territorially, it had to face new and intricate problems; to aid in their solution instructions of a pastoral and practical nature were issued by popes, bishops, and Fathers. St. Ignatius of Antioch in his letter to Polycarp reminded him of a bishop's duty to care for the sheep of his flock, to be vigilant for their spiritual and temporal welfare, to defend them and stand steadfast against heretics, to cultivate charity as the principle of union. St. Cyprian directed his clergy on their everyday conduct; he issued norms concerning the *lapsi* and for the administration of the Sacraments, especially of Penance. The *Didascalia Apostolorum,* a faint first attempt to form a code of ecclesiastical law, is a collection of moral and disciplinary norms and an enumeration of the duties of the hierarchy. It imitated an earlier Didache, which compiled moral, liturgical, and disciplinary rules. References to pastoral instruction are found *passim* in the works of St. Clement of Rome (Epistle to the Corinthians), of Polycarp (Epistle to the Philippians), and of Tertullian. St. Gregory of Nazianzus enumerated the qualifications of the pastor of souls in his *Oratio apologetica de fuga sua,* called also *De sacerdotio* (PG 35:407). He is credited with originating the phrase *Ars quaedam artium et scientia scientiarum mihi esse videtur hominem regere.* St. Ambrose, whose active episcopate was his best contribution to pastoral theology, described in his *De officiis ministrorum* (PL 16:25) the characteristics of the responsible cleric. St. Jerome in his letters (e.g., to

Nepotian, Rusticus, Heliodorus) commented on the life of the active priest. St. Augustine contributed his *De doctrina christiana, de moribus clericorum,* and *De catechizandis rudibus.* St. John Chrysostom's masterpiece, *De sacerdotio* (PG:68.387), was the first work of a truly pastoral nature; it defines the priest's mission and the requirements for it, offers practical and wise advice on preaching, on the exterior ministry, and on relations with other people.

St. Gregory the Great. However, the richest of the patristic contributions is the *Regulae pastoralis vitae* of St. Gregory the Great (PL 77.13). In four books he detailed a complete program of life for the good pastor, outlining the character, motives, and virtues of the director of souls; giving direction for teaching doctrine and preaching; and emphasizing the necessity of daily recollection and examination of conscience, because prayer and pastoral activity are complementary. He demanded holiness of the priest and listed humility, affability toward the good, firmness and wisdom in admonishing, and outstanding modesty as necessary virtues. His work was used as a standard text by the secular clergy during the Middle Ages and is still honored among priests.

Medieval Period. In the centuries that followed, corresponding roughly to the Middle Ages, pastoral theology was not distinct from other ecclesiastical sciences, but practical applications appended to dogmatic and moral treatises were pastoral in nature. Yet truly pastoral works appeared among the writings of St. Peter Damien; St. Bernard (*De officiis episcoporum; De consideratione*); St. Thomas Aquinas (*Opuscula* 17–20); St. Bonaventure (*De regimine animae Summa confessionalis*).

For at least 2 centuries before the Council of Trent, the Church felt the need of a devoted and zealous clergy; pastoral care was largely neglected, pastoral duties unattended, with disastrous results to the Church and its mission. The important work of the Council was the reform of the clergy and a renewal of pastoral endeavor. Inspired by Trent, bishops and priests set out with renewed zeal to recoup the losses of the Reformation and to restore fervor to the Church; and pastoral theology became a science in itself. During the post-Tridentine years a considerable number of formal treatises appeared, the products of the inspiration and zeal of the great churchmen of that period. Bl. *John of Avila wrote two treatises on the excellence of the priesthood and the sanctity demanded by it; St. Peter *Canisius introduced the pastoral spirit into Germany and was the first to use the term pastoral theology; Pedro de *Soto, Franz Neumayr, Tommaso de Vio *Cajetan, Luis de *Molina, Paolo *Segneri, G. B. *Scaramelli by their writings strengthened the new pastoral spirit of the Counter Reformation. The great reformers of the clergy flourished during this same era: St. *Vincent of Paul, Jean Jacques *Olier, St. John *Eudes, Cardinal de *Bérulle, Charles de *Condren, and St. Francis de Sales. All who followed the French school of *spirituality set as their chief goal the reform and sanctification of the clergy, endeavoring to make it the "type and likeness" of Christ both interiorly and exteriorly. Among the parochial clergy many who had been trained under the influence of these men became competent preachers, teachers of doctrine, catechists, and missionaries. Typical but preeminent was

St. Francis de Sales, himself a model of fruitful pastoral practice. He instituted catechetical instruction, made wise regulations for the guidance of the clergy, fortified his instructions with canonical visitation of the diocese, and undertook the reform of religious communities within his diocese.

St. *Alphonsus Liguori wrote his *Homo apostolicus* to renew the apostolic spirit in the lax clergy of his Diocese of Sant' Agata. It is a systematized treatise providing material for those giving priests' retreats and for the spiritual reading for the clergy. He applied his extensive knowledge of moral theology to the hearing of confessions and summed up the pastoral duties of directing souls, spiritual assistance of the dying, the knowledge required of priests in the ministry, the duty of self-sanctification for the clergy and of sanctifying the souls under their care. It has continued for many generations to inspire countless numbers of priests.

Benedict XIV, pope and scholar, added to pastoral literature by his letters to bishops, his instructions, and his pastoral letters, which were practically treatises on the care of souls. Outstanding among his contributions were *De synodo dioecesana* and *Institutiones ecclesiasticae*. The outstanding reformer of the clergy of this period, perhaps of all time, was St. Charles *Borromeo, whose characteristic virtue, mentioned in the Collect of his feast, was pastoral solicitude. He was the author of much of the reform legislation in Trent, and he was the first to put it into effect in his archdiocese. By his example, his direction, and his writings, all marked by eminent prudence and wisdom, he was a most effective pastoral guide for the clergy of Milan. He concerned himself with every phase of priestly work—the restoration of ecclesiastical ceremonies, Church music, and the Confraternity of Christian Doctrine. He implemented this by diocesan visitation, by synods, by introducing (the first to do so) regular and periodic clerical conferences, and by becoming the energetic promoter of seminaries. During the 18th and 19th centuries formal treatises on pastoral theology began to appear more frequently. In Germany they went under the general name of *Pastoraltheologie* and assumed an importance comparable to that of other branches of sacred science. In France the bishops issued instruction in pastoral letters and in the form of commentaries on the Ritual, these latter being expanded to include all pastoral duties. This work of the French bishops continued even during the exile at the time of the French Revolution and exercised a deep influence on the clergy during the next century. In Italy G. *Frassinetti, whose *Manuale pratico del parocho novello* (Novara 1863) was translated into English as the *Parish Priest's Manual,* and E. Berardi, whose *Praxis confessariorum* went through numerous reprintings, were most prominent and influential in the area of pastoral science. José Mach, a Spanish Jesuit, contributed an excellent systematic treatise, *Tesoro del sacerdote* (Barcelona 1861). Radlinsky gave Austria his *Theologia pastoralis*. In England and Ireland the work began slowly but progressed rapidly during the latter half of the 19th century. There is a multitude of writings on priestly life that, if not scientific treatises, have a pastoral format and have had significant influence in forming generations of priests with admirable pastoral spirit. Cardinal H. E. *Manning's *The Eternal Priesthood,* David Moriarty's *Allocutions to the Clergy,*

F. W. Keating's *The Priest, His Life and Duties* are thought of as classics.

In the U.S. an authoritative pastoral theology began with the Councils of Baltimore, whose legislation guided bishops and priests struggling to establish the Church in a country of rapidly growing population and beset by problems consequent upon immigration, multiplicity of nations and races, and expanding territorial growth. A pastoral literature began to form with such books as *Directorium pastorale* by F. Valuy; the *Catholic Priesthood* by F. Muller; and most influential of all, *The Ambassador of Christ* (Baltimore 1897) by Cardinal James Gibbons. Then appeared the first two formal textbooks in English, *Pastoral Theology* (Cincinnati 1903) by William Stang, who treated the subject from the parish priest's point of view, and *Manual of Pastoral Theology* (Milwaukee 1899) by Frederick Schulze, who viewed it as a professor. These have been used extensively in American seminaries.

Periodicals containing pastoral direction and information appeared in various parts of the world, and these have multiplied considerably in the 20th century. In the U.S., the *American Ecclesiastical Review* (Philadelphia 1889–   ) was begun; in other countries, *Irish Ecclesiastical Record* (Dublin 1865–   ), *Nouvelle revue théologique* (Tournai (1869–   ), *Theologisch-praktische Quartalschrift* (Linz), *Zeitschrift für katholische theologie* (Innsbruck 1877–   ). In the 20th century a large number of clerical reviews have appeared, less pretentious but useful in supplying information and direction in the pastoral endeavor.

Finally, side by side with modern developments in sociology, medicine, psychiatry, and pedagogy and under the impetus of the pastoral consciousness aroused in the Church, many books of unequal value appeared; they are concerned with the priesthood and the pastoral mission of the Church and endeavor to demonstrate how the apostolate of the Church is to be accomplished in the complex culture of today.

Sources. Before 1918 the sources of pastoral theology were many and varied, beginning with Scripture and tradition, in which the general councils took first place, then the decrees and decisions of the Roman congregations, the pronouncements of the popes; locally, the decrees of regional councils and synods, plus the pastoral letters of the ordinaries. The one authoritative source since 1918 is the Code of Canon Law, promulgated by Benedict XV, which became effective May 19, 1918. It collects and systematizes in a series of canons the position and relationship of bishops and priests in the care of diocese and parish. The duties of the priest, his obligations toward his flock, and his powers and privileges are precisely set down in the Code. The Code reproduces many past decrees and decisions, eliminates useless laws, frames new ones to meet modern situations. It remains, together with the interpretations of its laws, as the sole sourcebook of pastoral law. There has arisen an extensive new literature of interpretation and commentary.

From the beginning of the 20th century pastoral theology assumed new importance in the Church universal. It reached a climax in Vatican Council II, convened by Pope John XXIII for the specific purpose of pastoral renewal and *aggiornamento*. The renewal initiated by St. Pius X and effectively furthered by his successors began with the liturgical movement and the many forms of Catholic Action. In many European seminaries a "pastoral year" was added to the regular course, after ordination, devoted to pastoral study and the practice of pastoral activity. Some pastoral experiments, e.g., the *worker priests in France and the seminarian workers in Spain, exceeded the limits of prudent zeal and were eliminated by the Holy See. But despite some misdirection of zeal, pastoral theology has taken on a new spirit. Up to now it meant reviewing and teaching a few courses in the seminary to acquaint the priest with the problems of the ministry and to instruct him to discharge his duties faithfully and wisely; now it centers on the mystery of the Church. A new recognition of the dynamic mission of the Church has turned its sight inward to search for the secret of a vital, living, and expanding Church. The pastoral ministry becomes the "Church's self fulfillment in the ever changing situation." This spirit prompted Vatican Council II to issue the constitutions on communications, the Church, ecumenism, the liturgy, all decidedly pastoral in approach and direction; these will be the authoritative source and inspiration of pastoral theology.

Content. Pastoral theology includes all that is connected with the priestly ministry to souls. Traditionally the duties of the pastor have been adequately divided into those deriving from his threefold office of teacher, shepherd (ruler), and sanctifier (minister of the sacred mysteries). These duties are succinctly summed up by the Code of Canon Law, from which they take their obligatory force and direction. But it is axiomatic that a priest will be successful and effective in his work in proportion to his personal holiness and zeal. Indeed priestly holiness is described as the sanctified service of God and souls. Hence the study of pastoral is usually prefaced by a discussion on the qualities required of the pastor, the nature and necessity of sanctity of those in care of souls, the means to achieve the sanctity, and success, within the framework of pastoral activity. Also included in the preliminary treatise are the necessity of the spiritual exercises imposed by the Church and the method of profiting by them, the practice of various pastoral virtues, the priest's relations with his superiors and inferiors, the spirit of obedience, the charity that is the foundation of all zeal. Such problems as health and study are also treated so that nothing will be lacking in the pastoral formation and training of the priest.

As teacher the pastor must instruct the faithful in the truths of revelation and Christian doctrine. Under the leadership of the ordinary he must, at stated times during the year, instruct the children for the proper reception of the Sacraments of Confirmation and Penance (CIC c.1330); with exceptional care he must prepare children during Lent for the reception of their first Holy Communion (CIC c.1331); he must not neglect those who have already received their first Holy Communion or neglect to establish a branch of the *Confraternity of Christian Doctrine, whose members he will employ to help him with the instruction of the faithful. In the U.S. the confraternity and catechetical work have assumed such importance that *catechetics now occupies a separate course in the seminary curriculum.

The Code suggests, and the Council of Baltimore insists, that the pastor establish a Catholic school in his parish. On Sundays and greater holidays the pastor will teach by means of a homily at Mass in which he will acquaint his people with the "good news" and in which "the guiding principles of the Christian life are expounded from the sacred text" (Vatican II, *Constitution on the Liturgy*, 52). He is required to give advanced instruction in doctrine to adults; the task is usually accomplished in the U.S. by means of discussion groups and study clubs. Included in the duty of teaching is the obligation to warn his people against dangers to faith, especially in the form of bad and prohibited books (CIC c.1405); to instruct the faithful, particularly doctors, in the manner of baptizing in emergency (CIC c.743); to warn about the necessity of early Baptism (CIC c.770); to explain the sanctity and nature of marriage and its impediments (CIC c.1018) and the means of sanctifying married life (CIC c.1033).

As the "dispenser of the mysteries of God" and the minister of sanctity to his people, the priest must administer the Sacraments to the faithful when they reasonably ask for them. He intimately engages himself in the entire sacramental and liturgical life of his parish. He must know therefore not only the nature of the Sacraments and the requirements for their validity but how to aid his people to profit most by their reception, so that by communicating these supernatural means of grace he will justify and sanctify the souls committed to his care. Thus he will lead his people to that degree of union with Christ and to the height of sanctity of which they are capable and to which they are called. Hence he is reminded of his obligation not only to administer the Sacraments but also to dispose the recipients (CIC c.467).

A large section of pastoral theology is concerned with outlining the duties of the priest as the minister of the Eucharist, as both Sacrament and sacrifice, and his obligation to foster devotion to the Eucharistic Presence. Since the days of Pius X early first Communion and frequent Communion for all have been goals the pastor must endeavor to achieve. The instruction on the liturgy of Vatican II insists that he arouse his people to a fuller and more intelligent external participation in the liturgy and in the Mass. Visiting the sick and bringing Viaticum to the dying are important and difficult tasks of the pastor of souls. He must help the sick to sanctify their suffering, to profit by their infirmity, to prevent the depression that sometimes accompanies serious illness. Frequently during his care of the sick he will meet grave and intricate moral problems for which he must have prompt and adequate answers. The Sacrament of Orders is his concern insofar as he has an obligation to discover and stimulate vocations among the youth of his parish.

Another portion of pastoral theology deals with the efficient administration of the Sacrament of Penance. Attention is called to the virtues required and the qualities expected of the priest as judge, father, and physician (*see* CONFESSOR, SACRAMENTAL). Goodness of life and kindness, knowledge and prudence are needed for the proper discharge of the ministry of reconciliation. An extended treatment of casuistry is included in which the principles of all theology are brought together, synthesized, and applied to practical problems. Prudent suggestions are offered for dealing with diverse classes of penitents, such as children, the sincerely contrite, the obdurate, the undisposed, the sinner in the occasion of sin, and the relapsed sinner. Some penitents will be able to be inspired and encouraged to a higher way in the spiritual life, others will need realistic and effective means of overcoming the habit of sin or avoiding its occasion. Penances must be proportioned and practical in each case. The general rules for spiritual direction of pious penitents, especially those in the states of perfection, must be skillfully applied.

A closer link is necessary between pastoral theology and the developments in social and psychological sciences and medicine. These sciences have developed greatly since the late 19th century and have come to be effective helps for the mentally disturbed. Priests must be acquainted with them at least to the extent of being able to discern the necessity of referral to experts in these sciences. Frequently the priest is confronted with problems associated with obsessive-compulsive neuroses, scruples, and depression; he must recognize that guilt complexes and guilt feelings can interfere with the normal functioning of the personality. He must form a judgment regarding the extent to which misconduct is due to malice or is attributable to neurotic disposition or pathological tendencies. From the modern techniques of counseling he will receive help for his pastoral advice and direction. Pastoral medicine supplies the correct solution for the complicated medicomoral problems arising with regard to childbirth, pregnancy, use of steroids, etc.

The pastor, as administrator, faces a variety of situations that increase with the growing complexity of modern life. The modern parish in the U.S. especially must be wisely organized and prudently administered. The pastoral situation is complicated by varying conditions in city, country, and suburban parishes and by the constant ebb and flow of population. The building and maintaining of parish institutions; the material maintenance and the scholastic management of elementary and high schools; the formation of societies and organizations for young and old, the married and unmarried; parish visitation and census control; the various forms of the apostolate, the ecumenical movement, Catholic Action, cooperation with the laity, youth programs, and social charitable works—all these make heavy demands on the organizational and administrative abilities of the pastor; and pastoral theology helps him to cope with them.

Bibliography: Pastoral theologies. W. STANG, *Pastoral Theology* (New York 1896). F. SCHULZE, *Manual of Pastoral Theology* (9th ed. St. Louis 1936). A. MICHELETTI, *Epitome theologiae pastoralis*, 3 v. (Rome 1925–29). F. SCHUBERT, *Grundzüge der Pastoraltheologie* (Graz 1934). V. LITHARD, *Précis de théologie pastorale* (new ed. Paris 1941). F. MOUREY, *La Préparation au sacerdoce* (Paris 1943). F. X. ARNOLD, *Seelsorge aus der Mitte der Heilsgeschichte* (Freiburg 1956). *Dizionario di theologia pastorale* (Rome 1962).

Canon Law on pastors. C. J. KOUDELKA, *Pastors: Their Rights and Duties* (CUA CLS 11; 1921). P. REILLY, *Residence of Pastors* (ibid. 97; 1935). B. M. KELLY, *The Functions Reserved to Pastors* (ibid. 250; 1947). W. F. FITZGERALD, *The Paris Census and the "Liber status animarum"* (ibid. 339; 1954).

Other studies. H. BONZELET, *Pastoral Companion*, ed. and tr. L. ANLER (New York 1945). M. J. MATHIS and N. W. MEYER, eds., *The Pastoral Companion* (12th ed. Chicago 1961). T. F. Casey, *Pastoral Manual for New Priests* (Milwaukee 1962). J. R. CAVANAGH, *Fundamental Pastoral Counselling* (Milwaukee 1962). W. DEMAL, *Pastoral Psychology in Practice*, tr. J. W. CONWAY (New York 1955). A. SNOECK, *Confession and Pastoral Psychology*, tr. T. ZUYDWIJK (Westminster, Md. 1961). J. J. NAVAGH, *The Apostolic Parish* (New York 1950). C. R. WARD, *The Living Parish* (Notre Dame 1959). A. BLÖCHLINGER, *The Modern Parish Community*, tr. G. STEVENS (New York 1965). G. ANTONELLI, *Medicina pastoralis*, 3 v. (4th ed. Rome 1920). E. F HEALY, *Medical Ethics* (Chicago 1956). T. J. O'DONNELL, *Morals in Medicine* (2d ed. Westminster, Md. 1959). A. NIEDERMEYER, *Compendium of Pastoral Medicine*, tr. F. BUONANNO (New York 1960). J. A. JUNGMANN, *Pastoral Liturgy* (New York 1962). K. RAHNER, ed., *The Pastoral Mission of the Church* (Concilium 3; Glen Rock, N.J. 1965).

[J. H. BRENNAN]

PASTOUREAUX, CRUSADE OF THE.

The *Pastoureaux* were bands of peasants and laborers who swept through France in 1251 in a popular uprising similar to the Children's Crusade. Their aim was to free the King of France, *Louis IX, who was then a captive of the Moslems, and to reconquer Jerusalem. The *Pastoureaux* were led by a mysterious "Master of Hungary," a powerful and persuasive preacher about 60 years old. The "Master" also sent an emissary to England in an effort to raise other bands there, but his representative was torn to pieces by a mob. The movement was accompanied by violent attacks upon feudal lords and upon the clergy, particularly the *Franciscans and *Dominicans, who were held in some way responsible for the disasters that befell St. Louis's Crusade in Egypt. The Queen-Regent, *Blanche of Castile, was at first inclined to assist the *Pastoureaux,* but when news of their more violent outbreaks reached her, she ordered their suppression. The "Master of Hungary" was killed in battle near Villeneuve-sur-Cher and the main bands quickly broke up. Only a few of the *Pastoureaux* ever reached the Holy Land.

Bibliography: MATTHEW PARIS, *Chronica majora*, ed. H. R. LUARD, 7 v. (RollsS 57; 1872–83) 5:246–254. É. BERGER, *Histoire de Blanche de Castille* (Paris 1895). J. DELALANDE, *Les Extraordinaires croisades d'enfants et de pastoureaux au moyen âge* (Paris 1962).

[J. A. BRUNDAGE]

PATARINES

Constituents of a religious movement with social overtones originating among the laity and certain sections of the clergy, especially the lower clergy, in northern Italy in the early part of the second half of the 11th century.

Origin. The derivation of the term is unclear, but it probably has its origin in *Pataria,* a quarter of Milan where the group was particularly active. The earliest known "Patarine" preaching was that of the deacon of Milan, *Arialdo, at Varese (early 1057), and later in Milan. He was soon joined by Landulph Cotta, the notary of the church in Milan. Initially Patarine preaching was directed against priests' concubinage or marriage (*see* CELIBACY). However, it soon came to condemn, with equal vehemence, every kind of *simony, attacking specifically the Archbishop of Milan, Guido of Velate, but by extension, implicating the greater part of the clergy, most of whom were guilty of some personal simony or had, at least, been ordained by simoniac bishops. This antisimony movement struck also at the vested interests of the upper classes of the laity, for they had insinuated their own members into the ranks of the higher clergy precisely by means of simoniac practices.

The Patarine movement signified a more intense participation by the laity in the life of the Church, and the ethical standards demanded by that laity resulted in an active campaign to reform the morals of the clergy. In an age that drew its spiritual values from the evangelical counsels of perfection, i.e., apostolic poverty and virginity, it was natural that the laity demanded chastity of its clergy and condemned any traffic in sacred objects, as well as excessive wealth or power for clergymen. The Patarine movement was, in fact, but one facet of an age that produced at one and the same time the heretical *Cathari and the *Gregorian reform, new eremitical groups such as the *Camaldolese and *Vallombrosans, and the reform of both monks and canons. Thus, the Patarines of Florence were much influenced by the Vallombrosans, and Arialdo himself founded a reformed chapter of canons regular.

Milan remained the head of the Patarine movement, and after the death of Landulph Cotta, his brother *Erlembald, a layman, assumed its leadership. To the bishops, to the supporters of the Church's diocesan hierarchy, and to those faithful to local church traditions, the Patarines appeared to be a dangerous lay movement subversive of the sacramental hierarchy and of Holy Orders itself. It *was* such, in its extreme forms; for certain lay Patarines took upon themselves the duty of preaching, especially against corrupt clergy. Nor did they limit themselves to abstaining, as directed by decrees of the councils, from participation in rites celebrated by priests guilty of simony; they would even use force to prevent any of the other faithful from participating and would forcibly remove an unworthy cleric from the altar, from the church, and from his benefices, which he, as a simonist, had legally forfeited. The Patarines often did not act as the executors of a regular canonical sentence of condemnation of an unworthy churchman, but on their own initiative proclaimed to the people the cleric's guilt. Pope *Alexander II, even though he was a fellow townsman and supporter, reproved the Milanese Patarines for taking matters into their own hands in this way.

The Patarine movement did not go so far as to deny the special character and indispensable function of the priesthood. The Milanese Patarines, however, refused to attend rites celebrated by contumacious priests or to receive the Sacraments from such clerics, and they sought out priests and bishops free of every taint so that they might "freely" receive the Sacraments from them (*mente libera,* as one source puts it). To find such men they dispatched a mission to Vallombrosa and gladly welcomed a bishop, Rudolph, sent from the Vallombrosan area to minister to their needs in Milan. When the Patarines considered simonist ordinations as invalid and the Sacraments administered by such priests and bishops as sacrilegious, they were simply following the common teaching in the Church of the day, supported by Cardinal *Humbert of Silva Candida, who was not without Vallombrosan connections. *Peter Damian himself had allowed and promoted lay preaching, although he limited it to "earnest exhortation" and excluded doctrinal preaching.

Crisis in Milan. When the Milanese Patarines appealed to the Holy See against the diocesan bishop and clergy, Rome dispatched an exploratory mission in 1057. Two years later, a second mission composed of Peter Damian and the Milanese Bishop of Lucca, Anselm I of Baggio, later Pope Alexander II, reconciled Archbishop Guido to the Church along with any guilty priests who declared themselves willing to amend their ways and to do penance. But the traditionalist Ambrosian clergy was irritated by the Patarines' appeals to Rome, and Archbishop Guido soon reverted to his old ways, sided with antipope Cadalus of Parma, and persecuted the Patarines. Alexander II thereupon granted Erlembald the gonfalon of St. Peter (*see* BAN-

NER), entrusting this layman with exercising the physical coercive power of the Church; the Pope then excommunicated Guido (March 9, 1066), touching off a violent anti-Patarine reaction that led to the murder of Arialdo (June 28).

The Patarine movement spread to other Italian cities, notably Cremona, Piacenza, Lodi, and later Brescia. A religious movement in Florence had the essential characteristics of the Patarines if not their name; it united the laity and the lower clergy under *John Gualbert and his Vallombrosans against corrupt ecclesiastics and the simonist Bishop Peter Mezzabarba, a Pavian nobleman. The faithful appealed to the Pope, who sent Peter Damian to attempt a reconciliation: by the victory of their representative in an ordeal by fire, the insurgents convicted Mezzabarba of simony and persuaded him to resign.

In Milan itself the ephemeral reconciliation and futile reform effected by a third pontifical mission in 1067 were swept away by the schism that broke out after the resignation of Archbishop Guido in 1070, a schism between Godfrey, appointed and invested by the German king (*Henry IV), and *Atto of Milan, elected by the Patarines and recognized by the Holy See. Thus the campaign of the Patarines for Church reform became part of the vaster arena of the imperial-papal *investiture struggle. Pope *Gregory VII naturally gave strong support to Erlembald and to the Patarines in their fight against the corrupt clergy and the schismatic archbishop, who had received lay *investiture.

Erlembald was killed in a tumult triggered by his trampling on holy chrism that had been consecrated by a simoniac bishop. His death marked the end of Patarine agitations (1075). The Ambrosian Archbishop Anselm III submitted to Pope *Urban II, whose conciliatory policy toward the bishops of central and northern Italy smoothed the way for rooting out some of the worst evils of the Church in that area. And thus the chief cause of Patarine complaints disappeared in the atmosphere of the new enthusiasm for the Crusades. An important social result of the Patarine movement was the destruction of the network of vested interests and family contacts that had enabled a few powerful Lombard families to keep the most important Sees of central and northern Italy, especially Tuscany, for their own members. However, there remained in Lombardy, especially in Milan, a small group of Patarine extremists, dissatisfied with the compromise of a moderate and orderly reform. These smoldering resentments and the deluded aspirations for radical religious renewal later found expression in other reform movements or in new heretical currents.

Bibliography: Sources. *Arnulphi gesta archiepiscoporum mediolanensium,* in MGS 8:17–25. *Landulphi Senioris Mediolanensis historiae libri quatuor,* in Muratori RIS 4:81–128. *Vita sancti Arialdi auctore Andrea abbate Strumensi,* in MGS 30.2:1047–75. Literature. C. PELLEGRINI, *I ss. Arialdo ed Erlenbaldo* (Milan 1897). S. M. BROWN, "Movimenti politico-religiosi a Milano ai tempi della pataria," ArchStorIt 58 (1931) 227–278. C. VIOLANTE, *La pataria milanese e la riforma ecclesiastica,* v.1 *Le premesse, 1045–1057* (Rome 1955); "I movimenti patarini e la riforma ecclesiastica," *Annuario dell' Università Cattolica del S. Cuore . . . 1955–57* (Milan 1957) 209–223. E. WERNER," "Παταρηνοί—Patarini: Ein Beitrag zur Kirchen- und Sektengeschichte des 11. Jahrhunderts," *Vom Mittelalter zur Neuzeit* (Berlin 1956) 404–419. G. MICCOLI, "Per la storia della pataria milanese," *Bullettino dell' Istituto storico italiano per il medioevo e Archivio Muratoriano* 70 (1958) 43–123.

[C. VIOLANTE]

PATERNITY, DIVINE

What is designated in contemporary theological literature under the title divine paternity is perhaps a little ambiguous. On first glance, *paternity* would be simply the Latin derivative (from *paternitas*) corresponding to the more familiar Anglo-Saxon *fatherhood*. Thus, one might expect to see treated under the rubric divine paternity the entire Old and New Testament revelation bearing upon the fatherhood of God and the way this became assimilated and interpreted in the Judeo-Christian community ever since. Actually, however, such a wide and Biblically oriented use of *paternity* is rarely, if ever, encountered. Centuries of theological, and ultimately scholastic, convention have reserved this Latinism for the Father's unique relation to the eternal Son as grasped and expressed in the technicalities of Trinitarian doctrine and theology.

Historically, this technical usage grew out of a theological insight that can be traced back at least as far as the Cappadocian Fathers—Basil, Gregory of Nazianzus, and Gregory of Nyssa. This was the understanding that plurality within the Godhead was not a contradiction, because the three—Father, Son, and Holy Spirit—differed from one another not in respect to Godhead as such but in respect solely to what was proper to each, and this property (ἰδιότης) was something purely relative. Even earlier, Athanasius had written (*Or. 3 c. Arian.* 4; *De syn.* 49) that whatever is said of the Father is said likewise of the Son, excepting only the very name Father. Subsequently, with the schoolmen and especially Aquinas, the idea of the relative property first appearing with Athanasius and the Cappadocians was still further developed and refined by means of a carefully worked out doctrine of relations. The whole meaning of paternity is simply "to be with reference, or respect, to" son. There is no question, therefore, of the Father being more God than the Son or of having some perfection not shared by the Son. For Father and Son differ in no absolute way but only in what is exclusively relative.

Such a notion of divine paternity contributes by way of explanatory device to an extremely limited, yet fruitful, understanding of the noncontradictoriness of a plurality of Persons in the one and undivided Godhead. But the problematic of plurality is only one of many considerations pertinent to the fatherhood of God. Hence, the focus of attention under the concept of divine paternity, and in contradistinction to fatherhood, is quite restricted. This does not mean, however, and certainly should not mean, that what is still more basic to the larger question of the fatherhood of God will not be treated in Roman Catholic theology, but rather that it will be treated under different titles than paternity and that its detail will be presupposed, not ignored, by paternity.

See also GOD THE FATHER; AGENNĒTOS; PERSON (IN THEOLOGY); PERSON, DIVINE; RELATIONS, TRINITARIAN; TRINITY, HOLY; TRINITY, HOLY, ARTICLES ON.

Bibliography: For a fresh approach to the traditional notion, see B. LONERGAN, *De Deo Trino*, v.2, *Pars systematica* (3d ed. Rome 1964), esp. 115–185. For the historical origins of the notion, see the same author's companion volume *De Deo Trino*, v.1, *Pars dogmatica* (2d ed. Rome 1964) 195–204. J. N. D. KELLY, *Early Christian Doctrines* (2d ed. New York 1960) 263–269.

[R. L. RICHARD]

PATERSON, DIOCESE OF (PATERSONENSIS),

suffragan of the See of Newark, comprising the counties of Morris, Passaic, and Sussex in New Jersey, an area of 1,214 square miles containing 88 parishes. In 1963 it numbered more than 238,790 Catholics in a total population of about 717,400. From 1853 to 1937 this area was a part of the ecclesiastical Province of New York and the Diocese of Newark, N.J. On Dec. 10, 1937, Pius XI established New Jersey as a separate province, raised Newark to a metropolitan see, and created the Diocese of Paterson.

Bishop Thomas H. McLaughlin was appointed first ordinary of Paterson on Dec. 16, 1937, and served until his death, March 17, 1947. On June 21, 1947, he was succeeded by Bp. Thomas A. Boland, who served until Nov. 15, 1952, when he was appointed second archbishop of Newark. Bishop James A. McNulty was appointed to Paterson on April 9, 1953, the third auxiliary of Newark to be transferred to Paterson. When McNulty was appointed to the Diocese of Buffalo, N.Y., on Feb. 12, 1963, Bp. James J. Navagh of Ogdensburg, N.Y., succeeded him in Paterson.

The increase in the Catholic population of the diocese represents an expansion of 80 per cent in the first 25 years, and the number of infants baptized in the faith during an average year has almost trebled during the same period. The Sisters of Charity of Convent Station conduct *St. Elizabeth's College for Women there. *Seton Hall University, administered by priests of the Archdiocese of Newark, has a day and evening college at Paterson. High schools in the diocese numbered 16 by 1963, with an increase in enrollment of more than 300 per cent over that of 1940. There were 70 elementary schools in 1963 enrolling about 27,000 students, as well as 4 general hospitals, 2 homes for the aged, and an orphanage.

The cathedral of the diocese is St. John the Baptist, in Paterson. The offices of the Associated Catholic Charities and the Mt. Carmel Guild Social Service Center (for alcoholics) are located in the cathedral city. Three mission churches have been established in the diocese to care for the needs of Catholics from Puerto Rico. Two of these missions are administered by Chinese priests, and the third, by diocesan priests. The Sisters of the Good Shepherd conduct a training school for girls at Morristown. There are two Benedictine abbeys in the diocese, one at Morristown chiefly for educational purposes, and another at Newton, for missionary work. The motherhouse of the Sisters of Charity is located at Convent Station, and the provincial house of the Sisters of Christian Charity, Mallinkrodt Convent, is established at Mendham. Eleven religious communities of men and 25 of women serve the diocese, which in 1963 contained 372 priests, 1,327 nuns, and 341 seminarians.

Bibliography: Diocese of Paterson, *Records of the Chancery Office*. J. M. FLYNN, *The Catholic Church in New Jersey* (Morristown, N.J. 1904).

[G. L. A. REILLY]

PATIENCE

A moral virtue that disposes and inclines a man to suffer and endure present evils without unreasonable dejection. Patience is a perfection of the concupiscible appetite that disposes it to submit to the control of reason so that the difficulties of life will not overwhelm a man with sadness. The primary action that flows from this virtue is to endure; thus patience is annexed to the virtue of fortitude as a potential part. Since the acquisition of any virtue requires the endurance of some sorrow, generally on the sense level, patience is said to prepare the way for the acquisition of all of the other virtues.

Patience does not require the endurance of all present evils. Some can reasonably be avoided or mitigated, and to fail to take action to this end could be culpable. A mother, for example, with a family of small children to control cannot endure unlimited chaos and disorder with apathetic serenity; not infrequently she will be obliged to feel and express some measure of indignation and irritation.

Patience, motivated by man's willingness to endure unpleasant things in order to attain natural virtue and natural goods, is an acquired virtue. Beyond this there is infused into man's soul with sanctifying grace a supernatural virtue of patience that is motivated by a supernatural willingness to endure trouble and affliction in order to attain sanctity and union with God. This supernatural patience can be a joyous thing—suffering for love of God is a source of joy.

True patience possesses three special characteristics: it must be universal, humble, and supernatural. Patience endures every type of evil that should be borne, no matter what may be its kind, cause, or consequences. Patience is humble when it does not complain unduly or seek attention, sympathy, or compassion. Patience is supernatural when it is motivated by charity. St. Paul said: "Charity is patient" (1 Cor 13.4).

Two vices are opposed to the virtue of patience: insensibility and impatience. Insensibility is a lack of feeling that leaves a person stoical and unmoved by his own suffering or by that of others. Impatience is an unreasonable refusal to endure sorrow from present troubles necessary for the accomplishment of works of virtue. Impatience manifests itself externally by unreasonable anger, complaints, and evidences of depression or discouragement; internally, it shows itself in feelings of antipathy to trials and suffering, and in an excessive inclination to protect oneself against all discomfort. The vice of impatience leads a man to the feeling that there is no joy in loving and serving God; it inclines man to avoid the difficulties and the sorrows that often are the prelude to great joy and happiness.

Bibliography: Thomas Aquinas, ST 2a2ae, 136. E. Vansteenberghe, DTC 12.1:2247–51. Augustine, *Patientia.* Tertullian, "Patience," *Disciplinary, Moral, and Ascetical Works,* tr. R. Arbesmann et al. (New York 1959). A. Royo, *The Theology of Christian Perfection,* tr. and ed. J. Aumann (Dubuque 1962). EncDictBibl 1758–60. Francis de Sales, *Introduction to the Devout Life,* tr. M. Day (Westminster, Md. 1959).

[R. Doherty]

PATIENCE (IN THE BIBLE)

The quality or virtue of patience is presented as either forbearance or endurance. In the former sense it is a quality of self-restraint or of not giving way to anger, even in the face of provocation; it is attributed to both God and man and is closely related to mercy and compassion. In the latter sense it is a virtue by which one bears the trials of this life with resignation to God's will, and is therefore associated with hope [see HOPE (IN THE BIBLE)]; obviously in this sense it is predicated only of man. This article will discuss patience as forbearance,

patience as endurance, and will then go on to discuss the eschatological aspect of patience.

Patience as Forbearance. God's patience with men is one of His most frequently stressed attributes in the OT; compare especially the use of the Hebrew roots *rḥm* and *ḥnn.* He is called upon as "a merciful [*rāḥûm*] and gracious [*ḥannûn*] God, slow to anger and rich in kindness and fidelity" (Ex 34.6; see also Nm 14.18; Wis 11.24–12.1; Jl 2.13; Neh 9.17). The psalmists praise Him because He does not punish men harshly but is patient with them [Ps 77(78).38–39; 85(86).15; 102(103).8; 144(145).8–9]. The greatness of His patience exceeds that of man (Sir 18.8–13) and therefore is not easily understood by impatient man (e.g., Jer 15.15; Jon 4.2). The purpose of this patience is to bring man to repentance (Wis 11.23; 12.8–10); man remains free to abuse it—but he does so to his own detriment (Is 5.18; 57.11–13). The NT reflects the same doctrine; cf. especially the use of the Greek μακροθυμία. God "endures with great patience vessels of wrath" (Rom 9.22), and has shown his forbearance in condoning former sins in the vicarious death of Christ (Rom 3.25–26). Therefore, man should not misuse God's patience (Rom 2.4–5) but rather should come to repentance (1 Pt 3.9).

The OT praises the patient man because he possesses much good sense (Prv 14.29), allays discord (Prv 15.18), and is stronger than a warrior (Prv 16.32). According to the NT, patience purifies faith (1 Pt 1.6), fosters hope (Rom 8.25; 15.4), leads to perfection (Jas 1.4), and pertains to charity (1 Cor 13.4, 5, 7). Thus, it is a fruit of the Holy Spirit (Gal 5.22), deriving its power from God (Col 1.11). It is, moreover, God's own patience that Christians must imitate in dealing with others (Mt 5.45; 18.23–35). Therefore their patience must be universal (1 Thes 5.14) and prudent (2 Cor 11.19), and must pervade their daily conduct (Eph 4.2; Col 3.12). There should be no complaining against one another (Jas 5.8), because by bearing one another's burdens they can fulfill the law of Christ (Gal 6.2). Such patience is especially necessary for those who would spread the kingdom of God. St. Paul performed his apostolic work "in all patience" (2 Cor 12.12) in order not to give offense and in order to prove himself a worthy minister of God (2 Cor 6.4–6). He wished his patience to be an example to Timothy (2 Tm 3.10) and urged him to work patiently (1 Tm 6.11; 2 Tm 4.2) and to be a "forbearing teacher" in instructing others (2 Tm 2.24). Writing to Titus, he recommended the same virtue for the elders of the Church (Ti 2.2).

Patience as Endurance. The Christian's bearing of suffering (expressed especially in the Greek term ὑπομονή) has its precedent in the OT where the afflicted put all their trust in God [e.g., Ps 24(25).3; 26(27).14; 32(33).20] and where the Prophets call Yahweh "the Hope of Israel" (Jer 14.8; 17.13). Christ tells us that it is only through this patient endurance of suffering that our life will bear fruit (Lk 8.15). St. Peter exhorts the Christians to endure unjust suffering because it is of great value in the eyes of God (1 Pt 2.19–20). St. Paul, too, recommends patience in affliction (Rom 12.12), rejoices in his own sufferings (Rom 5.3; 1 Cor 4.12; 2 Cor 1.6), and praises the endurance of his recent converts (2 Thes 1.4), because through such endurance they will enter the kingdom of God (Acts 14.21).

Eschatological Aspect. The Christian's patience is also eschatological. Although the coming of Christ is certain, the day and the hour are not (cf. Mt 24.1–51; Mk 13.1–37; Lk 21.5–38; 1 Thes 4.13–5.11; 2 Thes 2.1–12). Hence, the life of Christians here on earth consists in "looking for the blessed hope and coming of the great God and our Savior Jesus Christ" (Ti 2.13). They should not be easily shaken from their right mind (2 Thes 2.2) but should patiently wait (Jas 5.7–8; Heb 10.36; 12.1), for only those who persevere till the end will be saved (Mt 10.22).

See also PAROUSIA, 1; SUFFERING.

Bibliography: EncDictBibl 1758–60. X. LÉON-DUFOUR, ed., *Vocabulaire de théologie biblique* (Paris 1962) 764–767. C. SPICQ, "Patientia," RevScPhilTh 19 (1930) 95–106. J. HORST, Kittel ThW 4:377–390. R. BULTMANN, *ibid.* 4:585–595.

[J. BUKOVSKY]

PATMORE, COVENTRY KERSEY DIGHTON,

poet and essayist; b. Woodford, Essex, England, July 23, 1823; d. Lymington, Hampshire, Nov. 26, 1896. He was the first of four children of Peter George Patmore and Eliza Robertson. Patmore had no formal education beyond 6 months at the age of 16 at the Collège de France. His *Poems* (1844) met with remarkable success. When financial losses forced his father to move to France, Coventry Patmore was left penniless. Monckton Milnes arranged for his appointment as an assistant librarian in the British Museum, where he worked for 20 years. In 1847 he married Emily Augusta Andrews, who gave him the inspiration of a deep love. They had three daughters and three sons.

Coventry Patmore, portrait by John Singer Sargent (1894).

Patmore's second book, *Tamerton Church-Tower and Other Poems* (1853), showed no advance in poetic power, though it was reminiscent of Wordsworth and Tennyson. Meanwhile, he was writing *The Angel in the House* (1854–62), his long "verse novel" celebrating the trials and joys of married love. This work sold almost a quarter of a million copies and was widely acclaimed.

Emily died in 1862; 2 years later Patmore accompanied Aubrey de Vere to Rome, where his interest in Catholicism deepened. There he also met Marianne Byles, a wealthy and devout Catholic, and, having been received into the Church, he returned to London and there married Miss Byles before Father Henry Manning (later cardinal). He retired from the British Museum, and purchased an estate in Sussex. There he read extensively in St. Thomas Aquinas and St. John of the Cross, and there he slowly produced his finest work, the 43 odes that form *The Unknown Eros* (1878), a profound exploration of human and divine love.

Patmore sold his estate in 1874 and lived in Hastings until 1891, when he moved to Lymington. His second wife died in 1880, and a year later he married Harriet Robson. "I have left the world nothing but my best," Patmore wrote. What he left is admittedly uneven—at worst, sentimental and dull; at best, alive with a true poetic passion.

Bibliography: *Poems,* ed. F. PAGE (New York 1949). B. CHAMPNEYS, *Memoirs and Correspondence of Coventry Patmore,* 2 v. (London 1900). F. PAGE, *Patmore: A Study in Poetry* (London 1933). J. C. REID, *The Mind and Art of Coventry Patmore* (London 1957), the most complete study. **Illustration credit:** National Portrait Gallery, London.

[A. D. BISCHOFF]

PATRIARCH

By the term patriarch the Jews indicated the father or the head of a family or tribe. It was used in the 4th and 5th centuries as an ecclesiastical title, designating sometimes even titular bishops. However, from the time of Justinian it was reserved to the incumbents of the five major sees (Rome, Constantinople, Alexandria, Antioch, and Jerusalem).

IN ORIENTAL CANON LAW

A patriarch is a "bishop on whom the canons confer jurisdiction over all the bishops, including metropolitans, and over the clergy and people of a territory or specified rite; such jurisdiction is to be exercised in conformity with the law and under the authority of the Roman pontiff" (ClerSanc c.216.2n1).

The patriarch is, therefore, a bishop to whom the sacred canons grant a superepiscopal jurisdiction: this indicates that the patriarchal institution finds its origin in the custom and practice of the Church; the canons have only recognized a situation already in existence. Futhermore, the patriarch exercises his jurisdiction on all the bishops and metropolitans and on the clergy and faithful of a certain territory or specified rite. Consequently, his authority is limited by the territory and by the community of people living within such a territory; this makes the ecclesiastical law, in the Oriental Church, personal rather than territorial.

When a large number of faithful of the same rite as the patriarch live outside the boundaries of his territory, the sacred canons grant the patriarch authority over them also; this is regulated, however, by the codified general law as well as by the particular law proper to each community or to each Oriental rite. Thus, the common law reserves to the patriarch the following rights: after obtaining approval from the Holy See, he may entrust to the care of a qualified priest the faithful of his rite living outside the patriarchate (ClerSanc c.261.1); he may conduct a pastoral and paternal visit (but not a canonical visit, this being reserved to the Holy See: ClerSanc c.262.2) to those faithful, by means of a qualified priest, secular or religious, delegated by him (ClerSanc c.262.1n1); he may designate a hierarch for the same faithful, after previous consent of the Holy See (ClerSanc c.260.1n2d). This threefold power presupposes, however, the prior and positive existence of the particular law authorizing the patriarch to act in these canonical matters. The particular law of the Melkites, for example, favors this power of the patriarch. Indeed, several synodal and even pontifical documents authorize him to watch over the faithful of his rite who have left the patriarchate, to care for a precise observance of the rite as well as for their spiritual welfare in general.

Precedence. A distinction is made between the so-called traditional or major patriarchs and the other so-called minor patriarchs (ClerSanc c.219). The order of precedence among the former, established many centuries ago (cf. in particular CorpIurCivNov 131) and confirmed by the above-mentioned canon, is the following: the patriarch of Constantinople precedes the patriarch of Alexandria; then follows the patriarch of Antioch; and last comes the patriarch of Jerusalem.

However, certain patriarchs of different rites have the same title; thus, three Catholic patriarchs, that of Melkite rite, that of Syrian rite, and the patriarch of Maronite rite, have now the same title of Antioch. The order of precedence among them, as well as among the other so-called patriarchs, namely, the patriarch of Chaldean rite and the patriarch of Armenian rite, is regulated according to the general norms established in ClerSanc c.37: the patriarch senior by promotion to the patriarchal dignity enjoys precedence over the others; if promotion took place at the same time, the most advanced in age has precedence.

In his churches and during divine services of his own rite a patriarch precedes the other patriarchs, even those of higher title or prior promotion. Likewise a patriarch that exercises jurisdiction enjoys precedence over titular patriarchs, regardless of their rite, except in the Roman Curia.

Selection. Not later than a month from the day of vacancy of the patriarchal see, unless particular law establishes a shorter time, the administrator of the patriarchate must prepare with scrupulous care all that is necessary for the synod in which the new patriarch will be elected. As a general rule he shall convoke the synod in the patriarchal residence itself, but should he deem it opportune to convoke it elsewhere, he must first consult by letter the other fathers of the synod.

Convocation of these fathers having been accomplished, only bishops enjoy active voice. Totally excluded from the electoral synod, therefore, are all who lack the episcopal character, those judged incapable of voting, according to the norms of ClerSanc c.109, and all laymen regardless of their rank or author-ity. Indeed, laymen must not interfere with the election of the patriarch, either by their intervention in the synod or by their presentation of candidates or in any other way. Such prohibition of intervention of laymen protects the electoral synod from politics and from rivalry between families.

Following a legitimate convocation, i.e., one in accordance with the canons applying to elections in general (ClerSanc cc.102–120) and to the election of the patriarch in particular, the bishops have a grave obligation of complying with the convocation. If they believe themselves prevented by an obstacle from attending, they shall manifest in writing their reasons to the synod and shall conform to its instructions.

Before proceeding to the election, the following acts must be provided for: (1) Ascertainment of the synod's canonical structure. If two-thirds of those who possess active voice and are not detained by any impediment are present, the synod shall be declared canonical. (2) Presidency of the synod. In general, the bishop senior by episcopal consecration presides over the synod. Yet, the Holy See could establish otherwise in a particular case and for special, adequate reasons. Also the particular law could determine a different procedure; indeed, for the Melkites, the presidency of this synod is reserved to the administrator of the patriarchate. (3) Election of two tellers. These must be selected, according to the norms of the particular law, from among the fathers of the synod or among the priests and must be elected by secret ballot. After taking an oath to discharge faithfully their duty and to preserve secrecy even after the election about all the proceedings of the electoral assembly, the tellers shall collect the votes of the fathers and, together with the presiding officer of the synod, shall see to it that the votes are given secretly, methodically, and according to the order of precedence of the fathers (ClerSanc c.113). (4) Selection of the secretary, or notary, of the synod. This must be done by the presiding officer of the synod, after consultation with the two bishops senior by episcopal consecration, from among the bishops present at the synod. The secretary must take an oath. (5) Preparation of the ballots. It must be done in accordance with the norms of the particular law; Melkites, for example, use an ordinary blank sheet of paper. (6) Taking of an oath. The fathers of the synod take an oath to elect the person whom they believe before God should be elected, namely, that person who is *hic et nunc* the worthiest to be at the head of the patriarchate.

Election. The patriarch is generally elected, that is, designated, by means of the legitimate votes of all those, and only those, who are present at the election; excluded, therefore, is the faculty of expressing one's own vote by letter or proxy. Election is the canonical title by which one becomes patriarch. The election in question may be made by ballots, and this is the most frequent method, or by compromise, namely, when the electors unanimously and in writing transfer their right of electing to one or more qualified persons belonging to the electoral college or even to outsiders. This is done with the provision that they, on behalf of all the electors and in force of the power received, perform the election. Election by quasi-inspiration is hardly possible since in conformity with ClerSanc c.111.2 it must be conducted secretly.

In order to be considered eligible for the patriarchal dignity, a candidate must: (1) have been born of lawful wedlock; it is not sufficient if he was legitimized, even by a subsequent marriage; (2) be free of any matrimonial bond; (3) be at least 40 years old; (4) have been ordained priest for at least 10 years; (5) be known for good morals, piety, zeal for souls, prudence, and for possessing all the other qualifications needed to govern a patriarchate; and (6) have been granted a doctorate in theology or in Canon Law by a university or by another institution of learning approved by the Holy See; or he must be at least thoroughly familiar or expert in said disciplines. If the candidate in question is a religious, he must possess from his major superiors either an equivalent title or a testimonial to his true proficiency (ClerSanc c.394.1nn1, 2, 5, 6).

The candidate who receives two-thirds of the valid votes shall be considered the elected patriarch. Thus, balloting is to go on until the two-thirds of the votes are obtained. Nevertheless, should the election not be accomplished after 15 days from the opening of the synod, the electoral college loses the right of electing a patriarch, and the designation of the same is made by the Roman pontiff.

Acceptance and Enthronement. Following the ballot, the fathers of the synod assist at the inspection of the ballot box while the presiding officer reads aloud the name of the candidate elected. The same officer notifies the elected of the result of the election, or, in case the president himself has been elected, the officer who must take his place makes the official notification. This is done on behalf of the whole synod by following the method and the formula used in each rite.

The elected must then manifest within 2 days of available time following the notification whether or not he accepts the election. If he renounces or fails to indicate his acceptance within 2 days of available time, a new synodal session must be held. If he accepts, the following acts take place: (1) If the elected is a bishop designated, confirmed, and duly consecrated, who has not canonically renounced his episcopal office, who has not been deposed, and is not one of those mentioned in ClerSanc c.109.1, the synod shall proceed with his proclamation and enthroning. (2) If the elected is a bishop designated, confirmed, but not consecrated, the synod shall proclaim him; his enthroning, however, must come only after his episcopal consecration. (3) If the elected has not been confirmed by the Roman pontiff, the synod can neither proclaim him, nor consecrate him, nor enthrone him before the pontifical confirmation. Should the elected be in one way or another notified of the election, the sacred canons forbid him from meddling, under pretext of his election, with the administration of the patriarchal office, either in spiritual or temporal matters. Acts performed by the elected before his confirmation would be void. In the meantime, the fathers of the synod and all those who have in any way taken part in it or have been in one way or another informed about the result of the election are bound to keep the secret until confirmation is given and is legitimately published. The fathers meanwhile may return to their residence, provided, however, that they come back to the synod upon arrival of the response of the Holy Father. (4) If the elected does not receive confirmation from the sovereign pontiff, the synod must proceed immediately with a new ballot.

All the proceedings having been terminated, the presiding officer, the fathers, the two tellers, and the notary of the synod must sign the acts and carefully place them in the secret archives of the patriarchate. The new patriarch shall receive a certificate of election signed by the presiding officer, the tellers, and the notary of the synod.

The new patriarch must write to the Roman pontiff and inform him of his canonical election; he shall forward the documents, signed by his own hand, of his profession of faith and of his oath of fidelity taken before the synod; he shall also petition for ecclesiastical communion and for the pallium, which is a sign of the fullness and of the jurisdiction of the pontifical office.

At the same time the synod must notify the Roman pontiff of the election, performed in accordance with the law, of the profession of faith, the signing of the formula, and the oath of fidelity taken by the patriarch before the synod. A request must also be forwarded for ecclesiastical communion and for the pallium. The sending of these letters concerning the newly elected patriarch to the pope and to the other patriarchs was strictly required in the past. It was a sign of communion and unity. Lack of response was considered an indication of disapproval and of denied recognition. Other signs of communion were the inscription of the name of the patriarch on the diptychs of the living and the representation of the patriarchs by nuncios.

The patriarch thus elected, confirmed, and enthroned acquires full rights to his office; he truly becomes the head of his Church. Nevertheless, as long as he has not received confirmation in consistory and the pallium has not been solemnly imposed on him, he is prevented from performing certain acts that are considered to be the full exercise of the patriarchal office: the convocation of a patriarchal synod and the election or consecration of bishops.

Rights. It may be said that ClerSanc preserved in substance the patriarchal prerogatives of the past centuries; however, it has suppressed even the semblance of complete self-government. It has the merit of having extended the Byzantine institution of the permanent synod to all the patriarchates.

Nature of the Patriarchal Power. The power of the patriarch is: (1) Superepiscopal. The patriarch enjoys a twofold juridical personality. He is first of all a bishop and, as such, is granted the same power as all residential bishops in his own eparchy and in all the places of the patriarchate wherein neither eparchies nor patriarchal exarchates are erected (ClerSanc c.282). What makes him a patriarch, however, is the jurisdiction he enjoys over all the bishops of his own patriarchate (ClerSanc c.240.1). (2) Direct and indirect. On the bishops of his patriarchate he exercises a direct power, that is, without intermediaries. On the clergy and faithful of his patriarchate he exercises, instead, an indirect power, namely, through hierarchs. However, in certain cases the sacred canons grant the patriarch a direct power also over his clergy and faithful, e.g., ClerSanc cc.246, 249.1n3, 258.2, 134.3, 145, 260.2. (3) Ordinary. A power of jurisdiction attached by the law itself to the patriarchal post in as stable a manner as the very office of the patriarchate is ordinary power. It is also a proper ordinary power since the patriarch exercises it in his own name and not in the name of the Holy See or another person. (4) Personal. The power of the patriarch is reserved to himself as patriarch in such a way that he cannot nominate a syncellus, an alter ego for the whole patriarchate (ClerSanc c.241).

Object of the Patriarchal Power. The patriarch's power has a broad range and it is manifested in three principal ways: in enacting and executing laws, in teaching, and in administrating.

The patriarch has the power to enact laws. He can issue edicts, orders, and general prescriptions on questions that concern his Church and his rite. He can, above all, enact laws either for the whole patriarchate or for a part of it or for a group of persons, but only in the patriarchal synod. Thus, the fathers of the synod become colegislators under the presidency of the patriarch. This legislative power must never be exercised against the common law of the Church or against laws enacted by the Apostolic See for the patriarchate but only *praeter ius* or *secundum ius.* In order to become effective, the laws must first be promulgated by the patriarch, who, until the convocation of the next synod and after consultation with his permanent synod, enjoys the exclusive right of interpreting them authentically.

The patriarch may grant dispensation from them in particular cases and for a just reason, the dispensation affecting even the whole patriarchate. Should a dispensation go beyond particular cases, the patriarch needs for the validity of the dispensation a grave reason as well as the consent of the permanent synod. Furthermore, he is able to dispense from a law of the patriarchal synod when a dispensation has previously been denied by the local hierarch, but only for a just reason and after consultation with the hierarch.

The patriarch also has the power to execute laws. He must see that his laws are enforced and that the will of the sovereign pontiff and his own legitimate orders are faithfully carried out. He must also punish the negligent and the reluctant if their cases warrant it. The patriarch does his utmost so that personal statutes are respected by the civil authority in those regions where they are in effect.

The patriarch possesses the power to teach, as he can and must be the light of his Church. The sacred canons grant him the privilege of preaching the word of God all over the world (ClerSanc c.283.2). He is, therefore, required to give instructions to the clergy and to the people in order to clarify sound doctrine, to promote piety, to correct abuses, and to approve and recommend those practices that further the spiritual good of the faithful. He also issues encyclical letters for the whole patriarchate and approves courses of preaching for the entire territory. Above all, the patriarch must do his utmost in order to maintain the faithful preservation and the strictest possible observance of his liturgical rite: it is mostly through liturgy that he must give his faithful the spiritual nourishment that is necessary to any soul seeking God.

The patriarch also has administrative powers for the general management of his patriarchate. Therefore, he provides for the election of the bishops of his patriarchate in the best possible way, for the erection of provinces and eparchies, or for the modification of their boundaries. His main concern, along with the local hierarch, is the pastoral service and the progress of the eparchies. He has the right and the duty of visiting his patriarchate, of convoking to conferences the bishops and other local hierarchs from the entire patriarchate, or from a province or region, for the purpose of studying in common the measures to be taken for a good government of the various eparchies. Moreover, he must see that his patriarchate's temporal goods are completely, faithfully, and diligently administered so that they may serve the purpose for which they were constituted.

Obligations. The patriarch must profess complete obedience to the pope and must commemorate him during divine services. Every 5 years he is obliged to make a report on the state of his patriarchate, and in the same year in which he must present this report, he is required to go to Rome for the purpose of paying veneration to the tombs of the Apostles Peter and Paul and of visiting the sovereign pontiff (ClerSanc cc.273, 274, 275).

The patriarch is bound by law to reside in the patriarchal see and cannot absent himself except for a canonical cause, that is, for a reason explicitly or implicitly contemplated by the canons (ClerSanc c.276).

The application of the Mass for a specified intention comes within the authentic tradition of the Oriental Church. In fact, at the Prothesis the priest commemorates those whom he has particularly in mind. However, the institution of the Mass *pro populo,* in its present form, is a Latin custom. In 1863 the Congregation for the Propagation of the Faith instructed Orientals to observe this usage. Considered an institution concerning an obligation of divine law, it has been put into Oriental practice and prescribed in Cler Sanc c.277. The patriarch must, therefore, apply the holy Mass for the faithful of his patriarchate on those solemn days mentioned in ClerSanc c.277.

The duty of maintaining purity of faith and morals falls primarily and directly on local hierarchs (Cler Sanc c.400). In virtue of his office, however, the patriarch is also responsible for the faithful of his patriarchate. If the hierarchs of places fail to fulfill their duties, the patriarch must not omit to warn them. If the warnings do not achieve the desired effect, he proceeds according to the provisions of the canons (ClerSanc c.278).

Although the first approval of liturgical books of Oriental rites is reserved to the Congregation for the *Oriental Church (ClerSanc c.195.1n2), nevertheless the patriarch has the duty of examining the various editions of liturgical books. Thus he must guarantee the fidelity and integrity of the texts, as well as their concordance with approved versions. Furthermore, only he may allow their publication.

Privileges. The patriarch enjoys the following privileges. He may hear confessions everywhere of all the faithful, including religious of both sexes, and may absolve from all sins and censures, even those that are reserved, with the sole exception of censures reserved most specially to the Apostolic See and those attached to the crime of revelation of a secret of the Holy Office. He may preach the word of God everywhere. He may bless objects destined for religious purposes (crosses, statues, medals, etc.) and grant indulgences of 300 days. In every church of his rite, even outside the patriarchate, he may declare one altar to be perpetually privileged every day (*privilegiatum perpetuum cotidianum*). Besides, he may make use of the crosier and pallium within his patriarchate, and of the crosier alone even outside his territory, provided he is in a church of his rite (ClerSanc c.283nn1–9).

According to law the administration of Baptism and Confirmation is reserved to the hierarch of the place and to the pastor; assistance at marriages is likewise reserved to them, and this is for the validity of the matrimonial contracts (CrebAllat c.85). The patriarch, even without being a local hierarch, enjoys the same powers by privilege.

The patriarch is granted precedence, even outside the Oriental territory, over all primates, archbishops, and other metropolitans; over bishops regardless of their Oriental rite and even though each of the bishops is in his own territory (ClerSanc c.283n11). He is given the title of Beatitude. He may appoint procurators to represent him or to act on his behalf in matters concerning the patriarchate (ClerSanc c.283nn10, 13). Unless otherwise provided by particular laws, the patriarch may delegate to a duly ordained priest the power of blessing churches and statues, of conferring minor Orders, and of consecrating chalices, etc. Furthermore, in case of urgent necessity and after consultation with their superiors, he may promote either to the first Order, or from one Order to another, and even to the priesthood, monks of any monastery, provided that it is not of pontifical right (ClerSanc c.285.1n1–2).

Vacancy of the Patriarchal See. The patriarchal see becomes vacant by death of the patriarch, by his renunciation (effective when he is notified of its acceptance by the Roman pontiff), by his tacit renunciation, by his transfer, or by deprivation of the see (effective only when notification of it has been given to the patriarch). Unless the Apostolic See establishes otherwise for grave reasons, the administration of the vacant see is conducted by a bishop of the patriarchate, who is called administrator. According to common law he may be the bishop senior by episcopal consecration among those who have office and residence in the patriarchal curia. However, the particular law prevails in this matter. Thus, in the Melkite particular law the dean of the bishops by episcopal consecration becomes administrator. In reference to the vacancy as such, the administrator of the patriarchate must see to it that the Holy See, all the bishops even titular of the patriarchate, and all the hierarchs of places are immediately notified of the vacancy. He must also prepare the synod for the election of the patriarch and convoke, at the prescribed time, the fathers of the synod. In general, he shall not fail to execute personally or by proxy whatever is prescribed by the common or particular law for such a circumstance. As for the government of the eparchy proper of the patriarch, of the other places of the patriarchate subject to the direct jurisdiction of the patriarch and exarchs, the norms to be followed are the same as for the administration of a vacant eparchy. With regard to the government of the whole patriarchate as such, the administrator generally enjoys the patriarch's ordinary jurisdiction in both spiritual and temporal matters and the usual faculties granted to the patriarch by the Apostolic See. However, the faculties listed in ClerSanc c.310.1n1 are granted to him by principle, but with exceptions according to the nature of things (e.g., ClerSanc cc.272, 273.2, 283, 285) or under the form of a juridical prescription that likewise admits limitations (e.g., Cler

Sanc c.311). Because of the transitory and provisional nature of his powers, the administrator shall not introduce any innovation that may appear as a diminution or deterioration of the patriarchate's juridical state rather than an improvement of it. Finally, the administrator shall give an account of his administration to the new patriarch.

Latin Patriarchs Compared. A patriarch of an Oriental Church differs considerably from a patriarch of the Latin Church. The latter enjoys no special jurisdiction (CIC c.271). The title of patriarch is given to a few archbishops of the Latin Church, such as the patriarchs of Venice, Lisbon, and Goa, and carries with it only a prerogative of honor and the right of precedence over primates (CIC c.280). They are two completely different institutions. One is purely nominal and honorific; the other is truly jurisdictional, and by it the patriarch becomes the highest authority within an ecclesiastical territory, the head and the crown glory of a Church.

Bibliography: A. COUSSA, *Epitome praelectionum de iure ecclesiastico orientali,* v.1 (Grottaferrata 1948); suppl. (1958). Pospishil PersOr. C. DE CLERCQ, DDC 6:1255–65. F. CLAEYS BOUUAERT, *ibid.* 1254–55. L. BRÉHIER, *Les Institutions de l'empire byzantin,* v.2 of *Le Monde byzantin,* 3 v. (Paris 1947–50). E. GERLAND, ed., *Corpus notitiarum episcopatuum ecclesiae orientalis graecae* (Le Patriarcat byzantin, 2d ser. Istanbul 1931–). É. EID, *La Figure juridique du patriarche* (2d ed. Rome 1962). G. EVERY, *The Byzantine Patriarchate, 451–1204* (2d ed. London 1962). MAXIMOS IV (Patriarch of Antioch), ed., *The Eastern Churches and Catholic Unity,* tr. J. DINGLE (New York 1963). A. WUYTS, "Le Droit des personnes dans l'église orientale," NouvRevTh 80 (1958) 359–383; "Il diritto delle persone nella nuova legislazione per la chiesa orientale," OrChrPer 24 (1958) 175–201. N. LOVER, "New Law Affecting Our Dealings with Oriental Catholics," AmEcclRev 139 (1958) 250. M. M. WOJNAR, "The Code of Oriental Canon Law *De ritibus orientalibus* and *De personis,*" Jurist 19 (1959) 212–245, 277–299, 413–464. T. A. KANE, *The Jurisdiction of the Patriarchs of the Major Sees in Antiquity and in the Middle Ages* (CUA CLS 276; 1949). G. MANESSO, "Il diritto degli orientali," *Studia patavina* 9 (1962) 218–241. S. A. MORÁN, "El nuevo derecho de la iglesia oriental," RevEspDC 13 (1958) 115–143.

[G. SALEM]

THEOLOGY AND HISTORY

In this section an effort will be made to assess the patriarchal structure in the light of history and of ecclesiological principles.

Ecclesiology. Truly the division of the Church into *patriarchates and the powers traditionally exercised by the ancient (major) patriarchs are not immediately of divine origin. The Code of Canon Law (c.108) declares that from the standpoint of divine institution the *hierarchy is composed (so far as *jurisdiction is concerned) of the supreme pontificate and a subordinate episcopate. Any intermediate grouping and any intermediate authority vested in bishops of certain sees are therefore of ecclesiastical origin. The extent to which the erection and continued existence of the patriarchates may be attributed to the guidance of the Holy Spirit is to be judged by the consonance of this structural form with the nature and needs of the Church.

It is in forming such a judgment that theologians of the East and West have even up to the present often been at odds. Catholic theologians, especially in the millennium that has passed since the split between East and West, in focusing on the note of unity that belongs to the Mystical Body, have tended to see in the broad autonomy enjoyed by the Eastern patriarchates the seedbed of schism. They are accustomed to appeal to Church history to show that the patriarchal structure and patriarchal loyalties were too often an invitation to or a cloak for a *de facto* independence of the divinely established center of unity. They see a natural and psychological development beginning as early as the Council of Chalcedon, 451 [cf. Jugie Theol Dog 4:450–463], in which the *de facto* recognition of the five patriarchates (Rome, Alexandria, Antioch, Constantinople, Jerusalem) led first to a theory of pentarchy uneasily compatible with the *primacy of the pope and then as time went on to a theory of pentarchy incompatible with that primacy.

Eastern theologians, both those of the Eastern dissident churches and quite generally those of the Oriental rites of the Catholic Church, have tended to judge the patriarchal structure in focusing on the note of *catholicity that equally marks the Mystical Body. This viewpoint, eloquently expressed in the 45th general congregation (Oct. 10, 1963) of Vatican Council II by Msgr. Isaac Ghattas, Catholic Coptic Bishop of Thebes in Egypt, holds as "providential" the institution of the patriarchates and maintains that it is due to this structure of ecclesiastical life that in extensive territories there have been conserved the Lord's presence and the Eucharistic Liturgy under the presidency of the patriarch, the high priest, chief and center of unity of the episcopal college in his region. "If we insist," Msgr. Ghattas added, "on the position and dignity of patriarchs, it is not out of some desire to maintain outmoded traditions, but out of a conception of the Church itself and of its catholic unity. Certainly the Church is universal, but this universality is not to be divorced from the multiplicity of the individual Churches: such is the perspective of the Pauline Epistles and of the Apocalypse. And the patriarchate is an element in this structure." The bishop insisted that the patriarchal institution represents a form and an instrument of the diversity that is inherent in the true unity of the Church, of the variety that is essential to authentic catholicity.

In the continuing dialogue that balances unity against catholicity and strives to find a mean between centralization and decentralization, it may perhaps be found that the patriarchal arrangement afforded in past times and may still today afford in certain parts of the Church a congenial grouping that prevents any monolithic uniformity in Catholic life and discipline, while impeding a decentralization that would issue in fragmentation. Vatican Council II officially acknowledged the patriarchate structure (*Constitution on the Church* n.23). Moreover, prelates of the Eastern rites felt that in it they already possessed what their colleagues of the West were striving to attain through large regional groupings in *episcopal conferences.

History of Patriarchates. The origins of the patriarchates are but dimly seen in the documentation of the period before the Peace of Constantine. The Council of Nicaea I (325), though it did not employ the term, recognized in its canons the reality of the patriarchal status of Alexandria and Antioch—and, by implication, of Rome. This Council, moreover, seems to have allowed a somewhat similar status for Caesarea (in Cappadocia) over the civil Diocese of Pontus, for Ephesus over the civil Diocese of Asia, and for Heraclea over the civil Diocese of Thrace—Churches that

lost their importance with the rise of the Church of Constantinople. Nicaea took cognizance also of the tradition that gave a special place of honor to the bishop of Jerusalem, but without prejudice to the rights of the bishop of Caesarea (in Palestine). It was not until the Council of Chalcedon that Jerusalem was recognized as a patriarchate.

Constantinople was from its beginning a suffragan see of the metropolitan of Heraclea. Its ecclesiastical importance began with its establishment as the civil capital of the Empire by Constantine in A.D. 324. The first Council of Constantinople (second ecumenical) in 381 recognized the "new Rome" as the second bishopric in Christendom, but historians and canonists are not agreed whether this Council gave to the bishop of Constantinople real patriarchal jurisdiction or conceded him merely an honorary precedence. Though Rome did not recognize the legislation of this Council in regard to the See of Constantinople nor the fuller legislation of the Council of Chalcedon, it cannot be denied that from the late 5th century Constantinople was acknowledged practically as a patriarchal center and, in fact, the second see in the Church, a situation that was officially recognized in the 21st canon of Constantinople IV (869–870).

The origin then of the rights attributed to these four Eastern sees (Alexandria, Antioch, Constantinople, Jerusalem) cannot be reduced to any single cause. One does better to allow the influence of several factors: (1) sacred character (especially for Jerusalem); (2) apostolic foundation (Alexandria and Antioch); (3) importance as centers from which Christianity spread in broad areas (again Alexandria and Antioch); and (4) civil importance (predominantly Constantinople).

Bibliography: E. VALTON, DTC 5.2:1704, s.v. "Évêques." M. JUGIE, *ibid.* 3.2:1291–94, s.v. "Constantinople (IVᵉ Concile de)." R. VANCOURT, *ibid.* 11.2:2253–97, s.v. "Patriarcats." K. MÖRSDORF, LexThK² 8:174–177. T. A. KANE, *The Jurisdiction of the Patriarchs of the Major Sees in Antiquity and in the Middle Ages* (CUA CLS 276; 1949).

[S. E. DONLON]

PATRIARCHATE, BYZANTINE

Chief ecclesiastical office in the Byzantine Church. This article deals with the nature of the office, the territory of the patriarchate, the *synodos endēmousa*, the subordinate officials and their duties.

Patriarch. Patriarch was a title of honor given at first to any bishop of advanced years or special dignity. In Justinian's legislation, patriarch takes on its technical sense, connoting a definite rank in the hierarchy, that of a chief bishop ruling over an extensive territory and subject only to the patriarch in Rome. The epithet "ecumenical" was employed in isolated cases in addressing Dioscurus of Alexandria, Pope St. Leo, and Acacius of Constantinople, but became the customary designation of the patriarchs of Constantinople after the Acacian schism. Scholars have reached no agreement on its meaning or original importance. It can be said only that as applied to the patriarch of Constantinople, it met with no objection until Popes Pelagius II (579–590) and Gregory the Great (590–604), who opposed it strongly and persistently; and it remained a bone of contention between Rome and Byzantium for centuries afterward. It was not made strict etiquette in communicating with a patriarch until the reign of the Patriarch *Photius (858–867; 877–886). The title was never used by the patriarch of himself, but only by others speaking to him or of him, until Michael I Cerularius (1043–58) placed it on his seal; and it finally became part of the official title under Manuel I (1217–22). It was never used by a patriarch in dealing with the papacy.

Pentarchy. To the three ancient Patriarchates, Rome, Alexandria and Antioch, the Council of Chalcedon added two more, by acknowledging the new Patriarchate of Jerusalem, and by formally recognizing Constantinople's right over the territory that it had ruled in fact for 50 years. These five sees emerged in the public consciousness as a distinct group, the pentarchy, through the legislation of Justinian. The pentarchy soon took on a theological aspect; the five patriarchs were believed to represent the moral universality of the Church, and it was maintained that a council could not be ecumenical without their presence either in person or by deputies. Actually, this doctrine served as a check on imperial control of the Church.

Further development was connected with the growing sense of the importance of apostolicity; just as the primitive Christian community had been governed by the college of the Apostles with Peter as their head, so the Church was governed by the pentarchy with Rome as the first see. Finally, sometime before the break under Cerularius (1054), it took a heretical turn: the five patriarchs are equals, the only head is Christ, and the majority rules.

The territory of Constantinople originally comprised Thrace (in the northeast part of the Balkans) and Asia Minor, with rights over Armenia and the cis-Caucasus. In 731 the rest of the Balkan Peninsula, with Sicily and southern Italy, was annexed to Byzantium and transferred by Emperor *Leo III, the iconoclast, from Rome, although Rome never acknowledged this as valid. Bulgaria never came into the patriarchate, remaining either independent or autocephalous, i.e., subject directly to the emperor and exempt from the patriarch's jurisdiction. In 1035 Constantinople gained all of Russia—a tremendous expansion beyond the empire's boundaries. In 1071 it sustained catastrophic losses—all southern Italy with Sicily fell to the Normans and Rome, and most of Asia Minor to the Seljuks. In the 14th century, however, Constantinople won Rumania's voluntary submission.

Synodos Endēmousa. The patriarch's rights were always intimately associated with the *synodos endēmousa,* and rested not on legislation either ecclesiastical or civil but on custom, to which according to Roman theory law was but the servant and supplement. During semi-Arian times the emperor would refer ecclesiastical matters to a synod of the many bishops in his retinue gathered under the presidency of the local ordinary. That this procedure would continue seems to have been taken for granted as something perfectly natural, e.g., by St. Gregory of Nazianzus and St. Ambrose, even after 381 when Theodosius the Great restored orthodoxy in the East and Constantinople became the permanent residence. Hence, from the very beginning we see St. John Chrysostom convoking the *synodos endēmousa* (literally, "stopping-over synod"). The bishops who were stopping over on business at Constantinople were called together into a synod by and under the patriarch to decide appeals either made directly to it or referred to it by the emperor from any part of the East regard-

less of patriarchal boundaries. About the 9th century membership in the synod was restricted to the metropolitans and autocephalous (i.e., exempt from the metropolitan) archbishops of the patriarchate, to whom were added the synod's five highest administrative officials.

Since the time of Theodosius the Great, patriarchs were appointed by the emperor, but Canon Law required certain formalities. In the earlier period, the patriarch was elected like any other bishop, but from about the end of the 9th century only the synod had the right of election; it nominated three candidates from whom the emperor chose one, or, if none pleased him, he selected another for the (automatic) approval of the synod. The successful candidate then received the same investiture as lay dignitaries from the emperor and was consecrated the following Sunday, always by the metropolitan of Heraclea. He held office for life and could be canonically deposed only by the synod; treason automatically terminated his tenure.

Once enthroned, the patriarch became the head of the Byzantine Church and the second person in the empire. In time, his powers developed in connection with his presidency of the synod, and it is impossible to distinguish his personal rights from those exercised conjointly with it. Furthermore, the emperor had greater authority in all matters not requiring orders, though he always consulted the patriarch before publishing any ordinance affecting religion and always addressed it to him. Actually, the patriarch could at times wield tremendous influence, e.g., one of strong character, particularly a monk, confronting a weak ruler, especially if the Church was in a position to throw its weight to either of two evenly balanced political parties. In general, the emperor kept nearly complete control of ecclesiastical geography and the rank of sees (which determined the precedence of bishops), usually by suggestion to the synod and with the consent of the patriarch. After the quarrel over the tetragamy, marriage legislation was more and more reserved to the Church. The spiritual head enjoyed most independence in the liturgy and in the maintaining of ecclesiastical discipline. He also had the final say in the choice of metropolitans, picking from three candidates presented by the synod. From the 9th century he possessed the very important privilege of *stauropegia* (planting of the cross), i.e., the canonical establishment of a religious house; this also entitled him to approve of a proposed abbot and to collect the *kanonikon,* a sort of tribute. At about the same time he acquired the exclusive right to consecrate the chrism.

Officials. The officials of the church of Holy Wisdom in Constantinople were the officials of the patriarchate. In the middle and late periods, they were five: (1) *megas oikonomos* (grand manager), who controlled the entire property of the patriarchate, both cash and real estate; (2) *megas sakkelarius* and (3) *ho sakkeliou,* of whom the one had charge of all monastic establishments and the other, of all parish churches throughout the patriarchate, but their functions were frequently interchanged; (4) *megas skeuophylax* (grand sacristan), who took care of all precious possessions of the Church and acted as sacristan of Holy Wisdom with general supervision of the lands that furnished materials used in the liturgy (wheat, wine, oil, wax, etc.); (5) *megas chartophylax* (grand archivist), who, though he ranked fourth and was always only a deacon, had by far the greatest power, since he was the vice-patriarch and the real ecclesiastical governor of Constantinople; he controlled all access personal or by mail to the patriarch, determined the worthiness of all candidates for priesthood or episcopacy, tried all clergy (not bishops) guilty of any offense, determined freedom to marry, and, as archivist, also acted as chief canonist, issuing interpretations, in the name of the synod, that had force of law. These five highest dignitaries were known as the *Exokatakoiloi* and were comparable to the Roman Cardinals; they were members of the synod outranking the metropolitans. Originally they were all deacons, but subsequently many were priests. Another important functionary often mentioned in the sources was the *apocrisiarius* (nuncio), a permanent representative that the patriarch kept at each of the other patriarchates. Metropolitans had permanent or temporary *apocrisiarii* in Constantinople, and each bishop with his metropolitan. From the earlier Byzantine period two offices ought to be mentioned: that of the archdeacon, head of the administration when all officials were deacons, later reduced to his purely liturgical duties, and the *synkellos* (cellmate), second in rank to the patriarch and successor designate; later on, the term became a purely honorary title of bishops. All of these dignitaries had many minor officials under them and office help at their disposal.

Bibliography: Beck KTLBR. L. Bréhier, *Les Institutions de l'Empire byzantin* (*Le Monde byzantin* 2; Paris 1949). F. Dvornik, *Byzance et la primauté romaine* (Paris 1964); *Idea of Apostolicity in Byzantium and the Legend of the Apostle Andrew* (Cambridge, Mass. 1958). S. Vailhé, ÉchosOr 11 (1908) 65–69. A. H. M. Jones, JThSt 11 (1960) 84–94. J. Hajjar, *Le Synode permanent dans l'Église byzantine des origines au XIe siècle* (OrChrAnal 164; 1962).

[M. J. HIGGINS]

PATRIARCHATES

A patriarchate (Gr. πατριαρχεία; Lat. *Patriarchatus*) is a patriarch's office, see, reign, or, most often, the territory he governs. The number of patriarchates was in the course of time enlarged from the original three to five, and subsequent historical factors caused a multiplication of patriarchates.

The Three Patriarchs. The oldest Canon Law admitted only three bishops as having what later ages called patriarchal rights—the bishops of Rome, Alexandria, and Antioch. The successor of St. Peter held the highest place as pope; however he was not only bishop, but metropolitan, primate, and patriarch. The pope combines the above positions, and each of them gives him a special relation to the faithful and the bishops in the territories corresponding. As pope he is visible head of the whole Church; no Christian is outside his papal jurisdiction. As bishop of Rome he is the diocesan bishop of that diocese only. As metropolitan he governs the Roman province. As primate he governs the Italian bishops. And as patriarch he rules only the West. As patriarch the pope has from the beginning ruled all the Western lands where Latin was once the civilized, and is still the liturgical, language; where the Roman rite is now used almost exclusively; and where the Roman Canon Law obtains. To Christians in the East he is supreme pontiff, not patriarch. Hence there has always been a closer relation between Western bishops and the pope than between him and their Eastern

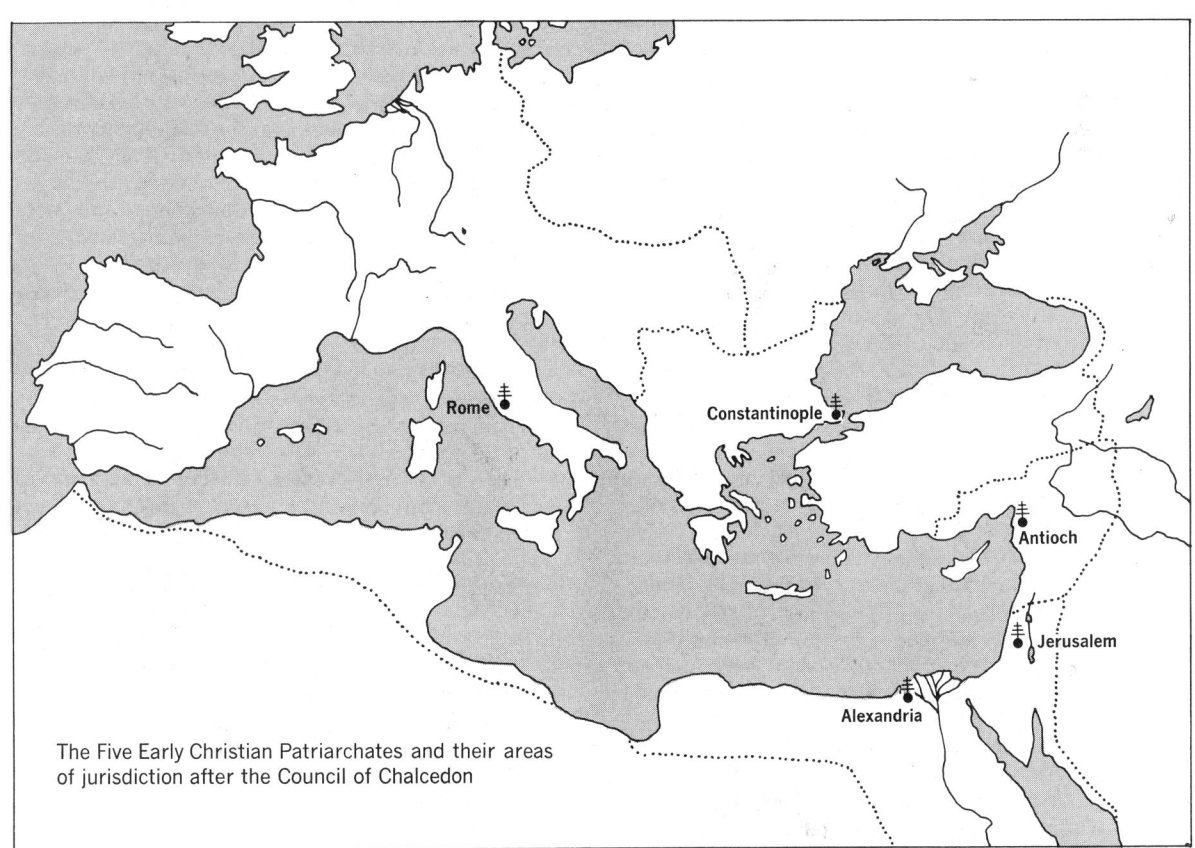

The Five Early Christian Patriarchates and their areas of jurisdiction after the Council of Chalcedon

brethren, just as there is a still closer relation between him and the suburban bishops of the Roman province, of which he is metropolitan.

Before the Council of Nicaea I (325) two bishops in the East had the same patriarchal authority over large territories, those of Alexandria and Antioch. It is difficult to say exactly how they obtained this position. The organization of provinces under metropolitans followed, as a matter of obvious convenience, the reorganization of the Empire made by Diocletian. In the new system the most important cities in the East were Alexandria in Egypt and Antioch in Syria. Consequently the bishop of Alexandria became the chief of all Egyptian bishops and metropolitans; the bishop of Antioch held the same place over Syria and at the same time extended his sway over Asia Minor, Greece, and the rest of the East. Diocletian had divided the Empire into four great prefectures. Three of these (Italy, Gaul, and Illyricum) made up the Roman patriarchate; the other, the East (*Praefectura Orientis*), had five (civil) "dioceses"—Thrace, Asia, Pontus, the Diocese of the East, and Egypt. Egypt was the Alexandrine patriarchate. The Antiochene patriarchate embraced the civil Diocese of the East. The other three civil divisions of Thrace, Asia, and Pontus would probably have developed into separate patriarchates but for the rise of Constantinople.

Later it became popular to connect all three patriarchates with the Prince of the Apostles. St. Peter had also reigned at Antioch, and he had founded the Church of Alexandria through his disciple St. Mark. At any rate the Council of Nicaea in 325 recognized the supreme place of the bishops of these three cities as related to an "ancient custom" (c.6). Rome, Alexandria, and Antioch are the three old patriarchates, whose unique position and order were disturbed by later developments.

The Five Patriarchates. When pilgrims began to flock to the Holy City, the bishop of Jerusalem, the guardian of the sacred shrines, began to be considered the head of more than a mere suffragan of Caesarea. The Council of Nicaea (325) gave him an honorary primacy, saving, however, the metropolitical rights of Caesarea (c.7). Juvenal of Jerusalem (420–458) succeeded finally, after much dispute, in changing this honorary position into official rule over a patriarchate. The Council of Chalcedon (451) severed Palestine and Arabia (Sinai) from Antioch and formed the Patriarchate of Jerusalem (sess. 7 and 8). Since that time Jerusalem has always been counted among the patriarchal sees.

The greatest change, the one that met most opposition, was the rise of Constantinople to patriarchal rank. Because Constantine had made Byzantium the "New Rome," its bishop, once the humble suffragan bishop of Heraclea, thought that he should become second only, if not almost equal, to the bishop of old Rome. For many centuries the popes opposed this ambition, not because any of them thought of disputing their first place, but because they were unwilling to change the old order of the hierarchy. In 381 the Council of Constantinople declared that "the Bishop of Constantinople shall have the primacy of honor after the Bishop of Rome, because it is New Rome" (c.3). The popes (Damasus, Gregory the Great) refused to confirm this

canon. Nevertheless Constantinople grew by favor of the Emperor, whose centralizing policy found a ready help in the authority of his court bishop. The Council of Chalcedon (451) established Constantinople as a patriarchate with jurisdiction over Asia Minor and Thrace and gave it the second place after Rome (c.28). Pope Leo I (440–461) refused to admit this canon, which was made in the absence of his legates; for centuries Rome still refused to give the second place to Constantinople. It was not until the Fourth Lateran Council (1215) that the Latin patriarch of Constantinople would be allowed this place; in 1439 the Council of Florence was to give it to the Greek patriarch. Meanwhile, however, in the East the Emperor's wish was powerful enough to obtain recognition for his patriarch; from the time of the Council of Chalcedon Constantinople was practically, if not legally, the second patriarchate. The new order of five patriarchs—Rome, Constantinople, Alexandria, Antioch, Jerusalem—seemed, to Eastern theologians especially, an essential element of the constitution of the Church. (*See* ROME, PATRIARCHATE OF; CONSTANTINOPLE, PATRIARCHATE OF; ALEXANDRIA, PATRIARCHATE OF; ANTIOCH, PATRIARCHATE OF; JERUSALEM, PATRIARCHATE OF.)

Multiplication of Patriarchates. At the time of Cerularius's schism (1054) the great Church of the Empire knew practically these five patriarchs only, though "minor" patriarchates had already begun in the West. The Council of Constantinople IV (869) had solemnly affirmed their position (c.11). The schism, and further distinctions that would not have existed but for it, considerably augmented the number of bishops who claimed the title of patriarch. But even before the great schism, the earlier Nestorian and Monophysite separations had resulted in the appearance of various heretical patriarchs. To be under a patriarch had come to be the normal, and apparently necessary, condition for any Church. So it was natural that these heretics, when they broke from the Catholic patriarchs, should sooner or later set up rivals of their own. But in most cases they have been neither consistent nor logical. Instead of being merely an honorable title for the occupants of the five chief sees, the name patriarch was looked upon as denoting a rank of its own. So the idea grew that a bishop might be patriarch of any place.

Developments in the five traditional patriarchates occasioned by nationalist tendencies and schism have resulted in expansion to seven Catholic patriarchs and seventeen patriarchs of the *Orthodox Churches and *Eastern Churches. (*See* MELCHITE RITE; COPTIC RITE; MARONITE RITE; SYRIAN RITE; CHALDEAN RITE; ARMENIAN RITE; ETHIOPIAN RITE; RUSSIAN RITE; GEORGIAN RITE; SERBIAN RITE; RUMANIAN RITE; BULGARIAN RITE.)

Bibliography: A. COUSSA, *Epitome praelectionum de iure ecclesiastico orientali*, 3 v. (Grottaferrata-Rome 1948–50; supp. 1958) 1:201–286. T. A. KANE, *The Jurisdiction of the Patriarchs of the Major Sees in Antiquity and in the Middle Age* (CUA CLS 276; Washington 1949). Pospishil PersOr 112–152. C. DE CLERCQ DDC 6:1254–65. A. FORTESCUE, CE 11:549–553. W. DE VRIES, "La S. Sede ed i patriarchati cattolici d'Oriente," OrChr Per 27 (1961) 313–361; "Die Entstehung der Patriarchate des Ostens und ihr Verhältnis zur päpstlichen Vollgewalt," *Scholastik* 37 (1962) 341–369; *Rom und die Patriarchate des Ostens* (Freiburg 1963). H. GROTZ, *Die Hauptkirchen des Ostens . . .* (OrChrAnal 169; 1964).

[J. J. MC GRATH]

PATRIARCHS, BIBLICAL

A condensed study of the Biblical patriarchs warrants the following plan: origin and uses of the word "patriarch," the pre-Abrahamic patriarchs, the structure of the genealogies, the problem of their long lives, and the similar lists in ancient Mesopotamia.

Origin of "Patriarch." In the Septuagint (LXX) version, πατριάρχης, from which patriarch is derived, first appears in Chronicles, where it is used for translating several Hebrew expressions. Some of its significations are: the heads of Israelite families (2 Chr 19.8; 26.12); in many Greek MSS, the priestly and Levitical family chiefs (1 Chr 24.31); the chiefs over the tribes of Israel (1 Chr 27.22); the captains of companies of 100 men (2 Chr 23.20; cf. 4 Kgs 11.19). It has a more restricted use in the apocryphal 4 Machabees 16.25, where it apparently refers to the 12 sons of Jacob. The same book, however, speaks of "our patriarchs, Abraham, Isaac, and Jacob" (7.19). The word also appears in the NT where it refers to the 12 sons of Jacob (Acts 7.8–9); to David (Acts 2.29); to Abraham (Heb 7.4).

In present-day exegesis "patriarch" properly refers to *Abraham, *Isaac, and *Jacob, although two other acceptations are acknowledged: the eponymous ancestors of the 12 tribes of Israel, Joseph and his brothers; the 10 antediluvian and 10 postdiluvian celebrities listed by the Pentateuchal *Priestly Writers in Gn 5.1–32 and 11.10–26, respectively. In the last case, one would not speak of "patriarchal times," which comprise only the period of Abraham, Isaac, and Jacob. In this article the term patriarchs is used only in the last acceptation, signifying the pre-Abrahamic patriarchs.

Pre-Abrahamic Patriarchs. The list of antediluvian patriarchs from Adam to Noe is attributed to the Priestly Writers. The *Yahwist too handed down parallel but incomplete lists (Gn 4.17–22, 25–26) containing only six generations after Cain and only one after Seth. The Priestly genealogy proceeds from Adam through *Seth, while the Yahwist proceeds from Adam through Cain in its major genealogy. Notwithstanding the variants, it can be established that the same names appear in both lists.

Structure of the Genealogies. The two Priestly lists of Gn 5.1–32 and 11.10–26 are almost identical in form. Stereotyped formulas, typical of this tradition, are used for each patriarch in both lists and include the name of the patriarch, his age when he begot his first son, and the number of years he lived after the birth of that son. The lists are only slightly divergent; ch. 5 totals the duration of the lifetime of each patriarch, while ch. 11 does not.

The fact that each genealogy contains 10 generations is not mere coincidence. It reveals the author's desire for symmetry in the periods that preceded and followed the *Deluge. This is all the more apparent when one considers the divergence between the Masoretic Text (MT) and the LXX. In the MT, one finds 10 patriarchs in each period provided that Noe figures in both periods. The LXX adds Cainan from Gn 5.9–14 to the second list in Gn 11.12–13, thus eliminating the necessity of counting Noe twice. The Greek interpolater of the addition sacrificed accuracy for perfect symmetry. His preference for literary perfection and his grasp of the original author's intentions are thus apparent.

Extraordinary Ages. The didactic rather than historical nature of the lists is further confirmed by the amazingly long lives of the patriarchs. All procreated at, and lived to, an age that today, despite our highly superior medical knowledge, would be preposterous. Among the antediluvian patriarchs, according to the MT, the shortest life span was 365 years and the earliest procreation age, 65 years. Most of them exceeded 900 years or were not far removed from that age at death except Henoch, 365 years, and Lamek, 777 years, both figures being symbols of perfection in Hebrew numerology. On the average, the postdiluvian patriarchs had a shorter life. Their ages range downward from 950 for Noe, and 600 for Sem, to 148 for Nahor.

Literal Interpretation. The historicity of the genealogies used to be a trying problem for scholars. One of the attempts at a solution was to ignore the problem and accept the strict historical character of the passages and the figures. Modern scholars unhesitatingly reject this position because it pays no attention to historical or literary criticism. Its advocates would be accused of Biblical *fundamentalism today, since they considered that anything contained in the Bible must be interpreted literally and is of necessity historically accurate. They also referred to the legends of other cultures that assert the great longevity of their early ancestors and concluded that the common accord implies a one-time reality. There is no scientific evidence, however, to corroborate this stand. On the contrary, the findings of science show that the life span of primitive man was shorter than ours today. Many favored a modified position but still inflexibly adhered to the historical accuracy of the figures. The year, they conjectured, lasted only 1 month or more—an erroneous assumption, since, in the Bible, the word "year" always means a span of 12 months and is clearly distinguished from shorter periods.

Didactic Literary Device. The solution admitted by most modern scholars takes the figures as didactic literary artifices without strict historical intent (*see* LITERARY GENRES, BIBLICAL). The genealogies and the ages of the patriarchs reflect ancient traditions and a system of computation for which a completely satisfactory explanation has not yet been found. Modern interpretation stresses the texts' etiological character as a function of religious teaching. Why is man's life span so limited? A long, fruitful life was considered an incomparable blessing, the reward of faithful service to God. The gradual shortening of man's life span was in keeping with the progress of evil in the world. In Noe's day, evil was so rampant that God said to Noe, "The end of all creatures of flesh is in my mind; . . . I will destroy them" (Gn 6.13). As a result, God punished man by the Deluge and reduced his life expectancy by hundreds of years (cf. Noe's, Sem's, Arphachsad's, and Phaleg's ages). This chastisement showed God's hatred of sin and gave a reason for the evil of man's short lifetime. The extraordinary ages of the patriarchs, therefore, have religious implications and are to be taken as didactic symbols.

Textual Discrepancies. There are notable discrepancies in the numbers of the lists in the MT, the Samaritan Pentateuch (the original Hebrew text of the first five books of the Bible handed down by the Samaritans and quite different in places from the MT; it dates, in its first form, from c. 300 B.C.), and the LXX. The

Cylinder (really a four-sided prism) of baked clay inscribed with eight columns of cuneiform text giving the "Sumerian King List," a traditional account of the early rulers of Sumeria. Beginning with the time "when kingship was lowered from heaven," it first lists the eight kings who reigned for 241,000 years before the Deluge. The list of rulers goes almost to the end of the First Dynasty of Isin (c. 1958–1733 B.C.), when the inscription was probably written (at Larsa), though based on several much earlier documents. For an English translation of the first part of the text, see Pritchard ANET, 265–266.

freedom with which the figures were altered indicates that they were known to be symbolic and could be modified to bring out more clearly the religious lesson. A comparison shows that the Samaritan Pentateuch agrees with the MT down to the fifth patriarch Malaleel but keeps to a decreasing amount of years for the following names, in contrast to the MT, which has the sixth and eighth patriarchs living longer than Adam. A corresponding lessening of the ages at which the patriarchs first generated a son leads to a discrepancy of 349 years less than the period between Adam and the Flood in the Samaritan Pentateuch.

The LXX adds 100 years to the first five names and to the seventh for the procreation age and thus lengthens the antediluvian period by 606 years and 955 years more than the MT and Samaritan versions. All three agree on the perfect age of Henoch, 365 years, but neither of the other two agrees with the MT on the perfect 777 years of Lamek. The LXX agrees with the MT on the age of the longest-lived patriarch, Mathusale,

both as to generating age and age at death, 187 and 969.

These variants are interesting but not very enlightening. The reason that procreation was delayed so long in all three, but especially in the LXX, is most puzzling. It may merely have been to underline the extraordinary characteristics of the men of old, who were closer to God and His original act of creation and who, therefore, could not have been like the ordinary men of the ancient writers' experience.

The case of Henoch is significant. He is described by a Hebrew idiom meaning that he was an extremely holy man. "Henoch walked with God; and he was seen no more because God took him" (Gn 5.24). One would expect him to have lived much longer than the other patriarchs, but his lifetime was only 365 years. However, this figure is a perfect number, the exact duration of the solar year. His mysterious disappearance without the mention of his death is also indicative of his unique position. Later Judaism did not miss these significant details; it made him a messianic figure comparable to Elia, who was also "taken up by God," and attributed to him apocryphal books that inspired at least one NT writer, Jude 14–15 (see HENOCH).

Mesopotamian Genealogies. The Babylonians had similar lists of antediluvian kings. Two cuneiform texts, W.B. 444 and W.B. 62 (*The Weld-Blundell Collection, Oxford Editions of Cuneiform Inscriptions*, v. 2, p. 8f and plate VI), and the Greek text of *Berossus, a Chaldaean priest of the time of Alexander the Great, are well known. Only eight names (given in Pritchard ANET 265) are contained in W.B. 444, whereas W.B. 62 and the text of Berossus, like the Genesis genealogy of the antediluvian patriarchs, contain 10 names. The names in the two cuneiform lists are nearly identical, though they do not appear in the same order; those of the Greek text can be identified with the kings in the cuneiform texts. The last name in W.B. 444 is Ubar-Tutu of Shuruppak, the father of the Deluge hero, Utnapishtim (in Akkadian), but the other two lists end with the hero himself, Ziusudra (in Sumerian), Xisouthros (in Greek). The life span of the antediluvian kings is very much longer than that of the Biblical patriarchs. Again the figures vary from one list to another and thus reveal the authors' indifference to historical chronology. A look at the list of W.B. 444 will exemplify the grossly exaggerated ages of the Mesopotamian kings: A-lulim of Eridu, 28,800 years; Alalgar of Eridu, 36,000 years; En-men-lu-Anna of Badtibira, 43,200 years, etc., with a total of 241,000 years for the eight kings before the Flood. In this list, the 241,000 years from the monarchy's institution, identified with Creation, to the death of the last antediluvian king contrasts with the 456,000 years of W.B. 62 and the 432,000 years of the Berossus text (the two last include the hero of the Flood plus another previous king). The figures, therefore, were subjected to alterations from one text to another.

Many critics have studied the resemblances and the differences between these lists and the Genesis genealogies. The differences are more striking. The Babylonian lists speak of kings and intend to show the unbroken succession of monarchs from the Creation onward; their perspective is decidedly national. The Biblical genealogies consider the patriarchs as the ancestors of all the races and nations; their perspective is universal and manifests God's supremacy over all of mankind. The chronological computations are very dissimilar, and it is unlikely that the Biblical system is based on the Babylonian. Efforts to identify the patriarchs' names with those of the antediluvian kings have been futile, save for that of Noe, which may possibly have the same meaning as Utnapishtim and its Sumerian equivalent Ziusudra. There may also be some relationship between Henoch's 365 years, as a solar year symbol, and the seventh king of W.B. 62 and the text of Berossus, the king of Sippar, the city of the sun. It appears, therefore, that the Priestly traditions concerning the antediluvian and postdiluvian patriarchs are only remotely non-Israelite traditions.

Bibliography: J. CHAINE, Le Livre de la Genèse (Paris 1951). J. SCHILDENBERGER, Vom Geheimnis des Gotteswortes (Heidelberg 1950) 261–303. H. CAZELLES, DBSuppl 1:745–754; 7:81–82. EncDictBibl 855–856, 1342, 1760, 1920–26. Illustration credit: Courtesy of the Ashmolean Museum, Oxford.

[N. VAILLANCOURT]

PATRICIAN BROTHERS,

popular name for the Congregation of the Brothers of St. Patrick (FSP), founded at Tullow, County Carlow, Ireland, in 1808 by Bp. Daniel Delany (1747–1814) of the Diocese of Kildare and Leighlin. The congregation, approved by Rome in 1893, engages in the apostolate of Christian education. Mt. St. Joseph, the motherhouse, is in Tullow, where the congregation is governed by a superior general, aided by four assistants. All are elected by a general chapter for 6-year terms. Members take simple, perpetual vows and are distinguished by a green sash worn with the habit. There are three provinces: Ireland and Africa, India and Pakistan, and Australia. Each province has a provincial superior appointed by the superior general. In 1963 the congregation had 305 brothers, 36 houses, 53 schools, and 14,900 students. The province of Ireland and Africa had 145 brothers, 18 schools and 3,800 students; India and Pakistan, 70 brothers, 15 schools and 5,600 students; and Australia, 63 brothers, 17 schools and 4,300 pupils. The 27 brothers in 3 houses in the Archdiocese of Los Angeles, Calif., had 3 schools and 1,200 students and were governed by a regional superior.

Bibliography: Dr. Delany and the Patrician Brothers (Tullow, Ire. 1955).

[D. LOMASNEY]

PATRICIUS ROMANORUM

Patrician of the Romans, an honorary title instituted by Emperor *Constantine I (306–337) as a personal distinction for his principal juridical and military officers. The emperors of the 5th and 6th centuries conferred it, with other honors such as the consulate, upon barbarian chieftains, as well as upon high imperial officials; individual kings of the Visigoths, Ostrogoths, Franks, and Burgundians all held the title. The patriciate remained honorific. In the West, it survived the imperial collapse of the 7th and 8th centuries only in Italy, where the fact that the effective imperial representative, the exarch of *Ravenna, was also patricius gave the title genuine political content. After the *Lombards suppressed the exarchate in the 8th century, the patriciate assumed a new character, which it retained until its extinction. In their search for a ruler to assume the duties of defense that the exarchs had formerly owed to the bishops of Rome, the popes of the late 8th century granted the patriciate to their chosen defenders, the Frankish kings. Pope *Stephen II conferred the title

upon *Pepin III the Short and his sons *Charlemagne and *Carloman in 754, when he also anointed and crowned them as kings of the Franks, specifically designating them as protectors of the Roman Church. In 781 Charlemagne likewise saw Pope *Adrian I anoint and crown his sons Pepin and Louis as kings and proclaim them patricii. The title thus came to be an ancillary distinction of the Frankish kings peculiarly expressive of their political and military obligations in Italy, and after the coronation of Charlemagne as emperor (800), it became an attribute of the imperial office itself. Some scholars have maintained that in bestowing the patriciate, Stephen II and Adrian I deliberately usurped prerogatives of the Byzantine emperors and moved to adapt to papal direction what had been the most powerful imperial office in Italy. The patriciate, however, retained the institutional independence of papal authority that it had held in the time of the exarchate, and, though it was frequently bestowed by medieval popes to secure temporal defenders, it was also assumed in other ways by persons hostile to the papacy. Thus, heads of the great Roman family, the *Crescentii, claimed the patriciate by popular election late in the 10th century and turned the official powers they attributed to the office toward undermining the alliance between the papacy and the Ottonian rulers at the same time that the emperors themselves used the title "by apostolic benediction." Likewise, Emperor *Henry IV, who wore the golden circlet of the patricius at least as early as 1061, commanded Pope Gregory VII to descend from the throne of St. Peter by virtue of the patriciate he held "through the bestowal of God and the sworn assent of the Romans" (1076). Still, because of its close association with papal prerogatives, the insurgent Roman commune abolished the office (1144–45).

Bibliography: L. VON HEINEMANN, Der Patriziat der deutschen Könige: Ein Beitrag zur Geschichte der Beziehungen zwischen Staat und Kirche im Mittelalter (Wolfenbüttel 1888). F. GREGOROVIUS, History of the City of Rome in the Middle Ages, tr. A. HAMILTON, 8 v. in 13 (London 1894–1902). L. HALPHEN, Charlemagne et l'empire carolingien (Paris 1947). L. BRÉHIER, Le Monde byzantine (Paris 1947–50) v.2, Les Institutions de l'empire byzantine. R. FOLZ, L'Idée d'empire en occident du Vᵉ au XIVᵉ siècle (Paris 1953); Le Couronnement impérial de Charlemagne (Paris 1964). P. E. SCHRAMM, Herrschaftszeichen und Staatssymbolik, 3 v. (Schriften der Monumenta Germaniae historica 13; Stuttgart 1954–56). O. TREITINGER, Die oströmische Kaiser-und Reichsidee nach ihrer Gestaltung im höfischen Zeremoniell (2d ed. Darmstadt 1956). J. DEÉR, "Die Vorrechte des Kaisers in Rom (772–800)," Schweizerische Beiträge zur allgemeinen Geschichte 15 (1957) 5–63. W. ULLMANN, The Growth of Papal Government in the Middle Ages (2d ed. New York 1962).

[K. F. MORRISON]

PATRICK, ST.

Apostle of Ireland; b. c. 389; d. c. 461? (feast, March 17). Patrick (Patricius), as he himself relates, was born in Roman Britain, son of the decurio (alderman), and later deacon, Calporn(i)us. The dates of his birth and death are disputed, as is his chronology generally. At the age of 16, while staying on his father's country estate (probably near Ravenglass), he was seized by Irish raiders and sold as a slave in Ireland. After 6 years' servitude as a shepherd, and encouraged by a voice in his sleep, he escaped, found a ship to take him on board, and eventually reached home. For the worldly youth that he had been, though a nominal Christian, captivity had become a means of spiritual conversion. A desire to preach the Christian faith to the Irish grew within him to the certainty of a vocation. Once in a dream he even heard the "voice of the Irish" calling him back. He went to the Continent to train for the priesthood and probably stayed for some time as disciple of St. *Germain at Auxerre. Perhaps he visited colonies of monks at Lérins and on the islands of the Tyrrhene Sea.

His desire for converting the Irish did not find favor with his superiors, mainly because of his defective education, for which he had never been able to compensate properly. Upon the death of Palladius, whom Pope *Celestine I had sent to the Irish as their first bishop in 431, Patrick was appointed his successor. His mission concentrated on the west and north of Ireland, where nobody had preached the gospel before. Having secured the protection of the local kings, he toured the country extensively and made numerous converts. Church organization had to be adapted to the political and social conditions of Ireland. Since there were no towns on the Roman pattern, Patrick established episcopal churches with quasi-monastic chapters as were found not infrequently on the Continent, especially in Gaul. Although he never mentions his own see, the claim of Armagh to be Patrick's church, though not recorded before the 7th century, seems to represent a genuine tradition. The clergy was originally recruited on the Continent (Gaul) and in Britain, but later increasingly from among the native converts. Patrick also propagated monasticism in the primitive form as practiced in the islands off the Mediterranean coast of Gaul.

In his missionary work he had to face frequent dangers to his freedom and even to his life. The Druids were probably his chief opponents. Patrick's conduct of

Remains of the so-called "Cross of St. Patrick," at Cashel, County Tipperary, Ireland.

the mission was severely criticized by the British clergy and also, it seems, by some persons in Ireland. Things would appear to have come to an issue when Patrick demanded the excommunication of the British Prince Coroticus, who during a retaliatory raid on Ireland had killed some of Patrick's converts and sold others into slavery. To his critics Patrick replied with his *Confessio*, written in his old age.

Writings. Of the writings that go under Patrick's name, his *Confessio* and the letter (*Epistola*) concerning the raid of Coroticus are commonly accepted as genuine. The *Confessio* is an account of Patrick's spiritual development and a justification of his mission, but above all it is a homage to God and thanksgiving for His grace, for having called Patrick, an unworthy sinner, to the apostolate. Autobiographical and historical detail are merely incidental and often difficult to interpret.

The letter is directed partly against the raiders and Coroticus, their leader, partly against the higher clergy of Britain and their scornful attitude toward the Irish bishop. Both works are written in an unusual mixture of Biblical and Vulgar Latin, which often results in strained and obscure language.

Opinion is divided about the authenticity of the *Dicta* (Sayings) of Patrick in the Book of Armagh, especially the first one, which refers to a sojourn on the Tyrrhene Islands, and the last one, which urges the chanting of Kyrie eleison, Christe eleison at all canonical hours. The canons of a circular letter issued by Bishops Patricius, Auxilius, and Iserninus after the so-called synod of St. Patrick, are probably substantially genuine. Ecclesiastical life as implied in this document, and in particular the frequent references to diocesan jurisdiction of bishops and to canonical discipline, are consistent with a 5th-century date and would not fit into the pattern of the Irish monastic Church of later times. A number of these canons are quoted under Patrick's name in the *Collectio Hibernensis* alongside others that are spurious. The beautiful Old Irish morning prayer known as "The Breastplate of St. Patrick" is of later date than the saint's lifetime.

Doctrine. Patrick was a man of action, with little inclination for learning. His writings are proof of his firm belief in his vocation, of his devotion to his cause, and of his courage and humility. His "voices"—foretelling his escape from captivity, calling him to the Irish apostolate, comforting him when in disgrace—are for the most part capable of a perfectly natural explanation; only the experiences related in the *Confessio* (ch. 24, 25) have the characteristics of mystical prayer.

Of his doctrine, little can be stated beyond its orthodoxy. A certain emphasis in his teaching regarding grace might possibly be interpreted as anti-Pelagian. The credal statements in his *Confessio* (ch. 4) echo a formal creed of Gallican type. Patrick's Biblical text, as far as can be judged, is also Gallican.

Chronology. The only contemporary sources for Patrick's life are his genuine writings and the entries concerning St. Germain and Palladius in the Chronicle of *Prosper of Aquitaine. The former are, unfortunately, not precise enough for even approximation of an absolute chronology of the events referred to; they merely place Patrick within the 5th century. The *Confessio* does contain elements of a relative chronology: capture at the age of 16; escape from slavery at 22; some form of ecclesiastical censure because of a sin he had committed when barely 15 years old, disclosed "after 30 years"—but the date upon which they are reckoned is not clear. On the other hand, the precise dates given by Prosper (delegation of St. Germain to Britain in 429, mission of Palladius to Ireland in 431) bear on the chronology of Patrick only on the assumption that a document from the church of Auxerre, embedded in some lives of St. Patrick, is a genuine record of the saint's life, which some scholars doubt. According to this document, Patrick succeeded Palladius after a very short time; this would bear out the Irish annals, which date the beginning of his mission as of 432. These annals, however, record the death of a *Patricius senex* in 457 or 461, and the death of the "apostle" Patrick in 493 or thereabouts. However, the value of the Irish annals as sources for the early Christian period has been questioned by J. V. Kelleher of Harvard.

The Latin and Irish Lives of St. Patrick from the 7th century onward are written mainly with a view to promoting the territorial and juridical claims of the See of *Armagh. They portray a powerful miracle worker, in the manner of Irish hagiographical legend, who has little in common with the author of the *Confessio.* How much genuine tradition in regard to persons and places they may contain is largely a matter of speculation. It has been observed that most of the persons with whom they bring Patrick into contact belong to the late rather than the middle decades of the 5th century and that the annalistic obits of many of Patrick's disciples fall in the first decades of the 6th century.

This conflicting evidence has been differently interpreted. J. Bury accepted 432 as the initial year of Patrick's mission and 461 as the date of his death. He was followed, in the main, by E. MacNeill, P. Grosjean, and L. Bieler. T. F. O'Rahilly believed that the mission of Palladius, whom he identified with *Patricius senex,* lasted from 432 to 461 and was continued by the British Patrick from 461 to *c.* 490. J. Carney allows for only one Patrick, whose mission he dates from 457 to 493. Accordingly he maintains that Palladius was sent to Scotland, not to Ireland, and the first mission to Ireland, including the foundation of Armagh, was the work of St. Secundinus (annalistic date of arrival: 439), to whom an early hymn on St. Patrick is ascribed in later manuscripts. M. Esposito would make Patrick precede rather than succeed Palladius. D. Binchy, weighing carefully the arguments on all sides, concludes that the balance of probability favors the opinion of O'Rahilly. C. Mohrmann, analyzing Patrick's Latin, inclines to accept the chronology of Bury. It does seem possible, without forcing the evidence, to vindicate the chronology of Bury in all essentials, except that 432 as the initial year of Patrick's mission is probably a little too early.

Cult and Relics. A cult of St. Patrick is attested in the 6th century. The day of his death is first recorded in the 7th-century Life of St. Gertrud, who died on March 17, 659. In the 9th century Ferdomnach, scribe of Armagh, testified to the celebration of St. Patrick's feast as a triduum. The cult of St. Patrick and some of his relics were brought to Péronne in Picardy by St. Fursa (middle of 7th century); the cult soon spread over France, Italy, and Germany. When the Anglo-Normans established themselves in Ireland, they took over the cult of St. Patrick and of other Irish saints.

Reliquary of bronze ornamented with gold, silver, and enamels, c. 1100, traditionally said to enshrine a handbell St. Patrick used during Mass.

In 1186 relics of SS. Patrick, Brigid, and Columcille were solemnly deposited in the cathedral of Down under the patronage of John de Courcy and Bishop Malachy. An English Cistercian of De Courcy's entourage, Jocelin of Furness, was commissioned to write a life of St. Patrick, and this became the standard text of later times. With the recent Irish emigration the cult has spread over many parts of the New World.

St. Patrick's Purgatory in Lough Derg, a place of penitential pilgrimages since the 12th century, has probably no connection with the saint. The earliest pictorial representation of St. Patrick dates from *c.* 900. The two most common ones—Patrick's expelling all poisonous snakes from Ireland and his symbolizing the Holy Trinity by the shamrock leaf—are based on legend.

Bibliography: St. Patrick's *Confessio,* the 7th-century Life by Muirchú, and the *Breviarum* by Tírechán have been collected in the Book of Armagh, an early 9th-century MS, now in Trinity College, Dublin. Editions. J. GWYNN, ed., *Liber Ardmachanus* (Dublin 1913). L. BIELER, ed., *Libri Epistolarum s. Patricii Episcopi* in *Classica et mediaevalia* 11 (1950) 1–150; 12 (1951) 79–214; repr. in 2 v. (Dublin 1952); *The Irish Penitentials* (Scriptores Latini Hiberniae 5; Dublin 1963), the canons; *The Works of St. Patrick* (AncChrWr 17; 1953), *Confessio,* letter, sayings, canons, hymn attributed to St. Secundus, Breastplate. E. I. HOGAN, ed., *Documenta de s. Patricio* (Brussels 1884). J. COLGAN, ed., *Trias thaumaturga* (Louvain 1647) 11–116; new eds. are being prepared by L. BIELER. W. STOKES, ed., *Tripartite Life of St. Patrick,* 2 v. (RollsS 89; 1888; repr. 1965), critical ed. and tr. K. MULCHRONE (Dublin 1939–   ).

Literature. J. B. BURY, *The Life of St. Patrick* (New York 1905). Kenney 319–356. E. MACNEILL, *St. Patrick, Apostle of Ireland* (London 1934; 2d ed., J. RYAN, 1964). T. F. O'RAHILLY, *The Two Patricks* (Dublin 1942). L. BIELER, *The Life and Legend of St. Patrick* (Dublin 1949). J. CARNEY, *The Problem of St. Patrick* (Dublin 1961). C. MOHRMANN, *The Latin of St. Patrick* (Dublin 1961). D. A. BINCHY, "Patrick and His Biographers," *Studia Hibernica* 2 (1962) 7–173. R. E. MCNALLY, CathHistRev 47 (1961–62) 305–324. **Illustration credit:** Fig. 1, Commissioners of Public Works in Ireland. Fig. 2, National Museum of Ireland.

[L. BIELER]

PATRIOTISM

The love of and devotion to one's country, having as its moral foundation the virtue of *piety. Benedict XV considered it a twin virtue with religion itself and a tie between the human person and his roots in nature.

Basis and Notion. Its social foundation is community. Man is bound to act in accordance with the divinely revealed and humanly confirmed truth that it is not good for him to be alone. Genesis attributes the statement of this truth to the Lord God before Eve's creation; it can be understood in an even stronger sense after the fact: given his social nature, it is impossible for man to be alone, and any pretension to independence from the human community must be disastrous because unrealistic and inhuman. Each man is compelled by nature to live in society for the attainment of his personal good, which good in turn provides the basis for society's growth and development toward a common good ordered in love and justice. To live humanly is to live in community; and to live morally, as a creature under God, is to love that community of which one forms a part.

Patriotism in the sense of a love of one's community is therefore a duty of man flowing from intelligent recognition and moral acceptance of the very form of creation: the creation not of the individual, man, who existed alone only long enough for God to confirm the fact of his incompleteness, but of the human family, mankind, which provides the social principle of the person's being and the necessary context for his truly personal growth.

But patriotism as a form of charity, or love, has a more specific object in its actuation than mankind or the human family as such. According to St. Thomas Aquinas, the particular love of one's fatherland is an important aspect of that preferential form of charity that is called *pietas* (ST 2a2ae, 101.1). Through piety the person has an obligation of love to God, parents, and fatherland. Each is in some sense a principle of man's being: God through creation; parents through procreation and education; fatherland through a formation of one's cultural and historical identity.

Patriotism, in its specific sense of love of fatherland, or of one's people, is a historical corollary of a natural demand of community. The love of community that is an imperative of man's created being gains only a vague and illusory existence if it is directed finally at nothing more specific than mankind. And again, love-in-community, when confined to family and friends, or even a local community, becomes a confinement, or limitation, of the person, if not even a "passion against" when it meets the larger communities of nation and world. To the love of hearth and of mankind, a love of country is the psychological and moral, as well as historical, mediary.

Patriotism can therefore be defined descriptively as the reverent acknowledgment of community as it is expressed in history in a form intermediate to home and world, a response in love to the people and milieu in which man exists because he is created not only as a member of a family or species but is bound to a particular cultural group in space, time, and tradition. Put more concisely, patriotism is a special form of piety binding a person to his historical and cultural sources. As such, it makes certain practical demands of the person: loyalty to his nation, collaboration in its political order, and the will to seek the moral perfection of his people.

Traditional Catholic teaching, notably as it is synthesized doctrinally and in practical applications by the modern popes, has insisted especially on the profoundly moral basis of rightly ordered patriotism. Pius XI reminded Christian citizens in *Ubi arcano Dei* that "it is never lawful, nor even wise, to dissociate morality from the affairs of practical life," so that "in the last analysis, it is 'justice which exalteth a nation: but sin maketh nations miserable'" (Prv 14.34). The citizen must seek the good of his nation according to the norms of a moral order rooted in nature itself, though confirmed by Old Testament precepts and New Testament counsels. The Catholic acknowledgment of natural law is nowhere more explicit or normative than in moral questions connected with the *ius gentium,* nationalism and internationalism, civic loyalty and patriotism.

National and International Dimensions. The understanding of this natural moral order in practical affairs, though often difficult and obscure, admits no concessions from political expediency or in the name of "moral ambiguity" to violations of justice. Thus, within a moral context, an act of civil disobedience may conceivably be the patriot's deepest expression of love, when other actions would only pass over or strengthen a process of injustice corroding the community. The Christian citizen is bound to his nation in a loyal but intelligent union, accepting gladly his national identity but freeing himself and his nation, by a continual reference to the supernatural values of charity and justice, for constant growth and reformation. For patriotism is love, and love wills the good of the other—in the case of a nation, a good dependent on its united response to the just claims of its citizens and, to whatever extent possible, to the human needs beyond its borders.

There is no contradiction in seeing a nation's own common good dependent on its contribution to the common good of other peoples in an international community, since, as Pius XII pointed out in *Summi pontificatus,* "legitimate and well-ordered love of our native country should not make us close our eyes to the all-embracing nature of Christian charity." This is so true that patriotism rightly understood, far from obstructing a love of mankind, becomes itself in modern papal teaching one of the bases for sane and salutary internationalism.

The charity of patriotism, while being preferential in its practical object, is at the same time universal in its ultimate aim. It is directed at the exaltation of one's nation under God and thus at its fulfillment in justice of the moral principles governing the relations among states. The devout patriot fears nothing so much for his nation as its following a course of injustices that, however "politically realistic," he recognizes as a way of self-destruction. Since patriotism is a form of charity directed toward a social order whose goal and perfection is justice, its concern for the nation's good extends naturally and harmoniously into the international order, where the nation's drive for global justice is its own exaltation. The aggressive character of political nationalism, the "immoderate nationalism" that Pius XI repeatedly distinguished from patriotism, is, on the other hand, the kind of sin that "maketh nations miserable."

The flowering of a rightly ordered patriotism is therefore wider than one's own fatherland alone and seeks relations of that land to the wider human community and world—hence the manner in which modern papal teaching emphasizes at every turn the balance between a sane nationalism and a humane internationalism. This integration of patriotic piety with international loyalty recent popes base on the fact that the preferential love that finds its object in the nation wills the good of that nation as realizable through its pursuit of a justice greater than itself and extending beyond its borders. Furthermore, since patriotism is a species of charity, its development involves the deepening of an unspecified power at its source in the human will. Man widens his family through love. Just as the father's deepening love for his family increases his capacity for love, so must the true patriot's love for his country grow naturally until it simultaneously embraces the world while yet remaining, alive and effective within the symphony of human loves and social loyalties, the special preferential piety that is patriotism.

Bibliography: General. J. C. BENNETT, The Christian as Citizen (New York 1955). M. CURTI, The Roots of American Loyalty (New York 1946). C. DAWSON, Religion and the Modern State (New York 1935). C. J. H. HAYES, Essays on Nationalism (New York 1926); Christianity and Western Civilization (Stanford 1954). J. L. SPALDING, Things of the Mind (Chicago 1894; 4th ed. 1901); Socialism and Labor and other Arguments, Social, Political and Patriotic (Chicago 1902) ch. 8, essay on "Patriotism." C. VAN DOREN, Patriotic Anthology (New York 1941). J. J. WRIGHT, National Patriotism in Papal Teaching (Westminster, Md. 1956).
Encyclicals. Leo XIII, "Sapientiae christianae" (Jan. 10, 1890) ActSS 22 (1890) 385–404; Eng., Tablet 75 (Jan. 25, 1890) 121–126; "Immortale Dei" (Nov. 1, 1885) ActSS 18 (1885) 161–180; Eng., Catholic Mind 34 (Nov. 8, 1936) 425–429. Pius XI, "Caritate Christi compulsi" (May 3, 1932) ActApS 24 (1932) 177–194; Eng. ibid. 30 (June 22, 1932) 228–243. John XXIII MatMagis. John XXIII PacTerr.

[J. J. WRIGHT]

PATRIPASSIANISM, a Trinitarian heresy that denied that the Logos, Jesus Christ, possessed subsistence and implied that God the Father Himself suffered and died on the cross in the guise of the Son. This term is thus synonymous with *Sabellianism and was invented by the Latin Fathers who called the propagators of *monarchianism patripassiani (attributors of suffering to the Father) while the Greeks called them Sabellians. *Tertullian, in his Treatise Against Praxeas 1, first insisted on this implication of Sabellianism, taking Praxeas to task not only for his monarchianism, but also for his opposition to *Montanism, which Praxeas persuaded the Pope (apparently Victor I) to condemn: Duo negotia diaboli Praxeas Romae procuravit: . . . Paracletum fugavit et Patrem crucifixit (Praxeas achieved two works of the devil in Rome: . . . he put the Holy Spirit to flight and crucified the Father).

Some scholars think that Tertullian misrepresented Praxeas's archaic Trinitarian formulations to make him the father of *modalism, and so discredit him, for the name Praxeas does not appear elsewhere in contemporary sources; others suggest that Tertullian is using the word Praxeas (busybody) as a nickname for Pope Callistus.

Bibliography: TERTULLIAN, Treatise Against Praxeas, ed. and tr. E. EVANS (SPCK; 1949). J. DANIÉLOU and H. MARROU, Des origines à saint Grégoire le Grand, v.1 of Nouvelle histoire de l'Église (Paris 1963–) 1:138. G. BARDY, DTC 10.2:2196–2200.

[P. LEBEAU]

PATRISTIC PHILOSOPHY

Patristic philosophy can be considered from the point of view of the history of Christianity—and it is then part of the science of *patrology—or from the point of view of the history of philosophy that began outside, and before, the Christian community. The point of view of this article is the history of philosophy.

The history of Western philosophy has three periods: ancient, medieval, and modern. The medieval is the period of the religious philosophies: Jewish, Christian, and Mohammedan. Though "medieval" designates the European period of the 11th to the 14th centuries A.D., the history of *Christian philosophy comprises the two periods of patristic and *scholastic philosophy. The patristic period extends from the beginnings of Christianity to the 8th century (or from St. *Justin Martyr, c. 100–164, to St. *John Damascene, d. c. 749) and is limited to the Mediterranean basin. The development of patristic thought begins with the apostolic Fathers and continues with the Apologists and the beginnings of theology and philosophy to the golden age of the 4th century (Nicaea, 325 to Chalcedon, 451); the final period concludes with Damascene.

The idea that patristic thought belongs to the history of philosophy except for its extrinsic influence has been challenged. The rationalist philosophers (E. Bréhier) maintained that patristic thought is not philosophy because it depends upon a revelation that cannot be questioned. Scholastic theologians have said that the Fathers did not adequately distinguish philosophy and theology and consequently their work was properly theology (P. Mandonnet). In response, some have admitted the actual fusion of philosophy and theology in the Fathers, but have maintained that the distinction was made in principle and that true philosophical work was done that prepared the way for scholastic philosophy (B. Geyer). Others have defended an intermediate concept of "Christian philosophy" and argued that though precisions were made later, there was a properly Christian philosophy in the Fathers as well as in the scholastics (É. Gilson).

On the other hand, rationalist historians have argued that the more philosophical of the Fathers (Origen, Gregory of Nyssa, Augustine) were not authentic Christians but really Gnostics or Neoplatonists. There is as a result an extensive literature studying the question, and in each case it has been resolved in favor of the Christianity of the patristic writer.

GENERAL MOVEMENTS OF PATRISTIC PHILOSOPHY

Not all the patristic writers were philosophers. Some were exegetes, preachers, poets, or theologians in the technical sense. Though there were some elements of philosophy in the apostolic Fathers, Justin was the first Christian "philosopher"—not only because he professed philosophy before his conversion and called himself a philosopher as a Christian, but especially because he made the basic distinction between the logos of revelation and the logos of Greek philosophy or of reason.

Greek. But the dominant and almost exclusive philosophical tradition among the Greek writers is that which originated with the school of *Clement of Alexandria (*c.* 150–219) and *Origen (*c.* 185–254). In the 4th century it moved to Cappadocia principally in *Gregory of Nyssa (*c.* 335–395), and then to Athens(?) with *Pseudo-Dionysius the Areopagite (*c.* 500). There are other figures of philosophical importance—such as *Nemesius of Emesa (*c.* 400), whose *De natura hominis* was mistakenly attributed to Gregory of Nyssa in the Middle Ages, and Damascene, who is important principally as a summit and transmitter of patristic teaching to the scholastics—but the Alexandrian tradition is the mainline of Greek patristic philosophy.

Latin. In the beginning Greek was the language of the writers in the Roman world also, but Latin began to be used toward the end of the 2d century by *Minucius Felix (*c.* 180) and *Tertullian (*c.* 155–245). However, though a certain amount of philosophy came to the Christians by way of Cicero and Varro, for the most part the development of philosophy among the Latin Fathers was the result of the influence of the Greek writers, both Christian and pagan. In the Roman spirit Tertullian and St. *Ambrose contributed to the development of moral philosophy, and Tertullian made some important beginnings in the definition of theologico-philosophical concepts. By far the most important Latin Father philosophically, however, was St. *Augustine. Augustine was an original thinker and the history of his doctrine followed the itinerary of his development from Manichaeism, through skepticism and Neoplatonism, to Christianity. But since the strongest philosophical influence on him was that of *Porphyry, *Plotinus, and the Greek Fathers, he may be assimilated to the Alexandrian tradition in philosophy.

Second in importance to Augustine is *Boethius, a layman. Though Augustinian and Neoplatonic at base, his thought is not as mystical and spiritual. His *Consolation of Philosophy* presents an example of lay philosophy, though he also wrote theological treatises that are philosophically important. He is especially significant for his effort to make both Plato and Aristotle available to the Latin world, and particularly for introducing Aristotelian logic into European philosophy. The work of translation of the Neoplatonists into Latin had been begun much earlier by *Marius Victorinus (b. *c.* 300).

NATURE OF PHILOSOPHY IN THE FATHERS

In the Western world philosophy means the type of rational understanding developed by the Greeks. For this reason the history of philosophy is in large part the history of the influence of Greek philosophy.

Influence of the Greeks. The influence of Hellenism on Christian origins is discernible in the Old Testament, e.g., in the Book of Wisdom. Greek influences are recognizable also in the New Testament, in John and Paul. But the first major effort to unite Greek speculation with the Bible was made by *Philo Judaeus (*c.*

St. Augustine dictating his works to a scribe, 13th-century fresco, upper church, Basilica of S. Francesco, Assisi.

A.D. 40). *Gnosticism likewise had much to do with initiating the movement among the Christians, since it professed to be able to discern in the Scriptures a secret, saving doctrine that had large elements of Greek philosophy in it. One of the motives of the Alexandrian school was to develop a true Christian Gnosticism, though Origen was undoubtedly stimulated also by the beginnings of Neoplatonism in which he seems to have taken part.

The history of pagan philosophy at the time of the beginning of Christianity is not very well known. It was a period of syncretism, not only between philosophies but also between religions, and there was no dominant school. Plotinus (d. A.D. 270) presented the first strong new philosophy since Stoicism and Epicureanism. The first Christians therefore tended to be eclectic. Plato (*Timaeus*), however, seemed closer to Moses (Genesis) than the others, while Epicurus and Aristotle were considered the most incompatible with Christianity. Even skepticism was significant, not only in the development of Augustine's thought, but also in provoking arguments for the necessity of faith. Once Neoplatonism developed, however, it had a preponderant influence on the Christians (Plotinus and Porphyry on Augustine, *Proclus on Dionysius).

Concept of Philosophy. The distinction and meanings of theology and philosophy as used in the postscholastic world were not operative in the patristic period. Among the pagans philosophy was a general term for the doctrine and way of life of a particular group of men. Theology meant simply the part of philosophy that treated of God. The patristic philosophers compared Christianity to the pagan philosophies, much as Christianity and communism might be contrasted. They distinguished between "our philosophy" and the philosophy of "those outside." Thus, philosophy could be considered as a way of human beatitude (Augustine), or a way of salvation through higher, speculative knowledge (Gnosticism), or a way of Christian perfection by the elevation of the mind of God (Alexandrians).

Thus the movement of philosophy among both the pagans and the Christians was toward beatifying knowledge. The Christians, however, insisted that the goal could not be achieved by finite reason alone. Faith is necessary from beginning to end. Thus the process goes from simple faith in revelation, through the hierarchy of human and divine sciences, to mystical contemplation and union with God. This process involves a dialectic of faith and reason that recognizes the validity of human reason proceeding from an analysis of creatures to the Creator (Wis 13; Rom 1.20; Greek philosophy) but considers this insufficient. Faith and reason are interrelated as teacher and pupil in the natural process of human learning (Augustine).

The desire for God did not exhaust all the causes of philosophical reasoning among the Christians. Philosophy was needed to meet the challenge of the pagans (e.g., *Celsus) and to clarify the meaning of the Christian revelation in the face of heretical views within. Moreover, philosophers such as Justin, when converted, could not resist philosophizing within Christianity. Neither did the intellectual mystical tradition present the only view of Christian perfection. There were those such as Basil and Ambrose who stressed the Biblical service of God and the life of the moral virtues.

GENERAL SYNTHESIS OF PATRISTIC PHILOSOPHY

A catalogue of the philosophical opinions of the individual patristic writers taken chronologically can be found in the Catholic histories of Christian or medieval philosophy (Gilson, Copleston). Some general lines of doctrine are sketched here.

When patristic philosophy is seen from the viewpoint of the history of philosophy, it is generally considered as a correction and development of Greek philosophy. Though there are merits in this procedure, it gives a false perspective. Patristic philosophy began with the Hebrew tradition and the Bible. Greek philosophy entered this tradition and taught the patristic philosophers how to develop the philosophical elements in revelation rationally (cf. C. Tresmontant). But the patristic philosophers also saw themselves as different from the Jews, who held strictly to the Old Testament. The difference, of course, was Christ, and though the mystery of Christ took them beyond the realm of rational understanding, nevertheless the theology of Christ forced a reconstruction of philosophy that can be called specifically Christian, at least in the historical sense.

Trinitarian Doctrine. Christ meant first of all the doctrine of the Trinity, the mystery of one divine nature but three Persons. This was anathema to the Jews, who saw it as a species of polytheism; but philosophically speaking, it forced against the Arians a distinction between generation (the Son) and creation that sharpened appreciably the notion of creation out of nothing derived from the Old Testament.

Creation and Divine Ideas. The Fathers found it easy to adapt the myth of Plato's *Timaeus* and understood God as an omnipotent artist who freely willed the world in time out of nothing according to patterns that He contemplates in His divine mind. But the break was made with Greek philosophy both by denying any kind of dualism of matter that is coeternal with the Creator and is shaped by Him, and by denying any kind of generationism whereby creatures proceed from God's substance in some way. To the Platonic division between the intelligible and the sensible a more embracing and radical division was added—between Creator and creature—in such a way that the division of creature contained the division of spiritual and material.

The nature of this last division was not always clear to the Fathers, and a certain reality was sometimes attributed to the divine ideas distinct from the being of God, as though God first created the intelligible world that the material world imitated, in a Platonic fashion. The Platonic myth of the fall of man into the body was also sometimes used, as in Gregory of Nyssa. But the ultimate pattern that prevailed was that of Dionysius, who made every creature apart from God a substance and made the intelligible creation the orders of the angels (as against the hypostases of Plotinus and Proclus). The question whether the angels were able to contribute to the creative process was asked but not definitely answered. They were granted some gubernatorial functions in the universe, which was conceived as one whole under God.

After Origen's thesis of multiple worlds, the patristic doctrine settled in the direction of one single creation in time, which, however, went through gradual stages of development until man appeared and the history of civilization began. Here the harmonization between Genesis and the *Timaeus* is again apparent. Augustine followed Gregory of Nyssa in making use of the theory of *seminal reasons to explain how it was possible that the whole of creation was produced "at once" (as they understood Sir 18.1 to teach) but nevertheless went through the stages of the 6 days. The theory of an eternal world was constantly rejected as contrary not only to revelation but also to Plato. The possibility of distinguishing between the conclusions of reason (which might leave the question of eternity open) and the affirmations of revelation (which does not) did not occur to the Christian world before *Maimonides suggested it in the 12th century. Hence, time and history were primary categories of patristic thought, and the world scheme of the Fathers came closer to the 20th-century evolutionary and historical world view than did that of the scholastics.

Psychology of Person. Another great influence of the Trinitarian doctrine on philosophy came in the development of the psychology of the *person. It was principally Augustine who reconstructed the Greek psychology into a new Christian synthesis. Christ is the Word of God. This teaching enabled the Fathers to join the Platonic and Stoic theories of the logos. In Augustine the interior word became the middle term of a process that came out of memory and completed itself in love. Plato's theory of reminiscence was changed into a doctrine of divine *illumination, which formed at once the basis for absolute knowledge and the ascent of the mind to God. Taken objectively as being, truth, and goodness, the triad joined the ontology of the Greeks and became a Christian doctrine of *participation whereby all things descend from, and exist by, the One Being who is the cause of all.

In patristic philosophy there are, then, two forms of participation, that of *exemplarism, or participation in the creative ideas by imitation, and an ontological participation whereby creatures derive from the Creator in descending grades of perfection. At the heart of this philosophy is the principle enunciated by Boethius that the imperfect presupposes the perfect (*Consol. phil.* 3.10).

Knowledge of God. The mystery of the Trinity brought forth yet another theme of patristic philosophy, the knowability yet incomprehensibility of God. The Arian, *Eunomius of Constantinople, had attempted to apply univocally to God the Aristotelian categories taken from the sensible world. It became clear in the debate that this could not be done, and the beginnings of the doctrine of *analogy were shaped. Moreover, though it is true that reason can apply names from creatures to the Creator in a transcendent manner, nevertheless God still remains incomprehensible and a mystery. This is the constant theme of the Greek Fathers. The negative theology of Dionysius is perhaps their strongest statement about God, though it is mitigated by Damascene's position that God is naturally and readily known by a kind of instinctive ascent from creatures to the Creator.

Teaching on the Incarnation. Christ also means the *Incarnation, that is, the mystery of the assumption of human nature by a divine Person so that the Second Person of the Trinity is both God and man. This forced the Fathers to establish their understanding of the human nature that the Word assumed. Christ did

not assume a soul without a body, or a body without a soul; He had all the powers and faculties of man. In terms of the division of creatures into spiritual and material, it became clear that man was a composite of both "natures" and mediated between both worlds. It was possible, then, with Gregory of Nyssa, to define him both as a rational animal and as a corporeal spirit.

Spirit. The notion of *spirit and of the spirituality of the human soul did not come easy for the early Fathers. Stoicism and Manichaeism had a developed materialism that included God and held thinkers such as Tertullian and Augustine in its grasp for a while. Scripture itself, especially the Old Testament, was not clear and forceful on this point. Thus it was probably Neoplatonism—in part a reaction to the materialism of Hellenistic philosophy—that did most to clarify the spiritual nature of the soul. But this left the Fathers with a certain dualism in man of soul and body that was not completely overcome. The soul was not conceived in a simple undifferentiated way, however, but rather as a hierarchy of powers and functions that stretched between the poles of spirit and matter. As the soul became more interior, it became more spiritual and also the center wherein God dwelt. This psychology was intimately connected with the theory of mystical contemplation, itself the Christian response to the immanentist doctrine of Plotinus. Within the Alexandrian tradition, at least, the ascetical and moral teaching of the Fathers was worked out from the point of view of this mystical psychology. Thus the life of virtue was structured toward union with God. The view of man's nature as composite made it relatively easy to defend the immortality of the human soul, though it was not as helpful regarding the question of the resurrection of the body.

Person and Nature. The Incarnation and the doctrine of the Trinity both forced a distinction between person and nature, though from opposite directions. The Incarnation presented an instance of one Person but two natures; the Trinity of one nature but three Persons. This led to new precisions about the Aristotelian category of *substance, but particularly it made important the problem of *universals and individuals. The question that Boethius bequeathed to the Middle Ages in his commentary on Porphyry's *Isagoge* was not merely a speculative question that intrigued the scholastics; it was very closely bound up with the doctrines of the Trinity and the Incarnation. The solutions of the Fathers tended to be a modification of Platonism and Stoicism and to stress the unity of a nature in all men that was nevertheless possessed by different individuals or persons. When their views were repeated in the early Middle Ages, they came under the sharp criticism of *Abelard, and the problem came into greater prominence.

Role of the Redemption. Christ finally also means redemption. This immediately engages the problem of *evil, which was probably the most absorbing problem in the syncretic period of the beginning of the patristic age. All the dualistic religions of the East and the Hellenistic philosophies revolved around the mystery of *good and evil, the freedom and determinism of man, the providence of God. It is in this context that the historical significance of Christianity can best be understood. Because of the patristic doctrine of creation of all beings by God, who is Being, any kind of absolute *dualism had to be rejected. There is nothing that did not proceed from God. In this there was a parallelism with the Plotinian doctrine of the emanation of all from the One. Because God is good only, everything He made was good, even matter, and in this the Plotinian doctrine was modified. But perhaps the greatest impulse toward the recognition of the goodness of matter came from the doctrine of the Incarnation; for it was early established against *Docetism that matter was assumed also by the Son.

Freedom. Consequently, the Christians moved in the direction of explaining evil metaphysically in the Platonic sense of nonbeing, but morally as having its possibility in the *freedom and finitude of man. The Fathers worked hard, therefore, to defend human freedom against Manichaeism. On the other hand, the mission of Christ as redeemer also taught them to fend off Pelagian optimism. Man's freedom, then, was seen in an ambivalent position, as drawn to determinism in the physical world and as elevated to freedom by the grace of Christ. The same dialectic that was mentioned above regarding faith and reason was operative also between grace and freedom. These questions absorbed much of Augustine's time, but Nemesius, and especially Damascene, worked to clarify the psychology of choice. In this area the positive help of Aristotle was finally apparent.

Image of God. The doctrine of redemption in patristic thought is closely related also to the doctrine of man as the *image of God. This doctrine was derived from Genesis, but it also fitted well with the Platonic scheme. For the Christians, however, the image of God meant the image of the Creator, and so it was the freedom of man and his position as lord of the world that characterized man's likeness to God. This position, developed by Gregory of Nyssa and others, was to be repeated by St. *Thomas Aquinas. It is this image that was dimmed by the Fall, that was brought back to its original intention by the redemptive grace of Christ, and that was given a new goal by the new reality of the Son of God made man. Thus, though the Christian doctrine of the Fall and Redemption resembles the Platonic cycle, the patristic doctrine of image also lays the theoretical foundations for man's creative and productive function in history and civilization. He is to be a second creator.

But because men are ultimately free, they are divided into two camps: those who struggle with Christ to redeem the world and those who do not. There is then a dualism of spirits in history, but it is the result of the freedom of creatures and not of two absolute and independent sources. This is the theme of Augustine's great *City of God,* which furnished the blueprint for the Christian Middle Ages.

Conclusion. Patristic philosophy is not a single tradition, nor is it a separate science apart from the totality of developing Christian life. It did not answer definitively all the questions it raised, but it did explore most of them and set themes and directions that formed the bases not only for medieval philosophy but for much of modern philosophy as well.

Bibliography: É. Bréhier, *Période Héllenistique et Romaine,* v.1.2 of *Histoire de la philosophie,* 2 v. (Paris 1926–32). Copleston v.2. Ueberweg v.2. Gilson HistChrPhil. B. Romeyer, *La Philosophie chrétienne jusqu'à Descartes,* 3 v. (Paris 1935–37). C. Tresmontant, *The Origins of Christian Philosophy,* tr. M. Pontifex (New York 1963); *A Study of Hebrew Thought,* tr. M. F. Gibson (New York 1960); *La Métaphysique du christianisme et la naissance de la philosophie chrétienne* (Paris 1961). R. Arnou, DTC 12.2:2258–2392. J. Daniélou, *Message évangélique et culture hellénistique aux IIᵉ et IIIᵉ siècles,* v.2 of *Histoire des doctrines chrétiennes avant Nicée* (Tournai 1961). M. Spanneut, *Le Stoïcisme des Pères de l'Église de Clément de Rome à Clément d'Alexandrie* (Paris 1957). H. A. Wolfson, *Philo,* 2 v. (Cambridge, Mass. 1947). A. J. Festugière, *L'Idéal religieux des Grecs et l'Évangile* (Paris 1932). **Illustration credit:** Alinari-Art Reference Bureau.

[R. F. Harvanek]

PATRISTIC THEOLOGY

The development of Christian thought about God and the mystery of man's destiny in the writings of the Fathers of the Church during the first 7 centuries A.D. constitutes patristic theology. It differs from Biblical theology in that it consciously reflects the philosophical and religious thought of the Hellenistic world, while its emphasis on a positive approach to Scripture and the Church's tradition and its lack of systematization distinguish it from scholastic and post-Tridentine theology.

Coincident with the Biblical approach, patristic theology is concerned primarily with an event: man's meeting with Christ, the Son of God, who suffered under Pontius Pilate, died, and rose again from the dead. This was the essential consideration of Christian thought, and from time to time threatened to be the Christian's sole interest. However in the annunciation and explanation of this event the Church's teachers were constrained to utilize contemporary philosophy, religious concepts, and cultural patterns in order to defend and clarify their message. Thus patristic theology is an amalgam of Judeo-Christian, Hellenistic, and some Oriental thought adapted to the singular facts enunciated in the Old and New Testaments about God, and enacted by Christ in His own life, and in the life of the Church, His Mystical Body.

It was *Eusebius of Caesarea, the great Church historian, who in the 4th century certified the legitimacy of the word theology for Christian usage. He described the Evangelist St. John as "The Theologian," since his Gospel is concerned primarily with the divinity of Christ (*De eccl. theol.* 1.20; 2.12), and announced the purpose of his Church history as a demonstration of the "theology and economy of salvation according to Christ" (*Hist. Eccl.* 1.1.7; *prol.* 2).

THE BEGINNINGS

Earlier Christian thinkers had hesitated to use the words *theologos, theologia, theologein* because, as St. Augustine, quoting the naturalist Varro, remarked, there were three kinds of pagan theology: rational, or an explanation of the gods in their myths; physical, or the explanation of the world in its causes; and civil, devoted to the essentially political religion and cult of the city-state or imperial dynasty (*Civ.* 6.5; Tertullian, *Ad nat.* 2.1, 2).

Greek thought associated theology with the theogonies of the poets, particularly Orpheus, Homer, and Hesiod. Aristotle contrasted these theologians with Thales and Anaximander who sought a physical explanation of things, while in his *Metaphysics* (bk. 12) he supplied a philosophy about God that is a solid natural theology. The Neoplatonists and some Church Fathers considered Plato a theologian, although he used the word theology to designate the educative value of mythology (*Rep.* 379A).

*Clement of Alexandria gave Christian recognition to theology as the knowledge of divine things. While Clement recognized the poetical function of ancient pagan theology, he credited the philosophers with a desire to achieve knowledge of the true God (*Strom.* 1.13; 5.9). Origen spoke of the "ancient theologians among the Greeks" and the "theology of the Persians" as devoted to an explanation of religion and the divinity; but gradually he limited *theologia* and *theologein* to the Christian sense of a true knowledge of God (*Cont. Cel.* 6.18; *Comm. in Jn* 2.34) and particularly of Christ the Savior (*ibid.* 1.24).

Despite the warnings of early Christians such as Tatian, Tertullian, and Lactantius against a speculative consideration of faith, an explanation of the fact of Christ's activities, and the mystery embodied in the *Christian way of life in the Church early proved a necessity. This was apparent to St. Paul, who experienced the shock caused by the preaching of "Christ crucified, a scandal to the Greeks, a stumbling block to the Jews." While he warned against "philosophy" and human deceit controlled by the demons (Col 2.8–20), he illustrated his teaching with parallels in nature and in Judeo-Hellenistic thought.

Jewish Theology. Jewish theological speculation embodied in the Apocalypses, Haggadah, Pescherim, and liturgical writings greatly influenced both the New Testament and the Judeo-Christian thought concerned with the nature of God, angelology, eschatology, and dualistic considerations of the problem of evil. These influences are apparent in the so-called *Apostolic Fathers from Clement and the Didache to the Pseudo-Barnabas and Ignatius of Antioch. But it was with the Apologists that true theological thinking began.

Converts from philosophy, convinced that in Christ the Logos they had finally achieved truth, they utilized the arguments and *topoi* in the handbooks and florilegia of the current Stoic, Pythagorean, and Platonic schools to ridicule the gods and counter the anti-Christian charges. While they addressed the public authorities in protest against persecution of the Christians, their primary function was a missionary effort aimed at converting their contemporaries. In this they had as precedent a considerable Judeo-Hellenistic literature in the *Letter of Aristeas*, the Judeo-Christian *Sibylline Books*, and *Philo Judaeus. They admitted that the philosophers had achieved some appreciation of truth which, since it was one, had to be homogeneous. Following Philo they claimed that Plato and the earlier thinkers had read Moses and the Prophets for their knowledge of monotheism or had retained a kernel of truth given in an original revelation and preserved among both Greeks and barbarians. But in any case the Christians now possessed the fullness of truth in Christ (Theophilus of Antioch, *Ad Autol.* 2.12; Justin, *1 Apol.* 20; Athenagoras, *Suppl.* 1.6).

The Apologists. The late 2d-century writers confronted their audience with the "unique, eternal, invisible God" (Athenagoras, *Resur.* 10), "Creator of the universe" (Justin, *2 Apol* 12.1), manifest in his works (Theophilus of Antioch, 1.6) and reminded them of the judgment facing all mankind (Justin, *ibid.*). Though differing in method, they presented the doctrine of the Resurrection with considerable argument following St. Paul (1 Cor) and St. John (Jn 12.24). They contrasted

the purity of the Christian life with the immorality of the pagan (Justin *1 Apol.* 14.1–4), utilizing the technique of the early catechesis in the *Didache and Letter of Barnabas.

Athenagoras stressed the Christian doctrine of love of neighbor, sanctity of marriage, and virginity (*Suppl.* 32–33); and the *Epistle to Diognetus* maintained that the Christians lived like their neighbors but kept the laws of God and man, serving as a leaven for society, giving it life as the soul does the body (5.6–13).

What the Christians took from the Greeks was a manner of explaining both monotheism and the divinity of Christ, leaning on amalgams of Platonic philosophy to establish God's oneness, and on Stoicism for speculation on the Logos. Later they turned to Middle Platonism and Neoplatonism. The danger in this process was illustrated by the Gnostics, who employed the Platonic philosophies to speculate about God and Christ, but without the Judaic insistence on the historical actuality of Christ and His eschatological setting. Their idealist concept of the divinity gave Him no concrete place in history, and only an apparent piercing of time and space in the salvationary work of Christ. Despising the material world, they called for an absolute spiritualizing of man. The Church rejected this teaching with its parallels in Manichaeism and Marcionism, which were combatted by Irenaeus of Lyons, Hippolytus of Rome, and Tertullian.

THEOLOGICAL SPECULATION

Theological advancement began with Justin and Irenaeus who spoke of the *oikonomia*, or economy of salvation, to designate the events in the life of Christ, "the Son of God who existed before the morning star and the moon, who consented to become flesh in order that by this economy, the serpent who from the beginning had acted evilly, and the angels who imitated him, might be destroyed" (Justin, *Dial.* 45.4).

Justin embodied the mysteries of Christ, particularly His virgin birth and His Passion, in the economy, comparing these glories to the Parousia, or second coming (*Dial.* 30.3). He included the events of the Old Testament, which he maintains are a *typology of the things accomplished by Christ (*Dial.* 134.2). They are thus part of his theology of the Word, who carries out the will of His Father (*Dial.* 67.6) in the theophanies of the Old Testament (*Dial.* 126.3, 5; 127.1) and operates through the Church in the Eucharist and the sacraments of His power (*1 Apol.* 66.2), which will be visible in the second coming (*Dial.* 54.1).

These fundamental ideas are developed by Irenaeus, who considered the Incarnation of Christ as the key to the history of salvation wherein God has approached man to bring man to God (*Adv. haer.* 4.20.1), an idea that will be emphasized by St. *Athanasius (*De Incarn.* 53). Again it is Christ who carried out His Father's will in the Old Testament encounters (*Demonst.* 45), and who is the Beginning and the Law, the Resurrection and the Life. He saw the two Testaments as two steps in the reeducation by grace of man who sinned from ignorance as a child (*nepios*), and portrayed Christ as the recapitulation of man, submitting to human experience, but conquering sin and the devil and effecting a recapitulation of all things in His Church by sending man the Holy Spirit in preparation for the final restoration of all things in God (*Adv. haer.* 3–5; *Demonst.* 31–33).

Development of Speculative Theology. True theological speculation began with the 3d-century Fathers, particularly Clement of Alexandria, Origen, Methodius of Olympus, Hippolytus of Rome, and Tertullian. The doctrine of ideas in the mind of God had been accepted by Philo Judaeus and combined with Jewish thought expressed in the Books of Wisdom, which saw God's wisdom not merely as an attribute, but as a mysterious entity, possibly personal, who in the beginning assisted God in creation. First-century Jewish speculation had concentrated further on powers, the names of God, and the angel of God, through whom He worked in dealing with the universe. Philo translated the Hebrew word *dabar* (the power, or word, of God) by the Greek word Logos, thus identifying the notion of knowledge or wisdom with the Hebrew idea of God's power. The Stoics employed logos for the fiery rational principle that formed the universe, while the Neoplatonists defined logos as "a power (*dynamis*) that represents a higher principle in action on a lower plane."

When St. John in the prologue of his Gospel named Christ the Logos who was with God and is God, he was reflecting common usage in both the Diasporic Jewish and Hellenistic milieu. But John gave the Logos a definite meaning: He is a person; and Heb 1.3 further identified Christ with God's wisdom, calling him the "shining out of His glory." In contrast to the cyclical concept of history based on the material world as merely a reflection of ideas in the divine mind, the Christian thinkers of the 3d century followed the Judaic unilinear concept of history, and insisted on the historical reality of Christ, a beginning to the universe, man's destiny with creation, the history of the Fall, Redemption through the Incarnation, and the Church as an eschatological setting.

The Alexandrians were able to locate speculation about the essence of divinity within the Biblical perspective. Hence in considering Neoplatonic doctrine of the One-in-Many—the transcendent being, from whom proceeds the first mind, or Demiurge, who in turn brings into existence the intelligent soul of the universe—they had at least a similitude for the doctrine of the Trinity. But it was a dangerous similitude, and caused some of the Christian thinkers to subordinate the Logos to the Father, and the Holy Spirit to the Logos.

Arius and Eunomius later made the Father the transcendent One; the Logos-Son, the Divine Mind; and the Holy Spirit, something equivalent to the world soul. In reaction to this tendency, the Monarchians (*see* MONARCHIANISM) denied a real distinction in the persons of the Trinity, seeing them as single phases in the divine life, or modes (*see* MODALISM) of the divine being. The latter were likewise influenced by Stoicism, which postulates an expanding and contracting Divinity who produces the universe out of His divine substance and periodically reabsorbs it into Himself.

Conciliar Definitions. Athanasius of Alexandria and the Council of *Nicaea I (325) clarified the issue of the Trinity by denying that there could be degrees of divinity, and defining the Son as *homoousios or consubstantial with the Father, thus likewise eliminating any idea of inferiority of the Son in relation to the Father. The definition of the consubstantiality of the

Holy Spirit with Father and Son was the result of subsequent discussion led by *Didymus the Blind, *Hilary of Poitiers, *Basil of Caesarea, and the Cappadocian fathers and consummated by the Council of *Constantinople I in 381.

SCRIPTURAL FOUNDATIONS AND INFLUENCE

The greater portion of this early Christian theology was represented by scriptural exegesis. Justin and Irenaeus had engaged in a typological explanation of the Old Testament in relation to the New, and Clement of Alexandria stressed the fact that the Old Testament was a preparation for the New. He utilized a collection of texts called *Testimonia* that were a continuation of the Jewish technique, to supply a series of types such as the tree of life planted in the world which represented the Divine Wisdom for Moses and Solomon (*Strom.* 5.2.75).

In the East: Clement and Origen. Clement's theology stemmed from his conception of the Logos as the divine reason and teacher of the world, and is developed in his exegesis by an insistence on Christ's activities as the mysteries or sacraments whose salvific effects originated before the creation of the universe, and are extended through time in the Church, in which the hierarchy is established on the pattern of the angelic choirs.

Origen most consciously used the allegorical techniques employed by the pagan teachers in the explanation of Homer and the poets. He worked out a threefold interpretation of the Scriptures: the literal or historical meaning, the moral, and the typological. This methodology was reflected in both Western and Eastern exegesis, rising to a fourfold interpretation—literal, allegorical, typological, and anagogic—with Hilary of Poitiers and *Rufinus of Aquileia (*De bened. patriarch.*).

Origen's *Peri Archon,* or First Principles, is actually an attempt at theological speculation rather than a systematic treatise. Its four books dealt with God, the world, freedom, and revelation, and were explicitly intended as "an examination into the reasons behind" the unalterable truths of the faith revealed by Christ and preached by the Apostles. Aided by the Holy Spirit, he desired "to form a connected series and a body of truths based on the Scriptures and deduced by drawing correct conclusions from those truths" (*Preface* 10). His errors regarding the preexistence of souls, a possible metempsychosis, and the *anakephalaiosis* or recapitulation arose from Neoplatonist influence in a realm of thought he felt was open to speculation.

The typological approach to theology is furthered by Hippolytus, who developed the relation between Joseph, David, Susanna, and Christ, and the Church. He is the first Father to compose a consecutive explanation of a book of Scripture—his Commentary on the Canticle of Canticles. His contribution to the catechesis of the Resurrection and the mystagogic significance of the Church and Sacraments influenced *Ambrose of Milan and *Cyril of Jerusalem, particularly in regard to the triple parousia of Christ in his Christology, ecclesiology and eschatology. *Methodius of Olympus pursued the typology of Christ as the new Adam, and of the Church as the new Eve. He gave a mystical explanation of the relation between Christ and the Virgin in an ecclesial sense, and indulged in number speculation certainly influenced by the Pythagoreans.

In the West: Tertullian and His Successors. In the West Tertullian, despite his disjoinder "What has Athens to do with Jerusalem?" (*De Idol.* 19), witnessed at once to the Church's theological tradition concerning the nature of God, the relationship between the two Testaments (*Adv. Marc.*), the Christology, and sacramental mysteries of the faith. He helped determine the Church's terminology, and more particularly the development of moral concepts based on free will and God's law, influenced at once by his legal background, the Stoic attitude toward nature, and the Church as an institution in competition with the imperial organization surrounding it.

The law of God and the law of the Gospel were explained as the guide to the Church's tradition and deposit of faith; the bishops were the official dispensers of the divine mysteries, and the Church was the Ark without which no one could be sanctified. In his soteriological thought, sin was a crime against God's sovereignty calling for satisfaction, and words such as debt, guilt, and merit are often employed. The redemption is seen as an intervention of God to vindicate His law through One who took man's sin upon Himself to achieve man's forgiveness.

In order to be the Mediator between God and man, Christ had to be both true God and true man (*Adv. Marc.* 2, 3; *De Resur.* 63). Thus soteriological thought gave rise to Christological precisions, and this is true of Novatian's *De Trinitate,* Ambrose's *De fide,* and Augustine's *De Trinitate,* and led directly to Leo's *Tome to Flavian* accepted at the Council of *Chalcedon, which "recognized the difference of the natures" united without admixture or confusion in the One Person of the Son of God.

The Problem of Grace. Western preoccupation with man's moral obligations brought about the problems of the nature of grace and its efficacy posed by the Pelagians (*see* PELAGIUS AND PELAGIANISM) and settled by Jerome, Augustine, and the Roman See; and, while the doctrine of man's deification was brought to the West by Irenaeus and echoes through Tertullian (*Adv. Marc.* 2.27) and Cyprian (*Epist.* 58.6), its appearance in Hilary of Poiters and Leo I is due to their contact with later Eastern ideas. This is likewise true of concern for freedom of the will, which Origen found necessary to assert against the astrologers of his day, and Tertullian defended against the Stoics and Marcion.

Cyprian of Carthage was involved in the controversy over penance and the rebaptism of heretics, problems that forced him to reconsider his doctrine on the unity of the Church, and which led in the 4th and 5th centuries to a development of the Roman understanding of the papal primacy that grew obviously from Siricius and Innocent I to Leo I and Gelasius, and was full-fledged with Gregory the Great.

There was a constant interchange of Western and Eastern ideas all during this period, aided by the exile of Hilary in the East and Athanasius in the West and a constant going back and forth of bishops, scholars, and monks. Athanasius was responsible for the flowering of a vast cenobitic and monastic movement in Italy and Gaul during the 4th century, stimulated by his *Life of St. Anthony the Hermit* (*see* ANTHONY OF EGYPT, ST.). Ambrose of Milan, Rufinus of Aquileia, and Jerome contributed to the furtherance of ascetical thought based upon the writings and experiences of St. Basil, St. *Pachomius, and the *Desert Fathers; they stressed the value of virginity and continence as well as the practice of austere virtue that is a consequence of participation in the mysteries of salvation.

THE GOLDEN AGE OF PATRISTIC THEOLOGY

In the East, theological speculation continued with the mystical tendencies embodied in the Alexandrian doctrine of man made in the image of God and called to the imitation of Christ, as it was developed particularly in *Gregory of Nyssa, *Evagrius Ponticus, and *Ephrem of Syria. At the same time, Antiochene preoccupation with the literal approach toward the Scriptures and a more Aristotelian anthropology represented by Diodore of Tarsus (d. 394), Flavian of Antioch (d. 404), *Theodore of Mopsuestia (d. 428), and *Theodoret of Cyr (d. *c.* 466) made them wary of the allegorical exegesis favored at Alexandria. In their Christology, they insisted upon the human factors in Christ's constitution, leading their Alexandrian opponents to accuse them of dividing Christ into "two sons" when Nestorius refused to apply the term *Theotokos to Mary, preferring to call her the *Christotokos,* or Mother of Christ.

Christology. The Christological problem arose in good part from the attempt to apply the Trinitarian concepts of substance and person directly to the person and natures in Christ. It was also the result of the Alexandrian ontological approach, seeing man's deification as his final goal, whereas the Antiocheans had a fear of breaking down the impassable distinction between the finite and the infinite and saw man's destiny in moral perfection that would be realized in the resurrection.

The quarrel came to a climax at the Council of *Ephesus in 431, when the Church defined the doctrine of the Theotokos; it reached a second climax at the Council of Chalcedon (451), when Antiochene, Alexandrian, and Western thought were amalgamated on the basis of Leo's *Tome to Flavian* and the *Letter of Union* signed by both Cyril of Alexandria and John of Antioch in 433. No great progress was made at Justinian's Council of *Constantinople II in 553, and as a consequence questions regarding Christ's human faculties returned to bother the Church down to modern times, though the question of two wills was settled at the Council of *Constantinople III in 681.

Heretical Views. The controversies during the later patristic period occasioned the rise of two separate heretical churches, the Monophysite and the Nestorian (*see* MONOPHYSITISM; NESTORIANISM), and involved the ecclesiastical and imperial authorities in a series of struggles that resulted in the domination of the Eastern Church by the State, with the emperors taking an active part in the theological controversies. Some of the emperors, such as Theodosius II and *Justinian I, demonstrated considerable theological ability.

The Monophysites, with *Severus of Antioch, *Philoxenus of Mabbugh, and their supporters, produced an enormous theological literature and were able to influence clergy, monks, and laity by their insistence on man's vocation to deification with a definite mystical tendency. Their opponents were equally productive, from *John the Grammarian and *Facundus of Hermiane, whose *Defense of the Three Chapters* was one of the finer theological productions of the 6th century, to *John of Scythopolis, the Chalcedonian who wrote the first commentary on the writings of the Pseudo-Dionysius, and *Leontius of Byzantium, who wrote against both the Nestorians and the Eutychians, employing Aristotelian logic and Neoplatonist psychology.

The two men who dominate the great productive period of patristic theology are *John Chrysostom in the East, and Augustine in the West. Chrysostom exhibited a reluctance to enter the intricacies of theological disputation, saying that the two natures in Christ are conjoined "by a union ineffable and past understanding; ask not how" (*Hom. in Joh.* 11.2). He devoted himself to a practical explanation of the whole of Scripture in his homilies and pastoral instruction that is unsurpassed in breadth of interest, social and psychological understanding, and witness to the traditional teaching of the Church.

Augustinian Theology. St. *Augustine insisted that the understanding of the faith (*intellectus*) is not merely a knowledge of the truths of revelation, but an encounter with God as an end to be loved. It is the *pia fides* that purifies the soul. He refused to separate knowledge from its moral obligations. The Augustinian theology of contemplation implies the use of all man's resources in soul and spirit, and the vision at Ostia was an immortal example of this experience.

In the *De Trinitate* he offered a systematic explanation: the movement toward God constituted by an exercise of wisdom forces the soul to use corporeal objects, then the memory for previous acquisitions, to find God in the superior portion of the mind. The use of sensible similitudes and the resources of science and the arts open the mind to a comprehension of divine things enhanced by faith and elevated by grace. Thus the first seven books of the *De Trinitate* were devoted to the process of *credere:* he established the existence of the Trinity, studied the divine attributes, and answered objections on evidence in the Scriptures and Church Fathers. In books 8 to 15 he proceeded *modo interiore,* by analogies taken from nature, man's moral life, and divine wisdom, to give an insight into the mystery. He thus justified the employment of profane studies and the technique of theology based on pagan disciplines.

In his numerous treatises Augustine covered the whole ambit of theological interest from grace and Christology to the intricacies of the ascetico-mystical life, incorporating the liberal arts, free will and concupiscence, marriage and virginity, and the Church and the Sacraments in a vast synthesis of life in Christ.

Patristic Heritage. The heritage of patristic theology was preserved through the effort of John *Cassian for the monks of the West, and of *Cassiodorus, *Isidore of Seville, and *Bede for the Western Church more generally. In the East, the return to the negative theology of the 1st-century Neoplatonist Albinus, combined with the emphasis of a hierarchical ascension toward mystical union with God, was propagated by the 6th-century mitigated Monophysite writer, *Pseudo-Dionysius the Areopagite. Eastern thought was summed up in the anonymous *De Sectis* and in the writings of the 7th-century Sophronius of Damascus, *Maximus the

Confessor, and particularly St. *John Damascene, whose *De fide orthodoxa* is a remarkable summary of Greek thought on the principle Christian doctrines and was taken over by the Western scholastics.

Whereas a polemical spirit characterized much of the patristic theological writings, equanimity had been practiced by Clement of Alexandria and Origen; in his five theological orations, Gregory of Nazianzus called for justice and charity in dealing with opponents, while St. Leo the Great insisted on moderation.

The scholastics made considerable use of the patristic writings, particularly in florilegia, or collections of texts that go back to the 3d and 4th centuries and are the continuations of the Biblical *Testimonia.* Their witness to the Church's tradition has never been unheeded; but a tendency to rationalize their teachings and theology generally prevailed in the late scholastic and post-Tridentine period, despite the call of Melchior *Cano, and above all *Petau, for a return to the Fathers, and the great work of rediscovery and edition that was undertaken by the humanist Churchmen of the 15th and early 16th century, and pursued assiduously by the *Maurists.

Since the middle of the 19th century there has been a reflowering of patristic thought, made possible by the comprehensive reprinting effort of J. P. *Migne, the critical editions of the Berlin and Vienna corpora, the more recent *Corpus Christianorum,* and translations such as the *Sources chrétiennes,* the *Ancient Christian Writers,* and others. The turn of the 20th century saw a reflowering of patristic theology in both Catholic and non-Catholic circles, which seems to have taken on new proportions in the post-World War II period and is a substantial factor in the ecumenical progress resulting from Vatican Council II.

Bibliography: Y. M. J. CONGAR, DTC 15.1:341–364. K. RAHNER, *Theological Investigations,* tr. C. ERNST (Baltimore 1961–) v.1. A. H. ARMSTRONG and R. A. MARKUS, *Christian Faith and Greek Philosophy* (New York 1964). J. DANIÉLOU, *Message évangélique et culture hellénistique aux II*^e *et III*^e *siècles* (Tournai 1961). G. EBELING, RGG³ 6:789–819. Ghellinck Patr v.1–3. Quasten Patr v.1–3. Altaner. A. VON HARNACK, *History of Dogma,* tr. N. BUCHANAN et al., 7 v. (London 1896–99). J. TIXERONT, *History of Dogmas,* tr. H. L. BRIANCEAU, 3 v. (St. Louis 1910–16).

[F. X. MURPHY]

PATRIZI, FRANCESCO SAVERIO, exegete; b. Rome, June 19, 1797; d. Rome, April 23, 1881. Eldest son and heir of the Roman Count Patrizi, he was ordained a Jesuit priest in 1824 and in the following year appointed professor of Sacred Scripture and Hebrew at the Roman College. Because of his noble ancestry, he was forced to abandon this post and seek refuge in England and later in Louvain during the Revolution of 1848. When peace was restored, he resumed his duties at the Roman College and lectured there until his career was ended by the Revolution of 1870. He took up residence at the German-Hungarian College at Rome and remained there until his death. Among his most significant works are the following: *De Interpretatione Scripturarum Sacrarum* (2 v. Rome 1844), *De Interpretatione Oraculorum ad Christum Pertinentium* (Rome 1853), *De Immaculata Mariae Origine* (Rome 1853), *De Consensu Utriusque Libri Machabaeorum* (Rome 1856), *Delle parole di San Paolo: In quo omnes peccaverunt* (Rome 1876). Also important are his commentaries on the Gospels, polemical in tone, directed against the rationalistic errors of his time.

Bibliography: J. SCHMID, LexThK² 8:181. S. ZEDDA, EncCatt 9:967–968.

[J. B. DONNELLY]

PATROLOGY

The study of the *Fathers of the Church. The term was used first by the Lutheran theologian Johannes Gerhard as the title of a posthumous work (1653). Although the terms patrology, patristics, and the history of ancient Christian literature are sometimes employed interchangeably, it seems advisable to distinguish three scholarly disciplines, covering on broad lines the same period of history and much the same authors, but eyeing their material from distinctive standpoints. Patrology normally has a more historical cast, setting forth the life, writings (genuine, doubtful, spurious), and significant doctrines (or doctrinal significance) of the various authors. Patristics concentrates on the content, primarily theological, of the writings of the Fathers and implies a systematic exposition of their doctrine in whole or in part. The term stems from the 17th century and was first used in Lutheran circles, where theology was divided into Biblical, positive, scholastic, symbolic, and speculative. (*See* PATRISTIC THEOLOGY.) The history of ancient Christian literature is more in conformity with the philological development and outlook of the 19th and 20th centuries; it puts the Fathers in the framework of the general history of literature, gives more play to the literary aspect of the works involved, and has legitimately introduced (as patrology itself has been compelled to do) a number of writers who are not technically Fathers or even orthodox Christians, but deserve a place in the treatment of the literature of the time. The controversy over the scope and character of early Christian literature initiated early in the 20th century by A. von *Harnack, O. *Bardenhewer, and others has long since been resolved, and "ancient Christian literature" is now universally recognized as a satisfactory expression.

The history of patrology goes back to the *Church History* of *Eusebius of Caesarea (early 4th century) and *Jerome's *De viris illustribus* (392). The latter was continued in the patristic era by *Gennadius of Marseilles, *Isidore of Seville, and *Ildefonsus of Toledo. In the Middle Ages the most significant "patrology" was *Photius's *Myriobiblon* or *Bibliotheca* (858). The catalogue (*c.* 1317–18) of the last great Nestorian writer *'Abdisho bar Berīkā is important for early Syriac literature. Other medieval compilers, such as *Sigebert of Gembloux, *Honorius of Autun, and Johannes *Trithemius, were content to rely on Jerome and Gennadius. Fresh impetus for patristic study came from the discovery of early Christian texts during the Renaissance, the return to antiquity sparked by the humanists, the Reformation thesis of a gradual deterioration of primitive Christianity, and theological discussions at the Council of *Trent. The studies of the 17th century and the first half of the 18th constitute a first flowering of high-level patristic scholarship on a vast expanse, with remarkable editions (preeminently by the *Maurists) distinguished for prolegomena and critical apparatus, the painstaking *De scriptoribus ecclesiasticis* of Robert

*Bellarmine, comprehensive historical productions such as L. S. le Nain de *Tillemont's 16-volume *Mémoires pour servir a l'histoire ecclésiastique des six premiers siècles* (1693–1712) and R. *Ceillier's 23-volume *Histoire générale des auteurs sacrés et ecclésiastiques* (1729–63), and the research of Denis *Petau, who gave to positive theology its rightful place in sacred science (notably in his 4-volume *Dogmata theologica*, 1644–50).

Stimulated in part by A. *Mai, J. A. *Möhler, and J. B. *Pitra, the 19th century inaugurated another productive period of patristic scholarship, marked by new discoveries, especially in the Oriental field; the establishment of university chairs of patrology; J. P. *Migne's comprehensive *Patrologiae cursus completus* (1844–66); the critical editions of the Latin Fathers (*Corpus scriptorum ecclesiasticorum latinorum*, 1866–   ) and the Greek (*Die griechischen christlichen Schriftsteller der ersten drei Jahrhunderte*, 1897–   ) undertaken with philological competence by the Vienna and the Prussian Academies of Sciences respectively; and the passage from vast histories to treatises, monographs, and manuals. This florescence produced, toward the end of the century, the extraordinary patristic research initiated by A. von Harnack and O. Bardenhewer, accompanied by scholars such as F. *Loofs and L. *Duchesne, F. X. von *Funk and P. *Batiffol—whose research was continued and intensified by F. J. *Dölger, H. *Lietzmann, A. *Baumstark, G. *Morin, G. *Bardy, B. *Altaner, and a host of others. Twentieth-century patrologists have shown a predilection for exploring more profoundly the doctrinal content of the Fathers, investigating the evolution of words and ideas, and plumbing the patristic stress on history and mystery. Since World War II, new interest in patristic study has been stimulated by striking discoveries (Tura, Nag' Ḥammâdi, Bodmer papyri) and by prolific production of texts and translations (cf. *Corpus christianorum*, 1953–   , ultimately to replace Migne; A. Hamman's *Supplementum* to PL v.1–96, 1958–   ; *Sources chrétiennes*, 1942–   ; *Corpus scriptorum christianorum orientalium*, 1903–   , but esp. since 1949; *Ancient Christian Writers*, 1946–   ). This renewed interest has been quickened by the quadrennial Oxford International Conference on Patristic Studies, the ecumenical movement, and an increasing awareness of the significance of doctrinal development.

Bibliography: Quasten Patr. F. L. CROSS, *The Early Christian Fathers* (London 1960). A. HAMMAN, LexThK² 8:183–187. B. ALTANER, MiscMercati 1:483–520. Ghellinck Patr 2, esp. 149–180. J. DE GHELLINCK, "Les Recherches patristiques: Progrès et problèmes," *Mélanges R. P. Ferdinand Cavallera* (Toulouse 1948) 65–85. J. MADOZ, ed., *Segundo decenio de estudios sobre patrística española, 1941–50* (Madrid 1951). A. BENOÎT, *L'Actualité des Pères de l'Église* (Neuchâtel 1961). K. ALAND, "Der gegenwärtige Stand der patristischen Arbeit in Deutschland," *Miscellanea historiae ecclesiasticae* (Louvain 1961) 119–136. (For additional bibliography, *see* FATHERS OF THE CHURCH; PATRISTIC THEOLOGY.)

[W. J. BURGHARDT]

PATRON SAINT, a saint or angel designated (by individuals, groups, or the Church) as the heavenly protector of individuals, institutions, or specialized activities. The example of the saint's life is proposed to those under his care (see 1 Cor 14.12), and it is customary that his intercession with God be specially invoked. Patrons of certain ecclesiastical and civic bodies receive liturgical honors; their nomination thus requires confirmation by the Holy See (CIC c.1278).

The practice of choosing patrons dates from the early Church. In the early 4th century Christians were already being named after Apostles and martyrs. Dedication of churches to saints soon followed. It is not known when angels were first chosen as patrons, but in 545 a church in Ravenna was dedicated to St. Michael the Archangel.

Patrons found their greatest popularity in the Middle Ages. Towns were named after saints, and nearly every circumstance of life had its heavenly protector. In the 14th and 15th centuries St. Catherine was the acknowledged patron of hospital chapels; St. George, of castle chapels; and St. Anne, of cemetery chapels; while St. Michael was held to protect bell-towers against lightning. To other saints was attributed the care of particular illnesses.

In recent years the popes have frequently named patrons, e.g., St. John Chrysostom, for preachers; St. Thomas, for Catholic schools; St. Camillus, for hospitals; St. Joseph (since 1870 patron of the universal Church), for the Vatican Council II.

Bibliography: H. Leclercq, DACL 13.2:2513–24. P. Molinari, *I santi e il loro culto* (Rome 1962). J. M. Senaveratna, *Patron Saints* (New York 1958). D. Attwater, comp., *A Dictionary of Saints* (New York 1938). Butler Th Attw.

[C. O'Neill]

PATRONAGE, CANON LAW OF

Patronage, according to the *Code of Canon Law, is defined as the sum total of the privileges that the Church concedes, along with certain burdens, to Catholic founders of a church, chapel, or benefice, or to those who have acquired the right of patronage from the founders (CIC c.1448).

History. At the time of the Council of Trent there still existed in many dioceses, cities, and country places, parochial churches without fixed boundaries and rectors without a flock of their own to govern. In the early Middle Ages, the problem had been more acute and initiatives had been taken to fulfill the needs of local Christians. Due to economic and political conditions, feudal lords had taken on themselves, often under the influence of local clergy, to build churches, chapels, or benefices. As benefactors (patrons, hence patronage), they could garner certain privileges in connection with the appointment of the priests who had the care of souls in these churches. Thus the origin of patronage gradually appeared in the Church as an offshoot of the privilege or the consideration shown to a benefactor.

The patronage of churches had its beginning in a number of usages that already existed prior to the first ecclesiastical canons that speak of it. In the East, one may find references in the Justinian Law (CorpIur CivNov 57.2; Nov 123.18); in the West, some mention is made of it in the Councils of Orange (441) and Toledo (633), but the most explicit are found in the 9th century. It was not really defined until the 12th century, and little change was made in later centuries. In brief, it consisted in the right of a patron to present someone to an ecclesiastical office and in some measure, the right of jurisdiction exercised by a benefactor in administration of church property. (*See* BENEFICES.)

In regard to appointment of bishops, patronage led to abuses that developed into the *investiture struggle that was finally ended with the solution of the conflict between the Teutonic emperors of the 11th and 12th centuries and the Church in the Concordat of *Worms. As far as parishes were concerned, the Church granted the privilege to founders or benefactors, but the privilege was transmitted, exchanged, and extended in various ways, particularly under the feudal system, so that the majority of parishes thus came to depend on patrons. The Church tolerated such privileges, but laid down the conditions under which they were to be exercised. Limitations concerning right to appointments were enacted by Pope Alexander III and the Fourth Council of Lateran; the same rules were stated more definitely in the decretals of Gregory IX and Boniface VIII as well as in the apostolic constitutions of Clement V, and finally in the Council of Trent.

Legislation. The Code of Canon Law did not change substantially the law of patronage. Besides abolishing henceforth the right of patronage, the new law stated more clearly the obligations of patrons, who were considered more as depositories of rights than as people subject to obligations. Traces of patronage are still found in some countries of Europe (Italy and Spain), but in France where it had been so strong, it was abolished in 1791. In the U.S. the Second Plenary Council of Baltimore, confirming former decrees of the Provincial Councils of Baltimore, denied the existence of the right of patronage. The Church does not grant the right of patronage any longer and even invites those in possession to renounce it, without, however, obliging them to do so. Wherever litigation arises, cases usually end in compromise that consists in withdrawing the privilege in favor of noncontroversial office holders.

The type of patronage depends on the *leges fundationis*—a kind of charter drawn up by the founder with the consent of the bishop. The right is real or personal according as it adheres to some object or is vested in some person; it may pass to the heirs (hereditary), to those of the family, tribe, or clan (CIC c.1449). In case of several patrons an agreement may anticipate and guarantee the exercise of the right in rotation (CIC c.1459). The privileges consist mainly in the right of presentation of a cleric to a vacant church or parish, together with some tokens of honor and respect (CIC c.1457). Presentation must be exercised within 4 months from the time of the vacancy of the office (CIC c.1457), and the local ordinary remains the judge whether the person presented is qualified (CIC c.1464). The obligations of a patron, besides vigilance over the goods of the church, deal mainly with the rebuilding of the church if it collapses, making the necessary repairs, and supplying the revenue in case of a church's insufficient income (CIC c.1469).

Bibliography: J. A. Godfrey, *The Right of Patronage According to the Code of Canon Law* (CUA CLS 21; Washington 1924). J. J. Coady, *The Appointment of Pastors* (CUA CLS 52; Washington 1929). E. Magnin, DDC 2:692–706. Wernz-Vidal 2:280–314.

[R. Chaput]

PATRONATO REAL

Royal patronage, a form of Church-State relationship in which the State played an active role in the administration and support of the Church, developed extensively in the colonial empires of Portugal and Spain. Papal grants were its foundation but it was extended through the centuries by the unilateral action of the State.

PADROADO OF PORTUGAL

Padroado or patronage is a form of ecclesiastical benefice.

Origin. From the 5th century, laymen were called upon by the Church to help in the building of churches and in the establishment of other pious foundations. In return they were offered several privileges. The Council of Trent was very outspoken on this matter. Two kinds of rights were assigned to the patron: *jus praesentandi* and *jura honorifica*. The first entitled him to appoint the person to the ecclesiastical benefice, whether bishop, parish priest, abbot, etc. Rights and duties of the patrons were summarized in the following Latin verses: *Patrono debetur honos, onus, emolumentum, Praesentet, praesit, defendat, alatur egenus.* Patronage was thus both binding and useful to the patron. In case of need he could even avail himself of the revenues of his church or ecclesiastical foundation.

Christianity developed throughout Europe by means of this system of patronage. Portugal was no exception. Kings and nobles were patrons to many churches, chapels, and other pious foundations. In the 15th century Portuguese patronage was extended overseas by the popes, as the building of churches and the formation and maintenance of missionaries entailed enormous expenses. It was the Order of Christ, established in Portugal in 1319 to replace the Order of the Temple, then about to be suppressed, that received this right of patronage. As the administrators of the Order of Christ were members of the royal family, the overseas patronage became known as the Royal Patronage. The Church realized that, although there were many misuses and complaints about European patronage, it was necessary to encourage the Portuguese to carry their Christian faith overseas. From then on patronage decayed in Europe, but flourished in Africa, India, Brazil, China, Japan, etc. The reaction of the popes, from the beginning of the Portuguese expansion, was most enthusiastic. Martin V in 1418 started a long list of graces and privileges granted by the Church to the Portuguese overseas patronage.

The system was duly carried out with good results. Bishops were presented by the kings of Portugal, as administrators of the Order of Christ, and later nominated by the Holy See. In 1580 Portugal fell under the Spanish crown and remained thus up to 1640, when a national revolution reestablished a Portuguese dynasty on the throne. In this period (1580–1640) something new had happened in Church organization. The Congregation for the Propagation of the Faith (Propaganda Fide) was established in 1622, and it immediately took command of all mission work. Its first "Instructions" ordered Propaganda missionaries to carry the gospel to regions other than those already under padroado personnel. From 1622 to 1640 Portuguese patronage cooperated with the Propaganda Fide. In 1640, however, after the victory of the Portuguese revolution, relations between the two missionary bodies were seriously undermined. Spain did not at once recognize Portuguese independence and influenced the Holy See to take the same position. Portuguese bishops died one

after the other, both in Europe and in the East, and were not replaced by the normal appointment of others. It was only in 1668, when both Spain and the Holy See recognized Lusitanian independence, that this sad state of affairs could be duly redressed.

Padroado versus Propaganda Fide. During this critical period of 28 years (1640–68) the long drawn-out clashes began between missionaries sent by the Propaganda and those under the padroado. They took place mainly in Cochin China, Tonkin, Siam, and India. The padroado missionaries had several flourishing missions in these regions, which had been entrusted by pontifical bulls to padroado dioceses. Taking advantage of the political situation then prevailing in Europe, Propaganda missionaries, instead of establishing themselves in other places, preferred to occupy positions close to the ones belonging to the padroado dioceses. In France, under Louis XIV, the Société des Missions Etrangères de Paris was founded in this period.

The Jesuit Alexander Rhodes, after an extensive tour of the East, came to the conclusion that the Church could not depend altogether on the decadent padroado dioceses. According to his opinion, the Holy See should appoint titular bishops or vicars apostolic, sent directly by Rome and independent from Lisbon. Portugal held the opinion that since the dioceses had been duly created and their boundaries properly marked in their respective bulls, any change would have to be agreed upon after mutual consultation. Besides, according to Portuguese officials, the vicars apostolic would be welcome in territories not assigned to the padroado dioceses; once within diocesan boundaries, such vicars apostolic would automatically fall under diocesan jurisdiction.

In 1658 the Holy See appointed the first two vicars apostolic, Francis Pallu, Bishop of Heliopolis, and Peter de la Motte Lambert, Bishop of Berith. They received from the Holy See the task of exercising their jurisdiction not only in Tonkin and Cochin China, but also over all adjoining territories. Now, Tonkin and Cochin China belonged to the padroado. The same thing happened in Siam. The missionaries sent by the Société des Missions Etrangères de Paris built a church only 4 or 5 miles away from the one under the padroado priests. In 1668 the Holy See declared that Siam belonged indeed to the Diocese of Malacca, but later on, in 1669, came a new statement from Rome to the effect that the French missionaries could hold jurisdiction over their own Christians. Thus originated the famous double jurisdiction. Clashes occurred, and in 1673 Siam was definitely taken out of the Malacca diocese. Tonkin belonged to the Macao diocese, but was also taken over by the Propaganda in 1696, as was Cochin China.

India, however, was the scene of the most deplorable misunderstanding between padroado and Propaganda missionaries. Portuguese padroado had the following dioceses in Indian territory: Goa, Cochin, Mylapur, and Cranganor. Bombay became an object of dispute between the Goanese clergy (padroado) and the Propaganda missionaries. Bombay had been given to the English as part of the dowry of the Portuguese Princess Catherine, when she married Charles II of England. The Bombay Catholic population, mainly composed of Goans, remained sympathetic toward their own missionaries (the Goan clergy), who were appointed by their ordinary, the archbishop of Goa. The new Protestant political authorities of Bombay did not rely on such priests and managed to have new missionaries sent them by the Vicar Apostolic of the Great Mogul, recently appointed, Father Mauritius of St. Theresa, an Italian Carmelite. In spite of Portuguese remonstrances, the Holy See agreed to the change and in 1720 the Goan fathers had to leave. As time went on, relations between Goa and Bombay authorities improved and in 1789 the Vicar Apostolic of the Great Mogul, Father Victory of St. Mary, received official notification to quit Bombay, which by then was the official residence of the same vicars apostolic. Thus the Goan priests came back, but Bombay Catholics were already deeply divided. The East India Company, in order to avoid any further breaches of the peace, decided to divide the then existent churches between the two groups: two for the padroado and two for the Propaganda missionaries.

Between 1834 and 1836, when Portugal had broken off her diplomatic relations with Rome, the Holy See under Gregory XVI reorganized the Indian missions. Three eminent theologians were consulted as to whether the Holy See could extinguish the Portuguese padroado outside non-Portuguese territories without consulting the patron. Gregory XVI acted immediately and published the brief *Multa praeclare* on April 24, 1838, in which it was solemnly stated that the padroado was to be exercised only in the Archdiocese of Goa and in the Diocese of Macao. All the other Indian territories would belong to the Propaganda. Now Bombay belonged to the archdiocese of Goa, but apparently in Rome it was taken for granted that it did not. It was this geographical error that was at the root of all future clashes. As there was no official new statement from the Holy See regarding Bombay, the padroado missionaries defended their presence in Bombay to their utmost. It was in fact during these years that the Church in India was shaken by most regrettable disputes. In 1841 diplomatic relations between Lisbon and Rome were renewed.

In the meantime, however, things went so far that three bishops became involved in the imbroglio: J. da Silva Torres, Archbishop of Goa; J. da Mata, Bishop of Macao; and A. Hartmann, Vicar Apostolic of Patna. Bombay was always the crucial question. While the padroado bishops maintained that until a new official decision by the Holy See was published, Bombay would continue to belong to the Archdiocese of Goa, Propaganda circles asserted that by the *Multa praeclare* it had ceased to belong to the padroado and there was no need for further official pronouncement. The Holy See came to the conclusion that the best solution was to conclude a concordat with Portugal.

Conclusion. The concordat was duly signed in 1857. In 1886 a new concordat was negotiated and remained valid until 1928. Portuguese padroado maintained in India, besides the Archdiocese of Goa, the Diocese of Damão (later attached to Goa), the titular Diocese of Cranganor, the Diocese of Cochin, and that of St. Thomas of Mylapur. Bombay remained under double jurisdiction. Other agreements were afterward signed with the effect of reducing more and more the field of the padroado missions. In 1950, after the independence of India and upon negotiations with the Holy See, Portugal renounced the padroado in Indian territory, but the Archdiocese of Goa kept some mission posts outside Portuguese Goa. A final agreement signed on Oct. 25, 1953, put an end to the padroado in India.

In Africa and in Brazil, the padroado system had no difficulties at all, for the Propaganda missionaries did not try to work in those territories. Conflicts burst out only in territories given first to the padroado but claimed afterward by the Propaganda. As other missionaries stepped in and as Portugal had lost influence in such territories, the padroado had to adapt itself to the new circumstances.

[A. DA SILVA REGO]

PATRONATO OF SPAIN

The origin and theories, operation, and effects of the patronato of Spain are similar to those of the Portuguese padroado.

Origin and Theories. Upon the return of Columbus from his first trip to America, the rulers of Spain, Ferdinand and Isabella, immediately asked Pope Alexander VI for documents affirming their right to the recently discovered territory (*see* ALEXANDRINE BULLS). Through letters issued in 1493 the Holy Father charged these rulers with the spiritual conquest of the natives of the New World, making concessions so broad and vague that they lent themselves to differing interpretations.

The first of these documents was the confidential *Inter caetera* (May 3) in which a grant was made, with exclusive rights to all the islands and land (the rights of the Portuguese rulers being respected) and with concession of apostolic privileges for the Christianizing enterprise to which the Spanish monarchs were obligated. Others followed: *Piis fidelium* (June 25), granting vicarial power to appoint the missionaries who were to go to the Indies, and various privileges to these and to the natives of the lands discovered; *Inter caetera* (probably June 28), broader than the bull of the same name, with some variations but with the same intent; *Eximiae devotionis* (probably July 2), granting *pleno jure* all the privileges that the Portuguese enjoyed; and *Dudum siquidem* (September 25), which annulled the previous concessions and made a new general grant, unconditional and unlimited, and broader so as to include India.

Since the rights acquired by the king over the territories of the Indies were not clarified, the grant of general patronage was issued again during the papacy of Julius II. Only July 28, 1508, the bull *Universalis ecclesiae* was issued; it gave the rulers of Castile and León the right in perpetuity to grant permission for the construction of "large churches" and to propose proper persons for the offices and benefices of the cathedrals, collegiate churches, monasteries, and other pious places. It stipulated that presentations for benefices decreed in consistory were to be made to the pope and all the rest of the bishops.

From the papal documents Spanish authors arrived at various theories as to the juridical nature of the royal right, which evolved historically as follows: (1) During the 16th century patronage properly speaking was considered an ecclesiastical juridical right that the king exercised by virtue of specific apostolic concession. (2) In the 17th century it was held that the royal vicariate that made the king a delegate of the pope for the Church in the Indies originated in the Church, but once granted, it was irrevocable, properly and exclusively the monarch's in full right (juridically it could be classified as a mixed right, ecclesiastical and civil). (3) The regalism of the 18th century maintained that it was the right of the monarch, inherent in the crown and as such juridically a purely civil right, which the monarch exercised over some ecclesiastical affairs. The reaction of the Church to the doctrines these theories proclaimed was to put the works of their authors on the Index of Prohibited Books, as was done with the *De indiarum iure* (Madrid 1641) of Juan de Solórzano Pereira, and the *Tractatus de regio patronata* (Madrid 1677) of Pedro Frasso.

Operation. In spite of theoretical distinctions, in practice the right of patronage was exercised in almost the same manner throughout the centuries of viceregal government in the Americas. Since presentation was the essential right of patronage, this aspect is most interesting to examine. Whenever the king had notice of a vacant see, he sent an order to the Cámara of the Council of the Indies to propose candidates. From all the information that had been accumulated on the ecclesiastics, the Cámara selected three names and suggested them to the king, who consulted the father confessor. The latter chose one, which the king invariably proposed to the Holy See for papal approval. The appointment of capitular prebendaries was made in the same way, without the intervention of the Roman Curia.

According to the legislative system of the Indies, the viceroys, the presidents of the audiencias, and the provincial governors were vice patrons; they were charged with proposing candidates for offices and benefices. In the case of vacancies in benefices held by secular clergy, the bishop, or the cabildo of the vacant see if the benefice was a bishopric, called the candidates together within a set time. When the examinations had been taken and the candidates approved, the three most suitable ones were proposed to the vice patron; he chose one and proposed him to the bishop for canonical bestowal of the benefice. For benefices held by the regular clergy, the religious superiors selected three of their subjects, in accord with their rights, and proposed them to the vice patron. The latter chose one and proposed him to the bishop, who had the right to examine the candidate before approving him for the appointment.

In spite of strict limitation of the right of patronage to the presentation of candidates, the kings arrogated to themselves derivative rights. These involved not only the bureaucratic procedures to which the nominees were subjected (the same as those applying to civil public officials), but also limitations on the autonomy of the Church and of the hierarchy. The Council of the Indies was given the right to examine all documents issued by the Holy See and to allow their free circulation (*regium exequatur*), to hold back those that it did not want to reach the Church in America, or to change their content in order that the king's right of patronage might not be infringed upon. The bishops were prohibited from making visits *ad limina* and from sending information about their dioceses to Rome; they were required to send it to the Council of the Indies. Through these measures the Church in the Indies was kept completely isolated from the Roman Curia during the 3 centuries of the colonial period.

The king also maintained the right to send the bishop-elect to govern the diocese while procedures were under

way to obtain papal approval, as well as the right of being represented in provincial councils and among the applicants for benefices by a royal delegate, who defended patronage. The holders of benefices did not receive inalienable possession of them; they were subject to removal *ad nutum* by the vice patron and the bishop, by common agreement, for just cause. In practice the patronato regulated the qualifications of candidates for the priesthood and for the religious life, as well as the erection of monasteries and the destruction of those built without royal permission. There was even legislation as to the place that the ecclesiastic judge and vicar-general of the diocese, not being prebendary, was to occupy in the meetings of the ecclesiastic chapter inside and outside the choir.

Effects. The methods of control established by the king—many of them not canonical—limited the action of the Church in America and hindered its full development during the viceregal period. The dioceses kept their original limits, which made spiritual government difficult. Permission was denied for building monasteries and other pious establishments; the ordination and profession of mestizos was prohibited (during the 17th century), contributing to the scarcity of secular and regular clergy and of nuns, which deprived the faithful of proper training. The anticanonical subjection of the religious orders to juridic decree and diocesan law limited the privileges and the autonomy which the Church grants to the orders to enable them to develop their apostleship in the most suitable manner; it made them virtually officials of the State.

Because of this system, which prevailed for 3 centuries, when independence was achieved in the American provinces the Church lacked the training necessary for establishing autonomy within the State. The new governments tried to obtain from the Holy See the same privileges of patronage that the rulers of Castile had enjoyed. Ferdinand VII prevented this through his representative to the Vatican, alleging his right of presentation, which he claimed had been granted to the person of the king, not because of his political bonds with the American people. The new republics systematically rejected nominees who arrived from Rome. In order to reconcile the interests of the various parties, the Holy See tried to provide bishops *in partibus* while the problem was being solved, but this effort met with protest and resistance on the part of the American hierarchy. Pius VII, Leo XII, and Pius VIII finally stopped making nominations. In Mexico all the bishoprics were vacant in April 1829.

The Spanish government continued to exercise the right of patronage in Cuba, Puerto Rico, and the Philippines during the 19th century.

See also LATIN AMERICA, CHURCH IN.

[W. M. PORRAS]

Bibliography: Portugal. A. DA SILVA REGO, *Le Patronage portugais de l'Orient: Aperçu historique* (Lisbon 1957). J. GODINHO, *The Padroado of Portugal in the Orient, 1454–1860* (Bombay 1924). E. HULL, *Bombay Mission History and the Padroado Question,* 2 v. (Bombay 1927–30). A. LOURENÇO, *Utrum fuerit Schisma Goanum post Breve "Multa praeclare" usque ad annum 1849* (Goa 1947). Spain. J. GARCÍA GUTIÉRREZ, *Apuntes para la historia del origen y desenvolvimiento del regio patronato indiano hasta 1857* (Mexico City 1941). A. DE LA HERA, *El regalismo borbónico en su proyección indiana* (Madrid 1963). P. DE LETURIA, *Relaciones entre la Santa Sede e Hispanoamérica,* 3 v. (AnalGreg 101–103; 1959–60).

PATUZZI, GIOVANNI VINCENZO, Dominican apologist and theologian; b. Conegliano near Verona, July 19, 1700; d. Vicenza, May 26, 1769. He entered the religious life in 1717 and taught philosophy and theology at Venice. Patuzzi attacked *probabilism (with *Concina) and the *equiprobabilism of St. Alphonsus. He also wrote in history and apologetics and in defense of St. Thomas and of Concina. At times he used the pen name Eusebio Eraniste. His works include: *De futuro impiorum statu* (1748), *Trattato della regola prossima delle azioni umane* (1758), and *La causa del probabilismo* (1764), which was written against St. Alphonsus.

Bibliography: Hurter Nomencl 5.1:226–228. J. Carreyre, DTC 11.2:2329–30.

[W. A. Hinnebusch]